DEPARTMENT OF DEFENSE LAW OF WAR MANUAL

OFFICE OF GENERAL COUNSEL
DEPARTMENT OF DEFENSE
THIRD EDITION, REVISED 2017

Cover photo: Photograph of John McCain After Being Released as Prisoner of War; General Black-and-White Photographic File of the Department of Navy, 1958 – 1981; General Records of the Department of Navy, 1941 – 2004, Record Group 241; National Archives at College Park, College Park MD [online version available through the Archival Research Catalog (ARC identifier 1633553) at *www.archives.gov*; January 12, 2017].

Note on Text: The text of this Third Edition is the updated version of the Department of Defense Law of War Manual publicly released in December 2016. An archived version of the electronic publication is available at *https://perma.cc/F9D7-HGL7*.

Library Cataloging Data

United States. Dept. of Defense. Office of General Counsel.
Department of Defense Law of War Manual / foreword by Stephen W. Preston.

xxiii, 1173 p. : ill.; 25 cm.

ISBN-13: [978-0-9978783-1-8] (pbk: alk. paper)

Includes bibliographic references.

1. War (International Law) -- Handbooks, manuals, etc. 2. United States. -- Department of Defense -- Handbook, manuals, etc. 3. Military Law -- United States -- Handbooks, manuals, etc. 4. United States -- Department of Defense. 5. Military law. 6. War (International law). 7. United States.

LIEBER

LIEBER & SONS // MAPLEWOOD, NJ

DEPARTMENT OF DEFENSE
OFFICE OF THE GENERAL COUNSEL
1600 DEFENSE PENTAGON
WASHINGTON, DC 20301-1600

December 13, 2016

The changes described in the attachment are hereby promulgated pursuant to Department of Defense Directive 2311.01E, *DoD Law of War Program* (May 9, 2006), Department of Defense Directive 5145.01, *General Counsel of the Department of Defense (GC DoD)* (Dec. 2, 2013), and 10 U.S.C. § 140(b) (2012).

The Department of Defense Law of War Manual (June 2015, Updated December 2016) incorporates the changes described in the attachment. Previous versions of this Manual (June 2015) and (June 2015, Updated May 2016) should no longer be used.

Jennifer M. O'Connor

Attachment
Description of Changes Promulgated on December 13, 2016

FOREWORD

The law of war is of fundamental importance to the Armed Forces of the United States.

The law of war is part of who we are. George Washington, as Commander in Chief of the Continental Army, agreed with his British adversary that the Revolutionary War would be "carried on agreeable to the rules which humanity formed" and "to prevent or punish every breach of the rules of war within the sphere of our respective commands." During the Civil War, President Lincoln approved a set of "Instructions for the Government of the Armies of the United States in the Field," which inspired other countries to adopt similar codes for their armed forces, and which served as a template for international codifications of the law of war.

After World War II, U.S. military lawyers, trying thousands of defendants before military commissions did, in the words of Justice Robert Jackson, "stay the hand of vengeance and voluntarily submit their captive enemies to the judgment of law" in "one of the most significant tributes that Power has ever paid to Reason." Reflecting on this distinctive history, one Chairman of the Joint Chiefs of Staff observed that "[t]he laws of war have a peculiarly American cast." And it is also true that the laws of war have shaped the U.S. Armed Forces as much as they have shaped any other armed force in the world.

The law of war is a part of our military heritage, and obeying it is the right thing to do. But we also know that the law of war poses no obstacle to fighting well and prevailing. Nations have developed the law of war to be fundamentally consistent with the military doctrines that are the basis for effective combat operations. For example, the self-control needed to refrain from violations of the law of war under the stresses of combat is the same good order and discipline necessary to operate cohesively and victoriously in battle. Similarly, the law of war's prohibitions on torture and unnecessary destruction are consistent with the practical insight that such actions ultimately frustrate rather than accomplish the mission.

This manual reflects many years of labor and expertise, on the part of civilian and military lawyers from every Military Service. It reflects the experience of this Department in applying the law of war in actual military operations, and it will help us remember the hard-learned lessons from the past. Understanding our duties imposed by the law of war and our rights under it is essential to our service in the nation's defense.

Stephen W. Preston
General Counsel of the Department of Defense

PREFACE

This manual is a Department of Defense (DoD)-wide resource for DoD personnel – including commanders, legal practitioners, and other military and civilian personnel – on the law of war.

This manual has many distinguished antecedents that have provided important guidance to the U.S. Armed Forces. For example, General Order No. 100, the Instructions for the Government of Armies of the United States in the Field, commonly known as the Lieber Code, was prepared by Professor Francis Lieber and approved by President Abraham Lincoln during the Civil War in 1863.[1] A similar code related to naval warfare titled The Law and Usages of War at Sea: A Naval War Code was prepared by then-Captain Charles H. Stockton and approved by President William McKinley in 1900.[2] The War Department published instructions for the armed land forces of the United States in a 1914 manual titled Rules of Land Warfare, which was updated in 1917, 1934, and 1940.[3]

After World War II, in connection with U.S. ratification of the 1949 Geneva Conventions, the Department of the Navy published Naval Warfare Information Publication 10-2, Law of Naval Warfare, in 1955,[4] and the Department of the Army published Field Manual 27-10, The Law of Land Warfare, in 1956, which was updated in 1976.[5] The Department of the Army also published pamphlets on international law applicable in peace and war in the 1960s, and, in 1979, an updated version of the pamphlet on the law of peace.[6] The Department of the Air Force published in 1976 Air Force Pamphlet 110-31, International Law – The Conduct of Armed Conflict and Air Operations, which was updated in 1980.[7] More recently, the Judge Advocate General of the Air Force's School has published a manual titled Air Force Operations and the Law in 2002, with new editions in 2009 and 2014.[8] The Navy, Marine Corps, and Coast

---

[1] E. D. Townsend, Assistant Adjutant General, *General Orders No. 100, Instructions for the Government of Armies of the United States in the Field,* Apr. 24, 1863, *reprinted in* INSTRUCTIONS FOR THE GOVERNMENT OF ARMIES OF THE UNITED STATES IN THE FIELD (Government Printing Office, 1898).

[2] John D. Long, Secretary of the Navy, *General Orders No. 551, The Laws and Usages of War at Sea*, Jun. 27, 1900, *reprinted as Appendix I in* U.S. Naval War College, *International Law Discussions, 1903: The United States Naval War Code of 1900*, 101 (1904).

[3] War Department, Office of the Chief of Staff, *Rules of Land Warfare* (Apr. 25, 1914); War Department, Office of the Chief of Staff, *Rules of Land Warfare* (Apr. 25, 1914 with Changes Nos. 1 and 2, corrected to Apr. 15, 1917); War Department, *Basic Field Manual, Volume VII, Military Law, Part Two: Rules of Land Warfare* (Jan. 2, 1934); War Department Field Manual 27-10, *Rules of Land Warfare* (Oct. 1, 1940).

[4] Department of the Navy, Office of the Chief of Naval Operations, Naval Warfare Information Publication 10-2, *Law of Naval Warfare* (Sept. 1955), *reprinted* as *Appendix in* ROBERT W. TUCKER, THE LAW OF WAR AND NEUTRALITY AT SEA (U.S. Naval War College International Law Studies, Volume 50, 1955).

[5] Department of the Army Field Manual 27-10, *The Law of Land Warfare* (Jul. 18, 1956 with Change 1, Jul. 15, 1976).

[6] Department of the Army Pamphlet 27-161-2, *II International Law* (Oct. 23, 1962); Department of the Army Pamphlet 27-161-1, *I International Law: The Law of Peace* (Sept. 1, 1979).

[7] Department of the Air Force Pamphlet 110-31, *International Law – The Conduct of Armed Conflict and Air Operations* (Nov. 19, 1976).

Guard have published several editions of The Commander's Handbook on the Law of Naval Operations starting in 1987 and most recently in 2007.[9] Helpful annotated supplements have also been published.[10]

In addition to these major publications, DoD components have produced many other publications that have supported DoD lawyers in giving advice on the law of war. For example, since 1895, the Naval War College has published its International Law Studies journal.[11] The Judge Advocate General of the Army's Legal Center & School has published many editions of a Law of Armed Conflict Deskbook, a Law of Armed Conflict Documentary Supplement, and an Operational Law Handbook.[12]

The preparation of this manual also has benefited greatly from consulting foreign experts and resources – for example, the 2004 edition of the Manual of the Law of Armed Conflict by United Kingdom Ministry of Defence.[13] In this way, the preparation of this manual is no different from its predecessors. For example, the 1956 Army Field manual benefited from considering a draft of what ultimately became the 1958 United Kingdom law of war manual, and the preparation of the 1914 War Department manual benefited from the Rules of Land Warfare prepared by officers of the English Army and Professor Lassa Oppenheim.[14] The law of war manuals of Germany, Australia, and Canada were also helpful resources in the preparation of this

---

[8] Department of the Air Force, The Judge Advocate General's School, *Air Force Operations and the Law* (3rd ed., 2014); Department of the Air Force, The Judge Advocate General's School, *Air Force Operations & the Law: A Guide for Air, Space, and Cyber Forces* (2nd ed., 2009); Department of the Air Force, Office of the Judge Advocate General, *Air Force Operations & the Law* (1st ed., 2002).

[9] Department of the Navy, Naval Warfare Publication 9, *The Commander's Handbook on the Law of Naval Operations* (Jul. 1987); Department of the Navy, Naval Warfare Publication 1-14M / Marine Corps Warfighting Publication 5-2.1 / Commandant Publication P5800.1, *The Commander's Handbook on the Law of Naval Operations* (Oct. 1995); Department of the Navy, Naval Warfare Publication 1-14M / Marine Corps Warfighting Publication 5-12.1 / Commandant Publication P5800.7A, *The Commander's Handbook on the Law of Naval Operations* (Jul. 2007).

[10] Department of the Navy, Office of the Judge Advocate General, *Annotated Supplement to the Commander's Handbook on the Law of Naval Operations, NWP (Rev.A)/FMFM 1-10* (1989); U.S. Naval War College, Center for Naval Warfare Studies, Oceans Law and Policy Department, *Annotated Supplement to the Commander's Handbook on the Law of Naval Operations* (1997).

[11] *See, e.g.*, U.S. Naval War College, International Law Studies, Vol. 88, *Non-International Armed Conflict in the Twenty-first Century* (2012).

[12] *See, e.g.*, The Judge Advocate General's Legal Center and School, U.S. Army, International and Operational Law Department, *Law of Armed Conflict Deskbook* (2014); The Judge Advocate General's Legal Center and School, U.S. Army, International and Operational Law Department, *Law of Armed Conflict Documentary Supplement* (2014); The Judge Advocate General's Legal Center and School, U.S. Army, International and Operational Law Department, *Operational Law Handbook* (2014).

[13] United Kingdom Ministry of Defence, Joint Service Publication 383, *The Joint Service Manual of the Law of Armed Conflict* (2004).

[14] *See* War Department, Office of the Chief of Staff, *Rules of Land Warfare*, Preface 7 (Apr. 25, 1914) ("Especial use was made of the Rules of Land Warfare, prepared by officers of the English Army and Prof. L. Oppenheim, LL.D., and of Prof. Nagao Ariga's book, 'La Guerre Russo-Japonaise,' which deals so carefully and thoroughly with the laws and usages of war during one of the greatest wars of recent times.").

manual.[15]

The preparation of this manual has also benefited from the participation of officers from the United Kingdom's Royal Air Force and the Royal Australian Air Force on exchange assignments with the U.S. Air Force. In addition, military lawyers from Canada, the United Kingdom, New Zealand, and Australia reviewed and commented on a draft of the manual in 2009 as part of review that also included comments from distinguished scholars.

Promulgating a DoD-wide manual on the law of war has been a long-standing goal of DoD lawyers. Memoranda and meeting notes from the 1970s reflect that the international law offices of the Department of the Army's Office of the Judge Advocate General and the Department of the Navy's Office of the Judge Advocate General generally agreed on a concept plan for a new all-Services law of war manual that would be a resource for implementing the 1977 Additional Protocols to the 1949 Geneva Conventions.[16] At the time, it was anticipated that the United States would ratify the Protocols, which has not occurred.

The origin of this manual may be traced to work in the late 1980s to update Department of the Army Field Manual 27-10, The Law of Land Warfare.[17] Then, in the mid-1990s, work began on an all-Services law of war manual to reflect the views of all DoD components. It was envisioned that the manual would provide not only the black letter rules, but also discussion, examples of State practice, and references to past manuals, treatises, and other documents to provide explanation, clarification, and elaboration. The present manual has sought to realize that vision and thus it falls within the tradition of the 1914 War Department manual, as well as the 1989 and 1997 Commander's Handbook on the Law of Naval Operations, which also adopted this general approach of an annotated manual.

This manual is an institutional publication and reflects the views of the Department of Defense, rather than the views of any particular person or DoD component. An effort has been made to reflect in this manual sound legal positions based on relevant authoritative sources of the law, including as developed by the DoD or the U.S. Government under such sources, and to show in the cited sources the past practice of DoD or the United States in applying the law of war.

This manual primarily has been prepared by the DoD Law of War Working Group, which is chaired by a representative of the DoD General Counsel and includes representatives of the Judge Advocates General of the Army, Navy, and Air Force; the Staff Judge Advocate to the

---

[15] Germany, Federal Ministry of Defence, Joint Service Regulation (ZDv) 15/2, *Law of Armed Conflict Manual* (May 1, 2013); Australian Defence Force, Australian Defence Doctrine Publication 06.4, *Law of Armed Conflict* (May 11, 2006); Canada, Department of National Defence, Joint Doctrine Manual B-GJ-005-104/FP-021, *Law of Armed Conflict at the Operational and Tactical Levels* (Aug. 13, 2001).

[16] Captain Bruce A. Harlow, JAGC, U.S. Navy, Memorandum for Mr. Waldemar H. Solf (DAJA-IA), *Preparation of New Law of War Manual* (Dec. 28, 1976).

[17] Remarks by W. Hays Parks, *Customary Law and Additional Protocol I to the Geneva Conventions for Protection of War Victims: Future Directions in Light of the U.S. Decision Not to Ratify*, 81 AMERICAN SOCIETY OF INTERNATIONAL LAW PROCEEDINGS 26 (Apr. 9, 1987) ("I have the job of writing the new U.S. Army Field Manual 27-10, The Law of Land Warfare, so this panel is of particular interest to me.").

Commandant of the Marine Corps; the offices of the General Counsels of the Military Departments; and the Legal Counsel to the Chairman of the Joint Chiefs of Staff.[18] This manual has been reviewed by principals of these offices. The preparation of this manual has also benefited significantly from the participation of experts from the Department of State, Office of the Legal Adviser, and the Department of Justice, Office of Legal Counsel, although the views in this manual do not necessarily reflect the views of those Departments or the U.S. Government as a whole.

Comments and suggestions from users of the DoD Law of War Manual are invited. All such correspondence should be addressed by email to:

osd.pentagon.ogc.mbx.ia-law-of-war-manual-comments@mail.mil.

[18] DoD Directive 2310.01E, *DoD Law of War Program* ¶5.1.4 (May 9, 2006, Certified Current as of Feb. 22, 2011) (providing for a "DoD Law of War Working Group, consisting of representatives, at the election by each of the GC, DoD; the General Counsel of each Military Department; the Counsel to the Commandant of the Marine Corps; the Judge Advocate General of each Military Department; the Staff Judge Advocate to the Commandant of the Marine Corps; and the Legal Counsel to the Chairman of the Joint Chiefs of Staff. The DoD Law of War Working Group shall develop and coordinate law of war initiatives and issues; support the research, preparation, review, and updating of the DoD Law of War Manual; manage other law of war matters as they arise; and provide advice to the General Counsel on legal matters covered by this Directive.").

TABLE OF CONTENTS

LIST OF ABBREVIATIONS

To make the manual easier to read, the use of abbreviations has often been avoided, especially in the main text. Nonetheless, the following abbreviations of the titles of documents have been used for frequently cited documents.

Abbreviation	Long Form
1899 Hague II	Convention with Respect to the Laws and Customs of War on Land, Jul. 29, 1899, 32 Stat. 1803
1899 Hague II Reg.	Regulations Respecting the Laws and Customs of War on Land, annexed to Convention with Respect to the Laws and Customs of War on Land, Jul. 29, 1899, 32 Stat. 1803, 1811
1909 Declaration of London	Declaration Concerning the Laws of Maritime War, Feb. 26, 1909, *reprinted in* James Brown Scott, *The Declaration of London, February 26, 1909: A Collection of Official Papers and Documents Relating to the International Naval Conference Held in London, December, 1908—February, 1909 (1919)*
1914 Rules of Land Warfare	War Department, Office of the Chief of Staff, *Rules of Land Warfare* (Apr. 25, 1914)
1925 Geneva Gas and Bacteriological Protocol	Protocol for the Prohibition of the Use in War of Asphyxiating, Poisonous, or Other Gases, and of Bacteriological Methods of Warfare, Jun. 17, 1925, 94 LNTS 65
1928 Pan American Maritime Neutrality Convention	Pan American Maritime Neutrality Convention, Feb. 20, 1928, 47 Stat. 1989
1929 GPW	Geneva Convention Relative to the Treatment of Prisoners of War, Jul. 27, 1929, 47 Stat. 2021
1929 GWS	Geneva Convention for the Amelioration of the Condition of the Wounded and Sick of Armies in the Field, Jul. 27, 1929, 47 Stat. 2074
1940 Rules of Land Warfare	War Department, Field Manual 27-10, *Rules of Land Warfare (1940)*
1944 Chicago Convention	Convention on International Civil Aviation, Dec. 7, 1944, 61 Stat. 1180
1954 Hague Cultural Property Convention	Convention for the Protection of Cultural Property in the Event of Armed Conflict, 249 UNTS 240
1955 NWIP 10-2	Department of the Navy, Office of the Chief of Naval Operations, Naval Warfare Information Publication 10-2, *Law of Naval Warfare* (Sept. 1955), *reprinted* as *Appendix in* Robert W. Tucker, The Law of War and Neutrality at Sea (U.S. Naval War College International Law Studies, Volume 50, 1955)
1956 FM 27-10 (Change No. 1 1976)	Department of the Army Field Manual 27-10, *The Law of Land Warfare* (Jul. 18, 1956 with Change 1, Jul. 15, 1976)
1958 UK Manual	United Kingdom War Office, *Manual of Military Law, Part III: The Law of War on Land* (1958)
1976 Air Force Pamphlet 110-31	Department of the Air Force Pamphlet 110-31, *International Law – The Conduct of Armed Conflict and Air Operations* (Nov. 19, 1976)

Abbreviation	Long Form
1989 NWP 9	Department of the Navy, Office of the Judge Advocate General, *Annotated Supplement to the Commander's Handbook on the Law of Naval Operations, NWP (Rev.A)/FMFM 1-10* (1989)
1997 Multi-Service Detention Regulation	Army Regulation 190-8 / Office of the Chief of Naval Operations Instruction 3461.6 / Air Force Joint Instruction 31-304 / Marine Corps Order 3461.1, *Enemy Prisoners of War, Retained Personnel, Civilian Internees and Other Detainees* (Oct. 1, 1997)
1997 NWP 9	U.S. Naval War College, Center for Naval Warfare Studies, Oceans Law and Policy Department, *Annotated Supplement to the Commander's Handbook on the Law of Naval Operations* (1997)
2001 Canadian Manual	Canada, Department of National Defence, Joint Doctrine Manual B-GJ-005-104/FP-021, *Law of Armed Conflict at the Operational and Tactical Levels* (Aug. 13, 2001)
2004 UK Manual	United Kingdom Ministry of Defence, Joint Service Publication 383, *The Joint Service Manual of the Law of Armed Conflict* (2004)
2006 Australian Manual	Australian Defence Force, Australian Defence Doctrine Publication 06.4, *Law of Armed Conflict* (May 11, 2006)
2007 NWP 1-14M	Department of the Navy, Naval Warfare Publication 1-14M / Marine Corps Warfighting Publication 5-12.1 / Commandant Publication P5800.7A, *The Commander's Handbook on the Law of Naval Operations* (Jul. 2007)
2013 German Manual	Germany, Federal Ministry of Defence, Joint Service Regulation (ZDv) 15/2, *Law of Armed Conflict Manual* (May 1, 2013)
AJIL	American Journal of International Law
AP I	Protocol (I) Additional to the Geneva Conventions of August 12, 1949, and Relating to the Protection of Victims of International Armed Conflicts, Jun. 8, 1977, 1125 UNTS 3
AP II	Protocol (II) Additional to the Geneva Conventions of 12 August 1949, and Relating to the Protection of Victims of Non-International Armed Conflicts, Jun. 8, 1977, 1125 UNTS 609
AP III	Protocol (III) Additional to the Geneva Conventions of 12 August 1949, and Relating to the Adoption of an Additional Distinctive Emblem, Dec. 8, 2005, 2404 UNTS 1
Appendix to 1985 CJCS Memo on AP I	Appendix to John W. Vessey, Jr., Chairman, Joint Chiefs of Staff, *Review of the 1977 First Additional Protocol to the Geneva Conventions of 1949*, May 3, 1985.
Bevans	Charles I. Bevans, Assistant Legal Adviser, Department of State, *Treaties and Other International Agreements of the United States of America, 1776-1949* (13 Volumes, 1968- 1976)

Abbreviation	Long Form
Biological Weapons Convention	Convention on the Prohibition of the Development, Production and Stockpiling of Bacteriological (Biological) and Toxin Weapons and on Their Destruction, Apr. 10, 1972, 1015 UNTS 163
Bothe, Partsch, & Solf, New Rules	Michael Bothe, Karl Josef Partsch, & Waldemar A. Solf, *New Rules for Victims of Armed Conflicts* (1982)
CCW	Convention on Prohibitions or Restrictions on the Use of Certain Conventional Weapons Which May be Deemed to be
CCW Amended	Amendment to Article I of the Convention on Prohibitions or Restrictions on the Use of Certain Conventional Weapons Which May be Deemed to be Excessively Injurious or to Have Indiscriminate Effects, Dec. 21, 2001, 2260 UNTS 82
CCW Amended Mines Protocol	Protocol (II) on Prohibitions or Restrictions on the Use of Mines, Booby-Traps and Other Devices, as Amended on May 3, 1996, Annexed to the Convention on Prohibitions or Restrictions on the Use of Certain Conventional Weapons Which May be Deemed to be Excessively Injurious or to Have Indiscriminate Effects, May 3, 1996, 2048 UNTS 93
CCW Protocol I	Protocol (I) on Non-Detectable Fragments, Annexed to the Convention on Prohibitions or Restrictions on the Use of Certain Conventional Weapons Which May be Deemed to be Excessively Injurious or to Have Indiscriminate Effects, Oct. 10, 1980, 1342 UNTS 137
CCW Protocol III on Incendiary Weapons	Protocol (III) on Prohibitions or Restrictions on the Use of Incendiary Weapons, Annexed to the Convention on Prohibitions or Restrictions on the Use of Certain Conventional Weapons Which May be Deemed to be Excessively Injurious or to Have Indiscriminate Effects, Oct. 10, 1980, 1342 UNTS 137
CCW Protocol IV on Blinding Laser Weapons	Protocol (IV) on Blinding Laser Weapons, Annexed to the Convention on Prohibitions or Restrictions on the Use of Certain Conventional Weapons Which May be Deemed to be Excessively Injurious or to Have Indiscriminate Effects, Oct. 13, 1995, 1380 UNTS 163
CCW Protocol V on Explosive Remnants of War	Protocol (V) on Explosive Remnants of War, Annexed to the Convention on Prohibitions or Restrictions on the Use of Certain Conventional Weapons Which May be Deemed to be Excessively Injurious or to Have Indiscriminate Effects, Nov. 28, 2003, 2399 UNTS 100
Chairman's Commentary to the Copenhagen Process: Principles and Guidelines	The Copenhagen Process on the Handling of Detainees in International Military Operations, *Chairman's Commentary to the Copenhagen Process: Principles and Guidelines* (Denmark, Ministry of Foreign Affairs, Oct. 19, 2012)
Chemical Weapons Convention	Convention on the Prohibition of the Development, Production, Stockpiling and Use of Chemical Weapons and on Their Destruction, Jan. 13, 1993, 1974 UNTS 317

Abbreviation	Long Form
Copenhagen Process: Principles and Guidelines	The Copenhagen Process on the Handling of Detainees in International Military Operations, *The Copenhagen Process: Principles and Guidelines* (Denmark, Ministry of Foreign Affairs, Oct. 19, 2012)
Digest of United States Practice in International Law	Digest of United States Practice in International Law (Department of State, Office of the Legal Adviser)
ENMOD Convention	Convention on the Prohibition of Military or Any Other Hostile Use of Environmental Modification Techniques, Dec. 10, 1976, 1108 UNTS 151
Final Record of 1949 Geneva Diplomatic Conference	Diplomatic Conference of Geneva, *Final Record of the Diplomatic Conference of Geneva of 1949* (Switzerland, Federal Political Department, 1949)
Final Report on the Persian Gulf War	Department of Defense, *Conduct of the Persian Gulf War: Final Report to Congress* (1992)
GC	Geneva Convention Relative to the Protection of Civilian Persons in Time of War, Aug. 12, 1949, 75 UNTS 287
GC Commentary	Jean S. Pictet, *Geneva Convention Relative to the Protection of Civilian Persons in Time of War: Commentary* (International Committee of the Red Cross, 1958)
GPW	Geneva Convention Relative to the Treatment of Prisoners of War, Aug. 12, 1949, 75 UNTS 135
GPW Commentary	Jean S. Pictet, *Geneva Convention Relative to the Treatment of Prisoners of War: Commentary* (International Committee of the Red Cross, 1960)
Greenspan, Modern Law of Land Warfare	Morris Greenspan, *The Modern Law of Land Warfare* (1959)
Grotius, Law of War & Peace	Hugo Grotius, *The Law of War and Peace: De Jure Belli ac Pacis Libri Tres* (translated by Francis W. Kelsey, 1925)
GWS	Geneva Convention for the Amelioration of the Condition of the Wounded and Sick in Armed Forces in the Field, Aug. 12,
GWS Commentary	Jean S. Pictet, *Geneva Convention for the Amelioration of the Condition of the Wounded and Sick in Armed Forces in the Field: Commentary* (International Committee of the Red Cross, 1952)
GWS-Sea	Geneva Convention for the Amelioration of the Condition of the Wounded, Sick and Shipwrecked Members of Armed Forces at Sea, Aug. 12, 1949, 75 UNTS 85
GWS-Sea Commentary	Jean S. Pictet, *Geneva Convention for the Amelioration of the Condition of the Wounded, Sick and Shipwrecked Members of Armed Forces at Sea: Commentary* (International Committee of the Red Cross, 1960)
Hague IV	Convention (IV) Respecting the Laws and Customs of War on Land, Oct. 18, 1907, 36 Stat. 2277
Hague IV Reg.	Regulations Respecting the Laws and Customs of War on Land, Annex to Convention (IV) Respecting the Laws and Customs of War on Land, Oct. 18, 1907, 36 Stat. 2295

Abbreviation	Long Form
Hague IX	Convention (IX) Concerning Bombardment by Naval Forces in Time of War, Oct. 18, 1907, 36 Stat. 2351
Hague V	Convention (V) Respecting the Rights and Duties of Neutral Powers and Persons in Case of War on Land, Oct. 18, 1907, 36 Stat. 2310
Hague VIII	Convention (VIII) Relative to the Laying of Automatic Submarine Contact Mines, Oct. 18, 1907, 36 Stat. 2332
Hague X	Convention (X) for the Adaptation to Maritime Warfare of the Principles of the Geneva Convention, Oct. 18, 1907, 36 Stat. 2371
Hague XI	Convention (XI) Relative to Certain Restrictions with Regard to the Exercise of the Right of Capture in Naval War, Oct. 18, 1907, 36 Stat. 2396
Hague XIII	Convention (XIII) Concerning the Rights and Duties of Neutral Powers in Naval War, Oct. 18, 1907, 36 Stat. 2415
ICJ Statute	Statute of the International Court of Justice (Annex to the Charter of the United Nations), Jun. 26, 1945, 59 Stat. 1055
ICRC AP Commentary	Jean S. Pictet et al., *Commentary on the Additional Protocols of 8 June 1977 to the Geneva Conventions of 12 August 1949* (International Committee of the Red Cross, 1987)
ICTR	International Criminal Tribunal for the Prosecution of Persons Responsible for Genocide and Other Serious Violations of International Humanitarian Law Committed in the Territory of Rwanda and Rwandan Citizens Responsible for Genocide and Other Such Violations Committed in the Territory of Neighbouring States, between 1 January 1994 and 31 December 1994
ICTR Statute	Statute of the ICTR, Annex to U.N. Security Council Resolution 955 (1994), U.N. Doc. S/RES/955(1994) (Nov. 8, 1994).
ICTY	International Tribunal for the Prosecution of Persons Responsible for Serious Violations of International Humanitarian Law Committed in the Territory of the Former Yugoslavia since 1991
ICTY Statute	Statute of the ICTY, Annex to *Report of the Secretary-General Pursuant to Paragraph 2 of Security Council Resolution 808 (1993)*, U.N. Doc. S/25704 (May 3, 1993), adopted by U.N. Security Council Resolution 827 (1993), U.N. Doc. S/RES/827(1993) (May 25, 1993).
J.A.G.S. Text No. 11, Law of Belligerent Occupation	U.S. Army, The Judge Advocate General's School Text No. 11, *Law of Belligerent Occupation* (Jun. 1, 1944, reissued Jul. 2, 1945)
Lauterpacht, II Oppenheim's International Law	Lassa Oppenheim, *International Law, Volume II: Disputes, War and Neutrality* (edited by H. Lauterpacht, 7th ed., 1952)
Levie, Documents on POWs	Howard S. Levie, *Documents on Prisoners of War* (U.S. Naval War College International Law Studies, Volume 60, 1979)
Levie, POWs	Howard Levie, *Prisoners of War in International Armed Conflicts* (U.S. Naval War College International Law Studies, Volume 59, 1978)

Abbreviation	Long Form
Lieber Code	E. D. Townsend, Assistant Adjutant General, General Orders No. 100, *Instructions for the Government of Armies of the United States in the Field*, Apr. 24, 1863, *reprinted in Instructions for the Government of Armies of the United States in the Field* (Government Printing Office, 1898).
LNTS	League of Nations Treaty Series
LOS Convention	United Nations Convention on the Law of the Sea, Dec.10, 1982, 1833 UNTS 396.
Message from the President Transmitting AP II	Message from the President of the United States Transmitting the Protocol II Additional to the Geneva Conventions of August 12, 1949, and Relating to the Protection of Victims of Noninternational Armed Conflicts, Concluded at Geneva on June 10, 1977, Treaty Doc. 100-2 (1987)
Message from the President Transmitting AP III, CCW Amended Article 1, and CCW Protocol V on Explosive Remnants of War	Message from the President of the United States transmitting Protocol Additional to the Geneva Conventions of 12 August 1949, and Relating to the Adoption of an Additional Distinctive Emblem (The "Geneva Protocol III"), Adopted at Geneva on December 8, 2005, and Signed by the United States on that date; The Amendment to Article 1 of the Convention on Prohibitions or Restrictions on the Use of Certain Conventional Weapons Which May Be Deemed to be Excessively Injurious or to Have Indiscriminate Effects ("The CCW Amendment"); and The CCW Protocol Explosive Remnants of War (The "CCW Protocol V"), Treaty Doc. 109-10 (2006)
Message from the President Transmitting LOS Convention	Message from the President of the United States transmitting the United Nations Convention on the Law of the Sea, with Annexes, and the Agreement Relating to the Implementation of Part XI of the United Nations Convention on the Law of the Sea, with Annex, Adopted at New York on July 28, 1994 and signed by the United States, Subject to Ratification on July 29, 1994, Treaty Doc. 103-09 (1994)
Message from the President Transmitting the 1925 Geneva Gas and Bacteriological Protocol	Message From the President of the United States Transmitting The Protocol for the Prohibition of the Use in War of Asphyxiating, Poisonous, or Other Gases, and of Bacteriological Methods of Warfare, Signed at Geneva June 17, 1925, Executive J (1970)
Message from the President Transmitting the 1954 Hague Cultural Property Convention	Message from the President of the United States Transmitting the Hague Convention for the Protection of Cultural Property in the Event of Armed Conflict (the Convention) and, for Accession, the Hague Protocol, Concluded on May 14, 1954, and Entered into Force on August 7, 1956 with Accompanying Report from the Department of State on the Convention and the Hague Protocol, Treaty Doc. 106-1 (1999)

Abbreviation	Long Form
Message from the President Transmitting the CCW Amended Mines Protocol, Protocol III on Incendiary Weapons, and Protocol IV on Blinding Laser Weapons	Message From the President of the United States Transmitting Protocols to the 1980 Convention on Prohibitions or Restrictions on the use of Certain Conventional Weapons which may be deemed to be excessively injurious or to Have Indiscriminate effects: The Amended Protocol on Prohibitions or Restrictions on the Use of Mines, Booby-traps or other devices (Protocol II or the Amended Mines Protocol); The Protocol On Prohibitions or Restrictions on the Use of Incendiary Weapons (Protocol III or the Incendiary Weapons Protocol); and the Protocol on Blinding Laser Weapons (Protocol IV), Treaty Doc. 105-1 (1997)
Message from the President Transmitting the Chemical Weapons Convention	Message from the President of the United States Transmitting the Convention on the Prohibition of Development, Production, Stockpiling, and use of Chemical Weapons and on their Destruction, Opened for Signature and Signed by the United States at Paris on Jan. 13, 1993, Treaty Doc. 103-21 (1993)
Message from the President Transmitting the VCLT	Message from the President of the United States Transmitting the Vienna Convention on the Law of Treaties Signed for the United States on April 24, 1970, Executive L (1971)
Moore's Digest	John Bassett Moore, *A Digest of International Law* (8 Volumes, 1906)
Official Records of the CDDH	Official Records of the Diplomatic Conference on the Reaffirmation and Development of International Humanitarian Law Applicable in Armed Conflicts, Geneva 1974-1977 (16 Volumes, 1978)
Outer Space Treaty	Treaty on Principles Governing the Activities of States in the Exploration and Use of Outer Space, Including the Moon and Other Celestial Bodies, Jan. 27, 1967, 610 UNTS 205
Public Papers of the Presidents	Public Papers of the Presidents of the United States (National Archives and Records Administration, Office of the Federal Register)
Regulations for the Execution of the 1954 Hague Cultural Property Convention	Regulations for the Execution of the Convention for the Protection of Cultural Property in the Event of Armed Conflict, Annexed to the Hague Cultural Property Convention, May 14, 1954, 249 UNTS 270
Roerich Pact	Treaty between the United States of America and other American Republics on the Protection of Artistic and Scientific Institutions and Historic Monuments, Apr. 15, 1935, 49 Stat. 3267
Rogers, Law on the Battlefield	A.P.V. Rogers, *Law on the Battlefield* (1996)
Rome Statute	Rome Statute of the International Criminal Court, July 17, 1998, 2187 UNTS 90
Spaight, Air Power and War Rights	James Maloney Spaight, *Air Power and War Rights* (3rd ed., 1947)
Spaight, War Rights on Land	James Maloney Spaight, *War Rights on Land* (1911)

Abbreviation	Long Form
Stat.	United States Statutes at Large
Technical Annex to CCW Protocol V On Explosive Remnants of War	Technical Annex to Protocol (V) on Explosive Remnants of War, Annexed to the Convention on Prohibitions or Restrictions on the Use of Certain Conventional Weapons Which May be Deemed to be Excessively Injurious or to Have Indiscriminate Effects, Nov. 28, 2003, 2399 UNTS 132
Trial of the Major War Criminals Before the IMT	Trial of the Major War Criminals Before the International Military Tribunal (42 Volumes, 1947-1949)
Trials of War Criminals Before the NMT	Trials of War Criminals Before the Nuernberg Military Tribunals Under Control Council Law No. 10 (15 Volumes, 1949-1953)
Tucker, The Law of War and Neutrality at Sea	Robert W. Tucker, *The Law of War and Neutrality at Sea* (U.S. Naval War College International Law Studies, Volume 50, 1955)
U.N. Charter	Charter of the United Nations, Jun. 26, 1945, 59 Stat. 1031
U.N. Law Reports	United Nations War Crimes Commission, Law Reports of the Trials of War Criminals (15 Volumes 1947-1949)
U.S. Response to ICRC CIHL Study	John B. Bellinger, III, Legal Adviser, Department of State, & William J. Haynes II, General Counsel, Department of Defense, *Letter to Dr. Jacob Kellenberger, President, International Committee of the Red Cross, Regarding Customary International Humanitarian Law Study*, Nov. 3, 2006, *reprinted in* 46 International Legal Materials 514 (2007).
U.S.C.	United States Code (as of the date of publication of this manual)
UNTS	United Nations Treaty Series
Vattel, The Law of Nations	Emer de Vattel, *The Law of Nations, or the Principles of the Law of Nature, Applied to the Conduct and Affairs of Nations and Sovereigns* (translated by Charles Fenwick, 1916)
VCLT	Vienna Convention on the Law of Treaties, May 23, 1969, 1155 UNTS 331
Von Glahn, The Occupation of Enemy Territory	Gerhard von Glahn, *The Occupation of Enemy Territory* (1957)
Whiteman's Digest	Marjorie M. Whiteman, Assistant Legal Adviser, Department of State, *Digest of International Law* (15 Volumes, 1963-1973)
Winthrop, Military Law & Precedents	William Winthrop, *Military Law and Precedents* (2nd. ed., 1920)

I – General Background

Chapter Contents

1.1 Purpose and Scope of This Manual

1.1.1 Purpose. The purpose of this manual is to provide information on the law of war to DoD personnel responsible for implementing the law of war and executing military operations.[1]

This manual represents the legal views of the Department of Defense. This manual does not, however, preclude the Department from subsequently changing its interpretation of the law. Although the preparation of this manual has benefited from the participation of lawyers from the Department of State and the Department of Justice, this manual does not necessarily reflect the views of any other department or agency of the U.S. Government or the views of the U.S. Government as a whole.

This manual is not intended to, and does not, create any right or benefit, substantive or procedural, enforceable at law or in equity against the United States, its departments, agencies, or other entities, its officers or employees, or any other person.

1.1.2 Scope. This manual is not a definitive explanation of all law of war issues. This manual focuses on *jus in bello* – law relating to the conduct of hostilities and the protection of war victims.

This manual seeks to address the law of war that is applicable to the United States, including treaties to which the United States is a Party, and applicable customary international law. It provides legal rules, principles, and discussion, particularly with respect to DoD practice. Although the views of other States may be referenced in this manual, it is not a purpose of this manual to describe the views of other States, which may differ from views expressed in this manual.

This manual is not a substitute for the careful practice of law. As specific legal issues

---

[1] *Refer to* § 1.3 (Definition of the Law of War).

arise, legal advisers should consider relevant legal and policy materials (*e.g.*, treaty provisions, judicial decisions, past U.S. practice, regulations, and doctrine), and should apply the law to the specific factual circumstances.

This manual is intended to be a description of the law as of the date of the manual's promulgation. In this vein, much of this manual has been written in the past tense to help ensure that the text remains accurate, even after subsequent developments have occurred. Every effort has been made to ensure the accuracy of the manual, but it must be read in the light of later developments in the law.

1.2 Use of Footnotes, Sources, Cross-References, and Signals in This Manual

1.2.1 Use of Footnotes in This Manual. This manual uses footnotes to provide sources or cross-references to other sections of the manual in order to clarify, elaborate on, or support the main text.

An effort has been made to avoid introducing discussion in the footnotes that addresses different propositions than those discussed in the main text. Although providing tangential information in footnotes is common in academic legal writing, this practice has been avoided to the extent possible for principally two reasons. First, it was desirable that this manual's main text convey as much information as possible without the reader needing to read the footnotes. For example, it was desirable to avoid the possibility that a reader might misunderstand a legal rule addressed in the main text because a notable exception to that rule was addressed only in a footnote accompanying the text. Second, tangential discussion on a given issue in footnotes would have made it much more difficult to keep the manual's treatment of that issue consistent from section to section and to allow the reader to find all the relevant information about a single topic. Thus, tangential discussion in footnotes has been avoided, to the extent possible, in favor of cross-references to the appropriate section of the manual that addresses that topic in more detail.

1.2.2 Use of Sources in This Manual. This manual cites sources in the footnotes to support or elaborate upon propositions in the main text. These sources are cited in the footnotes to help practitioners research particular topics discussed in the main text. Reviewing the cited sources in their entirety may provide additional contextual information, especially where sources are only partially quoted in the footnotes.

1.2.2.1 *Selection of Sources*. The sources cited in the footnotes have been chosen for a variety of reasons. For example, a source may contain a particularly helpful explanation or illustration. A source may have been chosen to illustrate U.S. practice or legal interpretation. A source may have been selected because its author was a particularly influential and respected international lawyer. For example, the 1956 Department of Army Field Manual 27-10, The Law of Land Warfare, has been a source of legal guidance for the U.S. armed forces for more than 50 years, and was published in connection with the U.S. ratification of the 1949 Geneva Conventions. One of the persons who helped prepare the 1956 manual was Richard Baxter, a highly respected DoD lawyer, who later became a judge on the International Court of Justice.

Citation to a particular source should not be interpreted to mean that the cited source represents an official DoD position, or to be an endorsement of the source in its entirety. For example, parts of a source, such as an opinion by the International Court of Justice or a commentary published by the International Committee of the Red Cross, may reflect the DoD legal interpretation, while other parts of the source may not. Similarly, the citation of the jurisprudence of the Inter-American Commission on Human Rights should not be understood to indicate that the United States has accepted the competence of the Inter-American Commission on Human Rights to apply the law of war.[2]

1.2.2.2 Use of Older Sources. Older sources are sometimes cited: (1) because that source is particularly influential; (2) to demonstrate the origin of a legal proposition; or (3) to illustrate that a particular rule or formulation has a long history.

The citation of an older source should not necessarily be interpreted as an endorsement that every aspect of that source remains current law. For example, the Lieber Code is a canonical law of war document for the United States, but parts of it no longer reflect current law.[3] Moreover, an older document produced by a State does not necessarily reflect its current legal views. For example, the 1958 UK Manual, although a particularly influential law of war manual prepared by distinguished experts Hersch Lauterpacht and Gerald Draper, has been superseded by subsequent UK Manuals, which reflect more recent developments in the law for the United Kingdom (*e.g.*, its ratification of AP I).

1.2.2.3 Quotes Provided From Sources. Quotes from sources are sometimes given in parentheticals within footnotes. These parentheticals are provided to help practitioners, such as by facilitating comparison between the main text of the manual and the language used in the sources. Every effort has been made to quote sources accurately. Practitioners, however, should verify quotations using the original source.

Certain formatting rules have been followed for quoted material. Two spaces have been placed after each period ending a sentence. Footnote numbers and carriage returns have been omitted from quoted text. Otherwise, quotes have not been changed unless noted through the use of ellipses, brackets, or parentheticals after the quotes indicating the changes made.

1.2.2.4 Citation of Policies and Regulations. Policies and regulations of the U.S. Government or particular DoD components are sometimes cited as examples of past practice.

This manual, however, seeks primarily to address the law and not to address applicable U.S. Government or DoD policies or regulations. Many policies and regulations are not addressed in this manual, and the discussion of some policies, where relevant, should not be understood to indicate that other pertinent policies or regulations do not exist. Moreover, policies and regulations are constantly updated, so practitioners are advised to ascertain whether

---

[2] *See, e.g., U.S. Additional Response to the Request for Precautionary Measures—Detention of Enemy Combatants at Guantanamo Bay, Cuba*, Inter-American Commission on Human Rights, Jul. 15, 2002, 2002 DIGEST OF UNITED STATES PRACTICE IN INTERNATIONAL LAW 1008, 1009 ("Put simply, the Commission's jurisdiction does not include the application of the law of armed conflict, the *lex specialis* governing the status and treatment of persons detained during armed conflict.").

[3] *Refer to* § 19.3 (Lieber Code).

more recent versions of cited policies and regulations have been issued.

In some cases, cancelled issuances or superseded policies or regulations are cited to show the past practice, and, at times, a series of issuances are cited to illustrate a continuity in practice.

Policies and regulations often exceed the requirements of applicable law, and the mere citation of a policy or regulation in this manual should not be understood to reflect the view that the policy or regulation's requirements have been promulgated out of a sense of legal obligation for the purposes of assessing customary international law or otherwise intending to reflect legal requirements.

1.2.2.5 *Citation Forms*. An effort has been made to make citations forms consistent throughout the manual, and to provide enough information about each cited source to reflect its significance and to enable readers to find it.[4] This manual has not strictly adhered to an established system of citation. Although certain citation systems were consulted, modifications were made as deemed appropriate for this type of resource, to make the citation forms straightforward and simple and relatively easy for readers to understand. In regard to abbreviations, for example, this manual generally does not abbreviate the names of academic journals. Moreover, it is hoped that the quotations from the cited sources that have been included in footnotes will help readers find the cited sources electronically.

1.2.3 Use of Cross-References in This Manual. This manual uses cross-references in the footnotes to point the reader to other sections of the manual containing relevant discussion of a particular topic. In particular, an effort has been made to use cross-references rather than to repeat discussion of a recurring issue or duplicate citation of legal sources. In sections in which a law of war rule is only mentioned tangentially or as an example, a cross-reference is used to direct the reader to the section of the manual in which a more in-depth discussion of that rule and supporting sources are provided.[5]

Cross-references are linked to enable the reader to access the referenced section quickly.

---

[4] *Cf.* Richard A. Posner, *The Bluebook Blues (reviewing Harvard Law Review Association, The Bluebook: A Uniform System of Citation (19th ed., 2010))*, THE YALE LAW JOURNAL 850, 852 (2011) ("A system of citation forms has basically two functions: to provide enough information about a reference to give the reader a general idea of its significance and whether it's worth looking up, and to enable the reader to find the reference if he decides that he does want to look it up. In *Goodbye to the Bluebook* I suggested four principles to guide the design of such a system: 'to spare the writer or editor from having to think about citation form,' 'to economize on space and the reader's time,' 'to provide information to the reader,' and 'to minimize distraction.'").

[5] *Refer to* § 1.2.1 (Use of Footnotes in This Manual).

1.2.4 Use of Signals in This Manual. This manual uses signals to introduce the sources and cross-references in the footnotes. The table below identifies the signals used in this manual, describes their function, and provides examples of their use.

Signal	Function and Examples of Use
[no signal]	Directly states the proposition If a person joins a *levée en masse*, he or she may be held as a POW even if he or she actually took no part in fighting.[1] [1] 1958 UK MANUAL ¶100 ("If it is shown that they joined the *levée en masse*, but took no part in the defence, they may be held as prisoners of war."). Identifies the source of a quotation As the Supreme Court has explained: "Lawful combatants are subject to capture and detention as prisoners of war by opposing military forces."[2] [2] Ex parte Quirin, 317 U.S. 1, 31 (1942). Identifies an authority referred to in the text There are additional provisions of the CCW Amended Mines Protocol addressing international exchanges of information and cooperation in this respect.[3] [3] CCW AMENDED MINES PROTOCOL art. 11.
See	Clearly supports the proposition but does not directly state it In addition, observers on military reconnaissance aircraft have not been regarded as acting clandestinely or under false pretenses.[4] [4] *See* HAGUE IV REG. art. 29 ("Persons sent in balloons for the purpose of carrying despatches and, generally, of maintaining communications between the different parts of an army or a territory" are not considered spies.).
See also	Elaborates on the proposition This means that a combatant's "killing, wounding, or other warlike acts are not individual crimes or offenses."[5] [5] LIEBER CODE art. 57. *See also* WINTHROP, MILITARY LAW & PRECEDENTS 778 ("The State is represented in active war by its contending army, and the laws of war justify the killing or disabling of members of the one army by those of the other in battle or hostile operations.").

Signal	Function and Examples of Use
Cf.	Supports the proposition by analogy, *i.e.*, discusses a different proposition that is sufficiently similar to support the original proposition A person must engage in acts of espionage in the zone of operations of a belligerent to be considered a spy. "Zone of operations" has been construed broadly to include areas supporting the war effort.[6] [6] *Cf.* Ex parte Quirin, 317 U.S. 1, 37 (1942) ("The law of war cannot rightly treat those agents of enemy armies who enter our territory, armed with explosives intended for the destruction of war industries and supplies, as any the less belligerent enemies than are agents similarly entering for the purpose of destroying fortified places or our Armed Forces.").
Refer to	Refers to another manual section that supports or elaborates on the proposition Certain categories of persons are not members of the armed forces, but are nonetheless authorized to support the armed forces in the fighting: • persons authorized to accompany the armed forces, but who are not members thereof;[7] [7] *Refer to* § 4.15 (Persons Authorized to Accompany the Armed Forces).
Compare	Refers to another manual section that is analogous to the proposition Persons authorized to accompany the armed forces who provide security against criminal elements generally would not be viewed as taking a direct part in hostilities (and do not forfeit their protection from being made the object of attack).[269] [269] *Compare* § 4.23.1 (Police as Civilians).
Consider	Identifies a treaty that relates to the proposition but to which the United States is not a Party (*e.g.*, AP I) Under international law, every treaty in force is binding upon the Parties to it and must be performed by them in good faith.[10] [10] *Consider* VCLT art. 26 ("Every treaty in force is binding upon the parties to it and must be performed by them in good faith.").

Signal	Function and Examples of Use
For example,	<u>Illustrates the proposition with an example drawn from historical practice</u> Adjusting the timing of an attack may reduce the risk of incidental harm. For example, attacking a military objective when civilians are less likely to be present may be appropriate.[11] [11] *For example,* Jennifer O'Connor, General Counsel, Department of Defense, *Remarks at New York University School of Law: Applying the Law of Targeting to the Modern Battlefield*, Nov. 28, 2016 ("Given the facts of this specific situation, including the intelligence that the cash was being used to pay ISIL fighters and conduct terrorist operations, the targeting authority determined that the bulk cash was a legitimate military objective. The next step then for the targeting authority before approving the strike was to conduct a proportionality analysis. This bulk cash storage site happened to be in an area where civilians were often present—as you might expect from a building that used to be a civilian bank before ISIL turned it into a cash storage site. As a result of the high number of civilians in the area, the targeting authority took specific steps to minimize potential harm to civilians by ordering the attack to occur at a time when the potential for any civilian casualties was deemed to be the lowest."); FINAL REPORT ON THE PERSIAN GULF WAR 100 (noting that during Operation DESERT STORM "attacks on known dual (i.e., military and civilian) use facilities normally were scheduled at night, because fewer people would be inside or on the streets outside.").
e.g.,	<u>Added to any of the other signals when the cited authority is one of several authorities (some of which remain uncited) that stand for the same proposition</u> International humanitarian law is an alternative term for the law of war that may be understood to have the same substantive meaning as the law of war.[12] [12] *See, e.g., Overview of the Amendment to the Convention on the Physical Protection of Nuclear Material*, 6, Enclosure to Condoleezza Rice, Letter of Submittal, Jun. 11, 2007, MESSAGE FROM THE PRESIDENT OF THE UNITED STATES TRANSMITTING AMENDMENT TO THE CONVENTION ON THE PHYSICAL PROTECTION OF NUCLEAR MATERIAL (THE "AMENDMENT"). A CONFERENCE OF STATES PARTIES TO THE CONVENTION ON THE PHYSICAL PROTECTION OF NUCLEAR MATERIAL, ADOPTED ON OCTOBER 28, 1979, ADOPTED THE AMENDMENT ON JULY 8, 2005, AT THE INTERNATIONAL ATOMIC ENERGY AGENCY IN VIENNA, TREATY DOC. 110-6, 6 (2007) ("(2) The United States of America understands that the term 'international humanitarian law' in Paragraph 5 of the Amendment (Article 2 of the Convention on the Physical Protection of Nuclear Material, as amended) has the same substantive meaning as the law of war.").

1.3 DEFINITION OF THE LAW OF WAR

For the purposes of this manual, the *law of war* is that part of international law that regulates the resort to armed force; the conduct of hostilities and the protection of war victims in both international and non-international armed conflict; belligerent occupation; and the relationships between belligerent, neutral, and non-belligerent States.[6]

For the purposes of this manual, the law of war comprises treaties and customary international law applicable to the United States.[7]

1.3.1 Law of War – Notes on Terminology.

1.3.1.1 *Different Definitions of the Law of War*. The law of war may be defined slightly differently in other publications. For example, DoD issuances have defined the law of war more narrowly than the definition discussed in this section (*e.g.*, by omitting reference to that part of international law that regulates the resort to armed force).[8]

1.3.1.2 *Law of War Versus International Humanitarian Law and Law of Armed Conflict*. The *law of war* is often called the *law of armed conflict*. Both terms can be found in DoD directives and training materials. *International humanitarian law* is an alternative term for the law of war that may be understood to have the same substantive meaning as the law of war.[9] In other cases, international humanitarian law is understood more narrowly than the law of war (*e.g.*, by understanding international humanitarian law not to include the law of neutrality).[10]

---

[6] *Refer to* § 3.2 (Situations to Which the Law of War Applies).

[7] *Refer to* § 1.7 (Treaties); § 1.8 (Customary International Law).

[8] *For example*, DoD DIRECTIVE 2310.01E, *DoD Detainee Program*, 14 (Aug. 19, 2014) ("law of war. The part of international law that regulates the conduct of hostilities and the protection of victims of armed conflict in both international and non-international armed conflict and occupation, and that prescribes the rights and duties of neutral, non-belligerent, and belligerent states. It is often called the 'law of armed conflict' or 'international humanitarian law,' and is specifically intended to address the circumstances of armed conflict. It encompasses all international law applicable to the conduct of military operations in armed conflicts that is binding on the United States or its individual citizens, including treaties and international agreements to which the United States is a party (e.g., the Geneva Conventions of 1949), and applicable customary international law."); DoD DIRECTIVE 2311.01E, *DoD Law of War Program*, ¶3.1 (May 9, 2006, Certified Current as of Feb. 22, 2011) ("Law of War. That part of international law that regulates the conduct of armed hostilities. It is often called the 'law of armed conflict.' The law of war encompasses all international law for the conduct of hostilities binding on the United States or its individual citizens, including treaties and international agreements to which the United States is a party, and applicable customary international law.").

[9] *See, e.g.*, *Overview of the Amendment to the Convention on the Physical Protection of Nuclear Material*, 6, Enclosure to Condoleezza Rice, *Letter of Submittal*, Jun. 11, 2007, MESSAGE FROM THE PRESIDENT OF THE UNITED STATES TRANSMITTING AMENDMENT TO THE CONVENTION ON THE PHYSICAL PROTECTION OF NUCLEAR MATERIAL (THE "AMENDMENT"). A CONFERENCE OF STATES PARTIES TO THE CONVENTION ON THE PHYSICAL PROTECTION OF NUCLEAR MATERIAL, ADOPTED ON OCTOBER 28, 1979, ADOPTED THE AMENDMENT ON JULY 8, 2005, AT THE INTERNATIONAL ATOMIC ENERGY AGENCY IN VIENNA, TREATY DOC. 110-6, 6 (2007) ("(2) The United States of America understands that the term 'international humanitarian law' in Paragraph 5 of the Amendment (Article 2 of the Convention on the Physical Protection of Nuclear Material, as amended) has the same substantive meaning as the law of war."); FRITS KALSHOVEN & LIESBETH ZEGVELD, CONSTRAINTS ON THE WAGING OF WAR: AN INTRODUCTION TO INTERNATIONAL HUMANITARIAN LAW 11 (International Committee of the Red Cross, 3rd ed., 2001) ("The law of war nowadays is often referred to by a phrase better suited to express its object and purpose, such as 'international humanitarian law applicable in armed conflict' or 'humanitarian law' – we shall be using these terms interchangeably, as we do with 'war' and 'armed conflict'.").

[10] Christopher Greenwood, *Historical Development and Legal Basis*, *in* DIETER FLECK, THE HANDBOOK OF HUMANITARIAN LAW IN ARMED CONFLICTS 9 (¶102) (1999) ("The term 'international humanitarian law' is of relatively recent origin and does not appear in the Geneva Conventions of 1949. ... International humanitarian law

1.3.2 The Law of War's Relationship to Other Bodies of Law. An issue that often confronts law of war practitioners is the relationship of the law of war to other bodies of law, especially when rules in those bodies of law may appear to conflict with rules reflected in the law of war. These apparent conflicts are often resolved by considering the principle that the law of war is the *lex specialis* governing armed conflict.[11] How a law of war rule relates to a particular rule that is not grounded in the law of war may depend on the specific legal rule in question.

In general, the law of war may relate to other bodies of law through: (1) law of war rules superseding rules in other bodies of law with respect to armed conflict; (2) construing the rules in other bodies of law to avoid conflict with law of war rules; (3) law of war rules informing the content of general standards in other bodies of law, should such standards be construed to apply to armed conflict; and (4) law of war treaties explicitly incorporating concepts from other bodies of law.

In some cases, it may be difficult to distinguish between these approaches, and different entities may apply different approaches to achieve the same result.[12] Although there are different approaches and although the ultimate resolution may depend on the specific rules and context, the law of war, as the *lex specialis* of armed conflict, is the controlling body of law with regard to the conduct of hostilities and the protection of war victims.[13]

1.3.2.1 *The Law of War as the Lex Specialis Governing Armed Conflict*. The maxim *lex specialis derogat legi generali* means that "[a]s a rule the special rule overrides the

---

thus includes most of what used to be known as the laws of war, although strictly speaking some parts of those laws, such as the law of neutrality, are not included since their primary purpose is not humanitarian.").

[11] *See, e.g.*, Mary McLeod, Acting Legal Adviser, Department of State, *Opening Statement at 53rd Session of the U.N. Committee Against Torture, Nov. 3 – 28, 2014*, Nov. 12, 2014 (noting that "the law of armed conflict is the controlling body of law with respect to the conduct of hostilities and the protection of war victims,"); U.S. Delegation to U.N. General Assembly Third Committee, *Statement Clarifying Legal Points of Importance*, 2004 DIGEST OF UNITED STATES PRACTICE IN INTERNATIONAL LAW 331 ("Third, with respect to [preambular paragraph ('PP')] 4 and PP6, references to human rights law during armed conflict by necessity refer only to those provisions, if any, that may be applicable. As may be well known, it is the position of the United States Government that the Law of War is the *lex specialis* governing armed conflict.") (amendment in original).

[12] *Report of the International Law Commission, Fifty-sixth session (3 May-4 June and 5 July-6 August 2004)*, U.N. Doc. A/59/10 ¶304 (2004) ("In introducing the part of the study concerning the function and scope of the *lex specialis* rule, the Chairman stressed several points. First, he emphasized that recourse to the *lex specialis* rule was an aspect of legal reasoning that was closely linked to the idea of international law as a legal system. The *lex specialis* maxim sought to harmonize conflicting standards through interpretation or establishment of definite relationships of priority between them. In fact, he said, it was often difficult to distinguish between these two aspects of the functioning of the technique: the interpretation of a special law in the light of general law, and the setting aside of the general law in view of the existence of a conflicting specific rule. ... The adoption of a systemic view was important precisely in order to avoid thinking of *lex specialis* in an overly formal or rigid manner. Its operation was always conditioned by its legal-systemic environment.").

[13] *Observations of the United States of America on the Human Rights Committee's Draft General Comment 35: Article 9*, June 10, 2014, ¶20 ("While the United States acknowledges that difficult questions arise regarding the applicability of international human rights law in situations of armed conflict, the draft does not accord sufficient weight to the well-established principle that international humanitarian law, as the *lex specialis* of armed conflict, is the controlling body of law with regard to the conduct of hostilities and the protection of war victims.").

general law."[14] The rule that is more specifically directed towards the action receives priority because it takes better account of the particular features of the context in which the law is to be applied, thus creating a more equitable result and better reflecting the intent of the authorities that have made the law.[15]

The law of war has been developed with special consideration of the circumstances of war and the challenges inherent in its regulation by law. Thus, for example, the exigencies of armed conflict cannot justify violating the law of war.[16] Moreover, lawmakers sometimes have considered peacetime rules appropriate to apply during armed conflict, and in certain of these cases, they have explicitly incorporated such concepts into the law of war.[17]

Thus, traditionally, the law of war has been described as the only "authoritative rules of action between hostile armies," or as superseding ordinary law in the actual theater of military operations.[18] Similarly, law of war treaties have been viewed as a clear example of a *lex specialis* in relation to treaties providing peacetime norms concerning the same subjects.[19]

1.3.2.2 <u>Construing Other Laws to Avoid Conflict With the Law of War</u>. Potential

---

[14] Colleanu v. German State, German-Rumanian Mixed Arbitral Tribunal, Jan. 12, 1929, *reprinted in* H. LAUTERPACHT, V INTERNATIONAL LAW REPORTS 438 (1929). *See also* GROTIUS, LAW OF WAR & PEACE 428 (2.16.29.1) ("[A]mong agreements which are equal in respect to the qualities mentioned, that should be given preference which is most specific and approaches most nearly to the subject at hand; for special provisions are ordinarily more effective than those that are general").

[15] U.N. International Law Commission, *Conclusions of the work of the Study Group on the Fragmentation of International Law: Difficulties arising from the Diversification and Expansion of International Law* 2(7) (2006) ("*Rationale of the principle.* That special law has priority over general law is justified by the fact that such special law, being more concrete, often takes better account of the particular features of the context in which it is to be applied than any applicable general law. Its application may also often create a more equitable result and it may often better reflect the intent of the legal subjects.").

[16] *Refer to* § 2.2.2 (Military Necessity and Law of War Rules).

[17] *Refer to* § 1.3.2.4 (Explicit Incorporation of Concepts From Other Bodies of Law Into the Law of War).

[18] *See* LIEBER CODE art. 40 ("There exists no law or body of authoritative rules of action between hostile armies, except that branch of the law of nature and nations which is called the law and usages of war on land."). *See also* WINTHROP, MILITARY LAW & PRECEDENTS 773-74 ("By the term LAW OF WAR is intended that branch of International Law which prescribes the rights and obligations of belligerents, or—more broadly—those principles and usages which, in time of war, define the status and relations not only of enemies—whether or not in arms—but also of persons under military government or martial law and persons simply resident or being upon the theatre of war, and which authorizes their trial and punishment when offenders. Unlike Military Law Proper, the Law of War *in this country* is not a formal written code, but consists mainly of general rules derived from International Law, supplemented by acts and orders of the military power and a few legislative provisions. In general it is quite independent of the ordinary law. 'On the actual theatre of military operations,' as is remarked by a learned judge, 'the ordinary laws of the land are superseded by the laws of war. The jurisdiction of the civil magistrate is there suspended, and military authority and force are substituted.' Finding indeed its original authority in the war powers of Congress and the Executive, and thus constitutional in its source, the Law of War may, in its exercise, substantially supersede for the time even the Constitution itself–as will be hereinafter indicated.").

[19] C. Wilfred Jenks, *The Conflict of Law-Making Treaties*, 30 BRITISH YEARBOOK OF INTERNATIONAL LAW 401, 446 (1953) ("A clear illustration of [the *lex specialis* principle's] applicability is afforded by instruments relating to the laws of war which, in the absence of evidence of a contrary intention or other special circumstances, must clearly be regarded as a *leges speciales* in relation to instruments laying down peace-time norms concerning the same subjects.").

conflicts between the law of war and other law may be resolved by construing such other law to avoid conflict with law of war rules.

Underlying this approach is the fact that the law of war is firmly established in customary international law as a well-developed body of law that is separate from the principles of law generally applicable in peace.[20] Lawmakers have been understood not to amend that well-developed body of law, absent affirmative evidence of an intention to do so.[21] In a similar fashion, for comparison, the GC deliberately excludes from its application the nationals of certain States in order to avoid creating complications or inconsistencies in procedures should both the GC and the law applicable to normal diplomatic representation apply.[22]

In some cases, treaties explicitly clarify that they do not affect States' rights under the law of war.[23] For example, the 1944 Chicago Convention on civil aviation explicitly provides that it does not affect the freedom of action of States during armed conflict.[24] However, even when not explicitly stated, infringements on the law of war through international agreements that primarily address situations other than armed conflict are not to be presumed.[25] For example, the

---

[20] Edwin D. Williamson, Agent of the United States of America, *Preliminary Objections Submitted by the United States of America*, Case Concerning the Aerial Incident of 3 July 1988, I.C.J. (Iran v. United States), 200-01 (Mar. 4, 1991) ("The laws of armed conflict are firmly established in customary international law as a well-developed body of law separate from the principles of law generally applicable in times of peace.").

[21] *See, e.g.*, Case Concerning Oil Platforms (Iran v. United States), Preliminary Objection, Judgment,1996 I.C.J. 874, 876 (Dissenting Opinion of Vice-President Schwebel) ("It is plain that this is a Treaty which is essentially concerned with encouraging mutually beneficial trade and investments and closer economic intercourse on the basis of reciprocal equality of treatment. There is no suggestion of regulating the use of armed force by one party against the other. ... None of these core provisions of the Treaty suggests that attacks by armed forces of one party against what it treats as military objectives within the jurisdiction of the other party are within the reach of the Treaty. It is significant as well that the Treaty contains none of the treaty provisions which typically do bear on the international use of force."); *Written Statement of the Government of the United States of America*, 34, Jun. 20, 1995, I.C.J., Request by the United Nations General Assembly for an Advisory Opinion on the Legality of the Threat or Use of Nuclear Weapons ("No international environmental instrument is expressly applicable in armed conflict. No such instrument expressly prohibits or regulates the use of nuclear weapons. Consequently, such an international environmental instrument could be applicable only by inference. Such an inference is not warranted because none of these instruments was negotiated with the intention that it would be applicable in armed conflict or to any use of nuclear weapons. Further, such an implication is not warranted by the textual interpretation of these instruments."); Edwin D. Williamson, Agent of the United States of America, *Preliminary Objections Submitted by the United States of America*, Case Concerning the Aerial Incident of 3 July 1988, I.C.J. (Iran v. United States), 207 (Mar. 4, 1991) ("When, 14 years later, the ICAO Assembly drafted Article 3 bis of the Chicago Convention, discussed above, it was careful to include in the Article a statement that it 'should not be interpreted as modifying in any way the rights and obligations of States set forth in the Charter of the United Nations;' which included the inherent right of self-defense. The participants at the Montreal conference would have included a similar provision if they had intended the Montreal Convention to modify the laws of armed conflict, and particularly if they had intended to address actions by military forces in armed conflict. There is no such provision in the Montreal Convention.").

[22] *Refer to* § 10.3.3.3 (Nationals of a Neutral State or Co-Belligerent State While Normal Diplomatic Representation Exists).

[23] *See, e.g.*, Convention on the Protection of Submarine Cables, art. 15, Mar. 14, 1884, 24 STAT. 989, 997 ("It is understood that the stipulations of this Convention shall in no wise affect the liberty of action of belligerents.").

[24] *Refer to* § 14.1.1.1 (1944 Chicago Convention and Freedom of Action of States During Armed Conflict).

[25] Edwin D. Williamson, Agent of the United States of America, *Preliminary Objections Submitted by the United States of America*, Case Concerning the Aerial Incident of 3 July 1988, I.C.J. (Iran v. United States), 203 (Mar. 4,

LOS Convention has been interpreted not to impair a State's rights during armed conflict, even though this principle is not explicitly stated in the treaty.[26] In addition, the International Convention for the Suppression of the Financing of Terrorism has been understood not to preclude any State Party to the Convention from conducting any legitimate activity against any lawful target in accordance with the law of armed conflict.[27]

In addition to treaties, domestic statutes have also been construed not to violate international law, including the law of war, if any other construction remains possible.[28] Certain domestic statutes have been interpreted not to apply to situations addressed by the law of war because such intention was not made clear and unequivocal.[29]

1991) ("Infringements on the laws of armed conflict through international agreements primarily addressing situations other than armed conflict are not to be presumed. There is no indication that the drafters of the Montreal Convention intended it to apply to military forces acting in armed conflict. If they had so intended, they would have had to address a myriad of issues relating to acts by military forces."); The S.S. Wimbledon, (United Kingdom, France, Japan v. Germany), Judgment (MM. Anzilotti and Huber, dissenting), 1923 P.C.I.J. (series A) 1, 35, 36 (¶3) ("In this respect, it must be remembered that international conventions and more particularly those relating to commerce and communications are generally concluded having regard to normal peace conditions. If, as the result of a war, a neutral or belligerent State is faced with the necessity of taking extraordinary measures temporarily affecting the application of such conventions in order to protect its neutrality or for the purposes of national defence, it is entitled to do so even if no express reservations are made in the convention. This right possessed by all nations, which is based on generally accepted usage, cannot lose its *raison d'être* simply because it may in some cases have been abused;").

[26] *Refer to* § 13.1.1 (The Law of the Sea During Armed Conflict).

[27] United States, *Statement on Ratification of International Convention for the Suppression of the Financing Terrorism*, Jun. 26, 2002, 2185 UNTS 611, 612 ("(1) Exclusion of legitimate activities against lawful targets. The United States of America understands that nothing in the Convention precludes any State Party to the Convention from conducting any legitimate activity against any lawful target in accordance with the law of armed conflict.").

[28] The Charming Betsy, 6 U.S. 64, 118 (1804) (Marshall, C.J.) ("It has also been observed that an act of Congress ought never to be construed to violate the law of nations if any other possible construction remains, and consequently can never be construed to violate neutral rights or to affect neutral commerce further than is warranted by the law of nations as understood in this country. These principles are believed to be correct, and they ought to be kept in view in construing the act now under consideration.").

[29] *See, e.g.*, Walter Dellinger, Assistant Attorney General, *United States Assistance to Countries that Shoot Down Civil Aircraft Involved in Drug Trafficking*, Jul. 14, 1994, 18 OPINIONS OF THE OFFICE OF LEGAL COUNSEL 148, 163-64 ("Specifically, we believe that the section would not apply to the actions of United States military forces acting on behalf of the United States during a state of hostilities. As discussed above, § 32(b)(2) was intended to implement the United States's obligations under the Montreal Convention. That Convention does not appear to apply to acts of armed forces that are otherwise governed by the laws of armed conflict. ... We do not think that § 32(b)(2) should be construed to have the surprising and almost certainly unintended effect of criminalizing actions by military personnel that are lawful under international law and the laws of armed conflict. We note specifically that the application of § 32(b)(2) to acts of United States military personnel in a state of hostilities could readily lead to absurdities: for example, it could mean in some circumstances that military personnel would not be able to engage in reasonable self-defense without subjecting themselves to the risk of criminal prosecution. Unless Congress by a clear and unequivocal statement declares otherwise, § 32(b)(2) should be construed to avoid such outcomes. Thus, we do not think the statute, as written, should apply to such incidents as the downing on July 3, 1988 of Iran Air Flight 655 by the United States Navy cruiser *Vincennes*."); France Biddle, Attorney General, *Procurements by Commanding Generals in Foreign Theaters of Operations*, Nov. 12, 1942, 40 OPINIONS OF THE ATTORNEY GENERAL 250, 253 (1949) ("The statutes in question do not expressly declare that their provisions are inapplicable to foreign theaters of operations. But there are conclusive reasons for inferring that the Congress did not intend them to apply to such theaters. The Supreme Court has long recognized that the power to conduct

1.3.2.3 *Using the Law of War to Determine the Content of General Standards if Applied to Armed Conflict*. Another way in which the law of war has been applied as *lex specialis* is to determine the content of a more general standard with respect to the situation of armed conflict. For example, the law of war has been used to inform the content of general authorizations to conduct military operations.[30]

As another example, to the extent that the concept of "due regard" for the safety of civil aircraft may be deemed to apply during armed conflict, what regard is due would be understood in terms of the requirements of the law of war.[31] Similarly, to the extent that the concept of "due regard" for the rights of other States under the law of the sea may be deemed to apply during armed conflict, what regard is due would be understood in terms of the requirements of the law of war.[32]

Lastly, even where international courts or commissions have characterized human rights obligations as applicable during armed conflict, they generally have characterized the content of those obligations as determined by standards and tests drawn from the law of war.[33]

1.3.2.4 *Explicit Incorporation of Concepts From Other Bodies of Law Into the Law of War*. In some cases, law of war treaties explicitly incorporate concepts from other bodies of law. For example, the peacetime property law concept of usufruct is made applicable to the duties of the Occupying States.[34] Similarly, the GC explicitly applies a peacetime rule with respect to the nationals of the Occupying Power who, before the outbreak of hostilities, have sought refuge in the occupied territory.[35] And as another example, Common Article 3 of the 1949 Geneva Conventions incorporates by reference those judicial guarantees that are

---

military campaigns includes power to procure needed supplies in theaters of operations by whatever methods are dictated by military necessity. Property may be taken summarily, even from a citizen, if military exigencies make its seizure reasonably appear to be necessary. It is unthinkable that the Congress attempted, by statutory restrictions, to abrogate this rule of military necessity, to handicap commanding generals waging war on foreign soil, to limit or encroach upon the power of the President as Commander in Chief to conduct, through his subordinates, military campaigns abroad.") (internal citations omitted).

[30] Hamdi v. Rumsfeld, 542 U.S. 507, 519 (2004) (plurality) ("In light of these principles, it is of no moment that the AUMF does not use specific language of detention. Because detention to prevent a combatant's return to the battlefield is a fundamental incident of waging war, in permitting the use of 'necessary and appropriate force,' Congress has clearly and unmistakably authorized detention in the narrow circumstances considered here."). *See also* In re Guantanamo Bay Litigation, *Respondents' Memorandum Regarding the Government's Detention Authority Relative to Detainees Held at Guantanamo Bay*, Misc. No. 08-442, 4 (D.D.C., Mar. 13, 2009) ("The United States bases its detention authority as to such persons on the Authorization for the Use of Military Force ('AUMF'), Pub. L. 107-40, 115 Stat. 224 (2001). The detention authority conferred by the AUMF is necessarily informed by principles of the laws of war.").

[31] *Refer to* § 14.1.1.4 (Due Regard for the Safety of Navigation of Civil Aircraft).

[32] *Refer to* § 13.1.1 (The Law of the Sea During Armed Conflict).

[33] *Refer to* § 1.6.3.1 (Relationship Between Human Rights Treaties and the Law of War).

[34] *Refer to* § 11.18.5.2 (Public Real (Immovable) Property That Is Essentially of a Non-Military Nature).

[35] *Refer to* § 11.11.7.2 (Protection of Nationals of the Occupying Power Who, Before the Outbreak of Hostilities, Have Sought Refuge in the Territory of the Occupied State).

recognized as indispensable by civilized peoples.[36]

1.3.3 Restrictive and Permissive Character of the Law of War. In certain respects, the law of war may be viewed as prohibitive; in other respects, the law of war may be viewed as permissive.[37]

1.3.3.1 *Law of War as Prohibitive Law*. The law of war that relates to the conduct of hostilities has generally been viewed as "prohibitive law," in the sense that it forbids rather than authorizes certain uses of force.[38] For example, the lawfulness of the use of a type of weapon does not depend on an absence of authorization, but, on the contrary, on whether the weapon is prohibited.[39]

One rationale for this view is that the rules binding upon States in treaties and customary law reflect restrictions that they have accepted, and that States are otherwise independent entities with freedom to act.[40] Thus, the authority to take actions under the law of war would be viewed as emanating from the State's rights as a sovereign entity rather than from any particular instrument of international law.

The prohibitive character of the law of war that relates to the conduct of hostilities is also consistent with the view that *jus in bello* applies to aggressors and defenders alike. The fact that an aggressor complies with *jus in bello* does not justify the legality of its military operations under *jus ad bellum*.[41]

The lack of an express prohibition in treaty law, however, does not necessarily mean that

---

[36] *Refer to* § 8.16 (Criminal Procedure and Punishment).

[37] VON GLAHN, THE OCCUPATION OF ENEMY TERRITORY 5 ("Throughout the pages of this study a basic fact will appear repeatedly: the laws of war, including the rules applicable to belligerent occupation, are in part permissive and in part prohibitive—a fact that has been overlooked frequently in treatments of the subject.").

[38] *See* Richard R. Baxter, *So-Called 'Unprivileged Belligerency': Spies, Guerillas, and Saboteurs*, 28 BRITISH YEAR BOOK OF INTERNATIONAL LAW 323, 324 (1951) ("The law of war is, in the descriptive words of a war crimes tribunal, 'prohibitive law' in the sense that it forbids rather than authorizes certain manifestations of force.") (quoting United States v. List, *et al.* (The Hostage Case), XI TRIALS OF WAR CRIMINALS BEFORE THE NMT 1252); Gherebi v. Obama, 609 F. Supp. 2d 43, 65 (D.D.C. 2009) (rejecting as "exactly backwards" the "notion that the Geneva Conventions must specifically enable its signatories to act in a specific manner for a signatory to have the authority necessary to take such action."); JOHN WESTLAKE, II INTERNATIONAL LAW 52 (1907) ("These rules are always restrictive, never permissive in any other sense than that of the absence of prohibition, for law can give no positive sanction to any act of force of which it cannot secure the employment on the side of justice alone, even if the particular act be not one which the law would prohibit both to the just and to the unjust if it could. Whenever therefore in speaking of the laws of war it is said that a belligerent may do this or that, it is always only the absence of prohibition that must be understood.").

[39] *Refer to* § 6.2.1 (Review of New Types of Weapons).

[40] The S.S. Lotus, (France v. Turkey) (Judgment), 1927 P.C.I.J. (series A) No. 10, at 18 ("International law governs relations between independent States. The rules of law binding upon States therefore emanate from their own free will as expressed in conventions or by usages generally accepted as expressing principles of law and established in order to regulate the relations between these co-existing independent communities or with a view to the achievement of common aims. Restrictions upon the independence of States cannot therefore be presumed.").

[41] *Refer to* § 3.5.2 (*Jus in Bello* and *Jus ad Bellum* Generally Operate Independently of One Another).

an action is lawful under *jus in bello*. When no specific rule applies, the principles of the law of war form the general guide for conduct during war.[42]

1.3.3.2 *Law of War as Permissive Law*. Although the law of war is generally viewed as "prohibitive law," in some respects, especially in the context of domestic law, the law of war may be viewed as permissive or even as a source of authority.[43]

For example, the principle of military necessity in the customary law of war may be viewed as justifying or permitting certain acts.[44] Similarly, under the law of belligerent occupation, the fact of occupation is the basis for the Occupying Power to exercise authority over the occupied territory.[45] In addition, law of war treaties also sometimes recognize States' authorities in war.[46]

1.3.4 Purposes of the Law of War. The main purposes of the law of war are:

- protecting combatants, noncombatants, and civilians from unnecessary suffering;[47]
- providing certain fundamental protections for persons who fall into the hands of the enemy, particularly prisoners of war, civilians, and military wounded, sick, and shipwrecked;[48]
- facilitating the restoration of peace;[49]
- assisting military commanders in ensuring the disciplined and efficient use of military

---

[42] *Refer to* § 2.1.2.2 (Law of War Principles as a General Guide).

[43] *See, e.g.*, Eric Holder, Attorney General, *Remarks at Northwestern University School of Law*, Mar. 5, 2012, 2012 DIGEST OF UNITED STATES PRACTICE IN INTERNATIONAL LAW 577, 581 ("It is preferable to capture suspected terrorists where feasible—among other reasons, so that we can gather valuable intelligence from them—but we must also recognize that there are instances where our government has the clear authority—and, I would argue, the responsibility—to defend the United States through the appropriate and lawful use of lethal force. This principle has long been established under both U.S. and international law. In response to the attacks perpetrated—and the continuing threat posed—by al Qaeda, the Taliban, and associated forces, Congress has authorized the President to use all necessary and appropriate force against those groups. Because the United States is in an armed conflict, we are authorized to take action against enemy belligerents under international law. The Constitution empowers the President to protect the nation from any imminent threat of violent attack. And international law recognizes the inherent right of national self-defense. None of this is changed by the fact that we are not in a conventional war.").

[44] *Refer to* § 2.2.1 (*Military Necessity* as a Justification).

[45] *Refer to* § 11.2.1 (Military Occupation as a Fact).

[46] *See, e.g.*, GPW art. 21 (recognizing that "[t]he Detaining Power may subject prisoners of war to internment."); HAGUE IV REG. art. 24 (recognizing that "[r]uses of war and the employment of measures necessary for obtaining information about the enemy and the country are considered permissible.").

[47] *Refer to* § 2.3 (Humanity).

[48] *Refer to* § 7.5 (Humane Treatment and Care of Enemy Military Wounded, Sick, and Shipwrecked in the Power of a Party to the Conflict); § 8.2 (Humane Treatment of Detainees); § 9.5 (Humane Treatment and Basic Protections for POWs); § 10.5 (Humane Treatment and Other Basic Protections for Protected Persons).

[49] *Refer to* § 12.1.2.2 (Non-Hostile Relations to Facilitate the Restoration of Peace).

force;[50] and

- preserving the professionalism and humanity of combatants.[51]

1.4 Object and Nature of War

Understanding the object and nature of war is important in understanding and applying the law of war.[52]

1.4.1 Object of War. The object of war has been understood to be the submission of the enemy as quickly and efficiently as possible.[53] The military defeat of the enemy in war is intended to advance political objectives.[54] Even where those political objectives are limited, the object of war is nonetheless to ensure the submission of the enemy as quickly and efficiently as possible.[55]

---

[50] *Refer to* § 18.2.1 (Reinforcing Military Effectiveness).

[51] *Refer to* § 2.6 (Honor).

[52] Department of the Army Pamphlet 27-161-2, *II International Law*, 1 (Oct. 23, 1962) ("An understanding of the laws of war necessitates an understanding of 'war' itself. It is the phenomenon of war which these laws are attempting in some manner to control."). *See also* Adam Roberts, *Land Warfare: From Hague to Nuremberg, in* Michael Howard, George J. Andreopoulous, & Mark A. Shulman, The Laws of War: Constraints on Warfare in The Western World 117 (1994) ("The laws of war are strange not only in their subject matter, which to many people seems a contradiction in terms, but also in their methodology. There is little tradition of disciplined and reasoned assessment of how the laws of war have operated in practice. Lawyers, academics, and diplomats have often been better at interpreting the precise legal meaning of existing accords, or at devising new law, than they have been at assessing the performance of existing accords or at generalizing about the circumstances in which they can or cannot work. In short, the study of law needs to be integrated with the study of history; if not, it is inadequate.").

[53] *See* 1940 Rules of Land Warfare ¶22 ("The object of war is to bring about the complete submission of the enemy as soon as possible by means of regulated violence."); 1914 Rules of Land Warfare ¶10 (same).

[54] George H. Aldrich, Deputy Legal Adviser, Department of State, *Human Rights in Armed Conflict: Development of the Law*, Apr. 13, 1973, 68 Department of State Bulletin, 876, 880 (Jun. 18, 1973) ("What we have seen is all too clearly a general acceptance of the view that modern war is aimed not merely at the enemy's military forces but at the enemy's willingness and ability to pursue its war aims. Thus, in the Second World War the enemy's will to fight and his capacity to produce weapons were primary targets; and saturation bombing, blockade of food supplies, and indiscriminate terror weapons such as the German V bombs, were all brought to bear on those targets. In Viet-Nam political, rather than military, objectives were even more dominant. Both sides had as their goal not the destruction of the other's military forces but the destruction of the will to continue the struggle."); United States v. von Leeb, *et al.* (The High Command Case), XI Trials of War Criminals Before the NMT 485 ("War is the exerting of violence by one state or politically organized body against another. In other words, it is the implementation of a political policy by means of violence."); Carl von Clausewitz, On War 87 (1989) ("We see, therefore, that war is not merely an act of policy but a true political instrument, a continuation of political intercourse, carried on with other means. What remains peculiar to war is simply the peculiar nature of its means. War in general, and the commander in any specific instance, is entitled to require that the trend and designs of policy shall not be inconsistent with these means. That, of course, is no small demand; but however much it may affect political aims in a given case, it will never do more than modify them. The political object is the goal, war is the means of reaching it, and means can never be considered in isolation from their purpose.").

[55] *For example*, General Colin L. Powell, Chairman of the Joint Chiefs of Staff, *U.S. Forces: Challenges Ahead*, 71 Foreign Affairs 32, 37 (1992) (explaining that despite the limited political objectives of the 1991 Gulf War, the United States "did use overwhelming force quickly and decisively.").

The object of war informs the principle of *military necessity* and what uses of force may be justified in war.[56] Nevertheless, the law of war limits what uses of force the object of war may justify.[57]

1.4.2 Nature of War.

1.4.2.1 *Nature of War – Violence and Suffering*. War has been described as a violent clash of interests characterized by the use of force.[58] The fact that violence is an essential element of war has been viewed as important in understanding the nature of war.[59] The violent nature of war has also meant that suffering has been an unfortunate and tragic, but unavoidable consequence of war.[60]

Law of war treaties such as the Hague and Geneva Conventions have been negotiated with the understanding that suffering and destruction are unavoidably part of war.[61] But these

---

[56] *Refer to* § 2.2.1 (*Military Necessity* as a Justification); § 2.2.3.1 (Consideration of the Broader Imperatives of Winning the War).

[57] *Refer to* § 2.2.2 (*Military Necessity* and Law of War Rules).

[58] DEPARTMENT OF THE ARMY FIELD MANUAL 3-24, *Counterinsurgency*, 1-1 (¶1-1) (Dec. 2006) ("Insurgency and counterinsurgency (COIN) are complex subsets of warfare. Globalization, technological advancement, urbanization, and extremists who conduct suicide attacks for their cause have certainly influenced contemporary conflict; however, warfare in the 21st century retains many of the characteristics it has exhibited since ancient times. Warfare remains a violent clash of interests between organized groups characterized by the use of force. Achieving victory still depends on a group's ability to mobilize support for its political interests (often religiously or ethnically based) and to generate enough violence to achieve political consequences. Means to achieve these goals are not limited to conventional forces employed by nation-states."); MARINE CORPS DOCTRINAL PUBLICATION 1, *Warfighting*, 3 (Jun. 20, 1997) (explaining that war is "a violent clash of interests between or among organized groups characterized by the use of military force.").

[59] MARINE CORPS DOCTRINAL PUBLICATION 1, *Warfighting*, 14 (Jun. 20, 1997) ("War is among the greatest horrors known to humanity; it should never be romanticized. The means of war is force, applied in the form of organized violence. It is through the use of violence, or a credible threat of violence, that we compel our enemy to do our will. Violence is an essential element of war, and its immediate result is bloodshed, destruction, and suffering. While the magnitude of violence may vary with the object and means of war, the violent essence of war will never change. Any study of war that neglects this basic truth is misleading and incomplete.").

[60] *For example*, Friedrich II, Letter to Lord Marischal, Nov. 23, 1758 *reprinted in* THOMAS CARLYLE, V HISTORY OF FRIEDERICH II OF PRUSSIA: CALLED FREDERICK THE GREAT 386 (1865) ("Our Campaign is over; and there has nothing come of it on one side or the other, but the loss of a great many worthy people, the misery of a great many poor soldiers crippled forever, the ruin of some Provinces, the ravage, pillage and conflagration of some flourishing Towns. Exploits these, which make humanity shudder: … .").

[61] Edward R. Cummings, Acting Assistant Legal Adviser for Politico-Military Affairs, *Remarks at Symposium at Brooklyn Law School*, Sept. 25, 1982, III CUMULATIVE DIGEST OF UNITED STATES PRACTICE IN INTERNATIONAL LAW 1981-88 3421, 3422 ("The Conventions referred to today, such as the Hague and Geneva Conventions, are important ones and are strongly supported by the United States. They have helped reduce the suffering caused by wars. But one should not ask the impossible of these agreements. They were not intended to make war 'humane' or to ban war, or to make wars more difficult to fight. They were modestly intended to reduce the inhumanity and barbarity of war when militarily possible. Anyone who has read the negotiating records of these old agreements will note that they were largely negotiated by the military. In fact, the first agreement of this kind, the St. Petersburg Declaration, was agreed to by a military commission. Unrealistic provisions which just would not be accepted or respected in battle were not favored.").

treaties and the principle of humanity seek to reduce unnecessary suffering and destruction.[62]

1.4.2.2 _Nature of War – Limited and Unreliable Information – "Fog of War"_. During war, information is often limited and unreliable.[63] The uncertainty of information in war results from the chaotic nature of combat and from the opposing sides' efforts to deceive one another, which generally is not prohibited by the law of war.[64]

The limited and unreliable nature of information available during war has influenced the development of the law of war. For example, it affects how the principle of military necessity is applied.[65] The limited and unreliable nature of information available during war also is recognized in the law of war's standards for how persons are to assess information.[66]

1.5 "WAR" AS A LEGAL CONCEPT

"War" is sometimes used as a legal concept, *i.e.*, the application or operation of a legal rule may depend on the existence of a "war," "armed conflict," or "hostilities." As a legal concept, "war" has traditionally been viewed as a condition in which a State is prosecuting its rights by military force, usually against another State. However, the precise definition of "war" often depends on the specific legal context in which it is used.

1.5.1 Traditional Conception of War Under International Law. As international law began to regulate "war," "hostilities," and "armed conflict," it became necessary to determine what "war" is for the purpose of triggering those legal obligations.[67]

As a legal concept, war has usually been described as a condition or state that applies more broadly than only the mere employment of force or the mere commission of acts of

[62] *Refer to* § 2.3 (Humanity).

[63] *See, e.g.*, United States v. List, *et al.* (The Hostage Case), XI TRIALS OF WAR CRIMINALS BEFORE THE NMT 1297 ("The course of a military operation by the enemy is loaded with uncertainties, such as the numerical strength of the enemy, the quality of his equipment, his fighting spirit, the efficiency and daring of his commanders, and the uncertainty of his intentions."); CARL VON CLAUSEWITZ, ON WAR 140 (1989) ("the general unreliability of all information presents a special problem in war: all action takes place so to speak, in a kind of twilight, which like fog or moonlight, often tends to make things grotesque and larger than they really are.").

[64] *Refer to* § 5.25 (Ruses of War and Other Lawful Deceptions).

[65] *Refer to* § 2.2.3 (Applying Military Necessity).

[66] *Refer to* § 5.3 (Assessing Information Under the Law of War).

[67] *See, e.g.*, Arnold D. McNair, *The Legal Meaning of War, and the Relation of War to Reprisals*, 11 TRANSACTIONS OF THE GROTIUS SOCIETY 29, 30 (1925) ("There exist many treaties and other international conventions under which important obligations arise upon the occurrence of a state of 'war,' and as regards which, therefore, either because the term 'war' or some other term connoting war, such as 'neutrality,' is used, it becomes essential to know whether or not a state of war exists at a given point of time. Thus most of the Hague Conventions only come into operation once a state of war has arisen—for instance, those relating to the Laws and Customs of War on Land, to the Rights and Duties of Neutrals in Land and Maritime War respectively, to the Bombardment of Ports, Towns and Villages by Naval Forces, and to the Status of Enemy Merchant Ships at the Outbreak of Hostilities.").

violence.[68]

When treated as a legal concept, "war" has been associated with a State's use of force to vindicate its rights (principally, its inherent right of self-defense) under international law.[69]

Traditionally, war has often been described as a legal condition between two or more States.[70] However, certain law of war rules apply to non-international armed conflicts (such as intrastate conflicts or conflicts between a State and a non-State armed group).[71]

1.5.2 Different Definitions of "War" for Different Legal Purposes. There is no single legal definition of "war," "hostilities," or "armed conflict," and the definition of these terms has varied in both domestic and international law.

In domestic law, "war," "hostilities," and "armed conflict" have been interpreted differently depending on the specific legal context at issue.[72] For example, under the

---

[68] 1956 FM 27-10 (Change No. 1 1976) ¶8 ("While it is usually accompanied by the commission of acts of violence, a state of war may exist prior to or subsequent to the use of force."); VII MOORE'S DIGEST 153 ("Much confusion may be avoided by bearing in mind the fact that by the term war is meant not the mere employment of force, but the existence of the legal condition of things in which rights are or may be prosecuted by force."); GROTIUS, LAW OF WAR & PEACE 33 (1.1.2.1) ("war is the condition of those contending by force").

[69] SPAIGHT, AIR POWER AND WAR RIGHTS 2 ("War, after all, is only a means to an end. It is a way of settling an international difference which diplomacy has failed to adjust and which is not susceptible of treatment by the other means of pacific settlement, such as inquiry commissions, arbitration, or submission to the Permanent Court of The Hague. When all else fails, there is no way in which a nation can assert its rights save by going to war. War is the means by which it vindicates a vital right threatened or infringed by the claim or act of another State. Its object is to cause the other State to desist from the action or abandon the claim which is the cause of offence. In other words, a war is fought in order to bring about a change of mind in another State."); The Prize Cases, 67 U.S. 635, 666 (1863) ("War has been well defined to be, 'That state in which a nation prosecutes its right by force.'") (quoting EMERICH DE VATTEL, DROIT DE GENS (LAW OF NATIONS) (1760)); LIEBER CODE art. 30 ("Ever since the formation and coexistence of modern nations, and ever since wars have become great national wars, war has come to be acknowledged not to be its own end, but the means to obtain great ends of state, or to consist in defense against wrong; and no conventional restriction of the modes adopted to injure the enemy is any longer admitted; but the law of war imposes many limitations and restrictions on principles of justice, faith, and honor.").

[70] 1956 FM 27-10 (Change No. 1 1976) ¶8a ("War may be defined as a legal condition of armed hostility between States. While it is usually accompanied by the commission of acts of violence, a state of war may exist prior to or subsequent to the use of force. The outbreak of war is usually accompanied by a declaration of war (see par. 20). Instances of armed conflict without declaration of war may include, but are not necessarily limited to, the exercise of armed force pursuant to a recommendation, decision, or call by the United Nations, in the exercise of the inherent right of individual or collective self-defense against armed attack, or in the performance of enforcement measures through a regional arrangement, or otherwise, in conformity with appropriate provisions of the United Nations Charter."); LAUTERPACHT, II OPPENHEIM'S INTERNATIONAL LAW 202 (§54) ("War is a contention between two or more States through their armed forces, for the purpose of overpowering each other and imposing such conditions of peace as the victor pleases."); LIEBER CODE art. 20 ("Public war is a state of armed hostility between sovereign nations or governments. It is a law and requisite of civilized existence that men live in political, continuous societies, forming organized units, called states or nations, whose constituents bear, enjoy, and suffer, advance and retrograde together, in peace and in war.").

[71] *Refer to* § 3.3.1 (International Armed Conflict and Non-International Armed Conflict).

[72] *See, e.g.*, Fred K. Green, *The Concept of "War" and the Concept of "Combatant" in Modern Conflicts*, 10 MILITARY LAW AND LAW OF WAR REVIEW 267, 269 (1971) ("[I]n US municipal law, the existence of "war" and its beginning and termination is a question of objective fact determined for different purposes by different agencies of

Constitution, Congress has the power to "declare war."[73] Thus, "war" might be interpreted to determine whether a military operation constitutes "war" in this sense.[74] Similarly, the War Powers Resolution states certain requirements that are triggered when U.S. forces are introduced into "hostilities."[75] Other statutes may require a determination that conduct has occurred "[w]hen the United States is at war" or during "time of war."[76]

Under international law, "war," "hostilities," and "armed conflict" may also be interpreted with different purposes in mind.[77] A state of "war" can affect what duties States that are not participating in the conflict have under the law of neutrality.[78] A state of "war" can affect whether peacetime treaties between two States continue to apply. Most importantly for the purposes of this manual, the terms "war" and "armed conflict" are used to describe when *jus in bello* rules apply.[79]

1.6 Law of War Distinguished From Certain Topics

The law of war may be distinguished from the following topics: (1) operational law; (2) arms control; (3) human rights treaties; (4) the Just War Tradition; (5) rules of engagement; and (6) the Code of Conduct for U.S. Armed Forces.

---

the sovereign. There has been no apparent effort to coordinate federal law so as to permit establishment of fixed criteria that would be identified and applicable for all purposes. The tremendous variations in result that this situation produces renders meaningless any attempt to generalize with respect to established criteria.").

[73] U.S. Constitution art. I, § 8.

[74] Caroline D. Krass, Principal Deputy Assistant Attorney General, *Authority to use Military Force in Libya*, 8 (Apr. 1, 2011) ("[T]he historical practice of presidential military action without congressional approval precludes any suggestion that Congress's authority to declare war covers every military engagement, however limited, that the President initiates. In our view, determining whether a particular planned engagement constitutes a 'war' for constitutional purposes instead requires a fact-specific assessment of the 'anticipated nature, scope, and duration' of the planned military operations. *Haiti Deployment*, 18 Op. O.L.C. at 179.").

[75] *See* 50 U.S.C. § 1543(a)(1) ("In the absence of a declaration of war, in any case in which United States Armed Forces are introduced— (1) into hostilities or into situations where imminent involvement in hostilities is clearly indicated by the circumstances; … the President shall submit within 48 hours to the Speaker of the House of Representatives and to the President pro tempore of the Senate a report, in writing, setting forth … .").

[76] *See, e.g.*, 10 U.S.C. § 843(f) ("When the United States is at war, the running of any statute of limitations applicable to [certain offenses]… is suspended until three years after the termination of hostilities as proclaimed by the President or by a joint resolution of Congress."); 10 U.S.C. § 906 ("Any person who in time of war is found lurking as a spy or acting as a spy in or about any place, vessel, or aircraft, within the control or jurisdiction of any of the armed forces, or in or about any shipyard, any manufacturing or industrial plant, or any other place or institution engaged in work in aid of the prosecution of the war by the United States, or elsewhere, shall be tried by a general court-martial or by a military commission and on conviction shall be punished by death. This section does not apply to a military commission established under chapter 47A of this title.").

[77] Julius Stone, Legal Controls of International Conflict 312 (1954) ("[T]he question 'War or No War?' may have to be answered differently according to the purposes for which an answer is sought. One answer, for example, may be indicated for the purposes of the rules for the mitigation of suffering; another for those governing war supplies to belligerents from neutral governments, or governing blockade or contraband.").

[78] *Refer to* § 15.2.1 (Armed Conflict and the Application of the Law of Neutrality).

[79] *Refer to* § 3.4 (When *Jus in Bello* Rules Apply).

1.6.1 Operational Law. The law of war is an important part of, but not the entirety of, operational law. Operational law consists of that body of domestic, foreign, and international law that specifically pertains to the activities of military forces across the entire conflict spectrum. Operational law includes diverse legal disciplines, such as military justice, administrative and civil law, legal assistance, claims, procurement law, national security law, fiscal law, and the law of war.[80]

1.6.2 Arms Control. Arms control is a broad term that includes a variety of efforts to reduce the numbers, types, performance characteristics, proliferation, testing, or other aspects of certain categories of weapons. Arms control usually proceeds through bilateral or multilateral treaties. Arms control can also include non-binding political commitments, as well as reciprocal unilateral statements of intention or policy. The overall goals of arms control are to reduce: (1) the likelihood of war; (2) the consequences of war, should it occur; and (3) the costs of preparing for war.

Arms control is closely related to other concepts. For example, "non-proliferation" refers specifically to efforts to restrict the spread of weapons (in particular, weapons of mass destruction). "Disarmament" refers to efforts to eliminate entirely, rather than to restrict, a particular category of weapon. And sometimes States accept "confidence-building measures" (or confidence, security, and transparency-building measures) that do not directly reduce the quantity or quality of armaments, but rather increase States' certainty that ambiguous activities by other States are not secret actions in violation of arms control obligations.

Arms control and the law of war frequently overlap in treaties. For example, the CCW Protocol IV on Blinding Laser Weapons has both arms control and law of war provisions.[81] Similarly, the Chemical Weapons Convention prohibits, *inter alia*, the development and stockpiling of chemical weapons, but it is also directly relevant to the law of war because it prohibits the use of chemical weapons in all circumstances.[82]

1.6.3 Human Rights Treaties.[83] Human rights treaties address primarily the obligations

---

[80] THE JUDGE ADVOCATE GENERAL'S SCHOOL, U.S. ARMY, OPERATIONAL LAW HANDBOOK JA 422 1-1 (1997) ("[Operational law is] [t]hat body of domestic, foreign, and international law that impacts specifically upon the activities of U.S. Forces across the entire operational spectrum. Operational law is the essence of the military legal practice. It is a collection of diverse legal and military skills, focused on military operations. It includes military justice, administrative and civil law, legal assistance, claims, procurement law, environmental law, national security law, fiscal law, international law, host nations law, and the law of war. In short, operational law is a unique blend of every source of law that has application within the operational context. ... Because the definition of operational law is so broad, ample statutory and regulatory references serve to establish the substance of the practice.").

[81] *Refer to* § 19.21.5 (CCW Protocol IV on Blinding Laser Weapons).

[82] *Refer to* § 6.8.3.2 (Prohibitions With Respect to Chemical Weapons).

[83] This section focuses on human rights treaties and not other sources of international human rights law. *See, e.g.*, Catherine Amirfar, Counselor for International Law, Department of State, *Statement at 53rd Session of the U.N. Committee Against Torture, Nov. 3 – 28, 2014*, Nov. 12, 2014 ("For example, the prohibition against torture is customary international law binding on all nations everywhere, at all times."); U.N. International Law Commission, *State responsibility: Comments and observations received from Governments*, U.N. Doc. A/CN.4/488, 133 (Mar. 25, 1998) ("**United States of America** Subparagraph (e) [which would reflect a prohibition against conduct by way of countermeasures in contravention of a peremptory norm of general international law] similarly does not provide useful guidance in determining whether a countermeasure would be permissible. Just as there is little agreement

of governments with respect to the rights of individuals, including their own nationals.[84] For example, governments must refrain from subjecting individuals to arbitrary detention, to arbitrary deprivation of life, or to cruel, inhuman, or degrading treatment or punishment.[85]

As a general matter, human rights treaties have been described as primarily applicable to the relationship between a State and individuals in peacetime.[86] Some human rights treaties also provide for derogation from certain provisions in emergency situations.[87]

Law of war treaties have been described as chiefly concerned with the conditions particular to armed conflict and the relationship between a State and nationals of the enemy State.[88] Law of war treaties generally do not provide for derogation because necessity is not a

---

with respect to 'basic' human rights and political and economic 'coercion', the content of peremptory norms is difficult to determine outside the areas of genocide, slavery and torture.").

[84] *See, e.g.*, Jimmy Carter, *United Nations Remarks on Signing International Covenants on Human Rights*, 1977-II PUBLIC PAPERS OF THE PRESIDENTS 1734 ("The Covenant on Civil and Political Rights concerns what governments must not do to their people, and the Covenant on Economic, Social and Cultural Rights concerns what governments must do for their people. By ratifying the Covenant on Civil and Political Rights, a government pledges, as a matter of law, to refrain from subjecting its own people to arbitrary imprisonment or execution or to cruel or degrading treatment. It recognizes the right of every person to freedom of thought, freedom of conscience, freedom of religion, freedom of opinion, freedom of expression, freedom of association, and the rights of peaceful assembly, and the right to emigrate from that country.").

[85] International Covenant on Civil and Political Rights, art. 9(1), Dec. 19, 1966, 999 UNTS 171, 175 ("Everyone has the right to liberty and security of person. No one shall be subjected to arbitrary arrest or detention. No one shall be deprived of his liberty except on such grounds and in accordance with such procedure as are established by law."); International Covenant on Civil and Political Rights, art. 6(1), Dec. 19, 1966, 999 UNTS 171, 174 ("Every human being has the inherent right to life. This right shall be protected by law. No one shall be arbitrarily deprived of his life."); International Covenant on Civil and Political Rights, art. 7, Dec. 19, 1966, 999 UNTS 171, 175 ("No one shall be subjected to torture or to cruel, inhuman or degrading treatment or punishment. In particular, no one shall be subjected without his free consent to medical or scientific experimentation.").

[86] *See, e.g.*, JEAN PICTET, HUMANITARIAN LAW AND THE PROTECTION OF WAR VICTIMS 15 (1975) ("Admittedly, human rights embody more general principles while the law of armed conflicts is of a specific and exceptional nature, coming as it does into operation at the very time when the exercise of human rights is prevented or restricted by war. But the two legal systems are fundamentally different, for humanitarian law is valid only in the case of an armed conflict while human rights are essentially applicable in peacetime, and contain derogation clauses in case of conflict. Moreover, human rights govern relations between the State and its own nationals, the law of war those between the State and enemy nationals.").

[87] *See, e.g.*, International Covenant on Civil and Political Rights, art. 4(1), Dec. 19, 1966, 999 UNTS 171, 174 ("In time of public emergency which threatens the life of the nation and the existence of which is officially proclaimed, the States Parties to the present Covenant may take measures derogating from their obligations under the present Covenant to the extent strictly required by the exigencies of the situation, provided that such measures are not inconsistent with their other obligations under international law and do not involve discrimination solely on the ground of race, colour, sex, language, religion or social origin.").

[88] Christopher Greenwood, *Historical Development and Legal Basis*, *in* DIETER FLECK, THE HANDBOOK OF HUMANITARIAN LAW IN ARMED CONFLICTS 9 (¶102) (1999) ("Human rights law is designed to operate primarily in normal peacetime conditions, and within the framework of the legal relationship between a state and its citizens. International humanitarian law, by contrast, is chiefly concerned with the abnormal conditions of armed conflict and the relationship between a state and the citizens of its adversary, a relationship otherwise based upon power rather than law.").

basis for derogating from law of war rules.[89]

1.6.3.1 Relationship Between Human Rights Treaties and the Law of War. In some circumstances, the rules in the law of war and the rules in human rights treaties may appear to conflict; these apparent conflicts may be resolved by the principle that the law of war is the *lex specialis* during situations of armed conflict, and, as such, is the controlling body of law with regard to the conduct of hostilities and the protection of war victims.[90]

For example, the right to challenge the lawfulness of an arrest before a court provided in Article 9 of the International Covenant on Civil and Political Rights (ICCPR) would appear to conflict with the authority under the law of war to detain certain persons without judicial process or criminal charge.[91] However, the United States has understood Article 9 of the ICCPR not to affect a State's authorities under the law of war, including a State's authority in both international and non-international armed conflicts to detain enemy combatants until the end of hostilities.[92] Some international courts or commissions have interpreted the rights conveyed by human rights treaties in light of the rules of the law of war, as the applicable *lex specialis,* when assessing situations in armed conflict.[93]

---

[89] *Refer to* § 2.2.2 (*Military Necessity* and Law of War Rules).

[90] *Refer to* § 1.3.2 (The Law of War's Relationship to Other Bodies of Law).

[91] International Covenant on Civil and Political Rights, art. 9(4), Dec. 19, 1966, 999 UNTS 171, 176 ("Anyone who is deprived of his liberty by arrest or detention shall be entitled to take proceedings before a court, in order that that court may decide without delay on the lawfulness of his detention and order his release if the detention is not lawful.").

[92] *Observations of the United States of America on the Human Rights Committee's Draft General Comment 35: Article 9*, ¶22, Jun. 10, 2014 ("Given that international humanitarian law is the controlling body of law in armed conflict with regard to the conduct of hostilities and the protection of war victims, the United States does not interpret references to 'detainees' and 'detention' in several paragraphs to refer to government action in the context of and associated with an armed conflict. For example, paragraph 15 incorrectly implies that the detention of enemy combatants in the context of a non-international armed conflict 'would normally amount to arbitrary detention as other effective measures addressing the threat, including the criminal justice system, would be available.' On the contrary, in both international and non-international armed conflicts, a State may detain enemy combatants consistent with the law of armed conflict until the end of hostilities. Similarly, to the extent paragraphs 15 and 66 are intended to address law-of-war detention in situations of armed conflict, it would be incorrect to state that there is a 'right to take proceedings before a court to enable the court to decide without delay on the lawfulness of detention' in all cases. In addition, to the extent the discussion of an individual right to compensation under Article 9 in paragraphs 49-52 is intended to extend to individuals detained in the context of an armed conflict, as a matter of international law, the rules governing available remedies for unlawful detention in the context of an armed conflict would be drawn from international humanitarian law.").

[93] Coard, *et al.* v. United States, Inter-American Commission on Human Rights, Organization of American States, Case 10.951, Report 109/99, ¶42 (Sept. 29, 1999) ("[I]n a situation of armed conflict, the test for assessing the observance of a particular right, such as the right to liberty, may, under given circumstances, be distinct from that applicable in a time of peace. For that reason, the standard to be applied must be deduced by reference to the applicable *lex specialis*."); Juan Carlos Abella v. Argentina, Inter-American Commission on Human Rights, Organization of American States, Case 11.137, OEA/Ser.L/V/II.98, ¶161 (Nov. 18, 1997) ("[T]he Commission must necessarily look to and apply definitional standards and relevant rules of humanitarian law as sources of authoritative guidance in its resolution of this and other kinds of claims alleging violations of the American Convention in combat situations."); Legality of the Threat or Use of Nuclear Weapons, Advisory Opinion, 1996 I.C.J. 226, 240 (¶25) ("In principle, the right not arbitrarily to be deprived of one's life applies also in hostilities.

On the other hand, during armed conflict, human rights treaties would clearly be controlling with respect to matters that are within their scope of application and that are not addressed by the law of war. For example, a time of war does not suspend the operation of the ICCPR with respect to matters within its scope of application. Therefore, as an illustration, participation in a war would in no way excuse a State Party to the ICCPR from respecting and ensuring the right and opportunity of every citizen to vote and to be elected at genuine periodic elections.[94]

1.6.3.2 *Different Views on the Applicability of Human Rights Treaties*. In conducting operations with coalition partners, it may be important to consider that some States may have different perspectives on the applicability of human rights treaties. Such differences may result from different legal interpretations or from the fact that the other State is a Party to different human rights treaties than the United States. For example, the European Court of Human Rights – as well as some European States – have construed certain obligations under the European Convention on Human Rights (ECHR) as applicable to their military forces abroad during occupation.[95]

1.6.3.3 *International Covenant on Civil and Political Rights (ICCPR)*. The United States is a Party to the International Covenant on Civil and Political Rights (ICCPR).

The ICCPR creates obligations for a State with respect to persons within its territory and subject to its jurisdiction.[96] The United States has long interpreted the ICCPR not to apply abroad.[97] The inclusion of the reference to "within its territory" in Article 2(1) of the ICCPR

The test of what is an arbitrary deprivation of life, however, then falls to be determined by the applicable *lex specialis*, namely, the law applicable to armed conflict which is designed to regulate the conduct of hostilities.").

94 *Fourth Periodic Report of the United States of America to the United Nations Committee on Human Rights Concerning the International Covenant on Civil and Political Rights*, Dec. 30, 2011, ¶506 ("With respect to the application of the Covenant and the international law of armed conflict (also referred to as international humanitarian law or 'IHL'), the United States has not taken the position that the Covenant does not apply 'in time of war.' Indeed, a time of war does not suspend the operation of the Covenant to matters within its scope of application. To cite but two obvious examples from among many, a State Party's participation in a war would in no way excuse it from respecting and ensuring rights to have or adopt a religion or belief of one's choice or the right and opportunity of every citizen to vote and to be elected at genuine periodic elections.").

95 Case of Al-Skeini and Others v. The United Kingdom, ECtHR, 55721/07, ¶149 (Jul. 7, 2011) ("It can be seen, therefore, that following the removal from power of the Ba'ath regime and until the accession of the Interim Government, the United Kingdom (together with the United States) assumed in Iraq the exercise of some of the public powers normally to be exercised by a sovereign government. In particular the United Kingdom assumed authority and responsibility for the maintenance of security in South East Iraq. In these exceptional circumstances the Court considers that the United Kingdom, through its soldiers engaged in security operations in Basrah during the period in question, exercised authority and control over individuals killed in the course of such security operations so as to establish a jurisdictional link between the deceased and the United Kingdom for the purposes of Article 1 of the (ECHR).").

96 International Covenant on Civil and Political Rights, art. 2(1), Dec. 19, 1966, 999 UNTS 171, 173 ("Each State Party to the present Covenant undertakes to respect and to ensure to all individuals within its territory and subject to its jurisdiction the rights recognized in the present Covenant, without distinction of any kind, such as race, colour, sex, language, religion, political or other opinion, national or social origin, property, birth or other status.").

97 *See, e.g.*, U.N. Human Rights Committee, Summary Record of the 1405th Meeting, U.N. Doc. CCPR/C/SR.1405 6-7 (¶20) (Apr. 24, 1995) ("Klein had asked whether the United States took the view that the Covenant did not apply

was adopted as a result of a proposal made by U.S. delegate Eleanor Roosevelt – specifically to ensure that a State Party's obligations would not apply to persons outside its territories, such as in occupied territory and leased territory.[98]

1.6.3.4 Convention Against Torture. The United States is a Party to the Convention Against Torture and Other Cruel, Inhuman or Degrading Treatment or Punishment.[99]

The Convention against Torture was not intended to supersede the prohibitions against torture already contained in customary international law and the 1949 Geneva Conventions or its Additional Protocols.[100] The law of war is the controlling body of law with respect to the conduct of hostilities and the protection of war victims. Nevertheless, a time of war does not suspend operation of the Convention Against Torture. The Convention Against Torture continues to apply even when a State is engaged in armed conflict.[101] For example, a state of war could not justify a State's torture of individuals during armed conflict.[102]

In addition, where the text of the Convention Against Torture provides that obligations apply to a State Party in "any territory under its jurisdiction," such obligations, including the obligations in Articles 2 and 16 to prevent torture and cruel, inhuman, or degrading treatment or punishment, extend to certain areas beyond the sovereign territory of the State Party, and more specifically to "all places that the State Party controls as a governmental authority."[103]

---

to government actions outside the United States. The Covenant was not regarded as having extraterritorial application. In general, where the scope of application of a treaty was not specified, it was presumed to apply only within a party's territory. Article 2 of the Covenant expressly stated that each State party undertook to respect and ensure the rights recognized 'to all individuals within its territory and subject to its jurisdiction'. That dual requirement restricted the scope of the Covenant to persons under United States jurisdiction and within United States territory. During the negotiating history, the words 'within its territory' had been debated and were added by vote, with the clear understanding that such wording would limit the obligations to within a Party's territory.").

[98] *Refer to* § 11.1.2.6 (Occupation and the ICCPR and Other Human Rights Treaties).

[99] Convention against Torture and Other Cruel, Inhuman or Degrading Treatment or Punishment, Dec. 10, 1984, 1465 UNTS 85.

[100] *Refer to* § 8.2.1 (Protection Against Violence, Torture, and Cruel Treatment).

[101] Mary McLeod, Acting Legal Adviser, Department of State, *Opening Statement at 53rd Session of the U.N. Committee Against Torture, Nov. 3 – 28, 2014*, Nov. 12, 2014 ("Although the law of armed conflict is the controlling body of law with respect to the conduct of hostilities and the protection of war victims, a time of war does not suspend operation of the Convention Against Torture, which continues to apply even when a State is engaged in armed conflict. The obligations to prevent torture and cruel, inhuman, and degrading treatment and punishment in the Convention remain applicable in times of armed conflict and are reinforced by complementary prohibitions in the law of armed conflict.").

[102] Convention against Torture and Other Cruel, Inhuman or Degrading Treatment or Punishment, art. 2(2), Dec. 10, 1984, 1465 UNTS 85, 114 ("No exceptional circumstances whatsoever, whether a state of war or a threat of war, internal political instability or any other public emergency, may be invoked as a justification of torture.").

[103] Mary McLeod, Acting Legal Adviser, Department of State, *Opening Statement at 53rd Session of the U.N. Committee Against Torture, Nov. 3 – 28, 2014*, Nov. 12, 2014 ("In brief, we understand that where the text of the Convention provides that obligations apply to a State Party in 'any territory under its jurisdiction,' such obligations, including the obligations in Articles 2 and 16 to prevent torture and cruel, inhuman or degrading treatment or punishment, extend to certain areas beyond the sovereign territory of the State Party, and more specifically to 'all places that the State Party controls as a governmental authority.' We have determined that the United States

1.6.4 Just War Tradition. The Just War Tradition describes customs, ethical codes, and moral teachings associated with warfare that military thinkers and philosophers have developed over centuries to seek the moral justification of and the limitations to war.[104]

The Just War Tradition provides part of the philosophical foundation for the modern law of war and has considered both *jus ad bellum* and *jus in bello*. The Just War Tradition developed criteria or principles that have provided the foundation for modern *jus ad bellum* rules.[105] Similarly, law of war treaties that provide *jus in bello* rules, such as the 1949 Geneva Conventions, are also rooted in the Just War Tradition. The Just War Tradition remains relevant for decisions to employ U.S. military forces and in warfighting.[106]

1.6.5 Rules of Engagement (ROE). *Rules of engagement* (ROE) have been defined as "[d]irectives issued by competent military authority that delineate the circumstances and limitations under which United States forces will initiate and/or continue combat engagement with other forces encountered."[107] ROE are used by States to tailor the rules for the use of force to the circumstances of a particular operation.[108]

---

currently exercises such control at the U.S. Naval Station at Guantanamo Bay, Cuba, and with respect to U.S. registered ships and aircraft.").

[104] WILLIAM O'BRIEN, THE CONDUCT OF JUST AND LIMITED WAR 4 (1981) ("The just-war tradition begins with the efforts of St. Augustine to justify Christian participation in Roman wars. From this foundation, St. Thomas Aquinas and other Scholastic thinkers developed the Scholastic just-war doctrine. This doctrine reached its mature form by the time of the writings of Vitoria and Suarez in the sixteenth and seventeenth centuries. Various Protestant moralists and secular writers dealt with just-war issues during the Reformation, but by the eighteenth century just-war doctrine was becoming a curiosity that was not taken seriously. It remained for the twentieth century reaction against total war to spark renewed studies in the just-war tradition.").

[105] *Refer to* § 1.11.1 (*Jus ad Bellum* Criteria).

[106] *See, e.g.*, Barack Obama, *Remarks on Accepting the Nobel Peace Prize in Oslo*, Dec. 10, 2009, 2009-II PUBLIC PAPERS OF THE PRESIDENTS 1799 ("And over time, as codes of law sought to control violence within groups, so did philosophers and clerics and statesmen seek to regulate the destructive power of war. The concept of a just war emerged, suggesting that war is justified only when certain conditions were met: if it is waged as a last resort or in self-defense; if the force used is proportional; and if, whenever possible, civilians are spared from violence."); George H. W. Bush, *Remarks at the Annual Convention of the National Religious Broadcasters*, Jan. 28, 1991, 1991-I PUBLIC PAPERS OF THE PRESIDENTS 70 ("Nowhere is this more true than in the Persian Gulf where -- despite protestations of Saddam Hussein -- it is not Iraq against the United States, it's the regime of Saddam Hussein against the rest of the world. Saddam tried to cast this conflict as a religious war, but it has nothing to do with religion per se. It has, on the other hand, everything to do with what religion embodies: good versus evil, right versus wrong, human dignity and freedom versus tyranny and oppression. The war in the Gulf is not a Christian war, a Jewish war, or a Moslem war; it is a just war. And it is a war with which good will prevail.").

[107] JOINT PUBLICATION 1-04, *Legal Support to Military Operations*, GL-3 (Aug. 17, 2011) ("**rules of engagement.** Directives issued by competent military authority that delineate the circumstances and limitations under which United States forces will initiate and/or continue combat engagement with other forces encountered. Also called **ROE.**").

[108] *For example*, Juan Carlos Gomez, *Twenty-First-Century Challenges: The Use of Military Forces to Combat Criminal Threats*, 88 INTERNATIONAL LAW STUDIES 279, 285-86 (2012) ("There must be clear, understandable rules provided to military forces on the circumstances under which force may be used and the type and degree of that force. This is dependent on the mission assigned to the forces. In Colombia, two differently colored cards are used. A blue card is used when the military unit is engaged in a law enforcement mission. The rules on the blue card are based on HRL. They provide for the use of force only when no other option is available to accomplish the mission

ROE reflect legal, policy, and operational considerations, and are consistent with the international law obligations of the United States, including the law of war.[109] ROE may restrict actions that would be lawful under the law of war, but may not permit actions prohibited by the law of war. States have used ROE as part of the implementation of their law of war obligations during military operations.[110]

1.6.6 Code of Conduct for U.S. Armed Forces. The Code of Conduct is a moral guide for U.S. forces to govern their conduct in resisting capture and their actions in the event they fall into hostile hands.[111] The Code of Conduct was developed after the Korean War and was promulgated by Executive Order.[112] The Code of Conduct is consistent with the law of war obligations of the United States, including obligations in the GPW.[113]

1.7 TREATIES

Treaties are generally defined as international agreements concluded between States in written form and governed by international law.[114] Under international law, a treaty is binding upon States that are Parties to it.[115]

The United States is a Party to a number of law of war treaties.[116] For many years, the Department of State has published annually a listing of treaties and other international agreements in force for the United States. This publication has provided helpful information about such treaties, including the date of U.S. ratification and a listing of other Parties to each treaty.

---

and in self-defense of the person and others. The red card is used in operations against military objectives. These cards are based on IHL and permit the offensive use of force, including lethal force if demanded by military necessity.").

[109] J. Fred Buzhardt, General Counsel, Department of Defense, Letter to Senator Edward Kennedy, Sept. 22, 1972, *reprinted in* 67 AJIL 124 (1973) ("With reference to your inquiry concerning the rules of engagement governing American military activity in Indochina, you are advised that rules of engagement are directives issued by competent military authority which delineate the circumstances and limitations under which United States Forces will initiate and/or continue combat engagement with the enemy. These rules are the subject of constant review and command emphasis. They are changed from time to time to conform to changing situations and the demands of military necessity. One critical and unchanging factor is their conformity to existing international law as reflected in the Hague Conventions of 1907 and the Geneva Conventions of 1949, as well as with the principles of customary international law of which UNGA Resolution 2444 (XXIII) is deemed to be a correct restatement.").

[110] *Refer to* § 5.1.2 (Implementation of Law of War Obligations in the Conduct of Hostilities During Military Operations).

[111] *Refer to* § 9.39 (Code of Conduct for U.S. Armed Forces).

[112] *Refer to* § 9.39.2 (Background on the U.S. Code of Conduct).

[113] *Refer to* § 9.39.1 (Text of the Code of Conduct and Discussion).

[114] *Consider, e.g.,* VCLT art. 1(a) ("'[T]reaty' means an international agreement concluded between States in written form and governed by international law, whether embodied in a single instrument or in two or more related instruments and whatever its particular designation;").

[115] *Refer to* § 1.10.1.1 (Legal Force of Treaties Among States).

[116] *Refer to* § 19.2.1 (Law of War Treaties to Which the United States Is a Party).

1.7.1 Treaties – Notes on Terminology. Treaties may be titled or referred to by several other terms in addition to "treaty" – including convention, protocol, or agreement. In the context of the law of war, "protocol" often refers to an agreement that supplements or updates an existing agreement.

1.7.1.1 *"Treaties" Under U.S. Constitutional Law*. Under the Constitution, a "treaty" must receive the advice and consent of the Senate before U.S. ratification or accession. Certain international agreements, such as Executive agreements, are not classified as "treaties" for the purposes of this requirement, although they may be characterized as "treaties" for the purposes of international law and impose obligations upon the United States.[117]

1.7.2 Reservations to Treaties. A State may limit the application of provisions of a treaty by reservation upon ratification of the treaty as long as the treaty does not prohibit such reservations and the reservation is compatible with the object and purpose of the treaty.[118] For example, the United States has taken a reservation to certain provisions of CCW Protocol III on Incendiary Weapons.[119] On the other hand, for example, the Chemical Weapons Convention expressly prohibits reservations to the Convention and prohibits reservations to the Convention's Annexes that are incompatible with its object and purpose.[120]

1.7.3 Withdrawal From Treaties. Under certain circumstances, States may withdraw from treaties.[121] Some law of war and arms control treaties specify the conditions under which Parties may withdraw from them.[122] Even upon denunciation of a treaty, States remain bound by

---

[117] *See, e.g.*, Weinberger v. Rossi, 456 U.S. 25, 29-30 (1982) ("The word 'treaty' has more than one meaning. Under principles of international law, the word ordinarily refers to an international agreement concluded between sovereigns, regardless of the manner in which the agreement is brought into force. Under the United States Constitution, of course, the word 'treaty' has a far more restrictive meaning. Article II, §2, cl. 2, of that instrument provides that the President 'shall have Power, by and with the Advice and Consent of the Senate, to make Treaties, provided two thirds of the Senators present concur.'") (internal citation omitted).

[118] *Consider* VCLT art. 19 ("A State may, when signing, ratifying, accepting, approving or acceding to a treaty, formulate a reservation unless: (a) the reservation is prohibited by the treaty; (b) the treaty provides that only specified reservations, which do not include the reservation in question, may be made; or (c) in cases not failing under subparagraphs (a) and (b), the reservation is incompatible with the object and purpose of the treaty."). *See also* William P. Rogers, *Letter of Submittal*, Oct. 18, 1971, MESSAGE FROM THE PRESIDENT TRANSMITTING THE VCLT 2 ("Part 2 of Section II sets forth the rules on reservations to treaties (Articles 19-23). The articles reflect flexible current treaty practice with regard to multilateral treaties as generally followed since World War II. The earlier traditional rule on reservations had been that in order for a State to become party to a multilateral treaty with a reservation the unanimous consent of the other parties was required. That rule has given way in practice to a more flexible approach particularly after the International Court of Justice in 1951 handed down its Advisory Opinion on Reservations to the Genocide Convention.").

[119] *Refer to* § 6.14.3.2 (U.S. Reservation to CCW Protocol III on Incendiary Weapons).

[120] *Refer to* § 19.22 (Chemical Weapons Convention).

[121] *Consider* VCLT art. 54 ("The termination of a treaty or the withdrawal of a party may take place: (a) in conformity with the provisions of the treaty; or (b) at any time by consent of all the parties after consultation with the other contracting States.").

[122] *See, e.g.*, CCW art. 9(1) ("Any High Contracting Party may denounce this Convention or any of its annexed Protocols by so notifying the Depositary."); GWS art. 63 ("Each of the High Contracting Parties shall be at liberty to denounce the present Convention.").

customary international law, including law of war principles.[123]

1.7.4 Use of Certain Subsequent Practice in Treaty Interpretation. Certain subsequent State practice in the application of a treaty provision may be taken into account when interpreting that provision.[124] Subsequent State practice is important as an element of interpretation when it constitutes objective evidence of the understanding of the Parties as to the meaning of the treaty.[125] For example, the subsequent practice of States in the application of the GWS-Sea's requirements for hospital ships has clarified that States may use hospital ships with the capability to conduct encrypted communications.[126]

1.7.5 Treaties and Domestic Implementing Legislation. States may enact domestic legislation to implement treaty provisions. Although such implementing legislation is not international law, it may reflect a State's interpretation of those provisions.[127]

A State's domestic implementing legislation, or lack of such legislation, however, does not justify that State's noncompliance with an international obligation as a matter of international law.[128]

1.8 Customary International Law

Customary international law results from a general and consistent practice of States that

---

[123] *Refer to* § 19.8.3 (Martens Clause).

[124] *Consider* VCLT art. 31(3) ("There shall be taken into account, together with the context: (*b*) Any subsequent practice in the application of the treaty which establishes the agreement of the parties regarding its interpretation;"). *See also* I Restatement (Third) of Foreign Relations Law of the United States 199 (§325(2)) (1987) ("Any subsequent agreement between the parties regarding the interpretation of the agreement, and subsequent practice between the parties in the application of the agreement, are to be taken into account in its interpretation."); I Restatement (Third) of Foreign Relations Law of the United States 203 (§325, comment c) (1987) (This "conforms to United States modes of interpretation, affirming that subsequent practice of the parties can be taken into account in interpreting international agreements.").

[125] *See* II Yearbook of the International Law Commission 221 (¶15) (1966) ("The importance of such subsequent practice in the application of the treaty, as an element of interpretation, is obvious; for it constitutes objective evidence of the understanding of the parties as to the meaning of the treaty. Recourse to it as a means of interpretation is well-established in the jurisprudence of international tribunals."). *See also* Case Concerning Kasikili/Sedudu Island (Botswana v. Namibia), Judgment, 1999 I.C.J. 1045, 1075-76 (¶49) (same); Russian Claim for Interest on Indemnities (The Russian Indemnity Case), Russia/Turkey, 11 R.I.A.A. 421, 433 (1912) Permanent Court of Arbitration Unofficial English Translation, 3 ("Whereas the fulfilment of obligations is, between States as between individuals, the surest commentary on the meaning of these obligations;"); Case Concerning The Temple of Preah Vihear (Cambodia v. Thailand), Merits, Judgment, 1962 I.C.J. 6, 34 (The map "was accepted by the Parties in 1908 and thereafter as constituting the result of the interpretation given by the two Governments to the delimitation which the Treaty itself required. In other words, the Parties at that time adopted an interpretation of the treaty settlement which caused the map line, in so far as it may have departed from the line of the watershed, to prevail over the relevant clause of the treaty.").

[126] *Refer to* § 7.12.2.7 (Use of Secret Codes for Communication).

[127] *See* United States v. Navarre, 173 U.S. 77, 79 (1899) (noting that "[i]f the meaning of the treaty was doubtful, it was competent for Congress to resolve the doubt" in its enactment of legislation).

[128] *Refer to* § 1.10.1.4 (Force of International Law Notwithstanding a State's Domestic Law).

is followed by them from a sense of legal obligation (*opinio juris*).[129] Customary international law is an unwritten form of law in the sense that it is not created through a written agreement by States.

Customary international law is generally binding on all States, but States that have been persistent objectors to a customary international law rule during its development are not bound by that rule.[130]

Assessing whether State practice and *opinio juris* have resulted in a rule of customary international law may be a difficult inquiry.[131]

1.8.1 Relationship Between Treaties and Customary International Law. Treaty provisions may, *inter alia*: (1) not reflect customary international law; (2) reflect customary international law; or (3) be based on customary law, but not precisely reflect it.

In most cases, treaty provisions do not reflect customary international law. For example, AP I's provisions changing which persons would be entitled to the privileges of combatant status were viewed as novel at the time of the adoption of AP I and as not reflecting customary international law.[132]

In some cases, a treaty provision may reflect customary international law. The rule reflected in the treaty would thus be understood to be binding, even if the treaty provision was not applicable, because the rule maintains a separate existence as a customary norm.[133] For example, provisions of Hague IV and the Hague IV Regulations have been found to reflect customary international law.[134] Law of war treaties have specified that customary law and

---

[129] *See* I RESTATEMENT (THIRD) OF FOREIGN RELATIONS LAW OF THE UNITED STATES 24 (§102(2)) (1987) ("Customary international law results from a general and consistent practice of states followed by them from a sense of legal obligation.").

[130] *Refer to* § 1.10.1.2 (Legal Force of Customary International Law Among States).

[131] Michael J. Matheson, Deputy Legal Adviser, Department of State, *Remarks on the United States Position on the Relation of Customary International Law to the 1977 Protocols Additional to the 1949 Geneva Conventions at the Sixth Annual American Red Cross-Washington College of Law Conference on International Humanitarian Law* (Jan. 22, 1987), 2 AMERICAN UNIVERSITY JOURNAL OF INTERNATIONAL LAW AND POLICY 419, 421-22 (1987) ("Having described the reasons why I believe that the topic of this Workshop is important and very relevant to decisions currently being taken with respect to Protocol I in the United States and other governments, it is of course much more difficult to say exactly which of the rules contained in the Protocol currently are in fact a part of customary law. As I am sure you all appreciate quite well, there is no clear line drawn in the dust for all to see between those principles that are now customary law and those which have not yet attained the degree of acceptance and observance that might make them customary law. Instead, there are degrees of acceptance and degrees of observance, and the judgment as to what degree of each is sufficient for establishment as customary law is inherently subjective and hard to define precisely.").

[132] *Refer to, e.g.*, § 4.6.1.2 (AP I and the GPW 4A(2) Conditions).

[133] Military and Paramilitary Activities in and Against Nicaragua (Nicaragua v. United States), Merits, Judgment, 1986 I.C.J. 14, 95 (¶178) ("[E]ven if two norms belonging to two sources of international law appear identical in content, and even if the States in question are bound by these rules both on the level of treaty-law and on that of customary international law, these norms retain a separate existence.").

[134] *Refer to* § 19.8.2.1 (Hague IV and Customary International Law).

principles continue to apply even if the treaty is not applicable.[135]

A treaty provision may be based on an underlying principle that is an accepted part of customary law, but the precise language of the treaty provision may not reflect customary international law because there may be considerable disagreement as to the precise statement of that underlying principle.[136] For example, the United States has expressed support for the customary principle on which Article 51(3) of AP I is based, but has noted that Article 51(3) of AP I, as drafted, does not reflect customary international law.[137]

1.8.2 State Practice. One part of determining whether a purported rule is customary international law is to analyze whether there is a general and consistent practice of States that supports the purported rule.

An analysis of State practice to determine whether a purported rule reflects the customary international law of war should include consideration of, *inter alia*: (1) whether the State practice is extensive and virtually uniform; (2) actual operational practice; (3) the practice of specially affected States; and (4) contrary practice.

1.8.2.1 *Extensive and Virtually Uniform*. State practice should be sufficiently dense and consistent to meet the "extensive and virtually uniform" standard generally required for existence of a customary rule.[138]

1.8.2.2 *Actual Operational Practice*. An analysis of State practice should include an analysis of actual operational practice by States during armed conflict. Although manuals or other official statements may provide important indications of State behavior, they cannot

---

[135] *Refer to* § 19.8.3 (Martens Clause).

[136] Michael J. Matheson, Deputy Legal Adviser, Department of State, *Remarks on the United States Position on the Relation of Customary International Law to the 1977 Protocols Additional to the 1949 Geneva Conventions at the Sixth Annual American Red Cross-Washington College of Law Conference on International Humanitarian Law* (Jan. 22, 1987), 2 AMERICAN UNIVERSITY JOURNAL OF INTERNATIONAL LAW AND POLICY 419, 422 (1987) ("In addition, it may be possible in many cases to say that a general principle is an accepted part of customary law, but to have considerable disagreement as to the precise statement of that general principle.").

[137] *Refer to* § 5.8.1.2 (AP I, Article 51(3) Provision on Direct Participation in Hostilities).

[138] *See, e.g.*, Harold Koh, Legal Adviser, Department of State, *Responses to Questions Submitted by Senator Richard G. Lugar*, in *Libya and War Powers: Hearing Before the Committee on Foreign Relations, U.S. Senate*, 112th Congress, First Session, 53, 57 (Jun. 28, 2011) ("Determining that a principle has become customary international law requires a rigorous legal analysis to determine whether such principle is supported by a general and consistent practice of states followed by them from a sense of legal obligation. Although there is no precise formula to indicate how widespread a practice must be, one frequently used standard is that state practice must be extensive and virtually uniform, including among States particularly involved in the relevant activity (i.e., specially affected States)."); North Sea Continental Shelf Cases (Federal Republic of Germany v. Denmark; Federal Republic of Germany v. Netherlands), 1969 I.C.J. 3, 43 (¶74) ("Although the passage of only a short period of time is not necessarily, or of itself, a bar to the formation of a new rule of customary international law on the basis of what was originally a purely conventional rule, an indispensable requirement would be that within the period in question, short though it might be, State practice, including that of States whose interests are specially affected, should have been both extensive and virtually uniform in the sense of the provision invoked; and should moreover have occurred in such a way as to show a general recognition that a rule of law or legal obligation is involved.").

replace a meaningful assessment of operational State practice.[139]

1.8.2.3 <u>*Specially Affected States*</u>. The practice of "States whose interests are specially affected," *e.g.*, States with a distinctive history of participation in the relevant matter, must support the purported rule.[140] States that have had a wealth of experience, or that have otherwise had significant opportunities to develop a carefully considered military doctrine, may be expected to have contributed a greater quantity and quality of State practice relevant to the law of war than States that have not.

For example, "specially affected States" could include, depending upon the relevant matter, the nuclear powers, other major military powers, and occupying or occupied States.[141] As a case in point, the United Kingdom has been viewed as a specially affected State with respect to the law of the sea.[142]

1.8.2.4 <u>*Contrary Practice*</u>. Evidence of contrary practice, *i.e.*, the practice of States that does not support the purported rule, must be considered in assessing whether that rule

---

[139] U.S. RESPONSE TO ICRC CIHL STUDY 515 ("Second, we are troubled by the type of practice on which the Study has, in too many places, relied. Our initial review of the State practice volumes suggests that the Study places too much emphasis on written materials, such as military manuals and other guidelines published by States, as opposed to actual operational practice by States during armed conflict. Although manuals may provide important indications of State behavior and *opinio juris*, they cannot be a replacement for a meaningful assessment of operational State practice in connection with actual military operations. We also are troubled by the extent to which the Study relies on non-binding resolutions of the General Assembly, given that States may lend their support to a particular resolution, or determine not to break consensus in regard to such a resolution, for reasons having nothing to do with a belief that the propositions in it reflect customary international law.").

[140] *See* U.S. RESPONSE TO ICRC CIHL STUDY 517 endnote 3 ("Not every State that has participated in an armed conflict is 'specially affected;' such States do generate salient practice, but it is those States that have a distinctive history of participation that merit being regarded as 'specially affected.'"); *Written Statement of the Government of the United States of America*, 28-29, Jun. 20, 1995, I.C.J., Request by the United Nations General Assembly for an Advisory Opinion on the Legality of the Threat or Use of Nuclear Weapons ("Evidence of a customary norm requires indication of 'extensive and virtually uniform' State practice, including States whose interests are 'specially affected.' ... With respect to the use of nuclear weapons, customary law could not be created over the objection of the nuclear-weapon States, which are the States whose interests are most specially affected.").

[141] Theodor Meron, *The Continuing Role of Custom in the Formation of International Humanitarian Law*, 90 AJIL 238, 249 (1996) ("A broader question, however, concerns the degree of weight to be assigned to the practice of various states in the formation of the international customary law of war. I find it difficult to accept the view, sometimes advanced, that all states, whatever their geographical situation, military power and interests, inter alia, have an equal role in this regard. Belligerency is only one factor here. The practice and opinion of Switzerland, for example, as a neutral state, surely have more to teach us about assessment of customary neutrality law than the practice of states that are not committed to the policy of neutrality and have not engaged in pertinent national practice. The practice of 'specially affected states' -such as nuclear powers, other major military powers, and occupying and occupied states-which have a track record of statements, practice and policy, remains particularly telling. I do not mean to denigrate state equality, but simply to recognize the greater involvement of some states in the development of the law of war, not only through operational practice but through policies expressed, for example, in military manuals.").

[142] *See, e g.*, The Paquete Habana, 175 U.S. 677, 719 (1900) (Fuller, J., dissenting) (noting that "[i]t is difficult to conceive of a law of the sea of universal obligation to which Great Britain has not acceded.").

exists as a rule of customary international law.[143]

In addition, the persistent objection of States may be relevant after the formation of that rule by preventing the application of that rule to States that have objected to that rule during its development.[144]

1.8.3 *Opinio Juris*. In addition to analyzing State practice, one must determine whether the State practice results from a sense of legal obligation (*opinio juris*) or merely reflects States' policy or practical interests. *Opinio juris* cannot simply be inferred from consistent State practice, which may exist for reasons other than *opinio juris*.[145] For example, the fact that nuclear weapons have not been used to conduct attacks during armed conflict since 1945 does not reflect a prohibition in customary international law against their use because such lack of use has not resulted from *opinio juris*.[146]

1.8.3.1 *Potential Sources of* Opinio Juris. It may be difficult to find evidence of *opinio juris*, and care should be exercised in assessing whether a source reflects *opinio juris* on the part of a State. For example, treaty provisions do not necessarily reflect *opinio juris*.[147] Similarly, rather than indicating a position expressed out of a sense of a customary legal

---

[143] *For example*, Legality of the Threat or Use of Nuclear Weapons, Advisory Opinion, 1996 I.C.J. 311, 311-12 (Dissenting Opinion of Vice-President Schwebel) ("One way of surmounting the antinomy between practice and principle would be to put aside practice. That is what those who maintain that the threat or use of nuclear weapons is unlawful in all circumstances do. … State practice demonstrates that nuclear weapons have been manufactured and deployed by States for some 50 years; that in that deployment inheres a threat of possible use; and that the international community, by treaty and through action of the United Nations Security Council, has, far from proscribing the threat or use of nuclear weapons in all circumstances, recognized in effect or in terms that in certain circumstances nuclear weapons may be used or their use threatened.").

[144] *Refer to* § 1.8.4 (Objection During Development).

[145] U.S. RESPONSE TO ICRC CIHL STUDY 515 ("Although the same action may serve as evidence both of State practice and opinio juris, we do not agree that opinio juris simply can be inferred from practice. Both elements instead must be assessed separately in order to determine the presence of a norm of customary international law.").

[146] *See* Legality of the Threat or Use of Nuclear Weapons, Advisory Opinion, 1996 I.C.J. 226, 253-54 (¶¶65-67) ("States which hold the view that the use of nuclear weapons is illegal have endeavoured to demonstrate the existence of a customary rule prohibiting this use. They refer to a consistent practice of non-utilization of nuclear weapons by States since 1945 and they would see in that practice the expression of an *opinio juris* on the part of those who possess such weapons. Some other States, which assert the legality of the threat and use of nuclear weapons in certain circumstances, invoked the doctrine and practice of deterrence in support of their argument. They recall that they have always, in concert with certain other States, reserved the right to use those weapons in the exercise of the right to self-defence against an armed attack threatening their vital security interests. In their view, if nuclear weapons have not been used since 1945, it is not on account of an existing or nascent custom but merely because circumstances that might justify their use have fortunately not arisen. The Court does not intend to pronounce here upon the practice known as the 'policy of deterrence.' It notes that it is a fact that a number of States adhered to that practice during the greater part of the Cold War and continue to adhere to it. Furthermore, the members of the international community are profoundly divided on the matter of whether non-recourse to nuclear weapons over the past 50 years constitutes the expression of an *opinio juris*. Under these circumstances the Court does not consider itself able to find that there is such an *opinio juris*.").

[147] U.S. RESPONSE TO ICRC CIHL STUDY 515 ("One therefore must be cautious in drawing conclusions as to *opinio juris* from the practice of States that are parties to conventions, since their actions often are taken pursuant to their treaty obligations, particularly *inter se*, and not in contemplation of independently binding customary international law norms.").

obligation, a State's military manual often recites requirements applicable to that State under treaties to which it is a Party, or provides guidance to its military forces for reasons of national policy.[148]

1.8.4 Objection During Development. Even if a rule otherwise reflects customary international law, the rule is not binding upon a State that has persistently objected to that rule during its development.[149] This principle is an accepted application of the traditional principle that international law essentially depends on the consent of States.[150]

1.9 Subsidiary Means of Determining International Law

As a subsidiary means, it may be helpful to consult judicial decisions and the teachings of the most highly qualified publicists of various nations in determining the applicable rules of international law. These means are subsidiary in the sense that they do not, in themselves, constitute sources of treaty or customary international law.

Discretion must be exercised in weighing sources, however, because sources vary significantly in their probative value. For example, the United States has said that it is not in a position to accept without further analysis the conclusions in a study on customary international humanitarian law published by the ICRC.[151]

1.9.1 Judicial Decisions. Judicial decisions have sometimes been used as a subsidiary

---

[148] U.S. Response to ICRC CIHL Study 516 ("We are troubled by the Study's heavy reliance on military manuals. We do not agree that *opinio juris* has been established when the evidence of a State's sense of legal obligation consists predominately of military manuals. Rather than indicating a position expressed out of a sense of a customary legal obligation, in the sense pertinent to customary international law, a State's military manual often (properly) will recite requirements applicable to that State under treaties to which it is a party. Reliance on provisions of military manuals designed to implement treaty rules provides only weak evidence that those treaty rules apply as a matter of customary international law in non-treaty contexts.").

[149] *See* Fisheries Case, (United Kingdom v. Norway), Judgment, 1951 I.C.J. 116, 131 ("In these circumstances the Court deems it necessary to point out that although the ten-mile rule has been adopted by certain States both in their national law and in their treaties and conventions, and although certain arbitral decisions have applied it as between these States, other States have adopted a different limit. Consequently, the ten-mile rule has not acquired the authority of a general rule of international law. In any event the ten-mile rule would appear to be inapplicable as against Norway inasmuch as she has always opposed any attempt to apply it to the Norwegian coast."); Asylum Case (Colombia v. Peru), 1950 I.C.J. 266, 277-78 ("The Court cannot therefore find that the Colombian Government has proved the existence of such a custom. But even if it could be supposed that such a custom existed between certain Latin-American States only, it could not be invoked against Peru which, far from having by its attitude adhered to it, has, on the contrary, repudiated it by refraining from ratifying the Montevideo Conventions of 1933 and 1939, which were the first to include a rule concerning the qualification of the offence in matters of diplomatic asylum."). *See also* U.S. Response to ICRC CIHL Study 529 endnote 38 ("We note that the Study raises doubts about the continued validity of the 'persistent objector' doctrine. Study, Vol. I, p. xxxix. The U.S. Government believes that the doctrine remains valid.").

[150] I Restatement (Third) of the Foreign Relations Law of the United States 32 (§102, Reporters' Note 2) (1987) ("That a rule of customary law is not binding on any state indicating its dissent during the development of the rule (Comment *d*) is an accepted application of the traditional principle that international law essentially depends on the consent of states.").

[151] *Refer to* § 19.25 (2005 ICRC Study on Customary International Humanitarian Law).

means of determining the rules of international law.[152]

Judicial decisions are generally consulted as only persuasive authority because a judgment rendered by an international court generally binds only the parties to the case in respect of that particular case.[153] The legal reasoning underlying the decisions of the International Court of Justice is not binding on States.[154] Similarly, the decisions of the International Criminal Tribunal for the Former Yugoslavia and the International Criminal Tribunal for Rwanda cannot, as a strictly legal matter, "bind" other courts.[155]

The legal principle of *stare decisis* does not generally apply between international tribunals, *i.e.*, customary international law does not require that one international tribunal follow the judicial precedent of another tribunal in dealing with questions of international law.[156] Moreover, depending on the international tribunal, a tribunal may not be bound by its prior decisions. Some international courts, however, may adhere to their own prior decisions in

---

[152] ICJ STATUTE art. 38(1) ("The Court, whose function is to decide in accordance with international law such disputes as are submitted to it, shall apply: ... d. subject to the provisions of Article 59, judicial decisions ... as subsidiary means for the determination of rules of law.").

[153] *See, e.g.*, ICJ STATUTE art. 59 ("The decision of the Court has no binding force except between the parties and in respect of that particular case.").

[154] John B. Bellinger, III, Legal Adviser, Department of State, 2006 DIGEST OF UNITED STATES PRACTICE IN INTERNATIONAL LAW 1024 ("We believe that these concerns were largely borne out in the advisory opinion rendered by the Court. In practice, the opinion has made little meaningful contribution to efforts to resolve issues between the Israelis and Palestinians. Also, the Court's opinion is open to criticism on its treatment of both factual and legal issues, in some cases due more to process than to any fault on the part of the Court. For example, the fact that the General Assembly had already declared itself on many of the issues, risks creating the impression that the Court was being used to advance a particular set of political claims. Also of concern are efforts in some quarters to suggest that aspects of the Court's advisory opinion, such as that relating to the extraterritorial application of the International Covenant on Civil and Political Rights, have binding force on member states in contexts that go beyond those addressed in the advisory opinion. This of course, is not the case. Under the ICJ statute, states are bound only by the decisions—and not by the Court's reasoning underlying those decisions—in contentious cases to which they are parties, and advisory opinions have no binding force at all, but rather serve to provide guidance on legal questions to the UN organ or specialized agency requesting them.").

[155] Harold Hongju Koh, Legal Adviser, Department of State, *Remarks on international criminal justice at the Vera Institute of Justice in New York and at Leiden University, Campus The Hague*, 2012 DIGEST OF UNITED STATES PRACTICE IN INTERNATIONAL LAW 61, 67 ("The ICTY and ICTR began developing a modern jurisprudence of criminal liability that was based on existing law as applied to a modern ethnic conflict. One of the ICTY's early accomplishments was the Dusko Tadic case, which involved a relatively low-level offender who -- had he been caught only a few years later -- would have been referred to Bosnia for domestic prosecution. The Tadic decision provided a reasoned basis for the seminal conclusions that (1) the UN Security Council had the authority to set up a criminal court under Chapter VII of the UN Charter; (2) the tribunal's jurisdiction extended to war crimes committed in the course of a non-international armed conflict; and (3) Tadic could be convicted for his association with a small group of offenders, articulating the concept of joint criminal enterprise ("JCE") that later became a central feature of the ICTY's work. ... The post-WWII tribunals had largely ignored sexual violence, but the ICTY and ICTR situated the issue within the existing law of war crimes, crimes against humanity, and genocide. Although these decisions cannot, as a strictly legal matter 'bind' other courts, there is no doubt that the jurisprudence of the ICTY and ICTR has been influential in the broader development of international criminal law.").

[156] I RESTATEMENT (THIRD) OF FOREIGN RELATIONS LAW OF THE UNITED STATES 36-37 (§103, comment b) (1987) ("That provision [Article 59 of the Statute of the ICJ] reflects the traditional view that there is no *stare decisis* in international law.").

resolving a case absent a sufficiently persuasive reason to reconsider the point of law.[157]

1.9.2 Legal Writings of Highly Qualified Publicists. The writings "of the most highly qualified publicists" have sometimes been used as a subsidiary means of determining the rules of international law.[158] For example, classical publicists, such as Hugo Grotius and Emmerich de Vattel, and recognized scholars, such as Francis Lieber and Hersch Lauterpacht, have been widely cited and relied upon as practitioners have sought to interpret and apply the law of war.

The standard for whose writings should be relied upon is high, and writings are only as authoritative as the evidence upon which they are based. The writings should only be relied upon to the degree they accurately reflect existing law, rather than the author's views about what the law should be.[159]

1.10 Legal Force of the Law of War

This section addresses the technical legal force of the law of war under international and U.S. domestic law. As a matter of policy, DoD personnel may be required to adhere to law of war rules, even where the rules do not technically apply as a matter of law.[160]

1.10.1 Legal Force of the Law of War Under International Law. The technical force of a law of war rule depends on whether it takes the form of a treaty or customary international law.

1.10.1.1 *Legal Force of Treaties Among States*. Under international law, every treaty in force is binding upon the Parties to it and must be performed by them in good faith.[161] A treaty enters into force for a State after, *inter alia*, it has provided its consent to be bound by the treaty.[162] In some cases, the terms of a treaty may cause it to expire, and in other cases,

---

157 *See, e.g.*, Prosecutor v. Aleksovski, ICTY Appeals Chamber, IT-95-14/1-A, *Judgment*, ¶¶107-109 (Mar. 24, 2000) ("[I]in the interests of certainty and predictability, the Appeals Chamber should follow its previous decisions, but should be free to depart from them for cogent reasons in the interests of justice. … It is necessary to stress that the normal rule is that previous decisions are to be followed, and departure from them is the exception. The Appeals Chamber will only depart from a previous decision after the most careful consideration has been given to it, both as to the law, including the authorities cited, and the facts.").

158 ICJ Statute art. 38(1) ("The Court, whose function is to decide in accordance with international law such disputes as are submitted to it, shall apply: … d. subject to the provisions of Article 59, … the teachings of the most highly qualified publicists of the various nations, as subsidiary means for the determination of rules of law.").

159 *See* The Paquete Habana, 175 U.S. 677, 700 (1900) ("For this purpose, where there is no treaty, and no controlling executive or legislative act or judicial decision, resort must be had to the customs and usages of civilized nations; and, as evidence of these, to the works of jurists and commentators, who by years of labor, research and experience, have made themselves peculiarly well acquainted with the subjects of which they treat. Such works are resorted to by judicial tribunals, not for the speculations of their authors concerning what the law ought to be, but for trustworthy evidence of what the law really is.").

160 *Refer to* § 3.1.1 (DoD Practice of Applying Law of War Rules Even When Not Technically Applicable).

161 *Consider* VCLT art. 26 ("Every treaty in force is binding upon the parties to it and must be performed by them in good faith.").

162 *Consider* VCLT art. 24 ("1. A treaty enters into force in such manner and upon such date as it may provide or as the negotiating States may agree. 2. Failing any such provision or agreement, a treaty enters into force as soon as consent to be bound by the treaty has been established for all the negotiating States. 3. When the consent of a State to be bound by a treaty is established on a date after the treaty has come into force, the treaty enters into force for

States may withdraw from a treaty.[163] In some cases, a reservation may also modify the obligations imposed by a treaty on that State.[164]

A treaty does not create either obligations or rights for a third State without its consent.[165] Thus, a treaty generally would not be binding on non-Parties to the treaty or create rights or obligations for a non-Party to the treaty with respect to a Party to the treaty. Instead, a treaty only creates law (*i.e.*, rights that may be invoked) as between the States that are Parties to it.[166]

1.10.1.2 *Legal Force of Customary International Law Among States*. The customary law of war generally binds all States. However, States that have objected to a customary international law rule during its development are not bound by that rule.[167]

1.10.1.3 *Predominately Inter-State Nature of International Obligations*. International obligations are generally viewed as running to other States, although individuals may have responsibility under international law.

Traditionally, international law has governed relations between States, although over time it has increasingly regulated the relationships between States and persons. Under the traditional view, a State's international law obligations run to other States, even when the obligations relate to an individual (*e.g.*, by protecting that individual), such that individuals' "place in international life depends largely on their status as nationals of states."[168] For example, the 1949 Geneva Conventions and the customary law of war do not provide a private right for individuals to claim compensation directly from a State for violations of the law of war; rather, such claims are made

---

that State on that date, unless the treaty otherwise provides. 4. The provisions of a treaty regulating the authentication of its text, the establishment of the consent of States to be bound by the treaty, the manner or date of its entry into force, reservations, the functions of the depositary and other matters arising necessarily before the entry into force of the treaty apply from the time of the adoption of its text."). *See also* DEPARTMENT OF THE ARMY PAMPHLET 27-161-1, *I International Law: Law of Peace*, ¶8-12 (Sept. 1, 1979) ("An international agreement is basically a contract between states, and elements of obligation akin to those found in municipal contract law are present. However, as discussed in Part I, a treaty is not a contract in the common law sense of an agreement requiring consideration. It is the *assent to be bound* and not reciprocity or *quid pro quo* that obligates the parties.").

[163] *Refer to* § 1.7.3 (Withdrawal From Treaties).

[164] *Refer to* § 1.7.2 (Reservations to Treaties).

[165] *Consider* VCLT art. 34 ("A treaty does not create either obligations or rights for a third State without its consent.").

[166] Case Concerning Certain German Interests in Polish Upper Silesia (Merits) (Germany v. Poland) 1925 P.C.I.J. (series A) No. 7, at 29 ("A treaty only creates law as between the States which are parties to it; in case of doubt, no rights can be deduced from it in favour of third States.").

[167] *Refer to* § 1.8.4 (Objection During Development).

[168] I RESTATEMENT (THIRD) OF FOREIGN RELATIONS LAW OF THE UNITED STATES 71 (1987). *See also* II RESTATEMENT (THIRD) OF FOREIGN RELATIONS LAW OF THE UNITED STATES 217 (§713, comment a) (1987) (explaining that in principle, state responsibility for injury to the nationals of other states "is to the state of the alien's nationality and gives that state a claim against the offending state. The claim derives from injury to an individual, but once espoused it is the state's claim, and can be waived by the state.").

by other States.[169]

International law has long prescribed certain rules regulating the conduct of individuals.[170] Under international law, there may be responsibility for individuals, apart from State responsibility.[171]

1.10.1.4 *Force of International Law Notwithstanding a State's Domestic Law*. A State's domestic law does not justify that State's noncompliance with an international obligation as a matter of international law.[172] Similarly, the fact that a State's domestic law does not provide for a penalty with respect to a violation of international law does not relieve a person from responsibility for that act under international law.[173]

1.10.2 Force of the Law of War Under U.S. Domestic Law. The specific legal force of a law of war rule under U.S. domestic law may depend on whether that rule takes the form of a self-executing treaty, non-self-executing treaty, or customary international law.

Longstanding DoD policy has been to require DoD personnel to comply with the law of war obligations of the United States.[174]

Even if a violation of a rule is not directly punishable under U.S. law, a variety of tools in U.S. domestic law may be used to enforce a law of war obligation of the United States. For example, a violation of a law of war obligation may be made punishable through implementation of the obligation in military instructions, regulations, and procedures.[175]

1.10.2.1 *Force of Self-Executing and Non-Self-Executing Treaties Under U.S. Domestic Law*. Under domestic law, treaties to which the United States is a Party are part of U.S. law.[176]

---

[169] *Refer to* § 18.16.4 (No Private Right to Compensation Under Customary International Law or the 1949 Geneva Conventions).

[170] *See* Sosa v. Alvarez-Machain, 542 U.S. 692, 715 (2004) (noting that international law has included "a body of judge-made law regulating the conduct of individuals situated outside domestic boundaries" and "rules binding individuals for the benefit of other individuals [that] overlapped with the norms of state relationships").

[171] *Refer to* § 18.22.1 (Individual Criminal Responsibility for Acts Constituting Crimes Under International Law).

[172] Secretary of State Bayard, Instruction to Mr. Connery, charge to Mexico, Nov. 1, 1887, II MOORE'S DIGEST 235 ("[A] government can not appeal to its municipal regulations as an answer to demands for the fulfillment of international duties. Such regulations may either exceed or fall short of the requirements of international law, and in either case that law furnishes the test of the nation's liability and not its own municipal rules."). *Consider* VCLT art. 27 ("A party may not invoke the provisions of its internal law as justification for its failure to perform a treaty. This rule is without prejudice to article 46.").

[173] *Refer to* § 18.22.2 (Absence of Penalty Under Domestic Law Does Not Relieve a Person of Responsibility).

[174] *Refer to* § 18.1.1 (DoD Policy on Implementing and Enforcing the Law of War).

[175] *Refer to* § 18.7 (Instructions, Regulations, and Procedures to Implement and Enforce the Law of War).

[176] *See* U.S. CONSTITUTION art. VI ("This Constitution, and the laws of the United States which shall be made in pursuance thereof; and all treaties made, or which shall be made, under the authority of the United States, shall be

The terms "self-executing" and "non-self-executing" may be used to explain how a treaty is to take effect in U.S. domestic law. A treaty may be classified as a self-executing treaty that "operates of itself, without the aid of any legislative provision," or as a non-self-executing treaty that would require "that the Legislature must execute the contract before it can become a rule for the Court."[177]

1.10.2.2 Force of Customary International Law Under U.S. Domestic Law. The customary law of war is part of U.S. law insofar as it is not inconsistent with any treaty to which the United States is a Party, or a controlling executive or legislative act.[178]

1.11 *JUS AD BELLUM*

The law of war has been categorized into *jus ad bellum* (law concerning the resort to force) and *jus in bello* (law concerning conduct during war).[179] Although *jus ad bellum* is an essential part of the law of war to consider in the political process of whether to resort to military force, this manual focuses on *jus in bello*.[180] Although *jus in bello* rules generally operate independently of whether a side has comported with *jus ad bellum* in the resort to force, parts of *jus ad bellum* are relevant to *jus in bello*.[181]

This section provides a brief overview of some basic aspects of *jus ad bellum*. *Jus ad bellum* issues might raise questions of national policy that, in the Executive Branch, would be

---

the supreme law of the land; and the judges in every state shall be bound thereby, anything in the Constitution or laws of any State to the contrary notwithstanding.").

[177] Foster & Elam v. Neilson 27 U.S. 253, 314 (1829) (Marshall, C.J.). *See also* Whitney v. Robertson, 124 U.S. 190, 194 (1888) ("A treaty is primarily a contract between two or more independent nations, and is so regarded by writers on public law. For the infraction of its provisions a remedy must be sought by the injured party through reclamations upon the other. When the stipulations are not self-executing, they can only be enforced pursuant to legislation to carry them into effect, and such legislation is as much subject to modification and repeal by Congress as legislation upon any other subject. If the treaty contains stipulations which are self-executing, that is, require no legislation to make them operative, to that extent they have the force and effect of a legislative enactment."); Medellin v. Texas, 552 U.S. 491, 525-26 (2008) ("The responsibility for transforming an international obligation arising from a non-self-executing treaty into domestic law falls to Congress.").

[178] The Paquete Habana, 175 U.S. 677, 700 (1900) ("International law is part of our law, … where there is no treaty and no controlling executive or legislative act or judicial decision, resort must be had to the customs and usages of civilized nations,").

[179] *See, e.g.*, WILLIAM O'BRIEN, THE CONDUCT OF JUST AND LIMITED WAR 9 (1981) (defining *jus ad bellum* as the "doctrines concerning permissible recourse to war" and *jus in bello* as "the just conduct of war"); MICHAEL WALZER, JUST AND UNJUST WARS 21 (1977) ("War is always judged twice, first with reference to the reasons states have for fighting, secondly with reference to the means they adopt. The first kind of judgment is adjectival in character: we say that a particular war is just or unjust. The second is adverbial: we say that a war is being fought justly or unjustly. Medieval writers made the difference a matter of prepositions, distinguishing *jus ad bellum*, the justice of war, from *jus in bello*, justice in war."). *But see* Robert Kolb, *Origin of the twin terms jus ad bellum/jus in bello*, 37 INTERNATIONAL REVIEW OF THE RED CROSS 553 (Sept.-Oct. 1997) ("The august solemnity of Latin confers on the terms *jus ad bellum* and *jus in bello* the misleading appearance of being centuries old. In fact, these expressions were only coined at the time of the League of Nations and were rarely used in doctrine or practice until after the Second World War, in the late 1940s to be precise.").

[180] *Refer to* § 1.1.2 (Scope).

[181] *Refer to* § 3.5 (Relationship Between *Jus in Bello* and *Jus ad Bellum*).

decided by the President. In U.S. practice, legal advice provided to national-level principal officials on such issues generally would need to be addressed through interagency discussions coordinated by the legal adviser to the National Security Council, including consultation and coordination among senior counsel of relevant U.S. departments and agencies.

1.11.1 *Jus ad Bellum* Criteria. Certain *jus ad bellum* criteria have, at their philosophical roots, drawn from principles that have been developed as part of the Just War Tradition.[182] These principles have included:

- a competent authority to order the war for a public purpose;
- a just cause (such as self-defense);
- the means must be proportionate to the just cause;
- all peaceful alternatives must have been exhausted; and
- a right intention on the part of the just belligerent.[183]

These principles may be reflected in modern law of war rules. For example, the Charter of the United Nations recognizes the inherent right of States to use force in individual or collective self-defense—a just cause for military action.[184]

These principles have also been incorporated into military doctrine.[185]

1.11.1.1 Competent Authority (Right Authority) to Wage War for a Public Purpose. One longstanding criterion for a just war is that war must be ordered by a competent authority for a public purpose. This *jus ad bellum* principle (sometimes called *right authority*) acknowledges that the resort to military force is a prerogative of the State.[186]

---

182 *Refer to* § 1.6.4 (Just War Tradition).

183 WILLIAM O'BRIEN, THE CONDUCT OF JUST AND LIMITED WAR 16 (1981) ("The decision to invoke the exceptional rights of war must be based on the following criteria: there must be competent authority to order the war for a public purpose; there must be a just cause (it may be self-defense or the protection of rights by offensive war) and the means must be proportionate to the just cause and all peaceful alternatives must have been exhausted; and there must be right intention on the part of the just belligerent.").

184 *Refer to* § 1.11.4.1 (Use of Force in Self-Defense).

185 MARINE CORPS DOCTRINAL PUBLICATION 1-1, *Strategy*, 93, 95 (1997) ("[T]he just war criteria provide objective measures from which to judge our motives. The effective strategist must be prepared to demonstrate to all sides why the defended cause meets the criteria of just war theory and why the enemy's cause does not. If a legitimate and effective argument on this basis cannot be assembled, then it is likely that both the cause and the strategy are fatally flawed.").

186 *See* Talbot v. Janson, 3 U.S. 133, 160-61 (1795) (Iredell, J., concurring) ("[N]o hostilities of any kind, except in necessary self-defence, can lawfully be practised by one individual of a nation, against an individual of any other nation at enmity with it, but in virtue of some public authority. War can alone be entered into by national authority; it is instituted for national purposes, and directed to national objects; and each individual on both sides is engaged in it as a member of the society to which he belongs, not from motives of personal malignity and ill will."); VATTEL, THE LAW OF NATIONS 235 (3.1.4) ("It is the sovereign power alone, therefore, which has the right to make war.");

The criterion that war must be ordered by a competent authority for a public purpose is reflected in the requirement that armed groups must belong to a State to receive the privileges of combatant status.[187] This criterion is also reflected in the general denial to private persons of the entitlement to the privileges of combatant status.[188] This criterion is also reflected in the condemnation under international law of certain types of private acts of hostility (such as piracy or terrorism) outside the context of patriotic resistance against an enemy State during international armed conflict.[189]

1.11.1.2 <u>*The Means Must Be Proportionate to the Just Cause (Proportionality – Jus ad Bellum)*</u>. *Proportionality* involves a weighing of the contemplated actions with the justification for taking action.[190] For example, the proportionality of the measures taken in self-defense is to be judged according to the nature of the threat being addressed.[191] Force may be used in self-defense, but only to the extent that it is required to repel the armed attack and to restore the security of the party attacked.[192] As an illustration, assessing the proportionality of measures taken in self-defense may involve considerations of whether an actual or imminent attack is part of an ongoing pattern of attacks or what force is reasonably necessary to discourage future armed attacks or threats thereof.[193]

GROTIUS, LAW OF WAR & PEACE 97 (1.3.4.2) ("But because the whole state is endangered by war, provision has been made by the laws of almost every state that war may be waged only under the authority of him who holds the sovereign power in the state.").

[187] *Refer to* § 4.6.2 (Belonging to a Party to the Conflict).

[188] *Refer to* § 4.18.3 (Private Persons Who Engage in Hostilities – Lack of the Privileges of Combatant Status).

[189] *Refer to* § 4.18.5 (Private Persons Who Engage in Hostilities and the Law of War).

[190] *Refer to* § 2.4 (Proportionality).

[191] William H. Taft IV, Legal Adviser, Department of State, *Self-Defense and the Oil Platforms Decision*, 29 YALE JOURNAL OF INTERNATIONAL LAW 295, 305-06 (2004) ("There is no requirement in international law that a State exercising its right of self-defense must use the same degree or type of force used by the attacking State in its most recent attack. Rather, the proportionality of the measures taken in self-defense is to be judged according to the nature of the threat being addressed… . A proper assessment of the proportionality of a defensive use of force would require looking not only at the immediately preceding armed attack, but also at whether it was part of an ongoing series of attacks, what steps were already taken to deter future attacks, and what force could reasonably be judged to be needed to successfully deter future attacks.").

[192] Counter-memorial and Counter-claim Submitted by the United States of America, International Court of Justice, Case Concerning Oil Platforms (Iran v. United States) 141 (¶4.31) (Jun. 23, 1997) ("Actions in self-defense must be proportionate. Force can be used in self-defense, but only to the extent that it is required to repel the armed attack and to restore the security of the party attacked.").

[193] Herbert S. Okun, *Letter Dated 14 April 1986 from the Acting Permanent Representative of the United States of America to the United Nations Addressed to the President of the Security Council*, U.N. Doc. S/17990 (Apr. 14, 1986) ("The United States objective was to destroy facilities used to carry out Libya's hostile policy of international terrorism and to discourage Libyan terrorist attacks in the future. These facilities constituted essential elements which have enabled Libyan agents to carry out deadly missions against U.S. installations and innocent individuals."); Madeleine Albright, *Letter Dated 26 June 1993 from the Permanent Representative of the United States of America to the United Nations Addressed to the President of the Security Council*, U.N. Doc. S/26003 (Jun. 26, 1993) ("Accordingly, as a last resort, the United States has decided that it is necessary to respond to the attempted attack and the threat of further attacks by striking at an Iraqi military and intelligence target that is involved in such attacks. … It is the sincere hope of the United States Government that such limited and

The *jus ad bellum* criterion of proportionality is different from the *jus in bello* principle of proportionality in conducting attacks.[194] These concepts should not be confused with one another.[195]

1.11.1.3 <u>*All Peaceful Alternatives Must Have Been Exhausted (Necessity – Jus ad Bellum)*</u>. The *jus ad bellum* condition of necessity requires that no reasonable alternative means of redress are available.[196] For example, in exercising the right of self-defense, diplomatic means must be exhausted or provide no reasonable prospect of stopping the armed attack or threat thereof.[197]

The *jus ad bellum* criterion of *necessity* is different from the *jus in bello* concept of *military necessity.*[198]

1.11.2 <u>U.N. Charter Framework and the U.N. Security Council</u>. The Charter of the United Nations provides the modern treaty framework for *jus ad bellum.* Under the Charter of the United Nations, the U.N. Security Council has primary responsibility for the maintenance of international peace and security.[199] The U.N. Security Council may determine the existence of any threat to the peace, breach of the peace, or act of aggression, and may decide what measures shall be taken under the Charter to maintain or restore international peace and security.[200] For

---

proportionate action may frustrate future unlawful actions on the part of the Government of Iraq and discourage or preempt such activities.").

[194] *Refer to* § 5.10 (Proportionality in Conducting Attacks).

[195] *Refer to* § 3.5.1 (General Distinction Between *Jus in Bello* and *Jus ad Bellum*).

[196] William H. Taft IV, Legal Adviser, Department of State, *Self-Defense and the Oil Platforms Decision*, 29 YALE JOURNAL OF INTERNATIONAL LAW 295, 304 (2004) ("The condition of 'necessity,' rather, requires that no reasonable alternative means of redress are available.").

[197] *For example*, Madeleine Albright, *Letter Dated 26 June 1993 from the Permanent Representative of the United States of America to the United Nations Addressed to the President of the Security Council*, U.N. Doc. S/26003 (Jun. 26, 1993) ("Based on the pattern of the Government of Iraq's behavior, including the disregard for international law and Security Council resolutions, the United States has concluded that there is no reasonable prospect that new diplomatic initiatives or economic measures can influence the current Government of Iraq to cease planning future attacks against the United States. Accordingly, as a last resort, the United States has decided that it is necessary to respond to the attempted attack and the threat of further attacks by striking at an Iraqi military and intelligence target that is involved in such attacks."); Thomas R. Pickering, *Letter Dated 20 December 1989 from the Permanent Representative of the United States of America to the United Nations Addressed to the President of the Security Council*, U.N. Doc. S/21035 (Dec. 20, 1989) ("The United States has exhausted every available diplomatic means to resolve peacefully disputes with Mr. Noriega, who has rejected all such efforts. Action by the United States was taken after Mr. Noriega declared on 15 December that a state of war existed with the United States, and following brutal attacks by forces of Mr. Noriega on lawfully present American personnel, murdering one American and injuring and threatening others.").

[198] *Refer to* § 2.2 (Military Necessity).

[199] U.N. CHARTER art. 24(1) ("In order to ensure prompt and effective action by the United Nations, its Members confer on the Security Council primary responsibility for the maintenance of international peace and security, and agree that in carrying out its duties under this responsibility the Security Council acts on their behalf.").

[200] U.N. CHARTER art. 39 ("The Security Council shall determine the existence of any threat to the peace, breach of the peace, or act of aggression and shall make recommendations, or decide what measures shall be taken in accordance with Articles 41 and 42, to maintain or restore international peace and security.").

example, the U.N. Security Council may recognize that a State is acting lawfully in self-defense or that another State is the aggressor in an armed conflict.[201] In addition, the U.N. Security Council may authorize the use of military force.[202]

1.11.2.1 *U.N. Member State Obligations With Respect to U.N. Security Council Decisions*. Members of the United Nations have agreed to give the United Nations every assistance in any action it takes in accordance with the Charter and to refrain from giving assistance to any State against which the United Nations is taking preventive or enforcement action.[203]

Members of the United Nations have agreed to accept and carry out the decisions of the U.N. Security Council in accordance with the Charter.[204] They have also agreed to join in affording mutual assistance in carrying out the measures decided upon by the U.N. Security Council.[205]

Moreover, in the event of a conflict between the obligations of the Members of the United Nations under the Charter and their obligations under any other international agreement, their obligations under the Charter prevail.[206]

1.11.3 Prohibition on Certain Uses of Force. Under Article 2(4) of the Charter of the United Nations, "[a]ll Members shall refrain in their international relations from the threat or use of force against the territorial integrity or political independence of any State, or in any other manner inconsistent with the Purposes of the United Nations.[207] Numerous other treaties also

---

[201] *For example*, U.N. SECURITY COUNCIL RESOLUTION 661, U.N. Doc. S/RES/661 (1990) ("*Affirming* the inherent right of individual or collective self-defence, in response to the armed attack of Iraq against Kuwait, in accordance with Article 51 of the Charter,"); U.N. SECURITY COUNCIL RESOLUTION 1368, U.N. Doc. S/RES/1368 (2001) ("*Determined* to combat by all means threats to international peace and security caused by terrorist acts, *Recognizing* the inherent right of individual or collective self-defence in accordance with the Charter, 1. *Unequivocally condemns* in the strongest terms the horrifying terrorist attacks which took place on 11 September 2001 in New York, Washington, D.C. and Pennsylvania and regards such acts, like any act of international terrorism, as a threat to international peace and security;").

[202] *Refer to* § 1.11.4.2 (Use of Force Authorized by the U.N. Security Council Acting Under Chapter VII of the Charter of the United Nations).

[203] U.N. CHARTER art. 2(5) ("All Members shall give the United Nations every assistance in any action it takes in accordance with the present Charter, and shall refrain from giving assistance to any state against which the United Nations is taking preventive or enforcement action.").

[204] U.N. CHARTER art. 25 ("The Members of the United Nations agree to accept and carry out the decisions of the Security Council in accordance with the present Charter.").

[205] U.N. CHARTER art. 49 ("The Members of the United Nations shall join in affording mutual assistance in carrying out the measures decided upon by the Security Council.").

[206] U.N. CHARTER art. 103 ("In the event of a conflict between the obligations of the Members of the United Nations under the present Charter and their obligations under any other international agreement, their obligations under the present Charter shall prevail.").

[207] U.N. CHARTER art. 2(4).

reflect these prohibitions on the threat or use of force.[208]

The resort to force must have a legal basis in order not to violate these prohibitions. The legality of the use of force must be assessed in light of the particular facts and circumstances at issue.[209]

1.11.3.1 Aggression. Aggression is the most serious and dangerous form of the illegal use of force.[210] Not every act of illegal use of force prohibited by Article 2(4) of the Charter constitutes aggression.[211] Initiating a war of aggression is a serious international crime.[212]

U.N. General Assembly Resolution 3314 suggested considerations that the Security Council should bear in mind in determining whether an act of aggression had occurred.[213]

---

[208] *See, e.g.*, Inter-American Treaty of Reciprocal Assistance, art. 1, Sept. 2, 1947, 62 STAT. 1681, 1700 ("The High Contracting Parties formally condemn war and undertake in their international relations not to resort to the threat or the use of force in any manner inconsistent with the provisions of the Charter of the United Nations or of this Treaty."); Treaty Providing for the Renunciation of War as an Instrument of National Policy, art. 1, Aug. 27, 1928, 46 STAT. 2343, 2345-46 ("The High Contracting Parties solemnly declare in the names of their respective peoples that they condemn recourse to war for the solution of international controversies, and renounce it as an instrument of national policy in their relations with one another.").

[209] *See, e.g.*, William H. Taft IV, Legal Adviser, Department of State, & Todd F. Buchwald, Assistant Legal Adviser for Political-Military Affairs, Department of State, *Preemption, Iraq, and International Law*, 97 AJIL 557 (2003) ("In the end, each use of force must find legitimacy in the facts and circumstances that the state believes have made it necessary. Each should be judged not on abstract concepts, but on the particular events that gave rise to it."); Daniel Webster, *Letter to Mr. Fox*, Apr. 24, 1841, *reprinted in* DANIEL WEBSTER, THE DIPLOMATIC AND OFFICIAL PAPERS OF DANIEL WEBSTER, WHILE SECRETARY OF STATE 105 (1848) ("It is admitted that a just right of self-defense attaches always to nations as well as to individuals, and is equally necessary for the preservation of both. But the extent of this right is a question to be judged of by the circumstances of each particular case;").

[210] *Definition of Aggression*, preamble ¶5, Annex to U.N. GENERAL ASSEMBLY RESOLUTION 3314 (XXIX), *Definition of Aggression*, U.N. Doc. A/RES/3314 (XXIX) (Dec. 14, 1974) ("*Considering also* that, since aggression is the most serious and dangerous form of the illegal use of force, being fraught, in the conditions created by the existence of all types of weapons of mass destruction, with the possible threat of a world conflict and all its catastrophic consequences, aggression should be defined at the present stage.").

[211] Joseph Sanders, Rapporteur, The Special Committee on the Question of Defining Aggression, *Report of the Special Committee on the Question of Defining Aggression, Annex 1: Views expressed by members of the Special Committee at the concluding stage of the Special Committee's session*, U.N. General Assembly Official Records: Twenty-Ninth Session Supplement No. 19, U.N. Doc. A/9619, 22-23 (Mar. 11-Apr. 12, 1974) ("Mr. ROSENSTOCK (United States of America) … The fifth preambular paragraph, while recognizing the dangers which would flow from an illegal use of force amounting to aggression, correctly stated the view that not every act of force in violation of the Charter constituted aggression.").

[212] United States, *et al.* v. Göring, *et al.*, *Judgment*, I TRIAL OF THE MAJOR WAR CRIMINALS BEFORE THE IMT 421 ("To initiate a war of aggression, therefore, is not only an international crime; it is the supreme international crime differing only from other war crimes in that it contains within itself the accumulated evil of the whole.").

[213] Joseph Sanders, Rapporteur, The Special Committee on the Question of Defining Aggression, *Report of the Special Committee on the Question of Defining Aggression, Annex 1: Views expressed by members of the Special Committee at the concluding stage of the Special Committee's session*, U.N. General Assembly Official Records: Twenty-Ninth Session Supplement No. 19, U.N. Doc. A/9619, 22-23 (Mar. 11-Apr. 12, 1974) ("Mr. ROSENSTOCK (United States of America) … The text that had been produced was a recommendation of the General Assembly for use by the Security Council. … In article 2, the definition suggested the considerations which the Security Council should bear in mind in determining whether an act of aggression had occurred.").

Although this resolution states basic principles as guidance for such determinations, it recognizes that whether an act of aggression has been committed must be considered in light of all the circumstances of each particular case.[214]

The United States has expressed the view that the definition of the act of aggression in the Kampala amendments to the Rome Statute does not reflect customary international law.[215]

1.11.4 Rationales for the Resort to Force.

1.11.4.1 *Use of Force in Self-Defense*. The right to use force in self-defense is an inherent right of States.[216]

1.11.4.2 *Use of Force Authorized by the U.N. Security Council Acting Under Chapter VII of the Charter of the United Nations*. Chapter VII of the Charter of the United Nations provides that the U.N. Security Council may take such action by air, sea, or land forces as may be necessary to maintain or restore international peace or security, including demonstrations, blockade, and other military operations.[217]

1.11.4.3 *Use of Force With the Consent of the Territorial State*. Military action in the territory of another State is not a violation of Article 2(4)'s prohibition against the use of force against that State where it consents to such military action.[218]

1.11.4.4 *Humanitarian Intervention*. Violations of law of war treaties applicable to non-international armed conflict generally have not been understood to provide an

---

[214] *Definition of Aggression*, preamble ¶10, Annex to U.N. GENERAL ASSEMBLY RESOLUTION 3314 (XXIX), *Definition of Aggression*, U.N. Doc. A/RES/3314 (XXIX) (Dec. 14, 1974) ("*Believing* that, although the question whether an act of aggression has been committed must be considered in the light of all the circumstances of each particular case, it is nevertheless desirable to formulate basic principles as guidance for such determination,").

[215] *Refer to* § 18.20.3.4 (ICC and the Crime of Aggression).

[216] *Refer to* § 1.11.5 (Use of Force in Self-Defense).

[217] U.N. CHARTER art. 42 ("Should the Security Council consider that measures provided for in Article 41 would be inadequate or have proved to be inadequate, it may take such action by air, sea, or land forces as may be necessary to maintain or restore international peace and security. Such action may include demonstrations, blockade, and other operations by air, sea, or land forces of Members of the United Nations.").

[218] *For example*, Davis R. Robinson, Legal Adviser, Department of State, *Letter to Professor Edward Gordon, Chairman of the Committee on Grenada Section on International Law and Practice American Bar Association on The Legal Position of the United States on the Action taken in Grenada* (Feb. 10, 1984), *reprinted in* 18 INTERNATIONAL LAWYERS 381 (1984) ("In the case of the action taken in Grenada, the legal position of the United States was based upon the application of a combination of three well established principles of international law… (1) the lawful governmental authorities of a State may invite the assistance in its territory of military forces of other states or collective organizations in dealing with internal disorder as well as external threats."); Statement of the U.S. Government, attached to Adlai E. Stevenson, *Letter Dated 24 November 1964 From the Permanent Representative of the United States of America Addressed to the President of the Security Council,* U.N. Doc. S/6062, Nov. 24, 1964 ("The United States Government has just received confirmation that a short time ago - early morning of 24 November in the Congo - a unit of Belgian paratroopers, carried by United States military transport planes, landed at Stanleyville in the Congo. This landing has been made (1) with the authorization of the Government of the Congo, (2) in conformity with our adherence to the Geneva Conventions, and (3) in exercise of our clear responsibility to protect United States citizens under the circumstances existing in the Stanleyville area.").

independent basis for intervening in a State.[219]

Although the United Kingdom and certain other States have argued that intervention for humanitarian reasons may be a legal basis for the resort to force, the United States has not adopted this legal rationale.[220] Consistent with this view, the United States did not adopt this theory as a legal rationale for NATO's military action to address the humanitarian catastrophe in Kosovo in 1999, but rather expressed the view that such action was justified on the basis of a number of factors.[221]

Military action for humanitarian reasons may, however, be authorized by the U.N. Security Council.[222]

1.11.5 Use of Force in Self-Defense. Article 51 of the Charter of the United Nations provides that "[n]othing in the present Charter shall impair the inherent right of individual or collective self-defence if an armed attack occurs against a Member of the United Nations, until the Security Council has taken measures necessary to maintain international peace and

---

[219] *Refer to* § 17.18.1 (Duty of Non-Belligerent States to Refrain From Supporting Hostilities by Non-State Armed Groups Against Other States).

[220] William H. Taft IV, Legal Adviser, Department of State, *Role and Significance of International Law Governing the Use of Force in the New Global Context Confronting the United States After 9/11: remarks regarding the use of force under international law* (Oct. 27, 2004) ("Of particular note, the idea that humanitarian catastrophes must be avoided has been asserted as a reason for rethinking what actions international law permits in a number of situations. NATO's intervention in Kosovo in 1999 is a case to consider in this connection. In defending the legality of NATO's actions, the United Kingdom and several other allies asserted a doctrine of humanitarian intervention, under which states have a right to use force if it is necessary to prevent genocide, a major loss of civilian life, or a large scale forced movement of a population, which would destabilize other states and threaten international peace and security. In this view, the humanitarian intervention doctrine is often presented as a necessary extension of humanitarian law as it has evolved since 1945. Significantly, the doctrine was invoked in the absence of authorization by the UN Security Council. The United States did not, however, adopt this theory as a basis for the NATO intervention in Kosovo, and instead pointed to a range of other factors to justify its participation in the Kosovo campaign.").

[221] David Andrews, Legal Adviser, Department of State, Oral Proceedings, May 11, 1999, Legality of Use of Force (Yugoslavia v. United States) I.C.J. 10 (¶1.7) ("As you have already heard, the actions of the Members of the NATO Alliance find their justification in a number of factors. These include: - The humanitarian catastrophe that has engulfed the people of Kosovo as a brutal and unlawful campaign of ethnic cleansing has forced many hundreds of thousands to flee their homes and has severely endangered their lives and well-being; - The acute threat of the actions of the Federal Republic of Yugoslavia to the security of neighbouring States, including threat posed by extremely heavy flows of refugees and armed incursions into their territories; - The serious violation of international humanitarian law and human rights obligations by forces under the control of the Federal Republic of Yugoslavia, including widespread murder, disappearances, rape, theft and destruction of property; and, finally - The resolutions of the Security Council, which have determined that the actions of the Federal Republic of Yugoslavia constitute a threat to peace and security in the region and, pursuant to Chapter VII of the Charter, demanded a halt to such actions.").

[222] *For example*, U.N. SECURITY COUNCIL RESOLUTION 1973, U.N. Doc. S/RES/1973, ¶4 (Mar. 17, 2011) ("[This Resolution] [a]uthorizes Member States that have notified the Secretary-General, acting nationally or through regional organizations or arrangements, and acting in cooperation with the Secretary-General, to take all necessary measures, notwithstanding paragraph 9 of resolution 1970 (2011), to protect civilians and civilian populated areas under threat of attack in the Libyan Arab Jamahiriya, including Benghazi, while excluding a foreign occupation force of any form on any part of Libyan territory … .").

security."[223]

The Charter of the United Nations was not intended to supersede a State's inherent right of individual or collective self-defense in customary international law.[224]

To constitute legitimate self-defense under customary international law, it is generally understood that the defending State's actions must be necessary.[225] For example, reasonably available peaceful alternatives must be exhausted.[226] In addition, the measures taken in self-defense must be proportionate to the nature of the threat being addressed.[227]

1.11.5.1 Responding to an Imminent Threat of an Attack. The text of Article 51 of the Charter of the United Nations refers to the right of self-defense "if an armed attack occurs against a Member of the United Nations."[228] Under customary international law, States had, and continue to have, the right to take measures in response to imminent attacks.[229]

1.11.5.2 Use of Force Versus Armed Attack. The United States has long taken the position that the inherent right of self-defense potentially applies against any illegal use of force.[230] Others, however, would be inclined to draw more of a distinction between "armed

---

[223] U.N. CHARTER art. 51.

[224] Abraham D. Sofaer, *Terrorism, the Law, and the National Defense*, 126 MILITARY LAW REVIEW 89, 94 (1989) ("The United States rejects the notion that the U.N. Charter supersedes customary international law on the right of self-defense. Article 51 characterizes that right as 'inherent' in order to prevent its limitation based on any provision in the Charter. We have always construed the phrase 'armed attack' in a reasonable manner, consistent with a customary practice that enables any State effectively to protect itself and its citizens from every illegal use of force aimed at the State.").

[225] William H. Taft IV, Legal Adviser, Department of State, *Self-Defense and the Oil Platforms Decision*, 29 YALE JOURNAL OF INTERNATIONAL LAW 295, 304 (2004) ("To constitute legitimate self-defense under customary international law, it is generally understood that the defending State's actions must be both 'necessary' and 'proportional.'").

[226] *Refer to* § 1.11.1.3 (All Peaceful Alternatives Must Have Been Exhausted (Necessity – Jus ad Bellum)).

[227] *Refer to* § 1.11.1.2 (The Means Must Be Proportionate to the Just Cause (Proportionality – Jus ad Bellum)).

[228] U.N. CHARTER art. 51.

[229] Lord Peter Henry Goldsmith, Attorney General, United Kingdom, *Oral Answers to Questions*, Apr. 21, 2004, HANSARD 660 HOUSE OF COMMONS DEBATES §§ 370-71 ("It is argued by some that the language of Article 51 provides for a right of self-defence only in response to an actual armed attack. However, it has been the consistent position of successive United Kingdom Governments over many years that the right of self-defence under international law includes the right to use force where an armed attack is imminent. It is clear that the language of Article 51 was not intended to create a new right of self-defence. Article 51 recognises the inherent right of self-defence that states enjoy under international law. ... It is not a new invention. The charter did not therefore affect the scope of the right of self-defence existing at that time in customary international law, which included the right to use force in anticipation of an imminent armed attack.").

[230] *See* Abraham D. Sofaer, *Terrorism, the Law, and the National Defense*, 126 MILITARY LAW REVIEW 89, 92-93 (1989) ("The United States has long assumed that the inherent right of self defense potentially applies against any illegal use of force, and that it extends to any group or State that can properly be regarded as responsible for such activities. These assumptions are supported in customary practice."). *See also* William H. Taft IV, Legal Adviser, Department of State, *Self-Defense and the Oil Platforms Decision*, 29 YALE JOURNAL OF INTERNATIONAL LAW 295, 300-01 (2004) ("A requirement that an attack reach a certain level of gravity before triggering a right of self-defense would make the use of force more rather than less likely, because it would encourage States to engage in a series of

attacks" and uses of force that do not give rise to the right to use force in self-defense.[231]

1.11.5.3 Use of Force to Protect Nationals Abroad. A State's right to use force in self-defense may be understood to include the right to use force to protect its nationals abroad.[232] The United States has taken action to protect U.S. nationals abroad when the government of the territory in which they are located was unwilling or unable to protect them.[233] A State need not await actual violence against its nationals before taking such action if an attack against them is imminent.[234]

1.11.5.4 Right of Self-Defense Against Non-State Actors. The inherent right of self-defense, recognized in Article 51 of the Charter of the United Nations, applies in response to any "armed attack," not just attacks that originate with States.[235] As with any other exercise of

---

small-scale military attacks, in the hope that they could do so without being subject to defensive responses. Moreover, if States were required to wait until attacks reached a high level of gravity before responding with force, their eventual response would likely be much greater, making it more difficult to prevent disputes from escalating into full-scale military conflicts.").

[231] *See, e.g.*, Military and Paramilitary Activities in and Against Nicaragua (Nicaragua v. United States), Merits, Judgment, 1986 I.C.J. 14, 101 (¶191) ("As regards certain particular aspects of the principle in question, it will be necessary to distinguish the most grave forms of the use of force (those constituting an armed attack) from other less grave forms."); *id.* at 126-27 (¶247) ("So far as regards the allegations of supply of arms by Nicaragua to the armed opposition in El Salvador, the Court has indicated that while the concept of an armed attack includes the despatch by one State of armed bands into the territory of another State, the supply of arms and other support to such bands cannot be equated with armed attack. Nevertheless, such activities may well constitute a breach of the principle of the non-use of force and an intervention in the internal affairs of a State, that is, a form of conduct which is certainly wrongful, but is of lesser gravity than an armed attack.").

[232] Ambassador William Scranton, U.S. Representative to the United Nations, *Statement in the U.N. Security Council* regarding Israeli action at Entebbe, Jul. 12, 1976, 1976 DIGEST OF UNITED STATES PRACTICE IN INTERNATIONAL LAW 150 ("[T]here is a well-established right to use limited force for the protection of one's own nationals from an imminent threat of injury or death in a situation where the State in whose territory they are located either is unwilling or unable to protect them. The right, flowing from the right of self defense, is limited to such use of force as is necessary and appropriate to protect threatened nationals from injury.").

[233] *For example*, Jimmy Carter, *Letter to Thomas P. O'Neal, Jr., Speaker of the House of Representatives, and Warren G. Magnuson, President pro tempore of the Senate regarding the rescue attempt for American hostages in Iran*, Apr. 26, 1980, 1980-I PUBLIC PAPERS OF THE PRESIDENTS 779 ("In carrying out this operation [to rescue the American hostages in the U.S. embassy in Tehran] the United States was acting wholly within its right, in accordance with Article 51 of the United Nations Charter, to protect and rescue its citizens where the government of the territory in which they are located is unwilling or unable to protect them.").

[234] Kenneth W. Dam, Deputy Secretary of State, *Statement before the House Committee on Foreign Affairs*, Nov. 2, 1983, *reprinted in* 78 AJIL 200, 203-04 (1984) ("U.S. actions have been based on three legal grounds: … Third, U.S. action to secure and evacuate endangered U.S. citizens on the island was undertaken in accordance with well-established principles of international law regarding the protection of one's nationals. That the circumstances warranted this action has been amply documented by the returning students themselves. There is absolutely no requirement of international law that compelled the United States to await further deterioration of the situation that would have jeopardized a successful operation. Nor was the United States required to await actual violence against U.S. citizens before rescuing them from the anarchic and threatening conditions the students have described.").

[235] *See, e.g.*, In re Guantanamo Bay Litigation, *Respondents' Memorandum Regarding the Government's Detention Authority Relative to Detainees Held at Guantanamo Bay*, Misc. No. 08-442, 4 (D.D.C., Mar. 13, 2009) ("Under international law, nations lawfully can use military force in an armed conflict against irregular terrorist groups such as al-Qaida. The United Nations Charter, for example, recognizes the inherent right of states to use force in self defense in response to any 'armed attack,' not just attacks that originate with states. United Nations Charter, art.

the right of self-defense, actions taken in self-defense against non-State actors must comply with applicable international law.[236]

1.11.5.5 Right of Collective Self-Defense. Article 51 of the Charter of the United Nations also recognizes a right of States to engage in collective self-defense with a State that can legitimately invoke its own right of national self-defense. Collective self-defense of a State must proceed with that State's consent, although this consent need not necessarily be expressed in the form of an explicit request.[237]

Some treaties include commitments by States to assist one another in collective self-defense.[238]

1.11.5.6 Reporting to the U.N. Security Council. Measures taken in the exercise of national self-defense shall be immediately reported to the U.N. Security Council.[239]

51."); *U.S. Additional Response to the Request for Precautionary Measures—Detention of Enemy Combatants at Guantanamo Bay, Cuba*, Inter-American Commission on Human Rights, Jul. 15, 2002, 2002 DIGEST OF UNITED STATES PRACTICE IN INTERNATIONAL LAW 1008, 1011-12 ("The terrorist attacks of September 11 were not ordinary criminal acts. ... The international community has clearly recognized the right of the United States and allied forces to resort to armed force in self-defense in response to these attacks. For instance, the United Nations explicitly recognized the 'inherent right of individual and collective self-defence' immediately following September 11. It is in this context that NATO and others recognized that the September 11 attacks constituted an 'armed attack,' a conclusion inherent in the UN Security Council's recognition of the right of self-defense.").

[236] *Refer to* § 17.18.2 (Duty of Belligerent States to Respect the Sovereignty of Other States).

[237] *See also* BRUNO SIMMA, THE CHARTER OF THE UNITED NATIONS: A COMMENTARY 675 (1994) ("Art. 51 of the Charter allows not only individual, but also collective self-defence. The latter is not, as the wording might suggest, restricted to a common, co-ordinated exercise of the right to individual self-defence by a number of states. ... It is not required for the exercise of the right of collective self-defence that the state invoking the right be under an obligation resulting from a treaty of assistance. Rather, it is sufficient, but also necessary, that the support be given with the consent of the attacked state. But this consent does not, as the ICJ states for the right of self-defence under customary law, need to be declared in the form of an explicit 'request'.").

[238] *For example*, The North Atlantic Treaty, Washington, D.C., Apr. 4, 1949, art. 5 ("The Parties agree that an armed attack against one or more of them in Europe or North America shall be considered an attack against them all and consequently they agree that, if such an armed attack occurs, each of them, in exercise of the right of individual or collective self-defense recognized by Article 51 of the Charter of the United Nations, will assist the Party or Parties so attacked by taking forthwith, individually and in concert with the other Parties, such action as it deems necessary, including the use of armed force, to restore and maintain the security of the North Atlantic area.").

[239] U.N. CHARTER art. 51 ("Measures taken by Members in the exercise of this right of self-defence shall be immediately reported to the Security Council and shall not in any way affect the authority and responsibility of the Security Council under the present Charter to take at any time such action as it deems necessary in order to maintain or restore international peace and security.").

II – Principles

Chapter Contents

2.1 INTRODUCTION

Three interdependent principles – *military necessity*, *humanity*, and *honor* – provide the foundation for other law of war principles, such as *proportionality* and *distinction*, and most of the treaty and customary rules of the law of war.

This Chapter briefly addresses certain specific rules to illustrate these foundational principles. For more information about a specific rule, practitioners should refer to the cross-referenced section that addresses that rule.[1]

2.1.1 Legal Principles as Part of International Law. General principles of law common to the major legal systems of the world are a recognized part of international law.[2] Law of war principles have been understood to be included in this category of international law.[3]

---

[1] *Refer to* § 1.2.3 (Use of Cross-References in This Manual).

[2] *See* ICJ STATUTE art. 38(1)(c) (providing that "the general principles of law recognized by civilized nations" are a source of applicable law for the court); I RESTATEMENT (THIRD) OF FOREIGN RELATIONS LAW OF THE UNITED STATES 24 (§102(1)(c)(4)) (1987) (including "general principles common to the major legal systems of the world," among sources of international law); Thirty Hogsheads of Sugar v. Boyle, 13 U.S. 191, 198 (1815) (Marshall, C.J.) (ascertaining international law includes "resort to the great principles of reason and justice").

[3] *See* BOTHE, PARTSCH, & SOLF, NEW RULES 44 (AP I art. 1, ¶2.10) ("Following the original clause in the preamble of the 1899 IV. Hague Convention on Land Warfare (para. 9) and para. 4 of the denunciation clause in the Conventions (63/62/142/158) these principles are stated in the present text to be *part of* international law. They are 'general principles of law' in the sense of Art. 38 of the Statute of the ICJ."); *Speech by Baron Descamps on the Rules of Law to be applied*, Annex No. 1 to *14th Meeting (Private), held at the Peace Palace, the Hague, on July 2nd, 1920*, PERMANENT COURT OF INTERNATIONAL JUSTICE, ADVISORY COMMITTEE OF JURISTS, PROCÈS-VERBAUX OF THE PROCEEDINGS OF THE COMMITTEE: JUNE 16TH – JULY 24TH 1920 WITH ANNEXES 322, 323-24 (1920) ("The only question is, -- how to make unerring rules for the judge's guidance. … I allow him to take into consideration the legal conscience of civilised nations, which is illustrated so strikingly on certain occasions. … [L]isten to this solemn declaration of the Powers, placed at the beginning of the Convention dealing with laws and customs of war on land: 'Until a more complete code of the laws of war has been issued, the high contracting Parties deem it expedient to declare that, in cases not included in the Regulations adopted by them, populations and belligerents remain under the protection and the rule of the principles of the law of nations, as they result from the usages established among civilised peoples, from the laws of humanity, and the dictates of the public conscience.' … I am convinced that the assembly of all the States does not and cannot intend, in dealing with the state of peace, to abjure principles which are clearly intended to be applied in war.").

2.1.2 Uses of Law of War Principles. Law of war principles provide the foundation for the specific law of war rules. Legal principles, however, are not as specific as rules, and thus interpretations of how principles apply to a given situation may vary.

Law of war principles: (1) help practitioners interpret and apply specific treaty or customary rules; (2) provide a general guide for conduct during war when no specific rule applies; and (3) work as interdependent and reinforcing parts of a coherent system.

2.1.2.1 *Law of War Principles as an Aid in Interpreting and Applying Law of War Rules*. Understanding law of war principles helps practitioners interpret and apply specific law of war rules. For example, the principle of *military necessity* has been incorporated into specific law of war rules.[4] Similarly, the principle of *humanity* can assist in the proper interpretation and application of law of war rules that are based on humanitarian considerations.[5]

2.1.2.2 *Law of War Principles as a General Guide*. When no specific rule applies, the principles of the law of war form the general guide for conduct during war.

States have reflected this idea in certain treaty provisions, including the "Martens Clause," which make clear that situations not covered by the treaty remain governed by principles of international law.[6]

The considerable progress States have made in developing specific law of war rules, however, has lessened the need to rely solely on these principles to guide conduct during war.[7]

2.1.2.3 *Law of War Principles as a Coherent System*. Law of war principles work as interdependent and reinforcing parts of a coherent system.

Military necessity justifies certain actions necessary to defeat the enemy as quickly and efficiently as possible.[8] Conversely, *humanity* forbids actions unnecessary to achieve that object.[9] *Proportionality* requires that even when actions may be justified by *military necessity*, such actions not be unreasonable or excessive.[10] *Distinction* underpins the parties' responsibility to comport their behavior with *military necessity*, *humanity*, and *proportionality* by requiring parties to a conflict to apply certain legal categories, principally the distinction between the

---

[4] *Refer to* § 2.2.2.2 (Incorporation of Military Necessity Into Law of War Rules).

[5] *Refer to* § 2.3.2 (Humanity and Law of War Rules).

[6] *Refer to* § 19.8.3 (Martens Clause).

[7] TUCKER, THE LAW OF WAR AND NEUTRALITY AT SEA 46-47 ("Where the general principles of the law of war have received—through the agreement of states—detailed application in the form of specific rules, the question of the proper interpretation of these general principles can only be answered by an examination of the former. Hence, to the extent that the conduct of war is increasingly subjected to such regulation resort to the general principles of the law of war must become, in turn, correspondingly less frequent. The reason for this is simply that the essential function of these general principles is to provide a guide for determining the legal status of weapons and methods of warfare *where no more specific rule is applicable*.").

[8] *Refer to* § 2.2 (Military Necessity).

[9] *Refer to* § 2.3 (Humanity).

[10] *Refer to* § 2.4 (Proportionality).

armed forces and the civilian population.[11] Lastly, *honor* supports the entire system and gives parties confidence in it.[12]

2.2 Military Necessity

Military necessity may be defined as the principle that justifies the use of all measures needed to defeat the enemy as quickly and efficiently as possible that are not prohibited by the law of war. *Military necessity* has been defined in military publications,[13] judicial decisions,[14] and scholarly works.[15]

2.2.1 Military Necessity as a Justification. *Military necessity* justifies actions, such as destroying and seizing persons and property.[16] Thus, *military necessity* underlies law of war

[11] *Refer to* § 2.5 (Distinction).

[12] *Refer to* § 2.6 (Honor).

[13] *See* LIEBER CODE art. 14 ("Military necessity, as understood by modern civilized nations, consists in the necessity of those measures which are indispensable for securing the ends of the war, and which are lawful according to the modern law and usages of war."); 1914 RULES OF LAND WARFARE ¶¶9-11 ("a belligerent is justified in applying any amount and any kind of force which is necessary for the purpose of the war; that is, the complete submission of the enemy at the earliest possible moment with the least expenditure of men and money. ... Military necessity justifies a resort to all measures which are indispensable for securing this object and which are not forbidden by the modern laws and customs of war."); 1940 RULES OF LAND WARFARE ¶4a ("a belligerent is justified in applying any amount and any kind of force to compel the complete submission of the enemy with the least possible expenditure of time, life, and money."); 1956 FM 27-10 (Change No. 1 1976) ¶3 ("that principle which justifies those measures not forbidden by international law which are indispensable for securing the complete submission of the enemy as soon as possible."); 1958 UK MANUAL ¶3 ("a belligerent is justified in applying compulsion and force of any kind, to the extent necessary for the realization of the purpose of war, that is, the complete submission of the enemy at the earliest possible moment with the least possible expenditure of men, resources, and money."); 2004 UK MANUAL ¶2.2 ("Military necessity is now defined as 'the principle whereby a belligerent has the right to apply any measures which are required to bring about the successful conclusion of a military operation and which are not forbidden by the laws of war.' Put another way, a state engaged in an armed conflict may use that degree and kind of force, not otherwise prohibited by the law of armed conflict, that is required in order to achieve the legitimate purpose of the conflict, namely the complete or partial submission of the enemy at the earliest possible moment with the minimum expenditure of life and resources."); NATO, Glossary of Terms and Definitions, AAP-6 at 2-M-6 (2009) (defining military necessity as "the principle whereby a belligerent has the right to apply any measures which are required to bring about the successful conclusion of a military operation and which are not forbidden by the laws of war.").

[14] *See* United States v. List, *et al.* (The Hostage Case), XI TRIALS OF WAR CRIMINALS BEFORE THE NMT 1253 ("Military necessity permits a belligerent, subject to the laws of war, to apply any amount and kind of force to compel the complete submission of the enemy with the least possible expenditure of time, life, and money.").

[15] *See* GREENSPAN, MODERN LAW OF LAND WARFARE 313-14 (military necessity is "the right to apply that amount and kind of force which is necessary to compel the submission of the enemy with the least possible expenditure of time, life, and money); CHARLES HENRY HYDE, II INTERNATIONAL LAW: CHIEFLY AS INTERPRETED AND APPLIED BY THE UNITED STATES 299-300 (1922) ("Military necessity, as understood by the United States, justifies a resort to all measures which are indispensable to bring about the complete submission of the enemy by means of regulated violence and which are not forbidden by the modern laws and customs of war."); WILLIAM EDWARD HALL, A TREATISE ON INTERNATIONAL LAW 63 (§17) (A. Pearce Higgins, ed., 7th ed., 1917) ("When violence is permitted at all, the amount which is permissible is that which is necessary to attain the object proposed. The measure of the violence which is permitted in war is therefore that which is required to reduce the enemy to terms.").

[16] *See* LIEBER CODE art. 15 ("Military necessity admits of all destruction of life or limb of armed enemies, ... it allows of the capturing of every armed enemy, and every enemy of importance to the hostile government, or of peculiar danger to the captor; it allows of all destruction of property, and obstruction of the ways and channels of

concepts that explain when persons and property may be the object of attack, *e.g.*, the concepts of "taking a direct part in hostilities"[17] and "military objective."[18]

Military necessity may justify not only violence and destruction, but also alternative means of subduing the enemy.[19] For example, military necessity may justify the capture of enemy persons,[20] or non-forcible measures, such as propaganda and intelligence-gathering.[21]

Military necessity also justifies certain incidental harms that inevitably result from the actions it justifies.[22] The extent to which *military necessity* justifies such harms is addressed by the principle of proportionality.[23]

2.2.2 Military Necessity and Law of War Rules.

2.2.2.1 *Military Necessity Does Not Justify Actions Prohibited by the Law of War*. *Military necessity* does not justify actions that are prohibited by the law of war.

From the late 19th Century through World War II, Germany asserted that *military necessity* could override specific law of war rules (*Kriegsraeson geht vor Kriegsmanier* – "necessity in war overrules the manner of warfare").[24] This view was strongly criticized.[25] Post-

---

traffic, travel, or communication, and of all withholding of sustenance or means of life from the enemy; of the appropriation of whatever an enemy's country affords necessary for the subsistence and safety of the army, and of such deception as does not involve the breaking of good faith either positively pledged, regarding agreements entered into during the war, or supposed by the modern law of war to exist."); United States v. List, *et al.* (The Hostage Case), XI TRIALS OF WAR CRIMINALS BEFORE THE NMT 1253-54 ("In general, [military necessity] sanctions measures by an occupant necessary to protect the safety of his forces and to facilitate the success of his operations. It permits the destruction of life of armed enemies and other persons whose destruction is incidentally unavoidable by the armed conflicts of the war; it allows the capturing of armed enemies and others of peculiar danger … . It is lawful to destroy railways, lines of communication, or any other property that might be utilized by the enemy. Private homes and churches even may be destroyed if necessary for military operations.").

[17] *Refer to* § 5.8 (Civilians Taking a Direct Part in Hostilities).

[18] *Refer to* § 5.6 (Military Objective).

[19] *For example*, Abraham Lincoln, The Emancipation Proclamation, Jan. 1, 1863, *reprinted in* 12 STAT. 1268 (justifying emancipation of slaves held in rebellious states as "warranted by the Constitution, upon military necessity").

[20] *Refer to* § 8.1.3.1 (Detention Authority).

[21] *Refer to* § 5.26 (Non-Forcible Means and Methods of Warfare).

[22] *See* LIEBER CODE art. 15 ("Military necessity admits of all destruction of life or limb of … persons whose destruction is incidentally unavoidable in the armed contests of the war;"); United States v. List, *et al.* (The Hostage Case), XI TRIALS OF WAR CRIMINALS BEFORE THE NMT 1253-54 (military necessity "permits the destruction of life of … persons whose destruction is incidentally unavoidable by the armed conflicts of the war;").

[23] *Refer to* § 2.4 (Proportionality).

[24] *See* LAUTERPACHT, II OPPENHEIM'S INTERNATIONAL LAW 231-32 (§69) ("In accordance with the German proverb, *Kriegsraeson geht vor Kriegsmanier* (*necessity in war overrules the manner of warfare*), many German authors before the First World War were maintaining that the laws of war lose their binding force in case of extreme necessity."); United States, *et al.* v. Göring, *et al.*, *Judgment*, I TRIAL OF THE MAJOR WAR CRIMINALS BEFORE THE IMT 227 ("The truth remains that War Crimes were committed on a vast scale, never before seen in the history of war. … There can be no doubt that the majority of them arose from the Nazi conception of 'total war', with which

World War II war crimes tribunals rejected it as well.[26]

Military necessity cannot justify departures from the law of war because States have crafted the law of war specifically with war's exigencies in mind.[27] In devising law of war rules, States considered military requirements.[28] Thus, prohibitions on conduct in the law of war may be understood to reflect States' determinations that such conduct is militarily unnecessary *per se*.

The fact that law of war rules are formulated specifically with military requirements in

---

the aggressive wars were waged. For in this conception of 'total war', the moral ideas underlying the conventions which seek to make war more humane are no longer regarded as having force or validity. Everything is made subordinate to the overmastering dictates of war. Rules, regulations, assurances, and treaties all alike are of no moment; and so, freed from the restraining influence of international law, the aggressive war is conducted by the Nazi leaders in the most barbaric way. Accordingly, War Crimes were committed when and wherever the Führer and his close associates thought them to be advantageous.").

[25] *See, e.g.*, Elihu Root, *Opening Address*, 15 PROCEEDINGS OF THE AMERICAN SOCIETY OF INTERNATIONAL LAW 1, 2 (1921) ("More important still is a fact which threatens the foundation of all international law. The doctrine of *kriegsraison* has not been destroyed. It was asserted by Bethman Hollweg at the beginning of the war when he sought to justify the plain and acknowledged violation of international law in the invasion of Belgium upon the ground of military necessity. The doctrine practically is that if a belligerent deems it necessary for the success of its military operations to violate a rule of international law, the violation is permissible. As the belligerent is to be the sole judge of the necessity, the doctrine really is that a belligerent may violate the law or repudiate it or ignore it whenever that is deemed to be for its military advantage. The alleged necessity in the case of the German invasion of Belgium was simply that Belgium was deemed to be the most advantageous avenue through which to attack France. Of course, if that doctrine is to be maintained, there is no more international law, for the doctrine cannot be confined to the laws specifically relating to war on land and sea. With a nation at liberty to declare war, there are few rules of peaceful intercourse, the violation of which may not be alleged to have some possible bearing upon a military advantage, and a law which may rightfully be set aside by those whom it is intended to restrain is no law at all.").

[26] *See, e.g.*, United States v. List, *et al.* (The Hostage Case), XI TRIALS OF WAR CRIMINALS BEFORE THE NMT 1255-56 ("It is apparent from the evidence of these defendants that they considered military necessity, a matter to be determined by them, a complete justification of their acts. We do not concur in the view that the rules of warfare are anything less than they purport to be. Military necessity or expediency do not justify a violation of positive rules."); United States v. Krupp, *et al.*, IX TRIALS OF WAR CRIMINALS BEFORE THE NMT 1340 (rejecting defense counsel argument that Hague IV and Hague IV Reg. rules did not apply in cases of "total war"). *See also* Trial of Gunther Thiele and Georg Steinert, III U.N. LAW REPORTS 58-59 (U.S. Military Commission, Augsberg, Germany, Jun. 13, 1945) (rejecting military necessity as a defense to the murder of a prisoner of war); United States v. Milch, II TRIALS OF WAR CRIMINALS BEFORE THE NMT 849-50 (Musmanno, J., concurring) (rejecting defense counsel argument that "total warfare" allowed suspension or abrogation of law of war rules).

[27] 1956 FM 27-10 (Change No. 1 1976) ¶3a ("Military necessity has been generally rejected as a defense for acts forbidden by the customary and conventional laws of war inasmuch as the latter have been developed and framed with consideration for the concept of military necessity."); United States v. Krupp, *et al.*, IX TRIALS OF WAR CRIMINALS BEFORE THE NMT 1347 ("In short these rules and customs of warfare are designed specifically for all phases of war. They comprise the law for such emergency."); Treaty of Amity and Commerce between His Majesty the King of Prussia and the United States of America, art. 24, Sept. 10, 1785, 18 STAT. 641, 647 (declaring that "neither the pretence that war dissolves all treaties, nor any other whatever, shall be considered as annulling or suspending this and next preceding article; but on the contrary, that the state of war is precisely that for which they are provided, and during which they are to be as sacredly observed as the most acknowledged articles in the law of nature or nations.").

[28] *See, e.g.*, HAGUE IV preamble ¶5 ("these provisions, the wording of which has been inspired by the desire to diminish the evils of war, as far as military requirements permit, are intended to serve as a general rule of conduct for the belligerents in their mutual relations and in their relations with the inhabitants.") (emphasis added).

mind has played an important part in the doctrine that the law of war is the *lex specialis* governing armed conflict.[29]

2.2.2.2 *Incorporation of Military Necessity Into Law of War Rules*. Although *military necessity* cannot justify actions that have been prohibited by the law of war, some law of war rules expressly incorporate *military necessity*.

For example, certain law of war rules specify that departures from what would otherwise be the rule are permissible when *absolutely* or *imperatively* necessary. In these cases, *military necessity* must not be conflated with mere convenience.[30] Examples of rules incorporating the concept of *absolute* or *imperative* necessity include the following:

- The activities of the representatives or delegates of the Protecting Powers shall only be restricted as an exceptional and temporary measure when this is rendered necessary by imperative military necessities.[31]
- The internment or placing in assigned residence of protected persons may be ordered only if the security of the Detaining Power makes it absolutely necessary.[32]
- If the Occupying Power considers it necessary, for imperative reasons of security, to take safety measures concerning protected persons, it may, at the most, subject them to assigned residence or to internment.[33]
- The seizure or destruction of enemy property must be imperatively demanded by the necessities of war.[34]

Certain law of war rules may direct that persons comply with an obligation, but only to the extent feasible or consistent with *military necessity*. Examples of rules incorporating the concept of *feasibility* or *necessity* include the following:

- Certain affirmative duties to take feasible precautions to reduce the risk of harm to the

[29] *Refer to* § 1.3.2.1 (The Law of War as the Lex Specialis Governing Armed Conflict).

[30] *See* United States v. List, *et al.* (The Hostage Case), XI TRIALS OF WAR CRIMINALS BEFORE THE NMT 1252 (rejecting defendants' "plea of military necessity, a term which they confuse with convenience and strategical interests."); General Dwight D. Eisenhower, Commander-in-Chief, U.S. Army, *Memorandum Regarding the Protection of Historical Monuments in Italy*, Dec. 29, 1943, X WHITEMAN'S DIGEST 438 (§13) (explaining that although "the phrase 'military necessity' is sometimes used where it would be more truthful to speak of military convenience or even personal convenience," *military necessity* should not "cloak slackness or indifference" to discerning whether law of war obligations, such as the protection of cultural property, may be fulfilled without any detriment to operational needs).

[31] *Refer to* § 4.25.3 (Restrictions on Representatives of the Protecting Powers).

[32] *Refer to* § 10.9.2.1 (Internment or Assigned Residence Only if Absolutely Necessary).

[33] *Refer to* § 10.9.3.1 (Internment or Assigned Residence for Imperative Reasons of Security).

[34] *Refer to* § 5.17.2 (Enemy Property – Military Necessity Standard); § 11.18.2 (Seizure or Destruction of Property During Occupation – Application of the Military Necessity Standard).

civilian population and other protected persons and objects.[35]

- Military medical and religious personnel, if their retention is not indispensable, are to be returned to the party to the conflict to which they belong as soon as a road is open for their return and military requirements permit.[36]

- Whenever military considerations permit, POW camps shall be indicated in the day time by the letters PW or PG, placed so as to be clearly visible from the air.[37]

- Should military necessity require the quantity of relief shipments to civilian internees to be limited, due notice thereof shall be given to the Protecting Power and to the International Committee of the Red Cross, or to any other organization giving assistance to the internees and responsible for the forwarding of such shipments.[38]

2.2.3 Applying Military Necessity. *Military necessity* is a difficult concept to define and apply.[39] What is necessary in war may depend closely on the specific facts and circumstances of a given situation, and different people often assess *military necessity* differently. The limited and unreliable nature of information available during war compounds this difficulty in evaluating what is necessary.[40] This difficulty runs throughout the law of war, since *military necessity* is itself important and is an element of many other principles and rules.

The law of war seeks to ameliorate these difficulties in applying *military necessity* by: (1) permitting consideration of the broader imperatives of winning the war as quickly and efficiently as possible; (2) recognizing that certain types of actions are, as a general matter, inherently militarily necessary; and (3) recognizing that persons must assess the *military necessity* of an action in good faith based on the information available to them at the relevant time and that they cannot be judged based on information that subsequently comes to light.

2.2.3.1 *Consideration of the Broader Imperatives of Winning the War*. In evaluating *military necessity*, one may consider the broader imperatives of winning the war as quickly and efficiently as possible and is not restricted to considering only the demands of the specific situation.

This is the case because *military necessity* justifies those measures necessary to achieve the object of war, and the object of war is not simply to prevail, but to prevail as quickly and efficiently as possible.[41] Thus, *military necessity* may consider the broader imperatives of

[35] *Refer to* § 5.2.3 (Affirmative Duties to Take Feasible Precautions for the Protection of Civilians and Other Protected Persons and Objects).

[36] *Refer to* § 7.9.4 (Return of Personnel Whose Retention Is Not Indispensable).

[37] *Refer to* § 9.11.4.3 (Marking of POW Camps).

[38] *Refer to* § 10.23.3 (Receipt of Individual and Collective Relief Shipments for Internees).

[39] *See* SPAIGHT, WAR RIGHTS ON LAND 113 ("There is no conception in International Law more elusive, protean, wholly unsatisfactory, than that of war necessity.").

[40] *Refer to* § 1.4.2.2 (Nature of War – Limited and Unreliable Information – "Fog of War").

[41] *Refer to* § 1.4.1 (Object of War).

winning the war and not only the demands of the immediate situation. For example, in assessing the military advantage of attacking an object, one may consider the entire war strategy rather than only the potential tactical gains from attacking that object.[42] An interpretation of *military necessity* that only permitted consideration of the immediate situation could prolong the fighting and increase the overall suffering caused by the war.[43]

Some commentators have argued that *military necessity* should be interpreted so as to permit only what is actually necessary in the prevailing circumstances, such as by requiring commanders, if possible, to seek to capture or wound enemy combatants rather than to make them the object of attack.[44] This interpretation, however, does not reflect customary international law or treaty law applicable to DoD personnel.[45] For example, the law of war does not require that enemy combatants be warned before being made the object of attack, nor does the law of war require that enemy combatants be given an opportunity to surrender before being made the object of attack.[46] Moreover, the law of war may justify the use of overwhelming force against enemy military objectives.[47]

2.2.3.2 *Recognizing Certain Types of Actions as Generally Inherently Militarily*

---

[42] *Refer to* § 5.6.7.3 (Definite Military Advantage); § 5.12.2.1 (Considering the Advantage From the Attack as a Whole – In the Operational and Strategic Context).

[43] *See, e.g.*, Department of Defense, *National Military Strategy of the United States*, 10 (Jan. 1992) ("Once a decision for military action has been made, half-measures and confused objectives extract a severe price in the form of a protracted conflict which can cause needless waste of human lives and material resources, a divided nation at home, and defeat. Therefore, one of the essential elements of our national military strategy is the ability to rapidly assemble the forces needed to win -- the concept of applying decisive force to overwhelm our adversaries and thereby terminate conflicts swiftly with a minimum loss of life."); LIEBER CODE art. 29 ("The more vigorously wars are pursued, the better it is for humanity. Sharp wars are brief."); Count von Moltke, letter to Professor Bluntschli, Dec. 11, 1880, *reprinted in* G. SHERSTON BAKER, II HALLECK'S INTERNATIONAL LAW 19 footnote 1 (1908) ("The greatest kindness in war is to bring it to a speedy conclusion.").

[44] *See, e.g.*, Nils Melzer, Legal Adviser, International Committee of the Red Cross, *Interpretive Guidance on the Notion of Direct Participation in Hostilities Under International Humanitarian Law*, 79 (May 2009) ("In conjunction, the principles of military necessity and of humanity reduce the sum total of permissible military action from that which IHL does not expressly prohibit to that which is actually necessary for the accomplishment of a legitimate military purpose in the prevailing circumstances.") (emphasis added); JEAN PICTET, DEVELOPMENT AND PRINCIPLES OF INTERNATIONAL HUMANITARIAN LAW 75-76 (1985) ("If we can put a soldier out of action by capturing him, we should not wound him; if we can obtain the same result by wounding him, we must not kill him.").

[45] *See, e.g.*, W. Hays Parks, Chief, International Law Branch, Office of the Judge Advocate General, Department of the Army, *Executive Order 12333 and Assassination*, Nov. 2, 1989, III CUMULATIVE DIGEST OF UNITED STATES PRACTICE IN INTERNATIONAL LAW 1981-1988 3411, 3419 ("In the employment of military forces, the phrase 'capture or kill' carries the same meaning or connotation in peacetime as it does in wartime. There is no obligation to attempt capture rather than attack of an enemy. In some cases, it may be preferable to utilize ground forces in order to capture, *e.g.*, a known terrorist. However, where the risk to U.S. forces is deemed too great, if the President has determined that the individual[s] in question pose such a threat to U.S. citizens or the national security interests of the United States as to require the use of military force, it would be legally permissible to employ, *e.g.*, an airstrike against that individual or group rather than attempt his, her, or their capture, and would not violate the prohibition on assassination.").

[46] *Refer to* § 5.4.6.1 (Surprise Attacks); § 5.4.6.2 (Attacks on Retreating Forces).

[47] *Refer to* § 5.4.6 (Force That May Be Applied Against Military Objectives).

Necessary. The law of war recognizes that certain types of actions are, as a general matter, inherently militarily necessary.[48] For example, attacking enemy combatants is generally lawful.[49] Similarly, the internment of enemy POWs is generally lawful.[50] Such rules may be viewed as an example of how, when specific rules are applicable, there is less need to resort to fundamental law of war principles as a general guide for conduct during war.[51]

2.2.3.3 Good Faith Evaluation of Military Necessity Based on the Available Information. In what is sometimes called the "Rendulic Rule," the law of war recognizes that persons must assess the *military necessity* of an action based on the information available to them at that time; they cannot be judged based on information that subsequently comes to light.[52]

2.3 HUMANITY

Humanity may be defined as the principle that forbids the infliction of suffering, injury, or destruction unnecessary to accomplish a legitimate military purpose.[53]

2.3.1 Humanity as a Prohibition. Although *military necessity* justifies certain actions necessary to defeat the enemy as quickly and efficiently as possible, *military necessity* cannot justify actions not necessary to achieve this purpose, such as cruelty or wanton violence.[54] Moreover, once a military purpose has been achieved, inflicting more suffering is unnecessary

---

[48] *See* VATTEL, THE LAW OF NATIONS 295 (3.9.173) (explaining that the law of war seeks to avoid contentious disputes between belligerents about whether actions are militarily necessary by establishing "general rules independent of circumstances and of certain and easy application" and thus "permits or tolerates every act which in its essential nature is adapted to attaining the end of war; and it does not stop to consider whether the act was unnecessary, useless, or superfluous in a given case unless there is the clearest evidence that an exception should be made in that instance").

[49] *Refer to* § 5.5.1 (Persons, Objects, and Locations That Are Not Protected From Being Made the Object of Attack).

[50] *Refer to* § 9.11.1 (Internment in POW Camps).

[51] *Refer to* § 2.1.2.2 (Law of War Principles as a General Guide).

[52] *Refer to* § 5.3 (Assessing Information Under the Law of War).

[53] *See, e.g.*, 2001 CANADIAN MANUAL ¶202(6) (humanity "forbids the infliction of suffering, injury or destruction not actually necessary for the accomplishment of legitimate military purposes."); 2004 UK MANUAL ¶2.4 ("Humanity forbids the infliction of suffering, injury, or destruction not actually necessary for the accomplishment of legitimate military purposes."); GREENSPAN, MODERN LAW OF LAND WARFARE 315 (humanity "forbids the employment of all such kinds and degrees of violence as are not necessary for the purpose of the war"); 1958 UK MANUAL ¶3 (humanity is the principle "according to which kinds and degrees of violence which are not necessary for the purpose of war are not permitted to a belligerent;"); LAUTERPACHT, II OPPENHEIM'S INTERNATIONAL LAW 227 (§67) (Humanity "postulates that all such kinds and degrees of violence as are not necessary for the overpowering of the opponent should not be permitted to a belligerent."); 1940 RULES OF LAND WARFARE ¶4b (defining the principle of humanity as "prohibiting employment of any such kind or degree of violence as is not actually necessary for the purpose of the war"); 1914 RULES OF LAND WARFARE ¶9 (The principle of humanity "says that all such kinds and degrees of violence as are not necessary for the purpose of war are not permitted to a belligerent.").

[54] United States v. List, *et al.* (The Hostage Case), XI TRIALS OF WAR CRIMINALS BEFORE THE NMT 1253-54 ("[Military necessity] does not permit the killing of innocent inhabitants for purposes of revenge or the satisfaction of a lust to kill. ... It does not admit the wanton devastation of a district or the willful infliction of suffering upon its inhabitants for the sake of suffering alone."); LIEBER CODE art. 16 ("Military necessity does not admit to cruelty -- that is, the infliction of suffering for the sake of suffering or for revenge, ...").

and should be avoided. For example, if an enemy combatant has been placed *hors de combat* (*e.g.*, incapacitated by being severely wounded or captured), no military purpose is served by continuing to attack him or her.[55] Thus, the principle of *humanity* forbids making enemy combatants who have been placed *hors de combat* the object of attack.[56] Similarly, the principle of *humanity* has been viewed as the source of the civilian population's immunity from being made the object of attack because their inoffensive and harmless character means that there is no military purpose served by attacking them.[57]

2.3.1.1 *Relationship Between the Principles of Humanity and Military Necessity*. Humanity is related to military necessity, and these principles logically complement one another.

Humanity may be viewed as the logical inverse of the principle of military necessity. If certain necessary actions are justified, then certain unnecessary actions are prohibited. The principle of humanity is an example of how the concept of necessity can function as a limitation as well as a justification.[58]

Because humanity forbids those actions that are unnecessary, the principle of humanity is not in tension with military effectiveness, but instead reinforces military effectiveness.[59]

2.3.2 Humanity and Law of War Rules. *Humanity* animates certain law of war rules, including:

- fundamental safeguards for persons who fall into the hands of the enemy;[60]
- protections for the civilian population and civilian objects;[61]
- protections for military medical personnel, units, and transports;[62]

---

[55] *See* 2004 UK MANUAL ¶2.4.1 ("The principle of humanity is based on the notion that once a military purpose has been achieved, the further infliction of suffering is unnecessary. Thus, if an enemy combatant has been put out of action by being wounded or captured, there is no military purpose to be achieved by continuing to attack him. For the same reason, the principle of humanity confirms the basic immunity of civilian populations and civilian objects from attack because civilians and civilian objects make no contribution to military action.").

[56] *Refer to* § 5.9 (Persons Placed *Hors de Combat*).

[57] *Refer to* § 4.2.1 (Development of the Distinction Between the Armed Forces and the Civilian Population).

[58] *Cf.* Ex parte Milligan, 71 U.S. 2, 127 (1866) ("If, in foreign invasion or civil war, the courts are actually closed, and it is impossible to administer criminal justice according to law, then, on the theatre of active military operations, where war really prevails, there is a necessity to furnish a substitute for the civil authority, thus overthrown, to preserve the safety of the army and society, and as no power is left but the military, it is allowed to govern by martial rule until the laws can have their free course. As necessity creates the rule, so it limits its duration, for, if this government is continued after the courts are reinstated, it is a gross usurpation of power.") (emphasis added).

[59] *Refer to* § 18.2.1 (Reinforcing Military Effectiveness).

[60] *Refer to* § 8.2 (Humane Treatment of Detainees); § 9.5 (Humane Treatment and Basic Protections for POWs); § 10.5 (Humane Treatment and Other Basic Protections for Protected Persons).

[61] *Refer to* § 5.2 (Overview of Rules for the Protection of Civilians).

- prohibitions on weapons that are calculated to cause superfluous injury;[63] and
- prohibitions on weapons that are inherently indiscriminate.[64]

The principle of *humanity* may help interpret or apply these and other law of war rules. For example, the requirement that POWs be interned only in premises located on land has been understood not to prohibit POW detention aboard ships pending the establishment of suitable facilities on land, if detention aboard ships provides the most appropriate living conditions for POWs.[65] Similarly, the U.S. reservation to CCW Protocol III on Incendiary Weapons makes clear that U.S. forces may use incendiary weapons against military objectives located in concentrations of civilians where it is judged that such use would cause fewer casualties and/or less collateral damage than alternative weapons.[66]

2.4 Proportionality

Proportionality may be defined as the principle that even where one is justified in acting, one must not act in a way that is unreasonable or excessive.[67]

Proportionality has also been viewed as a legal restatement of the military concept of economy of force.[68]

2.4.1 Proportionality as a Limit on the Exercise of a Right.

2.4.1.1 *Justification in Acting*. *Proportionality* is implicated in cases in which one is justified in acting. In *jus in bello*, for example, *military necessity* justifies making military objectives, such as enemy combatants, the object of attack. So, an attack on enemy combatants that incidentally damages civilian property would raise *proportionality* considerations. On the other hand, where there is no justification for acting, such as unlawful attacks directed against

---

[62] *Refer to* § 7.8 (Respect and Protection of Categories of Medical and Religious Personnel); § 7.10 (Military Medical Units and Facilities); § 7.11 (Ground Transport); § 7.12 (Hospital Ships, Sick-Bays in Warships, and Coastal Rescue Craft); § 7.14 (Military Medical Aircraft).

[63] *Refer to* § 6.6 (Weapons Calculated to Cause Superfluous Injury).

[64] *Refer to* § 6.7 (Inherently Indiscriminate Weapons).

[65] *Refer to* § 9.11.3.1 (Location on Land).

[66] *Refer to* § 6.14.3.2 (U.S. Reservation to CCW Protocol III on Incendiary Weapons).

[67] *See* Daniel Webster, *Letter to Mr. Fox*, Apr. 24, 1841, *reprinted in* DANIEL WEBSTER, THE DIPLOMATIC AND OFFICIAL PAPERS OF DANIEL WEBSTER, WHILE SECRETARY OF STATE 110 (1848) (explaining that even actions taken in self-defense should not be "unreasonable or excessive" since such actions "justified by the necessity of self-defense, must be limited by that necessity and kept clearly within it"). *See also* GROTIUS, LAW OF WAR & PEACE 601 (3.1.4.2) ("we must also beware of what happens, and what we foresee may happen, beyond our purpose, unless the good which our action has in view is much greater than the evil which is feared, or, greater than the fear of the evil."); VATTEL, THE LAW OF NATIONS 279 (3.8.137) (explaining that a Sovereign has "the right to make war upon his fellow-men as a matter of necessity, and as a remedy," but the Sovereign should not "push the remedy beyond its just limits," and should "be careful not to make it more severe or more disastrous to mankind than the care of his own safety and the defense of his rights require.").

[68] *Refer to* § 5.12.3.1 (The Military Concept of Economy of Force).

the civilian population, a *proportionality* analysis would not be necessary to reach the conclusion that the attack would be unlawful.

2.4.1.2 Unreasonable or Excessive. *Proportionality* generally weighs the justification for acting against the expected harms to determine whether the latter are disproportionate in comparison to the former. In war, incidental damage to the civilian population and civilian objects is unfortunate and tragic, but inevitable.[69] Thus, applying the principle of proportionality in conducting attacks does not require that no incidental damage result from attacks.[70] Rather, this principle creates obligations to refrain from attacks in which the expected harm incidental to such attacks would be excessive in relation to the concrete and direct military advantage anticipated to be gained and to take feasible precautions in planning and conducting attacks to reduce the risk of harm to civilians and other persons and objects protected from being made the object of attack.[71]

Under the law of war, judgments of *proportionality* often involve difficult and subjective comparisons.[72] Recognizing these difficulties, States have declined to use the term "proportionality" in law of war treaties because it could incorrectly imply an equilibrium between considerations or suggest that a precise comparison between them is possible.[73]

2.4.2 Examples Where Proportionality Is Reflected in Law of War Rules. The principle of proportionality is reflected in many areas in the law of war.

Proportionality is often used to refer to the *jus in bello* prohibition on attacks expected to cause excessive incidental harm.[74] However, the principle of proportionality described in a more general sense in this section also underlies the affirmative duties to take feasible precautions for the protection of civilians and other protected persons and objects.[75] These obligations apply both in conducting attacks and to the party subject to attack.[76] *Proportionality* also plays a role in assessing whether weapons are prohibited because they are calculated to cause unnecessary

---

[69] *Refer to* § 1.4.2 (Nature of War).

[70] *Refer to* § 5.10 (Proportionality in Conducting Attacks).

[71] *Refer to* § 5.12 (Proportionality – Prohibition on Attacks Expected to Cause Excessive Incidental Harm); § 5.11 (Proportionality – Feasible Precautions in Planning and Conducting Attacks to Reduce the Risk of Harm to Protected Persons and Objects).

[72] *Refer to* § 5.10.2.2 (Subjective Aspects of the Decisions and Judgments Required by the Principle of Proportionality). *Compare* § 2.2.3 (Applying *Military Necessity*).

[73] *See, e.g.*, BOTHE, PARTSCH, & SOLF, NEW RULES 309-10 (AP I art. 51, ¶2.6.2) (describing how some government delegations in the 1974-1977 Diplomatic Conference opposed incorporation of the term "proportionality" or acknowledgement of a law of war "rule" of proportionality in AP I and AP II).

[74] *Refer to* § 5.12 (Proportionality – Prohibition on Attacks Expected to Cause Excessive Incidental Harm).

[75] *Refer to* § 5.2.3 (Affirmative Duties to Take Feasible Precautions for the Protection of Civilians and Other Protected Persons and Objects).

[76] *Refer to* § 5.11 (Proportionality – Feasible Precautions in Planning and Conducting Attacks to Reduce the Risk of Harm to Protected Persons and Objects); § 5.14 (Feasible Precautions to Reduce the Risk of Harm to Protected Persons and Objects by the Party Subject to Attack).

suffering.[77]

In *jus ad bellum*, *proportionality* requires that the State's means in resorting to force be proportionate to its just cause in using force, such as the threat that the State seeks to address.[78] *Proportionality* is also a requirement for reprisals, which must respond in a proportionate manner to the preceding illegal act by the party against which they are taken.[79]

2.5 Distinction

Distinction, sometimes called *discrimination*, obliges parties to a conflict to distinguish principally between the armed forces and the civilian population, and between unprotected and protected objects.[80]

Distinction may be understood as encompassing two sets of reinforcing duties. Parties to a conflict must apply a framework of legal classes for persons and objects by: (1) discriminating in conducting attacks against the enemy; and (2) distinguishing a party's own persons and objects.

2.5.1 Distinction as a Framework of Legal Classes. *Distinction* requires parties to a conflict to apply a framework of legal classes for persons and objects, each class characterized by different rights, duties, and liabilities.

Principally, *distinction* seeks to separate the armed forces and the civilian population.[81] There are, however, certain special cases, such as military medical and religious personnel, who may be treated like a combatant for one purpose (*e.g.*, detention) but like a civilian for another purpose (*e.g.*, not being made the object of attack).[82] However, for any particular legal purpose, a person may not claim the distinct rights afforded to both combatants and civilians at the same

---

[77] *Refer to* § 6.6.3.3 (Clearly Disproportionate).

[78] *Refer to* § 1.11.1.2 (The Means Must Be Proportionate to the Just Cause (Proportionality – Jus ad Bellum)).

[79] *Refer to* § 18.18.2.4 (Proportionality in Reprisal).

[80] *See, e.g.*, J. Fred Buzhardt, General Counsel, Department of Defense, Letter to Senator Edward Kennedy, Sept. 22, 1972, *reprinted in* 67 AJIL 122 (1973) ("A summary of the laws of armed conflict, in the broadest terms, reveals certain general principles including the following: … (c). That a distinction must be made at all times between persons taking part in the hostilities and members of the civilian population to the effect that the civilians be spared as much as possible. These general principles were recognized in a resolution unanimously adopted by the United Nations General Assembly in its Resolution dated 13 January 1969 (Resolution 2444 (XXIII)). We regard them as declaratory of existing customary international law."); Ex parte Quirin, 317 U.S. 1, 30 (1942) ("By universal agreement and practice, the law of war draws a distinction between the armed forces and the peaceful populations of belligerent nations,"); 2004 UK MANUAL ¶2.5 ("Since military operations are to be conducted only against the enemy's armed forces and military objectives, there must be a clear distinction between the armed forces and civilians, or between combatants and non-combatants, and between objects that might legitimately be attacked and those that are protected from attack."). *Consider* AP I art. 48 ("In order to ensure respect for and protection of the civilian population and civilian objects, the Parties to the conflict shall at all times distinguish between the civilian population and combatants and between civilian objects and military objectives and accordingly shall direct their operations only against military objectives.").

[81] *Refer to* § 4.2 (The Armed Forces and the Civilian Population).

[82] *Refer to* § 4.2.3 (Mixed Cases).

time.[83]

2.5.2 Discriminating in Conducting Attacks Against the Enemy. *Distinction* requires parties to a conflict to discriminate in conducting attacks against the enemy.[84] On the one hand, consistent with *military necessity*, parties may make enemy combatants and other military objectives the object of attack.[85] On the other hand, consistent with *humanity*, parties may not make the civilian population and other protected persons and objects the object of attack.[86] Moreover, persons using force must discriminate between legitimate and illegitimate objects of attack in good faith based on the information available to them at the time.[87]

2.5.3 Distinguishing a Party's Own Persons and Objects. *Distinction* enjoins the party controlling the population[88] to use its best efforts to distinguish or separate its military forces and war-making activities from members of the civilian population to the maximum extent feasible so that civilian casualties and damage to civilian objects incidental to attacks on military objectives will be minimized as much as possible.[89]

Parties to a conflict must: (1) take certain measures to help ensure that military forces and civilians can be visually distinguished from one another; (2) physically separate, as feasible, their military objectives from the civilian population and other protected persons and objects; and (3) refrain from the misuse of protected persons and objects to shield military objectives.

2.5.3.1 *Measures to Help Ensure That Military Forces and Civilians Are Visually Distinguishable From One Another*. Parties to a conflict must take certain measures, in offense or defense, to help ensure that military forces and civilians can be visually distinguished from one another.

First, parties to a conflict must not disguise their armed forces as civilians or as other protected categories of persons in order to kill or wound opposing forces.[90] Second, other rules

---

[83] *Refer to* § 4.2.2 (No Person May Claim the Distinct Rights Afforded to Both Combatants and Civilians at the Same Time).

[84] *Refer to* § 5.5 (Discrimination in Conducting Attacks).

[85] *Refer to* § 5.5.1 (Persons, Objects, and Locations That Are Not Protected From Being Made the Object of Attack).

[86] *Refer to* § 5.5.2 (Persons, Objects, and Locations That Are Protected From Being Made the Object of Attack).

[87] *Refer to* § 5.3 (Assessing Information Under the Law of War).

[88] *Refer to* § 5.2.1 (Responsibility of the Party Controlling Civilian Persons and Objects).

[89] *See* J. Fred Buzhardt, General Counsel, Department of Defense, Letter to Senator Edward Kennedy, Sept. 22, 1972, *reprinted in* 67 AJIL 122 (1973) ("A summary of the laws of armed conflict, in the broadest terms, reveals certain general principles including the following: … (c). That a distinction must be made at all times between persons taking part in the hostilities and members of the civilian population to the effect that the civilians be spared as much as possible. … The principle in (c) addresses primarily the Party exercising control over members of the civilian population. This principle recognizes the interdependence of the civilian community with the overall war effort of a modern society. But its application enjoins the party controlling the population to use its best efforts to distinguish or separate its military forces and war making activities from members of the civilian population to the maximum extent feasible so that civilian casualties and damage to civilian objects incidental to attacks on military objectives, will be minimized as much as possible.").

[90] *Refer to* § 5.22 (Treachery or Perfidy Used to Kill or Wound).

obligate parties to mark protected persons and objects to help ensure they receive the protections of that status.[91] Third, certain rules encourage parties to a conflict to identify certain persons and objects as unprotected. For example, during international armed conflict, members of organized resistance movements must, *inter alia*, wear fixed distinctive signs visible at a distance and carry arms openly to distinguish themselves from the civilian population in order for members of their group to receive POW status.[92]

2.5.3.2 *Feasible Measures to Separate Physically a Party's Own Military Objectives From the Civilian Population and Other Protected Persons and Objects*. *Distinction* also creates obligations for parties to a conflict to take feasible measures to separate physically their own military objectives from the civilian population and other protected persons and objects.[93]

For example, it may be appropriate to evacuate civilians from danger areas.[94] Similarly, if feasible, military commanders should avoid placing military objectives in densely populated areas.[95] In addition, it may be appropriate to establish zones where civilians and other protected persons may seek refuge.[96]

2.5.3.3 *Refrain From the Misuse of Protected Persons and Objects to Shield Military Objectives*. Parties to a conflict must refrain from the misuse of civilians and other protected persons and objects to shield their own military objectives.[97] For example, it is prohibited to take hostages or otherwise to endanger deliberately protected persons or objects for the purpose of deterring enemy military operations.

Misusing protected persons and objects to shield military objectives also offends *honor* because it constitutes a breach of trust with the enemy and thus undermines respect for the law of war.[98]

2.5.4 Misconceptions About Distinction. *Distinction* seeks to ensure that protected and unprotected categories are distinct from one another, not distinct in the abstract. For example, using camouflage is consistent with *distinction* because foliage is not a protected category and because civilians generally do not wear camouflage.[99] Similarly, U.S. forces have worn non-standard uniforms to blend with local forces while remaining distinct from the civilian

---

[91] *Refer to* § 5.14.4 (Using Distinctive and Visible Signs to Identify Protected Persons and Objects as Such).

[92] *Refer to* § 4.6.4 (Having a Fixed Distinctive Sign Recognizable at a Distance); § 4.6.5 (Carrying Arms Openly).

[93] *Refer to* § 5.14 (Feasible Precautions to Reduce the Risk of Harm to Protected Persons and Objects by the Party Subject to Attack).

[94] *Refer to* § 5.14.2 (Removing Civilians and Civilian Objects From the Vicinity of Military Objectives).

[95] *Refer to* § 5.14.1 (Refraining From Placing Military Objectives in Densely Populated Areas).

[96] *Refer to* § 5.14.3 (Establishing Areas Where Civilians or the Wounded and Sick Are Protected).

[97] *Refer to* § 5.16 (Prohibition on Using Protected Persons and Objects to Shield, Favor, or Impede Military Operations).

[98] *Refer to* § 2.6.2 (Certain Amount of Fairness in Offense and Defense).

[99] *Refer to* § 5.25.2 (Examples of Ruses), footnote 799 and accompanying text.

population.[100]

Distinction addresses the different rights, duties, and liabilities of the categories; it does not require that a particular person or object fall within a particular category. For example, the principle of *distinction* does not prohibit an otherwise civilian object from being used for military purposes, thereby turning it into a military objective.[101] However, if such an object were seized from the enemy, such seizure would have to have been imperatively demanded by the necessities of war.[102] Similarly, persons with medical training or who provide medical care on the battlefield are not necessarily military medical personnel and need not be identified as such.[103] Rather, a State may reserve the ability to use these persons as combatants by refraining from designating them as exclusively engaged in medical activities.

2.5.5 Reinforcing Duties – Discriminating in Conducting Attacks and Distinguishing a Party's Own Persons and Objects. Discriminating in conducting attacks against the enemy and distinguishing a party's own persons and objects reinforce one another.

A party is not relieved of its obligations to discriminate in conducting attacks by the failures of its adversary to distinguish its military objectives from protected persons and objects.[104] Nonetheless, the practical ability of a party to a conflict to discriminate in conducting attacks often depends on the degree to which its enemy has distinguished its military objectives from its protected persons and objects. For example, if enemy forces intermingle with civilians, then a party may be less able to avoid incidentally harming the civilian population.

In addition, the degree to which an enemy force in fact discriminates in conducting attacks may affect whether a party distinguishes its protected persons and objects from its military objectives. For example, if enemy forces do not respect the red cross emblem, but instead specifically attack persons wearing it, then the party receiving these attacks is less likely to distinguish its medical personnel and transports.[105] Similarly, if insurgents seek to attack civilians in a non-international armed conflict, positioning military forces near the civilian population may be essential to protecting the civilian population.[106]

2.6 Honor

Honor demands a certain amount of fairness in offense and defense and a certain mutual

---

[100] *Refer to* § 5.25.2.1 (Mimicking Other Friendly Forces).

[101] *Refer to* § 5.16.1 (Protected Persons and Objects).

[102] *Refer to* § 5.17.2.2 (Seizure or Destruction of Enemy Property to Support Military Operations).

[103] *Refer to* § 4.9.2 (Requirements for Military Medical and Religious Status).

[104] *Refer to* § 5.4.4 (Failure by the Defender to Separate or Distinguish Does Not Relieve the Attacker of the Duty to Discriminate in Conducting Attacks).

[105] *Refer to* § 7.15.2.1 (Removal or Obscuration of the Distinctive Emblem).

[106] *Refer to* § 17.5.2.1 (Positioning Military Forces Near the Civilian Population to Win Their Support and to Protect Them).

respect between opposing military forces.[107]

2.6.1 Honor – Background and Notes on Terminology. *Honor* has been vital to the development of the law of war, which was preceded by warriors' codes of ethical behavior.[108] U.S. military canons of personal conduct continue to emphasize the importance of honor as a core value. Honor as a core value and other ethical norms continue to be vital as a medium for the implementation of the law of war.[109]

Honor has also been called *chivalry*. *Chivalry* is often associated with a specific historical context—a code of behavior for knights in Europe during the Middle Ages. Rather than refer to this specific context, the term *honor* is used in this manual to indicate more clearly that the law of war principle of *honor* draws from warriors' codes from a variety of cultures and time periods.

2.6.2 Certain Amount of Fairness in Offense and Defense. *Honor* requires a certain amount of fairness in offense and defense. *Honor* forbids resort to means, expedients, or conduct

---

[107] *See, e.g.*, LAUTERPACHT, II OPPENHEIM'S INTERNATIONAL LAW 227 (§67) (chivalry "arose in the Middle Ages and introduced a certain amount of fairness in offence and defence, and a certain mutual respect"); 1958 UK MANUAL ¶3 ("The development of the law of war has been determined by three principles: ... and thirdly, the principle of chivalry, which demands a certain amount of fairness in offence and defence, and a certain mutual respect between the opposing forces."); 1914 RULES OF LAND WARFARE ¶9 ("The development of the laws and usages of war is determined by three principles. ... *Third,* the principle of chivalry, which demands a certain amount of fairness in offense and defense and a certain mutual respect between opposing forces."); UNITED KINGDOM WAR OFFICE, MANUAL OF MILITARY LAW, *Chapter XIV, The Laws and Usages of War on Land*, 234 (¶3) (1914) ("The development of the laws and usages of war is determined by three principles. ... And there is, thirdly, the principle of chivalry, which demands a certain amount of fairness in offence and defence, and a certain mutual respect between the opposing forces.").

[108] *See, e.g.*, LESLIE C. GREEN, THE CONTEMPORARY LAW OF ARMED CONFLICT 20-23 (2000) (describing references to warrior codes from ancient Israel, China, India, Greece, Rome, and Islam).

[109] John Keegan, *If you won't, we won't: Honour and the decencies of battle*, THE TIMES LITERARY SUPPLEMENT, Issue 4834, 11 (Nov. 24, 1995; London, England) ("In the most perceptive sentence in *The Laws of War*, Adam Roberts observes, during his survey of the effect of the Hague Conventions of 1895 and 1907, that 'the experience of land war in two world wars must raise a question as to whether formal legal codification is necessarily superior to notions of custom, honour, professional standards, and natural law' in making for battlefield decencies. He might have made his point more emphatically. There is no substitute for honour as a medium of enforcing decency on the battlefield, never has been and never will be. There are no judges, more to the point, no policemen at the place where death is done in combat; that may be, in fact, the intended and all too often true, meaning of 'silent leges inter arma'. All turns on the values of the junior leader present at the moment when the opponent's capacity or will to resist fails, he ceases to be a combatant and he must hope for the mercy of the suddenly stronger."); *for example*, MORAL COURAGE IN COMBAT: THE MY LAI STORY, *Lecture by Hugh Thompson*, 26 (U.S. Naval Academy Center for Professional Military Ethics 2003) ("***Question*** Do you attribute your ability to see through the moral fog that day, better than those who made the massacre at My Lai happen, to any prior military training or experience? ***Mr. Thompson*** No, I don't believe it was any military training, because I had been through the training that everybody else had been. We had a 50-minute class of instruction on the Geneva Convention, a 50-minute class of instruction on the Code of Conduct, and a 50-minute class of instruction on the rules of engagement. ... But [my parents] always taught me to help the underdog. Don't be a bully and live by the golden rule. That golden rule says so much, and it's so simple and so basic. You know, I can't say it was a leadership 405 or whatever. I just think it was my parents, and they taught me right from wrong.").

that would constitute a breach of trust with the enemy.[110]

2.6.2.1 *Acceptance That Belligerent Rights Are Not Unlimited*. In requiring a certain amount of fairness in offense and defense, *honor* reflects the principle that parties to a conflict must accept that certain limits exist on their ability to conduct hostilities. For example, parties to the conflict must accept that the right of belligerents to adopt means of injuring the enemy is not unlimited.[111] Here, *honor* does not address what those limits are so much as requires that parties accept that there are legal limits that govern their conduct of hostilities.[112] This acceptance is a prerequisite for the existence and operation of the law of war in the way that the principle of *pacta sunt servanda* (treaties are binding on parties and must be performed by them in good faith) provides a necessary foundation for treaties to exist and operate as instruments that are legally binding on States.[113]

Thus, *honor* may be understood to provide a foundation for obligations that help enforce and implement the law of war or special agreements between belligerents during armed conflict.[114] For example, *honor* may be understood to provide the foundation for the requirement for persons to comply with the law of war in good faith.[115] Similarly, POWs are bound to adhere to paroles on their personal honor.[116]

2.6.2.2 *Prohibition on Conduct That Breaches Trust With the Enemy*. In requiring a certain amount of fairness in offense and defense, *honor* also forbids resort to means, expedients, or conduct that would constitute a breach of trust with the enemy. In particular, *honor* requires a party to a conflict to refrain from taking advantage of its opponent's adherence to the law by falsely claiming the law's protections.

Honor forbids such conduct because it may: (1) undermine the protections afforded by the law of war; (2) impair non-hostile relations between opposing belligerents; and (3) damage the basis for the restoration of peace short of complete annihilation of one belligerent by

---

[110] 1940 RULES OF LAND WARFARE ¶4(c) (chivalry "denounces and forbids resort to dishonorable means, expedients, or conduct"); 2001 CANADIAN MANUAL ¶202(7) ("An armed conflict is rarely a polite contest. Nevertheless, the concept of chivalry is reflected in specific prohibitions such as those against dishonourable or treacherous conduct and against misuse of enemy flags or flags of truce.").

[111] *See, e.g.*, 1899 HAGUE II REG. art. 22 ("The right of belligerents to adopt means of injuring the enemy is not unlimited."); HAGUE IV REG. art. 22 (same); CCW preamble (noting "the principle of international law that the right of the parties to an armed conflict to choose methods or means of warfare is not unlimited"). *Consider* AP I art. 35(1) ("In any armed conflict, the right of the Parties to the conflict to choose methods or means of warfare is not unlimited.").

[112] Legality of the Threat or Use of Nuclear Weapons, Advisory Opinion, 1996 I.C.J. 583, 585 (¶11) (Dissenting Opinion of Judge Higgins) ("The legal principle by which parties to an armed conflict do not have an unlimited choice of weapons or of methods of warfare... [is intended] to ensure that weapons, both in the context of their use, and in the methods of warfare, must comply with the other substantive rules.").

[113] *Refer to* § 1.10.1.1 (Legal Force of Treaties Among States).

[114] *Refer to* § 18.1.2 (National Obligations to Implement and Enforce the Law of War).

[115] *Refer to* § 18.3 (Duties of Individual Members of the Armed Forces).

[116] *Refer to* § 9.11.2 (Parole of POWs).

another.[117]

For example, enemies must deal with one another in good faith in their non-hostile relations.[118] And even in the conduct of hostilities, good faith prohibits: (1) killing or wounding enemy persons by resort to perfidy; (2) misusing certain signs; (3) fighting in the enemy's uniform; (4) feigning non-hostile relations in order to seek a military advantage; and (5) compelling nationals of a hostile party to take part in the operations of war directed against their own country.[119] *Honor*, however, does not forbid parties from using ruses and other lawful deceptions against which the enemy ought to take measures to protect itself.[120]

2.6.3 Certain Mutual Respect Between Opposing Military Forces. *Honor* demands a certain mutual respect between opposing military forces.

Opposing military forces should respect one another outside of the fighting because they share a profession and they fight one another on behalf of their respective States and not out of personal hostility.[121] For example, this principle is reflected in the rule that POWs are legally in the hands of the enemy State and not the individuals or military units who have captured them.[122]

2.6.3.1 *Honor and Rules for POW Captivity*. In demanding a certain mutual respect between opposing military forces, *honor* animates rules that relate to the treatment of POWs. For example, *honor* is one of the foundations for the humane treatment of POWs.[123] The principle of *honor* is also reflected in rules that require POWs and their captors to treat one another with respect. For example, POWs must be treated with respect for their honor and person.[124] As another example, POWs, with the exception of officers, must salute and show to all officers of the Detaining Power the external marks of respect provided for by the regulations

---

[117] *Refer to* § 5.21.1 (Harms From Breaches of Good Faith).

[118] *Refer to* § 12.2 (Principle of Good Faith in Non-Hostile Relations).

[119] *Refer to* § 5.21 (Overview of Good Faith, Perfidy, and Ruses).

[120] *Refer to* § 5.25 (Ruses of War and Other Lawful Deceptions).

[121] *See* JEAN-JACQUES ROUSSEAU, THE SOCIAL CONTRACT & DISCOURSES 12 (1920) ("The object of war being the destruction of the hostile State, the other side has a right to kill its defenders, while they are bearing arms; but as soon as they lay them down and surrender, they cease to be enemies or instruments of the enemy, and become once more merely men, whose life no one has any right to take.").

[122] *Refer to* § 9.2.2 (Responsibility of the Detaining Power).

[123] *See, e.g.*, Samuel Falle, *Chivalry*, 113 Proceedings Magazine, Jan. 1987 ("During World War II, the Japanese were portrayed as brutal, subhuman savages—the hordes of Attila or Genghis Khan. Certainly they did terrible things, but I was fortunate enough to see something different. It is called 'chivalry,' which the Oxford Dictionary defines as a 'medieval knightly system, with its religious, moral, and social code; ideal knight's characteristics.' I see it as compassion and magnanimity toward a beaten enemy."); United States, *et al.* v. Göring, *et al.*, *Judgment*, I TRIAL OF THE MAJOR WAR CRIMINALS BEFORE THE IMT 289 ("When, on 8 September 1941, OKW issued its ruthless regulations for Soviet POW's, Canaris wrote to [the defendant] Keitel that under international law the SD should have nothing to do with this matter. On this memorandum, in Keitel's handwriting, dated 23 September and initialed by him, is the statement: 'The objections arise from the military concept of chivalrous warfare. This is the destruction of an ideology. Therefore I approve and back the measures.'").

[124] *Refer to* § 9.5.1 (Respect for Their Persons and Honor).

applying in their own forces.[125] In addition, capitulations agreed upon between belligerents must take into account the rules of military honor.[126]

2.6.3.2 Honor and the Class of Military Forces. In demanding a certain mutual respect between opposing military forces, *honor* also reflects the premise that military forces are a common class of professionals who have undertaken to comport themselves honorably.[127]

Honor thus animates the rules that determine who qualifies for privileges of combatant status. For example, an armed group must, *inter alia*, be organized under a responsible command and conduct its operations in accordance with the law of war in order for its members to be entitled to POW status during international armed conflict.[128] On the other hand, private persons are generally denied the privileges of combatant status because they do not belong to this class of combatants.[129]

The principle that combatants share a common class has also been a foundation for the trial of enemy combatants by military tribunals.[130] For example, the GPW expresses a preference for POWs to be tried by military courts rather than civilian courts.[131]

---

[125] *Refer to* § 9.22.3 (Saluting Between POWs and Officers of the Detaining Power).

[126] *Refer to* § 12.8.3 (Rules of Military Honor).

[127] SPAIGHT, AIR POWER AND WAR RIGHTS 109-10 ("Chivalry is difficult to define but it means broadly, the waging of war in accordance with certain well-recognised formalities and courtesies. It is an influence quite distinct from the humanitarian one; indeed, it prevailed in its full vigour at a time in which humanitarian interests were otherwise entirely disregarded: witness the cruelty of the Black Prince to the people of Limoges. It is against free from any necessary connection with Christianity; Saladin was a chivalrous as Coeur-de-Lion. It is, indeed, the spirit pure and simple, of knighthood. It expresses in effect the feeling of the combatants that they belong to a caste, that their encounter in arms is a high ceremonial, that an opponent is entitled to all honour and respect, that your enemy, though he is your enemy, is at the same time a brother in the same noble family of knights-at-arms. Until gunpowder came to democratise war, chivalry and chivalry alone was an influence making for moderation in war. It was the first motive power for the creation of a restrictive law of war.").

[128] *Refer to* § 4.6.1 (GPW 4A(2) Conditions in General).

[129] *Refer to* § 4.18.3 (Private Persons Who Engage in Hostilities – Lack of the Privileges of Combatant Status).

[130] General Douglas MacArthur, *Action of the Confirming Authority*, Feb. 7, 1946, United States v. Yamashita (U.S. Military Commission, Manila, Dec. 7, 1945), LEVIE, DOCUMENTS ON POWS 298 ("It is not easy for me to pass penal judgment upon a defeated adversary in a major military campaign. I have reviewed the proceedings in vain search for some mitigating circumstance on his behalf. I can find none. Rarely has so cruel and wanton a record been spread to public gaze. Revolting as this may be in itself, it pales before the sinister and far reaching implication thereby attached to the profession of arms. The soldier, be he friend or foe, is charged with the protection of the weak and unarmed. It is the very essence and reason for his being. When he violates this sacred trust, he not only profanes his entire cult but threatens the very fabric of international society. The traditions of fighting men are long and honorable. They are based upon the noblest of human traits, - sacrifice. This officer, of proven field merit, entrusted with high command involving authority adequate to responsibility, has failed this irrevocable standard; has failed his duty to his troops, to his country, to his enemy, to mankind; has failed utterly his soldier faith. The transgressions resulting therefrom as revealed by the trial are a blot upon the military profession, a stain upon civilization and constitute a memory of shame and dishonor that can never be forgotten. Peculiarly callous and purposeless was the sack of the ancient city of Manila, with its Christian population and its countless historic shrines and monuments of culture and civilization, which with campaign conditions reversed had previously been spared.").

[131] *Refer to* § 9.26.3 (Trial by Military Courts).

III – Application of the Law of War

Chapter Contents

3.1 Introduction

Whether a particular law of war rule applies to a situation may depend on a variety of issues, such as (1) whether a state of "war," "hostilities," or "armed conflict" exists;[1] (2) whether a party is recognized as a belligerent or as a State;[2] or (3) whether an enemy State has accepted that law of war rule.[3] This Chapter addresses these and other broad issues underlying the application of law of war rules. Later chapters address issues in applying specific rules, including considerations specific to those rules. For example, whether a specific provision of the GPW applies to a particular person may depend on whether that person is entitled to POW status under the GPW.[4]

Many of the legal issues underlying the application of law of war rules may be confusing because they are complex and may appear to result in contradictory legal positions. For example, a State may be at "war" for some purposes, but not for other purposes.[5] The legal character of U.S. military operations may change rapidly. For example, some operations may begin as military operations other than war and later evolve into war, or an international armed conflict may change into a non-international armed conflict.

Although this Chapter addresses how rules apply as a matter of law, DoD practice has often been to act consistently with law of war rules, even in certain cases where these rules might not technically be applicable as a matter of law.

3.1.1 <u>DoD Practice of Applying Law of War Rules Even When Not Technically Applicable</u>. DoD policy and doctrine make clear the importance of compliance with,

---

[1] *Refer to* § 3.4 (When *Jus in Bello* Rules Apply).

[2] *Refer to* § 3.3 (Status of the Parties and the Law of War).

[3] *Refer to* § 3.6.1 (Treaty Provisions That Provide for Reciprocity in the Scope of Application of the Treaty).

[4] *Refer to* § 9.3 (POW Status).

[5] *Refer to* § 1.5 ("War" as a Legal Concept).

implementation of, and enforcement of the law of war.[6]

In addition, DoD practice has often been to act consistently with law of war rules, even in certain cases where these rules might not technically be applicable as a matter of law. This means, for example, that DoD practice has often been to act consistently with a particular law of war treaty rule, even if that rule might not apply as a matter of treaty law. Moreover, DoD practice has sometimes been to adhere to the standards in the law of war, even in situations that do not constitute "war" or "armed conflict," because these standards in the law of war reflect legal standards that must be adhered to in all circumstances (*i.e.*, whether there is a state of armed conflict or not).

3.1.1.1 *Reasons for Acting Consistent With a Treaty Rule, Even Though the Treaty Does Not Apply*. DoD practice has often been to act consistently with a treaty rule, even if that rule might not apply as a matter of treaty law. First, it may be appropriate to act consistently with the terms of a treaty (even as applied in dealings with a non-Party to a treaty) because the general principles of the treaty have been determined to be declaratory of customary international law.[7] In such cases, practice that is consistent with the treaty's terms with regard to a particular matter likewise would be in compliance with applicable customary international law.

In addition, it may be important to act consistently with the terms of the treaty because the treaty represents "modern international public opinion" as to how military operations should be conducted.[8] Other policy considerations, including efficacious training standards or close relations with coalition partners, may lead to a policy decision that DoD practice should be consistent with a particular law of war treaty rule, even if that rule does not apply to U.S. forces as a matter of law.

3.1.1.2 *Applying Law of War Standards as Reflecting Minimum Legal Standards*. DoD practice also has been to adhere to certain standards in the law of war, even in situations that do not constitute "war" or "armed conflict," because these law of war rules reflect standards that must be adhered to in all circumstances. Applying these standards provides assurance that the standards adhered to equal or exceed those required. This practice has been reflected in DoD policies to comply with the law of war, or to comply with the spirit and principles of the law of

---

[6] *Refer to* § 18.1.1 (DoD Policy on Implementing and Enforcing the Law of War).

[7] 1956 FM 27-10 (Change No. 1 1976) Foreword ("Moreover, even though States may not be parties to, or strictly bound by, the 1907 Hague Conventions and the 1929 Geneva Convention relative to the Treatment of Prisoners of War, the general principles of these conventions have been held declaratory of the customary law of war to which all States are subject. For this reason, the United States has adopted the policy of observing and enforcing the terms of these conventions in so far as they have not been superseded by the 1949 Geneva Conventions which necessarily govern the relations between the parties to the latter (see pars. 6 and 7 of the text).").

[8] 1956 FM 27-10 (Change No. 1 1976) ¶7a ("These treaty provisions are in large part but formal and specific applications of general principles of the unwritten law. While solemnly obligatory only as between the parties thereto, they may be said also to represent modern international public opinion as to how belligerents and neutrals should conduct themselves in the particulars indicated. For these reasons, the treaty provisions quoted herein will be strictly observed and enforced by United States forces without regard to whether they are legally binding upon this country. Military commanders will be instructed which, if any, of the written rules herein quoted are not legally binding as between the United States and each of the States immediately concerned, and which, if any, for that reason are not for the time being to be observed or enforced.").

war, during military operations outside the context of armed conflict.[9]

Certain prohibitions and certain other rules in the law of war that reflect customary international law have been described as reflecting "elementary considerations of humanity."[10] These "elementary considerations of humanity" have been understood to be "even more exacting in peace than in war."[11] Thus, these legal standards, at a minimum, must be adhered to in all circumstances.

In particular, Common Article 3 of the 1949 Geneva Conventions reflects a minimum yardstick of humane treatment protections for all persons taking no active part in hostilities, including members of armed forces who have laid down their arms and those placed *hors de combat* by sickness, wounds, detention, or any other cause.[12] The standards in Common Article 3 of the 1949 Geneva Conventions may be understood to reflect minimum humane treatment standards for detainees in any military operation, including those during international or non-international armed conflict or occupation, and those military operations that are not addressed by the law of war. Additional rules will apply depending on the particular context. For example, the United States has supported adherence to the guarantees in Article 75 of AP I during international armed conflict.[13]

3.2 Situations to Which the Law of War Applies

Although the law of war is commonly understood as applying to the conduct of hostilities and the protection of war victims, the law of war addresses other situations as well. The law of war establishes:

---

[9] *See* DoD Directive 2311.01E, *DoD Law of War Program*, ¶4.1 (May 9, 2006, Certified Current as of Feb. 22, 2011) ("Members of the DoD Components comply with the law of war during all armed conflicts, however such conflicts are characterized, and in all other military operations."); DoD Directive 5100.77, *DoD Law of War Program*, ¶5.3 (Dec. 9, 1998) ("The Heads of the DoD Components shall: 5.3.1. Ensure that the members of their DoD Components comply with the law of war during all armed conflicts, however such conflicts are characterized, and with the principles and spirit of the law of war during all other operations."). *Refer to* § 18.1.1 (DoD Policy on Implementing and Enforcing the Law of War).

[10] Legality of the Threat or Use of Nuclear Weapons, Advisory Opinion, 1996 I.C.J. 226, 257 (¶79) ("It is undoubtedly because a great many rules of humanitarian law applicable in armed conflict are so fundamental to the respect of the human person and 'elementary considerations of humanity' as the Court put it in its Judgment of 9 April 1949 in the Corfu Channel case (I.C.J. Reports 1949, p. 22), that the Hague and Geneva Conventions have enjoyed a broad accession. Further these fundamental rules are to be observed by all States whether or not they have ratified the conventions that contain them, because they constitute intransgressible principles of international customary law.").

[11] Corfu Channel Case (United Kingdom v. Albania), Merits, Judgment, 1949 I.C.J. 4, 22 ("The obligations incumbent upon the Albanian authorities consisted in notifying, for the benefit of shipping in general, the existence of a minefield in Albanian territorial waters and in warning the approaching British warships of the imminent danger to which the minefield exposed them. Such obligations are based, not on the Hague Convention of 1907, No. VIII, which is applicable in time of war, but on certain general and well-recognized principles, namely: elementary considerations of humanity, even more exacting in peace than in war; the principle of the freedom of maritime communication; and every State's obligation not to allow knowingly its territory to be used for acts contrary to the rights of other States.").

[12] *Refer to* § 8.1.4.1 (Common Article 3 of the 1949 Geneva Conventions).

[13] *Refer to* § 8.1.4.2 (Article 75 of AP I and Relevant AP II Provisions).

- rules governing the resort to force (*jus ad bellum*);[14]
- rules between enemies for the conduct of hostilities and the protection of war victims in international and non-international armed conflict;[15]
- rules between belligerents and neutrals;[16]
- rules for military occupation;[17] and
- duties during peacetime that help implement the above rules.[18]

In addition, these rules in the law of war can sometimes be applied by analogy to other contexts.[19]

3.3 Status of the Parties and the Law of War

The law of war distinguishes between: (1) international armed conflicts, *i.e.*, conflicts between States; and (2) other armed conflicts, typically called non-international armed conflicts.

Three situations—unrecognized governments, recognition of belligerency, and national liberation movements—merit further discussion because they may affect whether law of war rules relating to international armed conflict apply.

3.3.1 International Armed Conflict and Non-International Armed Conflict. The law of war treats situations of "war," "hostilities," or "armed conflict" differently based on the legal status of parties to the conflict. If two or more States oppose one another, then this type of armed conflict is known as an "international armed conflict" because it takes place between States. However, a state of war can exist when States are not on opposite sides of the conflict.[20] These other types of conflict are described as "not of an international character" or "non-international armed conflict."[21] For example, two non-State armed groups warring against one

---

[14] *Refer to* § 1.11 (*Jus ad Bellum*).

[15] Chapter V addresses the conduct of hostilities.

[16] Chapter XV addresses the law of neutrality.

[17] *Refer to* § 11.2 (When Military Occupation Law Applies).

[18] *Refer to* § 3.9 (Law of War Duties Also Applicable in Peace).

[19] *Refer to* § 3.7 (Applying Rules by Analogy).

[20] *See, e.g.*, Hamdan v. Rumsfeld, 548 U.S. 557, 630 (2006) (noting that an armed conflict described in Common Article 3 of the 1949 Geneva Conventions "does not involve a clash between nations."); The Prize Cases, 67 U.S. 635, 666 (1863) ("it is not necessary to constitute war, that both parties should be acknowledged as independent nations or sovereign States. A war may exist where one of the belligerents, claims sovereign rights as against the other.").

[21] *See, e.g.*, Hamdan v. Rumsfeld, 415 F.3d 33, 44 (D.C. Cir. 2005) (Williams, J., concurring) ("Non-state actors cannot sign an international treaty. Nor is such an actor even a 'Power' that would be eligible under Article 2 (P3) to secure protection by complying with the Convention's requirements. Common Article 3 fills the gap, providing some minimal protection for such non-eligibles in an 'armed conflict not of an international character occurring in the territory of one of the High Contracting Parties.' The gap being filled is the non-eligible party's failure to be a

another or States warring against non-State armed groups may be described as "non-international armed conflict," even if international borders are crossed in the fighting.[22]

The law of war rules applicable to non-international armed conflict are addressed in Chapter XVII.[23] There are a number of important differences between the law applicable to international armed conflict and the law applicable to non-international armed conflict.[24]

3.3.1.1 *Application of* Jus in Bello *Rules Does Not Necessarily Affect the Legal Status of Parties*. Although the legal status of an opponent affects the character of the conflict and what rules apply as a matter of law, the application of *jus in bello* rules does not necessarily affect the legal status of parties to a conflict. For example, a belligerent may, as a policy matter, afford a person POW protections and treatment without affording that person legal status as a POW.[25] Similarly, the application of humanitarian rules, such as those reflected in Common Article 3 of the 1949 Geneva Conventions, towards enemy non-State armed groups does not affect their legal status (*e.g.*, such application does not amount to recognizing the group as lawful belligerents or as the legitimate government of a State).[26]

3.3.1.2 *Mixed Conflicts Between Opposing States and Non-State Armed Groups*. Rather than viewing a situation as either an international armed conflict or a non-international armed conflict, it may be possible to characterize parts of a conflict as international in character, while other parts of that armed conflict may be regarded as non-international in character.[27] For example, under this view, during a situation involving conflict between a variety of States and non-State armed groups, as between the States, the rules of international armed conflict would apply, while as between the States and non-State armed groups, the rules of non-international armed conflicts would apply.[28]

---

nation. Thus the words 'not of an international character' are sensibly understood to refer to a conflict between a signatory nation and a non-state actor. The most obvious form of such a conflict is a civil war. But given the Convention's structure, the logical reading of 'international character' is one that matches the basic derivation of the word 'international,' i.e., between nations. Thus, I think the context compels the view that a conflict between a signatory and a non-state actor is a conflict 'not of an international character.'").

[22] *Refer to* § 17.1.1.2 (NIAC and Internal Armed Conflict).

[23] *Refer to* § 17.1 (Introduction).

[24] *Refer to* § 17.1.3 (Important Differences Between the Law Applicable to International Armed Conflict and the Law Applicable to Non-International Armed Conflict).

[25] *Refer to* § 9.3.1 (POW Status Versus POW Protections).

[26] *Refer to* § 17.2.3 (Application of Humanitarian Rules and the Legal Status of the Parties to the Conflict).

[27] Christopher Greenwood, *International Humanitarian Law and the Tadic Case*, 7 EUROPEAN JOURNAL OF INTERNATIONAL LAW 265, 271 (1996) ("[T]here is nothing intrinsically illogical or novel in characterizing some aspects of a particular set of hostilities as an international armed conflict while others possess an internal character. Conflicts have been treated as having such a dual aspect where a Government is simultaneously engaged in hostilities with a rebel movement and with another State which backs that movement.").

[28] *See, e.g.*, Military and Paramilitary Activities in and Against Nicaragua (Nicaragua v. United States), Merits, Judgment, 1986 I.C.J. 14, 114 (¶219) ("The conflict between the *contras'* forces and those of the Government of Nicaragua is an armed conflict which is 'not of an international character'. The acts of the *contras* towards the Nicaraguan Government are therefore governed by the law applicable to conflicts of that character; whereas the

3.3.2 Unrecognized Governments. Even if a State does not recognize an opponent as the legitimate government of a State, under certain circumstances, rules of international armed conflict may apply to a conflict between a State and a government that it does not recognize. For example, members of the regular armed forces who profess allegiance to a government or authority not recognized by the Detaining Power nonetheless would be entitled to POW status if they fall into the power of the enemy during international armed conflict.[29]

3.3.3 State Recognition of Armed Groups as Belligerents. In certain cases, States have recognized armed groups as belligerents for certain legal purposes.

For the purpose of applying humanitarian rules, recognition of the armed group as having belligerent rights is neither a prerequisite for nor a result of applying humanitarian rules.[30]

3.3.3.1 *Recognition by Outside States of a Rebel Faction as a Belligerent in a Civil War*. In the past, in cases of a major civil war in a State, other States have recognized the rebel faction as a belligerent with the effect of treating the rebels as though they were a State with belligerent rights under the law of neutrality.[31]

Historically, certain conditions had to be satisfied before outside States could recognize a non-State armed group as a belligerent:

---

actions of the United States in and against Nicaragua fall under the legal rules relating to international conflicts. Because the minimum rules applicable to international and to non-international conflicts are identical, there is no need to address the question whether those actions must be looked at in the context of the rules which operate for the one or for the other category of conflict."); Prosecutor v. Thomas Lubanga Dyilo, ICC Trial Chamber I, ICC-01/04-01/06, Judgment 258 (¶563) (Mar. 14, 2012) ("Similarly, although there is evidence of direct intervention on the part of Uganda, this intervention would only have internationalised the conflict between the two states concerned (viz. the DRC and Uganda). Since the conflict to which the UPC/FPLC [Lubanga's militia] was a party was not 'a difference arising between two states' but rather protracted violence carried out by multiple non-state armed groups, it remained a non-international conflict notwithstanding any concurrent international armed conflict between Uganda and the DRC.").

[29] *Refer to* § 4.5.3 (Regular Armed Forces Who Profess Allegiance to a Government or an Authority Not Recognized by the Detaining Power).

[30] *Refer to* § 17.2.3 (Application of Humanitarian Rules and the Legal Status of the Parties to the Conflict).

[31] *For example*, STEFAN TALMON, RECOGNITION OF GOVERNMENTS IN INTERNATIONAL LAW 309 (1998) ("Prior to its installation in Nicaraguan territory the PJNR [Provisional Junta of National Reconstruction] was recognized as the Government of Nicaragua by the following States: Panama (22 June 1979), Grenada (23 June 1979), Costa Rica (18 July 1969). In a rare case of recognition of belligerency in modern history, the members of the Andean Group (Bolivia, Colombia, Ecuador, Peru, and Venezuela) declared on 17 June 1979 that they had recognized both sides in the Nicaraguan conflict as 'belligerents'."); B.F. Butler, Attorney General, *Piracy Upon the High Seas*, May 17, 1836, 3 OPINIONS OF THE ATTORNEY GENERAL 120, 122 (1852) ("The existence of a civil war between the people of Texas and the authorities and people of the other Mexican States, was recognised by the President of the United States at an early day in the month of November last. Official notice of this fact, and of the President's intention to preserve the neutrality of the United States, was soon after given to the Mexican government."); The Santissima Trinidad, 20 U.S. 283, 337 (1822) ("The government of the United States has recognized the existence of a civil war between Spain and her colonies, and has avowed a determination to remain neutral between the parties, and to allow to each the same rights of asylum and hospitality and intercourse. Each party is, therefore, deemed by us a belligerent nation, having, so far as concerns us, the sovereign rights of war, and entitled to be respected in the exercise of those rights.").

- a general state of armed conflict within a territory;
- the armed group occupies and administers a significant portion of national territory;
- the armed group acts under responsible chain of command and respects the laws of war; and
- circumstances exist that make it necessary for outside States to define their attitude toward the conflict.[32]

This doctrine has not been invoked often, especially after the adoption of the Charter of the United Nations, and the unwarranted recognition of an insurgent group likely would, at least, be considered an unfriendly act against a State engaged in hostilities against that group.[33]

3.3.3.2 <u>Assertion of War Powers by a State Engaged in Hostilities Against a Non-State Armed Group</u>. Occasionally, a State that has been engaged in hostilities against a non-State armed group has taken actions that have recognized the belligerency of the non-State armed group, at least for certain purposes. For example, President Lincoln's proclamation of a blockade during the U.S. Civil War was viewed as recognizing the existence of a state of war, at least for the purposes of imposing the blockade on foreign vessels seeking to trade with the Confederacy.[34]

3.3.3.3 <u>Recognition of Friendly Armed Groups as Lawful Belligerents</u>. In some cases, a State has recognized an armed group that fights alongside it as a belligerent.[35] One

---

32 HERSCH LAUTERPACHT, RECOGNITION IN INTERNATIONAL LAW 175-76 (1947) ("There is general agreement as to the nature of the conditions which impose the duty of recognition of belligerency—or which, according to others, justify recognition of belligerency. These conditions are as follows: first, there must exist within the State an armed conflict of a general (as distinguished from a purely local) character; secondly, the insurgents must occupy and administer a substantial portion of national territory; thirdly, they must conduct the hostilities in accordance with the rules of war and through organized armed forces acting under a responsible authority; fourthly, there must exist circumstances which make it necessary for outside States to define their attitude by means of recognition of belligerency.").

33 *See, e.g.*, HERSCH LAUTERPACHT, RECOGNITION IN INTERNATIONAL LAW 239 (1947) ("If a distant continental State in no way directly concerned with the hostilities at sea were to recognize the insurgents as belligerents, it would lay itself open to the charge of a gratuitous gesture unfriendly to the lawful government and merely calculated to encourage the rebellion.").

34 The Prize Cases, 67 U.S. 635, 670 (1862) ("Whether the President, in fulfilling his duties as Commander-in-chief in suppressing an insurrection, has met with such armed hostile resistance and a civil war of such alarming proportions as will compel him to accord to them the character of belligerents is a question to be decided by him, and this Court must be governed by the decisions and acts of the political department of the Government to which this power was entrusted. 'He must determine what degree of force the crisis demands.' The proclamation of blockade is itself official and conclusive evidence to the Court that a state of war existed which demanded and authorized a recourse to such a measure under the circumstances peculiar to the case.").

35 *For example*, Case Concerning Certain German Interests in Polish Upper Silesia (Merits) (Germany v. Poland) P.C.I.J. (series A) No. 7, at 28 ("At the time of the conclusion of those two Conventions, Poland was not recognized as a belligerent by Germany; it is, however, only on the basis of such recognition that an armistice could have been concluded between those two Powers. The Principal Allied Powers had, it is true, recognized the Polish armed forces as an autonomous, allied and co-belligerent (or belligerent) army. This army was placed under the supreme political authority of the Polish National Committee with headquarters in Paris."); Statement of the Secretary of

reason for such recognition might be to seek to persuade other States that have not recognized the armed group as a belligerent, such as an enemy State, to grant the privileges of combatant status to members of those armed groups.[36] An armed group that has been recognized in this way by a friendly State may be viewed as analogous to an organized resistance movement that belongs to a State that is a party to a conflict.[37]

3.3.4 <u>AP I Provision on National Liberation Movements</u>. AP I treats as international armed conflicts "armed conflicts in which peoples are fighting against colonial domination and alien occupation and against racist regimes in the exercise of their right of self-determination."[38]

The United States has strongly objected to this provision as making the applicability of the rules of international armed conflict turn on subjective and politicized criteria that would eliminate the distinction between international and non-international conflicts.[39] The United States has understood these types of conflicts to be non-international armed conflicts.[40] Moreover, the United States has not accepted this provision in the context of the CCW.[41] The

---

State, September 1918, *reprinted in* Charles Henry Hyde, *The Recognition of the Czecho-Slovaks as Belligerents*, 13 AJIL 93-95 (1919) ("The Government of the United States recognizes that a state of belligerency exists between the Czecho-Slovaks thus organized and the German and Austro-Hungarian Empires. It also recognizes the Czecho-Slovak National Council as a *de facto* belligerent government, clothed with proper authority to direct the military and political affairs of the Czecho-Slovaks.").

[36] *For example, Declaration Concerning Czechoslovak Army*, Sept. 7, 1944, 11 DEPARTMENT OF STATE BULLETIN 263 (Sept. 10, 1944) ("The United States Government therefore declares: ... (3) In these circumstances reprisals by the German military authorities against the soldiers of the Czechoslovak Army violate the rules of war by which Germany is bound. The United States Government, therefore, solemnly warns all Germans who take part in or are in any way responsible for such violations that they do so at their peril and will be held answerable for their crimes.").

[37] *Compare* § 4.6.2 (Belonging to a Party to the Conflict).

[38] AP I art. 1(4) ("The situations referred to in the preceding paragraph [*i.e.*, the situations referred to in Article 2 common to those Conventions] include armed conflicts in which peoples are fighting against colonial domination and alien occupation and against racist regimes in the exercise of their right of self-determination, as enshrined in the Charter of the United Nations and the Declaration on Principles of International Law concerning Friendly Relations and Co-operation among States in accordance with the Charter of the United Nations.").

[39] *See* Ronald Reagan, *Letter of Transmittal*, Jan. 29, 1987, MESSAGE FROM THE PRESIDENT TRANSMITTING AP II III-IV ("But Protocol I is fundamentally and irreconcilably flawed. It contains provisions that would undermine humanitarian law and endanger civilians in war. One of its provisions, for example, would automatically treat as an international conflict any so-called 'war of national liberation.' Whether such wars are international or non-international should turn exclusively on objective reality, not on one's view of the moral qualities of each conflict. To rest on such subjective distinctions based on a war's alleged purposes would politicize humanitarian law and eliminate the distinction between international and non-international conflicts. It would give special status to 'wars of national liberation,' an ill-defined concept expressed in vague, subjective, politicized terminology.").

[40] *Detailed Analysis of Provisions*, Attachment 1 to George P. Shultz, *Letter of Submittal*, Dec. 13, 1986, MESSAGE FROM THE PRESIDENT TRANSMITTING AP II 1-2 ("This Article technically excludes four types of situations from the scope of the Protocol: ... (2) the so-called wars of 'national liberation' defined as international armed conflicts by Article 1(4) of Protocol I Additional to the 1949 Geneva Conventions; ... However, the exclusion of the second and third categories is inappropriate. The second category--so-called 'liberation wars' defined in Protocol I--are often in fact non-international conflicts, and are distinguished by Protocol I from other non-international conflicts only on the basis of highly politicized and undesirable criteria which detract from the integrity of international humanitarian law; the United States should therefore reject this distinction.").

[41] *Refer to* § 19.21.1.2 (U.S. Reservation to Article 7(4)(b) of the CCW).

United States has expressed the view that it would not be appropriate to treat this provision of AP I as customary international law.[42]

3.4 WHEN *JUS IN BELLO* RULES APPLY

Jus in bello treaties often provide that they apply in cases of "declared war or of any other armed conflict," even if the state of war is not recognized by them.[43] This standard has also been understood to result in the application of the customary law of war.[44]

A case of "declared war or any other armed conflict" for the purpose of determining whether parties must comply with *jus in bello* rules may be understood as arising in two ways: (1) when a party intends to conduct hostilities; or (2) when parties are actually conducting hostilities.

"War," "hostilities," and "armed conflict" may be defined differently for other legal purposes.[45] It must be emphasized that the discussion in this section is for the purpose of assessing whether *jus in bello* restrictions apply and not necessarily for other purposes. For example, the fact that *jus in bello* restrictions apply is not determinative of whether a State's actions are lawful under *jus ad bellum*.[46] Similarly, the fact that *jus in bello* restrictions apply is not determinative of whether the permissions that are sometimes viewed as inherent in *jus in bello* rules may be relied upon by a State or non-State actor.[47]

3.4.1 Intent-Based Test for Applying *Jus in Bello* Rules. *Jus in bello* rules apply when a party intends to conduct hostilities.

If a State chooses to go to war, then it is bound by *jus in bello* rules for the conduct of

---

[42] Memorandum submitted in United States v. Shakur, 690 F. Supp. 1291 (S.D.N.Y. 1988), III CUMULATIVE DIGEST OF UNITED STATES PRACTICE IN INTERNATIONAL LAW 1981-88 3436, 3441 ("The new provisions on wars of national liberation and prisoners of war in Protocol I clearly do not reflect the practice of states. Indeed, they were adopted precisely because states did not accord prisoner-of-war status in such conflicts. It is most unlikely that states will in the future choose to accord prisoner-of-war status in conflicts described as wars of national liberation. Accordingly, it is the view of the United States that it would be inappropriate to treat these provisions as part of customary international law under any circumstances.").

[43] *See, e.g.*, GWS art. 2 (The convention applies "to all cases of declared war or of any other armed conflict which may arise between two or more of the High Contracting Parties, even if the state of war is not recognized by them."); GWS-SEA art. 2 (same); GPW art. 2 (same); GC art. 2 (same); 1954 HAGUE CULTURAL PROPERTY CONVENTION art. 18 ("the present Convention shall apply in the event of declared war or of any other armed conflict which may arise between two or more of the High Contracting Parties, even if the state of war is not recognized by one or more of them."); CCW art. 1 ("This Convention and its annexed Protocols shall apply in the situations referred to in Article 2 common to the Geneva Conventions of 12 August 1949 for the Protection of War Victims,").

[44] 1956 FM 27-10 (Change No. 1 1976) ¶8b ("The customary law of war applies to all cases of declared war or any other armed conflict which may arise between the United States and other nations, even if the state of war is not recognized by one of them. The customary law is also applicable to all cases of occupation of foreign territory by the exercise of armed force, even if the occupation meets with no armed resistance.").

[45] *Refer to* § 1.5.2 (Different Definitions of "War" for Different Legal Purposes).

[46] *Refer to* § 3.5.2 (*Jus in Bello* and *Jus ad Bellum* Generally Operate Independently of One Another).

[47] *Refer to* § 1.3.3.2 (Law of War as Permissive Law).

those hostilities.[48] For example, if a State considers it necessary to respond to attacks with military force, then those military operations must comply with *jus in bello* rules.[49]

The fact that the intention to conduct hostilities gives rise to obligations to comply with the law of war is important because law of war obligations must be taken into account even before the fighting actually begins, such as in the planning of military operations.[50] Similarly, certain obligations under the GPW and the GC are triggered by the onset of hostilities, and it may be necessary to implement these obligations even before the fighting actually begins.[51] As another example, the party that is subject to attack is often in a position to take feasible precautions for the protection of the civilian population even before the fighting begins.[52]

3.4.1.1 Declarations of War or Other Official Recognition by States of a State of Hostilities. The application of the 1949 Geneva Conventions and other law of war treaties to cases of "declared war" is an example of how *jus in bello* restrictions apply when a party intends to conduct hostilities.[53] Traditionally, a State could create a state of hostilities with another State simply by providing objective evidence of its decision to resort to force through formal declarations that hostilities exist between them.[54]

---

[48] L. OPPENHEIM, II INTERNATIONAL LAW 66 (2nd ed., 1912) ("But if [States] choose to go to war they have to comply with the rules laid down by International Law regarding the conduct of war and the relations between belligerents and neutral States.").

[49] *For example*, Patrick F. Philbin, Deputy Assistant Attorney General, *Legality of the Use of Military Commissions to Try Terrorists*, Nov. 6, 2001, 25 OPINIONS OF THE OFFICE OF LEGAL COUNSEL 238, 276 ("In addition, the United States has determined that it is necessary to respond to the attacks with military force. That decision is significant because one element often cited for determining whether a situation involving a non-state actor rises to the level of an "armed conflict" (for example, for purposes of common Article 3 of the Geneva Conventions) is whether a state responds with its regular military forces. The United States has urged this position. See 3 U.S. Practice § 2, at 3443; see also G.I.A.D. Draper, The Red Cross Conventions 15-16 (1958) (under common Article 3, "armed conflict" exists when the government is "obliged to have recourse to its regular military forces"). Here, this criterion is overwhelmingly satisfied. As outlined above, the United States has found it necessary to respond with a massive use of military force. The current operations in Afghanistan and continuing preparations for a sustained campaign easily establish that the situation here involves an armed conflict for purposes of international law.").

[50] *Refer to* § 18.8 (Considering Law of War Obligations in the Planning of Military Operations).

[51] *Refer to* § 9.4 (National-Level GPW Implementation Measures); § 10.2 (National-Level GC Implementation Measures).

[52] *Refer to* § 5.14 (Feasible Precautions to Reduce the Risk of Harm to Protected Persons and Objects by the Party Subject to Attack).

[53] *See, e.g.*, GWS art. 2 (The convention applies "to all cases of declared war … between two or more of the High Contracting Parties"); GWS-SEA art. 2 (same); GPW art. 2 (same); GC art. 2 (same); 1954 HAGUE CULTURAL PROPERTY CONVENTION art. 18 ("the present Convention shall apply in the event of declared war ... between two or more of the High Contracting Parties"); CCW art. 1 ("This Convention and its annexed Protocols shall apply in the situations referred to in Article 2 common to the Geneva Conventions of 12 August 1949 for the Protection of War Victims,").

[54] *See, e.g.*, Convention (III) Relative to the Opening of Hostilities, art. 1, Oct. 18, 1907, 36 STAT. 2259, 2271 ("The Contracting Powers recognize that hostilities between themselves must not commence without previous and explicit warning, in the form either of a reasoned declaration of war or of an ultimatum with conditional declaration of war."); Eliza Ann and others, 1 DODSON 244, 247 (Mar. 9, 1813) (a declaration of war "proves the existence of

Although States generally no longer file formal declarations of war with one another, officials may make public statements that are like declarations of war in that they provide notice of a state of hostilities.[55] For example, States may make statements that indicate their view that they are engaged in armed conflict in the context of reporting measures taken in the exercise of their inherent right of self-defense to the U.N. Security Council.[56] Similarly, the authorization by Congress of the use of military force has been interpreted as triggering the application of certain parts of the law of war.[57]

These types of statements concerning *jus ad bellum* may be probative of the applicability of *jus in bello* restrictions. For example, a statement by a State indicating that it had suffered a wrongful attack under *jus ad bellum* would also indicate that the State viewed *jus in bello* restrictions as applicable to its adversary's operations against it and its own military operations against its adversary.[58]

Similarly, statements by States that justify the legality of their actions or assert authority under *jus in bello* rules may also provide evidence that States have the intention of conducting hostilities and that *jus in bello* restrictions apply to the activities that will effectuate those intentions.[59]

---

actual hostilities on one side at least, and puts the other party also into a state of war, though he may, perhaps, think proper to act on the defensive only.").

[55] *See, e.g.*, Navios Corp. v. The Ulysses II, 161 F. Supp. 932, 943 (D. Md. 1958) (concluding that a speech by President Nasser of Egypt "of November 1, confirmed by the statement of November 3, constituted a declaration of war even under the technical requirements of international law."), *affirmed*, 260 F.2d 959 (4th Cir. 1958).

[56] *Refer to* § 1.11.5.6 (Reporting to the U.N. Security Council).

[57] Talbot v. Seeman, 5 U.S. 1, 28 (1801) (Marshall, C.J.) ("It is not denied, nor in the course of the argument has it been denied, that congress may authorize general hostilities, in which case the general laws of war apply to our situation; or partial hostilities, in which case the laws of war, so far as they actually apply to our situation, must be noticed.").

[58] *For example*, John O. Brennan, Assistant to the President for Homeland Security and Counterterrorism, *Remarks at Harvard Law School: Strengthening Our Security by Adhering to Our Values and Laws*, Sept. 16, 2011 ("First, our definition of the conflict. As the President has said many times, we are at war with al-Qa'ida. In an indisputable act of aggression, al-Qa'ida attacked our nation and killed nearly 3,000 innocent people. And as we were reminded just last weekend, al-Qa'ida seeks to attack us again. Our ongoing armed conflict with al-Qa'ida stems from our right—recognized under international law—to self defense. An area in which there is some disagreement is the geographic scope of the conflict. The United States does not view our authority to use military force against al-Qa'ida as being restricted solely to 'hot' battlefields like Afghanistan. Because we are engaged in an armed conflict with al-Qa'ida, the United States takes the legal position that —in accordance with international law—we have the authority to take action against al-Qa'ida and its associated forces without doing a separate self-defense analysis each time. And as President Obama has stated on numerous occasions, we reserve the right to take unilateral action if or when other governments are unwilling or unable to take the necessary actions themselves. That does not mean we can use military force whenever we want, wherever we want. International legal principles, including respect for a state's sovereignty and the laws of war, impose important constraints on our ability to act unilaterally—and on the way in which we can use force—in foreign territories.").

[59] *Legal and Practical Consequences of a Blockade of Cuba*, Oct. 19, 1962, 1 SUPPLEMENTAL OPINIONS OF THE OFFICE OF LEGAL COUNSEL 486, 488-89 (2013) ("The declaration of a state of war was helpful in ascertaining the rights and obligations of neutrals in a given situation. Apart from this, however, it served little function. War itself, whatever its reason, was legal self-help, and so were lesser measures if such could be said to exist. Whether or not a nation declared a state of war it would be found by others to exist if that state were claiming rights, such as

3.4.1.2 *Non-State Armed Groups With the Intention of Conducting Hostilities*. A non-State armed group, such as a rebel group, might also intend to conduct hostilities.[60] Non-State armed groups are similarly bound by the restrictions in the law of war for the conduct of hostilities when they intend to conduct hostilities.[61] However, in contrast to States, non-State armed groups lack *competent authority*.[62] Thus, there would not be a basis for non-State armed groups to claim the permissions that may be viewed as inherent in parts of the law of war.[63] For example, members of a non-State group may be subject to prosecution under a State's domestic law for their participation in hostilities against it.[64]

3.4.2 Act-Based Test for Applying *Jus in Bello* Rules. *Jus in bello* rules apply when parties are actually conducting hostilities, even if the war is not declared or if the state of war is not recognized by them.[65] The *de facto* existence of an armed conflict is sufficient to trigger

---

blockade, normally associated with war."). *For example*, National Defense Authorization Act for Fiscal Year 2012 § 1021 ("Congress affirms that the authority of the President to use all necessary and appropriate force pursuant to the Authorization for Use of Military Force (Public Law 107–40; 50 U.S.C. 1541 note) includes the authority for the Armed Forces of the United States to detain covered persons (as defined in subsection (b)) pending disposition under the law of war."); Hugh J. Clausen & W. Hays Parks, *Geneva Conventions Status of Enemy Personnel Captured During URGENT FURY*, DAJA-IA 1983/7031 (Nov. 4, 1983), III CUMULATIVE DIGEST OF UNITED STATES PRACTICE IN INTERNATIONAL LAW 1981-1988 3452, 3454 (considering, *inter alia*, the fact that "[t]he Department of State, in a press release on 4 November 9 [1984], cited the GPW as authority for U.S. detention of Cuban Grenadan military personnel" in concluding that "*de facto* hostilities existed on Grenada and that the Geneva Conventions do apply.") (insertion reflect in the Digest).

[60] *For example*, Hamdan v. Rumsfeld, 548 U.S. 557, 687 (2006) (Thomas, J., dissenting) ("According to the State Department, al Qaeda *declared war* on the United States as early as August 1996. In February 1998, al Qaeda leadership issued another statement ordering the indiscriminate—and, even under the laws of war as applied to legitimate nation-states, plainly illegal—killing of American civilians and military personnel alike. This was not mere rhetoric; even before September 11, 2001, al Qaeda was involved in the bombing of the World Trade Center in New York City in 1993, the bombing of the Khobar Towers in Saudi Arabia in 1996, the bombing of the U. S. Embassies in Kenya and Tanzania in 1998, and the attack on the U. S. S. Cole in Yemen in 2000.") (internal citations omitted). *See also* United States v. Burr, 25 F. Cas. 201, 203 (C.C.D. Va. 1807) (Marshall, C.J.) (explaining in the context of a prosecution of rebels for treason that "war might be levied without a battle, or the actual application of force to the object on which it was designed to act; that a body of men assembled for the purpose of war, and being in a posture of war, do levy war; and from that opinion I have certainly felt no disposition to recede. But the intention is an indispensable ingredient in the composition of the fact; and if war may be levied without striking the blow, the intention to strike must be plainly proved.").

[61] *Refer to* § 17.2.4 (Binding Force of the Law of War on Insurgents and Other Non-State Armed Groups).

[62] *Refer to* § 1.11.1.1 (Competent Authority (Right Authority) to Wage War for a Public Purpose).

[63] *Refer to* § 1.3.3.2 (Law of War as Permissive Law).

[64] *Refer to* § 17.4.1 (Ability of a State to Use Its Domestic Law Against Non-State Armed Groups).

[65] *See, e.g.*, GWS art. 2 (The convention applies "to all cases of declared war or of any other armed conflict which may arise between two or more of the High Contracting Parties, even if the state of war is not recognized by them.") (emphasis added); GWS-SEA art. 2 (same); GPW art. 2 (same); GC art. 2 (same); 1954 HAGUE CULTURAL PROPERTY CONVENTION art. 18 ("the present Convention shall apply in the event of declared war or of any other armed conflict which may arise between two or more of the High Contracting Parties, even if the state of war is not recognized by one or more of them.") (emphasis added); CCW art. 1 ("This Convention and its annexed Protocols shall apply in the situations referred to in Article 2 common to the Geneva Conventions of 12 August 1949 for the Protection of War Victims,").

obligations for the conduct of hostilities.[66]

The United States has interpreted "armed conflict" in Common Article 2 of the 1949 Geneva Conventions to include "any situation in which there is hostile action between the armed forces of two parties, regardless of the duration, intensity or scope of the fighting."[67]

3.4.2.1 <u>*Reasons for States to Seek to Deny the Existence of Hostilities*</u>. States have specified that *jus in bello* rules apply even if a state of hostilities is not recognized by them because States have frequently denied that they are at "war." And, in some cases, this denial has resulted in a refusal to comply with *jus in bello* obligations.[68]

There are a variety of reasons why States might deny that they are at "war." For example, government officials may deny that an armed conflict exists: (1) to avoid an escalation in fighting and to facilitate a diplomatic resolution; (2) for reasons of domestic law; (3) to avoid economic costs (such as discouraging commerce and foreign investment); or (4) to avoid appearing to acknowledge the military effectiveness of an opposing force.

In particular, States have often been reluctant to acknowledge that operations by non-State armed groups have triggered the application of Common Article 3 of the 1949 Geneva

---

[66] GPW COMMENTARY 22-23 ("There is no need for a formal declaration of war, or for the recognition of the existence of a state of war, as preliminaries to the application of the Convention. The occurrence of *de facto* hostilities is sufficient."). *For example*, Hugh J. Clausen & W. Hays Parks, *Geneva Conventions Status of Enemy Personnel Captured During URGENT FURY*, DAJA-IA 1983/7031 (Nov. 4, 1983), III CUMULATIVE DIGEST OF UNITED STATES PRACTICE IN INTERNATIONAL LAW 1981-1988 3452, 3454 (concluding "that *de facto* hostilities existed on Grenada and that the Geneva Conventions do apply" despite the fact that "[n]o party to the hostilities in Grenada has suggested that a state of war exists; officials of Cuba and the United States publicly have announced they are not at war."); George Aldrich, Assistant Legal Adviser for Far Eastern Affairs, Department of State, *Entitlement of American Military Personnel Held by North Viet-Nam to Treatment as Prisoners of War Under the Geneva Convention of 1949 Relative to the Treatment of Prisoners of War*, Jul. 13, 1966, X WHITEMAN'S DIGEST 231-32 (§7) ("Although there have been no declarations of war, the present conflict in Vietnam is indisputably an 'armed conflict' between parties to the Geneva Conventions of 1949. In one aspect of the war, American aircraft are operating against military targets in North Vietnam, and North Vietnamese forces have engaged these aircraft. Under these circumstances, the Convention applies in its entirety to this conflict. … In this case, the state of war (under international law) is not disputed; it is merely undeclared.").

[67] Department of State, Telegram 348126 to American Embassy at Damascus, Dec. 8, 1983, III CUMULATIVE DIGEST OF UNITED STATES PRACTICE IN INTERNATIONAL LAW 1981-1988 3456, 3457 ("The Third Geneva Convention accords 'prisoner-of-war' status to members of the armed forces who are captured during 'armed conflict' between two or more parties to the Convention. 'Armed conflict' includes any situation in which there is hostile action between the armed forces of two parties, regardless of the duration, intensity or scope of the fighting and irrespective of whether a state of war exists between the two parties."). *Cf.* Bas v. Tingy, 4 U.S. 37, 40 (1800) (Washington, J., concurring) ("every contention by force between two nations, in external matters, under the authority of their respective governments, is not only war, but public war.").

[68] *For example*, United States, *et al.* v. Araki, *et al.*, *Majority Judgment*, International Military Tribunal for the Far East, 49,602, *reprinted in* NEIL BOISTER & ROBERT CRYER, DOCUMENTS ON THE TOKYO INTERNATIONAL MILITARY TRIBUNAL: CHARTER, INDICTMENT AND JUDGMENTS 535 (2008) ("Since the Government of Japan officially classified the China War as an 'Incident' and considered Chinese soldiers in Manchuria as 'bandits' the Army refused to accord to captives taken in the fighting the status and the rights of prisoners of war. MUTO says that it was officially decided in 1938 to continue to call the war in China an 'Incident' and to continue for that reason to refuse to apply the rules of war to the conflict. TOJO told us the same.").

Conventions.[69] This reluctance often stems from an unwillingness to take any action that could enhance the perceived status of rebels or give any appearance of legitimacy to their actions.[70] Nonetheless, the application of the humanitarian rules does not affect the legal status of parties to a conflict.[71]

3.4.2.2 Distinguishing Armed Conflict From Internal Disturbances and Tensions. In assessing whether *de facto* hostilities exist for the purpose of applying *jus in bello* restrictions, situations of internal disturbances and tensions, such as riots, isolated and sporadic acts of violence, and other acts of a similar nature do not amount to armed conflict.[72]

Any hostile action between the armed forces of different States (*i.e.*, international armed conflict) may readily be distinguished from an "internal disturbance or tension." However, it has been more difficult to distinguish "armed conflict not of an international character" from "internal disturbances or tensions."

"Armed conflict not of an international character" for the purpose of applying the obligations in Common Article 3 of the 1949 Geneva Conventions was not specifically defined

---

[69] *See, e.g.*, George H. Aldrich, Deputy Legal Adviser, Department of State, *Human Rights in Armed Conflict: Development of the Law*, Apr. 13, 1973, 68 DEPARTMENT OF STATE BULLETIN, 876, 878 (Jun. 18, 1973) ("I would note that Pakistan in Bangladesh and the United Kingdom in Northern Ireland have refused to acknowledge the applicability of article 3 common to the four Geneva Conventions concerning noninternational armed conflicts.").

[70] *See, e.g.*, George H. Aldrich, Deputy Legal Adviser, Department of State, *Human Rights in Armed Conflict: Development of the Law*, Apr. 13, 1973, 68 DEPARTMENT OF STATE BULLETIN, 876, 879 (Jun. 18, 1973) ("In the first place there is a general concern of governments that the acceptance of international standards for a civil war connotes international recognition of the insurgents. This concern results from the historical development of the law; in customary law the international laws of war become applicable to a civil war upon international recognition of the rebels as belligerents. This concern persists despite an explicit provision in common article 3 that its application shall not affect the legal status of the parties to the conflict. Personally, I deplore the fact that this concern so often effectively prevents official admission that an internal armed conflict is one to which article 3 applies, but we cannot ignore that political reality. Governments will predictably remain unwilling to do anything that could enhance the perceived status of rebels or give any appearance of legitimacy to their actions.").

[71] *Refer to* § 17.2.3 (Application of Humanitarian Rules and the Legal Status of the Parties to the Conflict).

[72] *See, e.g.*, CCW AMENDED art. 1 (2) ("This Convention and its annexed Protocols shall not apply to situations of internal disturbances and tensions, such as riots, isolated and sporadic acts of violence, and other acts of similar nature, as not being armed conflicts."); CCW AMENDED MINES PROTOCOL art. 1(2) ("This Protocol shall not apply to situations of internal disturbances and tensions, such as riots, isolated and sporadic acts of violence and other acts of a similar nature, as not being armed conflicts."); United States, *Statement on Ratification of the International Convention for the Suppression of the Financing of Terrorism*, Jun. 26, 2002, 2185 UNTS 611, 612 ("(2) Meaning of the term armed conflict. The United States of America understands that the term 'armed conflict' in Article 2 (1) (b) of the Convention does not include internal disturbances and tensions, such as riots, isolated and sporadic acts of violence, and other acts of a similar nature."). *Consider* AP II art. 1(2) ("This Protocol shall not apply to situations of internal disturbances and tensions, such as riots, isolated and sporadic acts of violence and other acts of a similar nature, as not being armed conflicts."); ROME STATUTE art. 8(2)(d) ("Paragraph 2(c) applies to armed conflicts not of an international character and thus does not apply to situations of internal disturbances and tensions, such as riots, isolated and sporadic acts of violence or other acts of a similar nature."); ROME STATUTE art. 8(2)(f) ("Paragraph 2(e) applies to armed conflicts not of an international character and thus does not apply to situations of internal disturbances and tensions, such as riots, isolated and sporadic acts of violence or other acts of a similar nature.").

in those conventions.[73] There has been a range of views on what constitutes an "armed conflict not of an international character" for this purpose.[74] The intensity of the conflict and the organization of the parties are criteria that have been assessed to distinguish between non-international armed conflict and "internal disturbances and tensions."[75] A variety of factors have been considered in assessing these criteria and in seeking to distinguish between armed conflict and internal disturbances and tensions.[76]

---

[73] GWS COMMENTARY 49 ("What is meant by 'armed conflict not of an international character'? That was the burning question which arose again and again at the Diplomatic Conference. The expression was so general, so vague, that many of the delegations feared that it might be taken to cover any act committed by force of arms—any form of anarchy, rebellion, or even plain banditry. For example, if a handful of individuals were to rise in rebellion against the State and attack a police station, would that suffice to bring into being an armed conflict within the meaning of the Article? In order to reply to questions of this sort, it was suggested that the term 'conflict' should be defined or, which would come to the same thing, that a certain number of conditions for the application of the Convention should be enumerated. The idea was finally abandoned—wisely, we think.").

[74] *See, e.g.*, Prosecutor v. Tadić, ICTY Appeals Chamber, IT-94-1-A, *Decision on the Defence Motion for Interlocutory Appeal on Jurisdiction*, ¶70 (Oct. 2, 1995) ("On the basis of the foregoing, we find that an armed conflict exists whenever there is a resort to armed force between States or protracted armed violence between governmental authorities and organized armed groups or between such groups within a State."); Juan Carlos Abella v. Argentina, Inter-American Commission on Human Rights, Organization of American States, Case 11.137, OEA/Ser.L/V/II.98, ¶152 (Nov. 18, 1997) ("Common Article 3 is generally understood to apply to low intensity and open armed confrontations between relatively organized armed forces or groups that take place within the territory of a particular State.").

[75] *See, e.g.*, Prosecutor v. Tadić, ICTY Trial Chamber, IT-94-1-A, *Judgment*, ¶562 (May 7, 1997) ("In an armed conflict of an internal or mixed character, these closely related criteria are used solely for the purpose, as a minimum, of distinguishing an armed conflict from banditry, unorganized and short-lived insurrections, or terrorist activities, which are not subject to international humanitarian law."); Prosecutor v. Akayesu, ICTR Trial Chamber, ICTR-96-4-T, *Judgment*, ¶625 (Sept. 2, 1998) ("The concept of armed conflict has already been discussed in the previous section pertaining to Common Article 3. It suffices to recall that an armed conflict is distinguished from internal disturbances by the level of intensity of the conflict and the degree of organization of the parties to the conflict.").

[76] *See, e.g.*, GPW COMMENTARY 35-36 (collecting conditions that States negotiating the 1949 Geneva Conventions viewed as indicative factors); Prosecutor v. Boskoski, ICTY Trial Chamber II, IT-04-82-T, *Judgment*, ¶177 (Jul. 10, 2008) ("Various indicative factors have been taken into account by Trial Chambers to assess the 'intensity' of the conflict. These include the seriousness of attacks and whether there has been an increase in armed clashes, the spread of clashes over territory and over a period of time, any increase in the number of government forces and mobilisation and the distribution of weapons among both parties to the conflict, as well as whether the conflict has attracted the attention of the United Nations Security Council, and whether any resolutions on the matter have been passed. Trial Chambers have also taken into account in this respect the number of civilians forced to flee from the combat zones; the type of weapons used, in particular the use of heavy weapons, and other military equipment, such as tanks and other heavy vehicles; the blocking or besieging of towns and the heavy shelling of these towns; the extent of destruction and the number of casualties caused by shelling or fighting; the quantity of troops and units deployed; existence and change of front lines between the parties; the occupation of territory, and towns and villages; the deployment of government forces to the crisis area; the closure of roads; cease fire orders and agreements, and the attempt of representatives from international organisations to broker and enforce cease fire agreements."); Prosecutor v. Dordevic, ICTY Trial Chamber II, IT-04-82-T, *Judgment*, ¶1526 (Feb. 23, 2011) ("Trial Chambers have taken into account a number of factors when assessing the organization of an armed group. These fall into five broad groups. First, are the factors signalling the presence of a command structure. Secondly, are factors indicating that an armed group could carry out operations in an organised manner. Thirdly, are factors indicating a level of logistics have been taken into account. Fourthly, are factors relevant to determining whether an armed group possessed a level of discipline and the ability to implement the basic obligations of Common Article 3. A fifth group includes factors indicating that the armed group was able to speak with one voice.").

A helpful rule of thumb may be that where parties are, in fact, engaged in activities that the law of war contemplates (*e.g.*, detention of enemy military personnel without criminal charge, bombardment of military objectives), those activities are subject to the law of war.[77]

3.4.2.3 Responding to Ordinary Crimes, Including Acts of Terrorism. States are not required to apply law of war rules when using domestic law enforcement tools to respond to ordinary crimes, including acts of terrorism.[78] For example, States may apply their domestic law and prosecute acts of terrorism by non-State armed groups.[79] States, however, have at times decided to resort to military force to counter a terrorist or similar threat that is beyond the capabilities of ordinary law enforcement to address.[80] If States intend to conduct hostilities, then they are also bound by the applicable *jus in bello* restrictions in the law of war.[81]

Acts of terrorism during armed conflict are prohibited by the law of war.[82]

---

[77] Juan Carlos Abella v. Argentina, Inter-American Commission on Human Rights, Organization of American States, Case 11.137, OEA/Ser.L/V/II.98, ¶155 (Nov. 18, 1997) ("What differentiates the events at the La Tablada base from these situations [of internal disturbances] are the concerted nature of the hostile acts undertaken by the attackers, the direct involvement of governmental armed forces, and the nature and level of the violence attending the events in question. More particularly, the attackers involved carefully planned, coordinated and executed an armed attack, i.e., a military operation, against a quintessential military objective - a military base."); GPW COMMENTARY 23 ("It makes no difference how long the conflict lasts, how much slaughter takes place, or how numerous are the participating forces; it suffices for the armed forces of one Power to have captured adversaries falling within the scope of Article 4. Even if there has been no fighting, the fact that persons covered by the Convention are detained is sufficient for its application. The number of persons captured in such circumstances is, of course, immaterial.").

[78] United Kingdom, *Statement on Ratification of AP I*, Jan. 28, 1998, 2020 UNTS 75, 76 ("It is the understanding of the United Kingdom that the term 'armed conflict' of itself and in its context denotes a situation of a kind which is not constituted by the commission of ordinary crimes including acts of terrorism whether concerted or in isolation.").

[79] *Refer to* § 17.4.1 (Ability of a State to Use Its Domestic Law Against Non-State Armed Groups).

[80] *For example*, William J. Clinton, *Address to the Nation on Military Action Against Terrorist Sites in Afghanistan and Sudan*, Aug. 20, 1998, 1998-II PUBLIC PAPERS OF THE PRESIDENTS 1460, 1461 ("America has battled terrorism for many years. Where possible, we've used law enforcement and diplomatic tools to wage the fight. … But there have been and will be times when law enforcement and diplomatic tools are simply not enough, when our very national security is challenged, and when we must take extraordinary steps to protect the safety of our citizens. With compelling evidence that the bin Ladin network of terrorist groups was planning to mount further attacks against Americans and other freedom-loving people, I decided America must act. And so this morning, based on the unanimous recommendation of my national security team, I ordered our armed forces to take action to counter an immediate threat from the bin Ladin network. Earlier today, the United States carried out simultaneous strikes against terrorist facilities and infrastructure in Afghanistan."); Public Committee against Torture in Israel, *et al.* v. Government of Israel, *et al.*, HCJ 769/02, Israel Supreme Court Sitting as the High Court of Justice, ¶21 (Dec. 11, 2005) ("Indeed, in today's reality, a terrorist organization is likely to have considerable military capabilities. At times they have military capabilities that exceed those of states. Confrontation with those dangers cannot be restricted within the state and its penal law.").

[81] *Refer to* § 3.4.1 (Intent-Based Test for Applying *Jus in Bello* Rules).

[82] *Refer to* § 10.5.3.2 (Collective Penalties and Measures of Intimidation or Terrorism); § 17.6.5 (Prohibition on Acts of Terrorism).

3.5 RELATIONSHIP BETWEEN *JUS IN BELLO* AND *JUS AD BELLUM*

3.5.1 General Distinction Between *Jus in Bello* and *Jus ad Bellum*. As a general matter, *jus in bello* and *jus ad bellum* address different legal issues and should not be conflated.[83]

Conflating *jus in bello* and *jus ad bellum* risks misunderstanding and misapplying these concepts. For example, in *jus ad bellum*, proportionality refers to the principle that the overall goal of the State in resorting to war should not be outweighed by the harm that the war is expected to produce.[84] However, the principle of proportionality in *jus in bello* generally refers to the obligations to take feasible precautions in planning and conducting attacks and to refrain from attacks in which the expected loss of civilian life, injury to civilians, and damage to civilian objects incidental to the attack would be excessive.[85] Therefore, although a *jus ad bellum* proportionality analysis might consider the harm suffered by enemy military forces in the fighting, a *jus in bello* proportionality analysis would not.[86]

3.5.2 *Jus in Bello* and *Jus ad Bellum* Generally Operate Independently of One Another. One important attribute of rules for conduct during war (*jus in bello*) is that, in general, they operate independently from rules regarding the resort to force (*jus ad bellum*).

3.5.2.1 *Compliance With* Jus in Bello *Is Required Regardless of Compliance With* Jus ad Bellum. States fighting against one another must adhere to rules relating to the conduct of hostilities (*jus in bello*), regardless of whether a State may be considered the aggressor or whether the initial resort to force was lawful under *jus ad bellum*. For example, the 1949 Geneva Conventions require States to undertake to respect and to ensure respect for the conventions in all circumstances.[87] The phrase "in all circumstances" has been interpreted to mean that a Party's obligations to respect and to ensure respect for the 1949 Geneva Conventions applies regardless of whether a Party to the Convention is the aggressor or lawfully using force in self-defense.[88] Similarly, once an occupation exists in fact, the law of occupation applies, regardless of whether the invasion was lawful under *jus ad bellum*.[89]

3.5.2.2 *Compliance With* Jus ad Bellum *Is Required Regardless of Compliance*

---

[83] *Refer to* § 1.11 (*Jus ad Bellum*).

[84] *Refer to* § 1.11.1.2 (The Means Must Be Proportionate to the Just Cause (Proportionality – Jus ad Bellum)).

[85] *Refer to* § 5.10 (Proportionality in Conducting Attacks).

[86] *Refer to* § 5.10.1.1 (Proportionality in Conducting Attacks and Military Objectives).

[87] GWS art. 1 ("The High Contracting Parties undertake to respect and to ensure respect for the present Convention in all circumstances.").

[88] GWS COMMENTARY 27 ("The words 'in all circumstances' mean in short that the application of the Convention does not depend on the character of the conflict. Whether a war is 'just' or 'unjust', whether it is a war of aggression or of resistance to aggression, the protection and care due to the wounded and sick are in no way affected."). *Consider* AP I preamble ("the provisions of the Geneva Conventions of 12 August 1949 and of this Protocol must be fully applied in all circumstances to all persons who are protected by those instruments, without any adverse distinction based on the nature or origin of the armed conflict or on the causes espoused by or attributed to the Parties to the conflict,").

[89] *Refer to* § 11.2.1 (Military Occupation as a Fact).

With Jus in Bello. Compliance with *jus ad bellum* is required regardless of compliance with *jus in bello*.[90] For example, a State that complies with *jus in bello* rules may nonetheless commit aggression under *jus ad bellum*.[91] In addition, violations of law of war treaties applicable to non-international armed conflict generally have not been understood to provide a basis in international law for a non-belligerent State to intervene against the State in that conflict.[92]

3.5.2.3 *Rationales for the Independent Operation of* Jus in Bello *and* Jus ad Bellum. The principle that *jus in bello* rules operate independently of *jus ad bellum* rules is based on principles of sovereignty and humanity, as well as practical considerations.

If the law of war only protected parties justly resorting to force, then both sides, believing their opponent's cause to be unjust, could consider themselves free to depart from *jus in bello* rules.[93] As a consequence, both sides could deny protections to their opponent, and no one would benefit from the law of war's humanitarian protections.[94] Moreover, there might not be a competent procedure for deciding which, if any, State has unlawfully resorted to force.[95]

The principle that *jus in bello* rules operate independently of *jus ad bellum* rules is also influenced by the fact that it would be unjust to punish individual military members based on *jus ad bellum* considerations when they have no influence on whether their State has resorted to

---

[90] *Consider* AP I preamble ("nothing in this Protocol or in the Geneva Conventions of 12 August 1949 can be construed as legitimizing or authorizing any act of aggression or any other use of force inconsistent with the Charter of the United Nations,").

[91] *Refer to* § 1.11.3.1 (Aggression)

[92] *Refer to* § 17.18.1 (Duty of Non-Belligerent States to Refrain From Supporting Hostilities by Non-State Armed Groups Against Other States).

[93] VATTEL, THE LAW OF NATIONS 305 (3.12.190) ("Moreover, since each Nation claims to have justice on its side, it will arrogate to itself all the rights of war and claim that its enemy has none, that his hostilities are but deeds of robbery, acts in violation of the Law of Nations, and deserving of punishment by all Nations. The decision of the rights at issue will not be advanced thereby, and the context will become more cruel, more disastrous in its effects, and more difficult of termination.").

[94] VATTEL, THE LAW OF NATIONS 305 (3.12.190) ("The first rule of that law [of nations], with respect to the subject under consideration, is that *regular war, as regards its effects, must be accounted just on both sides*. This principle, as we have just shown, is absolutely necessary if any law or order is to be introduced into a method of redress as violent as that of war, if any bounds are to be set to the disasters it occasions, and if a door is to be left at all times open for the return of peace. Moreover, any other rule would be impractical as between Nation and Nation, since they recognize no common judge.").

[95] LAUTERPACHT, II OPPENHEIM'S INTERNATIONAL LAW 218 (§61) ("Unless war is to degenerate into a savage contest of physical forces freed from all restraints of compassion, chivalry and respect for human life and dignity, it is essential that the accepted rules of war should continue to be observed. This is so in particular in view of the fact that in the present state of international judicial and political organisation there may be no means by which an authoritative judgment can be arrived at on the question as to which State is the aggressor. (It will be noted, for instance, that nothing short of an unanimous vote of the permanent members of the Security Council is sufficient for the determination that a particular State has resorted to war in violation of its obligations under the Charter.) Accordingly it must be held that during the war all belligerents are bound to respect and are entitled to insist as among themselves on the observance of rules of war as generally recognised.").

force lawfully under applicable international law.[96]

3.5.3 *Jus in Bello* and *Jus ad Bellum* Are Sometimes Related. Although as a general matter parties must comport with *jus in bello* rules, regardless of *jus ad bellum* considerations, sometimes *jus ad bellum* issues can affect how *jus in bello* rules operate.

For example, the *jus ad bellum* principle of *competent authority* (also called *right authority*) acknowledges that the resort to military force is a prerogative of the State.[97] *Competent authority* is reflected in the distinction between international armed conflict and non-international armed conflict; military operations against another State are fundamentally different as a matter of law than military operations against a non-State armed group.[98] *Competent authority* also is reflected in *jus in bello* rules relating to who is entitled to receive the privileges of combatant status. Private persons captured after engaging in hostilities generally are not entitled to receive the privileges of POW status under the law of war because they lack *competent authority*.[99]

As another example, the *jus ad bellum* issue of whether a disputed territory belongs to a State affects whether the law of belligerent occupation applies to that territory because the law of belligerent occupation only applies to territory that belongs to an enemy State.[100]

3.5.4 U.N. Security Council Decisions and *Jus in Bello*. The Charter of the United Nations provides the modern treaty framework for *jus ad bellum*, and assigns important responsibilities to the U.N. Security Council.[101]

In theory, decisions by the Security Council, acting under Chapter VII of the Charter of the United Nations, could create obligations that conflict with, and prevail over, obligations in law of war treaties or customary international law.[102] In practice, however, the U.N. Security Council frequently has affirmed the obligations of States and parties to conflicts to comply with the law of war, including military forces operating pursuant to U.N. Security Council decisions.[103]

---

[96] United States v. Josef Altstoetter, *et al.* (Justice Case), III TRIALS OF WAR CRIMINALS BEFORE THE NMT 1027 ("If we should adopt the view that by reason of the fact that the war was a criminal war of aggression every act which would have been legal in a defensive war was illegal in this one, we would be forced to the conclusion that every soldier who marched under orders into occupied territory or who fought in the homeland was a criminal and a murderer. The rules of land warfare upon which the prosecution has relied would not be the measure of conduct and the pronouncement of guilt in any case would become a mere formality.").

[97] *Refer to* § 1.11.1.1 (Competent Authority (Right Authority) to Wage War for a Public Purpose).

[98] *Refer to* § 3.3.1 (International Armed Conflict and Non-International Armed Conflict).

[99] *Refer to* § 4.18.3 (Private Persons Who Engage in Hostilities – Lack of the Privileges of Combatant Status).

[100] *Refer to* § 11.2.2.3 ("Of the Hostile Army" – Belligerent Occupation Applies to Enemy Territory).

[101] *Refer to* § 1.11.2 (U.N. Charter Framework and the U.N. Security Council).

[102] *Refer to* § 1.11.2.1 (U.N. Member State Obligations With Respect to U.N. Security Council Decisions).

[103] *For example*, U.N. SECURITY COUNCIL RESOLUTION 2011(2011), U.N. Doc. S/RES/2011 (2011) (Oct. 12, 2011) ("*Expressing* its serious concern with the increased high number of civilian casualties in Afghanistan, in particular women and children casualties, the increasingly large majority of which are caused by Taliban, Al-Qaida and other

The U.N. Security Council also has certain authorities to respond to situations involving violations of the law of war, including establishing commissions of inquiry or authorizing the use of force.[104]

Decisions of the Security Council, however, may alter the obligations of member States of the United Nations under the law of neutrality.[105] In addition, a U.N. Security Council authorization may provide additional authority for an Occupying Power to govern occupied territory.[106]

3.6 Reciprocity and Law of War Rules

"Reciprocity" sometimes refers to the idea that whether a law of war rule applies to a party to a conflict depends on whether its opponent has accepted and complies with that same rule or a corresponding rule. The requirement to comply with many law of war rules (such as the obligation to treat detainees humanely) does not depend on whether the enemy complies with that rule. Nonetheless, in the law of war, reciprocity may play a role in: (1) whether a rule applies; (2) enforcing a rule; or (3) how a rule operates.

3.6.1 Treaty Provisions That Provide for Reciprocity in the Scope of Application of the Treaty. Considerations of reciprocity – *i.e.*, the degree of confidence as to whether an adversary will, in fact, abide by a certain rule – may be a critical factor in the willingness of States to enter into treaty obligations.

Similarly, various treaty provisions also reflect, to varying degrees, the principle that whether a rule is legally binding on a party depends on whether its opponent has accepted and applied that same rule. For example, some law of war treaties have a "general participation clause" – *i.e.*, a clause specifying that the treaty only applies to an armed conflict if all the parties to the armed conflict are also Parties to the treaty.[107] A number of treaties on the law of

---

violent and extremist groups, *reaffirming* that all parties to armed conflict must take all feasible steps to ensure the protection of affected civilians, especially women, children and displaced persons, *calling* for all parties to comply with their obligations under international humanitarian and human rights law and for all appropriate measures to be taken to ensure the protection of civilians, and *recognizing* the importance of the ongoing monitoring and reporting to the United Nations Security Council, including by ISAF, of the situation of civilians and in particular civilian casualties, and noting in this regard the work of the ISAF Civilian Casualties Tracking Cell,").

[104] *Refer to* § 18.12 (U.N. Security Council and Enforcement of the Law of War).

[105] *Refer to* § 15.2.3 (The Law of Neutrality Under the Charter of the United Nations).

[106] *Refer to* § 11.1.2.5 (Occupation and U.N. Security Council Resolutions).

[107] *For example*, HAGUE IV art. 2 ("The provisions contained in the Regulations referred to in Article 1, as well as in the present Convention, do not apply except between Contracting Powers, and then only if all the belligerents are parties to the Convention."); HAGUE V art. 20 ("The provisions of the present Convention do not apply except between Contracting Powers, and then only if all the belligerents are parties to the Convention."); HAGUE IX art. 8 ("The provisions of the present Convention do not apply except between Contracting Powers, and then only if all the belligerents are parties to the Convention."); HAGUE XIII art. 28 ("The provisions of the present Convention do not apply except to the Contracting Powers, and then only if all the belligerents are parties to the Convention."); 1929 GPW art. 82 ("The provisions of the present Convention must be respected by the High Contracting Parties under all circumstances. In case, in time of war, one of the belligerents is not a party to the Convention, its provisions shall nevertheless remain in force as between the belligerents who are parties thereto."); 1929 GWS art. 25 ("The provisions of the present Convention shall be respected by the High Contracting Parties under all circumstances. If,

neutrality have such a clause.[108] Other treaties specify that if both Parties and non-Parties to a treaty are in an armed conflict, then Parties to the treaty remain bound by the treaty in their mutual relations, but not in relation to States that are not Parties to the treaty.[109] Treaties have also provided that if a State in an armed conflict is not a Party to the treaty, but it accepts and applies the treaty's provisions, then the Parties to the treaty are bound by the treaty in relation to that State.[110]

These provisions, however, only determine the application of the treaty as matter of treaty law and not as customary international law. For example, although not all parties to World War II were Parties to Hague IV (thus failing to satisfy the requirements of Hague IV's general participation clause), Hague IV's humanitarian protections were deemed applicable as a matter of customary international law.[111]

3.6.2 Reciprocity in the Enforcement of the Law of War. Reciprocity may be reflected in the enforcement of the law of war. For example, the principle of reciprocity is reflected in the concept of reprisal, which under very limited circumstances permits a belligerent to take action that would otherwise be unlawful in order to remedy an enemy's breach of the law.[112] However, the prohibitions on reprisal in the law of war also may be understood to reflect important limitations on the principle of reciprocity in enforcing the law of war.[113]

Reciprocity is also reflected in the principle of *tu quoque*, which may limit a State's ability to deem unlawful and punish certain conduct by its adversary when that State has chosen to allow its forces to engage in that same conduct.[114]

Even if the application of a law of war rule does not depend on reciprocity as a matter of

---

in time of war, a belligerent is not a party to the Convention, its provisions shall nevertheless remain in force as between all the belligerents who are parties to the Convention.").

[108] *Refer to* § 15.1.4 (Application of Treaties on Neutrality and Customary International Law).

[109] *See, e.g.*, GPW art. 2 ("Although one of the Powers in conflict may not be a party to the present Convention, the Powers who are parties thereto shall remain bound by it in their mutual relations."); GWS-SEA art. 2 (same); GPW art. 2 (same); GC art. 2 (same); CCW art. 7(1) ("When one of the parties to a conflict is not bound by an annexed Protocol, the parties bound by this Convention and that annexed Protocol shall remain bound by them in their mutual relations.").

[110] *See* CCW art. 7(2) ("Any High Contracting Party shall be bound by this Convention and any Protocol annexed thereto which is in force for it, in any situation contemplated by Article 1, in relation to any State which is not a party to this Convention or bound by the relevant annexed Protocol, if the latter accepts and applies this Convention or the relevant Protocol, and so notifies the Depositary."); GWS art. 2 ("Although one of the Powers in conflict may not be a party to the present Convention, the Powers who are parties thereto ... shall furthermore be bound by the Convention in relation to the said Power, if the latter accepts and applies the provisions thereof."); GWS-SEA art. 2 (same); GPW art. 2 (same); GC art. 2 (same).

[111] *Refer to* § 19.8.2.1 (Hague IV and Customary International Law).

[112] *Refer to* § 18.18 (Reprisals).

[113] *Refer to* § 18.18.3 (Treaty Prohibitions on Reprisals). *Consider also* VCLT art. 60(5) ("Paragraphs 1 to 3 do not apply to provisions relating to the protection of the human person contained in treaties of a humanitarian character, in particular to provisions prohibiting any form of reprisals against persons protected by such treaties.").

[114] *Refer to* § 18.21.2 (Tu Quoque).

law, reciprocity may be important as a practical way of encouraging compliance by the adversary with the law of war.[115]

3.6.3 Law of War Rules May Incorporate Reciprocity. Apart from affecting whether rules apply, reciprocity may be incorporated into the operation of particular law of war rules. In other words, a law of war rule may operate differently depending upon an opponent's behavior.

3.6.3.1 *Reciprocity – "Golden Rule"*. A principle of reciprocity may be understood to be reflected in law of war rules that reflect the golden rule.[116] For example, the treatment of POWs has been based on the principle that POWs should be treated as the Detaining Power would want its forces held by the enemy to be treated.[117] Similarly, during the process of releasing and repatriating POWs, it is proper to expect that each Party's conduct with respect to the repatriation of POWs will be reasonable and broadly commensurate with the conduct of the other.[118]

3.6.3.2 *Benefits-Burdens Principle in Law of War Rules*. In some cases, the law of war requires that those seeking to obtain certain benefits under the law of war also accept certain burdens as a condition for receiving those benefits.[119] For example, militia and volunteer corps that seek the privileges of combatant status during international armed conflict must meet certain conditions (*e.g.*, conducting their operations in accordance with the laws and customs of war) before receiving such privileges.[120] In addition, hospital ships and coastal rescue craft must not be used for military purposes in order to receive their protection from capture and from being made the object of attack.[121] Similarly, cultural property must not be used for military purposes in order to receive special protection.[122]

---

[115] *Refer to* § 18.2.2 (Encouraging Reciprocal Adherence by the Adversary).

[116] *See* J. Pictet, *The Principles of International Humanitarian Law*, 6 INTERNATIONAL REVIEW OF THE RED CROSS 455, 462 (Sept. 1966) ("Humanitarian law receives its impulse from moral science all of which can be summed up in one sentence, 'do to others what you would have done to yourself'. This crystallizes the wisdom of nations and is the secret of happiness, or at least, of the best order of society. This fundamental precept can be found, in an almost identical form, in all the great religions, Brahmin, Buddhist, Christian, Confucian, Islamic, Jewish and Taoist. It is also the main prop of the positivists who do not base themselves on precepts of any given religion, but on social facts, considered objectively, through their own reasoning alone.").

[117] *Refer to* § 9.2.5 (Reciprocity in the Treatment of POWs).

[118] *Refer to* § 9.37.1 (Agreements on POW Release and Repatriation).

[119] *See, e.g.*, Al Warafi v. Obama, 716 F.3d 627, 631-32 (D.C. Cir. 2013) ("The Geneva Conventions and their commentary provide a roadmap for the establishment of protected status. As the district court found, Al Warafi was serving as part of the Taliban. The Taliban has not followed the roadmap set forth in the Conventions, and it has not carried Al Warafi to the destination. … Without compliance with the requirements of the Geneva Conventions, the Taliban's personnel are not entitled to the protection of the Convention."); Jack L. Goldsmith III, Assistant Attorney General, *"Protected Person" Status in Occupied Iraq Under the Fourth Geneva Convention*, Mar. 18, 2004, 28 OPINIONS OF THE OFFICE OF LEGAL COUNSEL 35, 53-57 (explaining "the Geneva Conventions' fundamental principle that warring entities must accept the Conventions' burdens in order to claim their benefits.").

[120] *Refer to* § 4.6 (Other Militia and Volunteer Corps).

[121] *Refer to* § 5.18.8.2 (Conditions for the Granting of Special Protection – No Use for Military Purposes).

[122] *Refer to* § 7.12.2.2 (No Use for Military Purposes).

As another example, the rights and duties of belligerents and neutrals under the law of neutrality may be understood as correlative or reciprocal. For example, a neutral's valid assertion of its rights may depend on whether it has fulfilled its corresponding neutral duties.[123]

3.6.3.3 *Law of War Duties That Are Reinforced by Corresponding Duties for the Enemy*. Similarly, the ability of a party to comply with a particular duty may be affected by whether its opponent has complied with a corresponding duty. For example, the ability of a party to discriminate in conducting attacks may be affected by whether its adversary has properly distinguished its military objectives from the civilian population and other protected persons and objects.[124]

3.7 Applying Rules by Analogy

In some cases, a rule developed specifically for one situation may be a useful and appropriate standard to apply in a different situation. This is sometimes called an application of a rule by analogy.

In some cases, there is a treaty requirement to apply rules by analogy; in other cases, it may be appropriate to apply law of war rules by analogy without a treaty-based requirement to do so.

3.7.1 Treaty Requirement to Apply Rules by Analogy. The application of law of war rules by analogy is sometimes required by a treaty provision.

For example, under the 1949 Geneva Conventions, neutral or non-belligerent States must apply by analogy the rules relating to the treatment of the wounded and sick and of POWs when interning such persons under their duties of neutrality.[125] Similarly, the GC rules for penal procedures for protected persons in occupied territory apply by analogy to proceedings against internees who are in the national territory of the Detaining Power.[126]

3.7.2 Examples of Law of War Rules and Areas in Which Such Rules Have Been Applied by Analogy. There are other situations in which it may be appropriate to apply law of war rules by analogy, even though there is no treaty requirement to do so. For example, it may be appropriate to apply the GWS and GWS-Sea rules for the respectful treatment and handling of enemy military dead to all persons.[127] Other examples of law of war rules and situations in which it may be appropriate to apply those rules by analogy include: (1) applying *jus in bello* rules in certain situations involving neutral or non-belligerent States; (2) applying law of war rules with a humanitarian purpose in situations outside the context of armed conflict; (3)

---

[123] *Refer to* § 15.3.3 (Correlative or Reciprocal Nature of Rights and Duties Under the Law of Neutrality).

[124] *Refer to* § 2.5.5 (Reinforcing Duties – Discriminating in Conducting Attacks and Distinguishing a Party's Own Persons and Objects).

[125] *Refer to* § 15.16.3.1 (Provision of POW Treatment and Application of the GWS and GWS-Sea by Analogy).

[126] *Refer to* § 10.29 (Judicial Proceedings Regarding Protected Persons in Occupied Territory or Internees in a Belligerent's Home Territory).

[127] *Refer to* § 7.7 (Treatment and Handling of Enemy Military Dead).

applying occupation law provisions for the protection of the civilian population in situations not constituting belligerent occupation; and (4) applying certain international armed conflict rules in situations of non-international armed conflict.

3.7.2.1 Jus in Bello *Rules and Situations Involving Neutral or Non-Belligerent States*. Although States developed *jus in bello* rules to address relations between enemies, some *jus in bello* rules may be applied by analogy to other situations, such as relations between a belligerent and a neutral or between co-belligerents. For example, a belligerent might take feasible precautions to protect the civilian population of a neutral or co-belligerent State from its military operations, even though such actions might not be required by the law of war.[128] In addition, although the GC excludes certain persons from the definition of protected person based on their nationality, it may be appropriate to afford such persons the standards of treatment for protected persons.[129]

3.7.2.2 *Law of War Rules and Military Operations Outside the Context of Armed Conflict*. Because law of war rules often reflect elementary considerations of humanity, it may be appropriate to apply such standards to military operations occurring outside the context of armed conflict.[130]

3.7.2.3 *Occupation Law and Situations Not Constituting Belligerent Occupation*. Occupation law may also provide a useful framework for certain situations to which it may not be strictly applicable.[131] For example, it may be appropriate for a State that liberates its ally's territory from enemy control to apply by analogy rules from the law of belligerent occupation to the administration of such territory, pending an agreement with the allied government.[132]

3.7.2.4 *International Armed Conflict Rules and Situations of Non-International Armed Conflict*. Legal rules applicable to international armed conflict may sometimes be applied

---

[128] *For example*, DEPARTMENT OF THE AIR FORCE, HEADQUARTERS PACIFIC AIR FORCES, DIRECTORATE OF OPERATIONS ANALYSIS, *Project CHECO [Contemporary Historical Examination of Current Operations] Report, Rules of engagement, November 1969-September 1972* (Mar. 1, 1973), *reprinted in* CONGRESSIONAL RECORD S3011, S3014 (Mar. 18, 1985) ("The Cambodian incursion plan was a closely held secret timed to coincide with the President's announcement. It was not until 27 April [1970] that 7AF was told to start definitive planning. Thus, there was no time to coordinate a new set of ROE for [neutral] Cambodia. Instead 7AF instructed its pilots to follow the normal rules for South Vietnam and to exercise extreme vigilance to avoid dropping ordnance on the noncombatant populace."); Franklin Roosevelt, message to Winston Churchill, *reprinted in* WINSTON CHURCHILL, CLOSING THE RING 467-68 (1985) ("I share fully with you your distress at the loss of life among the French population incident to our air preparations for 'Overlord'. I share also with you a satisfaction that every possible care is being and will be taken to minimise civilian casualties. No possibility of alleviating adverse French opinion should be overlooked, always provided that there is no reduction of our effectiveness against the enemy at this crucial time. However regrettable the attendant loss of civilian lives is, I am not prepared to impose from this distance any restriction on military action by the responsible commanders that in their opinion might militate against the success of 'Overlord' or cause additional loss of life to our Allied forces of invasion.").

[129] *Refer to* § 10.3.3 (Categories of Nationals Specifically Excluded From the Definition of Protected Person Under the GC).

[130] *Refer to* § 3.1.1.2 (Applying Law of War Standards as Reflecting Minimum Legal Standards).

[131] *Refer to* § 11.1.3 (Application of Occupation Law to Situations Not Constituting Belligerent Occupation).

[132] *Refer to* § 11.1.3.2 (Liberation of Friendly Territory).

by analogy to non-international armed conflict.[133]

3.8 End of Hostilities and the Application of the Law of War

In general, law of war rules for the conduct of hostilities cease to apply when hostilities have ended. However, certain duties that have arisen during hostilities may continue after hostilities have ended, and certain new duties arise at the end of hostilities.

3.8.1 General Cessation of the Application of the Law of War at the End of Hostilities. Hostilities end when opposing parties decide to end hostilities and actually do so, *i.e.*, when neither the intent-based nor act-based tests for when hostilities exist are met.[134] Of course, if the test for the existence of hostilities continues to be met, then hostilities cannot be deemed to have ceased.[135] For example, hostilities may be terminated by:

- an agreement to end hostilities, normally in the form of a treaty of peace;
- unilateral declaration of one of the parties to end the war, provided the other party does not continue hostilities or otherwise decline to recognize the act of its enemy;
- the complete subjugation of an enemy State and its allies; or
- a simple cessation of hostilities.[136]

3.8.1.1 *Agreements to End Hostilities*. Parties to a conflict often have negotiated peace treaties to end hostilities.[137] Armistice agreements, *i.e.*, temporary cease-fires, are negotiated to suspend hostilities.[138] In addition, the U.N. Security Council may require certain

---

[133] *Refer to* § 17.2.2.3 (Application of IAC Rules by Analogy).

[134] *Refer to* § 3.4 (When *Jus in Bello* Rules Apply).

[135] David Kris, Assistant Attorney General, *Response to Questions Submitted by Members Post Hearing, Questions Submitted by Mr. Skelton, Reforming the Military Commissions Act of 2006 and Detainee Policy: Hearing Before the Committee on Armed Services, U.S. House of Representatives*, 111th Congress, 1st Session, 77 (Jul. 24, 2009) ("At a minimum, we believe active hostilities will continue--and detention of enemy forces will be authorized--as long as the United States is involved in active combat operations against such forces. In reaching the determination that active hostilities have ceased, we would likely consider factors that have been recognized in international law as relevant to the existence of an armed conflict, including the frequency and level of intensity of any continuing violence generated by enemy forces; the degree to which they maintain an organizational structure and operate according to a plan; the enemy's capacity to procure, transport and distribute arms; and the enemy's intent to inflict violence.").

[136] 1956 FM 27-10 (Change No. 1 1976) ¶10 ("The law of land warfare generally ceases to be applicable upon: *a*. The termination of a war by agreement, normally in the form of a treaty of peace; or *b*. The termination of a war by unilateral declaration of one of the parties, provided the other party does not continue hostilities or otherwise decline to recognize the act of its enemy; or *c*. The complete subjugation of an enemy State and its allies, if prior to *a* or *b*; or *d*. The termination of a declared war or armed conflict by simple cessation of hostilities.").

[137] *For example*, Agreement on Ending the War and Restoring Peace in Viet Nam signed between the Government of the Democratic Republic of Viet Nam and the Government of the United States, and the Protocols to this Agreement, Jan. 27, 1973, T.I.A.S. 7542, 935 UNTS 2, 6; General Agreement for Peace in Bosnia and Herzegovina, Bosn. & Herz.-Croat.-F.R.Y, December 14, 1995, 35 I.L.M. 75 (also known as the Dayton Accords).

[138] *Refer to* § 12.11.1.2 (Armistice as a Suspension of Hostilities and Not a Peace Treaty).

steps leading to the end of hostilities.[139]

In drafting and interpreting agreements for the cessation of hostilities, it is important to understand the rules normally applicable to the cessation of hostilities. These agreements may refer to provisions in the Geneva Conventions or other law of war instruments. These agreements may modify or supplement the rules normally applicable to the cessation of hostilities, *e.g.*, by specifying precisely when a legal obligation is triggered or satisfied.

3.8.1.2 *End of Hostilities Absent Written Agreement*. Although States often have concluded agreements to end hostilities, it is possible for hostilities to cease absent a written or formal agreement. For example, an armed conflict may end when a party is fully subjugated.

It may be difficult to determine when an armed conflict has ceased, as opposed, for example, to a lull in hostilities during which opposing forces may simply be reconstituting themselves.[140] Hostilities generally would not be deemed to have ceased without an agreement, unless the conditions clearly indicate that they are not be resumed or there has been a lapse of time indicating the improbability of resumption.[141]

3.8.2 Duties Continuing After Hostilities. Under the law of war, certain duties that have arisen during hostilities may continue after hostilities have ended. For example, POWs are protected by the GPW from the moment they fall into the power of the enemy until their final release and repatriation.[142] Similarly, protected persons whose release, repatriation, or re-establishment may take place after the general close of military operations continue to benefit from the protection of the GC.[143] In addition, duties under occupation law may continue after hostilities have ended.[144]

3.8.3 Duties Arising at the End of Hostilities. Certain obligations are triggered by the end of hostilities. For example, the end of hostilities triggers obligations regarding the marking of minefields, demining, and clearance of unexploded ordnance.[145] In addition, POWs and

---

[139] *Refer to* § 12.14 (U.N. Security Council Cease-Fires).

[140] Mr. Seward, Secretary of State, to Mr. Goni, Spanish Minister, Jul. 22, 1868, VII MOORE'S DIGEST 336 ("It is certain that a condition of war can be raised without an authoritative declaration of war, and, on the other hand, the situation of peace may be restored by the long suspension of hostilities without a treaty of peace being made. History is full of such occurrences. What period of suspension of war is necessary to justify the presumption of the restoration of peace has never yet been settled, and must in every case be determined with reference to collateral facts and circumstances.").

[141] Manley O. Hudson, *The Duration of the War Between the United States and Germany*, 39 HARVARD LAW REVIEW 1020, 1029-30 (1926) ("If a war may be ended by a mere cessation of hostilities, the cessation of hostilities must either be under such conditions that it is clear that they are not to be resumed or there must be a lapse of time indicating the improbability of resumption.").

[142] *Refer to* § 9.3.6 (Commencement and Duration of POW Status and Treatment).

[143] *Refer to* § 10.3.4 (Commencement and Duration of Protected Person Status).

[144] *Refer to* § 11.3.2 (Duration of GC Obligations in the Case of Occupied Territory).

[145] *Refer to* § 6.12.12.2 (Clearance of Minefields, Mined Areas, Mines, Booby-Traps, and Other Devices After Hostilities); § 6.20.5 (Obligations Under the CCW Protocol V on Explosive Remnants of War That Are Triggered by the Cessation of Active Hostilities).

protected persons, in general, must be released and returned to the party to the conflict to which they belong.[146]

3.9 Law of War Duties Also Applicable in Peace

Some law of war obligations also apply in peace, *i.e.*, even when a State is not engaged in an armed conflict. For example, States must:

- disseminate information regarding the law of war;[147]
- train their armed forces in accordance with the law of war;[148]
- issue instructions and regulations for their armed forces in conformity with the law of war;[149]
- review the legality of new weapons;[150]
- take appropriate measures to prepare for the safeguarding of cultural property;[151] and
- take other appropriate measures to ensure the implementation and enforcement of law of war treaties.[152]

States that are at peace have obligations under the law of neutrality in relation to States that are at war.[153]

---

[146] *Refer to* § 9.37 (Release and Repatriation After Hostilities); § 10.35 (Release, Return, Repatriation of Internees After the Close of Hostilities); § 11.11.8 (Disposition of Accused and Convicted Protected Persons Upon the Close of Occupation).

[147] *Refer to* § 18.6.1 (General Dissemination and Study of Treaties).

[148] *Refer to* § 18.6.2 (Special Instruction or Training).

[149] *Refer to* § 18.7 (Instructions, Regulations, and Procedures to Implement and Enforce the Law of War).

[150] *Refer to* § 6.2 (DoD Policy of Reviewing the Legality of Weapons).

[151] *Refer to* § 5.18.2.1 (Peacetime Obligations to Prepare for the Safeguarding of Cultural Property).

[152] *Refer to* § 18.1.2 (National Obligations to Implement and Enforce the Law of War).

[153] *Refer to* § 15.1.1 (Matters Addressed by the Law of Neutrality).

IV – Classes of Persons

Chapter Contents

4.1 Introduction

This Chapter addresses different classes of persons under the law of war. The law of war has created a framework of classes of persons to help confine the fighting between opposing military forces and thereby to help protect the civilian population from the effects of war.[1]

This Chapter addresses issues relating to various classes of people under the law of war including: (1) who is included in the various classes, such as "combatant" and "civilian"; (2) the rights, duties, and liabilities of the persons in each class; and (3) how certain factual categories of persons, such as journalists, police officers, or child soldiers, fall within various classes and are treated under the law of war.

---

[1] *Refer to* § 2.5.1 (Distinction as a Framework of Legal Classes).

This Chapter briefly addresses specific rules that relate to the rights, duties, and liabilities of persons in the various classes to illustrate and provide an overview of that class. For more information about specific rules, practitioners should refer to the cross-referenced sections that addresses those specific rules.[2]

4.1.1 General Notes on Terminology for Persons in the Law of War. The terms in the law of war that describe different classes of people are often used in confusing and contradictory ways. Although striving to use terms consistently within DoD reduces confusion, understanding the substantive standards that apply to a person in the applicable circumstances is more important than using a particular label or a particular system of classification.

4.1.1.1 *The Same Term Used With Different Meanings*. Sometimes different meanings are given to the same term. For example, someone might be considered a "combatant" in the sense that the person may be made the object of attack, but the person would not necessarily be a "combatant" in the sense that the person is privileged to engage in hostilities.[3]

Similarly, one source might use the term "noncombatant" to mean all persons who are not combatants, including persons placed *hors de combat* and civilians.[4] Alternatively, another source might use the term "noncombatant" to refer specifically to persons who are members of the armed forces, but who are not combatants.[5] In the past, some commentators have used "noncombatants" of the armed forces to refer to all members of the armed forces serving in combat service support or sustainment roles.[6] In contemporary parlance, however, the term "noncombatant" should generally be used to mean military medical and religious personnel,[7] but also can include those combatants placed *hors de combat*.[8]

---

[2] *Refer to* § 1.2.3 (Use of Cross-References in This Manual).

[3] *Refer to* § 4.3.2 (Combatant – Notes on Terminology).

[4] *See, e.g.*, L.C. GREEN, THE CONTEMPORARY LAW OF ARMED CONFLICT 88 (2nd ed., 2000) ("Nationals of the adverse party are normally classified as combatants and non-combatants, with the latter including some members of the armed forces – chaplains, medical personnel and those *hors de combat*."); LIEBER CODE art. 19 ("Commanders, whenever admissible, inform the enemy of their intention to bombard a place, so that the noncombatants, and especially the women and children, may be removed before the bombardment commences.").

[5] *See, e.g.*, HAGUE IV REG. art. 3 ("The armed forces of the belligerent parties may consist of combatants and noncombatants. In the case of capture by the enemy, both have the right to be treated as prisoners of war.").

[6] *See, e.g.*, GREENSPAN, MODERN LAW OF LAND WARFARE 56 ("The distinction between combatants and noncombatants within the armed forces must be taken to correspond to the distinction between fighting troops and troops in service units. The fighting troops of an army carry out the actual military operations, whereas the service troops minister to the needs of the former and supply their various requirements. The Hague Regulations do not define the elements in the two classes, but combatants would include infantry, cavalry, armored troops, and the like, whose function it is to engage with the enemy; as well as artillery, engineers, signals, and others, whose duty it is to support such action. Noncombatants would include personnel of the various 'services' comprising (*inter alia*) medical, chaplains, veterinary, graves, pay, postal, labor, supply, transport, ordnance, provost, legal, and military-government units."); GWS COMMENTARY 223 footnote 4 ("In correct terminology, however, 'armed forces' include 'combatants' (*i.e.* soldiers bearing arms) and 'non-combatants' (who comprise not only medical personnel but also various other army services not called upon to carry arms).").

[7] *Refer to* § 4.9 (Military Medical and Religious Personnel).

[8] *Refer to* § 5.9 (Persons Placed *Hors de Combat*).

4.1.1.2 *Different Terms Used to Describe the Same Concept*. Different legal sources may use different terms to refer to the same class of people under the law of war. For example, one source might use "belligerent," whereas another source might use "combatant" to refer to the same class of people under the law of war.[9]

4.1.2 Classes and Categories Are Only the Starting Point for Legal Analysis. When analyzing a person's rights, duties, and liabilities under the law of war, it is important to analyze the specific question in light of the applicable facts. Determining what class a person falls into, such as "combatant," "civilian," or "unprivileged belligerent," may be only the first step in a legal analysis. For example, whether a person may be the object of attack, may be detained, is entitled to POW status, or may be punished for their actions are all different questions. Although these questions are often related to one another and associated with the general classes of "combatant" and "civilian," each question requires its own specific analysis. This specific analysis should be done in each case, applying the legal rules to the facts, rather than deriving an answer based on a conclusory labeling of a person as, for example, an "enemy combatant."[10] Indeed, some persons might, for some purposes, be treated like "combatants," but for other purposes be treated like "civilians."[11]

4.2 THE ARMED FORCES AND THE CIVILIAN POPULATION

The law of war has recognized that the population of an enemy State is generally divided into two classes: the armed forces and the civilian population, also sometimes called, respectively, "combatants" and "civilians." This division results from the principle of distinction.[12]

4.2.1 Development of the Distinction Between the Armed Forces and the Civilian Population. A citizen or national of a State that is a party to a conflict, as one of the constituents of a State that is engaged in hostilities, may be subjected to the hardships of war by an enemy State.[13] However, because the ordinary members of the civilian population make no resistance, it has long been recognized that there is no right to make them the object of attack.[14] Thus,

---

[9] *Refer to* § 4.3.2 (Combatant – Notes on Terminology).

[10] *Refer to* § 4.18.1 (Private Persons Who Engage in Hostilities – Notes on Terminology).

[11] *Refer to* § 4.2.3 (Mixed Cases).

[12] *Refer to* § 2.5 (Distinction).

[13] *See, e.g.*, Johnson v. Eisentrager, 339 U.S. 763, 772-73 (1950) ("The alien enemy is bound by an allegiance which commits him to lose no opportunity to forward the cause of our enemy; hence the United States, assuming him to be faithful to his allegiance, regards him as part of the enemy resources. It therefore takes measures to disable him from commission of hostile acts imputed as his intention because they are a duty to his sovereign."); LIEBER CODE art. 21 ("The citizen or native of a hostile country is thus an enemy, as one of the constituents of the hostile state or nation, and as such is subjected to the hardships of the war.").

[14] *See* LAUTERPACHT, II OPPENHEIM'S INTERNATIONAL LAW 204 (§57) ("Those private subjects of the belligerents who do not directly or indirectly belong to the armed forces do not take part in it; they do not attack and defend; and no attack ought therefore to be made upon them."); G. SHERSTON BAKER, II HALLECK'S INTERNATIONAL LAW 15-16 (20.3) (1908) ("Feeble old men, women, and children, and sick persons, come under the general description of enemies, and we have certain rights over them as members of the community with which we are at war; but, as they are enemies who make no resistance, we have no right to maltreat their persons, or to use any violence toward them, much less to take their lives."); LIEBER CODE arts. 22, 23, 25 (explaining that protection of the "unarmed citizen,"

States have departed from ancient and medieval practices of war between entire peoples, and instead, as much as possible, have treated war as a contention between the professional military forces of warring States.[15] This separation of the armed forces and the civilian population has greatly mitigated the evils of war.[16]

4.2.2 No Person May Claim the Distinct Rights Afforded to Both Combatants and Civilians at the Same Time. The classes of combatants and civilians have distinct rights, duties, and liabilities; no person may claim the distinct rights afforded both classes at the same time.[17] For example, a person may not claim the combatant's right to attack enemy forces while also claiming the civilian's right not to be made the object of attack.[18]

4.2.3 Mixed Cases. Certain classes of persons do not fit neatly within the dichotomy of the armed forces and the civilian population, *i.e.*, combatants and civilians. Each of these

---

the "inoffensive individual," or the "inoffensive citizen of the hostile country" is the rule) (emphasis added); VATTEL, THE LAW OF NATIONS 282 (3.8.145) ("Women, children, feeble old men, and the sick … these are enemies who make no resistance, and consequently the belligerent has no right to maltreat or otherwise offer violence to them, much less to put them to death.").

[15] *See, e.g.*, LAUTERPACHT, II OPPENHEIM'S INTERNATIONAL LAW 204 (§57) ("During antiquity, and the greater part of the Middle Ages, war was a contention between the whole populations of the belligerent States. In time of war every subject of one belligerent, whether an armed and fighting individual or not, whether man or woman, adult or infant, could be killed or enslaved by the other belligerent at will. But gradually a milder and more discriminating practice grew up, and nowadays the life and liberty of such private subjects of belligerents as do not directly or indirectly belong to their armed forces, and, with certain exceptions, their private property, are protected by International Law."); LIEBER CODE art. 22 ("Nevertheless, as civilization has advanced during the last centuries, so has likewise steadily advanced, especially in war on land, the distinction between the private individual belonging to a hostile country and the hostile country itself, with its men in arms. The principle has been more and more acknowledged that the unarmed citizen is to be spared in person, property, and honor as much as the exigencies of war will admit.").

[16] *See* SPAIGHT, WAR RIGHTS ON LAND 37 ("The separation of armies and peaceful inhabitants into two distinct classes is perhaps the greatest triumph of International Law. Its effect in mitigating the evils of war has been incalculable."); G. SHERSTON BAKER, II HALLECK'S INTERNATIONAL LAW 20-22 (20.3) (1908) ("But afterwards in Italy, and more particularly during the lawless confusion of the feudal ages, hostilities were carried on by all classes of persons, and everyone capable of being a soldier was regarded as such, and all the rights of war attached to his person. But as wars are now carried on by regular troops, or, at least, by forces regularly organised, the peasants, merchants, manufacturers, agriculturists, and, generally, all public and private persons, who are engaged in the ordinary pursuits of life, and take no part in military operations, have nothing to fear from the sword of the enemy. So long as they refrain from all hostilities, pay the military contributions which may be imposed on them and quietly submit to the authority of the belligerent who may happen to be in the military possession of their country, they are allowed to continue in the enjoyment of their property, and in the pursuit of their ordinary avocations. This system has greatly mitigated the evils of war, … .").

[17] *See, e.g.*, 1956 FM 27-10 (Change No. 1 1976) ¶60 (dividing into "prisoners of war" and "the civilian population," and noting that "[p]ersons in each of the foregoing categories have distinct rights, duties, and disabilities."); 1940 RULES OF LAND WARFARE ¶8 ("The enemy population is divided in war into two general classes, known as, the armed forces and the peaceful population. Both classes have distinct rights, duties, and disabilities, and no person can belong to both classes at one and the same time."); 1934 RULES OF LAND WARFARE ¶8 (same); 1914 RULES OF LAND WARFARE ¶29 (same).

[18] *See* 1958 UK MANUAL ¶86 ("It is one of the purposes of the law of war to ensure that an individual who belongs to one class or the other shall not be permitted to enjoy the privileges of both. Thus he must not be allowed to kill or wound members of the army of the opposing belligerent and subsequently, if captured, to claim that he is a peaceful citizen.").

particular classes has some attributes of combatant status and some attributes of civilian status; in certain respects persons in these classes are treated like combatants, but in other respects they are treated like civilians. These classes may be classified into three groups: (1) certain personnel engaged in humanitarian duties; (2) certain authorized supporters of the armed forces; and (3) unprivileged belligerents.

4.2.3.1 *Certain Personnel Engaged Humanitarian Duties*. Certain categories of personnel have humanitarian duties that involve them in hostilities but also entitle them to special protections:

- military medical and religious personnel;[19]
- authorized staff of voluntary aid societies;[20]
- staff of a recognized aid society of a neutral country;[21]
- auxiliary medical personnel;[22] and
- personnel engaged in the protection of cultural property.[23]

4.2.3.2 *Certain Authorized Supporters of the Armed Forces*. Certain categories of persons are not members of the armed forces, but are nonetheless authorized to support the armed forces in the fighting:

- persons authorized to accompany the armed forces, but who are not members thereof;[24] and
- members of the crews of merchant marine vessels or civil aircraft of a belligerent.[25]

4.2.3.3 *Unprivileged Belligerents*. Unprivileged belligerents generally are subject to the liabilities of both combatant and civilian status, and include:[26]

- persons engaging in spying, sabotage, and similar acts behind enemy lines;[27] and
- private persons engaging in hostilities.[28]

---

[19] *Refer to* § 4.9 (Military Medical and Religious Personnel).

[20] *Refer to* § 4.11 (Authorized Staff of Voluntary Aid Societies).

[21] *Refer to* § 4.12 (Staff of a Recognized Aid Society of a Neutral Country).

[22] *Refer to* § 4.13 (Auxiliary Medical Personnel).

[23] *Refer to* § 4.14.1 (Personnel Engaged in the Protection of Cultural Property).

[24] *Refer to* § 4.15 (Persons Authorized to Accompany the Armed Forces).

[25] *Refer to* § 4.16 (Crews of Merchant Marine Vessels or Civil Aircraft).

[26] *Refer to* § 4.3.4 (Types of Unprivileged Belligerents).

[27] *Refer to* § 4.17 (Spies, Saboteurs, and Other Persons Engaging in Similar Acts Behind Enemy Lines).

4.3 Lawful Combatants and Unprivileged Belligerents

In addition to distinguishing between the armed forces and the civilian population, the law of war also distinguishes between "privileged" and "unprivileged," or "lawful" and "unlawful" combatants. As the Supreme Court has explained:

> Lawful combatants are subject to capture and detention as prisoners of war by opposing military forces. Unlawful combatants are likewise subject to capture and detention, but in addition they are subject to trial and punishment by military tribunals for acts which render their belligerency unlawful.[29]

"Unlawful combatants" or "unprivileged belligerents" are persons who, by engaging in hostilities, have incurred one or more of the corresponding liabilities of combatant status (*e.g.*, being made the object of attack and subject to detention), but who are not entitled to any of the distinct privileges of combatant status (*e.g.*, combatant immunity and POW status).[30]

4.3.1 <u>"Unprivileged Belligerents" as a Category in Treaty Law</u>. States have, in a few cases, explicitly recognized in treaties certain categories of unprivileged belligerents, such as spies and saboteurs.[31] However, States have generally refrained from explicitly recognizing unprivileged belligerents as a class in treaties in the way that classes of lawful combatants have been defined.[32]

Law of war treaties have been understood to reflect restrictions on the conduct of hostilities by States,[33] and States have been reluctant to conclude treaties to afford unprivileged enemy belligerents the distinct privileges of POW status or the full protections afforded civilians.[34]

---

[28] *Refer to* § 4.18 (Private Persons Who Engage in Hostilities).

[29] Ex parte Quirin, 317 U.S. 1, 31 (1942). *See also* Hamdi v. Rumsfeld, 542 U.S. 507, 518 (2004) (plurality) ("The capture and detention of lawful combatants and the capture, detention, and trial of unlawful combatants, by 'universal agreement and practice,' are 'important incident[s] of war.'") (quoting Ex parte Quirin at 28, 30).

[30] *Refer to* § 4.19 (Rights, Duties, and Liabilities of Unprivileged Belligerents).

[31] *See, e.g.*, Hague IV Reg. arts. 29-31 (defining the category of spy and regulating the treatment of captured spies); GC art. 5 (regulating the treatment of certain protected persons "detained as a spy or saboteur, or as a person under definite suspicion of activity hostile to the security of the Occupying Power"). *See also* GC Commentary 5 ("It may, nevertheless, seem rather surprising that a humanitarian Convention should tend to protect spies, saboteurs or irregular combatants. Those who take part in the struggle while not belonging to the armed forces are acting deliberately outside the laws of warfare. Surely they know the dangers to which they are exposing themselves. It might therefore have been simpler to exclude them from the benefits of the Convention, if such a course had been possible, but the terms espionage, sabotage, terrorism, banditry and intelligence with the enemy, have so often been used lightly, and applied to such trivial offences, that it was not advisable to leave the accused at the mercy of those detaining them.").

[32] *See, e.g.*, GWS art. 13; GWS-Sea art. 13; GPW art. 4.

[33] *Refer to* § 1.3.3.1 (Law of War as Prohibitive Law).

[34] *See, e.g.*, IIA Final Report of the Diplomatic Conference of Geneva of 1949 433 (ICRC representative explaining that "[t]he present Conference was engaged in framing a Convention to protect members of armed forces and similar categories of persons, such as members of organized resistance movements, and another convention to

Although seldom explicitly recognized as a class in law of war treaties, the category of unprivileged belligerent may be understood as an implicit consequence of creating the classes of lawful combatants and peaceful civilians.[35] The concept of unprivileged belligerency, *i.e.*, the set of legal liabilities associated with unprivileged belligerents, may be understood in opposition to the rights, duties, and liabilities of lawful combatants and peaceful civilians. Unprivileged belligerents include lawful combatants who have forfeited the privileges of combatant status by engaging in spying or sabotage, and private persons who have forfeited one or more of the protections of civilian status by engaging in hostilities.[36]

4.3.2 Combatant – Notes on Terminology.

4.3.2.1 *"Combatant" and "Belligerent"*. "Combatant" and "belligerent" have sometimes been used interchangeably and, in this usage, they generally describe individuals who are not "civilians."

"Belligerent," however, has also sometimes used to describe States and to contrast such States with "neutral" or "non-belligerent" States.[37] "Belligerent" has also been used to contrast armed groups that have "belligerent rights" with armed groups that lack such rights, such as "insurgents."[38]

4.3.2.2 *"Lawful," "Privileged," and "Qualified"*. The distinction between "lawful" and "unlawful" combatants has sometimes been called a distinction between

---

protect civilians. Although the two Conventions might appear to cover all the categories concerned, irregular belligerents were not actually protected."); *id.* at 612 (Swiss representative taking the view that "[i]n regard to the legal status of those who violated the laws of war, the [Civilians] Convention could not of course cover criminals or saboteurs."); *id.* at 621 (UK representative rejecting a draft which "would mean that persons who were not entitled to protection under the Prisoners of War Convention would receive exactly the same protection by virtue of the Civilians Convention, so that all persons participating in hostilities would be protected, whether they conformed to the laws of war or not. … The whole conception of the Civilians Convention was the protection of civilian victims of war and not the protection of illegitimate bearers of arms, who could not expect full protection under rules of war to which they did not conform. Such persons should no doubt be accorded certain standards of treatment, but should not be entitled to all the benefits of the Convention.").

[35] *See, e.g.*, 10 U.S.C. § 948a ("The term 'unprivileged enemy belligerent' means an individual (other than a privileged belligerent) who" engages in certain conduct); Ex parte Quirin, 317 U.S. 1, 35 (1942) ("Our Government, by thus defining lawful belligerents entitled to be treated as prisoners of war, has recognized that there is a class of unlawful belligerents not entitled to that privilege, including those who, though combatants, do not wear 'fixed and distinctive emblems.'").

[36] *Refer to* § 4.3.4 (Types of Unprivileged Belligerents).

[37] *Refer to* § 15.1.2 (Classification of States as Belligerent, Neutral, or Non-Belligerent).

[38] *See, e.g.*, Memorandum submitted in United States v. Shakur, 690 F. Supp. 1291 (S.D.N.Y. 1988), III CUMULATIVE DIGEST OF UNITED STATES PRACTICE IN INTERNATIONAL LAW 1981-88 3436, 3448 ("The concept of 'insurgency' was traditionally used to describe a conflict that did not meet the rigid standards of customary international law for recognition of belligerency."); Anthony Eden, Secretary of State for Foreign Affairs, United Kingdom, *Oral Answers to Questions*, Dec. 8, 1937, HANSARD 330 HOUSE OF COMMONS DEBATES § 357 ("His Majesty's Ambassador at Hendaye has been instructed to inform the Salamanca authorities that as belligerent rights have not been recognised to either party in the Spanish conflict. His Majesty's Government are not prepared to admit their right to declare any such blockade."). *Refer to* § 3.3.3 (State Recognition of Armed Groups as Belligerents).

"privileged" and "unprivileged" belligerents, *i.e.*, distinguishing between persons who are entitled to the privileges of combatant or belligerent status, and those who are not.[39] This distinction has also sometimes been called a distinction between "qualified" and "unqualified" belligerents, *i.e.*, distinguishing between persons who have met the qualifications to receive the privileges of combatant status and those who have not.[40]

4.3.2.3 *"Combatant" Used Without Modification*. "Combatant" and "belligerent," when used without modification (such as "lawful" or "unlawful," or "privileged" or "unprivileged"), have often referred implicitly to lawful or privileged combatants.[41] However, in some cases, "combatant" or "belligerent" has been used to refer to all persons who engage in hostilities, without taking a position as to whether they are entitled to receive the privileges of combatant status.

4.3.2.4 *General Usage of "Combatant" in This Manual*. This manual generally uses "combatant" to refer implicitly to lawful or privileged combatants.

This manual generally uses the term "unprivileged belligerent" (instead of, *e.g.*, "unlawful combatant," "unlawful belligerent," "unprivileged combatant," etc.) to refer to persons who are subject to one or more of the liabilities of combatant status, but are not entitled to receive its distinct privileges.

4.3.3 Types of Lawful Combatants. Three classes of persons qualify as "lawful" or "privileged" combatants:

- members of the armed forces of a State that is a party to a conflict, aside from certain categories of medical and religious personnel;[42]
- under certain conditions, members of militia or volunteer corps that are not part of the armed forces of a State, but belong to a State;[43] and
- inhabitants of an area who participate in a kind of popular uprising to defend against foreign invaders, known as a *levée en masse*.[44]

4.3.4 Types of Unprivileged Belligerents. Unprivileged belligerents may generally be

---

[39] *See, e.g.*, 1958 UK MANUAL ¶96 ("Should *regular* combatants fail to comply with these four conditions, they may in certain cases become unprivileged belligerents. This would mean that they would not be entitled to the status of prisoners of war upon their capture."); Richard R. Baxter, *So-Called 'Unprivileged Belligerency': Spies, Guerillas, and Saboteurs*, 28 BRITISH YEAR BOOK OF INTERNATIONAL LAW 323 (1951); LIEBER CODE art. 49 (describing who is "exposed to the inconveniences as well as entitled to the privileges of a prisoner of war").

[40] *See, e.g.*, JAMES M. SPAIGHT, AIRCRAFT IN WAR 51 (1914) (referring to "that outlaw of war law—the unqualified belligerent"); HAGUE IV REG. arts. 1-3 (describing who meets "[t]he Qualifications of Belligerents").

[41] *See, e.g.*, AP I art. 43(2) (describing "combatants" as those who "have the right to participate directly in hostilities.").

[42] *Refer to* § 4.5 (Armed Forces of a State).

[43] *Refer to* § 4.6 (Other Militia and Volunteer Corps).

[44] *Refer to* § 4.7 (*Levée en Masse*).

classified into two categories that may be distinguished from one another by the presence or absence of State authorization:

- persons who have initially qualified as combatants (*i.e.*, by falling into one of the three categories mentioned above), but who have acted so as to forfeit the privileges of combatant status by engaging in spying or sabotage;[45] and

- persons who never meet the qualifications to be entitled to the privileges of combatant status, but who have, by engaging in hostilities, incurred the corresponding liabilities of combatant status (*i.e.*, forfeited one or more of the protections of civilian status).[46]

These two categories of unprivileged belligerents generally receive the same treatment.[47] However, the distinction that the first category has State authorization, while the second category does not, may be important and create different legal results. For example, the combatant who spies regains the entitlement to the privileges of combatant status upon returning to friendly lines, but the private person who spies cannot regain a status to which the person was never entitled.[48] Similarly, acts of unprivileged belligerency on the high seas may constitute piracy, a crime under international law, although similar acts by persons acting under State authority, even if they were not members of the armed forces, could not constitute piracy.[49]

4.4 Rights, Duties, and Liabilities of Combatants

Combatants have a special legal status, *i.e.,* certain rights, duties, and liabilities. As discussed below, combatants may engage in hostilities and are liable to being made the object of attack by enemy combatants. Combatants must conduct their operations in accordance with the law of war. They have the right to POW status if they fall into the power of the enemy during international armed conflict. Combatants have legal immunity from domestic law for acts done under military authority and in accordance with the law of war.

4.4.1 Combatants – Conduct of Hostilities. In general, combatants may engage in hostilities and may be made the object of attack by enemy combatants.[50] However, combatants placed *hors de combat* must not be made the object of attack.[51]

Combatants must conduct their operations in accordance with the law of war. For example, combatants must take certain measures to distinguish themselves from the civilian population.[52] Combatants also may not kill or wound the enemy by resort to perfidy.[53]

---

[45] *Refer to* § 4.17 (Spies, Saboteurs, and Other Persons Engaging in Similar Acts Behind Enemy Lines).

[46] *Refer to* § 4.18 (Private Persons Who Engage in Hostilities).

[47] *Refer to* § 4.19 (Rights, Duties, and Liabilities of Unprivileged Belligerents).

[48] *Refer to* § 4.17.5 (Spying and Sabotage – Forfeiture of the Privileges of Combatant Status).

[49] *Refer to* § 4.18.5 (Private Persons Who Engage in Hostilities and the Law of War).

[50] *Refer to* § 5.7 (Combatants).

[51] *Refer to* § 5.9 (Persons Placed *Hors de Combat*).

[52] *Refer to* § 5.4.8 (Obligation of Combatants to Distinguish Themselves When Conducting Attacks).

Combatants may make enemy combatants and other military objectives the object of attack, but may not make the civilian population and other protected persons and objects the object of attack.[54] Combatants must exercise due regard to reduce the risk of incidental harm to the civilian population and other persons and objects that may not be made the object of attack.[55] Chapter V addresses in detail the rules that combatants must follow in the conduct of hostilities.

4.4.2 <u>Combatants – POW Status During Detention</u>. Combatants are liable to capture and detention by enemy combatants, but are entitled to POW status when they fall into the power of the enemy during international armed conflict. POWs, like all detained individuals, must be treated humanely.[56] In addition, POWs are afforded a variety of privileges in detention in accordance with the GPW, such as camp canteens, advances of pay, and permission to wear their badges of rank, nationality, or decorations.[57] POWs also have duties in detention, such as identifying themselves to their captors,[58] and they are subject to the laws, regulations, and orders of the Detaining Power.[59] Chapter IX addresses in detail the treatment of POWs and their duties.

In general, POWs shall be released and repatriated without delay after the cessation of active hostilities.[60] However, seriously wounded, injured, or sick POWs should be returned before the end of hostilities.[61] In addition, after the hostilities have ended, certain POWs may be held in connection with criminal proceedings.[62]

In general, combatants retain their right to POW status and treatment, even if they are alleged to have committed crimes before capture.[63] For example, POWs are entitled to a variety of rights in relation to judicial proceedings against them.[64] In addition, POWs serving disciplinary punishment shall continue to receive the benefits of the GPW, except insofar as these benefits are necessarily rendered inapplicable by the mere fact that the POW is confined.[65]

Combatants captured while engaged in spying or sabotage forfeit their entitlement to POW status.[66] In cases of doubt as to whether a detainee is entitled to POW status, that person

---

[53] *Refer to* § 5.22 (Treachery or Perfidy Used to Kill or Wound).

[54] *Refer to* § 5.5 (Discrimination in Conducting Attacks).

[55] *Refer to* § 5.10 (Proportionality in Conducting Attacks).

[56] *Refer to* § 9.5 (Humane Treatment and Basic Protections for POWs).

[57] *Refer to* § 9.17 (Canteens for POWs); § 9.18.3 (Advance of Pay); § 9.22.4 (Rank and Age of POWs).

[58] *Refer to* § 9.8 (Interrogation of POWs).

[59] *Refer to* § 9.26.1 (POWs Subject to the Laws, Regulations, and Orders in Force in the Armed Forces of the Detaining Power).

[60] *Refer to* § 9.37 (Release and Repatriation After Hostilities).

[61] *Refer to* § 9.36.1 (Direct Repatriation of Seriously Wounded, Injured, or Sick POWs).

[62] *Refer to* § 9.37.4.3 (POWs Undergoing Criminal Proceedings for an Indictable Offense).

[63] *Refer to* § 9.26.4 (Retention of Benefits of the GPW Even if Prosecuted for Pre-Capture Acts).

[64] *Refer to* § 9.28 (Judicial Proceedings and Punishment).

[65] *Refer to* § 9.27.6.2 (Retention of the Benefits of the GPW While Undergoing Disciplinary Punishment).

[66] *Refer to* § 4.17.5 (Spying and Sabotage – Forfeiture of the Privileges of Combatant Status).

should be afforded the protections of POW status until their status has been determined by a competent tribunal.[67]

4.4.3 Combatants - Legal Immunity From a Foreign State's Domestic Law. International law affords combatants a special legal immunity from the domestic law of the enemy State for their actions done in accordance with the law of war.[68] This legal immunity is sometimes called the "combatant's privilege" or "combatant immunity." This means that a combatant's "killing, wounding, or other warlike acts are not individual crimes or offenses,"[69] if they are done under military authority and are not prohibited by the law of war.[70] Similarly, a combatant's warlike acts done under military authority and in accordance with the law of war also do not create civil liability.[71]

Combatants lack legal immunity from an enemy State's domestic law for acts that are prohibited by the law of war.[72] Also, combatants lack legal immunity from an enemy State's domestic law while engaging in spying or sabotage.[73] Combatants, however, must receive a fair and regular trial before any punishment.[74]

---

[67] *Refer to* § 4.27.2 (POW Protections for Certain Persons Until Status Has Been Determined).

[68] This legal immunity would also be applicable with respect to neutral States to the extent they sought to exercise jurisdiction over the conduct of belligerents. Traditionally, however, neutral States generally did not assert jurisdiction over conduct committed between belligerents. *Refer to* § 18.21.1 (Jurisdiction Over War Crimes).

[69] LIEBER CODE art. 57. *See also* Johnson v. Eisentrager, 339 U.S. 763, 793 (1950) (Black, J., dissenting) (explaining that "legitimate 'acts of warfare,' however murderous, do not justify criminal conviction" and that "it is no 'crime' to be a soldier."); WINTHROP, MILITARY LAW & PRECEDENTS 778 ("The State is represented in active war by its contending army, and the laws of war justify the killing or disabling of members of the one army by those of the other in battle or hostile operations."); Arce v. State, 202 S.W. 951 (Texas Court of Criminal Appeals 1918) (reversing homicide conviction of Mexican soldiers prosecuted in connection with hostilities between the United States and Mexico). *Consider* AP I art. 43(2) ("combatants ... have the right to participate directly in hostilities.").

[70] *See* United States v. List, *et al.* (The Hostage Case), XI TRIALS OF WAR CRIMINALS BEFORE THE NMT 1236 ("acts done in time of war under the military authority of an enemy cannot involve criminal liability on the part of officers or soldiers if the acts are not prohibited by the conventional or customary rules of war."); Daniel Webster, Department of State, *Letter to John G. Crittenden, Attorney General*, Mar. 15, 1841, *reprinted in* THE DIPLOMATIC AND OFFICIAL PAPERS OF DANIEL WEBSTER, WHILE SECRETARY OF STATE 134-35 (1848) (explaining "[t]hat an individual forming part of a public force, and acting under the authority of his Government, is not to be held answerable, as a private trespasser or malefactor, is a principle of public law sanctioned by the usages of all civilized nations").

[71] *See* Freeland v. Williams, 131 U.S. 405, 416 (1889) ("Ever since the case of Dow v. Johnson, 100 U.S. 158, the doctrine has been settled in the courts that in our late civil war, each party was entitled to the benefit of belligerent rights, as in the case of public war, and that, for an act done in accordance with the usages of civilized warfare, under and by military authority of either party, no civil liability attached to the officers or soldiers who acted under such authority."); Dow v. Johnson, 100 U.S. 158, 165 (1879) ("There would be something singularly absurd in permitting an officer or soldier of an invading army to be tried by his enemy, whose country it had invaded. The same reasons for his exemption from criminal prosecution apply to civil proceedings.").

[72] *See* United States, *et al.* v. Göring, *et al.*, *Judgment*, I TRIAL OF THE MAJOR WAR CRIMINALS BEFORE THE IMT 223 ("He who violates the laws of war cannot obtain immunity while acting in pursuance of the authority of the state if the state in authorizing action moves outside its competence under international law.").

[73] *Refer to* § 4.17.3 (Spying and Sabotage – Forfeiture of the Privileges of Combatant Status).

[74] *Refer to* § 9.28.4 (Rights of Defense and Trial Procedure).

4.4.3.1 *Combatants - Legal Immunity and POW Status*. The "combatant's privilege" from liability under domestic law has been associated with POW status.[75] In that vein, U.S. courts have inferred from provisions of the GPW the combatant's privilege against being prosecuted by capturing States.[76] However, the legal immunity that combatants may be afforded is not the same as POW status. For example, a combatant's conduct may be protected by legal immunities even when that person is not in the power of the enemy and thus is not a POW. As another example of how POW status and legal immunity may differ, the GPW generally affords the same treatment to all classes of POWs identified in Article 4. However, not all the categories of POWs identified in Article 4 of the GPW, such as persons authorized to accompany the armed forces, receive the general license to commit belligerent acts that is afforded members of the armed forces.[77]

4.4.3.2 *Combatants – Legal Immunity and Sovereignty*. In addition to being associated with humanitarian principles governing the treatment of POWs, the combatant's privilege has also been viewed as an application of the immunity that international law affords States from each other's jurisdiction.[78] In this view, "the act of the soldier who conforms to the law of war and does not engage in private acts of warfare is an act of state depriving the enemy

---

[75] *See, e.g.*, Memorandum submitted in United States v. Shakur, 690 F. Supp. 1291 (S.D.N.Y. 1988), III CUMULATIVE DIGEST OF UNITED STATES PRACTICE IN INTERNATIONAL LAW 1981-88 3436, 3451 ("It is well-accepted that individuals who enjoy the status of prisoner of war are generally immune from prosecution for legitimate acts of war in international armed conflicts."); ALLAN ROSAS, THE LEGAL STATUS OF PRISONERS OF WAR: A STUDY IN INTERNATIONAL HUMANITARIAN LAW APPLICABLE IN ARMED CONFLICTS 305 (1976) ("there has traditionally been a close relationship between the concept of prisoners of war and that of lawful combatants."); LIEBER CODE art. 56 ("A prisoner of war is subject to no punishment for being a public enemy, nor is any revenge wreaked upon him by the intentional infliction of any suffering, or disgrace, by cruel imprisonment, want of food, by mutilation, death, or any other barbarity.").

[76] *See* United States v. Lindh, 212 F. Supp. 2d 541, 553 (E.D. Va. 2002) (memorandum opinion) (interpreting articles 87 and 99 of GPW to "make clear that a belligerent in a war cannot prosecute the soldiers of its foes for the soldiers' lawful acts of war"); United States v. Khadr, 717 F.Supp.2d. 1215, 1222 footnote 7 (USCMCR 2007) (same); United States v. Pineda, 2006 U.S. Dist. LEXIS 17509, 6-8 (D.D.C. Mar. 23, 2006) (D.D.C. 2006) (same). *See also* United States v. Noriega, 746 F. Supp. 1506, 1529 (S.D. Fla. 1990) ("As is evident from its text and construed as a whole, the essential purpose of the Geneva Convention Relative to the Treatment of Prisoners of War is to protect prisoners of war from prosecution for conduct which is customary in armed conflict.").

[77] ALLAN ROSAS, THE LEGAL STATUS OF PRISONERS OF WAR: A STUDY IN INTERNATIONAL HUMANITARIAN LAW APPLICABLE IN ARMED CONFLICTS 305 (1976) ("The relationship between the concepts of lawful combatants and prisoners of war has been said to arise from the fact that lawful combatants are always entitled to prisoner-of-war status, while the reverse is not necessarily true, as there are categories of persons entitled to the status of prisoners of war who as civilians enjoy no general license to commit belligerent acts.").

[78] *Cf.* United States v. Thierichens, 243 F. 419, 420 (E.D. Pa. 1917) ("The well-settled rule that, under the comity existing between nations, the public armed ship of a friendly nation, acting under the immediate and direct command of the sovereign power, is not to be interfered with by the courts of a foreign state, is based upon the principle that, if the courts did attempt to assume jurisdiction over such vessel, it would require the sovereign of the nation to which the vessel belongs to be impleaded in the court from which the process issued, and, by common consent of nations, such situations could not arise without interference with the power and dignity of the foreign sovereign. Therefore the courts will not assume jurisdiction over such vessel or its officers, while acting as such, but leave controversies arising out of the acts of the vessel, and its officers, while acting in their official character, for settlement through diplomatic channels.").

state of jurisdiction."[79] This view of the combatant's privilege requires that combatants act under the commission of a belligerent State.[80] This view also reflects the principle that only States may authorize the resort to force.[81]

4.4.4 Nationality and Combatant Status.

4.4.4.1 *Nationals of Neutral States in Enemy Forces*. Members of enemy armed forces may include nationals of neutral or non-belligerent States. For example, the U.S. armed forces include many foreign nationals, and the United States could be engaged in hostilities when those foreign nationals' home States are not. Nationals of a neutral or non-belligerent State who are members of the armed forces of a belligerent State should be treated like other members of that State's armed forces.[82] For example, such nationals are entitled to POW status if they fall into the power of the enemy during international armed conflict.[83]

4.4.4.2 *Nationals of a State Who Join Enemy Forces*. The special privileges that international law affords combatants generally do not apply between a national and his or her State of nationality.[84] For example, provisions of the GPW assume that POWs are not nationals of the Detaining Power.[85] Thus, international law does not prevent a State from punishing its

---

[79] Richard Baxter, *The Municipal and International Law Basis of Jurisdiction over War Crimes*, 28 BRITISH YEAR BOOK OF INTERNATIONAL LAW 382, 385 (1951). *See also* Hans Kelsen, *Collective and Individual Responsibility in International Law with Particular Regard to the Punishment of War Criminals*, 31 CALIFORNIA LAW REVIEW 530, 549 (1943) ("That a State violates international law if it punishes as a criminal, according to its national law, a member of the armed forces of the enemy for an act of legitimate warfare, can be explained only by the fact that the State by so doing makes an individual responsible for an act of another State. According to international law, the act in question must be imputed to the enemy State and not to the individual who in the service of his State has performed the act. It cannot be considered as a crime of the individual because it must not be considered as his act at all."); LIEBER CODE art. 41 ("All municipal law of the ground on which the armies stand, or of the countries to which they belong, is silent and of no effect between armies in the field.").

[80] *See* Wharton, *Com. Am. Law*, § 221, VII MOORE'S DIGEST 175 ("It is necessary in order to place the members of an army under the protection of the law of nations, that it should be commissioned by a state. … Hence, all civilized nations have agreed in the position that war to be a defence to an indictment for homicide or other wrong, must be conducted by a belligerent state, and that it can not avail voluntary combatants not acting under the commission of a belligerent.").

[81] *Refer to* § 1.11.1.1 (Competent Authority (Right Authority) to Wage War for a Public Purpose).

[82] *Refer to* § 15.6.2.1 (No More Severe Treatment Than Nationals of an Opposing Belligerent State).

[83] LEVIE, POWS 74-75 ("Normally, the nationality of the individual falling within one of the categories enumerated in Article 4 is that of the belligerent Power for which he is fighting. However, he may have the nationality of a neutral, or of an ally of the belligerent in whose armed forces he is serving at the time that he falls into the power of the enemy--or even of the adverse Party, or one of its allies. Does this affect his entitlement to prisoner-of-war status? Apparently there is no dispute with respect to the entitlement to prisoner-of-war status of an individual who is a national of a neutral State or of a State which is an ally of the belligerent in whose armed forces he is serving.").

[84] *Compare* § 10.3.3.1 (A State's Own Nationals).

[85] *See, e.g.*, GPW art. 87 ("When fixing the penalty, the courts or authorities of the Detaining Power shall take into consideration, to the widest extent possible, the fact that the accused, not being a national of the Detaining Power, is not bound to it by any duty of allegiance, and that he is in its power as the result of circumstances independent of his own will."). *Refer to* § 9.26.6 (Prohibited Penalties); § 9.28.6 (Death Sentences).

nationals whom it may capture among the ranks of enemy forces.[86] This rule is significant in non-international armed conflicts in which a State is fighting a rebel group composed of its own citizens.[87]

Although, as a matter of international law, nationals may not assert the privileges of combatant status against their own State, they may be subject to the liabilities of combatant status in relation to their own State under that State's domestic law. For example, under U.S. law, U.S. nationals who join enemy forces have been subject to the liabilities of combatant status, such as potentially being made the object of attack or detained.[88]

4.4.4.3 Nationals of Allied or Co-Belligerent States. Nationals of an allied or co-belligerent State who are serving with enemy forces are in a position that is similar to the position of nationals of a State who are serving with enemy forces. If the nationals of an allied or co-belligerent State who are serving with enemy forces are captured by a State, they may be transferred to their State of nationality (*i.e.*, the co-belligerent or allied State), which is not required to afford them POW status.[89] However, U.S. practice as the Detaining Power in this situation has been to afford POW treatment to such individuals if they claim such protection.[90]

---

[86] *See* Public Prosecutor v. Oie Hee Koi and Associated Appeals (UK Privy Council, Dec. 4 1967), LEVIE, DOCUMENTS ON POWS 737, 741 (quoting LAUTERPACHT, II OPPENHEIM'S INTERNATIONAL LAW) ("'The privileges of members of armed forces cannot be claimed by members of the armed forces of a belligerent who go over to the forces of the enemy and are afterwards captured by the former. They may be, and always are, treated as criminals. The same applies to traitorous subjects of a belligerent who, without having been members of his armed forces, fight in the armed forces of the enemy. Even if they appear under the protection of a flag of truce, deserters and traitors may be seized and punished.' This edition was published in 1951 after Aug. 12, 1949, the date of the Geneva Conventions, and in their lordships' opinion correctly states the relevant law.").

[87] *Refer to* § 17.12 (Use of Captured or Surrendered Enemy Personnel in NIAC).

[88] *See, e.g.*, Hamdi v. Rumsfeld 542 U.S. 507, 519 (2004) (plurality) ("There is no bar to this Nation's holding one of its own citizens as an enemy combatant."); Ex parte Quirin, 317 U.S. 1, 37 (1942) ("Citizenship in the United States of an enemy belligerent does not relieve him from the consequences of a belligerency which is unlawful because in violation of the law of war."); In re Territo, 156 F. 2d 142, 145 (9th Cir. 1946) (rejecting the argument of petitioner, an Italian army draftee, that he could not be subject to the liabilities of combatant status and detained because he was a U.S. citizen).

[89] *For example*, DEPARTMENT OF THE ARMY PAMPHLET 20-213, *History of Prisoner Of War Utilization By The United States Army, 1776-1945*, 198 (Jun. 24, 1955) ("During the [Second World] war many soldiers of a state of origin other than Germany were found in German uniform among German prisoners of war. Therefore when Allied forces captured these prisoners they segregated them by nationalities. The individual PW was then interrogated by representatives of his country's government in exile. If acceptable to that government and if he was willing, the PW was sent to Great Britain for service in an army unit of his national government. If the PW was rejected, he was treated in all respects as a German prisoner of war.").

[90] *For example, Announcement Concerning Soviet Allegations on Allied Prisoners of War*, May 3, 1945, 12 DEPARTMENT OF STATE BULLETIN 864 (May 6, 1945) ("In as much as the American Government has always insisted that all wearers of the American uniform, whether American citizens or not, are, as American soldiers, entitled to full protection of the [1929] Geneva convention and has so informed the enemy, these German prisoners of war of apparent Soviet nationality claiming such protection are being held as German prisoners of war in order to protect American soldiers in enemy hands.").

4.5 Armed Forces of a State

Members of the armed forces of a State, including members of all groups that are part of the armed forces of a State, but excluding certain medical and religious personnel,[91] receive combatant status (*i.e.*, its rights, duties, and liabilities) by virtue of that membership.[92] This section addresses various classes of persons within the armed forces of a State.

4.5.1 Components of Armed Forces. The armed forces of a State may include a variety of components, such as militia or volunteer corps that form part of those armed forces.[93]

The U.S. armed forces include members of the active duty military, the reserve forces, and the National Guard. U.S. armed forces also include the Coast Guard, which normally operates under the Department of Homeland Security.[94]

The U.S. armed forces may also include the Commissioned Corps of the U.S. Public Health Service, which normally operates under the Department of Health and Human Services.[95] Similarly, members of the Commissioned Corps of the National Oceanic and Atmospheric Administration, which normally operates under the Department of Commerce, may also become part of the U.S. armed forces.[96] Members of these and other organizations assigned to, and serving with, the U.S. armed forces may be subject to the Uniform Code of Military Justice.[97]

---

[91] *Refer to* § 4.9 (Military Medical and Religious Personnel).

[92] *See* GPW art. 4A(1) (defining "prisoners of war, in the sense of the present Convention," to include "(1) [m]embers of the armed forces of a Party to the conflict" who have fallen into the power of the enemy); HAGUE IV REG. art. 1 ("The laws, rights, and duties of war apply … to armies"); LIEBER CODE art. 57 ("So soon as a man is armed by a sovereign government and takes the soldier's oath of fidelity, he is a belligerent;"). *Cf.* sources cited in footnote 150 in § 4.6.1.3 (Application of GPW 4A(2) Conditions to the Armed Forces of a State).

[93] *See* GPW art. 4A(1) (defining "prisoners of war, in the sense of the present Convention," to include "members of militias or volunteer corps forming part of such armed forces" who have fallen into the power of the enemy); HAGUE IV REG. art. 1 ("In countries where militia or volunteer corps constitute the army, or form part of it, they are included under the denomination 'army.'").

[94] *See* 10 U.S.C. § 101(a)(4) (explaining that, for the purposes of U.S. domestic law, "the term 'armed forces' means the Army, Navy, Air Force, Marine Corps, and Coast Guard."); 14 U.S.C. § 1 ("The Coast Guard as established January 28, 1915, shall be a military service and a branch of the armed forces of the United States at all times. The Coast Guard shall be a service in the Department of Homeland Security, except when operating as a service in the Navy.").

[95] 42 U.S.C. § 217 ("In time of war, or of emergency involving the national defense proclaimed by the President, he may by Executive order declare the commissioned corps of the [Public Health] Service to be a military service.").

[96] 33 U.S.C. § 3061 ("The President may, whenever in the judgment of the President a sufficient national emergency exists, transfer to the service and jurisdiction of a military department such vessels, equipment, stations, and officers of the Administration as the President considers to be in the best interest of the country. … An officer of the Administration transferred under this section, shall, while under the jurisdiction of a military department, have proper military status and shall be subject to the laws, regulations, and orders for the government of the Army, Navy, or Air Force, as the case may be, insofar as the same may be applicable to persons whose retention permanently in the military service of the United States is not contemplated by law.").

[97] 10 U.S.C. § 802(a)(8) ("Members of the National Oceanic and Atmospheric Administration, Public Health Service, and other organizations, when assigned to and serving with the armed forces," are subject to the Uniform Code of Military Justice).

The U.S. armed forces may also include the volunteer auxiliary of the Air Force when the services of the Civil Air Patrol are used in certain missions.[98]

4.5.1.1 *Reserve Armed Forces*. Although domestic law sometimes differentiates between the reserve and active components of the armed forces for the purpose of entitlement to benefits and other matters, international law treats members of the reserve forces that are part of the armed forces of a State the same as other members of the armed forces.

In the United States, reserve armed forces include the reserve components of the Army, Navy, Air Force, Marine Corps, and Coast Guard, as well as the Army National Guard of the United States and the Air National Guard of the United States.[99]

4.5.2 Classes of Persons Within the Armed Forces.

4.5.2.1 *Special Operations Forces*. Special operations forces may be described as military forces specially organized, trained, and equipped to achieve military, political, economic, and psychological objectives by unconventional military means in hostile, denied, or politically sensitive areas.[100] As members of the armed forces, special operations forces have the same rights, duties, and liabilities as other members of the armed forces.[101]

Nonetheless, in the past, some States have illegitimately questioned whether special operations forces are entitled to the privileges of combatant status. For example, during World War II, Hitler directed that German forces summarily execute captured Allied special operations forces.[102] Post-World War II war crimes tribunals found that this order was not a legitimate reprisal, violated the prohibition against executions without a fair trial, and improperly denied POW status to soldiers wearing a uniform behind enemy lines.[103]

---

[98] *See* 10 U.S.C. § 9442(b)(1) ("The Secretary of the Air Force may use the services of the Civil Air Patrol to fulfill the noncombat programs and missions of the Department of the Air Force.").

[99] 10 U.S.C. § 10101 ("The reserve components of the armed forces are: (1) The Army National Guard of the United States. (2) The Army Reserve. (3) The Navy Reserve. (4) The Marine Corps Reserve. (5) The Air National Guard of the United States. (6) The Air Force Reserve. (7) The Coast Guard Reserve.").

[100] JOINT PUBLICATION 3-05, *Special Operations*, ix (Jul. 16, 2014) ("Special operations require unique modes of employment, tactics, techniques, procedures, and equipment. They are often conducted in hostile, denied, or politically and/or diplomatically sensitive environments, and are characterized by one or more of the following: time-sensitivity, clandestine or covert nature, low visibility, work with or through indigenous forces, greater requirements for regional orientation and cultural expertise, and a higher degree of risk. Special operations provide joint force commanders (JFCs) and chiefs of mission with discrete, precise, and scalable options that can be synchronized with activities of other interagency partners to achieve United States Government (USG) objectives.").

[101] *Refer to* § 4.4 (Rights, Duties, and Liabilities of Combatants).

[102] Adolf Hitler, Commando Order, *reprinted in* Trial of Generaloberst Nickolaus von Falkenhorst, XI U.N. LAW REPORTS 18, 20-21 (British Military Court, Brunswick, Jul. 29-Aug. 2, 1946); also *reprinted in* United States v. von Leeb, *et al.* (The High Command Case), XI TRIALS OF WAR CRIMINALS BEFORE THE NMT 525-27; also *reprinted in* The Dostler Case, Trial of General Anton Dostler, I U.N. LAW REPORTS 22, 33-34 (U.S. Military Commission, Rome, Oct. 8-12, 1945).

[103] *See* Trial of Generaloberst Nickolaus von Falkenhorst, XI U.N. LAW REPORTS 18, 28 (British Military Court, Brunswick, Jul. 29-Aug. 2, 1946) (reporter noting that Hitler's commando order was clearly illegal because it provided "that there should be no military courts, for even a war traitor is entitled to a trial," and because the

Special operations forces personnel, like other members of the armed forces, remain entitled to the privileges of combatant status, unless they temporarily forfeit such privileges by engaging in spying or sabotage.[104] In some cases, military personnel who do not wear the standard uniform of their armed forces may nonetheless remain entitled to the privileges of combatant status because the wearing of such uniforms does not constitute the element of "acting clandestinely or under false pretenses."[105] For example, special operations forces have sometimes dressed like friendly forces.[106] Special operations forces personnel remain entitled to the privileges of combatant status even when operating detached from the main body of forces behind enemy lines.[107]

4.5.2.2 Members Trained as Medical Personnel, but Not Attached to the Medical Service. Members of the armed forces might have medical training but not be designated as military medical personnel. For example, before joining the armed forces, a person might have been trained as a nurse or physician, and after joining the armed forces might not be designated as part of the medical corps.

Because such personnel have not been designated as military medical personnel, they are are combatants, like other members of the armed forces.[108] However, if they fall into the power of the enemy during international armed conflict, such personnel may be required to tend to fellow POWs, in light of their previous training. In particular, POWs who, though not attached to the medical service of their armed forces, are physicians, surgeons, dentists, nurses, or medical orderlies may be required by the Detaining Power to exercise their medical functions in the interests of POWs dependent on the same Power.[109] In that case, they shall continue to be POWs, but shall receive the same treatment as corresponding medical personnel retained by the

---

"commando order was to apply to troops engaged on commando operations whether in uniform or not"); The Dostler Case, Trial of General Anton Dostler, I U.N. LAW REPORTS 22, 27-33 (U.S. Military Commission, Rome, Oct. 8-12, 1945) (conviction of a German General for the murder of 15 U.S. Army personnel and rejection of his defense that the commando order was a valid and applicable superior order); Trial of Karl Adam Golkel and Thirteen Others, V U.N. LAW REPORTS 45-53 (British Military Court, Wuppertal, Germany, May 15-21, 1946) (trial of German soldiers for killing eight members of the British Special Air Service); United States v. von Leeb, *et al.* (The High Command Case), XI TRIALS OF WAR CRIMINALS BEFORE THE NMT 527 ("This order was criminal on its face. It simply directed the slaughter of these 'sabotage' troops.").

[104] *Refer to* § 4.17 (Spies, Saboteurs, and Other Persons Engaging in Similar Acts Behind Enemy Lines).

[105] *Refer to* § 4.17.2.1 (Acting Clandestinely or Under False Pretenses).

[106] *Refer to* § 5.25.2.1 (Mimicking Other Friendly Forces).

[107] *See* Trial of Generaloberst Nickolaus von Falkenhorst, XI U.N. LAW REPORTS 18, 28 (British Military Court, Brunswick, Jul. 29-Aug. 2, 1946) (reporter noting that "[i]t is not possible to say that troops who engage in acts of sabotage behind the enemy lines are bandits, as Hitler declared them. They carry out a legitimate act of war, provided the objective relates directly to the war effort and provided they carry it out in uniform."); LIEBER CODE art. 81 ("Partisans are soldiers armed and wearing the uniform of their army, but belonging to a corps which acts detached from the main body for the purpose of making inroads into the territory occupied by the enemy. If captured, they are entitled to all the privileges of the prisoner of war.").

[108] *Refer to* § 4.9.2.2 (Designated by Their Armed Forces).

[109] GPW art. 32 ("Prisoners of war who, though not attached to the medical service of their armed forces, are physicians, surgeons, dentists, nurses or medical orderlies, may be required by the Detaining Power to exercise their medical functions in the interests of prisoners of war dependent on the same Power.").

Detaining Power.[110] They shall be exempted from any other work under Article 49 of the GPW.[111]

4.5.2.3 *Members Who Are Ministers of Religion Without Having Officiated as Chaplains to Their Own Forces*. Members of the armed forces might be ministers of religion, but might not be designated as military religious personnel.[112] Because such personnel have not been designated as military religious personnel, they are combatants, like other members of the armed forces.[113] However, if they fall into the power of the enemy during international armed conflict, such personnel may minister to fellow POWs. In particular, POWs who are ministers of religion, without having officiated as chaplains to their own forces, shall be at liberty, whatever their denomination, to minister freely to the members of their community.[114] For this purpose, they shall receive the same treatment as chaplains retained by the Detaining Power.[115] They shall not be obliged to do any other work.[116]

4.5.2.4 *Draftees*. Some States require military service for categories of their nationals. The United States employs all-volunteer armed forces, although it has drafted its nationals into military service in prior conflicts.

Under international law, a draftee, *i.e.*, a person who has been compelled to join a State's armed forces, is to be treated the same as other members of the armed forces.[117]

4.5.2.5 *Deserters*. A deserter from the armed forces of a belligerent who falls into the power of the enemy in international armed conflict is a POW.[118] Similarly, a deserter who is interned by a neutral State would also be treated as a POW.[119] The deserter's relationship with his or her armed forces is a question of that State's domestic law and not international law. States generally forbid members of their armed forces from desertion and generally regard members of the armed forces who desert as continuing to be members of their armed forces.

---

[110] GPW art. 32 ("In that case they shall continue to be prisoners of war, but shall receive the same treatment as corresponding medical personnel retained by the Detaining Power.").

[111] GPW art. 32 ("They shall be exempted from any other work under Article 49.").

[112] *Refer to* § 4.9.2 (Requirements for Military Medical and Religious Status).

[113] *Refer to* § 4.9.2.2 (Designated by Their Armed Forces).

[114] GPW art. 36 ("Prisoners of war who are ministers of religion, without having officiated as chaplains to their own forces, shall be at liberty, whatever their denomination, to minister freely to the members of their community.").

[115] GPW art. 36 ("For this purpose, they shall receive the same treatment as the chaplains retained by the Detaining Power.").

[116] GPW art. 36 ("They shall not be obliged to do any other work.").

[117] *See* 1958 UK MANUAL ¶ 89(i) (noting that "[t]he members, male and female, of the land, sea and air forces are entitled to recognition as belligerent forces whether they have joined voluntarily or have been compelled to do so by their own law").

[118] *See* GREENSPAN, MODERN LAW OF LAND WARFARE 99 ("Deserters from the enemy do not thereby lose their right to be treated as prisoners of war if they fall into the hands of the opposing side.").

[119] *Refer to* § 15.16 (Belligerent Forces Taking Refuge in Neutral Territory).

Deserters who are subsequently captured by their own armed forces are not POWs because they are not in the power of the enemy and because the privileges of combatant status are generally understood not to apply, as a matter of international law, between nationals and their State of nationality.[120]

4.5.2.6 *Defectors*. Defectors are persons from one side's armed forces who voluntarily join the armed forces of the opposing side. They are generally not regarded as POWs while serving in their new armed force.[121]

Defectors serving in the forces of the enemy who are captured by the State to which they originally owed an allegiance generally would not be entitled to POW status because the privileges of combatant status are generally understood not to apply, as a matter of international law, between nationals and their State of nationality.[122]

States may not compel POWs, retained personnel, or protected persons in their power to defect and serve in their armed forces.[123]

4.5.3 Regular Armed Forces Who Profess Allegiance to a Government or an Authority Not Recognized by the Detaining Power. During international armed conflict, members of regular armed forces who profess allegiance to a Government or an authority not recognized by the Detaining Power are treated as members of the armed forces of a State.[124] Under Article 4A(3) of the GPW, they receive POW status, and they should also receive the rights, duties, and liabilities of combatants.[125]

Article 4A(3) of the GPW was developed to address situations like those that had occurred during World War II, when members of a military force continued fighting after their State had been occupied.[126] For example, military forces might continue to fight for a

---

[120] *Refer to* § 4.4.4 (Nationality and Combatant Status).

[121] *Refer to* § 9.3.4.1 (Having Fallen).

[122] *Refer to* § 4.4.4.2 (Nationals of a State Who Join Enemy Forces).

[123] *Refer to* § 9.19.2.3 (Labor Assignments That May Be Compelled); § 10.7.3 (Compulsory Work for Protected Persons in a Belligerent's Home Territory); § 11.20.1.1 (Prohibition on Compulsory Service in an Occupying Power's Armed Forces).

[124] GPW art. 4A(3) (defining "prisoners of war, in the sense of the present Convention," to include "[m]embers of regular armed forces who profess allegiance to a government or an authority not recognized by the Detaining Power" who have fallen into the power of the enemy).

[125] *Refer to* § 4.4 (Rights, Duties, and Liabilities of Combatants).

[126] *See* INTERNATIONAL COMMITTEE OF THE RED CROSS, *Report on the Work of the Conference of Government Exports for the Study of the Convention for the Protection of War Victims*, 106 (Geneva, Apr. 14-26, 1947) ("In its report, the ICRC stressed that certain States [during World War II] had denied the status of belligerents to combatant units subject to a Government or authority which these States did not recognise; this despite the fact that these units (e.g. the French forces constituted under General de Gaulle) fulfilled all the conditions required for the granting of PW status. The Commission approved the ICRC's proposal that these armed forces should enjoy PW status, irrespective of the Government or authority under whose orders they might claim to be.").

government-in-exile or for a government that had ceased to exist.[127] Such a government would provide the *right authority* for its regular armed forces to participate in the ongoing war and to receive POW status upon capture by the enemy.[128] Members of those forces were sometimes denied POW status by an enemy State, even though other States recognized the group to which they belonged as a co-belligerent force.[129]

4.5.4 Persons Belonging, or Having Belonged, to the Armed Forces of an Occupied State. Under Article 4B(1) of the GPW, persons belonging, or having belonged, to the armed forces of an occupied State should be treated as POWs if, while hostilities are continuing outside occupied territory, the Occupying Power considers it necessary, by reason of their allegiance to the armed forces, to intern them.[130]

Article 4B(1) of the GPW seeks to address the proper status of an army demobilized by the Occupying Power while a portion of those same armed forces continue the struggle. When the forces are demobilized, they are treated as civilians, but when recalled for internment based on their prior service, they are treated as POWs.[131] In particular, States developed this provision to address Germany's practice during World War II of arresting demobilized military personnel from occupied States.[132] These personnel were often interned and sought to escape to join the ongoing fighting. This provision was promulgated to ensure that individuals in similar circumstances would receive POW treatment if they were interned. For example, the rules for the parole of POWs would apply to them.[133] Similarly, the rules relating to POW escape would

---

[127] II-A FINAL RECORD OF THE DIPLOMATIC CONFERENCE OF GENEVA OF 1949 415 ("Mr. Lamarle (France) realized that cases might arise where combatants claiming allegiance to an authority which was not recognized by the Detaining Power might be deprived of the benefit of the Convention; but he thought the word 'authority' afforded sufficient safeguards to such combatants. After an exchange of views on the subject, the Committee agreed that the word 'authority' afforded sufficient safeguards to combatants claiming allegiance to Governments which had ceased to exist.").

[128] *Refer to* § 1.11.1.1 (Competent Authority (Right Authority) to Wage War for a Public Purpose).

[129] *Refer to* § 3.3.3.3 (Recognition of Friendly Armed Groups as Lawful Belligerents).

[130] GPW art. 4B(1) ("(1) Persons belonging, or having belonged, to the armed forces of the occupied country, if the occupying Power considers it necessary by reason of such allegiance to intern them, even though it has originally liberated them while hostilities were going on outside the territory it occupies, in particular where such persons have made an unsuccessful attempt to rejoin the armed forces to which they belong and which are engaged in combat, or where they fail to comply with a summons made to them with a view to internment.").

[131] GPW COMMENTARY 69 ("In fact, as one delegate to the Conference pointed out, the question relates to the proper status of an army demobilized by the Occupying Power, while a portion of those same armed forces continue the struggle. It is logical to treat its members as civilians until such time as they are recalled in order to be interned; but from that moment, it is equally logical to treat them as prisoners of war.").

[132] *See* GPW COMMENTARY 68 ("During the Second World War, the Occupying Power, for security reasons, frequently arrested demobilized military personnel in occupied territory, especially officers. These men were granted prisoner-of-war status but usually only after repeated representations by the International Committee of the Red Cross and the Governments concerned. In the report which the International Committee prepared for the Government Experts, it therefore proposed that the entitlement of such persons to prisoner-of-war status should be explicitly mentioned and the Conference supported this suggestion."). For further historical background *see* LEVIE, POWS 66-67, II-A FINAL RECORD OF THE DIPLOMATIC CONFERENCE OF GENEVA OF 1949 431-32, and the note appended to In re Siebers, Special Court of Cassation, Feb. 20, 1950, The Hague, in 1950 INTERNATIONAL LAW REPORTS, 399-400.

[133] *Refer to* § 9.11.2 (Parole of POWs).

also apply to them.[134] So, a demobilized person who disobeyed an internment order and attempted to escape to rejoin his or her armed force would, like a POW, be subject, at most, to disciplinary punishment in respect of the act of escape.[135]

Persons belonging, or having belonged, to the armed forces of an occupied State would only be entitled to receive POW treatment while an international armed conflict continues.[136] For example, this provision would not apply to a situation like the occupation of Japan after World War II because all hostilities had ended.[137]

4.6 Other Militia and Volunteer Corps

Under certain conditions, members of militia and volunteer corps that are not part of the armed forces of a State qualify as combatants and receive the rights, duties, and liabilities of combatant status.[138] More specifically, Article 4(A)(2) of the GPW defines prisoners of war to include:

> Members of other militias and members of other volunteer corps, including those of organized resistance movements, belonging to a Party to the conflict and operating in or outside their own territory, even if this territory is occupied, provided that such militias or volunteer corps, including such organized resistance movements, fulfil the following conditions:
>
> (a) that of being commanded by a person responsible for his subordinates;
>
> (b) that of having a fixed distinctive sign recognizable at a distance;
>
> (c) that of carrying arms openly;
>
> (d) that of conducting their operations in accordance with the laws and customs of war.[139]

---

[134] *Refer to* § 9.25 (POW Escapes).

[135] *Refer to* § 9.25.2.2 (Only Disciplinary Punishments in Respect of an Act of Escape).

[136] *See* LEVIE, POWS 67-68 ("It is important to bear in mind that the foregoing provisions explicitly contemplate that the government of the unoccupied part of the territory of the State the members of whose armed forces are in question, or that State's allies if it has been completely occupied, are continuing the hostilities. The mere existence of a government-in-exile after the complete cessation of hostilities would not suffice to make the provision applicable. In other words, this provision was not intended to apply to the situation which arises when the capitulation of a State is followed by the complete termination of armed hostilities.").

[137] *See* LEVIE, POWS 68 and footnote 261 ("[T]his provision was not intended to apply to the situation which arises when the capitulation of a State is followed by the complete termination of armed hostilities" and "would, therefore, not apply in a situation such as that which existed upon the capitulation of Japan in 1945.").

[138] *Refer to* § 4.4 (Rights, Duties, and Liabilities of Combatants).

[139] GPW art. 4(A)(2). *See also* HAGUE IV REG. art. 1 ("The laws, rights, and duties of war apply not only to armies, but also to militia and volunteer corps fulfilling the following conditions: -- 1. To be commanded by a person responsible for his subordinates; 2. To have a fixed distinctive emblem recognizable at a distance; 3. To carry arms openly; and 4. To conduct their operations in accordance with the laws and customs of war."); 1899 HAGUE II REG.

Under these conditions, which are discussed below, members of these armed groups may operate as combatants in or outside their own territory, even if this territory is occupied. By contrast, a *levée en masse* may only be formed on the approach of the enemy to non-occupied territory.[140]

4.6.1 GPW 4A(2) Conditions in General. The conditions set forth in Article 4A(2) of the GPW were derived from conditions found in the Regulations annexed to the 1899 Hague II and the 1907 Hague IV.[141] These conditions reflect the attributes common to regular armed forces of a State.[142] By seeking to ensure that participants in hostilities are sufficiently disciplined, law-abiding, and distinguishable from the civilian population, these conditions help protect the civilian population from the hardships of war. In addition, these conditions contribute to the military effectiveness of the force that satisfies the conditions.[143]

These conditions may be understood to reflect a burdens-benefits principle, *i.e.*, the receipt of certain benefits in the law of war (*e.g.*, privileges of combatant status) requires the assumption of certain obligations.[144]

4.6.1.1 *GPW 4A(2) Conditions Required on a Group Basis*. The armed group, as a whole, must fulfill these conditions for its members to be entitled to the privileges of combatant status. For example, if a member of an armed group met these requirements, but the armed group did not, that member would not be entitled to the privileges of combatant status because the armed group failed to satisfy the conditions.[145] Similarly, isolated departures from a

---

art. 1 ("The laws, rights, and duties of war apply not only to armies, but also to militia and volunteer corps, fulfilling the following conditions: 1. To be commanded by a person responsible for his subordinates; 2. To have a fixed distinctive emblem recognizable at a distance; 3. To carry arms openly; and 4. To conduct their operations in accordance with the laws and customs of war.").

[140] *Refer to* § 4.7.1.3 (Approach of the Enemy to Non-Occupied Territory).

[141] *See* GPW COMMENTARY 49 ("[T]here was unanimous agreement [at the 1949 Diplomatic Conference] that the categories of persons to whom the Convention is applicable must be defined, in harmony with the Hague Regulations.").

[142] *See* GPW COMMENTARY 58 (explaining that an organization satisfying the conditions of GPW art. 4A(2) "must have the principal characteristics generally found in armed forces throughout the world, particularly in regard to discipline, hierarchy, responsibility and honour.").

[143] JAMES BROWN SCOTT, THE PROCEEDINGS OF THE HAGUE PEACE CONFERENCES: THE CONFERENCE OF 1899 549 ("General **den Beer Poortugael**, while fully endorsing the considerations set forth by the PRESIDENT and his Excellency Mr. BEERNAERT, wishes to add a few words. ... But from a military standpoint also it must be recognized that it is to the benefit of the populations to impose on them the conditions contained in Articles 9 and 10 [predecessors to GPW art. 4A(2) and 4A(6) and], which they must satisfy if they wish to take up arms. For it is an undeniable fact that to lead undisciplined and unorganized troops into the fire is to lead them to butchery.").

[144] *Refer to* § 3.6.3.2 (Benefits-Burdens Principle in Law of War Rules).

[145] *See* G.I.A.D. Draper, *The Status of Combatants and the Question of Guerrilla Warfare*, 45 BRITISH YEAR BOOK OF INTERNATIONAL LAW 173, 197 (1971) ("the fate of the individual irregular is essentially linked with that of the group in which he operates. If the group's members, as a majority, always meet the legal conditions, the individual will answer only for his own misdoings, and then as a prisoner of war who had the right to participate in the combat. If, however, the individual were punctilious in a group in which the majority did not observe the conditions on any one occasion, he would not acquire combatant status or prisoner-of-war status upon capture, and will answer in law as an individual who participated in combat with no legal right to do so, i.e. answerable in municipal law or occupation law, or the law of war.").

condition by a member of the armed group (*e.g.*, a failure to comply with the conditions by a member of the armed group that was not directed by the armed group's leader) would not prevent the armed group from satisfying these conditions.

4.6.1.2 *AP I and the GPW 4A(2) Conditions*. AP I changed, for its Parties, the conditions under which armed groups that are not part of a State's armed forces may qualify for combatant status.[146] The United States has objected to the way these changes relaxed the requirements for obtaining the privileges of combatant status, and did not ratify AP I, in large part, because of them.[147] A chief concern has been the extent to which these changes would undermine the protection of the civilian population.[148] The United States has expressed the view that it would not be appropriate to treat this provision of AP I as customary international law.[149]

4.6.1.3 *Application of GPW 4A(2) Conditions to the Armed Forces of a State*. The text of the GPW does not expressly apply the conditions in Article 4A(2) of the GPW to the armed forces of a State.[150] Thus, under the GPW, members of the armed forces of a State

[146] *See* AP I, arts. 1(4), 43, 44.

[147] *See* Ronald Reagan, *Letter of Transmittal*, Jan. 29, 1987, MESSAGE FROM THE PRESIDENT TRANSMITTING AP II IV ("Another provision [of AP I] would grant combatant status to irregular forces even if they do not satisfy the traditional requirements to distinguish themselves from the civilian population and otherwise comply with the laws of war. This would endanger civilians among whom terrorists and other irregulars attempt to conceal themselves.").

[148] *See, e.g.*, John B. Bellinger, III, *Lawyers and Wars: A Symposium in Honor of Edward R. Cummings*, Sept. 30, 2005, 2005 DIGEST OF UNITED STATES PRACTICE IN INTERNATIONAL LAW 953, 955 ("More problematic from the lawyer's perspective—or at least this lawyer's perspective—is how law deals with the kind of situation where a would-be terrorist seeks to cloak his actions in the garb of legitimate combatant. This second factor working against civilian protection is fueled in part by Article 44 of Additional Protocol I, which suggests that combatants do not need to distinguish themselves from the civilian population except prior to and during an attack. To be fair, there is no doubt that a terrorist would not meet the combatancy definition of any instrument of international humanitarian law. But the very fact that Additional Protocol I allows greater flexibility in distinction undermines this fundamental protection. The principle of distinction, among the foundational principles of humanitarian law, exists for the purposes of civilian protection, to ensure that fighters can identify the combatant from the bystander. Article 44, pressed so strongly for largely political reasons in the 1970s, undermines it. And as a result, one has to lament that the process of negotiating international humanitarian law instruments has not always inured to the civilian population's benefit.").

[149] Memorandum submitted in United States v. Shakur, 690 F. Supp. 1291 (S.D.N.Y. 1988), III CUMULATIVE DIGEST OF UNITED STATES PRACTICE IN INTERNATIONAL LAW 1981-88 3436, 3441 ("Article 44 grants combatant status to irregular forces in certain circumstances even if they do not satisfy the traditional requirements to distinguish themselves from the civilian population and otherwise comply with the existing laws of war. This was not acceptable as a new norm of international law. It clearly does not reflect customary law. ... While the U.S. is of the view that certain provisions in Protocol I reflect customary international law (see, *e.g.*, Treaty Doc. 100-2, *supra*, at X), the provisions on wars of national liberation and combatant and prisoner-of-war status are definitely not in this category. ... Accordingly, it is the view of the United States that it would be inappropriate to treat these provisions as part of customary international law under any circumstances.").

[150] II-A FINAL RECORD OF THE DIPLOMATIC CONFERENCE OF GENEVA OF 1949 465-66 ("General SLAVIN (Union of Soviet Socialist Republics) said that according to the first paragraph, sub-paragraph I, of the working text it would appear that members of the Armed forces would have to fulfil the four traditional requirements mentioned in *(a)*, *(b)*, *(c)* and *(d)* in order to obtain prisoner of war status, which was contrary to the Hague Regulations (Article I of the Regulations concerning the Laws and Customs of War, 18 October 1907). General DEVIJVER (Belgium) pointed out that the above reproduced working text had been drafted with due regard to the Hague Regulations, and the first paragraph, sub-paragraph (I), of the working text carefully specified that only members of militia or volunteer corps should fulfil all four conditions."). *Cf.* In re Lewinski (called von Manstein) Case, *reprinted in* ANNUAL DIGEST

receive combatant status (including its privileges and liabilities) by virtue of their membership in the armed forces of a State.[151] Nonetheless, the GPW 4A(2) conditions were intended to reflect attributes of States' armed forces.[152] If an armed force of a State systematically failed to distinguish itself from the civilian population and to conduct its operations in accordance with the law of war, its members should not expect to receive the privileges afforded lawful combatants.[153] Similarly, members of the armed forces engaged in spying or sabotage forfeit their entitlement to the privileges of combatant status if captured while engaged in those activities.[154]

4.6.2 Belonging to a Party to the Conflict. The armed group must belong to a party to the conflict.[155] The requirement of "belonging" to a party establishes that the armed group fulfills a *jus ad bellum* requirement of *right authority, i.e.*, it is acting on the authority of a State.[156] This requirement recognizes that members of a non-State armed group are not entitled to the privileges of combatant status even if that armed group satisfies the other conditions.[157]

The State's authority may be granted by its representatives orally; it need not be granted in writing, such as through a commission or warrant. In all cases, however, opposing parties to

---

AND REPORTS OF PUBLIC INTERNATIONAL LAW CASES 509, 515-16 (H. Lauterpacht, ed., 1949) ("Regular soldiers are so entitled without any of the four requirements set out in Article 1 [of the Hague IV Reg.]: they are requisite in order to give the Militia and Volunteer Corps the same privileges as the Army.").

[151] *Refer to* § 4.5 (Armed Forces of a State).

[152] *Refer to* footnote 142 in § 4.6.1 (GPW 4A(2) Conditions in General).

[153] *See* Jay S. Bybee, Assistant Attorney General, *Status of Taliban Forces Under Article 4 of the Third Geneva Convention of 1949*, Feb. 7, 2002, 26 OPINIONS OF THE OFFICE OF LEGAL COUNSEL 1, 4 ("We conclude, however, that the four basic conditions that apply to militias must also apply, at a minimum, to members of armed forces who would be legally entitled to POW status. In other words, an individual cannot be a POW, even if a member of an armed force, unless forces also are: (a) 'commanded by a person responsible for his subordinates'; (b) 'hav[e] a fixed distinctive sign recognizable at a distance'; (c) 'carry[] arms openly'; and (d) 'conduct[] their operations in accordance with the laws and customs of war.' Thus, if the President has the factual basis to determine that Taliban prisoners are not entitled to POW status under Article 4(A)(2) as members of a militia, he therefore has the grounds to also find that they are not entitled to POW status as members of an armed force under either Article 4(A)(1) or Article 4(A)(3).") (brackets in original); BOTHE, PARTSCH, & SOLF, NEW RULES 234-35 (AP I art. 43, ¶2.1.2) ("It is generally assumed that these conditions were deemed, by the 1874 Brussels Conference and the 1899 and 1907 Hague Peace Conferences, to be inherent in the regular armed forces of States. Accordingly, it was considered to be unnecessary and redundant to spell them out in the Conventions.").

[154] *Refer to* § 4.17.5 (Spying and Sabotage – Forfeiture of the Privileges of Combatant Status).

[155] GPW art. 4A(2). *Cf.* LIEBER CODE art. 81 ("Partisans are soldiers armed and wearing the uniform of their army, but belonging to a corps which acts detached from the main body for the purpose of making inroads into the territory occupied by the enemy. If captured, they are entitled to all the privileges of the prisoner of war.").

[156] *Refer to* § 1.11.1.1 (Competent Authority (Right Authority) to Wage War for a Public Purpose).

[157] *See* The Military Prosecutor v. Omar Mahmud Kassem and Others (Israeli Military Court, Ramallah, Apr. 13, 1969), LEVIE, DOCUMENTS ON POWS 776 (explaining that "the most basic condition of the right of combatants to be considered upon capture as prisoners of war" is belonging to a belligerent State and that if persons "do not belong to the Government or State for which they fight, ... they do not possess the right to enjoy the status of prisoners of war upon capture."). *Cf.* BOTHE, PARTSCH, & SOLF, NEW RULES 237 (AP I art. 43, ¶2.3.1) ("gangs of terrorists acting on their own behalf and not linked to an entity subject to international law are excluded" from the definition of "armed forces of a Party to the Conflict" in AP I similar to how they would be excluded under Article 4A(2) of the GPW).

the conflict must be able to discern that the armed group enjoys such authority. A State's formal acknowledgement that an armed group "belongs" to it is sufficient. On the other hand, the bare claim by the armed group that it acts on behalf of a State would be insufficient. In some cases, State support and direction to the armed group may establish that it belongs to the State.[158]

4.6.3 Being Commanded by a Person Responsible for His or Her Subordinates. The armed group must be commanded by a person responsible for his or her subordinates; the armed group must have a commander with effective authority over the armed group.[159] This requirement helps ensure that the armed group has sufficient discipline and organization to conduct its operations in accordance with the law of war.[160]

The commander may derive his or her authority over the armed group by a regular or temporary commission from a State. However, a commander may derive his or her command from another position or authority. For example, the armed group may be formed informally and may have elected the commander as its leader. In practice, a State may provide members of the armed group with certificates or distinctive badges to show that they are officers, or military personnel responsible to higher authority, and not private persons acting on individual initiative.[161]

The authority of the commander over his or her subordinates gives rise to a corresponding duty to ensure that the armed group's members conduct their operations in accordance with the law of war.[162]

4.6.4 Having a Fixed Distinctive Sign Recognizable at a Distance. Members of the

---

[158] *See* The Military Prosecutor v. Omar Mahmud Kassem and Others (Israeli Military Court, Ramallah, Apr. 13, 1969), LEVIE, DOCUMENTS ON POWS 776-77 ("It is natural that, in international armed conflicts, the Government which previously possessed an occupied area should encourage and take under its wing the irregular forces which continue fighting within the borders of the country, give them protection and material assistance, and that therefore a 'command relationship' should exist between such Government and the fighting forces, with the result that a continuing responsibility exists of the Government and the commanders of its army for those who fight in its name and on its behalf.").

[159] *See* GREENSPAN, MODERN LAW OF LAND WARFARE 59 ("The commander must be a person responsible for his subordinates, that is, his authority over those in his command must be effective.").

[160] *See* G.I.A.D. Draper, *The Status of Combatants and the Question of Guerrilla Warfare*, 45 BRITISH YEAR BOOK OF INTERNATIONAL LAW 173, 201 (1971) (explaining that this condition "does probably mean that the commander must have sufficient authority to ensure that the conditions applicable to the members of the group, necessary for lawful combatancy, are observed."); 1958 UK MANUAL ¶91 note 1 (explaining that "Field Marshall Rundstedt, C.-in-C. of the German armed forces in the West, disclaimed all responsibilities for the atrocities by Waffen S.S. units on the ground that neither their commanders nor members were subject to military law" and that "he could take no disciplinary action against them," and thus German "Waffen S.S." paramilitary units used during World War II failed to meet this condition and were not lawful combatants).

[161] 1958 UK MANUAL ¶91 ("The first condition, 'to be commanded by a person responsible for his subordinates,' is fulfilled if the commander of the corps is regularly or temporarily commissioned as an officer or is a person of position and authority, or if the members are provided with certificates or badges granted by the government of the State to show that they are officers, or soldiers, so that there may be no doubt that they are not partisans acting on their own responsibility. State recognition, however, is not essential, and an organisation may be formed spontaneously and elect its own officers.").

[162] *Refer to* § 18.23.3 (Command Responsibility).

armed group should display a fixed distinctive sign or other device recognizable at a distance. The essence of this requirement is that members of the armed group are distinguishable from the civilian population.[163] By helping to ensure that members of the armed group can be visually distinguished from civilians, this requirement helps protect the civilian population from being erroneously made the object of attack.[164]

4.6.4.1 Distinctive Sign. The requirement does not specify a particular sign or emblem that persons must wear.[165] Wearing a military uniform satisfies this condition. However, a full uniform is not required.[166] The sign suffices if it enables the person to be distinguished from the civilian population. For example, a helmet or headdress that makes the silhouette of the individual readily distinguishable from that of a civilian can meet this requirement. Similarly, a partial uniform (such as a uniform jacket or trousers), load bearing vest, armband, or other device could suffice, so long as it served to distinguish the members from the civilian population. Formally notifying enemy forces of the distinctive sign is not required, and the proposal to add such a requirement was not accepted by States.[167] Such notification, however, may avoid misunderstanding and facilitate claims of POW status for captured members of the armed group.

---

[163] *See* GREENSPAN, MODERN LAW OF LAND WARFARE 59 ("Soldiers must be dressed in such a fashion that they are clearly distinguishable from the general population as members of the armed forces.").

[164] *See* Abraham Sofaer, Legal Adviser, Department of State, *The Rationale for the United States Decision*, 82 AJIL 784, 786 (1988) ("Inevitably, regular forces would treat civilians more harshly and with less restraint if they believed that their opponents were free to pose as civilians while retaining their right to act as combatants and their POW status if captured."). *For example*, LEVIE, POWS 50 footnote 187 ("In Vietnam individuals who were apparently civilian noncombatants (women, children, working farmers, etc.) would approach American servicemen in seeming innocence and then suddenly toss a hand grenade at them. After a very few such incidents the soldiers understandably came to distrust all civilians while they were in the field and frequently took definitive action upon suspicion and without waiting to ascertain the facts. Thus, the original illegal actions taken by the guerrillas subsequently endangered the members of the civilian population who, as noncombatants, were entitled to be protected in their status.") (internal citations omitted).

[165] *See* GPW COMMENTARY 52 ("The drafters of the 1949 Convention, like those of the Hague Conventions, considered it unnecessary to specify the sign which members of the armed forces should have for the purposes of recognition. It is the duty of each State to take steps so that members of its armed forces can be immediately recognized as such and to see to it that they are easily distinguishable from … civilians.").

[166] *See, e.g.*, 1958 UK MANUAL ¶92 ("The second condition, relating to a fixed distinctive sign recognisable at a distance, would be satisfied by the wearing of a military uniform, but something less than a complete uniform will suffice."); 1914 RULES OF LAND WARFARE ¶33 ("*The distinctive sign.* – This requirement will be satisfied by the wearing of a uniform or even less than a complete uniform."); SPAIGHT, WAR RIGHTS ON LAND 57 ("The 'distinctive emblem' does not mean a uniform."). *Cf.* ICRC AP COMMENTARY 468 (¶1577) ("What constitutes a uniform, and how can emblems or nationality be distinguished from each other? The Conference in no way intended to define what constitutes a uniform … . '[A]ny customary uniform which clearly distinguished the member wearing it from a non-member should suffice.' Thus a cap or an armlet, etc. worn in a standard way is actually equivalent to a uniform.").

[167] *See* JAMES BROWN SCOTT, THE PROCEEDINGS OF THE HAGUE PEACE CONFERENCES: III THE CONFERENCE OF 1907 6 (1921) ("The PRESIDENT first takes up the German amendment relating to Article 1, tending to require *previous notice* to the hostile party of *fixed distinctive emblems recognizable at a distance*. He recalls that this amendment was rejected by 23 votes to 11, and asks whether it is again advanced by the German delegation. On the negative answer of Major General VON GUNDELL, he considers it useless to put the question to discussion and passes to Article 2.").

4.6.4.2 *Fixed*. The text of the GPW indicates that the sign should be "fixed." This requirement has been interpreted to mean that the sign must be such that it cannot be easily removed and disposed of at the first sign of danger.[168] In practice, however, it would be important to assess whether members of the armed group are functionally distinguishable from the civilian population, even if the distinctive sign that they wear is not permanent and could be removed.[169]

4.6.4.3 *Visible at a Distance*. "Distance" has not been defined, but may be interpreted as requiring that the sign be easily distinguishable by the naked eye of ordinary people at a distance at which the form of the individual can be determined.[170]

4.6.5 Carrying Arms Openly. Members of the armed group must carry their arms openly.[171] This requirement is not satisfied if the armed group makes a practice of carrying only concealed weapons or of hiding weapons on the approach of enemy forces to avoid identification

---

[168] *See* LEVIE, POWS 48 (a resistance fighter "must wear some item which will identify him as a combatant, thereby distinguishing him from the general population, and that item must be such that he cannot remove and dispose of it at the first sign of danger. A handkerchief, or rag, or armband slipped onto or loosely pinned to the sleeve does not meet this definition. An armband sewed to the sleeve, a logotype of sufficient size displayed on the clothing, a unique type of jacket-these will constitute a fixed and distinctive identifying insignia, effectively separating the combatant of the moment from the rest of the population."); GREENSPAN, MODERN LAW OF LAND WARFARE 59 ("Where a complete uniform is not worn, and this is sometimes not possible because of the poverty of the country, sudden emergency or other reasons, the fixed distinctive sign should be something which cannot be instantly taken off or assumed at will, thus enabling a combatant to appear a peaceful citizen one moment and a soldier the next. The sign should be part of the clothing or sewn to it."); 1958 UK MANUAL ¶92 ("Something in the nature of a badge sewn on the clothing should therefore be worn in addition [to a distinctive helmet]" in order to meet the condition that the sign must be fixed.).

[169] *See* FRANCIS LIEBER, GUERRILLA PARTIES CONSIDERED WITH REFERENCE TO THE LAWS AND USAGES OF WAR 16-17 (1862) ("The Southern prisoners made at Fort Donelson, whom I have seen at the West, had no uniform. They were indeed dressed very much alike, but it was the uniform dress of the countryman in that region. Yet they were treated by us as prisoner of war, and well treated too. Nor would it be difficult to adopt something of a badge, easily put on and off, and to call it a uniform. It makes a great difference, however, whether the absence of the uniform is used for the purpose of concealment or disguise, in order to get by stealth within the lines of the invader, for destruction or life or property, or for pillage, and whether the parties have no organization at all, and are so small that they cannot act otherwise than by stealth.").

[170] *See* 1958 UK MANUAL ¶92 ("The distance at which the sign should be visible is necessarily vague, but it is reasonable to expect that the silhouette of an irregular combatant in the position of standing against the skyline should at once be distinguishable from the outline of a peaceful inhabitant, and this by the naked eye of an ordinary individual at a distance at which the form of the individual can be determined."); 1914 RULES OF LAND WARFARE ¶33 ("The distance that the sign must be visible is left vague and undetermined and the practice is not uniform. This requirement will be satisfied certainly if the sign is 'easily distinguishable by the naked eye of ordinary people' at a distance at which the form of the individual can be determined."); CHARLES HENRY HYDE, II INTERNATIONAL LAW: CHIEFLY AS INTERPRETED AND APPLIED BY THE UNITED STATES 291 footnote 3 (1922) (quoting the same provision in the 1917 U.S. Rules of Land Warfare); SPAIGHT, WAR RIGHTS ON LAND 57 (explaining that "[i]f the sign is recognizable at a distance at which the naked eye can distinguish the form and color of a person's dress, all reasonable requirements appear to be met" and noting the Japanese view during the Russo-Japanese War that a Russian free corps that "would wear no uniform but only a distinctive sign on the cap and sleeve" would only be considered belligerents "'if they can be *distinguishable by the naked eye from the ordinary people* or fulfill the conditions for militias or volunteers by the Hague *Réglement*'.").

[171] *See* GPW art. 4A(2)(c); HAGUE IV REG. art. 1(3).

as fighters.[172]

4.6.6 Conducting Their Operations in Accordance With the Laws and Customs of War. The armed group, as a whole, must conduct its operations in accordance with the law of war. Evidence that an armed group enforced the law of war (such as by promulgating instructions regarding law of war requirements and punishing violations by its members) would help establish that an armed group meets this condition.

4.7 *Levée en Masse*

A *levée en masse* is a spontaneous uprising of the inhabitants of non-occupied territory who, on the approach of the enemy in an international armed conflict, take up arms to resist the invading forces, without having time to form themselves into regular armed units.[173] Participants in a *levée en masse* are entitled to the privileges of combatant status, provided that they carry their arms openly and respect the laws and customs of war.[174]

4.7.1 Conditions for a *Levée en Masse*. The following discussion elaborates upon some of the conditions for a *levée en masse*.

4.7.1.1 *Spontaneous*. A *levée en masse* is a spontaneous uprising in which members have not had time to form into regular armed units.[175] Thus, unlike other categories of lawful combatants, persons who join a *levée en masse* need not wear a distinctive sign nor be organized under a responsible command. The spontaneity of their response generally precludes their being able to take such measures.

4.7.1.2 *Inhabitants*. A *levée en masse* is understood to reflect the right of inhabitants to resist approaching enemy forces. Non-inhabitants who travel to a territory to resist invading forces would not be entitled to participate in a *levée en masse*.[176]

---

[172] 1958 UK MANUAL ¶94 ("The third condition is that irregular combatants shall carry arms openly. They may therefore be refused the rights of the armed forces if it is found that their sole arm is a pistol, hand-grenade, or dagger concealed about the person, or a sword-stick or similar weapon, or if it is found that they have hidden their arms on the approach of the enemy.").

[173] GPW art. 4A(6) (defining "prisoners of war, in the sense of the present Convention," to include "[i]nhabitants of a non-occupied territory, who on the approach of the enemy spontaneously take up arms to resist the invading forces, without having had time to form themselves into regular armed units, provided they carry arms openly and respect the laws and customs of war" who have fallen into the power of the enemy); HAGUE IV REG. art. 2 ("The inhabitants of a territory which has not been occupied, who, on the approach of the enemy, spontaneously take up arms to resist the invading troops without having had time to organize themselves in accordance with Article 1, shall be regarded as belligerents if they carry arms openly and if they respect the laws and customs of war."); LIEBER CODE art. 51 ("If the people of that portion of an invaded country which is not yet occupied by the enemy, or of the whole country, at the approach of a hostile army, rise, under a duly authorized levy, *en masse* to resist the invader, they are now treated as public enemies, and, if captured, are prisoners of war.").

[174] For more background, *see* LEVIE, POWS 64-66.

[175] *See* GREENSPAN, MODERN LAW OF LAND WARFARE 63 ("the essence of a *levée en masse* is that it is unorganized.").

[176] *Compare* § 10.3.2.1 ("Find Themselves").

4.7.1.3 Approach of the Enemy to Non-Occupied Territory. A *levée en masse* may only be formed on the approach of the enemy to non-occupied territory. Once the belligerent has established an occupation, the local population should comply with the orders of the occupation force, and a *levée en masse* may not be formed.[177] Similarly, even before the establishment of an occupation, inhabitants of areas that have already been invaded may not form a *levée en masse.*[178]

By contrast, members of an organized resistance movement under Article 4A(2) of the GPW may operate as combatants in or outside their own territory, even if this territory is occupied.[179]

4.7.2 *Levée en Masse* – Discerning Participants. Should some inhabitants form a *levée en masse* to defend an area, it may be justifiable for the invading force to detain all persons of military age in that area and treat them as POWs.[180] Even if an inhabitant who joined or participated in the *levée en masse* lays down arms, if he or she is later captured, he or she may be detained as a POW.[181] If a person joins a *levée en masse*, he or she may be held as a POW even if he or she actually took no part in fighting.[182]

If detained, a person believed to have participated in a *levée en masse* should be treated as a POW until a determination is otherwise made by a competent tribunal.[183] If a competent tribunal determines that a person did not join the *levée en masse* but instead committed private acts of hostility against enemy military forces,[184] the person may be treated as an unprivileged belligerent.[185]

---

[177] *Refer to* § 11.7.1 (Inhabitants' Obedience to the Occupying Power).

[178] *See* LAUTERPACHT, II OPPENHEIM'S INTERNATIONAL LAW 258 (§81) ("Article 2 [of the HAGUE IV REG.] distinctly speaks of the *approach* of the enemy, and thereby sanctions only such a levy *en masse* as takes place in territory not yet *invaded* by the enemy. Once the territory is invaded, although the invasion has not yet ripened into occupation, a levy *en masse* is no longer legitimate. But, of course, the term *territory*, as used by Article 2, is not intended to mean the whole extent of the State of a belligerent, but only such parts of it as are not yet invaded. For this reason, if a town is already invaded, but not a neighbouring town, the inhabitants of the latter may, on the approach of the enemy, legitimately rise *en masse*.").

[179] *Refer to* § 4.6 (Other Militia and Volunteer Corps).

[180] 1956 FM 27-10 (Change No. 1 1976) ¶65 ("Should some inhabitants of a locality thus take part in its defense, it might be justifiable to treat all the males of military age as prisoners of war."); 1958 UK MANUAL ¶100 ("Where the majority of inhabitants of a locality have taken part in its defence in circumstances amounting to a *levée en masse*, it is justifiable and probably advisable to treat all the male inhabitants of military age as prisoners of war, leaving it to the individual concerned to claim that they took no part in the *levée en masse* or defence of the locality.").

[181] 1956 FM 27-10 (Change No. 1 1976) ¶65 ("Even if inhabitants who formed the *levee en masse* lay down their arms and return to their normal activities, they may be made prisoners of war.").

[182] 1958 UK MANUAL ¶100 ("If it is shown that they joined the *levée en masse*, but took no part in the defence, they may be held as prisoners of war.").

[183] *Refer to* § 4.27.3 (Competent Tribunal to Assess Entitlement to POW Status or Treatment).

[184] *Refer to* § 4.18 (Private Persons Who Engage in Hostilities).

[185] *Refer to* § 4.19 (Rights, Duties, and Liabilities of Unprivileged Belligerents).

4.8 RIGHTS, DUTIES, AND LIABILITIES OF CIVILIANS

Like combatants, members of the civilian population also have certain rights, duties, and liabilities under the law of war. Civilians may not be made the object of attack. If detained, civilians are entitled to humane treatment and a variety of additional protections. Civilians lack the combatant's privilege, and may be punished, after a fair trial, by an enemy State for engaging in hostilities against it.

4.8.1 Civilians – Notes on Terminology. Like other terms, "civilian" is used in a variety of different ways in the law of war.[186]

4.8.1.1 *"Civilian" Versus "Military"*. Sometimes, "civilian" is used to describe persons who are not military personnel. For example, persons authorized to accompany the armed forces are often called "civilians" in this sense, even though they are POWs if they fall into the power of the enemy during international armed conflict.[187]

4.8.1.2 *"Civilian" Versus "Combatant"*. "Civilian" is also often used to refer to persons who are not "combatants." Since "combatant" is often used in different ways, "civilian," correspondingly, is also used in different ways. For example, sometimes "civilians" is used to refer to persons who lack the right to participate in hostilities. Other times "civilian" is used to refer to persons who neither have the right to participate in hostilities nor have in fact participated in hostilities.[188] For example, "civilian" casualty reports generally exclude insurgents or terrorists, even though some might call such persons "civilians" because they are not entitled to participate in hostilities.

4.8.1.3 *"Civilian" in the GC*. The GC does not define "civilian," although it uses the word.[189] The GC uses the term "protected person" to refer to persons protected by the Convention.[190] The GC excludes from the definition of "protected person" those persons who are protected under the other 1949 Geneva Conventions, *e.g.*, POWs and retained personnel.[191] In some cases, "protected persons" can include a person "detained as a spy or saboteur, or as a person under definite suspicion of activity hostile to the security of the Occupying Power," although such persons are not entitled to all the protections applicable to protected persons.[192]

---

186 *Refer to* § 4.3.2 (Combatant – Notes on Terminology).

187 *Refer to* § 4.15.3 (Persons Authorized to Accompany the Armed Forces – Detention).

188 *See, e.g.*, GC COMMENTARY 134 ("These rules [for the protection of the wounded and sick] are even more essential when the wounded or sick person is a civilian, i.e. a person who, by definition, takes no part in the hostilities.").

189 *See, e.g.*, GC art. 10 ("The provisions of the present Convention constitute no obstacle to the humanitarian activities which the International Committee of the Red Cross or any other impartial humanitarian organization may, subject to the consent of the Parties to the conflict concerned, undertake for the protection of civilian persons and for their relief.").

190 *Refer to* § 10.3 (Protected Person Status).

191 *Refer to* § 10.3.2.3 (Not Protected by the GWS, GWS-Sea, or the GPW).

192 GC art. 5. *Refer to* § 10.3.2.4 (Unprivileged Belligerents Not Per Se Excluded From Protected Person Status).

4.8.1.4 *"Civilian" in AP I and AP II*. AP I defines "civilian" in opposition to "combatant"; under AP I, anyone who is not a "combatant" is, by definition, a "civilian."[193] The United States has objected to AP I's definition of combatant.[194] AP II uses the term "civilian" without providing a definition.[195]

4.8.1.5 *General Usage of "Civilian" in This Manual*. This manual generally uses "civilian" to mean a member of the civilian population, *i.e.*, a person who is neither part of nor associated with an armed force or group, nor otherwise engaging in hostilities.

4.8.2 Civilians – Conduct of Hostilities. Civilians may not be made the object of attack, unless they take direct part in hostilities.[196] The wounded and sick, as well as the infirm, and expectant mothers, shall be the object of particular protection and respect.[197] Civilians may be killed incidentally in military operations; however, the expected incidental harm to civilians may not be excessive in relation to the anticipated military advantage from an attack,[198] and feasible precautions must be taken to reduce the risk of harm to civilians during military operations.[199]

Civilians who engage in hostilities thereby forfeit the corresponding protections of civilian status and may be liable to treatment in one or more respects as unprivileged belligerents.[200]

4.8.3 Civilians – Detention. In general, civilians may be subject to non-violent measures that are justified by military necessity, such as searches, or temporary detention.[201] Belligerents or Occupying Powers may take necessary security measures in relation to civilians, including internment or assigned residence for imperative reasons of security.[202]

Enemy civilians who are interned during international armed conflict or occupation generally are classified as "protected persons" under the GC and receive a variety of protections.[203] Chapter X addresses in detail the required treatment of enemy civilian internees

---

193 *See* AP I art. 50(1) ("A civilian is any person who does not belong to one of the categories of persons referred to in Article 4 A (1), (2), (3) and (6) of the Third Convention and in Article 43 of this Protocol. In case of doubt whether a person is a civilian, that person shall be considered to be a civilian.").

194 *Refer to* § 4.6.1.2 (AP I and the GPW 4A(2) Conditions).

195 *See, e.g.*, AP II art. 13 ("1. The civilian population and individual civilians shall enjoy general protection against the dangers arising from military operations.").

196 *Refer to* § 5.8 (Civilians Taking a Direct Part in Hostilities).

197 GC art. 16 ("The wounded and sick, as well as the infirm, and expectant mothers, shall be the object of particular protection and respect.").

198 *Refer to* § 5.12 (Proportionality – Prohibition on Attacks Expected to Cause Excessive Incidental Harm).

199 *Refer to* § 5.11 (Proportionality – Feasible Precautions in Planning and Conducting Attacks to Reduce the Risk of Harm to Protected Persons and Objects); § 5.14 (Feasible Precautions to Reduce the Risk of Harm to Protected Persons and Objects by the Party Subject to Attack).

200 *Refer to* § 4.18 (Private Persons Who Engage in Hostilities).

201 *Refer to* § 5.2.2.1 (Non-Violent Measures That Are Militarily Necessary).

202 *Refer to* § 10.6 (Measures of Control and Security).

203 *Refer to* § 10.3 (Protected Person Status).

during international armed conflict and occupation. In all circumstances, detained civilians must be treated humanely.[204] Special categories of civilians, such as children, may require additional consideration during detention.[205]

4.8.4 Civilians – Legal Liability Under an Enemy State's Domestic Law. Unlike combatants, civilians lack the combatant's privilege excepting them from the domestic law of the enemy State. Civilians who engage in hostilities may, after a fair trial, be punished by an opposing State.[206]

A State that is an Occupying Power has additional authorities over enemy civilians that extend beyond the ability to punish their unauthorized participation in hostilities.[207]

Note, however, the special cases of persons authorized to accompany the armed forces,[208] members of the merchant marine and civil aircraft,[209] and participants in a *levée en masse*.[210]

4.9 Military Medical and Religious Personnel

"Medical personnel exclusively engaged in the search for, or the collection, transport or treatment of the wounded or sick, or in the prevention of disease, staff exclusively engaged in the administration of medical units and establishments, as well as chaplains attached to the armed forces" are treated as a special category under the law of war.[211] This manual generally refers to them as military medical and religious personnel.

Under certain circumstances, (1) the authorized staff of voluntary aid societies and (2) the staff of a recognized aid society of a neutral country are treated like military medical and religious personnel.[212]

4.9.1 Types of Military Medical and Religious Personnel. Military medical and religious personnel include: (1) medical personnel exclusively engaged in the search for, or the collection, transport, or treatment of the wounded or sick, or in the prevention of disease; (2) staff exclusively engaged in the administration of medical units and establishments; and (3) chaplains

---

[204] *Refer to* § 10.5 (Humane Treatment and Other Basic Protections for Protected Persons).

[205] *Refer to* § 4.20 (Children).

[206] *Refer to* § 4.18.3 (Private Persons Who Engage in Hostilities – Lack of the Privileges of Combatant Status).

[207] *Refer to* § 11.7 (Authority of the Occupying Power Over Inhabitants).

[208] *Refer to* § 4.15.4 (Persons Authorized to Accompany the Armed Forces – Liability Under Domestic Law for Participation in Hostilities).

[209] *Refer to* § 4.16 (Crews of Merchant Marine Vessels or Civil Aircraft).

[210] *Refer to* § 4.7 (*Levée en Masse*).

[211] GWS art. 24.

[212] *Refer to* § 4.11 (Authorized Staff of Voluntary Aid Societies); § 4.12 (Staff of a Recognized Aid Society of a Neutral Country).

attached to the armed forces.[213]

4.9.1.1 *Medical Personnel Exclusively Engaged in Medical Duties*. Medical personnel exclusively engaged in the search for, or the collection, transport, or treatment of the wounded or sick, or in the prevention of disease include military physicians, dentists, nurses, orderlies, stretcher-bearers, and other persons belonging to the armed forces who give direct care to the wounded and sick.[214]

Persons who are exclusively engaged in the prevention of disease also qualify as military medical personnel. For example, veterinary personnel qualify for military medical status, if they are exclusively engaged in providing health services for military personnel (*e.g.*, performing food safety inspections and ensuring that animal illnesses do not spread to humans). However, as a general matter, veterinary personnel would not qualify for military medical status based on being part of the veterinary service.[215]

4.9.1.2 *Staff Exclusively Engaged in Support to Medical Units and Establishments*. In addition to persons directly engaged in medical duties, medical personnel also include staff exclusively engaged in the administration of medical units and establishments. These persons also receive status as medical personnel provided that they are exclusively assigned to the Medical Service.[216] For example, Medical Service Corps personnel, and individuals with a non-medical Military Occupation Specialty permanently assigned to a medical unit or facility (such as its cooks, clerks and supply personnel, or crews operating permanent medical aircraft), would qualify for military medical status.

4.9.1.3 *Chaplains Attached to the Armed Forces*. Chaplains attached to the armed forces include any cleric, regardless of faith, who is attached to the armed forces of a belligerent and assigned duties exclusively of a religious or spiritual nature.[217]

---

[213] GWS art. 24 ("Medical personnel exclusively engaged in the search for, or the collection, transport or treatment of the wounded or sick, or in the prevention of disease, staff exclusively engaged in the administration of medical units and establishments, as well as chaplains attached to the armed forces, shall be respected and protected at all times.").

[214] GWS COMMENTARY 218 ("Medical personnel proper. – These are the doctors, surgeons, dentists, chemists, orderlies, nurses, stretcher-bearers, etc., who give direct care to the wounded and sick.").

[215] *See* GWS COMMENTARY 205 ("[GWS Article 22(4) of the GWS], which dates from 1929, was introduced at the suggestion of the United States Delegation, which pointed out that veterinary personnel were attached to medical units in the American Army. A proposal, made by another delegation in 1929, to place the Veterinary Service on the same footing as the Medical Service was, on the other hand, rejected.").

[216] GWS COMMENTARY 219 ("These are persons who look after the administration of medical units and establishments, without being directly concerned in the treatment of the wounded and sick. They include office staff, ambulance drivers, cooks (male or female), cleaners, etc. Like the previous category, they form part of the Medical Service of the armed forces, and accordingly had to be accorded the same immunity as medical personnel proper. They form an integral part of medical units and establishments, which could not function properly without their help. They too must be exclusively assigned to the Medical Service.").

[217] GWS art. 24. *Cf.* BOTHE, PARTSCH, & SOLF, NEW RULES 99 (AP I art. 8, ¶2.6) ("In the new definition [of 'religious personnel' in AP I], the Christian notion of "chaplain" is only used by way of an example. Religious personnel are ministers of any religion. What is a 'minister' will not always be easy to determine, because that concept varies from religion to religion. Again the word 'exclusively' adds some precision. A lay preacher, being,

4.9.2 Requirements for Military Medical and Religious Status. To acquire and retain military medical and religious status, members of the armed forces must (1) belong to a force whose members qualify for POW status; (2) be designated as exclusive medical or religious personnel by their armed forces; and (3) serve exclusively in a medical or religious capacity.

Underlying military medical and religious status is the principle that the armed forces have committed to use these personnel exclusively in a humanitarian role; thus, these personnel have a "supra-national" and "quasi-neutral character" because their humanitarian duties place them "above the conflict."[218]

4.9.2.1 *Belong to a Force Whose Members Qualify for POW Status*. To acquire military medical and religious status, a person must belong to an armed force whose members qualify for POW status, *i.e.*, the armed forces of a State, regular armed forces who profess allegiance to a government or an authority not recognized by the Detaining Power, or other militia and volunteer corps meeting the conditions in the GPW.[219] For example, medical personnel belonging to non-State armed groups would not be entitled to retained personnel status under the GWS, GWS-Sea, and GPW because their members do not qualify for POW status.

4.9.2.2 *Designated by Their Armed Forces*. To acquire military medical and religious status, members of the armed forces must be designated as such by their armed forces, usually by being part of the official medical or religious service.[220] A member of the armed forces cannot designate himself or herself as military medical or religious personnel.

Thus, members of the armed forces do not acquire military medical and religious status merely by performing medical or religious functions or by having medical or religious training. For example, a member of a special operations unit might be trained as a medical specialist, but not be designated as military medical personnel, because that person is expected to perform both

---

if a 'minister', a part-time minister, is not protected as religious personnel. Furthermore, the protection does not extend to every individual minister. The protection granted by the First and Second Conventions only applies to those attached to the armed forces or to a hospital ship.").

[218] GWS COMMENTARY 244 ("On the one hand, the Conference thought it necessary to affirm the supra-national and quasi-neutral character of personnel whose duties placed them above the conflict."). *See also* Vowinckel v. First Federal Trust Co., 10 F.2d 19, 21 (9th Cir. 1926) ("Red Cross surgeons and nurses, who are engaged exclusively in ameliorating the condition of the wounded of the armies in the field, and in alleviating the sufferings of mankind in general, are not enemies of the United States in any proper sense of that term."); WINTHROP, MILITARY LAW & PRECEDENTS 779 ("Another class who are to be exempt from violence, or seizure as prisoners, are the surgeons, assistants and employees charged with the care and transport of the wounded on the field and the attendance upon them in field ambulance or hospital. Persons of this class 'enjoy the rights of neutrality, provided they take no active part in the operations of war.'").

[219] *Refer to* § 4.5 (Armed Forces of a State); § 4.5.3 (Regular Armed Forces Who Profess Allegiance to a Government or an Authority Not Recognized by the Detaining Power); § 4.6 (Other Militia and Volunteer Corps).

[220] *See* GWS COMMENTARY 218 ("Article 24 refers to the official medical personnel and chaplains of the armed forces."); *id.* at 220 ("On the other hand, chaplains, to be accorded immunity, must be attached to the armed forces. They do not attach themselves. The decision will rest with the competent military authorities and the relationship must be an official one. Accordingly, ministers of religion who wish to serve in a non-official capacity, are not covered by the Convention, and, until such time as they have been regularly appointed, act at their own risk and peril."). *Cf.* GPW art. 32 (referring to POWs "who, though not attached to the medical service of their armed forces, are physicians, surgeons, dentists, nurses or medical orderlies," as not being entitled to retained personnel status).

combatant and medical duties. That person, therefore, would not receive the rights, duties, and liabilities related to military medical status. He or she, however, may be treated like military medical personnel while detained by the enemy by being required to perform medical duties.[221]

4.9.2.3 <u>*Exclusively Engaged in Humanitarian Duties*</u>. In order to establish and maintain their status as military medical or religious personnel, these personnel must serve exclusively in a humanitarian capacity. This assignment must generally be permanent.[222]

Military physicians or other medical specialist personnel who are not exclusively engaged in humanitarian duties, such as duties that involve committing acts harmful to the enemy, would not be entitled to military medical status.[223] For example, an Army Medical Corps or Medical Service Corps officer serving as the commander of a tactical convoy would not be entitled to military medical status.[224] Similarly, in general, persons who engage in combat search and rescue missions would not be exclusively engaged in humanitarian duties, since preventing the capture of combatants by the adversary constitutes an act harmful to the enemy.[225] However, these individuals may be treated like auxiliary medical personnel or members of the armed forces who are trained in medical care, but who are not attached to the medical service.[226]

The requirement that military medical and religious personnel serve exclusively in a humanitarian capacity not only requires that they refrain from acts harmful to the enemy, but also has been interpreted as an affirmative obligation to serve in a humanitarian capacity. For example, captured military medical personnel who refuse to perform their medical duties to care for fellow prisoners would not be entitled to retained personnel status.[227]

---

[221] *Refer to* § 4.5.2.2 (Members Trained as Medical Personnel, but Not Attached to the Medical Service); § 4.5.2.3 (Members Who Are Ministers of Religion Without Having Officiated as Chaplains to Their Own Forces).

[222] *See* GWS COMMENTARY 219 ("The words 'exclusively engaged' indicate that the assignment must be permanent, which is not the case in Article 25 dealing with auxiliary personnel.").

[223] *Refer to* § 7.8.3 (Loss of Protection for Medical and Religious Personnel From Being Made the Object of Attack).

[224] *See* W. Hays Parks, *Status of Certain Medical Corps and Medical Service Corps Officers under the Geneva Conventions, reprinted in* THE ARMY LAWYER 5 (¶8) (Apr. 1989) ("U.S. Army MSC officers, AMEDD noncommissioned officers, or other Medical Corps personnel serving in positions that do not meet the 'exclusively engaged' criteria of article 24 are not entitled to its protections but, under article 25, are entitled to protection from intentional attack during those times in which they are performing medical support functions. This would include physicians who, while serving as medical company commanders, might be detailed to perform the duties specified in paragraph 2b. [¶2b. The medical company commander, a physician, and the executive officer, an MSC officer, by nature of their positions and grade, may be detailed as convoy march unit commanders. In this position they would be responsible for medical and nonmedical unit routes of march, convoy control, defense, and repulsing attacks.]").

[225] *Refer to* § 7.10.3.1 (Acts Harmful to the Enemy).

[226] *Refer to* § 4.13 (Auxiliary Medical Personnel); § 4.5.2.2 (Members Trained as Medical Personnel, but Not Attached to the Medical Service).

[227] *See* LEVIE, POWS 74 ("But what of the physician in the power of the enemy who, perhaps for some ideological reason, refuses to perform any professional duties and will not provide medical treatment for the sick and wounded members of the armed forces of his own Power of Origin? This was the procedure followed by most of the North Vietnamese medical personnel captured in Vietnam. The South Vietnamese responded by treating them as ordinary prisoners of war. Once again, there was probably no specific legal basis for such action; but certainly, if a member

4.10 RIGHTS, DUTIES, AND LIABILITIES OF MILITARY MEDICAL AND RELIGIOUS PERSONNEL

Although military medical and religious personnel are members of, or attached to, the armed forces and are in many respects treated like combatants, they are afforded special privileges so that they may fulfill their humanitarian duties. They must be respected and protected in all circumstances. In turn, they generally may not commit acts harmful to the enemy. If they fall into the power of the enemy during international armed conflict, they may be retained to care for, or minister to, POWs.

4.10.1 Military Medical and Religious Personnel - Conduct of Hostilities. Military medical and religious personnel may not be made the object of attack.[228] However, military medical and religious personnel must accept the risks of incidental harm from military operations.[229]

Military medical and religious personnel generally may not commit acts harmful to the enemy (*e.g.*, resisting lawful capture by the enemy military forces).[230] Military medical and religious personnel, however, may employ arms in self-defense or in defense of their patients against unlawful attacks.[231]

Military medical and religious personnel who take actions outside their role as military medical and religious personnel forfeit the corresponding protections of their special status and may be treated as combatants or auxiliary medical personnel, as appropriate.[232]

4.10.2 Military Medical and Religious Personnel - Detention. If military medical and religious personnel fall into the power of the enemy during international armed conflict, they are not held as POWs, but instead are held as retained personnel.[233] They should present their identity cards to demonstrate their status as retained personnel.[234] They are retained so that they may fulfill their humanitarian duties to care for, or minister to, POWs.[235]

Although they are not held as POWs, military medical and religious personnel receive, at a minimum, the protections of POW status.[236] In addition, retained personnel shall be granted all

---

of the medical profession refuses to employ his professional abilities, even for the benefit of his own countrymen, he is denying his professional status and, under those circumstances, there is little that a Detaining Power can do except to remove him from the category of a retained person and to place him in a general prisoner-of-war status (unless his recalcitrance is to be rewarded by repatriation).").

[228] *Refer to* § 7.8.2 (Meaning of "Respect and Protection" of Medical and Religious Personnel).

[229] *Refer to* § 7.8.2.1 (Incidental Harm Not Prohibited).

[230] *Refer to* § 7.8.3 (Loss of Protection for Medical and Religious Personnel From Being Made the Object of Attack).

[231] *Refer to* § 7.10.3.5 (Use of Weapons in Self-Defense or Defense of the Wounded and Sick).

[232] *Refer to* § 4.9.2.3 (Exclusively Engaged in Humanitarian Duties).

[233] *Refer to* § 7.9.1.2 (Medical and Religious Personnel Who May Be Retained).

[234] *Refer to* § 7.9.2 (Use of Identification Card to Help Establish Retained Personnel Status).

[235] *Refer to* § 7.9.3 (Duties of Retained Personnel).

[236] *Refer to* § 7.9.5.1 (POW Treatment as a Minimum).

facilities necessary to provide for the medical care of, and religious ministration to, POWs.[237] For example, retained personnel may not be compelled to carry out any work other than that concerned with their medical or religious duties.[238] Retained personnel shall be authorized to visit periodically POWs situated in working detachments or in hospitals outside the camp.[239] Retained personnel, through their senior officer in each camp, have the right to deal with the competent authorities of the camp on all questions relating to their duties.[240]

If they are not needed to care for, or minister to, POWs, and if military requirements permit, retained personnel should be returned to the forces to which they belong so that they may continue to care for, or minister to, members of their armed forces.[241] The parties to the conflict would establish special agreements to establish the procedures for repatriation.[242]

4.11 Authorized Staff of Voluntary Aid Societies

States may choose to employ the staff of National Red Cross Societies and that of other Voluntary Aid Societies, like military medical and religious personnel. If States subject such staff to military laws and regulations, then such personnel are to be treated like military medical and religious personnel.[243] States must notify other Parties to the 1949 Geneva Conventions before actually employing such personnel.[244]

4.11.1 American National Red Cross. Under U.S. law, the American National Red Cross is a voluntary aid society authorized to support the U.S. armed forces in time of war.[245] American National Red Cross personnel who support the U.S. armed forces in military operations in this way are subject to the Uniform Code of Military Justice.[246]

---

237 *Refer to* § 7.9.5.2 (All Facilities Necessary to Provide for the Medical Care of, and Religious Ministration to, POWs).

238 *Refer to* § 7.9.5.6 (No Other Compulsory Duties).

239 *Refer to* § 7.9.5.3 (Visits of POWs Outside the Camp).

240 *Refer to* § 7.9.5.7 (Senior Medical Officer in the Camp).

241 *Refer to* § 7.9.4 (Return of Personnel Whose Retention Is Not Indispensable).

242 *Refer to* § 7.9.4.3 (Special Agreements on the Percentage of Personnel to Be Retained); § 7.9.5.8 (Agreements on Possible Relief of Retained Personnel).

243 *See* GWS art. 26 ("The staff of National Red Cross Societies and that of other Voluntary Aid Societies, duly recognized and authorized by their Governments, who may be employed on the same duties as the personnel named in Article 24, are placed on the same footing as the personnel named in the said Article, provided that the staff of such societies are subject to military laws and regulations.").

244 *See* GWS art. 26 ("Each High Contracting Party shall notify to the other, either in time of peace or at the commencement of or during hostilities, but in any case before actually employing them, the names of the societies which it has authorized, under its responsibility, to render assistance to the regular medical service of its armed forces.").

245 *See* 36 U.S.C. § 300102 (the purposes of the American National Red Cross include "to provide volunteer aid in time of war to the sick and wounded of the Armed Forces, in accordance with the spirit and conditions of … the treaties of Geneva, August 22, 1864, July 27, 1929, and August 12, 1949" and "to perform all the duties devolved on a national society by each nation that has acceded to any of those treaties, conventions, or protocols").

246 *Refer to* § 18.19.3.1 (Uniform Code of Military Justice Offenses).

4.12 Staff of a Recognized Aid Society of a Neutral Country

The 1949 Geneva Conventions recognize that neutral States may lend their recognized aid societies to a party to the conflict by placing those personnel and units under the control of that party to the conflict.[247] The neutral Government shall notify this consent to the adversary of the State that accepts such assistance, and the party to a conflict that accepts such assistance must notify enemy States before using it.[248] This assistance is not considered as interference in the conflict by the neutral State.[249]

The staff of a recognized aid society of a neutral country who have been lent to a party to the conflict must be furnished with an identity card similar to that provided to retained personnel before leaving their neutral State.[250] Such personnel who have fallen into the hands of the adverse party may not be detained.[251] Unless otherwise agreed, such personnel shall have permission to return to their country, or if this is not possible, to the territory of the party to the conflict in whose service they were, as soon as a route for their return is open and military considerations permit.[252] Pending their release, such personnel shall continue their work under the direction of the adverse party; they shall preferably be engaged in the care of the wounded and sick of the party to the conflict in whose service they were.[253] On their departure, they shall take with them their effects, personal articles and valuables and the instruments, arms, and if possible, the means of transport belonging to them.[254]

Such personnel, while in the power of a party to the conflict, should be treated on the same basis as corresponding personnel of the armed forces of that party to the conflict; food in particular must be sufficient as regards quantity, quality, and variety to keep them in a normal

---

[247] GWS art. 27 ("A recognized Society of a neutral country can only lend the assistance of its medical personnel and units to a Party to the conflict with the previous consent of its own Government and the authorization of the Party to the conflict concerned. That personnel and those units shall be placed under the control of that Party to the conflict.").

[248] GWS art. 27 ("The neutral Government shall notify this consent to the adversary of the State which accepts such assistance. The Party to the conflict who accepts such assistance is bound to notify the adverse Party thereof before making any use of it.").

[249] GWS art. 27 ("In no circumstances shall this assistance be considered as interference in the conflict.").

[250] GWS art. 27 ("The members of the personnel named in the first paragraph shall be duly furnished with the identity cards provided for in Article 40 before leaving the neutral country to which they belong."); GWS art. 40 (giving requirements with regard to the identification of "[t]he personnel designated in Article 24 and in Articles 26 and 27").

[251] GWS art. 32 ("Persons designated in Article 27 who have fallen into the hands of the adverse Party may not be detained.").

[252] GWS art. 32 ("Unless otherwise agreed, they shall have permission to return to their country, or if this is not possible, to the territory of the Party to the conflict in whose service they were, as soon as a route for their return is open and military considerations permit.").

[253] GWS art. 32 ("Pending their release, they shall continue their work under the direction of the adverse Party; they shall preferably be engaged in the care of the wounded and sick of the Party to the conflict in whose service they were.").

[254] GWS art. 32 ("On their departure, they shall take with them their effects, personal articles and valuables and the instruments, arms and if possible the means of transport belonging to them.").

state of health.[255] They may also fly their national flag.[256]

4.13 Auxiliary Medical Personnel

Auxiliary medical personnel are members of the armed forces specially trained for employment, should the need arise, as hospital orderlies, nurses, or auxiliary stretcher-bearers, in the search for or the collection, transport, or treatment of the wounded and sick in international armed conflict.[257] In general, auxiliary medical personnel are treated like combatants; however, while carrying out medical duties, they must distinguish themselves by wearing a white armlet bearing the distinctive sign (*e.g.*, the red cross), and they may not be made the object of attack.

4.13.1 Auxiliary Medical Personnel – U.S. Armed Forces. The recent practice of the United States has not been to employ persons as auxiliary medical personnel. Rather, the U.S. armed forces have employed military medical and religious personnel.[258] In addition, the U.S. armed forces have given members of the armed forces additional training in combat medicine but have not designated them as military medical personnel or as auxiliary medical personnel.[259] Thus, such personnel have not worn the distinctive emblem while engaging in medical duties, and they may be made the object of attack by the enemy.

Although the recent practice of the United States has not been to employ persons as auxiliary medical personnel, the United States may later decide to employ auxiliary medical personnel, and enemy military forces may employ such personnel. Moreover, certain members of the medical corps, who do not qualify as military medical personnel because they perform duties inconsistent with exclusive medical status, may be treated like auxiliary medical personnel.[260]

4.13.2 Acquiring Auxiliary Medical Status. As with military medical and religious

---

[255] GWS art. 32 ("The Parties to the conflict shall secure to this personnel, while in their power, the same food, lodging, allowances and pay as are granted to the corresponding personnel of their armed forces. The food shall in any case be sufficient as regards quantity, quality and variety to keep the said personnel in a normal state of health.").

[256] GWS art. 43 ("The medical units belonging to neutral countries, which may have been authorized to lend their services to a belligerent under the conditions laid down in Article 27, shall fly, along with the flag of the Convention, the national flag of that belligerent, wherever the latter makes use of the faculty conferred on him by Article 42. Subject to orders to the contrary by the responsible military authorities, they may on all occasions fly their national flag, even if they fall into the hands of the adverse Party.").

[257] GWS art. 25 ("Members of the armed forces specially trained for employment, should the need arise, as hospital orderlies, nurses or auxiliary stretcher-bearers, in the search for or the collection, transport or treatment of the wounded and sick shall likewise be respected and protected if they are carrying out these duties at the time when they come into contact with the enemy or fall into his hands.").

[258] *Refer to* § 4.9 (Military Medical and Religious Personnel).

[259] *Refer to* § 4.5.2.2 (Members Trained as Medical Personnel, but Not Attached to the Medical Service).

[260] *See, e.g.*, W. Hays Parks, *Status of Certain Medical Corps and Medical Service Corps Officers under the Geneva Conventions, reprinted in* THE ARMY LAWYER 5 (¶8) (Apr. 1989) ("U.S. Army MSC officers, AMEDD noncommissioned officers, or other Medical Corps personnel serving in positions that do not meet the 'exclusively engaged' criteria of article 24 are not entitled to its protection but, under article 25 are entitled to protection from intentional attack during those times in which they are performing medical support functions.").

status, members of the armed forces do not acquire auxiliary medical status simply by performing medical duties.[261] For example, a combatant who treats fellow combatants on the battlefield does not automatically acquire auxiliary medical status. Similarly, persons do not acquire auxiliary medical status only because they happen to have medical training.

In order to acquire auxiliary medical status, a person must receive appropriate training and be designated as such by his or her armed forces.[262] Those armed forces must provide proper identification to such persons, including an armband and a special identity document.[263]

4.13.3 Auxiliary Medical Personnel – Conduct of Hostilities. Auxiliary medical personnel may not be made the object of attack when carrying out their medical duties.[264] Auxiliary medical personnel shall wear, but only while carrying out medical duties, a white armlet bearing in its center the distinctive sign in miniature; the armlet shall be issued and stamped by the military authority.[265] In addition, auxiliary medical personnel must abstain from acts harmful to the enemy while carrying out their medical duties.[266]

When the above conditions are not present, auxiliary medical personnel may be made the object of attack on the same basis as other combatants.

4.13.4 Auxiliary Medical Personnel – Detention. Auxiliary medical personnel are POWs when detained by the enemy during international armed conflict, but may be required to perform their medical duties, as needed.[267] Auxiliary medical personnel are not subject to the repatriation provisions that apply specifically to retained personnel.[268]

4.14 Personnel Engaged in Duties Related to the Protection of Cultural Property

During armed conflict, different classes of persons may be engaged in duties related to

---

[261] *Refer to* § 4.9.2 (Requirements for Military Medical and Religious Status).

[262] GWS COMMENTARY 222 ("To be accorded immunity, auxiliary personnel must, as we have said, have received special medical training beforehand, the nature and duration of which are wisely not defined. If it is necessary to make good a deficiency in permanent personnel, such training may even take place in wartime; but personnel filling this temporary role must in any case have had a real training.").

[263] GWS COMMENTARY 223-24 ("To have immunity even on the battlefield, military personnel caring for the wounded had to form a distinct category—that of medical personnel—and enjoy a separate status, recognizable by a distinctive emblem and an identity card. If recourse was had to such safeguards, it was because military considerations demanded them. Otherwise the risk of abuse would have been too great. It is not straining the imagination to picture combatants approaching an enemy position, ostensibly to assist the wounded, and then opening fire in order to seize it: similarly, a fighting unit might suddenly transform itself into a medical unit, in order to avoid enemy fire.").

[264] *Refer to* § 7.8.1 (Categories of Persons Who Are Entitled to Respect and Protection as Medical and Religious Personnel on the Battlefield).

[265] *Refer to* § 7.8.4.2 (Wearing of Armlet With Miniature Distinctive Emblem).

[266] *Refer to* § 7.8.3 (Loss of Protection for Medical and Religious Personnel From Being Made the Object of Attack).

[267] *See* GWS art. 29 ("Members of the personnel designated in Article 25 who have fallen into the hands of the enemy, shall be prisoners of war, but shall be employed on their medical duties in so far as the need arises.").

[268] *Refer to* § 4.10.2 (Military Medical and Religious Personnel - Detention).

the protection of cultural property. These classes of persons may include: specialist personnel in the armed forces, armed custodians specially empowered to guard cultural property, as well as persons who are engaged in duties of control in accordance with the Regulations for the Execution of the 1954 Hague Cultural Property Convention. So far as consistent with the interests of security, such personnel should be respected and permitted to carry out their duties for the protection of cultural property.

4.14.1 Personnel Engaged in the Protection of Cultural Property. As far as is consistent with the interests of security, personnel engaged in the protection of cultural property shall, in the interests of such property, be respected and, if they fall into the hands of the opposing party, shall be allowed to continue to carry out duties whenever the cultural property for which they are responsible has also fallen into the hands of the opposing party.[269] Such personnel are analogous to military medical and religious personnel who also shall continue to carry out their medical and spiritual duties when they have fallen into the hands of the enemy.[270]

No special agreement may be concluded that would diminish the protection afforded by the 1954 Hague Cultural Property Convention to the personnel engaged in the protection of cultural property.[271]

4.14.1.1 *Specialist Personnel in the Armed Forces*. States, especially Parties to the 1954 Hague Cultural Property Convention, may have within their armed forces, services or specialist personnel whose purpose is to secure respect for cultural property and to cooperate with the civilian authorities responsible for safeguarding it.[272] The United States has long had such personnel in its armed forces.[273]

For example, during World War II, Allied forces dedicated a specific group of personnel who were tasked to save as much of the culture of Europe as they could during combat.[274] These

---

[269] 1954 HAGUE CULTURAL PROPERTY CONVENTION art. 15 ("As far as is consistent with the interests of security, personnel engaged in the protection of cultural property shall, in the interests of such property, be respected and, if they fall into the hands of the opposing Party, shall be allowed to continue to carry out duties whenever the cultural property for which they are responsible has also fallen into the hands of the opposing Party."); ROERICH PACT art. 1 (requiring respect and protection for personnel of "[t]he historic monuments, museums, scientific, artistic, educational and cultural institutions").

[270] *Refer to* § 7.9.3 (Duties of Retained Personnel).

[271] 1954 HAGUE CULTURAL PROPERTY CONVENTION art. 24(2) ("No special agreement may be concluded which would diminish the protection afforded by the present Convention to cultural property and to the personnel engaged in its protection.").

[272] 1954 HAGUE CULTURAL PROPERTY CONVENTION art. 7(2) ("The High Contracting Parties undertake to plan or establish in peacetime, within their armed forces, services or specialist personnel whose purpose will be to secure respect for cultural property and to co-operate with the civilian authorities responsible for safeguarding it.").

[273] *Section-by-Section Analysis of Provisions*, 4, Tab 1 to Strobe Talbot, *Letter of Submittal*, May 12, 1998, MESSAGE FROM THE PRESIDENT TRANSMITTING THE 1954 HAGUE CULTURAL PROPERTY CONVENTION 5 ("It is longstanding U.S. Army practice to maintain such personnel in their civil affairs reserve force. Marine Corps reserve civil affairs personnel receive training to perform similar functions if necessary.").

[274] R. M. EDSEL, THE MONUMENTS MEN 2 (2009) ("The Monuments Men were a group of men and women from thirteen nations, most of whom volunteered for service in the newly created Monuments, Fine Arts, and Archives section [of the Western Allied military effort], or MFAA. Most of the early volunteers had expertise as museum

personnel worked to mitigate combat damage to churches and museums and to locate moveable works of art that were stolen or missing.[275]

4.14.1.2 *Armed Custodians Specially Empowered to Protect Cultural Property*. States may use armed custodians who are specially empowered to protect cultural property. The guarding of cultural property under special protection by armed custodians specially empowered to do so, however, shall not be deemed to be a use for military purposes that would deprive cultural property of special protection.[276]

4.14.2 Persons Responsible for the Duties of Control in Accordance With the Regulations for the Execution of the 1954 Hague Cultural Property Convention. A number of persons are responsible for the duties of control in accordance with the Regulations for the Execution of the 1954 Hague Cultural Property Convention. These individuals may include: (1) the Director-General of the United Nations Educational, Scientific and Cultural Organization (UNESCO); (2) a State-appointed representative for cultural property; (3) delegates of the Protecting Powers; (4) a Commissioner-General for Cultural Property; and (5) inspectors and experts proposed by the Commissioner-General for Cultural Property.

The Commissioners-General for Cultural Property, delegates of the Protecting Powers, inspectors, and experts shall in no case exceed their mandates. In particular, they shall take account of the security needs of the Party to the 1954 Hague Cultural Property Convention to which they are accredited and shall in all circumstances act in accordance with the requirements of the military situation as communicated to them by that State.[277]

4.14.2.1 *Director-General of UNESCO*. Under the 1954 Hague Cultural Property Convention, the Director-General of the United Nations Educational, Scientific, and Cultural Organization (UNESCO) plays an important role. For example, among other duties, the Director-General compiles and periodically revises an international list consisting of all persons nominated by participating States as qualified to carry out the functions of Commissioner-

---

directors, curators, art scholars and educators, artists, architects, and archivists. Their job was simple: to save as much of the culture of Europe as they could during combat. The creation of the MFAA section was a remarkable experiment. It marked the first time an army fought a war while comprehensively attempting to mitigate cultural damage, and was performed without adequate transportation, supplies, personnel, or historical precedent. The men tasked with this mission were, on the surface, the most unlikely of heroes.").

[275] R. M. EDSEL, THE MONUMENTS MEN xiv (2009) ("Their initial responsibility was to mitigate combat damage, primarily to structures – churches, museums, and other important monuments. As the war progressed and the German border was breached, their focus shifted to locating moveable works of art and other cultural items stolen or otherwise missing.").

[276] *Refer to* § 5.18.8.2 (Conditions for the Granting of Special Protection – No Use for Military Purposes).

[277] REGULATIONS FOR THE EXECUTION OF THE 1954 HAGUE CULTURAL PROPERTY CONVENTION art. 8 ("The Commissioners-General for Cultural Property, delegates of the Protecting Powers, inspectors and experts shall in no case exceed their mandates. In particular, they shall take account of the security needs of the High Contracting Party to which they are accredited and shall in all circumstances act in accordance with the requirements of the military situation as communicated to them by that High Contracting Party.").

General for Cultural Property.[278]

4.14.2.2 *State-Appointed Representative for Cultural Property*. As soon as any Party to the 1954 Hague Cultural Property Convention is engaged in an international armed conflict, that Party shall appoint a representative for cultural property situated in its territory; if that Party is in occupation of another territory, it shall appoint a special representative for cultural property situated in that territory.[279]

4.14.2.3 *Delegates of the Protecting Powers*. A Protecting Power shall appoint delegates to perform certain functions in the protection of cultural property.[280] The delegates of the Protecting Powers shall take note of violations of the 1954 Hague Cultural Property Convention, investigate, with the approval of the Party to which they are accredited, the circumstances in which they have occurred, make representations locally to secure their cessation, and, if necessary, notify the Commissioner-General of such violations. They shall keep the Commissioner-General informed of their activities.[281]

4.14.2.4 *Commissioner-General for Cultural Property*. The Regulations for the Execution of the 1954 Hague Cultural Property Convention provide for the appointment of a Commissioner-General for cultural property, but always with the approval of the Party to which he or she will be accredited.[282]

---

[278] REGULATIONS FOR THE EXECUTION OF THE 1954 HAGUE CULTURAL PROPERTY CONVENTION art. 1 ("On the entry into force of the Convention, the Director-General of the United Nations Educational, Scientific and Cultural Organization shall compile an international list consisting of all persons nominated by the High Contracting Parties as qualified to carry out the functions of Commissioner-General for Cultural Property. On the initiative of the Director-General of the United Nations Educational, Scientific and Cultural Organization, this list shall be periodically revised on the basis of requests formulated by the High Contracting Parties.").

[279] REGULATIONS FOR THE EXECUTION OF THE 1954 HAGUE CULTURAL PROPERTY CONVENTION art. 2 ("As soon as any High Contracting Party is engaged in an armed conflict to which Article 18 of the Convention applies: (a) It shall appoint a representative for cultural property situated in its territory; if it is in occupation of another territory, it shall appoint a special representative for cultural property situated in that territory;").

[280] REGULATIONS FOR THE EXECUTION OF THE 1954 HAGUE CULTURAL PROPERTY CONVENTION art. 2 ("As soon as any High Contracting Party is engaged in an armed conflict to which Article 18 of the Convention applies: (b) The Protecting Power acting for each of the Parties in conflict with such High Contracting Party shall appoint delegates accredited to the latter in conformity with Article 3 below;"); REGULATIONS FOR THE EXECUTION OF THE 1954 HAGUE CULTURAL PROPERTY CONVENTION art. 3 ("The Protecting Power shall appoint its delegates from among the members of its diplomatic or consular staff or, with the approval of the Party to which they will be accredited, from among other persons.").

[281] REGULATIONS FOR THE EXECUTION OF THE 1954 HAGUE CULTURAL PROPERTY CONVENTION art. 5 ("The delegates of the Protecting Powers shall take note of violations of the Convention, investigate, with the approval of the Party to which they are accredited, the circumstances in which they have occurred, make representations locally to secure their cessation and, if necessary, notify the Commissioner-General of such violations. They shall keep him informed of their activities.").

[282] REGULATIONS FOR THE EXECUTION OF THE 1954 HAGUE CULTURAL PROPERTY CONVENTION art. 4 ("1. The Commissioner-General for Cultural Property shall be chosen from the international list of persons by joint agreement between the Party to which he will be accredited and the Protecting Powers acting on behalf of the opposing Parties. 2. Should the Parties fail to reach agreement within three weeks from the beginning of their discussions on this point, they shall request the President of the International Court of Justice to appoint the

The Commissioner-General exercises a number of functions, including proposing the appointment of inspectors and experts, ordering an investigation with the agreement of the Party to which he or she is accredited, and drawing up reports on the application of the Convention.[283]

4.14.2.5 *Inspectors and Experts Proposed by the Commissioner-General for Cultural Property*. The Commissioner-General for Cultural Property may propose, for the approval of the Party to which the Commissioner-General is accredited, inspectors of cultural property to be charged with specific missions.[284] The Commissioner-General, delegates, and inspectors may have recourse to the services of experts, who will also be proposed for the approval of the Party to which the Commissioner-General is accredited.[285]

In some cases, inspectors may be entrusted with the functions of delegates of the Protecting Powers.[286]

4.14.3 Identifying Personnel Engaged in Duties for the Protection of Cultural Property. Persons responsible for duties of control in accordance with the Regulations for the Execution of the 1954 Hague Cultural Property Convention, and persons engaged in duties for the protection of cultural property, are to carry a special identity card bearing the distinctive emblem.[287] In

---

Commissioner-General, who shall not take up his duties until the Party to which he is accredited has approved his appointment.").

[283] REGULATIONS FOR THE EXECUTION OF THE 1954 HAGUE CULTURAL PROPERTY CONVENTION art. 6 ("1. The Commissioner-General for Cultural Property shall deal with all matters referred to him in connexion with the application of the Convention, in conjunction with the representative of the Party to which he is accredited and with the delegates concerned. 2. He shall have powers of decision and appointment in the cases specified in the present Regulations. 3. With the agreement of the Party to which he is accredited, he shall have the right to order an investigation or to, conduct it himself. 4. He shall make any representations to the Parties to the conflict or to their Protecting Powers which he deems useful for the application of the Convention. 5. He shall draw up such reports as may be necessary on the application of the Convention and communicate them to the Parties concerned and to their Protecting Powers. He shall send copies to the Director-General of the United Nations Educational, Scientific and Cultural Organization, who may make use only of their technical contents. 6. If there is no Protecting Power, the Commissioner-General shall exercise the functions of the Protecting Power as laid down in Articles 21 and 22 of the Convention.").

[284] REGULATIONS FOR THE EXECUTION OF THE 1954 HAGUE CULTURAL PROPERTY CONVENTION art. 7(1) ("Whenever the Commissioner-General for Cultural Property considers it necessary, either at the request of the delegates concerned or after consultation with them, he shall propose, for the approval of the Party to which he is accredited, an inspector of cultural property to be charged with a specific mission. An inspector shall be responsible only to the Commissioner-General.").

[285] REGULATIONS FOR THE EXECUTION OF THE 1954 HAGUE CULTURAL PROPERTY CONVENTION art. 7(2) ("The Commissioner-General, delegates and inspectors may have recourse to the services of experts, who will also be proposed for the approval of the Party mentioned in the preceding paragraph.").

[286] REGULATIONS FOR THE EXECUTION OF THE 1954 HAGUE CULTURAL PROPERTY CONVENTION art. 9 ("If a Party to the conflict does not benefit or ceases to benefit from the activities of a Protecting Power, a neutral State may be asked to undertake those functions of a Protecting Power which concern the appointment of a Commissioner-General for Cultural Property in accordance with the procedure laid down in Article 4 above. The Commissioner-General thus appointed shall, if need be, entrust to inspectors the functions of delegates of Protecting Powers as specified in the present Regulations.").

[287] REGULATIONS FOR THE EXECUTION OF THE 1954 HAGUE CULTURAL PROPERTY CONVENTION art. 21(2) ("[The persons mentioned in Article 17, paragraph 2 (b) and (c) of the Convention] shall carry a special identity card bearing the distinctive emblem. This card shall mention at least the surname and first names, the date of birth, the

addition, such persons may wear an armlet bearing the distinctive emblem issued and stamped by the competent authorities.[288]

Such persons may not, without legitimate reason, be deprived of their identity card or of the right to wear the armlet.[289] The distinctive emblem displayed on an armlet or special identity card is to be displayed once (as opposed to repeated three times).[290]

4.15 Persons Authorized to Accompany the Armed Forces

Under the law of war, persons who are not members of the armed forces, but are authorized to accompany them, fall into a special category. Although they are often referred to as "civilians" because they are not military personnel, they differ materially from the civilian population because these persons are authorized – and in some cases, are ordered – to accompany military forces into a theater of operations to support the force.[291]

DoD policies have often addressed the use of non-military personnel to support military operations.[292]

---

title or rank, and the function of the holder. The card shall bear the photograph of the holder as well as his signature or his fingerprints, or both. It shall bear the embossed stamp of the competent authorities.").

[288] Regulations for the Execution of the 1954 Hague Cultural Property Convention art. 21(1) ("The persons mentioned in Article 17, paragraph 2 (b) and (c) of the Convention may wear an armlet bearing the distinctive emblem, issued and stamped by the competent authorities.").

[289] Regulations for the Execution of the 1954 Hague Cultural Property Convention art. 21(4) ("The said persons may not, without legitimate reason, be deprived of their identity card or of the right to wear the armlet.").

[290] *Refer to* § 5.18.7.2 (Display of the Distinctive Emblem for Cultural Property – Once Versus Three Times).

[291] Christian Damson (United States) v. Germany, 7 Reports of the International Arbitral Awards 184, 198 (1925) (concluding that a non-military employee of the U.S. Government whose activities were "directly in furtherance of a military operation" was not a "civilian" for the purposes of the Treaty of Berlin and thus was not entitled to assert a claim under the provisions of the Treaty of Berlin that provided for Germany to compensate for damages to the civilian population that it caused during World War I); Arthur Ellt Hungerford (United States) v. Germany, 7 Reports of the International Arbitral Awards 368, 371 (1926) ("From the foregoing it is apparent that the members of the Y.M.C.A. who served on the western front were, in the language of the Commander-in-Chief of the A.E.F., 'militarized and *** under the control and supervision of the American military authorities'. Or, to use the language of their own spokesman, they were 'a part of the military machine'. They rendered military service of a high order. The mere fact that they were not formally inducted into the Army or were not in the pay of the Government of the United States is immaterial so far as concerns the question here presented. They had voluntarily segregated themselves from 'the civilian population' as that term is used in the Treaty of Berlin. They had deliberately exposed themselves and their personal belongings to the risks of war which began at the port of embarkation. The provisions of the Treaty of Berlin obligating Germany to make compensation for damages to 'civilians' or to 'civilian victims' or to the 'civilian population' were manifestly intended to apply to the passive victims of warfare, not to those who entered the war zone, subjected themselves to risks to which members of the civilian population generally were immune, and participated in military activities, whether as combatants or noncombatants.").

[292] *For example*, DoD Instruction 3020.41, *Operational Contract Support (OCS)* (Dec. 20, 2011); DoD Instruction 1100.22, *Policies and Procedures for Determining Workforce Mix* (Apr. 12, 2010); DoD Directive 1404.10, *DoD Civilian Expeditionary Workforce* (Jan. 23, 2009); DoD Instruction 1400.32, *DoD Civilian Work Force Contingency and Emergency Planning Guidelines and Procedures* (Apr. 24, 1995); DoD Directive 1404.10,

Persons authorized to accompany the armed forces may not be made the object of attack unless they take direct part in hostilities. They may, however, be detained by enemy military forces, and are entitled to POW status if they fall into the power of the enemy during international armed conflict. They have legal immunity from the enemy's domestic law for providing authorized support services to the armed forces.

4.15.1 Persons Authorized to Accompany the Armed Forces – Notes on Terminology. In the past, the category of persons who "accompany" or "follow" the armed forces has referred to journalists, private clergy, and sutlers,[293] who traditionally were subject to the jurisdiction of the army that they accompanied.[294] These persons, to the extent that they were simply following the armed forces for their own purposes and not to provide support to military operations, were subject to detention, not as POWs, but like civilians, only if specifically necessary.[295] On the other hand, non-military persons who were serving the armed forces, such as civilian employees of the war department, were detained as POWs.[296]

Article 4A(4) of the GPW reflects the modern practice and rule.[297] Persons authorized to accompany the armed forces under Article 4A(4) include employees of the Department of

---

Emergency-Essential DoD U.S. Civilian Employees (Apr. 10, 1992); DoD INSTRUCTION 3020.37, *Continuation of Essential DoD Contractor Services During Crises* (Nov. 6, 1990 Incorporating Change 1, Jan. 26, 1996).

293 "Sutler" is an old term for a civilian provisioner to the army, whether in garrison or in the field.

294 *For example*, *Articles of War*, art. 2(d), Jun. 4, 1920, 41 STAT. 759, 787 ("All retainers to the camp and all persons accompanying or servicing with the armies of the United States without the territorial jurisdiction of the United States, and in time of war all such retainers and persons accompanying or serving with the armies of the United States in the field, both within and without the territorial jurisdiction of the United States, though not otherwise subject to these articles"); *American Articles of War of 1775*, art. 32, Jun. 30, 1775, *reprinted in* WINTHROP, MILITARY LAW & PRECEDENTS 953 ("All suttlers and retailers to a camp, and all persons whatsoever, serving with the continental army in the field, though not in-listed soldiers, are to be subject to the articles, rules, and regulations of the continental army.").

295 WINTHROP, MILITARY LAW & PRECEDENTS 789 ("Camp-followers, including members of soldiers' families, sutlers, contractors, newspaper correspondents, and others allowed with the army but not in the public employment, should, when taken, be treated similarly as prisoners of war, but should be held only so long as may be necessary.") (emphasis added).

296 *See, e.g.*, SPAIGHT, WAR RIGHTS ON LAND 304 ("[W]hat persons may be made prisoner of war" includes "persons not commissioned or enlisted, but employed permanently by an army as pay-clerks, telegraph-operators, engine drivers, or, generally, in any civilian capacity with an army in the field."); WINTHROP, MILITARY LAW & PRECEDENTS 789 ("The class of persons entitled upon capture to the privileges of prisoners of war comprises members of the enemy's armies, embracing both combatants and non-combatants, and the wounded and sick taken on the field and in hospital. It should comprise also civil persons engaged in military duty or in immediate connection with an army, such as clerks, telegraphists, aeronauts, teamsters, laborers, messengers, guides, scouts, and men employed on transports and military railways—the class indeed of civilians in the employment and service of the government such as are specified in our 63d Article of War as 'Persons serving with the armies in the field.'").

297 *See* GPW COMMENTARY 64 ("The Conference of Government Experts considered that the text of Article 81 of the 1929 Convention had become obsolete (in particular the word 'sutlers' is no longer appropriate) and should include a reference to certain other classes of persons who were more or less part of the armed forces and whose position when captured had given rise to difficulties during the Second World War. The list given is only by way of indication, however, and the text could therefore cover other categories of persons or services who might be called upon, in similar conditions, to follow the armed forces during any future conflict.").

Defense, employees of other government agencies sent to support the armed forces, and other authorized persons working on government contracts to support the armed forces. DoD practice has been to permit a broad range of civilians to be authorized to accompany U.S. forces.[298]

Persons authorized to accompany the armed forces are often referred to, and treated as, "civilians," since they are not members of the armed forces. However, as discussed below, persons authorized to accompany the armed forces are also treated like "combatants" in some respects.

4.15.2 Persons Authorized to Accompany the Armed Forces – Conduct of Hostilities. The rules relating to the conduct of hostilities for persons authorized to accompany the armed forces are similar in some respects to the rules relating to military medical and religious personnel. For example, persons in both classes: (1) generally may not be made the object of attack; (2) accept certain risks of incidental harm from enemy military operations; and (3) have the right of self-defense against unlawful attacks.[299]

4.15.2.1 *Liability to Being Made the Object of Attack*. For the purposes of determining whether they may be made the object of attack, persons authorized to accompany the armed forces are treated as civilians. They may not be made the object of attack unless they take direct part in hostilities.[300]

4.15.2.2 *Employment in Hostilities*. The law of war does not prohibit persons authorized to accompany the armed forces from providing authorized support that constitutes taking direct part in hostilities. Even if the authorized support that they provide constitutes taking a direct part in hostilities, such persons retain their entitlement to POW status under Article 4A(4) of the GPW.[301] Although international law does not prohibit States from using persons authorized to accompany the armed forces to provide support that constitutes direct participation in hostilities, commanders should exercise care in placing such personnel in situations in which an attacking enemy may consider their activities to constitute taking a direct part in hostilities, as there may be legal and policy considerations against such use.

Commanders may not employ persons authorized to accompany the armed forces to perform duties and functions traditionally performed by a military person if such action is taken

---

[298] *For example*, FINAL REPORT ON THE PERSIAN GULF WAR 599 ("In Operations Desert Shield and Desert Storm, the United States employed civilians both as career civil service employees and indirectly as contractor employees. Civilians performed as part of the transportation system, at the forward depot level repair and intermediate level maintenance activities and as weapon systems technical representatives. Civilians worked aboard Navy ships, at Air Force (USAF) bases, and with virtually every Army unit. Only the Marine Corps (USMC) did not employ significant numbers of civilians in theater. This civilian expertise was invaluable and contributed directly to the success achieved.").

[299] *Refer to* § 4.10.1 (Military Medical and Religious Personnel - Conduct of Hostilities).

[300] *Refer to* § 5.8 (Civilians Taking a Direct Part in Hostilities).

[301] *Refer to* § 4.15.4 (Persons Authorized to Accompany the Armed Forces – Liability Under Domestic Law for Participation in Hostilities).

for the purpose of shielding a military objective from attack.[302]

4.15.2.3 *Increased Risk of Incidental Harm*. Persons authorized to accompany the armed forces should expect that they have an increased risk of death or injury incidental to an enemy attack because of their deliberate proximity to military operations and military objectives.[303] For example, civilian members of military aircrews should expect that they might be incidentally injured in an attack against the military aircraft in which they are working.[304] Similarly, in some cases, the location at which persons authorized to accompany the armed forces are serving may itself be a military objective.[305] Furthermore, in some cases, an enemy could reasonably conclude that the mere presence of a person at a location (*e.g.*, a remote military base) indicates that they are a combatant or are directly participating in hostilities, and therefore could lawfully be made the object of attack.

4.15.2.4 *Self-Defense and Arming*. Persons authorized to accompany the armed forces have a right of self-defense against unlawful attacks, such as attacks by bandits. Persons authorized to accompany the armed forces should not resist capture by enemy military forces whom they expect to respect their status under the law of war. If persons authorized to accompany the armed forces make any resistance to enemy military forces, then they may be regarded as taking a direct part in hostilities, and may be made the object of attack.[306] Their resistance to capture by enemy military forces whom they expect to respect their status under the law of war would be incompatible with the principle that a person may not claim the distinct rights of both combatants and civilians at the same time.[307]

The arming of persons authorized to accompany the armed forces is analogous to the arming of military medical and religious personnel.[308] DoD practice has been to permit commanders to authorize persons authorized to accompany the armed forces to carry defensive weapons if necessary.[309]

A State may decide to arm persons authorized to accompany the armed forces for

---

[302] *Refer to* § 5.16 (Prohibition on Using Protected Persons and Objects to Shield, Favor, or Impede Military Operations).

[303] *Refer to* § 5.12.3.3 (Civilian Workers Who Support Military Operations In or On Military Objectives).

[304] *Refer to* § 14.4.2 (Civilian Members of Military Aircrew and Other Persons Authorized to Accompany the Armed Forces).

[305] *Refer to* § 5.6.8.4 (Examples of Military Objectives – Places of Military Significance).

[306] *Refer to* § 5.8.3.1 (Examples of Taking a Direct Part in Hostilities).

[307] *Refer to* § 4.2.2 (No Person May Claim the Distinct Rights Afforded to Both Combatants and Civilians at the Same Time).

[308] *Refer to* § 7.10.3.4 (Arming of Military Medical Units or Facilities).

[309] *See* DoD INSTRUCTION 1100.22, *Policy and Procedures for Determining Workforce Mix*, E-5 ¶2.d.(5)(a) (Apr. 12, 2010) ("It is not a violation of the law of war for DoD civilians and Defense contractor employees who are authorized to accompany the armed forces in the field during hostilities to be issued a weapon on the authority of the Combatant Commander for individual self-defense as addressed in References (n), (o), and (t)."); DoD INSTRUCTION 3020.41, *Operational Contract Support (OCS)*, E-2 ¶4.e (Dec. 20, 2011) (describing policy procedures for issuing weapons to contingency contractor personnel).

personal security and self-defense purposes without incorporating them into the armed forces or otherwise authorizing them to act as a combatant.

4.15.2.5 _Wearing of Uniform_. The law of war does not prohibit persons authorized to accompany the armed forces from wearing a uniform, including the uniform of armed forces that they accompany. Recent U.S. practice, however, has been to ensure that persons accompanying U.S. forces wear clothing that distinguishes them from members of the armed forces in order to prevent confusion about their status.[310]

Persons who wear a military uniform accept the risk of being made the object of attack by enemy forces, as the enemy would reasonably believe them to be lawful objects of attack. However, the mere wearing of a uniform or being authorized by a State to wear a uniform does not necessarily authorize that person to act as a combatant.

4.15.2.6 _Provision of Security Services_. Persons authorized to accompany the armed forces who provide security against criminal elements generally would not be viewed as taking a direct part in hostilities (and do not forfeit their protection from being made the object of attack).[311] However, providing such services to defend against enemy armed forces of a State would be regarded as taking a direct part in hostilities (and would forfeit their protection from being made the object of attack).[312]

DoD policies have addressed the use of non-military personnel to provide security services for DoD components.[313] Where there has been a significant risk of attack by enemy armed forces of a State, DoD practice generally has been to use military personnel to provide security.

4.15.3 Persons Authorized to Accompany the Armed Forces – Detention. For the purposes of detention, persons authorized to accompany the armed forces are treated like combatants. These persons may be detained by the enemy and are entitled to POW status during

---

[310] DoD Instruction 3020.41, *Operational Contract Support (OCS)*, E-2 ¶3.j (Dec. 20, 2011) ("Defense contractors or their personnel are responsible for providing their own personal clothing, including casual and working clothing required by the assignment. Generally, commanders shall not issue military clothing to contractor personnel or allow the wearing of military or military look-alike uniforms. However, a CCDR [Combatant Commander] or subordinate JFC [Joint Force Commander] deployed forward may authorize contractor personnel to wear standard uniform items for operational reasons. Contracts shall require that this authorization be in writing and maintained in the possession of authorized contractor personnel at all times. When commanders issue any type of standard uniform item to contractor personnel, care must be taken to ensure, consistent with force protection measures, that contractor personnel are distinguishable from military personnel through the use of distinctive patches, arm bands, nametags, or headgear.").

[311] *Compare* § 4.23.1 (Police as Civilians).

[312] *Refer to* § 5.8.3.1 (Examples of Taking a Direct Part in Hostilities).

[313] *For example*, DoD Instruction 3020.50, *Private Security Contractors Operating in Contingency Operations, Humanitarian or Peace Operations, or Other Military Operations or Exercises* (Jul. 22, 2009, Incorporating Change 1, Aug. 1, 2011).

international armed conflict.[314]

When held as POWs, persons authorized to accompany the armed forces are to receive advance of pay from the Detaining Power, and they should be assigned equivalent ranks to those of members of the armed forces for this purpose.[315]

Persons who are authorized to accompany the armed forces must be issued an identity card to confirm their status.[316] Presenting the identification card is not a prerequisite for POW status, but it helps captured persons establish to enemy forces that they are entitled to POW status.[317]

4.15.4 Persons Authorized to Accompany the Armed Forces – Liability Under Domestic Law for Participation in Hostilities. Unlike combatants, persons authorized to accompany the armed forces receive no general license to participate in hostilities. However, international law contemplates that persons authorized to accompany the armed forces may lawfully support armed forces in the conduct of hostilities. Such persons should not be liable under an enemy State's domestic law for providing authorized support services.[318] For example, they should not be prosecuted for offenses of aiding the enemy. Persons authorized to accompany the armed forces may not be punished by an enemy State for authorized support activities or for defending themselves against unlawful attacks. This protection would not apply with respect to acts by persons authorized to accompany the armed forces that are prohibited by the law of war.

---

[314] *See* GPW art. 4(A)(4) (defining "prisoners of war, in the sense of the present Convention," to include persons who have fallen into the power of the enemy and "who accompany the armed forces without actually being members thereof, such as civilian members of military aircraft crews, war correspondents, supply contractors, members of labour units or of services responsible for the welfare of the armed forces, provided that they have received authorization from the armed forces which they accompany,"); 1929 GPW art. 81 ("Persons who follow the armed forces without directly belonging thereto, such as correspondents, newspaper reporters, sutlers, or contractors, who fall into the hands of the enemy, and whom the latter think fit to detain, shall be entitled to be treated as prisoners of war, provided they are in possession of an authorization from the military authorities of the armed forces which they were following."); HAGUE IV REG. art. 13 ("Individuals who follow an army without directly belonging to it, such as newspaper correspondents and reporters, sutlers and contractors, who fall into the enemy's hands and whom the latter thinks expedient to detain, are entitled to be treated as prisoners of war, provided they are in possession of a certificate from the military authorities of the army which they were accompanying."); LIEBER CODE art. 50 ("Moreover, citizens who accompany an army for whatever purpose, such as sutlers, editors, or reporters of journals, or contractors, if captured, may be made prisoners of war, and be detained as such.").

[315] *Refer to* § 9.18.3 (Advance of Pay).

[316] *Refer to* § 9.4.3 (Issue of Identification Cards to Persons Liable to Become POWs).

[317] *Refer to* § 4.27.1 (Identification Cards Used to Help Clarify Status).

[318] *See* BOTHE, PARTSCH, & SOLF, NEW RULES 304 (AP I art. 51, ¶2.4.2.2) ("As civilians, they have no general right to take part in hostilities, but some activities of these persons could amount to direct participation if done in the midst of an ongoing engagement. For example, it is common practice to have civilian technical advisers assist and advise in the installation and maintenance of sophisticated command and control or target acquisition equipment. Repair of a target acquisition or missile guidance equipment in the midst of battle would probably be regarded as direct participation in hostilities. As in the case of a sick bay on a warship, the immunity from attack is academic, except with respect to individualized attack against the protected person within a military objective. The issue becomes practically significant only if an attempt is made to subject such a civilian to penal sanction for his unauthorized participation in hostilities. Under US practice support activities behind the lines of battle is not subject to penal sanction, although the support activity may be the legitimate object of attack.").

Persons authorized to accompany the armed forces should not engage in unauthorized participation in hostilities. Such activity would be treated like engagement in private acts of hostility,[319] and such persons would be in the position of unprivileged belligerents in relation to those activities.[320]

There may be additional considerations in determining which prosecution forum is appropriate because persons authorized to accompany the armed forces are not themselves members of the armed forces.[321]

Commanders who use persons authorized to accompany the armed forces could, under certain circumstances, be prosecuted for war crimes committed by such personnel under theories of command responsibility or other theories of individual liability.[322]

4.16 Crews of Merchant Marine Vessels or Civil Aircraft

Crews of merchant marine vessels or civil aircraft of a belligerent fall into a special category, and are in many respects treated like persons authorized to accompany the armed forces.[323] Under certain circumstances, crews of merchant marine vessels or civil aircraft of a neutral that engage in hostilities may be treated like the crews of belligerent vessels or aircraft.[324]

4.16.1 Merchant or Civil Crews - Conduct of Hostilities. Merchant vessels or civil aircraft of a belligerent may be used to support military operations, such as by conveying goods and military personnel to theaters of active military operations.

Enemy merchant vessels or civil aircraft may be captured.[325] Belligerent merchant vessels or civil aircraft may resist attacks by enemy forces, including by eventually seizing the attacking vessels or aircraft.[326] However, merchant vessels or civil aircraft should not commit hostile acts in offensive combat operations.[327]

---

[319] *Refer to* § 4.18 (Private Persons Who Engage in Hostilities).

[320] *Refer to* § 4.19 (Rights, Duties, and Liabilities of Unprivileged Belligerents).

[321] *Refer to* § 18.19.4.1 (Limits on Military Jurisdiction Over U.S. Citizens Who Are Not Members of the Armed Forces).

[322] *Refer to* § 18.23.3 (Command Responsibility); § 18.23 (Theories of Individual Criminal Liability).

[323] *Refer to* § 4.15 (Persons Authorized to Accompany the Armed Forces).

[324] *Refer to* § 15.14 (Acquisition of Enemy Character by Neutral-Flagged Merchant Vessels and Neutral-Marked Civil Aircraft).

[325] *Refer to* § 13.5 (Enemy Merchant Vessels).

[326] LAUTERPACHT, II OPPENHEIM'S INTERNATIONAL LAW 266 (§85) ("In a sense, the crews of merchantmen owned by subjects of a belligerent belong to its armed forces. For those vessels are liable to be seized by enemy men-of-war, and, if attacked for that purpose, they may defend themselves, may return the attack, and eventually seize the attacking men-of-war. The crews of merchant men become in such cases combatants, and enjoy all the privileges of the members of the armed forces.").

[327] LAUTERPACHT, II OPPENHEIM'S INTERNATIONAL LAW 266 (§85) ("But, unless attacked, they must not commit hostilities, and if they do so they are liable to be treated as criminals, just as are private individuals who commit hostilities in land warfare.").

4.16.2 Merchant or Civil Crews – Detention. Members of the crews of merchant marine vessels or civil aircraft of a belligerent are entitled to POW status, if they fall into the power of the enemy during international armed conflict.[328]

The GPW contemplates that certain members of the crews of merchant marine vessels or civil aircraft of a belligerent may benefit from more favorable treatment under international law; *i.e.*, they would not be detained as POWs. During wartime, enemy merchant seamen have customarily been subject to capture and detention.[329] However, the 1907 Hague XI provides that the crews of enemy merchant ships that did not take part in hostilities were not to be held as POWs provided "that they make a formal promise in writing, not to undertake, while hostilities last, any service connected with the operations of the war."[330] Although these provisions proved ineffective during World War I and World War II,[331] the GPW allows for the possibility that they might apply.[332]

4.17 Spies, Saboteurs, and Other Persons Engaging in Similar Acts Behind Enemy Lines

Spying, sabotage, and similar acts behind enemy lines have a dual character under the law of war; States are permitted to employ persons who engage in these activities, but these activities are punishable by the enemy State.

Belligerents may employ spies and saboteurs consistent with the law of war. However, any person (including individuals who would otherwise receive the privileges of lawful combatants) engaging in spying, sabotage, or similar acts behind enemy lines, is regarded as an unprivileged belligerent while doing so. These persons forfeit entitlement to the privileges of combatant status and may be punished after a fair trial if captured.

---

[328] GPW art. 4A(5) (defining "prisoners of war, in the sense of the present Convention," to include "[m]embers of crews, including masters, pilots and apprentices, of the merchant marine and the crews of civil aircraft of the Parties to the conflict, who do not benefit by more favourable treatment under any other provisions of international law" who have fallen into the power of the enemy).

[329] GPW COMMENTARY 65 ("In the past, it was generally recognized that in time of war merchant seamen were liable to capture.").

[330] *See* HAGUE XI art. 6 ("The captain, officers, and members of the crew, when nationals of the enemy State, are not made prisoners of war, on condition that they make a formal promise in writing, not to undertake, while hostilities last, any service connected with the operations of the war."); HAGUE XI art. 8 ("The provisions of the three preceding articles do not apply to ships taking part in the hostilities.").

[331] *See* LEVIE, POWS 63 (explaining that Articles 5-8 of Hague XI "proved ineffective during World War I" and "[d]uring World War II the provisions of the Eleventh Hague Convention of 1907 were again completely disregarded, with the result that there was no assurance as to exactly what the status of a captured merchant seaman would be."). Hague XI had fewer than 30 Parties at that time, and only technically applied when all the belligerents to a conflict were also parties to Hague XI. *See* HAGUE XI art. 9 ("The provisions of the present Convention do not apply except between Contracting Powers, and then only if all the belligerents are parties to the Convention."). Hague XI did not apply during World War II for this reason. *See* II-A FINAL RECORD OF THE DIPLOMATIC CONFERENCE OF GENEVA OF 1949 419 (UK representative noting that "[t]he provisions of the Eleventh Hague Convention were not applied during the last War, owing to the fact that all the belligerent States were not parties to it.").

[332] For further background *see* II-A FINAL RECORD OF THE DIPLOMATIC CONFERENCE OF GENEVA OF 1949 238-39, 418-19.

4.17.1 Spies, Saboteurs, and Other Persons Engaging in Similar Acts Behind Enemy Lines – Notes on Terminology. Spying has been given a technical definition in the Hague IV Regulations.[333] However, as discussed below, certain conduct, most notably sabotage, has been treated as having the same legal consequences as spying and has even been called spying, even though such acts do not meet the definition of spying in the Hague IV Regulations.[334]

In some cases, "saboteurs" has been used in a purely factual way to refer to those persons engaged in damaging or destroying enemy materiel.[335] In other cases, "saboteurs" has been used as a legal term of art to refer to those persons who are engaged in damaging or destroying enemy material and who, by definition, would not be entitled to receive the privileges of combatant status.[336]

4.17.1.1 *General Usage of "Spies and Saboteurs" in This Manual*. This manual generally uses the term "spying and sabotage" to refer to that general category of secretive, hostile activities that, when performed behind enemy lines, deprives that person of entitlement to the privileges of combatant status. In some places, the phrase "spying, sabotage, and similar acts behind enemy lines" is used to make more clear that this general category of acts is broader than only spying and sabotage.

4.17.2 Spies. A person may only be considered a spy when, (1) acting clandestinely or under false pretenses, (2) in the zone of operations of a belligerent, (3) he or she obtains, or endeavors to obtain, information, (4) with the intention of communicating it to the hostile party.[337] During war, any person—military or civilian—whose actions meet all of these elements may be considered a spy under the law of war.

---

[333] *Refer to* § 4.17.2 (Spies).

[334] *Refer to* § 4.17.3 (Saboteurs and Other Persons Engaging in Secretive, Hostile Acts Behind Enemy Lines).

[335] 1958 UK MANUAL ¶331 ("Whether saboteurs, *i.e.*, persons dropped or landed behind the lines of the belligerent in order to commit acts of destruction and terrorism, are to be treated as spies depends on whether they are caught in disguise or not. If they are disguised in civilian clothing or in the uniform of the army by which they are caught or that of an ally of that army, they are in the same position as spies. If caught in their own uniform, they are entitled to be treated as prisoners of war.").

[336] II-A FINAL REPORT OF THE DIPLOMATIC CONFERENCE OF GENEVA OF 1949 621 (Norwegian representative explaining that "[s]aboteurs could not of course claim protection under the Prisoners of War Convention; they should nevertheless be protected against criminal treatment and torture.").

[337] HAGUE IV REG. art. 29 ("A person can only be considered a spy when, acting clandestinely or on false pretences, he obtains or endeavours to obtain information in the zone of operations of a belligerent, with the intention of communicating it to the hostile party."); LIEBER CODE art. 88 ("A spy is a person who secretly, in disguise or under false pretense, seeks information with the intention of communicating it to the enemy."); *id.* at art. 83 ("Scouts, or single soldiers, if disguised in the dress of the country or in the uniform of the army hostile to their own, employed in obtaining information, if found within or lurking about the lines of the captor, are treated as spies, and suffer death."); WINTHROP, MILITARY LAW & PRECEDENTS 766-67 ("A spy is a person who, without authority and secretly, or under a false pretext, contrives to enter within the lines of an army for the purpose of obtaining material information and communicating it to the enemy; or one who, being by authority within the lines, attempts secretly to accomplish such purpose."). *Consider* AP I art. 46(3) ("A member of the armed forces of a Party to the conflict who is a resident of territory occupied by an adverse Party and who, on behalf of the Party on which he depends, gathers or attempts to gather information of military value within that territory shall not be considered as engaging in espionage unless he does so through an act of false pretences or deliberately in a clandestine manner.").

The following discussion elaborates upon the elements of spying.

4.17.2.1 <u>*Acting Clandestinely or Under False Pretenses*</u>. Acting "clandestinely or under false pretenses" means deliberately concealing or misrepresenting one's identity and conduct.[338] For example, a member of the armed forces fulfills this element when the person wears a disguise, such as civilian clothes or the uniform of the enemy, so that the enemy will fail to identify the person as a member of the opposing armed force.

Persons who act openly, such as by wearing the uniform of the armed forces to which they belong, do not meet this element.[339] For example, members of a ground reconnaissance team or couriers who wear their normal uniforms would not meet this element.[340] In addition, observers on military reconnaissance aircraft have not been regarded as acting clandestinely or under false pretenses.[341]

4.17.2.2 <u>*In the Zone of Operations of a Belligerent*</u>. A person must engage in acts of espionage in the zone of operations of a belligerent to be considered a spy.[342] "Zone of operations" has been construed broadly to include areas supporting the war effort.[343] However, a person who engages in surveillance or information gathering from outside territory controlled by

---

[338] *See* WINTHROP, MILITARY LAW & PRECEDENTS 767 ("The clandestine character of [the spy's] proceedings and the deception thus practised constitute the gist or rather aggravation of the offence of the spy."); 1958 UK MANUAL ¶330 ("The principal characteristic of the offence of espionage is disguise and secrecy in action."). *Consider* AP I art. 46(3) ("A member of the armed forces of a Party to the conflict who is a resident of territory occupied by an adverse Party and who, on behalf of the Party on which he depends, gathers or attempts to gather information of military value within that territory shall not be considered as engaging in espionage unless he does so through an act of false pretences or deliberately in a clandestine manner.").

[339] *See* HAGUE IV REG. art. 29 ("[S]oldiers not wearing a disguise who have penetrated into the zone of operations of the hostile army, for the purpose of obtaining information, are not considered spies."). *Consider* AP I art. 46(2) ("A member of the armed forces of a Party to the conflict who, on behalf of that Party and in territory controlled by an adverse Party, gathers or attempts to gather information shall not be considered as engaging in espionage if, while so acting, he is in the uniform of his armed forces.").

[340] *See* HAGUE IV REG. art. 29 ("Soldiers and civilians, carrying out their mission openly, intrusted with the delivery of despatches intended either for their own army or for the enemy's army" are not considered spies).

[341] *See* HAGUE IV REG. art. 29 ("Persons sent in balloons for the purpose of carrying despatches and, generally, of maintaining communications between the different parts of an army or a territory" are not considered spies.); WINTHROP, MILITARY LAW & PRECEDENTS 768-69 ("[T]he mere observing of the enemy, with a view to gain intelligence of his movements, does not constitute [spying], for this may be done, and in active service is constantly done, as a legitimate act of war … . Observing the enemy from a balloon is no more criminal than any other form of reconnaissance.").

[342] *See, e.g.*, Ex Parte Quirin, 317 U.S. 1, 31 (1942) (characterizing a spy as one "who secretly and without uniform <u>passes the military lines of a belligerent</u> in time of war, seeking to gather military information and communicate it to the enemy") (emphasis added).

[343] *See* United States ex rel. Wessels v. McDonald, 265 F. 754, 763-64 (E.D.N.Y. 1920) ("In this great World War through which we have just passed, the field of operations which existed after the United States entered the war, and, especially in regard to naval operations, brought the port of New York within the field of active operations."). *Cf.* Ex parte Quirin, 317 U.S. 1, 37 (1942) ("The law of war cannot rightly treat those agents of enemy armies who enter our territory, armed with explosives intended for the destruction of war industries and supplies, as any the less belligerent enemies than are agents similarly entering for the purpose of destroying fortified places or our Armed Forces.").

a hostile party would not meet this element, and would not be considered a spy.

4.17.2.3 *Obtains, or Endeavors to Obtain, Information*. A person may be punished as a spy regardless of whether that person succeeds in obtaining information or in transmitting it to the enemy.[344] A person, however, must obtain or attempt to obtain information to be considered a spy.

4.17.2.4 *With the Intention of Communicating It to the Hostile Party*. A person must act with the intention of communicating the sought-after information to a hostile party to the conflict to be considered a spy within the meaning of this rule.

However, a person who seeks to send information to a State not involved in the conflict may still commit acts punishable by the offended State, and that person's conduct may fall within the broader category of secretive, hostile acts behind enemy lines.[345]

4.17.3 Saboteurs and Other Persons Engaging in Secretive, Hostile Acts Behind Enemy Lines. In addition to spies, other persons acting clandestinely or under false pretenses with a hostile purpose behind enemy lines have also been treated like spies under the law of war.

Like spies, persons engaged in these secretive, hostile activities behind enemy lines have also been deprived of the privileges of combatant status and often been punished. For example, saboteurs[346] acting clandestinely or under false pretenses in the zone of operations of a belligerent are treated as spies.[347] However, activities besides sabotage that are helpful to one side's war effort that are done behind the other side's lines have been punishable as well, often under the rubric of "war treason,"[348] "secretly entering the lines,"[349] or "activities hostile to the

---

[344] *See* LIEBER CODE art. 88 ("The spy is punishable ... whether or not he succeed in obtaining the information or in conveying it to the enemy."); WINTHROP, MILITARY LAW & PRECEDENTS 768 ("The fact that [one] was 'lurking' or 'acting' with intent to obtain material information, to be communicated by himself or another to the enemy, is all that is required to complete the offence.").

[345] *Refer to* § 4.17.3 (Saboteurs and Other Persons Engaging in Secretive, Hostile Acts Behind Enemy Lines).

[346] 2001 CANADIAN MANUAL ¶610(1) ("Saboteurs are persons operating behind the lines of an adverse party to commit acts of destruction."); GC COMMENTARY 57 ("Sabotage is harder to define, as no definition of it is given in any text in international law. The term 'sabotage' [in article 5 of the GC] should be understood to mean acts whose object or effect is to damage or destroy material belonging to the army of occupation or utilized by it.").

[347] 2001 CANADIAN MANUAL ¶610(3) ("Civilian saboteurs or saboteurs not in uniform are not so protected [i.e., entitled to POW status] and are liable to be treated as spies. Such civilian saboteurs and saboteurs not in uniform may be tried in accordance with the law of the captor and may face the death penalty. They must not, however, be punished without a fair trial."); 1958 UK MANUAL ¶331 ("Whether saboteurs, *i.e.*, persons dropped or landed behind the lines of the belligerent in order to commit acts of destruction and terrorism, are to be treated as spies depends on whether they are caught in disguise or not. If they are disguised in civilian clothing or in the uniform of the army by which they are caught or that of an ally of that army, they are in the same position as spies. If caught in their own uniform, they are entitled to be treated as prisoners of war.").

[348] *See* GREENSPAN, MODERN LAW OF LAND WARFARE 330 ("The characteristic which unites all acts of war treason is that they are hostile acts committed inside the area controlled by the belligerent against whom the acts are directed by persons who do not possess the status of combatants."); LAUTERPACHT, II OPPENHEIM'S INTERNATIONAL LAW 575 (§255) ("So-called 'war treason' consists of all such acts (except hostilities in arms on the part of the civilian population, spreading of seditious propaganda by aircraft, and espionage) committed within the lines of a belligerent as are harmful to him and are intended to favour the enemy."); LIEBER CODE art. 90 ("A traitor under the law of war,

security of the State."[350]

These kinds of activities almost necessarily take on the character of spying.[351] In many cases, these actions have been reported as spying.[352] However, the actual purpose of these activities may not be to gain or transmit intelligence information, but to take other sorts of actions that would further the war effort.

Thus, a belligerent's presence on the territory controlled by an opposing State with a hostile purpose while clandestinely or under false pretenses, suffices to make that person liable to treatment as a spy under the law of war.[353]

4.17.4 Spying and Sabotage Permissible Under the Law of War. Under the law of war,

---

or a war-traitor, is a person in a place or district under Martial Law who, unauthorized by the military commander, gives information of any kind to the enemy, or holds intercourse with him.").

[349] Ex parte Quirin, 317 U.S. 1, 31 (1942) (giving as an example of an unprivileged belligerent "an enemy combatant who without uniform comes secretly through the lines for the purpose of waging war by destruction of life or property"); WINTHROP, MILITARY LAW & PRECEDENTS 786 ("A similar though less aggravated offence against the laws of war is that of officers, soldiers, or agents, of one belligerent who come secretly within the lines of the other, or within the territory held by his forces, for any unauthorized purpose other than that of the spy, as, for example, for the purpose of recruiting for their army, obtaining horses or supplies for the same, holding unlawful communication, &c.,--a class of offences of which instances were not unfrequent in the border States during our late civil war.").

[350] GC art. 5 ("Where in the territory of a Party to the conflict, the latter is satisfied that an individual protected person is definitely suspected of or engaged in activities hostile to the security of the State, such individual person shall not be entitled to claim such rights and privileges under the present Convention as would, if exercised in the favour of such individual person, be prejudicial to the security of such State.").

[351] 1958 UK MANUAL ¶331 note 1 ("A question may arise if a saboteur, being a member of the armed forces, is caught in civilian clothes worn over or under his military uniform. It may be difficult to accept the defence that the intention was to shed the civilian clothing before the commission of the offence. Sabotage operations behind the enemy lines are frequently carried out by members of the armed forces in uniform who, upon completion of their mission, make their way to the nearest neutral territory with a view to returning to their own country. If when engaged in sabotage or subsequent evading action they are discovered in civilian clothing worn over their uniform or underneath it they run the risk of being treated as spies and not merely as members of the armed forces engaged in a sabotage mission. … It may well be that a sabotage mission behind the enemy lines inevitably takes on the added character of espionage, unless uniform is worn throughout the stay in enemy territory.").

[352] L. Oppenheim, *On War Treason*, 33 LAW QUARTERLY REVIEW 266 (1917) ("Thus, in 1780, during the American War of Independence, Major André was convicted and hanged as a spy, although he was not seeking information but was returning after having negotiated treason with General Arnold; it was a case of war treason. And the Japanese Major Shozo Jakoga and Captain Teisuki Oki, who in the summer of 1904, during the Russo-Japanese War, were caught, disguised in Chinese clothes, in the attempt to destroy, with the aid of dynamite, a railway bridge in Manchuria in the rear of the Russian forces—a clear case of war treason—would previous to the Hague Regulations surely have been executed as spies; in fact the case was reported in the newspapers as one of espionage.").

[353] Ex parte Quirin, 317 U.S. 1, 38 (1942) ("[E]ach petitioner, in circumstances which gave him the status of an enemy belligerent, passed our military and naval lines and defenses or went behind those lines, in civilian dress and with hostile purpose. The offense was complete when with that purpose they entered — or, having so entered, they remained upon — our territory in time of war without uniform or other appropriate means of identification.").

belligerents may employ spies and saboteurs.[354]

Spying and sabotage are not prohibited by any law of war treaty to which the United States is a Party. For example, spying and sabotage are not prohibited by the 1949 Geneva Conventions, nor defined as a "grave breach" of those conventions.[355] Similarly, spying and sabotage also have not been listed as war crimes punishable under the statutes of international criminal tribunals.[356] In addition, law of war treaties that regulate, but do not prohibit, spying, recognize implicitly that belligerents may use this method of warfare.[357]

Although spying and sabotage are not prohibited by the law of war, acting clandestinely or under false pretenses could, in some circumstances, constitute "feigning a protected status," one of the elements of perfidy.[358] Persons engaged in these activities and commanders who employ them should take special care not to kill or wound by resort to perfidy.

4.17.5 Spying and Sabotage – Forfeiture of the Privileges of Combatant Status. Although the law of war allows belligerents to employ spies, saboteurs, and other persons engaged in secretive hostile activities behind enemy lines, the law of war also permits belligerents to take additional measures to defend against these persons.

These individuals, by acting clandestinely or under false pretenses, fail to distinguish themselves as combatants generally must do.[359] Thus, persons otherwise entitled to privileges of combatant status, including POW status, forfeit their entitlement to those privileges while engaged in spying, sabotage, or other hostile, secretive activities behind enemy lines.[360] Although not explicitly reflected in the GPW, this understanding was the general understanding at the 1949 Diplomatic Conference[361] and is reflected in other treaties,[362] judicial decisions,[363]

---

[354] *See* United States v. List, *et al.* (The Hostage Case), XI TRIALS OF WAR CRIMINALS BEFORE THE NMT 1245 ("By the law of war it is lawful to use spies."); Richard R. Baxter, *So-Called 'Unprivileged Belligerency': Spies, Guerillas, and Saboteurs*, 28 BRITISH YEAR BOOK OF INTERNATIONAL LAW 323, 333 (1951) (noting that "espionage is regarded a conventional weapon of war, being neither treacherous nor productive of unnecessary suffering").

[355] *Refer to* § 18.9.5 (War Crimes – Notes on Terminology).

[356] *See, e.g., Charter of the International Military Tribunal*, art. 6, annexed to Agreement by the Government of the United Kingdom of Great Britain and Northern Ireland, the Government of the United States of America, the Provisional Government of the French Republic and the Government of the Union of Soviet Socialist Republics for the Prosecution and Punishment of the Major War Criminals of the European Axis, Aug. 8, 1945, 82 UNTS 280, 288; ICTY STATUTE arts. 2-5; ICTR STATUTE arts. 2-4. *Consider* ROME STATUTE arts. 5-8.

[357] *See* HAGUE IV REG. arts. 24, 29-31 (governing the classification, conduct, and treatment of spies). *Consider* AP I art. 46 (same).

[358] *See* § 5.22.1 (Definition of Perfidy).

[359] *Refer to* § 5.14.5 (Carrying Arms Openly and Wearing of Distinctive Emblems by the Armed Forces to Distinguish Themselves From the Civilian Population).

[360] *Compare* § 4.6.1.3 (Application of GPW 4A(2) Conditions to the Armed Forces of a State).

[361] II-A FINAL RECORD OF THE DIPLOMATIC CONFERENCE OF GENEVA OF 1949 509 (noting the UK representative's statement that "spies ... according to general opinion, should not have the benefits of the privileges accorded by" the GPW); II-A FINAL REPORT OF THE DIPLOMATIC CONFERENCE OF GENEVA OF 1949 621 (Norwegian representative explaining that "Saboteurs could not of course claim protection under the Prisoners of War Convention; they should nevertheless be protected against criminal treatment and torture.").

military manuals,[364] and scholarly works.[365]

4.17.5.1 Liability of Persons Not Captured While Spying for Previous Acts of Espionage. Persons who qualify for the privileges of combatant status who engage in spying, and then return to friendly lines, incur no responsibility or liability for previous acts of espionage.[366] Persons who have never qualified for the privileges of combatant status would not

---

[362] *See* HAGUE IV REG. art. 31 (impliedly contrasting the position of a spy captured while spying with a "spy who, after rejoining the army to which he belongs, is subsequently captured by the enemy, is treated as a prisoner of war, and incurs no responsibility for his previous acts of espionage."). *Consider* AP I art. 46 (1) ("Notwithstanding any other provision of the Conventions or of this Protocol, any member of the armed forces of a Party to the conflict who falls into the power of an adverse Party while engaging in espionage shall not have the right to the status of prisoner of war and may be treated as a spy."); AP I art. 44(4) ("A combatant who falls into the power of an adverse Party while failing to meet the requirements set forth in the second sentence of paragraph 3 [certain obligations to distinguish himself during military engagements] shall forfeit his right to be a prisoner of war, but he shall, nevertheless, be given protections equivalent in all respects to those accorded to prisoners of war by the Third Convention and by this Protocol. This protection includes protections equivalent to those accorded to prisoners of war by the Third Convention in the case where such a person is tried and punished for any offences he has committed.").

[363] *See, e.g.*, Ex parte Quirin, 317 U.S. 1, 31 (1942) (describing spies as "familiar examples of belligerents who are generally deemed not to be entitled to the status of prisoners of war"); *Mohamad Ali and Another v. Public Prosecutor* [1969] A.C. 430 (P.C.) (appeal taken from U.K.), LEVIE, DOCUMENTS ON POWS 766 ("[A]ppellants, if they were members of the Indonesian armed forces, were not entitled to be treated on capture as prisoners of war under the Geneva Convention when they had landed to commit sabotage and had been dressed in civilian clothes both when they had placed the explosives and lit them and when they were arrested.").

[364] 2001 CANADIAN MANUAL ¶320(1) ("Generally speaking, persons engaging in espionage may be attacked and if captured while doing so shall NOT have the right to the status of prisoner of war."); 1992 GERMAN MANUAL ¶321 ("Even if they are members of their armed forces, they do not have the right to the status of prisoner of war."); 1958 UK MANUAL ¶96 (noting that "regular members of the armed forces who are caught as spies are not entitled to be treated as prisoners of war"); 1956 FM 27-10 (Change No. 1 1976) ¶74 ("Members of the armed forces of a party to the conflict and members of militias or volunteer corps forming part of such armed forces lose their right to be treated as prisoners of war whenever they deliberately conceal their status in order to pass behind the military lines of the enemy for the purpose of gathering military information or for the purpose of waging war by destruction of life or property.").

[365] LEVIE, POWS 82-83 (noting that "[e]ven individuals who fall within the categories specifically enumerated in Article 4 are not entitled to prisoner-of-war status if, at the time of capture by the enemy, they were dressed in civilian clothes and were engaged in an espionage or sabotage mission behind enemy lines"); WINTHROP, MILITARY LAW & PRECEDENTS 769 ("A spy, under capture, is not treated as a prisoner of war but as an outlaw, and is to be tried and punished as such.").

[366] *See* HAGUE IV REG. art. 31 ("A spy who, after rejoining the army to which he belongs, is subsequently captured by the enemy, is treated as a prisoner of war, and incurs no responsibility for his previous acts of espionage."); LIEBER CODE art. 104 (explaining that "[a] successful spy or war-traitor, safely returned to his own army, and afterwards captured as an enemy, is not subject to punishment for his acts as a spy or war-traitor"); Rieger, Dalloz Hebdomadaire (France, Cour de Cassation, Jul. 29, 1948), summarized in 44 AJIL 422 (1950) ("The court sustained the acquittal of a German national who, after mobilization as a German army officer, had been in France a spy and a recruiter of spies, but had not been apprehended until after he had rejoined the German Army and been demobilized in Germany."); In re Martin, 45 BARB. 142, 148 (New York County Supreme Court, Dec. 4, 1865) (Court directed the release of a prisoner who "was not taken in the act of committing the offense charged against him, of being a spy. He had returned within the lines of the confederate forces, or had otherwise escaped, so that he was not arrested till after the confederate armies had surrendered, been disbanded and sent to their homes, with the promise that they should not be further disturbed if they remained there and engaged in peaceful pursuits."). *Consider* AP I arts. 46(3), 46(4) (referring to persons who "engage in espionage in [the] territory" of a hostile party, and noting that a person "may not be treated as a spy unless he is captured while engaging in espionage").

benefit from this rule because they cannot regain a status that they did not receive in the first place.[367]

4.17.5.2 *Cases of Doubt*. During international armed conflict, should there be any doubt as to whether persons suspected of committing a belligerent act and having fallen into the hands of the enemy are entitled to POW status, such persons are entitled to have their status determined by a competent tribunal and should be treated as POWs pending that determination.[368]

4.18 PRIVATE PERSONS WHO ENGAGE IN HOSTILITIES

In general, private persons who engage in hostilities forfeit many of the protections to which members of the civilian population are entitled, and are liable to treatment in one or more respects as unprivileged belligerents.[369]

4.18.1 Private Persons Who Engage in Hostilities – Notes on Terminology. This section refers to "private persons" who engage in hostilities rather than "civilians" who engage in hostilities for three reasons. First, an emphasis on "private" persons is consistent with longstanding explanations of the principle of distinction.[370] Second, it may be analytically unhelpful to focus on "civilians" because private persons who engage in hostilities are liable to treatment in one or more respects as combatants. Third, non-military personnel belonging to a State (*e.g.*, persons authorized to accompany the armed forces), who are often called "civilians," raise a different set of issues that merit special consideration as opposed to the general case of a private person who decides to engage in hostilities.

For the purpose of applying different law of war rules, different formulations have been used to describe when a person has engaged in hostilities. Although these phrases often refer to the same conduct, the context in which each term is applied is important; whether a phrase includes a particular type of conduct may depend on the particular legal rule in question. Whether a particular person is liable as a consequence of his or her conduct to treatment as a combatant (*e.g.*, being made the object of attack, internment, or prosecution for acts of unprivileged belligerency) must be assessed with reference to the specific legal rule at issue rather than based on the use of a conclusory label, such as "enemy combatant."[371]

---

[367] *See* LAUTERPACHT, II OPPENHEIM'S INTERNATIONAL LAW 424-25 (§161) ("But Article 31 applies only to spies who belong to the armed forces of the enemy; civilians who act as spies, and are captured later, may be punished."). *Cf.* HAGUE IV REG. art. 31 (referring only to a spy who rejoins "the army to which he belongs" in connection with protection against subsequent prosecution).

[368] *Refer to* § 4.27.2 (POW Protections for Certain Persons Until Status Has Been Determined).

[369] *Refer to* § 4.19 (Rights, Duties, and Liabilities of Unprivileged Belligerents).

[370] *See, e.g.*, LIEBER CODE arts. 22 and 23 ("Nevertheless, as civilization has advanced during the last centuries, so has likewise steadily advanced, especially in war on land, the distinction between the private individual belonging to a hostile country and the hostile country itself, with its men in arms. ... Private citizens are no longer murdered, enslaved, or carried off to distant parts, and the inoffensive individual is as little disturbed in his private relations as the commander of the hostile troops can afford to grant In the overruling demands of a vigorous war.").

[371] *See* Harold Hongju Koh, Legal Adviser, Department of State, *Address at the Annual Meeting of the American Society of International Law: The Obama Administration and International Law*, Mar. 25, 2010, 2010 DIGEST OF

This manual generally uses the phrase "engaging in hostilities" in a broad sense to refer to any of those actions that could cause a person to forfeit one or more protections under the law of war. When discussing specific legal rules, on the other hand, this manual uses the particular language of the rule at issue, rather than the phrase "engaging in hostilities." For example, this manual generally reserves the use of the phrase "taking a direct part in hostilities" to address the rule applicable when a civilian forfeits his or her protection from being made the object of attack.[372]

4.18.2 Private Persons Who Engage in Hostilities – Denial of the Distinct Protections Afforded Peaceful Civilians. Private persons who engage in hostilities forfeit many of the protections afforded civilians under the law of war.[373] The principle of military necessity can justify taking military action (such as detention) to address the threat posed by such persons.[374] The forfeiture of many of the protections of civilian status is also reflected in the principle that a person may not claim the distinct rights of both combatants and civilians at the same time.[375]

4.18.3 Private Persons Who Engage in Hostilities – Lack of the Privileges of Combatant Status. Private persons who engage in hostilities are not entitled to the privileges of combatant status and may be punished, after a fair trial.[376] The law of war does not condone the "farmer by

---

UNITED STATES PRACTICE IN INTERNATIONAL LAW 749 ("Some commentators have criticized our decision to detain certain individuals based on their membership in a non-state armed group. But as those of you who follow the Guantánamo habeas litigation know, we have defended this position based on the AUMF, as informed by the text, structure, and history of the Geneva Conventions and other sources of the laws of war. Moreover, while the various judges who have considered these arguments have taken issue with certain points, they have accepted the overall proposition that individuals who are part of an organized armed group like Al Qaeda can be subject to law-of-war detention for the duration of the current conflict. In sum, we have based our authority to detain not on conclusory labels, like 'enemy combatant,' but on whether the factual record in the particular case meets the legal standard.").

372 *Refer to* § 5.8 (Civilians Taking a Direct Part in Hostilities).

373 *See* Joint Chiefs of Staff, Joint Pub. 3-60, *Joint Doctrine for Targeting*, A-2 (Jan. 17, 2002) ("The protection offered civilians carries a strict obligation on the part of civilians not to participate directly in armed combat, become combatants, or engage in acts of war. Civilians engaging in fighting or otherwise participating in combat operations, singularly or as a group, become unlawful combatants and lose their protected civilian status."); 1992 GERMAN MANUAL ¶517 ("Persons taking a direct part in hostilities are not entitled to claim the rights accorded to civilians by international humanitarian law (Art. 51 para 3 AP I; Art. 13 para 3 AP II). The same applies if they are they are definitely suspected of activities hostile to the security of the State (Art. 5 para 1 GC IV)."); 1956 FM 27-10 (Change No. 1 1976) ¶60 ("Persons who are not members of the armed forces, as defined in Article 4, *GPW*, who bear arms or engage in other conduct hostile to the enemy thereby deprive themselves of many of the privileges attaching to the members of the civilian population (see sec. II of this chapter).").

374 *Refer to* § 2.2.1 (Military Necessity as a Justification).

375 *Refer to* § 4.2.2 (No Person May Claim the Distinct Rights Afforded to Both Combatants and Civilians at the Same Time).

376 *See* 1958 UK MANUAL ¶88 (If civilian inhabitants "commit or attempt to commit hostile acts, they are liable to punishment, after a proper trial."); LAUTERPACHT, II OPPENHEIM'S INTERNATIONAL LAW 206 (§57) ("According to a generally recognised customary rule of International Law, hostile acts on the part of private individuals, not organised as compact movements operating under responsible authority, are not acts of legitimate wafare, and the offenders may be punished in accordance with International Law."); United States v. List, *et al.*, XI TRIALS OF WAR CRIMINALS BEFORE THE NMT 1246 ("[T]he rule is established that a civilian who aids, abets, or participates in the fighting is liable to punishment as a war criminal under the laws of war."); LIEBER CODE art. 82 ("Men, or squads of men, who commit hostilities, whether by fighting, or inroads for destruction or plunder, or by raids of any kind, without commission, without being part and portion of the organized hostile army, and without sharing continuously

day and guerilla by night."[377]

The denial of the privileges of combatant status to private persons engaging in hostilities may be justified on the basis that such persons act inconsistently with the *jus ad bellum* principle of competent authority, under which the resort to armed force is a prerogative of the State.[378] These individuals lack the principal qualification for entitlement to the privileges of combatant status—State authorization.[379] This requirement for State authorization has been traced to medieval law of arms.[380]

Denying private persons who engage in hostilities the privileges of combatant status has also been viewed as justified on humanitarian grounds. Private persons who engage in hostilities risk undermining the protections afforded the civilian population.[381] And, private persons who

---

in the war, but who do so with intermitting returns to their homes and avocations, or with the occasional assumption of the semblance of peaceful pursuits, divesting themselves of the character or appearance of soldiers -- such men, or squads of men, are not public enemies, and, therefore, if captured, are not entitled to the privileges of prisoners of war").

[377] BOTHE, PARTSCH, & SOLF, NEW RULES 252 (AP I art. 44, ¶2.7.1) ("[T]he pre-existing rule [*i.e.*, prior to AP I] precluded combatant status and PW status for the persons who engaged in civilian pursuits during the day but fought as a guerilla by night."); SENATE EXECUTIVE REPORT 84-9, *Geneva Conventions for the Protection of War Victims: Report of the Committee on Foreign Relations on Executives D, E, F, and G*, 82nd Congress, First Session, 5 (Jun. 27, 1955) ("In sum, extension of protection to "partisans" [in the GPW] does not embrace that type of partisan who performs the role of farmer by day, guerilla by night. Such individuals remain subject to trial and punishment as unlawful belligerents."); THEODORE WOOLSEY, INTRODUCTION TO THE STUDY OF INTERNATIONAL LAW 216 (§134) (1897) (explaining that "[g]uerilla parties [i.e., armed groups not called out by public authority], however, do not enjoy the full benefit of the laws of war" and instead "are apt to fare worse than either regular troops or an unarmed peasantry" because, inter alia, "they put on and off with ease the character of a soldier").

[378] *Refer to* § 1.11.1.1 (Competent Authority (Right Authority) to Wage War for a Public Purpose).

[379] *Refer to* § 4.6.2 (Belonging to a Party to the Conflict).

[380] G.I.A.D. Draper, *The Status of Combatants and the Question of Guerrilla Warfare*, 45 BRITISH YEAR BOOK OF INTERNATIONAL LAW 173, 175 (1971) ("With the break-up of Christendom the medieval law of arms took shape as the embryonic international law of war. The older idea of knights, men-at-arms and mercenaries 'avowed' by a prince changed to that of armed forces in the service of a territorial, secular state. However, many of the ideas and technical rules of the *jus militare* came through into the new international law of war, including the idea of a right or privilege to fight reserved for military classes and the requirement of a certain 'openness' in the manner of fighting. This 'openness' spells out the older idea of a 'public' war and the rejection of perfidy as abhorrent to the knightly classes. Conversely, those who had not the right to fight met short shrift at the hands of those who had. The marauder and the freebooter acted against, and were outside, 'faith and the law of nations' and were early forms of war criminals."). *See also* M. H. KEEN, THE LAWS OF WAR IN THE LATE MIDDLE AGES 246 (1965) (The medieval law of arms "was a formal and generally accepted law, and its currency helped to establish" the principle that "war, in its proper sense could only be waged by sovereigns.").

[381] GREENSPAN, MODERN LAW OF LAND WARFARE 55 ("If any and every citizen capable of bearing arms is entitled to use them then the distinction between the soldier and the remainder of the population disappears. The result could only expose the civilian element, regardless of sex, to massacre. The enemy soldier, unable to distinguish his foe, aware that any man, woman, boy, or girl in civilian clothes might produce at any moment a concealed weapon to be used against him, would inevitably be disposed to treat soldier and civilian alike, indiscriminately."); Raymund T. Yingling and Robert W. Ginnane, *The Geneva Conventions of 1949*, 46 AJIL 393, 402 (1953) ("While the conditions imposed by the convention for treatment as prisoners of war of members of resistance movements would not have covered many persons acting as 'partisans' during World War II, nevertheless, it is believed that such conditions are the minimum necessary if regular forces are to have any protection against attacks by the civilian population and if any distinction is to be made between combatants and noncombatants. The farmer by day,

engage in hostilities generally have not been trained in the law of war and are not subject to the same disciplinary regime as members of the armed forces.[382] Thus, their participation in hostilities has been associated with the commission of war crimes.[383]

4.18.4 Activities That Constitute "Engaging in Hostilities" by Private Persons. Certain activities constitute "engaging in hostilities," *i.e.*, when done by private persons, make them liable to treatment in one or more respects by the enemy State as unprivileged belligerents.

4.18.4.1 *Being Part of a Hostile, Non-State Armed Group*. Being part of a non-State armed group that is engaged in hostilities against a State is a form of engaging in hostilities that makes private persons liable to treatment in one or more respects as unprivileged belligerents by that State.[384] Being part of a non-State armed group may involve formally joining the group or simply participating sufficiently in its activities to be deemed part of it.

Whether a person has joined a non-State armed group may be a difficult factual question. Non-State armed groups may not use formal indicia of membership (*e.g.*, uniforms or identity cards), or members of these groups may seek to conceal their association with the group.[385] It may be appropriate to use circumstantial or functional information to assess whether a person is part of a non-State armed group.[386]

---

assassin by night, type of 'partisan' cannot be condoned by international law, whatever other justification circumstances may give him."). *Refer to* § 4.6.4 (Having a Fixed Distinctive Sign Recognizable at a Distance), footnote 164 and accompanying text.

[382] *Refer to* § 4.6.3 (Being Commanded by a Person Responsible for His or Her Subordinates).

[383] *See, e.g.*, CHARLES HENRY HYDE, II INTERNATIONAL LAW: CHIEFLY AS INTERPRETED AND APPLIED BY THE UNITED STATES 296 (1922) ("The law of nations, apart from the Hague Regulations above noted, denies belligerent qualifications to guerrilla bands. Such forces wage a warfare which is irregular in point of origin and authority, of discipline, of purpose and of procedure. They may be constituted at the beck of a single individual; they lack uniforms; they are given to pillage and destruction; they take few prisoners and are hence disposed to show slight quarter."); Wharton, *Com. Am. Law*, § 221, VII MOORE'S DIGEST 175 ("If war were to be waged by private parties, operating according to the whims of individual leaders, every place that was seized would be sacked and outraged; and war would be the pretence to satiate private greed and spite.").

[384] *See, e.g.*, In re Guantanamo Bay Litigation, *Respondents' Memorandum Regarding the Government's Detention Authority Relative to Detainees Held at Guantanamo Bay*, Misc. No. 08-442, 5-6 (D.D.C., Mar. 13, 2009) ("Because the use of force includes the power of detention, the United States has the authority to detain those who were part of al-Qaida and Taliban forces. Indeed, long-standing U.S. jurisprudence, as well as law-of-war principles, recognize that members of enemy forces can be detained even if 'they have not actually committed or attempted to commit any act of depredation or entered the theatre or zone of active military operations.' Accordingly, under the AUMF as informed by law-of-war principles, it is enough that an individual was part of al-Qaida or Taliban forces, the principal organizations that fall within the AUMF's authorization of force.") (internal citations omitted); Hamdan v. Rumsfeld, 548 U.S. 557, 693 (2006) (Thomas, J., dissenting) ("For well over a century it has been established that to unite with banditti, jayhawkers, guerillas, or any other unauthorized marauders is a high offence against the laws of war; the offence is complete when the band is organized or joined.") (internal emphasis and quotations omitted).

[385] *Refer to* § 17.5.1.1 (Increased Difficulty in Identifying Enemy Forces and Other Military Objectives).

[386] *See, e.g.*, Bensayah v. Obama, 610 F.3d 718, 725 (D.C. Cir. 2010) ("Although it is clear al Qaeda has, or at least at one time had, a particular organizational structure, … , the details of its structure are generally unknown, … , but it is thought to be somewhat amorphous, … . As a result, it is impossible to provide an exhaustive list of criteria for determining whether an individual is 'part of' al Qaeda. That determination must be made on a case-by-case basis

In addition, non-State armed groups may also rely on individuals who are not members of the groups, but who are functionally part of those organizations. Their support might be particularly important to enable the non-State armed group to conduct and sustain its operations.[387] For example, these individuals might participate sufficiently in the activities of the group or support its operations substantially in a way that is analogous to the support that persons authorized to accompany the armed forces provide to the armed forces.[388] These individuals may be regarded as constructively part of the group, even if they are, in fact, not formal members of the group.[389]

4.18.4.2 *Other Hostile Acts*. In addition to being part of or substantially supporting a hostile, non-State armed group, other hostile acts can make a person liable to treatment in one or more respects as an unprivileged belligerent under the law of war. For example, private persons who bear arms against enemy personnel or who attempt to kill or injure enemy personnel would become liable to being made the object of attack.[390] Performing spying, sabotage, and other hostile activities behind enemy lines would render a person liable to prosecution for such conduct.[391]

4.18.5 Private Persons Who Engage in Hostilities and the Law of War. As in the cases of spying and sabotage, under international law private enemy nationals are not generally regarded as being prohibited from engaging in hostilities during international armed conflict. International law does recognize, however, that opposing States may punish such persons.[392]

---

by using a functional rather than a formal approach and by focusing upon the actions of the individual in relation to the organization.") (internal citations omitted).

[387] *Refer to* § 17.5.1.2 (Different Support Structures for Non-State Armed Groups).

[388] *Refer to* § 4.15 (Persons Authorized to Accompany the Armed Forces).

[389] Hedges v. Obama, No. 12-3644, *Reply Brief for Defendant-Appellant*, 11-12 (2d Cir. Dec. 20, 2012) ("More generally, 'substantial support' encompasses individuals who, even if not considered part of the irregular enemy forces at issue in the current conflict, bear sufficiently close ties to those forces and provide them support that warrants their detention consistent with the law of war. The substantial support concept, as properly informed by the law of war, would include people whose support for al-Qaeda or the Taliban makes them analogous to those who 'accompany the armed forces without actually being members thereof, such as civilian members of military aircraft crews, war correspondents, supply contractors, members of labour units or of services responsible for the welfare of the armed forces.' Such substantial supporters are, in short, 'more or less part of the armed force' and subject to law-of-war detention for the duration of the conflict.") (internal citations omitted).

[390] *Refer to* § 5.8 (Civilians Taking a Direct Part in Hostilities).

[391] *Refer to* § 4.17 (Spies, Saboteurs, and Other Persons Engaging in Similar Acts Behind Enemy Lines).

[392] *See* GREENSPAN, MODERN LAW OF LAND WARFARE 61 ("Guerillas who do not comply with the provisions laid down [of GPW art. 4(A)(2)] may perform patriotic service for their country (just as espionage agents often do), yet such illegitimate hostilities come within the technical heading of war crimes, and their perpetrators must be prepared to take their punishment if captured."); United States v. List, *et al.* (The Hostage Case), XI TRIALS OF WAR CRIMINALS BEFORE THE NMT 1245 ("Just as the spy may act lawfully for his country and at the same time be a war criminal to the enemy, so guerrillas may render great service to their country and, in the event of success, become heroes even, still they remain war criminals in the eyes of the enemy and may be treated as such."); HERBERT C. FOOKS, PRISONERS OF WAR 40 (1924) ("Individuals who undertake to wage a war in their private capacity are not entitled to the treatment of prisoners of war. The enemy may punish them when captured as war criminals. The safety of the troops compels the enemy to punish such hostilities as acts of illegitimate warfare, and international law gives the right to do so. Nations do not prohibit its citizens from such acts, however, for they may be most helpful to it just as spying is helpful.").

Nonetheless, like other forms of unprivileged belligerency, private engagement in hostilities has been described in some contexts as a "war crime" or as a violation of international law or the law of war.[393]

In discussions of the status of private acts of hostility under international law, the point is often made that international law does not require States to prevent what they may regard as acts of patriotism and heroism.[394]

However, outside the context of patriotic acts of resistance by persons in international armed conflict, private acts of hostility often carry additional sanction under international law. For example, persons who set off in private military expeditions against a foreign State from a State that has peaceful relations with the foreign State, have been subject to punishment under the law of nations.[395] Similarly, private acts of hostility, under certain conditions, may be regarded as piracy.[396] In contemporary parlance, private acts of hostility are often punished as "terrorism."[397] The unauthorized use of violence by private persons to achieve political ends has been viewed as contrary to the principles of democratic States.[398] Moreover, States have obligations under international law to repress terrorism, especially when conducted on their territory against other States.[399]

4.19 Rights, Duties, and Liabilities of Unprivileged Belligerents

Unprivileged belligerents have certain rights, duties, and liabilities. In general,

---

[393] *See, e.g.*, James Speed, Attorney General, *Military Commissions*, July 1865, 11 OPINIONS OF THE ATTORNEY GENERAL 297, 314 (1869) ("A bushwhacker, a jayhawker, a bandit, a war rebel, an assassin, being public enemies, may be tried, condemned, and executed as offenders against the laws of war.").

[394] Richard R. Baxter, *So-Called 'Unprivileged Belligerency': Spies, Guerillas, and Saboteurs*, 28 BRITISH YEAR BOOK OF INTERNATIONAL LAW 323, 342 (1951) ("In both occupied and unoccupied areas, resistance activities, guerrilla warfare, and sabotage by private persons may be expected to continue on at least as widespread a basis in future warfare as they have in the past. More often than not, patriotism or some sort of political allegiance lies at the root of such activities. Consequently the law of nations has not ventured to require of states that they prevent the belligerent activities of their citizenry or that they refrain from the use of secret agents or that these activities upon the part of their military forces or civilian population be punished.").

[395] *Refer to* § 15.1.5 (Domestic Neutrality Laws).

[396] *Refer to* § 13.3.3.1 (Entitlement of Vessels to Conduct Attacks During Non-International Armed Conflict).

[397] *See, e.g.*, R. v. Khawaja, (Supreme Court of Canada, Dec. 14, 2012) (upholding the terrorism conviction of a defendant who provided support to terrorist groups in Afghanistan and rejecting his argument that his support for terrorist groups could not be punished because they were part of an armed conflict governed by international law).

[398] Public Prosecutor v. Folkerts, (The Netherlands, District Court of Utrecht, Dec. 20, 1977), *reprinted in* 74 INTERNATIONAL LAW REPORTS 695, 698 (1987) ("It is totally unacceptable in democratic countries such as those just mentioned [the United States and the Federal Republic of Germany], and also in the Netherlands, for individuals who disagree with their country's policy, for that reason to resort to acts of violence such as those which took place here. Such acts attack the most fundamental principles of the constitutional State.").

[399] *See, e.g.*, U.N. SECURITY COUNCIL RESOLUTION 1373, U.N. Doc. S/RES/1373 (2001) (deciding that all States shall, *inter alia*, "[e]nsure that any person who participates in the financing, planning, preparation or perpetration of terrorist acts or in supporting terrorist acts is brought to justice and ensure that, in addition to any other measures against them, such terrorist acts are established as serious criminal offences in domestic laws and regulations and that the punishment duly reflects the seriousness of such terrorist acts;").

unprivileged belligerents lack the distinct privileges afforded to combatants and civilians, and are subject to the liabilities of both classes. Unprivileged belligerents generally may be made the object of attack by enemy combatants. They, however, must be afforded fundamental guarantees of humane treatment if *hors de combat*. Unprivileged belligerents may be punished by enemy States for their engagement in hostilities if they are convicted after a fair trial.

4.19.1 Rules Applicable to the Treatment of Unprivileged Belligerents. Although unprivileged belligerents have not been recognized and protected in treaty law to the same extent as peaceful civilians and lawful combatants,[400] basic guarantees of humane treatment in customary international law (*i.e.*, elementary considerations of humanity) protect unprivileged belligerents.[401] Moreover, some treaty protections apply to certain unprivileged belligerents.[402]

In some cases, U.S. practice has, as a matter of domestic law or policy, afforded unprivileged belligerents more favorable treatment than they would be entitled to receive under international law.[403] Nonetheless, U.S. practice has also recognized that unprivileged belligerents should not be afforded the distinct privileges afforded lawful combatants and the protections afforded peaceful civilians under the law of war.[404]

4.19.2 Unprivileged Belligerents – Conduct of Hostilities. Although unprivileged belligerents lack the right to engage in hostilities, international law nevertheless requires that they observe the same duties as lawful combatants during their conduct of hostilities.[405]

In addition, unprivileged belligerents are generally subject to the same liabilities to which combatants are subject in the conduct of hostilities; *i.e.*, they may be made the object of attack by enemy combatants. Unprivileged belligerents placed *hors de combat*, however, may not be made the object of attack, and must be treated humanely.

4.19.3 Unprivileged Belligerents – Detention. Unprivileged belligerents are liable to capture and detention, like lawful combatants.

4.19.3.1 *Humane Treatment*. Although unprivileged belligerents are not entitled to the privileges of POW status, unprivileged belligerents, like all other detained persons, must be treated humanely. In particular, they, like all other detainees, must receive, at a minimum, the

---

[400] *Refer to* § 4.3.1 ("Unprivileged Belligerents" as a Category in Treaty Law).

[401] *Refer to* § 3.1.1.2 (Applying Law of War Standards as Reflecting Minimum Legal Standards).

[402] *See, e.g.*, GPW art. 3; GC art. 5.

[403] *See, e.g.*, Boumediene v. Bush, 553 U.S. 723 (2008) (affording the constitutional privilege of habeas corpus to aliens detained as unprivileged belligerents at Guantanamo); U.S. MILITARY ASSISTANCE COMMAND VIETNAM DIRECTIVE 381-46, *Military Intelligence: Combined Screening of Detainees* Annex A ¶4.a.(2)-(3) (Dec. 27, 1967), *reprinted in* 62 AJIL 766-67 (classifying as POWs members of certain categories of guerilla or insurgent units provided that they were not engaged in acts of terrorism, sabotage, or spying while captured).

[404] *Refer to, e.g.*, § 4.6.1.2 (AP I and the GPW 4A(2) Conditions); FRANCIS LIEBER, GUERRILLA PARTIES CONSIDERED WITH REFERENCE TO THE LAWS AND USAGES OF WAR 22 (1862) ("no army, no society, engaged in war, any more than a society at peace, can allow unpunished assassination, robbery, and devastation, without the deepest injury to itself and disastrous consequences, which might change the very issue of the war.").

[405] *Refer to* § 4.4.1 (Combatants – Conduct of Hostilities).

fundamental guarantees of humane treatment described in Common Article 3 of the 1949 Geneva Conventions.[406] In addition, the United States has explicitly supported, out of a sense of legal obligation, the fundamental guarantees reflected in Article 75 of AP I as minimum standards for the humane treatment of all persons detained during international armed conflict.[407]

4.19.3.2 *Cases of Doubt*. During international armed conflict, in cases of doubt as to whether a person held as an unprivileged belligerent is, in fact, a POW or entitled to POW treatment, that person should enjoy POW protections until their status is assessed by a competent tribunal.[408]

4.19.3.3 *Necessary Security Measures*. A State may take necessary security measures with regard to unprivileged belligerents.

Since they have engaged in hostilities, unprivileged belligerents, or persons suspected of being unprivileged belligerents, may be denied certain privileges to which they might otherwise be entitled under the law of war. For example, the rights of unprivileged belligerents who are entitled to "protected person" status under the GC would be subject to derogation for security reasons.[409] However, unprivileged belligerents who are protected by the GC should be afforded its full protections when feasible.[410]

4.19.3.4 *Duration of Detention*. Unprivileged belligerents who are detained in order to prevent their further participation in hostilities generally must be released when hostilities have ended, unless there is another legal basis for their detention.[411] DoD practice has been to review periodically the detention of all persons not afforded POW status or treatment.[412]

4.19.4 Unprivileged Belligerents – Liability for Participation in Hostilities. Although international law affords lawful combatants a privilege or immunity from prosecution,[413] unprivileged belligerents lack such protection.[414] A State may punish unprivileged enemy belligerents,[415] subject to applicable requirements, such as a fair trial.[416]

---

[406] *Refer to* § 8.1.4.1 (Common Article 3 of the 1949 Geneva Conventions).

[407] *Refer to* § 8.1.4.2 (Article 75 of AP I and Relevant AP II Provisions).

[408] *Refer to* § 4.27.2 (POW Protections for Certain Persons Until Status Has Been Determined).

[409] *Refer to* § 10.4 (Derogation for Security Reasons).

[410] *Refer to* § 10.4.4 (Limits on Derogation).

[411] *Refer to* § 8.14.3.1 (Participants in Hostilities or Persons Belonging to Armed Groups That Are Engaged in Hostilities).

[412] *Refer to* § 8.14.2 (Review of Continued Detention for Security Reasons).

[413] *Refer to* § 4.4.3 (Combatants - Legal Immunity From a Foreign State's Domestic Law).

[414] *Refer to* § 4.17.5 (Spying and Sabotage – Forfeiture of the Privileges of Combatant Status); § 4.18.3 (Private Persons Who Engage in Hostilities – Lack of the Privileges of Combatant Status).

[415] *See, e.g.*, 1956 FM 27-10 (Change No. 1 1976) ¶73 ("The foregoing provisions [of article 5 of the GC] impliedly recognize the power of a Party to the conflict to impose the death penalty and lesser punishments on spies, saboteurs, and other persons not entitled to be treated as prisoners of war, except to the extent that that power has

4.19.4.1 <u>*Unprivileged Belligerency and the Law of War – Notes on Terminology*</u>. In contemporary parlance, spying and other forms of unprivileged belligerency generally have not been referred to as "violations of the law of war" or "war crimes."[417] For example, spying is permissible under the law of war in the sense that belligerents are not prohibited from employing spies; these activities are punishable but not prohibited under international law.[418]

However, in some cases, offenses related to unprivileged belligerency have been characterized as violations of the law of war.[419] For example, spying has been called a violation of the law of war or "war crime."[420] Spying and other acts of unprivileged belligerency have been called offenses against the law of nations or law of war – the punishment of these offenders has been viewed as a recognized incident or exercise of a belligerent's war powers under the law of war.[421]

The difference in these characterizations may be traced to different definitions of "war crime" that have been used over time. The difference in these characterizations may also be traced to different definitions of the "law of war." If one views the law of war as only containing

---

been limited or taken away by Article 68, GC (par. 438)."); LIEBER CODE art. 88 ("The spy is punishable with death by hanging by the neck, whether or not he succeed in obtaining the information or in conveying it to the enemy.").

416 *See* HAGUE IV REG. art. 30 ("A spy taken in the act shall not be punished without previous trial.").

417 Richard R. Baxter, *So-Called 'Unprivileged Belligerency': Spies, Guerillas, and Saboteurs*, 28 BRITISH YEAR BOOK OF INTERNATIONAL LAW 323, 324 (1951) ("The correct legal formulation is, it is submitted, that armed and unarmed hostilities, wherever occurring, committed by persons other than those entitled to be treated as prisoners of war or peaceful civilians merely deprive such individuals of a protection they might otherwise enjoy under international law and place them virtually at the power of the enemy. 'Unlawful belligerency' is actually 'unprivileged belligerency'.").

418 *Refer to* § 4.17.4 (Spying and Sabotage Permissible Under the Law of War).

419 *See, e.g.*, 10 U.S.C. § 950t (27) (defining the offense of spying as "in violation of the law of war"); G.I.A.D. Draper, *The Status of Combatants and the Question of Guerrilla Warfare*, 45 BRITISH YEAR BOOK OF INTERNATIONAL LAW 173, 173, 176 (1971) ("On balance, the theory that illicit combatants may be killed after capture, as an act of warfare, subject to any restraint imposed by the law of war, is somewhat artificial. There may be some substance in the contention, and it may be more consonant with the war practices of belligerents, the official manuals on the law of war issued by States, and the decisions of national tribunals applying the law of war, that illegal participation in combat is a violation of the law of war exposing the offender to loss of immunity from attack, and, upon capture, to trial and punishment upon conviction. However, the matter is controversial, and there are certain passages in the classical writers on the law of war, such as Grotius, which lend support to the theory of 'unprivileged belligerency'.").

420 *See, e.g.*, U.N. SECRETARY-GENERAL, *Historical Survey of the Question of International Criminal Jurisdiction*, U.N. Doc. A/CN.4/7/Rev.1, 1 (1949) ("During the greater part of modern history customary law has also recognized so-called war crimes of various description. Perfidy, particularly that type of perfidy which is described as espionage, is the oldest example of such a war crime."); Ex parte Quirin, 317 U.S. 1, 31 (1942) (describing spies as "offenders against the law of war subject to trial and punishment by military tribunals."); WINTHROP, MILITARY LAW & PRECEDENTS 770 ("Under the law of nations and of war, [a spy's] offence is an exclusively military one, cognizable only by military tribunals."); G. SHERSTON BAKER, I HALLECK'S INTERNATIONAL LAW 628-29 (18.20) (1908) ("the act of spying is an offence against the laws of war alone"); James Speed, Attorney General, *Military Commissions*, July 1865, 11 OPINIONS OF THE ATTORNEY GENERAL 297, 312-13 (1869) ("to act as spy is an offence against the laws of war, ... every lawyer knows that a spy was a well-known offender under the laws of war,").

421 Ex parte Quirin, 317 U.S. 1, 28 (1942) (holding that the trial and punishment of enemy saboteurs by military commission was an "important incident to the conduct of war").

prohibitions, the punishment of unprivileged belligerents, like all exercises of the war powers, emanates from the domestic law of the belligerent State.[422] On the other hand, if one views the law of war as also including sources of authority, the punishment of unprivileged belligerents is also grounded in the international law of war.[423]

Although the relationship between unprivileged belligerency and the law of war has been characterized in different ways, it is well-accepted that States may punish unprivileged enemy belligerents after a fair trial.

4.20 CHILDREN

The GC provides special protection for children in order to protect them against the dangers of war. In addition, certain provisions of treaties and U.S. law seek to restrict the use or recruitment of children in armed conflict.

4.20.1 Specific Protections for All Children During International Armed Conflict.

4.20.1.1 *Children Under Fifteen Who Are Orphaned or Separated*. The parties to the conflict shall take the necessary measures to ensure that children under fifteen, who are orphaned or are separated from their families as a result of the war, are not left to their own resources, and that their maintenance, the exercise of their religion, and their education are facilitated in all circumstances.[424] The maintenance of the children concerned means their feeding, clothing, and accommodation, care for their health, and, where necessary, medical and hospital treatment.[425]

Their education shall, as far as possible, be entrusted to persons of a similar cultural tradition.[426] This provision is intended to exclude inappropriate religious or political propaganda designed to influence them.[427]

The parties to the conflict shall facilitate the reception of such children in a neutral country for the duration of the conflict with the consent of the Protecting Power, if any, and under due safeguards for the observance of the principles stated in the first paragraph of Article

---

[422] *Refer to* § 1.3.3.1 (Law of War as Prohibitive Law).

[423] *Refer to* § 1.3.3.2 (Law of War as Permissive Law).

[424] GC art. 24 ("The Parties to the conflict shall take the necessary measures to ensure that children under fifteen, who are orphaned or are separated from their families as a result of the war, are not left to their own resources, and that their maintenance, the exercise of their religion and their education are facilitated in all circumstances.").

[425] GC COMMENTARY 187 ("The maintenance of the children concerned means their feeding, clothing, and accommodation, care for their health and, where necessary medical and hospital treatment.").

[426] GC art. 24 ("Their education shall, as far as possible, be entrusted to persons of a similar cultural tradition.").

[427] GC COMMENTARY 187 ("That provision is most important. It is intended to exclude any religious or political propaganda designed to wean children from their natural milieu; for that would cause additional suffering to human beings already grievously stricken by the loss of their parents.").

24 of the GC.[428]

4.20.1.2 *Identification for Children Under Twelve*. The parties to the conflict shall endeavor to arrange for all children under twelve to be identified by the wearing of identity discs, or by some other means.[429] The age of twelve was chosen because it was considered that children over twelve are generally capable of stating their own identity.[430]

4.20.2 Protection for Alien Children in a Belligerent's Home Territory. In a belligerent's home territory, the GC provides that certain aliens (*i.e.*, those qualifying for protected person status under the GC) who are children under fifteen years, pregnant women, and mothers of children under seven years shall benefit from any preferential treatment to the same extent as the nationals of the State concerned.[431]

4.20.3 Protection for Children in Occupied Territory. Provisions of the GC address the protection of children in occupied territory.[432]

4.20.4 Protection for Children in the Context of Internment Under the GC. The GC provides certain protections for children in the context of internment. Provisions of the GC address:

- the internment of children with their parents;[433]
- special treatment for children during internment, including
  - ensuring the education of children and young people, including school attendance,[434]
  - additional food for children under fifteen in proportion to their physiological needs,[435] and

---

[428] GC art. 24 ("The Parties to the conflict shall facilitate the reception of such children in a neutral country for the duration of the conflict with the consent of the Protecting Power, if any, and under due safeguards for the observance of the principles stated in the first paragraph.").

[429] GC art. 24 ("They shall, furthermore, endeavour to arrange for all children under twelve to be identified by the wearing of identity discs, or by some other means.").

[430] GC COMMENTARY 189 ("It will be noticed that the age limit here is twelve, whereas in the first two paragraphs it was fifteen years of age: this is in accordance with a recommendation made at the XVIIth International Red Cross Conference in Stockholm, where it was considered that children over twelve were generally capable of stating their own identity.").

[431] *Refer to* § 10.7.1 (Regulation of the Situation of Protected Persons, in Principle, by Provisions Applicable to Aliens in Time of Peace).

[432] *Refer to* § 11.13 (Protection of Children in Occupied Territory).

[433] *Refer to* § 10.10.3 (Families Kept Together).

[434] *Refer to* § 10.16.2 (Education).

[435] *Refer to* § 10.13.1.2 (Additional Food for Certain Groups).

  - special playgrounds reserved for children and young people;[436] and

- special agreements for the release, the repatriation, the return to places of residence, or the accommodation in a neutral country of, among others, children, pregnant women, and mothers with infants and young children.[437]

4.20.5 <u>Child Soldiers</u>. Certain provisions of treaties and U.S. law seek to restrict the use or recruitment of children in armed conflict. If children are nonetheless employed in armed conflict, they generally are treated on the same basis as adults, although children may be subject to special treatment in detention because of their age.

Prohibitions on the use or recruitment of children also apply in non-international armed conflict.[438]

4.20.5.1 *<u>U.S. Offense of Recruiting or Using Child Soldiers</u>*. U.S. law makes it a crime, under certain circumstances, to recruit, enlist, or conscript a person to serve in an armed force or group, while such person is under 15 years of age.[439] U.S. law also makes it a crime to use a person under 15 years of age to participate actively in hostilities.[440] These restrictions in U.S. law are similar to provisions in treaties to which the United States is not a Party.[441]

4.20.5.2 *<u>Child Soldiers Protocol</u>*. As a Party to the Optional Protocol to the Convention on the Rights of the Child on the involvement of children in armed conflict,[442] the United States must "take all feasible measures to ensure that members of [its] armed forces who

---

[436] *Refer to* § 10.16.3 (Opportunities for Physical Exercise, Sports, and Outdoor Games).

[437] *Refer to* § 10.9.6 (Agreements for the Release, Return, or Accommodation in a Neutral Country of Certain Classes of Internees).

[438] *Refer to* § 17.10.2 (Children and Participation in Non-International Armed Conflict).

[439] 18 U.S.C. § 2442(a) (making punishable, under certain circumstances, "[w]hoever knowingly— (1) recruits, enlists, or conscripts a person to serve while such person is under 15 years of age in an armed force or group; … knowing such person is under 15 years of age").

[440] 18 U.S.C. § 2442(a) (making punishable, under certain circumstances, "[w]hoever knowingly … (2) uses a person under 15 years of age to participate actively in hostilities; knowing such person is under 15 years of age").

[441] *Consider* AP I art. 77(2) ("The Parties to the conflict shall take all feasible measures in order that children who have not attained the age of fifteen years do not take a direct part in hostilities and, in particular, they shall refrain from recruiting them into their armed forces. In recruiting among those persons who have attained the age of fifteen years but who have not attained the age of eighteen years the Parties to the conflict shall endeavour to give priority to those who are oldest."); Convention on the Rights of the Child, art. 38(2)-(3), Feb. 16, 1995, 1577 UNTS 3, 56 (providing that "States Parties shall take all feasible measures to ensure that persons who have not attained the age of fifteen years do not take a direct part in hostilities" and that "States Parties shall refrain from recruiting any person who has not attained the age of fifteen years into their armed forces"); ROME STATUTE art. 8(2)(b)(xxvi) (defining 'war crime' to include "[c]onscripting or enlisting children under the age of fifteen years into the national armed forces or using them to participate actively in hostilities" in international armed conflict).

[442] 2201 UNTS 311 ("*RATIFICATION (WITH DECLARATION AND UNDERSTANDINGS)* **United States of America** *Deposit of instrument with the Secretary-General of the United Nations: 23 December 2002*").

have not attained the age of 18 years do not take a direct part in hostilities."[443] The United States made a statement of understanding regarding the meaning of the phrase "direct part in hostilities" in the Child Soldiers Protocol.[444]

As a Party to the Child Soldiers Protocol, the United States also has an obligation to ensure that persons who have not attained the age of 18 years are not compulsorily recruited into its armed forces.[445] In a declaration deposited pursuant to Article 3(2) of the Child Soldiers Protocol,[446] the United States described its measures in place to comply with this obligation and stated that the minimum age at which it permitted persons to be voluntarily recruited in the U.S. Armed Forces is 17 years of age.[447]

4.20.5.3 _Treatment of Child Soldiers_. In general, children receive the rights, duties, and liabilities of combatant status on the same basis as other persons. For example, there is no age requirement for someone to receive POW status. Similarly, whether a civilian is considered to be taking a direct part in hostilities does not depend on that person's age.

Children who have participated in hostilities or been associated with an armed force who are detained might require additional consideration because of their age. For example, rules for

---

[443] Optional Protocol to the Convention on the Rights of the Child on the Involvement of Children in Armed Conflict, art. 1, May 25, 2000, 2173 UNTS 222, 237 ("States Parties shall take all feasible measures to ensure that members of their armed forces who have not attained the age of 18 years do not take a direct part in hostilities.").

[444] *See* United States, *Statement on Ratification of the Child Soldiers Protocol*, Dec. 23, 2002, 2201 UNTS 311, 312 ("(2) The United States understands that, with respect to Article 1 of the Protocol - ... (B) the phrase 'direct part in hostilities' - (i) means immediate and actual action on the battlefield likely to cause harm to the enemy because there is a direct causal relationship between the activity engaged in and the harm done to the enemy; and (ii) does not mean indirect participation in hostilities, such as gathering and transmitting military information, transporting weapons, munitions, or other supplies, or forward deployment;"). This statement of understanding was intended to address the usage of the phrase "direct part in hostilities" in the context of these treaty obligations relating to limiting the participation of children in armed conflict, and the phrase "direct part in hostilities" may be interpreted differently in other contexts, such as the circumstances in which civilians forfeit their protection from being made the object of attack. *Refer to* § 5.8 (Civilians Taking a Direct Part in Hostilities).

[445] Optional Protocol to the Convention on the Rights of the Child on the Involvement of Children in Armed Conflict, art. 2, May 25, 2000, 2173 UNTS 222, 237 ("States Parties shall ensure that persons who have not attained the age of 18 years are not compulsorily recruited into their armed forces.").

[446] Optional Protocol to the Convention on the Rights of the Child on the Involvement of Children in Armed Conflict, art. 3(2), May 25, 2000, 2173 UNTS 222, 237 ("Each State Party shall deposit a binding declaration upon ratification of or accession to this Protocol that sets forth the minimum age at which it will permit voluntary recruitment into its national armed forces and a description of the safeguards that it has adopted to ensure that such recruitment is not forced or coerced.").

[447] United States, *Statement on Ratification of the Child Soldiers Protocol*, Dec. 23, 2002, 2201 UNTS 311 ("(A) the minimum age at which the United States permits voluntary recruitment into the Armed Forces of the United States is 17 years of age; (B) The United States has established safeguards to ensure that such recruitment is not forced or coerced, including a requirement in section 505 (a) of title 10, United States Code, that no person under 18 years of age may be originally enlisted in the Armed Forces of the United States without the written consent of the person's parent or guardian, if the parent or guardian is entitled to the person's custody and control; (C) each person recruited into the Armed Forces of the United States receives a comprehensive briefing and must sign an enlistment contract that, taken together, specify the duties involved in military service; and (D) all persons recruited into the Armed Forces of the United States must provide reliable proof of age before their entry into military service.").

the additional provision for their education might be applicable.[448] Similarly, it might be appropriate to take into account the age of a defendant in determining liability or punishment for violations of the law of war.

4.21 Mercenaries

The act of being a mercenary is not a crime in customary international law nor in any treaty to which the United States is a Party.[449] Under the customary law of war and the GPW, "mercenaries" receive the rights, duties, and liabilities of combatant status on the same basis as other persons. For example, being a "mercenary" or paid for participating in hostilities does not deprive a person of POW status, if that person otherwise meets the requirements for POW status, such as by being a member of a militia that is part of the armed forces of a State.[450] Mercenaries must comply with the law of war and may be tried and punished for violations of the law of war on the same basis as other persons. States that employ mercenaries are responsible for their conduct, including their compliance with the law of war.

Mercenaries are often nationals of States that are not parties to a conflict. In general, a national of a neutral State who, during an international armed conflict, commits hostile acts against a State or who voluntarily enlists in the armed forces of one of the parties should not be more severely treated by the State against whom he or she has abandoned his or her neutrality than a national of the other belligerent State could be for the same act.[451]

4.21.1 Treaties on Mercenaries. A number of treaty provisions are intended to repress mercenary activities. The United States has not accepted any such provision because these efforts are not consistent with fundamental principles of the law of war.[452]

---

[448] *Refer to* § 9.16.2 (Education); § 10.16.2 (Education).

[449] *See* Edward R. Cummings, Attorney-Adviser, Department of State, *International Legal Rights of Captured Mercenaries*, Oct. 17, 1980, III CUMULATIVE DIGEST OF UNITED STATES PRACTICE IN INTERNATIONAL LAW 1981-1988 3457 ("The act of being a mercenary is not a crime under international law. An individual who is accused of being a mercenary and who is captured during an armed conflict is entitled to the basic humanitarian protections of the international law applicable in armed conflict, including those specified in the Geneva Convention Relative to the Protection of Civilian Persons in Time of War (Aug. 12, 1949; TIAS No. 3365; 6 UST 3516). The specific rights which such an individual would be entitled to vary depending on whether the conflict is an international conflict or an internal one and, in the case of international armed conflicts, on whether the person is entitled to prisoner-of-war status.").

[450] *Refer to* § 4.5 (Armed Forces of a State).

[451] *Refer to* § 15.6.2.1 (No More Severe Treatment Than Nationals of an Opposing Belligerent State).

[452] *See, e.g., The Position of the United States on Current Law of War Agreements: Remarks of Judge Abraham D. Sofaer, Legal Adviser, United States Department of State, January 22, 1987*, 2 AMERICAN UNIVERSITY JOURNAL OF INTERNATIONAL LAW AND POLICY 460, 469 (1987) ("[Article 47 of AP I] was included in the Protocol not for humanitarian reasons, but purely to make the political point that mercenary activity in the Third World is unwelcome. In doing so, this article disregards one of the fundamental principles of international humanitarian law by defining the right to combatant status, at least in part, on the basis of the personal or political motivations of the individual in question. This politicizing of the rules of warfare is contrary to Western interests and the interests of humanitarian law itself.").

AP I denies "mercenaries" the right to be lawful combatants or POWs.[453] This provision in AP I was adopted because certain States wanted to condemn mercenary groups that had played a role in armed conflicts that had taken place in Sub-saharan Africa since 1960.[454] However, AP I defines "mercenary" very narrowly.[455] For example, any member of the armed forces of a party to the conflict, or any member of the armed forces of any other State, who is sent on official duty as a member of its armed forces, is not a mercenary as defined by AP I.[456] In addition, although, under AP I, mercenaries lack the right to be a combatant or a POW, Parties to AP I may nonetheless decide as a matter of policy to treat enemy mercenaries as lawful combatants or POWs.

Shortly after the adoption of AP I, the Convention for the Elimination of Mercenarism in Africa was adopted, which uses the same definition of mercenary as AP I,[457] but creates greater obligations for Parties to punish and repress mercenarism.[458] The United States is not a Party to

---

[453] *See* AP I art. 47(1) ("A mercenary shall not have the right to be a combatant or a prisoner of war.").

[454] BOTHE, PARTSCH, & SOLF, NEW RULES 269 (AP I art. 47, ¶2.2) ("The condemnation and outlawing of mercenary groups and individual mercenaries who had played a substantial (and often unsavoury) role in the armed conflicts which took place in Sub-saharan Africa since 1960 was a high priority goal of African delegations, which was supported by other Third World delegations and by the Eastern European group.").

[455] *See* AP I art. 47(2) ("A mercenary is any person who: (*a*) Is specially recruited locally or abroad in order to fight in an armed conflict; (*b*) Does, in fact, take a direct part in the hostilities; (*c*) Is motivated to take part in the hostilities essentially by the desire for private gain and, in fact, is promised, by or on behalf of a Party to the conflict, material compensation substantially in excess of that promised or paid to combatants of similar ranks and functions in the armed forces of that Party; (*d*) Is neither a national of a Party to the conflict nor a resident of territory controlled by a Party to the conflict; (*e*) Is not a member of the armed forces of a Party to the conflict; and (*f*) Has not been sent by a State which is not a Party to the conflict on official duty as a member of its armed forces.").

[456] Edward R. Cummings, Attorney-Adviser, Department of State, *International Legal Rights of Captured Mercenaries*, Oct. 17, 1980, III CUMULATIVE DIGEST OF UNITED STATES PRACTICE IN INTERNATIONAL LAW 1981-1988 3457, 3461 ("This narrow definition of mercenaries in effect denies prisoner-of-war status to individuals who fight strictly for private gain. It does not affect any individual who is a member of the state's regular forces and other legitimate combatants.").

[457] *See* Organisation of African Unity Convention for the Elimination of Mercenarism in Africa, art. 1(1), Jul. 3, 1977, 1490 UNTS 89, 96 ("A mercenary is any person who: *a*) Is specially recruited locally or abroad in order to fight in an armed conflict; *b*) Does in fact take a direct part in the hostilities; *c*) Is motivated to take part in the hostilities essentially by the desire for private gain and in fact is promised by or on behalf of a party to the conflict material compensation; *d*) Is neither a national of a party to the conflict nor a resident of territory controlled by a party to the conflict; *e*) Is not a member of the armed forces of a party to the conflict; and *f*) Is not sent by a State other than a party to the conflict on official mission as a member of the armed forces of the said State.").

[458] *See* Organisation of African Unity Convention for the Elimination of Mercenarism in Africa, art. 6, Jul. 3, 1977, 1490 UNTS 89, 97-98 ("The contracting parties shall take all necessary measures to eradicate all mercenary activities in Africa. To this end, each contracting State shall undertake to: *a*) Prevent its nationals or foreigners on its territory from engaging in any of the acts mentioned in Article 1 of this Convention; *b*) Prevent entry into or passage through its territory of any mercenary or any equipment destined for mercenary use; *c*) Prohibit on its territory any activities by persons or organisations who use mercenaries against any African State member of the Organization of African Unity or the people of Africa in their struggle for liberation; *d*) Communicate to the other Member States of the Organization of African Unity either directly or through the Secretariat of the OAU any information related to the activities of mercenaries as soon as it comes to its knowledge; *e*) Forbid on its territory the recruitment, training, financing and equipment of mercenaries and any other form of activities likely to promote mercenarism; *f*) Take all the necessary legislative and other measures to ensure the immediate entry into force of this Convention.").

this treaty.

The International Convention against the Recruitment, Use, Financing and Training of Mercenaries of December 4, 1989, defines "mercenary" slightly more broadly than AP I, applies to both international and non-international armed conflicts, and defines various offenses related to the recruiting, use, financing, or training of mercenaries.[459] The United States is not a Party to this treaty.

4.22 AP I Provisions on Civil Defense Personnel

Articles 61-67 of AP I address "civil defence", *i.e.*, the performance of certain humanitarian tasks intended to benefit the civilian population.[460]

The United States has supported the principle that civilian civil defense organizations and their personnel be respected and protected as civilians and be permitted to perform their civil defense tasks except in cases of imperative military necessity.[461] However, a number of military operational problems have been identified with respect to the system of protection for civil defense established by AP I, and these provisions of AP I may be understood not to preclude an attack on an otherwise lawful military objective.[462]

4.23 Law Enforcement Officers

In general, police officers receive the rights, duties, and liabilities of civilian status.[463] However, law enforcement agencies are in many respects similar to military forces. They are authorized to use necessary force on behalf of the State, are generally distinguishable from

---

[459] *See* International Convention against the Recruitment, Use, Financing and Training of Mercenaries, Dec. 4, 1989, Annex to U.N. General Assembly Resolution 44/34, U.N. Doc. A/RES/44/34 (Dec. 4, 1989).

[460] AP I art. 61 ("For the purposes of this Protocol: (a) 'Civil defence' means the performance of some or all of the undermentioned humanitarian tasks intended to protect the civilian population against the dangers, and to help it to recover from the immediate effects, of hostilities or disasters and also to provide the conditions necessary for its survival. These tasks are: (i) Warning; (ii) Evacuation; (iii) Management of shelters; (iv) Management of blackout measures; (v) Rescue; (vi) Medical services, including first aid, and religious assistance; (vii) Fire-fighting; …").

[461] Michael J. Matheson, Deputy Legal Adviser, Department of State, *Remarks on the United States Position on the Relation of Customary International Law to the 1977 Protocols Additional to the 1949 Geneva Conventions at the Sixth Annual American Red Cross-Washington College of Law Conference on International Humanitarian Law* (Jan. 22, 1987), 2 American University Journal of International Law and Policy 419, 427 (1987) ("Turning now to the field of civil defense, we support the principle that civilian civil defense organizations and their personnel be respected and protected as civilians and be permitted to perform their civil defense tasks except in cases of imperative military necessity. We also support the principle that in occupied territories, civilians receive from the appropriate authorities, as practicable, the facilities necessary for the performance of their tasks. These principles reflect, in general terms, many of the detailed provisions in articles 62 and 63.").

[462] Appendix to 1985 CJCS Memo on AP I 69-71 ("In general, the system of protection for civil defense established by the Protocol is well-meaning, but creates a number of military operational problems. The main practical problems arise from the ambiguity of the definition of civil defense activities in Article 61. … An attacking force will often have difficulty deciding whether to respect the sign in a particular case. To lessen the risk of misuse of this sign and avoid placing an unacceptable burden on proof of an attacking force, an understanding is proposed that makes it clear that Articles 61-67 do not preclude an attack on an otherwise lawful military objective.").

[463] *Refer to* § 4.8 (Rights, Duties, and Liabilities of Civilians).

private citizens, and are often organized like military forces. In cases where States choose to use police officers as part of the armed forces, they receive the rights, duties, and liabilities of combatant status.[464]

4.23.1 Police as Civilians. In general, members of law enforcement agencies have civilian status.[465] Furthermore, routine domestic law enforcement is part of the general protection of the civilian population and does not constitute "taking a direct part in hostilities" that would deprive police officers of their protection from being made the object of attack.[466]

4.23.2 Police With a Military Role. Some States use police forces in a paramilitary capacity or use military forces in a police role. Members of the armed forces engaged in police roles are combatants.

The extent to which police officers are treated as combatants largely depends on whether the State decides to use them in that capacity. States may decide to make law enforcement agencies part of their armed forces.[467] Members of these law enforcement agencies, like other members of those armed forces, receive combatant status by virtue of their membership in the armed forces.[468] In addition, States may authorize members of the law enforcement agencies to accompany their armed forces without incorporating them into their armed forces. These persons have the legal status of persons authorized to accompany the armed forces.[469]

4.23.3 Police in Non-International Armed Conflict. Police officers may play a larger role in armed conflicts between States and insurgent or terrorist groups because in such conflicts the State may treat all enemy persons' participation in hostilities as criminal.[470]

4.24 JOURNALISTS

In general, journalists are civilians and are protected as such under the law of war.

---

[464] *Refer to* § 4.4 (Rights, Duties, and Liabilities of Combatants).

[465] Memorandum submitted in United States v. Shakur, 690 F. Supp. 1291 (S.D.N.Y. 1988), III CUMULATIVE DIGEST OF UNITED STATES PRACTICE IN INTERNATIONAL LAW 1981-88 3436, 3450 ("Members of the civilian police force are not deemed to be legitimate objects of attack during international wars unless they are incorporated into the armed forces. The 'status of police is generally that of civilians' for purposes of the law of war.").

[466] *Refer to* § 5.8.3.2 (Examples of Acts Not Considered Taking a Direct Part in Hostilities).

[467] *For example*, Belgium, *Statement on Ratification of AP I*, May 20, 1986, 1435 UNTS 367, 367-68 ("Considering paragraph 3 of article 43 (armed forces) and the special status of the Belgian *gendarmerie*, the Belgian Government has decided to notify the High Contracting Parties about the following duties which are entrusted to the Belgian *gendarmerie* during periods of armed conflict. It believes that this notification, in so far as is necessary, meets the requirements of article 43 in respect of the *gendarmerie*. (a) The Belgian *gendarmerie*, which was established to maintain order and enforce the law, is a public force which, under national legislation, constitutes one of the armed forces and which therefore corresponds to the concept of 'armed forces of a party to a conflict' within the meaning of article 43 of Protocol I. Thus, in times of international armed conflict the members of the *gendarmerie* have 'combatant' status within the meaning of that Protocol.").

[468] *Refer to* § 4.5 (Armed Forces of a State).

[469] *Refer to* § 4.15 (Persons Authorized to Accompany the Armed Forces).

[470] *Refer to* § 17.4.1 (Ability of a State to Use Its Domestic Law Against Non-State Armed Groups).

Journalists play a vital role in free societies and the rule of law and in providing information about armed conflict.[471] Moreover, the proactive release of accurate information to domestic and international audiences has been viewed as consistent with the objectives of U.S. military operations.[472] DoD operates under the policy that open and independent reporting is the principal means of coverage of U.S. military operations.[473] In addition to responding to press inquiries and providing briefings to members of the press on U.S. military operations, DoD practice has also been to embed journalists with units during military operations.[474] Embedded journalists are assigned to a unit, and they eat, sleep, and move with the unit.[475]

4.24.1 Status of Journalists – Generally Civilian. In general, journalists are protected as

---

[471] *See, e.g.*, Robert S. Taylor, Acting General Counsel, Department of Defense, *Letter to Christophe Deloire, Secretary-General, Reporters Without Borders*, Sept. 15, 2015 ("The Department supports and respects the vital work that journalists perform. Their work in gathering and reporting news is essential to a free society and the rule of law. The Department shares your deep concern about the risks faced by journalists in situations of armed conflict."); *Remarks by Ambassador Rosemary A. DiCarlo, Acting Permanent Representative to the United Nations, At a Security Council Open Debate on Protection of Civilians in Armed Conflict: Protection of Journalists*, July 17, 2013, 2013 DIGEST OF UNITED STATES PRACTICE IN INTERNATIONAL LAW 195 ("Journalists are literally our eyes and ears in every corner of the world. They sound the warning when local tensions threaten to erupt into war. They document the suffering of civilians in conflict areas. And they expose human rights violations and war crimes. Journalists are critical to this Council's ability to remain well informed so that it may fulfill its mandate to maintain international peace and security.").

[472] JOINT PUBLICATION 3-61, *Public Affairs*, I-1 (Nov. 17, 2015) ("b. The US military has an obligation to communicate with its members and the US public, and it is in the national interest to communicate with international publics. The proactive release of accurate information to domestic and international audiences puts joint operations in context, facilitates informed perceptions about military operations, undermines adversarial propaganda, and helps achieve national, strategic, and operational objectives.").

[473] DOD DIRECTIVE 5122.05, *Assistant Secretary of Defense for Public Affairs (ASD(PA))*, 9 (Sept. 5, 2008), Enclosure 3 - *Statement of DoD Principles for News Media Coverage of DoD Operations* ("1. Open and independent reporting shall be the principal means of coverage of U.S. military operations.").

[474] *For example*, Richard K. Wright, *Assessment of the DoD Embedded Media Program*, I-1 (Institute for Defense Analyses, Sept. 2004) ("The Department of Defense (DoD) Embedded Media Program resulted in an unprecedented opportunity for the media to report in real time on the military units and the soldiers, marines, sailors, and airmen who executed combat operations during Operation Iraqi Freedom (OIF). A total of 692 reporters, photographers, producers, cameramen, and technicians were embedded with ground units, on ships, and at air bases for an extended period of time.").

[475] *Public Affairs Guidance (PAG) On Embedding Media During Possible Future Operations/Deployments In The U.S. Central Command (CENTCOM) Area Of Responsibility (AOR)*, Feb. 10, 2003, ¶2.C, *reprinted as Appendix D in* Richard K. Wright, *Assessment of the DoD Embedded Media Program*, D-4 (Institute for Defense Analyses, Sept. 2004) ("A MEDIA EMBED IS DEFINED AS A MEDIA REPRESENTATIVE REMAINING WITH A UNIT ON AN EXTENDED BASIS – PERHAPS A PERIOD OF WEEKS OR EVEN MONTHS. COMMANDERS WILL PROVIDE BILLETING, RATIONS, AND MEDICAL ATTENTION, IF NEEDED, TO THE EMBEDDED MEDIA COMMENSURATE WITH THAT PROVIDED TO MEMBERS OF THE UNIT, AS WELL AS ACCESS TO MILITARY TRANSPORTATION AND ASSISTANCE WITH COMMUNICATIONS FILING/TRANSMITTING MEDIA PRODUCTS, IF REQUIRED."); DEPARTMENT OF THE ARMY FIELD MANUAL 46-1, *Public Affairs Operations*, 25-26 (May 30, 1997) ("PAOs should seek out those members of the media who are willing to spend extended periods of time with soldiers during an operation, embedding them into the unit they cover. Embedding is the act of assigning a reporter to a unit as a member of the unit. The reporter eats, sleeps, and moves with the unit. The reporter is authorized open access to all sections of the unit and is not escorted by public affairs personnel. Rather, the unit is the reporter's escort.").

civilians;[476] *i.e.*, engaging in journalism does not constitute taking a direct part in hostilities such that such a person would be deprived of protection from being made the object of attack.[477]

Journalists do not form a distinct class of persons under the law of war, but instead receive protection through the general protections afforded civilians.[478] Thus, in general, the rights, duties, and liabilities applicable to civilians also apply to journalists.[479]

Although journalism is regarded as a civilian activity, the fact that a person performs such work does not preclude that person from otherwise acquiring a different status under the law of war, such as the status of persons authorized to accompany the armed forces or of combatants.

4.24.1.1 War Correspondents and Other Journalists Authorized to Accompany the Armed Forces. Journalists authorized to accompany the armed forces have the status of such persons.[480] For example, if they fall into the power of the enemy during international armed conflict, they are entitled to POW status.[481] Such journalists are sometimes called "war

---

[476] *See* Hedges v. Obama, No. 12-3644, *Reply Brief for Defendant-Appellant*, 11 (2d Cir. Dec. 20, 2012) ("As an initial matter, it is an established law of war norm, which is reflected in Article 79 of Additional Protocol I to the Geneva Conventions, that 'journalists' are generally to be protected as 'civilians.' Although the United States is not a party to Additional Protocol I, it supports and respects this important principle."); Michael J. Matheson, Deputy Legal Adviser, Department of State, *Remarks on the United States Position on the Relation of Customary International Law to the 1977 Protocols Additional to the 1949 Geneva Conventions at the Sixth Annual American Red Cross-Washington College of Law Conference on International Humanitarian Law* (Jan. 22, 1987), 2 AMERICAN UNIVERSITY JOURNAL OF INTERNATIONAL LAW AND POLICY 419, 428 (1987) ("We also support the principle that journalists be protected as civilians under the Convention, provided they take no action adversely affecting such status."). *Consider* AP I art. 79 ("MEASURES OF PROTECTION FOR JOURNALISTS. 1. Journalists engaged in dangerous professional missions in areas of armed conflict shall be considered as civilians within the meaning of Article 50, paragraph 1. 2. They shall be protected as such under the Conventions and this Protocol, provided that they take no action adversely affecting their status as civilians, and without prejudice to the right of war correspondents accredited to the armed forces to the status provided for in Article 4 A (4) of the Third Convention.").

[477] *Refer to* § 5.8.3.2 (Examples of Acts Not Considered Taking a Direct Part in Hostilities).

[478] *See, e.g.*, U.N. SECURITY COUNCIL RESOLUTION 2222 (2015), U.N. Doc. S/RES/2222 (2015) ¶¶ 3, 7 (May 27, 2015) ("3. *Recalls* in this regard that journalists, media professionals and associated personnel engaged in dangerous professional missions in areas of armed conflict shall be considered as civilians and shall be respected and protected as such, provided that they take no action adversely affecting their status as civilians. … 7. *Recalls its demand* that all parties to an armed conflict comply fully with the obligations applicable to them under international law related to the protection of civilians in armed conflict, including journalists, media professionals and associated personnel;").

[479] *Refer to* § 4.8 (Rights, Duties, and Liabilities of Civilians).

[480] *Refer to* § 4.15 (Persons Authorized to Accompany the Armed Forces).

[481] *See* GPW art. 4A(4) (defining "prisoners of war, in the sense of the present Convention" to include "[p]ersons who accompany the armed forces without actually being members thereof, such as … war correspondents, … provided that they have received authorization from the armed forces which they accompany," who have fallen into the power of the enemy); HAGUE IV REG. art. 13 ("Individuals who follow an army without directly belonging to it, such as newspaper correspondents and reporters, … who fall into the enemy's hands and whom the latter thinks expedient to detain, are entitled to be treated as prisoners of war, provided they are in possession of a certificate from the military authorities of the army which they were accompanying.").

correspondents," which is a term used in Geneva Conventions of 1949.[482]

Since journalists authorized to accompany the armed forces are liable to become POWs, they must be issued identification cards so that they may establish their entitlement to POW status upon falling into the power of the enemy during international armed conflict.[483]

4.24.1.2 *Combatants Performing Journalistic Work*. Although generally journalists are civilians, journalists are not precluded from being considered combatants, whether privileged or unprivileged, if they otherwise acquire such status. For example, members of the armed forces sometimes serve as journalists or in some other public affairs capacity, and these persons have the same status as other privileged combatants.[484] Non-State armed groups sometimes use their members[485] for propaganda or other media activities, and such personnel are not precluded from being considered unprivileged belligerents.[486] In addition, although engaging in journalism would not be a basis to consider a person an unprivileged belligerent, an unprivileged belligerent would not be precluded from being considered as such because he or she works as a journalist.

4.24.2 General Rules for the Treatment of Civilian Journalists and Journalists Authorized to Accompany the Armed Forces. Although journalists generally are protected as civilians as a legal matter, the factual circumstances of armed conflict often expose journalists exercising their profession in such a situation to dangers not normally encountered by other civilians.[487]

4.24.2.1 *Journalists – Risks in Areas of Military Operations*. Journalists who enter areas of military operations assume a significant risk that they could be injured or killed incidental to an enemy attack or from other dangers.[488] Unfortunately, journalists have sometimes been killed while reporting in close proximity to combat operations.[489] To minimize

---

[482] GPW art. 4A(4); AP I art. 79(2).

[483] *Refer to* § 9.4.3 (Issue of Identification Cards to Persons Liable to Become POWs).

[484] *Refer to* § 4.5 (Armed Forces of a State).

[485] *Refer to* § 4.18.4.1 (Being Part of a Hostile, Non-State Armed Group).

[486] *For example*, United States v. Al Bahlul, 820 F. Supp. 2d 1141, 1261 (CMCR 2011) ("In his voluntary statements to investigators, appellant admitted on multiple occasions to traveling to Afghanistan with the intent to join al Qaeda, undergoing military-type training at an al Qaeda sponsored camp, and meeting with bin Laden following his training. During that meeting, appellant admitted discussing bin Laden's views on Islam and jihad against the United States, agreeing with those views, and then pledging personal loyalty to bin Laden. He then joined al Qaeda as a member, worked in al Qaeda's media office, and eventually took charge of that office, where he performed a number of acts to recruit, to incite others to join al Qaeda, and to indoctrinate prospective al Qaeda recruits into the al Qaeda Plan.").

[487] *See* ICRC AP COMMENTARY 918 (¶3245) ("The circumstances of armed conflict expose journalists exercising their profession in such a situation to dangers which often exceed the level of danger normally encountered by civilians. In some cases the risks are even similar to the dangers encountered by members of the armed forces, although they do not belong to the armed forces.").

[488] *Refer to* § 4.15.2.3 (Increased Risk of Incidental Harm).

[489] *For example*, Marc Warren, *The 'Fog of Law': The Law of Armed Conflict in Operation Iraqi Freedom*, 86 U.S. NAVAL WAR COLLEGE INTERNATIONAL LAW STUDIES 167, 196-97 endnote 20 (2010) ("Consider, e.g., the case of the Palestine Hotel in Baghdad, where two civilian cameramen were killed in an explosion caused by a round from

the risk of mistakenly being made the object of attack, journalists often seek to distinguish themselves from military forces.[490] Where possible, efforts should be made to distinguish between the activities of journalists and the activities of enemy forces, so that journalists' activities (*e.g.*, meetings or other contacts with enemy personnel for journalistic purposes) do not result in a mistaken conclusion that a journalist is part of enemy forces.

In addition, civilian journalists and journalists authorized to accompany the armed forces should not take any action adversely affecting their status as civilians if they wish to retain protection as a civilian.[491] For example, relaying target coordinates with the specific purpose of directing an artillery strike against opposing forces would constitute taking a direct part in hostilities that would forfeit protection from being made the object of attack.[492]

4.24.2.2 *Journalists – Reporting on Military Operations*. As noted above, DoD operates under the policy that open and independent reporting is the principal means of coverage of U.S. military operations. Under the law of war, there is no special right for journalists to access areas of military operations without the consent of the State conducting those operations.[493] The law of war does not prohibit States from taking security measures to reduce the risk of disclosure of sensitive military information, such as numbers of military personnel, types of on-hand equipment, unit locations, and plans for future operations.[494] For example,

---

the main gun of a US Abrams tank on April 8, 2003. The unit of which the tank was a part had been engaged in significant urban fighting, including repulsing an enemy counterattack on the day of the incident, and had received reports of enemy forward observers in high-rise buildings on the east side of the Tigris River. As the tank crossed the Al Jumhuriya Bridge, its crew spotted, and fired one round at, what appeared to be an enemy forward observer, but was in fact a civilian cameraman. The explosion killed Spanish cameraman Jose Couso and Reuters cameraman Taras Protsyuk, and wounded three other journalists. US forces conducted an investigation and determined that the Palestine Hotel had been fortified by the enemy and was occupied by the enemy. The cameraman had been misidentified as an enemy forward observer, which was a reasonable mistake under the circumstances."); *Ernie Pyle Is Killed on Ie Island; Foe Fired when All Seemed Safe*, THE NEW YORK TIMES, Apr. 19, 1945 ("GUAM, April 18—Ernie Pyle died today on Ie Island, just west of Okinawa, like so many of the doughboys he had written about. The nationally known war correspondent was killed instantly by Japanese machine-gun fire. The slight, graying newspaper man, chronicler of the average American soldier's daily round, in and out of foxholes in many war theatres, had gone forward early this morning to observe the advance of a well-known division of the Twenty-fourth Army Corps.").

[490] *For example*, Reporters Without Borders, *Safety Guide for Journalists: A handbook for reporters in high-risk environments*, 41 (2015) ("**To protect yourself against snipers:** ... • Indicate clearly that you are a journalist. Write PRESS or TV on everything. • Don't wear military-style clothing so as not to be confused with a combatant. And be careful with how you carry your equipment – cameras and zooms could look like weapons from afar."); Reporters Without Borders, *Handbook for Journalists*, 26 (2010) ("PASSING THROUGH AN AREA OF FIGHTING Only do so if you have no alternative. ... • Distinguish yourself from those fighting, for example by putting a 'press' sign on the vehicle.").

[491] *Consider* AP I art. 79 ("Journalists engaged in dangerous professional missions in areas of armed conflict" shall be protected as civilians from attack "provided that they take no action adversely affecting their status as civilians,").

[492] *Refer to* § 5.8.3.1 (Examples of Taking a Direct Part in Hostilities).

[493] *Compare* § 4.26.2 (Consent of the Parties to the Conflict Concerned).

[494] JOINT PUBLICATION 3-61, *Public Affairs*, C-3 (Nov. 17, 2015) ("In more general terms, information in the following categories should not be revealed because of potential jeopardy to future operations, the risk to human life, possible violation of HN and/or allied sensitivities, or the possible disclosure of intelligence methods and sources. ... (1) For US (or allied) units, specific numerical information on troop strength, aircraft, weapons systems, on-hand equipment, or supplies available for support of combat units. General terms should be used to describe

military security ground rules may be developed for media personnel.[495] The particular restrictions imposed by a State are likely to depend on its domestic law and policy.

Access to military operations that is afforded to media personnel must be consistent with law of war obligations,[496] including obligations to protect prisoners of war and other detainees against public curiosity.[497]

4.25 Delegates or Representatives of the Protecting Powers

4.25.1 Appointment of Delegates of the Protecting Powers. The Protecting Powers may appoint, apart from their diplomatic or consular staff, delegates from among their own nationals or the nationals of other neutral Powers to carry out its duties under the GPW and the GC.[498] These delegates shall be subject to the approval of the Power with which they are to carry out their duties.[499]

4.25.2 Duties of the Representatives or Delegates of the Protecting Power. The parties to the conflict shall facilitate to the greatest extent possible the task of the representatives or

---

units, equipment, and/or supplies. (2) Any information that reveals details of future plans, operations, or strikes, including postponed or canceled operations. (3) Information and VI [visual information] that would reveal the specific location of military forces or show the level of security at military installations or encampments.").

[495] DoD Directive 5122.05, *Assistant Secretary of Defense for Public Affairs (ASD(PA))*, 9 (Sept. 5, 2008), Enclosure 3 – *Statement of DoD Principles for News Media Coverage of DoD Operations* ("4. Journalists in a combat zone shall be credentialed by the U.S. military and shall be required to abide by a clear set of military security ground rules that protect U.S. Armed Forces and their operations. Violation of the ground rules may result in suspension of credentials and expulsion from the combat zone of the journalist involved. News organizations shall make their best efforts to assign experienced journalists to combat operations and to make them familiar with U.S. military operations."); *see also* Joint Publication 3-61, *Public Affairs*, III-17 (Nov. 17, 2015) ("Ground rules are developed to protect members of DOD from the release of information that could threaten their security or safety during ongoing operations while facilitating the media's access to timely, relevant information. Ground rules reconcile the desire of the media to cover military operations with DOD security and safety concerns and are in no way intended to prevent release of derogatory, embarrassing, negative, or non-complimentary information. Media ground rules include requirements designed to protect the security, health, and welfare of the media. Media ground rules should also include the process for release of information, media access to the commander, and access to the Internet if not commercially available, and the process for unintentional exposure to classified information.").

[496] *For example*, Center for Law and Military Operations, The Judge Advocate General's Legal Center & School, U.S. Army, I Legal Lessons Learned from Afghanistan and Iraq: Major Combat Operations (11 September 2001 - 1 May 2003) 138 (2004) ("The presence of embedded media resulted in various issues for the legal teams. For instance with hundreds of journalists traveling throughout Iraq looking for stories, JAs reported that they had to be vigilant in ensuring that EPWs and the bodies of deceased individuals were not photographed. Although journalists were warned not to film or photograph EPWs and the deceased, and in most cases they did not, some journalists had to be sent home for violating this guidance.").

[497] *Refer to* § 8.2.2.2 (Protection Against Public Curiosity); § 9.5.3 (Protection Against Insults and Public Curiosity).

[498] GPW art. 8 ("For this purpose, the Protecting Powers may appoint, apart from their diplomatic or consular staff, delegates from amongst their own nationals or the nationals of other neutral Powers."); GC art. 9 (same).

[499] GPW art. 8 ("The said delegates shall be subject to the approval of the Power with which they are to carry out their duties."); GC art. 9 (same).

delegates of the Protecting Powers.[500]

The representatives or delegates of the Protecting Powers shall not in any case exceed their mission under the 1949 Geneva Conventions.[501] They shall, in particular, take account of the imperative necessities of security of the State wherein they carry out their duties.[502]

4.25.3 Restrictions on Representatives of the Protecting Powers. A belligerent may impose legitimate security restrictions on the activities of the delegates or representatives of the Protecting Powers working in its territory or in its facilities. However, belligerents should only restrict the activities of the representatives or delegates of the Protecting Powers "as an exceptional and temporary measure when this is rendered necessary by imperative military necessities."[503] For example, a belligerent may postpone a visit by Protecting Power representatives to a POW camp for security or humanitarian reasons, such as tactical movement of its own forces or to protect Protecting Power personnel from explosive remnants of war being cleared from recent military operations along the route to the POW camp.

4.26 ICRC and Other Impartial Humanitarian Organizations

The 1949 Geneva Conventions contemplate that the ICRC and other impartial humanitarian organizations may, subject to the consent of the parties to the conflict concerned, provide humanitarian aid and seek to ensure the protection of war victims in armed conflict.[504] In some cases, the ICRC or another impartial humanitarian organization may assume the humanitarian functions performed by the Protecting Powers.[505]

4.26.1 "Impartial". To be an "impartial humanitarian organization" under the 1949 Geneva Conventions, a humanitarian organization must be impartial. The requirement of impartiality distinguishes these humanitarian organizations from those with an allegiance to a party to the conflict, such as national red cross societies.[506]

4.26.2 Consent of the Parties to the Conflict Concerned. The activities of the ICRC or other impartial humanitarian organizations in a State's sovereign territory, or in the area of a

---

[500] GPW art. 8 ("The Parties to the conflict shall facilitate to the greatest extent possible the task of the representatives or delegates of the Protecting Powers."); GC art. 9 (same).

[501] GPW art. 8 ("The representatives or delegates of the Protecting Powers shall not in any case exceed their mission under the present Convention."); GC art. 9 (same).

[502] GPW art. 8 ("They shall, in particular, take account of the imperative necessities of security of the State wherein they carry out their duties."); GC art. 9 (same).

[503] GWS art. 8; GWS-SEA art. 8 (same). *Refer to* § 9.33.1 (Access by Protecting Powers); § 10.33.1 (Access by Protecting Powers).

[504] *See, e.g.*, GWS art. 9 ("The provisions of the present Convention constitute no obstacle to the humanitarian activities which the International Committee of the Red Cross or any other impartial humanitarian organization may, subject to the consent of the Parties to the conflict concerned, undertake for the protection" and relief of persons protected by the Convention); GWS-SEA art. 9 (same); GPW art. 9 (same); GC art. 10 (same).

[505] *Refer to* § 18.15.2 (Appointment of a Protecting Power).

[506] *Refer to* § 4.11 (Authorized Staff of Voluntary Aid Societies).

State's military operations, are subject to the consent of that State.[507] The requirement of State consent is based on the State's sovereign right to control access to its territory and a belligerent's right to control access to its military operations or territory it occupies.[508] For example, members of impartial humanitarian organizations, like other civilians, may be removed from the vicinity of military objectives for their protection.[509]

States may grant access on a case-by-case basis; access granted to one impartial humanitarian organization does not constitute entitlement of access for other humanitarian organizations. Impartial humanitarian organizations that have been granted access must also act within the terms of this consent.[510] For comparison, the activities of the Protecting Power are also subject to the consent of the affected States.[511]

States should not arbitrarily withhold their consent to the activities of humanitarian organizations, even in non-international armed conflict.[512] Where a State has accepted the services of an impartial humanitarian organization, the State must not regard such service, such as the provision of medical care, as unlawful and subject to punishment.[513]

4.26.2.1 Impartial Humanitarian Organizations – Conditions on Access. States may attach conditions to their consent, including necessary security measures. For example, in the past, armed groups have sometimes attempted to use humanitarian organizations as cover for

---

[507] *U.S. Comments on the International Committee of the Red Cross's Memorandum on the Applicability of International Humanitarian Law in the Gulf Region*, Jan. 11, 1991, DIGEST OF UNITED STATES PRACTICE IN INTERNATIONAL LAW 1991-1999 2057, 2066 ("The obligations set forth in this paragraph generally are subject to the consent of the parties to the conflict, as noted in Article 9 of the GPW and 10 of the GC. Although the U.S. historically has called upon the ICRC to assist it in implementation of the provisions of the 1949 Geneva Conventions, ultimately any decision to seek assistance of the ICRC or any other humanitarian organization is subject to the consent of the parties to the conflict in general and the host nation in particular.").

[508] *Refer to* § 5.19.1.1 (Belligerent Authority to Exercise Control in the Immediate Vicinity of Military Operations); § 11.4.1 (Right of the Occupying Power to Govern the Enemy Territory Temporarily).

[509] *Refer to* § 5.14.2 (Removing Civilians and Civilian Objects From the Vicinity of Military Objectives).

[510] *See* U.S. RESPONSE TO ICRC CIHL STUDY 520 ("We do not believe that rule 31, as drafted, reflects customary international law applicable to international or non-international armed conflicts. The rule does not reflect the important element of State consent or the fact that States' obligations in this area extend only to HRP [Humanitarian Relief Personnel] who are acting within the terms of their mission - that is, providing humanitarian relief. To the extent that the authors intended to imply a 'terms of mission' requirement in the rule, the authors illustrated the difficulty of proposing rules of customary international law that have been simplified as compared to the corresponding treaty rules.").

[511] *Refer to* § 18.15.3 (Activities of the Protecting Power).

[512] *Refer to* § 17.8.1 (State Consent for Humanitarian Organizations).

[513] Principles Related to the Protection of Medical Care Provided by Impartial Humanitarian Organizations During Armed Conflict, ¶VI, attachment to Ash Carter, Secretary of Defense, *Memorandum re: Principles Related to the Protection of Medical Care Provided by Impartial Humanitarian Organizations During Armed Conflict*, Oct. 3, 2016 ("VI. Impartial humanitarian organizations may offer their services to any of the parties to the conflict. A. States should not arbitrarily withhold their consent to the activities of humanitarian organizations. B. Where a State has accepted the services of an impartial humanitarian organization, it must not regard such services, including the provision of medical care, as unlawful and subject to punishment.").

participation in hostilities.[514] In addition to legitimate military considerations, other considerations may also limit access by impartial humanitarian organizations to military operations. For example, the GPW obligates a Detaining Power to protect POWs from "public curiosity," which may entail limiting access to POWs by private organizations.[515]

4.26.2.2 *Impartial Humanitarian Organizations – CCW Amended Mines Protocol Obligation*. In certain cases, however, there may be an obligation to take measures to help protect the personnel of certain humanitarian organizations that are performing functions with the consent of the Party to the CCW Amended Mines Protocol on whose territory the functions are performed from the effects of mines, booby-traps, and other devices.[516]

4.26.3 Special Status of the ICRC. The 1949 Geneva Conventions explicitly recognize the special position of the ICRC among impartial humanitarian organizations.[517] Similarly, Congress has specifically authorized – and the President has designated – the ICRC to be extended the same privileges and immunities that are afforded to public international organizations in which the United States participates.[518] The President has also recognized the role of the ICRC in visiting individuals detained in armed conflict.[519] The United States has relied on the ICRC's capacity, particularly in conflict situations, and has contributed substantially to the ICRC's work.[520] The United States has maintained a very constructive

---

[514] U.S. RESPONSE TO ICRC CIHL STUDY 519-20 ("For example, during the 1982 Israeli incursion into Lebanon, Israel discovered ambulances marked with the Red Crescent, purportedly representing the Palestinian Red Crescent Society, carrying able-bodied enemy fighters and weapons. This misconduct reportedly was repeated during the 2002 seizure of Bethlehem's Church of the Nativity by members of the terrorist al Aqsa Martyrs Brigade. … Military commanders also have had to worry about individuals falsely claiming HRP [humanitarian relief personnel] status, as happened in Afghanistan when some members of Al Qaeda captured while fighting claimed to be working for a humanitarian relief organization. These examples demonstrate why States, in crafting treaty provisions on this topic, have created a 'terms of mission' condition for HRP in a way that rule 31 fails to do.").

[515] *Refer to* § 9.5.3 (Protection Against Insults and Public Curiosity).

[516] *Refer to* § 6.12.11 (Obligation to Seek to Protect Certain Groups From the Effects of Minefields, Mined Areas, Mines, Booby-Traps, and Other Devices).

[517] *See, e.g.*, GPW art. 125 ("The special position of the International Committee of the Red Cross in this field shall be recognized and respected at all times."); GC art. 142 (same).

[518] *See* 22 U.S.C. § 288f-3 ("The International Committee of the Red Cross, in view of its unique status as an impartial humanitarian body named in the Geneva Conventions of 1949 and assisting in their implementation, shall be considered to be an international organization for the purposes of this subchapter and may be extended the provisions of this subchapter in the same manner, to the same extent, and subject to the same conditions, as such provisions may be extended to a public international organization in which the United States participates pursuant to any treaty or under the authority of any Act of Congress authorizing such participation or making an appropriation for such participation."); Executive Order 12643, *International Committee of the Red Cross*, 53 FEDERAL REGISTER 24247 (Jun. 23, 1988) ("I hereby extend to the International Committee of the Red Cross the privileges, exemptions, and immunities provided by the International Organizations Immunities Act.").

[519] *Refer to* § 8.10.4 (ICRC Access to Detainees).

[520] Gary Robbins, Chargé d'Affaires, Department of State, U.S. Mission to the Organization for Security and Cooperation in Europe, *Response to Ambassador Peter Maurer, President of the International Committee of the Red Cross*, Jan. 30, 2014 ("We honor the work that the ICRC has done over the past 150 years. With its founding principles of impartiality, neutrality, and independence, the ICRC is able to carry out crucial work where others cannot. The United States values the ICRC's work and relies on its capacity, particularly in conflict situations. In fiscal year 2013, the United States contributed more than $280 million to the ICRC's work, which reflects our

dialogue with the ICRC.

The ICRC does important work in visiting detainees, facilitating communication between detainees and their families, organizing relief operations, and undertaking similar humanitarian activities during armed conflicts. For example, the ICRC has performed the functions of a Protecting Power during armed conflict.[521] In addition, the ICRC has performed the functions of the Central Information Agency for POWs and protected persons during international armed conflict.[522] In order to facilitate access, the ICRC conducts its visits to detention facilities on a confidential basis, a practice that DoD has sought to respect.[523]

The ICRC has issued policy proposals or interpretative guidance on a variety of international law issues. Although the ICRC's proposals and interpretations do not have binding legal effect, they have often been helpful to States. In some cases, the United States and other States have not accepted the ICRC's proposals or interpretations and instead expressed opposing views. For example, the United States has not accepted the ICRC's study on customary international humanitarian law nor its "interpretive guidance" on direct participation in hostilities.[524]

4.27 Determining the Status of Detainees in Cases of Doubt

4.27.1 Identification Cards Used to Help Clarify Status. The 1949 Geneva Conventions contemplate that identification cards will be used to help clarify the status of detainees in international armed conflict.[525] Parties to the GPW must provide identity cards to persons under their jurisdiction who are liable to become POWs.[526] Similarly, Parties to the GWS must provide retained personnel with a special identity card that denotes their status.[527] Capturing units should not take these identity cards from POWs or retained personnel.[528] In addition,

---

confidence in the organization. We look forward to supporting the ICRC in the future as we confront significant humanitarian need around the globe.").

[521] *Refer to* § 18.15.2.3 (Impartial Humanitarian Organizations Assuming Humanitarian Functions Performed by Protecting Powers Under the 1949 Geneva Conventions).

[522] *Refer to* § 9.31.3 (Central POW Information Agency); § 10.31.3 (Central Information Agency for Protected Persons).

[523] *See, e.g.*, American Civil Liberties Union v. Department of Defense, 389 F. Supp. 2d 547, 554 (S.D.N.Y. 2005) (noting that DoD policy "requires confidential treatment of all ICRC communications"). For discussion of the ICRC practice of confidentiality, *see* Prosecutor v. Blagoje Simic *et al.*, ICTY Trial Chamber, IT-95-9, *Decision on the Prosecution Motion Under Rule 73 for a Ruling Concerning the Testimony of a Witness*, ¶¶45-74 (Jul. 27, 1999); Prosecutor v. Blagoje Simic, *et al.*, ICTY Trial Chamber, IT-95-9, *Separate Opinion Of Judge David Hunt On Prosecutor's Motion For A Ruling Concerning The Testimony Of A Witness*, ¶¶14-33 (Jul. 27, 1999).

[524] *Refer to* § 19.25 (2005 ICRC Study on Customary International Humanitarian Law); § 5.8.1.2 (AP I, Article 51(3) Provision on Direct Participation in Hostilities).

[525] *See, e.g.*, GPW Commentary 52 ("If need be, any person to whom the provisions of Article 4 [of the GPW] are applicable can prove his status by presenting the identity card provided for in Article 17.").

[526] *Refer to* § 9.4.3 (Issue of Identification Cards to Persons Liable to Become POWs).

[527] *Refer to* § 7.9.2 (Use of Identification Card to Help Establish Retained Personnel Status).

[528] GPW art. 17 ("The identity card shall be shown by the prisoner of war upon demand, but may in no case be taken away from him."); GWS art. 40 ("In no circumstances may the said personnel be deprived of their insignia or

States should retain duplicate copies of identification cards that they issue.[529] In contemporary practice, modern storage systems, such as computer databases, are used rather than storing duplicates of the issued identification cards.[530]

Producing an identification card to capturing forces is not necessarily a prerequisite for a person to be entitled to a particular status. Identification cards may become lost, damaged, or stolen during military operations, so a failure to produce an identity card does not necessarily mean that person lacks a particular status.[531]

4.27.2 POW Protections for Certain Persons Until Status Has Been Determined. Capturing personnel may be unable to establish a detainee's status, including whether that person is entitled to POW status under the GPW. For example, a detainee might have lost his or her identity card or the detainee might be a deserter who does not wish to admit that he or she is a member of enemy armed forces.

During international armed conflict, should any doubt arise as to whether persons, having committed a belligerent act and having fallen into the hands of the enemy, belong to any of the categories enumerated in Article 4 of the GPW, such persons shall enjoy the protection of the GPW until such time as their status has been determined by a competent tribunal.[532]

4.27.3 Competent Tribunal to Assess Entitlement to POW Status or Treatment. The "competent tribunal" in Article 5 of the GPW is often called an "Article 5 tribunal." In some

---

identity cards nor of the right to wear the armlet. In case of loss, they shall be entitled to receive duplicates of the cards and to have the insignia replaced.").

[529] GWS art. 40 (Identity cards for military medical and religious personnel "should be made out, if possible, at least in duplicate, one copy being kept by the home country."); GPW art. 17 (Identity cards for prisoners of war "[a]s far as possible … shall be issued in duplicate.").

[530] *For example*, DoD INSTRUCTION 1000.01, *Identification (ID) Cards Required by the Geneva Conventions*, ¶3(a)(3) (Apr. 16, 2012) ("The duplicate ID card requirements of Article 17 of Reference (f), to facilitate identification of POWs with the Prisoner of War Information Bureau as delineated in Article 122 of Reference (f), are more adequately met by the information routinely maintained in the Defense Enrollment Eligibility Reporting System (DEERS). Accordingly, duplicate ID cards will not be required.").

[531] *See, e.g.*, GPW COMMENTARY 64-65 (noting that States at the Diplomatic Conference of Geneva of 1949 "considered that the capacity in which the person was serving should be a determining factor; the possession of a[n identification] card is not therefore an indispensable condition of the right to be treated as a prisoner of war, but a supplementary safeguard").

[532] GPW art. 5 ("Should any doubt arise as to whether persons, having committed a belligerent act and having fallen into the hands of the enemy, belong to any of the categories enumerated in Article 4, such persons shall enjoy the protection of the present Convention until such time as their status has been determined by a competent tribunal."). *Consider* AP I art. 45(1) ("A person who takes part in hostilities and falls into the power of an adverse Party shall be presumed to be a prisoner of war, and therefore shall be protected by the Third Convention, if he claims the status of prisoner of war, or if he appears to be entitled to such status, or if the Party on which he depends claims such status on his behalf by notification to the detaining Power or to the Protecting Power. Should any doubt arise as to whether any such person is entitled to the status of prisoner of war, he shall continue to have such status and, therefore, to be protected by the Third Convention and this Protocol until such time as his status has been determined by a competent tribunal.").

cases, courts have undertaken to assess whether a detainee is entitled to POW status,[533] but a "competent tribunal" generally entails the Detaining Power convening an administrative board.[534] The GPW affords the Detaining Power substantial discretion regarding the composition and procedures of an Article 5 tribunal.[535]

Article 5 only requires a tribunal if there is "any doubt" regarding a person's entitlement to POW status or treatment.[536] For example, if there was no doubt that the armed group to which a person belongs fails to qualify for POW status, then the GPW would not require a tribunal to adjudicate the person's claim to POW status by virtue of membership in that group.[537]

4.27.4 <u>Tribunals to Assess Other Detainee Issues</u>. By its terms, Article 5 of the GPW only addresses a person's entitlement to POW status or treatment. However, an administrative process may be appropriate to address status questions besides entitlement to POW status or treatment, such as whether detainees are retained personnel or civilians. DoD practice has been to use Article 5 tribunals or similar administrative tribunals to address those issues.[538] For example, DoD used administrative tribunals to address a variety of detainee issues during detention operations in Viet Nam,[539] Panama,[540] the Persian Gulf in 1991,[541] Iraq in 2003,[542]

---

[533] *See, e.g.*, United States v. Lindh, 212 F. Supp. 2d 541, 557-58 (E.D. Va. 2002) (assessing whether a captured Taliban fighter was entitled to POW status under GPW); United States v. Noriega, 808 F. Supp. 791, 794-96 (S.D. Fla. 1992) (assessing whether a captured Panamanian General was entitled to POW Status under GPW); Stanislaus Krofan & Anor. v. Public Prosecutor, (Singapore Federal Court, 1966), LEVIE, DOCUMENTS ON POWS 732-36 (assessing whether captured Indonesian saboteurs were entitled to POW status under GPW); The Military Prosecutor v. Omar Mahmud Kassem and Others (Israeli Military Court, Ramallah, Apr. 13, 1969), LEVIE, DOCUMENTS ON POWS 771-80 (assessing whether members of the Popular Front for the Liberation of Palestine were entitled to POW status under GPW).

[534] Denmark proposed the term "competent tribunal" instead of "military tribunal" because "[t]he laws of the Detaining Power may allow the settlement of this question by a civil court rather than by a military tribunal." II-B FINAL RECORD OF THE DIPLOMATIC CONFERENCE OF GENEVA OF 1949 270.

[535] For examples of the procedures of past U.S. tribunals, *see, e.g.*, U.S. CENTRAL COMMAND REGULATION 27-13, *Captured Persons: Determination of Eligibility for Enemy Prisoner of War Status* (Jan. 15, 1991); 1997 MULTI-SERVICE DETENTION REGULATION § 1-6.*e*.

[536] Jay S. Bybee, Assistant Attorney General, *Status of Taliban Forces Under Article 4 of the Third Geneva Convention of 1949*, Feb. 7, 2002, 26 OPINIONS OF THE OFFICE OF LEGAL COUNSEL 1, 9 ("Under Article 5 of GPW, '[s]hould any doubt arise as to whether persons ... belong to any of the categories enumerated in Article 4, such persons shall enjoy the protection of the present Convention until such time as their status has been determined by a competent tribunal.' As we understand it, DoD in the past has presumed prisoners to be entitled to POW status until a tribunal determines otherwise. The presumption and tribunal requirement are triggered, however, only if there is 'any doubt' as to a prisoner's Article 4 status.") (amendments in original).

[537] *Refer to* § 4.6.1.1 (GPW 4A(2) Conditions Required on a Group Basis).

[538] *See, e.g.*, 1997 MULTI-SERVICE DETENTION REGULATION § 1-6.*e*.(10) (boards making determinations pursuant to Article 5 of GPW may make, in addition to a determination that someone is an enemy prisoner of war, also determinations that an individuals is retained personnel, an "innocent civilian," or a civilian internee "who for reasons of operational security, or probable cause incident to criminal investigation, should be detained.").

[539] In Viet Nam, the U.S. Army used panels of three officers assisted by a judge advocate advisor to assess the status of detainees. *See, e.g.*, U.S. MILITARY ASSISTANCE COMMAND VIETNAM DIRECTIVE 381-46, *Military Intelligence: Combined Screening of Detainees* (Dec. 27, 1967); U.S. MILITARY ASSISTANCE COMMAND VIETNAM DIRECTIVE 20-5, *Prisoners of War -- Determination of Eligibility* (Mar. 15, 1968); Fred K. Green, *The Concept of "War" and the*

Afghanistan,[543] and Guantanamo.[544]

Concept of "Combatant" in Modern Conflicts, 10 THE MILITARY LAW AND THE LAW OF WAR REVIEW 267, 285 (1971) (discussing detainee status classifications under Military Assistance Command Vietnam Directive 20 5).

[540] *See* FRED BORCH, JUDGE ADVOCATES IN COMBAT 103-06 (2001) (describing detainee screening procedures in 1989-1990 Operation JUST CAUSE in Panama).

[541] *See* FINAL REPORT ON THE PERSIAN GULF WAR 577-78 (describing article 5 tribunals during Operation DESERT STORM).

[542] *See, e.g.*, CENTER FOR LAW AND MILITARY OPERATIONS, THE JUDGE ADVOCATE GENERAL'S LEGAL CENTER & SCHOOL, U.S. ARMY, I LEGAL LESSONS LEARNED FROM AFGHANISTAN AND IRAQ: MAJOR COMBAT OPERATIONS (11 SEPTEMBER 2001 - 1 MAY 2003) 41-47 (2004) (describing Article 5 tribunals conducted during Operation IRAQI FREEDOM in 2003).

[543] *See* Al Maqaleh v. Gates, 604 F. Supp. 2d 205, 227 (D.D.C., 2009) (describing detainee review procedures in Afghanistan); Detainee Review Procedures At Bagram Theater Internment, enclosed in Phillip Carter, Deputy Assistant Secretary of Defense for Detainee Policy, Letter to Senator Carl Levin, Jul. 14, 2009 (describing modified detainee review procedures in Afghanistan).

[544] *See, e.g.*, Executive Order 13567, *Periodic Review of Individuals Detained at Guantanamo Bay Naval Station Pursuant to the Authorization for Use of Military Force*, 76 FEDERAL REGISTER 13277 (Mar. 7, 2011) (establishing a process to review on a periodic basis the continued discretionary exercise of existing detention authority for certain individuals detained at Guantanamo Bay, Cuba); Paul Wolfowitz, Deputy Secretary of Defense, Order Establishing Combatant Status Review Tribunal, Jul. 7, 2004, as amended 2006 (establishing an administrative process to review the detention of foreign nationals held as enemy combatants at Guantanamo Bay, Cuba).

V – The Conduct of Hostilities

Chapter Contents

5.1 Introduction

The right of States engaged in armed conflict to adopt means and methods of warfare is not unlimited.[1] This Chapter addresses the law of war rules on the conduct of hostilities during international armed conflict, such as the rules applicable to conducting attacks, the seizure and destruction of enemy property, and deception.

---

[1] *Refer to* § 2.6.2.1 (Acceptance That Belligerent Rights Are Not Unlimited).

This Chapter, however, does not address all rules related to the conduct of hostilities. For example, rules on the use of certain types of weapons are addressed in Chapter VI.[2] In addition, later chapters address conduct of hostilities rules and issues specific to the Naval (Chapter XIII), Air (Chapter XIV), Space (Chapter XIV), and Cyber (Chapter XVI) domains, and Chapter XVIII addresses non-international armed conflict.[3]

Violations of the rules in the conduct of hostilities may be violations of criminal law, although it is not a purpose of this Chapter to address liability under criminal law.

5.1.1 Notes on Terminology – "Means and Methods of Warfare". In general, *method of warfare* has referred to how warfare is conducted, while *means of warfare* has referred to weapons or devices used to conduct warfare.[4]

For example, an analysis of a *method of warfare* might consider the way in which an artillery projectile may be employed, particularly where employment could have an adverse effect on the civilian population. On the other hand, an analysis of the legality of the *means of warfare* might consider the legality of the way in which the artillery projectile is designed to kill or injure enemy combatants.[5]

Although the terms *means of warfare* and *methods of warfare* lack an established, specific meaning, in some cases, the phrase "method of warfare" may be a term of art in a legal instrument that has been specifically interpreted by the United States. For example, the Chemical Weapons Convention obligates Parties to undertake not to use riot control agents as a "method of warfare," and the United States has interpreted that prohibition not to include certain uses of riot control agents.[6]

5.1.2 Implementation of Law of War Obligations in the Conduct of Hostilities During

---

[2] *Refer to* § 6.5.1 (Certain Types of Weapons With Specific Rules on Use).

[3] *Refer to* § 13.3 (Overview of Rules for Naval Engagements); § 14.8 (Attacks Against Military Objectives in the Air); § 14.9 (Air Attacks Against Military Objectives on the Ground); § 16.5 (Cyber Operations and Jus in Bello); § 17.7 (Rules on Conducting Attacks in NIAC).

[4] *See, e.g.*, W. Hays Parks, Special Assistant to The Judge Advocate General of the Army for Law of War Matters, *Memorandum of Law: Travaux Preparatoires and Legal Analysis of Blinding Laser Weapons Protocol, reprinted in* THE ARMY LAWYER 33, 34-35 (Jun. 1997) ("*Method of warfare* is one of two historic phrases in the law of war. Although neither phrase has an agreed definition, *means of warfare* traditionally has been understood to refer to the effect of weapons in their use against combatants, while *method of warfare* refers to the way weapons are used in a broader sense."); ICRC AP COMMENTARY 621 (¶1957) ("The term 'means of combat' or 'means of warfare' (*cf.* Article 35 – *Basic rules*) generally refers to the weapons being used, while the expression 'methods of combat' generally refers to the way in which such weapons are used.").

[5] *See* W. Hays Parks, Special Assistant to The Judge Advocate General of the Army for Law of War Matters, *Memorandum of Law: Travaux Preparatoires and Legal Analysis of Blinding Laser Weapons Protocol, reprinted in* THE ARMY LAWYER 33, 35 (Jun. 1997) ("Thus, *means* considers the legality of the way in which a projectile or its fragments, for example, kill or injure combatants. As an illustration, Protocol I of the UNCCW makes the use of fragments not detectable by X-ray a prohibited *means of warfare*. In contrast, *method* weighs the way in which weapons may be employed, particularly where employment may have an adverse effect on civilians not taking a direct part in the hostilities.").

[6] *Refer to* § 6.16.2 (Prohibition on Use of Riot Control Agents as a Method of Warfare).

<u>Military Operations</u>. The law of war rules for the conduct of hostilities have been implemented during military operations through rules of engagement and other military orders.[7]

5.1.2.1 *<u>Applying Standards in the Conduct of Hostilities That Pose More Restrictions on Military Operations and That Are More Protective of Civilians Than Required By the Law of War</u>*. U.S. military operations are routinely subject to more restrictions and apply standards that are more protective of civilians than required by the law of war.[8] For example, military commanders often seek to reduce the risk of civilian casualties by taking additional precautions even when such measures are not required by the law of war.[9] Similarly, there are cases in which, for military or policy reasons, an attack is not conducted, even though the attack would be legally permissible.[10]

As with other cases in which a higher standard is applied as a matter of policy, violations of such standards are not necessarily violations of the law of war.[11]

5.1.2.2 *<u>Applicability of International Obligations to Persons With the Domestic Authority to Implement the Obligations</u>*. As with other aspects of the law of war, the persons

---

[7] *Refer to* § 1.6.5 (Rules of Engagement (ROE)); § 18.7 (Instructions, Regulations, and Procedures to Implement and Enforce the Law of War).

[8] *For example*, Executive Order 13732, *United States Policy on Pre- and Post-Strike Measures To Address Civilian Casualties in U.S. Operations Involving the Use of Force*, 81 FEDERAL REGISTER 44485, § 1 (Jul. 1, 2016) ("The protection of civilians is fundamentally consistent with the effective, efficient, and decisive use of force in pursuit of U.S. national interests. Minimizing civilian casualties can further mission objectives; help maintain the support of partner governments and vulnerable populations, especially in the conduct of counterterrorism and counterinsurgency operations; and enhance the legitimacy and sustainability of U.S. operations critical to our national security. As a matter of policy, the United States therefore routinely imposes certain heightened policy standards that are more protective than the requirements of the law of armed conflict that relate to the protection of civilians.").

[9] *For example*, Brian Egan, Legal Adviser, Department of State, *Remarks to the American Society of International Law: International Law, Legal Diplomacy, and the Counter-ISIL Campaign*, Apr. 1, 2016 ("As a matter of international law, the United States is bound to adhere to the law of armed conflict. In many cases, the United States imposes standards on its direct action operations that go beyond the requirements of the law of armed conflict. For example, the U.S. military may impose an upper limit as a matter of policy on the anticipated number of non-combatant casualties that is much lower than that which would be lawful under the rule that prohibits attacks that are expected to cause excessive incidental harm.").

[10] *For example*, FINAL REPORT ON THE PERSIAN GULF WAR 615 ("Similar actions were taken by the Government of Iraq to use cultural property to protect legitimate targets from attack; a classic example was the positioning of two fighter aircraft adjacent to the ancient temple of Ur (as depicted in the photograph in Volume II, Chapter VI, 'Off Limits Targets' section) on the theory that Coalition respect for the protection of cultural property would preclude the attack of those aircraft. While the law of war permits the attack of the two fighter aircraft, with Iraq bearing responsibility for any damage to the temple, Commander-in-Chief, Central Command (CINCCENT) elected not to attack the aircraft on the basis of respect for cultural property and the belief that positioning of the aircraft adjacent to Ur (without servicing equipment or a runway nearby) effectively had placed each out of action, thereby limiting the value of their destruction by Coalition air forces when weighed against the risk of damage to the temple. Other cultural property similarly remained on the Coalition no-attack list, despite Iraqi placement of valuable military equipment in or near those sites.").

[11] *Refer to* § 18.7.2.3 (Setting Higher Standards as a Matter of Policy).

within a party to a conflict who are responsible for implementing an obligation, are those persons with the authority to make the decisions and judgments required by the law of war.[12]

For example, the decisions and judgments required by the principle of proportionality normally require authority over military operations, and ordinarily would not require military personnel to take actions, such as providing warnings, when a superior commander has already determined that such actions are not feasible.[13] As another example, a pilot generally would be entitled to rely on the determination by headquarters that a given target is, in fact, a military objective.[14]

5.1.3 Principles for the Conduct of Hostilities. The principles that provide the foundation for the law of war are discussed in Chapter II, and these principles apply to the conduct of hostilities. As noted in Chapter II, specific rules on the conduct of hostilities are derived from, and must be interpreted consistent with, the basic principles that underlie the law of war.[15] Moreover, where no specific rule applies, law of war principles provide a general guide for conduct during war, including the conduct of hostilities.[16]

5.2 OVERVIEW OF RULES FOR THE PROTECTION OF CIVILIANS

The protection of civilians[17] against the harmful effects of hostilities is one of the main purposes of the law of war.[18] Many of the rules for the protection of civilians are derived from the principles of distinction and proportionality.[19] Specific rules for the protection of civilians may be grouped into two categories: (1) essentially negative duties to respect civilians and to refrain from directing military operations against them; and (2) affirmative duties to take feasible precautions to protect civilians and other protected persons and objects.

5.2.1 Responsibility of the Party Controlling Civilian Persons and Objects. The party controlling civilians and civilian objects has the primary responsibility for the protection of civilians and civilian objects.[20] The party controlling the civilian population generally has the

---

[12] *Refer to* § 18.3.1.1 (Implementation of International Obligations by Persons With the Authority to Make the Necessary Decisions and Judgments Required by International Law).

[13] *Refer to* § 5.10.2 (Responsibility of Commanders for Implementing the Principle of Proportionality in Conducting Attacks).

[14] ICTY, *Final Report to the Prosecutor by the Committee Established to Review the NATO Bombing Campaign Against the Federal Republic of Yugoslavia*, ¶84 (Jun. 13, 2000) ("The building hit was clearly a civilian object and not a legitimate military objective. ... It is the opinion of the committee that the aircrew involved in the attack should not be assigned any responsibility for the fact they were given the wrong target ... .").

[15] *Refer to* § 2.1.2.1 (Law of War Principles as an Aid in Interpreting and Applying Law of War Rules).

[16] *Refer to* § 2.1.2.2 (Law of War Principles as a General Guide).

[17] *Refer to* § 4.8.1.5 (General Usage of "Civilian" in This Manual).

[18] *Refer to* § 1.3.4 (Purposes of the Law of War).

[19] *Refer to* § 2.5 (Distinction); § 2.4 (Proportionality).

[20] *See* J. Fred Buzhardt, General Counsel, Department of Defense, Letter to Senator Edward Kennedy, Sept. 22, 1972, *reprinted in* 67 AJIL 122 (1973) ("A summary of the laws of armed conflict, in the broadest terms, reveals certain general principles including the following: ... (c). That a distinction must be made at all times between

greater opportunity to minimize risk to civilians.[21] Civilians also may share in the responsibility to take precautions for their own protection.[22] For example, civilians may decide to take measures for their own protection upon receiving a warning to stay away from military objectives.[23]

5.2.2 Essentially Negative Duties to Respect Civilians and to Refrain From Directing Military Operations Against Them. In general, military operations must not be directed against enemy civilians.[24] In particular:

- Civilians must not be made the object of attack;[25]
- Military objectives may not be attacked when the expected incidental loss of civilian life,

---

persons taking part in the hostilities and members of the civilian population to the effect that the civilians be spared as much as possible. … The principle in (c) addresses primarily the Party exercising control over members of the civilian population."); BOTHE, PARTSCH, & SOLF, NEW RULES 284 (AP I art. 48, ¶2.2) (explaining that "an important share of the responsibility for implementing the principle of distinction rests on the Party which controls the civilian population."); United States, *Statement on Ratification of the 1954 Hague Cultural Property Convention*, Mar. 13, 2009, 2575 UNTS 7, 8 ("It is the understanding of the United States of America that, as is true for all civilian objects, the primary responsibility for protection of cultural objects rests with the party controlling that property, to ensure that it is properly identified and that it is not used for an unlawful purpose.").

[21] FINAL REPORT ON THE PERSIAN GULF WAR 614 ("In the effort to minimize collateral civilian casualties, a substantial responsibility for protection of the civilian population rests with the party controlling the civilian population. Historically, and from a common sense standpoint, the party controlling the civilian population has the opportunity and the responsibility to minimize the risk to the civilian population through the separation of military objects from the civilian population, evacuation of the civilian population from near immovable military objects, and development of air raid precautions. Throughout World War II, for example, both Axis and Allied nations took each of these steps to protect their respective civilian populations from the effects of military operations.").

[22] *U.S. Comments on the International Committee of the Red Cross's Memorandum on the Applicability of International Humanitarian Law in the Gulf Region*, Jan. 11, 1991, DIGEST OF UNITED STATES PRACTICE IN INTERNATIONAL LAW 1991-1999 2057, 2063 ("The obligation of distinguishing combatants and military objectives from civilians and civilian objects is a shared responsibility of the attacker, defender, and the civilian population as such. An attacker must exercise reasonable precautions to minimize incidental or collateral injury to the civilian population, consistent with mission accomplishment and allowable risk to the attacking force. A defender must exercise reasonable precaution to separate the civilian population and civilian objects from military objectives. Civilians must exercise reasonable precaution to remove themselves from the vicinity of military objectives or military operations. The force that has control over the civilians has an obligation to place them in a safe place."); Brigadier General George B. Davis, *Working Memoranda (Confidential for the United States Delegates): The Second Peace Conference (Paragraph 2 of Programme), The Rules of War on Land*, 28 (1907) ("It seems hardly necessary to say, however, that if any defense is attempted or if a town is occupied or held by the armed forces of the enemy, it ceases to be undefended and, for that reason, may be attacked or fired upon. The inhabitants of such a place, so soon as a garrison is established or military defense is attempted, become charged with the knowledge that the town is defended and, as such, liable to attack, and, if they desire to secure an immunity from acts of war, should remove their families and belongings from the zone of active military operations.").

[23] *Refer to* § 5.11.5 (Effective Advance Warning Before an Attack That May Affect the Civilian Population).

[24] *Consider* AP I art. 48 ("In order to ensure respect for and protection of the civilian population and civilian objects, the Parties to the conflict shall at all times distinguish between the civilian population and combatants and between civilian objects and military objectives and accordingly shall direct their operations only against military objectives.").

[25] *Refer to* § 5.5.2 (Persons, Objects, and Locations That Are Protected From Being Made the Object of Attack).

injury to civilians, and damage to civilian objects would be excessive in relation to the concrete and direct military advantage expected to be gained;[26]

- Civilians must not be used as shields or as hostages;[27] and
- Measures of intimidation or terrorism against the civilian population are prohibited, including acts or threats of violence, the primary purpose of which is to spread terror among the civilian population.[28]

5.2.2.1 Non-Violent Measures That Are Militarily Necessary. The principle that military operations must not be directed against civilians does not prohibit military operations short of violence that are militarily necessary. For example, such operations may include:

- stopping and searching civilians for weapons and to verify that they are civilians;[29]
- temporarily detaining civilians for reasons of mission accomplishment, self-defense, or for their own safety;[30]

---

[26] *Refer to* § 5.12 (Proportionality – Prohibition on Attacks Expected to Cause Excessive Incidental Harm).

[27] *Refer to* § 5.16 (Prohibition on Using Protected Persons and Objects to Shield, Favor, or Impede Military Operations).

[28] *Refer to* § 10.5.3.2 (Collective Penalties and Measures of Intimidation or Terrorism).

[29] *For example*, 101st Airborne ROE Card, Iraq (2003), *reprinted in* CENTER FOR LAW AND MILITARY OPERATIONS, THE JUDGE ADVOCATE GENERAL'S LEGAL CENTER & SCHOOL, U.S. ARMY, I LEGAL LESSONS LEARNED FROM AFGHANISTAN AND IRAQ: MAJOR COMBAT OPERATIONS (11 SEPTEMBER 2001 - 1 MAY 2003) 315 (2004) ("You may stop civilians and check their identities, search for weapons and seize any found."). *Compare* § 10.6.1 (General Authority of a Belligerent to Search and Secure Protected Persons and Their Property).

[30] *For example*, Detainee Review Procedures at Bagram Theater Internment Facility (BTIF), Afghanistan, *enclosure to* Phillip Carter, Deputy Assistant Secretary of Defense for Detainee Policy, Letter to Chairman Carl Levin, Jul. 14, 2009 ("(U) U.S. Forces operating under Operation Enduring Freedom (OEF) authority are authorized to detain persons temporarily, consistent with the laws and customs of war (e.g., in self-defense or for force protection)."); Coalition Forces Land Component Command (CFLCC) Rules of Engagement (ROE) Card, Iraq (2003), *reprinted in* CENTER FOR LAW AND MILITARY OPERATIONS, THE JUDGE ADVOCATE GENERAL'S LEGAL CENTER & SCHOOL, U.S. ARMY, I LEGAL LESSONS LEARNED FROM AFGHANISTAN AND IRAQ: MAJOR COMBAT OPERATIONS (11 SEPTEMBER 2001 - 1 MAY 2003) 314 (2004) ("Detain civilians if they interfere with mission accomplishment or if required for self-defense."); 101st Airborne ROE Card, Iraq (2003), *reprinted in* CENTER FOR LAW AND MILITARY OPERATIONS, THE JUDGE ADVOCATE GENERAL'S LEGAL CENTER & SCHOOL, U.S. ARMY, I LEGAL LESSONS LEARNED FROM AFGHANISTAN AND IRAQ: MAJOR COMBAT OPERATIONS (11 SEPTEMBER 2001 - 1 MAY 2003) 315 (2004) ("Detain civilians when necessary to accomplish your mission or for their own safety."); CENTER FOR LAW AND MILITARY OPERATIONS, THE JUDGE ADVOCATE GENERAL'S LEGAL CENTER & SCHOOL, U.S. ARMY, LAW AND MILITARY OPERATIONS IN KOSOVO, 1999-2001: LESSONS LEARNED FOR JUDGE ADVOCATES 102-03 (2001) ("Based on the KFOR [Kosovo Force] guidance, Task Force Falcon instructed U.S. soldiers and Marines to detain persons who committed criminal misconduct under a familiar standard, the Uniform Code of Military Justice (UCMJ). This was the standard to be applied during each of the 1,300 patrols that U.S. soldiers conducted per week in Kosovo. If soldiers or Marines witnessed an act that would be a crime under the UCMJ, they arrested the wrongdoer. COMKFOR and the SRSG augmented crimes under the military code with mission-specific unauthorized acts, such as weapons, uniform, and curfew violations. Soldiers were also authorized to detain local citizens who were considered a threat to the military or to the overall mission.").

- collecting intelligence from civilians, including interrogating civilians;[31]

- restricting the movement of civilians or directing their movement away from military operations for their own protection;[32] or

- seeking to influence enemy civilians with propaganda.[33]

5.2.2.2 *Military Operations Intended to Benefit Civilians*. The principle that military operations not be directed against civilians does not preclude military operations intended to benefit civilians. Such operations may include humanitarian assistance operations, noncombatant evacuation operations, civil affairs operations, or civil-military operations. During counter-insurgency operations, military operations to protect civilians and to help obtain their support may be particularly important.[34]

5.2.3 Affirmative Duties to Take Feasible Precautions for the Protection of Civilians and Other Protected Persons and Objects. Parties to a conflict must take feasible precautions to reduce the risk of harm to the civilian population and other protected persons and objects.[35] Feasible precautions to reduce the risk of harm to civilians and civilian objects must be taken when planning and conducting attacks.[36] Feasible precautions should be taken to mitigate the burden on civilians when seizing or destroying enemy property.[37] It is specifically provided that feasible precautions must be taken in connection with certain types of weapons.[38] Feasible precautions to reduce the risk of harm to civilians must also be taken by the party subject to

---

[31] *Refer to* § 5.26.2 (Information Gathering).

[32] *Refer to* § 5.14.2 (Removing Civilians and Civilian Objects From the Vicinity of Military Objectives).

[33] *Refer to* § 5.26.1.2 (Propaganda Generally Permissible).

[34] *Refer to* § 17.5.2.1 (Positioning Military Forces Near the Civilian Population to Win Their Support and to Protect Them).

[35] *See, e.g.*, Michael J. Matheson, Deputy Legal Adviser, Department of State, *Remarks on the United States Position on the Relation of Customary International Law to the 1977 Protocols Additional to the 1949 Geneva Conventions at the Sixth Annual American Red Cross-Washington College of Law Conference on International Humanitarian Law* (Jan. 22, 1987), 2 AMERICAN UNIVERSITY JOURNAL OF INTERNATIONAL LAW AND POLICY 419, 426-27 (1987) ("We support the principle that all practicable precautions, taking into account military and humanitarian considerations, be taken in the conduct of military operations to minimize incidental death, injury, and damage to civilians and civilian objects, and that effective advance warning be given of attacks which may affect the civilian population, unless circumstances do not permit."); U.N. GENERAL ASSEMBLY RESOLUTION 2675, *Basic Principles for the Protection of Civilian Populations in Armed Conflict*, U.N. Doc. A/8028 (Dec. 9, 1970) ("In the conduct of military operations, every effort should be made to spare civilian populations from the ravages of war, and all necessary precautions should be taken to avoid injury, loss or damage to civilian populations."). *Refer to* § 5.18.4 (Other Feasible Precautions to Reduce the Risk of Harm to Cultural Property).

[36] *Refer to* § 5.11 (Proportionality – Feasible Precautions in Planning and Conducting Attacks to Reduce the Risk of Harm to Protected Persons and Objects).

[37] *Refer to* § 5.17.5 (Feasible Precautions Should Be Taken to Mitigate the Burden on Civilians).

[38] *Refer to* § 5.2.3.4 (Requirements to Take Precautions Regarding Specific Weapons).

attack.[39]

5.2.3.1 Feasible Precautions – Notes on Terminology. Although this manual primarily uses "feasible," other adjectives have been used to describe the obligation to take feasible precautions during armed conflict. The words "practicable,"[40] "reasonable,"[41] "due,"[42] and "necessary"[43] have been used to describe this obligation.

Some sources may distinguish between whether a precaution is "feasible" or "reasonable" or "practical."[44] It is also possible to use these words interchangeably with one another, *e.g.*, such that feasible precautions are reasonable precautions.[45]

---

[39] *Refer to* § 5.14 (Feasible Precautions to Reduce the Risk of Harm to Protected Persons and Objects by the Party Subject to Attack).

[40] Michael J. Matheson, Deputy Legal Adviser, Department of State, *Remarks on the United States Position on the Relation of Customary International Law to the 1977 Protocols Additional to the 1949 Geneva Conventions at the Sixth Annual American Red Cross-Washington College of Law Conference on International Humanitarian Law* (Jan. 22, 1987), 2 AMERICAN UNIVERSITY JOURNAL OF INTERNATIONAL LAW AND POLICY 419, 426-27 (1987) ("We support the principle that all practicable precautions, taking into account military and humanitarian considerations, be taken in the conduct of military operations to minimize incidental death, injury, and damage to civilians and civilian objects, and that effective advance warning be given of attacks which may affect the civilian population, unless circumstances do not permit.").

[41] *See, e.g., U.S. Comments on the International Committee of the Red Cross's Memorandum on the Applicability of International Humanitarian Law in the Gulf Region*, Jan. 11, 1991, DIGEST OF UNITED STATES PRACTICE IN INTERNATIONAL LAW 1991-1999 2057, 2063 ("A defender must exercise reasonable precaution to separate the civilian population and civilian objects from military objectives."); 1956 FM 27-10 (Change No. 1 1976) ¶41 ("Those who plan or decide upon an attack, therefore, must take all reasonable steps to ensure not only that the objectives are identified as military objectives or defended places within the meaning of the preceding paragraph but also that these objectives may be attacked without probable losses in lives and damage to property disproportionate to the military advantage anticipated."); Neville Chamberlain, Prime Minster, United Kingdom, *Statement before the House of Commons*, Jun. 21, 1938, HANSARD, 337 HOUSE OF COMMONS DEBATES §§ 937 ("[R]easonable care must be taken in attacking those military objectives so that by carelessness a civilian population in the neighbourhood is not bombed.").

[42] United States, *Statement on Consent to Be Bound by the CCW Amended Mines Protocol,* May 24, 1999, 2065 UNTS 128, 129 ("The United States reserves the right to use other devices (as defined in Article 2(5) of the Amended Mines Protocol) to destroy any stock of food or drink that is judged likely to be used by an enemy military force, if due precautions are taken for the safety of the civilian population.").

[43] U.N. GENERAL ASSEMBLY RESOLUTION 2675, *Basic Principles for the Protection of Civilian Populations in Armed Conflict*, U.N. Doc. A/8028 (Dec. 9, 1970) ("In the conduct of military operations, every effort should be made to spare civilian populations from the ravages of war, and all necessary precautions should be taken to avoid injury, loss or damage to civilian populations."); HAGUE IX art. 5 ("In bombardments by naval forces all the necessary measures must be taken by the commander to spare as far as possible sacred edifices, buildings used for artistic, scientific, or charitable purposes, historic monuments, hospitals, and places where the sick or wounded are collected, on the understanding that they are not used at the same time for military purposes.").

[44] ICRC AP COMMENTARY 688 (¶2230) ("It should be noted that 'all reasonable precautions' must be taken, which is undoubtedly slightly different from and a little less far-reaching than the expression 'take all feasible precautions', used in paragraph 2. As the nuance is tenuous, the purpose of the provision appears to be to reaffirm the rules that exist to protect civilians in such situations.").

[45] *U.S. Comments on the International Committee of the Red Cross's Memorandum on the Applicability of International Humanitarian Law in the Gulf Region*, Jan. 11, 1991, DIGEST OF UNITED STATES PRACTICE IN

Insofar as these words are used to describe the legal obligation to take precautions, these words are used as terms of art that do not necessarily take their ordinary meaning and are subject to a substantial degree of interpretation and discretion in their application to a given circumstance.

Thus, this manual does not distinguish between, for example, the obligation to take "reasonable" precautions versus the obligation to take "feasible" precautions versus the obligation to take "practical" precautions. This manual uses "feasible" to mean the standard of precautions that are required by the law of war, and that standard is explained in more detail in this section.

Some sources describe the obligation to take precautions as one in which "all feasible" precautions must be taken or that "everything feasible" must be done. Stating the requirement in terms of "all feasible" precautions could entail articulating a narrower interpretation of what is considered "feasible" rather than articulating a difference in what the law ultimately requires. In any event, as discussed below, the obligation to take feasible precautions does not require everything that is capable of being done – a standard that would be almost impossible to meet if interpreted literally and that is inconsistent with the definition of feasible precautions that provides for taking into account humanitarian and military considerations. In addition, the fact that a precaution was taken does not necessarily mean that taking the precaution was required as a matter of law.

5.2.3.2 *What Precautions Are Feasible*. The standard for what precautions must be taken is one of due regard or diligence, not an absolute requirement to do everything possible.[46] A wanton disregard for civilian casualties or harm to other protected persons and objects is clearly prohibited.[47]

Feasible precautions are those that are practicable or practically possible, taking into account all circumstances ruling at the time, including humanitarian and military

---

INTERNATIONAL LAW 1991-1999 2057, 2063 ("'Feasible precautions' are reasonable precautions, consistent with mission accomplishment and allowable risk to attacking forces.").

[46] *See also* Neville Chamberlain, Prime Minster, United Kingdom, *Statement before the House of Commons*, Jun. 21, 1938, HANSARD, 337 HOUSE OF COMMONS DEBATES §§ 937-939 ("[R]easonable care must be taken in attacking those military objectives so that by carelessness a civilian population in the neighbourhood is not bombed. … I say that reasonable care must be taken, in attacking military objectives, not to go outside those objectives, but it is extremely difficult in practice to determine whether in fact the dropping of bombs which have killed civilians in the neighbourhood of military objectives is the result of want of care or not. Suppose a man makes a bad shot, which is not at all unlikely when machines are going at over 300 miles an hour and when, as I am informed, in taking aim you have to release the bomb miles away from its objective—it seems to me that it is extremely difficult to lay down exactly the point at which reasonable care turns into unreasonable want of care.").

[47] *U.S. Comments on the International Committee of the Red Cross's Memorandum on the Applicability of International Humanitarian Law in the Gulf Region*, Jan. 11, 1991, DIGEST OF UNITED STATES PRACTICE IN INTERNATIONAL LAW 1991-1999 2057, 2064 ("While it is difficult to weigh the possibility of collateral civilian casualties on a target-by-target basis, minimization of collateral civilian casualties is a continuing responsibility at all levels of the targeting process. Combat is a give-and-take between attacker and defender, and collateral civilian casualties are likely to occur notwithstanding the best efforts of either party. What is prohibited is wanton disregard for possible civilian casualties.").

considerations.[48] These circumstances may include:

- the effect of taking the precaution on mission accomplishment;[49]
- whether taking the precaution poses a risk to one's own forces or presents other security risks;
- the likelihood and degree of humanitarian benefit from taking the precaution;
- the cost of taking the precaution, in terms of time, money, or other resources; or
- whether taking the precaution forecloses alternative courses of action.

For example, a commander may determine that a precaution would not be feasible because it would result in increased operational risk (*i.e.*, a risk of failing to accomplish the

---

[48] *See* CCW PROTOCOL III ON INCENDIARY WEAPONS art. 1(5) ("'Feasible precautions' are those precautions which are practicable or practically possible taking into account all circumstances ruling at the time, including humanitarian and military considerations."); CCW AMENDED MINES PROTOCOL art. 3(10) ("Feasible precautions are those precautions which are practicable or practically possible taking into account all circumstances ruling at the time, including humanitarian and military considerations."); CCW PROTOCOL V ON EXPLOSIVE REMNANTS OF WAR art. 5(1) ("Feasible precautions are those precautions which are practicable or practicably possible, taking into account all circumstances ruling at the time, including humanitarian and military considerations."). *Cf.* United Kingdom, *Statement on Ratification of AP I*, Jan. 28, 1998, 2020 UNTS 75, 76 ("The United Kingdom understands the term 'feasible' as used in the Protocol to mean that which is practicable or practically possible, taking into account all circumstances ruling at the time, including humanitarian and military considerations."); Canada, *Statement on Ratification of AP I*, Nov. 20, 1990, 1591 UNTS 462, 464 ("It is the understanding of the Government of Canada that, in relation to Articles 41, 56, 57, 58, 78 and 86 the [word] 'feasible' means that which is practicable or practically possible, taking into account all circumstances ruling at the time, including humanitarian and military considerations."); Germany, *Statement on Ratification of AP I*, Feb. 14, 1991, 1607 UNTS 526, 529 ("The Federal Republic of Germany understands the word 'feasible' in Articles 41, 56, 57, 58, 78 and 86 of Additional Protocol I to mean that which is practicable or practically possible, taking into account all circumstances ruling at the time including humanitarian and military considerations."); Netherlands, *Statement on Ratification of AP I*, Jun. 26, 1987, 1477 UNTS 300 ("With regard to Article 41, paragraph 3, Article 56, paragraph 2, Article 57, paragraph 2, Article 58, Article 78, paragraph 1, and Article 86, paragraph 2 of Protocol I: It is the understanding of the Government of the Kingdom of the Netherlands that the word 'feasible' means that which is practicable or practically possible, taking into account all circumstances ruling at the time, including humanitarian and military considerations.").

[49] VI OFFICIAL RECORDS OF THE CDDH 241 (CDDH/SR.42, Explanations of Vote: United States) ("It is the understanding of the United States Government that the word 'feasible' when used in draft Protocol I, for example in Articles 50 and 51, refers to that which is practicable or practically possible, taking into account all circumstances at the time, including those relevant to the success of military operations."); VI OFFICIAL RECORDS OF THE CDDH 226 (CDDH/SR.42, Explanations of Vote: Germany) ("Finally, we interpret the word 'feasible' [in draft article 50 of Protocol I] as meaning what is practicable or practically possible, taking into account all circumstances at the time, including those relevant to the success of military operations."); VI OFFICIAL RECORDS OF THE CDDH 211 (CDDH/SR.42, ¶41) ("Mr. Soysal (Turkey) said that as far as his delegation was concerned, the word 'feasible' in Article 50 and other articles should be interpreted as related to what was practicable, taking into account all the circumstances at the time and those relevant to the success of military operations."); VI OFFICIAL RECORDS OF THE CDDH 224 (CDDH/SR.42, Explanations of Vote: Canada) ("It is the understanding of the Canadian delegation that the word 'feasible', when used in this Protocol, for example, in Articles 50 and 51, refers to that which is practicable or practically possible, taking into account all circumstances existing at the relevant time, including those circumstances relevant to the success of military operations.").

mission) or an increased risk of harm to his or her forces.[50]

Similarly, taking a precaution would not be required if it is assessed not to yield a humanitarian benefit. For example, issuing a warning before an attack would not be required when only military objectives are expected to be harmed and civilians are not present.[51] Moreover, it would not be required to use distinctive emblems to identify civilians and civilian objects as such, if enemy forces are likely to use that information to direct attacks against those civilians and civilian objects.[52]

Since what precautions are feasible depends greatly on the context and other military considerations,[53] it would be inaccurate to conclude that specific precautions are required as a general rule. For example, there is not a general requirement to use precision-guided munitions.[54] Nonetheless, military commanders must make reasonable efforts to reduce the risk of harm to civilians and civilian objects.

5.2.3.3 The Taking of Precautions and Law, Policy, and Practice. There may be questions about the extent to which precautions are legally required or are instead policy decisions.

The obligation to take feasible precautions is a legal requirement. However, the determination of whether a precaution is feasible involves significant policy, practical, and military judgments, which are committed to the responsible commander to make in good faith based on the available information. In assessing whether the obligation to take feasible precautions has been satisfied after the fact, it will be important to assess the situation that the commander confronted at the time of the decision and not to rely on hindsight.

As discussed above, it is not the case that the legal requirement to take feasible precautions requires whatever may be done. Rather, it is possible for precautions to be taken, as a matter of practice or policy, that are not required as a matter of law, and the U.S. military frequently has done so.

---

[50] *U.S. Comments on the International Committee of the Red Cross's Memorandum on the Applicability of International Humanitarian Law in the Gulf Region*, Jan. 11, 1991, DIGEST OF UNITED STATES PRACTICE IN INTERNATIONAL LAW 1991-1999 2057, 2063 ("'Feasible precautions' are reasonable precautions, consistent with mission accomplishment and allowable risk to attacking forces. While collateral damage to civilian objects should be minimized, consistent with the above, collateral damage to civilian objects should not be given the same level of concern as incidental injury to civilians. Measures to minimize collateral damage to civilian objects should not include steps that will place U.S. and allied lives at greater or unnecessary risk.").

[51] *Refer to* § 5.11.5 (Effective Advance Warning Before an Attack That May Affect the Civilian Population).

[52] *Refer to* § 5.14.4 (Using Distinctive and Visible Signs to Identify Protected Persons and Objects as Such).

[53] *See, e.g.*, VI OFFICIAL RECORDS OF THE CDDH 231 (CDDH/SR.42, Explanations of Vote: Italy) ("In several places Article 50 speaks of taking all 'feasible' precautions. This term is basic to the whole structure of Article 50. It indicates that the obligations it imposes are conditional on the actual circumstances really allowing the proposed precautions to be taken, on the basis of the available information and the imperative needs of national defence. I would like to emphasize that all the foregoing comments relate to all the articles in the section of the Protocol concerned, in particular Article 46 as regards the military advantage expected and Articles 46 and 51 as regards the meaning of the word 'feasible'.").

[54] *Refer to* § 5.11.6 (Weaponeering (E.g., Selecting Appropriate Weapons, Aim Points)).

In this connection, it should also be noted that mere poor military judgment (such as mistakes or accidents in conducting attacks that result in civilian casualties) is not by itself a violation of the obligation to take precautions.

5.2.3.4 *Requirements to Take Precautions Regarding Specific Weapons*. In addition to the general obligation to take feasible precautions to reduce the risk of harm to the civilian population and other protected persons and objects, it is specifically provided that precautions be taken in connection with certain types of weapons:

- mines, booby-traps, or other devices;[55]
- incendiary weapons;[56]
- laser systems;[57] and
- explosive ordnance.[58]

5.2.3.5 *AP I Obligation to Take Constant Care to Spare Civilians and Civilian Objects*. Parties to AP I have agreed that "[i]n the conduct of military operations, constant care shall be taken to spare the civilian population, civilians and civilian objects."[59] Although this obligation is susceptible to a range of interpretations, Parties to AP I may also interpret it in a manner that is consistent with the discussion in this section.

5.3 Assessing Information Under the Law of War

Commanders and other decision-makers must make decisions in good faith and based on the information available to them. Even when information is imperfect or lacking (as will frequently be the case during armed conflict), commanders and other decision-makers may direct and conduct military operations, so long as they make a good faith assessment of the information that is available to them at that time.[60]

5.3.1 Law of War Rules Often Depend on Difficult Factual Assessments. Many of the rules for the conduct of hostilities require determinations of fact that may be difficult to make.

The special circumstances of armed conflict often make an accurate determination of

---

[55] *Refer to* § 6.12.5.3 (Obligation to Take Feasible Precautions to Protect Civilians From the Effects of Mines, Booby-Traps, and Other Devices).

[56] *Refer to* § 6.14.3 (Restrictions on the Use of Incendiary Weapons).

[57] *Refer to* § 6.15.2 (Feasible Precautions in the Employment of Laser Systems to Avoid the Incident of Permanent Blindness).

[58] *Refer to* § 6.19.2 (Using Explosive Ordnance); § 6.19.3 (Abandoning Explosive Ordnance).

[59] AP I art. 57(1).

[60] Appendix to 1985 CJCS Memo on AP I 52 ("Commanders and other military personnel who make decisions in the fog of war must do so in good faith and on the basis of whatever information they have available at the time. Such decisions will almost never be free of 'doubt,' either subjective or objective.").

facts very difficult.[61] For example, combatants must make decisions while enemy forces are attempting to attack them[62] and while enemy forces are seeking to deceive them.[63] In addition, the importance of prevailing during armed conflict[64] often justifies taking actions based upon limited information that would be considered unreasonable outside armed conflict.[65]

Thus, for example, it may be difficult to discern whether a person is a combatant, a civilian, or a civilian taking a direct part in hostilities. Similarly, it may be difficult to assess the degree to which an object makes an effective contribution to the adversary's military action or to assess the concrete and direct military advantage anticipated from an attack.

5.3.2 Decisions Must Be Made in Good Faith and Based on Information Available at the Time. Decisions by military commanders or other persons responsible for planning, authorizing, or executing military action must be made in good faith and based on their assessment of the information available to them at the time.[66] A large number of States have recognized this principle.[67] This principle has also been reflected in the decisions of courts assessing individual

---

[61] *Refer to* § 1.4.2.2 (Nature of War – Limited and Unreliable Information – "Fog of War").

[62] *Cf.* Brown v. United States, 256 U.S. 335, 343 (1921) ("Detached reflection cannot be demanded in the presence of an uplifted knife. Therefore in this Court, at least, it is not a condition of immunity that one in that situation should pause to consider whether a reasonable man might not think it possible to fly with safety or to disable his assailant rather than to kill him.").

[63] *Refer to* § 5.25 (Ruses of War and Other Lawful Deceptions).

[64] *Refer to* § 1.4.1 (Object of War).

[65] Korematsu v. United States, 323 U.S. 214, 244 (1944) (Jackson, J., dissenting) ("The very essence of the military job is to marshal physical force, to remove every obstacle to its effectiveness, to give it every strategic advantage. Defense measures will not, and often should not, be held within the limits that bind civil authority in peace. No court can require such a commander in such circumstances to act as a reasonable man; he may be unreasonably cautious and exacting. Perhaps he should be.").

[66] *See* United States, *Statement on Consent to Be Bound by CCW Protocol III on Incendiary Weapons*, Jan. 21, 2009, 2562 UNTS 36, 37 ("[A]ny decision by any military commander, military personnel, or any other person responsible for planning, authorizing or executing military action shall only be judged on the basis of that person's assessment of the information reasonably available to the person at the time the person planned, authorized, or executed the action under review, and shall not be judged on the basis of information that comes to light after the action under review was taken.").

[67] *See, e.g.*, Australia, *Statement on Ratification of AP I*, Jun. 21, 1991, 1642 UNTS 473 ("In relation to Articles 51 to 58 inclusive it is the understanding of Australia that military commanders and others responsible for planning, deciding upon, or executing attacks, necessarily have to reach their decisions on the basis of their assessment of the information from all sources, which is available to them at the relevant time."); Austria, *Statement on Ratification of AP I*, Feb. 13, 1983, 1289 UNTS 303 ("Article 57, paragraph 2, of Protocol I shall be applied to the extent that, for any decision taken by a military commander, the information actually available at the time of the decision is the determining factor."); Canada, *Statement on Ratification of AP I*, Nov. 20, 1990, 1591 UNTS 462, 464 ("It is the understanding of the Government of Canada that, in relation to Articles 48, 51 to 60 inclusive, 62 and 67, military commanders and others responsible for planning, deciding upon or executing attacks have to reach decisions on the basis of their assessment of the information reasonably available to them at the relevant time and that such decisions cannot be judged on the basis of information which has subsequently come to light."); Italy, *Statement on Ratification of AP I*, Feb. 27, 1986, 1425 UNTS 438, 439 ("In relation to Articles 51 to 58 inclusive, the Italian Government understands that military commanders and others responsible for planning, deciding upon or executing attacks necessarily have to reach decisions on the basis of their assessment of the information from all sources which is available to them at the relevant time."); Netherlands, *Statement on Ratification of AP I*, Jun. 26, 1987, 1477 UNTS 300 ("With regard to Articles 51 to 58 inclusive of Protocol I: It is the understanding of the Government of

responsibility under the law of war, which have declined to second-guess military decisions with the benefit of hindsight.[68]

The requirement that military commanders and other decision-makers make decisions in good faith based on the information available to them recognizes that decisions may be made when information is imperfect or lacking, which will often be the case during armed conflict.

5.4 RULES ON CONDUCTING ASSAULTS, BOMBARDMENTS, AND OTHER ATTACKS

Combatants may conduct assaults, bombardments, and other attacks, but a number of rules apply to these operations.

5.4.1 Notes on Terminology – Protection From "Attack As Such," "Being Made the Object of Attack," "Direct Attack," and "Intentional Attack" Versus Protection From "Incidental" or "Collateral" Harm. A variety of formulations have been commonly used to distinguish between: (1) the protection from being made the object of attack (*i.e.*, the attack is purposefully directed against that person or object) and (2) the protection from the incidental effects of an attack (*i.e.*, the object or person is not the object of the attack, but is collaterally harmed by the attack).

These situations are treated quite differently under the law of war.[69] In the former case, it

---

the Kingdom of the Netherlands that military commanders and others responsible for planning, deciding upon or executing attacks necessarily have to reach decisions on the basis of their assessment of the information from all sources which is available to them at the relevant time;"); Spain, *Statement on Ratification of AP I*, Apr. 21, 1989, 1537 UNTS 389, 392 ("It is understood that decisions by military authorities or others with legal powers to plan or carry out attacks which might affect civilian personnel goods or other effects, necessarily shall not be made on any basis other than that of relevant information available at the time in question and obtained for that purpose."); Switzerland, *Statement on Ratification of AP I*, Feb. 17, 1982, 1271 UNTS 409 ("The provisions of article 57, paragraph 2, create obligations only for battalion or group commanders and higher-echelon commanders. The information available to the commanders at the time of the decision shall be the determining factor."); United Kingdom, *Statement on Ratification of AP I*, Jan. 28, 1998, 2020 UNTS 75, 76 ("Military commanders and others responsible for planning, deciding upon, or executing attacks necessarily have to reach decisions on the basis of their assessment of the information from all sources which is reasonably available to them at the relevant time.").

[68] United States v. List, *et al.* (The Hostage Case), XI TRIALS OF WAR CRIMINALS BEFORE THE NMT 1295-96 ("It was with this situation confronting him that he [the defendant, Rendulic] carried out the 'scorched earth' policy in the Norwegian province of Finmark which provided the basis for this charge [of wanton destruction of property] of the indictment. ... There is evidence in the record that there was no military necessity for this destruction and devastation. An examination of the facts in restrospect can well sustain this conclusion. But we are obliged to judge the situation as it appeared to the defendant at the time. If the facts were such as would justify the action by the exercise of judgment, after giving consideration to all the factors and existing possibilities, even though the conclusion reached may have been faulty, it cannot be said to be criminal.").

[69] *See, e.g.*, United States v. Ohlendorf, *et al.* (The Einsatzgruppen Case), IV TRIALS OF WAR CRIMINALS BEFORE THE NMT 411, 467 ("A city is bombed for tactical purposes; communications are to be destroyed, railroads wrecked, ammunition plants demolished, factories razed, all for the purpose of impeding the military. In these operations it inevitably happens that nonmilitary persons are killed. This is an incident, a grave incident to be sure, but an unavoidable corollary of battle action. The civilians are not individualized. The bomb falls, it is aimed at the railroad yards, houses along the tracks are hit and many of their occupants killed. But that is entirely different, both in fact and in law, from an armed force marching up to these same railroad tracks, entering those houses abutting thereon, dragging out the men, women, and children and shooting them.").

is often said that protected persons and objects are protected "as such,"[70] from "direct attack,"[71] from "intentional attack,"[72] "from attack directed exclusively against them,"[73] or from being made the "object of attack."[74] Sometimes a combination of these formulations has been used.

In some cases, a text may not use any qualification (*e.g.*, "direct attack" or "as such,"), but is understood to refer only to the first category of protection. For example, Article 52 of AP I provides that "[a]ttacks shall be limited strictly to military objectives."[75] However, this article has been understood to comprise only an obligation not to direct attacks against civilian objects and not to address the question of incidental harm resulting from attacks directed against military objectives.[76]

This manual generally uses the phrase "object of attack" to convey the idea that the attack is being purposefully directed against that person or object.

This manual generally uses the term "incidental harm" to refer to the death or injury to civilians, or the destruction of or damage to civilian objects, that is incidentally (but potentially knowingly) caused as a collateral consequence of an attack directed against a military objective.[77]

5.4.2 Overview of Rules in Conducting Attacks. Parties to a conflict must conduct attacks in accordance with the principles of distinction and proportionality. In particular, the following rules must be observed:

---

[70] *See, e.g.*, 1956 FM 27-10 (Change No. 1 1976) ¶40a ("Customary international law prohibits the launching of attacks (including bombardment) against either the civilian population as such or individual civilians as such.") (emphasis added).

[71] 2004 UK MANUAL ¶5.3.2 ("A civilian is a non-combatant. He is protected from direct attack and is to be protected against dangers arising from military operations.") (emphasis added).

[72] Department of Defense, *Report to the Senate and House Appropriations Committees regarding international policies and procedures regarding the protection of natural and cultural resources during times of war*, Jan. 19, 1993, *reprinted as Appendix VIII in* Patrick J. Boylan, *Review of the Convention for the Protection of Cultural Property in the Event of Armed Conflict (The Hague Convention of 1954)* 201, 204 (1993) ("Like any civilian object, cultural property is protected from intentional attack so long as it is not used for military purposes, or to shield military objectives from attack.").

[73] *See, e.g.*, 1956 FM 27-10 (Change No. 1 1976) ¶25 ("However, it is a generally recognized rule of international law that civilians must not be made the object of attack directed exclusively against them.") (emphasis added).

[74] AP I art. 51(2) ("The civilian population as such, as well as individual civilians, shall not be the object of attack.") (emphasis added).

[75] AP I art. 52(2).

[76] *See, e.g.*, United Kingdom, *Statement on Ratification of AP I*, Jan. 28, 1998, 2020 UNTS 75, 77 ("The first sentence of paragraph 2 prohibits only such attacks as may be directed against non-military objectives; it does not deal with the question of collateral damage resulting from attacks directed against military objectives."); Canada, *Statement on Ratification of AP I*, Nov. 20, 1990, 1591 UNTS 462, 465 ("The first sentence of paragraph 2 of the Article is not intended to, nor does it, deal with the question of incidental or collateral damage resulting from an attack directed against a military objective.").

[77] *Refer to* § 5.12 (Proportionality – Prohibition on Attacks Expected to Cause Excessive Incidental Harm).

- Combatants may make military objectives the object of attack, but may not direct attacks against civilians, civilian objects, or other protected persons and objects.[78]

- Combatants must refrain from attacks in which the expected loss of life or injury to civilians, and damage to civilian objects incidental to the attack, would be excessive in relation to the concrete and direct military advantage expected to be gained.[79]

- Combatants must take feasible precautions in planning and conducting attacks to reduce the risk of harm to civilians and other persons and objects protected from being made the object of attack.[80]

- In conducting attacks, combatants must assess in good faith the information that is available to them.[81]

- Combatants may not kill or wound the enemy by resort to perfidy.[82]

- Specific rules apply to the use of certain types of weapons.[83]

5.4.3 Assessing Information in Conducting Attacks. Persons who plan, authorize, or make other decisions in conducting attacks must make the judgments required by the law of war in good faith and on the basis of information available to them at the time.[84] For example, a commander must, on the basis of available information, determine in good faith that a target is a military objective before authorizing an attack against that target. Similarly, the expected incidental damage to civilians or civilian objects must be assessed in good faith, given the information available to the commander at the time.

In making the judgments that are required by the law of war rules governing attacks, persons may rely on information obtained from other sources, including human intelligence or other sources of information.[85] For example, in a long-distance attack, a commander may rely on information obtained from aerial reconnaissance and intelligence units in determining

---

[78] *Refer to* § 5.5 (Discrimination in Conducting Attacks).

[79] *Refer to* § 5.12 (Proportionality – Prohibition on Attacks Expected to Cause Excessive Incidental Harm).

[80] *Refer to* § 5.11 (Proportionality – Feasible Precautions in Planning and Conducting Attacks to Reduce the Risk of Harm to Protected Persons and Objects).

[81] *Refer to* § 5.4.3 (Assessing Information in Conducting Attacks).

[82] *Refer to* § 5.22 (Treachery or Perfidy Used to Kill or Wound).

[83] *Refer to* § 6.5.1 (Certain Types of Weapons With Specific Rules on Use).

[84] *Refer to* § 5.3 (Assessing Information Under the Law of War).

[85] ICTY, *Final Report to the Prosecutor by the Committee Established to Review the NATO Bombing Campaign Against the Federal Republic of Yugoslavia*, ¶84 (Jun. 13, 2000) ("The building hit was clearly a civilian object and not a legitimate military objective. … It is the opinion of the committee … that it is inappropriate to attempt to assign criminal responsibility for the incident to senior leaders because they were provided with wrong information by officials of another agency.").

whether to conduct an attack.[86]

5.4.3.1 *Heightened Identification Requirements in Conducting Attacks*. Although doing so would impose greater restrictions than the requirements of the law of war, applying heightened standards of identification may be a policy choice to reduce the risk of incidental harm in conducting an attack.[87]

5.4.3.2 *AP I Presumptions in Favor of Civilian Status in Conducting Attacks*. In the context of conducting attacks, certain provisions of AP I reflect a presumption in favor of civilian status in cases of doubt. Article 52(3) of AP I provides that "[i]n case of doubt whether an object which is normally dedicated to civilian purposes, such as a place of worship, a house or other dwelling or a school, is being used to make an effective contribution to military actions, it shall be presumed not to be so used."[88] Article 50(1) of AP I provides that "[i]n case of doubt whether a person is a civilian, that person shall be considered to be a civilian."

Under customary international law, no legal presumption of civilian status exists for persons or objects, nor is there any rule inhibiting commanders or other military personnel from

---

[86] ICRC AP COMMENTARY 681 (¶2195) ("In the case of long-distance attacks, information will be obtained in particular from aerial reconnaissance and from intelligence units, which will of course attempt to gather information about enemy military objectives by various means.").

[87] *For example*, The White House, Office of the Press Secretary, *Fact Sheet: U.S. Policy Standards and Procedures for the Use of Force in Counterterrorism Operations Outside the United States and Areas of Active Hostilities*, May 23, 2013 (In counterterrorism operations, "lethal force will be used outside areas of active hostilities only when the following preconditions are met: … *Third*, the following criteria must be met before lethal action may be taken: 1) Near certainty that the terrorist target is present; 2) Near certainty that non-combatants will not be injured or killed;"); Coalition Forces Land Component Command (CFLCC) Rules of Engagement (ROE) Card, Iraq (2003), *reprinted in* CENTER FOR LAW AND MILITARY OPERATIONS, THE JUDGE ADVOCATE GENERAL'S LEGAL CENTER & SCHOOL, U.S. ARMY, I LEGAL LESSONS LEARNED FROM AFGHANISTAN AND IRAQ: MAJOR COMBAT OPERATIONS (11 SEPTEMBER 2001 - 1 MAY 2003) 314 (2004) ("1. On order, enemy military and paramilitary forces are declared hostile and may be attacked subject to the following instructions: a. Positive Identification (PID) is required prior to engagement. PID is a reasonable certainty that the proposed target is a legitimate military target. If no PID, contact your next higher commander for decision."); FINAL REPORT ON THE PERSIAN GULF WAR 177 ("Attack procedures specified that if the pilot could not positively identify his target or was not confident the weapon would guide properly (because of clouds, for example), he could not deliver that weapon. Several attack sorties were forced to return with their bombs for this reason."); U.S. MILITARY ASSISTANCE COMMAND VIET-NAM DIRECTIVE 525-13, *Military Operations: Rules of Engagement for the Employment of Firepower in the Republic of Vietnam*, ¶6a (May 1971), *reprinted in* 1975 DIGEST OF UNITED STATES PRACTICE IN INTERNATIONAL LAW 814, 815 ("All possible means will be employed to limit the risk to the lives and property of friendly forces and civilians. In this respect, a target must be clearly identified as hostile prior to making a decision to place fire on it.") ("All possible means will be employed to limit the risk to the lives and property of friendly forces and civilians. In this respect, a target must be clearly identified as hostile prior to making a decision to place fire on it.").

[88] AP I art. 52(3). *See also* BOTHE, PARTSCH, & SOLF, NEW RULES 326 (AP I art. 52, ¶2.5.1) ("It should be noted that the presumption applies only as to objects which normally do not have any significant military use or purpose. The committee deleted from the illustrative list proposed by the ICRC in draft Art. 47, the phrase 'installations and means of transport', thus indicating an intent by the Conference that the presumption should not apply to objects which are of such a nature that their value to military action in combat situations is probable. Means of transport and of communication fall into a category where their use for military purposes cannot be excluded through a presumption.").

acting based on the information available to him or her in doubtful cases.[89] Attacks, however, may not be directed against civilians or civilian objects based on merely hypothetical or speculative considerations regarding their possible current status as a military objective. In assessing whether a person or object that normally does not have any military purpose or use is a military objective, commanders and other decision-makers must make the decision in good faith based on the information available to them in light of the circumstances ruling at the time.

A legal presumption of civilian status in cases of doubt may demand a degree of certainty that would not account for the realities of war.[90] Affording such a presumption could also encourage a defender to ignore its obligation to separate military objectives from civilians and civilian objects.[91] For example, unprivileged belligerents may seek to take advantage of a legal presumption of civilian status.[92] Thus, there is concern that affording such a presumption likely would increase the risk of harm to the civilian population and tend to undermine respect for the law of war.

In applying AP I rules on "doubt," some Parties to AP I have interpreted these rules in a more limited way (*e.g.*, applying a "substantial doubt" standard) than AP I's text would suggest.[93]

5.4.4 Failure by the Defender to Separate or Distinguish Does Not Relieve the Attacker of the Duty to Discriminate in Conducting Attacks. A party that is subject to attack might fail to take feasible precautions to reduce the risk of harm to civilians, such as by separating the civilian population from military objectives.[94] Moreover, in some cases, a party to a conflict might

---

[89] *See, e.g.*, Christopher Greenwood, *Customary international law and the First Geneva Protocol of 1977 in the Gulf conflict, in* PETER ROWE, THE GULF WAR 1990-91 IN INTERNATIONAL AND ENGLISH LAW 63, 75 (1993) ("[I]t is very doubtful that Article 52(3) represents customary international law."); BOTHE, PARTSCH, & SOLF, NEW RULES 327 (AP I art. 52, ¶2.5.2) (quoting a Rapporteur's observation at the Diplomatic Conference that a presumption "will be a significant new addition to the law").

[90] *Refer to* § 1.4.2.2 (Nature of War – Limited and Unreliable Information – "Fog of War").

[91] *See* FINAL REPORT ON THE PERSIAN GULF WAR 616 ("This language, which is not a codification of the customary practice of nations, causes several things to occur that are contrary to the traditional law of war. It shifts the burden for determining the precise use of an object from the party controlling that object (and therefore in possession of the facts as to its use) to the party lacking such control and facts, i.e., from defender to attacker. This imbalance ignores the realities of war in demanding a degree of certainty of an attacker that seldom exists in combat. It also encourages a defender to ignore its obligation to separate the civilian population, individual civilians and civilian objects from military objectives, as the Government of Iraq illustrated during the Persian Gulf War.").

[92] *See* APPENDIX TO 1985 CJCS MEMO ON AP I 53 (rejecting the presumption of civilian status in AP I because "[t]his presumption also provides an additional protection for guerillas and other irregulars who may find it advantageous to be presumed to be a civilian rather than a combatant.").

[93] *See, e.g.*, 2004 UK MANUAL ¶5.3.4 ("In the practical application of the principle of civilian immunity and the rule of doubt, (a) commanders and others responsible for planning, deciding upon, or executing attacks necessarily have to reach decisions on the basis of their assessment of the information from all sources which is available to them at the relevant time, (b) it is only in cases of substantial doubt, after this assessment about the status of the individual in question, that the latter should be given the benefit of the doubt and treated as a civilian, and (c) the rule of doubt does not override the commander's duty to protect the safety of troops under his command or to preserve the military situation.").

[94] *Refer to* § 5.14 (Feasible Precautions to Reduce the Risk of Harm to Protected Persons and Objects by the Party Subject to Attack).

attempt to use the presence or movement of the civilian population or individual civilians in order to shield military objectives from seizure or attack.[95]

When enemy persons engage in such behavior, commanders should continue to seek to discriminate in conducting attacks and to take feasible precautions to reduce the risk of harm to the civilian population and civilian objects.[96] However, the ability to discriminate and to reduce the risk of harm to the civilian population likely will be diminished by such enemy conduct. In addition, such conduct by the adversary does not increase the legal obligations of the attacking party to discriminate in conducting attacks against the enemy.[97] Violations by the defending party are not a basis for that party to assert additional legal rights against the attacking party.[98]

5.4.5 Permissible Location of Attacks. In general, attacks may be conducted against military objectives wherever located, outside neutral territory.[99] Attacks, however, may not be conducted in special zones established by agreement between the belligerents, such as hospital, safety, or neutralized zones.[100]

Attacks on military objectives in the enemy rear or diversionary attacks away from the current theaters or zones of active military operations are lawful.[101] The law of war does not require that attacks on enemy military personnel or objectives be conducted near ongoing fighting, in a theater of active military operations, or in a theater of active armed conflict.[102]

---

[95] *Refer to* § 5.16 (Prohibition on Using Protected Persons and Objects to Shield, Favor, or Impede Military Operations).

[96] *See* FINAL REPORT ON THE PERSIAN GULF WAR 615 ("As correctly stated in Article 51(8) of Protocol I, a nation confronted with callous actions by its opponent (such as the use of 'human shields') is not released from its obligation to exercise reasonable precaution to minimize collateral injury to the civilian population or damage to civilian objects. This obligation was recognized by Coalition forces in the conduct of their operations.").

[97] *See* W. Hays Parks, *Air War and the Law of War*, 32 AIR FORCE LAW REVIEW 1, 163 (1990) ("While an attacker facing a target shielded from attack by civilians is not relieved from his duty to exercise reasonable precautions to minimize the loss of civilian life, neither is he obligated to assume any additional responsibility as a result of the illegal acts of the defender. Were an attacker to do so, his erroneous assumption of additional responsibility with regard to protecting the civilians shielding a lawful target would serve as an incentive for a defender to continue to violate the law of war by exposing other innocent civilians to similar risk.").

[98] *See, e.g.*, Charles J. Dunlap Jr., *The DoD Law of War Manual and its Critics: Some Observations*, 92 U.S. NAVAL WAR COLLEGE INTERNATIONAL LAW STUDIES 99-100 (2016) ("To reward a belligerent for flaunting the LoW [law of war] in that way is flatly contrary to the principle of international law expressed in the axiom *ex injuria non jus oritur* or 'legal rights should not be understood to result from the commission of wrongful acts.' … Given that the law has proven almost totally impotent in restraining today's adversaries who routinely violate LoW in exquisitely barbaric ways, we should be very sensitive to—and resistant of—any reading of the LoW that seems to result in privileging such lawbreakers *because of their lawbreaking*.").

[99] *Refer to* § 15.3.1.2 (Inviolability of Neutral Territory - Prohibition on Hostile Acts or Other Violations of Neutrality).

[100] *Refer to* § 5.14.3 (Establishing Areas Where Civilians or the Wounded and Sick Are Protected).

[101] *Refer to* § 5.6.7.3 (Definite Military Advantage).

[102] John O. Brennan, Assistant to the President for Homeland Security and Counterterrorism, *Speech at the Wilson Center: The Ethics and Efficacy of the President's Counterterrorism Strategy*, Apr. 30, 2012, 2012 DIGEST OF UNITED STATES PRACTICE IN INTERNATIONAL LAW 584, 585 ("There is nothing in international law … that prohibits

There are many examples of lawful attacks taking place far from where the fighting was previously taking place.[103]

For policy or operational reasons, military orders, such as applicable rules of engagement, may limit the locations where attacks on otherwise lawful military objectives may be conducted.

5.4.6 Force That May Be Applied Against Military Objectives. In the absence of expected harm to civilians and civilian objects or of wanton destruction that is not justified by military necessity, the law of war imposes no limit on the degree of force that may be directed against enemy military objectives, including enemy military personnel (but not including enemy personnel who are placed *hors de combat*).[104] For example, the principle of military necessity does not require that only the minimum force that is actually necessary in a specific situation may be used against military objectives.[105] Instead, the broader imperatives of winning the war may be considered, and overwhelming force may be used against enemy military objectives.[106]

In addition, combatants need not offer opponents an opportunity to surrender before

---

us from using lethal force against our enemies outside of an active battlefield, at least when the country involved consents or is unable or unwilling to take action against the threat.").

[103] *For example*, John D. Negroponte, *Letter dated 7 October 2001 from the Permanent Representative of the United States of America to the United Nations addressed to the President of the Security Council*, U.N. Doc. No. S/2001/946 (Oct. 7, 2001) (informing the U.N. Security Council that "the United States of America, together with other States, has initiated actions in the exercise of its inherent right of individual and collective self-defence following the armed attacks that were carried out against the United States on 11 September 2001" including U.S. military operations against al-Qaida and the Taliban in Afghanistan); LOUIS MORTON, UNITED STATES ARMY IN WORLD WAR II, THE WAR IN THE PACIFIC, STRATEGY AND COMMAND: THE FIRST TWO YEARS, 269-74 (1962) (describing U.S. bombing raid led by Lt. Col. James H. Doolittle on April 18, 1942, against military objectives in Tokyo).

[104] *See Refresher Course for Battalion and Brigade Commanders*, ¶11, Appendix B in DEPARTMENT OF THE ARMY SUBJECT SCHEDULE 27-1, *The Geneva Conventions of 1949 and Hague Convention No. IV of 1907*, 16 (Aug. 29, 1975) ("Nowhere in the law of war will you find a prohibition on shooting—and shooting to kill—the enemy in a firefight. On the battlefield the regrettable but necessary reality is kill or be killed. Once the enemy has surrendered, however, or otherwise fallen into your hands, there is no need to kill him."); J. Fred Buzhardt, General Counsel, Department of Defense, Letter to Senator Edward Kennedy, Sept. 22, 1972, *reprinted in* 67 AJIL 122, 124 (1973) ("I would like to reiterate that it is recognized by all states that they may not lawfully use their weapons against civilian population or civilians as such, but there is no rule of international law that restrains them from using weapons against enemy armed forces or military targets. The correct rule of international law which has applied in the past and continued to apply to the conduct of our military operations in Southeast Asia is that 'the loss of life and damage to property must not be out of proportion to the military advantage to be gained.'"); ICRC AP COMMENTARY 620 (¶1953) ("The armed forces and their installations are objectives that may be attacked wherever they are, except when the attack could incidentally result in loss of human life among the civilian population, injuries to civilians, and damage to civilian objects which would be excessive in relation to the expected direct and specific military advantage.").

[105] *Refer to* § 2.2.3.1 (Consideration of the Broader Imperatives of Winning the War).

[106] *See, e.g.*, 2007 NWP 1-14M ¶5.3.1 ("It is important to note that the principle of military necessity does not prohibit the application of overwhelming force against enemy combatants, units and material consistent with the principles of distinction and proportionality."); AIR FORCE OPERATIONS & THE LAW 16 (2009) ("The prohibition of unnecessary suffering does not limit the bringing of overwhelming firepower on an opposing military force in order to subdue or destroy it.").

carrying out an attack.[107]

In particular, the following practices are not prohibited: (1) surprise attacks; (2) attacks on retreating forces; (3) harassing fires; and (4) attacks on specific individuals.

5.4.6.1 *Surprise Attacks*. The law of war does not prohibit the use of surprise to conduct attacks, such as the use of surprise in ambushes, sniper attacks, air raids, and attacks by special operations forces carried out behind enemy lines.[108] There is no requirement that an enemy combatant must be warned before being attacked.[109] Rather, warning requirements apply only with respect to the civilian population and certain other protected units, vessels, and facilities, such as military medical units and facilities.[110]

5.4.6.2 *Attacks on Retreating Forces*. Enemy combatants remain liable to attack when retreating.[111] Retreat is not the same as surrender. Retreating forces remain dangerous as the enemy force may recover to counterattack, consolidate a new defensive position, or assist the war effort in other ways.[112] Retreat may also be a ruse.[113] Retreating enemy combatants may

---

[107] *See* FINAL REPORT ON THE PERSIAN GULF WAR 629 ("A combatant force involved in an armed conflict is not obligated to offer its opponent an opportunity to surrender before carrying out an attack.").

[108] *For example*, 1958 UK MANUAL ¶115 note 2 ("It is not forbidden to send a detachment or individual members of the armed forces to kill, by sudden attack, members or a member of the enemy armed forces. Thus, for instance, the raid by a British commando party on the headquarters of General Rommel's African Army at Beda Littoria in 1943 was not contrary to the provisions of the Hague Rules. The operation was carried out by military personnel in uniform; it had as part of its objective the seizure of Rommel's operational headquarters, including his own residence, and the capture or killing of enemy personnel therein, … ."); SPAIGHT, WAR RIGHTS ON LAND 87-88 ("A surprise attack is a very different thing [from a treacherous one]. When a body of Federal cavalrymen made a sudden descent on 'Hickory Hill' farm, in which the young Confederate General, W. F. H. Lee (son of the great commander, R. E. Lee), was convalescing from a wound, and carried him off as a prisoner of war to Fortress Munroe, they were guilty of no treachery under the laws of war. It was a fair and open raid.").

[109] *See, e.g.*, W. Hays Parks, Special Assistant for Law of War Matters, Office of the Judge Advocate General, U.S. Army, *Memorandum re: Legality of Silencers/Suppressors* 6 (Jun. 9, 1995) ("There is no law of war requirement that a combatant must be 'warned' before he or she is subject to the application of lawful, lethal force. A landmine provides no warning; neither does an ambush, a sniper, a machinegun in a concealed defensive position, a Claymore munition in a defensive perimeter, a delayed action munition, a naval mine, or many other means or methods of warfare. A sentry or personnel in a listening or observation post lawfully may be killed quietly, preferably through surprise, by garrote or knife attack. A surface-to-air missile undetected by its targeted aircraft likewise kills by surprise."); W. Hays Parks, Special Assistant for Law of War Matters, *Memorandum of Law—Legality of Snipers* (Sept. 29, 1992), *reprinted in* THE ARMY LAWYER 3 (Dec. 1992) ("The element of surprise is a fundamental principle of war, and does not make an otherwise legitimate act of violence unlawful.").

[110] *Refer to* § 5.11.5.3 (That May Affect the Civilian Population); § 5.11.5.1 (Other Warning Requirements).

[111] FINAL REPORT ON THE PERSIAN GULF WAR 632 ("The law of war permits the attack of enemy combatants and enemy equipment at any time, wherever located, whether advancing, retreating, or standing still. Retreat does not prevent further attack. At the small-unit level, for example, once an objective has been seized and the position consolidated, an attacking force is trained to fire upon the retreating enemy to discourage or prevent a counterattack.").

[112] *See* FINAL REPORT ON THE PERSIAN GULF WAR 622 ("It is recognized by military professionals that a retreating force remains dangerous. The First Marine Division and its 4,000 attached U.S. Army forces and British Royal Marines, in the famous 1950 march out of the Chosin Reservoir in North Korea, fighting outnumbered by a 4:1 margin, turned its 'retreat' into a battle in which it defeated the 20th and 26th Chinese Armies trying to annihilate it, … .").

have the same amount of force brought to bear upon them as an attacking military force, and a military commander is under no obligation to limit force directed against enemy combatants because they are, or appear to be, in retreat.

5.4.6.3 *Harassing Fires*. Harassing fires against enemy combatants are not prohibited. (Such action is clearly distinguishable from attacks to terrorize or otherwise harm the civilian population, which are, of course, prohibited.) Harassing fires are delivered on enemy locations for the purpose of disturbing enemy forces' rest, curtailing their movement, or lowering their morale.[114]

5.4.6.4 *Attacks on Specific Individuals*. Military operations may be directed against specific enemy combatants.[115] U.S. forces have often conducted such operations.[116]

5.4.7 Prohibition Against Declaring That No Quarter Be Given. It is forbidden to declare that no quarter will be given.[117] This means that it is prohibited to order that legitimate offers of surrender will be refused or that detainees, such as unprivileged belligerents, will be summarily

---

[113] *Refer to* § 5.25.2 (Examples of Ruses).

[114] APPENDIX TO 1985 CJCS MEMO ON AP I 47 ("Harassing fires are delivered on enemy locations for the purpose of disturbing the rest, curtailing the movement, or lowering the morale of troops.").

[115] *See, e.g.*, Harold Hongju Koh, Legal Adviser, Department of State, *Address at the Annual Meeting of the American Society of International Law: The Obama Administration and International Law*, Mar. 25, 2010, 2010 DIGEST OF UNITED STATES PRACTICE IN INTERNATIONAL LAW 718 ("First, some have suggested that the *very act of targeting* a particular leader of an enemy force in an armed conflict must violate the laws of war. But individuals who are part of such an armed group are belligerents and, therefore, lawful targets under international law. … Indeed, targeting particular individuals serves to narrow the focus when force is employed and to avoid broader harm to civilians and civilian objects."); 1956 FM 27-10 (Change No. 1 1976) ¶31 ("[The prohibition on killing or wounding treacherously reflected the Hague IV Regulations] does not, however, preclude attacks on individual soldiers or officers of the enemy whether in the zone of hostilities, occupied territory, or elsewhere.").

[116] *For example*, Barack Obama, *Remarks by the President on Osama Bin Laden* (May 2, 2011) ("Today, at my direction, the United States launched a targeted operation against that compound [suspected of housing Osama Bin Laden] in Abbottabad, Pakistan. A small team of Americans carried out the operation with extraordinary courage and capability. No Americans were harmed. They took care to avoid civilian casualties. After a firefight, they killed Osama bin Laden and took custody of his body."); George W. Bush, *Remarks on the Death of Senior Al Qaeda Associate Abu Musab Al Zarqawi*, Jun. 8, 2006, 2006-I PUBLIC PAPERS OF THE PRESIDENTS 1099 (describing how after "work[ing] tirelessly with their Iraqi counterparts to track down this brutal terrorist," U.S. "special operation forces, acting on tips and intelligence from Iraqis, confirmed Zarqawi's location" and killed him); JOHN MILLER, CARTWHEEL: THE REDUCTION OF RABAUL 44 (Office of the Chief of Military History, Department of the Army 1959) ("American intelligence officers had discovered the exact time on 18 April [Admiral] Yamamoto[, Commander-in-Chief of the Japanese Combined Fleet,] was due to reach the Buin area … . [D]isposing of Yamamoto would advance the Allied cause, so the Commander, Aircraft, Solomons, was told to shoot him down [and did so successfully]."); Henry Pinckney McCain, Adjutant General of the U.S. Army, Telegram to General Frederick Funston (Mar. 10, 1916), *reprinted in* PAPERS RELATING TO THE FOREIGN RELATIONS OF THE UNITED STATES WITH THE ADDRESS OF THE PRESIDENT TO CONGRESS DECEMBER 5, 1916 (Department of State 1925) (relaying that the "President has directed that an armed force be sent into Mexico with the sole object of capturing [Pancho] Villa and preventing any further raids by his band").

[117] HAGUE IV REG. art. 23(d) (noting that it is especially forbidden "[t]o declare that no quarter will be given;"). *Consider* AP I art. 40 ("It is prohibited to order that there shall be no survivors, to threaten an adversary therewith or to conduct hostilities on this basis.").

executed.[118] Moreover, it is also prohibited to conduct hostilities on the basis that there shall be no survivors, or to threaten the adversary with the denial of quarter.[119]

This rule is based on both humanitarian and military considerations.[120] This rule also applies during non-international armed conflict.[121]

5.4.8 Obligation of Combatants to Distinguish Themselves When Conducting Attacks. Combatants have certain obligations to distinguish themselves that include, but are not limited to, those times when they conduct attacks.[122] For example, militia and volunteer corps must wear fixed, distinctive insignia, including when they are conducting attacks.[123] In addition, combatants may not kill or wound by resort to perfidy.[124] Combatants may not fight in the enemy's uniform.[125] Lastly, persons engaging in spying or sabotage risk additional penalties under the domestic law of enemy States.[126]

5.4.8.1 *Fighting Out of Uniform*. Although military operations generally are conducted while wearing a uniform or other distinctive emblems, there may be occasions, such as a surprise attack by enemy forces, when military personnel are unable to dress in their uniforms before resisting the enemy's assault.[127]

Military personnel not in uniform may resist an attack, so long as they are not wearing

---

[118] ICRC AP COMMENTARY 476 (¶1595) ("[A]ny order of 'liquidation' is prohibited, whether it concerns commandos, political or any other kind of commissars, irregular troops or so-called irregular troops, saboteurs, parachutists, mercenaries or persons considered to be mercenaries, or other cases.").

[119] ICRC AP COMMENTARY 476 (¶1595) ("It is not only the order to put them to death that is prohibited, but also the threat and the execution, with or without orders.").

[120] BOTHE, PARTSCH, & SOLF, NEW RULES 217 (AP I art. 40, ¶2.1) ("A declaration or order that there shall be no survivors, or that no prisoners shall be taken, tends to stiffen the adversary's will to resist and is therefore counterproductive to the achievement of the legitimate objectives of a military operations. Moreover, it incites the adversary to adopt a similar policy thus causing the conflict to degenerate into unrestrained savagery.").

[121] *Refer to* § 17.6.1 (Prohibition on Declaring That No Quarter Be Given).

[122] *See also* ALLAN ROSAS, THE LEGAL STATUS OF PRISONERS OF WAR: A STUDY IN INTERNATIONAL HUMANITARIAN LAW APPLICABLE IN ARMED CONFLICTS 351 (1976) ("What such proposals and statements [made in the context of the negotiations for the 1949 Geneva Conventions] do seem to imply, however, is that in areas where enemy forces are present (notably in occupied territory) members of independent (or of regular) forces are not allowed to appear as part of the peaceful civilian population (e.g., as peasants or workers) while occasionally committing hostile acts against the enemy (the 'day-time civilian, night-time combatant' -situation).").

[123] *Refer to* § 4.6.4 (Having a Fixed Distinctive Sign Recognizable at a Distance).

[124] *Refer to* § 5.22 (Treachery or Perfidy Used to Kill or Wound).

[125] *Refer to* § 5.23 (Use of Enemy Flags, Insignia, and Military Uniforms).

[126] *Refer to* § 4.17 (Spies, Saboteurs, and Other Persons Engaging in Similar Acts Behind Enemy Lines).

[127] *For example*, SPAIGHT, AIR POWER AND WAR RIGHTS 101 ("In the second world war, too, there were instances in which pilots fought *en dishabille*. For example, in Kenya a pilot of the South African Air Force happened to be wearing nothing but a singlet when Italian bombers approached, and so clad (or unclad) he dashed to his aircraft and joined in the fight.").

the enemy's uniform and do not kill or wound treacherously.[128] For example, military personnel not in uniform who resist an attack, and who do not purposefully seek to conceal their status as combatants, commit no violation of the law of war and remain entitled to the privileges of combatant status. The normal wearing of uniforms or other distinctive emblems, however, should resume as soon as practicable because such wear helps protect the civilian population from erroneous attack by helping to distinguish military forces from the civilian population.[129]

5.4.8.2 *AP I Obligation for Combatants to Distinguish Themselves During Attacks or Military Operations Preparatory to an Attack*. AP I provides that: "combatants are obliged to distinguish themselves from the civilian population while they are engaged in an attack or in a military operation preparatory to an attack."[130]

The AP I provision only partially describes the obligation under customary international law of combatants to distinguish themselves from the civilian population. Under customary international law, the obligation of combatants to distinguish themselves is a general obligation that the armed forces have as a group and is not limited to times when they are engaged in an attack or in a military operation preparatory to an attack.[131] Moreover, measures such as wearing insignia or other distinctive emblems may be of less practical significance during an attack. During an attack, combatants are likely to be distinguishable based on their activities more than any insignia or devices they are wearing.

5.5 Discrimination in Conducting Attacks

Under the principle of distinction, combatants may make enemy combatants and other military objectives the object of attack, but may not make the civilian population and other protected persons and objects the object of attack.[132]

5.5.1 Persons, Objects, and Locations That Are Not Protected From Being Made the Object of Attack. Combatants may make enemy combatants and other military objectives the object of attack.[133]

5.5.2 Persons, Objects, and Locations That Are Protected From Being Made the Object of Attack. Persons, objects, and locations that are not military objectives may not be made the object of attack. In particular, the following persons and objects may not be made the object of attack, unless that protection is specifically forfeited under the circumstances:

- Persons, such as

---

[128] *Refer to* § 5.23 (Use of Enemy Flags, Insignia, and Military Uniforms); § 5.22 (Treachery or Perfidy Used to Kill or Wound).

[129] *Refer to* § 5.14.5 (Carrying Arms Openly and Wearing of Distinctive Emblems by the Armed Forces to Distinguish Themselves From the Civilian Population).

[130] AP I art. 44(3).

[131] *Refer to* § 4.6.1.1 (GPW 4A(2) Conditions Required on a Group Basis).

[132] *Refer to* § 2.5.2 (Discriminating in Conducting Attacks Against the Enemy).

[133] *Refer to* § 5.6 (Military Objectives).

- individual civilians and the civilian population;[134]
- military medical and religious personnel, including military medical units;[135]
- combatants placed *hors de combat*;[136] and
- *parlementaires*;[137] and

- Objects and locations, provided they are not military objectives, such as
  - military medical transport, facilities, and equipment;[138]
  - cultural property;[139]
  - historic monuments, museums, scientific, artistic, educational and cultural institutions;[140]
  - places of worship;
  - undefended villages, towns, or cities;[141]
  - hospital and safety zones, and persons and objects within these zones;[142] and
  - neutralized zones, and persons and objects within neutralized zones.[143]

5.6 MILITARY OBJECTIVES

Military objectives refers to persons and objects that may be made the object of attack. Certain classes of persons and objects are categorically recognized as military objectives. Apart from these classes that are categorically military objectives, other objects are assessed as to

---

[134] *Refer to* § 4.8.2 (Civilians – Conduct of Hostilities).

[135] *Refer to* § 4.10.1 (Military Medical and Religious Personnel - Conduct of Hostilities); § 7.8 (Respect and Protection of Categories of Medical and Religious Personnel); § 7.10 (Military Medical Units and Facilities).

[136] *Refer to* § 5.9 (Persons Placed *Hors de Combat*).

[137] *Refer to* § 12.5.4 (Rights of Inviolability of the *Parlementaire*).

[138] *Refer to* § 7.10 (Military Medical Units and Facilities).

[139] *Refer to* § 5.18 (Protection of Cultural Property During Hostilities).

[140] ROERICH PACT art. 1 ("The historic monuments, museums, scientific, artistic, educational and cultural institutions shall be considered as neutral and as such respected and protected by belligerents. The same respect and protection shall be due to the personnel of the institutions mentioned above. The same respect and protection shall be accorded to the historic monuments, museums, scientific, artistic, educational and cultural institutions in time of peace as well as in war.").

[141] *Refer to* § 5.15 (Undefended Cities, Towns, and Villages).

[142] *Refer to* § 5.14.3.1 (Civilian Hospital and Safety Zones and Localities).

[143] *Refer to* § 5.14.3.3 (Neutralized Zones).

whether they meet the definition of "military objective."

5.6.1 Military Objective – Notes on Terminology. The term *military objective* has been used in various treaties as a term of art to mean a person or object that may lawfully be made the object of attack.[144]

5.6.1.1 *Persons and Objects as Military Objectives*. Although enemy combatants may be made the object of attack, some sources do not classify persons as *military objectives*, and limit the term *military objective* to objects.

Definitions of *military objectives* in treaties have defined the term *military objective* insofar as objects (rather than persons) are concerned.[145] In addition, the treaty definitions have been written with the purpose of explaining when objects that normally are civilian objects have become military objectives under the circumstances.

This manual uses the term *military objective* to include persons who may be made the object of attack.[146]

5.6.1.2 *Dual-Use Objects*. Sometimes, "dual-use" is used to describe objects that are used by both the armed forces and the civilian population, such as power stations or communications facilities. However, from the legal perspective, such objects are either military objectives or they are not; there is no intermediate legal category.[147] If an object is a military objective, it is not a civilian object and may be made the object of attack.[148] However, it will be appropriate to consider in applying the principle of proportionality the harm to the civilian population that is expected to result from the attack on such a military objective.[149]

5.6.2 Persons Who Are Military Objectives. Certain classes of persons are military

---

[144] *See, e.g.*, CCW PROTOCOL III ON INCENDIARY WEAPONS art. 2(4) (referring to "combatants or other military objectives"); 1954 HAGUE CULTURAL PROPERTY CONVENTION art. 8(1) (referring to "any important military objective constituting a vulnerable point"); GC art. 18 ("In view of the dangers to which hospitals may be exposed by being close to military objectives, it is recommended that such [civilian] hospitals be situated as far as possible from such objectives.").

[145] *See* CCW PROTOCOL III ON INCENDIARY WEAPONS art. 1(3) ("'Military objective' means, so far as objects are concerned, any object which … ."); CCW AMENDED MINES PROTOCOL art. 2(6) ("'Military objective' means, so far as objects are concerned, any object which … ."). *Consider* AP I art. 52(2) ("Attacks shall be limited strictly to military objectives. In so far as objects are concerned, military objectives are limited to those objects which … .").

[146] *Refer to* § 5.6.2 (Persons Who Are Military Objectives).

[147] Christopher Greenwood, *Customary international law and the First Geneva Protocol of 1977 in the Gulf conflict*, *in* PETER ROWE, THE GULF WAR 1990-91 IN INTERNATIONAL AND ENGLISH LAW 63, 73 (1993) ("If an object is a military objective, it may be attacked (subject to the requirements of the principle of proportionality which are discussed in the next section), while if it is a civilian object, it may not be attacked. There is no intermediate category of 'dual use' objects: either something is a military objective or it is not.").

[148] CCW AMENDED MINES PROTOCOL art. 2(7) ("'Civilian objects' are all objects which are not military objectives as defined in paragraph 6 of this Article.").

[149] *Refer to* § 5.10 (Proportionality in Conducting Attacks).

objectives and may be made the object of attack.[150] These classes of persons include:

- combatants, such as military ground, air, and naval units, or unprivileged belligerents;[151] and

- civilians taking a direct part in hostilities.[152]

However, the following classes of persons are not military objectives:

- military medical and religious personnel, unless they commit acts harmful to the enemy;[153]

- military medical units, unless they have forfeited their protected status;[154]

- combatants placed *hors de combat*;[155] and

- *parlementaires*.[156]

5.6.3 Objects That Are Military Objectives. Military objectives, insofar as objects are concerned, include "any object which by its nature, location, purpose or use makes an effective contribution to military action and whose total or partial destruction, capture or neutralization, in the circumstances ruling at the time, offers a definite military advantage."[157]

This definition of military objective may be viewed as a way of evaluating whether military necessity exists to attack an object.[158] It may also be applied outside the context of conducting attacks to assess whether the seizure or destruction of an object is justified by

---

[150] *See* CCW PROTOCOL III ON INCENDIARY WEAPONS art. 2(4) (referring to "combatants or other military objectives"); ICRC AP COMMENTARY 635 (¶2017) ("It should be noted that the definition [of military objective in AP I] is limited to objects but it is clear that members of the armed forces are military objectives, … .").

[151] *Refer to* § 5.7 (Combatants).

[152] *Refer to* § 5.8 (Civilians Taking a Direct Part in Hostilities).

[153] *Refer to* § 7.8.3 (Loss of Protection for Medical and Religious Personnel From Being Made the Object of Attack).

[154] *Refer to* § 7.10.3 (Loss of Protection of Military Medical Units and Facilities From Being Made the Object of Attack).

[155] *Refer to* § 5.9 (Persons Placed *Hors de Combat*).

[156] *Refer to* § 12.5.4 (Rights of Inviolability of the *Parlementaire*).

[157] CCW AMENDED MINES PROTOCOL art. 2(6). *See also* CCW PROTOCOL III ON INCENDIARY WEAPONS art. 1(3) (same); 10 U.S.C. § 950p(a)(1) ("The term 'military objective' means combatants and those objects during hostilities which, by their nature, location, purpose, or use, effectively contribute to the war-fighting or war-sustaining capability of an opposing force and whose total or partial destruction, capture, or neutralization would constitute a definite military advantage to the attacker under the circumstances at the time of an attack."). *Consider* AP I art. 52(2) ("In so far as objects are concerned, military objectives are limited to those objects which by their nature, location, purpose or use make an effective contribution to military action and whose total or partial destruction, capture or neutralization, in the circumstances ruling at the time, offers a definite military advantage.").

[158] *Refer to* § 2.2 (Military Necessity).

military necessity.[159]

5.6.4 Objects Categorically Recognized as Military Objectives. Two types of objects are categorically recognized as military objectives. In other words, the definition of military objective is always considered to be met as a matter of law with regard to these objects. Thus, these objects may be made the object of attack without specifically applying the analysis discussed in § 5.6.5 (Definition of Military Objective for Objects: A Two-Part Test).

5.6.4.1 *Military Equipment and Bases*. First, certain objects belonging to the armed forces and used in military operations are recognized as military objectives.[160] This includes:

- Military ground, air, and naval equipment (other than identifiable medical equipment or transport),[161] including vehicles, ships, weapons, munitions, and supplies, such as
  - strategic and tactical integrated air defense systems;
  - missile launching equipment and positions; and
  - command and control equipment.
- Military bases, such as army, air, and naval bases (other than military medical facilities, POW camps, and civilian internee camps), whether used for training, billeting, or staging, or offensive or defensive purposes, such as
  - headquarters or command and control facilities;
  - defense ministries; and
  - intelligence facilities.

5.6.4.2 *Objects Containing Military Objectives*. Second, objects that contain military objectives are military objectives.[162] For example,

---

[159] *Refer to* § 5.17 (Seizure and Destruction of Enemy Property); § 5.17.2.1 (Using the Military Objective Definition to Assess Whether the Seizure or Destruction of Enemy Property Is Justified by Military Necessity).

[160] 2004 UK MANUAL ¶5.4.1 ("The term 'military objective' includes combatant members of the enemy armed forces and their military weapons, vehicles, equipment, and installations."); 2006 AUSTRALIAN MANUAL ¶5.27 ("The term 'military objective' includes combatant members of the enemy armed forces and their military weapons, vehicles, equipment and installations."); 2001 CANADIAN MANUAL ¶407(1) ("The following are generally accepted as being military objectives: a. military bases, warehouses, petroleum storage areas, ports and airfields; and b. military aircraft, weapons, ammunition, buildings and objects that provide administrative and logistical support for military operations.").

[161] For devices to facilitate identification of military medical units, transport, and equipment, *refer to* § 7.15 (Display of the Distinctive Emblem to Facilitate Identification).

[162] ROGERS, LAW ON THE BATTLEFIELD 36 ("A civilian object which contains military personnel or things of military significance is considered a military objective."); 2001 CANADIAN MANUAL ¶407(2) ("Civilian vessels, aircraft, vehicles and buildings are military objectives if they contain combatants, military equipment or supplies."). *Cf.*

- Storage and production sites for military equipment, including
    - missile production and storage facilities; and
    - nuclear, biological, and chemical weapons research and production facilities; and
- Facilities in which combatants are sheltering or billeting.[163]

5.6.5 Definition of Military Objective for Objects: A Two-Part Test. The definition of military objective insofar as objects are concerned may be divided into two parts, both of which must be met for the object to be considered a military objective: (1) that the object somehow makes an effective contribution to military action; and (2) attacking, capturing, or neutralizing the object, in the circumstances, offers a definite military advantage.[164]

Generally, the reason why the object meets the first part of the definition also satisfies the second part of the definition. In other words, attacking the object in the circumstances will offer a definite military advantage because it seeks to preclude the object from effectively contributing to the enemy's military action. Moreover, the two parts are not necessarily connected because the concept of definite military advantage is broader than simply denying the adversary the benefit of an object's effective contribution to its military operations.[165] These broader aspects of "military advantage" may also be relevant in evaluating whether an attack is expected to be excessive under the principle of proportionality.[166]

The following discussion elaborates upon the definition of *military objective*.

5.6.6 By Its Nature, Location, Purpose, or Use Makes an Effective Contribution to Military Action. The first part of the test is whether the object, by its nature, location, purpose, or use makes an effective contribution to the enemy's military action.

5.6.6.1 *Nature, Location, Purpose, or Use*. The nature, location, purpose, or use of the object may contribute to the object making an effective contribution to the enemy's military action. The issue is whether, in total, an effective contribution is made; one factor alone

---

CCW PROTOCOL III ON INCENDIARY WEAPONS art. 2(4) (plants "used to cover, conceal, or camouflage combatants or other military objectives," may be attacked with incendiary weapons).

163 1956 FM 27-10 (Change No. 1 1976) ¶40 (giving as examples of legitimate objects of attack "a place which is occupied by a combatant military force or through which such a force is passing," as well as "[f]actories producing munitions and military supplies, military camps, warehouses storing munitions and military supplies, ports and railroads being used for the transportation of military supplies, and other places devoted to the support of military operations or the accommodation of troops"); ICRC AP COMMENTARY 701 (¶2265) ("If combat is taking place within a city or a town, and there is fighting from house to house, which is frequently the case, it is clear that the situation becomes very different and that any building sheltering combatants becomes a military objective.").

164 ICRC AP COMMENTARY 635 (¶2018) ("The definition comprises two elements: a) the nature, location, purpose or use which makes an effective contribution to military action; b) the total or partial destruction, capture or neutralization which in the circumstances ruling at the time offers a definite military advantage. Whenever these two elements are simultaneously present, there is a military objective in the sense of the Protocol.").

165 *Refer to* § 5.6.7.3 (Definite Military Advantage).

166 *Refer to* § 5.12.2 (Concrete and Direct Military Advantage Expected to Be Gained).

need not provide the effective contribution. In addition, nature, location, purpose, or use need not be viewed as mutually exclusive concepts; rather, these concepts may be understood to overlap.

"Nature" refers to the type of object and may be understood to refer to objects that are *per se* military objectives. For example, military equipment and facilities, by their nature, make an effective contribution to military action.[167] On the other hand, "nature" can also be understood to refer to objects that may be used for military purposes as discussed below.

The location of an object may provide an effective contribution to military action. For example, during military operations in urban areas, a house or other structure that would ordinarily be a civilian object may be located such that it provides cover to enemy forces or would provide a vantage point from which attacks could be launched or directed. The word "location" also helps clarify that an area of land can be militarily important and therefore a military objective.[168]

"Use" refers to the object's present function. For example, using an otherwise civilian building to billet combatant forces makes the building a military objective.[169] Similarly, using equipment and facilities for military purposes, such as using them as a command and control center or a communications station, would result in such objects providing an effective contribution to the enemy's military action.

"Purpose" means the intended or possible use in the future.[170] For example, runways at a civilian airport could qualify as military objectives because they may be subject to immediate military use in the event that runways at military air bases have been rendered unserviceable or inoperable.[171] Similarly, the possibility that bridges or tunnels would be used to assist in the adversary's military operations in the future could result in such objects providing an effective contribution to the enemy's military action, even though they are not being used at that moment for such purposes.

5.6.6.2 Make an Effective Contribution to Military Action. The object must make or be intended to make an effective contribution to military action; however, this contribution need not be "direct" or "proximate."[172] For example, an object might make an effective, but

---

[167] ICRC AP COMMENTARY 636 (¶2020) ("A closer look at the various criteria used [*i.e.*, nature, purpose, location, or use] reveals that the first refers to objects which, by their *nature*, make an effective contribution to military action. This category comprises all objects directly used by the armed forces: weapons, equipment, transports, fortifications, depots, buildings occupied by armed forces, staff headquarters, communications centres etc."). *Refer to* § 5.6.4 (Objects Categorically Recognized as Military Objectives).

[168] *Refer to* § 5.6.8.4 (Examples of Military Objectives – Places of Military Significance).

[169] *Refer to* § 5.6.4.2 (Objects Containing Military Objectives).

[170] *See, e.g.*, 2006 AUSTRALIAN MANUAL ¶5.29 ("**Purpose** means the future intended use of an object while 'use' means its present function."); 2004 UK MANUAL ¶5.4.4 ("e. 'Purpose' means the future intended use of an object while 'use' means its present function.").

[171] *Refer to* § 5.6.8.3 (Examples of Military Objectives – Transportation Objects).

[172] *Cf.* BOTHE, PARTSCH, & SOLF, NEW RULES 324 (AP I art. 52, ¶2.4.3) (noting that "[m]ilitary objectives must make an 'effective contribution to military action' … does not require a direct connection with combat operations"

remote, contribution to the enemy's military action and nonetheless meet this aspect of the definition. Similarly, an object might be geographically distant from most of the fighting and nonetheless satisfy this element.

Military action has a broad meaning and is understood to mean the general prosecution of the war.[173] It is not necessary that the object provide immediate tactical or operational gains or that the object make an effective contribution to a specific military operation. Rather, the object's effective contribution to the war-fighting or war-sustaining capability of an opposing force is sufficient.[174] Although terms such as "war-fighting," "war-supporting," and "war-sustaining" are not explicitly reflected in the treaty definitions of military objective, the United States has interpreted the military objective definition to include these concepts.[175]

5.6.7 <u>Whose Total or Partial Destruction, Capture, or Neutralization, in the Circumstances Ruling at the Time, Offers a Definite Military Advantage</u>. In addition to making an effective contribution to the adversary's military action, the attack of the object must also, in the circumstances ruling at the time, offer a definite military advantage for the object to be considered a "military objective."

5.6.7.1 <u>*Capture or Neutralization*</u>. The definition of military objective incorporates considerations beyond whether an object's destruction is justified. It also incorporates considerations of whether the object's capture and neutralization would offer a

---

and that "a civilian object may become a military objective and thereby lose its immunity from deliberate attack through use which is only indirectly related to combat action, but which nevertheless provides an effective contribution to the military phase of a Party's overall war effort.").

[173] ROGERS, LAW ON THE BATTLEFIELD 36 ("The term *military action* appears to have a wide meaning equating to the general prosecution of the war.").

[174] *See* APPENDIX TO 1985 CJCS MEMO ON AP I 51 ("Under this definition [of military objective in AP I], an area of land could, for example, be a military objective, as could political and economic activities that support the enemy's war effort."); BOTHE, PARTSCH, & SOLF, NEW RULES 324 (AP I art. 52, ¶2.4.2) (noting that military objectives may include "activities providing administrative and logistical support to military operations such as transportation and communications systems, railroads, airfields and port facilities and industries of fundamental importance for the conduct of the armed conflict."). *Cf.* 10 U.S.C. § 950p(a)(1) ("The term 'military objective' means … those objects during hostilities which, by their nature, location, purpose, or use, effectively contribute <u>to the war-fighting or war-sustaining capability of an opposing force</u>.") (emphasis added).

[175] Brian Egan, Legal Adviser, Department of State, *Remarks to the American Society of International Law: International Law, Legal Diplomacy, and the Counter-ISIL Campaign*, Apr. 1, 2016 ("In particular, I'd like to spend a few minutes walking through some of the targeting rules that the United States regards as customary international law applicable to all parties in a NIAC: … Insofar as objects are concerned, military objectives are those objects which by their nature, location, purpose or use make an effective contribution to military action and whose total or partial destruction, capture or neutralization, in the circumstances ruling at the time, offers a definite military advantage. The United States has interpreted this definition to include objects that make an effective contribution to the enemy's war-fighting or war-sustaining capabilities."). *See also* W. Hays Parks, *Asymmetries and the Identification of Legitimate Military Objectives,* in INTERNATIONAL HUMANITARIAN LAW FACING NEW CHALLENGES 100 (2007) ("*War-sustaining* and/or *war-fighting* reflect State practice. Historical evidence and the description of the target sets agreed upon by NATO governments in ALLIED FORCE support the idea that nations have, do, and will attack not only an enemy's war-fighting capability, but also his capacity to sustain the conflict."); Horace B. Robertson, *The Principle of the Military Objective in the Law of Armed Conflict*, 8 UNITED STATES AIR FORCE ACADEMY JOURNAL OF LEGAL STUDIES 35, 50-51 (1997) (comparing the definition of military objective in the 1995 Commander's Handbook on the Law of Naval Operations to the definition of military objective in AP I).

military advantage.

Capture refers to the possibility of seizure (rather than destruction), which would confer a military advantage. For example, the seizure of a city may be a military objective because of its strategic location.[176]

Neutralization refers to a military action that denies an object to the enemy without capturing or destroying it. For example, a specific area of land may be neutralized by planting landmines on or around it, and thus denying it to the enemy.[177]

5.6.7.2 _In the Circumstances Ruling at the Time_. The attack of the object must, "in the circumstances ruling at the time," offer a definite military advantage for the object to be considered a military objective.

Nonetheless, the purpose (*i.e.*, future use) of the object can be considered in whether an object provides an effective contribution to the adversary's military action.[178] In addition, the definite military advantage offered by the attack need not be immediate, but may be assessed in the full context of the war strategy.[179]

5.6.7.3 _Definite Military Advantage_. "Definite" means a concrete and perceptible military advantage, rather than one that is merely hypothetical or speculative.[180]

The advantage need not be immediate.[181] For example, the military advantage in the attack of an individual bridge may not be seen immediately (particularly if, at the time of the attack, there is no military traffic in the area), but can be established by the overall effort to isolate enemy military forces on the battlefield through the destruction of bridges.

"Military advantage" refers to the advantage anticipated from an attack when considered as a whole, and not only from its isolated or particular parts.[182] Similarly, "military advantage"

---

[176] *Refer to* § 5.6.8.4 (Examples of Military Objectives – Places of Military Significance).

[177] *Refer to* § 5.6.8.4 (Examples of Military Objectives – Places of Military Significance).

[178] *Refer to* § 5.6.6.1 (Nature, Location, Purpose, or Use).

[179] *Refer to* § 5.6.7.3 (Definite Military Advantage).

[180] *For example*, W. Hays Parks, *Asymmetries and the Identification of Legitimate Military Objectives*, in INTERNATIONAL HUMANITARIAN LAW FACING NEW CHALLENGES footnotes 88 and 170 and accompanying text (2007) (giving an example of a case in which objects did not meet this standard, "the 25 February 1991 recommendation by the U.S. Air Force component of US Central Command for an air attack on a Baghdad statue of Saddam Hussayn and another statue, consisting of matching sets of arms with crossed swords (modeled on the arms of Saddam Hussayn), called the Victory Arch or Crossed Swords Monument," because the military assessment was that such targets were worthless and any value from attacking them was too speculative).

[181] *See* J. Fred Buzhardt, General Counsel, Department of Defense, Letter to Senator Edward Kennedy, Sept. 22, 1972, *reprinted in* 67 AJIL 122, 124 (1973) ("Turning to the deficiencies in the Resolutions of the Institut de Droit International, and with the foregoing in view, it cannot be said that Paragraph 2, which refers to legal restraints that there must be an 'immediate' military advantage, reflects the law of armed conflict that has been adopted in the practices of States.").

[182] *See, e.g.*, France, *Statement on Ratification of AP I, translated in* SCHINDLER & TOMAN, THE LAWS OF ARMED CONFLICTS: A COLLECTION OF CONVENTIONS, RESOLUTIONS, AND OTHER DOCUMENTS 800 (2004) ("It is the

is not restricted to immediate tactical gains, but may be assessed in the full context of the war strategy.[183]

The definite military advantage offered by damaging, destroying, or neutralizing the object may result from denying the enemy the ability to use this object in its military operations (*i.e.*, to benefit from the object's effective contribution to the military action). For example, the attack or seizure of objects with a common military purpose, such as bridges used, or potentially available to be used, in lines of communication would offer a definite military advantage.

The military advantage from an attack is not limited to denying the enemy the benefit of that object's contribution to its military action. For example, in a diversionary attack, the military advantage to be gained from attacking an object would result from diverting enemy forces' resources and attention.[184] The military advantage from an attack may involve a variety of other considerations, including improving the security of the attacking force.

The military advantage from an attack may result from harm to the morale of enemy forces.[185] Diminishing the morale of the civilian population and their support for the war effort does not provide a definite military advantage.[186] However, attacks that are otherwise lawful are

---

understanding of the Government of the French Republic that the expression 'military advantage' contained in paragraphs 5(b) of Article 51, 2 of Article 52 and 2(a)(iii) of Article 57, is intended to refer to the advantage anticipated from the attack considered as a whole and not from isolated or particular parts of the attack."); Spain, *Statement on Ratification of AP I*, Apr. 21, 1989, 1537 UNTS 389, 392 ("Articles 51, 52 and 57. It is understood that the words 'military advantage' in these articles refer to the advantage expected from the attack as a whole and not from isolated parts of it.").

183 *See* FINAL REPORT ON THE PERSIAN GULF WAR 613 ("'Military advantage' is not restricted to tactical gains, but is linked to the full context of a war strategy, in this instance, the execution of the Coalition war plan for liberation of Kuwait."). *See also* Eritrea Ethiopia Claims Commission, *Partial Award: Western Front, Aerial Bombardment and Related Claims, Eritrea's Claims 1, 3, 5, 9-13, 14, 21, 25 & 26*, ¶113 (Dec. 19, 2005) ("The Commission is of the view that the term 'military advantage' can only properly be understood in the context of the military operations between the Parties taken as a whole, not simply in the context of a specific attack. Thus, with respect to the present claim, whether the attack on the power station offered a definite military advantage must be considered in the context of its relation to the armed conflict as a whole at the time of the attack.").

184 *For example*, BOTHE, PARTSCH, & SOLF, NEW RULES 325 (AP I art. 52, ¶2.4.4) ("Thus, prior to the 1944 cross channel operation, the Allies attacked a large number of bridges, fuel dumps, airfields and other targets in the *Pas de Calais*. These targets made an effective contribution to German military action in that area. The primary military advantage of these attacks anticipated by the Allies, however, was not to reduce German military strength in that area, but to deceive the Germans into believing that the Allied amphibious assault would occur in the *Pas de Calais* instead of the beaches of Normandy."); MILITARY ANALYSIS DIVISION, THE UNITED STATES STRATEGIC BOMBING SURVEY (PACIFIC): JAPANESE AIR POWER 10 (1946) ("The [Doolittle] raid was too small to do substantial physical damage, but its repercussions on the planning level of the high command were considerable. ... [A]ttention was focused on the eastern approaches to the home islands, and additional impetus given the prewar plan to attack Midway and the Aleutians. ... [T]he Japanese began to implement their plans for air defense of Japan which before that time had received scant consideration. ... A total of four Army fighter groups were held in Japan throughout 1942 and 1943 for the defense of the homeland when the Japanese Navy was urgently demanding that the Army send reinforcements to the Solomons.").

185 *Refer to* § 5.4.6.3 (Harassing Fires).

186 *Cf.* LAUTERPACHT, II OPPENHEIM'S INTERNATIONAL LAW 528-29 (§214eb) ("It is also probable that till the end of the War the aerial bombardment by the Allies did not assume the complexion of bombing for the exclusive purpose of spreading terror and shattering the morale of the population at large—though this was the inevitable concomitant

not rendered unlawful if they happen to result in diminished civilian morale.[187]

The military advantage expected to be gained from an attack might not be readily apparent to the enemy or to outside observers because, for example, the expected military advantage might depend on the commander's strategy or assessments of classified information.

5.6.8 Examples of Objects Often Regarded as Military Objectives. The following types of objects generally have met the definition of "military objective" in past conflicts, but may not be military objectives in all circumstances: (1) leadership facilities; (2) communications objects; (3) transportation objects; (4) places of military significance; and (5) economic objects associated with military operations or with war-supporting or war-sustaining industries.

This list of examples is not exclusive (*i.e.*, an object could fall in more than one category in this list), and this list is not exhaustive (*i.e.*, an object outside these categories may nonetheless meet the definition of military objective). Lastly, this list is not conclusive, *i.e.*, whether an example is, in fact, a military objective, must be assessed according to the definition of military objective.

5.6.8.1 *Examples of Military Objectives – Leadership Facilities*. Facilities used by enemy leaders as headquarters for military operations or otherwise to command military operations have often been regarded as military objectives.[188] In some cases, enemy leaders themselves may be made the object of attack.[189]

5.6.8.2 *Examples of Military Objectives – Communications Objects*. Communications objects, such as facilities, networks, and equipment that could be used for command and control of military operations or intelligence gathering, have often been regarded

---

of strategic target-bombing. Thus what remained of the protection afforded by International Law to the civilian population in the matter of aerial bombardment was the principle—generally acknowledged by the Allies, though not always capable of being adhered to in practice—that the bombing of towns or purely residential parts of towns which were not in any way related to the war efforts of the enemy was unlawful. At the same time abstention from such bombing could also be explained by reference to considerations of economy militating against costly operations for the sake of achieving purely psychological effect—considerations the disregard of which rendered the use by Germany of the flying bomb and long-range projectiles not only unlawful but, in the judgment of many, also detrimental to her own war effort.").

[187] *For example*, Judith A. Miller, *Commentary*, 78 U.S. NAVAL WAR COLLEGE INTERNATIONAL LAW STUDIES 107, 110 (2002) ("I will readily admit that, aside from directly damaging the military electrical power infrastructure, NATO wanted the civilian population to experience discomfort, so that the population would pressure Milosevic and the Serbian leadership to accede to UN Security Council Resolution 1244, but the intended effects on the civilian population were secondary to the military advantage gained by attacking the electrical power infrastructure."). *Refer to* § 5.2.2 (Essentially Negative Duties to Respect Civilians and to Refrain From Directing Military Operations Against Them).

[188] *For example*, 2006 AUSTRALIAN MANUAL ¶2.8, at 2-5 ("HISTORICAL EXAMPLE—AVOIDING COLLATERAL DAMAGE, AFGHANISTAN 2002-2003 ... **A major focus in Afghanistan was the leadership.** This meant targeting residences and road convoys, with difficulties of identification and the consequent acceptance of non-combatant casualties as a necessary proportionate risk to achieve the military objective.").

[189] *Refer to* § 5.7.4 (Leaders).

as military objectives.[190]

5.6.8.3 *Examples of Military Objectives – Transportation Objects*. Transportation objects, including facilities (*e.g.*, port facilities and airfields) and equipment that could be part of lines of communication (*e.g.*, highways, railroads, waterways, and bridges connecting military forces with logistics depots and storage areas), have often been regarded as military objectives.[191]

5.6.8.4 *Examples of Military Objectives – Places of Military Significance*. Areas of land that are militarily significant may constitute military objectives.[192] For example, anti-

---

[190] *For example*, ICTY, *Final Report to the Prosecutor by the Committee Established to Review the NATO Bombing Campaign Against the Federal Republic of Yugoslavia*, ¶¶71-72 (Jun. 13, 2000) ("On 23 April 1999, at 0220, NATO intentionally bombed the central studio of the RTS (state-owned) broadcasting corporation at 1 Aberdareva Street in the centre of Belgrade. … The bombing of the TV studio was part of a planned attack aimed at disrupting and degrading the C3 (Command, Control and Communications) network. In co-ordinated attacks, on the same night, radio relay buildings and towers were hit along with electrical power transformer stations.").

[191] *For example*, DoD statement, Dec. 26, 1966, X WHITEMAN'S DIGEST 427 ("U.S. policy is to target military targets only, particularly those which have a direct impact on the movement of men and supplies into South Vietnam. These targets include but are not limited to roads, railroads, bridges, road junctions, POL facilities, barracks and supply depots. … In the specific case of Nam Dinh and Phu Li, targets have been limited to railroad and highway bridges, railroad yards, POL dumps and air defense sites."); Report of the United Nations Command Operations in Korea for the Period 1 to 15 August 1950, enclosure to *Note Dated 2 September 1950 From the Permanent Representative of the United States of America to the President of the Security Council Transmitting the Third Report of the United Nations Command in Korea in Accordance with the Security Council Resolution of 7 July 1950 (S/1588)*, U.N. Doc. S/1756 (Sept. 2, 1950) ("United States Far East Air Force medium bombers struck heavy blows at north Korean industrial targets of military significance and at the north Korean transportation system. The Korean manufacturing complex, the largest in the Far East, and the oil refinery at Wonsan, have been extensively damaged by successive attacks. The marshalling yards in Pyongyang, Wonsan, and Seoul have been repeatedly attacked, as have yards of less consequence. A general transportation interdiction program continues with destruction of rail and highway bridges along principal lines of communication. The rail and port transportation center at Najin-dong was also bombed.").

[192] *See, e.g.*, Canada, *Statement on Ratification of AP I*, Nov. 20, 1990, 1591 UNTS 462, 465 ("It is the understanding of the Government of Canada in relation to Article 52 that: *a.* A specific area of land may be a military objective if, because of its location or other reasons specified in the Article as to what constitutes a military objective, its total or partial destruction, capture or neutralization in the circumstances governing at the time offers a definite military advantage, … ."); Germany, *Statement on Ratification of AP I*, Feb. 14, 1991, 1607 UNTS 526, 529 ("Article 52 of Additional Protocol I is understood by the Federal Republic of Germany to mean that a specific area of land may also be a military objective if it meets all requirements of Article 52, paragraph 2."); Netherlands, *Statement on Ratification of AP I*, Jun. 26, 1987, 1477 UNTS 300 ("It is the understanding of the Government of the Kingdom of the Netherlands that a specific area of land may also be a military objective if, because of its location or other reasons specified in paragraph 2, its total or partial destruction, capture, or neutralization in the circumstances ruling at the time, offers a definite military advantage;"); New Zealand, *Statement on Ratification of AP I*, Feb. 8, 1988, 1499 UNTS 358 ("In relation to Article 52, it is the understanding of the Government of New Zealand that a specific area of land may be a military objective if, because of its location or other reasons specified in the Article, its total or partial destruction, capture or neutralisation in the circumstances ruling at the time offers a definite military advantage."); United Kingdom, *Statement on Ratification of AP I*, Jan. 28, 1998, 2020 UNTS 75, 77 ("*Re: Article 52* It is the understanding of the United Kingdom that: A specific area of land may be a military objective if, because of its location or other reasons specified in this Article, its total or partial destruction, capture or neutralization in the circumstances ruling at the time offers definite military advantage; … .").

tank mines may be laid on such areas in order to block enemy forces' tanks.[193] Areas of land that have been regarded as military objectives have included, for example:

- road networks;[194]
- known or suspected enemy avenues of approach or withdrawal;
- mountain passes, hills, defiles, and bridgeheads;[195] and
- villages, towns, or cities whose seizure is militarily important.[196]

5.6.8.5 Examples of Military Objectives – Economic Objects Associated With Military Operations. Economic objects associated with military operations or with war-supporting or war-sustaining industries have been regarded as military objectives.

Electric power stations are generally recognized to be of sufficient importance to a State's capacity to meet its wartime needs of communication, transport, and industry so as usually to qualify as military objectives during armed conflicts.[197]

---

[193] United States, *Statement on Consent to Be Bound by the CCW Amended Mines Protocol,* May 24, 1999, 2065 UNTS 128, 130 ("The United States understands that an area of land itself can be a legitimate military objective for the purpose of the use of landmines, if its neutralization or denial, in the circumstances applicable at the time, offers a military advantage.").

[194] *See* FINAL REPORT ON THE PERSIAN GULF WAR 612 ("A bridge or highway vital to daily commuter and business traffic can be equally crucial to military traffic, or support for a nation's war effort. Railroads, airports, seaports, and the interstate highway system in the United States have been funded by the Congress in part because of US national security concerns, for example; each proved invaluable to the movement of US military units to various ports for deployment to Southwest Asia (SWA) for Operations Desert Shield and Desert Storm. Destruction of a bridge, airport, or port facility, or interdiction of a highway can be equally important in impeding an enemy's war effort.").

[195] ROGERS, LAW ON THE BATTLEFIELD 37.

[196] *For example*, MILAN N. VEGO, JOINT OPERATIONAL WARFARE: THEORY AND PRACTICE II-34-II-35 (Reprint of 1st ed., 2009) ("In purely military terms, a capital is normally an operational objective to be seized or defended. The reason is that no enemy's capital can possibly physically include the enemy's entire armed forces, or even most of the ground forces. Therefore, the defeat of enemy forces defending the capital (and most other large cities as well) would normally amount to the accomplishment of an operational objective that in some situations could have strategic consequences for the war's outcome. ... General Mark Clark, the Fifth Army's commander, was directed by President Franklin D. Roosevelt and General George Marshall to take Rome as quickly as possible, and in any event before the planned Normandy landing. The Allied troops entered Rome on 6 June 1944, the same day the Allied forces landed in Normandy.").

[197] Eritrea Ethiopia Claims Commission, *Partial Award: Western Front, Aerial Bombardment and Related Claims, Eritrea's Claims 1, 3, 5, 9-13, 14, 21, 25 & 26,* ¶117 (Dec. 19, 2005) ("The Commission agrees with Ethiopia that electric power stations are generally recognized to be of sufficient importance to a State's capacity to meet its wartime needs of communication, transport and industry so as usually to qualify as military objectives during armed conflicts. The Commission also recognizes that not all such power stations would qualify as military objectives, for example, power stations that are known, or should be known, to be segregated from a general power grid and are limited to supplying power for humanitarian purposes, such as medical facilities, or other uses that could have no effect on the State's ability to wage war."). *For example*, W. Hays Parks, *Air War and the Law of War*, 32 AIR FORCE LAW REVIEW 1, 168-69 (1990) ("In selecting North Vietnamese power sources for attack, target intelligence authorities identified the Lang Chi hydroelectric facility, a Soviet-built, 122,500-kilowatt electric generating plant

Oil refining and distribution facilities and objects associated with petroleum, oil, and lubricant products (including production, transportation, storage, and distribution facilities) have also been regarded as military objectives.[198]

5.7 Combatants

In general, combatants, whether privileged or unprivileged, may be made the object of attack, provided they have not been placed *hors de combat*.

5.7.1 Armed Forces and Groups and Liability to Being Made the Object of Attack. Membership in the armed forces or belonging to an armed group makes a person liable to being made the object of attack regardless of whether he or she is taking a direct part in hostilities.[199] This is because the organization's hostile intent may be imputed to an individual through his or her association with the organization. Moreover, the individual, as an agent of the group, can be assigned a combat role at any time, even if the individual normally performs other functions for the group.[200]

Thus, combatants may be made the object of attack at all times, regardless of the activities in which they are engaged at the time of attack.[201] For example, combatants who are

---

63 miles up the Red River Valley from Hanoi that was capable of supplying seventy-five percent of the electricity for Hanoi's industrial and defense needs. Without question, it was a valuable target. … The Lang Chi hydroelectric facility was attacked by Air Force F-4 Phantoms using LGB [laser-guided bombs] on 10 June 1972. They placed twelve 2000-pound LGB through the roof of the 50-by-100-foot building, thereby destroying the electric generating plant without breach of the dam, despite the fact that the roof of the power plant was 100 feet below the top of the dam.").

[198] *For example*, Department of Defense, *Report to Congress: Kosovo/Operation Allied Force, After-Action Report*, 82 (Jan. 31, 2000) ("Following the end of Operation Allied Force, NATO released an initial assessment of their attack effectiveness against a number of targets. These targets destroyed or significantly damaged include: … • Fifty-seven percent of petroleum reserves; • All Yugoslav oil refineries … ."); Department of Defense, *Report to the Senate and House Appropriations Committees regarding international policies and procedures regarding the protection of natural and cultural resources during times of war*, Jan. 19, 1993, *reprinted as Appendix VIII in* Patrick J. Boylan, *Review of the Convention for the Protection of Cultural Property in the Event of Armed Conflict (The Hague Convention of 1954)* 201, 204 (1993) ("Similarly, natural resources that may be of value to an enemy in his war effort are legitimate targets. The 1943 air raids on the Ploesti oil fields in Romania, and the Combined Bomber Offensive campaign against Nazi oil, were critical to allied defeat of Germany in World War II, for example. What is prohibited is unnecessary destruction, that is, destruction of natural resources that has no or limited military value.").

[199] *See, e.g.*, ICRC AP Commentary 1453 (¶4789) ("Those who belong to armed forces or armed groups may be attacked at any time."); Greenspan, Modern Law of Land Warfare 57 (explaining that "as members of the armed forces [non-combat military personnel except for medical personnel and chaplains] are legitimate objects of attack by the enemy,").

[200] Gherebi v. Obama, 609 F. Supp. 2d 43, 69 (D.D.C. 2009) (noting that "many members of the armed forces who, under different circumstances, would be 'fighters' may be assigned to non-combat roles at the time of their apprehension" and that "[t]hese individuals are no less a part of the military command structure of the enemy, and may assume (or resume) a combat role at any time because of their integration into that structure."), *abrogated on different grounds by* Uthman v. Obama, 637 F.3d 400, 403 (D.C. Cir. 2011).

[201] W. Hays Parks, Chief, International Law Branch, Office of the Judge Advocate General, Department of the Army, *Executive Order 12333 and Assassination*, Nov. 2, 1989, III Cumulative Digest of United States Practice in International Law 1981-1988 3411, 3413 ("Combatants are liable to attack at any time or place,

standing in a mess line, engaging in recreational activities, or sleeping remain the lawful object of attack, provided they are not placed *hors de combat*.[202]

5.7.1.1 U.S. Practice in Declaring Forces Hostile. In DoD practice, an armed force or group may be designated as hostile (also known as declaring the force hostile) in rules of engagement. This means that personnel to whom such rules of engagement apply are authorized to attack the members of the group. In DoD practice, the authority to designate a group as hostile has been limited to only certain officials.[203]

5.7.2 Categories of Persons Who Are Combatants for the Purpose of Assessing Their Liability to Attack. The following categories of persons are combatants who may be made the object of attack because they are sufficiently associated with armed forces or armed groups:

- members of the armed forces of a State;[204]
- members of militia and volunteer corps;[205]

---

regardless of their activity when attacked. Nor is a distinction made between combat and combat service support personnel with regard to the right to be attacked as combatants; combatants are subject to attack if they are participating in hostilities through fire, maneuver, and assault; providing logistic, communications, administrative, or other support; or functioning as staff planners. An individual combatant's vulnerability to lawful targeting (as opposed to assassination) is not dependent upon his or her military duties, or proximity to combat as such.") (citations omitted).

[202] *For example*, 101st Airborne ROE Card, Iraq (2003), *reprinted in* CENTER FOR LAW AND MILITARY OPERATIONS, THE JUDGE ADVOCATE GENERAL'S LEGAL CENTER & SCHOOL, U.S. ARMY, I LEGAL LESSONS LEARNED FROM AFGHANISTAN AND IRAQ: MAJOR COMBAT OPERATIONS (11 SEPTEMBER 2001 - 1 MAY 2003) 315-16 (2004) ("1. Fire at all members of forces DECLARED HOSTILE. You may immediately fire upon any force that you know to be hostile. ... **1. Facts**: An enemy unit maneuvers within your weapon range. **Response**: Shoot to eliminate the threat and accomplish the mission. **2. Facts**: An unarmed enemy soldier sees you and does nothing but stare at you. **Response**: Shoot to eliminate the threat. The soldier is a member of a Hostile Force and is lawful target.").

[203] *For example*, CHAIRMAN OF THE JOINT CHIEFS OF STAFF INSTRUCTION 3121.01B, *Standing Rules of Engagement/Standing Rules for the Use of Force for U.S. Forces*, A-2, ¶2(b) (June 13, 2005), *reprinted in* INTERNATIONAL AND OPERATIONAL LAW DEPARTMENT, THE JUDGE ADVOCATE GENERAL'S LEGAL CENTER & SCHOOL, U.S. ARMY, OPERATIONAL LAW HANDBOOK 94 (2014) ("Once a force is declared hostile by appropriate authority, U.S. forces need not observe a hostile act or demonstrated hostile intent before engaging the declared hostile force. Policy and procedures regarding the authority to declare forces hostile are provided in Appendix A to Enclosure A, paragraph 3."); CHAIRMAN OF THE JOINT CHIEFS OF STAFF INSTRUCTION 3121.01A, *Standing Rules of Engagement for US Forces*, A-12, ¶6 (Jan. 15, 2000), *reprinted in* CENTER FOR LAW AND MILITARY OPERATIONS, THE JUDGE ADVOCATE GENERAL'S LEGAL CENTER & SCHOOL, U.S. ARMY, *Rules of Engagement (ROE) Handbook for Judge Advocates* 96 (May 1, 2000) ("6. Declaring Forces Hostile. Once a force is declared hostile by appropriate authority, US units need not observe a hostile act or a demonstration of hostile intent before engaging that force. The responsibility for exercising the right and obligation of national self-defense and as necessary declaring a force hostile is a matter of the utmost importance. All available intelligence, the status of international relationships, the requirements of international law, an appreciation of the political situation, and the potential consequences for the United States must be carefully weighed. The exercise of the right and obligation of national self-defense by competent authority is separate from and in no way limits the commander's right and obligation to exercise unit self-defense. The authority to declare a force hostile is limited as amplified in Appendix A of this Enclosure.").

[204] *Refer to* § 4.5 (Armed Forces of a State).

[205] *Refer to* § 4.6 (Other Militia and Volunteer Corps).

- participants in a *levée en masse*;[206]

- persons belonging to non-State armed groups;[207] and

- leaders whose responsibilities include the operational command and control of the armed forces or of a non-State armed group.[208]

5.7.3 Persons Belonging to Non-State Armed Groups. Like members of an enemy State's armed forces, individuals who are formally or functionally part of a non-State armed group that is engaged in hostilities may be made the object of attack because they likewise share in their group's hostile intent.[209]

5.7.3.1 *Formal Membership*. Formal membership in an armed group might be indicated by formal or direct information or by other types of information.

In some cases, there might be formal or direct information indicating membership in the group. This might include:

- using a rank, title, or style of communication;

- taking an oath of loyalty to the group or the group's leader;

- wearing a uniform or other clothing, adornments, or body markings that identify members of the group; or

- documents issued or belonging to the group that identify the person as a member, such as membership lists, identity cards, or membership applications.[210]

Although in some cases this type of formal or direct information might be available, in many cases it will not be available because members of these groups seek to conceal their association with that group. In such cases, the following types of information might indicate that a person is a member of a non-State armed group:

---

206 *Refer to* § 4.7 (*Levée en Masse*).

207 *Refer to* § 5.7.3 (Persons Belonging to Non-State Armed Groups).

208 *Refer to* § 5.7.4 (Leaders).

209 *Cf.* Al-Adahi v. Obama, 613 F.3d 1102, 1108 (D.C. Cir. 2010) ("The district court seemed to think it important to determine Al-Adahi's motive for attending the al-Qaida training camp. We do not understand why. Whatever his motive, the significant points are that al-Qaida was intent on attacking the United States and its allies, that bin Laden had issued a *fatwa* announcing that every Muslim had a duty to kill Americans, and that Al-Adahi voluntarily affiliated himself with al-Qaida.").

210 *Cf.* Alsabri v. Obama, 684 F.3d 1298, 1304-05 (D.C. Cir. 2012) (upholding a district court's determination that petitioner was part of the Taliban, al-Qaida, or associated forces, including by considering "an English translation of a document appearing to be Alsabri's application to attend an al Qaeda training camp" and "an English-language translation of a 92-page collection of documents that the government maintains were internal Taliban or al Qaeda records" that "were captured by Coalition forces from the 'Director of Al-Qa'ida Security Training Office,'").

- acting at the direction of the group or within its command structure;
- performing a function for the group that is analogous to a function normally performed by a member of a State's armed forces;
- taking a direct part in hostilities, including consideration of the frequency, intensity, and duration of such participation;[211]
- accessing facilities, such as safehouses, training camps, or bases used by the group that outsiders would not be permitted to access;[212]
- traveling along specific clandestine routes used by those groups;[213] or
- traveling with members of the group in remote locations or while the group conducts operations.[214]

5.7.3.2 Functional Membership. Some non-State armed groups might not be organized in a formal command structure, as generally is required for POW status during international armed conflict.[215] Such groups might lack a formal distinction between those

---

[211] *Refer to* § 5.8.3 ("Taking a Direct Part in in Hostilities").

[212] *Cf.* Alsabri v. Obama, 684 F.3d 1298, 1306 (D.C. Cir. 2012) ("[I]t is difficult to believe that 'Taliban fighters would allow an individual to infiltrate their posts near a battle zone unless that person was understood to be a part of the Taliban.'") (quoting Alsabri v. Obama, 764 F.Supp.2d 60, 94 (D.D.C. 2011)); Uthman v. Obama, 637 F.3d 400, 406 (D.C. Cir. 2011) ("In two prior cases, this Court has stated that staying at an al Qaeda guesthouse is 'powerful—indeed 'overwhelming'—evidence' that an individual is part of al Qaeda. Al–Adahi, 613 F.3d at 1108 (quoting Al-Bihani v. Obama, 590 F.3d 866, 873 footnote 2 (D.C. Cir. 2010)) (alterations omitted). The reason for that assessment is plain: It is highly unlikely that a visitor to Afghanistan would end up at an al Qaeda guesthouse by mistake, either by the guest or by the host.").

[213] *Cf.* Suleiman v. Obama, 670 F.3d 1311, 1314 (D.C. Cir. 2012) ("There is no dispute that Suleiman's travel was initiated at the suggestion of and facilitated by a Taliban recruiter, and that he traveled a well-worn path to Afghanistan frequently used by Taliban recruits. We have stated that such travel may indicate that an individual traveled to Afghanistan to join the Taliban.") (citing Al Odah v. United States, 611 F.3d 8, 14 (D.C. Cir. 2010)); Uthman v. Obama, 637 F.3d 400, 405 (D.C. Cir. 2011) ("[T]raveling to Afghanistan along a distinctive path used by al Qaeda members can be probative evidence that the traveler was part of al Qaeda."); Al Odah v. United States, 611 F.3d 8, 16 (D.C. Cir. 2010) (finding it significant that "Al Odah traveled to Afghanistan on a series of one-way plane tickets purchased with cash in a manner consistent with travel patterns of those going to Afghanistan to join the Taliban and al Qaeda").

[214] *Cf.* Hussain v. Obama, 718 F.3d 964, 968-69 (D.C. Cir. 2013) ("Evidence that Hussain bore a weapon of war while living side-by-side with enemy forces on the front lines of a battlefield at least invites — and may very well compel — the conclusion that he was loyal to those forces. We have repeatedly affirmed the propriety of this common-sense inference."); Uthman v. Obama, 637 F.3d 400, 405 (D.C. Cir. 2011) ("Being captured in the company of a Taliban fighter and two al Qaeda members and Osama bin Laden bodyguards 12 miles from Tora Bora in December 2001 might not be precisely the same as being captured in a German uniform 12 miles from the Normandy beaches in June 1944. But it is still, at a minimum, highly significant. And absent a credible alternative explanation, the location and date of Uthman's capture, together with the company he was keeping, strongly suggest that he was part of al Qaeda.").

[215] *Refer to* § 4.6.3 (Being Commanded by a Person Responsible for His or Her Subordinates).

members and non-members who nonetheless participate in the hostile activities of the group.[216]

An individual who is integrated into the group such that the group's hostile intent may be imputed to him or her may be deemed to be functionally (*i.e.*, constructively) part of the group, even if not formally a member of the group. The integration of the person into the non-State armed group and the inference that the individual shares the group's intention to commit hostile acts distinguish such an individual from persons who are merely sympathetic to the group's goals.[217]

The following may indicate that a person is functionally a member of a non-State armed group:

- following directions issued by the group or its leaders;[218]
- taking a direct part in hostilities on behalf of the group on a sufficiently frequent or intensive basis;[219] or
- performing tasks on behalf of the group similar to those provided in a combat, combat support, or combat service support role in the armed forces of a State.

5.7.3.3 Dissociation or Renunciation. A person may not be made the object of attack based on his or her association with a non-State armed group if that association has clearly been severed. Relevant factors in determining when an individual has unambiguously ceased to be a member of a non-State armed group may include:

- whether the individual has formally ceased to be a member of the group, such as by filing relevant paperwork or by otherwise formally renouncing any allegiance to the group;
- whether there are concrete and verifiable facts or persuasive indicia that he or she has affirmatively returned to peaceful pursuits, such as by participating in a reconciliation program and swearing an oath of loyalty to the government; and
- the amount of time that has passed since the person participated in the activities of the group in question, if coupled with other indicia of dissociation or renunciation.[220]

---

[216] *Compare* § 4.7 (*Levée en Masse*).

[217] *Compare* § 5.8.3.2 (Examples of Acts Not Considered Taking a Direct Part in Hostilities).

[218] *Cf.* Uthman v. Obama, 637 F.3d 400, 403 (D.C. Cir. 2011) ("[D]emonstrating that someone is part of al Qaeda's command structure is sufficient to show that person is part of al Qaeda."); Al-Adahi v. Obama, 613 F.3d 1102, 1109 (D.C. Cir. 2010) ("When the government shows that an individual received and executed orders from al-Qaida members in a training camp, that evidence is sufficient (but not necessary) to prove that the individual has affiliated himself with al-Qaida."); Salahi v. Obama, 625 F.3d 745, 752 (D.C. Cir. 2010) ("Evidence that an individual operated within al-Qaida's command structure is 'sufficient but is not necessary to show he is 'part of' the organization.'" (quoting Bensayah v. Obama, 610 F.3d 718, 725 (D.C. Cir. 2010))).

[219] *Refer to* § 5.8.3 ("Taking a Direct Part in in Hostilities").

[220] Stephen Pomper, Assistant Legal Adviser for Political-Military Affairs, Department of State, *Toward a Limited Consensus on the Loss of Civilian Immunity in Non-International Armed Conflict: Making Progress Through*

The onus is on the person having belonged to the armed group to demonstrate clearly and affirmatively to the opposing forces that he or she will no longer participate in the activities of the group.[221] Moreover, if persons who have dissociated from an armed group rejoin the group or fail to cease permanently their participation in hostilities, they may be made the object of attack.[222]

5.7.4 Leaders. Military leaders are subject to attack on the same basis as other members of the armed forces. Similarly, leaders of non-State armed groups are also subject to attack on the same basis as other members of the group. There is no objection to making a specific enemy leader who is a combatant the object of attack.[223]

Leaders who are not members of an armed force or armed group (including heads of State, civilian officials, and political leaders) may be made the object of attack if their responsibilities include the operational command or control of the armed forces. For example, as the commander-in-chief of the U.S. armed forces, the President would be a legitimate target in wartime, as would, for example, the Prime Minister of a constitutional monarchy. In contrast, the reigning monarch of a constitutional monarchy with an essentially ceremonial role in State affairs may not be made the object of attack.

In addition to leaders who have a role in the operational chain of command, leaders taking a direct part in hostilities may also be made the object of attack.[224] Planning or authorizing a combat operation is an example of taking a direct part in hostilities.[225]

As a matter of practice, attacks on the national leadership of an enemy State have often been avoided on the basis of comity and to help ensure that authorities exist with whom peace agreements may be concluded.

Practice, 88 U.S. NAVAL WAR COLLEGE INTERNATIONAL LAW STUDIES 181, 189 (2012) ("Relevant factors in determining that an individual has ceased to be a member of an organized armed group include the amount of time that has passed since that individual has taken relevant action on behalf of the group in question, and whether he or she affirmatively has disassociated himself or herself from the organized armed group.").

[221] Wolff Heintschel von Heinegg & Peter Dreist, *The 2009 Kunduz Air Attack: The Decision of the Federal Prosecutor-General on the Dismissal of Criminal Proceedings Against Members of the German Armed Forces*, 53 GERMAN YEARBOOK OF INTERNATIONAL LAW 833, 844-45 (2010) ("Here, the Prosecutor-General takes the opportunity to identify different categories of lawful targets under the law of non-international armed conflict. As regards fighters belonging to a non-State party to the conflict, their qualification as lawful targets is not based on some form of legal status but on the mere fact of their functional integration into an organized armed group. If they are so integrated, they do not qualify as civilians even though they may eventually pursue civilian occupation. They only regain their civilian status if they clearly and irrevocably renounce their function in the organized armed group. Hence, the Prosecutor-General is not prepared to consider Taliban fighters to be lawful targets only insofar and for such time as they take a direct part in armed hostilities."). *Compare* § 5.9.3 (Persons Who Have Surrendered).

[222] *Refer to* § 5.8.4.2 (No "Revolving Door" Protection); § 5.8.4.1 (Permanently Ceased Participation in Hostilities).

[223] *Refer to* § 5.4.6.4 (Attacks on Specific Individuals).

[224] *Refer to* § 5.8.3 ("Taking a Direct Part in in Hostilities").

[225] *Refer to* § 5.8.3.1 (Examples of Taking a Direct Part in Hostilities).

5.8 Civilians Taking a Direct Part in Hostilities

Civilians who take a direct part in hostilities forfeit protection from being made the object of attack.

5.8.1 Civilians Taking a Direct Part in Hostilities – Notes on Terminology. This manual uses the phrase "direct part in hostilities" to indicate what activities cause a civilian to forfeit his or her protection from being made the object of attack. This usage does not mean that the United States has adopted the direct participation in hostilities rule that is expressed in Article 51 of AP I.

5.8.1.1 *"Active" Versus "Direct"*. The phrases "*active* part in hostilities" and "*direct* part in hostilities" have been used to describe when civilians forfeit their protection from being made the object of attack. As noted above, this manual uses "direct" rather than "active" in this context, although as discussed below, this usage should not be regarded as indicating a substantive difference between "active" and "direct."

Common Article 3 of the 1949 Geneva Conventions refers to "[p]ersons taking no active part in the hostilities." AP I and AP II use the phrase "direct part in hostilities."[226] In addition, AP I uses the phrase "direct part in hostilities" to address other situations apart from the protection of civilians.[227]

Although the words *active* and *direct* can mean different things in the English language, the terms have sometimes been treated as the same for the purpose of applying the direct participation in hostilities rule.[228] One of the reasons for treating the terms the same is that although the English language version of the 1949 Geneva Conventions uses "active," and the English language versions of AP I and AP II use "direct," the French language versions of these treaties use the same word, "*directement*."[229] Because the English and French language versions

---

[226] AP I art. 51(3) ("Civilians shall enjoy the protection [from being made the object of attack], unless and for such time as they take a direct part in hostilities."); AP II art. 13(3) ("Civilians shall enjoy the protection [from being made the object of attack], unless and for such time as they take a direct part in hostilities.").

[227] *See, e.g.*, AP I art. 43(2) ("Members of the armed forces of a Party to a conflict (other than medical personnel and chaplains covered by Article 33 of the Third Convention) are combatants, that is to say, they have the right to participate directly in hostilities"); AP I art. 47(2) ("A mercenary is any person who ... [*inter alia*] (*b*) Does, in fact, take a direct part in the hostilities ... .").

[228] *See, e.g.*, Prosecutor v. Tadić, ICTY Trial Chamber, IT-94-1-T, *Judgment*, ¶¶614-15 (May 7, 1997) ("The rules contained in paragraph 1 of Common Article 3 proscribe a number of acts which: ... (iii) are committed against persons taking no active part in hostilities ... the test the Trial Chamber has applied is to ask whether, at the time of the alleged offence, the alleged victim of the proscribed acts was directly taking part in hostilities, being those hostilities in the context of which the alleged offences are said to have been committed. If the answer to that question is negative, the victim will enjoy the protection of the proscriptions contained in Common Article 3."); Prosecutor v. Akayesu, ICTR Trial Chamber, ICTR-96-4-T, *Judgment*, ¶629 (Sept. 2, 1998) ("'The victims referred to in this Indictment were, at all relevant times, persons not taking an active part in the hostilities'. This is a material averment for charges involving Article 4 inasmuch as Common Article 3 is for the protection of 'persons taking no active part in the hostilities' (Common Article 3(1)), and Article 4 of Additional Protocol II is for the protection of, 'all persons who do not take a direct part or who have ceased to take part in hostilities.' These phrases are so similar that, for the Chamber's purposes, they may be treated as synonymous.").

[229] GC art. 3, 973 UNTS 289 ("*ne participant pas directement aux hostilitiés*").

of the 1949 Geneva Conventions, AP I, and AP II are equally authentic, States negotiating these treaties may not have intended a difference between "active" and "direct."[230]

Another reason for treating the terms "active" and "direct" the same in this context is that they are understood to be terms of art addressing a particular legal standard, and there are a range of views as to what that legal standard means. Thus, there may be different views about what the underlying standard means, even when there is agreement on the appropriate term to describe that standard. Accordingly, there seems to be little value in distinguishing between the two terms for the purposes of applying this legal rule.

5.8.1.2 *AP I, Article 51(3) Provision on Direct Participation in Hostilities*. Although, as drafted, Article 51(3) of AP I does not reflect customary international law, the United States supports the customary principle on which Article 51(3) is based.[231] Similarly, although parts of the ICRC's interpretive guidance on the meaning of direct participation in hostilities are consistent with customary international law, the United States has not accepted significant parts of the ICRC's interpretive guidance as accurately reflecting customary international law.[232] But some States that are Parties to AP I may interpret and apply Article 51(3) of AP I consistent with the customary international law standard.

5.8.2 Persons to Whom This Rule Applies. For the purpose of applying the rule discussed in this section, "civilians" are persons who do not fall within the categories of combatants listed in § 5.7.2 (Categories of Persons Who Are Combatants for the Purpose of Assessing Their Liability to Attack). Accordingly, for the purposes of this section, "civilians" include:

---

[230] *See, e.g.*, GC art. 150 ("The present Convention is established in English and in French. Both texts are equally authentic."); AP I art. 102 ("The original of this Protocol, of which the Arabic, Chinese, English, French, Russian and Spanish texts are equally authentic, shall be deposited with the depositary, which shall transmit certified true copies thereof to all the Parties to the Conventions."); AP II art. 28 (same).

[231] *See* John B. Bellinger, III, Legal Adviser, Department of State, *Unlawful Enemy Combatants*, Jan.17, 2007, DIGEST OF UNITED STATES PRACTICE IN INTERNATIONAL LAW 915-16 ("While we agree that there is a general principle of international law that civilians lose their immunity from attack when they engage in hostilities, we disagree with the contention that the provision as drafted in AP I [Article 51(3)] is customary international law."); Michael J. Matheson, Deputy Legal Adviser, Department of State, *Remarks on the United States Position on the Relation of Customary International Law to the 1977 Protocols Additional to the 1949 Geneva Conventions at the Sixth Annual American Red Cross-Washington College of Law Conference on International Humanitarian Law* (Jan. 22, 1987), 2 AMERICAN UNIVERSITY JOURNAL OF INTERNATIONAL LAW AND POLICY 419, 426 (1987) ("We also support the principle that the civilian population not be used to shield military objectives or operations from attack, and that immunity not be extended to civilians who are taking part in hostilities. This corresponds to provisions in articles 51 and 52[of AP I].").

[232] *See, e.g.*, Stephen Pomper, Assistant Legal Adviser for Political-Military Affairs, Department of State, *Toward a Limited Consensus on the Loss of Civilian Immunity in Non-International Armed Conflict: Making Progress Through Practice*, 88 U.S. NAVAL WAR COLLEGE INTERNATIONAL LAW STUDIES 181, 186 (2012) ("From the operational perspective, the feedback [on the ICRC's interpretive guidance] was that the report was too rigid and complex, and did not give an accurate picture of State practice or (in some respects) of a practice to which States could realistically aspire."); Al-Bihani v. Obama, 590 F.3d 866, 885 (D.C. Cir. 2010) (Williams, J., concurring) ("The work itself explicitly disclaims that it should be read to have the force of law. ... Even to the extent that Al Bihani's reading of the Guidance is correct, then, the best he can do is suggest that we should follow it on the basis of its persuasive force. As against the binding language of the AUMF and its necessary implications, however, that force is insubstantial.").

- members of the civilian population;[233]
- persons authorized to accompany the armed forces;[234] and
- members of the merchant marine and civil aircraft of parties to a conflict.[235]

5.8.2.1 Persons Belonging to Hostile, Non-State Armed Groups. Some States may choose to characterize persons who belong to hostile, non-State armed groups that do not qualify for status as lawful combatants as "civilians" who may not be attacked unless they are taking a direct part in hostilities. However, these States may also characterize the act of joining and remaining a member of an armed group that is engaged in hostilities as a form of taking a direct part in hostilities that continuously deprives these individuals of their protection from being made the object of attack.[236]

The U.S. approach has generally been to refrain from classifying those belonging to non-State armed groups as "civilians" to whom this rule would apply. The U.S. approach has been to treat the status of belonging to a hostile, non-State armed group as a separate basis upon which a person is liable to attack, apart from whether he or she has taken a direct part in hostilities.[237] Either approach may yield the same result: members of hostile, non-State armed groups may be made the object of attack unless they are placed *hors de combat*. However, practitioners, especially when working with coalition partners, should understand that different legal reasoning is sometimes applied in reaching that result.

5.8.3 "Taking a Direct Part in in Hostilities". Unlike the treaty definition of "military objective" for objects,[238] the United States is not a Party to a treaty with a comparable provision defining taking a direct part in hostilities for the purpose of assessing what conduct renders civilians liable to being made the object of attack.

At a minimum, taking a direct part in hostilities includes actions that are, by their nature and purpose, intended to cause actual harm to the enemy.[239] Taking a direct part in hostilities extends beyond merely engaging in combat and also includes certain acts that are an integral part of combat operations or that effectively and substantially contribute to an adversary's ability to

---

233 *Refer to* § 4.8.1.5 (General Usage of "Civilian" in This Manual).

234 *Refer to* § 4.15 (Persons Authorized to Accompany the Armed Forces).

235 *Refer to* § 4.16 (Crews of Merchant Marine Vessels or Civil Aircraft).

236 Stephen Pomper, Assistant Legal Adviser for Political-Military Affairs, Department of State, *Toward a Limited Consensus on the Loss of Civilian Immunity in Non-International Armed Conflict: Making Progress Through Practice*, 88 U.S. NAVAL WAR COLLEGE INTERNATIONAL LAW STUDIES 181, 193 endnote 22 (2012) ("As discussed below, there is a range of views on whether individuals who pass the membership threshold lose their civilian status (and are therefore unprivileged belligerents) or remain civilians but are deemed to be continuously taking a direct part in hostilities and accordingly continuously lose their protections from being made the object of attack.").

237 *Refer to* § 5.7.3 (Persons Belonging to Non-State Armed Groups).

238 *Refer to* § 5.6.3 (Objects That Are Military Objectives).

239 ICRC AP COMMENTARY 619 ("Thus 'direct' participation means acts of war which by their nature or purpose are likely to cause actual harm to the personnel and equipment of the enemy armed forces.").

conduct or sustain combat operations.[240] However, taking a direct part in hostilities does not encompass the general support that members of the civilian population provide to their State's war effort, such as by buying war bonds.[241]

Whether an act by a civilian constitutes taking a direct part in hostilities is likely to depend highly on the context, such as the weapon systems or methods of warfare employed by the civilian's side in the conflict.[242] For example, in some contexts, training and logistical support may be viewed as taking a direct part in hostilities, while in other contexts it might not.[243] The following considerations may be relevant:[244]

---

[240] *See* GUENTER LEWY, AMERICA IN VIETNAM 232 (1978) ("We know that on occasion in Vietnam women and children placed mines and booby traps, and that villagers of all ages and sexes, willingly or under duress, served as porters, built fortifications, or engaged in other acts helping the communist forces. It is well established that once civilians act as support personnel they cease to be noncombatants and are subject to attack.").

[241] Stephen Pomper, Assistant Legal Adviser for Political-Military Affairs, Department of State, *Toward a Limited Consensus on the Loss of Civilian Immunity in Non-International Armed Conflict: Making Progress Through Practice*, 88 U.S. NAVAL WAR COLLEGE INTERNATIONAL LAW STUDIES 181, 189 (2012) ("With respect to determining what it means to take 'direct part in hostilities,' as a threshold matter there seems to be a common view that direct participation in hostilities stands in contrast to support by a general population to a nation's war effort. Civilians who are contributing to a nation's war effort accordingly do not by dint of this alone lose their protection.").

[242] *See* Nils Melzer, *Third Expert Meeting on the Notion of Direct Participation in Hostilities: Summary Report*, 35 (2005) ("Since, currently, the qualification of a particular act as direct participation in hostilities often depends on the particular circumstances and the technology or weapons system employed, it is unlikely that an abstract definition of direct participation in hostilities applicable to every situation can be found.").

[243] *For example*, Kenneth Watkin, *Opportunity Lost: Organized Armed Groups and the ICRC "Direct Participation in Hostilities" Interpretive Guidance*, 42 N.Y.U. JOURNAL OF INTERNATIONAL LAW AND POLITICS 641, 680-81 (2010) ("For example in Iraq, it has been noted, 'IED and suicide-bomber cells are essentially combatant units themselves,' where the most technically skilled bomb builder 'also doubles as a training instructor.' Further, 'bombers do not 'just turn up to their target'. They need a logistical infrastructure, which consists of individuals ... who provide everything from reconnaissance of the potential target ... to the provision of a safe house and food, and the explosives-laden vehicle or suicide belt.' ... To limit direct participation to persons who place or detonate explosives is an artificial division of what is fundamentally a group activity. ... The person who is key in planning and facilitating such deadly attacks must be a valid target as a direct participant in hostilities ...") (first and second ellipses in original).

[244] Stephen Pomper, Assistant Legal Adviser for Political-Military Affairs, Department of State, *Toward a Limited Consensus on the Loss of Civilian Immunity in Non-International Armed Conflict: Making Progress Through Practice*, 88 U.S. NAVAL WAR COLLEGE INTERNATIONAL LAW STUDIES 181, 189 ("Any determination that a civilian is taking part in hostilities (and thus loses immunity from being made the object of attack) will be highly situational and needs to be made by a decisionmaker taking the following considerations into account: • Nature of the harm: Is the individual's activity directed at (i) adversely affecting one party's military capacity or operations or enhancing the capacity/operations of the other, or (ii) killing, injuring or damaging civilian objects or persons?
• Causation/integration between action and harm: Is there a sufficiently direct causal link between the individual's relevant act and the relevant harm, or does the act otherwise form an integral part of coordinated action resulting in that harm? (Although it is not enough that the act merely occurs during hostilities, there is no requirement that the act be only a single causal step removed from the harm.) • Nexus to hostilities: Is the individual's activity linked to an ongoing armed conflict and is it intended either to disadvantage one party, or advance the interests of an opposing party, in that conflict? ... There is also a range of views about whether each of the foregoing three factors must be present in order to make a determination that an individual is directly participating in hostilities (or whether a 'totality of the circumstances' approach should govern), ... Moreover, there is a range of views concerning the

- the degree to which the act causes harm to the opposing party's persons or objects, such as
  - whether the act is the proximate or "but for" cause of death, injury, or damage to persons or objects belonging to the opposing party; or
  - the degree to which the act is likely to affect adversely the military operations or military capacity of the opposing party;
- the degree to which the act is connected to the hostilities, such as
  - the degree to which the act is temporally or geographically near the fighting; or
  - the degree to which the act is connected to military operations;
- the specific purpose underlying the act, such as
  - whether the activity is intended to advance the war aims of one party to the conflict to the detriment of the opposing party;
- the military significance of the activity to the party's war effort, such as
  - the degree to which the act contributes to a party's military action against the opposing party;
  - whether the act is of comparable or greater value to a party's war effort than acts that are commonly regarded as taking a direct part in hostilities;[245]
  - whether the act poses a significant threat to the opposing party;
- the degree to which the activity is viewed inherently or traditionally as a military one, such as
  - whether the act is traditionally performed by military forces in conducting military operations against the enemy (including combat, combat support, and

---

relevance of geographic and temporal proximity of an individual's actions to particular hostile acts in ongoing hostilities.").

[245] W. Hays Parks, Chief, International Law Branch, Office of the Judge Advocate General, Department of the Army, *Executive Order 12333 and Assassination*, Nov. 2, 1989, III CUMULATIVE DIGEST OF UNITED STATES PRACTICE IN INTERNATIONAL LAW 1981-1988 3411, 3416 ("Finally, one rule of thumb with regard to the likelihood that an individual may be subject to lawful attack is his (or her) immunity from military service if continued service in his (or her) civilian position is of greater value to a nation's war effort than that person's service in the military. A prime example would be civilian scientists occupying key positions in a weapons program regarded as vital to a nation's national security or war aims. Thus, more than 900 of the World War II Project Manhattan personnel were civilians, and their participation in the U.S. atomic weapons program was of such importance as to have made them liable to legitimate attack. Similarly, the September 1944 Allied bombing raids on the German rocket sites at Peenemunde regarded the death of scientists involved in research and development at that facility to have been as important as destruction of the missiles themselves.").

combat service support functions);[246] or

- o whether the activity involves making decisions on the conduct of hostilities, such as determining the use or application of combat power.

5.8.3.1 <u>*Examples of Taking a Direct Part in Hostilities*</u>. The following acts are generally considered taking a direct part in hostilities that would deprive civilians who perform them of protection from being made the object of attack. These examples are illustrative and not exhaustive:

- taking up or bearing arms against the opposing party, or otherwise personally trying to kill, injure, or capture personnel or damage material belonging to the opposing party,[247] such as
  - o defending military objectives against enemy attack (*e.g.*, manning an antiaircraft gun, acting as a bodyguard for an enemy combatant);[248]
  - o acting as a member of a weapons crew;
  - o engaging in an act of sabotage; or
  - o emplacing mines or improvised explosive devices;
- preparing for combat and returning from combat;
- planning, authorizing, or implementing a combat operation against the opposing party, even if that person does not personally use weapons or otherwise employ destructive force in connection with the operation;[249]

---

[246] Kenneth Watkin, *Controlling the Use of Force: A Role for Human Rights Norms in Contemporary Armed Conflict*, 98 AJIL 1, 17 (2004) ("The argument that civilians are protected unless engaged in overtly aggressive acts like carrying weapons may be particularly difficult to maintain where armed groups are technically accorded civilian status by virtue of not being considered lawful combatants. To the extent that civilians fulfill the same function as combatants, either in the armed forces or as part of the organization of an 'illegitimate' nonstate actor, they are logically subject to targeting under the same provisions of international humanitarian law.").

[247] 2006 AUSTRALIAN MANUAL ¶5.36 ("Civilians are only protected as long as they refrain from taking a direct part in hostilities. … Civilians bearing arms and taking part in military operations are clearly taking part in hostilities;"); ICRC AP COMMENTARY 618-19 (¶1943) ("It seems that the word 'hostilities' covers not only the time that the civilian actually makes use of a weapon, but also, for example, the time that he is carrying it, as well as situations in which he undertakes hostile acts without using a weapon.").

[248] 2004 UK MANUAL ¶5.3.3 ("Whether civilians are taking a direct part in hostilities is a question of fact. Civilians manning an anti-aircraft gun or engaging in sabotage of military installations are doing so.").

[249] *See* Public Committee against Torture in Israel, *et al.* v. Government of Israel, *et al.*, HCJ 769/02, Israel Supreme Court Sitting as the High Court of Justice, ¶37 (Dec. 11, 2005) ("We have seen that a civilian causing harm to the army is taking 'a direct part' in hostilities. What says the law about those who enlist him to take a direct part in the hostilities, and those who send him to commit hostilities? Is there a difference between his direct commanders and those responsible for them? Is the 'direct' part taken only by the last terrorist in the chain of command, or by the entire chain? In our opinion, the 'direct' character of the part taken should not be narrowed merely to the person committing the physical act of attack. Those who have sent him, as well, take 'a direct part'. The same goes for the

- providing or relaying information of immediate use in combat operations, such as
  - acting as an artillery spotter or member of a ground observer corps or otherwise relaying information to be used to direct an airstrike, mortar attack, or ambush;[250] and
  - acting as a guide or lookout for combatants conducting military operations;[251]
- supplying weapons and ammunition, whether to conventional armed forces or non-state armed groups, or assembling weapons (such as improvised explosive devices) in close geographic or temporal proximity to their use,[252] such as
  - delivering ammunition to the front lines; or
  - outfitting and preparing a suicide bomber to conduct an attack.

5.8.3.2 Examples of Acts Not Considered Taking a Direct Part in Hostilities. The following acts are generally not considered taking a direct part in hostilities that would deprive civilians who perform them of protection from being made the object of attack. These examples are illustrative and not exhaustive:

- mere sympathy or moral support for a party's cause;
- general contributions made by citizens to their State's war effort (*e.g.*, buying war bonds or paying taxes to the government that will ultimately be used to fund the armed forces);
- police services (*e.g.*, police officers who maintain public order against common criminals

---

person who decided upon the act, and the person who planned it. It is not to be said about them that they are taking an indirect part in the hostilities. Their contribution is direct (and active) (*see* Schmitt, at p. 529).").

[250] 2013 GERMAN MANUAL ¶518 ("Accordingly, civilians who perform concrete actions that constitute direct participation in hostilities (e.g. conducting military operations, transporting weapons and ammunition to combat units, operating weapon systems, transmitting target data that leads immediately to the engagement of a military objective, etc.) can be engaged as military objectives while performing such actions.").

[251] *For example*, 101st Airborne ROE Card, Iraq (2003), *reprinted in* CENTER FOR LAW AND MILITARY OPERATIONS, THE JUDGE ADVOCATE GENERAL'S LEGAL CENTER & SCHOOL, U.S. ARMY, I LEGAL LESSONS LEARNED FROM AFGHANISTAN AND IRAQ: MAJOR COMBAT OPERATIONS (11 SEPTEMBER 2001 - 1 MAY 2003) 315, 316 (2004) ("**7. Facts**: Your unit comes under fire, you notice a young civilian woman who appears to be pointing to the location where friendly troops are concealed, based on her actions, those locations are then targeted. **Response**: Shoot to eliminate the threat … .").

[252] *See, e.g.*, United States v. Hamdan 6 (Dec. 19, 2007), *reversed on different grounds*, 696 F.3d 1238 (D.C. Cir. 2012) ("The Commission also finds that the accused directly participated in those hostilities by driving a vehicle containing two surface-to-air missiles in both temporal and spatial proximity to both ongoing combat operations [in the nearby town of Takta Pol and the more distant Kandahar]. … Although Kandahar was a short distance away, the accused's past history of delivering munitions to Taliban and al Qaeda fighters, his possession of a vehicle containing surface to air missiles, and his capture while driving in the direction of a battle already underway, satisfies the requirement of 'direct participation.'").

during armed conflict);[253]

- independent journalism or public advocacy (*e.g.*, opinion journalists who write columns supporting or criticizing a State's war effort);[254]

- working in a munitions factory or other factory that is not in geographic or temporal proximity to military operations but that is supplying weapons, materiel, and other goods useful to the armed forces of a State;[255] or

- providing medical care or impartial humanitarian assistance.[256]

Although performing these activities does not make a person liable to being made the object of attack, performing these activities also does not immunize a person from attack if that person takes a direct part in hostilities or is otherwise lawfully made the object of attack.

5.8.3.3 *Taking a Direct Part in Hostilities and Standards for the Use of Force in Self-Defense*. In the practice of the United States, the U.S. armed forces have been authorized to use necessary and proportional force in self-defense in response to hostile acts or demonstrated hostile intent.[257]

In some cases, hostile acts or demonstrated hostile intent may also constitute taking a

---

[253] *Refer to* § 4.23.1 (Police as Civilians).

[254] *Refer to* § 4.24.1 (Status of Journalists – Generally Civilian). *Cf.* ICTY, *Final Report to the Prosecutor by the Committee Established to Review the NATO Bombing Campaign Against the Federal Republic of Yugoslavia*, ¶47 (Jun. 13, 2000) ("Whether the media constitutes a legitimate target group is a debatable issue. If the media is used to incite crimes, as in Rwanda, then it is a legitimate target. If it is merely disseminating propaganda to generate support for the war effort, it is not a legitimate target.").

[255] BOTHE, PARTSCH, & SOLF, NEW RULES 303 (AP I art. 51, ¶2.4.2.2) (noting that during international armed conflict, "workers in defense plants or those engaged in distribution or storage of military supplies in rear areas, do not pose an immediate threat to the adversary and therefore would not be subject to deliberate individual attack"). However, these individuals assume the risk of incidental injury as a result of attacks against those factories. *Refer to* § 5.12.3.3 (Civilian Workers Who Support Military Operations In or On Military Objectives).

[256] Principles Related to the Protection of Medical Care Provided by Impartial Humanitarian Organizations During Armed Conflict, ¶I, attachment to Ash Carter, Secretary of Defense, *Memorandum re: Principles Related to the Protection of Medical Care Provided by Impartial Humanitarian Organizations During Armed Conflict*, Oct. 3, 2016 ("Medical care during armed conflict is an activity that is fundamentally of a neutral, humanitarian, and non-combatant character.").

[257] *For example*, CHAIRMAN OF THE JOINT CHIEFS OF STAFF INSTRUCTION 3121.01B, *Standing Rules of Engagement/Standing Rules for the Use of Force for U.S. Forces*, ¶6b(1) (June 13, 2005), *reprinted in* INTERNATIONAL AND OPERATIONAL LAW DEPARTMENT, THE JUDGE ADVOCATE GENERAL'S LEGAL CENTER & SCHOOL, U.S. ARMY, OPERATIONAL LAW HANDBOOK 95 (2007) ("Unit commanders always retain the inherent right and obligation to exercise unit self-defense in response to a hostile act or demonstrated hostile intent. Unless otherwise directed by a unit commander as detailed below, military members may exercise individual self-defense in response to a hostile act or demonstrated hostile intent."); CHAIRMAN OF THE JOINT CHIEFS OF STAFF INSTRUCTION 3121.01A, *Standing Rules of Engagement for US Forces*, Enclosure A, A-1 (Jan. 15, 2000), *reprinted in* INTERNATIONAL AND OPERATIONAL LAW DEPARTMENT, THE JUDGE ADVOCATE GENERAL'S SCHOOL, U.S. ARMY, JA, OPERATIONAL LAW HANDBOOK 102 (2006) ("US forces always retain the right to use necessary and proportional force for unit and individual self-defense in response to a hostile act or demonstrated hostile intent.").

direct part in hostilities. However, hostile acts and demonstrated hostile intent in some respects may be narrower than the concept of taking a direct part in hostilities. For example, although supplying weapons and ammunition in close geographic or temporal proximity to their use is a common example of taking a direct part in hostilities, it would not necessarily constitute a hostile act or demonstrated hostile intent.

On the other hand, hostile acts and demonstrated hostile intent in some respects may be broader than the concept of taking a direct part in hostilities. For example, the use of force in response to hostile acts and demonstrated hostile intent applies outside hostilities, but taking a direct part in hostilities is limited to acts that occur during hostilities. Thus, the concept of taking a direct part hostilities must not be understood to limit the use of force in response to hostile acts or demonstrated hostile intent.

In the practice of the United States, offensive combat operations against people who are taking a direct part in hostilities have been authorized through specific rules of engagement.

5.8.4 Duration of Liability to Attack. There has been a range of views about the duration for which civilians who have taken a direct part in hostilities forfeit protection from being made the object of attack.[258]

In the U.S. approach, civilians who have taken a direct part in hostilities must not be made the object of attack after they have permanently ceased their participation because there would be no military necessity for attacking them. Persons who take a direct part in hostilities, however, do not benefit from a "revolving door" of protection. There may be difficult cases not clearly falling into either of these categories, and in such situations a case-by-case analysis of the specific facts would be needed.[259]

5.8.4.1 *Permanently Ceased Participation in Hostilities*. If a civilian has permanently ceased participation in hostilities, then that person must not be made the object of attack because there is no military necessity for doing so.[260] The assessment of whether a person

---

[258] *See, e.g.*, Nils Melzer, *Background Paper – Direct Participation on Hostilities under International Humanitarian Law – Expert Meeting of Oct. 25-26, 2004* 34 ("At one end of the spectrum were experts who preferred narrowly defining temporal scope and favoured strictly limiting loss of protection to the period where DPH is actually being carried out. At the other end were experts who said that, once a person had undertaken an act constituting DPH, that person must clearly express a will to definitively disengage and offer assurances that he or she will not resume hostilities in order to regain protection against direct attack. However, opinions varied greatly and could not easily be divided into two groups supporting distinct positions.").

[259] Public Committee against Torture in Israel, *et al.* v. Government of Israel, *et al.*, HCJ 769/02, Israel Supreme Court Sitting as the High Court of Justice, ¶40 (Dec. 11, 2005) ("These examples point out the dilemma which the 'for such time' requirement presents before us. On the one hand, a civilian who took a direct part in hostilities once, or sporadically, but detached himself from them (entirely, or for a long period) is not to be harmed. On the other hand, the 'revolving door' phenomenon, by which each terrorist has 'horns of the alter' (1 Kings 1:50) to grasp or a 'city of refuge' (Numbers 35:11) to flee to, to which he turns in order to rest and prepare while they grant him immunity from attack, is to be avoided (*see* Schmitt, at p. 536; Watkin, at p. 12; Kretzmer, at p. 193; DINSTEIN, at p. 29; *and* Parks, at p. 118). In the wide area between those two possibilities, one finds the 'gray' cases, about which customary international law has not yet crystallized. There is thus no escaping examination of each and every case.").

[260] *Refer to* § 2.3 (Humanity).

has permanently ceased participation in hostilities must be based on a good faith assessment of the available information.[261]

For example, a civilian might have engaged in an isolated instance of taking a direct part in hostilities. This isolated instance is likely to have involved multiple acts, because taking a direct part in hostilities normally includes deploying or moving to a position of attack and exfiltrating from an attack.[262] However, if this participation was an isolated instance that will not be repeated, then no military necessity for attacking that person exists after he or she has ceased taking a direct part in hostilities. Accordingly, the civilian must not be made the object of attack after he or she has ceased taking a direct part in hostilities. However, there may be other legal consequences from this isolated instance of participation. For example, such civilians may, depending on the circumstances, be detained, interned, or prosecuted because of these actions.[263]

5.8.4.2 <u>*No "Revolving Door" Protection*</u>. The law of war, as applied by the United States, gives no "revolving door" protection; that is, the off-and-on protection in a case where a civilian repeatedly forfeits and regains his or her protection from being made the object of attack depending on whether or not the person is taking a direct part in hostilities at that exact time.[264] Thus, for example, persons who are assessed to be engaged in a pattern of taking a direct part in hostilities do not regain protection from being made the object of attack in the time period between instances of taking a direct part in hostilities.[265]

---

[261] *Refer to* § 5.3 (Assessing Information Under the Law of War).

[262] *Refer to* § 5.8.3.1 (Examples of Taking a Direct Part in Hostilities).

[263] *Refer to* § 4.18 (Private Persons Who Engage in Hostilities).

[264] *See also* Kenneth Watkin, *Opportunity Lost: Organized Armed Groups and the ICRC 'Direct Participation in Hostilities' Interpretive Guidance*, 42 NEW YORK UNIVERSITY JOURNAL OF INTERNATIONAL LAW AND POLITICS 641, 689 (2010) ("Further, on one level the term 'revolving door' evokes the idea of a form of carnival shooting gallery, where soldiers must wait until an opponent pops out from behind a door to be shot at. At some point, the credibility of the law begins to be undermined by suggesting an opponent can repeatedly avail themselves of such protection.").

[265] Kenneth Watkin, *Opportunity Lost: Organized Armed Groups and the ICRC 'Direct Participation in Hostilities' Interpretive Guidance*, 42 NEW YORK UNIVERSITY JOURNAL OF INTERNATIONAL LAW AND POLITICS 641, 692 (2010) ("However, given the lack of credibility associated with the term, there can be no 'revolving door' of protection. After the first involvement, any subsequent act demonstrating direct participation would start to provide the basis to believe that there is the beginning of a pattern of conduct that reflects an intention to regularly engage in the hostilities. Repetitious participation can be considered in determining if such persons are in reality continuously engaged in hostilities. When such participation occurs, affirmative disengagement would be required in order to establish that such persons are no longer direct participants in hostilities."). *Cf.* Bill Boothby, *"And For Such Time As": The Time Dimension to Direct Participation in Hostilities*, 42 NEW YORK UNIVERSITY JOURNAL OF INTERNATIONAL LAW AND POLITICS 741, 765-66 (2010) ("In my view, an alternative interpretation of the treaty language is equally valid. According to this alternative view, the temporal element in the provision lies both in the phrase 'unless and for such time' and in the word 'participates.' … If, however, a person engages in repeated acts of DPH, there is an evident artificiality in regarding that individual as having protected status during the intervals in between. Experience shows that during those periods a further act of direct participation by the persistent participator is likely to be in prospect, and the likelihood is that during those intervals he will be preparing himself for the next act, checking his equipment, obtaining any additional equipment or stores he may require, communicating with like-minded or otherwise involved individuals, refining his plan and so on. While some such activities may be DP in their own right, the more important point is that a person who is so engaged cannot be

A "revolving door" of protection would place these civilians who take a direct part in hostilities on a better footing than lawful combatants, who may be made the object of attack even when not taking a direct part in hostilities.[266] The United States has strongly disagreed with posited rules of international law that, if accepted, would operate to give the so-called "farmer by day, guerilla by night" greater protections than lawful combatants.[267] Adoption of such a rule would risk diminishing the protection of the civilian population.

5.8.5 Civilians Who Take a Direct Part in Hostilities and the Law of War. Although the concept of direct participation in hostilities may be discussed in contexts besides targeting, such as in the context of criminal liability or detention, there are often significant differences between "taking a direct part in hostilities" for targeting purposes and the standards used for assessing whether a civilian may be detained or prosecuted.

For example, whether someone may be made the object of attack for taking a direct part in hostilities is different from whether he or she may be prosecuted for his or her actions. In some cases, domestic criminal liability for support to enemy armed groups is much broader than what acts constitute "taking a direct part in hostilities."

Similarly, the authority to detain enemy persons during wartime extends beyond detaining those who have taken a direct part in hostilities.[268]

5.9 Persons Placed Hors de Combat

Persons, including combatants, placed *hors de combat* may not be made the object of attack. Persons placed *hors de combat* include the following categories of persons, provided they abstain from any hostile act and do not attempt to escape:

- persons in the power of an adverse party;
- persons not yet in custody, who have surrendered;
- persons who have been rendered unconscious or otherwise incapacitated by wounds, sickness, or shipwreck; and
- persons parachuting from aircraft in distress.

5.9.1 *Hors de Combat* – Notes on Terminology. *Hors de combat* is a French phrase that means "out of the battle." It is generally used as a term of art to mean persons who may not be made the object of attack because they are out of the fighting and who therefore must be treated humanely.

---

equated with a civilian who remains uninvolved in the conflict. To do so is to place at risk the respect, based on law, to be accorded to the civilian population.").

[266] *Refer to* § 5.7.1 (Armed Forces and Groups and Liability to Being Made the Object of Attack).

[267] *Refer to* § 4.18.3 (Private Persons Who Engage in Hostilities – Lack of the Privileges of Combatant Status).

[268] *Refer to* § 4.8.3 (Civilians – Detention); § 4.4.2 (Combatants – POW Status During Detention).

Hors de combat is used in Common Article 3 of the 1949 Geneva Conventions[269] and has been defined in Article 41 of AP I.[270]

5.9.2 Persons in the Power of an Adverse Party. Persons in the power of an adverse party include all persons detained by an adverse party, such as POWs, unprivileged belligerents, retained personnel, and civilian internees. As with other categories of persons *hors de combat*, detainees must refrain from hostile acts or attempts to escape in order to be considered *hors de combat*.[271]

5.9.3 Persons Who Have Surrendered. Persons who are not in custody but who have surrendered are *hors de combat* and may not be made the object of attack.[272] In order to make a person *hors de combat*, the surrender must be (1) genuine; (2) clear and unconditional; and (3) under circumstances where it is feasible for the opposing party to accept the surrender.[273]

5.9.3.1 *Genuine*. The offer to surrender must be genuine. In addition to being legally ineffective, feigning the intent to surrender can constitute perfidy.[274]

5.9.3.2 *Clear and Unconditional*. The offer to surrender must be clear and unconditional.

Any arms being carried should be laid down. All hostile acts or resistance, or manifestations of hostile intent, including efforts to escape or to destroy items, documents, or equipment to prevent their capture by the enemy, would need to cease immediately for the offer to be clear and unconditional. Raising one's hands above one's head to show that one is not preparing to fire a weapon or engage in combat is often a sign of surrender. Waving a white flag

---

[269] GWS art. 3(1) (requiring humane treatment for "[p]ersons taking no active part in the hostilities, including members of armed forces who have laid down their arms and those placed *hors de combat* by sickness, wounds, detention, or any other cause"); GWS-SEA art. 3(1) (same); GPW art. 3(1) (same); GC art. 3(1) (same).

[270] AP I art. 41(2) ("A person is *hors de combat* if: (a) He is in the power of an adverse Party; (b) He clearly expresses an intention to surrender; or (c) He has been rendered unconscious or is otherwise incapacitated by wounds or sickness, and therefore is incapable of defending himself; provided that in any of these cases he abstains from any hostile act and does not attempt to escape.").

[271] *Consider* AP I art. 41(2) ("A person is *hors de combat* if: (a) He is in the power of an adverse Party; ... provided that in any of these cases he abstains from any hostile act and does not attempt to escape.").

[272] HAGUE IV REG. art. 23(c) (it is especially forbidden "[t]o kill or wound an enemy who, having laid down his arms, or having no longer means of defence, has surrendered at discretion;"). *Consider* AP I art. 41(2) ("A person is *hors de combat* if: ... (b) He clearly expresses an intention to surrender; ... provided that in any of these cases he abstains from any hostile act and does not attempt to escape.").

[273] Harold Hongju Koh, Legal Adviser, Department of State, *The Lawfulness of the U.S. Operation Against Osama bin Laden*, May 19, 2011, 2011 DIGEST OF UNITED STATES PRACTICE IN INTERNATIONAL LAW 558-59 ("Finally, consistent with the laws of armed conflict and U.S. military doctrine, the U.S. forces were prepared to capture bin Laden if he had surrendered in a way that they could safely accept. The laws of armed conflict require acceptance of a genuine offer of surrender that is clearly communicated by the surrendering party and received by the opposing force, under circumstances where it is feasible for the opposing force to accept that offer of surrender. But where that is not the case, those laws authorize use of lethal force against an enemy belligerent, under the circumstances presented here.").

[274] *Refer to* § 5.22.3 (Examples of Killing or Wounding by Resort to Perfidy).

technically is not a sign of surrender, but signals a desire to negotiate.[275]

The surrender must be "at discretion," *i.e.*, unconditional.[276] A person who offers to surrender only if certain demands are met would not be *hors de combat* until that offer has been accepted.

5.9.3.3 *Under Circumstances in Which It Is Feasible to Accept*. For an offer of surrender to render a person *hors de combat*, it must be feasible for the opposing party to accept the offer.[277] By way of comparison, a city may not be declared "undefended" (and thus essentially surrendered) if it is not open for immediate physical occupation by opposing military forces.[278]

The feasibility of accepting the surrender refers to whether it is practical and safe for the opposing force to take custody of the surrendering persons in the circumstances. For example, consider the situation of enemy soldiers who man an antiaircraft gun and shoot at an enemy aircraft, and then who raise their hands as if to surrender seconds before a second aircraft attacks their position. In the circumstances, it would not be feasible for the crew of the attacking aircraft to land and accept their surrender.[279] Similarly, a soldier fifty meters from an enemy defensive position in the midst of an infantry assault by his unit could not throw down his weapon and raise his arms (as if to indicate his desire to surrender) and reasonably expect that the defending unit will be able to accept and accomplish his surrender while resisting the ongoing assault by his unit.[280]

Although the feasibility of accepting surrender includes consideration of whether it is feasible to take custody of the persons offering to surrender, this does not include consideration of whether it is feasible to care for detainees after taking custody. Offers to surrender may not be refused because it would be militarily inconvenient or impractical to guard or care for detainees.[281]

5.9.4 Persons Rendered Unconscious or Otherwise Incapacitated by Wounds, Sickness,

---

[275] *Refer to* § 12.4 (The White Flag of Truce to Initiate Negotiations).

[276] HAGUE IV REG. art. 23(c) (it is especially forbidden "[t]o kill or wound an enemy who, having laid down his arms, or having no longer means of defence, has surrendered at discretion;") (emphasis added).

[277] *See* FINAL REPORT ON THE PERSIAN GULF WAR 629 ("Surrender involves an offer by the surrendering party (a unit or an individual soldier) and an ability to accept on the part of his opponent. The latter may not refuse an offer of surrender when communicated, but that communication must be made at a time when it can be received and properly acted upon – an attempt at surrender in the midst of a hard-fought battle is neither easily communicated nor received. The issue is one of reasonableness.").

[278] *Refer to* § 5.15.3.1 (Open for Immediate Physical Occupation).

[279] *Refer to* § 14.9.3.2 (Feasibility of Air Units to Accept the Surrender of Ground Forces).

[280] *See* SPAIGHT, WAR RIGHTS ON LAND 92-93 ("A party in a trench must *all* surrender, genuinely and unmistakably, for a regiment, squadron, company or squad of men is not like a ship, which, when it 'hath its bellyful of fighting,' hauls down its colours and is clearly out of the fight. There is no such homogeneity in a unit in land war. … It is the safest rule for a commander to pay no heed to a white flag which is hoisted, in the midst of an action, by a few men who form part of a more considerable force which still resists.").

[281] *Refer to* § 9.5.2.1 (Prohibition on Killing of POWs).

or Shipwreck. Persons who have been rendered unconscious or otherwise incapacitated by wounds, sickness, or shipwreck, such that they are no longer capable of fighting, are *hors de combat*.[282]

Those "rendered unconscious" does not include persons who simply fall asleep. Sleeping combatants generally may be made the object of attack.[283]

Shipwrecked combatants include those who have been shipwrecked from any cause and includes forced landings at sea by or from aircraft.[284]

Persons who have been incapacitated by wounds, sickness, or shipwreck are in a helpless state, and it would be dishonorable and inhumane to make them the object of attack.[285] In order to receive protection as *hors de combat*, the person must be wholly disabled from fighting.[286] On the other hand, many combatants suffer from wounds and sickness, but nonetheless continue to fight and would not be protected.[287]

In many cases, the circumstances of combat may make it difficult to distinguish between persons who have been incapacitated by wounds, sickness, or shipwreck and those who continue to fight.[288] If possible, those seeking protection as wounded, sick, or shipwrecked, should make their condition clear.[289]

---

[282] *Consider* AP I art. 41(2) ("A person is hors de combat if: … (c) He has been rendered unconscious or is otherwise incapacitated by wounds or sickness, and therefore is incapable of defending himself; provided that in any of these cases he abstains from any hostile act and does not attempt to escape.").

[283] *For example*, Judy G. Endicott, *Raid on Libya: Operation ELDORADO CANYON*, *in* SHORT OF WAR: MAJOR USAF CONTINGENCY OPERATIONS 1947–1997 (A. Timothy Warnock, Air Force Historical Research Agency ed., 2000) (describing Operation ELDORADO CANYON, in which the United States responded to the Berlin discotheque bombing by conducting air strikes on multiple Libyan targets—including two military barracks—in the early hours of April 15, 1986).

[284] *Refer to* § 7.3.1.2 (Shipwrecked).

[285] GWS-SEA COMMENTARY 87 ("[I]t must be pointed out that the purpose of this provision [i.e., the first paragraph of Article 12 of the GWS-Sea], and indeed of the whole Convention, is to protect wounded, sick and shipwrecked persons who, if they were not in this helpless state, could rightfully be attacked.").

[286] *Cf.* LIEBER CODE art. 71 ("Whoever intentionally inflicts additional wounds on an enemy already wholly disabled, or kills such an enemy, or who orders or encourages soldiers to do so, shall suffer death, if duly convicted, whether he belongs to the Army of the United States, or is an enemy captured after having committed his misdeed.").

[287] GWS COMMENTARY 136 footnote 1 ("Cases are frequent of soldiers who have heroically continued to fight in spite of serious wounds. It goes without saying that in so doing they renounce any claim to protection under the Convention.").

[288] GWS-SEA COMMENTARY 90 ("[D]uring a landing by armed forces it will not always be possible while the attack is in progress to distinguish between an attacker trying to reach land and a soldier in danger of drowning. Similarly, in the case of persons specialized in under-water attacks, it may not always be evident when they are in peril and need assistance as shipwrecked. In such instances, persons in distress who renounce active combat can only expect the adversary to respect and rescue them if they make their situation clear, and of course provided the adversary sees their signals.").

[289] *Compare* § 5.9.3.2 (Clear and Unconditional).

5.9.5 Persons Parachuting From an Aircraft in Distress. In general, persons, such as aircrew or embarked passengers, parachuting from an aircraft in distress are treated as though they are *hors de combat*, *i.e.*, they must not be made the object of attack.[290]

This protection is provided because a person descending by parachute is temporarily *hors de combat* just like someone who is shipwrecked[291] or unconscious.[292]

5.9.5.1 *No Hostile Acts or Attempts to Evade Capture*. As with other categories of persons *hors de combat*, the protection from being made the object of attack is forfeited if the persons engage in hostile acts or attempt to evade capture.

Routine "slipping" to steer a parachute or similar actions to facilitate a safe parachute landing do not constitute acts of evasion.

5.9.5.2 *Persons Deploying Into Combat by Parachute*. Persons deploying into combat by parachute may be attacked throughout their descent, and upon landing.

Persons deploying into combat by parachute may include special operations or reconnaissance personnel, combat control teams, or airborne forces (*i.e.*, specialized combat forces trained to arrive at military objectives by parachute drops).

Persons deploying into combat by parachute may be attacked even if they deploy from an aircraft in distress (*e.g.*, the enemy has attacked the aircraft to resist the assault).

It may be the case, however, that airborne forces are parachuting from an aircraft in distress outside the context of an airborne assault. Since they would not be "deploying into combat," they would be *hors de combat* while descending by parachute.

---

[290] 1956 FM 27-10 (Change No. 1 1976) ¶30 ("The law of war does not prohibit firing upon paratroops or other persons who are or appear to be bound upon hostile missions while such persons are descending by parachute. Persons other than those mentioned in the preceding sentence who are descending by parachute from disabled aircraft may not be fired upon."); APPENDIX TO 1985 CJCS MEMO ON AP I 31 ("Article 42 of the Protocol prohibits attacks on aircrew members descending by parachute from disabled aircraft. The United States regards such attacks as prohibited under customary international law, and the US delegation argued for explicit recognition of such a rule at the diplomatic conference which negotiated the Protocol."). *Consider* AP I art. 42 ("1. No person parachuting from an aircraft in distress shall be made the object of attack during his descent. … 3. Airborne troops are not protected by this Article."); Commission of Jurists to Consider and Report Upon the Revision of the Rules of Warfare, *General Report, Part II: Rules of Aërial Warfare*, art. 20, Feb. 19, 1923, *reprinted in* 32 AJIL SUPPLEMENT: OFFICIAL DOCUMENTS 12, 21 (1938) ("When an aircraft has been disabled, the occupants, when endeavoring to escape by means of a parachute, must not be attacked in the course of their descent.").

[291] ICRC AP COMMENTARY 495 (¶1637) ("There is absolutely no doubt that the majority [of States at the diplomatic conference] considered that airmen in distress are comparable to the shipwrecked persons protected by the Second Convention.").

[292] ICRC AP COMMENTARY 497 (¶1644) ("The airman who parachutes from an aircraft in distress is therefore temporarily *hors de combat*, just as if he had lost consciousness, until the moment that he lands on the ground, and as long as he is incapacitated.").

5.10 PROPORTIONALITY IN CONDUCTING ATTACKS

In accordance with the principle of proportionality, combatants must not exercise the right to engage in attacks against military objectives in an unreasonable or excessive way.[293] Therefore, when prosecuting attacks against military objectives (*i.e.*, the persons and objects that may be made the object of attack), combatants must exercise due regard to reduce the risk of incidental harm to the civilian population and other persons and objects that may not be made the object of attack. In particular, the following rules apply:

- Combatants must take feasible precautions in planning and conducting attacks to reduce the risk of harm to civilians and other persons and objects protected from being made the object of attack;[294] and

- Combatants must refrain from attacks in which the expected loss of civilian life, injury to civilians, and damage to civilian objects incidental to the attack would be excessive in relation to the concrete and direct military advantage expected to be gained.[295]

5.10.1 Scope of Application of the Principle of Proportionality in Conducting Attacks. The principle of proportionality in conducting attacks imposes duties that apply to the protection of persons and objects that may not be made the object of attack. This principle does not impose obligations intended to reduce the risk of harm to military objectives (*i.e.*, persons and objects that may be made the object of attack).

Although the prohibition on attacks expected to cause excessive harm to civilians and civilian objects generally does not require consideration of military personnel and objects, feasible precautions must be taken to reduce the risk of harm to military personnel and objects that are protected from being made the object of attack, such as military personnel placed *hors de combat*.

5.10.1.1 *Proportionality in Conducting Attacks and Military Objectives*. The principle of proportionality in conducting attacks does not impose obligations intended to reduce the risk of harm to military objectives (*i.e.*, persons and objects that may be made the object of attack).[296] For example, an attack against an enemy combatant might also injure other enemy combatants who were not the specific targets of the attack. The principle of proportionality in conducting attacks would not require that efforts be made to reduce the likelihood of harm to other enemy combatants or damage to other military objectives, even if this harm were an unintended result of the attack.

5.10.1.2 *Proportionality in Conducting Attacks and Protected Military Personnel and Facilities*. The prohibition on attacks expected to cause excessive incidental harm requires

---

[293] *Refer to* § 2.4 (Proportionality).

[294] *Refer to* § 5.11 (Proportionality – Feasible Precautions in Planning and Conducting Attacks to Reduce the Risk of Harm to Protected Persons and Objects).

[295] *Refer to* § 5.12 (Proportionality – Prohibition on Attacks Expected to Cause Excessive Incidental Harm).

[296] *Refer to* § 5.4.6 (Force That May Be Applied Against Military Objectives).

consideration of civilians and civilian objects, but this prohibition generally does not require consideration of military personnel and objects, even if they may not be made the object of attack, such as military medical personnel, the military wounded and sick, and military medical facilities. For example, treaty provisions articulating a prohibition on attacks expected to cause excessive incidental harm do not reflect protections for military personnel who are protected from being made the object of attack.[297] Those planning or conducting attacks may consider such military personnel as a matter of practice or policy in applying the prohibition on attacks expected to cause excessive incidental harm.

The exclusion of protected military personnel and military medical facilities from this prohibition reflects such factors as, among others, the general impracticality of prohibiting attacks on this basis during combat operations.[298] For example, the expected incidental harm to a sick-bay on a warship would not serve to exempt that warship from being made the object of attack.

Nonetheless, feasible precautions must be taken to reduce the risk of harm to military personnel and objects that are protected from being made the object of attack.[299] For example, in the context of a deliberate, planned bombardment of a military objective near an identifiable military hospital, it may be feasible to take precautions to reduce the risk of harming the military hospital, and such precautions must be taken.

5.10.2 Responsibility of Commanders for Implementing the Principle of Proportionality in Conducting Attacks. Commanders, at all levels, have a great responsibility to exercise the leadership necessary to reduce the risk of harm to civilians and civilian objects.[300] Although the

---

[297] *Consider* AP I art. 57(2)(a) ("Those who plan or decide upon an attack shall: … (iii) Refrain from deciding to launch any attack which may be expected to cause incidental loss of civilian life, injury to civilians, damage to civilian objects, or a combination thereof, which would be excessive in relation to the concrete and direct military advantage anticipated;"); ROME STATUTE art. 8(2)(b)(iv) (defining war crimes in international armed conflict for the purposes of the Rome Statute to include "[i]ntentionally launching an attack in the knowledge that such attack will cause incidental loss of life or injury to civilians or damage to civilian objects or widespread, long-term and severe damage to the natural environment which would be clearly excessive in relation to the concrete and direct overall military advantage anticipated;").

[298] *Refer to* § 7.8.2.1 (Incidental Harm Not Prohibited); § 7.12.2.5 (Acceptance of the Risk From Proximity to Combat Operations).

[299] *See, e.g.*, TUCKER, THE LAW OF WAR AND NEUTRALITY AT SEA 133 footnote 17 ("It is clear that hospital ships act at their own risk whenever they place themselves in the immediate vicinity of legitimate military objectives. For even though every effort must be made to avoid firing upon—or bombing—hospital ships, the presence of the latter cannot serve to exempt nearby military objectives from attack for fear that a hospital vessel might thereby suffer incidental injury.").

[300] Defense Legal Policy Board, *Report of the Subcommittee on Military Justice in Combat Zones*, 60 (May 30, 2013) ("Virtually all witnesses agreed that a moral, ethical command climate in combat that inculcates and maintains U.S. values despite the difficulties of the mission or the particular area of operations is the single most important factor in preventing civilian casualties, ensuring civilian casualty reporting, and appropriately addressing reported incidents. Individual commanders, at all levels, together with their non-commissioned officers, have a great responsibility in this regard. No substitute exists for ethical leadership manifested by the provision of training in garrison and throughout deployments. Such training should demonstrate ethical responses to civilian engagements, including incident reporting and investigations, and engender trust that civilian casualty investigations are used to determine facts, and not just to uncover misconduct.").

specific responsibilities that individual combatants have to implement the principle of proportionality will depend on their role and assigned military duties in planning or conducting an attack, commanders are responsible for making the decisions and judgments required by the principle of proportionality in conducting attacks.[301]

5.10.2.1 *Need for Competent Authority to Make the Decisions and Judgments Required by the Principle of Proportionality*. As with other aspects of the law of war, the persons within a party to a conflict who are responsible for making the decisions and judgments required by the principle of proportionality are those who have the authority to make these decisions and judgments.[302] The specific responsibilities that individual combatants have to implement the principle of proportionality will depend on their role and assigned military duties in planning or conducting an attack.[303]

The decisions and judgments required by the principle of proportionality normally require authority over military operations. For example, assessing the military advantage expected to be gained from an attack may require knowing the broader strategy being employed by the attacking party or knowing intelligence information about the strategic and operational context in which the attack takes place.[304] Lower-level personnel may not be privy to the strategic or operational significance of a specific attack, and thus may not be competent to

---

[301] HAGUE IV REG. art. 26 ("The officer in command of an attacking force must, before commencing a bombardment, except in cases of assault, do all in his power to warn the authorities.") (emphasis added); HAGUE IX art. 6 ("If the military situation permits, the commander of the attacking naval force, before commencing the bombardment, must do his utmost to warn the authorities.") (emphasis added). *Cf.* United Kingdom, *Statement on Ratification of AP I*, Jan. 28, 1998, 2020 UNTS 75, 78 ("The United Kingdom understands that the obligation to comply with [art. 57] paragraph 2(b) only extends to those who have the authority and practical possibility to cancel or suspend the attack."); VI OFFICIAL RECORDS OF THE CDDH 212 (CDDH/SR.42, ¶43) ("Mr. BINDSCHEDLER (Switzerland) said that he was critical of paragraphs 2 and 3 of Article 50 because they lacked clarity, particularly the words 'Those who plan or decide upon an attack…' in paragraph 2(a). That ambiguous wording might well place a burden or responsibility on junior military personnel which ought normally to be borne by those of higher rank. The obligations set out in article 50 could concern the high commands only – the higher grade of the military hierarchy, and it was thus that Switzerland would interpret that provision.") (ellipsis shown in original); *id.* at ¶¶44-46 ("Mr. KUSSBACH (Austria) said that … His delegation considered that the precautions envisaged could only be taken at a higher level of military command, in other words by the high command. Junior military personnel could not be expected to take all the precautions prescribed, particularly that of ensuring respect for the principle of proportionality during an attack.").

[302] *Refer to* § 18.3.1.1 (Implementation of International Obligations by Persons With the Authority to Make the Necessary Decisions and Judgments Required by International Law).

[303] 2004 UK MANUAL ¶5.32.9 ("Those who plan or decide upon attacks are the planners and commanders and they have a duty to verify targets, take precautions to reduce incidental damage, and refrain from attacks that offend the proportionality principle. Whether a person will have this responsibility will depend on whether he has any discretion in the way the attack is carried out and so the responsibility will range from commanders-in-chief and their planning staff to single soldiers opening fire on their own initiative."); 2004 UK MANUAL ¶5.33.5 ("In assessing whether the proportionality rule has been violated, the effect of the whole attack must be considered. That does not, however, mean that an entirely gratuitous and unnecessary action within the attack as a whole would be condoned. Generally speaking, when considering the responsibility of a commander at any level, it is necessary to look at the part of the attack for which he was responsible in the context of the attack as a whole and in the light of the circumstances prevailing at the time the decision to attack was made.").

[304] *Refer to* § 5.12.2.1 (Considering the Advantage From the Attack as a Whole – In the Operational and Strategic Context).

evaluate the expected military advantage of the attack against the expected harm to civilians and civilian objects.[305] Similarly, determinations about the feasibility of taking a precaution may require the authority to direct and manage resources (*e.g.*, allocating weapons systems and intelligence assets) or judgments about the acceptable degree of risk (*e.g.*, to the lives of friendly forces and to mission accomplishment).[306] For example, the principle of proportionality ordinarily does not require military personnel to take actions, such as providing warnings, when a superior commander has already determined that such actions are not feasible because, for instance, such actions could endanger mission accomplishment and the safety of friendly forces.

In the absence of specific direction to the contrary, subordinate commanders or engagement authorities have the authority to make the corresponding decisions required by the law of war, such as the decision to cancel or suspend an attack in light of new information, in order to effectuate the commander's intent.[307]

5.10.2.2 *"Reasonable Military Commander" Standard for Proportionality Decisions and Judgments*. The commander's decisions on proportionality must be reasonable.[308] For example, the commander must be able to explain the expected military importance of the target and why the anticipated civilian collateral injury or damage is not expected to be excessive.[309]

5.10.2.3 *Subjective Aspects of the Decisions and Judgments Required by the Principle of Proportionality*. The decisions and judgments required by the principle of proportionality in conducting attacks have subjective aspects.[310]

---

[305] BOTHE, PARTSCH, & SOLF, NEW RULES 366-67 (AP I art. 57, ¶2.8.1.3) ("In co-ordinated military operation, the relative importance of the military objective under attack in relation to the concrete and direct military advantage anticipated is not a matter which can be determined by individual tank leaders, the commanders of lower echelon combat units or individual attacking bomber aircraft. If assigned a fire or bombing mission they must assume that an appropriate assessment has been made by those who assigned the mission. Thus, in this situation, the decision to cancel will have to be made at the level where the decision to initiate the attack was made.").

[306] *Refer to* § 5.2.3.2 (What Precautions Are Feasible).

[307] *Refer to* § 5.10.2.5 (Discretion of Subordinates in the Conduct of Attacks).

[308] ICTY, *Final Report to the Prosecutor by the Committee Established to Review the NATO Bombing Campaign Against the Federal Republic of Yugoslavia*, ¶50 (Jun. 13, 2000) ("It is suggested that the determination of relative values must be that of the 'reasonable military commander'. Although there will be room for argument in close cases, there will be many cases where reasonable military commanders will agree that the injury to noncombatants or the damage to civilian objects was clearly disproportionate to the military advantage gained.").

[309] *See* Department of the Air Force, The Judge Advocate General's School, *Air Force Operations and The Law*, 18 (3rd ed., 2014) ("If the commander can clearly articulate in a reasonable manner what the military importance of the target is and why the anticipated civilian collateral injury or damage is outweighed by the military advantage to be gained, this will generally satisfy a 'reasonable military commander' standard."); Department of the Air Force, The Judge Advocate General's School, *Air Force Operations and The Law*, 21 (2nd ed., 2009) (same); Department of the Air Force, The Judge Advocate General's School, *Air Force Operations and The Law*, 28 (1st ed., 2002) (substantially similar).

[310] BOTHE, PARTSCH, & SOLF, NEW RULES 368 (AP I art. 57, ¶2.10.1) ("Like subparas. 2(a) (ii) and (iii), implementation of this provision is dependent on upon the subjective judgment of the commanders concerned. In this case a subjective determination is expected as to whether two or more targets for attack, offer a similar military advantage.").

Although the decisions and judgments required by the principle of proportionality must be applied with common sense and good faith,[311] there nonetheless might be variation in how reasonable persons would apply the principle of proportionality in a given circumstance.[312] The principle of proportionality typically involves the comparison of "unlike quantities and values."[313] Moreover, there may be disagreements among experts as to the precise requirements of the law.

For example, it could often be the case that reasonable persons might disagree as to whether the expected civilian casualties from an attack would be excessive.[314] Similarly, reasonable commanders might make different decisions in applying the principle of proportionality.[315]

---

[311] ICRC AP COMMENTARY 683-84 (¶2208) ("Even if this system is based to some extent on a subjective evaluation, the interpretation must above all be a question of common sense and good faith for military commanders. In every attack they must carefully weigh up the humanitarian and military interests at stake."). *See also* ICRC AP COMMENTARY 395 (¶1393) ("Good faith is not a virtue which is the exclusive attribute of the interpreters of the law, but is also imposed on those who enjoy a certain degree of freedom of action in the field, even though the heat of battle does not favour an objective view of things.").

[312] Janina Dill, *Applying the Principle of Proportionality in Combat Operations*, 4 (Oxford Institute for Ethics, Law and Armed Conflict, December 2010) ("While the proportionality judgement call is thus pushed higher-up the chain of command as more civilian damage is expected to result from an attack, it remains an essentially subjective and personal matter. Interviews with practitioners suggest that professional experience and personal morality rather than a transparent and stable set of criteria determine what is considered proportionate. Military lawyers acknowledge that, as a result, different professionals are likely to come to different conclusions about whether an anticipated collateral damage is excessive in the same situation, when applying the law in good faith. Commanders suggest that, proportionality judgements, in reality, often boil down to asking 'can the estimated collateral damage be further reduced, through timing, choice of weapons or angle of attack.' If the answer is no, the principle is considered to be fulfilled.").

[313] *See, e.g.*, Brief of the United States as Amicus Curiae In Support of Defendants-Appellees, Vietnam Association for Victims of Agent Orange, *et al.*, v. Dow Chemical Co., *et al.*, 25-26 (Feb. 15, 2006) ("The plaintiffs argue that the U.S. military's use of herbicides was unlawful because the harm to persons and property caused by herbicide use was disproportionate to the anticipated military advantage. ... In order to adjudicate the plaintiffs' claims, a court would be required to balance the U.S. military's interests in protecting our forces from ambush or other attack, and in weakening enemy forces, with the anticipated harms that might be caused by exposure to herbicides. Even apart from the significant uncertainty about the effects of Agent Orange and other herbicides, this balancing would be inherently subjective since it would involve unlike quantities and values – e.g., the long-term health of civilians or enemy soldiers exposed to herbicides, with the death of U.S. forces and the accomplishment of military objectives.").

[314] *Refer to* § 5.12.3 (Determining Whether the Expected Incidental Harm Is Excessive).

[315] ICTY, *Final Report to the Prosecutor by the Committee Established to Review the NATO Bombing Campaign Against the Federal Republic of Yugoslavia*, ¶¶49-50 (Jun. 13, 2000) ("49. The questions which remain unresolved once one decides to apply the principle of proportionality include the following: a) What are the relative values to be assigned to the military advantage gained and the injury to non-combatants and or the damage to civilian objects? b) What do you include or exclude in totaling your sums? c) What is the standard of measurement in time or space? and d) To what extent is a military commander obligated to expose his own forces to danger in order to limit civilian casualties or damage to civilian objects? 50. The answers to these questions are not simple. It may be necessary to resolve them on a case by case basis, and the answers may differ depending on the background and values of the decision maker. It is unlikely that a human rights lawyer and an experienced combat commander would assign the same relative values to military advantage and to injury to noncombatants. Further, it is unlikely that military

A degree of deference should be given to commanders when assessing after the fact whether a decision-maker has complied with the principle of proportionality.[316] In addition, an assessment of whether a decision-maker has complied with the legal requirements must be based on the information available to that person at the time.[317]

5.10.2.4 _Duty Not to Comply With Clearly Illegal Orders and the Principle of Proportionality_. In the context of the principle of distinction, it would often be clear whether a given situation implicates the duty not to comply with clearly illegal orders to commit law of war violations – such as the duty of a subordinate to refrain from complying with an order to attack the civilian population. However, the nuances involved in applying the principle of proportionality could make it more difficult to know whether an order given is clearly illegal.

The duty not to comply with orders that are clearly illegal also applies to violations of the principle of proportionality, in particular, the case of a commander who orders subordinates to conduct an attack that is expected to result in civilian casualties that the commander himself or herself acknowledges would be excessive.

Nonetheless, this duty must be understood in light of application of the principle that law of war obligations are implemented by those with responsibility to make the decisions and judgments required by the law of war, and in particular the point that subordinates might not be competent to evaluate whether the requirements of proportionality had been met.[318]

Subordinates ordinarily do not have an obligation to second-guess the judgments of their superiors in relation to the principle of proportionality. As with other aspects of the law of war, subordinates are not required to screen the orders of superiors for questionable points of legality, and may, absent specific knowledge to the contrary, presume that orders have been lawfully

---

commanders with different doctrinal backgrounds and differing degrees of combat experience or national military histories would always agree in close cases.").

[316] *See, e.g.*, WILLIAM H. BOOTHBY, THE LAW OF TARGETING 126 (2012) ("There is a widely recognized margin of appreciation such that criminal liability, for example before the International Criminal Court, will only arise if an attack is intentionally launched in the knowledge that it will be clearly disproportionate."); ICRC AP COMMENTARY 684 (¶2210) ("Despite these clarifications, the provision allows for a fairly broad margin of judgment, as stated above; several delegations regretfully stressed this fact. In contrast, other delegations commended the fact that in [the] future military commanders would have a universally recognized guideline as regards their responsibilities to the civilian population during attacks against military objectives.").

[317] *Refer to* § 5.3.2 (Decisions Must Be Made in Good Faith and Based on Information Available at the Time).

[318] *See also* APPENDIX TO 1985 CJCS MEMO ON AP I 64-65 ("Under military law, members of the armed forces may, and should, refuse to obey an order to commit a crime, such as the shooting of prisoners of war or unarmed civilians. Article 57, however, goes considerably beyond this, in allowing each individual combatant to call off an 'attack' (or at least his participation in it) if it appears to him that collateral damage 'may' be excessive to whatever military advantage he is aware of. In order to overcome this defense in a trial by court-martial, the prosecution would have to prove, beyond a reasonable doubt, that the possible collateral damage would not be excessive to the military advantage gained. To do this would often require the declassification of information known to the accused's superiors and its discussion in a public trial. Finally, the accused might be able to prevail on this issue simply by demonstrating a reasonable mistake of fact on his part--a reasonable belief, perhaps formed in part on the basis of propaganda reports in the public media, that collateral damage was excessive to any expected military advantage. … If the United States ratifies Protocol I, therefore, it should do so subject to an understanding that this paragraph of Article 57 only applies to commanders who have authority to terminate attacks.").

issued.[319] If questions arise, service members should apply their training, refer to applicable policy and regulations, and direct questions through appropriate channels.[320]

5.10.2.5 *Discretion of Subordinates in the Conduct of Attacks*. Commanders often provide subordinates substantial discretion in the tactics of an attack, such as in the selection of individual targets and in the timing of the attack. In the absence of specific direction to the contrary, subordinate commanders or engagement authorities have the authority to make the corresponding decisions required by the law of war, such as the decision to cancel or suspend an attack in light of new information, in order to effectuate the commander's intent.[321] This is especially important in situations where the subordinate is not in direct communication with the commander and the commander does not have situational awareness. For example, a commander may provide subordinates broad discretion to conduct an attack in which subordinates discover an unanticipated risk of civilian casualties. If receiving updated instructions in light of this new information was not possible, the subordinates would be understood to have the authority to take additional precautions to mitigate this unanticipated risk or even to refrain from conducting the attack if the subordinates believe that such measures would best achieve the commander's intent if the commander had known such information.

5.10.3 Implementation of Proportionality Through Military Procedures. As with other aspects of the law of war, during U.S. military operations, commanders have implemented the requirements of the principle of proportionality through military procedures, such as rules of engagement, doctrine, standard operating procedures, and special instructions.[322] In U.S. practice, implementing procedures sometimes place more restrictions on military operations and are more protective of civilians than what would be required by the law of war.[323]

Military authorities have developed procedures to assess before an attack the expected collateral damage or effects of an attack.[324] For example, lists of sensitive objects for which

---

[319] *Refer to* § 18.3.2.1 (Clearly Illegal Orders to Commit Law of War Violations).

[320] *Refer to* § 18.3.1.2 (Practical Ways in Which the Requirement to Comply With the Law of War in Good Faith is Met by Individual Service Members).

[321] *Compare* § 18.3.2.2 (Commands and Orders Should Not Be Understood as Implicitly Authorizing Violations of the Law of War).

[322] *Refer to* § 18.7 (Instructions, Regulations, and Procedures to Implement and Enforce the Law of War).

[323] *Refer to* § 5.1.2.1 (Applying Standards in the Conduct of Hostilities That Pose More Restrictions on Military Operations and That Are More Protective of Civilians Than Required By the Law of War).

[324] *For example*, JOINT PUBLICATION 3-60, *Joint Targeting*, p. II-16 (Jan. 31, 2013) ("CDE is a critical part of the effects estimate step in the joint targeting process phase 3 (or in the 'track' step of phase 5 during dynamic targeting) when munitions are used on facilities. CJCSI 3160.01, No-Strike and the Collateral Damage Estimation Methodology details a specific CDE process followed Department of Defense (DOD)-wide."); JOINT PUBLICATION 3-60, *Joint Targeting*, p. II-16 (Apr. 13, 2007) ("CJCSM 3160.01A codifies the joint standards and methods for estimating collateral damage potential, provides mitigation techniques, and assists commanders with weighing collateral risk against military necessity and assessing proportionality within the framework of the military decision-making process. These joint standards and methods for conducting CDE apply across the range of military operations. In addition, the CDEs that result from CJCSM 3160.01A are meant to inform decision makers and commanders and are not decisions themselves. CDEs help senior leaders evaluate collateral risk against military necessity during the planning and execution of combat operations.").

responsible commanders have imposed requirements for additional review or higher-level approval before the objects may be attacked (sometimes referred to as "no-strike lists") have been developed,[325] as have procedures for presenting to more senior commanders for decision potential attacks on targets that involve higher risks of incidental harm.[326]

These procedures help ensure the sound implementation of the requirements of the principle of proportionality. As a case in point, procedures for requesting higher-level approval of targets that involve high risks of incidental harm allow for a better evaluation of the expected military advantage from the attack (as it is likely that more senior commanders have a more comprehensive understanding of the strategic and operational context), and allow more senior commanders to implement additional precautions with the greater resources under their control.[327] Similarly, rules of engagement and military orders can be used to delineate the

---

[325] *For example*, FINAL REPORT ON THE PERSIAN GULF WAR 100 ("To help strike planners, CENTCOM target intelligence analysts, in close coordination with the national intelligence agencies and the State Department, produced a joint no-fire target list. This list was a compilation of historical, archaeological, economic, religious and politically sensitive installations in Iraq and Kuwait that could not be targeted. Additionally, target intelligence analysts were tasked to look in a six-mile area around each master attack list target for schools, hospitals, and mosques to identify targets where extreme care was required in planning. Further, using imagery, tourist maps, and human resource intelligence (HUMINT) reports, these same types of areas were identified for the entire city of Baghdad."). *Refer to* § 5.18.4 (Other Feasible Precautions to Reduce the Risk of Harm to Cultural Property), especially footnote 606.

[326] *For example*, JOINT PUBLICATION 3-60, *Joint Targeting*, p. II-16 (Jan. 31, 2013) ("Targets with associated collateral damage concerns expected to exceed theater (combatant command) thresholds are referred either to SecDef or the President using the sensitive target approval and review (STAR) process, detailed in CJCSI 3122.06, *Sensitive Target Approval and Review (STAR) Process*."); JOINT PUBLICATION 3-60, *Joint Targeting*, pp. II-10-II-11 (Apr. 13, 2007) ("Targets with associated collateral damage concerns expected to exceed theater (combatant command) thresholds are referred either to the Secretary of Defense (SecDef) or President using the sensitive target approval and review process, detailed in Chairman of the Joint Chiefs of Staff Instruction (CJCSI) 3122.06B, *Sensitive Target Approval and Review (STAR) Process*. See also Appendix A, 'Time Sensitive Target Considerations' and Appendix G, 'Collateral Damage Estimation,' for more detail.").

[327] *See* Geoff Corn, *War, Law, and the Oft Overlooked Value of Process as a Precautionary Measure*, 42 PEPPERDINE LAW REVIEW 419, 463-64 (2015) ("There is another subtle, but perhaps most important, benefit of elevating certain proportionality judgments to higher echelons of command: an increasingly more expansive operational perspective. Commanders and staffs at all levels of command focus inherently on their operational situation. As a result, commanders' operational focuses will inevitably expand or contract depending on their level of command. Proportionality judgments have profound tactical and strategic consequences. Where a commander authorizes an attack anticipating it will produce civilian casualties and the attack does in fact do so, those casualties may become a source of condemnation by external observers, become a motivation for resistance by the enemy and civilian population, or become a source of motivation for enemy forces. Any of these consequences poses significant strategic risk for the overall military effort. In contrast, where a commander decides to forego an attack because of anticipated risk to the civilian population, the decision may compromise tactical effectiveness, increase the risk to friendly forces, and make mission accomplishment more difficult. Broadening the decision-making commander's operational perspective should logically enhance the ability to assess these tactical and strategic consequences inherent in proportionality judgments. Thus, as this perspective increases at each higher echelon of command, so too does the acceptable degree of risk associated with a proportionality judgment. Finally, it is a simple axiom of military organizations that the range of combat resources increases with each higher level of command. This is a highly significant benefit of reserving proportionality judgments to higher levels of command, because as the judgment is progressively elevated, the commander entrusted with the judgment will be able to consider a broader range of alternative targeting options. As a result, a difficult proportionality judgment for a lower level commander may be obviated at a higher level of command because that commander may utilize an alternate

circumstances and limitations under which subordinates will initiate and/or continue an attack.[328]

5.10.4 Time Constraints and the Application of Proportionality. The time available to make decisions and to take precautions is a major factor affecting the implementation of the requirements of the principle of proportionality. For example, the available time affects what precautions are feasible, and the available time is a constraint in assessing whether an attack is expected to cause excessive incidental harm. Thus, although the legal standard of proportionality does not distinguish as such between, *e.g.*, dynamic and deliberate targeting, the availability of more time in the context of deliberate targeting generally allows for more actions to be taken to reduce the risk of civilian casualties.

Training on, and application of, targeting procedures can help forces implement the requirements of the principle of proportionality even when there is little time to make targeting decisions or to take precautions. Moreover, as with other law of war requirements, the principle of proportionality does not preclude commanders from taking decisive action in doubtful cases, but commanders must make decisions in good faith on the basis of the information available to them.[329]

5.10.5 Relationship Between the Requirement to Take Feasible Precautions in Planning and Conducting Attacks and the Prohibition on Attacks Expected to Cause Excessive Incidental Harm. This manual describes the requirement to take feasible precautions in planning and conducting attacks and the prohibition on attacks expected to cause excessive incidental harm as rules that are based on the principle of proportionality. Other sources may describe the relationships between the rules differently.[330] But this manual adopts this approach because the requirement to take feasible precautions in planning and conducting attacks and the prohibition on attacks expected to cause excessive incidental harm are fundamentally connected and mutually reinforcing obligations.

U.S. military manuals reflect the fundamental connection between the requirement to take feasible precautions in planning and conducting attacks and the prohibition on attacks expected to cause excessive incidental harm.[331] This connection is also reflected in the

---

method or means of attack to avoid the proportionality issue altogether, an option that did not exist for the commander of the subordinate unit.") (footnotes omitted).

[328] *Refer to* § 1.6.5 (Rules of Engagement (ROE)); § 5.11.4 (Canceling or Suspending Attacks Based on New Information Raising Concerns of Expected Civilian Casualties).

[329] *Refer to* § 5.3.2 (Decisions Must Be Made in Good Faith and Based on Information Available at the Time).

[330] *E.g.*, Columbia, Constitutional Court, Plenary Chamber, Constitutional Case No. C-291/07, Judgment, Apr. 25, 2007, as reprinted and translated by the International Committee of the Red Cross at https://ihl-databases.icrc.org/customary-ihl/eng/docs/v2_cou_co_rule17 ("The precautionary principle is the cornerstone of a number of specific rules which are all considered to have attained customary status and to be applicable in internal armed conflicts … Among these rules is … the obligation of the parties to a conflict to take all feasible precautions in the choice of means and methods of warfare with a view to avoiding, and in any event to minimizing, incidental loss of civilian life, injury to civilians and damage to civilian objects. [footnote in original omitted]").

[331] *See, e.g.*, 2007 NWP 1-14M ¶8.3.1 ("It is not unlawful to cause incidental injury to civilians, or collateral damage to civilian objects, during an attack upon a legitimate military objective. The principle of proportionality requires that the anticipated incidental injury or collateral damage must not, however, be excessive in light of the military advantage expected to be gained. Naval commanders must take all reasonable precautions, taking into account

negotiating history of the treaty provisions that sought to codify the principle of proportionality.[332] For example, the obligation to take precautions has been viewed as following from the prohibition on attacks expected to result in excessive harm.[333] In addition, applying the prohibition on attacks expected to result in excessive harm has been viewed as a precaution.[334]

The requirement to take feasible precautions in planning and conducting attacks and the prohibition on attacks expected to cause excessive incidental harm are mutually reinforcing obligations. Taking precautions helps ensure that the prohibition is not violated, and ensuring that the precautionary obligation has been complied with may help with the assessment of whether a strike would be consistent with the prohibition.[335] However, feasible precautions must be taken even when the attack is not expected to cause excessive incidental harm, and, even when feasible precautions have been taken, an attack could still be prohibited as one expected to cause excessive incidental harm.

5.11 Proportionality – Feasible Precautions in Planning and Conducting Attacks to Reduce the Risk of Harm to Protected Persons and Objects

Combatants must take feasible precautions in planning and conducting attacks to reduce the risk of harm to civilians and other persons and objects protected from being made the object of attack.[336]

---

military and humanitarian considerations, to keep civilian casualties and damage to the minimum consistent with mission accomplishment and the security of the force."); Department of the Air Force Pamphlet 110-34, *Commander's Handbook on the Law of Armed Conflict*, ¶3-8 (Jul. 25, 1980) ("It is not unlawful to cause incidental injury or death to civilians or damage to civilian property during an attack on a legitimate military objective as defined in chapter 2. This collateral damage should not, however, be excessive in light of the military advantage anticipated from the attack, and in all operations, every feasible precaution should be taken to keep civilian casualties and damage to a minimum.").

332 XV Official Records of the CDDH 285 (CDDH/215/Rev. 1, ¶97) ("Paragraph 2 (a) of article 50 required much time and effort to work out, but the other paragraphs were fairly quickly agreed upon. <u>The so-called rule of proportionality in paragraph 2 (a) iii was found ultimately to be acceptable when it was preceded by paragraph 2 (a) i and paragraph 2 (a) ii which prescribe additional precautions</u> and phrased in terms of losses 'excessive in relation to the concrete and direct military advantage anticipated', and was supplemented by paragraph 5 to make clear that it may not be construed as authorization for attacks against civilians.") (emphasis added).

333 1956 FM 27-10 (Change No. 1 1976) ¶39 ("Particularly in the circumstances referred to in the preceding paragraph, loss of life and damage to property incidental to attacks must not be excessive in relation to the concrete and direct military advantage expected to be gained. Those who plan or decide upon an attack, <u>therefore</u>, must take all reasonable steps to ensure not only that the objectives are identified as military objectives or defended places within the meaning of the preceding paragraph but also that these objectives may be attacked without probable losses in lives and damage to property disproportionate to the military advantage anticipated.") (emphasis added).

334 *Consider* AP I art. 57(2) ("With respect to attacks, the following precautions shall be taken: … (a) Those who plan or decide upon an attack shall: … (iii) Refrain from deciding to launch any attack which may be expected to cause incidental loss of civilian life, injury to civilians, damage to civilian objects, or a combination thereof, which would be excessive in relation to the concrete and direct military advantage anticipated;").

335 *Refer to* § 5.12.3.2 (Feasibility of Taking Additional Precautions to Reduce the Risk of Incidental Harm).

336 *See* Executive Order 13732, *United States Policy on Pre- and Post-Strike Measures To Address Civilian Casualties in U.S. Operations Involving the Use of Force*, 81 Federal Register 44485, 44485-86 (§2) (Jul. 1, 2016) ("In particular, relevant agencies shall, consistent with mission objectives and applicable law, including the

As discussed in § 5.2.3.2 (What Precautions Are Feasible), what precautions are feasible depends greatly on the context.[337] Moreover, the requirement to take feasible precautions should be applied as part of the principle of proportionality in conducting attacks, and the discussion in this section should be considered in light of the discussion in § 5.10 (Proportionality in Conducting Attacks).[338]

Feasible precautions in planning and conducting attacks may include, but are not limited to, the following:

- assessing the risks to civilians;[339]
- identifying zones in which military objectives are more likely to be present or civilians are more likely to be absent;[340]
- providing effective advance warning before an attack that may affect the civilian population;[341]
- adjusting the timing of an attack;[342]

---

law of armed conflict: … (iv) take feasible precautions in conducting attacks to reduce the likelihood of civilian casualties, such as providing warnings to the civilian population (unless the circumstances do not permit), adjusting the timing of attacks, taking steps to ensure military objectives and civilians are clearly distinguished, and taking other measures appropriate to the circumstances;"); HAGUE IV REG. art. 27 ("In sieges and bombardments all necessary steps must be taken to spare, as far as possible, buildings dedicated to religion, art, science, or charitable purposes, historic monuments, hospitals, and places where the sick and wounded are collected, provided they are not being used at the time for military purposes."); HAGUE IX art. 5 ("In bombardments by naval forces all the necessary measures must be taken by the commander to spare as far as possible sacred edifices, buildings used for artistic, scientific, or charitable purposes, historic monuments, hospitals, and places where the sick or wounded are collected, on the understanding that they are not used at the same time for military purposes."); Harold Koh, Legal Adviser, Department of State, *Letter to Paul Seger, Legal Adviser of Switzerland regarding Switzerland's Position on the U.S. Reservation to Protocol III of the Convention on Certain Conventional Weapons*, Dec. 30, 2009 ("In particular, the U.S. reservation is consistent with article 57(2)(ii) and article 57(4) of the 1977 Additional Protocol I to the Geneva Conventions. Article 57(4) provides that governments shall 'take all reasonable precautions to avoid losses of civilian lives and damage to civilian objects.' Although the United States is not a party to Additional Protocol I, we believe these provisions are an accurate statement of the fundamental law of war principle of discrimination."). *Consider* AP I art. 57(2) ("With respect to attacks, the following precautions shall be taken: (a) Those who plan or decide upon an attack shall: … (ii) Take all feasible precautions in the choice of means and methods of attack with a view to avoiding, and in any event to minimizing, incidental loss of civilian life, injury to civilians and damage to civilian objects;"); AP I art. 57(4) ("In the conduct of military operations at sea or in the air, each Party to the conflict shall, in conformity with its rights and duties under the rules of international law applicable in armed conflict, take all reasonable precautions to avoid losses of civilian lives and damage to civilian objects.").

[337] *Refer to* § 5.2.3.2 (What Precautions Are Feasible).

[338] *Refer to* § 5.10 (Proportionality in Conducting Attacks).

[339] *Refer to* § 5.11.1 (Assessing the Risks to Civilians).

[340] *Refer to* § 5.11.2 (Identifying Zones in Which Military Objectives Are More Likely to Be Present or Civilians Are More Likely to Be Absent).

[341] *Refer to* § 5.11.5 (Effective Advance Warning Before an Attack That May Affect the Civilian Population).

[342] *Refer to* § 5.11.3 (Adjusting the Timing of the Attack).

- cancelling or suspending attacks based on new information raising concerns of expected civilian casualties;[343]
- weaponeering (*e.g.*, selecting appropriate weapons, aim points);[344] and
- selecting military objectives.[345]

5.11.1 Assessing the Risks to Civilians. Assessments of the risks to civilians can include: 1) general assessments of the risks to civilians and the effectiveness of efforts to reduce the risk to civilians; 2) pre-strike assessments of expected civilian casualties; and 3) after-action assessments and investigations.

5.11.1.1 *General Assessments of the Risks to Civilians and the Effectiveness of Efforts to Reduce the Risks to Civilians*. In the planning of military operations, general assessments (*i.e.*, assessments not necessarily done in relation to a particular attack) of the risks to civilians and efforts to reduce the risks to civilians can assist in efforts to reduce the risk of incidental harm. For example, military authorities could identify places or objects posing significant risks of incidental harm if struck and could compile them into a list. They could then use such information in planning efforts and when conducting specific attacks to reduce the risk of incidental harm.

5.11.1.2 *Pre-Strike Assessments of Expected Civilian Casualties*. Pre-strike assessments of expected civilian casualties can assist in determining what other precautions are feasible, as well as in determining whether a strike is expected to result in excessive incidental harm.[346]

5.11.1.3 *After-Action Assessments and Investigations*. Battle damage assessments, as well as other reviews or investigations of incidents involving civilian casualties, may be appropriate in order to identify measures to mitigate the likelihood of future incidents of civilian casualties.[347] Similarly, review or investigation may be appropriate after "close call" incidents that do not cause civilian casualties but in which post-incident reporting reveals that a

---

[343] *Refer to* § 5.11.4 (Canceling or Suspending Attacks Based on New Information Raising Concerns of Expected Civilian Casualties).

[344] *Refer to* § 5.11.6 (Weaponeering (E.g., Selecting Appropriate Weapons, Aim Points)).

[345] *Refer to* § 5.11.7 (Selecting Military Objective).

[346] *Refer to* § 5.12.1 (Expected Loss of Civilian Life, Injury to Civilians, and Damage to Civilian Objects Incidental to the Attack).

[347] Executive Order 13732, *United States Policy on Pre- and Post-Strike Measures To Address Civilian Casualties in U.S. Operations Involving the Use of Force*, 81 FEDERAL REGISTER 44485, 44485-86 (§2) (Jul. 1, 2016) ("In particular, relevant agencies shall, consistent with mission objectives and applicable law, including the law of armed conflict: … (v) conduct assessments that assist in the reduction of civilian casualties by identifying risks to civilians and evaluating efforts to reduce risks to civilians.").

high risk of causing such casualties was not fully understood when relevant decisions were made.[348]

After such reviews, appropriate actions should be taken to reduce the risk of such incidents in the future.[349] For example, such actions could include repairing or inspecting equipment, retraining personnel, or changing applicable rules of engagement or operational procedures.

Although battle damage assessments or other after-action reviews or investigations of whether and how many civilians were harmed by an attack may serve a number of useful purposes, the actual results of an attack do not always provide useful information in assessing whether the requirements of the principle of proportionality were met in conducting the attack. The requirements of the principle of proportionality in conducting attacks are to be met based on the information available at the time, and the responsibility of commanders is not to be assessed on the basis of information known only after the fact.

5.11.2 Identifying Zones in Which Military Objectives Are More Likely to Be Present or Civilians Are More Likely to Be Absent. Identifying and designating zones in which military objectives are more likely to be present or in which civilians are more likely to be absent may also reduce the risk of harm to civilians or other protected persons and objects.

For example, a commander could decide to impose greater restrictions on attacks in areas in which civilians are known to be present.[350] Similarly, it may be possible to identify areas in

---

[348] ARMY TECHNIQUES PUBLICATION 3-07.6, *Protection of Civilians*, ¶5-49 (Oct. 29, 2015) ("Civilian casualty lessons do not come solely from actual civilian casualty incidents, but also from incidents that posed a high risk of civilian casualties which did not actually happen. Such near misses can offer valuable lessons and best practices. While collecting information on near misses can be a challenge, Soldiers may be more willing to discuss these experiences more openly than those involving actual casualties. Leaders should ensure that these incidents are also used for training, mentoring, and learning.").

[349] Ash Carter, Secretary of Defense, *Memorandum Re: Investigation Review – Secretary of Defense Guidance*, Apr. 28, 2016 ("Following the airstrike in Kunduz, Afghanistan, on October 3, 2015, that resulted in civilian casualties at the Doctors Without Borders Trauma Center, the investigation identified causal factors and specific deficiencies. I am committed to ensuring that similar incidents do not occur in the future. Therefore, after consulting with the Chairman, I am directing the Combatant Commands and the Services to take the following actions within the next 120 days to improve the Joint Force and mitigate the potential for similar incidents in the future: Conduct a comprehensive review of relevant policies, tactical directives, and rules of engagement (ROE) to clarify conflicting or confusing directives. Ensure they provide appropriate guidance for mission accomplishment, including the prevention of civilian casualties, in the complex, changing operational environment. … Incorporate lessons learned from the Kunduz strike in leadership development and operational training to emphasize the role of individual judgment and accountability in the execution of mission command.").

[350] *For example*, General Petraeus, *Unclassified Excerpts from Tactical Directive*, Aug. 1, 2010, *reprinted in* International Security Assistance Force – Afghanistan, Headquarters, *General Petraeus Issues Updated Tactical Directive: Emphasizes "Disciplined Use of Force,"* Aug. 4, 2010 ("Prior to the use of fires, the commander approving the strike must determine that no civilians are present. If unable to assess the risk of civilian presence, fires are prohibited, except under of the following two conditions (specific conditions deleted due to operational security; however, they have to do with the risk to ISAF and Afghan forces). (NOTE) This directive, as with the previous version, does not prevent commanders from protecting the lives of their men and women as a matter of self-defense where it is determined no other options are available to effectively counter the threat.)."); U.S. MILITARY ASSISTANCE COMMAND VIET-NAM DIRECTIVE 525-13, *Military Operations: Rules of Engagement for the Employment of Firepower in the Republic of Vietnam*, ¶5g (May 1971), *reprinted in* 1975 DIGEST OF UNITED

which objects of the greatest military importance are located and to place additional restrictions on attacks conducted outside these areas in order to limit unnecessary destruction.[351]

5.11.3 Adjusting the Timing of the Attack. Adjusting the timing of an attack may reduce the risk of incidental harm. For example, attacking a military objective when civilians are less likely to be present may be appropriate.[352] Similarly, it may be appropriate to wait until enemy forces have departed from populated areas before attacking such forces in order to reduce the risk of civilian casualties.[353]

STATES PRACTICE IN INTERNATIONAL LAW 814, 815 ("Specified Strike Zones (SSZ). An area designated for a specific period of time by Government of South Viet-Nam (G.V.N.) RVNAF [Republic of Vietnam Armed Forces] in which there are no friendly forces or populace and in which targets may be attacked on the initiative of U.S./FWMAF/RVNAF commanders. SSZ will not be referred to as 'Free Fire Zones.' Furthermore, the term 'Free Fire Zone' will not be used under any circumstances.").

351 *For example*, MALCOLM W. CAGLE & FRANK A. MANSON, THE SEA WAR IN KOREA 97 (1957) ("Vice Admiral Struble's orders to the bombardment forces clearly specified that there should be no promiscuous firing at the city itself or at civilian installations. To achieve this, the entire objective area had been divided into 60 sub-areas. Known military targets had been previously assigned, and those which offered the greatest potential hazard to our landing troops were circled in red. It had been agreed that any ship could fire into a red-circle area with or without a 'spot.' In the uncircled areas, however, firing was permitted only if definite targets were found and an air spot was available. This differentiation between types of areas was adopted to reduce destruction of nonmilitary targets to a minimum, to save the city of Inchon for occupation forces, and to avoid injury to civilian personnel. 'The Seoul-Inchon area is inhabited by our South Korean Allies,' said Struble in an order to his forces, 'and our forces plan to utilize facilities in this area. Unnecessary destruction will impede our progress. Bombing and gunfire will be confined to targets whose destruction will contribute to the conduct of operations – accurate gunfire and pinpoint bombing against specific targets, rather than area destruction, is contemplated.'").

352 *For example*, Jennifer O'Connor, General Counsel, Department of Defense, *Remarks at New York University School of Law: Applying the Law of Targeting to the Modern Battlefield*, Nov. 28, 2016 ("Given the facts of this specific situation, including the intelligence that the cash was being used to pay ISIL fighters and conduct terrorist operations, the targeting authority determined that the bulk cash was a legitimate military objective. The next step then for the targeting authority before approving the strike was to conduct a proportionality analysis. This bulk cash storage site happened to be in an area where civilians were often present—as you might expect from a building that used to be a civilian bank before ISIL turned it into a cash storage site. As a result of the high number of civilians in the area, the targeting authority took specific steps to minimize potential harm to civilians by ordering the attack to occur at a time when the potential for any civilian casualties was deemed to be the lowest."); FINAL REPORT ON THE PERSIAN GULF WAR 100 (noting that during Operation DESERT STORM "attacks on known dual (i.e., military and civilian) use facilities normally were scheduled at night, because fewer people would be inside or on the streets outside.").

353 *For example*, Joby Warrick, *ISIS's Second-in-Command Hid in Syria for Months. The Day He Stepped Out, the U.S. Was Waiting*, THE WASHINGTON POST, Nov. 28, 2016 ("The Syrian who exhorted thousands of young Muslims to don suicide belts appeared increasingly obsessed with his own safety, U.S. officials say. He banished cellphones, shunned large meetings and avoided going outdoors in the daytime. He began sleeping in crowded tenements in a northern Syrian town called al-Bab, betting on the presence of young children to shield him from the drones prowling the skies overhead. But in late August, when a string of military defeats suffered by the Islamic State compelled Adnani to briefly leave his hiding place, the Americans were waiting for him. A joint surveillance operation by the CIA and the Pentagon tracked the 39-year-old as he left his al-Bab sanctuary and climbed into a car with a companion. They were headed north on a rural highway a few miles from town when a Hellfire missile struck the vehicle, killing both of them."); FINAL REPORT ON THE PERSIAN GULF WAR 631 ("The concentration of Iraqi military personnel and vehicles, including tanks, invited attack. CINCCENT decided against attack of the Iraqi forces in Kuwait City, since it could lead to substantial collateral damage to Kuwaiti civilian property and could cause surviving Iraqi units to decide to mount a defense from Kuwait City rather than depart. Iraqi units remaining in Kuwait City would cause the Coalition to engage in military operations in urban terrain, a form of fighting that is

5.11.4 Canceling or Suspending Attacks Based on New Information Raising Concerns of Expected Civilian Casualties. Commanders may decide to cancel or suspend attacks based on new information of expected civilian casualties or authorize subordinates to do so, in order to reduce the risk of harm to civilians and civilian objects.[354]

Subordinates generally would not be authorized to suspend or cancel attacks contrary to specific military orders because they disagree with the commander's decisions and judgments in relation to the principle of proportionality.[355] However, subordinate commanders or engagement authorities would be required to report promptly new information of expected civilian casualties or to cancel or suspend attacks in appropriate circumstances. For example, aircrews have refrained from conducting an attack or have redirected a munition toward a different impact location when concerns about civilian harm have become unexpectedly apparent.[356]

Subordinates should also generally be understood to have the authority to make decisions required by the law of war, such as the decision to cancel or suspend an attack in light of new information, in order to effectuate the commander's intent.[357] This is especially true when those commanders will not be able to maintain situational awareness of the risks of civilian casualties.

The decision to cancel or suspend an attack based on new information raising concerns of expected civilian casualties does not necessarily mean that the attack would have been unlawful, such as by violating the prohibition against attacks expected to cause excessive incidental harm.[358]

5.11.5 Providing Effective Advance Warning Before an Attack That May Affect the Civilian Population. Unless circumstances do not permit, effective advance warning must be

---

costly to attacker, defender, innocent civilians, and civilian objects. The decision was made to permit Iraqi forces to leave Kuwait City and engage them in the unpopulated area to the north.").

[354] *Consider* AP I art. 57(2) ("With respect to attacks, the following precautions shall be taken: ... (*b*) An attack shall be cancelled or suspended if it becomes apparent that the objective is not a military one or is subject to special protection or that the attack may be expected to cause incidental loss of civilian life, injury to civilians, damage to civilian objects, or a combination thereof, which would be excessive in relation to the concrete and direct military advantage anticipated;").

[355] *Refer to* § 5.10.2.3 (Duty Not to Comply With Clearly Illegal Orders and the Principle of Proportionality).

[356] *For example*, BBC NEWS, *How 'Shift Cold' Works*, Sept. 12, 2016 ("On 9 September 2015, an unmanned coalition aircraft targeted a checkpoint, controlled by the so-called Islamic State, near Shaddadi in Syria. According to the US Department of Defense: 'After the aircraft's weapon was released, a transient motorcycle approached the checkpoint. The aircrew elected to 'shift cold,' or identify an alternate location for the weapon to impact, in flight to avoid any effects from the impact on the civilians on the motorcycle. The aircrew identified a nearby empty field where the weapon impacted.'").

[357] *Refer to* § 5.10.2.4 (Provision of Substantial Discretion by Commanders to Subordinates).

[358] Note that AP I art. 57(2) is framed differently and provides for the cancellation or suspension of attacks as a precaution "if it becomes apparent that the objective is not a military one or is subject to special protection or that the attack may be expected to cause incidental loss of civilian life, injury to civilians, damage to civilian objects, or a combination thereof, which would be excessive in relation to the concrete and direct military advantage anticipated." AP I art. 57(2).

given of an attack that may affect the civilian population.[359]

5.11.5.1 _Other Warning Requirements_. In addition, warning requirements exist before certain medical units, vessels, or facilities forfeit their protection from being made the object of attack:

- military medical units and facilities;[360]
- ground medical transports;[361]
- hospital ships and sick-bays in warships;[362]
- civilian hospitals;[363] and
- civilian hospital convoys.[364]

5.11.5.2 _Effective Advance Warning_. The purpose of a warning is to facilitate the protection of the civilian population so that civilians and the authorities in control of the civilian population can take measures to reduce the risk that civilians will be harmed by military operations. Although there is no set form for warnings, a warning should be designed to accomplish this purpose to the extent feasible.

Warnings may be communicated to the authorities in control of the civilian population, such as the national leadership of the enemy State.[365] Warnings may also be delivered directly to the civilian population through military information support operations (*e.g.*, broadcasts,[366]

---

[359] HAGUE IV REG. art. 26 ("The officer in command of an attacking force must, before commencing a bombardment, except in cases of assault, do all in his power to warn the authorities."); HAGUE IX art. 6 ("If the military situation permits, the commander of the attacking naval force, before commencing the bombardment, must do his utmost to warn the authorities."); LIEBER CODE art. 19 ("Commanders, whenever admissible, inform the enemy of their intention to bombard a place, so that the noncombatants, and especially the women and children, may be removed before the bombardment commences. But it is no infraction of the common law of war to omit thus to inform the enemy. Surprise may be a necessity."). *Consider* AP I art. 57(2)(c) ("Effective advance warning shall be given of attacks which may affect the civilian population, unless circumstances do not permit.").

[360] *Refer to* § 7.10.3.2 (Due Warning Before Cessation of Protection).

[361] *Refer to* § 7.11.1 (Protection of Ground Medical Transports on the Same Basis as That of Medical Units).

[362] *Refer to* § 7.12.6.1 (Due Warning Before Cessation of Protection).

[363] *Refer to* § 7.17.1.2 (Due Warning Before Cessation of Protection).

[364] *Refer to* § 7.18.1 (Protection of Civilian Hospital Convoys on the Same Basis as That of Civilian Hospitals).

[365] HAGUE IV REG. art. 26 ("The officer in command of an attacking force must, before commencing a bombardment, except in cases of assault, do all in his power to warn the authorities.") (emphasis added); HAGUE IX art. 6 ("If the military situation permits, the commander of the attacking naval force, before commencing the bombardment, must do his utmost to warn the authorities.") (emphasis added).

[366] *For example*, Jim Garamone, *U.S. Commando Solo II Takes Over Afghan Airwaves*, AMERICAN FORCES PRESS SERVICE, Oct. 29, 2001 (describing the Commando Solo II flights that use broadcasts "to warn the Afghan population to stay away from Taliban and Al Qaeda targets," including one broadcast that warns civilians to "'[s]tay away from military installations, government buildings, terrorist camps, roads, factories or bridges'"); SPAIGHT, AIR POWER AND WAR RIGHTS 242 ("An hour and a half before the Skoda armament works at Pilsen in Czechoslovakia

leaflets[367]) advising the civilian population of risk of harm if they are near military objectives. Low passes of aircraft or warning shots may also be appropriate in certain circumstances.[368]

The warnings may be general in nature; giving the specific time and place of an attack is not required.[369]

---

were attacked by Flying Fortresses of the 8th U.S.A.A.F. on 25 April, 1945, Supreme Allied Headquarters broadcast the following warning: 'Allied bombers are out in great strength to-day. Their destination may be the Skoda works. Skoda workers get out and stay out until the afternoon.'").

[367] *For example*, Jim Garamone, *Coalition Aircraft "Paper" Iraq With Leaflets*, AMERICAN FORCES PRESS SERVICE, Mar. 19, 2003 (stating that Coalition forces "dropped almost 2 million leaflets over Iraq" that "warned Iraqis to stay away from military targets"); *Report of the United Nations Command Operations in Korea for the Period 1-15 July 1952*, enclosure to *Note Dated 8 October 1952 From the Representative of the United States Addressed to the Secretary-General Transmitting the Forty-Ninth Report of the United Nations Command Operations in Korea in Accordance with the Security Council Resolution of 7 July 1950 (S/1588)*, U.N. Doc. S/2805 (Oct. 9, 1952) ("For approximately one month prior to the raid on Pyongyang and other main supply targets, the United Nations Command aircraft had dropped leaflets warning civilians to stay away from military targets. Immediately after the strikes more leaflets were dropped telling civilians to beware of delayed action bombs and to stay away from bomb craters. Every precaution was taken to attack only military targets and to prevent injury to non-combatants. … In consonance with the United Nations policy of taking every possible step both to restore peace and to prevent needless loss of life, United Nations Command leaflets and radio broadcasts are being used continually to warn civilians in enemy-occupied northern Korea to move away from places where the Communists have concentrated war material factories and military equipment, supplies and personnel. These warnings are a humanitarian measure taken to minimize civilian loss of life in United Nations Command attacks on military targets.").

[368] *For example*, Department of Defense Briefing by Operation Inherent Resolve Spokesman Col. Warren (Nov. 18, 2015) ("In Al-Bukamal, we destroyed 116 tanker trucks, which we believe will reduce ISIL's ability to transport its stolen oil products. This is our first strike against tanker trucks, and to minimize risks to civilians, we conducted a leaflet drop prior to the strike. We did a show of force, by -- we had aircraft essentially buzz the trucks at low altitude. So, I do have copy of the leaflet, and I have got some videos, so why don't you pull the leaflet up. Let me take a look at it so I can talk about it. As you can see, it's a fairly simple leaflet, it says, 'Get out of your trucks now, and run away from them.' A very simple message. And then, also, 'Warning: airstrikes are coming. Oil trucks will be destroyed. Get away from your oil trucks immediately. Do not risk your life.' And so, these are the leaflets that we dropped -- about 45 minutes before the airstrikes actually began. Again, we combine these leaflet drops with very low altitude passes of some of our attack aviation, which sends a very powerful message."); Major Thomas A. Wagoner, Staff Judge Advocate, 15th Marine Expeditionary Unit (Special Operations Capable), *After Action Report for Operation Iraqi Freedom*, 7 (2003), *reprinted in* CENTER FOR LAW AND MILITARY OPERATIONS, THE JUDGE ADVOCATE GENERAL'S LEGAL CENTER & SCHOOL, U.S. ARMY, I LEGAL LESSONS LEARNED FROM AFGHANISTAN AND IRAQ: MAJOR COMBAT OPERATIONS (11 SEPTEMBER 2001 - 1 MAY 2003) 108 (2004) ("The one group that reported success with warning shots was the LAR [Light Armored Reconnaissance] Company. They explained that the warning shots fired from their chain guns at vehicles coming towards them with unknown intentions tended to stop the vehicles so they could be searched. They surmised that the size of the LAR was a large part of the success in that vehicles clearly saw who was firing at them and rather than risk getting shot they stopped for Marine forces. This as compared to infantry forces who were usually unable to see the intended beneficiaries of the warning shots and vice versa."); SPAIGHT, AIR POWER AND WAR RIGHTS 243 ("Before objectives in the French town of Annecy were bombed on the night of 9 May, 1944, the alert was sounded by an Allied plane equipped with a siren. It cruised over the town for twenty minutes before the first bombers arrived, with the result that the inhabitants had time to seek shelter and only those who disregarded the warning were injured.").

[369] *U.S. Comments on the International Committee of the Red Cross's Memorandum on the Applicability of International Humanitarian Law in the Gulf Region*, Jan. 11, 1991, DIGEST OF UNITED STATES PRACTICE IN INTERNATIONAL LAW 1991-1999 2057, 2064 ("A warning need not be specific. It may be a blanket warning, delivered by leaflets and/or radio, advising the civilian population of an enemy nation to avoid remaining in proximity to military objectives.").

5.11.5.3 _That May Affect the Civilian Population_. The purpose of a warning to facilitate the protection of the civilian population is so that civilians and the authorities in control of the civilian population can take measures to reduce the risk that civilians will be harmed by military operations. If the civilian population will not be affected by an attack, then there is no obligation to provide a warning to facilitate its protection.[370]

5.11.5.4 _Unless Circumstances Do Not Permit_. Circumstances not permitting the giving of advance warning include where giving a warning would be incompatible with legitimate military requirements, such as exploiting the element of surprise in order to provide for mission accomplishment and preserving the security of the attacking force.[371]

5.11.6 Weaponeering (E.g., Selecting Appropriate Weapons, Aim Points). Depending on the circumstances, the process of "weaponeering" in a strike against a target can be used to reduce the risk of harm to civilians and civilian objects by selecting munitions of appropriate size and type, as well as appropriate aim points, while offering the same or superior military advantage in neutralizing or destroying a military objective.[372] For example, it may be advantageous to employ incendiary weapons in attacking an adversary's repository of biological weapons so as to prevent the biological agents from adversely affecting the civilian population.[373]

As with other precautions, the decision of which weapon to use will be subject to many practical considerations.[374] For example, a commander may decide not to use precision-guided munitions or cyber tools[375] because he or she determines it is necessary to preserve those capabilities for other engagements.[376]

---

[370] GREENSPAN, MODERN LAW OF LAND WARFARE 338-39 ("Naturally, there is no obligation to give notice where no civilians remain, and only the military will come under fire.").

[371] *U.S. Comments on the International Committee of the Red Cross's Memorandum on the Applicability of International Humanitarian Law in the Gulf Region*, Jan. 11, 1991, DIGEST OF UNITED STATES PRACTICE IN INTERNATIONAL LAW 1991-1999 2057, 2064 ("The 'unless circumstances do not permit' recognizes the importance of the element of surprise. Where surprise is important to mission accomplishment and allowable risk to friendly forces, a warning is not required.").

[372] *For example*, Jim Michaels, *Exclusive: Inside the Anti-Islamic State Air Campaign Command Center*, USA TODAY, Sept. 13, 2016 ("Analysts assign the target a collateral damage estimate based on its proximity to civilians and the extent that danger to them can be lessened. If there is a risk of hitting nearby buildings, they mitigate the risk by choosing smaller bombs or a fuse that can delay the explosion, so, for example, a bomb would only detonate after it penetrates the target. Military officers plot each bomb's point of impact on a building or other target, allowing them to measure precisely the blast radius of each explosive they will drop. The selection of munitions can produce a precise impact. Recently, a communications tower near a school was hit so that when it collapsed, it fell away from a cluster of nearby buildings.").

[373] *Refer to* § 6.14.3.2 (U.S. Reservation to CCW Protocol III on Incendiary Weapons).

[374] *Refer to* § 5.2.3.2 (What Precautions Are Feasible).

[375] *Refer to* § 14.9.2 (Selection of Weapons in Conducting Attacks From the Air Against Ground Military Objectives); § 16.5.3.1 (Cyber Tools as Potential Measures to Reduce the Risk of Harm to Civilians or Civilian Objects).

[376] *See, e.g.*, 2013 GERMAN MANUAL ¶1117 ("The law of armed conflict (LOAC) contains no obligation to use precision guided ammunition. There may however be situations in which the obligation to discriminate between

5.11.7 Selecting Military Objectives. In planning or conducting an attack, the selection of a military objective may reduce the risk of incidental harm. In particular, when attempting to achieve a particular military advantage through an attack, a commander may confront a choice among several military objectives for achieving that advantage. When facing such a choice, provided that all other factors are equal, the object to be selected for attack shall be the object the attack on which may be expected to cause the least danger to civilian lives and to civilian objects. For example, in seeking to deny an adversary the ability to use a railroad network, it may be possible to disable the railroad network just as effectively by striking the railroad lines away from inhabited areas as by striking the railroad station located near civilians.[377]

This rule does not dictate what choices a commander should consider, but presupposes that the commander is confronted with a choice of potential military objectives to attack to achieve the desired military advantage. In other words, this rule does not prevent the commander from attacking multiple military objectives or pursuing every military advantage he or she believes warrants pursuit.

When the choice of military objectives involves different risks and benefits potentially yielding different military advantages, this rule does not require that the object that may be expected to cause the least danger to civilian lives and to civilian objects be chosen for attack. For example, a commander could decide to attack a military objective involving higher risks of civilian casualties because the attack on that objective affords a greater likelihood of achieving the military advantage.

5.11.7.1 *AP I Provision on Choice Possible Between Several Military Objectives*. AP I provides that "[w]hen a choice is possible between several military objectives for obtaining a similar military advantage, the objective to be selected shall be that the attack on which may be expected to cause the least danger to civilian lives and to civilian objects."[378] The United States

---

military targets and civilians/civilian objects or the obligation to avoid or minimise collateral damage cannot be fulfilled without the use of such weapons.") (internal cross-reference omitted); 2006 AUSTRALIAN MANUAL ¶8.38 ("The existence of precision-guided weapons, such as GBU 10 and Harpoon missiles, in a military inventory does not mean that they must necessarily be used in preference to conventional weapons even though the latter may cause collateral damage. In many cases, conventional weapons may be used to bomb legitimate military targets without violating the LOAC requirements. It is a command decision as to which weapon to use. This decision will be guided by the basic principles of the LOAC: military necessity, avoidance of unnecessary suffering and proportionality."); 2001 CANADIAN MANUAL ¶527(1) ("With the advent of modern technology many armed forces are now able to deliver weapons on target with much greater precision. However, states are not limited to the use of precision weapons and munitions. An attack by conventional, free-fall weapons or 'dumb' bombs is lawful provided that the overriding principles of proportionality and superfluous injury/unnecessary suffering as well as other applicable rules are not violated.").

[377] *See* ICRC AP COMMENTARY 687 (¶¶2227-28) ("In this field mention could be made of attacks launched against enemy road and rail traffic; some belligerents have tried to attack the adversary only when this would not result in severe damage for the population. Instead of attacking railway stations, which are usually located in towns, the railway lines were hit at crucial points, but away from inhabited areas; the same action was taken with respect to roads. Such examples show that it is possible to choose objectives so that their destruction does not imperil the population and civilian objects, while still gaining the same military advantage. There is no doubt with regard to [an] economic target of military importance, that it is possible to attack only certain parts the destruction of which will result in paralyzing the whole structure.").

[378] AP I art. 57(3).

has expressed the view that this language is not a part of customary international law.[379] Whether this AP I provision is consistent with customary international law would depend on how AP I Parties interpret it. If this AP I provision is interpreted as described in § 5.11.7 (Selecting Military Objectives), then this provision could be understood to be consistent with customary international law.

5.12 PROPORTIONALITY – PROHIBITION ON ATTACKS EXPECTED TO CAUSE EXCESSIVE INCIDENTAL HARM

Combatants must refrain from attacks in which the expected loss of civilian life, injury to civilians, and damage to civilian objects incidental to the attack would be excessive in relation to the concrete and direct military advantage expected to be gained.[380]

This prohibition should be applied as part of the principle of proportionality in conducting attacks, and the discussion in this section should be considered in light of the discussion in § 5.10 (Proportionality in Conducting Attacks).[381]

5.12.1 <u>Expected Loss of Civilian Life, Injury to Civilians, and Damage to Civilian Objects Incidental to the Attack</u>. The totality of the expected loss of civilian life, injury to civilians, and damage to civilian objects incidental to the attack must be considered. AP I uses the phrase "a combination thereof" and an "or" to convey that the totality of the expected loss of civilian life, injury to civilians, and damage to civilian objects incidental to the attack is to be considered.[382]

---

[379] *U.S. Comments on the International Committee of the Red Cross's Memorandum on the Applicability of International Humanitarian Law in the Gulf Region*, Jan. 11, 1991, DIGEST OF UNITED STATES PRACTICE IN INTERNATIONAL LAW 1991-1999 2057, 2064 ("Paragraph 4B(4) contains the language of Article 57(3) of Protocol I, and is not a part of customary law. The provision applies 'when a choice is possible … ;' it is not mandatory. An attacker may comply with it if it is possible to do so, subject to mission accomplishment and allowable risk, or he may determine that it is impossible to make such a determination.") (amendment shown in Digest).

[380] 1956 FM 27-10 (Change No. 1 1976) ¶41 ("[L]oss of life and damage to property incidental to attacks must not be excessive in relation to the concrete and direct military advantage expected to be gained. Those who plan or decide upon an attack, therefore, must take all reasonable steps to ensure not only that the objectives are identified as military objectives or defended places within the meaning of the preceding paragraph but also that these objectives may be attacked without probable losses in lives and damage to property disproportionate to the military advantage anticipated."). *Consider* AP I art. 51(5)(b) (considering as a prohibited indiscriminate attack "[a]n attack which may be expected to cause incidental loss of civilian life, injury to civilians, damage to civilian objects, or a combination thereof, which would be excessive in relation to the concrete and direct military advantage anticipated."); AP I art. 57(2)(a)(iii) (requiring that those who plan or decide upon an attack "[r]efrain from deciding to launch any attack which may be expected to cause incidental loss of civilian life, injury to civilians, damage to civilian objects, or a combination thereof, which would be excessive in relation to the concrete and direct military advantage anticipated;").

[381] *Refer to* § 5.10 (Proportionality in Conducting Attacks).

[382] *Consider* AP I art. 51(5)(b) (considering as a prohibited indiscriminate attack "[a]n attack which may be expected to cause incidental loss of civilian life, injury to civilians, damage to civilian objects, or a combination thereof, which would be excessive in relation to the concrete and direct military advantage anticipated."); AP I art. 57(2)(a)(iii) (requiring that those who plan or decide upon an attack "[r]efrain from deciding to launch any attack which may be expected to cause incidental loss of civilian life, injury to civilians, damage to civilian objects, or a

5.12.1.1 *Priority in Considering the Loss of Civilian Life and Damage to Civilian Objects*. In light of the humanitarian objectives of the law of war, the expected loss of civilian life and injury to civilians should be given greater consideration than the expected damage to civilian objects.[383] Similarly, the expected damage to civilian objects (such as schools, hospitals, and religious facilities) should be given greater consideration when such damage is expected to involve the risk of harming civilians present inside such objects.

In light of the great importance of cultural property, expected damage to cultural property should be afforded greater consideration than expected damage to ordinary property.[384]

5.12.1.2 *Loss of Life, Injury, and Damage Versus Mere Inconveniences or Temporary Disruptions*. Expected loss of civilian life, injury to civilians, and damage to civilian objects must be considered. Mere inconveniences or temporary disruptions to civilian life need not be considered in applying this rule.[385]

For example, although the actual damage to a civilian marketplace from an attack on a nearby military objective would be considered, the temporary disruption to commerce from the closure of the marketplace due to the nearby attack would not need to be considered.

5.12.1.3 *Foreseeable Harms Versus Remote Harms*. The expected loss of civilian life, injury to civilians, and damage to civilian objects is generally understood to mean such immediate or direct harms foreseeably resulting from the attack. Remote harms that could result from the attack do not need to be considered in applying this prohibition. The exclusion of remote harms is based on the difficulty in accurately predicting the myriad of remote harms from

---

combination thereof, which would be excessive in relation to the concrete and direct military advantage anticipated;").

[383] *U.S. Comments on the International Committee of the Red Cross's Memorandum on the Applicability of International Humanitarian Law in the Gulf Region*, Jan. 11, 1991, DIGEST OF UNITED STATES PRACTICE IN INTERNATIONAL LAW 1991-1999 2057, 2063-64 ("While collateral damage to civilian objects should be minimized, consistent with the above, collateral damage to civilian objects should not be given the same level of concern as incidental injury to civilians."). *Cf.* BOTHE, PARTSCH, & SOLF, NEW RULES 368-69 (AP I art. 57, ¶2.10.2) ("Humanitarian inclinations would tend to suggest that the avoidance of danger to civilian lives should be preferred over that of property. This conclusion is supported by other provisions of Protocol I. For example, a higher standard is established by Art. 51, para. 3, for loss of protection by civilians than that which is applicable under the two pronged test of Art. 52, para. 2, defining when objects may become military objectives and thus be subject to attack. Moreover, while an indiscriminate attack which causes excessive loss of civilian life or injury to civilians may be a grave breach under Art. 85, para. 3, the excessive damage to civilian property can support a grave breach only if the indiscriminate attack causes death or serious injury to civilian persons.").

[384] *Refer to* § 5.18.1 (Definition of Cultural Property).

[385] *See* Yoram Dinstein, *Distinction and Loss of Civilian Protection in International Armed Conflicts*, 84 U.S. NAVAL WAR COLLEGE INTERNATIONAL LAW STUDIES, 183, 186 (2008) ("Yet it must be borne in mind that not every inconvenience to civilians ought to be considered relevant. In war-time, there are inevitable scarcities of foodstuffs and services. Indeed, food, clothing, petrol and other essentials may actually be rationed; buses and trains may not run on time; curfews and blackouts may impinge on the quality of life; etc. These do not count in the calculus of proportionality."). *Cf.* WILLIAM H. BOOTHBY, THE LAW OF TARGETING 370 (2012) ("Issues of proportionality do not of course arise where there is no attack. Thus where soft attack methods are adopted resulting, perhaps, in inconvenience but neither injury nor damage, there is no requirement to consider that inconvenience when deciding whether, and if so how, to undertake the military operation.").

the attack (including the possibility of unrelated or intervening actions that might prevent or exacerbate such harms) as well as the primary responsibility of the party controlling the civilian population to take measures to ensure that population's protection.[386]

For example, if the destruction of a power plant would be expected to cause the loss of civilian life or injury to civilians very soon after the attack due to the loss of power at a connected hospital, then such harm should be considered in assessing whether an attack is expected to cause excessive harm. On the other hand, the attacker would not be required to consider the economic harm that the death of an enemy combatant would cause to his or her family, or the loss of jobs due to the destruction of a tank factory.[387] Similarly, in determining the expected loss of civilian life, injury to civilians, and damage to civilian objects, the attacker would not be required to consider the possibility that a munition might not detonate as intended and might injure civilians much later after the attack. This is due to the difficulty in assessing such risks and the responsibility of the party controlling the territory and the civilian population to take steps with regard to the protection of the civilian population from unexploded ordnance.[388]

5.12.1.4 _Harms Caused by the Attacking Force Versus Harms Caused by Enemy Action or Beyond the Control of Either Party_. The harm caused by the attacking forces' actions in conducting the attack must be considered. Harm caused by enemy action, or beyond the control of either party, need not be considered.

For example, a commander directing an air operation would not need to consider civilians injured or killed by counter-attacks from enemy air defense measures, such as spent surface-to-

---

386 *Refer to* § 5.2.1 (Responsibility of the Party Controlling Civilian Persons and Objects).

387 *For example*, Rear Admiral Thomas Wilson, Director of Intelligence, Joint Staff, *DoD News Briefing*, Apr. 22, 1999 ("Krusevac tractor plant in Serbia was a new target. You can see here assembly and engineering buildings which were involved in manufacturing support or parts for tanks and APCs as well as for civilian vehicles, and we had moderate to severe physical damage to these facilities with functional damage assessments being made at this time. ... Q: At the Yugo factory there are tens of thousands of Yugoslav workers that can't work. I take it the tractor factory will put thousands out of work. Is that an intended strike against the economy of Milosevic? Rear Admiral Wilson: The intent of the strike was to destroy their ability to sustain and repair military vehicles. It's an unfortunate consequence of the leadership's decision to pursue their policies that's impacting the Yugoslav people.").

388 Christopher Greenwood, *Legal Issues Regarding Explosive Remnants Of War*, Group of Government Experts of States Parties to the Convention on Prohibitions or Restrictions on the Use of Certain Conventional Weapons, CCW/GGE/I/WP.10 (2002) 8 ("If, for example, cluster weapons are used against military targets in an area where there are known to be civilians, then the proportionality test may require that account be taken both of the risk to the civilians from sub-munitions exploding during the attack and of the risk from unexploded sub-munitions in the hours immediately after the attack. It is an entirely different matter, however, to require that account be taken of the longer-term risk posed by [Explosive Remnants of War (ERW)], particularly of the risk which ERW can pose after a conflict has ended or after civilians have returned to an area from which they had fled. The degree of that risk turns on too many factors which are incapable of assessment at the time of the attack, such as when and whether civilians will be permitted to return to an area, what steps the party controlling that area will have taken to clear unexploded ordnance, what priority that party gives to the protection of civilians and so forth. The proportionality test has to be applied on the basis of information reasonably available at the time of the attack. The risks posed by ERW once the immediate aftermath of an attack has passed are too remote to be capable of assessment at that time."). *Refer to* § 6.20.3 (Taking Feasible Precautions to Protect Civilians From Explosive Remnants of War).

air measures or antiaircraft projectiles.[389] Similarly, the risk to the civilian population from the legitimate deception activities of the defending force, such as jamming, smoke, or chaff, would not need to be considered by the attacking force, although the defending force should consider such risks as part of its obligations to take feasible precautions in defense.[390]

When the attacking force causes harms that are the responsibility of the defending force due to its use of voluntary human shields or due to the employment of civilian personnel in or on military objectives, the responsibility of the defending force is a factor that may be considered in determining whether such harm is excessive.[391]

5.12.2 Concrete and Direct Military Advantage Expected to Be Gained. The "concrete and direct military advantage expected to be gained" must be considered.

The considerations in assessing a "definite military advantage" in the definition of "military objective" are also relevant in assessing the "concrete and direct military advantage expected to be gained."[392] For example, the military advantage may not be merely hypothetical or speculative, although there is no requirement that the military advantage be "immediate."

There must be a good faith expectation that the attack will make a relevant and proportional contribution to the goal of the military attack involved.[393] Such goals may include: (1) denying the enemy the ability to benefit from the object's effective contribution to its military action (*e.g.*, using this object in its military operations); (2) improving the security of the

---

[389] *See, e.g.*, FINAL REPORT ON THE PERSIAN GULF WAR 177-78 (During the 1991 Gulf War, "[t]here is also a probability that some [incidental civilian] casualties occurred when unexploded Iraqi SAMs [surface-to-air missiles] or AAA [antiaircraft artillery] fell back to earth. The often dense fire the Iraqis expended in attempts to shoot down Coalition aircraft and cruise missiles almost certainly caused some destruction on the ground from malfunctioning fuses or self-destruction features, as well as the simple impact of spent rounds.").

[390] *Refer to* § 5.14 (Feasible Precautions to Reduce the Risk of Harm to Protected Persons and Objects by the Party Subject to Attack).

[391] *Refer to* § 5.12.3.3 (Civilian Workers Who Support Military Operations In or On Military Objectives); § 5.12.3.4 (Enemy Use of Human Shields).

[392] New Zealand, *Statement on Ratification of AP I*, Feb. 8, 1988, 1499 UNTS 358 ("3. In relation to paragraph 5(*b*) of Article 51 and to paragraph 2(*a*)(iii) of Article 57, the Government of New Zealand understands that the military advantage anticipated from an attack is intended to refer to the advantage anticipated from the attack considered as a whole and not only from isolated or particular parts of that attack and that the term 'military advantage' involves a variety of considerations, including the security of attacking forces."). *Refer to* § 5.6.7.3 (Definite Military Advantage).

[393] Australia, *Statement on Ratification of AP I*, Jun. 21, 1991, 1642 UNTS 474 ("It is further the understanding of Australia that the term 'concrete and direct military advantage anticipated', used in Articles 51 and 57, means a bona fide expectation that the attack will make a relevant and proportional contribution to the objective of the military attack involved."); New Zealand, *Statement on Ratification of AP I*, Feb. 8, 1988, 1499 UNTS 358 ("It is further the understanding of the Government of New Zealand that the term 'concrete and direct military advantage anticipated', used in Articles 51 and 57, means a bona fide expectation that the attack will make a relevant and proportional contribution to the objective of the military attack involved."). *See also* 2001 CANADIAN MANUAL ¶415(2) ("A concrete and direct military advantage exists if the commander has an honest and reasonable expectation that the attack will make a relevant contribution to the success of the overall operation.").

attacking force;[394] and (3) diverting enemy forces' resources and attention.

5.12.2.1 *Considering the Advantage From the Attack as a Whole – In the Operational and Strategic Context*. The military advantage expected from an attack is intended to refer to the advantage gained from the attack considered as a whole, rather than only from isolated or particular parts of an attack.[395] Similarly, "military advantage" is not restricted to immediate tactical gains, but may be assessed in the full context of the war strategy.[396] The military importance of a target often turns on its relationship to other targets within an operational system, and the effect that disabling the target will have on the functions that comprise the adversary's ability to wage war.[397] For example, an attack against a

---

[394] Australia, *Statement on Ratification of AP I*, Jun. 21, 1991, 1642 UNTS 473-74 ("In relation to paragraph 5(b) of Article 51 and to paragraph 2(a)(iii) of Article 57, it is the understanding of Australia … that the term 'military advantage' involves a variety of considerations including the security of attacking forces."); New Zealand, *Statement on Ratification of AP I*, Feb. 8, 1988, 1499 UNTS 358 ("3. In relation to paragraph 5(*b*) of Article 51 and to paragraph 2(*a*)(iii) of Article 57, the Government of New Zealand understands … that the term 'military advantage' involves a variety of considerations, including the security of attacking forces."); 2001 CANADIAN MANUAL ¶415(2) ("Military advantage may include a variety of considerations including the security of the attacking forces.").

[395] United Kingdom, *Statement on Ratification of AP I*, Jan. 28, 1998, 2020 UNTS 75, 77 ("*Re: Article 51 and Article 57* In the view of the United Kingdom, the military advantage anticipated from an attack is intended to refer to the advantage anticipated from the attack considered as a whole and not only from isolated or particular parts of the attack."); Australia, *Statement on Ratification of AP I*, Jun. 21, 1991, 1642 UNTS 473 ("In relation to paragraph 5(b) of Article 51 and to paragraph 2(a)(iii) of Article 57, it is the understanding of Australia that references to the 'military advantage' are intended to mean the advantage anticipated from the military attack considered as a whole and not only from isolated or particular parts of that attack … ."); Germany, *Statement on Ratification of AP I*, Feb. 14, 1991, 1607 UNTS 526, 529 ("In applying the rule of proportionality in Article 51 and Article 57, 'military advantage' is understood to refer to the advantage anticipated from the attack considered as a whole and not only from isolated or particular parts of the attack."); Netherlands, *Statement on Ratification of AP I*, Jun. 26, 1987, 1477 UNTS 300 ("With regard to Article 51, paragraph 5 and Article 57, paragraphs 2 and 3 of Protocol I: It is the understanding of the Government of the Kingdom of the Netherlands that military advantage refers to the advantage anticipated from the attack considered as a whole and not only from isolated or particular parts of the attack … .").

[396] *U.S. Comments on the International Committee of the Red Cross's Memorandum on the Applicability of International Humanitarian Law in the Gulf Region*, Jan. 11, 1991, DIGEST OF UNITED STATES PRACTICE IN INTERNATIONAL LAW 1991-1999 2057, 2064 ("The concept of 'incidental loss of life excessive in relation to the military advantage anticipated' generally is measured against an overall campaign."). *For example*, FINAL REPORT ON THE PERSIAN GULF WAR 611 ("An uncodified but similar provision is the principle of proportionality. It prohibits military action in which the negative effects (such as collateral civilian casualties) clearly outweigh the military gain. This balancing may be done on a target-by-target basis, as frequently was the case during Operation Desert Storm, but also may be weighed in overall terms against campaign objectives.").

[397] *See, e.g.*, JOINT PUBLICATION 3-60, *Joint Targeting*, pp. II-5-II-6 (Jan. 31, 2013) ("While a single target may be significant because of its own characteristics, the target's real importance lies in its relationship to other targets within an operational system. A target system is most often considered as a collection of assets directed to perform a specific function or series of functions (see Figure II-4). While target systems are intra-dependent to perform a specific function, they are also interdependent in support of adversary capabilities (e.g., the electric power system may provide energy to run the adversary's railroads that are a key component of their military logistic system). System level target development links these multiple target systems and their components to reflect both their intra- and interdependency that, in aggregate, contribute to the adversary capabilities. JIPOE helps target developers prioritize an adversary's target systems based on how much each contributes to the adversary's ability to wage war."); JOINT PUBLICATION 3-05.5, *Joint Special Operations Targeting and Mission Planning Procedures*, p. II-5 (Aug. 10, 1993) ("A single target may be significant because of its own characteristics. Most often, its importance lies in its relationship to other targets.").

communications relay that was a military objective might be expected to yield a much greater military advantage when the attack was part of a strategy of coordinated attacks to disable the adversary's command and control network than as an isolated attack.[398]

Consideration of the military advantage of the entire attack in its operational and strategic context ensures the proper consideration and allocation of responsibility to the appropriate levels within the military hierarchy.[399] Lower-level personnel may not be competent to evaluate the broader strategic and operational implications of the entire attack.[400]

5.12.3 Determining Whether the Expected Incidental Harm Is Excessive. A potential attack against a military objective is prohibited by this rule only when the expected incidental harm is excessive in relation to the concrete and direct military advantage expected to be gained.

Determining whether the expected incidental harm is excessive does not necessarily lend itself to quantitative analysis because the comparison is often between unlike quantities and values.[401] The evaluation of expected incidental harm in relation to expected military advantage intrinsically involves both professional military judgments as well as moral and ethical judgments evaluating the risks to human life (*e.g.*, civilians at risk from the attack, friendly forces or civilians at risk if the attack is not taken).

On the one hand, striking an ammunition depot or a terrorist training camp would not be prohibited because a farmer is plowing a field in the area.[402] On the other hand, an extraordinary

---

[398] *For example*, ICTY, *Final Report to the Prosecutor by the Committee Established to Review the NATO Bombing Campaign Against the Federal Republic of Yugoslavia*, ¶78 (Jun. 13, 2000) ("The FRY command and control network was alleged by NATO to comprise a complex web and that could thus not be disabled in one strike. … The proportionality or otherwise of an attack should not necessarily focus exclusively on a specific incident. (See in this regard para. 52, above, referring to the need for an overall assessment of the totality of civilian victims as against the goals of the military campaign). With regard to these goals, the strategic target of these attacks was the Yugoslav command and control network. The attack on the RTS building must therefore be seen as forming part of an integrated attack against numerous objects, including transmission towers and control buildings of the Yugoslav radio relay network which were 'essential to Milosevic's ability to direct and control the repressive activities of his army and special police forces in Kosovo' (NATO press release, 1 May 1999) and which comprised 'a key element in the Yugoslav air-defence network' (*ibid*, 1 May1999).").

[399] 2013 GERMAN MANUAL ("In accordance with a statement made by the Federal Republic of Germany upon the deposit of the instrument of ratification of the Additional Protocols, a military advantage is the advantage expected to result from the entire attack and not from the individual acts that constitute the attack (**46**). This ensures the proper consideration and allocation of responsibility to the appropriate levels within the military hierarchy.").

[400] *Refer to* § 5.10.2.1 (Need for Competent Authority to Make the Decisions and Judgments Required by the Principle of Proportionality).

[401] ICTY, *Final Report to the Prosecutor by the Committee Established to Review the NATO Bombing Campaign Against the Federal Republic of Yugoslavia*, ¶48 (Jun. 13, 2000) ("The main problem with the principle of proportionality is not whether or not it exists but what it means and how it is to be applied. It is relatively simple to state that there must be an acceptable relation between the legitimate destructive effect and undesirable collateral effects. … Unfortunately, most applications of the principle of proportionality are not quite so clear cut. It is much easier to formulate the principle of proportionality in general terms than it is to apply it to a particular set of circumstances because the comparison is often between unlike quantities and values. One cannot easily assess the value of innocent human lives as opposed to capturing a particular military objective.").

[402] ICTY, *Final Report to the Prosecutor by the Committee Established to Review the NATO Bombing Campaign Against the Federal Republic of Yugoslavia*, ¶48 (Jun. 13, 2000) ("For example, bombing a refugee camp is

military advantage would be necessary to justify an operation posing risks of collateral death or injury to thousands of civilians.[403] In less clear-cut cases, the legal question of whether the expected incidental harm is excessive may be a "highly open-ended" inquiry, and the answer may be "subjective and imprecise."[404] For this reason, States have chosen to apply a "clearly excessive" standard for determining whether a criminal violation has occurred.[405]

---

obviously prohibited if its only military significance is that people in the camp are knitting socks for soldiers. Conversely, an air strike on an ammunition dump should not be prohibited merely because a farmer is plowing a field in the area."); ROGERS, LAW ON THE BATTLEFIELD 64-65 ("Accepting at face value for the sake of legal analysis a press report of a pilot whose attack on an army lorry and a busload of soldiers also killed a small boy in a civilian car, this could not be said to have violated the proportionality principle.").

[403] *See, e.g.*, GREENSPAN, MODERN LAW OF LAND WARFARE 335 ("[A]n attack on a war factory which is known to be of minor importance cannot justify the incidental destruction of the whole town where it is situated."). *For example*, W. Hays Parks, *The 1977 Protocols to the Geneva Convention of 1949*, 68 U.S. NAVAL WAR COLLEGE INTERNATIONAL LAW STUDIES 467, 470 (1995) ("During the Vietnam War, for example, the North Vietnamese installed substantial concentrations of antiaircraft guns and missiles on the earthware dikes and dams surrounding Haiphong and Hanoi. *Military necessity* warranted airstrikes against these positions. However, attack of the positions with conventional ordnance would destroy not only the enemy positions but the dams as well. This would result in massive flooding and in the probable deaths of several hundred thousand civilians, a cost U.S. authorities concluded was disproportionate to the military advantage to be gained. When the mission finally was approved by President Nixon, it was executed with a clear proviso that only antipersonnel bombs, capable of neutralization of the positions without substantial damage to the dikes, would be used.").

[404] *Statement of Interest of the United States of America*, Matar v. Dichter, 05 Civ. 10270 (WHP) (S.D.N.Y. Nov. 17, 2006), 2006 DIGEST OF UNITED STATES PRACTICE IN INTERNATIONAL LAW 465, 471-72 ("Along similar lines, plaintiffs cite Article 57 of Additional Protocol I, which provides, *inter alia*, that '[t]hose who plan or decide upon an attack shall … [r]efrain from deciding to launch any attack which may be expected to cause incidental loss of civilian life, injury to civilians, damage to civilian objects, or a combination thereof, which would be excessive in relation to the concrete and direct military advantage anticipated.' Additional Protocol I, Art. 57, cl. 2(a)(iii). Again, the rub lies in determining what counts as 'excessive.' Any number of intangibles must be [c]onsidered: How important is the military objective sought to be achieved? What are the pros and cons of each option available to achieve that objective? For each option, what is the probability of success? What are the costs of failure? What are the risks of civilian casualties involved in each option? What are the risks of military casualties involved in each option? How are casualties of either kind to be weighed against the benefits of the operation? In short, questions of proportionality are highly open-ended, and the answers to them tend to be subjective and imprecise.").

[405] *See, e.g.*, III OFFICIAL RECORDS OF THE UNITED NATIONS DIPLOMATIC CONFERENCE OF PLENIPOTENTIARIES ON THE ESTABLISHMENT OF AN INTERNATIONAL CRIMINAL COURT 229, 232 (2002) (United States of America: proposal regarding an annex on definitional elements for part 2 crimes, A/CONF.183/C.1/L.10) ("*Proportionality*. The principle of proportionality prohibits attacks which are expected to cause incidental loss of civilian life, injury to civilians, damage to civilian objects, or a combination thereof, which would be clearly excessive in relation to the overall advantage anticipated;"); Germany, Federal Court of Justice, Federal Prosecutor General, Fuel Tankers Case, Decision, Apr. 16, 2010, as reprinted and translated by the International Committee of the Red Cross at https://ihl-databases.icrc.org/customary-ihl/eng/docs/v2_cou_de_rule14_sectionb ("Even if the killing of several dozen civilians would have had to be anticipated (which is assumed here for the sake of the argument), from a tactical-military perspective this would not have been out of proportion to the anticipated military advantages. The literature consistently points out that general criteria are not available for the assessment of specific proportionality because unlike legal goods, values and interests are juxtaposed which cannot be 'balanced' … Therefore, considering the particular pressure at the moment when the decision had to be taken, an infringement is only to be assumed in cases of obvious excess where the commander ignored any considerations of proportionality and refrained from acting 'honestly', 'reasonably' and 'competently' … This would apply to the destruction of an entire village with hundreds of civilian inhabitants in order to hit a single enemy fighter, but not if the objective was to destroy artillery positions in the village … There is no such obvious disproportionality in the present case. Both the destruction of the fuel tankers and the destruction of high-level Taliban had a military importance which is not to be underestimated, not

In determining whether the expected incidental harm would be excessive, the totality of the circumstances must be considered. This holistic judgment should consider any relevant moral, legal, and military factors.

5.12.3.1 The Military Concept of Economy of Force. As with the obligation to take feasible precautions, the prohibition on attacks expected to cause excessive incidental harm involves military judgments.[406] Use of excessive and indiscriminate force is costly, highly inefficient, and wasteful of scarce resources.

The principle of proportionality has been viewed as a legal restatement of the military concept of economy of force.[407] Economy of force seeks to allocate the maximum possible combat power on primary efforts through the judicious employment and distribution of forces and the measured allocation of available combat power.[408]

---

least because of the thereby considerably reduced risk of attacks by the Taliban against own troops and civilians. There is thus no excess."). *Consider* ROME STATUTE art. 8(2)(b)(iv) (defining "war crimes" for the purposes of the Statute to include, in the context of international armed conflict, "[i]ntentionally launching an attack in the knowledge that such attack will cause incidental loss of life or injury to civilians or damage to civilian objects or widespread, long-term and severe damage to the natural environment which would be clearly excessive in relation to the concrete and direct overall military advantage anticipated;"). *See also* U.S. RESPONSE TO ICRC CIHL STUDY 528 endnote 30 ("One of the U.S. concerns has been that Articles 35(3) and 55 [of AP I] fail to acknowledge that use of such weapons is prohibited only if their use is clearly excessive in relation to the concrete and direct overall military advantage anticipated."); FINAL REPORT ON THE PERSIAN GULF WAR 611 ("An uncodified but similar provision is the principle of proportionality. It prohibits military action in which the negative effects (such as collateral civilian casualties) clearly outweigh the military gain."); BOTHE, PARTSCH, & SOLF, NEW RULES 309-10 footnote 30 (AP I art. 51, ¶2.6.2) ("As the two sides of the equation cannot be quantified, it seems that only an obvious imbalance can be considered 'disproportionate' or 'excessive'."); APPENDIX TO 1985 CJCS MEMO ON AP I, *Annex: Draft Reservations and Understandings*, 3 (providing a draft understanding that "in relation to Articles 51(5)(b), 52(2), and 57(2)(a)(iii) that the military advantage anticipated from an attack must be considered as a whole and not only from isolated or particular parts of the attack and that incidental civilian losses are excessive only when tantamount to the total disregard for the safety of the civilian population.").

406 *Refer to* § 5.2.3.3 (The Taking of Precautions and Law, Policy, and Practice).

407 General George S. Brown, Chairman of the Joint Chiefs of Staff, *Address: Duke University School of Law*, Oct. 10, 1974, *reprinted in* ADDRESSES AND STATEMENTS BY GENERAL GEORGE S. BROWN, USAF, CHAIRMAN, JOINT CHIEF OF STAFF 1974-1978 (1978) ("We recognize that wanton destruction and unnecessary suffering are both violations of these military developed legal principles and counterproductive to the political military goals of the Nation. The law of 'proportionality' is simply a legal restatement of the time honored military concept of 'economy of force.'"); 1989 NWP 9 ¶5.2 footnote 8, p. 5-8 ("Economy of force means that no more--or less--effort should be devoted to a task than is necessary to achieve the objective. This implies the correct selection and use of weapons and weapon systems, maximum productivity from available weapons platforms, and careful balance in the allocation of tasks. This principle is embodied in the fundamental legal principle of proportionality.").

408 JOINT PUBLICATION 3-0, *Joint Operations*, A-2 (Aug. 11, 2011) ("e. **Economy of Force** (1) The purpose of economy of force is to expend minimum essential combat power on secondary efforts in order to allocate the maximum possible combat power on primary efforts. (2) Economy of force is the judicious employment and distribution of forces. It is the measured allocation of available combat power to such tasks as limited attacks, defense, delays, deception, or even retrograde operations to achieve mass elsewhere at the decisive point and time."). *See also* CARL VON CLAUSEWITZ, ON WAR 213 (1989) ("If a segment of one's force is located where it is not sufficiently busy with the enemy, or if troops are on the march—that is, idle—while the enemy is fighting, then these forces are being managed uneconomically. When the time for action comes, the first requirement should be that all parts must act: even the least appropriate task will occupy some of the enemy's forces and reduce his overall strength, while completely inactive troops are neutralized for the time being.").

Although mere poor military judgment or substandard operational practice is not by itself unlawful, if a strike would be so wasteful of resources as to be inconsistent with the principle of economy of force, this is a factor counseling against taking the contemplated strike.

5.12.3.2 Feasibility of Taking Additional Precautions to Reduce the Risk of Incidental Harm. Incidental harm is more likely to be regarded as excessive in attacks in which it would be feasible to take additional precautions and those precautions are not taken.[409]

The obligation to take feasible precautions is fundamentally connected to the prohibition on attacks expected to cause excessive incidental harm, and the two obligations are mutually reinforcing.[410] Thus, although the obligation to take feasible precautions applies even if an attack is expected not to cause excessive incidental harm, incidental harm expected to result from strikes in which additional precautions are feasible, but have not been taken, would be more likely to be considered excessive.

5.12.3.3 Civilian Workers Who Support Military Operations In or On Military Objectives. In general, reasonable steps must be taken to separate the civilian population from military objectives, such as by removing members of the civilian population from the vicinity of military objectives and combat operations.[411] However, sometimes civilian personnel work in or on military objectives in order to support military operations. For example, civilian workers sometimes serve as members of military aircrews, as technical advisers on warships, and as workers in munitions factories. Such persons assume a certain risk of injury.[412] Provided such workers are not taking a direct part in hostilities, those determining whether a planned attack would be excessive must consider such workers, and feasible precautions must be taken to

---

[409] *Refer to* § 5.11 (Proportionality – Feasible Precautions in Planning and Conducting Attacks to Reduce the Risk of Harm to Protected Persons and Objects).

[410] *Refer to* § 5.10.5 (Relationship Between the Requirement to Take Feasible Precautions in Planning and Conducting Attacks and the Prohibition on Attacks Expected to Cause Excessive Incidental Harm).

[411] *Refer to* § 5.14 (Feasible Precautions to Reduce the Risk of Harm to Protected Persons and Objects by the Party Subject to Attack).

[412] *U.S. Comments on the International Committee of the Red Cross's Memorandum on the Applicability of International Humanitarian Law in the Gulf Region*, Jan. 11, 1991, DIGEST OF UNITED STATES PRACTICE IN INTERNATIONAL LAW 1991-1999 2057, 2063 ("Likewise, civilians working within or in the immediate vicinity of a legitimate military objective assume a certain risk of injury."). *See also* BOTHE, PARTSCH, & SOLF, NEW RULES 295 (AP I art. 50, ¶2.2.2) ("By being within, or in the vicinity of a military objective, these civilians assume the risk of collateral injury from the effects of attack. It is also doubtful that incidental injury to persons serving the armed forces within a military objective will weigh as heavily in the application of the rule of proportionality as that part of the civilian population which is not so closely linked to military operations."); *The Sixth Annual American Red Cross-Washington College of Law Conference on International Humanitarian Law: A Workshop on Customary International Law and the 1977 Protocols Additional to the 1949 Geneva Conventions: Remarks of Lieutenant Colonel Burrus M. Carnahan*, 2 AMERICAN UNIVERSITY JOURNAL OF INTERNATIONAL LAW AND POLICY 505, 510 ("State practice, on the other hand, suggests the existence of at least one intermediate category: persons who, while not taking a direct part in hostilities, are so intimately connected with a military objective that they have forfeited the right to be free from risk of collateral damage."); Waldemar A. Solf, *Protection of Civilians Against the Effects of Hostilities under Customary International law and Under Protocol I*, 1 AMERICAN UNIVERSITY INTERNATIONAL LAW REVIEW 117, 131 (1986) ("Thus, while a civilian may not lose his protection against individualized attack while working in a munitions plant, he assumes the risk of collateral injury when he is in the vicinity of the munitions plant, although he continues to retain full protection while at home.").

reduce the risk of harm to them. Those making such determinations may consider all relevant facts and circumstances.

The expected harm to civilian members of military aircrews on military aircraft or civilian technical advisers on warships does not render military aircraft or warships immune from attack.[413] Similarly, munitions factories have not been deemed to be immune from attack just because of the presence of civilian workers inside the factory.[414]

5.12.3.4 Enemy Use of Human Shields. Adversary use of human shields can present complex moral, ethical, legal, and policy considerations.[415] Use of civilians as human shields violates the rule that protected persons may not be used to shield, favor, or impede military operations.[416] The party that employs human shields in an attempt to shield military

---

[413] 2001 CANADIAN MANUAL ¶425 ("For targeting purposes, the presence of civilians who are authorized to accompany the armed forces without actually being members thereof (such as crews of military aircraft, war correspondents, supply contractors or members of services responsible for the welfare of the armed forces) does not render a legitimate target immune from attack. Such persons run the risk of being attacked as part of a legitimate target.").

[414] *See, e.g.*, Spain, Orientaciones. El Derecho de los Conflictos Armadas, Tomo 1, Publicacion OR7-0004 (Edicion Segunda), Mando de adiestramiento y Doctrina, Direccion de Doctrina, Organica y Materiales, Nov. 2, 2007, § 4.4e, as reprinted and translated by the International Committee of the Red Cross at https://www.icrc.org/customary-ihl/eng/docs/v2_rul_rule8_sectioni ("Indirect objectives are those that cannot be directly attacked, but may suffer the consequences of an attack on a military objective. Civilians … are considered to be indirect objectives that may suffer the effects of an attack on a legitimate military target in the following cases: - presence in the vicinity of a military objective, with a view to shielding it from attacks; - activities that support military operations (labour units, workers in weapons factories, etc.).") (ellipsis in ICRC reprint); Spain, Orientaciones. El Derecho de los Conflictos Armados, Publicacion OR7-004, 2 Tomos, aprobado por el Estado Mayor del Ejercito, Division de Operaciones, Mar. 18, 1996, Vol. I, §4.4e, as reprinted and translated by the International Committee of the Red Cross at https://www.icrc.org/customary-ihl/eng/docs/v2_rul_rule8_sectioni ("indirect objectives" are objectives "which may not be the object of a direct attack but which can suffer the consequences of an attack upon a military objective. Such is the case for civilians … who may suffer the effects of an attack upon a legitimate military objective due to: – their proximity to a military objective aimed at shielding that objective against attack; – their carrying out activities supporting military operations (units of workers, workers in arms factories, etc.") (ellipsis in ICRC reprint); Federal Republic of Germany, Federal Ministry of Defence, Humanitarian law in Armed Conflicts Manual ¶445 (August 1992) ("**Civilians present in military objectives** are not protected against attacks directed at these objectives; the presence of civilian workers in an arms production plant, for instance, will not prevent opposing armed forces from attacking this military objective."); Switzerland, *Lois et coutumes de la guerre (Extrait et commentaire)*, Reglement 51.7/II f, Armee Suisse, 1987, Article 28 and commentary, as reprinted and translated by the International Committee of the Red Cross at https://www.icrc.org/customary-ihl/eng/docs/v2_cou_ch_rule8_sectioni ("Civilians who are inside or in the immediate vicinity of military objectives run the risks to which the military objectives are exposed. For example, the presence of civilian workers inside a weapons factory does not prevent the enemy from attacking this military objective.").

[415] *Cf.* Presidential Policy Directive 30, *U.S. Nationals Taken Hostage Abroad and Personnel Recovery Efforts*, June 24, 2015 ("The United States will use every appropriate resource to gain the safe return of U.S. nationals who are held hostage. But the United States Government will make no concessions to individuals or groups holding U.S. nationals hostage. It is United States policy to deny hostage-takers the benefits of ransom, prisoner releases, policy changes, or other acts of concession. This policy protects U.S. nationals and strengthens national security by removing a key incentive for hostage-takers to target U.S. nationals, thereby interrupting the vicious cycle of hostage-takings, and by helping to deny terrorists and other malicious actors the money, personnel, and other resources they need to conduct attacks against the United States, its nationals, and its interests.").

[416] *Refer to* § 5.16 (Prohibition on Using Protected Persons and Objects to Shield, Favor, or Impede Military Operations).

objectives from attack assumes responsibility for their injury, although the attacker may share this responsibility if it fails to take feasible precautions.[417]

If civilians are being used as human shields, provided they are not taking a direct part in hostilities, they must be considered as civilians in determining whether a planned attack would be excessive, and feasible precautions must be taken to reduce the risk of harm to them.[418] However, the enemy use of voluntary human shields may be considered as a factor in assessing the legality of an attack. Based on the facts and circumstances of a particular case, the commander may determine that persons characterized as voluntary human shields are taking a direct part in hostilities.[419]

5.13 Attacks on Facilities, Works, or Installations Containing Dangerous Forces

Certain facilities containing dangerous forces, such as dams, nuclear power plants, or facilities producing weapons of mass destruction, may constitute military objectives. There may be a number of reasons for their attack, such as denial of electric power to military sources, use of a dangerous facility (*e.g.*, by causing release from a dam) to damage or destroy other military objectives, or to pre-empt enemy release of the dangerous forces to hamper the movement or advance of U.S. or allied forces.[420]

Attack of facilities, works, or installations containing dangerous forces, such as dams, nuclear power plants, or facilities producing weapons of mass destruction, is permissible so long as it is conducted in accordance with other applicable rules, including the rules of discrimination and proportionality.[421] In light of the increased potential magnitude of incidental harm, additional precautions, such as weaponeering or timing the attack such that weather conditions would minimize dispersion of dangerous materials, may be appropriate to reduce the risk that the release of these dangerous forces may pose to the civilian population.[422]

5.13.1 AP I Provisions on Works and Installations Containing Dangerous Forces. Article

---

[417] *Refer to* § 5.16.5 (Responsibility for Harm to Human Shields). *See also* 2004 UK MANUAL ¶2.7.2 ("Even where human shields are being used, the proportionality rule must be considered. However, if the defenders put civilians or civilian objects at risk by placing military objectives in their midst or by placing civilians in or near military objectives, this is a factor to be taken into account in favour of the attackers in considering the legality of attacks on those objectives.") (footnote omitted).

[418] *Refer to* § 5.11 (Proportionality – Feasible Precautions in Planning and Conducting Attacks to Reduce the Risk of Harm to Protected Persons and Objects).

[419] *Refer to* § 5.8.3 ("Taking a Direct Part in in Hostilities").

[420] *For example*, Mark L. Evans and C. Ross Bloodsworth, *The Dambusters at Hwachon*, NAVAL AVIATION NEWS 22, 23 (May-Jun. 2001) (explaining the military significance of Hwachon Dam during the Korean war by noting that the enemy's control of the facility allowed them to "flood the valley and stop further UN advances" or "[i]f they held back the water by closing the gates, the river would be lowered to fordable depths and enable communist infiltration across the river against the exposed allied flanks.").

[421] *Refer to* § 5.5 (Discrimination in Conducting Attacks); § 5.12 (Proportionality – Prohibition on Attacks Expected to Cause Excessive Incidental Harm).

[422] *Refer to* § 5.11 (Proportionality – Feasible Precautions in Planning and Conducting Attacks to Reduce the Risk of Harm to Protected Persons and Objects).

56 of AP I provides special rules for works and installations containing dangerous forces. For example, "[w]orks or installations containing dangerous forces, namely dams, dykes and nuclear electrical generating stations, shall not be made the object of attack, even where these objects are military objectives, if such attack may cause the release of dangerous forces and consequent severe losses among the civilian population." In addition, Article 56 of AP I provides immunity from attack to combatants and military equipment stationed or placed around works and installations containing dangerous forces "for the sole purpose of defending the protected works."

The United States has objected to this article of AP I.[423] In ratifying AP I, other States have taken reservations from this article.[424] Insofar as Article 56 of AP I deviates from the regular application of the principles of distinction and proportionality, the U.S. view has been that it does not reflect customary international law applicable in international and non-international armed conflicts.

5.14 Feasible Precautions to Reduce the Risk of Harm to Protected Persons and Objects by the Party Subject to Attack

Outside the context of conducting attacks (such as when conducting defense planning or other military operations), parties to a conflict should also take feasible precautions to reduce the risk of harm to protected persons and objects from the effects of enemy attacks.[425] In particular,

---

[423] *See The Position of the United States on Current Law of War Agreements: Remarks of Judge Abraham D. Sofaer, Legal Adviser, United States Department of State, Jan. 22, 1987*, 2 AMERICAN UNIVERSITY JOURNAL OF INTERNATIONAL LAW AND POLICY 460, 468 (1987) ("Article 56 of Protocol I is designed to protect dams, dikes, and nuclear power plants against attacks that could result in 'severe' civilian losses. As its negotiating history indicates, this article would protect objects that would be considered legitimate military objectives under customary international law. Attacks on such military objectives would be prohibited if 'severe' civilian casualties might result from flooding or release of radiation. The negotiating history throws little light on what level of civilian losses would be 'severe.' It is clear, however, that under this article, civilian losses are not to be balanced against the military value of the target. If severe losses would result, then the attack is forbidden, no matter how important the target. It also appears that article 56 forbids any attack that raises the possibility of severe civilian losses, even though considerable care is taken to avoid them.").

[424] *See, e.g.*, United Kingdom, *Statement on Ratification of AP I*, Jan. 28, 1998, 2020 UNTS 75, 78 ("*Re. Articles 56 and 85, paragraph 3 (c)* The United Kingdom cannot undertake to grant absolute protection to installations which may contribute to the opposing Party's war effort, or to the defenders of such installations, but will take all due precautions in military operations at or near the installations referred to in paragraph 1 of Article 56 in the light of the known facts, including any special marking which the installation may carry, to avoid severe collateral losses among civilian populations; direct attacks on such installations will be launched only on authorization at a high level of command."); France, *Statement on Ratification of AP I, translated in* SCHINDLER & TOMAN, THE LAWS OF ARMED CONFLICTS: A COLLECTION OF CONVENTIONS, RESOLUTIONS, AND OTHER DOCUMENTS 801 (2004) ("The Government of the French Republic cannot guarantee an absolute protection to the works and installations containing dangerous forces which may contribute to the opposing Party's war effort, or to the defenders of such installations, but will take all precautions referred to the provisions of Article 56, of Article 57, paragraph 2(a)(iii) and of paragraph 3(c) of Article 85 in order to avoid severe collateral losses among the civilian populations, including possible direct attacks.").

[425] *Consider* AP I art. 58 ("The Parties to the conflict shall, to the maximum extent feasible: (a) Without prejudice to Article 49 of the Fourth Convention, endeavour to remove the civilian population, individual civilians and civilian objects under their control from the vicinity of military objectives; (b) Avoid locating military objectives within or near densely populated areas; (c) Take the other necessary precautions to protect the civilian population, individual civilians and civilian objects under their control against the dangers resulting from military operations.").

military commanders and other officials responsible for the safety of the civilian population must take reasonable steps to separate the civilian population from military objectives and to protect the civilian population from the effects of combat. As discussed in § 5.2.3.2 (What Precautions Are Feasible), what precautions are feasible depends greatly on the context.[426] Feasible precautions by the party subject to attack may include the following:

5.14.1 Refraining From Placing Military Objectives in Densely Populated Areas. It may be appropriate to avoid placing military objectives, such as the armed forces, in urban or other densely populated areas, in order to reduce the risk of incidental harm to the civilian population.[427]

However, it often may not be feasible to refrain from placing military objectives in densely populated areas. Legitimate military reasons often require locating or billeting military forces in urban areas or other areas where civilians are present. For example, forces may be housed in populated areas to take advantage of existing facilities, such as facilities for shelter, health and sanitation, communications, or power. In some cases, especially during counter-insurgency operations or in non-international armed conflict generally, the protection of the civilian population may be increased by placing military forces in densely populated areas to protect the civilian population from enemy attack and influence.[428]

5.14.2 Removing Civilians and Civilian Objects From the Vicinity of Military Objectives. It may be appropriate to remove civilians and civilian objects from the vicinity of military objectives.[429] In particular, civilian hospitals should be situated as far as possible from military objectives.[430]

The evacuation of civilians from areas likely to be attacked is advisable when there is immediate danger and where it would be likely to involve less hardship and danger to civilians than leaving them in place.[431]

Voluntary removal of civilians may be accomplished through the use of warnings.[432] When removing civilians from the vicinity of military objectives, it may be appropriate to establish safety, hospital, or neutralized zones so that civilians have safe places to move

---

[426] *Refer to* § 5.2.3.2 (What Precautions Are Feasible).

[427] *Consider* AP I art. 58 ("The Parties to the conflict shall, to the maximum extent feasible: ... (b) Avoid locating military objectives within or near densely populated areas;").

[428] *Refer to* § 17.5.2.1 (Positioning Military Forces Near the Civilian Population to Win Their Support and to Protect Them).

[429] *Consider* AP I art. 58 ("The Parties to the conflict shall, to the maximum extent feasible: (a) Without prejudice to Article 49 of the Fourth Convention, endeavour to remove the civilian population, individual civilians and civilian objects under their control from the vicinity of military objectives;").

[430] *Refer to* § 7.17.3 (Location of Civilian Hospitals).

[431] 2004 UK MANUAL ¶5.36.1 ("The evacuation of civilians from areas likely to be attacked is advisable when there is immediate danger and where it would be likely to involve less hardship and danger to civilians than leaving them in place.").

[432] *Refer to* § 5.11.5 (Effective Advance Warning Before an Attack That May Affect the Civilian Population).

toward.[433]

It also may be appropriate to conclude local agreements for the removal of civilians from besieged or encircled areas.[434]

During international armed conflict, the forcible transfer or deportation of protected persons from occupied territory is prohibited.[435]

5.14.3 Establishing Areas Where Civilians or the Wounded and Sick Are Protected. Certain zones or localities may be established through the agreement of parties to a conflict to shelter civilians or wounded and sick combatants from the effects of attacks.[436]

In this context, "locality" means a specific place of limited area, generally containing buildings, while "zone" means a relatively large area of land and may include one or more localities.[437]

5.14.3.1 *Civilian Hospital and Safety Zones and Localities*. During international armed conflict, States may establish hospital and safety zones and localities to protect certain persons from the effects of war, namely, wounded, sick, and aged persons, children under fifteen, expectant mothers, and mothers of children under seven.[438] Parties to a conflict may conclude agreements on the mutual recognition of the hospital zones and localities they have created, drawing upon model agreements that are annexed to the 1949 Geneva Conventions.[439] The establishment of a zone only binds an adverse party when it agrees to recognize the zone.[440]

---

[433] *Refer to* § 5.14.3 (Establishing Areas Where Civilians or the Wounded and Sick Are Protected).

[434] *Refer to* § 5.19.2 (Removal and Passage of Certain Personnel – Vulnerable Civilians, Diplomatic and Consular Personnel, the Wounded and Sick, and Medical Personnel).

[435] *Refer to* § 11.12.3 (Prohibition Against Forcible Transfers and Deportations).

[436] *For example*, SYLVIE-STOYANKA JUNOD, INTERNATIONAL COMMITTEE OF THE RED CROSS, PROTECTION OF THE VICTIMS OF ARMED CONFLICT FALKLAND-MALVINAS ISLANDS: INTERNATIONAL HUMANITARIAN LAW AND HUMANITARIAN ACTION (1982) 26 (1984) ("At Britain's suggestion, and without any special agreement in writing, the Parties to the conflict established a neutral zone at sea. This zone, called the Red Cross Box, with a diameter of approximately twenty nautical miles, was located on the high seas to the north of the islands. Without hampering military operations, it enabled hospital ships to hold position, in particular the UGANDA, and exchange British and Argentine wounded.").

[437] GC COMMENTARY 120-21 ("*Locality* should be taken to mean a specific place of limited area, generally containing buildings. The term *zone* is used to describe a relatively large area of land and may include one or more localities.").

[438] GC art. 14 ("In time of peace, the High Contracting Parties and, after the outbreak of hostilities, the Parties thereto, may establish in their own territory and, if the need arises, in occupied areas, hospital and safety zones and localities so organized as to protect from the effects of war, wounded, sick and aged persons, children under fifteen, expectant mothers and mothers of children under seven.").

[439] GC art. 14 ("Upon the outbreak and during the course of hostilities, the Parties concerned may conclude agreements on mutual recognition of the zones and localities they have created. They may for this purpose implement the provisions of the Draft Agreement annexed to the present Convention, with such amendments as they may consider necessary.").

[440] GC COMMENTARY 127 ("The zones will not, strictly speaking, have any legal existence, or enjoy protection under the Convention, until such time as they have been recognized by the adverse Party. This will entail the

These zones and localities may be combined with hospital zones established for the wounded and sick of the armed forces.[441]

Protecting Powers and the ICRC may seek to facilitate the institution and recognition of civilian hospital and safety zones and localities.[442]

5.14.3.2 Military Hospital Zones and Localities. States may establish in their own territory, and if the need arises, in occupied areas, hospital zones and localities so organized as to protect the wounded and sick (as defined in the GWS[443]) from the effects of war, as well as the personnel entrusted with the organization and administration of these zones and localities and with the care of the persons assembled within them.[444]

5.14.3.3 Neutralized Zones. It may be appropriate to conclude agreements with opposing forces to establish neutralized zones in regions where fighting is taking place.[445] Neutralized zones differ from civilian hospital and safety zones in that they are intended to protect a broader group of persons and in that they are generally established on a temporary basis in regions where fighting is taking place.[446]

---

conclusion of an agreement between the Power which has established zones in its territory and the Powers with which it is at war. It is only an agreement of this kind, concluded, as a general rule, after the outbreak of hostilities, which gives legal form to the obligation on States which have accorded recognition to zones to respect those zones. An agreement recognizing the zones is thus a *sine qua non* of their legal existence from the international point of view. It should contain all the provisions, particularly in regard to control procedure, required to prevent disputes arising later in regard to its interpretation.").

[441] GC COMMENTARY 125 ("As has already been pointed out, the provisions relating to hospital and safety zones in the First and Fourth Geneva Conventions are sufficiently flexible to make various combinations possible. There is, for instance, no reason why a hospital zone should not combine the two types and provide shelter for both soldiers and civilians in need of treatment, since once a soldier is wounded or sick, he may be said to be no longer a combatant on either side, but simply a suffering, inoffensive human being.").

[442] GC art. 14 ("The Protecting Powers and the International Committee of the Red Cross are invited to lend their good offices in order to facilitate the institution and recognition of these hospital and safety zones and localities.").

[443] *Refer to* § 7.3.2 (Persons Entitled to Protection as Wounded, Sick, or Shipwrecked Under the GWS and GWS-Sea).

[444] GWS art. 23 ("In time of peace, the High Contracting Parties and, after the outbreak of hostilities, the Parties thereto, may establish in their own territory and, if the need arises, in occupied areas, hospital zones and localities so organized as to protect the wounded and sick from the effects of war, as well as the personnel entrusted with the organization and administration of these zones and localities and with the care of the persons therein assembled.").

[445] *For example*, 2004 UK MANUAL ¶5.40.1 footnote 258 ("During the Falklands conflict of 1982, a neutralized zone was set up in the centre of Port Stanley, comprising the cathedral and a clearly defined area around it. This was done at the suggestion of the ICRC representative and with the consent of the Argentine and British authorities."); SPAIGHT, AIR POWER AND WAR RIGHTS 256 ("With the consent of both the Chinese and Japanese military authorities a district known as Nantao, lying between the French concession and a densely populated part of the old Chinese city, was selected and cleared of all troops, munition factories and other military establishments, and its boundaries were marked by flags. … 'The outstanding success of this scheme at Shanghai … led very quickly to the adoption of similar arrangements at Hankow and other great Chinese cities that were liable to bombardment, and it may be accepted that the lives of tens, if not of hundreds, of thousands of hapless Chinese have thus been saved.'").

[446] GC COMMENTARY 129 ("[N]eutralized zones differ from hospital and safety zones in that they are established in the actual regions where fighting is taking place and are intended to give shelter to both civilian and military wounded and sick, as well as all civilian persons who take no part in hostilities. Furthermore, they are generally set

These neutralized zones are to shelter: (a) wounded and sick combatants or noncombatants; and (b) civilian persons who take no part in hostilities, and who, while they reside in the zones, perform no work of a military character.[447]

Agreements should be made in writing, signed by representatives of the parties to the conflict, and should establish: (a) the location of the zone; (b) the administration of the zone; (c) the food supply of the zone; (d) the supervision of the zone; and (e) the beginning and duration of the neutralization of the zone.[448]

5.14.4 Using Distinctive and Visible Signs to Identify Protected Persons and Objects as Such. It may be appropriate to identify protected persons and objects, as such, through the use of distinctive and visible signs. For example, it may be appropriate to identify civilian hospitals[449] or civilian air raid shelters in order to facilitate their protection during enemy bombardment.[450] Signs indicating civilian objects, as such, should be notified to the opposing party so that the opposing party knows to refrain from bombarding places or buildings bearing these signs.

Where enemy forces seek to make peaceful civilians the object of attack, then it would not be appropriate to distinguish civilian objects. Such precautions would not be feasible because they would not be expected to yield a humanitarian benefit.[451]

5.14.5 Carrying Arms Openly and Wearing of Distinctive Emblems by the Armed Forces to Distinguish Themselves From the Civilian Population. Although the practices of carrying arms openly and wearing uniforms and distinctive emblems by armed forces predates

---

up on a temporary basis to meet the tactical situation at a particular moment, whereas hospital and safety zones tend to be more permanent in character.").

[447] GC art. 15 ("Any Party to the conflict may, either direct or through a neutral State or some humanitarian organization, propose to the adverse Party to establish, in the regions where fighting is taking place, neutralized zones intended to shelter from the effects of war the following persons, without distinction: (a) wounded and sick combatants or non-combatants; (b) civilian persons who take no part in hostilities, and who, while they reside in the zones, perform no work of a military character.").

[448] GC art. 15 ("When the Parties concerned have agreed upon the geographical position, administration, food supply and supervision of the proposed neutralized zone, a written agreement shall be concluded and signed by the representatives of the Parties to the conflict. The agreement shall fix the beginning and the duration of the neutralization of the zone.").

[449] *Refer to* § 7.17.2.2 (Markings of Civilian Hospitals With the Distinctive Emblem).

[450] *See, e.g.*, HAGUE IV REG. art. 27 ("In sieges and bombardments all necessary steps must be taken to spare, as far as possible, buildings dedicated to religion, art, science, or charitable purposes, historic monuments, hospitals, and places where the sick and wounded are collected, provided they are not being used at the time for military purposes. It is the duty of the besieged to indicate the presence of such buildings or places by distinctive and visible signs, which shall be notified to the enemy beforehand."); HAGUE IX art. 5 ("In bombardments by naval forces all the necessary measures must be taken by the commander to spare as far as possible sacred edifices, buildings used for artistic, scientific, or charitable purposes, historic monuments, hospitals, and places where the sick or wounded are collected, on the understanding that they are not used at the same time for military purposes. It is the duty of the inhabitants to indicate such monuments, edifices, or places by visible signs, which shall consist of large stiff rectangular panels divided diagonally into two coloured triangular portions, the upper portion black, the lower portion white.").

[451] *Refer to* § 5.2.3.2 (What Precautions Are Feasible).

contemporary doctrines of feasible precautions, these practices may be viewed as feasible precautions that help protect the civilian population from being erroneously made the object of attack.[452]

This requirement of armed forces to wear distinctive emblems has been understood as a requirement for the armed forces as a group.[453] However, it applies, to some extent, on an individual basis in the context of liability for spying or sabotage.[454] The obligation of armed forces to distinguish themselves includes, but is not limited to, those times when they conduct attacks.[455] However, the requirement to wear distinctive emblems is not an absolute one, even during combat.[456]

5.15 Undefended Cities, Towns, and Villages

Attack, by whatever means, of a village, town, or city that is undefended is prohibited.[457] Undefended villages, towns, or cities may, however, be captured.

5.15.1 "Undefended" – Notes on Terminology. The term *undefended city* (or *town* or *village*, or any other populated area) is a term of art in the law of war and should not be confused with a place that simply lacks defensive capabilities. Historically, open or undefended status for a town, village, or city would be sought as opposing military forces approached and the military forces previously controlling the city abandoned it.[458] Undefended or open status would essentially surrender the city to the opposing force; this minimized injury to the inhabitants and damage to civilian objects within the city because the city could be occupied without resistance or bypassed.[459]

---

[452] *Refer to* § 4.6.4 (Having a Fixed Distinctive Sign Recognizable at a Distance); § 4.6.5 (Carrying Arms Openly).

[453] *Refer to* § 4.6.1.1 (GPW 4A(2) Conditions Required on a Group Basis).

[454] *Refer to* § 4.17 (Spies, Saboteurs, and Other Persons Engaging in Similar Acts Behind Enemy Lines).

[455] *Refer to* § 5.4.8 (Obligation of Combatants to Distinguish Themselves When Conducting Attacks).

[456] *Refer to* § 5.4.8.1 (Fighting Out of Uniform).

[457] *See* HAGUE IV REG. art. 25 ("The attack or bombardment, by whatever means, of towns, villages, dwellings, or buildings which are undefended is prohibited."); HAGUE IX art. 1 ("The bombardment by naval forces of undefended ports, towns, villages, dwellings, or buildings is forbidden."). *Consider* AP I art. 59(1) ("It is prohibited for the Parties to the conflict to attack, by any means whatsoever, non-defended localities.").

[458] *For example*, H. Wayne Elliot, *Open Cities and (Un)defended Places*, THE ARMY LAWYER 39, 41 (Apr. 1995) ("When the military forces had abandoned the city, the city's civic leaders normally had the burden of meeting with the opposing commander and informing him that the city was open. Accordingly, the mayor of Columbia, South Carolina, went to the Union lines as General Sherman approached the city and informed him that the Confederate forces had left and that the city was open for the Union army's entry. When the Confederate government was forced to abandon Richmond, Virginia, the mayor met the advancing Union forces and informed General Grant's commanders that the city was open. Once the capturing forces entered the city, they were obligated to refrain from looting and pillaging and were responsible for the safety of the city's residents. Nonetheless, war materials still in the city could be destroyed.").

[459] H. Wayne Elliot, *Open Cities and (Un)defended Places*, THE ARMY LAWYER 39, 41 (Apr. 1995) ("Surrender usually meant the complete submission of the military forces defending an area to the enemy. However, when the opposing military forces simply abandoned the city, the city was considered to be undefended and 'open.' That is, the attacking force could enter the city at will and without fear of attack. Under these circumstances destroying the

5.15.1.1 <u>*Non-defended Versus Undefended*</u>. Article 59 of AP I uses the term "non-defended" rather than "undefended," but uses essentially the same criteria as FM 27-10's discussion of "undefended" places within the meaning of Article 25 of the Hague IV Regulations. The change from "undefended" in the Hague IV Regulations and Hague IX, to "non-defended" in AP I, appears to reflect a difference in translation from French to English rather than a substantive difference.

The original text of the Hague IV Regulations and Hague IX is French.[460] In the French versions of the text, both the Hague IV Regulations and Hague IX use a dependent clause "that are not defended" in order to modify the list of places.[461] Rather than a dependent clause, AP I uses an adjective -- "non-defended" modifying the word "localities."[462] The difference in English terms seems to reflect this underlying change in the French phrasing.

Moreover, the title of the chapter in Hague IX—"Du bombardement des ports, villes, villages, habitations ou bâtiments <u>non défendus</u>" (emphasis added)—uses the same French phrase as is used in AP I, yet the last two words of the title of the chapter in Hague IX have typically been translated as "undefended" rather than "non-defended."

Thus, the consistency in terminology across the French texts suggests that even though the English terminology has varied slightly, no substantive change has been intended.

5.15.1.2 <u>*Open Versus Undefended*</u>. If "undefended" is simply understood in a factual sense to mean a lack of defenses and "open" is simply understood in a factual sense to mean "open" for entry by the enemy, then distinctions could be drawn between "open" cities and "undefended" cities, because not all cities lacking defenses would be open for entry by enemy forces. For example, a city that did not itself have defenses, but was located deep behind the State's defensive lines would not be "open" for entry by enemy forces.

Most sources, however, use "open" and "undefended" interchangeably.[463] It appears that these terms tend to be used interchangeably because both terms generally refer to a specific legal

---

entire city was unnecessary, although individual military targets in the city might be destroyed, either before or after entry.").

[460] William H. Taft, *Proclamation Regarding the Hague IX*, Feb. 28, 1910, 36 STAT. 2351 ("Whereas a Convention concerning bombardment by naval forces in time of war was concluded … the original of which Convention, being in the French language, is word for word as follows:"); William H. Taft, *Proclamation Regarding the Hague IV*, Feb. 28, 1910, 36 STAT. 2277 ("Whereas a Convention respecting the laws and customs of war on land was concluded … the original of which Convention, being in the French language, is word for word as follows:").

[461] *See* HAGUE IV REG. art. 25 ("Il est interdit d'attaquer ou de bombarder, par quelque moyen que ce soit, des villes, villages, habitations, ou bâtiments <u>qui ne sont pas défendus</u>.") (emphasis added); HAGUE IX art. 1 ("Il est interdit de bombarder, par des forces navales, des ports, villes, villages, habitations ou bâtiments, <u>qui ne sont pas défendus</u>.") (emphasis added).

[462] *See* AP I art. 59, 1125 UNTS 299 ("Il est interdit aux Parties au conflit d'attaquer, par quelque moyen que ce soit, des localités <u>non défendues</u>.") (emphasis added).

[463] *See, e.g.*, 1958 UK MANUAL ¶290 ("An undefended or 'open' town is a town which is so completely undefended from within or without that the enemy may enter and take possession of it without fighting or incurring casualties.").

category of populated areas that are protected by the law of war from attack.[464]

5.15.2 "By Whatever Means". The phrase "by whatever means" was inserted in the Hague IV Regulations to clarify that bombing attacks by air were included in the rule.[465]

5.15.3 Declaration of a City as "Undefended". An undefended city may be established through negotiations with opposing forces,[466] or unilaterally by the party to the conflict in control of it. If the latter, the intent and actions of that party should be communicated to opposing military forces through a declaration. A town, village, or city may be declared "undefended" when it is near, or in, a zone where opposing armed forces are in contact with one another and it is open for immediate physical occupation by an adverse party without resistance.[467]

5.15.3.1 *Open for Immediate Physical Occupation*. The area in question must be open for immediate physical occupation by opposing military ground forces.[468] Thus, a city in rear areas behind enemy lines cannot be "undefended." For example, a party to a conflict cannot declare a city or other population center to be undefended if it is several hundred miles behind the area of ground conflict where it would not be feasible for opposing ground forces to occupy it. By way of comparison, it would not be effective for a person to seek to surrender to an opposing force's aircraft that could not physically take custody of that person.[469]

5.15.3.2 *Necessity for a Declaration of Undefended Status*. Although there is no explicit treaty requirement that a city be declared undefended before achieving that status, the practice has been to make such declarations to the opposing party. Without them, a belligerent

---

[464] *See* R.Y. Jennings, *Open Towns*, 22 BYIL 258, 260-61 (1945) ("There can be little doubt that the land warfare rules exempted the 'open and undefended' town from bombardment because, being undefended, it was, under the conditions of contemporary warfare, open for the enemy to enter and take possession of, or destroy, its military resources. This quality of being open to entry by the enemy is the essence of the rule. … It is impossible to conceive of a truly undefended town which is not also open in every sense of the word.").

[465] *See* JAMES BROWN SCOTT, THE PROCEEDINGS OF THE HAGUE PEACE CONFERENCES: I THE CONFERENCE OF 1907 104 (1920) ("The Russian and Italian proposals had the same design, and were calculated to supplement Article 25 of the 1899 Regulations with a provision securing to undefended towns, villages, dwellings or buildings absolute immunity from all attack or bombardment, 'even by aid of balloons or other new methods of a similar nature.' … The delegation of France then observed that the prohibition contemplated by the new Russian text, while entirely conforming to its opinion as previously expressed, is already contained in the text now in force in Article 25, and that consequently it is sufficient, if deemed necessary to avoid misunderstanding by rendering its terms precise, to insert the words 'by any means whatever' after 'to attack or bombard.'").

[466] *Refer to* § 5.15.5 (Agreements to Establish Undefended Cities).

[467] 1956 FM 27-10 (Change No. 1 1976) ¶39b ("An undefended place, within the meaning of Article 25, HR, is any inhabited place near or in a zone where opposing armed forces are in contact which is open for occupation by an adverse party without resistance."). *Consider* AP art. 59(2) ("The appropriate authorities of a Party to the conflict may declare as a non-defended locality any inhabited place near or in a zone where armed forces are in contact which is open for occupation by an adverse Party.").

[468] BOTHE, PARTSCH, & SOLF, NEW RULES 382 (AP I art. 59, ¶2.5.1) ("The concept intended is that it is sufficiently close to the adverse Party's forces that tactical movement to occupy it is a feasible course of action by the advancing force.").

[469] *Refer to* § 5.9.3.3 (Under Circumstances in Which It Is Feasible to Accept).

would have no way of knowing whether a city was truly open for occupation without resistance. For example, a city may not satisfy the conditions described below for undefended status, or it may contain defenses that are concealed or that are operated from other areas.[470]

5.15.3.3 *Refusal to Recognize a Declaration*. Belligerents may refuse to recognize a declaration that a city is undefended if they assess that it does not satisfy all of the necessary conditions, although they should notify the opposing belligerent of that decision.[471] Absent or until recognition, military objectives in a city unilaterally designated as undefended remain subject to attack.[472]

5.15.3.4 *Authority to Make a Declaration or to Recognize a Declaration*. Declaration of a city being open or recognition of an opposing party's declaration may only be accomplished by those with authority to enforce the corresponding obligations, which may be the immediate military commander, theater commander, or national command authorities.[473] These obligations may extend more broadly than control over the city itself as, for example, when the city's defenses are operated from a different location.

5.15.4 Conditions Necessary for a Place to Maintain Undefended Status. Once a party to a conflict has validly declared a city to be undefended, the city must also satisfy certain conditions. If the city fails to satisfy these conditions, it would not be entitled to undefended status, or, if previously granted, it would lose that status.[474] Persons and objects within that city,

---

[470] R.Y. Jennings, *Open Towns*, 22 BYIL 258, 261 (1945) ("But it is ludicrous to suppose that a town shielded by an army holding a line in front of it is undefended. Moreover, even the defences peculiarly appropriate to aerial warfare are no longer purely or even mainly local defences. Defending fighter planes may be based miles from the town. A screen of anti-aircraft guns sited on the route to the town, even though many miles away from it, may be a more effective defence than anti-aircraft guns sited in or around the town itself.").

[471] *Consider* AP I art. 59(4) ("The Party to the conflict to which the declaration is addressed shall ackowledge [sic] its receipt and shall treat the locality as a non-defended locality unless the conditions laid down in paragraph 2 are not in fact fullfilled, in which event it shall immediately so inform the Party making the declaration.").

[472] *Cf. Sansolini and Others v. Bentivegna and Others*, Italian Court of Cassation, Jul. 19, 1957 ("The declaration that Rome was an open city was made by the Italian Government before the armistice, *viz.*, on July 31, 1943. It was made to the British and the Americans but never accepted by them. It follows from this lack of acceptance that the declaration could not create any legal obligation for the Italian Government vis-à-vis the British and the Americans. … We must therefore reject the contention that there was any violation of an undertaking to respect Rome as an open city because there were not agreements to this effect … ."); BOTHE, PARTSCH, & SOLF, NEW RULES 383 (AP I art. 59, ¶2.5.2) ("Drawing on the World War II experience, the Canadian delegation pointed out that the decision not to defend Paris and Rome had been made while defending forces still had possession of these urban centres. Accordingly, the Canadian delegation proposed that a mechanism be developed under which the defending Party would declare that it did not intend to defend the locality and to initiate negotiations for permitting an orderly withdrawal. The locality was not to be attacked while such negotiation was taking place. Other delegations pointed out that the Canadian proposal would amount to a unilateral cease fire enabling the defending force to extricate itself from a precarious situation. This matter was left for mutual agreement between the Parties under para. 5.").

[473] *For example*, R.Y. Jennings, *Open Towns*, 22 BYIL 258, 263 (1945) ("The declaration of Rome as an open city by the Italian Government in August 1943 was little more than a public request to the Allies to state the conditions under which they would discontinue their bombing attacks on the city. The Allies were unable to comply with the request for the very good reason that however anxious the Italian Government might have been to comply with any conditions, they were in fact powerless to prevent the German Army from using the city as a military centre.").

[474] *Consider* AP I art. 59(7) ("A locality loses its status as a non-defended locality when it ceases to fulfil the conditions laid down in paragraph 2 or in the agreement referred to in paragraph 5.").

however, may still receive other protections for civilians and civilian objects.[475]

5.15.4.1 *Combatants and Mobile Military Equipment Have Been Evacuated*. All combatants, as well as their mobile weapons and mobile military equipment, must have been evacuated.[476] However, the presence of military medical personnel, the wounded and sick, and civilian police forces for the purpose of maintaining local law and order would not cause a city designated as undefended to lose that status.[477]

5.15.4.2 *No Hostile Use of Fixed Military Facilities*. No hostile use shall be made of fixed military installations or establishments within the city.[478]

5.15.4.3 *No Hostile Acts Against the Occupying Force*. Hostile acts may not be committed by the local civilian authorities or the civilian population against the occupying military force.[479]

5.15.4.4 *No Activities in Support of Military Operations*. No activities in support of military operations may be undertaken.[480] For example, factories in the city should not be used to manufacture munitions, and ports or railroads should not be used to transport military supplies.[481]

---

[475] *Consider* AP I art. 59(7) ("In such an eventuality, the locality shall continue to enjoy the protection provided by the other provisions of this Protocol and the other rules of international law applicable in armed conflict.").

[476] *See* 1956 FM 27-10 (Change No. 1 1976) ¶39b ("In order to be considered as undefended, the following conditions should be fulfilled: (1) Armed forces and all other combatants, as well as mobile weapons and mobile military equipment, must have been evacuated, or otherwise neutralized;"). *Consider* AP I art. 59(2) (requiring that in a non-defended locality "(a) All combatants, as well as mobile weapons and mobile military equipment, must have been evacuated;").

[477] 1956 FM 27-10 (Change No. 1 1976) ¶39b ("The presence, in the place, of medical units, wounded and sick, and police forces retained for the sole purpose of maintaining law and order does not change the character of such an undefended place."). *Consider* AP I art. 59(3) ("The presence, in this locality, of persons specially protected under the Conventions and this Protocol, and of police forces retained for the sole purpose of maintaining law and order, is not contrary to the conditions laid down in paragraph 2."). *Compare* § 4.23.1 (Police as Civilians).

[478] *See* 1956 FM 27-10 (Change No. 1 1976) ¶39b ("In order to be considered as undefended, the following conditions should be fulfilled: … (2) no hostile use shall be made of fixed military installations or establishments;"). *Consider* AP I art. 59(2) (requiring that in a non-defended locality "(b) No hostile use shall be made of fixed military installations or establishments;").

[479] *See* 1956 FM 27-10 (Change No. 1 1976) ¶39b ("In order to be considered as undefended, the following conditions should be fulfilled: … (3) no acts of warfare shall be committed by the authorities or by the population;"). *Consider* AP I art. 59(2) (requiring that in a non-defended locality "(c) No acts of hostility shall be committed by the authorities or by the population;").

[480] *See* 1956 FM 27-10 (Change No. 1 1976) ¶39b ("In order to be considered as undefended, the following conditions should be fulfilled: … (4) no activities in support of military operations shall be undertaken."). *Consider* AP I art. 59(2) (requiring that in a non-defended locality "(d) No activities in support of military operations shall be undertaken.").

[481] *For example*, F.D. ROOSEVELT & S. ROSENMAN, THE PUBLIC PAPERS AND ADDRESSES OF FRANKLIN D. ROOSEVELT: 1943 VOLUME 309 (1950) ("The Nine Hundred and Tenth Press Conference (Excerpts) July 23, 1943 (Rome as a military center - Bombing of Rome) Q. Mr. President, is there any comment you can make, sir, upon establishing Rome as an open city? THE PRESIDENT: I think the easiest thing is to tell you in general what has

5.15.5 Agreements to Establish Undefended Cities. Even if the conditions described above are not met, parties to a conflict may agree between themselves to treat an area as an undefended city.[482] The agreement should be in writing and should define and describe, as precisely as possible, the limits of the undefended city (such as the exact geographic limits of the locality, when the location is to begin to receive protection as undefended, and the duration of undefended status). If necessary, methods of supervision to ensure that the city continues to fulfill the conditions should be specified.[483] It may also be appropriate for agreements to specify: (1) rules on marking the city and agreed signs;[484] (2) persons authorized to enter the city; and (3) whether and under what conditions the city may be occupied by enemy forces.

5.15.6 Actions of the Occupying Force. The occupying force may use the city, town, or village for military operations, including by establishing defenses to prevent its recapture by the enemy.[485] In such cases, the city would lose its undefended status, and, for example, military objectives within the city may be attacked.[486]

However, if the occupying force acts in a manner consistent with the conditions necessary for the inhabited place to maintain undefended status,[487] the place would remain undefended for the purpose of protecting it against military operations by all parties to the conflict.

---

been happening for over a year. We have been very anxious to have Rome declared an open city. However, the Fascists would not do it; and on the contrary, it has become—probably was then—a very important military center. That means they were making munitions, and using airports very close to Rome-actually in Rome, and the use of Rome because it's a railroad center for transportation of troops, guns, and ammunition down to the south of Rome. And we used every argument, and pleaded that it be made an open city. But it didn't work. We did our best. And we still hope that the Germans and the Fascists will make it an open city.").

[482] *Consider* AP I art. 59(5) ("The Parties to the conflict may agree on the establishment of non-defended localities even if such localities do not fulfil the conditions laid down in paragraph 2.").

[483] *Consider* AP I art. 59(5) ("The agreement should define and describe, as precisely as possible, the limits of the non-defended locality; if necessary, it may lay down the methods of supervision.").

[484] *Consider* AP I art. 59(6) ("The Party which is in control of a locality governed by such an agreement shall mark it, so far as possible, by such signs as may be agreed upon with the other Party, which shall be displayed where they are clearly visible, especially on its perimeter and limits and on highways.").

[485] BOTHE, PARTSCH, & SOLF, NEW RULES 382 (AP I art. 59, ¶2.4) ("Once in possession of a previously non-defended locality a Party is not bound to refrain from organizing its defense to maintain the security of the locality against an attempt to recapture the locality.").

[486] *See* The Legal Adviser (Hackworth) to Secretary of State Hull, memorandum, Aug. 19, 1943, X WHITEMAN'S DIGEST 437 ("If our troops were in Rome [after the United States had recognized it as an open city] or passing through Rome, they would be subject to bombardment by Germany and hence the city would be in the same position as French cities, including Paris, were after they were occupied by German forces or were being used for military purposes. It appears that in the last war French cities, such as Vouziers, Charleville, and Mézières, regarded as open cities were bombarded by the French after they had been occupied by Germany. The sum and substance of these examples is that the status of a city may change from an undefended to a defended place as military operations change, and that recognition by use of Rome as an open city would mean only that we could not bomb it while it was so recognized, but that if we later used it ourselves, it would again become subject to bombardment.").

[487] *Refer to* § 5.15.4 (Conditions Necessary for a Place to Maintain Undefended Status).

5.16 Prohibition on Using Protected Persons and Objects to Shield, Favor, or Impede Military Operations

Parties to a conflict may not use the presence or movement of protected persons[488] or objects[489]: (1) to attempt to make certain points or areas immune from seizure or attack; (2) to shield military objectives from attack; or (3) otherwise to shield or favor one's own military operations or to impede the adversary's military operations.

5.16.1 Protected Persons and Objects. In particular, the civilian population,[490] protected persons under the GC,[491] POWs,[492] fixed medical establishments and medical units, *parlementaires* and other persons protected by a flag of truce,[493] and cultural property are protected persons and objects that may not be used for the above purposes.

Although persons and objects that are protected by the law of war may not be used in these ways, this rule does not prohibit a party from using what would otherwise be a civilian object for military purposes and thereby converting it to a military objective that is not protected by the law of war. For example, a building that previously was a civilian object could be used for military purposes (including as cover) and would not implicate this rule because it would no longer be a protected object. Similarly, this rule does not prohibit persons who would otherwise be civilians from participating in hostilities or otherwise assuming the risks inherent in

---

[488] *Cf.* 10 U.S.C. § 950t ("(9) Using protected persons as a shield.—Any person subject to this chapter who positions, or otherwise takes advantage of, a protected person with the intent to shield a military objective from attack. [sic] or to shield, favor, or impede military operations, shall be punished, if death results to one or more of the victims, by death or such other punishment as a military commission under this chapter may direct, and, if death does not result to any of the victims, by such punishment, other than death, as a military commission under this chapter may direct."); 10 U.S.C. § 950p (a)(3) ("The term 'protected person' means any person entitled to protection under one or more of the Geneva Conventions, including civilians not taking an active part in hostilities, military personnel placed out of combat by sickness, wounds, or detention, and military medical or religious personnel.").

[489] *Cf.* 10 U.S.C. § 950t ("(10) Using protected property as a shield.—Any person subject to this chapter who positions, or otherwise takes advantage of the location of, protected property with the intent to shield a military objective from attack, or to shield, favor, or impede military operations, shall be punished as a military commission under this chapter may direct."); 10 U.S.C. § 950p(a)(3) ("The term 'protected property' means any property specifically protected by the law of war, including buildings dedicated to religion, education, art, science, or charitable purposes, historic monuments, hospitals, and places where the sick and wounded are collected, but only if and to the extent such property is not being used for military purposes or is not otherwise a military objective. The term includes objects properly identified by one of the distinctive emblems of the Geneva Conventions, but does not include civilian property that is a military objective.").

[490] *Consider* AP I 51(7) ("The presence or movements of the civilian population or individual civilians shall not be used to render certain points or areas immune from military operations, in particular in attempts to shield military objectives from attacks or to shield, favour or impede military operations. The Parties to the conflict shall not direct the movement of the civilian population or individual civilians in order to attempt to shield military objectives from attacks or to shield military operations.").

[491] GC art. 28 ("The presence of a protected person may not be used to render certain points or areas immune from military operations.").

[492] *Refer to* § 9.5.2.3 (No Exposure to a Combat Zone or Use as a Human Shield).

[493] *Refer to* § 12.4.2.1 (Prohibition on Improper Use of the Flag of Truce).

supporting military operations.[494]

5.16.2 Intent to Endanger Protected Persons or Objects to Deter Enemy Military Operations. The essence of this rule is to refrain from deliberately endangering protected persons or objects for the purpose of deterring enemy military operations.[495] This absolute duty to refrain from purposeful misconduct may be contrasted with the affirmative obligation that parties have to take feasible precautions to separate the civilian population,[496] civilian internees,[497] POWs,[498] fixed medical establishments and medical units,[499] and cultural property,[500] from the dangers of military operations.

An adversary's intention to violate this rule is likely to be clear because that adversary normally would make it apparent to the opposing party that attacks against the military objective being shielded would risk harming protected persons or objects.[501]

On the other hand, in the absence of purposeful action to put protected persons and objects at risk of harm from enemy military operations, there would be no violation of this rule. For example, this rule would not prohibit restricting the movement of civilians in order to conduct military operations without their interference. In addition, it would also not prohibit the

---

[494] *Refer* § 4.15.2.2 (Employment in Hostilities); § 4.18.5 (Private Persons Who Engage in Hostilities and the Law of War); § 5.12.3.3 (Civilian Workers Who Support Military Operations In or On Military Objectives).

[495] BOTHE, PARTSCH, & SOLF, NEW RULES 316 (AP I art. 51, ¶2.8.2) ("The mandatory provisions of para. 7 are intended to prohibit any deliberate use of the physical presence or physical movement of civilians for the purpose of shielding or favouring friendly military operations against enemy action or to impede enemy military operations. … In practice this means that in some close cases the location of a military objective in the midst of a populated town may violate para. 7 *if the purpose of the location* is to shield the military unit or facility from attack. On the other hand, the same act could be innocent if it were militarily necessary to so situate the unit or facility. Thus the subjective intent of military commander is the controlling element in determining whether there has been a breach of para. 7, a negligent failure to take the precautions urged by Art. 58, or a legitimate act of war.").

[496] *Refer to* § 5.14 (Feasible Precautions to Reduce the Risk of Harm to Protected Persons and Objects by the Party Subject to Attack).

[497] *Refer to* § 10.11.1.1 (Avoidance of Particularly Dangerous Areas).

[498] *Refer to* § 9.11.3 (Location of POW Camps).

[499] *Refer to* § 7.10.2 (Obligation to Situate Military Medical Units and Facilities Relative to Military Objectives).

[500] *Refer to* § 5.18.3 (Refraining From Any Use for Purposes That Are Likely to Expose It to Destruction or Damage).

[501] *For example*, STUART I. ROCHESTER & FREDERICK KILEY, HONOR BOUND: THE HISTORY OF AMERICAN PRISONERS OF WAR IN SOUTHEAST ASIA, 1961-1973 316-21 (1998) ("Between June and October 1967 the North Vietnamese confined more than 30 U.S. PWs in the vicinity of the Yen Phu thermal power plant in northern Hanoi. … Although the Communists would deny it, their conspicuous display and virtual announcement of the PWs' presence at the power plant evidenced a transparent attempt to use the prisoners as hostages to discourage U.S. bombing of the facility. … Through calculated disclosures to visiting journalists and diplomats, local placard publicity, and exhibiting the captives in full view of civilians—all sharp departures from their normal practice—the Vietnamese could be certain the PWs' presence would be reported to the U.S. government. … The hostage charade did not deter U.S. strikes on the target. The plant was attacked regularly after 13 August, with apparently no casualties and conflicting reports on the extent of damage to the power facility and PW cellblocks.").

evacuation of civilians for their own security or for imperative military reasons.[502]

In addition, this rule must not be understood to alter the rules on spying and sabotage. In other words, this rule does not prohibit a spy from hiding among civilians in order to gather intelligence. However, the spy runs the risk of prosecution by the enemy State if he or she is discovered and captured while spying.

5.16.3 Prohibition on Taking Hostages. The taking of hostages is prohibited.[503] This prohibition is understood to include a prohibition against threatening to harm detainees whose lives are valued by the adversary in order to induce the adversary not to attack, but is also understood to include the prohibition against using hostages as human shields.[504]

The taking of hostages is also prohibited in non-international armed conflict.[505]

5.16.4 Use of Human Shields by Defenders Does Not Relieve Attackers of Duties in Conducting Attacks. Violations by the adversary of the prohibition on using protected persons and objects to shield, favor, or impede military operations do not relieve those conducting attacks from their obligation to seek to discriminate between lawful and unlawful objects of attack.[506] However, such violations by the adversary may impair the attacking force's ability to discriminate and increase the risk of harm to protected persons and objects.[507]

---

[502] *Cf.* BOTHE, PARTSCH, & SOLF, NEW RULES 317 (AP I art. 51, ¶2.8.3) ("Paragraph 7 [of Article 51 of AP I] does not prohibit measures to restrict the movement of civilians so as to avoid their interference with military movement, nor does it prohibit ordering their evacuation if their security or imperative military reasons so demand.").

[503] GC art. 34 ("The taking of hostages is prohibited."). *Cf.* 18 U.S.C. § 2441(d)(1)(I) (defining "Taking hostages" as "The act of a person who, having knowingly seized or detained one or more persons, threatens to kill, injure, or continue to detain such person or persons with the intent of compelling any nation, person other than the hostage, or group of persons to act or refrain from acting as an explicit or implicit condition for the safety or release of such person or persons."); 10 U.S.C. § 950t(7) ("TAKING HOSTAGES.—Any person subject to this chapter who, having knowingly seized or detained one or more persons, threatens to kill, injure, or continue to detain such person or persons with the intent of compelling any nation, person other than the hostage, or group of persons to act or refrain from acting as an explicit or implicit condition for the safety or release of such person or persons, shall be punished, if death results to one or more of the victims, by death or such other punishment as a military commission under this chapter may direct, and, if death does not result to any of the victims, by such punishment, other than death, as a military commission under this chapter may direct.").

[504] GC COMMENTARY 230 (giving as examples of hostage taking: (1) "taking as hostages persons generally selected from among prominent persons in a city or a district in order to prevent disorders or attacks on occupation troops"; (2) "arresting after an attack a certain number of inhabitants of the occupied territory and announcing that they will be kept captive or executed if the guilty are not given up"; and (3) "the practice of taking so-called accompanying hostages consists of placing inhabitants of occupied territory on board lorry convoys or trains in order to prevent attacks by their compatriots").

[505] *Refer to* § 17.6.2 (Prohibition on the Taking of Hostages).

[506] *Refer to* § 5.4.4 (Failure by the Defender to Separate or Distinguish Does Not Relieve the Attacker of the Duty to Discriminate in Conducting Attacks).

[507] FINAL REPORT ON THE PERSIAN GULF WAR 613 ("Another reason for collateral damage to civilian objects and injury to civilians during Operation Desert Storm lay in the policy of the Government of Iraq, which purposely used both Iraqi and Kuwaiti civilian populations and civilian objects as shields for military objects. Contrary to the admonishment against such conduct contained in Article 19, GWS, Articles 18 and 28, GC, Article 4(1), 1954 Hague, and certain principles of customary law codified in Protocol I (discussed below), the Government of Iraq

Although human shields who are civilians are to be considered as civilians in determining whether a planned attack would be excessive, enemy use of voluntary human shields may be considered as a factor in assessing the legality of an attack.[508] Feasible precautions must be taken to reduce the risk of harm to human shields.

5.16.5 Responsibility for Harm to Human Shields. The party that employs human shields in an attempt to shield military objectives from attack assumes responsibility for their injury, although the attacker may share this responsibility if it fails to take feasible precautions.[509]

5.17 SEIZURE AND DESTRUCTION OF ENEMY PROPERTY

Outside the context of attacks, certain rules apply to the seizure and destruction of enemy property:

- Enemy property may not be seized or destroyed unless imperatively demanded by the necessities of war;
- Public movable property and certain types of private movable property may customarily be captured as war booty;
- Enemy private movable property that is not susceptible of direct military use may be appropriated only to the extent that such taking is permissible in occupied areas;
- Pillage is prohibited; and
- Feasible precautions should be taken to mitigate the burden on civilians, but there is no obligation to compensate the owners of enemy property that is lawfully damaged.

---

placed military assets (personnel, weapons, and equipment) in civilian populated areas and next to protected objects (mosques, medical facilities, and cultural sites) in an effort to protect them from attack. For this purpose, Iraqi military helicopters were dispersed into residential areas; and military supplies were stored in mosques, schools, and hospitals in Iraq and Kuwait. Similarly, a cache of Iraqi Silkworm surface-to-surface missiles was found inside a school in a populated area in Kuwait City. UN inspectors uncovered chemical bomb production equipment while inspecting a sugar factory in Iraq. The equipment had been moved to the site to escape Coalition air strikes. This intentional mingling of military objects with civilian objects naturally placed the civilian population living nearby, working within, or using those civilian objects at risk from legitimate military attacks on those military objects.").

[508] *Refer to* § 5.12.3.4 (Enemy Use of Human Shields).

[509] *U.S. Comments on the International Committee of the Red Cross's Memorandum on the Applicability of International Humanitarian Law in the Gulf Region*, Jan. 11, 1991, DIGEST OF UNITED STATES PRACTICE IN INTERNATIONAL LAW 1991-1999 2057, 2063 ("In no case may a combatant force utilize individual civilians or the civilian population to shield a military objective from attack. A nation that utilizes civilians to shield a target from attack assumes responsibility for their injury, so long as an attacker exercises reasonable precaution in executing its operations. Likewise, civilians working within or in the immediate vicinity of a legitimate military objective assume a certain risk of injury."); *Instructor Training Course*, ¶3g, Appendix C in DEPARTMENT OF THE ARMY SUBJECT SCHEDULE 27-1, *The Geneva Conventions of 1949 and Hague Convention No. IV of 1907*, 18 (Aug. 29, 1975) ("(4) ***Question:*** Suppose we are receiving fire from the enemy, and they are using unarmed civilians as shields. May we fire back, knowing that we will be killing many of these unarmed civilians? ***Answer:*** Yes. We may fire since we have the right to defend ourselves. The responsibility for innocent casualties falls upon those who would violate the law of war by using innocents as shields.").

During occupation, other rules relating to the treatment of enemy property apply.[510]

5.17.1 Definition of Enemy Property. All property located in enemy territory is regarded as enemy property regardless of its ownership.[511]

5.17.2 Enemy Property – Military Necessity Standard. Enemy property may not be seized or destroyed unless imperatively demanded by the necessities of war.[512] In particular, devastation or destruction may not be pursued as an end in itself.[513] The measure of permissible seizure or destruction of enemy property is found in the strict necessities of war.[514] There must be some reasonable connection between the seizure or destruction of the enemy property and the overcoming of enemy forces.[515]

Extensive destruction and appropriation of property protected by the GC, not justified by military necessity and carried out unlawfully and wantonly, constitutes a grave breach of the GC.[516]

5.17.2.1 *Using the Military Objective Definition to Assess Whether the Seizure or Destruction of Enemy Property Is Justified by Military Necessity*. The definition of military objective (that has been developed to assess whether objects may be made the object of attack) may be applied outside the context of attacks to assess whether an object's seizure or destruction is justified by imperative military necessity.[517] After all, if sufficient military necessity exists to justify attacking an object as reflected by that object meeting the definition of military objective, then imperative military necessity would also exist to justify seizing or destroying that object by measures short of attack.

On the other hand, if imperative military necessity justifies the seizure or destruction of an object, that object does not necessarily satisfy the definition of a military objective. Rather, the object must be assessed as to whether it meets the definition of military objective and may be

---

510 *Refer to* § 11.18 (Enemy Property During Occupation).

511 *See, e.g.*, Aris Gloves, Inc. v. United States, 420 F.2d 1386, 1391 (Ct. Cl. 1970) (collecting cases and describing "the general rule that all property located in enemy territory, regardless of its ownership, is in time of war regarded as enemy property subject to the laws of war").

512 HAGUE IV REG. art. 23(g) ("[I]t is especially forbidden: … (g.) To destroy or seize the enemy's property, unless such destruction or seizure be imperatively demanded by the necessities of war;"). For general discussion of military necessity, *refer to* § 2.2 (Military Necessity).

513 1956 FM 27-10 (Change No. 1 1976) ¶56 ("Devastation as an end in itself or as a separate measure of war is not sanctioned by the law of war."); United States v. List, *et al.* (The Hostage Case), XI TRIALS OF WAR CRIMINALS BEFORE THE NMT 1253 ("Destruction as an end in itself is a violation of international law."). *Refer to* § 2.3.1 (*Humanity as a Prohibition*).

514 1956 FM 27-10 (Change No. 1 1976) ¶56 ("The measure of permissible devastation is found in the strict necessities of war.").

515 United States v. List, *et al.* (The Hostage Case), XI TRIALS OF WAR CRIMINALS BEFORE THE NMT 1253-54 ("There must be some reasonable connection between the destruction of property and the overcoming of the enemy forces.").

516 *Refer to* § 18.9.3.1 (Acts Constituting Grave Breaches).

517 *Refer to* § 5.6.5 (Definition of Military Objective for Objects: A Two-Part Test).

made the object of attack.

5.17.2.2 <u>*Seizure or Destruction of Enemy Property to Support Military Operations*</u>. It may be imperatively demanded by the necessities of war to seize or destroy enemy property in order to support military operations. These examples are illustrative and not exhaustive:

- using enemy land for the construction of military bases, air fields, and other facilities to support military operations;[518]

- using enemy buildings to billet military personnel and others supporting them, to house the wounded and sick, for observation and reconnaissance, for concealment and cover, and for defensive purposes;[519]

- demolishing, cutting down, or removing enemy walls, forests, and buildings to clear a field of fire or to provide construction material;[520] or

- seizing means of transportation for use in military operations.[521]

5.17.2.3 <u>*Destruction of Enemy Property to Diminish the Enemy's Ability to Conduct or Sustain Operations*</u>. It may be imperatively demanded by the necessities of war to seize or destroy enemy property in order to diminish the enemy's ability to conduct or sustain operations, such as railways, lines of communication, and other war fighting and war sustaining infrastructure.[522] For instance, Union forces destroyed the Confederacy's cotton during the Civil

---

[518] 1956 FM 27-10 (Change No. 1 1976) ¶56 ("[R]eal estate may be used for marches, camp sites, construction of field fortifications, etc.").

[519] 1956 FM 27-10 (Change No. 1 1976) ¶56 ("Buildings may be destroyed for sanitary purposes or used for shelter for troops, the wounded and sick and vehicles and for reconnaissance, cover, and defense."); LAUTERPACHT, II OPPENHEIM'S INTERNATIONAL LAW 398 (§136) ("So far as the necessities of war demand, a belligerent may make use of public enemy buildings for all kinds of purposes. Troops must be housed, horses stabled, the sick and wounded looked after. Public buildings may in the first instance, therefore, be made use of for such purposes, although they may thereby be considerably damaged."); LAUTERPACHT, II OPPENHEIM'S INTERNATIONAL LAW 403 (§140) ("What has been said above with regard to utilisation of public buildings applies equally to private buildings.").

[520] 1956 FM 27-10 (Change No. 1 1976) ¶56 ("Fences, woods, crops, buildings, etc., may be demolished, cut down, and removed to clear a field of fire, to clear the ground for landing fields, or to furnish building materials or fuel if imperatively needed for the army.").

[521] *For example*, Interview by Robert K. Wright, Jr., Department of the Army, with Col. Barry S. Baer, Commander, 18th Finance Group, in Fort Bragg, N.C. (Mar. 15, 1990), *available at* http://www.history.army.mil/documents/panama/JCIT/JCIT31.htm (recounting how U.S. forces commandeered rental cars in Panama to increase tactical mobility in Operation JUST CAUSE).

[522] United States v. List, *et al.* (The Hostage Case), XI TRIALS OF WAR CRIMINALS BEFORE THE NMT 1254 ("It is lawful to destroy railways, lines of communication, or any other property that might be utilized by the enemy. Private homes and churches even may be destroyed if necessary for military operations."); LIEBER CODE art. 15 ("Military necessity … allows of all destruction of property, and obstruction of the ways and channels of traffic, travel, or communication, and of all withholding of sustenance or means of life from the enemy."). *Compare* § 5.6.6.2 (Make an Effective Contribution to Military Action).

War in order to deprive the Confederacy of the ability to fund its military operations.[523] Similarly, coalition forces during Operation ENDURING FREEDOM destroyed narcotics in order to weaken the Taliban and al Qaeda's ability to finance their operations.[524]

5.17.2.4 *Incidental Damage to Enemy Property*. Military necessity also justifies damage to property incidental to combat operations that is reasonably related to overcoming enemy forces.[525] For example, the movement of armed forces and equipment may damage roads or fields.[526]

5.17.3 Enemy Movable Property on the Battlefield (War Booty). Any enemy public movable property on the battlefield may be seized.[527] Property is public if it belongs to the enemy State or an agency of that State.[528]

---

523 In re Mrs. Alexander's Cotton, 69 U.S. 404, 419-20, 421 (1864) (holding that 72 bales of cotton taken from a barn by Union naval forces could lawfully be captured as enemy property based on "the peculiar character of the property" as "one of [the rebels'] main sinews of war," but that the cotton was not a maritime prize because it had been captured on land).

524 International Security Assistance Force (ISAF) Joint Command – Afghanistan, *Press Release: Combined Force Finds, Destroys Drugs, Weapons Cache* (Sept. 7, 2010) (describing a patrol's destruction of a cache of opium and weapons in order to "significantly reduce[] the insurgent's ability to ... procure financial resources"); April Campbell, *Afghan Forces Becoming Increasingly Effective Against Drug Producers*, AFGHANISTAN INTERNATIONAL SECURITY ASSISTANCE FORCE – NEWS (Sept. 29, 2011) (describing Afghan counter-narcotics forces' seizure and destruction of narcotics laboratories and narcotics as "dealing a significant blow to the insurgency's ability to fund operations").

525 *See also* GREENSPAN, MODERN LAW OF LAND WARFARE 282-83 ("While the seizure or destruction of enemy personnel and war material are actual objectives of warfare, the operations of war must also result in the incidental destruction and seizure of much property, not as the prime object of attack, but which becomes involved in the struggle. ... Troops march, ride, and fight wherever the battle takes them, whether over fields of growing crops or in the streets of cities, towns, or villages. Land is used for camp sites, entrenchments, and other defenses constructed in or on it, streets may be torn up, bridges demolished, dwellings and factories converted into strong points, furniture and bedding may provide the cover for a sharpshooter hidden in some dwelling. Practically every shell or bomb that explodes damages property in one form or another, whether or not it attains its objective. Most bullets that are fired strike, not humans, but property. Each missile that is launched must finally come to earth somewhere.").

526 *See, e.g.*, 1956 FM 27-10 (Change No. 1 1976) ¶56 (explaining that "the rule requiring respect for private property is not violated through damage resulting from operations, movements, or combat activity of the army"); 1958 UK MANUAL ¶589 ("The rule that private property must be respected admits, however, of exceptions necessitated by the exigencies of war. In the first instance, practically every operation, movement or combat occasions damage to private property."); LAUTERPACHT, II OPPENHEIM'S INTERNATIONAL LAW 414 (§151) ("Destruction of enemy property in marching troops, in conducting military transport, and in reconnoitring, is lawful if unavoidable. A reconnoitring party need not keep on the road if they can better serve their purpose by riding across tilled fields. Troops may be marched, and transport may be conducted, over crops when necessary. A humane commander will not unnecessarily allow his troops and transport to march and ride over tilled fields and crops. But if the purpose of war necessitates it, he is justified in so doing.").

527 1956 FM 27-10 (Change No. 1 1976) ¶59a ("All enemy public movable property captured or found on a battlefield becomes the property of the capturing State."); LAUTERPACHT, II OPPENHEIM'S INTERNATIONAL LAW 402 (§139) ("[Movable] public enemy property on the battlefield may be appropriated by belligerents.").

528 *See, e.g.*, William Gerald Downey, Jr., *Captured Enemy Property: Booty of War and Seized Enemy Property*, 44 AJIL 488, 489 (1950) ("Enemy *public* property is defined as chattels, the title to which is vested in a state or in any agency of such state.").

In general, enemy private movable property on the battlefield may be seized if the property is susceptible to direct military use, *i.e.*, it is necessary and indispensable for the conduct of war.[529] This includes arms, ammunition, military papers, or property that can be used as military equipment (*e.g.*, as a means of transportation or communication).[530] However, certain types of military equipment used for clothing, feeding, or personal protection (*e.g.*, helmets and gas masks) may not be seized from POWs, and should remain in their possession.[531]

5.17.3.1 *Private Military Property Not Susceptible to Direct Military Use*. Private enemy property that is not susceptible to direct military use (*e.g.*, arms, ammunition, military papers, or military equipment) may be appropriated only to the extent such taking is permissible in occupied areas.[532] In particular, receipts should be given and compensation paid, when feasible.[533]

5.17.3.2 *Ownership of Captured or Found Property on the Battlefield*. All enemy property that is captured or found on the battlefield becomes the property of the capturing State.[534] During international armed conflict, personal property recovered from enemy dead becomes the property of the capturing State for the purpose of returning it to the next-of-kin of the deceased.[535] The individual military member or person accompanying the armed forces who captures or finds enemy property acquires no title or claim.[536]

---

529 *See* Menzel v. List, 267 N.Y.S.2d 804, 820 (N.Y. Sup. Ct. 1966) ("*Booty* is defined as property necessary and indispensable for the conduct of war, such as food, means of transportation, and means of communication; and is lawfully taken.").

530 1958 UK MANUAL ¶615 ("Private enemy property on the battlefield is not (as it was in former times) in every case booty. Arms and ammunition and military equipment and papers are booty, even if they are the property of individuals, but cash, jewellery, and other private articles of value are not."); GREENSPAN, MODERN LAW OF LAND WARFARE 281 ("Private property in the following categories belonging to members of the enemy forces falls within the description of booty: arms, horses, military equipment, and military documents."); LAUTERPACHT, II OPPENHEIM'S INTERNATIONAL LAW 406 (§144) ("Private enemy property on the battlefield is no longer in every case an object of booty. Arms, horses, and military papers may indeed be appropriated, even if they are private property, as may also private means of transport, such as cars and other vehicles which an enemy may make use of.").

531 *Refer to* § 9.7 (POW Effects and Articles of Personal Use).

532 *See* 1956 FM 27-10 (Change No. 1 1976) ¶59b ("Enemy private movable property, other than arms, military papers, horses, and the like captured or found on a battlefield, may be appropriated only to the extent that such taking is permissible in occupied areas."). *Refer to* § 11.18.6 (Treatment of Enemy Private Property).

533 *Refer to* § 11.18.6.2 (Seizure of Private Property Susceptible to Direct Military Use).

534 1956 FM 27-10 (Change No. 1 1976) ¶59a-b (providing that "[a]ll enemy public movable property captured or found on a battlefield becomes the property of the capturing State" and that "[e]nemy private movable property, other than arms, military papers, horses, and the like captured or found on a battlefield, may be appropriated only to the extent that such taking is permissible in occupied areas (see pars. 405-411)."); 1956 FM 27-10 (Change No. 1 1976) ¶396 ("Public property captured or seized from the enemy, as well as private property validly captured on the battlefield and abandoned property, is property of the United States … ."); 1958 UK MANUAL ¶615 ("Public enemy property found or captured on a battlefield becomes, as a general rule, the property of the opposing belligerent.").

535 *Refer to* § 7.7.2.2 (Forwarding Valuable Articles Found on the Dead).

536 Foster v. United States, 98 F. Supp. 349, 352 (Ct. Cl. 1951) ("[A] soldier may not make a profit out of the disorder and flight which ensues from war. In the abandoned property which he comes upon, and which he must

Failure to turn over such property to the proper authorities, or disposal of such property for personal profit, is punishable under Article 103 of the Uniform Code of Military Justice.[537]

5.17.4 Pillage Prohibited. Pillage is prohibited, both in general[538] and specifically with respect to:

- the wounded, sick, shipwrecked, and dead;[539]
- POWs;[540]
- protected persons under the GC;[541]
- persons in occupied territory[542] and in areas of non-international armed conflict;[543] and
- cultural property.[544]

In certain cases, there is an affirmative obligation to prohibit and prevent pillage.[545]

5.17.4.1 *Pillage – Definition and Notes on Terminology*. *Pillage* is the taking of private or public movable property (including enemy military equipment) for private or personal

---

turn over to the proper authority without delay, he does not acquire any proprietary interest. His taking possession of it is done as an agent of the Government, and if it is not reclaimed by the owner who abandoned it, it belongs to the Government.").

[537] *See* 10 U.S.C. § 903 ("(a) All persons subject to this chapter shall secure all public property taken from the enemy for the service of the United States, and shall give notice and turn over to the proper authority without delay all captured or abandoned property in their possession, custody, or control. (b) Any person subject to this chapter who—(1) fails to carry out the duties prescribed in subsection (a); (2) buys, sells, trades, or in any way deals in or disposes of captured or abandoned property, whereby he receives or expects any profit, benefit, or advantage to himself or another directly or indirectly connected with himself; or (3) engages in looting or pillaging; shall be punished as a court-martial may direct.").

[538] *See, e.g.*, HAGUE IV REG. art. 28 ("The pillage of a town or place, even when taken by assault, is prohibited."); 1899 HAGUE II art. 28 (same); LIEBER CODE art. 44 ("[A]ll robbery, all pillage or sacking, even after taking a place by main force … are prohibited under the penalty of death, or such other severe punishment as may seem adequate for the gravity of the offense.").

[539] *Refer to* § 7.4.2 (Affirmative Measures to Protect Against Pillage and Ill-Treatment); § 7.7.2.1 (Measures to Prevent the Dead From Being Despoiled); § 17.14.3 (Search, Collection, and Protection of the Wounded, Sick, Shipwrecked, and Dead).

[540] *Refer to* § 9.7 (POW Effects and Articles of Personal Use).

[541] *Refer to* § 10.5.3.3 (Pillage Against Protected Persons).

[542] *Refer to* § 11.18.1 (Prohibition Against Pillage in Occupied Territory).

[543] *Refer to* § 17.6.4 (Prohibition on Pillage).

[544] *Refer to* § 5.18.6 (Prohibition Against and Prevention of Theft, Pillage, Misappropriation, or Acts of Vandalism, and Prohibition Against Requisition of Foreign Cultural Property).

[545] *Refer to* § 5.18.6.1 (Obligation to Stop or Prevent Theft, Pillage, or Misappropriation of, and Acts of Vandalism Against, Cultural Property); § 7.4.2 (Affirmative Measures to Protect Against Pillage and Ill-Treatment); § 17.14.3 (Search, Collection, and Protection of the Wounded, Sick, Shipwrecked, and Dead).

use.[546] It does not include an appropriation of property justified by military necessity.[547] For example, if ordinary requisitions are unavailable, the taking of food does not constitute pillage.[548] Pillage also has been referred to as "looting"[549] and "plunder."[550]

5.17.4.2 *History of Pillage*. In the medieval era, pillage served as a form of compensation for private armies, but it ceased to be regarded as lawful with the widespread adoption of standing armies at the end of the Eighteenth Century. The prohibition on pillage has, in part, been intended to maintain discipline among the armed forces.[551] For example, a member of the armed forces who before or in the presence of the enemy quits his or her place of duty to plunder or pillage is guilty of the offense of misbehavior before the enemy.[552]

5.17.5 Feasible Precautions Should Be Taken to Mitigate the Burden on Civilians. In seizing or destroying enemy property, feasible precautions should be taken to mitigate the burdens imposed on civilians.

For example, in the practice of the United States, religious buildings, shrines, and consecrated places employed for worship are used only for aid stations, medical installations, or

---

[546] 10 U.S.C. § 950t(5) ("(5) PILLAGING.--Any person subject to this chapter who intentionally and in the absence of military necessity appropriates or seizes property for private or personal use, without the consent of a person with authority to permit such appropriation or seizure, shall be punished…."). *Consider* ROME STATUTE, ELEMENTS OF CRIMES, art. 8(2)(b)(xvi), Official Records of the Assembly of States Parties to the Rome Statute of the International Criminal Court, First session, New York, ICC-ASP/1/3, 112, 145-6 (Sept. 3-10, 2002) (defining the elements of the war crime of pillaging as including (1) appropriation of property, (2) intent "to deprive the owner of the property and to appropriate it for private or personal use," and (3) "appropriation … without the consent of the owner").

[547] *Consider* ROME STATUTE, ELEMENTS OF CRIMES art. 8(2)(b)(xvi), Official Records of the Assembly of States Parties to the Rome Statute of the International Criminal Court, First session, New York, ICC-ASP/1/3, 112, 146 footnote 47 (Sept. 3-10, 2002) ("As indicated by the use of the term 'private or personal use', appropriations justified by military necessity cannot constitute the crime of pillaging.").

[548] LAUTERPACHT, II OPPENHEIM'S INTERNATIONAL LAW 405 (§143) ("If there is no time for ordinary requisitions to provide food, forage, clothing, and fuel, or if the inhabitants of a locality have fled so that ordinary requisitions cannot be made, a belligerent must take these articles wherever he can get them, and he is justified in so doing."). *Refer to* § 11.18.7 (Requisitions of Private Enemy Property).

[549] 10 U.S.C. § 903 ("(b) Any person subject to this chapter who- ... (3) engages in looting or pillaging; shall be punished as a court-martial may direct."); MANUAL FOR COURTS-MARTIAL IV-40 (¶27.c.(4)) (2012) ("'Looting or pillaging' means unlawfully seizing or appropriating property which is located in enemy or occupied territory.").

[550] *See, e.g.*, MANUAL FOR COURTS-MARTIAL IV-35 (¶23.c.(6)(b)) (2012) ("'Plunder or pillage' means to seize or appropriate public or private property unlawfully."); Prosecutor v. Jelisić, ICTY Trial Chamber, IT-95-10-T, *Judgment*, ¶¶48-49 (Dec. 14, 1999) (noting that "[p]lunder is defined as the fraudulent appropriation of public or private funds belonging to the enemy or the opposing party perpetrated during an armed conflict and related thereto" and confirming the guilt of the accused on the charge of plunder because he "stole money, watches, jewellery and other valuables from the detainees upon their arrival at Luka camp by threatening those who did not hand over their possessions with death").

[551] 1958 UK MANUAL ¶589 (noting that the prohibitions contained in Hague IV Regulations "did not constitute new rules at the time they were promulgated" and that "it has for a long time past been embodied in the regulations of every civilized army, for nothing is more demoralizing to troops or more subversive of discipline than plundering.").

[552] 10 U.S.C. § 899 ("Any member of the armed forces who before or in the presence of the enemy— … (6) quits his place of duty to plunder or pillage; … shall be punished by death or such other punishment as a court-martial may direct.").

the housing of wounded personnel awaiting evacuation, provided in each case that a situation of emergency requires such use.[553]

Similarly, if armed forces use a private residence, they must treat its inhabitants and owners humanely and with as much consideration as the circumstances permit.[554] In particular, the armed forces should generally allow the inhabitants to continue to live in part of their own homes, and should not expel them in the absence of alternate shelter.[555] But if imperative military necessity requires the removal of the inhabitants, then efforts should be made to give them notice and to aid them in taking their essential possessions.[556] If the armed forces take anything, they should leave a note to this effect.[557]

However, there is no obligation to protect abandoned property in the area of active operations.[558]

5.17.5.1 <u>*Compensation for Property Seizure or Damage*</u>. Although reasonable efforts should be made to spare civilians from unnecessary harm when seizing or destroying enemy property, the law of war imposes no obligation to compensate for loss of, or damage to, private property imperatively demanded by the necessities of war, including damage incidental to combat operations.[559] However, if time allows, a record of the use or damage should be kept, or given to the owner, so that in the event of funds being provided by either belligerent at the

---

[553] *Refer to* § 11.18.6.4 (Municipal, Religious, Charitable, and Cultural Property).

[554] GREENSPAN, MODERN LAW OF LAND WARFARE 283 ("Where private dwellings are taken over by troops, the inhabitants must be treated humanely and afforded as much consideration as the circumstances permit."). *For example*, DICK COUCH, THE SHERIFF OF RAMADI 69 (2008) ("'On yet another SR [special reconnaissance] mission, we had intelligence that a restaurant was being used as a meeting place for insurgents, but there were a lot of other Iraqis coming and going there as well. We needed an OP [observation post] that was close to the restaurant but not too close -- a secure perch from which we could observe the target for several days and still be safe from informers. We found this three-story house that was several hundred yards from the restaurant entrance. It was perfect. We sent one of our interpreters to speak with the residents and to make arrangements to use one of their upper-floor rooms for a few days. We paid them well, but the key was that after being coached by the terp and our scouts, we were very polite and respectful of their customs.'") (second alteration in original).

[555] 1958 UK MANUAL ¶615 ("When troops are quartered in private dwellings some rooms should be left to the inhabitants; the latter should not be driven into the streets and left without shelter.").

[556] 1958 UK MANUAL ¶615 ("If for military reasons, whether for operational purposes or to protect men and animals from the weather, it is imperative to remove the inhabitants, efforts should be made to give them notice and provide them with facilities for taking essential baggage with them.").

[557] 1958 UK MANUAL ¶615 ("A note should be left if anything is taken."); GREENSPAN, MODERN LAW OF LAND WARFARE 284 ("For anything validly taken, a note to this effect should be left.").

[558] 1958 UK MANUAL ¶615 ("There is … no obligation to protect abandoned property."); GREENSPAN, MODERN LAW OF LAND Warfare 284 ("[T]here is no obligation on the part of the invader to protect abandoned property in the area of active operations … .").

[559] *See, e.g.*, 1958 UK MANUAL ¶593 ("The owner of property may claim neither rent for its use nor compensation for damage caused by the necessities of war.").

close of hostilities to compensate the owners, there may be evidence to assist the assessors.[560]

As a matter of practice, during counter-insurgency operations, U.S. forces have often made payments to, or taken other actions on behalf of, civilians suffering loss.[561]

5.18 Protection of Cultural Property During Hostilities

Certain types of property receive additional protection as cultural property. Cultural property, the areas immediately surrounding it, and appliances in use for its protection should be safeguarded and respected.

Some obligations with respect to cultural property apply during non-international armed conflict.[562] There are also obligations with respect to cultural property during occupation[563] and peacetime.[564] Certain treaty obligations with respect to cultural property may only apply on the territory of Parties to the 1954 Hague Cultural Property Convention,[565] but the United States has previously identified some of these obligations as customary international law.[566] DoD personnel, therefore, in the absence of contrary guidance by competent authority, should act as if they were legally bound by the rules for the protection of cultural property in the 1954 Hague Cultural Property Convention during hostilities even when conducting operations in the territory of a State that is not a Party to the 1954 Hague Cultural Property Convention.[567]

5.18.1 Definition of Cultural Property. For the purpose of the 1954 Hague Cultural Property Convention and this manual, cultural property includes, irrespective of origin or ownership:[568]

---

[560] 1958 UK Manual ¶593 ("If time allows, however, a note of the use or damage should be kept, or given to the owner, so that in the event of funds being provided by either belligerent at the close of hostilities to compensate the inhabitants, there may be evidence to assist the assessors.").

[561] *For example*, Department of the Army Field Manual 3-24.2, *Tactics in Counterinsurgency*, ¶7-89 (Apr. 2009) ("Recent experiences have shown the effectiveness of using money to win popular support and further the interests and goals of units conducting counterinsurgency operations. … A counterinsurgency force can use money to … • Repair damage resulting from combined and coalition operations. • Provide condolence payments to civilians for casualties from combined and coalition operations.").

[562] *Refer to* § 17.11 (Protection of Cultural Property in NIAC).

[563] *Refer to* § 11.19 (Protection of Cultural Property During Occupation).

[564] *Refer to* § 5.18.2.1 (Peacetime Obligations to Prepare for the Safeguarding of Cultural Property).

[565] *See, e.g.*, 1954 Hague Cultural Property Convention art. 4(1) ("The High Contracting Parties undertake to respect cultural property situated within their own territory as well as within the territory of other High Contracting Parties.").

[566] *Refer to* § 5.18.8 (Special Protection for Certain Cultural Property).

[567] *Refer to* § 3.1.1 (DoD Practice of Applying Law of War Rules Even When Not Technically Applicable).

[568] 1954 Hague Cultural Property Convention art. 1 ("For the purposes of the present Convention, the term 'cultural property' shall cover, irrespective of origin or ownership: (a) movable or immovable property of great importance to the cultural heritage of every people, such as monuments of architecture, art or history, whether religious or secular; archaeological sites; groups of buildings which, as a whole, are of historical or artistic interest; works of art; manuscripts, books and other objects of artistic, historical or archaeological interest; as well as

- movable or immovable property of great importance to the cultural heritage of every people;[569]
- buildings intended to shelter cultural property;[570] and
- centers containing monuments.[571]

5.18.1.1 Definition of Cultural Property – Notes on Terminology. "Cultural property" is a term of art that is defined in the 1954 Hague Cultural Property Convention. The definition in the 1954 Hague Cultural Property Convention may be more limited than cultural property described and protected by other instruments.

For example, the Lieber Code contemplates protection for property belonging to "establishments of an exclusively charitable character, to establishments of education, or foundations for the promotion of knowledge, whether public schools, universities, academies of learning or observatories, museums of the fine arts, or of a scientific character," as well as "[c]lassical works of art, libraries, scientific collections, or precious instruments, such as astronomical telescopes."[572] The Hague IV Regulations seek to protect "buildings dedicated to religion, art, science, or charitable purposes, historic monuments."[573] Hague IX seeks to protect "sacred edifices, buildings used for artistic, scientific, or charitable purposes, [and] historic monuments."[574] The Roerich Pact seeks to protect "historic monuments, museums, scientific, artistic, educational and cultural institutions."[575] AP I seeks to protect "historic monuments, works of art or places of worship which constitute the cultural or spiritual heritage of peoples."[576]

Because the definition of cultural property in the 1954 Hague Cultural Property Convention is different from the categories of property protected by other instruments, the scope of objects being protected by each instrument is not the same (although there may be overlap). Nevertheless, the protections afforded cultural property by the 1954 Hague Cultural Property Convention are supplementary to those afforded by earlier treaties, although the distinctive

---

scientific collections and important collections of books or archives or of reproductions of the property defined above; (b) buildings whose main and effective purpose is to preserve or exhibit the movable cultural property defined in sub-paragraph (a) such as museums, large libraries and depositories of archives, and refuges intended to shelter, in the event of armed conflict, the movable cultural property defined in subparagraph (a); (c) centres containing a large amount of cultural property as defined in sub-paragraphs (a) and (b), to be known as 'centres containing monuments'.").

569 *Refer to* § 5.18.1.2 (Movable or Immovable Property of Great Importance to the Cultural Heritage of Every People).

570 *Refer to* § 5.18.1.3 (Buildings Intended to Preserve Cultural Property).

571 *Refer to* § 5.18.1.4 (Centers Containing Monuments).

572 LIEBER CODE arts. 34-36.

573 HAGUE IV REG. art. 27.

574 HAGUE IX art. 5.

575 ROERICH PACT art. 1.

576 AP I art. 53.

emblem for cultural property established in the 1954 Hague Cultural Property Convention is to be used where appropriate instead of emblems established in earlier treaties.[577]

5.18.1.2 Movable or Immovable Property of Great Importance to the Cultural Heritage of Every People. Property must be "of great importance to the cultural heritage of every people" to qualify as cultural property. Ordinary property (such as churches or works of art) that are not of great importance to the cultural heritage of every people would not qualify as cultural property, although such property may benefit from other protections, such as those afforded civilian objects or enemy property.[578]

The question of whether cultural property is "of great importance to the cultural heritage of every people" may involve delicate and somewhat subjective judgments.[579] Items that can easily be replaced would not qualify as being of great importance.[580] On the other hand, irreplaceable items may be of great cultural importance, even if they have little monetary value.[581]

Cultural property may include, but is not limited to, the following types of property (provided the property is of great importance to the cultural heritage of every people):

- monuments of architecture, art, or history, whether religious or secular;[582]
- archaeological sites;
- groups of buildings that, as a whole, are of historical or artistic interest;[583]

---

[577] *Refer to* § 19.17.1 (Relationship Between the 1954 Hague Cultural Property Convention and Earlier Treaties).

[578] *Refer to* § 5.5.2 (Persons, Objects, and Locations That Are Protected From Being Made the Object of Attack); § 5.17 (Seizure and Destruction of Enemy Property).

[579] *See* ROGERS, LAW ON THE BATTLEFIELD 90 ("It must be property of great importance to the cultural heritage of every people. This may involve delicate decisions about whether, for example, an original manuscript by a minor composer, say Spohr, was of great importance to the cultural heritage of every people, perhaps not. The situation would be different if it were an original manuscript by one of the great composers, say Schubert.").

[580] *See* JIRI TOMAN, CULTURAL PROPERTY IN WARTIME 50 (1996) ("Certain objects, although of limited value, may be important for the national culture while others, even though of great value, can be replaced and are therefore less important.").

[581] *For example*, JIRI TOMAN, CULTURAL PROPERTY IN WARTIME 49-50 (1996) ("[A] papyrus reporting a marriage that took place three thousand years ago, although it was of no intrinsic cultural value, was of very great cultural importance because of the fact that it enabled an institution, on which no such ancient information existed, to be studied.") (internal quotation marks omitted).

[582] *See also* JIRI TOMAN, CULTURAL PROPERTY IN WARTIME 50-51 (1996) ("[W]orks of architecture, sculpture, specially designed to perpetuate the memory of a person, action, period, event or thing, or as buildings, structures, edifices remarkable for their archaeological, historical or aesthetic interest or intended to commemorate a notable person, action or event.").

[583] *See also* JIRI TOMAN, CULTURAL PROPERTY IN WARTIME 51 (1996) (During the drafting of the 1954 Hague Cultural Property Convention "the Scandinavian countries proposed the protection of certain sites which, although not containing particularly remarkable monuments, were of undoubted value from a cultural point of view and for that reason had a right to be protected. It was explained that the Scandinavian countries had very little cultural

- works of art;
- manuscripts, books, and other objects of artistic, historical, or archaeological interest;
- scientific collections;[584] and
- important collections of books or archives or of reproductions of the property defined above.[585]

Natural sites of great beauty are not included within the definition of cultural property.[586]

5.18.1.3 _Buildings Intended to Preserve Cultural Property_. Cultural property is also understood to include buildings whose main and effective purpose is to preserve or exhibit movable cultural property, such as museums, large libraries, and depositories of archives, and refuges intended to shelter cultural property in the event of armed conflict.[587]

For these types of buildings, protection is gained from the structure's purpose and contents as opposed to the physical structure itself constituting immovable property of great importance to the cultural heritage of every people. The building must be intended to contain and, in fact, contain, conserve, or exhibit movable cultural property as its primary purpose.[588] Alternatively, the structure may be intended to store movable cultural property for protection in the event of armed conflict. Some of these refuges may be subject to special protection.[589]

---

property and that their gift to culture consisted mainly in distant mediaeval villages or lonely farms.") (internal quotation marks omitted).

[584] *See also* JIRI TOMAN, CULTURAL PROPERTY IN WARTIME 52 (1996) (Scientific "collections are made up of scientific books but also cover other objects such as Boissier's herbarium in Geneva or the collections of important laboratories ... [and] national monuments that were objects of valuable scientific research, such as rare animals or plants that were becoming extinct.").

[585] *See also* JIRI TOMAN, CULTURAL PROPERTY IN WARTIME 52 (1996) ("[P]rotection is accorded to important collections of books without their necessarily having to be of artistic, historical or archaeological interest. Any important library is thus protected, probably in the spirit of protecting human knowledge.").

[586] *See* JIRI TOMAN, CULTURAL PROPERTY IN WARTIME 53 (1996) ("The [1954 Hague Cultural Property] Conference also discussed the protection of 'natural sites of great beauty' (United States of America and Japan), but appears to have given up the idea for reasons mentioned by the delegation of France, who considered that 'it was probably difficult to define the protection of natural sites as their value was of a subjective nature. At best, only a diluted form of protection could result. Finally, it had been observed that natural sites could often be restored very quickly.").

[587] 1954 HAGUE CULTURAL PROPERTY CONVENTION art. 1(b) (defining the term cultural property to include, *inter alia*, "buildings whose main and effective purpose is to preserve or exhibit the movable cultural property defined in sub-paragraph (a) such as museums, large libraries and depositories of archives, and refuges intended to shelter, in the event of armed conflict, the movable cultural property defined in subparagraph (a)").

[588] *See* JIRI TOMAN, CULTURAL PROPERTY IN WARTIME 53-54 (1996) ("According to subparagraph (b), such buildings are protected not because of their own historical value but because of their purpose and their content. The purpose must be the primary one, the very aim and *raison d'etre* of such a building; it must also be effectively true -- the building must in fact contain, conserve or exhibit movable cultural property.").

[589] *Refer to* § 5.18.8 (Special Protection for Certain Cultural Property).

5.18.1.4 *Centers Containing Monuments*. Cultural property also includes centers containing monuments, *i.e.*, centers containing a large amount of cultural property or buildings intended to preserve cultural property.[590] This includes monument complexes or major groups of buildings containing movable and immovable cultural property.

5.18.2 Respect and Safeguarding of Cultural Property. The protection of cultural property comprises the safeguarding of and respect for such property.[591] Safeguarding consists of the affirmative acts that are to be taken to ensure the protection of cultural property.[592] On the other hand, respect essentially requires parties to refrain from certain acts, such as placing cultural property in peril or causing damage to it.[593]

Safeguarding and respect are mutually reinforcing obligations that help ensure the protection of cultural property.

5.18.2.1 *Peacetime Obligations to Prepare for the Safeguarding of Cultural Property*. Parties to 1954 Hague Cultural Property Convention are obliged to undertake to prepare in time of peace for the safeguarding of cultural property situated within their own territory against the foreseeable effects of an armed conflict, by taking such measures as they consider appropriate.[594] This obligation reflects the opinion that measures for the protection of cultural property during armed conflict, in order to be effective, must begin in peacetime.[595]

The failure of a State to fulfill its obligations in peacetime to safeguard cultural property during armed conflict does not relieve other States of their obligation to respect cultural

---

[590] 1954 HAGUE CULTURAL PROPERTY CONVENTION art. 1(c) (defining the term cultural property to include, *inter alia*, "centres containing a large amount of cultural property as defined in sub-paragraphs (a) and (b) to be known as 'centres containing monuments'"). *See also* JIRI TOMAN, CULTURAL PROPERTY IN WARTIME 54 (1996) ("The term 'centres containing monuments' was preferred to the terms 'groups' or 'groups of buildings' when the reference was to larger areas containing a considerable amount of cultural property coming under subparagraphs (a) and (b). The term comprises a group of historical or artistic monuments situated in the same vicinity, such as the districts of certain cities or even entire cities.").

[591] 1954 HAGUE CULTURAL PROPERTY CONVENTION art. 2 ("For the purposes of the present Convention, the protection of cultural property shall comprise the safeguarding of and respect for such property.").

[592] JIRI TOMAN, CULTURAL PROPERTY IN WARTIME 57 (1996) ("'Safeguarding' consists of all the positive measures (defining the action to be taken) which are designed to ensure the best possible material conditions for the protection of cultural property.").

[593] JIRI TOMAN, CULTURAL PROPERTY IN WARTIME 57 (1996) ("Respect ... has an essentially negative character: it represents an obligation not to commit a number of prohibited acts. Respect therefore implies a requirement to refrain from certain acts, such as placing cultural property in peril or causing damage to it.").

[594] 1954 HAGUE CULTURAL PROPERTY CONVENTION art. 3 ("The High Contracting Parties undertake to prepare in time of peace for the safeguarding of cultural property situated within their own territory against the foreseeable effects of an armed conflict, by taking such measures as they consider appropriate.").

[595] 1954 HAGUE CULTURAL PROPERTY CONVENTION preamble ("Guided by the principles concerning the protection of cultural property during armed conflict, as established in the Conventions of The Hague of 1899 and of 1907 and in the Washington Pact of 15 April, 1935; Being of the opinion that such protection cannot be effective unless both national and international measures have been taken to organize it in time of peace;").

property.[596]

5.18.3 Refraining From Any Use for Purposes That Are Likely to Expose It to Destruction or Damage. In general, no use should be made of cultural property, its immediate surroundings, or appliances in use for its protection, for purposes that are likely to expose it to destruction or damage in the event of armed conflict.[597] However, such use is permissible when military necessity imperatively requires such use.[598]

Uses that would be likely to expose cultural property to destruction or damage in the event of armed conflict would include: (1) using the cultural property for military purposes;[599] (2) placing military objectives near cultural property; or (3) using the cultural property in such a way that an adversary would likely regard it as a military objective.[600] For example, such uses would include billeting military personnel in buildings that constitute cultural property, or emplacing artillery, mortars, or anti-air systems on the grounds of cultural property.

In addition, it is prohibited to use deliberately the threat of potential harm to cultural property to shield military objectives from attack, or otherwise to shield, favor, or impede military operations.[601] There is no waiver of this obligation in cases of imperative military necessity.

5.18.3.1 *Imperative Military Necessity Waiver*. Cultural property, its immediate surroundings, and appliances in use for its protection may be used for purposes that are likely to expose it to destruction or damage if military necessity imperatively requires such use. The requirement that military necessity imperatively require such acts should not be confused with convenience or be used to cloak slackness or indifference to the preservation of cultural property.[602] This waiver of obligations with respect to cultural property is analogous to the

---

[596] 1954 HAGUE CULTURAL PROPERTY CONVENTION art. 4(5) ("No High Contracting Party may evade the obligations incumbent upon it under the present Article, in respect of another High Contracting Party, by reason of the fact that the latter as not applied the measures of safeguard referred to in Article 3.").

[597] 1954 HAGUE CULTURAL PROPERTY CONVENTION art. 4(1) ("The High Contracting Parties undertake to respect cultural property situated within their own territory as well as within the territory of other High Contracting Parties by refraining from any use of the property and its immediate surroundings or of the appliances in use for its protection for purposes which are likely to expose it to destruction or damage in the event of armed conflict … .").

[598] 1954 HAGUE CULTURAL PROPERTY CONVENTION art. 4(2) ("The obligations mentioned in paragraph 1 of the present Article may be waived only in cases where military necessity imperatively requires such a waiver.").

[599] *Compare* § 5.18.8.2 (Conditions for the Granting of Special Protection – No Use for Military Purposes).

[600] *Refer to* § 5.6 (Military Objectives).

[601] *Refer to* § 5.16 (Prohibition on Using Protected Persons and Objects to Shield, Favor, or Impede Military Operations).

[602] *See* General Dwight D. Eisenhower, Commander-in-Chief, U.S. Army, *Memorandum Regarding the Protection of Historical Monuments in Italy*, Dec. 29, 1943, X WHITEMAN'S DIGEST 438 (§13) ("If we have to choose between destroying a famous building and sacrificing our own men, then our men's lives count infinitely more and the building must go. But the choice is not always so clear-cut as that. In many cases the monuments can be spared without any detriment to operational needs. Nothing can stand against the argument of military necessity. That is an accepted principle. But the phrase 'military necessity' is sometimes used where it would be more truthful to speak of military convenience or even personal convenience. I do not want it to cloak slackness or indifference.").

requirement that enemy property may only be seized or destroyed if imperatively required by the necessities of war.[603]

5.18.4 Other Feasible Precautions to Reduce the Risk of Harm to Cultural Property. Other feasible precautions should be taken to reduce the risk of harm to cultural property.[604] Such precautions may include:

- determining the location of cultural property and disseminating that information among the armed forces;[605]
- compiling and promulgating lists of cultural property and areas that are not to be attacked;[606]
- establishing civil authorities to assume responsibility for planning and acting to ensure respect for cultural property under its control;[607]
- physically shielding cultural property from harm; and
- establishing refuges and evacuating movable cultural property to them.[608]

5.18.5 Refraining From Any Act of Hostility. In general, acts of hostility may not be directed against cultural property, its immediate surroundings, or appliances in use for its

---

[603] *Refer to* § 5.17.2 (Enemy Property – Military Necessity Standard). For general discussion of military necessity *refer to* § 2.2 (Military Necessity).

[604] *Refer to* § 5.2.3 (Affirmative Duties to Take Feasible Precautions for the Protection of Civilians and Other Protected Persons and Objects).

[605] *For example*, General Dwight D. Eisenhower, Commander-in-Chief, U.S. Army, *Memorandum Regarding the Protection of Historical Monuments in Italy*, Dec. 29, 1943, X WHITEMAN'S DIGEST 438 (§13) ("It is a responsibility of higher commanders to determine through A.M.G. Officers the locations of historical monuments whether they be immediately ahead of our front lines or in areas occupied by us. This information passed to lower echelons through normal channels places the responsibility on all Commanders of complying with the spirit of this letter.").

[606] *For example*, Strobe Talbot, *Letter of Submittal*, May 12, 1998, MESSAGE FROM THE PRESIDENT TRANSMITTING THE 1954 HAGUE CULTURAL PROPERTY CONVENTION VIII (1999) ("During Operation Desert Storm, for example, intelligence resources were utilized to look for cultural property in order to properly identify it. Target intelligence officers identified cultural property or cultural property sites in Iraq; a 'no-strike' target list was prepared, placing known cultural property off limits from attack, as well as some otherwise legitimate targets if their attack might place nearby cultural property at risk of damage."); 7th Air Force Operations Order 71-17 (Rules of Engagement), *reprinted in* 121 CONGRESSIONAL RECORD 17555 (Jun. 6, 1975) (specifying during the Vietnam War "Angkor Wat Park: This area will not be attacked for any reason. Under no circumstances will [forward air controllers] control or assist air strikes of any nation within the Angkor Wat area. Should a [forward air controller] observe such a strike being made, he will advise the [Forces Armée Nationale Khmer] ground commander and depart the area immediately. Other Areas of Cultural Value: Except during [combat search and rescue] operations, no U.S. air strikes will be made within 1,000 meters of any of the areas of cultural value [nearly 100 other sites specifically listed in the directive]. U.S. [forward air controllers] will not control or assist air strikes of any nation within 1,000 meters of these areas regardless of [Forces Armée Nationale Khmer] request of validation.").

[607] These include museum curators and staff, local fire and law enforcement authorities, and civil defense personnel.

[608] *Refer to* § 5.18.1.3 (Buildings Intended to Preserve Cultural Property).

protection.[609] Acts of hostility may, however, be directed against cultural property, its immediate surroundings, or appliances in use for its protection, when military necessity imperatively requires such acts.[610]

5.18.5.1 _Imperative Military Necessity Waiver_. Acts of hostility may be directed against cultural property, its immediate surroundings, or appliances in use for its protection when military necessity imperatively requires such acts. The requirement that military necessity imperatively require such acts should not be confused with convenience or be used to cloak slackness or indifference to the preservation of cultural property.[611] This waiver of obligations with respect to cultural property is analogous to the requirement that enemy property may only be seized if imperatively required by the necessities of war.[612]

For example, if cultural property is being used by an opposing force for military purposes, then military necessity generally would imperatively require its seizure or destruction.[613]

Similarly, if an opposing force uses cultural property and its immediate surroundings to protect military objectives, then the attack of those military objectives may be imperatively required by military necessity.[614] Or, if a military objective was located near cultural property, the protection afforded the area surrounding the cultural property could be subject to waiver for reasons of imperative military necessity such that the attack of the military objective would be permissible, despite its proximity to cultural property.[615]

---

[609] 1954 HAGUE CULTURAL PROPERTY CONVENTION art. 4(1) ("The High Contracting Parties undertake to respect cultural property situated within their own territory as well as within the territory of other High Contracting Parties … by refraining from any act of hostility directed against such property.").

[610] 1954 HAGUE CULTURAL PROPERTY CONVENTION art. 4(2) ("The obligations mentioned in paragraph 1 of the present Article may be waived only in cases where military necessity imperatively requires such a waiver.").

[611] *Refer to* footnote 602 in § 5.18.3.1 (Imperative Military Necessity Waiver).

[612] *Refer to* § 5.17.2 (Enemy Property – Military Necessity Standard). For general discussion of military necessity, *refer to* § 2.2 (Military Necessity).

[613] *Cf.* ROERICH PACT art. 5 ("The monuments and institutions mentioned in article I shall cease to enjoy the privileges recognized in the present treaty in case they are made use of for military purposes."); HAGUE IV REG. art. 27 ("In sieges and bombardments all necessary steps must be taken to spare, as far as possible, buildings dedicated to religion, art, science, or charitable purposes, historic monuments, hospitals, and places where the sick and wounded are collected, _provided they are not being used at the time for military purposes_.") (emphasis added); HAGUE IX art. 5 ("In bombardments by naval forces all the necessary measures must be taken by the commander to spare as far as possible sacred edifices, buildings used for artistic, scientific, or charitable purposes, historic monuments, hospitals, and places where the sick or wounded are collected, _on the understanding that they are not used at the same time for military purposes_.") (emphasis added). *Compare* § 5.18.8.2 (Conditions for the Granting of Special Protection – No Use for Military Purposes).

[614] FINAL REPORT ON THE PERSIAN GULF WAR 610 ("While Article 4(1) of the 1954 Hague Convention provides specific protection for cultural property, Article 4(2) permits waiver of that protection where military necessity makes such a waiver imperative; such 'imperative military necessity' can occur when an enemy uses cultural property and its immediate surroundings to protect legitimate military targets, in violation of Article 4(1).").

[615] Strobe Talbot, *Letter of Submittal*, May 12, 1998, MESSAGE FROM THE PRESIDENT TRANSMITTING THE 1954 HAGUE CULTURAL PROPERTY CONVENTION VIII (1999) (During Operation DESERT STORM, when "attacking legitimate targets in the vicinity of cultural objects, to the extent possible, weapons were selected that would

Even where the waiver of the protection afforded cultural property, its immediate surroundings, or appliances in use for its protection may be warranted for reasons of imperative military necessity, the risk of harm to the cultural property must be considered in a proportionality analysis[616] and feasible precautions should be taken to reduce the risk of harm to the cultural property.[617] And, even where waiver of the protection of cultural property may be warranted as a matter of law, as a matter of policy, decision-makers may still seek to refrain from harming cultural property.[618]

5.18.6 Prohibition Against and Prevention of Theft, Pillage, Misappropriation, or Acts of Vandalism, and Prohibition Against Requisition of Foreign Cultural Property. Any form of theft, pillage, or misappropriation of, and any acts of vandalism directed against, cultural property are prohibited.[619] In addition, Parties to the 1954 Hague Cultural Property Convention shall refrain from requisitioning movable cultural property situated in the territory of another Party to the 1954 Hague Cultural Property Convention.

There are no "imperative military necessity" waivers from these obligations.

Pillage is prohibited, even if the property does not constitute cultural property.[620]

5.18.6.1 *Obligation to Stop or Prevent Theft, Pillage, or Misappropriation of, and Acts of Vandalism Against, Cultural Property*. Military commanders have an obligation to take reasonable measures to prevent or stop any form of theft, pillage, or misappropriation of, and any acts of vandalism directed against, cultural property. This obligation may also be viewed as part of the obligation to take feasible precautions to reduce the risk of harm to cultural property.[621]

What efforts would be reasonable would depend on a variety of factors, such as availability of forces, the commander's mission, and enemy threats. What efforts would be

---

accomplish destruction of the target while minimizing the risk of collateral damage to nearby cultural or civilian property. However, the proximity of military objectives to cultural property did not render those military objectives immune from attack, nor would it under the [1954 Hague Cultural Property] Convention.").

616 *Refer to* § 5.12 (Proportionality – Prohibition on Attacks Expected to Cause Excessive Incidental Harm).

617 *Refer to* § 5.11 (Proportionality – Feasible Precautions in Planning and Conducting Attacks to Reduce the Risk of Harm to Protected Persons and Objects).

618 *For example*, H. STIMSON, ON SERVICE IN PEACE AND WAR 625 (1948) ("With President Truman's warm support I struck off the list of suggest targets the city of Kyoto. Although it was a target of considerable military importance, it had been the ancient capital of Japan and was a shrine of Japanese art and culture. We determined that it should be spared. I approved four other targets including the cities of Hiroshima and Nagasaki.").

619 1954 HAGUE CULTURAL PROPERTY CONVENTION art. 4(3) ("The High Contracting Parties further undertake to prohibit, prevent and, if necessary, put a stop to any form of theft, pillage or misappropriation of, and any acts of vandalism directed against, cultural property."). *See also* LIEBER CODE art. 36 ("In no case shall [classical works of art, libraries, scientific collections, or precious instruments] be sold or given away, if captured by the armies of the United States, nor shall they ever be privately appropriated, or wantonly destroyed or injured.").

620 *Refer to* § 5.17.4 (Pillage Prohibited).

621 *Refer to* § 5.18.4 (Other Feasible Precautions to Reduce the Risk of Harm to Cultural Property).

reasonable would also depend on the information available to the commander at the time.[622]

Some measures to ensure adherence to this obligation may include training members of the armed forces and persons authorized to accompany the armed forces on the protection of cultural property in general (and the prohibition of theft, pillage, or vandalism in particular) as part of general procedures for the dissemination and implementation of the law of war.[623] Other measures may include: (1) issuing and enforcing orders to the same effect;[624] (2) investigating alleged or suspected offenses and taking disciplinary or punitive action, as appropriate under U.S. law;[625] and (3) taking measures to facilitate the recovery and return of stolen or misappropriated cultural property.

Although it may not always be feasible to prevent or stop theft, pillage, or misappropriation of, or acts of vandalism against, cultural property, efforts to identify cultural property within an area of operations and to secure it from theft or pillage are a prudent part of the planning process of military operations. For example, such efforts may deny opposing forces the opportunity to exploit harm to cultural property for propaganda purposes.

5.18.6.2 *Prohibition Against Requisition of Movable Cultural Property Situated in the Territory of Another Party to the 1954 Hague Cultural Property Convention*. Parties to the 1954 Hague Cultural Property Convention shall refrain from requisitioning movable cultural property situated in the territory of another Party to the 1954 Hague Cultural Property Convention.[626]

This rule makes no distinction between movable property of nationals of the country in which it is located and property of nationals of another High Contracting Party. As such, it would also protect from requisition any movable property from a third State temporarily on loan for an exhibition within the territory of a State participating in an armed conflict.[627]

5.18.7 Marking of Cultural Property With the Distinctive Emblem. Cultural property

---

[622] *Refer to* § 5.3 (Assessing Information Under the Law of War).

[623] *Refer to* § 18.6 (Dissemination, Study, and Other Measures to Facilitate Understanding of Duties Under the Law of War).

[624] *For example*, General John P. Abizaid, U.S. Central Command, General Order 1B (GO-1B), Prohibited Activities for U.S. Department of Defense Personnel Present Within the United States Central Command (USCENTCOM) Area of Responsibility (AOR), ¶2h (Mar. 13, 2006) (prohibiting "[r]emoving, possessing, selling, defacing or destroying archaeological artifacts or national treasures.").

[625] *Refer to* § 18.19 (Discipline in National Jurisdictions of Individuals for Violations of the Law of War).

[626] 1954 HAGUE CULTURAL PROPERTY CONVENTION art. 4(3) ("They [the High Contracting Parties] shall, refrain from requisitioning movable cultural property situated in the territory of another High Contracting Party.").

[627] JIRI TOMAN, CULTURAL PROPERTY IN WARTIME 71 (1996) ("[T]he prohibition of requisitioning should also apply to property existing on the territory of a High Contracting Party but belonging to the nationals of another High Contracting Party, as in the case of the collections of the historical or scientific institutes in Athens, Cairo, Paris, and Rome. The same guarantee would also apply in respect of movable cultural property made available on loan for an exhibition … .").

may bear a distinctive emblem so as to facilitate its recognition.[628] This distinctive emblem is described in Article 16 of the 1954 Hague Cultural Property Convention.[629] There is a degree of discretion as to the placing of the distinctive emblem and its degree of visibility.[630] The emblem may be displayed on flags or armlets, and it may be painted on an object or represented in any other appropriate form.[631]

5.18.7.1 *Distinctive Emblem Facilitates Identification Rather Than Confers Status as Such*. As is the case with distinctive emblems for medical personnel, units, transport, and facilities, the distinctive emblem for cultural property facilitates identification, rather than confers cultural property status as such.[632] For example, cultural property may be protected, even though it is not marked with the distinctive emblem. On the other hand, a distinctive emblem placed on property does not make that property cultural property (and grant corresponding protections) if that property does not meet the criteria for cultural property (or the corresponding criteria for protection).[633]

5.18.7.2 *Display of the Distinctive Emblem for Cultural Property – Once Versus Three Times*. In some cases, the distinctive emblem for cultural property is to be used once, while in other cases, the distinctive emblem for cultural property is to be displayed three times in a triangular formation (one shield below the other two shields).[634]

The distinctive emblem for cultural property used once may only be used as a means of identification of:

- cultural property not under special protection;
- the persons responsible for the duties of control in accordance with the Regulations for the Execution of the 1954 Hague Cultural Property Convention;[635]

---

[628] 1954 HAGUE CULTURAL PROPERTY CONVENTION art. 6 ("In accordance with the provisions of Article 16, cultural property may bear a distinctive emblem so as to facilitate its recognition.").

[629] 1954 HAGUE CULTURAL PROPERTY CONVENTION art. 16(1) ("The distinctive emblem of the Convention shall take the form of a shield, pointed below, per saltire blue and white (a shield consisting of a royal-blue square, one of the angles of which forms the point of the shield, and of a royal-blue triangle above the square, the space on either side being taken up by a white triangle).").

[630] REGULATIONS FOR THE EXECUTION OF THE 1954 HAGUE CULTURAL PROPERTY CONVENTION art. 20(1) ("The placing of the distinctive emblem and its degree of visibility shall be left to the discretion of the competent authorities of each High Contracting Party.").

[631] REGULATIONS FOR THE EXECUTION OF THE 1954 HAGUE CULTURAL PROPERTY CONVENTION art. 20(1) ("It may be displayed on flags or armlets; it may be painted on an object or represented in any other appropriate form.").

[632] *Compare* § 7.15 (Display of the Distinctive Emblem to Facilitate Identification).

[633] *Refer to* § 5.18.1 (Definition of Cultural Property).

[634] 1954 HAGUE CULTURAL PROPERTY CONVENTION art. 16(2) ("The emblem shall be used alone, or repeated three times in a triangular formation (one shield below), under the conditions provided for in Article 17.").

[635] *Refer to* § 4.14 (Personnel Engaged in Duties Related to the Protection of Cultural Property).

- the personnel engaged in the protection of cultural property;[636] and
- the identity cards mentioned in the Regulations for the Execution of the 1954 Hague Cultural Property Convention.[637]

The distinctive emblem, repeated three times, may be used only as a means of identification of:[638]

- immovable cultural property under special protection;[639]
- the transport of cultural property under the special protection or in urgent cases;[640] and
- improvised refuges, under the conditions provided for in the Regulations for the Execution of the 1954 Hague Cultural Property Convention.[641]

5.18.7.3 *Display of the Distinctive Emblem on Immovable Cultural Property*. The distinctive emblem for cultural property may not be placed on any immovable cultural property unless at the same time there is displayed an authorization duly dated and signed by the competent authority of the relevant State.[642]

5.18.7.4 *Other Uses of the Distinctive Emblem for Cultural Property Prohibited During Armed Conflict*. During armed conflict, the use of the distinctive emblem for cultural property in any other cases than those mentioned in the 1954 Hague Cultural Property Convention, and the use for any purpose whatsoever of a sign resembling the distinctive emblem, is forbidden.[643]

---

[636] *Refer to* § 4.14 (Personnel Engaged in Duties Related to the Protection of Cultural Property).

[637] 1954 HAGUE CULTURAL PROPERTY CONVENTION art. 17(2) ("The distinctive emblem may be used alone only as a means of identification of: (a) cultural property not under special protection; (b) the persons responsible for the duties of control in accordance with the Regulations for the execution of the Convention; (c) the personnel engaged in the protection of cultural property; (d) the identity cards mentioned in the Regulations for the execution of the Convention.").

[638] 1954 HAGUE CULTURAL PROPERTY CONVENTION art. 17(1) ("The distinctive emblem repeated three times may be used only as a means of identification of: (a) immovable cultural property under special protection; (b) the transport of cultural property under the conditions provided for in Articles 12 and 13; (c) improvised refuges, under the conditions provided for in the Regulations for the execution of the Convention.").

[639] *Refer to* § 5.18.8 (Special Protection for Certain Cultural Property).

[640] *Refer to* § 5.18.9 (Transport of Cultural Property).

[641] *Refer to* § 5.18.8 (Special Protection for Certain Cultural Property).

[642] 1954 HAGUE CULTURAL PROPERTY CONVENTION art. 17(4) ("The distinctive emblem may not be placed on any immovable cultural property unless at the same time there is displayed an authorization duly dated and signed by the competent authority of the High Contracting Party.").

[643] 1954 HAGUE CULTURAL PROPERTY CONVENTION art. 17(3) ("During an armed conflict, the use of the distinctive emblem in any other cases than those mentioned in the Cultural Property Convention, and the use for any purpose whatever of a sign resembling the distinctive emblem, shall be forbidden."). *Consider* AP I art. 38(1)(a) ("It is also prohibited to misuse deliberately in an armed conflict other internationally recognized protective emblems, signs or signals, including the flag of truce, and the protective emblem of cultural property.").

5.18.8 Special Protection for Certain Cultural Property. A highly limited category of cultural property receives special protection by its entry in an International Register.[644]

The standards governing the protection of such cultural property are essentially the same as the standards governing the protection of cultural property under customary law[645] and the protection afforded all cultural property under the 1954 Hague Cultural Property Convention.[646] However, the special procedures applicable to cultural property under special protection facilitate its protection beyond that afforded cultural property that is not under special protection.

Special protection can apply to:[647]

- a limited number of refuges intended to shelter movable cultural property in the event of armed conflict;
- a limited number of centers containing monuments and other immovable property of very great importance; and
- improvised refuges under the procedures specified in the Regulations for the Execution of the 1954 Hague Cultural Property Convention.[648]

---

[644] 1954 HAGUE CULTURAL PROPERTY CONVENTION art. 8(6) ("Special protection is granted to cultural property by its entry in the 'International Register of Cultural Property under Special Protection'. This entry shall only be made, in accordance with the provisions of the present Convention and under the conditions provided for in the Regulations for the execution of the Convention.").

[645] *See* United States, *Statement on Ratification of the 1954 Hague Cultural Property Convention*, Mar. 13, 2009, 2575 UNTS 7, 8 ("It is the understanding of the United States of America that 'special protection', as defined in Chapter II of the Convention, codifies customary international law in that it, first, prohibits the use of any cultural property to shield any legitimate military targets from attack and, second, allows all property to be attacked using any lawful and proportionate means, if required by military necessity and notwithstanding possible collateral damage to such property.").

[646] *Compare* 1954 HAGUE CULTURAL PROPERTY CONVENTION art. 9 ("The High Contracting Parties undertake to ensure the immunity of cultural property under special protection by refraining, from the time of entry in the International Register, from any act of hostility directed against such property and, except for the cases provided for in paragraph 5 of Article 8, from any use of such property or its surroundings for military purposes.") *with* 1954 HAGUE CULTURAL PROPERTY CONVENTION art. 4(1) ("The High Contracting Parties undertake to respect cultural property situated within their own territory as well as within the territory of other High Contracting Parties by refraining from any use of the property and its immediate surroundings or of the appliances in use for its protection for purposes which are likely to expose it to destruction or damage in the event of armed conflict; and by refraining from any act of hostility directed against such property.").

[647] 1954 HAGUE CULTURAL PROPERTY CONVENTION art. 8(1) ("There may be placed under special protection a limited number of refuges intended to shelter movable cultural property in the event of armed conflict, of centres containing monuments and other immovable cultural property of very great importance, provided that they: (a) are situated at an adequate distance from any large industrial centre or from any important military objective constituting a vulnerable point, such as, for example, an aerodrome, broadcasting station, establishment engaged upon work of national defence, a port or railway station of relative importance or a main line of communication; (b) are not used for military purposes.").

[648] REGULATIONS FOR THE EXECUTION OF THE 1954 HAGUE CULTURAL PROPERTY CONVENTION art. 11 ("1. If, during an armed conflict, any High Contracting Party is induced by unforeseen circumstances to set up an improvised refuge and desires that it should be placed under special protection, it shall communicate this fact

Property granted special protection must be marked with the distinctive emblem for special protection, and opened to international control as provided for in the Regulations for the Execution of the 1954 Hague Cultural Property Convention.[649]

5.18.8.1 *Conditions for the Granting of Special Protection – Adequate Distance From Military Objectives*. In order to qualify for special protection, these categories of property must: (1) be situated an adequate distance from any large industrial center, or from any important military objective constituting a vulnerable point; and (2) not be used for military purposes.

The property must be situated at an adequate distance from any large industrial center or from any important military objective, such as an airport, railway station, or marshalling yards, port facilities, key lines of communication, command and control activity, or other defense facility.[650] The term "adequate distance" is not defined within the 1954 Hague Cultural Property Convention, but relies upon determinations and actions by the State Party requesting "special protection" status, and by States Parties in determining whether the distance set forth by the requesting nation is sufficient to support approval of the request.

Immovable cultural property of very great importance adjacent to a military objective may retain its special protection status provided, in the event of armed conflict, all use of the military objective ceases.[651] For example, if the military objective in question is an airport, port facility, or railway station or marshaling yards, all activity must cease, and military traffic must be diverted, in order for the site to maintain its protected status.

A refuge for storing and protecting movable cultural property may also be placed under

---

forthwith to the Commissioner-General accredited to that Party. 2. If the Commissioner-General considers that such a measure is justified by the circumstances and by the importance of the cultural property sheltered in this improvised refuge, he may authorize the High Contracting Party to display on such refuge the distinctive emblem defined in Article 16 of the Convention. He shall communicate his decision without delay to the delegates of the Protecting Powers who are concerned, each of whom may, within a time-limit of 30 days, order the immediate withdrawal of the emblem. 3. As soon as such delegates have signified their agreement or if the time-limit of 30 days has passed without any of the delegates concerned having made an objection, and if, in the view of the Commissioner-General, the refuge fulfils the conditions laid down in Article 8 of the Convention, the Commissioner-General shall request the Director-General of the United Nations Educational, Scientific and Cultural Organization to enter the refuge in the Register of Cultural Property under Special Protection.").

[649] 1954 HAGUE CULTURAL PROPERTY CONVENTION art. 10 ("During an armed conflict, cultural property under special protection shall be marked with the distinctive emblem described in Article 16, and shall be open to international control as provided for in the Regulations for the execution of the Convention.").

[650] 1954 HAGUE CULTURAL PROPERTY CONVENTION art. 8(1) (Refuges and centers may only be placed under special protection if "they: (a) are situated at an adequate distance from any large industrial centre or from any important military objective constituting a vulnerable point, such as, for example, an aerodrome, broadcasting station, establishment engaged upon work of national defence, a port or railway station of relative importance or a main line of communication."). *Refer to* § 5.6 (Military Objectives).

[651] 1954 HAGUE CULTURAL PROPERTY CONVENTION art. 8(5) ("If any cultural property mentioned in paragraph 1 of the present Article is situated near an important military objective as defined in the said paragraph, it may nevertheless be placed under special protection if the High Contracting Party asking for that protection undertakes, in the event of armed conflict, to make no use of the objective and particularly, in the case of a port, railway station or aerodrome, to divert all traffic therefrom. In that event, such diversion shall be prepared in time of peace.").

special protection, whatever its location, if it is so constructed that, in all probability, it will not be damaged by bombs.[652]

5.18.8.2 *Conditions for the Granting of Special Protection – No Use for Military Purposes*. A "center containing monuments"[653] shall be deemed to be used for military purposes whenever it is used for the movement of military personnel or material, even in transit. The same shall apply whenever activities directly connected with military operations, the stationing of military personnel, or the production of war material are carried on within the center.[654]

The guarding of cultural property under special protection by armed custodians specially empowered to do so, or the presence, in the vicinity of such cultural property, of police forces normally responsible for the maintenance of public order, however, shall not be deemed to be use for military purposes.[655] Such activities may fulfill the obligation to safeguard cultural property, especially against looters.[656] Employment of law enforcement personnel to protect cultural property is analogous to activities of armed military medical personnel deployed in and around military medical units and facilities in order to provide security from criminal acts.[657]

5.18.8.3 *Marking of Cultural Property Under Special Protection*. The distinctive emblem for cultural property is to be displayed three times in a triangular formation to indicate cultural property under special protection.[658]

The emblem shall be visible from the ground: (a) at regular intervals sufficient to indicate clearly the perimeter of a center containing monuments under special protection; and (b) at the entrance to other immovable cultural property under special protection.[659]

5.18.8.4 *Withdrawal of Special Protection*. If a Party to 1954 Hague Cultural

---

652 1954 HAGUE CULTURAL PROPERTY CONVENTION art. 8(2) ("A refuge for movable cultural property may also be placed under special protection, whatever its location, if it is so constructed that, in all probability, it will not be damaged by bombs.").

653 *Refer to* § 5.18.1.4 (Centers Containing Monuments).

654 1954 HAGUE CULTURAL PROPERTY CONVENTION art. 8(3) ("A centre containing monuments shall be deemed to be used for military purposes whenever it is used for the movement of military personnel or material, even in transit. The same shall apply whenever activities directly connected with military operations, the stationing of military personnel, or the production of war material are carried on within the centre.").

655 1954 HAGUE CULTURAL PROPERTY CONVENTION art. 8(4) ("The guarding of cultural property mentioned in paragraph 1 above by armed custodians specially empowered to do so, or the presence, in the vicinity of such cultural property, of police forces normally responsible for the maintenance of public order shall not be deemed to be used for military purposes."). *Compare* § 4.23.1 (Police as Civilians).

656 *Refer to* § 5.18.6.1 (Obligation to Stop or Prevent Theft, Pillage, or Misappropriation of, and Acts of Vandalism Against, Cultural Property).

657 *Refer to* § 7.10.3.5 (Use of Weapons in Self-Defense or Defense of the Wounded and Sick).

658 *Refer to* § 5.18.7.2 (Display of the Distinctive Emblem for Cultural Property – Once Versus Three Times).

659 REGULATIONS FOR THE EXECUTION OF THE 1954 HAGUE CULTURAL PROPERTY CONVENTION art. 20(2) ("The emblem shall be visible from the ground: (a) at regular intervals sufficient to indicate clearly the perimeter of a centre containing monuments under special protection; (b) at the entrance to other immovable cultural property under special protection.").

Property Convention commits, in respect of any item of cultural property under special protection, a violation of its obligations to refrain from any act of hostility directed against such property and from use of such property or its surroundings for military purposes, the opposing Party shall, so long as this violation persists, be released from the obligation to ensure the immunity of the property concerned.[660] Nevertheless, whenever possible, the latter Party shall first request the cessation of such violation within a reasonable time.[661]

Apart from violations by the opposing Party, immunity shall be withdrawn from cultural property under special protection only in exceptional cases of unavoidable military necessity, and only for such time as that necessity continues.[662] Such necessity can be established only by an officer commanding a force the equivalent of a division in size or larger.[663] However, such necessity should not be construed to impose an unreasonable and disproportionate responsibility on the attacker to avoid damage to cultural property.[664] Moreover, all property may be attacked using any lawful and proportionate means if required by military necessity and notwithstanding possible collateral damage to such property.[665]

Whenever circumstances permit, the opposing Party shall be notified, a reasonable time in advance, of the decision to withdraw immunity.[666] The Party withdrawing immunity is also to notify the Commissioner-General for Cultural Property as soon as possible as provided for in the Regulations for the Execution of the 1954 Hague Cultural Property Convention, in writing,

---

[660] 1954 HAGUE CULTURAL PROPERTY CONVENTION art. 11(1) ("If one of the High Contracting Parties commits, in respect of any item of cultural property under special protection, a violation of the obligations under Article 9, the opposing Party shall, so long as this violation persists, be released from the obligation to ensure the immunity of the property concerned.").

[661] 1954 HAGUE CULTURAL PROPERTY CONVENTION art. 11(1) ("Nevertheless, whenever possible, the latter Party shall first request the cessation of such violation within a reasonable time.").

[662] 1954 HAGUE CULTURAL PROPERTY CONVENTION art. 11(2) ("Apart from the case provided for in paragraph I of the present Article, immunity shall be withdrawn from cultural property under special protection only in exceptional cases of unavoidable military necessity, and only for such time as that necessity continues.").

[663] 1954 HAGUE CULTURAL PROPERTY CONVENTION art. 11(2) ("Such necessity can be established only by the officer commanding a force the equivalent of a division in size or larger.").

[664] *Section-by-Section Analysis of Provisions*, 6, Tab 1 to Strobe Talbot, *Letter of Submittal*, May 12, 1998, MESSAGE FROM THE PRESIDENT TRANSMITTING THE 1954 HAGUE CULTURAL PROPERTY CONVENTION 7 ("Due to ambiguous modifiers such as those in the Article 11 phrase ''exceptional cases of 'unavoidable' military necessity,'' the provisions may be misconstrued to impose an unreasonable and disproportionate responsibility on the attacker to avoid damage to cultural property. Clarification would help avoid a suggestion that strict compliance with the Convention would mean that any collateral damage would constitute a violation of the Convention.").

[665] *See* United States, *Statement on Ratification of the 1954 Hague Cultural Property Convention,* Mar. 13, 2009, 2575 UNTS 7, 8 ("It is the understanding of the United States of America that 'special protection', as defined in Chapter II of the Convention, … allows all property to be attacked using any lawful and proportionate means, if required by military necessity and notwithstanding possible collateral damage to such property.").

[666] 1954 HAGUE CULTURAL PROPERTY CONVENTION art. 11(2) ("Whenever circumstances permit, the opposing Party shall be notified, a reasonable time in advance, of the decision to withdraw immunity.").

stating the reasons for withdrawing immunity.[667]

5.18.9 Transport of Cultural Property. The transport of cultural property may take place: (1) under special protection through procedures provided in the Regulations for the Execution of the 1954 Hague Cultural Property Convention; and (2) in urgent cases without such procedures. Additional rules apply to the transport of cultural property in occupied territory.[668]

The distinctive emblem for cultural property should be placed on vehicles of transport so as to be clearly visible in daylight from the air as well as from the ground.[669]

5.18.9.1 *Transport Under Special Protection*. Transport exclusively engaged in the transfer of cultural property, whether within a territory or to another territory, may, at the request of the State concerned, take place under special protection in accordance with the conditions specified in the Regulations for the Execution of the 1954 Hague Cultural Property Convention.[670] No acts of hostility may be directed against transport under special protection.[671]

A request for such transport should be addressed to the Commissioner-General for Cultural Property and should contain all relevant information, including the reason for the transfer, the approximate number and importance of objects to be transferred, their present location, the intended destination, the means of transport to be used, the route to be followed, and the date proposed for transfer.[672] The Commissioner-General for Cultural Property determines whether such transfer is justified and notifies parties to the conflict concerned of the transfer.[673]

---

[667] 1954 HAGUE CULTURAL PROPERTY CONVENTION art. 11(3) ("The Party withdrawing immunity shall, as soon as possible, so inform the Commissioner-General for cultural property provided for in the Regulations for the execution of the Convention, in writing, stating the reasons.").

[668] *Refer to* § 11.19 (Protection of Cultural Property During Occupation).

[669] REGULATIONS FOR THE EXECUTION OF THE 1954 HAGUE CULTURAL PROPERTY CONVENTION art. 20(2) ("However, without prejudice to any possible fuller markings, the emblem shall, in the event of armed conflict and in the cases mentioned in Articles 12 and 13 of the Convention, be placed on vehicles of transport so as to be clearly visible in daylight from the air as well as from the ground.").

[670] 1954 HAGUE CULTURAL PROPERTY CONVENTION art. 12(1) ("Transport exclusively engaged in the transfer of cultural property, whether within a territory or to another territory, may, at the request of the High Contracting Party concerned, take place under special protection in accordance with the conditions specified in the Regulations for the execution of the Convention.").

[671] 1954 HAGUE CULTURAL PROPERTY CONVENTION art. 12(3) ("The High Contracting Parties shall refrain from any act of hostility directed against transport under special protection.").

[672] REGULATIONS FOR THE EXECUTION OF THE 1954 HAGUE CULTURAL PROPERTY CONVENTION art. 17(1) ("The request mentioned in paragraph 1 of Article 12 of the Convention shall be addressed to the Commissioner-General for Cultural Property. It shall mention the reasons on which it is based and specify the approximate number and the importance of the objects to be transferred, their present location, the location now envisaged, the means of transport to be used, the route to be followed, the date proposed for the transfer, and any other relevant information.").

[673] REGULATIONS FOR THE EXECUTION OF THE 1954 HAGUE CULTURAL PROPERTY CONVENTION art. 17(2) ("If the Commissioner-General, after taking such opinions as he deems fit, considers that such transfer is justified, he shall consult those delegates of the Protecting Powers who are concerned, on the measures proposed for carrying it out. Following such consultation, he shall notify the Parties to the conflict concerned of the transfer, including in such notification all useful information.").

Transport under special protection shall take place under the international supervision provided for in the Regulations for the Execution of the 1954 Hague Cultural Property Convention and shall display the distinctive emblem described in Article 16.[674] The distinctive emblem for cultural property is to be displayed repeated three times in a triangular formation to indicate that the transport occurs under special protection.[675]

The transport of cultural property to the territory of another State is subject to additional rules.[676]

5.18.9.2 Transport in Urgent Cases. If a State that is a Party to the 1954 Hague Cultural Property Convention considers that the safety of certain cultural property requires transfer, and that the matter is of such urgency that the request procedure to the Commissioner-General for Cultural Property cannot be followed, the transport may display the distinctive emblem for cultural property, provided that a request for transport under special protection has not already been made and refused.[677] As far as possible, notification of transfer should be made to the opposing Parties.[678] Nevertheless, transport conveying cultural property to the territory of another State may not display the distinctive emblem unless immunity has been expressly granted to it.[679]

---

[674] 1954 HAGUE CULTURAL PROPERTY CONVENTION art. 12(2) ("Transport under special protection shall take place under the international supervision provided for in the aforesaid Regulations and shall display the distinctive emblem described in Article 16."). *See also* REGULATIONS FOR THE EXECUTION OF THE 1954 HAGUE CULTURAL PROPERTY CONVENTION art. 17(3) ("The Commission-General shall appoint one or more inspectors, who shall satisfy themselves that only the property stated in the request is to be transferred and that the transport is to be by the approved methods and bears the distinctive emblem. The inspector or inspectors shall accompany the property to its destination.").

[675] *Refer to* § 5.18.7.2 (Display of the Distinctive Emblem for Cultural Property – Once Versus Three Times).

[676] *See* REGULATIONS FOR THE EXECUTION OF THE 1954 HAGUE CULTURAL PROPERTY CONVENTION art. 18 ("(a) [W]hile the cultural property remains on the territory of another State, that State shall be its depositary and shall extend to it as great a measure of care as that which it bestows upon its own cultural property of comparable importance; (b) the depositary State shall return the property only on the cessation of the conflict; such return shall be effected within six months from the date on which it was requested; (c) during the various transfer operations, and while it remains on the territory of another State, the cultural property shall be exempt from confiscation and may not be disposed of either by the depositor or by the depositary. Nevertheless, when the safety of the property requires it, the depositary may, with the assent of the depositor, have the property transported to the territory of a third country, under the conditions laid down in the present article; (d) the request for special protection shall indicate that the State to whose territory the property is to be transferred accepts the provisions of the present Article [of the Regulations for the Execution of the 1954 Hague Cultural Property Convention].").

[677] 1954 HAGUE CULTURAL PROPERTY CONVENTION art. 13(1) ("If a High Contracting Party considers that the safety of certain cultural property requires its transfer and that the matter is of such urgency that the procedure laid down in Article 12 cannot be followed, especially at the beginning of an armed conflict, the transport may display the distinctive emblem described in Article 16, provided that an application for immunity referred to in Article 12 has not already been made and refused.").

[678] 1954 HAGUE CULTURAL PROPERTY CONVENTION art. 13(1) ("As far as possible, notification of transfer should be made to the opposing Parties.").

[679] 1954 HAGUE CULTURAL PROPERTY CONVENTION art. 13(1) ("Nevertheless, transport conveying cultural property to the territory of another country may not display the distinctive emblem unless immunity has been expressly granted to it.").

As far as possible, necessary precautions shall be taken to avoid acts of hostility directed against transport of cultural property under the protection provided in urgent cases and while displaying the distinctive emblem.[680]

5.18.9.3 Immunity From Seizure, Capture, and Prize. Transport of cultural property under special protection or under the protection provided in urgent cases is immune from seizure, placing in prize, or capture.[681] Means of transport exclusively engaged in the transport of such property is similarly immune.[682] However, such immunity does not limit the right of visit and search of such transportation or property.[683]

5.18.10 AP I Provision on the Protection of Objects Which Constitute the Cultural or Spiritual Heritage of Peoples. Article 53 of AP I provides certain protections to "historic monuments, works of art or places of worship which constitute the cultural or spiritual heritage of peoples."[684] This provision has been interpreted in a more limited fashion than its text would suggest.

For example, based on the statements of national delegations, including the U.S. delegation, during the negotiations of this provision, it appears that objects that qualify for special protection under Article 53 of AP I are substantially those that qualify for special protection under the 1954 Hague Cultural Property Convention.[685]

In addition, protection is waived when an object is used in support of the military effort or for military purposes.[686] In addition, Canada has interpreted Article 53 to permit waiver of its

---

[680] 1954 HAGUE CULTURAL PROPERTY CONVENTION art. 13(2) ("The High Contracting Parties shall take, so far as possible, the necessary precautions to avoid acts of hostility directed against the transport described in paragraph 1 of the present Article and displaying the distinctive emblem.").

[681] 1954 HAGUE CULTURAL PROPERTY CONVENTION art. 14(1) ("Immunity from seizure, placing in prize, or capture shall be granted to: (a) cultural property enjoying the protection provided for in Article 12 or that provided for in Article 13; (b) the means of transport exclusively engaged in the transfer of such cultural property.").

[682] *Compare* § 4.9.2.3 (Exclusively Engaged in Humanitarian Duties).

[683] 1954 HAGUE CULTURAL PROPERTY CONVENTION art. 14(2) ("Nothing in the present Article shall limit the right of visit and search."). *Refer to* § 15.13 (Belligerent Right of Visit and Search of Merchant Vessels).

[684] AP I art. 53 ("Without prejudice to the provisions of the Hague Convention for the Protection of Cultural Property in the Event of Armed Conflict of 14 May 1954, and of other relevant international instruments, it is prohibited: (a) to commit any acts of hostility directed against the historic monuments, works of art or places of worship which constitute the cultural or spiritual heritage of peoples; (b) to use such objects in support of the military effort; (c) to make such objects the object of reprisals.").

[685] BOTHE, PARTSCH, & SOLF, NEW RULES 333 (AP I art. 53, ¶2.5.1) ("In light of this understanding [by the U.S. delegation], it appears that the objects which qualify for special protection under Art. 53 are substantially those which would qualify for special protection under Art. 8 of the Hague Convention of 1954 without, however, imposing a requirement for the procedural measures required by that Convention to effect such special protection.").

[686] *See, e.g.*, France, *Statement on Ratification of AP I, translated in* SCHINDLER & TOMAN, THE LAWS OF ARMED CONFLICTS: A COLLECTION OF CONVENTIONS, RESOLUTIONS, AND OTHER DOCUMENTS 801 (2004) ("The Government of the French Republic declares that if the objects protected by Article 53 are used for military purposes, they will lose protection which they would otherwise have according to the provisions of the Protocol."); Ireland, *Statement on Ratification of AP I*, Nov. 19, 1999, 2073 UNTS 28, 30 ("It is the understanding of Ireland in relation to the protection of cultural objects in Article 53 that if the objects protected by this Article are unlawfully used for military purposes they will thereby lose protection from attacks directed against such unlawful military

obligations when military necessity imperatively requires such waiver.[687]

5.19 SIEGES AND ENCIRCLED AREAS

It is lawful to besiege enemy forces. Commanders must seek to make arrangements to permit the passage of certain consignments and should seek to make arrangements for the passage of certain categories of civilians, and of religious and medical personnel. Different rules apply to blockade.[688]

5.19.1 Siege and Encirclement Permissible. It is lawful to besiege enemy forces, *i.e.*, to encircle them with a view towards inducing their surrender by cutting them off from reinforcements, supplies, and communications with the outside world.[689] In particular, it is permissible to seek to starve enemy forces into submission.[690]

5.19.1.1 *Belligerent Authority to Exercise Control in the Immediate Vicinity of Military Operations*. The conduct of a siege or encirclement may require the imposition of measures of control to ensure that outsiders may not deliver supplies to enemy forces. Thus, the right to conduct a siege or encirclement impliedly recognizes the authority of the military commander to exercise control (*e.g.*, stopping, searching, and diverting traffic) over civilians and other persons in the immediate vicinity of military operations. For example, commanders may also impose certain restrictions on neutral vessels or aircraft (such as restricting communications) within the immediate vicinity of the belligerent's operations.[691]

5.19.2 Removal and Passage of Certain Personnel – Vulnerable Civilians, Diplomatic and Consular Personnel, the Wounded and Sick, and Medical Personnel. Although the commander of the force laying siege has the right to forbid all communications and access between the besieged place and the outside, the parties to the conflict should attempt to conclude local

---

use."); Italy, *Statement on Ratification of AP I*, Feb. 27, 1986, 1425 UNTS 438, 439 ("If and so long as the objectives protected by Article 53 are unlawfully used for military purposes, they will thereby lose protection."); United Kingdom, *Statement on Ratification of AP I*, Jan. 28, 1998, 2020 UNTS 75, 77 ("The United Kingdom declares that if the objects protected by this Article are unlawfully used for military purposes they will thereby lose protection from attacks directed against such unlawful military uses.").

[687] Canada, *Statement on Ratification of AP I*, Nov. 20, 1990, 1591 UNTS 462, 465 ("It is the understanding of the Government of Canada in relation to Article 53 that: *a*. Such protection as is afforded by the Article will be lost during such time as the protected property is used for military purposes, and *b*. The prohibitions contained in subparagraphs (a) and (b) of this Article can only be waived when military necessity imperatively requires such a waiver.").

[688] *Refer to* § 13.10 (Blockade).

[689] 1956 FM 27-10 (Change No. 1 1976) ¶40 ("Investment, bombardment, assault, and siege have always been recognized as legitimate means of land warfare."). *See also* 2004 UK MANUAL ¶5.34.1 ("Attacks can be costly in casualties and incidental loss or damage. A more effective method may be to encircle enemy forces, cutting them off from supplies and communications with the outside world and forcing their surrender. The same is true of besieging a town or stronghold. Siege is a legitimate method of warfare as long as it is directed against enemy armed forces. It would be unlawful to besiege an undefended town since it could be occupied without resistance.").

[690] *Refer to* § 5.20 (Starvation).

[691] *Refer to* § 13.8 (Belligerent Control of the Immediate Area of Naval Operations); § 14.6 (Belligerent Control of Aviation in the Immediate Vicinity of Hostilities).

agreements for the removal of wounded, sick, infirm and aged persons, children, and maternity cases, or for the passage of ministers of all religions, medical personnel, and medical equipment on their way to such areas.[692] Concluding such agreements is not compulsory. A commander of an encircling force is not required to agree to the passage of medical or religious personnel, supplies, and equipment if he or she has legitimate military reasons denying such requests (*e.g.*, if denying passage may increase the likelihood of surrender of enemy forces in the encircled area). Nonetheless, commanders should make reasonable, good-faith efforts to do so when possible.[693]

Diplomatic and consular personnel of a neutral State should not be prevented from leaving a besieged place before hostilities commence, but this privilege cannot be claimed while hostilities are in progress. If diplomatic and consular personnel of a neutral State voluntarily decide to remain, they are subject to the same risks as other inhabitants.[694]

5.19.3 Passage of Relief Consignments. Commanders should make arrangements to permit the free passage of certain consignments:

- all consignments of medical and hospital stores and objects necessary for religious worship intended only for civilians; and
- all consignments of essential foodstuffs, clothing, and tonics (*i.e.*, medicine) intended for children under fifteen, expectant mothers, and maternity cases.[695]

However, allowing passage of these items is not required by the party controlling the area unless that party is satisfied that there are no serious reasons for fearing that:

- the consignments may be diverted from their destination;

---

[692] GC art. 17 ("The Parties to the conflict shall endeavour to conclude local agreements for the removal from besieged or encircled areas, of wounded, sick, infirm, and aged persons, children and maternity cases, and for the passage of ministers of all religions, medical personnel and medical equipment on their way to such areas."); GWS art. 15 ("Likewise, local arrangements may be concluded between Parties to the conflict for the removal or exchange of wounded and sick from a besieged or encircled area, and for the passage of medical and religious personnel and equipment on their way to that area."); GWS-SEA art. 18 ("Whenever circumstances permit, the Parties to the conflict shall conclude local arrangements for the removal of the wounded and sick by sea from a besieged or encircled area and for the passage of medical and religious personnel and equipment on their way to that area.").

[693] GC COMMENTARY 139 ("The words 'The Parties to the conflict shall endeavor' show that under the Convention evacuation is not compulsory; belligerents should nevertheless regard this provision as a very strong recommendation to arrange for evacuation whenever it is in the interest of the civilian population and the military situation makes it possible.").

[694] 1956 FM 27-10 (Change No. 1 1976) ¶44b ("Diplomatic and consular personnel of a neutral State should not be prevented from leaving a besieged place before hostilities commence, but this privilege cannot be claimed while hostilities are in progress. Should they voluntarily decide to remain, they must undergo the same risks as other inhabitants.").

[695] GC art. 23 ("Each High Contracting Party shall allow the free passage of all consignments of medical and hospital stores and objects necessary for religious worship intended only for civilians of another High Contracting Party, even if the latter is its adversary. It shall likewise permit the free passage of all consignments of essential foodstuffs, clothing and tonics intended for children under fifteen, expectant mothers and maternity cases.").

- the control may not be effective; or
- a definite advantage may accrue to the military efforts or economy of the enemy.[696]

5.19.3.1 *Technical Arrangements for the Passage and Distribution of Relief Consignments*. Commanders may require, as a condition for allowing the passage of consignments listed above, that the consignments be distributed under the local supervision of the Protecting Powers.[697] Commanders may prescribe other rules and regulations for how consignments are to be distributed, although consignments should be forwarded as rapidly as possible.[698]

5.19.4 Attacks by Forces Laying Siege. The general rules that apply to conducting attacks also apply to attacks by forces laying siege.[699]

5.19.4.1 *Use of Force to Drive Fleeing Civilians Back to Besieged Areas*. In the past, it was permissible, but an extreme measure, to refuse to allow civilians to leave a besieged locality and to use force to drive any who attempted to flee back to the besieged locality.[700] However, such actions would now be prohibited because they would not be consistent with the duty to take feasible precautions for the protection of civilians.[701] Permitting civilians to flee may also be militarily advantageous.[702]

---

[696] GC art. 23 ("The obligation of a High Contracting Party to allow the free passage of the consignments indicated in the preceding paragraph is subject to the condition that this Party is satisfied that there are no serious reasons for fearing: (a) that the consignments may be diverted from their destination, (b) that the control may not be effective, or (c) that a definite advantage may accrue to the military efforts or economy of the enemy through the substitution of the above-mentioned consignments for goods which would otherwise be provided or produced by the enemy or through the release of such material, services or facilities as would otherwise be required for the production of such goods.").

[697] GC art. 23 ("The Power which allows the passage of the consignments indicated in the first paragraph of this Article may make such permission conditional on the distribution to the persons benefited thereby being made under the local supervision of the Protecting Powers.").

[698] GC art. 23 ("Such consignments shall be forwarded as rapidly as possible, and the Power which permits their free passage shall have the right to prescribe the technical arrangements under which such passage is allowed.").

[699] *Refer to* § 5.4 (Rules on Conducting Assaults, Bombardments, and Other Attacks).

[700] *See, e.g.*, United States v. von Leeb, *et al.* (The High Command Case), XI TRIALS OF WAR CRIMINALS BEFORE THE NMT 563 ("Leningrad was encircled and besieged. Its defenders and the civilian population were in great straits and it was feared the population would undertake to flee through the German lines. Orders were issued to use artillery to 'prevent any such attempt at the greatest possible distance from our own lines by opening fire as early as possible, so that the infantry, if possible, is spared shooting on civilians.' … It is said that if the commander of a besieged place expels the noncombatants, in order to lessen the number of those who consume his stock of provisions, it is lawful, though an extreme measure, to drive them back so as to hasten the surrender.' We might wish the law were otherwise but we must administer it as we find it. Consequently, we hold no criminality attached on this charge.").

[701] *Refer to* § 5.2.3 (Affirmative Duties to Take Feasible Precautions for the Protection of Civilians and Other Protected Persons and Objects).

[702] *See* ROGERS, LAW ON THE BATTLEFIELD 62 ("In fact, the besieging commander would be better advised to allow all civilians and the wounded and sick to leave the besieged area. He would then legitimately be able to prevent all supplies from reaching the enemy forces and bombardment and assault would be considerably eased.").

5.19.5 Duties of Forces Under Siege to Take Feasible Precautions to Reduce the Risk of Incidental Harm. Besieged forces should take feasible precautions to reduce the risk of incidental harm.[703] For example, it may be appropriate to mark protected buildings to indicate their protected status to enemy forces.[704] Similarly, it may be appropriate to concentrate the wounded and sick and civilians in areas remote from military objectives[705] or in areas neutralized by arrangement with the enemy.[706]

5.20 STARVATION

Starvation is a legitimate method of warfare, but it must be conducted in accordance with the principles of distinction and proportionality, as well as other law of war rules. Starvation of civilians as a method of combat is also prohibited in non-international armed conflict.[707]

5.20.1 Starvation – Distinction. It is a legitimate method of war to starve enemy forces.[708] For example, it is permitted to destroy food intended as sustenance for enemy forces with a view towards weakening them and diverting their resources.[709] Enemy forces, for the purpose of this rule, means those persons constituting military objectives.[710]

Starvation specifically directed against the enemy civilian population, however, is prohibited.[711] For example, it would be prohibited to destroy food or water supplies for the purpose of denying sustenance to the civilian population.

---

[703] *Refer to* § 5.14 (Feasible Precautions to Reduce the Risk of Harm to Protected Persons and Objects by the Party Subject to Attack).

[704] *Refer to* § 5.14.4 (Using Distinctive and Visible Signs to Identify Protected Persons and Objects as Such).

[705] *Refer to* § 5.14.2 (Removing Civilians and Civilian Objects From the Vicinity of Military Objectives).

[706] *Refer to* § 5.14.3 (Establishing Areas Where Civilians or the Wounded and Sick Are Protected).

[707] *Refer to* § 17.9.2 (Prohibition on Starvation of Civilians as a Method of Combat).

[708] *See* LIEBER CODE art. 17 ("It is lawful to starve the hostile belligerent, armed or unarmed, so that it leads to the speedier subjection of the enemy."). *Consider* AP I art. 54(3) ("The prohibitions in paragraph 2 shall not apply to such of the objects covered by it as are used by an adverse Party: (a) As sustenance solely for the members of its armed forces; or (b) If not as sustenance, then in direct support of military action, provided, however, that in no event shall actions against these objects be taken which may be expected to leave the civilian population with such inadequate food or water as to cause its starvation or force its movement.").

[709] *For example*, Department of the Air Force, Headquarters Pacific Air Forces, Directorate of Operations Analysis, *Project CHECO [Contemporary Historical Examination of Current Operations] Report, "Ranch Hand: Herbicide Operations in SEA [Southeast Asia]"* 19 (Jul. 13, 1971) ("The enemy documents revealed that the VC [Viet Cong] had suffered serious personnel losses due to the lack of food. Troops normally used in fighting had to be detailed to crop raising, and in one case the 95th North Vietnamese Army (NVA) regiment had to fast for one or two days on several occasions due to a lack of food. The overall conclusion of the PACOM report was that crop destruction was 'an integral, essential and effective part of the total effort in South Vietnam.'").

[710] *Refer to* § 5.6.2 (Persons Who Are Military Objectives).

[711] *See* J. Fred Buzhardt, General Counsel, Department of Defense, Letter to Chairman Fulbright, Senate Committee on Foreign Relations, Apr. 5, 1971, 10 INTERNATIONAL LEGAL MATERIALS 1300, 1302 (1971) ("But an attack by any means against crops intended solely for consumption by noncombatants not contributing to the enemy's war effort would be unlawful for such would not be an attack upon a legitimate military objective."). *Consider* AP I art. 54(1) ("Starvation of civilians as a method of warfare is prohibited.").

5.20.2 Starvation – Proportionality. Military action intended to starve enemy forces, however, must not be taken where it is expected to result in incidental harm to the civilian population that is excessive in relation to the military advantage anticipated to be gained.[712]

Feasible precautions to reduce the risk of harm to the civilian population or other reasonable measures to mitigate the burden to the civilian population may also be warranted when seeking to starve enemy forces.[713] For example, it may be appropriate to seek to compensate civilians whose food has been inadvertently destroyed.[714] Moreover, an Occupying Power would have additional duties to ensure food and water for the civilian population.[715]

5.20.3 Starvation and Other Law of War Rules. Starvation as a method of warfare must comply with other applicable law of war rules. For example, it would be unlawful to poison food or water.[716] Additionally, starvation, for example, may involve sieges or encirclement, blockades, attacks, or the seizure and destruction of enemy property.[717] In each case, the rules applicable to those situations must be followed.

5.20.4 AP I Provision on Objects Indispensable to the Survival of the Civilian Population. Article 54(2) of AP I makes it prohibited for Parties to AP I "to attack, destroy, remove or render useless objects indispensable to the survival of the enemy civilian population, such as foodstuffs, agricultural areas for the production of foodstuffs, crops, livestock, drinking water installations, and supplies for irrigation works, for the specific purpose of denying them for their sustenance value to the civilian population or to the adverse party, whatever the motive,

---

712 *Cf.* J. Fred Buzhardt, General Counsel, Department of Defense, Letter to Chairman Fulbright, Senate Committee on Foreign Relations, Apr. 5, 1971, 10 INTERNATIONAL LEGAL MATERIALS 1300, 1302 (1971) ("Where it cannot be determined whether crops were intended solely for consumption by the enemy's armed forces, crop destruction would be lawful if a reasonable inquiry indicated that the intended destruction is justified by military necessity under the principles of Hague Regulation Article 23(g), and that the devastation occasioned is not disproportionate to the military advantage gained.").

713 *Refer to* § 5.2.3 (Affirmative Duties to Take Feasible Precautions for the Protection of Civilians and Other Protected Persons and Objects).

714 *For example*, Department of State, *Telegram From the Department of State to the Embassy in Vietnam*, Washington, May 7, 1963, *reprinted in* III FOREIGN RELATIONS OF THE UNITED STATES, 1961–1963, VIETNAM, JANUARY–AUGUST 1963, DOCUMENT 110, p. 275 ("All herbicide operations [including crop destruction] to be undertaken only after it is clear both PsyWar preparations and compensation and relief machinery [for peasants whose crops are inadvertently destroyed] are adequate. Would appear GVN [Government of Vietnam] should increase compensation efforts."); Memorandum Prepared in the Department of State, *Chemical Defoliation and Crop Destruction in South Viet-Nam*, Washington, Apr. 18, 1963, *reprinted in* III FOREIGN RELATIONS OF THE UNITED STATES, 1961–1963, VIETNAM, JANUARY–AUGUST 1963, DOCUMENT 96, pp. 240 ("The GVN [Government of Vietnam] has set up a mechanism for compensating peasants whose crops are inadvertently destroyed. We do not have much information on the results of the compensation program, but there are indications that it was not adequately carried out, in part because of security difficulties.").

715 *Refer to* § 11.14 (Food and Medical Supplies for the Civilian Population).

716 *Refer to* § 6.8 (Poison).

717 *Refer to* § 5.19 (Sieges and Encircled Areas); § 13.10 (Blockade); § 5.4 (Rules on Conducting Assaults, Bombardments, and Other Attacks); § 5.17 (Seizure and Destruction of Enemy Property).

whether in order to starve out civilians, cause them to move away, or for any other motive."[718]

This rule would not apply to attacks that are carried out for specific purposes other than to deny sustenance.[719] For example, this rule would not prohibit destroying a field of crops to prevent it from being used as concealment by the enemy or destroying a supply route that is used to move military supplies but is also used to supply the civilian population with food.[720]

Similarly, this AP I prohibition does not apply to objects that would otherwise be covered by it if those objects are used by an adverse party "as sustenance solely for the members of its armed forces" or "if not as sustenance, then in direct support of military action."[721] Actions against this latter category of objects forfeiting protection, however, may not be taken if they "may be expected to leave the civilian population with such inadequate food or water as to cause its starvation or force its movement."[722]

Further exception is made for a State to engage in a "scorched earth" defense of a party's own territory.[723]

When adopted, this AP I prohibition was novel and the product of extensive diplomatic negotiation. Given the intricacy of this provision of AP I, it would be difficult to conclude that all of its particulars reflect customary international law. Nonetheless, the United States has supported the underlying principle that starvation of civilians may not be used as a method of

---

718 AP I art. 54(2).

719 *See, e.g.*, APPENDIX TO 1985 CJCS MEMO ON AP I 56 (The restrictions of Article 54(2) "do not apply to attacks that are not for the specific purpose of denying sustenance;"); United Kingdom, *Statement on Ratification of AP I*, Jan. 28, 1998, 2020 UNTS 75, 77 (Article 54(2) of AP I "has no application to attacks that are carried out for a specific purpose other than denying sustenance to the civilian population or the adverse party.").

720 2004 UK MANUAL ¶5.27.2 ("The law is not violated if military operations are not intended to cause starvation but have that incidental effect, for example, by cutting off enemy supply routes which are also used for the transportation of food, or if civilians through fear of military operations abandon agricultural land or are not prepared to risk bringing food supplies into areas where fighting is going on."); BOTHE, PARTSCH, & SOLF, NEW RULES 339 (AP I art. 54, ¶2.3) ("This paragraph does not prohibit the incidental distress of civilians resulting from otherwise lawful military operations. It would not, for example, be unlawful to attack or destroy a railroad line simply because the railroad was used to transport food needed to supply the population of a city, if the railroad was otherwise a military objective under Art. 52 [of AP I].").

721 AP I art. 54(3) ("The prohibitions in paragraph 2 shall not apply to such of the objects covered by it as are used by an adverse Party: (*a*) As sustenance solely for the members of its armed forces; or (*b*) If not as sustenance, then in direct support of military action, provided, however, that in no event shall actions against these objects be taken which may be expected to leave the civilian population with such inadequate food or water as to cause its starvation or force its movement.").

722 AP I art. 54(3) ("The prohibitions in paragraph 2 shall not apply to such of the objects covered by it as are used by an adverse Party: ... (*b*) If not as sustenance, then in direct support of military action, provided, however, that in no event shall actions against these objects be taken which may be expected to leave the civilian population with such inadequate food or water as to cause its starvation or force its movement.").

723 AP I art. 54(5) ("In recognition of the vital requirements of any Party to the conflict in the defence of its national territory against invasion, derogation from the prohibitions contained in paragraph 2 may be made by a Party to the conflict within such territory under its own control where required by imperative military necessity.").

warfare, as discussed in the sub-sections above.[724]

5.21 Overview of Good Faith, Perfidy, and Ruses

Absolute good faith with the enemy must be observed as a rule of conduct.[725] The line between those deceptions that good faith permits and those that good faith prohibits may appear indistinct and has varied according to State practice.[726] Good faith prohibits:

- killing or wounding enemy persons by resort to perfidy;[727]
- misusing certain signs;[728]
- fighting in the enemy's uniform;[729]
- feigning non-hostile relations in order to seek a military advantage;[730] and
- compelling nationals of a hostile party to take part in the operations of war directed against their own country.[731]

However, good faith permits:

- ruses of war or other lawful deceptive activities;[732]

---

[724] Michael J. Matheson, Deputy Legal Adviser, Department of State, *Remarks on the United States Position on the Relation of Customary International Law to the 1977 Protocols Additional to the 1949 Geneva Conventions at the Sixth Annual American Red Cross-Washington College of Law Conference on International Humanitarian Law* (Jan. 22, 1987), 2 American University Journal of International Law and Policy 419, 426 (1987) ("We support the principle that starvation of civilians not be used as a method of warfare, and subject to the requirements of imperative military necessity, that impartial relief actions necessary for the survival of the civilian population be permitted and encouraged. These principles can be found, though in a somewhat different form, in articles 54 and 70.").

[725] 1956 FM 27-10 (Change No. 1 1976) ¶49 ("Absolute good faith with the enemy must be observed as a rule of conduct; but this does not prevent measures such as using spies and secret agents, encouraging defection or insurrection among the enemy civilian population, corrupting enemy civilians or soldiers by bribes, or inducing the enemy's soldiers to desert, surrender, or rebel.").

[726] 1958 UK Manual ¶310 ("The borderline between legitimate ruses and forbidden treachery has varied at different times, and it is difficult to lay down hard and fast rules in the matter. Many of the doubtful cases, however, which arose at a time when, from the nature of their weapons, troops could only engage at close range, can now seldom or never occur.").

[727] *Refer to* § 5.22 (Treachery or Perfidy Used to Kill or Wound).

[728] *Refer to* § 5.24 (Improper Use of Certain Signs).

[729] *Refer to* § 5.23 (Use of Enemy Flags, Insignia, and Military Uniforms).

[730] *Refer to* § 12.2 (Principle of Good Faith in Non-Hostile Relations).

[731] *Refer to* § 5.27 (Prohibition Against Compelling Enemy Nationals to Take Part in the Operations of War Directed Against Their Own Country).

[732] *Refer to* § 5.25 (Ruses of War and Other Lawful Deceptions).

- intelligence collection;[733]
- military information support operations, including propaganda;[734] and
- certain types of bribery.[735]

5.21.1 Harms From Breaches of Good Faith. Breaches of good faith may: (1) undermine the protections afforded by the law of war to classes of persons and objects; (2) impair non-hostile relations between opposing belligerents; and (3) damage the basis for the restoration of peace short of complete annihilation of one belligerent by another.

Breaches of good faith, principally perfidious conduct, may undermine the protections afforded by the law of war to civilians, persons who are *hors de combat*, or certain other classes of persons and objects.[736]

Breaches of good faith also impair other non-hostile relations between opposing belligerents during the war. For example, such breaches may diminish the legitimate activities that depend upon a degree of mutual respect and trust between hostile forces, such as effecting surrender or collection of the dead, wounded, or sick (enemy or friendly force) on the battlefield. It also may make it more difficult for military commanders to ensure that their forces comply with the law of war where treacherous acts by the enemy have resulted in casualties among their own forces.

Breaches of good faith also damage, and may destroy, the basis for restoration of peace short of the complete annihilation of one belligerent by another.[737] A degree of mutual respect and trust is essential for the negotiation of cease-fires, truces, surrenders, and other agreements necessary to bring an end to hostilities.

5.22 Treachery or Perfidy Used to Kill or Wound

During international armed conflict, it is prohibited to kill or wound the enemy by resort to perfidy.[738]

---

[733] *Refer to* § 5.26.1 (Propaganda).

[734] *Refer to* § 5.26.2 (Information Gathering).

[735] *Refer to* § 5.26.3 (Bribery or Offering of Rewards).

[736] BOTHE, PARTSCH, & SOLF, NEW RULES 202 (AP I art. 37, ¶2.1) ("Combatants, in practice, find it difficult to respect protected persons and objects if experience causes them to believe or suspect that their adversaries are abusing their claim to protection under the rules of international law applicable in armed conflict in order to achieve a military advantage. The prohibitions of perfidy are thus directly related to protection for the wounded and sick, hors de combat combatants, prisoners of war and civilians."). *See also* footnote 164, § 4.6.4 (Having a Fixed Distinctive Sign Recognizable at a Distance).

[737] 1956 FM 27-10 (Change No. 1 1976) ¶50 ("Treacherous or perfidious conduct in war is forbidden because it destroys the basis for a restoration of peace short of the complete annihilation of one belligerent by the other.").

[738] HAGUE IV REG. art. 23(b) (It is especially forbidden "[t]o kill or wound treacherously individuals belonging to the hostile nation or army"); LIEBER Code art. 101 (noting that "the common law of war allows even capital punishment for clandestine or treacherous attempts to injure an enemy"). *Consider* ROME STATUTE art. 8(2)(b)(xi)

5.22.1 Definition of Perfidy. Acts of *perfidy* are acts that invite the confidence of enemy persons to lead them to believe that they are entitled to, or are obliged to accord, protection under the law of war, with intent to betray that confidence.[739]

The key element in perfidy is the false claim to protections under the law of war in order to secure a military advantage over the opponent.[740] The claim must be to legal protections.[741]

5.22.1.1 *Perfidy and Treachery – Notes on Terminology*. "Treachery" and "perfidy" have been used interchangeably.[742] Article 23(b) of the Hague IV Regulations uses the word "treacherously," which was also used in Article 13(b) of the 1874 Brussels Declaration.[743]

Sometimes, "perfidy" is used to refer to conduct that is, by definition, prohibited.[744] Other times, as, for example, in AP I, "perfidy" is used to refer to a certain type of deception, which might not, by itself, be prohibited (*e.g.*, feigning death would not be prohibited in order to facilitate escape).[745] It will be important to examine closely the context to determine which usage is intended. This manual generally uses "perfidy" in the latter sense.

5.22.2 Perfidy - "Kill or Wound". It is prohibited to use perfidy to kill or wound the enemy. It may not be prohibited to invite the confidence of the adversary that he or she is obligated to accord protection under the law of war, for certain purposes (*e.g.*, to facilitate

---

(defining war crimes in international armed conflict to include "[k]illing or wounding treacherously individuals belonging to the hostile nation or army").

739 *Consider* AP I art. 37(1) ("Acts inviting the confidence of an adversary to lead him to believe that he is entitled to, or is obliged to accord, protection under the rules of international law applicable in armed conflict, with intent to betray that confidence, shall constitute perfidy."); APPENDIX TO 1985 CJCS MEMO ON AP I 26 ("Rather than 'treachery,' paragraph 1 of Article 37 uses the modern term 'perfidy,' and defines it as 'acts inviting the confidence of an adversary to lead him to believe that he is entitled to, or is obliged to accord, protection under the rules of international law applicable in armed conflict, with the intent to betray that confidence.' This definition, and the examples provided, are an accurate and helpful clarification of existing law.").

740 ICRC AP COMMENTARY 435 (¶1500) ("The central element of the definition of perfidy is the deliberate claim to legal protection for hostile purposes.").

741 BOTHE, PARTSCH, & SOLF, NEW RULES 204-05 (AP I art. 37, ¶2.4.2) ("The ICRC draft of the article referred to 'confidence' without elaborating that confidence must be based on a norm of international law. It would have involved confidence in moral obligations as well as in binding legal obligations. This was considered to be overly abstract and ambiguous by delegations representing several regional groups.").

742 *For example*, XV OFFICIAL RECORDS OF THE CDDH 99 (CDDH/III/SR.47 ¶78) ("Mr. Reed (United States of America) said that article 35, paragraph 1, was a reaffirmation and development of Article 23 b) of The Hague Regulations respecting the Laws and Customs of War on Land annexed to The Hague Convention No. IV of 1907 concerning the Laws and Customs of War on Land. The word 'treacherously' in Article 23 b) was synonymous with 'perfidy' in article 35 of draft Protocol I.").

743 SPAIGHT, WAR RIGHTS ON LAND 86 ("The word 'Treachery' in Article XXIII(b) seems hardly applicable to an enemy's act, and one of the Brussels delegates proposed to substitute 'perfidy' for it. The original word was, however, retained, as being the equivalent of the German *Meuchelmord* ('murder by treachery')").

744 1956 FM 27-10 (Change No. 1 1976) ¶50 (providing that "[t]reacherous or perfidious conduct in war is forbidden").

745 BOTHE, PARTSCH, & SOLF, NEW RULES 203 (AP I art. 37, ¶2.4) ("It should be noted that Art. 37 [of AP I] does not prohibit perfidy *per se*, although the term is defined with precision.").

spying, sabotage, capturing enemy personnel, or evading enemy forces). However, such deception may not rely on certain signs and symbols.[746] Moreover, persons who use perfidy to engage in spying and sabotage may forfeit POW status or be liable to certain penalties under the domestic law of enemy States.[747]

5.22.2.1 *AP I Prohibition on "Capture" by Resort to Perfidy*. In addition to killing or wounding, Article 37 of AP I prohibits "capture" by resort to perfidy. The Department of Defense has not interpreted customary international law to prohibit U.S. forces from seeking to capture by resort to perfidy.

5.22.3 Examples of Killing or Wounding by Resort to Perfidy. Examples of killing or wounding by resort to perfidy include:

- feigning an intent to negotiate under a flag of truce and then attacking,[748] which takes advantage of the rule that flags of truce may not be used to shield military operations.[749]

- feigning surrender and then attacking,[750] which takes advantage of the rule that the enemy may not attack those who have surrendered;[751]

- feigning of death or incapacitation by wounds or sickness[752] and then attacking, which takes advantage of the respect afforded the dead[753] or the protection afforded those who are *hors de combat*;[754]

- feigning civilian status and then attacking;[755] and

---

[746] *Refer to* § 5.24 (Improper Use of Certain Signs).

[747] *Refer to* § 4.17 (Spies, Saboteurs, and Other Persons Engaging in Similar Acts Behind Enemy Lines).

[748] *For example*, William Gerald Downey, *The Law of War and Military Necessity*, 47 AJIL 251, 260 (1953) ("A good example of the use of deception which involved a breach of good faith is one that happened in this writer's presence during the Battle of Metz in 1944. At that time the German forces held several forts south and east of Metz. One November morning, just as our attack was getting under way, a German unit of some 20 men came out of one of the forts under a white flag. The American battalion commander gave the order to cease fire, and the Germans marched under the protection of the white flag down the road toward our lines. As they came abreast of a large bunker they pulled down their white flag, ran into the bunker and immediately opened fire on our positions.").

[749] *Refer to* § 5.24.7 (Flags of Truce).

[750] *See* FINAL REPORT ON THE PERSIAN GULF WAR 621 ("During the same battle, an Iraqi officer approached Coalition forces with his hands in the air, indicating his intention to surrender. When near his would-be captors, he drew a concealed pistol from his boot, fired, and was killed during the combat that followed.").

[751] *Refer to* § 5.9.3 (Persons Who Have Surrendered).

[752] 1958 UK MANUAL ¶115 note 2 ("For instance, it would be treachery for a soldier to sham wounded or dead and then to attack enemy soldiers who approached him without hostile intent, or to pretend he had surrendered and afterwards to open fire upon or attack an enemy who was treating him as *hors de combat* or a prisoner.).

[753] *Refer to* § 7.7 (Treatment and Handling of Enemy Military Dead).

[754] *Refer to* § 5.9.4 (Persons Rendered Unconscious or Otherwise Incapacitated by Wounds, Sickness, or Shipwreck).

[755] *Refer to* § 5.4.8 (Obligation of Combatants to Distinguish Themselves When Conducting Attacks).

- calling out "do not fire; we are friends" and then attacking.[756]

5.23 Use of Enemy Flags, Insignia, and Military Uniforms

During international armed conflict, improper use of enemy flags, military emblems, insignia, or uniforms, is prohibited.[757]

5.23.1 Improper Use of Enemy Flags, Insignia, and Military Uniforms Prohibited. In general, the use of enemy flags, insignia, and military uniforms is prohibited during combat, but is permissible outside of combat.[758]

A similar rule is applied during naval operations.[759]

5.23.1.1 *Improper Use of Enemy Uniforms and "Perfidy"*. The prohibition on the use of enemy uniforms in combat has been described as a prohibition against using enemy uniforms to kill or wound treacherously.[760] However, feigning enemy military status is not technically "perfidy" as the term is used in this manual because perfidy requires the feigning of protected status, and the law of war generally does not protect enemy military personnel from being made the object of attack.[761]

5.23.1.2 *Use of Enemy Uniforms and Other Equipment Without the Intent to Deceive*. Uses of enemy uniforms and other equipment without any intention to deceive the enemy are not prohibited. For example, if there is a shortage of clothing it may be necessary to use enemy uniforms.[762] Similarly, the immediate use of captured enemy weapons or equipment

---

[756] 2004 UK MANUAL ¶5.9 footnote 35 ("Examples of treachery included calling out 'Do no fire, we are friends' and then firing at enemy troops who had lowered their guard, especially if coupled with the wearing of enemy uniforms or civilian clothing;"); 1958 UK MANUAL ¶311 note 1 (giving as an example of treacherous killing or wounding "calling out 'Do not fire, we are friends', and then firing" which "is often accompanied by the use of enemy uniforms or civilian clothing"); 1914 1914 RULES OF LAND WARFARE ¶178 note 1 ("It would be treacherous to call out, 'Do not fire; we are friends,' and then fire a volley.").

[757] HAGUE IV REG. art. 23(f) (making it especially forbidden "[t]o make improper use … of the national flag, or of the military insignia and uniform of the enemy,").

[758] APPENDIX TO 1985 CJCS MEMO ON AP I 28 ("Existing international law prohibits 'improper' use of the enemy uniform or insignia. The United States interprets this rule to prohibit their use in combat, but not in situations preceding or following combat."); 1956 FM 27-10 (Change No. 1 1976) ¶54 ("It is certainly forbidden to employ [national flags, insignia, and uniforms] during combat, but their use at other times is not forbidden.").

[759] *Refer to* § 13.13.1 (Belligerent Warship's Use of False Colors and Other Disguises).

[760] *For example*, Trial of Otto Skorzeny and Others, IX U.N. LAW REPORTS 90 (General Military Government Court of the U.S. Zone of Germany, Aug. 18-Sept. 9, 1947) ("The ten accused involved in this trial were all officers in the 150th Panzer Brigade commanded by the accused Skorzeny. They were charged with participating in the improper use of American uniforms by entering into combat disguised therewith and treacherously firing upon and killing members of the armed forces of the United States.").

[761] *Refer to* § 5.22.1 (Definition of Perfidy).

[762] *See* 1958 UK MANUAL ¶322 ("If, owing to shortage of clothing, it becomes necessary to utilise apparel captured from the enemy, the badges should be removed before the articles are worn."); 1958 UK MANUAL ¶322 note 1 ("Articles of uniform which are distinctive of a particular army—such as the beret of the French Chasseurs des Alpes or the coloured berets of certain British troops, the kilt of some regiments, or the Turkish fez—should not be used except in cases of absolute necessity.").

during combat is permissible. When circumstances permit, however, enemy insignia should generally be removed or alternative measures taken to distinguish U.S. forces from the enemy.[763]

5.23.1.3 Deceptive Use of Enemy Flags, Insignia, and Military Uniforms Outside of Combat. It is a legitimate ruse to use enemy flags, insignia, and military uniforms outside of combat.[764]

5.23.1.4 Use of Enemy Uniforms to Evade Capture or Escape. Military personnel, such as aircrew downed behind enemy lines, may use enemy uniforms to evade capture. Similarly, escaping prisoners of war may use enemy military uniforms to facilitate their escape from a POW camp to return to friendly lines.[765]

However, those using enemy uniforms to evade capture or escape must not engage in combat while in the enemy's uniform, and, if they are not escaping POWs, they may be liable to treatment as spies and saboteurs if caught behind enemy lines.[766]

5.23.1.5 Use of Enemy Codes, Passwords, and Countersigns Not Restricted. The prohibition on misuse of enemy flags, insignia, and military uniforms refers only to concrete visual objects, rather than enemy codes, passwords, and countersigns.[767] Enemy codes, passwords, and countersigns may be used as a ruse to aid military operations.[768] Enemy use of these measures is permissible because military forces are expected to take measures to guard against the use of their codes, passwords, and countersigns by the enemy.

5.23.2 Persons Using Enemy Uniforms May Be Liable to Treatment as Spies and Saboteurs. Although the use of enemy uniforms outside of combat generally is neither prohibited by the customary law of war nor by law of war treaties to which the United States is a Party, combatants captured by an opposing party behind the opposing party's lines while wearing

---

[763] *See* LIEBER CODE art. 64 ("If American troops capture a train containing uniforms of the enemy, and the commander considers it advisable to distribute them for use among his men, some striking mark or sign must be adopted to distinguish the American soldier from the enemy.").

[764] *For example*, 1958 UK MANUAL ¶320 note 3 ("During the Second World War the German intelligence service in Belgium used German soldiers disguised as British airmen 'to discover the attitude of the Belgian population towards individual British airmen landing in Belgium. The operation was completely successful. Active assistance was rendered by an organised network which was uncovered. The mass of the population was not involved'. (Extract from a captured German teleprint dated 9th January, 1943.) It would seem that this use of enemy uniform outside of battle operations is a legitimate ruse.").

[765] *Refer to* § 9.25.2.3 (Disciplinary Punishment for Certain Offenses Committed in Connection With Escape).

[766] *Refer to* § 4.17 (Spies, Saboteurs, and Other Persons Engaging in Similar Acts Behind Enemy Lines).

[767] *Cf.* BOTHE, PARTSCH, & SOLF, NEW RULES 214 (AP I art. 29, ¶2.3.3) ("The term 'emblem, insignia, or uniforms' [in AP I art. 39(2)] refers only to concrete visual objects, including the national symbols marked on military vehicles and aircraft. This prohibition does not apply to the ruse of using the adversary's codes, passwords and countersigns to aid military operations.").

[768] *See, e.g.*, BOTHE, PARTSCH, & SOLF, NEW RULES 207 footnote 25 (AP I art. 37, ¶2.5) ("It would be a legitimate ruse to use the electronic transponder aboard a combatant aircraft to respond with the code used for identifying friendly aircraft,"); SPAIGHT, AIR POWER AND WAR RIGHTS 176 ("The greatly developed use of wireless telephony afforded opportunities for deception of which the airmen were not slow to avail themselves. The feigning of orders to enemy machines to return to their base, for instance, was a common ruse.").

the uniform of the opposing party may be liable to treatment as spies and saboteurs.[769]

5.23.3 AP I and the Use of Enemy Flags, Insignia, or Uniforms to Shield, Favor, Protect, or Impede Military Operations. In addition to prohibiting the use of enemy uniforms while engaging in attacks, AP I also prohibits the use of flags, military emblems, insignia, or uniforms of an enemy in order to shield, favor, protect, or impede military operations.[770] Canada has taken a reservation from this rule.[771]

This provision of AP I is unclear as to what uses would be permissible and what uses would be prohibited.[772] However, because the United States is not a Party to AP I and because the rule is not part of customary international law, U.S. military personnel are not subject to this more restrictive rule.

5.24 Improper Use of Certain Signs

Certain signs, symbols, or signals reflect a status that receives special protection under the law of war, and thus these signs may not be improperly used. They may not be used: (1) while engaging in attacks; (2) in order to shield, favor, or protect one's own military operations; or (3) to impede enemy military operations. Thus, their use may be improper even when that use does not involve killing or wounding, and they may not be used to facilitate espionage (except for signs, emblems, or uniforms of a neutral or non-belligerent State). The following types of signs are subject to this broader rule against improper use:

5.24.1 Signs, Emblems, or Uniforms of a Neutral or Non-Belligerent State. During international armed conflict, the use of signs, emblems, or uniforms of a neutral or other nation not a party to the conflict is prohibited.[773]

However, recognized exceptions exist concerning espionage[774] and warfare at sea.[775]

---

769 *Refer to* § 4.17 (Spies, Saboteurs, and Other Persons Engaging in Similar Acts Behind Enemy Lines).

770 AP I art. 39(2) ("It is prohibited to make use of the flags or military emblems, insignia or uniforms of adverse Parties while engaging in attacks or in order to shield, favour, protect or impede military operations.").

771 Canada, *Statement on Ratification of AP I*, Nov. 20, 1990, 1591 UNTS 462, 463 ("The Government of Canada does not intend to be bound by the prohibitions contained in paragraph 2 of Article 39 to make use of military emblems, insignia or uniforms of adverse parties in order to shield, favour, protect or impede military operations.").

772 BOTHE, PARTSCH, & SOLF, NEW RULES 214 (AP I art. 39, ¶2.3) (Article 39(2) of AP I "suggests that some uses [of the enemy uniform] are not breaches of the Protocol, but the boundary between forbidden and permissible uses is not very distinct.").

773 *Consider* AP I art. 39(1) ("It is prohibited to make use in an armed conflict of the flags or military emblems, insignia or uniforms of neutral or other States not Parties to the conflict."); AP I art. 37(1)(d) (giving as an example of perfidy the feigning of protected status by the use of signs, emblems or uniforms "of neutral or other States not Parties to the conflict."); BOTHE, PARTSCH, & SOLF, NEW RULES 213 (AP I art. 39, ¶2.2) ("The purpose behind the rule is to avoid escalation of armed conflict to neutral countries in the mistaken belief that the neutral State had abandoned its neutrality.").

774 *See* SPAIGHT, WAR RIGHTS ON LAND 203-04 ("The spy in modern war is usually a soldier who dons civilian dress, or the uniform of the enemy, or of a neutral country; and in all these cases, he would be liable to punishment, apart from this article, for assuming a disguise to further a hostile act."). Although Article 37(1)(d) of AP I lists

5.24.2 Distinctive Emblems of the Geneva Conventions (*e.g.*, Red Cross). The distinctive emblems of the red cross, red crescent, and red crystal are symbols that identify military medical and religious personnel, medical units, and medical transports, or certain other categories of persons engaged in humanitarian work as personnel and objects entitled to special protection.[776] These emblems may not be used except to identify these protected persons and objects.[777]

5.24.3 Markings for POW or Civilian Internee Camps. Only POW camps under the GPW should be marked using internationally agreed symbols, such as the PW or PG designation.[778]

Only civilian internee camps under the GC should be marked with an IC designation.[779]

5.24.4 Markings for Hospital, Safety, or Neutralized Zones. Markings that distinguish hospital or safety zones or neutralized zones established under the 1949 Geneva Conventions may not be used for other purposes.[780]

5.24.5 Distinctive and Visible Signs to Identify Civilian Objects as Such. Certain distinctive and visible signs that are intended to identify that an object is protected as a civilian object under the law of war must not be used for other purposes.[781]

5.24.6 Markings for Cultural Property. The distinctive emblem for cultural property may not be used for other purposes.[782]

5.24.7 Flags of Truce. The improper use of a flag of truce is strictly prohibited.[783]

"[t]he feigning of protected status by the use of signs, emblems or uniforms ... of neutral or other States not Parties to the conflict" as an example of perfidy, and Article 39(1) prohibits the "use in an armed conflict of the flags or military emblems, insignia or uniforms of neutral or other States not Parties to the conflict," Article 39(3) of AP I clarifies that "[n]othing in this Article or in Article 37, paragraph 1 (d), shall affect the existing generally recognized rules of international law applicable to espionage ... ."

[775] APPENDIX TO 1985 CJCS MEMO ON AP I 28 ("Article 39, paragraph 1, of the Protocol prohibits the use of neutral flags, uniforms or emblems in armed conflict. This is already a rule of customary law, to which recognized exceptions exists governing espionage and warfare at sea. The exceptions are preserved by paragraph 3 of the Article."). *Refer to* § 13.13.1 (Belligerent Warship's Use of False Colors and Other Disguises).

[776] *Refer to* § 7.15 (Display of the Distinctive Emblem to Facilitate Identification).

[777] *Refer to* § 7.15.4 (Prohibitions on Unauthorized Uses of the Distinctive Emblem).

[778] *Refer to* § 9.11.4.3 (Marking of POW Camps).

[779] *Refer to* § 10.11.1.3 (Marking of Internment Camps).

[780] *Refer to* § 5.14.3 (Establishing Areas Where Civilians or the Wounded and Sick Are Protected).

[781] *Refer to* § 5.14.4 (Using Distinctive and Visible Signs to Identify Protected Persons and Objects as Such).

[782] *Refer to* § 5.18.7.4 (Other Uses of the Distinctive Emblem for Cultural Property Prohibited During Armed Conflict).

[783] *Refer to* § 12.4.2.1 (Prohibition on Improper Use of the Flag of Truce).

5.25 Ruses of War and Other Lawful Deceptions

Ruses of war are considered permissible.[784] In general, a belligerent may resort to those measures for mystifying or misleading the enemy against which the enemy ought to take measures to protect itself.[785] Apart from ruses of war, certain other deceptions are not prohibited, but may expose combatants employing them to liability as spies and saboteurs.

5.25.1 Definition of Ruses of War. Ruses of war are acts that are intended to mislead an adversary or to induce him to act recklessly, but that do not infringe upon any rule of international law applicable in armed conflict and that are not perfidious because they do not invite the confidence of an adversary with respect to protection under that law.[786]

Ruses of war are methods, resources, and techniques that can be used either to convey false information or deny information to opposing forces. They can include physical, technical, or administrative means, such as electronic warfare measures, flares, smoke, chaff, aerosol material, or dissemination devices.

5.25.1.1 *Acts That Are Intended to Mislead an Adversary or to Induce an Adversary to Act Recklessly*. Ruses may be used for a variety of purposes, such as:

- facilitating surprise attacks or ambushes,[787] such as by
    - misleading the enemy as to the planned targets or locations of military operations;[788]

---

[784] Hague IV Reg. 24 ("Ruses of war and the employment of measures necessary for obtaining information about the enemy and the country are considered permissible."). *Consider* AP I art. 37(2) ("Ruses of war are not prohibited.).

[785] 1956 FM 27-10 (Change No. 1 1976) ¶49 ("In general, a belligerent may resort to those measures for mystifying or misleading the enemy against which the enemy ought to take measures to protect himself.").

[786] *Consider* AP I art. 37(2) ("Such ruses are acts which are intended to mislead an adversary or to induce him to act recklessly but which infringe no rule of international law applicable in armed conflict and which are not perfidious because they do not invite thé confidence of an adversary with respect to protection under that law."). *Refer to* § 5.22.1 (Definition of Perfidy).

[787] *Refer to* § 5.4.6.1 (Surprise Attacks).

[788] *For example*, Final Report on the Persian Gulf War 247 ("CINCCENT [Commander-in-Chief, U.S. Central Command] placed a high priority on deception operations which were intended to convince Iraq that the main attack would be directly into Kuwait, supported by an amphibious assault. All components contributed to the deception operation. Aggressive ground force patrolling, artillery raids, amphibious feints and ship movements, and air operations all were part of CINCCENT's orchestrated deception operation."); Spaight, Air Power and War Rights 185 ("'The greatest hoax in military history' was the description officially applied to the scheme of deception used to induce the Germans to believe that the invasion of the Continent in June, 1944, was coming in the Pas de Calais and not in Normandy. It was carried out by a force of 105 aircraft of the R.A.F., by 34 ships of the Royal Navy, and by 'R.C.M.' (Radio Counter-Measures). On the night of 5 June, 18 small ships of the Navy steamed towards Cap d'Antifer to give the impression of an intended landing, while a bomber squadron, No. 617, under G/Capt. G. L. Chesire, V.C., circled over them, dropping bundles of 'Window,' the thin metallised strips which produce false echoes on the enemy's radar screens and so confuse their plotting. Another squadron, No. 218, with 16 ships, made a similar feint towards Boulogne, and other methods of deception were practised elsewhere

- baiting the enemy into a trap; or
- distracting or disorienting the enemy;

- inducing enemy forces to waste their resources;
- inducing enemy forces to surrender by falsely alleging military superiority;
- provoking friendly fire among enemy forces; or
- causing confusion among enemy forces.

5.25.1.2 *But That Do Not Infringe Upon Any Rule of International Law Applicable in Armed Conflict*. According to the definition in AP I, *ruses* do not infringe upon any rule of international law applicable in armed conflict. For example, misusing certain signs and symbols would not constitute ruses.[789] Similarly, although fighting in the enemy's uniform would not be perfidy since enemy military personnel are not generally protected by the law of war, fighting in the enemy's uniform also would not be a ruse, since such action would infringe upon the rule against improper use of the enemy's uniform.[790]

5.25.1.3 *And That Are Not Perfidious Because They Do Not Invite the Confidence of an Adversary With Respect to Protection Under That Law*. The ruses described in AP I do not invite the confidence of the enemy with respect to protection under the law of war.[791] For example, pretending to be a civilian would not constitute a ruse, although it may be a permissible deception in certain circumstances.[792]

5.25.1.4 *Ruses – Notes on Terminology*. The term "ruse" is sometimes used as a legal term of art to mean deceptions that are not prohibited by the law of war. In other cases, "ruse" may be used as a factual term to mean a deception that may or may not be prohibited by the law of war, and thus the distinction is made between "lawful" and "unlawful" ruses.[793]

In this manual, the term "ruse" is used to indicate a certain category of permissible deceptions.

5.25.2 Examples of Ruses. Often, ruses of war operate by misleading the enemy as to the identity, strength, position, or disposition of one's own forces. Ruses of war include, but are not

---

along the Channel. The result was that the enemy were led to believe that convoys were moving to points other than that at which the landing was in fact made with complete success and without opposition by air or sea.").

789 *Refer to* § 5.24 (Improper Use of Certain Signs).

790 *Refer to* § 5.23.1 (Improper Use of Enemy Flags, Insignia, and Military Uniforms Prohibited).

791 *Refer to* § 5.22.1 (Definition of Perfidy).

792 *Refer to* § 5.25.3 (Examples of Other Deceptions That Are Not Prohibited).

793 1956 FM 27-10 (Change No. 1 1976) ¶50 ("Ruses of war are legitimate so long as they do not involve treachery or perfidy on the party of the belligerent resorting to them.").

limited to:[794]

- decoys or dummy materials, such as dummy weapons, equipment, ships, aircraft, and buildings;[795]
- feigned activity or inactivity, such as
  - simulating quiet;
  - feigned flights, retreats, attacks, marches,[796] movements (*e.g.*, approaching a destination indirectly[797]), supply movements, operations, withdrawals, or camp;
- mimicking other friendly forces;[798]
- camouflage or deceptive lighting;[799]
- removing or altering identifying information, including moving identifying landmarks;
- planting false information in a manner that allows enemy forces to intercept it,[800] such as

---

[794] *Consider* AP I art. 37 (giving as examples of lawful ruses "the use of camouflage, decoys, mock operations and misinformation").

[795] *For example*, SPAIGHT, WAR RIGHTS ON LAND 153-54 ("The 'Quaker guns'—logs shaped like ordinary cannon and mounted on wheels—which the Confederates used at Vicksburg to induce the besieging Federals to credit them with an heavier armament than they possessed…[were a] legitimate ruse[] of war.").

[796] *For example*, SPAIGHT, AIR POWER AND WAR RIGHTS 186 ("The ruse of reversing temporarily the direction of a march was used on both sides in the first world war. 'Aeroplane observers can easily be deceived by a body of the enemy who, on sighting the aeroplane, move at once in a contrary direction to that of the real march, and turn back as soon as the machine has gone to give the news.'…[A] Turkish order which was captured in the Kara Tepe operations in Mesopotamia in December, 1917, instruct[ed] the Turkish infantry to try to deceive the British aeroplanes by setting out at once upon the march towards Jebel Hamrin if the aeroplanes came into sight and only to return to Kara Tepe upon the withdrawal of the aeroplanes.").

[797] *For example*, SPAIGHT, AIR POWER AND WAR RIGHTS 187 ("The outstanding example of the technique of indirect approach is to be found in the raid on Munich on the night of 24 April, 1944. A force of Lancasters left England in the evening and made for north Italy; they crossed the French Alps and flew nearly to Milan; then they suddenly changed direction to the north-east and flew to Munich, which was heavily bombed. The feint took the Germans completely by surprise and the raiders' losses were extremely low. The bewilderment of the defences was increased by the fact that Karlsruhe was attacked, after direct approach, on the same night.").

[798] *Refer to* § 5.25.2.1 (Mimicking Other Friendly Forces).

[799] *For example*, SPAIGHT, WAR RIGHTS ON LAND 154 ("The concealment of cannon in deftly arranged branches or brushwood is a common device of gunners, but the Japanese reached a dizzy and dramatic height of stratagem when they actually transformed the face of nature as a means of masking their batteries. On the night before the battle of the Yalu they transplanted trees to hide the tell-tale discharge of their artillery, choosing those growing either directly in front or directly behind the entrenchment that was to be concealed. Thus next morning the landscape appeared unchanged from the Russian side of the river, as the fact that a tree of a particular shape had advanced or retired 200 or 300 yards during the night was naturally imperceptible.") (internal quotations omitted).

[800] *For example*, ALBERT N. GARLAND & HOWARD M. SMYTH, SICILY AND THE SURRENDER OF ITALY 64-65 (1993) ("One part of this plan, known as Operation Mincemeat, was designed to convince the enemy high command that the objectives of the impending Allied offensive in the Mediterranean were Sardinia and the Peloponnesus rather than Sicily. The plan itself was simple but highly imaginative. With painstaking care a counterfeit letter from

through the use of

- o false messages among one's own forces;
- o intensifying or minimizing message traffic; or
- o bogus messages, dispatches, or newspapers;

- lying in the course of a POW interrogation in answering questions where no obligation to answer correctly exists;
- feigning enemy military status by using enemy flags, insignia, or military uniforms outside of combat;[801] or
- using enemy codes, signals, or passwords.[802]

5.25.2.1 _Mimicking Other Friendly Forces_. It is a permissible ruse of war for combatant forces to mimic other friendly forces. For example, small forces may simulate larger units.[803] Units of one type may pretend to be units of another type.[804] Markings that identify equipment or personnel as belonging to a particular unit may be removed. Individuals or units may also dress like friendly forces.[805]

'Archie Nye' of the British War Office in London was drawn up....[i]ndicating that a feint against Sicily would be a deception maneuver to screen an invasion of Sardinia.... To get this letter into Axis hands, British intelligence obtained with great difficulty the body of a service man who had been a victim of pneumonia.... With a courier's briefcase realistically chained to the wrist, the body was cast adrift at a predesignated spot where tide and current would carry it to [the Axis-controlled] shore.... The information reached the Germans who accepted it as authentic.").

[801] *Refer to* § 5.23.1.3 (Deceptive Use of Enemy Flags, Insignia, and Military Uniforms Outside of Combat).

[802] *Refer to* § 5.23.1.5 (Use of Enemy Codes, Passwords, and Countersigns Not Restricted).

[803] *For example*, HUGH M. COLE, THE LORRAINE CAMPAIGN 162 (1993) ("General Walker asked for a 'deception team' to simulate a stronger force in the cavalry sector. This team finally arrived from 12th Army Group headquarters and operated for some weeks in the area as an 'armored division.' (The Germans seem to have been well deceived for the OB WEST maps show the '14th Armored Division' in this area.)").

[804] *For example*, R. FRANK FUTRELL, ET AL., ACES AND AERIAL VICTORIES: THE UNITED STATES AIR FORCE IN SOUTHEAST ASIA 1965-1973, 37-43 (1976) ("The West Force used an elaborate ruse to make the Phantoms appear to the enemy as an F-105 Rolling Thunder strike force. The F4C's used F-105 tanker anchors, refueling altitudes, approach routes, approach altitudes, airspeeds, and radio call signs and communications to simulate a normal Thunderchief strike force. This was intended to deceive the enemy on NVN [North Vietnamese] radars. ... An opportunity to perpetuate another ruse presented itself a few days later, when RF-4C weather reconnaissance aircraft were forced to abort their planned weather reconnaissance missions in North Vietnam because of MIG attacks on 3 and 4 January 1967. To lure the MIG's into the air, two F4C's on the following day flew, in close formation, a route similar to that normally flown by weather reconnaissance aircraft. The intent of the F4C's was to deceive the enemy radar operators into believing that only one aircraft was flying a weather reconnaissance mission.").

[805] *For example*, W. Hays Parks, *Special Forces' Wear of Non-Standard Uniform*, 4 CHICAGO JOURNAL OF INTERNATIONAL LAW 493, 554 (2003) ("In response to the September 11, 2001 al Qaeda terrorist attacks against the World Trade Center and the Pentagon, US and Coalition Special Forces began operations in Afghanistan in late September 2001. At the request— initially insistence—of the leaders of the indigenous forces they supported, they dressed in indigenous attire. For identification purposes within the Northern Alliance, this included the Massoud

5.25.3 Examples of Other Deceptions That Are Not Prohibited. Certain deceptions may not meet the definition of "ruses" because they may invite the confidence of an adversary with respect to protection under the law of war. Nevertheless, these deceptions are not technically prohibited by the law of war, even though, in some cases, they may expose the persons performing them to liability under an enemy State's domestic law.[806] These include:

- feigning incapacitation or death in order to escape the enemy,[807] such as
    - a soldier who feigns death in the hope that he or she will be left alone by enemy forces, permitting him or her subsequently to take evasive actions to return to friendly forces without engaging the enemy;[808] and
    - an aircraft crew that feigns loss of control and the appearance that the aircraft was about to crash in order to dissuade further enemy attack and to break contact with enemy forces;[809]
- feigning civilian status to facilitate spying or sabotage, such as
    - false use of journalist credentials; and
- using an informal ceasefire for the purpose of collecting wounded and dead and to withdraw unseen by the enemy.[810]

---

pakol (a round brownish-tan or gray wool cap) and Massoud checkered scarf, each named for former Northern Alliance leader Ahmad Shah Massoud, who was assassinated days before the al Qaeda attacks on the World Trade Center and Pentagon. This attire was not worn to appear as civilians, or to blend in with the civilian population, but rather to lower the visibility of US forces vis-à-vis the forces they supported.").

[806] *Refer to* § 4.17 (Spies, Saboteurs, and Other Persons Engaging in Similar Acts Behind Enemy Lines).

[807] ICRC AP COMMENTARY 438 (¶1505) ("[P]erfidious use always involves the abuse of the adversary's confidence. Thus, for example, feigning death simply to save one's life would not be an act of perfidy, while feigning death to kill an enemy once his back is turned, would constitute an act of perfidy.").

[808] *For example*, SPAIGHT, AIR POWER AND WAR RIGHTS 173 ("A ruse which is mentioned by Major C. J. Biddle, American Aviation, appears to have been a legitimate one. An American pilot was forced down in the German lines. 'When he landed he left his motor turning over slowly and lay over in his cockpit, as though he had been shot, the Huns all the time circling above his head. They evidently thought he was done for, for after looking him over they flew away, whereupon our pilot took off and came home.").

[809] SPAIGHT, AIR POWER AND WAR RIGHTS 170-71 ("The chief ruse practised in air fighting in the first world war was the vertical nose-dive or spin, used by a pilot who was outfought or outnumbered, or whose gun had jammed or engine failed, to escape by simulating a fall out of control.").

[810] *For example*, 1958 UK MANUAL ¶319 note 1 ("[A]t 1 p.m. on 7th March, 1905, during the battle of Mukden, a group of Russians bearing Red Cross and white flags advanced towards the 1st Japanese Army and asked for a suspension of arms for several hours to remove the wounded and dead. The Japanese agreed, as they themselves had many wounded, but the suspension was made without any formal agreement (*sans entente bien dèfinie*). In the evening, when the Japanese reopened fire, there was no reply and it was found that the Russians had retired during the suspension of arms.").

5.26 Non-Forcible Means and Methods of Warfare

In general, propaganda, information gathering, and bribery are permissible means and methods of warfare.

5.26.1 Propaganda. In general, the use of propaganda is permissible under the law of war, even when it encourages acts that violate an enemy State's domestic law or is directed towards civilian or neutral audiences. However, certain types of propaganda are prohibited.

5.26.1.1 *Propaganda – Notes on Terminology*. Propaganda has been referred to as psychological warfare, psychological operations (PSYOP), or military information support operations (MISO).[811] The word "propaganda" often has been used with a pejorative connotation to refer to misleading or false statements, but "propaganda" is used in this section without intending any such connotation.

5.26.1.2 *Propaganda Generally Permissible*. In general, propaganda is a permissible means of warfare.[812] Propaganda has been disseminated through a variety of communications media, including printed materials, loudspeakers, radio or television broadcast, aircraft, or the internet. Propaganda is sometimes used with bribery[813] or to support intelligence gathering.[814] Propaganda may be directed at enemy civilians and neutrals.[815]

Propaganda may encourage enemy persons to commit acts that would violate the domestic law of the enemy State.[816] For example, it would be permissible to encourage enemy

---

[811] Robert Gates, Secretary of Defense, *Memorandum: Changing the Term Psychological Operations (PSYOP) to Military Information Support Operations (MISO)*, OSD 1012-10 (Dec. 3, 2010) ("Since the 1940s, military information activities, undertaken both in wartime and peacetime, have been described as 'psychological warfare,' 'psychological operations,' or PSYOP. These terms helped draw a useful distinction between lethal military operations, on the one hand, and military efforts to change minds and reduce or prevent conflict through truthful, persuasive information, on the other. Today, however, the term 'Psychological Operations' has become anachronistic and misleading. Although PSYOP activities rely on truthful information, credibly conveyed, the term PSYOP tends to connote propaganda, brainwashing, manipulation, and deceit.").

[812] GREENSPAN, MODERN LAW OF LAND WARFARE 323 ("Propaganda must be considered a legal means of warfare, since there are no specific rules of war which forbid its use, nor is it as such incompatible with the existing rules of war.").

[813] 1976 AIR FORCE PAMPHLET 110-31 ¶5-6 ("In World War I, Austrian airmen dropped leaflets over Italian lines inviting desertion with the promise of compensation for every airplane surrendered intact. In the Korean conflict, an award was offered to any enemy flier who would defect with his plane intact to the United Nations Command. In fact $100,000 was paid to a North Korean pilot for such a defection.").

[814] Robert Gates, Secretary of Defense, *Memorandum: Changing the Term Psychological Operations (PSYOP) to Military Information Support Operations (MISO)*, OSD 1012-10 (Dec. 3, 2010) ("In Iraq and Afghanistan, U.S. military information programs urging civilians to report possible insurgent activity led to valuable information, enabling our forces to disarm hundreds of improvised explosive devices safely and capture numerous key insurgent leaders.").

[815] *For example*, 1958 UK MANUAL ¶313 note 3 ("In the Second World War both sides established regular wireless services for spreading war news among both the enemy and neutrals. They also resorted on a large scale to propaganda disseminated from aircraft and from the ground.").

[816] *See* SPAIGHT, AIR POWER AND WAR RIGHTS 333 ("To drop a pamphlet inciting to assassination would no doubt be an offence under the laws of war, assassination being forbidden by those laws. It is an entirely different matter

combatants to defect, desert, or surrender.[817] Similarly, it is generally permissible to encourage insurrection among the enemy civilian population.[818]

5.26.1.3 _Prohibited Types of Propaganda_. Propaganda must not: (1) incite violations of the law of war; nor (2) itself violate a law of war rule.

Propaganda must not incite acts that are prohibited by the law of war.[819] For example, propaganda intended to incite attacks against civilians is prohibited. In certain cases, individuals may be liable for instigating or inciting violations of the law of war.[820]

Propaganda is also prohibited when it would violate other law of war rules. For example, it is specifically prohibited for an Occupying Power to use propaganda that aims at securing voluntary enlistment of protected persons in its armed or auxiliary forces.[821] Similarly, it is prohibited to declare that no quarter will be given, and propaganda in the form of a declaration to the adversary that no quarter will be given would be prohibited.[822] In addition, propaganda would be prohibited if it constituted a measure of intimidation or terrorism against the civilian population, such as the threats of violence whose primary purpose is to spread terror among the civilian population.[823] Similarly, propaganda may not be used to subject a detainee to public curiosity or other humiliating or degrading treatment.[824] Additionally, the delivery of the

---

when the act which the message seeks to accomplish is one not repugnant to natural law, not *malum in se*, but merely contrary to the law (because to the interest) of the State affected, or *malum prohibitum*. It cannot be held that to try to persuade a modern civilized nation to change its form of government is to incite to an act of the former category.").

[817] *For example*, FINAL REPORT ON THE PERSIAN GULF WAR xxvi ("Coalition strategy also benefitted immensely from psychological operations, the success of which is evidenced primarily by the large number of Iraqi soldiers who deserted Iraqi ranks or surrendered without putting up any resistance during the ground offensive. Our efforts built on, among other factors, the disheartening effect on Iraqi troops of the unanswered and intensive Coalition aerial bombardment, the privations they suffered due to the degradation of the Iraqi logistics system, and the threat of the impending ground campaign. Radio transmissions and leaflets exploited this demoralization by explaining to the Iraqi troops how to surrender and assuring them of humane treatment if they did. More specific messages reduced Iraqi readiness by warning troops to stay away from their equipment (which was vulnerable to attack by precision munitions) and induced desertions by warning troops that their positions were about to be attacked by B-52s.").

[818] *For example*, LAUTERPACHT, II OPPENHEIM'S INTERNATIONAL LAW 426-27 (§162a) ("The legitimacy, formerly controversial, of inciting enemy subjects to rise against the Government in power is now no longer disputed. … While, in the Second World War, both sides established regular wireless services for spreading war news among both the enemy and the neutrals, the Allies resorted on a large scale to propaganda disseminated from aircraft as a means of inducing the population of Germany to remove a dictatorial régime which, it was asserted, was solely responsible for the war.").

[819] 1976 AIR FORCE PAMPHLET 110-31 ¶5-6 ("Propaganda which would incite illegal acts of warfare, as for example killing civilians, killing or wounding by treachery or the use of poison or poisonous weapons, is forbidden.").

[820] *Refer to* § 18.23.2 (Instigating or Directly Inciting).

[821] *Refer to* § 11.20.1.1 (Prohibition on Compulsory Service in an Occupying Power's Armed Forces).

[822] *Refer to* § 5.4.7 (Prohibition Against Declaring That No Quarter Be Given).

[823] *Refer to* § 10.5.3.2 (Collective Penalties and Measures of Intimidation or Terrorism).

[824] *Refer to* § 8.2.2 (Protection Against Humiliating or Degrading Treatment).

propaganda should be consistent with other law of war obligations.[825]

5.26.2 Information Gathering. The employment of measures necessary for obtaining information about the enemy and their country is considered permissible.[826]

Information gathering measures, however, may not violate specific law of war rules.[827] For example, it would be unlawful, of course, to use torture or abuse to interrogate detainees for purposes of gathering information. Similarly, it is prohibited to make improper use of a flag of truce to obtain information.[828]

Some forms of deception used to gather information, although not prohibited by the law of war, may put the persons engaging in them at risk of being treated as spies.[829]

5.26.3 Bribery or Offering of Rewards. In general, it is permissible to offer rewards for assistance in the conduct of hostilities, including rewards intended to corrupt enemy combatants or civilians.[830] Rewards, however, may not be offered for the commission of violations of the law of war, and rewards may not be offered for the killing of enemy persons.

5.26.3.1 *Prohibition on Offering Rewards for Enemy Persons Dead or Alive*. It is forbidden to place a price on the head of enemy persons or to offer a reward for enemy persons "dead or alive."[831] Such actions encourage the denial of quarter or encourage private persons to take up arms whose participation in hostilities is often undisciplined and associated with the commission of war crimes.[832] This prohibition extends to offers of rewards for the killing or wounding of all enemies, including specific individuals or a class of enemy persons (*e.g.*, officers).

However, this rule would not prohibit offering rewards for the capture of unharmed enemy personnel generally or of particular enemy personnel.[833] Similarly, this rule does not

---

[825] *See, e.g.*, GREENSPAN, MODERN LAW OF LAND WARFARE 324 ("It would appear to be improper to induce enemy nationals to listen to propaganda emanating from the opposing side by such methods as doling out a few names of prisoners of war on the occasion of each broadcast and deliberately holding other next of kin in suspense, instead of transmitting such information by the most rapid means possible.").

[826] HAGUE IV REG. 24 ("[T]he employment of measures necessary for obtaining information about the enemy and the country are considered permissible.").

[827] GREENSPAN, MODERN LAW OF LAND WARFARE 325 ("In obtaining information, a belligerent must not contravene specific rules of war.").

[828] *Refer to* § 5.24.7 (Flags of Truce).

[829] *Refer to* § 4.17 (Spies, Saboteurs, and Other Persons Engaging in Similar Acts Behind Enemy Lines).

[830] 1958 UK MANUAL ¶313 ("It is not unlawful to employ spies; or to corrupt enemy civilians or soldiers by bribes in order to induce them to give information, to desert with or without technical equipment, new weapons, vehicles or aircraft, to surrender, to rebel, or to mutiny; or to give false information to the enemy.").

[831] 1956 FM 27-10 (Change No. 1 1976) ¶31 (Article 23 of the Hague IV Regulations "is construed as prohibiting … putting a price upon an enemy's head, as well as offering a reward for an enemy 'dead or alive.'").

[832] *Refer to* § 4.18.3 (Private Persons Who Engage in Hostilities – Lack of the Privileges of Combatant Status).

[833] *See* 2004 UK MANUAL ¶5.14.1 ("[O]ffers of rewards for the capture unharmed of enemy personnel generally or of particular enemy personnel would be lawful.").

prohibit offering rewards for information that may be used by combatants to conduct military operations that attack enemy combatants.

5.27 Prohibition Against Compelling Enemy Nationals to Take Part in the Operations of War Directed Against Their Own Country

During international armed conflict, it is prohibited to compel the nationals of the hostile party to take part in the operations of war directed against their own country, even if they were in the belligerent's service before the commencement of the war.[834] Underlying this prohibition is the principle that States must not compel foreign nationals to commit treason or otherwise to violate their allegiance to their country.[835]

Additional restrictions are applicable with respect to POWs, retained personnel, protected persons in the home territory of a belligerent, and protected persons in occupied territory.[836]

5.27.1 Compel. This prohibition applies to attempts to compel enemy nationals, rather than measures short of compulsion, such as bribing enemy nationals or seeking to influence them through propaganda.[837] However, it is specifically prohibited for an Occupying Power to use propaganda that aims at securing voluntary enlistment of protected persons in its armed or auxiliary forces.[838]

5.27.2 Nationals of a Hostile Party … Against Their Own Country. This rule applies to nationals of a hostile party; States are not prohibited by the law of war from compelling their nationals to serve in the armed forces.[839] Similarly, this rule would not prohibit States from

---

[834] HAGUE IV REG. art. 23 ("A belligerent is likewise forbidden to compel the nationals of the hostile party to take part in the operations of war directed against their own country, even if they were in the belligerent's service before the commencement of the war.").

[835] *See* Johnson v. Eisentrager, 339 U.S. 763, 773 (1950) ("The United States does not invoke this enemy allegiance only for its own interest, but respects it also when to the enemy's advantage. In World War I, our conscription act did not subject the alien enemy to compulsory military service. 40 Stat. 885, c. XII, § 4. The Selective Service Act of 1948, 62 Stat. 604, 50 U.S.C. Appendix, § 454(a), exempts aliens who have not formally declared their intention to become citizens from military training, service and registration, if they make application, but if so relieved, they are barred from becoming citizens. Thus, the alien enemy status carries important immunities, as well as disadvantages. The United States does not ask him to violate his allegiance or to commit treason toward his own country for the sake of ours. This also is the doctrine and the practice of other states comprising our Western Civilization.").

[836] *Refer to* § 9.19.2.3 (Labor Assignments That May Be Compelled); § 7.9.5.6 (No Other Compulsory Duties); § 10.7.3 (Compulsory Work for Protected Persons in a Belligerent's Home Territory); § 11.20.1.1 (Prohibition on Compulsory Service in an Occupying Power's Armed Forces).

[837] United States v. Weizsaecker, *et al.* (The Ministries Case), XIV TRIALS OF WAR CRIMINALS BEFORE THE NMT 549 ("As the war progressed Germany suffered severe losses of manpower. It adopted conscription as to its own nationals and in many instances of foreign nationals living within its borders. We hold that it is not illegal to recruit prisoners of war who volunteer to fight against their own country, but pressure or coercion to compel such persons to enter into the armed services obviously violates international law."). *Refer to* § 5.26.1 (Propaganda); § 5.26.3 (Bribery or Offering of Rewards).

[838] *Refer to* § 11.20.1.1 (Prohibition on Compulsory Service in an Occupying Power's Armed Forces).

[839] *Refer to* § 4.5.2.4 (Draftees).

compelling persons to betray an allegiance to a non-State armed group during non-international armed conflict.[840]

[840] *Refer to* § 17.12.1 (Compelling Captured or Surrendered Enemy Personnel to Take Part in the Conflict).

VI – Weapons

Chapter Contents

6.1 Introduction

This Chapter addresses the legal review of new weapons and legal rules specific to certain types of weapons, including whether certain weapons are illegal *per se*, specific rules for the use of certain other weapons, and obligations that may arise after certain weapons are used.

In addition to the law of war, other law, policy, and regulation may apply to certain weapons. Such law, policy, or regulation may include arms control agreements, U.S. domestic law, U.S. policy, applicable rules of engagement, and other military orders. This Chapter notes some provisions of such law, policy, and regulation where relevant, but does not seek to address exhaustively all of them.[1] In advising on the legality of specific weapons, one must take care to identify all applicable restrictions and not rely unduly on the absence of discussion in this Chapter as reflecting the absence of any such restrictions.

6.1.1 Legality of the Weapon Itself (Per Se) Distinguished From the Legality of the Use of the Weapon. A weapon may be illegal *per se* if a treaty to which the United States is a Party

[1] *Refer to* § 1.2.2.4 (Citation of Policies and Regulations).

or customary international law has prohibited its use under all circumstances.[2] For example, the use of "blinding laser" weapons is prohibited, regardless of how they are used.[3]

On the other hand, most weapons are not illegal *per se*. That is, their use may be lawful in some circumstances, although unlawful in others, such as if they are used to attack combatants placed *hors de combat*.[4]

Law of war issues related to targeting (*e.g.*, the requirement that an attack may only be directed against a military objective) generally are not determinative of the lawfulness of a weapon. However, weapons that are inherently indiscriminate are prohibited.[5] In addition, certain weapons, such as mines, are subject to specific rules on their use in order to reduce the risk of harm to the civilian population.[6]

6.2 DoD Policy of Reviewing the Legality of Weapons

As provided in DoD issuances, DoD policy for many years has required the legal review of the intended acquisition or procurement of weapons or weapon systems; this review includes ensuring that such acquisition or procurement is consistent with the law of war.[7] These DoD policy requirements have been implemented in Military Department regulations.[8]

The fact that the legality of a weapon is discussed in this manual does not obviate the

---

[2] 1976 Air Force Pamphlet 110-31 ¶6-2 ("A weapon may be illegal *per se* if either international custom or treaty has forbidden its use under all circumstances."). *Refer to* § 6.4.2 (Specifically Prohibited Types of Weapons).

[3] *Refer to* § 6.15.1 (Prohibition on "Blinding Laser" Weapons).

[4] *Refer to* § 5.9 (Persons Placed *Hors de Combat*).

[5] *Refer to* § 6.7 (Inherently Indiscriminate Weapons).

[6] *Refer to* § 6.12.5.3 (Obligation to Take Feasible Precautions to Protect Civilians From the Effects of Mines, Booby-Traps, and Other Devices).

[7] *For example*, DoD Directive 5000.01, *The Defense Acquisition System*, ¶E1.1.15 (May 12, 2003, certified current as of Nov. 20, 2007) ("The acquisition and procurement of DoD weapons and weapon systems shall be consistent with all applicable domestic law and treaties and international agreements (for arms control agreements, see DoD Directive 2060.1 (Reference (m), customary international law, and the law of armed conflict (also known as the laws and customs of war)[)]. An attorney authorized to conduct such legal reviews in the Department shall conduct the legal review of the intended acquisition of weapons or weapons systems."); DoD Directive 5000.01, *The Defense Acquisition System*, ¶4.2.10 (Mar. 15, 1996, cancelled by DoD Directive 5000.1 Oct. 23, 2000) ("DoD acquisition and procurement of weapons shall be consistent with *applicable domestic law and* all applicable treaties, customary international law, and the law of armed conflict (also known as the laws and customs of war)."); DoD Instruction 5500.15, *Review of Legality of Weapons Under International Law*, ¶II (Oct. 16, 1974, cancelled by DoD Instruction 5000.2 Feb. 23, 1991) ("All actions of the Department of Defense with respect to the acquisition and procurement of weapons, and their intended use in armed conflict, shall be consistent with the obligations assumed by the United States Government under all applicable treaties, with customary international law, and, in particular, with the laws of war.").

[8] *For example*, Department of the Army Regulation 27-53, *Review of Legality of Weapons Under International Law* (Jan. 1, 1979); Secretary of the Navy Instruction 5000.2E, *Department of the Navy Implementation and Operation of the Defense Acquisition System and the Joint Capabilities Integration and Development System* (Sept. 1, 2011); Department of the Air Force Instruction 51-402, *Legal Reviews of Weapons and Cyber Capabilities* (Jul. 27, 2011).

requirement under applicable directives or regulations for a legal review of a weapon or weapon system that is to be acquired or procured.

6.2.1 Review of New Types of Weapons. The development of new types of weapons has often resulted in public denunciation of their allegedly cruel effects and in attempts to prohibit their use in armed conflict.[9] This has been true of the crossbow, siege engines for hurling projectiles, firearms, gunpowder, bayonets, and other weapons that have since been widely recognized as not prohibited by the law of war.

Like other aspects of the law of war, the rules relating to weapons are generally characterized as prohibitive law forbidding certain weapons or the use of weapons in certain instances rather than positive law authorizing the weapon or its use.[10] The lawfulness of the use of a type of weapon does not depend on the presence or absence of authorization, but, on the contrary, on whether the weapon is prohibited.[11] Thus, the mere fact that a weapon is novel or employs new technology does not mean that the weapon is illegal.[12] The law of war does not require States to establish a general practice of using a weapon before it is to be regarded as legal. Moreover, it would appear absurd to suggest that a new type of weapon should automatically be prohibited because there is no State practice supporting such use, or to suggest that States must continue using a weapon in each conflict simply to maintain its legality.

6.2.2 Questions Considered in the Legal Review of Weapons for Consistency With U.S. Law of War Obligations. The review of the acquisition or procurement of a weapon for consistency with U.S. law of war obligations should consider three questions to determine whether the weapon's acquisition or procurement is prohibited:

- whether the weapon's intended use is calculated to cause superfluous injury;[13]
- whether the weapon is inherently indiscriminate;[14] and
- whether the weapon falls within a class of weapons that has been specifically

---

[9] 1976 AIR FORCE PAMPHLET 110-31 ¶6-7a ("The development of new weapons or methods of warfare has often resulted in public denunciation of their allegedly cruel effects, and attempts to prohibit their use in warfare. This has been true of the crossbow, siege engines for hurling projectiles, firearms, gunpowder, bayonets and other less efficient methods of warfare.").

[10] *Refer to* § 1.3.3.1 (Law of War as Prohibitive Law).

[11] Legality of the Threat or Use of Nuclear Weapons, Advisory Opinion, 1996 I.C.J. 226, 247 (¶52) ("Nor, however, is there any principle or rule of international law which would make the legality of the threat or use of nuclear weapons or of any other weapons dependent on a specific authorization. State practice shows that the illegality of the use of certain weapons as such does not result from an absence of authorization but, on the contrary, is formulated in terms of prohibition.").

[12] 1976 AIR FORCE PAMPHLET 110-31 ¶6-7a ("A weapon or method of warfare may not be considered illegal solely because it is new or has not previously been used in warfare.").

[13] *Refer to* § 6.6 (Weapons Calculated to Cause Superfluous Injury).

[14] *Refer to* § 6.7 (Inherently Indiscriminate Weapons).

prohibited.[15]

If the weapon is not prohibited, the review should also consider whether there are legal restrictions on the weapon's use that are specific to that type of weapon.[16] If any specific restrictions apply, then the intended concept of employment of the weapon should be reviewed for consistency with those restrictions.

Lastly, it may be appropriate to advise whether other measures should be taken that would assist in ensuring compliance with law of war obligations related to the type of weapon being acquired or procured. For example, it may be appropriate to advise on the need for training programs and other practical measures, such as promulgating doctrine and rules of engagement related to that type of weapon.[17]

6.2.3 AP I Requirement for Legal Review of a New Weapon, Means, or Method of Warfare. Article 36 of AP I provides:

> In the study, development, acquisition or adoption of a new weapon, means or method of warfare, a High Contracting Party is under an obligation to determine whether its employment would, in some or all circumstances, be prohibited by this Protocol or by any other rule of international law applicable to the High Contracting Party.

The DoD policy and practice of conducting legal reviews of weapons preceded this AP I provision.[18]

6.2.4 Policy and Processes for Review of Applicable Arms Control Obligations. DoD has had a separate, but complementary, policy and practice requiring review of its activities (*e.g.*, research, development, and testing of weapons) to ensure that these activities are consistent with the arms control agreements to which the United States is a Party.[19]

---

[15] *Refer to* § 6.4.2 (Specifically Prohibited Types of Weapons).

[16] *Refer to* § 6.5.1 (Certain Types of Weapons With Specific Rules on Use).

[17] *Refer to* § 6.15.2 (Feasible Precautions in the Employment of Laser Systems to Avoid the Incident of Permanent Blindness).

[18] *For example*, DOD INSTRUCTION 5500.15, *Review of Legality of Weapons Under International Law*, ¶II (Oct. 16, 1974, cancelled by DoD Instruction 5000.2 Feb. 23, 1991) ("All actions of the Department of Defense with respect to the acquisition and procurement of weapons, and their intended use in armed conflict, shall be consistent with the obligations assumed by the United States Government under all applicable treaties, with customary international law, and, in particular, with the laws of war.").

[19] DOD DIRECTIVE 2060.1, *Implementation of, and Compliance with, Arms Control Agreements*, ¶4.6.7 (Jan. 9, 2001, certified current Nov. 24, 2003) ("For specific DoD-planned activities, [Heads of DoD components are to] seek clearance from the USD(AT&L), through the appropriate CRG [Compliance Review Group], on a timely basis, before taking any action, including but not limited to research, tests, development, exercises and operations that reasonably raises an issue of DoD compliance with an arms control agreement. For other compliance issues requiring resolution (such as those arising from an on-site inspection), seek resolution from the USD(AT&L), through the appropriate CRG. When there is doubt whether clearance or resolution is necessary, it shall be sought. If the issue involves a DoD SAP [Special Access Program], contact the Director of the cognizant DoD SAP Central

6.3 Other Practices to Help Implement Law of War Obligations With Respect to Weapons

A number of practices contribute to the effective implementation of law of war obligations with respect to weapons (although these practices are not necessarily required by the law of war): (1) using weapons in accordance with their design intent and the doctrine that has been promulgated for their use; (2) refraining from modifying weapons without proper authorization; (3) refraining from using personal firearms during military operations; and (4) refraining from using captured weapons in combat, except on a field-expedient basis.

6.3.1 Using Weapons in Accordance With Their Design Intent and Promulgated Doctrine. The use of weapons in accordance with their design intent and the doctrine that has been promulgated for their use contributes to compliance with law of war obligations with respect to weapons because the legality of the weapon would have been reviewed based on its intended use.[20] However, the use of weapons outside their design intent does not necessarily violate the law of war.

Certain weapon systems may also be subject to law of war restrictions on how they are to be used, such as incendiary weapons or mines.[21] In such cases, the use of the weapon in accordance with doctrine and policy is required by international law because that doctrine and policy incorporates certain international obligations.

6.3.1.1 *Using Weapons for Purposes Other Than Those for Which a Weapon or Tool Is Designed*. Although in some cases military orders may restrict the use of certain weapons to only certain authorized purposes, there is not a law of war rule that requires that weapons or tools only be used for the purposes for which they were designed.

For example, an entrenching tool may be designed for digging fighting positions. However, its use as a weapon is not prohibited by the law of war.[22] Similarly, it is not prohibited to use a laser that is not designed to blind enemy persons as a weapon to blind an attacking enemy.[23] It also generally would not be prohibited to use a weapon that has been designed to destroy enemy material, such as a large-caliber machine gun, against enemy personnel.[24]

6.3.2 Refraining From Modifying Weapons Without Proper Authorization. For a variety of reasons, DoD practice has been not to permit the modification of weapons without proper authorization.

Office and the Chairman of the DoD SAP Senior Review Group (SRG). The SRG Chairman will effect coordination with the appropriate CRG.").

[20] *Refer to* § 6.6.3.4 (Superfluous Injury Rule – the Circumstances to Be Assessed and Design Intent); § 6.7.2 (Inherently Indiscriminate Weapons – Circumstances to Be Assessed and Design Intent).

[21] *Refer to* § 6.5.1 (Certain Types of Weapons With Specific Rules on Use).

[22] *Refer to* § 6.5.3.2 (Use of Tools to Stab or Cut).

[23] *Refer to* § 6.15.2.1 (Use of Non-Prohibited Laser Systems to Blind Is Not Absolutely Prohibited).

[24] *Refer to* § 6.5.4.7 (Anti-Personnel Use of Larger (e.g., .50) Caliber Guns or Cannons).

In particular, weapons must not be modified in the field for the purposes of aggravating the harm inflicted on incapacitated persons.[25] For example, substances designed to inflame wounds must not be added to bullets or edged weapons for the purpose of making wounds more painful or difficult to treat.

6.3.3 Refraining From the Use of Personal Firearms and Ammunition. DoD personnel have normally not been permitted to deploy with, or use, personal firearms or ammunition during military operations.[26] This practice is based on a variety of reasons, including to help ensure compliance with the law of war and U.S. domestic law.

6.3.4 Refraining From the Use of Captured Weapons, Except on a Field-Expedient Basis. Under DoD practice, captured or other foreign weapons have been used on a field-expedient basis, but otherwise have not been used in combat unless they have undergone the required legal review and have been duly issued to personnel.

Any weapon, ammunition, or munition captured, found, or recovered on the battlefield by DoD personnel is the property of the United States and not the individual who recovered it, regardless of whether the property is of U.S., enemy, allied, or unknown origin.[27]

6.4 Prohibited Weapons

Two general prohibitions apply to all types of weapons. In addition, certain types of weapons are specifically prohibited.

6.4.1 General Prohibitions Applicable to All Types of Weapons. Two fundamental prohibitions based in customary international law apply to all weapons. It is prohibited to use:

- weapons calculated to cause superfluous injury;[28] or
- inherently indiscriminate weapons.[29]

6.4.2 Specifically Prohibited Types of Weapons. In addition, the use of the following types of weapons is prohibited by treaty or customary international law:

---

25 *Refer to* § 6.6.4 (Weapons Modified for the Purpose of Aggravating the Harm Inflicted on Incapacitated Persons).

26 *For example*, General John P. Abizaid, U.S. Central Command, General Order 1B (GO-1B), *Prohibited Activities for U.S. Department of Defense Personnel Present Within the United States Central Command (USCENTCOM) Area of Responsibility (AOR)*, ¶2a (Mar. 13, 2006) (prohibiting "[p]urchase, possession, use or sale of privately owned firearms, ammunition, explosives or the introduction of these items into the USCENTCOM AOR."); General Tommy R. Franks, U.S. Central Command, General Order 1A (GO-1A), *Prohibited Activities for U.S. Department of Defense Personnel Present Within the United States Central Command (USCENTCOM) AOR*, ¶2a (Dec. 19, 2000) (prohibiting "[p]urchase, possession, use or sale of privately owned firearms, ammunition, explosives, or the introduction of these items into the USCENTCOM AOR.").

27 *Refer to* § 5.17.3 (Enemy Movable Property on the Battlefield (War Booty)).

28 *Refer to* § 6.6 (Weapons Calculated to Cause Superfluous Injury).

29 *Refer to* § 6.7 (Inherently Indiscriminate Weapons).

- poison, poisoned weapons, poisonous gases, and other chemical weapons;[30]
- biological weapons;[31]
- certain environmental modification techniques;[32]
- weapons that injure by fragments that are non-detectable by X-rays;[33]
- certain types of mines, booby-traps, and other devices;[34] and
- blinding lasers.[35]

6.4.3 Relationship Between the Specific Prohibitions and the General Prohibitions. When a specific prohibition on a weapon is viewed as reflecting customary international law, such prohibition may sometimes be viewed as, in effect, a declaration that the weapon is prohibited as one calculated to cause superfluous injury or as one that is inherently indiscriminate.[36]

However, a specific treaty prohibition on a weapon does not necessarily reflect a State Party's view that the weapon is prohibited by customary international law (*e.g.*, that the weapon is calculated to cause superfluous injury or is inherently indiscriminate). For example, the mere prohibition or restriction of a weapon in the CCW or its Protocols does not necessarily reflect the conclusion that the weapon is calculated to cause superfluous injury or is inherently indiscriminate.[37]

6.5 Lawful Weapons

Apart from the categories of weapons described in § 6.4 (Prohibited Weapons), all other types of weapons are lawful for use by the U.S. armed forces; that is, they are not illegal *per se*. In other words, other types of weapons are prohibited only to the extent that they fall under the categories of weapons described in § 6.4 (Prohibited Weapons). For example, a landmine is not

---

[30] *Refer to* § 6.8 (Poison, Poisoned Weapons, Poisonous Gases, and Other Chemical Weapons).

[31] *Refer to* § 6.9 (Biological Weapons).

[32] *Refer to* § 6.10 (Certain Environmental Modification Techniques).

[33] *Refer to* § 6.11 (Weapons Injuring by Fragments Not Detectable by X-Rays).

[34] *Refer to* § 6.12.4 (Prohibited Classes of Mines, Booby-Traps, and Other Devices).

[35] *Refer to* § 6.15.1 (Prohibition on "Blinding Laser" Weapons).

[36] J. Fred Buzhardt, General Counsel, Department of Defense, Letter to Chairman Fulbright, Senate Committee on Foreign Relations, Apr. 5, 1971, 10 International Legal Materials 1300, 1302 (1971) ("The thrust of the phrase 'harmless to man' made part of the discussion of the rules draws attention to Article 23(e) of the Hague Regulations of 1907, wherein combatants are forbidden to employ weapons 'calculated to cause unnecessary suffering.' However, the provision in Hague Regulation Article 23(a) concerning the prohibition against using poison or poisoned weapons is a special case of this rule since it, in effect, declares that any use of a lethal substance against human beings is, per se, a use which is calculated to cause unnecessary suffering.").

[37] *Refer to* § 19.21.1.3 (CCW and Customary International Law).

necessarily a legally prohibited weapon; it is only prohibited if it falls under one of the specific classes of prohibited mines listed in § 6.12.4 (Prohibited Classes of Mines, Booby-Traps, and Other Devices).

The rules that apply to the use of all weapons are addressed in § 5.4.2 (Overview of Rules in Conducting Attacks).

6.5.1 Certain Types of Weapons With Specific Rules on Use. Certain types of weapons, however, are subject to specific rules that apply to their use by the U.S. armed forces. These rules may reflect U.S. obligations under international law or national policy. These weapons include:

- mines, booby-traps, and other devices (except certain specific classes of prohibited mines, booby-traps, and other devices);[38]
- cluster munitions;[39]
- incendiary weapons;[40]
- laser weapons (except blinding lasers);[41]
- riot control agents;[42]
- herbicides;[43]
- nuclear weapons;[44] and
- explosive ordnance.[45]

6.5.2 Other Examples of Lawful Weapons. In particular, aside from the rules prohibiting weapons calculated to cause superfluous injury and inherently indiscriminate weapons,[46] there are no law of war rules specifically prohibiting or restricting the following types of weapons by the U.S. armed forces:

---

[38] *Refer to* § 6.12 (Landmines, Booby-Traps, and Other Devices).

[39] *Refer to* § 6.13 (Cluster Munitions).

[40] *Refer to* § 6.14 (Incendiary Weapons).

[41] *Refer to* § 6.15.2 (Feasible Precautions in the Employment of Laser Systems to Avoid the Incident of Permanent Blindness).

[42] *Refer to* § 6.16 (Riot Control Agents).

[43] *Refer to* § 6.17 (Herbicides).

[44] *Refer to* § 6.18 (Nuclear Weapons).

[45] *Refer to* § 6.19 (Explosive Ordnance).

[46] *Refer to* § 6.6 (Weapons Calculated to Cause Superfluous Injury); § 6.7 (Inherently Indiscriminate Weapons).

- edged or pointed weapons, including weapons with serrated edges or entrenching tools used as weapons;[47]

- small arms, cannons, and other guns, including shotguns, exploding bullets, expanding bullets, suppressors, or large-caliber guns;[48]

- blast weapons;[49]

- fragmentation weapons;[50]

- depleted uranium munitions;[51]

- remotely piloted aircraft;[52]

- autonomy in weapons systems;[53] and

- non-lethal weapons.[54]

6.5.3 Edged or Pointed Weapons. Stabbing or cutting weapons (*e.g.*, knives, bayonets, swords, lances, and tomahawks) are not specifically prohibited or restricted by the law of war. Like other weapons, however, they must not be calculated to cause superfluous injury.[55] Thus, it is prohibited to modify the weapon for the purpose of making wounds more difficult to treat, such as by adding a barbed head to a lance or by applying to the blade or point a poison or substance that is designed to inflame wounds.[56]

6.5.3.1 *Serrated Edges*. The law of war does not prohibit the use of serrated-edged weapons by military forces, including against enemy personnel.

Many bayonets or knives have a serrated edge (a formation resembling the toothed edge of a saw). Provided that the design intent of the serrated edge is not to aggravate suffering unnecessarily, such as by making the wound more difficult to treat, the serrated edge is not prohibited. For example, a serrated edge may improve the capabilities of the blade as a multi-purpose field utility tool, rather than be intended to increase the pain and suffering of enemy personnel injured by the blade.

---

[47] *Refer to* § 6.5.3 (Edged or Pointed Weapons).

[48] *Refer to* § 6.5.4 (Small Arms, Cannons, and Other Guns).

[49] *Refer to* § 6.5.5 (Blast Weapons).

[50] *Refer to* § 6.5.6 (Fragmentation Weapons).

[51] *Refer to* § 6.5.7 (Depleted Uranium Munitions).

[52] *Refer to* § 6.5.8 (Remotely Piloted Aircraft).

[53] *Refer to* § 6.5.9 (Autonomy in Weapon Systems).

[54] *Refer to* § 6.5.10 (Non-Lethal (Less-Lethal) Weapons).

[55] *Refer to* § 6.6 (Weapons Calculated to Cause Superfluous Injury).

[56] *Refer to* § 6.6.4 (Weapons Modified for the Purpose of Aggravating the Harm Inflicted on Incapacitated Persons).

6.5.3.2 _Use of Tools to Stab or Cut_. Edged tools, such as over-size knives, machetes, and entrenching tools, have often been employed both as tools and as weapons. Such tools are not prohibited by the law of war, and the law of war does not prohibit the use of tools as weapons to bludgeon, stab, or cut.

6.5.4 Small Arms, Cannons, and Other Guns. Small arms, cannons, and other guns are not specifically restricted or prohibited by the law of war. In particular, there are no specific rules against shotguns, exploding bullets, expanding bullets, suppressors, or anti-personnel use of larger caliber guns or cannons.

6.5.4.1 _Small Arms, Cannons, and Other Guns – Other Rules on Weapons, as Applicable_. Although no law of war rule regulates small arms, cannons, and other guns as a specific category, these weapons are subject to other law of war rules on weapons, as applicable.

For example, the use of ammunition, the primary effect of which is to injure by fragments that in the human body escape detection by X-rays, is prohibited.[57] In addition, poison must not be added to bullets or other projectiles.[58] As with other weapons, small arms, cannons, and other guns must not be calculated to cause superfluous injury.[59] For example, modifying guns or ammunition for the purpose of aggravating the harm inflicted upon incapacitated persons would be prohibited (*e.g.*, adding a substance to bullets with the intent to inflame wounds).[60]

Guns that fall under the definition of incendiary weapons would be regulated as incendiary weapons.[61] However, tracer ammunition is not an "incendiary weapon" because any incendiary effects are incidental.[62] In addition, even certain projectiles designed to have incendiary effects that are combined with other effects (*e.g.*, penetration, blast, or fragmentation effects) would not be regulated as incendiary weapons.[63]

6.5.4.2 _Shotguns_. There is no law of war prohibition on the use (including anti-personnel use) of the shotgun in combat.[64] The fact that multiple fragments are used in many

---

[57] *Refer to* § 6.11 (Weapons Injuring by Fragments Not Detectable by X-Rays).

[58] *Refer to* § 6.8.1 (Poison and Poisoned Weapons).

[59] *Refer to* § 6.6 (Weapons Calculated to Cause Superfluous Injury).

[60] *Refer to* § 6.6.4 (Weapons Modified for the Purpose of Aggravating the Harm Inflicted on Incapacitated Persons).

[61] *Refer to* § 6.14 (Incendiary Weapons).

[62] *Refer to* § 6.14.1.3 (Excluded From the Definition of Incendiary Weapons – Weapons With Incidental Incendiary Effects).

[63] *Refer to* § 6.14.1.4 (Excluded From the Definition of Incendiary Weapons – Certain Combined-Effects Munitions).

[64] *For example,* The Secretary of State to the Swiss Chargé (Oderlin) (Sept. 28, 1918), *reprinted in* PAPERS RELATING TO THE FOREIGN RELATIONS OF THE UNITED STATES, 1918, SUPPLEMENT 2, THE WORLD WAR 785-86 (1933) ("In reply to the German protest, the Government of the United States has to say that the provision of the Hague convention [*Hague IV Reg.* art. 23(e)], cited in the protest, does not in its opinion forbid the use of this kind of weapon. Moreover, in view of the history of the shotgun as a weapon of warfare, and in view of the well-known effects of its present use, and in the light of a comparison of it with other weapons approved in warfare, the shotgun now in use by the American Army cannot be the subject of legitimate or reasonable protest.").

shotgun rounds to wound does not prohibit their use.[65]

Shotguns have been used as anti-personnel weapons for close-combat, for guarding enemy prisoners of war, and for anti-materiel purposes during armed conflict for many years.[66] Shotgun munitions may include, for example, buckshot ammunition, flechette ammunition, non-lethal projectiles, and breaching rounds.

Breaching rounds are an anti-materiel munition designed to dislodge door hinges or door locks and are used to enable military forces to enter a room or building. As with other weapons designed for anti-material use, the use of an anti-material round against enemy personnel is not prohibited.[67] For example, a breaching round may be used against an enemy combatant who opens the door or appears in the doorway just as the door is about to be breached.

6.5.4.3 *Exploding Bullets*. The use of exploding bullets, including use against enemy personnel, is not prohibited by the law of war. For example, explosive bullets have been lawfully used during armed conflict, against both enemy material and enemy combatants.[68]

Exploding bullets, like all weapons, however, are subject to the superfluous injury rule.[69] For example, without a valid military reason, bullets that are specifically designed to explode within the human body would be prohibited, since a non-exploding bullet would be just as effective and efficient at incapacitating an enemy combatant.[70]

On the other hand, an explosive bullet that was designed to explode in order to increase the probability of striking an enemy combatant or to strike an enemy combatant behind cover

---

[65] *Refer to* § 6.5.6 (Fragmentation Weapons).

[66] *For example*, W. Hays Parks, Special Assistant for Law of War Matters, Office of The Judge Advocate General, U.S. Army, *Joint Service Combat Shotgun Program*, THE ARMY LAWYER 16, 17-18 (Oct. 1997) ("The combat shotgun or military rifle with a shotgun-type munition continued to be used in the United States. In the American Revolution, General George Washington encouraged his troops to load their muskets with 'buck and ball,' a load consisting of one standard musket ball and three to six buckshot, in order to increase the probability of achieving a hit. … United States Air Force security police employed shotguns in base security operations in Saudi Arabia during Operations Desert Shield and Desert Storm (1990-91) to protect them from attack by terrorists or Iraqi military units, and some personnel in British armored units were armed with shotguns as individual weapons during that conflict.").

[67] *Refer to* § 6.3.1.1 (Using Weapons for Purposes Other Than Those for Which a Weapon or Tool Is Designed).

[68] *For example*, SPAIGHT, AIR POWER AND WAR RIGHTS 213 ("In the second world war projectiles of the kind referred to [in the 1868 St. Petersburg Declaration] were freely used by all the belligerent air forces. The explosive bullet gave place to the small cannon shell, but the latter, fired normally from a gun of 20 mm. bore, was equally within the prohibited limit, since its weight was only 130 grammes as compared with the 400 grammes specified in the Declaration. Cannon guns of 40 mm. were also mounted in aircraft and the projectiles were outside the ban. The incendiary bullets used were usually fired from machine guns with bores of .303 inch and .5 inch.").

[69] *Refer to* § 6.6 (Weapons Calculated to Cause Superfluous Injury).

[70] *For example*, ULYSSES S. GRANT, I PERSONAL MEMOIRS OF U.S. GRANT 538 (1892) ("The enemy used in their defence explosive musket-balls, no doubt thinking that, bursting over our men in the trenches, they would do some execution; but I do not remember a single case where a man was injured by a piece of one of these shells. When they were hit and the ball exploded, the wound was terrible. In these cases a solid ball would have hit as well. Their use is barbarous, because they produce increased suffering without any corresponding advantage to those using them.").

would not be prohibited.[71] Similarly, bullets that explode in order to neutralize enemy material more effectively are not prohibited, and there is no objection to using these bullets also against enemy combatants.[72]

The United States is not a Party to the 1868 St. Petersburg Declaration on Exploding Bullets, and its prohibition on the use of certain projectiles does not reflect customary international law.[73]

6.5.4.4 *Expanding Bullets*. The law of war does not prohibit the use of bullets that expand or flatten easily in the human body. Like other weapons, such bullets are only prohibited if they are calculated to cause superfluous injury.[74] The U.S. armed forces have used expanding bullets in various counterterrorism and hostage rescue operations, some of which have been conducted in the context of armed conflict.

The 1899 Declaration on Expanding Bullets prohibits the use of expanding bullets in armed conflicts in which all States that are parties to the conflict are also Party to the 1899 Declaration on Expanding Bullets.[75] The United States is not a Party to the 1899 Declaration on Expanding Bullets, in part because evidence was not presented at the diplomatic conference that expanding bullets produced unnecessarily severe or cruel wounds.[76]

---

[71] *For example*, C. Todd Lopez, *Army wants 36 more "Punisher" weapons in 2012*, ARMY NEWS SERVICE, Feb. 3, 2011 ("The XM25 allows Soldiers to engage defilade targets -- those behind a barrier, protected from oncoming weapons fire. The XM25 measures the distance to the enemy's protective barrier, and can then program the round to detonate a user-adjustable distance past that -- allowing Soldiers to put an air-bursting round directly above the enemy's head, inside their protected area. … The five prototype weapons entered theater in November, and were first used in combat Dec. 3.").

[72] U.S. RESPONSE TO ICRC CIHL STUDY 524 ("States widely have employed bullets that may detonate on impact with materiel for both anti-materiel and anti-personnel purposes. Such ammunition was in common use by all States that participated in World War II, and in conflicts thereafter including in widespread aircraft strafing of enemy forces, a practice common to every conflict since World War I in which aircraft were employed."). *See also* Commission of Jurists to Consider and Report Upon the Revision of the Rules of Warfare, *General Report*, Feb. 19, 1923, *reprinted in* 32 AJIL SUPPLEMENT: OFFICIAL DOCUMENTS 1, 20-21 (1938) ("In the form in which the proposal was first brought forward its provisions were limited to a stipulation that the use of tracer bullets against aircraft generally was not prohibited. Various criticisms were, however, made about the proposed text, chiefly founded on the impracticability for an airman while in flight to change the ammunition which he is using in the machine-gun in his aircraft. He cannot employ different bullets in accordance with the target at which he is aiming, one sort of ammunition for other aircraft and another sort for land forces by whom he may be attacked. The Commission, therefore, came to the conclusion that the most satisfactory solution of the problem would be to state specifically that the use of tracer, incendiary or explosive projectiles by or against aircraft is not prohibited.").

[73] *Refer to* § 19.6 (1868 St. Petersburg Declaration).

[74] *Refer to* § 6.6 (Weapons Calculated to Cause Superfluous Injury).

[75] *Refer to* § 19.7.1 (1899 Declaration on Expanding Bullets).

[76] William Crozier, Captain of Ordnance, U.S. Army, *Report of Captain Crozier to the American Delegation to the First Hague Conference, Regarding the Work of the First Committee of the Conference and its Subcommittee*, *reprinted in* INSTRUCTIONS TO THE AMERICAN DELEGATES TO THE HAGUE PEACE CONFERENCES AND THEIR OFFICIAL REPORTS 34 (1916) (noting the objection of the U.S. representative that the 1899 Declaration "condemned by designed implication, without even the introduction of any evidence against it, the use of a bullet actually employed by the army of a civilized nation").

In 2013, a review conducted by DoD in coordination with the Department of State reconfirmed that the prohibition in the 1899 Declaration on Expanding Bullets did not reflect customary international law.[77] The findings of this review were consistent with the longstanding position of the United States not to become a Party to the 1899 Declaration and not to apply a distinct prohibition against expanding bullets, but instead to regard expanding bullets as prohibited only to the extent that such bullets are calculated to cause unnecessary suffering.[78]

In the past, expanding bullets have been viewed as ineffective for military and technical reasons.[79] Non-expanding bullets that were widely used in armed conflict produced wounds comparable to, or more severe than, wounds produced by expanding bullets.[80] In addition,

---

[77] Portions of the analysis in this review are presented in the following paragraphs.

[78] William Crozier, Captain of Ordnance, U.S. Army, *Report of Captain Crozier to the American Delegation to the First Hague Conference, Regarding the Work of the First Committee of the Conference and its Subcommittee*, *reprinted in* INSTRUCTIONS TO THE AMERICAN DELEGATES TO THE HAGUE PEACE CONFERENCES AND THEIR OFFICIAL REPORTS 33-34 (1916); JAMES BROWN SCOTT, THE PROCEEDINGS OF THE HAGUE PEACE CONFERENCES: III THE CONFERENCE OF 1907 15 (1921) (Brigadier General George B. Davis recalling the U.S. delegation's proposal in 1907 to amend the 1899 Declaration to prohibit 'bullets that inflict unnecessarily cruel wounds'); 1914 RULES OF LAND WARFARE ¶3 note 2 (explaining that the 1899 Declaration "has never been ratified by the United States but see paragraph 'e,' Article XXIII, convention IV, Hague Rules, 1907, infra, par., 184"); U.S. ARMY ORDNANCE, HISTORY OF SMALL-ARMS AMMUNITION, NO. 1940, 15 (1920) ("The Judge Advocate General's Office has given the opinion that the armor-piercing ammunition [with a soft lead nose that mushrooms] is a lawful weapon"); 1934 RULES OF LAND WARFARE ¶34 (1934) (giving no separate rule against expanding bullets, but providing that certain types of bullets may be prohibited under the rule against weapons calculated to cause unnecessary suffering); 1940 RULES OF LAND WARFARE ¶34 (1940) (same); 1956 FM 27-10 (Change No. 1 1976) ¶34(b) (same); *Use of Expanding Ammunition by U.S. Military Forces in Counterterrorist Incidents*, 45 (reiterating that the United States is not a party to the 1899 Hague Declaration on expanding bullets but is a party to the Hague Convention IV, which includes the prohibition against weapons calculated to cause unnecessary suffering); W. Hays Parks for The Judge Advocate General, U.S. Army, *Memorandum of Law—Sniper Use of Open-Tip Ammunition*, Oct. 12, 1990, *reprinted in* THE ARMY LAWYER 86, 87 (Feb. 1991) ("The United States is not a party to [the 1899 Hague Declaration], but United States officials over the years have taken the position that the armed forces of the United States will adhere to its terms to the extent that its application is consistent with the object and purpose of article 23e of the Annex to Hague Convention IV"); W. Hays Parks, *Joint Service Combat Shotgun Program*, THE ARMY LAWYER 16, 22 (Oct. 1997) (same).

[79] *See, e.g.*, Alfons Vanheusden, W. Hays Parks, and William H. Boothby, *The Use of Expanding Bullets in Military Operations: Examining the Kampala Consensus*, 50 MILITARY LAW AND LAW OF WAR REVIEW 535, 537 (2011) ("[L]ack of use of expanding ammunition by armed forces could be attributed equally to the increased risk of weapon malfunction (specifically, failure to feed) through its use, particularly in machineguns"); P. R. COURTNEY-GREEN, AMMUNITION FOR THE LAND BATTLE 33 (1991) (noting that expanding bullets "may not cause a sufficiently incapacitating wound, particularly in a military context,"); WILLY LEY, SHELLS AND SHOOTING 39-41 (1942) ("[D]umdum bullets find too much air resistance. Roughly speaking, their power of penetration is only one-quarter that of other bullets, and the 'dumdum effect' does not take place if the velocity is low. Ranges of more than 600 yards ruin the 'dumdum effect,' and over 1200 yards the bullet may be so slow that it cannot penetrate a heavy uniform with overcoat."); Charles Frederick Carter, *"Atrocities" in War*, Nov. 1914, 29 THE WORLD'S WORK 65, 66 (1915) ("But since the first Hague Conference no nation has used dum-dum bullets for a compelling reason that has nothing to do with the Hague nor with considerations of humanity. Experience has taught that when a modern high powered rifle, such as is used in all armies to-day, is hot and dirty, conditions common to battle, the dum-dum bullet is liable to 'strip'; that is, the leaden core is apt to squirt out, leaving the jacket in the barrel, so that when the next shot is fired the gun blows back, or bursts.").

[80] *See, e.g.*, *High-speed Bullets and Dumdums*, 79 SCIENTIFIC AMERICAN SUPPLEMENT NO. 2053, 304 (May 8, 1915) ("But the modern spitzer, at its still higher velocities and its unsteady performance in tissue, gives results that are more frightful than any dumdum."); *Medical News: The Explosive Effect of Bullets*, 46 JOURNAL OF THE AMERICAN

expanding bullets are widely used by law enforcement agencies today, which also supports the conclusion that States do not regard such bullets are inherently inhumane or needlessly cruel.[81]

6.5.4.5 *Rome Statute of the International Criminal Court War Crime Regarding the Use of Expanding Bullets*. The war crime of using expanding bullets that is reflected in the Rome Statute of the International Criminal Court has been interpreted by States only to criminalize the use of expanding bullets that are also calculated to cause superfluous injury and not to create or reflect a prohibition against expanding bullets as such.

The Rome Statute of the International Criminal Court lists as a war crime "[e]mploying bullets which expand or flatten easily in the human body, such as bullets with a hard envelope which does not entirely cover the core or is pierced with incisions."[82]

Elements of Crimes have been adopted by the Assembly of States Parties to the Rome Statute to assist the ICC in its interpretation and application of the Article 8 of the Rome Statute, which includes this war crime.[83] The Elements of Crimes explain that this rule is not violated unless, *inter alia*, "[t]he perpetrator was aware that the nature of the bullets was such that their employment would uselessly aggravate suffering or the wounding effect."[84] When adopting an amendment at the Review Conference in 2010 that would apply this crime to non-international armed conflict, Parties to the Rome Statute reiterated this understanding and explained that "the crime is committed only if the perpetrator employs the bullets to uselessly aggravate suffering or the wounding effect upon the target of such bullets, as reflected in customary international law."[85]

MEDICAL ASSOCIATION 66 (Jan. 2, 1915) ("[T]he instability of flight and tendency of the [pointed modern] bullet to revolve around a transverse axis give it a capacity for wounding the soft part greater than that of any expanding or soft-nosed bullet."); George B. Davis, *The Amelioration of the Rules of War on Land*, 2 AJIL 63, 75-76 (1908) ("Small-arm projectiles having the mechanical construction, or causing the wounds which are particularly described in the declaration, have ceased to be manufactured; and the forms now in use, some of which inflict wounds of great and unnecessary severity, are no longer within the narrow and illogical terms of the prohibition. Had the Crozier amendment been adopted, it is highly probable that a type of small-arm projectile would have been developed which would have met all reasonable requirements in respect to velocity, range, and flatness of trajectory, without the needless and inhuman laceration of tissues which attend those now in use, or which are proposed for adoption in the armies of some civilized powers.").

[81] *For example*, NILS MELZER, TARGETED KILLING IN INTERNATIONAL LAW 417 and note 103 (2009) ("A model example in this respect [*i.e.*, a situation governed by the law enforcement paradigm] is the case of Ewald K., which occurred in Chur, Switzerland, in 2000. In this case, although there was no risk to innocent bystanders, Swiss Police snipers deliberately used expanding rifle bullets in order to ensure that Ewald K. had no opportunity to return fire, but would be killed instantly. ... This motivation was accepted by the Cantonal Court as sufficient to justify the use of expanding rifle bullets. See Cantonal Court Grisons, *Ewald K. Case*, Deliberation 13(d).").

[82] ROME STATUTE art. 8(2)(b)(xix).

[83] ROME STATUTE art. 9 ("1. Elements of Crimes shall assist the Court in the interpretation and application of articles 6, 7 and 8. They shall be adopted by a two-thirds majority of the members of the Assembly of States Parties.").

[84] ROME STATUTE, ELEMENTS OF CRIMES, art. 8(2)(b)(xix), Official Records of the Assembly of States Parties to the Rome Statute of the International Criminal Court, First session, New York, ICC-ASP/1/3, 112, 146 (Sept. 3-10, 2002).

[85] Resolution RC/Res. 5, First ICC Review Conference: Resolutions and Declarations, 49 INTERNATIONAL LEGAL MATERIALS 1328, 1333 (2010).

Thus, this crime only applies to expanding bullets that are also calculated to cause superfluous injury and does not create or reflect a prohibition against expanding bullets as such.[86]

6.5.4.6 *Suppressors (Silencers)*. A suppressor or silencer is a device that is intended to reduce or disguise the sound of a firearm's discharge without affecting its ability to fire. There is no law of war prohibition on the use of a suppressor, and silenced weapons have been a part of the inventory of military forces and law enforcement agencies in many States, including the United States.[87]

6.5.4.7 *Anti-Personnel Use of Larger (e.g., .50) Caliber Guns or Cannons*. The law of war does not prohibit the use of .50 caliber machineguns or other large-caliber guns against enemy personnel.[88] Such use has been widespread and long-standing.[89]

Similarly, cannons and other artillery (*e.g.*, the M242 25mm Bushmaster in the Bradley Fighting Vehicle or the 30mm GAU-8 in the A-10 aircraft) have often been used during armed conflict against enemy material and may also be used against enemy combatants. Although use against individual enemy combatants may not necessarily reflect the most efficient use of resources, such use is not prohibited by the law of war.

6.5.5 Blast Weapons. Blast weapons rely upon the pressure wave caused by an explosion, rather than fragmentation, to cause damage to objects and injury to enemy military personnel. Inflicting blast injury is not prohibited by the law of war.[90]

---

[86] *Refer to* § 6.6 (Weapons Calculated to Cause Superfluous Injury).

[87] W. Hays Parks, Special Assistant for Law of War Matters, Office of the Judge Advocate General, U.S. Army, *Memorandum re: Legality of Silencers/Suppressors* 3 (Jun. 9, 1995) ("Today, silenced weapons are a standard part of the inventory of military forces and law enforcement agencies throughout the world. For example, the Heckler and Koch MP5SD, an integrally suppressed 9x19mm Parabellum submachinegun, is in use by law enforcement and military forces in more than forty nations; in the United States, local, state and federal law enforcement agencies and each of the four armed services are equipped with the MP5SD. The H&K MP5SD was employed by U.S. Army, Navy and Marine Corps units during the 1991 liberation of Kuwait.").

[88] U.S. Army, Office of the Judge Advocate General, International Law Division, Opinion DAJA-IA 1986/8044, *Use of the .50-Caliber Machinegun*, Nov. 21, 1986, *reprinted in* THE ARMY LAWYER 36, 37 (Apr. 1987) ("Employment of the .50 caliber machinegun or other .50 caliber weapons against enemy personnel does not violate the law of war.").

[89] U.S. Army, Office of the Judge Advocate General, International Law Division, Opinion DAJA-IA 1986/8044, *Use of the .50-Caliber Machinegun*, Nov. 21, 1986, *reprinted in* THE ARMY LAWYER 36 (Apr. 1987) ("Larger-caliber weapons have remained in the inventories of virtually every nation. For example, the Soviet Union mounts the NSV .50 caliber machinegun on its tanks; it can be removed and employed on a tripod in a ground mode. Nations generally employ .50-caliber machineguns as antiaircraft, antimaterial, and antipersonnel weapons. On occasion, they have been employed specifically as long-range sniper weapons. The Soviet PTRD was a 14.5mm (.58 caliber) bolt-action, single-shot antitank weapon employed during World War II; because of its long-range accuracy, it was frequently employed as a sniper weapon against German troops. Similarly, the Browning Machinegun Caliber .50 HB, M2 currently in use by U.S. forces, was employed as a single-shot sniper rifle during the Vietnam War.").

[90] W. Hays Parks, Special Assistant to The Judge Advocate General, U.S. Army, *Memorandum re: 40mm Thermobaric Munition; Legal Review*, Apr. 2, 2003 ("Blast is and has been an inherent part of high explosive munitions, and combatants have died solely from the blast effects of conventional HE munitions. Pioneers, sappers

6.5.6 Fragmentation Weapons. Some munitions operate by projecting a large number of fragments or projectiles on detonation. Such weapons may include fragmenting artillery shells, the Claymore munition, "grape shot," grenades, flechettes,[91] and shotgun buckshot.[92]

The fragments or projectiles in such weapons must be detectable by X-rays.[93] However, the use of multiple fragments or projectiles to injure enemy personnel is not prohibited by the law of war.[94] The fact that enemy military personnel in the path of fragment dispersion are likely to suffer multiple wounds does not render the weapon unlawful. Multiple fragments may be necessary to increase the probability of incapacitating enemy combatants.

6.5.7 Depleted Uranium Munitions. Depleted uranium (DU) is used in some munitions because its density and physical properties create a particularly effective penetrating combination to defeat enemy armored vehicles, including tanks.[95]

States have regarded the use of depleted uranium weapons as consistent with their law of war obligations.[96]

---

and combat engineers engaged in tunneling operations under enemy lines in the American Civil War, World War I, and Korea employed substantial amounts of high explosives. Enemy personnel above the detonation became blast casualties. Artillery barrages generally will produce a number of enemy casualties, including fatalities, from blast alone, as will heavy aerial bombardment.").

[91] *See* SPAIGHT, AIR POWER AND WAR RIGHTS 201 (1947) ("Reference has been made above to *flêchettes* and it is desirable to explain what these were. They were small arrows of steel which were dropped in bundles of fifty at a time from aeroplanes upon ground targets or observation balloons. They were used on both the Allies' and the German sides, but were originally an Italian invention, having been first used in Tripoli in 1911-12."). *See also* W. Hays Parks, *Conventional Weapons and Weapons Reviews*, 8 YEARBOOK OF INTERNATIONAL HUMANITARIAN LAW 55, 81 (2005) ("Flechettes are steel darts of varying sizes fired at high velocities in large quantities in munitions as small as a shotgun shell to as large as a 90mm tank round, 105mm artillery round and 106mm recoilless rifle round, enabling a uniform dispersion of flechettes to increase the probability of wounding enemy combatants within their path. These munitions had proved particularly effective as a close-range final defensive fire against massed attacking forces.").

[92] *Refer to* § 6.5.4.2 (Shotguns).

[93] *Refer to* § 6.11 (Weapons Injuring by Fragments Not Detectable by X-Rays).

[94] 1976 AIR FORCE PAMPHLET 110-31 ¶6-6b ("Where a military purpose is apparent and suffering is incidental to the military necessities involved, the use of explosives and fragmentation particles such as those contained in projectiles, mines, bombs, rockets, missiles and hand grenades is not prohibited under the law of armed conflict. This result is confirmed by an extensive practice of nations in using such weapons during periods of armed conflict in the 20th Century and previously.").

[95] Col. James Naughton, Army Materiel Command, *Special Department of Defense Briefing: Update on Depleted Uranium* (Mar. 14, 2003) ("[T]he depleted uranium is a material that has a characteristic that allows it to sharpen itself as it penetrates the target. The uranium shreds off the sides of the penetrator instead of squashing or mushrooming. If you look at the lower picture, which is what happens with tungsten, the tungsten mushrooms. The result is the depleted uranium will penetrate more armor of a given character and type at a given range than tungsten will, no matter how we design the penetrators.").

[96] *For example*, DAILY HANSARD, HOUSE OF COMMONS DEBATES, Jul. 12, 2012, Written Ministerial Statements, Column 40WS-41WS ("**The Minister for the Armed Forces (Nick Harvey)**: I informed the House on 31 October 2011 that I had commissioned officials to undertake a legal weapons review of our depleted uranium (DU) anti-armour tank rounds, known as Charm-3. … The review is now complete and has concluded that Charm-3 is capable of being used lawfully by UK armed forces in an international armed conflict. … The use of DU in weapon systems

The U.S. armed forces have fielded and used depleted uranium munitions. Extensive efforts have been made to study whether there are harmful health effects from exposure to depleted uranium from weapons that use it, but no such effects have been found.[97]

6.5.8 Remotely Piloted Aircraft. There is no prohibition in the law of war on the use of remotely piloted aircraft (also called "unmanned aerial vehicles").[98] Such weapons may offer certain advantages over other weapons systems.[99]

---

is not prohibited by any treaty provision. There have been extensive scientifically based studies, undertaken by the World Health Organisation in relation to the long-term environmental and other health effects allegedly attributable to the use of DU munitions. In the light of the reassuring conclusions drawn by such scientific studies, and noting the continuing military imperative underpinning retention of Charm-3 as a weapon system, it was concluded that use of Charm-3 does not offend the principle prohibiting superfluous injury or unnecessary suffering in armed conflict. … Finally, it was concluded that DU continues to be a material of choice used by states in the manufacture of anti-armour munitions. To date no inter-state consensus has emerged that DU munitions should be banned and the available scientific evidence (developed in the aftermath of the Gulf war in 1991) continues to support the view held by the UK that such munitions can be retained for the limited role envisaged for their employment. The UK policy remains that DU can be used within weapons; it is not prohibited under current or likely future international agreements.").

[97] Ambassador Robert Wood, United States Mission to the United Nations, *Remarks at the Sixty-Ninth UNGA First Committee Cluster Five: Explanation of Vote Before the Vote on L.43, Agenda Item 96 (e) "Effects of the use of armaments and ammunitions containing depleted uranium,"* Oct. 31, 2014 ("I am speaking on behalf of France, the United Kingdom and the United States to explain our negative vote on draft resolution L.43 'Effects of the use of armaments and ammunitions containing depleted uranium'. Mr. Chairman, this is not a new issue. The environmental and long-term health effects of the use of depleted uranium munitions have been thoroughly investigated by the World Health Organization, the United Nations Environmental Program, the International Atomic Energy Agency, NATO, the Centres for Disease Control, the European Commission, and others. None of these inquiries has documented long-term environmental or health effects attributable to use of these munitions."); Dr. Michael Kilpatrick, DoD Deployment Health Support Directorate, *Special Department of Defense Briefing: Update on Depleted Uranium* (Mar. 14, 2003) ("We looked at some 90 Gulf War veterans who were in or on an armored vehicle when it was struck by depleted uranium in friendly fire. And those individuals have been followed on an annual basis now we are talking 12 years post-incident. And we do not see any kidney damage in those individuals … . They were also followed for other medical problems, and … they've had no other medical consequences of that depleted uranium exposure. Now, some of these individuals had amputations, were burned, had deep wounds, so that these individuals, some of them of course do have medical problems. But as far as a consequence of the depleted uranium exposure, we are not seeing anything related to that either from a chemical or radiological effect.").

[98] John O. Brennan, Assistant to the President for Homeland Security and Counterterrorism, *Speech at the Wilson Center: The Ethics and Efficacy of the President's Counterterrorism Strategy*, Apr. 30, 2012, 2012 DIGEST OF UNITED STATES PRACTICE IN INTERNATIONAL LAW 584, 585 ("As a matter of international law, the United States is in an armed conflict with al-Qa'ida, the Taliban, and associated forces, in response to the 9/11 attacks, and we may also use force consistent with our inherent right of national self-defense. There is nothing in international law that bans the use of remotely piloted aircraft for this purpose… ."); Harold Hongju Koh, Legal Adviser, Department of State, *Address at the Annual Meeting of the American Society of International Law: The Obama Administration and International Law*, Mar. 25, 2010, 2010 DIGEST OF UNITED STATES PRACTICE IN INTERNATIONAL LAW 715, 718-19 ("[T]here is no prohibition under the laws of war on the use of technologically advanced weapons systems in armed conflict -- such as pilotless aircraft … .").

[99] John O. Brennan, Assistant to the President for Homeland Security and Counterterrorism, *Speech at the Wilson Center: The Ethics and Efficacy of the President's Counterterrorism Strategy*, Apr. 30, 2012, 2012 DIGEST OF UNITED STATES PRACTICE IN INTERNATIONAL LAW 584, 586 ("Targeted strikes are wise. Remotely piloted aircraft in particular can be a wise choice because of geography, with their ability to fly hundreds of miles over the most treacherous terrain, strike their targets with astonishing precision, and then return to base. They can be a wise

6.5.9 Autonomy in Weapon Systems. The law of war does not prohibit the use of autonomy in weapon systems. DoD has developed policy on the use of autonomy in weapon systems.[100]

6.5.9.1 *Description and Examples of the Use of Autonomy in Weapon Systems*. Some weapons may have autonomous functions. For example, mines may be regarded as rudimentary autonomous weapons because they are designed to explode by the presence, proximity, or contact of a person or vehicle, rather than by the decision of the operator.[101] Other weapons may have more sophisticated autonomous functions and may be designed such that the weapon is able to select targets or to engage targets automatically after being activated by the user. For example, the United States has used weapon systems for local defense with autonomous capabilities designed to counter time-critical or saturation attacks. These weapon systems have included the Aegis ship defense system and the Counter-Rocket, Artillery, and Mortar (C-RAM) system.

6.5.9.2 *No Law of War Prohibition on the Use of Autonomy in Weapon Systems*. The law of war does not specifically prohibit or restrict the use of autonomy to aid in the operation of weapons.

In fact, in many cases, the use of autonomy could enhance the way law of war principles are implemented in military operations. For example, some munitions have homing functions that enable the user to strike military objectives with greater discrimination and less risk of incidental harm. As another example, some munitions have mechanisms to self-deactivate or to self-destruct, which helps reduce the risk they may pose generally to the civilian population or after the munitions have served their military purpose.[102]

Although no law of war rule specifically restricts the use of autonomy in weapon systems, other rules may apply to weapons with autonomous functions. For example, to the extent a weapon system with autonomous functions falls within the definition of a "mine" in the CCW Amended Mines Protocol, it would be regulated as such.[103] In addition, the general rules applicable to all weapons would apply to weapons with autonomous functions. For example, autonomous weapon systems must not be calculated to cause superfluous injury or be inherently indiscriminate.[104]

6.5.9.3 *Law of War Obligations of Distinction and Proportionality Apply to Persons Rather Than the Weapons Themselves*. The law of war rules on conducting attacks

---

choice because of time, when windows of opportunity can close quickly and there may be just minutes to act. They can be a wise choice because they dramatically reduce the danger to U.S. personnel, even eliminating the danger altogether. Yet they are also a wise choice because they dramatically reduce the danger to innocent civilians, especially considered against massive ordnance that can cause injury and death far beyond its intended target.").

[100] *Refer to* § 6.5.9.4 (DoD Policy on Autonomy in Weapon Systems).

[101] *Refer to* § 6.12.1.2 (Designed to Be Exploded by the Presence, Proximity, or Contact of a Person or Vehicle).

[102] *Refer to* § 6.12.1.6 (Mines With Compliant Self-Destruction and Self-Deactivation (SD/SDA) Mechanisms).

[103] *Refer to* § 6.12.1 (Definition of Mine).

[104] *Refer to* § 6.6 (Weapons Calculated to Cause Superfluous Injury); § 6.7 (Inherently Indiscriminate Weapons).

(such as the rules relating to discrimination and proportionality) impose obligations on persons. These rules do not impose obligations on the weapons themselves; of course, an inanimate object could not assume an "obligation" in any event. Thus, it is not the case that the law of war requires that a weapon determine whether its target is a military objective. Similarly, the law of war does not require that a weapon make other legal determinations such as whether an attack may be expected to result in incidental harm that is excessive in relation to the concrete and direct military advantage expected to be gained. The law of war does not require weapons to make legal determinations, even if the weapon (*e.g.*, through computers, software, and sensors) may be characterized as capable of making factual determinations, such as whether to fire the weapon or to select and engage a target. Rudimentary autonomous weapons, such as mines, have been employed for many years, and there has never been a requirement that such weapons themselves determine that legal requirements are met.

Rather, it is persons who must comply with the law of war. For example, persons may not use inherently indiscriminate weapons.[105] In addition, in the situation in which a person is using a weapon that selects and engages targets autonomously, that person must refrain from using that weapon where it is expected to result in incidental harm that is excessive in relation to the concrete and direct military advantage expected to be gained.[106] In addition, the obligation on the person using the weapon to take feasible precautions in order to reduce the risk of civilian casualties may be more significant when the person uses weapon systems with more sophisticated autonomous functions.[107] For example, such feasible precautions a person is obligated to take may include monitoring the operation of the weapon system or programming or building mechanisms for the weapon to deactivate automatically after a certain period of time.

6.5.9.4 <u>DoD Policy on Autonomy in Weapon Systems</u>. DoD policy has addressed the use of autonomy in certain types of weapon systems.[108] Under a 2012 policy, certain types of autonomous weapon systems require an additional review by senior DoD officials before formal development and fielding.[109] In addition, the policy establishes rigorous standards for system design, testing of hardware and software, and training of personnel on the proper use of autonomous and semi-autonomous systems. Among other things, the policy requires that military commanders use autonomous and semi-autonomous weapon systems in a manner consistent with their design, testing, certification, operator training, and doctrine.[110]

---

[105] *Refer to* § 6.7 (Inherently Indiscriminate Weapons).

[106] *Refer to* § 5.12 (Proportionality – Prohibition on Attacks Expected to Cause Excessive Incidental Harm).

[107] *Refer to* § 5.11 (Proportionality – Feasible Precautions in Planning and Conducting Attacks to Reduce the Risk of Harm to Protected Persons and Objects).

[108] DoD Directive 3000.09, *Autonomy in Weapons Systems* (Nov. 21, 2012).

[109] DoD Directive 3000.09, *Autonomy in Weapons Systems*, ¶4d (Nov. 21, 2012) ("Autonomous or semi-autonomous weapon systems intended to be used in a manner that falls outside the policies in subparagraphs 4.c.(1) through 4.c.(3) must be approved by the Under Secretary of Defense for Policy (USD(P)); the Under Secretary of Defense for Acquisition, Technology, and Logistics (USD(AT&L)); and the CJCS before formal development and again before fielding in accordance with the guidelines in Enclosure 3, References (b) and (c), and other applicable policies and issuances.").

[110] DoD Directive 3000.09, *Autonomy in Weapons Systems*, Enclosure 4 ¶10 (Nov. 21, 2012) ("The Commanders of the Combatant Commands shall: a. Use autonomous and semi-autonomous weapon systems in accordance with

U.S. domestic law may also be applicable to the development of autonomous functions in certain weapon systems.[111]

6.5.10 Non-Lethal (Less-Lethal) Weapons. The law of war does not prohibit or specifically address non-lethal weapons as a class of weapons. DoD policies regulate non-lethal weapons and require the legal review of their acquisition, as with other types of weapons. There is no requirement to use non-lethal weapons before using lethal weapons against military objectives.

6.5.10.1 *Non-Lethal Weapons – Notes on Terminology*. The United States is not a Party to any law of war treaty that regulates "non-lethal weapons" as a class or category of weapons. Thus, there is no applicable treaty definition of "non-lethal weapons" for the purpose of applying rules related to such weapons. Accordingly, in practice, the contours of the definition of "non-lethal weapons" have been developed as a matter of policy for the purpose of applying DoD policies with respect to "non-lethal weapons."

6.5.10.2 *Description and Examples of Non-Lethal Weapons*. *Non-lethal weapons*, sometimes called "less-lethal weapons," have been defined as weapons, devices, and munitions that are explicitly designed and primarily employed to incapacitate targeted personnel or materiel immediately, while minimizing fatalities, permanent injury to personnel, and undesired damage to property in the target area or environment.[112]

Non-lethal weapons are less lethal than conventional military weapons, and they use means other than gross physical destruction to defeat targets (whether enemy vehicles or personnel). Non-lethal weapons are intended to have reversible effects on personnel and materiel.

Non-lethal weapons, however, do not have a zero probability of producing fatalities or permanent injuries, which is why these weapons are sometimes referred to as less-lethal weapons.[113] The use of non lethal weapons may still present risks of serious injury or loss of

---

this Directive and in a manner consistent with their design, testing, certification, operator training, doctrine, TTPs, and approval as autonomous or semi-autonomous systems.").

[111] *See, e.g.*, PUBLIC LAW 100-180, § 224 (Dec. 4, 1987) ("No agency of the Federal Government may plan for, fund, or otherwise support the development of command and control systems for strategic defense in the boost or post-boost phase against ballistic missile threats that would permit such strategic defenses to initiate the directing of damaging or lethal fire except by affirmative human decision at an appropriate level of authority."). This statute may, however, be an unconstitutional intrusion on the President's authority, as Commander in Chief, to determine how weapons are to be used in military operations.

[112] DOD DIRECTIVE 3000.03E, *DoD Executive Agent for Non-Lethal Weapons (NLW), and NLW Policy*, Glossary (Apr. 25, 2013) ("NLW. Weapons, devices, and munitions that are explicitly designed and primarily employed to incapacitate targeted personnel or materiel immediately, while minimizing fatalities, permanent injury to personnel, and undesired damage to property in the target area or environment. NLW are intended to have reversible effects on personnel and materiel.").

[113] *See* NATO RESEARCH AND TECHNOLOGY ORGANISATION TECHNICAL REPORT RTO-TR-HFM-073, *The Human Effects of Non-Lethal Technologies*, §6-4 (August 2006) ("Terminology options have referred to 'non-lethal', 'less than lethal', or 'less-lethal'. These first two terms imply that death will not result following the use of these weapons but plainly, this is not always the case in spite of the reassuring connotation. … The military forces of the North Atlantic Treaty Organisation (NATO) use the descriptor 'non-lethal'. This term in the military context does

life.

Non-lethal weapons include, but are not limited to:[114]

- riot control agents;[115]
- blunt impact projectiles, such as stingball grenades, beanbag rounds, and rubber bullets;
- dazzling lasers that cause temporary loss of sight;
- the active denial system, a directed energy weapon that uses millimeter wave energy to penetrate 1/64th of an inch into the surface of the skin, causing a rapid and intense heating sensation;
- electrical stun guns that incapacitate by disrupting the body's electrical signals (also called human electro-muscular incapacitation devices or tasers); and
- counter-material weapons, such as the vehicle lightweight arresting device or the portable vehicle arresting barrier, that are designed to stop vehicles without harming the occupants of the vehicles.

6.5.10.3 *No Law of War Prohibitions or Restrictions on Non-Lethal Weapons as Such*. The law of war does not prohibit or specifically address non-lethal weapons as a class of weapons. Rather, such weapons are governed by the general customary rules applicable to weapons and other specific rules, insofar as those rules are applicable. For example, the use of riot control agents is prohibited as a method of warfare.[116]

Weapons designed to use the minimum amount of force and to preserve life are, consistent with the principle of humanity, often less likely to be prohibited or restricted by the law of war.

6.5.10.4 *DoD Policy Requiring a Legal Review of the Acquisition of Non-Lethal*

---

not imply nil casualties or damage, but is a statement of intent to achieve the lowest achievable probability of casualties and physical damage. The term has often been challenged as being inappropriate, but an alternative descriptor that can provide a better interpretation has yet to be widely adopted within international circles.").

[114] *For example*, David A. Koplow, *Tangled Up in Khaki and Blue: Lethal and Non-Lethal Weapons in Recent Confrontations*, 36 GEORGETOWN JOURNAL OF INTERNATIONAL LAW 703, 727 (2005) ("In 1995, the thirteenth Marine Expeditionary Unit was assigned the daunting mission of covering the withdrawal of 2,500 United Nations peacekeepers from chaotic Somalia, while providing protection against native war lords, disorganized military, and paramilitary units. Lieutenant General Anthony C. Zinni boldly decided to include a variety of NLW in the Marines' training and equipment for this operation 'United Shield,' and his departure from standard operation procedures garnered a substantial amount of publicity. Among the unconventional tools deployed to Somalia were: sticky foam, used to create temporary, immediate barriers; caltrops, sharp-edged pyramids that could puncture the tires of vehicles following too closely; flash-bang and stinger grenades; low-kinetic-energy rounds which fired beanbags or wooden plugs; laser dazzlers and target designators; and chemical riot control agents.").

[115] *Refer to* § 6.16 (Riot Control Agents).

[116] *Refer to* § 6.16.2 (Prohibition on Use of Riot Control Agents as a Method of Warfare).

Weapons. DoD policy has addressed non-lethal weapons.[117] Like lethal weapons, non-lethal weapons have been subject to legal review to ensure their compliance with U.S. law of war and arms control obligations.[118]

If acquisition of a non-lethal weapon is being considered, the command seeking to acquire the weapon should inquire through command or service channels whether the applicable legal reviews have been conducted.

6.5.10.5 *No Requirement to Use Non-Lethal Weapons Before Using Lethal Weapons Where Deadly Force Is Warranted.* Where the use of deadly force is warranted, such as against enemy combatants, the law of war does not create a legal obligation to use non-lethal weapons before using lethal weapons.[119] Moreover, under the law of war, the availability of non-lethal weapons does not create the obligation to use these weapons instead of lethal weapons or create a higher standard for the use of force.[120]

In addition, the availability of non-lethal weapons does not limit the authority to use force in self-defense.[121]

6.6 Weapons Calculated to Cause Superfluous Injury

It is especially forbidden to use weapons that are calculated to cause superfluous

---

[117] *For example*, DoD Directive 3000.03E, *DoD Executive Agent for Non-Lethal Weapons (NLW), and NLW Policy* (Apr. 25, 2013); DoD Directive 3000.3, *Policy for Non-Lethal Weapons* (Jul. 9, 1996).

[118] *For example*, DoD Directive 3000.03E, *DoD Executive Agent for Non-Lethal Weapons (NLW), and NLW Policy*, Enclosure 2 ¶11 (Apr. 25, 2013) ("The Secretaries of the Military Departments and the Commander, USSOCOM, through the CJCS: … c. Require, as appropriate, that a legal review of the acquisition of all NLW is conducted in accordance with Reference (h) and an arms control compliance review is completed in accordance with DoDD 2060.1 (Reference (l))."); DoD Directive 3000.3, *Policy for Non-Lethal Weapons*, ¶E6 (Jul. 9, 1996) ("The Secretaries of the Military Departments and the Commander in Chief of the United States Special Operations Command shall: ... (b) Ensure that a legal review of the acquisition of all non-lethal weapons is conducted. The review should ensure consistency with the obligations assumed by the U.S. Government under all applicable treaties, with customary international law, and, in particular, the laws of war.").

[119] *Refer to* § 5.4.6 (Force That May Be Applied Against Military Objectives).

[120] DoD Directive 3000.03E, *DoD Executive Agent for Non-Lethal Weapons (NLW), and NLW Policy*, ¶3h (Apr. 25, 2013) ("The presence of NLW will not constitute an obligation for their use, or create a higher standard for the use of force, under the applicable law, rules of engagement, or other rules for the use of force."); DoD Directive 3000.3, *Policy for Non-Lethal Weapons*, ¶4.5 (Jul. 9, 1996) ("Neither the presence nor the potential effect of non-lethal weapons shall constitute an obligation for their employment or a higher standard for employment of force than provided for by applicable law. In all cases, the United States retains the option for immediate use of lethal weapons, when appropriate, consistent with international law.").

[121] DoD Directive 3000.03E, *DoD Executive Agent for Non-Lethal Weapons (NLW), and NLW Policy*, ¶3g (Apr. 25, 2013) ("The availability of NLW will not limit the commander's inherent right or obligation to exercise unit self-defense in response to a hostile act of [sic] demonstrated hostile intent, or to use lethal force when authorized by competent authority pursuant to the standing rules of engagement or standing rules for the use of force."); DoD Directive 3000.3, *Policy for Non-Lethal Weapons*, ¶4.4 (Jul. 9, 1996) ("The availability of non-lethal weapons shall not limit a commander's inherent authority and obligation to use all necessary means available and to take all appropriate action in self-defense.").

injury.[122]

6.6.1 Superfluous Injury or Unnecessary Suffering – Notes on Terminology. The prohibition against weapons calculated to cause superfluous injury or of a nature to cause unnecessary suffering has been formulated in a variety of ways both in treaties to which the United States is a Party and in other treaties. The United States is not a Party to a treaty that provides a definition of "superfluous injury."

Article 23(e) of the 1899 Hague II Regulations prohibits weapons "of a nature to cause superfluous injury." Article 23(e) of the 1907 Hague IV Regulations prohibits weapons "calculated to cause unnecessary suffering." The official texts of both the 1899 and 1907 treaties are French, and the French text of that paragraph is exactly the same in both treaties, even though English translations of the treaties are different. The title of the CCW refers to "Weapons Which May be Deemed to Be Excessively Injurious," and the CCW Preamble also recognizes "the principle that prohibits the employment in armed conflicts of weapons, projectiles and material and methods of warfare of a nature to cause superfluous injury or unnecessary suffering."

Treaties that the United States has not ratified have also included this prohibition. The Preamble to the 1868 Declaration of St. Petersburg noted that "the employment of arms which uselessly aggravate the sufferings of disabled men, or render their death inevitable" would be "be contrary to the laws of humanity."[123] AP I Article 35(2) prohibits the use of "weapons, projectiles and material and methods of warfare of a nature to cause superfluous injury or unnecessary suffering."

Although the various formulations may be regarded as describing the same underlying prohibition, the phrase "calculated to cause superfluous injury" may be regarded as the more accurate translation of the French rule stated in the 1907 Hague IV Regulations and as more precisely conveying the intent of the rule.[124]

---

[122] CCW preamble (recognizing "the principle that prohibits the employment in armed conflicts of weapons, projectiles and material and methods of warfare of a nature to cause superfluous injury or unnecessary suffering"); HAGUE IV REG. art. 23 ("[I]t is especially forbidden … (e) To employ arms, projectiles, or material calculated to cause unnecessary suffering … ."); 1899 HAGUE II REG. art. 23 (prohibits employing "arms, projectiles, or material of a nature to cause superfluous injury"). *Consider* AP I art. 35(2) ("It is prohibited to employ weapons, projectiles and material and methods of warfare of a nature to cause superfluous injury or unnecessary suffering.").

[123] The Declaration of St. Petersburg, 1868, *reprinted in* 1 AJIL SUPPLEMENT: OFFICIAL DOCUMENTS 95 (1907).

[124] R.R. Baxter, *Conventional Weapons Under Legal Prohibitions*, 1 INTERNATIONAL SECURITY 42, 43 (1977) ("This last expression [calculated to cause unnecessary suffering] has been the source of a vast amount of confusion because the English translation from the authentic French text is inaccurate. The expression used in French was *propres a causer des maux superflus*, which might be more accurately translated as 'calculated to cause superfluous (or excessive) injury.' In the metaphysical atmosphere in which the legality of certain weapons is often discussed, such niceties count."); W. Hays Parks, *Conventional Weapons and Weapons Reviews*, 8 YEARBOOK OF INTERNATIONAL HUMANITARIAN LAW 55, 86-87 footnote 123 (2005) ("This argument [about superfluous injury or unnecessary suffering] was based upon a novel ICRC interpretation of the original 1899 Hague language in Art. 23(g) of the Annex prohibiting 'arms, projectiles or material *of a nature to cause* superfluous injury', as compared to the language in the subsequent 1907 Hague Convention, '*calculated to cause* unnecessary suffering'. The latter phrase is a clearer expression of the intent of governments to focus on design and intended purpose rather than every remote possibility of weapon injury.").

This manual generally uses the formulation "weapons calculated to cause superfluous injury" or refers to the "superfluous injury rule."

6.6.2 Superfluous Injury Rule – the Principle of Humanity. The superfluous injury rule is an application of the principle of humanity in the context of weapons.[125] The superfluous injury rule prohibits weapons that are designed to increase the injury or suffering of the persons attacked beyond that justified by military necessity.[126]

Thus, the principle of humanity may assist in understanding and applying the rule.[127] For example, weapons that are regarded as lawful in peacetime or that apply only the minimum force necessary in order to avoid death or injury to civilians would not be prohibited under the superfluous injury rule.[128]

6.6.3 Applying the Superfluous Injury Rule. The test for whether a weapon is prohibited by the superfluous injury rule is whether the suffering caused by the weapon provides no military advantage or is otherwise clearly disproportionate to the military advantage reasonably expected from the use of the weapon.[129] Thus, the suffering must be assessed in relation to the military utility of the weapon.[130] Weapons that may cause great injury or suffering or inevitable death are not prohibited, if the weapon's effects that cause such injury are necessary to enable users to

---

[125] Prosecutor v. Tadić, ICTY Appeals Chamber, IT-94-1-AR72, *Decision on the Defence Motion for Interlocutory Appeal on Jurisdiction*, ¶119 (Oct. 2, 1995) (explaining that the prohibitions on weapons in the customary law of war applicable to international and non-international armed conflicts are based on "elementary considerations of humanity and common sense").

[126] *Written Statement of the Government of the United States of America*, 28-29, Jun. 20, 1995, I.C.J., Request by the United Nations General Assembly for an Advisory Opinion on the Legality of the Threat or Use of Nuclear Weapons ("This prohibition was intended to preclude weapons designed to increase the injury or suffering of the persons attacked beyond that necessary to accomplish the military objective. It does not prohibit weapons that may cause great injury or suffering if the use of the weapon is necessary to accomplish the military mission. For example, it does not prohibit the use of anti-tank munitions which must penetrate armor by kinetic-energy or incendiary effects, even though such weapons can produce severe and painful injuries.").

[127] *Refer to* § 2.3 (Humanity).

[128] *Cf. Statement by Secretary Rusk*, Mar. 24, 1965, 52 DEPARTMENT OF STATE BULLETIN 529 (Apr. 12, 1965) (defending the legality of riot control agents by explaining that "[w]hat has been involved has been well-known, traditional agents, in the hands of police forces in many parts of the world. And under the circumstances in which this gas was used in Viet-Nam, the desire was to use the minimum force required to deal with the situation to avoid death or injury to innocent people."). *Refer to* § 6.16 (Riot Control Agents).

[129] WINTHROP, MILITARY LAW & PRECEDENTS 784 ("An illegitimate weapon of war would be one which, in disabling or causing death, inflicted a needless, unusual and unreasonable amount of torture or injury and the deliberate use of such a weapon would properly be treated as a violation of the laws of war."); SPAIGHT, WAR RIGHTS ON LAND 75 ("Hence commanders are quite ready to admit the claims of humanity to the extent of forgoing the use of any engine of war whose military effect is disproportioned to the suffering it entails.").

[130] Ronald J. Bettauer, Deputy Assistant Legal Adviser, Department of State, *Statement at the Conference of Government Experts on Weapons which may Cause Unnecessary Suffering or have Indiscriminate Effects, held in Lucerne from Sept. 24 to Oct. 18, 1974*, Sept. 25, 1974, 1974 DIGEST OF UNITED STATES PRACTICE IN INTERNATIONAL LAW 707 ("It is the U.S. view that the 'necessity' of the suffering must be judged in relation to the military utility of the weapons. The test is whether the suffering is needless, superfluous, or disproportionate to the military advantage reasonably expected from the use of the weapon.").

accomplish their military missions.[131]

6.6.3.1 Military Necessity. The legitimate military necessity that may be considered in assessing the legality of a weapon includes its capability to disable or incapacitate enemy combatants, including, for example:

- the probability of striking a person against whom the weapon is aimed or directed;
- the probability that a person who is struck by the weapon will be incapacitated;
- the speed at which a person who is struck by the weapon will be incapacitated; and
- the number of persons the weapon could strike.[132]

However, the military utility of the weapon is often broader than its capacity to disable enemy combatants.[133] It may include other factors, such as:[134]

- the destruction or neutralization of military materiel;
- the restriction of military movement;
- the interdiction of military lines of communication;
- the effects on the morale, command and control, stamina, and cohesion of opposing forces;

---

131 *Written Statement of the Government of the United States of America*, 32-33, Jun. 20, 1995, I.C.J., Request by the United Nations General Assembly for an Advisory Opinion on the Legality of the Threat or Use of Nuclear Weapons ("This argument is based on a misconception of the St. Petersburg principle, which was directed at anti-personnel weapons that were deliberately designed to kill when that design feature was not needed to disable enemy combatants. This does not mean that it is unlawful to use a weapon that has a high probability of killing persons in its immediate vicinity if that design feature is required to fulfill a legitimate military mission. For example, any large high-explosive or fragmentation weapon has a high probability of killing exposed persons within a certain distance of the detonation. An effective anti-submarine, anti-aircraft or anti-tank weapon has a high probability of killing the crews of these vehicles. This fact does not make these weapons unlawful, since these lethal effects are necessary for the effective accomplishment of their legitimate mission.").

132 SPAIGHT, AIR POWER AND WAR RIGHTS 203 ("[A]lthough a shell [fired by a cannon] may kill or mutilate—and mutilate horribly—only one man, it may also be compensated by the possible 'bag' of a projectile of widely radiating effect.").

133 BOTHE, PARTSCH, & SOLF, NEW RULES 196 (AP I art. 35, ¶2.3.3) ("The problem cannot be simplified by restating the preamble of the 1968 [sic] St. Petersburg Declaration that to weaken the enemy's military forces it is sufficient to disable the greatest possible number of men (i.e., to render enemy combatants *hors de combat*). This test is valid only for weapons designed for antipersonnel purposes. However, weapons are designed and produced to be used to fulfill a variety of military requirements other than merely disabling enemy combatants.").

134 BOTHE, PARTSCH, & SOLF, NEW RULES 196-97 (AP I art. 35, ¶2.3.3) ("Some examples of such requirements include the destruction or neutralization of military material, restriction of military movement, the interdiction of military lines of communications, the weakening of the enemy's war making resources and capabilities, and the enhancement of the security of friendly forces. ... Factors which must also be taken into account are the availability of alternate weapon systems (and their effects), the logistics of providing the weapon and its ammunition at the place where it is to be used when needed, and the security of the troops involved.").

- the weakening of the enemy's war-making resources and capabilities;
- the enhancement of the security of forces employing the weapon or other friendly forces;
- the effectiveness of the weapon against particular types of targets;
- the availability of alternative weapons and their effects;
- the logistics of providing the weapon and its ammunition where and when it is needed;
- the amount of ammunition required;
- the cost of using the weapon in terms of time, money, and other resources;
- the efficacy of the weapon compared to the adversary's defenses;
- the efficacy of the weapon in light of the weapons and tactics of the adversary; or
- the risk to the civilian population when the weapon is used for its intended purposes.[135]

These other factors can justify weapons that inflict injuries on enemy combatants that are much greater than the minimum needed to render them *hors de combat*. For example, an artillery shell designed to destroy field fortifications or heavy material causes injuries to enemy personnel that are much greater than those necessary to make enemy combatants *hors de combat*. However, the artillery shell is not prohibited because these military advantages are not clearly disproportionate to the injuries it inflicts.[136]

6.6.3.2 Suffering and Injury Inflicted. The superfluous injury rule addresses the harm inflicted upon the persons who are struck by the weapon. The types of harm addressed by the superfluous rule include: mortality rates, the painfulness of wounds, the severity of wounds, and the ease with which they may be treated (including the incidence of permanent damage or disfigurement).[137] Weapons that have been modified only for the purpose of increasing these

---

[135] Christopher Greenwood, *Legal Aspects of current Regulations,* KEYNOTE SPEECHES, THIRD INTERNATIONAL WORKSHOP ON WOUND BALLISTICS (Thun, Switzerland, Mar. 28-29, 2001) ("Moreover, there are circumstances, particularly in street warfare and in counter terrorist operations where it may be necessary to make a trade, in effect, between the principle of the protection of civilian life and the principle of 'unnecessary suffering' to combatants. What I would like to suggest is that where that trade has to be made – and I accept that it is not one which has to be made in all, or even most types of combat – one cannot regard suffering as unnecessary if it is inflicted for the purpose of protecting the civilian population. In other words, if the civilian population's protection is enhanced by the use of a particular weapon, then the adverse effects of that weapon on combatants cannot properly be regarded as unnecessary.").

[136] BOTHE, PARTSCH, & SOLF, NEW RULES 196-97 (AP I art. 35, ¶2.3.3) ("[A]n artillery projectile or missile designed to destroy field fortifications or heavy material may be expected to cause injuries to personnel in the vicinity of the target which would be more severe than necessary to render these combatants *hors de combat*, but no authority has questioned the lawfulness of such projectiles despite the gravity of the incidental effect on personnel.").

[137] *See* INTERNATIONAL COMMITTEE OF THE RED CROSS, CONFERENCE OF GOVERNMENT EXPERTS ON THE USE OF CERTAIN CONVENTIONAL WEAPONS: LUCERNE, SEPT. 24- OCT. 18, 1974, 8 (¶23) (Geneva, 1975) ("The concept of

types of harms for persons who have already been incapacitated are prohibited by the superfluous injury rule.[138]

6.6.3.3 Clearly Disproportionate. A weapon is only prohibited by the superfluous injury rule if the suffering it inflicts is clearly disproportionate to its military utility. This excessiveness should be assessed in light of the State practice and *opinio juris* and the principle of humanity.

Because of the difficulty of comparing the military necessity for the weapon and the suffering it is likely to cause, a weapon is only prohibited if the suffering is clearly or manifestly disproportionate to the military necessity.[139] The suffering likely to result from the use of the weapon and its military effectiveness are likely to be difficult to assess, much less to compare to one another.[140]

Like other determinations of customary international law, whether a weapon is calculated to cause superfluous injury is to be determined in light of the practice of States, and in particular, whether States have declined to use the weapon or similar weapons because they are believed to

---

'injury' or 'suffering' evoked some further comment. It was generally considered that this comprised such factors as mortality rates, the painfulness or severeness of wounds, or the incidence of permanent damage or disfigurement.").

[138] *Refer to* § 6.6.4 (Weapons Modified for the Purpose of Aggravating the Harm Inflicted on Incapacitated Persons).

[139] BOTHE, PARTSCH, & SOLF, NEW RULES 197 (AP I art. 35, ¶2.3.3) ("Because of the impossibility of quantifying either side of the equation it is important that military advantage be qualified by such words as 'definite', and also that the disproportionate suffering be 'manifest' or 'clear'."). *See also* W. Hays Parks, Special Assistant for Law of War Matters, Office of The Judge Advocate General, U.S. Army, *Joint Service Combat Shotgun Program*, THE ARMY LAWYER 16, 18 (Oct. 1997) ("In determining whether a weapon causes superfluous injury, a balancing test is applied between the force dictated by military necessity to achieve a legitimate objective vis-a-vis injury that may be considered superfluous to the achievement of the stated or intended objective (in other words, whether the suffering caused is out of proportion to the military advantage to be gained). The test is not easily applied; a weapon that can incapacitate or wound lethally at, for example, 300 meters or longer ranges may result in a greater degree of incapacitation or greater lethality at lesser ranges. For this reason, the degree of 'superfluous' injury must be clearly disproportionate to the intended objective(s) for development of the weapon (that is, the suffering must outweigh substantially the military necessity for the weapon)."); W. Hays Parks, Chief, International Law Branch, International Affairs Division, Office of the Judge Advocate General, U.S. Army, *Memorandum re: Sniper Use of Open-Tip Ammunition*, Oct. 12, 1990, *reprinted in* THE ARMY LAWYER 86, 87 (Feb. 1991) (similar).

[140] BOTHE, PARTSCH, & SOLF, NEW RULES 196 (AP I art. 35, ¶2.3.3) ("In applying para. 2 of Art. 35, the suffering or injury caused by a weapon must be judged in relation to the military utility of the weapon. The test is whether the suffering is needless, superfluous, or manifestly disproportionate to the military advantage reasonably expected from the use of the weapon. On the humanitarian side of the equation against which military advantage is to be balanced are such factors as the painfulness or severity of wounds, mortality rates, and the incidence of permanent damage or disfigurement and the feasibility of treatment under field conditions. Neither element of the equation can be taken in isolation. All such comparative judgments logically lead to an inquiry into how much suffering various weapons cause and whether available alternate weapons can achieve the same military advantage effectively but cause less suffering. The comparison of, and balancing between, suffering and military effectiveness is difficult in practice because neither side of the equation is easy to quantify. Inevitably, the assessment will be subjective even when sufficient agreed factual data are available on wound effects and military effectiveness.").

have this effect.[141] The consideration of the military utility of the weapon and the suffering the weapon inflicts should be compared to other destructive mechanisms that States have used or retained for use and consider to be lawful.

A State's acceptance of a treaty prohibition against a weapon should not be understood as necessarily reflecting that State's conclusion that the weapon is calculated to cause superfluous injury. For example, the CCW and its Protocols generally do not reflect a conclusion that the weapons prohibited or restricted by them are calculated to cause superfluous injury.[142] On the other hand, a prohibition or restriction in a treaty can be relevant in determining that a weapon is not calculated to cause superfluous injury. For example, the CCW Amended Mines Protocol prohibits mines, booby-traps, and other devices that are designed or of a nature to cause unnecessary suffering.[143] Thus, this prohibition implicitly recognizes that not all mines, booby-traps, and other devices are calculated to cause superfluous injury.[144] In addition, even if a treaty that declared that certain weapons were calculated to cause superfluous injury, such treaty language would not necessarily mean that the weapon was prohibited by customary international law. For example, specially affected States might decline to ratify the treaty and decide to retain the right to use the weapon.[145]

6.6.3.4 *Superfluous Injury Rule – the Circumstances to Be Assessed and Design Intent*. In determining a weapon's legality, the weapon's planned uses and the normal circumstances in which it would be used should be considered.[146] It is not necessary to assess all possible uses or all possible circumstances.

6.6.4 Weapons Modified for the Purpose of Aggravating the Harm Inflicted on Incapacitated Persons. Weapons that have been modified for the purpose of aggravating the harm inflicted upon incapacitated persons are weapons that are prohibited by the superfluous

---

[141] 1956 FM 27-10 (Change No. 1 1976) ¶34b ("What weapons cause 'unnecessary injury' [within the meaning of Hague IV Reg. art. 23(e)] can only be determined in light of the practice of States in refraining from the use of a given weapon because it is believed to have that effect.").

[142] *Refer to* § 19.21.1.3 (CCW and Customary International Law).

[143] *Refer to* § 6.12.4.1 (Mines, Booby-Traps, and Other Devices Calculated to Cause Superfluous Injury).

[144] *Article-by-Article Analysis of CCW Amended Mines Protocol*, 11, Enclosure A to Warren Christopher, *Letter of Submittal*, Dec. 7, 1996, MESSAGE FROM THE PRESIDENT TRANSMITTING THE CCW AMENDED MINES PROTOCOL, PROTOCOL III ON INCENDIARY WEAPONS, AND PROTOCOL IV ON BLINDING LASER WEAPONS 11 (CCW Amended Mines Protocol art. 3(3) "reiterates a proscription already in place as a matter of customary international law applicable to all weapons. It also implicitly makes clear that mines, booby-traps and other devices are not, per se, of a nature to cause unnecessary suffering, for if that were considered to be the case, no such rule would be necessary and they would be prohibited entirely.").

[145] *Refer to* § 1.8.2.3 (Specially Affected States).

[146] WILLIAM BOOTHBY, WEAPONS AND THE LAW OF ARMED CONFLICT 62 (2009) ("So, in the context of superfluous injury and unnecessary suffering, the comparator [or excessiveness] must be determined by 'the generic purpose or purposes for which the weapon has been designed or adapted, or the purpose or purposes for which that weapon will generally be used'. The word 'generic' is used here to show that we are specifically not referring to the use of the weapon on a particular occasion in prosecution of a specific mission. The word 'generally' indicates that it is the normal applications of the weapon that are to be considered, not some unusual application, or misapplication, of it which lies outside the scope of purposes for which it was procured or adapted.").

injury rule.[147]

For example, adding poison to bullets or other substances to weapons for the purpose of increasing the pain caused by the wound, to make wounds more difficult to treat, or to make death inevitable, would be prohibited. Such a substance would not increase the military utility of the weapon to incapacitate the enemy (*i.e.*, it would have no corresponding military advantage); thus, the additional injury would be superfluous when compared to the injury caused by the weapon without such a substance.

Weapons that have been modified are readily assessed under the superfluous injury rule because the unmodified version of the weapon provides a clear point of comparison. It is difficult to compare, in the abstract, the military utility of a weapon against the suffering it causes. But, by comparing an existing weapon to a proposed modification, one can evaluate more easily whether the proposed changes are warranted by legitimate military reasons (*e.g.*, to increase the ability of the weapon to incapacitate the enemy) or illegitimate reasons (*e.g.*, cruelty) because, in considering a modification to the weapon, one would expect that a number of relevant factors would be the same as between the existing weapon and the proposed modification.

6.7 Inherently Indiscriminate Weapons

Inherently indiscriminate weapons, *i.e.*, weapons that are incapable of being used in accordance with the principles of distinction and proportionality, are prohibited. Such weapons include weapons that are specifically designed to conduct attacks against the civilian population as well as weapons that, when used, would necessarily cause incidental harm that is excessive compared the military advantage expected to be gained from their use.

6.7.1 Inherently Indiscriminate Weapons – Principles of Distinction and Proportionality. The prohibition against inherently indiscriminate weapons results from the principles of distinction and proportionality.[148] Attacks must be conducted in accordance with the principles of distinction and proportionality.[149] Consequently, a weapon that, when used, would necessarily violate these rules, would be prohibited.[150]

---

[147] *Consider* The Declaration of St. Petersburg, 1868, *reprinted in* 1 AJIL Supplement: Official Documents 95 (1907) (considering that it would "be contrary to the laws of humanity" to use "arms which uselessly aggravate the sufferings of disabled men, or render their death inevitable;").

[148] *Refer to* § 2.5 (Distinction); § 2.4 (Proportionality).

[149] *Refer to* § 5.5 (Discrimination in Conducting Attacks); § 5.12 (Proportionality – Prohibition on Attacks Expected to Cause Excessive Incidental Harm).

[150] *See* Legality of the Threat or Use of Nuclear Weapons, Advisory Opinion, 1996 I.C.J. 226, 257 (¶78) ("The cardinal principles contained in the texts constituting the fabric of humanitarian law are the following. The first is aimed at the protection of the civilian population and civilian objects and establishes the distinction between combatants and non-combatants; States must never make civilians the object of attack and must consequently never use weapons that are incapable of distinguishing between civilian and military targets."); Greenspan, Modern Law of Land Warfare 359 ("[I]t must be borne in mind that indiscriminate bombardment of the civilian population is prohibited, so that weapons which must necessarily have that effect when used are also illegal.").

Few weapons have been understood to be inherently indiscriminate weapons.[151] This may be the case because weapons that are more accurate and precise are more militarily effective; the military and humanitarian interests coincide.[152] On the other hand, the few weapons that have been understood to violate this rule have been directed at illegitimate objectives, such as attacking and terrorizing the civilian population.[153]

6.7.2 Inherently Indiscriminate Weapons – Circumstances to Be Assessed and Design Intent. The test for whether a weapon is inherently indiscriminate is whether its use necessarily violates the principles of distinction and proportionality, *i.e.*, whether its use is expected to be illegal in all circumstances.

Special consideration should be given to the planned or intended uses of the weapon, *i.e.*, those that are reasonably foreseeable. For example, a practitioner conducting a legal review of the proposed acquisition or procurement of a weapon should consider the uses of the weapon that are planned and reflected in the design documents. Practitioners should advise if the planned uses of the weapon are not consistent with the principles of distinction and proportionality, with a view towards ensuring that either the weapon or the planned uses are modified accordingly.

The wide range of circumstances in which weapons can lawfully be used should also be considered before concluding that a weapon is prohibited as inherently indiscriminate. For example, in some circumstances, an area of land can be a military objective.[154] Thus, even if it would not be possible for the weapon to be directed against enemy combatants, if the weapon could be directed at specific areas, it would be unlikely that the weapon would be considered inherently indiscriminate. As another example, in some circumstances, feasible precautions can mitigate the incidental harm expected to be caused so that it is not excessive.[155] Whether such precautions could be taken to mitigate the expected incidental harm caused by the weapon under review should be considered before concluding that a weapon is prohibited as inherently indiscriminate.

6.7.3 Weapons Designed to Conduct Attacks Against the Civilian Population. Inherently

---

[151] Christopher Greenwood, *Legal Aspects of current Regulations*, KEYNOTE SPEECHES, THIRD INTERNATIONAL WORKSHOP ON WOUND BALLISTICS (Thun, Switzerland, Mar. 28-29, 2001) ("There are virtually no cases of weapons which are inherently indiscriminate. The United States Naval Commander's Handbook, one of the most modern texts and an important piece of State practice, gives in its annotations an illustration of an inherently indiscriminate weapon – a proposal during the Second World War to tie tiny incendiary bombs around the necks of bats. The bats would then be released from aircraft over enemy targets, would glide down into the trees and into the rafters of buildings and set fire to those buildings when the incendiaries exploded. If that is the best example that can be given of an inherently indiscriminate weapon, there are not very many inherently indiscriminate weapons in existence.").

[152] ICRC AP COMMENTARY 621 (¶1958) ("It should be noted that most armies endeavour to use accurate weapons as attacks which do not strike the intended objective result in a loss of time and equipment without giving a corresponding advantage. ... Here the military interests and humanitarian requirements coincide.").

[153] *Refer to* § 6.7.3 (Weapons Designed to Conduct Attacks Against the Civilian Population).

[154] *Refer to* § 5.6.8.4 (Examples of Military Objectives – Places of Military Significance).

[155] *Refer to* § 5.11 (Proportionality – Feasible Precautions in Planning and Conducting Attacks to Reduce the Risk of Harm to Protected Persons and Objects).

indiscriminate weapons include those that are specifically designed to be used to conduct attacks against the civilian population, including attacks to terrorize the civilian population. For example, Japanese bombs attached to free-floating, long-range balloons used during World War II were unlawful for this reason.[156] Also, German long-range rockets without guidance systems used during World War II were similarly illegal.[157]

6.7.4 Weapons That Necessarily Cause Excessive Incidental Harm. Indiscriminate weapons also include weapons whose anticipated incidental effects are necessarily excessive compared to the military advantages expected to be gained from using the weapon.[158] To be clear, the principle of proportionality does not prohibit the use of weapons whose destructive force cannot be limited to a specific military objective.[159] Such weapons may be used when their use is required against a target of sufficient military importance to outweigh the incidental harm

---

[156] *For example*, ROBERT C. MIKESH, JAPAN'S WORLD WAR II BALLOON BOMB ATTACKS ON NORTH AMERICA 1 (1973) ("In a desperate attempt to find a means of reprisal [for the Doolittle raid], the Japanese conceived a method to strike directly at the American continent. Their plan was simple; launch balloons with incendiary and antipersonnel bombs attached, let them travel across the Pacific with the prevailing winds, and drop on American cities, forests, and farmlands. It took over two years to design the balloons, bombs, and automatic dropping mechanism. … Finally, on 3 November 1944, the first of more than nine thousand bomb-bearing balloons was released. It is estimated that nearly one thousand of the death-dealing balloons must have reached the North American continent.").

[157] *For example*, SPAIGHT, AIR POWER AND WAR RIGHTS 214-15 ("As used by the Germans in 1944-45, [the V-2 long-range rocket] was simply a crude instrument of random bombardment, utterly lacking in precision, and its military value was *nil*. While such a weapon is not banned in terms by any international convention, the use of it could not be regarded as compatible with the observance of certain rules which are the subject of definite international agreement, such as those forbidding the bombardment 'by any means' of undefended towns and villages, and those enjoining the sparing, as far as possible, of 'buildings dedicated to religious, art, science or charitable purposes, historic monuments, hospitals and places where the sick and wounded are collected.' … The flying [V-1] bomb is another abominable projectile which might well be prohibited at the same time. It is, again, a weapon which cannot really be aimed at all.").

[158] 1976 AIR FORCE PAMPHLET 110-31 ¶6-3c ("In addition, some weapons, though capable of being directed only at military objectives, may have otherwise uncontrollable effects so as to cause disproportionate civilian injuries or damage. Biological warfare is a universally agreed illustration of such an indiscriminate weapon. Uncontrollable effects, in this context, may include injury to the civilian population of other states as well as injury to an enemy's civilian population. Uncontrollable refers to effects which escape in time or space from the control of the user as to *necessarily* create risk to civilian persons or objects excessive in relation to the military advantage anticipated. International law does not require that a weapon's effects be strictly confined to the military objectives against which it is directed, but it does restrict weapons whose foreseeable effects result in unlawful disproportionate injury to civilians or damage to civilian objects.").

[159] J. Fred Buzhardt, General Counsel, Department of Defense, Letter to Senator Edward Kennedy, Sept. 22, 1972, *reprinted in* 67 AJIL 122, 124 (1973) ("The existing laws of armed conflict do not prohibit the use of weapons whose destructive force cannot be limited to a specific military objective. The use of such weapons is not proscribed when their use is necessarily required against a military target of sufficient importance to outweigh inevitable, but regrettable, incidental casualties to civilians and destruction of civilian objects."). *See also* Edward Cummings, Head of the U.S. Delegation to CCW Group of Government Experts, *Statement*, Jul. 17, 2002 ("On proportionality. As the paper noted, the law of armed conflict does not require the effects of weapons to be limited such that they cause no civilian casualties. This would, unfortunately, be impossible. It does however, as Professor Greenwood points out, require compliance with the principle of proportionality with respect to the use of weapons and thus requires an assessment of the risks posed to civilians in the context of the military advantage hoped for.").

that is expected to result.[160]

As with the superfluous injury rule, in assessing whether weapons necessarily cause excessive incidental harm, it will be important to consider whether the practice of States demonstrates that they are prohibited as such.[161] For example, the United States regards nuclear weapons not to be inherently disproportionate weapons.[162]

Weapons that necessarily cause excessive incidental harm include "blind" or essentially random weapons that are incapable of being controlled, and thus, cannot, with any degree of certainty, be directed against a military objective.[163] The expected incidental harm from the use of such weapons outweighs the little, if any, military utility of such weapons.[164]

Weapons that necessarily cause excessive incidental harm also include weapons whose uncontrollable nature is such that, even when directed against military objectives, they otherwise are expected invariably to cause excessive incidental harm. For example, using communicable diseases such as the plague as weapons has been prohibited, in part because such use would almost inevitably cause excessive incidental harm among the civilian population compared to the military advantages from their use.[165]

6.8 Poison, Poisoned Weapons, Poisonous Gases, and Other Chemical Weapons

The use of poison, poisoned weapons, poison and asphyxiating gases, and other chemical weapons is prohibited.

6.8.1 Poison and Poisoned Weapons. It is especially forbidden to use poison or poisoned weapons.[166] For example, poisoning the enemy's food or water supply is prohibited.[167]

---

[160] *Refer to* § 5.12 (Proportionality – Prohibition on Attacks Expected to Cause Excessive Incidental Harm).

[161] *Refer to* § 6.6.3.3 (Clearly Disproportionate).

[162] *Written Statement of the Government of the United States of America*, 23, Jun. 20, 1995, I.C.J., Request by the United Nations General Assembly for an Advisory Opinion on the Legality of the Threat or Use of Nuclear Weapons ("Whether an attack with nuclear weapons would be disproportionate depends entirely on the circumstances, including the nature of the enemy threat, the importance of destroying the objective, the character, size and likely effects of the device, and the magnitude of the risk to civilians. Nuclear weapons are not inherently disproportionate.").

[163] 1976 Air Force Pamphlet 110-31 ¶6-3c ("Indiscriminate weapons are those incapable of being controlled, through design or function, and thus they can not, with any degree of certainty be directed against military objectives."); Bothe, Partsch, & Solf, New Rules 305 (AP I art. 51, ¶2.5.2.2) ("The provision of subpara. 4.b. to methods which cannot be directed at a specific military objective prohibits 'blind' weapons which cannot, with any reasonable assurance, be directed against a military objective. Attaching incendiary or antipersonnel bombs to free floating balloons, or using long range missiles with only a rudimentary guidance system are examples of this type of weapon.").

[164] 1976 Air Force Pamphlet 110-31 ¶6-3c ("Use of such essentially unguided weapons could be expected to cause unlawful excessive injury to civilians and damage to civilian objects.").

[165] *Refer to* § 6.9.1 (Biological Weapons – Prohibition on Use as a Method of Warfare).

[166] *See* Hague IV Reg. art. 23(a) (it is especially forbidden "[t]o employ poison or poisoned weapons;"); 1899 Hague II Reg. art. 23(a) (same); Lieber Code art. 16 (military necessity "does not admit of the use of poison in any

Similarly, adding poison to weapons is prohibited. The rule against poison and poisoned weapons reflected in the 1899 Hague II Regulations has been interpreted not to include poison gas weapons that were developed during the modern era, which were subsequently prohibited.[168]

Poisons are understood to be substances that cause death or disability with permanent effects when, in even small quantities, they are ingested, enter the lungs or bloodstream, or touch the skin.[169]

The longstanding prohibition against poison is based on: (1) their uncontrolled character; (2) the inevitability of death or permanent disability; and (3) the traditional belief that it is treacherous to use poison.[170]

6.8.1.1 Designed to Injure by Poison. This prohibition on poison applies to weapons that are designed to injure or kill by poison. It does not apply to weapons that injure or cause destruction by other means that also produce toxic byproducts.[171]

6.8.1.2 Death or Permanent Disability to Persons. The prohibition on using poison applies to use against human beings.[172] Thus, the prohibition on the use of poison has been understood not to prohibit the use of chemical herbicides that are harmless to human

---

way,"); LIEBER CODE art. 70 ("The use of poison in any manner, be it to poison wells, or food, or arms, is wholly excluded from modern warfare. He that uses it puts himself out of the pale of the law and usages of war.").

[167] 1958 UK MANUAL ¶112 ("Water in wells, pumps, pipes, reservoirs, lakes, rivers, and the like, from which the enemy may draw drinking water, must not be poisoned or contaminated. The poisoning or contamination of water is not made lawful by posting up a notice informing the enemy that the water has been thus polluted. There is, however, no rule to prevent measures being taken to dry up springs and to divert rivers and aqueducts.").

[168] WILLIAM H. BOOTHBY, WEAPONS AND THE LAW OF ARMED CONFLICT 122 (2009) ("The Hague Peace Conference of 1899 tackled the problem [of poison gas attacks]. The delegates at that conference made no direct association between poison, which they considered to be an ancient and barbarous form of warfare, and poison gas, which was seen as a novel weapon the product of scientific advance.").

[169] 1976 AIR FORCE PAMPHLET 110-31 ¶6-4f ("Poisons are biological or chemical substances causing death or disability with permanent effects when, in even small quantities, they are ingested, enter the lungs or bloodstream, or touch the skin.").

[170] 1976 AIR FORCE PAMPHLET 110-31 ¶6-4f ("The longstanding customary prohibition against poison is based on their uncontrolled character and the inevitability of death or permanent disability as well as on a traditional belief that it is treacherous to use poison.").

[171] *Written Statement of the Government of the United States of America*, 24, Jun. 20, 1995, I.C.J., Request by the United Nations General Assembly for an Advisory Opinion on the Legality of the Threat or Use of Nuclear Weapons ("This prohibition was established with particular reference to projectiles that carry poison into the body of the victim. It was not intended to apply, and has not been applied, to weapons that are designed to injure or cause destruction by other means, even though they also may create toxic byproducts. For example, the prohibition on poison weapons does not prohibit conventional explosives or incendiaries, even though they may produce dangerous fumes. By the same token, it does not prohibit nuclear weapons, which are designed to injure or cause destruction by means other than poisoning the victim, even though nuclear explosions may also create toxic radioactive byproducts.").

[172] 1956 FM 27-10 (Change No. 1 1976) ¶37b (explaining that the prohibition against poison or poison weapons in the Hague IV Regulations "prohibits the use in war of poison or poisoned weapons against human beings.").

beings.[173] Other rules, however, may apply to the use of herbicides.[174]

6.8.2 Asphyxiating, Poisonous, or Other Gases, and All Analogous Liquids, Materials, or Devices. It is prohibited to use in war asphyxiating, poisonous, or other gases, and all analogous liquids, materials, or devices.[175] The United States has determined that this rule is part of customary international law.[176]

Although the rule appears quite broad, it has been understood only to apply to the use of gases that are designed to kill or injure human beings.[177] Thus, herbicides and riot control agents

---

[173] J. Fred Buzhardt, General Counsel, Department of Defense, Letter to Chairman Fulbright, Senate Committee on Foreign Relations, Apr. 5, 1971, 10 INTERNATIONAL LEGAL MATERIALS 1300, 1302 (1971) (explaining the DoD view that it does "not regard chemical herbicides, harmless to man, as poison or poisoned weapons, for if they had been so considered, their use against crops intended solely for the consumption by the enemy's armed forces would clearly have been prohibited by Article 23(a) of the Hague Regulations.").

[174] *Refer to* § 6.17 (Herbicides).

[175] 1925 GENEVA GAS AND BACTERIOLOGICAL PROTOCOL ("Whereas the use in war of asphyxiating, poisonous or other gases, and of all analogous liquids materials or devices, has been justly condemned by the general opinion of the civilised world; and Whereas the prohibition of such use has been declared in Treaties to which the majority of Powers of the world are Parties; and To the end that this prohibition shall be universally accepted as part of International Law, binding alike the conscience and the practice of nations; DECLARE: That the High Contracting Parties, so far as they are not already Parties to Treaties prohibiting such use, accept this prohibition, agree to extend this prohibition to the use of bacteriological methods of warfare and agree to be bound as between themselves according to the terms of this declaration."). *Consider* Treaty in Relation to the Use of Submarines and Noxious Gases in Warfare, art. 5, Feb. 6, 1922, *reprinted in* 16 AJIL SUPPLEMENT: OFFICIAL DOCUMENTS 57, 59 (1922) ("The use in war of asphyxiating, poisonous or other gases, and all analogous liquids, materials or devices, having been justly condemned by the general opinion of the civilized world and a prohibition of such use having been declared in treaties to which a majority of the civilized Powers are parties, The Signatory Powers, to the end that this prohibition shall be universally accepted as a part of international law binding alike the conscience and practice of nations, declare their assent to such prohibition, agree to be bound thereby as between themselves and invite all other civilized nations to adhere thereto."); Declaration to Abstain From the Use of Projectiles the Object of Which Is the Diffusion of Asphyxiating or Deleterious Gases, Jul. 29, 1899, *reprinted in* 1 AJIL SUPPLEMENT: OFFICIAL DOCUMENTS 157 (1907) ("The Contracting Powers agree to abstain from the use of projectiles the object of which is the diffusion of asphyxiating or deleterious gases.").

[176] Franklin D. Roosevelt, *Statement Warning the Axis Against Using Poison Gas*, Jun. 8, 1943 ("From time to time since the present war began there have been reports that one or more of the Axis powers were seriously contemplating use of poisonous or noxious gases or other inhumane devices of warfare. ... Use of such weapons has been outlawed by the general opinion of civilized mankind."); Myron C. Cramer, The Judge Advocate General, U.S. Army, *Memorandum re: Destruction of Crops by Chemicals,* ¶2, Mar. 1945, 10 INTERNATIONAL LEGAL MATERIALS 1304, 1305 (1971) (noting that "[a]n exhaustive study of the source materials, however, warrants the conclusion that a customary rule of international law has developed by which poisonous gases and those causing unnecessary suffering are prohibited").

[177] Myron C. Cramer, The Judge Advocate General, U.S. Army, *Memorandum re: Destruction of Crops by Chemicals,* ¶3, Mar. 1945, 10 INTERNATIONAL LEGAL MATERIALS 1304, 1305 (1971) ("Nevertheless, the scope of this prohibition is restricted. It does not constitute a complete ban on all gases and chemical substances. A distinction exists between the employment of poisonous and deleterious gases against enemy human beings, and the use of chemical agents to destroy property, such as natural vegetation, crop cultivations, and the like. ... The true motive behind the movement to outlaw poison gas is that it is considered a barbarous and inhumane weapon against human beings, because it inflicts unnecessary suffering upon them.").

are not prohibited by this rule.[178] In addition, the rule is understood only to prohibit weapons whose prime, or even exclusive, effect is to poison or asphyxiate.[179] Thus, for example, smoke, flame, napalm, conventional explosives, and nuclear weapons are not covered by this rule, even though these weapons may produce asphyxiating or poisonous byproducts.[180]

6.8.3 Chemical Weapons. Chemical weapons are subject to a number of prohibitions.

6.8.3.1 *Definition of Chemical Weapons*. Under the Chemical Weapons Convention, chemical weapons mean the following, together or separately:

> (a) Toxic chemicals and their precursors, except where intended for purposes not prohibited under this Convention, as long as the types and quantities are consistent with such purposes;
>
> (b) Munitions and devices, specifically designed to cause death or other harm through the toxic properties of those toxic chemicals specified in subparagraph (a), which would be released as a result of the employment of such munitions and devices;
>
> (c) Any equipment specifically designed for use directly in connection with the employment of munitions and devices specified in subparagraph (b).[181]

Toxic chemicals refer to any chemical that through its chemical action on life processes can cause death, temporary incapacitation, or permanent harm to humans or animals. This includes all such chemicals, regardless of their origin or of their method of production, and regardless of whether they are produced in facilities, in munitions, or elsewhere.[182] Chemicals

---

[178] William P. Rogers, *Letter of Submittal*, Aug. 11, 1970, MESSAGE FROM THE PRESIDENT TRANSMITTING THE 1925 GENEVA GAS AND BACTERIOLOGICAL PROTOCOL VI ("It is the United States understanding of the Protocol that it does not prohibit the use in war of riot-control agents and chemical herbicides.").

[179] Legality of the Threat or Use of Nuclear Weapons, Advisory Opinion, 1996 I.C.J. 226, 248 (¶55) ("The Court will observe that the Regulations annexed to the Hague Convention IV do not define what is to be understood by 'poison or poisoned weapons' and that different interpretations exist on the issue. Nor does the 1925 Protocol specify the meaning to be given to the term 'analogous materials or devices'. The terms have been understood, in the practice of States, in their ordinary sense as covering weapons whose prime, or even exclusive, effect is to poison or asphyxiate. This practice is clear, and the parties to those instruments have not treated them as referring to nuclear weapons.").

[180] *See* William P. Rogers, *Letter of Submittal*, Aug. 11, 1970, MESSAGE FROM THE PRESIDENT TRANSMITTING THE 1925 GENEVA GAS AND BACTERIOLOGICAL PROTOCOL VI ("Smoke, flame, and napalm are also not covered by the Protocol."); *Written Statement of the Government of the United States of America*, 25, Jun. 20, 1995, I.C.J., Request by the United Nations General Assembly for an Advisory Opinion on the Legality of the Threat or Use of Nuclear Weapons ("Once again, the [1925 Geneva Gas and Bacteriological] Protocol does not prohibit conventional explosives or incendiary weapons, even though they may produce asphyxiating or poisonous byproducts, and it likewise does not prohibit nuclear weapons."); GREENSPAN, MODERN LAW OF LAND WARFARE 359 ("The use of smoke for smoke screens concealing movements and operations could not be considered an infringement of the law against gas warfare.").

[181] CHEMICAL WEAPONS CONVENTION art. 2(1).

[182] CHEMICAL WEAPONS CONVENTION art. 2(2) ("'Toxic Chemical' means: Any chemical which through its chemical action on life processes can cause death, temporary incapacitation or permanent harm to humans or

that only cause harm to plants, such as herbicides, are not covered.[183] In addition, toxic chemicals intended for purposes not prohibited by the Chemical Weapons Convention are also excluded, so long as they are of a type and quantity consistent with these purposes that are not prohibited.[184]

Precursor means any chemical reactant (including any key component of a binary or multicomponent chemical system) that takes part at any stage in the production by whatever method of a toxic chemical.[185] *Key component of a binary or multicomponent chemical system* means the precursor that plays the most important role in determining the toxic properties of the final product and reacts rapidly with other chemicals in the binary or multicomponent system.[186]

Equipment specifically designed for use directly in connection with the employment of such munitions and devices only applies to equipment designed solely for use with chemical weapons and does not, for example, include equipment that is designed also for purposes that are not prohibited.[187]

6.8.3.2 Prohibitions With Respect to Chemical Weapons. Chemical weapons are subject to a number of prohibitions. It is prohibited:

- to use chemical weapons;
- to develop, produce, otherwise acquire, stockpile or retain chemical weapons, or transfer,

---

animals. This includes all such chemicals, regardless of their origin or of their method of production, and regardless of whether they are produced in facilities, in munitions or elsewhere. (For the purpose of implementing this Convention, toxic chemicals which have been identified for the application of verification measures are listed in Schedules contained in the Annex on Chemicals.)"). *See also Article-by-Article Analysis of the Chemical Weapons Convention*, 9, Attachment to Peter Tarnoff, Acting, *Letter of Submittal*, Nov. 20, 1993, MESSAGE FROM THE PRESIDENT TRANSMITTING THE CHEMICAL WEAPONS CONVENTION 9 ("The wording of this definition [in paragraph 2 of Article 2] is intended to cover toxins, as well as organic and inorganic chemicals, and chemicals produced by binary and multicomponent weapons.").

183 *Refer to* § 6.17 (Herbicides).

184 *Refer to* § 6.8.3.4 (Certain Uses of Toxic Chemicals Not Prohibited).

185 CHEMICAL WEAPONS CONVENTION art. 2(3) ("'Precursor' means: Any chemical reactant which takes part at any stage in the production by whatever method of a toxic chemical. This includes any key component of a binary or multicomponent chemical system.").

186 CHEMICAL WEAPONS CONVENTION art. 2(4) ("'Key Component of Binary or Multicomponent Chemical Systems' (hereinafter referred to as 'key component') means: The precursor which plays the most important role in determining the toxic properties of the final product and reacts rapidly with other chemicals in the binary or multicomponent system.").

187 *See Article-by-Article Analysis of the Chemical Weapons Convention*, 9, Attachment to Peter Tarnoff, Acting, *Letter of Submittal*, Nov. 20, 1993, MESSAGE FROM THE PRESIDENT TRANSMITTING THE CHEMICAL WEAPONS CONVENTION 9 ("Note that the term 'directly' in subparagraph 1(c) is intended to mean 'solely.' Thus, dual-use munitions and their components are not considered to be chemical weapons provided they do not otherwise meet this definition. For example, dual-use munitions may be used to disperse chemicals not prohibited by the Convention, such as smoke, provided the munitions have not been specifically designed to cause death through the release of toxic chemicals. Also, dual-use weapons systems such as artillery or aircraft that are capable of employing chemical weapons are not covered by this definition, and so are not subject to the destruction requirements.").

directly or indirectly, chemical weapons to anyone;

- to engage in any military preparations to use chemical weapons; and
- to assist, encourage, or induce, in any way, anyone to engage in any activity prohibited to a Party to the Chemical Weapons Convention.[188]

These prohibitions apply in any circumstances. For example, chemical weapons may not be used in international armed conflict and non-international armed conflicts.[189] Similarly, chemical weapons may not be used in retaliation after a State has suffered from a chemical weapons attack, even if that attack has been conducted by a State that is not a Party to the Chemical Weapons Convention.[190]

6.8.3.3 *Obligation to Destroy Certain Chemical Weapons and Chemical Weapons Production Facilities*. In addition, a Party to the Chemical Weapons Convention has an obligation to destroy chemical weapons or chemical weapon production facilities it owns or possesses or that are located in a place under its jurisdiction or control.[191] If U.S. armed forces encounter chemical weapons or chemical weapon production facilities during armed conflict, U.S. national authorities should be notified as soon as practicable. In addition, with due regard for safety and security considerations, reasonable efforts should be made to secure and retain information regarding the chemical weapons.[192]

6.8.3.4 *Certain Uses of Toxic Chemicals Not Prohibited*. The Chemical Weapons

---

[188] CHEMICAL WEAPONS CONVENTION art. 1(1) ("Each State Party to this Convention undertakes never under any circumstances: (a) To develop, produce, otherwise acquire, stockpile or retain chemical weapons, or transfer, directly or indirectly, chemical weapons to anyone; (b) To use chemical weapons; (c) To engage in any military preparations to use chemical weapons; (d) To assist, encourage or induce, in any way, anyone to engage in any activity prohibited to a State Party under this Convention.").

[189] *Article-by-Article Analysis of the Chemical Weapons Convention*, 4, Attachment to Peter Tarnoff, Acting, *Letter of Submittal*, Nov. 20, 1993, MESSAGE FROM THE PRESIDENT TRANSMITTING THE CHEMICAL WEAPONS CONVENTION 4 ("Moreover, the prohibition on the use of chemical weapons extends beyond solely their use in international armed conflicts, i.e. chemical weapons may not be used in any type of situation, including purely domestic conflicts, civil wars or state-sponsored terrorism. As such, this article closes a loophole in the Geneva Protocol of 1925, which covered only uses in war, i.e. international armed conflicts.").

[190] *Article-by-Article Analysis of the Chemical Weapons Convention*, 4, Attachment to Peter Tarnoff, Acting, *Letter of Submittal*, Nov. 20, 1993, MESSAGE FROM THE PRESIDENT TRANSMITTING THE CHEMICAL WEAPONS CONVENTION 4 ("The prohibitions are phrased as undertakings 'never under any circumstances' to engage in certain activities related to chemical weapons. … Thus, the prohibitions apply to a State Party even if chemical weapons are used against it and even if those chemical weapons are used by a State not Party to the Convention, i.e. even 'retaliatory use' of chemical weapons is banned.").

[191] CHEMICAL WEAPONS CONVENTION art. 1(2) ("Each State Party undertakes to destroy chemical weapons it owns or possesses, or that are located in any place under its jurisdiction or control, in accordance with the provisions of this Convention."); CHEMICAL WEAPONS CONVENTION art. 1(4) ("Each State Party undertakes to destroy any chemical weapons production facilities it owns or possesses, or that are located in any place under its jurisdiction or control, in accordance with the provisions of this Convention.").

[192] *See* Ireland, Facilitator's Paper, Concerning the Mandate Created by the Executive Council at its Fifty-Eighth Sessions Under the Heading 'Other Destruction-Related Issues,' Oct. 8, 2010, Organization for the Prohibition of Chemical Weapons Doc. No. EC-62/NAT.11.

Convention does not prohibit the use of toxic chemicals and their precursors for certain purposes.[193] Toxic chemicals and their precursors that are used for these purposes are not considered chemical weapons, so long as they are of a type and quantity consistent with these permitted purposes.[194] These purposes include:

- industrial, agricultural, research, medical, pharmaceutical, or other peaceful purposes;
- protective purposes, namely those purposes directly related to protection against toxic chemicals and to protection against chemical weapons;
- military purposes not connected with the use of chemical weapons and not dependent on the use of the toxic properties of chemicals as a method of warfare; and
- law enforcement, including domestic riot control purposes.[195]

Seeking to develop and use means of protection against chemical weapons is permissible, provided such protection is not intended to facilitate the use of chemical weapons or for other purposes prohibited by the Chemical Weapons Convention.[196]

6.9 Biological Weapons

Biological weapons, including bacteriological and toxin weapons, are subject to a number of prohibitions and restrictions.

6.9.1 Biological Weapons – Prohibition on Use as a Method of Warfare. It is prohibited to use bacteriological methods of warfare.[197] This prohibition includes all biological methods of

[193] CHEMICAL WEAPONS CONVENTION art. 6(1) ("Each State Party has the right, subject to the provisions of this Convention, to develop, produce, otherwise acquire, retain, transfer and use toxic chemicals and their precursors for purposes not prohibited under this Convention.").

[194] *Article-by-Article Analysis of the Chemical Weapons Convention*, 13, Attachment to Peter Tarnoff, Acting, *Letter of Submittal*, Nov. 20, 1993, MESSAGE FROM THE PRESIDENT TRANSMITTING THE CHEMICAL WEAPONS CONVENTION 13 ("Paragraph 9 of Article II defines, in four subparagraphs, the phrase 'purposes not prohibited under this Convention.' This phrase is important because it forms the basis for many exceptions to obligations or prohibited activities. … This provision means that toxic chemicals and their precursors that are used for one or more of these enumerated purposes are not chemical weapons, so long as they are of a type and quantity consistent with these permitted purposes.").

[195] CHEMICAL WEAPONS CONVENTION art. 2(9) ("'Purposes Not Prohibited Under this Convention' means: (a) Industrial, agricultural, research, medical, pharmaceutical or other peaceful purposes; (b) Protective purposes, namely those purposes directly related to protection against toxic chemicals and to protection against chemical weapons; (c) Military purposes not connected with the use of chemical weapons and not dependent on the use of the toxic properties of chemicals as a method of warfare; (d) Law enforcement including domestic riot control purposes.").

[196] CHEMICAL WEAPONS CONVENTION art. 10(2) ("Nothing in this Convention shall be interpreted as impeding the right of any State Party to conduct research into, develop, produce, acquire, transfer or use means of protection against chemical weapons, for purposes not prohibited under this Convention.").

[197] Richard Nixon, *Statement on Chemical and Biological Defense Policies and Programs*, Nov. 25, 1969, 1969 PUBLIC PAPERS OF THE PRESIDENTS 968 ("The United States shall renounce the use of lethal biological agents and weapons, and all other methods of biological warfare."); 1925 GENEVA GAS AND BACTERIOLOGICAL PROTOCOL

warfare and the use in warfare of toxin weapons.[198] For example, it is prohibited to use plague as a weapon.[199]

A prohibition against the use of biological weapons may be understood to result from U.S. obligations in the Biological Weapons Convention to refrain from developing, acquiring, or retaining biological weapons.[200]

Bacteriological or biological warfare is prohibited, at least in part, because it can have massive, unpredictable, and potentially uncontrollable consequences.[201]

6.9.1.1 Toxin Weapons. The term *toxin* refers to poisonous chemical substances that are naturally produced by living organisms, and that, if present in the body, produce effects similar to disease in the human body.[202] Toxins are not living organisms and thus are not

---

(The High Contracting Parties agree to prohibit "the use of bacteriological methods of warfare and agree to be bound as between themselves according to the terms of this declaration.").

[198] William P. Rogers, *Letter of Submittal*, Aug. 11, 1970, MESSAGE FROM THE PRESIDENT TRANSMITTING THE 1925 GENEVA GAS AND BACTERIOLOGICAL PROTOCOL VI ("The United States considers the term 'bacteriological methods of warfare' as used in the Protocol encompasses all biological methods of warfare and the use in warfare of toxins however produced.").

[199] *For example*, *Verdict of the Military Tribunal*, MATERIALS ON THE TRIAL OF FORMER SERVICEMEN OF THE JAPANESE ARMY CHARGED WITH MANUFACTURING AND EMPLOYING BACTERIOLOGICAL WEAPONS 529-30 (1950) ("The Japanese imperialists employed bacteriological weapons in the war against China and in sabotage raids against the U.S.S.R. In 1940 a special expedition of Detachment 731 commanded by General **Ishii** was despatched to the theatre of hostilities in Central China, where, by dropping plague-infected fleas from aircraft with special apparatus, it caused a plague epidemic in the Nimpo area. This criminal operation which brought in its wake thousands of victims among the peaceful Chinese population was filmed, and this film was later demonstrated in Detachment 731 to representatives of the High Command of the Japanese Army, among the accused **Yamada**.").

[200] William P. Rogers, *Report of the Secretary of State*, Jun. 21, 1972, MESSAGE FROM THE PRESIDENT OF THE UNITED STATES TRANSMITTING THE CONVENTION ON THE PROHIBITION OF THE DEVELOPMENT, PRODUCTION, AND STOCKPILING OF BACTERIOLOGICAL (BIOLOGICAL) AND TOXIN WEAPONS, AND ON THEIR DESTRUCTION, OPENED FOR SIGNATURE AT WASHINGTON, LONDON AND MOSCOW ON APRIL 10, 1972, EXECUTIVE Q, 3 (1972) ("While this Convention does not explicitly ban the use of biological weapons, no Party to the Convention would be permitted to possess such weapons even in wartime. There is no possibility that a Party could use biological or toxin weapons without being in violation of Articles I and II of this Convention."). *Refer to* § 6.9.2 (Biological Weapons – Prohibition on Development, Acquisition, or Retention).

[201] Richard Nixon, *Statement on Chemical and Biological Defense Policies and Programs*, Nov. 25, 1969, 1969 PUBLIC PAPERS OF THE PRESIDENTS 968 ("Biological weapons have massive, unpredictable and potentially uncontrollable consequences. They may produce global epidemics and impair the health of future generations."); 1976 AIR FORCE PAMPHLET 110-31 ¶6-4(b) ("The wholly indiscriminate and uncontrollable nature of biological weapons has resulted in the condemnation of biological weapons by the international community, and the practice of states in refraining from their use in warfare has confirmed this rule."); ICRC AP COMMENTARY 623 (¶1965) ("There are some weapons which by their very nature have an indiscriminate effect. The example of bacteriological means of warfare is an obvious illustration of this point.").

[202] William P. Rogers, *Report of the Secretary of State*, Jun. 21, 1972, MESSAGE FROM THE PRESIDENT OF THE UNITED STATES TRANSMITTING THE CONVENTION ON THE PROHIBITION OF THE DEVELOPMENT, PRODUCTION, AND STOCKPILING OF BACTERIOLOGICAL (BIOLOGICAL) AND TOXIN WEAPONS, AND ON THEIR DESTRUCTION, OPENED FOR SIGNATURE AT WASHINGTON, LONDON AND MOSCOW ON APRIL 10, 1972, EXECUTIVE Q, 3 (1972) ("Toxins are poisonous chemical substances which are naturally produced by living organisms and which, if present in the body, produce effects comparable to those of infection by hostile organisms.").

capable of reproducing themselves and transmissible from one person to another.[203]

Toxin weapons have been regulated in connection with biological weapons because they have been produced in facilities similar to those used for the production of biological agents.[204] However, even toxins that are produced synthetically, and not through biological processes, fall within these prohibitions. Substances that are classified as "toxins" for the purpose of applying the requirements of the Biological Weapons Convention may also be classified as "chemical weapons" that are subject to the requirements of the Chemical Weapons Convention.[205]

6.9.2 Biological Weapons – Prohibition on Development, Acquisition, or Retention. It is also prohibited to develop, produce, stockpile, or otherwise acquire or retain:

- microbial or other biological agents, or toxins whatever their origin or method of production, of types and in quantities that have no justification for prophylactic, protective, or other peaceful purposes; or

- weapons, equipment or means of delivery designed to use such agents or toxins for hostile purposes or in armed conflict.[206]

6.9.3 Biological Weapons – Prohibition on Transfer or Assisting, Encouraging, or Inducing the Manufacture or Acquisition. It is also prohibited to transfer or to assist, encourage, or induce others to acquire biological weapons.[207]

---

[203] Office of the White House Press Secretary, *The United States renounces offensive preparations for and the use of toxins as a method of warfare*, Feb. 14, 1970, *reprinted in* DEPARTMENT OF STATE, FOREIGN RELATIONS OF THE UNITED STATES, 1969-1976, VOLUME E-2, DOCUMENTS ON ARMS CONTROL, 1969-1972, Document 189 (2007) ("Toxins are chemical substances, not living organisms, and are so regarded by the U.N. Secretary General and the World Health Organization. Although the effects of some toxins are commonly described as disease, they are not capable of reproducing themselves and are not, transmissible from one person to another.").

[204] Office of the White House Press Secretary, *The United States renounces offensive preparations for and the use of toxins as a method of warfare*, Feb. 14, 1970, *reprinted in* DEPARTMENT OF STATE, FOREIGN RELATIONS OF THE UNITED STATES, 1969-1976, VOLUME E-2, DOCUMENTS ON ARMS CONTROL, 1969-1972, Document 189 (2007) ("However, the production of toxins in any significant quantity would require facilities similar to those needed for the production of biological agents. If the United States continued to operate such facilities, it would be difficult for others to know whether they were being used to produce only toxins but not biological agents. Moreover, though toxins of the type useful for military purposes could conceivably be produced by chemical synthesis in the future, the end products would be the same and their effects would be indistinguishable from toxins produced by bacteriological or other biological processes.").

[205] *Refer to* § 6.8.3.1 (Definition of Chemical Weapons).

[206] BIOLOGICAL WEAPONS CONVENTION art. 1 ("Each State Party to this Convention undertakes never in any circumstances to develop, produce, stockpile or otherwise acquire or retain: (1) microbial or other biological agents, or toxins whatever their origin or method of production, of types and in quantities that have no justification for prophylactic, protective or other peaceful purposes; (2) weapons, equipment or means of delivery designed to use such agents or toxins for hostile purposes or in armed conflict.").

[207] BIOLOGICAL WEAPONS CONVENTION art. 3 ("Each State Party to this Convention undertakes not to transfer to any recipient whatsover [sic], directly or indirectly, and not in any way to assist, encourage, or induce any State, group of States or international organisations to manufacture or otherwise acquire any of the agents, toxins, weapons, equipment or means of delivery specified in Article I of the Convention.").

The exchange of equipment, materials, and scientific and technological information for the use of bacteriological and biological agents and toxins for peaceful purposes, such as the prevention of disease, however, is not restricted.[208]

6.10 Certain Environmental Modification Techniques

It is prohibited to use environmental modification techniques having widespread, long-lasting, or severe effects as a means of destruction, damage, or injury to another Party to the ENMOD Convention.[209] In addition, it is prohibited to assist, encourage, or induce others to use such environmental modification techniques against a Party to the ENMOD Convention.[210]

6.10.1 Environmental Modification Techniques. "Environmental modification techniques" refers to any technique for changing through the deliberate manipulation of natural processes the dynamics, composition, or structure of the earth, including its biota, lithosphere, hydrosphere and atmosphere, or of outer space.[211]

6.10.2 Having Widespread, Long-Lasting, or Severe Effects. The techniques must have widespread, long-lasting, or severe effects. These terms are interpreted as follows:

(a) "widespread": encompassing an area on the scale of several hundred square kilometers;

(b) "long-lasting": lasting for a period of months, or approximately a season;

(c) "severe": involving serious or significant disruption or harm to human life,

---

[208] BIOLOGICAL WEAPONS CONVENTION art. 10(1) ("The States Parties to this Convention undertake to facilitate, and have the right to participate in, the fullest possible exchange of equipment, materials and scientific and technological information for the use of bacteriological (biological) agents and toxins for peaceful purposes. Parties to the Convention in a position to do so shall also co-operate in contributing individually or together with other States or international organisations to the further development and application of scientific discoveries in the field of bacteriology (biology) for the prevention of disease, or for other peaceful purposes."); BIOLOGICAL WEAPONS CONVENTION art. 10(2) ("This Convention shall be implemented in a manner designed to avoid hampering the economic or technological development of States Parties to the Convention or international co-operation in the field of peaceful bacteriological (biological) activities, including the international exchange of bacteriological (biological) agents and toxins and equipment for the processing, use or production of bacteriological (biological) agents and toxins for peaceful purposes in accordance with the provisions of the Convention.").

[209] ENMOD CONVENTION art. 1(1) ("Each State Party to this Convention undertakes not to engage in military or any other hostile use of environmental modification techniques having widespread, long-lasting or severe effects as the means of destruction, damage or injury to any other State Party.").

[210] ENMOD CONVENTION art. 1(2) ("Each State Party to this Convention undertakes not to assist, encourage or induce any State, group of States or international organization to engage in activities contrary to the provisions of paragraph 1 of this article.").

[211] ENMOD CONVENTION art. 2 ("The term 'Environmental modification techniques' refers to any technique for changing through the deliberate manipulation of natural processes the dynamics, composition or structure of the earth, including its biota, lithosphere, hydrosphere and atmosphere, or of outer space.").

natural and economic resources, or other assets.[212]

For example, earthquakes, tsunamis, and cyclones are environmental effects likely to be widespread, long-lasting, or severe that could be caused by the use of environmental modification techniques.[213] On the other hand, dispelling fog to facilitate military or combat operations may involve the use of environmental modification techniques that would not have widespread, long-lasting, or severe effects.[214]

6.10.3 As a Means of Destruction, Damage, or Injury. In order to fall within the ENMOD Convention's prohibitions, the environmental modification techniques must be used as a means of destruction, damage, or injury to another Party to the ENMOD Convention. The ENMOD Convention does not prohibit damage to the environment, but reflects the idea that the environment itself should not be used as an instrument of war.[215]

Weapons or military operations may incidentally have widespread, long-lasting, or severe

---

212 Cyrus Vance, *Letter of Submittal*, Aug. 31, 1978, MESSAGE FROM THE PRESIDENT OF THE UNITED STATES TRANSMITTING THE CONVENTION ON THE PROHIBITION OF MILITARY OR ANY OTHER HOSTILE USE OF ENVIRONMENTAL MODIFICATION TECHNIQUES, SIGNED AT GENEVA ON MAY 18, 1977, EXECUTIVE K, 4 (1978) ("According to the Understanding related to this Article the terms 'widespread, long-lasting and severe', for purposes of this Convention only, are to be interpreted as follows: (a) 'widespread': encompassing an area on the scale of several hundred square kilometers; (b) 'long-lasting': lasting for a period of months, or approximately a season; (c) 'severe': involving serious or significant disruption or harm to human life, natural and economic resources or other assets."). *See also* U.N. Conference of the Committee on Disarmament, New York, U.S., Dec. 10, 1976, *Report of the Conference of the Committee on Disarmament: Official records: Thirty-first session, Supplement No. 27* 92 U.N. Doc A/31/27 (Vol I) (1976) ("Referring to suggestions at the previous year's session and at the General Assembly that the phrase 'having widespread, long-lasting or severe effects' be eliminated, the delegation of the United States held that the phrase was necessary to ensure that the ban could be implemented successfully and would not give rise to friction over trivial issues: the phrase served to avoid the risk of unprovable claims of violation while eliminating the use of techniques with significant effects.").

213 *See* U.N. Conference of the Committee on Disarmament, *Report of the Conference of the Committee on Disarmament*, U.N. Official records: Thirty-First Session, Supplement No. 27, U.N. Doc A/31/27 (Vol I) 92 (Dec. 10, 1976) ("It is the understanding of the Committee that the following examples are illustrative of phenomena that could be caused by the use of environmental modification techniques as defined in article II of the Convention: earthquakes; tsunamis; an upset in the ecological balance of a region; changes in weather patterns (clouds, precipitation, cyclones of various types and tornadic storms); changes in climate patterns; changes in ocean currents; changes in the state of the ozone layer; and changes in the state of the ionosphere.").

214 Rear Admiral Edward F. Welch, Jr., Deputy Director for International Negotiations, Plans and Policy Directorate, Joint Chiefs of Staff, *Environmental Modication Treaty: Hearing Before the Committee on Foreign Relations, U.S. Senate*, Ninety-Fifth Congress, Second Session, 31 (Oct. 3, 1978) ("I think the Joint Chiefs of Staff prefer to have this threshold treaty with these stipulations in it rather than a complete foreclosure of any military options. The example I might cite, that was in the testimony given to this committee in 1974 was the case of the situation in Belgium during the Battle of the Bulge where they had the opportunity and, had the technique been available for cutting and dispelling the fog that attended that battle, it could have been done in 30 to 40 minutes. Dispelling the fog that was there preventing the resupply of our units is now within the technology of limiting fog.").

215 Michael Moodie, United States Arms Control and Disarmament Agency, *Statement before the Second Review Conference of the Convention on the Prohibition of Military or Any Other Hostile Use of Environmental Modification Techniques* (Sept. 15, 1992) ("The Environmental Modification Convention is not an Environmental Protection Treaty; it is not a treaty to prohibit damage to the environment resulting from armed conflict. Rather, the Environmental Modification Convention fills a special, but important niche reflecting the international community's consensus that the environment itself should not be used as an instrument of war.").

effects on the environment. Such weapons and military operations are not prohibited by the ENMOD Convention because the harm to the environment is incidental and not intended to be used as a means of destruction, damage, or injury to another Party to the ENMOD Convention. For example, nuclear weapons are not prohibited by the ENMOD Convention because their effects on the environment are a by-product of their use rather than intended as a means of injuring the enemy.[216]

6.10.3.1 <u>*AP I Provisions on Environmental Protection*</u>. In contrast to the ENMOD Convention's prohibition against using certain environmental modification techniques as a means of destruction, damage, or injury, two provisions of AP I specifically address the protection of the environment. Article 35(3) of AP I provides that "[i]t is prohibited to employ methods or means of warfare which are intended, or may be expected, to cause widespread, long-term and severe damage to the natural environment." Article 55 of AP I provides:

> Protection of the natural environment: (1) Care shall be taken in warfare to protect the natural environment against widespread, long-term and severe damage. This protection includes a prohibition of the use of methods or means of warfare which are intended or may be expected to cause such damage to the natural environment and thereby to prejudice the health or survival of the population. (2) Attacks against the natural environment by way of reprisals are prohibited.

The United States has not accepted these provisions[217] and has repeatedly expressed the view that these provisions are "overly broad and ambiguous and 'not a part of customary law.'"[218] Articles 35(3) and 55 of AP I "fail to acknowledge that use of such weapons is

---

[216] *Written Statement of the Government of the United States of America*, 29, Jun. 20, 1995, I.C.J., Request by the United Nations General Assembly for an Advisory Opinion on the Legality of the Threat or Use of Nuclear Weapons ("Although one might imagine a hypothetical use of nuclear weapons to create an environmental modification technique (for example, to cause an earthquake or tidal wave), the Convention does not prohibit other uses of nuclear weapons (or any other weapon), even if they cause serious damage to the environment. Only the 'deliberate manipulation' of environmental forces to cause destruction is covered.").

[217] *See, e.g.*, Mark Simonoff, Minister Counselor, U.S. Mission to the United Nations, *Remarks at the 70th UN General Assembly Sixth Committee on Agenda Item 83: Report of the International Law Commission on the Work of its 67th Session*, Nov. 11, 2015, 2015 DIGEST OF UNITED STATES PRACTICE IN INTERNATIONAL LAW 287 ("Relatedly, we are troubled by the presence among the principles of rules extracted from certain treaties that we do not believe reflect customary law. For example, draft principle II-4 repeats a prohibition in Additional Protocol I, AP I, on attacks against the natural environment by way of reprisals that we do not believe exists as a matter of customary international law. To the extent the rule is offered to encourage normative development, we remain in disagreement with it, consistent with the objections we have stated on other occasions."); United States, *Statement on Ratification of the CCW, Accepting Protocols I & II*, Mar. 24, 1995, 1861 UNTS 482, 483 ("The United States considers that the fourth paragraph of the preamble to the Convention, which refers to the substance of provisions of article 35 (3) and article 55 (1) of additional Protocol I to the Geneva Conventions for the Protection of War Victims of August 12, 1949, applies only to States which have accepted those provisions.").

[218] U.S. RESPONSE TO ICRC CIHL STUDY 521 ("France and the United States repeatedly have declared that Articles 35(3) and 55 of AP I, from which the Study derives the first sentence of rule 45, do not reflect customary international law. In their instruments of ratification of the 1980 CCW, both France and the United States asserted that the preambular paragraph in the CCW treaty, which refers to the substance of Articles 35(3) and 55, applied only to States that have accepted those articles. The U.S. State Department Principal Deputy Legal Adviser stated

prohibited only if their use is clearly excessive in relation to the concrete and direct overall military advantage anticipated."[219]

6.10.4 Environmental Modification Techniques for Peaceful Purposes. The ENMOD Convention does not hinder the use of environmental modification techniques for peaceful purposes.[220]

6.11 Weapons Injuring by Fragments Not Detectable by X-Rays

It is prohibited to use any weapon the primary effect of which is to injure by fragments that in the human body escape detection by X-rays.[221]

6.11.1 Primary Effect. The prohibition requires that the fragments that are intended to cause injury be made of materials that are detectable in the human body by X-rays.

Portions of many munitions, such as the casing, detonator, or timing mechanism, may be made of nonmetallic parts or other substances that are not detectable by X-rays in order to reduce weight, manufacturing costs, etc. These munitions are not prohibited because their primary effect is not to injure by fragments that in the human body escape detection by X-rays.[222]

6.11.2 Fragments That Injure by Penetrating the Human Body. The prohibition applies only to weapons that are intended to injure by penetrating the human body. Thus, for example, a weapon that employs rubber projectiles that are unlikely to penetrate the skin need not be detectable by X-rays.

---

during a conference in 1987 that the United States considered Articles 35 and 55 to be overly broad and ambiguous and 'not a part of customary law.'").

[219] U.S. RESPONSE TO ICRC CIHL STUDY 528 endnote 30 ("An example illustrates why States – particularly those not party to AP I – are unlikely to have supported rule 45. Suppose that country A has hidden its chemical and biological weapons arsenal in a large rainforest, and plans imminently to launch the arsenal at country B. Under such a rule, country B could not launch a strike against that arsenal if it expects that such a strike may cause widespread, long-term, and severe damage to the rainforest, even if it has evidence of country A's imminent launch, and knows that such a launch itself would cause environmental devastation.").

[220] ENMOD CONVENTION art. 3(1) ("The provisions of this Convention shall not hinder the use of environmental modification techniques for peaceful purposes and shall be without prejudice to the generally recognized principles and applicable rules of international law concerning such use.").

[221] CCW PROTOCOL I ("It is prohibited to use any weapon the primary effect of which is to injure by fragments which in the human body escape detection by X-rays.").

[222] Canada, *Statement on Ratification of CCW, Accepting Protocols I, II, & III*, Jun. 24, 1994, 1787 UNTS 501 ("With respect to Protocol I, it is the understanding of the Government of Canada that the use of plastics or similar materials for detonators or other weapons parts not designed to cause injury is not prohibited."). *For example*, W. Hays Parks, *Memorandum re: Advanced Combat Rifle; Request for Legal Review*, ¶6 (May 21, 1990), *reprinted in* THE ARMY LAWYER 18, 20 (Jul. 1990) ("[B]oth the AAI and Steyr-Mannlicher ammunition employ liquid crystal polymers in the sabot that holds the flechette in place. It is not necessary to determine whether liquid crystal polymers are detectable by x-ray, as the sabot in each round is employed for effects other than injury to combatants. (The wounding capability of the sabot is extremely limited, as it separates from the flechette, quickly loses its force, and falls to the ground within one hundred feet of the muzzle.) The negotiation history of the UNCCW Protocol I is clear that its prohibition would not extend to the polymer sabot in the AAI and Steyr ammunition.").

6.11.3 Fragments Escaping Detection by X-Rays. The fragments must not be such that they escape detection by X-rays. For example, a member of the armed forces engaged in the authorized construction and/or employment of field-improvised booby-traps may not use glass for fragments for the purpose of wounding enemy personnel.[223]

In some cases, the fragments that otherwise would not be detectable by X-rays may be modified in order to ensure that they would be detectable by X-rays. For example, projectiles may be modified with a substance, such as barium sulfate, so that they are readily detectable by X-rays if they happen to penetrate the skin.[224]

6.12 LANDMINES, BOOBY-TRAPS, AND OTHER DEVICES

As a class of weapons, landmines, booby-traps, and other devices are not specifically prohibited under the law of war. However, certain landmines, booby-traps, and other devices are prohibited. In addition, the use of landmines, booby-traps, and other devices is subject to certain restrictions that the United States has accepted in the CCW Amended Mines Protocol.

6.12.1 Definition of Mine. The CCW Amended Mines Protocol defines a "mine" as "a munition placed under, on, or near the ground or other surface area and designed to be exploded by the presence, proximity or contact of a person or vehicle."[225] The term "mine" thus includes both anti-personnel and anti-vehicle mines, including anti-tank mines.

The mines to which the CCW Amended Mines Protocol relate are those used on land, including those laid to interdict beaches, waterway crossings, or river crossings, but do not include the use of anti-ship mines at sea or in inland waterways.[226] The rules on naval mines are addressed in § 13.11 (Naval Mines).

The term "mine" does not include hand grenades.[227] A trip-wired hand grenade is not

---

[223] *Refer to* § 6.12.4.1 (Mines, Booby-Traps, and Other Devices Calculated to Cause Superfluous Injury).

[224] W. Hays Parks, *Means and Methods of Warfare*, 38 THE GEORGE WASHINGTON INTERNATIONAL LAW REVIEW 511, 524 note 53 (2006) ("In 1998, the author conducted the legal review of the Modular Crowd Control Munition, a less-lethal version of the M18 Claymore mine containing rubber instead of steel projectiles. While the chance of the rubber projectiles penetrating the skin was negligible, the rubber projectiles were implanted with 5 percent Barium Sulfate to make them detectable by x-ray and compliant with Protocol I of the UNCCW. *See* Office of The Judge Advocate General of the Army, Memorandum of Law: Legal Review of Modular Crowd Control Munition (MCCM) (Oct. 13, 1998) [hereinafter DAJA-IO: Modular Crowd Control Munition].") (insertion in original).

[225] CCW AMENDED MINES PROTOCOL art. 2(1) ("'Mine' means a munition placed under, on or near the ground or other surface area and designed to be exploded by the presence, proximity or contact of a person or vehicle.").

[226] CCW AMENDED MINES PROTOCOL art. 1(1) ("This Protocol relates to the use on land of the mines, booby-traps and other devices, defined herein, including mines laid to interdict beaches, waterway crossings or river crossings, but does not apply to the use of anti-ship mines at sea or in inland waterways.").

[227] United States, *Statement on Consent to Be Bound by the CCW Amended Mines Protocol,* May 24, 1999, 2065 UNTS 128, 130 ("For the purposes of the Amended Mines Protocol, the United States understands that - ... (C) none of the provisions of the Amended Mines Protocol, including Article 2 (5), applies to hand grenades other than trip-wired hand grenades.").

considered a mine, but is considered a booby-trap under the CCW Amended Mines Protocol.[228]

6.12.1.1 Notes on Terminology - *"Landmines" Versus "Mines"*. The CCW Amended Mines Protocol uses the term "mines," but does not address naval mines. This section uses the term "mines" to refer to landmines, including both anti-personnel and anti-vehicle mines.

6.12.1.2 *Designed to Be Exploded by the Presence, Proximity, or Contact of a Person or Vehicle*. An important characteristic of a mine is its designed function of being exploded by the presence, proximity, or contact of a person or vehicle.[229] Command-detonated munitions (*i.e.*, munitions whose explosion is triggered by a decision of an operator) are not "mines" under the CCW Amended Mines Protocol, but may be regulated under the CCW Amended Mines Protocol as "other devices."[230]

Some munitions, such as the Claymore, may be configured for detonation by command, or by trip-wire. When used in trip-wire mode, they are mines and subject to corresponding restrictions. When used in command-detonated mode, they are subject to the restrictions applicable to "other devices."[231]

The design function of being activated by the target also distinguishes a mine from unexploded ordnance that results from the malfunction of a munition.[232] Other rules address

---

[228] United States, *Statement on Consent to Be Bound by the CCW Amended Mines Protocol,* May 24, 1999, 2065 UNTS 128, 130 ("For the purposes of the Amended Mines Protocol, the United States understands that - ... (B) a trip-wired hand grenade shall be considered a 'booby-trap' under Article 2(4) of the Amended Mines Protocol and shall not be considered a 'mine' or an 'anti-personnel mine' under Article 2(1) or 2(3), respectively;"). *Refer to* § 6.12.2 (Definition of Booby-Trap).

[229] *Article-by-Article Analysis of CCW Amended Mines Protocol*, 5, Enclosure A to Warren Christopher, *Letter of Submittal*, Dec. 7, 1996, MESSAGE FROM THE PRESIDENT TRANSMITTING THE CCW AMENDED MINES PROTOCOL, PROTOCOL III ON INCENDIARY WEAPONS, AND PROTOCOL IV ON BLINDING LASER WEAPONS 5 ("The definition also contemplates that mines can be emplaced in a variety of ways -- under, on or near the ground or other surface area. This makes clear that the critical defining characteristic of a mine is not its relationship to the ground or other surface area but rather its design function of being exploded by the presence, proximity or contact of a target, be that target a person or a vehicle. (This applies whether a munition is designed for this purpose in the factory, or adapted for this purpose in the field.)").

[230] *Refer to* § 6.12.10 (Rule for Using Booby-Traps and Other Devices).

[231] *Article-by-Article Analysis of CCW Amended Mines Protocol*, 7, Enclosure A to Warren Christopher, *Letter of Submittal*, Dec. 7, 1996, MESSAGE FROM THE PRESIDENT TRANSMITTING THE CCW AMENDED MINES PROTOCOL, PROTOCOL III ON INCENDIARY WEAPONS, AND PROTOCOL IV ON BLINDING LASER WEAPONS 7 ("With respect to anti-personnel mines which have the potential to be either trip-wired or command-detonated, the definition applies when such mines are used with a trip-wire or are otherwise target-activated. When such mines are command-detonated, that is, exploded not by the target itself, but by an operator, they do not meet the definition of antipersonnel mine and are therefore not subject to the restrictions imposed on anti-personnel mines. They do, however, fall within the definition of 'other devices' in paragraph 7.").

[232] *Article-by-Article Analysis of CCW Amended Mines Protocol*, 5, Enclosure A to Warren Christopher, *Letter of Submittal*, Dec. 7, 1996, MESSAGE FROM THE PRESIDENT TRANSMITTING THE CCW AMENDED MINES PROTOCOL, PROTOCOL III ON INCENDIARY WEAPONS, AND PROTOCOL IV ON BLINDING LASER WEAPONS 5 ("It is also this characteristic, i.e. that the munition is designed to be activated by the target, that distinguishes a mine from so-called unexploded ordinance [sic] or UXO. UXO is not covered by the Protocol, either the 1980 or the amended version. Unexploded ordinance [sic] is a result of a malfunction of a munition; UXO is not 'designed' in any sense, and, in

unexploded ordnance.[233]

6.12.1.3 *Anti-Personnel Mines*. Under the CCW Amended Mines Protocol, an "anti-personnel mine" is a mine primarily designed to be exploded by the presence, proximity, or contact of a person and that will incapacitate, injure, or kill one or more persons.[234]

"Primarily" was added to ensure that anti-vehicle mines equipped with anti-handling devices (which often cause the mine to detonate by contact of a person) are not treated as anti-personnel mines under the CCW Amended Mines Protocol.[235]

Another element in the definition of "anti-personnel mine" is its effect of incapacitating, injuring, or killing one or more persons. This description was understood to be broad enough to cover the range of hazards posed by anti-personnel mines, but the term "incapacitating" means permanent incapacity.[236] Thus, the definition of "mine" for the purposes of the CCW Amended Mines Protocol does not include non-lethal weapon technology that is designed temporarily to disable, stun, or signal the presence of a person, but not to cause permanent incapacity.[237]

---

particular, is not designed to be detonated by the presence, proximity or contact of person. Although UXO presents a serious problem that requires concerted attention, it is a problem outside the scope of Protocol II.").

[233] *Refer to* § 6.20 (Explosive Remnants of War).

[234] CCW AMENDED MINES PROTOCOL art. 2(3) ("'Anti-personnel mine' means a mine primarily designed to be exploded by the presence, proximity or contact of a person and that will incapacitate, injure or kill one or more persons.").

[235] *Article-by-Article Analysis of CCW Amended Mines Protocol*, 6-7, Enclosure A to Warren Christopher, *Letter of Submittal*, Dec. 7, 1996, MESSAGE FROM THE PRESIDENT TRANSMITTING THE CCW AMENDED MINES PROTOCOL, PROTOCOL III ON INCENDIARY WEAPONS, AND PROTOCOL IV ON BLINDING LASER WEAPONS 6-7 ("The first is the word 'primarily' in the phrase 'primarily designed'. This element was added to ensure that anti-tank mines equipped with anti-handling devices are not treated as anti-personnel mines. This was an important consideration for U.S. military operations. Anti-personnel mines are frequently used in conjunction with anti-tank mines to protect anti-tank mines against enemy removal during military operations. With increasing restrictions on the use of anti-personnel mines, it was clear, from a military perspective, that alternative means of protecting anti-tank mines against enemy removal during combat operations would be increasingly important. One such common alternative is to equip anti-tank mines with anti-handling devices. But since such devices are, as a practical matter, intended to cause an anti-tank mine to detonate if handled by a person, there was concern that an anti-tank mine equipped with an anti-handling device would inadvertently fall within the definition of an anti-personnel mine, and be subject, therefore, to the additional constraints imposed on anti-personnel mines. Adding the word 'primarily' before 'designed' clarified that anti-tank mines that are equipped with anti-handling devices are not considered anti-personnel mines as a result of being so equipped. This language was not intended to exclude from the restrictions on anti-personnel mines any munition designed to perform the function of an anti-personnel mine.").

[236] *Article-by-Article Analysis of CCW Amended Mines Protocol*, 7, Enclosure A to Warren Christopher, *Letter of Submittal*, Dec. 7, 1996, MESSAGE FROM THE PRESIDENT TRANSMITTING THE CCW AMENDED MINES PROTOCOL, PROTOCOL III ON INCENDIARY WEAPONS, AND PROTOCOL IV ON BLINDING LASER WEAPONS 7 ("The second additional element in the anti-personnel mine definition is the reference to incapacitating, injuring or killing one or more persons. This description was understood to be broad enough to cover the range of hazards posed by anti-personnel mines. Additionally, the term 'incapacitating' does not restrict non-lethal weapon technology that may temporarily disable, stun or signal the presence of person but not cause permanent incapacity.").

[237] United States, *Statement on Consent to Be Bound by the CCW Amended Mines Protocol,* May 24, 1999, 2065 UNTS 128, 130 ("The United States understands that nothing in the Amended Mines Protocol may be construed as

6.12.1.4 _Mines Other Than Anti-Personnel Mines_. The CCW Amended Mines Protocol uses the term "mines other than anti-personnel mines" to refer to anti-vehicle mines. "Anti-vehicle mines" or "mines other than anti-personnel mines" are also sometimes referred to as anti-tank mines.[238]

The CCW Amended Mines Protocol defines "mine" in terms of a munition that is designed to be exploded by a person or vehicle.[239] Thus, "mines other than anti-personnel mines" are anti-vehicle mines.[240]

6.12.1.5 _Remotely Delivered Mines_. "Remotely-delivered mine" means a mine that is not directly emplaced, but is instead delivered by artillery, missile, rocket, mortar, or similar means, or dropped from an aircraft.[241]

Mines delivered from a land-based system from less than 500 meters, however, are not considered to be remotely delivered, provided that they are used in accordance with Article 5 and other relevant articles of the CCW Amended Mines Protocol.[242] These mines were excluded from the definition of remotely delivered mines because, when delivered in the prescribed manner, they can be accurately marked and precautions to protect civilians can be reliably maintained.

6.12.1.6 _Mines With Compliant Self-Destruction and Self-Deactivation (SD/SDA) Mechanisms_. Certain types of mines may be equipped with self-destruction or self-neutralization mechanisms, or be self-deactivating.

"Self-destruction [SD] mechanism" means an incorporated or externally attached automatically functioning mechanism that secures the destruction of the munition into which it is

---

restricting or affecting in any way non-lethal weapon technology that is designed to temporarily disable, stun, signal the presence of a person, or operate in any other fashion, but not to cause permanent incapacity.").

[238] *Article-by-Article Analysis of CCW Amended Mines Protocol*, 8, Enclosure A to Warren Christopher, *Letter of Submittal*, Dec. 7, 1996, MESSAGE FROM THE PRESIDENT TRANSMITTING THE CCW AMENDED MINES PROTOCOL, PROTOCOL III ON INCENDIARY WEAPONS, AND PROTOCOL IV ON BLINDING LASER WEAPONS 8 ("Finally, the term 'anti-tank mine' is not used or defined in the amended Protocol; such mines are referred to by the use of the phrase 'mines other than anti-personnel mines,' which includes all mines designed to be exploded by the presence, proximity or contact of a vehicle. This formulation flows from the definitions for 'mine' and 'anti-personnel mine' when read in light of each other. Throughout this analysis mines other than anti-personnel mines are also referred to as anti-tank mines.").

[239] CCW AMENDED MINES PROTOCOL art. 2(1) ("'Mine' means a munition placed under, on or near the ground or other surface area and designed to be exploded by the presence, proximity or contact of a person or vehicle.").

[240] *See* CCW AMENDED MINES PROTOCOL art. 2(3) ("'Anti-personnel mine' means a mine primarily designed to be exploded by the presence, proximity or contact of a person and that will incapacitate, injure or kill one or more persons.").

[241] CCW AMENDED MINES PROTOCOL art. 2(2) ("'Remotely-delivered mine' means a mine not directly emplaced but delivered by artillery, missile, rocket, mortar, or similar means, or dropped from an aircraft.").

[242] CCW AMENDED MINES PROTOCOL art. 2(2) ("Mines delivered from a land-based system from less than 500 metres are not considered to be 'remotely delivered', provided that they are used in accordance with Article 5 and other relevant Articles of this Protocol.").

incorporated or to which it is attached.[243]

"Self-neutralization mechanism" means an incorporated automatically functioning mechanism that renders inoperable the munition into which it is incorporated.[244] The term is used in Article 6 of the CCW Amended Mines Protocol in relation to remotely delivered mines other than anti-personnel mines. There are no technical specifications for self-neutralization mechanisms in the Technical Annex to the CCW Amended Mines Protocol.[245]

"Self-deactivating" (SDA) means automatically rendering a munition inoperable by means of the irreversible exhaustion of a component; for example, a battery that is essential to the operation of the munition could be exhausted as part of a self-deactivating mine.[246]

6.12.2 Definition of Booby-Trap. Under the CCW Amended Mines Protocol, a "booby-trap" means any device or material that is designed, constructed, or adapted to kill or injure, and that functions when a person disturbs or approaches an apparently harmless object or performs an apparently safe act.[247]

This includes field-expedient devices, *e.g.*, a hand grenade attached to a door and rigged to explode when the door is opened (as opening a door is an apparently safe act), as well as devices designed in advance to function as booby-traps (such as explosive devices designed to resemble civilian objects).[248]

6.12.3 Definition of "Other Devices" Similar to Mines. "Other devices" in the CCW Amended Mines Protocol means manually emplaced munitions and devices, including improvised explosive devices, designed to kill, injure, or damage, and which are actuated

---

[243] CCW AMENDED MINES PROTOCOL art. 2(10) ("'Self-destruction mechanism' means an incorporated or externally attached automatically-functioning mechanism which secures the destruction of the munition into which it is incorporated or to which it is attached.").

[244] CCW AMENDED MINES PROTOCOL art. 2(11) ("'Self-neutralization mechanism' means an incorporated automatically-functioning mechanism which renders inoperable the munition into which it is incorporated.").

[245] *Article-by-Article Analysis of CCW Amended Mines Protocol*, 9, Enclosure A to Warren Christopher, *Letter of Submittal*, Dec. 7, 1996, MESSAGE FROM THE PRESIDENT TRANSMITTING THE CCW AMENDED MINES PROTOCOL, PROTOCOL III ON INCENDIARY WEAPONS, AND PROTOCOL IV ON BLINDING LASER WEAPONS 9 ("The term is used in Article 6 in relation to remotely-delivered mines other than anti-personnel mines. There are no technical specifications for self-neutralization mechanisms in the Technical Annex.").

[246] CCW AMENDED MINES PROTOCOL art. 2(12) ("'Self-deactivating' means automatically rendering a munition inoperable by means of the irreversible exhaustion of a component, for example, a battery, that is essential to the operation of the munition.").

[247] CCW AMENDED MINES PROTOCOL art. 2(4) ("'Booby-trap' means any device or material which is designed, constructed or adapted to kill or injure, and which functions unexpectedly when a person disturbs or approaches an apparently harmless object or performs an apparently safe act.").

[248] *Article-by-Article Analysis of CCW Amended Mines Protocol*, 8, Enclosure A to Warren Christopher, *Letter of Submittal*, Dec. 7, 1996, MESSAGE FROM THE PRESIDENT TRANSMITTING THE CCW AMENDED MINES PROTOCOL, PROTOCOL III ON INCENDIARY WEAPONS, AND PROTOCOL IV ON BLINDING LASER WEAPONS 8 ("[Paragraph 4 of Article 2 of the CCW Amended Mines Protocol] is understood to include, for example, a hand-grenade when attached to a door and rigged to explode when the door opens, as well as devices designed in advance to function as booby-traps.").

manually, by remote control, or automatically after a lapse of time.[249]

"Other devices" do not include munitions and devices that are not manually emplaced, such as munitions that are remotely delivered.

"Other devices" do not include hand grenades.[250] However, trip-wired hand grenades are regulated as booby traps.[251]

6.12.4 Prohibited Classes of Mines, Booby-Traps, and Other Devices. Certain types of mines, booby-traps, and other devices are prohibited. These types include:

- mines, booby-traps, and other devices calculated to cause superfluous injury;[252]
- mines, booby-traps, and other devices specifically designed to detonate during detection operations;[253]
- self-deactivating mines with anti-handling devices designed to function after the mine's operation;[254]
- non-detectable anti-personnel mines;[255]
- remotely delivered mines without compliant self-destruction and self-deactivation mechanisms;[256]
- remotely delivered mines other than anti-personnel mines without a feasible SD/SDA mechanism;[257]

---

[249] CCW AMENDED MINES PROTOCOL art. 2(5) ("'Other devices' means manually-emplaced munitions and devices including improvised explosive devices designed to kill, injure or damage and which are actuated manually, by remote control or automatically after a lapse of time.").

[250] United States, *Statement on Consent to Be Bound by the CCW Amended Mines Protocol,* May 24, 1999, 2065 UNTS 128, 130 ("For the purposes of the Amended Mines Protocol, the United States understands that - … (C) none of the provisions of the Amended Mines Protocol, including Article 2 (5), applies to hand grenades other than trip-wired hand grenades.").

[251] *Refer to* § 6.12.2 (Definition of Booby-Trap).

[252] *Refer to* § 6.12.4.1 (Mines, Booby-Traps, and Other Devices Calculated to Cause Superfluous Injury).

[253] *Refer to* § 6.12.4.2 (Mines, Booby-Traps, and Other Devices Specifically Designed to Detonate During Detection Operations).

[254] *Refer to* § 6.12.4.3 (Self-Deactivating Mines With Anti-Handling Devices Designed to Function After the Mine's Operation).

[255] *Refer to* § 6.12.4.4 (Non-Detectable Anti-Personnel Mines).

[256] *Refer to* § 6.12.4.5 (Remotely Delivered Anti-Personnel Mines Not in Compliance With Self-Destruction and Self-Deactivation Requirements).

[257] *Refer to* § 6.12.4.6 (Remotely Delivered Mines Other Than Anti-Personnel Mines Without a Feasible SD/SDA Mechanism).

- mines produced after December 3, 1998, without identifying information;[258]
- booby-traps and other devices in the form of apparently harmless portable objects specifically designed to explode;[259] and
- certain types of prohibited booby-traps and other devices.[260]

6.12.4.1 *Mines, Booby-Traps, and Other Devices Calculated to Cause Superfluous Injury*. As with other weapons, it is prohibited in all circumstances to use any mine, booby trap, or other device that is designed or of a nature to cause superfluous injury or unnecessary suffering.[261]

For example, mines and booby-traps filled with shards of glass as their primary wounding mechanism would violate this prohibition. Such a weapon would be regarded as calculated to cause superfluous injury because the shards would be undetectable by X-rays and would hinder the medical treatment of the wound without offering any corresponding military advantage.[262] In addition, such a weapon would be prohibited on the grounds that it used fragments non-detectable by X-rays.[263]

6.12.4.2 *Mines, Booby-Traps, and Other Devices Specifically Designed to Detonate During Detection Operations*. It is prohibited to use mines, booby-traps, and other devices that employ a mechanism or device specifically designed to detonate the munition by the presence of commonly available mine detectors as a result of their magnetic or other non-contact influence during normal use in detection operations.[264]

This rule only applies to mines, booby-traps, and other devices that are specifically

---

[258] *Refer to* § 6.12.4.7 (Mines Produced After December 3, 1998, Without Identifying Information).

[259] *Refer to* § 6.12.4.8 (Booby-Traps and Other Devices in the Form of Apparently Harmless Portable Objects Specifically Designed to Explode).

[260] *Refer to* § 6.12.4.9 (Certain Types of Prohibited Booby-Traps and Other Devices).

[261] CCW AMENDED MINES PROTOCOL art. 3(3) ("It is prohibited in all circumstances to use any mine, booby-trap or other device which is designed or of a nature to cause superfluous injury or unnecessary suffering."). *Refer to* § 6.6 (Weapons Calculated to Cause Superfluous Injury).

[262] *Article-by-Article Analysis of CCW Amended Mines Protocol*, 11, Enclosure A to Warren Christopher, *Letter of Submittal*, Dec. 7, 1996, MESSAGE FROM THE PRESIDENT TRANSMITTING THE CCW AMENDED MINES PROTOCOL, PROTOCOL III ON INCENDIARY WEAPONS, AND PROTOCOL IV ON BLINDING LASER WEAPONS 11 ("Which types of such weapons might cause 'unnecessary suffering' can only be determined on a case-by-case basis, weighing the suffering caused against the military necessity for its use. One example of a prohibited device might be a mine or booby-trap that is filled with shards of glass. Such a weapon would likely be regarded as unnecessarily injurious because the shards would be undetectable by X-ray in the victim's body, and this would cause suffering that would be wholly unnecessary for its military purpose. (In any case, the device would be prohibited by Protocol I of the Convention on non-detectable fragments).").

[263] *Refer to* § 6.11 (Weapons Injuring by Fragments Not Detectable by X-Rays).

[264] CCW AMENDED MINES PROTOCOL art. 3(5) ("It is prohibited to use mines, booby-traps or other devices which employ a mechanism or device specifically designed to detonate the munition by the presence of commonly available mine detectors as a result of their magnetic or other non-contact influence during normal use in detection operations.").

designed to detonate through the normal use of non-contact mine detectors during mine detection operations. Thus, mines, booby-traps, and other devices specifically designed to detonate upon actual physical contact are permissible.[265] Similarly, anti-handling devices that are designed to detonate a mine upon attempts to defuse or deactivate the mine are not prohibited by this rule.

6.12.4.3 *Self-Deactivating Mines With Anti-Handling Devices Designed to Function After the Mine's Operation*. It is prohibited to use a self-deactivating mine equipped with an anti-handling device that is designed in such a manner that the anti-handling device is capable of functioning after the mine has ceased to be capable of functioning.[266]

The intent is to avoid situations where a self-deactivating mine, the "life" of which is normally limited by the life of its battery, remains dangerous indefinitely as a result of a long-lived anti-handling device. This would defeat the purpose of the self-deactivation function by leaving a hazardous mine in place.[267]

6.12.4.4 *Non-Detectable Anti-Personnel Mines*. It is prohibited to use anti-personnel mines that are not detectable as specified in paragraph 2 of the Technical Annex to the CCW Amended Mines Protocol.[268] Paragraph 2 of the Technical Annex specifies that:

> (a) With respect to anti-personnel mines produced after 1 January 1997, such mines shall incorporate in their construction a material or device that enables the mine to be detected by commonly-available technical mine detection equipment and provides a response signal equivalent to a signal from 8 grammes or more of iron in a single coherent mass.
>
> (b) With respect to anti-personnel mines produced before 1 January 1997, such mines shall either incorporate in their construction, or have attached prior to their emplacement, in a manner not easily removable, a material or device that enables the mine to be detected by commonly-available technical mine detection

---

[265] *Article-by-Article Analysis of CCW Amended Mines Protocol*, 12, Enclosure A to Warren Christopher, *Letter of Submittal*, Dec. 7, 1996, MESSAGE FROM THE PRESIDENT TRANSMITTING THE CCW AMENDED MINES PROTOCOL, PROTOCOL III ON INCENDIARY WEAPONS, AND PROTOCOL IV ON BLINDING LASER WEAPONS 12 ("The provision clearly excludes situations where actual physical contact with mine detectors or abnormal use of mine detectors is required to detonate the mine. For example, a mine's trip-wire or tilt-rod (a type of vertical trip-wire) may be pulled or pushed in a sweep of a mine detector, setting off the mine. This would not constitute the use of a mine in contravention of this provision.").

[266] CCW AMENDED MINES PROTOCOL art. 3(6) ("It is prohibited to use a self-deactivating mine equipped with an anti-handling device that is designed in such a manner that the anti-handling device is capable of functioning after the mine has ceased to be capable of functioning.").

[267] *Article-by-Article Analysis of CCW Amended Mines Protocol*, 15, Enclosure A to Warren Christopher, *Letter of Submittal*, Dec. 7, 1996, MESSAGE FROM THE PRESIDENT TRANSMITTING THE CCW AMENDED MINES PROTOCOL, PROTOCOL III ON INCENDIARY WEAPONS, AND PROTOCOL IV ON BLINDING LASER WEAPONS 15 ("The intent is to avoid situations where a self-deactivating mine, the 'life' of which is normally limited by the life of its battery, is dangerous indefinitely as a result of a long-lived anti-handling device. This would defeat the purpose of the self-deactivation function by leaving a hazardous mine in place.").

[268] CCW AMENDED MINES PROTOCOL art. 4 ("It is prohibited to use anti-personnel mines which are not detectable, as specified in paragraph 2 of the Technical Annex.").

> equipment and provides a response signal equivalent to a signal from 8 grammes or more of iron in a single coherent mass.
>
> (c) In the event that a High Contracting Party determines that it cannot immediately comply with sub-paragraph (b), it may declare at the time of its notification of consent to be bound by this Protocol that it will defer compliance with sub-paragraph (b) for a period not to exceed 9 years from the entry into force of this Protocol. In the meantime it shall, to the extent feasible, minimize the use of anti-personnel mines that do not so comply.[269]

6.12.4.5 *Remotely Delivered Anti-Personnel Mines Not in Compliance With Self-Destruction and Self-Deactivation Requirements*. It is prohibited to use remotely delivered anti-personnel mines that are not in compliance with the provisions on self-destruction and self-deactivation in the Technical Annex to the CCW Amended Mines Protocol.[270]

All remotely delivered anti-personnel mines shall be designed and constructed so that no more than 10% of activated mines will fail to self-destruct within 30 days after emplacement, and each mine shall have a back-up self-deactivation feature designed and constructed so that, in combination with the self-destruction mechanism, no more than one in one thousand activated mines will function as a mine 120 days after emplacement.[271]

6.12.4.6 *Remotely Delivered Mines Other Than Anti-Personnel Mines Without a Feasible SD/SDA Mechanism*. It is prohibited to use remotely delivered mines other than anti-personnel mines, unless, to the extent feasible, they are equipped with an effective self-destruction or self-neutralization mechanism and have a back-up self-deactivation feature, which is designed so that the mine will no longer function as a mine when the mine no longer serves the military purpose for which it was placed in position.[272]

6.12.4.7 *Mines Produced After December 3, 1998, Without Identifying Information*. Subparagraph 1(d) of the Technical Annex to the CCW Amended Mines Protocol provides:

> The use of mines produced after the entry into force of this Protocol is prohibited unless they are marked in English or in the respective national language or languages with the following information:

---

[269] TECHNICAL ANNEX TO CCW AMENDED MINES PROTOCOL ¶2.

[270] CCW AMENDED MINES PROTOCOL art. 6(2) ("It is prohibited to use remotely-delivered anti-personnel mines which are not in compliance with the provisions on self-destruction and self-deactivation in the Technical Annex.").

[271] TECHNICAL ANNEX TO CCW AMENDED MINES PROTOCOL ¶3(a) ("All remotely-delivered anti-personnel mines shall be designed and constructed so that no more than 10% of activated mines will fail to self-destruct within 30 days after emplacement, and each mine shall have a back-up self-deactivation feature designed and constructed so that, in combination with the self-destruction mechanism, no more than one in one thousand activated mines will function as a mine 120 days after emplacement.").

[272] CCW AMENDED MINES PROTOCOL art. 6(3) ("It is prohibited to use remotely-delivered mines other than anti-personnel mines, unless, to the extent feasible, they are equipped with an effective self-destruction or self-neutralization mechanism and have a back-up self-deactivation feature, which is designed so that the mine will no longer function as a mine when the mine no longer serves the military purpose for which it was placed in position.").

(i) name of the country of origin;

(ii) month and year of production; and

(iii) serial number or lot number.

The marking should be visible, legible, durable and resistant to environmental effects, as far as possible.

The CCW Amended Mines Protocol entered into force on December 3, 1998.[273]

6.12.4.8 *Booby-Traps and Other Devices in the Form of Apparently Harmless Portable Objects Specifically Designed to Explode*. It is prohibited in all circumstances to use booby-traps or other devices in the form of apparently harmless portable objects that are specifically designed and constructed to contain explosive material.[274] This prohibition relates to booby-traps manufactured to resemble items, such as watches, personal audio players, cameras, toys, and the like. This prohibition is intended to prevent the production of large quantities of dangerous objects that can be scattered around and are likely to be attractive to civilians, especially children.[275]

This rule does not prohibit the use of booby-traps in connection with non-portable objects, such as a door or gate.

This rule does not prohibit field-expedient adaptation, or adaptation in advance, of objects for use as booby-traps or other devices that are not designed or constructed for such use.[276] For example, it would not be prohibited to improvise a booby-trap using a trip-wired hand grenade in the form of an apparently harmless portable object. Such improvisation of booby-traps, for example, to retard an enemy advance, does not pose the same sort of danger to the civilian population as the mass production of objects specifically designed as booby-traps.[277]

---

[273] *Refer to* § 19.21.3 (CCW Amended Mines Protocol).

[274] CCW AMENDED MINES PROTOCOL art. 7(2) ("It is prohibited to use booby-traps or other devices in the form of apparently harmless portable objects which are specifically designed and constructed to contain explosive material.").

[275] During World War II, such devices were manufactured and intended to be used by guerilla forces operating in denied areas or forces withdrawing from territory about to be occupied by enemy forces. *See* DEPARTMENT OF THE ARMY FIELD MANUAL 5-31, *Land Mines and Booby Traps*, ¶1(d) (1943) ("Factory-produced booby-traps (dirty trick devices) are described. Most of these have been developed and used in the field by foreign armies."); *id.* at. ¶50(d)(4-5) (1943) ("The Japanese manufactured a [tobacco] pipe boobytrap with a charge, detonator, and spring-loaded striker. The Italians had a booby-trapped headset containing an electric detonator connected to the terminals on the back. The connection of the headset into the line communication line initiated detonation.").

[276] United States, *Statement on Consent to Be Bound by the CCW Amended Mines Protocol,* May 24, 1999, 2065 UNTS 128, 130 ("For the purposes of the Amended Mines Protocol, the United States understands that - … (A) the prohibition contained in Article 7(2) of the Amended Mines Protocol does not preclude the expedient adaptation or adaptation in advance of other objects for use as booby-traps or other devices;").

[277] *Article-by-Article Analysis of CCW Amended Mines Protocol*, 27, Enclosure A to Warren Christopher, *Letter of Submittal*, Dec. 7, 1996, MESSAGE FROM THE PRESIDENT TRANSMITTING THE CCW AMENDED MINES PROTOCOL, PROTOCOL III ON INCENDIARY WEAPONS, AND PROTOCOL IV ON BLINDING LASER WEAPONS 27 ("Such

6.12.4.9 *Certain Types of Prohibited Booby-Traps and Other Devices*. It is prohibited to use booby-traps and other devices that are in any way attached to or associated with:[278]

- internationally recognized protective emblems, signs, or signals;
    - This includes the distinctive emblem of the red cross and red crescent and the distinctive emblem for cultural property.[279]
- sick, wounded, or dead persons;
- burial or cremation sites or graves;
- medical facilities, equipment, supplies, or transportation;
- children's toys or other portable objects or products specially designed for the feeding, health, hygiene, clothing, or education of children;
- food or drink;
    - The United States has reserved the right to use other devices to destroy any stock of food or drink that is judged likely to be used by an enemy military force, if due precautions are taken for the safety of the civilian population.[280]
- kitchen utensils or appliances, except in military establishments, military locations, or military supply depots;
    - This does not authorize kitchen utensils or appliances in military hospitals, POW

---

improvisation of booby-traps, for example to retard an enemy advance, does not pose the same sort of danger to the civilian population as the mass production of objects specifically designed as booby-traps toward which the provision was directed.").

[278] CCW AMENDED MINES PROTOCOL art. 7(1) ("Without prejudice to the rules of international law applicable in armed conflict relating to treachery and perfidy, it is prohibited in all circumstances to use booby-traps and other devices which are in any way attached to or associated with: (a) internationally recognized protective emblems, signs or signals; (b) sick, wounded or dead persons; (c) burial or cremation sites or graves; (d) medical facilities, medical equipment, medical supplies or medical transportation; (e) children's toys or other portable objects or products specially designed for the feeding, health, hygiene, clothing or education of children; (f) food or drink; (g) kitchen utensils or appliances except in military establishments, military locations or military supply depots; (h) objects clearly of a religious nature; (i) historic monuments, works of art or places of worship which constitute the cultural or spiritual heritage of peoples; or (j) animals or their carcasses.").

[279] *Refer to* § 7.15.1 (The Distinctive Emblems: Red Cross, Crescent, and Crystal); § 5.18.7 (Marking of Cultural Property With the Distinctive Emblem).

[280] United States, *Statement on Consent to Be Bound by the CCW Amended Mines Protocol,* May 24, 1999, 2065 UNTS 128, 129 ("The United States reserves the right to use other devices (as defined in Article 2(5) of the Amended Mines Protocol) to destroy any stock of food or drink that is judged likely to be used by an enemy military force, if due precautions are taken for the safety of the civilian population.").

camps, or military chapels to be booby-trapped.[281]

- objects clearly of a religious nature;
- historic monuments, works of art, or places of worship that constitute the cultural or spiritual heritage of peoples;[282] or
- animals or their carcasses.

6.12.5 General Rules for Using Mines, Booby-Traps, and Other Devices. The use of mines, booby traps, and other devices is subject to the same rules and principles that govern the use of other weapons to conduct attacks.[283] However, because mines, booby-traps, and other devices explode only after their emplacement, there have been different views as to when the use of a mine constitutes an "attack."[284] Thus, the CCW Amended Mines Protocol seeks to clarify how these principles apply to the use of mines, booby-traps, and other devices. These rules include:

- a prohibition against directing mines, booby-traps, and other devices against the civilian population;
- a prohibition against the indiscriminate use of mines, booby-traps, and other devices;
- an obligation to take feasible precautions to protect civilians from the effects of mines, booby-traps, and other devices;
- an obligation to give effective advance warning of the emplacement of mines, booby-

[281] *Article-by-Article Analysis of CCW Amended Mines Protocol*, 26, Enclosure A to Warren Christopher, *Letter of Submittal*, Dec. 7, 1996, MESSAGE FROM THE PRESIDENT TRANSMITTING THE CCW AMENDED MINES PROTOCOL, PROTOCOL III ON INCENDIARY WEAPONS, AND PROTOCOL IV ON BLINDING LASER WEAPONS 26 ("The exception in paragraph 1(g) of Article 7 does not, however, authorize kitchen utensils or appliances in military hospitals, military POW camps or military chapels to be booby-trapped.").

[282] United States, *Statement on Consent to Be Bound by the CCW Amended Mines Protocol*, May 24, 1999, 2065 UNTS 128, 129 ("The United states [sic] understands that Article 7(1)(i) of the Amended Mines Protocol refers only to a limited class of objects that, because of their clearly recognizable characteristics and because of their widely recognized importance, constitute a part of the cultural or spiritual heritage of peoples."). *Refer to* § 5.18.1 (Definition of Cultural Property).

[283] *Refer to* § 5.4 (Rules on Conducting Assaults, Bombardments, and Other Attacks).

[284] *See, e.g.*, A.P.V. Rogers, *Mines, Booby-traps and Other Devices*, 30 INTERNATIONAL REVIEW OF THE RED CROSS 521, 524-25 (Nov.-Dec. 1990) ("One of the difficulties of the conference [that negotiated the Original Mines Protocol] was to apply to mine warfare the provisions of Additional Protocol I dealing with attacks. Agreement could not be reached as to what stage in the mine-laying process amounts to an attack: when the mine is laid, when it is armed, when somebody is endangered by it or when it actually explodes. To avoid these difficulties it was necessary to draw up special rules relating to the use of mines."); ICRC AP COMMENTARY 622 (¶1960) ("However, the question may arise at what point the use of mines constitutes an attack in the sense of this provision [AP I art. 51(4)(b)]. Is it when the mine is laid, when it is armed, when a person is endangered by it, or when it finally explodes? The participants at the meeting of the International Society of Military Law and the Law of War (Lausanne, 1982) conceded that from the legal point of view the use of mines constituted an attack in the sense of the Protocol when a person was directly endangered by such a mine.").

traps, and other devices, unless circumstances do not permit; and

- obligations with respect to the recording of the placement of mines, booby-traps, and other devices.

6.12.5.1 *Prohibition Against Directing Mines, Booby-Traps, and Other Devices Against Civilians*. As with other weapons, mines, booby-traps, and other devices may not be directed against the civilian population, individual civilians, or civilian objects.[285]

6.12.5.2 *Prohibition Against Indiscriminate Use of Mines, Booby-Traps, or Other Devices*. Indiscriminate use of mines, booby-traps, or other devices is prohibited.[286]

This prohibition on indiscriminate use of mines, booby-traps, or other devices prohibits any placement of mines, booby-traps, or other devices that is not on, or directed against, a military objective.[287] On the other hand, it would be permissible to direct mines against enemy forces that are expected to pass through an area. Similarly, it would be permissible to direct mines against a piece of land that is a military objective.[288] In addition, it would be permissible to place mines on land or objects that belong to friendly forces and that the adversary would regard as a military objective, in order to protect such land or objects from interference or attack.

This prohibition on indiscriminate use of mines, booby-traps, or other devices also prohibits placing mines, booby-traps, or other devices using a method or means of delivery that cannot be directed at a specific military objective.[289] For example, it would be prohibited to deliver mines using unguided long-distance balloons.[290]

This prohibition on indiscriminate use of mines, booby-traps, or other devices also prohibits placing mines, booby-traps, or other devices that may be expected to cause incidental loss of civilian life, injury to civilians, damage to civilian objects, or a combination thereof, which would be excessive in relation to the concrete and direct military advantage anticipated.[291]

---

[285] CCW AMENDED MINES PROTOCOL art. 3(7) ("It is prohibited in all circumstances to direct weapons to which this Article applies, either in offence, defence or by way of reprisals, against the civilian population as such or against individual civilians or civilian objects."). *Refer to* § 5.5 (Discrimination in Conducting Attacks).

[286] CCW AMENDED MINES PROTOCOL art. 3(8) ("The indiscriminate use of weapons to which this Article applies is prohibited.").

[287] CCW AMENDED MINES PROTOCOL art. 3(8) ("Indiscriminate use is any placement of such weapons: (a) which is not on, or directed against, a military objective. In case of doubt as to whether an object which is normally dedicated to civilian purposes, such as a place of worship, a house or other dwelling or a school, is being used to make an effective contribution to military action, it shall be presumed not to be so used;").

[288] *Refer to* § 5.6.8.4 (Examples of Military Objectives – Places of Military Significance).

[289] CCW AMENDED MINES PROTOCOL art. 3(8) ("Indiscriminate use is any placement of such weapons: … (b) which employs a method or means of delivery which cannot be directed at a specific military objective;").

[290] *Refer to* § 6.7 (Inherently Indiscriminate Weapons).

[291] CCW AMENDED MINES PROTOCOL art. 3(8) ("Indiscriminate use is any placement of such weapons: … (c) which may be expected to cause incidental loss of civilian life, injury to civilians, damage to civilian objects, or a combination thereof, which would be excessive in relation to the concrete and direct military advantage

6.12.5.3 *Obligation to Take Feasible Precautions to Protect Civilians From the Effects of Mines, Booby-Traps, and Other Devices*. All feasible precautions shall be taken to protect civilians from the effects of mines, booby-traps, and other devices.[292] This obligation corresponds to a more general obligation to take feasible precautions.[293] Feasible precautions are those precautions that are practicable or practically possible, taking into account all circumstances ruling at the time, including humanitarian and military considerations.[294] These circumstances include, but are not limited to:

- the short- and long-term effect of mines, booby-traps, and other devices upon the local civilian population for the duration of their use;
- possible measures to protect civilians (*e.g.*, fencing, signs, warning, and monitoring);
- the availability and feasibility of using alternatives; and
- the short- and long-term military requirements for a minefield, or for the use of booby-traps or other devices.[295]

6.12.5.4 *Effective Advance Warning of Any Emplacement*. Effective advanced warning shall be given of any emplacement of mines, booby-traps, and other devices that may affect the civilian population, unless circumstances do not permit doing so.[296]

6.12.5.5 *Recording of Minefields, Mined Areas, Mines, Booby-Traps, and Other Devices*. All information concerning minefields, mined areas, mines, booby-traps, and other devices shall be recorded in accordance with the provisions of the Technical Annex to the CCW

---

anticipated."). *Refer to* § 5.12 (Proportionality – Prohibition on Attacks Expected to Cause Excessive Incidental Harm).

[292] CCW AMENDED MINES PROTOCOL art. 3(10) ("All feasible precautions shall be taken to protect civilians from the effects of weapons to which this Article applies.").

[293] *Refer to* § 5.2.3 (Affirmative Duties to Take Feasible Precautions for the Protection of Civilians and Other Protected Persons and Objects).

[294] CCW AMENDED MINES PROTOCOL art. 3(10) ("Feasible precautions are those precautions which are practicable or practically possible taking into account all circumstances ruling at the time, including humanitarian and military considerations."). *Refer to* § 5.2.3.2 (What Precautions Are Feasible).

[295] CCW AMENDED MINES PROTOCOL art. 3(10) ("These circumstances include, but are not limited to: (a) the short- and long-term effect of mines upon the local civilian population for the duration of the minefield; (b) possible measures to protect civilians (for example, fencing, signs, warning and monitoring); (c) the availability and feasibility of using alternatives; and (d) the short- and long-term military requirements for a minefield."). *See also Article-by-Article Analysis of CCW Amended Mines Protocol*, 14, Enclosure A to Warren Christopher, *Letter of Submittal*, Dec. 7, 1996, MESSAGE FROM THE PRESIDENT TRANSMITTING THE CCW AMENDED MINES PROTOCOL, PROTOCOL III ON INCENDIARY WEAPONS, AND PROTOCOL IV ON BLINDING LASER WEAPONS 14 ("These general considerations [described in CCW Amended Mines Protocol art. 3(10)] are relevant to all mines, both anti-personnel and anti-tank, as well as the other weapons to which the amended Protocol applies.").

[296] CCW AMENDED MINES PROTOCOL art. 3(11) ("Effective advance warning shall be given of any emplacement of mines, booby-traps and other devices which may affect the civilian population, unless circumstances do not permit."). *Refer to* § 5.11.5 (Effective Advance Warning Before an Attack That May Affect the Civilian Population).

Amended Mines Protocol.[297]

"Minefield" is a defined area in which mines have been emplaced (including areas free of mines that simulate a minefield), and a "mined area" is an area that is dangerous due to the presence of mines.[298] "Recording" means a physical, administrative, and technical operation designed to obtain, for the purpose of registration in official records, all available information facilitating the location of minefields, mined areas, booby-traps, and other devices.[299]

Subparagraph 1(a) of the Technical Annex to the CCW Amended Mines Protocol specifies that the recording of the location of non-remotely delivered mines, minefields, mined areas, booby-traps, and other devices shall be carried out in accordance with the following provisions:

> (i) the location of the minefields, mined areas and areas of booby-traps and other devices shall be specified accurately by relation to the coordinates of at least two reference points and the estimated dimensions of the area containing these weapons in relation to those reference points;
>
> (ii) maps, diagrams or other records shall be made in such a way as to indicate the location of minefields, mined areas, booby-traps and other devices in relation to reference points, and these records shall also indicate their perimeters and extent;
>
> (iii) for purposes of detection and clearance of mines, booby-traps and other devices, maps, diagrams or other records shall contain complete information on the type, number, emplacing method, type of fuse and life time, date and time of laying, antihandling devices (if any) and other relevant information on all these weapons laid. Whenever feasible the minefield record shall show the exact location of every mine, except in row minefields where the row location is sufficient. The precise location and operating mechanism of each booby-trap laid shall be individually recorded.[300]

Records shall be retained by the parties to the conflict.[301] Copies of records shall be held

---

[297] CCW AMENDED MINES PROTOCOL art. 9(1) ("All information concerning minefields, mined areas, mines, booby-traps and other devices shall be recorded in accordance with the provisions of the Technical Annex.").

[298] CCW AMENDED MINES PROTOCOL art. 2(8) ("'Minefield' is a defined area in which mines have been emplaced and 'mined area' is an area which is dangerous due to the presence of mines. 'Phoney minefield' means an area free of mines that simulates a minefield. The term 'minefield' includes phoney minefields.").

[299] CCW AMENDED MINES PROTOCOL art. 2(9) ("'Recording' means a physical, administrative and technical operation designed to obtain, for the purpose of registration in official records, all available information facilitating the location of minefields, mined areas, mines, booby-traps and other devices.").

[300] TECHNICAL ANNEX TO CCW AMENDED MINES PROTOCOL ¶1(c).

[301] CCW AMENDED MINES PROTOCOL art. 9(2) (providing that "[a]ll such records [mentioned in paragraph 1 of Article 9] shall be retained by the parties to a conflict").

at a level of command sufficient to guarantee their safety as far as possible.[302]

6.12.6 Rules for Using Non-Remotely Delivered Anti-Personnel Mines With Compliant SD/SDA Mechanisms. Non-remotely delivered anti-personnel mines that comply with the requirements for self-destruction and self-deactivation in the Technical Annex to the CCW Amended Mines Protocol may be used outside of marked areas.[303]

6.12.7 Rules for Using Non-Remotely Delivered Anti-Personnel Mines Without Compliant SD/SDA Mechanisms. Anti-personnel mines other than remotely delivered mines that are not in compliance with the provisions on self-destruction and self-deactivation in the Technical Annex to the CCW Amended Mines Protocol may be used subject to certain requirements. For a number of years, U.S. forces maintained minefields that met these standards.[304] The United States, however, no longer maintains any minefields.[305]

First, such weapons are to be placed within a perimeter-marked area that is monitored by military personnel and protected by fencing or other means, to ensure the effective exclusion of civilians from the area. The marking must be of a distinct and durable character, and must be visible to a person who is about to enter the perimeter-marked area.[306] The State Party controlling a minefield is obligated to take all feasible measures to prevent the unauthorized removal, defacement, destruction, or concealment of any device, system, or material used to establish the perimeter of a permanently marked area.[307]

Second, such weapons are to be cleared before the area is abandoned, unless the area is turned over to the forces of another State that accepts responsibility for the maintenance of the

---

[302] TECHNICAL ANNEX TO CCW AMENDED MINES PROTOCOL ¶1(c) ("Copies of records shall be held at a level of command sufficient to guarantee their safety as far as possible.").

[303] TECHNICAL ANNEX TO CCW AMENDED MINES PROTOCOL ¶3(b) ("All non-remotely delivered anti-personnel mines, used outside marked areas, as defined in Article 5 of this Protocol, shall comply with the requirements for self-destruction and self-deactivation stated in sub-paragraph (a).").

[304] *Article-by-Article Analysis of CCW Amended Mines Protocol*, 16-17, Enclosure A to Warren Christopher, *Letter of Submittal*, Dec. 7, 1996, MESSAGE FROM THE PRESIDENT TRANSMITTING THE CCW AMENDED MINES PROTOCOL, PROTOCOL III ON INCENDIARY WEAPONS, AND PROTOCOL IV ON BLINDING LASER WEAPONS 16-17 ("The U.S. military has maintained minefields for a number of years in Guantanamo and Korea that meet these standards, and is confident that these requirements are feasible and realistic.").

[305] Department of State, Bureau of Political-Military Affairs, *Fact Sheet: Frequently Asked Questions on the New United States Landmine Policy* (Feb. 27, 2004) ("The United States … currently maintains no minefields anywhere in the world, including Korea.").

[306] CCW AMENDED MINES PROTOCOL art. 5(2)(a) ("It is prohibited to use weapons to which this Article applies which are not in compliance with the provisions on self-destruction and self-deactivation in the Technical Annex, unless: … such weapons are placed within a perimeter-marked area which is monitored by military personnel and protected by fencing or other means, to ensure the effective exclusion of civilians from the area. The marking must be of a distinct and durable character and must at least be visible to a person who is about to enter the perimeter-marked area;").

[307] CCW AMENDED MINES PROTOCOL art. 5(5) ("All feasible measures shall be taken to prevent the unauthorized removal, defacement, destruction or concealment of any device, system or material used to establish the perimeter of a perimeter-marked area.").

protections stated above, and the subsequent clearance of those weapons.[308] This requirement does not preclude agreement, in connection with peace treaties or similar arrangements, to allocate responsibilities under Article 5 of the CCW Amended Mines Protocol in a manner that respects the essential spirit and purpose of Article 5.[309]

A party to a conflict is relieved from compliance with these obligations if compliance is not feasible due to forcible loss of control of the area as a result of enemy military action, including situations where direct enemy military action makes it impossible to comply. If the party that laid the minefield regains control of the area, it must re-assume its responsibilities.[310] The forces of a party to the conflict gaining control of an area assume the responsibilities, to the maximum extent feasible, until the mines have been cleared.[311]

6.12.8 Rules for Using Non-Remotely Delivered Anti-Personnel Mines That Propel Fragments in a Horizontal Arc of Less Than 90 Degrees (*e.g.*, Claymores). Anti-personnel mines other than remotely delivered mines that propel fragments in a horizontal arc of less than 90 degrees may be used on or above the ground outside of marked areas for up to 72 hours if:

- they are located in immediate proximity to the military unit that emplaced them; and
- the area is monitored by military personnel to ensure the effective exclusion of civilians.[312]

The maintenance of observation over avenues of approach where such mines are deployed constitutes one acceptable form of monitoring to ensure the effective exclusion of civilians.[313]

---

[308] CCW AMENDED MINES PROTOCOL art. 5(2)(b) ("such weapons are cleared before the area is abandoned, unless the area is turned over to the forces of another State which accept responsibility for the maintenance of the protections required by this Article and the subsequent clearance of those weapons.").

[309] United States, *Statement on Consent to Be Bound by the CCW Amended Mines Protocol,* May 24, 1999, 2065 UNTS 128, 130 ("The United States understands that the allocation of responsibilities for landmines in Article 5(2)(b) of the Amended Mines Protocol does not preclude agreement, in connection with peace treaties or similar arrangements, to allocate responsibilities under that Article in a manner that respects the essential spirit and purpose of the Article.").

[310] CCW AMENDED MINES PROTOCOL art. 5(3) ("A party to a conflict is relieved from further compliance with the provisions of subparagraphs 2 (a) and 2 (b) of this Article only if such compliance is not feasible due to forcible loss of control of the area as a result of enemy military action, including situations where direct enemy military action makes it impossible to comply. If that party regains control of the area, it shall resume compliance with the provisions of sub-paragraphs 2 (a) and 2 (b) of this Article.").

[311] CCW AMENDED MINES PROTOCOL art. 5(4) ("If the forces of a party to a conflict gain control of an area in which weapons to which this Article applies have been laid, such forces shall, to the maximum extent feasible, maintain and, if necessary, establish the protections required by this Article until such weapons have been cleared.").

[312] CCW AMENDED MINES PROTOCOL art. 5(6) ("Weapons to which this Article applies which propel fragments in a horizontal arc of less than 90 degrees and which are placed on or above the ground may be used without the measures provided for in sub-paragraph 2 (a) of this Article for a maximum period of 72 hours, if: (a) they are located in immediate proximity to the military unit that emplaced them; and (b) the area is monitored by military personnel to ensure the effective exclusion of civilians.").

[313] United States, *Statement on Consent to Be Bound by the CCW Amended Mines Protocol,* May 24, 1999, 2065 UNTS 128, 129 ("The United States understands that, for the purposes of Article 5(6)(b) of the Amended Mines

A Claymore munition used in trip-wire mode is an example of this type of mine.[314] A Claymore used in command-detonated mode is regulated as an "other device."[315]

6.12.9 Rules for Using Remotely Delivered Mines. Remotely delivered mines are subject to special, additional restrictions because their location cannot be marked as accurately as mines placed by hand or by mechanical mine layers. In addition, because remotely delivered mines are often emplaced by long-range means, it may be difficult to ensure that civilians are absent or excluded from areas containing such mines. Remotely delivered mines may not be used unless they have compliant self-destruction and self-deactivation mechanisms.[316]

6.12.9.1 *Effective Advance Warning of the Delivery of Mines Unless Circumstances Do Not Permit*. As with other weapons, effective advance warning shall be given of any delivery or dropping of remotely delivered mines that may affect the civilian population, unless circumstances do not permit doing so.[317]

6.12.9.2 *Recording of Remotely Delivered Mines*. It is prohibited to use remotely delivered mines unless they are recorded in accordance with subparagraph 1(b) of the Technical Annex to the CCW Amended Mines Protocol.[318] Subparagraph 1(b) of the Technical Annex requires that the estimated location and area of remotely delivered mines be specified by coordinates of reference points (normally corner points) and shall be ascertained and, when feasible, marked on the ground at the earliest opportunity. In addition, the total number and type of mines laid, the date and time of laying, and the self-destruction time periods shall also be recorded.[319]

6.12.10 Rule for Using Booby-Traps and Other Devices. Booby-traps may not be of the

---

Protocol, the maintenance of observation over avenues of approach where mines subject to that Article are deployed constitutes one acceptable form of monitoring to ensure the effective exclusion of civilians.").

[314] *Article-by-Article Analysis of CCW Amended Mines Protocol*, 7 8, Enclosure A to Warren Christopher, *Letter of Submittal*, Dec. 7, 1996, MESSAGE FROM THE PRESIDENT TRANSMITTING THE CCW AMENDED MINES PROTOCOL, PROTOCOL III ON INCENDIARY WEAPONS, AND PROTOCOL IV ON BLINDING LASER WEAPONS 7-8 ("In a trip-wired mode, the Claymore is not excluded from the restrictions applicable to anti-personnel mines by reason of the definition in paragraph 3. Specifically, such mines, when used in a trip-wired mode, are covered by the definition but special, less restrictive rules in Article 5 apply to their use for a limited time -- 72 hours -- from their emplacement.").

[315] *Refer to* § 6.12.10 (Rule for Using Booby-Traps and Other Devices).

[316] *Refer to* § 6.12.4.5 (Remotely Delivered Anti-Personnel Mines Not in Compliance With Self-Destruction and Self-Deactivation Requirements).

[317] CCW AMENDED MINES PROTOCOL art. 6(4) ("Effective advance warning shall be given of any delivery or dropping of remotely-delivered mines which may affect the civilian population, unless circumstances do not permit."). *Refer to* § 5.11.1 (Warning Before Attack).

[318] CCW AMENDED MINES PROTOCOL art. 6(1) ("It is prohibited to use remotely-delivered mines unless they are recorded in accordance with sub-paragraph I (b) of the Technical Annex.").

[319] TECHNICAL ANNEX TO CCW AMENDED MINES PROTOCOL ¶1(b) ("The estimated location and area of remotely-delivered mines shall be specified by coordinates of reference points (normally corner points) and shall be ascertained and when feasible marked on the ground at the earliest opportunity. The total number and types of mines laid, the date and time of laying and the self-destruction time periods shall also be recorded.").

prohibited type discussed in § 6.12.4.8 (Booby-Traps and Other Devices in the Form of Apparently Harmless Portable Objects Specifically Designed to Explode) and § 6.12.4.9 (Certain Types of Prohibited Booby-Traps and Other Devices).

In addition, as with mines, there are recording obligations with respect to the use of booby-traps and other devices, including the obligation to record the precise location and operating mechanism of each booby-trap laid.[320]

6.12.10.1 *Use of Booby-Traps and Other Devices in Populated Areas When Combat Between Ground Forces Is Not Taking Place or Does Not Appear Imminent*. In addition, booby-traps and other devices may not be used in any city, town, village, or other area containing a similar concentration of civilians in which combat between ground forces is not taking place or does not appear to be imminent, unless either:

- "they are placed on or in the close vicinity of a military objective;"[321] or
- "measures are taken to protect civilians from their effects, for example, the posting of warning [signs, the posting of] sentries, the issue of warnings or the provision of fences."[322]

6.12.11 Obligation to Seek to Protect Certain Groups From the Effects of Minefields, Mined Areas, Mines, Booby-Traps, and Other Devices. Article 12 of the CCW Amended Mines Protocol creates certain obligations to take measures to help protect certain groups from the effects of minefields, mined areas, mines, booby-traps, and other devices. Such obligations may apply with respect to:

- Any United Nations force or mission performing peace-keeping, observation, or similar functions in any area in accordance with the Charter of the United Nations; or
- Any of the following, if they have the consent of the State in whose territory they are operating:[323]
    - missions established pursuant to Chapter VIII of the Charter of the United Nations and performing its functions in the area of a conflict;

---

[320] *Refer to* § 6.12.5.5 (Recording of Minefields, Mined Areas, Mines, Booby-Traps, and Other Devices).

[321] CCW AMENDED MINES PROTOCOL art. 7(3)(a).

[322] CCW AMENDED MINES PROTOCOL art. 7(3) ("Without prejudice to the provisions of Article 3, it is prohibited to use weapons to which this Article applies in any city, town, village or other area containing a similar concentration of civilians in which combat between ground forces is not taking place or does not appear to be imminent, unless either: (a) they are placed on or in the close vicinity of a military objective; or (b) measures are taken to protect civilians from their effects, for example, the posting of warning sentries, the issuing of warnings or the provision of fences."). The words in square brackets appeared in Original CCW Protocol II Article 4(2)(b). Their omission in the CCW Amended Mines Protocol is an apparent error overlooked by the Drafting Committee.

[323] CCW AMENDED MINES PROTOCOL art. 12(a) ("With the exception of the forces and missions referred to in sub-paragraph 2(a) (i) of this Article, this Article applies only to missions which are performing functions in an area with the consent of the High Contracting Party on whose territory the functions are performed.").

- o humanitarian or fact-finding missions of the United Nations System;
- o missions of the ICRC;
- o humanitarian missions of a national Red Cross or Red Crescent Society or of their International Federation; and
- o missions of inquiry established pursuant to the provisions of the Geneva Conventions of 12 August 1949 and, where applicable, their Additional Protocols.

The obligations to take affirmative measures under Article 12 are subject to practical considerations.[324] In addition, the forces and missions that are afforded protection under Article 12 have corresponding obligations to keep information confidential, to respect applicable laws and regulations, and to refrain from activities that are incompatible with the impartial and international nature of their duties.[325]

6.12.12 Obligations Arising After the Cessation of Active Hostilities. Certain obligations with respect to mines, booby-traps, and other devices are triggered after the cessation of active hostilities.

6.12.12.1 *Take Measures to Protect Civilians From the Effects of Minefields, Mined Areas, Mines, Booby-Traps, and Other Devices in Areas Under Their Control After Hostilities*. Without delay after the cessation of active hostilities, a party to a conflict is to take

---

[324] CCW AMENDED MINES PROTOCOL art. 12(2)(b) ("Each High Contracting Party or party to a conflict, if so requested by the head of a force or mission to which this paragraph applies, shall: (i) so far as it is able, take such measures as are necessary to protect the force or mission from the effects of mines, booby-traps and other devices in any area under its control; (ii) if necessary in order effectively to protect such personnel, remove or render harmless, so far as it is able, all mines, booby-traps and other devices in that area; and (iii) inform the head of the force or mission of the location of all known minefields, mined areas, mines, booby-traps and other devices in the area in which the force or mission is performing its functions and, so far as is feasible, make available to the head of the force or mission all information in its possession concerning such minefields, mined areas, mines, booby-traps and other devices.") (emphasis added); CCW AMENDED MINES PROTOCOL art. 12(3)(b) ("Each High Contracting Party or party to a conflict, if so requested by the head of a mission to which this paragraph applies, shall: (i) provide the personnel of the mission with the protections set out in sub-paragraph 2(b) (i) of this Article; and (ii) if access to or through any place under its control is necessary for the performance of the mission's functions and in order to provide the personnel of the mission with safe passage to or through that place: (aa) unless on-going hostilities prevent, inform the head of the mission of a safe route to that place if such information is available; or (bb) if information identifying a safe route is not provided in accordance with sub-paragraph (aa), so far as is necessary and feasible, clear a lane through minefields.") (emphasis added); CCW Amended Mines Protocol art. 12(5)(b) ("Each High Contracting Party or party to a conflict, if so requested by the head of a mission to which this paragraph applies, shall, so far as is feasible: (i) provide the personnel of the mission with the protections set out in sub-paragraph 2(b) (i) of this Article, and (ii) take the measures set out in sub-paragraph 3(b) (ii) of this Article.") (emphasis added).

[325] CCW AMENDED MINES PROTOCOL art. 12 ("6. Confidentiality All information provided in confidence pursuant to this Article shall be treated by the recipient in strict confidence and shall not be released outside the force or mission concerned without the express authorization of the provider of the information. 7. Respect for laws and regulations Without prejudice to such privileges and immunities as they may enjoy or to the requirements of their duties, personnel participating in the forces and missions referred to in this Article shall: (a) respect the laws and regulations of the host State; and (b) refrain from any action or activity incompatible with the impartial and international nature of their duties.").

all necessary and appropriate measures, including the use of records kept in accordance with the CCW Amended Mines Protocol, to protect civilians from the effects of minefields, mined areas, mines, booby-traps, and other devices in areas under their control.[326] Information is to be shared with the other party or parties to the conflict and with the Secretary-General of the United Nations regarding mines laid by the party's forces in areas no longer under their control, subject to reciprocity and security requirements.[327]

6.12.12.2 Clearance of Minefields, Mined Areas, Mines, Booby-Traps, and Other Devices After Hostilities. Each Party to the CCW Amended Mines Protocol or party to a conflict is, in accordance with the provisions of the CCW Amended Mines Protocol, responsible for all mines, booby-traps, and other devices employed by it and undertakes to clear, remove, destroy, or maintain them as specified in Article 10 of the CCW Amended Mines Protocol.[328]

Without delay after the cessation of active hostilities, a Party to the CCW Amended Mines Protocol or a party to a conflict has an obligation to ensure that all minefields, mined areas, mines, booby-traps, and other devices in areas under its control are cleared, removed, destroyed, or maintained in accordance with Article 3 and Paragraph 2 of Article 5 of the CCW Amended Mines Protocol.[329]

With respect to mines laid by a Party to the CCW Amended Mines Protocol or a party to a conflict in areas over which the party no longer exercises control, the party is to provide to the party that is now in control of the area, to the extent permitted by such party, technical and material assistance necessary to fulfill its responsibility to ensure that all minefields are cleared, removed, destroyed, or maintained.[330] For example, such assistance may include maps and other

---

[326] CCW AMENDED MINES PROTOCOL art. 9(2) ("All such records shall be retained by the parties to a conflict, who shall, without delay after the cessation of active hostilities, take all necessary and appropriate measures, including the use of such information, to protect civilians from the effects of minefields, mined areas, mines, booby-traps and other devices in areas under their control.").

[327] CCW AMENDED MINES PROTOCOL art. 9(2) ("At the same time, they shall also make available to the other party or parties to the conflict and to the Secretary-General of the United Nations all such information in their possession concerning minefields, mined areas, mines, booby-traps and other devices laid by them in areas no longer under their control; provided, however, subject to reciprocity, where the forces of a party to a conflict are in the territory of an adverse party, either party may withhold such information from the Secretary-General and the other party, to the extent that security interests require such withholding, until neither party is in the territory of the other. In the latter case, the information withheld shall be disclosed as soon as those security interests permit. Wherever possible, the parties to the conflict shall seek, by mutual agreement, to provide for the release of such information at the earliest possible time in a manner consistent with the security interests of each party.").

[328] CCW AMENDED MINES PROTOCOL art. 3(2) ("Each High Contracting Party or party to a conflict is, in accordance with the provisions of this Protocol, responsible for all mines, booby-traps, and other devices employed by it and undertakes to clear, remove, destroy or maintain them as specified in Article 10 of this Protocol.").

[329] CCW AMENDED MINES PROTOCOL art. 10(1) ("Without delay after the cessation of active hostilities, all minefields, mined areas, mines, booby-traps and other devices shall be cleared, removed, destroyed or maintained in accordance with Article 3 and paragraph 2 of Article 5 of this Protocol."); CCW AMENDED MINES PROTOCOL art. 10(2) ("High Contracting Parties and parties to a conflict bear such responsibility with respect to minefields, mined areas, mines, booby-traps and other devices in areas under their control.").

[330] CCW AMENDED MINES PROTOCOL art. 10(3) ("With respect to minefields, mined areas, mines, booby-traps and other devices laid by a party in areas over which it no longer exercises control, such party shall provide to the party

information regarding the mines and minefields.

In addition, the parties have an obligation to endeavor to reach agreement among themselves and, where appropriate, with other States and with international organizations, on the provision of technical and material assistance, including, in appropriate circumstances, the undertaking of joint operations necessary to fulfill such responsibilities.[331] There are additional provisions of the CCW Amended Mines Protocol addressing international exchanges of information and cooperation in this respect.[332] However, no provision of the CCW Amended Mines Protocol is to be construed as affecting the discretion of the United States to refuse assistance or to restrict or deny permission for the export of equipment, material, or scientific or technological information for any reason, and the CCW Amended Mines Protocol may not be used as a pretext for the transfer of weapons technology or the provision of assistance to the military mining or military counter-mining capabilities of a State Party to the CCW Amended Mines Protocol.[333]

6.12.13 U.S. Policy on Landmines. Landmines have been addressed by U.S. national policy. The United States has announced a policy: (1) not to use anti-personnel landmines outside the Korean Peninsula; (2) not to assist, encourage, or induce anyone outside the Korean Peninsula to engage in activity prohibited by the Ottawa Convention; (3) to undertake to destroy anti-personnel landmine stockpiles not required for the defense of the Republic of Korea; and (4) not to produce or otherwise acquire any anti-personnel munitions that are not compliant with the Ottawa Convention.[334] The United States has also previously committed not to emplace new persistent anti-personnel or anti-vehicle landmines (*i.e.*, landmines without self-destruction mechanisms and self-deactivation features).[335] U.S. landmines will continue to meet or exceed

---

in control of the area pursuant to paragraph 2 of this Article, to the extent permitted by such party, technical and material assistance necessary to fulfil such responsibility.").

[331] CCW AMENDED MINES PROTOCOL art. 10(4) ("At all times necessary, the parties shall endeavour to reach agreement, both among themselves and, where appropriate, with other States and with international organizations, on the provision of technical and material assistance, including, in appropriate circumstances, the undertaking of joint operations necessary to fulfil such responsibilities.").

[332] CCW AMENDED MINES PROTOCOL art. 11.

[333] United States, *Statement on Consent to Be Bound by the CCW Amended Mines Protocol,* May 24, 1999, 2065 UNTS 128, 130 ("The United States understands that - (A) no provision of the Protocol may be construed as affecting the discretion of the United States to refuse assistance or to restrict or deny permission for the export of equipment, material, or scientific or technological information for any reason; and (B) the Amended Mines Protocol may not be used as a pretext for the transfer of weapons technology or the provision of assistance to the military mining or military counter-mining capabilities of a State Party to the Protocol.").

[334] Department of State, Bureau of Political-Military Affairs, *Fact Sheet: Changes to U.S. Anti-Personnel Landmine Policy* (Sept. 23, 2014) ("This means that [the] United States will: not use APL outside the Korean Peninsula; not assist, encourage, or induce anyone outside the Korean Peninsula to engage in activity prohibited by the Ottawa Convention; and undertake to destroy APL stockpiles not required for the defense of the Republic of Korea. This change to U.S. APL policy builds on the announcement that the U.S. delegation made in June at the Third Review Conference of the Ottawa Convention in Maputo, Mozambique, that the United States will not produce or otherwise acquire any anti-personnel munitions that are not compliant with the Ottawa Convention, including to replace such munitions as they expire in the coming years.").

[335] Department of State, Bureau of Political-Military Affairs, *Fact Sheet: New United States Policy on Landmines: Reducing Humanitarian Risk and Saving Lives of United States Soldiers* (Feb. 27, 2004) ("The United States has committed to eliminate persistent landmines of all types from its arsenal.").

international standards for self-destruction and self-deactivation.[336] In addition, the United States no longer has any non-detectable mine of any type in its arsenal.[337]

The United States has a long practice of contributing significantly to humanitarian demining efforts and other conventional weapons destruction programs.[338]

6.12.14 Ottawa Convention on Anti-Personnel Landmines. The United States is not a Party to the Convention on the Prohibition of the Use, Stockpiling, Production and Transfer of Anti-Personnel Mines and on Their Destruction.[339] This Convention is commonly called the Ottawa Convention.

The United States has announced policy changes that align U.S. anti-personnel landmine policy outside the Korean Peninsula with the key requirements of the Ottawa Convention.[340] Among other reasons, because the practice of the United States and other States remains inconsistent with the prohibitions of the Ottawa Convention, its prohibitions do not reflect customary international law.[341]

---

[336] Department of State, Bureau of Political-Military Affairs, *Fact Sheet: New United States Policy on Landmines: Reducing Humanitarian Risk and Saving Lives of United States Soldiers* (Feb. 27, 2004) ("The United States will continue to develop non-persistent anti-personnel and anti-tank landmines. As with the current United States inventory of non-persistent landmines, these mines will continue to meet or exceed international standards for self-destruction and self-deactivation. This ensures that, after they are no longer needed for the battlefield, these landmines will detonate or turn themselves off, eliminating the threat to civilians.").

[337] Department of State, Bureau of Political-Military Affairs, *Fact Sheet: New United States Policy on Landmines: Reducing Humanitarian Risk and Saving Lives of United States Soldiers* (Feb. 27, 2004) ("Within one year, the United States will no longer have any non-detectable mine of any type in its arsenal.").

[338] Department of State, Bureau of Political-Military Affairs, *To Walk the Earth in Safety: Documenting the United States' 20 Year Commitment to Conventional Weapons Destruction*, 6 (August 2013) ("In 1993, the United States established the Demining Assistance Program and the Interagency Working Group (IWG) on Demining and Landmine Control, initiating a coordinated interagency aid effort to support international humanitarian mine action (HMA). Though the United States first provided HMA assistance in 1988, a coordinated and sustained U.S. Government effort began with this IWG. Over the past two decades, the U.S. approach to mine action has expanded to meet related needs in post-conflict environments, such as threats from ERW and at-risk SA/LW [small arms and light weapons], including manportable air-defense systems (MANPADS). … Since 1993, the United States has invested more than $2 billion in CWD programs in over 90 countries.").

[339] Convention on the Prohibition of the Use, Stockpiling, Production and Transfer of Anti-Personnel Mines and on their Destruction, Sept. 18, 1997, 2056 UNTS 211.

[340] Department of State, Bureau of Political-Military Affairs, *Fact Sheet: Changes to U.S. Anti-Personnel Landmine Policy* (Sept. 23, 2014) ("President Clinton, in his 1994 address to the United Nations General Assembly, called for the eventual elimination of anti-personnel landmines (APL). Today, the Obama Administration is announcing new policy changes that bring the United States closer to that goal. Specifically, the United States is aligning our APL policy outside the Korean Peninsula with the key requirements of the Ottawa Convention, the international treaty prohibiting the use, stockpiling, production, and transfer of APL, which more than 160 countries have joined, including all of our NATO Allies.").

[341] *See, e.g.*, Eritrea Ethiopia Claims Commission, *Partial Award: Central Front, Ethiopia's Claim 2*, ¶95 (Apr. 28, 2004) ("Landmines. As with other weredas [*i.e.*, geographic districts], the evidence indicates that Eritrea made extensive use of anti-personnel landmines, but it does not demonstrate a pattern of their unlawful use. For liability, the Commission would have to conclude that landmines were used in ways that intentionally targeted civilians or were indiscriminate. However, the available evidence suggests that landmines were extensively used as part of the

Many U.S. allies and coalition partners, including Australia, Canada, and the United Kingdom, are parties to the Ottawa Convention. Article 1 of the Ottawa Convention prohibits States Parties from using, developing, producing, otherwise acquiring, stockpiling, retaining, or transferring to anyone, directly or indirectly, anti-personnel landmines, or to assist, encourage, or induce, in any way, anyone to engage in any activity prohibited to a State Party under the Convention. Australia, Canada, and the United Kingdom have taken the position that its armed forces would not violate the Ottawa Convention merely by reason of taking part in joint operations with forces of an ally that is not bound by the Ottawa Convention and that uses anti-personnel mines.[342]

6.13 Cluster Munitions

Cluster munitions are not specifically prohibited or restricted by the law of war. DoD has policies on cluster munitions. The use of cluster munitions, in certain circumstances, is likely to reduce the risk of incidental harm as compared to other weapons.

6.13.1 Description of Cluster Munitions. Cluster munitions may be described as munitions composed of a non-reusable canister or delivery body containing multiple, conventional explosive submunitions.[343] Some munitions that may contain submunitions are not considered cluster munitions. For example, nuclear, chemical, and biological weapons, as well as obscurants, pyrotechnics, non-lethal systems (*e.g.*, leaflets), non-explosive kinetic effect submunitions (*e.g.*, flechettes or rods), and landmines, generally are not considered cluster munitions.

---

defenses of Eritrea's trenches and field fortifications. Thus, the declarations citing landmine use also frequently refer to the presence of Eritrean trenches in the area/kushet concerned. In principle, the defensive use of minefields to protect trenches would be a lawful use under customary international law.").

[342] Australia, *Statement on Ratification of the Convention on the Prohibition of the Use, Stockpiling, Production and Transfer of Anti-Personnel Mines and on Their Destruction,* Jan. 14, 1999, 2057 UNTS 214, 218 ("It is the understanding of Australia that, in the context of operations, exercises or other military activity authorized by the United Nations or otherwise conducted in accordance with international law, the participation by the ADF, or individual Australian citizens or residents, in such operations, exercises or other military activity conducted in combination with the armed forces of States not party to the Convention which engage in activity prohibited under the Convention would not, by itself, be considered to be in violation of the Convention."); Canada, *Statement on Signature of the Convention on the Prohibition of the Use, Stockpiling, Production and Transfer of Anti-Personnel Mines and on Their Destruction*, Dec. 3, 1997, 2056 UNTS 211, 310 ("It is the understanding of the Government of Canada that, in the context of operations, exercises or other military activity sanctioned by the United Nations or otherwise conducted in accordance with international law, the mere participation by the Canadian Forces, or individual Canadians, in operations, exercises or other military activity conducted in combination with the armed forces of States not party to the Convention which engage in activity prohibited under the Convention would not, by itself, be considered to be assistance, encouragement or inducement in accordance with the meaning of those terms in article 1, paragraph 1 (c)."); 2004 UK MANUAL ¶6.13 ("Members of the United Kingdom armed forces, will not, however, be guilty of an offence merely by reason of taking part in joint operations with forces of an ally not bound by the Ottawa Convention which deploy landmines.").

[343] Robert Gates, Secretary of Defense, *Memorandum re: DoD Policy on Cluster Munitions and Unintended Harm to Civilians*, Jun. 19, 2008 ("For the purposes of this policy, cluster munitions are defined as munitions composed of a non-reusable canister or delivery body containing multiple, conventional explosive submunitions. Excluded from the definition are nuclear, chemical, and biological weapons as well as obscurants, pyrotechnics, non-lethal systems (e.g., leaflets), non-explosive kinetic effect submunitions (e.g., flechettes or rods), or electronic effects. Landmine submunitions are also excluded since they are covered by existing policy and international agreements.").

6.13.2 Use of Cluster Munitions to Reduce the Risk of Incidental Harm. As with incendiary weapons, the use of cluster munitions, in certain circumstances, is likely to result in less incidental harm than the use of other weapons.[344] For example, cluster munitions have been used against military objectives containing dangerous forces, such as dams, in order to reduce the risk that bombardment of these objectives would release such forces and cause incidental harm to the civilian population.[345]

6.13.3 DoD Policy on Cluster Munitions. DoD has developed policies to minimize the negative humanitarian consequences that can sometimes be associated with cluster munitions.[346] Under a 2008 policy, the U.S. armed forces will, after 2018, only employ cluster munitions containing submunitions that, after arming, do not result in more than 1% unexploded ordnance (UXO) across the range of intended operational environments.[347] Until the end of 2018, cluster munitions that exceed the 1% UXO rate may not be used unless approved by the Combatant Commander.[348]

6.13.4 Convention on Cluster Munitions. The United States is not a Party to the Convention on Cluster Munitions.[349] The United States has determined that its national security interests cannot be fully ensured consistent with the terms of the Convention on Cluster

---

[344] Robert Gates, Secretary of Defense, *Memorandum re: DoD Policy on Cluster Munitions and Unintended Harm to Civilians*, Jun. 19, 2008 ("DoD recognizes that blanket elimination of cluster munitions is unacceptable due not only to negative military consequences but also due to potential negative consequences for civilians. Large-scale use of unitary weapons, as the only alternative to achieve military objectives, could result, in some cases, in unacceptable collateral damage and explosive remnants of war (ERW) issues."). *Refer to* § 5.11.6 (Weaponeering (E.g., Selecting Appropriate Weapons, Aim Points)).

[345] *For example*, W. Hays Parks, *Linebacker and the Law of War*, AIR UNIVERSITY REVIEW (Jan.-Feb. 1983) (During the Vietnam War, the North Vietnamese placed "AAA gun positions, ground-controlled intercept (GCI) radar, and surface-to-air missile (SAM) sites atop or adjacent to dikes, and storing POL [petroleum, oil, and lubricants] alongside or on top of dikes as a shield against attack. All were legitimate targets. ... When [the air defenses] were finally authorized for attack during Linebacker I, it was with the stipulation that the targets were to be attacked with weapons that would minimize the risk of structural damage to the dikes. This was accomplished through the use of napalm, strafing, cluster munitions, and other antipersonnel weapons.").

[346] Robert Gates, Secretary of Defense, *Memorandum re: DoD Policy on Cluster Munitions and Unintended Harm to Civilians*, Jun. 19, 2008 ("The DoD policy above is intended to minimize the potential unintended harm to civilians and civilian infrastructure of U.S. cluster munitions employment to the extent possible."); William Cohen, *Memorandum re: DoD Policy on Submunition Reliability*, Jan. 10, 2001 ("Submunition weapons employment in Southwest Asia and Kosovo, and major theater war modeling, have revealed a significant unexploded ordnance (UXO) concern. ... It is the policy of the DoD to reduce overall UXO through a process of improvement in submunition system reliability-the desire is to field future submunitions with a 99% or higher functioning rate. Submunition functioning rates may be lower under operational conditions due to environmental factors such as terrain and weather.").

[347] Robert Gates, Secretary of Defense, *Memorandum re: DoD Policy on Cluster Munitions and Unintended Harm to Civilians*, Jun. 19, 2008 ("After 2018, the Military Departments and Combatant Commands will only employ cluster munitions containing submunitions that, after arming, do not result in more than 1% unexploded ordnance (UXO) across the range of intended operational environments.").

[348] Robert Gates, Secretary of Defense, *Memorandum re: DoD Policy on Cluster Munitions and Unintended Harm to Civilians*, Jun. 19, 2008 ("Until the end of 2018, use of cluster munitions that exceed the 1% UXO rate must be approved by the Combatant Commander.").

[349] Convention on Cluster Munitions, May 30, 2008, 2688 UNTS 39.

Munitions.[350] The United States has expressed the view that the Convention on Cluster Munitions does not represent an emerging norm or reflect customary international law that would prohibit the use of cluster munitions in armed conflict.[351]

The Convention on Cluster Munitions establishes for its States Parties a number of prohibitions and restrictions on certain types of cluster munitions.[352] These rules include prohibitions on assisting, encouraging, or inducing anyone to engage in any activity prohibited to a State Party.[353] Despite these restrictions, States Parties and their military personnel and nationals may engage in military cooperation and operations with States that are not Parties to the Convention on Cluster Munitions that might engage in activities prohibited to a State Party.[354] Yet, even during such military operations, the Convention on Cluster Munitions does not authorize a State Party:

(a) To develop, produce or otherwise acquire cluster munitions;

(b) To itself stockpile or transfer cluster munitions;

(c) To itself use cluster munitions; or

(d) To expressly request the use of cluster munitions in cases where the choice of

---

[350] Harold Hongju Koh, Legal Adviser, Department of State, *Opening Statement for the United States Delegation to the Third Conference of the High Contracting Parties to CCW Protocol V on Explosive Remnants of War*, Nov. 9, 2009 ("We realize many delegations here are parties to the Convention on Cluster Munitions (CCM). However, many States, including the United States, have determined that their national security interests cannot be fully ensured consistent with the terms of the CCM.").

[351] Ambassador Robert Wood, U.S. Permanent Representative to the Conference on Disarmament, Explanation of Vote at the 70th UN General Assembly First Committee on Draft Resolution L.49/Rev.1, "Implementation of the Convention on Cluster Munitions," Nov. 4, 2015, 2015 DIGEST OF UNITED STATES PRACTICE IN INTERNATIONAL LAW 763, 764 ("In general, the lawfulness of the use of a type of weapon under international law does not depend on an absence of authorization, but instead depends upon whether the weapon is prohibited. The United States does not accept by this or any other standard that the Convention on Cluster Munitions represents an emerging norm or reflects customary international law that would prohibit the use of cluster munitions in armed conflict.").

[352] Convention on Cluster Munitions, art. 2(2), May 30, 2008, 2688 UNTS 39, 95 ("'**Cluster munition**' means a conventional munition that is designed to disperse or release explosive submunitions each weighing less than 20 kilograms, and includes those explosive submunitions. It does not mean the following: … (c) A munition that, in order to avoid indiscriminate area effects and the risks posed by unexploded submunitions, has all of the following characteristics: (i) Each munition contains fewer than ten explosive submunitions; (ii) Each explosive submunition weighs more than four kilograms; (iii) Each explosive submunition is designed to detect and engage a single target object; (iv) Each explosive submunition is equipped with an electronic self-destruction mechanism; (v) Each explosive submunition is equipped with an electronic self-deactivating feature;").

[353] *See, e.g.*, Convention on Cluster Munitions, art. 1(1), May 30, 2008, 2688 UNTS 39, 94 ("Each State Party undertakes never under any circumstances to: (a) Use cluster munitions; (b) Develop, produce, otherwise acquire, stockpile, retain or transfer to anyone, directly or indirectly, cluster munitions; (c) Assist, encourage or induce anyone to engage in any activity prohibited to a State Party under this Convention.").

[354] Convention on Cluster Munitions, art. 21(3), May 30, 2008, 2688 UNTS 39, 113 ("Notwithstanding the provisions of Article 1 of this Convention and in accordance with international law, States Parties, their military personnel or nationals, may engage in military cooperation and operations with States not party to this Convention that might engage in activities prohibited to a State Party.").

munitions used is within its exclusive control.[355]

6.14 Incendiary Weapons

The use of incendiary weapons is permissible, but subject to certain restrictions in order to reduce the risk of incidental harm to civilians.

6.14.1 Definition of an Incendiary Weapon. An "incendiary weapon" is any weapon or munition that is primarily designed to set fire to objects or to cause burn injury to persons through the action of flame, heat, or combination thereof, produced by a chemical reaction of a substance on the target.[356] Only "pure" incendiaries, such as napalm or the type of incendiary bombs used in World War II and Korea, are regulated as incendiary weapons.[357]

6.14.1.1 *Fire or Burn Injury Produced by Chemical Reaction of a Substance on the Target*. Incendiary weapons use a chemical reaction of a substance on the target to create flame or heat that destroys or injures.

On the other hand, laser weapons, even if their primary effect is to set fire to objects or cause burn injuries, do not constitute "incendiary weapons" under CCW Protocol III on Incendiary Weapons because the fire or burn injuries are not produced by a chemical reaction of a substance that is delivered to the target.[358] Similarly, chemical weapons cause death or other harm through the toxic properties of chemicals themselves, rather than the chemicals causing a fire or burn injury.[359]

6.14.1.2 *Examples of Incendiary Weapons*. Examples of incendiary weapons include:[360]

---

[355] Convention on Cluster Munitions, art. 21(4), May 30, 2008, 2688 UNTS 39, 113.

[356] CCW PROTOCOL III ON INCENDIARY WEAPONS art. 1(1) (defining *incendiary weapon* as "any weapon or munition which is primarily designed to set fire to objects or to cause burn injury to persons through the action of flame, heat, or combination thereof, produced by a chemical reaction of a substance delivered on the target.").

[357] *Article-by-Article Analysis of CCW Protocol III on Incendiary Weapons*, 2, Enclosure B to Warren Christopher, *Letter of Submittal*, Dec. 7, 1996, MESSAGE FROM THE PRESIDENT TRANSMITTING THE CCW AMENDED MINES PROTOCOL, PROTOCOL III ON INCENDIARY WEAPONS, AND PROTOCOL IV ON BLINDING LASER WEAPONS 38 ("As a result, the Protocol only covers 'pure' incendiaries, such as napalm or the type of incendiary bombs used in World War II and Korea.").

[358] *Article-by-Article Analysis of CCW Protocol III on Incendiary Weapons*, 2, Enclosure B to Warren Christopher, *Letter of Submittal*, Dec. 7, 1996, MESSAGE FROM THE PRESIDENT TRANSMITTING THE CCW AMENDED MINES PROTOCOL, PROTOCOL III ON INCENDIARY WEAPONS, AND PROTOCOL IV ON BLINDING LASER WEAPONS 38 ("Similarly, laser weapons are not covered even if their primary effect is to set fire to objects or cause burn injuries, since they do not deliver burning substances on the target.").

[359] *Refer to* § 6.8.3.1 (Definition of Chemical Weapons).

[360] CCW PROTOCOL III ON INCENDIARY WEAPONS art. 1(a) ("Incendiary weapons can take the form of, for example, flame throwers, fougasses, shells, rockets, grenades, mines, bombs and other containers of incendiary substances.").

- flame throwers;[361]
- fougasse;[362] and
- shells, rockets, grenades, mines, bombs, and other containers of incendiary substances, such as napalm and thermite.[363]

6.14.1.3 *Excluded From the Definition of Incendiary Weapons – Weapons With Incidental Incendiary Effects*. Incendiary weapons do not include munitions that may have incidental incendiary effects, such as illuminants, tracers, or smoke or signaling systems.[364]

For example, white phosphorous is a munition that contains fragments of white phosphorous. It is intended primarily for marking or illuminating a target or masking friendly force movement by creating smoke.

Similarly, tracer rounds are not incendiary weapons as they are designed to enable a gunner to direct his or her rounds onto a target rather than to set fire to objects.

6.14.1.4 *Excluded From the Definition of Incendiary Weapons – Certain Combined-Effects Munitions*. Certain combined-effects munitions are excluded from the definition of incendiary weapons. These munitions are designed to combine penetration, blast, or fragmentation effects with an additional incendiary effect, in which the incendiary effect is not specifically designed to cause burn injury to persons, but to be used against objects that are military objectives, such as armored vehicles, aircraft, and installations or facilities. Such

[361] *See also* International Committee of the Red Cross, *Conference of Government Experts on the Use of Certain Conventional Weapons (Lucerne, 24.9–18.10.1974): Report*, ¶¶69-70 (1975) ("Experts referred to three different types of flamethrower: portable, mechanized and emplaced. Emplaced flamethrowers, and such things as flame fougasses and incendiary landmines, find their principal application in perimeter defence, both of fixed and of temporary positions. … Portable and mechanized flamethrowers were seen to have several applications of which the two most important were the attack on pillboxes, and other such strongpoints, and the burning away of vegetation from positions suspected of concealing enemy units.").

[362] *For example*, DEPARTMENT OF THE ARMY FIELD MANUAL 3-11 / MARINE CORPS WARFIGHTING PUBLICATION 3-3.7.2, *Flame, Riot Control Agents and Herbicide Operations* (Aug. 19, 1996) ("The flame fougasse is a variation of an exploding FFE [flame field expedient] in which the flame is projected by explosive means over a preselected area. An excellent defensive weapon, the fougasse can also provide illumination as well as produce casualties. On Defensive Line Wyoming, during the Korean Conflict, elements of the 1st Cavalry Division emplaced 1,000 drums of FFEs in front of fighting positions. The drums were set in the ground at a 45-degree angle with the opening toward the enemy. Two examples of flame fougasses are the propellant charge container and the 55-gallon container.").

[363] W. Hays Parks, *The Protocol on Incendiary Weapons*, 30 INTERNATIONAL REVIEW OF THE RED CROSS 543-44 (Nov.-Dec. 1990) ("Thermite weapons, which contain a mixture of powdered ferric oxide and powdered or granular aluminium, are antimateriel and fire-sustaining. Thermite bombs, which burn at temperatures of about 2,400 degrees Centigrade, were the primary antimateriel incendiaries used by air forces of both sides in World Wars I and II. A later version contained barium nitrate and is called thermate, while a more recent variant is triethylaluminium (TEA). There has been little use of thermite-type bombs since 1945, in part because there have been few air campaigns directed against industrial targets.").

[364] CCW PROTOCOL III ON INCENDIARY WEAPONS art. 1(b) ("Incendiary weapons do not include: (i) Munitions which may have incidental incendiary effects, such as illuminants, tracers, smoke or signalling systems;").

weapons may include armor-piercing projectiles, fragmentation shells, explosive bombs, and similar combined-effects munitions.[365]

6.14.2 Use of Incendiary Weapons Is Permissible. Although subject to certain specific restrictions described in § 6.14.3 (Restrictions on the Use of Incendiary Weapons), the use of incendiary weapons, including anti-personnel use, is not prohibited.

6.14.2.1 *Use of Non-Incendiary Weapons to Set Fire to Objects or Cause Burn Injury to Persons*. The use of non-incendiary weapons to set fire to objects or to cause burn injury is technically not subject to the additional restrictions described in § 6.14.3 (Restrictions on the Use of Incendiary Weapons). For example, white phosphorus may be used as an anti-personnel weapon.[366] However, such use must comply with the general rules for the conduct of hostilities, including the principles of discrimination and proportionality.[367] In addition, feasible precautions to reduce the risk of harm to civilians must be taken.[368]

As a practical matter, however, it may be more effective to attack enemy combatants through other means, rather than seeking to cause them burn injury.[369]

6.14.3 Restrictions on the Use of Incendiary Weapons. As with other weapons, it is prohibited to make the civilian population as such, individual civilians, or civilian objects the object of attack by incendiary weapons.[370] In addition, it is specifically prohibited to make forests or other kinds of plant cover the object of attack by incendiary weapons, except when such natural elements are used to cover, conceal, or camouflage combatants or other military

---

[365] CCW PROTOCOL III ON INCENDIARY WEAPONS art. 1(b) ("Incendiary weapons do not include: … (ii) Munitions designed to combine penetration, blast or fragmentation effects with an additional incendiary effect, such as armour-piercing projectiles, fragmentation shells, explosive bombs and similar combined-effects munitions in which the incendiary effect is not specifically designed to cause burn injury to persons, but to be used against military objectives, such as armoured vehicles, aircraft and installations or facilities.").

[366] *For example*, Captain James T. Cobb, First Lieutenant Christopher A. LaCour, and Sergeant First Class William H. Hight, *After-Action Review (AAR) for the Battle of Fallujah*, ¶9b, *reprinted in* FIELD ARTILLERY 23, 26 (Mar.-Apr. 2005) ("White Phosphorous [WP]. WP proved to be an effective and versatile munition. We used it for screening missions at two breeches and, later in the fight, as a potent psychological weapon against the insurgents in trench lines and spider holes when we could not get effects on them with HE [High Explosive]. We fired 'shake and bake' missions at the insurgents, using WP to flush them out and HE to take them out.").

[367] *Refer to* § 5.5 (Discrimination in Conducting Attacks); § 5.12 (Proportionality – Prohibition on Attacks Expected to Cause Excessive Incidental Harm).

[368] *Refer to* § 5.11 (Proportionality – Feasible Precautions in Planning and Conducting Attacks to Reduce the Risk of Harm to Protected Persons and Objects).

[369] *For example*, Peter Pace, Chairman of the Joint Chiefs of Staff, *News Briefing with Secretary of Defense Donald Rumsfeld and Gen. Peter Pace*, Nov. 29, 2005 ("No armed force in the world goes to greater effort than your armed force to protect civilians and to be very precise in the way we apply our power. A bullet goes through skin even faster than white phosphorus does. So I would rather have the proper instrument applied at the proper time as precisely as possible to get the job done in a way that kills as many of the bad guys as possible and does as little collateral damage as possible. That is just the nature of warfare.").

[370] CCW PROTOCOL III ON INCENDIARY WEAPONS art. 2(1) ("It is prohibited in all circumstances to make the civilian population as such, individual civilians or civilian objects the object of attack by incendiary weapons.").

objectives, or are themselves military objectives.[371]

Similarly, the risks that the use of an incendiary weapon may pose to the civilian population should be considered in a proportionality analysis.[372]

As with the use of other weapons, commanders must take feasible precautions to reduce the risk of incidental harm to civilians when using incendiary weapons.[373]

6.14.3.1 <u>Use Against Military Objectives Located in Concentrations of Civilians</u>. Subject to a reservation by the United States discussed below, two additional rules apply to the use of incendiary weapons against military objectives that are located within a concentration of civilians. A "concentration of civilians" means any concentration of civilians, be it permanent or temporary, such as in inhabited parts of cities, in inhabited towns or villages, or in camps or columns of refugees or evacuees, or groups of nomads.[374]

First, subject to the U.S. reservation discussed below, it is prohibited to use air-delivered incendiary weapons to make any military objective located within a concentration of civilians the object of attack.[375]

Second, subject to the U.S. reservation discussed below, it is also prohibited to use incendiary weapons other than air-delivered incendiary weapons (*e.g.*, ground artillery) to make any military objective located within a concentration of civilians the object of attack. However, it is not prohibited to use such incendiary weapons against a military objective located within a concentration of civilians, when such military objective is clearly separated from the concentration of civilians and all feasible precautions are taken with a view to limiting the incendiary effects to the military objective and to avoiding, and in any event to minimizing, incidental loss of civilian life, injury to civilians, and damage to civilian objects.[376]

6.14.3.2 <u>U.S. Reservation to CCW Protocol III on Incendiary Weapons</u>. The

---

[371] CCW PROTOCOL III ON INCENDIARY WEAPONS art. 2(4) ("It is prohibited to make forests or other kinds of plant cover the object of attack by incendiary weapons except when such natural elements are used to cover, conceal or camouflage combatants or other military objectives, or are themselves military objectives.").

[372] *Refer to* § 5.12 (Proportionality – Prohibition on Attacks Expected to Cause Excessive Incidental Harm).

[373] *Refer to* § 5.11 (Proportionality – Feasible Precautions in Planning and Conducting Attacks to Reduce the Risk of Harm to Protected Persons and Objects).

[374] CCW PROTOCOL III ON INCENDIARY WEAPONS art. 1(2) ("A 'concentration of civilians' means any concentration of civilians, be it permanent or temporary, such as in inhabited parts of cities, or inhabited towns or villages, or as in camps or columns of refugees or evacuees, or groups of nomads.").

[375] CCW PROTOCOL III ON INCENDIARY WEAPONS art. 2(2) ("It is prohibited in all circumstances to make any military objective located within a concentration of civilians the object of attack by air-delivered incendiary weapons.").

[376] CCW PROTOCOL III ON INCENDIARY WEAPONS art. 2(3) (prohibiting making "any military objective located within a concentration of civilians the object of attack by means of incendiary weapons other than air-delivered incendiary weapons, except when such military objective is clearly separated from the concentration of civilians and all feasible precautions are taken with a view to limiting the incendiary effects to the military objective and to avoiding, and in any event to minimizing, incidental loss of civilian life, injury to civilians and damage to civilian objects.").

United States has taken a reservation to CCW Protocol III on Incendiary Weapons for the purpose of improving the protection of the civilian population.[377] Thus, for the U.S. armed forces, incendiary weapons may be used against military objectives located in concentrations of civilians where it is judged that such use would cause fewer casualties and/or less collateral damage than alternative weapons. However, in such cases, all feasible precautions should be taken with a view to limiting the incendiary effects to the military objective and to avoiding, and in any event minimizing, incidental loss of civilian life, injury to civilians, and damage to civilian objects.[378]

For example, the use of incendiary weapons might be the means of attacking enemy biological weapons facilities that poses the least risk of incidental harm to the civilian population.[379] Similarly, the use of incendiary weapons might reduce the number of sorties or attacks, and thereby further reduce the risk of incidental harm to the civilian population.[380]

6.15 LASER WEAPONS

In general, laser weapons are permissible. They may be used against enemy combatants, including to kill and injure them. However, the use of "blinding laser" weapons is prohibited. In addition, feasible precautions shall be taken in the employment of laser systems to avoid causing permanent blindness.

---

[377] Harold Koh, Legal Adviser, Department of State, *Letter to Paul Seger, Legal Adviser of Switzerland regarding Switzerland's Position on the U.S. Reservation to Protocol III of the Convention on Certain Conventional Weapons*, Dec. 30, 2009 ("In our view, this reservation is compatible with the object and purpose of Protocol III. We take the view that the object and purpose of Protocol III is to protect civilians from the collateral damage associated with the use of incendiary weapons. The narrow reservation taken by the United States is not incompatible with this object and purpose. In fact, this reservation ensures that the United States has the ability to provide for even greater protection of the civilian population, consistent with Protocol III.").

[378] United States, *Statement on Consent to Be Bound by CCW Protocol III on Incendiary Weapons*, Jan. 21, 2009, 2562 UNTS 36 ("The United States of America, with reference to Article 2, paragraphs 2 and 3, reserves the right to use incendiary weapons against military objectives located in concentrations of civilians where it is judged that such use would cause fewer casualties and/or less collateral damage than alternative weapons, but in so doing will take all feasible precautions with a view to limiting the incendiary effects to the military objective and to avoiding, and in any event to minimizing, incidental loss of civilian life, injury to civilians and damage to civilian objects."). *Refer to* § 5.11 (Proportionality – Feasible Precautions in Planning and Conducting Attacks to Reduce the Risk of Harm to Protected Persons and Objects).

[379] *Article-by-Article Analysis of CCW Protocol III on Incendiary Weapons*, 3, Enclosure B to Warren Christopher, *Letter of Submittal*, Dec. 7, 1996, MESSAGE FROM THE PRESIDENT TRANSMITTING THE CCW AMENDED MINES PROTOCOL, PROTOCOL III ON INCENDIARY WEAPONS, AND PROTOCOL IV ON BLINDING LASER WEAPONS 39 ("Incendiaries are the only weapons which can effectively destroy certain counter-proliferation targets such as biological weapons facilities which require high heat to eliminate bio-toxins. To use only high explosives would risk the widespread release of dangerous contaminants with potentially disastrous consequences for the civilian population.").

[380] *Article-by-Article Analysis of CCW Protocol III on Incendiary Weapons*, 3-4, Enclosure B to Warren Christopher, *Letter of Submittal*, Dec. 7, 1996, MESSAGE FROM THE PRESIDENT TRANSMITTING THE CCW AMENDED MINES PROTOCOL, PROTOCOL III ON INCENDIARY WEAPONS, AND PROTOCOL IV ON BLINDING LASER WEAPONS 39-40 ("Certain flammable military targets are also more readily destroyed by incendiaries. For example, a fuel depot could require up to eight times the bombs and sorties to destroy using only high explosives rather than incendiaries. Such an increase means a significantly greater humanitarian risk of collateral damage.").

6.15.1 Prohibition on "Blinding Laser" Weapons. It is prohibited to employ laser weapons specifically designed, as their sole combat function or as one of their combat functions, to cause permanent blindness to unenhanced vision, that is, to the naked eye or to the eye with corrective eyesight devices.[381]

Any use of such weapons is prohibited, including uses that are not intended to blind.

Although the U.S. armed forces and other militaries use lasers in a variety of roles, such as range-finding or causing temporary loss of sight, the United States has not developed or fielded a "blinding laser" weapon.

6.15.1.1 *Laser Weapon Specifically Designed, as Its Sole Combat Function or One of Its Combat Functions*. To fall under the above prohibition, the laser device must be specifically designed, as a combat function, to cause permanent blindness to unenhanced vision.

On the other hand, blinding as an incidental or collateral effect of the legitimate military employment of laser systems, including laser systems used against optical equipment, is not prohibited.[382] Thus, laser systems and devices used for rangefinding, target designation, jamming, dazzling, communications, and weapons guidance do not fall under this prohibition, even if serious eye injury or permanent blindness may incidentally occur through their use.[383] Similarly, incidental blinding from the use of lasers that are designed to attack or destroy material or injure persons as a combat function (but are not specifically designed to blind) would be permissible.

6.15.1.2 *Permanent Blindness to Unenhanced Vision*. "Permanent blindness" is defined as irreversible and uncorrectable loss of vision that is seriously disabling with no prospect of recovery. Serious disability is equivalent to visual acuity of less than 20/200 Snellen measured using both eyes.[384]

Lasers that are designed to cause a temporary loss of sight, such as laser "dazzlers,"

---

[381] CCW PROTOCOL IV ON BLINDING LASER WEAPONS art. 1 ("It is prohibited to employ laser weapons specifically designed, as their sole combat function or as one of their combat functions, to cause permanent blindness to unenhanced vision, that is to the naked eye or to the eye with corrective eyesight devices.").

[382] CCW PROTOCOL IV ON BLINDING LASER WEAPONS art. 3 ("Blinding as an incidental or collateral effect of the legitimate military employment of laser systems, including laser systems used against optical equipment, is not covered by the prohibition of this Protocol.").

[383] W. Hays Parks, Special Assistant to The Judge Advocate General of the Army for Law of War Matters, *Memorandum of Law: Travaux Preparatoires and Legal Analysis of Blinding Laser Weapons Protocol, reprinted in* THE ARMY LAWYER 33, 36 (Jun. 1997) ("Choice of the term *weapon* was intentional to distinguish the prohibited system from lasers which are used for rangefinding, jamming, dazzling, communications, weapons guidance, and similar purposes.").

[384] CCW PROTOCOL IV ON BLINDING LASER WEAPONS art. 4 ("For the purpose of this protocol 'permanent blindness' means irreversible and uncorrectable loss of vision which is seriously disabling with no prospect of recovery. Serious disability is equivalent to visual acuity of less than 20/200 Snellen measured using both eyes.").

would not fall under this prohibition.[385]

Unenhanced vision means the naked eye or the eye with corrective eyesight devices, such as ordinary glasses or contact lenses.[386] For example, unenhanced vision does not mean vision through direct-view optics, such as binoculars, a telescopic sight, night-vision goggles, or similar devices used to increase vision beyond that of an ordinary person without such enhancement. Persons using direct-view optics may have an increased risk of eye injury from lasers.

6.15.2 Feasible Precautions in the Employment of Laser Systems to Avoid the Incident of Permanent Blindness. In the employment of laser systems, all feasible precautions shall be taken to avoid the incidence of permanent blindness to unenhanced vision.[387] Feasible precautions may be understood to include those that are practicable or practically possible taking into account all circumstances ruling at the time, including humanitarian and military considerations.[388] Such precautions include training of the armed forces and other practical measures, such as promulgating doctrine and rules of engagement.[389]

6.15.2.1 *Use of Non-Prohibited Laser Systems to Blind Is Not Absolutely Prohibited*. Although feasible precautions should be taken to avoid blinding, the use of laser systems (that are not prohibited as blinding laser weapons) to blind enemy combatants is not prohibited if avoiding such harm is not feasible, *i.e.*, if such harm is militarily necessary. For example, it would not be prohibited for a soldier to use a non-prohibited laser system to blind an enemy combatant to save the user's life.[390]

---

385 *For example*, Defense Science Board, *Defense Science Board Task Force on Directed Energy Weapons*, 13 (Dec. 2007) ("Laser-based optical incapacitation devices have been deployed to Iraq in response to urgent fielding requirements for a non-lethal means to warn or temporarily incapacitate individuals. Marines employing these devices have reported that 'they consistently defuse potential escalation of force incidents.' Laser devices currently employed by the Marine Corps are green laser (532 nm) systems emitting a strong beam that can temporarily reduce visual acuity at a distance of 300m or more. It has a nominal ocular hazard minimum distance that the operator must avoid to preclude risk of eye injury. The lasers have been successfully used in convoy operations, mounted and dismounted patrols, vehicle check points, and entry control points. Army units have also purchased laser optical incapacitation devices of various types, principally for use in escalation of force situations and to warn or deter drivers of cars approaching checkpoints, U.S. convoys, or fixed-site installations.").

386 CCW PROTOCOL IV ON BLINDING LASER WEAPONS art. 1 (defining "unenhanced vision" as "the naked eye or … the eye with corrective eyesight devices.").

387 CCW PROTOCOL IV ON BLINDING LASER WEAPONS art. 2 ("In the employment of laser systems, the High Contracting Parties shall take all feasible precautions to avoid the incidence of permanent blindness to unenhanced vision.").

388 *Refer to* § 5.2.3.2 (What Precautions Are Feasible).

389 CCW PROTOCOL IV ON BLINDING LASER WEAPONS art. 2 ("Such precautions shall include training of their armed forces and other practical measures.").

390 W. Hays Parks, Special Assistant to The Judge Advocate General of the Army for Law of War Matters, *Memorandum of Law: Travaux Preparatoires and Legal Analysis of Blinding Laser Weapons Protocol, reprinted in* THE ARMY LAWYER 33, 36 (Jun. 1997) ("Finally, although Article 2 requires use of a laser device in a manner consistent with the spirit and intent of the Protocol, the delegations could not agree that a soldier should be criminally responsible if, in an *in extremis* situation, he employs a laser device against an enemy combatant to save the user's life.").

6.16 Riot Control Agents

The use of riot control agents is subject to certain prohibitions and restrictions. Riot control agents are widely used by governments for law enforcement purposes (such as crowd control), but are prohibited as a method of warfare.

6.16.1 Definition of Riot Control Agents. *Riot control agents* mean any chemical not listed in a Schedule Annexed to the Chemical Weapons Convention, which can produce rapidly in humans sensory irritation or disabling physical effects that disappear within a short time following termination of exposure.[391] Riot control agents include, for example, tear gas and pepper spray, but generally are understood to exclude the broader class of non-lethal weapons that may sometimes be used for riot control or other similar purposes, such as foams, water cannons, bean bags, or rubber bullets.[392]

The United States does not consider riot control agents to be "chemical weapons,"[393] or otherwise to fall under the prohibition against asphyxiating, poisonous, or other gases, and all analogous liquids, materials, or devices.[394]

6.16.2 Prohibition on Use of Riot Control Agents as a Method of Warfare. It is prohibited to use riot control agents as a method of warfare.[395] The United States has understood this prohibition not to prohibit the use of riot control agents in war in defensive military modes to save lives, such as use of riot control agents:

- in riot control situations in areas under direct and distinct U.S. military control, including

---

[391] Chemical Weapons Convention art. 2(7) ("'Riot Control Agent' means: Any chemical not listed in a Schedule, which can produce rapidly in humans sensory irritation or disabling physical effects which disappear within a short time following termination of exposure.").

[392] Joseph Benkert, Principal Deputy Assistant Secretary of Defense for International Security Policy, *Testimony on U.S. policy and practice with respect to the use of riot control agents by the U.S. Armed Forces before the Senate Committee on Armed Services, Subcommittee on Readiness and Management Support*, Sept. 27, 2006, 2006 Digest of United States Practice in International Law 1224 ("[W]hen I refer to 'riot control agents' in my testimony today I am referring to chemicals not listed in a Chemical Weapons Convention schedule which can produce rapidly in humans sensory irritation or disabling physical effects which disappear within a short time following termination of exposure. This includes for example, tear gas and pepper spray. I am not referring to the broader class of non-chemical non-lethal weapons that may sometimes be used for riot control or other similar purposes such as foams, water cannons, bean bags, or rubber bullets.").

[393] Joseph Benkert, Principal Deputy Assistant Secretary of Defense for International Security Policy, *Testimony on U.S. policy and practice with respect to the use of riot control agents by the U.S. Armed Forces before the Senate Committee on Armed Services, Subcommittee on Readiness and Management Support*, Sept. 27, 2006, 2006 Digest of United States Practice in International Law 1223-24 ("The Administration agrees with the policy statement in the National Defense Authorization Act for FY2006, section 1232 (the 'Ensign Amendment'); namely, 'It is the policy of the United States that riot control agents are not chemical weapons … .'").

[394] *See Statement by Secretary Rusk*, Mar. 24, 1965, 52 Department of State Bulletin 528 (Apr. 12, 1965) (explaining that tear gas used by U.S. forces in Vietnam is not "gas that is prohibited by the Geneva convention of 1925 or any other understandings about the use of gas"). *Refer to* § 6.8.2 (Asphyxiating, Poisonous, or Other Gases, and All Analogous Liquids, Materials, or Devices).

[395] Chemical Weapons Convention art. 1(5) ("Each State Party undertakes not to use riot control agents as a method of warfare.").

controlling rioting POWs;[396]

- in situations in which civilians are used to mask or screen attacks and civilian casualties can be reduced or avoided;[397]
- in rescue missions in remotely isolated areas, of downed aircrews and passengers, and escaping prisoners; and
- in rear echelon areas outside the zone of immediate combat to protect convoys from civil disturbances, terrorists, and paramilitary organizations.

These uses are as articulated in Executive Order 11850.[398] Even though Executive Order 11850 predated the Chemical Weapons Convention (which could have created legal obligations that were inconsistent with Executive Order 11850), interpreting the Chemical Weapons Convention consistent with Executive Order 11850 was a condition of the Senate giving its advice and consent to ratification of the Chemical Weapons Convention.[399] Thus, Executive Order 11850 has remained an important part of U.S. policy on the use of riot control agents.[400]

---

[396] *For example*, WALTER G. HERMES, UNITED STATES ARMY IN THE KOREAN WAR: TRUCE TENT AND FIGHTING FRONT 256-57 (1992) ("Armed with stones, flails, sharpened tent poles, steel pipes, and knives, the defiant prisoners [held during the Korean War] screamed insults and challenges. The infantry maintained excellent discipline, using tear gas and concussion grenades to break up the prisoners' opposition. Herding the prisoners into a corner, the U.N. troops forced them into their new compound. Only one prisoner was killed and twenty-nine were wounded as against one U.S. injury.").

[397] *For example*, JACK SHULIMSON & MAJOR CHARLES M. JOHNSON, U.S. MARINES IN VIETNAM: THE LANDING AND THE BUILDUP 1965, 91 (1978) ("Operation STOMP unfolded according to plan. Company H made its LVT assault through the mud flats of Qui Nhon bay while Company F landed by helicopter to cut off the VC avenues of retreat. The two companies closed their cordon around the Viet Cong, killing 26 and capturing three. With escape denied, the enemy went underground, taking many local peasants with them for use as human shields. During the mop-up of the area, a much-publicized action occurred. As the Marines slowly and methodically searched out a complex of tunnels, they threw in tear gas grenades to flush out the occupants. Seventeen VC were forced from hiding in this fashion, as well as more than 300 women, children, and old men, not one of whom was harmed.").

[398] Executive Order 11850, *Renunciation of Certain Uses in War of Chemical Herbicides and Riot Control Agents*, 40 FEDERAL REGISTER 16187 (Apr. 8, 1975) ("The United States renounces, as a matter of national policy, … first use of riot control agents in war except in defensive military modes to save lives such as: (a) Use of riot control agents in riot control situations in areas under direct and distinct U.S. military control, to include controlling rioting prisoners of war. (b) Use of riot control agents in situations in which civilians are used to mask or screen attacks and civilian casualties can be reduced or avoided. (c) Use of riot control agents in rescue missions in remotely isolated areas, of downed aircrews and passengers, and escaping prisoners. (d) Use of riot control agents in rear echelon areas outside the zone of immediate combat to protect convoys from civil disturbances, terrorists and paramilitary organizations.").

[399] Senate, *Conditions to Ratification of the Chemical Weapons Convention*, Senate Resolution 75, 105th Congress 143 CONGRESSIONAL RECORD S3651, S3657 (1997) ("The President shall take no measure, and prescribe no rule or regulation, which would alter or eliminate Executive Order 11850 of April 8, 1975.").

[400] Joseph Benkert, Principal Deputy Assistant Secretary of Defense for International Security Policy, *Testimony on U.S. policy and practice with respect to the use of riot control agents by the U.S. Armed Forces before the Senate Committee on Armed Services, Subcommittee on Readiness and Management Support*, Sept. 27, 2006, 2006 DIGEST OF UNITED STATES PRACTICE IN INTERNATIONAL LAW 1223-24 ("The policy governing the use of riot control agents by the U.S. Armed Forces is expressed principally in the Chemical Weapons Convention, the resolution of ratification of the Chemical Weapons Convention, and Executive Order 11850 [Renunciation of Certain Uses in

In addition to being permitted in war in defensive military modes to save lives, it is not prohibited to use riot control agents in military operations outside of war or armed conflict. Specifically, the United States has taken the position that riot control agents may be used in the conduct of:

- peacetime military operations within an area of ongoing armed conflict when the United States is not a party to the conflict;
- consensual peacekeeping operations when the use of force is authorized by the receiving state, including operations pursuant to Chapter VI of the United Nations Charter; and
- peacekeeping operations when force is authorized by the Security Council under Chapter VII of the United Nations Charter.[401]

6.17 HERBICIDES

The United States has renounced, as a matter of national policy, first use of herbicides in war except use, under regulations applicable to their domestic use, for control of vegetation within U.S. bases and installations or around their immediate defensive perimeters.[402]

6.17.1 Definition of Herbicide. An herbicide is a chemical compound that will kill or damage plants. Herbicides that are harmless to human beings are not prohibited under the rule

---

War of Chemical Herbicides and Riot Control Agents (1975)]. The Administration agrees with the policy statement in the National Defense Authorization Act for FY2006, section 1232 (the 'Ensign Amendment'); namely, 'It is the policy of the United States that riot control agents are not chemical weapons and that the President may authorize their use as legitimate, legal, and nonlethal alternatives to the use of force that, as provided in Executive Order 11850 (40 Fed. Reg. 16187) and consistent with the resolution of ratification of the Chemical Weapons Convention, may be employed by members of the Armed Forces in war in defensive military modes to save lives, including the illustrative purposes cited in Executive Order 11850.'") (insertions in original).

[401] Senate, *Conditions to Ratification of the Chemical Weapons Convention*, Senate Resolution 75, 105th Congress 143 CONGRESSIONAL RECORD S3651, S3657 (1997) ("Prior to the deposit of the United States instrument of ratification, the President shall certify to Congress that the United States is not restricted by the Convention in its use of riot control agents, including the use against combatants who are parties to a conflict, in any of the following cases: (i) UNITED STATES NOT A PARTY. — The conduct of peacetime military operations within an area of ongoing armed conflict when the United States is not a party to the conflict (such as recent use of the United States Armed Forces in Somalia, Bosnia, and Rwanda). (ii) CONSENSUAL PEACEKEEPING. — Consensual peacekeeping operations when the use of force is authorized by the receiving state, including operations pursuant to Chapter VI of the United Nations Charter. (iii) CHAPTER VII PEACEKEEPING. — Peacekeeping operations when force is authorized by the Security Council under Chapter VII of the United Nations Charter."); William J. Clinton, *Message to the Senate on the Chemical Weapons Convention*, Apr. 25, 1997, 1997-I PUBLIC PAPERS OF THE PRESIDENTS 495, 497 ("In accordance with Condition (26) on Riot Control Agents, I have certified that the United States is not restricted by the Convention in its use of riot control agents in various peacetime and peacekeeping operations. These are situations in which the United States is not engaged in a use of force of a scope, duration and intensity that would trigger the laws of war with respect to U.S. forces.").

[402] Executive Order 11850, *Renunciation of Certain Uses in War of Chemical Herbicides and Riot Control Agents*, 40 FEDERAL REGISTER 16187 (Apr. 8, 1975) ("The United States renounces, as a matter of national policy, first use of herbicides in war except use, under regulations applicable to their domestic use, for control of vegetation within U.S. bases and installations or around their immediate defensive perimeters.").

against the use of poison or poisoned weapons.[403]

6.17.2 Chemical Weapons Convention and Herbicides. The Chemical Weapons Convention does not add any new constraints on the use of herbicides.[404] The Chemical Weapons Convention addresses toxic chemicals that cause death, temporary incapacitation, or permanent harm to humans or animals, rather than plants.[405] Moreover, even if an herbicide were such a toxic chemical, its use would likely be for a purpose not prohibited by the Chemical Weapons Convention.[406]

6.17.3 ENMOD Convention and Herbicides. Under certain circumstances, the use of herbicides could be prohibited by the ENMOD Convention.[407] However, the use of herbicides to control vegetation within U.S. bases and installations or around their immediate defensive perimeters has been understood by the United States to be permitted under international law.[408]

6.17.4 Authority Under Domestic Law to Employ Herbicides in War. Use of herbicides in war by the U.S. armed forces requires advance Presidential approval.[409] Additional regulations govern the use of herbicides.

6.18 Nuclear Weapons

There is no general prohibition in treaty or customary international law on the use of nuclear weapons.[410] The United States has not accepted a treaty rule that prohibits the use of

---

[403] *Refer to* § 6.8.1.2 (Death or Permanent Disability to Persons).

[404] *Article-by-Article Analysis of the Chemical Weapons Convention*, 2-3, Attachment to Peter Tarnoff, Acting, *Letter of Submittal*, Nov. 20, 1993, MESSAGE FROM THE PRESIDENT TRANSMITTING THE CHEMICAL WEAPONS CONVENTION 2-3 ("The seventh preambular paragraph, although not legally binding, nevertheless recognizes the prohibition, embodied in the pertinent agreements and relevant principles of international law, of the use of herbicides as a method of warfare. Thus, the Convention does not add any new constraints on the use of herbicides.").

[405] *Refer to* § 6.8.3.1 (Definition of Chemical Weapons).

[406] *Refer to* § 6.8.3.4 (Certain Uses of Toxic Chemicals Not Prohibited).

[407] Second Review Conference of the Parties to the ENMOD Convention in September 1992, Final Declaration, ("The Conference confirms that the military or any other hostile use of herbicides as an environmental modification technique in the meaning of Article II [of the ENMOD Convention] is a method of warfare prohibited by Article I [of the ENMOD Convention] if such use of herbicides upsets the ecological balance of a region, thus causing widespread, long-lasting or severe effects as the means of destruction, damage or injury to any other State Party [to the ENMOD Convention].").

[408] *Article-by-Article Analysis of the Chemical Weapons Convention*, 3, Attachment to Peter Tarnoff, Acting, *Letter of Submittal*, Nov. 20, 1993, MESSAGE FROM THE PRESIDENT TRANSMITTING THE CHEMICAL WEAPONS CONVENTION 3 ("It is the understanding of the United States that the uses of herbicides proscribed [sic] in Executive Order 11850 do not cause such effects [that would violate the ENMOD Convention] and are allowed under international law.").

[409] Executive Order 11850, *Renunciation of Certain Uses in War of Chemical Herbicides and Riot Control Agents*, 40 FEDERAL REGISTER 16187 (Apr. 8, 1975) ("The Secretary of Defense shall take all necessary measures to ensure that the use by the Armed Forces of the United States of any ... chemical herbicides in war is prohibited unless such use has Presidential approval, in advance.").

[410] *Written Statement of the Government of the United States of America*, 21, Jun. 20, 1995, I.C.J., Request by the United Nations General Assembly for an Advisory Opinion on the Legality of the Threat or Use of Nuclear

nuclear weapons *per se*, and thus nuclear weapons are lawful weapons for the United States.

The law of war governs the use of nuclear weapons, just as it governs the use of conventional weapons.[411] For example, nuclear weapons must be directed against military objectives.[412] In addition, attacks using nuclear weapons must not be conducted when the expected incidental harm to civilians is excessive compared to the military advantage expected to be gained.[413]

6.18.1 U.S. Policy on the Use of Nuclear Weapons. The United States has developed national policy on the use of nuclear weapons. For example, the United States has stated that it would only consider the use of nuclear weapons in extreme circumstances to defend the vital interests of the United States or its allies and partners.[414] In addition, the United States has stated that it will not use or threaten to use nuclear weapons against non-nuclear weapons States that are party to the Nuclear Non-Proliferation Treaty and in compliance with their nuclear non-proliferation obligations.[415]

6.18.2 Nuclear Weapons and Arms Control Obligations. Nuclear weapons are regulated by a number of arms control agreements restricting their development, testing, production, proliferation, deployment, use, and, with respect to specific types, possession. Some of these agreements may not apply in times of war. Guidance on nuclear arms control agreements is beyond the scope of this manual.

6.18.3 AP I Provisions and Nuclear Weapons. Parties to AP I have expressed the

---

Weapons (noting that "there is no general prohibition in conventional or customary international law on the use of nuclear weapons,").

[411] *See, e.g.*, Secretary of Defense, *Report on Nuclear Employment Strategy of the United States Specified in Section 491 of 10 U.S.C.*, 4-5 (Jun. 2013) ("The new guidance makes clear that all plans must also be consistent with the fundamental principles of the Law of Armed Conflict. Accordingly, plans will, for example, apply the principles of distinction and proportionality and seek to minimize collateral damage to civilian populations and civilian objects. The United States will not intentionally target civilian populations or civilian objects."); *Written Statement of the Government of the United States of America*, 21, Jun. 20, 1995, I.C.J., Request by the United Nations General Assembly for an Advisory Opinion on the Legality of the Threat or Use of Nuclear Weapons ("The United States has long taken the position that various principles of the international law of armed conflict would apply to the use of nuclear weapons as well as to other means and methods of warfare. This in no way means, however, that the use of nuclear weapons is precluded by the law of war."); Edward R. Cummings, *The Role of Humanitarian Law*, Sept. 25, 1982, III CUMULATIVE DIGEST OF UNITED STATES PRACTICE IN INTERNATIONAL LAW 1981-1988 3421, 3422 (As far back as 1965 the U.S. supported a UN Resolution that essentially stated "that all governments and other authorities responsible for action in armed conflicts should conform at least to the following principle[] ... that the general principles of the Law of War apply to nuclear and similar weapons.").

[412] *Refer to* § 5.5 (Discrimination in Conducting Attacks).

[413] *Refer to* § 5.12 (Proportionality – Prohibition on Attacks Expected to Cause Excessive Incidental Harm).

[414] Department of Defense, *Nuclear Posture Review Report* 17 (Apr. 2010) ("The United States would only consider the use of nuclear weapons in extreme circumstances to defend the vital interests of the United States or its allies and partners.").

[415] Department of Defense, *Nuclear Posture Review Report* 17 (Apr. 2010) ("The United States will not use or threaten to use nuclear weapons against non-nuclear weapons states that are party to the NPT and in compliance with their nuclear non-proliferation obligations.").

understanding that the rules relating the use of weapons introduced by AP I were intended to apply exclusively to conventional weapons.[416] Thus, Parties to AP I have understood AP I provisions not to regulate or prohibit the use of nuclear weapons.[417] Although the United States is not a Party to AP I, the United States participated in the diplomatic conference that negotiated AP I based upon this understanding.[418]

6.18.4 Authority to Launch Nuclear Weapons. The authority to launch nuclear weapons generally is restricted to the highest levels of government. The domestic law and procedures concerning nuclear weapons employment are beyond the scope of this manual.

---

[416] Belgium, *Statement on Ratification of AP I*, May 20, 1986, 1435 UNTS 367 ("The Belgian Government, bearing in mind the preparatory work on the international instrument which is hereby ratified, wishes to stress that the Protocol was drawn up in order to expand the protection conferred by humanitarian law exclusively when conventional weapons are used in armed conflicts, without prejudice to the provisions of international law relating to the use of other types of weapons."); Germany, *Statement on Ratification of AP I*, Feb. 14, 1991, 1607 UNTS 526, 529 ("It is the understanding of the Federal Republic of Germany that the rules relating to the use of weapons introduced by Additional Protocol I were intended to apply exclusively to conventional weapons without prejudice to any other rules of international law applicable to other types of weapons."); Italy, *Statement on Ratification of AP I*, Feb. 27, 1986, 1425 UNTS 438 ("It is the understanding of the Government of Italy that the rules relating to the use of weapons introduced by Additional Protocol I were intended to apply exclusively to conventional weapons. They do not prejudice any other rule of international law applicable to other types of weapons."); Netherlands, *Statement on Ratification of AP I*, Jun. 26, 1987, 1477 UNTS 300 ("With regard to Protocol I as a whole: It is the understanding of the Government of the Kingdom of the Netherlands that the rules introduced by Protocol I relating to the use of weapons were intended to apply and consequently do apply solely to conventional weapons, without prejudice to any other rules of international law applicable to other types of weapons;"); Spain, *Statement on Ratification of AP I*, Apr. 21, 1989, 1537 UNTS 390, 391 ("This Protocol shall be understood to apply in its particular field, exclusively to conventional weapons and without prejudice to the norms of international law applicable to weapons of any other type.").

[417] *See, e.g.*, United Kingdom, *Statement on Ratification of AP I*, Jan. 28, 1998, 2020 UNTS 75, 76 ("It continues to be the understanding of the United Kingdom that the rules introduced by the Protocol apply exclusively to conventional weapons without prejudice to any other rules of international law applicable to other types of weapons. In particular, the rules so introduced do not have any effect on and do not regulate or prohibit the use of nuclear weapons."); France, *Statement on Ratification of AP I, translated in* SCHINDLER & TOMAN, THE LAWS OF ARMED CONLFICTS: A COLLECTION OF CONVENTIONS, RESOLUTIONS, AND OTHER DOCUMENTS 800 (2004) ("Referring to the draft protocol drawn up by the International Committee of the Red Cross which constituted the basis of 1974-1977 Diplomatic Conference, the Government of the French Republic continues to consider that the Protocol's provisions concern exclusively conventional weapons and do not regulate or prohibit the use of nuclear weapons, nor should they constitute a prejudice to any other rules of international law applicable to other activities necessary for the exercise by France of its inherent right of self-defense."); Canada, *Statement on Ratification of AP I*, Nov. 20, 1990, 1591 UNTS 462, 463 ("It is the understanding of the Government of Canada that the rules introduced by Protocol I were intended to apply exclusively to conventional weapons. In particular, the rules so introduced do not have any effect on and do not regulate or prohibit the use of nuclear weapons.").

[418] APPENDIX TO 1985 CJCS MEMO ON AP I 89 ("The United States participated in the negotiation of the Protocol on the assumption that its rules on the conduct of combat operations would not apply to the use of nuclear weapons, a position based on statements in the introduction to the original draft of the Protocol tabled by the Red Cross."); United States, *Statement on Signature of AP I*, 1125 UNTS 434 ("1. It is the understanding of the United States of America that the rules established by this Protocol were not intended to have any effect on and do not regulate or prohibit the use of nuclear weapons."). *See also* International Committee of the Red Cross, Introduction, *Draft Additional Protocols to the Geneva Conventions of August 12, 1949*, June 1973, 2, *reprinted in* I OFFICIAL RECORDS OF THE CDDH Part Three ("Problems relating to atomic, bacteriological and chemical warfare are subjects of international agreements or negotiations by governments, and in submitting these draft Additional Protocols, the ICRC does not intend to broach those problems.").

6.19 Explosive Ordnance

Information should be kept on the use of explosive ordnance in order to reduce the risk posed by explosive remnants of war once the conflict has ended.[419] If possible, explosive ordnance that must be abandoned should be left in a safe and secure manner, and information should be recorded and retained on its abandonment.[420] In addition, generic preventive measures should be taken during the life-cycle of explosive ordnance in order to minimize the occurrence of explosive remnants of war.[421]

6.19.1 Definitions of Explosive Ordnance, Unexploded Ordnance, and Abandoned Ordnance.

6.19.1.1 *Definition of Explosive Ordnance*. "Explosive ordnance" means conventional munitions containing explosives, with the exception of mines, booby-traps, and other devices as defined in the CCW Amended Mines Protocol.[422]

As a factual matter, mines, booby-traps, and other devices may constitute explosive ordnance, but the legal definition of explosive ordnance in the CCW Protocol V on Explosive Remnants of War excludes these items because they are addressed by the CCW Amended Mines Protocol.[423]

The reference to conventional munitions in the definition of "explosive ordnance" means that chemical, biological, and nuclear weapons are not covered by the CCW Protocol V on Explosive Remnants of War.[424]

6.19.1.2 *Definition of Unexploded Ordnance (UXO)*. "Unexploded ordnance" means explosive ordnance that has been primed, fused, armed, or otherwise prepared for use and used in an armed conflict.[425] "Explosive ordnance" is defined in § 6.19.1.1 (Definition of Explosive Ordnance). UXO may have been fired, dropped, launched, or projected, and should have exploded, but failed to do so.[426] For example, UXO does not include weapons that have

---

[419] *Refer to* § 6.19.2 (Using Explosive Ordnance).

[420] *Refer to* § 6.19.3 (Abandoning Explosive Ordnance).

[421] *Refer to* § 6.19.5 (Generic Preventive Measures During the Life-Cycle of Explosive Ordnance Aimed at Minimizing the Occurrence of Explosive Remnants of War).

[422] CCW PROTOCOL V ON EXPLOSIVE REMNANTS OF WAR art. 2(1) ("*Explosive ordnance* means conventional munitions containing explosives, with the exception of mines, booby traps and other devices as defined in Protocol II of this Convention as amended on 3 May 1996.").

[423] *Refer to* § 6.12.1 (Definition of Mine); § 6.12.2 (Definition of Booby-Trap); § 6.12.3 (Definition of "Other Devices" Similar to Mines).

[424] WILLIAM H. BOOTHBY, WEAPONS AND THE LAW OF ARMED CONFLICT 303 (2009) ("Specifically, the Protocol does not apply to chemical, biological, or nuclear weapons.").

[425] CCW PROTOCOL V ON EXPLOSIVE REMNANTS OF WAR art. 2(2) ("*Unexploded ordnance* means explosive ordnance that has been primed, fused, armed, or otherwise prepared for use and used in an armed conflict.").

[426] CCW PROTOCOL V ON EXPLOSIVE REMNANTS OF WAR art. 2(2) ("It may have been fired, dropped, launched or projected and should have exploded but failed to do so.").

remained in the armory or arsenal and that have not been prepared for firing.[427] UXO are sometimes called "duds."

6.19.1.3 *Definition of Abandoned Explosive Ordnance (AXO)*. "Abandoned explosive ordnance" means explosive ordnance that has not been used during an armed conflict, that has been left behind or dumped by a party to an armed conflict, and that is no longer under control of the party that left it behind or dumped it.[428] AXO may or may not have been primed, fused, armed, or otherwise prepared for use.[429] For example, mortar rounds in a supply point that is abandoned as a result of a quick departure would constitute AXO.

6.19.2 Using Explosive Ordnance. To the maximum extent possible and as far as practicable, information should be recorded and retained on the use of explosive ordnance during armed conflict in order to reduce the risks posed by explosive remnants of war.[430] The best practice is to record and retain, as accurately as possible, the following information regarding explosive ordnance that may have become unexploded ordnance:

- the location of areas targeted using explosive ordnance;
- the approximate number, type, and nature of explosive ordnance used in these areas; and
- the general location of known and probable unexploded ordnance.[431]

6.19.3 Abandoning Explosive Ordnance. Where it has been necessary to abandon explosive ordnance in the course of operations, the best practice, if possible, is to leave it in a safe and secure manner.[432] In addition, to the maximum extent possible and as far as practicable,

---

[427] WILLIAM H. BOOTHBY, WEAPONS AND THE LAW OF ARMED CONFLICT 303 (2009) ("[Unexploded ordnance as defined the CCW Protocol V on Explosive Remnants of War] also does not include weapons that have remained in the armoury or arsenal and that have not been prepared for firing. The definition is quite specific. The ordnance must have been prepared for use and must have been actually used in an armed conflict.").

[428] CCW PROTOCOL V ON EXPLOSIVE REMNANTS OF WAR art. 2(3) ("*Abandoned explosive ordnance* means explosive ordnance that has not been used during an armed conflict, that has been left behind or dumped by a party to an armed conflict, and which is no longer under control of the party that left it behind or dumped it.").

[429] CCW PROTOCOL V ON EXPLOSIVE REMNANTS OF WAR art. 2(3) ("Abandoned explosive ordnance may or may not have been primed, fused, armed or otherwise prepared for use.").

[430] CCW PROTOCOL V ON EXPLOSIVE REMNANTS OF WAR art. 4(1) ("High Contracting Parties and parties to an armed conflict shall to the maximum extent possible and as far as practicable record and retain information on the use of explosive ordnance … to facilitate the rapid marking and clearance, removal or destruction of explosive remnants of war, risk education and the provision of relevant information to the party in control of the territory and to civilian populations in that territory.").

[431] TECHNICAL ANNEX TO CCW PROTOCOL V ON EXPLOSIVE REMNANTS OF WAR part 1(a) ("Recording of information: Regarding explosive ordnance which may have become UXO a State should endeavour to record the following information as accurately as possible: (i) the location of areas targeted using explosive ordnance; (ii) the approximate number of explosive ordnance used in the areas under (i); (iii) the type and nature of explosive ordnance used in areas under (i); (iv) the general location of known and probable UXO;").

[432] TECHNICAL ANNEX TO CCW PROTOCOL V ON EXPLOSIVE REMNANTS OF WAR part 1(a) ("Where a State has been obliged to abandon explosive ordnance in the course of operations, it should endeavour to leave AXO in a safe and secure manner … .").

information should be recorded and retained on the abandonment of explosive ordnance in order to reduce the risks posed by explosive remnants of war.[433] The best practice is to record as accurately as possible and retain the following information regarding abandoned explosive ordnance:

- the location of AXO;
- the approximate amount of AXO at each specific site; and
- the types of AXO at each specific site.[434]

6.19.4 Storing Records on the Use or Abandonment of Explosive Ordnance. Information regarding the use or abandonment of explosive ordnance should be stored in such a manner as to allow for its subsequent retrieval in accordance with § 6.20.6 (Making Available Information on Used or Abandoned Explosive Ordnance That May Have Become Explosive Remnants of War).

6.19.5 Generic Preventive Measures During the Life-Cycle of Explosive Ordnance Aimed at Minimizing the Occurrence of Explosive Remnants of War. Generic preventive measures aimed at minimizing the occurrence of explosive remnants of war are described in part 3 of the Technical Annex to the CCW Protocol V on Explosive Remnants of War.[435] Such measures include munitions manufacturing management, munitions management, training, transfer, and future production. When producing or procuring explosive ordnance, to the extent possible, and as appropriate, these best practice measures should be implemented and respected during the life-cycle of explosive ordnance.[436]

6.19.5.1 *Munitions Manufacturing Management*. The following best practices should be applied during munitions manufacturing management:

- Production processes should be designed to achieve the greatest reliability of munitions.
- Production processes should be subject to certified quality control measures.

---

[433] CCW PROTOCOL V ON EXPLOSIVE REMNANTS OF WAR art. 4(1) ("High Contracting Parties and parties to an armed conflict shall to the maximum extent possible and as far as practicable record and retain information on the use of explosive ordnance or abandonment of explosive ordnance, to facilitate the rapid marking and clearance, removal or destruction of explosive remnants of war, risk education and the provision of relevant information to the party in control of the territory and to civilian populations in that territory.").

[434] TECHNICAL ANNEX TO CCW PROTOCOL V ON EXPLOSIVE REMNANTS OF WAR part 1(a) ("Where a State has been obliged to abandon explosive ordnance in the course of operations, it should endeavour to leave AXO in a safe and secure manner and record information on this ordnance as follows: (v) the location of AXO; (vi) the approximate amount of AXO at each specific site; (vii) the types of AXO at each specific site.").

[435] CCW PROTOCOL V ON EXPLOSIVE REMNANTS OF WAR art. 9(1) ("Bearing in mind the different situations and capacities, each High Contracting Party is encouraged to take generic preventive measures aimed at minimizing the occurrence of explosive remnants of war, including, but not limited to, those referred to in part 3 of the Technical Annex.").

[436] TECHNICAL ANNEX TO CCW PROTOCOL V ON EXPLOSIVE REMNANTS OF WAR part 3 ("States producing or procuring explosive ordnance should to the extent possible and as appropriate endeavour to ensure that the following measures are implemented and respected during the life-cycle of explosive ordnance.").

- During the production of explosive ordnance, certified quality assurance standards that are internationally recognized should be applied.

- Acceptance testing should be conducted through live-fire testing over a range of conditions or through other validated procedures.

- High reliability standards should be required in the course of explosive ordnance transactions and transfers.[437]

6.19.5.2 *Munitions Management*. In order to ensure the best possible long-term reliability of explosive ordnance, best practice norms and operating procedures with respect to its storage, transport, field storage, and handling should be applied in accordance with the following guidance.[438]

- Explosive ordnance, where necessary, should be stored in secure facilities or appropriate containers that protect the explosive ordnance and its components in a controlled atmosphere, if necessary.[439]

- Explosive ordnance should be transported to and from production facilities, storage facilities, and the field in a manner that minimizes the risk of damage to the explosive ordnance.[440]

- Appropriate containers and controlled environments, where necessary, should be used when stockpiling and transporting explosive ordnance.[441]

- The risk of explosions in stockpiles should be minimized by the use of appropriate

---

[437] TECHNICAL ANNEX TO CCW PROTOCOL V ON EXPLOSIVE REMNANTS OF WAR part 3(a) ("(i) Production processes should be designed to achieve the greatest reliability of munitions. (ii) Production processes should be subject to certified quality control measures. (iii) During the production of explosive ordnance, certified quality assurance standards that are internationally recognised should be applied. (iv) Acceptance testing should be conducted through live-fire testing over a range of conditions or through other validated procedures. (v) High reliability standards should be required in the course of explosive ordnance transactions and transfers.").

[438] TECHNICAL ANNEX TO CCW PROTOCOL V ON EXPLOSIVE REMNANTS OF WAR part 3(b) ("In order to ensure the best possible long-term reliability of explosive ordnance, States are encouraged to apply best practice norms and operating procedures with respect to its storage, transport, field storage, and handling in accordance with the following guidance.").

[439] TECHNICAL ANNEX TO CCW PROTOCOL V ON EXPLOSIVE REMNANTS OF WAR part 3(b)(i) ("Explosive ordnance, where necessary, should be stored in secure facilities or appropriate containers that protect the explosive ordnance and its components in a controlled atmosphere, if necessary.").

[440] TECHNICAL ANNEX TO CCW PROTOCOL V ON EXPLOSIVE REMNANTS OF WAR part 3(b)(ii) ("A State should transport explosive ordnance to and from production facilities, storage facilities and the field in a manner that minimizes damage to the explosive ordnance.").

[441] TECHNICAL ANNEX TO CCW PROTOCOL V ON EXPLOSIVE REMNANTS OF WAR part 3(b)(iii) ("Appropriate containers and controlled environments, where necessary, should be used by a State when stockpiling and transporting explosive ordnance.").

stockpile arrangements.[442]

- Appropriate explosive ordnance logging, tracking, and testing procedures should be applied. These procedures should include information on: (1) the date of manufacture of each number, lot, or batch of explosive ordnance; (2) where the explosive ordnance has been; (3) under what conditions the explosive ordnance has been stored; and (4) to what environmental factors the explosive ordnance has been exposed.[443]

- Periodically, stockpiled explosive ordnance should undergo, where appropriate, live-fire testing to ensure that munitions function as desired.[444]

- Sub-assemblies of stockpiled explosive ordnance should, where appropriate, undergo laboratory testing to ensure that munitions function as desired.[445]

- Where necessary, appropriate action (including adjustment to the expected shelf-life of ordnance) should be taken as a result of information acquired by logging, tracking, and testing procedures, in order to maintain the reliability of stockpiled explosive ordnance.[446]

6.19.5.3 _Training_. All personnel who are involved in handling, transporting, and using explosive ordnance should be properly trained through suitable training programs on the munitions that they will be required to handle.[447]

6.19.5.4 _Transfer_. When contemplating transfers of explosive ordnance to another State that did not previously possess that type of explosive ordnance, reasonable efforts should be made to ensure that the receiving State has the capability to store, maintain, and use

---

[442] TECHNICAL ANNEX TO CCW PROTOCOL V ON EXPLOSIVE REMNANTS OF WAR part 3(b)(iv) ("The risk of explosions in stockpiles should be minimised by the use of appropriate stockpile arrangements.").

[443] TECHNICAL ANNEX TO CCW PROTOCOL V ON EXPLOSIVE REMNANTS OF WAR part 3(b)(v) ("States should apply appropriate explosive ordnance logging, tracking and testing procedures, which should include information on the date of manufacture of each number, lot or batch of explosive ordnance, and information on where the explosive ordnance has been, under what conditions it has been stored, and to what environmental factors it has been exposed.").

[444] TECHNICAL ANNEX TO CCW PROTOCOL V ON EXPLOSIVE REMNANTS OF WAR part 3(b)(vi) ("Periodically, stockpiled explosive ordnance should undergo, where appropriate, live-firing testing to ensure that munitions function as desired.").

[445] TECHNICAL ANNEX TO CCW PROTOCOL V ON EXPLOSIVE REMNANTS OF WAR part 3(b)(vii) ("Sub-assemblies of stockpiled explosive ordnance should, where appropriate, undergo laboratory testing to ensure that munitions function as desired.").

[446] TECHNICAL ANNEX TO CCW PROTOCOL V ON EXPLOSIVE REMNANTS OF WAR part 3(b)(viii) ("Where necessary, appropriate action, including adjustment to the expected shelf-life of ordnance, should be taken as a result of information acquired by logging, tracking and testing procedures, in order to maintain the reliability of stockpiled explosive ordnance.").

[447] TECHNICAL ANNEX TO CCW PROTOCOL V ON EXPLOSIVE REMNANTS OF WAR part 3(c) ("The proper training of all personnel involved in the handling, transporting and use of explosive ordnance is an important factor in seeking to ensure its reliable operation as intended. States should therefore adopt and maintain suitable training programmes to ensure that personnel are properly trained with regard to the munitions with which they will be required to deal.").

that explosive ordnance correctly.[448]

6.19.5.5 *Future Production*. When producing, procuring, or developing explosive ordnance, ways and means of improving the reliability of explosive ordnance should be considered with a view to achieving the highest possible reliability.[449]

6.20 EXPLOSIVE REMNANTS OF WAR

There are certain obligations with respect to explosive remnants of war on territory under U.S. control. Most of these obligations are trigged upon the cessation of active hostilities.

6.20.1 Definition of Explosive Remnants of War. Under the CCW Protocol V on Explosive Remnants of War, "explosive remnants of war" means: (1) unexploded ordnance (UXO); and (2) abandoned explosive ordnance (AXO).[450]

"Unexploded ordnance" is defined in § 6.19.1.2 (Definition of Unexploded Ordnance (UXO)). "Abandoned explosive ordnance" is defined in § 6.19.1.3 (Definition of Abandoned Explosive Ordnance (AXO)).

6.20.2 Scope of the Obligations Created by the CCW Protocol V on Explosive Remnants of War. The CCW Protocol V on Explosive Remnants of War applies to explosive remnants of war on the land territory, including internal waters, of States that are Parties to the Protocol.[451]

The CCW Protocol V on Explosive Remnants of War applies to situations resulting from armed conflict and occupation.[452]

Certain obligations in the CCW Protocol V on Explosive Remnants of War only apply to explosive remnants of war that were created after the entry into force of the Protocol for the High Contracting Party on whose territory the explosive remnants of war exist.[453] These obligations

---

[448] TECHNICAL ANNEX TO CCW PROTOCOL V ON EXPLOSIVE REMNANTS OF WAR part 3(d) ("A State planning to transfer explosive ordnance to another State that did not previously possess that type of explosive ordnance should endeavour to ensure that the receiving State has the capability to store, maintain and use that explosive ordnance correctly.").

[449] TECHNICAL ANNEX TO CCW PROTOCOL V ON EXPLOSIVE REMNANTS OF WAR part 3(e) ("A State should examine ways and means of improving the reliability of explosive ordnance that it intends to produce or procure, with a view to achieving the highest possible reliability.").

[450] CCW PROTOCOL V ON EXPLOSIVE REMNANTS OF WAR art. 2(4) ("*Explosive remnants of war* means unexploded ordnance and abandoned explosive ordnance.").

[451] CCW PROTOCOL V ON EXPLOSIVE REMNANTS OF WAR art. 1(2) ("This Protocol shall apply to explosive remnants of war on the land territory including internal waters of High Contracting Parties.").

[452] CCW PROTOCOL V ON EXPLOSIVE REMNANTS OF WAR art. 1(3) ("This Protocol shall apply to situations resulting from conflicts referred to in Article 1, paragraphs 1 to 6, of the Convention, as amended on 21 December 2001.").

[453] CCW PROTOCOL V ON EXPLOSIVE REMNANTS OF WAR art. 1(4) ("Articles 3, 4, 5 and 8 of this Protocol apply to explosive remnants of war other than existing explosive remnants of war as defined in Article 2, paragraph 5 of this Protocol."); CCW PROTOCOL V ON EXPLOSIVE REMNANTS OF WAR art. 2(5) ("*Existing explosive remnants of war* means unexploded ordnance and abandoned explosive ordnance that existed prior to the entry into force of this Protocol for the High Contracting Party on whose territory it exists.").

include obligations discussed in:

- § 6.20.3 (Taking Feasible Precautions to Protect Civilians From Explosive Remnants of War);
- § 6.20.6 (Making Available Information on Used or Abandoned Explosive Ordnance That May Have Become Explosive Remnants of War);
- § 6.20.7 (Clearance, Removal, or Destruction of Explosive Remnants of War From Territory Under a Party's Control); and
- § 6.20.8 (Providing Assistance to Facilitate the Removal of Explosive Remnants of War From a Party's Military Operations in Areas Outside Its Control).

6.20.3 Taking Feasible Precautions to Protect Civilians From Explosive Remnants of War. Parties to the CCW Protocol V on Explosive Remnants of War and parties to an armed conflict shall take all feasible precautions in the territory under their control affected by explosive remnants of war to protect the civilian population, individual civilians, and civilian objects from the risks and effects of explosive remnants of war.[454]

Feasible precautions are those precautions that are practicable or practically possible, taking into account all circumstances ruling at the time, including humanitarian and military considerations.[455]

These precautions may include warnings, risk education to the civilian population, and marking, fencing, and monitoring of territory affected by explosive remnants of war, as set out in Part 2 of the Technical Annex to CCW Protocol V on Explosive Remnants of War.[456]

6.20.3.1 *Best Practice Elements on Warnings and Risk Education*. Warnings are the punctual provision of cautionary information to the civilian population, intended to minimize risks caused by explosive remnants of war in affected territories.[457]

Risk education to the civilian population should consist of risk education programs to facilitate information exchange between affected communities, government authorities, and

---

[454] CCW PROTOCOL V ON EXPLOSIVE REMNANTS OF WAR art. 5(1) ("High Contracting Parties and parties to an armed conflict shall take all feasible precautions in the territory under their control affected by explosive remnants of war to protect the civilian population, individual civilians and civilian objects from the risks and effects of explosive remnants of war.").

[455] CCW PROTOCOL V ON EXPLOSIVE REMNANTS OF WAR art. 5(1) ("Feasible precautions are those precautions which are practicable or practicably possible, taking into account all circumstances ruling at the time, including humanitarian and military considerations."). *Refer to* § 5.2.3.2 (What Precautions Are Feasible).

[456] CCW PROTOCOL V ON EXPLOSIVE REMNANTS OF WAR art. 5(1) ("These precautions may include warnings, risk education to the civilian population, marking, fencing and monitoring of territory affected by explosive remnants of war, as set out in Part 2 of the Technical Annex.").

[457] TECHNICAL ANNEX TO CCW PROTOCOL V ON EXPLOSIVE REMNANTS OF WAR part 2(a) ("Warnings are the punctual provision of cautionary information to the civilian population, intended to minimise risks caused by explosive remnants of war in affected territories.").

humanitarian organizations so that affected communities are informed about the threat from explosive remnants of war. Risk education programs are usually long-term activities.[458]

All programs of warnings and risk education should, where possible, take into account prevailing national and international standards, including the International Mine Action Standards.[459]

Warnings and risk education should be provided to the affected civilian population, which comprises civilians living in or around areas containing explosive remnants of war and civilians who transit such areas.[460]

Warnings should be given as soon as possible, depending on the context and the information available. A risk education program should replace a warnings program as soon as possible. Warnings and risk education always should be provided to the affected communities at the earliest possible time.[461]

Third parties, such as international organizations and non-governmental organizations, should be used when there are insufficient resources and skills to deliver efficient risk education.[462]

If possible, additional resources for warnings and risk education should be provided. Such items might include: provision of logistical support, production of risk education materials, financial support, and general cartographic information.[463]

6.20.3.2 *Best Practices on Marking, Fencing, and Monitoring Areas Containing Explosive Remnants of War*. When possible, at any time during the course of a conflict and at

---

[458] Technical Annex to CCW Protocol V on Explosive Remnants of War part 2(b) ("Risk education to the civilian population should consist of risk education programmes to facilitate information exchange between affected communities, government authorities and humanitarian organisations so that affected communities are informed about the threat from explosive remnants of war. Risk education programmes are usually a long term activity.").

[459] Technical Annex to CCW Protocol V on Explosive Remnants of War part 2(c) ("All programmes of warnings and risk education should, where possible, take into account prevailing national and international standards, including the International Mine Action Standards.").

[460] Technical Annex to CCW Protocol V on Explosive Remnants of War part 2(d) ("Warnings and risk education should be provided to the affected civilian population which comprises civilians living in or around areas containing explosive remnants of war and civilians who transit such areas.").

[461] Technical Annex to CCW Protocol V on Explosive Remnants of War part 2(e) ("Warnings should be given, as soon as possible, depending on the context and the information available. A risk education programme should replace a warnings programme as soon as possible. Warnings and risk education always should be provided to the affected communities at the earliest possible time.").

[462] Technical Annex to CCW Protocol V on Explosive Remnants of War part 2(f) ("Parties to a conflict should employ third parties such as international organisations and non-governmental organisations when they do not have the resources and skills to deliver efficient risk education.").

[463] Technical Annex to CCW Protocol V on Explosive Remnants of War part 2(g) ("Parties to a conflict should, if possible, provide additional resources for warnings and risk education. Such items might include: provision of logistical support, production of risk education materials, financial support and general cartographic information.").

the earliest possible time and to the maximum extent possible, the best practice is for areas containing explosive remnants of war to be marked, fenced, and monitored so as to ensure the effective exclusion of civilians, in accordance with the following provisions.[464]

Warning signs based on methods of marking recognized by the affected community should be used in the marking of suspected hazardous areas. Signs and other hazardous area boundary markers should as far as possible be visible, legible, durable, and resistant to environmental effects and should clearly identify which side of the marked boundary is considered safe and which side is considered to be within the area affected by explosive remnants of war.[465]

An appropriate structure should be put in place with responsibility for the monitoring and maintenance of permanent and temporary marking systems, integrated with national and local risk education programs.[466]

6.20.4 Protecting, as Far as Feasible, Humanitarian Missions and Organizations From the Effects of Explosive Remnants of War. Each Party to the CCW Protocol V on Explosive Remnants of War and party to an armed conflict shall protect, as far as feasible, from the effects of explosive remnants of war, humanitarian missions and organizations that are or will be operating in the area under the control of the Party to the CCW Protocol V on Explosive Remnants of War or party to an armed conflict and with that party's consent.[467]

In addition, each Party to the CCW Protocol V on Explosive Remnants of War and party to an armed conflict shall, upon request by such a humanitarian mission or organization, provide, as far as feasible, information on the location of all explosive remnants of war that it is aware of in territory where the requesting humanitarian mission or organization will operate or is operating.[468] Other treaties or certain U.N. Security Council resolutions may provide a higher

---

[464] TECHNICAL ANNEX TO CCW PROTOCOL V ON EXPLOSIVE REMNANTS OF WAR part 2(h) ("When possible, at any time during the course of a conflict and thereafter, where explosive remnants of war exist the parties to a conflict should, at the earliest possible time and to the maximum extent possible, ensure that areas containing explosive remnants of war are marked, fenced and monitored so as to ensure the effective exclusion of civilians, in accordance with the following provisions.").

[465] TECHNICAL ANNEX TO CCW PROTOCOL V ON EXPLOSIVE REMNANTS OF WAR part 2(i) ("Warning signs based on methods of marking recognised by the affected community should be utilised in the marking of suspected hazardous areas. Signs and other hazardous area boundary markers should as far as possible be visible, legible, durable and resistant to environmental effects and should clearly identify which side of the marked boundary is considered to be within the explosive remnants of war affected area and which side is considered to be safe.").

[466] TECHNICAL ANNEX TO CCW PROTOCOL V ON EXPLOSIVE REMNANTS OF WAR part 2(j) ("An appropriate structure should be put in place with responsibility for the monitoring and maintenance of permanent and temporary marking systems, integrated with national and local risk education programmes.").

[467] CCW PROTOCOL V ON EXPLOSIVE REMNANTS OF WAR art. 6(1) ("Each High Contracting Party and party to an armed conflict shall: (a) Protect, as far as feasible, from the effects of explosive remnants of war, humanitarian missions and organizations that are or will be operating in the area under the control of the High Contracting Party or party to an armed conflict and with that party's consent.").

[468] CCW PROTOCOL V ON EXPLOSIVE REMNANTS OF WAR art. 6(1) ("Each High Contracting Party and party to an armed conflict shall: … (b) Upon request by such a humanitarian mission or organization, provide, as far as feasible, information on the location of all explosive remnants of war that it is aware of in territory where the requesting humanitarian mission or organization will operate or is operating.").

level of additional protection.[469]

6.20.5 Obligations Under the CCW Protocol V on Explosive Remnants of War That Are Triggered by the Cessation of Active Hostilities. Certain obligations under the CCW Protocol V on Explosive Remnants of War are triggered by the cessation of active hostilities. These obligations include those obligations addressed in:

- § 6.20.6 (Making Available Information on Used or Abandoned Explosive Ordnance That May Have Become Explosive Remnants of War);
- § 6.20.7 (Clearance, Removal, or Destruction of Explosive Remnants of War From Territory Under a Party's Control); and
- § 6.20.8 (Providing Assistance to Facilitate the Removal of Explosive Remnants of War From a Party's Military Operations in Areas Outside Its Control).

The determination that active hostilities have ceased for the purposes of triggering these obligations would be made at the national level.

In addition, peace treaties or similar agreements negotiated in connection with the settlement of armed conflicts may also allocate responsibilities with respect to explosive remnants of war.[470] Nothing in the CCW Protocol V on Explosive Remnants of War precludes future arrangements in connection with the settlement of armed conflicts, or assistance connected thereto, to allocate responsibilities with respect to explosive remnants of war in a manner that respects the essential spirit and purpose of the CCW Protocol V on Explosive Remnants of War.[471]

---

[469] CCW PROTOCOL V ON EXPLOSIVE REMNANTS OF WAR art. 6(2) ("The provisions of this Article are without prejudice to existing International Humanitarian Law or other international instruments as applicable or decisions by the Security Council of the United Nations which provide for a higher level of protection.").

[470] *For example*, Protocol to the Agreement on Ending the War and Restoring Peace in Viet-Nam Concerning the Cease-fire in South Viet-Nam and the Joint Military Commissions, art. 5(a), Jan. 27, 1972, 935 UNTS 251, 253 ("Within fifteen days after the cease-fire comes into effect, each party shall do its utmost to complete the removal or deactivation of all demolition objects, mine-fields, traps, obstacles or other dangerous objects placed previously, so as not to hamper the population's movement and work, in the first place on waterways, roads and railroads in South Viet-Nam. Those mines which cannot be removed or deactivated within that time shall be clearly marked and must be removed or deactivated as soon as possible."); Protocol to the Agreement on Ending the War and Restoring Peace in Viet-Nam Concerning the Removal, Permanent Deactivation, or Destruction of Mines in the Territorial Waters, Ports, Harbors, and Waterways of the Democratic Republic of Viet-Nam, art. 5, Jan. 27, 1973, 935 UNTS 393, 395 ("The United States shall be responsible for the mine clearance on inland waterways of the Democratic Republic of Viet-Nam. The Democratic Republic of Viet-Nam shall, to the full extent of its capabilities, actively participate in the mine clearance with the means of surveying, removal and destruction and technical advice supplied by the United States.").

[471] United States, *Statement on Consent to Be Bound by CCW Protocol V on Explosive Remnants of War*, Jan. 21, 2009, 2562 UNTS 39, 40 ("It is the understanding of the United States of America that nothing in Protocol V would preclude future arrangements in connection with the settlement of armed conflicts, or assistance connected thereto, to allocate responsibilities under Article 3 in a manner that respects the essential spirit and purpose of Protocol V"). *See also Overview and Article-by-Article Analysis of CCW Protocol V on Explosive Remnants of War* 3-4, MESSAGE FROM THE PRESIDENT TRANSMITTING AP III, CCW AMENDED ARTICLE 1, AND CCW PROTOCOL V ON EXPLOSIVE

6.20.6 Making Available Information on Used or Abandoned Explosive Ordnance That May Have Become Explosive Remnants of War. Without delay after the cessation of active hostilities and as far as practicable, Parties to the CCW Protocol V on Explosive Remnants of War and parties to an armed conflict have an obligation, subject to their legitimate security interests, to make available certain information on used or abandoned explosive ordnance, which may have become explosive remnants of war, to certain recipients.[472]

6.20.6.1 *Timing of the Release of Information*. The best practice is for the information to be released as soon as possible, taking into account such matters as any ongoing military and humanitarian operations in the affected areas, the availability and reliability of information, and relevant security issues.[473]

6.20.6.2 *Recipients of the Released Information*. The information shall be made available to the party or parties in control of the affected territory and, upon request, to other relevant organizations that the party providing the information believes are, or will be, undertaking risk education and the marking and clearance, removal, or destruction of explosive remnants of war in the affected area.[474]

The best practice is to release this information to the party or parties in control of the affected territory and to those persons or institutions that the releasing State is satisfied are, or will be, involved in UXO or AXO clearance in the affected area, or in the education of the civilian population on the risks of UXO or AXO.[475]

REMNANTS OF WAR 13-14 ("During the negotiations, the United States and other delegations raised the need to reconcile this Protocol with other international agreements or arrangements related to the settlement of armed conflict, in order to avoid unintended consequences in connection with peace treaties or similar arrangements. In the context of armed conflict, the parties to the conflict themselves will be in the best position to determine how the responsibilities for ERW should fit into an overall settlement.").

[472] CCW PROTOCOL V ON EXPLOSIVE REMNANTS OF WAR art. 4(2) ("High Contracting Parties and parties to an armed conflict which have used or abandoned explosive ordnance which may have become explosive remnants of war shall, without delay after the cessation of active hostilities and as far as practicable, subject to these parties' legitimate security interests, make available such information to the party or parties in control of the affected area, bilaterally or through a mutually agreed third party including *inter alia* the United Nations or, upon request, to other relevant organizations which the party providing the information is satisfied are or will be undertaking risk education and the marking and clearance, removal or destruction of explosive remnants of war in the affected area.").

[473] TECHNICAL ANNEX TO CCW PROTOCOL V ON EXPLOSIVE REMNANTS OF WAR part 1(c)(iv) ("Timing: The information should be released as soon as possible, taking into account such matters as any ongoing military and humanitarian operations in the affected areas, the availability and reliability of information and relevant security issues.").

[474] CCW PROTOCOL V ON EXPLOSIVE REMNANTS OF WAR art. 4(2) (information shall be made available "to the party or parties in control of the affected area, … or, upon request, to other relevant organizations which the party providing the information is satisfied are or will be undertaking risk education and the marking and clearance, removal or destruction of explosive remnants of war in the affected area.").

[475] TECHNICAL ANNEX TO CCW PROTOCOL V ON EXPLOSIVE REMNANTS OF WAR part 1(c)(ii) ("Recipient: The information should be released to the party or parties in control of the affected territory and to those persons or institutions that the releasing State is satisfied are, or will be, involved in UXO or AXO clearance in the affected area, in the education of the civilian population on the risks of UXO or AXO.").

6.20.6.3 Mechanism for the Release of Information. This information may be made available bilaterally (*e.g.*, directly from the United States to the recipient) or through a mutually agreed third party (*e.g.*, the United Nations).[476] In addition, a best practice would be to make use of those mechanisms established internationally or locally for the release of such information, such as through the United Nations Mine Action Service (UNMAS), the Information Management System for Mine Action (IMSMA), and other expert agencies, as considered appropriate by the releasing State.[477]

6.20.6.4 Best Practices for the Content of Released Information on UXO. The best practice is for the released information on UXO to contain details on:

- the general location of known and probable UXO;
- the types and approximate number of explosive ordnance used in the targeted areas;
- the method of identifying the explosive ordnance including color, size, and shape, and other relevant markings; and
- the method for safe disposal of the explosive ordnance.[478]

This information may be drawn from the information recorded and retained when using explosive ordnance.[479]

6.20.6.5 Best Practices for the Content of Released Information on AXO. The best practice is for the released information on AXO to contain details on:

- the location of the AXO;
- the approximate number of AXO at each specific site;
- the types of AXO at each specific site;
- the method of identifying the AXO, including color, size, and shape;

---

476 CCW PROTOCOL V ON EXPLOSIVE REMNANTS OF WAR art. 4(2) (information shall be made available "bilaterally or through a mutually agreed third party including inter alia the United Nations").

477 TECHNICAL ANNEX TO CCW PROTOCOL V ON EXPLOSIVE REMNANTS OF WAR part 1(c)(iii) ("Mechanism: A State should, where feasible, make use of those mechanisms established internationally or locally for the release of information, such as through UNMAS, IMSMA, and other expert agencies, as considered appropriate by the releasing State.").

478 TECHNICAL ANNEX TO CCW PROTOCOL V ON EXPLOSIVE REMNANTS OF WAR part 1(c)(i) ("On UXO the released information should contain details on: (1) the general location of known and probable UXO; (2) the types and approximate number of explosive ordnance used in the targeted areas; (3) the method of identifying the explosive ordnance including colour, size and shape and other relevant markings; (4) the method for safe disposal of the explosive ordnance.").

479 *Refer to* § 6.19.2 (Using Explosive Ordnance); § 6.19.4 (Storing Records on the Use or Abandonment of Explosive Ordnance).

- information on type and methods of packing for AXO;
- the state of readiness; and
- the location and nature of any booby traps known to be present in the area of AXO.[480]

This information may be drawn from the information recorded and retained when abandoning explosive ordnance.[481]

6.20.7 Clearance, Removal, or Destruction of Explosive Remnants of War From Territory Under a Party's Control. After the cessation of active hostilities and as soon as feasible, each Party to the CCW Protocol V on Explosive Remnants of War and party to an armed conflict shall mark and clear, remove, or destroy explosive remnants of war in affected territories under its control.[482] This obligation is consistent with long-established customary international law principles of sovereignty and responsibility.[483] In particular, the following measures are to be taken in such territories:

- surveying and assessing the threat posed by explosive remnants of war;
- assessing and prioritizing the needs and practicability in terms of marking and clearance, removal, or destruction;
- marking and clearing, removing, or destroying explosive remnants of war; and
- taking steps to mobilize resources to carry out these activities.[484]

---

[480] TECHNICAL ANNEX TO CCW PROTOCOL V ON EXPLOSIVE REMNANTS OF WAR part 1(c)(i) ("On AXO the released information should contain details on: (5) the location of the AXO; (6) the approximate number of AXO at each specific site; (7) the types of AXO at each specific site; (8) the method of identifying the AXO, including colour, size and shape; (9) information on type and methods of packing for AXO; (10) state of readiness; (11) the location and nature of any booby traps known to be present in the area of AXO.").

[481] *Refer to* § 6.19.3 (Abandoning Explosive Ordnance); § 6.19.4 (Storing Records on the Use or Abandonment of Explosive Ordnance).

[482] CCW PROTOCOL V ON EXPLOSIVE REMNANTS OF WAR art. 3(2) ("After the cessation of active hostilities and as soon as feasible, each High Contracting Party and party to an armed conflict shall mark and clear, remove or destroy explosive remnants of war in affected territories under its control.").

[483] *Overview and Article-by-Article Analysis of CCW Protocol V on Explosive Remnants of War* 3, MESSAGE FROM THE PRESIDENT TRANSMITTING AP III, CCW AMENDED ARTICLE 1, AND CCW PROTOCOL V ON EXPLOSIVE REMNANTS OF WAR 13 ("During the negotiations [about CCW Protocol V on Explosive Remnants of War], some delegations proposed that the responsibility to clear unexploded munitions should be shifted to the party that used the munitions. Such a provision would have been contrary to the long-established customary principle of the rights and responsibilities of a sovereign state over its territory; responsibility should be assigned to the entity in the best position to exercise it.").

[484] CCW PROTOCOL V ON EXPLOSIVE REMNANTS OF WAR art. 3(3) ("After the cessation of active hostilities and as soon as feasible, each High Contracting Party and party to an armed conflict shall take the following measures in affected territories under its control, to reduce the risks posed by explosive remnants of war: (a) survey and assess the threat posed by explosive remnants of war; (b) assess and prioritize needs and practicability in terms of marking

In conducting these activities, international standards, including the International Mine Action Standards, should be taken into account.[485] Areas affected by explosive remnants of war that are assessed to pose a serious humanitarian risk are to be accorded priority status for clearance, removal, or destruction.[486]

Territories under its control include territory over which the State is an Occupying Power. An Occupying Power assumes responsibility for the safety of the civilian population, including responsibilities associated with explosive remnants of war.[487]

6.20.8 Providing Assistance to Facilitate the Removal of Explosive Remnants of War From a Party's Military Operations in Areas Outside Its Control. In cases where a user of explosive ordnance that has become explosive remnants of war does not exercise control of the territory, the user shall, after the cessation of active hostilities, provide where feasible, *inter alia*, technical, financial, material or human resources assistance, bilaterally or through a mutually agreed third party, including, *inter alia*, through the United Nations system or other relevant organizations, to facilitate the marking and clearance, removal, or destruction of such explosive remnants of war.[488]

---

and clearance, removal or destruction; (c) mark and clear, remove or destroy explosive remnants of war; (d) take steps to mobilize resources to carry out these activities.").

[485] CCW Protocol V on Explosive Remnants of War art. 3(4) ("In conducting the above activities High Contracting Parties and parties to an armed conflict shall take into account international standards, including the International Mine Action Standards.").

[486] CCW Protocol V on Explosive Remnants of War art. 3(2) ("Areas affected by explosive remnants of war which are assessed pursuant to paragraph 3 of this Article as posing a serious humanitarian risk shall be accorded priority status for clearance, removal or destruction.").

[487] *Refer to* § 11.5 (Duty of the Occupying Power to Ensure Public Order and Safety).

[488] CCW Protocol V on Explosive Remnants of War art. 3(1) ("Each High Contracting Party and party to an armed conflict shall bear the responsibilities set out in this Article with respect to all explosive remnants of war in territory under its control. In cases where a user of explosive ordnance which has become explosive remnants of war, does not exercise control of the territory, the user shall, after the cessation of active hostilities, provide where feasible, inter alia technical, financial, material or human resources assistance, bilaterally or through a mutually agreed third party, including inter alia through the United Nations system or other relevant organizations, to facilitate the marking and clearance, removal or destruction of such explosive remnants of war.").

VII –Wounded, Sick, Shipwrecked, Dead, and the Medical Services

Chapter Contents

7.1 Introduction

This Chapter addresses the protection of the wounded, sick, shipwrecked, and dead, both on the battlefield and after having fallen into the hands of the enemy during international armed conflict. It also addresses the rights, duties, and liabilities of military medical and religious personnel, and the protection of military medical units, facilities, and transports. Lastly, it addresses the protection of civilians who are wounded, sick, infirm, or maternity cases, and civilian hospitals.

Hospital and safety zones are addressed in Chapter V.[1] Rights and obligations of neutral States with respect to the wounded, sick, and shipwrecked are addressed in Chapter XV.[2] Rules for the protection of medical personel and the wounded, sick, and shipwrecked during non-

---

[1] *Refer to* § 5.14.3 (Establishing Areas Where Civilians or the Wounded and Sick Are Protected).

[2] *Refer to* § 15.3.2.4 (Authorized Humanitarian Assistance Is Not a Violation of Neutrality); § 15.5.2.1 (Exception for Authorized Medical Personnel); § 15.16.2 (Neutral Reception of the Wounded, Sick, and Shipwrecked); § 15.18 (Authorized Passage of Wounded and Sick Combatants Through Neutral Territory).

international armed conflict are addressed in Chapter XVII.[3]

7.1.1 Interpretation and Application of Provisions Relating to Medical Issues in the GWS, GWS-Sea, GPW, and GC. The GWS and GWS-Sea underlie most of the international law rules applicable to the United States for: (1) the protection of the wounded, sick, shipwrecked, and dead; (2) the rights, duties, and liabilities of military medical and religious personnel; and (3) the protection of military medical units, facilities, and transports.

In addition to the rules of the GWS and GWS-Sea, the GPW also has rules on the medical treatment of POWs that may apply to persons who are wounded and sick.[4] The GWS and GWS-Sea, however, have rules for the protection of the wounded, sick, shipwrecked, and dead who are not POWs (*e.g.*, they are on the battlefield and not in the power of the adverse party, they died without being captured).

The GC has provisions relating to the protection of civilians who are wounded, sick, infirm, or maternity cases, and civilian hospitals.[5] The GC also has rules addressing medical care for civilians in occupied territory.[6]

7.1.1.1 *Interpretation of the GWS and GWS-Sea*. As with the GPW and GC, the provisions of the GWS and GWS-Sea should be interpreted in light of the principles that underlie the treatment of the wounded, sick, shipwrecked, dead, and the medical services, and, in particular, in light of the goal of promoting the care of the wounded and sick.[7] The subsequent practice of States in applying the GWS and GWS-Sea could also assist in interpreting their provisions because States' decades of experience in applying the GWS and GWS-Sea may be very helpful in understanding their requirements.[8]

7.1.1.2 *Special Agreements Under the GWS and GWS-Sea*. Under the GWS and GWS-Sea, States may conclude a variety of special agreements during international armed conflict to facilitate the protection of the wounded, sick, shipwrecked, and others protected by the GWS and GWS-Sea. The GWS and GWS-Sea specifically provide for agreements:

- to entrust to an effective and impartial organization the duties of the Protecting Powers;[9]
- to establish an armistice or suspension of fire, or local arrangement to permit the removal,

---

[3] *Refer to* § 17.14 (Protection of the Wounded, Sick, Shipwrecked, and Dead in NIAC); § 17.15 (Protection of Medical and Religious Personnel and Medical Transports in NIAC).

[4] *Refer to* § 9.14 (Medical Attention for Interned POWs).

[5] *Refer to* § 7.16 (Protection of Civilians Who Are Wounded, Sick, Infirm, or Expectant Mothers); § 7.17 (Civilian Hospitals and Their Personnel).

[6] *Refer to* § 11.15 (Public Health and Hygiene).

[7] *Refer to* § 9.1.2 (Interpretation and Application of the GPW); § 10.1.1 (Interpretation and Application of the GC).

[8] *Refer to* § 1.7.4 (Use of Certain Subsequent Practice in Treaty Interpretation).

[9] *Refer to* § 18.15.2.1 (Agreement for an Impartial and Effective Organization to Perform Protecting Power Duties Under the 1949 Geneva Conventions).

exchange, and transport of the wounded, sick, and shipwrecked;[10]

- to establish and recognize hospital zones and localities;[11]
- to establish the corresponding ranks for the medical personnel, including the staff of any authorized voluntary aid societies, in order to help determine the senior retained medical officer in POW camps;[12]
- to put neutral observers on board ships to verify the strict observation of provisions of the GWS-Sea or verify the equipment carried on board is exclusively for the treatment of the wounded and sick, or for the prevention of disease;[13]
- to determine the percentage of personnel to be retained, in proportion to the number of POWs, and the distribution of the retained personnel in POW camps;[14]
- to establish flights or additional markings for medical aircraft;[15]
- to approve chartered medical transport ships;[16]
- between the belligerent parties and a neutral Power on the wounded, sick, and shipwrecked who are disembarked onto the neutral Power's territory;[17]
- to use the most modern methods available to facilitate the identification of hospital ships;[18] and
- on the procedure, or to select an umpire who will decide the procedure, to be followed for an inquiry concerning any alleged violation of the GWS or GWS-Sea.[19]

In addition to these agreements expressly provided for in the GWS and GWS-Sea, Parties to the GWS or GWS-Sea may conclude other special agreements for all matters concerning

---

[10] *Refer to* § 7.4.3.1 (Armistices and Local Arrangements to Permit the Removal, Exchange, or Transport of the Wounded).

[11] *Refer to* § 5.14.3 (Establishing Areas Where Civilians or the Wounded and Sick Are Protected).

[12] *Refer to* § 7.9.5.7 (Senior Medical Officer in the Camp).

[13] *Refer to* § 7.13.1 (Agreement to Place Neutral Observers on Chartered Medical Transports); § 7.12.2.6 (Control and Search of Hospital Ships and Coastal Rescue Craft).

[14] *Refer to* § 7.9.4.3 (Special Agreements on the Percentage of Personnel to Be Retained).

[15] *Refer to* § 7.14 (Military Medical Aircraft).

[16] *Refer to* § 7.13 (Chartered Medical Transport Ships).

[17] *Refer to* § 7.14.6.2 (Detention of the Wounded, Sick, or Shipwrecked).

[18] *Refer to* § 7.12.3.5 (Agreements to Facilitate the Identification of Hospital Ships).

[19] *Refer to* § 18.14.1 (Inquiry Procedure in the 1949 Geneva Conventions).

which they may deem it suitable to make separate provision.[20]

No special agreement shall adversely affect the situation of wounded, sick, and shipwrecked persons, of members of the medical personnel, or of chaplains, as defined by the GWS or the GWS-Sea, nor restrict the rights that the GWS or GWS-Sea confer upon them.[21]

Wounded, sick, and shipwrecked persons, as well as medical personnel and chaplains, shall continue to have the benefit of such agreements as long as the GWS or GWS-Sea is applicable to them, except where express provisions to the contrary are contained in these or in subsequent agreements, or where more favorable measures have been taken with regard to them by one or other of the parties to the conflict.[22]

7.2 Application of the Protections of the GWS and GWS-Sea

7.2.1 Circumstances and Duration of Application of the GWS and GWS-Sea. In general, the GWS-Sea addresses the protection of persons at sea, while the GWS applies to persons on land. In case of hostilities between land and naval forces of parties to the conflict, the provisions of the GWS-Sea shall apply only to forces on board ship.[23]

For the wounded and sick, the GWS and GWS-Sea provide corresponding protections until these persons no longer suffer from that condition. For example, the GWS would no longer cover a detained member of the armed forces who recovers from his or her wounds, although the GPW would continue to apply to that person because he or she is a POW.[24]

---

[20] GWS art. 6 ("In addition to the agreements expressly provided for in Articles 10, 15, 23, 28, 31, 36, 37 and 52, the High Contracting Parties may conclude other special agreements for all matters concerning which they may deem it suitable to make separate provision."); GWS-SEA art. 6 ("In addition to the agreements expressly provided for in Articles 10, 18, 31, 38, 39, 40, 43 and 53, the High Contracting Parties may conclude other special agreements for all matters concerning which they may deem it suitable to make separate provision.").

[21] GWS art. 6 ("No special agreement shall adversely affect the situation of the wounded and sick, of members of the medical personnel or of chaplains, as defined by the present Convention, nor restrict the rights which it confers upon them."); GWS-SEA art. 6 ("No special agreement shall adversely affect the situation of wounded, sick and shipwrecked persons, of members of the medical personnel or of chaplains, as defined by the present Convention, nor restrict the rights which it confers upon them.").

[22] GWS art. 6 ("Wounded and sick, as well as medical personnel and chaplains, shall continue to have the benefit of such agreements as long as the Convention is applicable to them, except where express provisions to the contrary are contained in the aforesaid or in subsequent agreements, or where more favourable measures have been taken with regard to them by one or other of the Parties to the conflict."); GWS-SEA art. 6 ("Wounded, sick and shipwrecked persons, as well as medical personnel and chaplains, shall continue to have the benefit of such agreements as long as the Convention is applicable to them, except where express provisions to the contrary are contained in the aforesaid or in subsequent agreements, or where more favourable measures have been taken with regard to them by one or other of the Parties to the conflict.").

[23] GWS-SEA art. 4 ("In case of hostilities between land and naval forces of Parties to the conflict, the provisions of the present Convention shall apply only to forces on board ship.").

[24] GWS COMMENTARY 65 ("It is clear, however, that the Convention will cease to apply to the wounded and sick from the moment they are cured. This does not result from the actual Article under review, but from the general structure of the Convention. While in enemy hands, the wounded and sick—who are also prisoners of war—enjoy protection under both the First and Third Conventions. Once they have regained their health, only the Third Convention, relative to the treatment of prisoners of war, applies.").

For protected persons who have fallen into the hands of the enemy, the GWS shall apply until their final repatriation.[25] The GWS-Sea does not specify when it ceases to apply, but once persons who are covered by its provisions reach land, the GWS applies. Forces put ashore shall immediately become subject to the provisions of the GWS.[26] If dead persons are landed, the provisions of the GWS shall be applicable.[27] Retained personnel at sea shall be subject, on landing, to the provisions of the GWS.[28]

7.2.2 Non-Renunciation of Rights Secured by the GWS or GWS-Sea. Wounded, sick, and shipwrecked persons, as well as military medical and religious personnel, may in no circumstances renounce in part or in entirety the rights secured to them by the GWS or the GWS-Sea, or by special agreements, if any, referred to in Article 6 of the GWS or the GWS-Sea.[29] A similar provision of the GPW applies to POWs, and a similar provision of the GC applies to protected persons.[30]

This rule is intended to prevent States from evading their obligations by coercing enemy nationals in their power to waive their rights.[31] The prohibition on the non-renunciation of rights is based on a recognition that: (1) persons in the hands of the enemy are in a vulnerable position; (2) it would be difficult to establish whether they had voluntarily renounced their rights; and (3) an absolute prohibition would best serve the interests of the majority.[32]

---

[25] GWS art. 5 ("For the protected persons who have fallen into the hands of the enemy, the present Convention shall apply until their final repatriation."). *Compare* § 9.3.6 (Commencement and Duration of POW Status and Treatment).

[26] GWS-SEA art. 4 ("Forces put ashore shall immediately become subject to the provisions of the Geneva Convention for the Amelioration of the Condition of the Wounded and Sick in Armed Forces in the Field of August 12, 1949.").

[27] GWS-SEA art. 20 ("If dead persons are landed, the provisions of the Geneva Convention for the Amelioration of the Condition of the Wounded and Sick in Armed Forces in the Field of August 12, 1949, shall be applicable.").

[28] GWS-SEA art. 37 ("Retained personnel shall be subject, on landing, to the provisions of the Geneva Convention for the Amelioration of the Condition of the Wounded and Sick in Armed Forces in the Field of August 12, 1949.").

[29] GWS art. 7 ("Wounded and sick, as well as members of the medical personnel and chaplains, may in no circumstances renounce in part or in entirety the rights secured to them by the present Convention, and by the special agreements referred to in the foregoing Article, if such there be."); GWS-SEA art. 7 ("Wounded, sick and shipwrecked persons, as well as members of the medical personnel and chaplains, may in no circumstances renounce in part or in entirety the rights secured to them by the present Convention, and by the special agreements referred to in the foregoing Article, if such there be.").

[30] *Refer to* § 9.3.7 (Non-Renunciation of Rights Secured by the GPW); § 10.3.6 (Non-Renunciation of Rights Secured by the GC).

[31] GWS COMMENTARY 78-79 ("When a State offers to persons detained by it the choice of another status, such a step is usually dictated by its own interest. Experience has proved that such persons may be subjected to pressure in order to influence their choice. The pressure may vary in its intensity and be either more or less apparent; but it nevertheless constitutes a violation of their moral and sometimes even of their physical integrity. The inevitable result of such practices is to expose the protected persons to a two-fold series of what may on occasion be very serious drawbacks, first from the fact that they are under pressure, and secondly, as already indicated, from their partial or total renunciation of the protection accorded to them by the Convention.").

[32] *See* GWS COMMENTARY 79-80 ("But in the end the Diplomatic Conference unanimously adopted the present wording—mainly for the reasons given above, that is to say, the danger of allowing the persons concerned the

This rule does not prohibit States from reassigning their own military medical and religious personnel to non-medical duties or from transferring their own personnel outside of the medical service. Similarly, this rule constitutes an obligation on States and does not directly bind individuals.[33]

7.2.3 Reprisals Prohibited. Reprisals against the wounded, sick, or shipwrecked persons, personnel, buildings, vessels, or equipment protected by the GWS or GWS-Sea are prohibited.[34]

7.3 Respect and Protection of the Wounded, Sick, and Shipwrecked

Members of the armed forces and other persons mentioned in Article 13 of the GWS and the GWS-Sea, who are wounded, sick, or shipwrecked, shall be respected and protected in all circumstances.[35] Such persons are among the categories of persons placed *hors de combat*; making them the object of attack is strictly prohibited.[36]

7.3.1 Definitions of Wounded, Sick, and Shipwrecked.

7.3.1.1 *Wounded or Sick*. The meanings of "wounded" and "sick" are a matter of common sense and good faith.[37] They include:

---

choice of renouncing their rights, and the difficulty, and even impossibility, of proving the existence of duress or pressure. Among the reasons given in favour of the present Article 7, two points call for notice. The Conference did not overlook the fact that the absolute character of the rule drafted might entail for some persons what one delegate termed 'unfortunate' results. It adopted the rule, because it seemed to safeguard the interests of the majority. If provision were made for exceptions in the case of certain individuals, would that not at once open a breach which others, in much greater numbers, would, perhaps, have cause to regret?").

[33] GWS COMMENTARY 85 ("One last question remains to be considered. Rights entail obligations. With the focus on the individual under Article 7, can the rules of the Conventions, or certain of them, be considered as obligations which are directly incumbent on the persons protected? There can be no doubt that certain stipulations, such as the respect due to the wounded and sick, are also incumbent on persons who can claim protection under the Convention. For example, a member of the medical personnel who, profiting by his duties, plundered the wounded or dead on the battlefield, would be liable to the punishment which the law of his country or of the enemy stipulates in of the obligation by which every contracting State is bound to repress such breaches. This question arises in connection with Article 7, which appears to take the form of an obligation on the persons protected, stating, as it does, that the latter 'may in no circumstances renounce …'. It was for this reason that, in their 'Remarks and Proposals' submitted to the Diplomatic Conference, the International Committee of the Red Cross pointed out that the general effect of the Conventions was to impose obligations on the States parties to the Conventions rather than on individuals, and proposed to draft Article 7 in that sense.").

[34] *Refer to* § 18.18.3.2 (Reprisals Prohibited by the 1949 Geneva Conventions).

[35] GWS art. 12 ("Members of the armed forces and other persons mentioned in the following Article, who are wounded or sick, shall be respected and protected in all circumstances."); GWS-SEA art. 12 ("Members of the armed forces and other persons mentioned in the following Article, who are at sea and who are wounded, sick or shipwrecked, shall be respected and protected in all circumstances, it being understood that the term 'shipwreck' means shipwreck from any cause and includes forced landings at sea by or from aircraft.").

[36] *Refer to* § 5.9 (Persons Placed *Hors de Combat*).

[37] *See also* GWS COMMENTARY 136 ("No attempt has ever been made in the Geneva Convention to define what is meant by a 'wounded or sick' combatant; nor has there ever been any definition of the degree of severity of a wound or a sickness entitling the wounded or sick combatant to respect. That is as well; for any definition would necessarily be restrictive in character, and would thereby open the door to every kind of misinterpretation and abuse.

- combatants who have been rendered unconscious or otherwise have been incapacitated because of their wounds or sickness;[38] and
- combatants who have surrendered as a consequence of their health.[39]

To merit respect and protection as "wounded" or "sick" under the law of war, combatants must abstain from hostile acts or attempts to evade capture.[40]

7.3.1.2 *Shipwrecked*. For the purpose of applying the protections afforded by the GWS-Sea, the term "shipwreck" means shipwreck from any cause and includes forced landings at sea by or from aircraft.[41]

The shipwrecked may be understood to include those in distress at sea or stranded on the coast who are also helpless.[42] To be considered "shipwrecked," persons must be in need of assistance and care, and they must refrain from any hostile act.[43] For example, shipwrecked persons do not include combatant personnel engaged in amphibious, underwater, or airborne attacks who are proceeding ashore.[44]

7.3.2 Persons Entitled to Protection as Wounded, Sick, or Shipwrecked Under the GWS and GWS-Sea. The GWS and GWS-Sea apply to the wounded, sick, and shipwrecked belonging

---

The meaning of the words 'wounded and sick' is a matter of common sense and good faith. They cover combatants who have fallen by reason of a wound or sickness of any kind, or who have ceased to fight and laid down their arms as a consequence of what they themselves think about their health. It is the fact of falling or laying down of arms which constitutes the claim to protection. It is only the soldier who is himself seeking to kill who may be killed. The abandonment of all aggressiveness should put an end to aggression.").

[38] *Refer to* § 5.9.4 (Persons Rendered Unconscious or Otherwise Incapacitated by Wounds, Sickness, or Shipwreck).

[39] *Refer to* § 5.9.3 (Persons Who Have Surrendered).

[40] *Refer to* § 5.9 (Persons Placed *Hors de Combat*).

[41] GWS-SEA art. 12 ("Members of the armed forces and other persons mentioned in the following Article, who are at sea and who are wounded, sick or shipwrecked, shall be respected and protected in all circumstances, it being understood that the term 'shipwreck' means shipwreck from any cause and includes forced landings at sea by or from aircraft.").

[42] GWS-SEA COMMENTARY 89 ("Article 11 of the Brussels Convention of 1910 defines a shipwrecked person as being a person found at sea in danger of perishing. That definition, however, does not introduce the concept of need, and does not cover a shipwrecked person who manages to reach the coast or an island, or one who is not really in danger of losing his life. For our part, we prefer the following definition: 'a person in distress at sea or stranded on the coast'.").

[43] GWS-SEA COMMENTARY 89 ("Another factor is involved here: the shipwrecked persons must be in need of assistance and care, and they must naturally refrain from any hostile act.").

[44] 2007 NWP 1-14M ¶8.2.3.2 ("Shipwrecked persons do not include combatant personnel engaged in amphibious, underwater, or airborne attacks who are proceeding ashore, unless they are clearly in distress and require assistance. In the latter case they may qualify as shipwrecked persons only if they cease all active combat activity and the enemy has an opportunity to recognize their condition of distress."). *Compare* § 5.9.5.2 (Persons Deploying Into Combat by Parachute).

to the following categories:[45]

- members of the armed forces of a party to the conflict, as well as members of militias or volunteer corps forming part of such armed forces;[46]
- members of other militias and members of other volunteer corps meeting certain conditions;[47]
- members of regular armed forces who profess allegiance to a Government or an authority not recognized by the Detaining Power;[48]
- persons who are authorized to accompany the armed forces;[49]
- members of the crews of the merchant marine and the crews of civil aircraft of the parties to the conflict;[50] and
- participants in a *levée en masse*.[51]

These categories are the same categories of persons to whom the GPW affords POW status if they fall into the hands of the enemy during international armed conflict.[52] Thus, the

---

[45] GWS art. 13 ("The present Convention shall apply to the wounded and sick belonging to the following categories: (1) Members of the armed forces of a Party to the conflict, as well as members of militias or volunteer corps forming part of such armed forces. (2) Members of other militias and members of other volunteer corps, including those of organized resistance movements, belonging to a Party to the conflict and operating in or outside their own territory, even if this territory is occupied, provided that such militias or volunteer corps, including such organized resistance movements, fulfil the following conditions: a. That of being commanded by a person responsible for his subordinates; b. That of having a fixed distinctive sign recognizable at a distance; c. That of carrying arms openly; d. That of conducting their operations in accordance with the laws and customs of war. (3) Members of regular armed forces who profess allegiance to a Government or an authority not recognized by the Detaining Power. (4) Persons who accompany the armed forces without actually being members thereof, such as civil members of military aircraft crews, war correspondents, supply contractors, members of labour units or of services responsible for the welfare of the armed forces, provided that they have received authorization from the armed forces which they accompany. (5) Members of crews, including masters, pilots and apprentices of the merchant marine and the crews of civil aircraft of the Parties to the conflict, who do not benefit by more favourable treatment under any other provisions in international law. (6) Inhabitants of a non-occupied territory who, on the approach of the enemy, spontaneously take up arms to resist the invading forces, without having had time to form themselves into regular armed units, provided they carry arms openly and respect the laws and customs of war."); GWS-SEA art. 13 ("The present Convention shall apply to the wounded, sick and shipwrecked at sea belonging to the following categories: [identical to those covered in GWS].").

[46] *Refer to* § 4.5 (Armed Forces of a State).

[47] *Refer to* § 4.6 (Other Militia and Volunteer Corps).

[48] *Refer to* § 4.5.3 (Regular Armed Forces Who Profess Allegiance to a Government or an Authority Not Recognized by the Detaining Power).

[49] *Refer to* § 4.15 (Persons Authorized to Accompany the Armed Forces).

[50] *Refer to* § 4.16 (Crews of Merchant Marine Vessels or Civil Aircraft).

[51] *Refer to* § 4.7 (*Levée en Masse*).

[52] *Refer to* § 9.3.2 (Persons Entitled to POW Status).

GWS and GWS-Sea recognize that such persons who fall into enemy hands during international armed conflict shall be POWs, and the provisions of international law concerning POWs (such as the GPW) shall also apply to them.[53]

The categories of persons entitled to POW status under the GPW and protection as wounded, sick, and shipwrecked under the GWS and GWS-Sea were drafted to be the same, but the GWS or GWS-Sea do not refer specifically to Article 4 of the GPW so that the GWS and GWS-Sea could operate as stand-alone legal instruments if a State ratified either the GWS or the GWS-Sea, but not the GPW.[54]

Civilians who are wounded and sick are protected under the GC.[55]

7.3.3 Meaning of "Respect and Protection" of the Wounded, Sick, and Shipwrecked. The wounded, sick, and shipwrecked must be respected and protected at all times. This means that they should not be knowingly attacked, fired upon, or unnecessarily interfered with.[56]

7.3.3.1 *Incidental Harm Not Prohibited*. The respect and protection due to the wounded, sick, and shipwrecked do not prohibit incidental damage or casualties due to their proximity to military objectives or to a justifiable mistake. Combatants who are wounded, sick, or shipwrecked on the battlefield are deemed to have accepted the risk of death or further injury due to their proximity to military operations.[57] Although the presence of the wounded, sick, or shipwrecked on the battlefield does not serve to exempt military objectives from attack due to the risk that such personnel would be incidentally harmed, feasible precautions must be taken to

---

[53] GWS art. 14 ("Subject to the provisions of Article 12, the wounded and sick of a belligerent who fall into enemy hands shall be prisoners of war, and the provisions of international law concerning prisoners of war shall apply to them."); GWS-SEA art. 16 ("Subject to the provisions of Article 12, the wounded, sick and shipwrecked of a belligerent who fall into enemy hands shall be prisoners of war, and the provisions of international law concerning prisoners of war shall apply to them.").

[54] GWS COMMENTARY 144-45 ("When the Diplomatic Conference set out to define the categories of persons, to whom, on their being wounded or falling sick, the First Geneva Convention was to apply, it noted that the categories in question were precisely those which were entitled, on falling into the enemy's hands, to be treated as prisoners of war. The Conference was thus logically led to refer to the contents of Article 4 of the Third Convention. There were two ways of doing this in practice. It was possible merely to refer to the Article in question, or alternatively to repeat its substance in the First Convention. The second of these solutions was the one adopted, in accordance with the general principle, to which the Conference adhered wherever possible, of endeavouring to make each of the four Geneva Conventions an independent diplomatic instrument. The course thus adopted also covered the possible case of a Power being a party to the First Convention without having ratified the Third."). *Refer to* § 19.16.1 (Common Provisions in the 1949 Geneva Conventions).

[55] *Refer to* § 7.16 (Protection of Civilians Who Are Wounded, Sick, Infirm, or Expectant Mothers).

[56] *Cf.* APPENDIX TO 1985 CJCS MEMO ON AP I 5-6 ("Articles 10, 12, and 15 [of AP I] then extend the provisions of the First and Second Geneva Conventions of 1949 to civilian sick, wounded, and shipwrecked and to civilian medical personnel and units and associated civilian religious personnel, all of whom would be 'respected and protected' by the parties to the conflict, the sick and wounded to receive required care 'to the fullest extent practicable.' As used in the Protocol [I to the 1949 Geneva Conventions], the term 'respected and protected' means that an activity should not be knowingly attacked, fired upon, or unnecessarily interfered with; it does not cover accidental damage or casualties due to proximity to military objectives or to a justifiable mistake in identifying the activity."). *Compare* § 7.8.2 (Meaning of "Respect and Protection" of Medical and Religious Personnel).

[57] *Compare* § 7.12.2.5 (Acceptance of the Risk From Proximity to Combat Operations).

reduce the risk of harm to the wounded, sick, or shipwrecked.[58]

7.3.3.2 *Search and Other Security Measures Not Prohibited*. The wounded, sick, and shipwrecked are not immune from search or other necessary security measures by the enemy.[59] Searches of the wounded, sick, and shipwrecked, and other security measures applied to them, should be consistent with those applicable to other POWs.[60]

7.3.3.3 *Capture of Wounded, Sick, and Shipwrecked Not Prohibited*. The respect and protection afforded the wounded, sick, and shipwrecked do not immunize them from detention.[61] When they fall into enemy hands, they are POWs.[62]

It is not prohibited to capture the wounded and sick, even if they are in the care of military medical units or facilities, or civilian hospitals.[63] However, upon taking custody, the Detaining Power is required to ensure that they continue to receive the necessary medical care.[64]

All warships of a belligerent party shall have the right to demand that the wounded, sick, or shipwrecked on board military hospital ships, and hospital ships belonging to relief societies or to private individuals, as well as merchant vessels, yachts, and other craft shall be surrendered, whatever their nationality, provided that the wounded and sick are in a fit state to be moved and that the warship can provide adequate facilities for necessary medical treatment.[65]

In cases of capture at sea, the captor may decide, according to circumstances, whether it is expedient to hold the wounded, sick, or shipwrecked, or to convey them to a port in the captor's own country, to a neutral port, or even to a port in enemy territory. In the last case,

---

[58] *Refer to* § 5.10.1.2 (Proportionality in Conducting Attacks and Protected Military Personnel and Facilities).

[59] *Refer to* § 7.10.1.2 (Search Not Prohibited).

[60] *Refer to* § 9.6 (Security Measures With Respect to POWs).

[61] *Refer to* § 7.9 (Captured Medical and Religious Personnel).

[62] *Refer to* § 7.3.2 (Persons Entitled to Protection as Wounded, Sick, or Shipwrecked Under the GWS and GWS-Sea).

[63] *For example*, J.C. Massop, *Hospital Ships in the Second World War*, 24 BRITISH YEAR BOOK OF INTERNATIONAL LAW 398, 405 (1947) ("In 1944 and 1945 the Germans decided to pass the hospital ships Tübingen and Gradisca through the Allied patrol lines in the Adriatic to embark sick and wounded in Salonica. In accordance with the requirements of the Convention the ships were allowed to pass on the outward voyage, but they were diverted to Allied ports on the homeward trip and some 4,000 prisoners were made: a high percentage were only slightly wounded and the great majority were considered likely to be fit for active service within twelve months. This action brought forth no protest from the German Government, who considered it justified by the terms of the Convention.").

[64] *Refer to* § 7.5 (Humane Treatment and Care of Enemy Military Wounded, Sick, and Shipwrecked in the Power of a Party to the Conflict).

[65] GWS-SEA art. 14 ("All warships of a belligerent Party shall have the right to demand that the wounded, sick or shipwrecked on board military hospital ships, and hospital ships belonging to relief societies or to private individuals, as well as merchant vessels, yachts and other craft shall be surrendered, whatever their nationality, provided that the wounded and sick are in a fit state to be moved and that the warship can provide adequate facilities for necessary medical treatment.").

POWs thus returned to their home country may not serve for the duration of the war.[66]

7.3.3.4 *Prohibition Against Use in Booby-Traps*. Booby trapping the wounded or sick is expressly prohibited.[67]

7.4 SEARCH, COLLECTION, AND AFFIRMATIVE PROTECTION OF THE WOUNDED, SICK, SHIPWRECKED, AND DEAD

At all times, and particularly after an engagement, parties to the conflict shall, without delay, take all possible measures to search for and collect the wounded and sick on land, to protect them against pillage and ill-treatment, to ensure their adequate care, and to search for the dead and prevent their being despoiled.[68]

The GC provides for the obligation to search for, collect, protect, and care for, civilians who are wounded, sick, shipwrecked, and dead.[69]

7.4.1 GWS-Sea Obligation Regarding the Search, Collection, and Affirmative Protection of the Wounded, Sick, Shipwrecked, and Dead. After each engagement, parties to the conflict shall, without delay, take all possible measures to search for and collect the wounded, sick, and shipwrecked at sea, to protect them against pillage and ill-treatment, to ensure their adequate care, and to search for the dead and prevent their being despoiled.[70]

The obligation in the GWS-Sea to search for, and collect, certain persons is written differently than the comparable obligation in the GWS. Instead of a general obligation to take measures "at all times," in Article 15 of the GWS, in Article 18 of the GWS-Sea, the obligation to search for and collect the wounded, sick, and shipwrecked applies only "after each engagement."

7.4.2 Affirmative Measures to Protect Against Pillage and Ill-Treatment. If practicable, affirmative measures (including, in some cases, the use of force) must be taken to protect the wounded, sick, and shipwrecked, from pillage or ill-treatment by any person, whether military or

---

[66] GWS-SEA art. 16 ("The captor may decide, according to circumstances, whether it is expedient to hold them, or to convey them to a port in the captor's own country, to a neutral port or even to a port in enemy territory. In the last case, prisoners of war thus returned to their home country may not serve for the duration of the war.").

[67] *Refer to* § 6.12.4.9 (Certain Types of Prohibited Booby-Traps and Other Devices).

[68] GWS art. 15 ("At all times, and particularly after an engagement, Parties to the conflict shall, without delay, take all possible measures to search for and collect the wounded and sick, to protect them against pillage and ill-treatment, to ensure their adequate care, and to search for the dead and prevent their being despoiled.").

[69] *Refer to* § 7.16.1 (Obligation to Facilitate Efforts to Search for Civilians Who Are Wounded, Killed, Shipwrecked, or Exposed to Grave Danger).

[70] GWS-SEA art. 18 ("After each engagement, Parties to the conflict shall, without delay, take all possible measures to search for and collect the shipwrecked, wounded and sick, to protect them against pillage and ill-treatment, to ensure their adequate care, and to search for the dead and prevent their being despoiled.").

civilian, seeking to harm them.[71]

7.4.3 Range of Measures to Search for, Collect, and Protect the Wounded, Sick, and Shipwrecked. A range of measures may be taken to fulfill the obligation to search for, collect, and protect the wounded, sick, and shipwrecked. Military forces may directly engage in these activities.[72]

In addition to searching for, collecting, and protecting the wounded, sick, and shipwrecked directly, commanders may take other measures to fulfill this obligation. For example, commanders may request the help of civilian volunteers.[73] As another example, if a warship is unable to collect the shipwrecked after an engagement, it might be able to alert a hospital ship in the vicinity or provide the shipwrecked with a lifeboat.[74]

7.4.3.1 *Armistices and Local Arrangements to Permit the Removal, Exchange, or Transport of the Wounded*. Whenever circumstances permit, an armistice or a suspension of fire shall be arranged, or local arrangements made, to permit the removal, exchange, and transport of the wounded left on the battlefield.[75] Such arrangements may take the form of or include a protected or neutral zone.[76]

Likewise, local arrangements may be concluded between parties to the conflict for the removal or exchange of wounded and sick by land or sea from a besieged or encircled area, or for the passage of medical and religious personnel and equipment on their way to that area.[77] For example, parties to a conflict may agree to a temporary cease-fire to permit evacuation of the

---

[71] GWS COMMENTARY 152 ("In other words, the wounded and the dead must be guarded and, if necessary, defended against all parties, whether military or civilian, who may seek to lay hands on them. Combatants, like medical personnel, are called upon to prevent this, going, if necessary, to the length of using their arms for the purpose.").

[72] *For example*, George W. Bush, *Remarks to the Community at Camp Lejeune, North Carolina*, Apr. 3, 2003, 2003-I PUBLIC PAPERS OF THE PRESIDENTS 404, 406 ("American forces and our allies are treating innocent civilians with kindness and showing proper respect to soldiers who surrender. Many Americans have seen the picture of Marine Lance Corporal Marcco Ware carrying a wounded Iraqi soldier on his shoulders to safety for medical treatment.").

[73] *Refer to* § 7.4.5.1 (Requests for Civilian Volunteers to Collect and Care for the Wounded, Sick, and Shipwrecked).

[74] GWS-SEA COMMENTARY 131 ("The 'possible measures' which may be taken by the belligerents to collect the shipwrecked are, on the other hand, many and varied and in nearly all cases they should enable the purpose of the present paragraph to be achieved. Thus, a warship which was unable to collect the victims of an engagement should, for instance, alert a hospital ship if there is one in the vicinity, or even a ship of any kind better equipped than itself; otherwise, it should resort to the possibility provided in Article 21, and appeal to neutral vessels. It can also alert the nearest coastal authorities, or request assistance from the air forces. Generally speaking, if a warship is forced to leave shipwrecked persons to their fate, it will endeavour to provide them with the means to enable them to await rescue or reach the coast: life-boats, food, water, a compass, charts, etc.").

[75] GWS art. 15 ("Whenever circumstances permit, an armistice or a suspension of fire shall be arranged, or local arrangements made, to permit the removal, exchange and transport of the wounded left on the battlefield.").

[76] *Refer to* § 5.14.3 (Establishing Areas Where Civilians or the Wounded and Sick Are Protected).

[77] *Refer to* § 5.19.2 (Removal and Passage of Certain Personnel – Vulnerable Civilians, Diplomatic and Consular Personnel, the Wounded and Sick, and Medical Personnel).

wounded from the fighting area.[78]

7.4.4 Practical Limitations on the Obligation to Search for, Collect, and Take Measures to Protect the Wounded, Sick, and Shipwrecked. The obligations to search for, collect, and take affirmative steps to protect the wounded, sick, and shipwrecked are subject to practical limitations.

Military commanders are to judge what is possible, and to what extent they can commit their personnel to these duties.[79] In some cases, commanders might designate specific units or personnel to engage in such missions.

7.4.4.1 *Risk of Harm*. For example, personnel performing rescue and recovery missions need not place their lives at undue risk in an effort to search for, collect, or protect the wounded, sick, shipwrecked, or dead (*e.g.*, recovery of a body from a minefield, or entry into a disabled enemy armored vehicle that might contain unexploded ordnance or other hazards). Similarly, a commander of a naval ship need not increase the risk to his or her vessel from threats (*e.g.*, by slowing his or her transit, or by placing his or her ship dead in the water) in order to recover shipwrecked enemy military personnel from a sunken vessel or crashed aircraft.[80]

7.4.4.2 *Military Necessity*. Similarly, the requirements of ongoing military operations may render rescue efforts impractical. For example, during a fast-tempo operation (offensive or defensive), it might not be possible to devote resources to the search and collection of the wounded, sick, and shipwrecked. In other cases, the rescue of enemy personnel may exceed the abilities of the force and its medical personnel. For example, a small patrol operating behind enemy lines or a submarine may not have the capability to receive and care for large numbers of injured personnel.[81]

---

[78] *For example*, MARTIN MIDDLEBROOK, ARNHEM 1944: THE AIRBORNE BATTLE, 17-26 SEPTEMBER 383 (1994) ("After consulting Major-General Urquhart, Colonel Warrack decided to ask the Germans if they would allow the wounded to be evacuated from the fighting area. He was driven with the Dutch officer, Commander Woters, who would act as interpreter, and eventually met General Bittrich, who agreed to a truce and an evacuation. ... The evacuation commenced that afternoon, but only in the Main Dressing Stations. ... All went well, much credit being given to the Germans for their humane treatment of the wounded.").

[79] GWS COMMENTARY 151 ("But there are times when military operations will make the obligation to search for the fallen impracticable. There will be cases which exceed the limits of what the medical personnel can be expected to do, however great their courage and devotion. It was not possible, therefore, to make the obligation absolute. It was accordingly provided that 'Parties to the conflict shall, without delay, take all possible measures...' The obligation to act without delay is strict; but the action to be taken is limited to what is possible, and it is left to the military command to judge what is possible, and to decide to what extent it can commit its medical personnel.") (ellipsis in original).

[80] *For example*, W.T. MALLISON, JR., STUDIES IN THE LAW OF NAVAL WARFARE: SUBMARINES IN GENERAL AND LIMITED WARS 136 (1968) ("It should be mentioned also that there were apparently numerous instances when it was not feasible for surface warships to make rescue attempts even though they had adequate passenger facilities. The British heavy cruiser *Devonshire*, operating in the South Atlantic, sank the German raider *Atlantis* on November 22, 1941 and the German supply ship *Python* on November 30, 1941. In neither case was rescue attempted since it was thought that U-boats might be in the vicinity.").

[81] *See also* GWS-SEA COMMENTARY 131 ("Of course, one cannot always require certain fighting ships, such as fast torpedo-boats and submarines, to collect in all circumstances the crews of ships which they have sunk, for they will

7.4.5 Collection and Care of the Wounded, Sick, and Shipwrecked by Civilians.

7.4.5.1 *Requests for Civilian Volunteers to Collect and Care for the Wounded, Sick, and Shipwrecked*. The military authorities may appeal to the charity of the inhabitants voluntarily to collect and care for, under their direction, the wounded, sick, and shipwrecked, granting persons who have responded to this appeal the necessary protection and facilities.[82] Should the adverse party take or retake control of the area, that party shall likewise grant these persons the same protection and the same facilities.[83]

7.4.5.2 *Spontaneous Collection and Care for the Wounded, Sick, and Shipwrecked by Inhabitants and Relief Societies*. The military authorities shall permit the inhabitants and relief societies, even in invaded or occupied areas, spontaneously to collect and care for wounded or sick of whatever nationality.[84] The civilian population shall respect these wounded and sick, and in particular abstain from offering them violence.[85]

7.4.5.3 *Prohibition on Molestation or Conviction for Nursing the Wounded or Sick*. No one shall ever be molested or convicted for having nursed the wounded or sick.[86] For example, persons should not be prosecuted for offenses of aiding the enemy because they tended to wounded members of enemy military forces.

7.4.6 Collection and Care of the Wounded, Sick, and Shipwrecked by Neutral Vessels. The parties to the conflict may appeal to the charity of commanders of neutral merchant vessels, yachts, or other craft, to take on board and care for wounded, sick, or shipwrecked persons, and to collect the dead.[87]

Vessels of any kind responding to this appeal, and those having of their own accord collected wounded, sick, or shipwrecked persons, shall enjoy special protection and facilities to

---

often have inadequate equipment and insufficient accommodation. Submarines stay at sea for a long time and sometimes they neither wish nor are able to put in at a port where they could land the persons whom they have collected. Generally speaking, one cannot lay down an absolute rule that the commander of a warship must engage in rescue operations if, by doing so, he would expose his vessel to attack."). *Refer to* § 13.7.2 (Different Application of Law of War Rules in the Context of Submarine Warfare).

[82] GWS art. 18 ("The military authorities may appeal to the charity of the inhabitants voluntarily to collect and care for, under their direction, the wounded and sick, granting persons who have responded to this appeal the necessary protection and facilities.").

[83] GWS art. 18 ("Should the adverse Party take or retake control of the area, he shall likewise grant these persons the same protection and the same facilities.").

[84] GWS art. 18 ("The military authorities shall permit the inhabitants and relief societies, even in invaded or occupied areas, spontaneously to collect and care for wounded or sick of whatever nationality.").

[85] GWS art. 18 ("The civilian population shall respect these wounded and sick, and in particular abstain from offering them violence.").

[86] GWS art. 18 ("No one shall ever be molested or convicted for having nursed the wounded or sick.").

[87] GWS-SEA art. 21 ("The Parties to the conflict may appeal to the charity of commanders of neutral merchant vessels, yachts or other craft, to take on board and care for wounded, sick or shipwrecked persons, and to collect the dead.").

carry out such assistance.[88]

They may, in no case, be captured on account of any such transport; but, in the absence of any promise to the contrary, they shall remain liable to capture for any violations of neutrality they may have committed.[89]

7.5 Humane Treatment and Care of Enemy Military Wounded, Sick, and Shipwrecked in the Power of a Party to the Conflict

The wounded, sick, and shipwrecked who are protected by the GWS and GWS-Sea shall be treated humanely and cared for by the party to the conflict in whose power they may be, without any adverse distinction founded on sex, race, nationality, religion, political opinions, or any other similar criteria.[90] Any attempts upon their lives, or violence to their persons, shall be strictly prohibited; in particular, they shall not be murdered or exterminated or subjected to torture or to biological experiments; they shall not willfully be left without medical assistance and care, nor shall conditions exposing them to contagion or infection be created.[91]

7.5.1 Humane Treatment of the Wounded, Sick, and Shipwrecked Without Adverse Distinction. The wounded, sick, and shipwrecked who are protected by the GWS or GWS-Sea who are in the power of a party to the conflict are also POWs. Thus, their humane treatment is required by the GPW as well.[92]

For example, the prohibition on subjecting the wounded, sick, or shipwrecked to biological experiments is also reflected in the GPW.[93] Similarly, the wounded, sick, and shipwrecked who are women shall be treated with all consideration due to their sex.[94]

7.5.2 Medical Care of the Wounded and Sick. Below are general rules for the medical care of the wounded and sick, including both those on the battlefield and those who are POWs.

---

[88] GWS-SEA art. 21 ("Vessels of any kind responding to this appeal, and those having of their own accord collected wounded, sick or shipwrecked persons, shall enjoy special protection and facilities to carry out such assistance.").

[89] GWS-SEA art. 21 ("They may, in no case, be captured on account of any such transport; but, in the absence of any promise to the contrary, they shall remain liable to capture for any violations of neutrality they may have committed.").

[90] GWS art. 12 ("They shall be treated humanely and cared for by the Party to the conflict in whose power they may be, without any adverse distinction founded on sex, race, nationality, religion, political opinions, or any other similar criteria."); GWS-SEA art. 12 ("Such persons shall be treated humanely and cared for by the Parties to the conflict in whose power they may be, without any adverse distinction founded on sex, race, nationality, religion, political opinions, or any other similar criteria.").

[91] GWS art. 12 ("Any attempts upon their lives, or violence to their persons, shall be strictly prohibited; in particular, they shall not be murdered or exterminated, subjected to torture or to biological experiments; they shall not wilfully be left without medical assistance and care, nor shall conditions exposing them to contagion or infection be created."); GWS-SEA art. 12 (same).

[92] *Refer to* § 9.5 (Humane Treatment and Basic Protections for POWs).

[93] *Refer to* § 9.5.2.4 (No Physical Mutilation or Medical, Scientific, or Biological Experiments).

[94] GWS art. 12 ("Women shall be treated with all consideration due to their sex."); GWS-SEA art. 12 (same). *Refer to* § 9.5.6 (Due Regard for Women POWs).

POWs shall be provided necessary medical attention during evacuation, although they may be temporarily kept back in a danger zone if they would face greater risks by being evacuated than by remaining where they are.[95] Additional rules provide for the medical attention and care for POWs who have been interned in POW camps.[96]

7.5.2.1 *Prohibitions Against Willful Medical Neglect or Deliberate Endangerment*. The wounded, sick, and shipwrecked shall not willfully be left without medical assistance and care. In addition, conditions exposing them to contagion or infection shall not be willfully created.

7.5.2.2 *Affirmative Obligation to Provide Adequate Care*. In addition to the prohibitions against willful neglect or deliberate endangerment, the parties to a conflict shall take all possible measures to ensure the adequate care of the wounded, sick, and shipwrecked.[97] The obligation to care for enemy combatants who are wounded and sick is a longstanding law of war obligation.[98]

The obligation to provide medical care incorporates practical considerations; whether resources may be committed to medical care may depend on military necessity, such as the requirements of the mission or the immediate tactical situation.[99]

7.5.2.3 *Priority of Treatment Based on Medical Urgency*. Only urgent medical reasons will authorize priority in the order of treatment to be administered.[100]

For example, in addressing an influx of wounded that include both friends and enemies, doctors should attend to those patients for whom delay might be fatal or at any rate prejudicial, proceeding afterwards to those whose condition is not such as to necessitate immediate attention.[101]

---

[95] *Refer to* § 9.9.2 (Conditions of Evacuation); § 9.9.1 (Delay in Evacuation for Medical Reasons).

[96] *Refer to* § 9.14 (Medical Attention for Interned POWs).

[97] *Refer to* § 7.4 (Search, Collection, and Affirmative Protection of the Wounded, Sick, Shipwrecked, and Dead).

[98] *See, e.g.*, LIEBER CODE art. 79 ("Every captured wounded enemy shall be medically treated, according to the ability of the medical staff."); Convention for the Amelioration of the Wounded in Armies in the Field, art. 6, Aug. 22, 1864, 22 STAT. 940, 944 ("Wounded or sick soldiers shall be entertained and taken care of, to whatever nation they may belong.").

[99] *For example*, OFFICE OF THE SURGEON GENERAL OF THE ARMY, EMERGENCY WAR SURGERY 30 (2014) ("The decision to withhold care from a casualty who in another less overwhelming situation might be salvaged is difficult for any physician, nurse, or medic. Decisions of this nature are unusual, even in mass casualty situations. Nonetheless, the overarching goal of providing the greatest good to the greatest number must guide these difficult decisions. Commitment of resources should be decided first based on the mission and immediate tactical situation and then by medical necessity, irrespective of a casualty's national or combatant status.").

[100] GWS art. 12 ("Only urgent medical reasons will authorize priority in the order of treatment to be administered."); GWS-SEA art. 12 (same).

[101] GWS COMMENTARY 140 ("Let us suppose that the Medical Service in some place is overwhelmed by an influx of wounded, both friends and enemies. The doctors, in such a case, will attend first to those patients for whom delay might be fatal or at any rate prejudicial, proceeding afterwards to those whose condition is not such as to necessitate immediate attention.").

7.5.2.4 *Compulsory Medical Treatment*. The wounded, sick, and shipwrecked, and other POWs, may be ordered to receive medical treatment or care that is warranted by their medical condition.

Because POWs are subject to the laws, regulations, and orders in force in the armed forces of the Detaining Power, POWs may be ordered to receive medical treatment just as Detaining Power military personnel may be ordered to do so.[102] However, the wounded, sick, and shipwrecked, and other POWs, may not be subjected to medical or biological experiments, even if Detaining Power military personnel could be ordered to be subjected to such procedures.[103]

The Detaining Power's authority to order POWs to receive medical treatment also derives from the Detaining Power's duty to ensure the well-being of POWs.[104] For example, the Detaining Power's duty to take all sanitary measures necessary to prevent epidemics in the POW camp may require the Detaining Power to order POWs to receive certain measures, such as vaccinations.[105]

AP I, Article 11, paragraph 5 provides for a "right to refuse any surgical operation."[106] However, this rule could operate in an inhumane manner in some circumstances, and the United States has not accepted it.[107]

7.5.2.5 *Medical Attention Free of Charge*. The Power detaining POWs shall be bound to provide free of charge for the medical attention required by POWs' state of health.[108]

7.5.3 Abandonment of the Wounded or Sick on the Battlefield. In an extreme case, military forces in an international armed conflict may be compelled to abandon wounded or sick

---

[102] *Refer to* § 9.26.1 (POWs Subject to the Laws, Regulations, and Orders in Force in the Armed Forces of the Detaining Power).

[103] *Refer to* § 9.5.2.4 (No Physical Mutilation or Medical, Scientific, or Biological Experiments).

[104] *For example*, 1958 UK MANUAL ¶154 note 3 ("Again, if prisoners in British military custody resort to a hunger strike, it would seem that they may under medical direction be forcibly fed if their lives are in danger. This is permissible by English law and may in certain cases be a duty. If British military prisoners are allowed to die from the effects of a hunger strike, the camp commandant and medical officer are liable to be prosecuted for manslaughter, *Leigh v. Gladstone and Others*, 26 T.L.R. 139.").

[105] *Refer to* § 9.11.5.1 (Necessary Sanitary Measures).

[106] AP I art. 11(5) ("The persons described in paragraph 1 have the right to refuse any surgical operation. In case of refusal, medical personnel shall endeavour to obtain a written statement to that effect, signed or acknowledged by the patient.").

[107] APPENDIX TO 1985 CJCS MEMO ON AP I 8 ("The provision [in AP I art. 11] specifying an absolute right to refuse any surgery could, however, operate in an inhumane manner in some circumstances. A detainee might, for example, refuse surgery necessary to save his own life in order to make a political point or because of ignorance or mental incompetence.").

[108] GPW art. 15 ("The Power detaining prisoners of war shall be bound to provide free of charge for their maintenance and for the medical attention required by their state of health.").

to the enemy.[109] The party to the conflict that is compelled to abandon wounded or sick to the enemy shall, as far as military considerations permit, leave with them a part of its medical personnel and material to assist in their care.[110]

Unlike the obligations to provide humane treatment for the wounded and sick who are in custody, the obligation to provide medical personnel and material for the care of abandoned wounded or sick is a strong recommendation, rather than an absolute requirement.[111]

The party that encounters and captures the wounded and sick who have been abandoned by another party to the conflict is not relieved of its duties because the party that has abandoned wounded and sick personnel has not left medical personnel and material to assist in the care of those wounded and sick.[112] On the other hand, the party that encounters and captures the wounded and sick also is not relieved of its duties when the party that has abandoned wounded and sick personnel has left medical personnel and material to assist in the care of those wounded and sick.[113]

In addition to providing for the medical care of wounded and sick abandoned to the enemy, other feasible precautions should be taken to ensure their safety.[114]

7.6 ACCOUNTABILITY INFORMATION FROM THE ENEMY MILITARY WOUNDED, SICK, SHIPWRECKED, AND DEAD

The GWS and GWS-Sea impose certain obligations to gather and report information in order to gain as full an accounting as possible for captured enemy personnel and enemy dead recovered from the battlefield. These obligations complement similar obligations in the GPW to

---

[109] *For example*, STEPHEN BADSEY, ARNHEM 1944: OPERATION 'MARKET GARDEN' 85 (1993) ("At Arnhem itself, 10,300 men of 1st British Airborne Division and 1st Polish Parachute Brigade landed from air. Some 2,587 men escaped across the Rhine in Operation 'Berlin' (1,741 of 1st British Airborne, 422 of the Gilder Pilot Regiment, 160 Poles and 75 from the Dorsetshire Regiment), and 240 more returned later with the aid of the PAN. About 1,600 wounded were left behind in the Oosterbeek pocket, together with 204 medical officers and chaplains who volunteered to stay. The Germans claimed 6,450 prisoners taken, wounded or not, and 1st British Airborne therefore lost about 1,300 killed.").

[110] GWS art. 12 ("The Party to the conflict which is compelled to abandon wounded or sick to the enemy shall, as far as military considerations permit, leave with them a part of its medical personnel and material to assist in their care.").

[111] GWS COMMENTARY 142 ("If this provision [paragraph 5 of Article 12 of the GWS] cannot, therefore, be considered imperative, it represents none the less a clear moral obligation which the responsible authority cannot evade except in cases of urgent necessity. ... Paragraph 2 [of Article 12 of the GWS] imposes an absolute obligation to which there are no exceptions; paragraph 5 is a recommendation, but an urgent and forcible one.").

[112] GWS COMMENTARY 142 ("It should, moreover, be noted that this provision is in no way bound up with the obligation, imposed upon the Parties to the conflict by paragraph 2, to care for the wounded. A belligerent can never refuse to care for enemy wounded he has picked up, on the pretext that his adversary has abandoned them without medical personnel and equipment. On the contrary, he is bound to give to them the same care as he gives the wounded of his own army.").

[113] *Refer to* § 7.9.6 (No Relief of Obligations of the Detaining Power).

[114] *Compare* § 9.9.3.2 (Feasible Precautions to Ensure Safety).

maintain accountability for POWs.[115]

7.6.1 Recording Identifying Information. Parties to the conflict shall record as soon as possible, in respect of each wounded, sick, shipwrecked, or dead person of the adverse party falling into their hands, any particulars that may assist in his or her identification.[116] These records should, if possible, include:[117]

- designation of the Power on which the person depends;
- surname (*i.e.*, last name) and first name or names (*i.e.*, first and middle names);
- army, regimental, personal, or serial number;
- date of birth;
- any other particulars shown on the person's identity card or disc;[118]
- date and place of capture or death; and
- particulars concerning wounds or illness, or cause of death.

The GPW requires the collection of a similar set of information for all POWs.[119]

In order to implement these obligations, as part of their initial processing, the recovering or capturing unit should endeavor to obtain this information from each living POW.[120] POWs who, owing to their physical or mental condition, are unable to state their identity, shall be handed over to the medical service.[121]

Other sources of information should be used to establish the identity of the wounded, sick, shipwrecked, and dead. For example, items associated with the person (*e.g.*, personal effects, a life jacket bearing the name of the ship on which that person served) should be examined, and other members of the person's unit should be questioned.

---

[115] *Refer to* § 9.31 (National Accounting of the Detention of POWs).

[116] GWS art. 16 ("Parties to the conflict shall record as soon as possible, in respect of each wounded, sick or dead person of the adverse Party falling into their hands, any particulars which may assist in his identification."); GWS-SEA art. 19 ("The Parties to the conflict shall record as soon as possible, in respect of each shipwrecked, wounded, sick or dead person of the adverse Party falling into their hands, any particulars which may assist in his identification.").

[117] GWS art. 16 ("These records should if possible include: (a) designation of the Power on which he depends; (b) army, regimental, personal or serial number; (c) surname; (d) first name or names; (e) date of birth; (f) any other particulars shown on his identity card or disc; (g) date and place of capture or death; (h) particulars concerning wounds or illness, or cause of death."); GWS-SEA art. 19 (same).

[118] *Refer to* § 9.4.3 (Issue of Identification Cards to Persons Liable to Become POWs).

[119] *Refer to* § 9.31.1 (Accountability Information That the Detaining Power Should Collect).

[120] *Refer to* § 9.8.4 (Accountability Information That POWs Are Bound to Provide Upon Questioning).

[121] *Refer to* § 9.8.4.1 (POWs Unable to State Their Identity).

An examination of a deceased person's body may also facilitate identification by gathering information that can be used to identify the person later (*e.g.*, measurements and description of the body and its physical features, examination of the teeth, fingerprints, photograph, DNA samples).[122] This examination should be conducted before burial or cremation.[123]

7.6.2 Forwarding Identifying Information. As soon as possible, the above mentioned identifying information shall be forwarded to the National POW Information Bureau described in Article 122 of the GPW, which shall transmit this information to the Power on which these persons depend through the intermediary of the Protecting Power and of the Central POW Agency.[124]

7.6.2.1 *Military Necessity to Delay Reporting*. As the phrase "as soon as possible" reflects, reporting may be delayed due to practical considerations, including security risks.[125]

7.6.3 U.S. Practice in Reporting Through the ICRC Central Tracing Agency. In U.S. practice, information has been provided to the Theater Detainee Reporting Center, which in turn processes it and reports it to the National Detainee Reporting Center, which has then transmitted it to the ICRC Central Tracing Agency, acting as the Central POW Information Agency.[126]

7.7 Treatment and Handling of Enemy Military Dead

The GWS and GWS-Sea address the treatment and handling of enemy dead who have been collected from the battlefield.[127] However, the provisions of the GWS and GWS-Sea relating to the treatment and handling of enemy dead may also be interpreted to include wounded and sick combatants who have died shortly after having been collected.[128] The GPW provides

---

[122] *See* GWS COMMENTARY 177 ("In the absence of papers recourse must be had to other methods which will make it possible for the adverse Party itself to establish his identity, *e.g.* measurements and description of the body and its physical features, examination of the teeth, fingerprints, photograph, etc.").

[123] *Refer to* § 7.7.4.1 (Examination of Bodies Before Burial or Cremation).

[124] GWS art. 16 ("As soon as possible the above mentioned information shall be forwarded to the Information Bureau described in Article 122 of the Geneva Convention relative to the Treatment of Prisoners of War of August 12, 1949, which shall transmit this information to the Power on which these persons depend through the intermediary of the Protecting Power and of the Central Prisoners of War Agency."); GWS-SEA art. 19 (same).

[125] *See, e.g.*, GWS-SEA COMMENTARY 138 ("A warship always has good reasons for communicating by radio as little as possible, and one cannot therefore expect it to transmit by that means sundry information about the shipwrecked or sick whom it may have picked up. It will delay doing so until it has arrived at a port in its home country, and the authorities on land will then have to notify the enemy.").

[126] *Refer to* § 9.31.4 (U.S. Practice in Reporting to the ICRC Central Tracing Agency).

[127] GWS COMMENTARY 179 (noting that "the First Convention was essentially concerned with the dead picked up on the battlefield").

[128] GWS COMMENTARY 176 ("In the first place the present Article (Article 17) is essentially concerned with the dead picked up by the enemy on the battlefield, that is to say, with the mortal remains of combatants who have never for one moment been prisoners of war. Again, combatants who have died shortly after having been picked up wounded or sick, will have succumbed to the wounds or sickness which brought them under the protection of the

other rules relating to POWs who have died while in detention.[129] Thus, certain enemy dead may be addressed by both the GPW and GWS.

Although the provisions of the GWS and GWS-Sea are not applicable to civilian dead, in many cases it may be appropriate and practical to apply those rules by analogy. The GC provides rules relating to protected persons who have died while interned.[130]

7.7.1 Treatment of Enemy Military Dead. Subject to the tactical situation and sanitation requirements, the handling and burial of enemy military dead must be discharged with the same respect as would be afforded to, or expected for, friendly military dead. The respectful treatment of the dead is one of the oldest rules in the law of war.[131]

7.7.1.1 *No Disrespectful or Degrading Treatment of the Dead*. Enemy military dead must be protected from disrespectful or degrading acts.[132] For example, mutilation or cannibalism of dead bodies is prohibited.[133] In addition, posing with bodies for photographs or

---

First Convention, and it is therefore only natural that they should remain subject to the provisions of that Convention.").

[129] *Refer to* § 9.34 (Death of POWs).

[130] *Refer to* § 10.34 (Death of Internees).

[131] *See, e.g*, GROTIUS, LAW OF WAR & PEACE 455-56 (2.19.3.1) ("Consequently, all agree that even public enemies are entitled to burial. Appian calls this 'a common right of wars'; Philo, 'the common interchange in war'. Says Tacitus: 'Not even enemies begrudge burial.' Dio Chrysostom says that this right is observed even 'among enemies'; he adds, 'even though hatred has reached the utmost limit.' In treating of the same matter, Lucan says that the laws and customs of humanity must be observed in the case of an enemy. The same Sopater, who was cited above, asks: 'What war has deprived the human race of this last honour? What enmity has extended the memory of evil deeds to such a point that it would dare to violate this law?' And Dio Chrysostom, whom I have just cited, in his oration On the Law, says: 'For this reason no one judges enemies after death, and wrath and insult are not extended to their bodies.'").

[132] *For example*, Trial of Max Schmid, *Outline of the Proceedings*, XIII U.N. LAW REPORTS 151 (U.S. General Military Government Court, Dachau, Germany, May 19, 1947) ("The third charge against the accused was that he did 'wilfully, deliberately and wrongfully encourage, aid, abet and participate in the maltreatment of a dead unknown member of the United States Army.' … The evidence showed that shortly before the time of the allied invasion of France the body of a dead U.S. airman was brought to his dispensary by a detail whose duty it was to collect dead bodies, and to remove them from the battlefield. The accused severed the head from the body, boiled it and removed the skin and flesh and bleached the skull which he kept on his desk for several months. The prosecution alleged that he eventually sent it to his wife in Germany as a souvenir.").

[133] *For example*, H. Wayne Elliott, *The Third Priority: The Battlefield Dead*, ARMY LAWYER 3, 14 (Jul. 1996) ("Reports of the mutilation of bodies, particularly cutting the ears off dead enemy soldiers, also circulated. One such incident was filmed and shown on the CBS Evening News in 1967. In another incident which occurred in 1967, an Army sergeant was court-martialed for 'conduct to the prejudice of good order and discipline,' a violation of Article 134 of the Uniform Code of Military Justice (UCMJ). The sergeant was convicted of decapitating two enemy corpses and posing for a photograph with the heads. The disciplinary or judicial action taken in these incidents is proof that such conduct was not sanctioned by the command in Vietnam. In October 1967, General Westmoreland, United States Commander in Vietnam, described the practice of cutting ears and fingers off the dead as 'subhuman' and 'contrary to all policy and below the minimum standards of human decency.'"); Trial of Max Schmid, *Notes on the Case: Mutilation of Dead Bodies and Refusal of Honourable Burial*, XIII U.N. LAW REPORTS 151, 152 (U.S. General Military Government Court, Dachau, Germany, May 19, 1947) ("Another United States Military Commission at the Mariana Islands (2nd-15th August, 1946) tried and convicted Tachibana Yochio, a Lieutenant-General in the Japanese Army and 13 others, of murdering 8 prisoners of war. Some of the accused were also charged with 'preventing an honourable burial due to the consumption of parts of the bodies of prisoners of war

leaving a "calling card" on a body are also inconsistent with the respectful treatment of the dead.

7.7.1.2 *Prohibition Against Booby-Trapping Dead Bodies*. The dead may not be booby-trapped.[134]

7.7.2 Handling of Personal Effects Belonging to Enemy Dead. During international armed conflict, personal property recovered from enemy dead becomes the property of the recovering State for the purpose of returning it to the next-of-kin of the deceased.

7.7.2.1 *Measures to Prevent the Dead From Being Despoiled*. At all times, and particularly after an engagement, parties to the conflict shall, without delay, take all possible measures to prevent the dead from being despoiled.[135] This means that the personal effects of deceased persons may not be pillaged or otherwise taken without proper authorization.[136]

Individuals are not entitled to retain the personal effects of a deceased person as "booty"; the individual military member or person accompanying the armed forces who captures or finds enemy property acquires no title or claim.[137]

7.7.2.2 *Forwarding Valuable Articles Found on the Dead*. Parties to the conflict shall collect and forward, through the National POW Information Bureau, one-half of the double identity disc, last wills or other documents of importance to the next of kin, money, and in general all articles of an intrinsic or sentimental value, which are found on the dead.[138]

If there is only a single identity disc, it should remain with the body if the body is to be buried on land, so that the body may subsequently be identified as needed.[139] If the body is to be buried at sea, then the single identity disc itself should be collected and forwarded through the

---

by the accused during a special meal in the officers' mess.' They were found guilty of these charges; sentences ranging from death to imprisonment for 5 years were imposed. (3) An Australian Military Court at Wewak (30th November, 1945) sentenced Tazaki Takehiko, a First Lieutenant in the Japanese Army to death for 'mutilating the dead body of a prisoner of war' and for 'cannibalism.' The sentence was commuted to 5 years' imprisonment by the confirming officer.").

[134] *Refer to* § 6.12.4.9 (Certain Types of Prohibited Booby-Traps and Other Devices).

[135] GWS art. 15 ("At all times, and particularly after an engagement, Parties to the conflict shall, without delay, take all possible measures to search for and collect the wounded and sick, to protect them against pillage and ill-treatment, to ensure their adequate care, and to search for the dead and prevent their being despoiled.").

[136] GWS COMMENTARY 152 footnote 2 ("Although this Article speaks only of measures to prevent the 'despoiling' (French, *dépouillement*) of the dead, it incontestably involves a prohibition of 'pillage' (French, *pillage*) of the dead.").

[137] *Refer to* § 5.17.3.2 (Ownership of Captured or Found Property on the Battlefield).

[138] GWS art. 16 ("They shall likewise collect and forward through the same bureau one half of a double identity disc, last wills or other documents of importance to the next of kin, money and in general all articles of an intrinsic or sentimental value, which are found on the dead."); GWS-SEA art. 19 ("They shall likewise collect and forward through the same bureau one half of the double identity disc, or the identity disc itself if it is a single disc, last wills or other documents of importance to the next of kin, money and in general all articles of an intrinsic or sentimental value, which are found on the dead.").

[139] *Refer to* § 7.7.4.2 (Burial on Land).

National POW Information Bureau.[140]

These articles, together with unidentified articles, shall be sent in sealed packets, accompanied by statements giving all particulars necessary for the identification of the deceased owners, as well as by a complete list of the contents of the parcel.[141]

The GPW also requires the forwarding of wills and all personal valuables left by POWs, including those who have died.[142]

7.7.3 Preparation and Forwarding of Death Certificates and Lists of the Dead. Parties to the conflict shall prepare and forward to each other, through the National POW Information Bureau, certificates of death or duly authenticated lists of the dead.[143] Where applicable, these certificates or lists shall state the circumstances and reasons for cremation.[144]

The GPW provides further requirements for death certificates and lists of persons who died as POWs.[145]

7.7.4 Handling of Enemy Battlefield Dead – Burial and Cremation.

7.7.4.1 *Examination of Bodies Before Burial or Cremation*. Parties to the conflict shall ensure that burial (whether on land or at sea) or cremation of the dead, carried out individually as far as circumstances permit, is preceded by a careful examination, if possible by a medical examination, of the bodies, with a view to confirming death, establishing identity, and enabling a report to be made.[146]

An examination helps ensure that persons who are still living are not mistakenly buried or cremated. An examination also helps ensure that accountability information can be gathered and

---

140 *See* GWS-SEA COMMENTARY 144 ("Provision is still made for the possibility of military personnel being issued with single discs only, inscribed with the bare particulars. In the case of burial on land, such a disc must remain with the body, so that the latter may be identifiable at any time. In the case of burial at sea, it must be removed and sent to the deceased's home country, for a body buried at sea is usually wrapped in a weighted sailcloth bag and we know of no instance of one having been washed ashore; there is therefore no question of subsequent identification.").

141 GWS art. 16 ("These articles, together with unidentified articles, shall be sent in sealed packets, accompanied by statements giving all particulars necessary for the identification of the deceased owners, as well as by a complete list of the contents of the parcel."); GWS-SEA art. 19 (same).

142 *Refer to* § 9.31.2.3 (Collection of Personal Valuables Left by POWs).

143 GWS art. 16 ("Parties to the conflict shall prepare and forward to each other through the same bureau, certificates of death or duly authenticated lists of the dead."); GWS-SEA art. 19 (same).

144 *Refer to* § 7.7.4.4 (Cremation).

145 *Refer to* § 9.34.1 (Transmittal of Wills); § 9.34.2 (Death Certificates).

146 GWS art. 17 ("Parties to the conflict shall ensure that burial or cremation of the dead, carried out individually as far as circumstances permit, is preceded by a careful examination, if possible by a medical examination, of the bodies, with a view to confirming death, establishing identity and enabling a report to be made."); GWS-SEA art. 20 ("Parties to the conflict shall ensure that burial at sea of the dead, carried out individually as far as circumstances permit, is preceded by a careful examination, if possible by a medical examination, of the bodies, with a view to confirming death, establishing identity and enabling a report to be made.").

forwarded in accordance with other requirements.[147]

7.7.4.2 Burial on Land. Parties to the conflict shall further ensure that the dead are honorably interred, if possible according to the rites of the religion to which they belonged, and that their graves are respected, grouped if possible according to the nationality of the deceased, properly maintained, and marked so that they may always be found.[148] The use of collective graves should be avoided.[149]

One-half of the double identity disc, or the identity disc itself if it is a single disc, should remain on the body.[150]

7.7.4.3 Burial at Sea. Burial at sea is contemplated by the GWS-Sea. Burial at sea shall be conducted honorably and, if possible, according to the rites of the religion to which the dead belonged.

Where a double identity disc is used, one-half of the disc should remain on the body.[151] On the other hand, if a single identity disc is used, then it should be collected and forwarded through the National POW Information Bureau along with other valuable articles.[152]

An examination and report are especially important in such cases in order to ensure that accountability information is collected and forwarded.[153] The position (latitude and longitude) and the date should be recorded in the death certificate.[154]

7.7.4.4 Cremation. Bodies shall not be cremated except for imperative reasons of hygiene or for motives based on the religion of the deceased.[155] For example, hygiene reasons may include the risk of contamination to recovery personnel or other personnel from disease or exposure to chemical or biological warfare agents.

In case of cremation, the circumstances and reasons for cremation shall be stated in detail

---

[147] *Refer to* § 7.6 (Accountability Information From the Enemy Military Wounded, Sick, Shipwrecked, and Dead); § 7.7.3 (Preparation and Forwarding of Death Certificates and Lists of the Dead).

[148] GWS art. 17 ("They shall further ensure that the dead are honourably interred, if possible according to the rites of the religion to which they belonged, that their graves are respected, grouped if possible according to the nationality of the deceased, properly maintained and marked so that they may always be found.").

[149] *Refer to* § 9.34.3.2 (Burial).

[150] GWS art. 17 ("One half of the double identity disc, or the identity disc itself if it is a single disc, should remain on the body.").

[151] GWS-SEA art. 20 ("Where a double identity disc is used, one half of the disc should remain on the body.").

[152] *Refer to* § 7.7.2.2 (Forwarding Valuable Articles Found on the Dead).

[153] *Refer to* § 7.7.4.1 (Examination of Bodies Before Burial or Cremation).

[154] GWS-SEA COMMENTARY 143 ("If, as will more often be the case, they are buried at sea, then the position (latitude and longitude) and date alone need be mentioned.").

[155] GWS art. 17 ("Bodies shall not be cremated except for imperative reasons of hygiene or for motives based on the religion of the deceased.").

in the death certificate or on the authenticated list of the dead.[156]

7.7.5 Graves Registration Service. In order to ensure that graves may always be found, parties to the conflict shall organize at the commencement of hostilities an Official Graves Registration Service to allow subsequent exhumations and to ensure the identification of bodies, whatever the site of the graves, and the possible transportation to the home country.[157] The Graves Registration Service shall also identify, record, and respectfully keep the ashes until they can be disposed of in accordance with the wishes of the home country.[158]

The GPW provides additional requirements for the Graves Registration Service with respect to POWs who have died while POWs.[159]

7.7.5.1 *Exchange of Information Regarding Battlefield Graves*. As soon as circumstances permit, and at the latest at the end of hostilities, the Graves Registration Services of the belligerents shall exchange, through the National POW Information Bureaus, lists showing the exact location and markings of the graves, together with particulars of the dead interred therein.[160]

7.8 Respect and Protection of Categories of Medical and Religious Personnel

Certain categories of medical and religious personnel shall be respected and protected during military operations.

7.8.1 Categories of Persons Who Are Entitled to Respect and Protection as Medical and Religious Personnel on the Battlefield. The categories of persons who are entitled to respect and protection as medical and religious personnel during military operations include:

- military medical and religious personnel, including[161]

---

[156] GWS art. 17 ("In case of cremation, the circumstances and reasons for cremation shall be stated in detail in the death certificate or on the authenticated list of the dead.").

[157] GWS art. 17 ("They shall further ensure that the dead are honourably interred, if possible according to the rites of the religion to which they belonged, that their graves are respected, grouped if possible according to the nationality of the deceased, properly maintained and marked so that they may always be found. For this purpose, they shall organize at the commencement of hostilities an Official Graves Registration Service, to allow subsequent exhumations and to ensure the identification of bodies, whatever the site of the graves, and the possible transportation to the home country.").

[158] GWS art. 17 ("These provisions shall likewise apply to the ashes, which shall be kept by the Graves Registration Service until proper disposal thereof in accordance with the wishes of the home country.").

[159] *Refer to* § 9.34.4.1 (Records Held by the Graves Registration Service).

[160] GWS art. 17 ("As soon as circumstances permit, and at latest at the end of hostilities, these Services shall exchange, through the Information Bureau mentioned in the second paragraph of Article 16, lists showing the exact location and markings of the graves, together with particulars of the dead interred therein.").

[161] GWS art. 24 ("Medical personnel exclusively engaged in the search for, or the collection, transport or treatment of the wounded or sick, or in the prevention of disease, staff exclusively engaged in the administration of medical units and establishments, as well as chaplains attached to the armed forces, shall be respected and protected in all circumstances."). *Refer to* § 4.9 (Military Medical and Religious Personnel).

  - medical personnel exclusively engaged in medical duties;[162]
  - administrative staff exclusively engaged in support to medical units;[163] and
  - chaplains attached to the armed forces;[164]

- auxiliary medical personnel, if they are carrying out their medical duties at the time when they come into contact with the enemy or fall into the enemy's hands;[165]
- authorized staff of voluntary aid societies;[166]
- staff of a recognized aid society of a neutral country;[167] and
- the religious, medical, and hospital personnel of hospital ships and their crews.[168]

7.8.2 Meaning of "Respect and Protection" of Medical and Religious Personnel. The respect and protection accorded medical and religious personnel by the GWS and GWS-Sea mean that they must not knowingly be attacked, fired upon, or unnecessarily prevented from discharging their proper functions.[169]

7.8.2.1 *Incidental Harm Not Prohibited*. The incidental killing or wounding of such personnel, due to their presence among or in proximity to combatant elements actually engaged by fire directed at the latter, gives no just cause for complaint.[170] Medical and religious personnel are deemed to have accepted the risk of death or injury due to their proximity to military operations.[171] Although the presence of medical and religious personnel does not serve

---

162 *Refer to* § 4.9.1.1 (Medical Personnel Exclusively Engaged in Medical Duties).

163 *Refer* to § 4.9.1.2 (Staff Exclusively Engaged in Support to Medical Units and Establishments).

164 *Refer to* § 4.9.1.3 (Chaplains Attached to the Armed Forces).

165 GWS art. 25 ("Members of the armed forces specially trained for employment, should the need arise, as hospital orderlies, nurses or auxiliary stretcher-bearers, in the search for or the collection, transport or treatment of the wounded and sick shall likewise be respected and protected if they are carrying out these duties at the time when they come into contact with the enemy or fall into his hands."). *Refer to* § 4.13 (Auxiliary Medical Personnel).

166 *Refer to* § 4.11 (Authorized Staff of Voluntary Aid Societies).

167 *Refer to* § 4.12 (Staff of a Recognized Aid Society of a Neutral Country).

168 GWS-SEA art. 36 ("The religious, medical and hospital personnel of hospital ships and their crews shall be respected and protected; they may not be captured during the time they are in the service of the hospital ship, whether or not there are wounded and sick on board.").

169 1956 FM 27-10 (Change No. 1 1976) ¶225 ("*b. What is Meant by Respect and Protection.* The respect and protection accorded personnel of certain categories by Articles 19 (par. 220), 24 (par. 67), and 25 (par. 226), *GWS*, mean that they must not knowingly be attacked, fired upon, or unnecessarily prevented from discharging their proper functions. The accidental killing or wounding of such personnel, due to their presence among or in proximity to combatant elements actually engaged, by fire directed at the latter, gives no just cause for complaint.").

170 *See* GREENSPAN, MODERN LAW OF LAND WARFARE 57 (Medical personnel and chaplains "must accept the risks of accidental death or injury as a result of war operations.").

171 *Compare* § 7.12.2.5 (Acceptance of the Risk From Proximity to Combat Operations).

to exempt nearby military objectives from attack due to the risk that military medical and religious personnel would be incidentally harmed, feasible precautions must be taken to reduce the risk of harm to military medical and religious personnel.[172]

7.8.2.2 _Search and Other Security Measures Not Prohibited_. Medical and religious personnel are not immune from search or other necessary security measures by the enemy.[173] Searches of medical and religious personnel, and other security measures applied to them, should be consistent with the rules applicable when such actions are taken with respect to POWs.[174]

7.8.2.3 _Capture Not Prohibited_. The respect and protection afforded medical and religious personnel do not immunize them from detention.[175] However, certain classes of medical and religious personnel are, under other rules, exempt from detention or capture.[176]

7.8.3 Loss of Protection for Medical and Religious Personnel From Being Made the Object of Attack. Medical and religious personnel forfeit their protected status and therefore may be made the object of attack if they, outside of their humanitarian duties, participate in hostilities or otherwise commit acts harmful to the enemy.[177]

For example, weapons may not be used by medical and religious personnel against enemy military forces except in self-defense or defense of their patients.[178] Similarly, medical or religious personnel who, during combat, drive vehicles carrying able-bodied combatants or ammunition for able-bodied combatants, forfeit their protection from being made the object of attack by enemy military forces.[179] Hampering or impeding enemy military operations also would be a basis for finding that medical or religious personnel have forfeited protection.[180]

Acts that are part of their humanitarian duties, such as caring for the wounded and sick, are not a basis for depriving medical and religious personnel of their protection.[181]

7.8.4 Use of the Distinctive Emblem to Facilitate the Respect and Protection of Military

---

[172] _Refer to_ § 5.10.1.2 (Proportionality in Conducting Attacks and Protected Military Personnel and Facilities).

[173] _Refer to_ § 7.10.1.2 (Search Not Prohibited).

[174] _Refer to_ § 9.6 (Security Measures With Respect to POWs).

[175] _Refer to_ § 7.9 (Captured Medical and Religious Personnel).

[176] _Refer to_ § 7.9.1.1 (Medical and Religious Personnel Who Are Exempt From Capture and Detention).

[177] GWS COMMENTARY 221 ("Nevertheless, to enjoy immunity, they must naturally abstain from any form of participation—even indirect—in hostile acts. We saw in Article 21 that the protection to which medical units are entitled ceases if they are used to commit acts 'harmful to the enemy'. This proviso obviously applies to medical personnel also."). _Refer to_ § 7.10.3 (Loss of Protection of Military Medical Units and Facilities From Being Made the Object of Attack).

[178] _Refer to_ § 7.10.3.5 (Use of Weapons in Self-Defense or Defense of the Wounded and Sick).

[179] _Compare_ § 7.12.2.2 (No Use for Military Purposes).

[180] _Compare_ § 7.12.2.3 (No Hampering the Movement of Combatants).

[181] _Refer to_ § 7.10.3.1 (Acts Harmful to the Enemy).

Medical and Religious Personnel. The GWS contemplates the use of the distinctive emblem, including through wearing an armlet bearing the emblem, to facilitate the identification of protected medical and religious personnel, as such.

Claiming protected medical status (including feigning such status) in order to deceive the adversary into affording protection so as then to kill or wound the enemy is prohibited.[182]

As with other instances of the display of the distinctive emblem, the wearing of the armlet with the distinctive emblem is controlled by the competent military authority, and the armlet may be obscured or removed at the competent military authority's direction.[183] The fact that military medical and religious personnel do not wear an armlet does not deprive them of their protection from being made the object of attack if they are recognized as such.[184]

7.8.4.1 *Wearing of Armlet With the Distinctive Emblem*. The GWS contemplates that

- military medical and religious personnel;[185]
- authorized staff of voluntary aid societies;[186] and
- staff of a recognized aid society of a neutral country;[187]

shall wear, affixed to the left arm, a water-resistant armlet bearing the distinctive emblem, issued and stamped by the military authority.[188] In no circumstances may these personnel be deprived of the right to wear the armlet.[189]

7.8.4.2 *Wearing of Armlet With Miniature Distinctive Emblem*. Auxiliary medical personnel shall wear, but only while carrying out medical duties, a white armlet bearing in its center the distinctive sign in miniature; the armlet shall be issued and stamped by the military

---

[182] *Refer to* § 5.22 (Treachery or Perfidy Used to Kill or Wound).

[183] *Refer to* § 7.15.2 (Control of Display by the Competent Military Authority); § 7.15.2.1 (Removal or Obscuration of the Distinctive Emblem).

[184] *Refer to* § 7.15.3 (Significance of the Display of the Distinctive Emblem).

[185] *Refer to* § 4.9 (Military Medical and Religious Personnel).

[186] *Refer to* § 4.11 (Authorized Staff of Voluntary Aid Societies).

[187] *Refer to* § 4.12 (Staff of a Recognized Aid Society of a Neutral Country).

[188] GWS art. 40 ("The personnel designated in Article 24 and in Articles 26 and 27 shall wear, affixed to the left arm, a water-resistant armlet bearing the distinctive emblem, issued and stamped by the military authority."); GWS-SEA art. 42 ("The personnel designated in Articles 36 and 37 shall wear, affixed to the left arm, a water-resistant armlet bearing the distinctive emblem, issued and stamped by the military authority.").

[189] GWS art. 40 ("In no circumstances may the said personnel be deprived of their insignia or identity cards nor of the right to wear the armlet."); GWS-SEA art. 42 ("In no circumstances may the said personnel be deprived of their insignia or identity cards nor of the right to wear the armlet.").

authority.[190]

7.9 Captured Medical and Religious Personnel

The treatment of captured persons who perform medical or religious duties depends on their legal status. Identification cards are used to help determine the correct status of medical and religious personnel. Retained personnel are subject to certain duties, rights, and privileges during detention.

7.9.1 Different Classes of Persons Performing Medical or Religious Duties. Persons who perform medical or religious duties may be grouped into three categories based on their treatment with respect to detention: (1) medical and religious personnel who are exempt from capture; (2) medical and religious personnel who may be retained; and (3) persons who perform medical and religious duties who are held as POWs.

7.9.1.1 *Medical and Religious Personnel Who Are Exempt From Capture and Detention*. Certain classes of medical and religious personnel are exempt from capture and detention. These classes of personnel include:

- staff of a recognized aid society of a neutral country;[191] and
- the religious, medical, and hospital personnel of hospital ships and their crews during the time they are in service of the hospital ship, whether or not there are wounded and sick on board.[192]

Such individuals may be held temporarily pending determination of their status or until conditions permit their safe return or release.[193]

7.9.1.2 *Medical and Religious Personnel Who May Be Retained*. Certain classes of medical and religious personnel who fall into the hands of the adverse party shall be retained only in so far as the state of health, the spiritual needs, and the number of POWs require.[194] Personnel who are retained in this way are not considered POWs.[195]

---

[190] GWS art. 41 ("The personnel designated in Article 25 shall wear, but only while carrying out medical duties, a white armlet bearing in its centre the distinctive sign in miniature; the armlet shall be issued and stamped by the military authority.").

[191] *Refer to* § 4.12 (Staff of a Recognized Aid Society of a Neutral Country).

[192] GWS-Sea art. 36 ("The religious, medical and hospital personnel of hospital ships and their crews shall be respected and protected; they may not be captured during the time they are in service of the hospital ship, whether or not there are wounded and sick on board.").

[193] *Refer to* § 4.12 (Staff of a Recognized Aid Society of a Neutral Country).

[194] GWS art. 28 ("Personnel designated in Articles 24 and 26 who fall into the hands of the adverse Party, shall be retained only in so far as the state of health, the spiritual needs and the number of prisoners of war require.").

[195] GPW art. 33 ("Members of the medical personnel and chaplains while retained by the Detaining Power with a view to assisting prisoners of war, shall not be considered as prisoners of war."); GWS art. 28 ("Personnel thus retained shall not be deemed prisoners of war."). *See also* GPW art. 4C ("This Article shall in no way affect the status of medical personnel and chaplains as provided for in Article 33 of the present Convention.").

These classes of personnel include:

- military medical and religious personnel, including[196]
    - medical personnel exclusively engaged in medical duties;[197]
    - administrative staff exclusively engaged in support to medical units;[198] and
    - chaplains attached to the armed forces;[199] and
- authorized staff of voluntary aid societies.[200]

7.9.1.3 *Persons Performing Medical or Religious Duties Who Are Held as POWs*. Certain classes of persons who perform medical or religious duties are held as POWs if they fall into the hands of the enemy during international armed conflict. These classes of personnel include:

- auxiliary medical personnel, if they are carrying out their medical duties at the time when they come into contact with the enemy or fall into the enemy's hands;[201]
- members of the armed forces who are trained as medical personnel, but not attached to the medical service;[202]
- members of the armed forces who are ministers of religion without having officiated as chaplains to their own forces;[203] and
- military medical and religious personnel who forfeit their status as retained personnel because they are not exclusively engaged in medical and religious duties.[204]

7.9.2 Use of Identification Card to Help Establish Retained Personnel Status. The 1949 Geneva Conventions contemplate that identification cards will be used to help establish the proper status of persons, including the entitlement to retained personnel status.[205]

---

[196] *Refer to* § 4.9 (Military Medical and Religious Personnel).

[197] *Refer to* § 4.9.1.1 (Medical Personnel Exclusively Engaged in Medical Duties).

[198] *Refer to* § 4.9.1.2 (Staff Exclusively Engaged in Support to Medical Units and Establishments).

[199] *Refer to* § 4.9.1.3 (Chaplains Attached to the Armed Forces).

[200] *Refer to* § 4.11 (Authorized Staff of Voluntary Aid Societies).

[201] *Refer to* § 4.13 (Auxiliary Medical Personnel).

[202] *Refer to* § 4.5.2.2 (Members Trained as Medical Personnel, but Not Attached to the Medical Service).

[203] *Refer to* § 4.5.2.3 (Members Who Are Ministers of Religion Without Having Officiated as Chaplains to Their Own Forces).

[204] *Refer to* § 4.9.2.3 (Exclusively Engaged in Humanitarian Duties).

[205] *Refer to* § 4.27.1 (Identification Cards Used to Help Clarify Status).

Persons entitled to retained personnel status, in addition to wearing the identity disc mentioned in Article 16 of the GWS or Article 19 of the GWS-Sea, shall also carry a special identity card bearing the distinctive emblem.[206]

This card shall be water-resistant and of such size that it can be carried in the pocket. It shall be worded in the national language; shall mention at least the surname and first names, the date of birth, the rank, and the service number of the bearer; and shall state in what capacity the bearer is entitled to the protection of the GWS or GWS-Sea. The card shall bear the photograph of the owner and also either the bearer's signature or fingerprints or both. It shall be embossed with the stamp of the military authority.[207]

The identity card shall be uniform throughout the same armed forces and, as far as possible, of a similar type in the armed forces of the Parties to the GWS and GWS-Sea. The parties to the conflict may be guided by the model, which is annexed, by way of example, to the GWS and GWS-Sea. Parties to the conflict shall inform each other, at the outbreak of hostilities, of the model they are using. Identity cards should be made out, if possible, at least in duplicate, one copy being kept by the home country.[208]

In no circumstances may retained personnel be deprived of their insignia or identity cards nor of the right to wear the armlet.[209] In case of loss, they shall be entitled to receive duplicates of the cards and to have the insignia replaced.[210]

7.9.3 <u>Duties of Retained Personnel</u>. Within the framework of the military laws and regulations of the Detaining Power, and under the authority of its competent service, retained personnel shall continue to carry out, in accordance with their professional ethics, their medical and spiritual duties on behalf of POWs, preferably those of the armed forces to which they themselves belong.[211] This preference for retained personnel to treat the POWs of the armed

---

[206] GWS art. 40 ("Such personnel, in addition to wearing the identity disc mentioned in Article 16, shall also carry a special identity card bearing the distinctive emblem."); GWS-SEA art. 42 ("Such personnel, in addition to wearing the identity disc mentioned in Article 19, shall also carry a special identity card bearing the distinctive emblem.").

[207] GWS art. 40 ("This card shall be water-resistant and of such size that it can be carried in the pocket. It shall be worded in the national language, shall mention at least the surname and first names, the date of birth, the rank and the service number of the bearer, and shall state in what capacity he is entitled to the protection of the present Convention. The card shall bear the photograph of the owner and also either his signature or his finger-prints or both. It shall be embossed with the stamp of military authority."); GWS-SEA (same).

[208] GWS art. 40 ("The identity card shall be uniform throughout the same armed forces and, as far as possible, of a similar type in the armed forces of the High Contracting Parties. The Parties to the conflict may be guided by the model which is annexed, by way of example, to the present Convention. They shall inform each other, at the outbreak of hostilities, of the model they are using. Identity cards should be made out, if possible, at least in duplicate, one copy being kept by the home country."); GWS-SEA art. 42 (same).

[209] GWS art. 40 ("In no circumstances may the said personnel be deprived of their insignia or identity cards nor of the right to wear the armlet."); GWS-SEA art. 42 (same).

[210] GWS art. 40 ("In case of loss, they shall be entitled to receive duplicates of the cards and to have the insignia replaced."); GWS-SEA art. 42 (same).

[211] GWS art. 28 ("Within the framework of the military laws and regulations of the Detaining Power, and under the authority of its competent service, they shall continue to carry out, in accordance with their professional ethics, their medical and spiritual duties on behalf of prisoners of war, preferably those of the armed forces to which they

forces to which the retained personnel belong is also reflected in the provisions of the GPW related to the medical treatment of POWs.[212]

Like POWs, retained personnel may be subject to disciplinary or judicial proceedings for violations of the laws and regulations of the Detaining Power.[213]

If retained personnel refuse to perform their medical duties on behalf of POWs, they are liable to forfeit their status as retained personnel.[214]

7.9.4 Return of Personnel Whose Retention Is Not Indispensable. Personnel whose retention is not indispensable to provide for the health and spiritual needs of POWs shall be returned to the party to the conflict to whom they belong, as soon as a road is open for their return and military requirements permit.[215] As a historical matter, such return has been exceptional while hostilities are ongoing.[216]

7.9.4.1 *Treatment Pending Return*. Pending their return, such personnel whose retention is not indispensable shall not be deemed POWs; nevertheless, they shall at least benefit from all the provisions of the GPW.[217] They shall continue to fulfill their duties under the orders of the adverse party and shall preferably be engaged in the care of the wounded and sick of the party to the conflict to which they themselves belong.[218]

On their departure, they shall take with them the effects, personal belongings, valuables, and instruments belonging to them.[219]

---

themselves belong."); GPW art. 33 ("Members of the medical personnel and chaplains while retained by the Detaining Power with a view to assisting prisoners of war, shall … continue to exercise their medical and spiritual functions for the benefit of prisoners of war, preferably those belonging to the armed forces upon which they depend, within the scope of the military laws and regulations of the Detaining Power and under the control of its competent services, in accordance with their professional etiquette.").

212 *Refer to* § 9.14.2.2 (Treatment by Medical Personnel of the Power on Which They Depend).

213 *Refer to* § 9.26 (General Principles Applicable to POW Discipline); § 9.27 (Disciplinary Proceedings and Punishment); § 9.28 (Judicial Proceedings and Punishment).

214 *Refer to* § 4.9.2.3 (Exclusively Engaged in Humanitarian Duties).

215 GWS art. 30 ("Personnel whose retention is not indispensable by virtue of the provisions of Article 28 shall be returned to the Party to the conflict to whom they belong, as soon as a road is open for their return and military requirements permit.").

216 *See* Lewis C. Vollmar, Jr., *Military Medicine in War: The Geneva Conventions Today*, Chapter 23 in II MILITARY MEDICAL ETHICS 739, 746 (2003) ("As it always has been throughout the development of the Geneva Conventions, retention of medical personnel remains subordinate to their repatriation. But, if history is any indication of the future, it is likely that retention will become the rule and repatriation will remain the exception.").

217 GWS art. 30 ("Pending their return, they shall not be deemed prisoners of war. Nevertheless they shall at least benefit by all the provisions of the Geneva Convention relative to the Treatment of Prisoners of War of August 12, 1949.").

218 GWS art. 30 ("They shall continue to fulfil their duties under the orders of the adverse Party and shall preferably be engaged in the care of the wounded and sick of the Party to the conflict to which they themselves belong.").

219 GWS art. 30 ("On their departure, they shall take with them the effects, personal belongings, valuables and instruments belonging to them.").

7.9.4.2 *Selection of Personnel for Return*. The selection of personnel for return under Article 30 of the GWS shall be made irrespective of any consideration of race, religion, or political opinion, but preferably according to the chronological order of their capture and their state of health.[220]

7.9.4.3 *Special Agreements on the Percentage of Personnel to Be Retained*. As from the outbreak of hostilities, parties to the conflict may determine by special agreement the percentage of personnel to be retained, in proportion to the number of POWs and the distribution of these medical and religious personnel in the camps.[221]

7.9.5 Rights and Privileges of Retained Personnel.

7.9.5.1 *POW Treatment as a Minimum*. Retained personnel shall receive, as a minimum, the benefits and protection of the GPW.[222]

7.9.5.2 *All Facilities Necessary to Provide for the Medical Care of, and Religious Ministration to, POWs*. Retained personnel shall also be granted all facilities necessary to provide for the medical care of, and religious ministration to, POWs.[223]

7.9.5.3 *Visits of POWs Outside the Camp*. Retained personnel, including chaplains, shall be authorized to visit periodically POWs situated in working detachments or in hospitals outside the camp.[224] For this purpose, the Detaining Power shall place at their disposal the necessary means of transport.[225]

7.9.5.4 *Correspondence by Chaplains*. Chaplains shall be free to correspond,

---

[220] GWS art. 31 ("The selection of personnel for return under Article 30 shall be made irrespective of any consideration of race, religion or political opinion, but preferably according to the chronological order of their capture and their state of health.").

[221] GWS art. 31 ("As from the outbreak of hostilities, Parties to the conflict may determine by special agreement the percentage of personnel to be retained, in proportion to the number of prisoners and the distribution of the said personnel in the camps.").

[222] GWS art. 28 (Retained personnel "shall at least benefit by all the provisions of the Geneva Convention relative to the Treatment of Prisoners of War of 12 August 1949."); GPW art. 33 ("Members of the medical personnel and chaplains while retained by the Detaining Power with a view to assisting prisoners of war, shall … receive as a minimum the benefits and protection of the present Convention,").

[223] GPW art. 33 ("Members of the medical personnel and chaplains while retained by the Detaining Power with a view to assisting prisoners of war, shall not be considered as prisoners of war. They shall, however, receive as a minimum the benefits and protection of the present Convention, and shall also be granted all facilities necessary to provide for the medical care of, and religious ministration to prisoners of war."); GWS art. 28 ("Personnel thus retained shall not be deemed prisoners of war. Nevertheless they shall at least benefit from the provisions of the Geneva Convention relative to the Treatment of Prisoners of War of August 12, 1949.").

[224] GPW art. 33 ("They shall be authorized to visit periodically prisoners of war situated in working detachments or in hospitals outside the camp."); GWS art. 28 ("They shall be authorized to visit periodically the prisoners of war in labour units or hospitals outside of the camp."); GPW art. 35 ("[Chaplains] shall enjoy the necessary facilities, including the means of transport provided for in Article 33, for visiting the prisoners of war outside their camp.").

[225] GPW art. 33 ("For this purpose, the Detaining Power shall place at their disposal the necessary means of transport."); GWS art. 28 ("The Detaining Power shall put at their disposal the means of transport required.").

subject to censorship, on matters concerning their religious duties with the ecclesiastical authorities in the country of detention and with international religious organizations.[226] Letters and cards, which they may send for this purpose, shall be in addition to the quota provided for in Article 71 of the GPW.[227]

7.9.5.5 Proposal of POWs for Examination by Mixed Medical Commissions. Retained medical personnel may propose wounded and sick POWs for examination by Mixed Medical Commissions with a view towards repatriation or accommodation in a neutral country and the entitlement to attend examinations conducted by Mixed Medical Commissions.[228]

7.9.5.6 No Other Compulsory Duties. Although they shall be subject to the internal discipline of the camp in which they are retained, such personnel may not be compelled to carry out any work other than that concerned with their medical or religious duties.[229]

7.9.5.7 Senior Medical Officer in the Camp. The senior medical officer in each camp shall be responsible to the camp military authorities for everything connected with the activities of retained medical personnel.[230] For this purpose, parties to the conflict shall agree at the outbreak of hostilities on the subject of the corresponding ranks of the medical personnel, including that of societies mentioned in Article 26 of the GWS.[231]

In all questions arising out of their duties, the senior medical officer, and chaplains, shall have direct access to the military and medical authorities of the camp, who shall grant them the facilities they may require for correspondence relating to these questions.[232]

---

[226] GPW art. 35 ("They shall be free to correspond, subject to censorship, on matters concerning their religious duties with the ecclesiastical authorities in the country of detention and with international religious organizations.").

[227] GPW art. 35 ("Letters and cards which they may send for this purpose shall be in addition to the quota provided for in Article 71."). *Refer to* § 9.20.2.1 (POW Correspondence Quota).

[228] *Refer to* § 9.36.5.2 (POWs Entitled to Present Themselves for Examination Before the Commission); § 9.36.5.3 (Observers at the Examination).

[229] GPW art. 33 ("Although they shall be subject to the internal discipline of the camp in which they are retained, such personnel may not be compelled to carry out any work other than that concerned with their medical or religious duties."); GWS art. 28 ("Although retained personnel in a camp shall be subject to its internal discipline, they shall not, however, be required to perform any work outside their medical or religious duties.").

[230] GPW art. 33 ("The senior medical officer in each camp shall be responsible to the camp military authorities for everything connected with the activities of retained medical personnel."); GWS art. 28 ("In each camp, the senior medical officer of the highest rank shall be responsible to the military authorities of the camp for the professional activity of the retained military medical personnel.").

[231] GPW art. 33 ("For this purpose, Parties to the conflict shall agree at the outbreak of hostilities on the subject of the corresponding ranks of the medical personnel, including that of societies mentioned in Article 26 of the Geneva Convention for the Amelioration of the Condition of the Wounded and Sick in Armed Forces in the Field of August 12, 1949."); GWS art. 28 ("For this purpose, from the outbreak of hostilities, the Parties to the conflict shall agree regarding the corresponding seniority of the ranks of their medical personnel, including those of the societies designated in Article 26.").

[232] GWS art. 28 ("In all questions arising out of their duties, this medical officer, and the chaplains, shall have direct access to the military and medical authorities of the camp who shall grant them the facilities they may require for correspondence relating to these questions."); GPW art. 33 ("This senior medical officer, as well as chaplains, shall

7.9.5.8 *Agreements on Possible Relief of Retained Personnel*. During hostilities, the parties to the conflict shall agree concerning the possible relief of retained personnel and shall settle the procedure to be followed.[233] This provision arose from limited practice in World War II where retained personnel were repatriated and replaced by medical personnel from their home country.[234]

7.9.6 No Relief of Obligations of the Detaining Power. None of the provisions of Article 28 of the GWS or Article 33 of the GPW shall relieve the Detaining Power of its obligations with regard to POWs from the medical or spiritual point of view.[235] In other words, the fact that the Detaining Power permits and enables retained personnel to care for POWs does not relieve the Detaining Power of its own responsibilities to care for POWs.

7.10 Military Medical Units and Facilities

Fixed establishments and mobile medical units of the Medical Service (*i.e.*, military medical units and facilities) may in no circumstances be attacked, but shall at all times be respected and protected by the parties to the conflict.[236] In addition, establishments ashore that are entitled to the protection of the GWS shall be protected from bombardment or attack from the sea.[237]

7.10.1 Meaning of "Respect and Protection" of Military Medical Units and Facilities. The respect and protection accorded by the GWS to military medical units and facilities mean that they must not knowingly be attacked, fired upon, or unnecessarily prevented from discharging their proper functions.[238]

7.10.1.1 *Incidental Harm Not Prohibited*. The incidental harm to military

---

have the right to deal with the competent authorities of the camp on all questions relating to their duties. Such authorities shall afford them all necessary facilities for correspondence relating to these questions.").

[233] GPW art. 33 ("During hostilities, the Parties to the conflict shall agree concerning the possible relief of retained personnel and shall settle the procedure to be followed."); GWS art. 28 ("During hostilities the Parties to the conflict shall make arrangements for relieving where possible retained personnel, and shall settle the procedure of such relief.").

[234] GWS Commentary 257 ("During the last World War certain belligerents planned to relieve doctors retained in enemy camps, by personnel from the home country. On being replaced the doctors in question were to be repatriated. A beginning was made in the case of some Yugoslav doctors and a larger number of French doctors retained in Germany.").

[235] GPW art. 33 ("None of the preceding provisions shall relieve the Detaining Power of its obligations with regard to prisoners of war from the medical or spiritual point of view."); GWS art. 28 ("None of the preceding provisions shall relieve the Detaining Power of the obligations imposed upon it with regard to the medical and spiritual welfare of the prisoners of war.").

[236] GWS art. 19 ("Fixed establishments and mobile medical units of the Medical Service may in no circumstances be attacked, but shall at all times be respected and protected by the Parties to the conflict.").

[237] GWS-Sea art. 23 ("Establishments ashore entitled to protection of the Geneva Convention for the Amelioration of the Condition of the Wounded and Sick in Armed Forces in the Field of August 12, 1949, shall be protected from bombardment or attack from the sea.").

[238] *Refer to* § 7.8.2 (Meaning of "Respect and Protection" of Medical and Religious Personnel).

medical units or facilities, due to their presence among or in proximity to combatant elements actually engaged, by fire directed at the latter, gives no just cause for complaint.[239] Commanders are obligated to situate military medical units and facilities such that they are not in danger from attack against military objectives.[240] Military medical units and facilities that are positioned near military objectives are deemed to have accepted the risk of harm due to their proximity to military operations.[241] Although the presence of military medical units and facilities does not serve to exempt nearby military objectives from attack due to the risk that military medical units and facilities would be incidentally harmed, feasible precautions must be taken to reduce the risk of harm to military medical units and facilities.[242]

7.10.1.2 *Search Not Prohibited*. Military medical units and facilities are not immune from search by the enemy.[243] For example, search may be necessary to verify that these units and facilities are not being used, outside their humanitarian duties, to commit acts harmful to the enemy.

7.10.1.3 *Capture Not Prohibited*. The respect and protection afforded military medical units and facilities do not immunize them from capture.[244]

7.10.2 Obligation to Situate Military Medical Units and Facilities Relative to Military Objectives. Responsible authorities shall ensure that military medical establishments and units are, as far as possible, situated in such a manner that attacks against military objectives cannot imperil their safety.[245]

In no case may a military medical unit or facility be used for the purpose of shielding military objectives from attack.[246]

---

[239] *Compare* § 7.12.2.5 (Acceptance of the Risk From Proximity to Combat Operations). *For example*, Col. Robert D. Heinl, Jr., *Military Writer Charges: Reds Dupe Doves On Hanoi Hospital*, THE PITTSBURGH PRESS, Jan. 10, 1973 ("Bach Mai Hospital, outside Hanoi, appears to have replaced North Vietnam's inconveniently intact dike systems as Exhibit A in the Communist propaganda campaign to convict the United States of war crimes, atrocities and what is called 'terror bombing.' Bach Mai, or what is left of it, has been regularly shown to visiting American antiwar activists as evidence that we are singling out hospitals, orphanages and similar illegal targets in the air war against Hanoi. … Examination of current aerial photographs shows the hospital to be sited by the Communists in the very bull's-eye of a ring of military targets. … Besides being virtually astride the Communists' main logistic artery for support of the war, the damaged hospital lies just across the road from Bach Mai Airfield, one of North Vietnam's most important military airdromes. **Within a few hundred yards of Bach Mai Hospital, the Communists maintain their main command center for the air defense of the North.**").

[240] *Refer to* § 7.10.2 (Obligation to Situate Military Medical Units and Facilities Relative to Military Objectives).

[241] *Compare* § 7.12.2.5 (Acceptance of the Risk From Proximity to Combat Operations).

[242] *Refer to* § 5.10.1.2 (Proportionality in Conducting Attacks and Protected Military Personnel and Facilities).

[243] 1956 FM 27-10 (Change No. 1 1976) ¶221 ("*GWS* does not confer immunity from search by the enemy on medical units, establishments, or transports.").

[244] *Refer to* § 7.10.5 (Capture of Military Medical Units and Facilities).

[245] GWS art. 19 ("The responsible authorities shall ensure that the said medical establishments and units are, as far as possible, situated in such a manner that attacks against military objectives cannot imperil their safety.").

[246] *Refer to* § 5.16 (Prohibition on Using Protected Persons and Objects to Shield, Favor, or Impede Military Operations).

7.10.2.1 *Necessity for the Intermingling of Military Objectives and Military Medical Units and Facilities*. The obligation to situate medical units and facilities so that attacks against military objectives cannot imperil their safety is limited by practical considerations.

For example, in order to perform their medical duties effectively, medical units and facilities must, to some degree, be intermingled with military objectives (such as combatants or vehicles that constitute military objectives). In addition, medical units and facilities may be faced with threats of unlawful attacks (*e.g.*, from criminal elements or enemy combatants not abiding by the law of war) that may warrant the placement of medical units and facilities in a more secure location (*e.g.*, within the perimeter of a military base) so that they may be guarded by combatant units. Logistical considerations (*e.g.*, access to roads, water, power, or communications) may also limit the implementation of this obligation.

7.10.2.2 *Implementation of the Obligation to Situate Medical Units and Facilities*. Implementing the obligation to ensure that military medical units and facilities are, as far as possible, situated in such a manner that attacks against military objectives cannot imperil their safety is a responsibility of commanders of military medical units, as well as commanders of combatant units.

Commanders of military medical units and facilities should, as far as possible, place their units and facilities so as to protect them from the effects of enemy attacks on military objectives. Commanders of combatant units should also avoid placing their units in proximity to medical units and facilities to the extent feasible. For example, procedures should be established to ensure that, during international armed conflict, non-medical vehicles or personnel do not remain unnecessarily within or near medical facilities.

7.10.3 Loss of Protection of Military Medical Units and Facilities From Being Made the Object of Attack. The protection from being made the object of attack, to which fixed establishments and mobile medical units of the Medical Service are entitled, shall not cease unless they are used to commit, outside their humanitarian duties, acts harmful to the enemy.[247]

7.10.3.1 *Acts Harmful to the Enemy*. Medical establishments and units must refrain from all interference, direct or indirect, in military operations.[248] For example, a hospital may not be used as a shelter for able-bodied combatants or fugitives, as an arms or ammunition depot, or as a military observation post.[249] A medical unit must not be deliberately situated so as

---

[247] GWS art. 21 ("The protection to which fixed establishments and mobile medical units of the Medical Service are entitled shall not cease unless they are used to commit, outside their humanitarian duties, acts harmful to the enemy. Protection may, however, cease only after a due warning has been given, naming, in all appropriate cases, a reasonable time limit, and after such warning has remained unheeded.").

[248] GWS COMMENTARY 201 ("Medical establishments and units must observe, towards the opposing belligerent, the neutrality which they claim for themselves and which is their right under the Convention. Being placed outside the struggle, they must loyally refrain from all interference, direct or indirect, in military operations.").

[249] GWS COMMENTARY 200-01 ("Such harmful acts would, for example, include the use of a hospital as a shelter for able-bodied combatants or fugitives, as an arms or ammunition dump, or as a military observation post; another instance would be the deliberate siting of a medical unit in a position where it would impede an enemy attack.").

to hamper or impede an enemy attack.[250]

Acts that are part of their humanitarian duties, such as caring for the wounded and sick, are not a basis for depriving medical units and facilities of their protection.[251]

7.10.3.2 Due Warning Before Cessation of Protection. Protection may, however, cease only after a due warning has been given, naming, in all appropriate cases, a reasonable time limit, and after such warning has remained unheeded.[252]

The obligation to refrain from use of force against a medical unit acting in violation of its mission and protected status without due warning does not prohibit the exercise of the right of self-defense. There may be cases in which, in the exercise of the right of self-defense, a warning is not "due" or a reasonable time limit is not appropriate. For example, forces receiving heavy fire from a hospital may exercise their right of self-defense and return fire.[253] Such use of force in self-defense against medical units or facilities must be proportionate.[254] For example, a single enemy rifleman firing from a hospital window would warrant a response against the rifleman only, rather than the destruction of the hospital.

7.10.3.3 Conditions Not Depriving Military Medical Units or Facilities of Protection. The following conditions shall not be considered as depriving a medical unit or establishment of the protection guaranteed by Article 19 of the GWS:

- That the personnel of the unit or establishment are armed, and that they use the arms in their own defense, or in that of the wounded and sick in their charge.
- That in the absence of armed orderlies, the unit or establishment is protected by a picket, by sentries, or by an escort.
- That small arms and ammunition taken from the wounded and sick and not yet handed to the proper service are found in the unit or establishment.

---

[250] *Compare* § 7.12.2.3 (No Hampering the Movement of Combatants).

[251] GWS COMMENTARY 201 ("The Diplomatic Conference of 1949 stated specifically that protection could only cease in the case of harmful acts committed by the units 'outside their humanitarian duties'. It is possible for a humane act to be harmful to the enemy, or for it to be wrongly interpreted as so being by an enemy lacking in generosity. Thus the presence or activities of a medical unit might interfere with tactical operations; so might its lights at night. It was stated, for example, at the Conference, that the waves given off by an X-ray apparatus could interfere with the transmission or reception of wireless messages by a military set, or with the working of a radar unit.").

[252] GWS art. 21 ("The protection to which fixed establishments and mobile medical units of the Medical Service are entitled shall not cease unless they are used to commit, outside their humanitarian duties, acts harmful to the enemy. Protection may, however, cease only after a due warning has been given, naming, in all appropriate cases, a reasonable time limit, and after such warning has remained unheeded.").

[253] *See* GWS COMMENTARY 202 ("As we have seen, a time limit is to be named 'in all appropriate cases'. There might obviously be cases where no time limit could be allowed. Suppose, for example, that a body of troops approaching a hospital were met by heavy fire from every window. Fire would be returned without delay.").

[254] *Refer to* § 2.4 (Proportionality).

- That personnel and material of the veterinary service are found in the unit or establishment, without forming an integral part thereof; and

- That the humanitarian activities of medical units and establishments or of their personnel extend to the care of civilian wounded or sick.[255]

7.10.3.4 Arming of Military Medical Units or Facilities. The GWS contemplates that the personnel of medical units or establishments may be armed, and it does not specifically restrict the weapons that medical units or facilities may have.[256]

Military medical units and facilities may be armed to the extent necessary to enable them to defend themselves or their patients against unlawful attacks.[257] For example, military medical and religious personnel may be equipped with weapons to meet internal security needs, to maintain discipline, to protect staff and patients from criminal threats of violence, and to prevent the theft of medical supplies. On the other hand, medical units or establishments should not be armed such that they would appear to an enemy military force to present an offensive threat.[258] The type of weapon that is necessary for defensive or other legitimate purposes may depend on the anticipated threats against the medical unit or facility.

7.10.3.5 Use of Weapons in Self-Defense or Defense of the Wounded and Sick. Although medical personnel may carry arms for self-defense, they may not employ such arms against enemy forces acting in conformity with the law of war.[259] Medical personnel must refrain from all aggressive action and may not use force to resist the advance of enemy forces (*e.g.*, to prevent the search or capture of their unit or the wounded and sick in their care by

---

[255] GWS art. 22 ("The following conditions shall not be considered as depriving a medical unit or establishment of the protection guaranteed by Article 19: (1) That the personnel of the unit or establishment are armed, and that they use the arms in their own defence, or in that of the wounded and sick in their charge. (2) That in the absence of armed orderlies, the unit or establishment is protected by a picket or by sentries or by an escort. (3) That small arms and ammunition taken from the wounded and sick and not yet handed to the proper service, are found in the unit or establishment. (4) That personnel and material of the veterinary service are found in the unit or establishment, without forming an integral part thereof. (5) That the humanitarian activities of medical units and establishments or of their personnel extend to the care of civilian wounded or sick.").

[256] *See* GWS art. 22 ("The following conditions shall not be considered as depriving a medical unit or establishment of the protection guaranteed by Article 19: (1) That the personnel of the unit or establishment are armed, and that they use the arms in their own defence, or in that of the wounded and sick in their charge. (2) That in the absence of armed orderlies, the unit or establishment is protected by a picket or by sentries or by an escort.").

[257] For example, U.S. military medical and religious personnel have been armed with the M9 pistol, M16 rifle, or M4 carbine.

[258] For example, U.S. military medical and religious personnel have generally not been authorized to carry or employ crew-served weapons, hand grenades, grenade launchers, antitank weapons, or Claymore munitions.

[259] 1956 FM 27-10 (Change No. 1 1976) ¶223b ("Although medical personnel may carry arms for self-defense, they may not employ such arms against enemy forces acting in conformity with the law of war. These arms are for their personal defense and for the protection of the wounded and sick under their charge against marauders and other persons violating the law of war.").

enemy military forces).[260]

Medical personnel may use force to defend themselves or the wounded and sick in their care from unlawful attacks, such as those from unprivileged belligerents or other persons violating the law of war.[261]

Medical personnel who use their arms in circumstances not justified by the law of war expose themselves to penalties for violation of the law of war and, provided they have been given due warning to cease such acts, may also forfeit the protection of the medical unit or facility of which they form part or that they are protecting.[262]

7.10.3.6 *Temporary Presence of Combatants or Other Military Objectives Within a Medical Unit or Facility*. In some cases, combatants or other military objectives may be temporarily present within a medical unit or facility. For example, a military vehicle that is not protected as medical aircraft or transport may deliver the wounded or sick to a medical facility. Similarly, a commander may visit a hospital to visit wounded or sick members of the commander's unit for the benefit of their morale, or to award medals.

The temporary presence of combatants or other military objectives within a medical unit or facility does not automatically constitute an act harmful to the enemy that forfeits its protection from being made the object of attack. More facts would be necessary to establish that the medical unit or facility was somehow being used to commit acts harmful to the enemy, such as if a unit or facility were being used for the purpose of sheltering able-bodied combatants or providing a base from which military operations were being planned or conducted.

7.10.4 Use of the Distinctive Emblem to Facilitate the Identification of Medical Units and Facilities. The GWS contemplates that the distinctive emblem will be used to facilitate the identification of medical units and facilities as such.

7.10.4.1 *Flying of the Distinctive Flag of the GWS Over Medical Units and Facilities*. The distinctive flag of the GWS shall be hoisted only over such medical units and establishments as are entitled to be respected under the GWS, and only with the consent of the

---

[260] *See, e.g.*, DoD INSTRUCTION 1300.21, *Code of Conduct (CoC) Training and Education*, Enclosure 2 ¶E.2.3.2 (Jan. 8, 2001) ("[M]edical personnel and chaplains are subject to lawful capture. They may only resort to arms in self-defense or in defense of the wounded and sick in their charge when attacked in violation of the Geneva Convention (I). They must refrain from all aggressive action and may not use force to prevent their capture or that of their unit by the enemy."); GWS COMMENTARY 203 ("But such personnel may only resort to arms for purely defensive purposes, and in cases where it is obviously necessary. They must refrain from all aggressive action and may not use force to prevent the capture of their unit by the enemy.").

[261] GWS COMMENTARY 203 ("If a medical unit is attacked, in violation of the Convention, its personnel cannot be asked to sacrifice themselves without resistance. Quite apart from the above extreme case, it is clearly necessary for medical personnel to be in a position to ensure the maintenance of order and discipline in the units under their charge.").

[262] 1956 FM 27-10 (Change No. 1 1976) ¶223b ("Medical personnel who use their arms in circumstances not justified by the law of war expose themselves to penalties for violation of the law of war and, provided they have been given due warning to cease such acts, may also forfeit the protection of the medical unit or establishment of which they form part or which they are protecting.").

military authorities.[263] In mobile units, as in fixed establishments, it may be accompanied by the national flag of the party to the conflict to which the unit or establishment belongs.[264]

Nevertheless, medical units that have fallen into the hands of the enemy shall not fly any flag other than that of the GWS.[265]

7.10.4.2 *Necessary Steps to Make the Distinctive Emblems Clearly Visible*. Parties to the conflict shall take the necessary steps, in so far as military considerations permit, to make the distinctive emblems indicating medical units and establishments clearly visible to the enemy land, air, and naval forces, in order to obviate the possibility of any hostile action.[266]

7.10.5 Capture of Military Medical Units and Facilities. Military medical units and facilities may be captured. Should they fall into the hands of the adverse party, their personnel shall be free to pursue their duties, as long as the capturing Power has not itself ensured the necessary care of the wounded and sick found in such establishments and units.[267]

7.10.5.1 *Disposition of Buildings, Material, and Stores of Captured Medical Units and Facilities*. The material of mobile medical units of the armed forces that fall into the hands of the enemy shall be reserved for the care of wounded and sick.[268]

The buildings, material, and stores of fixed medical establishments of the armed forces shall remain subject to the laws of war (*e.g.*, they may be captured and used by the enemy military force[269]), but may not be diverted from their purpose as long as they are required for the care of wounded and sick.[270] Nevertheless, the commanders of forces in the field may make use of them, in case of urgent military necessity, provided that they make previous arrangements for

---

[263] GWS art. 42 ("The distinctive flag of the Convention shall be hoisted only over such medical units and establishments as are entitled to be respected under the Convention, and only with the consent of the military authorities.").

[264] GWS art. 42 ("In mobile units, as in fixed establishments, it may be accompanied by the national flag of the Party to the conflict to which the unit or establishment belongs.").

[265] GWS art. 42 ("Nevertheless, medical units which have fallen into the hands of the enemy shall not fly any flag other than that of the Convention.").

[266] GWS art. 42 ("Parties to the conflict shall take the necessary steps, in so far as military considerations permit, to make the distinctive emblems indicating medical units and establishments clearly visible to the enemy land, air or naval forces, in order to obviate the possibility of any hostile action.").

[267] GWS art. 19 ("Should they fall into the hands of the adverse Party, their personnel shall be free to pursue their duties, as long as the capturing Power has not itself ensured the necessary care of the wounded and sick found in such establishments and units.").

[268] GWS art. 33 ("The material of mobile medical units of the armed forces which fall into the hands of the enemy, shall be reserved for the care of wounded and sick.").

[269] *Refer to* § 5.17 (Seizure and Destruction of Enemy Property).

[270] GWS art. 33 ("The buildings, material and stores of fixed medical establishments of the armed forces shall remain subject to the laws of war, but may not be diverted from their purpose as long as they are required for the care of wounded and sick.").

the welfare of the wounded and sick who are being cared for in them.[271]

The material and stores of mobile medical units and fixed medical establishments of the armed forces that fall into the hands of the enemy shall not be intentionally destroyed.[272]

7.11 Ground Transports of the Wounded and Sick, or of Medical Equipment

Ground transports of wounded and sick, or of medical equipment, shall be respected and protected in the same way as mobile medical units.[273]

7.11.1 Protection of Ground Medical Transports on the Same Basis as That of Medical Units. The protection to which these transports are entitled shall not cease unless they are used to commit, outside their humanitarian duties, acts harmful to the enemy.[274]

As with medical units, these ground transports must refrain from all interference, direct or indirect, in military operations in order to retain protection.[275] For example, these ground transports must not be used to transport able-bodied combatants or to carry ammunition to combat forces.[276]

The protection for ground transports of the wounded and sick, or of medical equipment, may cease only after due warning has been given, naming, in all appropriate cases, a reasonable time limit, and after such warning has remained unheeded.[277]

7.11.2 Captured Medical Transport. Should these ground medical transports or vehicles fall into the hands of the adverse party, they shall be subject to the laws of war, on condition that the party to the conflict who captures them shall in all cases ensure the care of the wounded and sick they contain.[278] The reference to the laws of war means that the adverse party may seize and dispose of the property as enemy property.[279] Thus, the adverse party may use or dispose of such transports (including by removing the distinctive emblem and using the vehicle for a hostile purpose), provided that the capturing party ensures the care of the wounded and sick being

---

271 GWS art. 33 ("Nevertheless, the commanders of forces in the field may make use of them, in case of urgent military necessity, provided that they make previous arrangements for the welfare of the wounded and sick who are nursed in them.").

272 GWS art. 33 ("The material and stores defined in the present Article shall not be intentionally destroyed.").

273 GWS art. 35 ("Transports of wounded and sick or of medical equipment shall be respected and protected in the same way as mobile medical units."). *Refer to* § 7.10 (Military Medical Units and Facilities).

274 *Compare* § 7.10.3 (Loss of Protection of Military Medical Units and Facilities From Being Made the Object of Attack).

275 *Compare* § 7.10.3.1 (Acts Harmful to the Enemy).

276 *Compare* § 7.12.2.2 (No Use for Military Purposes).

277 *Compare* § 7.10.3.2 (Due Warning Before Cessation of Protection).

278 GWS art. 35 ("Should such transports or vehicles fall into the hands of the adverse Party, they shall be subject to the laws of war, on condition that the Party to the conflict who captures them shall in all cases ensure the care of the wounded and sick they contain.").

279 *Refer to* § 5.17 (Seizure and Destruction of Enemy Property).

carried in such transports.[280]

The civilian personnel and all means of transport obtained by requisition shall be subject to the general rules of international law.[281] This rule is stated broadly to account for a variety of situations. For example, if the civilian personnel and vehicles have been requisitioned in occupied territory by the Occupying Power and then captured by a State that is adverse to the Occupying Power, the persons and property would likely belong to the capturing State or a State that is friendly to the capturing State and thus likely would not fall under the GC.[282] On the other hand, the civilian personnel and vehicles could have been requisitioned by a belligerent State within in its own territory and, upon capture by enemy forces, the persons and property likely would fall under the protection of the GC.[283]

7.12 HOSPITAL SHIPS, SICK-BAYS IN WARSHIPS, AND COASTAL RESCUE CRAFT

7.12.1 Types of Hospital Ships and Coastal Rescue Craft.

7.12.1.1 *Military Hospital Ships*. Military hospital ships, that is to say, ships built or equipped by the Powers specially and solely with a view to assisting the wounded, sick, and shipwrecked, to treating them, and to transporting them, may in no circumstances be attacked or captured, but shall at all times be respected and protected on condition that their names and descriptions have been notified to the parties to the conflict ten days before those ships are employed.[284]

The characteristics, which must appear in the notification, shall include registered gross tonnage, the length from stem to stern, and the number of masts and funnels.[285]

Many States have employed ships that are equipped or converted into hospital ships,

---

[280] GWS COMMENTARY 282 ("Medical vehicles—like the material of fixed medical establishments—are to be subject to the laws of war. The captor may thus dispose of these vehicles, and may even use them as military transport. Naturally, in the latter case, the emblem must be at once removed.").

[281] GWS art. 35 ("The civilian personnel and all means of transport obtained by requisition shall be subject to the general rules of international law.").

[282] *Refer to* § 10.3.3 (Categories of Nationals Specifically Excluded From the Definition of Protected Person Under the GC).

[283] GWS COMMENTARY 284 ("The general rules of international law must needs apply to such persons and vehicles. These rules cannot be specified as they will vary with the evolution of international law. There are two possible cases to be considered. In the first place, the persons and vehicles may have been requisitioned in occupied territory by the Occupying Power; on being captured, they will be released automatically. On the other hand, the persons and vehicles may have been requisitioned by the belligerent within his own territory. On capture, the persons concerned will have the benefit of the provisions of the Fourth Geneva Convention of 1949. The disposal of the vehicles is governed by Articles 52 and 53 of the Hague Regulations.").

[284] GWS-SEA art. 22 ("Military hospital ships, that is to say, ships built or equipped by the Powers specially and solely with a view to assisting the wounded, sick and shipwrecked, to treating them and to transporting them, may in no circumstances be attacked or captured, but shall at all times be respected and protected, on condition that their names and descriptions have been notified to the Parties to the conflict ten days before those ships are employed.").

[285] GWS-SEA art. 22 ("The characteristics which must appear in the notification shall include registered gross tonnage, the length from stem to stern and the number of masts and funnels.").

rather than building them specifically as hospital ships.[286]

7.12.1.2 Commissioned Civilian Hospital Ships. Hospital ships used by the National Red Cross Societies, by officially recognized relief societies, or by private persons shall have the same protection as military hospital ships and shall be exempt from capture, if the party to the conflict on which they depend has given them an official commission and in so far as the provisions of Article 22 of the GWS-Sea concerning notification have been complied with.[287] These ships must be provided with certificates from the responsible authorities, stating that the vessels have been under their control while fitting out and on departure.[288]

7.12.1.3 Authorized Neutral Civilian Hospital Ships. Civilian hospital ships may also be sent from neutral countries.[289]

Hospital ships utilized by National Red Cross Societies, officially recognized relief societies, or private persons of neutral countries shall have the same protection as military hospital ships and shall be exempt from capture, on condition that they have placed themselves under the control of one of the parties to the conflict, with the previous consent of their own governments and with the authorization of the party to the conflict concerned, in so far as the provisions of Article 22 of the GWS-Sea concerning notification have been complied with.[290]

7.12.1.4 Size of Hospital Ships. The protection for military hospital ships, commissioned civilian hospital ships, and authorized neutral civilian hospital ships mentioned in

---

[286] *For example*, Department of State, Diplomatic Note given to the Iraqi Chargé d'affairs in Washington, D.C., Jan. 19, 1991, *reprinted as* Annex II to Thomas R. Pickering, *Letter Dated 21 January 1991 From the Permanent Representative of the United States of America to the United Nations Addressed to President of the Security Council*, U.N. Doc. S/22122 (Jan. 21, 1991) ("The two hospital ships are 'USNS Mercy' (T-AH 19) and 'USNS Comfort' (T-AH 20). These two converted San Clemente class tankers, ex-SS Worth ex-SS Rose City, have identical characteristics: … . Both ships are equipped specially and solely to assist, treat, and transport wounded, sick, and shipwrecked.").

[287] GWS-SEA art. 24 ("Hospital ships utilized by National Red Cross Societies, by officially recognized relief societies or by private persons shall have the same protection as military hospital ships and shall be exempt from capture, if the Party to the conflict on which they depend has given them an official commission and in so far as the provisions of Article 22 concerning notification have been complied with.").

[288] GWS-SEA art. 24 ("These ships must be provided with certificates from the responsible authorities, stating that the vessels have been under their control while fitting out and on departure.").

[289] *For example*, LIEUTENANT GENERAL STANLEY ROBERT LARSEN AND BRIGADIER GENERAL JAMES LAWTON COLLINS, JR., ALLIED PARTICIPATION IN VIETNAM 163-64 (1985) ("German economic and humanitarian aid, beginning in 1966, averaged about $7.5 million annually and more than 200 technical and medical personnel served in Vietnam. In 1966 the Federal Republic of Germany also contributed the 3,000-ton hospital ship S.S. *Helgoland* to provide medical assistance to the civilian population. With eight doctors, thirty other medical personnel, and a 130-bed capacity, the ship was initially stationed near Saigon where more than 21,000 out-patient treatments were given to approximately 6,700 patients from September 1966 until 30 June 1967. Over 850 major surgical cases were also treated. In October of 1967 the Helgoland shifted its operations to Da Nang.").

[290] GWS-SEA art. 25 ("Hospital ships utilized by National Red Cross Societies, officially recognized relief societies, or private persons of neutral countries shall have the same protection as military hospital ships and shall be exempt from capture, on condition that they have placed themselves under the control of one of the Parties to the conflict, with the previous consent of their own governments and with the authorization of the Party to the conflict concerned, in so far as the provisions of Article 22 concerning notification have been complied with.").

Articles 22, 24, and 25 of the GWS-Sea, respectively, shall apply to hospital ships of any tonnage and to their lifeboats, wherever they are operating.[291] Nevertheless, to ensure the maximum comfort and security, the parties to the conflict shall endeavor to use, for the transport of the wounded, sick, and shipwrecked over long distances and on the high seas, only hospital ships of more than 2,000 tons gross.[292] For example, U.S. military hospital ships have adhered to this recommendation by a large margin.[293]

7.12.1.5 Coastal Rescue Craft and Fixed Coastal Installations Used Exclusively by Them. Under the same conditions as those provided for in Articles 22 and 24 of the GWS-Sea, small craft employed by the State, or by the officially recognized lifeboat institutions for coastal rescue operations, shall also be respected and protected, so far as operational requirements permit.[294] The same shall apply so far as possible to fixed coastal installations used exclusively by these craft for their humanitarian missions.[295]

The phrase, "so far as operational requirements permit," has been used to acknowledge the risks incurred by such craft, because of their small size, in a zone of military operations.[296]

As provided in Articles 22 and 24 of the GWS-Sea, the names and descriptions of these small craft (including registered gross tonnage, the length from stem to stern, and the number of

---

[291] GWS-SEA art. 26 ("The protection mentioned in Articles 22, 24 and 25 shall apply to hospital ships of any tonnage and to their lifeboats, wherever they are operating.").

[292] GWS-SEA art. 26 ("Nevertheless, to ensure the maximum comfort and security, the Parties to the conflict shall endeavor to utilize, for the transport of wounded, sick and shipwrecked over long distances and on the high seas, only hospital ships of over 2,000 tons gross.").

[293] *For example*, Department of State, Diplomatic Note given to the Iraqi Chargé d'affairs in Washington, D.C., Jan. 19, 1991, *reprinted as* Annex II to Thomas R. Pickering, *Letter Dated 21 January 1991 From the Permanent Representative of the United States of America to the United Nations Addressed to President of the Security Council*, U.N. Doc. S/22122 (Jan. 21, 1991) ("The two hospital ships are 'USNS Mercy' (T-AH 19) and 'USNS Comfort' (T-AH 20). These two converted San Clemente class tankers, ex-SS Worth ex-SS Rose City, have identical characteristics: tonnage 54,367, gross, 35,958 net; dimensions feet (meters) 894 length, 105.6 width 32.8 draft, i.e. depth, (272.6 x 32.2 x 10 meters); one mast forward, one funnel aft.").

[294] GWS-SEA art. 27 ("Under the same conditions as those provided for in Articles 22 and 24, small craft employed by the State or by the officially recognized lifeboat institutions for coastal rescue operations, shall also be respected and protected, so far as operational requirements permit.").

[295] GWS-SEA art. 27 ("The same shall apply so far as possible to fixed coastal installations used exclusively by these craft for their humanitarian missions.").

[296] *See* GWS-SEA COMMENTARY 172 ("Coastal rescue craft must be respected and protected in the same way as hospital ships, wherever they are operating. Article 30 refers to their use, and the commentary on that provision should be consulted. The protection is not absolute, however; it is afforded 'so far as operational requirements permit'. This wording was used in order to take account of the risks incurred by such craft, because of their small size, in a zone of military operations. The limitation also has regard to past events and to the requirements of military security. Thus, although lifeboats may in practice be exposed to certain risks, a belligerent which has recognized them will never be allowed to make a deliberate attack on them, unless they have committed a grave breach of neutrality."). *See also* II-A FINAL RECORD OF THE DIPLOMATIC CONFERENCE OF GENEVA OF 1949 202 ("It was, however, understood that the protection promised to these low tonnage craft as well as to coastal installations could not be absolute. Such protection can only be afforded within the measure of operational necessities. A belligerent face to face with an oponent [sic] in a restricted maritime area would find it difficult to tolerate the traffic of a large number of very fast, small craft belonging to the adverse party.").

masts and funnels) must be notified to the parties to the conflict ten days before such craft are employed.[297] In addition, if the craft are not military craft belonging to a party to the conflict, they must be provided an official commission from the party to the conflict on which they depend and with certificates from the responsible authorities.[298]

7.12.2 Duties and Liabilities of Hospital Ships and Coastal Rescue Craft. The following duties and liabilities apply to hospital ships and coastal rescue craft.

7.12.2.1 *Relief and Assistance Without Distinction of Nationality*. The military hospital ships, commissioned civilian hospital ships, authorized neutral civilian hospital ships, and coastal rescue craft described in Articles 22, 24, 25, and 27 of the GWS-Sea, respectively, shall afford relief and assistance to the wounded, sick, and shipwrecked without distinction of nationality.[299] In other words, these vessels should help friendly and enemy personnel without distinction.[300]

7.12.2.2 *No Use for Military Purposes*. Parties to the GWS-Sea undertake not to use these vessels for any military purpose.[301] These vessels must not participate in any way in the armed conflict or the war effort.[302] For example, these vessels may not be used to relay military orders, transport able-bodied combatants or military equipment, or engage in reconnaissance.[303] Such acts constitute acts harmful to the enemy that forfeit a vessel's

---

[297] *Refer to* § 7.12.1.1 (Military Hospital Ships).

[298] *Refer to* § 7.12.1.2 (Commissioned Civilian Hospital Ships).

[299] GWS-SEA art. 30 ("The vessels described in Articles 22, 24, 25 and 27 shall afford relief and assistance to the wounded, sick and shipwrecked without distinction of nationality.").

[300] *For example*, Vice Admiral Timothy Keating, *News Briefing with Vice Admiral Timothy Keating*, Apr. 12, 2003 ("The United States Naval Ship Comfort, our hospital ship, is providing care not only to our wounded but to Iraqi civilians and Iraqi military. This morning, there are over 80 Iraqi enemy prisoners of war who are in a significantly serious medical condition that they have been airlifted out to the United States ship Comfort, which is on station in the north Arabian Gulf. Eighty Iraqi military personnel and 40 Iraqi civilians, displaced civilians, all of them in significant -- who have suffered injuries significantly enough that they are out on the Comfort.").

[301] GWS-SEA art. 30 ("The High Contracting Parties undertake not to use these vessels for any military purpose.").

[302] GWS-SEA COMMENTARY 179 ("*Paragraph 2* [of Article 30 of the GWS-Sea] is self-explanatory. In return for the immunity which they enjoy, hospital ships must refrain from participating in any way in the armed conflict or war effort. This refers to acts even more serious than the 'acts harmful to the enemy' referred to in Articles 34 and 35. What sanction is applied if a hospital ship commits a flagrant violation of its neutral status? It simply loses its right to protection.").

[303] *For example, The "Orel," reported in* C. J. B. HURST AND F. E. BRAY, II RUSSIAN AND JAPANESE PRIZE CASES, VII INTERNATIONAL MILITARY LAW & HISTORY 354, 356-57 (1910) ("A hospital ship is only exempt from capture if she fulfils certain conditions and is engaged solely in the humane work of aiding the sick and wounded. That she is liable to capture, should she be used by the enemy for military purposes, is admitted by International Law, and is clearly laid down by the stipulations of the Hague Convention No. 3 of July 29th, 1899, for the adaptation to maritime warfare of the principles of the Geneva Convention of August 22nd, 1864. Although the 'Orel' had been lawfully equipped and due notification concerning her had been given by the Russian Government to the Japanese Government, yet her action in communicating the orders of the Commander-in-Chief of the Russian Pacific Second Squadron to other vessels during her eastward voyage with the squadron, and her attempt to carry persons in good health, i.e. the master and three others of British steamship captured by the Russian fleet, to Vladivostock, which is a naval port in enemy territory, were evidently acts in aid of the military operations of the enemy. Further, when the facts that she was instructed by the Russian squadron to purchase munitions of war, and that she occupied the

protection from being made the object of attack and capture.[304]

7.12.2.3 <u>No Hampering the Movement of Combatants</u>. Such vessels shall in no way hamper the movement of combatants.[305] Any deliberate attempt by a hospital vessel to hamper the movement of combatants would constitute an act harmful to the enemy, although inadvertent actions might also put those vessels at increased of harm (*e.g.*, if enemy forces mistakenly believe that the vessel is acting deliberately to impede their movements).[306]

For example, hospital ships and coastal rescue craft belonging to one State must not interfere with opposing forces' efforts to capture shipwrecked personnel, nor otherwise interfere with enemy military operations.[307] Therefore, hospital ships and coastal rescue craft should not engage in such activities lest they forfeit the special protection afforded by the GWS-Sea. Special agreements between the opposing forces, however, may provide protection to ships engaged in search, rescue, or other recovery missions.

---

position usually assigned to a ship engaged in reconnaissance, are taken in consideration, it is reasonable to assume that she was constantly employed for military purposes on behalf of the Russian squadron. She is, therefore, not entitled to the exemptions laid down in The Hague Convention for the adaptation to maritime warfare of the principles of the Geneva Convention, and may be condemned according to International Law."); John D. Long, Secretary of the Navy, General Orders No. 487, Apr. 27, 1898, *reprinted in* PAPERS RELATING TO THE FOREIGN RELATIONS OF THE UNITED STATES WITH THE ANNUAL MESSAGE OF THE PRESIDENT TRANSMITTED TO CONGRESS DECEMBER 5, 1898 1153 (1901) ("The *Solace* having been fitted and equipped by the Department as an ambulance ship for the naval service under the terms of the Geneva Convention [of 1868] is about to be assigned to service. … The neutrality of the vessel will, under no circumstances, be changed, nor will any changes be made in her equipment without the authority of the Secretary of the Navy. No guns, ammunition, or articles contraband of war, except coal or stores necessary for the movement of the vessel, shall be placed on board; nor shall the vessel be used as a transport for the carrying of dispatches, or officers or men not sick or disabled, other than those belonging to the medical department.").

304 *Refer to* § 7.12.6 (Forfeiture of Protection of Hospital Ships and Sick Bays).

305 GWS-SEA art. 30 ("Such vessels shall in no wise hamper the movements of the combatants.").

306 GWS-SEA COMMENTARY 179-80 ("During an engagement, hospital ships must not hamper the movements of other vessels, and the authors might have added that they must not get in the line of fire. Any deliberate breach of the present provision would constitute an act harmful to the enemy, in the sense of Article 34, and the hospital ship committing it would then lose its right to protection under the Convention, according to the procedure laid down in that clause. If, on the other hand, it had not acted with intent, the case would then be very close to that dealt with in the following paragraph, which should be referred to. The hospital ship would not lose its right to protection, but it would in fact be deprived of security."). *Refer to* § 7.12.2.5 (Acceptance of the Risk From Proximity to Combat Operations).

307 SPAIGHT, AIR POWER AND WAR RIGHTS 361-62 ("German Red Cross rescue vessels.—In August a further attempt was made by the German Government to apply to the Red Cross to a purpose never contemplated in the Convention of 1929. It notified His Majesty's Government, through the Swiss Government, that it proposed to make use of a number of vessels—sixty-four in all—marked with the Red Cross to rescue airmen who came down in the sea. His Majesty's Government replied that the use of such vessels would interfere with the conduct of naval and military operations and could not be accepted. It then went on to refer to Germany's attacks on British hospital ships and to the sinking of the Maid of Kent, Brighton and Paris. 'His Majesty's Government do not place their own boats employed in rescuing airmen under the Red Cross, even though they have on several occasions been deliberately attacked by the Germans while actually engaged in saving both British and German airmen, and they regard the claim of the German Government to invest rescue boats with the privileges of the Red Cross as wholly inadmissible.' It may be added that such privileges were never claimed for the Walrus amphibians or the other R.A.F. machines employed in the Air/Sea Rescue Service.").

7.12.2.4 *Merchant Vessels Transformed Into Hospital Ships*. Merchant vessels that have been transformed into hospital ships cannot be put to any other use throughout the duration of hostilities.[308]

7.12.2.5 *Acceptance of the Risk From Proximity to Combat Operations*. During and after an engagement, such vessels will act at their own risk.[309] A hospital ship or coastal rescue craft operating in proximity to combat operations assumes a certain risk of damage as a result of lawful enemy operations, including misidentification by enemy or friendly forces. Although the presence of hospital ships or coastal rescue craft does not serve to exempt nearby military objectives from attack due to the risk that the hospital ships or coastal rescue craft would be incidentally damaged, feasible precautions must be taken to reduce the risk of harm to hospital ships or coastal rescue craft.[310]

7.12.2.6 *Control and Search of Hospital Ships and Coastal Rescue Craft*. The parties to the conflict shall have the right to control and search military hospital ships, commissioned civilian hospital ships, authorized neutral civilian hospital ships, and costal rescue craft mentioned in Articles 22, 24, 25, and 27 of the GWS-Sea, respectively.[311] They may refuse assistance from these vessels, order them off, make them take a certain course, control the use of their wireless and other means of communication, and even detain them for a period not exceeding seven days from the time of interception, if the gravity of the circumstances so requires.[312] For example, a belligerent may delay the passage of a hospital ship belonging to its adversary in order to avoid interference with its military operations.[313]

Parties to a conflict may put a commissioner temporarily on board such vessels whose sole task shall be to see that these orders are carried out.[314]

---

[308] GWS-SEA art. 33 ("Merchant vessels which have been transformed into hospital ships cannot be put to any other use throughout the duration of hostilities.").

[309] GWS-SEA art. 30 ("During and after an engagement, they will act at their own risk.").

[310] *Refer to* § 5.10.1.2 (Proportionality in Conducting Attacks and Protected Military Personnel and Facilities).

[311] GWS-SEA art. 31 ("The Parties to the conflict shall have the right to control and search the vessels mentioned in Articles 22, 24, 25 and 27.").

[312] GWS-SEA art. 31 ("They can refuse assistance from these vessels, order them off, make them take a certain course, control the use of their wireless and other means of communication, and even detain them for a period not exceeding seven days from the time of interception, if the gravity of the circumstances so requires.").

[313] *For example*, J.C. Massop, *Hospital Ships in the Second World War*, 24 BRITISH YEAR BOOK OF INTERNATIONAL LAW, 398, 405-06 (1947) ("The limitation imposed on the immunity of a hospital ship has by Article 12 is flanked by the right conferred on a belligerent by Article 4 to control the movements of a hospital ship on grounds of operational necessity. Such a situation arose at least twice during the 1939 war, when the German High Command wished to pass a hospital ship through the Allied patrol lines to a besieged part. As noted above, no obstacle was placed in the way of the voyages to Salonica, but when the Germans sought permission to send a hospital ship to Brest—then invested by Allied forces—it was apparent that it could not pass into the port without serious inconvenience to the attacking forces, and it was decided to refuse the request until the tactical situation had clarified.").

[314] GWS-SEA art. 31 ("They may put a commissioner temporarily on board whose sole task shall be to see that orders given in virtue of the provisions of the preceding paragraph are carried out.").

As far as possible, the parties to the conflict shall enter in the log of the hospital ship, in a language he or she can understand, the orders they have given the captain of the vessel.[315]

Parties to the conflict may, either unilaterally or by particular agreements, put on board their ships neutral observers who shall verify the strict observation of the provisions contained in the GWS-Sea.[316]

7.12.2.7 Use of Secret Codes for Communication. The GWS-Sea provides that hospital ships may not possess or use a secret code for their wireless or other means of communication.[317] The lack of secret codes for communication was intended to afford belligerents a guarantee that hospital ships were not improperly participating in hostilities.[318] This rule was formulated before developments in modern communications technology made encryption more common.[319] Substantial practical difficulties have arisen in construing this rule in a way that would prohibit any use of encrypted communications by hospital ships.[320]

In light of the requirement for encryption in modern communications systems (*e.g.*, satellite communications and video teleconference systems) and navigational technology (*e.g.*, global positioning systems) and the goal of ensuring that hospital ships can effectively fulfill their humanitarian mission, the United States has employed hospital ships with the capability to

---

[315] GWS-SEA art. 31 ("As far as possible, the Parties to the conflict shall enter in the log of the hospital ship, in a language he can understand, the orders they have given the captain of the vessel.").

[316] GWS-SEA art. 31 ("Parties to the conflict may, either unilaterally or by particular agreements, put on board their ships neutral observers who shall verify the strict observation of the provisions contained in the present Convention.").

[317] GWS-SEA art. 34 ("In particular, hospital ships may not possess or use a secret code for their wireless or other means of communication.").

[318] GWS-SEA COMMENTARY 193 ("The fact that the use of any secret code is prohibited affords a guarantee to the belligerents that hospital ships will not make improper use of their transmitting apparatus or any other means of communication. Hospital ships may only communicate in clear, or at least in a code which is universally known, and rightly so, for the spirit of the Geneva Conventions requires that there should be nothing secret in their behaviour vis-à-vis the enemy.").

[319] Richard J. Grunawalt, *Hospital Ships in the War on Terror: Sanctuaries or Targets?*, 58 NAVAL WAR COLLEGE REVIEW 108-09 (Winter 2005) ("The genesis of these constraints [on hospital ships and secret codes] involves a few isolated incidents many years ago when hospital ships were alleged to have used coded wireless communications capability to transmit operational intelligence, a 'military purpose' use inconsistent with their protected status and in violation of the 1899 Hague (III) Convention and the 1907 Hague (X) Convention. ... Obviously, the conventional and customary rules mandating that hospital ships not be used for any military purpose other than the care and transport of the wounded, sick, and shipwrecked must remain inviolable. However, the likelihood that a hospital ship would be employed to collect and promulgate military intelligence in this age of satellite sensors, over-the-horizon radar, and fixed and mobile long-range hydrophones is extremely remote; it strains the imagination to conjure up a scenario where it would have any utility whatsoever.").

[320] *For example*, 2004 UK MANUAL ¶13.125 footnote 142 ("GC II, Art 34(2), states that hospital ships may not possess or use a secret code for their wireless or other means of communication. This general wording has caused difficulties. British forces in the Falklands conflict 1982 found that having to give orders to their hospital ships 'in the clear' risked giving away their own positions or likely movements. The rule stated in paragraph 13.128 is a legitimate interpretation of Art 34(2).").

conduct encrypted communications.[321] Other States have not objected to this practice.[322] Some States have taken the same view.[323] Scholarly commentators have also supported this view.[324]

Hospital ships may not use encrypted communications for military purposes (*e.g.*, transmitting intelligence data) or in any way that is harmful to an adversary.[325] Commissioners or neutral observers may be placed on board hospital ships to verify compliance with this rule.[326]

7.12.3 Distinctive Marking and Other Identification of Hospital Ships and Coastal Rescue Craft. The ships designated for protection by Articles 22, 24, 25, and 27 of the GWS-Sea (*i.e.*, military hospital ships, commissioned civilian hospital ships, authorized neutral civilian hospital

---

[321] *For example*, Michael Sirak, *US Navy seeks to revise laws of war on hospital ships*, Jane's Defense Weekly 1-3 (Aug. 19, 2003) ("The USN installed both encrypted communications devices ... on the USNS Comfort (T-AH 20), one of its two dedicated hospital ships, before it deployed in January to the Middle East theatre to support the US-led Operation 'Iraqi Freedom', a US Department of Defense spokesman told Jane's Defence Weekly. USN officials argue that the rules preventing hospital ships from using encrypted communications devices - contained principally in the Second Geneva Convention of 1949 - do not adequately account for technological advancements, such as satellite communications, which are today regarded as vital for these vessels to function effectively. 'The way most naval warships communicate now is done on a level that even the most simple communications have some level of encryption,' said one navy official. 'Even the actual navigation of the ship can sometimes be in jeopardy if you cannot use these encrypted forms of communication.' According to this official, the US position is that the international community could allow the capability for encrypted communications, while maintaining confidence among belligerents that a party is not exploiting it to gather and transmit intelligence on the enemy. A belligerent retains the right under international law to place an observer on the ship, or request a neutral observer, such as from the International Committee of the Red Cross (ICRC), to verify compliance, the official notes.").

[322] *See* Wolff Heintschel Von Heinegg, *The Law of Armed Conflict at Sea*, *in* Dieter Fleck, The Handbook of International Humanitarian Law 463, 543 (¶1058) (3rd ed., 2013) ("Moreover, Article 34, para. 2, GC II can be considered to have become obsolete by the subsequent practice of the states parties. Today, hospital ships, like all warships and the majority of merchant vessels, communicate via satellite. The use of satellite communications implies encryption for both sending and receiving messages. The only two remaining hospital ships–the USS *Comfort* and the USS *Mercy*–do not dispose of traditional radio equipments [sic] but communicate over satellite communications only. This fact is known to the states parties to GC II. Still, there have been no protests so far. Hence, there are good reasons to believe that the other states parties have acquiesced in the US practice. Again, it should not be left of out of consideration that abandoning the prohibition of using encryption for emissions would better serve the humanitarian purposes hospital ships are to serve.").

[323] 2006 Australian Manual ¶6.72 ("In order to fulfil their humanitarian mission, hospital ships should be permitted to use cryptographic equipment provided such equipment is not used to transmit intelligence data nor in any other way to acquire military advantage."); 2004 UK Manual ¶13.125 ("In order to fulfil most effectively their humanitarian mission, hospital ships should be permitted to use cryptographic equipment. The equipment shall not be used in any circumstances to transmit intelligence data nor in any other way to acquire any military advantage.").

[324] *See, e.g.*, Jane G. Dalton, *Future Navies – Present Issues*, 59 Naval War College Review 17, 26 (Winter 2006) ("There is no need to belabor here the point that the prohibition on use of a 'secret code' by hospital ships is anachronistic, unrealistic, and unworkable in today's high-technology environment, where satellite communications are both routinely encrypted and routinely employed by military systems."); Louise Doswald-Beck, *Vessels, Aircraft and Persons Entitled to Protection During Armed Conflicts at Sea*, 65 British Yearbook of International Law 211, 219 (1994) ("The participants working on the *San Remo Manual* were of the opinion that hospital ships should be allowed to use cryptographic equipment, with a specification that it must not be used for transmitting intelligence or put to any other use incompatible with the humanitarian mission of the hospital ship. This could be verified by a qualified neutral observer on board as foreseen in Article 31(4) of GC2.").

[325] *Refer to* § 7.12.2.2 (No Use for Military Purposes); § 7.10.3.1 (Acts Harmful to the Enemy).

[326] *Refer to* § 7.12.2.6 (Control and Search of Hospital Ships and Coastal Rescue Craft).

ships, and coastal rescue craft, respectively) shall be distinctively marked as follows:

- all exterior surfaces shall be white; and
- one or more dark red crosses, as large as possible, shall be painted and displayed on each side of the hull and on the horizontal surfaces, so placed as to afford the greatest possible visibility from the sea and from the air.[327]

7.12.3.1 *Rules for Flying the National Flag, the Flag of the Party to the Conflict, and the Distinctive Emblem Flag*. All hospital ships must make themselves known by hoisting their national flag and, further, if they belong to a neutral State, the flag of the party to the conflict whose direction they have accepted.[328] A white flag with a red cross shall be flown at the mainmast as high as possible.[329]

Hospital ships that, in accordance with Article 31 of the GWS-Sea, are provisionally detained by the enemy, must haul down the flag of the party to the conflict in whose service they are or whose direction they have accepted.[330]

Coastal lifeboats, if they continue to operate with the consent of the Occupying Power from a base that is occupied, may be allowed, when away from their base, to continue to fly their own national colors along with a flag carrying a red cross on a white ground, subject to prior notification to all the parties to the conflict concerned.[331]

7.12.3.2 *Lifeboats and All Small Craft Used by the Medical Service*. Lifeboats of hospital ships, coastal lifeboats, and all small craft used by the Medical Service shall be painted white with dark red crosses prominently displayed and shall, in general, comply with the identification system prescribed above for hospital ships.[332]

7.12.3.3 *Night-Time Identification Measures*. The above-mentioned ships and

---

[327] GWS-SEA art. 43 ("The ships designated in Articles 22, 24, 25 and 27 shall be distinctively marked as follows: (a) All exterior surfaces shall be white. (b) One or more dark red crosses, as large as possible, shall be painted and displayed on each side of the hull and on the horizontal surfaces, so placed as to afford the greatest possible visibility from the sea and from the air.").

[328] GWS-SEA art. 43 ("All hospital ships shall make themselves known by hoisting their national flag and further, if they belong to a neutral state, the flag of the Party to the conflict whose direction they have accepted.").

[329] GWS-SEA art. 43 ("A white flag with a red cross shall be flown at the mainmast as high as possible.").

[330] GWS-SEA art. 43 ("Hospital ships which, in accordance with Article 31, are provisionally detained by the enemy, must haul down the flag of the Party to the conflict in whose service they are or whose direction they have accepted.").

[331] GWS-SEA art. 43 ("Coastal lifeboats, if they continue to operate with the consent of the Occupying Power from a base which is occupied, may be allowed, when away from their base, to continue to fly their own national colours along with a flag carrying a red cross on a white ground, subject to prior notification to all the Parties to the conflict concerned.").

[332] GWS-SEA art. 43 ("Lifeboats of hospital ships, coastal lifeboats and all small craft used by the Medical Service shall be painted white with dark red crosses prominently displayed and shall, in general, comply with the identification system prescribed above for hospital ships.").

craft, which may wish to ensure by night and in times of reduced visibility the protection to which they are entitled, must, subject to the assent of the party to the conflict under whose power they are, take the necessary measures to render their painting and distinctive emblems sufficiently apparent.[333]

7.12.3.4 *Other Emblems Instead of the Red Cross*. All the provisions in Article 43 of the GWS-Sea relating to the red cross apply equally to the other emblems mentioned in Article 41 of the GWS-Sea.[334]

The distinctive emblem of the red crystal also may be used for the same purposes as the red cross.[335]

7.12.3.5 *Agreements to Facilitate the Identification of Hospital Ships*. Parties to the conflict shall at all times endeavor to conclude mutual agreements in order to use the most modern methods available to facilitate the identification of hospital ships.[336]

7.12.4 Rights and Privileges of Hospital Ships and Coastal Rescue Craft. Military hospital ships, commissioned civilian hospital ships, and authorized neutral civilian hospital ships that meet the applicable requirements shall be respected and protected and are exempt from capture. Coastal rescue craft shall also be respected and protected so far as operational requirements permit.

In addition, the following protections apply:

7.12.4.1 *Protection From Attacks From Land*. Hospital ships entitled to the protection of the GWS-Sea shall not be attacked from land.[337]

7.12.4.2 *Authority to Leave Ports Held by the Enemy*. Any hospital ship in a port that falls into the hands of the enemy shall be authorized to leave that port.[338]

7.12.4.3 *Relief From Taxation in Time of War*. In time of war, military hospital ships, commissioned civilian hospital ships, and authorized neutral civilian hospital ships are

---

[333] GWS-SEA art. 43 ("The above-mentioned ships and craft, which may wish to ensure by night and in times of reduced visibility the protection to which they are entitled, must, subject to the assent of the Party to the conflict under whose power they are, take the necessary measures to render their painting and distinctive emblems sufficiently apparent.").

[334] GWS-SEA art. 43 ("All the provisions in this Article relating to the red cross shall apply equally to the other emblems mentioned in Article 41.").

[335] *Refer to* § 7.15.1.3 (Red Crystal).

[336] GWS-SEA art. 43 ("Parties to the conflict shall at all times endeavour to conclude mutual agreements in order to use the most modern methods available to facilitate the identification of hospital ships.").

[337] GWS art. 20 ("Hospital ships entitled to the protection of the Geneva Convention for the Amelioration of the Condition of Wounded, Sick and Shipwrecked Members of Armed Forces at Sea of August 12, 1949, shall not be attacked from the land.").

[338] GWS-SEA art. 29 ("Any hospital ship in a port which falls into the hands of the enemy shall be authorized to leave the said port.").

exempt from all dues and taxes imposed for the benefit of the State in the ports of the Parties to a particular 1904 Hague treaty. Article 1 of this 1904 Hague treaty provides that certain categories of hospital ships listed in an 1899 Hague treaty receive this benefit.[339] These categories of hospital ships listed in the 1899 Hague treaty are the same categories of hospital ships that are used in the GWS-Sea.[340] Some States may be Parties to the GWS-Sea but not to the 1904 Hague treaty that creates this exemption.

7.12.4.4 *Stay in Neutral Ports*. Vessels described in Articles 22, 24, 25, and 27 of the GWS-Sea (*i.e.*, military hospital ships, commissioned civilian hospital ships, authorized neutral civilian hospital ships, and coastal rescue craft, respectively), are not classed as warships as regards their stay in a neutral port.[341] Thus, these vessels are not subject to the restrictions that belligerent warships staying in a neutral port are subject to by neutral Powers.[342]

7.12.5 Protection of Sick-Bays in Warships. Should fighting occur on board a warship, the sick-bays shall be respected and spared as far as possible.[343]

7.12.5.1 *Use of Seized Sick-Bays and Their Equipment*. Sick-bays and their equipment shall remain subject to the laws of warfare, but may not be diverted from their purpose so long as they are required for the wounded and sick.[344] Nevertheless, the commander into whose power they have fallen may, after ensuring the proper care of the wounded and sick who are accommodated therein, apply them to other purposes in case of urgent military

---

[339] Convention Regarding Hospital Ships, art. 1, Dec. 21, 1904, 35 STAT. 1854, 1857 ("Hospital ships, concerning which the conditions set forth in Articles 1, 2 & 3 of the Convention concluded at The Hague on July 29, 1899, for the adaptation to Maritime Warfare of the principles of the Geneva Convention of August 22, 1864, are fulfilled shall be exempted, in time of war, from all dues and taxes imposed on vessels for the benefit of the State, in the ports of the Contracting Parties.").

[340] *See* Convention for the Adaptation to Maritime Warfare of the Principles of the Geneva Convention of August 22, 1864, arts. 1-3, Jul. 29, 1899, 32 STAT. 1827, 1831-32 ("Article 1 Military hospital ships, that is to say, ships constructed or assigned by States specially and solely for the purpose of assisting the wounded, sick or shipwrecked, and the names of which shall have been communicated to the belligerent Powers at the beginning or during the course of hostilities, and in any case before they are employed, shall be respected and cannot be captured while hostilities last. … Article 2 Hospital ships, equipped wholly or in part at the cost of private individuals or officially recognized relief Societies, shall likewise be respected and exempt from capture, provided the belligerent Power to whom they belong has given them an official commission and has notified their names to the hostile Power at the commencement of or during hostilities, and in any case before they are employed. … Article 3 Hospital-ships, equipped wholly or in part at the cost of private individuals or officially recognized Societies of neutral countries, shall be respected and exempt from capture, if the neutral Power to whom they belong has given them an official commission and notified their names to the belligerent powers at the commencement of or during hostilities, and in any case before they are employed.").

[341] GWS-SEA art. 32 ("Vessels described in Articles 22, 24, 25 and 27 are not classed as warships as regards their stay in a neutral port.").

[342] *Refer to* § 15.9 (Additional Rules Applicable to Neutral Ports, Roadsteads, and Internal Waters).

[343] GWS-SEA art. 28 ("Should fighting occur on board a warship, the sick-bays shall be respected and spared as far as possible.").

[344] GWS-SEA art. 28 ("Sick-bays and their equipment shall remain subject to the laws of warfare, but may not be diverted from their purpose so long as they are required for the wounded and sick.").

necessity.[345]

7.12.6 Forfeiture of Protection of Hospital Ships and Sick Bays. The protection to which hospital ships and sick-bays are entitled shall not cease unless the vessels are used to commit, outside their humanitarian duties, acts harmful to the enemy.[346] In particular, hospital ships and coastal rescue craft may not be used for military purposes nor to hamper the movements of combatants.[347]

7.12.6.1 *Due Warning Before Cessation of Protection*. Protection may, however, cease only after due warning has been given, naming in all appropriate cases a reasonable time limit, and after such warning has remained unheeded.[348]

The obligation to refrain from use of force against a medical vessel or sick-bay acting in violation of its mission and protected status without due warning does not prohibit the exercise of the right of self-defense. There may be cases in which, in the exercise of the right of self-defense, a warning is not "due" or a reasonable time limit is not appropriate. For example, forces receiving heavy fire may exercise their right of self-defense and return fire. Such use of force in self-defense must also be proportionate.[349]

7.12.6.2 *Conditions That Do Not Deprive Hospital Ships and Sick-Bays of Vessels of Their Protection*. The following conditions shall not be considered as depriving hospital ships or sick-bays of vessels of the protection due to them:

- the fact that the crews of ships or sick-bays are armed for the maintenance of order, for their own defense, or for the defense of the sick and wounded;
- the presence on board of apparatus exclusively intended to facilitate navigation or communication;
- the discovery on board hospital ships or in sick-bays of portable arms and ammunition taken from the wounded, sick, and shipwrecked, and not yet handed over to the proper service;
- the fact that the humanitarian activities of hospital ships and sick-bays of vessels or of the crews extend to the care of wounded, sick, or shipwrecked civilians; and
- the transport of equipment and of personnel intended exclusively for medical duties, over

---

[345] GWS-SEA art. 28 ("Nevertheless, the commander into whose power they have fallen may, after ensuring the proper care of the wounded and sick who are accommodated therein, apply them to other purposes in case of urgent military necessity.").

[346] GWS-SEA art. 34 ("The protection to which hospital ships and sick-bays are entitled shall not cease unless they are used to commit, outside their humanitarian duties, acts harmful to the enemy.").

[347] *Refer to* § 7.12.2.2 (No Use for Military Purposes); § 7.12.2.3 (No Hampering the Movement of Combatants).

[348] GWS-SEA art. 34 ("Protection may, however, cease only after due warning has been given, naming in all appropriate cases a reasonable time limit, and after such warning has remained unheeded.").

[349] *Compare* § 7.10.3.2 (Due Warning Before Cessation of Protection).

and above the normal requirements.[350]

7.12.6.3 *Arming of Hospital Ships and Equipping Them With Defensive Devices*. The GWS-Sea contemplates that the crews of hospital ships may be armed and does not specifically restrict the weapons that they may have.

The crews of hospital ships may be armed to the extent necessary to enable them to defend themselves or their patients against unlawful attacks. Such arming is viewed as consistent with the ship's humanitarian purpose and the crew's duty to safeguard the wounded and sick. For example, crews of hospital ships may be equipped with weapons to meet internal security needs, to maintain discipline, to protect staff and patients from criminal threats of violence, and to prevent the theft of medical supplies. The type of weapon that is necessary for defensive or other legitimate purposes may depend on the nature of the threats against the hospital ship.[351] For example, hospital ships may be armed with defensive weapon systems, including when necessary certain crew-served weapons, as a prudent anti-terrorism/force protection (AT/FP) measure to defend against small boat attacks.[352] On the other hand, crews of hospital ships should not be armed such that they would appear to an enemy military force to present an offensive threat.

Equipping hospital ships with other defensive devices – such as chaff for protection against over-the-horizon weapons or similar threats – is not prohibited.[353] However, such devices, like weapons, must not be used to commit acts harmful to enemy military forces acting in conformity with the law of war.[354]

---

[350] GWS-SEA art. 35 ("The following conditions shall not be considered as depriving hospital ships or sick-bays of vessels of the protection due to them: (1) The fact that the crews of ships or sick-bays are armed for the maintenance of order, for their own defence or that of the sick and wounded. (2) The presence on board of apparatus exclusively intended to facilitate navigation or communication. (3) The discovery on board hospital ships or in sick-bays of portable arms and ammunition taken from the wounded, sick and shipwrecked and not yet handed to the proper service. (4) The fact that the humanitarian activities of hospital ships and sick-bays of vessels or of the crews extend to the care of wounded, sick or shipwrecked civilians. (5) The transport of equipment and of personnel intended exclusively for medical duties, over and above the normal requirements.").

[351] *For example*, Michael Sirak, *US Navy seeks to revise laws of war on hospital ships*, Jane's Defense Weekly 1-3 (Aug. 19, 2003) ("The USN installed both encrypted communications devices and 50-cal machine guns on the USNS Comfort (T-AH 20), one of its two dedicated hospital ships, before it deployed in January to the Middle East theatre to support the US-led Operation 'Iraqi Freedom', a US Department of Defense spokesman told Jane's Defence Weekly. … Furthermore, USN officials say the small arms currently allowed on hospital ships, such as sidearms and rifles, are not enough to thwart an attack by a non-state actor like a terrorist group. They say the limited protection afforded to these vessels under international law would be unlikely to deter terrorists and, unlike lawful belligerents, terrorists would consider them an attractive 'soft' target. Therefore, they argue that it is necessary to place 'crew-served' weapons like 30-cal and 50-cal machine guns on them, exclusively for defence, to fend off attacks by swarming, heavily armed speed boats or suicide craft.").

[352] Jane G. Dalton, *Future Navies – Present Issues*, 59 NAVAL WAR COLLEGE REVIEW 17, 27 (Winter 2006) (noting that a problem "facing hospital ships is the need to arm them for force protection against *USS Cole*-type attacks" and that "chaff and flares [would be] ineffective against a determined suicide attack like that launched against *Cole,*").

[353] *See* 2004 UK MANUAL ¶13.124 ("Hospital ships may be equipped with purely deflective means of defence, such as chaff and flares.").

[354] *Refer to* § 7.12.6 (Forfeiture of Protection of Hospital Ships and Sick Bays).

7.13 Chartered Medical Transport Ships

Ships chartered for medical transport purposes shall be authorized to transport equipment exclusively intended for the treatment of wounded and sick members of armed forces or for the prevention of disease, provided that the particulars regarding their voyage have been notified to the adverse Power and approved by the latter.[355] The adverse Power shall preserve the right to board the carrier ships, but not to capture them or seize the equipment carried.[356]

7.13.1 Agreement to Place Neutral Observers on Chartered Medical Transports. By agreement among the parties to the conflict, neutral observers may be placed on board such ships to verify the equipment carried.[357] For this purpose, free access to the equipment shall be given.[358]

7.14 Military Medical Aircraft

Medical aircraft – that is to say, aircraft exclusively employed for the removal of the wounded, sick, and shipwrecked, and for the transport of medical personnel and equipment – shall not be attacked, but shall be respected by the belligerents, while flying at heights and times, and on routes, specifically agreed upon by the belligerents concerned.[359]

7.14.1 Medical Aircraft Not Flying at Heights and Times and on Routes Specifically Agreed Upon by Belligerents Concerned. The use of protected medical aircraft generally depends on an agreement between the belligerents.[360]

However, known medical aircraft, when performing their humanitarian functions, must

---

[355] GWS-Sea art. 38 ("Ships chartered for that purpose shall be authorized to transport equipment exclusively intended for the treatment of wounded and sick members of armed forces or for the prevention of disease, provided that the particulars regarding their voyage have been notified to the adverse Power and approved by the latter.").

[356] GWS-Sea art. 38 ("The adverse Power shall preserve the right to board the carrier ships, but not to capture them or seize the equipment carried.").

[357] GWS-Sea art. 38 ("By agreement amongst the Parties to the conflict, neutral observers may be placed on board such ships to verify the equipment carried.").

[358] GWS-Sea art. 38 ("For this purpose, free access to the equipment shall be given.").

[359] GWS art. 36 ("Medical aircraft, that is to say, aircraft exclusively employed for the removal of wounded and sick and for the transport of medical personnel and equipment, shall not be attacked, but shall be respected by the belligerents, while flying at heights, times and on routes specifically agreed upon between the belligerents concerned."); GWS-Sea art. 39 ("Medical aircraft, that is to say, aircraft exclusively employed for the removal of the wounded, sick and shipwrecked, and for the transport of medical personnel and equipment, may not be the object of attack, but shall be respected by the Parties to the conflict, while flying at heights, at times and on routes specifically agreed upon between the Parties to the conflict concerned.").

[360] GWS-Sea Commentary 216-17 ("The solution adopted makes any future use of protected medical aircraft dependent on the conclusion of an agreement between the belligerents. As it will be a matter of fixing routes and times of flights, such agreements will no doubt usually be made for each specific case and by a simple exchange of communications between the military commands. But there might also be an agreement of longer duration. If there is no agreement, belligerents will be able to use medical aircraft only at their own risk. It is, however, to be hoped that in such cases the enemy will not resort to extreme measures until he has exhausted all other means of control at his disposal.").

be respected and protected.[361] Such aircraft does not constitute a military objective that is liable to being made the object of attack.[362] Thus, even if not flying pursuant to an agreement, such aircraft shall not be deliberately attacked or fired upon, if identified as protected medical aircraft. For example, if there is no agreement and a military force happens upon a medical aircraft belonging to an enemy State, the aircraft must not be made the object of attack until all other means of control (such as directing the aircraft to land and submit to search) have been exhausted.[363]

A medical aircraft that is not flying pursuant to a special agreement that seeks to claim protection as medical aircraft shall make every effort to identify itself and to inform the enemy State of its status and its operations, such as its flight times and routes.[364] For example, an unknown aircraft within a theater of military operations would often be reasonably presumed to be a military objective, and the aircraft must take affirmative steps to rebut this presumption.[365] In order to maintain its entitlement to protection, such aircraft must obey the directions of the enemy State, such as directions to land and to submit to search.

7.14.2 <u>Exclusively Employed for the Removal of the Wounded, Sick, or Shipwrecked, and for the Transport of Medical Personnel and Equipment</u>. In order to receive protection as medical aircraft, the aircraft must be exclusively employed for the removal of wounded, sick, or shipwrecked combatants and for the transport of medical personnel and equipment.

For example, such aircraft, while designated or operating as medical aircraft, may not be used also for military purposes, such as to transport able-bodied combatants or to carry

---

[361] Michael J. Matheson, Deputy Legal Adviser, Department of State, *Remarks on the United States Position on the Relation of Customary International Law to the 1977 Protocols Additional to the 1949 Geneva Conventions at the Sixth Annual American Red Cross-Washington College of Law Conference on International Humanitarian Law* (Jan. 22, 1987), 2 AMERICAN UNIVERSITY JOURNAL OF INTERNATIONAL LAW AND POLICY 419, 423-24 (1987) ("We support the principle that known medical aircraft be respected and protected when performing their humanitarian functions. That is a rather general statement of what is reflected in many, but not all, aspects of the detailed rules in articles 24 through 31, which include some of the more useful innovations in the Protocol.").

[362] *Refer to* § 5.6.4.1 (Military Equipment and Bases).

[363] 1976 AIR FORCE PAMPHLET 110-31 ("Generally, a medical aircraft (identified as such) should not be attacked unless under the circumstances at the time it represents an immediate military threat and other methods of control are not available.").

[364] *Consider* AP I art. 27(2) ("A medical aircraft which flies over an area physically controlled by an adverse Party without, or in deviation from the terms of, an agreement provided for in paragraph 1, either through navigational error or because of an emergency affecting the safety of the flight, shall make every effort to identify itself and to inform the adverse Party of the circumstances. As soon as such medical aircraft has been recognized by the adverse Party, that Party shall make all reasonable efforts to give the order to land or to alight on water, referred to in Article 30, paragraph 1, or to take other measures to safeguard its own interests, and, in either case, to allow the aircraft time for compliance, before resorting to an attack against the aircraft").

[365] *Cf.* BOTHE, PARTSCH, & SOLF, NEW RULES 155 (AP I art. 27, ¶2.2) ("The question then arises whether an aircraft which is operating without such agreement (or in deviation from the terms of such agreement) is a legitimate target, a military objective within the meaning of Art. 52, para. 2. Article 27, *para.* 2, is based on the (correct) assumption that it is, even if it is a true medical aircraft. ... An aircraft flying over areas controlled by an adverse Party is, in case of doubt, a military objective. Anything else is unrealistic.").

ammunition to combat forces.[366]

7.14.2.1 *Conversion of Aircraft To and From Use Under a Special Agreement for Medical Purposes*. If medical aircraft are flying pursuant to an agreement, it is not necessary that the aircraft should have been specially built and equipped for medical purposes.[367] There is no objection to converting ordinary aircraft into medical aircraft for use under a special agreement or to using medical aircraft that have been used under a special agreement for other purposes, provided the distinctive markings are removed.[368]

7.14.2.2 *Search, Rescue, or Other Recovery Excluded*. Medical aircraft may engage in the removal of wounded, sick, or shipwrecked combatants. However, medical aircraft may neither prevent the capture of combatants by enemy military forces nor otherwise interfere with enemy military operations.[369] Therefore, medical aircraft do not include combat search and rescue aircraft, and medical aircraft should not engage in such activities lest they forfeit the special protection afforded by the GWS or GWS-Sea.[370] Special agreements between the opposing forces, however, may provide protection to aircraft engaged in search, rescue, or other recovery missions.

7.14.3 Markings on Medical Aircraft. Medical aircraft shall bear, clearly marked, the distinctive emblem (prescribed in Article 38 of the GWS and Article 41 of the GWS-Sea), together with their national colors, on their lower, upper, and lateral surfaces.[371]

---

366 *Compare* § 7.12.2.2 (No Use for Military Purposes). *For example*, First Lieutenant Edward R. Cummings, *The Juridical Status of Medical Aircraft Under the Conventional Laws of War*, 66 MILITARY LAW REVIEW 105, 115 (1974) ("It has been said that during the Second World War 'Article 18 [of the 1929 GWS] was … more or less a dead letter,' even though air evacuation flights were used extensively during the war. One and a half million Americans alone were evacuated by air during the war. The United States primarily used aircraft that were not devoted exclusively to the care or the wounded and sick. It was able to do so because of its air supremacy. Even though these aircraft would not have been entitled to juridical protection under the 1929 Geneva Convention, none of the aircraft used to convey casualties 'suffered any mishap during the war.'") (ellipsis in original).

367 1956 FM 27-10 (Change No. 1 1976) ¶237b ("It is not necessary that the aircraft should have been specially built and equipped for medical purposes.").

368 1956 FM 27-10 (Change No. 1 1976) ¶237b ("There is no objection to converting ordinary aircraft into medical aircraft or to using former medical aircraft for other purposes, provided the distinctive markings are removed.").

369 *Compare* § 7.12.2.3 (No Hampering the Movement of Combatants); § 4.9.2.3 (Exclusively Engaged in Humanitarian Duties).

370 XI OFFICIAL RECORDS OF THE CDDH 503 (CDDH/II/SR.45, ¶10) ("Mr. SOLF (United States of America) recalled that 105 years previously, 160 wounded soldiers of France had been successfully evacuated from besieged Paris by balloon, thus for the first time making rapid medical evacuation by air a reality. It was an undisputed medical fact that the sooner a badly wounded person came under a surgeon's care, the better were his chances of recovery and survival. It was also recognized as an undisputed military fact that medical aircraft posed a security threat if they were used for military reconnaissance. Accordingly, throughout the history of the development of medical aircraft, their role in the search of the battlefield for wounded had been restricted."). *Consider* AP I art. 28(4) ("While carrying out the flights referred to in Articles 26 and 27, medical aircraft shall not, except by prior agreement with the adverse Party, be used to search for the wounded, sick and shipwrecked.").

371 GWS art. 36 ("They shall bear, clearly marked, the distinctive emblem prescribed in Article 38, together with their national colours, on their lower, upper and lateral surfaces."); GWS-SEA art. 39 ("They shall be clearly marked

They shall be provided with any other markings or means of identification that may be agreed upon between the belligerents upon the outbreak or during the course of hostilities.[372]

7.14.4 Prohibition on Flights Over Enemy or Enemy-Occupied Territory. Unless otherwise agreed, flights over enemy or enemy-occupied territory are prohibited.[373] If flying pursuant to an agreement, however, medical aircraft are to receive protection when flying over enemy or enemy-occupied territory.[374]

7.14.5 Landing and Inspection of Military Medical Aircraft. Medical aircraft shall obey every summons to land (including water landings if the aircraft is equipped for them).[375] In the event of a landing thus imposed, the aircraft with its occupants may continue its flight after examination, if any.[376]

7.14.5.1 *Treatment of Personnel in the Event of Involuntary Landing in Enemy or Enemy-Occupied Territory*. In the event of an involuntary landing in enemy or enemy-occupied territory (including a water landing), the wounded and sick, as well as the crew of the aircraft, shall be POWs.[377] The medical personnel shall be treated according to Article 24 and the Articles following of the GWS, and Articles 36 and 37 of the GWS-Sea.[378]

7.14.6 Belligerent Military Medical Aircraft in Neutral Territory. Subject to conditions set by the neutral Powers, medical aircraft of parties to the conflict may fly over the territory of neutral Powers, land on it in case of necessity, or use it as a port of call.[379] They shall give

---

with the distinctive emblem prescribed in Article 41, together with their national colours, on their lower, upper and lateral surfaces.").

[372] GWS art. 36 ("They shall be provided with any other markings or means of identification that may be agreed upon between the belligerents upon the outbreak or during the course of hostilities."); GWS-SEA art. 39 ("They shall be provided with any other markings or means of identification which may be agreed upon between the Parties to the conflict upon the outbreak or during the course of hostilities.").

[373] GWS art. 36 ("Unless agreed otherwise, flights over enemy or enemy-occupied territory are prohibited."); GWS-SEA art. 39 (same).

[374] *Consider* AP I art. 27 (1) ("The medical aircraft of a Party to the conflict shall continue to be protected while flying over land or sea areas physically controlled by an adverse Party, provided that prior agreement to such flights has been obtained from the competent authority of that adverse Party.").

[375] GWS art. 36 ("Medical aircraft shall obey every summons to land."); GWS-SEA art. 39 ("Medical aircraft shall obey every summons to alight on land or water.").

[376] GWS art. 36 ("In the event of a landing thus imposed, the aircraft with its occupants may continue its flight after examination, if any."); GWS-SEA art. 39 ("In the event of having thus to alight, the aircraft with its occupants may continue its flight after examination, if any.").

[377] GWS art. 36 ("In the event of an involuntary landing in enemy or enemy-occupied territory, the wounded and sick, as well as the crew of the aircraft shall be prisoners of war."); GWS-SEA art. 39 ("In the event of alighting involuntarily on land or water in enemy or enemy occupied territory, the wounded, sick and shipwrecked, as well as the crew of the aircraft shall be prisoners of war.").

[378] GWS art. 36 ("The medical personnel shall be treated according to Article 24 and the Articles following."); GWS-SEA art. 39 ("The medical personnel shall be treated according to Articles 36 and 37.").

[379] GWS art. 37 ("Subject to the provisions of the second paragraph, medical aircraft of Parties to the conflict may fly over the territory of neutral Powers, land on it in case of necessity, or use it as a port of call."); GWS-SEA art. 40

neutral Powers prior notice of their passage over the said territory, and obey every summons to alight, on land or water.[380] They will be immune from attack only when flying on routes, at heights, and at times specifically agreed upon between the parties to the conflict and the neutral Power concerned.[381]

7.14.6.1 *Conditions Set by Neutral Powers*. The neutral Powers may, however, place conditions or restrictions on the passage or landing of medical aircraft on their territory.[382] Such possible conditions or restrictions shall be applied equally to all parties to the conflict.[383]

7.14.6.2 *Detention of the Wounded, Sick, or Shipwrecked*. Unless otherwise agreed between the neutral Powers and the parties to the conflict, the wounded, sick, or shipwrecked who are disembarked with the consent of the local authorities on neutral territory by medical aircraft shall be detained by the neutral Power, where so required by international law, in such a manner that they cannot again take part in operations of war.[384] The cost of their accommodation and internment shall be borne by the Power on which they depend.[385]

7.15 Display of the Distinctive Emblem to Facilitate Identification

The GWS and GWS-Sea contemplate that the distinctive emblem, usually a red cross on a white background, will be used to facilitate the identification of the persons and objects protected by the GWS and GWS-Sea.[386] It helps identify protected persons and objects (*e.g.*, medical and religious personnel, medical transports, and medical facilities), but does not itself confer on them, or by its absence deprive them of, legal protection. The use of the distinctive emblem to facilitate protection is to take place under the direction of the competent military

---

("Subject to the provisions of the second paragraph, medical aircraft of Parties to the conflict may fly over the territory of neutral Powers, land thereon in case of necessity, or use it as a port of call.").

380 GWS art. 37 ("They shall give the neutral Powers previous notice of their passage over the said territory and obey all summons to alight, on land or water."); GWS-Sea art. 40 ("They shall give neutral Powers prior notice of their passage over the said territory, and obey every summons to alight, on land or water.").

381 GWS art. 37 ("They will be immune from attack only when flying on routes, at heights and at times specifically agreed upon between the Parties to the conflict and the neutral Power concerned."); GWS-Sea art. 40 (same).

382 GWS art. 37 ("The neutral Powers may, however, place conditions or restrictions on the passage or landing of medical aircraft on their territory."); GWS-Sea art. 40 (same).

383 GWS art. 37 ("Such possible conditions or restrictions shall be applied equally to all Parties to the conflict."); GWS-Sea art. 40 (same).

384 GWS art. 37 ("Unless agreed otherwise between the neutral Power and the Parties to the conflict, the wounded and sick who are disembarked, with the consent of the local authorities, on neutral territory by medical aircraft, shall be detained by the neutral Power, where so required by international law, in such a manner that they cannot again take part in operations of war."); GWS-Sea art. 40 ("Unless otherwise agreed between the neutral Powers and the Parties to the conflict, the wounded, sick or shipwrecked who are disembarked with the consent of the local authorities on neutral territory by medical aircraft shall be detained by the neutral Power, where so required by international law, in such a manner that they cannot again take part in operations of war.").

385 GWS art. 37 ("The cost of their accommodation and internment shall be borne by the Power on which they depend."); GWS-Sea art. 40 (same).

386 *See* GWS-Sea Commentary 235 ("In principle, a red cross on a white ground should be displayed on the buildings, persons, vehicles and objects protected by the Convention.").

authority. The misuse of the distinctive emblem is prohibited.

7.15.1 <u>The Distinctive Emblems: Red Cross, Crescent, and Crystal</u>. To facilitate visual identification of medical and religious personnel, and medical units, facilities, transports, and equipment, four distinctive emblems have been recognized in treaties to which the United States is a Party. As displayed below, they are 1) a red cross; 2) a red crescent; 3) a red crystal; and 4) a red lion and sun. Each is displayed on a white background.

The Distinctive Emblems

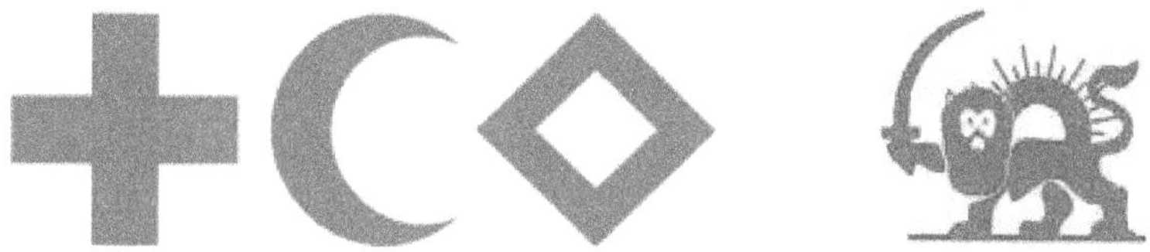

Red Cross Red Crescent Red Crystal Red Lion and Sun (withdrawn)

7.15.1.1 *<u>Red Cross</u>*. "As a compliment to Switzerland," the heraldic emblem of the red cross on a white ground formed by reversing the Federal colors is retained as the emblem and distinctive sign of the Medical Services of armed forces.[387] The explanation that the red cross is used as a compliment to Switzerland was added to emphasize that the red cross is not intended to have religious significance.[388] The red cross has long been used to identify medical personnel during armed conflict.[389]

7.15.1.2 *<u>Red Crescent, and Red Lion and Sun</u>*. In the case of countries that already use, in place of the red cross, the emblem of the red crescent or the emblem of the red lion and sun on a white ground, those emblems are also recognized by the terms of the GWS and GWS-Sea.[390]

---

[387] GWS art. 38 ("As a compliment to Switzerland, the heraldic emblem of the red cross on a white ground formed by reversing the Federal colours, is retained as the emblem and distinctive sign of the Medical Services of armed forces.").

[388] GWS COMMENTARY 303 ("The phrase stating that the red cross emblem was formed, as a compliment to Switzerland, by reversing the Federal colours was introduced into the Geneva Convention by the Diplomatic Conference of 1906. 'This tribute in 1906', wrote Paul Des Gouttes, the eminent commentator on the Geneva Convention, 'had also another object: to confirm officially and explicitly that the emblem had no religious significance'."). *See also* AP III preamble ("Stressing that the distinctive emblems are not intended to have any religious, ethnic, racial, regional or political significance,").

[389] *See, e.g.*, Convention for the Amelioration of the Wounded in Armies in the Field, art. 7, Aug. 22, 1864, 22 STAT. 940, 944 ("A distinctive and uniform flag shall be adopted for hospitals, ambulances and evacuations. It must, on every occasion, be accompanied by the national flag. An arm-badge (brassard) shall also be allowed for individuals neutralized, but the delivery thereof shall be left to military authority. The flag and arm-badge shall bear a red cross on a white ground.").

[390] GWS art. 38 ("Nevertheless, in the case of countries which already use as emblem, in place of the red cross, the red crescent or the red lion and sun on a white ground, those emblems are also recognized by the terms of the

7.15.1.3 <u>*Red Crystal*</u>. AP III recognizes an additional distinctive emblem in addition to, and for the same purposes as, the distinctive emblems of the Geneva Conventions, which, for parties to AP III, shall enjoy equal status to the other emblems.[391]

This additional distinctive emblem, composed of a red frame in the shape of a square on edge on a white ground, shall conform to the illustration in the Annex to AP III.[392]

This distinctive emblem is referred to in AP III as the "third Protocol emblem"[393] but is often called the red crystal.

The conditions for use of and respect for the third Protocol emblem are identical to those for the distinctive emblems established by the 1949 Geneva Conventions and, where applicable, AP I and AP II.[394]

AP III further provides for use of the Red Crystal for indicative purposes by national societies of the Parties to AP III. Such uses for indicative purposes by national societies are uses of the red crystal that do not indicate protection under the AP III, the GWS, or the GWS-Sea, but that indicate an association with the Red Cross movement.[395]

7.15.1.4 <u>*State Discretion Among Emblems*</u>. Although the GWS contemplates that the emblem of the red crescent and the emblem of the red sun and lion will be used only in States that already used them before ratifying the 1949 Geneva Conventions, AP III provides that the

---

present Convention."); GWS-SEA art. 41 ("Nevertheless, in the case of countries which already use as emblem, in place of the red cross, the red crescent or the red lion and sun on a white ground, these emblems are also recognized by the terms of the present Convention.").

[391] AP III art. 2(1) ("This Protocol recognizes an additional distinctive emblem in addition to, and for the same purposes as, the distinctive emblems of the Geneva Conventions. The distinctive emblems shall enjoy equal status.").

[392] AP III art. 2(2) ("This additional distinctive emblem, composed of a red frame in the shape of a square on edge on a white ground, shall conform to the illustration in the Annex to this Protocol.").

[393] AP III art. 2(2) ("This distinctive emblem is referred to in this Protocol as the 'third Protocol emblem'.").

[394] AP III art. 2(3) ("The conditions for use of and respect for the third Protocol emblem are identical to those for the distinctive emblems established by the Geneva Conventions and, where applicable, the 1977 Additional Protocols.").

[395] AP III art. 3 ("1. National Societies of those High Contracting Parties which decide to use the third Protocol emblem may, in using the emblem in conformity with relevant national legislation, choose to incorporate within it, for indicative purposes: a) a distinctive emblem recognized by the Geneva Conventions or a combination of these emblems; or b) another emblem which has been in effective use by a High Contracting Party and was the subject of a communication to the other High Contracting Parties and the International Committee of the Red Cross through the depositary prior to the adoption of this Protocol. Incorporation shall conform to the illustration in the Annex to this Protocol. 2. A National Society which chooses to incorporate within the third Protocol emblem another emblem in accordance with paragraph 1 above, may, in conformity with national legislation, use the designation of that emblem and display it within its national territory. 3. National Societies may, in accordance with national legislation and in exceptional circumstances and to facilitate their work, make temporary use of the distinctive emblem referred to in Article 2 of this Protocol. 4. This Article does not affect the legal status of the distinctive emblems recognized in the Geneva Conventions and in this Protocol, nor does it affect the legal status of any particular emblem when incorporated for indicative purposes in accordance with paragraph 1 of this Article.").

distinctive emblems of the Geneva Conventions shall enjoy equal status.[396] In addition, AP III provides that the medical services and religious personnel of armed forces of Parties to AP III may, without prejudice to their current emblems, make temporary use of any distinctive emblems where this may enhance protection.[397]

Some States have adopted the red crescent, without objection by other States Parties, even though their use of the red crescent did not predate the adoption of the GWS.[398] Israel ratified the 1949 Geneva Conventions with the reservation that it will use a Red Shield of David as its distinctive sign.[399]

7.15.2 Control of Display by the Competent Military Authority. Under the direction of the competent military authority, the emblem shall be displayed on the flags, armlets, and on all equipment employed in the Medical Service.[400] For example, under military regulations, helmets or vehicles used by the Medical Service might bear the distinctive emblem to facilitate

---

[396] AP III art. 2(1) ("The distinctive emblems shall enjoy equal status.").

[397] AP III art. 2(4) ("The medical services and religious personnel of armed forces of High Contracting Parties may, without prejudice to their current emblems, make temporary use of any distinctive emblem referred to in paragraph 1 of this Article where this may enhance protection.").

[398] *For example*, H. Beer, Secretary General, League of Red Cross Societies, and J. Moreillon, Department of Principles and Law, International Committee of the Red Cross, *Adoption of the Red Crescent by the Islamic Republic of Iran*, Circular No. 72 (Nov. 5, 1980), *reprinted in* 20 INTERNATIONAL REVIEW OF THE RED CROSS, 316-17 (1980) ("On 4 July 1980 the Islamic Republic of Iran informed the International Committee of the Red Cross and the League of Red Cross Societies of its decision to adopt the red crescent instead of the red lion and sun as the distinctive sign of its armed forces' medical service. ... On 4 September the Iranian Authorities notified the Swiss Government, the depositary of the Geneva Conventions, of the adoption by the Islamic Republic of Iran of the red crescent, and asked it to convey its decision to the States parties to the Geneva Conventions. This the Swiss Government did on 20 October.").

[399] *See* Israel, *Statement on Signature of the GWS*, Aug. 12, 1949, 75 UNTS 436 ("Subject to the reservation that, while respecting the inviolability of the distinctive signs and emblems of the Convention, Israel will use the Red Shield of David as the emblem and distinctive sign of the medical services of her armed forces."); Israel, *Statement on Ratification of the GWS*, Jul. 6, 1952, 96 UNTS 323 ("The instrument confirms the reservations made by Israel upon signature of the Convention."); Israel, *Statement on Signature of the GWS-Sea*, Aug. 12, 1949, 75 UNTS 438 ("Subject to the reservation that, while respecting the inviolability of the distinctive signs and emblems of the Convention, Israel will use the Red Shield of David on the flags, armlets and on all equipment (including hospital ships), employed in the medical service."); Israel, *Statement on Ratification of the GWS-Sea*, 96 UNTS 324 (Jul. 6, 1952) ("The instrument confirms the reservations made by Israel upon signature of the Convention."); Israel, *Statement on Signature of the GC*, Aug. 12, 1949, 75 UNTS 438 ("Subject to the reservation that, while respecting the inviolability of the distinctive signs and emblems provided for in Article 38 of the Geneva Convention for the Amelioration of the Condition of the Wounded and Sick in Armed Forces in the Field of August 12, 1949, Israel will use the Red Shield of David as the emblem and distinctive sign provided for in this Convention."); Israel, *Statement on Ratification of the GC*, Jul. 6, 1952, 96 UNTS 326 ("The instrument confirms the reservations made by Israel upon signature of the Convention.").

[400] GWS art. 39 ("Under the direction of the competent military authority, the emblem shall be displayed on the flags, armlets and on all equipment employed in the Medical Service."); GWS-SEA art. 41 ("Under the direction of the competent military authority, the emblem of the red cross on a white ground shall be displayed on the flags, armlets and on all equipment employed in the Medical Service.").

the respect and protection of medical personnel by the enemy.[401]

7.15.2.1 *Removal or Obscuration of the Distinctive Emblem*. The display of the distinctive emblem is under the direction of the competent military authority.[402] Thus, the military command may authorize the removal or obscuring of the distinctive emblem for tactical purposes, such as camouflage.[403] Similarly, it would be appropriate for the distinctive emblem to be removed if it is assessed that enemy forces will fail to respect the emblem and seek to attack medical personnel; display of the emblem in such circumstances would not be considered "feasible" because in that instance it would not result in a humanitarian benefit.[404]

In the practice of the United States, removal or obscuration of the distinctive emblem has generally been controlled by the responsible major tactical commander, such as a brigade commander or higher.[405]

7.15.3 Significance of the Display of the Distinctive Emblem.

7.15.3.1 *Distinctive Emblem Facilitates Protection*. The purpose of the display of the distinctive emblem is to facilitate the identification of protected status.[406] The absence of the

---

[401] *Consider* AP I Amended Annex I art. 5(4) ("Medical and religious personnel carrying out their duties in the battle area shall, as far as possible, wear headgear and clothing bearing the distinctive emblem.").

[402] GWS-SEA COMMENTARY 230 ("The initial phrase of the present Article is most important: use of the emblem is to be 'under the direction of the competent military authority'. This wording shows that it is the military command which controls the emblem and can give or withhold permission to use it. Moreover, only that command can order a medical unit to be camouflaged."). *See also* Frederic de Mulinen, Head of Division, International Committee of the Red Cross, *Signalling and Identification of Medical Personnel and Material*, 12 INTERNATIONAL REVIEW OF THE RED CROSS 479, 481 (1972) ("Distinctive emblems may not be displayed without the authorization of the State or of a State authority. … The State or, by the delegation of its competency, the military command therefore 'controls the emblem' and is free to permit or prohibit the use of the distinctive emblem. It may even prohibit its use entirely without thereby violating the Conventions. In that event, actual protection would obviously be very small.").

[403] GWS-SEA COMMENTARY 228-29 ("In the first place there is no obligation on a belligerent to mark his medical units with the emblem. Sometimes military commanders have camouflaged such units—i.e. have abstained from marking them and even tried to conceal them—in order to conceal the presence or real strength of their forces. This is more likely to occur on land than at sea.").

[404] *Refer to* § 5.2.3.2 (What Precautions Are Feasible).

[405] *For example*, DEPARTMENT OF THE ARMY REGULATION 750-1, *Army Material Maintenance Policy*, ¶8-9c(17) (Sept. 2013) ("Under tactical conditions, when requirements for concealment outweigh those for recognition, all conspicuous markings may be obscured or removed by the authority and at the discretion of the major organization commander present. Protective red cross markings may be obscured only at the direction of the responsible major tactical commander."); DEPARTMENT OF THE ARMY TECHNICAL MANUAL 43-0139, *Painting Instructions for Army Material*, ¶1-3g (Jan. 1990) ("Under tactical conditions, when requirements for concealment outweigh those for recognition, all conspicuous markings may be obscured or removed by the authority and at the discretion of the major organization commander present. Protective red cross markings may be obscured only at the direction of the responsible major tactical commander.").

[406] AP III preamble ("Recalling that the obligation to respect persons and objects protected by the Geneva Conventions and the Protocols additional thereto derives from their protected status under international law and is not dependent on use of the distinctive emblems, signs or signals,"). *Consider* AP I Amended Annex I art. 1(1) ("The regulations concerning identification in this Annex implement the relevant provisions of the Geneva Conventions and the Protocol; they are intended to facilitate the identification of personnel, material, units, transports and installations protected under the Geneva Conventions and the Protocol.").

distinctive emblem may increase the risk that enemy forces will not recognize the protected status of military medical and religious personnel and other protected persons and objects, and attack them in error.

7.15.3.2 *Distinctive Emblem Does Not in and of Itself Establish the Right to Protection*. The distinctive emblem does not in and of itself establish the right to protection.[407] Rather, the right to protection is established by the fact that the units, facilities, or personnel, have met the applicable requirements for protected status.[408]

Thus, if the distinctive emblem is displayed by forces not entitled to protection, the display of the emblem does not confer protection and those forces may be made the object of attack. On the other hand, if personnel who are entitled to protection are recognized as such, they remain entitled to respect and protection even if the distinctive emblem is not displayed.[409]

7.15.4 Prohibitions on Unauthorized Uses of the Distinctive Emblem. With the exception of certain cases mentioned in Article 44 of the GWS (discussed below), the emblem of the Red Cross on a white ground and the words "Red Cross" or "Geneva Cross" may not be employed, either in time of peace or in time of war, except to indicate or to protect the medical units and establishments, the personnel, and material protected by the GWS and other Conventions dealing with similar matters (*e.g.*, the GWS-Sea).[410] The same shall apply to the emblems mentioned in the second paragraph of Article 38 of the GWS (*i.e.*, the emblem of red crescent and the emblem of the red lion and sun), in respect of the countries that use them.[411]

The distinguishing signs referred to in Article 43 of the GWS-Sea (*i.e.*, certain red crosses on white backgrounds) may only be used, whether in time of peace or war, for indicating or protecting the ships mentioned in Article 43, except as may be provided in any other international Convention (*e.g.*, the GWS) or by agreement between all the parties to the conflict

---

[407] *See* GWS COMMENTARY 307, 312, 330. *Consider* AP I Amended Annex I art. 1(2) ("These rules do not in and of themselves establish the right to protection. This right is governed by the relevant articles in the Conventions and the Protocol.").

[408] *Refer to, e.g.*, § 4.9.2 (Requirements for Military Medical and Religious Status); § 7.12.1.1 (Military Hospital Ships); § 7.14.2 (Exclusively Employed for the Removal of the Wounded, Sick, or Shipwrecked, and for the Transport of Medical Personnel and Equipment).

[409] GWS-SEA COMMENTARY 229 ("Obviously, respect for camouflaged units will be purely theoretical. The enemy can respect a medical unit only if he knows of its presence. If the unit is exposed to long-range enemy fire, it will thus lose a large part of its security. If however, the enemy approaches, for instance, and recognizes the the [sic] medical unit as such, he must obviously respect it.").

[410] GWS art. 44 ("With the exception of the cases mentioned in the following paragraphs of the present Article, the emblem of the Red Cross on a white ground and the words 'Red Cross', or 'Geneva Cross' may not be employed, either in time of peace or in time of war, except to indicate or to protect the medical units and establishments, the personnel and material protected by the present Convention and other Conventions dealing with similar matters.").

[411] GWS art. 44 ("The same shall apply to the emblems mentioned in Article 38, second paragraph, in respect of the countries which use them.").

concerned.[412]

In particular, it is prohibited to use the distinctive emblem: (1) while engaging in attacks; (2) in order to shield, favor, or protect one's own military operations; or (3) to impede enemy military operations.[413] For example, using an ambulance marked with the Red Cross to mount a surprise attack against enemy forces would be prohibited.[414]

Certain non-military uses of the distinctive emblem are authorized under the GWS and GWS-Sea: (1) use by National Red Cross Societies and other Authorized Voluntary Aid Societies; (2) use by international Red Cross organizations and their duly authorized personnel; and (3) use by ambulances and free aid stations.

7.15.4.1 Use by National Red Cross Societies and Other Authorized Voluntary Aid Societies. The National Red Cross Societies and other Authorized Voluntary Aid Societies designated in Article 26 of the GWS shall have the right to use the distinctive emblem conferring the protection of the GWS only within the framework of paragraph 1 of Article 44 of the GWS.[415]

Furthermore, National Red Cross (Red Crescent, Red Lion and Sun) Societies may, in time of peace, in accordance with their national legislation, make use of the name and emblem of the Red Cross for their other activities that are in conformity with the principles laid down by the International Red Cross Conferences.[416] When those activities are carried out in time of war, the conditions for the use of the emblem shall be such that it cannot be considered as conferring the protection of the GWS; the emblem shall be comparatively small in size and may not be placed on armlets or on the roofs of buildings.[417] This use of the emblem is simply to indicate an

---

[412] GWS-SEA art. 44 ("The distinguishing signs referred to in Article 43 can only be used, whether in time of peace or war, for indicating or protecting the ships therein mentioned, except as may be provided in any other international Convention or by agreement between all the Parties to the conflict concerned.").

[413] *Refer to* § 5.24 (Improper Use of Certain Signs).

[414] *For example*, Trial of Heinz Hagendorf, XIII U.N. LAW REPORTS 146 (U.S. Intermediate Military Government Court, Dachau, Germany, Aug. 8-9, 1946) ("The accused, Heinz Hagendorf, a German soldier, was tried by a United states Intermediate Military Government Court at Dachau, Germany, being charged with having 'wrongfully used the Red Cross emblem in a combat zone by firing a weapon at American soldiers from an enemy ambulance displaying such emblem.'").

[415] GWS art. 44 ("With the exception of the cases mentioned in the following paragraphs of the present Article, the emblem of the Red Cross on a white ground and the words 'Red Cross', or 'Geneva Cross' may not be employed, either in time of peace or in time of war, except to indicate or to protect the medical units and establishments, the personnel and material protected by the present Convention and the other Conventions dealing with similar matters. The same shall apply to the emblems mentioned in Article 38, second paragraph, in respect of the countries which use them. The National Red Cross Societies and other Societies designated in Article 26 shall have the right to use the distinctive emblem conferring the protection of the Convention only within the framework of the present paragraph.").

[416] GWS art. 44 ("Furthermore, National Red Cross (Red Crescent, Red Lion and Sun) Societies may, in time of peace, in accordance with their national legislation, make use of the name and emblem of the Red Cross for their other activities which are in conformity with the principles laid down by the International Red Cross Conferences.").

[417] GWS art. 44 ("When those activities are carried out in time of war, the conditions for the use of the emblem shall be such that it cannot be considered as conferring the protection of the Convention; the emblem shall be comparatively small in size and may not be placed on armlets or on the roofs of buildings.").

association with the Red Cross movement.[418]

7.15.4.2 *Use by International Red Cross Organizations and Their Duly Authorized Personnel*. The international Red Cross organizations and their duly authorized personnel shall be permitted to make use, at all times, of the emblem of the Red Cross on a white ground.[419]

7.15.4.3 *Use by Ambulances and Free Aid Stations*. As an exceptional measure, in conformity with national legislation and with the express permission of one of the National Red Cross (Red Crescent, Red Lion and Sun) Societies, the emblem of the GWS may be employed in time of peace to identify vehicles used as ambulances and to mark the position of aid stations exclusively assigned to the purpose of giving free treatment to the wounded or sick.[420]

7.16 Protection of Civilians Who Are Wounded, Sick, Infirm, or Expectant Mothers

Wounded and sick civilians, as well as the infirm, and expectant mothers, shall be the object of particular protection and respect.[421] The infirm and expectant mothers are given special consideration along with the wounded and sick because they are vulnerable and also do not take part in hostilities.[422]

7.16.1 Obligation to Facilitate Efforts to Search for Civilians Who Are Wounded, Killed, Shipwrecked, or Exposed to Grave Danger. As far as military considerations allow, each party to the conflict shall facilitate the steps taken to search for the killed and wounded, to assist the shipwrecked and other persons exposed to grave danger, and to protect them against pillage and ill-treatment.[423]

---

[418] GWS COMMENTARY 325 ("In the second case, the sign is *purely indicatory*. It is only used to show that a person or object is connected with the Red Cross, without implying the protection of the Convention or any intention to invoke it. It is, for example, used in this way to draw public attention to premises or publications. The emblem should then, as a rule, be small in size, and the conditions under which it is used should preclude all risk of its being confused with the protective sign.").

[419] GWS art. 44 ("The international Red Cross organizations and their duly authorized personnel shall be permitted to make use, at all times, of the emblem of the Red Cross on a white ground.").

[420] GWS art. 44 ("As an exceptional measure, in conformity with national legislation and with the express permission of one of the National Red Cross (Red Crescent, Red Lion and Sun) Societies, the emblem of the Convention may be employed in time of peace to identify vehicles used as ambulances and to mark the position of aid stations exclusively assigned to the purpose of giving free treatment to the wounded or sick.").

[421] GC art. 16 ("The wounded and sick, as well as the infirm, and expectant mothers, shall be the object of particular protection and respect.").

[422] GC COMMENTARY 134-35 ("In addition to the wounded and sick the Diplomatic Conference mentions the infirm and also expectant mothers, as those persons are in a state of weakness which demands special consideration. Their being placed on the same footing as the wounded and sick is fully justified by the fact that they belong to categories of the population which do not take part in hostilities.").

[423] GC art. 16 ("As far as military considerations allow, each Party to the conflict shall facilitate the steps taken to search for the killed and wounded, to assist the shipwrecked and other persons exposed to grave danger, and to protect them against pillage and ill-treatment.").

The obligation with respect to civilians who are killed, wounded, shipwrecked, and exposed to grave danger is framed slightly differently from the corresponding obligation with respect to military personnel who are wounded, sick, and shipwrecked. These differences may be attributed to the fact that civilian authorities would often be responsible for collecting and bringing in civilian casualties.[424] However, as a practical matter, the armed forces may be asked to lead such efforts or to carry out a joint relief operation with civilian authorities.[425] For example, the U.S. armed forces often have undertaken to care for the civilian wounded and sick.[426]

7.17 Civilian Hospitals and Their Personnel

During international armed conflict, civilian hospitals organized to give care to the wounded and sick, the infirm, and maternity cases, may in no circumstances be the object of attack, but shall at all times be respected and protected by the parties to the conflict.[427]

7.17.1 Loss of Protection for Civilian Hospitals Used to Commit Acts Harmful to the Enemy. The protection to which civilian hospitals are entitled shall not cease unless they are used to commit, outside their humanitarian duties, acts harmful to the enemy.[428]

7.17.1.1 *Acts Harmful to the Enemy*. Civilian hospitals must avoid any

---

[424] GC Commentary 135 ("It is true that saving civilians is the responsibility of the civilian authorities rather than of the military. That is why the wording of Article 16 ('each Party to the conflict shall facilitate the steps' ...) is slightly different from the corresponding Article in the First Geneva Convention ('Parties to the conflict shall, without delay ... take all possible measures ...').").

[425] GC Commentary 135-36 ("In actual practice, however, when it is necessary to search devastated areas, the military and civilian bodies will usually carry out a joint relief operation covering all war casualties, civilians and members of the armed forces, friends and enemies. This is the only attitude to adopt in work of this description which consists, in short, not in helping soldiers on the one hand and civilians on the other, but simply in assisting human beings plunged into suffering by a common destiny-human beings among whom all distinctions have been wiped out by suffering.").

[426] *For example*, Sanders Marble, Skilled and Resolute: A History of the 12th Evacuation Hospital and the 212th MASH, 1917-2006, 69-70 (2013) ("About two-thirds of patients cared for by the 12th were US military; the other third were mainly Vietnamese but also included nonmilitary Americans and Free World Military Assistance Forces personnel. Staff regularly dealt with the Vietnamese, both military and civilian, enemy and friendly. There were wards set aside for enemy prisoners (who were stabilized, then transferred to hospitals at POW camps) and civilians. Wounded South Vietnamese Army soldiers were also stabilized and transferred to hospitals run by the Army of the Republic of Vietnam (ARVN). Civilian patients often stayed longer because the war swamped the available hospitals for Vietnamese civilians. Some local civilians came to the hospital for care of conditions not related to the war."); *id.* at. 104 ("Almost immediately after the ground fighting ended [during the 1991 Persian Gulf War], more patients arrived: civilians, enemy prisoners, and Coalition and US troops. Despite the influx, the 12th had to staff only 104 beds of its 400-bed maximum. At first the civilians were Kuwaitis, but by March 23 Iraqi civilians began arriving, victims of the southern Iraqi rebellion against Saddam Hussein. The civilians arrived in large batches, Chinook loads of 30 or 40 at a time. Not all were patients; families often accompanied an injured member.").

[427] GC art. 18 ("Civilian hospitals organized to give care to the wounded and sick, the infirm and maternity cases, may in no circumstances be the object of attack, but shall at all times be respected and protected by the Parties to the conflict.").

[428] GC art. 19 ("The protection to which civilian hospitals are entitled shall not cease unless they are used to commit, outside their humanitarian duties, acts harmful to the enemy.").

interference, direct or indirect, in military operations, such as the use of a hospital as a shelter for able-bodied combatants or fugitives, as an arms or ammunition store, as a military observation post, or as a center for liaison with combat forces.[429] However, the fact that sick or wounded members of the armed forces are nursed in these hospitals, or the presence of small arms and ammunition taken from such combatants and not yet handed to the proper service, shall not be considered acts harmful to the enemy.[430]

7.17.1.2 *Due Warning Before Cessation of Protection*. In addition, protection for civilian hospitals may cease only after due warning has been given, naming, in all appropriate cases, a reasonable time limit, and after such warning has remained unheeded.[431]

The obligation to refrain from use of force against a civilian medical facility acting in violation of its mission and protected status without due warning does not prohibit the exercise of the right of self-defense. There may be cases in which, in the exercise of the right of self-defense, a warning is not "due" or a reasonable time limit is not appropriate. For example, forces receiving heavy fire from a hospital may exercise their right of self-defense and return fire. Such use of force in self-defense against medical units or facilities must be proportionate. For example, a single enemy rifleman firing from a hospital window would warrant a response against the rifleman only, rather than the destruction of the hospital.[432]

7.17.2 Identification of Protected Civilian Hospitals. The GC provides for civilian hospitals to be identified with certificates and the distinctive emblem.

7.17.2.1 *State-Issued Certificates for Civilian Hospitals*. States that are parties to a conflict shall provide all civilian hospitals with certificates showing that they are civilian hospitals and that the buildings that they occupy are not used for any purpose that would deprive these hospitals of protection in accordance with Article 19 of the GC.[433]

7.17.2.2 *Markings of Civilian Hospitals With the Distinctive Emblem*. Civilian hospitals shall be marked by means of the distinctive emblem provided for in Article 38 of the

---

[429] GC COMMENTARY 155 ("Such harmful acts would, for example, include the use of a hospital as a shelter for able-bodied combatants or fugitives, as an arms or ammunition store, as a military observation post, or as a centre for liaison with fighting troops. The sense will become still clearer when paragraph 2, below is considered, which mentions two specific acts which are not to be regarded as being harmful to the enemy. One thing is certain. Civilian hospitals must observe, towards the enemy, the neutrality which they claim for themselves and which is their right under the Convention. Standing outside the struggle, they must steadfastly refrain from any interference, direct or indirect, in military operations.").

[430] GC art. 19 ("The fact that sick or wounded members of the armed forces are nursed in these hospitals, or the presence of small arms and ammunition taken from such combatants and not yet handed to the proper service, shall not be considered to be acts harmful to the enemy.").

[431] GC art. 19 ("Protection may, however, cease only after due warning has been given, naming, in all appropriate cases, a reasonable time limit, and after such warning has remained unheeded.").

[432] *Compare* § 7.10.3.2 (Due Warning Before Cessation of Protection).

[433] GC art. 18 ("States which are Parties to a conflict shall provide all civilian hospitals with certificates showing that they are civilian hospitals and that the buildings which they occupy are not used for any purpose which would deprive these hospitals of protection in accordance with Article 19.").

GWS, but only if authorized by the State.[434]

The parties to the conflict shall, in so far as military considerations permit, take the necessary steps to make the distinctive emblems indicating civilian hospitals clearly visible to the enemy land, air, and naval forces in order to obviate the possibility of any hostile action.[435]

7.17.3 Location of Civilian Hospitals. In view of the dangers to which civilian hospitals may be exposed by being close to military objectives, it is recommended that such hospitals be situated as far as possible from such objectives.[436]

This provision of the GC was drafted because the protection for civilian hospitals in the GC does not confer immunity on military objectives situated close to the hospital or restrict the right to make such military objectives the object of attack.[437]

7.17.4 Protection of Civilian Hospital Personnel.

7.17.4.1 *Civilian Hospital Personnel Who Are Regularly and Solely Engaged*. Persons regularly and solely engaged in the operation and administration of civilian hospitals, including the personnel engaged in the search for, removal and transporting of, and caring for wounded and sick civilians, the infirm, and maternity cases, shall be respected and protected at all times.[438] For example, a surgeon who works regularly in a hospital, but is not exclusively employed there, would not be engaged "solely" in hospital duties and would consequently not be covered by this provision, but could fall under the category of "other civilian hospital personnel."[439]

In occupied territory and in zones of military operations, civilian hospital personnel who

---

[434] GC art. 18 ("Civilian hospitals shall be marked by means of the emblem provided for in Article 38 of the Geneva Convention for the Amelioration of the Condition of the Wounded and Sick in Armed Forces in the Field of August 12, 1949, but only if so authorized by the State.").

[435] GC art. 18 ("The Parties to the conflict shall, in so far as military considerations permit, take the necessary steps to make the distinctive emblems indicating civilian hospitals clearly visible to the enemy land, air and naval forces in order to obviate the possibility of any hostile action.").

[436] GC art. 18 ("In view of the dangers to which civilian hospitals may be exposed by being close to military objectives, it is recommended that such hospitals be situated as far as possible from such objectives.").

[437] GC COMMENTARY 153 ("The last paragraph shows clearly that wide as that scope is, it is not intended to confer immunity on military objectives situated close to a hospital or to restrict the right to attack them as such. It is for that reason that the legal protection accorded to military hospitals must be accompanied by practical measures to ensure that they are situated as far as possible from military objectives and to protect them from the accidental consequences of attacks on such objectives. If that is not done the protection is very likely to be illusory, even if the hospitals are clearly marked.").

[438] GC art. 20 ("Persons regularly and solely engaged in the operation and administration of civilian hospitals, including the personnel engaged in the search for, removal and transporting of and caring for wounded and sick civilians, the infirm and maternity cases, shall be respected and protected.").

[439] GC COMMENTARY 159 ("For example, a surgeon who works regularly in a hospital, but is not exclusively employed there because he devotes part of his time to his private practice, or again, voluntary laboratory assistants or auxiliaries, who only work at the hospital for part of the day, or for one or two days a week, would not be engaged 'solely' in hospital duties and would consequently not be covered by paragraph 1.").

are regularly and solely engaged in hospital duties shall be recognizable by means of an identity card certifying their status, bearing the photograph of the holder and embossed with the stamp of the responsible authority, and also by means of a stamped, water-resistant armlet that they shall wear on the left arm while carrying out their duties.[440] This armlet shall be issued by the State and shall bear the emblem provided for in Article 38 of the GWS.[441]

7.17.4.2 Other Civilian Hospital Personnel. Other personnel who are engaged in the operation and administration of civilian hospitals shall also be entitled to respect and protection and to wear the armlet while they are employed on such duties.[442] The identity card shall state the duties on which they are employed.[443]

7.17.4.3 List of Permanent and Temporary Civilian Hospital Personnel. The management of each hospital shall at all times hold at the disposal of the competent national or occupying authorities an up-to-date list of such personnel.[444] This list should provide the names of all hospital personnel, both permanent and temporary, and specify the duties of each of them.[445]

7.18 Land and Sea Civilian Hospital Convoys

Convoys of vehicles or hospital trains on land or specially provided vessels on sea, conveying wounded and sick civilians, the infirm, and maternity cases, shall be respected and protected in the same manner as the hospitals provided for in Article 18 of the GC, and shall be marked, with the consent of the State, by the display of the distinctive emblem provided for in Article 38 of the GWS.[446]

The vehicles in a medical convoy need not be used permanently for medical purposes,

---

[440] GC art. 20 ("In occupied territory and in zones of military operations, the above personnel shall be recognizable by means of an identity card certifying their status, bearing the photograph of the holder and embossed with the stamp of the responsible authority, and also by means of a stamped, water-resistant armlet which they shall wear on the left arm while carrying out their duties.").

[441] GC art. 20 ("This armlet shall be issued by the State and shall bear the emblem provided for in Article 38 of the Geneva Convention for the Amelioration of the Condition of the Wounded and Sick in Armed Forces in the Field of August 12, 1949.").

[442] GC art. 20 ("Other personnel who are engaged in the operation and administration of civilian hospitals shall be entitled to respect and protection and to wear the armlet, as provided in and under the conditions prescribed in this Article, while they are employed on such duties.").

[443] GC art. 20 ("The identity card shall state the duties on which they are employed.").

[444] GC art. 20 ("The management of each hospital shall at all times hold at the disposal of the competent national or occupying authorities an up-to-date list of such personnel.").

[445] GC COMMENTARY 169 ("The management of every civilian hospital must keep an up-to-date nominal list of all the hospital staff, both permanent and temporary, specifying the duties of each of them.").

[446] GC art. 21 ("Convoys of vehicles or hospital trains on land or specially provided vessels on sea, conveying wounded and sick civilians, the infirm and maternity cases, shall be respected and protected in the same manner as the hospitals provided for in Article 18, and shall be marked, with the consent of the State, by the display of the distinctive emblem provided for in Article 38 of the Geneva Convention for the Amelioration of the Condition of the Wounded and Sick in Armed Forces in the Field of August 12, 1949.").

but while they are in the convoy, they are not to be used for other purposes.[447]

7.18.1 Protection of Civilian Hospital Convoys on the Same Basis as That of Civilian Hospitals. The protection to which these convoys are entitled shall not cease unless they are used to commit, outside their humanitarian duties, acts harmful to the enemy.[448]

As with civilian hospitals, medical convoys must maintain a strict abstention from any direct or indirect participation in a hostile act in order to retain protection.[449] However, the fact that sick or wounded members of the armed forces are transported by these convoys, or the presence of small arms and ammunition taken from such combatants and not yet handed to the proper service, shall not be considered acts harmful to the enemy.[450]

In addition, protection for civilian medical convoys may cease only after due warning has been given, naming, in all appropriate cases, a reasonable time limit, and after such warning has remained unheeded.[451]

7.19 Civilian Medical Aircraft

Aircraft exclusively employed for the removal of wounded and sick civilians, the infirm, and maternity cases, or for the transport of medical personnel and equipment, shall not be attacked, but shall be respected while flying at heights, times, and on routes specifically agreed upon between all the parties to the conflict concerned.[452]

7.19.1 Civilian Medical Aircraft Not Flying at Heights and Times and on Routes Specifically Agreed Upon by Belligerents Concerned. As with medical aircraft for military personnel, the use of protected medical aircraft for civilians generally depends on an agreement between the belligerents.[453]

However, as with medical aircraft for military personnel, known civilian medical aircraft, when performing their humanitarian functions, must be respected and protected, provided they

---

[447] GC Commentary 170 ("The word 'vehicle' must be taken in the broadest possible sense: it covers any means of transport by land; it need not necessarily be used solely for medical purposes. It will be enough if it is so used occasionally and temporarily, provided, of course, that while so employed it is not used for any other purpose. A medical convoy composed of horse drawn vehicles normally used for transporting agricultural produce and occasionally used in the service of the wounded, must, therefore, be protected in the same way as a convoy of specially designed ambulances.").

[448] *Compare* § 7.17.1 (Loss of Protection for Civilian Hospitals Used to Commit Acts Harmful to the Enemy).

[449] GC Commentary 171 ("As in the case of civilian hospitals and their staff, the protection of medical transport depends on strict abstention from any direct or indirect participation in a hostile act.").

[450] *Compare* § 7.17.1.1 (Acts Harmful to the Enemy).

[451] *Compare* § 7.17.1.2 (Due Warning Before Cessation of Protection).

[452] GC art. 22 ("Aircraft exclusively employed for the removal of wounded and sick civilians, the infirm and maternity cases, or for the transport of medical personnel and equipment, shall not be attacked, but shall be respected while flying at heights, times and on routes specifically agreed upon between all the Parties to the conflict concerned.").

[453] *Refer to* § 7.14 (Military Medical Aircraft).

identify themselves as such and comply with the directions of the enemy State.[454]

7.19.2 Marking of Civilian Medical Aircraft With the Distinctive Emblem. The aircraft may be marked with the distinctive emblem provided for in Article 38 of the GWS.[455]

7.19.3 Prohibition of Flight Over Enemy Territory. Unless otherwise agreed, flights over enemy or enemy-occupied territory are prohibited.[456]

7.19.4 Summons to Land. Such aircraft shall obey every summons to land.[457] If the aircraft refuses to obey, it does so at its own risk.[458]

In the event of a landing thus imposed, the aircraft with its occupants may continue its flight after examination, if any.[459] However, if examination reveals that an act "harmful to the enemy" has been committed, *e.g.*, if the aircraft is carrying munitions or has been used for military observation, it loses the benefit of the GC; the aircraft may be seized and the crew and passengers detained.[460]

7.20 AP I Provisions on the Wounded, Sick, and Shipwrecked

Part II of AP I has a number of provisions regarding the wounded, sick, and shipwrecked. These provisions have generally not been discussed in this Chapter because the United States is not a Party to AP I. These provisions, however, are summarized in this section to familiarize service members with them in case U.S. forces are engaged in multinational operations with, or are engaged in armed conflict against, States that are Parties to AP I.

---

[454] *Refer to* § 7.14.1 (Medical Aircraft Not Flying at Heights and Times and on Routes Specifically Agreed Upon by Belligerents Concerned).

[455] GC art. 22 ("They may be marked with the distinctive emblem provided for in Article 38 of the Geneva Convention for the Amelioration of the Condition of the Wounded and Sick in Armed Forces in the Field of August 12, 1949.").

[456] GC art. 22 ("Unless agreed otherwise, flights over enemy or enemy-occupied territory are prohibited.").

[457] GC art. 22 ("Such aircraft shall obey every summons to land."). *See also* GC COMMENTARY 176 ("The summons to land provides the adverse party with a safeguard; it is the one real means of defence against abuse. This extremely important provision has also been taken from the First Geneva Convention of 1949; it states explicitly that medical aircraft must obey every summons to land. It applies in the first place to aircraft flying over enemy or enemy-occupied territory whether or not they are authorized to do so. It also applies to aircraft which are over their own territory but close to the enemy lines.").

[458] GC COMMENTARY 176 ("If the aircraft refuses to obey, it does so at its own risk and it is lawful to open fire on it. If the machine is already out of range, the summons obviously becomes a mere formality. It should not be forgotten however that if the plane refuses to obey the summons and is pursued it loses the protection of the Convention, having failed to comply with its own obligations.").

[459] GC art. 22 ("In the event of a landing thus imposed, the aircraft with its occupants may continue its flight after examination, if any.").

[460] GC COMMENTARY 177 ("If—and it is to be hoped that such cases will be the exception—if examination reveals that an act 'harmful to the enemy', in the sense of Article 19, has been committed, i.e. if the plane is carrying munitions or has been used for military observation, it loses the benefit of the Convention; the enemy may seize it and intern the crew and passengers or, should occasion arise, treat them in accordance with Article 5 of the Convention.").

7.20.1 AP I Provisions on General Protection of the Wounded, Sick, and Shipwrecked Persons. Section I of Part II of AP I seeks to elaborate upon and change the protections afforded the wounded, sick, and shipwrecked. For example, AP I provides protection for certain civilian medical units.[461] The obligations in AP I also cover both combatants and civilians. For the purpose of applying AP I, Article 8 of AP I defines "wounded" and "sick" to include persons "whether military or civilian" and "maternity cases, new-born babies and other persons who may be in need of immediate medical assistance or care, such as the infirm or expectant mothers, and who refrain from any act of hostility."[462] On the other hand, in the 1949 Geneva Conventions, the protections for civilians who are wounded and sick are addressed in the GC, and the protections for combatants who are wounded and sick are addressed in the GWS, GWS-Sea, and GPW.[463]

7.20.2 AP I Provisions on Medical Transportation. Section II of AP I has a number of articles that are intended to expand upon the protection afforded to medical transports. For example, under AP I, the respect and protection of medical aircraft of a party to the conflict in and over land areas physically controlled by friendly forces or in and over sea areas not physically controlled by an adverse party are not dependent on any agreement with an adverse party.[464] Similarly, the protection of small craft described in Article 27 of the GWS-Sea is afforded, even if the notification envisaged by that Article has not been made.[465]

7.20.3 AP I Provisions on Missing and Dead Persons. Section III of Part II of AP I has three articles that are intended to help families know the fate of their relatives.[466] For example, as soon as circumstances and the relations between adverse parties permit, the States that are Parties to AP I in whose territories graves may be shall conclude agreements: (1) to facilitate access to gravesites by relatives of the deceased and by representatives of official Graves

---

[461] AP I art. 12(2) ("2. Paragraph 1 shall apply to civilian medical units, provided that they: a) belong to one of the Parties to the conflict; b) are recognized and authorized by the competent authority of one of the Parties to the conflict; or c) are authorized in conformity with Article 9, paragraph 2, of this Protocol or Article 27 of the First Convention.").

[462] AP I art. 8(a) ("'Wounded' and 'sick' mean persons, whether military or civilian, who, because of trauma, disease or other physical or mental disorder or disability, are in need of medical assistance or care and who refrain from any act of hostility. These terms also cover maternity cases, new-born babies and other persons who may be in need of immediate medical assistance or care, such as the infirm or expectant mothers, and who refrain from any act of hostility;").

[463] *Refer to* § 7.3.2 (Persons Entitled to Protection as Wounded, Sick, or Shipwrecked Under the GWS and GWS-Sea); § 7.16 (Protection of Civilians Who Are Wounded, Sick, Infirm, or Expectant Mothers).

[464] AP I art. 25 ("In and over land areas physically controlled by friendly forces, or in and over sea areas not physically controlled by an adverse Party, the respect and protection of medical aircraft of a Party to the conflict is not dependent on any agreement with an adverse Party. For greater safety, however, a Party to the conflict operating its medical aircraft in these areas may notify the adverse Party, as provided in Article 29, in particular when such aircraft are making flights bringing them within range of surface-to-air weapons systems of the adverse Party.").

[465] AP I art. 22(3) ("Small craft described in Article 27 of the Second Convention shall be protected even if the notification envisaged by that Article has not been made. The Parties to the conflict are, nevertheless, invited to inform each other of any details of such craft which will facilitate their identification and recognition.").

[466] AP I art. 32 ("In the implementation of this Section, the activities of the High Contracting Parties, of the Parties to the conflict and of the international humanitarian organizations mentioned in the Conventions and in this Protocol shall be prompted mainly by the right of families to know the fate of their relatives.").

Registration Services and to regulate the practical arrangements for such access; (2) to protect and maintain such gravesites permanently; and (3) to facilitate the return of the remains of the deceased and of personal effects to the home country upon its request or, unless that country objects, upon the request of the next of kin.[467]

---

[467] *Consider* AP I art. 34(2) ("As soon as circumstances and the relations between the adverse Parties permit, the High Contracting Parties in whose territories graves and, as the case may be, other locations of the remains of persons who have died as a result of hostilities or during occupation or in detention are situated, shall conclude agreements in order: (a) to facilitate access to the gravesites by relatives of the deceased and by representatives of official graves registration services and to regulate the practical arrangements for such access; (b) to protect and maintain such gravesites permanently; (c) to facilitate the return of the remains of the deceased and of personal effects to the home country upon its request or, unless that country objects, upon the request of the next of kin.").

VIII – Detention: Overview and Baseline Rules

Chapter Contents

8.1 INTRODUCTION

8.1.1 Overview of Detention Rules in This Manual and the Scope of Chapter VIII. The internment of POWs is addressed in Chapter IX. The internment of protected persons in the home territory of a belligerent or in occupied territory is addressed in Chapter X.

Detention may occur outside these contexts. For example, the detention of civilians may occur outside a belligerent's home territory but before the establishment of occupation. Similarly, detention may occur in non-international armed conflict or other military operations, such as non-combatant evacuation operations, peace operations, or humanitarian assistance operations. There are no "law-free zones" in which detainees are outside the protection of the law. Where no more specific rules apply, the rules in this Chapter apply as baseline rules addressing the detention of persons during military operations. For example, the following situations are covered by the rules in this Chapter:

- detention of persons who have participated in hostilities or who belong to armed groups, but who are not entitled to POW status or protected person status in international armed conflict;
- detention of persons held for reasons related to a non-international armed conflict; and
- any other detentions.

8.1.2 DoD Policies and Regulations Regarding the Treatment of Detainees. DoD policies and regulations regarding the treatment of detainees provide authoritative guidance for DoD personnel and fill an important role in implementing the requirements of Common Article 3 of the 1949 Geneva Conventions and applicable customary international law.[1] Practitioners are advised to consult all applicable policies and regulations, as these, in many cases, exceed the requirements of international law, U.S. statutes, and Executive Orders.

The practice of the U.S. armed forces has been to go beyond a minimalist approach of complying with the baseline rules of Common Article 3 of the 1949 Geneva Conventions and instead to endeavor to enhance conditions so as to ensure that treatment of detainees exceeds the requirements of humane treatment standards under international law, consistent with security concerns.[2]

8.1.3 Ad Hoc Legal Instruments or Frameworks That May Be Applicable to Detention Outside the Context of POW or Civilian Internment. The detention of persons under the law of war, outside the context of the regimes specified in Chapters IX (POWs under the GPW) and X (protected persons under the GC who are interned in a belligerent's home territory or occupied territory) may be addressed in ad hoc legal instruments or frameworks.

Such legal instruments may include, for example, an international agreement between the State conducting detention operations and the State on whose territory the operations are being conducted.[3] As another example, a U.N. Security Council Resolution may provide a basis for detention operations.[4]

8.1.3.1 *Detention Authority*. The legal authority to detain outside the context of

---

[1] *Refer to* § 18.7 (Instructions, Regulations, and Procedures to Implement and Enforce the Law of War).

[2] *For example*, Admiral Patrick Walsh, *et al*., Department of Defense, *Review of Department Compliance with President's Executive Order on Detainee Conditions of Confinement*, 4 (2009) ("While we conclude that conditions at Guantánamo are in conformity with Common Article 3, from our review, it was apparent that the chain of command responsible for the detention mission at Guantánamo consistently seeks to go beyond a minimalist approach to compliance with Common Article 3, and endeavors to enhance conditions in a manner as humane as possible consistent with security concerns.").

[3] *For example*, Agreement Between the United States and the Republic of Iraq on the Withdrawal of United States Forces from Iraq and the Organization of their Activities during their Temporary Presence in Iraq, Nov. 17, 2008, art. 22(1) ("No detention or arrest may be carried out by the United States Forces (except with respect to detention or arrest of members of the United States Forces and of the civilian component) except through an Iraqi decision issued in accordance with Iraqi law and pursuant to Article 4.").

[4] *For example*, U.N. SECURITY COUNCIL RESOLUTION 1546 (2004), U.N. Doc. S/RES/1546(2004), ¶10 (Jun. 8, 2004) ("*Decides* that the multinational force shall have the authority to take all necessary measures to contribute to the maintenance of security and stability in Iraq in accordance with the letters annexed to this resolution expressing, inter alia, the Iraqi request for the continued presence of the multinational force and setting out its tasks, including by preventing and deterring terrorism, so that, inter alia, the United Nations can fulfil its role in assisting the Iraqi people as outlined in paragraph seven above and the Iraqi people can implement freely and without intimidation the timetable and programme for the political process and benefit from reconstruction and rehabilitation activities;"). *See also* Colin L. Powell, Secretary of State, *Letter to the Lauro L. Baja, Jr., President of the Security Council*, Jun. 5, 2004, annexed to U.N. SECURITY COUNCIL RESOLUTION 1546 (2004), U.N. Doc. S/RES/1546(2004), 10, 11 (Jun. 8, 2004) ("Under the agreed arrangement, the MNF stands ready to continue to undertake a broad range of tasks to contribute to the maintenance of security and to ensure force protection. These include activities necessary to counter ongoing security threats posed by forces seeking to influence Iraq's political future through violence. This will include combat operations against members of these groups, internment where this is necessary for imperative reasons of security, and the continued search for and securing of weapons that threaten Iraq's security.").

the internment of POWs or protected persons may be addressed in ad hoc international instruments. Even if not specifically addressed in an international legal instrument, the legal authority to detain may sometimes be understood as an incident of general authorities conferred by that instrument, such as a U.N. Security Council Resolution authorizing military operations or an agreement authorizing one State to conduct military operations on the territory of another State.[5]

In many cases, the legal authority to detain would be understood as an exercise of the Detaining Power's sovereign rights under international law rather than, or in addition to, authorities arising from an international legal instrument.[6]

The authority to detain is often understood as an incident to more general authorities because detention is fundamental to waging war or conducting other military operations (*e.g.*, noncombatant evacuation operations, peacekeeping operations).[7] Detention operations may be militarily necessary to achieve the object of those operations.[8] In addition, the right to use force in self-defense during such operations includes at least a limited right to detain for security reasons.[9] In fact, it may be inhumane to conduct military operations without some provision for those who are detained incident to the operations (*e.g.*, being prepared to conduct detention operations, and provision for transfer of captured persons to coalition partners who are

---

[5] *For example*, Brigadier General Bantz J. Craddock, Task Force Falcon, Policy Letter #TFF-04, *Detention Processing* ¶1 (Aug. 3, 1999), *reprinted in* CENTER FOR LAW AND MILITARY OPERATIONS, THE JUDGE ADVOCATE GENERAL'S LEGAL CENTER & SCHOOL, U.S. ARMY, LAW AND MILITARY OPERATIONS IN KOSOVO, 1999-2001: LESSONS LEARNED FOR JUDGE ADVOCATES 281 (2001) ("Pursuant to United Nations Security Council Resolution 1244, KFOR [Kosovo Force] has the responsibility to ensure public safety and order until the international civil presence can take responsibility for this task. Sergio Vieira de Mello reiterated that, 'In performing this task, KFOR has the right to apprehend and detain persons who are suspected of having committed offenses against public safety and order, including the commission of such serious offenses as murder, rape, kidnapping or arson, or war crimes (enclosure).' This memorandum outlines the procedures to be employed in the Multi-National Brigade-East Area of Responsibility (MNB-E AOR) for the detention and release of civilians.").

[6] *Refer to* § 1.3.3.1 (Law of War as Prohibitive Law).

[7] *See, e.g.*, Hamdi v. Rumsfeld, 542 U.S. 507, 518 (2004) (plurality) ("The AUMF authorizes the President to use 'all necessary and appropriate force' against 'nations, organizations, or persons' associated with the September 11, 2001, terrorist attacks. 115 Stat. 224. There can be no doubt that individuals who fought against the United States in Afghanistan as part of the Taliban, an organization known to have supported the al Qaeda terrorist network responsible for those attacks, are individuals Congress sought to target in passing the AUMF. We conclude that detention of individuals falling into the limited category we are considering, for the duration of the particular conflict in which they were captured, is so fundamental and accepted an incident to war as to be an exercise of the 'necessary and appropriate force' Congress has authorized the President to use."); Moyer v. Peabody, 212 U.S. 78, 84 (1909) (Holmes, J.) ("The constitution [of the State of Colorado] is supplemented by an act providing that 'when an invasion of or insurrection in the state is made or threatened, the Governor shall order the national guard to repel or suppress the same.' Laws of 1897, c. 63, Art. 7, § 2, p. 204. That means that he shall make the ordinary use of the soldiers to that end; that he may kill persons who resist, and, of course, that he may use the milder measure of seizing the bodies of those whom he considers to stand in the way of restoring peace.").

[8] *See, e.g.*, *Copenhagen Process: Principles and Guidelines* ¶3 ("Participants recognised that detention is a necessary, lawful and legitimate means of achieving the objectives of international military operations;").

[9] *For example*, Detainee Review Procedures at Bagram Theater Internment Facility (BTIF), Afghanistan, *enclosure to* Phillip Carter, Deputy Assistant Secretary of Defense for Detainee Policy, Letter to Chairman Carl Levin, Jul. 14, 2009 ("(U) U.S. Forces operating under Operation Enduring Freedom (OEF) authority are authorized to detain persons temporarily, consistent with the laws and customs of war (e.g., in self-defense or for force protection).").

conducting humane detention operations).[10]

8.1.3.2 *Specific Procedures or Restrictions Applicable to Detention Outside the Context of POW or Protected Person Internment*. Ad hoc legal instruments may provide additional procedures or restrictions applicable to detention outside the context of the internment of POWs or protected persons. For example, special agreements between opposing non-State parties to a conflict could be used to bring into force provisions of the GPW or GC for the purposes of that conflict.[11] As another example, agreements among coalition partners regarding the transfer of detainees between one another might prescribe additional requirements.

8.1.4 Sources of Baseline Standards for the Treatment of Detainees. The baseline standards for the treatment of detainees by U.S. armed forces addressed in this Chapter are derived from Common Article 3 of the 1949 Geneva Conventions, applicable customary international law, and applicable U.S. law and national policy. The principle of humanity animates the rules discussed in this Chapter.[12] In addition, analogous provisions of the GPW and the GC may also be helpful in understanding the baseline rules for detention.

8.1.4.1 *Common Article 3 of the 1949 Geneva Conventions*. Although Common Article 3 of the 1949 Geneva Conventions provides that it applies "[i]n the case of armed conflict not of an international character occurring in the territory of one of the High Contracting Parties," Common Article 3 reflects minimum standards for humane treatment that apply to all military operations.[13] Thus, during both international and non-international armed conflict, Common Article 3 reflects a minimum yardstick of humane treatment protections for "all persons taking no active part in hostilities, including members of armed forces who have laid down their arms and those placed *hors de combat* by sickness, wounds, detention, or any other cause."[14]

DoD policy has explicitly incorporated the standards in Common Article 3 as minimum standards.[15]

---

[10] *Refer to* § 5.4.7 (Prohibition Against Declaring That No Quarter Be Given).

[11] *Refer to* § 17.3 (Special Agreements Between Parties to the Conflict).

[12] *Refer to* § 2.3 (Humanity).

[13] *Refer to* § 3.1.1.2 (Applying Law of War Standards as Reflecting Minimum Legal Standards).

[14] GWS art. 3; GWS-SEA art. 3 (same); GPW art. 3 (same); GC art. 3 (same). *See* Hamdan v. Rumsfeld, 548 U.S. 557, 630-31 (2006) (explaining that Common Article 3 provides "some minimal protection" in all armed conflicts); Military and Paramilitary Activities in and Against Nicaragua (Nicaragua v. United States), Merits, Judgment, 1986 I.C.J. 14, 114 (¶218) (explaining that the rules in Common Article 3 of the 1949 Geneva Conventions "constitute a minimum yardstick," in all armed conflicts and reflect "elementary considerations of humanity") (quoting Corfu Channel Case (United Kingdom v. Albania), Merits, Judgment, 1949 I.C.J. 4, 22).

[15] *For example*, DOD DIRECTIVE 2310.01E, *DoD Detainee Program*, ¶3a (Aug. 19, 2014) ("Until a detainee's release, repatriation, or transfer from DoD custody or control, all persons subject to this directive will, without regard to a detainee's legal status, at a minimum apply: (1) The standards established in Common Article 3 to References (b) through (e)."); DOD DIRECTIVE 2310.01E, *The Department of Defense Detainee Program*, ¶¶4.1-4.2 (Sept. 5, 2006) (requiring that all detainees "be treated humanely" and "shall receive, at a minimum, the standard of treatment discussed in Common Article 3 of the Geneva Conventions").

8.1.4.2 *Article 75 of AP I and Relevant AP II Provisions*. Article 75 of AP I reflects fundamental guarantees for the treatment of persons detained during international armed conflict. Although not a Party to AP I, the United States has stated that the U.S. Government will choose out of a sense of legal obligation to treat the principles set forth in Article 75 as applicable to any individual it detains in an international armed conflict, and expects all other nations to adhere to these principles as well.[16] This statement was intended to contribute to the crystallization of the principles contained in Article 75 as rules of customary international law applicable in international armed conflict.[17]

AP II also contains provisions that expand on Common Article 3's protections for persons held for reasons related to non-international armed conflict. Although the United States has not ratified AP II, President Reagan submitted AP II to the Senate for its advice and consent to ratification, and the Executive Branch has urged the Senate to act as soon as practicable on AP II, noting further that reviews have determined that relevant U.S. military practices are consistent with AP II.[18]

8.1.4.3 *U.S. Domestic Law and National Policy*. In addition to international law, the requirements in this Chapter are also based on the requirements of applicable U.S. statutes, such as the Detainee Treatment Act of 2005, or national policy, such as the requirements stated in applicable Executive Orders.

8.1.4.4 *Analogous GPW and GC Provisions*. In some cases, analogous provisions of the GPW and the GC may also be helpful in understanding the baseline rules for detention. For example, it may be appropriate to apply the principles of the GPW and GC, even when the relevant provisions do not apply as a matter of law.[19]

---

[16] *See* The White House, Office of the Press Secretary, *Fact Sheet: New Actions on Guantánamo and Detainee Policy*, Mar. 7, 2011 ("Article 75 of Additional Protocol I, which sets forth fundamental guarantees for persons in the hands of opposing forces in an international armed conflict, is similarly important to the international legal framework. Although the Administration continues to have significant concerns with Additional Protocol I, Article 75 is a provision of the treaty that is consistent with our current policies and practice and is one that the United States has historically supported. Our adherence to these principles is also an important safeguard against the mistreatment of captured U.S. military personnel. The U.S. Government will therefore choose out of a sense of legal obligation to treat the principles set forth in Article 75 as applicable to any individual it detains in an international armed conflict, and expects all other nations to adhere to these principles as well.").

[17] Harold Koh, Legal Adviser, Department of State, *Responses to Questions Submitted by Senator Richard G. Lugar, Libya and War Powers: Hearing Before the Committee on Foreign Relations, U.S. Senate*, 112th Congress, First Session, 53, 57 (Jun. 28, 2011) ("As a matter of international law, the administration's statement is likely to be received as a statement of the U.S. Government's opinio juris as well as a reaffirmation of U.S. practice in this area. The statement is therefore also likely to be received as a significant contribution to the crystallization of the principles contained in Article 75 as rules of customary international law applicable in international armed conflict. … The U.S. statement, coupled with a sufficient density of State practice and opinio juris, would contribute to creation of the principles reflected in Article 75 as rules of customary international law, which all States would be obligated to apply in international armed conflict.").

[18] *Refer to* § 19.20.2.1 (The United States and AP II).

[19] *For example*, George W. Bush, *Memorandum: Humane Treatment of Taliban and al Qaeda Detainees* ¶5 (Feb. 7, 2002) ("I hereby reaffirm the order previously issued by the Secretary of Defense to the United States Armed Forces requiring that the detainees be treated humanely and, to the extent appropriate and consistent with military necessity, in a manner consistent with the principles of Geneva.").

In addition, as a general matter, analogous provisions of the GPW and GC may be helpful for understanding the requirements in international law for conducting detention operations because the baseline standards for such operations during armed conflict are not more restrictive upon States than the requirements with respect to POWs and civilian internees under the GPW and GC, respectively.[20]

In this Chapter, cross-references to sections that address analogous GPW and GC requirements are used for the purposes described above.

8.1.4.5 Copenhagen Process on the Handling of Detainees in International Military Operations. From 2007 to 2012, U.S. representatives participated, along with those of 23 other States and from several international organizations, in a process led by the Government of Denmark to formulate principles and guidelines on the handling of detainees in international military operations.[21] Participants in the Copenhagen Process sought to develop principles to guide the implementation of the existing obligations with respect to detention in international military operations and to promote best practices.[22] The Copenhagen Process Principles and Guidelines is not a text of a legally binding nature.[23]

---

[20] *For example*, In re Guantanamo Bay Litigation, *Respondents' Memorandum Regarding the Government's Detention Authority Relative to Detainees Held at Guantanamo Bay*, Misc. No. 08-442, 1 (D.D.C., Mar. 13, 2009) ("The laws of war have evolved primarily in the context of international armed conflicts between the armed forces of nation states. This body of law, however, is less well-codified with respect to our current, novel type of armed conflict against armed groups such as al-Qaida and the Taliban. Principles derived from law-of-war rules governing international armed conflicts, therefore, must inform the interpretation of the detention authority Congress has authorized for the current armed conflict. … The President also has the authority under the AUMF [Authorization for the Use of Military Force] to detain in this armed conflict those persons whose relationship to al-Qaida or the Taliban would, in appropriately analogous circumstances in a traditional international armed conflict, render them detainable.").

[21] *Copenhagen Process: Principles and Guidelines* ¶I ("The Copenhagen Process on the Handling of Detainees in International Military Operations (The Copenhagen Process) was launched on 11 October 2007 and was concluded in Copenhagen on 19 October 2012. Representatives from Argentina, Australia, Belgium, Canada, China, Denmark, Finland, France, Germany, India, Malaysia, New Zealand, Nigeria, Norway, Pakistan, Russia, South Africa, Sweden, Tanzania, the Netherlands, Turkey, Uganda, the United Kingdom, and the United States of America participated in The Copenhagen Process meetings. Representatives of the African Union (AU), the European Union (EU), the North Atlantic Treaty Organisation (NATO), the United Nations (UN), and the International Committee of the Red Cross (ICRC) also attended The Copenhagen Process meetings as observers. Representatives of civil society were also consulted at various stages of The Copenhagen Process;").

[22] *Copenhagen Process: Principles and Guidelines* ¶II ("During The Copenhagen Process meetings participants – while not seeking to create new legal obligations or authorizations under international law – confirmed the desire to develop principles to guide the implementation of the existing obligations with respect to detention in international military operations; … Participants were also inspired by the good practices that States and organisations have developed in international military operations;").

[23] *Chairman's Commentary to the Copenhagen Process: Principles and Guidelines*, ¶16.2 ("This savings clause also recognises that *The Copenhagen Process Principles and Guidelines* is not a text of a legally binding nature and thus, does not create new obligations or commitments. Furthermore, The *Copenhagen Process Principles and Guidelines* cannot constitute a legal basis for detention. Although some language, e.g., Principle 2, may reflect legal obligations in customary and treaty law, *The Copenhagen Process Principles and Guidelines* are intended to reflect generally accepted standards. In such instances, the applicability and binding nature of those obligations is established by treaty law or customary international law, as applicable, and not by *The Copenhagen Process Principles and Guidelines*. Since *The Copenhagen Process Principles and Guidelines* were not written as a

The Copenhagen Process Principles and Guidelines are intended to apply to international military operations in the context of non-international armed conflicts and peace operations; they are not intended to address international armed conflicts.[24]

8.2 Humane Treatment of Detainees

Detainees shall in all circumstances be treated humanely and protected against any cruel, inhuman, or degrading treatment. This requirement has been reflected in international law,[25] domestic law,[26] national policy,[27] and DoD policies.[28] Violations of the requirement to treat detainees humanely may be violations of criminal law, although it is not a purpose of this section to address liability under criminal law.

8.2.1 Protection Against Violence, Torture, and Cruel Treatment. Detainees must be protected against violence to life and person, in particular murder of all kinds, mutilation, cruel treatment, torture, and any form of corporal punishment.[29]

---

restatement of customary international law, the mere inclusion of a practice in *The Copenhagen Process Principles and Guidelines* should not be taken as evidence that States regard the practice as required out of a sense of legal obligation.").

[24] *Copenhagen Process: Principles and Guidelines* ¶IX ("The Copenhagen Process Principles and Guidelines are intended to apply to international military operations in the context of non-international armed conflicts and peace operations; they are not intended to address international armed conflicts;").

[25] GWS art. 3 (requiring that "[p]ersons taking no active part in the hostilities, including members of armed forces who have laid down their arms and those placed hors de combat by sickness, wounds, detention, or any other cause, shall in all circumstances be treated humanely"); GWS-SEA art. 3 (same); GPW art. 3 (same); GC art. 3 (same).

[26] 42 U.S.C. § 2000dd ("No individual in the custody or under the physical control of the United States Government, regardless of nationality or physical location, shall be subject to cruel, inhuman, or degrading treatment or punishment.").

[27] *See, e.g.*, Executive Order 13491, *Ensuring Lawful Interrogations*, 74 FEDERAL REGISTER 4893, 4894 (Jan. 22, 2009) ("Consistent with the requirements of the Federal torture statute, 18 U.S.C. 2340–2340A, section 1003 of the Detainee Treatment Act of 2005, 42 U.S.C. 2000dd, the Convention Against Torture, Common Article 3, and other laws regulating the treatment and interrogation of individuals detained in any armed conflict, such persons shall in all circumstances be treated humanely and shall not be subjected to violence to life and person (including murder of all kinds, mutilation, cruel treatment, and torture), nor to outrages upon personal dignity (including humiliating and degrading treatment), whenever such individuals are in the custody or under the effective control of an officer, employee, or other agent of the United States Government or detained within a facility owned, operated, or controlled by a department or agency of the United States."); George W. Bush, *Memorandum: Humane Treatment of Taliban and al Qaeda Detainees* ¶5 (Feb. 7, 2002) ("I hereby reaffirm the order previously issued by the Secretary of Defense to the United States Armed Forces requiring that the detainees be treated humanely and, to the extent appropriate and consistent with military necessity, in a manner consistent with the principles of Geneva.").

[28] *For example*, DOD DIRECTIVE 2310.01E, *DoD Detainee Program*, ¶3b (Aug. 19, 2014) ("All detainees will be treated humanely and with respect for their dignity, in accordance with applicable U.S. law and policy and the law of war. The humane treatment requirements in this section apply during all military operations, however characterized."); DOD DIRECTIVE 2310.01E, *The Department of Defense Detainee Program*, ¶4.1 (Sept. 5, 2006) ("All detainees shall be treated humanely and in accordance with U.S. law, the law of war, and applicable U.S. policy."); 1997 MULTI-SERVICE DETENTION REGULATION § 1-5.*b* ("All prisoners will receive humane treatment without regard to race, nationality, religion, political opinion, sex, or other criteria.").

[29] *See* GWS art. 3 (prohibiting with respect to persons taking no active part in the hostilities "violence to life and person, in particular murder of all kinds, mutilation, cruel treatment and torture"); GWS-SEA art. 3 (same); GPW art.

8.2.2 Protection Against Humiliating or Degrading Treatment. Detainees must be protected against outrages upon personal dignity, in particular, humiliating and degrading treatment.[30]

8.2.2.1 *Protection Against Rape, Enforced Prostitution, and Other Indecent Assault*. Detainees must be protected against rape, forced prostitution, and other indecent assault.[31] Indecent assault is generally referred to today as sexual assault.[32]

8.2.2.2 *Protection Against Public Curiosity*. Detainees must be protected against insults and public curiosity.[33] For example, displaying detainees publicly with the purpose of exposing them to ridicule and humiliation is prohibited.[34]

8.2.2.3 *DoD Practice of Generally Prohibiting Taking Photographs Without Authorization*. In order to protect detainees against public curiosity, among other reasons, DoD policy has generally prohibited the taking of photographs of detainees except for authorized purposes.[35]

8.2.3 Prohibition Against Biological or Medical Experiments. Medical or biological

---

3 (same); GC art. 3 (same). *Consider* AP I art. 75(2)(a) (prohibiting with respect to persons who are in the power of a Party to the conflict "[v]iolence to the life, health, or physical or mental well-being of persons, in particular: (i) Murder; (ii) Torture of all kinds, whether physical or mental; (iii) Corporal punishment; and (iv) [Mutilation];") (brackets in original); AP II art. 4(2) (prohibiting with respect to persons who do not take a direct part or who have ceased to take part in hostilities "[v]iolence to the life, health and physical or mental well-being of persons, in particular murder as well as cruel treatment such as torture, mutilation or any form of corporal punishment;").

[30] *See* GWS art. 3 (prohibiting with respect to persons taking no active part in the hostilities "outrages upon personal dignity, in particular, humiliating and degrading treatment;"); GWS-SEA art. 3 (same); GPW art. 3 (same); GC art. 3 (same).

[31] *Consider* AP I art. 75(2)(b) (prohibiting with respect to persons who are in the power of a Party to the conflict "[o]utrages upon personal dignity, in particular humiliating and degrading treatment, enforced prostitution and any form of indecent assault"); AP II art. 4(2)(e) (prohibiting "[o]utrages upon personal dignity, in particular humiliating and degrading treatment, rape, enforced prostitution and any form of indecent assault;"). *Compare* § 9.5.1 (Respect for Their Persons and Honor); § 10.5.1.2 (Protection for Women Against Rape or Other Indecent Assault).

[32] BLACK'S LAW DICTIONARY (9th ed., 2009) ("indecent assault. See sexual assault (2) under assault.").

[33] DOD DIRECTIVE 2310.01E, *DoD Detainee Program*, ¶3b(2) (Aug. 19, 2014) ("All detainees will be respected as human beings … . They will be protected against … public curiosity, … ."); DOD DIRECTIVE 2310.01E, *The Department of Defense Detainee Program*, ¶E4.1.1.3 (Sept. 5, 2006) ("All detainees will be respected as human beings. They will be protected against … public curiosity … ."); *Chairman's Commentary to the Copenhagen Process: Principles and Guidelines*, ¶2.3 ("Furthermore, humane treatment implies that detainees will be protected from insults and public curiosity.").

[34] *Compare* § 9.5.3 (Protection Against Insults and Public Curiosity).

[35] *For example*, 1997 MULTI-SERVICE DETENTION REGULATION § 1-5.*d* ("Photographing, filming, and video taping of individual EPW, CI and RP for other than internal Internment Facility administration or intelligence/counterintelligence purposes is strictly prohibited. No group, wide area or aerial photographs of EPW, CI and RP or facilities will be taken unless approved by the senior Military Police officer in the Internment Facility commander's chain of command.").

experiments on detainees are prohibited.[36]

8.2.4 Threats to Commit Inhumane Treatment. Threats to commit the unlawful acts described above (*i.e.*, violence against detainees, or humiliating or degrading treatment, or biological or medical experiments) are also prohibited.[37] This prohibition may be understood to arise separately (*i.e.*, as a distinct prohibition against certain threats), or it may be understood to result when such threats themselves constitute a form of torture or other abuse.[38]

8.2.5 Duty to Protect Detainees. Detainees should be protected not only against unlawful acts by agents of the Detaining Power, but also against unlawful acts from others, including other detainees or the civilian population.[39]

8.2.6 No Adverse Distinction. Detainees shall be treated humanely without any adverse distinction founded on race, color, religion or faith, sex, birth or wealth, national or social origin, political or other opinion, or any other similar criteria.[40]

---

[36] *See Chairman's Commentary to the Copenhagen Process: Principles and Guidelines*, ¶2.1 ("[The principle requiring humane treatment of detainees] also incorporates the prohibition against torture and other forms of cruel, inhuman or degrading treatment or punishment, the prohibition against corporal and collective punishment and medical experiments; and includes threats to commit the foregoing acts."). *Compare* § 9.5.2.4 (No Physical Mutilation or Medical, Scientific, or Biological Experiments); § 10.5.1.1 (Measures of Physical Suffering, Extermination, or Other Brutality).

[37] *Consider* AP I art. 75(2)(e) (prohibiting with respect to persons who are in the power of a Party to the conflict "[t]hreats to commit any of the foregoing acts," which include "(*a*) Violence to the life, health, or physical or mental well-being of persons, in particular: (i) Murder; (ii) Torture of all kinds, whether physical or mental; (iii) Corporal punishment; and (iv) [Mutilation]; (*b*) Outrages upon personal dignity, in particular humiliating and degrading treatment, enforced prostitution and any form of indecent assault;"); AP II art. 4(2)(h) (prohibiting with respect to persons who do not take a direct part or who have ceased to take part in hostilities "[t]hreats to commit any of the foregoing acts," which include (a) violence to the life, health and physical or mental well-being of persons, in particular murder as well as cruel treatment such as torture, mutilation or any form of corporal punishment and (b) outrages upon personal dignity, in particular humiliating and degrading treatment, rape, enforced prostitution and any form of indecent assault).

[38] *See, e.g.*, 18 U.S.C. § 2340 (defining "torture" to include "severe mental pain or suffering" caused by or resulting from "(A) the intentional infliction or threatened infliction of severe physical pain or suffering; (B) the administration or application, or threatened administration or application, of mind-altering substances or other procedures calculated to disrupt profoundly the senses or the personality; (C) the threat of imminent death; or (D) the threat that another person will imminently be subjected to death, severe physical pain or suffering, or the administration or application of mind-altering substances or other procedures calculated to disrupt profoundly the senses or personality;") (emphasis added).

[39] *Compare* § 9.5.2 (Protection Against Acts of Violence or Intimidation).

[40] GWS art. 3 ("Persons taking no active part in the hostilities, including members of armed forces who have laid down their arms and those placed hors de combat by sickness, wounds, detention, or any other cause, shall in all circumstances be treated humanely, without any adverse distinction founded on race, colour, religion or faith, sex, birth or wealth, or any other similar criteria."); GWS-SEA art. 3 (same); GPW art. 3 (same); GC art. 3 (same). *Consider* AP I art. 75(1) ("In so far as they are affected by a situation referred to in Article 1 of this Protocol, persons who are in the power of a Party to the conflict and who do not benefit from more favourable treatment under the Conventions or under this Protocol shall be treated humanely in all circumstances and shall enjoy, as a minimum, the protection provided by this Article without any adverse distinction based upon race, colour, sex, language, religion or belief, political or other opinion, national or social origin, wealth, birth or other status, or on any other similar criteria."); AP II art. 2(1) ("This Protocol shall be applied without any adverse distinction founded

Special consideration for more vulnerable categories of detainees is consistent with the requirement that detainees must be humanely treated without adverse distinction.[41]

Distinction based on the above criteria may also be made so long as it is not adverse and it is made to advance legitimate interests, such as maintaining order in the camp.[42]

8.3 Security Measures

8.3.1 Searches. Although detainees must always be treated humanely, detainees and their property may be searched and secured, when necessary for security reasons and intelligence purposes.[43]

The dignity and honor of the detainee being searched should be protected to the greatest degree possible under the circumstances.[44] The person conducting the search should avoid doing or saying anything likely to be regarded as indecent. In some circumstances, it may be appropriate for a witness to observe the search so as to protect both the person being searched from abuse and the person conducting the search from unfounded accusations of abuse.

8.3.1.1 *Search of Female Detainees*. It is appropriate for female detainees to be searched by female personnel. This practice helps reduce the risk of accusations of indecent behavior.

8.3.2 Search of Detainee Property. Items in the possession of detainees may be removed and searched for security and intelligence purposes.[45]

8.3.3 Securing Detainees With Handcuffs and Other Security Devices. When necessary for security reasons, detainees may be secured temporarily with handcuffs, flex cuffs, blindfolds, or other security devices.[46]

---

on race, colour, sex, language, religion or belief, political or other opinion, national or social origin, wealth, birth or other status, or on any other similar criteria (hereinafter referred to as 'adverse distinction') to all persons affected by an armed conflict as defined in Article 1.").

[41] *See also Chairman's Commentary to the Copenhagen Process: Principles and Guidelines*, ¶2.4 ("The principle of humane treatment of all persons requires that special consideration be given to the treatment of detainees who may be vulnerable in this context, such as women, children, the aged and those with disabilities. Such special consideration is consistent with the requirement that detainees should be humanely treated without adverse distinction.").

[42] *Compare* § 7.5.1 (Humane Treatment of the Wounded, Sick, and Shipwrecked Without Adverse Distinction); § 9.5.5 (No Adverse Distinction Based on Race, Nationality, Religion, or Political Belief); § 10.5.5 (No Adverse Distinction Based on Race, Religion, or Political Opinion).

[43] *Compare* § 9.6 (Security Measures With Respect to POWs).

[44] *Refer to* § 10.5 (Humane Treatment and Other Basic Protections for Protected Persons).

[45] *Refer to* § 10.18.2 (Articles of Personal or Sentimental Value).

[46] *See also Copenhagen Process: Principles and Guidelines*, ¶2.2 ("Sensory deprivation of persons who are detained may in some circumstances amount to ill-treatment if used as a form of punishment or to inflict suffering. However, sensory deprivation may not in itself amount to ill-treatment as such if the purpose is to ensure the safety of the detainee or of others. For example, using earmuffs during transportation to protect a detainee's hearing will

8.3.4 Use of Force to Maintain Order and to Prevent Escape. Physical force is not to be used against a detained person except in circumstances where such force is necessary and proportionate.[47]

As with POWs, the use of weapons against detainees, especially against those who are escaping or attempting to escape, shall constitute an extreme measure, which shall always be preceded by warnings appropriate to the circumstances.[48] For example, detainees should not be fired upon if they are apprehended within the camp limits while making preparations to escape, and there is no risk of escape or harm to anyone.

8.3.4.1 *Use of Non-Lethal Weapons (Including Riot Control Agents)*. Non-lethal weapons may be employed to control rioting detainees or to prevent their escape. In particular, the use of riot control agents to control rioting detainees is not prohibited.[49]

If the use of deadly force is warranted and authorized against detainees, there is no legal requirement to employ non-lethal weapons before resort to deadly force.[50]

8.4 Interrogation

The law of war does not prohibit interrogation of detainees, but interrogation must be conducted in accordance with the requirements for humane treatment.

8.4.1 Humane Treatment During Interrogation. Interrogation must be carried out in a manner consistent with the requirements for humane treatment, including the prohibitions against torture, cruelty, degrading treatment, and acts or threats of violence.[51]

In addition to the legal prohibitions on torture or other illegal methods of interrogation, practical considerations have also strongly counseled against such methods.[52]

---

not amount to ill-treatment. Similarly, sensory deprivation undertaken as a reasonable security measure such as blindfolding temporarily a detainee to protect the identity of another detainee or for reasons of operational safety will not amount to ill-treatment."). *Compare* § 9.6.2 (Securing POWs With Handcuffs and Other Security Devices).

[47] *See Copenhagen Process: Principles and Guidelines*, ¶6 ("Physical force is not to be used against a detained person except in circumstances where such force is necessary and proportionate.").

[48] *Compare* § 9.22.6 (Use of Force to Maintain Order and to Prevent Escape).

[49] *Refer to* § 6.16.2 (Prohibition on Use of Riot Control Agents as a Method of Warfare).

[50] *Refer to* § 6.5.10.5 (No Requirement to Use Non-Lethal Weapons Before Using Lethal Weapons Where Deadly Force Is Warranted).

[51] *Refer to* § 8.2 (Humane Treatment of Detainees).

[52] *For example*, DEPARTMENT OF THE ARMY FIELD MANUAL 34-52, *Intelligence Interrogation*, 1-8 (Sept. 28, 1992) ("Experience indicates that the use of prohibited techniques is not necessary to gain the cooperation of interrogation sources. Use of torture and other illegal methods is a poor technique that yields unreliable results, may damage subsequent collection efforts and can induce the source to say what he thinks the interrogator wants to hear. Revelation of use of torture by US personnel will bring discredit upon the US and its armed forces while undermining domestic and international support for the war effort. It also may place US and allied personnel in enemy hands at a greater risk of abuse by their captors.").

8.4.2 Additional U.S. Law and Policy on Interrogation. U.S. law and policy impose additional requirements on the interrogation of detainees.

8.4.2.1 *Only Treatment or Techniques of Interrogation Authorized by and Listed in the U.S. Army Field Manual on Intelligence Interrogation*. No person in the custody or under the effective control of the Department of Defense or under detention in a Department of Defense facility shall be subject to any treatment or technique of interrogation not authorized by and listed in the United States Army Field Manual on Intelligence Interrogation.[53] The Army has published field manuals on interrogation for many years.[54]

8.5 Adequate Food, Drinking Water, and Clothing

Detainees shall be provided with adequate food, drinking water, and clothing.

8.5.1 Food for Detainees. Daily food rations for detainees shall be sufficient in quantity, quality, and variety to keep detainees in a good state of health or in any event no worse than that afforded the local civilian population.[55]

8.5.1.1 *Accounting for the Customary Diet*. DoD practice has been to take account of the customary diet of the internees.[56] For example, the detainee's cultural and religious requirements have been considered in determining and ensuring the appropriate diet.

8.5.2 Drinking Water. Sufficient drinking water shall be supplied to detainees.[57]

8.5.3 Clothing. As needed, detainees shall be supplied with sufficient clothing, underwear, and footwear that is appropriate for the climate.[58]

8.6 General Conditions of Detention Facilities

Detainees shall be afforded, to the same extent as the local civilian population, safeguards as regards health and hygiene and protection against the rigors of the climate and the dangers of

---

[53] PUBLIC LAW 109-163, § 1402(a) (Jan. 6, 2006), *codified at* 10 U.S.C. § 801 note ("No person in the custody or under the effective control of the Department of Defense or under detention in a Department of Defense facility shall be subject to any treatment or technique of interrogation not authorized by and listed in the United States Army Field Manual on Intelligence Interrogation."); PUBLIC LAW 109-148, § 1002(a) (Dec. 30, 2005), *codified at* 10 U.S.C. § 801 note (same).

[54] *For example*, DEPARTMENT OF THE ARMY FIELD MANUAL 2-22.3, *Human Intelligence Collector Operations* (Sept. 6, 2006); DEPARTMENT OF THE ARMY FIELD MANUAL 34-52, *Intelligence Interrogation* (Sept. 28, 1992); DEPARTMENT OF THE ARMY FIELD MANUAL 34-52, *Intelligence Interrogation* (May 8, 1987).

[55] *Consider* AP II art. 5(1)(b) ("The persons referred to in this paragraph shall, to the same extent as the local civilian population, be provided with food and drinking water and be afforded safeguards as regards health and hygiene and protection against the rigours of the climate and the dangers of the armed conflict;"). *Compare* § 9.13.1 (Food for POWs); § 10.13.1 (Food for Internees).

[56] *Compare* § 9.13.1.1 (Accounting for the Habitual Diet); § 10.13.1.1 (Accounting for the Customary Diet).

[57] *Compare* § 9.13.2 (Drinking Water); § 10.13.2 (Drinking Water).

[58] *Compare* § 9.13.4 (Clothing for POWs); § 10.13.4 (Clothing of Internees).

the armed conflict.[59]

8.6.1 Safeguards as Regards Health and Hygiene. The obligation to afford safeguards as regards health and hygiene would include taking sanitary measures necessary to ensure the cleanliness and healthfulness of camps and to prevent epidemics. For example, the DoD practice has been to give detainees medical examinations upon arrival at an internment facility, disinfect them, and provide them with any necessary inoculations. In addition, quarters should be kept free from vermin, and detainees suffering from contagious diseases should be placed in quarantine as needed.[60]

8.6.2 Protection Against the Rigors of Climate. The obligation to afford protection against the rigors of climate would include ensuring that detention facilities are adequately heated, lighted, and protected against dampness.[61]

8.6.3 Protection From the Dangers of Armed Conflict. Detention facilities shall not be located close to the combat zone.[62]

8.6.4 No Prohibition Against Detention Aboard Ships. Provided the above requirements are met, there is no prohibition against the humane detention of persons on ships.[63] The GPW generally requires that POWs be interned on premises located on land.[64]

8.7 Segregation of Detainees

Detainees may be segregated into camps or camp compounds according to their nationality, language, and customs, and the Detaining Power may use other criteria to segregate detainees for administrative, security, intelligence, medical, or law enforcement purposes.[65]

8.7.1 Gender and Family Segregation. Except when men and women of a family are accommodated together, women shall be held in quarters separated from those of men and shall

---

[59] *Consider* AP II art. 5(1)(b) ("The persons referred to in this paragraph shall, to the same extent as the local civilian population, be provided with food and drinking water and be afforded safeguards as regards health and hygiene and protection against the rigours of the climate and the dangers of the armed conflict;").

[60] *Compare* § 9.11.5.1 (Necessary Sanitary Measures).

[61] *Compare* § 10.11.3 (Conditions of Buildings and Quarters).

[62] *Consider* AP II art. 5(2)(c) ("Places of internment and detention shall not be located close to the combat zone."). *Compare* § 9.11.4.1 (Avoidance of the Combat Zone); § 10.11.1.1 (Avoidance of Particularly Dangerous Areas).

[63] *For example*, Charlie Savage, *U.S. Tests New Approach to Terrorism Cases on Somali Suspect*, THE NEW YORK TIMES, Jul. 6, 2011 ("In interrogating a Somali man for months aboard a Navy ship before taking him to New York this week for a civilian trial on terrorism charges, the Obama administration is trying out a new approach for dealing with foreign terrorism suspects. … The administration notified the International Committee of the Red Cross of his capture, and a Red Cross representative flew out to the ship and met with him. That visit came about two months after his capture, during a four-day break between his interrogation for intelligence purposes and separate questioning for law-enforcement purposes.").

[64] *Refer to* § 9.11.3.1 (Location on Land).

[65] *Compare* § 9.12 (Segregation of POWs); § 10.10 (Segregation of Internees).

be under the immediate supervision of women.[66]

8.8 Medical Attention

Wounded and sick detainees shall be cared for.[67] They should receive the medical care and attention required by their condition.[68] Medical or biological experiments on detainees are prohibited.[69]

8.8.1 Consent. Medical care should, wherever possible, be undertaken with the consent of the wounded or sick detainee.[70] However, medical actions to preserve the health of the detainee may be justified even where the detainee refuses to provide consent.[71] For example, it is not prohibited to administer vaccinations to detainees in order to preserve their health and to prevent epidemics. Similarly, it is not prohibited to order detainees to be fed, if they undertake a hunger strike.[72]

8.8.2 Blood Donation and Skin Grafting. Detainees may voluntarily consent to give blood for transfusion or skin for grafting for therapeutic purposes; such procedures should take place under conditions consistent with generally accepted medical standards and controls

---

[66] *Consider* AP II art. 5(2) ("Except when men and women of a family are accommodated together, women shall be held in quarters separated from those of men and shall be under the immediate supervision of women;"); AP I art. 75(5) ("Women whose liberty has been restricted for reasons related to the armed conflict shall be held in quarters separated from men's quarters. They shall be under the immediate supervision of women. Nevertheless, in cases where families are detained or interned, they shall, whenever possible, be held in the same place and accommodated as family units.").

[67] GWS art. 3 ("The wounded and sick shall be collected and cared for."); GWS-SEA art. 3 (same); GPW art. 3 (same); GC art. 3 (same). *Compare* § 7.5 (Humane Treatment and Care of Enemy Military Wounded, Sick, and Shipwrecked in the Power of a Party to the Conflict); § 7.16 (Protection of Civilians Who Are Wounded, Sick, Infirm, or Expectant Mothers).

[68] *See, e.g., Copenhagen Process: Principles and Guidelines* ¶9 ("Wounded and sick detainees are to receive the medical care and attention required by their condition.").

[69] *Refer to* § 8.2.3 (Prohibition Against Biological or Medical Experiments).

[70] *For example*, DoD INSTRUCTION 2310.08E, *Medical Program Support for Detainee Operations*, ¶4.7 (Jun. 6, 2006) ("In general, health care will be provided with the consent of the detainee. To the extent practicable, standards and procedures for obtaining consent will be consistent with those applicable to consent from other patients. Standard exceptions for lifesaving emergency medical care provided to a patient incapable of providing consent or for care necessary to protect public health, such as to prevent the spread of communicable diseases, shall apply.").

[71] *See Chairman's Commentary to the Copenhagen Process: Principles and Guidelines*, ¶9.5 ("Medical assistance should, wherever possible, be undertaken with the consent of the wounded or sick detainee. However, medical actions to preserve the health of the detainee may be justified even where the detainee refuses to provide consent."). *Compare* § 7.5.2.4 (Compulsory Medical Treatment).

[72] *For example*, DoD INSTRUCTION 2310.08E, *Medical Program Support for Detainee Operations*, ¶4.7.1 (Jun. 6, 2006) ("In the case of a hunger strike, attempted suicide, or other attempted serious self-harm, medical treatment or intervention may be directed without the consent of the detainee to prevent death or serious harm. Such action must be based on a medical determination that immediate treatment or intervention is necessary to prevent death or serious harm, and, in addition, must be approved by the commanding officer of the detention facility or other designated senior officer responsible for detainee operations.").

designed for the benefit of both the donor and the recipient.[73]

8.9 Administration and Discipline in Detention Facilities

Detention facility commanders may establish rules for detainees in the detention facility and conduct disciplinary proceedings, subject to the requirements for humane treatment.[74]

8.9.1 Complaints. Detainees should be permitted to submit, without reprisal, complaints regarding their treatment or conditions of detention to the detaining authorities.[75] Investigatory procedures and a practice of timely and effective investigations of credible complaints of maltreatment also help ensure that allegations regarding treatment or conditions of detention that may arise years after the detention can be addressed.[76]

8.10 Contacts With the Outside World

Subject to security measures, practical considerations, and other military necessities, detainees should be afforded appropriate contact with the outside world, including: (1) receipt of individual or collective relief; (2) correspondence; (3) communication with family; and (4) ICRC access.

8.10.1 Receipt of Individual or Collective Relief. Detainees shall be allowed to receive individual or collective relief.[77]

8.10.2 Correspondence. Detainees shall be allowed to send and receive letters and cards,

---

[73] *Consider* AP I art. 11 ("3. Exceptions to the prohibition in paragraph 2 (c) [against removal of tissue or organs for transplantation except where these acts are justified] may be made only in the case of donations of blood for transfusion or of skin for grafting, provided that they are given voluntarily and without any coercion or inducement, and then only for therapeutic purposes, under conditions consistent with generally accepted medical standards and controls designed for the benefit of both the donor and the recipient.").

[74] *Compare* § 9.27 (Disciplinary Proceedings and Punishment); § 10.28 (Disciplinary Proceedings and Punishment).

[75] *See Copenhagen Process: Principles and Guidelines* ¶14 ("Detainees or their representatives are to be permitted to submit, without reprisal, oral or written complaints regarding their treatment or conditions of detention. All complaints are to be reviewed and, if based on credible information, be investigated by the detaining authority."). *Compare* § 9.23.1 (POW Right to Make Requests and Complaints); § 10.21.1 (Internee Right to Present Petitions and Complaints).

[76] *See also Chairman's Commentary to the Copenhagen Process: Principles and Guidelines*, ¶14.2 ("The investigation of complaints permits the detaining authority to verify the validity of the complaint and, if verified, to rectify the situation giving rise to the complaint. Investigatory procedures and a practice of timely and effective investigations of credible complaints also helps ensure that allegations regarding treatment or conditions of detention that may arise years after the detention can be addressed. An independent and impartial authority should carry out such investigations, and the results of an investigation should be reported back to the complainant and the detaining authority. The investigator may be members of the military and should make recommendations based on the investigation it has carried out.").

[77] *Consider* AP II art. 5(1)(c) ("They shall be allowed to receive individual or collective relief;").

the number of which may be limited by a competent authority if it deems necessary.[78]

8.10.3 Communication With Family. DoD practice has been, where practicable, to grant detainees the means to communicate with family members (*e.g.*, exchange of letters, phone calls, and video teleconferences with family, family visits).[79]

8.10.4 ICRC Access to Detainees. An impartial humanitarian body, such as the ICRC, may offer its services to the parties to the conflict.[80]

All departments and agencies of the Federal Government shall provide the International Committee of the Red Cross with notification of, and timely access to, any individual detained in any armed conflict in the custody or under the effective control of an officer, employee, or other agent of the U.S. Government or detained within a facility owned, operated, or controlled by a department or agency of the U.S. Government, consistent with Department of Defense regulations and policies.[81]

8.11 Religious Exercise

Detainees shall be granted free exercise of religion, consistent with the requirements of detention.[82] Detainees' religious practices shall be respected.[83] They shall be allowed to

---

[78] *Consider* AP II art. 5(2)(b) ("They shall be allowed to send and receive letters and cards, the number of which may be limited by competent authority if it deems necessary;"). *Compare* § 9.20.2 (POW Correspondence Rights and Quota); § 10.23.2 (Internees' Correspondence Rights and Quota).

[79] *For example*, DoD Directive 2310.01E, *DoD Detainee Program*, ¶3b(1) (Aug. 19, 2014) ("Humane treatment includes: … (b) … appropriate contacts with the outside world (including, where practicable, exchange of letters, phone calls, and video teleconferences with immediate family or next of kin, as well as family visits)."). *Compare* § 9.20.2.3 (More Rapid Means of Correspondence in Appropriate Cases); § 10.23.2.3 (More Rapid Means of Correspondence in Appropriate Cases).

[80] GWS art. 3 ("An impartial humanitarian body, such as the International Committee of the Red Cross, may offer its services to the Parties to the conflict"); GWS-Sea art. 3 (same); GPW art. 3 (same); GC art. 3 (same).

[81] Executive Order 13491, *Ensuring Lawful Interrogations*, §4(b), 74 Federal Register 4893, 4894 (Jan. 22, 2009) ("All departments and agencies of the Federal Government shall provide the International Committee of the Red Cross with notification of, and timely access to, any individual detained in any armed conflict in the custody or under the effective control of an officer, employee, or other agent of the United States Government or detained within a facility owned, operated, or controlled by a department or agency of the United States Government, consistent with Department of Defense regulations and policies.").

[82] *For example*, DoD Directive 2310.01E, *DoD Detainee Program*, ¶3b (Aug. 19, 2014) ("All detainees will be treated humanely and with respect for their dignity, in accordance with applicable U.S. law and policy and the law of war. The humane treatment requirements in this section apply during all military operations, however characterized. (1) Humane treatment includes: … (e) Free exercise of religion, consistent with the requirements of detention."); DoD Directive 2310.01E, *The Department of Defense Detainee Program*, ¶E4.1.1 (Sept. 5, 2006) ("All persons captured, detained, interned, or otherwise in the control of DoD personnel during the course of military operations will be given humane care and treatment from the moment they fall into the hands of DoD personnel until release, transfer out of DoD control, or repatriation, including: … E4.1.1.2. Free exercise of religion, consistent with the requirements of detention;"). *Compare* § 9.15 (Religious Exercise by POWs); § 10.15 (Religious Exercise by Internees).

[83] *Consider* AP I art. 75(1) ("Each Party shall respect the person, honour, convictions and religious practices of all such persons.").

practice their religion and, if requested and appropriate, to receive spiritual assistance from persons, such as chaplains, performing religious functions.[84]

DoD practice has been for detainees to be provided religious materials of their faith (*e.g.*, copies of religious texts) as well as time and other accommodations for religious exercise.[85]

8.12 Intellectual, Physical, and Recreational Activities

Detainees should be provided with reasonable access to intellectual, physical, and recreational activities.[86] Such opportunity is increasingly important as detention occurs for longer periods of time.

Access to additional facilities for intellectual, physical, and recreational activities may be made contingent on compliance with camp rules.[87] Education programs may be offered to discourage violent extremism.[88]

---

[84] *Consider* AP II art. 5(1)(d) ("They shall be allowed to practise their religion and, if requested and appropriate, to receive spiritual assistance from persons, such as chaplains, performing religious functions;").

[85] *For example*, Admiral Patrick Walsh *et al.*, Department of Defense, *Review of Department Compliance with President's Executive Order on Detainee Conditions of Confinement*, 25 (2009) ("All detainees [at Guantanamo] are provided one Koran in the language of their choice, in addition to an Arabic Koran and TafSeer. All detainees are provided prayer beads, cap, rug, and current prayer schedule. These items are retained by all detainees regardless of disciplinary status, unless deliberately used for self-harm or as a weapon. … Guards observe silence during all prayer times. A monthly prayer schedule is published and call to prayer is sounded five times daily in all camps. Prayer is led within each camp and block by a detainee-selected prayer leader. In Camps 2, 3, 5, 6, and Echo group prayer is typically conducted by detainees from their individual cells. When this occurs, the food tray access doors of the prayer leaders are lowered to facilitate call to prayer on each block/tier. At times when detainees are engaged in group or communal activities and prayer call sounds, prayer is led by prayer leaders in person. In Camps 4 and Iguana, group prayer is conducted in communal areas of the camps. At Camp 7, prayer is conducted individually in their cells. Guard movement and activity is limited to only those actions required to maintain security. Visual signals are placed on each block/tier signifying quiet time. Each detainee cell and common area includes an arrow pointing towards Mecca.").

[86] *For example*, DoD Directive 2310.01E, *DoD Detainee Program*, ¶3b(1) (Aug. 19, 2014) ("Humane treatment includes: … (b) Reasonable access to the open air, reasonable educational and intellectual activities, … ."); *Chairman's Commentary to the Copenhagen Process: Principles and Guidelines*, ¶9.3 ("Health and hygiene factors that need to be addressed include … ensuring that detainees are permitted to engage in exercise regimes, including in the open air, … ."). *Compare* § 9.16 (Intellectual, Physical, and Recreational Activities); § 10.16 (Intellectual, Physical, and Recreational Activities).

[87] *For example*, Admiral Patrick Walsh *et al.*, Department of Defense, *Review of Department Compliance with President's Executive Order on Detainee Conditions of Confinement*, 11 (2009) ("Camp 4 [at Guantanamo], first occupied in February 2003, offers communal living, numerous recreation facilities, education and intellectual stimulation programs, and houses detainees considered the most compliant with camp rules. Unlike other camps, Camp 4 offers communal living in open-bay barracks with open access to fresh air in outdoor recreation and communal facilities throughout the day. It includes additional access to large recreation areas equipped with a basketball court, volleyball court, and soccer facility, during a specified four-hour period each day. Camp 4 has a media center equipped with satellite television, bench seating, and a classroom used to teach literacy and art.").

[88] *For example*, Charles A. Allen, Deputy General Counsel, Department of Defense, *Alternatives to Prosecution for War Crimes in the War on Terrorism*, 17 Transnational Law & Contemporary Problems 121, 137 (2008) ("For persons in detention in Iraq, MNF-I [Multi-National Force-Iraq] has a reintegration program to try to influence detainees not to join or rejoin the insurgency, but rather to reintegrate peacefully into society. This effort focuses on

8.13 Adequate Working Conditions

If made to work, detainees shall have the benefit of working conditions and safeguards similar to those enjoyed by the local civilian population.[89]

8.13.1 Prohibition on Slavery. Slavery and the slave trade in all their forms are prohibited.[90] For example, enforced prostitution is prohibited.[91]

8.14 Procedures for Detention

8.14.1 Informing of Reasons for Detention. Detainees shall be informed promptly of the reasons for their detention in a language that they understand.[92]

A prompt notification should generally occur within 10 days of detention.[93] The notification should ensure that the detainee adequately understands the general reason for detention (*e.g.*, security reasons, participation in hostilities or association with an armed group that is engaged in hostilities, suspect or witness in law enforcement proceedings).[94] When feasible, more specific information should be provided to the detainee so that he or she may participate in subsequent review procedures from an informed position.[95]

---

education. Detainees are provided access to moderate television, radio, and newspaper alternatives to extremist messages. The reintegration program for adults includes instruction in reading, writing, and mathematics. The program for juveniles includes both primary and secondary school instruction. In addition, detainees are offered classes on democracy, the Iraqi constitution, and the Iraqi government.").

[89] *Consider* AP II art. 5(1) (Persons deprived of their liberty for reasons related to an non-international armed conflict "shall, if made to work, have the benefit of working conditions and safeguards similar to those enjoyed by the local civilian population.").

[90] *Consider* AP II art. 4(2)(f) (prohibiting "slavery and the slave trade in all their forms;").

[91] *Refer to* § 8.2.2.1 (Protection Against Rape, Enforced Prostitution, and Other Indecent Assault).

[92] *See Copenhagen Process: Principles and Guidelines*, ¶7 ("Persons detained are to be promptly informed of the reasons for their detention in a language that they understand."). *Consider* AP I art. 75(3) ("Any person arrested, detained or interned for actions related to the armed conflict shall be informed promptly, in a language he understands, of the reasons why these measures have been taken.").

[93] ICRC AP COMMENTARY 876 (¶3072) ("'Promptly': unfortunately this expression is rather imprecise. ... [I]t is difficult to determine a precise time limit, but ten days would seem the maximum period.").

[94] *See Chairman's Commentary to the Copenhagen Process: Principles and Guidelines* ¶1.3 ("A person may be detained for a number of different reasons, including, posing a threat to the security of the military operation, for participating in hostilities, for belonging to an enemy organised armed group, for his or her own protection, or if the person is accused of committing a serious criminal offence.").

[95] *See also Chairman's Commentary to the Copenhagen Process: Principles and Guidelines*, ¶7.1 ("Informing the detainee of the reasons for detention seeks to ensure that the detainee adequately understands the basis of detention, and enables the detainee's participation in subsequent review procedures from an informed position. To the fullest extent feasible the reasons for detention should provide the detainee with information regarding the circumstances that form the basis for detention. Operational necessities or resource constraints, such as force protection or the availability of interpreters, may sometimes make it difficult to advise the detainee of the specific reasons for the detention at the precise moment of detention. The term 'promptly' is used to suggest that detainees should be advised of the reasons for detention in a reasonable time, taking into account other essential tasks and resource limitations that may affect the detaining authority's ability to inform the detainee. When feasible, more specific

8.14.2 Review of Continued Detention for Security Reasons. DoD practice has been to review periodically the detention of all persons not afforded POW status or treatment.[96] A detainee who has been deprived of liberty for security reasons is to have, in addition to a prompt initial review, the decision to detain reconsidered periodically by an impartial and objective authority that is authorized to determine the lawfulness and appropriateness of continued detention.[97]

The authority conducting the review is not necessarily outside the military, and often would be a military commander.[98]

There is no fixed requirement regarding how often the review must occur, and the period between reviews will depend on a variety of factors, including: (1) operational necessities or resource constraints, such as force protection, the availability of interpreters, or large numbers of detainees; (2) the thoroughness of the review process; and (3) whether there is a true prospect that the legal or factual predicates justifying detention have changed.[99]

8.14.3 Release When the Circumstances Justifying Detention Have Ceased to Exist.

---

information should be provided to the detainee so that he or she may participate in subsequent review procedures from an informed position.").

[96] *For example*, DoD DIRECTIVE 2310.01E, *DoD Detainee Program*, ¶3i (Aug. 19, 2014) ("DoD personnel will review periodically the detention of all individuals in DoD custody or control who do not receive the protections afforded POWs."); DoD DIRECTIVE 2310.01E, *The Department of Defense Detainee Program*, ¶4.8 (Sept. 5, 2006) ("Detainees under DoD control who do not enjoy prisoner of war protections under the law of war shall have the basis for their detention reviewed periodically by a competent authority.").

[97] *See Copenhagen Process: Principles and Guidelines* ¶12 ("A detainee whose liberty has been deprived for security reasons is to, in addition to a prompt initial review, have the decision to detain reconsidered periodically by an impartial and objective authority that is authorised to determine the lawfulness and appropriateness of continued detention."). *Compare* § 10.9.2.3 (Reconsideration and Periodic Review); § 10.9.3.1 (Internment or Assigned Residence for Imperative Reasons of Security).

[98] *See also Chairman's Commentary to* the *Copenhagen Process: Principles and Guidelines* ¶12.2 ("The 'authority' conducting the review must be objective and impartial but not necessarily outside the military. Although there is no requirement for the authority to be a judge or lawyer, he or she should be supported by a legal adviser. The authority must have sufficient information available to make an assessment of the legality and propriety of continued detention; and must consider both the legal and factual basis for detention. The authority must also be able to evaluate the relevant information and make relevant conclusions such as whether the detainee continues to constitute a threat to security. Furthermore, the authority must make decisions based on the circumstances of each specific case; and each decision must be taken with respect to the individual involved. The authority must have sufficient freedom to make a good faith judgment without any outside interference. In order for the review to be effective it is necessary that the reviewing authority has the power to determine the lawfulness and appropriateness of continued detention of the detainee.").

[99] *See also Chairman's Commentary to* the *Copenhagen Process: Principles and Guidelines* ¶12.3 ("Security detainees are to have their continued detention reviewed periodically or, where practicable, when new information becomes available. It is, however, difficult to provide a precise time limit to indicate when the decision to detain should be reconsidered or further reviewed. Operational necessities or resource constraints, such as force protection, the limited availability of interpreters or large case-loads of review sometimes make it difficult to reconsider the decision to detain frequently or at short intervals. Reviews should, however, occur as often as necessary, generally every six months. The length of time between reviews may also depend on the thoroughness of the review process and on whether there is a true prospect that the legal or factual predicates justifying detention have changed. More thorough reviews may require more resources and take place over longer intervals.").

Except in cases of arrest or detention for penal offenses, such persons shall be released with the minimum delay possible and in any event as soon as the circumstances justifying the arrest, detention, or internment have ceased to exist.[100]

8.14.3.1 *Participants in Hostilities or Persons Belonging to Armed Groups That Are Engaged in Hostilities*. For persons who have participated in hostilities or belong to armed groups that are engaged in hostilities, the circumstance that justifies their continued detention is the continuation of hostilities.[101] Thus, release of such persons is generally only required after the conflict has ceased.[102] As a matter of policy, release of lawfully detained persons often occurs before the conclusion of hostilities.[103]

However, even after hostilities have ceased, other circumstances may warrant continued detention of such persons. For example, persons who have participated in hostilities on behalf of non-State armed groups might be detained pending law enforcement proceedings and, after a conviction, pursuant to a lawful sentence.[104]

8.14.3.2 *Safe and Orderly Release*. If it is decided to release persons deprived of their liberty, necessary measures to ensure their safety shall be taken by those so deciding.[105] For example, detainees should not be released into a situation in which the detainee would be attacked by hostile elements upon release.[106]

---

[100] *Consider* AP I art. 75(3) ("Except in cases of arrest or detention for penal offences, such persons shall be released with the minimum delay possible and in any event as soon as the circumstances justifying the arrest, detention or internment have ceased to exist."). *Compare* § 9.37 (Release and Repatriation After Hostilities); § 10.9.5 (Release As Soon As Reasons for Internment No Longer Exist).

[101] *See, e.g.*, Hamdi v. Rumsfeld, 542 U.S. 507, 521 (2004) (plurality) ("we understand Congress' grant of authority [under the AUMF] for the use of 'necessary and appropriate force' to include the authority to detain for the duration of the relevant conflict, and our understanding is based on longstanding law-of-war principles."); Al-Bihani v. Obama, 590 F.3d 866, 874 (2010) (rejecting the argument that Taliban fighters must be released because the conflict had formally concluded as a principle that "would make each successful campaign of a long war but a Pyrrhic prelude to defeat" and under which "the victors would be commanded to constantly refresh the ranks of the fledgling democracy's most likely saboteurs."). *Cf.* Stewart v. Kahn, 78 U.S. 493, 507 (1870) ("In the latter case, the [war] power is not limited to victories in the field and the dispersion of the insurgent forces. It carries with it inherently the power to guard against the immediate renewal of the conflict and to remedy the evils which have arisen from its rise and progress.").

[102] *Compare* § 9.37 (Release and Repatriation After Hostilities).

[103] *For example*, DOD DIRECTIVE 2310.01E, *DoD Detainee Program*, ¶3m(2) (Aug. 19, 2014) ("Unprivileged belligerents may be released or transferred while active hostilities are ongoing if a competent authority determines that the threat the individual poses to the security of the United States can be mitigated by other lawful means. Such mitigation may involve credible assurances that a receiving country will take appropriate steps to mitigate any threat the detainee poses to the security of the United States and its interests, parole agreements by the detainee, or other agreements with the government of the receiving State.").

[104] *Compare* § 9.37.4.3 (POWs Undergoing Criminal Proceedings for an Indictable Offense).

[105] *Consider* AP II art. 5(4) ("If it is decided to release persons deprived of their liberty, necessary measures to ensure their safety shall be taken by those so deciding.").

[106] *See Chairman's Commentary to* the *Copenhagen Process: Principles and Guidelines* ¶4.10 ("Detaining authorities are to ensure that necessary measures are taken to ensure the safety of released detainees. For example, a

The obligation to release detainees in a safe and orderly manner, as well as operational necessities (*e.g.*, force protection) and logistical constraints (*e.g.*, the limited availability of transport), may make it difficult to release a detainee at the precise moment that the circumstances justifying detention cease.[107] Continued detention in order to facilitate a safe and orderly release may be necessary.[108]

8.14.4 Transfers of Detainees. Because the transfer of a detainee from U.S. custody to another entity or State may implicate certain U.S. legal obligations or policies, detainees should not be transferred to another State or entity without proper authorization.[109]

8.14.4.1 *U.S. Policy Prohibiting Transfers in Cases in Which Detainees Would Likely Be Tortured*. U.S. policy provides that no person shall be transferred to another State if it is more likely than not that the person would be tortured in the receiving country, regardless of whether the person is physically present in the United States or whether such transfer would otherwise be consistent with applicable law.[110]

8.15 National Accountability for Detention

A proper accounting of detainees is an important part of a State's implementation of the requirements of humane treatment.

8.15.1 Registration of Detainees. The detaining authority should register detainees

---

detainee is not to be released in a location where the conditions are such that the detainee may be threatened or attacked by hostile or malign elements upon release.").

[107] *See Chairman's Commentary to* the *Copenhagen Process: Principles and Guidelines* ¶4.8 ("It is difficult to provide a precise time limit to indicate how soon a detainee should be released after the circumstances justifying detention have ceased to exist. Operational necessities, such as force protection, the safety of a detainee, or the limited availability of transport sometimes make it difficult to release a detainee at the precise moment that the circumstances justifying detention cease.").

[108] *Compare* § 9.37.3 (Without Delay).

[109] *For example*, DoD Directive 2310.01E, *DoD Detainee Program*, ¶3m (Aug. 19, 2014) ("No detainee will be released, repatriated, or transferred out of DoD custody or control except in accordance with applicable law, regulation, policy, and other issuances."); DoD Directive 2310.01E, *The Department of Defense Detainee Program*, ¶4.6 (Sept. 5, 2006) ("No detainee shall be released or transferred from the care, custody, or control of a DoD Component except in accordance with applicable law, regulation, policy, and other issuances.").

[110] *See, e.g.*, Munaf v. Geren, 553 U.S. 674, 702 (2008) ("Indeed, the Solicitor General states that it is the policy of the United States not to transfer an individual in circumstances where torture is likely to result."); Public Law 105-277, § 2242(a) (Oct. 21, 1998), *codified at* 8 U.S.C. § 1231 note ("It shall be the policy of the United States not to expel, extradite, or otherwise effect the involuntary return of any person to a country in which there are substantial grounds for believing the person would be in danger of being subjected to torture, regardless of whether the person is physically present in the United States."). One of the formal understandings of the United States made upon ratification of the Convention Against Torture provided that "the United States understands the phrase, 'where there are substantial grounds for believing that he would be in danger of being subjected to torture,' as used in article 3 of the Convention, to mean 'if it is more likely than not that he would be tortured.'" United States, *Statement on Ratification of the Convention Against Torture and Other Cruel, Inhuman or Degrading Treatment or Punishment, Dec. 10, 1984*, Oct. 21, 1994, 1830 UNTS 320, 322.

promptly.[111] Detainees should be registered within a reasonable time, taking into account other essential tasks and resource limitations that may affect the detaining authority's ability to register detainees.[112]

Registration of detainees assists in ensuring that all detainees can be accounted for and that allegations of illegal detention can be addressed.[113] DoD practice has been to register detainees with the National Detainee Reporting Center that is also used to account for the detention of POWs under the GPW and protected persons under the GC.[114]

8.15.2 Records of Detainee Property. DoD practice has been for property in the possession of detainees to be inventoried, and for records of such property to be maintained in order to maintain accountability of it (*e.g.*, to prevent theft) and to ensure its lawful disposition.[115]

8.16 CRIMINAL PROCEDURE AND PUNISHMENT

The passing of sentences and the carrying out of executions without previous judgment pronounced by a regularly constituted court affording all the judicial guarantees that are recognized as indispensable by civilized peoples are prohibited.[116]

---

[111] *See Chairman's Commentary to* the *Copenhagen Process: Principles and Guidelines* ¶8 ("Persons detained are to be promptly registered by the detaining authority."). *For example*, DOD DIRECTIVE 2310.01E, *DoD Detainee Program*, ¶3d (Aug. 19, 2014) ("Detainees will be registered, and property in their possession will be inventoried. Records of their detention and such property will be maintained according to applicable law, regulation, policy, and other issuances. (1) DoD Components will maintain full accountability for all detainees under DoD control. Detainees will be assigned an Internment Serial Number (ISN) normally within 14 days after their capture by, or transfer to, the custody or control of DoD personnel, barring exceptional circumstances."); DOD DIRECTIVE 2310.01E, *The Department of Defense Detainee Program*, ¶4.4.1 (Sept. 5, 2006) ("Detainees shall be assigned an Internment Serial Number (ISN) as soon as possible after coming under DoD control, normally within 14 days of capture. DoD Components shall maintain full accountability for all detainees under DoD control.").

[112] *See also Chairman's Commentary to* the *Copenhagen Process: Principles and Guidelines* ¶8.3 ("It is difficult to provide a precise time limit to indicate when a detainee should be registered. Operational necessities or resource constraints, such as force protection, or the limited availability of interpreters sometimes make it difficult to register a detainee at the precise moment of detention. The term 'promptly' is used to suggest that detainees should be registered within a reasonable time, taking into account other essential tasks and resource limitations that may affect the detaining authority's ability to register detainees.").

[113] *See Chairman's Commentary to* the *Copenhagen Process: Principles and Guidelines* ¶8.1 ("Registration of detainees assists in ensuring that all detainees can be accounted for and that allegations of (illegal) detention can be addressed.").

[114] *For example*, Declaration of Vice Admiral Robert S. Harward, ¶8 (Dec. 17, 2010), *attached to* Hamidullah v. Gates, Response to Order to Show Cause and Motion to Dismiss, Civil Action No. 10-CV-758 (D.D.C. Dec. 17, 2010) ("DoD has registered individuals held under its control at the DFIP with the National Detainee Reporting Center ('NDRC') -- which accounts for persons who receive Internment Serial Numbers issued by DoD while in DoD's custody -- and with the International Committee of the Red Cross ('ICRC')."). *Compare* § 9.31.4 (U.S. Practice in Reporting to the ICRC Central Tracing Agency); § 10.31.4 (U.S. Practice in Reporting to the ICRC Central Tracing Agency).

[115] *Compare* § 9.7.4 (Money and Articles of Value); § 10.19.1 (Money and Valuables in the Internee's Possession).

[116] *See* GWS art. 3 (prohibiting with respect to persons taking no active part in the hostilities "the passing of sentences and the carrying out of executions without previous judgment pronounced by a regularly constituted court

The specific rules addressed in this section may be understood as examples of such guarantees.[117]

8.16.1 No Private Rights Created by This Section in Particular. As with all other sections of this manual, Section 8.16 does not create any private rights.[118] The competent prosecuting authorities shall ensure that the requirements reflected in this section are met.

8.16.2 General Limits on Punishments.

8.16.2.1 *Individual Penal Responsibility and No Collective Punishment*. No one shall be convicted of an offense except on the basis of individual penal responsibility.[119]

Collective punishments are prohibited. Collective punishments have been specifically prohibited with respect to POWs, protected persons under the GC, and inhabitants of occupied territory, and also in connection with non-international armed conflict.[120] This prohibition includes penalties of any kind inflicted upon persons or groups of persons for acts that these persons have not committed, including administrative penalties.[121] Punishment on the basis of conspiracy, joint criminal enterprise, and other theories of secondary liability are not prohibited by this rule.[122]

8.16.2.2 *No Crime or Punishment Without Prior Law*. No one shall be accused or convicted of a criminal offense on account of any act or omission that did not constitute a criminal offense under the national or international law to which he or she was subject at the time when it was committed; nor shall a heavier penalty be imposed than that which was

---

affording all the judicial guarantees which are recognized as indispensable by civilized peoples."); GWS-SEA art. 3 (same); GPW art. 3 (same); GC art. 3 (same). *Consider* AP I art. 75(4) ("No sentence may be passed and no penalty may be executed on a person found guilty of a penal offence related to the armed conflict except pursuant to a conviction pronounced by an impartial and regularly constituted court respecting the generally recognized principles of regular judicial procedure, which include the following:"); AP II art. 6(2) ("No sentence shall be passed and no penalty shall be executed on a person found guilty of an offence except pursuant to a conviction pronounced by a court offering the essential guarantees of independence and impartiality.").

[117] ICRC AP COMMENTARY 878 (¶3084) ("Article 3 [of the 1949 Geneva Conventions] relies on the 'judicial guarantees which are recognized as indispensable by civilized peoples', while Article 75 [of AP I] rightly spells out these guarantees. Thus this article, and to an even greater extent, Article 6 of Protocol II (*Penal prosecutions*), gives valuable indications to help explain the terms of Article 3 on guarantees.").

[118] *Refer to* § 1.1.1 (Purpose).

[119] *Consider* AP I art. 75(4)(a) ("No one shall be convicted of an offence except on the basis of individual penal responsibility;"); AP II art. 6(2)(b) ("No one shall be convicted of an offence except on the basis of individual penal responsibility;").

[120] *Refer to* § 9.26.6 (Prohibited Penalties); § 10.5.3.2 (Collective Penalties and Measures of Intimidation or Terrorism); § 11.6.2.2 (Prohibition Against General Penalties in Occupied Territory); § 17.6.7 (Prohibition on Collective Punishment).

[121] GC COMMENTARY 225 ("This paragraph then lays a prohibition on collective penalties. This does not refer to punishments inflicted under penal law, i.e. sentences pronounced by a court after due process of law, but penalties of any kind inflicted on persons or entire groups of persons, in defiance of the most elementary principles of humanity, for acts that these persons have not committed.").

[122] *Refer to* § 18.23 (Theories of Individual Criminal Liability).

applicable at the time when the criminal offense was committed; if, after the commission of the offense, provision is made by law for the imposition of a lighter penalty, the offender shall benefit thereby.[123]

8.16.2.3 *No Repetition of Punishment*. No one shall be prosecuted or punished by the same party for an offense in respect of which a final judgment acquitting or convicting that person has been previously pronounced under the same law and judicial procedure.[124]

8.16.2.4 *Limitations on the Death Penalty*. The death penalty shall not be pronounced on persons who were under the age of eighteen years at the time of the offense and shall not be carried out on pregnant women or mothers of young children.[125]

8.16.3 Rights of Defense and Trial Procedure. The procedure shall provide for an accused to be informed without delay of the particulars of the notice alleged against him or her and shall afford the accused before and during his or her trial all necessary rights and means of defense.[126]

8.16.3.1 *Presumption of Innocence*. Anyone charged with an offense is presumed innocent until proved guilty according to law.[127]

8.16.3.2 *Right to Trial in Presence*. Anyone charged with an offense shall have

---

[123] *Consider* AP I art. 75(4)(c) ("No one shall be accused or convicted of a criminal offence on account of any act or omission which did not constitute a criminal offence under the national or international law to which he was subject at the time when it was committed; nor shall a heavier penalty be imposed than that which was applicable at the time when the criminal offence was committed; if, after the commission of the offence, provision is made by law for the imposition of a lighter penalty, the offender shall benefit thereby;"); AP II art. 6(2)(c) ("No one shall be accused or convicted of a criminal offence on account of any act or omission which did not constitute a criminal offence under the national or international law to which he was subject at the time when it was committed; nor shall a heavier penalty be imposed than that which was applicable at the time when the criminal offence was committed; if, after the commission of the offence, provision is made by law for the imposition of a lighter penalty, the offender shall benefit thereby;").

[124] *Consider* AP I art. 75(4)(h) ("No one shall be prosecuted or punished by the same Party for an offence in respect of which a final judgement acquitting or convicting that person has been previously pronounced under the same law and judicial procedure;").

[125] *Consider* AP II art. 6(4) ("The death penalty shall not be pronounced on persons who were under the age of eighteen years at the time of the offence and shall not be carried out on pregnant women or mothers of young chidren [sic].").

[126] *Consider* AP I art. 75(4)(a) ("The procedure shall provide for an accused to be informed without delay of the particulars of the offence alleged against him and shall afford the accused before and during his trial all necessary rights and means of defence;"); AP II art. 6(2)(a) ("The procedure shall provide for an accused to be informed without delay of the particulars of the offence alleged against him and shall afford the accused before and during his trial all necessary rights and means of defence;").

[127] *Consider* AP I art. 75(4)(d) ("Anyone charged with an offence is presumed innocent until proved guilty according to law;"); AP II art. 6(2)(d) ("Anyone charged with an offence is presumed innocent until proved guilty according to law;").

the right to be tried in his or her presence.[128]

8.16.3.3 _No Compulsory Self-Incrimination_. No one shall be compelled to testify against himself or herself or to confess guilt.[129]

8.16.3.4 _Right to Obtain and Examine Witnesses_. Anyone charged with an offense shall have the right to examine, or have examined, the witnesses against him or her and to obtain the attendance and examination of witnesses on his or her behalf under the same conditions as witnesses against him or her.[130]

8.16.3.5 _Right to Have a Public Judgment_. Anyone prosecuted for an offense shall have the right to have the judgment pronounced publicly.[131]

8.16.3.6 _Advice on Appellate Procedure_. A convicted person shall be advised on conviction of his or her judicial and other remedies, and of the time-limits within which they may be exercised.[132]

---

[128] *Consider* AP I art. 75(4)(e) ("Anyone charged with an offence shall have the right to be tried in his presence;"); AP II art. 6(2)(e) ("Anyone charged with an offence shall have the right to be tried in his presence;").

[129] *Consider* AP I art. 75(4)(f) ("No one shall be compelled to testify against himself or to confess guilt;"); AP II art. 6(2)(f) ("No one shall be compelled to testify against himself or to confess guilt.").

[130] *Consider* AP I art. 75(4)(g) ("Anyone charged with an offence shall have the right to examine, or have examined, the witnesses against him and to obtain the attendance and examination of witnesses on his behalf under the same conditions as witnesses against him;").

[131] *Consider* AP I art. 75(4)(i) ("Anyone prosecuted for an offence shall have the right to have the judgement pronounced publicly;").

[132] *Consider* AP I art. 75(4)(j) ("A convicted person shall be advised on conviction of his judicial and other remedies and of the time-limits within which they may be exercised."); AP II art. 6(3) ("A convicted person shall be advised on conviction of his judicial and other remedies and of the time-limits within which they may be exercised.").

IX – Prisoners of War (POWs)

Chapter Contents

9.1 INTRODUCTION

This Chapter addresses the treatment of prisoners of war (POWs).

9.1.1 Brief History of POW Law. States have made significant humanitarian advances in the international law relating to the treatment of POWs.[1] Before the modern law of war, POWs were often put to death, held for ransom or as hostages, or sold into slavery.

Gradually, protections for POWs, such as providing for their repatriation at the end of conflict without ransom, were concluded in treaties.[2] The United States concluded bilateral treaties for the humane treatment and protection of POWs, written with a view towards forbidding abuses that occurred during the Revolutionary War.[3] Eventually multilateral treaties for the protection of POWs were concluded, which also drew from the experience of POWs during prior conflicts.[4] War crimes trials after World War II for POW mistreatment recognized that the humane treatment of POWs was required under customary international law.[5]

After World War II, the 1949 Geneva Conventions were concluded, and more than 190 States, including the United States, are Parties to the GPW.[6]

9.1.2 Interpretation and Application of the GPW. The GPW underlies most of the international law rules applicable to the United States for the treatment of POWs.

The GPW's provisions should be interpreted in light of the principles that underlie POW detention and, in particular, in light of the goal of advancing the humane treatment of POWs.[7]

---

[1] WINTHROP, MILITARY LAW & PRECEDENTS 788 ("Modern sentiment and usage have induced in the practice of war few changes so marked as that which affects the status of prisoners of war. The time has long passed when 'no quarter' was the rule on the battlefield, or when a prisoner could be put to death by virtue simply of his capture.").

[2] *See, e.g.*, Treaty of Peace Between Spain and the Netherlands, Signed at Munster, in Westphalia, on 30 January 1648, LEVIE, DOCUMENTS ON POWS 5 ("LXIII. All prisoners of war shall be delivered up by both sides, without the payment of any ransom, and without any distinction and without exception with respect to the prisoners who served outside of the Low Countries and under other standards and flags than those of the said Sovereign States.").

[3] *For example*, Treaty of Amity and Commerce between His Majesty the King of Prussia and the United States of America, art. 24, Sept. 10, 1785, 18 STAT. 641, 647.

[4] *Refer to* § 19.8.1 (1899 Hague II); § 19.13.2 (1929 GPW).

[5] *See, e.g.*, United States, *et al.* v. Göring, *et al.*, *Judgment*, I TRIAL OF THE MAJOR WAR CRIMINALS BEFORE THE IMT 232 ("The argument in defense of the charge with regard to the murder and ill-treatment of Soviet prisoners of war, that the U.S.S.R. was not a party to the [1929] Geneva Convention, is quite without foundation."); United States v. von Leeb, *et al.* (The High Command Case), XI TRIALS OF WAR CRIMINALS BEFORE THE NMT 495 (quoting the International Military Tribunal at Nuremberg's discussion of the murder and maltreatment of Soviet POWs and noting: "All of these unlawful acts, as well as employment under inhumane conditions and at prohibited labor, is shown by the record in this case. They were deliberate, gross and continued violations of the customs and usages of war as well as the Hague Regulations (1907) and the Geneva Convention (1929) and of international common law.").

[6] *Refer to* § 19.16 (1949 Geneva Conventions).

[7] *See* Jack L. Goldsmith III, Assistant Attorney General, *"Protected Person" Status in Occupied Iraq Under the Fourth Geneva Convention*, Mar. 18, 2004, 28 OPINIONS OF THE OFFICE OF LEGAL COUNSEL 35, 55 ("Our recourse to fundamental principles to address an ambiguity in article 4 is not unusual. In the context of the law of armed conflict, interpreters faced with changed or unexpected circumstances have not hesitated to resort to a treaty's

The subsequent practice of States in applying the GPW could assist in interpreting its provisions because States' decades of experience in applying the GPW may be very helpful in understanding its requirements.[8]

9.1.2.1 *GPW – Notes on Terminology*. "Prisoner of war" (abbreviated POW in this manual) does not refer to any person who is held prisoner in connection with a war; rather, POW is term of art that is defined and used in the GPW.[9]

In the GPW, the *Detaining Power* refers to the State that holds the POW.

In the GPW, the *Power on which the POWs depend* means the State that the POWs served before falling into the power of the enemy. (In some cases, this State might be different from the POW's State of nationality.)

In the GPW, the *Protecting Power* refers to a neutral State that helps implement the GPW.[10]

9.1.2.2 *Special Agreements Under the GPW*. Under the GPW, States may conclude a variety of special agreements during international armed conflict to facilitate the protection of POWs.

The GPW specifically provides for agreements:

- to entrust to an effective and impartial organization the duties of the Protecting Powers;[11]
- to establish a system for marking POW camps;[12]
- on how to allocate the profits made by camp canteens in case of a general repatriation;[13]
- to establish the corresponding ranks for their medical personnel and staff of National Red Cross Societies and other Voluntary Aid Services in order to help determine the senior medical officer in POW camps;[14]

---

fundamental principles to avoid a non-contextual reading of a treaty term that, wrenched from its original context, might lead to a conclusion that does violence to the treaty's object and purpose. And they have done so even when construing treaty text far less ambiguous than article 4."). *Refer to* § 9.2 (General Principles Applicable to the Treatment of POWs).

[8] *Refer to* § 1.7.4 (Use of Certain Subsequent Practice in Treaty Interpretation).

[9] *Refer to* § 9.3 (POW Status).

[10] *Refer to* § 18.15.1.1 (Protecting Power Under the 1949 Geneva Conventions).

[11] *Refer to* § 18.15.2.1 (Agreement for an Impartial and Effective Organization to Perform Protecting Power Duties Under the 1949 Geneva Conventions).

[12] *Refer to* § 9.4.2.3 (Location and Marking of POW Camps).

[13] *Refer to* § 9.17.3.2 (Disposition of Canteen Profits Upon Camp Closure).

[14] *Refer to* § 7.9.5.7 (Senior Medical Officer in the Camp).

- for the relief of retained personnel and the procedure for relief;[15]
- to modify the amount of advances of pay due to POWs based on their military rank during and at the close of hostilities;[16]
- to notify periodically, through the Protecting Power, the account balances of POWs;[17]
- to vary the required information provided for in the list of all appropriate particulars of all POWs whose captivity has been terminated;[18]
- regarding individual parcels and collective relief shipments to POWs;[19]
- for the accommodation in neutral countries of seriously wounded and sick POWs;[20]
- for the direct repatriation or internment in a neutral country of able-bodied POWs who have undergone a long period of captivity;[21]
- to determine the conditions that POWs who are accommodated in a neutral country must fulfill in order to permit their repatriation, and to establish the status of POWs accommodated in a neutral country;[22]
- to determine the equitable apportionment of costs of and a plan for repatriation for when hostilities have ceased;[23]
- to regulate the conditions of the transport of personal effects and the payment of the costs associated with the repatriation of POWs;[24]
- to establish a commission to search for dispersed POWs and to ensure their repatriation with the least possible delay;[25] and
- on the procedure, or to select an umpire who will decide the procedure, to be followed for

---

[15] *Refer to* § 7.9.5.8 (Agreements on Possible Relief of Retained Personnel).

[16] *Refer to* § 9.18.3 (Advance of Pay).

[17] *Refer to* § 9.18.6.3 (Periodic Notification of the Amount of the Accounts of POWs).

[18] *Refer to* § 9.18.6.4 (Statements of Credit Balance on Termination of Captivity).

[19] *Refer to* § 9.20.3.3 (Special Agreements Concerning Relief Shipments).

[20] *Refer to* § 9.36.2 (Accommodation in Neutral Countries).

[21] *Refer to* § 9.36.2 (Accommodation in Neutral Countries).

[22] *Refer to* § 9.36.3.1 (Repatriation From a Neutral State).

[23] *Refer to* § 9.37.6 (Costs of Repatriation at the Close of Hostilities).

[24] *Refer to* § 9.38.3 (Personal Property); § 9.31.2.3 (Collection of Personal Valuables Left by POWs).

[25] *Refer to* § 9.37.5 (Commissions to Search for Dispersed POWs).

an inquiry concerning any alleged violation of the GPW.[26]

In addition to the agreements expressly provided for in Articles 10, 23, 28, 33, 60, 65, 66, 67, 72, 73, 75, 109, 110, 118, 119, 122, and 132 of the GPW, Parties to the GPW may conclude other special agreements for all matters concerning which they may deem it suitable to make separate provision.[27] No special agreement shall adversely affect the situation of POWs, as defined by the GPW, nor restrict the rights that it confers upon them.[28]

POWs shall continue to have the benefit of such agreements as long as the GPW is applicable to them, except where express provisions to the contrary are contained in these or subsequent agreements, or where more favorable measures have been taken with regard to them by one or other of the parties to the conflict.[29]

9.1.3 <u>DoD Policies and Regulations for the Treatment of POWs</u>. DoD policies and regulations regarding the treatment of POWs provide authoritative guidance for DoD personnel and fill an important role in implementing the complex requirements of the GPW.[30] Practitioners are advised to consult all applicable policies and regulations, as these, in many cases, exceed the requirements of the GPW, U.S. statutes, and Executive Orders.

9.2 General Principles Applicable to the Treatment of POWs

Certain principles provide the foundation for the rules governing the treatment of POWs.

9.2.1 <u>Detention Is Non-Punitive in Character</u>. The detention of POWs is not punishment, and is devoid of all penal character.[31] It is intended to disable the POW and to prevent him or her from further participation in hostilities.[32]

---

[26] *Refer to* § 18.14.1 (Inquiry Procedure in the 1949 Geneva Conventions).

[27] GPW art. 6 ("In addition to the agreements expressly provided for in Articles 10, 23, 28, 33, 60, 65, 66, 67, 72, 73, 75, 109, 110, 118, 119, 122 and 132, the High Contracting Parties may conclude other special agreements for all matters concerning which they may deem it suitable to make separate provision.").

[28] GPW art. 6 ("No special agreement shall adversely affect the situation of prisoners of war, as defined by the present Convention, nor restrict the rights which it confers upon them.").

[29] GPW art. 6 ("Prisoners of war shall continue to have the benefit of such agreements as long as the Convention is applicable to them, except where express provisions to the contrary are contained in the aforesaid or in subsequent agreements, or where more favourable measures have been taken with regard to them by one or other of the Parties to the conflict.").

[30] *Refer to* § 18.7 (Instructions, Regulations, and Procedures to Implement and Enforce the Law of War).

[31] WINTHROP, MILITARY LAW & PRECEDENTS 788 ("It is now recognized that—'Captivity is neither a punishment nor an act of vengeance,' but 'merely a temporary detention which is devoid of all penal character.'"); Francis Lieber, *The Status of Rebel Prisoners of War, reprinted in* II THE MISCELLANEOUS WRITINGS OF FRANCIS LIEBER 293 (1881) ("A belligerent is not a criminal, and the imprisonment of a captured belligerent is not a punishment. A prisoner of war is no convict; his imprisonment is a simple war measure.").

[32] United States, *et al.* v. Göring, *et al.*, *Judgment*, I TRIAL OF THE MAJOR WAR CRIMINALS BEFORE THE IMT 232 (quoting approvingly a German Admiral who argued for the humane treatment of POWs during World War II, "war captivity is neither revenge nor punishment, but solely protective custody, the only purpose of which is to prevent the prisoners of war from further participation in the war.").

9.2.2 Responsibility of the Detaining Power. POWs are in the hands of the enemy Power, and not of the individuals or military units who have captured them.[33] Irrespective of the individual responsibilities that may exist, the Detaining Power is responsible for the treatment given POWs.[34]

9.2.3 Responsibility of POWs. Just as the Detaining Power is responsible for the treatment of POWs, POWs also have certain responsibilities related to their detention.

POWs continue to have obligations to the Power on which they depend.[35] POWs are also obliged to obey the laws, regulations, and orders of the Detaining Power.[36] Despite this general obligation, POWs may not be punished in respect of their successful escape, if recaptured by the Detaining Power.[37]

9.2.4 Humane Treatment. Humane treatment is a fundamental principle underlying the GPW; it is always required.[38] Moreover, interpretations of the GPW that provide for humane treatment should be favored over rigid interpretations of the GPW that lead to results that would be detrimental to the welfare of POWs.

9.2.5 Reciprocity in the Treatment of POWs. The rules for the treatment of POWs have long been based on the principle that POWs should be treated as the Detaining Power would want its forces held by the enemy to be treated.[39] Aside from being legally required, the

---

[33] GPW art. 12 ("Prisoners of war are in the hands of the enemy Power, but not of the individuals or military units who have captured them."); 1929 GPW art. 2 ("Prisoners of war are in the power of the hostile Power, but not of the individuals or corps who have captured them."); HAGUE IV REG. art. 4 ("Prisoners of war are in the power of the hostile Government, but not of the individuals or corps who capture them."); LIEBER CODE art. 74 ("A prisoner of war, being a public enemy, is the prisoner of the government, and not of the captor.").

[34] GPW art. 12 ("Irrespective of the individual responsibilities that may exist, the Detaining Power is responsible for the treatment given them.").

[35] *Refer to* § 9.22.2 (POWs' Status With Respect to Their Armed Forces).

[36] *Refer to* § 9.26.1 (POWs Subject to the Laws, Regulations, and Orders in Force in the Armed Forces of the Detaining Power).

[37] *Refer to* § 9.25.1 (No Punishment for Successful Escape).

[38] *Refer to* § 9.5 (Humane Treatment and Basic Protections for POWs).

[39] *For example, Basic Course in the Geneva Conventions of 1949 and Hague Convention No. IV of 1907: Lesson Plan—First Hour*, ¶6, Appendix A in DEPARTMENT OF THE ARMY SUBJECT SCHEDULE 27-1, *The Geneva Conventions of 1949 and Hague Convention No. IV of 1907*, 6 (Aug. 29, 1975) ("Although we shall presently discuss the most important of the many specific rules set out in these [1949 Geneva] Conventions, you should always keep in mind that these rules are embodied in one general principle: treat all prisoners of war, civilians, or other detained personnel *humanely*. … But, you ask, what does it mean to treat someone humanely? If you treat such people as you would like to be treated were you captured or detained, you will be treating them humanely. Remember that a PW is in your protective custody, and you cannot harm him."); George Washington, Commander-in-Chief of the Continental Army, *Letter to Lieutenant General Thomas Gage*, Head Quarters, Cambridge (Aug. 11, 1775), *reprinted in* JARED SPARKS, THE WRITINGS OF GEORGE WASHINGTON; PART SECOND, III 60 (1837) ("My Duty now makes it necessary to apprize you, that for the future I shall regulate my Conduct towards those Gentlemen, who are or may be in our Possession, exactly by the Rule you shall observe towards those of ours, now in your Custody. If severity and hardship mark the line of your conduct, painful as it may be to me, your prisoners will feel its effects. But if kindness and humanity are shown to ours, I shall with pleasure consider those in our hands only as unfortunate, and they shall receive from me that treatment to which the unfortunate are entitled.").

favorable treatment of POWs held by the U.S. armed forces can promote the favorable treatment of members of the U.S. armed forces held by enemy States.[40]

A similar concept may also be found in provisions of the GPW that provide for the treatment of POWs with reference to the treatment of the armed forces of the Detaining Power. For example, POWs shall be quartered under conditions as favorable as those for the forces of the Detaining Power who are billeted in the same area.[41] Similarly, in judicial proceedings, POWs should benefit from the same courts and same procedures as the members of the armed forces of the Detaining Power.[42]

9.3 POW STATUS

9.3.1 <u>POW Status Versus POW Protections</u>. In some cases, the policy of the United States has been to afford detainees certain POW protections even when they may not apply as a matter of law.[43] Certain POW protections may be afforded to an individual without affecting the legal status of that individual or the legal status of a group to which that person belongs.[44]

9.3.2 <u>Persons Entitled to POW Status</u>. During international armed conflict, persons entitled to POW status, if they fall into the power of the enemy, include:[45]

---

[40] *For example*, Martin Tollefson, *Enemy Prisoners of War*, 31 IOWA LAW REVIEW 51, 56 footnote 8 (1946) ("The writer of this law review article was a member of a committee of three officers sent by the Secretary of War to inspect concentration camps, civilian internee camps, and prisoner-of-war camps in Germany immediately upon their liberation. Testimony was frequently and freely given to these committee members by Americans held as prisoners of war (not in concentration camps where American servicemen were not interned) to the effect that they had been given better treatment as a result of the fair treatment given by the United States to German prisoners. Occasionally testimony was given by interned Americans that they were of the opinion that the reason they survived prisoner of war internment in Germany was the result of fair treatment of German prisoners.").

[41] *Refer to* 9.11.6 (Conditions of Living Quarters).

[42] *Refer to* § 9.28.2 (Same Courts and Same Procedures).

[43] *For example*, MAJOR GENERAL GEORGE S. PRUGH, LAW AT WAR: VIETNAM 1964-1973 66 (1975) ("The classification of Viet Cong combatants and Viet Cong suspects posed an interesting legal problem. Because it believed the Viet Cong were traitors and criminals, the Vietnam government was reluctant to accord prisoner of war status to Viet Cong captives. Furthermore it was certainly arguable that many Viet Cong did not meet the criteria of guerrillas entitled to prisoner of war status under Article 4, Geneva Prisoner of War Conventions. However, civil incarceration and criminal trial of the great number of Viet Cong was too much for the civil resources at hand. In addition, Article 22 prohibited the mingling of civil defendants with prisoners of war. By broadly construing Article 4, so as to accord full prisoner of war status to Viet Cong Main Force and Local Force troops, as well as regular North Vietnamese Army troops, any Viet Cong taken in combat would be detained for a prisoner of war camp rather than a civilian jail. The MACV policy was that all combatants captured during military operations were to be accorded prisoner of war status, irrespective of the type of unit to which they belonged. Terrorists, spies, and saboteurs were excluded from consideration as prisoners of war. Suspected Viet Cong captured under circumstances not warranting their treatment as prisoners of war were handled as civilian defendants.").

[44] *Compare* § 17.2.3 (Application of Humanitarian Rules and the Legal Status of the Parties to the Conflict).

[45] GPW art. 4A ("Prisoners of war, in the sense of the present Convention, are persons belonging to one of the following categories, who have fallen into the power of the enemy: (1) Members of the armed forces of a Party to the conflict, as well as members of militias or volunteer corps forming part of such armed forces. (2) Members of other militias and members of other volunteer corps, including those of organized resistance movements, belonging to a Party to the conflict and operating in or outside their own territory, even if this territory is occupied, provided

- members of the armed forces of a State that is a party to the conflict, including;[46]
    - deserters;[47] and
    - military medical and religious personnel not entitled to retained personnel status (*e.g.*, those not exclusively engaged in medical duties at the time of their capture);[48]
- members of certain militia and volunteer corps;[49]
- members of regular armed forces who profess allegiance to a government or authority not recognized by Detaining Power;[50]
- persons authorized to accompany the armed forces;[51]
- members of crews of merchant marine vessels or civil aircraft;[52] and
- participants in a *levée en masse*.[53]

9.3.2.1 Persons Who Are Not Entitled to POW Status. Certain categories of persons are not entitled to POW status:

- spies, saboteurs, and other persons engaging in similar acts behind enemy lines;[54] and

---

that such militias or volunteer corps, including such organized resistance movements, fulfil the following conditions: (a) that of being commanded by a person responsible for his subordinates; (b) that of having a fixed distinctive sign recognizable at a distance; (c) that of carrying arms openly; (d) that of conducting their operations in accordance with the laws and customs of war. (3) Members of regular armed forces who profess allegiance to a government or an authority not recognized by the Detaining Power. (4) Persons who accompany the armed forces without actually being members thereof, such as civilian members of military aircraft crews, war correspondents, supply contractors, members of labour units or of services responsible for the welfare of the armed forces, provided that they have received authorization from the armed forces which they accompany, who shall provide them for that purpose with an identity card similar to the annexed model. (5) Members of crews, including masters, pilots and apprentices, of the merchant marine and the crews of civil aircraft of the Parties to the conflict, who do not benefit by more favourable treatment under any other provisions of international law. (6) Inhabitants of a non-occupied territory, who on the approach of the enemy spontaneously take up arms to resist the invading forces, without having had time to form themselves into regular armed units, provided they carry arms openly and respect the laws and customs of war.").

[46] *Refer to* § 4.5 (Armed Forces of a State).

[47] *Refer to* § 4.5.2.5 (Deserters).

[48] *Refer to* § 4.9.2 (Requirements for Military Medical and Religious Status).

[49] *Refer to* § 4.6 (Other Militia and Volunteer Corps).

[50] *Refer to* § 4.5.3 (Regular Armed Forces Who Profess Allegiance to a Government or an Authority Not Recognized by the Detaining Power).

[51] *Refer to* § 4.15 (Persons Authorized to Accompany the Armed Forces).

[52] *Refer to* § 4.16 (Crews of Merchant Marine Vessels or Civil Aircraft).

[53] *Refer to* § 4.7 (*Levée en Masse*).

- persons who are nationals of the Detaining Power or its co-belligerents,[55] such as a defector who subsequently is captured by the force from which he or she defected.[56]

9.3.2.2 *Examples of Categories of Persons Who Are Not Necessarily Excluded From POW Status*. The following categories of persons are not necessarily excluded from POW status simply because they belong to one of these categories:

- mercenaries;[57]

- persons who are alleged to have committed war crimes;[58]

- nationals of neutral or non-belligerent States serving in the armed forces of an enemy State;[59] and

- persons whose capture has not been acknowledged by the Power to which they belong.[60]

9.3.3 Persons Entitled to POW Treatment. Certain persons, although not entitled to POW status, shall likewise be treated as POWs under the GPW:

- persons belonging, or having belonged, to the armed forces of an Occupied State if it is deemed necessary to intern them;[61] and

- persons belonging to one of the categories enumerated in Article 4 of the GPW who have been received by neutral or non-belligerent Powers on their territory and whom these Powers are required to intern under international law.[62]

9.3.4 Fallen Into the Power of the Enemy.

9.3.4.1 *Having Fallen*. Persons must have "fallen" into the power of the enemy to receive POW status.[63]

The person need not have been captured to have "fallen" into the power of the enemy; it

---

[54] *Refer to* § 4.17 (Spies, Saboteurs, and Other Persons Engaging in Similar Acts Behind Enemy Lines).

[55] *Refer to* § 4.4.4 (Nationality and Combatant Status).

[56] *Refer to* § 4.5.2.6 (Defectors).

[57] *Refer to* § 4.21 (Mercenaries).

[58] *Refer to* § 9.26.4 (Retention of Benefits of the GPW Even if Prosecuted for Pre-Capture Acts).

[59] *Refer to* § 4.4.4.1 (Nationals of Neutral States in Enemy Forces).

[60] *For example*, 2004 UK MANUAL ¶8.3 footnote 20 ("During the Gulf conflict 1991, the Iraqi action in declaring that captured aircrew would only be treated as prisoners of war (PW) if the coalition forces admitted that they had been captured was a clear breach of GC III, Art 4.").

[61] *Refer to* § 4.5.4 (Persons Belonging, or Having Belonged, to the Armed Forces of an Occupied State).

[62] *Refer to* § 15.16.3.1 (Provision of POW Treatment and Application of the GWS and GWS-Sea by Analogy).

[63] *Compare* § 10.3.2.1 ("Find Themselves").

may be the case that he or she became a prisoner without fighting, *e.g.*, by surrendering.[64]

Although defectors serving with their new armed force may be viewed as being in "the power of the enemy," they are not regarded as "hav[ing] fallen into" that condition, since they have voluntarily chosen to switch sides.[65] Thus, defectors are not considered by their new armed forces to be entitled to POW status.[66]

9.3.4.2 _Into the Power_. A person is considered to have fallen into the power of the enemy when that person has been captured by, or surrendered to, members of the military forces, the civilian police, or local civilian defense organizations or other enemy civilians who have taken that person into custody.[67] The person need not be captured by the armed forces of the opposing State.

9.3.4.3 _Of the Enemy_. Persons who have been captured by States that are not adversaries in the armed conflict are not technically in the hands of the enemy.[68] However, persons who are entitled to POW status or treatment and are interned by a neutral State under its duties under international law are generally entitled to POW treatment, as a minimum, under Article 4B(2) of the GPW.[69] Similarly, for example, military forces engaged in peace operations who are detained by the forces of a State that is a party to a conflict should, at a minimum, be afforded POW treatment by analogy.

9.3.5 _Treatment and Determination of POW Status in Case of Doubt_. Should any doubt arise as to whether persons, having committed a belligerent act and having fallen into the hands of the enemy, belong to any of the categories enumerated in Article 4 of the GPW, such persons shall enjoy the protection of the GPW until such time as their status has been determined by a

---

[64] GPW COMMENTARY 50 ("The words 'fallen into the power of the enemy' replace the word 'captured' which appeared in the 1929 Convention, the first expression having a wider significance and also covering the case of soldiers who became prisoners without fighting, for example following a surrender.").

[65] *See* U.N. GENERAL ASSEMBLY, *Report of the Secretary-General: Respect for Human Rights in Armed Conflicts*, U.N. Doc. A/7720 ¶88 (Nov. 20, 1969) ("One of the requirements of the acquisition of prisoner of war status is that the persons concerned must 'have fallen into the power of the enemy.' The view has been expressed that persons who defect from their own forces and give themselves up to the enemy and therefore do not have prisoner of war status, are not subject to the provisions of Geneva Convention III and are therefore neither entitled to the rights nor bound by the obligations of prisoners of war."); 1958 UK MANUAL ¶126 note 1 ("Defectors are not considered to have 'fallen' into the power of the enemy within the meaning of Art. 4A. ... The term 'fallen' clearly shows that it concerns combatants who pass into enemy hands, not of their own free will but by a force beyond their control because they are under its restraint,'").

[66] *Refer to* § 4.5.2.6 (Defectors).

[67] 1956 FM 27-10 (Change No. 1 1976) ¶84b ("A person is considered to have fallen into the power of the enemy when he has been captured by, or surrendered to members of the military forces, the civilian police, or local civilian defense organizations or enemy civilians who have taken him into custody.").

[68] *See* GPW COMMENTARY 50 ("The existence of a state of belligerence is no longer officially in question; the term 'enemy' covers any adversary during an 'armed conflict which may arise between two or more of the High Contracting Parties' pursuant to the first paragraph of Article 2.").

[69] *Refer to* § 15.16.3.1 (Provision of POW Treatment and Application of the GWS and GWS-Sea by Analogy).

competent tribunal.[70]

9.3.6 Commencement and Duration of POW Status and Treatment. The GPW applies to persons referred to in Article 4 of the GPW from the time they fall into the power of the enemy until their final release and repatriation.[71]

9.3.7 Non-Renunciation of Rights Secured by the GPW. POWs may in no circumstances renounce, in part or in entirety, the rights secured to them by the GPW, or by special agreements, if any, that are referred to in Article 6 of the GPW.[72] A similar provision of the GC applies to protected persons, and similar provisions of the GWS and GWS-Sea apply to the wounded, sick, shipwrecked, and military medical and religious personnel.[73]

This rule is intended to prevent States from evading their obligations by coercing enemy nationals in their power to waive their rights. The prohibition on the non-renunciation of rights is based on a recognition that: (1) POWs are in a vulnerable position; (2) it would be difficult to establish whether a POW had voluntarily renounced his or her rights; and (3) an absolute prohibition would best serve the interests of the majority of POWs.[74]

The non-renunciation of rights, in particular, prevents a POW from being compelled to serve in the armed forces of the Detaining Power.[75] The non-renunciation of POW rights, however, applies only to those who have fallen into the power of the enemy, and thus would not prevent persons from defecting to the enemy's side before capture.[76]

The non-renunciation of rights by the GPW does not prohibit States from affording POWs the right to refuse repatriation at the conclusion of the conflict.[77]

---

[70] *Refer to* § 4.27.2 (POW Protections for Certain Persons Until Status Has Been Determined); § 4.27.3 (Competent Tribunal to Assess Entitlement to POW Status or Treatment).

[71] GPW art. 5 ("The present Convention shall apply to the persons referred to in Article 4 from the time they fall into the power of the enemy and until their final release and repatriation.").

[72] GPW art. 7 ("Prisoners of war may in no circumstances renounce in part or in entirety the rights secured to them by the present Convention, and by the special agreements referred to in the foregoing Article, if such there be."). *Refer to* § 9.1.2.2 (Special Agreements Under the GPW).

[73] *Refer to* § 10.3.6 (Non-Renunciation of Rights Secured by the GC); § 7.2.2 (Non-Renunciation of Rights Secured by the GWS or GWS-Sea).

[74] *See* GPW COMMENTARY 89 ("In the end, however, the Diplomatic Conference unanimously adopted the absolute prohibition mainly because it is difficult, if not impossible, to prove the existence of duress or pressure [against a POW for him or her to renounce rights]. ... [The Diplomatic Conference] adopted the rule because it seemed to safeguard the interests of the majority. ... The Conference also accepted the view that in war-time prisoners in the hands of the enemy are not really in a sufficiently independent and objective state of mind to realize fully the implications of a renunciation of their rights."). *See also* LEVIE, POWS 91 ("Obviously, prisoners of war can never negotiate on a basis of equality with the Detaining Power.").

[75] *Refer to* § 9.19.2.3 (Labor Assignments That May Be Compelled).

[76] *Refer to* § 4.5.2.6 (Defectors).

[77] *Refer to* § 9.37.4.2 (POWs Who Resist Repatriation).

9.4 National-Level GPW Implementation Measures

The GPW requires a number of measures at the national level to facilitate protection for POWs.

9.4.1 Appointment or Establishment of Entities. The GPW provides for certain bodies or entities to be appointed or established.

9.4.1.1 *Appointment of a Protecting Power*. The GPW contemplates that a Protecting Power will have been appointed to assist in the implementation of the GPW.[78] A Protecting Power has a variety of roles under the GPW related to the protection of POWs.[79]

9.4.1.2 *Establishment of a National POW Information Bureau*. A National POW Information Bureau shall be established by each of the Powers concerned.[80]

9.4.1.3 *Establishment of a Central POW Information Agency*. A Central POW Information Agency shall be established in a neutral country by the Power concerned jointly.[81]

9.4.1.4 *Appointment of Mixed Medical Commissions*. Mixed Medical Commissions shall be appointed to examine sick and wounded POWs and to make all appropriate decisions regarding them.[82]

9.4.1.5 *Graves Registration Service*. A Graves Registration Service shall be established by each of the Powers concerned.[83]

9.4.2 Notification of Certain Laws or Policies Between Belligerents. Parties to a conflict must notify opposing belligerents or the Protecting Power of certain matters relating to POWs.

9.4.2.1 *Notification of Parole Policy*. Upon the outbreak of hostilities, each party to a conflict shall notify the adverse party or parties of its laws or regulations allowing or forbidding its armed forces to accept parole.[84] U.S. policy has prohibited the acceptance of parole.[85]

9.4.2.2 *Notification of Offenses Punishable by Death*. Information on what offenses are punishable by death should be communicated to the Protecting Power and the

---

[78] *Refer to* § 18.15.1.1 (Protecting Power Under the 1949 Geneva Conventions).

[79] *Refer to* § 9.32 (Role of the Protecting Power in the GPW).

[80] *Refer to* § 9.31.2 (National POW Information Bureau).

[81] *Refer to* § 9.31.3 (Central POW Information Agency).

[82] *Refer to* § 9.36.5 (Mixed Medical Commissions).

[83] *Refer to* § 9.34.4 (Maintenance and Records of Graves and Ashes).

[84] *Refer to* § 9.11.2 (Parole of POWs).

[85] *Refer to* § 9.39.1.3 (Code of Conduct – Article III).

POWs.[86]

9.4.2.3 *Location and Marking of POW Camps*. The Detaining Power should provide the Powers concerned useful information regarding the geographic location of POW camps, and agreements on their markings may be reached.[87]

9.4.2.4 *Requirements for the Validity of Wills*. Information on the requirements for the validity of wills should be communicated to the opposing party so that POWs in enemy custody may prepare valid wills.[88]

9.4.2.5 *Communication or Agreement Between the Powers Concerned on Ranks*. Titles and ranks of persons entitled to POW status or treatment shall be communicated to one another by the parties to the conflict.[89] Ranks of persons entitled to retained personnel status or treatment should also be communicated and agreed upon so that the senior medical officer in a POW Camp may be determined.[90]

9.4.2.6 *Arrangements Made for POWs to Write Correspondence and Receive Collective Relief*. Immediately upon POWs falling into its power, the Detaining Power shall inform them and the Powers on which they depend, through the Protecting Power, of the measures taken to carry out the provisions of the Section V of the GPW, which relates to POW correspondence and relief shipments.[91] The Detaining Power shall likewise inform the parties concerned of any subsequent modifications of such measures.[92]

9.4.3 Issue of Identification Cards to Persons Liable to Become POWs. Parties to the GPW must provide persons under their jurisdiction who are liable to become POWs with identity cards.[93] This card must show:

- the owner's surname (*i.e.*, last name), first names (*i.e.*, first and middle names);
- rank, army, regimental, personal or serial number or equivalent information; and
- date of birth.

---

[86] *Refer to* § 9.28.6 (Death Sentences).

[87] *Refer to* § 9.11.4.2 (Sharing Information on the Location of POW Camps); § 9.11.4.3 (Marking of POW Camps).

[88] *Refer to* § 9.21.2.1 (Preparation of Wills).

[89] *Refer to* § 9.22.4.1 (Communication of Titles and Ranks).

[90] *Refer to* § 7.9.5.7 (Senior Medical Officer in the Camp).

[91] GPW art. 69 ("Immediately upon prisoners of war falling into its power, the Detaining Power shall inform them and the Powers on which they depend, through the Protecting Power, of the measures taken to carry out the provisions of the present Section.").

[92] GPW art. 69 ("They shall likewise inform the parties concerned of any subsequent modifications of such measures.").

[93] GPW art. 17 ("Each Party to a conflict is required to furnish the persons under its jurisdiction who are liable to become prisoners of war, with an identity card showing the owner's surname, first names, rank, army, regimental, personal or serial number or equivalent information, and date of birth.").

In accordance with this requirement, DoD practice has been to issue all members of the U.S. armed forces identification cards that indicate their status under the Geneva Conventions.[94]

An individual's loss of the identification card issued by a State Party is not a basis for denial of POW status.[95]

9.5 HUMANE TREATMENT AND BASIC PROTECTIONS FOR POWS

POWs must at all times be humanely treated.[96] POWs are entitled in all circumstances to respect for their persons and their honor.[97] Likewise, POWs must at all times be protected, particularly against acts of violence or intimidation and against insults and public curiosity.[98]

Any unlawful act or omission by the Detaining Power causing death or seriously endangering the health of a POW in its custody is prohibited, and will be regarded as a serious breach of the GPW.[99]

9.5.1 Respect for Their Persons and Honor. POWs are entitled in all circumstances to respect for their persons and their honor.[100] For example, the rape or other indecent assault of POWs is forbidden.[101]

9.5.2 Protection Against Acts of Violence or Intimidation. POWs must at all times be protected, particularly against acts of violence or intimidation.[102] For example, the murder of POWs is forbidden.[103]

---

[94] *For example*, DoD INSTRUCTION 1000.01, *Identification (ID) Cards Required by the Geneva Conventions* (Apr. 16, 2012); DoD INSTRUCTION 1000.1, *Identity Cards Required by the Geneva Convention* (Jan. 30, 1974).

[95] *Refer to* § 4.27.1 (Identification Cards Used to Help Clarify Status).

[96] GPW art. 13 ("Prisoners of war must at all times be humanely treated."); HAGUE IV REG. art. 4 ("[Prisoners of war] must be humanely treated.").

[97] GPW art. 14 ("Prisoners of war are entitled in all circumstances to respect for their persons and their honour.").

[98] GPW art. 13 ("Likewise, prisoners of war must at all times be protected, particularly against acts of violence or intimidation and against insults and public curiosity.").

[99] GPW art. 13 ("Any unlawful act or omission by the Detaining Power causing death or seriously endangering the health of a prisoner of war in its custody is prohibited, and will be regarded as a serious breach of the present Convention.").

[100] GPW art. 14 ("Prisoners of war are entitled in all circumstances to respect for their persons and their honour.").

[101] *Compare* § 8.2.2.1 (Protection Against Rape, Enforced Prostitution, and Other Indecent Assault); § 10.5.1.2 (Protection for Women Against Rape or Other Indecent Assault).

[102] GPW art. 13 ("Likewise, prisoners of war must at all times be protected, particularly against acts of violence or intimidation and against insults and public curiosity.").

[103] *For example*, Trial of the Rear-Admiral Nisuke Masuda and Four Others of the Imperial Japanese Navy (The Jaluit Atoll Case), I U.N. LAW REPORTS 71, 72 (U.S. Military Commission, U.S. Naval Air Base, Kwajalein Island, Kwajalein Atoll, Marshall Islands, Dec. 7-13, 1945) ("The charge against the five accused, as approved by the Convening Authority, was one of murder. The specification stated that they 'did, on or about 10th March, 1944, on the Island of Aineman, Jaluit Atoll, Marshall Islands, at a time when a state of war existed between the United States of America and the Japanese Empire, wilfully, feloniously, with malice aforethought without justifiable cause, and

9.5.2.1 Prohibition on Killing of POWs. A commander of a force may not put enemy prisoners to death because their presence retards the force's movements or diminishes the force's power of resistance by necessitating a large guard, or by reason of the prisoners consuming supplies, or because it appears certain that they will regain their liberty through the impending success of enemy forces. It is likewise unlawful for a commander to kill enemy prisoners in the force's custody on grounds of self-preservation, even in the case of airborne or commando operations, although the circumstances of the operation may make necessary rigorous supervision of and restraint upon the movement of POWs.[104]

Older sources that permitted commanders in dire circumstances to deny quarter do not reflect the current law.[105]

9.5.2.2 Protection Against Violence by the Civilian Population or Others. POWs must be protected against violence by the civilian population.[106] POWs should be protected not only against unlawful acts by the agents of the Detaining Power, but also against violence from other POWs.[107]

---

without trial or other due process, assault and kill, by shooting and stabbing to death, three American fliers, then and there attached to the Armed forces of the United States of America, and then and there captured and unarmed prisoners of war in the custody of the said accused, all in violation of the dignity of the United States of America, the International rules of warfare and the moral standards of civilised society.'").

[104] 1956 FM 27-10 (Change No. 1 1976) ¶85 ("A commander may not put his prisoners to death because their presence retards his movements or diminishes his power of resistance by necessitating a large guard, or by reason of their consuming supplies, or because it appears that they will regain their liberty through the impending success of their forces. It is likewise unlawful for a commander to kill his prisoners on the grounds of self-preservation, even in the case of airborne or commando operations, although the circumstances of the operation may make necessary rigorous supervision of and restraint upon the movement of prisoners of war."); 1958 UK MANUAL ¶137 ("A commander may not put his prisoners of war to death because their presence retards his movements or diminishes his power of resistance by necessitating a large guard, or by reason of their consuming supplies, or because it appears that they will regain their liberty through the impending success of the forces to which they belong. It is unlawful for a commander to kill prisoners of war on grounds of self-preservation. This principle admits of no exception, even in the case of airborne or so-called commando operations—although the circumstances of the operation may make necessary rigorous supervision of and restraint upon their movement.").

[105] *See, e.g.*, LIEBER CODE art. 65 ("[A] commander is permitted to direct his troops to give no quarter, in great straits, when his own salvation makes it impossible to cumber himself with prisoners.").

[106] *See, e.g.*, Trial of Erich Heyer and Six Others (The Essen Lynch Case), I U.N. LAW REPORTS 88, 89 (British Military Court for the Trial of War Criminals, Essen, Dec. 18-19 and 21-22, 1945) ("[P]risoners of war were marched through one of the main streets of Essen, the crowd around grew bigger, started hitting them and throwing sticks and stones at them. An unknown German corporal actually fired a revolver at one of the airmen and wounded him in the head. When they reached the bridge, the airmen were eventually thrown over the parapet of the bridge; one of the airmen was killed by the fall; the others were not dead when they landed, but were killed by shots from the bridge and by members of the crowd who beat and kicked them to death."); United States, *et al.* v. Göring, *et al.*, *Judgment*, I TRIAL OF THE MAJOR WAR CRIMINALS BEFORE THE IMT 229 ("When Allied airmen were forced to land in Germany, they were sometimes killed at once by the civilian population. The Police were instructed not to interfere with these killings, and the Ministry of Justice was informed that no one should be prosecuted for taking part in them.").

[107] GPW COMMENTARY 143 ("Respect for physical integrity generally means that it is prohibited to kill, wound or even endanger prisoners of war. As we have seen above, Article 13 defines this obligation in a positive manner by specifying certain acts which constitute grave breaches. It should be emphasized that this protection must be

9.5.2.3 <u>No Exposure to a Combat Zone or Use as a Human Shield</u>. No POW may at any time be sent to or detained in areas where he or she may be exposed to the fire of the combat zone, nor may his or her presence be used to render certain points or areas immune from military operations.[108]

9.5.2.4 <u>No Physical Mutilation or Medical, Scientific, or Biological Experiments</u>. In particular, no POW may be subjected to physical mutilation or to medical or scientific experiments of any kind that are not justified by the medical, dental, or hospital treatment of the POW concerned and carried out in his or her interest.[109] The GWS and GWS-Sea also prohibit biological experiments on the wounded, sick, and shipwrecked.[110]

This prohibition was established in the 1949 Geneva Conventions in order to prohibit expressly criminal practices that occurred during World War II and to prevent the wounded, sick, or shipwrecked in captivity from being used as "guinea pigs" for medical experiments.[111]

The prohibition on subjecting the wounded, sick, or shipwrecked to biological experiments does not prevent doctors from trying new treatments that are justified on medical grounds and are employed solely for therapeutic purposes.[112]

<u>enforced</u> not only in regard to the agents of the Detaining Power, but also, <u>should the occasion arise, in regard to fellow prisoners</u>. Any infraction should be liable to punishment.") (emphasis added).

[108] GPW art. 23 ("No prisoner of war may at any time be sent to, or detained in areas where he may be exposed to the fire of the combat zone, nor may his presence be used to render certain points or areas immune from military operations."); United States v. von Leeb, *et al.* (The High Command Case), XI TRIALS OF WAR CRIMINALS BEFORE THE NMT 588 ("To use prisoners of war as a shield for the troops is contrary to international law."). *Refer to* § 5.16 (Prohibition on Using Protected Persons and Objects to Shield, Favor, or Impede Military Operations).

[109] GPW art. 13 ("In particular, no prisoner of war may be subjected to physical mutilation or to medical or scientific experiments of any kind which are not justified by the medical, dental or hospital treatment of the prisoner concerned and carried out in his interest.").

[110] GWS art. 12 ("Any attempts upon their lives, or violence to their persons, shall be strictly prohibited; in particular, they shall not be murdered or exterminated, subjected to torture or to biological experiments;").

[111] *See* GWS COMMENTARY 139 ("It was intended, by prohibiting the subjection of wounded and sick to biological experiments, to put an end for all time to criminal practices of which certain prisoners have been the victims, and also to prevent wounded or sick in captivity from being used as 'guinea-pigs' for medical experiments."). *See, e.g.*, United States v. Karl Brandt, *et. al* (The Medical Case), II TRIALS OF WAR CRIMINALS BEFORE THE NMT 171, 175-78 ("(A) High-Altitude Experiments. From about March 1942 to about August 1942 experiments were conducted at the Dachau concentration camp, for the benefit of the German Air Force, to investigate the limits of human endurance and existence at extremely high altitudes. The experiments were carried out in a low-pressure chamber in which the atmospheric conditions and pressures prevailing at high altitude (up to 68,000 feet) could be duplicated. The experimental subjects were placed in the low-pressure chamber and thereafter the simulated altitude therein was raised. Many victims died as a result of these experiments and others suffered grave injury, torture, and ill-treatment. … (L) Incendiary Bomb Experiments. From about November 1943 to about January 1944 experiments were conducted at the Buchenwald concentration camp to test the effect of various pharmaceutical preparations on phosphorus burns. These burns were inflicted on experimental subjects with phosphorus matter taken from incendiary bombs, and caused severe pain, suffering, and serious bodily injury.").

[112] GWS COMMENTARY 139 ("But the provision refers only to 'biological experiments'. Its effect is not to prevent the doctors in charge of wounded and sick from trying new therapeutic methods which are justified on medical grounds and are dictated solely by a desire to improve the patient's condition. Doctors must be free to resort to the

POWs may voluntarily consent to give blood for transfusion or skin for grafting for therapeutic purposes; such procedures should take place under conditions consistent with generally accepted medical standards and controls designed for the benefit of both the donor and the recipient.[113]

9.5.3 Protection Against Insults and Public Curiosity. POWs must at all times be protected against insults and public curiosity.[114] For example, organizing a parade of POWs through the civilian population, thereby exposing them to assault, ridicule, and insults, would be prohibited.[115] Displaying POWs in a humiliating fashion on television or on the internet would also be prohibited.[116] For this reason and others, DoD policy has prohibited the taking of

---

new remedies which science offers, provided always that such remedies have first been satisfactorily proved to be innocuous and that they are administered for purely therapeutic purposes.").

[113] *Consider* AP I art. 11 ("3. Exceptions to the prohibition in paragraph 2 (c) [against removal of tissue or organs for transplantation except where these acts are justified] may be made only in the case of donations of blood for transfusion or of skin for grafting, provided that they are given voluntarily and without any coercion or inducement, and then only for therapeutic purposes, under conditions consistent with generally accepted medical standards and controls designed for the benefit of both the donor and the recipient.").

[114] GPW art. 13 ("Likewise, prisoners of war must at all times be protected, particularly against acts of violence or intimidation and against insults and public curiosity.").

[115] *See, e.g.*, Trial of Lieutenant General Kurt Maelzer, XI U.N. LAW REPORTS 53 (U.S. Military Commission, Florence, Italy, Sept. 9-14, 1946) ("Some time in January, 1944, Field Marshal Kesselring, commander-in-chief of the German forces in Italy, ordered the accused who was commander of Rome garrison to hold a parade of several hundreds of British and American prisoners of war in the streets of the Italian capital. This parade, emulating the tradition of the triumphal marches of ancient Rome, was to be staged to bolster the morale of the Italian population in view of the recent allied landings, not very far from the capital. The accused ordered the parade which took place on 2nd February, 1944. 200 American prisoners of war were marched from the Coliseum, through the main streets of Rome under armed German escort. ... A film was made of the parade and a great number of photographs taken which appeared in the Italian press under the caption 'Anglo Americans enter Rome after all ... flanked by German bayonettes.'") (ellipses in original); United States, *et al.* v. Araki, *et al.*, *Majority Judgment*, International Military Tribunal for the Far East, 49,708, *reprinted in* NEIL BOISTER & ROBERT CRYER, DOCUMENTS ON THE TOKYO INTERNATIONAL MILITARY TRIBUNAL: CHARTER, INDICTMENT AND JUDGMENTS 574 (2008) ("About 1,000 prisoners captured in the fighting in Malaya arrived in Korea and were marched through the streets of Seoul, Fusan, and Jinsen where they were paraded before 120,000 Koreans and 57,000 Japanese. These prisoners had previously been subjected to malnutrition, ill-treatment and neglect so that their physical condition would elicit contempt from those who saw them."); STUART I. ROCHESTER & FREDERICK KILEY, HONOR BOUND: THE HISTORY OF AMERICAN PRISONERS OF WAR IN SOUTHEAST ASIA, 1961-1973 196 (1998) ("[H]oping to win increased support from Hanoi's patrons, [the North Vietnamese] deliberately marched the group [of POWs] past the Soviet and Chinese embassies to impress officials there with the numbers of PWs the DRV held. As the column turned onto the main avenue, the prisoners were met by larger and noisier crowds, in some places massed 10 deep (John McKamey estimated as many as a hundred thousand altogether). Cued by a chanting [Northern Vietnamese POW interrogator-indoctrinator] and incited by blaring loudspeakers and marshals with bullhorns, the throng erupted into a frenzy as the PWs filed past. The hostile galleries cursed the prisoners, hurled bricks and bottles, and pressed close enough to pummel them with outstretched arms while guards grabbed the men by the hair or used rifle butts to force them to lower their heads. Scores of spectators broke through the makeshift barriers, darting in between the Americans—kicking, screaming, spitting, striking the defenseless men with clenched fists as they stumbled along dazed and now frightened.").

[116] WILLIAM M. HAMMOND, THE UNITED STATES ARMY IN VIETNAM: PUBLIC AFFAIRS, THE MILITARY AND THE MEDIA, 1962-1968, 272 (1990) ("Hanoi itself diverted public attention in the United States by releasing photographs showing an angry mob of North Vietnamese jeering a parade of captured American pilots-a blatant violation of the 1949 Geneva Conventions which prohibited the exposure of prisoners of war to public curiosity and abuse.").

photographs of detainees except for authorized purposes.[117]

9.5.4 Reprisals Prohibited. Measures of reprisal against POWs are prohibited.[118]

9.5.5 No Adverse Distinction Based on Race, Nationality, Religion, or Political Belief. Taking into consideration the provisions of the GPW relating to rank and sex, and subject to any privileged treatment that may be accorded to them by reason of their state of health, age, or professional qualifications, all POWs shall be treated alike by the Detaining Power, without any adverse distinction based on race, nationality, religious belief, or political opinions, or any other distinction founded on similar criteria.[119]

Distinction based on nationality, political opinion, or other similar criteria may be made so long as it is not adverse and it is made to advance legitimate interests, such as maintaining order in the camp.[120]

In some cases, the Detaining Power must make distinctions between POWs as to rank or age,[121] state of health,[122] or professional status,[123] as well as to provide specific protection for women.

9.5.6 Due Regard for Women POWs. Women POWs shall be treated with all the regard due to their sex and shall in all cases benefit from treatment as favorable as that granted to men.[124] This principle also applies under the GWS and GWS-Sea to women who are wounded, sick, and shipwrecked.[125]

The GPW provides specifically for separate dormitories for women POWs in camps with both men and women and for separate bathroom facilities for women POWs.[126] The GPW also

---

[117] *Refer to* § 8.2.2.3 (DoD Practice of Generally Prohibiting Taking Photographs Without Authorization).

[118] *Refer to* § 18.18.3.2 (Reprisals Prohibited by the 1949 Geneva Conventions).

[119] GPW art. 16 ("Taking into consideration the provisions of the present Convention relating to rank and sex, and subject to any privileged treatment which may be accorded to them by reason of their state of health, age or professional qualifications, all prisoners of war shall be treated alike by the Detaining Power, without any adverse distinction based on race, nationality, religious belief or political opinions, or any other distinction founded on similar criteria.").

[120] *Refer to* § 9.12.1 (Assembling According to Nationality, Language, and Customs).

[121] *Refer to* § 9.22.4 (Rank and Age of POWs); § 9.19.1.2 (Labor Assignment – Officers and Persons of Equivalent Status).

[122] *Refer to* § 9.14.2.1 (Persons Requiring Special Treatment); § 9.36.1 (Direct Repatriation of Seriously Wounded, Injured, or Sick POWs).

[123] *Refer to* § 4.5.2.2 (Members Trained as Medical Personnel, but Not Attached to the Medical Service); § 4.5.2.3 (Members Who Are Ministers of Religion Without Having Officiated as Chaplains to Their Own Forces).

[124] GPW art. 14 ("Women shall be treated with all the regard due to their sex and shall in all cases benefit by treatment as favourable as that granted to men.").

[125] *Refer to* § 7.5.1 (Humane Treatment of the Wounded, Sick, and Shipwrecked Without Adverse Distinction).

[126] *Refer to* § 9.11.6.1 (Separate Dormitories for Women); § 9.11.5.2 (Sanitary Conveniences (e.g., latrines, bathrooms)).

provides for women POWs undergoing disciplinary punishment or serving a sentence to be confined in separate quarters under the supervision of women.[127] Although the GPW does not specifically provide for this, female POWs should be under the immediate supervision of women.[128]

9.6 Security Measures With Respect to POWs

Although POWs must always be treated humanely, the confinement and mode of treating a POW may be varied during captivity for security purposes.[129] For example, POWs and their property may be searched and secured, when operationally necessary (*e.g.*, immediately upon capture).[130]

9.6.1 Search of POWs. POWs may be searched for security reasons, intelligence purposes, and other administrative reasons. For example, POWs may be searched for concealed weapons, items of intelligence value, or contraband, such as cameras and cell phones.[131]

The dignity and honor of the POW being searched should be protected to the greatest degree possible under the circumstances.[132] The person conducting the search should avoid doing anything unnecessary or saying anything likely to be regarded as indecent or inappropriate. In some circumstances, it may be appropriate for a witness to observe the search so as to protect

---

[127] *Refer to* § 9.27.6.1 (Premises Where Disciplinary Punishments Are to Be Served); § 9.28.7.2 (Confinement of Women POWs Who Have Been Sentenced).

[128] *Refer to* § 8.7.1 (Gender and Family Segregation).

[129] LIEBER CODE art. 75 ("Prisoners of war are subject to confinement and imprisonment such as may be deemed necessary on account of safety, but they are to be subjected to no other intentional suffering or indignity. The confinement and mode of treating a prisoner may be varied during his captivity according to the demands of safety."). *See also* GPW COMMENTARY 140 ("The requirement of humane treatment and the prohibition of certain acts inconsistent with it are general and absolute in character. They are valid at all times, and apply, for example, to cases where repressive measures are legitimately imposed on a protected person, since the dictates of humanity must be respected even if measures of security or repression are being applied.").

[130] *See* Trial of Erich Weiss and Wilhelm Mundo, *Relevance of the Plea of Self-Defence in War Crime Trials*, XIII U.N. LAW REPORTS 149, 150 (U.S. General Military Government Court, Ludwigsburg, Germany, Nov. 9-10, 1945) ("In the light of the foregoing the rules contained in Articles 2 and 3 of the Geneva Convention, 1929, would appear to be subject to the principle that, given faithful observation of these provisions by the detaining authorities, the latter are generally entitled to use the force reasonably necessary to secure the custody of the prisoners or to protect themselves from an attack by the prisoners.").

[131] *For example*, 1997 MULTI-SERVICE DETENTION REGULATION § 2-1.*a*.(1) ("The commanding officer of the capturing unit will ensure that: ... (a) Each EPW/RP will be searched immediately after capture. ... Weapons, ammunition, and equipment or documents with intelligence value will be confiscated and turned over to the nearest intelligence unit. Propaganda and other Psychological Operations (PSYOP) materials will be confiscated, identified by the EPW/RP name and ISN and turned over to the supporting EPW/CI PSYOP unit through intelligence channels."); Office of the Provost Marshal General, *World War II - A Brief History* 492-93 (1946) ("Each prisoner was searched and disarmed immediately upon capture and contraband articles were taken from him, including all equipment issued to him by his government, except clothing. He was permitted to retain his helmet and gas mask in combat zones. Contraband included cameras, binoculars, signalling devices, compasses, and such other articles as might be useful to him in an escape. All military papers, documents, maps, and diaries were retained for intelligence examination.").

[132] *Refer to* § 9.5 (Humane Treatment and Basic Protections for POWs).

both the person being searched from abuse and the person conducting the search from unfounded accusations of abuse.

It is appropriate for female POWs to be searched by female personnel of the Detaining Power, if possible.[133] This practice helps reduce the risk of accusations of indecent behavior.

9.6.2 Securing POWs With Handcuffs and Other Security Devices. When necessary for security reasons (*e.g.*, to prevent escape or destruction of documents), POWs may be secured temporarily with handcuffs, flex cuffs, blindfolds, or other security devices.[134]

9.6.3 Search of POW Property. Items in the possession of POWs may be removed and searched for security and intelligence purposes, but certain items of personal or sentimental value must be returned as soon as possible.[135]

9.7 POW Effects and Articles of Personal Use

9.7.1 POW Effects and Articles of Personal Use. All effects and articles of personal use, except arms, horses, military equipment, and military documents, shall remain in the possession of POWs, likewise their metal helmets and gas masks and like articles issued for personal protection.[136] Effects and articles used for their clothing or feeding shall likewise remain in their possession, even if such effects and articles are part of their regulation military equipment.[137]

These rules do not prohibit the search of POW effects and articles of personal use.[138]

Items that may otherwise be legitimately impounded (*e.g.*, articles of value being withdrawn for reasons of security) are not precluded from being impounded because they may be characterized as an effect or article of personal use or an effect or article used for clothing or feeding.[139]

9.7.2 Identity Documents. At no time should POWs be without identity documents.[140]

---

133 *For example*, 1997 MULTI-SERVICE DETENTION REGULATION § 2-1.*a*.(1) ("The commanding officer of the capturing unit will ensure that: … (*a*) Each EPW/RP will be searched immediately after capture. Use males to search males and females to search female prisoners, when possible.").

134 *See* Winston Churchill, Prime Minster, United Kingdom, *Oral Answers to Questions,* Oct. 13, 1942, HANSARD, 383 HOUSE OF COMMONS DEBATES § 1500 ("His Majesty's Government have never countenanced any general order for the tying up of prisoners on the field of battle. Such a process, however, may be necessary from time to time under stress of circumstances, and may indeed be in the best interest of the safety of the prisoners themselves.").

135 *Refer to* § 9.7.3 (Badges, Decorations, and Articles Having Above All a Personal or Sentimental Value).

136 GPW art. 18 ("All effects and articles of personal use, except arms, horses, military equipment and military documents, shall remain in the possession of prisoners of war, likewise their metal helmets and gas masks and like articles issued for personal protection.").

137 GPW art. 18 ("Effects and articles used for their clothing or feeding shall likewise remain in their possession, even if such effects and articles belong to their regulation military equipment.").

138 *Refer to* § 9.6.3 (Search of POW Property).

139 *Refer to* § 9.7.4 (Money and Articles of Value).

140 GPW art. 18 ("At no time should prisoners of war be without identity documents.").

The Detaining Power shall supply such documents to POWs who possess none.[141]

Identity documents may be seized when necessary (*e.g.*, intelligence purposes), provided that the Detaining Power supplies a replacement identity document.[142]

9.7.3 Badges, Decorations, and Articles Having Above All a Personal or Sentimental Value. Badges of rank and nationality, decorations, and articles having "above all" a personal or sentimental value may not be taken from POWs.[143] Such items might include a ring, wristwatch, personal correspondence, or family photographs.

This rule does not prohibit the search of items, including a search in order to determine whether the items in question have above all a personal or sentimental value.[144]

Items that may otherwise be legitimately impounded (*e.g.*, articles of value being withdrawn for reasons of security) are not precluded from being impounded because of their personal or sentimental value to the POW.[145]

9.7.4 Money and Articles of Value. Sums of money carried by POWs may not be taken away from them except by order of an officer, and after the amount and particulars of the owner have been recorded in a special register and an itemized receipt has been given, legibly inscribed with the name, rank, and unit of the person issuing this receipt.[146]

Sums in the currency of the Detaining Power, or that are changed into such currency at the POW's request, shall be placed to the credit of the POW's account as provided for in Article 64 of the GPW.[147]

The Detaining Power may withdraw articles of value from POWs only for reasons of security; when such articles are withdrawn, the procedure laid down for sums of money

---

[141] GPW art. 18 ("The Detaining Power shall supply such documents to prisoners of war who possess none.").

[142] GPW COMMENTARY 168 ("It is obvious, however, that no Detaining Power would undertake not to seize the individual service records of combatants immediately following capture, since valuable information might be contained therein. The Convention does not, therefore, restrict the right of the Detaining Power to seize military documents; in this respect it departs from the 1929 text but also stipulates that at no time should prisoners of war be without identity documents. As we have already seen in connection with Article 17, the Detaining Power must therefore supply an identity document in place of any individual service record which it impounds.").

[143] GPW art. 18 ("Badges of rank and nationality, decorations and articles having above all a personal or sentimental value may not be taken from prisoners of war.").

[144] *Refer to* § 9.6.3 (Search of POW Property).

[145] *Refer to* § 9.7.4 (Money and Articles of Value).

[146] GPW art. 18 ("Sums of money carried by prisoners of war may not be taken away from them except by order of an officer, and after the amount and particulars of the owner have been recorded in a special register and an itemized receipt has been given, legibly inscribed with the name, rank and unit of the person issuing the said receipt.").

[147] GPW art. 18 ("Sums in the currency of the Detaining Power, or which are changed into such currency at the prisoner's request, shall be placed to the credit of the prisoner's account as provided in Article 64."). *Refer to* § 9.18.6.1 (Cash in POW Hands Taken at the Time of Capture); § 9.18.6 (POW Accounts).

impounded shall apply.[148] For example, an article of value may be impounded for reasons of security, even if it constitutes an article of personal use or an article having above all a personal or sentimental value.[149]

Such objects, likewise sums taken away in any currency other than that of the Detaining Power and the conversion of which has not been asked for by the owners, shall be kept in the custody of the Detaining Power and shall be returned in their initial shape to POWs at the end of their captivity.[150]

9.7.4.1 *Unexplained Possession of Large Sums of Money by POWs*. The unexplained possession by a POW of a large sum of money justifiably leads to the inference that such funds are not his or her own property and are in fact either property of the enemy government or property that has been looted or otherwise stolen.[151]

9.7.5 No Bartering With POWs for Personal Effects. It is not proper for members of the forces of the Detaining Power to engage in bartering and other transactions with POWs concerning their personal effects.[152]

9.7.6 Accountability for Impounded Personal Effects. In addition to the specific requirements for seized money or articles of value, it is a best practice for other items taken from POWs to be itemized and separated (packaged) with the name, unit, service number of the POW, and other identifying information to permit accountability, safekeeping, and return when appropriate to the POW.

9.8 Interrogation of POWs

The law of war does not prohibit interrogation of POWs, but specifies conditions and limitations for conducting interrogation.

9.8.1 Humane Treatment During Interrogation. Interrogation must be carried out in a manner consistent with the requirements for humane treatment, including the prohibition against

---

[148] GPW art. 18 ("The Detaining Power may withdraw articles of value from prisoners of war only for reasons of security; when such articles are withdrawn, the procedure laid down for sums of money impounded shall apply.").

[149] LEVIE, POWS 113 ("[A] prisoner of war might have an antique pocket watch with a compass in the stem. Even though such a watch falls within the category of 'articles of personal use' [Article 18, first paragraph] or of 'articles having above all a personal or sentimental value' [Article 18, third paragraph], which prisoners of war may normally retain, no Detaining Power could be censured for taking the watch and placing it in safekeeping until the owner is repatriated.").

[150] GPW art. 18 ("Such objects, likewise sums taken away in any currency other than that of the Detaining Power and the conversion of which has not been asked for by the owners, shall be kept in the custody of the Detaining Power and shall be returned in their initial shape to prisoners of war at the end of their captivity.").

[151] 1956 FM 27-10 (Change No. 1 1976) ¶94c ("The unexplained possession by a prisoner of war of a large sum of money justifiably leads to the inference that such funds are not his own property and are in fact either property of the enemy government or property which has been looted or otherwise stolen.").

[152] 1956 FM 27-10 (Change No. 1 1976) ¶94b ("It is not proper for members of the forces of the Detaining Power to engage in bartering and other transactions with prisoners of war concerning their personal effects.").

acts of violence or intimidation, and insults.[153]

No physical or mental torture, nor any other form of coercion, may be inflicted on POWs to secure from them information of any kind whatever.[154] POWs who refuse to answer may not be threatened, insulted, or exposed to unpleasant or disadvantageous treatment of any kind.[155] Prohibited means include imposing inhumane conditions,[156] denial of medical treatment, or the use of mind-altering chemicals.[157]

9.8.2 Language of Interrogation. The questioning of POWs shall be carried out in a language that they understand.[158]

9.8.3 Additional U.S. Law and Policy on Interrogation. U.S. law and policy impose additional requirements on the interrogation of POWs.[159]

9.8.4 Accountability Information That POWs Are Bound to Provide Upon Questioning. Every POW, when questioned on the subject, is bound to give only his or her surname, first names and rank, date of birth, and army, regimental, personal or serial number, or, failing this, equivalent information.[160] If POWs willfully infringe this rule, they may render themselves liable to a restriction of the privileges accorded to their rank or status.[161] However, POWs who refuse to provide this information may not be coerced or exposed to any other unpleasant or

---

[153] *Refer to* § 9.5 (Humane Treatment and Basic Protections for POWs).

[154] GPW art. 17 ("No physical or mental torture, nor any other form of coercion, may be inflicted on prisoners of war to secure from them information of any kind whatever.").

[155] GPW art. 17 ("Prisoners of war who refuse to answer may not be threatened, insulted, or exposed to unpleasant or disadvantageous treatment of any kind.").

[156] Trial of Erich Killinger and Four Others (The Dulag Luft Case), III U.N. Law REPORTS 67 (British Military Court, Wuppertal, Nov. 26-Dec. 3, 1945) ("The function of Dulag Luft was, shortly, to obtain information of an operational and vital nature from the captured crews of Allied machines. The allegation was that excessive heating of the prisoners cells took place at Dulag Luft between the dates laid in the charge for the deliberate purpose of obtaining from prisoners of war information of a kind which under the Geneva Convention they were not bound to give, and that the accused were concerned in that ill-treatment. The Prosecution also alleged a 'lack of and refusal of required medical attention' and 'in some cases, blows.' ... Killinger, Junge and Eberhardt were found guilty and sentenced to imprisonment for five, five and three years respectively. The remaining two accused were found not guilty.").

[157] U.S. Army, Office of The Judge Advocate General, JAGW 1961/1157, *Memo re: Use of "Truth Serum" in Questioning Prisoners of War,* Jun. 21, 1961, LEVIE, DOCUMENTS ON POWS 708, 709 ("3. In view of the foregoing, it is the opinion of this division that the suggested use of a chemical 'truth serum' during the questioning of prisoners of war would be in violation of the obligations of the United States under the Geneva Convention Relative to the Treatment of Prisoners of War.").

[158] GPW art. 17 ("The questioning of prisoners of war shall be carried out in a language which they understand.").

[159] *Refer to, e.g.,* § 8.4.2 (Additional U.S. Law and Policy on Interrogation).

[160] GPW art. 17 ("Every prisoner of war, when questioned on the subject, is bound to give only his surname, first names and rank, date of birth, and army, regimental, personal or serial number, or failing this, equivalent information.").

[161] GPW art. 17 ("If he wilfully infringes this rule, he may render himself liable to a restriction of the privileges accorded to his rank or status.").

disadvantageous treatment of any kind for failing to respond.

The provision of accountability information is important because it allows the Detaining Power to fulfill its obligations under the GPW. For example, the Detaining Power requires this information to establish lists of POWs for evacuation.[162] In addition, the Detaining Power is required to gather further information on POWs to facilitate notification of their families.[163]

9.8.4.1 *POWs Unable to State Their Identity*. POWs who, owing to their physical or mental condition, are unable to state their identity, shall be handed over to the medical service.[164] The identity of such POWs shall be established by all possible means, subject to the prohibition on physical or mental torture, or coercion, as well as the prohibition on threats, insults, or exposure to unpleasant or disadvantageous treatment.[165]

9.9 Evacuation From Combat Areas

POWs shall be evacuated, as soon as possible after their capture, to camps situated in an area far enough from the combat zone for them to be out of danger.[166] POWs shall not be unnecessarily exposed to danger while awaiting evacuation from a fighting zone.[167]

9.9.1 Delay in Evacuation for Medical Reasons. Only those POWs who, owing to wounds or sickness, would run greater risks by being evacuated than by remaining where they are, may be temporarily kept back in a danger zone.[168]

9.9.2 Conditions of Evacuation. The evacuation of POWs shall always be effected humanely and in conditions similar to those for the forces of the Detaining Power in their changes of station.[169] The Detaining Power shall supply POWs who are being evacuated with sufficient food and potable water, and with the necessary clothing and medical attention.[170] The Detaining Power shall take all suitable precautions to ensure their safety during evacuation, and

---

[162] *Refer to* § 9.9.2 (Conditions of Evacuation).

[163] *Refer to* § 9.31.1 (Accountability Information That the Detaining Power Should Collect).

[164] GPW art. 17 ("Prisoners of war who, owing to their physical or mental condition, are unable to state their identity, shall be handed over to the medical service.").

[165] GPW art. 17 ("The identity of such prisoners shall be established by all possible means, subject to the provisions of the preceding paragraph.").

[166] GPW art. 19 ("Prisoners of war shall be evacuated, as soon as possible after their capture, to camps situated in an area far enough from the combat zone for them to be out of danger.").

[167] GPW art. 20 ("Prisoners of war shall not be unnecessarily exposed to danger while awaiting evacuation from a fighting zone.").

[168] GPW art. 19 ("Only those prisoners of war who, owing to wounds or sickness, would run greater risks by being evacuated than by remaining where they are, may be temporarily kept back in a danger zone.").

[169] GPW art. 20 ("The evacuation of prisoners of war shall always be effected humanely and in conditions similar to those for the forces of the Detaining Power in their changes of station.").

[170] GPW art. 20 ("The Detaining Power shall supply prisoners of war who are being evacuated with sufficient food and potable water, and with the necessary clothing and medical attention.").

shall establish as soon as possible a list of the POWs who are evacuated.[171]

Provided that the requirements of humane treatment are met, the Detaining Power may subject POWs to security measures while evacuating them away from the combat zone. For example, POWs may be handcuffed, flex-cuffed, or blindfolded for security reasons.[172]

9.9.3 Release Under Unusual Conditions Rather Than Evacuation. When persons entitled to protection as POWs have fallen into the power of an adverse party under unusual conditions of combat that prevent their evacuation as provided for in Part III, Section I, of the GPW, they may be released, provided that feasible precautions are taken to ensure their safety.[173]

Release in such circumstances is permissible, but is not required.[174] In some cases, enemy forces may give their parole.[175]

9.9.3.1 *Unusual Conditions of Combat Preventing Evacuation*. Unusual conditions of combat may include airborne operations, commando raids, and long-range reconnaissance patrols.[176]

9.9.3.2 *Feasible Precautions to Ensure Safety*. POWs may be released in these circumstances only if feasible precautions are taken to ensure their safety.[177] For example, a long-range reconnaissance patrol need not make itself militarily ineffective by handing over all

---

[171] GPW art. 20 ("The Detaining Power shall take all suitable precautions to ensure their safety during evacuation, and shall establish as soon as possible a list of the prisoners of war who are evacuated.").

[172] *Refer to* § 9.6 (Security Measures With Respect to POWs).

[173] *Consider* AP I art. 41(3) ("When persons entitled to protection as prisoners of war have fallen into the power of an adverse Party under unusual conditions of combat which prevent their evacuation as provided for in Part III, Section I, of the Third Convention, they shall be released and all feasible precautions shall be taken to ensure their safety.").

[174] *Cf.* APPENDIX TO 1985 CJCS MEMO ON AP I, ANNEX-3 (providing a draft proposed understanding to AP I: "9. It is the understanding of the United States that Article 41, paragraph 3 [of AP I], does not obligate a Detaining Power to release prisoners of war simply because these individuals cannot be immediately evacuated from a combat zone. The United States continues to recognize, however, an obligation to provide for the safety of such personnel."); 2004 UK MANUAL ¶8.32.1 ("If, because of unusual conditions of combat, it is not possible to evacuate prisoners of war, they are to be released and all feasible precautions taken to ensure their safety. There is no obligation to release prisoners of war in circumstances in which safe evacuation is temporarily impossible. In such cases, prisoners of war may be held until release or evacuation is possible. There is, however, a continuing obligation to take all feasible measures to provide for the safety of such prisoners of war so long as they remain in the custody of the detaining power. This principle admits of no exception even in the case of airborne, commando, or special forces operations, although the circumstances of the operation may necessitate rigorous supervision of and restraint upon the movement of prisoners of war.").

[175] *Refer to* § 9.11.2 (Parole of POWs).

[176] BOTHE, PARTSCH, & SOLF, NEW RULES 224 (AP I art. 41, ¶2.4) ("Articles 19 and 20 of the Third Convention require the prompt and humane evacuation of prisoners of war from the combat zone to places out of the danger area. In certain types of operations, particularly airborne operations, commando raids, and long range reconnaissance patrols, compliance with these articles is clearly impractical, and there has been dispute as to what is required in such cases.").

[177] *Refer to* § 5.2.3.2 (What Precautions Are Feasible).

its supplies to POWs whom it has captured.[178] However, the patrol should take reasonable steps under the circumstances to help ensure the POWs' safety and survival, such as providing them with a modicum of food and water.[179]

9.9.3.3 *Accountability Measures*. In addition, it is a best practice to take feasible measures to account for the persons captured and released, such as recording: (1) full names, (2) serial numbers, (3) unit affiliation, and (4) the time, date, and location of capture and release.

9.10 TRANSIT OR SCREENING FACILITIES

POWs may be sent to transit or screening facilities before internment in a POW camp. For example, special interrogation centers have been used as screening facilities to interrogate POWs before their internment in the POW camp.[180]

9.10.1 Sending of Capture Cards in Transit or Screening Camps. Even in transit or screening camps, POWs are to be enabled to send capture cards within one week after arrival at a camp.[181]

9.10.2 Transit or Screening Camps Near Military Operations. Facilities within a zone of military operations are often established in order to house POWs captured during military operations in that particular zone that, due to their proximity to the fighting, are not able to meet all the requirements of the GPW.[182] Transit or screening facilities must, however, provide

---

[178] *Cf.* XV OFFICIAL RECORDS OF THE CDDH 384 (Committee III Report, CDDH/236/Rev.1, ¶24) ("Paragraph 3 dealing with the release of prisoners who could not be evacuated proved quite difficult. The phrase 'unusual conditions of combat' was intended to reflect the fact that that circumstance would be abnormal. What, in fact, most representatives referred to was the situation of the long distance patrol which is not equipped to detain and evacuate prisoners. The requirement that all 'feasible precautions' be taken to ensure the safety of released prisoners was intended to emphasize that the detaining power, even in those extraordinary circumstances, was expected to take all measures that were practicable in the light of the combat situation. In the case of the long distance patrol, it need not render itself ineffective by handing the bulk of its supplies over to the released prisoners, but it should do all that it reasonably can do, in view of all the circumstances, to ensure their safety.").

[179] 1958 UK MANUAL ¶137 note 1 ("Whether a commander may release prisoners of war in the circumstances stated in the text [commando operations and other situations in which it is not feasible to care for POWs] is not clear. No provision is made in the Convention [the GPW] for such release, and there may well be occasions when such a release will deprive the prisoners of war of such maintenance and food as is available, as, for example, if they are released in a desert or jungle or in mountainous districts. If such a release be made, it would seem clear that the commander should supply the prisoners with that modicum of food, water, and weapons as would give them a chance of survival.").

[180] *For example*, John Brown Mason, *German Prisoners of War in the United States*, 39 AJIL 198, 203 (1945) ("In American practice [during World War II], the prisoners are questioned at special interrogation centers. Practically no complaint has been made by the prisoners to the Swiss Legation about the treatment in these transient centers.").

[181] *Refer to* § 9.20.1 (Capture, Health, or Transfer Card).

[182] GPW COMMENTARY 176 ("The camps mentioned in the present paragraph are those which the military authorities may have to establish in a combat zone in order to house prisoners captured during military operations in that particular zone. In view of the fact that they are near the fighting zone, it is not always possible to require that such camps should fulfil all the material conditions specified in the Convention.").

POWs reasonable protection from the effects of combat, basic sanitation, and food and water.[183]

If POWs must, during evacuation, pass through transit camps, their stay in such camps shall be as brief as possible.[184]

9.10.3 Facilities of a Permanent Nature. Transit or screening camps of a permanent kind shall be fitted out under conditions similar to those described in Section II of the GPW for regular internment camps for POWs, and the POWs in those camps shall have the same treatment as in other camps.[185]

9.10.4 Use of Ships for Temporary Detention. POWs may be detained temporarily on board a ship if operational or humanitarian needs dictate, pending a reasonable opportunity to transfer them to a shore facility, or to another vessel for evacuation to a shore facility.[186] For example, they may be temporarily detained on board naval vessels: (a) while being transported between land facilities; or (b) if such action would appreciably improve their safety or health prospects, such as avoidance of exposure to severe environmental or combat conditions, or improved access to medical care for those requiring it. Such limited detention does not violate the requirement for internment of POWs on land.[187]

9.11 General Conditions in POW Camps: Location, Safety, Hygiene, and Living Conditions

9.11.1 Internment in POW Camps. The Detaining Power may subject POWs to internment.[188] It may impose on them the obligation of not leaving, beyond certain limits, the camp where they are interned, or if that camp is fenced in, of not going outside its perimeter.[189]

9.11.1.1 *Prohibition on Close Confinement*. Subject to the provisions of the GPW

---

[183] *Refer to* § 9.9.2 (Conditions of Evacuation).

[184] GPW art. 20 ("If prisoners of war must, during evacuation, pass through transit camps, their stay in such camps shall be as brief as possible.").

[185] GPW art. 24 ("Transit or screening camps of a permanent kind shall be fitted out under conditions similar to those described in the present Section, and the prisoners therein shall have the same treatment as in other camps.").

[186] *For example*, 1997 MULTI-SERVICE DETENTION REGULATION § 2-1.*b* ("Special policy pertaining to the temporary detention of EPW, CI, RP and other detained persons aboard United States Naval Vessels: (1) Detention of EPW/RP on board naval vessels will be limited. (2) EPW recovered at sea may be temporarily held on board as operational needs dictate, pending a reasonable opportunity to transfer them to a shore facility, or to another vessel for transfer to a shore facility. (3) EPW/RP may be temporarily held aboard naval vessels while being transported between land facilities. They may also be treated and temporarily quartered aboard naval vessels incidental to their treatment, to receive necessary and appropriate medical attention if such detention would appreciably improve their health or safety prospects. (4) Holding of EPW/RP on vessels must be temporary, limited to the minimum period necessary to evacuate them from the combat zone or to avoid significant harm that would be faced if detained on land. (5) Use of immobilized vessels for temporary holding of EPW/RP is not authorized without SECDEF approval.").

[187] *Refer to* § 9.11.3.1 (Location on Land).

[188] GPW art. 21 ("The Detaining Power may subject prisoners of war to internment.").

[189] GPW art. 21 ("It may impose on them the obligation of not leaving, beyond certain limits, the camp where they are interned, or if the said camp is fenced in, of not going outside its perimeter.").

relative to penal and disciplinary sanctions, POWs may not be held in close confinement except where necessary to safeguard their health and then only during the continuation of the circumstances that make such confinement necessary.[190]

9.11.2 Parole of POWs. POWs may be partially or wholly released on parole or promise, in so far as is allowed by the laws of the Power on which they depend.[191] Such measures shall be taken particularly in cases where this may contribute to the improvement of their state of health.[192] No POW shall be compelled to accept liberty on parole or promise.[193]

Upon the outbreak of hostilities, each party to the conflict shall notify the adverse party of the laws and regulations allowing or forbidding its own nationals to accept liberty on parole or promise.[194] U.S. policy prohibits U.S. servicemembers from accepting parole or special favors from the enemy.[195]

POWs who are paroled or who have given their promise in conformity with the laws and regulations so notified are bound on their personal honor scrupulously to fulfill, both towards the Power on which they depend and towards the Power that has captured them, the engagements of their paroles or promises.[196] In such cases, the Power on which they depend is bound neither to require nor to accept from them any service incompatible with the parole or promise given.[197]

9.11.3 Location of POW Camps.

9.11.3.1 *Location on Land*. POWs may be interned only in premises located on land.[198] This rule is intended to ensure that POWs are interned in a relatively safe and healthy

---

[190] GPW art. 21 ("Subject to the provisions of the present Convention relative to penal and disciplinary sanctions, prisoners of war may not be held in close confinement except where necessary to safeguard their health and then only during the continuation of the circumstances which make such confinement necessary.").

[191] GPW art. 21 ("Prisoners of war may be partially or wholly released on parole or promise, in so far as is allowed by the laws of the Power on which they depend.").

[192] GPW art. 21 ("Such measures shall be taken particularly in cases where this may contribute to the improvement of their state of health.").

[193] GPW art. 21 ("No prisoner of war shall be compelled to accept liberty on parole or promise.").

[194] GPW art. 21 ("Upon the outbreak of hostilities, each Party to the conflict shall notify the adverse Party of the laws and regulations allowing or forbidding its own nationals to accept liberty on parole or promise.").

[195] *Refer to* § 9.39.1.3 (Code of Conduct – Article III).

[196] GPW art. 21 ("Prisoners of war who are paroled or who have given their promise in conformity with the laws and regulations so notified, are bound on their personal honour scrupulously to fulfil, both towards the Power on which they depend and towards the Power which has captured them, the engagements of their paroles or promises."); HAGUE IV REG. art. 10 ("Prisoners of war may be set at liberty on parole if the laws of their country allow, and in such cases, they are bound, on their personal honour, scrupulously to fulfil, both towards their own Government and the Government by whom they were made prisoners, the engagements they have contracted. In such cases their own Government is bound neither to require of nor accept from them any service incompatible with the parole given.").

[197] GPW art. 21 ("In such cases, the Power on which they depend is bound neither to require nor to accept from them any service incompatible with the parole or promise given.").

[198] GPW art. 22 ("Prisoners of war may be interned only in premises located on land and affording every guarantee of hygiene and healthfulness.").

environment. For example, in prior conflicts, POWs interned on ships were not held in hygienic and humane conditions. Similarly, POWs held on ships faced increased risk from the dangers of war.

Because the purpose of the rule is to provide for the detention of POWs in a relatively safe and healthy environment, detention aboard ship for POWs captured at sea or pending the establishment of suitable facilities on land is nonetheless consistent with the GPW if detention on a ship provides the most appropriate living conditions for POWs.[199] Ships may also be used to transport POWs or for screening.[200]

9.11.3.2 Use of Penitentiaries as POW Camps. Except in particular cases that are justified by the interests of the POWs themselves, POWs shall not be interned in penitentiaries.[201] This rule reflects the principle that POW detention is not punitive, but also recognizes that penitentiaries may sometimes provide the most appropriate lodging.[202]

9.11.3.3 Location Outside the Theater of Military Operations. The GPW does not prohibit locating POW camps outside the theater of military operations, and there is much State practice in conducting detention operations outside of the theater in which POWs were captured.[203] Although the GC imposes geographic restrictions on the transfer of protected

---

[199] *For example*, Gregory P. Noone, Christian P. Fleming, Robert P. Morean, John V. Danner, Jr., Philip N. Fluhr, Jr., Jonathan I. Shapiro, Sandra L. Hodgkinson, Edward J. Cook, & Dillon L. Ross IV, *Prisoners of War in the 21st Century: Issues in Modern Warfare*, 50 NAVAL LAW REVIEW 1, 16 (2004) ("During OIF [Operation Iraqi Freedom], a U.S. naval vessel in the Persian Gulf served as a temporary detention facility for EPWs. EPW internment camps in Iraq were not yet ready for prisoners. Additionally, Kuwait refused to allow Coalition forces to build EPW camps in Kuwait and they would not allow Coalition forces to bring EPWs into Kuwait. The cavernous hold of USS DUBUQUE (LPD-8), an amphibious assault ship, was converted into a detention facility where prisoners were held and interrogated as EPWs until camps were operational on shore."); Joint Chiefs of Staff, *Memo re: Policy Concerning Temporary Detention of Prisoners of War, Civilian Internees, and Other Detained Persons Aboard Naval Vessels*, ¶2a.(3) -¶2b (Aug. 24, 1984) ("PW/CI/DET may be temporarily held on board naval vessels if such detention would appreciably improve the safety or health prospects for the PW/CI/DET. b. Holding of PW/CI/DET on board vessels must be truly temporary, limited to the minimum period necessary to evacuate the PW/CI/DET from the combat zone or to avoid the significant harm the PW/CI/DET would face if detained on land."); 2004 UK MANUAL ¶8.37.1 footnote 123 ("[Temporary internment on board ship for the purpose of evacuation from the combat zone] was done during the Falklands conflict 1982, with the concurrence of the ICRC, because there was nowhere suitable to hold PW on the Falklands Islands and the intention was to repatriate them as quickly as possible.").

[200] *Refer to* § 9.10.4 (Use of Ships for Temporary Detention).

[201] GPW art. 22 ("Except in particular cases which are justified by the interest of the prisoners themselves, they shall not be interned in penitentiaries.").

[202] *For example*, I REPORT OF THE INTERNATIONAL COMMITTEE OF THE RED CROSS ON ITS ACTIVITIES DURING THE SECOND WORLD WAR (SEPTEMBER 1, 1939 – JUNE 30, 1947) 248 (1948) ("Experience in the recent War showed that a great variety of buildings and quarters were put into service. A converted penitentiary, for example, proved a better lodging than many other buildings.").

[203] *For example*, Martin Tollefson, *Enemy Prisoners of War*, 32 IOWA LAW REVIEW 51, 59 (1946) ("The total number of enemy prisoners of war interned within the United States [during World War II] was 435,788. Included were 378,898 Germans, 51,455 Italians, and 5,435 Japanese. The number of prisoners of war in the United States was somewhat negligible prior to January 1943. It increased rapidly beginning with May of that year, largely as a result of the success of the African campaign. The increase continued irregularly but speedily until it reached its peak shortly after the surrender of Germany, when the influx of prisoners of war from Europe ceased.").

persons held in occupied territory, the GPW does not impose such restrictions on the transfer of POWs from the territory in which they were captured.[204]

Locating POW camps outside the theater of operations may be necessary for security (such as to discourage escape or reduce risk of enemy raids to release POWs) or other military reasons, such as improving the safety of POWs.

9.11.4 Safety of POW Camps.

9.11.4.1 *Avoidance of the Combat Zone*. POW camps should be situated in an area far enough from the combat zone for POWs to be out of danger.[205]

9.11.4.2 *Sharing Information on the Location of POW Camps*. Detaining Powers shall give the Powers concerned, through the intermediary of the Protecting Powers, all useful information regarding the geographic location of POW camps.[206]

9.11.4.3 *Marking of POW Camps*. Whenever military considerations permit, POW camps shall be indicated in the daytime by the letters "PW" or "PG," placed so as to be clearly visible from the air.[207] The Powers concerned may, however, agree upon any other system of marking.[208] No place, other than an internment camp, shall be marked as such.[209]

The caveat that POW camps need to be marked, as such, only when military considerations permit was intended to allow for camps not to be marked, *e.g.*, if marking camps would provide landmarks that would facilitate aerial bombardment by the enemy.[210]

9.11.4.4 *Air-Raid Shelters and Protective Measures for POWs*. POWs shall have shelters against air bombardment and other hazards of war, to the same extent as the local civilian population.[211] With the exception of those engaged in the protection of their quarters against these hazards, they may enter such shelters as soon as possible after the giving of the

---

[204] *Refer to* § 11.12.3 (Prohibition Against Forcible Transfers and Deportations).

[205] *Cf.* GPW art. 19 ("Prisoners of war shall be evacuated, as soon as possible after their capture, to camps situated in an area far enough from the combat zone for them to be out of danger.").

[206] GPW art. 23 ("Detaining Powers shall give the Powers concerned, through the intermediary of the Protecting Powers, all useful information regarding the geographical location of prisoner of war camps.").

[207] GPW art. 23 ("Whenever military considerations permit, prisoner of war camps shall be indicated in the day-time by the letters PW or PG, placed so as to be clearly visible from the air.").

[208] GPW art. 23 ("The Powers concerned may, however, agree upon any other system of marking.").

[209] GPW art. 23 ("Only prisoner of war camps shall be marked as such.").

[210] II-A FINAL RECORD OF THE DIPLOMATIC CONFERENCE OF GENEVA OF 1949 254 ("Miss BECKETT (United Kingdom) said that her Delegation was opposed to any mandatory provision regarding the marking of prisoner of war camps, owing to the small area of the United Kingdom. Camps so marked would provide excellent landmarks in the event of aerial bombardment. Large countries might conclude special agreements on the matter.").

[211] GPW art. 23 ("Prisoners of war shall have shelters against air bombardment and other hazards of war, to the same extent as the local civilian population.").

alarm.[212] Any other protective measure taken in favor of the population shall also apply to POWs.[213]

9.11.4.5 *Fire Precautions*. All precautions must be taken in POW camps against the danger of fire.[214]

9.11.5 Hygiene of POW Camps. POWs may be interned only in premises affording every guarantee of hygiene and healthfulness.[215] POWs interned in unhealthy areas, or where the climate is injurious for them, shall be removed as soon as possible to a more favorable climate.[216]

9.11.5.1 *Necessary Sanitary Measures*. The Detaining Power shall be bound to take all sanitary measures necessary to ensure the cleanliness and healthfulness of camps and to prevent epidemics.[217] For example, the Detaining Power should give POWs medical examinations upon arrival, disinfect them, and provide them with any necessary inoculations.[218] In addition, quarters should be kept free from vermin, and POWs suffering from contagious diseases should be placed in quarantine as needed.[219]

Although the Detaining Power is ultimately responsible for sanitary conditions, the Detaining Power may require POWs to assist in ensuring that POW camps are clean and healthy. For example, POWs may be assigned cleaning duties.[220] Additionally, POWs may be required to take baths or showers if necessary for health reasons.[221] Similarly, POWs may be required to receive inoculations to prevent the spread of contagious diseases.

---

[212] GPW art. 23 ("With the exception of those engaged in the protection of their quarters against the aforesaid hazards, they may enter such shelters as soon as possible after the giving of the alarm.").

[213] GPW art. 23 ("Any other protective measure taken in favour of the population shall also apply to them.").

[214] GPW art. 25 ("All precautions must be taken against the danger of fire.").

[215] GPW art. 22 ("Prisoners of war may be interned only in premises located on land and affording every guarantee of hygiene and healthfulness.").

[216] GPW art. 22 ("Prisoners of war interned in unhealthy areas, or where the climate is injurious for them, shall be removed as soon as possible to a more favourable climate.").

[217] GPW art. 29 ("The Detaining Power shall be bound to take all sanitary measures necessary to ensure the cleanliness and healthfulness of camps and to prevent epidemics.").

[218] GPW COMMENTARY 206 ("Among the special measures which the Detaining Power must take in regard to prisoners of war, we would mention first very strict examination upon entry into the camp, thorough disinfection and inoculation with all necessary vaccines.").

[219] GPW COMMENTARY 207 ("Prisoners suffering from contagious diseases must be placed in quarantine. Careful attention must also be paid to quarters, and all necessary measures taken to keep them free of vermin."). *Refer to* § 9.14.1.1 (Camp Infirmary).

[220] *Refer to* § 9.19.2.3 (Labor Assignments That May Be Compelled).

[221] GPW COMMENTARY 208 ("Baths and showers may be made compulsory for prisoners of war, provided no risk to their health is involved. This interpretation is not based on the present provision [paragraph 3 of GPW art. 29], but on paragraph 1 of this Article, which requires the Detaining Power to take all necessary sanitary measures. If baths and showers are considered necessary to ensure healthfulness in the camps and to prevent epidemics, they must be compulsory.").

9.11.5.2 *Sanitary Conveniences (e.g., latrines, bathrooms)*. POWs shall have for their use, day and night, conveniences that conform to the rules of hygiene and are maintained in a constant state of cleanliness.[222] The term "sanitary conveniences" should be taken to mean primarily the latrines. Access to the latrines at night is specified in the 1949 Geneva Conventions because lack of access was a frequent problem in POW camps in World War II.[223]

In any camps in which women POWs are accommodated, separate conveniences shall be provided for them.[224]

9.11.5.3 *Showers, Baths, Personal Toilet, and Laundry*. Also, apart from the baths and showers with which the camps shall be furnished, POWs shall be provided with sufficient water and soap for their personal toilet and for washing their personal laundry; the necessary installations, facilities, and time shall be granted them for that purpose.[225] For example, the POW camp may have camp laundry facilities that the POWs may use to wash their clothes, or the POWs may have access to a laundry service outside the camp.[226]

Although the frequency with which baths or showers may be taken is not specified, a reasonable opportunity (*e.g.*, considering the available resources, the POWs' cultural practices, the activities in which they are engaged) should be afforded.[227]

9.11.6 Conditions of Living Quarters. POWs shall be quartered under conditions as favorable as those for the forces of the Detaining Power who are billeted in the same area.[228] These conditions shall make allowance for the habits and customs of the POWs and shall in no

---

[222] GPW art. 29 ("Prisoners of war shall have for their use, day and night, conveniences which conform to the rules of hygiene and are maintained in a constant state of cleanliness.").

[223] *See* GPW COMMENTARY 207 ("During the Second World War, prisoners of war sometimes had no access to the conveniences during the night. The new Convention makes an express stipulation in this respect."); I REPORT OF THE INTERNATIONAL COMMITTEE OF THE RED CROSS ON ITS ACTIVITIES DURING THE SECOND WORLD WAR (SEPTEMBER 1, 1939 – JUNE 30, 1947) 263 (1948) ("Delegates of the ICRC frequently drew the attention of camp commandants to the fact that sanitary conveniences were insufficient in number and often inaccessible to PW at night.").

[224] GPW art. 29 ("In any camps in which women prisoners of war are accommodated, separate conveniences shall be provided for them.").

[225] GPW art. 29 ("Also, apart from the baths and showers with which the camps shall be furnished, prisoners of war shall be provided with sufficient water and soap for their personal toilet and for washing their personal laundry; the necessary installations, facilities and time shall be granted them for that purpose.").

[226] *See* GPW COMMENTARY 208 ("The time allowed must also be sufficient for the washing of personal laundry. In camps where other ranks are interned, this task is usually performed by the prisoners themselves; in camps for officers, it is usually done outside the camp against payment.").

[227] *See also* GPW COMMENTARY 208 ("In the first place, this paragraph [of article 29 of the GPW] provides that the camps must be furnished with baths and showers. Taking into account the difficulties which the Detaining Power may have in providing hot baths and showers for a large number of prisoners, one bath or shower per week for each prisoner may be considered reasonable.").

[228] GPW art. 25 ("Prisoners of war shall be quartered under conditions as favourable as those for the forces of the Detaining Power who are billeted in the same area.").

case be prejudicial to their health.[229] In particular, the dormitories of POWs as regards both total surface and minimum cubic space, and the general installations, bedding, and blankets for POWs, should be as favorable as those of the forces of the Detaining Power in that area and should allow for their habits and customs.[230]

The premises provided for the use of POWs individually or collectively shall be entirely protected from dampness and adequately heated and lighted, in particular between dusk and lights out.[231]

9.11.6.1 *Separate Dormitories for Women*. In any camps in which women POWs, as well as men, are accommodated, separate dormitories shall be provided for women POWs.[232]

Although the GPW refers only to separate dormitories and the quarters as a whole need not necessarily be separated, the Detaining Power may provide separate quarters or even camps for men and women POWs, as appropriate.[233]

9.12 Segregation of POWs

Although the Detaining Power must treat POWs without any adverse distinction based upon race, nationality, religion, or political belief, or any other distinction based upon similar criteria,[234] the Detaining Power shall assemble POWs in camps or camp compounds according to their nationality, language, and customs, and may use other similar criteria to segregate detainees in order to maintain order in the camps or to impose punishment, or for medical reasons.

9.12.1 Assembling According to Nationality, Language, and Customs. The Detaining Power shall assemble POWs in camps or camp compounds according to their nationality, language, and customs, provided that such POWs shall not be separated from POWs belonging to the armed forces with which they were serving at the time of their capture, except with their consent.[235] For example, unless they otherwise consent, POWs who are serving in the armed forces of a State of which they are not nationals should be quartered with POWs from that State

---

229 GPW art. 25 ("The said conditions shall make allowance for the habits and customs of the prisoners and shall in no case be prejudicial to their health.").

230 GPW art. 25 ("The foregoing provisions shall apply in particular to the dormitories of prisoners of war as regards both total surface and minimum cubic space, and the general installations, bedding and blankets.").

231 GPW art. 25 ("The premises provided for the use of prisoners of war individually or collectively, shall be entirely protected from dampness and adequately heated and lighted, in particular between dusk and lights out.").

232 GPW art. 25 ("In any camps in which women prisoners of war, as well as men, are accommodated, separate dormitories shall be provided for them.").

233 GPW Commentary 195 ("Strictly speaking, this paragraph refers only to dormitories and the quarters as a whole need not necessarily be separated; the Detaining Power is, however, at liberty to provide separate quarters if it deems fit and in order more easily to fulfil the other requirements of the Convention with regard to women prisoners.").

234 *Refer to* § 9.5.5 (No Adverse Distinction Based on Race, Nationality, Religion, or Political Belief).

235 GPW art. 22 ("The Detaining Power shall assemble prisoners of war in camps or camp compounds according to their nationality, language and customs, provided that such prisoners shall not be separated from prisoners of war belonging to the armed forces with which they were serving at the time of their capture, except with their consent.").

as opposed to with POWs of their nationality.

The assembling of POWs on the basis of nationality, language, and customs is intended to ameliorate the possibility of cultural conflicts within POW camps, such as those that occurred during World War I.[236]

9.12.1.1 Other Permissible Criteria for Segregating POWs. In addition to nationality, language, and customs, the Detaining Power may segregate POWs along the basis of other criteria to advance legitimate interests, such as maintaining order in camps or imposing punishment, or for medical reasons.[237] For example, it may be appropriate to segregate POWs on the basis of political opinion.[238] POWs who are deserters or who fear attacks by other POWs may also be segregated.[239] In addition, it may be appropriate to segregate POWs based on whether they are connected with potential war crimes proceedings.[240] POWs may be segregated according to their known or suspected security risk level. A combination of classifications may be used to ensure an orderly and secure POW camp.[241]

---

[236] GPW COMMENTARY 183 ("The First World War was the first occasion on which soldiers of every race and nationality fought on the same battlefields, and the very varied composition of armed forces sometimes raised difficult problems for the Detaining Powers. It was difficult to expect men to live side by side solely because they had belonged to the same armed forces when not only their culture and civilization were very different, but also they had customs and habits which differed very much, for instance in matters of hygiene.").

[237] 1956 FM 27-10 (Change No. 1 1976) ¶92b ("The foregoing provision [GPW art. 16] does not preclude the segregation of prisoners of war to maintain order in camps, to impose punishment, or for medical reasons.").

[238] *For example*, LEVIE, POWS 178 ("The incidents which occurred in the prisoner-of-war camps there [during the Korean War] demonstrated that where ideology is concerned, and where there is a major schism within the prisoner-of-war group itself, segregation by political opinion may be an absolute requirement in order to ensure the safety of many of the prisoners of war. Once again, it is necessary to state that there is no valid objection to this procedure as long as there is, nevertheless, compliance with the provisions of the third paragraph of Article 22 and as long as there is no discrimination in the treatment received by the individuals confined in different camps or compounds.").

[239] *For example*, Gordon Risius, *Prisoners of War in the United Kingdom*, *in* PETER ROWE, THE GULF WAR 1990-91 IN INTERNATIONAL AND ENGLISH LAW 289, 298 (1993) ("Four [Iraqi] prisoners [of war held in the United Kingdom] were accommodated separately at their own request. They considered themselves to be deserters, and were concerned that they might be attacked by the other prisoners if they were not segregated.").

[240] *For example*, DEPARTMENT OF THE ARMY PAMPHLET 20-213, *History of Prisoner Of War Utilization By The United States Army, 1776-1945*, 253 (Jun. 24, 1955) ("All Japanese PW's were divided into two classes after screening—processed and categorized. A processed prisoner of war was one who had been questioned and found not to be connected with any war crime. His name was recorded, a serial number assigned, and he was sent to a branch PW labor camp pending repatriation. A categorized prisoner of war was one held as a war criminal or as a material witness to atrocities committed by members of the Japanese forces. These were segregated from the other prisoners, but were eligible for use as laborers under adequate security.").

[241] *For example*, Martin Tollefson, *Enemy Prisoners of War*, 32 IOWA LAW REVIEW 51, 59 (1946) ("The most effective means, however, of stopping the crime wave [of murder and forced suicides in U.S.-run POW camps in World War II] and other troubles, among prisoners of war, was the adoption of a well-planned program of segregation. Prisoners were carefully screened and re-screened, classified, segregated, and transferred to camps accordingly. At the one extreme were found the rabid Nazis, and at the other the confirmed anti-Nazis, with the great mass of German prisoners falling in a middle category. In addition, there were many finer classifications and segregations. The trouble makers, the Gestapo agents, and the SS and SA men, for instance, had to be segregated from those who were willing to cooperate irrespective of their political views. Those who were inclined to be

9.13 FOOD, WATER, TOBACCO, AND CLOTHING FOR POWS

9.13.1 Food for POWs. The basic daily food rations shall be sufficient in quantity, quality, and variety to keep POWs in good health and to prevent loss of weight or the development of nutritional deficiencies.[242]

9.13.1.1 *Accounting for the Habitual Diet*. Account shall also be taken of the habitual diet of the POWs.[243] For example, the POWs' cultural and religious requirements should be considered in determining and ensuring the appropriate diet.[244] The preparation of the food by the POWs themselves also helps conform the food to the POWs' habitual diet.[245]

9.13.1.2 *Additional Food for Certain Groups*. The Detaining Power shall supply POWs who work with such additional rations as are necessary for the labor on which they are employed.[246]

9.13.1.3 *No Collective Disciplinary Measures Affecting Food*. Collective disciplinary measures affecting food are prohibited.[247] The use of food as an inducement to recalcitrant POWs to restore order in a POW camp is permissible.[248]

9.13.1.4 *Messing and Means for Preparing Additional Food*. Adequate premises shall be provided for messing.[249] Supervision of messes by the POWs themselves shall be

---

particularly cooperative had to be given protection. Approximately one dozen different classes of camps were maintained to make the segregation effective.").

242 GPW art. 26 ("The basic daily food rations shall be sufficient in quantity, quality and variety to keep prisoners of war in good health and to prevent loss of weight or the development of nutritial deficiencies.").

243 GPW art. 26 ("Account shall also be taken of the habitual diet of the prisoners.").

244 *For example*, FINAL REPORT ON THE PERSIAN GULF WAR 585 ("Rations for EPW were nourishing. The usual menu consisted of: Four slices of bread w/jam, cheese, 1/4 liter milk or juice for breakfast; 1 US meal ready to eat, North Atlantic Treaty Organization, or Saudi rations for lunch; and, beans, tomatoes, rice, meat (lamb or chicken), and tea for supper. Items prohibited by local and regional religious beliefs were not served to EPWs. US personnel removed these items from ration packets and replaced them with acceptable substitutes.").

245 GPW COMMENTARY 198 ("The present provision, which is additional to the requirements in the first sentence, should ensure that prisoners are provided with food corresponding to their needs, their taste and their habits. Paragraph 4 of this same Article [Article 26 of the GPW], which provides that prisoners of war may be associated with the preparation of their meals, will facilitate the application of this clause.").

246 GPW art. 26 ("The Detaining Power shall supply prisoners of war who work with such additional rations as are necessary for the labour on which they are employed.").

247 GPW art. 26 ("Collective disciplinary measures affecting food are prohibited.").

248 LEVIE, POWS 130 footnote 115 ("During the rioting at Koje-do in Korea in 1952 (*see* note V-8 *infra*), in order to move recalcitrant Communist prisoners of war to smaller, more manageable, prisoner-of-war compounds where control by the Detaining Power could be reestablished, the military authorities of the United Nations Command made food available in the new, small compounds and refused to make it available in the old, large compounds. If the prisoner of war wanted to eat, he had to move to the new compound. The ICRC Delegate took the position that this was collective punishment involving food. The United Nations Command took the position that as food was available in the new compounds, to which the prisoners of war were free to move, there was no denial of food to them.").

249 GPW art. 26 ("Adequate premises shall be provided for messing.").

facilitated in every way.[250]

POWs shall, as far as possible, be associated with the preparation of their meals; they may be employed for that purpose in the kitchens.[251] Furthermore, they shall be given the means of preparing, themselves, the additional food in their possession.[252] For example, the POWs should have access to facilities to prepare food purchased at the canteen or received in relief packages.

9.13.2 Drinking Water. Sufficient drinking water shall be supplied to POWs.[253]

9.13.3 Use of Tobacco. The use of tobacco shall be permitted.[254] The Detaining Power is not required to give tobacco to POWs, but should offer it for sale at the canteen.[255] The Detaining Power may impose reasonable restrictions on smoking to ensure that the camp is a healthful and safe environment.

9.13.4 Clothing for POWs. Clothing, underwear, and footwear shall be supplied to POWs in sufficient quantities by the Detaining Power, which shall make allowance for the climate of the region where the POWs are detained.[256] The regular replacement and repair of these articles shall be assured by the Detaining Power.[257]

9.13.4.1 *Uniforms for POWs*. Uniforms of enemy armed forces captured by the Detaining Power should, if suitable for the climate, be made available to clothe POWs.[258] The Power to which the POWs belong may send uniforms to the POWs through the Protecting Powers or ICRC.[259]

---

[250] GPW art. 44 ("Supervision of the mess by the officers themselves shall be facilitated in every way."); GPW art. 45 ("Supervision of the mess by the prisoners themselves shall be facilitated in every way.").

[251] GPW art. 26 ("Prisoners of war shall, as far as possible, be associated with the preparation of their meals; they may be employed for that purpose in the kitchens.").

[252] GPW art. 26 ("Furthermore, they shall be given the means of preparing, themselves, the additional food in their possession.").

[253] GPW art. 26 ("Sufficient drinking water shall be supplied to prisoners of war.").

[254] GPW art. 26 ("The use of tobacco shall be permitted.").

[255] *Refer to* § 9.17 (Canteens for POWs).

[256] GPW art. 27 ("Clothing, underwear and footwear shall be supplied to prisoners of war in sufficient quantities by the Detaining Power, which shall make allowance for the climate of the region where the prisoners are detained.").

[257] GPW art. 27 ("The regular replacement and repair of the above articles shall be assured by the Detaining Power.").

[258] GPW art. 27 ("Uniforms of enemy armed forces captured by the Detaining Power should, if suitable for the climate, be made available to clothe prisoners of war.").

[259] *For example*, I REPORT OF THE INTERNATIONAL COMMITTEE OF THE RED CROSS ON ITS ACTIVITIES DURING THE SECOND WORLD WAR (SEPTEMBER 1, 1939 – JUNE 30, 1947) 258 (1948) ("As in the case of food, countries whose economic conditions were considerably impaired by the war could not make adequate provision of the clothing of the prisoners in their hands. The Powers to which these PW belonged thereupon sent large quantities of uniforms to the camps through the ICRC. The object was not only to ensure that PW should have enough clothing, but also to give them uniforms of their national forces, which in any case could not be supplied by the detaining Power.").

The GPW does not prohibit providing POWs with uniforms of the armed forces of the Detaining Power. If this were necessary, it would be appropriate to remove insignia or alter the uniforms, which would reduce the risk that POWs might be mistaken for members of the armed forces of the Detaining Power.[260]

Similarly, uniforms or other clothing for POWs may contain markings denoting the individuals as POWs because the absence of any such markings may facilitate escape.[261] Any markings on clothing for POWs must be consistent with the principle of respect for the person and honor of the POW and, therefore, may not be humiliating or degrading.[262]

9.13.4.2 *Appropriate Clothing for Work*. POWs who work shall receive appropriate clothing, wherever the nature of the work demands.[263]

9.14 Medical Attention for Interned POWs

In addition to the rules relating to the general rules applicable to the medical care of the wounded and sick,[264] the following rules also apply to the medical care of POWs who have been interned in POW camps.

The GPW and the GWS contemplate that POWs will benefit from the services of retained medical personnel or POWs who are trained as medical personnel but not attached to the medical service.[265] However, the provision in the GPW and the GWS for such personnel does not relieve the Detaining Power of its obligations to provide for the medical care of POWs.[266]

9.14.1 Access to Medical Attention.

9.14.1.1 *Camp Infirmary*. Every camp shall have an adequate infirmary where POWs may have the attention they require, as well as an appropriate diet.[267] Isolation wards shall, if necessary, be set aside for cases of contagious or mental disease.[268]

---

[260] *Cf.* GPW COMMENTARY 201 ("Prisoners may in no case be obliged to wear the uniform of the Detaining Power if they consider that their honour does not so permit (Article 14, paragraph 1). The Detaining Power must therefore, as a minimum, alter those uniforms, in particular by removing all badges of nationality.").

[261] GPW COMMENTARY 201 ("Detaining Powers have never been willing to allow prisoners of war to wear civilian clothing, in order not to make escape easier.").

[262] *Refer to* § 9.5.3 (Protection Against Insults and Public Curiosity). *Compare* § 10.13.4.1 (No Humiliating Clothing).

[263] GPW art. 27 ("In addition, prisoners of war who work shall receive appropriate clothing, wherever the nature of the work demands.").

[264] *Refer to* § 7.5.2 (Medical Care of the Wounded and Sick).

[265] *Refer to* § 7.9 (Captured Medical and Religious Personnel).

[266] *Refer to* § 7.9.6 (No Relief of Obligations of the Detaining Power).

[267] GPW art. 30 ("Every camp shall have an adequate infirmary where prisoners of war may have the attention they require, as well as appropriate diet.").

[268] GPW art. 30 ("Isolation wards shall, if necessary, be set aside for cases of contagious or mental disease.").

9.14.1.2 *Right of POWs to Present Themselves for Examination*. POWs may not be prevented from presenting themselves to the medical authorities for examination.[269]

The GPW contemplates that POWs would have daily sick call in which they could present themselves for medical examination, even when undergoing disciplinary punishment.[270]

The right of POWs to present themselves for examination does not mean that POWs must necessarily be examined every day by a doctor, nor does it preclude disciplinary punishment if POWs abusively make groundless requests for medical examination.[271]

9.14.1.3 *Monthly Medical Inspections*. Medical inspections of POWs shall be held at least once a month.[272] They shall include the checking and the recording of the weight of each POW.[273] Their purpose shall be, in particular, to supervise the general state of health, nutrition, and cleanliness of POWs, and to detect contagious diseases, especially tuberculosis, malaria, and venereal disease.[274] For this purpose, the most efficient methods available shall be employed.[275] The GPW gives as an example periodic mass miniature radiography for early detection of tuberculosis, but medical experts should be consulted for the best practices.

9.14.2 Medical Treatment for Interned POWs.

9.14.2.1 *Persons Requiring Special Treatment*. POWs suffering from serious disease, or whose condition necessitates special treatment, a surgical operation, or hospital care, must be admitted to any military or civilian medical unit where such treatment can be given, even if their repatriation is contemplated in the near future.[276] Special facilities shall be afforded for the care to be given to the disabled, in particular to the blind, and for their rehabilitation, pending repatriation.[277]

9.14.2.2 *Treatment by Medical Personnel of the Power on Which They Depend*. POWs shall have the attention, preferably, of medical personnel of the Power on which they

---

[269] GPW art. 30 ("Prisoners of war may not be prevented from presenting themselves to the medical authorities for examination.").

[270] *Refer to* § 9.27.6.4 (Attendance at Daily Medical Inspection and Medical Attention).

[271] *Compare* § 10.14.1.2 (Right of Internees to Present Themselves for Examination).

[272] GPW art. 31 ("Medical inspections of prisoners of war shall be held at least once a month.").

[273] GPW art. 31 ("They shall include the checking and the recording of the weight of each prisoner of war.").

[274] GPW art. 31 ("Their purpose shall be, in particular, to supervise the general state of health, nutrition and cleanliness of prisoners and to detect contagious diseases, especially tuberculosis, malaria and venereal disease.").

[275] GPW art. 31 ("For this purpose the most efficient methods available shall be employed, e. g. periodic mass miniature radiography for the early detection of tuberculosis.").

[276] GPW art. 30 ("Prisoners of war suffering from serious disease, or whose condition necessitates special treatment, a surgical operation or hospital care, must be admitted to any military or civilian medical unit where such treatment can be given, even if their repatriation is contemplated in the near future.").

[277] GPW art. 30 ("Special facilities shall be afforded for the care to be given to the disabled, in particular to the blind, and for their rehabilitation, pending repatriation.").

depend and, if possible, of their nationality.[278] The preference for POWs to have the attention of the medical personnel of the Power on which they depend is also reflected in the provisions of the GPW and GWS on the duties of retained personnel.[279]

These medical personnel may be retained personnel or persons who are trained as medical personnel but not attached to the medical service in their armed forces.[280]

9.14.2.3 *Certification Recording Treatment*. The detaining authorities shall, upon request, issue to every POW who has undergone treatment an official certificate indicating the nature of his or her illness or injury, and the duration and kind of treatment received.[281] A duplicate of this certificate shall be forwarded to the Central POW Information Agency.[282]

9.14.2.4 *Cost of Treatment*. The costs of treatment, including those of any apparatus necessary for the maintenance of POWs in good health, particularly dentures and other artificial appliances, and eyeglasses, shall be borne by the Detaining Power.[283]

9.14.3 Receipt of Medical Supplies. POWs may receive individual parcels and collective shipments containing medical supplies.[284] However, medical supplies generally are to be sent in collective shipments so that they may be properly administered by the camp doctors.[285]

9.14.4 Inquiry in Certain Cases of Death or Serious Injury. In certain cases of death or serious injury of a POW, an official inquiry shall be conducted by the Detaining Power.[286]

9.15 Religious Exercise by POWs

POWs shall enjoy complete latitude in the exercise of their religious duties, including attendance at the service of their faith, on condition that they comply with the disciplinary

---

[278] GPW art. 30 ("Prisoners of war shall have the attention, preferably, of medical personnel of the Power on which they depend and, if possible, of their nationality.").

[279] *Refer to* § 7.9.3 (Duties of Retained Personnel).

[280] *Refer to* § 4.9 (Military Medical and Religious Personnel); § 4.5.2.2 (Members Trained as Medical Personnel, but Not Attached to the Medical Service).

[281] GPW art. 30 ("The detaining authorities shall, upon request, issue to every prisoner who has undergone treatment, an official certificate indicating the nature of his illness or injury, and the duration and kind of treatment received.").

[282] GPW art. 30 ("A duplicate of this certificate shall be forwarded to the Central Prisoners of War Agency.").

[283] GPW art. 30 ("The costs of treatment, including those of any apparatus necessary for the maintenance of prisoners of war in good health, particularly dentures and other artificial appliances, and spectacles, shall be borne by the Detaining Power.").

[284] *Refer to* § 9.20.3 (Receipt of Individual and Collective Relief Shipments for POWs).

[285] *Refer to* § 9.20.3.2 (Medical Supplies in Relief Shipments).

[286] *Refer to* § 9.34.5 (Inquiries Into Death or Serious Injury of POWs in Certain Cases).

routine prescribed by the military authorities.[287]

The GPW and the GWS contemplate that POWs will benefit from the services of retained chaplains or POWs who are ministers of religion without having officiated as chaplains to their own forces.[288] However, the provision in the GPW and the GWS for such personnel does not relieve the Detaining Power of its obligations to provide for the exercise of religion by POWs.[289]

9.15.1 Premises for Religious Services for POWs. Adequate premises shall be provided where religious services may be held.[290] The premises where services are held should be sufficiently spacious and clean, and should provide effective shelter to those attending services, but need not be set aside exclusively for religious services.[291]

9.15.2 Chaplains. Chaplains who fall into the hands of the enemy Power and who remain or are retained with a view to assisting POWs shall be allowed to minister to them and to exercise freely their ministry among POWs of the same religion, in accordance with their religious conscience.[292] They shall be allocated among the various camps and labor detachments containing POWs belonging to the same forces, speaking the same language, or practicing the same religion.[293]

9.15.3 Appointment of Other Ordained Ministers or Qualified Laypersons. When POWs do not have the assistance of a retained chaplain or of a POW minister of their faith, a minister belonging to the POWs' or a similar denomination, or in his or her absence a qualified layperson, if such a course is feasible from a confessional point of view, shall be appointed, at the request of the POWs concerned, to fill this office.[294] This appointment, subject to the approval of the Detaining Power, shall take place with the agreement of the community of POWs concerned and,

---

[287] GPW art. 34 ("Prisoners of war shall enjoy complete latitude in the exercise of their religious duties, including attendance at the service of their faith, on condition that they comply with the disciplinary routine prescribed by the military authorities.").

[288] *Refer to* § 7.9 (Captured Medical and Religious Personnel).

[289] *Refer to* § 7.9.6 (No Relief of Obligations of the Detaining Power).

[290] GPW art. 34 ("Adequate premises shall be provided where religious services may be held.").

[291] GC COMMENTARY 388 ("It does not seem essential that these premises should be set aside exclusively for religious services. The parallel text in the Prisoners of War Convention (Article 34, paragraph 2) speaks of 'adequate' premises. In both cases, it should be understood that the premises where services are held should be sufficiently spacious and clean and so built as to give effective shelter to those attending the services.").

[292] GPW art. 35 ("Chaplains who fall into the hands of the enemy Power and who remain or are retained with a view to assisting prisoners of war, shall be allowed to minister to them and to exercise freely their ministry amongst prisoners of war of the same religion, in accordance with their religious conscience.").

[293] GPW art. 35 ("They shall be allocated among the various camps and labour detachments containing prisoners of war belonging to the same forces, speaking the same language or practising the same religion.").

[294] GPW art. 37 ("When prisoners of war have not the assistance of a retained chaplain or of a prisoner of war minister of their faith, a minister belonging to the prisoners' or a similar denomination, or in his absence a qualified layman, if such a course is feasible from a confessional point of view, shall be appointed, at the request of the prisoners concerned, to fill this office.").

wherever necessary, with the approval of the local religious authorities of the same faith.[295] The person thus appointed shall comply with all regulations established by the Detaining Power in the interests of discipline and military security.[296]

9.16 Intellectual, Physical, and Recreational Activities

While respecting the individual preferences of every POW, the Detaining Power shall encourage the practice of intellectual, educational, and recreational pursuits, and sports and games, among POWs, and shall take the measures necessary to ensure the exercise thereof by providing them with adequate premises and necessary equipment.[297] Adequate premises and necessary equipment may include, for example, musical instruments, theatrical accessories, books, language courses, recreation rooms, or soccer fields.[298]

9.16.1 Voluntariness of the Activities. The Detaining Power should seek to encourage the POWs in engaging in these activities, while respecting their individual preferences. For example, it would be prohibited to compel POWs to listen to propaganda or to punish them if they do not participate.[299]

On the other hand, as reflected in U.S. practice, censoring educational or intellectual materials for security reasons or to refrain from providing POWs with anti-democratic political

---

[295] GPW art. 37 ("This appointment, subject, to the approval of the Detaining Power, shall take place with the agreement of the community of prisoners concerned and, wherever necessary, with the approval of the local religious authorities of the same faith.").

[296] GPW art. 37 ("The person thus appointed shall comply with all regulations established by the Detaining Power in the interests of discipline and military security.").

[297] GPW art. 38 ("While respecting the individual preferences of every prisoner, the Detaining Power shall encourage the practice of intellectual, educational, and recreational pursuits, sports and games amongst prisoners, and shall take the measures necessary to ensure the exercise thereof by providing them with adequate premises and necessary equipment.").

[298] *For example*, GPW COMMENTARY 237 ("During the Second World War the problem was often solved to the complete satisfaction of the prisoners of war. They were provided with musical instruments, theatrical accessories, books, language courses, recreation rooms, football fields, etc. The necessary equipment was usually supplied by relief societies or purchased by the prisoners themselves.").

[299] GPW COMMENTARY 237 ("[W]here propaganda involves inhuman treatment, it is *ipso facto* contrary to the Conventions, since such treatment is expressly prohibited. Where no inhuman treatment is involved, propaganda is nevertheless usually dangerous for prisoners of war and contrary to the Conventions, since it may be inconsistent with equality of treatment, respect for honour and, in particular, the present provision which affirms the right of prisoners to use their leisure time according to their own preferences."). *For example*, The Secretary of Defense's Advisory Committee on Prisoners of War, *POW The Fight Continues After The Battle: The Report of the Secretary of Defense's Advisory Committee on Prisoners of War* 10-11 (Aug. 1955) ("[T]he enemy had established a system of indoctrination courses. The prisoner might start the hard way—and be punished by restricted rations and other privations. If he began to show the 'proper spirit'—to cooperate with his captors—he was lectured and handed Communist literature. A docile prisoner who read the literature and listened politely to the lectures, was graduated to a better class. Finally he might be sent to 'Peaceful Valley.' In this lenient camp the food was relatively good. Prisoners might even have tobacco. And here they were given all sorts of Marxian propaganda. The graduates from 'Peaceful Valley' and others who accepted Communist schooling were called 'Progressives.' Prisoners who refused to go along with the program often remained in tougher circumstances. They were considered 'Reactionaries.'").

propaganda would be permissible.[300] Such censorship would be consistent with the general authority of the Detaining Power to censor POW correspondence and shipments with a view towards deleting or confiscating matter prejudicial to its military security.[301]

9.16.2 Education. The GPW does not provide specifically for the Detaining Power to grant facilities for POWs to continue their studies or to take up new subjects as the GC does for internees.[302] Nonetheless, as the duration of detention increases, the Detaining Power should make an effort to do so as part of its general obligation to encourage intellectual and educational pursuits among POWs.[303]

To advance educational opportunities for POWs, the Detaining Power may seek ways to encourage and assist them in teaching one another.[304]

9.16.3 Opportunities for Physical Exercise and for Being Outdoors. POWs shall have opportunities for taking physical exercise, including sports and games, and for being outdoors.[305] Sufficient open spaces shall be provided for this purpose in all camps.[306]

9.16.4 Contributions by Sources Apart From the Detaining Power. Apart from the Detaining Power, POWs may receive assistance from a variety of sources that allow them to engage in intellectual, physical, and recreational activities.

---

[300] *For example*, Office of the Provost Marshal General, *World War II - A Brief History* 443 (1946) ("Libraries and reading rooms were permitted to be maintained by prisoners, subject to censorship of the reading material. This censorship was exercised largely at the camp level. As time went on, however, increasing staff supervision was exercised by the Office of The Provost Marshal General, since quantities of reading material were available from welfare agencies and other sources, and censorship at the camp level was often impractical. Supervision was exercised by directives, correspondence with camps, and extensive liaison with welfare agencies and the Office of Censorship. Publications which related to military matters or which contained anti-democratic political propaganda were excluded.").

[301] *Refer to* § 9.20.6 (Censorship and Security Review of POW Correspondence and Shipments).

[302] *Refer to* § 10.16.2 (Education).

[303] *For example*, Office of the Provost Marshal General, *World War II - A Brief History* 443 (1946) ("The need of educating prisoners became, progressively, of increasing importance and was reflected in additional coverage in the official regulations and directives. Opportunities developed for prisoners to receive further education, subject to certain limitations which were required because of the prisoners' status. At the beginning the prisoners themselves took the initiative, aided by relief societies. Once launched, their efforts were given all necessary aid from the War Department, whether the courses were at elementary, secondary, or collegiate level.").

[304] DEPARTMENT OF THE ARMY PAMPHLET 20-213, *History of Prisoner Of War Utilization By The United States Army, 1776-1945*, 160 (Jun. 24, 1955) ("The War Department encouraged the PW's to organize formal study courses and allowed them to select a director of studies from their group to organize and promote educational and recreational activities. The PW's also selected qualified teachers and instructors who were given sufficient free time to carry out their educational work. These were paid the standard rate for their educational duties when the work excluded them from other paid labor. The expenses of the educational program, including the pay of the director and teachers, came from the PW fund of the camp served.").

[305] GPW art. 38 ("Prisoners shall have opportunities for taking physical exercise, including sports and games, and for being out of doors.").

[306] GPW art. 38 ("Sufficient open spaces shall be provided for this purpose in all camps.").

For example, relief organizations, including the ICRC, may contribute to ensuring that POWs have opportunities for intellectual, physical, and recreational activities.[307] In addition, POWs may receive shipments that are intended to allow them to engage in these activities.[308] Profits from the canteen may also be used for this purpose.[309]

9.17 CANTEENS FOR POWS

Canteens shall be established in all camps, where POWs may procure foodstuffs, soap and tobacco, and ordinary articles for daily use.[310] The purpose is to improve the morale of POWs by offering goods that are beyond the minimum necessities.[311]

9.17.1 Establishment of Canteens. Canteens should be established within a reasonable period of time, such as after more basic camp facilities have been established and similar facilities have been established for U.S. forces in the area. In conflicts of short duration or where POWs are to be transferred to another party to the conflict for longer-term internment, it may be unnecessary to establish a canteen.

9.17.1.1 *"Comfort Pack" Instead of Canteen and Advance of Pay*. Before canteens can be established, the need for a canteen may be mitigated if POWs are provided a free "comfort pack." The "comfort pack" was developed during Operation DESERT STORM for U.S. military personnel during the period before opening of exchanges in which such items were available for purchase. Comfort packs were provided to enemy POWs for similar reasons.[312]

9.17.2 Canteen Stock and Prices. Canteens are like a base or post exchange for POWs. The canteen stock should include foodstuffs, soap, tobacco, and other ordinary articles for daily use, but need not include luxury items. Ordinary articles for daily use may include, but are not limited to, items such as correspondence materials (*e.g.*, stationary, pencils, pens, ink, stamps), supplies for repairing personal effects (*e.g.*, buttons, thread, shoe laces), personal hygiene articles, tobacco, water, soft drinks, other non-alcoholic beverages, and reading materials.[313]

---

[307] *Refer to* § 9.33.2 (Access by Relief Societies and Other Organizations).

[308] *Refer to* § 9.20.3 (Receipt of Individual and Collective Relief Shipments for POWs).

[309] *Refer to* § 9.17.3 (Camp Canteen Management and Profits).

[310] GPW art. 28 ("Canteens shall be installed in all camps, where prisoners of war may procure foodstuffs, soap and tobacco and ordinary articles in daily use.").

[311] LEVIE, POWS 143 ("The existence of the canteen and the availability for sale of canteen-type articles has an affirmative effect on morale the extent of which is incalculable.").

[312] *For example*, W. Hays Parks, Special Assistant for Law of War Matters, Office of the Judge Advocate General of the Army, *Enemy Prisoner of War Health and Comfort Pack* (Oct. 28, 1994) ("In the 1991 Gulf War, the U.S. Army issued Iraqi EPW health and comfort packs provided by the ICRC or from U.S. stocks (that is, sundry packs for U.S. soldiers), but did not establish canteens within the EPW camps due to the short duration of the conflict and EPW transfer to Saudi Arabian authorities. Tobacco was provided separately, *gratis*.").

[313] GPW COMMENTARY 203 ("The term 'ordinary articles in daily use' means, in addition to soap and tobacco, which are specifically mentioned: (a) all necessary supplies for correspondence (paper, pencils, pens, ink, stamps, etc.); (b) all necessary toilet articles (towels, brushes, razors, combs, nail scissors, etc.); (c) all necessary supplies for

The canteen need not stock alcoholic beverages.[314]

The prices at canteens shall never be in excess of local market prices.[315]

9.17.3 Camp Canteen Management and Profits. Canteen profits shall be used for the benefit of the POWs, and a special fund shall be created for this purpose.[316] The POW Representative shall have the right to collaborate in the management of the canteen and of this fund.[317] The wishes expressed by the POWs should be considered to the extent consistent with camp regulations, and the profits should be used whenever needed to improve the conditions for POWs.[318]

9.17.3.1 *Use of Canteen Profits for Working Pay of the POW Representative*. Canteen profits should also be used for working pay of the POW Representative, of his or her advisers, if any, and of his or her assistants.[319]

9.17.3.2 *Disposition of Canteen Profits Upon Camp Closure*. When a camp is closed, the credit balance of the special fund shall be handed to an international welfare foundation, to be employed for the benefit of POWs of the same nationality as those who have contributed to the fund.[320] In case of a general repatriation, the profits shall be kept by the Detaining Power, subject to any agreement to the contrary between the Powers concerned.[321]

9.18 Financial Resources of POWs

9.18.1 Detaining Power Regulations on the Maximum Amount of Money in POW Possession. Upon the outbreak of hostilities, and pending an arrangement on this matter with the

---

repairing personal effects (buttons, thread, needles, shoe-laces, etc.); (d) miscellaneous articles (pocket torches and batteries, string, pen-knives, handkerchiefs, etc.).").

[314] GPW COMMENTARY 203 ("The camp authorities may prohibit the sale of alcoholic drinks, but must permit the sale of all other health-giving, refreshing or fortifying beverages, hot or cold, and, if possible, milk.").

[315] GPW art. 28 ("The tariff shall never be in excess of local market prices.").

[316] GPW art. 28 ("The profits made by camp canteens shall be used for the benefit of the prisoners; a special fund shall be created for this purpose.").

[317] GPW art. 28 ("The prisoners' representative shall have the right to collaborate in the management of the canteen and of this fund.").

[318] GPW COMMENTARY 204 ("It must be emphasized that, in accordance with the present paragraph, the fund must be used for the benefit of the prisoners. The wishes expressed by the prisoners must therefore be taken into consideration, to the extent that they do not run contrary to the regulations ensuring good administration and discipline in the camp. The Detaining Power may not utilize canteen profits to make up any shortcomings for which it is responsible. On the other hand, it is also recommended that canteen profits should not be hoarded, but should be utilized whenever needed in order to improve the lot of the prisoners.").

[319] *Refer to* § 9.24.4.5 (Working Pay of POW Representatives, Advisers, and Assistants).

[320] GPW art. 28 ("When a camp is closed down, the credit balance of the special fund shall be handed to an international welfare organization, to be employed for the benefit of prisoners of war of the same nationality as those who have contributed to the fund.").

[321] GPW art. 28 ("In case of a general repatriation, such profits shall be kept by the Detaining Power, subject to any agreement to the contrary between the Powers concerned.").

Protecting Power, the Detaining Power may determine the maximum amount of money in cash or in any similar form that POWs may have in their possession.[322] Any amount in excess, which was properly in their possession and which has been taken or withheld from them, shall be placed to their account, together with any monies deposited by them, and shall not be converted into any other currency without their consent.[323]

9.18.2 Purchases Outside the POW Camp. If POWs are permitted to purchase services or commodities outside the camp "against payment in cash," such payments shall be made by the POW himself or herself or by the camp administration who will charge them to the accounts of the POWs concerned.[324] The Detaining Power will establish the necessary rules in this respect.[325]

9.18.3 Advance of Pay. The Detaining Power shall grant all POWs a monthly advance of pay, the amount of which shall be fixed by conversion into the currency of the Detaining Power.[326]

This money allows POWs to purchase items at the canteen. This money may be paid in scrip or vouchers that can be used only in the POW camp, to prevent POWs from having or hoarding currency that might facilitate their escape.

Since the promulgation of the GPW, advances of pay to POWs by the Detaining Power have been infrequent.[327]

9.18.3.1 *GPW Specified Amounts for Monthly Advances of Pay*. Article 60 of the

---

322 GPW art. 58 ("Upon the outbreak of hostilities, and pending an arrangement on this matter with the Protecting Power, the Detaining Power may determine the maximum amount of money in cash or in any similar form, that prisoners may have in their possession.").

323 GPW art. 58 ("Any amount in excess, which was properly in their possession and which has been taken or withheld from them, shall be placed to their account, together with any monies deposited by them, and shall not be converted into any other currency without their consent.").

324 GPW art. 58 ("If prisoners of war are permitted to purchase services or commodities outside the camp against payment in cash, such payments shall be made by the prisoner himself or by the camp administration who will charge them to the accounts of the prisoners concerned.").

325 GPW art. 58 ("The Detaining Power will establish the necessary rules in this respect.").

326 GPW art. 60 ("The Detaining Power shall grant all prisoners of war a monthly advance of pay, the amount of which shall be fixed by conversion, into the currency of the said Power, of the following amounts: …").

327 *For example*, W. Hays Parks, Special Assistant for Law of War Matters, Office of the Judge Advocate General of the Army, *Enemy Prisoner of War Health and Comfort Pack* (Oct. 28, 1994) ("U.S. and allied or Coalition personnel held as prisoners of war during the Korean, Vietnam and 1991 Gulf Wars were not provided an advance of pay by their captors. Although members of the Panamanian Defense Force were not entitled to EPW status, the United States Army provided an advance of pay during Operation Just Cause (1989-90); the process proved cumbersome and unnecessarily complicated, as there was no budget or budget item designated for EPW advance of pay. The money was not recouped from the Government of Panama. No record could be found of the establishment of an advance of pay system by any nation in any conflict since promulgation of the 1949 GPW.").

GPW specifies the following amounts for monthly advances of pay:[328]

- Category I: POWs ranking below sergeants: eight Swiss francs.[329]
- Category II: Sergeants and other non-commissioned officers, or POWs of equivalent rank: twelve Swiss francs.[330]
- Category III: Warrant officers and commissioned officers below the rank of major or POWs of equivalent rank: fifty Swiss francs.[331]
- Category IV: Majors, lieutenant-colonels, colonels, or POWs of equivalent rank: sixty Swiss francs.[332]
- Category V: General officers or POWs of equivalent rank: seventy-five Swiss francs.[333]

"POWs of equivalent rank" refers to POWs, such as persons authorized to accompany the armed forces, who are not members of the armed forces and thus do not have a military rank.[334]

9.18.3.2 *Special Agreement to Modify the Amount of Advances of Pay*. The parties to the conflict concerned may, by special agreement, modify the amount of advances of pay due to POWs of the categories specified in Article 60 of the GPW.[335]

9.18.3.3 *Procedure for Limiting Amounts Drawn From Accounts Pending Special Agreement*. If the amounts indicated in Article 60 of the GPW would be unduly high compared with the pay of the Detaining Power's armed forces or would, for any reason, seriously embarrass the Detaining Power, then, pending the conclusion of a special agreement with the Power on which the POWs depend to vary the amounts indicated above, the Detaining Power:[336]

---

[328] GPW art. 60 ("The Detaining Power shall grant all prisoners of war a monthly advance of pay, the amount of which shall be fixed by conversion, into the currency of the said Power, of the following amounts:").

[329] GPW art. 60 ("Category I: Prisoners ranking below sergeants: eight Swiss francs.").

[330] GPW art. 60 ("Category II: Sergeants and other non-commissioned officers, or prisoners of equivalent rank: twelve Swiss francs.").

[331] GPW art. 60 ("Category III: Warrant officers and commissioned officers below the rank of major or prisoners of equivalent rank: fifty Swiss francs.").

[332] GPW art. 60 ("Category IV: Majors, lieutenant-colonels, colonels or prisoners of equivalent rank: sixty Swiss francs.").

[333] GPW art. 60 ("Category V: General officers or prisoners of war of equivalent rank: seventy-five Swiss francs.").

[334] *Refer to* § 9.22.4.1 (Communication of Titles and Ranks).

[335] GC art. 60 ("However, the Parties to the conflict concerned may by special agreement modify the amount of advances of pay due to prisoners of the preceding categories.").

[336] GPW art. 60 ("Furthermore, if the amounts indicated in the first paragraph above would be unduly high compared with the pay of the Detaining Power's armed forces or would, for any reason, seriously embarrass the Detaining Power, then, pending the conclusion of a special agreement with the Power on which the prisoners depend to vary the amounts indicated above, the Detaining Power:").

- shall continue to credit the accounts of the POWs with the amounts indicated in the first paragraph of Article 60 of the GPW;[337]

- may temporarily limit the amount made available from these advances of pay to POWs for their own use, to sums that are reasonable, but that, for Category I, shall never be inferior to the amount that the Detaining Power gives to the members of its own armed forces.[338]

The reasons for any limitations will be given without delay to the Protecting Power.[339]

9.18.3.4 *Reimbursement by the Power on Which the POWs Depend*. Advances of pay, issued to POWs in conformity with Article 60 of the GPW, shall be considered as made on behalf of the Power on which they depend.[340]

Such advances of pay, as well as all payments made by the Power on which the POWs depend under the third paragraph of Article 63 of the GPW (payments made by the POW in their own country[341]) and Article 68 of the GPW (claims by POWs for compensation for personal loss[342]), shall form the subject of arrangements between the Powers concerned, at the close of hostilities.[343]

9.18.4 Supplementary Pay From the Power on Which the POWs Depend. The Detaining Power shall accept for distribution as supplementary pay to POWs sums that the Power on which the POWs depend may forward to them, on condition that the sums to be paid shall be the same for each POW of the same category, shall be payable to all POWs of that category depending on that Power, and shall be placed in their separate accounts, at the earliest opportunity, in accordance with the provisions of Article 64 of the GPW.[344] Such supplementary pay shall not

---

[337] GPW art. 60 ("(a) shall continue to credit the accounts of the prisoners with the amounts indicated in the first paragraph above;").

[338] GPW art. 60 ("(b) may temporarily limit the amount made available from these advances of pay to prisoners of war for their own use, to sums which are reasonable, but which, for Category I, shall never be inferior to the amount that the Detaining Power gives to the members of its own armed forces.").

[339] GPW art. 60 ("The reasons for any limitations will be given without delay to the Protecting Power.").

[340] GPW art. 67 ("Advances of pay, issued to prisoners of war in conformity with Article 60, shall be considered as made on behalf of the Power on which they depend.").

[341] *Refer to* § 9.18.5.1 (Payments Made in the POW's Own Country).

[342] *Refer to* § 9.19.6.1 (Claims for Compensation From Injury or Other Disability Arising Out of Work); § 9.18.7 (Claims by POWs in Respect of Personal Loss).

[343] GPW art. 67 ("Such advances of pay, as well as all payments made by the said Power under Article 63, third paragraph, and Article 68, shall form the subject of arrangements between the Powers concerned, at the close of hostilities.").

[344] GPW art. 61 ("The Detaining Power shall accept for distribution as supplementary pay to prisoners of war sums which the Power on which the prisoners depend may forward to them, on condition that the sums to be paid shall be the same for each prisoner of the same category, shall be payable to all prisoners of that category depending on that Power, and shall be placed in their separate accounts, at the earliest opportunity, in accordance with the provisions of Article 64.").

relieve the Detaining Power of any obligation under the GPW.[345]

9.18.5 Remittances and Other Money Transfers. POWs shall be permitted to receive remittances of money addressed to them individually or collectively.[346]

Every POW shall have at his or her disposal the credit balance of his or her account as provided for in the Article 64 of the GPW, within the limits fixed by the Detaining Power, which shall make such payments as are requested.[347] Subject to financial or monetary restrictions that the Detaining Power regards as essential, POWs may also have payments made abroad.[348] In this case, payments addressed by POWs to dependents shall be given priority.[349]

9.18.5.1 *Payments Made in the POW's Own Country*. In any event, and subject to the consent of the Power on which they depend, POWs may have payments made in their own country, as follows:

- The Detaining Power shall send to the Power on which the POWs depend, through the Protecting Power, a notification giving all the necessary particulars concerning the POWs, the beneficiaries of the payments, and the amount of the sums to be paid, expressed in the Detaining Power's currency.[350]
- This notification shall be signed by the POWs and countersigned by the camp commander.[351]
- The Detaining Power shall debit the POWs' accounts by a corresponding amount; the sums thus debited shall be placed by it to the credit of the Power on which the POWs depend.[352]

---

[345] GPW art. 61 ("Such supplementary pay shall not relieve the Detaining Power of any obligation under this Convention.").

[346] GPW art. 63 ("Prisoners of war shall be permitted to receive remittances of money addressed to them individually or collectively.").

[347] GPW art. 63 ("Every prisoner of war shall have at his disposal the credit balance of his account as provided for in the following Article, within the limits fixed by the Detaining Power, which shall make such payments as are requested.").

[348] GPW art. 63 ("Subject to financial or monetary restrictions which the Detaining Power regards as essential, prisoners of war may also have payments made abroad.").

[349] GPW art. 63 ("In this case payments addressed by prisoners of war to dependents shall be given priority.").

[350] GPW art. 63 ("In any event, and subject to the consent of the Power on which they depend, prisoners may have payments made in their own country, as follows: the Detaining Power shall send to the aforesaid Power through the Protecting Power, a notification giving all the necessary particulars concerning the prisoners of war, the beneficiaries of the payments, and the amount of the sums to be paid, expressed in the Detaining Power's currency.").

[351] GPW art. 63 ("The said notification shall be signed by the prisoners and countersigned by the camp commander.").

[352] GPW art. 63 ("The Detaining Power shall debit the prisoners' account by a corresponding amount; the sums thus debited shall be placed by it to the credit of the Power on which the prisoners depend.").

To apply the foregoing provisions, the Detaining Power may usefully consult the Model Regulations in Annex V of the GPW.[353]

9.18.6 <u>POW Accounts</u>. The Detaining Power shall hold an account for each POW, showing at least the following:[354]

- the amounts due to the POW or received by him or her as advances of pay, as working pay or derived from any other source;
- the sums in the currency of the Detaining Power that were taken from him or her;
- the sums taken from the POW and converted at his or her request into the currency of that Power;
- the payments made to the POW in cash, or in any other similar form;
- the payments made on his or her behalf and request; and
- the sums transferred for payments made in a POW's own country under the third paragraph of Article 63 of the GPW.[355]

Every item entered in the account of a POW shall be countersigned or initialed by the POW, or by the POW Representative acting on his or her behalf.[356]

POWs shall at all times be afforded reasonable facilities for consulting and obtaining copies of their accounts, which may likewise be inspected by the representatives of the Protecting Powers at the time of visits to the camp.[357]

9.18.6.1 *<u>Cash in POW Hands Taken at the Time of Capture</u>*. Cash that was taken from POWs, in accordance with Article 18 of the GPW, at the time of their capture, and that is in the currency of the Detaining Power, shall be placed to their separate accounts, in accordance

---

[353] GPW art. 63 ("To apply the foregoing provisions, the Detaining Power may usefully consult the Model Regulations in Annex V of the present Convention.").

[354] GPW art. 64 ("The Detaining Power shall hold an account for each prisoner of war, showing at least the following: (1) The amounts due to the prisoner or received by him as advances of pay, as working pay or derived from any other source; the sums in the currency of the Detaining Power which were taken from him; the sums taken from him and converted at his request into the currency of the said Power. (2) The payments made to the prisoner in cash, or in any other similar form; the payments made on his behalf and at his request; the sums transferred under Article 63, third paragraph.").

[355] *Refer to* § 9.18.5.1 (Payments Made in the POW's Own Country).

[356] GPW art. 65 ("Every item entered in the account of a prisoner of war shall be countersigned or initialled by him, or by the prisoners' representative acting on his behalf.").

[357] GPW art. 65 ("Prisoners of war shall at all times be afforded reasonable facilities for consulting and obtaining copies of their accounts, which may likewise be inspected by the representatives of the Protecting Powers at the time of visits to the camp.").

with the Article 64 of the GPW.[358]

The amounts, in the currency of the Detaining Power, due to the conversion of sums in other currencies that are taken from the POWs at the same time, shall also be credited to their separate accounts.[359]

9.18.6.2 *Personal Account in the Event of Transfers to Another POW Camp*. When POWs are transferred from one camp to another, their personal accounts will follow them.[360] In case of transfer from one Detaining Power to another, the monies that are their property and are not in the currency of the Detaining Power will follow them.[361] POWs shall be given certificates for any other monies standing to the credit of their accounts.[362]

9.18.6.3 *Periodic Notification of the Amount of the Accounts of POWs*. The parties to the conflict concerned may agree to notify to each other at specific intervals, through the Protecting Power, the amount of the accounts of the POWs.[363]

9.18.6.4 *Statements of Credit Balance on Termination of Captivity*. On the termination of captivity, through the release of a POW or the POW's repatriation, the Detaining Power shall give him or her a statement, signed by an authorized officer of that Power, showing the credit balance then due to the POW.[364]

The Detaining Power shall also send through the Protecting Power to the government upon which the POWs depend lists giving all appropriate particulars of all POWs whose captivity has been terminated by repatriation, release, escape, death, or any other means, and showing the amount of their credit balances.[365] Such lists shall be certified on each sheet by an

---

[358] GPW art. 59 ("Cash which was taken from prisoners of war, in accordance with Article 18, at the time of their capture, and which is in the currency of the Detaining Power, shall be placed to their separate accounts, in accordance with the provisions of Article 64 of the present Section."). *Refer to* § 9.7.4.1 (Unexplained Possession of Large Sums of Money by POWs); § 9.18.1 (Detaining Power Regulations on the Maximum Amount of Money in POW Possession).

[359] GPW art. 59 ("The amounts, in the currency of the Detaining Power, due to the conversion of sums in other currencies that are taken from the prisoners of war at the same time, shall also be credited to their separate accounts.").

[360] GPW art. 65 ("When prisoners of war are transferred from one camp to another, their personal accounts will follow them.").

[361] GPW art. 65 ("In case of transfer from one Detaining Power to another, the monies which are their property and are not in the currency of the Detaining Power will follow them.").

[362] GPW art. 65 ("They shall be given certificates for any other monies standing to the credit of their accounts.").

[363] GPW art. 65 ("The Parties to the conflict concerned may agree to notify to each other at specific intervals through the Protecting Power, the amount of the accounts of the prisoners of war.").

[364] GPW art. 66 ("On the termination of captivity, through the release of a prisoner of war or his repatriation, the Detaining Power shall give him a statement, signed by an authorized officer of that Power, showing the credit balance then due to him.").

[365] GPW art. 66 ("The Detaining Power shall also send through the Protecting Power to the government upon which the prisoner of war depends, lists giving all appropriate particulars of all prisoners of war whose captivity has been terminated by repatriation, release, escape, death or any other means, and showing the amount of their credit balances.").

authorized representative of the Detaining Power.[366]

These rules may be varied by mutual agreement between any two parties to the conflict.[367]

9.18.6.5 *Responsibility for Credit Balance Due From the Detaining Power on the Termination of Captivity*. The Power on which the POWs depend shall be responsible for settling with each POW any credit balance due to him or her from the Detaining Power on the termination of the POW's captivity.[368]

9.18.7 Claims by POWs in Respect of Personal Loss. Any claim by a POW for compensation in respect of personal effects, monies, or valuables impounded by the Detaining Power under Article 18 of the GPW and not forthcoming on his or her repatriation, or in respect of loss alleged to be due to the fault of the Detaining Power or any of its servants, shall likewise be referred to the Power on which the POW depends.[369] Nevertheless, any such personal effects required for use by the POW while in captivity shall be replaced at the expense of the Detaining Power.[370]

The Detaining Power will, in all cases, provide the POW with a statement, signed by a responsible officer, showing all available information regarding the reasons why such effects, monies, or valuables have not been restored to him or her.[371] A copy of this statement will be forwarded to the Power on which he or she depends through the Central POW Information Agency provided for in Article 123 of the GPW.[372]

9.19 POW LABOR

The Detaining Power may use the labor of POWs who are physically fit, taking into account their age, sex, rank, and physical aptitude, and with a view particularly to maintaining

---

[366] GPW art. 66 ("Such lists shall be certified on each sheet by an authorized representative of the Detaining Power.").

[367] GPW art. 66 ("Any of the above provisions of this Article may be varied by mutual agreement between any two Parties to the conflict.").

[368] GPW art. 66 ("The Power on which the prisoner of war depends shall be responsible for settling with him any credit balance due to him from the Detaining Power on the termination of his captivity.").

[369] GPW art. 68 ("Any claim by a prisoner of war for compensation in respect of personal effects, monies or valuables impounded by the Detaining Power under Article 18 and not forthcoming on his repatriation, or in respect of loss alleged to be due to the fault of the Detaining Power or any of its servants, shall likewise be referred to the Power on which he depends.").

[370] GPW art. 68 ("Nevertheless, any such personal effects required for use by the prisoners of war whilst in captivity shall be replaced at the expense of the Detaining Power.").

[371] GPW art. 68 ("The Detaining Power will, in all cases, provide the prisoner of war with a statement, signed by a responsible officer, showing all available information regarding the reasons why such effects, monies or valuables have not been restored to him.").

[372] GPW art. 68 ("A copy of this statement will be forwarded to the Power on which he depends through the Central Prisoners of War Agency provided for in Article 123.").

them in a good state of physical and mental health.[373]

9.19.1 Determining the Appropriate Labor Assignment. In determining whether labor should be compelled, as well as the appropriate labor assignment for a POW, the POW's age, gender, rank, and physical aptitude should be considered.[374]

9.19.1.1 *Labor Assignment – Non-Commissioned Officers*. Noncommissioned officers shall only be required to do supervisory work.[375] Noncommissioned officers who are not required to do supervisory work may ask for other suitable work, which shall, so far as possible, be found for them.[376]

9.19.1.2 *Labor Assignment – Officers and Persons of Equivalent Status*. If officers or persons of equivalent status ask for suitable work, it shall be found for them, so far as possible, but they may in no circumstances be compelled to work.[377]

9.19.1.3 *Labor Assignment – POWs Who May Not Be Compelled to Do Other Work*. Retained personnel and persons treated like retained personnel (*e.g.*, POWs trained as medical personnel who are directed to provide medical care for fellow POWs), however, may not be compelled to carry out any work other than that concerned with their medical or religious duties.[378]

POW Representatives and their assistants also shall not be required to perform any other work, if the accomplishment of their duties is thereby made more difficult.[379]

9.19.2 Types of Labor Assignments.

9.19.2.1 *Unhealthy or Dangerous Labor*. Unless the POW is a volunteer, he or

---

[373] GPW art. 49 ("The Detaining Power may utilize the labour of prisoners of war who are physically fit, taking into account their age, sex, rank and physical aptitude, and with a view particularly to maintaining them in a good state of physical and mental health.").

[374] LEVIE, POWS 218-19 ("[T]he Detaining Power must take into account the age, sex, and physical aptitude of each prisoner of war as an individual. It may be assumed that these criteria are to be considered not only in determining whether a prisoner of war should be compelled to work, but also in determining the type of work to which the particular prisoner of war should be assigned.").

[375] GPW art. 49 ("Non-commissioned officers who are prisoners of war shall only be required to do supervisory work.").

[376] GPW art. 49 ("Those not so required may ask for other suitable work which shall, so far as possible, be found for them.").

[377] GPW art. 49 ("If officers or persons of equivalent status ask for suitable work, it shall be found for them, so far as possible, but they may in no circumstances be compelled to work.").

[378] *Refer to* § 7.9.5.6 (No Other Compulsory Duties); § 4.5.2.2 (Members Trained as Medical Personnel, but Not Attached to the Medical Service); § 4.5.2.3 (Members Who Are Ministers of Religion Without Having Officiated as Chaplains to Their Own Forces).

[379] *Refer to* § 9.24.4.1 (Limitations on Other Work Assignments); § 9.24.4.2 (Assistants for the POW Representatives).

she may not be employed on labor that is of an unhealthy or dangerous nature.[380]

For example, the removal of landmines or similar devices is considered dangerous labor.[381] "Similar devices" may be understood to include booby-traps and other devices that are similar to landmines.[382]

When employing POWs on dangerous or unhealthy activities, the Protecting Power or the ICRC should assist in verifying the voluntariness of the employment, and the suitability of the POW for such hazardous activities (*e.g.*, any special skills or training in relation to the hazards) should be considered.[383]

9.19.2.2 Prohibited Labor Assignments. No POW shall be assigned to labor that would be looked upon as humiliating for a member of the Detaining Power's own forces.[384]

9.19.2.3 Labor Assignments That May Be Compelled. POWs, like other enemy nationals, may not be compelled to take part in operations of war directed against their own country.[385] POWs may be compelled to do only such work as is included in the following classes:

- POW camp administration, installation, and maintenance;
- agriculture;
- industries connected with the production or the extraction of raw materials, and manufacturing industries, with the exception of metallurgical, machinery, and chemical industries;
- public works and building operations having no military character or purpose;
- transport and handling of stores not of a military character or purpose;
- commercial businesses, including arts and crafts;
- domestic services; and

---

380 GPW art. 52 ("Unless he be a volunteer, no prisoner of war may be employed on labour which is of an unhealthy or dangerous nature.").

381 GPW art. 52 ("The removal of mines or similar devices shall be considered as dangerous labour.").

382 *Refer to* § 6.12.2 (Definition of Booby-Trap); § 6.12.3 (Definition of "Other Devices" Similar to Mines).

383 *For example*, 2004 UK MANUAL ¶8.85 footnote 251 ("Argentinian PW who were specialist engineers were used in mine-clearance operations at the end of the Falklands conflict, but all were confirmed by the ICRC to be volunteers.").

384 GPW art. 52 ("No prisoner of war shall be assigned to labour which would be looked upon as humiliating for a member of the Detaining Power's own forces.").

385 *Refer to* § 5.27 (Prohibition Against Compelling Enemy Nationals to Take Part in the Operations of War Directed Against Their Own Country).

- public utilities having no military character or purpose.[386]

Should the above provisions be infringed, POWs shall be allowed to exercise their right of complaint, in conformity with Article 78 of the GPW.[387]

9.19.3 Suitable Work Conditions. POWs must be granted suitable working conditions, especially as regards accommodation, food, clothing, and equipment.[388] For example, POWs must be given additional rations or appropriate clothing, as necessary, for their work.[389]

POWs' working conditions shall not be inferior to those enjoyed by nationals of the Detaining Power employed in similar work.[390] Account shall also be taken of climatic conditions.[391]

9.19.3.1 *Application of National Legislation for the Protection of Labor and Regulations for Worker Safety*. The Detaining Power, in utilizing the labor of POWs, shall ensure that in areas in which such POWs are employed, the national legislation concerning the protection of labor, and, more particularly, the regulations for the safety of workers, are duly applied.[392] For example, labor conditions for POWs working in the United States would be determined by U.S. Federal labor and safety laws.

Conditions of labor shall in no case be rendered more arduous by disciplinary measures.[393] For example, the Detaining Power may not lower safety standards or disregard the requirements for protective equipment as a punishment for misbehavior.[394]

---

[386] GPW art. 50 ("Besides work connected with camp administration, installation or maintenance, prisoners of war may be compelled to do only such work as is included in the following classes: (a) agriculture; (b) industries connected with the production or the extraction of raw materials, and manufacturing industries, with the exception of metallurgical, machinery and chemical industries; public works and building operations which have no military character or purpose; (c) transport and handling of stores which are not military in character or purpose; (d) commercial business, and arts and crafts; (e) domestic service; (f) public utility services having no military character or purpose.").

[387] GPW art. 50 ("Should the above provisions be infringed, prisoners of war shall be allowed to exercise their right of complaint, in conformity with Article 78."). *Refer to* § 9.23 (POW Requests, Complaints).

[388] GPW art. 51 (providing that "[p]risoners of war must be granted suitable working conditions, especially as regards accommodation, food, clothing and equipment;").

[389] *Refer to* § 9.13.1.2 (Additional Food for Certain Groups); § 9.13.4.2 (Appropriate Clothing for Work).

[390] GPW art. 51 (providing that "such conditions shall not be inferior to those enjoyed by nationals of the Detaining Power employed in similar work;").

[391] GPW art. 51 ("[A]ccount shall also be taken of climatic conditions.").

[392] GPW art. 51 ("The Detaining Power, in utilizing the labour of prisoners of war, shall ensure that in areas in which such prisoners are employed, the national legislation concerning the protection of labour, and, more particularly, the regulations for the safety of workers, are duly applied.").

[393] GPW art. 51 ("Conditions of labour shall in no case be rendered more arduous by disciplinary measures.").

[394] *See also* LEVIE, POWS 244 ("Thus, a Detaining Power may not lower safety standards, disregard requirements for protective equipment, lengthen working hours, withhold required extra rations, etc., as punishment for misbehavior. On the other hand, 'fatigue details' of not more than two hours a day, or a monetary fine, or the withdrawal of extra privileges, all of which are authorized as disciplinary punishment by Article 89, undoubtedly

9.19.3.2 _Training and Means of Protection_. POWs shall receive training and be provided with the means of protection suitable to the work they will have to do and similar to those accorded to the nationals of the Detaining Power.[395] Subject to the provisions of Article 52 of the GPW, POWs may be submitted to the normal risks run by these civilian workers.[396]

9.19.3.3 _Limits on the Duration of Labor_. The duration of the daily labor of POWs, including any travel time, shall not be excessive, and must in no case exceed that permitted for civilian workers in the district, who are nationals of the Detaining Power and employed on the same work.[397]

POWs must be allowed, in the middle of the day's work, a rest of not less than one hour.[398] This rest will be the same as that to which workers of the Detaining Power are entitled, if the latter is of longer duration.[399] POWs shall be allowed, in addition, a rest of 24 consecutive hours every week, preferably on Sunday or the day of rest in their country of origin.[400] Furthermore, every POW who has worked for one year shall be granted a rest of eight consecutive days, during which his or her working pay shall be paid to him or her.[401]

If methods of labor, such as piece work, are employed, the length of the working period shall not be rendered excessive thereby.[402] Piece work refers to the practice of assigning and compensating for tasks as opposed to compensating based on the amount of time worked.[403]

---

could be imposed, as they obviously do not fall within the ambit of the prohibition; and the extra rations to which prisoners of war are entitled under Article 26, when they are engaged in heavy manual labor, could undoubtedly be withheld from a prisoner of war who refuses to work, inasmuch as he would no longer meet the requirement for entitlement to such extra rations.").

[395] GPW art. 51 ("Prisoners of war shall receive training and be provided with the means of protection suitable to the work they will have to do and similar to those accorded to the nationals of the Detaining Power.").

[396] GPW art. 51 ("Subject to the provisions of Article 52, prisoners may be submitted to the normal risks run by these civilian workers."). _See also_ GPW art. 52 ("Unless he be a volunteer, no prisoner of war may be employed on labour which is of an unhealthy or dangerous nature. No prisoner of war shall be assigned to labour which would be looked upon as humiliating for a member of the Detaining Power's own forces. The removal of mines or similar devices shall be considered as dangerous labour."). _Refer to_ § 9.19.2.1 (Unhealthy or Dangerous Labor).

[397] GPW art. 53 ("The duration of the daily labour of prisoners of war, including the time of the journey to and fro, shall not be excessive, and must in no case exceed that permitted for civilian workers in the district, who are nationals of the Detaining Power and employed on the same work.").

[398] GPW art. 53 ("Prisoners of war must be allowed, in the middle of the day's work, a rest of not less than one hour.").

[399] GPW art. 53 ("This rest will be the same as that to which workers of the Detaining Power are entitled, if the latter is of longer duration.").

[400] GPW art. 53 ("They shall be allowed in addition a rest of twenty-four consecutive hours every week, preferably on Sunday or the day of rest in their country of origin.").

[401] GPW art. 53 ("Furthermore, every prisoner who has worked for one year shall be granted a rest of eight consecutive days, during which his working pay shall be paid him.").

[402] GPW art. 53 ("If methods of labour such as piece work are employed, the length of the working period shall not be rendered excessive thereby.").

[403] DEPARTMENT OF THE ARMY PAMPHLET 20-213, _History of Prisoner Of War Utilization By The United States Army, 1776-1945_, 120 (Jun. 24, 1955) ("On 26 April 1944, the Secretary of War approved an incentive pay plan for

Thus, the limits on the number of hours of daily work cannot be circumvented by assigning work on the basis of tasks completed as opposed to requiring POWs to work a certain number of hours.[404]

9.19.4 Working Pay. The working pay due to POWs shall be fixed in accordance with the provisions of Article 62 of the GPW.[405]

POWs shall be paid a fair working rate of pay by the detaining authorities directly.[406] The rate shall be fixed by these authorities, but shall at no time be less than one-fourth of one Swiss franc for a full working day.[407] The Detaining Power shall inform POWs, as well as the Power on which they depend, through the intermediary of the Protecting Power, of the rate of daily working pay that it has fixed.[408]

Working pay shall likewise be paid by the detaining authorities to POWs permanently detailed to duties, or to a skilled or semi-skilled occupation, in connection with the administration, installation, or maintenance of camps, and to the POWs who are required to carry out spiritual or medical duties on behalf of their comrades.[409]

Working pay of POW Representatives, their advisers, if any, or assistants, also is provided for in the GPW.[410]

9.19.5 Medical Fitness to Work. The fitness of POWs for work shall be periodically verified by medical examinations, at least once a month.[411] The examinations shall have

---

piecework which compensated the PW's according to the number of units completed, up to a maximum of $1.20 per day. The objectives of this plan were to reward hard workers; to penalize laggards; and to encourage a greater degree of teamwork among PW laborers.").

404 LEVIE, POWS 248 ("With respect to hours of daily work, it must be noted, too, that the limitations contained in the Article cannot be circumvented by the adoption of piecework, or some other task system, in lieu of a stated number of working hours, the third paragraph of Article 53 of the Convention specifically prohibiting the rendering of the length of the working day excessive by the use of this method.").

405 GPW art. 54 ("The working pay due to prisoners of war shall be fixed in accordance with the provisions of Article 62 of the present Convention.").

406 GPW art. 62 ("Prisoners of war shall be paid a fair working rate of pay by the detaining authorities direct.").

407 GPW art. 62 ("The rate shall be fixed by the said authorities, but shall at no time be less than one-fourth of one Swiss franc for a full working day.").

408 GPW art. 62 ("The Detaining Power shall inform prisoners of war, as well as the Power on which they depend, through the intermediary of the Protecting Power, of the rate of daily working pay that it has fixed.").

409 GPW art. 62 ("Working pay shall likewise be paid by the detaining authorities to prisoners of war permanently detailed to duties or to a skilled or semi-skilled occupation in connection with the administration, installation or maintenance of camps, and to the prisoners who are required to carry out spiritual or medical duties on behalf of their comrades.").

410 *Refer to* § 9.24.4.5 (Working Pay of POW Representatives, Advisers, and Assistants).

411 GPW art. 55 ("The fitness of prisoners of war for work shall be periodically verified by medical examinations at least once a month.").

particular regard to the nature of the work that the POWs are required to do.[412]

If any POW considers himself or herself incapable of working, he or she shall be permitted to appear before the medical authorities of the camp.[413] Physicians or surgeons may recommend that the POWs who are, in their opinion, unfit for work, be exempted therefrom.[414]

9.19.6 Accidents or Disease in Connection With Work. POWs who sustain accidents in connection with work, or who contract a disease in the course or in consequence of their work, shall receive all the care their condition may require.[415] The Detaining Power shall furthermore deliver to such POWs a medical certificate enabling them to submit their claims to the Power on which they depend, and shall send a duplicate to the Central POW Information Agency provided for in Article 123 of the GPW.[416]

In certain cases, POWs who meet with accidents in connection with work would receive the benefit of the provisions of the GPW as regards repatriation or accommodation in a neutral country.[417]

9.19.6.1 *Claims for Compensation From Injury or Other Disability Arising Out of Work*. Any claim by a POW for compensation in respect of any injury or other disability arising out of work shall be referred to the Power on which he or she depends, through the Protecting Power.[418] In accordance with Article 54 of the GPW, the Detaining Power will, in all cases, provide the POW concerned with a statement showing the nature of the injury or disability, the circumstances in which it arose, and the particulars of medical or hospital treatment given for it.[419] This statement will be signed by a responsible officer of the Detaining Power and the medical particulars certified by a medical officer.[420]

---

[412] GPW art. 55 ("The examinations shall have particular regard to the nature of the work which prisoners of war are required to do.").

[413] GPW art. 55 ("If any prisoner of war considers himself incapable of working, he shall be permitted to appear before the medical authorities of his camp.").

[414] GPW art. 55 ("Physicians or surgeons may recommend that the prisoners who are, in their opinion, unfit for work, be exempted therefrom.").

[415] GPW art. 54 ("Prisoners of war who sustain accidents in connection with work, or who contract a disease in the course, or in consequence of their work, shall receive all the care their condition may require.").

[416] GPW art. 54 ("The Detaining Power shall furthermore deliver to such prisoners of war a medical certificate enabling them to submit their claims to the Power on which they depend, and shall send a duplicate to the Central Prisoners of War Agency provided for in Article 123.").

[417] *Refer to* § 9.36 (Direct Repatriation and Accommodation in Neutral Countries During Hostilities).

[418] GPW art. 68 ("Any claim by a prisoner of war for compensation in respect of any injury or other disability arising out of work shall be referred to the Power on which he depends, through the Protecting Power.").

[419] GPW art. 68 ("In accordance with Article 54, the Detaining Power will, in all cases, provide the prisoner of war concerned with a statement showing the nature of the injury or disability, the circumstances in which it arose and particulars of medical or hospital treatment given for it.").

[420] GPW art. 68 ("This statement will be signed by a responsible officer of the Detaining Power and the medical particulars certified by a medical officer.").

9.19.7 Labor Detachments. The organization and administration of labor detachments shall be similar to those of POW camps.[421]

Every labor detachment shall remain under the control of, and administratively part of, a POW camp.[422] The military authorities and the commander of the POW camp shall be responsible, under the direction of their government, for the observance of the provisions of the GPW in labor detachments that are dependent upon the POW camp.[423]

The camp commander shall keep an up-to-date record of the labor detachments dependent on the camp, and shall communicate it to the delegates of the Protecting Power, of the ICRC, or of other agencies giving relief to POWs, who may visit the camp.[424]

9.19.8 POWs Working for Private Persons. The treatment of POWs who work for private persons, even if the latter are responsible for guarding and protecting them, shall not be inferior to that which is provided for by the GPW.[425] The Detaining Power, the military authorities, and the commander of the camp to which such POWs belong shall be entirely responsible for the maintenance, care, treatment, and payment of the working pay of such POWs.[426]

Such POWs shall have the right to remain in communication with the POW Representatives in the camps on which they depend.[427]

9.20 POW Correspondence and Relief Shipments

POWs may send and receive mail and relief shipments, subject to security requirements. In addition, POWs benefit from certain postage exemptions.

9.20.1 Capture, Health, or Transfer Card. Immediately upon capture, or not more than one week after arrival at a camp, even if it is a transit camp, likewise in case of sickness or

[421] GPW art. 56 ("The organization and administration of labour detachments shall be similar to those of prisoner of war camps.").

[422] GPW art. 56 ("Every labour detachment shall remain under the control of and administratively part of a prisoner of war camp.").

[423] GPW art. 56 ("The military authorities and the commander of the said camp shall be responsible, under the direction of their government, for the observance of the provisions of the present Convention in labour detachments.").

[424] GPW art. 56 ("The camp commander shall keep an up-to-date record of the labour detachments dependent on his camp, and shall communicate it to the delegates of the Protecting Power, of the International Committee of the Red Cross, or of other agencies giving relief to prisoners of war, who may visit the camp.").

[425] GPW art. 57 ("The treatment of prisoners of war who work for private persons, even if the latter are responsible for guarding and protecting them, shall not be inferior to that which is provided for by the present Convention.").

[426] GPW art. 57 ("The Detaining Power, the military authorities and the commander of the camp to which such prisoners belong shall be entirely responsible for the maintenance, care, treatment, and payment of the working pay of such prisoners of war.").

[427] GPW art. 57 ("Such prisoners of war shall have the right to remain in communication with the prisoners' representatives in the camps on which they depend.").

transfer to a hospital or to another camp, every POW shall be enabled to write directly to his or her family, on the one hand, and to the Central POW Information Agency provided for in Article 123 of the GPW, on the other hand, a card similar, if possible, to the model annexed to the GPW (GPW Annex IV B), informing his or her relatives of his or her capture, address, and state of health.[428]

These cards shall be forwarded as rapidly as possible and may not be delayed in any manner.[429]

9.20.2 POW Correspondence Rights and Quota. POWs shall be allowed to send and receive letters and cards.[430]

9.20.2.1 *POW Correspondence Quota*. If the Detaining Power deems it necessary to limit the number of letters and cards sent by each POW, this number shall not be less than two letters and four cards monthly, exclusive of the capture cards provided for in Article 70 of the GPW (GPW Annex IV B), and conforming as closely as possible to the models annexed to the GPW (GPW Annex IV C).[431] In addition, the following correspondence also does not count toward this quota:

- formal requests and complaints;[432]
- correspondence between a duly appointed POW Representative at a principal camp and a POW Representative at a labor camp;[433]
- authorized correspondence by chaplains;[434] and
- correspondence by the senior medical officer in a camp with the competent authorities of the camp regarding the duties of retained medical personnel.[435]

Further limitations on POW correspondence may be imposed only if the Protecting

---

[428] GPW art. 70 ("Immediately upon capture, or not more than one week after arrival at a camp, even if it is a transit camp, likewise in case of sickness or transfer to hospital or to another camp, every prisoner of war shall be enabled to write direct to his family, on the one hand, and to the Central Prisoners of War Agency provided for in Article 123, on the other hand, a card similar, if possible, to the model annexed to the present Convention, informing his relatives of his capture, address and state of health.").

[429] GPW art. 70 ("The said cards shall be forwarded as rapidly as possible and may not be delayed in any manner.").

[430] GPW art. 71 ("Prisoners of war shall be allowed to send and receive letters and cards.").

[431] GPW art. 71 ("If the Detaining Power deems it necessary to limit the number of letters and cards sent by each prisoner of war, the said number shall not be less than two letters and four cards monthly, exclusive of the capture cards provided for in Article 70, and conforming as closely as possible to the models annexed to the present Convention.").

[432] *Refer to* § 9.23.2 (Communication of Requests and Complaints).

[433] *Refer to* § 9.24.4.6 (Facilities for Communication).

[434] *Refer to* § 7.9.5.4 (Correspondence by Chaplains).

[435] *Refer to* § 7.9.5.7 (Senior Medical Officer in the Camp).

Power is satisfied that it would be in the interests of the POWs concerned to do so owing to difficulties of translation caused by the Detaining Power's inability to find sufficient qualified linguists to carry out the necessary censorship.[436] If limitations must be placed on the correspondence addressed to POWs, they may be ordered only by the Power on which the POWs depend, possibly at the request of the Detaining Power.[437] Such letters and cards must be conveyed by the most rapid method at the disposal of the Detaining Power.[438]

9.20.2.2 *No Delay in Correspondence for Disciplinary Reasons*. Cards and letters may not be delayed or retained for disciplinary reasons.[439]

9.20.2.3 *More Rapid Means of Correspondence in Appropriate Cases*. POWs who have been without news for a long period, or who are unable to receive news from their next of kin or to give them news by the ordinary postal route, as well as those who are at a great distance from their homes, shall be permitted to send telegrams, the fees being charged against the POWs' accounts with the Detaining Power or paid in the currency at their disposal.[440] They shall likewise benefit from this measure in cases of urgency.[441]

More modern means of communication, such as email, should be considered for POW correspondence, as appropriate.[442]

9.20.2.4 *Language of POW Correspondence*. As a general rule, the correspondence of POWs shall be written in their native language.[443] The parties to the conflict may allow correspondence in other languages.[444]

9.20.2.5 *Handling of Sacks of POW Mail*. Sacks containing POW mail must be securely sealed and labeled so as clearly to indicate their contents, and must be addressed to

---

[436] GPW art. 71 ("Further limitations may be imposed only if the Protecting Power is satisfied that it would be in the interests of the prisoners of war concerned to do so owing to difficulties of translation caused by the Detaining Power's inability to find sufficient qualified linguists to carry out the necessary censorship.").

[437] GPW art. 71 ("If limitations must be placed on the correspondance addressed to prisoners of war, they may be ordered only by the Power on which the prisoners depend, possibly at the request of the Detaining Power.").

[438] GPW art. 71 ("Such letters and cards must be conveyed by the most rapid method at the disposal of the Detaining Power; they may not be delayed or retained for disciplinary reasons.").

[439] GPW art. 71 ("Such letters and cards must be conveyed by the most rapid method at the disposal of the Detaining Power; they may not be delayed or retained for disciplinary reasons.").

[440] GPW art. 71 ("Prisoners of war who have been without news for a long period, or who are unable to receive news from their next of kin or to give them news by the ordinary postal route, as well as those who are at a great distance from their homes, shall be permitted to send telegrams, the fees being charged against the prisoners of war's accounts with the Detaining Power or paid in the currency at their disposal.").

[441] GPW art. 71 ("They shall likewise benefit by this measure in cases of urgency.").

[442] *Refer to* § 8.10.3 (Communication With Family).

[443] GPW art. 71 ("As a general rule, the correspondence of prisoners of war shall be written in their native language.").

[444] GPW art. 71 ("The Parties to the conflict may allow correspondence in other languages.").

"offices of destination."[445]

9.20.3 Receipt of Individual and Collective Relief Shipments for POWs. POWs shall be allowed to receive by post, or by any other means, individual parcels or collective shipments containing, in particular, foodstuffs, clothing, medical supplies, and articles of a religious, educational, or recreational character, which may meet their needs, including books, devotional articles, scientific equipment, examination papers, musical instruments, sports outfits, and materials allowing POWs to pursue their studies or their cultural activities.[446] Such shipments shall in no way free the Detaining Power from the obligations imposed upon it by virtue of the GPW.[447]

The only limits that may be placed on these shipments shall be those proposed by the Protecting Power in the interest of the POWs themselves, or by the ICRC or any other organization giving assistance to the POWs, in respect of their own shipments only, on account of exceptional strain on transport or communications.[448]

9.20.3.1 *Separation of Books From Other Relief Supplies*. Parcels of clothing and foodstuffs may not include books.[449] Books should be separated because the time required for censorship of books would likely delay the distribution of other relief supplies.[450]

9.20.3.2 *Medical Supplies in Relief Shipments*. Medical supplies shall, as a rule, be sent in collective parcels.[451] This rule is meant to ensure that medical supplies can be administered by the camp doctors and not by the POWs themselves without medical supervision.[452] This rule, however, would not prohibit, in exceptional cases, for example, special

---

[445] GPW art. 71 ("Sacks containing prisoner of war mail must be securely sealed and labelled so as clearly to indicate their contents, and must be addressed to offices of destination.").

[446] GPW art. 72 ("Prisoners of war shall be allowed to receive by post or by any other means individual parcels or collective shipments containing, in particular, foodstuffs, clothing, medical supplies and articles of a religious, educational or recreational character which may meet their needs, including books, devotional articles, scientific equipment, examination papers, musical instruments, sports outfits and materials allowing prisoners of war to pursue their studies or their cultural activities.").

[447] GPW art. 72 ("Such shipments shall in no way free the Detaining Power from the obligations imposed upon it by virtue of the present Convention.").

[448] GPW art. 72 ("The only limits which may be placed on these shipments shall be those proposed by the Protecting Power in the interest of the prisoners themselves, or by the International Committee of the Red Cross or any other organization giving assistance to the prisoners, in respect of their own shipments only, on account of exceptional strain on transport or communications.").

[449] GPW art. 72 ("Books may not be included in parcels of clothing and foodstuffs.").

[450] GPW COMMENTARY 377 ("As in the first paragraph, it is specified here [in the second paragraph of Article 76 of the GPW] that delivery must not be delayed under the pretext of difficulties of censorship; the conditions are usually different, however. Except in the case of books, examination requires no linguistic ability and all delay can therefore be avoided. This is particularly important in the case of parcels containing perishable goods."). *Compare* § 10.23.3.1 (Separation of Books From Other Relief Supplies).

[451] GPW art. 72 ("Medical supplies shall, as a rule, be sent in collective parcels.").

[452] *See* GPW COMMENTARY 356 ("From the beginning of the Second World War, parcels of medical supplies addressed by name were always sent to the chief medical officer of a camp or hospital or, if there was none, to a head nurse, welfare officer or a representative of the local Red Cross. The question is now settled by paragraph 4 of

medication being sent from family members to a POW.[453]

9.20.3.3 *Special Agreements Concerning Relief Shipments*. The conditions for the sending of individual parcels and collective shipments shall, if necessary, be the subject of special agreements between the Powers concerned, which may in no case delay the receipt by the POWs of relief supplies.[454]

9.20.3.4 *Collective Relief for POWs*. In the absence of special agreements between the Powers concerned on the conditions for the receipt and distribution of collective relief shipments, the rules and regulations concerning collective relief that are annexed to the GPW shall be applied (GPW Annex III).[455]

The special agreements referred to above shall in no case restrict the right of POW Representatives to take possession of collective relief shipments intended for POWs, to proceed to their distribution, or to dispose of them in the interest of the POWs.[456] Nor shall such agreements restrict the right of representatives of the Protecting Power, the ICRC, or any other organization giving assistance to POWs and responsible for the forwarding of collective shipments, to supervise their distribution to the recipients.[457]

9.20.4 Exemptions From Postal and Shipping Charges. Relief shipments for POWs and mail sent by POWs or to them benefit from certain exemptions under international law.

9.20.4.1 *Exemption From Dues for Relief Shipments*. All relief shipments for POWs shall be exempt from import, customs, or other dues.[458]

9.20.4.2 *GPW Postal Dues Exemption*. Under the GPW, correspondence, relief shipments, and authorized remittances of money addressed to POWs or sent by them through the

---

the present Article, which states that, as a rule, medical supplies are to be sent in collective parcels. This solution was adopted in the interest of the prisoners of war, who should not have access to medical supplies except under medical supervision.").

[453] *Compare* § 10.23.3.2 (Medical Supplies in Relief Shipments).

[454] GPW art. 72 ("The conditions for the sending of individual parcels and collective relief shall, if necessary, be the subject of special agreements between the Powers concerned, which may in no case delay the receipt by the prisoners of relief supplies.").

[455] GPW art. 73 ("In the absence of special agreements between the Powers concerned on the conditions for the receipt and distribution of collective relief shipments, the rules and regulations concerning collective shipments, which are annexed to the present Convention, shall be applied.").

[456] GPW art. 73 ("The special agreements referred to above shall in no case restrict the right of prisoners' representatives to take possession of collective relief shipments intended for prisoners of war, to proceed to their distribution or to dispose of them in the interest of the prisoners.").

[457] GPW art. 73 ("Nor shall such agreements restrict the right of representatives of the Protecting Power, the International Committee of the Red Cross or any other organization giving assistance to prisoners of war and responsible for the forwarding of collective shipments, to supervise their distribution to the recipients.").

[458] GPW art. 74 ("All relief shipments for prisoners of war shall be exempt from import, customs and other dues."). *See also* HAGUE IV REG. art. 16 ("Presents and relief in kind for prisoners of war shall be admitted free of all import or other duties, as well as of payments for carriage by the State railways.").

post office, either directly or through the National POW Information Bureau provided for in Article 122 of the GPW and the Central POW Information Agency provided for in Article 123 of the GPW, shall be exempt from any postal dues, both in the countries of origin and destination, and in intermediate countries.[459]

9.20.4.3 Exemption From Postal Charges Under the Universal Postal Convention. Under the Universal Postal Convention, with the exception of air surcharges for airmail, letter-post items, postal parcels, and monetary articles addressed to or sent by POWs, either directly or through the National POW Information Bureau and the Central POW Information Agency, shall be exempt from all postal charges.[460] This exemption also applies to belligerents captured and interned in neutral countries.[461]

Parcels shall be admitted free of postage up to a weight of 5 kg.[462] The weight limit shall be increased to 10 kg in the case of parcels the contents of which cannot be split up and of parcels addressed to a camp or the POW Representatives there for distribution to the POWs.[463]

Items exempt from postal charges and POW parcels shall bear "Service des prisonniers

---

[459] GPW art. 74 ("Correspondence, relief shipments and authorized remittances of money addressed to prisoners of war or despatched by them through the post office, either direct or through the Information Bureaux provided for in Article 122 and the Central Prisoners of War Agency provided for in Article 123, shall be exempt from any postal dues, both in the countries of origin and destination, and in intermediate countries.").

[460] Universal Postal Convention, art. 17(1), Dec. 14, 1989, 1687 UNTS 241, 251-52 ("Subject to article 21, paragraph 1, letter-post items, postal parcels and monetary articles addressed to or sent by prisoners of war, either direct or through the Information Bureaux and the Central Prisoner-of-War Information Agency provided for in articles 122 and 123 respectively of the Geneva Convention of 12 August 1949 relative to the treatment of prisoners of war, shall be exempt from all postal charges."). *Consider* Universal Postal Convention, art. 7(2.1), Oct. 11, 2012, *reprinted in* INTERNATIONAL BUREAU OF THE UNIVERSAL POSTAL UNION, LETTER POST MANUAL, page C.8 (Berne 2013, Update 2 – Jan. 2015) ("Letter-post items, postal parcels and postal payment services items addressed to or sent by prisoners of war, either direct or through the offices mentioned in the Regulations of the Convention and of the Postal Payment Services Agreement, shall be exempt from all postal charges, with the exception of air surcharges.").

[461] Universal Postal Convention, art. 17, Dec. 14, 1989, 1687 UNTS 241, 251-52 ("Belligerents apprehended and interned in a neutral country shall be classed with prisoners of war proper so far as the application of the foregoing provisions is concerned."). *Consider* Universal Postal Convention, art. 7(2.1), Oct. 11, 2012, *reprinted in* INTERNATIONAL BUREAU OF THE UNIVERSAL POSTAL UNION, LETTER POST MANUAL, page C.8 (Berne 2013, Update 2 – Jan. 2015) (same).

[462] Universal Postal Convention, art. 17(4), Dec. 14, 1989, 1687 UNTS 241, 252 ("Parcels shall be admitted free of postage up to a weight of 5 kg."). *Consider* Universal Postal Convention, art. 7(2.4), Oct. 11, 2012, *reprinted in* INTERNATIONAL BUREAU OF THE UNIVERSAL POSTAL UNION, LETTER POST MANUAL, page C.8 (Berne 2013, Update 2 – Jan. 2015) ("Parcels shall be admitted free of postage up to a weight of 5 kilogrammes.").

[463] Universal Postal Convention, art. 17(4), Dec. 14, 1989, 1687 UNTS 241, 252 ("The weight limit shall be increased to 10 kg in the case of parcels the contents of which cannot be split up and of parcels addressed to a camp or the prisoners' representatives there ('*hommes de confiance*') for distribution to the prisoners."). *Consider* Universal Postal Convention, art. 7(2.4), Oct. 11, 2012, *reprinted in* INTERNATIONAL BUREAU OF THE UNIVERSAL POSTAL UNION, LETTER POST MANUAL, page C.8 (Berne 2013, Update 2 – Jan. 2015) ("The weight limit shall be increased to 10 kilogrammes in the case of parcels the contents of which cannot be split up and of parcels addressed to a camp or the prisoners' representatives there ('hommes de confiance') for distribution to the prisoners.").

de guerre" ("Prisoner-of-war Service) and a translation in another language, if appropriate.[464]

Postal administrations shall not be liable for the loss of, theft from, or damage to parcels in the case of POW parcels.[465]

9.20.4.4 *Costs of Transporting Relief Shipments Outside the Post Office*. If relief shipments intended for POWs cannot be sent through the post office by reason of weight or for any other cause, the cost of transportation shall be borne by the Detaining Power in all the territories under its control.[466] The other Parties to the GPW shall bear the cost of transport in their respective territories.[467]

In the absence of special agreements between the Parties concerned, the costs connected with transport of such shipments, other than costs covered by the above exemption, shall be charged to the senders.[468]

9.20.4.5 *Rates Charged for Telegrams*. The Parties to the GPW shall endeavor to reduce, so far as possible, the rates charged for telegrams sent by POWs, or addressed to them.[469]

9.20.5 Special Means of Transport of Shipments to POWs. Should military operations prevent the Powers concerned from fulfilling their obligation to ensure the transport of the shipments referred to in Articles 70, 71, 72, and 77 of the GPW, the Protecting Powers concerned, the ICRC, or any other organization duly approved by the parties to the conflict may undertake to ensure the conveyance of such shipments by suitable means (railway wagons, motor vehicles, vessels, or aircraft, etc.).[470] For this purpose, the Parties to the GPW shall endeavor to

---

[464] *Consider* Letter Post Regulations, Article RL 112 to Article 7 of the Universal Postal Convention of Oct. 11, 2012, *reprinted in* INTERNATIONAL BUREAU OF THE UNIVERSAL POSTAL UNION, LETTER POST MANUAL, page C.11 (2015) ("Items exempt from postal charges shall bear, on the address side in the top right-hand corner, the following indications, which may be followed by a translation: 'Service des prisonniers de guerre' (Prisoners-of-war service) or 'Servicedes internés civils' (Civilian internees service) for the items mentioned in article 7.2 of the Convention and article RL 111 and the forms relating to them;"); Parcel Post Regulations, Article RC 112(2), *reprinted in* INTERNATIONAL BUREAU OF THE UNIVERSAL POSTAL UNION, PARCEL POST MANUAL, page D.10 (2015) ("Every prisoner-of-war and civilian internee parcel and its dispatch note shall bear, the former beside the address, one of the indications 'Service des prisonniers de guerre' (Prisoner-of-war Service) or 'Service des internés civils' (Civilian Internees Service); these indications may be followed by a translation in another language.").

[465] Postal Parcels Agreement, art. 41(2)(f), Dec. 14, 1989, 1687 UNTS 346, 369 ("Postal administrations shall not be liable for the loss of, theft from or damage to parcels in the case of prisoner-or-war or civilian internee parcels.").

[466] GPW art. 74 ("If relief shipments intended for prisoners of war cannot be sent through the post office by reason of weight or for any other cause, the cost of transportation shall be borne by the Detaining Power in all the territories under its control.").

[467] GPW art. 74 ("The other Powers party to the Convention shall bear the cost of transport in their respective territories.").

[468] GPW art. 74 ("In the absence of special agreements between the Parties concerned, the costs connected with transport of such shipments, other than cost covered by the above exemption, shall be charged to the senders.").

[469] GPW art. 74 ("The High Contracting Parties shall endeavour to reduce, so far as possible, the rates charged for telegrams sent by prisoners of war, or addressed to them.").

[470] GPW art. 75 ("Should military operations prevent the Powers concerned from fulfilling their obligation to assure the transport of the shipments referred to in Articles 70, 71, 72 and 77, the Protecting Powers concerned, the International Committee of the Red Cross or any other organization duly approved by the Parties to the conflict may

supply them with such transport, and to allow its circulation, especially by granting the necessary safe-conducts.[471]

Such transport may also be used to convey:

- correspondence, lists, and reports exchanged between the Central POW Information Agency referred to in Article 123 of the GPW and the National POW Information Bureau referred to in Article 122 of the GPW; and
- correspondence and reports relating to POWs that the Protecting Powers, the ICRC, or any other body assisting the POWs exchange either with their own delegates or with the parties to the conflict.[472]

These provisions in no way detract from the right of any party to the conflict to arrange other means of transport, if it should so prefer, nor preclude the granting of safe-conducts, under mutually agreed conditions, to such means of transport.[473]

In the absence of special agreements, the costs occasioned by the use of such means of transport shall be borne proportionally by the parties to the conflict whose nationals are benefited thereby.[474] Expenses in setting up the special transport system are not specifically addressed by the GPW, and presumably would be addressed by an agreement between the body that takes the initiative in establishing the system and the Powers concerned.[475]

9.20.6 Censorship and Security Review of POW Correspondence and Shipments. The Detaining Power may examine and censor all communications sent to or by POWs, including correspondence, telegrams, parcels, newspapers, periodicals, and books, with a view to deleting or confiscating matter prejudicial to its military security.[476] The Detaining Power's general right

---

undertake to ensure the conveyance of such shipments by suitable means (railway wagons, motor vehicles, vessels or aircraft, etc.)").

[471] GPW art. 75 ("For this purpose, the High Contracting Parties shall endeavour to supply them with such transport and to allow its circulation, especially by granting the necessary safe-conducts.").

[472] GPW art. 75 ("Such transport may also be used to convey: (*a*) correspondence, lists and reports exchanged between the Central Information Agency referred to in Article 123 and the National Bureaux referred to in Article 122; (*b*) correspondence and reports relating to prisoners of war which the Protecting Powers, the International Committee of the Red Cross or any other body assisting the prisoners, exchange either with their own delegates or with the Parties to the conflict.").

[473] GPW art. 75 ("These provisions in no way detract from the right of any Party to the conflict to arrange other means of transport, if it should so prefer, nor preclude the granting of safe-conducts, under mutually agreed conditions, to such means of transport.").

[474] GPW art. 75 ("In the absence of special agreements, the costs occasioned by the use of such means of transport shall be borne proportionally by the Parties to the conflict whose nationals are benefited thereby.").

[475] *See* GPW COMMENTARY 468 ("This paragraph deals with the expenditure involved in the use of special transport, but not the expenditure incurred in setting up the special transport system. On this latter point the Convention says nothing and it is therefore to be supposed that such expenses will be covered by agreement between the body which takes the initiative in the matter and the Powers concerned.").

[476] *Compare* § 10.23.6 (Censorship and Security Review of Internee Correspondence and Shipments).

to conduct censorship is an implicit assumption in the GPW, as it is in the GC.[477] POWs' complaints, petitions, and reports may be subject to security review and censorship to ensure that they are not misused.[478]

The censoring of correspondence addressed to POWs or sent by them shall be done as quickly as possible.[479] Mail shall be censored only by the State from which the mail is sent and the State that receives the mail, and only once by each State.[480]

9.20.6.1 _Examination of Consignments_. The examination of consignments intended for POWs shall not be carried out under conditions that will expose the goods contained in them to deterioration; except in the case of written or printed matter, it shall be done in the presence of the addressee, or of a fellow POW duly delegated by him or her.[481]

The delivery to POWs of individual or collective consignments shall not be delayed under the pretext of difficulties of censorship.[482]

9.20.6.2 _Prohibitions of Correspondence_. Any prohibition of correspondence ordered by parties to the conflict, either for military or political reasons, shall be only temporary and its duration shall be as short as possible.[483]

9.21 Private Legal Matters of POWs

9.21.1 Civil Capacity. POWs shall retain their full civil capacity that they enjoyed at the time of their capture.[484] Their retention of their full civil capacity at the time of capture means that the law that applied to them before becoming a POW would continue to apply to them.[485]

---

[477] *Refer to* § 10.23.6 (Censorship and Security Review of Internee Correspondence and Shipments).

[478] *Refer to* § 9.23.2.1 (Review and Censorship of Requests and Complaints by the Detaining Power); § 9.23.3 (Periodic Reports by the POW Representatives).

[479] GPW art. 76 ("The censoring of correspondence addressed to prisoners of war or despatched by them shall be done as quickly as possible.").

[480] GPW art. 76 ("Mail shall be censored only by the despatching State and the receiving State, and once only by each.").

[481] GPW art. 76 ("The examination of consignments intended for prisoners of war shall not be carried out under conditions that will expose the goods contained in them to deterioration; except in the case of written or printed matter, it shall be done in the presence of the addressee, or of a fellow-prisoner duly delegated by him.").

[482] GPW art. 76 ("The delivery to prisoners of individual or collective consignments shall not be delayed under the pretext of difficulties of censorship.").

[483] GPW art. 76 ("Any prohibition of correspondence ordered by Parties to the conflict, either for military or political reasons, shall be only temporary and its duration shall be as short as possible.").

[484] GPW art. 14 ("Prisoners of war shall retain the full civil capacity which they enjoyed at the time of their capture.").

[485] GPW Commentary 149 ("The 1949 Diplomatic Conference considered it necessary to clarify the 1929 text establishing the civil capacity of prisoners of war. It was recalled that this capacity is always determined by law, whether the legislation of the country of origin of the internee or that of his country of domicile. But the prisoner will never be considered as 'resident' in the country of detention solely by virtue of the fact that he is in captivity.

The Detaining Power may not restrict the exercise, either within or without its own territory, of the rights such capacity confers, except in so far as the captivity requires.[486] Thus, POWs may, to the extent consistent with their detention, continue to exercise the civil capacity that they would have in their own country under that country's law.[487] For example, to the degree permitted by captivity, POWs may take legal steps that they were able to take before captivity, such as disposing of property, making wills, giving consent to marriage, voting, or executing a power of attorney.[488]

9.21.2 Legal Documents and Assistance. The Detaining Powers shall provide all facilities for the transmission, through the Protecting Power or the Central POW Information Agency provided for in Article 123 of the GPW, of instruments, papers, or documents intended for POWs or sent by them, especially powers of attorney and wills.[489] In all cases, the Detaining Power shall facilitate the preparation and execution of such documents on behalf of POWs; in particular, they shall allow them to consult a lawyer and shall take what measures are necessary for the authentication of their signatures.[490]

9.21.2.1 *Preparation of Wills*. Wills of POWs shall be drawn up so as to satisfy the conditions of validity required by the legislation of their country of origin, which will take steps to inform the Detaining Power of its requirements in this respect.[491] For States with federal systems like the United States in which the requirements of wills may vary according to jurisdictions within the State, the will should satisfy those provincial or state law requirements.

The legislation of his country of origin will, therefore, be applicable in most cases as that is also the country of domicile of the majority of prisoners. There are other possibilities, however, and for that reason the Stockholm draft, which only referred to the law of the country of origin, was amended by the Geneva Conference, so as to refer instead to the 'civil capacity which they enjoyed at the time of their capture'.").

486 GPW art. 14 ("The Detaining Power may not restrict the exercise, either within or without its own territory, of the rights such capacity confers except in so far as the captivity requires.").

487 II A FINAL RECORD OF THE DIPLOMATIC CONFERENCE OF GENEVA OF 1949 249 ("General DILLON (United States of America) fully agreed with the United Kingdom Delegate's observations regarding the second paragraph. As regards the third paragraph, he felt that a prisoner of war should be accorded all the civil rights that he would have in his own country, under his own country's legislation. He could not exercise them in the country of the Detaining Power, but could, on the other hand, exercise them in a prisoner of war camp. If he was a notary public, for instance, he could draw up authentic documents for his fellow prisoners and transmit them through the Protecting Power.").

488 2004 UK MANUAL ¶8.70 ("It means that prisoners of war are free, so far as captivity permits, to take legal steps in their state of origin, for example to dispose of property, make wills, give consent to marriage, or vote. Such action will normally be taken by appointment of an attorney or proxy.").

489 GPW art. 77 ("The Detaining Powers shall provide all facilities for the transmission, through the Protecting Power or the Central Prisoners of War Agency provided for in Article 123, of instruments, papers or documents intended for prisoners of war or despatched by them, especially powers of attorney and wills.").

490 GPW art. 77 ("In all cases they shall facilitate the preparation and execution of such documents on behalf of prisoners of war; in particular, they shall allow them to consult a lawyer and shall take what measures are necessary for the authentication of their signatures.").

491 GPW art. 120 ("Wills of prisoners of war shall be drawn up so as to satisfy the conditions of validity required by the legislation of their country of origin, which will take steps to inform the Detaining Power of its requirements in this respect.").

At the request of the POW, the will shall be transmitted without delay to the Protecting Power; a certified copy shall be sent to the Central POW Information Agency.[492]

9.22 Internal Discipline of POW Camps

9.22.1 <u>POW Camp Commander</u>. Every POW camp shall be put under the immediate authority of a responsible commissioned officer belonging to the regular armed forces of the Detaining Power.[493] For example, a non-commissioned officer, a contractor, a civilian, a member of a paramilitary force, or an enemy POW may not be the camp commander.[494] The POW camp commander has disciplinary powers over POWs.[495]

9.22.2 <u>POWs' Status With Respect to Their Armed Forces</u>. Although POWs are not subject to the judicial or disciplinary procedures of the Power to which they belong while they are POWs, POWs remain subject to the law, disciplinary authority, and regulations of the Power on which they depend.[496] For example, while they are POWs, they may not conduct disciplinary proceedings against one another; however, they are liable to punishment for violations committed during captivity, once they have been released and repatriated.[497]

9.22.3 <u>Saluting Between POWs and Officers of the Detaining Power</u>. POWs, with the

---

[492] GPW art. 120 ("At the request of the prisoner of war and, in all cases, after death, the will shall be transmitted without delay to the Protecting Power; a certified copy shall be sent to the Central Agency.").

[493] GPW art. 39 ("Every prisoner of war camp shall be put under the immediate authority of a responsible commissioned officer belonging to the regular armed forces of the Detaining Power.").

[494] *See* GPW COMMENTARY 239-40 ("The principle that a responsible commander should be appointed in each camp was already set forth in the 1929 Convention, Article 18, paragraph 1: "Each prisoners-of-war camp shall be placed under the authority of a responsible officer". The brevity of that text led to considerable abuse of the provision when disciplinary powers were delegated to non-commissioned officers and even to prisoners of war.").

[495] *Refer to* § 9.27.1 (POW Camp Authorities Who May Order Disciplinary Punishment).

[496] *See* GPW COMMENTARY 408-09 ("Although the legislation of the Detaining Power is applicable to him during his captivity, he remains subject to the military law of his State of origin, as a member of its armed forces. He may therefore be made answerable before the courts of his country for his acts, and cannot plead in defence that national legislation is inapplicable because it is suspended by Article 82.").

[497] *See, e.g.*, 10 U.S.C. § 905 ("Misconduct as a prisoner. Any person subject to this chapter who, while in the hands of the enemy in time of war-- (1) for the purpose of securing favorable treatment by his captors acts without proper authority in a manner contrary to law, custom, or regulation, to the detriment of others of whatever nationality held by the enemy as civilian or military prisoners; or (2) while in a position of authority over such persons maltreats them without justifiable cause; shall be punished as a court-martial may direct."); United States v. Dickenson 17 C.M.R. 438, 442 U.S. Army Board of Review (1954) (U.S. POW during the Korean War was found guilty of committing offense when he "for the purpose of securing favorable treatment by his captors, report[ed] to the enemy officials in command of Prisoner of War Camp Number Five, Pyoktong, North Korea, the preparations by Edward M. Gaither, then Private First Class Edward M. Gaither, United States Army, a prisoner of war at said camp, to escape, as a result of which report the said Edward M. Gaither was placed by the enemy before a mock firing squad on three occasions, placed by the enemy in solitary confinement for approximately seven months and severely kicked and beaten with clubs by the enemy."); United States v. Garwood, 16 M.J. 863, 865 United States Navy-Marine Corps Court of Military Review (1983) (U.S. POW during the Vietnam War was found guilty of committing offenses "of aiding enemy forces within prisoner of war camps in the Republic of South Vietnam, in violation of Article 104, Uniform Code of Military Justice (UCMJ), 10 U.S.C. § 904, and of assault of an American prisoner of war interned in an enemy prisoner of war camp, in violation of Article 128, UCMJ, 10 U.S.C. § 928.").

exception of officers, must salute and show to all officers of the Detaining Power the external marks of respect provided for by the regulations applying in their own forces.[498] POWs need not salute Detaining Power non-commissioned officers or persons of equivalent status to officers belonging to the Detaining Power.[499]

The form and conditions for saluting and showing external marks of respect are to be determined by the regulations applying in the armed forces to which the POWs belong.[500] Other external marks of respect may include, for example, standing at attention when an officer enters the room.[501]

Officer POWs are bound to salute only Detaining Power officers of higher rank and the camp commander, regardless of his or her rank.[502]

Although not required by the GPW, Detaining Power officers should return salutes as a matter of courtesy.[503] Members of the armed forces of the Detaining Power are not required to salute POWs of superior rank.[504]

9.22.4 Rank and Age of POWs. POWs shall be treated with the regard due to their rank and age.[505] POWs shall be permitted to wear their badges of rank, nationality, or decorations.[506] For example, rank insignia or similar devices may be worn by POWs.

---

[498] GPW art. 39 ("Prisoners of war, with the exception of officers, must salute and show to all officers of the Detaining Power the external marks of respect provided for by the regulations applying in their own forces.").

[499] GPW COMMENTARY 240-41 ("This provision requires prisoners of war to show the relevant external marks of respect to all officers; at the same time, it automatically excludes from this privilege any representative of the Detaining Power who is not an officer or does not wear officer's uniform. Similarly, it excludes all non-commissioned officers, regardless of the laws and regulations of the Detaining Power.").

[500] GPW COMMENTARY 241 ("The present provision does not merely state to whom prisoners of war must give the salute and show external marks of respect; it also determines the form and conditions for doing so, by referring explicitly to the regulations applying in the armed forces to which the prisoners belong. This provision is likely to prevent any recurrence of incidents such as those which took place during the Second World War, when certain belligerents insisted on prisoners conforming to the regulations for saluting applicable in the armed forces of the Detaining Power.").

[501] LEVIE, POWS 171, footnote 299 ("Other external marks of respect would include standing when the officer enters the room, remaining at attention while conversing with the officer, etc. These are not marks of obsequiousness, but of disciplined training.").

[502] GPW art. 39 ("Officer prisoners of war are bound to salute only officers of a higher rank of the Detaining Power; they must, however, salute the camp commander regardless of his rank.").

[503] *See* GPW COMMENTARY 241 ("There is one more question, in this connection, which gave rise to some difficulty: that of officers of the Detaining Power returning the salute of prisoners of war. The Conference of Government Experts considered that this was a matter of courtesy and did not call for precise ruling.").

[504] LEVIE, POWS 170 ("Members of the armed forces of the Detaining Power are not required to salute prisoners of war of superior rank.").

[505] GPW art. 44 ("Officers and prisoners of equivalent status shall be treated with the regard due to their rank and age."); GPW art. 45 ("Prisoners of war other than officers and prisoners of equivalent status shall be treated with the regard due to their rank and age.").

[506] GPW art. 40 ("The wearing of badges of rank and nationality, as well as of decorations, shall be permitted.").

The rank of POWs also determines the amount of the advances of pay that they are entitled to receive.[507] In addition, POWs awarded disciplinary punishment may not be deprived of the prerogatives of rank.[508]

9.22.4.1 *Communication of Titles and Ranks*. Upon the outbreak of hostilities, the parties to the conflict shall communicate to one another the titles and ranks of all the persons mentioned in Article 4 of the GPW, in order to ensure equality of treatment between POWs of equivalent rank.[509] Titles and ranks that are subsequently created shall form the subject of similar communications.[510]

9.22.4.2 *Recognition of Promotions in Rank*. Promotions in rank of POWs that have been accorded to POWs and that have been duly notified by the Power on which the POWs depend shall be recognized.[511]

9.22.5 Posting of Convention and Camp Orders. In every POW camp the text of the GPW and its Annexes, and the contents of any applicable special agreements, shall be posted, in the POWs' own language, in places where all may read them.[512] The POWs' own language means an official language of the State to which they belong.[513] Copies shall be supplied, on request, to the POWs who cannot have access to the posted copy.[514]

Regulations, orders, notices, and publications of every kind relating to the conduct of POWs shall be issued to them in a language that they understand.[515] Such regulations, orders, and publications shall be posted in the same manner as the GPW, and copies shall be handed to

---

[507] *Refer to* § 9.18.3.1 (GPW Specified Amounts for Monthly Advances of Pay).

[508] *Refer to* § 9.27.6.3 (Disciplinary Punishment - Retention of Prerogatives of Rank).

[509] GPW art. 43 ("Upon the outbreak of hostilities, the Parties to the conflict shall communicate to one another the titles and ranks of all the persons mentioned in Article 4 of the present Convention, in order to ensure equality of treatment between prisoners of equivalent rank.").

[510] GPW art. 43 ("Titles and ranks which are subsequently created shall form the subject of similar communications.").

[511] GPW art. 43 ("The Detaining Power shall recognize promotions in rank which have been accorded to prisoners of war and which have been duly notified by the Power on which these prisoners depend.").

[512] GPW art. 41 ("In every camp the text of the present Convention and its Annexes and the contents of any special agreement provided for in Article 6, shall be posted, in the prisoners' own language, in places where all may read them.").

[513] *See* GPW COMMENTARY 244 ("The 1929 Convention made the situation still more difficult by stipulating that the text must be posted 'in the native language of the prisoners of war'; the present Article refers merely to 'the prisoners' own language', this being the official language of the prisoners' country of origin-the language used in that country for official records and the publication of legislation. Where there is more than one official language in the country of origin, the Convention should, if possible, be posted in the language actually used by the prisoners concerned.").

[514] GPW art. 41 ("Copies shall be supplied, on request, to the prisoners who cannot have access to the copy which has been posted.").

[515] GPW art. 41 ("Regulations, orders, notices and publications of every kind relating to the conduct of prisoners of war shall be issued to them in a language which they understand.").

the POW Representative.[516] Every order and command addressed to POWs individually must likewise be given in a language that they understand.[517]

9.22.6 Use of Force to Maintain Order and to Prevent Escape. The use of weapons against POWs, especially against those who are escaping or attempting to escape, shall constitute an extreme measure, which shall always be preceded by warnings appropriate to the circumstances.[518] For example, POWs should not be fired upon if they are apprehended within the camp limits while making preparations to escape and there is no risk of escape or harm to anyone.[519]

9.22.6.1 *Use of Non-Lethal Weapons (Including Riot Control Agents)*. Non-lethal weapons may be employed to control rioting POWs or to prevent their escape.[520] In particular, the use of riot control agents to control rioting POWs is not prohibited.[521]

If the use of deadly force is warranted and authorized against POWs, there is no legal requirement to employ non-lethal weapons before resort to deadly force.[522]

9.23 POW Requests, Complaints, and Reports About Conditions of Captivity

9.23.1 POW Right to Make Requests and Complaints. POWs shall have the right to make known, to the military authorities in whose power they are, their requests regarding the conditions of captivity to which they are subjected.[523] The commander of a POW camp may issue regulations that establish procedures about how POWs are to make these requests.[524]

---

[516] GPW art. 41 ("Such regulations, orders and publications shall be posted in the manner described above and copies shall be handed to the prisoners' representative.").

[517] GPW art. 41 ("Every order and command addressed to prisoners of war individually must likewise be given in a language which they understand.").

[518] GPW art. 42 ("The use of weapons against prisoners of war, especially against those who are escaping or attempting to escape, shall constitute an extreme measure, which shall always be preceded by warnings appropriate to the circumstances.").

[519] GPW Commentary 246 ("It is also important, however, to make a distinction between escape proper and acts or phases preparatory thereto. If a prisoner is surprised within the camp limits while making preparations to escape, there is no justification for opening fire on him.").

[520] GPW Commentary 247 ("Before resorting to weapons of war, sentries can use others which do not cause fatal injury and may even be considered as warnings--tear-gas, truncheons, etc. These measures may prove inadequate, however, and from the moment when the guards and sentries are about to be overwhelmed, or are obliged to act in legitimate self-defence, they are justified in opening fire.").

[521] *Refer to* § 6.16.2 (Prohibition on Use of Riot Control Agents as a Method of Warfare).

[522] *Refer to* § 6.5.10.5 (No Requirement to Use Non-Lethal Weapons Before Using Lethal Weapons Where Deadly Force Is Warranted).

[523] GPW art. 78 ("Prisoners of war shall have the right to make known to the military authorities in whose power they are, their requests regarding the conditions of captivity to which they are subjected.").

[524] GPW Commentary 383 ("This right [under Article 78 of the GPW to make requests] must obviously be exercised in a manner compatible with the normal requirements of discipline and camp administration and may not be used for purposes other than those arising under the Convention. If need be, the camp commander will issue regulations concerning the exercise of this right.").

POWs shall also have the unrestricted right to apply to the representatives of the Protecting Powers, either through their POW Representative or, if they consider it necessary, directly, in order to draw their attention to any points on which they may have complaints to make regarding their conditions of captivity.[525]

9.23.1.1 *Making Requests and Complaints to the ICRC*. Such complaints may also be made to the delegates of the ICRC who enjoy the same prerogatives of access as the representatives of the Protecting Power.[526] In the past, the ICRC has been able to take appropriate measures besides merely forwarding the complaint to the Power on which the POWs depend, including measures on a confidential basis that help improve the situations of POWs.[527]

9.23.2 Communication of Requests and Complaints. These requests and complaints shall neither be limited nor considered to be part of the correspondence quota referred to in Article 71 of the GPW.[528] They must be transmitted immediately.[529]

9.23.2.1 *Review and Censorship of Requests and Complaints by the Detaining Power*. Complaints and requests by the POWs that are to be transmitted to the representatives of the Protecting Power may be reviewed and censored for security reasons by the Detaining Power, although the right of the POWs to make complaints about their conditions of captivity to the representatives of the Protecting Power must not be restricted.[530] In addition, security review and censorship must be conducted in accordance with the general rules on censoring POW

---

[525] GPW art. 78 ("They shall also have the unrestricted right to apply to the representatives of the Protecting Powers either through their prisoners' representative or, if they consider it necessary, direct, in order to draw their attention to any points on which they may have complaints to make regarding their conditions of captivity.").

[526] *Refer to* § 9.33.1.2 (ICRC Delegates Enjoying the Same Prerogatives of Access).

[527] *For example*, I REPORT OF THE INTERNATIONAL COMMITTEE OF THE RED CROSS ON ITS ACTIVITIES DURING THE SECOND WORLD WAR (SEPTEMBER 1, 1939 – JUNE 30, 1947) 342 (1948) ("On receiving a complaint [from POWs], the ICRC sought the most appropriate means in its power to put right the matter complained of, first verifying as far as possible the genuine foundation of the grievance. … The Committee was more concerned with finding some practical remedy for the deficiencies complained of than with bringing them to the notice of the PW's own country, as there was always a possible risk of provoking reprisals. In some cases, it made immediate representations, usually to the person or officials of the Detaining Power directly concerned, but sometimes also to higher authority. In other cases it instructed its delegates to take appropriate steps on the spot to bring about an improvement. These constant daily efforts, though often never heard of, are probably among the most useful services that the Committee was able to render to PW.").

[528] GPW art. 78 ("These requests and complaints shall not be limited nor considered to be a part of the correspondence quota referred to in Article 71."). *Refer to* § 9.20.2 (POW Correspondence Rights and Quota).

[529] GPW art. 78 ("They must be transmitted immediately.").

[530] GPW COMMENTARY 384 ("The problem is to reconcile the Detaining Power's own security requirements with the need to ensure that the right of complaint can be effectively exercised. For reasons of security, the Detaining Power must obviously make sure that prisoners of war do not use it as a means of communication with the outside world. The Conference of Government Experts therefore rejected the suggestion that the words 'without amendment' should be added to the obligation to transmit complaints. Such an addition would have resulted in doing away with censorship, and the Detaining Power could not agree to that. The authors of the Convention considered, however, that matters concerning only the 'conditions of captivity' could be mentioned without restriction, and the wording adopted seemed best suited to take into account both the interests of the prisoners of war and the Detaining Power's own security requirements.").

correspondence.[531]

9.23.2.2 <u>*No Punishment for Making Complaints*</u>. Even if the complaints are recognized to be unfounded, they may not give rise to any punishment.[532] This rule departs from the usual practice in armed forces, in which excessive use of the right of complaint within a State's armed forces may be punished.[533] The GPW provision against punishment for unfounded complaints arose after POWs were tortured for complaining to the representatives of the Protecting Power.[534] In any event, it could be contrary to POWs' interests to abuse this right by making groundless complaints because complaints that are justified might not, as a result, receive the appropriate attention.[535]

9.23.3 <u>Periodic Reports by the POW Representatives</u>. POW Representatives may send periodic reports on the situation in the camps and the needs of the POWs to the representatives of the Protecting Powers.[536] POW Representatives have discretion about how and when to submit their reports.[537] The Detaining Power may subject these reports to security review and censorship to ensure that these reports are not misused.[538]

9.24 POW REPRESENTATIVES

The GPW contemplates that certain POWs will serve as representatives of the POWs before the Detaining Power, the Protecting Power, and other entities. These persons have certain prerogatives that enable them to carry out their duties to further the well-being of the POWs.

In the GPW, these persons are called "prisoners' representatives." This manual refers to them as POW Representatives.

---

[531] *Refer to* § 9.20.6 (Censorship and Security Review of POW Correspondence and Shipments).

[532] GPW art. 78 ("Even if they are recognized to be unfounded, they may not give rise to any punishment.").

[533] GPW COMMENTARY 386 ("Lastly, the present paragraph establishes the impunity of prisoners of war in regard to any unfounded complaints or requests. Here the Convention departs from the regulations applied in national armed forces, which usually punish any excessive use of the right of complaint as being an attack on authority and an act of indiscipline.").

[534] United States, *et al.* v. Araki, *et al.*, *Majority Judgment*, International Military Tribunal for the Far East, 49,757, *reprinted in* NEIL BOISTER & ROBERT CRYER, DOCUMENTS ON THE TOKYO INTERNATIONAL MILITARY TRIBUNAL: CHARTER, INDICTMENT AND JUDGMENTS 592 (2008) ("After a visit to the prisoner of war camp at Motoyama in Japan in the spring of 1943, the senior prisoner at the camp, who had dared to complain of the working conditions to which the prisoners had been subjected, was tortured. He was forced to kneel for five hours before a Japanese guard. The next time this camp was visited, this senior prisoner was placed in confinement and was not allowed to speak to the representative although that representative demanded to interview him.").

[535] GPW COMMENTARY 386 ("It is to be hoped that prisoners of war will realize that in their own interest they should make judicious use of the right of complaint and request, and refrain from making complaints which they know to be groundless so that those which are justified can receive the attention they deserve.").

[536] GPW art. 78 ("Prisoners' representatives may send periodic reports on the situation in the camps and the needs of the prisoners of war to the representatives of the Protecting Powers.").

[537] *Compare* § 10.21.3 (Periodic Reports by the Internee Committees).

[538] *Refer to* § 9.20.6 (Censorship and Security Review of POW Correspondence and Shipments).

9.24.1 General Qualifications of the POW Representative. In all cases, the POW Representative must have the same nationality, language, and customs as the POWs whom he or she represents.[539] Thus, POWs distributed in different sections of a camp, according to their nationality, language, or customs, shall have for each section their own POW Representative.[540]

In practice, it is advisable for the POW Representative to be a POW as opposed to a retained person. Medical personnel have their own representative for issues related to their activities.[541] In addition, the duties of the POW Representative and the duties of retained personnel could interfere with one another, and special provision is made in the GPW to ensure that other duties not interfere with the duties of retained personnel or the duties of the POW Representative.[542]

9.24.2 Procedure for Selecting POW Representatives, Advisers, and Assistants. The procedure for selecting POW Representatives, and their advisers (POWs who are officers) and assistants (POWs who are not officers), depends on the rank of the POWs in the camp.

9.24.2.1 *Camps With Officer POWs*. In camps for officers and persons of equivalent status or in mixed camps, the senior officer among the POWs shall be recognized as the camp POW Representative.[543] A mixed camp refers to camps composed of both officers and other ranks.[544]

The senior officer is the officer of highest rank, not the oldest officer.[545] The senior officer is also a member of the armed forces, as opposed to a person of equivalent status (*e.g.*, such as a person authorized to accompany the armed forces who is of senior status).[546]

In camps for officers, the POW Representative shall be assisted by one or more advisers chosen by the officers.[547] These advisers may assist the POW Representative if his or her health

---

[539] GPW art. 79 ("In all cases the prisoners' representative must have the same nationality, language and customs as the prisoners of war whom he represents.").

[540] GPW art. 79 ("Thus, prisoners of war distributed in different sections of a camp, according to their nationality, language or customs, shall have for each section their own prisoners' representative, in accordance with the foregoing paragraphs.").

[541] *Refer to* § 7.9.5.7 (Senior Medical Officer in the Camp).

[542] *Refer to* § 7.9.5.6 (No Other Compulsory Duties); § 9.24.4.1 (Limitations on Other Work Assignments).

[543] GPW art. 79 ("In camps for officers and persons of equivalent status or in mixed camps, the senior officer among the prisoners of war shall be recognized as the camp prisoners' representative.").

[544] *See* GPW COMMENTARY 393 ("As may be seen from the record of the discussions at the Diplomatic Conference, the expression ["mixed camp"] refers to camps comprising both officers and other ranks.").

[545] *See* GPW COMMENTARY 392 ("In camps for officers, the prisoners' representative is appointed according to seniority and not by election. The term 'the senior officer' (in French, 'le plus ancien dans le grade le plus élevé') has sometimes been taken as meaning the oldest officer with the highest rank. If the words are to have a precise meaning, however, as they must have, it should be what the English text says, viz. the senior officer of the highest rank. Age will only be the determining factor where two officers of the same rank were promoted on the same date.").

[546] *Refer to* § 4.15 (Persons Authorized to Accompany the Armed Forces).

[547] GPW art. 79 ("In camps for officers, he shall be assisted by one or more advisers chosen by the officers;").

makes it difficult to carry out the duties of the POW Representative and also may assist the POW Representative in gauging the wishes of other POWs.[548]

In mixed camps, the POW Representative's assistants shall be chosen from among the POWs who are not officers and shall be elected by them.[549]

9.24.2.2 Labor Camps With Officers Who Carry Out Camp Administration Duties for POWs. Officer POWs of the same nationality shall be stationed in labor camps for POWs, for the purpose of carrying out the camp administration duties for which the POWs are responsible.[550] These officers may be elected as POW Representatives under the first paragraph of Article 79 of the GPW.[551] In such a case, the assistants to the POW Representatives shall be chosen from among those POWs who are not officers.[552]

9.24.2.3 Places Without Officer POWs. In all places where there are POWs, except in those where there are officers, the POWs shall freely elect POW Representatives by secret ballot, every six months, and also in case of vacancies.[553] These POW Representatives shall be eligible for re-election.[554]

9.24.2.4 Approval of Elected POW Representatives by the Detaining Power. Every elected POW Representative must be approved by the Detaining Power before he or she

---

[548] *See* GPW COMMENTARY 392 ("Thus it is clearly established that, like other prisoners of war, officers have a prisoners' representative. Serious difficulties may result, however, from the fact that he is appointed according to rank, particularly if his state of health makes it difficult for him to carry out the wide range of tasks incumbent on the prisoners' representative. The 1949 text therefore provides a possibility which did not exist in Article 43 of the 1929 Convention: the officer who is the prisoners' representative will be 'assisted' by one or more advisers chosen by the prisoners themselves. The intention of the authors of this new provision was that such assistants should be able to help the senior officer of the highest rank by expressing the wishes and opinions of all the prisoners.").

[549] GPW art. 79 ("[I]n mixed camps, his assistants shall be chosen from among the prisoners of war who are not officers and shall be elected by them.").

[550] GPW art. 79 ("Officer prisoners of war of the same nationality shall be stationed in labour camps for prisoners of war, for the purpose of carrying out the camp administration duties for which the prisoners of war are responsible.").

[551] GPW art. 79 ("These officers may be elected as prisoners' representatives under the first paragraph of this Article."). *See also* LEVIE, POWS 298 ("[E]ven though the labor detachment will, to a certain extent, be a 'mixed' camp, the senior officer detailed to it to perform the administrative details will not automatically be the prisoners' representative, but he will be eligible for election to that office.").

[552] GPW art. 79 ("In such a case the assistants to the prisoners' representatives shall be chosen from among those prisoners of war who are not officers.").

[553] GPW art. 79 ("In all places where there are prisoners of war, except in those where there are officers, the prisoners shall freely elect by secret ballot, every six months, and also in case of vacancies, prisoners' representatives entrusted with representing them before the military authorities, the Protecting Powers, the International Committee of the Red Cross and any other organization which may assist them."). *See also* GPW COMMENTARY 390 ("In view of the general wording of the phrase 'in all places where there are prisoners of war', there is no need to wait until they are actually in a camp. If circumstances permit, prisoners of war will be able to appoint a prisoners' representative in transit camps. The general wording of the provision therefore enables prisoners' representatives to be elected not only in the main camps which are usually situated on the outskirts of built-up areas, but also in labour detachments.").

[554] GPW art. 79 ("These prisoners' representatives shall be eligible for re-election.").

has the right to commence his or her duties.[555] Where the Detaining Power refuses to approve a POW elected by fellow POWs, it must inform the Protecting Power of the reason for such refusal.[556]

9.24.3 <u>Duties of POW Representatives</u>. The POW Representatives are entrusted with representing the POWs before the military authorities, the Protecting Powers, the ICRC, and any other organization that may assist them.[557] POW Representatives shall further the physical, spiritual, and intellectual well-being of POWs.[558]

The POW Representative's general duties imply that the POW Representatives will undertake a variety of activities to ensure that POWs receive proper treatment by the Detaining Power and to advance their welfare, even activities that are not specified in the GPW as constituting their duties.

9.24.3.1 <u>*POW Representatives and Mutual Assistance Among POWs*</u>. In particular, where the POWs decide to organize among themselves a system of mutual assistance, this organization will be within the province of the POW Representative, in addition to the special duties entrusted to him or her by other provisions of the GPW.[559]

9.24.3.2 <u>*Other Specific Duties*</u>. In addition to the general duties that the GPW imposes on the POW Representative, the GPW also imposes specific duties on POW Representatives in three areas: (1) relief activities; (2) relations between the POWs and the authorities; and (3) verification that the guarantees provided under GPW are respected.[560]

The POW Representative's duties in relation to relief activities include:

- assisting in the transport of the POWs' community property and luggage in cases of transfers of POWs;[561]

---

[555] GPW art. 79 ("Every representative elected must be approved by the Detaining Power before he has the right to commence his duties.").

[556] GPW art. 79 ("Where the Detaining Power refuses to approve a prisoner of war elected by his fellow prisoners of war, it must inform the Protecting Power of the reason for such refusal.").

[557] GPW art. 80 ("In all places where there are prisoners of war, except in those where there are officers, the prisoners shall freely elect by secret ballot, every six months, and also in case of vacancies, prisoners' representatives entrusted with representing them before the military authorities, the Protecting Powers, the International Committee of the Red Cross and any other organization which may assist them.").

[558] GPW art. 80 ("Prisoners' representatives shall further the physical, spiritual and intellectual wellbeing of prisoners of war.").

[559] GPW art. 80 ("In particular, where the prisoners decide to organize amongst themselves a system of mutual assistance, this organization will be within the province of the prisoners' representative, in addition to the special duties entrusted to him by other provisions of the present Convention.").

[560] *See* GPW COMMENTARY 397 ("The role of prisoners' representatives falls under three main headings: relief activities, relations with prisoners of war and the authorities, verification that the guarantees provided under the Convention are being respected.").

[561] *Refer to* § 9.29.3.4 (Disposition of Community Property and Remaining Property).

- managing the distribution of collective relief;[562]

- receiving parcels and remittances of money for POWs undergoing disciplinary punishment, and handing over to the infirmary any perishable goods;[563] and

- signing receipts for relief supplies or materials to the relief society or organization making the shipment.[564]

The POW Representative's duties in facilitating relations between the POWs and the authorities include:

- remaining in communication with POWs who work for private employers;[565]

- transmitting requests and complaints, and sending periodic reports on the needs of POWs;[566] and

- interviewing with delegates of the Protecting Powers.[567]

The POW Representative's duties in verifying that the guarantees provided under GPW are respected include:

- collaborating in the management of the canteen and its special fund;[568]

- receiving copies of regulations, orders, notices, and publications relating to the conduct of POWs issued by the Detaining Power for communication to POWs;[569]

- countersigning for entries entered in a POW's account on his or her behalf, or for notifications of payments sent by POWs to their own country;[570]

- monitoring decisions announced from any disciplinary proceeding against a POW;[571]

- receiving notifications of judicial proceedings instituted against POWs, and of any

---

[562] *Refer to* § 9.20.3.4 (Collective Relief for POWs).

[563] *Refer to* § 9.27.6.6 (Reading, Writing, Correspondence, and Packages).

[564] *Refer to* § 9.33.2.2 (Receipts for Relief Consignments).

[565] *Refer to* § 9.19.8 (POWs Working for Private Persons).

[566] *Refer to* § 9.23 (POW Requests, Complaints).

[567] *Refer to* § 9.33.1 (Access by Protecting Powers).

[568] *Refer to* § 9.17.3 (Camp Canteen Management and Profits).

[569] *Refer to* § 9.22.5 (Posting of Convention and Camp Orders).

[570] *Refer to* § 9.18 (Financial Resources of POWs).

[571] *Refer to* § 9.27.3 (Rights of POWs in Disciplinary Proceedings).

judgment or sentences pronounced upon them;[572] and

- proposing repatriation for certain POWs and participating in Mixed Medical Commissions.[573]

9.24.4 Prerogatives of POW Representatives. In order to accomplish their duties, POW Representatives are afforded certain prerogatives.

9.24.4.1 *Limitations on Other Work Assignments*. POW Representatives shall not be required to perform any other work, if the accomplishment of their duties is thereby made more difficult.[574] Officers, in any event, may not be required to work.[575]

9.24.4.2 *Assistants for the POW Representatives*. In addition to the advisers and assistants for the POW Representatives that are provided for in camps with officers, POW Representatives may appoint from among the POWs such assistants as they may require.[576] Assistants, like the POW Representative, should be exempted from any other work to the extent that the accomplishment of their duties would thereby be made more difficult.[577]

9.24.4.3 *Material Facilities, Including Certain Freedom of Movement*. All material facilities shall be granted to POW Representatives, particularly a certain freedom of movement necessary for the accomplishment of their duties (inspection of labor detachments, receipt of supplies, etc.).[578] This freedom of movement does not mean complete freedom.[579]

9.24.4.4 *Visiting Premises Where POWs Are Detained and Consultation With POWs*. POW Representatives shall be permitted to visit premises where POWs are detained, and every POW shall have the right to consult freely with his or her POW Representative.[580] The

---

[572] *Refer to* § 9.28.3.1 (Notification of Proceedings); § 9.28.4.6 (Notification of Trial Outcome).

[573] *Refer to* § 9.36.5 (Mixed Medical Commissions).

[574] GPW art. 81 ("Prisoners' representatives shall not be required to perform any other work, if the accomplishment of their duties is thereby made more difficult.").

[575] *Refer to* § 9.19.1.2 (Labor Assignment – Officers and Persons of Equivalent Status).

[576] GPW art. 81 ("Prisoners' representatives may appoint from amongst the prisoners such assistants as they may require."). *See also* GPW COMMENTARY 401 (Assistants "will be interpreters, legal advisers, secretaries, assistants competent in matters of storage and handling.").

[577] *See* GPW COMMENTARY 401 (All assistants "like the prisoners' representative himself, will be exempted from any other work to the extent that the accomplishment of their duties would 'thereby be made more difficult'.").

[578] GPW art. 81 ("All material facilities shall be granted them, particularly a certain freedom of movement necessary for the accomplishment of their duties (inspection of labour detachments, receipt of supplies, etc.).").

[579] *See* GPW COMMENTARY 402 (The authors of GPW "did not think fit to grant 'complete freedom', but only 'a certain freedom.' This freedom must be granted whenever 'necessary'. Two cases are expressly mentioned: inspection of labour detachments and receipt of relief supplies."). *For example*, GPW COMMENTARY 402 ("During the Second World War, prisoners' representatives were released on parole by some Detaining Powers in order to enable them to travel from one camp to another.").

[580] GPW art. 81 ("Prisoners' representatives shall be permitted to visit premises where prisoners of war are detained, and every prisoner of war shall have the right to consult freely his prisoners' representative.").

premises that may be visited will include the kitchen, infirmary, and other annexes to the POW Camp.[581]

9.24.4.5 *Working Pay of POW Representatives, Advisers, and Assistants*. The working pay of POW Representatives, advisers, if any, and assistants, shall be paid out of the fund maintained by canteen profits.[582] The scale of this working pay shall be fixed by the POW Representative and approved by the camp commander.[583] If there is no such fund, the detaining authorities shall pay these POWs a fair working rate of pay.[584]

9.24.4.6 *Facilities for Communication*. All facilities shall likewise be accorded to POW Representatives for communication by post and telegraph with the detaining authorities, the Protecting Powers, the ICRC and their delegates, the Mixed Medical Commissions, and the bodies that give assistance to POWs.[585]

POW Representatives of labor detachments shall enjoy the same facilities for communication with the POW Representatives of the principal camp.[586] Such communications shall not be restricted, nor considered as forming a part of the quota mentioned in Article 71 of the GPW.[587]

The facilities to be granted do not, however, include freedom from censorship, but correspondence may not be withheld.[588]

9.24.4.7 *No Responsibility for Offenses Committed by POWs by Reason of Their Duties*. POW Representatives shall not be held responsible, simply by reason of their duties, for

---

[581] GPW COMMENTARY 403 ("The premises which may be visited will include the kitchen, infirmary and other annexes.").

[582] GPW art. 62 ("The working pay of the prisoners' representative, of his advisers, if any, and of his assistants, shall be paid out of the fund maintained by canteen profits."). *Refer to* § 9.17.3.1 (Use of Canteen Profits for Working Pay of the POW Representative).

[583] GPW art. 62 ("The scale of this working pay shall be fixed by the prisoners' representative and approved by the camp commander.").

[584] GPW art. 62 ("If there is no such fund, the detaining authorities shall pay these prisoners a fair working rate of pay.").

[585] GPW art. 81 ("All facilities shall likewise be accorded to the prisoners' representatives for communication by post and telegraph with the detaining authorities, the Protecting Powers, the International Committee of the Red Cross and their delegates, the Mixed Medical Commissions and the bodies which give assistance to prisoners of war.").

[586] GPW art. 81 ("Prisoners' representatives of labour detachments shall enjoy the same facilities for communication with the prisoners' representatives of the principal camp.").

[587] GPW art. 81 ("Such communications shall not be restricted, nor considered as forming a part of the quota mentioned in Article 71."). *Refer to* § 9.20.2 (POW Correspondence Rights and Quota).

[588] GPW COMMENTARY 404 ("The facilities to be granted do not, however, include freedom from censorship, but correspondence may not be withheld. If circumstances so demand, a special censorship service must therefore be instituted or, at least, the correspondence of prisoners' representatives must be given priority.").

any offenses committed by POWs.[589] For example, POW Representatives may not be held responsible for escape attempts by other POWs, unless they personally participated in such activities.[590]

9.24.4.8 *Turnover for Successor POW Representatives Upon Transfer*. POW Representatives who are transferred shall be allowed a reasonable time to acquaint their successors with current affairs.[591]

9.24.5 Dismissal of POW Representative. In case of dismissal, the reason for the dismissal shall be communicated to the Protecting Power.[592]

The GPW does not provide a procedure for POWs to dismiss POW Representatives aside from not re-electing them.[593] However, the Detaining Power may withdraw its approval of a POW Representative and request that POWs hold new elections.[594]

9.25 POW ESCAPES

POWs who escape successfully are not liable to any punishment in respect of their previous escape. A number of rules limit the punishment of POWs who do not escape successfully. Notifications of POW escape and recapture should also be made. POWs punished as a result of an unsuccessful escape may be subjected to special surveillance.

9.25.1 No Punishment for Successful Escape. POWs who have made good their escape in the sense of Article 91 of the GPW, and who are recaptured, shall not be liable to any

---

[589] GPW art. 80 ("Prisoners' representatives shall not be held responsible, simply by reason of their duties, for any offences committed by prisoners of war.").

[590] *See* LEVIE, POWS 304 ("This is particularly relevant with respect to incidents such as the construction of a tunnel to be used for the purpose of escape. The military authorities of the Detaining Power will probably assume, and with some justification, that this could not have occurred unknown to the prisoners' representative--but whether he knew of it or not, he is not to be held responsible if he did not personally participate in it.").

[591] GPW art. 81 ("Prisoners' representatives who are transferred shall be allowed a reasonable time to acquaint their successors with current affairs.").

[592] GPW art. 81 ("In case of dismissal, the reasons therefore shall be communicated to the Protecting Power.").

[593] *See* GPW COMMENTARY 405 (GPW "Article 79, paragraph 1, enables [POWs] to show disapproval by not re-electing the prisoners' representative, since elections must be held every six months. The Convention provides no procedure, however, for a case where prisoners of war have grounds to demand that their representative should resign immediately; it makes provision only for dismissal of a prisoners' representative by the Detaining Power.").

[594] *See* GPW COMMENTARY 405 ("One solution would be for the prisoners of war to submit a request to the military authorities for recognition to be withdrawn from the prisoners' representative. If the Detaining Power is satisfied that that is the wish of the majority of prisoners, it may arrange for fresh elections to be held, and the results thereof will justify or not, as the case may be, the request made by the prisoners of war. The Detaining Power may at any time withdraw its approval and request prisoners of war to hold new elections. It must advise the Protecting Power of the actual reasons for its decision and may not merely state that there is no longer mutual confidence between the prisoners' representative and its own representatives.").

punishment in respect of their previous escape.[595]

In this way, POWs who have escaped successfully are treated similarly to persons who have engaged in espionage and returned safely to friendly lines.[596] Escaping POWs must not kill or wound the enemy by resort to perfidy.[597]

9.25.1.1 *Types of Successful Escapes*. Under Article 91 of the GPW, the escape of a POW shall be deemed to have succeeded when the POW has:

- joined the armed forces of the Power on which he or she depends, or those of an allied Power;
- left the territory under the control of the Detaining Power, or of an ally of the Detaining Power; or
- joined a ship flying the flag of the Power on which he or she depends, or of an allied Power, in the territorial waters of the Detaining Power, this ship not being under the control of the Detaining Power.[598]

The general principle is that the POW must have actually gone beyond the reach of the Detaining Power.[599] Thus, for example, a POW who escapes from the territory of the Detaining Power to the territory of one of the Detaining Power's allies will not be deemed to have escaped successfully. On the other hand, if the POW reaches neutral territory or the high seas, he or she will have escaped successfully.[600]

The situation of POWs who have successfully escaped into neutral territory is addressed under the law of neutrality.[601]

---

[595] GPW art. 91 ("Prisoners of war who have made good their escape in the sense of this Article and who are recaptured, shall not be liable to any punishment in respect of their previous escape.").

[596] *Refer to* § 4.17.5.1 (Liability of Persons Not Captured While Spying for Previous Acts of Espionage).

[597] *Refer to* § 5.22 (Treachery or Perfidy Used to Kill or Wound).

[598] GPW art. 91 ("The escape of a prisoner of war shall be deemed to have succeeded when: (1) he has joined the armed forces of the Power on which he depends, or those of an allied Power; (2) he has left the territory under the control of the Detaining Power, or of an ally of the said Power; (3) he has joined a ship flying the flag of the Power on which he depends, or of an allied Power, in the territorial waters of the Detaining Power, the said ship not being under the control of the last named Power.").

[599] GPW COMMENTARY 446 ("As Scheidl has pointed out, it is not sufficient for a prisoner attempting to escape to throw off immediate pursuit and hide among the population of the territory; he must actually succeed in escaping beyond the reach of the Detaining Power.").

[600] *See* 1958 UK MANUAL ¶238 note 3 ("The effect of Art. 91 [of the GPW] is that the escape is to be considered successful not only if the prisoner rejoins the armed forces of the State with which he was previously serving, or those of its allies, but also if he has left the territory of or occupied by the Detaining Power, *e.g.*, by reaching neutral territory. If he were picked up by a ship of the Detaining Power outside its territorial waters it would seem that he would not be liable to disciplinary punishment having already made a successful escape by leaving its territory.").

[601] *Refer to* § 15.17.1 (Escaped POWs Received by a Neutral State).

9.25.2 Unsuccessful Escapes. POWs who do not escape successfully retain their entitlement to POW status upon recapture. In particular, the wearing of civilian clothes does not deny escaping POWs their status as POWs.[602]

A number of rules limit the punishment of POWs who do not escape successfully. By limiting the punishment in respect of the act of escape, the GPW recognizes that POWs may legitimately try to escape from their captors.[603] In some cases, POWs may even be under an obligation to escape.[604] For example, U.S. military personnel have a duty to make every effort to escape captivity.[605]

9.25.2.1 *Handover of a Recaptured POW to Competent Military Authority*. A POW who is recaptured shall be handed over without delay to the competent military authority.[606] For example, if recaptured by private persons or by civilian law enforcement authorities, POWs should be handed over to competent military authority without delay. This rule makes certain practices used by Germany during World War II clearly unlawful.[607]

9.25.2.2 *Only Disciplinary Punishments in Respect of an Act of Escape*. A POW who attempts to escape and is recaptured before having made good his or her escape in the sense of Article 91 of the GPW shall be liable only to a disciplinary punishment in respect of this act,

---

602 GPW COMMENTARY 454 ("Additional difficulties have sometimes arisen from the wearing of civilian clothing; during the Second World War, some Detaining Powers stated their intention of considering prisoners of war in civilian clothing as spies and no longer as prisoners of war. This matter is settled by the present provision: a prisoner of war retains that legal status until such time as he has made good his escape.").

603 GPW COMMENTARY 445 ("A prisoner of war can legitimately try to escape from his captors. It is even considered by some that prisoners of war have a moral obligation to try to escape, and in most cases such attempts are of course motivated by patriotism. Conversely, in its own interest, the Detaining Power will endeavour to prevent escape whenever possible. This results in the paradox of escape to which A. R. Werner refers: an attempt to escape is considered by the Detaining Power as a breach of discipline and therefore punishable, while the adverse Party considers it as an act which cannot be held to be a crime. Attempted escape is therefore liable only to disciplinary punishment, and not to judicial proceedings.").

604 Rex v. Guenther Krebs (Magistrate's Court of the County of Renfrew, Ontario, Oct. 7, 1943), *reprinted in* 38 AJIL, 505, 507-08 (1944) ("This accused owes no allegiance to the Crown. He is an open and avowed enemy of the Crown, a man taken in war and a man who, if it is not his duty, may quite reasonably feel that it is his duty to escape from the domains of his captor state, and, if he can, return to the state to which he owes allegiance and perform his duty to that state. Whatever may be finally decided in this matter, my opinion is that a prisoner of war is not punishable for anything he may reasonably do to escape, or having escaped, to preserve his liberty. My opinion also is that what the accused did was done with a view to facilitating his escape. He, therefore is not guilty of any crime.").

605 *Refer to* § 9.39.1.3 (Code of Conduct – Article III).

606 GPW art. 92 ("A prisoner of war who is recaptured shall be handed over without delay to the competent military authority.").

607 1958 UK MANUAL ¶240 note 1 ("One of the purposes of these articles [of the GPW] is to render clearly unlawful the practice resorted to by Germany during the Second World War of handing over recaptured prisoners of war to non-military agencies such as the German *Gestapo* or the concentration camp service.").

even if it is a repeated offense.[608]

9.25.2.3 *Disciplinary Punishment for Certain Offenses Committed in Connection With Escape*. In conformity with the principle stated in Article 83 of the GPW (*i.e.*, leniency in favor of disciplinary rather than judicial proceedings), offenses committed by POWs with the sole intention of facilitating their escape and that do not entail any violence against life or limb, such as offenses against public property, theft without intention of self-enrichment, the drawing up or use of false papers, or the wearing of civilian clothing, shall occasion disciplinary punishment only.[609]

For example, if a POW steals food, money, or means of transport; wears civilian clothing; or fabricates false documents in order to facilitate his or her escape and is caught before escaping successfully, such acts may only incur disciplinary punishment.

9.25.2.4 *Escape Not an Aggravating Circumstance in Respect of a Judicial Offense Committed During Escape*. Escape or attempt to escape, even if it is a repeated offense, shall not be deemed an aggravating circumstance if the POW is subjected to trial by judicial proceedings in respect of an offense committed during his or her escape or attempt to escape.[610]

For example, an escaping POW who kills or injures a Detaining Power guard while escaping could be liable to judicial punishment for that offense. However, the circumstance of escape shall not be deemed to aggravate the sentence of the POW, even if the POW is one who frequently attempts to escape.

9.25.3 Liability of POWs for Other POWs' Escape or Attempts to Escape. POWs who aid or abet an escape or an attempt to escape are liable on this count to disciplinary punishment only.[611]

Collective punishment of POWs for an escape attempt by other POWs is also

---

[608] GPW art. 92 ("A prisoner of war who attempts to escape and is recaptured before having made good his escape in the sense of Article 91 shall be liable only to a disciplinary punishment in respect of this act, even if it is a repeated offence.").

[609] GPW art. 93 ("In conformity with the principle stated in Article 83, offences committed by prisoners of war with the sole intention of facilitating their escape and which do not entail any violence against life or limb, such as offences against public property, theft without intention of self-enrichment, the drawing up or use of false papers, or the wearing of civilian clothing, shall occasion disciplinary punishment only.").

[610] GPW art. 93 ("Escape or attempt to escape, even if it is a repeated offence, shall not be deemed an aggravating circumstance if the prisoner of war is subjected to trial by judicial proceedings in respect of an offence committed during his escape or attempt to escape.").

[611] GPW art. 93 ("Prisoners of war who aid or abet an escape or an attempt to escape shall be liable on this count to disciplinary punishment only."). *See also* GPW COMMENTARY 455 ("At the 1929 Conference, some delegations maintained that accomplices should be exempt from any punishment, even disciplinary. This proposal was rightly rejected. Furthermore, the punishment of accomplices is consistent with the principles of penal law. Escape is an offence against the Detaining Power. The privilege of impunity which is granted to a prisoner of war who commits this offence is based solely on the fact that captivity is interrupted and this is not so in the case of accomplices.").

prohibited.[612]

9.25.4 Special Surveillance of POWs as a Result of Unsuccessful Escape. Despite Article 88 of the GPW, which articulates the principle that POWs who have served disciplinary or judicial sentences may not be treated differently from other POWs,[613] POWs punished as a result of an unsuccessful escape may be subjected to special surveillance.[614] Such surveillance: (1) must not affect the state of their health; (2) must be undergone in a POW camp; and (3) must not entail the suppression of any of the safeguards granted to them by the GPW.[615]

9.25.5 Notification of Escape and Recapture. If a POW escapes, the State on which the POW depends should be notified by the Detaining Power's National POW Information Bureau through the intermediary of the Protecting Powers and Central Tracing Agency.[616]

If an escaped POW is recaptured, the Power on which the POW depends shall be notified of the recapture in the manner prescribed in Article 122 of the GPW (*i.e.*, by the Detaining Power's National POW Information Bureau through the intermediary of the Protecting Powers and Central Tracing Agency), provided notification of the POW's escape has been made.[617]

9.26 General Principles Applicable to POW Discipline

In the GPW, the rules on POW discipline are provided under three sub-headings:

- General principles applicable at all times.[618]
- "Disciplinary measures," which means punishment by the commander of the POW camp, and is equivalent to summary disposal by a commanding officer.[619]
- "Judicial proceedings," which means trial and punishment by a court having jurisdiction to try POWs, and is equivalent to trial by court-martial.[620]

This section addresses the general principles applicable to both disciplinary and judicial proceedings against POWs.

---

[612] *Refer to* § 9.26.6 (Prohibited Penalties).

[613] *Refer to* § 9.26.7 (Treatment of POWs Undergoing Punishment).

[614] GPW art. 92 ("Article 88, fourth paragraph, notwithstanding, prisoners of war punished as a result of an unsuccessful escape may be subjected to special surveillance.").

[615] GPW art. 92 ("Such surveillance must not affect the state of their health, must be undergone in a prisoner of war camp, and must not entail the suppression of any of the safeguards granted them by the present Convention.").

[616] *Refer to* § 9.31.1 (Accountability Information That the Detaining Power Should Collect).

[617] GPW art. 94 ("If an escaped prisoner of war is recaptured, the Power on which he depends shall be notified thereof in the manner defined in Article 122, provided notification of his escape has been made.").

[618] GPW arts. 82-88.

[619] GPW arts. 89-98. *Refer to* § 9.27 (Disciplinary Proceedings and Punishment).

[620] GPW arts. 99-108. *Refer to* § 9.28 (Judicial Proceedings and Punishment).

9.26.1 POWs Subject to the Laws, Regulations, and Orders in Force in the Armed Forces of the Detaining Power. A POW shall be subject to the laws, regulations, and orders in force in the armed forces of the Detaining Power; the Detaining Power shall be justified in taking judicial or disciplinary measures in respect of any offense committed by a POW against such laws, regulations, or orders.[621] For example, POWs in custody of the U.S. armed forces are subject to the Uniform Code of Military Justice.[622] However, no proceedings or punishments contrary to the provisions of Chapter III of the GPW shall be allowed.[623]

POWs also remain subject to the laws of the State to which they claim allegiance, and may be prosecuted by that State following release and repatriation for misconduct committed during their captivity.[624]

9.26.2 Leniency in Favor of Disciplinary Rather Than Judicial Proceedings. In deciding whether proceedings in respect of an offense alleged to have been committed by a POW shall be judicial or disciplinary, the Detaining Power shall ensure that the competent authorities exercise the greatest leniency and adopt, wherever possible, disciplinary rather than judicial measures.[625]

This requirement does not compel the competent authorities to choose disciplinary over judicial proceedings in any particular case.

9.26.3 Trial by Military Courts. A POW shall be tried only by a military court, unless the existing laws of the Detaining Power expressly permit the civil courts to try a member of the armed forces of the Detaining Power in respect of the particular offense alleged to have been committed by the POW.[626]

In no circumstances whatever shall a POW be tried by a court of any kind that does not offer the essential guarantees of independence and impartiality as generally recognized and, in particular, the procedure of which does not afford the accused the rights and means of defense provided for in Article 105 of the GPW.[627]

---

[621] GPW art. 82 ("A prisoner of war shall be subject to the laws, regulations and orders in force in the armed forces of the Detaining Power; the Detaining Power shall be justified in taking judicial or disciplinary measures in respect of any offence committed by a prisoner of war against such laws, regulations or orders.").

[622] 10 U.S.C. § 802 ("(a) The following persons are subject to this chapter [47 – Uniform Code of Military Justice]: … (9) Prisoners of war in custody of the armed forces.").

[623] GPW art. 82 ("However, no proceedings or punishments contrary to the provisions of this Chapter shall be allowed.").

[624] *Refer to* § 9.22.2 (POWs' Status With Respect to Their Armed Forces).

[625] GPW art. 83 ("In deciding whether proceedings in respect of an offence alleged to have been committed by a prisoner of war shall be judicial or disciplinary, the Detaining Power shall ensure that the competent authorities exercise the greatest leniency and adopt, wherever possible, disciplinary rather than judicial measures.").

[626] GPW art. 84 ("A prisoner of war shall be tried only by a military court, unless the existing laws of the Detaining Power expressly permit the civil courts to try a member of the armed forces of the Detaining Power in respect of the particular offence alleged to have been committed by the prisoner of war.").

[627] GPW art. 84 ("In no circumstances whatever shall a prisoner of war be tried by a court of any kind which does not offer the essential guarantees of independence and impartiality as generally recognized, and, in particular, the

9.26.4 Retention of Benefits of the GPW Even if Prosecuted for Pre-Capture Acts. POWs prosecuted under the laws of the Detaining Power for acts committed prior to capture shall retain, even if convicted, the benefits of the GPW.[628] For example, POWs prosecuted for pre-capture acts are entitled to the fair trial protections provided by the GPW.[629] POWs' fair trial protections could not be ensured if the mere allegation of a war crime could deny them POW status.[630]

9.26.5 Repetition of Punishment. No POW may be punished more than once for the same act, or on the same charge.[631]

9.26.6 Prohibited Penalties. POWs may not be sentenced by the military authorities and courts of the Detaining Power to any penalties except those provided for in respect of members of the armed forces of the Detaining Power who have committed the same acts.[632] The following punishments are expressly prohibited:

- collective punishments for individual acts;[633]
- corporal punishment;
- imprisonment in premises without daylight;
- any form of torture or cruelty; and
- deprivation of rank or of the right to wear badges.[634]

---

procedure of which does not afford the accused the rights and means of defence provided for in Article 105."). *Refer to* § 9.28.4 (Rights of Defense and Trial Procedure).

[628] GPW art. 85 ("Prisoners of war prosecuted under the laws of the Detaining Power for acts committed prior to capture shall retain, even if convicted, the benefits of the present Convention.").

[629] *Refer to* § 9.28.4 (Rights of Defense and Trial Procedure).

[630] George Aldrich, Assistant Legal Adviser for Far Eastern Affairs, Department of State, *Entitlement of American Military Personnel Held by North Viet-Nam to Treatment as Prisoners of War Under the Geneva Convention of 1949 Relative to the Treatment of Prisoners of War*, Jul. 13, 1966, X WHITEMAN'S DIGEST 231, 232-33 (§7) ("No nation has reserved the right to nullify its obligations under the Convention by a simple declaration that it regards members of the armed forces of an opposing party in an international conflict as war criminals. … While a number of Communist parties to the Convention, including North Viet Nam, have indicated, by reservations, that they will not comply with Article 85, these reservations (1) apply only to prisoners guilty of war crimes as opposed to recognized acts of warfare and (2) apply only *after* a prisoner has been tried in accordance with all the judicial guarantees which the Convention provides, and only after conviction.").

[631] GPW art. 86 ("No prisoner of war may be punished more than once for the same act, or on the same charge.").

[632] GPW art. 87 ("Prisoners of war may not be sentenced by the military authorities and courts of the Detaining Power to any penalties except those provided for in respect of members of the armed forces of the said Power who have committed the same acts.").

[633] *Refer to* § 8.16.2.1 (Individual Penal Responsibility and No Collective Punishment).

[634] GPW art. 87 ("Collective punishment for individual acts, corporal punishment, imprisonment in premises without daylight and, in general, any form of torture or cruelty, are forbidden. No prisoner of war may be deprived of his rank by the Detaining Power, or prevented from wearing his badges.").

The courts and authorities of the Detaining Power, in reaching decisions on punishment, must at all times remember that the accused:

- does not owe any allegiance to the Detaining Power and may be, for example, under a duty to escape;[635] and
- is in its power through circumstances beyond his or her control so that, for example, depression brought on by captivity should not be regarded as self-induced.

Courts and disciplinary authorities shall have the discretion to reduce the penalty below the minimum prescribed for members of the armed forces of the Detaining Power.[636]

9.26.7 Treatment of POWs Undergoing Punishment. Officers, non-commissioned officers, and men and women who are POWs undergoing a disciplinary or judicial punishment, shall not be subjected to more severe treatment than that applied in respect of the same punishment to members of the armed forces of the Detaining Power of equivalent rank.[637]

A woman POW shall not be awarded or sentenced to a punishment more severe, or treated while undergoing punishment more severely, than either a female or male member of the armed forces of the Detaining Power dealt with for a similar offense.[638]

POWs who have served disciplinary or judicial sentences may not be treated differently from other POWs.[639] However, POWs who have been punished as a result of an attempted escape may nonetheless be subjected to special surveillance.[640]

9.27 Disciplinary Proceedings and Punishment

In addition to the general principles applicable to POW punishment, the following rules address disciplinary proceedings and punishment.

---

[635] *Refer to* § 4.4.4.2 (Nationals of a State Who Join Enemy Forces).

[636] GPW art. 87 ("When fixing the penalty, the courts or authorities of the Detaining Power shall take into consideration, to the widest extent possible, the fact that the accused, not being a national of the Detaining Power, is not bound to it by any duty of allegiance, and that he is in its power as the result of circumstances independent of his own will. The said courts or authorities shall be at liberty to reduce the penalty provided for the violation of which the prisoner of war is accused, and shall therefore not be bound to apply the minimum penalty prescribed.").

[637] GPW art. 88 ("Officers, non-commissioned officers and men who are prisoners of war undergoing a disciplinary or judicial punishment, shall not be subjected to more severe treatment than that applied in respect of the same punishment to members of the armed forces of the Detaining Power of equivalent rank.").

[638] GPW art. 88 ("A woman prisoner of war shall not be awarded or sentenced to a punishment more severe, or treated whilst undergoing punishment more severely, than a woman member of the armed forces of the Detaining Power dealt with for a similar offence."); GPW art. 88 ("In no case may a woman prisoner of war be awarded or sentenced to a punishment more severe, or treated whilst undergoing punishment more severely, than a male member of the armed forces of the Detaining Power dealt with for a similar offence.").

[639] GPW art. 88 ("Prisoners of war who have served disciplinary or judicial sentences may not be treated differently from other prisoners of war.").

[640] *Refer to* § 9.25.4 (Special Surveillance of POWs as a Result of Unsuccessful Escape).

9.27.1 POW Camp Authorities Who May Order Disciplinary Punishment. Apart from judicial authorities or superior military authorities, only the camp commander, the officer acting in the commander's place, or an officer to whom the commander has delegated his or her disciplinary powers, may order disciplinary punishment.[641] A camp commander's power to order disciplinary punishment of POWs may not be delegated to POWs.[642]

9.27.2 Confinement of POWs Pending Disposal of Offense. A POW accused of an offense against discipline shall not be kept in confinement pending his or her hearing (*e.g.*, during the investigation of the accusation), unless (1) a member of the armed forces of the Detaining Power would be so confined if he or she were accused of a similar offense, or (2) if confinement is otherwise essential in the interests of camp order and discipline.[643]

Any period spent in confinement awaiting disposal of an offense against discipline shall be reduced to the absolute minimum and shall not exceed fourteen days.[644]

The provisions of Articles 97 and 98 of the GPW shall apply to a POW's confinement while awaiting the disposal of offenses against discipline.[645] Thus, the conditions of any confinement before the hearing should be at least as good as that afforded POWs who are confined as part of disciplinary punishment.[646]

9.27.3 Rights of POWs in Disciplinary Proceedings. Before any disciplinary award is pronounced, the accused shall be given (1) precise information regarding the offenses of which he or she is accused; (2) an opportunity to explain his or her conduct; and (3) an opportunity to defend himself or herself.[647] He or she shall be permitted, in particular, to call witnesses and to have recourse, if necessary, to the services of a qualified interpreter.[648]

---

641 GPW art. 96 ("Without prejudice to the competence of courts and superior military authorities, disciplinary punishment may be ordered only by an officer having disciplinary powers in his capacity as camp commander, or by a responsible officer who replaces him or to whom he has delegated his disciplinary powers.").

642 GPW art. 96 ("In no case may such powers be delegated to a prisoner of war or be exercised by a prisoner of war.").

643 GPW art. 95 ("A prisoner of war accused of an offence against discipline shall not be kept in confinement pending the hearing unless a member of the armed forces of the Detaining Power would be so kept if he were accused of a similar offence, or if it is essential in the interests of camp order and discipline.").

644 GPW art. 95 ("Any period spent by a prisoner of war in confinement awaiting the disposal of an offence against discipline shall be reduced to an absolute minimum and shall not exceed fourteen days.").

645 GPW art. 95 ("The provisions of Articles 97 and 98 of this Chapter shall apply to prisoners of war who are in confinement awaiting the disposal of offences against discipline.").

646 *Refer to* § 9.27.6 (Conditions for POWs Serving Disciplinary Punishments).

647 GPW art. 96 ("Before any disciplinary award is pronounced, the accused shall be given precise information regarding the offences of which he is accused, and given an opportunity of explaining his conduct and of defending himself.").

648 GPW art. 96 ("He shall be permitted, in particular, to call witnesses and to have recourse, if necessary, to the services of a qualified interpreter.").

The decision shall be announced to the accused POW and to the POW Representative.[649]

9.27.4 Record of Disciplinary Punishments. A record of disciplinary punishments shall be maintained by the camp commander and shall be open to inspection by representatives of the Protecting Power.[650]

9.27.5 Types of Disciplinary Punishments and Procedures for Dispensing Punishment. In no case shall disciplinary punishments be inhuman, brutal, or dangerous to the health of POWs.[651] The disciplinary punishments applicable to POWs are the following:

- a fine that shall not exceed 50 percent of the advances of pay and working pay that the POW would receive under Articles 60 and 62 of the GPW during a period of not more than thirty days;
- discontinuance of privileges granted over and above the treatment provided for by the GPW;
- fatigue duties, not exceeding two hours daily;
    - "Fatigue duties" refers to details of extra-duty chores (*e.g.*, such as policing of the POW camp grounds, kitchen duty).[652]
    - The punishment of fatigue duties shall not be applied to officers.[653] In addition, fatigue details should meet normal standards for working conditions and must not be made more arduous as a disciplinary measure.[654]
- confinement.[655]

The duration of any single punishment shall in no case exceed thirty days.[656] The

---

[649] GPW art. 96 ("The decision shall be announced to the accused prisoner of war and to the prisoners' representative.").

[650] GPW art. 96 ("A record of disciplinary punishments shall be maintained by the camp commander and shall be open to inspection by representatives of the Protecting Power.").

[651] GPW art. 89 ("In no case shall disciplinary punishments be inhuman, brutal or dangerous to the health of prisoners of war.").

[652] LEVIE, POWS 327 ("This punishment consists of extra-duty chores (beyond regular work hours and beyond normal duty-roster assignments), such as policing of the prisoner-of-war camp grounds, kitchen police, etc. The imposition of such extra fatigue duty as disciplinary punishment is limited to 2 hours per day; and Article 90 limits the overall duration to 30 days.").

[653] GPW art. 89 ("The punishment referred to under (3) shall not be applied to officers.").

[654] *Refer to* § 9.19.3 (Suitable Work Conditions).

[655] GPW art. 89 ("The disciplinary punishment applicable to prisoners of war are the following: (1) A fine which shall not exceed 50 per cent of the advances of pay and working pay which the prisoner of war would otherwise receive under the provisions of Articles 60 and 62 during a period of not more than thirty days. (2) Discontinuance of privileges granted over and above the treatment provided for by the present Convention. (3) Fatigue duties not exceeding two hours daily. (4) Confinement.").

maximum of thirty days may not be exceeded, even if the POW is answerable for several acts when punishment is awarded, regardless of whether such acts are related.[657]

Any period of confinement awaiting the hearing of a disciplinary offense or the award of disciplinary punishment shall be deducted from an award pronounced against a POW.[658]

The period between the pronouncing of an award of disciplinary punishment and its execution shall not exceed one month.[659] When a POW is awarded a further disciplinary punishment, a period of at least three days shall elapse between the execution of any two of the punishments, if the duration of one of these punishments is ten days or more.[660]

9.27.6 Conditions for POWs Serving Disciplinary Punishments. Conditions for disciplinary punishments must comply with the requirements for humane treatment.[661] In addition, the following rules apply:

9.27.6.1 *Premises Where Disciplinary Punishments Are to Be Served*. POWs shall not in any case be transferred to penitentiary establishments (prisons, penitentiaries, convict prisons, etc.) to undergo disciplinary punishment.[662]

Officers and persons of equivalent status shall not be lodged in the same quarters as non-commissioned officers or enlisted personnel.[663]

Women POWs undergoing disciplinary punishment shall be confined in separate quarters from male POWs and shall be under the immediate supervision of women.[664]

9.27.6.2 *Retention of the Benefits of the GPW While Undergoing Disciplinary Punishment*. A POW undergoing confinement as a disciplinary punishment shall continue to receive the benefits of the GPW, except insofar as these benefits are necessarily rendered

---

[656] GPW art. 90 ("The duration of any single punishment shall in no case exceed thirty days.").

[657] GPW art. 90 ("The maximum of thirty days provided above may not be exceeded, even if the prisoner of war is answerable for several acts at the same time when he is awarded punishment, whether such acts are related or not.").

[658] GPW art. 90 ("Any period of confinement awaiting the hearing of a disciplinary offence or the award of disciplinary punishment shall be deducted from an award pronounced against a prisoner of war.").

[659] GPW art. 90 ("The period between the pronouncing of an award of disciplinary punishment and its execution shall not exceed one month.").

[660] GPW art. 90 ("When a prisoner of war is awarded a further disciplinary punishment, a period of at least three days shall elapse between the execution of any two of the punishments, if the duration of one of these is ten days or more.").

[661] *Refer to* § 9.5 (Humane Treatment and Basic Protections for POWs).

[662] GPW art. 97 ("Prisoners of war shall not in any case be transferred to penitentiary establishments (prisons, penitentiaries, convict prisons, etc.) to undergo disciplinary punishment therein.").

[663] GPW art. 97 ("Officers and persons of equivalent status shall not be lodged in the same quarters as non-commissioned officers or men.").

[664] GPW art. 97 ("Women prisoners of war undergoing disciplinary punishment shall be confined in separate quarters from male prisoners of war and shall be under the immediate supervision of women.").

inapplicable by the mere fact that the POW is confined.[665]

In no case, however, may POWs undergoing disciplinary punishments be deprived of the benefits of the provisions of Articles 78 and 126 of the GPW.[666] Thus, POWs undergoing disciplinary punishments may not be deprived of the right to make requests and complaints, or to deal with representatives of the Protecting Power (including representatives of an impartial humanitarian organization performing the functions of the Protecting Power).[667]

9.27.6.3 Disciplinary Punishment - Retention of Prerogatives of Rank. A POW awarded disciplinary punishment may not be deprived of prerogatives attached to his or her rank.[668] The prerogatives referred to are those provided by the GPW, such as the right not to be required to work or the right to wear the insignia of their rank.[669]

9.27.6.4 Attendance at Daily Medical Inspection and Medical Attention. POWs awarded disciplinary punishment shall be allowed, on their request, to be present at the daily medical inspection.[670] They shall receive the attention that their state of health requires and, if necessary, shall be removed to the camp infirmary or to a hospital.[671]

9.27.6.5 Exercise and Access to the Open Air. POWs awarded disciplinary punishment shall be allowed to exercise and to stay in the open air at least two hours daily.[672]

9.27.6.6 Reading, Writing, Correspondence, and Packages. POWs awarded disciplinary punishment shall have permission to read and write, and to send and receive letters.[673] Parcels and remittances of money, however, may be withheld from them until the completion of the punishment; such parcels and remittances of money shall meanwhile be entrusted to the POW Representative, who will hand over to the infirmary the perishable goods

---

[665] GPW art. 98 ("A prisoner of war undergoing confinement as a disciplinary punishment, shall continue to enjoy the benefits of the provisions of this Convention except in so far as these are necessarily rendered inapplicable by the mere fact that he is confined.").

[666] GPW art. 98 ("In no case may he be deprived of the benefits of the provisions of Articles 78 and 126.").

[667] *Refer to* § 9.23 (POW Requests, Complaints); § 9.32 (Role of the Protecting Power in the GPW).

[668] GPW art. 98 ("A prisoner of war awarded disciplinary punishment may not be deprived of the prerogatives attached to his rank.").

[669] *See* GPW COMMENTARY 467 ("Officers retain the right to wear the insignia of their rank (Article 44). They may not be required to work (Article 49, paragraph 3) or to provide their own service (Article 44, paragraph 2), for that would amount to making them perform fatigue duties, which is forbidden under Article 89, paragraph 2. In accordance with Article 97, paragraph 3, officers will be lodged in quarters separate from those of non-commissioned officers and other ranks. These provisions were in the main observed during the Second World War.").

[670] GPW art. 98 ("[POWs awarded disciplinary punishment] shall be allowed, on their request, to be present at the daily medical inspections.").

[671] GPW art. 98 ("[POWs awarded disciplinary punishment] shall receive the attention which their state of health requires and, if necessary, shall be removed to the camp infirmary or to a hospital.").

[672] GPW art. 98 ("Prisoners of war awarded disciplinary punishment shall be allowed to exercise and to stay in the open air at least two hours daily.").

[673] GPW art. 98 ("They shall have permission to read and write, likewise to send and receive letters.").

contained in such parcels.[674]

9.27.7 Disciplinary Punishment and Repatriation or Accommodation in a Neutral Country. No POW on whom a disciplinary punishment has been imposed and who is eligible for repatriation or for accommodation in a neutral country may be kept back because he or she has not undergone his or her punishment.[675]

9.28 Judicial Proceedings and Punishment

In addition to the general principles applicable to POW punishment, the following rules address judicial proceedings and punishment.

9.28.1 No Trial or Sentence Without Pre-Existing Law. No POW may be tried or sentenced for an act that is not forbidden by the law of the Detaining Power or by international law in force at the time that act was committed.[676]

9.28.2 Same Courts and Same Procedures. A POW can be validly sentenced only if the sentence has been pronounced by the same courts according to the same procedure as in the case of members of the armed forces of the Detaining Power, and if, furthermore, the provisions of Chapter III of the GPW have been observed.[677] For example, evidence laws used in the trial of a POW will be the same as those applicable in the trial of a member of the Detaining Power's military forces.

9.28.3 Notification of Proceedings, Investigation of Offenses, and Confinement Before Trial.

9.28.3.1 *Notification of Proceedings*. In any case in which the Detaining Power decides to institute judicial proceedings against a POW, the Detaining Power shall notify the Protecting Power and the POW Representative as soon as possible and at least three weeks before the opening of the trial.[678] This period of three weeks shall run from the day on which such notification reaches the Protecting Power at the address previously indicated by the latter to

---

[674] GPW art. 98 ("Parcels and remittances of money however, may be withheld from them until the completion of the punishment; they shall meanwhile be entrusted to the prisoners' representative, who will hand over to the infirmary the perishable goods contained in such parcels.").

[675] GPW art. 115 ("No prisoner of war on whom a disciplinary punishment has been imposed and who is eligible for repatriation or for accommodation in a neutral country, may be kept back on the plea that he has not undergone his punishment.").

[676] GPW art. 99 ("No prisoner of war may be tried or sentenced for an act which is not forbidden by the law of the Detaining Power or by international law, in force at the time the said act was committed.").

[677] GPW art. 102 ("A prisoner of war can be validly sentenced only if the sentence has been pronounced by the same courts according to the same procedure as in the case of members of the armed forces of the Detaining Power, and if, furthermore, the provisions of the present Chapter have been observed.").

[678] *See* GPW art. 104 ("In any case in which the Detaining Power has decided to institute judicial proceedings against a prisoner of war, it shall notify the Protecting Power as soon as possible and at least three weeks before the opening of the trial. … The same communication shall be made by the Detaining Power to the prisoners' representative.").

the Detaining Power.[679] This notification shall contain the following information:

- surname and first names of the POW, his or her rank, his or her army, regimental, personal or serial number, his or her date of birth, and his or her profession or trade, if any;
- place of internment or confinement;
- specification of the charge or charges on which the POW is to be arraigned, giving the legal provisions applicable; and
- designation of the court that will try the case, and the date and place fixed for the opening of the trial.[680]

If no evidence is submitted at the opening of a trial that the notification referred to above was received by the Protecting Power, by the POW, and by the POW Representative concerned at least three weeks before the opening of the trial, then the trial may not take place and must be adjourned.[681]

9.28.3.2 *Rapid Investigations*. Judicial investigations relating to a POW shall be conducted as rapidly as circumstances permit so that his or her trial may take place as soon as possible.[682]

9.28.3.3 *Pre-Trial Confinement*. A POW shall not be confined while awaiting trial unless a member of the armed forces of the Detaining Power would be so confined if he or she were accused of a similar offense, or if it is essential to do so in the interests of national security.[683]

In no circumstances, however, may a POW be confined for more than three months.[684]

---

[679] GPW art. 104 ("This period of three weeks shall run as from the day on which such notification reaches the Protecting Power at the address previously indicated by the latter to the Detaining Power.").

[680] GPW art. 104 ("The said notification shall contain the following information: (1) surname and first names of the prisoner of war, his rank, his army, regimental, personal or serial number, his date of birth, and his profession or trade, if any; (2) place of internment or confinement; (3) specification of the charge or charges on which the prisoner of war is to be arraigned, giving the legal provisions applicable; (4) designation of the court which will try the case, likewise the date and place fixed for the opening of the trial.").

[681] GPW art. 104 ("If no evidence is submitted, at the opening of a trial, that the notification referred to above was received by the Protecting Power, by the prisoner of war and by the prisoners' representative concerned, at least three weeks before the opening of the trial, then the latter cannot take place and must be adjourned.").

[682] GPW art. 103 ("Judicial investigations relating to a prisoner of war shall be conducted as rapidly as circumstances permit and so that his trial shall take place as soon as possible.").

[683] GPW art. 103 ("A prisoner of war shall not be confined while awaiting trial unless a member of the armed forces of the Detaining Power would be so confined if he were accused of a similar offence, or if it is essential to do so in the interests of national security.").

[684] GPW art. 103 ("In no circumstances shall this confinement exceed three months.").

Any period spent by a POW in confinement awaiting trial shall be deducted from any sentence of imprisonment passed upon him or her and taken into account in fixing any penalty.[685]

Articles 97 and 98 of the GPW apply to a POW's confinement while awaiting trial.[686] Thus, the conditions of any confinement before trial should be at least as good as that afforded POWs who are confined as part of disciplinary punishment.[687]

9.28.4 Rights of Defense and Trial Procedure.

9.28.4.1 *No Moral or Physical Coercion to Induce Admissions of Guilt*. No moral or physical coercion may be exerted on a POW in order to induce him or her to admit himself or herself guilty of the act of which he or she is accused.[688]

9.28.4.2 *Opportunity to Present Defense and Assistance of Counsel*. No POW may be convicted without having had an opportunity to present his or her defense and to have the assistance of a qualified advocate or counsel.[689]

In judicial proceedings against a POW, the POW shall be entitled to:

- assistance by one of his or her POW comrades;
- defense by a qualified advocate or counsel of his or her own choice;
- the calling of witnesses; and
- if he or she deems necessary, the services of a competent interpreter.[690]

The POW shall be advised of these rights by the Detaining Power in due time before the trial to enable him or her to exercise them.[691]

---

[685] GPW art. 103 ("Any period spent by a prisoner of war in confinement awaiting trial shall be deducted from any sentence of imprisonment passed upon him and taken into account in fixing any penalty.").

[686] GPW art. 103 ("The provisions of Articles 97 and 98 of this Chapter shall apply to a prisoner of war whilst in confinement awaiting trial.").

[687] *Refer to* § 9.27.6 (Conditions for POWs Serving Disciplinary Punishments).

[688] GPW art. 99 ("No moral or physical coercion may be exerted on a prisoner of war in order to induce him to admit himself guilty of the act of which he is accused.").

[689] GPW art. 99 ("No prisoner of war may be convicted without having had an opportunity to present his defence and the assistance of a qualified advocate or counsel.").

[690] GPW art. 105 ("The prisoner of war shall be entitled to assistance by one of his prisoner comrades, to defence by a qualified advocate or counsel of his own choice, to the calling of witnesses and, if he deems necessary, to the services of a competent interpreter. He shall be advised of these rights by the Detaining Power in due time before the trial.").

[691] GPW art. 105 ("The prisoner of war shall be entitled to assistance by one of his prisoner comrades, to defence by a qualified advocate or counsel of his own choice, to the calling of witnesses and, if he deems necessary, to the

Failing a choice by the POW, the Protecting Power shall find him or her an advocate or counsel, and shall have at least one week at its disposal for this purpose.[692] The Detaining Power shall deliver to the Protecting Power, on request, a list of persons qualified to present the defense.[693] Failing a choice of an advocate or counsel by the POW or the Protecting Power, the Detaining Power shall appoint a competent advocate or counsel to conduct the defense.[694]

9.28.4.3 *Facilities for Defense Counsel*. The advocate or counsel conducting the defense on behalf of the POW shall have at his or her disposal a period of two weeks at least before the opening of the trial, as well as the necessary facilities to prepare the defense of the accused.[695] He or she may, in particular, freely visit the accused and interview him or her in private.[696] He or she may also confer with any witnesses for the defense, including POWs.[697] He or she shall have the benefit of these facilities until the term of appeal or petition has expired.[698]

9.28.4.4 *Rights of the Accused to Particulars of Charge*. Particulars of the charge or charges on which the POW is to be arraigned, as well as the documents that are generally communicated to the accused by virtue of the laws in force in the armed forces of the Detaining Power, shall be communicated to the accused POW in a language that he or she understands, and in good time before the opening of the trial.[699] The same communication in the same circumstances shall be made to the advocate or counsel conducting the defense on behalf of the POW.[700]

9.28.4.5 *Right of the Protecting Power to Attend Trial*. Representatives of the Protecting Power shall be entitled to attend the trial of the case unless, exceptionally, the trial is

---

services of a competent interpreter. He shall be advised of these rights by the Detaining Power in due time before the trial.").

[692] GPW art. 105 ("Failing a choice by the prisoner of war, the Protecting Power shall find him an advocate or counsel, and shall have at least one week at its disposal for the purpose.").

[693] GPW art. 105 ("The Detaining Power shall deliver to the said Power, on request, a list of persons qualified to present the defence.").

[694] GPW art. 105 ("Failing a choice of an advocate or counsel by the prisoner of war or the Protecting Power, the Detaining Power shall appoint a competent advocate or counsel to conduct the defence.").

[695] GPW art. 105 ("The advocate or counsel conducting the defence on behalf of the prisoner of war shall have at his disposal a period of two weeks at least before the opening of the trial, as well as the necessary facilities to prepare the defence of the accused.").

[696] GPW art. 105 ("He may, in particular, freely visit the accused and interview him in private.").

[697] GPW art. 105 ("He may also confer with any witnesses for the defence, including prisoners of war.").

[698] GPW art. 105 ("He shall have the benefit of these facilities until the term of appeal or petition has expired.").

[699] GPW art. 105 ("Particulars of the charge or charges on which the prisoner of war is to be arraigned, as well as the documents which are generally communicated to the accused by virtue of the laws in force in the armed forces of the Detaining Power, shall be communicated to the accused prisoner of war in a language which he understands, and in good time before the opening of the trial.").

[700] GPW art. 105 ("The same communication in the same circumstances shall be made to the advocate or counsel conducting the defence on behalf of the prisoner of war.").

held *in camera* in the interest of State security.[701] In such a case, the Detaining Power shall advise the Protecting Power accordingly.[702]

9.28.4.6 *Notification of Trial Outcome*. Any judgment and sentence pronounced upon a POW shall be immediately reported to the Protecting Power and the POW Representative concerned in the form of a summary communication, which shall also indicate whether the POW has the right of appeal with a view to the quashing of the sentence or the reopening of the trial.[703] This communication shall also be sent to the accused POW in a language he or she understands, if the sentence was not pronounced in his or her presence.[704]

9.28.5 Appeals and Notice of Final Conviction or Death Sentence.

9.28.5.1 *Appeals*. Every POW shall have, in the same manner as the members of the armed forces of the Detaining Power, the right of appeal or petition from any sentence pronounced upon him or her, with a view to the quashing or revising of the sentence or the reopening of the trial.[705]

He or she shall be fully informed of his or her right to appeal or petition and of the time limit within which he or she may do so.[706]

The Detaining Power shall immediately communicate to the Protecting Power the decision of the POW to use or to waive his or her right of appeal.[707]

9.28.5.2 *Notification of Final Conviction or Death Sentence*. If a POW is finally convicted or if a sentence pronounced on a POW in the first instance is a death sentence, the Detaining Power shall as soon as possible address to the Protecting Power a detailed communication containing:

- the precise wording of the finding and sentence;

---

[701] GPW art. 105 ("The representatives of the Protecting Power shall be entitled to attend the trial of the case, unless, exceptionally, this is held *in camera* in the interest of State security.").

[702] GPW art. 105 ("In such a case the Detaining Power shall advise the Protecting Power accordingly.").

[703] GPW art. 107 ("Any judgment and sentence pronounced upon a prisoner of war shall be immediately reported to the Protecting Power in the form of a summary communication, which shall also indicate whether he has the right of appeal with a view to the quashing of the sentence or the reopening of the trial. This communication shall likewise be sent to the prisoners' representative concerned.").

[704] GPW art. 107 ("It shall also be sent to the accused prisoner of war in a language he understands, if the sentence was not pronounced in his presence.").

[705] GPW art. 106 ("Every prisoner of war shall have, in the same manner as the members of the armed forces of the Detaining Power, the right of appeal or petition from any sentence pronounced upon him, with a view to the quashing or revising of the sentence or the reopening of the trial.").

[706] GPW art. 106 ("He shall be fully informed of his right to appeal or petition and of the time limit within which he may do so.").

[707] GPW art. 107 ("The Detaining Power shall also immediately communicate to the Protecting Power the decision of the prisoner of war to use or to waive his right of appeal.").

- a summarized report of any preliminary investigation and of the trial, emphasizing in particular the elements of the prosecution and the defense; and
- notification, where applicable, of the establishment where the sentence will be served.[708]

These communications shall be sent to the Protecting Power at the address previously made known to the Detaining Power.[709]

9.28.6 Death Sentences. POWs and the Protecting Powers shall be informed, as soon as possible, of the offenses that are punishable by death sentence under the laws of the Detaining Power.[710] Other offenses shall not thereafter be made punishable by the death penalty without the concurrence of the Power on which the POWs depend.[711]

The death sentence may not be pronounced on a POW unless the attention of the court has, in accordance with the second paragraph of Article 87 of the GPW, been particularly called to the fact:

- that since the accused is not a national of the Detaining Power, he or she is not bound to it by any duty of allegiance; and
- that he or she is in the power of the Detaining Power as the result of circumstances independent of his or her own will.[712]

If the death penalty is pronounced on a POW, the sentence shall not be executed before the expiration of a period of at least six months from the date when the Protecting Power receives, at an indicated address, the detailed communication provided for in Article 107 of the GPW.[713]

---

[708] GPW art. 107 ("Furthermore, if a prisoner of war is finally convicted or if a sentence pronounced on a prisoner of war in the first instance is a death sentence, the Detaining Power shall as soon as possible address to the Protecting Power a detailed communication containing: (1) the precise wording of the finding and sentence; (2) a summarized report of any preliminary investigation and of the trial, emphasizing in particular the elements of the prosecution and the defence; (3) notification, where applicable, of the establishment where the sentence will be served. The communications provided for in the foregoing sub-paragraphs shall be sent to the Protecting Power at the address previously made known to the Detaining Power.").

[709] GPW art. 107 ("The communications provided for in the foregoing sub-paragraphs shall be sent to the Protecting Power at the address previously made known to the Detaining Power.").

[710] GPW art. 100 ("Prisoners of war and the Protecting Powers shall be informed as soon as possible of the offences which are punishable by the death sentence under the laws of the Detaining Power.").

[711] GPW art. 100 ("Other offences shall not thereafter be made punishable by the death penalty without the concurrence of the Power on which the prisoners of war depend.").

[712] GPW art. 100 ("The death sentence cannot be pronounced on a prisoner of war unless the attention of the court has, in accordance with Article 87, second paragraph, been particularly called to the fact that since the accused is not a national of the Detaining Power, he is not bound to it by any duty of allegiance, and that he is in its power as the result of circumstances independent of his own will.").

[713] GPW art. 101 ("If the death penalty is pronounced on a prisoner of war, the sentence shall not be executed before the expiration of a period of at least six months from the date when the Protecting Power receives, at an indicated

9.28.7 Conditions for POWs Serving Judicial Punishments.

9.28.7.1 *Establishments and Conditions Where Sentences Are Served*. A sentence pronounced on a POW after a conviction has become duly enforceable shall be served in the same establishments and under the same conditions as in the case of members of the armed forces of the Detaining Power.[714] These conditions shall in all cases conform to the requirements of health and humanity.[715]

9.28.7.2 *Confinement of Women POWs Who Have Been Sentenced*. A woman POW on whom such a sentence has been pronounced shall be confined in separate quarters and shall be under the supervision of women.[716]

9.28.7.3 *Complaints and Access to ICRC and the Protecting Power During Confinement*. In any case, POWs sentenced to a penalty depriving them of their liberty shall retain the benefit of the provisions of Articles 78 and 126 of the GPW.[717] Thus, they may make requests and complaints and deal with representatives of the Protecting Power or the ICRC.[718]

9.28.7.4 *Correspondence, Relief Parcels, Exercise, Medical Care, and Spiritual Assistance*. Furthermore, POWs sentenced to a penalty depriving them of their liberty shall be entitled to receive and send correspondence, to receive at least one relief parcel monthly, to take regular exercise in the open air, to have the medical care required by their state of health, and to have the spiritual assistance they may desire.[719]

9.28.7.5 *Prohibited Penalties*. Penalties to which POWs may be subjected shall be in accordance with the provisions of the third paragraph of Article 87 of the GPW.[720] Thus, collective punishment for individual acts, corporal punishment, imprisonment in premises without daylight, and, in general, any form of torture or cruelty, are forbidden for POWs serving

address, the detailed communication provided for in Article 107."). *Refer to* § 9.28.5.2 (Notification of Final Conviction or Death Sentence).

714 GPW art. 108 ("Sentences pronounced on prisoners of war after a conviction has become duly enforceable, shall be served in the same establishments and under the same conditions as in the case of members of the armed forces of the Detaining Power.").

715 GPW art. 108 ("These conditions shall in all cases conform to the requirements of health and humanity.").

716 GPW art. 108 ("A woman prisoner of war on whom such a sentence has been pronounced shall be confined in separate quarters and shall be under the supervision of women.").

717 GPW art. 108 ("In any case, prisoners of war sentenced to a penalty depriving them of their liberty shall retain the benefit of the provisions of Articles 78 and 126 of the present Convention.").

718 *Refer to* § 9.23 (POW Requests, Complaints, and Reports About Conditions of Captivity); § 9.33 (Access to POWs by the Protecting Powers, ICRC, and Relief Organizations).

719 GPW art. 108 ("Furthermore, they shall be entitled to receive and despatch correspondence, to receive at least one relief parcel monthly, to take regular exercise in the open air, to have the medical care required by their state of health, and the spiritual assistance they may desire.").

720 GPW art. 108 ("Penalties to which they may be subjected shall be in accordance with the provisions of Article 87, third paragraph.").

judicial penalties.[721]

9.29 Transfer of POWs From the POW Camp

9.29.1 Determining Whether to Transfer POWs. The Detaining Power, when deciding upon the transfer of POWs, shall take into account the interests of the POWs themselves, more especially so as not to increase the difficulty of their repatriation.[722]

Sick or wounded POWs shall not be transferred as long as their recovery may be endangered by the journey, unless their safety imperatively demands it.[723]

If the combat zone draws closer to a camp, the POWs in that camp shall not be transferred unless their transfer can be carried out in adequate conditions of safety, or unless they are exposed to greater risks by remaining on the spot than by being transferred.[724]

9.29.2 Conditions for the Transfer of POWs. The transfer of POWs shall always be effected humanely and in conditions not less favorable than those under which the forces of the Detaining Power are transferred.[725] Account shall always be taken of the climatic conditions to which the POWs are accustomed, and the conditions of transfer shall in no case be prejudicial to their health.[726]

The Detaining Power shall supply POWs during transfer with sufficient food and drinking water to keep them in good health, and shall supply them with the necessary clothing, shelter, and medical attention.[727] The Detaining Power shall take adequate precautions, especially in case of transport by sea or by air, to ensure their safety during transfer, and shall draw up a complete list of all transferred POWs before their departure.[728]

---

721 *Refer to* § 9.26.6 (Prohibited Penalties).

722 GPW art. 46 ("The Detaining Power, when deciding upon the transfer of prisoners of war, shall take into account the interests of the prisoners themselves, more especially so as not to increase the difficulty of their repatriation.").

723 GPW art. 47 ("Sick or wounded prisoners of war shall not be transferred as long as their recovery may be endangered by the journey, unless their safety imperatively demands it.").

724 GPW art. 47 ("If the combat zone draws closer to a camp, the prisoners of war in the said camp shall not be transferred unless their transfer can be carried out in adequate conditions of safety, or unless they are exposed to greater risks by remaining on the spot than by being transferred.").

725 GPW art. 46 ("The transfer of prisoners of war shall always be effected humanely and in conditions not less favourable than those under which the forces of the Detaining Power are transferred.").

726 GPW art. 46 ("Account shall always be taken of the climatic conditions to which the prisoners of war are accustomed and the conditions of transfer shall in no case be prejudicial to their health.").

727 GPW art. 46 ("The Detaining Power shall supply prisoners of war during transfer with sufficient food and drinking water to keep them in good health, likewise with the necessary clothing, shelter and medical attention.").

728 GPW art. 46 ("The Detaining Power shall take adequate precautions especially in case of transport by sea or by air, to ensure their safety during transfer, and shall draw up a complete list of all transferred prisoners before their departure.").

9.29.3 Procedures for Transfer of POWs From the Camp.

9.29.3.1 *Notification of Transfer*. In the event of transfer, POWs shall be officially advised of their departure and of their new postal address.[729] Such notifications shall be given in time for them to pack their luggage and inform their next of kin.[730]

9.29.3.2 *Baggage*. POWs shall be allowed to take with them their personal effects and the correspondence and parcels that have arrived for them.[731] The weight of such baggage may be limited, if the conditions of transfer so require, to what each POW can reasonably carry, which shall in no case be more than 25 kilograms (approximately 55 pounds) per person.[732]

9.29.3.3 *Forwarding of Mail*. Mail and parcels addressed to their former camp shall be forwarded to POWs without delay.[733]

9.29.3.4 *Disposition of Community Property and Remaining Property*. The camp commander shall take, in agreement with the POW Representative, any measures needed to ensure the transport of the POWs' community property and of the luggage they are unable to take with them in consequence of restrictions imposed by virtue of the second paragraph of Article 48 of the GPW (*i.e.*, restrictions on the weight of baggage).[734]

9.29.3.5 *Costs of Transfers*. The costs of transfers shall be borne by the Detaining Power.[735]

9.30 Transfer of POWs to the Custody of Another Detaining Power

The GPW specifies a number of rules that apply to the transfer of POWs by the Detaining Power to the custody of another Detaining Power.

9.30.1 Requirements for Transfer to the Custody of Another Detaining Power. POWs may only be transferred by the Detaining Power to a Power that is a Party to the GPW and after the Detaining Power has satisfied itself of the willingness and ability of such receiving Power to

---

[729] GPW art. 48 ("In the event of transfer, prisoners of war shall be officially advised of their departure and of their new postal address.").

[730] GPW art. 48 ("Such notifications shall be given in time for them to pack their luggage and inform their next of kin.").

[731] GPW art. 48 ("They shall be allowed to take with them their personal effects, and the correspondence and parcels which have arrived for them.").

[732] GPW art. 48 ("The weight of such baggage may be limited, if the conditions of transfer so require, to what each prisoner can reasonably carry, which shall in no case be more than twenty-five kilograms per head.").

[733] GPW art. 48 ("Mail and parcels addressed to their former camp shall be forwarded to them without delay.").

[734] GPW art. 48 ("The camp commander shall take, in agreement with the prisoners' representative, any measures needed to ensure the transport of the prisoners' community property and of the luggage they are unable to take with them in consequence of restrictions imposed by virtue of the second paragraph of this Article.").

[735] GPW art. 48 ("The costs of transfers shall be borne by the Detaining Power.").

apply the GPW.[736] U.S. policy may prescribe additional requirements.[737]

To ensure accountability, a POW should not be transferred before his or her formal processing and submission of all required information to the National POW Information Bureau.[738]

9.30.2 Responsibility When Transferred to the Custody of Another Detaining Power. When POWs are transferred under such circumstances, responsibility for the application of the GPW rests on the Power accepting them while they are in its custody.[739]

Nevertheless, if that Power fails to carry out the provisions of the GPW in any important respect, the Power by whom the POWs were transferred shall, upon being notified by the Protecting Power, take effective measures to correct the situation or shall request the return of the POWs.[740] Such requests must be complied with.[741]

9.30.3 Special Agreements on Transfers to the Another Detaining Power. Special agreements may be concluded with respect to POW transfers to the custody of another Detaining Power. U.S. policy has been to require a written agreement or arrangement before transferring POWs to a coalition partner.[742] For example, the receiving State may agree to inspections by the transferring State to verify compliance with the GPW.[743]

---

[736] GPW art. 12 ("Prisoners of war may only be transferred by the Detaining Power to a Power which is a party to the Convention and after the Detaining Power has satisfied itself of the willingness and ability of such transferee Power to apply the Convention.").

[737] *Refer to, e.g.*, § 8.14.4.1 (U.S. Policy Prohibiting Transfers in Cases in Which Detainees Would Likely Be Tortured).

[738] *Refer to* § 9.31.2 (National POW Information Bureau).

[739] GPW art. 12 ("When prisoners of war are transferred under such circumstances, responsibility for the application of the Convention rests on the Power accepting them while they are in its custody.").

[740] GPW art. 12 ("Nevertheless, if that Power fails to carry out the provisions of the Convention in any important respect, the Power by whom the prisoners of war were transferred shall, upon being notified by the Protecting Power, take effective measures to correct the situation or shall request the return of the prisoners of war.").

[741] GPW art. 12 ("Such requests must be complied with.").

[742] *For example*, FINAL REPORT ON THE PERSIAN GULF WAR 578-79 ("US policy requires approval of a formal international agreement by the Assistant Secretary of Defense for International Security Affairs (ASD/ISA) and the State Department as a prerequisite to transferring EPWs to a Coalition partner. A government-to-government agreement was negotiated between Saudi Arabia and the United States authorizing the transfer of EPWs to Saudi custody. This document was signed formally on 15 January. Separate military-to-military agreements, authorized by the ASD/ISA and the State Department, were also negotiated. These negotiations resulted in the US/UK EPW transfer agreement of 31 January and US/French transfer agreement of 24 February. The agreements outlined the actions to be taken by capturing forces in processing EPWs and displaced civilians through US theater camps, and medical channels to Saudi facilities. The agreement between the United States and Saudi governments provided the United States would transfer custody of EPW to Saudi control after EPW registration by US forces. This agreement also was applicable to EPW captured by the French and British and processed by the US.").

[743] *For example*, *An Arrangement for the Transfer of Enemy Prisoners of War and Civilian Internees from the Custody of British Forces to the Custody of American Forces*, Jan. 31, 1991, *reprinted as Appendix 1 in* PETER ROWE, THE GULF WAR 1990-91 IN INTERNATIONAL AND ENGLISH LAW 348 (1993) ("6 The British Forces will retain a right of access to prisoners of war and civilian internees transferred from British custody while such persons are in

9.31 National Accounting of the Detention of POWs

A proper accounting of the detention of POWs is an important responsibility of the Detaining Power.[744] In order to provide as full an accounting as possible, and in order to minimize misidentification of POWs in its custody, the Detaining Power shall obtain detailed information about each POW for forwarding through its National POW Information Bureau to the Protecting Powers and the Central POW Information Agency.

9.31.1 Accountability Information That the Detaining Power Should Collect. The following information regarding POWs should be collected by the Detaining Power and given to its National POW Information Bureau for forwarding to the Powers concerned through the intermediary of the Protecting Powers and the Central POW Information Agency. This information shall make it possible quickly to advise the next of kin concerned.[745]

This information includes, in respect of each POW:

- indication of the Power on which he or she depends;
- surname (*i.e.*, last name) and first names (*i.e.*, first and middle names);
- army, regimental, personal, or serial number;
- rank;
- place and full date of birth;
- first name of the father and maiden name of the mother;
- name and address of the person to be informed; and
- the address to which correspondence for the POW may be sent.[746]

In addition to this information, information regarding transfers, releases, repatriations,

---

the custody of the American Forces."); FINAL REPORT ON THE PERSIAN GULF WAR 578 ("Trained Reserve Component (RC) EPW units were activated, and camp advisory teams were sent to Saudi Arabia to establish liaison with Saudi units to provide technical assistance, and to maintain accountability for EPWs and displaced civilians transferred to the Saudis. (In accordance with Article 12, GPW, the United States retained residual responsibility for EPWs transferred to the Saudi Arabian government.)").

744 *Refer to* § 9.2.2 (Responsibility of the Detaining Power).

745 GPW art. 122 ("This information shall make it possible quickly to advise the next of kin concerned.").

746 GPW art. 122 ("Subject to the provisions of Article 17, the information shall include, in so far as available to the Information Bureau, in respect of each prisoner of war, his surname, first names, rank, army, regimental, personal or serial number, place and full date of birth, indication of the Power on which he depends, first name of the father and maiden name of the mother, name and address of the person to be informed and the address to which correspondence for the prisoner may be sent.").

escapes, admissions to a hospital, and deaths shall also be collected and transmitted.[747] Likewise, information regarding the state of health of POWs who are seriously ill or seriously wounded shall be supplied regularly, every week if possible.[748]

In addition to notices of death, wills and records of death of POWs may be forwarded in accordance with Article 120 of the GPW.[749] Lists of graves and the particulars of POWs interred in cemeteries and elsewhere may also be forwarded in accordance with Article 120 of the GPW.[750]

9.31.1.1 *Difference Between the Accountability Information the Detaining Power Must Seek and the Information the POW Must Provide*. Although POWs are required to provide full name, rank, date of birth, and service (or equivalent) number, and POWs are required to show their identity card upon demand, POWs are not required to inform the Detaining Power of their places of birth, the first name of fathers, the maiden name of mothers, or the names and addresses of persons to be informed of capture.[751]

9.31.2 National POW Information Bureau. Upon the outbreak of a conflict and in all cases of occupation, each of the parties to the conflict shall institute an official National POW Information Bureau for POWs who are in its power.[752] Neutral or non-belligerent Powers, who may have received within their territory persons belonging to one of the categories referred to in Article 4 of the GPW, shall take the same action with respect to such persons.[753]

The Power concerned shall ensure that the National POW Information Bureau is provided with the necessary accommodation, equipment, and staff to ensure its efficient working.[754] It shall be at liberty to employ POWs in the National POW Information Bureau under the conditions laid down in Section III of the GPW dealing with work by POWs.[755]

Within the shortest possible period, each of the parties to the conflict shall give its National POW Information Bureau the information referred to in the fourth, fifth, and sixth

---

[747] GPW art. 122 ("The Information Bureau shall receive from the various departments concerned information regarding transfers, releases, repatriations, escapes, admissions to hospital, and deaths, and shall transmit such information in the manner described in the third paragraph above.").

[748] GPW art. 122 ("Likewise, information regarding the state of health of prisoners of war who are seriously ill or seriously wounded shall be supplied regularly, every week if possible.").

[749] *Refer to* § 9.34.1 (Transmittal of Wills); § 9.34.2 (Death Certificates).

[750] *Refer to* § 9.34.4 (Maintenance and Records of Graves and Ashes).

[751] *Refer to* § 9.8.4 (Accountability Information That POWs Are Bound to Provide Upon Questioning).

[752] GPW art. 122 ("Upon the outbreak of a conflict and in all cases of occupation, each of the Parties to the conflict shall institute an official Information Bureau for prisoners of war who are in its power.").

[753] GPW art. 122 ("Neutral or non-belligerent Powers who may have received within their territory persons belonging to one of the categories referred to in Article 4, shall take the same action with respect to such persons.").

[754] GPW art. 122 ("The Power concerned shall ensure that the Prisoners of War Information Bureau is provided with the necessary accommodation, equipment and staff to ensure its efficient working.").

[755] GPW art. 122 ("It shall be at liberty to employ prisoners of war in such a Bureau under the conditions laid down in the Section of the present Convention dealing with work by prisoners of war."). *Refer to* § 9.19 (POW Labor).

paragraphs of Article 122 of the GPW regarding any enemy person belonging to one of the categories referred to in Article 4 who has fallen into its power.[756] Neutral or non-belligerent Powers shall take the same action with regard to persons belonging to such categories whom they have received within their territory.[757]

All written communications made by the National POW Information Bureau shall be authenticated by a signature or a seal.[758]

The National POW Information Bureau: (1) receives and forwards certain information to the Powers concerned through the intermediary of the Protecting Powers and the Central POW Information Agency; (2) replies to inquiries; and (3) collects personal valuables left by POWs.

9.31.2.1 _Receiving and Forwarding Certain Information_. The National POW Information Bureau receives certain information regarding POWs from other departments of the State to which it belongs.[759]

The National POW Information Bureau shall immediately forward such information by the most rapid means to the Powers concerned through the intermediary of the Protecting Powers and likewise of the Central POW Information Agency provided for in Article 123 of the GPW.[760]

9.31.2.2 _Replying to Inquiries Regarding POWs_. The National POW Information Bureau shall also be responsible for replying to all inquiries sent to it concerning POWs, including those who have died in captivity; it will make any inquiries necessary to obtain the information that is asked for if the information is not in its possession.[761] Responses to inquiries

---

[756] GPW art. 122 ("Within the shortest possible period, each of the Parties to the conflict shall give its Bureau the information referred to in the fourth, fifth and sixth paragraphs of this Article regarding any enemy person belonging to one of the categories referred to in Article 4, who has fallen into its power.").

[757] GPW art. 122 ("Neutral or non-belligerent Powers shall take the same action with regard to persons belonging to such categories whom they have received within their territory.").

[758] GPW art. 122 ("All written communications made by the Bureau shall be authenticated by a signature or a seal.").

[759] GPW art. 122 ("Within the shortest possible period, <u>each of the Parties to the conflict shall give its Bureau</u> the information referred to in the fourth, fifth and sixth paragraphs of this Article regarding any enemy person belonging to one of the categories referred to in Article 4, who has fallen into its power. Neutral or non-belligerent Powers shall take the same action with regard to persons belonging to such categories whom they have received within their territory. … <u>The Information Bureau shall receive from the various departments concerned</u> information regarding transfers, releases, repatriations, escapes, admissions to hospital, and deaths, and shall transmit such information in the manner described in the third paragraph above. Likewise, information regarding the state of health of prisoners of war who are seriously ill or seriously wounded shall be supplied regularly, every week if possible.") (emphasis added).

[760] GPW art. 122 ("The Bureau shall immediately forward such information by the most rapid means to the Powers concerned, through the intermediary of the Protecting Powers and likewise of the Central Agency provided for in Article 123.").

[761] GPW art. 122 ("The Information Bureau shall also be responsible for replying to all enquiries sent to it concerning prisoners of war, including those who have died in captivity; it will make any enquiries necessary to obtain the information which is asked for if this is not in its possession.").

must be made consistent with the protection of POWs against insults and public curiosity.[762]

9.31.2.3 *Collection of Personal Valuables Left by POWs*. The National POW Information Bureau shall furthermore be charged with collecting all personal valuables including sums in currencies other than that of the Detaining Power and documents of importance to the next of kin that have been left by POWs who have been repatriated or released, or who have escaped or died, and shall forward these valuables to the Powers concerned.[763] Such articles shall be sent by the National POW Information Bureau in sealed packets, which shall be accompanied by statements giving clear and full particulars of the identity of the person to whom the articles belonged, and by a complete list of the contents of the parcel.[764] Other personal effects of such POWs shall be transmitted under arrangements agreed upon between the parties to the conflict concerned.[765]

9.31.3 Central POW Information Agency. The GPW contemplates that a Central POW Information Agency shall be created in a neutral country.[766] This organization may be the same as that provided for in the GC.[767]

The function of the Central POW Information Agency shall be to collect all the information it may obtain through official or private channels respecting POWs, and to transmit it as rapidly as possible to the country of origin of the POWs or to the Power on which they depend.[768] The Central POW Information Agency shall receive from the parties to the conflict all facilities for effecting such transmissions.[769] Parties to the GPW, and in particular those States whose nationals benefit from the services of the Central POW Information Agency, are requested to give the Central POW Information Agency the financial aid it may require.[770]

---

762 *Refer to* § 9.5.3 (Protection Against Insults and Public Curiosity).

763 GPW art. 122 ("The Information Bureau shall furthermore be charged with collecting all personal valuables including sums in currencies other than that of the Detaining Power and documents of importance to the next of kin, left by prisoners of war who have been repatriated or released, or who have escaped or died, and shall forward the said valuables to the Powers concerned.").

764 GPW art. 122 ("Such articles shall be sent by the Bureau in sealed packets which shall be accompanied by statements giving clear and full particulars of the identity of the person to whom the articles belonged, and by a complete list of the contents of the parcel.").

765 GPW art. 122 ("Other personal effects of such prisoners of war shall be transmitted under arrangements agreed upon between the Parties to the conflict concerned.").

766 GPW art. 123 ("A Central Prisoners of War Information Agency shall be created in a neutral country. The International Committee of the Red Cross shall, if it deems necessary, propose to the Powers concerned the organization of such an Agency.").

767 *Refer to* § 10.31.3 (Central Information Agency for Protected Persons).

768 GPW art. 123 ("The function of the Agency shall be to collect all the information it may obtain through official or private channels respecting prisoners of war, and to transmit it as rapidly as possible to the country of origin of the prisoners of war or to the Power on which they depend.").

769 GPW art. 123 ("It shall receive from the Parties to the conflict all facilities for effecting such transmissions.").

770 GPW art. 123 ("The High Contracting Parties, and in particular those whose nationals benefit by the services of the Central Agency, are requested to give the said Agency the financial aid it may require.").

The provisions of the GPW establishing the Central POW Information Agency do not restrict the humanitarian activities of the ICRC and of the relief societies described in Article 125 of the GPW.[771]

The GPW contemplates that the ICRC shall, if it deems necessary, propose to the Powers concerned the organization of a Central POW Information Agency.[772] The role of the Central POW Information Agency has been performed by the ICRC Central Tracing Agency, which has also performed this role for protected persons under the GC.

9.31.4 U.S. Practice in Reporting to the ICRC Central Tracing Agency. For the United States, the National POW Information Bureau, which has been established and managed by the Secretary of the Army, has been referred to at different times as the National Prisoner of War Information Center (NPWIC) in Operation DESERT STORM in 1991,[773] and as the National Detainee Reporting Center (NDRC) in Operation IRAQI FREEDOM in 2003. The NPWIC/NDRC has performed the same function for certain protected persons under the GC.

In general, the Theater Prisoner of War Information Center (TPWIC) has received reports from all subordinate POW facilities, regardless of Military Service, consolidated them and reconciled any discrepancies, and then forwarded its report to the NPWIC/NDRC. The NPWIC/NDRC, on behalf of the United States, has further reviewed and reconciled reports as needed, and forwarded its report to the ICRC Central Tracing Agency, which has acted as the Central POW Information Agency. The release of POW accountability information outside this process (such as directly from field components to ICRC field representatives) has been avoided so as to reduce the likelihood of erroneous, conflicting, or duplicate reporting.

9.31.5 Exemption of National POW Information Bureau and Central POW Information Agency From Certain Charges. The National POW Information Bureau and the Central POW Information Agency shall enjoy free postage for mail, all the exemptions provided for in Article 74 of the GPW,[774] and, further, so far as possible, exemption from telegraphic charges or, at

---

[771] GPW art. 123 ("The foregoing provisions shall in no way be interpreted as restricting the humanitarian activities of the International Committee of the Red Cross, or of the relief societies provided for in Article 125.").

[772] GPW art. 123 ("The International Committee of the Red Cross shall, if it deems necessary, propose to the Powers concerned the organization of such an Agency.").

[773] *For example*, FINAL REPORT ON THE PERSIAN GULF WAR 579-80 ("HQDA [Headquarters, Department of the Army] also operates the NPWIC, the central agency for all information pertaining to prisoners of war. Article 122, GPW, and Article 136, GC, require captors to establish a national information bureau as quickly as possible after the start of hostilities. The NPWIC, manned by Army Reserve (USAR) individual mobilization augmentees, volunteer Reservists, and retired personnel, served as a central repository for information related to EPW and displaced civilians captured or transferred to US forces. It also coordinated information with the ICRC pertaining to EPW held by Coalition forces and provided information pertaining to Americans (POW) in Iraqi hands. Additionally, the NPWIC consolidated information from the theater for dissemination to appropriate government agencies, Congress, and the ICRC.").

[774] *Refer to* § 9.20.4 (Exemptions From Postal and Shipping Charges).

least, greatly reduced rates.[775]

In addition, the National POW Information Bureau and the Central POW Information Agency shall also enjoy exemption from postal charges in respect of letter-post items, postal parcels, and monetary articles that concern POWs, which they send or receive, either directly or as intermediaries under the conditions laid down in the Universal Postal Convention.[776] Such items exempt from postal charges should be marked appropriately.[777]

9.32 ROLE OF THE PROTECTING POWER IN THE GPW

The Protecting Power is an organ for ensuring implementation of the GPW. The Protecting Power has extensive duties under the GPW. It transmits information between belligerents, monitors Detaining Power compliance with the GPW, and takes an active role in promoting the welfare of POWs.

9.32.1 Transmission of Information Between Belligerents. The Protecting Power helps transmit information between belligerents, including:

- information concerning the geographic location of camps;[778]
- financial information, including working rates of pay, notifications of payment, lists of credit balances, and claims for compensation;[779]
- notification of arrangements made for POW correspondence and relief shipments;[780]
- legal documents of POWs;[781]
- death certificates of POWs;[782]

---

[775] GPW art. 124 ("The national Information Bureaux and the Central Information Agency shall enjoy free postage for mail, likewise all the exemptions provided for in Article 74, and further, so far as possible, exemption from telegraphic charges or, at least, greatly reduced rates.").

[776] Universal Postal Convention, art. 17(3), Dec. 14, 1989, 1687 UNTS 241, 252 ("The national Information Bureaux and the Central Information Agencies mentioned above shall also enjoy exemption from postal charges in respect of letter-post items, postal parcels and monetary articles which concern the persons referred to in paragraphs 1 and 2, which they send or receive, either direct or as intermediaries, under the conditions laid down in those paragraphs."). *Consider* Letter Post Regulations, Article RL 111 to Article 7 of the Universal Postal Convention of Oct. 11, 2012, *reprinted in* INTERNATIONAL BUREAU OF THE UNIVERSAL POSTAL UNION, LETTER POST MANUAL, page C.10, C.10-11 (Berne 2013, Update 2 – Jan. 2015) ("The following shall enjoy exemption from postal charges within the meaning of article 7.2 of the Convention: 1.1 the Information Bureaux provided for in article 122 of the Geneva Convention of 12 August 1949 relative to the treatment of prisoners of war; 1.2 the Central Prisoner-of-War Information Agency provided for in article 123 of the same Convention;").

[777] *Refer to* § 9.20.4.3 (Exemption From Postal Charges Under the Universal Postal Convention).

[778] *Refer to* § 9.11.4.2 (Sharing Information on the Location of POW Camps).

[779] *Refer to* § 9.18 (Financial Resources of POWs).

[780] *Refer to* § 9.4.2.6 (Arrangements Made for POWs to Write Correspondence and Receive Collective Relief).

[781] *Refer to* § 9.21.2 (Legal Documents and Assistance).

- accountability information for the detention of POWs;[783] and

- official translations of the GPW, and laws and regulations that parties to the conflict have adopted to implement it.[784]

9.32.2 Monitoring or Inspecting Compliance With the GPW. The Protecting Power monitors or inspects the Detaining Power's compliance with the GPW, including by:

- visiting all places where POWs may be;[785]

- receiving complaints and requests by POWs, and periodic reports from the POW Representatives;[786]

- communicating with POW Representatives, and receiving the rationale in cases in which the Detaining Power refuses to approve an elected POW Representative or chooses to dismiss a POW Representative;[787]

- inspecting records of disciplinary punishments;[788]

- receiving communications and subsequent reports of death or serious injury of a POW in certain cases;[789]

- receiving the reasons for the limitations imposed by the Detaining Power on advances of pay;[790]

- inspecting POW accounts;[791]

- receiving records of labor detachments;[792] and

---

782 *Refer to* § 9.34.2 (Death Certificates).

783 *Refer to* § 9.31 (National Accounting of the Detention of POWs).

784 GPW art. 128 ("The High Contracting Parties shall communicate to one another through the Swiss Federal Council and, during hostilities, through the Protecting Powers, the official translations of the present Convention, as well as the laws and regulations which they may adopt to ensure the application thereof.").

785 *Refer to* § 9.33.1 (Access by Protecting Powers).

786 *Refer to* § 9.23.1 (POW Right to Make Requests and Complaints); § 9.23.3 (Periodic Reports by the POW Representatives).

787 *Refer to* § 9.24.2.4 (Approval of Elected POW Representatives by the Detaining Power); § 9.24.5 (Dismissal of POW Representative).

788 *Refer to* § 9.27.4 (Record of Disciplinary Punishments).

789 *Refer to* § 9.34.5 (Inquiries Into Death or Serious Injury of POWs in Certain Cases).

790 *Refer to* § 9.18.3.3 (Procedure for Limiting Amounts Drawn From Accounts Pending Special Agreement).

791 *Refer to* § 9.18.6 (POW Accounts).

792 *Refer to* § 9.19.7 (Labor Detachments).

- observing trials of POWs if security permits and receiving notification of: (1) judicial proceedings, (2) trial outcome, (3) whether the POW has decided to appeal, and (4) final conviction or death sentence.[793]

9.32.3 Actively Working to Improve the Welfare of POWs. In many other instances, the GPW contemplates that the Protecting Power will actively work to improve the welfare of POWs, such as by:

- helping the Detaining Power determine the maximum amount of money that POWs have in their possession;[794]

- approving any limitation on correspondence beyond two letters and four cards per month;[795]

- proposing any necessary limitations on relief shipments;[796]

- supervising the distribution of collective relief;[797]

- setting up special means of transport to ensure the conveyance of relief shipments to POWs;[798]

- finding POWs defense counsel when necessary;[799]

- notifying the transferring State in the event that a receiving State fails to carry out its obligations;[800]

- participating in the appointment of members of a Mixed Medical Commission;[801] and

- lending its good offices to assist in dispute resolution.[802]

---

[793] *Refer to* § 9.28.4.5 (Right of the Protecting Power to Attend Trial); § 9.28.3.1 (Notification of Proceedings); § 9.28.4.6 (Notification of Trial Outcome); § 9.28.5.1 (Appeals); § 9.28.5.2 (Notification of Final Conviction or Death Sentence).

[794] *Refer to* § 9.18.1 (Detaining Power Regulations on the Maximum Amount of Money in POW Possession).

[795] *Refer to* § 9.20.6 (Censorship and Security Review of POW Correspondence and Shipments).

[796] *Refer to* § 9.20.3 (Receipt of Individual and Collective Relief Shipments for POWs).

[797] *Refer to* § 9.20.3.4 (Collective Relief for POWs).

[798] *Refer to* § 9.20.5 (Special Means of Transport of Shipments to POWs).

[799] *Refer to* § 9.28.4.2 (Opportunity to Present Defense and Assistance of Counsel).

[800] *Refer to* § 9.30.2 (Responsibility When Transferred to the Custody of Another Detaining Power).

[801] *Refer to* § 9.36.5 (Mixed Medical Commissions).

[802] *Refer to* § 18.15.4 (Lending of Good Offices to Assist in Dispute Resolution).

9.33 Access to POWs by the Protecting Powers, ICRC, and Relief Organizations

9.33.1 Access by Protecting Powers. Representatives or delegates of the Protecting Powers shall have permission to go to all places where POWs may be, particularly to places of internment, imprisonment, and labor, and shall have access to all premises occupied by POWs; they also shall be allowed to go to the places of departure, passage, and arrival of POWs who are being transferred.[803] They shall be able to interview POWs, and in particular POW Representatives, without witnesses, either personally or through an interpreter.[804]

Representatives and delegates of the Protecting Powers shall have full liberty to select the places they wish to visit.[805] The duration and frequency of these visits shall not be restricted.[806] Visits may not be prohibited except for reasons of imperative military necessity, and then only as an exceptional and temporary measure.[807]

9.33.1.1 *Participation of Compatriots of POWs in Visits*. The Detaining Power and the Power on which these POWs depend may agree, if necessary, that compatriots of these POWs be permitted to participate in the visits.[808]

9.33.1.2 *ICRC Delegates Enjoying the Same Prerogatives of Access*. The delegates of the ICRC shall enjoy the same prerogatives as those of the representatives and delegates of the Protecting Powers described in Article 126 of the GPW.[809]

The appointment of such delegates shall be submitted to the approval of the Power detaining the POWs to be visited.[810]

9.33.2 Access by Relief Societies and Other Organizations. Subject to the measures that the Detaining Powers may consider essential to ensure their security or to meet any other reasonable need, the representatives of religious organizations, relief societies, or any other organization assisting POWs shall receive from these Powers, for themselves and their duly

---

[803] GPW art. 126 ("Representatives or delegates of the Protecting Powers shall have permission to go to all places where prisoners of war may be, particularly to places of internment, imprisonment and labour, and shall have access to all premises occupied by prisoners of war; they shall also be allowed to go to the places of departure, passage and arrival of prisoners who are being transferred.").

[804] GPW art. 126 ("They shall be able to interview the prisoners, and in particular the prisoners' representatives, without witnesses, either personally or through an interpreter.").

[805] GPW art. 126 ("Representatives and delegates of the Protecting Powers shall have full liberty to select the places they wish to visit.").

[806] GPW art. 126 ("The duration and frequency of these visits shall not be restricted.").

[807] GPW art. 126 ("Visits may not be prohibited except for reasons of imperative military necessity, and then only as an exceptional and temporary measure.").

[808] GPW art. 126 ("The Detaining Power and the Power on which the said prisoners of war depend may agree, if necessary, that compatriots of these prisoners of war be permitted to participate in the visits.").

[809] GPW art. 126 ("The delegates of the International Committee of the Red Cross shall enjoy the same prerogatives.").

[810] GPW art. 126 ("The appointment of such delegates shall be submitted to the approval of the Power detaining the prisoners of war to be visited.").

accredited agents, all necessary facilities for visiting the POWs; for distributing relief supplies and material, from any source, intended for religious, educational, or recreative purposes; and for assisting them in organizing their leisure time within the POW camps.[811] Such societies or organizations may be constituted in the territory of the Detaining Power or in any other country, or they may have an international character.[812]

9.33.2.1 *Limitations on the Number of Relief Organizations*. The Detaining Power may limit the number of societies and organizations whose delegates are allowed to carry out their activities in its territory and under its supervision, on condition, however, that such limitation shall not hinder the effective operation of adequate relief to all POWs.[813] The special position of the ICRC in this field shall be recognized and respected at all times.[814]

9.33.2.2 *Receipts for Relief Consignments*. As soon as relief supplies or material intended for religious, educational, or recreative purposes are handed over to POWs, or very shortly afterwards, receipts for each consignment, signed by the POW Representative, shall be forwarded to the relief society or organization making the shipment.[815] At the same time, receipts for these consignments shall be supplied by the administrative authorities responsible for guarding the POWs.[816]

9.34 Death of POWs

This section addresses rules relating to the death of POWs. The GWS and GWS-Sea also have rules relating to the treatment of the dead; however, the GWS and GWS-Sea provisions are broader in application, *e.g.*, they address members of the armed forces who have died on the battlefield and thus were not held as POWs.[817]

9.34.1 Transmittal of Wills. The Detaining Power has an obligation to help POWs with

---

[811] GPW art. 125 ("Subject to the measures which the Detaining Powers may consider essential to ensure their security or to meet any other reasonable need, the representatives of religious organizations, relief societies, or any other organization assisting prisoners of war, shall receive from the said Powers, for themselves and their duly accredited agents, all necessary facilities for visiting the prisoners, for distributing relief supplies and material, from any source, intended for religious, educational or recreative purposes, and for assisting them in organizing their leisure time within the camps.").

[812] GPW art. 125 ("Such societies or organizations may be constituted in the territory of the Detaining Power or in any other country, or they may have an international character.").

[813] GPW art. 125 ("The Detaining Power may limit the number of societies and organizations whose delegates are allowed to carry out their activities in its territory and under its supervision, on condition, however, that such limitation shall not hinder the effective operation of adequate relief to all prisoners of war.").

[814] GPW art. 125 ("The special position of the International Committee of the Red Cross in this field shall be recognized and respected at all times.").

[815] GPW art. 125 ("As soon as relief supplies or material intended for the above-mentioned purposes are handed over to prisoners of war, or very shortly afterwards, receipts for each consignment, signed by the prisoners' representative, shall be forwarded to the relief society or organization making the shipment.").

[816] GPW art. 125 ("At the same time, receipts for these consignments shall be supplied by the administrative authorities responsible for guarding the prisoners.").

[817] *Refer to* § 7.7 (Treatment and Handling of Enemy Military Dead).

their wills.[818] In all cases, after death, POWs' wills shall be transmitted without delay to the Protecting Power, and a certified copy shall be sent to the Central POW Information Agency.[819]

9.34.2 <u>Death Certificates</u>. Death certificates in the form given in Annex IV D to the GPW, or lists certified by a responsible officer, of all persons who die as POWs shall be forwarded as rapidly as possible to the National POW Information Bureau established in accordance with Article 122 of the GPW.[820]

The death certificates or certified lists shall show:

- particulars of identity, as set out in the third paragraph of Article 17 of the GPW, that are listed on the POW's identity card;
  - such as, surname; first names; rank; date of birth; and army, regimental, personal, or serial number or equivalent information;[821]
- the date and place of death;
- the cause of death;
- the date and place of burial;
- where applicable, the fact of, and reasons for, cremation;[822] and
- all particulars necessary to identify the graves or inurnment/columbarium location.[823]

9.34.3 <u>Burial or Cremation and Inurnment</u>.

9.34.3.1 <u>*Medical Examination Before Burial or Cremation*</u>. The burial or cremation of a POW shall be preceded by a medical examination of the body with a view to confirming death and enabling a report to be made and, where necessary, establishing identity.[824] For example, if a POW's identity was not established before death, and the identity cannot be

---

[818] *Refer to* § 9.21.2 (Legal Documents and Assistance).

[819] GPW art. 120 ("[I]n all cases, after death, the will shall be transmitted without delay to the Protecting Power; a certified copy shall be sent to the Central Agency.").

[820] GPW art. 120 ("Death certificates in the form annexed to the present Convention, or lists certified by a responsible officer, of all persons who die as prisoners of war shall be forwarded as rapidly as possible to the Prisoner of War Information Bureau established in accordance with Article 122.").

[821] *Refer to* § 9.4.3 (Issue of Identification Cards to Persons Liable to Become POWs).

[822] *Refer to* § 9.34.3.3 (Cremation).

[823] GPW art. 120 ("The death certificates or certified lists shall show particulars of identity as set out in the third paragraph of Article 17, and also the date and place of death, the cause of death, the date and place of burial and all particulars necessary to identity the graves.").

[824] GPW art. 120 ("The burial or cremation of a prisoner of war shall be preceded by a medical examination of the body with a view to confirming death and enabling a report to be made and, where necessary, establishing identity.").

established, the report should include information that will enable the Power on which the POW depended to establish his or her identity (*e.g.*, examination of teeth, fingerprints, photograph, DNA samples).[825]

9.34.3.2 *Burial*. The detaining authorities shall ensure that POWs who have died in captivity are honorably buried, if possible according to the rites of the religion to which they belonged.[826]

Wherever possible, deceased POWs who depended on the same Power shall be interred in the same place.[827] Deceased POWs shall be buried in individual graves unless unavoidable circumstances require the use of collective graves.[828] For example, an epidemic or military operations may require the Detaining Power to undertake collective burials in the interest of public health because individual graves are not possible due to lack of time and resources.[829]

9.34.3.3 *Cremation*. Bodies of POWs may be cremated only for imperative reasons of hygiene, on account of the religion of the deceased, or in accordance with his or her express wish to this effect.[830] In case of cremation, the fact shall be stated and the reasons given in the death certificate of the deceased.[831]

9.34.4 Maintenance and Records of Graves and Ashes. The detaining authorities shall ensure that the graves of POWs who have died in captivity are respected, suitably maintained, and marked so as to be found at any time.[832]

9.34.4.1 *Records Held by the Graves Registration Service*. In order that graves may always be found, all particulars of burials and graves shall be recorded with a Graves

---

[825] GPW COMMENTARY 564-65 ("If, however, a prisoner's identity remains in doubt (for instance, if he has not yet been questioned as provided in Article 17), the doctor will follow the same procedure as for those who have fallen on the battlefield: examination of papers found in the clothing of the dead man, questioning of his comrades or, if that is not possible, other methods must be adopted in order to enable the adverse Party to establish his identity, e.g. measurement and description of the body and its physical features, examination of the teeth, finger-prints, photograph, etc..").

[826] GPW art. 120 ("The detaining authorities shall ensure that prisoners of war who have died in captivity are honourably buried, if possible according to the rites of the religion to which they belonged, and that their graves are respected, suitably maintained and marked so as to be found at any time.").

[827] GPW art. 120 ("Wherever possible, deceased prisoners of war who depended on the same Power shall be interred in the same place.").

[828] GPW art. 120 ("Deceased prisoners of war shall be buried in individual graves unless unavoidable circumstances require the use of collective graves.").

[829] *Compare* § 10.34.3 (Burial or Cremation and Inurnment).

[830] GPW art. 120 ("Bodies may be cremated only for imperative reasons of hygiene, on account of the religion of the deceased or in accordance with his express wish to this effect.").

[831] GPW art. 120 ("In case of cremation, the fact shall be stated and the reasons given in the death certificate of the deceased.").

[832] GPW art. 120 ("The detaining authorities shall ensure … that their graves are respected, suitably maintained and marked so as to be found at any time.").

Registration Service established by the Detaining Power.[833] Lists of graves and particulars of the POWs interred in cemeteries and elsewhere shall be transmitted to the Power on which such POWs depended.[834] Responsibility for the care of these graves and for records of any subsequent moves of the bodies shall rest on the Power controlling the territory, if that Power is a Party to the GPW.[835]

The Graves Registration Service shall also identify, record, and respectfully keep the ashes until they can be disposed of in accordance with the wishes of the home country.[836]

The GWS also provides for the Graves Registration Service to record graves of persons belonging to enemy military forces who died but were never held as POWs.[837]

9.34.5 Inquiries Into Death or Serious Injury of POWs in Certain Cases. Every death or serious injury of a POW caused or suspected to have been caused by a sentry, another POW, or any other person, as well as any death the cause of which is unknown, shall be immediately followed by an official inquiry by the Detaining Power.[838] A communication on this subject shall be sent immediately to the Protecting Power.[839]

Serious injury, in many cases, may be understood to mean an injury that requires in-patient treatment in a hospital or infirmary.[840]

---

[833] GPW art. 120 ("In order that graves may always be found, all particulars of burials and graves shall be recorded with a Graves Registration Service established by the Detaining Power.").

[834] GPW art. 120 ("Lists of graves and particulars of the prisoners of war interred in cemeteries and elsewhere shall be transmitted to the Power on which such prisoners of war depended.").

[835] GPW art. 120 ("Responsibility for the care of these graves and for records of any subsequent moves of the bodies shall rest on the Power controlling the territory, if a Party to the present Convention.").

[836] GPW art. 120 ("These provisions shall also apply to the ashes, which shall be kept by the Graves Registration Service until proper disposal thereof in accordance with the wishes of the home country.").

[837] *Refer to* § 7.7.5 (Graves Registration Service).

[838] GPW art. 121 ("Every death or serious injury of a prisoner of war caused or suspected to have been caused by a sentry, another prisoner of war, or any other person, as well as any death the cause of which is unknown, shall be immediately followed by an official enquiry by the Detaining Power."). *For example*, FINAL REPORT ON THE PERSIAN GULF WAR 578 ("Eight EPW died in US custody; all as a result of injuries or sickness contracted prior to capture. Five died from combat injuries, one from malnutrition/dehydration, and two from unknown causes. Three US transferred prisoners died in Saudi camps due to wounds received while interned in the Saudi controlled camps. These deaths were investigated and reported through command channels to the ICRC, as required by Articles 120, 122, and 123, GPW."); 2004 UK MANUAL ¶8.176, footnote 452 ("In the Falklands conflict, an Argentinean PW was shot and killed to prevent an attempt to sabotage the captured submarine *Santa Fé*. The British notified the Argentinian authorities through the ICRC and established a board of inquiry to establish the facts.").

[839] GPW art. 121 ("A communication on this subject shall be sent immediately to the Protecting Power.").

[840] GPW COMMENTARY 570 ("What is meant by 'serious injury'? At the 1949 Diplomatic Conference one delegation suggested that it should be made clear that the term referred to an injury 'as a result of which the prisoner requires in-patient treatment in a hospital or infirmary'; this definition was not approved, however, and it might indeed have made the application of the Article too rigid. An injury may be not at all serious and nevertheless require treatment in the infirmary. Furthermore, it would have been dangerous to make the opening of an enquiry depend on whether or not the patient had been admitted to hospital for treatment. The two things must remain quite separate."). *Compare* § 10.34.5 (Inquiries Into Death or Serious Injury of Internees in Certain Cases).

Statements shall be taken from witnesses, especially from those who are POWs, and a report including such statements shall be forwarded to the Protecting Power.[841]

If the inquiry indicates the guilt of one or more persons, the Detaining Power shall take all measures for the prosecution of the person or persons responsible.[842]

9.35 EXCHANGES AND OTHER RELEASE AND REPATRIATION OF POWS DURING HOSTILITIES

9.35.1 Exchange of POWs During Hostilities Through Cartel Agreements. The exchange of POWs, other than those whose repatriation is required by the GPW, may be effected by agreement between the belligerents.[843] Such agreements have been called cartels.[844]

The modern practice in this area has been infrequent.[845]

As a general principle, the exchange of POWs, other than those whose repatriation is required by the GPW, is an act of convenience to both belligerents.[846]

The conditions for exchange are generally prescribed in the cartel, and exchanges need not be on the basis of number-for-number, or rank-for-rank.[847]

---

[841] GPW art. 121 ("Statements shall be taken from witnesses, especially from those who are prisoners of war, and a report including such statements shall be forwarded to the Protecting Power.").

[842] GPW art. 121 ("If the enquiry indicates the guilt of one or more persons, the Detaining Power shall take all measures for the prosecution of the person or persons responsible.").

[843] *For example*, Edward Bates, Attorney General, *Construction of a Cartel*, Oct. 18, 1862, 10 OPINIONS OF THE ATTORNEY GENERAL 357 (1868) ("Following your verbal direction, I have carefully examined the cartel for the exchange of prisoners of war, agreed to by the parties on the 22d of July, 1862, at Haxall's Landing, on James river, Virginia, and signed, respectively, by Major General Dix and Major General Hill, as the same is embodied in 'General Order No. 142' issued from the War Department, September 25, 1862.").

[844] *Refer to* § 12.7 (Cartels).

[845] *For example*, 1958 UK MANUAL ¶250 and note 3(b) ("In modern war between civilised States, an exchange of prisoners will rarely be carried out except by agreement between the governments concerned. ... In the First and Second World War no such exchanges took place. During the latter war some measured agreement was reached between Germany, the United Kingdom, the U.S.A. and Switzerland, whereby a number of prisoners of war of the three belligerent States interned in Switzerland were repatriated. No formal agreement was drawn up, and the negotiations were conducted by the diplomatic representatives of the belligerents direct with the Swiss Government. Germany insisted on a distinction between interned aircrews and other prisoners of war so that a certain number of German prisoners of war could be repatriated for every United States airman repatriated. Switzerland as a neutral State refused to permit repatriation except on a basis agreeable to all the belligerents concerned. Agreement was reached and repatriation was carried out on the basis of the German demand.").

[846] LIEBER CODE art. 109 ("The exchange of prisoners of war is an act of convenience to both belligerents. If no general cartel has been concluded, it can not be demanded by either of them. No belligerent is obliged to exchange prisoners of war.").

[847] 1956 FM 27-10 (Change No. 1 1976) ¶197 ("Exchange of prisoners of war, other than those whose repatriation is required by GPW, may be effected by agreement between the belligerents. No belligerent is obliged to exchange prisoners of war, except if a general cartel requiring such exchange has been concluded. The conditions for exchange are as prescribed by the parties thereto, and exchanges need not necessarily be on the basis of number for number or rank for rank.").

9.35.2 Release and Repatriation of POWs Not on the Basis of Exchange. Even when not required by the GPW or done on the basis of an exchange, a Detaining Power may release and repatriate POWs during hostilities to the Power to which they belong.[848]

Such release and repatriation of POWs during hostilities may be accomplished between governments through agreements. In any case, POWs subject to release and repatriation should be interviewed by representatives of the Protecting Power or the ICRC to ensure that their return is voluntary.[849]

9.36 Direct Repatriation and Accommodation in Neutral Countries During Hostilities

The GPW provides for the direct repatriation or accommodation in neutral countries of certain wounded and sick POWs during hostilities.

POWs who meet with accidents shall, unless the injury is self-inflicted, have the benefit of the provisions of the GPW as regards repatriation or accommodation in a neutral country.[850]

States may also conclude agreements with a view to the direct repatriation or internment in a neutral country of able-bodied POWs who have undergone a long period of captivity.[851]

9.36.1 Direct Repatriation of Seriously Wounded, Injured, or Sick POWs. Parties to a conflict have an obligation to send back to their own country, regardless of number or rank, certain seriously wounded and seriously sick POWs, after having cared for them until they are fit enough to travel.[852] Before the 1929 GPW, such repatriations occurred in accordance with specific agreements.[853] Under the GPW, such repatriations have been conducted as part of

---

[848] *For example*, SYLVIE-STOYANKA JUNOD, INTERNATIONAL COMMITTEE OF THE RED CROSS, PROTECTION OF THE VICTIMS OF ARMED CONFLICT FALKLAND-MALVINAS ISLANDS: INTERNATIONAL HUMANITARIAN LAW AND HUMANITARIAN ACTION (1982) 31 (1984) ("The Falkland-Malvinas Islands' conflict provides a rare example of prisoners being released even before the end of active hostilities. The British soldiers and the group of civilians captured by the Argentine forces when they landed on the island of South Georgia and on the Falkland-Malvinas archipelago were released almost immediately, via Montevideo, without the ICRC's participation. In May and June, the ICRC took part in several release operations: … . At the end of the hostilities, i.e. after 14 June 1982, a great number of prisoners were released in several groups over one month.").

[849] *Compare* § 9.37.4.2 (POWs Who Resist Repatriation).

[850] GPW art. 114 ("Prisoners of war who meet with accidents shall, unless the injury is self-inflicted, have the benefit of the provisions of this Convention as regards repatriation or accommodation in a neutral country.").

[851] GPW art. 109 ("They may, in addition, conclude agreements with a view to the direct repatriation or internment in a neutral country of able-bodies prisoners of war who have undergone a long period of captivity.").

[852] GPW art. 109 ("Subject to the provisions of the third paragraph of this Article, Parties to the conflict are bound to send back to their own country, regardless of number or rank, seriously wounded and seriously sick prisoners of war, after having cared for them until they are fit to travel, in accordance with the first paragraph of the following Article.").

[853] *For example*, 1958 UK MANUAL ¶255 note 1 ("In June, 1918, an agreement for the repatriation of prisoners of war on a large scale was concluded between Lord Cave's mission and a German military mission. During the Second World War repatriation of the sick and wounded was carried out by the belligerents in western Europe in accordance with the provisions of the 1929 Convention. There was no repatriation of sick and wounded between Germany and the U.S.S.R., or between Japan and the Allies.").

exchanges or on a unilateral basis.[854]

No sick or injured POW who is eligible for repatriation under the first paragraph of Article 109 of the GPW may be repatriated against his or her will during hostilities.[855]

9.36.1.1 *Categories of POWs Eligible for Direct Repatriation*. The following categories of POWs shall be repatriated directly:

- incurably wounded and sick whose mental or physical fitness seems to have been gravely diminished;

- wounded and sick who, according to medical opinion, are not likely to recover within one year, whose condition requires treatment, and whose mental or physical fitness seems to have been gravely diminished; and

- wounded and sick who have recovered, but whose mental or physical fitness seems to have been gravely and permanently diminished.[856]

9.36.2 Accommodation in Neutral Countries. Throughout the duration of hostilities, parties to the conflict shall endeavor, with the cooperation of the neutral Powers concerned, to make arrangements for the accommodation in neutral countries of certain sick and wounded POWs as discussed below.[857] This provision of the GPW reflected prior State practice.[858]

---

[854] *For example*, LEVIE, POWS, 409-10 ("Subsequent to 1949 a number of occasions arose warranting the implementation of the provisions of the first paragraph of Article 109. In February 1953 the United Nations Command in Korea proposed the exchange of seriously wounded and seriously sick prisoners of war pursuant to that Article, a proposal which the North Koreans and Chinese Communists accepted. During April and May 1953, some 6,640 North Korean and Chinese prisoners of war who had been found to be seriously wounded or seriously sick within the meaning of those terms as used in the Convention were exchanged for 684 members of the armed forces composing the United Nations Command. During the 1956 Middle East conflict, Israel repatriated a number of seriously wounded Egyptian prisoners of war in the course of the hostilities. During the 1962 Sino-Indian conflict, the People's Republic of China repatriated a number of seriously wounded or seriously sick Indian prisoners of war.").

[855] GPW art. 109 ("No sick or injured prisoner of war who is eligible for repatriation under the first paragraph of this Article, may be repatriated against his will during hostilities.").

[856] GPW art. 110 ("The following shall be repatriated direct: (1) Incurably wounded and sick whose mental or physical fitness seems to have been gravely diminished. (2) Wounded and sick who, according to medical opinion, are not likely to recover within one year, whose condition requires treatment and whose mental or physical fitness seems to have been gravely diminished. (3) Wounded and sick who have recovered, but whose mental or physical fitness seems to have been gravely and permanently diminished.").

[857] GPW art. 109 ("Throughout the duration of hostilities, Parties to the conflict shall endeavour, with the cooperation of the neutral Powers concerned, to make arrangements for the accommodation in neutral countries of the sick and wounded prisoners of war referred to in the second paragraph of the following Article.").

[858] *For example*, 1958 UK MANUAL ¶255 note 1 ("During the First World War agreements were arrived at between the Allies and Germany early in 1916 whereby all wounded prisoners of war held by their respective Governments, as well as those suffering from any one of twenty specified diseases or infirmities, were to be transferred to Switzerland. Later, agreements were arrived at whereby those who had been in captivity for not less than eighteen months and who fulfilled certain conditions as regards age and citizenship were to be repatriated or interned in a neutral country. Some 16,000 British and German prisoners of war were interned in Holland. In March, 1918, it

9.36.2.1 *Categories of Wounded, Injured, or Sick to Be Accommodated in a Neutral State*. The following categories of POWs may be accommodated in a neutral country:

- wounded, injured, or sick whose recovery may be expected within one year of the date of the wound or the beginning of the illness, if treatment in a neutral country might increase the prospects of a more certain and speedy recovery; and

- POWs whose mental or physical health, according to medical opinion, is seriously threatened by continued captivity, but whose accommodation in a neutral country might remove such a threat.[859]

9.36.3 Agreements to Intern POWs in Neutral Territory. The Detaining Power, the Power on which the POWs depend, and a neutral Power agreed upon by these two Powers, shall endeavor to conclude agreements that will enable POWs to be interned in the territory of that neutral Power until the close of hostilities.[860] For example, if the Detaining Power were unable to comply with the minimum standards in the GPW for the treatment of POWs, then it would seek to negotiate such agreements with the Power on which the POWs depend and a neutral Power.[861]

9.36.3.1 *Repatriation From a Neutral State*. The conditions that POWs accommodated in a neutral country must fulfill in order to permit their repatriation shall be fixed, as shall likewise their status, by agreement between the Powers concerned.[862] In general, POWs who have been accommodated in a neutral country, and who belong to the following categories, should be repatriated:

- those whose health has deteriorated so far as to fulfill the conditions for direct

---

was stated that 26,000 prisoners of war of the several belligerents were being cared for in Switzerland. Of these, 16,000 were British, French and Belgian, while 10,000 were German; besides these, some 500,000 invalid and sick prisoners of war of various nationalities had been exchanged and repatriated through Switzerland since the beginning of the war.").

[859] GPW art. 110 ("The following may be accommodated in a neutral country: (1) Wounded and sick whose recovery may be expected within one year of the date of the wound or the beginning of the illness, if treatment in a neutral country might increase the prospects of a more certain and speedy recovery. (2) Prisoners of war whose mental or physical health, according to medical opinion, is seriously threatened by continued captivity, but whose accommodation in a neutral country might remove such a threat.").

[860] GPW art. 111 ("The Detaining Power, the Power on which the prisoners of war depend, and a neutral Power agreed upon by these two Powers, shall endeavour to conclude agreements which will enable prisoners of war to be interned in the territory of the said neutral Power until the close of hostilities.").

[861] *See* II-A FINAL RECORD OF THE DIPLOMATIC CONFERENCE OF GENEVA OF 1949 365 ("The Committee considered that it was necessary to insert a new Article between Articles 101 and 102, in order to provide for the possibility of agreements between the Detaining Power, the Power on which the prisoners of war depend, and a neutral Power, permitting the internment of prisoners of war on neutral territory. This decision, which arose out of a proposal by the Canadian Delegation, aims at ensuring a reasonable standard of living for all prisoners of war, in the event of the Detaining Power being unable, for any reason, to comply with the minimum standards regarding the treatment of prisoners of war laid down in the Convention.").

[862] GPW art. 110 ("The conditions which prisoners of war accommodated in a neutral country must fulfil in order to permit their repatriation shall be fixed, as shall likewise their status, by agreement between the Powers concerned.").

repatriation;[863] and

- those whose mental or physical powers remain, even after treatment, considerably impaired.[864]

9.36.4 Lack of Special Agreements to Determine Cases of Disablement or Sickness Entailing Direct Repatriation or Accommodation in a Neutral Country. If no special agreements are concluded between the parties to the conflict concerned to determine the cases of disablement or sickness entailing direct repatriation or accommodation in a neutral country, such cases shall be settled in accordance with the principles laid down in the Model Agreement concerning direct repatriation and accommodation in neutral countries of wounded and sick POWs and in the Regulations concerning Mixed Medical Commissions annexed to the GPW (GPW Annex II).[865]

9.36.5 Mixed Medical Commissions. Upon the outbreak of hostilities, Mixed Medical Commissions shall be appointed to examine sick and wounded POWs, and to make all appropriate decisions regarding them.[866] The appointment, duties, and functioning of these Commissions shall be in conformity with the provisions of the Regulations annexed to the GPW (GPW Annex II).[867]

9.36.5.1 *Examination Not Necessary for Manifestly Seriously Injured or Sick POWs*. POWs who, in the opinion of the medical authorities of the Detaining Power, are manifestly seriously injured or seriously sick may be repatriated without having to be examined by a Mixed Medical Commission.[868]

9.36.5.2 *POWs Entitled to Present Themselves for Examination Before the Commission*. Besides those who are designated by the medical authorities of the Detaining Power, wounded or sick POWs belonging to the categories listed below shall be entitled to present themselves for examination by the Mixed Medical Commissions provided for in Article 112 of the GPW:

---

[863] *Refer to* § 9.36.1.1 (Categories of POWs Eligible for Direct Repatriation).

[864] GPW art. 110 ("In general, prisoners of war who have been accommodated in a neutral country, and who belong to the following categories, should be repatriated: (1) those whose state of health has deteriorated so as to fulfil the conditions laid down for direct repatriation; (2) those whose mental or physical powers remain, even after treatment, considerably impaired.").

[865] GPW art. 110 ("If no special agreements are concluded between the Parties to the conflict concerned, to determine the cases of disablement or sickness entailing direct repatriation or accommodation in a neutral country, such cases shall be settled in accordance with the principles laid down in the Model Agreement concerning direct repatriation and accommodation in neutral countries of wounded and sick prisoners of war and in the Regulations concerning Mixed Medical Commissions annexed to the present Convention.").

[866] GPW art. 112 ("Upon the outbreak of hostilities, Mixed Medical Commissions shall be appointed to examine sick and wounded prisoners of war, and to make all appropriate decisions regarding them.").

[867] GPW art. 112 ("The appointment, duties and functioning of these Commissions shall be in conformity with the provisions of the Regulations annexed to the present Convention.").

[868] GPW art. 112 ("However, prisoners of war who, in the opinion of the medical authorities of the Detaining Power, are manifestly seriously injured or seriously sick, may be repatriated without having to be examined by a Mixed Medical Commission.").

- Wounded and sick proposed by a physician or surgeon who is of the same nationality, or a national of a party to the conflict allied with the Power on which these POWs depend, and who exercises his or her functions in the camp;
- Wounded and sick proposed by their POW Representative; and
- Wounded and sick proposed by the Power on which they depend, or by an organization duly recognized by this Power and giving assistance to the POWs.[869]

POWs who do not belong to one of the three foregoing categories may nevertheless present themselves for examination by Mixed Medical Commissions, but shall be examined only after those belonging to the three foregoing categories.[870]

9.36.5.3 *Observers at the Examination*. The physician or surgeon of the same nationality as the POWs who present themselves for examination by the Mixed Medical Commission, and the POW Representative of these POWs, shall have permission to be present at the examination.[871]

9.36.6 Costs of Repatriation or Transportation to a Neutral Country During Hostilities. The costs of repatriating POWs or of transporting them to a neutral country are borne, from the frontiers of the Detaining Power, by the Power on which the POWs depend.[872]

9.36.7 Employment of Persons Who Have Been Repatriated. No repatriated person may be employed on active military service.[873]

9.36.7.1 *No Repatriated Person*. The rule against employment on active military service only applies to POWs repatriated by the Detaining Power pursuant to Articles 109 and 110 of the GPW.[874] For example, able-bodied POWs who are voluntarily repatriated by the

---

[869] GPW art. 113 ("Besides those who are designated by the medical authorities of the Detaining Power, wounded or sick prisoners of war belonging to the categories listed below shall be entitled to present themselves for examination by the Mixed Medical Commissions provided for in the foregoing Article: (1) Wounded and sick proposed by a physician or surgeon who is of the same nationality, or a national of a Party to the conflict allied with the Power on which the said prisoners depend, and who exercises his functions in the camp. (2) Wounded and sick proposed by their prisoners' representative. (3) Wounded and sick proposed by the Power on which they depend, or by an organization duly recognized by the said Power and giving assistance to the prisoners.").

[870] GPW art. 113 ("Prisoners of war who do not belong to one of the three foregoing categories may nevertheless present themselves for examination by Mixed Medical Commissions, but shall be examined only after those belonging to the said categories.").

[871] GPW art. 113 ("The physician or surgeon of the same nationality as the prisoners who present themselves for examination by the Mixed Medical Commission, likewise the prisoners' representative of the said prisoners, shall have permission to be present at the examination.").

[872] GPW art. 116 ("The cost of repatriating prisoners of war or of transporting them to a neutral country shall be borne, from the frontiers of the Detaining Power, by the Power on which the said prisoners depend.").

[873] GPW art. 117 ("No repatriated person may be employed on active military service.").

[874] *See* 1958 UK MANUAL ¶262 note 1 ("This article repeats the provisions of the 1929 Convention, Art. 74, which was considered to apply only to prisoners who were repatriated sick or wounded and not to exchanges by agreements made outside the Convention. This would also seem to be the proper scope of Art. 117."); GPW

unilateral decision of the Detaining Power during hostilities may be employed on active military service.[875]

9.36.7.2 Active Military Service. Not all military service is "active military service." Repatriated persons may remain employed on military service.[876] What "active military service" they may engage in after repatriation may be the subject of agreements pursuant to Articles 109 and 110 of the GPW. Absent such agreements, active military service may be understood as broadly covering any participation, whether direct or indirect, in armed operations against the former Detaining Power or its allies, but to exclude medical work or strictly administrative duties.[877]

9.37 Release and Repatriation After Hostilities

POWs shall be released and repatriated without delay after the cessation of active hostilities.[878]

9.37.1 Agreements on POW Release and Repatriation. The release and repatriation of POWs generally have been addressed by peace treaties or other agreements among belligerents

---

COMMENTARY 538 ("The Article covers prisoners of war repatriated by the Detaining Power pursuant to Articles 109 and 110, that is to say seriously wounded or seriously sick prisoners of war whom the Detaining Power is required to repatriate regardless of number or rank (Article 109, paragraph 1), prisoners of war accommodated in a neutral country and subsequently repatriated following an agreement between the Powers concerned (Article 110, paragraph 2), and lastly, able-bodied prisoners of war who have undergone a long period of captivity and are repatriated by agreement between the Powers concerned (Article 109, paragraph 2).").

[875] 2004 UK MANUAL ¶8.155.1 footnote 417 ("Despite its apparent general application, Art 117 is taken to apply only to PW repatriated under the special rules laid down in Arts 109 110 (see Pictet, *Commentary*, vol III, 538). It does not apply to able-bodied PW who are voluntarily repatriated by the unilateral decision of the detaining power during hostilities. The UK sent members of the Royal Marine garrison of the Falkland Islands, who had been captured and then repatriated by Argentina, back into combat with the Task Force that re-took the Islands in 1982.").

[876] *See* II-A FINAL RECORD OF THE DIPLOMATIC CONFERENCE OF GENEVA OF 1949 573 ("Articles 106 (Costs) and 107 (Activity after repatriation) reproduce the corresponding provisions of the 1929 Convention. It may be mentioned, however, that the word 'active' in the expression 'active military service' in Article 107 gave rise to long discussion. Some Delegations wished to see it deleted; others were in favour of keeping it because it is usual for many repatriated prisoners of war to depend on the administrative service of armies. Finally, the proposal to delete the word was rejected by the Committee by a small majority.").

[877] *See* GPW COMMENTARY 539 ("In interpreting this phrase, the spirit of the Convention rather than national legislation should serve as a guide. It is, of course, difficult to give a precise definition, but the expression may be considered as broadly covering any participation, whether direct or indirect, in armed operations against the former Detaining Power or its allies. In effect, Article 117 forbids any repatriated person to serve in units which form part of the armed forces but does not prevent their enrolment in unarmed military units engaged solely in auxiliary, complementary or similar work. In concluding agreements pursuant to Articles 109 and 110, the Parties concerned are at liberty to stipulate what is meant by 'active' service in the particular case concerned."); 1956 FM 27-10 (Change No. 1 1976) ¶196b ("Although it is not possible to frame any comprehensive rule concerning what constitutes 'active military service,' Article 117 does not preclude a repatriated person from performing medical or strictly administrative duties but does foreclose service in combat against the power formerly detaining the individual or an ally thereof.").

[878] GPW art. 118 ("Prisoners of war shall be released and repatriated without delay after the cessation of active hostilities.").

at the end of the war.[879] For example, agreements may address the apportionment of costs or commissions to search for dispersed POWs.[880]

In the absence of stipulations to the above effect in any agreement concluded between the parties to the conflict with a view to the cessation of hostilities, or failing any such agreement, each of the Detaining Powers shall itself establish and execute without delay a plan of repatriation in conformity with the principle laid down in paragraph 1 of the Article 118 of the GPW.[881] Thus, once active hostilities have ceased, the Detaining Powers must release and repatriate POWs, even if there is no specific agreement regarding the release and repatriation of POWs, or even if a formal peace agreement ending the war has not yet been concluded.[882]

During the process of releasing and repatriating POWs, it is proper to expect that each party's conduct with respect to the repatriation of POWs will be reasonable and broadly commensurate with the conduct of the other.[883] For example, it would not be reasonable to expect that a State would release all of the POWs it holds without assurance that its own

---

879 *For example*, FINAL REPORT ON THE PERSIAN GULF WAR 586 ("In March [of 1991], Coalition forces and Iraq signed a memorandum of understanding detailing administrative procedures for the repatriation of the remaining EPW, under ICRC auspices. On 4 March, Iraq released the first group of 10 Coalition POWs, six of whom were American. On 6 March, the US reciprocated by releasing 294 EPWs to the ICRC for repatriation to Iraq."); Agreement between the Commander-in-Chief, United Nations Command, on the one hand, and the Supreme Commander of the Korean People's Army and the Commander of the Chinese People's Volunteers, on the other hand, Concerning a Military Armistice in Korea art. 51, Jul. 27, 1953, 29 DEPARTMENT OF STATE BULLETIN 132, 137 (Aug. 3, 1953) ("The release and repatriation of all prisoners of war held in the custody of each side at the time this armistice agreement becomes effective shall be effected in conformity with the following provisions agreed upon by both sides prior to the signing of this Armistice Agreement.").

880 *Refer to* § 9.37.6 (Costs of Repatriation at the Close of Hostilities); § 9.37.5 (Commissions to Search for Dispersed POWs).

881 GPW art. 118 ("In the absence of stipulations to the above effect in any agreement concluded between the Parties to the conflict with a view to the cessation of hostilities, or failing any such agreement, each of the Detaining Powers shall itself establish and execute without delay a plan of repatriation in conformity with the principle laid down in the foregoing paragraph.").

882 LAUTERPACHT, II OPPENHEIM'S INTERNATIONAL LAW 613 (§275) ("That provision [of Article 118 of the GPW] was inspired by the experience of the situation as it developed after the Second World War when, following upon the unconditional surrender of Italy, Germany, and Japan, no treaty of peace was concluded between the principal belligerents for some years and when public opinion in many countries viewed with disapproval the continued detention of prisoners of war at a time when there was no longer any reasonable possibility that hostilities might be resumed.").

883 Eritrea Ethiopia Claims Commission, *Partial Award: Prisoners of War, Eritrea's Claim 17*, ¶149 (Jul. 1, 2003) ("The Commission finds that, given the character of the repatriation obligation and state practice, it is appropriate to consider the behavior of both Parties in assessing whether or when Ethiopia failed to meet its obligations under Article 118. In the Commission's view, Article 118 does not require precisely equivalent behavior by each Party. However, it is proper to expect that each Party's conduct with respect to the repatriation of POWs will be reasonable and broadly commensurate with the conduct of the other. Moreover, both Parties must continue to strive to ensure compliance with the basic objective of Article 118 – the release and repatriation of POWs as promptly as possible following the cessation of active hostilities. Neither Party may unilaterally abandon the release and repatriation process or refuse to work in good faith with the ICRC to resolve any impediments.").

personnel held by the enemy will also be released.[884]

9.37.2 Cessation of Active Hostilities. According to Lauterpacht, the phrase "cessation of active hostilities" probably does not refer to a situation that leaves open the possibility of a resumption of struggle, but to a situation in which it is out of the question for hostilities to resume.[885] It is the complete end of the fighting with clearly no probability of resumption of hostilities in the near future.[886] The cessation of active hostilities may also be understood as describing the point in time when belligerents feel sufficiently at ease about the future that they are willing to release and repatriate all POWs.[887] The cessation of active hostilities may result from a capitulation or agreement, but such an agreement is not required if there is no prospect that hostilities will resume.

9.37.3 Without Delay. The GPW provides that release and repatriation take place without delay. This requirement, however, does not affect the practical arrangements that must be made to ensure that repatriation takes place in a safe and orderly manner in accordance with the requirements of the GPW.[888]

---

[884] Eritrea Ethiopia Claims Commission, *Partial Award: Prisoners of War, Eritrea's Claim 17*, ¶148 (Jul. 1, 2003) ("There is also a fundamental question whether and to what extent each Party's obligation to repatriate depends upon the other's compliance with its repatriation obligations. The language of Article 118 is absolute. Nevertheless, as a practical matter, and as indicated by state practice, any state that has not been totally defeated is unlikely to release all the POWs it holds without assurance that its own personnel held by its enemy will also be released, and it is unreasonable to expect otherwise. At the hearing, distinguished counsel for Eritrea suggested that the obligation to repatriate should be seen as unconditional but acknowledged the difficulty of the question and the contrary arguments under general law.").

[885] LAUTERPACHT, II OPPENHEIM'S INTERNATIONAL LAW 613 (§275) ("Probably the phrase 'cessation of active hostilities' in the sense of Article 118 [of the GPW] refers not to suspension of hostilities in pursuance of an ordinary armistice which leaves open the possibility of a resumption of the struggle, but to a cessation of hostilities as the result of total surrender or of such circumstances or conditions of an armistice as render it out of the question for the defeated party to resume hostilities.").

[886] CHRISTIANE SHIELDS DELESSERT, RELEASE AND REPATRIATION OF PRISONERS OF WAR AT THE END OF ACTIVE HOSTILITIES: A STUDY OF ARTICLE 118, PARAGRAPH 1 OF THE THIRD GENEVA CONVENTION RELATIVE TO THE TREATMENT OF PRISONERS OF WAR 71-72 (1977) ("Is the phrase 'end of active hostilities' to be interpreted as referring to situations where it is clear that active hostilities have definitely stopped and will not be resumed, for example, as the result of surrender, or can it be interpreted in a more flexible way so as to take account of situations where the pattern has been an alternation of military operations and peaceful periods? If, once again, one refers to the Second World War which directly influenced the specific wording of Article 118, it would seem that what was envisaged was a situation of complete end of the war, if not in a legal sense, at least in a material one with *clearly no probability of resumption of hostilities in a near future*. The end of war for the purpose of the application of Article 118, meant the end of military operations. In the light of the history of Article 118, this would seem to be the proper interpretation to be given to it.").

[887] Edward R. Cummings, Acting Assistant Legal Adviser for African Affairs, *Memorandum of Law to Chester A. Crocker, Assistant Secretary of State for African Affairs*, Sept. 21, 1984, III CUMULATIVE DIGEST OF UNITED STATES PRACTICE IN INTERNATIONAL LAW 1981-1988, 3471, 3474 (Under the GPW, "the 'cessation' concept describes the point in time that belligerents feel sufficiently … [at ease] about the future that they are willing to release all prisoners of war and civilian internees.") (alterations to the quote in original).

[888] GPW COMMENTARY 550 ("The text as finally adopted states that the repatriation must take place 'without delay after the cessation of active hostilities'. This requirement does not, of course, affect the practical arrangements which must be made so that repatriation may take place in conditions consistent with humanitarian rules and the

For example, the availability of manpower and transportation to conduct the repatriation, continuing military operations in other theaters, or the ability of countries to receive POWs in large numbers, may all increase the time required to conduct the release and repatriation.[889] The security situation in the country in which POWs are to be released may also be an important factor.[890] In addition, time may be needed based on the medical condition of the POWs or in order to conduct interviews to ensure that repatriation is voluntary.

9.37.4 POWs Whom the Detaining Power Is Not Required to Repatriate.

9.37.4.1 *Persons Illegally Enrolled in Enemy Forces and Deserters*. The obligation to repatriate does not apply to persons who have been illegally enrolled in the armed forces of the enemy (for example, the inhabitants of occupied territories who have been forced to enlist in the military of the Occupying Power), or to persons who have deserted to the other side.[891]

9.37.4.2 *POWs Who Resist Repatriation*. The Detaining Power is not required to repatriate forcibly POWs who do not wish to be repatriated.

Although the GPW provides that POWs may not renounce the rights secured to them by the GPW,[892] this principle is not violated by the POW rejecting repatriation and requesting asylum, if it is established in a satisfactory manner that the POW is making an informed,

---

requirements of the Convention, as defined in Article 119, paragraph 1, below, which refers to Articles 46 to 48 (relating to transfer).").

[889] *For example*, FINAL REPORT ON THE PERSIAN GULF WAR 586 ("After the cease fire, expeditious repatriation of EPWs was a high priority and Coalition officials promptly began talks with Iraqi representatives on EPW exchanges. Iraq said it was anxious to return Coalition POWs, but was unwilling to accept large numbers of EPWs in return, saying it was not prepared to receive them."); Martin Tollefson, *Enemy Prisoners of War*, 32 IOWA LAW REVIEW 51, 74 (1946) ("Because of manpower and transportation shortages, because the war was still being fought against Japan, and because of the inability on the part of the European and Mediterranean theaters to receive prisoners of war from the United States in large numbers, the prisoner-of-war repatriation program did not assume large proportions until after V-J Day.").

[890] *For example*, EARL F. ZIEMKE, THE U.S. ARMY IN THE OCCUPATION OF GERMANY, 1944-1946, 293 (1975) ("SHAEF could not authorize a 'blanket release' of German forces, Eisenhower replied, because their discharge had to be 'strictly controlled in order to prevent widespread disorder, or other conditions which military government agencies will be unable to cope with'; the release of the categories already approved (see below) would 'tax the administrative machinery for a considerable time . . . . Until such time as indigenous resources can meet the needs,' he concluded, 12th Army Group could use imported military government food for the disarmed forces.") (ellipsis in original).

[891] GPW COMMENTARY 549 ("Enemy military personnel who have been illegally enrolled in the armed forces cannot be treated on the same basis as other prisoners of war, nor can those who go over to the other side. Although many countries, for instance Great Britain, treated the latter as prisoners of war, this does not mean that they are entitled to that status. The Detaining Power is under no obligation to repatriate persons who have deserted to the other side. Similarly, their names are not usually notified to their country of origin. It should, however, be noted that the status of a deserter who has gone over to the other side must be determined by the way in which he surrendered or by his statements during initial questioning. A prisoner of war does not become a deserter merely because he makes a statement in the course of captivity.").

[892] *Refer to* § 9.3.7 (Non-Renunciation of Rights Secured by the GPW).

voluntary, and personal choice.[893] Thus, the GPW does not itself change accepted principles of international law under which asylum is applicable to POWs, and the Detaining Power may, but is not required to, grant asylum.[894] The policy of the United States has been not to conduct forcible repatriation of POWs and, in particular, not to transfer any person when torture is more likely than not to result.[895]

The voluntariness of POWs' decisions may be established through interviews by an impartial intermediary, such as a neutral State or the ICRC.[896]

9.37.4.3 *POWs Undergoing Criminal Proceedings for an Indictable Offense*. The repatriation of a POW may not be delayed on the basis that the POW has not undergone

---

[893] LEVIE, POWS 93 ("The question of the extent of the coverage of Article 7 was directly raised during the armistice negotiations in Korea in connection with the problem of repatriation under Article 118. Is it a violation of Article 7 to permit a prisoner of war to reject repatriation and to seek asylum either in the territory of the Detaining Power, or elsewhere, when hostilities cease? The decision ultimately reached in that controversy, one that had the support of a large majority of the United Nations General Assembly as then composed, was that Article 7 was not violated if it could be established in a satisfactory manner that the prisoner of war was actually making an informed, voluntary, and personal choice.").

[894] SENATE EXECUTIVE REPORT 84-9, *Geneva Conventions for the Protection of War Victims: Report of the Committee on Foreign Relations on Executives D, E, F, and G*, 82nd Congress, First Session, 5 (Jun. 27, 1955) ("Members of the committee, exploring the problem of involuntary repatriation with the executive branch, were informed at the hearing that the United States official position continues to be that maintained in Korea and overwhelmingly supported in the resolution of the General Assembly, and that article 118 does nothing to change accepted principles of international law under which asylum is applicable to prisoners of war. The committee unqualifiedly concurs. It finds nothing in the Geneva conventions of 1949 which will compel the United States forcibly to repatriate prisoners of war who fear political persecution, personal injury, or death should they return to their homeland. That article, being intended for the benefit and the well-being of prisoners, will permit the United States to continue the policy of nonforceable repatriation, while at the same time leaving it free, where necessary, to refuse requests for asylum. The interpretation which has thus prevailed gives due weight to the word 'release' in article 118, is faithful to precedent and legislative history, and is fully consistent with the great humanitarian purposes which underlie all four of the conventions.").

[895] *Refer to* § 8.14.4.1 (U.S. Policy Prohibiting Transfers in Cases in Which Detainees Would Likely Be Tortured).

[896] *For example*, FINAL REPORT ON THE PERSIAN GULF WAR 587 ("By international convention, no EPW was forcibly repatriated. Coalition forces identified to the ICRC Iraqi EPW not desiring repatriation. When an Iraqi reached the exchange site, the ICRC reconfirmed willingness to be repatriated. Those who indicated they no longer desired to return to Iraq were returned to the custody of Saudi Arabia. ... On 2 May 1991, the last EPW in US custody was transferred to the Saudi Arabian government. The Coalition repatriation began on 6 March and ended on 22 August. A total of 13,418 EPWs refused repatriation (13,227 remain at Camp Al-Artawiyah and 191 officer EPWs remain at Camp Tabuk)."); R. R. Baxter, *Asylum to Prisoners of War*, 30 BRITISH YEAR BOOK OF INTERNATIONAL LAW 489, 489-90 (1953) ("After hostilities had ended in Korea and those prisoners of war who desired to be repatriated had been restored to the forces of which they were members, there remained over 22,000 prisoners of war in the custody of the United Nations Command and several hundreds in the hands of the Command of the Korean People's Army and Chinese People's Volunteers who had not elected to return. In accordance with the Resolution of the United Nations General Assembly of 3 December 1952, the Terms of Reference for the Neutral Nations Repatriation Commission annexed to the Korean Armistice Agreement provided that prisoners who had not 'exercised their right to be repatriated' should be placed in the custody of a Neutral Nations Repatriation Commission (N.N.R.C.), composed of members appointed by Sweden, Switzerland, Poland, Czechoslovakia, and India. ... Commissions with neutral representation had in a number of previous instances been employed to supervise the repatriation of prisoners.").

disciplinary proceedings or punishment.[897]

POWs against whom criminal proceedings for an indictable offense are pending may be detained until the end of such proceedings, and, if necessary, until the completion of the punishment.[898] The same shall apply to POWs already convicted for an indictable offense.[899]

In fact, in most instances, as the Supreme Court has observed, the practical administration of the system of military justice under the law of war would fail if such authority were thought to end with the cessation of hostilities because only after their cessation could the greater number of offenders and the principal ones be apprehended and tried.[900]

Parties to the conflict shall communicate to each other the names of any POWs who are detained until the end of the proceedings or until punishment has been completed.[901]

The GPW does not prohibit the extradition of POWs to other Parties to the GPW to face criminal charges.[902]

POWs held after the cessation of active hostilities on this basis, even if they have been convicted, remain entitled to the benefits of the GPW until they are released and repatriated.[903]

9.37.5 Commissions to Search for Dispersed POWs. By agreement between the parties to the conflict, commissions shall be established for the purpose of searching for dispersed POWs and of ensuring their repatriation with the least possible delay.[904]

9.37.6 Costs of Repatriation at the Close of Hostilities. The costs of repatriation of

---

[897] *Compare* § 9.27.7 (Disciplinary Punishment and Repatriation or Accommodation in a Neutral Country).

[898] GPW art. 119 ("Prisoners of war against whom criminal proceedings for an indictable offence are pending may be detained until the end of such proceedings, and, if necessary, until the completion of the punishment.").

[899] GPW art. 119 ("The same shall apply to prisoners of war already convicted for an indictable offence.").

[900] *See* In re Yamashita, 327 U.S. 1, 12 (1946) ("We cannot say that there is no authority to convene a commission after hostilities have ended to try violations of the law of war committed before their cessation, at least until peace has been officially recognized by treaty or proclamation of the political branch of the Government. In fact, in most instances the practical administration of the system of military justice under the law of war would fail if such authority were thought to end with the cessation of hostilities. For only after their cessation could the greater number of offenders and the principal ones be apprehended and subjected to trial.").

[901] GPW art. 119 ("Parties to the conflict shall communicate to each other the names of any prisoners of war who are detained until the end of the proceedings or until punishment has been completed.").

[902] *See* Noriega v. Pastrana, 564 F.3d 1290, 1298 (11th Cir. Fla. 2009) ("As a result of Noriega's conviction in the United States, article 119 authorized the United States to prolong his detention for the duration of his sentence—beyond the cessation of hostilities between the United States and Panama. Nowhere, however, is it suggested that a prisoner of war may not be extradited from one party to the Convention to face criminal charges in another. Nor do the stated purposes of articles 118 and 119, as reflected by their commentary, preclude detention in these circumstances: article 118 is intended to prohibit 'prolong[ed] war captivity,' while article 119 unambiguously reflects the intention of the drafters to permit detention of prisoners of war subject to criminal proceedings.").

[903] *Refer to* § 9.3.6 (Commencement and Duration of POW Status and Treatment).

[904] GPW art. 119 ("By agreement between the Parties to the conflict, commissions shall be established for the purpose of searching for dispersed prisoners of war and of assuring their repatriation with the least possible delay.").

POWs shall in all cases be equitably apportioned between the Detaining Power and the Power on which the POWs depend.[905]

If the two Powers are contiguous, then the Power on which the POWs depend shall bear the costs of repatriation from the frontiers of the Detaining Power.[906]

If the two Powers are not contiguous, the Detaining Power shall bear the costs of transport of POWs over its own territory as far as its frontier or its port of embarkation nearest to the territory of the Power on which the POWs depend.[907] The Parties concerned shall agree between themselves on the equitable apportionment of the remaining costs of the repatriation, but the conclusion of such agreement shall in no circumstances justify any delay in the repatriation of the POWs.[908]

9.38 Procedure on Release and Repatriation After Hostilities

9.38.1 Conditions During Release and Repatriation. Repatriation shall be effected in conditions similar to those laid down in Articles 46 through 48 of the GPW for the transfer of POWs, having regard to the provisions of Article 118 of the GPW and to those of Article 119 of the GPW.[909]

9.38.1.1 *Conditions of Movement*. The conditions of repatriation must be humane and not less favorable than those under which the forces of the Detaining Power are transferred.[910] Adequate precautions must be taken for the health and safety of POWs, including provision of sufficient food, drinking water, clothing, shelter, and medical attention.[911]

9.38.2 Notification of Repatriation Plan and Departure. POWs should be informed of the plan for their repatriation.[912] For example, this may take place through notices posted in the camps and provided to the POW Representatives, or a public announcement.[913]

---

[905] GPW art. 118 ("The costs of repatriation of prisoners of war shall in all cases be equitably apportioned between the Detaining Power and the Power on which the prisoners depend.").

[906] GPW art. 118 ("If the two Powers are continguous, the Power on which the prisoners of war depend shall bear the costs of repatriation from the frontiers of the Detaining Power.").

[907] GPW art. 118 ("If the two Powers are not contiguous, the Detaining Power shall bear the costs of transport of prisoners of war over its own territory as far as its frontier or its port of embarkation nearest to the territory of the Power on which the prisoners of war depend.").

[908] GPW art. 118 ("The parties concerned shall agree between themselves as to the equitable apportionment of the remaining costs of the repatriation. The conclusion of this agreement shall in no circumstances justify any delay in the repatriation of the prisoners of war.").

[909] GPW art. 119 ("Repatriation shall be effected in conditions similar to those laid down in Articles 46 to 48 inclusive of the present Convention for the transfer of prisoners of war, having regard to the provisions of Article 118 and to those of the following paragraphs.").

[910] *Refer to* § 9.29.2 (Conditions for the Transfer of POWs).

[911] *Refer to* § 9.29.2 (Conditions for the Transfer of POWs).

[912] GPW art. 118 ("In either case, the measures adopted shall be brought to the knowledge of the prisoners of war.").

[913] *Refer to* § 9.22.5 (Posting of Convention and Camp Orders).

POWs who are to be moved must be identified and listed before departure, and both the National POW Information Bureau and the POWs themselves officially notified in advance, so that they can pack their baggage and inform their next of kin.[914]

9.38.3 Personal Property. On repatriation, any articles of value impounded from POWs under Article 18 of the GPW,[915] and any foreign currency that has not been converted into the currency of the Detaining Power, shall be restored to them.[916] Articles of value and foreign currency that, for any reason whatever, are not restored to POWs on repatriation, shall be sent to the National POW Information Bureau set up under Article 122 of the GPW.[917]

POWs shall be allowed to take with them their personal effects and any correspondence and parcels that have arrived for them.[918] The weight of such baggage may be limited, if the conditions of repatriation so require, to what each POW can reasonably carry.[919] Each POW shall in all cases be authorized to carry at least 25 kilograms (approximately 55 pounds).[920] The other personal effects of the repatriated POW shall be left in the charge of the Detaining Power, which shall have them forwarded to him or her as soon as it has concluded an agreement to this effect, regulating the conditions of transport and the payment of the costs involved, with the Power on which the POW depends.[921]

9.38.4 POW Accounts and Financial Matters. POW accounts should be addressed in accordance with Article 66 of the GPW.[922]

In addition, the Powers concerned should make arrangements concerning advances of pay, compensation payments, and remittances.[923]

9.38.5 Canteen Profits. The profits of the canteen should be disposed of in accordance

---

[914] *Refer to* § 9.29.3.1 (Notification of Transfer).

[915] *Refer to* § 9.7.4 (Money and Articles of Value).

[916] GPW art. 119 ("On repatriation, any articles of value impounded from prisoners of war under Article 18, and any foreign currency which has not been converted into the currency of the Detaining Power, shall be restored to them.").

[917] GPW art. 119 ("Articles of value and foreign currency which, for any reason whatever, are not restored to prisoners of war on repatriation, shall be despatched to the Information Bureau set up under Article 122.").

[918] GPW art. 119 ("Prisoners of war shall be allowed to take with them their personal effects, and any correspondence and parcels which have arrived for them.").

[919] GPW art. 119 ("The weight of such baggage may be limited, if the conditions of repatriation so require, to what each prisoner can reasonably carry.").

[920] GPW art. 119 ("Each prisoner shall in all cases be authorized to carry at least twenty-five kilograms.").

[921] GPW art. 119 ("The other personal effects of the repatriated prisoner shall be left in the charge of the Detaining Power which shall have them forwarded to him as soon as it has concluded an agreement to this effect, regulating the conditions of transport and the payment of the costs involved, with the Power on which the prisoner depends.").

[922] *Refer to* § 9.18.6.4 (Statements of Credit Balance on Termination of Captivity).

[923] GPW art. 67 ("Such advances of pay, as well as all payments made by the said Power under Article 63, third paragraph, and Article 68, shall form the subject of arrangements between the Powers concerned, at the close of hostilities.").

with Article 28 of the GPW.[924]

9.39 CODE OF CONDUCT FOR U.S. ARMED FORCES

The Code of Conduct is a moral code designed to provide U.S. military personnel with a standard of conduct.[925] Although designed for situations in which members of the U.S. armed forces may be held as POWs, the spirit and intent of the Code apply to service members subjected to other types of hostile detention, such as hostage scenarios.[926]

9.39.1 Text of the Code of Conduct and Discussion. The Code of Conduct was written to be consistent with the requirements imposed by the GPW. Violations of the Code of Conduct are not criminally punishable as such, but conduct that violates the Code of Conduct may also violate the Uniform Code of Military Justice.

9.39.1.1 *Code of Conduct – Article I.*

> I am an American, fighting in the forces which guard my country and our way of life. I am prepared to give my life in their defense.

9.39.1.2 *Code of Conduct – Article II.*

> I will never surrender of my own free will. If in command, I will never surrender the members of my command while they still have the means to resist.

Under Article II of the Code of Conduct, the responsibility and authority of a commander never extends to the surrender of command, even if isolated, cut off, or surrounded, while the unit has a reasonable power to resist, break out, or evade to rejoin friendly forces.[927]

Under the Uniform Code of Military Justice, a U.S. commander who shamefully surrenders to the enemy any command or place that is his or her duty to defend is subject to

---

[924] *Refer to* § 9.17.3.2 (Disposition of Canteen Profits Upon Camp Closure).

[925] *See* Executive Order 10631, *Code of Conduct for Members of the Armed Forces of the United States*, 20 FEDERAL REGISTER 6057 (Aug. 17, 1955), as amended by Executive Order 12017, *Amending the Code of Conduct for Members of the Armed Forces of the United States*, 42 FEDERAL REGISTER 57941 (Nov. 3, 1977), and as amended by Executive Order 12633, *Amending the Code of Conduct for Members of the Armed Forces of the United States*, 53 FEDERAL REGISTER 10355 (Mar. 28, 1988).

[926] *See, e.g.*, DOD INSTRUCTION 1300.21, *Code of Conduct (CoC) Training and Education,* ¶E2.1.1 (Jan. 8, 2001) ("Although designed for evasion and prisoner of war (POW) situations, the spirit and intent of the CoC are applicable to Service members subjected to other hostile detention, and such Service members should conduct themselves consistently in a manner that avoids discrediting themselves and their country."); Joint Chiefs of Staff Memorandum 290-81, *Code of Military in Hostage Situations* (Aug. 5, 1981) ("a. All U.S. military personnel are subject to being taken hostage under circumstances short of war. In such situations, the conduct of military personnel will be guided by the Code of Conduct.").

[927] DOD INSTRUCTION 1300.21, *Code of Conduct (CoC) Training and Education,* ¶ E2.2.2.1.2 (Jan. 8, 2001) ("The responsibility and authority of a commander never extends to the surrender of command, even if isolated, cut off, or surrounded, while the unit has a reasonable power to resist, break out, or evade to rejoin friendly forces.").

punishment.[928] In addition, any person subject to the Uniform Code of Military Justice who compels or attempts to compel a commander of any place, vessel, aircraft, or other military property, or of any body of members of the armed forces, to give it up to an enemy or to abandon it, or who strikes the colors or flag to an enemy without proper authority, is subject to punishment.[929]

Article II of the Code of Conduct is consistent with the authority of commanders under the law of war to conclude capitulation agreements for the surrender of forces under their command.[930]

9.39.1.3 Code of Conduct – Article III.

> If I am captured I will continue to resist by all means available. I will make every effort to escape and to aid others to escape. I will accept neither parole nor special favors from the enemy.

By limiting the punishment of POWs with respect to an unsuccessful escape, the GPW acknowledges that POWs may have a duty to seek to escape, as reflected in Article III of the Code of Conduct.[931]

Although the GPW contemplates that POWs may accept parole,[932] U.S. policy, as reflected in Article III of the Code of Conduct, prohibits accepting parole.

9.39.1.4 Code of Conduct – Article IV.

> If I become a prisoner of war, I will keep faith with my fellow prisoners. I will give no information [n]or take part in any action which might be harmful to my comrades. If I am senior, I will take command. If not, I will obey the lawful orders of those appointed over me and will back them up in every way.

Article IV of the Code of Conduct exemplifies the spirit of comradeship that many POWs have exhibited in past conflicts.[933] It reflects a higher standard of conduct than that punishable

---

928 10 U.S.C. § 899 ("Any member of the armed forces who before or in the presence of the enemy— … (2) shamefully abandons, surrenders, or delivers up any command, unit, place, or military property which it is his duty to defend; … shall be punished by death or such other punishment as a court-martial may direct.").

929 10 U.S.C. § 900 ("Any person subject to this chapter who compels or attempts to compel the commander of any place, vessel, aircraft, or other military property, or of any body of members of the armed forces, to give it up to an enemy or to abandon it, or who strikes the colors or flag to an enemy without proper authority, shall be punished by death or such other punishment as a court-martial may direct.").

930 *Refer to* § 12.8.2 (Authority of Commanders to Conclude Capitulation Agreements).

931 *Refer to* § 9.25 (POW Escapes).

932 *Refer to* § 9.11.2 (Parole of POWs).

933 *For example*, The Secretary of Defense's Advisory Committee on Prisoners of War, *POW The Fight Continues After The Battle: The Report of the Secretary of Defense's Advisory Committee on Prisoners of War*, 14 (Aug. 1955) ("Many servicemen exhibited pride in themselves and their units. This was particularly pronounced where they had belonged to the same unit for years. They stood by one another like that 'band of brothers' inspired by Nelson. If a soldier were sick, his fellow soldiers took care of him. They washed his clothes, bathed him, and

under Article 105 of the Uniform Code of Military Justice regarding misconduct towards fellow POWs.[934] The senior POW in command is not necessarily the POW Representative.[935] In POW camps containing only enlisted personnel, the POW Representative is elected.[936]

9.39.1.5 *Code of Conduct – Article V*.

> When questioned, should I become a prisoner of war, I am required to give name, rank, service number and date of birth. I will evade answering further questions to the utmost of my ability. I will make no oral or written statements disloyal to my country and its allies or harmful to their cause.

Article V of the Code of Conduct reflects the obligations of the POW to provide accountability information.[937] The Detaining Power may have further obligations to collect additional accountability information relating to POWs.[938]

Article V of the Code of Conduct also underscores one aspect of Article 104 of the Uniform Code of Military Justice regarding aiding the enemy by specifically forbidding oral or written statements disloyal to the United States or harmful to its cause.[939]

9.39.1.6 *Code of Conduct – Article VI*.

> I will never forget that I am an American, fighting for freedom, responsible for my actions, and dedicated to the principles which made my country free. I will trust in my God and in the United States of America.

---

pulled him through. They exhibited true fraternal spirit comradeship, military pride. These soldiers did not let each other down. Nor could the Korean Reds win much cooperation from them.").

[934] *See* DEPARTMENT OF THE ARMY PAMPHLET 27-161-2, *II International Law*, 99-100 (Oct. 23, 1962) ("The provisions of the Code of Conduct are not as restrictive in their application as in Article 105(1), U.C.M.J. There is no requirement that the act be motivated by the desire to secure favorable treatment or that an actual detriment be inflicted on the other PWs as a direct result of the act.").

[935] *See* DOD INSTRUCTION 1300.21, *Code of Conduct (CoC) Training and Education*, ¶E2.2.4.1.6 (Jan. 8, 2001) ("U.S. policy on POW camp organization requires that the senior military POW assume command. The Geneva Convention on POWs (reference (g)) provides additional guidance to the effect that in POW camps containing only enlisted personnel, a prisoners' representative shall be elected. POWs should understand that such an elected representative is regarded by U.S. policy as only a spokesperson for the senior POW. The prisoners' representative does not have command, unless the POWs elect the senior POW to be the prisoners' representative. The senior POW shall assume and retain actual command, covertly if necessary.").

[936] *Refer to* § 9.24.2.3 (Places Without Officer POWs).

[937] *Refer to* § 9.8.4 (Accountability Information That POWs Are Bound to Provide Upon Questioning).

[938] *Refer to* § 9.31.1.1 (Difference Between the Accountability Information the Detaining Power Must Seek and the Information the POW Must Provide).

[939] DEPARTMENT OF THE ARMY PAMPHLET 27-161-2, *II International Law*, 99 (Oct. 23, 1962) ("The Uniform Code continues to apply to an American serviceman after his capture by the enemy. A prisoner of war is often in a better position then before capture to 'aid the enemy.' The Code of Conduct underscores one aspect of Article 104 U.C.M.J. by specifically forbidding oral or written statements disloyal to the U.S. or harmful to its cause. Such statements may materially aid the enemy in its propaganda efforts.").

9.39.2 Background on the U.S. Code of Conduct. Although misconduct by POWs was not unique to the Korean War, the Code of Conduct was introduced after public awareness of instances of misconduct by U.S. servicemembers during their captivity as POWs during the Korean War. The Secretary of Defense established a committee that recommended that a unified and purposeful standard of conduct for Americans who become POWs be promulgated.[940] President Dwight D. Eisenhower promulgated the Code of Conduct on August 17, 1955.[941] A review of the Code of Conduct after the return of U.S. POWs from the Vietnam War confirmed the value of the Code of Conduct.[942]

---

[940] The Secretary of Defense's Advisory Committee on Prisoners of War, *POW The Fight Continues After The Battle: The Report of the Secretary of Defense's Advisory Committee on Prisoners of War*, vii (Aug. 1955) ("[T]he Committee unanimously agreed that Americans require a unified and purposeful standard of conduct for our prisoners of war backed up by a first class training program. This position is also wholeheartedly supported by the concensus [sic] of opinion of all those who consulted with the Committee. From no one did we receive stronger recommendations on this point than from the former American prisoners of war in Korea-officers and enlisted men.").

[941] Executive Order 10631, *Code of Conduct for Members of the Armed Forces of the United States*, 20 FEDERAL REGISTER 163 (Aug. 20, 1955).

[942] DoD, Report of the Defense Review Committee for the Code of Conduct 6-7 (1976) ("There was consistent agreement throughout Committee proceedings that the Code of Conduct has served as a useful guide to the American Serviceman through a wide spectrum of circumstances during normal service, on the battlefield and in captivity. It represents the high standard of behavior which is expected of the individual and which he may expect of all other members of the Armed Forces. There was never any question that the Code is needed, and some POW returnees attributed their very survival to the inspiration provided by the Code of Conduct.").

X – Civilians in the Hands of a Party to the Conflict

Chapter Contents

10.1 Introduction

This Chapter addresses protection of civilians in the hands of a party to an international armed conflict. In particular, the Chapter addresses civilians who are interned in the home territory of a belligerent or occupied territory.

Rules for the protection of civilians in the conduct of hostilities are addressed in Chapter V. Rules for the protection of civilians that are specific to occupied territory are addressed in Chapter XI, while rules that apply to both civilians in occupied territory and civilians in a belligerent's home territory are addressed in this Chapter.

10.1.1 Interpretation and Application of the GC. The GC underlies most of the international law rules applicable to the United States for the treatment of civilians in the hands of a party to the conflict.

As with the GPW, the GC's provisions should be interpreted in light of the principles that underlie the treatment of civilians and, in particular, in light of the goal of advancing the humane treatment of protected persons.[1] The subsequent practice of States in applying the GC could also assist in interpreting its provisions because States' decades of experience in applying the GC may be very helpful in understanding its requirements.[2]

10.1.1.1 *GC – Notes on Terminology*. In the GC, *protected persons* does not simply refer to persons who are "civilians" in the sense of not being members of the military; rather, *protected persons* refers to persons who are protected by the GC in connection with international armed conflict or occupation.[3]

In the GC, *internees* refers to protected persons who are interned.

In the GC, the *Detaining Power* refers to the State that holds the internee.

In the GC, the *Protecting Power* refers to a neutral State that helps implement the GC.[4]

10.1.1.2 *Special Agreements Under the GC*. Under the GC, States may conclude a variety of special agreements during international armed conflict to facilitate the protection of civilians. The GC specifically provides for agreements:

- to entrust to an effective and impartial organization the duties of the Protecting Powers;[5]
- to establish and recognize civilian hospital zones and localities;[6]

---

[1] *Refer to* § 9.1.2 (Interpretation and Application of the GPW).

[2] *Refer to* § 1.7.4 (Use of Certain Subsequent Practice in Treaty Interpretation).

[3] *Refer to* § 10.3.1 (Protected Person – Notes on Terminology).

[4] *Refer to* § 18.15.1.1 (Protecting Power Under the 1949 Geneva Conventions).

[5] *Refer to* § 18.15.2.1 (Agreement for an Impartial and Effective Organization to Perform Protecting Power Duties Under the 1949 Geneva Conventions).

- to establish and determine the conditions of neutralized zones;[7]

- for the removal of wounded, sick, infirm, and aged persons, children, and maternity cases, from besieged or encircled areas or for the passage of medical and religious personnel on their way to such areas;[8]

- to settle practical details regarding the departure of protected persons from a belligerent's home territory;[9]

- to establish the conditions for the sending of individual parcels and collective relief shipments;[10]

- for the release, repatriation, the return to places of residence or the accommodation in a neutral country of certain classes of internees, in particular children, pregnant women and mothers with infants and young children, wounded and sick, and internees who have been detained for a long time;[11] and

- on the procedure, or to select an umpire who will decide the procedure, to be followed for an inquiry concerning any alleged violation of the GC.[12]

In addition to the agreements expressly provided for in Articles 11, 14, 15, 17, 36, 108, 109, 132, 133, and 149 of the GC, Parties to the GC may conclude other special agreements for all matters concerning which they may deem it suitable to make separate provision.[13] No special agreement shall adversely affect the situation of protected persons, as defined by the GC, nor restrict the rights that it confers upon them.[14]

Protected persons shall continue to have the benefit of such agreements as long as the GC is applicable to them, except where express provisions to the contrary are contained in these agreements or in subsequent agreements, or where more favorable measures have been taken

---

[6] *Refer to* § 5.14.3.1 (Civilian Hospital and Safety Zones and Localities).

[7] *Refer to* § 5.14.3.3 (Neutralized Zones).

[8] *Refer to* § 5.19.2 (Removal and Passage of Certain Personnel – Vulnerable Civilians, Diplomatic and Consular Personnel, the Wounded and Sick, and Medical Personnel).

[9] *Refer to* § 10.8.2 (Departures of Protected Persons From a Belligerent's Home Territory).

[10] *Refer to* § 10.23.3.3 (Special Agreements Concerning Relief Shipments).

[11] *Refer to* § 10.9.6 (Agreements for the Release, Return, or Accommodation in a Neutral Country of Certain Classes of Internees).

[12] *Refer to* § 18.14.1 (Inquiry Procedure in the 1949 Geneva Conventions).

[13] GC art. 7 ("In addition to the agreements expressly provided for in Articles 11, 14, 15, 17, 36, 108, 109, 132, 133 and 149, the High Contracting Parties may conclude other special agreements for all matters concerning which they may deem it suitable to make separate provision.").

[14] GC art. 7 ("No special agreement shall adversely affect the situation of protected persons, as defined by the present Convention, nor restrict the rights which it confers upon them.").

with regard to them by one or other of the parties to the conflict.[15]

10.1.2 DoD Policies and Regulations for the Treatment of Internees. DoD policies and regulations regarding the treatment of internees provide authoritative guidance for DoD personnel and fill an important role in implementing the complex requirements of the GC.[16] Practitioners are advised to consult all applicable policies and regulations, as these, in many cases, exceed the requirements of the GC, U.S. statutes, and Executive Orders.

10.2 National-Level GC Implementation Measures

The GC requires a number of measures at the national level to facilitate protection for protected persons.

10.2.1 Appointment or Establishment of Entities. The GC provides for certain bodies or entities to be appointed or established.

10.2.1.1 *Appointment of a Protecting Power*. The GC contemplates that a Protecting Power has been appointed to assist in the implementation of the GC.[17] A Protecting Power has a variety of roles under the GC related to the protection of protected persons.[18]

10.2.1.2 *Establishment of a National Protected Person Information Bureau*. A National Protected Person Information Bureau shall be established by each of the parties to the conflict.[19]

10.2.1.3 *Establishment of a Central Information Agency for Protected Persons*. A Central Information Agency for protected persons shall be established in a neutral country.[20]

10.2.2 Notification of Certain Laws or Policies Between Belligerents. Parties to a conflict must notify opposing belligerents or the Protecting Power of certain matters relating to protected persons.

10.2.2.1 *Location and Marking of Places of Internment Camps*. The Detaining Power shall provide the Powers concerned useful information regarding the geographic location of places of internment, and agreements on their markings may be reached.[21]

---

[15] GC art. 7 ("Protected persons shall continue to have the benefit of such agreements as long as the Convention is applicable to them, except where express provisions to the contrary are contained in the aforesaid or in subsequent agreements, or where more favourable measures have been taken with regard to them by one or other of the Parties to the conflict.").

[16] *Refer to* § 18.7 (Instructions, Regulations, and Procedures to Implement and Enforce the Law of War).

[17] *Refer to* § 18.15.1.1 (Protecting Power Under the 1949 Geneva Conventions).

[18] *Refer to* § 10.32 (Role of the Protecting Power in the GC).

[19] *Refer to* § 10.31.2 (National Protected Person Information Bureau).

[20] *Refer to* § 10.31.3 (Central Information Agency for Protected Persons).

[21] *Refer to* § 10.11.1.2 (Sharing Information on the Location of Places of Internment); § 10.11.1.3 (Marking of Internment Camps).

10.2.2.2 *Notification of Measures Taken for Implementing GC Provisions That Address Relations Between Internees and the Exterior*. Immediately upon interning protected persons, the Detaining Power shall inform them, the Power to which they owe allegiance, and their Protecting Power of the measures taken for executing the provisions of Chapter VIII of Section IV of the GC, which address the relations between internees and the exterior (*e.g.*, correspondence, relief shipments, family visits).[22] The Detaining Power shall likewise inform the Parties concerned of any subsequent modifications of such measures.[23]

10.3 Protected Person Status

In general, the GC uses the concept of *protected person* to define the individuals who are entitled to receive its protections. Principally, *protected persons* include persons of enemy nationality living in the territory of a belligerent State and the inhabitants of occupied territories.[24] Even if persons are not protected persons under the GC, other rules may be applicable to them. For example, certain baseline rules apply to the treatment of all detainees, including those who are not protected persons or POWs.[25]

10.3.1 Protected Person – Notes on Terminology. *Protected persons* is used in the GC as a term to refer to persons who are protected by the GC in connection with international armed conflict or occupation.

Protected persons is often understood as a term that is specific to the GC. In a few places, however, the GPW, the GWS, and the GWS-Sea also refer to "protected persons" or "persons protected."[26] In such cases, "protected persons" and "persons protected" refer to persons protected by that respective convention, as opposed to *protected persons* for purposes of the GC.

Although the GC addresses the protection of civilians, *protected persons* may include certain unprivileged belligerents. Certain rights and privileges that protected persons who are

---

[22] GC art. 105 ("Immediately upon interning protected persons, the Detaining Powers shall inform them, the Power to which they owe allegiance and their Protecting Power of the measures taken for executing the provisions of the present Chapter.").

[23] GC art. 105 ("The Detaining Powers shall likewise inform the Parties concerned of any subsequent modifications of such measures.").

[24] GC COMMENTARY 45 ("When work was begun on the preparation of the texts, it became clear—as early as the time of the Tokyo Draft—that there were two main classes of civilian to whom protection against arbitrary action on the part of the enemy was essential in time of war—on the one hand, persons of enemy nationality living in the territory of a belligerent State, and on the other, the inhabitants of occupied territories. The idea that the Convention should cover these two categories was accepted from the first and has never really been disputed. Any discussions which have taken place on the subject have been concerned with points of detail which we shall consider later. This Article [4 of the GC] is, in a sense, the key to the Convention; for it defines the people to whom it refers.").

[25] *Refer to* § 8.1.1 (Overview of Detention Rules in This Manual and the Scope of Chapter VIII).

[26] *See, e.g.*, GPW art. 11 ("In cases where they deem it advisable in the interest of protected persons, particularly in cases of disagreement between the Parties to the conflict as to the application or interpretation of the provisions of the present Convention, the Protecting Powers shall lend their good offices with a view to settling the disagreement.").

unprivileged belligerents receive, however, are subject to derogation for security reasons.[27]

10.3.2 Persons Who Receive Protected Person Status Under the GC. Subject to certain exceptions addressed below, persons protected by the GC are those who, at a given moment and in any manner whatsoever, find themselves, in case of a conflict or occupation, in the hands of a party to the conflict or Occupying Power of which they are not nationals.[28]

Because the definition of protected person is framed negatively in terms of persons who are in the hands of a State of which they are not nationals, the definition of protected person allows for the possibility that persons without any nationality may be protected persons.[29]

10.3.2.1 *"Find Themselves"*. The persons must "find themselves" in the hands of a party to the conflict or Occupying Power, which suggests an element of happenstance or coincidence.[30] For example, nationals of a neutral or non-belligerent State who travel to an occupied State to fight the Occupying Power cannot be said to have "found themselves" within that occupied territory within the meaning of Article 4 of the GC.

10.3.2.2 *In Occupied Territory or the Home Territory of a Party to the Conflict*. To be entitled to the protections provided under the GC for "protected persons," a person must be located in either (1) occupied territory or (2) the home territory of a party to the conflict.[31] The references in the GC that limit the scope of protections for protected persons to those "in the territory of a Party to the conflict" refer to the *home territory* of the party to the conflict in whose

---

[27] *Refer to* § 10.4 (Derogation for Security Reasons).

[28] GC art. 4 ("Persons protected by the Convention are those who, at a given moment and in any manner whatsoever, find themselves, in case of a conflict or occupation, in the hands of a Party to the conflict or Occupying Power of which they are not nationals.").

[29] GC COMMENTARY 47 ("It will be observed that owing to its negative form the definition covers persons without any nationality. The Rapporteur to Committee III pointed out that it thus complied with the recommendation made to the Diplomatic Conference by the representative of the International Refugee Organization. In the actual course of the discussions, however, certain speakers observed that the term 'nationals' (*ressortissants*, in the French version) did not cover all cases, in particular cases where men and women had fled from their homeland and no longer considered themselves, or were no longer considered, to be nationals of that country. Such cases exist, it is true, but it will be for the Power in whose hands they are to decide whether the persons concerned should or should not be regarded as citizens of the country from which they have fled. The problem presents so many varied aspects that it was difficult to deal with it fully in the Convention.").

[30] Jack L. Goldsmith III, Assistant Attorney General, *"Protected Person" Status in Occupied Iraq Under the Fourth Geneva Convention*, Mar. 18, 2004, 28 OPINIONS OF THE OFFICE OF LEGAL COUNSEL 35, 51 ("Alternatively, the phrase "find themselves" [in Article 4 of the GC] can be read more narrowly to suggest an element of happenstance or coincidence, and to connote a lack of deliberate action relating to the circumstances that leave the persons in question in the hands of an occupying power.").

[31] *See* Jack L. Goldsmith III, Assistant Attorney General, *"Protected Person" Status in Occupied Iraq Under the Fourth Geneva Convention*, Mar. 18, 2004, 28 OPINIONS OF THE OFFICE OF LEGAL COUNSEL 35, 41 ("To receive the protections provided for 'protected persons,' one must be located in either (1) 'occupied territory,' or (2) the 'territory of a party to the conflict.' This limitation does not emerge from article 4 itself, but rather from other provisions in GC."); GC COMMENTARY 46 ("Nevertheless, disregarding points of detail, it will be seen that there are two main classes of protected person: (1) *enemy nationals* within the national territory of each of the Parties to the conflict and (2) *the whole population* of occupied territories (excluding nationals of the Occupying Power). The other distinctions and, exceptions extend or restrict these limits, but not to any appreciable extent.").

hands the protected person finds himself or herself.[32] For example, Section II of Part III of the GC, which applies to "Aliens in the Territory of a Party to the Conflict," addresses the protection of aliens present on the home territory of a party to the conflict in relation to that State.

10.3.2.3 *Not Protected by the GWS, GWS-Sea, or the GPW*. Persons protected by the GWS, the GWS-Sea, or the GPW shall not be considered as *protected persons* within the meaning of the GC.[33] For example, persons who receive POW status under the GPW are not considered as *protected persons* within the meaning of the GC.[34]

10.3.2.4 *Unprivileged Belligerents Not Per Se Excluded From Protected Person Status*. The fact that a person has engaged in hostile or belligerent conduct does not *per se* exclude that person from protected person status under the GC.[35]

Certain rights and privileges of the GC that a protected person who has engaged in such conduct would otherwise receive are, however, subject to derogation for security reasons.[36]

10.3.3 Categories of Nationals Specifically Excluded From the Definition of Protected Person Under the GC. As discussed in this subsection, the GC specifically excludes certain

---

[32] Jack L. Goldsmith III, Assistant Attorney General, *"Protected Person" Status in Occupied Iraq Under the Fourth Geneva Convention*, Mar. 18, 2004, 28 OPINIONS OF THE OFFICE OF LEGAL COUNSEL 35, 41 ("The meaning of the phrase 'territory of a Party to the conflict,' considered in isolation, is not self-evident. At first glance, one might think that the phrase includes occupied territory, because the occupied power (to whom the territory belongs) is a party to the conflict. But in the context of the entire Convention, the phrase clearly refers to the *home territory* of the party to the conflict in whose hands the 'protected person' finds himself. This is evident from several provisions in GC4.").

[33] GC art. 4 ("Persons protected by the Geneva Convention for the Amelioration of the Condition of the Wounded and Sick in Armed Forces in the Field of August 12, 1949, or by the Geneva Convention for the Amelioration of the Condition of Wounded, Sick and Shipwrecked Members of Armed Forces at Sea of August 12, 1949, or by the Geneva Convention relative to the Treatment of Prisoners of War of August 12, 1949, shall not be considered as protected persons within the meaning of the present Convention.").

[34] *Refer to* § 9.3.2 (Persons Entitled to POW Status).

[35] *See* Jack L. Goldsmith III, Assistant Attorney General, *"Protected Person" Status in Occupied Iraq Under the Fourth Geneva Convention*, Mar. 18, 2004, 28 OPINIONS OF THE OFFICE OF LEGAL COUNSEL 35, 48 ("GC4's full title—'Geneva Convention Relative to the Protection of *Civilian* Persons in Time of War,' (emphasis added)—suggests that '[t]he main object of the Convention is to protect a strictly defined category of *civilians*.' 4 Pictet, *Commentary* at 10 (emphasis added). Consistent with this title, article 4(4) of GC expressly excludes lawful combatants who enjoy POW status from 'protected person' status. These factors, combined with the fact that unlawful combatants generally receive less favorable treatment than lawful combatants under the Geneva Convention system, see, e.g., Memorandum for Alberto R. Gonzales, Counsel to the President, from Jay S. Bybee, Assistant Attorney General, *Re: Status of Taliban Forces Under Article 4 of the Third Geneva Convention of 1949* at 1-7 (Feb. 7, 2002) (concluding that GPW withholds protections from persons who engage in hostilities but fail to satisfy criteria for lawful combatancy), might lead one to assume that unlawful combatants are categorically excluded from 'protected person' status under GC. GC's text, however, contemplates that persons who 'find themselves' in occupied territory within the meaning of article 4 may engage in at least some forms of unlawful belligerency without forfeiting all of the benefits of 'protected person' status."); 1956 FM 27-10 (Change No. 1 1976) ¶247b ("Subject to qualifications set forth in paragraph 248 [relating to derogations], those protected by GC also include all persons who have engaged in hostile or belligerent conduct but who are not entitled to treatment as prisoners of war.").

[36] *Refer to* § 10.4 (Derogation for Security Reasons).

classes of persons from the definition of protected person.[37]

The provisions of Part II of the GC, which address the general protection of populations against certain consequences of war, are, however, wider in application, as defined in Article 13 of the GC.[38] These provisions cover the whole of the populations in conflict without any adverse distinction based, in particular, on race, nationality, religion, or political opinion, and are intended to alleviate the sufferings caused by war.[39] Thus, persons excluded by reason of their nationality from the definition of protected person may nonetheless receive the protections of Part II of the GC.

10.3.3.1 *A State's Own Nationals*. In general, a State's own nationals who are in its hands are not *protected persons* under the GC.[40] This exclusion from the definition of "protected person" in the GC is consistent with a traditional principle of international law—the GC "does not interfere in a State's relations with its own nationals."[41] However, the GC does limit the arrest, prosecution, conviction, or deportation of nationals of any Occupying Power who, before the outbreak of hostilities, have sought refuge in the territory of the occupied State.[42]

10.3.3.2 *Nationals of a State That Is Not Bound by the GC*. Nationals of a State that is not bound by the GC are not protected by it.[43] This provision of the GC reflects a legal principle underlying the GC: a State must accept the burdens of the GC in order to receive its benefits.[44]

---

[37] *Compare* § 4.4.4 (Nationality and Combatant Status).

[38] *See* GC art. 4 ("The provisions of Part II are, however, wider in application, as defined in Article 13.").

[39] GC art. 13 ("The provisions of Part II cover the whole of the populations of the countries in conflict, without any adverse distinction based, in particular, on race, nationality, religion or political opinion, and are intended to alleviate the sufferings caused by war.").

[40] GC art. 4 ("Persons protected by the Convention are those who, at a given moment and in any manner whatsoever, find themselves, in case of a conflict or occupation, in the hands of a Party to the conflict or Occupying Power of which they are not nationals.") (emphasis added).

[41] GC COMMENTARY 46 ("The definition has been put in a negative form; as it is intended to cover anyone who is not a national of the Party to the conflict or Occupying Power in whose hands he is. The Convention thus remains faithful to a recognized principle of international law: it does not interfere in a State's relations with its own nationals. The only exception to this rule is the second paragraph of Article 70, which refers to nationals of the Occupying Power who sought refuge in the territory of the occupied State before the outbreak of hostilities. This is a very special case, based on the position such people have taken up with regard to their own country.").

[42] *Refer to* § 11.11.7 (Limitation on Criminal Jurisdiction With Respect to Pre-Occupation Acts).

[43] GC art. 4 ("Nationals of a State which is not bound by the Convention are not protected by it.").

[44] Jack L. Goldsmith III, Assistant Attorney General, *"Protected Person" Status in Occupied Iraq Under the Fourth Geneva Convention*, Mar. 18, 2004, 28 OPINIONS OF THE OFFICE OF LEGAL COUNSEL 35, 54 ("The benefits-burdens principle also finds expression in article 4(2), which provides: 'Nationals of a State which is not bound by the Convention are not protected by it.' The ICRC's Official Commentary states that article 4(2)'s exception to the definition of "protected person" in article 4(1) is a 'truism' and an 'unnecessary addition' that follows naturally from article 2(1) even in the absence of article 4(2). *See* 4 Pictet, *Commentary* at 48. Whether or not this is true, article 4(2) makes this much clear: persons in occupied territory, including those who commit hostile acts there, are not 'protected persons' under GC if the State that represents them has not formally accepted the Convention's burdens.").

10.3.3.3 *Nationals of a Neutral State or Co-Belligerent State While Normal Diplomatic Representation Exists*. Nationals of a neutral State who find themselves in the territory of a belligerent State, and nationals of a co-belligerent State, shall not be regarded as protected persons while the State of which they are nationals has normal diplomatic representation in the State in whose hands they are.[45]

These persons were omitted from the GC's definition of "protected person" in order to avoid creating complications or inconsistencies in procedures should both the GC and the law applicable to normal diplomatic representation apply.[46]

Nationals of a neutral State in occupied territory, however, are regarded as protected persons under the GC.[47]

10.3.4 Commencement and Duration of Protected Person Status. As with the general application of the GC, protected persons shall receive their protections from the outset of any conflict or occupation mentioned in Article 2 of the GC.[48] In general, the application of protected person status also ceases when the GC ceases to apply.

In the territory of parties to the conflict, the application of the GC shall cease on the general close of military operations.[49] In most cases, the general close of military operations will be the final end of all fighting between all those concerned.[50]

---

[45] GC art. 4 ("Nationals of a neutral State who find themselves in the territory of a belligerent State, and nationals of a co-belligerent State, shall not be regarded as protected persons while the State of which they are nationals has normal diplomatic representation in the State in whose hands they are.").

[46] *See* II-A FINAL RECORD OF THE DIPLOMATIC CONFERENCE OF GENEVA OF 1949 814 ("At the first reading several Delegates argued that the Convention should merely regulate the relations between a belligerent State and the nationals of an enemy State, and that it should not include relations between the State and nationals of a neutral country. Other delegates, however, argued that stateless persons should be borne in mind and that, moreover, there might be, in the territory of a belligerent State, nationals of foreign States who did not benefit by any diplomatic representation either because their home country had broken off diplomatic relations with the country where they were or because they had themselves broken away from their country of origin. Our Committee gave the most careful consideration to this problem and the majority recognized the weight of the reasons put forward by States sheltering a large number of aliens: the superposition of normal diplomatic representation and of the protection ensured by the Convention, would lead to complications and would be indefensible from the point of view of consistency of procedure.").

[47] *Refer to* § 15.6.4.1 (Protected Person Status of Neutral Persons in Occupied Territory).

[48] GC art. 6 ("The present Convention shall apply from the outset of any conflict or occupation mentioned in Article 2.").

[49] GC art. 6 ("In the territory of Parties to the conflict, the application of the present Convention shall cease on the general close of military operations.").

[50] GC COMMENTARY 62 ("What should be understood by the words 'general close of military operations'? In the opinion of the Rapporteur of Committee III, the general close of military operations was 'when the last shot has been fired'. There are, however, a certain number of other factors to be taken into account. When the struggle takes place between two States the date of the close of hostilities is fairly easy to decide: it will depend either on an armistice, a capitulation or simply on debellatio. On the other hand, when there are several States on one or both of the sides, the question is harder to settle. It must be agreed that in most cases the general close of military operations will be the final end of all fighting between all those concerned.").

In the case of occupied territory, the application of the GC shall cease one year after the general close of military operations; however, the Occupying Power shall be bound, for the duration of the occupation, to the extent that such Power exercises the functions of government in such territory, by the provisions of the following Articles of the GC: 1 through 12, 27, 29 through 34, 47, 49, 51, 52, 53, 59, 61 through 77, and 143.[51]

Protected persons whose release, repatriation, or re-establishment may take place after such dates shall meanwhile continue to benefit from the protection of the GC.[52] "Re-establishment" refers to protected persons who cannot be repatriated because, for example, they would be liable to persecution in their own country or because their homes have been destroyed.[53]

10.3.5 State Responsibility for Its Agents' Treatment of Protected Persons. A party to the conflict is responsible for the treatment accorded to protected persons by its agents, irrespective of any individual responsibility that may be incurred.[54]

10.3.6 Non-Renunciation of Rights Secured by the GC. Protected persons may in no circumstances renounce in part or in entirety the rights secured to them by the GC or by special agreements, if any, referred to in Article 7 of the GC.[55] A similar provision of the GPW applies to POWs, and similar provisions of the GWS and GWS-Sea apply to the wounded, sick, shipwrecked, and military medical and religious personnel.[56]

10.4 Derogation for Security Reasons

Certain rights and privileges of the GC that protected persons receive are subject to derogation for security reasons.

---

[51] *Refer to* § 11.3.2 (Duration of GC Obligations in the Case of Occupied Territory).

[52] GC art. 6 ("Protected persons whose release, repatriation or re-establishment may take place after such dates shall meanwhile continue to benefit by the present Convention.").

[53] 1956 FM 27-10 (Change No. 1 1976) ¶249b ("*Reestablishment of Protected Persons*. The word 'reestablishment,' as used in *a*, refers to protected persons who cannot be repatriated because, for example, they would be liable to persecution in their own country, or because their homes have been destroyed."). *See also* GC COMMENTARY 64 ("The time when the Convention as a whole ceases to apply, both in the territory of the Parties to the conflict and in occupied territory, may quite conceivably come before the protected persons have been able to resume a normal existence, especially if they have to be repatriated or assisted to resettle. … The word 'resettlement' is used in regard to protected persons who cannot be repatriated for one reason or another and are not allowed to settle permanently in the country where they are living. In such cases another country must be found where they will be received and allowed to settle. It was in particular the experience gained at the end of the Second World War which led to the adoption of this clause.").

[54] GC art. 29 ("The Party to the conflict in whose hands protected persons may be, is responsible for the treatment accorded to them by its agents, irrespective of any individual responsibility which may be incurred."). *Refer to* § 18.9.1 (State Responsibility for Violations of the Law of War by Its Armed Forces).

[55] GC art. 8 ("Protected persons may in no circumstances renounce in part or in entirety the rights secured to them by the present Convention, and by the special agreements referred to in the foregoing Article, if such there be."). *Refer to* § 10.1.1.2 (Special Agreements Under the GC).

[56] *Refer to* § 7.2.2 (Non-Renunciation of Rights Secured by the GWS or GWS-Sea); § 9.3.7 (Non-Renunciation of Rights Secured by the GPW).

10.4.1 Derogation in Home Territory. Where, in the territory of a party to the conflict, the latter is satisfied that an individual protected person is definitely suspected of or engaged in activities hostile to the security of the State, such individual person shall not be entitled to claim such rights and privileges under the GC as would, if exercised in the favor of such individual person, be prejudicial to the security of such State.[57]

10.4.2 Derogation in Occupied Territory. Where in occupied territory an individual protected person is detained as a spy or saboteur, or as a person under definite suspicion of activity hostile to the security of the Occupying Power, such person shall, in those cases where absolute military security so requires, be regarded as having forfeited rights of communication under the GC.[58] For example, it may be necessary to keep the fact of detention secret temporarily so as not to compromise an ongoing operation against a conspiracy or network of spies.[59]

The derogation provisions relating to the home territory of a belligerent are not applicable in occupied territory, even though the occupied territory may arguably be characterized as the home territory of the opposing belligerent (*i.e.*, the country being occupied).

10.4.3 Derogation in Other Areas. To the extent that the rights and privileges of protected persons afforded by the GC are applied outside the home territory of a party to the conflict or outside occupied territory, it would be reasonable for such rights and privileges similarly to be subject to derogation. Thus, if a party to the conflict is satisfied that an individual protected person is definitely suspected of or engaged in activities hostile to the security of the State in other contexts, such individual person similarly could be deemed not entitled to claim such rights and privileges under the GC as would, if exercised in favor of such individual person, be prejudicial to the security of such State.[60]

10.4.4 Limits on Derogation. In each case, such persons shall nevertheless be treated with humanity, and in case of trial, shall not be deprived of the rights of fair and regular trial prescribed by the GC.[61] No derogation from the provision of humane treatment and the rights of

---

[57] GC art. 5 ("Where, in the territory of a Party to the conflict, the latter is satisfied that an individual protected person is definitely suspected of or engaged in activities hostile to the security of the State, such individual person shall not be entitled to claim such rights and privileges under the present Convention as would, if exercised in the favour of such individual person, be prejudicial to the security of such State.").

[58] GC art. 5 ("Where in occupied territory an individual protected person is detained as a spy or saboteur, or as a person under definite suspicion of activity hostile to the security of the Occupying Power, such person, shall, in those cases where absolute military security so requires, be regarded as having forfeited rights of communication under the present Convention.").

[59] GC COMMENTARY 53 ("There may of course be occasions when it is desirable to keep the fact of an arrest secret in the hope of capturing a whole organization or spy ring.").

[60] 1956 FM 27-10 (Change No. 1 1976) ¶248b ("Where, in territories other than those mentioned in a above, a Party to the conflict is satisfied that an individual protected person is definitely suspected of or engaged in activities hostile to the security of the State, such individual person is similarly not entitled to claim such rights and privileges under GC as would, if exercised in favor of such individual person, be prejudicial to the security of such State.").

[61] GC art. 5 ("In each case, such persons shall nevertheless be treated with humanity, and in case of trial, shall not be deprived of the rights of fair and regular trial prescribed by the present Convention.").

fair and regular trial is permitted.[62]

Such persons shall also be granted the full rights and privileges of a protected person under the GC at the earliest date consistent with the security of the State or Occupying Power, as the case may be.[63]

10.5 Humane Treatment and Other Basic Protections for Protected Persons

Protected persons are entitled, in all circumstances, to respect for their persons, their honor, their family rights, their religious convictions and practices, and their manners and customs. They shall at all times be humanely treated, and shall be protected especially against all acts of violence or threats of violence, and against insults and public curiosity.[64]

10.5.1 Protection Against Violence or Threats. Protected persons must at all times be protected, particularly against acts or threats of violence. For example, the murder of protected persons is forbidden.

Protected persons should be protected not only against unlawful acts by the agents of the Detaining Power, but also against violence from other protected persons, such as during internment or, in the case of protected persons in a belligerent's home territory, violence from members of the civilian population.

10.5.1.1 *Measures of Physical Suffering, Extermination, or Other Brutality*. The Parties to the GC specifically agree that each of them is prohibited from taking any measure of such a character as to cause the physical suffering or extermination of protected persons in their hands.[65] This prohibition applies not only to murder, torture, corporal punishment, mutilation, and medical or scientific experiments not necessitated by the medical treatment of a protected person, but also to any other measures of brutality whether applied by civilian or military

---

[62] *Refer to* § 10.5 (Humane Treatment and Other Basic Protections for Protected Persons); § 10.29 (Judicial Proceedings Regarding Protected Persons in Occupied Territory or Internees).

[63] GC art. 5 ("They shall also be granted the full rights and privileges of a protected person under the present Convention at the earliest date consistent with the security of the State or Occupying Power, as the case may be.").

[64] GC art. 27 ("Protected persons are entitled, in all circumstances, to respect for their persons, their honour, their family rights, their religious convictions and practices, and their manners and customs. They shall at all times be humanely treated, and shall be protected especially against all acts of violence or threats thereof and against insults and public curiosity."). *See also* GC COMMENTARY 199-200 ("Article 27, placed at the head of Part III, occupies a key position among the Articles of the Convention. It is the basis of the Convention, proclaiming as it does the principles on which the whole of 'Geneva Law' is founded. It proclaims the principle of respect for the human person and the inviolable character of the basic rights of individual men and women. The statement of these principles in an international convention gives them the character of legal obligations and marks an essential stage in the history of international law -- in particular international humanitarian law, which is concerned above all with man as man.").

[65] GC art. 32 ("The High Contracting Parties specifically agree that each of them is prohibited from taking any measure of such a character as to cause the physical suffering or extermination of protected persons in their hands.").

agents.[66]

10.5.1.2 *Protection for Women Against Rape or Other Indecent Assault*. Women shall be especially protected against any attack on their honor, in particular against rape, enforced prostitution, or any form of indecent assault.[67]

Although the GC provides special protection for women against these offenses, all individuals, including children and men, should also be protected against these offenses. Indecent assault is generally referred to today as sexual assault.

10.5.1.3 *Presence May Not Be Used to Render Places Immune From Military Operations*. The presence of a protected person may not be used to render certain points or areas immune from military operations.[68]

10.5.1.4 *Taking of Hostages*. The taking of hostages is prohibited.[69]

10.5.2 Protection Against Insults and Public Curiosity. Internees must at all times be protected against insults and public curiosity. For example, displaying internees in a humiliating fashion on television or on the internet would be prohibited.[70] For this reason and others, DoD policy has prohibited the taking of photographs of detainees except for authorized purposes.[71]

10.5.3 Other Prohibited Measures.

10.5.3.1 *No Physical or Moral Coercion*. No physical or moral coercion shall be exercised against protected persons, in particular to obtain information from them or from third parties.[72] For example, protected persons in occupied territory may not be compelled to provide information about their State's military defenses.[73] Other requirements, including the requirements of U.S. law and policy, would apply to the interrogation of protected persons.[74]

The GC's prohibition against the use of coercion does not apply to those measures

---

[66] GC art. 32 ("This prohibition applies not only to murder, torture, corporal punishment, mutilation and medical or scientific experiments not necessitated by the medical treatment of a protected person, but also to any other measures of brutality whether applied by civilian or military agents.").

[67] GC art. 27 ("Women shall be especially protected against any attack on their honour, in particular against rape, enforced prostitution, or any form of indecent assault.").

[68] GC art. 28 ("The presence of a protected person may not be used to render certain points or areas immune from military operations.").

[69] GC art. 34 ("The taking of hostages is prohibited.").

[70] *Compare* § 9.5.3 (Protection Against Insults and Public Curiosity).

[71] *Refer to* § 8.2.2.3 (DoD Practice of Generally Prohibiting Taking Photographs Without Authorization).

[72] GC art. 31 ("No physical or moral coercion shall be exercised against protected persons, in particular to obtain information from them or from third parties.").

[73] *Refer to* § 11.20.1.4 (Prohibition Against Forcing Inhabitants to Provide Information About the Opposing Army or Its Means of Defense).

[74] *Refer to* § 10.6.2 (Interrogation of Protected Persons).

implicitly or explicitly authorized by the GC (such as the use of force to prevent one internee from harming another) or other lawful measures that are otherwise consistent with the GC (such as the use of force to prevent internees from escaping internment).[75]

10.5.3.2 *Collective Penalties and Measures of Intimidation or Terrorism*. No protected person may be punished for an offense he or she has not personally committed.[76] Collective penalties and likewise all measures of intimidation or of terrorism are prohibited.[77]

Collective penalties are prohibited as a general matter.[78]

10.5.3.3 *Pillage Against Protected Persons*. Pillage is prohibited.[79] In addition to this specific prohibition in the GC, pillage is prohibited as a general matter.[80]

10.5.4 Reprisals Against Protected Persons and Their Property. Reprisals against protected persons and their property are prohibited.[81]

10.5.5 No Adverse Distinction Based on Race, Religion, or Political Opinion. Without prejudice to the provisions of the GC relating to their state of health, age, and sex, all protected persons shall be treated with the same consideration by the party to the conflict in whose power they are, without any adverse distinction based, in particular, on race, religion, or political opinion.[82]

Distinctions are permitted, and in some cases required, for humanitarian reasons.[83] For

---

[75] GC COMMENTARY 220 ("The general nature of the new provision marks an important step forward in international law. For its exact significance to be appreciated, it should not be considered in isolation but rather in the light of the other provisions of the Convention. It will then be seen that there is no question of absolute prohibition, as might be thought at first sight. The prohibition only applies in so far as the other provisions of the Convention do not implicitly or explicitly authorize a resort to coercion. Thus, Article 31 is subject to the unspoken reservation that force is permitted whenever it is necessary to use it in the application of measures taken under the Convention. This power is embodied and expressed particularly in penal legislation and in the control and security regulations enacted by the belligerents and to which protected persons are subject.").

[76] GC art. 33 ("No protected person may be punished for an offence he or she has not personally committed.").

[77] GC art. 33 ("Collective penalties and likewise all measures of intimidation or of terrorism are prohibited."). *Consider* AP I art. 51(2) ("Acts or threats of violence the primary purpose of which is to spread terror among the civilian population are prohibited.").

[78] *Refer to* § 8.16.2.1 (Individual Penal Responsibility and No Collective Punishment).

[79] GC art. 33 ("Pillage is prohibited.").

[80] *Refer to* § 5.17.4 (Pillage Prohibited).

[81] *Refer to* § 18.18.3.2 (Reprisals Prohibited by the 1949 Geneva Conventions).

[82] GC art. 27 ("Without prejudice to the provisions relating to their state of health, age and sex, all protected persons shall be treated with the same consideration by the Party to the conflict in whose power they are, without any adverse distinction based, in particular, on race, religion or political opinion.").

[83] GC COMMENTARY 426 ("All discrimination contrary to Article 27 is prohibited. On the other hand implicit authority is given for the discrimination permitted by that Article for humanitarian reasons, in order to favour classes of people who are in particular need of help (the infirm, the sick, pregnant women, etc.). All this is an example of the application of the principle of non-discrimination, as understood in humanitarian law--that is to say the rule

example, the GC provides for special treatment for children during internment.[84]

Distinction based on religion, political opinion, or other similar criteria may also be made so long as it is not adverse and it is made to advance legitimate interests, such as maintaining order in a place of internment.[85]

10.5.6 Facility for Applying to the Protecting Powers and Assistance Organizations Such as the ICRC. Protected persons shall have every facility for making application to the Protecting Powers, the ICRC, the National Red Cross (Red Crescent, Red Lion and Sun) Society of the country where they may be, as well as to any organization that might assist them.[86]

These several organizations shall be granted all facilities for that purpose by the authorities, within the bounds set by military or security considerations.[87]

Apart from the visits of the delegates of the Protecting Powers and of the ICRC, provided for by Article 143 of the GC, the Detaining or Occupying Powers shall facilitate as much as possible visits to protected persons by the representatives of other organizations whose object is to give spiritual aid or material relief to such persons.[88]

10.6 Measures of Control and Security

The parties to the conflict may take such measures of control and security in regard to protected persons as may be necessary as a result of the war.[89] For example, in a belligerent's

---

which forbids all differentiation based on race, political opinions, religion or social class, but at the same time demands that the different degrees of suffering should be alleviated by different degrees of assistance.").

84 *Refer to* § 4.20.4 (Protection for Children in the Context of Internment Under the GC).

85 *Compare* § 9.5.5 (No Adverse Distinction Based on Race, Nationality, Religion, or Political Belief).

86 GC art. 30 ("Protected persons shall have every facility for making application to the Protecting Powers, the International Committee of the Red Cross, the National Red Cross (Red Crescent, Red Lion and Sun) Society of the country where they may be, as well as to any organization that might assist them.").

87 GC art. 30 ("These several organizations shall be granted all facilities for that purpose by the authorities, within the bounds set by military or security considerations."). *See also* GC COMMENTARY 218 ("The Convention requires the Parties to the conflict to grant all facilities to the Protecting Powers and relief organizations. That means that it will not be enough merely to authorize them to carry out their work; their task must be facilitated and promoted. It is the duty of the authorities to take all necessary steps to allow approved organizations to take rapid and effective action wherever they are asked to give assistance. Among examples of such measures can be mentioned the provision of facilities for delegates to move about and carry on correspondence, to have free access to all places where protected persons are living, transport facilities and facilities for distributing relief, etc. The obligation to facilitate this work is limited however by military or security considerations, as stated in the reservation at the end of the paragraph. It is essential, however, that the belligerents, who will be sole judges o [sic] the validity of the reasons put forward, should show moderation in the use they make of this reservation and only apply it in cases of real necessity").

88 GC art. 30 ("Apart from the visits of the delegates of the Protecting Powers and of the International Committee of the Red Cross, provided for by Article 143, the Detaining or Occupying Powers shall facilitate as much as possible visits to protected persons by the representatives of other organizations whose object is to give spiritual aid or material relief to such persons.").

89 GC art. 27 ("However, the Parties to the conflict may take such measures of control and security in regard to protected persons as may be necessary as a result of the war.").

home territory, measures of control are normally taken with respect to, at the very least, persons known to be active or reserve members of a hostile army, persons who would be liable to service in the enemy forces, and persons who it is expected would furnish information or other aid to a hostile State.[90]

These measures may include, for example, requiring protected persons: (1) to register with and report periodically to the police authorities; (2) to carry identity cards or special papers; (3) to refrain from carrying weapons; (4) to refrain from changing their place of residence without permission; (5) to refrain from accessing certain areas; (6) to have an assigned residence; and (7) to be interned.[91]

This section addresses searches, interrogation, and general rules for measures of control and security applied to protected persons, which must be applied consistent with humane treatment requirements.[92]

10.6.1 General Authority of a Belligerent to Search and Secure Protected Persons and Their Property. The measures of control and security that a belligerent may take in regard to protected persons include searching and securing protected persons and their property when necessary as a result of the war (*e.g.*, for security reasons and intelligence purposes).[93]

10.6.1.1 *Searches of Protected Persons*. The dignity and honor of the protected person being searched should be protected to the greatest degree possible under the circumstances.[94] The person conducting the search should avoid doing or saying anything likely to be regarded as indecent. In some circumstances, it may be appropriate for a witness to observe the search so as to protect both the person being searched from abuse and the person conducting the search from unfounded accusations of abuse.

10.6.1.2 *Search of Female Protected Persons*. It is appropriate for female protected persons to be searched by female personnel, if possible. This practice helps reduce the risk of accusations of indecent behavior.

---

[90] 1956 FM 27-10 (Change No. 1 1976) ¶26 ("Measures of control are normally taken with respect to at least persons known to be active or reserve members of a hostile army, persons who would be liable to service in the enemy forces, and persons who it is expected would furnish information or other aid to a hostile State.").

[91] GC COMMENTARY 207 ("The various security measures which States might take are not specified; the Article merely lays down a general provision. There are a great many measures, ranging from comparatively mild restrictions such as the duty of registering with and reporting periodically to the police authorities, the carrying of identity cards or special papers, or a ban on the carrying of arms, to harsher provisions such as a prohibition on any change in place of residence without permission, prohibition of access to certain areas, restrictions of movement, or even assigned residence and internment (which, according to Article 41, are the two most severe measures a belligerent may inflict on protected persons). A great deal is thus left to the discretion of the Parties to the conflict as regards the choice of means. What is essential is that the measures of constraint they adopt should not affect the fundamental rights of the persons concerned.").

[92] *Refer to* § 10.5 (Humane Treatment and Other Basic Protections for Protected Persons).

[93] *Compare* § 9.6 (Security Measures With Respect to POWs).

[94] *Refer to* § 10.5 (Humane Treatment and Other Basic Protections for Protected Persons).

A woman internee shall not be searched except by a woman.[95]

10.6.1.3 *Securing Protected Persons With Handcuffs and Other Security Devices*. When necessary for security reasons, protected persons may be secured temporarily with handcuffs, flex cuffs, blindfolds, or other security devices.[96]

10.6.1.4 *Search of the Property of Protected Persons*. When necessary as a result of the war, items in the possession of protected persons may be removed and searched, but property should be returned as soon as possible, absent a legal basis for the seizure of the property.[97]

10.6.2 Interrogation of Protected Persons. The law of war does not prohibit interrogation of protected persons, but specifies conditions and limitations for conducting interrogation.

10.6.2.1 *Humane Treatment During Interrogation*. Interrogation must be carried out in a manner consistent with the requirements for humane treatment, including the prohibition against acts of violence or intimidation, and insults.[98]

No physical or moral coercion shall be exercised against protected persons to obtain information from them or from third parties.[99]

10.6.2.2 *Additional U.S. Law and Policy on Interrogation*. U.S. law and policy impose additional requirements on the interrogation of protected persons.[100]

10.6.3 No Measures of Control More Severe Than Assigned Residence or Internment. If the measures of control mentioned in the GC for protected persons are considered to be inadequate by the Power imposing them, that Power may not have recourse to any other measure of control more severe than that of assigned residence or internment, in accordance with the provisions of Articles 42 and 43 of the GC.[101]

Similarly, if the Occupying Power considers it necessary, for imperative reasons of security, to take safety measures concerning protected persons, it may, at the most, subject them to assigned residence or to internment.[102]

---

[95] GC art. 97 ("A woman internee shall not be searched except by a woman.").

[96] *Compare* § 9.6.2 (Securing POWs With Handcuffs and Other Security Devices).

[97] *Refer to* § 5.17 (Seizure and Destruction of Enemy Property).

[98] *Refer to* § 10.5 (Humane Treatment and Other Basic Protections for Protected Persons).

[99] *Refer to* § 10.5.3.1 (No Physical or Moral Coercion).

[100] *Refer to, e.g.*, § 8.4.2 (Additional U.S. Law and Policy on Interrogation).

[101] GC art. 41 ("Should the Power in whose hands protected persons may be consider the measures of control mentioned in the present Convention to be inadequate, it may not have recourse to any other measure of control more severe than that of assigned residence or internment, in accordance with the provisions of Articles 42 and 43.").

[102] GC art. 78 ("If the Occupying Power considers it necessary, for imperative reasons of security, to take safety measures concerning protected persons, it may, at the most, subject them to assigned residence or to internment.").

10.6.4 Support to Persons Who Are Assigned Residence Should Be Guided by Internment Standards. In applying the provisions of the second paragraph of Article 39 of the GC to the cases of persons required to leave their usual places of residence by virtue of a decision placing them in assigned residence elsewhere, the Detaining Power shall be guided as closely as possible by the standards of welfare set forth in Part III, Section IV of the GC.[103] In other words, if the State assigns residence to a protected person in its home territory that results in the protected person being unable to support himself or herself and his or her dependents, the State shall provide support to that protected person and his or her dependents, being guided as closely as possible by the standards of welfare set forth in Part III, Section IV of the GC, which provides regulations for the treatment of internees.

Similarly, in occupied territory, protected persons made subject to assigned residence and thus required to leave their homes shall enjoy the full benefit of Article 39 of the GC.[104] For example, the internment standards in the GC should also be a guide for support to protected persons and their dependents who are subject to assigned residence in occupied territory.

10.6.5 Refugees Who Do Not Enjoy the Protection of Any Government. In applying the measures of control mentioned in the GC to protected persons in its home territory, the Detaining Power shall not treat as enemy aliens exclusively on the basis of their nationality *de jure* of an enemy State, refugees who do not, in fact, enjoy the protection of any government.[105] For example, a refugee who is not actually protected by his or her government should not be automatically subject to control measures simply on the basis of enemy nationality, but may be subject to any other recognized control measure if there are additional reasons for such action.[106]

10.7 General Treatment of Protected Persons in a Belligerent's Home Territory

10.7.1 Regulation of the Situation of Protected Persons, in Principle, by Provisions Applicable to Aliens in Time of Peace. With the exception of special measures authorized by the GC, in particular by Articles 27 and 41 of the GC (*i.e.*, measures of control and security, such as internment), the situation of protected persons shall continue to be regulated, in principle, by the

---

[103] GC art. 41 ("In applying the provisions of Article 39, second paragraph, to the cases of persons required to leave their usual places of residence by virtue of a decision placing them in assigned residence elsewhere, the Detaining Power shall be guided as closely as possible by the standards of welfare set forth in Part III, Section IV of this Convention.").

[104] GC art. 78 ("Protected persons made subject to assigned residence and thus required to leave their homes shall enjoy the full benefit of Article 39 of the present Convention.").

[105] GC art. 44 ("In applying the measures of control mentioned in the present Convention, the Detaining Power shall not treat as enemy aliens exclusively on the basis of their nationality *de jure* of an enemy State, refugees who do not, in fact, enjoy the protection of any government.").

[106] *See* 1956 FM 27-10 (Change No. 1 1976) ¶283b ("The purpose of the foregoing article [37 of the GC] is to insure that refugees who may only technically remain enemy aliens are not on that basis automatically subject to control measures, notwithstanding the fact they actually are not protected by their government. However, the quoted provision does not in any way deny the right of a State to intern any such person or subject him to any other recognized measure of control when there is any additional reason that renders necessary the taking of such action as may be required for the security of the State in a moment of national crisis.").

provisions concerning aliens in time of peace.[107] In any case, the following rights shall be granted to them:

- They shall be enabled to receive the individual or collective relief that may be sent to them (*e.g.*, by their home country or national or international relief organizations, such as the ICRC).

- They shall, if their state of health so requires, receive medical attention and hospital treatment to the same extent as the nationals of the State concerned.

- They shall be allowed to practice their religion and to receive spiritual assistance from ministers of their faith.

- If they reside in an area particularly exposed to the dangers of war, they shall be authorized to move from that area to the same extent as the nationals of the State concerned.

- Children under fifteen years, pregnant women, and mothers of children under seven years shall benefit from any preferential treatment to the same extent as the nationals of the State concerned.[108]

10.7.2 Opportunity for Employment and Other Support. Protected persons who, as a result of the war, have lost their gainful employment, shall be granted the opportunity to find paid employment.[109] That opportunity shall, subject to security considerations and to the provisions of Article 40, be equal to that enjoyed by the nationals of the Power in whose territory they are.[110]

10.7.2.1 *Support When Measures of Control Are Applied*. Where a party to the conflict applies to a protected person methods of control that result in that person being unable to support himself or herself, and especially if such a person is prevented for reasons of security from finding paid employment on reasonable conditions, that party shall ensure his or her

---

[107] GC art. 38 ("With the exception of special measures authorized by the present Convention, in particular by Articles 27 and 41 thereof, the situation of protected persons shall continue to be regulated, in principle, by the provisions concerning aliens in time of peace.").

[108] GC art. 38 ("In any case, the following rights shall be granted to them: (1) They shall be enabled to receive the individual or collective relief that may be sent to them. (2) They shall, if their state of health so requires, receive medical attention and hospital treatment to the same extent as the nationals of the State concerned. (3) They shall be allowed to practise their religion and to receive spiritual assistance from ministers of their faith. (4) If they reside in an area particularly exposed to the dangers of war, they shall be authorized to move from that area to the same extent as the nationals of the State concerned. (5) Children under fifteen years, pregnant women and mothers of children under seven years shall benefit by any preferential treatment to the same extent as the nationals of the State concerned.").

[109] GC art. 39 ("Protected persons who, as a result of the war, have lost their gainful employment, shall be granted the opportunity to find paid employment.").

[110] GC art. 39 ("That opportunity shall, subject to security considerations and to the provisions of Article 40, be equal to that enjoyed by the nationals of the Power in whose territory they are.").

support and that of his or her dependents.[111]

10.7.2.2 *Receipt of Allowances*. Protected persons may in any case receive allowances from their home country, the Protecting Power, or the relief societies referred to in Article 30 of the GC (*e.g.*, the ICRC).[112]

10.7.3 Compulsory Work for Protected Persons in a Belligerent's Home Territory. Protected persons may be compelled to work only to the same extent as nationals of the party to the conflict in whose territory they are.[113]

If protected persons are of enemy nationality, they may only be compelled to do work that is normally necessary to ensure the feeding, sheltering, clothing, transport, and health of human beings and that is not directly related to the conduct of military operations.[114]

In the cases mentioned in the two preceding paragraphs, protected persons compelled to work shall have the benefit of the same working conditions and of the same safeguards as national workers, in particular as regards wages, hours of labor, clothing and equipment, previous training, and compensation for occupational accidents and diseases.[115]

If the above provisions are infringed, protected persons shall be allowed to exercise their right of complaint in accordance with Article 30 of the GC.[116]

10.7.4 Cancellation of Restrictive Measures After Hostilities. In so far as they have not been previously withdrawn, restrictive measures taken regarding protected persons shall be cancelled as soon as possible after the close of hostilities.[117] Restrictive measures affecting their property shall be cancelled, in accordance with the law of the Detaining Power, as soon as

---

[111] GC art. 39 ("Where a Party to the conflict applies to a protected person methods of control which result in his being unable to support himself, and especially if such a person is prevented for reasons of security from finding paid employment on reasonable conditions, the said Party shall ensure his support and that of his dependents.").

[112] GC art. 39 ("Protected persons may in any case receive allowances from their home country, the Protecting Power, or the relief societies referred to in Article 30.").

[113] GC art. 40 ("Protected persons may be compelled to work only to the same extent as nationals of the Party to the conflict in whose territory they are.").

[114] GC art. 40 ("If protected persons are of enemy nationality, they may only be compelled to do work which is normally necessary to ensure the feeding, sheltering, clothing, transport and health of human beings and which is not directly related to the conduct of military operations.").

[115] GC art. 40 ("In the cases mentioned in the two preceding paragraphs, protected persons compelled to work shall have the benefit of the same working conditions and of the same safeguards as national workers, in particular as regards wages, hours of labour, clothing and equipment, previous training and compensation for occupational accidents and diseases.").

[116] GC art. 40 ("If the above provisions are infringed, protected persons shall be allowed to exercise their right of complaint in accordance with Article 30."). *Refer to* § 10.5.6 (Facility for Applying to the Protecting Powers and Assistance Organizations Such as the ICRC).

[117] GC art. 46 ("In so far as they have not been previously withdrawn, restrictive measures taken regarding protected persons shall be cancelled as soon as possible after the close of hostilities.").

possible after the close of hostilities.[118]

10.8 Expulsion From Areas Within a Belligerent's Home Territory and Departure and Transfers of Protected Persons From a Belligerent's Home Territory

10.8.1 Expulsion From Areas Within a Belligerent's Home Territory. At the outbreak of hostilities, a State may expel or bar the citizens or subjects of the enemy State from its seaports, the area surrounding airbases, airports, and fortified places, areas of possible attack, and the actual or contemplated theaters of operation.

When such expulsion is decreed, the persons expelled should be given such reasonable notice, consistent with public safety, as will enable them to arrange for the collection, disposal, and removal of their goods and property, and for the settlement of their personal affairs.[119]

Although such expulsion must be implemented in a humane manner, the provisions of the GC addressing a State's internment or assigned residence of civilians of an enemy State in its home territory (Articles 41-45), including the transfer of internees to other countries, do not apply to such expulsion.[120]

10.8.2 Departures of Protected Persons From a Belligerent's Home Territory. All protected persons who may desire to leave the territory at the outset of or during a conflict shall be entitled to do so, unless their departure is contrary to the national interests of the State.[121] The applications of such persons to leave shall be decided in accordance with regularly established procedures, and the decision shall be taken as rapidly as possible.[122] Those persons permitted to leave may provide themselves with the necessary funds for their journey and take with them a reasonable amount of their effects and articles of personal use.[123]

---

[118] GC art. 46 ("Restrictive measures affecting their property shall be cancelled, in accordance with the law of the Detaining Power, as soon as possible after the close of hostilities.").

[119] *See* 1956 FM 27-10 (Change No. 1 1976) ¶27 ("In modern practice at the outbreak of hostilities the expulsion of the citizens or subjects of the enemy is generally decreed from seaports, the area surrounding airbases, airports, and fortified places, areas of possible attack, and the actual or contemplated theaters of operation. When expulsion is decreed, the persons expelled should be given such reasonable notice, consistent with public safety, as will enable them to arrange for the collection, disposal, and removal of their goods and property and for the settlement of their personal affairs. Such persons do not, however, benefit from the provisions of Articles 41 through 45, *GC* (pars. 280-284).").

[120] *See* II-A Final Record of the Diplomatic Conference of Geneva of 1949 826 ("The internment procedure laid down in *Article 40* is similar to that provided for in Article 32 with regard to the authorization to leave the territory. Article 40 also empowers a court or administrative board, to be selected by the Detaining Power, to take decisions in cases of appeal against internment or assigned residence. The term 'assigned residence' obviously denotes a measure applicable to one person or one family, not the prohibition to enter or reside in a specified zone imposed upon an anonymous body of people such as all the nationals of a certain State.").

[121] GC art. 35 ("All protected persons who may desire to leave the territory at the outset of, or during a conflict, shall be entitled to do so, unless their departure is contrary to the national interests of the State.").

[122] GC art. 35 ("The applications of such persons to leave shall be decided in accordance with regularly established procedures and the decision shall be taken as rapidly as possible.").

[123] GC art. 35 ("Those persons permitted to leave may provide themselves with the necessary funds for their journey and take with them a reasonable amount of their effects and articles of personal use.").

If any such person is refused permission to leave the territory, he or she shall be entitled to have such refusal reconsidered as soon as possible by an appropriate court or administrative board designated by the Detaining Power for that purpose.[124]

Upon request, representatives of the Protecting Power shall, unless reasons of security prevent it, or the persons concerned object, be furnished with the reasons for refusal of any request for permission to leave the territory and be given, as expeditiously as possible, the names of all persons who have been denied permission to leave.[125]

Departures permitted under Article 35 of the GC shall be carried out in satisfactory conditions as regards safety, hygiene, sanitation, and food.[126] All costs in connection therewith, from the point of exit in the territory of the Detaining Power, shall be borne by the country of destination or, in the case of accommodation in a neutral country, by the Power whose nationals are benefited.[127] The practical details of such movements may, if necessary, be settled by special agreements between the Powers concerned.[128]

The foregoing shall not prejudice such special agreements as may be concluded between parties to the conflict concerning the exchange and repatriation of their nationals in enemy hands.[129]

Protected persons who are confined pending proceedings or serving a sentence involving loss of liberty shall be treated humanely during their confinement.[130] As soon as they are released, they may ask to leave the territory in conformity with Articles 35 and 36 of the GC.[131]

10.8.3 Transfers of Protected Persons From a Belligerent's Home Territory.

---

[124] GC art. 35 ("If any such person is refused permission to leave the territory, he shall be entitled to have such refusal reconsidered as soon as possible by an appropriate court or administrative board designated by the Detaining Power for that purpose.").

[125] GC art. 35 ("Upon request, representatives of the Protecting Power shall, unless reasons of security prevent it, or the persons concerned object, be furnished with the reasons for refusal of any request for permission to leave the territory and be given, as expeditiously as possible, the names of all persons who have been denied permission to leave.").

[126] GC art. 36 ("Departures permitted under the foregoing Article shall be carried out in satisfactory conditions as regards safety, hygiene, sanitation and food.").

[127] GC art. 36 ("All costs in connection therewith, from the point of exit in the territory of the Detaining Power, shall be borne by the country of destination, or, in the case of accommodation in a neutral country, by the Power whose nationals are benefited.").

[128] GC art. 36 ("The practical details of such movements may, if necessary, be settled by special agreements between the Powers concerned.").

[129] GC art. 36 ("The foregoing shall not prejudice such special agreements as may be concluded between Parties to the conflict concerning the exchange and repatriation of their nationals in enemy hands.").

[130] GC art. 37 ("Protected persons who are confined pending proceedings or serving a sentence involving loss of liberty, shall during their confinement be humanely treated.").

[131] GC art. 37 ("As soon as they are released, they may ask to leave the territory in conformity with the foregoing Articles.").

10.8.3.1 *Requirements for Transfer*. Protected persons shall not be transferred to a Power that is not a Party to the GC.[132] This provision shall in no way constitute an obstacle to the repatriation of protected persons, or to their return to their country of residence after the cessation of hostilities.[133]

Protected persons may be transferred by the Detaining Power only to a Power that is a Party to the GC and after the Detaining Power has satisfied itself of the willingness and ability of such receiving Power to apply the GC.[134]

In no circumstances shall a protected person be transferred to a country where he or she may have reason to fear persecution for his or her political opinions or religious beliefs.[135] In addition, U.S. policy provides that no detainee shall be transferred to another State if it is more likely than not that the detainee would be tortured in the receiving country.[136]

The provisions of Article 45 of the GC do not constitute an obstacle to the extradition, under extradition treaties concluded before the outbreak of hostilities, of protected persons accused of offenses against ordinary criminal law.[137]

10.8.3.2 *Responsibility Upon Transfer*. If protected persons are transferred under such circumstances, responsibility for the application of the GC rests on the Power accepting them, while they are in its custody.[138] Nevertheless, if that Power fails to carry out the provisions of the GC in any important respect, the Power by which the protected persons were transferred shall, upon being so notified by the Protecting Power, take effective measures to correct the situation or shall request the return of the protected persons.[139] Such request must be complied with.[140]

---

[132] GC art. 45 ("Protected persons shall not be transferred to a Power which is not a party to the Convention.").

[133] GC art. 45 ("This provision shall in no way constitute an obstacle to the repatriation of protected persons, or to their return to their country of residence after the cessation of hostilities.").

[134] GC art. 45 ("Protected persons may be transferred by the Detaining Power only to a Power which is a party to the present Convention and after the Detaining Power has satisfied itself of the willingness and ability of such transferee Power to apply the present Convention.").

[135] GC art. 45 ("In no circumstances shall a protected person be transferred to a country where he or she may have reason to fear persecution for his or her political opinions or religious beliefs.").

[136] *Refer to* § 8.14.4.1 (U.S. Policy Prohibiting Transfers in Cases in Which Detainees Would Likely Be Tortured).

[137] GC art. 45 ("The provisions of this Article do not constitute an obstacle to the extradition, in pursuance of extradition treaties concluded before the outbreak of hostilities, of protected persons accused of offences against ordinary criminal law.").

[138] GC art. 45 ("If protected persons are transferred under such circumstances, responsibility for the application of the present Convention rests on the Power accepting them, while they are in its custody.").

[139] GC art. 45 ("Nevertheless, if that Power fails to carry out the provisions of the present Convention in any important respect, the Power by which the protected persons were transferred shall, upon being so notified by the Protecting Power, take effective measures to correct the situation or shall request the return of the protected persons.").

[140] GC art. 45 ("Such request must be complied with.").

10.9 Internment

The parties to the conflict shall not intern protected persons, except in accordance with the provisions of Articles 41, 42, 43, 68, and 78 of the GC.[141]

10.9.1 Principles Underlying the Internment of Protected Persons Compared to Those Underlying POW Internment. In some respects, the principles underlying the internment of protected persons are similar to the principles underlying the internment of POWs.[142] For example, the internment of protected persons is non-punitive, the Detaining Power is responsible for the treatment of internees in its custody, and humane treatment is required.

However, the GC recognizes that the internment of protected persons is quite different in character from that of POWs by requiring the separation of internees from POWs.[143] Protected persons interned for security reasons, in theory, have not participated in hostilities.[144] Thus, their internment shall cease when the reasons that have necessitated it have ceased, which may occur before the end of the conflict.[145] In practice, however, internment for security reasons may involve persons who have participated in hostilities, and such persons' continued detention for the duration of the conflict may be justified in order to prevent their further participation in the conflict.

On the other hand, internees are not members of the armed forces and, thus, in certain respects, have not earned the special privileges that POWs have earned.[146] For example, although internees receive allowances, internees do not receive specified advances of pay like POWs.[147] Similarly, internees who have successfully escaped do not benefit from the immunity from punishment applicable to POWs who have successfully escaped.[148]

10.9.2 Procedure for Internment or Assigned Residence on Home Territory.

10.9.2.1 *Internment or Assigned Residence Only if Absolutely Necessary*. The internment or placing in assigned residence of protected persons may be ordered only if the

---

[141] GC art. 79 ("The Parties to the conflict shall not intern protected persons, except in accordance with the provisions of Articles 41, 42, 43, 68 and 78.").

[142] *Refer to* § 9.2 (General Principles Applicable to the Treatment of POWs).

[143] *Refer to* § 10.10.1 (Segregation From Other Types of Detainees).

[144] GC COMMENTARY 368 ("The persons subjected to these measures [of assigned residence or internment in accordance with Article 78 of the GC] are not, in theory, involved in the struggle. The precautions taken with regard to them cannot, therefore, be in the nature of a punishment.").

[145] *Refer to* § 10.9.5 (Release As Soon As Reasons for Internment No Longer Exist).

[146] *See, e.g.*, II-A FINAL RECORD OF THE DIPLOMATIC CONFERENCE OF GENEVA OF 1949 681 ("Mr. WERSHOF (Canada) suggested that the first paragraph should be deleted. He failed to see why the Detaining Power should make an allowance of any kind to enemy aliens whom it considered dangerous. He was of the opinion that the analogy between internees and prisoners of war had been carried too far. Prisoners of war had earned a standard of treatment which had not been earned by internees.").

[147] *Refer to* § 10.19.2 (Internee Allowances); § 9.18.3 (Advance of Pay).

[148] *Refer to* § 10.26 (Internee Escapes); § 9.25.1 (No Punishment for Successful Escape).

security of the Detaining Power makes it absolutely necessary.[149]

10.9.2.2 *Voluntary Internment*. If any person, acting through the representatives of the Protecting Power, voluntarily demands internment, and if his or her situation renders this step necessary, he or she shall be interned by the Power in whose hands he or she may be.[150]

10.9.2.3 *Reconsideration and Periodic Review*. Any protected person who has been interned or placed in assigned residence shall be entitled to have such action reconsidered as soon as possible by an appropriate court or administrative board designated by the Detaining Power for that purpose.[151] If the internment or placing in assigned residence is maintained, the court or administrative board shall periodically, and at least twice yearly, give consideration to his or her case, with a view to the favorable amendment of the initial decision, if circumstances permit.[152]

10.9.2.4 *Notification to the Protecting Power*. Unless the protected persons concerned object, the Detaining Power shall, as rapidly as possible, give the Protecting Power the names of any protected persons who have been interned or subjected to assigned residence, or who have been released from internment or assigned residence.[153] The decisions of the courts or boards mentioned in the first paragraph of Article 43 of the GC shall also, subject to the same conditions, be notified as rapidly as possible to the Protecting Power.[154]

10.9.3 Procedure for Internment or Assigned Residence in Occupied Territory. The requirements in the GC for the procedure for assigned residence or internment of protected persons in occupied territory are not as elaborate as those applicable in a belligerent's home territory because of concerns that it would not be practicable to implement the requirements applicable in a belligerent's home territory in view of the disorder that might prevail in occupied territory.[155]

---

[149] GC art. 42 ("The internment or placing in assigned residence of protected persons may be ordered only if the security of the Detaining Power makes it absolutely necessary.").

[150] GC art. 42 ("If any person, acting through the representatives of the Protecting Power, voluntarily demands internment, and if his situation renders this step necessary, he shall be interned by the Power in whose hands he may be.").

[151] GC art. 43 ("Any protected person who has been interned or placed in assigned residence shall be entitled to have such action reconsidered as soon as possible by an appropriate court or administrative board designated by the Detaining Power for that purpose.").

[152] GC art. 43 ("If the internment or placing in assigned residence is maintained, the court or administrative board shall periodically, and at least twice yearly, give consideration to his or her case, with a view to the favourable amendment of the initial decision, if circumstances permit.").

[153] GC art. 43 ("Unless the protected persons concerned object, the Detaining Power shall, as rapidly as possible, give the Protecting Power the names of any protected persons who have been interned or subjected to assigned residence, or who have been released from internment or assigned residence.").

[154] GC art. 43 ("The decisions of the courts or boards mentioned in the first paragraph of the present Article shall also, subject to the same conditions, be notified as rapidly as possible to the Protecting Power.").

[155] *See* II-A FINAL RECORD OF THE DIPLOMATIC CONFERENCE OF GENEVA OF 1949 773 ("[T]he Drafting Committee had felt that in view of the disorder which might prevail in occupied territory, it would not be practicable to lay down an elaborate procedure for internement, similar to that provided for the territory of a Party to the conflict.

10.9.3.1 *Internment or Assigned Residence for Imperative Reasons of Security*. If the Occupying Power considers it necessary, for imperative reasons of security, to take safety measures concerning protected persons, it may, at the most, subject them to assigned residence or to internment.[156]

Decisions regarding such assigned residence or internment shall be made according to a regular procedure to be prescribed by the Occupying Power in accordance with the provisions of the GC.[157] This procedure shall include the right of appeal for the parties concerned.[158] Appeals shall be decided with the least possible delay.[159] In the event of the decision being upheld, it shall be subject to periodic review, if possible every six months, by a competent body set up by the Occupying Power.[160] "Competent bodies" to review the internment or assigned residence of protected persons may be created with advisory functions only, leaving the final decision to a high official of the Government.[161]

10.9.3.2 *Internment for Minor Offenses Directed Against the Occupying Power*. Protected persons who commit an offense that is solely intended to harm the Occupying Power, but that does not constitute an attempt on the life or limb of members of the occupying forces or administration, nor a grave collective danger, nor seriously damage the property of the occupying forces or administration or the installations used by them, shall be liable to internment or simple imprisonment, provided the duration of such internment or imprisonment is proportionate to the offense committed.[162] Furthermore, internment or imprisonment shall, for

---

They had felt that it would be wiser to content themselves with making the Occupying Power responsible for establishing a regular and systematic procedure to suit the circumstances. The Occupying Power would then have no excuse for making arbitrary decisions regarding internment.").

[156] GC art. 78 ("If the Occupying Power considers it necessary, for imperative reasons of security, to take safety measures concerning protected persons, it may, at the most, subject them to assigned residence or to internment.").

[157] GC art. 78 ("Decisions regarding such assigned residence or internment shall be made according to a regular procedure to be prescribed by the Occupying Power in accordance with the provisions of the present Convention.").

[158] GC art. 78 ("This procedure shall include the right of appeal for the parties concerned.").

[159] GC art. 78 ("Appeals shall be decided with the least possible delay.").

[160] GC art. 78 ("In the event of the decision being upheld, it shall be subject to periodical review, if possible every six months, by a competent body set up by the said Power.").

[161] 1956 FM 27-10 (Change No. 1 1976) ¶433b ("'Competent bodies' to review the internment or assigned residence of protected persons may be created with advisory functions only, leaving the final decision to a high official of the Government."); SENATE EXECUTIVE REPORT 84-9, *Geneva Conventions for the Protection of War Victims: Report of the Committee on Foreign Relations on Executives D, E, F, and G*, 82nd Congress, First Session, 22 (Jun. 27, 1955) ("In article 78 it is likewise provided that persons who have been placed in internment or assigned residence in occupied territory, shall be entitled to review or reconsideration by a 'competent body.' From information furnished to the committee by the executive branch it appears that the administrative boards and the competent bodies contemplated by the three articles to reconsider decisions in these cases may be created with advisory functions only, leaving the final decision to a high official or officer of the government. This understanding of the provisions appears to be a reasonable one to the committee.").

[162] *Refer to* § 11.11.4 (Limitations on Penalties for Certain, Non-Serious Offenses Solely Intended to Harm the Occupying Power).

such offenses, be the only measure adopted for depriving protected persons of liberty.[163] The courts provided for under Article 66 of the GC may at their discretion convert a sentence of imprisonment to one of internment for the same period.[164]

10.9.4 Maintenance of Internees. Parties to the conflict who intern protected persons shall be bound to provide free of charge for their maintenance, and to grant them also the medical attention required by their state of health.[165] No deduction from the allowances, salaries, or credits due to the internees shall be made for the repayment of these costs.[166] The Detaining Power shall provide for the support of those dependent on the internees, if such dependents are without adequate means of support or are unable to earn a living.[167]

10.9.5 Release As Soon As Reasons for Internment No Longer Exist. Each interned person shall be released by the Detaining Power as soon as the reasons that necessitated his or her internment no longer exist.[168]

10.9.6 Agreements for the Release, Return, or Accommodation in a Neutral Country of Certain Classes of Internees. The parties to the conflict shall endeavor during the course of hostilities to conclude agreements for the release, the repatriation, the return to places of residence, or the accommodation in a neutral country of certain classes of internees, in particular children, pregnant women, and mothers with infants and young children, wounded and sick, and internees who have been detained for a long time.[169]

10.10 Segregation of Internees

10.10.1 Segregation From Other Types of Detainees. Internees shall be accommodated and administered separately from POWs and from persons deprived of liberty for any other reason.[170] This rule reflects the difference in character between the internment of internees from

---

[163] *Refer to* § 11.11.4.1 (Internment or Imprisonment as the Only Measure Adopted for Depriving Protected Persons of Liberty for Such Offenses).

[164] *Refer to* § 11.11.4.2 (Discretion of Non-Political, Military Courts to Convert Sentences of Imprisonment to Sentences of Internment).

[165] GC art. 81 ("Parties to the conflict who intern protected persons shall be bound to provide free of charge for their maintenance, and to grant them also the medical attention required by their state of health.").

[166] GC art. 81 ("No deduction from the allowances, salaries or credits due to the internees shall be made for the repayment of these costs.").

[167] GC art. 81 ("The Detaining Power shall provide for the support of those dependent on the internees, if such dependents are without adequate means of support or are unable to earn a living.").

[168] GC art. 132 ("Each interned person shall be released by the Detaining Power as soon as the reasons which necessitated his internment no longer exist.").

[169] GC art. 132 ("The Parties to the conflict shall, moreover, endeavour during the course of hostilities, to conclude agreements for the release, the repatriation, the return to places of residence or the accommodation in a neutral country of certain classes of internees, in particular children, pregnant women and mothers with infants and young children, wounded and sick, and internees who have been detained for a long time.").

[170] GC art. 84 ("Internees shall be accommodated and administered separately from prisoners of war and from persons deprived of liberty for any other reason.").

other types of detention or confinement.[171]

10.10.2 Accommodation According to Nationality, Language, and Customs. The Detaining Power shall, as far as possible, accommodate the internees according to their nationality, language, and customs.[172] Unlike the comparable rule in the GPW, this provision has the qualification "as far as possible" because of the competing interest in leaving internees near their families and because POWs are generally automatically grouped by nationality as a consequence of the circumstances of their capture.[173] Internees who are nationals of the same country shall not be separated merely because they speak different languages.[174]

10.10.3 Families Kept Together. Throughout the duration of their internment, members of the same family, and in particular parents and children, shall be lodged together in the same place of internment, except when separation of a temporary nature is necessitated for reasons of employment or health or for the purposes of enforcement of the provisions of Chapter IX (Penal and Disciplinary Sanctions) of Section IV of the GC.[175] Keeping families together during internment is intended to improve the morale and welfare of internees.[176]

Internees may request that their children who are left at liberty without parental care shall be interned with them.[177] For example, two parents who are interned together may request that

---

[171] GC COMMENTARY 384 ("This provision shows once more that the detention of internees is quite different in character from that of prisoners of war or common criminals. Internment is simply a precautionary measure and should not be confused with the penalty of imprisonment.").

[172] GC art. 82 ("The Detaining Power shall, as far as possible, accommodate the internees according to their nationality, language and customs.").

[173] GC COMMENTARY 380 ("This paragraph corresponds to paragraph 3 of Article 22 of the Convention relative to the Treatment of Prisoners of War. It states, but in less mandatory form, the principle that internees should be grouped, adding the words 'as far as possible' which do not occur in the Prisoners of War Convention. Indeed, prisoners of war generally fall into groups of the same nationality as a natural consequence of being captured together and grouping can be organized to a certain extent automatically. The grouping of civilians, on the other hand, who are taken into custody separately and sometimes coming from places distant from one another, presents some difficulties. It is better in certain cases to leave the internees near their families rather than to send them to a distance, in order to reunite them with persons of the same language and nationality. It is for this reason that Article 82 of the Fourth Convention is not mandatory."). *Refer to* § 9.12.1 (Assembling According to Nationality, Language, and Customs).

[174] GC art. 82 ("Internees who are nationals of the same country shall not be separated merely because they have different languages.").

[175] GC art. 82 ("Throughout the duration of their internment, members of the same family, and in particular parents and children, shall be lodged together in the same place of internment, except when separation of a temporary nature is necessitated for reasons of employment or health or for the purposes of enforcement of the provisions of Chapter IX of the present Section.").

[176] *See* GC COMMENTARY 380-81 ("The experience of the Second World War showed that internment was far less difficult to bear whenever internees could be grouped together in families. In India, Rhodesia, Kenya, Uganda, Tanganyika, Eritrea and France (at Vittel), such groups were successfully organized and the morale of the internees was better in those places than in other places of internment. Children benefited from the presence of their parents and were able to attend the school set up inside the camp. It is to the results of this experience which paragraphs 2 and 3 try to give permanent form in accordance with the recommendations of the experts.").

[177] GC art. 82 ("Internees may request that their children who are left at liberty without parental care shall be interned with them.").

their children be interned with them, but one of the parents would not be able to request the internment of a child being cared for by a parent who was not being interned.[178]

Wherever possible, interned members of the same family shall be housed in the same premises and given separate accommodation from other internees, together with facilities for leading a proper family life.[179]

10.11 Safety, Hygiene, and Living Conditions in Places of Internment

10.11.1 Safety of Places of Internment.

10.11.1.1 *Avoidance of Particularly Dangerous Areas*. The Detaining Power shall not set up places of internment in areas particularly exposed to the dangers of war.[180]

10.11.1.2 *Sharing Information on the Location of Places of Internment*. Detaining Powers shall give enemy Powers, through the intermediary of the Protecting Powers, all useful information regarding the geographic location of places of internment.[181]

10.11.1.3 *Marking of Internment Camps*. Whenever military considerations permit, internment camps shall be indicated by the letters "IC," placed so as to be clearly visible in the daytime from the air.[182] The Powers concerned may, however, agree upon any other system of marking.[183] No place, other than an internment camp, shall be marked as such.[184]

The caveat that internment camps need to be marked, as such, only when military considerations permit was intended to allow for camps not to be marked, *e.g.*, if such identification would enable an Enemy Power to instigate a revolt in the camp, provide weapons to the internees, enable escape attempts, etc.[185]

---

[178] GC Commentary 381 ("The report of the Third Committee indicates that the addition of the words 'without parental care' is intended to show that if only one of the parents is interned, he or she would not have the right, under the Convention, to demand the internment of a child being cared for by the other parent. On the other hand, the father and mother would have the right to demand such internment if they were interned together.").

[179] GC art. 82 ("Wherever possible, interned members of the same family shall be housed in the same premises and given separate accommodation from other internees, together with facilities for leading a proper family life.").

[180] GC art. 83 ("The Detaining Power shall not set up places of internment in areas particularly exposed to the dangers of war.").

[181] GC art. 83 ("The Detaining Power shall give the enemy Powers, through the intermediary of the Protecting Powers, all useful information regarding the geographical location of places of internment.").

[182] GC art. 83 ("Whenever military considerations permit, internment camps shall be indicated by the letters IC, placed so as to be clearly visible in the daytime from the air.").

[183] GC art. 83 ("The Powers concerned may, however, agree upon any other system of marking.").

[184] GC art. 83 ("No place other than an internment camp shall be marked as such.").

[185] GC Commentary 383 ("At the very beginning of hostilities during the Second World War, the International Committee of the Red Cross appealed to belligerents to mark their prisoner-of-war camps to protect them against bombing. Fearing that this would provide landmarks for the enemy air force, the Powers rejected the appeal. However, prisoners adopted the habit of displaying markings during the day consisting of large panels bearing the letters PG or PW. This method was approved by the Diplomatic Conference. It is, however, subject to an important

10.11.1.4 *Air-Raid Shelters and Protective Measures for Internees*. In all places of internment exposed to air raids and other hazards of war, shelters adequate in number and structure to ensure the necessary protection shall be installed.[186] In case of alarms, the internees shall be free to enter such shelters as quickly as possible, excepting those who remain for the protection of their quarters against these hazards.[187] Any protective measures taken in favor of the population shall also apply to the internees.[188]

10.11.1.5 *Fire Precautions*. All due precautions must be taken in places of internment against the danger of fire.[189]

10.11.2 Hygiene of Places of Internment. In no case shall permanent places of internment be situated in unhealthy areas, or in districts the climate of which is injurious to the internees.[190] In all cases where the district in which a protected person is temporarily interned is in an unhealthy area, or has a climate that is harmful to his or her health, he or she shall be removed to a more suitable place of internment as rapidly as circumstances permit.[191]

10.11.2.1 *Sanitary Conveniences (e.g., latrines, bathrooms)*. Internees shall have for their use, day and night, sanitary conveniences that conform to the rules of hygiene and are constantly maintained in a state of cleanliness.[192] The term "sanitary conveniences" should be taken to mean primarily the latrines.[193] Access to the latrines at night is specified in the 1949 Geneva Conventions because this was a frequent problem in POW camps in World War II.[194]

---

reservation drafted in the same way in the case of prisoners of war and of civilian internees: 'whenever military considerations permit'. This means that in the case of civilian internment camps, the daytime marking by means of the letters IC could be discontinued if the Detaining Power feared, for example, a parachute drop of arms to help the internees to revolt.").

[186] GC art. 88 ("In all places of internment exposed to air raids and other hazards of war, shelters adequate in number and structure to ensure the necessary protection shall be installed.").

[187] GC art. 88 ("In case of alarms, the internees shall be free to enter such shelters as quickly as possible, excepting those who remain for the protection of their quarters against the aforesaid hazards.").

[188] GC art. 88 ("Any protective measures taken in favour of the population shall also apply to them.").

[189] GC art. 88 ("All due precautions must be taken in places of internment against the danger of fire.").

[190] GC art. 85 ("In no case shall permanent places of internment be situated in unhealthy areas, or in districts the climate of which is injurious to the internees.").

[191] GC art. 85 ("In all cases where the district, in which a protected person is temporarily interned, is in an unhealthy area or has a climate which is harmful to his health, he shall be removed to a more suitable place of internment as rapidly as circumstances permit.").

[192] GC art. 85 ("Internees shall have for their use, day and night, sanitary conveniences which conform to the rules of hygiene and are constantly maintained in a state of cleanliness.").

[193] GC COMMENTARY 387 ("The term 'sanitary conveniences' should be taken to mean primarily the latrines, in conformity with the similar provision contained in paragraph 2 of Article 29 of the Third Convention. These conveniences should be so constructed as to preserve decency and cleanliness and must be sufficiently numerous. They should be inspected periodically by the health authorities.").

[194] *See* GC COMMENTARY 387 ("During the Second World War prisoners of war were sometimes forbidden to leave their quarters during the night. The Convention relative to the Protection of Civilian Persons in Time of War, like

In certain circumstances, women internees shall be provided separate sanitary conveniences for their use.[195]

10.11.2.2 *Showers, Baths, Personal Toilet, and Laundry*. Internees shall be provided with sufficient water and soap for their daily personal toilet and for washing their personal laundry; installations and facilities necessary for this purpose shall be granted to them.[196]

Showers or baths shall also be available.[197] The necessary time shall be set aside for washing and for cleaning.[198] Although the frequency of baths or showers is not specified in the GC, a reasonable opportunity (*e.g.*, considering the available resources, the internees' cultural practices, the activities in which they are engaged) should be afforded.[199]

10.11.3 Conditions of Buildings and Quarters. The Detaining Power is bound to take all necessary and possible measures to ensure that protected persons shall, from the outset of their internment, be accommodated in buildings or quarters that afford every possible safeguard in regard to hygiene and health, and provide efficient protection against the rigors of the climate and the effects of the war.[200]

The premises shall be fully protected from dampness and adequately heated and lighted, in particular between dusk and lights out.[201] The sleeping quarters shall be sufficiently spacious and well ventilated, and the internees shall have suitable bedding and sufficient blankets, with account being taken of the climate and of the age, sex, and state of health of the internees.[202]

10.11.3.1 *Separate Sleeping Quarters and Latrines for Women*. Whenever it is necessary, as an exceptional and temporary measure, to accommodate women internees who are not members of a family unit in the same place of internment as men, women internees shall be

---

the Prisoners of War Convention, stipulates that internees should have sanitary conveniences for their use day and night."). *Refer to* § 9.11.5.2 (Sanitary Conveniences (e.g., latrines, bathrooms)).

[195] *Refer to* § 10.11.3.1 (Separate Sleeping Quarters and Latrines for Women).

[196] GC art. 85 ("They shall be provided with sufficient water and soap for their daily personal toilet and for washing their personal laundry; installations and facilities necessary for this purpose shall be granted to them.").

[197] GC art. 85 ("Showers or baths shall also be available.").

[198] GC art. 85 ("The necessary time shall be set aside for washing and for cleaning.").

[199] GC COMMENTARY 387 ("The Government Experts had wished to lay down definitely the frequency with which baths could be taken. This idea was not accepted, but one bath or shower per week can be considered reasonable.").

[200] GC art. 85 ("The Detaining Power is bound to take all necessary and possible measures to ensure that protected persons shall, from the outset of their internment, be accommodated in buildings or quarters which afford every possible safeguard as regards hygiene and health, and provide efficient protection against the rigours of the climate and the effects of the war.").

[201] GC art. 85 ("The premises shall be fully protected from dampness, adequately heated and lighted, in particular between dusk and lights out.").

[202] GC art. 85 ("The sleeping quarters shall be sufficiently spacious and well ventilated, and the internees shall have suitable bedding and sufficient blankets, account being taken of the climate, and the age, sex, and state of health of the internees.").

provided separate sleeping quarters and sanitary conveniences for their use.[203]

10.12 Canteens for Internees

Canteens shall be installed in every place of internment, except where other suitable facilities are available.[204] As with canteens for POWs, the purpose of the canteen is to increase the morale and comfort of the internees.[205]

10.12.1 Establishment of the Canteen. Although canteens for POWs are required, canteens for civilian internees are not required if other suitable facilities, such as local shops, are available.[206]

If other suitable facilities are not available, and before canteens can be established, the need for a canteen may be mitigated if internees are provided a free "comfort pack."[207]

10.12.2 Canteen Stock and Prices. The purpose of the canteens shall be to enable internees to make purchases, at prices not higher than local market prices, of foodstuffs and articles of everyday use, including soap and tobacco, such as would increase their personal well-being and comfort.[208]

Internees are not entitled to more favorable treatment than the population at large with respect to canteen facilities, and are equally subject to regulations, such as those pertaining to rationing, which are applied to the population generally.[209]

10.12.3 Canteen Management and Profits. Canteen profits shall be credited to a welfare fund to be set up for each place of internment, and administered for the benefit of the internees

---

203 GC art. 85 ("Whenever it is necessary, as an exceptional and temporary measure, to accommodate women internees who are not members of a family unit in the same place of internment as men, the provision of separate sleeping quarters and sanitary conveniences for the use of such women internees shall be obligatory.").

204 GC art. 87 ("Canteens shall be installed in every place of internment, except where other suitable facilities are available.").

205 *Refer to* § 9.17 (Canteens for POWs).

206 GC Commentary 389 ("Whereas the establishment of canteens for prisoners of war is obligatory (Third Convention, Article 28, paragraph I), civilian internees will only be provided with canteens where other suitable facilities are not available. Indeed, there could be no question of establishing canteens if, for example, the internees were permitted to go to local shops to make purchases.").

207 *Compare* § 9.17.1.1 ("Comfort Pack" Instead of Canteen and Advance of Pay).

208 GC art. 87 ("Their purpose shall be to enable internees to make purchases, at prices not higher than local market prices, of foodstuffs and articles of everyday use, including soap and tobacco, such as would increase their personal well-being and comfort.").

209 *See* II-A Final Record of the Diplomatic Conference of Geneva of 1949 837 ("The general view was, however, that Article 76 was simply a 'morale-sustaining' Article, and that the internee was simply to be given the chance of purchasing, for example, a particular kind of soap, of his own choice, in substitution for a corresponding amount of the kind which the Detaining Power would normally provide under Article 75. It would be unreasonable in any case to contend that the provision of canteens was intended to put the internee in a superior position to the population at large.").

attached to such place of internment.[210] The Internee Committee shall have the right to check the management of the canteen and of the fund.[211]

When a place of internment is closed down, the balance of the welfare fund shall be transferred to the welfare fund of a place of internment for internees of the same nationality, or, if such a place does not exist, to a central welfare fund that shall be administered for the benefit of all internees remaining in the custody of the Detaining Power.[212] In case of a general release, the profits shall be kept by the Detaining Power, subject to any agreement to the contrary between the Powers concerned.[213]

10.13 Food, Water, Tobacco, and Clothing for Internees

10.13.1 Food for Internees. Daily food rations for internees shall be sufficient in quantity, quality, and variety to keep internees in a good state of health and prevent the development of nutritional deficiencies.[214]

10.13.1.1 *Accounting for the Customary Diet*. Account shall also be taken of the customary diet of the internees.[215] For example, the internee's cultural and religious requirements should be considered in determining and ensuring the appropriate diet.

10.13.1.2 *Additional Food for Certain Groups*. Internees who work shall receive additional rations in proportion to the kind of labor that they perform.[216] Expectant and nursing mothers, and children under fifteen years of age, shall be given additional food, in proportion to their physiological needs.[217]

10.13.1.3 *No Disciplinary Reductions in Food Rations*. The reduction in food

---

[210] GC art. 87 ("Profits made by canteens shall be credited to a welfare fund to be set up for each place of internment, and administered for the benefit of the internees attached to such place of internment.").

[211] GC art. 87 ("The Internee Committee provided for in Article 102 shall have the right to check the management of the canteen and of the said fund.").

[212] GC art. 87 ("When a place of internment is closed down, the balance of the welfare fund shall be transferred to the welfare fund of a place of internment for internees of the same nationality, or, if such a place does not exist, to a central welfare fund which shall be administered for the benefit of all internees remaining in the custody of the Detaining Power.").

[213] GC art. 87 ("In case of a general release, the said profits shall be kept by the Detaining Power, subject to any agreement to the contrary between the Powers concerned.").

[214] GC art. 89 ("Daily food rations for internees shall be sufficient in quantity, quality and variety to keep internees in a good state of health and prevent the development of nutritional deficiencies.").

[215] GC art. 89 ("Account shall also be taken of the customary diet of the internees.").

[216] GC art. 89 ("Internees who work shall receive additional rations in proportion to the kind of labour which they perform.").

[217] GC art. 89 ("Expectant and nursing mothers, and children under fifteen years of age, shall be given additional food, in proportion to their physiological needs.").

rations as a disciplinary punishment is specifically prohibited.[218]

10.13.1.4 *Means for Preparing Additional Food*. Internees shall be given the means by which they can prepare for themselves any additional food in their possession.[219]

10.13.2 Drinking Water. Sufficient drinking water shall be supplied to internees.[220]

10.13.3 Use of Tobacco. The use of tobacco shall be permitted.[221] The Detaining Power is not required to give tobacco to internees, but should offer it for sale at the canteen, if one is established.[222] The Detaining Power may impose reasonable restrictions on smoking to ensure that the camp is a healthful and safe environment.

10.13.4 Clothing of Internees. When taken into custody, internees shall be given all facilities to provide themselves with the necessary clothing, footwear, and change of underwear, and, later on, to procure further supplies, if required.[223] Should any internees not have sufficient clothing, account being taken of the climate, and be unable to procure any, it shall be provided free of charge to them by the Detaining Power.[224]

10.13.4.1 *No Humiliating Clothing*. The clothing supplied by the Detaining Power to internees and the outward markings placed on their own clothes shall not be ignominious nor expose them to ridicule.[225] For example, clothing provided to them should not resemble convicts' uniforms or be intended to humiliate them.[226]

10.13.4.2 *Clothing for Work*. Workers shall receive suitable working outfits,

---

[218] *Refer to* § 10.20.3.2 (Prohibition Against Prolonged Standing, Roll-Calls, Punishment Drill, Military Drill and Manuevers, or the Reduction of Food Rations).

[219] GC art. 89 ("Internees shall also be given the means by which they can prepare for themselves any additional food in their possession.").

[220] GC art. 89 ("Sufficient drinking water shall be supplied to internees.").

[221] GC art. 89 ("The use of tobacco shall be permitted.").

[222] *Refer to* § 10.12.2 (Canteen Stock and Prices).

[223] GC art. 90 ("When taken into custody, internees shall be given all facilities to provide themselves with the necessary clothing, footwear and change of underwear, and later on, to procure further supplies if required.").

[224] GC art. 90 ("Should any internees not have sufficient clothing, account being taken of the climate, and be unable to procure any, it shall be provided free of charge to them by the Detaining Power.").

[225] GC art. 90 ("The clothing supplied by the Detaining Power to internees and the outward markings placed on their own clothes shall not be ignominious nor expose them to ridicule.").

[226] *See* GC COMMENTARY 397 ("These provisos are connected with Articie 27 of the Convention stating that protected persons are entitled, in all circumstances, to respect for their persons and their honour. It is essential to prevent internees from being forced to wear convicts' uniforms or other uniforms of a similar nature, as was the case in certain concentration camps of hateful memory. The plenipotentiaries were unanimous in 1949 in disapproving of such practices and although paragraph 1 had already, as it were, implied that disapproval, they felt that they should reaffirm it explicitly at this point. It must, indeed, always be remembered that internment is not a punishment and cannot in any way besmirch anyone's honour.").

including protective clothing, whenever the nature of their work so requires.[227]

10.14 Medical Attention for Internees

Parties to the conflict who intern protected persons shall be bound to grant them the medical attention required by their state of health.[228]

10.14.1 Access to Medical Attention.

10.14.1.1 *Camp Infirmary*. Every place of internment shall have an adequate infirmary, under the direction of a qualified doctor, where internees may have the attention they require, as well as an appropriate diet.[229] Isolation wards shall be set aside for cases of contagious or mental diseases.[230]

10.14.1.2 *Right of Internees to Present Themselves for Examination*. Internees may not be prevented from presenting themselves to the medical authorities for examination.[231] The GC appears to contemplate that the internees would have daily sick call in which they could present themselves for medical examination, because it provides for internees who are undergoing disciplinary punishment to request to attend this inspection.[232] The right of internees to present themselves for examination does not mean that the internees must necessarily be examined every day by a doctor, nor does it preclude disciplinary punishment if internees abusively (on the basis of the doctor's report) make groundless requests for medical examination.[233]

10.14.1.3 *Monthly Medical Inspections*. Medical inspections of internees shall be made at least once a month.[234] Their purpose shall be, in particular, to supervise the general state

[227] GC art. 90 ("Workers shall receive suitable working outfits, including protective clothing, whenever the nature of their work so requires.").

[228] GC art. 81 ("Parties to the conflict who intern protected persons shall be bound to provide free of charge for their maintenance, and to grant them also the medical attention required by their state of health.").

[229] GC art. 91 ("Every place of internment shall have an adequate infirmary, under the direction of a qualified doctor, where internees may have the attention they require, as well as an appropriate diet.").

[230] GC art. 91 ("Isolation wards shall be set aside for cases of contagious or mental diseases.").

[231] GC art. 91 ("Internees may not be prevented from presenting themselves to the medical authorities for examination.").

[232] GC COMMENTARY 401 ("Although the fact is not mentioned in this paragraph [4 of Article 91 of the GC], a daily medical inspection will take place in places of internment. This follows, as will be seen further on, from Article 125. Internees will thus be able to report sick when they are ill, so as to receive medical attention without delay."). *Refer to* § 10.28.6.3 (Attendance at Daily Medical Inspection and Medical Attention).

[233] GC COMMENTARY 495-96 ("It was only logical to consider that the Detaining Power should arrange in every place of internment for a daily medical inspection and this paragraph [paragraph 2 of Article 125 of the GC] makes this important point quite clear. This does not mean, however, that internees must necessarily be examined every day by the doctor. The guards will not be entitled to forbid the internees to present themselves for daily medical examination; if the request to go on sick parade turns out to be groundless and upsets the maintenance of discipline, the offence may be considered as calling for disciplinary punishment by the commandant of the place of internment on the basis of the doctor's report.").

[234] GC art. 92 ("Medical inspections of internees shall be made at least once a month.").

of health, nutrition, and cleanliness of internees, and to detect contagious diseases, especially tuberculosis, malaria, and venereal diseases.[235] Such inspections shall include, in particular, the checking of weight of each internee and, at least once a year, radioscopic examination.[236]

10.14.2 Compulsory Medical Treatment. Because internees are subject to the laws in force in the territory in which they are detained,[237] internees may be ordered to undergo medical treatment to the extent that other persons in that territory may be so ordered.

10.14.3 Medical Treatment for Internees.

10.14.3.1 *Persons Requiring Special Treatment*. Maternity cases and internees suffering from serious diseases, or whose condition requires special treatment, a surgical operation, or hospital care, must be admitted to any institution where adequate treatment can be given and shall receive care not inferior to that provided for the general population.[238]

10.14.3.2 *Treatment by Medical Personnel of Their Own Nationality*. Internees shall, for preference, have the attention of medical personnel of their own nationality.[239]

10.14.3.3 *Certificate Recording Treatment*. The medical authorities of the Detaining Power shall, upon request, issue to every internee who has undergone treatment an official certificate showing the nature of his or her illness or injury, and the duration and nature of the treatment given.[240] A duplicate of this certificate shall be forwarded to the Central Information Agency for protected persons.[241]

10.14.3.4 *Cost of Medical Treatment*. Treatment, including the provision of any apparatus necessary for the maintenance of internees in good health, particularly dentures and other artificial appliances and spectacles, shall be free of charge to the internee.[242]

10.14.4 Receipt of Medical Shipments. Internees may receive individual parcels and

---

[235] GC art. 92 ("Their purpose shall be, in particular, to supervise the general state of health, nutrition and cleanliness of internees, and to detect contagious diseases, especially tuberculosis, malaria, and venereal diseases.").

[236] GC art. 92 ("Such inspections shall include, in particular, the checking of weight of each internee and, at least once a year, radioscopic examination.").

[237] *Refer to* § 10.27.1 (Applicability of the Laws in Force to Internees).

[238] GC art. 91 ("Maternity cases and internees suffering from serious diseases, or whose condition requires special treatment, a surgical operation or hospital care, must be admitted to any institution where adequate treatment can be given and shall receive care not inferior to that provided for the general population.").

[239] GC art. 91 ("Internees shall, for preference, have the attention of medical personnel of their own nationality.").

[240] GC art. 91 ("The medical authorities of the Detaining Power shall, upon request, issue to every internee who has undergone treatment an official certificate showing the nature of his illness or injury, and the duration and nature of the treatment given.").

[241] GC art. 91 ("A duplicate of this certificate shall be forwarded to the Central Agency provided for in Article 140.").

[242] GC art. 91 ("Treatment, including the provision of any apparatus necessary for the maintenance of internees in good health, particularly dentures and other artificial appliances and spectacles, shall be free of charge to the internee.").

collective shipments containing medical supplies.[243] However, medical supplies are generally to be sent in collective shipments so that they may be properly administered by the camp doctors.[244]

10.14.5 Inquiry in Certain Cases of Death or Serious Injury. In certain cases of death or serious injury of an internee, an official inquiry shall be conducted by the Detaining Power.[245]

10.15 Religious Exercise by Internees

Internees shall enjoy complete latitude in the exercise of their religious duties, including attendance at the services of their faith, on condition that they comply with the disciplinary routine prescribed by the detaining authorities.[246]

10.15.1 Premises for Religious Services for Internees. The Detaining Power shall place at the disposal of interned persons, of whatever denomination, premises suitable for the holding of their religious services.[247] The premises where services are held should be sufficiently spacious and clean, and should provide effective shelter to those attending services, but need not be set aside exclusively for religious services.[248]

10.15.2 Interned Ministers of Religion. Ministers of religion who are interned shall be allowed to minister freely to the members of their community.[249] For this purpose, the Detaining Power shall ensure their equitable allocation among the various places of internment in which there are internees speaking the same language and belonging to the same religion.[250] Should such ministers be too few in number, the Detaining Power shall provide them with the necessary facilities, including means of transport, for moving from one place to another, and they shall be authorized to visit any internees who are hospitalized.[251]

---

[243] *Refer to* § 10.23.3 (Receipt of Individual and Collective Relief Shipments for Internees).

[244] *Refer to* § 10.23.3.2 (Medical Supplies in Relief Shipments).

[245] *Refer to* § 10.34.5 (Inquiries Into Death or Serious Injury of Internees in Certain Cases).

[246] GC art. 93 ("Internees shall enjoy complete latitude in the exercise of their religious duties, including attendance at the services of their faith, on condition that they comply with the disciplinary routine prescribed by the detaining authorities.").

[247] GC art. 86 ("The Detaining Power shall place at the disposal of interned persons, of whatever denomination, premises suitable for the holding of their religious services.").

[248] GC COMMENTARY 388 ("It does not seem essential that these premises should be set aside exclusively for religious services. The parallel text in the Prisoners of War Convention (Article 34, paragraph 2) speaks of 'adequate' premises. In both cases, it should be understood that the premises where services are held should be sufficiently spacious and clean and so built as to give effective shelter to those attending the services.").

[249] GC art. 93 ("Ministers of religion who are interned shall be allowed to minister freely to the members of their community.").

[250] GC art. 93 ("For this purpose, the Detaining Power shall ensure their equitable allocation amongst the various places of internment in which there are internees speaking the same language and belonging to the same religion.").

[251] GC art. 93 ("Should such ministers be too few in number, the Detaining Power shall provide them with the necessary facilities, including means of transport, for moving from one place to another, and they shall be authorized to visit any internees who are in hospital.").

10.15.2.1 *Correspondence by Ministers of Religion*. Ministers of religion shall be at liberty to correspond on matters concerning their ministry with the religious authorities in the country of detention and, as far as possible, with the international religious organizations of their faith.[252] Such correspondence shall not be considered as forming a part of the quota mentioned in Article 107 of the GC.[253] It shall, however, be subject to the provisions of Article 112 of the GC.[254] In other words, such correspondence may be censored, but such censorship shall be done as quickly as possible.[255]

10.15.3 Appointment of Other Ministers or Qualified Laypersons. When internees do not have at their disposal the assistance of ministers of their faith, or should these latter be too few in number, the local religious authorities of the same faith may appoint, in agreement with the Detaining Power, a minister of the internees' faith or, if such a course is feasible from a denominational point of view, a minister of a similar religion or a qualified layperson.[256] The latter shall enjoy the facilities granted to the ministry he or she has assumed.[257] Persons so appointed shall comply with all regulations laid down by the Detaining Power in the interests of discipline and security.[258]

10.16 Intellectual, Physical, and Recreational Activities

The Detaining Power shall encourage intellectual, educational, and recreational pursuits, and sports and games among internees, while leaving them free to take part in them or not.[259] It shall take all practicable measures to ensure the exercise thereof, in particular by providing suitable premises for such purposes.[260]

10.16.1 Voluntariness of the Activities. The Detaining Power should seek to encourage the internees in engaging in these activities, while leaving them free to take part or not. For example, it would be prohibited to compel internees to listen to propaganda, such as by

---

[252] GC art. 93 ("Ministers of religion shall be at liberty to correspond on matters concerning their ministry with the religious authorities in the country of detention and, as far as possible, with the international religious organizations of their faith.").

[253] GC art. 93 ("Such correspondence shall not be considered as forming a part of the quota mentioned in Article 107."). *Refer to* § 10.23.2.1 (Internee Correspondence Quota).

[254] GC art. 93 ("It shall, however, be subject to the provisions of Article 112.").

[255] *Refer to* § 10.23.6 (Censorship and Security Review of Internee Correspondence and Shipments).

[256] GC art. 93 ("When internees do not have at their disposal the assistance of ministers of their faith, or should these latter be too few in number, the local religious authorities of the same faith may appoint, in agreement with the Detaining Power, a minister of the internees' faith or, if such a course is feasible from a denominational point of view, a minister of similar religion or a qualified layman.").

[257] GC art. 93 ("The latter shall enjoy the facilities granted to the ministry he has assumed.").

[258] GC art. 93 ("Persons so appointed shall comply with all regulations laid down by the Detaining Power in the interests of discipline and security.").

[259] GC art. 94 ("The Detaining Power shall encourage intellectual, educational and recreational pursuits, sports and games amongst internees, whilst leaving them free to take part in them or not.").

[260] GC art. 94 ("It shall take all practicable measures to ensure the exercise thereof, in particular by providing suitable premises.").

punishing them or giving them harsher conditions of confinement if they do not participate. On the other hand, censoring educational or intellectual materials for security reasons or to refrain from providing internees with anti-democratic political propaganda would be permissible.[261]

10.16.2 Education. All possible facilities shall be granted to internees to continue their studies or to take up new subjects.[262] The education of children and young people shall be ensured; they shall be allowed to attend schools either within the place of internment or outside.[263]

To advance educational opportunities for internees, the Detaining Power may seek ways to encourage and assist them in teaching one another.[264]

10.16.3 Opportunities for Physical Exercise, Sports, and Outdoor Games. Internees shall be given opportunities for physical exercise, sports, and outdoor games.[265] For this purpose, sufficient open spaces shall be set aside in all places of internment.[266] Special playgrounds shall be reserved for children and young people.[267]

10.16.4 Contributions by Sources Apart From the Detaining Power. Apart from the Detaining Power, internees may receive assistance from a variety of sources that allow them to engage in intellectual, physical, and recreational activities.

For example, relief organizations, including the ICRC, may contribute to the ensuring that internees have opportunities for intellectual, physical, and recreational activities.[268] In addition, internees may receive shipments that are intended to allow them to engage in these activities.[269] Lastly, the profits from the canteen may be used in this area.[270]

10.17 INTERNEE LABOR

The rules described in this section govern the use of internee labor. Additional rules apply to the use of the labor of protected persons depending on whether they are present in a

---

[261] *Compare* § 9.16.1 (Voluntariness of the Activities).

[262] GC art. 94 ("All possible facilities shall be granted to internees to continue their studies or to take up new subjects.").

[263] GC art. 94 ("The education of children and young people shall be ensured; they shall be allowed to attend schools either within the place of internment or outside.").

[264] *Compare* § 9.16.2 (Education).

[265] GC art. 94 ("Internees shall be given opportunities for physical exercise, sports and outdoor games.").

[266] GC art. 94 ("For this purpose, sufficient open spaces shall be set aside in all places of internment.").

[267] GC art. 94 ("Special playgrounds shall be reserved for children and young people.").

[268] *Refer to* § 10.33.2 (Access by Relief Societies and Other Organizations).

[269] *Refer to* § 10.23.3 (Receipt of Individual and Collective Relief Shipments for Internees).

[270] *Refer to* § 10.12.3 (Canteen Management and Profits).

belligerent's home territory or in occupied territory.[271]

10.17.1 General Rules on Internee Labor. The Detaining Power shall not employ internees as workers, unless the internees so desire.[272]

Employment that, if undertaken under compulsion by a protected person not in internment, would involve a breach of Articles 40 or 51 of the GC, and employment on work that is of a degrading or humiliating character, are in any case prohibited.[273]

After a working period of six weeks, internees shall be free to give up work at any moment, subject to eight days' notice.[274]

10.17.2 Compulsory Work for the Benefit of the Internee Community. The first two paragraphs of Article 95 of the GC constitute no obstacle to the right of the Detaining Power to employ interned doctors, dentists, and other medical personnel in their professional capacity on behalf of their fellow internees, or to employ internees for administrative and maintenance work in places of internment and to detail such persons for work in the kitchens or for other domestic tasks, or to require such persons to undertake duties connected with the protection of internees against aerial bombardment or other war risks.[275] Thus, although internees generally may not be compelled to work, there is an exception for tasks that benefit the internee community as a whole.[276]

No internee may, however, be required to perform tasks for which he or she is, in the opinion of a medical officer, physically unsuited.[277]

---

[271] *Refer to* § 10.7.3 (Compulsory Work for Protected Persons in a Belligerent's Home Territory); § 11.20 (Labor of Protected Persons in Occupied Territory).

[272] GC art. 95 ("The Detaining Power shall not employ internees as workers, unless they so desire.").

[273] GC art. 95 ("Employment which, if undertaken under compulsion by a protected person not in internment, would involve a breach of Articles 40 or 51 of the present Convention, and employment on work which is of a degrading or humiliating character are in any case prohibited.").

[274] GC art. 95 ("After a working period of six weeks, internees shall be free to give up work at any moment, subject to eight days' notice.").

[275] GC art. 95 ("These provisions constitute no obstacle to the right of the Detaining Power to employ interned doctors, dentists and other medical personnel in their professional capacity on behalf of their fellow internees, or to employ internees for administrative and maintenance work in places of internment and to detail such persons for work in the kitchens or for other domestic tasks, or to require such persons to undertake duties connected with the protection of internees against aerial bombardment or other war risks.").

[276] GC COMMENTARY 416 ("The commentary on Article 91 showed that internees must for preference be treated by medical personnel of their own nationality, and Article 88 refers to detained persons taking part in the protection of their quarters. The fact is that nobody could work more zealously on this task than the internees themselves. Such tasks represent work of human fellowship which they are bound to carry out on behalf of their companions. If they sought to avoid it they would be failing in an elementary duty and it would be right to force them to do it. A similar line of argument led to the inclusion of administrative work and domestic tasks (work in the kitchen, cleaning and camp maintenance) among the duties which internees may be forced to carry out.").

[277] GC art. 95 ("No internee may, however, be required to perform tasks for which he is, in the opinion of a medical officer, physically unsuited.").

In addition, members of the Internee Committee may not be compelled to do other work, if the accomplishment of their duties is thereby rendered more difficult.[278]

10.17.2.1 *Wages and Working Conditions for Internees Permanently Detailed for Work on Behalf of the Internee Community*. Internees permanently detailed for categories of work mentioned in the third paragraph of Article 95 of the GC shall be paid fair wages by the Detaining Power.[279] The working conditions and the scale of compensation for occupational accidents and diseases to internees thus detailed shall not be inferior to those applicable to work of the same nature in the same district.[280]

10.17.3 Working Conditions. The Detaining Power shall take entire responsibility for all working conditions, for medical attention, for the payment of wages, and for ensuring that all employed internees receive compensation for occupational accidents and diseases.[281] The standards prescribed for said working conditions and for compensation shall be in accordance with national laws and regulations, and with existing practice; they shall in no case be inferior to those obtaining for work of the same nature in the same district.[282]

In addition, internees who work shall receive additional rations in proportion to the kind of labor that they perform.[283]

10.17.4 Wage Agreement With Internees. Wages for work done shall be determined on an equitable basis by special agreements between the internees, the Detaining Power, and, if the case arises, employers other than the Detaining Power, due regard being paid to the obligation of the Detaining Power to provide for free maintenance of internees, and for the medical attention that their state of health may require.[284]

10.17.5 Labor Detachments of Internees. All labor detachments shall remain part of, and dependent upon, a place of internment.[285] The competent authorities of the Detaining Power and

---

[278] *Refer to* § 10.22.3.1 (Limitations on Other Work Assignments).

[279] GC art. 95 ("Internees permanently detailed for categories of work mentioned in the third paragraph of this Article, shall be paid fair wages by the Detaining Power.").

[280] GC art. 95 ("The working conditions and the scale of compensation for occupational accidents and diseases to internees thus detailed, shall not be inferior to those applicable to work of the same nature in the same district.").

[281] GC art. 95 ("The Detaining Power shall take entire responsibility for all working conditions, for medical attention, for the payment of wages, and for ensuring that all employed internees receive compensation for occupational accidents and diseases.").

[282] GC art. 95 ("The standards prescribed for the said working conditions and for compensation shall be in accordance with the national laws and regulations, and with the existing practice; they shall in no case be inferior to those obtaining for work of the same nature in the same district.").

[283] *Refer to* § 10.13.1.2 (Additional Food for Certain Groups).

[284] GC art. 95 ("Wages for work done shall be determined on an equitable basis by special agreements between the internees, the Detaining Power, and, if the case arises, employers other than the Detaining Power, due regard being paid to the obligation of the Detaining Power to provide for free maintenance of internees and for the medical attention which their state of health may require.").

[285] GC art. 96 ("All labour detachments shall remain part of and dependent upon a place of internment.").

the commandant of a place of internment shall be responsible for the observance of the provisions of the GC in a labor detachment.[286]

The commandant shall keep an up-to-date list of the labor detachments subordinate to him or her, and shall communicate it to the delegates of the Protecting Power, of the ICRC, and of other humanitarian organizations who may visit the places of internment.[287]

10.18 Internees' Articles of Personal Use

10.18.1 Internees' Articles of Personal Use. Internees shall be permitted to retain articles of personal use.[288]

Internees, however, are not entitled to retain items that could be put to a use prejudicial to the legitimate interests of the Detaining Power, such as items that may pose a risk to security (*e.g.*, knives or devices that may be used as weapons) or items that may facilitate escape (*e.g.*, flares, flare pistols, compasses, maps, radios, or cell phones).[289]

10.18.2 Articles of Personal or Sentimental Value. Articles that have "above all" a personal or sentimental value may not be taken away.[290] Items that may otherwise be legitimately impounded (*e.g.*, for security reasons) are not precluded from being impounded because of their personal or sentimental value to the internee.[291]

10.18.3 Family or Identity Documents for Internees. Family or identity documents in the possession of internees may not be taken away without a receipt being given.[292] At no time shall

---

[286] GC art. 96 ("The competent authorities of the Detaining Power and the commandant of a place of internment shall be responsible for the observance in a labour detachment of the provisions of the present Convention.").

[287] GC art. 96 ("The commandant shall keep an up-to-date list of the labour detachments subordinate to him and shall communicate it to the delegates of the Protecting Power, of the International Committee of the Red Cross and of other humanitarian organizations who may visit the places of internment.").

[288] GC art. 97 ("Internees shall be permitted to retain articles of personal use.").

[289] GC Commentary 420 ("Cameras should no doubt be regarded as an exception [to the permitted articles of personal use], because of the Detaining Power's special interest in removing anything which might promote espionage or perhaps be used for unfavourable propaganda. … The Detaining Power is free, however, to protect itself against efforts to put the resources retained by the internees—and above all their financial resources—to a use prejudicial to its interests.").

[290] GC art. 97 ("Articles which have above all a personal or sentimental value may not be taken away.").

[291] GC Commentary 422 ("The essential part of the clause is the words 'above all'. The clause formulates an exception to the right of the Detaining Power to take articles of value from internees; that exception applies to articles which have above all a personal or sentimental value. That means that the importance attached to their possession does not depend on their commercial value, but rather on what they represent in the sentimental sphere. A wedding ring would be one such example --a plain golden ring which costs little; its sale would not furnish the owner with large resources with which to make preparations for an escape or to take part in subversive propaganda. On the other hand jewels of great commercial value may be taken away, in spite of their sentimental value. It will be for the Detaining Power to judge in all fairness the appropriate course to take. It must be in accordance with the stipulation of paragraph 1 (in accordance with established procedure and against a receipt).").

[292] GC art. 97 ("Family or identity documents in the possession of internees may not be taken away without a receipt being given.").

internees be left without identity documents.[293] If they have none, they shall be issued special documents drawn up by the detaining authorities, which will serve as their identity papers until the end of their internment.[294]

10.19 Financial Resources of Internees

10.19.1 Money and Valuables in the Internee's Possession. Monies, checks, bonds, etc., and valuables in the possession of internees may not be taken from them, except in accordance with established procedure.[295] Detailed receipts shall be given for such valuables.[296]

The amounts shall be paid into the account of every internee, as provided for in Article 98 of the GC.[297] Such amounts may not be converted into any other currency unless legislation in force in the territory in which the owner is interned so requires or the internee gives his or her consent.[298]

10.19.1.1 *Pocket Money for Purchases*. Internees may keep on their persons a certain amount of money, in cash or in the form of purchase coupons, to enable them to make purchases.[299] For example, internees could use this money or scrip to purchase items at the canteen.[300]

For security reasons, the amount of money retained by internees generally will be small.[301]

10.19.2 Internee Allowances. All internees shall receive regular allowances, sufficient to enable them to purchase goods and articles, such as tobacco, toilet requisites, etc.[302] Such

---

[293] GC art. 97 ("At no time shall internees be left without identity documents.").

[294] GC art. 97 ("If they have none, they shall be issued with special documents drawn up by the detaining authorities, which will serve as their identity papers until the end of their internment.").

[295] GC art. 97 ("Monies, cheques, bonds, etc., and valuables in their possession may not be taken from them except in accordance with established procedure.").

[296] GC art. 97 ("Detailed receipts shall be given therefor.").

[297] GC art. 97 ("The amounts shall be paid into the account of every internee as provided for in Article 98.").

[298] GC art. 97 ("Such amounts may not be converted into any other currency unless legislation in force in the territory in which the owner is interned so requires or the internee gives his consent.").

[299] GC art. 97 ("Internees may keep on their persons a certain amount of money, in cash or in the shape of purchase coupons, to enable them to make purchases.").

[300] *Refer to* § 10.12 (Canteens for Internees).

[301] GC Commentary 424 ("It follows that the amount of money in question will be fairly small. If the Detaining Power considers that it must for security reasons limit very strictly the amount of cash held by the internees, it should provide them with purchase coupons of sufficient value to enable them to make purchases in the canteens it runs.").

[302] GC art. 98 ("All internees shall receive regular allowances, sufficient to enable them to purchase goods and articles, such as tobacco, toilet requisites, etc.").

allowances may take the form of credits or purchase coupons.[303]

Furthermore, internees may receive allowances from the Power to which they owe allegiance, the Protecting Powers, the organizations that may assist them, or their families, as well as the income on their property in accordance with the law of the Detaining Power.[304]

The amount of allowances granted by the Power to which an internee owes allegiance shall be the same for each category of internees (*e.g.*, infirm, sick, pregnant women), but may not be allocated by that Power or distributed by the Detaining Power on the basis of discrimination between internees that is prohibited by Article 27 of the GC.[305]

10.19.3 Internee Accounts. The Detaining Power shall open a regular account for every internee, to which shall be credited:

- allowances named in Article 98 of the GC;
- wages earned;
- remittances received; and
- such sums taken from the internee as may be available under the legislation in force in the territory in which he or she is interned.[306]

10.19.3.1 *Drawing Upon Accounts*. Internees may draw from their accounts the amounts necessary for their personal expenses, within the limits fixed by the Detaining Power.[307]

Internees shall be granted all facilities consistent with the legislation in force in such territory to make remittances to their families and to other dependents.[308]

10.19.3.2 *Account Statement*. Internees shall at all times be afforded reasonable

---

303 GC art. 98 ("Such allowances may take the form of credits or purchase coupons.").

304 GC art. 98 ("Furthermore, internees may receive allowances from the Power to which they owe allegiance, the Protecting Powers, the organizations which may assist them, or their families, as well as the income on their property in accordance with the law of the Detaining Power.").

305 GC art. 98 ("The amount of allowances granted by the Power to which they owe allegiance shall be the same for each category of internees (infirm, sick, pregnant women, etc.), but may not be allocated by that Power or distributed by the Detaining Power on the basis of discriminations between internees which are prohibited by Article 27 of the present Convention.").

306 GC art. 98 ("The Detaining Power shall open a regular account for every internee, to which shall be credited the allowances named in the present Article, the wages earned and the remittances received, together with such sums taken from him as may be available under the legislation in force in the territory in which he is interned.").

307 GC art. 98 ("They may draw from their accounts the amounts necessary for their personal expenses, within the limits fixed by the Detaining Power.").

308 GC art. 98 ("Internees shall be granted all facilities consistent with the legislation in force in such territory to make remittances to their families and to other dependants.").

facilities for consulting and obtaining copies of their accounts.[309] A statement of accounts shall be furnished to the Protecting Power on request, and shall accompany the internee in case of transfer.[310]

10.19.3.3 *Settlement of Account on Release or Repatriation*. On release or repatriation, internees shall be given all articles, monies, or other valuables taken from them during internment and shall receive in currency the balance of any credit to their accounts kept in accordance with Article 98 of the GC, with the exception of any articles or amounts withheld by the Detaining Power by virtue of its legislation in force.[311] If the property of an internee is so withheld, the owner shall receive a detailed receipt.[312]

10.20 ADMINISTRATION OF PLACES OF INTERNMENT AND DISCIPLINE

10.20.1 Responsible Officer and Staff. Every place of internment shall be put under the authority of a responsible officer, chosen from the regular military forces or the regular civil administration of the Detaining Power.[313]

The officer in charge of the place of internment must have in his or her possession a copy of the GC in the official language, or one of the official languages, of his or her country and shall be responsible for its application.[314] The staff in control of internees shall be instructed in the provisions of the GC and of the administrative measures adopted to ensure its application.[315]

10.20.2 Posting of Convention and Camp Orders. The text of the GC and the texts of special agreements concluded under the GC shall be posted inside the place of internment, in a language that the internees understand, or shall be in the possession of the Internee Committee.[316]

---

[309] GC art. 98 ("They shall at all times be afforded reasonable facilities for consulting and obtaining copies of their accounts.").

[310] GC art. 98 ("A statement of accounts shall be furnished to the Protecting Power on request, and shall accompany the internee in case of transfer.").

[311] GC art. 97 ("On release or repatriation, internees shall be given all articles, monies or other valuables taken from them during internment and shall receive in currency the balance of any credit to their accounts kept in accordance with Article 98, with the exception of any articles or amounts withheld by the Detaining Power by virtue of its legislation in force.").

[312] GC art. 97 ("If the property of an internee is so withheld, the owner shall receive a detailed receipt.").

[313] GC art. 99 ("Every place of internment shall be put under the authority of a responsible officer, chosen from the regular military forces or the regular civil administration of the Detaining Power.").

[314] GC art. 99 ("The officer in charge of the place of internment must have in his possession a copy of the present Convention in the official language, or one of the official languages, of his country and shall be responsible for its application.").

[315] GC art. 99 ("The staff in control of internees shall be instructed in the provisions of the present Convention and of the administrative measures adopted to ensure its application.").

[316] GC art. 99 ("The text of the present Convention and the texts of special agreements concluded under the said Convention shall be posted inside the place of internment, in a language which the internees understand, or shall be in the possession of the Internee Committee.").

Regulations, orders, notices, and publications of every kind shall be communicated to the internees and posted inside the places of internment, in a language that the internees understand.[317]

Every order and command addressed to internees individually must likewise be given in a language that they understand.[318]

10.20.3 Humane Disciplinary Regime. The disciplinary regime in places of internment shall be consistent with humanitarian principles, and shall in no circumstances include regulations imposing on internees any physical exertion dangerous to their health or involving physical or moral victimization.[319]

10.20.3.1 *Prohibition Against Tattooing or Imprinting Signs or Markings on the Body*. Identification by tattooing or imprinting signs or markings on the body is prohibited.[320]

10.20.3.2 *Prohibition Against Prolonged Standing, Roll-Calls, Punishment Drill, Military Drill and Manuevers, or the Reduction of Food Rations*. In particular, prolonged standing and roll-calls, punishment drill, military drill and maneuvers, or the reduction of food rations are prohibited.[321]

10.20.4 Use of Force to Maintain Order and to Prevent Escape. As with POWs, the use of weapons against protected persons, especially against those who are escaping or attempting to escape, shall constitute an extreme measure, which shall always be preceded by warnings appropriate to the circumstances.[322] For example, internees should not be fired upon if they are apprehended within the camp limits while making preparations to escape, and there is no risk of escape or harm to anyone.

It should be noted that, although the GC has no provision corresponding to Article 42 of the GPW, the above principle is equally valid in the internee context.

10.20.4.1 *Use of Non-Lethal Weapons (Including Riot Control Agents)*. Non-lethal weapons may be employed to control rioting protected persons or to prevent their escape. In particular, the use of riot control agents to control rioting protected persons is not

---

[317] GC art. 99 ("Regulations, orders, notices and publications of every kind shall be communicated to the internees and posted inside the places of internment, in a language which they understand.").

[318] GC art. 99 ("Every order and command addressed to internees individually, must likewise be given in a language which they understand.").

[319] GC art. 100 ("The disciplinary regime in places of internment shall be consistent with humanitarian principles, and shall in no circumstances include regulations imposing on internees any physical exertion dangerous to their health or involving physical or moral victimization.").

[320] GC art. 100 ("Identification by tattooing or imprinting signs or markings on the body, is prohibited.").

[321] GC art. 100 ("In particular, prolonged standing and roll-calls, punishment drill, military drill and manoeuvres, or the reduction of food rations, are prohibited.").

[322] *Compare* § 9.22.6 (Use of Force to Maintain Order and to Prevent Escape).

prohibited.[323]

If the use of deadly force is warranted and authorized against protected persons, there is no legal requirement to employ non-lethal weapons before resort to deadly force.[324]

10.21 Internee Petitions, Complaints, and Reports About Conditions of Internment

10.21.1 Internee Right to Present Petitions and Complaints. Internees shall have the right to present to the authorities in whose power they are, any petition with regard to the conditions of internment to which they are subjected.[325] The commandant of an internment facility may issue regulations that establish procedures about how internees are to exercise this right to petition.[326]

Internees shall also have the right to apply without restriction through the Internee Committee or, if they consider it necessary, directly to the representatives of the Protecting Power, in order to indicate to them any points on which they may have complaints to make with regard to the conditions of internment.[327]

10.21.1.1 *Making Requests and Complaints to the ICRC*. Such complaints may also be made to the delegates of the ICRC, who enjoy the same prerogatives of access to internees as the representatives of the Protecting Power.[328] In the past, the ICRC has been able to take appropriate measures besides merely forwarding the complaint to the Power on which the POWs depend, including measures on a confidential basis that help to improve the situation of internees.[329]

10.21.2 Communication of Petitions and Complaints. Such petitions and complaints shall be transmitted forthwith and without alteration, and even if the latter are recognized to be unfounded, they may not occasion any punishment.[330]

10.21.2.1 *Review and Censorship of Requests and Complaints by the Detaining*

---

[323] *Refer to* § 6.16.2 (Prohibition on Use of Riot Control Agents as a Method of Warfare).

[324] *Refer to* § 6.5.10.5 (No Requirement to Use Non-Lethal Weapons Before Using Lethal Weapons Where Deadly Force Is Warranted).

[325] GC art. 101 ("Internees shall have the right to present to the authorities in whose power they are, any petition with regard to the conditions of internment to which they are subjected.").

[326] GC COMMENTARY 434 ("The Convention does not state in detail the procedure for submitting petitions, but obviously it must be compatible with the normal requirements of discipline and the administration of the place of internment and petitions must not be used for purposes other than those arising under the Convention. It will be for the commandant of the place of internment to issue regulations concerning the exercise of this right, and particularly to say whether petitions can be submitted orally or in writing and in what form.").

[327] GC art. 101 ("They shall also have the right to apply without restriction through the Internee Committee or, if they consider it necessary, direct to the representatives of the Protecting Power, in order to indicate to them any points on which they may have complaints to make with regard to the conditions of internment.").

[328] *Refer to* § 10.33.1.2 (ICRC Delegates Enjoying the Same Prerogatives of Access).

[329] *Compare* § 9.23.1.1 (Making Requests and Complaints to the ICRC).

[330] GC art. 101 ("Such petitions and complaints shall be transmitted forthwith and without alteration, and even if the latter are recognized to be unfounded, they may not occasion any punishment.").

Power. Although petitions and complaints shall be transmitted forthwith and without alteration, the Detaining Power has the right to examine and censor petitions and complaints for security reasons.[331] Communications for transmittal may be examined to determine whether they legitimately contain petitions or complaints.[332] Security review and censorship must be conducted in accordance with the general rules on censoring internee correspondence.[333]

10.21.2.2 No Punishment for Making Complaints. Even if the petitions and complaints are recognized to be unfounded, they may not occasion any punishment.[334] In any event, as in the case of POWs, it could be contrary to internees' interests to abuse this right by making groundless complaints because complaints that are justified might not, as a result, receive the appropriate attention.[335]

10.21.3 Periodic Reports by the Internee Committees. Periodic reports on the situation in places of internment and as to the needs of the internees may be sent by the Internee Committees to the representatives of the Protecting Powers.[336] Internee Committees have discretion about how and when to submit their reports.[337] The Detaining Power may subject these reports to security review and censorship to ensure that these reports are not misused.[338]

10.22 Internee Committees

10.22.1 Election of Internee Committees. In every place of internment, the internees shall freely elect, by secret ballot every six months, the members of a Committee empowered to represent them before the Detaining and the Protecting Powers, the ICRC, and any other

---

[331] *See* 1956 FM 27-10 (Change No. 1 1976) ¶308b ("The Detaining Power has the right to examine and censor the complaints, petitions, and reports referred to above in the same manner as correspondence addressed to internees or dispatched by them. It may also examine such complaints and reports to the representatives of the Protecting Power to verify that they are what they purport to be and to delete matter not constituting either a complaint or a report within the meaning of the foregoing provision.").

[332] GC Commentary 435-36 ("The transmission 'forthwith' of complaints and petitions and the absence of punishment even when they are not well founded is in conformity with the procedure established with regard to prisoners of war during the two world wars. The Fourth Convention of 1949 has introduced a particularly important idea by stating that the transmission shall take place 'without alteration'. This wording was rejected by the authors of the Third Geneva Convention in order to respect the Detaining Power's right of censorship. The discussions at the Diplomatic Conference concerning the Fourth Convention showed that there was a specific wish to avoid any suggestion of censorship with regard to civilians. It was nevertheless said that some supervision by the Detaining Power must be allowed 'for security reasons'.").

[333] *Refer to* § 10.23.6 (Censorship and Security Review of Internee Correspondence and Shipments).

[334] GC art. 101 ("Such petitions and complaints shall be transmitted forthwith and without alteration, and even if the latter are recognized to be unfounded, they may not occasion any punishment.").

[335] *Compare* § 9.23.2.2 (No Punishment for Making Complaints).

[336] GC art. 101 ("Periodic reports on the situation in places of internment and as to the needs of the internees, may be sent by the Internee Committees to the representatives of the Protecting Powers.").

[337] GC Commentary 436 ("Some of the Government Experts who met in 1947 had envisaged making it obligatory to transmit periodically to the Protecting Power reports drafted on a model form. This opinion did not prevail in the sense that it was given mandatory form; the idea of periodical reports was retained, but the Convention leaves it to the Internee Committees to submit their reports when and how they think fit.").

[338] *Refer to* § 10.23.6 (Censorship and Security Review of Internee Correspondence and Shipments).

organization that may assist them.[339] The members of the Committee shall be eligible for re-election.[340]

10.22.1.1 *Approval of Internee Committee Members by the Detaining Authorities*. Internees so elected shall enter upon their duties after their election has been approved by the detaining authorities.[341] The reasons for any refusals or dismissals shall be communicated to the Protecting Powers concerned.[342]

10.22.2 Duties of Internee Committees. Internee Committees shall further the physical, spiritual, and intellectual well-being of the internees.[343] Internee Committees have duties similar to the duties of POW Representatives.[344]

The Internee Committee's general duties imply that the Internee Committee will undertake a variety of activitics to cnsurc that intcrnccs rcccivc propcr trcatmcnt by thc Detaining Power and to advance their welfare, even activities that are not specified in the GC as constituting their duties.

10.22.2.1 *Internee Committees and Mutual Assistance Among the Internees*. In case the internees decide, in particular, to organize a system of mutual assistance among themselves, this organization would be within the competence of the Internee Committees, in addition to the special duties entrusted to them under other provisions of the GC.[345] This provision of the GC is based on experience during World War II, when camp leaders allowed POWs to assist one another.[346]

---

[339] GC art. 102 ("In every place of internment, the internees shall freely elect by secret ballot every six months, the members of a Committee empowered to represent them before the Detaining and the Protecting Powers, the International Committee of the Red Cross and any other organization which may assist them.").

[340] GC art. 102 ("The members of the Committee shall be eligible for re-election.").

[341] GC art. 102 ("Internees so elected shall enter upon their duties after their election has been approved by the detaining authorities.").

[342] GC art. 102 ("The reasons for any refusals or dismissals shall be communicated to the Protecting Powers concerned.").

[343] GC art. 103 ("The Internee Committees shall further the physical, spiritual and intellectual well-being of the internees.").

[344] GC COMMENTARY 441 ("This general clause could therefore be regarded as giving the Internee Committees the right to take any action likely to further the internees' well-being. In the same way as the camp leader in the prisoner-of-war camp enjoys considerable latitude in assisting his comrades and is allowed to correspond with relief organizations, subscribe to newspapers, organize concerts and theatricals, initiate study courses, set up a legal advice bureau, transmit legal documents and suggest the sending to hospital or repatriation of certain men, so the Internee Committees have the general task of ensuring the application of the Convention on behalf of their fellow-internees."). *Compare* § 9.24.3 (Duties of POW Representatives).

[345] GC art. 103 ("In case the internees decide, in particular, to organize a system of mutual assistance amongst themselves, this organization would be within the competence of the Committees in addition to the special duties entrusted to them under other provisions of the present Convention.").

[346] GC COMMENTARY 441 ("The experience of two world wars has shown that the activities of the camp leaders have made it possible for the poorest of prisoners of war to be helped by their own comrades. In some cases the camp leader organized collections and his office became a real social welfare bureau. The second paragraph adapts

10.22.2.2 *Other Specific Duties*. In addition to the general duties that the GC imposes on the Internee Committees, the GC also imposes specific duties on the Internee Committees in the following matters:

- managing the distribution of collective relief;[347]
- assisting in the transport of the internees' community property and luggage in cases of transfers of internees;[348]
- receiving parcels and remittances of money for internees undergoing disciplinary punishment, and handing over to the infirmary any perishable goods;[349]
- checking on the management of the canteen and its special fund;[350]
- transmitting complaints and petitions, and making periodic reports on the needs of internees;[351]
- retaining a copy of the GC and any applicable special agreements under the GC, if a copy is not publicly posted;[352]
- monitoring decisions announced from any disciplinary proceeding against an internee;[353] and
- receiving information about all judicial proceedings against internees whom they represent, and of their result.[354]

10.22.3 Prerogatives of Internee Committees. In order to accomplish their duties, members of Internee Committtees are afforded certain prerogatives.

10.22.3.1 *Limitations on Other Work Assignments*. Members of Internee Committees shall not be required to perform any other work, if the accomplishment of their

---

the results of this experience to the case of internees and in particular gives the Internee Committees the task of organizing a mutual assistance scheme. In view of the variation in conditions and resources among the internees, such a scheme can be very useful, for among them there will certainly be heads of family who, in losing their normal work, will have left their dear ones in serious difficulty.").

347 *Refer to* § 10.23.3.4 (Collective Relief for Internees).

348 *Refer to* § 10.30.3.3 (Disposition of Community Property and Remaining Property).

349 *Refer to* § 10.28.6.4 (Reading, Writing, Correspondence, and Packages).

350 *Refer to* § 10.12.3 (Canteen Management and Profits).

351 *Refer to* § 10.21 (Internee Petitions, Complaints).

352 *Refer to* § 10.20.2 (Posting of Convention and Camp Orders).

353 *Refer to* § 9.27.3 (Rights of POWs in Disciplinary Proceedings).

354 *Refer to* § 10.29.1 (Information to Internee Committees).

duties is thereby rendered more difficult.[355] Because internees are generally exempted from compulsory work, this means that members of Internee Committees are generally exempted from maintenance work.[356]

10.22.3.2 *Assistants for the Members of Internee Committtees*. Members of Internee Committees may appoint from among the internees such assistants as they may require.[357]

10.22.3.3 *Material Facilities, Including Certain Freedom of Movement*. All material facilities shall be granted to members of Internee Committees, particularly a certain freedom of movement necessary for the accomplishment of their duties (*e.g.*, visits to labor detachments, receipt of supplies).[358] For example, members of Internee Committees may need to go to stations or other arrival points where relief supplies are sent.[359]

10.22.3.4 *Facilities for Communication*. All facilities shall likewise be accorded to members of Internee Committees for communication by post and telegraph with the detaining authorities, the Protecting Powers, the ICRC and their delegates, and the organizations that give assistance to internees.[360] Internee Committee members in labor detachments shall enjoy similar facilities for communication with their Internee Committee in the principal place of internment.[361] Such communications shall not be limited nor considered as forming a part of the quota mentioned in Article 107 of the GC.[362]

---

[355] GC art. 104 ("Members of Internee Committees shall not be required to perform any other work, if the accomplishment of their duties is rendered more difficult thereby.").

[356] *See* GC COMMENTARY 442-43 ("The desire to make this Convention parallel to the Prisoners of War Convention has led in this paragraph to a somewhat illogical result, which was pointed out during the discussions in Geneva. In the case of prisoners of war who may be made to work under the provisions of the Convention, it is reasonable that camp leaders should be given exemption; but is a similar provision necessary in the case of civilians who are covered by Article 95 stating that they may not be compelled to work? The reply was that Article 95 also contains a clause exempting maintenance work in the camp, which internees may be compelled to do, so that paragraph 1 would be justified as referring to this."). *Refer to* § 10.17 (Internee Labor).

[357] GC art. 104 ("Members of Internee Committees may appoint from amongst the internees such assistants as they may require.").

[358] GC art. 104 ("All material facilities shall be granted to them, particularly a certain freedom of movement necessary for the accomplishment of their duties (visits to labour detachments, receipt of supplies, etc.).").

[359] GC COMMENTARY 443 ("It should be noted, with regard to the 'freedom of movement' which is mentioned, that the text says 'a certain freedom', not 'complete freedom'. Article 3 of the Draft Rules concerning Collective Relief annexed to the Convention in a way provides a commentary on this provision by stating that members of Internee Committees shall be permitted to go to stations or other arrival points near their place of internment where the relief supplies are sent.").

[360] GC art. 104 ("All facilities shall likewise be accorded to members of Internee Committees for communication by post and telegraph with the detaining authorities, the Protecting Powers, the International Committee of the Red Cross and their delegates, and with the organizations which give assistance to internees.").

[361] GC art. 104 ("Committee members in labour detachments shall enjoy similar facilities for communication with their Internee Committee in the principal place of internment.").

[362] GC art. 104 ("Such communications shall not be limited, nor considered as forming a part of the quota mentioned in Article 107."). *Refer to* § 10.23.2 (Internees' Correspondence Rights and Quota).

Censorship of communications with the Protecting Powers, ICRC, etc., is not prohibited, but the Detaining Power should ensure that delays do not occur to the disadvantage of the internees.[363]

10.22.3.5 *Turnover for Successor Members of the Internee Committee Upon Transfer*. Members of Internee Committees who are transferred shall be allowed a reasonable time to acquaint their successors with current affairs.[364]

10.23 Internee Correspondence and Relief Shipments

Internees may send and receive mail and relief shipments, subject to security requirements. In addition, internees benefit from certain postage exemptions.

10.23.1 Internment, Health, or Transfer Card. As soon as he or she is interned, or at the latest not more than one week after his or her arrival in a place of internment, and likewise in cases of sickness or transfer to another place of internment or to a hospital, every internee shall be enabled to send direct to his or her family, on the one hand, and to the Central Information Agency for protected persons, on the other, an internment card that is similar, if possible, to the model annexed to the GC (GC Annex III.I), informing his or her relatives of his or her detention, address, and state of health.[365]

These cards shall be forwarded as rapidly as possible and may not be delayed in any way.[366]

10.23.2 Internees' Correspondence Rights and Quota. Internees shall be allowed to send and receive letters and cards.[367]

10.23.2.1 *Internee Correspondence Quota*. If the Detaining Power deems it necessary to limit the number of letters and cards sent by each internee, this number shall not be fewer than two letters and four cards monthly; these letters and cards shall be drawn up so as to conform as closely as possible to the models annexed to the GC (GC Annexes III.II & III.III).[368]

---

[363] GC Commentary 444 ("It is not stated that these communications are free from censorship. However, the granting of all facilities lays an obligation on the Detaining Power, if it subjects this correspondence to censorship, to ensure that delays do not occur to the disadvantage of the internees.").

[364] GC art. 104 ("Members of Internee Committees who are transferred shall be allowed a reasonable time to acquaint their successors with current affairs.").

[365] GC art. 106 ("As soon as he is interned, or at the latest not more than one week after his arrival in a place of internment, and likewise in cases of sickness or transfer to another place of internment or to a hospital, every internee shall be enabled to send direct to his family, on the one hand, and to the Central Agency provided for by Article 140, on the other, an internment card similar, if possible, to the model annexed to the present Convention, informing his relatives of his detention, address and state of health.").

[366] GC art. 106 ("The said cards shall be forwarded as rapidly as possible and may not be delayed in any way.").

[367] GC art. 107 ("Internees shall be allowed to send and receive letters and cards.").

[368] GC art. 107 ("If the Detaining Power deems it necessary to limit the number of letters and cards sent by each internee, the said number shall not be less than two letters and four cards monthly; these shall be drawn up so as to conform as closely as possible to the models annexed to the present Convention.").

If limitations must be placed on the correspondence addressed to internees, they may be ordered only by the Power to which such internees owe allegiance, possibly at the request of the Detaining Power.[369] If the Detaining Power can censor and transport more than the minimum stated, in a reasonable time-frame, it should permit more correspondence.[370]

10.23.2.2 *No Delay in Correspondence for Disciplinary Reasons*. Such letters and cards must be conveyed with reasonable dispatch; they may not be delayed or retained for disciplinary reasons.[371]

10.23.2.3 *More Rapid Means of Correspondence in Appropriate Cases*. Internees who have been a long time without news, or who find it impossible to receive news from their relatives, or to give them news by the ordinary postal route, as well as those who are at a considerable distance from their homes, shall be allowed to send telegrams, the charges being paid by them in the currency at their disposal.[372] Internees shall likewise benefit from this provision in cases that are recognized to be urgent.[373]

More modern means of communication, such as email, may be considered for internee correspondence, as appropriate.[374]

10.23.2.4 *Language of Internee Correspondence*. As a rule, internees' mail shall be written in their own language.[375] The parties to the conflict may authorize correspondence in other languages.[376]

10.23.3 Receipt of Individual and Collective Relief Shipments for Internees. Internees shall be allowed to receive, by post or by any other means, individual parcels or collective shipments containing in particular foodstuffs, clothing, medical supplies, as well as books and

---

369 GC art. 107 ("If limitations must be placed on the correspondence addressed to internees, they may be ordered only by the Power to which such internees owe allegiance, possibly at the request of the Detaining Power.").

370 *See* GC COMMENTARY 449 ("The minimum of two letters and four cards per month laid down by the Convention seems to be best suited to the possibilities of rapid censorship. This is the minimum which, after representations by the International Committee of the Red Cross, most of the belligerents had accepted from December 1940 onwards. It remained the same until the end of hostilities. The results of this experience are embodied in the Convention, but it goes without saying that these figures represent only a minimum and that if it can be done without overtaxing the normal capacity of the postal service they can be exceeded.").

371 GC art. 107 ("Such letters and cards must be conveyed with reasonable despatch; they may not be delayed or retained for disciplinary reasons.").

372 GC art. 107 ("Internees who have been a long time without news, or who find it impossible to receive news from their relatives, or to give them news by the ordinary postal route, as well as those who are at a considerable distance from their homes, shall be allowed to send telegrams, the charges being paid by them in the currency at their disposal.").

373 GC art. 107 ("They shall likewise benefit by this provision in cases which are recognized to be urgent.").

374 *Refer to* § 8.10.3 (Communication With Family).

375 GC art. 107 ("As a rule, internees' mail shall be written in their own language.").

376 GC art. 107 ("The Parties to the conflict may authorize correspondence in other languages.").

objects of a devotional, educational, or recreational character that may meet their needs.[377] Such shipments shall in no way free the Detaining Power from the obligations imposed upon it by virtue of the GC.[378]

Should military necessity require the quantity of such shipments to be limited, due notice thereof shall be given to the Protecting Power and to the ICRC, or to any other organization giving assistance to the internees and responsible for the forwarding of such shipments.[379] Such a case of military necessity may be, for example, when military operations could be hindered through the blocking of means of communication by large consignments of relief supplies.[380]

10.23.3.1 *Separation of Books From Other Relief Supplies*. Parcels of clothing and foodstuffs may not include books.[381] Books should be separated because the time required for censorship of books would likely delay the distribution of other relief supplies.[382]

10.23.3.2 *Medical Supplies in Relief Shipments*. Medical relief supplies shall, as a rule, be sent in collective parcels.[383] This rule is meant to ensure that medical supplies can be administered by the camp doctors and not by the internees themselves without medical advice.[384] However, this rule would not prohibit, in exceptional cases, for example, special medication being sent from family members to an internee.[385]

10.23.3.3 *Special Agreements Concerning Relief Shipments*. The conditions for

---

[377] GC art. 108 ("Internees shall be allowed to receive, by post or by any other means, individual parcels or collective shipments containing in particular foodstuffs, clothing, medical supplies, as well as books and objects of a devotional, educational or recreational character which may meet their needs.").

[378] GC art. 108 ("Such shipments shall in no way free the Detaining Power from the obligations imposed upon it by virtue of the present Convention.").

[379] GC art. 108 ("Should military necessity require the quantity of such shipments to be limited, due notice thereof shall be given to the Protecting Power and to the International Committee of the Red Cross, or to any other organization giving assistance to the internees and responsible for the forwarding of such shipments.").

[380] GC COMMENTARY 454-55 ("The Detaining Power may only limit the quantity of shipments for reasons of military necessity. This should be understood to mean cases where operations may be hindered through the blocking of means of communication by large consignments of relief supplies. In that case, the Protecting Power and the relief societies must be notified; the societies must indeed be able to regulate the frequency of consignments themselves and thus avoid perishable goods being held up. In the case of the Protecting Power, the notification is to enable it to discuss whether the restrictive measures are justified; as the military operations develop, the measures in any case must only be temporary and can be justified only by exceptional strain on transport or communications.").

[381] GC art. 108 ("Parcels of clothing and foodstuffs may not include books.").

[382] *See* GC COMMENTARY 455 ("Parcels of clothing and foodstuff must not contain books, so that they will not be delayed for censorship, … .").

[383] GC art. 108 ("Medical relief supplies shall, as a rule, be sent in collective parcels.").

[384] GC COMMENTARY 455 ("[M]edical supplies, as a rule, will only be sent in collective parcels. It would, indeed, be dangerous to let the internees themselves decide what medicaments to use. For preference they should only be used on medical advice.").

[385] GC COMMENTARY 455 footnote 2 ("'As a rule' was inserted [into the GC] because it was not wished to prohibit, as an exceptional case, the inclusion in a family parcel of a medicament required because of the state of health of the recipient and which might not be included in collective medical relief.").

the sending of individual parcels and collective shipments shall, if necessary, be the subject of special agreements between the Powers concerned, which may in no case delay the receipt by the internees of relief supplies.[386]

10.23.3.4 *Collective Relief for Internees*. In the absence of special agreements between parties to the conflict regarding the conditions for the receipt and distribution of collective relief shipments, the regulations concerning collective relief that are annexed to the GC (GC Annex II) shall be applied.[387]

The special agreements provided for above shall in no case restrict the right of Internee Committees to take possession of collective relief shipments intended for internees, to undertake their distribution, and to dispose of them in the interests of the recipients.[388]

Nor shall such agreements restrict the right of representatives of the Protecting Powers, the ICRC, or any other organization giving assistance to internees and responsible for the forwarding of collective shipments, to supervise their distribution to the recipients.[389]

10.23.4 Exemption From Postal and Shipping Charges for Shipments To and From Internees. Relief shipments for internees and mail sent by internees or to them benefit from certain exemptions in international law.

10.23.4.1 *Exemption From Dues for Relief Shipments*. All relief shipments for internees shall be exempt from import, customs, and other dues.[390]

10.23.4.2 *GC Postal Dues Exemption*. Under the GC, all matter sent by mail, including relief parcels sent by parcel post and remittances of money, addressed from other countries to internees or sent by them through the post office, either directly or through the National Protected Person Information Bureau and the Central Information Agency for protected persons, shall be exempt from all postal dues both in the countries of origin and destination, and in intermediate countries.[391]

---

[386] GC art. 108 ("The conditions for the sending of individual parcels and collective shipments shall, if necessary, be the subject of special agreements between the Powers concerned, which may in no case delay the receipt by the internees of relief supplies.").

[387] GC art. 109 ("In the absence of special agreements between Parties to the conflict regarding the conditions for the receipt and distribution of collective relief shipments, the regulations concerning collective relief which are annexed to the present Convention shall be applied.").

[388] GC art. 109 ("The special agreements provided for above shall in no case restrict the right of Internee Committees to take possession of collective relief shipments intended for internees, to undertake their distribution and to dispose of them in the interests of the recipients.").

[389] GC art. 109 ("Nor shall such agreements restrict the right of representatives of the Protecting Powers, the International Committee of the Red Cross, or any other organization giving assistance to internees and responsible for the forwarding of collective shipments, to supervise their distribution to the recipients.").

[390] GC art. 110 ("All relief shipments for internees shall be exempt from import, customs and other dues.").

[391] GC art. 110 ("All matter sent by mail, including relief parcels sent by parcel post and remittances of money, addressed from other countries to internees or despatched by them through the post office, either direct or through the Information Bureaux provided for in Article 136 and the Central Information Agency provided for in Article

To this end, in particular, the exemption provided by the Universal Postal Convention of 1947 and by the agreements of the Universal Postal Union in favor of civilians of enemy nationality detained in camps or civilian prisons, shall be extended to the other interned persons protected by the GC.[392] The countries not signatory to the above-mentioned agreements shall be bound to grant freedom from charges in the same circumstances.[393]

10.23.4.3 Exemption From Postal Charges Under the Universal Postal Convention. Under the Universal Postal Convention, with the exception of air surcharges for airmail, letter-post items, postal parcels, and monetary articles originating in other countries and addressed to, or sent by internees, either directly or through the National Protected Person Information Bureau and the Central Information Agency for protected persons, shall be exempt from all postal charges.[394]

Parcels shall be admitted free of postage up to a weight of 5 kg.[395] The weight limit shall be increased to 10 kg in the case of parcels the contents of which cannot be split up and of parcels addressed to a camp or the Internee Committee there for distribution to the internees.[396]

Items exempt from postal charges and internee parcels shall bear "*Service des internés*

140, shall be exempt from all postal dues both in the countries of origin and destination and in intermediate countries.").

[392] GC art. 110 ("To this end, in particular, the exemption provided by the Universal Postal Convention of 1947 and by the agreements of the Universal Postal Union in favour of civilians of enemy nationality detained in camps or civilian prisons, shall be extended to the other interned persons protected by the present Convention.").

[393] GC art. 110 ("The countries not signatory to the above-mentioned agreements shall be bound to grant freedom from charges in the same circumstances.").

[394] *See* Universal Postal Convention, art. 17(2), Dec. 14, 1989, 1687 UNTS 241, 252 ("Paragraph 1 [of Article 17] shall apply to letter-post items, postal parcels and monetary articles originating in other countries and addressed to or sent by civilian internees as defined by the Geneva Convention of 12 August 1949 relative to the protection of civilian persons in time of war, either direct or through the Information Bureaux and the Central Information Agency prescribed in articles 136 and 140 respectively of that Convention."). *Consider* Universal Postal Convention, art. 7(2.2), Oct. 11, 2012, *reprinted in* INTERNATIONAL BUREAU OF THE UNIVERSAL POSTAL UNION, LETTER POST MANUAL, page C.8 (Berne 2013, Update 2 – Jan. 2015) ("The provisions set out under 2.1 shall also apply to letter-post items, postal parcels and postal payment services items originating in other countries and addressed to or sent by civilian internees as defined by the Geneva Convention of 12 August 1949 relative to the protection of civilian persons in time of war, either direct or through the offices mentioned in the Regulations of the Convention and of the Postal Payment Services Agreement.").

[395] Universal Postal Convention, art. 17(4), Dec. 14, 1989, 1687 UNTS 241, 252 ("Parcels shall be admitted free of postage up to a weight of 5 kg."). *Consider* Universal Postal Convention, art. 7(2.4), Oct. 11, 2012, *reprinted in* INTERNATIONAL BUREAU OF THE UNIVERSAL POSTAL UNION, LETTER POST MANUAL, page C.8 (Berne 2013, Update 2 – Jan. 2015) ("Parcels shall be admitted free of postage up to a weight of 5 kilogrammes.").

[396] Universal Postal Convention, art. 17(4), Dec. 14, 1989, 1687 UNTS 241, 252 ("The weight limit shall be increased to 10 kg in the case of parcels the contents of which cannot be split up and of parcels addressed to a camp or the prisoners' representatives there ('*hommes de confiance*') for distribution to the prisoners."). *Consider* Universal Postal Convention, art. 7(2.4), Oct. 11, 2012, *reprinted in* INTERNATIONAL BUREAU OF THE UNIVERSAL POSTAL UNION, LETTER POST MANUAL, page C.8 (Berne 2013, Update 2 – Jan. 2015) ("The weight limit shall be increased to 10 kilogrammes in the case of parcels the contents of which cannot be split up and of parcels addressed to a camp or the prisoners' representatives there ("hommes de confiance") for distribution to the prisoners.").

civils" (Civilian internees service) and a translation in another language if appropriate.[397]

Postal administrations shall not be liable for the loss of, theft from, or damage to parcels in the case of internee parcels.[398]

10.23.4.4 *Costs of Transporting Relief Shipments Outside the Post Office*. The cost of transporting relief shipments that are intended for internees and that, by reason of their weight or any other cause, cannot be sent through the post office, shall be borne by the Detaining Power in all the territories under its control.[399] Other Powers that are Parties to the GC shall bear the cost of transport in their respective territories.[400]

Costs connected with the transport of such shipments that are not covered by the above paragraphs shall be charged to the senders.[401]

10.23.4.5 *Charges for Telegrams*. The Parties to the GC shall endeavor to reduce, so far as possible, the charges for telegrams sent by internees, or addressed to them.[402]

10.23.5 Special Means of Transport of Shipments to Internees. Should military operations prevent the Powers concerned from fulfilling their obligation to ensure the conveyance of the mail and relief shipments provided for in Articles 106, 107, 108, and 113 of the GC, the Protecting Powers concerned, the ICRC, or any other organization duly approved by the parties to the conflict, may undertake the conveyance of such shipments by suitable means (*e.g.*, rail, motor vehicles, vessels, or aircraft).[403] For this purpose, the Parties to the GC shall

---

[397] *Consider* Letter Post Regulations, Article RL 112 to Article 7 of the Universal Postal Convention of Oct. 11, 2012, *reprinted in* INTERNATIONAL BUREAU OF THE UNIVERSAL POSTAL UNION, LETTER POST MANUAL, page C.11 (2015) ("Items exempt from postal charges shall bear, on the address side in the top right-hand corner, the following indications, which may be followed by a translation: 'Service des prisonniers de guerre' (Prisoners-of-war service) or 'Service des internés civils' (Civilian internees service) for the items mentioned in article 7.2 of the Convention and article RL 111 and the forms relating to them;"); Parcel Post Regulations, Article RC 112(2) to Article 8 of the Universal Postal Convention of Oct. 11, 2012, *reprinted in* INTERNATIONAL BUREAU OF THE UNIVERSAL POSTAL UNION, PARCEL POST MANUAL, page D.10 (2015) ("Every prisoner-of-war and civilian internee parcel and its dispatch note shall bear, the former beside the address, one of the indications 'Service des prisonniers de guerre' (Prisoner-of-war Service) or 'Service des internés civils' (Civilian Internees Service); these indications may be followed by a translation in another language.").

[398] Postal Parcels Agreement, art. 41(2)(f), Dec. 14, 1989, 1687 UNTS 346, 369 ("Postal administrations shall not be liable for the loss of, theft from or damage to parcels in the case of prisoner-of-war or civilian internee parcels.").

[399] GC art. 110 ("The cost of transporting relief shipments which are intended for internees and which, by reason of their weight or any other cause, cannot be sent through the post office, shall be borne by the Detaining Power in all the territories under its control.").

[400] GC art. 110 ("Other Powers which are Parties to the present Convention shall bear the cost of transport in their respective territories.").

[401] GC art. 110 ("Costs connected with the transport of such shipments, which are not covered by the above paragraphs, shall be charged to the senders.").

[402] GC art. 110 ("The High Contracting Parties shall endeavour to reduce, so far as possible, the charges for telegrams sent by internees, or addressed to them.").

[403] GC art. 111 ("Should military operations prevent the Powers concerned from fulfilling their obligation to ensure the conveyance of the mail and relief shipments provided for in Articles 106, 107, 108 and 113, the Protecting Powers concerned, the International Committee of the Red Cross or any other organization duly approved by the

endeavor to supply them with such transport, and to allow its circulation, especially by granting the necessary safe-conducts.[404]

Such transport may also be used to convey:

- correspondence, lists, and reports exchanged between the Central Information Agency for protected persons and the National Protected Person Information Bureau; and
- correspondence and reports relating to internees that the Protecting Powers, the ICRC, or any other organization assisting the internees exchange either with their own delegates or with the parties to the conflict.[405]

These provisions in no way detract from the right of any party to the conflict to arrange other means of transport if it should so prefer, nor preclude the granting of safe-conducts, under mutually agreed conditions, to such means of transport.[406]

The costs occasioned by the use of such means of transport shall be borne, in proportion to the importance of the shipments, by the parties to the conflict whose nationals are benefited thereby.[407] Expenses in setting up the special transport system are not specifically addressed by the GC, and presumably would be addressed by an agreement between the body that takes the initiative in establishing the system and the Powers concerned.[408]

10.23.6 Censorship and Security Review of Internee Correspondence and Shipments. The Detaining Power may examine and censor all communications sent to or by internees, including correspondence, telegrams, parcels, newspapers, periodicals, and books, with a view to

---

Parties to the conflict may undertake the conveyance of such shipments by suitable means (rail, motor vehicles, vessels or aircraft, etc.).").

[404] GC art. 111 ("For this purpose, the High Contracting Parties shall endeavour to supply them with such transport, and to allow its circulation, especially by granting the necessary safe-conducts.").

[405] GC art. 111 ("Such transport may also be used to convey: (*a*) correspondence, lists and reports exchanged between the Central Information Agency referred to in Article 140 and the National Bureaux referred to in Article 136; (*b*) correspondence and reports relating to internees which the Protecting Powers, the International Committee of the Red Cross or any other organization assisting the internees exchange either with their own delegates or with the Parties to the conflict.").

[406] GC art. 111 ("These provisions in no way detract from the right of any Party to the conflict to arrange other means of transport if it should so prefer, nor preclude the granting of safe-conducts, under mutually agreed conditions, to such means of transport.").

[407] GC art. 111 ("The costs occasioned by the use of such means of transport shall be borne, in proportion to the importance of the shipments, by the Parties to the conflict whose nationals are benefited thereby.").

[408] *See* GC COMMENTARY 468 ("This paragraph deals with the expenditure involved in the use of special transport but not the expenditure incurred in setting up the special transport system. On this latter point, the Convention says nothing that is not contained in paragraph 1 of this Article-i.e., that the Contracting Powers will make every effort to procure the means of transport. It is therefore to be supposed that these expenses will be covered by agreement between the body which takes the initiative in the matter and the Power concerned.").

deleting or confiscating matter prejudicial to its military security.[409] The Detaining Power's general right to conduct censorship is an implicit assumption in the GC.[410] Internees' complaints, petitions, and reports may be subject to security review and censorship to ensure that they are not misused.[411]

The censoring of correspondence addressed to internees or sent by them shall be done as quickly as possible.[412]

10.23.6.1 <u>*Examination of Consignments*</u>. The examination of consignments intended for internees shall not be carried out under conditions that will expose the goods in them to deterioration.[413] It shall be done in the presence of the addressee, or of a fellow-internee duly delegated by him or her.[414] This measure is intended to prevent any misappropriation; the fellow-internee would generally be a member of the Internee Committee.[415]

The delivery to internees of individual or collective consignments shall not be delayed under the pretext of difficulties of censorship.[416]

10.23.6.2 <u>*Limitation on Prohibition of Correspondence*</u>. Any prohibition of

---

[409] 1956 FM 27-10 (Change No. 1 1976) ¶319b ("The Detaining Power may examine and censor all communications sent to or by internees, including correspondence and telegrams (*GC, art. 107*; par. 314 herein) and relief shipments (*GC, art, 108*; par. 315 herein) with a view to deleting matter prejudicial to its military security.").

[410] II-A FINAL RECORD OF THE DIPLOMATIC CONFERENCE OF GENEVA OF 1949 839-40 ("It was suggested by one Delegation that it would be desirable specifically to reserve the right of censorship in this Article, particularly in view of the insertion at Stockholm of the words 'and without alteration'. The view of the Committee generally was that to state a reservation on one Article might make it necessary to state a reserve on several others, since the first insertion would have created doubt as to the general right of censorship which otherwise is implicit in the Convention. It was generally accepted that a duty to transmit requests and complaints necessarily implied a right to read the documents in question to see whether they were in fact requests and complaints. Moreover, since there was no obligation to transmit without alteration a matter which was not a complaint and not a request, there could be no breach of the Convention if such matter were deleted from communications to representatives, for example, of the Protecting Power.").

[411] *Refer to* § 10.21.2.1 (Review and Censorship of Requests and Complaints by the Detaining Power); § 10.21.3 (Periodic Reports by the Internee Committees).

[412] GC art. 112 ("The censoring of correspondence addressed to internees or despatched by them shall be done as quickly as possible.").

[413] GC art. 112 ("The examination of consignments intended for internees shall not be carried out under conditions that will expose the goods contained in them to deterioration.").

[414] GC art. 112 ("It shall be done in the presence of the addressee, or of a fellow-internee duly delegated by him.").

[415] GC COMMENTARY 470 ("Parcels which cannot be examined by the Detaining Power in the presence of the internee, would be examined in the presence of a fellow-internee duly delegated by him. This measure is intended to prevent any misappropriation. In general, the fellow-internee duly delegated by the addressee will be the member of the Internee Committee entrusted with the task of receiving and distributing relief supplies in accordance with Article 109. A reference to the competence of the Internee Committee was, however, avoided in the Convention, because it was wished to leave the person concerned the opportunity of appointing someone as his delegate who was not a member of the Internee Committee, to cover cases where he did not have complete confidence in any of its members.").

[416] GC art. 112 ("The delivery to internees of individual or collective consignments shall not be delayed under the pretext of difficulties of censorship.").

correspondence ordered by the parties to the conflict for either military or political reasons shall be only temporary, and its duration shall be as short as possible.[417]

10.24 Private Legal Matters of Internees

10.24.1 Civil Capacity. Internees shall retain their full civil capacity and shall exercise such attendant rights as may be compatible with their status.[418] Their civil capacity continues to be governed by the laws that applied to them before they were interned (*e.g.*, the domestic laws of their home country or the laws governing the place where they were detained).[419]

10.24.2 Legal Documents and Assistance. The Detaining Power shall provide all reasonable facilities for the transmission, through the Protecting Power or the Central Information Agency for protected persons, or as otherwise required, of wills, powers of attorney, letters of authority, or any other documents intended for internees or sent by them.[420] In all cases, the Detaining Power shall facilitate the execution and authentication in due legal form of such documents on behalf of internees, in particular by allowing them to consult a lawyer.[421]

10.24.2.1 *Safekeeping of Wills*. In particular, the wills of internees shall be received for safe-keeping by the responsible authorities, *e.g.*, the commandant of the place of internment or, on the responsibility of the commandant, a public notary.[422] Upon the internee's death, the will shall be sent to a person whom the internee had designated.[423]

10.24.3 Management of Internee Property. Because internment is not punishment, enabling internees to manage their property is of major importance.[424]

---

[417] GC art. 112 ("Any prohibition of correspondence ordered by the Parties to the conflict either for military or political reasons, shall be only temporary and its duration shall be as short as possible.").

[418] GC art. 80 ("Internees shall retain their full civil capacity and shall exercise such attendant rights as may be compatible with their status.").

[419] GC Commentary 375 ("It must be realized, in fact, that the civil capacity of internees continues to be governed by the laws which applied to them before they were interned. That means that circumstances which modify it or cancel it in normal times (divorce, lunacy, etc.) continue to produce the same effects.").

[420] GC art. 113 ("The Detaining Powers shall provide all reasonable facilities for the transmission, through the Protecting Power or the Central Agency provided for in Article 140, or as otherwise required, of wills, powers of attorney, letters of authority, or any other documents intended for internees or despatched by them.").

[421] GC art. 113 ("In all cases the Detaining Powers shall facilitate the execution and authentication in due legal form of such documents on behalf of internees, in particular by allowing them to consult a lawyer.").

[422] *See* GC art. 129 ("The wills of internees shall be received for safe-keeping by the responsible authorities;"); GC Commentary 504 ("It was seen in Article 113 that in every case the Detaining Power would facilitate the execution and the authentication in due legal form of wills. These documents will be handed to the responsible authorities i.e. to the commandant of the place of internment or, on the responsibility of the commandant, to a public notary who will ensure their safe-keeping.").

[423] *Refer to* § 10.34.1 (Transmittal of Wills).

[424] GC Commentary 473 ("Internment, it must be insisted, is not a punishment. It would therefore be unjust if, through the restrictions on freedom which it imposes, it involved disastrous consequences for the internee himself and the members of his family. In this respect, the granting of permission to internees to manage their property is of major importance.").

The Detaining Power shall afford internees all facilities to enable internees to manage their property, provided such facilities are not incompatible with the conditions of internment and the law that is applicable.[425] The law that is applicable may include the Detaining Power's war regulations relating to enemy property.[426]

For the purpose of enabling internees to manage their property, the Detaining Power may give internees permission to leave the place of internment in urgent cases and if circumstances allow.[427] In general, however, the internee would act only by delegating his or her powers.[428]

10.24.4 Court Cases in Which Internees Are Parties. In all cases in which an internee is a party to proceedings in any court, the Detaining Power shall, if the internee so requests, cause the court to be informed of the internee's detention and shall, within legal limits, ensure that all necessary steps are taken to prevent the internee from being in any way prejudiced, by reason of his or her internment, as regards the preparation and conduct of his or her case, or as regards the execution of any judgment of the court.[429]

10.25 Internees and Visits of Family and Friends

Every internee shall be allowed to receive visitors, especially near relatives, at regular intervals and as frequently as possible.[430] The frequency of the visits will depend on practical considerations, including security needs.[431] The visitors need not be family members, but may be, for example, close friends.[432]

---

[425] GC art. 114 ("The Detaining Power shall afford internees all facilities to enable them to manage their property, provided this is not incompatible with the conditions of internment and the law which is applicable.").

[426] GC COMMENTARY 473 ("This Article, however, must not be interpreted in such a way as to give the internee a privileged position by making him not subject to the war regulations relating to enemy property. Clearly, a person delegated by him could not have greater power than himself and it is for this reason that the text expressly mentions the application of the laws in force.").

[427] GC art. 114 ("For this purpose, the said Power may give them permission to leave the place of internment in urgent cases and if circumstances allow.").

[428] GC COMMENTARY 473 ("It, however, remains a rule that the internee may act only by delegating his powers, since as one delegation to the Geneva Conference declared, 'it would not be reasonable to expect that an internee should be enabled to conduct a whole business from his place of internment'. In this case again, the Protecting Power will often have its services in demand.").

[429] GC art. 115 ("In all cases where an internee is a party to proceedings in any court, the Detaining Power shall, if he so requests, cause the court to be informed of his detention and shall, within legal limits, ensure that all necessary steps are taken to prevent him from being in any way prejudiced, by reason of his internment, as regards the preparation and conduct of his case or as regards the execution of any judgment of the court.").

[430] GC art. 116 ("Every internee shall be allowed to receive visitors, especially near relatives, at regular intervals and as frequently as possible.").

[431] *See* GC COMMENTARY 475 ("The frequency of visits was not stated because it was important to leave the detaining authorities discretion to appraise their security needs. Experience in the last war showed the advantage of monthly or bi-monthly visits which, in places of internment far away from urban centres, could last from one to three days.").

[432] *See* GC COMMENTARY 475 ("It is not only members of their families who are allowed to visit internees. In Kenya [during World War II], for example, internees without a family had been authorized, at the request of the

As far as is possible, internees shall be permitted to visit their homes in urgent cases, particularly in cases of death or serious illness of relatives.[433]

10.26 Internee Escapes

Similar to the rules on POW escape,[434] a number of provisions of the GC limit punishment of internees with respect to escape. However, unlike POWs,[435] internees are not afforded any protection from punishment for successful escapes.

10.26.1 Punishment for the Escape Itself. Internees who are recaptured after having escaped, or when attempting to escape, shall be liable only to disciplinary punishment in respect of this act, even if it is a repeated offense.[436]

10.26.1.1 *Punishment for Aiding and Abetting an Escape*. Internees who aid and abet an escape, or an attempt to escape, shall be liable on this count to disciplinary punishment only.[437]

10.26.2 Offenses Committed in Connection With, or During, Escape.

10.26.2.1 *Escape Not an Aggravating Circumstance for Offenses Committed During Escape*. Escape, or attempt to escape, even if it is a repeated offense, shall not be deemed an aggravating circumstance in cases where an internee is prosecuted for offenses committed during his or her escape.[438]

10.26.2.2 *Leniency in Favor of Disciplinary Punishments for Offenses Committed in Connection With Escape*. The parties to the conflict shall ensure that the competent authorities exercise leniency in deciding whether punishment inflicted for an offense shall be of a disciplinary or judicial nature, especially in respect of acts committed in connection with an escape, whether successful or not.[439] Thus, offenses that are committed in connection with an escape that are not serious should be punished in disciplinary as opposed to judicial

---

delegate of the International Committee of the Red Cross, to have visits from friends to whom they were in no way related. The results of this experience are embodied in the wording of this paragraph [of Article 116 of the GC].").

[433] GC art. 116 ("As far as is possible, internees shall be permitted to visit their homes in urgent cases, particularly in cases of death or serious illness of relatives.").

[434] *Refer to* § 9.25 (POW Escapes).

[435] *Refer to* § 9.25.1 (No Punishment for Successful Escape).

[436] GC art. 120 ("Internees who are recaptured after having escaped or when attempting to escape, shall be liable only to disciplinary punishment in respect of this act, even if it is a repeated offence.").

[437] GC art. 120 ("Internees who aid and abet an escape, or attempt to escape, shall be liable on this count to disciplinary punishment only.").

[438] GC art. 121 ("Escape, or attempt to escape, even if it is a repeated offence, shall not be deemed an aggravating circumstance in cases where an internee is prosecuted for offences committed during his escape.").

[439] GC art. 121 ("The Parties to the conflict shall ensure that the competent authorities exercise leniency in deciding whether punishment inflicted for an offence shall be of a disciplinary or judicial nature, especially in respect of acts committed in connection with an escape, whether successful or not.").

proceedings.[440]

This requirement does not compel the competent authorities to choose disciplinary over judicial proceedings in any particular case.[441]

10.26.3 Special Surveillance of Internees Who Have Previously Escaped or Attempted to Escape. Although paragraph 3 of Article 118 of the GC provides that internees who have served disciplinary or judicial sentences shall not be treated differently from other internees,[442] internees punished as a result of escape or attempt to escape may be subjected to special surveillance, on condition that such surveillance: (1) does not affect the state of their health; (2) is exercised in a place of internment; and (3) does not entail the abolition of any of the safeguards granted by the GC.[443]

10.26.4 Notification of Escape and Recapture. If an internee escapes, the State of which the internee was a national or in which the national resided should be notified by the Detaining Power's National Protected Person Information Bureau through the intermediary of the Protecting Powers and Central Information Agency for protected persons.[444]

10.27 General Provisions Applicable to Both Judicial and Disciplinary Sanctions Regarding Internees

This section addresses the rules that apply to both judicial and disciplinary sanctions regarding internees.

10.27.1 Applicability of the Laws in Force to Internees. Subject to the provisions of Chapter IX of the GC, the laws in force in the territory in which they are detained will continue to apply to internees who commit offenses during internment.[445]

10.27.2 Only Disciplinary Punishments for Internee-Specific Offenses. If general laws, regulations, or orders declare acts committed by internees to be punishable, whereas the same acts are not punishable when committed by persons who are not internees, such acts shall entail

[440] GC Commentary 488 ("It must be considered that whenever connected offences are not serious, they may only be punished as breaches of discipline. If there is any doubt, the authorities should give the accused the benefit of it.").

[441] *Compare* § 9.26.2 (Leniency in Favor of Disciplinary Rather Than Judicial Proceedings).

[442] *Refer to* § 10.27.5 (Treatment of Internees Who Have Served Sentences).

[443] GC art. 120 ("Article 118, paragraph 3, notwithstanding, internees punished as a result of escape or attempt to escape, may be subjected to special surveillance, on condition that such surveillance does not affect the state of their health, that it is exercised in a place of internment and that it does not entail the abolition of any of the safeguards granted by the present Convention.").

[444] *Refer to* § 10.31.1 (Accountability Information That Parties to a Conflict Should Collect).

[445] GC art. 117 ("Subject to the provisions of the present Chapter, the laws in force in the territory in which they are detained will continue to apply to internees who commit offences during internment.").

disciplinary punishments only.[446]

10.27.3 No Repetition of Punishment. No internee may be punished more than once for the same act, or on the same count.[447]

10.27.4 Penalties Imposed on Internees. The courts or authorities shall, in passing sentence, take as far as possible into account the fact that the defendant is not a national of the Detaining Power.[448] They shall be free to reduce the penalty prescribed for the offense with which the internee is charged and shall not be obliged, to this end, to apply the minimum sentence prescribed.[449]

10.27.4.1 *Prohibited Penalties*. Imprisonment in premises without daylight and, in general, all forms of cruelty without exception are forbidden.[450]

Collective punishments of internees are also prohibited.[451]

10.27.4.2 *Deduction From Penalty for Duration of Preventive Detention*. The duration of preventive detention undergone by an internee shall be deducted from any disciplinary or judicial penalty involving confinement to which he or she may be sentenced.[452]

10.27.5 Treatment of Internees Who Have Served Sentences. Internees who have served disciplinary or judicial sentences shall not be treated differently from other internees.[453]

10.28 Disciplinary Proceedings and Punishment

In addition to the general principles applicable to the punishment of internees, the following rules address disciplinary proceedings and punishment.

10.28.1 Internment Camp Authorities Who May Order Disciplinary Punishment. Without prejudice to the competence of courts and higher authorities, disciplinary punishment may be ordered only by the commandant of the place of internment, or by a responsible officer

---

[446] GC art. 117 ("If general laws, regulations or orders declare acts committed by internees to be punishable, whereas the same acts are not punishable when committed by persons who are not internees, such acts shall entail disciplinary punishments only.").

[447] GC art. 117 ("No internee may be punished more than once for the same act, or on the same count.").

[448] GC art. 118 ("The courts or authorities shall in passing sentence take as far as possible into account the fact that the defendant is not a national of the Detaining Power.").

[449] GC art. 118 ("They shall be free to reduce the penalty prescribed for the offence with which the internee is charged and shall not be obliged, to this end, to apply the minimum sentence prescribed.").

[450] GC art. 118 ("Imprisonment in premises without daylight and, in general, all forms of cruelty without exception are forbidden.").

[451] *Refer to* § 10.5.3.2 (Collective Penalties and Measures of Intimidation or Terrorism).

[452] GC art. 118 ("The duration of preventive detention undergone by an internee shall be deducted from any disciplinary or judicial penalty involving confinement to which he may be sentenced.").

[453] GC art. 118 ("Internees who have served disciplinary or judicial sentences shall not be treated differently from other internees.").

or official who replaces him or her, or to whom the commandant has delegated his or her disciplinary powers.[454] The delegation of disciplinary authorities by the commandant, however, does not absolve the commandant of his or her own responsibility and of his or her duty of supervision.[455]

10.28.2 Confinement of Internees Awaiting Trial. Acts that constitute offenses against discipline shall be investigated immediately.[456] This rule shall be applied, in particular, in cases of escape or attempt to escape.[457] Recaptured internees shall be handed over to the competent authorities as soon as possible.[458] Competent authorities are those directly responsible for the person concerned before the escape and who are entitled to direct that the internee receive a disciplinary punishment.[459]

In cases of offenses against discipline, confinement awaiting trial shall be reduced to an absolute minimum for all internees, and shall not exceed fourteen days.[460] Although the words "awaiting trial" are used in the GC, the GC does not require that this period of investigation before the disciplinary proceedings have the complicated character of pre-trial discovery and involve motions, for example, as in the judicial context.[461]

The provisions of Articles 124 and 125 of the GC shall apply to internees who are in confinement awaiting trial for offenses against discipline.[462] Thus, the conditions of any

---

[454] GC art. 123 ("Without prejudice to the competence of courts and higher authorities, disciplinary punishment may be ordered only by the commandant of the place of internment, or by a responsible officer or official who replaces him, or to whom he has delegated his disciplinary powers.").

[455] GC COMMENTARY 490 ("In very large places of internment, however, the need to place before the commandant every case involving disciplinary punishment would lead to delays and complications. The Government Experts had already noted this and, at their suggestion, the Stockholm Draft included a provision that disciplinary powers could be delegated. This delegation of powers, authorized in the paragraph under discussion, does not however absolve the commandant from his own responsibility nor his duty of supervision. Since, under Article 99, he is responsible for the application of the Convention, he assumes responsibility for any abuses of which his subordinates might become guilty in exercising the disciplinary power he has delegated to them.").

[456] GC art. 122 ("Acts which constitute offences against discipline shall be investigated immediately.").

[457] GC art. 122 ("This rule shall be applied, in particular, in cases of escape or attempt to escape.").

[458] GC art. 122 ("Recaptured internees shall be handed over to the competent authorities as soon as possible.").

[459] *See* GC COMMENTARY 488 ("With regard to handing over the recaptured internee to the 'competent' authorities, this text should be compared with paragraph 2 of Article 92 of the Third Convention, which provides that an escaped prisoner of war must be handed over to the competent military authorities. In both cases the competent authorities are those directly responsible for the person concerned before the escape-i.e. either the camp commandant (or the commander of the labour detachment), or the commandant of the place of internment. In short, the competent authority is the authority entitled to inflict a disciplinary punishment on the internee.").

[460] GC art. 122 ("In case of offences against discipline, confinement awaiting trial shall be reduced to an absolute minimum for all internees, and shall not exceed fourteen days.").

[461] *See* GC COMMENTARY 488 ("While an investigation to establish the facts must always precede the infliction of a punishment, it will not in this case have the complicated character of a judicial enquiry.").

[462] GC art. 122 ("The provisions of Articles 124 and 125 shall apply to internees who are in confinement awaiting trial for offences against discipline."). *Refer to* § 10.28.6 (Conditions for Internees Serving Disciplinary Punishments).

confinement before the trial should be at least as good as those afforded internees who are confined as part of disciplinary punishment.[463]

10.28.3 Rights of Internees in Disciplinary Proceedings. Before any disciplinary punishment is awarded, the accused internee shall be given: (1) precise information regarding the offenses of which he or she is accused; (2) an opportunity to explain his or her conduct; and (3) an opportunity to defend himself or herself.[464] The internee shall be permitted, in particular, to call witnesses and to have recourse, if necessary, to the services of a qualified interpreter.[465]

The decision shall be announced in the presence of the accused and of a member of the Internee Committee.[466]

10.28.4 Record of Disciplinary Punishments. A record of disciplinary punishments shall be maintained by the commandant of the place of internment and shall be open to inspection by representatives of the Protecting Power.[467]

10.28.5 Types of Disciplinary Punishments and Procedures for Dispensing Punishment. In no case shall disciplinary penalties be inhuman, brutal, or dangerous for the health of internees.[468]

In addition, prolonged standing and roll-calls, punishment drill, military drill and maneuvers, and the reduction of food rations are prohibited.[469]

Account shall be taken of the internee's age, sex, and state of health.[470] The disciplinary punishments applicable to internees shall be the following:

- a fine that shall not exceed 50 percent of the wages that the internee would otherwise receive under Article 95 of the GC during a period of not more than thirty days;

---

[463] *See* GC COMMENTARY 489 ("This solution, moreover, is logical and conforms to the traditional procedure in penal matters. Deprivation of liberty while awaiting trial indeed takes place before the guilt of the accused has been established. Detention must not, therefore, be harsher for a man who is merely accused than for a guilty person.").

[464] GC art. 123 ("Before any disciplinary punishment is awarded, the accused internee shall be given precise information regarding the offences of which he is accused, and given an opportunity of explaining his conduct and of defending himself.").

[465] GC art. 123 ("He shall be permitted, in particular, to call witnesses and to have recourse, if necessary, to the services of a qualified interpreter.").

[466] GC art. 123 ("The decision shall be announced in the presence of the accused and of a member of the Internee Committee.").

[467] GC art. 123 ("A record of disciplinary punishments shall be maintained by the commandant of the place of internment and shall be open to inspection by representatives of the Protecting Power.").

[468] GC art. 119 ("In no case shall disciplinary penalties be inhuman, brutal or dangerous for the health of internees.").

[469] *Refer to* § 10.20.3.2 (Prohibition Against Prolonged Standing, Roll-Calls, Punishment Drill, Military Drill and Manuevers, or the Reduction of Food Rations).

[470] GC art. 119 ("Account shall be taken of the internee's age, sex and state of health.").

- discontinuance of privileges granted over and above the treatment provided for by the GC;
- fatigue duties, not exceeding two hours daily, in connection with the maintenance of the place of internment; and
- confinement.[471]

The duration of any single punishment shall in no case exceed a maximum of thirty consecutive days, even if the internee is answerable for several breaches of discipline when his or her case is dealt with, regardless of whether such breaches are connected.[472]

The duration of confinement awaiting trial shall in any case be deducted from any sentence of confinement.[473]

The period elapsing between the time of award of a disciplinary punishment and its execution shall not exceed one month.[474] When an internee is awarded a further disciplinary punishment, a period of at least three days shall elapse between the execution of any two of the punishments, if the duration of one of these punishments is ten days or more.[475]

10.28.6 Conditions for Internees Serving Disciplinary Punishments. Conditions for disciplinary punishments must comport with the requirements for humane treatment. In addition, the following rules apply:

10.28.6.1 *Premises Where Disciplinary Punishments Are to Be Served*. Internees shall not, in any case, be transferred to penitentiary establishments (*e.g.*, prisons, penitentiaries, convict prisons) to undergo disciplinary punishments.[476]

The premises in which disciplinary punishments occur shall conform to sanitary requirements; they shall, in particular, be provided with adequate bedding.[477] Internees

---

[471] GC art. 119 ("The disciplinary punishments applicable to internees shall be the following: (1) A fine which shall not exceed 50 per cent of the wages which the internee would otherwise receive under the provisions of Article 95 during a period of not more than thirty days. (2) Discontinuance of privileges granted over and above the treatment provided for by the present Convention. (3) Fatigue duties, not exceeding two hours daily, in connection with the maintenance of the place of internment. (4) Confinement.").

[472] GC art. 119 ("The duration of any single punishment shall in no case exceed a maximum of thirty consecutive days, even if the internee is answerable for several breaches of discipline when his case is dealt with, whether such breaches are connected or not.").

[473] GC art. 122 ("Its duration shall in any case be deducted from any sentence of confinement.").

[474] GC art. 123 ("The period elapsing between the time of award of a disciplinary punishment and its execution shall not exceed one month.").

[475] GC art. 123 ("When an internee is awarded a further disciplinary punishment, a period of at least three days shall elapse between the execution of any two of the punishments, if the duration of one of these is ten days or more.").

[476] GC art. 124 ("Internees shall not in any case be transferred to penitentiary establishments (prisons, penitentiaries, convict prisons, etc.) to undergo disciplinary punishment therein.").

[477] GC art. 124 ("The premises in which disciplinary punishments are undergone shall conform to sanitary requirements; they shall in particular be provided with adequate bedding.").

undergoing punishment shall be enabled to keep themselves in a state of cleanliness.[478]

Women internees undergoing disciplinary punishment shall be confined in separate quarters from male internees and shall be under the immediate supervision of women.[479]

10.28.6.2 *Exercise and Access to the Open Air*. Internees awarded disciplinary punishment shall be allowed to exercise and to stay in the open air at least two hours daily.[480] Exercising and staying in the open air should be given as an opportunity and should not be compelled.[481]

10.28.6.3 *Attendance at Daily Medical Inspection and Medical Attention*. Internees awarded disciplinary punishment shall be allowed, if they so request, to be present at daily medical inspections.[482] They shall receive the attention that their state of health requires and, if necessary, shall be removed to the infirmary of the place of internment or to a hospital.[483]

10.28.6.4 *Reading, Writing, Correspondence, and Packages*. Internees awarded disciplinary punishment shall have permission to read and write, and to send and receive letters.[484] Parcels and remittances of money, however, may be withheld from them until the completion of their punishment; such consignments shall meanwhile be entrusted to the Internee Committee, who will hand over to the infirmary the perishable goods contained in the parcels.[485]

No internee given a disciplinary punishment may be deprived of the benefit of the provisions of Articles 101 and 143 of the GC.[486] Thus, internees undergoing disciplinary

---

[478] GC art. 124 ("Internees undergoing punishment shall be enabled to keep themselves in a state of cleanliness.").

[479] GC art. 124 ("Women internees undergoing disciplinary punishment shall be confined in separate quarters from male internees and shall be under the immediate supervision of women.").

[480] GC art. 125 ("Internees awarded disciplinary punishment shall be allowed to exercise and to stay in the open air at least two hours daily.").

[481] *See* GC COMMENTARY 495 ("It should be made quite clear, moreover, that exercise in the open air is a possibility offered to the internee; whether he takes advantage of it or not is according to his wishes. It would not be right, indeed, if, under the pretext of applying this rule, certain commandants of places of internment made the punishment more severe by compulsory exercise, keeping the internees in the full sun or the snow for two hours at a stretch as sometimes happened during the Second World War.").

[482] GC art. 125 ("They shall be allowed, if they so request, to be present at the daily medical inspections."). *Refer to* § 10.14.1.3 (Monthly Medical Inspections).

[483] GC art. 125 ("They shall receive the attention which their state of health requires and, if necessary, shall be removed to the infirmary of the place of internment or to a hospital.").

[484] GC art. 125 ("They shall have permission to read and write, likewise to send and receive letters."). *Refer to* § 10.23.2 (Internees' Correspondence Rights and Quota).

[485] GC art. 125 ("Parcels and remittances of money, however, may be withheld from them until the completion of their punishment; such consignments shall meanwhile be entrusted to the Internee Committee, who will hand over to the infirmary the perishable goods contained in the parcels.").

[486] GC art. 125 ("No internee given a disciplinary punishment may be deprived of the benefit of the provisions of Articles 107 and 143 of the present Convention."). Article 125 of the GC specifies Article 107 instead of Article 101. However, considering (1) the legislative history; (2) the parallel provision in Article 98 of the GPW that refers to the right of making complaints; (3) the fact that the right to send or receive letters is already given in paragraph 3

punishments may not be deprived of the right to make requests and complaints, or to deal with representatives of the Protecting Power (including representatives of an impartial humanitarian organization performing the functions of the Protecting Power).[487]

10.29 Judicial Proceedings Regarding Protected Persons in Occupied Territory or Internees in a Belligerent's Home Territory

In addition to the general principles applicable to the punishment of internees, the following rules address judicial proceedings against internees in a belligerent's home territory and protected persons in occupied territory.

The provisions of Articles 71 through 76 of the GC shall apply, by analogy, to proceedings against internees who are in the national territory of the Detaining Power.[488] Articles 71-76 of the GC address the penal procedures for protected persons in occupied territory. Thus, this section has been written with a view towards describing both situations.

10.29.1 Information to Internee Committees. Internee Committees shall be informed of all judicial proceedings instituted against internees whom they represent, and of their result.[489]

10.29.2 Pre-Trial Matters.

10.29.2.1 *Prompt Information of the Charges and Brought to Trial as Rapidly as Possible*. Accused persons who are prosecuted by the Occupying or Detaining Power shall be promptly informed, in writing, in a language that they understand, of the particulars of the charges preferred against them, and shall be brought to trial as rapidly as possible.[490]

10.29.2.2 *Notification of Proceeding in Respect of Charges Involving the Death Penalty or Imprisonment for Two or More Years*. The Protecting Power shall be informed of all proceedings instituted by the Occupying or Detaining Power against protected persons in respect of charges involving the death penalty or imprisonment for two years or more, and shall be enabled, at any time, to obtain information regarding the state of such proceedings.[491] Furthermore, the Protecting Power shall be entitled, on request, to be furnished with all

---

of Article 125 of the GC; and (4) the principles underlying the GC; "[i]t may therefore be deduced that the last paragraph refers to Article 107 in error for Article 101." GC Commentary 497.

[487] *Refer to* § 10.21 (Internee Petitions, Complaints); § 10.33 (Access to Internees by Protecting Powers, ICRC, and Other Relief Organizations).

[488] GC art. 126 ("The provisions of Articles 71 to 76 inclusive shall apply, by analogy, to proceedings against internees who are in the national territory of the Detaining Power.").

[489] GC art. 118 ("Internee Committees shall be informed of all judicial proceedings instituted against internees whom they represent, and of their result.").

[490] GC art. 71 ("Accused persons who are prosecuted by the Occupying Power shall be promptly informed, in writing, in a language which they understand, of the particulars of the charges preferred against them, and shall be brought to trial as rapidly as possible.").

[491] GC art. 71 ("The Protecting Power shall be informed of all proceedings instituted by the Occupying Power against protected persons in respect of charges involving the death penalty or imprisonment for two years or more; it shall be enabled, at any time, to obtain information regarding the state of such proceedings.").

particulars of these and of any other proceedings instituted by the Occupying or Detaining Power against protected persons.[492]

The notification to the Protecting Power, as provided for in the second paragraph of Article 71 of the GC, shall be sent immediately, and shall in any case reach the Protecting Power three weeks before the date of the first hearing.[493] Unless, at the opening of the trial, evidence is submitted that the provisions of Article 71 of the GC are fully complied with, the trial shall not proceed.[494] The notification shall include the following particulars:

- description of the accused;
- place of residence or detention;
- specification of the charge or charges (with mention of the penal provisions under which it is brought);
- designation of the court that will hear the case; and
- place and date of the first hearing.[495]

10.29.3 Right of Defense and Trial Procedure. Accused persons shall have the right to present evidence necessary to their defense and may, in particular, call witnesses.[496] They shall have the right to be assisted by a qualified advocate or counsel of their own choice, who shall be able to visit them freely and shall enjoy the necessary facilities for preparing the defense.[497]

10.29.3.1 *Additional Provision for Defense Counsel and Interpreter*. Failing a choice by the accused, the Protecting Power may provide him or her with an advocate or counsel.[498] Where the accused person is facing a serious charge and the Protecting Power is not functioning, the Occupying or Detaining Power, subject to the consent of the accused, shall

---

[492] GC art. 71 ("Furthermore, the Protecting Power shall be entitled, on request, to be furnished with all particulars of these and of any other proceedings instituted by the Occupying Power against protected persons.").

[493] GC art. 71 ("The notification to the Protecting Power, as provided for in the second paragraph above, shall be sent immediately, and shall in any case reach the Protecting Power three weeks before the date of the first hearing.").

[494] GC art. 71 ("Unless, at the opening of the trial, evidence is submitted that the provisions of this Article are fully complied with, the trial shall not proceed.").

[495] GC art. 71 ("The notification shall include the following particulars: (a) description of the accused; (b) place of residence or detention; (c) specification of the charge or charges (with mention of the penal provisions under which it is brought); (d) designation of the court which will hear the case; (e) place and date of the first hearing.").

[496] GC art. 72 ("Accused persons shall have the right to present evidence necessary to their defence and may, in particular, call witnesses.").

[497] GC art. 72 ("They shall have the right to be assisted by a qualified advocate or counsel of their own choice, who shall be able to visit them freely and shall enjoy the necessary facilities for preparing the defence.").

[498] GC art. 72 ("Failing a choice by the accused, the Protecting Power may provide him with an advocate or counsel.").

provide an advocate or counsel.[499] Accused persons shall, unless they freely waive such assistance, be aided by an interpreter, both during preliminary investigation and during the hearing in court.[500] They shall have the right at any time to object to the interpreter and to ask for the interpreter to be replaced.[501]

10.29.3.2 *Attendance by the Protecting Power in the Proceedings*. Representatives of the Protecting Power shall have the right to attend the trial of any protected person, unless the hearing, as an exceptional measure, has to be held *in camera* in the interests of the security of the Occupying or Detaining Power, which shall then notify the Protecting Power.[502] A notification in respect of the date and place of trial shall be sent to the Protecting Power.[503]

10.29.3.3 *Regular Trial*. No sentence shall be pronounced by the competent courts of the Occupying or Detaining Power except after a regular trial.[504]

10.29.3.4 *Notification of Judgment Involving Sentence of Death or Imprisonment*. Any judgment involving a sentence of death, or imprisonment for two years or more, shall be communicated, with the relevant grounds, as rapidly as possible to the Protecting Power.[505] The notification shall contain a reference to the notification made under Article 71 of the GC and, in the case of sentences of imprisonment, the name of the place where the sentence is to be served.[506] A record of judgments other than those referred to above shall be kept by the court and shall be open to inspection by representatives of the Protecting Power.[507] Any period allowed for appeal in the case of sentences involving the death penalty, or imprisonment of two years or more, shall not run until notification of judgment has been received by the Protecting Power.[508]

---

[499] GC art. 72 ("When an accused person has to meet a serious charge and the Protecting Power is not functioning, the Occupying Power, subject to the consent of the accused, shall provide an advocate or counsel.").

[500] GC art. 72 ("Accused persons shall, unless they freely waive such assistance, be aided by an interpreter, both during preliminary investigation and during the hearing in court.").

[501] GC art. 72 ("They shall have the right at any time to object to the interpreter and to ask for his replacement.").

[502] GC art. 74 ("Representatives of the Protecting Power shall have the right to attend the trial of any protected person, unless the hearing has, as an exceptional measure, to be held in camera in the interests of the security of the Occupying Power, which shall then notify the Protecting Power.").

[503] GC art. 74 ("A notification in respect of the date and place of trial shall be sent to the Protecting Power.").

[504] GC art. 71 ("No sentence shall be pronounced by the competent courts of the Occupying Power except after a regular trial.").

[505] GC art. 74 ("Any judgment involving a sentence of death, or imprisonment for two years or more, shall be communicated, with the relevant grounds, as rapidly as possible to the Protecting Power.").

[506] GC art. 74 ("The notification shall contain a reference to the notification made under Article 71, and, in the case of sentences of imprisonment, the name of the place where the sentence is to be served.").

[507] GC art. 74 ("A record of judgments other than those referred to above shall be kept by the court and shall be open to inspection by representatives of the Protecting Power.").

[508] GC art. 74 ("Any period allowed for appeal in the case of sentences involving the death penalty, or imprisonment of two years or more, shall not run until notification of judgment has been received by the Protecting Power.").

10.29.4 Right of Appeal. A convicted person shall have the right of appeal provided for by the laws applied by the court.[509] The convicted person shall be fully informed of his or her right to appeal or petition, and of the time limit within which he or she may do so.[510]

The penal procedure in Section III of the GC shall apply, as far as it is applicable, to appeals.[511] Where the laws applied by the court make no provision for appeals, the convicted person shall have the right to petition against the finding and sentence to the competent authority of the Occupying or Detaining Power.[512]

10.29.5 Death Sentences. In no case shall persons condemned to death be deprived of the right of petition for pardon or reprieve.[513]

No death sentence shall be carried out before the expiration of a period of at least six months from the date of receipt by the Protecting Power of the notification of the final judgment confirming such death sentence, or of an order denying pardon or reprieve.[514]

The six-month period of suspension of the death sentence prescribed in Article 75 of the GC may be reduced in individual cases in circumstances of grave emergency involving an organized threat to the security of the Occupying or Detaining Power or its forces, provided always that the Protecting Power is notified of such reduction and is given reasonable time and opportunity to make representations to the competent occupying or domestic authorities in respect of such death sentences.[515]

10.29.6 Conditions for Accused or Convicted Protected Persons Who Are Detained. If found in occupied territory, protected persons accused of offenses shall be detained in the occupied country, and, if convicted, they shall serve their sentences therein.[516] This provision does not preclude the appearance of convicted persons before appeal courts outside the occupied

---

[509] GC art. 73 ("A convicted person shall have the right of appeal provided for by the laws applied by the court.").

[510] GC art. 73 ("He shall be fully informed of his right to appeal or petition and of the time limit within which he may do so.").

[511] GC art. 73 ("The penal procedure provided in the present Section shall apply, as far as it is applicable, to appeals.").

[512] GC art. 73 ("Where the laws applied by the Court make no provision for appeals, the convicted person shall have the right to petition against the finding and sentence to the competent authority of the Occupying Power.").

[513] GC art. 75 ("In no case shall persons condemned to death be deprived of the right of petition for pardon or reprieve.").

[514] GC art. 75 ("No death sentence shall be carried out before the expiration of a period of at least six months from the date of receipt by the Protecting Power of the notification of the final judgment confirming such death sentence, or of an order denying pardon or reprieve.").

[515] GC art. 75 ("The six months period of suspension of the death sentence herein prescribed may be reduced in individual cases in circumstances of grave emergency involving an organized threat to the security of the Occupying Power or its forces, provided always that the Protecting Power is notified of such reduction and is given reasonable time and opportunity to make representations to the competent occupying authorities in respect of such death sentences.").

[516] GC art. 76 ("Protected persons accused of offences shall be detained in the occupied country, and if convicted they shall serve their sentences therein.").

territory, or the possibility of protected persons receiving medical care outside the occupied territory.[517]

Accused or convicted protected persons who are detained shall, if possible, be separated from other detainees and shall enjoy conditions of food and hygiene that will be sufficient to keep them in good health, and that will be at least equal to those obtaining in prisons in that country.[518]

10.29.6.1 Medical Attention and Spiritual Assistance. Accused or convicted protected persons who are detained shall receive the medical attention required by their state of health.[519] They shall also have the right to receive any spiritual assistance that they may require.[520]

10.29.6.2 Separate Confinement for Women and Special Treatment for Minors. Women shall be confined in separate quarters and shall be under the direct supervision of women.[521] Proper regard shall be paid to the special treatment due to minors.[522]

10.29.6.3 Visits by the Protecting Power and ICRC and Right to Receive Relief Parcel. Accused or convicted protected persons who are detained shall have the right to be visited by delegates of the Protecting Power and the ICRC, in accordance with the provisions of Article 143 of the GC.[523] Accused or convicted protected persons who are detained also shall have the right to receive at least one relief parcel monthly.[524]

10.30 Transfers of Internees From the Place of Internment

The rules in this section apply to transfers of internees from the place of internment.

Additional rules apply to the transfer of protected persons from the belligerent's home

[517] *See* II-A Final Record of the Diplomatic Conference of Geneva of 1949 835 ("A provision appeared in Article 67 of the Stockholm text that protected persons indicted or convicted by the courts in occupied territory shall in no case be taken outside the said territory. The Committee felt this prohibition to be too emphatic since it would preclude the appearance of convicted persons before appeal courts outside the occupied territory, or the possibility of their receiving health treatment outside the territory. The Committee considered that the principle behind this provision could be preserved by including in Article 66 a provision to the effect that protected persons indicted shall be detained in the occupied country and if convicted shall serve their sentence therein.").

[518] GC art. 76 ("They shall, if possible, be separated from other detainees and shall enjoy conditions of food and hygiene which will be sufficient to keep them in good health, and which will be at least equal to those obtaining in prisons in the occupied country.").

[519] GC art. 76 ("They shall receive the medical attention required by their state of health.").

[520] GC art. 76 ("They shall also have the right to receive any spiritual assistance which they may require.").

[521] GC art. 76 ("Women shall be confined in separate quarters and shall be under the direct supervision of women.").

[522] GC art. 76 ("Proper regard shall be paid to the special treatment due to minors.").

[523] GC art. 76 ("Protected persons who are detained shall have the right to be visited by delegates of the Protecting Power and of the International Committee of the Red Cross, in accordance with the provisions of Article 143.").

[524] GC art. 76 ("Such persons shall have the right to receive at least one relief parcel monthly.").

territory.[525] Individual or mass forcible transfers of protected persons from occupied territory are prohibited.[526]

10.30.1 Determining Whether to Transfer Internees. When making decisions regarding the transfer of internees, the Detaining Power shall take their interests into account and, in particular, shall not do anything to increase the difficulties of repatriating them or returning them to their own homes.[527]

Sick, wounded, or infirm internees, and maternity cases, shall not be transferred if the journey would be seriously detrimental to them, unless their safety imperatively so demands.[528]

If the combat zone draws close to a place of internment, the internees in that place shall not be transferred unless their removal can be carried out in adequate conditions of safety, or unless they are exposed to greater risks by remaining on the spot than by being transferred.[529]

10.30.2 Conditions for the Transfer of Internees. The transfer of internees shall always be effected humanely.[530] As a general rule, it shall be carried out by rail or other means of transport, and under conditions at least equal to those obtaining for the forces of the Detaining Power in their changes of station.[531] If, as an exceptional measure, such removals have to be effected on foot, they may not take place unless the internees are in a fit state of health, and may not in any case expose them to excessive fatigue.[532] This provision seeks to prevent abuses such as the forced "death marches" that occurred during World War II.[533] When considering movement by foot, the Detaining Power must assess the fitness of each individual, not the

---

[525] *Refer to* § 10.8.3 (Transfers of Protected Persons From a Belligerent's Home Territory).

[526] *Refer to* § 11.12.3 (Prohibition Against Forcible Transfers and Deportations).

[527] GC art. 127 ("When making decisions regarding the transfer of internees, the Detaining Power shall take their interests into account and, in particular, shall not do anything to increase the difficulties of repatriating them or returning them to their own homes.").

[528] GC art. 127 ("Sick, wounded or infirm internees and maternity cases shall not be transferred if the journey would be seriously detrimental to them, unless their safety imperatively so demands.").

[529] GC art. 127 ("If the combat zone draws close to a place of internment, the internees in the said place shall not be transferred unless their removal can be carried out in adequate conditions of safety, or unless they are exposed to greater risks by remaining on the spot than by being transferred.").

[530] GC art. 127 ("The transfer of internees shall always be effected humanely.").

[531] GC art. 127 ("As a general rule, it shall be carried out by rail or other means of transport, and under conditions at least equal to those obtaining for the forces of the Detaining Power in their changes of station.").

[532] GC art. 127 ("If, as an exceptional measure, such removals have to be effected on foot, they may not take place unless the internees are in a fit state of health, and may not in any case expose them to excessive fatigue.").

[533] II-A FINAL RECORD OF THE DIPLOMATIC CONFERENCE OF GENEVA OF 1949 269 ("Mr. GARDNER (United Kingdom) submitted the three following amendments: … It had been proved that during the Second World War over ten thousand prisoners lost their lives while being transferred by sea; but a very much larger number lost their lives while being transferred by land. He referred not only to the Bataan march, but also to a march in Borneo where some four thousand prisoners had started out, and only six or seven survived. There were also the forced marches carried out by prisoners in Central Europe towards the end of the war; it was certainly not due to any efforts by the Detaining Power that the number of deaths during those marches was comparatively small.").

condition of the majority.[534]

The Detaining Power shall supply internees during transfer with drinking water and food sufficient in quantity, quality, and variety to maintain them in good health, and also with the necessary clothing, adequate shelter, and the necessary medical attention.[535] The Detaining Power shall take all suitable precautions to ensure their safety during transfer, and shall establish before their departure a complete list of all internees transferred.[536]

10.30.3 Procedures for the Transfer of Internees. In the event of transfer, internees shall be officially advised of their departure and of their new postal address.[537] Such notification shall be given in time for them to pack their luggage and inform their next of kin.[538]

10.30.3.1 *Baggage*. Internees shall be allowed to take with them their personal effects, and the correspondence and parcels that have arrived for them.[539] The weight of such baggage may be limited if the conditions of transfer so require, but in no case may be limited to less than 25 kilograms (approximately 55 pounds) per internee.[540]

10.30.3.2 *Forwarding of Mail*. Mail and parcels addressed to their former place of internment shall be forwarded to internees without delay.[541]

10.30.3.3 *Disposition of Community Property and Remaining Property*. The commandant of the place of internment shall take, in agreement with the Internee Committee, any measures needed to ensure the transport of the internees' community property and of the luggage the internees are unable to take with them in consequence of restrictions that may be

---

[534] GC COMMENTARY 499 ("It is stated expressly that transfers on foot are only permissible in exceptional cases and if the internees are in a fit state of health. It is not the physical fitness of the majority of the internees which is to decide whether the transfer will be made on foot or not. The fitness of each individual must be considered and those who cannot walk must be taken in some sort of transport.").

[535] GC art. 127 ("The Detaining Power shall supply internees during transfer with drinking water and food sufficient in quantity, quality and variety to maintain them in good health, and also with the necessary clothing, adequate shelter and the necessary medical attention.").

[536] GC art. 127 ("The Detaining Power shall take all suitable precautions to ensure their safety during transfer, and shall establish before their departure a complete list of all internees transferred.").

[537] GC art. 128 ("In the event of transfer, internees shall be officially advised of their departure and of their new postal address.").

[538] GC art. 128 ("Such notification shall be given in time for them to pack their luggage and inform their next of kin.").

[539] GC art. 128 ("They shall be allowed to take with them their personal effects, and the correspondence and parcels which have arrived for them.").

[540] GC art. 128 ("The weight of such baggage may be limited if the conditions of transfer so require, but in no case to less than twenty-five kilograms per internee.").

[541] GC art. 128 ("Mail and parcels addressed to their former place of internment shall be forwarded to them without delay.").

imposed on baggage that internees may take with them.[542]

10.31 National Accounting for Protected Persons in Its Power

A proper accounting of the detention or assigned residence of protected persons is an important responsibility of States in relation to protected persons in their power. In order to provide as full an accounting as possible, and in order to minimize misidentification, a State must obtain detailed information about certain protected persons in its power for forwarding through its National Protected Person Information Bureau to the Central Information Agency for protected persons.

10.31.1 Accountability Information That Parties to a Conflict Should Collect. Each of the parties to the conflict shall, within the shortest possible period, give its National Protected Person Information Bureau information of any measure taken by it concerning any protected persons who are: (1) kept in custody for more than two weeks; (2) subjected to assigned residence; or (3) interned.[543]

The information received by the National Protected Person Information Bureau and transmitted by it shall be of such a character as to make it possible to identify the protected person exactly and to advise his or her next of kin quickly.[544] The information in respect of each person shall include at least:

- surname (*i.e.*, last name) and first names (*i.e.*, first and middle names);
- place and date of birth;
- nationality;
- last residence;
- any distinguishing characteristics;
- first name of the father and the maiden name of the mother;
- the date, place, and nature of the action taken with regard to the individual;
- the address at which correspondence may be sent to him or her; and
- the name and address of the person designated by the protected person to be informed of

[542] GC art. 128 ("The commandant of the place of internment shall take, in agreement with the Internee Committee, any measures needed to ensure the transport of the internees' community property and of the luggage the internees are unable to take with them in consequence of restrictions imposed by virtue of the second paragraph.").

[543] GC art. 136 ("Each of the Parties to the conflict shall, within the shortest possible period, give its Bureau information of any measure taken by it concerning any protected persons who are kept in custody for more than two weeks, who are subjected to assigned residence or who are interned.").

[544] GC art. 138 ("The information received by the national Bureau and transmitted by it shall be of such a character as to make it possible to identify the protected person exactly and to advise his next of kin quickly.").

information concerning him or her.[545]

In addition to this information, information regarding all changes pertaining to these protected persons, such as transfers, releases, repatriations, escapes, admittances to hospitals, births, and deaths, shall also be collected and transmitted.[546]

In addition to admittances to hospitals, information regarding the state of health of internees who are seriously ill or seriously wounded must be supplied to the National Protected Person Information Bureau regularly and, if possible, every week.[547]

In addition to notices of death, copies of records of death of internees shall be forwarded in accordance with Article 129 of the GC.[548] Lists of graves of deceased internees shall be forwarded, as soon as circumstances permit, in accordance with Article 130 of the GC.[549]

10.31.2 <u>National Protected Person Information Bureau</u>. Upon the outbreak of an international armed conflict and in all cases of occupation of the territory of one State by another State, each of the parties to the conflict shall establish an official National Protected Person Information Bureau responsible for receiving and transmitting information in respect of the protected persons who are in its power.[550] The State has discretion about the nature, composition, and working methods of the National Protected Person Information Bureau.[551]

All communications in writing made by any National Protected Person Information Bureau shall be authenticated by a signature or a seal.[552]

---

[545] GC art. 138 ("The information in respect of each person shall include at least his surname, first names, place and date of birth, nationality, last residence and distinguishing characteristics, the first name of the father and the maiden name of the mother, the date, place and nature of the action taken with regard to the individual, the address at which correspondence may be sent to him and the name and address of the person to be informed.").

[546] GC art. 136 ("It shall, furthermore, require its various departments concerned with such matters to provide the aforesaid Bureau promptly with information concerning all changes pertaining to these protected persons, as, for example, transfers, releases, repatriations, escapes, admittances to hospitals, births and deaths.").

[547] GC art. 138 ("Likewise, information regarding the state of health of internees who are seriously ill or seriously wounded shall be supplied regularly and if possible every week.").

[548] *Refer to* § 10.34.2 (Death Certificates).

[549] *Refer to* § 10.34.4 (Maintenance and Records of Graves and Ashes).

[550] GC art. 136 ("Upon the outbreak of a confict and in all cases of occupation, each of the Parties to the conflict shall establish an official Information Bureau responsible for receiving and transmitting information in respect of the protected persons who are in its power.").

[551] GC COMMENTARY 523 ("[Paragraph 1 of Article 136 of the GC] does not state in detail the nature, composition and working methods of the Bureau, all these matters being left to the free decision of each Party, nor does it state what authority will be responsible for establishing and conducting the Bureau. … During the Second World War, the Bureaux which had the task of transmitting information concerning civilian internees to the Central Agency were varied in nature and origin. In some cases, they were the same as the Bureaux responsible for prisoners of war; in others, they were established by the National Red Cross Society; most often, however, they depended directly on government authorities, such as the Ministry of the Interior or the Ministry of Security.").

[552] GC art. 137 ("All communications in writing made by any Bureau shall be authenticated by a signature or a seal.").

The National Protected Person Information Bureau: (1) receives and forwards certain information to the Powers concerned, through the intermediary of the Protecting Powers and the Central Information Agency for protected persons; (2) replies to inquiries; (3) withholds certain information from the Powers concerned, but not the Central Information Agency for protected persons, in the interest of protected persons or their relatives; (4) collects personal valuables left by certain protected persons; and (5) in occupied territory, has a special section that is responsible for identifying children whose identity is in doubt.

10.31.2.1 _Receiving and Forwarding Certain Information_. The National Protected Person Information Bureau receives certain information regarding protected persons from other departments of the State to which it belongs.[553]

Each National Protected Person Information Bureau shall immediately forward information concerning protected persons by the most rapid means to the Powers of whom these persons are nationals, or to Powers in whose territory they resided, through the intermediary of the Protecting Powers and likewise through the Central Information Agency for protected persons.[554]

10.31.2.2 _Replying to Inquiries Regarding Protected Persons_. The National Protected Person Information Bureau shall also reply to all inquiries that may be received regarding protected persons.[555] Responses to inquiries must be made consistent with the protection of protected persons against insults and public curiosity.[556]

10.31.2.3 _Withholding of Information When Detrimental to the Person or His or Her Relatives_. The National Protected Person Information Bureau shall transmit information concerning a protected person unless its transmission might be detrimental to the person concerned or to his or her relatives.[557] Even in such a case, the information may not be withheld from the Central Information Agency for protected persons, which, upon being notified of the circumstances, will take the necessary precautions indicated in Article 140 of the GC.[558] This rule seeks to protect persons who have fled persecution from their home governments, as well as

---

[553] GC art. 136 ("Each of the Parties to the conflict shall, within the shortest possible period, give its Bureau information of any measure taken by it concerning any protected persons who are kept in custody for more than two weeks, who are subjected to assigned residence or who are interned. It shall, furthermore, require its various departments concerned with such matters to provide the aforesaid Bureau promptly with information concerning all changes pertaining to these protected persons, as, for example, transfers, releases, repatriations, escapes, admittances to hospitals, births and deaths.").

[554] GC art. 137 ("Each national Bureau shall immediately forward information concerning protected persons by the most rapid means to the Powers of whom the aforesaid persons are nationals, or to Powers in whose territory they resided, through the intermediary of the Protecting Powers and likewise through the Central Agency provided for in Article 140.").

[555] GC art. 137 ("The Bureaux shall also reply to all enquiries which may be received regarding protected persons.").

[556] *Refer to* § 10.5.2 (Protection Against Insults and Public Curiosity).

[557] GC art. 137 ("Information Bureaux shall transmit information concerning a protected person unless its transmission might be detrimental to the person concerned or to his or her relatives.").

[558] GC art. 137 ("Even in such a case, the information may not be withheld from the Central Agency which, upon being notified of the circumstances, will take the necessary precautions indicated in Article 140.").

the family members of such persons.[559]

10.31.2.4 *Collection of Personal Valuables Left by Protected Persons*. Each National Protected Person Information Bureau shall be responsible for collecting all personal valuables left by protected persons mentioned in Article 136 of the GC, in particular those who have been repatriated or released, or who have escaped or died.[560] The National Protected Person Information Bureau shall forward these valuables to those concerned, either directly or, if necessary, through the Central Information Agency for protected persons.[561] Personal valuables may include wills, articles of sentimental value, or sums of money.[562] Such articles shall be sent by the National Protected Person Information Bureau in sealed packets, which shall be accompanied by statements giving clear and full identity particulars of the person to whom the articles belonged, and by a complete list of the contents of the parcel.[563] Detailed records shall be maintained of the receipt and sending of all such valuables.[564]

10.31.2.5 *Special Section for the Identification of Children in Occupied Territory*. In occupation, a special section of the National Protected Person Information Bureau shall be responsible for taking all necessary steps to identify children whose identity is in doubt.[565]

---

[559] GC COMMENTARY 531 ("This paragraph contains a provision not included in the Third Convention. It seeks to protect civilians in enemy hands and particularly their families in their country of origin, against the authorities of that country if they should have any reason for particular animosity towards them. This exceptional provision is based on the confused situations which occurred during the First World War. Civilians who have fled from persecution generally have an interest in remaining unknown to the authorities of their former country. They must therefore judge for themselves the expediency of notification to the authorities, even in the case of the forwarding of information to members of their family.").

[560] GC art. 139 ("Each national Information Bureau shall, furthermore, be responsible for collecting all personal valuables left by protected persons mentioned in Article 136, in particular those who have been repatriated or released, or who have escaped or died;").

[561] GC art. 139 ("[I]t shall forward the said valuables to those concerned, either direct, or, if necessary, through the Central Agency.").

[562] GC COMMENTARY 538 ("The term 'personal valuables' should be understood to mean all the articles which belonged to the person who is no longer there--whether he has been repatriated or has died--which are of any commercial worth or sentimental value. It must always be remembered that an article of absolutely no intrinsic worth may often have very great sentimental value for the next of kin of the deceased person. In practice, therefore, almost all the articles found on the spot will be collected and forwarded. The corresponding provision of the Third Convention (Article 122, paragraph 9) adds to the expression 'personal valuables' the words 'including sums in currencies other than that of the Detaining Power and documents of importance to the next of kin'. This expression has not been retained in the Fourth Convention mainly because it was considered that the term 'valuables' covered sums of money and that since the value of papers could be judged only by the next of kin, they should be forwarded to those persons, particularly if they seemed to be of a legal nature. It will be for the Detaining Power to decide what foreign currency may be sent if any. Among the documents which should be carefully kept are wills, which are particularly important.").

[563] GC art. 139 ("Such articles shall be sent by the Bureau in sealed packets which shall be accompanied by statements giving clear and full identity particulars of the person to whom the articles belonged, and by a complete list of the contents of the parcel.").

[564] GC art. 139 ("Detailed records shall be maintained of the receipt and despatch of all such valuables.").

[565] GC art. 50 ("A special section of the Bureau set up in accordance with Article 136 shall be responsible for taking all necessary steps to identify children whose identity is in doubt.").

Particulars of their parents or other near relatives should always be recorded if available.[566]

10.31.3 Central Information Agency for Protected Persons. A Central Information Agency for protected persons, in particular for internees, shall be created in a neutral country.[567] This agency may be the same as that provided for in Article 123 of the GPW.[568]

The function of the Central Information Agency for protected persons shall be to collect all information of the type set forth in Article 136 of the GC, which it may obtain through official or private channels, and to transmit it as rapidly as possible to the countries of origin or of residence of the persons concerned, except in cases where such transmissions might be detrimental to the persons whom this information concerns, or to their relatives.[569] The Central Information Agency for protected persons shall receive from the parties to the conflict all reasonable facilities for effecting such transmissions.[570] Parties to the GC, and in particular those States whose nationals benefit from the services of the Central Information Agency for protected persons, are requested to give the Central Information Agency for protected persons the financial aid it may require.[571]

The provisions of the GC establishing the Central Information Agency for protected persons do not restrict the humanitarian activities of the ICRC and of the relief societies described in Article 142 of the GC.[572]

The GC contemplates that the ICRC shall, if it deems necessary, propose to the Powers concerned the organization of a Central Information Agency for protected persons.[573] In fact, the role of the Central Information Agency for protected persons has been performed in many conflicts by the ICRC Central Tracing Agency, which has also performed this role for POWs.[574]

---

[566] GC art. 50 ("Particulars of their parents or other near relatives should always be recorded if available.").

[567] GC art. 140 ("A Central Information Agency for protected persons, in particular for internees, shall be created in a neutral country. The International Committee of the Red Cross shall, if it deems necessary, propose to the Powers concerned the organization of such an Agency, which may be the same as that provided for in Article 123 of the Geneva Convention relative to the Treatment of Prisoners of War of August 12, 1949.").

[568] *Refer to* § 9.31.3 (Central POW Information Agency).

[569] GC art. 140 ("The function of the Agency shall be to collect all information of the type set forth in Article 136 which it may obtain through official or private channels and to transmit it as rapidly as possible to the countries of origin or of residence of the persons concerned, except in cases where such transmissions might be detrimental to the persons whom the said information concerns, or to their relatives.").

[570] GC art. 140 ("It shall receive from the Parties to the conflict all reasonable facilities for effecting such transmissions.").

[571] GC art. 140 ("The High Contracting Parties, and in particular those whose nationals benefit by the services of the Central Agency, are requested to give the said Agency the financial aid it may require.").

[572] GC art. 140 ("The foregoing provisions shall in no way be interpreted as restricting the humanitarian activities of the International Committee of the Red Cross and of the relief societies described in Article 142.").

[573] GC art. 140 ("The International Committee of the Red Cross shall, if it deems necessary, propose to the Powers concerned the organization of such an Agency, which may be the same as that provided for in Article 123 of the Geneva Convention relative to the Treatment of Prisoners of War of August 12, 1949.").

[574] *Refer to* § 9.31.3 (Central POW Information Agency).

10.31.4 U.S. Practice in Reporting to the ICRC Central Tracing Agency. For the United States, the functions of the National Protected Person Information Bureau have been performed by the same entity that performs the functions of the National POW Information Bureau: the National Prisoner of War Information Center or the National Detainee Reporting Center.[575] This organization has provided information to the ICRC Central Tracing Agency, acting as the Central Information Agency for protected persons under the GC.

10.31.5 Exemption of National Protected Person Information Bureau and Central Information Agency for Protected Persons From Certain Charges. The National Protected Person Information Bureau and the Central Information Agency for protected persons shall enjoy free postage for mail, all the exemptions provided for in Article 110 of the GC,[576] and, further, so far as possible, exemption from telegraphic charges or, at least, greatly reduced rates.[577]

The National Protected Person Information Bureau and the Central Information Agency for protected persons shall also enjoy exemption from postal charges in respect of letter-post items, postal parcels, and monetary articles that concern internees, which they send or receive, either directly or as intermediaries, under the conditions laid down in the Universal Postal Convention.[578] Such items exempt from postal charges should be marked appropriately.[579]

10.32 Role of the Protecting Power in the GC

The Protecting Power is an organ for ensuring implementation of the GC. The Protecting Power has extensive duties under the GC. It transmits information between belligerents, monitors compliance with the GC, and takes an active role in promoting the welfare of protected persons.

10.32.1 Transmission of Information Between Belligerents. The Protecting Power helps transmit information between belligerents, including:

---

[575] *Refer to* § 9.31.4 (U.S. Practice in Reporting to the ICRC Central Tracing Agency).

[576] *Refer to* § 10.23.4 (Exemption From Postal and Shipping Charges for Shipments To and From Internees).

[577] GC art. 141 ("The national Information Bureaux and the Central Information Agency shall enjoy free postage for all mail, likewise the exemptions provided for in Article 110, and further, so far as possible, exemption from telegraphic charges or, at least, greatly reduced rates.").

[578] Universal Postal Convention, art. 17(3), Dec. 14, 1989, 1687 UNTS 241, 252 ("The national Information Bureaux and the Central Information Agencies mentioned above shall also enjoy exemption from postal charges in respect of letter-post items, postal parcels and monetary articles which concern the persons referred to in paragraphs 1 and 2, which they send or receive, either direct or as intermediaries, under the conditions laid down in those paragraphs."). *Consider* Letter Post Regulations, Article RL 111 to Article 7 of the Universal Postal Convention of Oct. 11, 2012, *reprinted in* International Bureau of the Universal Postal Union, Letter Post Manual, page C.10, C.10-11 (Berne 2013, Update 2 – Jan. 2015) ("The following shall enjoy exemption from postal charges within the meaning of article 7.2 of the Convention: … 1.3 the Information Bureaux provided for in article 136 of the Geneva Convention of 12 August 1949 relative to the protection of civilian persons in time of war; 1.4 the Central Information Agency provided for in article 140 of the latter Convention.").

[579] *Refer to* § 10.23.4.3 (Exemption From Postal Charges Under the Universal Postal Convention).

- useful information regarding the geographic location of places of internment;[580]

- accountability information concerning measures that States have taken with respect to protected persons in their power;[581]

- legal documents of internees;[582]

- copies of the records of the death of internees;[583]

- notification of measures taken by the Detaining Powers, immediately upon interning protected persons, for executing the provisions of the GC that address relations between internees and the exterior;[584] and

- official translations of the GC and of laws and regulations that parties to the conflict have adopted to implement it.[585]

10.32.2 Monitoring or Inspecting Compliance With the GC. The Protecting Power monitors or inspects the Detaining Power's compliance with the GC, including by:

- visiting places where protected persons are and interviewing them;[586]

- receiving petitions and complaints from internees and periodic reports from the Internee Committees;[587]

- communicating with members of the Internee Committees and receiving the reasons for any refusal or dismissal of a member of an Internee Committee;[588]

- receiving up-to-date lists of labor detachments so its representatives may visit them;[589]

- inspecting records of disciplinary punishments maintained by the commandant of the

---

[580] *Refer to* § 10.11.1.2 (Sharing Information on the Location of Places of Internment).

[581] *Refer to* § 10.31 (National Accounting for Protected Persons in Its Power).

[582] *Refer to* § 10.24.2 (Legal Documents and Assistance).

[583] *Refer to* § 10.34.2 (Death Certificates).

[584] *Refer to* § 10.2.2.2 (Notification of Measures Taken for Implementing GC Provisions That Address Relations Between Internees and the Exterior).

[585] GC art. 145 ("The High Contracting Parties shall communicate to one another through the Swiss Federal Council and, during hostilities, through the Protecting Powers, the official translations of the present Convention, as well as the laws and regulations which they may adopt to ensure the application thereof.").

[586] *Refer to* § 10.33.1 (Access by Protecting Powers).

[587] *Refer to* § 10.21.1 (Internee Right to Present Petitions and Complaints); § 10.21.3 (Periodic Reports by the Internee Committees).

[588] *Refer to* § 10.22.1.1 (Approval of Internee Committee Members by the Detaining Authorities).

[589] *Refer to* § 10.17.5 (Labor Detachments of Internees).

place of internment;[590]

- receiving notice if military necessity should require that the quantity of individual parcels or collective shipments be limited;[591]
- receiving statements of internee accounts;[592] and
- receiving communications and subsequent reports of death or serious injury of an internee in certain cases.[593]

10.32.3 Actively Working to Improve the Welfare of Protected Persons. In other instances, the GC contemplates that the Protecting Power will actively work to improve the welfare of protected persons, such as by:

- providing internees with allowances;[594]
- setting up special means of transport to ensure the conveyance of relief shipments to internees;[595] and
- lending its good offices with a view towards settling disagreements as to application or interpretation of the provisions of the GC between parties to the conflict.[596]

10.33 Access to Internees by Protecting Powers, ICRC, and Other Relief Organizations

10.33.1 Access by Protecting Powers. Representatives or delegates of the Protecting Powers shall have permission to go to all places where protected persons are, particularly to places of internment, detention, and work.[597] They shall have access to all premises occupied by protected persons and shall be able to interview the latter without witnesses, personally or through an interpreter.[598] Such visits may not be prohibited except for reasons of imperative military necessity, and then only as an exceptional and temporary measure.[599] Their duration

---

[590] *Refer to* § 10.28.4 (Record of Disciplinary Punishments).

[591] *Refer to* § 10.23.3 (Receipt of Individual and Collective Relief Shipments for Internees).

[592] *Refer to* § 10.19.3.2 (Account Statement).

[593] *Refer to* § 10.34.5 (Inquiries Into Death or Serious Injury of Internees in Certain Cases).

[594] *Refer to* § 10.19.2 (Internee Allowances).

[595] *Refer to* § 10.23.5 (Special Means of Transport of Shipments to Internees).

[596] *Refer to* § 18.15.4 (Lending of Good Offices to Assist in Dispute Resolution).

[597] GC art. 143 ("Representatives or delegates of the Protecting Powers shall have permission to go to all places where protected persons are, particularly to places of internment, detention and work.").

[598] GC art. 143 ("They shall have access to all premises occupied by protected persons and shall be able to interview the latter without witnesses, personally or through an interpreter.").

[599] GC art. 143 ("Such visits may not be prohibited except for reasons of imperative military necessity, and then only as an exceptional and temporary measure.").

and frequency must not be restricted.[600]

Such representatives and delegates shall have full liberty to select the places they wish to visit.[601]

10.33.1.1 *Participation of Compatriots of Internees in Visits*. The Detaining or Occupying Power, the Protecting Power, and, when the occasion arises, the Power of origin of the persons to be visited, may agree that compatriots of the internees shall be permitted to participate in the visits.[602]

10.33.1.2 *ICRC Delegates Enjoying the Same Prerogatives of Access*. The delegates of the ICRC shall also enjoy the prerogatives as those of the representatives and delegates of the Protecting Powers described in Article 143 of the GC.[603]

The appointment of such delegates shall be submitted to the approval of the Power governing the territories where they will carry out their duties.[604]

10.33.2 Access by Relief Societies and Other Organizations. Subject to the measures that the Detaining Powers may consider essential to ensure their security, or to meet any other reasonable need, the representatives of religious organizations, relief societies, or any other organizations assisting the protected persons shall receive from these Powers all facilities for visiting the protected persons; for distributing relief supplies and material from any source intended for educational, recreational, or religious purposes; or for assisting them in organizing their leisure time within the places of internment.[605] Such societies or organizations may be constituted in occupied territory, in the territory of the Detaining Power, or in any other country, or they may have an international character.[606]

10.33.2.1 *Limitations on the Number of Relief Organizations*. The Detaining Power may limit the number of societies and organizations whose delegates are allowed to carry

---

[600] GC art. 143 ("Their duration and frequency shall not be restricted.").

[601] GC art. 143 ("Such representatives and delegates shall have full liberty to select the places they wish to visit.").

[602] GC art. 143 ("The Detaining or Occupying Power, the Protecting Power and when occasion arises the Power of origin of the persons to be visited, may agree that compatriots of the internees shall be permitted to participate in the visits.").

[603] GC art. 143 ("The delegates of the International Committee of the Red Cross shall also enjoy the above prerogatives.").

[604] GC art. 143 ("The appointment of such delegates shall be submitted to the approval of the Power governing the territories where they will carry out their duties.").

[605] GC art. 142 ("Subject to the measures which the Detaining Powers may consider essential to ensure their security or to meet any other reasonable need, the representatives of religious organizations, relief societies, or any other organizations assisting the protected persons, shall receive from these Powers, for themselves or their duly accredited agents, all facilities for visiting the protected persons, for distributing relief supplies and material from any source, intended for educational, recreational or religious purposes, or for assisting them in organizing their leisure time within the places of internment.").

[606] GC art. 142 ("Such societies or organizations may be constituted in the territory of the Detaining Power, or in any other country, or they may have an international character.").

out their activities in its territory and under its supervision, on condition, however, that such limitation shall not hinder the supply of effective and adequate relief to all protected persons.[607] The special position of the ICRC in this field shall be recognized and respected at all times.[608]

10.34 DEATH OF INTERNEES

10.34.1 Transmittal of Wills. The Detaining Power has an obligation to help internees with their wills, such as by receiving them for safe-keeping.[609] In the event of the death of an internee, his or her will shall be transmitted without delay to a person whom he or she has previously designated.[610]

10.34.2 Death Certificates. Deaths of internees shall be certified in every case by a doctor, and a death certificate shall be made out, showing the causes of death and the conditions under which it occurred.[611]

An official record of the death, duly registered, shall be drawn up in accordance with the procedure relating thereto in force in the territory where the place of internment is situated, and a duly certified copy of such record shall be transmitted without delay to the Protecting Power and to the Central Information Agency for protected persons.[612]

10.34.3 Burial or Cremation and Inurnment. The detaining authorities shall ensure that internees who die while interned are honorably buried, if possible according to the rites of the religion to which they belonged.[613]

Deceased internees shall be buried in individual graves unless unavoidable circumstances require the use of collective graves.[614] For example, an epidemic or military operations may require the Detaining Power to undertake collective burials in the interest of public health

---

[607] GC art. 142 ("The Detaining Power may limit the number of societies and organizations whose delegates are allowed to carry out their activities in its territory and under its supervision, on condition, however, that such limitation shall not hinder the supply of effective and adequate relief to all protected persons.").

[608] GC art. 142 ("The special position of the International Committee of the Red Cross in this field shall be recognized and respected at all times.").

[609] *Refer to* § 10.24.2 (Legal Documents and Assistance).

[610] GC art. 129 ("[I]n the event of the death of an internee his will shall be transmitted without delay to a person whom he has previously designated.").

[611] GC art. 129 ("Deaths of internees shall be certified in every case by a doctor, and a death certificate shall be made out, showing the causes of death and the conditions under which it occurred.").

[612] GC art. 129 ("An official record of the death, duly registered, shall be drawn up in accordance with the procedure relating thereto in force in the territory where the place of internment is situated, and a duly certified copy of such record shall be transmitted without delay to the Protecting Power as well as to the Central Agency referred to in Article 140.").

[613] GC art. 130 ("The detaining authorities shall ensure that internees who die while interned are honourably buried, if possible according to the rites of the religion to which they belonged, … .").

[614] GC art. 130 ("Deceased internees shall be buried in individual graves unless unavoidable circumstances require the use of collective graves.").

because individual graves are not possible due to lack of time and resources.[615]

10.34.3.1 _Cremation_. Bodies of internees may be cremated only for imperative reasons of hygiene, on account of the religion of the deceased, or in accordance with his or her expressed wish to this effect.[616] In case of cremation, the fact shall be stated and the reasons given in the death certificate of the deceased.[617] The ashes shall be retained for safe-keeping by the detaining authorities and shall be transferred as soon as possible to the next of kin on their request.[618]

10.34.4 Maintenance and Records of Graves and Ashes. The detaining authorities shall ensure that the graves of internees who die while interned are respected, properly maintained, and marked in such a way that they can always be recognized.[619] Ideally, the markings on the graves should contain at least the surname, first name, and date of birth of the dead person in detail and in a durable fashion.[620]

As soon as circumstances permit, and not later than the close of hostilities, the Detaining Power shall forward lists of graves of deceased internees to the Powers on whom the deceased internees depended, through the National Protected Person Information Bureau.[621] Such lists shall include all particulars necessary for the identification of the deceased internees, as well as the exact location of their graves.[622]

10.34.5 Inquiries Into Death or Serious Injury of Internees in Certain Cases. Every death or serious injury of an internee, caused or suspected to have been caused by a sentry, another

---

[615] GC COMMENTARY 507 ("However desirable it may be to have individual graves properly marked, advocated as the general practice by the Convention, the Article does allow of exceptions. These would be valid for reasons of *force majeure*, during an epidemic, for example, if the death of an excessively large number of persons created a danger of infection which did not allow time for the digging of individual graves, or again if warlike operations obliged the Detaining Power to retreat and before retreating and from lack of time it undertook collective burials in the interests of public health.").

[616] GC art. 130 ("Bodies may be cremated only for imperative reasons of hygiene, on account of the religion of the deceased or in accordance with his expressed wish to this effect.").

[617] GC art. 130 ("In case of cremation, the fact shall be stated and the reasons given in the death certificate of the deceased.").

[618] GC art. 130 ("The ashes shall be retained for safe-keeping by the detaining authorities and shall be transferred as soon as possible to the next of kin on their request.").

[619] GC art. 130 ("The detaining authorities shall ensure … that their graves are respected, properly maintained, and marked in such a way that they can always be recognized.").

[620] GC COMMENTARY 506-07 ("The Convention does not state how graves should be marked. The practice of placing individual markings on the grave showing the surname, first name and date of birth of the dead person in detail and in a durable fashion, is, however, particularly to be recommended to belligerents wishing to fulfill their obligations. The same applies to ashes in the case of cremation, as mentioned in the following paragraph.").

[621] GC art. 130 ("As soon as circumstances permit, and not later than the close of hostilities, the Detaining Power shall forward lists of graves of deceased internees to the Powers on whom the deceased internees depended, through the Information Bureaux provided for in Article 136.").

[622] GC art. 130 ("Such lists shall include all particulars necessary for the identification of the deceased internees, as well as the exact location of their graves.").

internee, or any other person, as well as any death the cause of which is unknown, shall be immediately followed by an official inquiry by the Detaining Power.[623] A communication on this subject shall be sent immediately to the Protecting Power.[624]

Serious injury, in many cases, may be understood to mean a wound that requires in-patient treatment at a hospital or infirmary.[625]

The evidence of any witnesses shall be taken, and a report including such evidence shall be prepared and forwarded to the Protecting Power.[626]

If the inquiry indicates the guilt of one or more persons, the Detaining Power shall take all necessary steps to ensure the prosecution of the person or persons responsible.[627] For example, depending on the circumstances, prosecutions could take place in the civil or military courts of the Detaining Power or in accordance with the laws in force in the territory where they happen to be interned.[628]

10.35 RELEASE, RETURN, REPATRIATION OF INTERNEES AFTER THE CLOSE OF HOSTILITIES

10.35.1 Cessation of Internment After the Close of Hostilities. Internment shall cease as soon as possible after the close of hostilities.[629] The GC, however, does not preclude internment after the close of hostilities.[630] For example, internment may be necessary during occupation after hostilities have ended.

---

[623] GC art. 131 ("Every death or serious injury of an internee, caused or suspected to have been caused by a sentry, another internee or any other person, as well as any death the cause of which is unknown, shall be immediately followed by an official enquiry by the Detaining Power.").

[624] GC art. 131 ("A communication on this subject shall be sent immediately to the Protecting Power.").

[625] GC COMMENTARY 509 ("What is meant by 'serious injury'? During the discussion of the corresponding text concerning prisoners of war, one delegation suggested that it should be made clear that what was referred to was a wound as a result of which a prisoner required in-patient treatment in a hospital or an infirmary. This definition was considered too rigid and was therefore not inserted in the Convention, but it could usefully be adopted in most cases."). *Compare* § 9.34.5 (Inquiries Into Death or Serious Injury of POWs in Certain Cases).

[626] GC art. 131 ("The evidence of any witnesses shall be taken, and a report including such evidence shall be prepared and forwarded to the said Protecting Power.").

[627] GC art. 131 ("If the enquiry indicates the guilt of one or more persons, the Detaining Power shall take all necessary steps to ensure the prosecution of the person or persons responsible.").

[628] GC COMMENTARY 510 ("If the enquiry leads to responsibility being laid at the door of one or more persons, whoever they may be, they must be prosecuted before a court of law. If they are nationals of the Detaining Power, that Power will not be able to exempt them from prosecution before its own civil or military courts. In the case of internees, they will be prosecuted in accordance with the laws in force in the teritory [sic] where they happen to be (Article 117, paragraph 1).").

[629] GC art. 133 ("Internment shall cease as soon as possible after the close of hostilities.").

[630] *See* II-A FINAL RECORD OF THE DIPLOMATIC CONFERENCE OF GENEVA OF 1949 844 ("The only change effected in the Stockholm text is the deletion of the words 'and, in occupied territories, at the close of occupation' in the first paragraph. The reason for the deletion was that the close of occupation necessarily means that internment by the Occupying Power comes to an end. The Committee did not accept the view that the retention of the remainder of the paragraph, i.e. the phrase 'Internment shall cease as soon as possible after the close of hostilities' bore the implication that no person could be interned after the close of hostilities.").

10.35.1.1 *Close of Hostilities*. The phrase "close of hostilities" should be understood in the same sense as the phrase "cessation of active hostilities" in the GPW.[631]

10.35.1.2 *Internees Subject to Penal Proceedings or Punishment*. Internees in the territory of a party to the conflict, against whom penal proceedings are pending for offenses not exclusively subject to disciplinary penalties, may be detained until the close of such proceedings and, if circumstances require, until the completion of the penalty.[632] The same shall apply to internees who have been previously sentenced to a punishment depriving them of liberty.[633]

10.35.2 Return to the Last Place of Residence or Repatriation. The Parties to the GC shall endeavor, upon the close of hostilities or occupation, to ensure the return of all internees to their last place of residence, or to facilitate their repatriation.[634]

10.35.2.1 *Internees Who Resist Repatriation*. Internees who resist repatriation need not be forcibly repatriated.[635] A similar rule applies to POWs.[636] U.S. policy provides that no person shall be transferred to another State if it is more likely than not that the person would be tortured in the receiving country.[637]

10.35.3 Committees to Search for Dispersed Internees. By agreement between the Detaining Power and the Powers concerned, committees may be set up after the close of hostilities, or after the close of the occupation of territories, to search for dispersed internees.[638]

10.35.4 Costs of Returning Internees. The Detaining Power shall bear the expense of returning released internees to the places where they were residing when interned, or, if it took them into custody while they were in transit or on the high seas, the cost of completing their

---

[631] GC COMMENTARY 514-15 ("The expression 'the close of hostilities' should be taken to mean a state of fact rather than the legal situation covered by laws or decrees fixing the date of cessation of hostilities. The similar provision concerning prisoners of war speaks of 'the cessation of active hostilities' and the wording of the paragraph here should be understood in the same sense."). *Refer to* § 9.37.2 (Cessation of Active Hostilities).

[632] GC art. 133 ("Internees in the territory of a Party to the conflict, against whom penal proceedings are pending for offences not exclusively subject to disciplinary penalties, may be detained until the close of such proceedings and, if circumstances require, until the completion of the penalty.").

[633] GC art. 133 ("The same shall apply to internees who have been previously sentenced to a punishment depriving them of liberty.").

[634] GC art. 134 ("The High Contracting Parties shall endeavour, upon the close of hostilities or occupation, to ensure the return of all internees to their last place of residence, or to facilitate their repatriation.").

[635] GC COMMENTARY 519 ("[I]t would be contrary to the spirit of the Convention if an internee could be forcibly repatriated when he feared persecution in his country of origin for his political opinions or his religious beliefs. In such a case he would become a refugee, obliged to seek a new domicile in a country different from the one in which he is living.").

[636] *Refer to* § 9.37.4.2 (POWs Who Resist Repatriation).

[637] *Refer to* § 8.14.4.1 (U.S. Policy Prohibiting Transfers in Cases in Which Detainees Would Likely Be Tortured).

[638] GC art. 133 ("By agreement between the Detaining Power and the Powers concerned, committees may be set up after the close of hostilities, or of the occupation of territories, to search for dispersed internees.").

journey or of their return to their point of departure.[639]

Where a Detaining Power refuses permission to reside in its territory to a released internee who previously had his or her permanent domicile there, such Detaining Power shall pay the cost of this internee's repatriation.[640] If, however, the internee elects to return to his or her country on his or her own responsibility or in obedience to the Government of the Power to which he or she owes allegiance, the Detaining Power need not pay the expenses of his or her journey beyond the point of his or her departure from its territory.[641]

The Detaining Power need not pay the costs of repatriation of an internee who was interned at his or her own request.[642]

If internees are transferred in accordance with Article 45 of the GC, the transferring and receiving Powers shall agree on the portion of the above costs to be borne by each.[643]

The foregoing discussion shall not prejudice such special agreements as may be concluded between parties to the conflict concerning the exchange and repatriation of their nationals in enemy hands.[644]

---

[639] GPW art. 135 ("The Detaining Power shall bear the expense of returning released internees to the places where they were residing when interned, or, if it took them into custody while they were in transit or on the high seas, the cost of completing their journey or of their return to their point of departure.").

[640] GPW art. 135 ("Where a Detaining Power refuses permission to reside in its territory to a released internee who previously had his permanent domicile therein, such Detaining Power shall pay the cost of the said internee's repatriation.").

[641] GPW art. 135 ("If, however, the internee elects to return to his country on his own responsibility or in obedience to the Government of the Power to which he owes allegiance, the Detaining Power need not pay the expenses of his journey beyond the point of his departure from its territory.").

[642] GPW art. 135 ("The Detaining Power need not pay the costs of repatriation of an internee who was interned at his own request.").

[643] GPW art. 135 ("If internees are transferred in accordance with Article 45, the transferring and receiving Powers shall agree on the portion of the above costs to be borne by each.").

[644] GC art. 135 ("The foregoing shall not prejudice such special agreements as may be concluded between Parties to the conflict concerning the exchange and repatriation of their nationals in enemy hands.").

XI – Military Occupation

Chapter Contents

11.1 Introduction

This Chapter addresses military occupation. The GC provides specific rules for the internment of protected persons in occupation, which are addressed in Chapter X.

Military occupation is a temporary measure for administering territory under the control of invading forces, and involves a complicated, trilateral set of legal relations between the Occupying Power, the temporarily ousted sovereign authority, and the inhabitants of occupied territory.[1]

The law of belligerent occupation seeks to account for both military and humanitarian imperatives. The Occupying Power's primary objective in conducting military occupation is to further the purpose of the war in which the occupying forces are engaged and to ensure the maintenance and security of those forces, but the Occupying Power is also bound to provide for

---

[1] *Refer to* § 11.4 (Legal Position of the Occupying Power).

the interests and welfare of the civilian population of the occupied territory.[2] The Occupying Power has obligations related to the maintenance of public order and safety, and the protection of civilians and property in occupied territory.[3]

11.1.1 Military Occupation – Notes on Terminology.

11.1.1.1 *Military Occupation, Military Government, Belligerent Occupation, and Martial Law*. The practice of conducting military occupation is very old, and the law of military occupation has long been part of the law of war.[4] Military occupation is also called belligerent occupation. The conduct of military occupation has also been characterized as an exercise of "military government"[5] or "martial law."[6]

---

[2] GREENSPAN, THE MODERN LAW OF LAND WARFARE 213 ("In considering the law on military occupation the dual nature of such an occupation must be borne in mind. Its primary objective is to further the purpose of the war in which the occupying forces are engaged and to ensure the maintenance and security of those forces; yet at the same time the occupant is bound to provide for the interests and welfare of the civilian population of the occupied territory.").

[3] *Refer to* § 11.5 (Duty of the Occupying Power to Ensure Public Order and Safety).

[4] *See, e.g.*, American Ins. Co. v. 356 Bales of Cotton, 26 U.S. 511, 542 (1828) (Marshall, C.J.) ("The usage of the world is, if a nation be not entirely subdued, to consider the holding of conquered territory as a mere military occupation, until its fate shall be determined at the treaty of peace."); Thirty Hogsheads of Sugar v. Boyle, 13 U.S. 191, 195 (1815) (Marshall, C.J.) ("Some doubt has been suggested whether Santa Cruz, while in the possession of Great Britain, could properly be considered as a British island. But for this doubt there can be no foundation. Although acquisitions made during war are not considered as permanent until confirmed by treaty, yet to every commercial and belligerent purpose, they are considered as a part of the domain of the conqueror, so long as he retains the possession and government of them. The island of Santa Cruz, after its capitulation, remained a British island until it was restored to Denmark."). *See also* WINTHROP, MILITARY LAW & PRECEDENTS 800-01 ("Instances in our history of military government are presented in our Revolutionary war during the occupancy by the British of Boston, New York and Philadelphia; at Castine, Maine, when taken and held by the British in 1814-15; and in the provinces of Mexico in the course of the conquest of the same by our forces in 1846-7. It was however during the late civil war, which, by reasons of its exceptional proportions, was assimilated to an international war, that Military Government was more generally and variously exercised, and its nature more fully illustrated than at any previous period of our history.").

[5] WINTHROP, MILITARY LAW & PRECEDENTS 799 ("By *military government* is meant that dominion exercised in war by a belligerent power over territory of the enemy invaded and occupied by him and over the inhabitants thereof. By most writers, prior to the appearance of the dissenting opinion of Chase, C.J., in *Ex parte* Milligan, this species of government was designated in general terms as 'martial law,' and thus was confused with or not properly distinguished from the *martial law proper* exerted at home under circumstances of emergency, and yet to be considered."); Ex parte Milligan, 71 U.S. 2, 141-42 (1866) (Chase, C.J., separate opinion) ("There are under the Constitution three kinds of military jurisdiction: one to be exercised both in peace and war; another to be exercised in time of foreign war without the boundaries of the United States, or in time of rebellion and civil war within states or districts occupied by rebels treated as belligerents; and a third to be exercised in time of invasion or insurrection within the limits of the United States, or during rebellion within the limits of states maintaining adhesion to the National Government, when the public danger requires its exercise. The first of these may be called jurisdiction under MILITARY LAW, and is found in acts of Congress prescribing rules and articles of war, or otherwise providing for the government of the national forces; the second may be distinguished as MILITARY GOVERNMENT, superseding, as far as may be deemed expedient, the local law, and exercised by the military commander under the direction of the President, with the express or implied sanction of Congress; while the third may be denominated MARTIAL LAW PROPER, and is called into action by Congress, or temporarily, when the action of Congress cannot be invited, and in the case of justifying or excusing peril, by the President, in times of

This manual uses the terms "military occupation," "belligerent occupation," and "occupation" to refer to situations governed by the law of belligerent occupation.

11.1.1.2 *Occupying Power, Occupant, and Occupying State*. Treaties or other legal documents may refer to the State conducting the occupation as the "Occupying Power," "Occupying State," or "occupant." This manual uses the term "Occupying Power" to refer to a State conducting an occupation.

In some cases, multiple States may conduct an occupation together, and each State may be considered an Occupying Power.[7]

11.1.2 Military Occupation and Bodies of International Law.

11.1.2.1 *Military Occupation and Other Law of War Rules*. In general, the law of war rules that are not specific to the occupation of enemy territory continue to apply to situations that are addressed by those rules that may arise during occupation. For example, the rules for the conduct of hostilities and the humane treatment of detainees apply also to combat operations and detention operations, respectively, during occupation.

However, the fact of occupation triggers the application of additional rules specific to occupation.[8]

11.1.2.2 *Occupation and the Hague IV Regulations*. Articles 42 through 56 of the Hague IV Regulations address military occupation.

When the GC and the Hague IV Regulations are both applicable, the provisions of the GC regarding occupation supplement the provisions of the Hague IV Regulations regarding occupation.[9]

When the 1954 Hague Cultural Property Convention and the Hague IV Regulations are both applicable, the provisions of the 1954 Hague Cultural Property Convention regarding

---

insurrection or invasion, or of civil or foreign war, within districts or localities where ordinary law no longer adequately secures public safety and private rights.").

[6] LIEBER CODE art. 1 ("A place, district, or country occupied by an enemy stands, in consequence of the occupation, under the Martial Law of the invading or occupying army, whether any proclamation declaring Martial Law, or any public warning to the inhabitants, has been issued or not. Martial Law is the immediate and direct effect and consequence of occupation or conquest. The presence of a hostile army proclaims its Martial Law.").

[7] *For example*, Supplemental Brief of the United States, Apr. 22, 2005, United States of America ex rel. DR, Inc. v. Custer Battles, LLC, 376 F. Supp. 2d 617 (E.D. Va. 2005), 2005 DIGEST OF UNITED STATES PRACTICE IN INTERNATIONAL LAW 228, 232 ("The United States and the United Kingdom, and other member states of the Coalition were the occupying powers in Iraq under the laws and usages of war. The CPA was the administrative device that the Coalition created under the laws and usages of war to perform civil government functions in liberated Iraq during the brief period of occupation. As an active member of the Coalition, the United States played an important role in, and had certain responsibilities for, the occupation, which it chose to fulfill through creation of and participation in the CPA.").

[8] *Refer to* § 11.2 (When Military Occupation Law Applies).

[9] *Refer to* § 19.16.5.2 (Relationship Between the GC and the 1899 Hague II and the 1907 Hague IV Conventions).

occupation supplement the provisions of the Hague IV Regulations regarding occupation.[10]

Although in some cases the Hague IV Regulations would not be applicable as a matter of treaty law because belligerent States might not be Parties to Hague IV, many of the provisions in Articles 42 through 56 of the Hague IV Regulations reflect customary international law.[11] For example, Article 42 of the Hague IV Regulations, which provides a standard for when the law of belligerent occupation applies, is regarded as customary international law.[12]

11.1.2.3 Occupation and the 1949 Geneva Conventions. Common Article 2 of the 1949 Geneva Conventions provides that "[t]he Convention shall also apply to all cases of partial or total occupation of the territory of a High Contracting Party, even if the said occupation meets with no armed resistance."[13]

Articles 47 through 78 of the GC specifically address occupied territories.[14] Other provisions of the GC also apply to occupied territory. For example, Articles 27 through 34 of the GC contain provisions common to the territories of parties to the conflict and to occupied territories.[15]

11.1.2.4 Occupation and the 1954 Hague Cultural Property Convention. The 1954 Hague Cultural Property Convention applies to all cases of partial or total occupation of the territory of a High Contracting Party, even if this occupation meets with no armed resistance.[16]

The 1954 Hague Cultural Property Convention and the Regulations for the Execution of the 1954 Hague Cultural Property Convention also have provisions that explicitly address occupation.[17]

---

[10] *Refer to* § 19.17.1.1 (Relationship Between the 1954 Hague Cultural Property Convention and Certain 1899 and 1907 Hague Conventions).

[11] *See, e.g.*, United States, *et al.* v. Göring, *et al.*, *Judgment*, I TRIAL OF THE MAJOR WAR CRIMINALS BEFORE THE IMT 253-54 ("With respect to War Crimes, however, as has already been pointed out, the crimes defined by Article 6, Section (b), of the Charter were already recognized as War Crimes under international law. They were covered by Articles 46, 50, 52, and 56 of the Hague Convention of 1907, and Articles 2, 3, 4, 46, and 51 of the Geneva Convention of 1929. … But it is argued that the Hague Convention does not apply in this case, because of the 'general participation' clause in Article 2 of the Hague Convention of 1907. … The rules of land warfare expressed in the Convention undoubtedly represented an advance over existing international law at the time of their adoption. But the convention expressly stated that it was an attempt 'to revise the general laws and customs of war', which it thus recognized to be then existing, but by 1939 these rules laid down in the Convention were recognized by all civilized nations, and were regarded as being declaratory of the laws and customs of war which are referred to in Article 6 (b) of the Charter.").

[12] *Refer to* § 11.2.2 (Standard for Determining When Territory Is Considered Occupied).

[13] GWS art. 2; GWS-SEA art. 2; GPW art. 2; GC art. 2.

[14] *Refer to* § 19.16.5.1 (Application of Different Parts of the GC).

[15] *Refer to* § 19.16.5.1 (Application of Different Parts of the GC).

[16] 1954 HAGUE CULTURAL PROPERTY CONVENTION art. 18 ("The Convention shall also apply to all cases of partial or total occupation of the territory of a High Contracting Party, even if the said occupation meets with no armed resistance.").

[17] *Refer to* § 11.19 (Protection of Cultural Property During Occupation).

11.1.2.5 <u>Occupation and U.N. Security Council Resolutions</u>. The U.N. Security Council may call upon Occupying Powers to comply with existing international law.[18]

Acting under the Charter of the United Nations, the U.N. Security Council may also establish authorities or limitations that might interact with those otherwise applicable under occupation law.[19] For example, a U.N. Security Council authorization may provide additional authority for an Occupying Power to govern occupied territory.[20]

In cases of conflict with obligations in other treaties or under customary international law, such obligations provided by the U.N. Security Council may prevail.[21] Thus, such authority may be used to take action that would not otherwise be permissible under the law of belligerent occupation.

11.1.2.6 <u>Occupation and the ICCPR and Other Human Rights Treaties</u>. It has been the U.S. view that the International Covenant on Civil and Political Rights (ICCPR) does not create obligations for an Occupying Power with respect to occupied territory because a contracting State's obligations under the ICCPR only extend to persons within its territory and subject to its jurisdiction.[22] Although persons within occupied territory are subject to the jurisdiction of the Occupying Power for certain purposes, they are not within the Occupying Power's national territory. This limit to the scope of the ICCPR's obligations was proposed by the United States to preclude the creation of obligations for States with respect to territories that

---

[18] *For example*, U.N. SECURITY COUNCIL RESOLUTION 1483, U.N. Doc. S/RES/1483, ¶5 (May 22, 2003) ("*Calls upon* all concerned to comply fully with their obligations under international law including in particular the Geneva Conventions of 1949 and the Hague Regulations of 1907;").

[19] *For example*, John B. Bellinger, III, Legal Adviser, Department of State, *United Nations Security Council Resolutions and the Application of International Humanitarian Law, Human Rights and Refugee Law*, Sept. 9, 2005, 2005 DIGEST OF UNITED STATES PRACTICE IN INTERNATIONAL LAW 957-58 ("Prior to the Iraq intervention, lawyers for the United States and its Coalition partners thoroughly analyzed a complex range of issues related to the expected occupation of Iraq. This review involved developing an understanding of how the law of occupation—in particular the Hague Regulations and Geneva Convention—would likely apply to Coalition activities. At the same time, there already existed a broad and complex range of Chapter VII Security Council resolutions addressing a number of issues, including Iraqi requirements to disarm, economic and arms embargos, and restrictions related to the production and sale of Iraqi petroleum products. As the Coalition analyzed the principles of occupation law, we were careful also to analyze the extent to which pre-existing Chapter VII resolutions included provisions that might themselves establish authorities or limitations that might interact with those otherwise applicable under occupation law.").

[20] *For example*, U.N. SECURITY COUNCIL RESOLUTION 1483, U.N. Doc. S/RES/1483, ¶4 (May 22, 2003) ("*Calls upon* the Authority, consistent with the Charter of the United Nations and other relevant international law, to promote the welfare of the Iraqi people through the effective administration of the territory, including in particular working towards the restoration of conditions of security and stability and the creation of conditions in which the Iraqi people can freely determine their own political future;"); Coalition Provisional Authority Regulation No. 1, §1(1) (May 16, 2003) ("The CPA is vested with all executive, legislative and judicial authority necessary to achieve its objectives, to be exercised under relevant U.N. Security Council resolutions, including Resolution 1483 (2003), and the laws and usages of war. This authority shall be exercised by the CPA Administrator.").

[21] *Refer to* § 1.11.2.1 (U.N. Member State Obligations With Respect to U.N. Security Council Decisions); § 3.5.4 (U.N. Security Council Decisions and *Jus in Bello*).

[22] *Refer to* § 1.6.3.3 (International Covenant on Civil and Political Rights (ICCPR)).

they occupied, such as post-World War II Germany and Japan.[23]

In addition, the law of belligerent occupation is specially crafted to address the situation of belligerent occupation. Thus, in cases of apparent conflict with other provisions of law that are not intended to address the situation of belligerent occupation, there might be a presumption that such provisions would not conflict with occupation law, or that occupation law likely would prevail when addressing the situation of belligerent occupation.[24]

Other States, such as some coalition partners, may interpret their human rights treaty obligations to create obligations for their military operations outside their home territory in the context of belligerent occupation.[25]

Subject to the Occupying Power's authority to change local law,[26] an occupied State's domestic law that has been enacted pursuant to its human rights treaty obligations or that meets the requirements of the occupied State's human rights treaty obligations may continue to apply during an occupation.

11.1.3 Application of Occupation Law to Situations Not Constituting Belligerent Occupation. The law of belligerent occupation is only applicable as a matter of law when certain conditions have been met.[27] The law of belligerent occupation generally does not apply to (1) mere invasion; (2) liberation of friendly territory; (3) non-international armed conflict; or (4) post-war situations (except for certain provisions of the GC). Nonetheless, it may be appropriate to apply rules from the law of belligerent occupation in such situations.

11.1.3.1 *Mere Invasion*. Mere physical presence of a belligerent's military forces in the territory of its enemy alone does not constitute military occupation. Such presence might not constitute an effective and firm possession of enemy territory, or the belligerent State might

---

[23] Eleanor Roosevelt, Chairman, U.N. Economic and Social Council, Commission on Human Rights, Sixth Session, Summary Record of the Hundred and Thirty-Eighth Meeting, U.N. Doc. E/CN.4/SR.138 ¶34 (Apr. 6, 1950) ("The purpose of the proposed addition was to make it clear that the draft Covenant would apply only to persons within the territory and subject to the jurisdiction of contracting States. The United States was afraid that without such an addition the draft Covenant might be construed as obliging the contracting States to enact legislation concerning persons who, although outside its territory were technically within its jurisdiction for certain purposes. An illustration would be the occupied territories of Germany, Austria and Japan: persons within those countries were subject to the jurisdiction of the occupying States in certain respects, but were outside the scope of the legislation of those States. Another illustration would be the case of leased territories: some countries leased certain territories from others for limited purposes, and there might be questions of conflicting authority between the lessor nation and the lessee nation."). *See also* Eleanor Roosevelt, Chairman, U.N. Economic and Social Council, Commission on Human Rights, Sixth Session, Summary Record of the Hundred and Ninety-Fourth Meeting, U.N. Doc. E/CN.4/SR.194 ¶14 (May 16, 1950) ("That [insertion of language] would limit the application of the covenant only to persons within its territory and subject to its jurisdiction. By this amendment the United States Government would not, by ratifying the covenant, be assuming an obligation to ensure the rights recognized in it to the citizens of countries under United States occupation.").

[24] *Refer to* § 1.3.2 (The Law of War's Relationship to Other Bodies of Law).

[25] *Refer to* § 1.6.3.2 (Different Views on the Applicability of Human Rights Treaties).

[26] *Refer to* § 11.9 (Local Law and Legislation).

[27] *Refer to* § 11.2 (When Military Occupation Law Applies).

lack the intention to displace and substitute the enemy State's authority with its own.[28]

Guidance for the U.S. armed forces has sought, to the extent possible, to apply the rules of the law of occupation as a matter of policy to areas through which U.S. forces are passing, and even on the battlefield.[29]

11.1.3.2 *Liberation of Friendly Territory*. The law of belligerent occupation does not apply to the liberation of friendly territory.[30] Indeed, a belligerent occupation presupposes that the Occupying Power is hostile in relation to the State whose territory is being occupied.[31]

The administration of liberated territory may be conducted in accordance with a civil affairs agreement between the co-belligerent States.[32] In the absence of such an agreement, a military government may be established in the area as a provisional and interim measure.[33] The law of belligerent occupation may provide appropriate rules to apply by analogy, pending an agreement with the lawful government.[34]

11.1.3.3 *Occupation and Non-International Armed Conflict*. The law of

---

[28] *Refer to* § 11.2.2.1 ("Actually Placed" – Effectiveness of Occupation); § 11.2.2.2 ("Under the Authority" – Suspension and Substitution of Governmental Authority).

[29] 1956 FM 27-10 (Change No. 1 1976) ¶352 ("*b. Application of Law of Occupation.* The rules set forth in this chapter apply of their own force only to belligerently occupied areas, but they should, as a matter of policy, be observed as far as possible in areas through which troops are passing and even on the battlefield.").

[30] *See* FM 27-10 (Change No. 1 1976) ¶354 ("Civil affairs administration is that form of administration established in friendly territory whereby a foreign government pursuant to an agreement, expressed or implied, with the government of the area concerned, may exercise certain authority normally the function of the local government. Such administration is often established in areas which are freed from enemy occupation. It is normally required when the government of the area concerned is unable or unwilling to assume full responsibility for its administration. Territory subject to civil affairs administration is not considered to be occupied."); Raymund T. Yingling and Robert W. Ginnane, *The Geneva Conventions of 1949*, 46 AJIL 393, 417 (1953) ("While the Civilian Convention contains no definition of 'occupation,' probably nothing could be added to the principle in Hague Article 42 that 'Territory is considered occupied when it is actually placed under the authority of the hostile army. 'The convention will not apply in liberated territory of an allied country such as France in 1944 in relation to the United States and the United Kingdom.").

[31] *Refer to* § 11.2.2.3 ("Of the Hostile Army" – Belligerent Occupation Applies to Enemy Territory).

[32] *For example*, Directives and Agreements in Civil Affairs in France, Aug. 25, 1944, *reprinted in* U.S. ARMY, JUDGE ADVOCATE GENERAL SCHOOL, CIVIL AFFAIRS MILITARY GOVERNMENT: SELECTED CASES AND MATERIALS 10 (1958) ("As a result of discussions between American, British, and French representatives, agreement has been reached on the practical arrangements for civil affairs administration in Continental France.").

[33] 1956 FM 27-10 (Change No. 1 1976) ¶354 ("If circumstances have precluded the conclusion of a civil affairs agreement with the lawful government of allied territory recovered from enemy occupation or of other territory liberated from the enemy, military government may be established in the area as a provisional and interim measure (see par. 12*b* and *c*). A civil affairs agreement should, however, be concluded with the lawful government at the earliest possible opportunity.").

[34] 1958 UK MANUAL ¶499 note 3(b) ("Where it is not possible to conclude 'Civil Affairs' agreement before the liberation of allied territory, there may be an interregnum between invasion of such territory and the assumption of authority on the part of the domestic civilian government. In such a situation the powers and restraints applicable to an occupant by international law ought to apply as a minimum standard until such time as a 'Civil Affairs' agreement can be concluded.").

belligerent occupation does not address non-international armed conflict as such because a belligerent occupation presupposes that the Occupying Power is hostile in relation to the State whose territory is being occupied.[35] A State's military forces controlling its own territory would not be regarded as conducting an occupation; similarly, foreign forces conducting operations with the consent of the territorial State would also not be regarded as conducting an occupation.[36]

However, the law of belligerent occupation may be applicable to a non-international armed conflict when a non-State party to the conflict has been recognized as a belligerent.[37] In addition, a non-international armed conflict could be regarded as taking place in the context of, or alongside, an occupation.[38]

11.1.3.4 Occupation and Post-War Situations. Before the GC was adopted and entered into force, the law of belligerent occupation was not applicable when a state of hostilities had completely ceased.[39] The general inapplicability of the law of belligerent occupation to post-war situations may be viewed as resulting from the law of belligerent occupation presupposing that a hostile relationship exists between the invading force's State and the State of the occupied territory.[40] For example, if the State of the occupied territory unconditionally surrendered and any international armed conflict completely ended, the law of belligerent occupation was not applicable.[41]

---

[35] *Refer to* § 17.1.3.1 (Nationality and Territoriality Exclusions in the Law of International Armed Conflict).

[36] *Refer to* § 11.2.2.3 ("Of the Hostile Army" – Belligerent Occupation Applies to Enemy Territory).

[37] *Refer to* § 3.3.3.1 (Recognition by Outside States of a Rebel Faction as a Belligerent in a Civil War).

[38] *For example*, Jack L. Goldsmith III, Assistant Attorney General, *"Protected Person" Status in Occupied Iraq Under the Fourth Geneva Convention*, Mar. 18, 2004, 28 OPINIONS OF THE OFFICE OF LEGAL COUNSEL 35, 36 ("The United States is currently involved in two armed conflicts that are relevant to our analysis: the armed conflict with and occupation of Iraq, and the armed conflict with al Qaeda. In this Part we analyze how article 2 applies to each conflict *considered independently*. This analysis is not conclusive as to how GC applies when the two conflicts become intertwined, as they may when al Qaeda operatives carry on their armed conflict against the United States in occupied Iraq. This latter issue is addressed in Part III, *infra*."). *Compare* § 3.3.1.2 (Mixed Conflicts Between Opposing States and Non-State Armed Groups).

[39] *For example*, Forrest Hannaman, Chief of the Legal Service Division of the Office of the United States High Commissioner for Germany, Letter to the Judge Advocate Division of EUCOM (Jan. 28, 1952), X WHITEMAN'S DIGEST 595-96 ("The position of the United States that the Hague Regulations do not apply to the post-capitulation period of the present occupation of German [was noted by] the Military Governor in a First Indorsement to the Commander-in-Chief, European Command, dated January 7, 1948 (AG 386.3LD), [which] stated *inter alia*: '... it appears that the French authorities are interested in the policy of the United States in regard to the treatment of property owned or used by the Wehrmacht and in the applicability of the Annex to Hague Convention IV of 1907 to that question ... With respect to the applicability at the present time of the Annex ... the Legal Division of this Headquarters has expressed the view ... that since the period of hostilities has ended, the provisions of Section III of the Annex to Hague Convention IV of 1907 'do not literally apply to the present occupation of Germany' ...'") (amendments shown in Digest).

[40] *Refer to* § 11.2.2.3 ("Of the Hostile Army" – Belligerent Occupation Applies to Enemy Territory).

[41] *For example*, United States v. Altstoetter, *et al.*, III TRIALS OF WAR CRIMINALS BEFORE THE NMT 960 ("It is this fact of the complete disintegration of the government in Germany, followed by unconditional surrender and by occupation of the territory, which explains and justifies the assumption and exercise of supreme governmental power by the Allies. The same fact distinguishes the present occupation of Germany from the type of occupation

The GC, however, continues to apply in occupied territory until one year after the general close of military operations, and the Occupying Power is bound, for the duration of the occupation, to the extent that such State exercises the functions of government in such territory, by the provisions of certain articles of the GC.[42] Additionally, protected persons under the GC who remain in the custody of the Occupying Power following the end of occupation retain that protection until their release, repatriation, or re-establishment.[43]

In addition, it may be appropriate to adhere to the rules of belligerent occupation or to apply those rules by analogy even if not applicable as a matter of law in post-conflict situations.[44] The rules of belligerent occupation may reflect fundamental safeguards applicable to a wider range of situations.[45]

---

which occurs when, in the course of actual warfare, an invading army enters and occupies the territory of another state, whose government is still in existence and is in receipt of international recognition, and whose armies, with those of its allies, are still in the field. In the latter case the occupying power is subject to the limitations imposed upon it by the Hague Convention and by the laws and customs of war. In the former case (the occupation of Germany) the Allied Powers were not subject to those limitations. By reason of the complete breakdown of government, industry, agriculture, and supply, they were under an imperative humanitarian duty of far wider scope to reorganize government and industry and to foster local democratic governmental agencies throughout the territory.").

[42] *Refer to* § 11.3.2 (Duration of GC Obligations in the Case of Occupied Territory).

[43] *Refer to* § 10.3.4 (Commencement and Duration of Protected Person Status).

[44] *For example*, Forrest Hannaman, Chief Legal Advice Division, Memorandum to Office of Economic Affairs – Finance Division on Revenues from Laender-Owned Property (Mar. 30, 1951), *reprinted in* XX SELECTED OPINIONS JANUARY 1, 1951 – APRIL 30, 1951 OF OFFICE OF THE UNITED STATES HIGH COMMISSIONER FOR GERMANY, OFFICE OF GENERAL COUNSEL, FRANKFURT, GERMANY, 57-58 ("The Hague Regulations were designed to define the powers of a belligerent occupant of enemy territory during, or shortly after, hostilities. As such, they cannot be considered literally applicable to the situation in Germany today, and we cannot consider without reflection that the occupying powers may exercise to their full extent powers which a belligerent occupant might rightfully exercise under the Regulations. Insofar as there exists an accepted custom and practice of nations relevant to our situation it is largely our own practice, since our present situation is without international precedent. In determining any concrete problem of this nature it has consistently been the position of the legal advisors to OMGUS and HICOG that whenever, in light of the actual problem and all of the relevant factors, the Hague Regulations may be considered as expressing principles of international law which are pertinent to our situation, those principles should be observed by us."); Major G.B. Crook and Major W.G. Downey, Memorandum for the Judge Advocate General, *Present Applicability of Hague and Geneva Conventions in Germany, reprinted in* Ernst H. Feilchenfeld and Members of the Institute of World Polity, *Status of Germany*, 1 WORLD POLITY 182, 196 (1958) ("We conclude, therefore, that: a. The authority of the Allied Control Council and of the United States zone commander in occupied Germany is not limited by the provisions of Section III of the Regulations annexed to the Hague Convention IV (1907) and such Regulations have not been applicable to the occupation of Germany since 5 June 1945. … The general rules expressed in the Hague Regulations will be considered as guiding principles unless and until specific U.S. or Allied occupation policies require deviation.").

[45] 1956 FM 27-10 (Change No. 1 1976) ¶10 ("However, certain designated provisions of the Geneva Conventions of 1949 (see *GC*, art. *6;* par 249 herein) continue to be operative, notwithstanding the termination of any antecedent hostilities, during the continuance of a military occupation. Insofar as the unwritten law of war and the Hague Regulations extend certain fundamental safeguards to the persons and property of the populations of occupied territory, their protection continues until the termination of any occupation having its origin in the military supremacy of the occupant, notwithstanding the fact the Geneva Convention relative to the Protection of Civilian Persons may have ceased to be applicable.").

11.2 When Military Occupation Law Applies

The law of military occupation applies when a military occupation exists in fact.

Even if the requirements of the law of belligerent occupation do not apply as a matter of law, general law of war principles and rules, such as those for the conduct of hostilities, continue to apply.[46]

11.2.1 Military Occupation as a Fact. Military occupation is a question of fact.[47] The legal consequences arising from the fact of occupation (*i.e.*, that this fact is the basis for both rights and duties) illustrates how the law of war may be viewed as both permissive and restrictive in nature.[48]

The fact of occupation is the basis for the Occupying Power to exercise authority over the occupied territory.[49] The fact of occupation, as a requirement for the exercise of authority over the occupied territory, prevents a State from simply claiming the authorities of military government over an enemy territory without actually controlling such territory.[50]

The fact of occupation also imposes certain duties on the Occupying Power with respect to occupied territory.[51] The fact of occupation, as a requirement for triggering the duties of an Occupying Power, means that a State that does not, in fact, occupy an area, does not incur the obligations of an Occupying Power.

Once an occupation exists in fact, regardless of whether the invasion was lawful or

---

[46] Eritrea-Ethiopia Claims Commission, *Partial Award – Western Front, Aerial Bombardment and Related Claims, Eritrea's Claims 1, 3, 5, 9-13, 14, 21, 25 & 26*, ¶27 (Dec. 19, 2005) ("The Commission agrees that the Ethiopian military presence was more transitory in most towns and villages on the Western Front than it was on the Central Front, where the Commission found Ethiopia to be an occupying power. The Commission also recognizes that not all of the obligations of Section III of Part III of Geneva Convention IV (the section that deals with occupied territories) can reasonably be applied to an armed force anticipating combat and present in an area for only a few days. Nevertheless, a State is obligated by the remainder of that Convention and by customary international humanitarian law to take appropriate measures to protect enemy civilians and civilian property present within areas under the control of its armed forces. Even in areas where combat is occurring, civilians and civilian objects cannot lawfully be made objects of attack.").

[47] 1956 FM 27-10 (Change No. 1 1976) ¶355 ("Military occupation is a question of fact.").

[48] *Refer to* § 1.3.3 (Restrictive and Permissive Character of the Law of War).

[49] *See, e.g.*, WINTHROP, MILITARY LAW & PRECEDENTS 799 ("The authority for military government is the fact of occupation. Not a mere temporary occupation of enemy's country on the march, but a settled and established one. Mere invasion, the presence of the hostile army in the country, is not sufficient. There must be a full possession, a firm holding, a government *de facto*."); MacLeod v. United States, 229 U.S. 416, 425 (1913) ("There has been considerable discussion in the cases and in works of authoritative writers upon the subject of what constitutes an occupation which will give the right to exercise governmental authority. Such occupation is not merely invasion, but is invasion plus possession of the enemy's country for the purpose of holding it temporarily at least."); United States v. Rice, 17 U.S. 246, 254 (1819) (Story, J.) ("By the conquest and military occupation of Castine, the enemy acquired that firm possession which enabled him to exercise the fullest rights of sovereignty over that place.").

[50] *Compare* § 13.10.2.3 (Effectiveness of the Blockade).

[51] *Refer to* § 11.5 (Duty of the Occupying Power to Ensure Public Order and Safety).

unlawful under *jus ad bellum*, the rights and duties of the Occupying Power and the population in relation to each other apply.[52] This application of the law of belligerent occupation is an example of how *jus in bello* rules and *jus ad bellum* rules generally operate independently of one another.[53]

11.2.2 Standard for Determining When Territory Is Considered Occupied. Territory is considered occupied when it is actually placed under the authority of the hostile forces.[54]

This standard for when the law of belligerent occupation applies is reflected in Article 42 of the Hague IV Regulations and is regarded as customary international law.[55]

11.2.2.1 *"Actually Placed" – Effectiveness of Occupation*. Military occupation must be actual and effective; that is, the organized resistance must have been overcome, and the Occupying Power must have taken measures to establish its authority.[56]

It is sufficient that the occupying force can, within a reasonable time, send detachments of forces to enforce its authority within the occupied district. Military occupation does not require the presence of military forces in every populated area, although the occupying force must, *inter alia*, control the most important places.[57]

The type of forces used to maintain the authority of the Occupying Power is not material.

---

[52] *See, e.g.*, United States v. List, *et al.* (The Hostage Case), XI TRIALS OF WAR CRIMINALS BEFORE THE NMT 1247 ("At the outset, we desire to point out that international law makes no distinction between a lawful and an unlawful occupant in dealing with the respective duties of occupant and population in occupied territory. There is no reciprocal connection between the manner of the military occupation of territory and the rights and duties of the occupant and population to each other after the relationship has in fact been established. Whether the invasion was lawful or criminal is not an important factor in the consideration of this subject.").

[53] *Refer to* § 3.5.2 (*Jus in Bello* and *Jus ad Bellum* Generally Operate Independently of One Another).

[54] HAGUE IV REG. art. 42 ("Territory is considered occupied when it is actually placed under the authority of the hostile army. The occupation extends only to the territory where such authority has been established and can be exercised.").

[55] *See, e.g.*, Jack L. Goldsmith III, Assistant Attorney General, *"Protected Person" Status in Occupied Iraq Under the Fourth Geneva Convention*, Mar. 18, 2004, 28 OPINIONS OF THE OFFICE OF LEGAL COUNSEL 35, 37 footnote 1 ("The Hague Regulations do not apply to the United States' conflict with and occupation of Iraq *as a matter of treaty law* because Iraq is not a party to the Hague Convention. ... But as the citations in the text make clear, article 42(1) of the Hague Regulations, which provides that occupation begins 'when [territory] is actually placed under the authority of the hostile army,' reflects customary international law."); Armed Activities on the Territory of the Congo (Democratic Republic of the Congo v. Uganda), Judgment, 2005 I.C.J. 168, 229 (¶172) ("[U]nder customary international law, as reflected in Article 42 of the Hague Regulations of 1907, territory is considered to be occupied when it is actually placed under the authority of the hostile army, and the occupation extends only to the territory where such authority has been established and can be exercised … .").

[56] 1956 FM 27-10 (Change No. 1 1976) ¶356 ("It follows from the definition that belligerent occupation must be both actual and effective, that is, the organized resistance must have been overcome and the force in possession must have taken measures to establish its authority.").

[57] Keely v. Sanders, 99 U.S. 441, 447 (1878) ("No conquering army occupies the entire territory conquered. Its authority is established when it occupies and holds securely the most important places, and when there is no opposing governmental authority within the territory. The inability of any other power to establish and maintain governmental authority therein is the test.").

For example, the occupation might be maintained by permanently based units or mobile forces, either of which would be able to send detachments of forces to enforce the authority of the Occupying Power within the occupied district.[58] However, air superiority alone would not constitute an effective occupation.

Similarly, as long as the occupation is effective, there is no precise number of forces that are considered necessary to constitute an effective occupation. The number of forces necessary to maintain effective occupation will depend on various considerations, such as the disposition of the inhabitants, the number and density of the population, the nature of the terrain, and similar factors.[59]

An occupation may be effective despite the existence of areas in the enemy State that are temporarily controlled by enemy forces or pockets of resistance. For example, the fact that a defended location (such as a city or town) still controlled by enemy forces exists within an area declared occupied by the Occupying Power does not render the occupation of the remainder of the area invalid, provided that continued resistance in such place or defended zone does not render the occupier unable to exercise control over the remainder of the occupied territory.[60] Similarly, an occupation may continue to be effective despite intermittent insurgent attacks or temporary seizures of territory by resistance forces.[61]

11.2.2.2 *"Under the Authority" – Suspension and Substitution of Governmental Authority*. Occupation also requires the suspension of the territorial State's authority and the substitution of the Occupying Power's authority for the territorial State's authority.[62]

The territorial State must be rendered incapable of publicly exercising its authority in the

---

[58] 1956 FM 27-10 (Change No. 1 1976) ¶356 ("It is sufficient that the occupying force can, within a reasonable time, send detachments of troops to make its authority felt within the occupied district. It is immaterial whether the authority of the occupant is maintained by fixed garrisons or flying columns, whether by small or large forces, so long as the occupation is effective.").

[59] 1956 FM 27-10 (Change No. 1 1976) ¶356 ("The number of troops necessary to maintain effective occupation will depend on various considerations such as the disposition of the inhabitants, the number and density of the population, the nature of the terrain, and similar factors. The mere existence of a fort or defended area within the occupied district, provided the fort or defended area is under attack, does not render the occupation of the remainder of the district ineffective. Similarly, the mere existence of local resistance groups does not render the occupation ineffective.").

[60] 1958 UK MANUAL ¶502 ("The fact that there is a defended place or zone still in possession of the national forces within an occupied district does not make the occupation of the remainder invalid, provided that such place or defended zone is surrounded and effectively cut off from the rest of the occupied district.").

[61] United States v. List, *et al.* (The Hostage Case), XI TRIALS OF WAR CRIMINALS BEFORE THE NMT 1243 ("It is clear that the German armed forces were able to maintain control of Greece and Yugoslavia until they evacuated them in the fall of 1944. While it is true that the partisans were able to control sections of these countries at various times, it is established that the Germans could at any time they desired assume physical control of any part of the country. The control of the resistance forces was temporary only and not such as would deprive the German armed forces of its status of an occupant.").

[62] LIEBER CODE art. 3 ("Martial Law in a hostile country consists in the suspension, by the occupying military authority, of the criminal and civil law, and of the domestic administration and government in the occupied place or territory, and in the substitution of military rule and force for the same, as well as in the dictation of general laws, as far as military necessity requires this suspension, substitution, or dictation.").

territory, and the Occupying Power must substitute its authority for that of the territorial State.[63] Invading forces in possession of the territory must have taken measures to establish their authority.[64] For example, such measures may include establishing its own governmental authority for that area and making regulations for the conduct of temporary government.[65] The suspension and substitution of authority may take place with local authorities continuing to administer territory subject to the paramount authority of the Occupying Power.[66] On the other hand, routine measures necessary to provide for unit security (*e.g.*, warning private persons not to threaten or interfere with military operations) would not necessarily constitute measures to establish authority over enemy territory.

The substitution of authority by the Occupying Power may be shown by a proclamation of occupation, although such a proclamation is not required.[67]

11.2.2.3 *"Of the Hostile Army" – Belligerent Occupation Applies to Enemy Territory*. Occupation occurs when territory is actually placed under the authority of the hostile army. Thus, the existence of an occupation presupposes a hostile relationship between the invading force's State and the State of the occupied territory, although the occupation need not

---

[63] 1956 FM 27-10 (Change No. 1 1976) ¶355 ("Military occupation is a question of fact. It presupposes a hostile invasion, resisted or unresisted, as a result of which the invader has rendered the invaded government incapable of publicly exercising its authority, and that the invader has successfully substituted its own authority for that of the legitimate government in the territory invaded."). *See also* Armed Activities on the Territory of the Congo (Democratic Republic of the Congo v. Uganda), Judgment, 2005 I.C.J. 165, 230 (¶¶173-74) ("In order to reach a conclusion as to whether a State, the military forces of which are present on the territory of another State as a result of an intervention, is an 'occupying Power' in the meaning of the term as understood in *jus in bello*, the Court must examine whether there is sufficient evidence to demonstrate that the said authority was in fact established and exercised by the intervening State in the areas in question. In the present case the Court will need to satisfy itself that the Ugandan armed forces in the DRC were not only stationed in particular locations, but also that they had substituted their own authority for that of the Congolese Government .... [T]he territorial limits of any zone of occupation by Uganda in the DRC cannot be determined by simply drawing a line connecting the geographical locations where Ugandan troops were present as has been done on the sketch-map presented by the DRC (see paragraphs 55 and 73 above).").

[64] GREENSPAN, THE MODERN LAW OF LAND WARFARE 213-14 ("An occupant sets up some form of administration in the territory, an invader merely passing through it does not.").

[65] *For example*, MacLeod v. United States, 229 U.S. 416, 424-25 (1913) ("When the Spanish fleet was destroyed at Manila, May 1, 1898, it became apparent that the Government of the United States might be required to take the necessary steps to make provision for the government and control of such part of the Philippines as might come into the military occupation of the forces of the United States. The right to thus occupy an enemy's country and temporarily provide for its government has been recognized by previous action of the executive authority and sanctioned by frequent decisions of this court. The local government being destroyed, the conqueror may set up its own authority and make rules and regulations for the conduct of temporary government, and to that end may collect taxes and duties to support the military authority and carry on operations incident to the occupation. Such was the course of the Government with respect to the territory acquired by conquest and afterwards ceded by the Mexican Government to the United States.").

[66] *Refer to* § 11.8.2 (Continued Performance of Duties by Civil Servants and Other Officials of Local Governments).

[67] *Refer to* § 11.2.4 (Proclamation of Occupation).

be met with armed resistance.[68]

For example, the law of belligerent occupation would not apply to the use of military forces to control a State's own territory, such as in cases of domestic emergency, insurrection, or non-international armed conflict.[69]

Similarly, the law of belligerent occupation would not apply to the liberation of friendly territory that was previously occupied by the enemy.[70]

The requirement of a hostile relationship between the invading force's State and the State of the occupied territory also prevents the law of belligerent occupation from applying to post-conflict situations (except for certain provisions of the GC).[71]

11.2.3 Scope of Occupied Territory. The occupation extends only to the territory where such authority has been established and can be exercised.[72]

For example, a State may remain in control of part of its territory while the remainder of its territory is under occupation. The 1949 Geneva Conventions apply in cases of partial or total occupation of a State.[73]

The end of occupation in one part of occupied territory does not end the occupation in other parts of the occupied territory where the Occupying Power maintains its authority.

11.2.4 Proclamation of Occupation. Due to the special relations established between the civilian population of the occupied territory and the Occupying Power, the fact of military occupation and the territory over which it extends should be made known to the citizens of the occupied territory and to other States.

However, there is no specific legal requirement that the Occupying Power issue a proclamation of military occupation.[74]

---

[68] GWS art. 2 ("The Convention shall also apply to all cases of partial or total occupation of the territory of a High Contracting Party, even if the said occupation meets with no armed resistance."); GWS-SEA art. 2 (same); GPW art. 2 (same); GC art. 2 (same).

[69] *Refer to* § 11.1.3.3 (Occupation and Non-International Armed Conflict).

[70] *Refer to* § 11.1.3.2 (Liberation of Friendly Territory).

[71] *Refer to* § 11.1.3.4 (Occupation and Post-War Situations).

[72] HAGUE IV REG. art. 42 ("Territory is considered occupied when it is actually placed under the authority of the hostile army. The occupation extends only to the territory where such authority has been established and can be exercised.").

[73] *Refer to* § 11.1.2.3 (Occupation and the 1949 Geneva Conventions).

[74] 1956 FM 27-10 (Change No. 1 1976) ¶357 ("In a strict legal sense no proclamation of military occupation is necessary. However, on account of the special relations established between the inhabitants of the occupied territory and the occupant by virtue of the presence of occupying forces, the fact of military occupation, with the extent of territory affected, should be made known. The practice of the United States is to make this fact known by proclamation."); 1914 RULES OF LAND WARFARE ¶292 ("In a strict legal sense no proclamation of military occupation is necessary. On account of the special relations established between the inhabitants of the occupied

The question of whether territory is occupied does not depend upon the issuance of any particular proclamation or other instrument. Territory may be occupied even though no proclamation of occupation has been issued. Conversely, the issuance of proclamation of occupation does not empower a State with the rights of an Occupying Power if it does not control such territory in fact.

A proclamation may help fix the date of the beginning of the occupation.[75] The proclamation may also advise inhabitants of occupied territory of the rules with which they must comply.[76] In particular, the proclamation may be used to advise inhabitants of changes to law, including penal law.[77]

The general practice of the United States has been to make the fact of occupation known by proclamation or similar notice.[78] In addition to giving notice to the inhabitants of occupied

---

territory and the occupant, by virtue of the presence of the invading force, the fact of military occupation, with the extent of terrritorry [sic] affected by the same, should be made known. The practice in this country is to make this fact known by proclamation."); LIEBER CODE art. 1 ("A place, district, or country occupied by an enemy stands, in consequence of the occupation, under the Martial Law of the invading or occupying army, whether any proclamation declaring Martial Law, or any public warning to the inhabitants, has been issued or not. Martial Law is the immediate and direct effect and consequence of occupation or conquest. The presence of a hostile army proclaims its Martial Law.").

[75] *For example*, Jack L. Goldsmith III, Assistant Attorney General, *"Protected Person" Status in Occupied Iraq Under the Fourth Geneva Convention*, Mar. 18, 2004, 28 OPINIONS OF THE OFFICE OF LEGAL COUNSEL 35, 37 ("Applying this standard, the United States became an occupying power no later than April 16, 2003, the date on which General Tommy Franks announced the creation of the 'Coalition Provisional Authority to exercise powers of government temporarily, and as necessary, especially to provide security, to allow the delivery of humanitarian aid and to eliminate weapons of mass destruction.' See Tommy R. Franks, Freedom Message to the Iraqi People (Apr. 16, 2003)"); The Venice, 69 U.S. 258, 276 (1865) ("The transports conveying the troops under the command of Major-General Butler, commanding the Department of the Gulf, arrived on the 1st of May, and the actual occupation of the city was begun. There was no armed resistance, but abundant manifestations of hostile spirit and temper both by the people and the authorities. The landing of the troops was completed on the 2d of May, and on the 6th a proclamation of General Butler, which had been prepared and dated on the 1st, and the next day printed by some soldiers, in an office seized for the purpose, was published in the newspapers of the city. Some copies of the proclamation had been previously distributed to individuals, but it was not made known to the population generally until thus published. There was no hostile demonstration, and no disturbance afterwards; and we think that the military occupation of the city of New Orleans may be considered as substantially complete from the date of this publication; and that all the rights and obligations resulting from such occupation, or from the terms of the proclamation, may be properly regarded as existing from that time. This proclamation declared the city to be under martial law, and announced the principles by which the commanding general would be guided in its administration.").

[76] *For example*, 1958 UK MANUAL ¶504 note 1 ("The practice in this matter in past wars appears to have been variable. Frequently the inhabitants were only warned to behave peaceably, not to communicate with the enemy, and to comply with requisitions; as for instance when the British troops entered France in 1813 and 1815. In 1870, in France, the Germans generally, but not always, proclaimed military jurisdiction directly[;] they took possession of a locality, by posting a notice which gave a list of offences against the troops for which the penalty of death would be inflicted.").

[77] *Refer to* § 11.9.3 (Procedural Obligation – Notification to the Population of Changes in Law); § 11.11.2.1 (Publication of Penal Provisions Before Coming Into Force).

[78] *For example*, Coalition Provisional Authority Regulation No. 1, §1(1) (May 16, 2003) ("The CPA shall exercise powers of government temporarily in order to provide for the effective administration of Iraq during the period of transitional administration … .").

territory, notice may be given to other governments.[79] In some cases, the U.N. Security Council has recognized the fact of occupation.[80]

11.3 END OF OCCUPATION AND DURATION OF GC OBLIGATIONS

The status of belligerent occupation ends when the conditions for its application are no longer met. Certain GC obligations with respect to occupied territory continue for the duration of the occupation after the general close of military operations.

11.3.1 End of Occupation. Belligerent occupation ceases when the conditions for its application are no longer met.[81] In particular, as discussed below, the status of belligerent occupation ceases when the invader no longer factually governs the occupied territory or when a hostile relationship no longer exists between the State of the occupied territory and the Occupying Power.[82]

Belligerent occupation ends when the Occupying Power no longer has effectively placed the occupied territory under its control.[83] For example, an uprising by the local population may prevent the Occupying Power from actually enforcing its authority over occupied territory. Similarly, the Occupying Power's expulsion or complete withdrawal from the territory would also suffice because the former Occupying Power generally would not be able to control sufficiently the occupied territory.

Belligerent occupation also may end when a hostile relationship no longer exists between the Occupying Power and the State of the occupied territory (although, as discussed in the following subsection, certain GC obligations may continue to apply).[84] For example, if a new,

---

[79] *For example*, John D. Negroponte & Jeremy Greenstock, *Letter Dated 8 May 2003 from the Permanent Representatives of the United Kingdom of Great Britain and Northern Ireland and the United States of America to the United Nations Addressed to the President of the Security Council*, U.N. Doc. S/2003/538 ("the United States, the United Kingdom, and Coalition partners, acting under existing command and control arrangements through the Commander of Coalition Forces, have created the Coalition Provisional Authority, which includes the Office of Reconstruction and Humanitarian Assistance, to exercise the powers of government temporarily, and, as necessary, especially to provide security, to allow the delivery of humanitarian aid, and to eliminate weapons of mass destruction. The United States, the United Kingdom and Coalition partners, working through the Coalition Provisional Authority, shall inter alia, provide for security in and for the provisional administration of Iraq … .").

[80] *For example*, U.N. SECURITY COUNCIL RESOLUTION 1483, U.N. Doc. S/RES/1483, 2 (May 22, 2003) ("Noting the letter of 8 May 2003 from the Permanent Representatives of the United States of America and the United Kingdom of Great Britain and Northern Ireland to the President of the Security Council (S/2003/538) and recognizing the specific authorities, responsibilities, and obligations under applicable international law of these states as occupying powers under unified command (the 'Authority'),"); U.N. SECURITY COUNCIL RESOLUTION 661, U.N. Doc. S/RES/661 (1990) (Aug. 6, 1990) ("Determined to bring the invasion and occupation of Kuwait by Iraq to an end and to restore the sovereignty, independence and territorial integrity of Kuwait,").

[81] *Refer to* § 11.2.2 (Standard for Determining When Territory Is Considered Occupied).

[82] WINTHROP, MILITARY LAW & PRECEDENTS 801 ("The status of military government continues from the inception of the actual occupation till the invader is expelled by force of arms, or himself abandons the conquest, or till, under a treaty of peace, the country is restored to its original allegiance or becomes incorporated with the domain of the prevailing belligerent.").

[83] *Refer to* § 11.2.2.1 ("Actually Placed" – Effectiveness of Occupation).

[84] *Refer to* § 11.2.2.3 ("Of the Hostile Army" – Belligerent Occupation Applies to Enemy Territory).

independent government of the previously occupied territory assumes control of the territory and consents to the presence of the previously occupying forces, then such a situation would no longer be considered a belligerent occupation. Similarly, if a peace treaty legitimately transfers the territory to the sovereignty of the Occupying Power, then the Occupying Power would no longer be characterized as such. However, an Occupying Power is not permitted, under the law of belligerent occupation, to annex occupied territory.[85]

11.3.2 <u>Duration of GC Obligations in the Case of Occupied Territory</u>. In the home territory of parties to the conflict, the application of the GC shall cease on the general close of military operations.[86]

In the case of occupied territory, the application of the GC shall cease one year after the general close of military operations; however, the Occupying Power shall be bound, for the duration of the occupation, to the extent that such State exercises the functions of government in such territory, by the provisions of the following Articles of the GC:

- 1 through 12 (general provisions and common articles, *e.g.*, the Protecting Power continues to function, and the derogation for security reasons continues to apply);
- 27, 29 through 34 (humane treatment);
- 47 (preserves rights as against change by annexation or arrangement with the local authorities so long as occupation lasts);
- 49 (transfers, evacuation, and deportation);
- 51, 52 (prohibitions against certain compulsory service and protection of workers);
- 53 (respect for property);
- 59, 61 through 63 (facilitating relief programs);
- 64 through 77 (criminal proceedings); and
- 143 (access by Protecting Powers and the ICRC).[87]

The one-year time limit for the cessation of the application of the GC (apart from the provisions that continue to apply to the extent that the Occupying Power exercises the functions of government in occupied territory) was proposed to account for situations like those of

---

[85] *Refer to* § 11.4.2 (Limitations on the Power of the Occupying Power Stemming From Its Lack of Sovereignty Over Occupied Territory).

[86] *Refer to* § 10.3.4 (Commencement and Duration of Protected Person Status).

[87] GC art. 6 ("In the case of occupied territory, the application of the present Convention shall cease one year after the general close of military operations; however, the Occupying Power shall be bound, for the duration of the occupation, to the extent that such Power exercises the functions of government in such territory, by the provisions of the following Articles of the present Convention: 1 to 12, 27, 29 to 34, 47, 49, 51, 52, 53, 59, 61 to 77, 143.").

Germany and Japan after World War II.[88] AP I provides that the 1949 Geneva Conventions and AP I shall cease to apply, in the case of occupied territories, on the termination of the occupation;[89] coalition partners that are Occupying Powers and Parties to AP I would be bound by this rule.

In any case, individuals entitled to GC protection who remain in the custody of the Occupying Power following the end of occupation retain that protection until their release, repatriation, or re-establishment.[90] In addition, it may be appropriate following the end of occupation to continue to apply by analogy certain rules from the law of belligerent occupation, even if such rules do not apply as a matter of law.[91]

11.4 Legal Position of the Occupying Power

Military occupation of enemy territory involves a complicated, trilateral set of legal relations between the Occupying Power, the temporarily ousted sovereign authority, and the inhabitants of occupied territory.[92] The fact of occupation gives the Occupying Power the right to govern enemy territory temporarily, but does not transfer sovereignty over occupied territory

---

[88] II-A Final Record of the Diplomatic Conference of Geneva of 1949 623 ("Mr. Clattenburg (United States of America) said that his Delegation would propose an amendment to Article 4 to provide that the Civilians Convention should cease to apply not earlier than one year after the termination of hostilities. It would be noted that the Convention did not define the terms 'occupied territory' or 'military occupation'. It was the view of the United States Delegation that the obligations imposed by the Convention on an Occupying Power should be applicable to the period of hostilities and to the period of disorganization following on the hostilities; these obligations would vary according to the nature and duration of the occupation. Experience had shown that an Occupying Power did, in fact, exercise the majority of the governmental functions in occupied territory. A prolonged military occupation was, however, also characterized by a progressive return of governmental responsibility to local authorities. The Occupying Power should be bound by the obligations of the Convention only during such time as the institutions of the occupied territory were unable to provide for the needs of the inhabitants. The ultimate solution of such problems as revictualling, sanitation and war damage was not the responsibility of the Occupying Power. He quoted the case of the Allied occupation of Germany and Japan to show that the responsibility of the Occupying Powers for the welfare of the local populations was far less at present than during the period immediately following hostilities.").

[89] AP I art. 3 ("Without prejudice to the provisions which are applicable at all times: (a) The Conventions and this Protocol shall apply from the beginning of any situation referred to in Article 1 of this Protocol; (b) The application of the Conventions and of this Protocol shall cease, in the territory of Parties to the conflict, on the general close of military operations and, in the case of occupied territories, on the termination of the occupation, except, in either circumstance, for those persons whose final release, repatriation or reestablishment takes place thereafter. These persons shall continue to benefit from the relevant provisions of the Conventions and of this Protocol until their final release, repatriation or re-establishment.").

[90] *Refer to* § 10.3.4 (Commencement and Duration of Protected Person Status).

[91] *Refer to* § 11.1.3.4 (Occupation and Post-War Situations).

[92] Julius Stone, Legal Controls on International Conflict 694 (1954) ("Whether belligerent occupation has been established depends not merely on the will of the belligerent, but whether his actual control satisfies the standards of range and stability laid down by international law. If it does not, he is a mere invader enjoying a comparatively narrow legal authority. If it does, international law attributes to him legal powers which *merely as a belligerent* he does not have, touching almost all aspects of the government of the territory and the lives of its inhabitants. Since, moreover, the ousted sovereign still retains all the residue of legal authority not attributed to the Occupant, it is apparent that belligerent occupation involves at its core a complicated trilateral set of legal relations between the Occupant, the temporarily ousted sovereign and the inhabitants.").

to the Occupying Power.

11.4.1 Right of the Occupying Power to Govern the Enemy Territory Temporarily. The right to govern the territory of the enemy during its military occupation is one of the incidents of war.[93] By the fact of occupation (*i.e.*, the Occupying Power's established power over occupied territory), the Occupying Power is conferred the authority to exercise some of the rights of sovereignty.[94] The exercise of these sovereign rights also results from the necessity of maintaining law and order, indispensable both to the inhabitants and to the occupying force, and the failure or inability of the legitimate government to exercise its functions, or the undesirability of allowing it to do so.[95]

11.4.2 Limitations on the Power of the Occupying Power Stemming From Its Lack of Sovereignty Over Occupied Territory. Belligerent occupation in a foreign war, being based upon the possession of enemy territory, necessarily implies that the sovereignty of the occupied territory is not vested in the Occupying Power.[96] Occupation is essentially provisional.[97]

Because sovereignty is not vested in the Occupying Power, the fact of military occupation does not authorize the Occupying Power to take certain actions. For example, the Occupying Power is not authorized by the fact of belligerent occupation to annex occupied territory or to create a new State.[98] In addition, the Occupying Power may not compel the

---

[93] Coleman v. Tennessee, 97 U.S. 509, 517 (1879) ("The doctrine of international law on the effect of military occupation of enemy's territory upon its former laws is well established. Though the late war was not between independent nations, but between different portions of the same nation, yet having taken the proportions of a territorial war, the insurgents having become formidable enough to be recognized as belligerents, the same doctrine must be held to apply. The right to govern the territory of the enemy during its military occupation is one of the incidents of war, being a consequence of its acquisition; and the character and form of the government to be established depend entirely upon the laws of the conquering State or the orders of its military commander.").

[94] 1956 FM 27-10 (Change No. 1 1976) ¶358 ("Being an incident of war, military occupation confers upon the invading force the means of exercising control for the period of occupation. It does not transfer the sovereignty to the occupant, but simply the authority or power to exercise some of the rights of sovereignty. The exercise of these rights results from the established power of the occupant and from the necessity of maintaining law and order, indispensable both to the inhabitants and to the occupying force.").

[95] 1956 FM 27-10 (Change No. 1 1976) ¶362 ("Military government is the form of administration by which an occupying power exercises governmental authority over occupied territory. The necessity for such government arises from the failure or inability of the legitimate government to exercise its functions on account of the military occupation, or the undesirability of allowing it to do so.").

[96] 1956 FM 27-10 (Change No. 1 1976) ¶353 ("Belligerent occupation in a foreign war, being based upon the possession of enemy territory, necessarily implies that the sovereignty of the occupied territory is not vested in the occupying power. Occupation is essentially provisional.").

[97] *See, e.g.*, VON GLAHN, THE OCCUPATION OF ENEMY TERRITORY 31 ("The consensus of the opinions of writers on international law is that the legitimate government of the territory retains its sovereignty but that the latter is suspended during the period of belligerent occupation."); EYAL BENVENISTI, THE INTERNATIONAL LAW OF OCCUPATION 6 (2004) ("The power exercising effective control within another's sovereign territory has only temporary managerial powers, for the period until a peaceful solution is reached. During that limited period, the occupant administers the territory on behalf of the sovereign. Thus the occupant's status is conceived to be that of a trustee.").

[98] 1956 FM 27-10 (Change No. 1 1976) ¶358 ("It is therefore unlawful for a belligerent occupant to annex occupied territory or to create a new State therein while hostilities are still in progress."). *Refer to* § 11.6.3 (Occupying Power's Duty to Respect the Rights of Protected Persons Secured by the GC).

inhabitants of occupied territory to become its nationals or otherwise to swear allegiance to it.[99] Similarly, in view of the provisional nature of belligerent occupation, the authority of the Occupying Power under occupation law has been interpreted as being subject to limitations on the ability of the Occupying Power to alter institutions of government permanently or change the constitution of a country.[100]

11.5 DUTY OF THE OCCUPYING POWER TO ENSURE PUBLIC ORDER AND SAFETY

The authority of the legitimate power having in fact passed into the hands of the Occupying Power, the latter shall take all the measures in its power to restore, and ensure, as far as possible, public order and safety, while respecting, unless absolutely prevented, the laws in force in the country.[101] This principle has been recognized as customary international law.[102]

The Occupying Power has a general duty to maintain public order and to provide for the

---

[99] *Refer to* § 11.6.2.1 (Prohibition on Compelling Inhabitants of Occupied Territory to Swear Allegiance to the Hostile State).

[100] John B. Bellinger, III, Legal Adviser, Department of State, *United Nations Security Council Resolutions and the Application of International Humanitarian Law, Human Rights and Refugee Law*, Sept. 9, 2005, 2005 DIGEST OF UNITED STATES PRACTICE IN INTERNATIONAL LAW 958-59 ("Some commentators take the position that occupation law establishes limitations on the ability of the occupying power to alter institutions of government permanently or change the constitution of a country."). *See also* 2004 UK MANUAL ¶11.25.1 ("Since the occupying power has a duty to look after the welfare of the inhabitants, regulations, for example, fixing prices and securing the equitable distribution of food and other commodities, are permissible. The occupying power should make no more changes to the law than are absolutely necessary, particularly where the occupied territory already has an adequate legal system."); 2001 CANADIAN MANUAL ¶1205(1) ("During occupation by the enemy, the sovereignty of the legitimate government continues to exist but it is temporarily latent. The powers of the occupant are of a provisional nature and it should only take measures, which are necessary for the purposes of the armed conflict, the maintenance of order and safety and the proper administration of the occupied territory. Generally speaking, the occupant is not entitled to alter the existing form of government, to upset the constitution and domestic laws of the occupied territory, or to set aside the rights of the inhabitants."); JULIUS STONE, LEGAL CONTROLS OF INTERNATIONAL CONFLICT 698 (1954) ("The limits on the legislative and regulatory power are as vague as the authority is general. The Occupant's authority is 'military authority'. Clearly this is not full sovereignty, but equally clearly it extends under the regulations to civil matters. His authority, of course, is limited like all his other powers to the occupied territory, under Article 42, paragraph 2; and by Article 43 the Occupant must respect the laws in force unless 'absolutely prevented'. But this last limitation has never been taken literally; and unless it is so taken, the boundaries of the Occupant's legislative power are still to be drawn. The most widely approved line of distinction is that the Occupant, in view of his merely provisional position, cannot make permanent changes in regard to fundamental institutions, for instance, change a republic into a monarchy. It becomes, however, increasingly difficult to say with confidence what is a fundamental institution.").

[101] HAGUE IV REG. art. 43 ("The authority of the legitimate power having in fact passed into the hands of the occupant, the latter shall take all the measures in his power to restore, and ensure, as far as possible, public order and safety, while respecting, unless absolutely prevented, the laws in force in the country.").

[102] *Opinion on the Legality of the Issuance of AMG (Allied Military Government) Currency in Sicily*, Sept. 23, 1943, *reprinted in Occupation Currency Transactions: Hearings Before the Committees on Appropriations Armed Services and Banking and Currency, U.S. Senate*, 80th Congress, First Session, 73, 75 (Jun. 17-18, 1947) ("The Hague Convention clearly enunciated the principle that the laws applicable in an occupied territory remain in effect during the occupation, subject to change by the military authorities within the limitations of the Convention. Article 43 provides: ... This declaration of the Hague Convention amounts only to a reaffirmation of the recognized international law prior to that time.").

preservation of rights of the inhabitants, including rights to their private property.[103]

11.5.1 Authority Conferred by the Occupying Power's Duty to Ensure Public Order and Safety. The Occupying Power's duty to take all the measures in its power to restore and ensure, as far as possible, public order and safety also provides it authority take such actions. For example, the Occupying Power may enact provisions to maintain the orderly government of the territory.[104]

11.5.2 Duty to Respect, Unless Absolutely Prevented, the Laws in Force in the Country. The duty to respect, unless absolutely prevented, the laws in force in the country prohibits the Occupying Power from arbitrarily exercising its authority to suspend, repeal, or change the municipal law applicable to occupied territory.[105]

The duty to respect, unless absolutely prevented, the laws in force in the country has been interpreted not to apply to local administrative laws, such as regulations, executive orders, ordinances, and decrees.[106]

11.6 Protection of the Population of an Occupied Territory

Under the law of belligerent occupation, the Occupying Power has certain duties with respect to the population of an occupied territory, including protected persons under the GC.

11.6.1 General Protections, Including Humane Treatment, of the Population of an

---

[103] Aboitiz & Co. v. Price, 99 F. Supp. 602, 610 (D. Utah 1951) ("[I]international law has recognized the right of the protection of [the Occupying Power's] military interests and the exercise of police powers. However, such law also imposes upon the occupant the duty to maintain public order and to provide for the preservation of the rights of the inhabitants. The emphasis is upon public order and safety, and the welfare of the inhabitants."). *See also* Ochoa v. Hernandez y Morales, 230 U.S. 139, 159 (1913) ("The protocol of August 12, 1898 (30 Stat. 1742), the purport of which has already been given, left our Government, by its military forces, in the occupation and control of Porto Rico as a colony of Spain, and bound by the principles of international law to do whatever was necessary to secure public safety, social order, and the guaranties of private property.").

[104] *Refer to* § 11.9.2 (Authority for the Occupying Power to Suspend, Repeal, or Change the Municipal Law Applicable to Occupied Territory).

[105] *See* GC COMMENTARY 335-36 ("Article 64 expresses, in a more precise and detailed form, the terms of Article 43 of the Hague Regulations, which lays down that the Occupying Power is to respect the laws in force in the country 'unless absolutely prevented'. ... The principle that the penal laws in force in the occupied territory must be maintained is subject to two reservations. The first relates to the security of the Occupying Power, which must obviously be permitted to cancel provisions such as those concerning recruiting or urging the population to resist the enemy. The second reservation is in the interests of the population and makes it possible to abrogate any discriminatory measures incompatible with humane requirements. ... These two exceptions are of a strictly limitative nature. The occupation authorities cannot abrogate or suspend the penal laws for any other reason—and not, in particular, merely to make it accord with their own legal conceptions.").

[106] VON GLAHN, THE OCCUPATION OF ENEMY TERRITORY 99 ("In sharp contrast to the 'restricted' view concerning civil laws, the occupant is generally conceded very extensive powers to change, alter, or suspend the ordinances and decrees (as distinct from laws) of the legitimate sovereign of an occupied territory. It is held that administrative regulations and executive orders are quite sharply distinct from the constitutional and statute law of a country and that they do not constitute as important or vital a part of the latter's legal structure. Hence the occupant is held to have the power to interfere and to enact such regulations and ordinances as are deemed fitting and proper in his interests and in the interests of his armed forces.").

Occupied Territory. The population of an occupied territory, like other protected persons under the GC, are entitled, in all circumstances, to respect for their persons, their honor, their family rights, their religious convictions and practices, and their manners and customs.[107] They shall at all times be humanely treated, and shall be protected especially against all acts of violence or threats of violence, and against insults and public curiosity.

Other provisions for the humane treatment of protected persons set forth in Articles 27 through 34 of the GC apply to the population of an occupied territory. For example, women must be especially protected against any attack on their honor, in particular against rape, enforced prostitution, or any form of indecent assault.[108] Reprisals against protected persons and their property are prohibited.[109] The taking of hostages is prohibited.[110]

In addition, protected persons in occupied territory shall have every facility for making application to the Protecting Powers, the ICRC, the National Red Cross (Red Crescent, Red Lion and Sun) Society of the country where they may be, as well as to any organization that might assist them.[111]

11.6.2 Overview of Additional Protections for the Population That Are Specific to Occupation. There are a number of protections for the population of occupied territory that are specific to occupation. For example, specific provision exists for the protection of children in occupied territory.[112] Specific constraints exist on the authority of the Occupying Power to punish protected persons, direct their movement, or compel them to perform labor.[113] Provision also is made with respect to: (1) food and medical supplies of the population; (2) public health and hygiene; (3) spiritual assistance; and (4) relief efforts and consignments.[114]

The following prohibitions also apply with respect to the inhabitants of occupied territory:

11.6.2.1 *Prohibition on Compelling Inhabitants of Occupied Territory to Swear Allegiance to the Hostile State*. It is forbidden to compel the inhabitants of occupied territory to

---

107 *Refer to* § 10.5 (Humane Treatment and Other Basic Protections for Protected Persons). *See also* HAGUE IV REG. art. 46 ("Family honour and rights, the lives of persons, and private property, as well as religious convictions and practice, must be respected.").

108 *Refer to* § 10.5.1.2 (Protection for Women Against Rape or Other Indecent Assault).

109 *Refer to* § 10.5.4 (Reprisals Against Protected Persons and Their Property).

110 *Refer to* § 10.5.1.4 (Taking of Hostages).

111 *Refer to* § 10.5.6 (Facility for Applying to the Protecting Powers and Assistance Organizations Such as the ICRC).

112 *Refer to* § 11.13 (Protection of Children in Occupied Territory).

113 *Refer to* § 11.11 (Criminal Law in Occupied Territory); 11.12 (Movement of Persons in Occupied Territory); 11.20.1 (Types of Labor That May Not Be Compelled).

114 *Refer to* § 11.14 (Food and Medical Supplies for the Civilian Population); § 11.15 (Public Health and Hygiene); § 11.16 (Spiritual Assistance); § 11.17 (Relief Efforts and Consignments).

swear allegiance to the hostile State.[115]

11.6.2.2 *Prohibition Against General Penalties in Occupied Territory*. No general penalty, pecuniary or otherwise, shall be inflicted upon the population on account of the acts of individuals for which they cannot be regarded as jointly and severally responsible.[116] Such penalties are prohibited, even if authorized under the law of the occupied territory.

Collective penalties are prohibited as a general matter.[117]

11.6.3 Occupying Power's Duty to Respect the Rights of Protected Persons Secured by the GC. The Occupying Power has certain obligations to respect the rights of protected persons secured by the GC.

Protected persons who are in occupied territory shall not be deprived, in any case or in any manner whatsoever, of the benefits of the GC by any change introduced, as the result of the occupation of a territory, into the institutions or government of the occupied territory, nor by any agreement concluded between the authorities of the occupied territories and the Occupying Power, nor by any annexation by the latter of the whole or part of the occupied territory.[118] For example, an Occupying Power may not purport to annex occupied territory in order to avoid its responsibilities as an Occupying Power.[119]

The Occupying Power may not enter into any special agreements that would adversely affect the situation of protected persons, as defined by the GC, nor restrict the rights that the GC confers upon them.[120]

---

[115] HAGUE IV REG. art. 45 ("It is forbidden to compel the inhabitants of occupied territory to swear allegiance to the hostile Power."); 1899 HAGUE II REG. art. 45 ("Any pressure on the population of occupied territory to take the oath to the hostile Power is prohibited.").

[116] HAGUE IV REG. art. 50 ("No general penalty, pecuniary or otherwise, shall be inflicted upon the population on account of the acts of individuals for which they cannot be regarded as jointly and severally responsible.").

[117] *Refer to* § 8.16.2.1 (Individual Penal Responsibility and No Collective Punishment).

[118] GC art. 47 ("Protected persons who are in occupied territory shall not be deprived, in any case or in any manner whatsoever, of the benefits of the present Convention by any change introduced, as the result of the occupation of a territory, into the institutions or government of the said territory, nor by any agreement concluded between the authorities of the occupied territories and the Occupying Power, nor by any annexation by the latter of the whole or part of the occupied territory.").

[119] *See* Trial of Robert Wagner, Gauleiter and Head of the Civil Government of Alsace during the Occupation, and Six Others, III U.N. LAW REPORTS 23, 45 (Permanent Military Tribunal at Strasbourg, Apr. 23-May 3, 1946, and Court of Appeal, Jul. 24, 1946) ("Wagner put forward a plea based upon an alleged violation by false application of the Ordinance of 28th August, 1944, claiming that the acts alleged were committed in Alsace, which was annexed by Germany, and on territory over which French sovereignty had ceased to operate. The purported declaration of annexation of Alsace by Germany on which reliance was placed in the plea was deemed by the Court of Appeal to be nothing more than a unilateral act which could not legally modify the clauses of the treaty signed at Versailles on 28th June, 1919, by the representatives of Germany. Therefore the acts alleged to have been committed by Wagner were committed in Alsace, French territory, and constituted war crimes in the sense of Art. 1 of the Ordinance of 28th August, 1944.").

[120] *Refer to* § 10.1.1.2 (Special Agreements Under the GC).

The Occupying Power may also not evade its responsibilities through the purported renunciation by protected persons of the rights secured to them by the GC and by any special agreements referred to in Article 7 of the GC.[121]

In certain cases, a protected person's rights of communication under the GC may be forfeited for security reasons.[122]

11.6.4 <u>Citizens of Neutral States in Occupied Territory</u>. Citizens of neutral States residing within an occupied territory are generally treated the same as other residents of occupied territory.[123]

11.7 Authority of the Occupying Power Over Inhabitants

The Occupying Power's authority over inhabitants of occupied territory derives from its war powers and from its duty to ensure public order and safety in occupied territory. The Occupying Power, as a belligerent State, may take such measures of control and security in regard to protected persons as may be necessary as a result of the war.[124] In addition, the Occupying Power may take measures necessary to fulfill its duty to ensure public order and safety.[125]

11.7.1 <u>Inhabitants' Obedience to the Occupying Power</u>. It is the duty of the inhabitants to carry on their ordinary peaceful pursuits, to behave in an absolutely peaceful manner, to take no part whatever in the hostilities carried on, to refrain from all injurious acts toward the forces or in respect to their operations, and to render strict obedience to the orders of the occupant.[126]

Subject to the restrictions imposed by international law, the Occupying Power may demand and enforce from the inhabitants of occupied territory such obedience as may be necessary for the security of its forces, for the maintenance of law and order, and for the proper administration of the country.[127]

The inhabitant's obedience to the Occupying Power is generally distinguished from a duty of allegiance.[128] The inhabitant's duty of allegiance to his or her State of nationality is not

---

[121] *Refer to* § 10.3.6 (Non-Renunciation of Rights Secured by the GC).

[122] *Refer to* § 10.4.2 (Derogation in Occupied Territory).

[123] *Refer to* § 15.6.4 (Neutral Persons Resident in Occupied Territory).

[124] *Refer to* § 10.6 (Measures of Control and Security).

[125] *Refer to* § 11.5.1 (Authority Conferred by the Occupying Power's Duty to Ensure Public Order and Safety).

[126] 1956 FM 27-10 (Change No. 1 1976) ¶432 ("It is the duty of the inhabitants to carry on their ordinary peaceful pursuits, to behave in an absolutely peaceful manner, to take no part whatever in the hostilities carried on, to refrain from all injurious acts toward the troops or in respect to their operations, and to render strict obedience to the orders of the occupant.").

[127] 1956 FM 27-10 (Change No. 1 1976) ¶432 ("Subject to the restrictions imposed by international law, the occupant can demand and enforce from the inhabitants of occupied territory such obedience as may be necessary for the security of its forces, for the maintenance of law and order, and for the proper administration of the country.").

[128] Brigadier General George B. Davis, *Working Memoranda (Confidential for the United States Delegates): The Second Peace Conference (Paragraph 2 of Programme), The Rules of War on Land*, 37 (1907) ("But the control

severed.[129] The inhabitants, however, are not bound to obey their State of nationality.[130]

11.7.1.1 *Enforcement of Obedience*. The Occupying Power's enforcement of obedience must comply with the law of war. For example, measures prohibited by the law of war, such as collective punishments, acts of torture, or reprisals, may not be used.

11.7.2 Censorship and Other Regulation of the Media. Under the law of belligerent occupation,[131] for the purposes of security, an Occupying Power may establish censorship or regulation of any or all forms of media (*e.g.*, press, radio, television) and entertainment (*e.g.*, theater, movies), of correspondence, and of other means of communication.[132] For example, an Occupying Power may prohibit entirely the publication of newspapers that pose a threat to security, or it may prescribe regulations for the publication or circulation of newspapers of other media for the purpose of fulfilling its obligations to restore public order.[133]

The Occupying Power is not required to furnish facilities for postal service, but may take charge of them itself, especially if the officials of the occupied district fail to act or to obey its

---

which the commanding general exercises over the inhabitants of occupied territory is not based upon any theory of allegiance, their relation to him being out of constrained obedience to his commands. As the allegiance of the population has not been changed, the occupying commander can not compel the individuals composing it to commit acts of treason; that is, to take part in acts of hostility against their own government.").

[129] GC COMMENTARY 346 ("The words 'duty of allegiance' [in Article 68 of the GC] constitute an acknowledgment of the fundamental principle according to which the occupation does not sever the bond existing between the inhabitants and the conquered State. Protected persons must nevertheless obey legitimate orders issued by the Occupying Power."); GC COMMENTARY 305 ("It may be mentioned in this connection that public officials and judges act under the superintendence and control of the occupant to whom legal power has passed in actual practice and to whom they, like any other protected person, owe obedience. But this duty of obedience does not cancel out the duty of allegiance which subsists during the period of occupation.").

[130] United States v. Rice, 17 U.S. 246, 254 (1819) (Story, J.) ("By the conquest and military occupation of Castine, the enemy acquired that firm possession which enabled him to exercise the fullest rights of sovereignty over that place. The sovereignty of the United States over the territory was, of course, suspended, and the laws of the United States could no longer be rightfully enforced there, or be obligatory upon the inhabitants who remained and submitted to the conquerors. By the surrender, the inhabitants passed under a temporary allegiance to the British government, and were bound by such laws, and such only, as it chose to recognise and impose. From the nature of the case, no other laws could be obligatory upon them, for where there is no protection or allegiance or sovereignty, there can be no claim to obedience. Castine was, therefore, during this period, so far as respected our revenue laws, to be deemed a foreign port; and goods imported into it by the inhabitants, were subject to such duties only as the British government chose to require. Such goods were in no correct sense imported into the United States.").

[131] The discussion in this sub-section focuses solely on what is permitted under the law of war and does not address possible implications of censorship under the First Amendment of the Constitution.

[132] 1956 FM 27-10 (Change No. 1 1976) ¶377 ("The belligerent occupant may establish censorship of the press, radio, theater, motion pictures, and television, of correspondence, and of all other means of communication. It may prohibit entirely the publication of newspapers or prescribe regulations for their publication and circulation.").

[133] *For example*, Coalition Provisional Authority Public Notice, *Towards a Responsible Iraqi Media*, Jun. 10, 2003 ("Disseminating material that incites violence, however poses a direct threat to personal freedoms, and is therefore banned under the terms of this order, as it is in any civilized society. Equally, advocating the return to power of the repressive and criminal Ba'athist regime would undermine civil order and the freedom from fear of political repression, both of which are necessary for the development of a free and democratic Iraq. Thus the CPA is issuing an Order that prohibits Iraqi media organizations from broadcasting or publishing material that would seriously undermine security and civil order in Iraq.").

orders.[134]

11.7.3 Control of Means of Transportation. An Occupying Power is entitled to exercise authority over all means of public and private transportation, whether land, waterborne, or air, within the occupied territory, and may seize them and regulate their operation.[135]

11.7.4 Limits on Safety Measures. If the Occupying Power considers it necessary, for imperative reasons of security, to take safety measures concerning protected persons, it may, at the most, subject them to assigned residence or to internment.[136] The Occupying Power must comply with certain procedural requirements (*e.g.*, appeal, periodic review) when conducting assigned residence or internment of protected persons in occupied territory based on imperative reasons of security.[137] The Occupying Power also has an obligation to support persons who are assigned residence and thus are required to leave their homes, consistent with the standards for the treatment of internees.[138]

11.8 Administration of Occupied Territory

11.8.1 Paramount Authority of the Occupying Power Over Government Functions in Occupied Territory. The functions of the hostile government—whether of a general, provincial, or local character—continue only to the extent they are sanctioned by the Occupying Power.[139]

11.8.2 Continued Performance of Duties by Civil Servants and Other Officials of Local Governments. The Occupying Power may, while retaining its paramount authority, permit the government of the country to perform some or all of its normal functions.[140] It may, for example, call upon the local authorities to administer designated rear areas, subject to the

[134] 1956 FM 27-10 (Change No. 1 1976) ¶377 ("The occupant is not required to furnish facilities for postal service, but may take charge of them itself, especially if the officials of the occupied district fail to act or to obey its orders.").

[135] 1956 FM 27-10 (Change No. 1 1976) ¶378 ("The belligerent occupant exercises authority over all means of transportation, both public and private, within the occupied district, and may seize them and regulate their operation.").

[136] *Refer to* § 10.6.3 (No Measures of Control More Severe Than Assigned Residence or Internment).

[137] *Refer to* § 10.9.3 (Procedure for Internment or Assigned Residence in Occupied Territory).

[138] *Refer to* § 10.6.4 (Support to Persons Who Are Assigned Residence Should Be Guided by Internment Standards).

[139] 1956 FM 27-10 (Change No. 1 1976) ¶367a ("The functions of the hostile government—whether of a general, provincial, or local character—continue only to the extent they are sanctioned by the occupant."). *For example*, Coalition Provisional Authority Regulation No. 1, §2 (May 16, 2003) ("Unless suspended or replaced by the CPA or superseded by legislation issued by democratic institutions of Iraq, laws in force in Iraq as of April 16, 2003 shall continue to apply in Iraq insofar as the laws do not prevent the CPA from exercising its rights and fulfilling its obligations, or conflict with the present or any other Regulation or Order issued by the CPA.").

[140] 1956 FM 27-10 (Change No. 1 1976) ¶367b ("The occupant may, while retaining its paramount authority, permit the government of the country to perform some or all of its normal functions. It may, for example, call upon the local authorities to administer designated rear areas, subject to the guidance and direction of the occupying power. Such action is consistent with the status of occupation, so long as there exists the firm possession and the purpose to maintain paramount authority.").

guidance and direction of the Occupying Power.[141] Such action is consistent with the status of occupation, so long as there exists the firm possession of territory and the purpose to maintain paramount authority.[142] Similarly, for example, courts are generally to continue the ordinary administration of justice during occupation.[143]

The compulsion of civil servants and other officials of local governments to continue to perform their duties must be justified by military necessity and consistent with applicable provisions of the GC.[144]

11.8.3 Local Governments Under Duress or Surrogate Governments. The restrictions placed upon the authority of a belligerent State cannot be avoided by a system of using a puppet government, central or local, to carry out acts that would be unlawful if performed directly by the Occupying Power. Acts induced or compelled by the Occupying Power are nonetheless its acts.[145]

11.8.4 Responsibility of the Occupying Power for Treatment Accorded to Protected Persons by Its Agents. An Occupying Power, like belligerent States, is responsible for the treatment accorded to protected persons by its agents, irrespective of any individual responsibility that may be incurred.[146] The responsibility of the Occupying Power for its agents includes those agents that are not its nationals, such as locally recruited agents of the nationality of the State whose territory is occupied.[147]

11.8.5 Immunity of Occupation Personnel From Local Law. Military and civilian personnel of the occupying forces and occupation administration and persons accompanying them are not subject to the local law or to the jurisdiction of the local civil or criminal courts of the occupied territory, unless expressly made subject thereto by a competent officer of the

---

[141] *For example*, Reports of General MacArthur, *in* I Supplement MacArthur in Japan: The Occupation: Military Phase 25-26 (1966) ("While the air lift of the main initial force was in progress on 30 August, GHQ, AFPAC, issued an amendment to Operations Instructions No. 4, which materially altered the missions assigned to the Army commanders who soon would be arriving on the Nippon homeland. Instead of actually instituting 'military government,' Army commanders were to supervise the execution of the policies relative to government functions which GHQ, AFPAC, was to issue directly to the Japanese Government;").

[142] *Refer to* § 11.2.2.2 ("Under the Authority" – Suspension and Substitution of Governmental Authority).

[143] *Refer to* § 11.10 (Ordinary Courts in Occupied Territory).

[144] *Refer to* § 11.21.1 (Continued Service of Judges and Other Public Officials).

[145] 1956 FM 27-10 (Change No. 1 1976) ¶366 ("The restrictions placed upon the authority of a belligerent government cannot be avoided by a system of using a puppet government, central or local, to carry out acts which would be unlawful if performed directly by the occupant. Acts induced or compelled by the occupant are nonetheless its acts.").

[146] *Refer to* § 10.3.5 (State Responsibility for Its Agents' Treatment of Protected Persons); § 18.9.1 (State Responsibility for Violations of the Law of War by Its Armed Forces).

[147] GC COMMENTARY 212 ("The nationality of the agents does not affect the issue. That is of particular importance in occupied territories, as it means that the occupying authorities are responsible for acts committed by their locally recruited agents of the nationality of the occupied country.").

Occupying Power.[148]

It is important for the Occupying Power to ensure that an appropriate system of substantive law applies to such persons and that tribunals are in existence to deal with civil litigation to which they are parties and with offenses committed by them.[149] In the past, provost courts have been used for these purposes.[150] In recent practice, the Uniform Code of Military Justice and the Military Extraterritorial Jurisdiction Act, among others, have been used to address offenses committed by military and civilian personnel in the context of occupation.[151]

11.8.6 Civilian or Military Nature of the Occupation Government. It is immaterial whether the government over an enemy's territory consists in a military or civil or mixed administration. Its character is the same and the source of its authority the same. It is a government imposed by force, and the legality of its acts is determined by the law of war.[152]

For example, the governing authority established by the Occupying Power may be composed of civilian personnel.[153]

---

[148] 1956 FM 27-10 (Change No. 1 1976) ¶374 ("Military and civilian personnel of the occupying forces and occupation administration and persons accompanying them are not subject to the local law or to the jurisdiction of the local courts of the occupied territory unless expressly made subject thereto by a competent officer of the occupying forces or occupation administration."). *For example*, Coleman v. Tennessee, 97 U.S. 509, 518-19 (1878) ("The laws of Tennessee with regard to offenses and their punishment, which were allowed to remain in force during its military occupation, did not apply to the defendant, as he was at the time a soldier in the army of the United States and subject to the Articles of War. He was responsible for his conduct to the laws of his own government only as enforced by the commander of its army in that state, without whose consent he could not even go beyond its lines. Had he been caught by the forces of the enemy after committing the offense, he might have been subjected to a summary trial and punishment by order of their commander, and there would have been no just ground of complaint, for the marauder and the assassin are not protected by any usages of civilized warfare. But the courts of the state, whose regular government was superseded and whose laws were tolerated from motives of convenience, were without jurisdiction to deal with him.").

[149] 1956 FM 27-10 (Change No. 1 1976) ¶374 ("The occupant should see to it that an appropriate system of substantive law applies to such persons and that tribunals are in existence to deal with civil litigation to which they are parties and with offenses committed by them.").

[150] *Refer to* § 11.11.3.1 (U.S. Practice for Properly Constituted, Non-Political Military Courts).

[151] *Refer to* § 18.19.3.1 (Uniform Code of Military Justice Offenses); § 18.19.3.5 (Extraterritorial Application of Certain Federal Offenses Through MEJA).

[152] 1956 FM 27-10 (Change No. 1 1976) ¶368 ("It is immaterial whether the government over an enemy's territory consists in a military or civil or mixed administration. Its character is the same and the source of its authority the same. It is a government imposed by force, and the legality of its acts is determined by the law of war.").

[153] *For example*, E. ZIEMKE, THE U.S. ARMY IN THE OCCUPATION OF GERMANY 1944-1946 404 (1975) ("From the beginning the US Group Control Council had been considered more a vehicle for future civilian authority than an element of Army-administered military government. In April 1945, in his first outline for military government organization, Clay proposed also to bring civilians into the theater G-5 so that both it and the US Group Control Council could be 'carved out of' the military command when the shift to civilian responsibility occurred. A month later, in the organizational directive for military government, Clay stated, 'This organization must become civilian in character as rapidly as consistent with efficient performance so that it may become at the earliest possible date a framework for the administration of political control in Germany by the appropriate US civil agencies.'").

11.9 LOCAL LAW AND LEGISLATION

11.9.1 General Continuation of Municipal Law of the Occupied Territory as Between Inhabitants. In general, the municipal law of the occupied territory (*i.e.*, the ordinary domestic civil and criminal law) and their administration remain in full force so far as the inhabitants of occupied territory are concerned, unless changed by the Occupying Power.[154] For example, the penal laws of the occupied territory generally continue in force.[155]

As a foreign State and as the paramount authority in the occupied territory, the Occupying Power is not bound by the municipal law of the occupied territory.[156] For example, the Occupying Power would not be bound by a municipal law that had been enacted by the State of the occupied territory to prevent trading with the enemy.[157] Similarly, the Occupying Power's personnel are immune from the application of local law.[158]

11.9.2 Authority for the Occupying Power to Suspend, Repeal, or Change the Municipal Law Applicable to Occupied Territory. The duty of the Occupying Power to respect, unless absolutely prevented, the laws in force in the country prohibits it from arbitrarily exercising its authority to suspend, repeal, or change the municipal law applicable to occupied territory.[159] As with other authorities under the law of war, the Occupying Power must use its power with respect to the municipal law of occupied territory in good faith and not for the purpose of oppressing the population.[160]

---

[154] Coleman v. Tennessee, 97 U.S. 509, 517 (1879) ("By such occupation the political relations between the people of the hostile country and their former government or sovereign are for the time severed; but the municipal laws -- that is, the laws which regulate private rights, enforce contracts, punish crime, and regulate the transfer of property -- remain in full force, so far as they affect the inhabitants of the country among themselves, unless suspended or superseded by the conqueror. And the tribunals by which the laws are enforced continue as before, unless thus changed. In other words, the municipal laws of the State, and their administration, remain in full force so far as the inhabitants of the country are concerned, unless changed by the occupying belligerent."). *See also* Ho Tung & Co. v. United States, 42 Ct. Cl. 213, 227 (Ct. Cl. 1907) ("It is unquestioned that upon the occupation by our military forces of the port of Manila it was their duty to respect and assist in enforcing the municipal laws then in force there until the same might be changed by order of the military commander, called for by the necessities of war.").

[155] *Refer to* § 11.11.1 (General Continuation of Penal Laws of the Occupied Territory).

[156] *Refer to* § 11.8.1 (Paramount Authority of the Occupying Power Over Government Functions in Occupied Territory).

[157] *For example*, N.V. De Bataafsche Petroleum Maatschappli & Ors. v. The War Damage Commission (Court of Appeal, Singapore, April 13, 1956), *reprinted in* 51 AJIL 802, 807 (1957) ('The provisions of the [Netherlands Indies] Wartime Legal Relations Ordinance were, no doubt, very appropriate when applied to 'persons,' as defined in section 1 of the Ordinance, but to contend that they apply to a belligerent occupant, that is to say, to an International Person, who is thereby placed under a statutory obligation to seek the permission of the Director of Economic Affairs before doing any act which might benefit the enemy (which is, of course, himself) is, to my mind, an untenable proposition.").

[158] *Refer to* § 11.8.5 (Immunity of Occupation Personnel From Local Law).

[159] *Refer to* § 11.5.2 (Duty to Respect, Unless Absolutely Prevented, the Laws in Force in the Country).

[160] GC COMMENTARY 337 ("It will be seen that the powers which the Occupying Power is recognized to have are very extensive and complex, but these varied measures must not under any circumstances serve as a means of oppressing the population. The legislative and penal jurisdiction exercised by the occupation authorities, as holder of public power, is therefore hedged about with numerous safeguards set forth in the following Articles.").

The Occupying Power may subject the population of the occupied territory to provisions: (1) that are essential to enable the Occupying Power to fulfill its obligations under the GC; (2) to maintain the orderly government of the territory; and (3) to ensure the security of the Occupying Power, of the members and property of the occupying forces or administration, and likewise of the establishments and lines of communication used by them.[161]

Broader authority for the Occupying Power to change the laws of the occupied territory may be provided by the U.N. Security Council.[162]

After the Occupying Power's occupation has ended, its changes to the municipal law of the occupied territory may be changed, subject to the requirements of applicable international law.

11.9.2.1 *Distinction Between Suspension, Repeal, Change, or Enactment of Municipal Laws*. The distinction between the suspension, repeal, change, or enactment of a new law may be of little practical consequence.

Implicit in the authority to enact new laws is the authority to suspend or repeal existing laws. Thus, the repeal or suspension of a law may be accomplished by the Occupying Power subjecting the population of the occupied territory to additional provisions of law that are inconsistent with the earlier law. For example, a law permitting discrimination may be effectively suspended by the Occupying Power requiring officials to apply the law impartially.[163]

The power to suspend or repeal laws may also include the power to amend laws. For example, the partial suspension of a tax imposed on the population may also be viewed as a change in the tax rate.[164]

However, new penal provisions may not come into force before they have been published.[165]

11.9.2.2 *Examples of Laws That May Be Suspended, Repealed, Changed, or Enacted by the Occupying Power*. Examples of provisions that may, depending on the circumstances, be suspended, repealed, changed, or enacted by the Occupying Power include legal provisions:

---

[161] GC art. 64 ("The Occupying Power may, however, subject the population of the occupied territory to provisions which are essential to enable the Occupying Power to fulfil its obligations under the present Convention, to maintain the orderly government of the territory, and to ensure the security of the Occupying Power, of the members and property of the occupying forces or administration, and likewise of the establishments and lines of communication used by them.").

[162] *Refer to* § 11.1.2.5 (Occupation and U.N. Security Council Resolutions).

[163] *For example*, Coalition Provisional Authority Order No. 7, *Penal Code*, §4 (Jun. 10, 2003) ("In exercising their official functions, all persons undertaking public duties or holding public office, including all police, prosecutors, and judges, must apply the law impartially. No person will be discriminated against on the basis of sex, race, color, language, religion, political opinion, national, ethnic or social origin, or birth.").

[164] *Refer to* § 11.22.1.2 (Changes in Taxes or New Taxes).

[165] *Refer to* § 11.11.2.1 (Publication of Penal Provisions Before Coming Into Force).

- relating to serious offenses that pose a threat to public order, such as kidnapping, rape, and forcible vehicle larceny;[166]

- relating to the sale or possession of weapons by members of the civilian population;[167]

- relating to measures for the protection of the Occupying Power's forces or administration (*e.g.*, laws relating to the recruitment of persons into the occupied State's armed forces or insurgent groups, relating to curfews or restricted areas);[168]

- relating to political process, such as laws regarding the rights of suffrage and of assembly;[169]

- relating to the supply of food and other items essential to the survival of the civilian population, and the prevention of illicit trade in, or hoarding of, such items;[170]

---

[166] *For example*, Coalition Provisional Authority Order No. 31, *Modifications of Penal Code and Criminal Proceedings Law*, preamble, §§2-3, 5 (Sept. 10, 2003) (modifying sentences for certain offenses in the Iraqi Penal Code based on the recognition that "instances of kidnapping, rape, and forcible vehicle larceny represent a serious threat to the security and stability of the Iraqi population").

[167] *For example*, COLONEL I. L. HUNT, AMERICAN MILITARY GOVERNMENT OF OCCUPIED GERMANY, 1918-1920: REPORT OF THE OFFICER IN CHARGE OF CIVIL AFFAIRS, THIRD ARMY AND AMERICAN FORCES IN GERMANY 107 (1943) ("'The carrying of arms or deadly weapons is forbidden except by the local police. Every person in possession of arms and ammunition of any kind must deliver them to the American authorities at such time or place as may be appointed. A receipt for each weapon will be given at the time of delivery and the weapon tagged with the name of the owner.' Precedents for forbidding the civil population to carry arms and ammunition during a military occupation are so numerous that the publication of such regulations by the American army in this instance cannot be considered a severe restriction. During the march to the Rhine, the Commanding General of the Third Army had recognized the necessity of a regulation of this nature, and in Memorandum No. 4 had instructed unit commanders to forbid civilians to carry deadly weapons.").

[168] GC COMMENTARY 337 ("(c) It is, lastly, authorized to promulgate penal provisions for its own protection. This power has long been recognized by international law. The provision is sufficiently comprehensive to cover all civilian and military organizations which an Occupying Power normally maintains in occupied territory. The Convention mentions 'the Occupying Power' itself besides referring to the members and property of the occupying forces or administration, so that general activities such as activities on behalf of enemy armed forces are covered. The Occupying Power is entitled to use establishments and lines of communication for its own needs; it is therefore entitled to take appropriate measures to ensure their security.").

[169] 1956 FM 27-10 (Change No. 1 1976) ¶371 ("The occupant may alter, repeal, or suspend laws of the following types: *a*. Legislation constituting a threat to its security, such as laws relating to recruitment and the bearing of arms. *b*. Legislation dealing with political process, such as laws regarding the rights of suffrage and of assembly. *c*. Legislation the enforcement of which would be inconsistent with the duties of the occupant, such as laws establishing racial discrimination.").

[170] *For example*, COLONEL I. L. HUNT, AMERICAN MILITARY GOVERNMENT OF OCCUPIED GERMANY, 1918-1920: REPORT OF THE OFFICER IN CHARGE OF CIVIL AFFAIRS, THIRD ARMY AND AMERICAN FORCES IN GERMANY 164-65 (1943) ("Sale of American foodstuffs was by the ticket system. … The method of using the food tickets, was, in brief, as follows. Each person or head of family was issued the number of coupons to which he was entitled, each coupon authorizing him to buy a certain quantity of a certain food, within a certain period of time. There were also coupons, not bearing the name of any particular food, but numbered, to be used for foods not regularly issued. The coupons entitled the holder to register with some merchant of his own choice, who in turn registered his total requirements with the local Food Office. When the food arrived, each merchant was allotted the amount necessary to provide for the persons registered with him. Announcements of distribution were made in the daily papers. The

- relating to the administration of the law, such as repealing laws establishing racial discrimination or promulgating laws requiring the impartial application of the law by local officials;[171] and

- relating to the Occupying Power's obligations under the GC, such as legislation to help provide for child welfare, labor, food, hygiene, and public health of the occupied territory.[172]

11.9.3 Procedural Obligation – Notification to the Population of Changes in Law. The Occupying Power is not required to adhere to the local procedure for amending municipal law. However, the population of the occupied territory must be informed of the alteration, suspension, or repeal of existing laws, and of the enactment of new laws. In particular, penal provisions must be published before entering into force.[173]

In practice, to ensure that all inhabitants are on notice of what is expected, the Occupying Power is to publish a decree or order at, or immediately after, the beginning of the occupation, in order to clarify the applicable laws and orders, and the punishments that can be imposed if the inhabitants fail to comply. Such notification may be provided as part of a proclamation of occupation.[174]

11.10 Ordinary Courts in Occupied Territory

In general, the courts and other tribunals of the occupied territory, like other governmental functions, should continue to operate.[175] For example, ordinary crimes that do not affect the security of the Occupying Power or its personnel should continue to be administered by the courts in the occupied territory.[176]

---

merchant kept the coupons to indicate the amounts and regularity of his sales. Any allotment not entirely sold, might be returned to the food authorities or debited against the next allotment. The system seemed simple enough, but there was considerable traffic in tickets. Well-to-do people seldom suffered for lack of food, though they may often not have been able to get the variety they wanted.").

[171] *For example*, Coalition Provisional Authority Order No. 7, *Penal Code*, §4 (Jun. 10, 2003) ("In exercising their official functions, all persons undertaking public duties or holding public office, including all police, prosecutors, and judges, must apply the law impartially. No person will be discriminated against on the basis of sex, race, color, language, religion, political opinion, national, ethnic or social origin, or birth.").

[172] GC Commentary 337 ("The legislative power of the occupant as the Power responsible for applying the Convention and the temporary holder of authority is limited to the matters set out in a limitative list below. (a) It may promulgate provisions required for the application of the Convention in accordance with the obligations imposed on it by the latter in a number of spheres: child welfare, labour, food, hygiene and public health etc.").

[173] *Refer to* § 11.11.2.1 (Publication of Penal Provisions Before Coming Into Force).

[174] *Refer to* § 11.2.4 (Proclamation of Occupation).

[175] Lieber Code art. 6 ("All civil and penal law shall continue to take its usual course in the enemy's places and territories under Martial Law, unless interrupted or stopped by order of the occupying military power; but all the functions of the hostile government – legislative, executive, or administrative – whether of a general, provincial, or local character, cease under Martial Law, or continue only with the sanction, or, if deemed necessary, the participation of the occupier or invader.").

[176] *Refer to* § 11.11.1.4 (Continued Administration of Penal Law by Courts in the Occupied Territory).

However, the administration of justice in the occupied territory, like the performance of other governmental functions, is subject to the direction of the Occupying Power.[177]

11.10.1 Authority to Suspend Ordinary Courts. The ordinary courts in occupied territory should be suspended only if: (1) judges and magistrates are unable or unwilling to perform their duties; (2) the courts are corrupt or unfairly constituted; or (3) the local judicial administration has collapsed due to the hostilities preceding the occupation.[178]

In such cases, the Occupying Power may use its own properly constituted, non-political military courts to ensure that offenses against the local laws are properly tried.[179] The Occupying Power may also reform local courts, including by establishing new criminal courts under the law of the occupied State.[180]

11.10.1.1 *Judicial Inability or Unwillingness to Perform Their Duties*. Judges and magistrates may abstain from fulfilling their functions for reasons of conscience.[181] An inability to perform their normal duties may result from a failure of public services, such as public transportation, or threats by insurgents.

11.10.1.2 *Corruption and Unfairness in the Judicial System*. Corruption and unfairness in the judicial system may constitute a serious obstacle to public order and safety, and an obstacle to the Occupying Power's application of the fundamental fair trial protections guaranteed by the GC.[182] The Occupying Power may take appropriate measures to remedy such corruption or unfairness. For example, committees may be established to review the suitability of judges and prosecutors.[183] Similarly, a facility may be established to help resolve conflicting property claims on a voluntary basis.[184]

---

[177] *For example*, Coalition Provisional Authority Order No. 7, *Penal Code*, §1 (Jun. 10, 2003) ("All judges, police and prosecutors shall perform their duties in accordance with CPA Regulation No. 1 (CPA/REG/23 May 2003/01) and in accordance with any other Regulations, Orders, Memoranda or instructions issued by the CPA.").

[178] 1956 FM 27-10 (Change No. 1 1976) ¶373 ("The ordinary courts of justice should be suspended only if: *a*. Judges and magistrates abstain from fulfilling their functions (see *GC, art. 54;* par. 422 herein); or *b*. The courts are corrupt or unfairly constituted; or *c*. Local judicial administration has collapsed during the hostilities preceding the occupation and the occupant must set up its own courts to ensure that offenses against the local laws are properly tried. In such cases, the occupant may establish courts of its own and make this measure known to the inhabitants.").

[179] *Refer to* § 11.11.3 (Properly Constituted, Non-Political Military Courts in Occupied Territory).

[180] *Refer to* § 11.11.1.4 (Continued Administration of Penal Law by Courts in the Occupied Territory).

[181] *Refer to* § 11.21.1 (Continued Service of Judges and Other Public Officials).

[182] *Refer to* § 11.5 (Duty of the Occupying Power to Ensure Public Order and Safety); § 10.29 (Judicial Proceedings Regarding Protected Persons in Occupied Territory or Internees in a Belligerent's Home Territory).

[183] *For example*, Coalition Provisional Authority Order No. 15, *Establishment of the Judicial Review Committee*, §4(1) (Jun. 23, 2003) ("The Committee shall investigate and gather information on the suitability of Judges and Prosecutors to hold office. It shall have the power to remove judges and prosecutors from office, confirm their continued holding of office, appoint replacements for judges and prosecutors removed from office and resolve the claims of judges and prosecutors who assert that they were improperly removed from office.").

[184] *For example*, Coalition Provisional Authority Regulation No. 4, *Establishment of the Iraqi Property Reconciliation Facility*, §1(1) (Jun. 26, 2003) ("There shall be established an Iraqi Property Reconciliation Facility

11.10.2 Prohibition Against Extinguishing Rights and Actions of Enemy Nationals. It is especially forbidden to declare abolished, suspended, or inadmissible in a court of law the rights and actions of the nationals of a hostile party.[185]

This rule has been interpreted to apply solely to enemy areas occupied by a belligerent.[186] It has been interpreted to prohibit a military commander from arbitrarily annulling the results of civil proceedings between private parties.[187]

11.11 Criminal Law in Occupied Territory

This section addresses criminal law in occupied territory. Additional rules apply to judicial proceedings against protected persons in occupied territory, which are also applied by analogy to judicial proceedings against internees in a belligerent's home territory.[188]

(IPRF) that shall commence operation at a time to be fixed by the Administrator, for the purpose of collecting real property claims and promptly resolving such claims on a voluntary basis in a fair and judicious manner.").

[185] HAGUE IV REG. art. 23 ("[I]t is especially forbidden … (h) To declare abolished, suspended, or inadmissible in a court of law the rights and actions of the nationals of a hostile party.").

[186] Ex parte Kumezo Kawato, 317 U.S. 69, 72 footnote 1 (1942) ("Petitioner argues that his case is covered by article 23 h of the Annex to the IVth Hague Convention of 1907: 'It is especially prohibited . . . to declare abolished, suspended, or inadmissible in a Court of law the rights and action of the nationals of the hostile party.' This clause, which was added to the convention of 1899 without substantial discussion either by the Delegates in General Assembly or by the committee and sub-committee which dealt with it, III Proceedings of the Hague Convention of 1907, 12, 107, 136, 240; and I ibid. 83, was construed by an English Court to apply solely in enemy areas occupied by a belligerent. Porter v. Freudenberg, [1915] 1 K. B. 857. The question has not been raised in the courts in this country, but the English interpretation was repeated with approval by Representative Montague of the Interstate Commerce Committee in his address to the House when he presented to it the Trading with the Enemy Act. 55 Cong. Rec. 4842 (1917).").

[187] *For example*, 1958 UK MANUAL ¶524 note 1 ("Hague Rules 23 (*h*). The following example of the relevance of that article may be mentioned: during the British occupation of Cyrenaica in the course of the Second World War, in order to avoid disturbances, pressure was put upon the British administration to prevent the execution of a local judgment restoring to its Italian owner a mill in the occupation of an Arab trustee. The legal adviser of the Administration expressed the view that a failure to enforce the judgment would be contrary to this article, see Watts in Grotius Society, vol. 37, pp. 69-82."). *Cf.* Ochoa v. Hernandez y Morales, 230 U.S. 139, 154-61 (1912) ("In order to determine the extent of the authority of General Henry, and the limitations upon it, we must look to the orders under which the military government was established and maintained. … Under all the circumstances we deem it clear that the Governor was without authority from the President to make any order, judicial in its nature, that would have the effect of depriving any person of his property without due process of law. … Whatever else may be uncertain about the definition of the term 'due process of law,' all authorities agree that it inhibits the taking of one man's property and giving it to another, contrary to settled usages and modes of procedure, and without notice or an opportunity for a hearing.); Raymond v. Thomas, 91 U.S. 712, 715-16 (1876) ("We have looked carefully through the acts of March 2, 1867, and July 19, 1867. They give very large governmental powers to the military commanders designated, within the States committed respectively to their jurisdiction; but we have found nothing to warrant the order here in question. It was not an order for mere delay. It did not prescribe that the proceeding should stop until credit and confidence were restored, and business should resume its wonted channels. It wholly annulled a decree in equity regularly made by a competent judicial officer in a plain case clearly within his jurisdiction, and where there was no pretense of any unfairness, of any purpose to wrong or oppress, or of any indirection whatsoever. … It was an arbitrary stretch of authority, needful to no good end that can be imagined.").

[188] *Refer to* § 10.29 (Judicial Proceedings Regarding Protected Persons in Occupied Territory or Internees in a Belligerent's Home Territory).

11.11.1 General Continuation of Penal Laws of the Occupied Territory. The general principle that the Occupying Power must respect, unless absolutely prevented, the laws in force in the occupied territory also applies to the penal laws of the occupied territory.[189]

In particular, the penal laws of the occupied territory shall remain in force during the occupation, with the exception that they may be repealed or suspended by the Occupying Power where they constitute a threat to its security or an obstacle to the application of the GC.[190] Subject to the latter consideration and to the necessity of ensuring the effective administration of justice, the courts of the occupied territory shall continue to function in respect of all offenses covered by these laws.[191]

11.11.1.1 *Types of Laws That Are Considered Penal Laws*. Penal laws addressed by this rule may be understood to include all laws, regulations, decrees, orders, and similar measures intended to repress offenses, including the rules of criminal procedure.[192]

11.11.1.2 *Laws Constituting an Obstacle to the Application of the GC*. The Occupying Power may repeal or suspend penal laws constituting an obstacle to the application of the GC. For example, the Occupying Power may abrogate discriminatory measures that are incompatible with humane requirements.[193]

11.11.1.3 *Method of Repeal or Suspension of Penal Laws*. The repeal or suspension of the penal laws of the occupied territory may be achieved directly through an order suspending or repealing the law.[194] The suspension of a penal law may also be done by requiring that a penal law may only be enforced with the approval of the Occupying Power.[195] The repeal

---

[189] *Refer to* § 11.9.1 (General Continuation of Municipal Law of the Occupied Territory as Between Inhabitants).

[190] GC art. 64 ("The penal laws of the occupied territory shall remain in force, with the exception that they may be repealed or suspended by the Occupying Power in cases where they constitute a threat to its security or an obstacle to the application of the present Convention.").

[191] GC art. 64 ("Subject to the latter consideration and to the necessity for ensuring the effective administration of justice, the tribunals of the occupied territory shall continue to function in respect of all offences covered by the said laws.").

[192] GC COMMENTARY 335 ("The words 'penal laws' mean all legal provisions in connection with the repression of offenses: the penal code and rules of procedure proper, subsidiary penal laws, laws in the strict sense of the term, decrees, orders, the penal clauses of administrative regulations, penal clauses of financial laws, etc.").

[193] GC COMMENTARY 335 ("The second reservation is in the interests of the population and makes it possible to abrogate any discriminatory measures incompatible with humane requirements. It refers in particular, to provisions which adversely affect racial or religious minorities, such provisions being contrary to the spirit of the Convention (Article 27), which forbids all adverse distinction based, in particular, on race, religion, and political opinion.").

[194] *For example*, Coalition Provisional Authority Order No. 7, *Penal Code*, §2(1) (Jun. 10, 2003) ("Without prejudice to the continuing review of Iraqi laws, the Third Edition of the 1969 Iraqi Penal Code with amendments, registered in Baghdad on the fifth day of Jumada I 1389 or the nineteenth day of July 1969, shall apply, with the exception that i) Part Two, Chapter Two, Paragraph 200, and ii) Part Two, Chapter Three, Section One, Paragraph 225 are hereby suspended.").

[195] *For example*, Coalition Provisional Authority Order No. 7, *Penal Code*, §2(2) (Jun. 10, 2003) ("Legal proceedings may be brought with respect to the following offenses only with the written permission of the Administrator of the CPA: a) Part One, Chapter Four, Paragraphs 81-84, publication offenses. b) Part Two, Chapter One, Paragraphs 156-189, offenses against the external security of the state. c) Part Two, Chapter Two, Paragraphs

or suspension of a penal law may also be done by the Occupying Power's subjecting the population of the occupied territory to additional provisions of law that are inconsistent with application of that penal law.[196]

11.11.1.4 *Continued Administration of Penal Law by Courts in the Occupied Territory*. In general, ordinary crimes that do not affect the security of the Occupying Power or its personnel would be left to the jurisdiction of the courts in the occupied territory.[197]

The continued administration of local and national penal law by the courts in occupied territory is subject to certain modifications by the Occupying Power, such as modifications necessary for ensuring the effective administration of justice.[198]

The Occupying Power may reform or establish new criminal courts in occupied territory as part of its authority to subject the population of the occupied territory to additional provisions of law and its duty to restore and maintain public order.[199] In addition, the Occupying Power may use its properly constituted, non-political military courts in occupied territory for certain types of offenses.[200]

11.11.2 Penal Provisions Enacted by the Occupying Power. As with other types of legal provisions, the Occupying Power may subject the population of the occupied territory to penal provisions: (1) that are essential to enable the Occupying Power to fulfill its obligations under the GC; (2) to maintain the orderly government of the territory; and (3) to ensure the security of the Occupying Power, of the members and property of the occupying forces or administration, and likewise of the establishments and lines of communication used by them.[201]

11.11.2.1 *Publication of Penal Provisions Before Coming Into Force*. The penal provisions enacted by the Occupying Power shall not come into force before they have been

---

190-195; 198-199; 201-219, offenses against the internal security of the state. d) Part Two, Chapter Three, Section One, Paragraphs 223-224; 226-228, offenses against public authorities. e) Part Two, Chapter Three, Section Two, Paragraph 229, offense of insulting a public official.").

[196] *Refer to* § 11.9.2.1 (Distinction Between Suspension, Repeal, Change, or Enactment of Municipal Laws).

[197] 1956 FM 27-10 (Change No. 1 1976) ¶370 ("Crimes not of a military nature and not affecting the occupant's security are normally left to the jurisdiction of the local courts.").

[198] 1956 FM 27-10 (Change No. 1 1976) ¶370 ("In restoring public order and safety, the occupant will continue in force the ordinary civil and penal (criminal) laws of the occupied territory except to the extent it may be authorized by Article 64, *GC* (par 369), and Article 43, *HR* (par. 363), to alter, suspend, or repeal such laws (see also *HR art. 23 (h)*; par. 372 herein; and *GC, art. 51*; par. 418 herein). These laws will be administered by the local officials as far as practicable.").

[199] *For example*, Coalition Provisional Authority Order No. 13, *The Central Criminal Court of Iraq (Revised), (Amended)*, §1(1) (Apr. 22, 2004) ("There shall be established a Central Criminal Court of Iraq (hereinafter 'the CCCI'), which shall sit in the city of Baghdad and in such sessions in other locations in Iraq as provided for in this Order. The CCCI shall have national jurisdiction over all matters set forth in Section 18.").

[200] *Refer to* § 11.11.3 (Properly Constituted, Non-Political Military Courts in Occupied Territory).

[201] *Refer to* § 11.9.2 (Authority for the Occupying Power to Suspend, Repeal, or Change the Municipal Law Applicable to Occupied Territory).

published and brought to the knowledge of the inhabitants in their own language.[202] When more than one language is used by the local population, the Occupying Power may adhere to the local practice regarding official publication of legislation.[203]

The effect of these penal provisions shall not be retroactive.[204]

11.11.3 Properly Constituted, Non-Political Military Courts in Occupied Territory. In case of a breach of the penal provisions promulgated by the Occupying Power by virtue of the second paragraph of Article 64 of the GC, the Occupying Power may hand over the accused to its properly constituted, non-political military courts, on condition that these courts sit in the occupied country. Courts of appeals shall preferably sit in the occupied country.[205]

These courts must be regularly constituted courts affording all the judicial guarantees that are recognized as indispensable by civilized peoples.[206] These courts must also comply with requirements for judicial proceedings regarding protected persons in occupied territory.[207]

11.11.3.1 *U.S. Practice for Properly Constituted, Non-Political Military Courts.* The United States has a long history of using provost courts in occupied territory.[208] In U.S. practice, provost courts have been used as properly constituted, non-political military courts.

---

[202] GC art. 65 ("The penal provisions enacted by the Occupying Power shall not come into force before they have been published and brought to the knowledge of the inhabitants in their own language.").

[203] GC COMMENTARY 338 footnote 3 ("In countries which have more than one official language the Occupying Power will follow local practice and publish the penal provisions it enacts, in either one or more than one language, according to whether the country's legislation was published in one or in more than one language before the occupation.").

[204] GC art. 65 ("The effect of these penal provisions shall not be retroactive.").

[205] GC art. 66 ("In case of a breach of the penal provisions promulgated by it by virtue of the second paragraph of Article 64, the Occupying Power may hand over the accused to its properly constituted, non-political military courts, on condition that the said courts sit in the occupied country. Courts of appeal shall preferably sit in the occupied country.").

[206] *Refer to* § 8.16 (Criminal Procedure and Punishment).

[207] *Refer to* § 10.29 (Judicial Proceedings Regarding Protected Persons in Occupied Territory or Internees in a Belligerent's Home Territory).

[208] *For example*, EARL F. ZIEMKE, THE U.S. ARMY IN THE OCCUPATION OF GERMANY, 1944-1946, 144 (1975) ("As instruments for shaping relations between the population and the occupation forces, military government courts were regarded as most important. They were expected, on the one hand, to enforce sternly the authority claimed in the proclamation and ordinances and, on the other, to point up for the Germans the difference between nazism and democracy by giving fair and impartial trials to all accused. Modeled after Army courts martial, the military government courts convened on three levels: summary (one officer), intermediate (one or more officers), and general (not less than three officers). Summary courts could impose up to one year in prison and fines in marks up to $1,000; intermediate courts, ten years in prison and fines to $10,000; and general courts, the death penalty and unlimited fines."); WINTHROP, MILITARY LAW & PRECEDENTS 803-04 ("In the late civil war there was established at New Orleans by the President, by an order of October 20, 1862, a civil court entitled the 'Provisional Court of Louisiana,' with both civil and criminal jurisdiction. … As to its jurisdiction of crimes, this appears maintained in an extended opinion of its judge, Hon. C.A. Peabody, in the cases of U.S. *v.* Reiter and Louis, charged with murder and arson. … Other Provost Courts, with a jurisdiction assimilated in general to that of justices' or police courts, were established from time to time by military commanders during the war;").

Service regulations have addressed the use of provost courts.[209]

11.11.3.2 *Applicable Law in Properly Constituted, Non-Political Military Courts*. Properly constituted, non-political military courts shall apply only those provisions of law that were applicable prior to the offense, and that are in accordance with general principles of law, in particular the principle that the penalty shall be proportionate to the offense.[210] The requirement that properly constituted, non-political military courts shall apply only those provisions of law that were applicable prior to the offense reflects the general rule that penal laws cannot be retroactive and that there cannot be an offense or penalty unless the act in question was punishable under the law in force at the time the act was committed.[211] The requirement that properly constituted, non-political military courts shall apply only those provisions of law that are in accordance with general principles of law includes the rule that punishments must be based on individual responsibility.[212]

These courts shall also take into consideration the fact that the accused is not a national of the Occupying Power.[213]

These courts also may, at their discretion, convert a sentence of imprisonment to one of internment for the same period.[214]

11.11.4 Limitations on Penalties for Certain, Non-Serious Offenses Solely Intended to Harm the Occupying Power. Protected persons who commit an offense that is solely intended to harm the Occupying Power, but that is not an attempt on the life or limb of members of the occupying forces or administration, nor a grave collective danger, nor seriously damage the property of the occupying forces or administration, or the installations used by them, shall be

---

[209] *See, e.g.*, DEPARTMENT OF THE ARMY PAMPHLET 27-9-2, *Military Judges' Benchbook for Provost Courts* (Oct. 4, 2004).

[210] GC art. 67 ("The courts shall apply only those provisions of law which were applicable prior to the offence, and which are in accordance with general principles of law, in particular the principle that the penalty shall be proportionate to the offence."); GC COMMENTARY 341 ("Article 67 relates to the military courts before which the Occupying Power may bring accused persons under the terms of the preceding Article.").

[211] GC COMMENTARY 341 ("The objet [sic] of the provision is to limit the possibility of arbitrary action by the Occupying Power by ensuring that penal jurisdiction is exercised on a sound basis of universally recognized legal principles. The rule that penal laws cannot be retroactive, which is stated here in general terms, had already been mentioned at the end of Article 65. *Nullum crimen, nulla poena sine lege* is a traditional principle of penal law. There can be no offence, and consequently no penalty, if the act in question is not referred to in a law in force at the time it was committed and subject to punishment under that law."). *Refer to* § 8.16.2.2 (No Crime or Punishment Without Prior Law); § 11.11.2.1 (Publication of Penal Provisions Before Coming Into Force).

[212] GC COMMENTARY 342 ("The 'general principles of law', which are not set out individually here but are referred to as a whole, include the rule concerning the personal nature of punishments, under which nobody may be punished for an offence committed by someone else. This rule is also laid down in Article 33 mentioned above."). *Refer to* § 8.16.2.1 (Individual Penal Responsibility and No Collective Punishment); § 10.5.3.2 (Collective Penalties and Measures of Intimidation or Terrorism).

[213] GC art. 67 ("They shall take into consideration the fact that the accused is not a national of the Occupying Power.").

[214] *Refer to* § 11.11.4.2 (Discretion of Non-Political, Military Courts to Convert Sentences of Imprisonment to Sentences of Internment).

liable to internment or simple imprisonment, provided the duration of such internment or imprisonment is proportionate to the offense committed.[215]

The minor offense must have been solely intended to harm the Occupying Power in order to trigger these restrictions.[216] For example, offenses such as traveling without a permit or violating exchange control regulations would not fall under this restriction, but, nonetheless, may result in internment or simple imprisonment.

11.11.4.1 *Internment or Imprisonment as the Only Measure Adopted for Depriving Protected Persons of Liberty for Such Offenses*. Furthermore, internment or imprisonment shall, for such offenses, be the only measure adopted for depriving protected persons of liberty.[217]

Penalties that do not deprive the protected person of liberty, such as fines, or less severe measures, such as arrest, are not addressed by this rule.[218]

11.11.4.2 *Discretion of Non-Political, Military Courts to Convert Sentences of Imprisonment to Sentences of Internment*. Properly constituted non-political military courts may, at their discretion, convert a sentence of imprisonment to one of internment for the same period.[219]

11.11.5 Imposing the Death Penalty for Offenses Committed by Protected Persons in Occupied Territory. The GC provides that the penal provisions promulgated by the Occupying Power in accordance with Articles 64 and 65 of the GC may impose the death penalty against a protected person only in cases where the person is guilty of espionage, or serious acts of sabotage against the military installations of the Occupying Power, or of intentional offenses that have caused the death of one or more persons, provided that such offenses were punishable by death under the law of the occupied territory in force before the occupation began.[220]

---

[215] GC art. 68 ("Protected persons who commit an offence which is solely intended to harm the Occupying Power, but which does not constitute an attempt on the life or limb of members of the occupying forces or administration, nor a grave collective danger, nor seriously damage the property of the occupying forces or administration or the installations used by them, shall be liable to internment or simple imprisonment, provided the duration of such internment or imprisonment is proportionate to the offence committed.").

[216] GC COMMENTARY 343 ("The minor offences must have been 'solely' intended to harm the Occupying Power. The inclusion of the word 'solely' excludes acts which harm the Occupying Power indirectly.").

[217] GC art. 68 ("Furthermore, internment or imprisonment shall, for such offences, be the only measure adopted for depriving protected persons of liberty.").

[218] GC COMMENTARY 344 ("It should be noted that internment and imprisonment are only mentioned as maximum penalties, and less severe penalties still, such as placing under arrest or fines, may be applied in the case of persons accused of minor offences.").

[219] GC art. 68 ("The courts provided for under Article 66 of the present Convention may at their discretion convert a sentence of imprisonment to one of internment for the same period.").

[220] GC art. 68 ("The penal provisions promulgated by the Occupying Power in accordance with Articles 64 and 65 may impose the death penalty on a protected person only in cases where the person is guilty of espionage, of serious acts of sabotage against the military installations of the Occupying Power or of intentional offences which have

However, the United States has reserved the right to impose the death penalty in accordance with the provisions of Article 68, paragraph 2, of the GC without regard to whether the offenses referred to in that paragraph are punishable by death under the law of the occupied territory at the time the occupation begins.[221] The United States expressed the position that an Occupying Power would be unable to protect its own forces adequately against the activities of illegal combatants unless it retained the authority to apply the death penalty, and the rule in Article 68 of the GC would be subject to manipulation in that an adversary on the verge of being occupied might repeal the death penalty to encourage subversive activities against an Occupying Power.[222]

The death penalty may not be pronounced against a protected person unless the attention of the court has been particularly called to the fact that since the accused is not a national of the Occupying Power, he or she is not bound to it by any duty of allegiance.[223]

In any case, the death penalty may not be pronounced against a protected person who was under eighteen years of age at the time of the offense.[224]

In practice, if an occupation is undertaken with coalition partners, the death penalty may be suspended in order to address requests of these States.[225]

11.11.6 Deduction From Sentences of Period Under Arrest. In all cases, the duration of

---

caused the death of one or more persons, provided that such offences were punishable by death under the law of the occupied territory in force before the occupation began.").

[221] United States, *Statement on Ratification of the GC*, Aug. 2, 1955, 213 UNTS 384 ("The United States reserves the right to impose the death penalty in accordance with the provisions of Article 68, paragraph 2, without regard to whether the offenses referred to therein are punishable by death under the law of the occupied territory at the time the occupation begins.").

[222] SENATE EXECUTIVE REPORT 84-9, *Geneva Conventions for the Protection of War Victims: Report of the Committee on Foreign Relations on Executives D, E, F, and G*, 82nd Congress, First Session, 23 (Jun. 27, 1955) ("Adoption of this limitation upon the death penalty was due to the efforts of a number of countries, some of which had experienced whole-sale imposition of this extreme measure under military occupation, and others of which have abolished the death penalty in their legal systems. Our own Government, while willing to agree not to impose it except in the three categories of cases listed in article 68, was unable to accept the proviso further limiting its use. Along with the United Kingdom, we took the position that an occupying power would be unable to protect its own forces adequately against the activities of illegal combatants unless it retained the power to take drastic legal action to meet the situation. From a practical standpoint, moreover, the limitation in article 68 would permit an enemy on the point of being dislodged from the national territory to repeal a death penalty law previously applicable, thus opening the way to all kinds of subversive activities against the occupant which would not be punishable by death.").

[223] GC art. 68 ("The death penalty may not be pronounced against a protected person unless the attention of the court has been particularly called to the fact that since the accused is not a national of the Occupying Power, he is not bound to it by any duty of allegiance."). *Compare* § 9.28.6 (Death Sentences); § 10.29.5 (Death Sentences).

[224] GC art. 68 ("In any case, the death penalty may not be pronounced against a protected person who was under eighteen years of age at the time of the offense.").

[225] *For example*, Coalition Provision Authority Order No. 7, *Penal Code*, §3(1) (Jun. 10, 2003) ("Capital punishment is suspended. In each case where the death penalty is the only available penalty prescribed for an offense, the court may substitute the lesser penalty of life imprisonment, or such other lesser penalty as provided for in the Penal Code.").

the period during which a protected person accused of an offense is under arrest awaiting trial or punishment shall be deducted from any period of imprisonment awarded.[226]

11.11.7 Limitation on Criminal Jurisdiction With Respect to Pre-Occupation Acts. The GC provides for certain limitations on the criminal jurisdiction of the Occupying Power with respect to the pre-occupation acts of protected persons and of nationals of the Occupying Power, who, before the outbreak of hostilities, have sought refuge in the territory of the occupied State.

11.11.7.1 *Pre-Occupation Acts of Protected Persons*. Protected persons shall not be arrested, prosecuted, or convicted by the Occupying Power for acts committed or opinions expressed before the occupation, or during a temporary interruption thereof, with the exception of breaches of the laws and customs of war.[227]

11.11.7.2 *Protection of Nationals of the Occupying Power Who, Before the Outbreak of Hostilities, Have Sought Refuge in the Territory of the Occupied State*. Nationals of the Occupying Power who, before the outbreak of hostilities, have sought refuge in the territory of the occupied State, shall not be arrested, prosecuted, convicted, or deported from the occupied territory, except for offenses committed after the outbreak of hostilities, or for offenses under common law committed before the outbreak of hostilities that, according to the law of the occupied State, would have justified extradition in time of peace.[228]

Thus, although protected persons may not be forcibly transferred or deported to another country,[229] nationals of the Occupying Power may be involuntarily removed under certain circumstances.[230]

This rule is an exception to the general principle that a State's own nationals are excluded from the protection of the GC.[231]

11.11.8 Disposition of Accused and Convicted Protected Persons Upon the Close of Occupation. Protected persons who have been accused of offenses or convicted by courts in

---

[226] GC art. 69 ("In all cases, the duration of the period during which a protected person accused of an offence is under arrest awaiting trial or punishment shall be deducted from any period of imprisonment awarded.").

[227] GC art. 70 ("Protected persons shall not be arrested, prosecuted or convicted by the Occupying Power for acts committed or for opinions expressed before the occupation, or during a temporary interruption thereof, with the exception of breaches of the laws and customs of war.").

[228] GC art. 70 ("Nationals of the Occupying Power who, before the outbreak of hostilities, have sought refuge in the territory of the occupied State, shall not be arrested, prosecuted, convicted or deported from the occupied territory, except for offences committed after the outbreak of hostilities, or for offences under common law committed before the outbreak of hostilities which, according to the law of the occupied State, would have justified extradition in time of peace.").

[229] *Refer to* § 11.12.3 (Prohibition Against Forcible Transfers and Deportations).

[230] GC COMMENTARY 351-52 ("When criminals again fall into the hands of their State of origin, as a result of the occupation of the territory in which they are living, they must answer for their actions; the occupying authorities may therefore arrest them, take them back to their home country and bring them before its courts, provided the law of the occupied State would have justified their extradition in time of peace.").

[231] *Refer to* § 10.3.3.1 (A State's Own Nationals).

occupied territory shall be handed over at the close of occupation, with the relevant records, to the authorities of the liberated territory.[232]

Pending their transfer to such authorities, such protected persons continue to be protected by the GC because protected persons whose release, repatriation, or re-establishment may take place after such dates continue to benefit from the protections of the GC.[233]

The practical arrangements for the handing over of such protected persons will depend on the circumstances, including whether the liberation of occupied territory is accompanied by fighting and whether the local administration is able to function.[234]

If occupying forces will remain in occupied territory after the end of occupation, it is permissible, with the consent of the formerly occupied State, for the occupying forces to retain custody, in the formerly occupied territory, of protected persons accused or convicted of offenses.

11.12 Movement of Persons in Occupied Territory

11.12.1 Authority of the Occupying Power to Restrict Freedom of Movement. As a general matter, the Occupying Power assumes the authority of the State whose territory is occupied in controlling the movement of persons within the occupied territory, as well as the movement of persons entering and exiting occupied territory. For example, private persons, members of non-governmental organizations, or representatives of foreign States or international organizations seeking to enter occupied territory generally would not be able to do so without authorization from the Occupying Power.

The Occupying Power may withdraw from individuals the right to change their residence, restrict freedom of internal movement, forbid visits to certain districts, prohibit emigration and immigration by protected persons who are nationals of the State whose territory is occupied, and require that all individuals carry identification documents.[235]

11.12.2 Departure of Protected Persons Who Are Not Nationals of the State Whose Territory Is Occupied. Protected persons who are not nationals of the State whose territory is occupied may avail themselves of the right to leave occupied territory subject to the provisions of Article 35 of the GC, and decisions thereon shall be taken according to the procedure that the

---

[232] GC art. 77 ("Protected persons who have been accused of offenses or convicted by the courts in occupied territory, shall be handed over at the close of occupation, with the relevant records, to the authorities of the liberated territory.").

[233] *Refer to* § 10.3.4 (Commencement and Duration of Protected Person Status).

[234] GC COMMENTARY 367 ("The Convention does not lay down any rules concerning the practical arrangements for handing over detainees, because they will depend on circumstances and on whether the liberation of the occupied territory is accompanied by fighting or not, and whether the local administration has been able to continue to function or not.").

[235] 1956 FM 27-10 (Change No. 1 1976) ¶375 ("The occupant may withdraw from individuals the right to change their residence, restrict freedom of internal movement, forbid visits to certain districts, prohibit emigration and immigration (but see *GC art. 48;* par. 381 herein), and require that all individuals carry identification documents.").

Occupying Power shall establish in accordance with the Article 35 of the GC.[236]

Article 35 of the GC sets forth rules regarding the departure of protected persons from the home territory of a belligerent State and provides protected persons with a right to depart. But, Article 35 allows a belligerent to prevent such departure if such departure is contrary to the belligerent's national interests, and Article 35 specifies certain procedural requirements.[237]

Thus, for example, an Occupying Power may prevent the departure of protected persons who are not nationals of the State whose territory is occupied if such departure is contrary to the Occupying Power's national interests. The Occupying Power must comply with the requirements of Article 35 of the GC if it does so (*e.g.*, providing for the reconsideration of its refusal of permission to depart by an appropriate court or administrative board).[238]

11.12.3 Prohibition Against Forcible Transfers and Deportations. Individual or mass forcible transfers, as well as deportations of protected persons from occupied territory to the territory of the Occupying Power, or of any other country, occupied or not, are prohibited, regardless of their motive.[239]

The unlawful deportation or transfer of protected persons in violation of this rule constitutes a grave breach of the GC.[240]

11.12.3.1 *Exception for Certain Transfers and Evacuations*. Nevertheless, the Occupying Power may undertake total or partial evacuation of a given area if required for the security of the population or for imperative military reasons. Such evacuations may not involve the displacement of protected persons outside the bounds of the occupied territory except when, for material reasons, it is impossible to avoid such displacement. Persons thus evacuated shall be transferred back to their homes as soon as hostilities in the area in question have ceased.[241]

For example, in some cases, the whole of occupied territory, such as an island, may be

---

[236] GC art. 48 ("Protected persons who are not nationals of the Power whose territory is occupied, may avail themselves of the right to leave the territory subject to the provisions of Article 35, and decisions thereon shall be taken according to the procedure which the Occupying Power shall establish in accordance with the said Article.").

[237] *Refer to* § 10.8.2 (Departures of Protected Persons From a Belligerent's Home Territory).

[238] GC COMMENTARY 277 ("For the procedure to be followed, Article 48 refers expressly to Article 35. Persons who wish to leave the occupied territory therefore enjoy the same safeguards as protected persons living in the territory of a party to the conflict, i.e. they will have the right to appeal to a court or administrative board and to ask for a Protecting Power to intervene. On the other hand, under paragraph 1 of Article 35, the Occupying Power is entitled to object to the departure of a protected person when its national interests make this absolutely necessary.").

[239] GC art. 49 ("Individual or mass forcible transfers, as well as deportations of protected persons from occupied territory to the territory of the Occupying Power or to that of any other country, occupied or not, are prohibited, regardless of their motive.").

[240] *Refer to* § 18.9.3.1 (Acts Constituting Grave Breaches).

[241] GC art. 49 ("Nevertheless, the Occupying Power may undertake total or partial evacuation of a given area if the security of the population or imperative military reasons so demand. Such evacuations may not involve the displacement of protected persons outside the bounds of the occupied territory except when for material reasons it is impossible to avoid such displacement. Persons thus evacuated shall be transferred back to their homes as soon as hostilities in the area in question have ceased.").

dangerous, and it may be safer for the protected person to be transferred from occupied territory.[242]

The Occupying Power undertaking such transfers or evacuations shall ensure, to the greatest practicable extent: (1) that proper accommodation is provided to receive the protected persons; (2) that evacuations or transfers are effected with satisfactory conditions of hygiene, health, safety, and nutrition; and (3) that members of the same family are not separated.[243]

11.12.3.2 *Transfer Prohibition Only Applicable to Protected Persons*. Persons in occupied territory who do not receive protected person status under the GC are not subject to this prohibition on forcible transfers.[244] For example, POWs may be transferred from occupied territory to POW camps in the home territory of a belligerent.[245] Similarly, a person who is not entitled to protected person status, such as a national of a neutral or non-belligerent State who travels to an occupied State to fight the Occupying Power, would not be covered by this prohibition.[246]

11.12.3.3 *Notification of Transfers and Evacuations to the Protecting Power*. The Protecting Power shall be informed of any transfers and evacuations as soon as they have taken place.[247]

11.12.3.4 *Voluntary Transfers Not Prohibited*. Only forcible transfers are prohibited; voluntary transfers from occupied territory, such as voluntary transfers of persons belonging to a minority group that had been persecuted by the occupied State, would not be prohibited.[248]

---

[242] II-A FINAL RECORD OF THE DIPLOMATIC CONFERENCE OF GENEVA OF 1949 759 ("As regards the proposed suppression of the words 'except in cases of physical necessity', there were cases where, owing to the limited size of the territory, it was physically impossible to evacuate the population otherwise than to places outside the occupied territory. That was the case, for example, in the islands of Wake and Guam, where the whole of the territory could be considered as dangerous.").

[243] GC art. 49 ("The Occupying Power undertaking such transfers or evacuations shall ensure, to the greatest practicable extent, that proper accommodation is provided to receive the protected persons, that the removals are effected in satisfactory conditions of hygiene, health, safety and nutrition, and that members of the same family are not separated.").

[244] *Refer to* § 10.3.2 (Persons Who Receive Protected Person Status Under the GC); § 10.3.3 (Categories of Nationals Specifically Excluded From the Definition of Protected Person Under the GC).

[245] *Refer to* § 9.11.3.3 (Location Outside the Theater of Military Operations).

[246] *Refer to* § 10.3.2.1 ("Find Themselves").

[247] GC art. 49 ("The Protecting Power shall be informed of any transfers and evacuations as soon as they have taken place."). *Consider* AP I art. 78 ("Any such evacuation [of children] shall be supervised by the Protecting Power in agreement with the Parties concerned, namely the Party arranging the evacuation, the Party receiving the children and any Parties whose nationals are being evacuated.").

[248] II-A FINAL RECORD OF THE DIPLOMATIC CONFERENCE OF GENEVA OF 1949 827 ("Although there was general unanimity in condemning such deportations as took place during the recent war, the phrase at the beginning of Article 45 caused some trouble in view of the difficulty in reconciling exactly the ideas expressed with the various terms in French, English and Russian. In the end the Committee have decided on a wording which prohibits individual or mass forcible removals as well as deportations of protected persons from occupied territory to any

11.12.4 General Prohibition Against Detaining Protected Persons in Dangerous Areas. The Occupying Power shall not detain protected persons in an area particularly exposed to the dangers of war unless the security of the population or imperative military reasons so demand.[249]

11.12.5 Prohibition Against Deporting or Transferring the Occupied State's Civilian Population Into Occupied Territory. The Occupying Power shall not deport or transfer parts of its own civilian population into the territory it occupies.[250]

11.13 Protection of Children in Occupied Territory

Article 50 of the GC provides for certain duties of an Occupying Power with respect to children in occupied territory. "Children" for the purposes of Article 50 of the GC and its obligations with respect to the protection of children in occupied territory may be understood generally to refer to children under fifteen years of age.[251]

Other duties that are not specific to occupied territory exist with regard to children.[252]

11.13.1 Obligation With Respect to the Care and Education of Children. The Occupying Power shall, with the cooperation of the national and local authorities, facilitate the proper working of all institutions devoted to the care and education of children.[253] This obligation goes beyond merely not interfering with such institutions, but also includes the affirmative duty to

---

other country, but which permits voluntary transfers."). *See also id.* at 759 ("Mr. CLATTENBURG (United States of America) believed that the addition (suggested by the Soviet Delegation) of the words 'any other transfer' would have hampered the evacuation of the religious and political minorities which the Allies, on entering Germany, had discovered in labour and concentration camps.").

[249] GC art. 49 ("The Occupying Power shall not detain protected persons in an area particularly exposed to the dangers of war unless the security of the population or imperative military reasons so demand."). *Consider* AP I art. 78 ("In each case [of the evacuation of children], all Parties to the conflict shall take all feasible precautions to avoid endangering the evacuation.").

[250] GC art. 49 ("The Occupying Power shall not deport or transfer parts of its own civilian populations into the territory it occupies.").

[251] GC COMMENTARY 285 ("What should the word 'children' be considered to mean for the purposes of Article 50? Although the conception of 'children' has an important place in the Convention there is, as has already been pointed out, no general definition of the word. On the other hand the Convention has fixed various age limits in the provisions prescribing preferential treatment for children: fifteen years of age, in Articles 14 (hospital and safety zones), 23 (consignment of relief supplies), 24 and 38 (5) (measures relating to child welfare); twelve years of age in Article 24, paragraph 3 (identification); and, as will be seen, eighteen years of age in Articles 51, paragraph 2 (compulsory labour) and 68, paragraph 4 (death penalty). Article 50, unlike those just mentioned, does not specify any age limit for the children to whom it refers, except in the last paragraph. Since, however, the establishments and institutions which paragraph 1 is intended to protect are generally for children and young people up to the age of fifteen, that appears to be a reasonable upper limit and might therefore serve here as a criterion. The application of Article 50, however, cannot depend on any formal and often too rigid rule; its application must be governed by the degree of development of the physical and mental faculties of the persons concerned; it may therefore be applied to young people until such time as they attain their majority. The meaning given to the term 'children' will also, of course, depend on the legislation of the occupied country, particularly in respect of identification.").

[252] *Refer to* § 4.20 (Children).

[253] GC art. 50 ("The Occupying Power shall, with the cooperation of the national and local authorities, facilitate the proper working of all institutions devoted to the care and education of children.").

support them when the responsible authorities of the country fail to do so.[254]

Should the local institutions be inadequate for the purpose, the Occupying Power shall make arrangements for the maintenance and education – if possible, by persons of their own nationality, language, and religion – of children who are orphaned or separated from their parents as a result of the war, and who cannot be adequately cared for by a near relative or friend.[255]

11.13.2 Obligation With Respect to the Identification of Children. The Occupying Power shall take all necessary steps to facilitate the identification of children and the registration of their parentage.[256]

A special section of the National Protected Person Information Bureau set up in accordance with Article 136 of the GC shall be responsible for taking all necessary steps to identify children whose identity is in doubt.[257]

11.13.3 Prohibition Against Changing the Personal Status of Children or Enlisting Them. The Occupying Power may not, in any case, change the personal status of children, nor enlist them in formations or organizations subordinate to it.[258]

11.13.4 Obligation Not to Hinder Preferential Measures for Children and Mothers. The Occupying Power shall not hinder the application of any preferential measures in regard to food, medical care, and protection against the effects of war that may have been adopted prior to the occupation in favor of children under fifteen years, expectant mothers, and mothers of children under seven years.[259]

11.14 FOOD AND MEDICAL SUPPLIES FOR THE CIVILIAN POPULATION

11.14.1 Duty of Ensuring the Food and Medical Supplies for the Population. To the fullest extent of the means available to it, the Occupying Power has the duty of ensuring the sufficiency of food and medical supplies for the population; it should, in particular, bring in the

---

[254] GC COMMENTARY 286 ("The Occupying Powers must, with the co-operation of the national and local authorities, facilitate the proper working of children's institutions. That means that the occupying authorities are bound not only to avoid interfering with their activities, but also to support them actively and even encourage them if the responsible authorities of the country fail in their duty.").

[255] GC art. 50 ("Should the local institutions be inadequate for the purpose, the Occupying Power shall make arrangements for the maintenance and education, if possible by persons of their own nationality, language and religion, of children who are orphaned or separated from their parents as a result of the war and who cannot be adequately cared for by a near relative or friend.").

[256] GC art. 50 ("The Occupying Power shall take all necessary steps to facilitate the identification of children and the registration of their parentage.").

[257] *Refer to* § 10.31.2.5 (Special Section for the Identification of Children in Occupied Territory).

[258] GC art. 50 ("The Occupying Power shall take all necessary steps to facilitate the identification of children and the registration of their parentage. It may not, in any case, change their personal status, nor enlist them in formations or organizations subordinate to it.").

[259] GC art. 50 ("The Occupying Power shall not hinder the application of any preferential measures in regard to food, medical care and protection against the effects of war, which may have been adopted prior to the occupation in favour of children under fifteen years, expectant mothers, and mothers of children under seven years.").

necessary foodstuffs, medical stores, and other articles if the resources of the occupied territory are inadequate.[260] Other articles may be understood to include all urgently required goods that may be essential to the "life of the territory."[261]

11.14.2 Limitation on Requisition of Food and Medical Supplies. The Occupying Power may not requisition foodstuffs, articles, or medical supplies available in the occupied territory, except for use by the occupation forces and administration personnel, and then only if the requirements of the civilian population have been taken into account.[262] Subject to the provisions of other international conventions, the Occupying Power shall make arrangements to ensure that fair value is paid for any requisitioned goods.[263]

11.14.3 Verification of the State of Food and Medical Supplies by the Protecting Power. The Protecting Power shall, at any time, be at liberty to verify the state of the food and medical supplies in occupied territories, except where temporary restrictions are made necessary by imperative military requirements.[264]

11.15 PUBLIC HEALTH AND HYGIENE

11.15.1 General Duty With Respect to Public Health. To the fullest extent of the means available to it, the Occupying Power has the duty of ensuring and maintaining, with the cooperation of national and local authorities, medical and hospital establishments, medical services, and public health and hygiene in the occupied territory, with particular reference to the

---

[260] GC art. 55 ("To the fullest extent of the means available to it, the Occupying Power has the duty of ensuring the food and medical supplies of the population; it should, in particular, bring in the necessary foodstuffs, medical stores and other articles if the resources of the occupied territory are inadequate.").

[261] 1956 FM 27-10 (Change No. 1 1976) ¶384 ("*b. Other Articles To Be Supplied.* The other articles which the occupant is required to provide under the above provision include all urgently required, goods which may be essential to the life of the territory."). *See also* GC COMMENTARY 309-10 ("Article 55 is concerned exclusively with the question of food and medical supplies for the population of an occupied territory. … Supplies for the population are not limited to food, but include medical supplies and any article necessary to support life.").

[262] GC art. 55 ("The Occupying Power may not requisition foodstuffs, articles or medical supplies available in the occupied territory, except for use by the occupation forces and administration personnel, and then only if the requirements of the civilian population have been taken into account."). *Consider* AP I art. 14 ("Limitations on requisition of civilian medical units – … 2. The Occupying Power shall not, therefore, requisition civilian medical units, their equipment, their materiel or the services of their personnel, so long as these resources are necessary for the provision of adequate medical services for the civilian population and for the continuing medical care of any wounded and sick already under treatment. 3. Provided that the general rule in paragraph 2 continues to be observed, the Occupying Power may requisition the said resources, subject to the following particular conditions: (a) that the resources necessary for the adequate and immediate medical treatment of the wounded and sick members of the armed forces of the Occupying Power or of prisoners of war; (b) that the requisition continues only while such necessity exists; and (c) that immediate arrangements are made to ensure that the medical needs of the civilian population, as well as those of any wounded and sick under treatment who are affected by the requisition, continue to be satisfied.").

[263] GC art. 55 ("Subject to the provisions of other international Conventions, the Occupying Power shall make arrangements to ensure that fair value is paid for any requisitioned goods.").

[264] GC art. 55 ("The Protecting Power shall, at any time, be at liberty to verify the state of the food and medical supplies in occupied territories, except where temporary restrictions are made necessary by imperative military requirements.").

adoption and application of the prophylactic and preventive measures necessary to combat the spread of contagious diseases and epidemics.[265] The responsibility for providing and maintaining health services falls primarily on the national and local authorities, but where such authorities are unable to provide adequately for the health needs of the civilian population, the Occupying Power then has the duty described above.[266]

11.15.2 Respect for the Work of Civilian Medical Personnel. Medical personnel of all categories must be allowed to carry out their duties.[267] "Medical personnel of all categories" includes a wide range of persons engaged in medical work.[268] It includes even those who are not affiliated with civilian hospitals who qualify for protection under Article 20 of the GC.[269]

11.15.3 Recognition of New Hospitals, Medical Personnel, and Transports. If new hospitals are set up in occupied territory and if the competent organs of the occupied State are not operating there, the occupying authorities must, if necessary, grant them the recognition provided for in Article 18 of the GC.[270] This recognition allows the civilian hospitals to show that they are civilian hospitals and that the buildings that they occupy are not used for any purpose that would deprive these hospitals of protection.[271] In similar circumstances, the occupying authorities must also grant recognition to hospital personnel and transport vehicles under the provisions of Articles 20 and 21 of the GC.[272] This recognition also allows such

---

[265] GC art. 56 ("To the fullest extent of the means available to it, the Occupying Power has the duty of ensuring and maintaining, with the cooperation of national and local authorities, the medical and hospital establishments and services, public health and hygiene in the occupied territory, with particular reference to the adoption and application of the prophylactic and preventive measures necessary to combat the spread of contagious diseases and epidemics.").

[266] GC COMMENTARY 313-14 ("[T]here can be no question of making the Occupying Power alone responsible for the whole burden of organizing hospitals and health services and taking measures to control epidemics. The task is above all one for the competent services of the occupied country itself. It is possible that in certain cases the national authorities will be perfectly well able to look after the health of the population; in such cases the Occupying Power will not have to intervene; it will merely avoid hampering the work of the organizations responsible for the task. In most cases, however, the invading forces will be occupying a country suffering severely from the effects of war; hospitals and medical services will be disorganized, without the necessary supplies and quite unable to meet the needs of the population. The Occupying Power must then, with the co-operation of the authorities and to the fullest extent of the means available to it, ensure that hospital and medical services can work properly and continue to do so.").

[267] GC art. 56 ("Medical personnel of all categories shall be allowed to carry out their duties.").

[268] GC COMMENTARY 314 ("'Medical personnel of all categories' should be taken to mean all people engaged in a branch of medical work: doctors, surgeons, dentists, pharmacists, midwives, medical orderlies and nurses, stretcher bearers, ambulance drivers, etc., whether such persons are or are not attached to a hospital. On that point the provision differs from Article 20 of the Convention, which refers only to hospital staff, who are alone authorized to wear the armlet bearing the red cross emblem.").

[269] *Refer to* § 7.17.4 (Protection of Civilian Hospital Personnel).

[270] GC art. 56 ("If new hospitals are set up in occupied territory and if the competent organs of the occupied State are not operating there, the occupying authorities shall, if necessary, grant them the recognition provided for in Article 18. In similar circumstances, the occupying authorities shall also grant recognition to hospital personnel and transport vehicles under the provisions of Articles 20 and 21.").

[271] *Refer to* § 7.17.2.1 (State-Issued Certificates for Civilian Hospitals).

[272] GC art. 56 ("In similar circumstances, the occupying authorities shall also grant recognition to hospital personnel and transport vehicles under the provisions of Articles 20 and 21.").

personnel and vehicles to display their entitlement to protection.[273]

11.15.4 Consideration of Cultural Traditions of the Population in Adopting Public Health Measures. In adopting measures of health and hygiene, and in their implementation, the Occupying Power must take into consideration the moral and ethical susceptibilities of the population of the occupied territory.[274] The Occupying Power should respect the sentiments and traditions of the population, and should not introduce new methods if they are liable to cause deep disquiet among the population.[275]

11.15.5 Requisition of Civilian Hospitals. The Occupying Power may requisition civilian hospitals only temporarily and only in cases of urgent necessity for the care of military wounded and sick, and then on the condition that suitable arrangements are made in due time for the care and treatment of the hospital's current patients, and for the future needs of the civilian population for hospital accommodation. The material and stores of civilian hospitals cannot be requisitioned so long as they are necessary for the needs of the civilian population.[276]

If the requisition of medical supplies is required for the occupying force, they must take the needs of the civilian population into account and resupply the materials as soon as possible.[277]

11.16 Spiritual Assistance

The Occupying Power shall permit ministers of religion to give spiritual assistance to the members of their religious communities. The Occupying Power shall also accept consignments of books and articles required for religious needs and shall facilitate their distribution in occupied territory.[278]

Religious assistance addressed by the GC, however, does not include activities that are a

---

[273] *Refer to* § 7.17.4 (Protection of Civilian Hospital Personnel); § 7.18 (Land and Sea Civilian Hospital Convoys).

[274] GC art. 56 ("In adopting measures of health and hygiene and in their implementation, the Occupying Power shall take into consideration the moral and ethical susceptibilities of the population of the occupied territory.").

[275] GC Commentary 315 ("The purpose of this provision is to ensure respect for sentiments and traditions, which must not be disregarded. The occupation must not involve the sudden introduction of new methods, if they are liable to cause deep disquiet among the population.").

[276] GC art. 57 ("The Occupying Power may requisition civilian hospitals only temporarily and only in cases of urgent necessity for the care of military wounded and sick, and then on condition that suitable arrangements are made in due time for the care and treatment of patients and the needs of the civilian population for hospital accommodation. The material and stores of civilian hospitals cannot be requisitioned so long as they are necessary for the needs of the civilian population.").

[277] GC Commentary 318 ("When so doing, it will take the needs of the population into account and it will replace the material used as soon as possible, usually by importing medical supplies in accordance with Article 55.").

[278] GC art. 58 ("The Occupying Power shall permit ministers of religion to give spiritual assistance to the members of their religious communities. The Occupying Power shall also accept consignments of books and articles required for religious needs and shall facilitate their distribution in occupied territory.").

pretext for political agitation against the Occupying Power.[279]

11.17 RELIEF EFFORTS AND CONSIGNMENTS

Special rules address relief efforts in occupied territory. Other rules address relief efforts outside the context of occupation.[280]

11.17.1 Collective Relief. If the whole or part of the population of an occupied territory is inadequately supplied, the Occupying Power shall agree to relief schemes on behalf of the affected population, and shall facilitate them by all the means at its disposal. Such schemes, which may be undertaken either by States or by impartial humanitarian organizations such as the ICRC, shall consist, in particular, of the provision of consignments of foodstuffs, medical supplies, and clothing.[281]

All Parties to the GC shall permit the free passage of these consignments and shall guarantee their protection.[282]

A State granting free passage to consignments on their way to territory occupied by an adverse party to the conflict shall, however, have the right to search the consignments, to regulate their passage according to prescribed times and routes, and to be reasonably satisfied (through the Protecting Power) that these consignments are to be used for the relief of the needy population, and are not to be used for the benefit of the Occupying Power.[283]

11.17.1.1 *Diversion of Relief Consignments*. The Occupying Power shall in no way whatsoever divert relief consignments from the purpose for which they are intended, except in cases of urgent necessity, in the interests of the population of the occupied territory, and with

[279] GC COMMENTARY 318 ("[R]eligious assistance must in no case serve as a pretext for political agitation against the Occupying Power. Should occasion arise, the Occupying Power would be entitled to take appropriate action, since the provision under discussion authorizes only spiritual assistance, and not activities which have nothing to do with religion.").

[280] *Refer to* § 5.19.3 (Passage of Relief Consignments); § 8.10.1 (Receipt of Individual or Collective Relief); § 9.20 (POW Correspondence and Relief Shipments); § 10.23 (Internee Correspondence and Relief Shipments).

[281] GC art. 59 ("If the whole or part of the population of an occupied territory is inadequately supplied, the Occupying Power shall agree to relief schemes on behalf of the said population, and shall facilitate them by all the means at its disposal. Such schemes, which may be undertaken either by States or by impartial humanitarian organizations such as the International Committee of the Red Cross, shall consist, in particular, of the provision of consignments of foodstuffs, medical supplies and clothing. All Contracting Parties shall permit the free passage of these consignments and shall guarantee their protection.").

[282] GC art. 59 ("All Contracting Parties shall permit the free passage of these consignments and shall guarantee their protection.").

[283] GC art. 59 ("A Power granting free passage to consignments on their way to territory occupied by an adverse Party to the conflict shall, however, have the right to search the consignments, to regulate their passage according to prescribed times and routes, and to be reasonably satisfied through the Protecting Power that these consignments are to be used for the relief of the needy population and are not to be used for the benefit of the Occupying Power.").

the consent of the Protecting Power.[284]

11.17.1.2 *Distribution of Collective Relief Consignments*. The distribution of collective relief consignments referred to in Articles 59 and 60 of the GC shall be carried out with the cooperation and under the supervision of the Protecting Power. This duty may also be delegated, by agreement between the Occupying Power and the Protecting Power, to a neutral State, the ICRC, or any other impartial humanitarian body.[285]

The Occupying Power shall facilitate the rapid distribution of these consignments.[286] For example, it may be necessary for the occupation authorities to remove administrative impediments (*e.g.*, granting permits) to relief organizations distributing consignments.[287]

11.17.1.3 *Charges, Taxes, and Customs Duties on Collective Relief Consignments for Occupied Territories*. Collective relief consignments referred to in Articles 59 and 60 of the GC shall be exempt in occupied territory from all charges, taxes, or customs duties unless such charges, taxes, or customs duties are necessary in the interests of the economy of the territory.[288] All Parties to the GC shall endeavor to permit the transit and transport, free of charge, of such relief consignments on their way to occupied territories.[289]

11.17.2 Individual Relief Consignments. Subject to imperative reasons of security, protected persons in occupied territories shall be permitted to receive individual relief consignments sent to them.[290]

An individual relief consignment is a shipment that is addressed to a particular person.[291]

---

[284] GC art. 60 ("The Occupying Power shall in no way whatsoever divert relief consignments from the purpose for which they are intended, except in cases of urgent necessity, in the interests of the population of the occupied territory and with the consent of the Protecting Power.").

[285] GC art. 61 ("The distribution of the relief consignments referred to in the foregoing Articles shall be carried out with the cooperation and under the supervision of the Protecting Power. This duty may also be delegated, by agreement between the Occupying Power and the Protecting Power, to a neutral Power, to the International Committee of the Red Cross or to any other impartial humanitarian body.").

[286] GC art. 61 ("The Occupying Power shall facilitate the rapid distribution of these consignments.").

[287] GC COMMENTARY 328 ("The second sentence in paragraph 2 says that the Occupying Power is to facilitate the rapid distribution of the consignments. The effect of a relief scheme will depend above all on the time the consignments take to reach the recipients; it is therefore important for the occupation authorities to take all necessary steps to facilitate their despatch and distribution (cutting out red tape, making transport available, granting permits allowing freedom of movement, facilities of all kinds for the staff of the distributing and supervising bodies, etc.).").

[288] GC art. 61 ("Such consignments shall be exempt in occupied territory from all charges, taxes or customs duties unless these are necessary in the interests of the economy of the territory.").

[289] GC art. 61 ("All Contracting Parties shall endeavour to permit the transit and transport, free of charge, of such relief consignments on their way to occupied territories.").

[290] GC art. 62 ("Subject to imperative reasons of security, protected persons in occupied territories shall be permitted to receive the individual relief consignments sent to them.").

[291] GC COMMENTARY 329 ("Unlike the three previous Articles which refer to relief supplies for a group of protected persons (collective consignments), Article 62 deals with consignments addressed to individuals (individual consignments).").

The occupation authorities may limit or temporarily forbid the entry of individual relief supplies for imperative reasons of security, such as if the volume of relief consignments prevents security screening.[292]

11.17.3 Continuing Responsibilities of the Occupying Power. Relief consignments shall in no way relieve the Occupying Power of any of its responsibilities under Articles 55, 56, and 59 of the GC.[293] The responsibilities of the Occupying Power under Articles 55, 56, and 59 of the GC relate to ensuring the provision of food, medical supplies, and medical services to the population.[294]

11.17.4 National Red Cross or Red Crescent Societies and Other Relief Organizations. Subject to temporary and exceptional measures imposed for urgent reasons of security by the Occupying Power:

- recognized National Red Cross (Red Crescent, Red Lion and Sun) Societies shall be able to pursue their activities in accordance with Red Cross principles, as prescribed by the International Red Cross Conferences. Other relief societies shall be permitted to continue their humanitarian activities under similar conditions;

- the Occupying Power may not require any changes in the personnel or structure of these societies that would prejudice these activities.[295]

The same principles shall apply to the activities and personnel of special organizations of a non-military character that already exist or that may be established for the purpose of ensuring the living conditions of the civilian population by the maintenance of the essential public utility services, by the distribution of relief, and by the organization of rescues.[296]

---

[292] GC COMMENTARY 329 ("[T]he occupation authorities have the right to refuse to receive individual relief consignments if imperative reasons of security so demand. A similar reservation in regard to collective relief was put forward during the preparatory work on Article 59, but was not adopted. The reservation was kept in Article 62 in order that efficient verification should not be rendered impossible by the arrival of huge quantities of individual parcels. Under such circumstances the Occupying Power could avoid importing articles detrimental to its security by limiting or temporarily forbidding the entry of individual relief supplies.").

[293] GC art. 60 ("Relief consignments shall in no way relieve the Occupying Power of any of its responsibilities under Articles 55, 56 and 59.").

[294] *Refer to* § 11.14 (Food and Medical Supplies for the Civilian Population); § 11.15 (Public Health and Hygiene); § 11.17.1 (Collective Relief).

[295] GC art. 63 ("Subject to temporary and exceptional measures imposed for urgent reasons of security by the Occupying Power: (*a*) recognized National Red Cross (Red Crescent, Red Lion and Sun) Societies shall be able to pursue their activities in accordance with Red Cross principles, as defined by the International Red Cross Conferences. Other relief societies shall be permitted to continue their humanitarian activities under similar conditions; (*b*) the Occupying Power may not require any changes in the personnel or structure of these societies, which would prejudice the aforesaid activities.").

[296] GC art. 63 ("The same principles shall apply to the activities and personnel of special organizations of a non-military character, which already exist or which may be established, for the purpose of ensuring the living conditions of the civilian population by the maintenance of the essential public utility services, by the distribution of relief and by the organization of rescues.").

11.18 Enemy Property During Occupation

Pillage is prohibited. Enemy property in occupied territory may not be seized or destroyed unless imperatively demanded by the necessities of war. The Occupying Power may take certain control measures with respect to property in occupied territory. Other rules apply to the treatment of public enemy property and private enemy property in occupied territory.

11.18.1 Prohibition Against Pillage in Occupied Territory. Pillage is forbidden.[297] In addition to this specific prohibition in the context of occupied territory, pillage is prohibited as a general matter.[298]

11.18.2 Seizure or Destruction of Property During Occupation – Application of the Military Necessity Standard. The general rule that enemy property may not be seized or destroyed unless imperatively demanded by the necessities of war also applies to property during the occupation of enemy territory.[299] In particular, any destruction by the Occupying Power of real (immovable) or personal (movable) property belonging individually or collectively to private persons, to the State of the occupied territory, to other public authorities, or to social or cooperative organizations, is prohibited, except where such destruction is rendered absolutely necessary by military operations.[300]

11.18.2.1 *Assessment of Military Necessity for Seizure or Destruction*. The evaluation of whether destruction of property is militarily necessary in the context of occupation is undertaken by applying the standards that also are applied in the context of combat operations.[301] For example, the evaluation of whether the destruction of property is militarily necessary is made by the responsible commander or other authority of the Occupying Power.[302] However, such assessment must be made in good faith based on the information available at the time.[303]

11.18.2.2 *Temporary Possession for Direct Military Use*. An Occupying Power may always take temporary possession of enemy property (real or personal, and public or

---

[297] HAGUE IV REG. art. 47 ("Pillage is formally forbidden.").

[298] *Refer to* § 5.17.4 (Pillage Prohibited).

[299] *Refer to* § 5.17.2 (Enemy Property – Military Necessity Standard).

[300] GC art. 53 ("Any destruction by the Occupying Power of real or personal property belonging individually or collectively to private persons, or to the State, or to other public authorities, or to social or cooperative organizations, is prohibited, except where such destruction is rendered absolutely necessary by military operations.").

[301] *Refer to* § 5.17.2 (Enemy Property – Military Necessity Standard).

[302] GC COMMENTARY 302 ("Furthermore, it will be for the Occupying Power to judge the importance of such military requirements. It is therefore to be feared that bad faith in the application of the reservation may render the proposed safeguard valueless; for unscrupulous recourse to the clause concerning military necessity would allow the Occupying Power to circumvent the prohibition set forth in the Convention. The Occupying Power must therefore try to interpret the clause in a reasonable manner: whenever it is felt essential to resort to destruction, the occupying authorities must try to keep a sense of proportion in comparing the military advantages to be gained with the damage done.").

[303] *Refer to* § 5.3.2 (Decisions Must Be Made in Good Faith and Based on Information Available at the Time).

private) where required for direct military use in military operations. In the case of private property, an Occupying Power, where possible, should requisition the property and offer compensation to the owner.[304]

11.18.2.3 *Capture or Seizure and Vesting of Title in the Occupying Power*. In the case of real (immovable) property that is captured or seized, the Occupying Power may use such property for the duration of the occupation but does not take title to the property.[305]

Public property captured or seized from the enemy, as well as private property validly captured on the battlefield and abandoned property, is the property of the capturing State.[306]

Valid capture or seizure of property requires both an intent to take such action and a physical act of capture or seizure. The mere presence within occupied territory of property that is subject to appropriation under international law does not operate to vest title thereto in the Occupying Power.[307]

11.18.2.4 *Seizure or Destruction of Submarine Cables Connecting an Occupied Territory With a Neutral Territory*. Submarine cables connecting an occupied territory with a neutral territory shall not be seized or destroyed except in the case of absolute necessity. Such cables must likewise be restored and compensation fixed when peace is made.[308]

This rule applies only to activities on land and does not deal with seizure or destruction of cables in the open sea.[309]

11.18.3 Property Control Measures. Public and private property within occupied territory may be controlled by the Occupying Power to the degree necessary to prevent its use by or for

---

[304] *Refer to* § 11.18.7 (Requisitions of Private Enemy Property).

[305] *Refer to* § 11.18.5.1 (Public Real (Immovable) Property Susceptible of Direct Military Use); § 11.18.5.2 (Public Real (Immovable) Property That Is Essentially of a Non-Military Nature).

[306] 1956 FM 27-10 (Change No. 1 1976) ¶396 ("Public property captured or seized from the enemy, as well as private property validly captured on the battlefield and abandoned property, is property of the United States (see *U.S. Const., Art. I, sec. 8, cl. 11*), and failure to turn over such property to the proper authorities or disposal thereof for personal profit is a violation of Article 103 of the Uniform Code of Military Justice."). *Refer to* § 5.17.3.2 (Ownership of Captured or Found Property on the Battlefield).

[307] 1956 FM 27-10 (Change No. 1 1976) ¶395 ("Valid capture or seizure of property requires both an intent to take such action and a physical act of capture or seizure. The mere presence within occupied territory of property which is subject to appropriation under international law does not operate to vest title thereto in the occupant.").

[308] HAGUE IV REG. art. 54 ("Submarine cables connecting an occupied territory with a neutral territory shall not be seized or destroyed except in the case of absolute necessity. They must likewise be restored and compensation fixed when peace is made.").

[309] JAMES BROWN SCOTT, THE PROCEEDINGS OF THE HAGUE PEACE CONFERENCES: III THE CONFERENCE OF 1907 13 (1921) ("Mr. Louis Renault observes that this amendment has reference only to what takes place on land, without touching the question of seizure or destruction of submarine cables in the open sea. The President thanks him for having given the text an interpretation that leaves no room for doubt.").

the benefit of hostile forces, or in a manner harmful to the Occupying Power.[310] For example, in the case of persons who have acted against the security of the Occupying Power, the Occupying Power may freeze their accounts to prevent such funds from being used against the interests of the Occupying Power.[311]

Conservators may be appointed to manage the property of absent persons (including nationals of the United States and of friendly States) and of internees, property managed by such persons, and property of persons whose activities are deemed to be prejudicial to the Occupying Power. However, when the owners or managers of such property are again able to resume control of their property and the risk of its hostile use no longer exists, it must be returned to them.[312]

Measures of property control must not extend to confiscation of private property.[313] For example, if the Occupying Power controls a private business and earns a profit, the owner must be indemnified.[314]

However, the authority of the Occupying Power to impose such controls does not limit its power to seize or requisition property or take such other action with respect to it as may be authorized by other provisions of law.[315]

11.18.4 Determination Whether Property Is Public or Private. The rules for the treatment of enemy property may depend on whether the property is public or private.

For example, private property may not be confiscated, and there is an obligation to pay compensation for requisitions of private property.[316] On the other hand, public property

---

[310] 1956 FM 27-10 (Change No. 1 1976) ¶399 ("Property within occupied territory may be controlled by the occupant to the degree necessary to prevent its use by or for the benefit of the hostile forces or in a manner harmful to the occupant.").

[311] VON GLAHN, THE OCCUPATION OF ENEMY TERRITORY 207 ("This control includes not only the steps mentioned above in connection with central banks and commercial banks but covers such things as the freezing of accounts where the owner of the funds in question has acted against the interests of the occupying power, control of large cash deposits, control over safe deposit boxes, and, of course, the removal of personnel held to be undesirable from the viewpoint of the occupant.").

[312] 1956 FM 27-10 (Change No. 1 1976) ¶399 ("Conservators may be appointed to manage the property of absent persons (including nationals of the United States and of friendly States) and of internees, property managed by such persons, and property of persons whose activities are deemed to be prejudicial to the occupant. However, when the owners or managers of such property are again able to resume control of their property and the risk of its hostile use no longer exists, it must be returned to them.").

[313] *Refer to* § 11.18.6.1 (Prohibition on Confiscation of Private Property in Occupied Territory).

[314] *Refer to* § 11.23.3 (Control of Business in Occupied Territory).

[315] 1956 FM 27-10 (Change No. 1 1976) ¶399 ("Measures of property control must not extend to confiscation. However, the authority of the occupant to impose such controls does not limit its power to seize or requisition property or take such other action with respect to it as may be authorized by other provisions of law.").

[316] *Refer to* § 11.18.6.1 (Prohibition on Confiscation of Private Property in Occupied Territory); § 11.18.7.3 (Prices and Compensation for Requisitioned Articles and Services).

generally may be seized or captured without any obligation to pay compensation.[317]

11.18.4.1 Beneficial Ownership Test. Under modern conditions, the distinction between public and private property is not always easy to draw. For the purpose of treatment of property under military occupation, it is often necessary to look beyond strict legal title and to ascertain the character of the property on the basis of the beneficial ownership thereof. Thus, for example, trust funds, pension funds, and bank deposits generated by private persons are not to be regarded as public property simply by reason of their being held by a State-owned bank.[318]

11.18.4.2 Property of Mixed Ownership. For the purpose of determining what type of control the Occupying Power may exercise over property (by way of confiscation, seizure, requisition, etc.), the most cogent evidence of public character is such a complete or partial assumption by the State of the economic risk involved in the holding and management of the property in question that the enemy State, rather than private individuals or corporations, would be subjected to a substantial portion of the loss were the property to be appropriated for the use of the Occupying Power.[319] Should property that is ostensibly private be subjected to a large measure of governmental control and management, or perform functions that are essentially public, these facts would tend to indicate that the property should be regarded in practice as public.[320]

If property that is appropriated by the Occupying Power is beneficially owned in part by the enemy State and in part by private interests, the occupation authorities should compensate the private owners to the extent of their interest. Such compensation should bear the same relationship to the compensation that would be paid if the property were entirely privately owned. The Occupying Power may take those measures it deems necessary to ensure that no portion of the compensation paid on account of private interests accrues to the enemy State.[321]

---

[317] *Refer to* § 11.18.5 (Treatment of Enemy Public Property).

[318] 1956 FM 27-10 (Change No. 1 1976) ¶394a ("*Beneficial Ownership.* Under modern conditions, the distinction between public and private property is not always easy to draw. For the purpose of treatment of property under belligerent occupation, it is often necessary to look beyond strict legal title and to ascertain the character of the property on the basis of the beneficial ownership thereof. Thus, for example, trust funds, pension funds, and bank deposits generated by private persons are not to be regarded as public property simply by reason of their being held by a State-owned bank.").

[319] 1956 FM 27-10 (Change No. 1 1976) ¶394b ("*Property of Mixed Ownership.* For the purpose of determining what type of control the occupant may exercise over property (by way of confiscation, seizure, requisition, etc.), the most cogent evidence of public character is such a complete or partial assumption by the State of the economic risk involved in the holding and management of the property in question that the State, rather than private individuals or corporation, would be subjected to a substantial portion of the loss were the property to be appropriated for the use of the occupant.").

[320] 1956 FM 27-10 (Change No. 1 1976) ¶394b ("Should property which is ostensibly private be subjected to a large measure of governmental control and management or perform functions which are essentially public, these facts would tend to indicate that the property should be regarded in practice as public.").

[321] 1956 FM 27-10 (Change No. 1 1976) ¶394b ("If property which is appropriated by the occupant is beneficially owned in part by the State and in part by private interests, the occupation authorities should compensate the private owners to the extent of their interest. Such compensation should bear the same relationship to the full compensation which would be paid if the property were entirely privately owned as their interest bears to the total value of the

11.18.4.3 *Property of Unknown Ownership*. If it is unknown whether certain property is public or private, it should be treated as public property until its ownership is ascertained.[322]

11.18.5 Treatment of Enemy Public Property. In general, an Occupying Power may capture or seize the real (immovable) and personal (movable) property of the occupied State and use it for military operations or the administration of the occupied territory. No compensation needs to be paid to the occupied State for the use or taking of such property.

11.18.5.1 *Public Real (Immovable) Property Susceptible of Direct Military Use*. Real property of the occupied State that is of direct military use, such as forts, arsenals, dockyards, magazines, barracks, railways, bridges, piers, wharves, airfields, and other military facilities, may remain in the hands of the Occupying Power until the close of the hostilities, and may be destroyed or damaged by the Occupying Power, if it deems it necessary to military operations.[323]

11.18.5.2 *Public Real (Immovable) Property That Is Essentially of a Non-Military Nature*. The Occupying Power shall be regarded only as administrator and usufructuary of public buildings, real estate, forests, and agricultural estates belonging to the hostile State, and situated in the occupied territory. It must safeguard the capital of these properties, and administer them in accordance with the rules of usufruct.[324] This real (immovable) property that is essentially of a non-military nature may not be damaged or destroyed unless such destruction is rendered absolutely necessary by military operations.[325]

The term usufruct means literally "to use the fruit."[326] The Occupying Power may use

---

property concerned. The occupant may take what measures it deems necessary to assure that no portion of the compensation paid on account of private interests accrues to the State.").

[322] 1956 FM 27-10 (Change No. 1 1976) ¶394c ("*Property of Unknown Ownership*. If it is unknown whether certain property is public or private, it should be treated as public property until its ownership is ascertained.").

[323] 1956 FM 27-10 (Change No. 1 1976) ¶401 ("Real property of a State which is of direct military use, such as forts, arsenals, dockyards, magazines, barracks, railways, bridges, piers, wharves, airfields, and other military facilities, remains in the hands of the occupant until the close of the war, and may be destroyed or damaged, if deemed necessary to military operations.").

[324] HAGUE IV REG. art. 55 ("The occupying State shall be regarded only as administrator and usufructuary of public buildings, real estate, forests, and agricultural estates belonging to the hostile State, and situated in the occupied country. It must safeguard the capital of these properties, and administer them in accordance with the rules of usufruct.").

[325] 1956 FM 27-10 (Change No. 1 1976) ¶402 ("Real property of the enemy State which is essentially of a non-military nature, such as public buildings and offices, land, forests, parks, farms, and mines, may not be damaged or destroyed unless such destruction is rendered absolutely necessary by military operations (see *Art. 63, GC;* par. 393 herein)."). *Refer to* § 11.18.2 (Seizure or Destruction of Property During Occupation – Application of the Military Necessity Standard).

[326] *See* DEPARTMENT OF THE ARMY PAMPHLET 27-161-2, *II International Law*, 183 (Oct. 23, 1962) ("The term 'usufruct' means literally 'to use the fruit.' The occupant can therefore enjoy the benefits of public real property, but he cannot interfere with the substantive rights still possessed by the displaced sovereign."); Brigadier General George B. Davis, *Working Memoranda (Confidential for the United States Delegates): The Second Peace Conference (Paragraph 2 of Programme), The Rules of War on Land*, 43 (1907) ("In the meaning which has been assigned to the term 'usufruct' in both the common and civil law, the usufructuary is entitled to the enjoyment of the

and enjoy the benefits of public real (immovable) property belonging to an enemy State, but does not have the right of sale or unqualified use of such property. As administrator or usufructuary, the Occupying Power should not exercise its rights in such a wasteful and negligent manner as seriously to impair the property's value.[327]

The Occupying Power may, however, lease or utilize public lands or buildings, sell the crops, cut and sell timber, and work the mines. The term of a lease or contract should not extend beyond the conclusion of the war.[328]

11.18.5.3 *Public Personal (Movable) Property*. An army of occupation may only take possession of cash, funds, and realizable securities that are strictly the property of an enemy State, depots of arms, means of transport, stores and supplies, and, generally, all personal (movable) property belonging to the State that may be used for military operations.[329]

Thus, all personal (movable) property belonging to an enemy State susceptible of military use may be taken possession of, and utilized for, the benefit of the Occupying Power. Under modern conditions of warfare, a large proportion of State property may be regarded as capable of being used for military purposes. However, personal (movable) property that is not susceptible of military use must be respected and may not be appropriated.[330]

11.18.6 Treatment of Enemy Private Property. Private property may not be confiscated.[331]

Private personal (movable) property susceptible to direct military use may be seized, with a receipt to be given to allow for compensation to be paid at the conclusion of the war.[332]

Other private property may be subject to requisition, with payment in cash given as soon

---

revenue so long as he preserves the substance or capital of which he appropriates and uses the usufruct. In its application to the commanding general of occupied territory this means that, so long as he maintains the properties thus unimpaired, he may apply the usufructuary revenue to the necessary expenses of the military occupation.").

327 1956 FM 27-10 (Change No. 1 1976) ¶402 ("The occupant does not have the right of sale or unqualified use of such property. As administrator or usufructuary he should not exercise his rights in such a wasteful, and negligent manner as seriously to impair its value.").

328 1956 FM 27-10 (Change No. 1 1976) ¶402 ("He may, however, lease or utilize public lands or buildings, sell the crops, cut and sell timber, and work the mines. The term of a lease or contract should not extend beyond the conclusion of the war.").

329 HAGUE IV REG. art. 53 ("An army of occupation can only take possession of cash, funds, and realizable securities which are strictly the property of the State, depots of arms, means of transport, stores and supplies, and, generally, all movable property belonging to the State which may be used for military operations.").

330 1956 FM 27-10 (Change No. 1 1976) ¶404 ("All movable property belonging to the State susceptible of military use may be taken possession of and utilized for the benefit of the occupant's government. Under modern conditions of warfare, a large proportion of State property may be regarded as capable of being used for military purposes. However, movable property which is *not* susceptible of military use must be respected and cannot be appropriated.").

331 *Refer to* § 11.18.6.1 (Prohibition on Confiscation of Private Property in Occupied Territory).

332 *Refer to* § 11.18.6.2 (Seizure of Private Property Susceptible to Direct Military Use).

as possible.[333]

Private property may be forfeited to the Occupying Power as a result of the valid imposition of penalties.[334] For example, a regulation closing a road for security reasons could specify that, as a penalty, unauthorized private vehicles found on the road would be subject to forfeiture without any compensation.[335]

11.18.6.1 *Prohibition on Confiscation of Private Property in Occupied Territory*. Private property may not be confiscated.[336]

The prohibition against confiscation of private property extends not only to outright taking in violation of the law of war, but also to any acts that, through the use of threats, intimidation, or pressure, or by actual exploitation of the power of the Occupying Power, permanently or temporarily deprive the owner of the use of such property without the owner's consent, or without authority under international law.[337]

The prohibition against confiscation of private property does not extend to takings by way of contribution, requisition, or the valid imposition of penalties.[338]

11.18.6.2 *Seizure of Private Property Susceptible to Direct Military Use*. All

---

[333] *Refer to* § 11.18.7 (Requisitions of Private Enemy Property).

[334] *See* Philip C. Jessup, *A Belligerent Occupant's Power over Property*, 38 AJIL 457, 459 (1944) ("3) Seizure and confiscation. This case is not spelled out in the Hague Regulations but it is important. Private property of any kind may be forfeited as a penalty. For example, a military regulation may forbid civilian carts to cross a certain bridge under penalty of forfeiture of the cart and its contents and the draft animal. A regulation may forbid the sale of intoxicating liquors under penalty of forfeiture of all stocks on hand. Especially in agrarian communities of rather primitive economy, fines may be imposed in terms of farm produce, articles of native manufacture, or any other commodities. Property taken by the occupant in this way is acquired with a clear title and may be used in any way the occupant sees fit.").

[335] VON GLAHN, THE OCCUPATION OF ENEMY TERRITORY 188 ("Private property may also have to be forfeited to an occupant as a penalty: fines for a great number of minor offenses may be lawfully exacted in terms of products or goods. For instance, vehicles found on closed roads may be confiscated, clothing over and above a stated maximum might well be seized, and so on. A lawful occupant could utilize all property thus acquired in any manner he saw fit, since he would have a clear title to the goods without having paid any compensation.").

[336] HAGUE IV REG. art. 46 ("Private property cannot be confiscated.").

[337] 1956 FM 27-10 (Change No. 1 1976) ¶406b ("*Prohibited Acts*. The foregoing prohibition extends not only to outright taking in violation of the law of war but also to any acts which, through the use of threats, intimidation, or pressure or by actual exploitation of the power of the occupant, permanently or temporarily deprive the owner of the use of his property without his consent or without authority under international law.").

[338] Brigadier General George B. Davis, *Working Memoranda (Confidential for the United States Delegates): The Second Peace Conference (Paragraph 2 of Programme), The Rules of War on Land*, 38 (1907) ("Article XVLI. ... Private property may be taken by way of contribution or requisition, in order to compel the enemy to bear his share of the burdens and hardships of war, but it can not be confiscated—that is, it can not be seized by way of punishment for a breach of allegiance, for no tie of allegiance exists between the inhabitants of the occupied territory and the invading enemy. It is not understood that in the operation of a penalty which may be imposed by a military commission or other tribunal with jurisdiction to try cases in occupied territory the private property of an individual may not be taken. It is rather a taking without compensation—a taking which is not in conformity to the laws of war which is here made the subject of the express prohibition.").

appliances, whether on land, at sea, or in the air, adapted for the transmission of news, or for the transport of persons or things, exclusive of cases governed by naval law, depots of arms, and, generally, all kinds of ammunition of war, may be seized, even if they belong to private individuals, but must be restored and compensation fixed when peace is made.[339]

Private property susceptible of direct military use includes cables, telephone and telegraph facilities, radio, television, telecommunications and computer networks and equipment, motor vehicles, railways, railway plants, port facilities, ships in port, barges and other watercraft, airfields, aircraft, depots of arms (whether military or sporting), documents connected with the conflict, all varieties of military equipment (including that in the hands of manufacturers), component parts of, or material suitable only for use in, the foregoing, and, in general, all kinds of war material.[340]

If private property is seized on the grounds that is it susceptible to direct military use, a receipt should be given the owner, or a record made of the nature and quantity of the property and the name of the owner or person in possession of it, in order that restoration and compensation may be made at the conclusion of the war.[341]

11.18.6.3 *Private Real (Immovable) Property*. Private real (immovable) property may under no circumstances be seized. It may, however, be requisitioned.[342]

11.18.6.4 *Municipal, Religious, Charitable, and Cultural Property*. The property of municipalities, that of institutions dedicated to religion, charity, and education, and the arts and sciences, even when State property, shall be treated as private property. All seizure of, destruction of, or willful damage done to institutions of this character, historic monuments, works of art, and science, is forbidden, and should be made the subject of legal proceedings.[343]

The reference to "property of municipalities" above has been interpreted as not granting

---

339 HAGUE IV REG. art. 53 ("All appliances, whether on land, at sea, or in the air, adapted for the transmission of news, or for the transport of persons or things, exclusive of cases governed by naval law, depots of arms, and, generally, all kinds of ammunition of war, may be seized, even if they belong to private individuals, but must be restored and compensation fixed when peace is made.").

340 1956 FM 27-10 (Change No. 1 1976) ¶410a ("*Seizure*. The rule stated in the foregoing paragraph includes everything susceptible of direct military use, such as cables, telephone and telegraph plants, radio, television, and telecommunications equipment, motor vehicles, railways, railway plants, port facilities, ships in port, barges and other watercraft, airfields, aircraft, depots of arms, whether military or sporting, documents connected with the war, all varieties of military equipment, including that in the hands of manufacturers, component parts of or material suitable only for use in the foregoing, and in general all kinds of war material.").

341 *See* 1956 FM 27-10 (Change No. 1 1976) ¶409 ("If private property is seized in conformity with the preceding paragraph, a receipt therefor should be given the owner or a record made of the nature and quantity of the property and the name of the owner or person in possession in order that restoration and compensation may be made at the conclusion of the war.").

342 *Refer to* § 11.18.7 (Requisitions of Private Enemy Property).

343 HAGUE IV REG. art. 56 ("The property of municipalities, that of institutions dedicated to religion, charity and education, the arts and sciences, even when State property, shall be treated as private property. All seizure of, destruction or willful damage done to institutions of this character, historic monuments, works of art, and science, is forbidden, and should be made the subject of legal proceedings.").

preferential treatment for all types of property owned by municipalities, but as referring to communal property, such as poor houses, asylums, park buildings, museums, and public records, whether owned by a parish, a town, or a province.[344]

Just as private property may be subject to requisitions and contribution and certain other purposes during a military occupation, the types of property referred to in Article 56 of the Hague IV Regulations may also be subject to such demands.[345] For example, such property may be requisitioned in case of necessity for quartering the forces and the sick and wounded, storage of supplies and material, housing of vehicles and equipment, and generally as prescribed for private property.[346] Such property must, however, be secured against all avoidable injury, even when located in fortified places that are subject to seizure or bombardment.[347]

Additional rules apply to cultural property.[348]

In the practice of the United States, religious buildings, shrines, and consecrated places employed for worship are used only for aid stations, for medical installations, or for the housing of wounded personnel awaiting evacuation, provided in each case that a situation of emergency requires such use.[349]

11.18.7 Requisitions of Private Enemy Property. Although private enemy property may not be confiscated, it may be subject to requisition, which is the method of taking private enemy

---

[344] William M. Franklin, *Municipal Property Under Belligerent Occupation*, 28 AJIL 383, 395-96 (1944) ("3. It was not the intention of the drafters of the article to grant the highly preferential treatment of Article 56 to all types of property owned by municipalities, simply on the basis of their ownership. Military installations maintained by municipalities and all other types of property owned by municipalities which would be susceptible of direct military use and were not dedicated to humanitarian, educational, scientific or artistic purposes do not enjoy the protection of Article 56. 4. For this reason it was never thought necessary to define the word '*communes*' in terms of any specific unit of local government. The expression was intended to include communal property, such as poor houses, asylums, park buildings, museums and public records, whether owned by a parish, a town or a province.").

[345] VON GLAHN, THE OCCUPATION OF ENEMY TERRITORY 192 ("It has to be remembered, in this connection, that municipal property is subject to requisitions and contributions.... While an occupant is prevented from confiscating the various kinds of property listed in Article 56, the rules of international law do not prevent him, on the other hand, from utilizing these properties for certain purposes during military occupation. He is entitled to lodge troops, animals, stores, supplies, and the like in buildings belonging to exempt or immune institutions, and may convert such buildings into hospitals for the care of this wounded. In other words, municipal and other exempt property may be used by the occupying forces in the same manner and to the same extent as in the case of private property.").

[346] 1956 FM 27-10 (Change No. 1 1976) ¶405 ("*b. Use of Such Premises.* The property included in the foregoing rule may be requisitioned in case of necessity for quartering the troops and the sick and wounded, storage of supplies and material, housing of vehicles and equipment, and generally as prescribed for private property. Such property must, however, be secured against all avoidable injury, even when located in fortified places which are subject to seizure or bombardment.").

[347] *Refer to* § 5.17.5 (Feasible Precautions Should Be Taken to Mitigate the Burden on Civilians).

[348] *Refer to* § 11.19 (Protection of Cultural Property During Occupation).

[349] 1956 FM 27-10 (Change No. 1 1976) ¶405c ("*Religious Buildings, Shrines, and Consecrated Places.* In the practice of the United States, religious buildings, shrines, and consecrated places employed for worship are used only for aid stations, medical installations, or for the housing of wounded personnel awaiting evacuation, provided in each case that a situation of emergency requires such use.").

real (immovable) and personal (movable) property for the needs of the army of occupation.[350]

Requisitions in kind and services shall not be demanded from municipalities or inhabitants except for the needs of the army of occupation. They shall be in proportion to the resources of the country, and of such a nature as not to involve the inhabitants in the obligation of taking part in military operations against their own country.[351]

11.18.7.1 *Method of Requisitioning*. Requisitions must be made under the authority of the commander in the locality.[352] No prescribed method is fixed, but if practicable, requisitions should be accomplished through the local authorities by systematic collection in bulk. They may be made direct by detachments if local authorities fail or if circumstances preclude resort to such authorities.[353]

11.18.7.2 *Types of Property That May Be Requisitioned*. Goods and services that are necessary for the maintenance of the occupation army (*e.g.*, fuel, food, clothing, building materials, machinery, tools, vehicles, furnishings for quarters) may be requisitioned. Billeting of forces in occupied areas is also authorized.[354]

Special additional rules apply to the requisition of foodstuffs, articles necessary to support life, or medical supplies available in the occupied territory.[355] Similarly, additional rules apply to the requisition of civilian hospitals and their supplies.[356]

11.18.7.3 *Prices and Compensation for Requisitioned Articles and Services*. Contributions in kind shall as far as possible be paid for in cash; if not, a receipt shall be given,

---

[350] DEPARTMENT OF THE ARMY PAMPHLET 27-161-2, *II International Law*, 181 (Oct. 23, 1962) ("Requisition is the method of taking private enemy movable and immovable property for the needs of the army of occupation."); VON GLAHN, THE OCCUPATION OF ENEMY TERRITORY 165 ("Requisition is the term used for the demand of a supply of all kinds of articles needed by an army such as foodstuffs, clothing, horses, transportation and means of transportation, and buildings.").

[351] HAGUE IV REG. art. 52 ("Requisitions in kind and services shall not be demanded from municipalities or inhabitants except for the needs of the army of occupation. They shall be in proportion to the resources of the country, and of such a nature as not to involve the inhabitants in the obligation of taking part in military operations against their own country.").

[352] HAGUE IV REG. art. 52 ("Such requisitions and services shall only be demanded on the authority of the commander in the locality occupied.").

[353] 1956 FM 27-10 (Change No. 1 1976) ¶415 ("Requisitions must be made under the authority of the commander in the locality. No prescribed method is fixed, but if practicable requisitions should be accomplished through the local authorities by systematic collection in bulk. They may be made direct by detachments if local authorities fail or if circumstances preclude resort to such authorities.").

[354] 1956 FM 27-10 (Change No. 1 1976) ¶412b ("*What May Be Requisitioned*. Practically everything may be requisitioned under this article that is necessary for the maintenance of the army, such as fuel, food, clothing, building materials, machinery, tools, vehicles, furnishings for quarters, etc. Billeting of troops in occupied areas is also authorized.").

[355] *Refer to* § 11.14.2 (Limitation on Requisition of Food and Medical Supplies).

[356] *Refer to* § 11.15.5 (Requisition of Civilian Hospitals).

and the payment of the amount due shall be made as soon as possible.[357]

The prices of articles and services requisitioned will be fixed by agreement if possible, otherwise by military authority.[358]

11.18.7.4 *Method of Enforcing Requisition*. Coercive measures may be used to enforce requisitions, but will be limited to the amount and kind necessary to secure the articles requisitioned.[359]

11.19 Protection of Cultural Property During Occupation

The following rules address the protection of cultural property during occupation. The general rules for the protection of cultural property during hostilities also apply during occupation.[360] For example, military commanders have an obligation to take reasonable measures to prevent or stop any form of theft, pillage, or misappropriation of, and any acts of vandalism directed against, cultural property.[361]

11.19.1 Obligation With Respect to the Safeguarding and Preservation of Cultural Property. Any Party to the 1954 Hague Cultural Property Convention in occupation of the whole or part of the territory of another Party to the 1954 Hague Cultural Property Convention shall as far as possible support the competent national authorities of the occupied country in safeguarding and preserving its cultural property.[362]

Should it prove necessary to take measures to preserve cultural property situated in occupied territory and damaged by military operations, and should the competent national authorities be unable to take such measures, the Occupying Power shall, as far as possible, and in close co-operation with such authorities, take the most necessary measures of preservation.[363]

11.19.2 Respect for Cultural Property by Members of a Legitimate Resistance

---

[357] HAGUE IV REG. art. 52 ("Contributions in kind shall as far as possible be paid for in cash; if not, a receipt shall be given and the payment of the amount due shall be made as soon as possible.").

[358] 1956 FM 27-10 (Change No. 1 1976) ¶416 ("The prices of articles and services requisitioned will be fixed by agreement if possible, otherwise by military authority. Receipts should be taken up and compensation paid promptly.").

[359] 1956 FM 27-10 (Change No. 1 1976) ¶417 ("Coercive measures will be limited to the amount and kind necessary to secure the articles requisitioned.").

[360] *Refer to* § 5.18 (Protection of Cultural Property During Hostilities).

[361] *Refer to* § 5.18.6.1 (Obligation to Stop or Prevent Theft, Pillage, or Misappropriation of, and Acts of Vandalism Against, Cultural Property).

[362] 1954 HAGUE CULTURAL PROPERTY CONVENTION art. 5(1) ("Any High Contracting Party in occupation of the whole or part of the territory of another High Contracting Party shall as far as possible support the competent national authorities of the occupied country in safeguarding and preserving its cultural property.").

[363] 1954 HAGUE CULTURAL PROPERTY CONVENTION art. 5(2) ("Should it prove necessary to take measures to preserve cultural property situated in occupied territory and damaged by military operations, and should the competent national authorities be unable to take such measures, the Occupying Power shall, as far as possible, and in close co-operation with such authorities, take the most necessary measures of preservation.").

Movement. Any Party to 1954 Hague Cultural Property Convention whose government is considered by members of a resistance movement as their legitimate government shall, if possible, draw the resistance movement members' attention to the obligation to comply with those provisions of the 1954 Hague Cultural Property Convention dealing with respect for cultural property.[364]

11.19.3 Special Representative for Cultural Property in Occupied Territory and Application for Special Protection. An Occupying Power shall appoint a special representative for cultural property situated in that territory.[365]

The Occupying Power is competent to submit an application for immovable cultural property to be entered into the International Register of Cultural Property Under Special Protection.[366]

11.19.4 Transfers of Cultural Property From and Within Occupied Territory. The requisition of movable cultural property situated in the territory of another Party to the 1954 Hague Cultural Property Convention is prohibited.[367]

If necessary under its obligation to take measures to preserve damaged cultural property, the Occupying Power may arrange for the transport of cultural property to a refuge within occupied territory in accordance with other provisions of the 1954 Hague Cultural Property Convention.[368] Whenever a High Contracting Party occupying territory of another High Contracting Party transfers cultural property to a refuge situated elsewhere in that territory, without being able to follow the procedure for the transport of cultural property under special protection provided for in Article 17 of the Regulations, the transfer in question shall not be regarded as misappropriation within the meaning of Article 4 of the Convention, provided that the Commissioner-General for Cultural Property certifies in writing, after having consulted the

---

[364] 1954 HAGUE CULTURAL PROPERTY CONVENTION art. 5(3) ("Any High Contracting Party whose government is considered their legitimate government by members of a resistance movement, shall, if possible, draw their attention to the obligation to comply with those provisions of the Conventions dealing with respect for cultural property.").

[365] REGULATIONS FOR THE EXECUTION OF THE 1954 HAGUE CULTURAL PROPERTY CONVENTION art. 2 ("As soon as any High Contracting Party is engaged in an armed conflict to which Article 18 of the Convention applies: (a) It shall appoint a representative for cultural property situated in its territory; if it is in occupation of another territory, it shall appoint a special representative for cultural property situated in that territory;").

[366] REGULATIONS FOR THE EXECUTION OF THE 1954 HAGUE CULTURAL PROPERTY CONVENTION art. 13 ("1. Any High Contracting Party may submit to the Director General of the United Nations Educational, Scientific and Cultural Organization an application for the entry in the Register of certain refuges, centres containing monuments or other immovable cultural property situated within its territory. Such application shall contain a description of the location of such property and shall certify that the property complies with the provisions of Article 8 of the Convention. 2. In the event of occupation, the Occupying Power shall be competent to make such application."). *Refer to* § 5.18.8 (Special Protection for Certain Cultural Property).

[367] *Refer to* § 5.18.6.2 (Prohibition Against Requisition of Movable Cultural Property Situated in the Territory of Another Party to the 1954 Hague Cultural Property Convention).

[368] *Refer to* § 5.18.9.1 (Transport Under Special Protection).

usual custodians, that such transfer was rendered necessary by circumstances.[369]

11.20 Labor of Protected Persons in Occupied Territory

11.20.1 Types of Labor That May Not Be Compelled. The Occupying Power may not compel protected persons to perform certain types of labor.

11.20.1.1 *Prohibition on Compulsory Service in an Occupying Power's Armed Forces*. The Occupying Power may not compel protected persons to serve in its armed or auxiliary forces. No pressure or propaganda that aims at securing voluntary enlistment is permitted.[370]

Compelling protected persons to serve in its armed or auxiliary forces would in most cases also violate the prohibition against compelling inhabitants of occupied territory to swear allegiance to the hostile State.[371] Compelling a protected person to serve in the forces of a hostile Power is a grave breach of the GC.[372]

11.20.1.2 *Prohibition Against Compelling Protected Persons as Guards for Compulsory Work Installations*. The Occupying Power may not compel protected persons to employ forcible means to ensure the security of the installations where protected persons are performing compulsory labor.[373]

11.20.1.3 *Prohibition Against Requisition Labor Such That Workers Are Mobilized in a Military or Semi-Military Organization*. In no case shall requisition of labor lead to a mobilization of workers in an organization of a military or semi-military character.[374]

11.20.1.4 *Prohibition Against Forcing Inhabitants to Provide Information About the Opposing Army or Its Means of Defense*. A belligerent is forbidden to force the inhabitants of territory occupied by it to furnish information about the army of the other belligerent, or about its means of defense.[375] This obligation also results from the general prohibition against use of

---

[369] REGULATIONS FOR THE EXECUTION OF THE 1954 HAGUE CULTURAL PROPERTY CONVENTION art. 19 ("Whenever a High Contracting Party occupying territory of another High Contracting Party transfers cultural property to a refuge situated elsewhere in that territory, without being able to follow the procedure provided for in Article 17 of the Regulations, the transfer in question shall not be regarded as misappropriation within the meaning of Article 4 of the Convention, provided that the Commissioner-General for Cultural Property certifies in writing, after having consulted the usual custodians, that such transfer was rendered necessary by circumstances.").

[370] GC art. 51 ("The Occupying Power may not compel protected persons to serve in its armed or auxiliary forces. No pressure or propaganda which aims at securing voluntary enlistment is permitted.").

[371] *Refer to* § 11.6.2.1 (Prohibition on Compelling Inhabitants of Occupied Territory to Swear Allegiance to the Hostile State).

[372] *Refer to* § 18.9.3.1 (Acts Constituting Grave Breaches).

[373] GC art. 51 ("The Occupying Power may not compel protected persons to employ forcible means to ensure the security of the installations where they are performing compulsory labour.").

[374] GC art. 51 ("In no case shall requisition of labour lead to a mobilization of workers in an organization of a military or semi-military character.").

[375] HAGUE IV REG. art. 44 ("A belligerent is forbidden to force the inhabitants of territory occupied by it to furnish information about the army of the other belligerent, or about its means of defence.").

physical or moral coercion against protected persons.[376]

11.20.1.5 _Prohibition Against Other Work That Would Involve Protected Persons in the Obligation of Taking Part in Military Operations_. Protected persons may not be compelled to undertake any work that would involve them in the obligation of taking part in military operations.[377] This rule is formulated more broadly than the general rule against compelling a national to take part in operations against his or her own country[378] because it prohibits compulsory service in any military operation.[379]

The purpose of this rule, at least in part, is to ensure that civilians in occupied territory are not required to engage in activities that would forfeit their protections as civilians under the law of war.[380]

The prohibition against forcing the inhabitants of an occupied territory to take part in military operations against their own country precludes requisitioning their services in work directly promoting the ends of the war, such as construction of fortifications, entrenchments, and military airfields, or the transportation of supplies or ammunition in the zone of operations.[381]

---

376 GC COMMENTARY 220 ("Furthermore, coercion is forbidden for any purpose or motive whatever. The authors of the Convention had mainly in mind coercion aimed at obtaining information, work or support for an ideological or political idea. The scope of the text is more general than that of Article 44 of the Hague Regulations of 1907, under which 'a belligerent is forbidden to force the inhabitants of a territory occupied by it to furnish information about the army of the other belligerent, or about its means of defence'; Article 31 prohibits coercion for any purpose or reason and the obtaining of information is only given as an example. Thus, the custom, hitherto accepted in practice but disputed in theory, that an invasion army may force the inhabitants of an occupied territory to serve as 'guides' is now forbidden."). *Refer to* § 10.5.3.1 (No Physical or Moral Coercion).

377 GC art. 51 ("Protected persons may not be compelled to undertake any work which would involve them in the obligation of taking part in military operations."). *See also* HAGUE IV REG. art. 52 ("Requisitions in kind and services shall not be demanded from municipalities or inhabitants except for the needs of the army of occupation. They shall be in proportion to the resources of the country, and of such a nature as not to involve the inhabitants in the obligation of taking part in military operations against their own country.").

378 *Refer to* § 5.27 (Prohibition Against Compelling Enemy Nationals to Take Part in the Operations of War Directed Against Their Own Country).

379 GC COMMENTARY 296-97 ("The prohibition in this sentence is even more general than that contained in Article 52 of the Hague Regulations; for it does not only embrace work involving the participation of the inhabitants in 'military operations against their own country', but refers in a general way to any work 'which would involve them in the obligation of taking part in military operations'. The importance of the distinction will be realised if the mind is cast back to cases when the occupying authorities have tried to circumvent the law of war by pretending that they are no longer engaged in military operations against the home country of the persons whose services they are requisitioning.").

380 GC COMMENTARY 297 ("One point must not be forgotten: the Fourth Convention applies to civilians and civilians are by definition outside the fighting. Any action on the part of the Occupying Power which had the effect of involving them, directly or indirectly, in the fighting and so preventing them from benefiting by special protection under the Convention must be regarded as unlawful. The application of this clause depends very largely on the good faith of the occupant, who must judge in each individual case, with a full sense of his responsibility in the matter, whether or not the work demanded is compatible with the conditions here laid down.").

381 1956 FM 27-10 (Change No. 1 1976) ¶420 ("The prohibition against forcing the inhabitants to take part in military operations against their own country precludes requisitioning their services upon works directly promoting

11.20.2 Types of Work That May Be Compelled. The Occupying Power may not compel protected persons to work unless they are over eighteen years of age, and then only on work that is necessary for: (1) the needs of the army of occupation; (2) the public utility services; or (3) the feeding, sheltering, clothing, transportation, or health of the population of the occupied country.[382]

Thus, the Occupying Power may compel protected persons to engage in these three types of work, provided that such work is consistent with the other prohibitions against employing protected persons.[383] For example, even if it is permitted to compel civilian engineers in occupied territory to provide information about the telecommunications system of an occupied country in order to facilitate restoration of service, they may not be required to provide such information where it will be used to locate and attack the armed forces of the occupied territory.

11.20.2.1 *Examples of Services That May Be Requisitioned From Inhabitants*. The services that may be obtained from inhabitants by requisition include those of professionals, such as engineers, physicians, and nurses; and of artisans and laborers, such as clerks, carpenters, butchers, bakers, and truck drivers. The officials and employees of:

- railways, trucking companies, airlines, canals, and river or coastal steamship companies;
- cable, telegraph, telephone, radio, postal, and similar services;
- gas, electric, and water works; and
- sanitary authorities;

whether employed by the State or private companies, may be requisitioned to perform their duties only so long as the duties required do not directly concern the operations of war against their own country.[384]

The Occupying Power may also requisition labor to restore the general condition of the public works to that of peace, including the repair of roads, bridges, railways, and telecommunication networks, and to perform services on behalf of the local population, such as

---

the ends of the war, such as construction of fortifications, entrenchments, and military airfields or the transportation of supplies or ammunition in the zone of operations.").

[382] GC art. 51 ("The Occupying Power may not compel protected persons to work unless they are over eighteen years of age, and then only on work which is necessary either for the needs of the army of occupation, or for the public utility services, or for the feeding, sheltering, clothing, transportation or health of the population of the occupied country.").

[383] *Refer to* § 11.20.1 (Types of Labor That May Not Be Compelled).

[384] 1956 FM 27-10 (Change No. 1 1976) ¶419 ("The services which may be obtained from inhabitants by requisition include those of professional men, such as engineers, physicians and nurses and of artisans and laborers, such as clerks, carpenters, butchers, bakers, and truck drivers. The officials and employees of railways, trucklines, airlines, canals, river or coastwise steamship companies, telegraph, telephone, radio, postal and similar services, gas, electric, and water works, and sanitary authorities, whether employed by the State or private companies, may be requisitioned to perform their professional duties only so long as the duties required do not directly concern the operations of war against their own country.").

the care of the wounded and sick, and the burial of the dead.[385]

In addition, inhabitants over eighteen years of age may be compelled to perform work necessary to meet the maintenance needs of the occupation forces (as opposed to its strategic or tactical needs), such as providing telephone, water, or electricity services to the facilities of the occupation army from which the occupied territory is administered, or providing support to prisons, police stations, and other facilities necessary for the maintenance of order among the civilian population.[386]

11.20.2.2 *Requisition of Police and Other Services Essential to Good Order*. In general, police, firefighters, prison guards, and others who provide services essential to good order and security in occupied territory may be compelled by an Occupying Power to continue to provide those services.[387] Such a requirement is consistent with the Occupying Power's obligation to maintain public order in occupied territory.[388]

These officials may not be required to participate in military operations or other measures aimed at countering belligerent acts against the Occupying Power that are performed by privileged combatants under the law of war.[389] For example, civilian police forces in occupied territory may not be compelled to provide security for an occupying force against attacks in compliance with the law of war launched by lawful combatants, including resistance fighters who, if captured, would be entitled to POW status under GPW Article 4.

On the other hand, such police forces may be required to continue to perform their normal policing functions with respect to actual or threatened criminal acts, even where the victim of such acts is the Occupying Power.[390] Similarly, civilian firefighters may be required to

---

385 1956 FM 27-10 (Change No. 1 1976) ¶419 ("The occupant may also requisition labor to restore the general condition of the public works to that of peace, including the repair of roads, bridges, and railways, and to perform services on behalf of the local population, such as the care of the wounded and sick and the burial of the dead.").

386 GC COMMENTARY 294 ("The wording 'work which is necessary for the needs of the army of occupation' is very comprehensive and its interpretation is open to discussion. It will be enough to note here that the clause covers a wide variety of services—those connected with billeting and the provision of fodder, transport services, the repairing of roads, bridges, ports and railways and laying telephone and telegraph lines. On the other hand it is generally agreed that the inhabitants of the occupied territory cannot be requisitioned for such work as the construction of fortifications, trenches or aerial bases. It is the maintenance needs of the army of occupation and not its strategic or tactical requirements which are referred to here. The distinction is essential and should be emphasized. It is confirmed by a provision, to be examined further on, laying down that the Occupying Power cannot compel protected persons to do work which would involve their participation in military operations.").

387 *See* VON GLAHN, THE OCCUPATION OF ENEMY TERRITORY 68 ("[I]n fact, all able-bodied native inhabitants may be called upon to perform police duties, to assist the regular native police in the maintenance of public order, to help in fire-fighting organizations, or to perform any other duty for the public good.").

388 *Refer to* § 11.5 (Duty of the Occupying Power to Ensure Public Order and Safety).

389 *Refer to* § 11.20.1.5 (Prohibition Against Other Work That Would Involve Protected Persons in the Obligation of Taking Part in Military Operations).

390 *See* GC COMMENTARY 307 ("The reference to Article 51 relates not only to the list of different types of work, but also to the conditions and safeguards contained in that Article, in particular the prohibition on the use of compulsion to make protected persons take part in military operations. This is particularly important in the case of police officers, who cannot under any circumstances be required to participate in measures aimed at opposing legitimate belligerent acts, whether committed by armed forces hostile to the Occupying Power, by corps of volunteers or by

extinguish fires endangering the Occupying Power's military property that result from attacks by unprivileged combatants.

11.20.3 Working Conditions for Laborers Performing Requisitioned Work. Requisitioned work shall be carried out only in the occupied territory where the persons whose services have been requisitioned are resident, and such persons shall, so far as possible, be kept in their usual places of employment.[391]

Workers shall be paid a fair wage, and the work shall be proportionate to their physical and intellectual capacities.[392]

The legislation in force in the occupied country concerning working conditions, and safeguards as regards, in particular, such matters as wages, hours of work, equipment, preliminary training, and compensation for occupational accidents and diseases, shall be applicable to the protected persons assigned to the work.[393]

11.20.4 Voluntary Work Not Prohibited by the GC. Although the GC prohibits protected persons from being compelled to provide certain types of work related to military operations, there is no prohibition in the law of war to such persons being employed voluntarily and for pay in such work.[394] For example, there is no law of war prohibition against civilian firefighters putting out fires endangering civilian property resulting from attacks by lawful combatants against the Occupying Power's military property.

However, no pressure or propaganda that aims at securing voluntary enlistment in the armed or auxiliary forces of the Occupying Power is permitted.[395]

In addition, certain voluntary humanitarian work is recognized and protected by the

---

organized resistance movements. On the other hand it would certainly appear that the Occupying Power is entitled to require the local police to take part in tracing and punishing hostile acts committed under circumstances other than those laid down in Article 4 of the Third Geneva Convention. Such acts may in fact be regarded as offences under common law, whatever ideas may have inspired their authors, and the occupation authorities, being responsible for maintaining law and order, are within their rights in claiming the co-operation of the police.").

[391] GC art. 51 ("The work shall be carried out only in the occupied territory where the person whose services have been requisitioned are. Every such person shall, so far as possible, be kept in his usual place of employment.").

[392] GC art. 51 ("Workers shall be paid a fair wage and the work shall be proportionate to their physical and intellectual capacities.").

[393] GC art. 51 ("The legislation in force in the occupied country concerning working conditions, and safeguards as regards, in particular, such matters as wages, hours of work, equipment, preliminary training and compensation for occupational accidents and diseases, shall be applicable to the protected persons assigned to the work referred to in this Article.").

[394] 1956 FM 27-10 (Change No. 1 1976) ¶420 ("The prohibition against forcing the inhabitants to take part in military operations against their own country precludes requisitioning their services upon works directly promoting the ends of the war, such as construction of fortifications, entrenchments, and military airfields or the transportation of supplies or ammunition in the zone of operations. There is no objection in law to their being employed voluntarily and for pay in such work.").

[395] *Refer to* § 11.20.1.1 (Prohibition on Compulsory Service in an Occupying Power's Armed Forces).

GWS.[396]

11.20.5 General Protections Applicable to Workers in Occupied Territory.

11.20.5.1 *Access to Protecting Power*. No contract, agreement, or regulation shall impair the right of any worker, whether voluntary or not and wherever he or she may be, to apply to the representatives of the Protecting Power in order to request the Protecting Power's intervention.[397]

For example, it would be prohibited to forbid workers who are protected persons from applying to the Protecting Power. It would also be prohibited to require any protected persons who are workers, as a condition of work, to renounce their right to apply for assistance to the Protecting Power concerning work conditions or any other matter.[398]

11.20.5.2 *No Use of Measures to Create Unemployment to Induce Work for the Occupying Power*. All measures aiming at creating unemployment or at restricting the opportunities offered to workers in an occupied territory, in order to induce them to work for the Occupying Power, are prohibited.[399]

Measures intended to reduce unemployment would not be prohibited by this rule.[400]

11.21 Judges and Other Public Officials

11.21.1 Continued Service of Judges and Other Public Officials. The Occupying Power may not alter the status of public officials or judges in the occupied territories, or in any way apply sanctions to or take any measures of coercion or discrimination against them, should they abstain from fulfilling their functions for reasons of conscience.[401]

Public officials may be understood to include officials at both the national and local levels who fulfill public duties.[402]

---

[396] *Refer to* § 7.4.5 (Collection and Care of the Wounded, Sick, and Shipwrecked by Civilians).

[397] GC art. 52 ("No contract, agreement or regulation shall impair the right of any worker, whether voluntary or not and wherever he may be, to apply to the representatives of the Protecting Power in order to request the said Power's intervention.").

[398] *Refer to* § 10.5.6 (Facility for Applying to the Protecting Powers and Assistance Organizations Such as the ICRC).

[399] GC art. 52 ("All measures aiming at creating unemployment or at restricting the opportunities offered to workers in an occupied territory, in order to induce them to work for the Occupying Power, are prohibited.").

[400] *For example*, Coalition Provisional Authority Order No. 39, *Foreign Investment*, preamble (Sept. 19, 2003) ("*Determined* to improve the conditions of life, technical skills, and opportunities for all Iraqis and to fight unemployment with its associated deleterious effect on public security,").

[401] GC art. 54 ("The Occupying Power may not alter the status of public officials or judges in the occupied territories, or in any way apply sanctions to or take any measures of coercion or discrimination against them, should they abstain from fulfilling their function for reasons of conscience.").

[402] GC Commentary 304 ("[T]he term public official generally designates people in State or local government service, who fulfill public duties.").

This prohibition does not prejudice the application of the second paragraph of Article 51 of the GC.[403] Thus, a public official may be compelled to work to meet the needs of the army of occupation or for the public utility services, such as water, electricity, or sanitation.[404] Similarly, a public official may be compelled to provide certain police services.[405]

This prohibition does not affect the right of the Occupying Power to remove public officials from their posts.[406] For example, the Occupying Power may remove the political leadership and other political agents from their posts to prevent them from undermining the Occupying Power's administration.[407]

11.21.2 Oath of Public Officials. An Occupying Power may not require the inhabitants of occupied territory, including officials, to swear allegiance to it.[408] However, the Occupying Power may require such officials as are continued in their offices to take an oath to perform their duties conscientiously and not to act to its prejudice.[409] Any official who declines to take the oath may be removed; but, regardless of whether the official takes the oath, the official is required to obey the legitimate orders of the Occupying Power.[410]

11.21.3 Salaries of Public Officials. The salaries of civil officials of the hostile government who remain in the occupied territory and continue the work of their offices, especially those who can properly continue it under the circumstances arising out of the war – such as judges, administrative or police officers, and officers of city or communal governments – are paid from the public revenues of the occupied territory, until the military government has

---

[403] GC art. 54 ("This prohibition does not prejudice the application of the second paragraph of Article 51.").

[404] *Refer to* § 11.20.2 (Types of Work That May Be Compelled).

[405] *Refer to* § 11.20.2.2 (Requisition of Police and Other Services Essential to Good Order).

[406] GC art. 54 ("It does not affect the right of the Occupying Power to remove public officials from their posts.").

[407] GC COMMENTARY 308 ("The provision refers primarily to government officials and other political agents who are generally removed from their posts by the occupation authorities."). *For example*, Coalition Provisional Authority Order No. 1, *De-Ba`athification of Iraqi Society*, §1(1) (May 16, 2003) ("On April 16, 2003 the Coalition Provisional Authority disestablished the Ba`ath Party of Iraq. This order implements the declaration by eliminating the party's structures and removing its leadership from positions of authority and responsibility in Iraqi society.").

[408] *Refer to* § 11.6.2.1 (Prohibition on Compelling Inhabitants of Occupied Territory to Swear Allegiance to the Hostile State).

[409] 1956 FM 27-10 (Change No. 1 1976) ¶423 ("The occupant may require such officials as are continued in their offices to take an oath to perform their duties conscientiously and not to act to its prejudice. Every such official who declines to take such oath may be removed; but, whether he does so or not, he owes strict obedience to the occupant as long as he remains in office."). *For example*, Military Government, Germany, Supreme Commander's Area of Control, Law No. 2, *German Courts*, art. V, *reprinted as Appendix 9 in* VON GLAHN, THE OCCUPATION OF ENEMY TERRITORY 305, 306 ("QUALIFICATIONS OF JUDGES, PROSECUTORS, NOTARIES, AND LAWYERS No person shall be qualified to act as a of judge, prosecutor, notary or lawyer, until he shall have taken an oath in the following form: Oath 'I swear by almighty God that I will at all times apply and administer the law without fear or favour and with justice and equity to all persons of whatever creed, race, color or political opinion they may be, that I will obey the laws of Germany, and all enactments of the Military Government, in spirit as well as in letter, and will constantly endeavour to establish equal justice under the law for all persons. So help me God.'").

[410] *Refer to* § 11.7.1 (Inhabitants' Obedience to the Occupying Power).

reason wholly or partially to dispense with their services.[411]

Based on consistent practice, salaries or incomes connected with purely honorary titles would be suspended.[412] Similarly, the Occupying Power need not continue to pay salaries that are rewards for loyalty to the prior regime, and may reform the pay system of public servants to increase transparency and fairness, as well as to create incentives for meritorious service.[413]

11.22 Public Finances and Taxes

As a result of assuming the functions of government of the occupied territory, the financial administration of the occupied territory passes into the hands of the Occupying Power. During the occupation, the fiscal laws of the enemy State remain in effect, but may be changed or suspended by the Occupying Power under certain circumstances, as discussed below.

11.22.1 Taxes. If, in the occupied territory, the Occupying Power collects the taxes, dues, and tolls imposed for the benefit of the State, it shall do so, as far as is possible, in accordance with the rules of assessment and incidence in force, and shall in consequence be bound to defray the expenses of the administration of the occupied territory to the same extent as the legitimate Government was so bound.[414]

11.22.1.1 *Supervision of Taxes Collected by Local Authorities*. The words "for the benefit of the State" were inserted in Article 48 of the Hague IV Regulations to exclude local taxes, dues, and tolls collected by local authorities for local purposes.[415] The Occupying Power

[411] 1956 FM 27-10 (Change No. 1 1976) ¶424 ("The salaries of civil officials of the hostile government who remain in the occupied territory and continue the work of their offices, especially those who can properly continue it under the circumstances arising out of the war – such as judges, administrative or police officers, officers of city or communal governments – are paid from the public revenues of the occupied territory, until the military government has reason wholly or partially to dispense with their services."). *For example*, Coalition Provisional Authority Regulation No. 2, *Development Fund for Iraq*, §6(3) (Jun. 15, 2003) ("Purposes. Sums may be disbursed from the Fund to meet the humanitarian needs of the Iraqi people and for the economic reconstruction and repair of Iraq's infrastructure; for the continued disarmament of Iraq; for the costs of Iraq's civilian administration; and for other purposes the Administrator determines to be for the benefit of the people of Iraq.").

[412] 1956 FM 27-10 (Change No. 1 1976) ¶424 ("Salaries or incomes connected with purely honorary titles are always suspended.").

[413] *For example*, Coalition Provisional Authority Order No. 30, *Reform of Salaries and Employment Conditions of State Employees*, preamble (Sept. 8, 2003) ("*Understanding* that the salaries of public workers under the former regime were paid through a complicated system largely composed of incentive pay that rewarded loyalty to the former regime over meritorious service, ... *Noting* that salary and conditions of employment reform is essential to guarantee fairness within the public system to ensure that state employees receive appropriate compensation for their efforts, but also to provide incentives for meritorious service or sanctions for failure to perform appropriately,").

[414] Hague IV Reg. art. 48 ("If, in the territory occupied, the occupant collects the taxes, dues, and tolls imposed for the benefit of the State, he shall do so, as far as is possible, in accordance with the rules of assessment and incidence in force, and shall in consequence be bound to defray the expenses of the administration of the occupied territory to the same extent as the legitimate Government was so bound.").

[415] J.A.G.S. Text No. 11, Law of Belligerent Occupation 185 ("Taxes raised by local authorities for local purposes may not be diverted by the occupant from the purpose for which they were raised although the occupant may supervise their collection. It would seem that state taxes collected by local bodies and not used for local purposes but transmitted to the state treasury are taxes 'imposed for the benefit of the state.'"). *See also* Spaight, War Rights on Land 378 ("The words 'imposed for the benefit of the State' in Article XLVIII are intended to

may supervise the expenditure of such revenue and prevent its hostile use.[416]

11.22.1.2 *Changes in Taxes or New Taxes*. The Occupying Power shall collect taxes, as far as is possible, in accordance with the rules of assessment and incidence in force. This is an example of the general rule that the Occupying Power shall respect the laws in force in the occupied territory unless absolutely prevented.[417] Modifications to the tax laws may be justified by practical considerations and considerations of public order and safety.

If, due to the flight or unwillingness of local officials, it is impracticable to follow the rules of incidence and assessment in force, then the total amount of taxes to be paid may be allotted among the districts, towns, etc., and the local authorities may be required to collect it.[418]

The Occupying Power may suspend the tax laws of the occupied territory.[419] Similarly, the Occupying Power may also reduce the rate of taxes under the existing tax laws.

Unless required to do so by considerations of public order and safety, the Occupying Power must not create new taxes.[420] Additional revenue may be raised in some other form, such

---

exclude provincial and parochial taxes, or 'rates' as they are called in England. The latter the occupant must not intercept; he can only supervise the expenditure of such revenue, to see that it is not devoted to a hostile purpose.").

[416] 1956 FM 27-10 (Change No. 1 1976) ¶427 ("The words 'for the benefit of the State' were inserted in the foregoing article (*HR, art. 48;* par. 425 herein) to exclude local taxes, dues, and tolls collected by local authorities. The occupant may supervise the expenditure of such revenue and prevent its hostile use."). *See also* JAMES BROWN SCOTT, THE PROCEEDINGS OF THE HAGUE PEACE CONFERENCES: THE CONFERENCE OF 1899 523 (1920) ("Jonkheer van Karnebeek remarks that as the fundamental purport of this article is that the authority of the occupant is substituted for that of the invaded State, it cannot be admitted that the occupant, by assuming a right which the occupied State does not possess, may take possession of the municipal taxes, which the invaded State itself would not think of appropriating in normal circumstances. Mr. Veljkovitch remarks that in this eventuality the municipal authorities, being no longer able to discharge their duties, can likewise not collect the municipal taxes and especially the county rate; it is therefore proper for the occupant, whose power is substituted for that of the authorities, to take possession of the said taxes.").

[417] J.A.G.S. TEXT NO. 11, LAW OF BELLIGERENT OCCUPATION 186 ("The occupant in collecting taxes must follow the rules of procedure as well as the law of the country with regard to the distribution of the tax burden. This is an instance of the general rule that the occupant shall respect the laws in force in the occupied territory unless absolutely prevented.").

[418] 1956 FM 27-10 (Change No. 1 1976) ¶426a ("*When Existing Rules May Be Disregarded.* If, due to the flight or unwillingness of the local officials, it is impracticable to follow the rules of incidence and assessment in force, then the total amount of taxes to be paid may be allotted among the districts, towns, etc., and the local authorities required to collect it.").

[419] VON GLAHN, THE OCCUPATION OF ENEMY TERRITORY 151-52 ("Just as an occupant may collect taxes, so he may suspend existing taxes if the unaffected levies are sufficient to cover administrative expenses and if he does not desire to enrich himself out of possible surplus revenues."). *For example*, Coalition Provisional Authority Order No. 37, *Tax Strategy for 2003*, §2 (Sept. 19, 2003) ("Subject to Section 6 of this Order, the following taxes are suspended from April 16, 2003 to the end of calendar year 2003:").

[420] 1956 FM 27-10 (Change No. 1 1976) ¶426b ("*New Taxes.* Unless required to do so by considerations of public order and safety, the occupant must not create new taxes."); Bassil Abu Aita *et al.* v. The Regional Commander of Judea and Samaria and Staff Officer in Charge of Matters of Custom and Excise, HCJ 69/81; Omar Abdu Kadar Kanzil, *et al.* v. Officer in Charge of Customs, Gaza Strip Region and the Regional Commander of the Gaza Strip, HCJ 493/81, Israel Supreme Court Sitting as the High Court of Justice, 200, 270-71 (Apr. 5, 1983) ("Since the power of imposing ordinary taxes are within the domain of the sovereign alone, accordingly, it is argued, it does not

as monetary contributions or customs duties.[421]

U.N. Security Council resolutions may provide additional authority for the Occupying Power to amend the tax laws.[422]

11.22.1.3 Spending of Tax Revenue. The first charge upon such taxes is for the cost of the administration of the occupied territory. The balance may be used for the purposes of the Occupying Power.[423]

The Occupying Power may use tax revenue to defray the costs of maintaining order in the occupied territory or for expenditures that benefit the local population (*e.g.*, infrastructure improvements).[424]

The Occupying Power may refrain from spending money for the support of any activity opposed to its military interests or to the restoration of order in the occupied territory, even if the State whose territory is occupied formerly allocated tax revenues to such activity.[425]

11.22.1.4 Exemption of the Occupying Power From Local Taxation. As the paramount authority in the occupied territory,[426] the Occupying Power is exempt from indigenous taxation in the occupied territory unless it specifically waives its sovereign immunity

---

pertain to anyone whose authority is temporary and military, as described. However, while no one disputes the theoretical base of this doctrine, it does not of necessity create a limitation on the power to impose taxation *if the benefit and requirements of the territory deem it necessary*, since the maintenance of proper balance between them and the requirements of the ruling army is a constant central guiding principle of military government. This character of military government indeed explains why taxes may be imposed only for the requirements of the territory (or requirements of the army when army contributions are involved), but it does not necessarily lead to the conclusion that the limitation on the imposition of taxes also takes precedence over the obligation to satisfy the needs of the territory and its inhabitants, and as far as possible, to restore normal life, including the economic aspect thereof.").

421 *Refer to* § 11.22.2 (Contributions); § 11.22.3 (Customs Duties).

422 *Refer to* § 11.1.2.5 (Occupation and U.N. Security Council Resolutions).

423 1956 FM 27-10 (Change No. 1 1976) ¶425b ("*Surplus*. The first charge upon such taxes is for the cost of the administration of the occupied territory. The balance may be used for the purposes of the occupant.").

424 *See also* VON GLAHN, THE OCCUPATION OF ENEMY TERRITORY 151 ("It should be pointed out in this connection that as long as it is a duty of the occupant to restore order and public safety in the territory, the expenditures incurred by him as administrator for the benefit of the territory and its inhabitants should be paid for by the beneficiaries. This appears to be particularly true in the case of capital expenditures. Normally an occupant would be unwilling to permit heavy capital outlays in occupied enemy territory (such as the construction of dams, power stations, canals, and public buildings), but if, in rare instances, permission would be granted for such extraordinary outlays over and above normal operating expenses of the native administration, then the necessary funds should come from any excess revenues collected by the indigenous agencies, not from the occupant's own reserves.").

425 VON GLAHN, THE OCCUPATION OF ENEMY TERRITORY 150 ("Obviously no occupant need spend money for the support of any activity opposed to his military interests or to the restoration of order in the area, even if the absent legitimate sovereign formerly allocated tax revenues to such activity.").

426 *Refer to* § 11.8.1 (Paramount Authority of the Occupying Power Over Government Functions in Occupied Territory).

and consents to be taxed.[427] Its personnel are also generally exempt from local taxation, as part of their immunity from local law.[428]

In practice, the Occupying Power often issues an order specifying that no direct taxes of any kind may be levied or assessed within the occupied territory on the persons, agencies, property, instrumentalities, or transactions of the Occupying Power.[429]

11.22.1.5 *Scope of the Occupying Power's Power to Collect Taxes*. The power of the Occupying Power to collect taxes extends only to persons or property under its actual control.[430] For example, persons and property wholly outside occupied territory generally may not be taxed,[431] but the property of the absent inhabitants that is within the occupied territory may be taxed.

11.22.1.6 *Social Welfare Taxes*. An Occupying Power is often an employer of local civilian labor. Local law may provide that employers are responsible for the deduction and transfer to indigenous agencies of unemployment, health insurance, pensions, and similar welfare contributions. However, generally the agencies of the Occupying Power do not act as a collector for the local authorities, and will not be responsible for the employer's share of such welfare taxes. On the other hand, the inhabitants retain their obligation to pay their share of such contributions out of their remuneration.[432]

11.22.2 Contributions. If, in addition to continuing to collect taxes under the existing law of the occupied territory as permitted by Article 48 of the Hague IV Regulations, the Occupying

---

[427] VON GLAHN, THE OCCUPATION OF ENEMY TERRITORY 153-54 ("[A]n occupant is virtually exempt from indigenous taxation in an occupied territory unless he takes the rather unlikely step of waiving his sovereign immunity and consents to be taxed. In actual practice the occupation authorities normally issue an order to the effect that no direct taxes of any kind may be levied within the occupied area on the persons, agencies, or property of the armed forces of the invader and that no direct taxes may be assessed against the property, instrumentalities or transactions of the occupying authorities themselves.").

[428] *Refer to* § 11.8.5 (Immunity of Occupation Personnel From Local Law).

[429] *For example*, Coalition Provisional Authority Order No. 17, *Status of the Coalition Provisional Authority, MNF-Iraq, Certain Missions and Personnel in Iraq*, §10(1) (Jun. 27, 2004) ("The MNF, Sending States and Contractors shall be exempt from general sales taxes, Value Added Tax (VAT), and any similar taxes in respect of all local purchases for official use or for the performance of Contracts in Iraq.").

[430] J.A.G.S. TEXT NO. 11, LAW OF BELLIGERENT OCCUPATION 197 ("It must be remembered that the power of the occupant to collect taxes is purely de facto and territorial, i.e., it extends only to persons or property under his actual control.").

[431] *Cf.* MacLeod v. United States, 229 U.S. 416, 432-33 (1913) ("A state of war as to third persons continued until the exchange of treaty ratifications, and, although rice, not being contraband of war, might have been imported, the authority of the military commander, until the exchange of ratifications, may have included the right to control vessels sailing from Manila to trade in the enemy's country and to penalize violations of orders in that respect. But whatever the authority of the commander at Manila or those acting under his direction to control shipments by persons trading at Manila and in vessels sailing from there of American registration, such authority did not extend to the second collection of duties upon a cargo from a foreign port to a port occupied by a de facto government which had compulsorily required the payment of like duties.").

[432] VON GLAHN, THE OCCUPATION OF ENEMY TERRITORY 153 ("An inhabitant of the occupied territory will retain his obligation to pay such contributions out of his remuneration as approved local law demands, but must pay the amounts due from his take-home pay to whatever native agency is responsible for the collection of the funds.").

Power levies other money contributions in the occupied territory, this shall only be for the needs of the army or the administration of the territory in question.[433]

11.22.2.1 Prohibited Purposes for Levying Contributions. Contributions may not be levied for other than the needs of the occupying forces and the administration of the occupied territory. For example, contributions may not be levied:

- for the enrichment of the Occupying Power;
- for the payment of war expenses generally;[434]
- for the purposes of collective punishment;[435] or
- for the purposes of impoverishing the population in order to pressure the enemy to sue for peace.[436]

11.22.2.2 Methods of Levying Contributions. No contribution shall be collected except under a written order, and on the responsibility of a "Commander-in-chief."[437] The term "Commander-in-chief" may be understood to refer to the highest military officer charged with the administration of the occupied territory.[438] Commanders of small units or detachments may not order the collection of contributions.[439]

The collection of contributions shall only be effected as far as possible in accordance with the rules of assessment and incidence of the taxes in force.[440]

For every contribution, a receipt shall be given to the contributors.[441] The receipt is intended to secure for the contributors the possibility of being indemnified afterward by their

[433] HAGUE IV REG. art. 49 ("If, in addition to the taxes mentioned in the above article, the occupant levies other money contributions in the occupied territory, this shall only be for the needs of the army or the administration of the territory in question.").

[434] 1956 FM 27-10 (Change No. 1 1976) ¶428b ("*Prohibited Purposes.* Contributions may not be levied for the enrichment of the occupant, for the payment of war expenses generally, or for other than the needs of the occupying forces and the administration of the occupied territory.").

[435] *Refer to* § 11.6.2.2 (Prohibition Against General Penalties in Occupied Territory).

[436] J.A.G.S. TEXT NO. 11, LAW OF BELLIGERENT OCCUPATION 177 ("They may not be imposed for the purpose of enriching the occupant or for impoverishing the population and thus exerting pressure on it to sue for peace.").

[437] HAGUE IV REG. art. 51 ("No contribution shall be collected except under a written order, and on the responsibility of a Commander-in-chief.").

[438] J.A.G.S. TEXT NO. 11, LAW OF BELLIGERENT OCCUPATION 182 ("Seemingly the term 'commander in chief' refers to the highest military officer charged with the administration of the occupied territory.").

[439] J.A.G.S. TEXT NO. 11, LAW OF BELLIGERENT OCCUPATION 181 ("Levies of contributions by commanders of small units or detachments are prohibited.").

[440] HAGUE IV REG. art. 51 ("The collection of the said contribution shall only be effected as far as possible in accordance with the rules of assessment and incidence of the taxes in force."). *Compare* § 11.22.1.2 (Changes in Taxes or New Taxes).

[441] HAGUE IV REG. art. 51 ("For every contribution a receipt shall be given to the contributors.").

own government, and does not imply a promise of reimbursement by the Occupying Power.[442]

11.22.2.3 *Forced Loans*. The Occupying Power may seek contributions from the inhabitants of an occupied territory in the form of forced loans. The Occupying Power is required to repay such loans. As forced loans are viewed as a form of contribution, they are governed by the rules applicable to contributions.[443]

11.22.2.4 *Non-Cash Contributions*. As contributions are money demands, commodities may not be exacted as contributions. However, if the inhabitants of the occupied territory use certain commodities, rather than money, as a medium of exchange and receivable in payment of tax obligations, contributions in-kind limited to such commodities would be permissible.[444] Additionally, if the Occupying Power finds it difficult to secure prompt money payment, it may accept securities and bills of exchange from contributors in lieu of money.[445]

11.22.3 Customs Duties. The Occupying Power has the right to continue to exact existing duties, as part of its right to collect existing taxes.[446] Such collection must comply with the rules for the collection of existing taxes.[447]

The Occupying Power may also exact new duties as a form of contributions levied against the enemy or its trade.[448] Such new duties must comply with the rules for

---

[442] J.A.G.S. TEXT NO. 11, LAW OF BELLIGERENT OCCUPATION 183-84 ("There is no obligation imposed by the Hague Regulations for the reimbursement of contributions. The receipt required to be given the contributors is evidence that money has been exacted but implies no promise to pay by the occupant. The receipt is intended to secure to the contributors 'the possibility of being indemnified afterwards by their own government'.").

[443] J.A.G.S. TEXT NO. 11, LAW OF BELLIGERENT OCCUPATION 184 ("A forced loan is an involuntary exaction of money imposed on the inhabitants by the occupant which the latter is bound to repay. It is a form of contribution and differs from the latter only in that there is a duty of returning the money exacted. The same rules that govern contributions apply to forced loans.").

[444] J.A.G.S. TEXT NO. 11, LAW OF BELLIGERENT OCCUPATION 182-83 ("In primitive communities some commodities may be the medium of exchange and receivable in payment of tax obligations. In such circumstances contributions in kind limited to such commodities would seemingly be permissible as being contributions in money.").

[445] J.A.G.S. TEXT NO. 11, LAW OF BELLIGERENT OCCUPATION 183 ("An occupant who finds it difficult to secure prompt money payments may accept securities and bills of exchange from the contributors in lieu of money. This practice was used by the Germans in the Franco-German War of 1870.").

[446] Dooley v. United States, 182 U.S. 222, 230 (1901) ("Upon the occupation of the country by the military forces of the United States, the authority of the Spanish Government was superseded, but the necessity for a revenue did not cease. The government must be carried on, and there was no one left to administer its functions but the military forces of the United States. Money is requisite for that purpose, and money could only be raised by order of the military commander. The most natural method was by the continuation of existing duties. In adopting this method, General Miles was fully justified by the laws of war.").

[447] *Refer to* § 11.22.1 (Taxes).

[448] *For example*, Coalition Provisional Authority Order No. 38, *Reconstruction Levy*, §1 (Sept. 19, 2003) ("1) Notwithstanding CPA Order Number 12 or any other CPA Order suspending a tax, levy, duty, charge, withholding, fee or tariff, there shall be created a levy known as the Reconstruction Levy. 2) For the purpose of calculating the Reconstruction Levy, the taxable value of goods shall consist of their total customs value assessed in accordance with international practice. 3) The Reconstruction Levy shall be imposed at a rate of 5% of the taxable value of goods. The revenues from the Reconstruction Levy shall be used only to assist the Iraqi people and support the

contributions.[449]

11.22.3.1 *Exemptions for Certain Relief Shipments*. Relief shipments for POWs, relief shipments for internees, and other relief consignments intended for occupied territory are exempt from customs duties.[450]

11.22.3.2 *Power to Suspend Customs Duties and Tariffs or Exempt Certain Goods*. The Occupying Power may suspend customs duties and tariffs for shipment of goods into the occupied territory.[451] It may also exempt certain types of goods (*e.g.*, humanitarian goods, goods for its forces) from customs duties and tariffs.[452]

11.22.4 Enemy Public Debts.

11.22.4.1 *Debts Owed to Occupied Territory*. Many jurists have taken the view that the Occupying Power is generally not permitted to collect pre-occupation debts owed to the sovereign of the occupied territory, as it is not a party to the agreement originating the debt.[453]

---

reconstruction of Iraq. It shall expire two years from the date that this Order enters into force. 4) Unless exempted under this Order, the Reconstruction Levy shall be imposed on all goods imported into Iraq from all countries beginning 1 January 2004."); Fleming v. Page, 50 U.S. 603, 616 (1850) ("The person who acted in the character of collector in this instance, acted as such under the authority of the military commander, and in obedience to his orders; and the duties he exacted, and the regulations he adopted, were not those prescribed by law, but by the President in his character of commander-in-chief. The custom-house was established in an enemy's country, as one of the weapons of war. … The duties required to be paid were regulated with this view, and were nothing more than contributions levied upon the enemy, which the usages of war justify when an army is operating in the enemy's country.").

449 *Refer to* § 11.22.2 (Contributions).

450 *Refer to* § 9.20.4.1 (Exemption From Dues for Relief Shipments): § 10.23.4.1 (Exemption From Dues for Relief Shipments); § 11.17.1.3 (Charges, Taxes, and Customs Duties on Collective Relief Consignments for Occupied Territories).

451 *For example*, Coalition Provisional Authority Order No. 12, *Trade Liberalization Policy*, §1 (Jun. 8, 2003) ("All tariffs, customs duties, import taxes, licensing fees and similar surcharges for goods entering or leaving Iraq, and all other trade restrictions that may apply to such goods, are suspended until December 31, 2003."); Coalition Provisional Authority Order No. 54, *Trade Liberalization Policy 2004*, §1 (Feb. 26, 2004) ("All customs tariffs, duties, import taxes (not including the Reconstruction Levy imposed by CPA Order Number 38), and similar surcharges for goods entering or leaving Iraq are suspended until the sovereign transitional Iraqi administration imposes such charges following the CPA's transfer of full governance authority to that administration.").

452 Coalition Provisional Authority Order No. 38, *Reconstruction Levy*, §2 (Sept. 19, 2003) ("1) The following humanitarian goods shall be exempt from the Reconstruction Levy: … e. Goods imported to be delivered as humanitarian assistance to the people of Iraq or in support of reconstruction of Iraq. … 2) The Reconstruction Levy shall not apply to the following persons or entities: … b) Coalition Forces;").

453 *See* VON GLAHN, THE OCCUPATION OF ENEMY TERRITORY 156 ("[T]he majority of jurists concur in the view that the occupant cannot legally collect pre-occupation debts owed to the legitimate sovereign of the territory and at the same time act in accordance with the prevailing rules of international law."); U.S. ARMY, THE JUDGE ADVOCATE GENERAL'S SCHOOL, CIVIL AFFAIRS MILITARY GOVERNMENT: SELECTED CASES AND MATERIALS 108 (1958) ("The first paragraph of Article 53, HR (par. 403, FM 27-10), raises, rather than answers, the question whether the occupant may collect debts due the ousted sovereign. The question is complicated by the argument that as state debts constitute obligations between the debtors and the ousted sovereign and as occupation does not transfer sovereignty, the occupant does not succeed to the privity enjoyed by the ousted sovereign. Some authorities accept this rationale and take the position that the occupant cannot legally collect any debts due the state. See, Von Glahn,

However, the Occupying Power may collect the debts owed to the sovereign, provided that the debts may be legitimately characterized as realizable securities that are strictly the property of the State (*e.g.*, bearer instruments).[454] In addition, the Occupying Power may seize debts owed to insurgent forces.[455]

11.22.4.2 Existing Debts Owed by the Occupied Territory. The Occupying Power is under no obligation to pay the debts owed by the occupied territory, although it may choose to do so as a matter of policy.[456]

The Occupying Power may prevent payments from being made from occupied territory to a hostile belligerent.[457]

11.22.4.3 Contracting New Debt on Behalf of the Occupied Territory. In general, the Occupying Power may not contract new debts (including through the issuance of debt securities) on behalf of the occupied territory or collect taxes to pay interest on such debt.[458]

The Occupation of Enemy Territory 156-159 (1957). Other authorities, resorting to Article 48 HR (par. 425a, FM 27-10), contend that as the occupant is obliged to defray the expenses of administration of the territory, he ought to be authorized to collect those debts falling due during the period of his occupation. See, Stone, Legal Controls of International Conflict 717 (1954).").

[454] *Refer to* § 11.18.5.3 (Public Personal (Movable) Property).

[455] *For example, In Re, Order of Major-General Otis Requiring Smith, Bell & Co., A Banking House at Manila, to Turn Over to the American Authorities One Hundred Thousand Dollars, Held by Said House as the Property of the Insurgent Forces in the Philippines*, Submitted October 10, 1899, Case No. 738, Division of Insular Affairs, War Department *in* CHARLES E. MAGOON, LAW OFFICER, BUREAU OF INSULAR AFFAIRS, WAR DEPARTMENT, REPORTS ON THE LAW OF CIVIL GOVERNMENT IN TERRITORY SUBJECT TO MILITARY OCCUPATION BY THE MILITARY FORCES OF THE UNITED STATES 261, 262 (2nd ed., 1902) ("It is conceded that the fund seized was intended to be used for promoting the insurrection and that the insurgents sought to utilize the bank as a means of transfer for said funds. Under the laws and usages of war the United States may lawfully seize and retain such funds, and to that end may compel the person having such funds, in his possession to pay over the same to the military authorities. The most favorable view of the conduct of the bank in attempting to perform the service rendered the insurgents herein, is to consider the obligation assumed by the bank as creating an indebtedness to the persons associated in the insurrection and the draft as an evidence thereof. Such indebtedness may properly be collected by the United States as a military measure calculated to weaken the insurrection.").

[456] VON GLAHN, THE OCCUPATION OF ENEMY TERRITORY 158-59 ("Most authorities concur in the belief that an occupant is under no obligation to pay interest on or the principal of any public debt owed by the territory, that is, by the lawful sovereign. The occupant may, of course, choose to do so, as a matter of public policy, just as he may decide to pay pensions hitherto charged against the absent sovereign, but ordinarily all such payments are not considered to constitute proper administrative expenses obligating the occupying power.").

[457] VON GLAHN, THE OCCUPATION OF ENEMY TERRITORY 156 ("The occupant may rightfully prevent all payments from the area under his control to the hostile government.").

[458] VON GLAHN, THE OCCUPATION OF ENEMY TERRITORY 159 ("Second, it is generally accepted that an occupant may *not* contract new debts on behalf of the occupied territory or collect taxes to pay interest on such unlawful debt. Some authorities differ with this conclusion and maintain that there exists an exception, based on necessity and on the occupant's obligation to restore and maintain order and public safety. This latter view appears reasonable, *provided* that it could be demonstrated convincingly that the new indebtedness was not only required by the welfare of the native population but also constituted a fair and reasonable transaction."). *For example*, Coalition Provisional Authority Order No. 95, *Financial Management Law and Public Debt Law*, §4(2) (Jun. 4, 2004) ("Until such time as the Iraqi Interim Government assumes full governance authority in accordance with Article (2)(B)(1) of the Law of

However, new debt may be undertaken on behalf of the occupied territory if immediately necessary for the welfare of the inhabitants of occupied territory, and if undertaking such debt constitutes a fair and reasonable transaction.[459]

11.22.4.4 *Refinancing or Consolidating Existing Public Debt*. The Occupying Power may refinance or consolidate already existing public debt of the occupied territory if it is clearly in the interest of sound financial administration of that territory, and therefore of direct benefit to the inhabitants.[460]

11.22.5 Currency and Exchange Rates. The Occupying Power may leave the local currency of the occupied area in circulation. The Occupying Power may also authorize domestic authorities to re-issue currency if necessary for ensuring public order and safety.[461]

The Occupying Power may introduce its own currency into the occupied area or issue special currency for use in the occupied area territory, should the introduction or issuance of such currency be necessary.[462] There is a long history of issuing such war currency.[463] The issuance

---

the Administration for the State of Iraq for the Transitional Period, the Ministry of Finance is prohibited from issuing new debt securities if the issuance of such securities would increase the total level of Iraq's public debt, including obligations to the Central Bank, beyond the current level of such debt.").

[459] John W. Griggs, Attorney General, *Cuba—Claims—Contracts*, Jan. 19, 1899, 22 OPINIONS OF THE ATTORNEY GENERAL 310, 311 (1900) ("The completion of the proposed contract between Dady & Co. and the city of Havana would involve an expenditure for the benefit of that city of $14,000,000, to be secured by an issue of municipal bonds. It is manifest that a matter of such great importance to the city of Havana, its citizens and taxpayers, ought not to be determined without a full and complete understanding of all the facts and a thorough knowledge of the civil law applicable thereto under the system prevailing in Cuba. ... The administration of the United States in Cuba is of a military nature, and merely temporary. No action binding the island or any of its municipalities to large expenditures and continuing debt ought to be made, except upon grounds of immediate necessity, which in this case do not appear to be present.").

[460] *For example*, Coalition Provisional Authority Order No. 95, *Financial Management Law and Public Debt Law*, §1(2) (Jun. 4, 2004) ("This Order promulgates the Public Debt Law, which authorizes the Ministry of Finance to issue and pay debt securities guaranteed by the Government, and establishes certain related authorities and duties, for the purposes of financing Government operations and promoting a stable Iraqi economy."). *See also* VON GLAHN, THE OCCUPATION OF ENEMY TERRITORY 159 ("[A]n occupant appears to be entitled to refinance or to consolidate already existing public debts of an occupied territory if such a step is clearly in the interest of sound financial administration and thus for the direct benefit of the inhabitants of the area."); J.A.G.S. TEXT NO. 11, LAW OF BELLIGERENT OCCUPATION 232 ("Seemingly, the occupant acting as administrator of the occupied territory may refinance or consolidate the existing indebtedness of the occupied state in the interest of sound public administration.").

[461] *For example*, Coalition Provisional Authority Order No. 43, *New Iraqi Dinar Banknotes*, §3(1) (Oct. 14, 2003) ("The CBI [Central Bank of Iraq] is, pursuant to Article 34 of the Central Bank of Iraq Law No. 64 of 1976, as amended, the sole authority in the Republic of Iraq vested with the power to issue legal tender currency. The CBI, under the supervision of the CPA, shall issue New Iraqi dinar banknotes and determine the denominations, designs, technical specifications, and other characteristics of New Iraqi dinar banknotes.").

[462] 1956 FM 27-10 (Change No. 1 1976) ¶430 ("The occupying power may leave the local currency of the occupied area in circulation. It is also authorized to introduce its own currency or to issue special currency for use only in the occupied area, should the introduction or issuance of such currency become necessary."); Abotiz & Co. v. Price, 99 F. Supp. 602, 611-12 (D. Utah 1951) ("Some recognized medium of exchange was necessary to keep the economic life of the community going. And, the power of a military government in occupied enemy territory to issue military currency cannot seriously be questioned.").

of occupation currency may be necessary to counteract the enemy State's practice of engaging in economic sabotage.[464]

The Occupying Power may also set exchange rates for currency in occupied territory.[465]

The Occupying Power's powers to regulate currency must not be used to confiscate private property.[466] For example, intentional debasement of currency by the establishment of fictitious valuation or exchange rates, or like devices, as well as failure to take reasonable steps to prevent inflation, with the result of enrichment of the Occupying Power, would violate international law.[467]

---

[463] Aboitiz & Co. v. Price, 99 F. Supp. 602, 614-15 (D. Utah 1951) ("The validity of such war currency is not only supported by these principles of international law, to which our own country has given its assent, but, it is supported by the dictates of a sound public policy, and, there is back of it a long history of the use of war money by many nations. During our own Revolutionary War, the Continental Congress issued currency for use in British territory occupied by the colonial troops before the Declaration of Independence. The rebel government of the Confederate States issued a war currency which, as we have seen, was held valid by the Supreme Court of the United States. Moreover, the United States and her allies in World War II issued occupation currency in Sicily, Germany, and Austria. The Combined Chief of Staffs of the Supreme Allied Commander issued a directive June 24, 1943, that the task forces use, besides regular United States coins, yellow seal dollars and besides regular British coins, British Military Authority (BMA) notes, to supplement lire currency. The Combined Directive for Military Government in Germany, April 28, 1944, directed the Allied forces to use yellow seal dollars and British Military Authority notes (BMA), if the Reichs mark currency became inadequate. The American Directive on Military Government of Austria, June 27, 1945, ordered our forces to use for military purposes only Allied Military Schillings.").

[464] *For example*, *Opinion on the Legality of the Issuance of AMG (Allied Military Government) Currency in Sicily*, Sept. 23, 1943, *reprinted in Occupation Currency Transactions: Hearings Before the Committees on Appropriations Armed Services and Banking and Currency, U.S. Senate*, 80th Congress, First Session, 73, 81-82 (Jun. 17-18, 1947) ("The currency policies deliberately followed by the Axis in retreat were designed to make the maintenance of 'public order and safety' by the Allied powers as difficult as possible. The variety of forms of economic sabotage which the Germans might use is illustrated by the seemingly opposite practices followed in Tunisia and in Sicily. In Tunisia, the Germans distributed Bank of France notes on a grand scale, increasing wage rates to some classes of employees manifold, patronizing the black market freely, and paying collaborationists lavishly. ... In Sicily, Mussolini went even further [than in Italy] and ordered the banks to be substantially depleted to the point where additional new currency was urgently needed for immediate use to permit the resumption of normal commercial activity. ... Thus, the Axis practices made a ready supply of new currency even more essential than otherwise, and provide a complete justification for the use of such currency under the test of the Hague Convention.").

[465] *For example*, Coalition Provisional Authority Order No. 43, *New Iraqi Dinar Banknotes*, §5 (Oct. 14, 2003) ("The 1990 dinar banknotes and the Swiss dinar banknotes and coins shall be exchanged against New Iraqi dinar banknotes at the official conversion rates of one (1) 1990 dinar to one (1) New Iraqi dinar, and of one (1) Swiss dinar to one-hundred-and-fifty (150) New Iraqi dinars.").

[466] *Refer to* § 11.18.6.1 (Prohibition on Confiscation of Private Property in Occupied Territory).

[467] 1956 FM 27-10 (Change No. 1 1976) ¶430 ("Intentional debasement of currency by the establishment of fictitious valuation or exchange rates, or like devices, as well as failure to take reasonable steps to prevent inflation, are violative of international law."). *See also Opinion on the Legality of the Issuance of AMG (Allied Military Government) Currency in Sicily*, Sept. 23, 1943, *reprinted in Occupation Currency Transactions: Hearings Before the Committees on Appropriations Armed Services and Banking and Currency, U.S. Senate*, 80th Congress, First Session, 73, 82 (Jun. 17-18, 1947) ("The Germans were roundly criticized during the First World War, and again in this war, for introducing occupation marks and similar currency devices. ... The vice of the German practice is not in the use of currency, but in the excessive issue of valueless currency as a device for stripping the occupied area of its good and its labor for the benefit of Germany.").

11.23 Other Economic Regulation of Occupied Territory

11.23.1 General Authority of the Occupying Power to Regulate Commercial Intercourse. The Occupying Power has the right to regulate commercial intercourse within, into, or out of the occupied territory. It may subject such intercourse to such prohibitions or restrictions as are essential to the purposes of the occupation.[468] The Occupying Power also may remove existing commercial restrictions or regulations when essential to the purposes of the occupation.[469] For example, the Occupying Power may suspend existing customs tariffs.[470]

The purposes of the occupation that justify economic regulation may include the military interest of the Occupying Power, the needs of the inhabitants of occupied territory, and applicable law of war obligations.

For example, for its military purposes, the Occupying Power may impose a moratorium on business payments until an effective occupation government is in place in order to safeguard financial institutions, to preserve records, and to ensure that funds and other assets of the enemy government are not transferred without the knowledge and approval of the Occupying Power. Similarly, for purposes of security and restoration of public order, the Occupying Power may also take steps to prevent hoarding of supplies, to curb or prevent black markets, and to regulate labor conditions, including strikes.[471] As another case in point, in order to fulfill its obligations with respect to the preservation of cultural property in occupied territory, the Occupying Power may issue commercial regulations intended to prevent illegal traffic in, and looting of, such property.[472]

Additional authority to regulate the economy of occupied territory may be provided by U.N. Security Council resolutions.[473]

---

[468] 1956 FM 27-10 (Change No. 1 1976) ¶376 ("The occupant has the right to regulate commercial intercourse in the occupied territory. It may subject such intercourse to such prohibitions and restrictions as are essential to the purposes of the occupation."). *See also* WILLIAM E. BIRKHIMER, MILITARY GOVERNMENT AND MARTIAL LAW 268 (1914) ("One of the most important incidents of military government is the regulation of trade with the subjugated state. The Occupying State has an unquestioned right to regulate commercial intercourse with conquered territory. It may be absolutely prohibited, or permitted to be unrestricted, or such limitations may be imposed thereon as either policy or a proper attention to military measures may justify.").

[469] 2004 UK MANUAL ¶11.32 ("The occupying power may place on the occupied territory such restrictions and conditions in respect of commercial dealings as may be necessary for military purposes. For the same reasons it may remove existing restrictions, such as current customs tariffs."); 1958 UK MANUAL ¶530 ("The Occupant may place such restrictions and conditions upon all commercial intercourse with the occupied territory as he may deem suitable for his military purpose. He may likewise remove existing restrictions; for instance, he may suspend the customs tariff in force.").

[470] *Refer to* § 11.22.3.2 (Power to Suspend Customs Duties and Tariffs or Exempt Certain Goods).

[471] VON GLAHN, THE OCCUPATION OF ENEMY TERRITORY 208 ("The occupant also appears to possess other powers over private business, including the right to prevent hoarding of supplies and raw materials, the prevention of black markets, the regulation of labor conditions, including strikes, and, in general, the power to return business conditions in the territory to nearly normal conditions as speedily as possible.").

[472] *Refer to* § 11.19.1 (Obligation With Respect to the Safeguarding and Preservation of Cultural Property).

[473] *Refer to* § 11.1.2.5 (Occupation and U.N. Security Council Resolutions).

11.23.2 <u>Limit on the Overall Burdens Placed on the Economy of the Occupied Territory</u>. The economy of an occupied territory can only be required to bear the expenses of the occupation, and these should not be greater than the economy of the occupied territory can reasonably be expected to bear.[474] For example, requisitions must be in proportion to the resources of the occupied territory.[475]

11.23.3 <u>Control of Business in Occupied Territory</u>. The Occupying Power may exercise controls over private business for the purpose of addressing the needs of the inhabitants of the occupied territory or for military purposes, including by: (1) compelling the continued operation of a business; (2) granting of business subsidies; (3) closing down a business; or (4) assuming control and management of a business.

The Occupying Power may compel a business to continue operations if necessary to serve the needs of the local population or for military purposes.[476] Compulsory work of protected persons, however, must comply with the GC.[477]

The Occupying Power may take steps to increase production from private business, such as by granting subsidies out of available governmental revenues from the occupied territory.[478]

If the Occupying Power determines that the continued operation of a business is detrimental to the interests of the local population or to the Occupying Power, the Occupying Power may close down the business.[479]

The Occupying Power may assume control and management of such a business if necessary to serve the needs of the local population or for military purposes.[480] Title to the business in such circumstances remains with the legal owner, and if the Occupying Power earns

---

[474] 1956 FM 27-10 (Change No. 1 1976) ¶364 ("The economy of an occupied country can only be required to bear the expenses of the occupation, and these should not be greater than the economy of the country can reasonably be expected to bear."). *See also* United States, *et al.* v. Göring, *et al.*, *Judgment*, I TRIAL OF THE MAJOR WAR CRIMINALS BEFORE THE IMT 239 ("The evidence in this case has established, however, that the territories occupied by Germany were exploited for the German war effort in the most ruthless way, without consideration of the local economy, and in consequence of a deliberate design and policy. There was in truth a systematic 'plunder of public or private property', which was criminal under Article 6(b) of the Charter… . Raw materials and finished products alike were confiscated for the needs of the German industry.").

[475] *Refer to* § 11.18.7 (Requisitions of Private Enemy Property).

[476] VON GLAHN, THE OCCUPATION OF ENEMY TERRITORY 207 ("If the operations of a given enterprise appear necessary to the occupant, he may compel the continuation of such operations.").

[477] *Refer to* § 11.20 (Labor of Protected Persons in Occupied Territory).

[478] VON GLAHN, THE OCCUPATION OF ENEMY TERRITORY 207-08 ("If existing private industries fail to supply in required quantities such commodities as may be urgently needed by the native inhabitants or by occupants own forces in the occupied territory, it appears to be permissible for him to undertake steps to increase production, if necessary by subsidization out of available government revenues of the occupied area.").

[479] VON GLAHN, THE OCCUPATION OF ENEMY TERRITORY 207 ("If, on the other hand, such continued operations appear to be against the interests of the population or of the occupying power, the latter may close down the enterprise in question.").

[480] *Refer to* § 11.18.3 (Property Control Measures).

a profit from the operation of the business, the legal owner must be indemnified, to avoid a prohibited confiscation of private property.[481]

11.23.4 Regulation of External Trade. The Occupying Power may also regulate foreign trade, including completely suspending such trade.[482] For example, the Occupying Power may halt the export of precious metals and other valuable items that are readily converted or exchanged on the international market, including metals such as copper, jewels, and securities.[483]

Commercial relations between the occupied territory and the remaining territory of the enemy and its allies are also normally suspended.[484] Such suspension may be relaxed through licenses to trade.[485]

11.23.5 Exchange Controls, Including Clearing Arrangements, and Asset Controls. The Occupying Power may also institute exchange controls, including clearing arrangements, and, if necessary, the freezing or blocking of certain assets, in order to conserve the monetary assets of the occupied territory, as well as for security purposes.[486] For example, the Occupying Power

---

481 VON GLAHN, THE OCCUPATION OF ENEMY TERRITORY 207 ("An occupant apparently may also lawfully place under his direct control and management any enterprise which is held by him to be vital for his needs or the needs of the indigenous population. Such an assumption of management is not expropriation, for title to the property in question remains vested in its former owner-operator; the occupant merely assumes a temporary control and has to return the firm when the need for his control has passed. If the occupant earns a profit during his operation of a private enterprise seized by him he should indemnify the owner in full for the amount of the profit, since the Hague regulations prohibit the confiscation of private property.").

482 VON GLAHN, THE OCCUPATION OF ENEMY TERRITORY 211-12 ("The occupant possesses a right, based on logic, to regulate all trade between an occupied area and the outside world. ... [N]ormally, also, all commercial relations between the area and its allies as well as the remainder of the sovereign's territory are suspended as soon as occupation becomes effective.").

483 *For example*, Coalition Provisional Authority Order No. 12, *Trade Liberalization Policy*, Annex – Prohibited Exports (Jun. 8, 2003); Coalition Provisional Authority Order No. 54, *Trade Liberalization Policy 2004*, Annex – Restricted Exports (Feb. 26, 2004); Coalition Provisional Authority Memorandum No. 8, *Exportation of Scrap Metal Under Order Number 12, Trade Liberalization Policy (CPA/ORD/7 June2003/12)*, §3 (Jan. 25, 2004) ("Effective February 1, 2004, metal, including scrap metal, shall not be exported without authorization from the Ministry of Trade. Prior to February 1, 2004, scrap metal, excluding copper and lead, may be exported without a license.").

484 1956 FM 27-10 (Change No. 1 1976) ¶376 ("The commander of the occupying forces will usually find it advisable to forbid intercourse between the occupied territory and the territory still in the possession of the enemy."). *Refer to* § 12.1.1 (Traditional Rule of Non-Intercourse During War).

485 *Refer to* § 12.6.3.2 (Licenses to Trade).

486 1956 FM 27-10 (Change No. 1 1976) ¶430 ("The occupant may also institute exchange controls, including clearing arrangements, in order to conserve the monetary assets of the occupied territory."). *For example*, Coalition Provisional Authority Order No. 93, *Anti-Money Laundering Act of 2004*, §1 (Jun. 3, 2004) ("The purpose of the Anti-Money Laundering Law is to secure financial institutions and combat instability by criminalizing the acts of laundering money, financing crime, financing terrorism, and structuring certain transactions."); Haw Pia v. China Banking Corp. (Supreme Ct., Philippines 1949), Annual Digest, 1951, Case No. 203, *reprinted in* 43 AJIL 821-23 (1949) ("As to the first question, we … hold, that the Japanese military authorities had power, under the international law, to order the liquidation of the China Banking Corporation and to appoint and authorize the Bank of Taiwan as liquidator to accept the payment in question, because such liquidation is not a confiscation of the properties of the bank appellee, but a mere sequestration of its assets which require the liquidation or winding up of the business of said bank.") (amendment in AJIL).

may regulate, or even prohibit, the flow of funds between the occupied territory and other countries, under the theory that preventing flight of capital assets is critical to maintaining order and stability.[487] Such measures must not, however, be used to enrich the Occupying Power or otherwise circumvent the restrictions placed on requisitions, contributions, seizures, and other measures dealing with property.[488]

11.23.6 Price Controls in Occupied Territory. The Occupying Power may regulate prices in the occupied territory. For example, shortages of commodities and increased demand for certain commodities in the occupied territory may result in a rise in price fluctuations requiring the Occupying Power to resort to measures designed to maintain prices at a reasonable maximum level.[489] However, the Occupying Power may not use its power over price controls for the purpose of exploiting the occupied territory to its own illegal advantage.[490]

[487] VON GLAHN, THE OCCUPATION OF ENEMY TERRITORY 203-04 ("Thus an occupant would appear to possess the right to regulate and even to prohibit a flow of funds between an occupied territory and other countries, in view of the likely possibility that a capital flight would disrupt the monetary system and hence the order and safety to be preserved by the occupant.").

[488] 1956 FM 27-10 (Change No. 1 1976) ¶430 ("Such measures must not, however, be utilized to enrich the occupant or otherwise circumvent the restrictions place on requisitions, contributions, seizures, and other measures dealing with property."). *For example*, JUDGMENT OF THE INTERNATIONAL MILITARY TRIBUNAL FOR THE TRIAL OF THE GERMAN MAJOR WAR CRIMINALS (Indictment Count 3(E)(6) ("By a variety of financial mechanisms, they despoiled all of the occupied countries of essential commodities and accumulated wealth, debased the local currency systems and disrupted the local economies. They financed extensive purchases in occupied countries through clearing arrangements by which they exacted loans from the occupied countries. They imposed occupation levies, exacted financial contributions, and issued occupation currency, far in excess of occupation costs. They used these excess funds to finance the purchase of business properties and supplies in the occupied countries.").

[489] VON GLAHN, THE OCCUPATION OF ENEMY TERRITORY 209 ("A majority of jurists writing on the law of occupation and most military manuals on the subject approve the right of an occupant to regulate prices in occupied territory. Shortages of every kind of commodity, ruined or damaged crops, lack of imported goods, increased demands through requisitions or purchases by occupation forces – all these contribute to a rise in the general price level unless the occupant resorts to measures designed to maintain prices at a reasonable maximum.").

[490] VON GLAHN, THE OCCUPATION OF ENEMY TERRITORY 209-10 ("Yet an unscrupulous occupant may easily misuse his power over price controls to exploit the occupied territory to his own illegal advantage—as shown repeatedly during the Second World War.").

XII – Non-Hostile Relations Between Belligerents

Chapter Contents

12.1 Introduction

This Chapter addresses the legal principles for non-hostile relations between belligerents and the basic mechanisms for implementing them.

More specifically, this Chapter addresses the rules for the protection of certain personnel engaged in non-hostile relations, such as *parlementaires*, and persons protected by military passports, safe-conducts, or safeguards. In addition, this Chapter addresses certain agreements between opposing belligerents, such as cartels, capitulations, and armistices.

12.1.1 Traditional Rule of Non-Intercourse During War. The traditional rule during international armed conflict is that, even without any special proclamation, all intercourse between the territories occupied by belligerent forces, including communication, transportation, and commerce, would cease.[1]

The traditional rule of non-intercourse reflects a belligerent's authority under the law of war to limit and regulate intercourse between persons and territory controlled by or belonging to that belligerent and persons and territory controlled by or belonging to the enemy.[2] For example,

[1] *See* 1956 FM 27-10 (Change No. 1 1976) ¶449 ("All intercourse between the territories occupied by belligerent armies, whether by traffic, communication, travel, or in any other way, ceases. This is the general rule to be observed without special proclamation."); LIEBER CODE art. 86 ("All intercourse between the territories occupied by belligerent armies, whether by traffic, by letter, by travel, or in any other way, ceases. This is the general rule, to be observed without special proclamation.").

[2] *See* Hamilton v. Dillin, 88 U.S. 73, 97 (1874) ("As before stated, the power of the government to impose such conditions upon commercial intercourse with an enemy in time of war as it sees fit is undoubted. It is a power which every other government in the world claims and exercises, and which belongs to the government of the United States as incident to the power to declare war and to carry it on to a successful termination. We regard the

States may authorize their military commanders to limit travel and trade within their areas of operations for security purposes. During armed conflict, States have exercised their authority to limit intercourse with the enemy in order to avoid supporting the enemy's war effort and in order to speak with one voice in communications with the enemy State.

In particular, the traditional rule of non-intercourse notifies a State's nationals and other persons subject to its jurisdiction that they may be liable to punishment by that State under its domestic law and war powers if they communicate with or support the State's enemies in war without proper authorization.[3]

Exceptions to the general rule of non-intercourse (such as communication with enemy forces or permission to trade or travel between territories that are controlled by forces hostile to one another) have been granted on behalf of individuals only with the approval of the Government or the highest military authority.[4]

12.1.1.1 Limitations on the Belligerent's Authority to Regulate Intercourse. A belligerent's authority to regulate intercourse between territory it controls and territory controlled by the enemy is subject to certain limitations.

Insofar as restrictions on travel and trade imposed by a belligerent affect neutral rights, such restrictions may be limited by the law of neutrality. An Occupying Power's authority to control travel and trade during belligerent occupation is addressed by the law of occupation.[5]

Under the GC, however, protected persons in a belligerent's home country, or in territory

---

regulations in question as nothing more than the exercise of this power. It does not belong to the same category as the power to levy and collect taxes, duties, and excises. It belongs to the war powers of the government, just as much so as the power to levy military contributions, or to perform any other belligerent act.").

[3] *For example*, 10 U.S.C. § 904 ("Any person who-- (1) aids, or attempts to aid, the enemy with arms, ammunition, supplies, money, or other things; or (2) without proper authority, knowingly harbors or protects or gives intelligence to, or communicates or corresponds with or holds any intercourse with the enemy, either directly or indirectly; shall suffer death or such other punishment as a court-martial or military commission may direct. This section does not apply to a military commission established under chapter 47A of this title."); Amos T. Akerman, Attorney General, *Unlawful Traffic with Indians*, Jul. 19, 1871, 13 OPINIONS OF THE ATTORNEY GENERAL 470, 471-72 (1873) ("But I observe that General Sherman, in his letter, refers to the parties apprehended by the military as having been captured 'while engaged in unlawful traffic with *hostile* Indians;' and the papers submitted show that a portion of the property employed in this trade consisted of ammunition. Now, if the Indians to whom the captured persons were thus supplying ammunition, &c., were in open and notorious hostility to the United States at the time, and, therefore, properly came within the description of public enemies, the parties apprehended would seem to be amenable to trial and punishment by court-martial under the 56th article of war, which applies to persons who are not, as well as to persons who are, in the military service."); LIEBER CODE art. 86 ("Contraventions of this rule [of non-intercourse] are highly punishable.").

[4] 1956 FM 27-10 (Change No. 1 1976) ¶450 ("Exceptions to this rule, whether by safe-conduct, license to trade, exchange of mails, or travel from one territory into the other, are made on behalf of individuals only with the approval of the Government or the highest military authority."); LIEBER CODE art. 86 ("Exceptions to this rule, whether by safe-conduct, or permission to trade on a small or large scale, or by exchanging mails, or by travel from one territory into the other, can take place only according to agreement approved by the government, or by the highest military authority.").

[5] *Refer to* § 11.12 (Movement of Persons in Occupied Territory); § 11.23.4 (Regulation of External Trade).

occupied by a belligerent, are entitled to leave unless such departure is contrary to the interests of the State.[6]

12.1.2 Necessity for Non-Hostile Relations. Despite the general rule of non-intercourse during war, the conduct of war and the restoration of peace require certain non-hostile relations between belligerents.[7]

12.1.2.1 *Non-Hostile Relations to Facilitate Humanitarian Activities During Armed Conflict*. Non-hostile relations, including local communication between belligerent forces, may be necessary to facilitate the conclusion and implementation of special agreements contemplated by the 1949 Geneva Conventions. These include:

- special agreements to facilitate the protection of the wounded, sick, shipwrecked, and medical personnel,[8] such as
  - armistices or local arrangements to permit the removal, exchange, or transport of the wounded and sick;[9]
- special agreements to facilitate the protection of POWs,[10] such as
  - agreements to effect the direct repatriation or accommodation in neutral countries of certain seriously wounded and sick POWs during hostilities;[11] and
- special agreements to facilitate the protection of civilians,[12] such as
  - agreements to establish areas where civilians or the wounded and sick are protected.[13]

Relatedly, non-hostile relations, including local communication between belligerent forces, may also be necessary:

- to obtain the necessary consent for the appointment of Protecting Powers;[14]

---

[6] *Refer to* § 10.8.2 (Departures of Protected Persons From a Belligerent's Home Territory); § 11.12.2 (Departure of Protected Persons Who Are Not Nationals of the State Whose Territory Is Occupied).

[7] 1956 FM 27-10 (Change No. 1 1976) ¶451 ("The conduct of war and the restoration of peace require certain nonhostile relations between belligerents.").

[8] *Refer to* § 7.1.1.2 (Special Agreements Under the GWS and GWS-Sea).

[9] *Refer to* § 7.4.3.1 (Armistices and Local Arrangements to Permit the Removal, Exchange, or Transport of the Wounded).

[10] *Refer to* § 9.1.2.2 (Special Agreements Under the GPW).

[11] *Refer to* § 9.36 (Direct Repatriation and Accommodation in Neutral Countries During Hostilities).

[12] *Refer to* § 10.1.1.2 (Special Agreements Under the GC).

[13] *Refer to* § 5.14.3 (Establishing Areas Where Civilians or the Wounded and Sick Are Protected).

[14] *Refer to* § 18.15.2 (Appointment of a Protecting Power).

- to establish safe-conduct protections for certain persons or property under the 1949 Geneva Conventions;[15] and

- to conclude special agreements applicable to a non-international armed conflict to bring into effect treaty provisions that would normally only apply during international armed conflict.[16]

12.1.2.2 Non-Hostile Relations to Facilitate the Restoration of Peace. Non-hostile relations, including local communication between belligerent forces, may also be important in facilitating the restoration of peace, including by facilitating:

- ceasefires or local armistices that implement a general armistice;

- armistices that are a prelude to a peace treaty;[17]

- the permanent cessation of hostilities through a peace treaty;

- agreements on the repatriation of POWs or retained personnel after the cessation of hostilities;[18]

- measures to protect civilians from the effects of minefields, mined areas, mines, booby-traps, and other devices, such as information sharing with another party or parties to the conflict;[19] and

- the provision of certain assistance to facilitate the marking and clearance, removal, or destruction of explosive remnants of war, in cases where a user of explosive ordnance that has become explosive remnants of war does not exercise control of the territory.[20]

12.2 Principle of Good Faith in Non-Hostile Relations

Absolute good faith with the enemy must be observed as a rule of conduct, including in non-hostile relations between opposing belligerents.[21] In particular, in the context of non-hostile relations, the principle of good faith requires that:

- compacts between enemies, such as truces and capitulations, shall be faithfully adhered

---

[15] *Refer to* § 12.6.3.3 (Safe-Conducts Contemplated by the 1949 Geneva Conventions).

[16] *Refer to* § 17.3 (Special Agreements Between Parties to the Conflict).

[17] *Refer to* § 12.11.1.2 (Armistice as a Suspension of Hostilities and Not a Peace Treaty).

[18] *Refer to* § 9.37.1 (Agreements on POW Release and Repatriation).

[19] *Refer to* § 6.12.12 (Obligations Arising After the Cessation of Active Hostilities).

[20] *Refer to* § 6.20.8 (Providing Assistance to Facilitate the Removal of Explosive Remnants of War From a Party's Military Operations in Areas Outside Its Control).

[21] *Refer to* § 5.21 (Overview of Good Faith, Perfidy, and Ruses).

to;[22]

- no advantage not intended to be given by the adversary shall be taken;[23] and
- the means of conducting non-hostile relations (such as flags of truce) must not be misused.[24]

On the other hand, the principle of good faith does not prohibit belligerents from:

- continuing their military operations while negotiations are ongoing;[25] or
- declining to respond to offers to negotiate, refusing offers to negotiate, or refusing specific offers from the adversary for reasons of military expediency.[26]

12.3 Methods for Communication Between Belligerents

Belligerents may communicate with one another through a variety of methods, including:

- directly by telecommunications;[27]

---

[22] Daniel Webster, Secretary of State, *Letter to Waddy Thompson, Esq., Envoy Extraordinary and Minister Plenipotentiary of the United States to the Mexican Republic*, Apr. 15, 1842, *reprinted in* THE DIPLOMATIC AND OFFICIAL PAPERS OF DANIEL WEBSTER, WHILE SECRETARY OF STATE 321, 331 (1848) ("If there is one rule of the law of war more clear and peremptory than another, it is that compacts between enemies, such as truces and capitulations, shall be faithfully adhered to; and their non-observance is denounced as being manifestly at variance with the true interest and duty; not only of the immediate parties, but of all mankind.").

[23] 1956 FM 27-10 (Change No. 1 1976) ¶453 ("It is absolutely essential in all nonhostile relations that the most scrupulous good faith shall be observed by both parties, and that no advantage not intended to be given by the adversary shall be taken.").

[24] 2004 UK MANUAL ¶10.2 ("Whenever there are non-hostile relations between parties to an armed conflict, those relations must be conducted with the utmost good faith and any agreement reached scrupulously observed. In particular, there should be no abuse of a flag of truce or emblems of identification in dealings between belligerents.").

[25] *For example*, Donald W. Boose, Jr., *Fighting While Talking: The Korean War Truce Talks*, OAH MAGAZINE OF HISTORY, 25, 27 (Spring 2000) ("The truce talks resumed on 26 April [1953], and the two sides quickly agreed on the broad outlines of a plan to deal with the POW issue through a Neutral Nations Repatriation Commission composed of the same members as the Neutral Nations Supervisory Commission, in addition to India. There were still unresolved issues, however. The U.S. leadership, losing patience with the slow pace of negotiations, now attempted to use military action to pressure the Chinese and North Koreans. In May U.S. aircraft attacked irrigation dams near Pyongyang, disrupting rail lines and roads and further straining the North Korean infrastructure. Then on 20 May Eisenhower and his advisors decided that if no progress were made, the UNC would initiate a military offensive that might include attacks on China and the use of nuclear weapons.").

[26] *Refer to* § 12.5.2 (Refusal or Reception of a *Parlementaire*).

[27] *For example*, James Reston, *Ridgway in Offer; Key Figure in Truce Plan Receives a Visitor U.S. Asks Command of Reds to Parley*, THE NEW YORK TIMES, Jun. 30, 1951 ("In accordance with Presidential instructions recommended by the National Security Council and dispatched from the Pentagon at 1:27 o'clock this afternoon, Gen. Matthew B. Ridgway of the United States broadcast the following message at 6 P.M. to 'The Commander in Chief, Communist Forces in Korea':").

- through the traditional mechanism of a display of a flag of truce and the sending of *parlementaires*;[28]
- in conferences between belligerent representatives in an agreed neutral zone;[29]
- through international organizations, such as the United Nations;
- indirectly through another State, such as a Protecting Power;[30] and
- indirectly through the ICRC or other impartial humanitarian organization.[31]

12.4 The White Flag of Truce to Initiate Negotiations

In the past, the normal means of initiating negotiations between belligerents has been the display of the white flag of truce.[32]

12.4.1 Meaning of the White Flag—a Desire to Communicate. As a legal matter, the white flag, when used by military forces, indicates a desire to communicate with the enemy. The hoisting of a white flag has no other legal meaning in the law of war.[33]

The hoisting of a white flag may indicate that the party hoisting it desires to open communication with a view to an armistice (*e.g.*, to enable forces to collect the wounded) or a surrender.[34] If hoisted during a military action by an individual combatant or a small party of combatants, it may signify merely that those persons or forces wish to surrender.[35] Although the white flag has been used with this intent, the display of the white flag does not necessarily mean that the person or forces displaying it are prepared to surrender. Moreover, enemy forces in the immediate area might not have the same intent as the individual or forces displaying the white flag, especially where the display of the white flag was not authorized by the individual or

---

[28] *Refer to* § 12.4 (The White Flag of Truce to Initiate Negotiations); § 12.5 (Rules for Parlementaires).

[29] *Refer to* § 12.5.5 (Neutral Zone and Other Appropriate Measures to Facilitate Negotiations).

[30] *For example*, *Acceptance of Germany's Offer Concerning Prisoners of War*, Apr. 23, 1945, 12 DEPARTMENT OF STATE BULLETIN 810 (Apr. 29, 1945) ("The Department of State and the War Department announced on April 23 that the Government of the United States has accepted an offer of the German Government to leave in camps all prisoners of war as the Allies advance. The proposal of the German Government was made to the United States through the Swiss Government as protecting power.").

[31] 1956 FM 27-10 (Change No. 1 1976) ¶452 ("One belligerent may communicate with another directly by radio, through parlementaires, or in a conference, and indirectly through a Protecting Power, a third State other than a Protecting Power, or the International Committee of the Red Cross.").

[32] 1956 FM 27-10 (Change No. 1 1976) ¶458 ("In the past, the normal means of initiating negotiations between belligerents has been the display of a white flag.").

[33] 1956 FM 27-10 (Change No. 1 1976) ¶458 ("The white flag, when used by troops, indicates a desire to communicate with the enemy. The hoisting of a white flag has no other signification in international law.").

[34] 1956 FM 27-10 (Change No. 1 1976) ¶458 ("It may indicate that the party hoisting it desires to open communication with a view to an armistice or a surrender.").

[35] 1956 FM 27-10 (Change No. 1 1976) ¶458 ("If hoisted in action by an individual soldier or a small party, it may signify merely the surrender of that soldier or party.").

force's commander.

12.4.2 Rules for the Party Displaying the White Flag. Forces displaying a flag of truce must show clearly that they intend to engage in non-hostile relations. They bear the burden of communicating their intent to the adversary.

To indicate that the hoisting of the white flag is authorized by its commander, the appearance of the flag should be accompanied or followed promptly by a complete cessation of fire from that side.[36]

The commander authorizing the hoisting of the flag should also promptly send a *parlementaire* to communicate the commander's intent.[37]

12.4.2.1 *Prohibition on Improper Use of the Flag of Truce*. It is especially forbidden to make improper use of a flag of truce.[38] It would be improper to use a flag of truce to feign an intention to negotiate, surrender, or otherwise suspend hostilities when there is no such intention.[39]

It is an abuse of the flag of truce if the force that sends a *parlementaire* does not halt and cease fire while the *parlementaire* is approaching, or is being received by, the other party.[40]

Improper use of a flag of truce also includes its use while engaging in attacks or in order to shield, favor, or protect one's own military operations, or otherwise to impede enemy military operations.[41] For example, flags of truce may not be used surreptitiously to obtain military information, or with the purpose of obtaining time to effect a withdrawal, secure reinforcements,

---

[36] 1956 FM 27-10 (Change No. 1 1976) ¶458 ("To indicate that the hoisting is authorized by its commander, the appearance of the flag should be accompanied or followed promptly by a complete cessation of fire from that side."); 1958 UK MANUAL ¶395 ("It is essential, however, that the troops who hoist the white flag to indicate a wish to enter into communication with the enemy, should halt and cease firing, for otherwise the enemy cannot be certain that the hoisting of the white flag is authorised.").

[37] 1956 FM 27-10 (Change No. 1 1976) ¶458 ("The commander authorizing the hoisting of the flag should also promptly send a parlementaire or parlementaires.").

[38] HAGUE IV REG. art. 23(f) (it is especially forbidden "[t]o make improper use of a flag of truce"). *Consider* AP I art. 38(1)(a) ("It is also prohibited to misuse deliberately in an armed conflict other internationally recognized protective emblems, signs or signals, including the flag of truce, and the protective emblem of cultural property.").

[39] *Cf.* 10 U.S.C. § 950t (18) ("Any person subject to this chapter who uses a flag of truce to feign an intention to negotiate, surrender, or otherwise suspend hostilities when there is no such intention shall be punished as a military commission under this chapter may direct.").

[40] 1958 UK MANUAL ¶415 ("The improper use of a flag of truce is forbidden. It is an abuse of the flag of truce if the force which sends a *parlementaire* does not halt and cease fire whilst the *parlementaire* is approaching, or is being received by, the other party."); 1956 FM 27-10 (Change No. 1 1976) ¶467 ("It is an abuse of the flag of truce, forbidden as an improper ruse under Article 23 (f), HR (par. 52), for an enemy not to halt and cease firing while the parlementaire sent by him is advancing and being received by the other party;").

[41] *Refer to* § 5.16 (Prohibition on Using Protected Persons and Objects to Shield, Favor, or Impede Military Operations).

resupply, or conduct other operations.[42]

12.4.3 Rules for the Party to Whom the White Flag Is Displayed. A party is not required to cease firing or other military operations when a white flag is raised by the other side.[43]

It is essential to determine with reasonable certainty that the flag is shown by actual authority of the enemy commander before basing important action upon that assumption.[44] For example, forces should not assume that all enemy forces in the locality intend to surrender and expose themselves to hostile fire based on the enemy's display of a white flag.[45]

Fire must not be directed intentionally on the person carrying the white flag or on persons near him or her unless there is a clear manifestation of hostile intent by those persons.[46]

12.5 RULES FOR *PARLEMENTAIRES*

After the display of the white flag, a *parlementaire* would be sent to conduct negotiations, traveling under the display and protection of the white flag of truce.

12.5.1 The *Parlementaire* and Party. *Parlementaires* ordinarily are agents employed by commanders of belligerent forces in the field, to go in person within the enemy lines, for the

---

[42] LIEBER CODE art. 114 ("If it be discovered, and fairly proved, that a flag of truce has been abused for surreptitiously obtaining military knowledge, the bearer of the flag thus abusing his sacred character is deemed a spy. So sacred is the character of a flag of truce, and so necessary is its sacredness, that while its abuse is an especially heinous offense, great caution is requisite, on the other hand, in convicting the bearer of a flag of truce as a spy."); 1958 UK MANUAL ¶416 ("It is also an abuse of the flag of truce to use a white flag for the purpose of making the enemy believe that a *parlementaire* is about to be sent when there is no such intention, and to carry out operations under the protection granted by the enemy to the pretended flag of truce.").

[43] 1956 FM 27-10 (Change No. 1 1976) ¶458 ("The enemy is not required to cease firing when a white flag is raised."); LIEBER CODE art. 112 ("Firing is not required to cease on the appearance of a flag of truce in battle.").

[44] 1956 FM 27-10 (Change No. 1 1976) ¶458 ("It is essential, therefore, to determine with reasonable certainty that the flag is shown by actual authority of the enemy commander before basing important action upon that assumption.").

[45] *For example*, 2004 UK MANUAL ¶10.5.2 footnote 10 ("A British officer was killed at Goose Green during the Falklands conflict 1982 when moving towards a white flag. The shots were not fired by those displaying the white flag, but by others in the vicinity."); SPAIGHT, WAR RIGHTS ON LAND 92-93 ("At Spion-Kop, some of the British troops in an advanced trench on the mountain held up handkerchiefs in token of surrender, and the Boers came forward to take them prisoners; they were fired upon by the other British soldiers, and some of them and also some of the prisoners were shot. Presidents Kruger and Steyn protested against this 'abuse of the white flag,' but the protest cannot be upheld. For the particular men who put up the signal of surrender to have fired on their captors would have been treachery, but their comrades were not bound by their action; the surrender was not authorised and the main body of the British troops on the hill were perfectly entitled to disregard it and to fire both on their own men who surrendered and on the enemy disarming them.").

[46] 1956 FM 27-10 (Change No. 1 1976) ¶461 ("Fire should not be intentionally directed on parlementaires or those accompanying them."); 1958 UK MANUAL ¶396 ("Fire must not be directed intentionally on the person carrying the white flag or on persons near him.").

purpose of communicating or negotiating openly and directly with the enemy commander.[47]

12.5.1.1 Parlementaire – *Notes on Terminology*. The term *parlementaire* is derived from "parley" and was adopted by governments at the First Hague Peace Conference in 1899.[48] These provisions were repeated in the 1907 Hague IV Regulations.

Article 32 of the Hague IV Regulations provides that "a person is regarded as bearing a flag of truce who has been authorized by one of the belligerents to enter into communication with the other, and who advances bearing a white flag."[49] Although the word *parlementaire* has been translated as a person bearing a flag of truce, the *parlementaire* need not physically carry the white flag.[50]

12.5.1.2 *Authorization and Credentials of the* Parlementaire. A *parlementaire* must be authorized by a belligerent to enter into communications with the other side.[51] To demonstrate the authorization to negotiate, a *parlementaire* must be duly authorized in a written instrument signed by the commander of his or her forces.[52]

12.5.1.3 *Members of a* Parlementaire *Party*. A *parlementaire* may come alone, or he or she may request to have others, such as an interpreter, accompany him or her. In the past, flag-bearers or drummers accompanied *parlementaires* to reduce the risk that the *parlementaires* would be inadvertently attacked.[53] In modern warfare, members of a *parlementaire's* party may include, for example, a driver and communications personnel, and they would take similar

---

[47] 1956 FM 27-10 (Change No. 1 1976) ¶459 ("Parlementaires are agents employed by commanders of belligerent forces in the field, to go in person within the enemy lines, for the purpose of communicating or negotiating openly and directly with the enemy commander.").

[48] 1958 UK MANUAL ¶389 ("The usual agents in the non-hostile intercourse of belligerent armies are known as *parlementaires*."); 1958 UK MANUAL ¶389 note 1 ("It has been thought desirable to adopt this term, for which the ancient verb 'to parley' would seem good authority, from the Hague Rules; it is current in other armies, in addition to the expression 'flag of truce'. The use of the latter term by British manuals in the past to mean sometimes both the envoy and the emblem, sometimes only the envoy, and at other times the envoy and his attendants, has given rise to some confusion. The use of the expression 'bearer of a flag of truce' to signify the principal agent is also misleading, as he is seldom the actual bearer of the flag.").

[49] HAGUE IV REG. art. 32.

[50] 1914 RULES OF LAND WARFARE ¶235 note 1 ("The adoption of the word 'parlementaire' to designate and distinguish the agent or envoy seems absolutely essential in order to avoid confusion and because all other nations, including Great Britain, utilize the word. In the past this word has been translated at times to mean the agent or envoy only, at other times the agent and emblem, or both. To call the *parlementaire* 'the bearer of a flag of truce' is not in reality correct, because he seldom, if ever, actually carries it.").

[51] HAGUE IV REG. art. 32 ("A person is regarded as bearing a flag of truce who has been authorized by one of the belligerents to enter into communication with the other, and who advances bearing a white flag.").

[52] 1956 FM 27-10 (Change No. 1 1976) ¶462 ("Parlementaires must be duly authorized in a written instrument signed by the commander of the forces.").

[53] HAGUE IV REG. art. 32 ("A person is regarded as bearing a flag of truce who has been authorized by one of the belligerents to enter into communication with the other, and who advances bearing a white flag. He has a right to inviolability, as well as the trumpeter, bugler or drummer, the flag-bearer and interpreter who may accompany him.").

measures to make their status and purpose clear to the other side.[54]

12.5.2 Refusal or Reception of a *Parlementaire*. The commander to whom a flag of truce is sent is not in all cases obliged to receive it.[55] A commander may decline to receive a *parlementaire* for reasons of military necessity, such as if the reception of the *parlementaire* would interfere with the commander's operations.[56] However, a belligerent may not declare beforehand, even for a specified period – except in case of reprisal for abuses of the flag of truce – that it will not receive *parlementaires*.[57]

A commander may declare the formalities and conditions upon which he or she will receive a *parlementaire* and fix the hour and place at which the *parlementaire* must appear.[58] The receiving commander may set the details of the meeting, such as the time, place, number of persons accompanying the *parlementaire*, authorized method of transport (*e.g.*, foot or vehicle), and the frequency of meetings if more than one will take place. For example, the receiving commander may limit the size of the *parlementaire*'s party and need not allow an unnecessary repetition of *parlementaire* visits.[59]

Although commanders may refuse to receive *parlementaires* and other enemy envoys seeking to negotiate, commanders may not refuse the unconditional surrender of the adversary or declare that they will refuse unconditional surrender.[60]

12.5.3 Duties and Liabilities of the *Parlementaire*. Persons who display a white flag during combat accept the risk that they might be inadvertently wounded or killed while attempting to communicate with opposing forces.[61] *Parlementaires* bear the burden of

---

[54] *See also* 2004 UK MANUAL ¶10.4 footnote 5 ("Although the reference here is to 'trumpeter, bugler or drummer, the flag bearer and interpreter who may accompany him', in modern warfare, the party is more likely to consist of a driver and radio operator, together with an interpreter. The interpreter will not necessarily be a member of the armed forces and may be a civilian. The white flag will most likely be attached to the vehicle conveying the party.").

[55] HAGUE IV REG. art. 33 ("The commander to whom a flag of truce is sent is not in all cases obliged to receive it."). *See also* LIEBER CODE art. 111 ("The bearer of a flag of truce cannot insist upon being admitted. He must always be admitted with great caution. Unnecessary frequency is carefully to be avoided.").

[56] 1958 UK MANUAL ¶398 ("The commander to whom a *parlementaire* is sent is not obliged to receive him in every case. There may be a movement in progress the success of which depends on secrecy, or owing to the state of the defences, it may be considered undesirable to allow an envoy to approach a besieged locality.").

[57] 1956 FM 27-10 (Change No. 1 1976) ¶464 ("The present rule is that a belligerent may not declare beforehand, even for a specified period -- except in case of reprisal for abuses of the flag of truce -- that he will not receive parlementaires.").

[58] 1956 FM 27-10 (Change No. 1 1976) ¶464 ("A commander may declare the formalities and conditions upon which he will receive a parlementaire and fix the hour and place at which he must appear.").

[59] *See, e.g.*, 1956 FM 27-10 (Change No. 1 1976) ¶464 ("An unnecessary repetition of visits need not be allowed."); LIEBER CODE art. 111 ("Unnecessary frequency is carefully to be avoided.").

[60] *Refer to* § 5.4.7 (Prohibition Against Declaring That No Quarter Be Given); § 5.9.3 (Persons Who Have Surrendered).

[61] 1956 FM 27-10 (Change No. 1 1976) ¶461 ("If, however, the parlementaires or those near them present themselves during an engagement and are killed or wounded, it furnishes no ground for complaint."); LIEBER CODE

communicating their status to the enemy.[62] They should take appropriate measures to help clarify their status to enemy forces. For example, the *parlementaire's* party should move slowly and deliberately so that it is not inadvertently attacked.[63]

While within the lines of the enemy, the *parlementaire* must obey all instructions given to him or her. The *parlementaire* may be required to deliver his or her message to a subordinate of the commander.[64]

12.5.4 Rights of Inviolability of the *Parlementaire*. A *parlementaire* and members of the *parlementaire's* party (*e.g.*, an interpreter) have a right to inviolability.[65] For example, it would be a serious violation of good faith to attack deliberately a *parlementaire's* party that has been received and acknowledged.[66]

12.5.4.1 *Security Measures Are Consistent With Inviolability*. The receiving commander, however, may take all the necessary steps to prevent the envoy from taking advantage of his or her mission to obtain information.[67] For example, the envoy and the envoy's interpreter may be blindfolded or hooded for security purposes.[68]

12.5.4.2 *Loss of Rights of Inviolability of* Parlementaire. A *parlementaire* loses his or her rights of inviolability if it is proved in a clear and uncontestable manner that he or she has taken advantage of his or her privileged position to provoke or commit an act of treachery.[69] Such acts of treachery include sabotage or the secret gathering of information about the

---

art. 113 ("If the bearer of a flag of truce, presenting himself during an engagement, is killed or wounded, it furnishes no ground of complaint whatever.").

[62] *See* 1956 FM 27-10 (Change No. 1 1976) ¶461 ("It is the duty of the parlementaire to select a propitious moment for displaying his flag, such as during the intervals of active operations, and to avoid dangerous zones by making a detour."); 1958 UK MANUAL ¶396 ("It is for the *parlementaire* to wait until there is a propitious moment, or to make a detour to avoid a dangerous zone.").

[63] *See* 1958 UK MANUAL ¶402 note 1 ("Unfortunate incidents may occur if the parlementaire arrives at or leaves the enemy lines at speed as he may draw fire before he is recognised.").

[64] 1956 FM 27-10 (Change No. 1 1976) ¶464 ("While within the lines of the enemy, the parlementaire must obey all instructions given him. He may be required to deliver his message to a subordinate of the commander.").

[65] HAGUE IV REG. art. 32 ("A person is regarded as bearing a flag of truce who has been authorized by one of the belligerents to enter into communication with the other, and who advances bearing a white flag. He has a right to inviolability, as well as the trumpeter, bugler or drummer, the flag-bearer and interpreter who may accompany him.").

[66] George H. Williams, Attorney General, *The Modoc Indian Prisoners*, Jun. 7, 1873, 14 OPINIONS OF THE ATTORNEY GENERAL 249, 250 (1875) ("According to the laws of war there is nothing more sacred than a flag of truce dispatched in good faith, and there can be no greater act of perfidy and treachery than the assassination of its bearers after they have been acknowledged and received by those to whom they are sent.").

[67] HAGUE IV REG. art. 33 ("[The commander to whom a flag of truce is sent] may take all the necessary steps to prevent the envoy taking advantage of his mission to obtain information.").

[68] SPAIGHT, WAR RIGHTS ON LAND 217-18 ("[I]t is no indignity for a *parlementaire*, however high his rank, to have his eyes bandaged.").

[69] HAGUE IV REG. art. 34 ("The envoy loses his rights of inviolability if it is proved in a clear and incontestable manner that he has taken advantage of his privileged position to provoke or commit an act of treachery.").

adversary while under the adversary's protection.[70]

A *parlementaire* does not commit an act of treachery if he or she reports what he or she observed in plain sight during his or her mission.[71]

12.5.4.3 Detention of Parlementaire. In case of abuse of a flag of truce, a commander to whom a flag of truce is sent has the right to detain the envoy temporarily.[72]

In addition to the right of detention for abuse of his or her position, a *parlementaire* may be detained for other imperative security reasons. For example, a *parlementaire* admitted during an engagement may be detained pending the conclusion of the immediate fighting.[73] In addition, a *parlementaire* may be detained in case he or she has seen anything that may be detrimental to the enemy, or otherwise obtained such knowledge, or if the envoy's departure would reveal information on the movement of forces.[74]

A *parlementaire* should be detained only so long as circumstances imperatively require, and information regarding the *parlementaire*'s detention, as well as any other action against the *parlementaire* or against any member of the *parlementaire*'s party, should be sent to his or her commander.[75]

12.5.5 Neutral Zone and Other Appropriate Measures to Facilitate Negotiations. If it is anticipated that negotiations between belligerents may be prolonged, a neutralized area may by

---

[70] 1958 UK MANUAL ¶410 note 1 ("Examples of a *parlementaire* abusing his position are the making of sketch maps or taking photographs of defense positions and the secret gathering of information.").

[71] 1958 UK MANUAL ¶408 ("A *parlementaire* is not, however, forbidden to observe, and afterwards report, what his enemy does not hide."); SPAIGHT, WAR RIGHTS ON LAND 219 ("It is for the commander who receives the flag of truce to ensure that the bearer gains no information, whether by sight or speech, and if he fails to take the requisite precautions, it is palpably unjust to treat the envoy's offense, for which his (the commander's) contributory negligence is partly to blame, as the very grave offence of spying.").

[72] HAGUE IV REG. art. 33 ("The commander to whom a flag of truce is sent is not in all cases obliged to receive it. He may take all the necessary steps to prevent the envoy taking advantage of his mission to obtain information. In case of abuse, he has the right to detain the envoy temporarily.").

[73] LIEBER CODE art. 112 ("If the bearer of a flag of truce offer himself during an engagement, he can be admitted as a very rare exception only. It is no breach of good faith to retain such flag of truce, if admitted during the engagement.").

[74] 1956 FM 27-10 (Change No. 1 1976) ¶465 ("In addition to the right of detention for abuse of his position, a parlementaire may be detained in case he has seen anything or obtained knowledge which may be detrimental to the enemy, or if his departure would reveal information on the movement of troops."); 1958 UK MANUAL ¶412 ("According to the Hague Rules a commander has the right to detain a *parlementaire* temporarily if the latter abuses his position. In addition, a commander has, by a customary rule of international law, the right to retain a *parlementaire* so long as circumstances require, if the latter has seen anything, knowledge of which might have adverse consequences for the receiving forces, or if his departure would coincide with movements of forces whose destination or employment he might guess. See Hague Rules 33.").

[75] 1956 FM 27-10 (Change No. 1 1976) ¶465 ("He should be detained only so long as circumstances imperatively demand, and information should be sent at once to his commander as to such detention, as well as of any other action taken against him or against his party.").

agreement of the parties be set aside for the site of the negotiations.[76] The belligerents may agree that no combat activity will take place within or over the area, and that forces will be detailed to maintain the security of the area.[77] The area designated as neutral on maps interchanged by representatives of the belligerents may be marked with searchlights, balloons, and other devices to ensure that it will not be attacked.[78]

Other appropriate measures may also be agreed upon to facilitate negotiations. For example, special signals that the *parlementaire's* party should give or routes that the *parlementaire's* party must take may be agreed upon to help identify the *parlementaire's* party to the opposing forces.

12.6 Military Passports, Safe-Conducts, and Safeguards

Persons within an area occupied by a belligerent may be protected from molestation or interference through military passports, safe-conducts, and safeguards. These devices are a matter of international law only when granted or posted by arrangement with the enemy or with a neutral State.[79]

12.6.1 Military Passports, Safe-Conducts, and Safeguards – Notes on Terminology. The terms *pass* or *permit* may be used instead of *passport*. *Pass* has sometimes been used for a general permission to do certain things, while *permit* has sometimes been used like *safe-conduct*, to signify permission to do a particular thing.[80]

The terms *military passport* and *safe-conduct* have to some degree been used

---

[76] 1956 FM 27-10 (Change No. 1 1976) ¶468 ("If it is anticipated that negotiations between belligerents may be prolonged, a neutralized area may by agreement of the parties be set aside for the site of the negotiations."). *For example*, Howard S. Levie, *How it All Started – and How it Ended: A Legal Study of the Korean War*, 35 AKRON LAW REVIEW 205, 223 (2002) ("Negotiations for an armistice began at Kaesong on July 10, 1951. Shortly thereafter, the negotiations were moved to Panmunjom at the insistence of the UNC because Kaesong, which had been between the two lines at the time of the negotiations of the liaison officers, had been occupied by the Communists and they presumed to dictate who could enter the area, while Panmunjom was located in a zone between territories occupied by the two sides. It was declared a neutral zone as were Kaesong (the Communist Armistice Delegation headquarters), Munsan-ni (the UNC Armistice Delegation headquarters), and the roads leading from each Delegation headquarters to Panmunjom.").

[77] 1956 FM 27-10 (Change No. 1 1976) ¶468 ("The belligerents may agree that no combat activity will take place within or over the area and that forces will be detailed to maintain the security of the area.").

[78] 1956 FM 27-10 (Change No. 1 1976) ¶468 ("The area designated as neutral on maps interchanged by representatives of the belligerents may be marked with searchlights, balloons, and other devices to insure that it will not be attacked.").

[79] 1956 FM 27-10 (Change No. 1 1976) ¶454 ("Persons within an area occupied by a belligerent may be protected from molestation or interference through military passports, safe-conducts, and safeguards. These devices are a matter of international law only when granted or posted by arrangement with the enemy."); 1958 UK MANUAL ¶495 ("Safeguards, like passports and safe-conducts, fall within the scope of international law only when posted by arrangement with the enemy.").

[80] 1958 UK MANUAL ¶490 ("The expressions 'pass' and 'permit' have in recent years been employed in the place of the older terms 'passport' and 'safe-conduct,' with, as a rule, the same distinction, although 'pass' has sometimes meant a general permission to do certain things, while 'permit' has been confined to permission to do a particular act.").

interchangeably, but *military passport* generally has been used in a broader sense than *safe-conduct*.[81]

Ultimately, however, the purpose of the document will be more important than the nomenclature in deciding the nature of the document issued.[82]

12.6.2 Military Passport. A military passport is a document issued by order of a commander of belligerent forces, authorizing a person or persons named therein residing or sojourning within territory occupied by such forces to travel unmolested within such territory, with or without permission to pass, or to pass and return by designated routes through the lines, subject to such further conditions and limitations as the commander may prescribe.[83]

Unlike a passport for peacetime travel, such as a passport issued by the U.S. State Department, a military passport would be issued under a commander's authority to regulate commerce and travel within territory controlled by his or her forces.[84]

12.6.3 Safe Conduct. Documents like passports, issued by the same authority and for similar purposes to persons residing or traveling outside of the occupied areas who desire to enter and remain within or pass through such areas, are called safe-conducts.[85] Similar documents issued by the same authority to persons residing within or without the occupied areas to permit them to carry specified goods to or from designated places within those areas, and to engage in trade otherwise forbidden by the general rule of non-intercourse, are also called safe-conducts.[86] Safe-conducts for goods in which the grantee is given a continuing right for a

---

[81] SPAIGHT WAR RIGHTS ON LAND 230 ("A 'safe-conduct' or 'passport' is a written authority issued by a commander to one or more individuals, allowing him or them to pass through districts occupied by his forces. The terms appear to be convertible, though some would make the 'passport' confer a more extended liberty of movement than the 'safe-conduct,' which they would confine to an authority to come to a specified place for a specified object.").

[82] 2004 UK MANUAL ¶10.35.1 ("Arrangements are sometimes made between a military commander and an individual national or group of nationals belonging to the adverse party or to a neutral state. Such arrangements may be in the form of passports or safe conducts. Nomenclature is not significant in deciding the nature of the document issued. In fact, occasionally, the term 'pass' or 'permit' has been used. The decisive factor is the purpose for which the document has been issued, and not its terminology.").

[83] 1956 FM 27-10 (Change No. 1 1976) ¶455 ("A military passport is a document issued by order of a commander of belligerent forces, authorizing a person or persons named therein, residing or sojourning within territory occupied by such forces, to travel unmolested within such territory, with or without permission to pass, or to pass and return, by designated routes, through the lines, subject to such further conditions and limitations as the commander may prescribe.").

[84] *Refer to* § 5.19.1.1 (Belligerent Authority to Exercise Control in the Immediate Vicinity of Military Operations); § 11.4.1 (Right of the Occupying Power to Govern the Enemy Territory Temporarily).

[85] 1956 FM 27-10 (Change No. 1 1976) ¶456 ("Documents like passports, issued by the same authority and for similar purposes, to persons residing or sojourning outside of the occupied areas, who desire to enter and remain within or pass through such areas, are called safe-conducts.").

[86] 1956 FM 27-10 (Change No. 1 1976) ¶456 ("Similar documents, issued by the same authority, to persons residing within or without the occupied areas, to permit them to carry specified goods to or from designated places within those areas, and to engage in trade otherwise forbidden by the general rule of nonintercourse, are also called safe-conducts.").

prescribed period, or until further orders, to engage in the specified trade, are sometimes called licenses to trade.[87]

12.6.3.1 Safe-Conduct Pass for Ambassadors and Diplomatic Agents of Neutral Governments Accredited to the Enemy. Ambassadors and other diplomatic agents of neutral governments accredited to the opposing party to the conflict may receive a safe-conduct pass through territory under the opposing force's control, unless there are military or other security reasons to the contrary, including the safety of the personnel in question, and unless they may reach their destination conveniently by another route.[88] There is no international law requirement, however, for issuing such a safe-conduct pass; such passes usually would be granted by national-level authorities and not subordinate officers.[89]

12.6.3.2 Licenses to Trade. Licenses to trade must, as a general rule, emanate from the supreme authority of the State.[90] In an international armed conflict, a State controlling territory of the enemy may grant licenses to trade that relax its prohibitions on trading with the enemy.[91]

Licenses to trade issued by military authorities may be either general or special. A *general license* generally or partially relaxes the exercise of the rights of war in regard to trade in relation to any community or individuals liable to be affected by their operation.[92] A *special license* is one given to individuals for a particular voyage or journey for the importation or exportation of particular goods.[93]

12.6.3.3 Safe-Conducts Contemplated by the 1949 Geneva Conventions. Certain safe-conduct protection may be granted by special agreements contemplated in the 1949 Geneva

---

[87] 1956 FM 27-10 (Change No. 1 1976) ¶456 ("Safe-conducts for goods in which the grantee is given a continuing right for a prescribed period, or until further orders, to engage in the specified trade, are sometimes called licenses to trade."); 1958 UK MANUAL ¶489 ("A safe-conduct may, however, also be given for goods, and it then comprises permission for such good to be carried unmolested from or to a certain place, for instance from or into a besieged town.").

[88] 1956 FM 27-10 (Change No. 1 1976) ¶456 ("Ambassadors and other diplomatic agents of neutral powers, accredited to the enemy, may receive safe-conducts through the territories occupied by the belligerents, unless there are military reasons to the contrary and unless they may reach the place of their destination conveniently by another route."); LIEBER CODE art. 87 ("Ambassadors, and all other diplomatic agents of neutral powers, accredited to the enemy, may receive safe-conducts through the territories occupied by the belligerents, unless there are military reasons to the contrary, and unless they may reach the place of their destination conveniently by another route.").

[89] 1956 FM 27-10 (Change No. 1 1976) ¶456 ("There is, however, no legal requirement that such safe-conducts be issued. Safe-conducts of this nature are usually given by the supreme authority of the State and not by subordinate officers."); LIEBER CODE art. 87 ("It implies no international affront if the safe-conduct is declined. Such passes are usually given by the supreme authority of the State, and not by subordinate officers.").

[90] 1914 RULES OF LAND WARFARE ¶281 note 1 ("Licenses to trade must, as a general rule, emanate from the supreme authority of the State.").

[91] *Refer to* § 12.1.1 (Traditional Rule of Non-Intercourse During War).

[92] 1914 RULES OF LAND WARFARE ¶281 ("A general license relaxes the exercise of the rights of war, generally or partially, in relation to any community or individuals liable to be affected by their operation.").

[93] 1914 RULES OF LAND WARFARE ¶281 ("A special license is one given to individuals for a particular voyage or journey for the importation or exportation of particular goods.").

Conventions. Such agreements include:

- agreements for the removal and passage of certain personnel, such as vulnerable civilians, from besieged areas;[94]
- agreements for the passage of consignments;[95]
- agreements for the removal or transport of the wounded and sick;[96]
- agreements for the passage of medical aircraft for the transport of the military or civilian wounded and sick;[97]
- agreements for the safe passage of chartered medical transport ships;[98] and
- agreements for the special transport of relief shipments for POWs or civilian internees.[99]

12.6.4 Safeguard. A safeguard may refer to a detachment of forces posted for the protection of, or a written instrument affording protection by a belligerent to, enemy or neutral persons or property.

A safeguard falls within the law of war, however, only when granted and posted by arrangement with the enemy or a neutral. For example, guards or written orders posted by a belligerent for the protection of its own personnel or property would not be governed by the law of war.[100]

The effect of a safeguard is to pledge the honor of the nation that the person or property will be respected by its armed forces.[101] It does not commit the government to its protection or defense against attacks by enemy armed forces or other hostile elements.

Safeguards have been used to protect cultural property or other civilian property or

---

[94] *Refer to* § 5.19.2 (Removal and Passage of Certain Personnel – Vulnerable Civilians, Diplomatic and Consular Personnel, the Wounded and Sick, and Medical Personnel).

[95] *Refer to* § 5.19.3 (Passage of Relief Consignments).

[96] *Refer to* § 7.4.3.1 (Armistices and Local Arrangements to Permit the Removal, Exchange, or Transport of the Wounded).

[97] *Refer to* § 7.14 (Military Medical Aircraft); § 7.19 (Civilian Medical Aircraft).

[98] *Refer to* § 7.13 (Chartered Medical Transport Ships).

[99] *Refer to* § 9.20.5 (Special Means of Transport of Shipments to POWs); § 10.23.5 (Special Means of Transport of Shipments to Internees).

[100] MANUAL FOR COURTS-MARTIAL IV-39 (¶26.c.(1)) (2012) ("A safeguard is not a device adopted by a belligerent to protect its own property or nationals or to ensure order within its own forces, even if those forces are in a theater of combat operations, and the posting of guards or of off-limits signs does not establish a safeguard unless a commander takes those actions to protect enemy or neutral persons or property.").

[101] 1956 FM 27-10 (Change No. 1 1976) ¶457 ("The effect of a safeguard is to pledge the honor of the nation that the person or property shall be respected by the national armed forces.").

personnel meriting special protection.[102]

12.6.4.1 *Personnel Serving as a Safeguard*. A safeguard is a detachment, guard, or detail posted by a commander for the protection of persons, places, or property of the enemy or of a neutral.[103]

Combatants serving as safeguards occupy a protected status.[104] They may not be attacked, and it is customary to send them back, together with their equipment and arms, to their own armed forces when the locality is occupied by the enemy and as soon as military exigencies permit.[105]

12.6.4.2 *Written Safeguard*. The term safeguard also refers to a written order left by a commander with an enemy subject, or posted upon enemy property, for the protection of that person or property.[106] It is usually directed to the succeeding commander and requests a grant of protection.[107]

12.6.4.3 *Uniform Code of Military Justice Offense of Forcing a Safeguard*. The violation of a safeguard is a serious violation of the law of war.[108] The Uniform Code of Military Justice makes forcing a safeguard punishable.[109] "Forcing a safeguard" means to perform an act or acts in violation of the protection of the safeguard.[110]

12.6.5 Revocation of Passports, Safe-Conducts, and Similar Documents. In general, passports, as well as safe-conducts, may be revoked for good reasons of military expediency by

---

[102] *For example*, SPAIGHT, WAR RIGHTS ON LAND 231 ("The object of a safeguard is generally to protect museums, historic monuments or the like; occasionally to show respect for a distinguished enemy, as in the case of the safeguard which McClellan placed over Mrs. R. E. Lee's residence, White House, Virginia, in 1862. When allies invaded France in 1814, the Emperor Alexander of Russia honoured himself and Poland by his graceful act in assigning a guard of honour of Polish soldiers to protect the house of Kosciusko -- then living, almost as a peasant, near Troyes -- from pillage and contribution.").

[103] 1956 FM 27-10 (Change No. 1 1976) ¶457 ("A safeguard is a detachment, guard, or detail posted by a commander for the protection of persons, places, or property of the enemy, or of a neutral.").

[104] 1956 FM 27-10 (Change No. 1 1976) ¶457 ("Soldiers on duty as safeguards occupy a protected status.").

[105] 1956 FM 27-10 (Change No. 1 1976) ¶457 ("They may not be attacked, and it is customary to send them back, together with their equipment and arms, to their own army when the locality is occupied by the enemy and as soon as military exigencies permit.").

[106] 1956 FM 27-10 (Change No. 1 1976) ¶457 ("The term also includes a written order left by a commander with an enemy subject or posted upon enemy property for the protection of the individual or property concerned.").

[107] 1956 FM 27-10 (Change No. 1 1976) ¶457 ("It is usually directed to the succeeding commander and requests the grant of protection.").

[108] 1956 FM 27-10 (Change No. 1 1976) ¶457 ("The violation of a safeguard is a grave violation of the law of war and, if committed by a person subject to the Uniform Code of Military Justice, is punishable under Article 102 thereof with death or such other punishment as a court-martial may direct.").

[109] *See* 10 U.S.C. § 902 ("Any person subject to this chapter who forces a safeguard shall suffer death or such other punishment as a court-martial may direct.").

[110] MANUAL FOR COURTS-MARTIAL IV-39 (¶26.c.(2)) (2012) ("'Forcing a safeguard' means to perform an act or acts in violation of the protection of the safeguard.").

the person who issued them or that person's superior officer. Revocation must never be used as a means of detaining the holder, who is always allowed to withdraw in safety.[111]

In addition, if the holder commits any wrongful act, such as using the opportunity given by a passport or safe-conduct to obtain military information or if the holder exceeds its terms, the privilege may be withdrawn.[112]

12.7 Cartels

In its narrower sense, a cartel is an agreement entered into by opposing belligerents for the exchange of POWs.[113] In its broader sense, it is any convention concluded between belligerents for the purpose of arranging or regulating certain kinds of non-hostile intercourse that would otherwise be prohibited by reason of the existence of the armed conflict (*e.g.*, postal communication or trade in certain goods or commodities).[114]

Both parties to a cartel are honor bound to observe its provisions scrupulously. A cartel is voidable by a party upon definite proof that it has been intentionally violated in an important particular by the other party.[115]

12.8 Capitulations – Negotiated Instruments of Surrender

12.8.1 Definition of Capitulation. A capitulation is an agreement (sometimes with certain conditions) entered into between commanders of belligerent forces for the surrender of a body of forces, a fortress, or other defended locality, or of a district of the theater of operations.[116] For

---

[111] 1958 UK MANUAL ¶493 ("Passports, as well as safe-conducts, may be revoked for good reasons of military expediency by the person who issued them or his superior officer. Until revoked, however, they are binding not only upon the person who granted them, but also upon his successors. The reasons for revocation need not be given, but revocation must never be used as a means of detaining the holder, who is always allowed to withdraw in safety. Such passports and safe-conducts as have been granted only for a limited time cease to be valid with the expiration of the period designated.").

[112] 1958 UK MANUAL ¶494 ("If the holder commits any wrongful act, such as using the opportunity given by a passport or safe-conduct to obtain military information or if he exceeds its terms, the privilege may be withdrawn.").

[113] *Refer to* § 9.35.1 (Exchange of POWs During Hostilities Through Cartel Agreements).

[114] 1956 FM 27-10 (Change No. 1 1976) ¶469 ("In its narrower sense, a cartel is an agreement entered into by belligerents for the exchange of prisoners of war. In its broader sense, it is any convention concluded between belligerents for the purpose of arranging or regulating certain kinds of nonhostile intercourse otherwise prohibited by reason of the existence of the war.").

[115] 1956 FM 27-10 (Change No. 1 1976) ¶469 ("Both parties to a cartel are in honor bound to observe its provisions with the most scrupulous care, but it is voidable by either party upon definite proof that it has been intentionally violated in an important particular by the other party.").

[116] 1956 FM 27-10 (Change No. 1 1976) ¶470 ("A capitulation is an agreement entered into between commanders of belligerent forces for the surrender of a body of troops, a fortress, or other defended locality, or of a district of the theater of operations."); 1958 UK MANUAL ¶462 ("Capitulations are agreements entered into between the commanders of armed forces or belligerents concerning the terms of surrender of a body of troops, of a defended town or place, or of a particular district of the theatre of war. Surrenders of territory are sometimes designated as evacuations."); SPAIGHT, WAR RIGHTS ON LAND 249 ("A capitulation is a military convention which puts an end, with or without conditions, to the resistance of a body of troops shut up in a fortress or surrounded in the field.").

example, a capitulation agreement could involve the surrender of a small unit, such as a squad, platoon, company, or battalion, or the surrender of larger forces, such as a division or corps.[117]

The surrender of military forces also may be arranged between belligerents at national levels without the involvement of military commanders, and possibly through third parties. A capitulation agreement may be negotiated between opposing military forces in local implementation of a surrender negotiated at national levels.

12.8.1.1 *Capitulation Compared to Armistice*. A *capitulation* surrenders the capitulating unit, while an *armistice* suspends fighting between opposing forces.

12.8.1.2 *Capitulation Compared to Unconditional Surrender*. A *capitulation* is a surrender pursuant to an agreement. A surrender may be effected without resort to a capitulation agreement.[118] For example, individuals or units may surrender themselves unconditionally to the opposite side without a specific capitulation agreement.[119]

On the other hand, an unconditional surrender may be effected through a capitulation instrument.[120] Such an instrument would lack any conditions on the surrender, but may specify the way in which the surrender is to be implemented or may clarify for all concerned that the surrender is to be conducted on an unconditional basis.

12.8.2 Authority of Commanders to Conclude Capitulation Agreements. Commanders are generally presumed to have the authority to conclude capitulation agreements with respect to forces under their command and areas under their control.[121] For example, if a commander of military forces concludes that continued fighting has become impossible and is unable to communicate with his or her superiors, under the law of war he or she may assume that he or she

---

[117] *For example*, Captain M. Scott Holcomb, *View from the Legal Frontlines*, 4 CHICAGO JOURNAL OF INTERNATIONAL LAW 561, 568 (2003) ("As of this writing, at the end of April 2003, only a few capitulation agreements have been signed. All of them were entered into after combat began, instead of before. Most noteworthy, Colonel Curtis Potts, Commander of the Fourth Brigade of the Third Infantry Division, entered into a capitulation agreement with Iraqi General Mohamad Jarawi for the surrender of the Iraqi Army's Anbar sector command, which encompassed sixteen thousand soldiers.").

[118] 1956 FM 27-10 (Change No. 1 1976) ¶470 ("A surrender may be effected without resort to a capitulation.").

[119] 1956 FM 27-10 (Change No. 1 1976) ¶478 ("An unconditional surrender is one in which a body of troops gives itself up to its enemy without condition. It need not be effected on the basis of an instrument signed by both parties. Subject to the restrictions of the law of war, the surrendered troops are governed by the directions of the State to which they surrender.").

[120] *For example*, Japan, Instrument of Surrender, Sept. 2, 1945, 59 STAT. 1733, 1734 ("We hereby proclaim the unconditional surrender to the Allied Powers of the Japanese Imperial General Headquarters and of all Japanese armed forces and all armed forces under Japanese control wherever situated."); German High Command, Act of Military Surrender, May 7, 1945, 59 STAT. 1857, 1858 ("1. We the undersigned, acting by authority of the German High Command, hereby surrender unconditionally to the Supreme Commander, Allied Expeditionary Force and simultaneously to the Soviet High Command all forces on land, sea, and in the air who are at this date under German control.").

[121] 1956 FM 27-10 (Change No. 1 1976) ¶472 ("Subject to the limitations hereinafter indicated, the commander of troops is presumed to be duly authorized to enter into capitulations.").

has authority to surrender his or her forces or position.[122]

However, a commanding officer's powers generally do not extend beyond the forces and territory under his or her command.[123] Thus, a commander may not surrender forces that are not under his or her command. Similarly, unless so authorized by his or her government, a commander lacks the authority to bind his or her government to a permanent cession of the place or places under his or her command, to surrender sovereignty over territory, or to agree to other terms of a political nature or such as will take effect after the termination of hostilities.[124] However, capitulation agreements that have been concluded by political authorities may include such terms.[125]

A State is not bound by the terms of a capitulation agreement that it has not authorized its commanders to conclude and may repudiate such terms.[126] For example, a State would not be bound to honor political conditions accepted by a capitulating commander or by a commander accepting capitulation, if those commanders lack such authority.[127]

12.8.2.1 *Surrenders Contrary to Domestic Law or Superior Orders*. The fact that a commander surrenders in violation of orders or the law of his or her own State does not impair

---

[122] 1956 FM 27-10 (Change No. 1 1976) ¶472 ("In the case of a commander of a military force of the United States, if continued battle has become impossible and he cannot communicate with his superiors, these facts will constitute proper authority to surrender.").

[123] 1956 FM 27-10 (Change No. 1 1976) ¶472 ("A commanding officer's powers do not extend beyond the forces and territory under his command."); 1958 UK MANUAL ¶466 ("The competence of a commander to accept conditions of capitulation is limited to the troops immediately under his command and does not necessarily extend to detached forces.").

[124] 1956 FM 27-10 (Change No. 1 1976) ¶472 ("Unless so authorized by his government, he does not possess power to bind his government to a permanent cession of the place or places under his command, or to any surrender of sovereignty over territory, or to any cessation of hostilities in a district beyond his command, or to agree to terms of a political nature or such as will take effect after the termination of hostilities."); Trial of Hans Albin Rauter, *Judgment*, XIV U.N. LAW REPORTS 89, 125 (Netherlands Special Court in 'S-Gravenhage (The Hague), May 4, 1948) ("According to international law a capitulation treaty is a pact between commanders of belligerent forces for the surrender of certain troops or certain parts of the country, towns or fortresses, and as such must be scrupulously fulfilled; the commander who concludes such a pact cannot, however, be considered empowered to bind his government to a permanent cession of territory, to a cessation of hostilities in territories which do not come under his command or, in general, to provisions of a political nature; such provisions are binding in a capitulation treaty *only if they are ratified by the governments of both belligerents*.").

[125] 1956 FM 27-10 (Change No. 1 1976) ¶473 ("The surrender of a place or force may also be arranged by the political authorities of the belligerents without the intervention of the military authorities. In this case the capitulation may contain other than military stipulations.").

[126] 1958 UK MANUAL ¶467 ("Similarly, the competence of a commander to grant conditions of capitulation is limited to those the fulfilment of which depends entirely upon the forces under his command. If he agrees, without the instruction of his government, to conditions the granting of which is not implied in his powers, or the fulfilment of which depends upon forces other than his own, and upon superior officers, the conditions may be repudiated.").

[127] WINTHROP, MILITARY LAW & PRECEDENTS 787 ("A capitulation is of course subject to be disapproved and annulled by the Government of either commander. Thus the Sherman-Johnston capitulation of April, 1865, was repudiated by the Government at Washington because of its assuming to deal with *political* issues.").

the validity of the surrender.[128] Commanders who surrender in violation of orders or the law of their own State may be punished by their State.

Under the Code of Conduct for U.S. armed forces, a commander must never surrender the members of his or her command while they still have the means to resist.[129] Under the Uniform Code of Military Justice, shameful surrenders are punishable. In addition, compelling or attempting to compel a commander to surrender or striking colors or flag to an enemy without proper authority is punishable.[130]

12.8.3 Rules of Military Honor. Capitulations agreed upon between belligerents must take into account the rules of military honor.[131]

Conditions involving unnecessary disgrace or ignominy should not be insisted upon.[132] Capitulations may include the right of the capitulating forces to surrender with colors displayed or other indications of professional respect for the capitulating forces.[133] For example, it may be appropriate to allow surrendering officers to keep their side arms.[134]

Even if the capitulation does not explicitly have such provisions, the capitulation agreement should be executed with honor and respect for the adversary. Treating the adversary honorably diminishes psychological stigma from capitulation and thereby provides an incentive for the adversary to capitulate rather than fight on without any chance of success.

12.8.4 Form of Capitulation Agreement or Instrument. There is no specified form for capitulation instruments. They may be concluded either orally or in writing, but in order to avoid disputes, they should be reduced to writing. The agreement should contain in precise terms every condition to be observed on either side, excepting such conditions as are clearly imposed by the law of war. Details of time and procedure should be prescribed in exact and unequivocal language. Even in case of an unconditional surrender, when the terms are dictated by the victor, they should nevertheless be embodied in a written capitulation as soon as practicable.[135]

---

[128] 1956 FM 27-10 (Change No. 1 1976) ¶472 ("The fact that any commander surrenders in violation of orders or the law of his own State does not impair the validity of the surrender.").

[129] *Refer to* § 9.39.1.2 (Code of Conduct – Article II).

[130] *Refer to* § 9.39.1.2 (Code of Conduct – Article II).

[131] HAGUE IV REG. art. 35 ("Capitulations agreed upon between the contracting parties must take into account the rules of military honour.").

[132] WINTHROP, MILITARY LAW & PRECEDENTS 786 ("Capitulation. This is an agreement for the surrender of an army, or of a fortified place, of which the terms are settled by the belligerent commanders. In the Project of the Brussels Conference it is prescribed that 'these conditions should not be contrary to military honor.' That is to say, conditions involving unnecessary disgrace or ignominy should not be insisted upon.").

[133] 1958 UK MANUAL ¶475 ("The expression 'with the honors of war,' which is sometimes used in capitulations, is usually construed to include the right to march out with colors displayed, bayonets fixed, etc., but the details of such arrangements should be precisely stated in the articles [of capitulation].").

[134] *Refer to* § 12.9.2.2 (Disarmament of Surrendered Forces).

[135] 1956 FM 27-10 (Change No. 1 1976) ¶474 ("There is no specified form for capitulations. They may be concluded either orally or in writing, but in order to avoid disputes, they should be reduced to writing. The

12.8.5 General Effect of Capitulation. The general effect of concluding a capitulation agreement is that of an unconditional surrender. In other words, absent specific terms in the capitulation agreement to the contrary, the capitulation agreement should be understood to create the effect of an unconditional surrender by the capitulating party.[136]

The capitulating party must generally cease operations and maintain the military status quo at the time in which the capitulation becomes effective.[137] For example, the capitulating forces must not engage in offensive operations against opposing forces.[138] Similarly, although forces may destroy their own weapons and intelligence information to prevent them from falling into the hands of the enemy before they capitulate, after the capitulation is effective, the capitulating forces must abstain from all destruction and damage to their own facilities and equipment, unless expressly permitted by the capitulation agreement.[139] The capturing side is free to confiscate as war booty or, at its discretion, destroy the weapons, ammunition, and military equipment of the capitulating side.[140]

12.9 CAPITULATIONS – SUBJECTS USUALLY ADDRESSED

In general, a capitulation agreement is understood to have the effect of an unconditional surrender under the law of war. However, specific topics may be addressed in the capitulation agreement that attach conditions to the surrender or specify the way in which the surrender is to be effected.

12.9.1 Scope of Surrendered Forces and Territory and Time of Surrender. The capitulation agreement may specify the force or territory that is surrendered and the exact time when the surrender is to take effect. If a place or area is surrendered, provisions relative to the withdrawal of the defenders from it and the entering into possession of it by the victorious forces may also be specified in the agreement.

A commander's competence to capitulate is limited to forces under his or her

---

agreement should contain in precise terms every condition to be observed on either side, excepting such conditions as are clearly imposed by the laws of war. Details of time and procedure should be prescribed in the most exact and unequivocal language. Even in case of an unconditional surrender, when the terms are dictated by the victor, they should nevertheless be embodied in a written capitulation as soon as practicable.").

[136] *Refer to* § 5.9.3 (Persons Who Have Surrendered).

[137] SPAIGHT, WAR RIGHTS ON LAND 253-54 ("The same principles which apply to the *matériel* of a fortress which has capitulated are applicable also in the case of the *personnel*. Once the capitulation is signed, the position is stereotyped and fixed; the *status quo* of the moment of signature must be honourably maintained. The victorious belligerent is justified in expecting that not only the *matériel* but the *personnel* of the capitulating force shall be handed over to him in accordance with the terms of the convention.").

[138] *Refer to* § 5.9.3.2 (Clear and Unconditional).

[139] SPAIGHT, WAR RIGHTS ON LAND 251-52 ("A commander who has brought a fortress to the point of capitulating, may make the non-destruction of property during the negotiations a condition for granting better terms, and it may suit the besieged's interests to meet him in the matter. In the absence of such a special arrangement, the commandant has a perfect right to dispose as he chooses of his *matériel* up to the moment of the signing of the act of capitulation.").

[140] *Refer to* § 5.17.3 (Enemy Movable Property on the Battlefield (War Booty)).

command.[141] To avoid misunderstandings, capitulation should state the forces to be surrendered and to what extent detached forces and personnel are included in the surrender of the main body.[142]

12.9.2 Disposition of Surrendered Forces. The capitulation instrument may specify the movements and administration of the surrendered forces after the surrender.

In general, surrendering military forces and others entitled to POW status who fall into the power of the enemy during international armed conflict become POWs under the GPW. Similarly, the disposition of surrendered medical personnel and the wounded and sick belonging to the surrendered party would be addressed by the GWS and GWS-Sea. Insofar as matters are addressed by those treaties, there is little need for similar provisions in a capitulation instrument.

However, special circumstances, such as inability of the victor to guard, evacuate, and maintain large numbers of POWs or to occupy the area in which enemy military forces are present, may justify the victorious commander in allowing the defeated force to remain in its present positions, to withdraw, or to disperse after having been disarmed and having given their paroles, provided that the giving of paroles is not forbidden by the laws of their own country and that they are willing to give their paroles.[143]

12.9.2.1 *Orders Given by the Victor*. It is normally stipulated that the orders of the victorious commander will be scrupulously carried out by the surrendered forces and that those who fail to comply with such orders or with the terms of the surrender itself may be punished.[144]

12.9.2.2 *Disarmament of Surrendered Forces*. Normally provisions are included to govern the disposition of enemy arms, equipment, and other property in the hands of the force

---

[141] *Refer to* § 12.8.2 (Authority of Commanders to Conclude Capitulation Agreements).

[142] 1958 UK MANUAL ¶466 ("To avoid misunderstandings, capitulations should invariably state to what extent detached forces and outlying defences are included in the surrender of the main body.").

[143] 1956 FM 27-10 (Change No. 1 1976) ¶475b ("However, special circumstances, such as inability of the victor to guard, evacuate, and maintain large numbers of prisoners of war or to occupy the area in which enemy military forces are present, may justify the victorious commander in allowing the defeated force to remain in its present positions, to withdraw, or to disperse after having been disarmed and having given their paroles, provided that the giving of paroles is not forbidden by the laws of their own country and that they are willing to give their paroles (see par. 185).").

[144] 1956 FM 27-10 (Change No. 1 1976) ¶475j ("Orders given by the victor. It is normally stipulated that the orders of the victorious commander will be scrupulously carried out by the surrendered forces and that those who fail to comply with such orders or with the terms of the surrender itself will be severely punished."). *For example, Instrument of Surrender of all German armed forces in Holland, in North West Germany, including all islands, and in Denmark*, May 4, 1945, ¶¶3-4, *reprinted in* The Scuttled U-Boats Case, Trial of Oberleutnant Gerhard Grumpelt, I U.N. LAW REPORTS 55, 57 (British Military Court Held at Hamburg, Germany, Feb. 12-13, 1946) ("3. The German Command to carry out at once, and without argument or comment, all further orders that will be issued by the Allied Powers on any subject. 4. Disobedience of orders, or failure to comply with them, will be regarded as a breach of these surrender terms and will be dealt with by the Allied Powers in accordance with the accepted laws and usages of war.").

that has surrendered. Officers have sometimes been allowed to retain their side arms.[145] In addition, POWs are allowed to keep certain articles under the GPW.[146]

12.9.2.3 *Prohibitions on Acts of Destruction by the Surrendered Forces*. Although a capitulation, like an unconditional surrender, generally has the effect of prohibiting acts of destruction by surrendered forces, the capitulation may also specifically prohibit destruction by the surrendered forces of their materiel or installations, or communications, transportation facilities, and other public utilities in the area concerned.

12.9.3 Disposition of Detainees Held by the Surrendered Forces. The disposition of POWs, civilian internees, and other persons held in the custody of the surrendered forces may be addressed in a capitulation.[147]

12.9.4 Minefields and Other Defensive Measures. The provision of facilities and of information on such matters as minefields and other defensive measures may be addressed in a capitulation.[148]

12.9.5 Civil Administration of the Area Concerned. The civil administration of the area concerned, if a place or area is surrendered, may also be addressed in a capitulation.

12.10 CAPITULATIONS – VIOLATIONS AND DENUNCIATION

Once capitulation agreements have been made, they must be scrupulously observed by all parties.[149]

12.10.1 Denunciation of Capitulation Agreements Based on Directed Violations. If violations of a capitulation agreement have been directed by the commander who capitulated or by higher authority, the other belligerent may denounce the capitulation and resume hostilities.[150]

---

[145] *For example*, WINTHROP, MILITARY LAW & PRECEDENTS 787 ("In the capitulation between Gens. Grant and Lee, of April, 1865, in providing for the surrender of military property, it is added—'This will not embrace the side arms of the officers, nor their private horses nor baggage.'").

[146] *Refer to* § 9.7 (POW Effects and Articles of Personal Use).

[147] *For example*, Japan, Instrument of Surrender, Sept. 2, 1945, 59 STAT. 1733, 1734 ("We hereby command the Japanese Imperial Government and the Japanese Imperial General Headquarters at once to liberate all allied prisoners of war and civilian internees now under Japanese control and to provide for their protection, care, maintenance and immediate transportation to places as directed.").

[148] *For example*, Instrument of Surrender of Italy, Sept. 29, 1943, 61 STAT. 2742, 2743-44 ("10. The Italian Supreme Command will make available all information about naval, military and air devices, installations, and defences, about all transport and inter-communication systems established by Italy or her allies on Italian territory or in the approaches thereto, about minefields or other obstacles to movement by land, sea or air and such other particulars as the United Nations may require in connection with the use of Italian bases, or with the operations, security, or welfare of the United Nations Land, Sea or Air Forces. Italian forces and equipment will be made available as required by the United Nations for the removal of the above mentioned obstacles.").

[149] HAGUE IV REG. art. 35 ("Capitulations agreed upon between the contracting parties must take into account the rules of military honour. Once settled, they must be scrupulously observed by both parties.").

[150] 1956 FM 27-10 (Change No. 1 1976) ¶477 ("If the violation is directed by the commander who capitulated or by higher authority, the other belligerent may denounce the capitulation and resume hostilities.").

Like action may also be taken if the capitulation was obtained through a breach of faith.[151]

A capitulation may not, however, be denounced because one of the parties has been induced to agree to it by a means consistent with the law of war, such as a ruse, or by that party's own incapacity, such as through mistake of fact.[152]

12.10.2 Violation of Capitulation Agreements by Individuals. Deliberate violations of the terms of a capitulation by individuals are punishable as a war crime.[153] For example, a member of the capitulated force may be punished by his or her State or the enemy State for carrying out attacks on enemy military equipment or personnel in violation of the terms of the capitulation agreement. Similarly, destroying one's own military equipment in violation of the terms of the capitulation agreement would also be punishable.[154]

Unwitting violations of a capitulation agreement, however, are not punishable. For example, individuals who return from a patrol and find their unit to have surrendered and, lacking knowledge of capitulation, continue to fight, would not be committing a war crime.

12.10.2.1 *Violation of Capitulation Agreements and POW Status*. Violation of a capitulation agreement, like other pre-capture law of war violations, is not a basis for denying a person POW status, if that person otherwise qualifies for POW status under the GPW.[155]

12.10.2.2 *Violation of Capitulation Agreements by POWs*. Members of the armed forces who have capitulated may become POWs. Violations of the terms of a capitulation agreement by a POW may also be punishable as misconduct as a POW, either by the Detaining Power or the State to which the POW belongs when that POW has been repatriated.[156]

12.11 ARMISTICES AND OTHER CEASE-FIRE AGREEMENTS

12.11.1 Definition of Armistice. An armistice may also be described as the cessation of

---

[151] 1956 FM 27-10 (Change No. 1 1976) ¶477 ("Like action may also be taken if the capitulation was obtained through a breach of faith.").

[152] 1958 UK MANUAL ¶484 ("A capitulation may be denounced if a party to it formally refuses to execute a clause which has been agreed upon, and it may be cancelled if it was obtained by a breach of faith. It may not, however, be annulled because one of the parties has been induced to agree to it by ruse, or from motives for which there is no justification, or by his own incapacity or feebleness.").

[153] 1956 FM 27-10 (Change No. 1 1976) ¶477 ("Violation of the terms of a capitulation by individuals is punishable as a war crime."); Johnson v. Eisentrager, 339 U.S. 763, 787 (1950) ("Breach of the terms of an act of surrender is no novelty among war crimes.").

[154] *For example*, The Scuttled U-Boats Case, Trial of Oberleutnant Gerhard Grumpelt, I U.N. LAW REPORTS 55-70 (British Military Court, Hamburg, Germany, Feb. 12-13, 1946) (First Lieutenant Grumpelt was convicted "of having scuttled two U-boats which had been surrendered by the German Command to the Allies" in violation of the Instrument of Surrender of 4th May, 1945.).

[155] *Refer to* § 9.26.4 (Retention of Benefits of the GPW Even if Prosecuted for Pre-Capture Acts).

[156] *Refer to* § 9.26.1 (POWs Subject to the Laws, Regulations, and Orders in Force in the Armed Forces of the Detaining Power); § 9.22.2 (POWs' Status With Respect to Their Armed Forces).

active hostilities for a period agreed upon by the belligerents.[157] An armistice suspends military operations by mutual agreement between the belligerent parties.[158]

12.11.1.1 Armistice as an Agreement. An armistice is an agreed suspension of hostilities. For example, a unilateral suspension of operations by one party would not be an armistice.

12.11.1.2 Armistice as a Suspension of Hostilities and Not a Peace Treaty. An armistice is not a partial or a temporary peace; it is only the suspension of military operations to the extent agreed upon by the parties to the conflict.[159] War as a legal state of hostilities between parties may continue, despite the conclusion of an armistice agreement.[160]

In some cases, however, armistice agreements may be intended to be a prelude to peace treaties.[161] In some cases, armistice agreements may persist for a long time.[162]

12.11.1.3 Armistice – Notes on Terminology. An armistice also has been referred to as a *truce, local truce*, *ceasefire*, *cessation of hostilities*, and *suspension of arms*.[163]

---

[157] 1956 FM 27-10 (Change No. 1 1976) ¶479 ("An armistice (or truce, as it is sometimes called) is the cessation of active hostilities for a period agreed upon by the belligerents."); LIEBER CODE art. 135 ("An armistice is the cessation of active hostilities for a period agreed between belligerents.").

[158] HAGUE IV REG. art. 36 ("An armistice suspends military operations by mutual agreement between the belligerent parties.").

[159] 1956 FM 27-10 (Change No. 1 1976) ¶479 ("It is not a partial or temporary peace; it is only the suspension of military operations to the extent agreed upon by the parties."); LIEBER CODE art. 142 ("An armistice is not a partial or a temporary peace; it is only the suspension of military operations to the extent agreed upon by the parties.").

[160] *See, e.g.*, Kahn v. Anderson, 255 U.S. 1, 9 (1921) ("That complete peace, in the legal sense, had not come to pass by the effect of the Armistice and the cessation of hostilities, is not disputable."); Commercial Cable Co. v. Burleson, 255 F. 99, 104-05 (S.D.N.Y. 1919) (Hand, J.) ("It is the treaty which terminates the war. An armistice effects nothing but a suspension of hostilities; the war still continues. It is true that a war may end by the cessation of hostilities, or by subjugation; but that is not the normal course, and neither had hostilities ceased, nor had the enemy been subjugated in the sense in which that term is used.") (citations omitted) *reversed on other grounds and vacated as moot*, Commercial Cable Co. v. Burleson, 250 U.S. 360 (1919).

[161] *For example*, Protocol of Agreement Between the United States and Spain, art. V, Aug. 12, 1898, 30 STAT. 1742, 1743 ("The United States and Spain will each appoint not more than five commissioners to treat of peace, and the commissioners so appointed shall meet at Paris not later than October 1, 1898, and proceed to the negotiation and conclusion of a treaty of peace, which treaty shall be subject to ratification according to the respective constitutional forms of the two countries.").

[162] *For example*, DEPARTMENT OF STATE, *Treaties in Force: A List of Treaties and Other International Agreements of the United States in Force on January 1, 2013*, 411 (2013) ("Agreement concerning a military armistice in Korea, with annex. *Signed at Panmunjon July 27, 1953, by the Commander-in-Chief, United Nations Command; the Supreme Commander of the Korean People's Army; and the Commander of the Chinese People's Volunteers. Entered into force July 27, 1953.* 4 UST 346; TIAS 2782.").

[163] *See, e.g.*, Richard Baxter, *Armistices and Other Forms of Suspension of Hostilities, in* HUMANIZING THE LAWS OF WAR: SELECTED WRITINGS OF RICHARD BAXTER 310 (2013) ("In military usage, as reflected in particular in manuals on the law of war, the older expression 'armistice' seems to be used quite generally to describe agreements which in these days go under the name of 'cease-fires' or 'truces' or 'suspensions of arms'. Very often when we speak today of 'cease-fire', our predecessors, at least up to the Second World War, would have been inclined to use the term 'general armistice' or 'local armistice'. These are largely terminological differences and the employment

Although in some cases distinctions may be drawn between these different terms, *armistice* may also be used in a general sense to encompass these terms.[164]

12.11.2 Types of Armistice and the Authority to Conclude Armistice Agreements. Armistice agreements have been categorized based on the degree to which they suspend hostilities.

An armistice may be general or local. The first suspends the military operations of the belligerent States everywhere; the second only between certain fractions of the belligerent armies and within a fixed radius.[165]

The degree to which the parties wish to suspend hostilities affects what authorities are needed to conclude the armistice agreement. An armistice agreement must be concluded by authorities who are competent to agree to and to enforce its terms. Thus, armistices that include more substantive and expansive terms must be approved by more senior authorities. For example, a commander would not have the authority to conclude an armistice agreement that binds units or areas that are not under his or her command. Similarly, if an armistice contains political terms, it must be made under authorization from the governments concerned or subject to approval by them.[166]

12.11.2.1 *General Armistice*. A *general armistice* suspends all military operations between opposing forces.

General armistices are usually of a combined political and military character. They usually precede the negotiations for peace, but may be concluded for other purposes. Due to its

---

of one expression or another does not normally of itself have operative legal consequences."); 1958 UK MANUAL ¶418 note 1 ("Six expressions have in the past been used in the British army to signify a cessation of hostilities falling short of peace: truce, local truce, armistice, cessation of hostilities (as in the Convention made after Majuba in 1881), cessation of arms (as in the negotiations preceding the surrender at Saratoga in 1777), and suspension of arms. Yet they do not appear to have been employed with any exactitude. Moreover, other expressions, such as 'a cease fire for three hours,' have not been unknown. Neither do other languages follow an exact terminology in the matter; the Germans speak of *Waffenruhe* and *Waffenstillstand*, without distinguishing precisely between them. The French instructions distinguish between amistices and suspensions d'armes. It has been found advisable to follow the practice of the more authoritative writers in distinguishing three different kinds of armistice as in the text above.").

[164] *See, e.g.*, WALTER G. HERMES, UNITED STATES ARMY IN THE KOREAN WAR: TRUCE TENT AND FIGHTING FRONT 15 footnote 1 (1992) ("For literary reasons, the terms 'armistice,' 'truce,' and 'cease-fire' have been used interchangeably throughout this volume. According to the Office of the Judge Advocate General, 'truce' signifies a temporary interruption of fighting between local forces for some reason such as the collection of the dead and wounded. The word 'armistice' has a similar connotation, but is utilized to cover a temporary cessation of hostilities on a broader scale. 'Cease-fire' applies when all acts of war are halted, bringing about an informal end to the war and stabilizing the situation until formal negotiations can be completed.").

[165] HAGUE IV REG. art. 37 ("An armistice may be general or local. The first suspends the military operations of the belligerent States everywhere; the second only between certain fractions of the belligerent armies and within a fixed radius."); LIEBER CODE art. 137 ("An armistice may be general, and valid for all points and lines of the belligerents, or special, that is, referring to certain troops or certain localities only.").

[166] 1956 FM 27-10 (Change No. 1 1976) ¶483 ("If an armistice contains political terms, it must be made under authorization from the governments concerned or subject to approval by them.").

political importance and the fact that it would be binding on all of a belligerent's forces, a general armistice is normally negotiated by senior officials and is subject to approval by each State.[167] For example, an armistice agreement may be negotiated by senior military commanders and be subject to approval of each State.[168]

12.11.2.2 *Local or Partial Armistice*. A local armistice (also called a partial armistice) suspends operations between certain portions of the belligerent forces or within a specified area.[169] In some cases, a local armistice has been distinguished from a suspension of arms as implicating a large number of forces, a greater geographic area, and broader interests than the local military requirements that are addressed in a suspension of arms.[170]

12.11.2.3 *Suspension of Arms*. A suspension of arms is a form of local armistice concluded between commanders of military forces for some local military purpose, such as to bury the dead, to collect the wounded, to arrange for exchange of detainees, or to enable a commander to communicate with his or her government or superior officer.[171]

Commanders are presumed to have the authority to conclude suspensions of arms for forces and areas within their control.

12.11.3 Form of Armistice Agreements. No special form for an armistice is prescribed. If possible, armistice agreements should be reduced to writing to avoid misunderstandings and for the purpose of reference should differences of opinion arise. Armistice agreements should be

---

[167] 1956 FM 27-10 (Change No. 1 1976) ¶483 ("General armistices are usually of a combined political and military character. They usually precede the negotiations for peace, but may be concluded for other purposes. Due to its political importance, a general armistice is normally concluded by senior military officers or by diplomatic representatives or other high civilian officials.").

[168] *For example*, Barbara Salazar Torreon, *U.S. Periods of War and Dates of Current Conflicts*, 5-6 (Congressional Research Service, Dec. 28, 2012) ("Cease-fire terms [of the 1991 Persian Gulf War] negotiated at Safwan, Iraq, March 1, 1991. Iraq officially accepted cease-fire terms, April 6, 1991. Cease-fire took effect April 11, 1991."); *id.* at footnote 8 ("This agreement is actually a transcript of the discussion held at Safwan Airfield, Iraq, between Coalition participants, U.S. Gen. M. Norman Schwarzkopf and Lt. Gen. Khalid of the Joint Arab Forces, and Iraqi participants, Lt. Gen. Sultan Kasim Ahmad, Chief of Staff of the Ministry of Defense, and Lt. Gen. Sala Abud Mahmud, III Corps Commander.").

[169] 1956 FM 27-10 (Change No. 1 1976) ¶484 ("A local armistice suspends operations between certain portions of the belligerent forces or within a designated district of the theater of operations.").

[170] 1958 UK MANUAL ¶425 ("It is, however, always a condition of the [partial] armistice that a considerable part of the forces and of the region of war must be included, and that the cause for which it has been concluded is not only some pressing local interests, as in the case of a suspension of arms, but one of a more general character, such as a general exhaustion of the opposing belligerent forces in one part of the theatre of war; the outbreak of a virulent infectious disease in the opposing camps; or any other cause the requirements of which cannot be satisfied by a mere suspension of arms, but do not demand a general armistice.").

[171] 1956 FM 27-10 (Change No. 1 1976) ¶485 ("A suspension of arms is a form of armistice concluded between commanders of military forces for some local military purpose, such as to bury the dead, to collect the wounded, to arrange for exchange of prisoners, or to enable a commander to communicate with his government or superior officer.").

drafted with the greatest possible precision and clarity.[172]

12.11.3.1 *Languages*. Unless agreement is possible for an armistice to be drawn up in one language, an armistice should be drawn up in the language of each belligerent force, with each side retaining a copy in its language. Each belligerent should confirm the text in each version to ensure consistency in each language.

12.11.4 General Effects of an Armistice Agreement. The precise effect of an armistice agreement may depend on the terms of the agreement. In the absence of specific provisions to the contrary, the following effects should be understood to result from an armistice agreement.

12.11.4.1 *Commencement, Notification, and Effective Time of the Armistice*. An armistice must be notified officially and in good time to the competent authorities and to the forces. Hostilities are suspended immediately after the notification, or on the date fixed.[173]

An armistice for the parties commences at the moment it is signed, in the absence of specific provision to the contrary.[174] For example, an armistice agreement may specify that hostilities are suspended for the parties upon receipt of notification by their commanders, rather than upon signing.[175]

Although an armistice is binding upon the belligerents from the time agreed for commencement of the armistice (or the time of signature if the time of commencement is not specified), officers of the armed forces are responsible for adhering to the armistice only from the time when they receive official information of its existence from their State.[176]

12.11.4.2 *Duration of an Armistice and the Resumption of Operations*. If the duration of an armistice is not prescribed, belligerents may resume operations at any time, provided always that the enemy is warned within the time agreed upon, in accordance with the

[172] 1956 FM 27-10 (Change No. 1 1976) ¶486 ("No special form for an armistice is prescribed. It should, if possible, be reduced to writing, in order to avoid misunderstandings and for the purpose of reference should differences of opinion arise. It should be drafted with the greatest precision and with absolute clearness.").

[173] HAGUE IV REG. art. 38 ("An armistice must be notified officially and in good time to the competent authorities and to the troops. Hostilities are suspended immediately after the notification, or on the date fixed.").

[174] 1956 FM 27-10 (Change No. 1 1976) ¶487a ("An armistice commences, in the absence of express mention to the contrary, at the moment it is signed.").

[175] *For example*, 1958 UK MANUAL ¶485 note 1 ("The capitulation of Manila was signed by the local commanders-in-chief on 4 August 1898, but a general armistice had been agreed to by the Governments of Spain and the U.S.A. on 12 August. Notice of this, however, did not reach the Philippines until 16 August, owing to a breakdown in signal communications. The Spaniards contended that the capitulation had become void, but the United States Government denied, maintaining that the protocol concerning the armistice had stipulated suspension of hostilities, not from the date of signature, but from the date of receipt of notification on the part of the respective commanders.").

[176] 1956 FM 27-10 (Change No. 1 1976) ¶491 ("An armistice is binding upon the belligerents from the time of the agreed commencement, but the officers of the armies are responsible only from the time when they receive official information of its existence."); LIEBER CODE art. 139 ("An armistice is binding upon the belligerents from the day of the agreed commencement; but the officers of the armies are responsible from the day only when they receive official information of its existence.").

terms of the armistice.[177]

If the duration is for a definite period of time and there is no positive agreement to the contrary, hostilities may be resumed without notice after the prescribed period of time.

12.11.4.3 General Prohibition on Offensive Military Operations. An armistice agreement generally would be understood to prohibit offensive military operations, such as conducting attacks or seizing territory.[178] Such acts would be examples of serious violations of an armistice.[179]

12.11.4.4 Armistice No Excuse for Relaxing Vigilance. The existence of an armistice does not warrant relaxation of vigilance in the service of security and protection, or in the preparedness of forces for action or exposing positions to the enemy.[180] For example, belligerents may continue to gather intelligence during an armistice, and may rely on that intelligence after the armistice has ended.[181]

12.11.4.5 Preparations for Resuming Hostilities and Espionage Generally Not Prohibited. During an armistice, in the absence of stipulations to the contrary, each belligerent is authorized:

- to make movements of forces within its own lines;
- to receive reinforcements;

---

[177] HAGUE IV REG. art. 36 ("If [an armistice's] duration is not defined, the belligerent parties may resume operations at any time, provided always that the enemy is warned within the time agreed upon, in accordance with the terms of the armistice."); LIEBER CODE art. 137 ("An armistice may be concluded for a definite time; or for an indefinite time, during which either belligerent may resume hostilities on giving the notice agreed upon to the other.").

[178] *See* 1958 UK MANUAL ¶446 ("If an armistice is declared without conditions, nothing more than a total cessation of hostilities along the front of both positions is required.") (emphasis added); LIEBER CODE art. 136 ("If an armistice be declared, without conditions, it extends no further than to require a total cessation of hostilities along the front of both belligerents.") (emphasis added); 1914 RULES OF LAND WARFARE ¶261 ("*What may be done during an armistice.*—An armistice need not in terms prohibit actual hostilities [in order to have the effect of prohibiting actual hostilities]. Anything else [beyond conducting actual hostilities] may be done during an armistice that is not in express terms prohibited by the agreement."). *See also* 1914 RULES OF LAND WARFARE ¶261 note 1 ("Actual hostilities will provide, of course, that firing shall cease; that the belligerents must not gain ground to the front; and, during siege operations, 'that the besieger must cease all extension, perfection, or advance of his attack works, as much so as from attacks by main force.' (G.O. 100, 1863, art. 142.)").

[179] *Refer to* § 12.13.1.1 (Examples of Serious Violations of an Armistice).

[180] 1956 FM 27-10 (Change No. 1 1976) ¶481 ("The existence of an armistice does not warrant relaxation of vigilance in the service of security and protection, or in the preparedness of troops for action, or exposing positions to the enemy."); 1958 UK MANUAL ¶460 ("The existence of an armistice is no reason for relaxing either vigilance or the readiness of troops for action, or for exhibiting positions to the enemy which he could not detect during combat.").

[181] *For example*, 1914 RULES OF LAND WARFARE ¶273 note 1 ("At the second battle of Fredericksburg, May 5, 1863, the Federals discovered the weakness of Gen. Barksdale's force during a suspension of hostilities to collect the wounded after the second repulse. Memoirs, Alexander, p. 351. In the suspension of arms at Wynnes Hill, during the relief of Ladysmith, many of the burghers stood up and disclosed the position of their trenches, which until then had not been located by the enemy. South African War, Vol. II, p. 602.").

- to construct new fortifications, installations, and bases;
- to build and repair transportation and communications facilities;
- to seek information about the enemy;
- to bring up supplies and equipment; and
- in general, to take advantage of the time and means at its disposal to prepare for resuming hostilities.[182]

Belligerents are not bound to discontinue espionage during an armistice, but the risks incurred by spies are the same as at other times.[183] For example, spies may be punished by an opposing belligerent if captured.[184]

12.11.4.6 *Armistice and Besieged Localities*. Absent express provision in the armistice agreement to the contrary, an armistice does not give authorities of a besieged place the right to receive food, water, or other supplies.[185]

However, armistice negotiations may be an opportunity for belligerents to attempt to conclude local agreements for the removal of wounded, sick, infirm and aged persons, children, and maternity cases, or for the passage of ministers of all religions, medical personnel, and medical equipment on their way to such areas.[186] In addition, armistice negotiations may be an opportunity for commanders to seek to make arrangements to permit the free passage of certain consignments.[187]

12.12 Armistices – Subjects Usually Addressed

The following topics are often addressed in an armistice agreement: (1) the scope of the armistice, including start time and duration; (2) what military activities are prohibited by the armistice; (3) the relations between forces and the local populations during the armistice; (4) humanitarian activities to occur during the armistice; and (5) mechanisms for implementing the

---

[182] 1956 FM 27-10 (Change No. 1 1976) ¶487e ("In the absence of stipulations to the contrary, each belligerent is authorized to make movements of troops within his own lines, to receive reinforcements, to construct new fortifications, installations, and bases, to build and repair transportation and communications facilities, to seek information about the enemy, to bring up supplies and equipment, and, in general, to take advantage of the time and means at his disposal to prepare for resuming hostilities.").

[183] 1958 UK Manual ¶449 ("Belligerents are not bound to discontinue espionage during an armistice, but the risks incurred by spies are the same as at other times.").

[184] *Refer to* § 4.17 (Spies, Saboteurs, and Other Persons Engaging in Similar Acts Behind Enemy Lines).

[185] 1958 UK Manual ¶445 ("The conclusion of an armistice gives the authorities of a besieged place no right to introduce provisions either for the garrison or for the civil population. Arrangements may, however, be made to supply them so that at the end of the armistice the forces are in the same position as at the beginning.").

[186] *Refer to* § 5.19.2 (Removal and Passage of Certain Personnel – Vulnerable Civilians, Diplomatic and Consular Personnel, the Wounded and Sick, and Medical Personnel).

[187] *Refer to* § 5.19.3 (Passage of Relief Consignments).

armistice.

Armistice provisions may address a range of political and military issues, provided that belligerents agree upon the terms and provided that the approving authorities are competent to address them.[188]

12.12.1 Scope of an Armistice, Including Start Time and Duration. The armistice should specify its scope—when and where it applies. The start time and duration of an armistice should be specified as precisely as possible (*e.g.*, date, time, and applicable time zone) to avoid misunderstanding and an unintentional resumption of hostilities.[189]

It may be appropriate for the armistice to specify that it starts at a later time to allow all forces to receive notification of the armistice before it becomes effective.[190]

If the armistice is of an indefinite duration, the terms and manner of giving notice that that armistice is to be ended (including the length of time between the delivery of the notice and when combat operations may recommence) should be specified in the armistice agreement.[191]

12.12.2 What Military Activities Are Prohibited by an Armistice. Although an armistice is generally understood to prohibit offensive operations, the armistice agreement may specify the extent to which offensive operations are prohibited and other military activities that are also prohibited during the armistice.[192]

12.12.3 Relations Between Forces and the Local Population During an Armistice. It rests with the Contracting Parties to settle, in the terms of the armistice, what intercourse may be held in the theater of war with the inhabitants of one belligerent State and those of the other.[193]

---

[188] 1956 FM 27-10 (Change No. 1 1976) ¶488 ("In addition to the provisions set forth in the preceding paragraph, general armistices normally contain a number of political and military stipulations concerning such matters as the evacuation of territory; disposition of aircraft and shipping; cooperation in the punishment of war crimes; restitution of captured or looted property; communications facilities and public utilities; civil administration; displaced persons; and the dissolution of organizations which may subvert public order.").

[189] 1956 FM 27-10 (Change No. 1 1976) ¶487a ("The precise date, day, and hour for the suspension of hostilities should also be stipulated. The effective times may be different in different geographical areas. An armistice commences, in the absence of express mention to the contrary, at the moment it is signed.").

[190] *For example*, Treaty of Armistice with Germany, Nov. 11, 1918, 2 BEVANS 9 ("An armistice has been concluded on the following conditions: ... (A) CLAUSES RELATING TO THE WESTERN FRONT I. Cessation of hostilities by land and in the air six hours after the signing of the armistice.").

[191] *Refer to* § 12.11.4.2 (Duration of an Armistice and the Resumption of Operations).

[192] *Refer to* § 12.11.4.3 (General Prohibition on Offensive Military Operations).

[193] HAGUE IV REG. art. 39 ("It rests with the Contracting Parties to settle, in the terms of the armistice, what communications may be held in the theater of war with the inhabitants of one belligerent State and those of the other."); LIEBER CODE art. 141 ("It is incumbent upon the contracting parties of an armistice to stipulate what intercourse of persons or traffic between the inhabitants of the territories occupied by the hostile armies shall be allowed, if any."). *See also* 1914 RULES OF LAND WARFARE ¶268 note 1 ("Of course, what is intended [by Article 29 of the Hague IV Regulations] to be regulated is the intercourse of the population of the *occupied* territory with the population of the country still held by the enemy (in both cases nationals of the State), and also between each belligerent force and the inhabitants of the localities held by the other.").

If nothing is stipulated, intercourse (*e.g.*, communication, movement, or commerce) remains suspended, as during actual hostilities.[194] For example, absent explicit agreement, a belligerent retains the right to control all communications or movement of members of the civilian population between its lines and enemy lines (*e.g.*, denying movement to reduce the risk of enemy espionage activities, denying trade to avoid strengthening enemy armed forces).[195]

The armistice agreement may also stipulate responsibilities of each party for civil administration of areas under its respective control (*e.g.*, public safety and public health needs, maintenance of public utilities including communications facilities). The armistice agreement may also specify the responsibilities of each belligerent for civil administration of neutral areas or areas where control is shared.[196]

12.12.4 Humanitarian Activities to Occur During an Armistice. An armistice agreement may arrange for a variety of humanitarian activities, such as:

- search for and collection of the sick and wounded from the battlefield, by, for example, medical personnel or authorized civilians (such as non-governmental organizations); and
- the provision or transport of medical care or food supplies intended for the civilian population, including displaced persons.

12.12.4.1 *Disposition of Detainees*. Because armistice agreements are generally only a temporary suspension of hostilities and not a complete cessation of active hostilities, POWs generally need not be repatriated upon the conclusion of an armistice agreement.[197] If it is desired that detainees, such as POWs, retained personnel, or civilian internees, should be released or exchanged, specific provisions in this regard should be made in the armistice agreement.[198]

---

194 1956 FM 27-10 (Change No. 1 1976) ¶487d ("If it is desired to make any change during the armistice in the relations between the opposing forces and the peaceable inhabitants, this must be accomplished by express provision. Otherwise these relations remain unchanged, each belligerent continuing to exercise the same rights as before, including the right to prevent or control all intercourse between the inhabitants within his lines and persons within the enemy lines."); LIEBER CODE art. 141 ("If nothing is stipulated the intercourse remains suspended, as during actual hostilities.").

195 *Refer to* § 5.19.1.1 (Belligerent Authority to Exercise Control in the Immediate Vicinity of Military Operations); § 11.4.1 (Right of the Occupying Power to Govern the Enemy Territory Temporarily).

196 *For example*, Agreement Between the Governments of the United States of America, the Soviet Union, and the United Kingdom on the One Hand and the Government of Rumania on the Other Concerning an Armistice, Sept. 12, 1944, 59 STAT. 1712, 1715 ("17. Rumanian civil administration is restored in the whole area of Rumania separated by not less than 50-100 kilometres (depending upon conditions of terrain) from the front line, Rumanian administrative bodies undertaking to carry out, in the interests of the reestablishment of peace and security, instructions and orders of the Allied (Soviet) High Command issued by them for the purpose of securing the execution of these armistice terms.").

197 *Refer to* § 9.37 (Release and Repatriation After Hostilities).

198 1956 FM 27-10 (Change No. 1 1976) ¶487f ("If it is desired that prisoners of war and civilian internees should be released or exchanged, specific provisions in this regard should be made."). *For example*, Agreement between the Commander-in-Chief, United Nations Command, on the one hand, and the Supreme Commander of the Korean People's Army and the Commander of the Chinese People's Volunteers, on the other hand, Concerning a Military

12.12.5 Mechanisms for Implementing an Armistice. An armistice agreement may specify mechanisms to help implement it.

12.12.5.1 *Neutral Zone Created by an Armistice*. An armistice may create a "neutral zone," situated in order to minimize risk of unintentional confrontation between opposing forces.[199] It may be necessary for forces to withdraw in order to establish the zone.[200] It is usually agreed that these lines are not to be crossed or the neutral zone entered except by *parlementaires* or other parties by special agreement for specified purposes, such as to bury the dead and collect the wounded.[201]

12.12.5.2 *Consultative Mechanism*. The armistice agreement may provide for the establishment of a commission composed of representatives of the opposing forces to supervise the implementation of the armistice agreement.[202] The agreement may specify that other representatives, such as representatives from neutral States or representatives from local authorities, are included on the commission.[203]

12.12.5.3 *Signals*. The belligerents may agree to use certain signals to help implement the armistice. For example, signals may be agreed upon to indicate the passage of *parlementaires*, the start or end of the armistice, or for other reasons.

12.12.5.4 *Maps Showing Boundaries or the Location of Forces*. An armistice agreement may also include an exchange of maps or other imagery showing the lines of

---

Armistice in Korea art. 52, Jul. 27, 1953, 29 DEPARTMENT OF STATE BULLETIN 132, 137 (Aug. 3, 1953) ("Each side insures [sic] that it will not employ in acts of war in the Korean conflict any prisoner of war released and repatriated incident to the coming into effect of this Armistice Agreement.").

[199] *For example*, *Protocol of Armistice between Japan and Russia*, Sept. 1, 1905, *reprinted in* I TREATIES AND AGREEMENTS WITH AND CONCERNING CHINA 1894-1919, 527 (1921) ("The undersigned Plenipotentiaries of Japan and Russia duly authorised to that effect by their Governments have agreed upon the following terms of armistice between the belligerents, pending the coming into force of the Treaty of Peace: -- 1. A certain distance (zone of demarcation) shall be fixed between the fronts of the armies of the two Powers in Manchuria as well as in the region of the Tomamko (Tumen).").

[200] *For example*, Dayton Accords, Annex 1A, art. IV (OHR Doc. 14/12/1995) ("The Parties immediately after this Annex enters into force shall begin promptly and proceed steadily to withdraw all Forces behind a Zone of Separation which shall be established on either side of the Agreed Cease-Fire Line that represents a clear and distinct demarcation between any and all opposing Forces.").

[201] 1956 FM 27-10 (Change No. 1 1976) ¶487c ("Provision may be included for a neutral zone between the two armies. It is usually agreed that these lines are not to be crossed or the neutral zone entered except by parlementaires or other parties by special agreement for specified purposes, such as to bury the dead and collect the wounded.").

[202] 1956 FM 27-10 (Change No. 1 1976) ¶487g ("It is generally desirable to provide for the establishment of a commission, composed of representatives of the opposing forces, to supervise the implementation of the armistice agreement.").

[203] *For example*, Egyptian-Israeli General Armistice Agreement, art. 10(1) Feb. 24, 1949, 42 UNTS 251, 264 ("The execution of the provisions of this Agreement shall be supervised by a Mixed Armistice Commission composed of seven members, of whom each Party to this Agreement shall designate three, and whose Chairman shall be the United Nations Chief of Staff of the Truce Supervision Organization or a senior officer from the Observer personnel of that Organization designated by him following consultation with both Parties to this Agreement.").

opposing forces (or the location of forces) at the time of the start of the armistice.[204] Such maps may facilitate understanding of applicable boundaries, such as the location of neutral zones, as well as reduce the risk of unintended confrontation.

12.13 ARMISTICES – VIOLATIONS AND DENUNCIATION

An armistice, like other formal arrangements between belligerents, engages the honor of all parties for the exact and complete fulfillment of every obligation thereby imposed.[205] Serious violations of the armistice by one of the parties gives an opposing party the right of denouncing the armistice, and deliberate violations of the armistice by individuals are punishable.

12.13.1 Serious Violations as a Basis for Denouncing an Armistice. Any serious violation of the armistice by one of the parties gives an opposing belligerent the right of denouncing the armistice, and even, in cases of urgency, of recommencing hostilities immediately.[206]

12.13.1.1 *Examples of Serious Violations of an Armistice*. Serious violations of an armistice include acts in contravention of the terms of the agreement or acts that are wholly inconsistent with the status of the suspension of hostilities.[207] Such acts may include:

- conducting attacks against the enemy;
- a deliberate advance or construction of works beyond the line agreed upon;
- the seizure of any point outside the lines; and
- the utilization of the occasion to withdraw forces from an unfavorable position commanded by the enemy.[208]

---

[204] *For example*, Egyptian-Israeli Agreement on Disengagement of Forces in Pursuance of the Geneva Peace Conference, Annex to Kurt Waldheim, *Letter Dated 18 January 1974 From the Secretary-General Addressed to President of the Security Council*, U.N. Doc. S/11198, 2 (Jan. 18, 1974) ("A. Egypt and Israel will scrupulously observe the cease-fire on land, sea and air called for by the United Nations Security Council and will refrain from the time of the signing of this document from all military or para-military actions against each other. B. The military forces of Egypt and Israel will be separated in accordance with the following principles: 1. All Egyptian forces on the east side of the canal will be deployed west of the line designated as line A on the attached map. All Israeli forces, including those west of the Suez Canal and the Bitter Lakes, will be deployed east of the line designated as line B on the attached map.").

[205] 1956 FM 27-10 (Change No. 1 1976) ¶493 ("An armistice, like other formal agreements between belligerents, engages the honor of both parties for the exact and complete fulfillment of every obligation thereby imposed.").

[206] HAGUE IV REG. art. 40 ("Any serious violation of the armistice by one of the parties gives the other party the right of denouncing it, and even, in cases of urgency, of recommencing hostilities immediately.").

[207] *Cf.* WINTHROP, MILITARY LAW & PRECEDENTS 787 ("The offence of violation of an armistice may consist in an act in contravention of the terms of the agreement, or in an act wholly inconsistent with the status of suspension.").

[208] 1958 UK MANUAL ¶456 ("A deliberate advance or construction of works beyond the line agreed upon, the seizure of any point outside the lines, or the utilization of the occasion to withdraw troops from an unfavourable position commanded by the enemy, or any violation of an express condition would, as a rule, constitute a grave breach [of an armistice].").

12.13.1.2 *Process of Denunciation – Warning Requirement*. Absent urgent necessity, a delay should occur between denunciation of the armistice and the resumption of hostilities.[209] This delay allows the denunciation to act as warning and to ensure that the party recommencing hostilities does not rely on the other party's compliance with the armistice as a way of facilitating its offensive military operations.

It would be dishonorable and perfidious for either party, without warning, to resume hostilities during the period of an armistice, with or without a formal denunciation thereof, except in case of urgency and upon convincing proof of intentional and serious violation of its terms by the other party.[210]

Nevertheless, under Article 40 of the Hague IV Regulations, upon definite proof of such a violation of an armistice, if the delay incident to formal denunciation and warning seems likely to give the violator a substantial advantage of any kind, the other party is free to resume hostilities without warning and with or without a formal denunciation.[211] For example, the law of war does not prohibit armed forces that reasonably believe an adversary is committing armistice violations from taking necessary and proportionate action in self-defense immediately in response.

12.13.1.3 *Process of Denunciation – Approval of Co-Belligerents Not Required*. A belligerent faced with serious violations of an armistice is not required to obtain the permission of its co-belligerents, even though those States may be parties to the armistice agreement, before recommencing hostilities.[212]

12.13.2 Violations of an Armistice by Individuals. A violation of the terms of an armistice by private persons acting on their own initiative only entitles the injured party to demand the punishment of the offenders or, if necessary, compensation for the losses sustained.[213]

---

[209] 1958 UK MANUAL ¶458 (Unless there be great urgency, there should always be a delay between denunciation of the armistice and resumption of hostilities.").

[210] 1956 FM 27-10 (Change No. 1 1976) ¶493 ("It would be an outrageous act of perfidy for either party, without warning, to resume hostilities during the period of an armistice, with or without a formal denunciation thereof, except in case of urgency and upon convincing proof of intentional and serious violation of its terms by the other party.").

[211] 1956 FM 27-10 (Change No. 1 1976) ¶493 ("Nevertheless, under the article last above quoted, upon definite proof of such a violation of the armistice, if the delay incident to formal denunciation and warning seems likely to give the violator a substantial advantage of any kind, the other party is free to resume hostilities without warning and with or without a formal denunciation.").

[212] *For example*, Jay S. Bybee, Assistant Attorney General, *Authority of the President Under Domestic and International Law to Use Military Force Against Iraq*, 26 OPINIONS OF THE OFFICE OF LEGAL COUNSEL 143, 174-75 (Oct. 23, 2002) ("The missile strikes in 1993 and 1998 serve as clear examples of the suspension of a cease-fire and a resumption of hostilities due to serious violations by Iraq. … It is our understanding based on information supplied by the Department of Defense that in neither case did the United States obtain the express agreement of all of the other members of the Persian Gulf War coalition before suspending the cease-fire and using force.").

[213] HAGUE IV REG. art. 41 ("A violation of the terms of the armistice by private persons acting on their own initiative only entitles the injured party to demand the punishment of the offenders or, if necessary, compensation for the losses sustained.").

12.13.2.1 *"Private Persons" Defined for the Purposes Article 41 of the Hague IV Regulations*. A private person, in the sense of Article 41 of the Hague IV Regulations, refers to any person, including a member of the armed forces, who acts on his or her own responsibility.[214]

12.13.2.2 *Effect of Violations of an Armistice by Individuals*. Deliberate violation of the terms of an armistice by individuals is punishable as a war crime. Such violations by individual members of the armed forces or subordinate officers do not justify denunciation of the armistice unless they are proved to have been committed with the knowledge and actual or tacit consent of their own government or commander. Consent may be inferred in the event of a persistent failure to punish such offenders.[215]

12.13.2.3 *Violation of Armistice Agreements and POW Status*. Violations of an armistice agreement, like other pre-capture law of war violations, are not a basis for denying a person POW status, if that person otherwise qualifies for POW status under the GPW.[216]

12.14 U.N. SECURITY COUNCIL CEASE-FIRES

The U.N. Security Council may call upon or demand that hostilities be ceased.[217] In addition, the U.N. Security Council may call upon or demand that members of the United Nations conclude cease-fire or armistice agreements.[218] The U.N. Security Council may also establish a formal cease-fire.[219]

Cease-fires established by the U.N. Security Council may be interpreted in accordance

---

[214] 1956 FM 27-10 (Change No. 1 1976) ¶494b ("A private individual, in the sense of the foregoing article, refers to any person, including a member of the armed forces, who acts on his own responsibility.").

[215] 1956 FM 27-10 (Change No. 1 1976) ¶494c ("Violation of the terms of an armistice by individuals is punishable as a war crime. Such violations by individual soldiers or subordinate officers do not justify denunciation of the armistice unless they are proved to have been committed with the knowledge and actual or tacit consent of their own government or commander. Consent may be inferred in the event of a persistent failure to punish such offenders.").

[216] *Refer to* § 9.26.4 (Retention of Benefits of the GPW Even if Prosecuted for Pre-Capture Acts).

[217] *For example*, U.N. SECURITY COUNCIL RESOLUTION 1199, U.N. Doc S/RES/1199, ¶1 (Sept. 23, 1998) ("Acting under Chapter VII of the Charter of the United Nations, 1. Demands that all parties, groups and individuals immediately cease hostilities and maintain a ceasefire in Kosovo, Federal Republic of Yugoslavia, which would enhance the prospects for a meaningful dialogue between the authorities of the Federal Republic of Yugoslavia and the Kosovo Albanian leadership and reduce the risks of a humanitarian catastrophe;"); U.N. SECURITY COUNCIL RESOLUTION 338, U.N. Doc. S/RES/338 (Oct. 22, 1973) ("Calls upon all parties to the present fighting to cease all firing and terminate all military activity immediately, no later than 12 hours after the moment of the adoption of this decision, in the positions they now occupy.").

[218] *For example*, U.N. SECURITY COUNCIL RESOLUTION 27, U.N. Doc S/RES/27 (Aug. 1, 1947) ("The Security Council, *Noting with concern* the hostilities in progress between the armed forces of the Netherlands and the Republic of Indonesia, *Calls upon* the parties: (a) To cease hostilities forthwith, and (b) To settle their dispute by arbitration or by other peaceful means and keep the Security Council informed about the progress of the settlement.").

[219] *For example*, U.N. SECURITY COUNCIL RESOLUTION 687, U.N. Doc S/RES/687 ¶33 (Apr. 3, 1991) ("*Declares* that, upon official notification by Iraq to the Secretary-General and to the Security Council of its acceptance of the above provisions, a formal cease-fire is effective between Iraq and Kuwait and the Member States cooperating with Kuwait in accordance with resolution 678 (1990);").

with the general principles of international law governing armistices.[220]

[220] *For example*, Jay S. Bybee, Assistant Attorney General, *Authority of the President Under Domestic and International Law to Use Military Force Against Iraq*, 26 OPINIONS OF THE OFFICE OF LEGAL COUNSEL 143, 175 (Oct. 23, 2002) ("Under general principles of armistice law, therefore, because the initial use of force in response to the invasion of Kuwait—Operation Desert Storm—was authorized under UNSCR 678, subsequent uses of force against Iraq in response to serious violations of the terms of the cease-fire established by UNSCR 687 would be authorized as well, provided either that Iraq has been warned, or that such a warning may be avoided because it would be likely to give Saddam Hussein a substantial advantage.").

XIII – Naval Warfare

Chapter Contents

13.1 Introduction

This Chapter addresses the law of war rules that apply to naval operations, especially those aspects of naval warfare that differ from warfare on land or in the air. This Chapter also briefly addresses the legal boundaries of the ocean, which may be relevant to the application of the law of war.

Navy publications have provided discussion of other public international law relating to naval operations, including discussion of the law of the sea applicable during peacetime.[1]

Some topics that are related to neutrality law and that are relevant to the conduct of both naval and air warfare, such as the conduct of visit and search and neutral commerce, are addressed in Chapter XV, the Law of Neutrality.[2]

13.1.1 The Law of the Sea During Armed Conflict. The law of the sea is a body of treaty and customary international law. Its rules have been developed principally with peacetime situations in mind. Nothing in the law of the sea impairs a State's inherent right of individual or collective self-defense, or rights during armed conflict.[3]

---

[1] *See, e.g.*, 2007 NWP 1-14M; 1997 NWP 9; 1989 NWP 9.

[2] *Refer to* § 15.13 (Belligerent Right of Visit and Search of Merchant Vessels and Civil Aircraft); § 15.12 (Neutral Commerce and Carriage of Contraband).

[3] *Responses of Rear Admiral John E. Crowley, Chief Counsel and Judge Advocate General, U.S. Coast Guard, to Additional Questions for the Record Submitted by Senator Joseph R. Biden, Jr.*, SENATE EXECUTIVE REPORT 108-10, *United Nations Convention on the Law of the Sea,* 108th Congress, Second Session, 170, 172 (Mar. 11, 2004) ("It should also be noted that nothing in the Convention restricts the inherent right of individual or collective self-defense or rights during armed conflict, and the administration is recommending that the United States express such

For example, the law of the sea provides that the high seas are reserved for peaceful purposes.[4] However, the use of the high seas for peaceful purposes is understood not to impose restraints upon military operations that would otherwise be consistent with international law, or to impair a State's inherent right of self-defense.[5] The use of outer space for peaceful purposes also has been interpreted in this way.[6]

As another example, certain rights under the law of the sea (*e.g.*, certain rights of navigation of vessels, or rights of States with respect to exclusive economic zones) must be exercised with due regard for the rights and duties of other States.[7] To the extent this obligation applies during armed conflict, what regard would be due would depend on military necessity and other principles and rules of the law of war, which are specially adapted to the circumstances of armed conflict.[8]

13.1.2 The United States and the LOS Convention. The U.N. Convention on the Law of the Sea (LOS Convention) was opened for signature on December 10, 1982.[9]

The United States is not a Party to the LOS Convention. The United States did not sign the LOS Convention when it opened for signature because of several major problems in the Convention's deep seabed mining provisions.[10] However, in 1983, the United States announced that it was prepared to accept and act in accordance with the balance of interests reflected in the LOS Convention relating to traditional uses of the oceans – such as navigation and overflight – and that the United States would exercise and assert its navigation and overflight rights and

---

an understanding."); William H. Taft, Legal Adviser, Department of State, *Response to an Additional Question from Senator Inhofe, United Nations Convention on the Law of the Sea: Hearing Before the Committee on Environment and Public Works, U.S. Senate*, 108th Congress, Second Session, 77 (Mar. 23, 2004) ("As stated in the resolution of advice and consent now before the Senate, nothing in the Convention impairs the inherent right of individual or collective self-defense or rights during armed conflict.").

[4] *Consider* LOS CONVENTION art. 88 ("The high seas shall be reserved for peaceful purposes.").

[5] *Commentary—The 1982 United Nations Convention on the Law of the Sea and the Agreement on Implementation of Part XI*, 94 in MESSAGE FROM THE PRESIDENT TRANSMITTING LOS CONVENTION ("Article 88 reserves the high seas for peaceful purposes, while articles 141 and 155(2) reserves the Area [which is defined in the LOS Convention art. 1(1) as "the seabed and ocean floor and subsoil thereof, beyond the limits of national jurisdiction;"] for peaceful purposes. … None of these provisions creates new rights or obligations, imposes restraints upon military operations, or impairs the inherent right of self-defense, enshrined in article 51 of the United Nations Charter. More generally, military activities which are consistent with principles of international law are not prohibited by these, or any other provisions of the Convention.").

[6] *Refer to* § 14.10.4 (General Use of Outer Space for Peaceful Purposes).

[7] *Refer to* § 13.2.3.3 (Exclusive Economic Zones (EEZs)); § 13.2.3.4 (High Seas).

[8] *Refer to* § 1.3.2 (The Law of War's Relationship to Other Bodies of Law).

[9] United Nations Convention on the Law of the Sea, Dec. 10, 1982, 1833 UNTS 397.

[10] Ronald Reagan, *Statement on United States Oceans Policy,* Mar. 10, 1983, 1983-I PUBLIC PAPERS OF THE PRESIDENTS 378 ("Last July, I announced that the United States will not sign the United Nations Law of the Sea Convention that was opened for signature on December 10. We have taken this step because several major problems in the Convention's deep seabed mining provisions are contrary to the interests and principles of industrialized nations and would not help attain the aspirations of developing countries. However, the convention also contains provisions with respect to traditional uses of the oceans which generally confirm existing maritime law and practice and fairly balance the interests of all states.").

freedoms on a worldwide basis in a manner that is consistent with the balance of interests reflected in the LOS Convention.[11] For example, consistent with the LOS Convention, the United States has claimed a 12-nautical mile territorial sea.[12] Similarly, the United States has established a contiguous zone extending 24 nautical miles from the baselines of the United States determined in accordance with international law, but in no case within the territorial sea of another nation.[13]

The Agreement on the Implementation of Part XI of the LOS Convention was adopted on August 17, 1994.[14] Because this agreement addressed the objections that the United States previously expressed to Part XI of the LOS Convention, President Clinton recommended that the Senate give its advice and consent to accession to the LOS Convention and to ratification of the Agreement on the Implementation of Part XI.[15] Subsequent administrations have also supported U.S. accession to the LOS Convention and the ratification of the Agreement on the Implementation of Part XI of the LOS Convention.[16]

13.2 Legal Boundaries of the Oceans

The legal classifications of ocean areas may be relevant to the application of the law of war and therefore affect military operations during armed conflict by, for example:

---

[11] Ronald Reagan, *Statement on United States Oceans Policy,* Mar. 10, 1983, 1983-I Public Papers of the Presidents 378, 379 ("First, the United States is prepared to accept and act in accordance with the balance of interests relating to traditional uses of the oceans - such as navigation and overflight. In this respect, the United States will recognize the rights of other States in the waters off their coasts, as reflected in the Convention, so long as the rights and freedoms of the United States and others under international law are recognized by such coastal states. Second, the United States will exercise and assert its navigation and overflight rights and freedoms on a worldwide basis in a manner that is consistent with the balance of interests reflected in the Convention. The United States will not, however, acquiesce in unilateral acts of other States designed to restrict the rights and freedoms of the international community in navigation and overflight and other related high seas uses.").

[12] *Refer to* § 13.2.2.2 (Territorial Seas).

[13] *Refer to* § 13.2.3.2 (Contiguous Zones).

[14] Agreement relating to the implementation of Part XI of the United Nations Convention on the Law of the Sea of 10 December 1982, *annex to* U.N. General Assembly Resolution 48/263, U.N. Doc. A/RES/48/263 (Aug. 17, 1994).

[15] William J. Clinton, *Letter of Transmittal*, Oct. 7, 1994, Message from the President Transmitting LOS Convention 1 ("As described in the report by the Secretary of State, the Agreement meets the objections the United States and other industrialized nations previously expressed to Part XI. It promises to provide a stable and internationally recognized framework for mining to proceed in response to future demand for minerals.... I therefore recommend that the Senate give early and favorable consideration to the Convention and to the Agreement and give its advice and consent to accession to the Convention and to ratification of the Agreement.").

[16] *See, e.g.*, George W. Bush, *Statement on the Advancement of United States Maritime Interests*, May 15, 2007, 2007-I Public Papers of the Presidents 583 ("First, I urge the Senate to act favorably on U.S. accession to the United Nations Convention on the Law of the Sea during this session of Congress. Joining will serve the national security interests of the United States, including the maritime mobility of our armed forces worldwide. It will secure U.S. sovereign rights over extensive marine areas, including the valuable natural resources they contain. Accession will promote U.S. interests in the environmental health of the oceans. And it will give the United States a seat at the table when the rights that are vital to our interests are debated and interpreted."); Barack Obama, *National Security Strategy* 50 (May 2010) ("As one key effort in the sea domain, for example, we will pursue ratification of the United Nations Convention on the Law of the Sea.").

- determining the legal boundaries of airspace above those waters;[17]
- determining whether waters are neutral waters;[18]
- determining the authority that a belligerent State has with respect to neutral vessels in an area;[19] or
- determining the authority that a neutral State has with respect to belligerent vessels in an area.[20]

Waters are often divided analytically between *national waters* (*i.e.*, internal waters, territorial seas, and archipelagic waters), which are subject to the sovereignty of a State, and *international waters*, which are not subject to the sovereignty of any State.[21] In addition, special rules apply to international straits and archipelagic sea lanes.[22]

13.2.1 Territory – Notes on Terminology. In some cases, the word "territory" is used to describe the land, waters, and airspace subject to the sovereignty of a State.[23] In other cases, the word "territory" is used to describe only the land that is subject to the sovereignty of a State.[24]

Thus, in describing waters that are not subject to the sovereignty of a State (*e.g.*, the exclusive economic zone and continental shelf, and high seas), the word "territory" should not be used. Coastal States may exercise limited "sovereign rights" over specific functional areas in the exclusive economic zone and on the continental shelf, but these rights do not imply sovereignty over these areas.[25]

---

[17] *Refer to* § 14.2 (Legal Boundaries of Airspace).

[18] *Refer to* § 15.7.1 (Waters That Are Considered Neutral).

[19] *Refer to, e.g.*, § 13.11.3.5 (Restrictions on Where Naval Mines May Be Placed); § 13.10.2.5 (Limitations on the Scope of the Blockade).

[20] *Refer to, e.g.*, § 15.8 (Passage of Belligerent Vessels and Aircraft Through International Straits and Archipelagic Sea Lanes).

[21] *Refer to* § 13.2.2 (National Waters); § 13.2.3 (International Waters).

[22] *Refer to* § 15.8 (Passage of Belligerent Vessels and Aircraft Through International Straits and Archipelagic Sea Lanes).

[23] *See, e.g.*, The Ann, 1 F. Cas. 926, 926-27 (C.C.D. Mass. 1812) (Story, J.) ("As the Ann arrived off Newburyport, and within three miles of the shore, it is clear that she was within the acknowledged jurisdiction of the United States. All the writers upon public law agree that every nation has exclusive jurisdiction to the distance of a cannon shot, or marine league, over the waters adjacent to its shores, and this doctrine has been recognized by the supreme court of the United States. Indeed such waters are considered as a part of the territory of the sovereign.") (internal citations omitted).

[24] *See, e.g.*, 1955 NWIP 10-2 ¶421 ("According to established international law, each State has exclusive legal control (jurisdiction) in the air space above its territory, internal waters, and territorial sea.").

[25] *See Commentary—The 1982 United Nations Convention on the Law of the Sea and the Agreement on Implementation of Part XI*, 24, MESSAGE FROM THE PRESIDENT TRANSMITTING LOS CONVENTION ("Article 56 enumerates the rights of the coastal State in the EEZ. Article 56(1)(a) establishes the sovereign rights of the coastal State. Article 56(1)(b) sets forth the nature and scope of coastal State jurisdiction with respect to specific matters.

13.2.2 National Waters. National waters, which are subject to the sovereignty of a State, include internal waters, territorial seas, and archipelagic waters.

13.2.2.1 *Internal Waters*. A State has sovereignty over its internal waters.[26] Internal waters are generally understood to be those waters on the landward side of the baseline of the territorial sea.[27] The coastal baseline must be defined in accordance with specific rules of international law as reflected in the LOS Convention.[28]

13.2.2.2 *Territorial Seas*. The sovereignty of a State extends, beyond its land territory and its internal waters, to a belt of sea adjacent to its coast, described as the territorial sea.[29]

The United States has claimed a 12-nautical mile territorial sea and recognizes territorial sea claims of other nations up to a maximum breadth of 12 nautical miles.[30] Previously, the

---

The terms 'sovereign rights' and 'jurisdiction' are used to denote functional rights over these matters and do not imply sovereignty. A claim of sovereignty in the EEZ would be contradicted by the language of articles 55 and 56 and precluded by article 58 and the provisions it incorporates by reference."); *id.* at 55 ("Article 77 reiterates that the coastal State has sovereign rights over the continental shelf for the purpose of exploring it and exploiting its natural resources. The sovereign rights of the coastal State are balanced with provisions protecting the freedom of navigation and the other rights and freedoms of other States from infringement or unjustifiable interference by the coastal State. Under article 78, rights of the coastal State over the continental shelf do not affect the legal status of the superjacent waters or of the airspace above those waters.").

[26] Convention on the Territorial Sea and Contiguous Zone, art. 1, Apr. 29, 1958, 516 UNTS 205, 207-08 ("1. The sovereignty of a State extends, beyond its land territory and its internal waters, to a belt of sea adjacent to its coast, described as the territorial sea. 2. This sovereignty is exercised subject to the provisions of these articles and to other rules of international law."). *Consider* LOS CONVENTION art. 2 ("1. The sovereignty of a coastal State extends, beyond its land territory and internal waters and, in the case of an archipelagic State, its archipelagic waters, to an adjacent belt of sea, described as the territorial sea. 2. This sovereignty extends to the air space over the territorial sea as well as to its bed and subsoil. 3. The sovereignty over the territorial sea is exercised subject to this Convention and to other rules of international law.").

[27] Convention on the Territorial Sea and Contiguous Zone, art. 5, Apr. 29, 1958, 516 UNTS 205, 210 ("1.Waters on the landward side of the baseline of the territorial sea form part of the internal waters of the State."). *Consider* LOS CONVENTION art. 8(1) ("Except as provided in Part IV, waters on the landward side of the baseline of the territorial sea form part of the internal waters of the State.").

[28] *Consider* LOS CONVENTION art. 5 ("Except where otherwise provided in this Convention, the normal baseline for measuring the breadth of the territorial sea is the low-water line along the coast as marked on large-scale charts officially recognized by the coastal State.").

[29] Convention on the Territorial Sea and Contiguous Zone, art. 1, Apr. 29, 1958, 516 UNTS 205, 207-08 ("1. The sovereignty of a State extends, beyond its land territory and its internal waters, to a belt of sea adjacent to its coast, described as the territorial sea. 2. This sovereignty is exercised subject to the provisions of these articles and to other rules of international law."). *Consider* LOS CONVENTION art. 2 ("1. The sovereignty of a coastal State extends, beyond its land territory and internal waters and, in the case of an archipelagic State, its archipelagic waters, to an adjacent belt of sea, described as the territorial sea. 2. This sovereignty extends to the air space over the territorial sea as well as to its bed and subsoil. 3. The sovereignty over the territorial sea is exercised subject to this Convention and to other rules of international law.").

[30] *See* Ronald Reagan, *Proclamation 5928: Territorial Sea of the United States of America*, Dec. 27, 1988, 54 FEDERAL REGISTER 777 (Jan. 9, 1989) ("The territorial sea of the United States henceforth extends to 12 nautical miles from the baselines of the United States determined in accordance with international law."). *Consider* LOS CONVENTION art. 3 ("Every State has the right to establish the breadth of its territorial sea up to a limit not exceeding 12 nautical miles, measured from baselines determined in accordance with this Convention.").

United States claimed a three-nautical mile territorial sea.[31] This claim was made in the context of asserting the rights of the United States as a neutral State.[32]

Coastal States often make specific maritime claims, but the United States does not recognize those maritime claims that are not in conformity with customary international law, as reflected in the LOS Convention.[33]

13.2.2.3 *Archipelagic Waters*. An archipelagic State's sovereignty extends to certain waters enclosed by archipelagic baselines drawn in accordance with the LOS Convention.[34]

An "archipelago" means a group of islands, including parts of islands, interconnecting water, and other natural features that are so closely interrelated that they form an intrinsic

---

[31] Thomas Jefferson, Secretary of State, Letter to the British Minister Mr. Hammond (Nov. 8, 1793), I MOORE'S DIGEST 702-03 ("The President of the United States thinking that before it shall be finally decided to what distance from our sea shores the territorial protection of the United States shall be exercised, it will be proper to enter into friendly conferences and explanations with the powers chiefly interested in the navigation of the seas on our coasts, and relying that convenient occasions may be taken for these hereafter, finds it necessary in the mean time, to fix provisionally on some distance for the present government of these questions. ... Reserving, however, the ultimate extent of this for future deliberation, the President gives instructions to the officers acting under his authority to consider those heretofore given them as restrained for the present to the distance of one sea league or three geographical miles from the sea-shores. This distance can admit of no opposition, as it is recognized by treaties between some of the powers with whom we are connected in commerce and navigation, and is as little, or less, than is claimed by any of them on their own coasts.").

[32] *See, e.g.*, Douglas W. Kmiec, Acting Assistant Attorney General, *Legal Issues Raised by the Proposed Presidential Proclamation to Extend the Territorial Sea*, Oct. 4, 1988, 12 OPINIONS OF THE OFFICE OF LEGAL COUNSEL 238, 244 (1988) ("The primary example, of course, is the first claim of a three-mile territorial sea made on behalf of the United States by then-Secretary of State Jefferson in 1793. France, Great Britain, and Spain -- all of which held territory in North America -- were engaged in maritime hostilities off our Atlantic coast, an extension of wars ongoing in Europe. As part of an effort to undermine our policy of neutrality, France pressured us to state the extent of our territorial sea."); United States v. California, 332 U.S. 19, 33 note 16 (1947) ("[S]hortly after we became a nation our statesmen became interested in establishing national dominion over a definite marginal zone to protect our neutrality. Largely as a result of their efforts, the idea of a definite three-mile belt in which an adjacent nation can, if it chooses, exercise broad, if not complete dominion, has apparently at last been generally accepted throughout the world, although as late as 1876 there was still considerable doubt in England about its scope and even its existence.").

[33] DEPARTMENT OF DEFENSE MANUAL 2005.1-M, *Maritime Claims Reference*, 2 (Jun. 23, 2005) ("The maritime claims references in this Manual represent claims made by the coastal nations. Some of the claims are inconsistent with international law. The United States does not recognize those maritime claims that are not in conformity with customary international law, as reflected in the 1982 United Nations Law of the Sea Convention. Examples include excessive straight baseline claims, territorial sea claims in excess of 12 nautical miles (nm), and other claims that unlawfully impede freedom of navigation and overflight.").

[34] *Consider* LOS CONVENTION art. 49(1) ("The sovereignty of an archipelagic State extends to the waters enclosed by the archipelagic baselines drawn in accordance with article 47, described as archipelagic waters, regardless of their depth and distance from the coast."); LOS CONVENTION art. 47 ("An archipelagic State may draw straight archipelagic baselines joining the outermost posts of the outermost islands and drying reefs of the archipelago provided that within such baselines are included the main islands and an area in which the ratio of the area of the water to the area of the land, including atolls, is between 1 to 1 and 9 to 1.").

geographic, economic, and political entity or that historically have been regarded as such.[35] An "archipelagic State" means a State constituted wholly by one or more archipelagos and may include other islands.[36] The Philippines and Indonesia are examples of archipelagic States.[37]

13.2.2.4 *Innocent Passage of Foreign Vessels Through Territorial Seas and Archipelagic Waters*. During peacetime, all ships enjoy a right of innocent passage through territorial seas and archipelagic waters.[38] A Coastal State, however, has a right of protection, which includes the right to suspend temporarily in specified areas of its territorial sea the innocent passage of foreign ships if such suspension is essential for the protection of its security.[39]

During armed conflict, the right of innocent passage would not apply between belligerent States. During armed conflict, belligerent States may restrict the right of neutral vessels to conduct innocent passage through territorial seas and archipelagic waters belonging to a belligerent State, such as by establishing maritime zones.[40] During armed conflict, neutral States may regulate, and even prohibit, belligerent warships and prizes from entering their territorial seas and archipelagic waters.[41]

13.2.3 International Waters. International waters, which are not subject to the sovereignty of any State, include contiguous zones, exclusive economic zones (EEZs), and the high seas. These waters, which are seaward of the territorial sea, are waters in which States have certain freedoms, such as freedom of navigation and overflight.

13.2.3.1 *High Seas Freedoms*. States may exercise certain freedoms on the high

---

[35] *Consider* LOS CONVENTION art. 46(b) ("'archipelago' means a group of islands, including parts of islands, interconnecting water and other natural features which are so closely interrelated that [they] form an intrinsic geographic, economic, and political entity or which historically have been regarded as such.").

[36] *Consider* LOS CONVENTION art. 46(a) ("'archipelagic State' means a State constituted wholly by one or more archipelagos and may include other islands;").

[37] *Commentary—The 1982 United Nations Convention on the Law of the Sea and the Agreement on Implementation of Part XI*, 22, MESSAGE FROM THE PRESIDENT TRANSMITTING LOS CONVENTION ("A State may enclose archipelagic waters within archipelagic baselines that satisfy the criteria specified in Article 47. Depending on how the archipelagic baseline system is established, the following 20 States could legitimately claim archipelagic waters: Antigua & Barbuda, The Bahamas, Cape Verde, Comoros, Fiji, Grenada, Indonesia, Jamaica, Kiribati (in part), Maldives, Marshall Islands (in part), Papua New Guinea, Philippines, Saint Vincent and the Grenadines, Sao Tome & Principe, Seychelles, Solomon Islands (five archipelagos), Tonga, Trinidad & Tobago, and Vanuatu.").

[38] *Consider* LOS CONVENTION art. 17 ("Subject to this Convention, ships of all States, whether coastal or land-locked, enjoy the right of innocent passage through the territorial sea."); LOS CONVENTION art. 52 ("1. Subject to article 53 and without prejudice to article 50, ships of all States enjoy the right of innocent passage through archipelagic waters, in accordance with Part II, section 3.").

[39] *Consider* LOS CONVENTION art. 25(3) ("The coastal State may, without discrimination in form or in fact among foreign ships, suspend temporarily in specified areas of its territorial sea the innocent passage of foreign ships if such suspension is essential for the protection of its security, including weapons exercises. Such suspension shall take effect only after having been duly published.").

[40] *Refer to* § 13.9.4 (Use of Zones to Prevent Movement – Exclusion Zones).

[41] *Refer to* § 15.7.2 (A Neutral State's Regulations Concerning Belligerent Warships and Prizes in Its Waters).

seas, such as freedom of navigation and freedom of overflight.[42] For example, the high seas freedoms that warships may exercise include: task force maneuvering, flight operations, military exercises, surveillance, intelligence gathering activities, and ordnance testing and firing.[43] These rights and freedoms must be exercised with due regard for the interests of other States in their exercise of the freedom of the high seas and other applicable rights.[44]

Within a State's EEZ, other States enjoy high seas freedoms of navigation and overflight, and other rights, but must exercise those rights with due regard for the rights and duties of the coastal State.[45]

13.2.3.2 Contiguous Zones. A contiguous zone is an area extending seaward from the territorial sea to a maximum distance of 24 nautical miles from the baseline, in which the coastal State may exercise the control necessary to prevent or punish infringement of its customs, fiscal, immigration, and sanitary laws and regulations that occurs within its territory or territorial sea.[46]

---

[42] Convention on the High Seas, art. 2, Apr. 29, 1958, 450 UNTS 82, 83-84 ("Freedom of the high seas is exercised under the conditions laid down by these articles and by the other rules of international law. It comprises, *inter alia*, both for coastal and non coastal states: (1) Freedom of navigation; (2) Freedom of fishing; (3) Freedom to lay submarine cables and pipelines; (4) Freedom to fly over the high seas."). *Consider* LOS CONVENTION art. 87(1) ("The high seas are open to all States, whether coastal or land-locked. Freedom of the high seas is exercised under the conditions laid down by this Convention and by other rules of international law. It comprises, inter alia, both for coastal and land-locked States: (a) freedom of navigation; (b) freedom of overflight; (c) freedom to lay submarine cables and pipelines, subject to Part VI; (d) freedom to construct artificial islands and other installations permitted under international law, subject to Part VI; (e) freedom of fishing, subject to the conditions laid down in section 2; (f) freedom of scientific research, subject to Parts VI and XIII.").

[43] 2007 NWP 1-14M ¶2.6.3 ("All ships and aircraft, including warship and military aircraft, enjoy complete freedom of movement and operation on and over the high seas. For warships, this includes task force maneuvering, flight operations, military exercises, surveillance, intelligence gathering activities, and ordnance testing and firing."); 1997 NWP 9 ¶2.4.3 (same); 1989 NWP 9 ¶2.4.3 (same).

[44] Convention on the High Seas, art. 2, Apr. 29, 1958, 450 UNTS 82, 84 ("These freedoms, and others which are recognized by the general principles of international law, shall be exercised by all States with reasonable regard to the interests of other States in their exercise of the freedom of the high seas."). *Consider* LOS CONVENTION art. 87(2) ("These freedoms shall be exercised by all States with due regard for the interests of other States in their exercise of the freedom of the high seas, and also with due regard for the rights under this Convention with respect to activities in the Area.").

[45] *Consider* LOS CONVENTION art. 58 ("1. In the exclusive economic zone, all States, whether coastal or land-locked, enjoy, subject to the relevant provisions of this Convention, the freedoms referred to in article 87 of navigation and overflight and of the laying of submarine cables and pipelines, and other internationally lawful uses of the sea related to these freedoms, such as those associated with the operation of ships, aircraft and submarine cables and pipelines, and compatible with the other provisions of this Convention. 2. Articles 88 to 115 and other pertinent rules of international law apply to the exclusive economic zone in so far as they are not incompatible with this Part. 3. In exercising their rights and performing their duties under this Convention in the exclusive economic zone, States shall have due regard to the rights and duties of the coastal State and shall comply with the laws and regulations adopted by the coastal State in accordance with the provisions of this Convention and other rules of international law in so far as they are not incompatible with this Part.").

[46] Convention on the Territorial Sea and Contiguous Zone, art. 24, Apr. 29, 1958, 516 UNTS 205, 220 ("1. In a zone of the high seas contiguous to its territorial sea, the coastal State may exercise the control necessary to: (a) Prevent infringement of its customs, fiscal, immigration or sanitary regulations within its territory or territorial sea; (b) Punish infringement of the above regulations committed within its territory or territorial sea."). *Consider* LOS

The United States has established a contiguous zone extending 24 nautical miles from the baselines of the United States determined in accordance with international law, but in no case within the territorial sea of another nation.[47]

13.2.3.3 *Exclusive Economic Zones (EEZs)*. An Exclusive Economic Zone (EEZ) is a zone of limited, generally resource-related rights and jurisdiction adjacent to the territorial sea and may not extend beyond 200 nautical miles from the baseline.[48] The United States has established an exclusive economic zone.[49]

Although a coastal State does not have sovereignty over its EEZ, it has certain, generally economic rights over these areas that must be exercised with due regard for the rights and duties of other States, such as the high seas freedoms of other States.[50]

13.2.3.4 *High Seas*. International law regarding the high seas applies to all parts of the sea that are not included in the EEZ, territorial sea, internal waters, or archipelagic waters

---

CONVENTION art. 33 ("1. In a zone contiguous to its territorial sea, described as the contiguous zone, the coastal State may exercise the control necessary to: (a) prevent infringement of its customs, fiscal, immigration or sanitary laws and regulations within its territory or territorial sea; (b) punish infringement of the above laws and regulations committed within its territory or territorial sea. 2. The contiguous zone may not extend beyond 24 nautical miles from the baselines from which the breadth of the territorial sea is measured.").

[47] William J. Clinton, *Proclamation 7219: Contiguous Zone of the United States*, Aug. 2, 1999, 64 FEDERAL REGISTER 48701 (Aug. 8, 1999) ("The contiguous zone of the United States extends to 24 nautical miles from the baselines of the United States determined in accordance with international law, but in no case within the territorial sea of another nation.").

[48] *Consider* LOS CONVENTION art. 55 ("The exclusive economic zone is an area beyond and adjacent to the territorial sea, subject to the specific legal regime established in this Part, under which the rights and jurisdiction of the coastal State and the rights and freedoms of other States are governed by the relevant provisions of this Convention."); LOS CONVENTION art. 57 ("The exclusive economic zone shall not extend beyond 200 nautical miles from the baselines from which the breadth of the territorial sea is measured.").

[49] Ronald Reagan, *Proclamation 5030: Exclusive Economic Zone of the United States of America*, Mar. 10, 1983, 97 STAT. 1557 ("The Exclusive Economic Zone of the United States is a zone contiguous to the territorial sea, including zones contiguous to the territorial sea of the United States, the Commonwealth of Puerto Rico, the Commonwealth of the Northern Mariana Islands (to the extent consistent with the Covenant and the United Nations Trusteeship Agreement), and United States overseas territories and possessions. The Exclusive Economic Zone extends to a distance 200 nautical miles from the baseline from which the breadth of the territorial sea is measured. In cases where the maritime boundary with a neighboring State remains to be determined, the boundary of the Exclusive Economic Zone shall be determined by the United States and other State concerned in accordance with equitable principles.").

[50] *Consider* LOS CONVENTION art. 56 ("1. In the exclusive economic zone, the coastal State has: (a) sovereign rights for the purpose of exploring and exploiting, conserving and managing the natural resources, whether living or non-living, of the waters superjacent to the seabed and of the seabed and its subsoil, and with regard to other activities for the economic exploitation and exploration of the zone, such as the production of energy from the water, currents and winds; (b) jurisdiction as provided for in the relevant provisions of this Convention with regard to: (i) the establishment and use of artificial islands, installations and structures; (ii) marine scientific research; (iii) the protection and preservation of the marine environment; (c) other rights and duties provided for in this Convention. 2. In exercising its rights and performing its duties under this Convention in the exclusive economic zone, the coastal State shall have due regard to the rights and duties of other States and shall act in a manner compatible with the provisions of this Convention. 3. The rights set out in this article with respect to the seabed and subsoil shall be exercised in accordance with Part VI.").

of an archipelagic State.[51] No State may validly purport to subject any part of the high seas to its sovereignty.[52] States may exercise certain freedoms on the high seas, such as freedom of navigation and freedom of overflight.[53]

13.2.4 Chart Illustrating the Legal Boundaries of the Oceans and Airspace. This chart, reproduced from the 2007 Commander's Handbook on the Law of Naval Operations, seeks to summarize the maximum permissible claims of States with respect to the boundaries of the oceans and airspace, as reflected in the LOS Convention.[54]

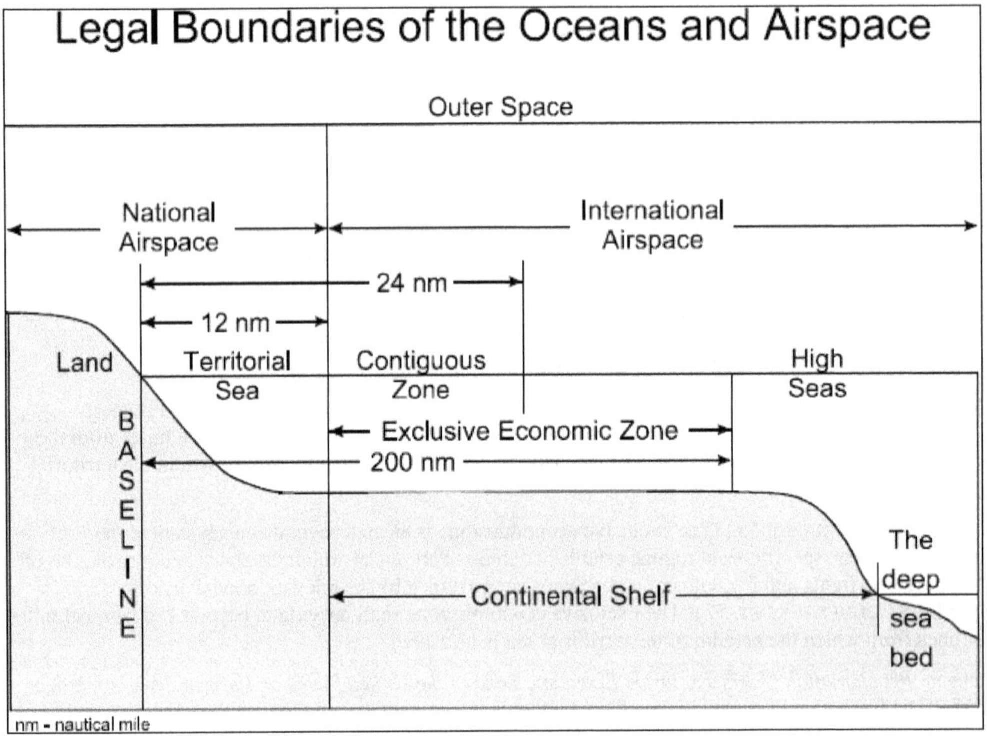

[51] Convention on the High Seas, art. 1, Apr. 29, 1958, 450 UNTS 82 ("The term 'high seas' means all parts of the sea that are not included in the territorial sea or in the internal waters of a State."). *Consider* LOS CONVENTION art. 86 ("The provisions of this Part apply to all parts of the sea that are not included in the exclusive economic zone, in the territorial sea or in the internal waters of a State, or in the archipelagic waters of an archipelagic State. This article does not entail any abridgement of the freedoms enjoyed by all States in the exclusive economic zone in accordance with article 58.").

[52] Convention on the High Seas, art. 2, Apr. 29, 1958, 450 UNTS 82 ("The high seas being open to all nations, no State may validly purport to subject any part of them to its sovereignty."). *Consider* LOS CONVENTION art. 89 ("No State may validly purport to subject any part of the high seas to its sovereignty.").

[53] *Refer to* § 13.2.3.1 (High Seas Freedoms).

[54] 2007 NWP 1-14M ¶1.3, Figure 1-1. *See also Commentary—The 1982 United Nations Convention on the Law of the Sea and the Agreement on Implementation of Part XI*, 4, Figure 1, MESSAGE FROM THE PRESIDENT TRANSMITTING LOS CONVENTION; JOINT PUBLICATION 3-32, *Command and Control for Joint Maritime Operations*, I-7, Figure I-1 (Aug. 7, 2013); JUDGE ADVOCATE GENERAL'S LEGAL CENTER & SCHOOL, INTERNATIONAL AND OPERATIONAL LAW DEPARTMENT, OPERATIONAL LAW HANDBOOK 160 (2013).

13.3 OVERVIEW OF RULES FOR NAVAL ENGAGEMENTS

In general, the rules for conducting attacks, such as bombardments, by naval forces are the same as those for land or air forces.[55]

13.3.1 Areas of Naval Warfare. As a general rule, naval forces may attack military objectives wherever located outside neutral territory.[56] In certain cases (*e.g.*, involving belligerent use of neutral territory as a base of operations), hostilities may be conducted in neutral territory to redress violations of neutrality.[57]

13.3.2 Classification of Vessels. The law of land warfare has divided enemy nationals into different categories in order to facilitate the protection of the civilian population from hostilities.[58] Similarly, the law of naval warfare has sought to classify enemy vessels to protect those that are civilian or non-combatant in character.

In general, all vessels of an enemy State may be understood to fall into one of three classes: (1) warships and naval and military auxiliaries; (2) merchant vessels; and (3) exempt vessels.

Warships and naval and military auxiliaries are generally liable to attack and capture.[59] Merchant vessels are generally liable to capture, but are liable to attack if they forfeit their protection.[60] Exempt vessels are not liable to capture or attack, unless they forfeit their protection.[61]

13.3.3 Vessels Entitled to Conduct Attacks. During international armed conflict at sea, warships are the only vessels that are entitled to conduct attacks.[62]

Other vessels, such as auxiliary vessels and merchant vessels, are not entitled to conduct attacks in offensive combat operations.[63] All vessels, however, may defend themselves

---

[55] *Refer to* § 5.4 (Rules on Conducting Assaults, Bombardments, and Other Attacks).

[56] *Refer to* § 15.3.1.2 (Inviolability of Neutral Territory - Prohibition on Hostile Acts or Other Violations of Neutrality).

[57] *Refer to* § 15.4.2 (Belligerent Use of Self-Help When Neutral States Are Unable or Unwilling to Prevent Violations of Neutrality).

[58] *Refer to* § 4.2 (The Armed Forces and the Civilian Population).

[59] *Refer to* § 13.4 (Enemy Warships).

[60] *Refer to* § 13.5 (Enemy Merchant Vessels).

[61] *Refer to* § 13.6 (Enemy Vessels Exempt From Capture or Destruction).

[62] *See* 1955 NWIP 10-2 ¶500e ("At sea, only warships and military aircraft may exercise belligerent rights.").

[63] 2013 GERMAN MANUAL ¶1020 ("The following vessels and persons may not perform acts of naval warfare: - state ships other than warships, even when carrying out support services for the naval forces, - merchant ships, - fishing vessels and other civilian ships, - prize crews of captured ships, - state aircraft other than military aircraft and - civilian aircraft. The crews of all ships and aircraft are, however, entitled to defend themselves against attacks by enemy armed forces."); 1992 GERMAN MANUAL ¶1016 ("The following vessels and persons may not perform

(including resisting attacks by enemy forces).[64]

13.3.3.1 *Entitlement of Vessels to Conduct Attacks During Non-International Armed Conflict*. The United States is not a Party to any treaties that would prohibit the use of warships and auxiliaries in non-international armed conflict, nor has the United States recognized such a prohibition in customary international law. Accordingly, State vessels other than warships may be used to conduct attacks against non-State armed groups during non-international armed conflict.[65] For example, international law does not prohibit auxiliaries from conducting attacks in a non-international armed conflict. Similarly, a State may use its law enforcement authorities to address insurgent groups, and there would be no objection to using a law enforcement vessel as part of operations against insurgents.[66]

In some cases, the acts of hostility by insurgents on the high seas may be regarded as piracy.[67]

13.3.4 Shipwrecked Persons. Shipwrecked persons are *hors de combat*, and may not be made the object of attack.[68] Shipwrecked persons include personnel involved in forced landings at sea by or from aircraft, but do not include, for example, combatant personnel engaged in attacks.[69]

---

acts of naval warfare: - state ships other than warships, even when carrying out support Services for the naval forces, - state aircraft other than military aircraft, - merchant ships, - fishing boats and other civil ships, - civil aircraft, and - prize crews of captured ships. The crews of all ships and aircraft are, however, entitled to defend themselves against attacks by enemy forces.").

[64] *See* Institute of International Law, *Manual of the Laws of Naval War*, art. 12 (1913) ("Apart from the conditions laid down in Articles 3 [regarding the conversion of public and private vessels into war-ships] and following, neither public nor private vessels, nor their personnel, may commit acts of hostility against the enemy. Both may, however, use force to defend themselves against the attack of an enemy vessel."). *Refer to* § 4.16.1 (Merchant or Civil Crews - Conduct of Hostilities).

[65] *Wolff Heintschel von Heinegg, Methods and Means of Naval Warfare in Non-International Armed Conflicts*, 88 U.S. NAVAL WAR COLLEGE INTERNATIONAL LAW STUDIES 211, 219 (2012) ("Under the law of international armed conflict, only warships are entitled to exercise belligerent rights. This rule goes back to the prohibition of privateering under the 1856 Paris Declaration. Warships are those vessels that meet the criteria set forth in Articles 2-5 of the 1907 Hague Convention VII, Article 8(2) of the 1958 High Seas Convention and Article 29 of the LOS Convention. Limitations on the exercise of belligerent rights are most important with regard to interference with neutral navigation and aviation; thus, neutral vessels and aircraft must accede to such interference only if the measures are taken by warships. No such limitation applies to non-international armed conflicts vis-à-vis the parties. It follows from the object and purpose of the rule limiting the exercise of belligerent rights under the law of naval warfare—i.e., the transparent entitlement of the warship—that the non-State actor will obviously not have ships that meet the criteria for classification as a warship since one of the criteria is that it be a State vessel. The government forces may make use of any vessel or aircraft, including, for example, those used for law enforcement and customs enforcement, in the conduct of hostilities.").

[66] *Refer to* § 17.4.1 (Ability of a State to Use Its Domestic Law Against Non-State Armed Groups).

[67] The Three Friends, 166 U.S. 1 (1897) ("Belligerency is recognized when a political struggle has attained a certain magnitude and affects the interests of the recognizing power; and in the instance of maritime operations, recognition may be compelled, or the vessels of the insurgents, if molesting third parties, may be pursued as pirates.").

[68] *Refer to* § 5.9.4 (Persons Rendered Unconscious or Otherwise Incapacitated by Wounds, Sickness, or Shipwreck).

[69] *Refer to* § 7.3.1.2 (Shipwrecked).

As far as military exigencies permit, after each naval engagement, all possible measures should be taken without delay to search for and collect the wounded, sick, and shipwrecked, and to recover the dead.[70]

13.3.5 Surrender by Enemy Vessels. The general rules on the protection of persons *hors de combat*, including the rule prohibiting the attack of persons who have surrendered, also apply to enemy vessels.[71] In particular, it is forbidden to make an enemy vessel the object of attack if it has genuinely, clearly, and unconditionally surrendered, in circumstances in which it is feasible to accept such surrender.[72]

Once an enemy vessel has clearly indicated a readiness to surrender, the attack must be discontinued.[73] Indicia of surrender by vessels may include:

- hauling down her flag;
- hoisting a white flag;[74]
- surfacing (in the case of submarines);[75]
- stopping engines and responding to the attacker's signals;[76] or
- taking to lifeboats.

---

[70] *Refer to* § 7.4.1 (GWS-Sea Obligation Regarding the Search, Collection, and Affirmative Protection of the Wounded, Sick, Shipwrecked, and Dead).

[71] *Refer to* § 5.9.3 (Persons Who Have Surrendered).

[72] 2007 NWP ¶8.6.1 ("It is forbidden, however, to target an enemy warship or military aircraft that in good faith unambiguously and effectively conveys a timely offer of surrender."); 1955 NWIP ¶511c ("It is forbidden to refuse quarter to any enemy who has surrendered in good faith. In particular, it is forbidden either to continue to attack enemy warships and military aircraft which have clearly indicated a readiness to surrender or to fire upon the survivors of such vessels and aircraft who no longer have the means to defend themselves.").

[73] 2007 NWP 1-14M ¶8.6.1 ("Once an enemy warship has clearly indicated a readiness to surrender, such as by hauling down her flag, by hoisting a white flag, by surfacing (in the case of submarines), by stopping engines and responding to the attacker's signals, or by taking to lifeboats, the attack must be discontinued.").

[74] *Refer to* § 12.4 (The White Flag of Truce to Initiate Negotiations).

[75] W.T. MALLISON, JR., STUDIES IN THE LAW OF NAVAL WARFARE: SUBMARINES IN GENERAL AND LIMITED WARS 134 (1968) ("The duty to give quarter is, of course, the same in submarine warfare as it is in other naval warfare. There are undoubtedly unusual problems which occur concerning manifestations of surrender in submarine warfare. A submarine even when fully surfaced lies low in the water. There may be, consequently, particular difficulties in observing a submarine's manifestation of surrender. Where a submarine is forced to the surface following depth charging, it seems reasonable that the submarine's commander should be given an opportunity to surrender unless an unequivocal intention of fighting it out on the surface is manifested. The attempt of a surface ship to indicate surrender to a submerged submarine also raises problems. For example, it is clear that the submerged submarine at periscope depth has only limited visibility.").

[76] Trial of Helmuth von Ruchteschell, *Outline of the Proceedings*, IX U.N. LAW REPORTS 82 (British Military Court, Hamburg, May 5-21, 1947) ("The captain of the *Davisian* stopped his engines, hoisted an answering pennant and acknowledged the signal. In spite of this, the raider's firing continued for 15 minutes, wounding 8 or 10 of the crew of the *Davisian*, whilst they were trying to abandon ship [by taking to lifeboats].").

13.4 Enemy Warships

Enemy warships and naval and military auxiliaries are subject to attack, destruction, or capture anywhere beyond neutral territory.

13.4.1 Character of Warships. A warship is generally understood to be a ship belonging to the armed forces of a State bearing the external markings distinguishing the character and nationality of such ships, under the command of an officer duly commissioned by the government of that State and whose name appears in the appropriate service list of officers, and manned by a crew that is under regular armed forces discipline.[77]

Warships are generally understood to possess certain privileges and immunities from the jurisdiction of other States.[78]

13.4.2 Attacks Against Enemy Warships. In general, enemy warships are military objectives.[79] However, warships that have surrendered or that are exempt vessels may not be made the object of attack.[80]

13.4.3 Captured Enemy Warships – No Prize Procedure. Prize procedures are not used for captured enemy warships because their ownership vests immediately in the captor's government by the fact of capture.[81] As public movable property, warships are seizable as war booty.[82] Similarly, prize procedures are not used for captured enemy military aircraft.[83]

---

[77] Convention on the High Seas, art. 8, Apr. 29, 1958, 450 UNTS 82, 86 ("1. Warships on the high seas have complete immunity from the jurisdiction of any State other than the flag State. 2. For the purposes of these articles, the term 'warship' means a ship belonging to the naval forces of a State and bearing the external marks distinguishing warships of its nationality, under the command of an officer duly commissioned by the government and whose name appears in the Navy List, and manned by a crew who are under regular naval discipline."). *Consider* LOS CONVENTION art. 29 ("For the purposes of this Convention, 'warship' means a ship belonging to the armed forces of a State bearing the external marks distinguishing such ships of its nationality, under the command of an officer duly commissioned by the government of the State and whose name appears in the appropriate service list or its equivalent, and manned by a crew which is under regular armed forces discipline.").

[78] *See, e.g.*, The Schooner Exch. v. McFaddon, 11 U.S. 116, 144 (1812) ("But in all respects different is the situation of a public armed ship. She constitutes a part of the military force of her nation; acts under the immediate and direct command of the sovereign; is employed by him in national objects. He has many and powerful motives for preventing those objects from being defeated by the interference of a foreign state. Such interference cannot take place without affecting his power and his dignity. The implied license therefore under which such vessel enters a friendly port, may reasonably be construed, and it seems to the Court, ought to be construed, as containing an exemption from the jurisdiction of the sovereign, within whose territory she claims the rites of hospitality."). *Consider* LOS CONVENTION art. 95 ("Warships on the high seas have complete immunity from the jurisdiction of any State other than the flag State.").

[79] *Refer to* § 5.6.4 (Objects Categorically Recognized as Military Objectives).

[80] *Refer to* § 13.3.5 (Surrender by Enemy Vessels); § 13.6 (Enemy Vessels Exempt From Capture or Destruction).

[81] 1955 NWIP 10-2 ¶503a(2) ("Enemy warships and military aircraft may be captured outside neutral jurisdiction. Prize procedure is not used for such captured vessels and aircraft because their ownership immediately vests in the captor's government by the fact of capture.").

[82] *Refer to* § 5.17.3 (Enemy Movable Property on the Battlefield (War Booty)).

[83] *Refer to* § 14.5.3 (Capture of Aircraft and Goods on Board Aircraft).

13.5 Enemy Merchant Vessels

13.5.1 Capture of Enemy Merchant Vessels. Enemy merchant vessels may be captured wherever located beyond neutral territory. Prior exercise of visit and search is not required, provided positive determination of enemy status can be made by other means.[84]

13.5.1.1 *Captured Enemy Merchant Vessels – Notes on Terminology*. A captured neutral or enemy merchant vessel is called a *prize*.

13.5.1.2 *Use of Prize Procedures to Complete Transfer of Title*. Prize procedures are usually used to complete the transfer of title of captured property, such as enemy merchant ships.[85]

13.5.1.3 *Destruction of Captured Enemy Merchant Vessels*. When military circumstances preclude sending or taking in such vessel or aircraft for adjudication as an enemy prize, it may be destroyed after all possible measures are taken to provide for the safety of passengers and crew.[86] Documents and papers relating to the prize should be safeguarded and, if practicable, the personal effects of passengers should be saved.[87] Every case of destruction of a captured enemy prize should be reported promptly to higher command.[88]

The destruction of neutral prizes involves similar procedures, but a more serious responsibility.[89]

13.5.2 Attack of Enemy Merchant Vessels. Enemy merchant vessels may be made the

---

[84] 2007 NWP 1-14M ¶8.6.2.1 ("Enemy merchant vessels and civil aircraft may be captured wherever located beyond neutral territory. Prior exercise of visit and search is not required, provided positive determination of enemy status can be made by other means.").

[85] *See, e.g.*, LAUTERPACHT, II OPPENHEIM'S INTERNATIONAL LAW 482 (§192) ("It has already been stated above that the capture of a private enemy vessel has to be confirmed by a Prize Court, and that it is only through its adjudication that the vessel becomes finally appropriated."); Oakes v. United States, 174 U.S. 778, 786-87 (1899) ("By the law of nations, recognized and administered in this country, when movable property in the hands of the enemy, used, or intended to be used, for hostile purposes, is captured by land forces, the title passes to the captors as soon as they have reduced the property to firm possession; but when such property is captured by naval forces, a judicial decree of condemnation is usually necessary to complete the title of the captors.").

[86] 2007 NWP 1-14M ¶8.6.2.1 ("When military circumstances preclude sending or taking in such vessel or aircraft for adjudication as an enemy prize, it may be destroyed after all possible measures are taken to provide for the safety of passengers and crew."); 1955 NWIP 10-2 ¶503b(2) ("Enemy merchant vessels and aircraft which have been captured may, in case of military necessity, be destroyed by the capturing officer when they cannot be sent or escorted in for adjudication. Should the necessity for the destruction of an enemy prize arise, it is the duty of the capturing officer to take all possible measures to provide for the safety of passengers and crew.").

[87] 1955 NWIP 10-2 ¶503b(2) ("All documents and papers relating to an enemy prize should be saved. If practicable, the personal effects of passengers should be saved.").

[88] 1955 NWIP 10-2 ¶503b(2) ("Every case of destruction of an enemy prize should be reported promptly to higher command.").

[89] *Refer to* § 15.15.3 (Destruction of Neutral Prizes).

object of attack, outside neutral territory, if they constitute a military objective.[90]

In particular, enemy merchant vessels may be attacked and destroyed by warships, either with or without prior warning, in any of the following circumstances:[91]

- persistently refusing to stop upon being duly summoned to do so;
- actively resisting visit and search or capture;
- sailing under convoy of enemy warships or enemy military aircraft;
- armed with systems or weapons beyond that required for self-defense against terrorist, piracy, or like threats;
- if incorporated into, or assisting, the enemy's military intelligence system;
- if acting in any capacity as a naval or military auxiliary to an enemy's armed forces; or
- if otherwise integrated into the enemy's war-fighting/war-sustaining effort such that a belligerent warship's compliance with the rules of the 1936 London Protocol would, under the circumstances of the specific encounter, subject the warship to imminent danger or would otherwise preclude mission accomplishment.

The 1936 London Protocol provides that "except in the case of persistent refusal to stop on being duly summoned, or of active resistance to visit or search, a warship, whether surface vessel or submarine, may not sink or render incapable of navigation a merchant vessel without having first placed passengers, crew and ship's papers in a place of safety."[92] Merchant vessels

---

[90] *Refer to* § 5.6 (Military Objectives).

[91] 2007 NWP 1-14M ¶8.6.2.2 ("Accordingly, enemy merchant vessels may be attacked and destroyed by surface warships, either with or without prior warning, in any of the following circumstances: 1. Persistently refusing to stop upon being duly summoned to do so 2. Actively resisting visit and search or capture 3. Sailing under convoy of enemy warships or enemy military aircraft 4. If armed with systems or weapons beyond that required for self-defense against terrorist, piracy, or like threats 5. If incorporated into, or assisting in any way, the intelligence system of the enemy's armed forces 6. If acting in any capacity as a naval or military auxiliary to an enemy's armed forces 7. If integrated into the enemy's war-fighting/war-sustaining effort and compliance with the rules of the 1936 London Protocol would, under the circumstances of the specific encounter, subject the surface warship to imminent danger or would otherwise preclude mission accomplishment."); 1955 NWIP 10-2 ¶503b(3) ("Destruction of Enemy Merchant Vessels Prior to Capture. Enemy merchant vessels may be attacked and destroyed, either with or without prior warning, in any of the following circumstances: 1. Actively resisting visit and search or capture. 2. Refusing to stop upon being duly summoned. 3. Sailing under convoy of enemy warships or enemy military aircraft. 4. If armed, and there is reason to believe that such armament has been used, or is intended for use, offensively against an enemy. 5. If incorporated into, or assisting in any way, the intelligence system of an enemy's armed forces. 6. If acting in any capacity as a naval or military auxiliary to an enemy's armed forces.").

[92] *Procès-Verbal* Relating to the Rules of Submarine Warfare Set Forth in Part IV of the Treaty of London of April 22, 1930, Nov. 6, 1936, 173 LNTS 353, 357. *See* Treaty for the Limitation and Reduction of Naval Armament, art. 22, Apr. 22, 1930, 46 STAT. 2858, 2881-82 ("In particular, except in the case of persistent refusal to stop on being duly summoned, or of active resistance to visit or search, a warship, whether surface vessel or submarine, may not sink or render incapable of navigation a merchant vessel without having first placed passengers, crew and ship's papers in a place of safety. For this purpose the ship's boats are not regarded as a place of safety unless the safety of

in the sense of this rule, however, do not include merchant vessels that constitute military objectives.[93]

13.5.2.1 *Attack of Civilian Passenger Vessels*. If a civilian passenger vessel constitutes a military objective and thus is liable to attack, any attack must comply with other applicable rules related to attacks.[94]

In particular, attacks against civilian passenger vessels engaged in passenger service must comply with the requirement that the expected loss of life or injury to civilians, and damage to civilian objects incidental to the attack, must not be excessive in relation to the concrete and direct military advantage expected to be gained.[95]

13.5.3 Detention of Personnel From Enemy Merchant Vessels. Officers and crews of captured enemy merchant ships may be detained.[96] If detained, such persons are POWs.[97]

Other civilian enemy nationals on board such captured ships as private passengers are subject to the discipline of the captor.[98] If detained, such persons must, at a minimum, be afforded certain fundamental guarantees of humane treatment.[99]

Nationals of a neutral State on board captured enemy merchant vessels should not be detained unless they have participated in acts of hostility or resistance against the captor, or are

---

the passengers and crew is assured, in the existing sea and weather conditions, by the proximity of land, or the presence of another vessel which is in a position to take them on board.").

[93] Wolff Heintschel von Heinegg, *The Law of Armed Conflict at Sea, in* DIETER FLECK, THE HANDBOOK OF HUMANITARIAN LAW IN ARMED CONFLICTS 428-29 (¶1025) (1999) ("The rules laid down in that document formed part of the 1922 Washington Treaty and were reaffirmed by the 1930 London Conference. During that conference a committee of legal experts presented a report in which the matter was clarified as follows: 'The Committee wish to place it on record that the expression 'merchant vessel', where it is employed in the declaration, is not to be understood as including a merchant vessel which is at the moment participating in hostilities in such a manner as to cause her to lose her right to the immunities of a merchant vessel.' Whereas it remains unclear what is meant by 'participating in hostilities' it is obvious that merchant vessels are not in all circumstances protected by the 1936 London Protocol. This was confirmed by the judgment of the Nuremberg Tribunal. Hence, enemy merchant vessels that, by their conduct, qualify as legitimate military objectives are not protected by the 1936 London Protocol and may—as an exceptional measure—be attacked and sunk.").

[94] *Refer to* § 5.4 (Rules on Conducting Assaults, Bombardments, and Other Attacks).

[95] *Refer to* § 5.12 (Proportionality – Prohibition on Attacks Expected to Cause Excessive Incidental Harm).

[96] 2007 NWP 1-14M ¶8.6.2.1 ("Officers and crews of captured enemy merchant ships and civilian aircraft may be detained."); 1955 NWIP 10-2 ¶512 ("The officers and crews of captured enemy merchant vessels and aircraft may be made prisoners of war.").

[97] *Refer to* § 4.16.2 (Merchant or Civil Crews – Detention).

[98] 2007 NWP 1-14M ¶8.6.2.1 ("Other enemy nationals on board such captured ships and aircraft as private passengers are subject to the discipline of the captor."); 1955 NWIP 10-2 ¶512 ("Other enemy nationals on board captured enemy merchant vessels and aircraft as private passengers are subject to the discipline of a captor.").

[99] *Refer to* § 8.1.1 (Overview of Detention Rules in This Manual and the Scope of Chapter VIII).

otherwise in the service of the enemy.[100]

13.6 ENEMY VESSELS EXEMPT FROM CAPTURE OR DESTRUCTION

Certain classes of enemy vessels are exempt from capture or destruction, provided they are innocently and solely employed in the activities that enjoy exempted status.

Exempt vessels may not be used for purposes outside their innocent role while taking advantage of their harmless appearance. Warships may not be disguised as exempt vessels.[101]

13.6.1 Duties of Exempt Vessels. These specially protected vessels must not take part in hostilities or assist the enemy's military effort in any manner.

Such vessels and boats are subject to the regulations of a belligerent naval commander operating in the area.[102] They must not hamper the movement of combatants, must submit to identification and inspection procedures, and may be ordered out of harm's way. Refusal to provide immediate identification upon demand is ordinarily sufficient legal justification for capture or destruction.

13.6.2 Classes of Exempt Vessels. Specifically exempt vessels include: (1) cartel vessels; (2) hospital ships; (3) vessels charged with religious, non-military scientific, or philanthropic missions; (4) vessels granted safe conduct; and (5) small fishing and trade vessels.[103]

13.6.2.1 *Cartel Vessels*. Vessels and aircraft designated for, and engaged in, the exchange of POWs are privileged from capture.[104]

---

[100] 2007 NWP 1-14M ¶8.6.2.1 ("Nationals of a neutral nation on board captured enemy merchant vessels and civilian aircraft should not be detained unless they have participated in acts of hostility or resistance against the captor or are otherwise in the service of the enemy."); 1955 NWIP 10-2 ¶512 ("The nationals of a neutral state on board captured enemy merchant vessels and aircraft as private passengers should not be made prisoners of war."). *Refer to* § 15.6.2 (Forfeiture of Protections of Neutral Status by a Neutral Person).

[101] *Refer to* § 13.13 (Deception by Naval Forces, Including the Use of Enemy or Neutral Flags).

[102] *Refer to* § 13.8 (Belligerent Control of the Immediate Area of Naval Operations).

[103] 1955 NWIP 10-2 ¶503c ("The following enemy vessels and aircraft, when innocently employed, are exempt from destruction or capture: 1. Cartel vessels and aircraft, i.e., vessels and aircraft designated for and engaged in the exchange of prisoners. 2. Properly designated hospital ships, medical transports, and medical aircraft. 3. Vessels charged with religious, scientific, or philanthropic missions. 4. Vessels and aircraft guaranteed safe conduct by prior arrangement between the belligerents. 5. Vessels and aircraft exempt by proclamation, operation plan, order, or other directive. 6. Small costal (not deep-sea) fishing vessels and small boats engaged in local coastal trade and not taking part in hostilities. Such vessels and boats are subject to the regulations of a belligerent naval commander operating in the area.").

[104] *See, e.g.*, The Brig "Betsey", 49 Ct. Cl. 125, 132 (Ct. Cl. 1913) ("What is a cartel in warfare of the nations? An agreement between belligerents for the exchange of prisoners. What is a cartel ship except a vessel of belligerents duly commissioned for the carriage by sea of exchanged prisoners from enemy country to their own country or for the carriage of official communications to and from enemies?"); The Adula, 176 U.S. 361, 379-80 (1900) ("While the mission of the Adula was not an unfriendly one to this Government, she was not a cartel ship, privileged from capture as such, but one employed in a commercial enterprise for the personal profit of the charterer, and only

13.6.2.2 *Hospital Ships That Meet the Requirements of the GWS-Sea*. Hospital ships, including military hospital ships, commissioned civilian hospital ships, and authorized neutral hospital ships, that meet the requirements of the GWS-Sea are exempt from capture.[105] Hospital ships do not forfeit their exempt status if they are armed for self-defense purposes or if they possess or use communications equipment with encryption.

Hospital ships may be armed with defensive weapon systems, including when necessary certain crew-served weapons, as a prudent anti-terrorism/force protection (AT/FP) measure to defend against small boat attacks.[106] The 1949 Geneva Conventions do not directly address weapons systems for hospital ships, but they do expressly provide for the arming of crew members with small arms for the maintenance of order and for the self-defense of the crew or the sick and wounded.[107] The arming of the ship with crew-served weapons for self-defense of the ship is not prohibited and is consistent with the ship's humanitarian purpose and the crew's duty to safeguard the wounded and sick.

The GWS-Sea provides that hospital ships may not use or possess "secret codes" as means of communication; however, state practice has evolved to accept that modern communications systems (*e.g.*, satellite communications and video teleconference systems) and navigational technology (*e.g.*, global positioning systems) require encryption.[108] Such systems must not be used for military purposes or in any way that is harmful to an adversary.[109]

13.6.2.3 *Vessels Charged With Religious, Nonmilitary Scientific, or Philanthropic Missions*. Vessels charged with religious, nonmilitary scientific, or philanthropic missions are exempt from capture.[110] Vessels engaged in the collection of scientific data of potential military application, however, would not be included within this exemption.

13.6.2.4 *Vessels Granted Safe Conduct*. Vessels and aircraft guaranteed safe

---

secondarily, if at all, for the purpose of humanity."); Crawford v. The William Penn., 6 F. Cas. 778, 780-81 (C.C.D.N.J. 1815) ("What is the character of a cartel vessel, and of the persons concerned in her navigation? The flag of truce which she carries, throws over her and them the mantle of peace. She is, pro hac vice, a neutral licensed vessel; and all persons concerned in her navigation, upon the particular service in which both belligerents have employed her, are neutral, in respect to both, and under the protection of both. She cannot carry on commerce under the protection of her flag, because this was not the business for which she was employed, and for which the immunities of that flag were granted to her. She is engaged in a special service, to carry prisoners from one place to another; and, whilst so engaged, she is under the protection of both belligerents, in relation to every act necessarily connected with that service.").

[105] *Refer to* § 7.12.1.1 (Military Hospital Ships); § 7.12.1.2 (Commissioned Civilian Hospital Ships); § 7.12.1.3 (Authorized Neutral Civilian Hospital Ships).

[106] *Refer to* § 7.12.6.2 (Conditions That Do Not Deprive Hospital Ships and Sick-Bays of Vessels of Their Protection).

[107] *Refer to* § 7.12.6.3 (Arming of Hospital Ships and Equipping Them With Defensive Devices).

[108] *Refer to* § 7.12.2.7 (Use of Secret Codes for Communication).

[109] *Refer to* § 7.12.2.2 (No Use for Military Purposes); § 7.10.3.1 (Acts Harmful to the Enemy).

[110] HAGUE XI art. 4 ("Vessels charged with religious, scientific, or philanthropic missions are likewise exempt from capture.").

conduct by prior arrangement between the belligerents are exempt from capture.[111]

13.6.2.5 *Small Coastal Fishing Vessels and Small Boats Engaged in Local Coastal Trade*. Small coastal (not deep-sea) fishing vessels and small boats engaged in local coastal trade are exempt from capture.[112]

13.7 Submarine Warfare

13.7.1 General Principle – Same Rules Applicable to Both Submarine and Surface Warships. Submarine warships must comply with the same law of war rules that apply to surface warships.[113] For example, in their action with regard to merchant ships, submarines must conform to the law of war rules to which surface vessels are subject.[114] In general, submarines must provide for the safety of passengers, crew, and ship's papers before destruction of an enemy merchant vessel.[115] However, the same exceptions to this rule that permit surface ships to attack enemy merchant vessels that are military objectives also permit submarines to conduct such attacks.[116]

13.7.2 Different Application of Law of War Rules in the Context of Submarine Warfare. Although submarines must comply with the same law of war rules as surface ships, a law of war rule may apply differently in the context of submarine warfare because of the different circumstances of submarine warfare as compared to surface warfare.

For example, like surface warships, submarine warships also have an obligation to search

[111] *Refer to* § 12.6.3 (Safe Conduct).

[112] HAGUE XI art. 3 ("Vessels used exclusively for fishing along the coast or small boats employed in local trade are exempt from capture, as well as their appliances, rigging, tackle, and cargo. They cease to be exempt as soon as they take any part whatever in hostilities. The Contracting Powers agree not to take advantage of the harmless character of the said vessels in order to use them for military purposes while preserving their peaceful appearance."); The Paquete Habana, 175 U.S. 677, 708 (1900) ("This review of the precedents and authorities on the subject appears to us abundantly to demonstrate that at the present day, by the general consent of the civilized nations of the world, and independently of any express treaty or other public act, it is an established rule of international law, founded on considerations of humanity to a poor and industrious order of men, and of the mutual convenience of belligerent States, that coast fishing vessels, with their implements and supplies, cargoes and crews, unarmed, and honestly pursuing their peaceful calling of catching and bringing in fresh fish, are exempt from capture as prize of war. The exemption, of course, does not apply to coast fishermen or their vessels, if employed for a warlike purpose, or in such a way as to give aid or information to the enemy; nor when military or naval operations create a necessity to which all private interests must give way. Nor has the exemption been extended to ships or vessels employed on the high sea in taking whales or seals, or cod or other fish which are not brought fresh to market, but are salted or otherwise cured and made a regular article of commerce.").

[113] 2007 NWP 1-14M ¶8.7 ("The law of armed conflict imposes essentially the same rules on submarines as apply to surface warships."); 1997 NWP 9 ¶8.3 (same); 1989 NWP 9 ¶8.3 (same).

[114] Treaty for the Limitation and Reduction of Naval Armament, art. 22, Apr. 22, 1930, 46 STAT. 2858, 2881 ("In their action with regard to merchant ships, submarines must conform to the rules of International Law to which surface vessels are subject."). *Consider Procès-Verbal* Relating to the Rules of Submarine Warfare Set Forth in Part IV of the Treaty of London of April 22, 1930, Nov. 6, 1936, 173 LNTS 353, 357 (same).

[115] *Refer to* § 13.5.1.3 (Destruction of Captured Enemy Merchant Vessels).

[116] *Refer to* § 13.5.2 (Attack of Enemy Merchant Vessels).

for and collect the shipwrecked, wounded, and sick after an engagement.[117] This obligation, however, is subject to certain practical limitations, and the practical limitations faced by submarines may be different than those faced by surface vessels.[118] For example, although a surface warship might be able to take on board survivors after an engagement, a submarine may have limited passenger carrying capabilities. Thus, it may be necessary to rely on other measures (*e.g.*, such as passing the location of possible survivors to a surface ship, aircraft, or shore facility capable of rendering assistance) to comply with the law of war obligation.[119]

13.8 Belligerent Control of the Immediate Area of Naval Operations

13.8.1 Belligerent Right to Establish Special Restrictions in the Immediate Area of Naval Operations. Within the immediate area or vicinity of naval operations, to ensure proper battle space management and self-defense objectives, a belligerent State may establish special restrictions upon the activities of neutral vessels and aircraft, and may prohibit altogether such vessels and aircraft from entering the area.[120]

The immediate area or vicinity of naval operations is that area within which hostilities are taking place, or belligerent State forces are actually operating.[121]

---

[117] *Refer to* § 7.4.1 (GWS-Sea Obligation Regarding the Search, Collection, and Affirmative Protection of the Wounded, Sick, Shipwrecked, and Dead).

[118] *Refer to* § 7.4.4 (Practical Limitations on the Obligation to Search for, Collect, and Take Measures to Protect the Wounded, Sick, and Shipwrecked).

[119] Affidavit subscribed by Chester W. Nimitz, Fleet Admiral, Chief of Naval Operations, U.S. Navy from Joseph L. Broderick, Lieutenant Commander, U.S. Naval Reserve, of the International Law Section, Office of the Judge Advocate General, Navy Department (11 May 1946), *in* XVII TRIAL OF THE MAJOR WAR CRIMINALS BEFORE THE IMT 379-80 ("13. Q: 'Were, by order or on general principles, the U.S. submarines prohibited from carrying out rescue measures toward passengers and crews of ships sunk without warning in those cases where by doing so the safety of their own boat was endangered?' 'A: 'On general principles, the U.S. submarines did not rescue enemy survivors if undue additional hazard to the submarine resulted or the submarine would thereby be prevented from accomplishing its further mission. U.S. submarines were limited in rescue measures by small passenger-carrying facilities combined with the known desperate and suicidal character of the enemy. Therefore, it was unsafe to pick up many survivors. Frequently survivors were given rubber boats and/or provisions. Almost invariably survivors did not come aboard the submarine voluntarily, and it was necessary to take them prisoner by force.'").

[120] 2007 NWP 1-14M ¶7.8 ("Within the immediate area or vicinity of naval operations, to ensure proper battle space management and self-defense objectives, a belligerent may establish special restrictions upon the activities of neutral vessels and aircraft and may prohibit altogether such vessels and aircraft from entering the area."); 1955 NWIP ¶430b ("Within the immediate area or vicinity of naval operations, a belligerent may establish special restrictions (see, for example, paragraph 520a) upon the activities of neutral vessels and aircraft and may prohibit altogether such vessels and aircraft from entering the area."); 2006 AUSTRALIAN MANUAL ¶6.16 ("Within the immediate area or vicinity of naval operations, a belligerent may establish special restrictions upon the activities of neutral vessels and aircraft and may prohibit altogether such vessels and aircraft from entering the area."); 2004 UK MANUAL ¶13.80 ("Nothing in paragraphs 13.65 to 13.79 [on blockades and security zones] should be deemed to derogate from the customary belligerent right to control neutral vessels and aircraft in the immediate vicinity of naval operations.").

[121] 2007 NWP 1-14M ¶7.8 ("The immediate area or vicinity of naval operations is that area within which hostilities are taking place or belligerent forces are actually operating."); 1997 NWP 9 ¶7.8 (same); 1989 NWP 9 ¶7.8 (substantially similar); TUCKER, THE LAW OF WAR AND NEUTRALITY AT SEA 300 ("It should be emphasized, though,

Belligerent State control over neutral vessels and aircraft within the immediate area of naval operations is based upon a belligerent State's right to ensure the security of its forces and its right to conduct hostilities without interference from neutrals.[122]

A belligerent State may not purport to deny access to neutral States, or to close an international strait to neutral shipping, pursuant to this authority unless another route of similar convenience remains open to neutral traffic.[123]

13.8.2 <u>Belligerent Right to Control Communication of Neutral Merchant Vessels or Aircraft at Sea</u>. A belligerent warship may exercise control over the communications of any neutral merchant vessel or civil aircraft whose presence in the immediate vicinity of naval operations might otherwise endanger or jeopardize those operations.[124]

A neutral merchant ship or civil aircraft within that area that fails to conform to a belligerent warship's directions concerning communications may thereby assume enemy character and risk being fired upon or captured.[125] Any transmission to an opposing belligerent State of information concerning military operations or military forces is inconsistent with the neutral State's duties of abstention and impartiality, and renders the neutral State's vessel or aircraft making such a communication liable to capture or destruction.[126]

---

that the immediate area of naval operations refers to an area within which naval hostilities are taking place or within which belligerent forces are actually operating.").

[122] TUCKER, THE LAW OF WAR AND NEUTRALITY AT SEA 301 ("The claim to control neutral vessels and aircraft within the immediate vicinity of operating forces is essentially a limited and transient one and is based not only upon the right of a belligerent to insure the security of his forces but upon the right to attack and to defend himself without interference from neutrals.").

[123] 2007 NWP 1-14M ¶7.8 ("A belligerent may not, however, purport to deny access to neutral nations, or to close an international strait to neutral shipping, pursuant to this authority unless another route of similar convenience remains open to neutral traffic."); 1997 NWP 9 ¶7.8 (same); 1989 NWP 9 ¶7.8 (same). *Compare* § 13.10.2.5 (Limitations on the Scope of the Blockade).

[124] 2007 NWP 1-14M ¶7.8 ("The commanding officer of a belligerent warship may exercise control over the communication of any neutral merchant vessel or civil aircraft whose presence in the immediate area of naval operations might otherwise endanger or jeopardize those operations."); 1955 NWIP 10-2 ¶520a ("Within the immediate vicinity of his forces, a belligerent commanding officer may exercise control over the communications of any neutral merchant vessel or aircraft whose presence might otherwise endanger the success of the operations."); 2006 AUSTRALIAN MANUAL ¶6.17 ("Within the immediate area or vicinity of naval operations, a commanding officer of a belligerent warship may exercise control over the communications of any neutral merchant vessel or aircraft whose presence might otherwise endanger the success of the belligerent operation.").

[125] 2007 NWP 1-14M ¶7.8 ("A neutral merchant ship or civil aircraft within that area that fails to conform to a belligerent's directions concerning communications may thereby assume enemy character and risk being fired upon or captured."); 1955 NWIP 10-2 ¶430b ("Neutral vessels and aircraft which fail to comply with a belligerent's orders expose themselves to the risk of being fired upon. Such vessels and aircraft are also liable to capture (see subparagraph 503d7).").

[126] 2007 NWP 1-14M ¶7.8 ("Any transmission to an opposing belligerent of information concerning military operations or military forces is inconsistent with the neutral duties of abstention and impartiality and renders the neutral vessel or aircraft liable to capture or destruction."). *Consider* Commission of Jurists to Consider and Report Upon the Revision of the Rules of Warfare, *General Report, Part I: Rules for the Control of Radio in Time of War*, art. 6, Feb. 19, 1923, *reprinted in* 32 AJIL SUPPLEMENT: OFFICIAL DOCUMENTS 2, 7-8 (1938) ("1. The transmission by radio by a vessel or an aircraft, whether enemy or neutral, when on or over the high seas of military intelligence

Legitimate distress communications should be permitted to the extent that the success of the operation is not prejudiced thereby.[127]

13.9 Maritime and Airspace Zones: Exclusion, War, Operational, Warning, and Safety

Belligerent States may establish various maritime and airspace zones during armed conflict. The legal rules that apply to the establishment and enforcement of a zone may depend on the function of the zone and, in particular, whether additional belligerent rights are asserted as a consequence of vessels entering the zone.

Neutral or non-belligerent States have established such zones.[128]

13.9.1 Authority to Establish Zones. The authority necessary to establish a zone may depend on the location of the zone and the belligerent rights that are asserted as a consequence of vessels entering the zone.

The establishment of a zone in a State's waters may rely on its sovereignty over those waters.[129] Similarly, the establishment of a zone in a State's airspace may rely on its sovereignty over that airspace.[130] The right of a belligerent State to establish a zone outside its territory may rely on the belligerent State's: (1) right to interdict contraband; (2) right to control the immediate area of operations; or (3) right of blockade.[131]

Exclusion zones may also be established in accordance with an appropriate resolution adopted by the U.N. Security Council.

13.9.2 Use of Zones to Warn Vessels or Aircraft – War, Operational, Warning, and

---

for the immediate use of a belligerent is to be deemed a hostile act and will render the vessel or aircraft liable to be fired upon. 2. A neutral vessel or neutral aircraft which transmits when on or over the high seas information destined for a belligerent concerning military operations or military forces shall be liable to capture. The prize court may condemn the vessel or aircraft if it considers that the circumstances justify condemnation.").

[127] 2007 NWP 1-14M ¶7.8 ("Legitimate distress communications should be permitted to the extent that the success of the operation is not prejudiced thereby."); 1955 NWIP 10-2 ¶520a ("Legitimate distress communications by neutral vessels and aircraft should be permitted if they do not prejudice the success of such operations.").

[128] *For example*, The Nyon Arrangement Between the United Kingdom of Great Britain and Northern Ireland, Bulgaria, Egypt, France, Greece, Roumania, Turkey, the Union of Soviet Socialist Republics and Yugoslavia, Sept.14, 1937, 181 LNTS 135.

[129] *Refer to* § 13.2.2 (National Waters). *For example*, L.F.E. Goldie, *Maritime War Zones & Exclusion Zones*, 64 U.S. Naval War College International Law Studies 156, 189-90 (1991) ("At this point it may be noted in passing that 'Operation Market Time,' which was enforced by the United States Navy during the Vietnamese War was legally valid since it was a law-enforcement operation limited to a distance of twelve miles from the low water mark of South Vietnam (it did not extend north beyond the DMZ) and so within the domestic competence of South Vietnam, which legislated to empower the activity. Since that operation was conducted entirely within the territorial sea and contiguous zone of South Vietnam, it does not come within the perspective of the present paper.").

[130] *Refer to* § 14.2.1.1 (National Airspace).

[131] *Refer to* 15.12 (Neutral Commerce and Carriage of Contraband); § 13.8 (Belligerent Control of the Immediate Area of Naval Operations); § 13.10 (Blockade).

Safety Zones. A zone may be issued to advise vessels or aircraft to remain clear of an area of naval operations. Such a zone may also provide procedures to reduce the risk of neutral vessels being mistakenly attacked.[132]

Such zones have been used: (1) to identify a particularly dangerous operational area;[133] (2) to assist in the defense of a particular area;[134] or (3) to assist in the defense of particular naval forces (*i.e.*, a defensive bubble).[135]

The establishment of such a zone does not relieve the proclaiming belligerent State of its obligation under the law of war to refrain from attacking vessels and aircraft that do not constitute military objectives. Thus, a vessel or aircraft that is otherwise protected does not forfeit its protection from being made the object of attack simply by entering a zone of the ocean

---

[132] *For example*, HYDROLANT 597/03 (54,56) EASTERN MEDITERRANEAN SEA (202135Z MAR 2003), *reprinted in* 2007 NWP 1-14M, Appendix A ("2. ALL VESSELS SHOULD MAINTAIN A SAFE DISTANCE FROM U.S. FORCES SO THAT INTENTIONS ARE CLEAR AND UNDERSTOOD BY U.S. FORCES. VESSELS THAT ENTER THE MARITIME SAFETY ZONE WHICH ARE APPROACHING U.S. FORCES, OR VESSELS WHOSE INTENTIONS ARE UNCLEAR ARE SUBJECT TO BOARDING AND VISIT BY U.S. FORCES. ALL VESSELS APPROACHING U.S. FORCES ARE REQUESTED TO MAINTAIN RADIO CONTACT WITH U.S. FORCES ON BRIDGE-TO-BRIDGE CHANNEL 16. 3. U.S. FORCES WILL EXERCISE APPROPRIATE MEASURES IN SELF-DEFENSE IF WARRANTED BY THE CIRCUMSTANCES. VESSELS APPROACHING U.S. FORCES WILL HELP MAKE THEIR INTENTIONS CLEAR AND AVOID UNNECESSARY INITIATION OF SUCH DEFENSIVE MEASURES BY MAKING PRIOR CONTACT AS DESCRIBED ABOVE.").

[133] *For example*, HYDROLANT 597/03 (54,56) EASTERN MEDITERRANEAN SEA (202135Z MAR 2003), *reprinted in* 2007 NWP 1-14M, Appendix A ("U.S. FORCES IN THE EASTERN MEDITERRANEAN HAVE ESTABLISHED A MARITIME SAFETY ZONE AND ARE CONDUCTING COMBAT OPERATIONS IN INTERNATIONAL WATERS THAT POSE A HAZARD TO NAVIGATION. ALL VESSELS ARE ADVISED TO EXERCISE EXTREME CAUTION AND TO REMAIN CLEAR OF THE FOLLOWING DESIGNATED OPERATION AREA BOUND BY 32-28.0N 033-22.0E, 31-40.0N 033-22.0E, 31-55.0N 032-20.0E, 32-46.8N 032-20.0E.").

[134] *For example*, Woodrow Wilson, Executive Order Establishing Defensive Sea Areas, No. 2584, Apr. 5, 1917, *reprinted in* 12 AJIL SUPPLEMENT: OFFICIAL DOCUMENTS 13, 16 (1918) ("I, WOODROW WILSON, President of the United States of America, do order that defensive sea areas are hereby established, to be maintained until further notification, at the places and within the limits prescribed as follows, … The responsibility of the United States of America for any damage inflicted by force of arms with the object of detaining any person or vessel proceeding in contravention to Regulations duly promulgated in accordance with this Executive order shall cease from this date.").

[135] *For example*, A.D. Parsons, *Letter Dated 24 April 1982 from the Permanent Representative of the United Kingdom of Great Britain and Northern Ireland to the United Nations Addressed to the President of the Security Council*, U.N. Doc. S/14997 ("Further to Mr. Whyte's letter dated 9 April 1982 (S/14963), I have the honour, on instructions from my Government, to inform you that the following communication was conveyed to the Government of Argentina on 23 April 1982: In announcing the establishment of a maritime exclusion zone around the Falkland Islands, Her Majesty's Government made it clear that this measure was without prejudice to the right of the United Kingdom to take whatever additional measures may be needed in the exercise of its right of self-defence under Article 51 of the United Nations Charter. In this connection, Her Majesty's Government now wishes to make clear that any approach on the part of Argentine warships, including submarines, naval auxiliaries, or military aircraft which could amount to a threat to interfere with the mission of the British forces in the South Atlantic, will encounter the appropriate response. All Argentine aircraft including civil aircraft engaging in surveillance of these British forces will be regarded as hostile and are liable to be dealt with accordingly.").

on the high seas established by a belligerent State.[136]

In some cases, however, the fact that a vessel or aircraft enters a zone without authorization may be probative in assessing whether it is entitled to protection (*e.g.*, whether it is an enemy military vessel or aircraft, or whether it has acquired the character of enemy military vessels or aircraft).[137] For example, the notification of the zone in advance may mean that most neutral or protected vessels and aircraft have departed the area. Similarly, the entry into the zone of an unidentified vessel without authorization may be probative of whether the vessel constitutes a military objective.

13.9.3 Use of Zones to Counter Enemy Logistics. Zones may be used to assist in the implementation of the belligerent's strategy to counter the adversary's logistics.[138] For example, zones may be established to facilitate the interdiction of contraband.[139] As a case in point, a zone may be established to warn neutral vessels and aircraft that they will be subject to visit and search if they attempt to enter the zone without authorization.

Zones may not be employed for the purpose of starving the civilian population.[140] Such zones must not impose an unreasonable burden on neutral commerce in free goods.[141]

---

[136] John H. McNeil, *Neutral Rights and Maritime Sanctions: The Effects of Two Gulf Wars*, 31 VIRGINIA JOURNAL OF INTERNATIONAL LAW 631, 635-36 (1991) ("Iraq replied to these Iranian declarations by proclaiming a series of escalating exclusion zones, beginning with a 'prohibited war zone;' Iraq declared that it would 'attack all vessels' appearing within these zones, and stated that 'all tankers, regardless of nationality, docking at Kharg Island are targets for the Iraqi Air Force." As noted earlier, Iraq launched the Tanker War in 1984 in an apparent bid to internationalize the war. During the first months of this new offensive, some seventy ships were hit, many of which were neutral-flag tankers bound to or from the massive Iranian oil terminal at Kharg Island. But international law has never legitimized attacks upon neutral merchant vessels simply because they ventured into a specified area of the high seas.").

[137] *Refer to* § 15.14.2.1 (Acquiring the Character of an Enemy Warship or Military Aircraft).

[138] *For example*, L.F.E. Goldie, *Maritime War Zones & Exclusion Zones*, 64 U.S. NAVAL WAR COLLEGE INTERNATIONAL LAW STUDIES 156, 185-86 (1991) ("*(a) The Exclusion Zone of the Skaggerak* The Skaggerak is an arm of the North Sea on its eastern side and lies between Denmark and Norway. It is some 150 nautical miles in length and 85 miles in width. … The argument vindicating the British proclamation of the Skaggerak as a maritime exclusion zone under emerging customary international law may be accepted, since the strategy for enforcing the exclusion of the adversary from the zone was an apparently successful one. It was a persisting logistical strategy enforced by both aircraft and submarines providing an adequate ratio of force to space. This proposition can be analyzed out into the following elements. (i) The zone was reasonable in area, and despite German surface naval power, the logistical strategy was persistently maintained and was made effective through submarine and aerial warfare; (ii) The object, while not primarily one of self-defense, was for the related purposes of: … (b) encumbering Germany's reinforcements and supplies destined for its oppressive occupation of Norway—a victim of Nazi aggression; (c) the target shipping had military objectives and purposes and could not be viewed as carrying supplies which had the object of benefitting the civilian population of Norway;").

[139] *Refer to* § 15.12 (Neutral Commerce and Carriage of Contraband).

[140] *Refer to* § 5.20 (Starvation).

[141] *See* 2007 NWP 1-14M ¶7.9 ("To the extent that such zones serve to warn neutral vessels and aircraft away from belligerent activities and thereby reduce their exposure to collateral damage and incidental injury (see paragraph 8.3.1), and to the extent that they do not unreasonably interfere with legitimate neutral commerce, they are undoubtedly lawful.").

13.9.4 Use of Zones to Prevent Movement – Exclusion Zones. Belligerents may establish exclusion zones that prohibit the entry of vessels or aircraft without authorization from that belligerent.[142] Such zones may suspend the right of innocent passage through non-neutral waters.[143]

The extent, location, and duration of the exclusion zone and the measures imposed should not exceed what is required by military necessity.[144]

Belligerents establishing such zones must provide safe passage through the zone for neutral vessels and aircraft where the geographical extent of the zone significantly impedes free and safe access to the ports and coasts of a neutral State and, unless military requirements do not permit, in other cases where normal navigation routes are affected.[145]

13.9.5 Procedures for Declaring a Zone. As a matter of practice, maritime and/or aerial warnings (*e.g.*, HYDROLANT, HYDROPAC, Notice to Airmen (NOTAM)) would ordinarily be promulgated as part of the establishment of a maritime or airspace zone.

---

[142] *For example*, 2004 UK MANUAL ¶12.58 footnote 76 ("During the Falklands conflict 1982, a total exclusion zone of 200 nautical miles was established around the Islands. It applied, *inter alia,* to any aircraft, military or civil, operating in support of the illegal occupation by the Argentine forces, and any aircraft (military or civil) found within the zone without authority from the Ministry of Defence would be regarded as operating in support of the illegal occupation and thus hostile and liable to be attacked by the British forces.").

[143] *For example*, HYDROPAC 795/2004 (62) PERSIAN GULF (030850Z MAY 2004), *reprinted in* 2007 NWP 1-14M, Appendix C ("8. ADDITIONALLY, EFFECTIVE IMMEDIATELY, EXCLUSION ZONES ARE ESTABLISHED AND THE RIGHT OF INNOCENT PASSAGE IS TEMPORARILY SUSPENDED IN ACCORDANCE WITH INTERNATIONAL LAW AROUND THE KAAOT AND ABOT OIL TERMINALS WITHIN IRAQI TERRITORIAL WATERS. THE EXCLUSION ZONES EXTEND 2000 METERS FROM THE OUTER EDGES OF THE TERMINAL STRUCTURES IN ALL DIRECTIONS. 9. ONLY TANKERS AND SUPPORT VESSELS AUTHORIZED BY TERMINAL OPERATORS OR COALITION MARITIME SECURITY FORCES ARE ALLOWED TO ENTER THE EXCLUSION ZONES. VESSELS ATTEMPTING TO ENTER THE ZONES WITHOUT AUTHORIZATION MAY BE SUBJECT TO DEFENSIVE MEASURES, INCLUDING WHEN NECESSARY, THE USE OF DEADLY FORCE. ALL REASONABLE EFFORTS WILL BE TAKEN TO WARN VESSELS AWAY BEFORE EMPLOYING DEADLY FORCE. HOWEVER, DEADLY FORCE WILL BE EMPLOYED WHEN NECESSARY TO PROTECT COALITION MARITIME SECURITY FORCES, LEGITIMATE SHIPPING PRESENT IN THE EXCLUSION ZONES AND THE OIL TERMINALS.").

[144] *For example*, Wolff Heintschel von Heinegg, *The Law of Armed Conflict at Sea*, *in* DIETER FLECK, THE HANDBOOK OF HUMANITARIAN LAW IN ARMED CONFLICTS 467 (¶1049) ("On 28 April 1982 Great Britain proclaimed a 'Total Exclusion Zone' (TEZ) in the South Atlantic. Beside deterring the Argentine naval forces from leaving their ports, its main purpose was to facilitate the early identification of military objectives and to prevent vessels flying neutral flags from conveying information to Argentina. … On one hand, the British TEZ covered an area of 200 nautical miles measured from the centre of the main island. On the other hand, the TEZ was situated far from any main shipping lanes. Moreover, its duration was comparatively short. It did not serve economic warfare purposes but was aimed at facilitating military operations, including identification. Vessels and aircraft flying flags of states not parties to the conflict suffered no damage whatsoever. For these reasons, only the former USSR officially protested against the British TEZ.").

[145] 2007 NWP 1-14M ¶7.9 ("Belligerents creating such zones must provide safe passage through the zone for neutral vessels and aircraft where the geographical extent of the zone significantly impedes free and safe access to the ports and coasts of a neutral state and, unless military requirements do not permit, in other cases where normal navigation routes are affected.").

13.10 Blockade

A blockade is an operation by a belligerent State to prevent vessels and/or aircraft of all States, enemy as well as neutral, from entering or exiting specified ports, airfields, or coastal areas belonging to, occupied by, or under the control of an enemy belligerent State.[146]

13.10.1 Purpose of Blockade and Belligerent Rights Associated With Blockade. The purpose of a blockade is to deprive the adversary of supplies needed to conduct hostilities.[147]

A blockade enables the blockading State to control traffic in the blockaded area. A blockade also enables the blockading State to take measures on the high seas to deny supplies to a blockaded area.[148] For example, a blockading State has the right to visit and search vessels on the high seas to enforce its blockade.[149]

13.10.2 Criteria for Blockades. In order to be binding, a blockade must meet certain criteria.

13.10.2.1 *Authority for the Establishment of a Blockade*. A blockade must be established by proper legal authority. The establishment of a blockade has been accomplished by a declaration of the belligerent State, or by the commander of the blockading force acting on behalf of the belligerent State.[150]

The U.N. Security Council is also expressly given the authority by the Charter of the United Nations to authorize blockades.[151] A blockade of the ports or coasts of a State is generally regarded as a measure involving force against that State for the purposes of the Charter

---

[146] 2007 NWP 1-14M ¶7.7.1 ("Blockade is a belligerent operation to prevent vessels and/or aircraft of all nations, enemy as well as neutral, from entering or exiting specified ports, airfields, or coastal areas belonging to, occupied by, or under the control of an enemy nation."); 1997 NWP 9 ¶7.7.1 (same); 1989 NWP 9 ¶7.7.1 (same); 1955 NWIP 10-2 ¶632a ("A blockade is a belligerent operation intended to prevent vessels of all States from entering or leaving specified coastal areas which are under the sovereignty, under the occupation, or under the control of an enemy.").

[147] ICRC AP COMMENTARY 654 (¶2095) ("It should be emphasized that the object of a blockade is to deprive the adversary of supplies needed to conduct hostilities, and not to starve civilians.").

[148] John Reese Stevenson, Legal Adviser, Department of State, Letter dated June 6, 1972, *reprinted in* Steven C. Nelson, *Contemporary Practice of the United States Relating to International Law*, 66 AJIL 836, 837 (1972) ("To have declared a blockade could have implied, under traditional international law, a whole range of actions which would have extended the area of hostilities and risked grave dangers of widening the conflict. The traditional law of blockade requires a formal declaration of the establishment of the blockade and notification of it to all states. A blockade must be 'effective' in preventing all ingress or egress—including commercial trade and activities—from or to the enemy's coast. The blockading state would have the right to stop vessels of any nation anywhere on the high seas, to inspect and search such vessels, to seize them if they are bound to or from the blockaded ports, and eventually to condemn them and their cargos in a prize court. Ships attempting to violate the blockade could be taken under fire should they fail to stop on order.").

[149] *Refer to* § 15.13.1 (Purposes of Visit and Search).

[150] *Consider* DECLARATION OF LONDON art. 9 (1909) ("A declaration of a blockade is made either by the blockading Power or by the naval authorities acting in its name.").

[151] *Refer to* § 1.11.4.2 (Use of Force Authorized by the U.N. Security Council Acting Under Chapter VII of the Charter of the United Nations).

of the United Nations.[152]

13.10.2.2 <u>Notification of the Blockade</u>. It is customary for the belligerent State establishing the blockade to notify all affected States of its imposition.[153] The commander of the blockading forces will usually also notify local authorities in the blockaded area.[154]

Notification should include, as a minimum, the date the blockade is to begin, its geographic limits, and the grace period granted neutral vessels and aircraft to leave the area to be blockaded.[155]

The form of the notification is not material so long as it is effective, and a variety of methods may be used.[156]

---

[152] *See, e.g.*, *Legal and Practical Consequences of a Blockade of Cuba*, Oct. 19, 1962, 1 SUPPLEMENTAL OPINIONS OF THE OFFICE OF LEGAL COUNSEL 486, 490 (2013) ("The legality today of a blockade unilaterally imposed by one state upon another depends upon its compatibility with the language and principles of the Charter. Ordinarily it, like other measures involving force, is reserved to the United Nations or to regional organizations such as the OAS. If imposed unilaterally without prior approval it must be considered a reasonable measure under the circumstances, proportional to the threat posed, and limited to a legitimate purpose. It does not become more or less lawful on the basis of declaration of war or a failure to declare war."); *Definition of Aggression*, arts. 1, 3, Annex to U.N. GENERAL ASSEMBLY RESOLUTION 3314 (XXIX), *Definition of Aggression*, U.N. Doc. A/RES/3314 (XXIX) (Dec. 14, 1974) ("Aggression is the use of armed force by a State against the sovereignty, territorial integrity or political independence of another State, or in any other manner inconsistent with the Charter of the United Nations, as set out in this Definition. … Any of the following acts, regardless of a declaration of war, shall, subject to and in accordance with the provisions of article 2, qualify as an act of aggression: ... (c) The blockade of the ports or coasts of a State by the armed forces of another State.").

[153] 2007 NWP 1-14M ¶7.7.2.2 ("It is customary for the belligerent nation establishing the blockade to notify all affected nations of its imposition."); 1955 NWIP 10-2 ¶632b ("It is customary for the blockade to be notified in a suitable manner to the governments of all States."). *Consider* 1909 DECLARATION OF LONDON art. 11 ("A declaration of blockade is notified– (1) to neutral Powers, by the blockading Power, by means of a communication addressed to the Governments direct, or to their representatives accredited to it.").

[154] 2007 NWP 1-14M ¶7.7.2.2 ("The commander of the blockading forces will usually also notify local authorities in the blockaded area."); 1955 NWIP 10-2 ¶632b ("The commander of the blockading force usually makes notification to local authorities in the blockaded area."). *Consider* 1909 DECLARATION OF LONDON art. 11 ("A declaration of blockade is notified– … (2) to the local authorities, by the officer commanding the blockading force. The local authorities will, in turn, inform the foreign consular officers at the port or on the coastline under blockade as soon as possible.").

[155] 2007 NWP 1-14M ¶7.7.2.1 ("The declaration should include, as a minimum, the date the blockade is to begin, its geographic limits, and the grace period granted neutral vessels and aircraft to leave the area to be blockaded."); 1955 NWIP 10-2 ¶632b ("The declaration should include the date the blockade begins, the geographical limits of the blockade, and the period granted neutral vessels and aircraft to leave the blockaded area."). *Consider* 1909 DECLARATION OF LONDON art. 9 ("A declaration of blockade is made either by the blockading Power or by the naval authorities acting in its name. It specifies– (1) The date when the blockade begins; (2) The geographical limits of the coastline under blockade; (3) The period within which neutral vessels may come out.").

[156] *For example*, The Public Commission to Examine the Maritime Incident of 31 May 2010, *et. al* (The Turkel Commission), Report: Part one, 162-63 (¶58) (Jan. 2010) ("In the case at hand, the State of Israel took the following steps in order to give notice of the naval blockade: from the testimony of the Military Advocate-General, Major-General Avichai Mendelblit, it can be seen that the Military Advocate-General's Office asked the Ministry of Transport to transmit information regarding the imposition of the naval blockade by all methods at its disposal, in order to ensure that the notice would reach all vessels in the Mediterranean Sea. This was also done. The notice was also published on the Internet sites of the IDF, the Shipping Authority, the Military Advocate-General, and the

The notification of the blockade may establish a presumption of knowledge of the blockade that is required in the offense of breach or attempted breach of a blockade.[157]

13.10.2.3 *Effectiveness of the Blockade*. In order to be binding, a blockade must be effective.[158] This requirement of effectiveness is intended to prevent "paper" blockades.[159]

The requirement of effectiveness means that the blockade must be maintained by forces that are sufficient to render ingress or egress of the blockaded area dangerous.[160] The requirement of effectiveness does not preclude temporary absence of the blockading force, if such absence is due to stress of weather or to some other reason connected with the blockade (*e.g.*, pursuit of a blockade runner).[161]

The forces that are necessary to make a blockade effective depend on the specific military

---

Ministry of Transport, and, as noted above, via several international channels. The announcement was also transmitted twice a day via the emergency channel for maritime communication to all ships within a distance of up to 300 kilometers from the Israeli coast. In addition, notices were also sent to the flag States and the States that Israel knew intended to send ships to the area. These steps clearly satisfy the requirement of 'notice.'").

[157] *Refer to* § 13.10.4.2 (Knowledge of the Existence of Blockade).

[158] *Consider* 1909 DECLARATION OF LONDON art. 2 ("In accordance with the Declaration of Paris of 1856, a blockade, in order to be binding must be effective – that is to say, it must be maintained by a force sufficient really to prevent access to the enemy coastline."); Declaration respecting maritime law signed by the Plenipotentiaries of Great Britain, Austria, France, Prussia, Russia, Sardinia, and Turkey, assembled in Congress at Paris, Apr. 16, 1856, *reprinted in* 1 AJIL SUPPLEMENT: OFFICIAL DOCUMENTS 89 (1907) ("4. Blockades, in order to be binding, must be effective, that is to say, maintained by a force sufficient really to prevent access to the coast of the enemy.").

[159] The Peterhoff, 72 U.S. 28, 50 (1867) ("It must be premised that no paper or constructive blockade is allowed by international law. When such blockades have been attempted by other nations, the United States have ever protested against them and denied their validity. Their illegality is now confessed on all hands. It was solemnly proclaimed in the Declaration of Paris of 1856, to which most of the civilized nations of the world have since adhered; and this principle is nowhere more fully recognized than in our own country, though not a party to that declaration."); The Olinde Rodrigues, 174 U.S. 510, 513-14 (1899) ("The fourth maxim of the Declaration of Paris (April 16, 1856) was: 'Blockades, in order to be binding, must be effective, that is to say, maintained by a force sufficient really to prevent access to the coast of the enemy.' Manifestly this broad definition was not intended to be literally applied. The object was to correct the abuse, in the early part of the century, of paper blockades, where extensive coasts were put under blockade by proclamation, without the presence of any force, or an inadequate force; and the question of what might be sufficient force was necessarily left to be determined according to the particular circumstances.").

[160] *See* 2007 NWP 1-14M ¶7.7.2.3 ("To be valid, a blockade must be effective—that is, it must be maintained by a surface, air, or subsurface force or other legitimate methods and means of warfare that is sufficient to render ingress or egress of the blockaded area dangerous."); 1955 NWIP 10-2 ¶632d ("A blockade, in order to be binding, must be effective. This means that a blockade must be maintained by a force sufficient to render ingress and egress to or from the blockaded area dangerous."); The Olinde Rodrigues, 174 U.S. 510, 515 (1899) ("Such is the settled doctrine of the English and American courts and publicists, and it is embodied in the second of the instructions issued by the Secretary of the Navy, June 20, 1898, General Order No. 492: 'A blockade to be effective and binding must be maintained by a force sufficient to render ingress to or egress from the port dangerous.'").

[161] 2007 NWP 1-14M ¶7.7.2.3 ("The requirement of effectiveness does not preclude temporary absence of the blockading force, if such absence is due to stress of weather or to some other reason connected with the blockade (e.g., pursuit of a blockade runner)."). *Consider* 1909 DECLARATION OF LONDON art. 4 ("A blockade is not regarded as raised if the blockading force is temporarily withdrawn on account of stress of weather.").

circumstances.[162] The blockade may be maintained by forces that are some distance from the shore.[163]

13.10.2.4 *Impartial Application of the Blockade*. A blockade must be applied impartially to the vessels and aircraft of all States.[164] The requirement that a belligerent must apply a blockade impartially to the vessels and aircraft of all States is intended to prevent measures of discrimination by the blockading belligerent in favor of or against the vessels and aircraft of particular States, including its own or allied vessels and aircraft.[165]

13.10.2.5 *Limitations on the Scope of the Blockade*. A blockade must not bar access to, or departure from, neutral ports and coasts.[166]

A blockade may not be used for the purpose of starving the civilian population, and the expected incidental harm to the civilian population may not be excessive in relation to the expected military advantage to be gained from employing the blockade.[167]

13.10.3 Special Entry and Exit Authorization. In certain cases, vessels or aircraft may enter or exit a blockaded area.

13.10.3.1 *Neutral Warships and Military Aircraft*. Although neutral warships and military aircraft enjoy no positive right of access to blockaded areas, the belligerent State imposing the blockade may authorize their entry and exit. Such special authorization may be made subject to such conditions as the blockading force considers necessary and expedient.[168]

---

[162] *See* The Olinde Rodrigues, 174 U.S. 510, 516-18 (1899) ("As we hold that an effective blockade is a blockade so effective as to make it dangerous in fact for vessels to attempt to enter the blockaded port, it follows that the question of effectiveness is not controlled by the number of the blockading force. In other words, the position cannot be maintained that one modern cruiser though sufficient in fact is not sufficient as matter of law. … The question of effectiveness must necessarily depend on the circumstances. We agree that the fact of a single capture is not decisive of the effectiveness of a blockade, but the case made on this record does not rest on that ground. We are of opinion that if a single modern cruiser blockading a port renders it in fact dangerous for other craft to enter the port, that is sufficient, since thereby the blockade is made practically effective.").

[163] 2013 GERMAN MANUAL ¶1062 ("A blockade, in order to be binding, must be **effective** (**25** Principle 4). It must be maintained by armed forces sufficient to prevent access to the blockaded coast. **Long distance blockades** are also permissible, i.e. the blockade and control of an enemy coast by armed forces at a greater distance from the blockaded coast as a result of military requirements."); 2004 UK MANUAL ¶13.68 ("The force maintaining the blockade may be stationed at a distance determined by military requirements.").

[164] 1955 NWIP 10-2 ¶632f ("A blockade must be applied equally (impartially) to the vessels and aircraft of all states."). *Consider* 1909 DECLARATION OF LONDON art. 5 ("A blockade must be applied impartially to the ships of all nations.").

[165] 1955 NWIP 10-2 ¶632f note 35 ("The requirement that a belligerent must apply a blockade impartially to the vessels and aircraft of all states is intended to prevent measures of discrimination by the blockading belligerent in favor of or against the vessels and aircraft of particular states, including its own or allied vessels and aircraft.").

[166] 1955 NWIP 10-2 ¶632e ("A blockade must not bar access or departure from neutral ports or coasts."). *Consider* 1909 DECLARATION OF LONDON art. 18 ("The blockading forces must not bar access to neutral ports or coasts.").

[167] *Refer to* § 5.20 (Starvation).

[168] *See* 2007 NWP 1-14M ¶7.7.3 ("Although neutral warships and military aircraft enjoy no positive right of access to blockaded areas, the belligerent imposing the blockade may authorize their entry and exit. Such special

13.10.3.2 *Neutral Vessels and Aircraft in Evident Distress*. Neutral vessels and aircraft in evident distress should be authorized entry into a blockaded area, and subsequently authorized to depart, under conditions prescribed by the officer in command of the blockading force or responsible for maintenance of the blockading instrumentality (*e.g.*, mines).[169]

13.10.3.3 *Passage of Relief Consignments Under the GC*. Similarly, neutral vessels and aircraft engaged in the carriage of qualifying relief supplies for the civilian population and the sick and wounded should be authorized to pass through the blockade cordon, subject to the right of the blockading force to prescribe the technical arrangements, including search, under which passage is permitted.[170]

13.10.4 Breach and Attempted Breach of Blockade. Breach or attempted breach of a blockade subjects a neutral vessel or aircraft to capture.[171]

13.10.4.1 *Acts of Breach or Attempted Breach of Blockade*. Breach of blockade is the passage of a vessel or aircraft through a blockade without special entry or exit authorization from the blockading belligerent.[172]

Attempted breach of a blockade occurs from the time a vessel or aircraft leaves a port or airfield with the intention of evading the blockade and, for vessels exiting the blockaded area, continues until the voyage is completed.[173] A temporary anchorage in waters occupied by the

---

authorization may be made subject to such conditions as the blockading force considers to be necessary and expedient."); 1955 NWIP 10-2 ¶632h(1) ("Neutral warships and neutral military aircraft have no positive right of entry to a blockaded area. However, they may be allowed to enter or leave a blockaded area as a matter of courtesy. Permission to visit a blockaded area is subject to any conditions, such as the length of stay, that the senior officer of the blockading force may deem necessary and expedient."). *Consider* 1909 DECLARATION OF LONDON art. 6 ("The commander of a blockading force may give permission to a warship to enter, and subsequently leave, a blockaded port.").

[169] *See* 2007 NWP 1-14M ¶7.7.3 ("Neutral vessels and aircraft in evident distress should be authorized entry into a blockaded area, and subsequently authorized to depart, under conditions prescribed by the officer in command of the blockading force or responsible for maintenance of the blockading instrumentality (e.g., mines)."); 1955 NWIP 10-2 ¶632h(2) ("Neutral vessels and aircraft in urgent distress may be permitted to enter a blockaded area, and subsequently to leave it, under conditions prescribed by the commander of the blockading force."). *Consider* 1909 DECLARATION OF LONDON art. 7 ("In circumstances of distress, acknowledged by an officer of the blockading force, a neutral vessel may enter a place under blockade and subsequently leave it, provided that she has neither discharged nor shipped any cargo there.").

[170] 2007 NWP 1-14M ¶7.7.3 ("Similarly, neutral vessels and aircraft engaged in the carriage of qualifying relief supplies for the civilian population and the sick and wounded should be authorized to pass through the blockade cordon, subject to the right of the blockading force to prescribe the technical arrangements, including search, under which passage is permitted."). *Refer to* § 5.19.3 (Passage of Relief Consignments).

[171] *Refer to* § 15.15.1 (Grounds for the Capture of Neutral Vessels and Aircraft).

[172] 2007 NWP 1-14M ¶7.7.4 ("Breach of blockade is the passage of a vessel or aircraft through a blockade without special entry or exit authorization from the blockading belligerent."); 1997 NWP 9 ¶7.7.4 (same); 1989 NWP 9 ¶7.7.4 (same); 1955 NWIP 10-2 ¶632g ("Breach of blockade is the passage of a vessel or aircraft through the blockade.").

[173] 2007 NWP 1-14M ¶7.7.4 ("Attempted breach of blockade occurs from the time a vessel or aircraft leaves a port or airfield with the intention of evading the blockade, and for vessels exiting the blockaded area, continues until the voyage is completed."); 1997 NWP 9 ¶7.7.4 (same); 1989 NWP 9 ¶7.7.4 (substantially similar); 1955 NWIP 10-2

blockading vessels does not justify capture, in the absence of other grounds.[174]

A presumption arises that certain merchant vessels or aircraft are attempting to breach a blockade where those vessels or aircraft are bound for a neutral port or airfield serving as a point of transit to the blockaded area.[175]

13.10.4.2 Knowledge of the Existence of Blockade. Knowledge of the existence of the blockade is essential to the offenses of breach of blockade and attempted breach of blockade; presumed knowledge is sufficient.[176]

Knowledge may be presumed once a blockade has been declared and appropriate notification provided to affected governments.[177] For example, a vessel in a blockaded port is presumed to have notice of the blockade as soon as it commences.[178]

A vessel sailing ignorantly (*i.e.*, with neither presumptive nor actual knowledge) to a blockaded port is not liable to capture, although it may be turned away from the blockaded area.[179]

¶632g(2) ("Attempted breach of blockade occurs from the time a vessel or aircraft leaves a port or air take-off point with the intent of evading the blockade.").

[174] The Teresita, 72 U.S. 180, 182 (1867) ("We are of opinion that, under such circumstances, temporary anchorage in waters occupied by the blockading vessels, does not justify capture, in the absence of other grounds.").

[175] 2007 NWP 1-14M ¶7.7.4 ("There is a presumption of attempted breach of blockade where vessels or aircraft are bound for a neutral port or airfield serving as a point of transit to the blockaded area."); 1955 NWIP 10-2 ¶632g(1) ("There is a presumption of attempted breach of blockade where vessels and aircraft are bound to a neutral port or airfield serving as a point of transit to the blockaded area."); The Peterhoff, 72 U.S. 28, 55 (1867) ("It is an undoubted general principle, recognized by this court in the case of The Bermuda, and in several other cases, that an ulterior destination to a blockaded port will infect the primary voyage to a neutral port with liability for intended violation of blockade."). *Compare* § 15.12.2 (Requirement of Enemy Destination).

[176] 2007 NWP 1-14M ¶7.7.4 ("Knowledge of the existence of the blockade is essential to the offenses of breach of blockade and attempted breach of blockade."); 1997 NWP 9 ¶7.7.4 (same); 1989 NWP 9 ¶7.7.4 (same); 1955 NWIP 10-2 ¶632g ("Knowledge of the existence of a blockade is essential to the offenses of breach of blockade and attempted breach of blockade; presumed knowledge is sufficient."). *Consider* 1909 DECLARATION OF LONDON art. 14 ("The liability of a neutral vessel to capture for breach of blockade is contingent on her knowledge, actual or presumptive, of the blockade.").

[177] 2007 NWP 1-14M ¶7.7.4 ("Knowledge may be presumed once a blockade has been declared and appropriate notification provided to affected governments."); 1997 NWP 9 ¶7.7.4 (same); 1989 NWP 9 ¶7.7.4 (same). *Consider* 1909 DECLARATION OF LONDON art. 15 ("Failing proof to the contrary, knowledge of the blockade is presumed if the vessel left a neutral port subsequently to the notification of the blockade to the Power to which such port belongs, provided that such notification was made in sufficient time.").

[178] The Prize Cases, 67 U.S. 635, 677 (1863) ("A vessel being in a blockaded port is presumed to have notice of the blockade as soon as it commences. This is a settled rule in the law of nations.").

[179] Yeaton v. Fry, 9 U.S. 335, 342-43 (1809) (Marshall, C.J.) ("Hispaniola is excepted absolutely from the policy; but other ports are within the terms of the voyage insured, if they be not blockaded. It is their character, as blockaded ports, which excludes them from the insurance. Their being excepted by this character is thought to justify the opinion, that it is the risk attending this character which produces the exception, and which is the risk excepted. The risk of a blockaded port, as a blockaded port, is the risk incurred by breaking the blockade. This is defined by public law. Sailing from Tobago for Curracoa, knowing Curracoa to be blockaded, would have incurred this risk, but sailing for that port, without such knowledge, did not incur it.").

13.11 Naval Mines

Naval mines are lawful weapons, *i.e.*, they are not illegal *per se*.[180] However, specific rules apply to their use. These rules have developed largely to mitigate the risk these mines pose to neutral vessels.[181] Different rules apply to landmines.[182]

13.11.1 Background on Naval Mines. Naval mines have been used for area denial, coastal and harbor defense, anti-surface and anti-submarine warfare, and blockade.

Naval mines are sometimes classified as either armed or controlled mines, with controlled mines having no destructive capability until affirmatively activated by an arming order (thereby becoming armed mines).[183]

13.11.2 Peacetime Mining. Naval mines may not be emplaced in internal waters, the territorial sea, or archipelagic waters of another State in peacetime without that State's consent.[184]

---

[180] *Refer to* § 6.5 (Lawful Weapons).

[181] *For example*, A. PEARCE HIGGINS, THE HAGUE PEACE CONFERENCES AND OTHER INTERNATIONAL CONFERENCES CONCERNING THE LAWS AND USAGES OF WAR. TEXT OF CONVENTIONS WITH COMMENTARIES 328-29 (1909) ("The Russo-Japanese War drew the attention of the world to the deadly results produced by floating mines. Though not expressly mentioned in Count Benckendorff's Circular, the laying of torpedoes, etc. (pose de torpilles, etc.) was included among the subjects for consideration. Mines were employed in the Russo-Japanese War by both belligerents, and hundreds either broke adrift from their moorings or, not be anchored at all, floated into the high seas and caused serious loss of life to neutrals long after the conclusion of the war. In the course of the discussion of the British proposal in Committee, the Chinese delegate made the following declaration which brings out strongly the dangers to which neutral shipping is exposed by their employment: 'At the same time, the Delegation [of China] desires to bring to the knowledge of the delegates certain facts which it ventures to hope will suggest the examination of this important proposition in a widely humanitarian sense. The Chinese Government is even to-day obliged to furnish vessels engaged in coastal navigation with special apparatus to raise and destroy floating mines which are found not only on the open sea but even in its territorial waters. In spite of the precautions which have been taken a very considerable number of coasting vessels, fishing boats, junks and sampans have been lost with all hands without the details of these disasters being known to the western world. It is calculated from five to six hundred of our countrymen engaged in their peaceful occupations have there met a cruel death in consequence of these dangerous engines of war.'") (amendment in original).

[182] *Refer to* § 6.12 (Landmines, Booby-Traps, and Other Devices).

[183] 2007 NWP 1-14M ¶9.2.1 ("For purposes of this publication, naval mines are classified as armed or controlled mines. Armed mines are either emplaced with all safety devices withdrawn, or are armed following emplacement, so as to detonate when preset parameters (if any) are satisfied. Controlled mines have no destructive capability until affirmatively activated by some form of arming order (whereupon they become armed mines)."); 1989 NWP 9 ¶9.2.1 ("For purposes of this publication, naval mines are classified as armed or controlled mines. *Armed mines* are either emplaced with all safety devices withdrawn, or are armed following emplacement, so as to detonate when preset parameters (if any) are satisfied. *Controlled mines* have no destructive capability until affirmatively activated by some form of controlled arming order (whereupon they become armed mines).").

[184] 2007 NWP 1-14M ¶9.2.2 ("Naval mines may not be emplaced in internal waters, territorial seas, or archipelagic waters of another nation in peacetime without that nation's consent."). *See also* Military and Paramilitary Activities in and Against Nicaragua (Nicaragua v. United States), Merits, Judgment, 1986 I.C.J. 14, 111-12 (¶¶213-15) ("The legal rules in the light of which these acts of mining should be judged depend upon where they took place. The laying of mines within the ports of another State is governed by the law relating to internal waters, which are subject to the sovereignty of the coastal State. The position is similar as regards mines placed in the territorial sea. It is

13.11.2.1 *A State's Archipelagic Waters and Territorial Sea*. A State's right to mine its archipelagic waters and territorial sea during peacetime is subject to the right of innocent passage of foreign vessels.[185]

If armed mines are emplaced in a State's own archipelagic waters or territorial sea, appropriate international notification of the existence and location of such mines is required.[186] Because the right of innocent passage may be suspended only temporarily,[187] armed mines must be removed or rendered harmless as soon as the security threat that prompted their emplacement has terminated.[188]

Armed mines may not be emplaced in international straits or archipelagic sea lanes during peacetime.[189]

Emplacement of controlled mines in a State's own archipelagic waters or territorial sea is not subject to notification or removal requirements.[190]

13.11.2.2 *International Waters*. Controlled mines may be emplaced in international waters (*i.e.*, beyond the territorial sea of any State) if they do not unreasonably interfere with other lawful uses of the oceans. What constitutes an "unreasonable interference" may involve a number of factors, including:

- the rationale for their emplacement (*e.g.*, the self-defense requirements of the emplacing State);
- the extent of the area to be mined;

---

therefore the sovereignty of the coastal State which is affected in such cases. … It has already been made clear above that in peacetime for one State to lay mines in the internal or territorial waters of another is an unlawful act;").

[185] *Refer to* § 13.2.2.4 (Innocent Passage of Foreign Vessels Through Territorial Seas and Archipelagic Waters).

[186] Corfu Channel Case (United Kingdom v. Albania), Merits, Judgment, 1949 I.C.J. 4, 22 ("The obligations incumbent upon the Albanian authorities consisted in notifying, for the benefit of shipping in general, the existence of a minefield in Albanian territorial waters and in warning the approaching British warships of the imminent danger to which the minefield exposed them. Such obligations are based, not on the Hague Convention of 1907, No. VIII, which is applicable in time of war, but on certain general and well-recognized principles, namely: elementary considerations of humanity, even more exacting in peace than in war; the principle of the freedom of maritime communication; and every State's obligation not to allow knowingly its territory to be used for acts contrary to the rights of other States.").

[187] *Refer to* § 13.2.2.4 (Innocent Passage of Foreign Vessels Through Territorial Seas and Archipelagic Waters).

[188] 2007 NWP 1-14M ¶9.2.2 ("Because the right of innocent passage can be suspended only temporarily, armed mines must be removed or rendered harmless as soon as the security threat that prompted their emplacement has terminated."); 1997 NWP 9 ¶9.2.2 (same); 1989 NWP 9 ¶9.2.2 (same).

[189] 2007 NWP 1-14M ¶9.2.2 ("Armed mines may not be emplaced in international straits or archipelagic sea lanes during peacetime."); 1997 NWP 9 ¶9.2.2 (same).

[190] 2007 NWP 1-14M ¶9.2.2 ("Emplacement of controlled mines in a nation's own archipelagic waters or territorial sea is not subject to such notification or removal requirements."); 1997 NWP 9 ¶9.2.2 (same); 1989 NWP 9 ¶9.2.2 (same).

- the hazard (if any) to other lawful ocean uses; and
- the duration of their emplacement.[191]

Because controlled mines do not constitute a hazard to navigation, international notice of their emplacement is not required.[192]

Armed mines may not be emplaced in international waters prior to the outbreak of armed conflict, except under the most demanding requirements of individual or collective self-defense. Should armed mines be emplaced in international waters under such circumstances, prior notification of their location must be provided. A State emplacing armed mines in international waters during peacetime must maintain an on-scene presence in the area sufficient to ensure that appropriate warning is provided to ships approaching the danger area. All armed mines must be expeditiously removed or rendered harmless when the imminent danger that prompted their emplacement has passed.[193]

13.11.3 Naval Mining During Armed Conflict. Belligerent States may lawfully employ naval mines subject to certain restrictions.

Neutral States that lay automatic contact mines off their coasts must observe the same rules and take the same precautions as those that are imposed on belligerents.[194] In addition, a neutral State must inform ship owners, by a notice issued in advance, where automatic contact mines have been laid. This notice must be communicated at once to the Governments through the diplomatic channel.[195]

13.11.3.1 *General Obligation to Take Feasible Precautions When Using Naval Mines*. The general obligation to take feasible precautions for the protection of civilians applies

---

[191] 2007 NWP 1-14M ¶9.2.2 ("The determination of what constitutes an 'unreasonable interference' involves a balancing of a number of factors, including the rationale for their emplacement (i.e., the self-defense requirements of the emplacing nation), the extent of the area to be mined, the hazard (if any) to other lawful ocean uses, and the duration of their emplacement.").

[192] 2007 NWP 1-14M ¶9.2.2 ("Because controlled mines do not constitute a hazard to navigation, international notice of their emplacement is not required."); 1997 NWP 9 ¶9.2.2 (same); 1989 NWP 9 ¶9.2.2 (same).

[193] 2007 NWP 1-14M ¶9.2.2 ("Armed mines may not be emplaced in international waters prior to the outbreak of armed conflict, except under the most demanding requirements of individual or collective self-defense. Should armed mines be emplaced in international waters under such circumstances, prior notification of their location must be provided. A nation emplacing armed mines in international waters during peacetime must maintain an on-scene presence in the area sufficient to ensure that appropriate warning is provided to ships approaching the danger area. All armed mines must be expeditiously removed or rendered harmless when the imminent danger that prompted their emplacement has passed.").

[194] HAGUE VIII art. 4 ("Neutral Powers which lay automatic contact mines off their coasts must observe the same rules and take the same precautions as are imposed on belligerents.").

[195] HAGUE VIII art. 4 ("The neutral Power must inform ship-owners, by a notice issued in advance, where automatic contact mines have been laid. This notice must be communicated at once to the Governments through the diplomatic channel.").

when using naval mines.[196] In particular, when anchored automatic contact mines are employed, every possible precaution must be taken for the security of peaceful shipping.[197]

13.11.3.2 *International Notification When Using Armed Mines*. International notification of the location of emplaced armed mines must be made as soon as military exigencies permit.[198] Such notification may be conducted through official public announcements, communications to the United Nations, bilateral diplomatic notification, or notices to mariners.[199]

In particular, when anchored automatic contact mines are employed, belligerents undertake to do their utmost to render these mines harmless within a limited time and, should they cease to be under surveillance, to notify the danger zones as soon as military exigencies permit, by a notice addressed to ship owners, which must also be communicated to the Governments through the diplomatic channel.[200]

13.11.3.3 *Surveillance of Minefields*. Surveillance or monitoring of minefields may be an appropriate precaution to reduce the risk of harm to peaceful vessels by permitting warning to be given to peaceful vessels that unwittingly venture near the minefield.[201]

13.11.3.4 *Recording of Minefield Locations*. The location of minefields must be carefully recorded to ensure accurate notification and to facilitate subsequent removal and/or deactivation.[202]

13.11.3.5 *Restrictions on Where Naval Mines May Be Placed*. Mines may not be

---

[196] *Refer to* § 5.2.3 (Affirmative Duties to Take Feasible Precautions for the Protection of Civilians and Other Protected Persons and Objects).

[197] HAGUE VIII art. 3 ("When anchored automatic contact mines are employed, every possible precaution must be taken for the security of peaceful shipping.").

[198] 2007 NWP 1-14M ¶9.2.3 ("International notification of the location of emplaced mines must be made as soon as military exigencies permit."); 1997 NWP 9 ¶9.2.3 (same); 1989 NWP 9 ¶9.2.3 ("International notification of the location of emplaced armed mines must be made as soon as military exigencies permit.").

[199] *For example*, HOWARD S. LEVIE, MINE WARFARE AT SEA 146-47 (1992) ("The mining was announced by President Nixon on radio and television on the evening of 8 May 1972. Appropriate notification was also given to all other nations concerned, both by a letter to the President of the United Nations Security Council, and by direct bilateral diplomatic notification, as well as by notices to mariners. That same day (9 May 1972, in Hanoi), mines were dropped by aircraft in Haiphong harbor (and in Cam Pha and Hon Gai harbors), three days in advance of the mines becoming armed, thus permitting the ships in the harbor three periods of daylight in which to leave if they so desired.").

[200] HAGUE VIII art. 3 ("The belligerents undertake to do their utmost to render these mines harmless within a limited time, and, should they cease to be under surveillance, to notify the danger zones as soon as military exigencies permit, by a notice addressed to ship owners, which must also be communicated to the Governments through the diplomatic channel.").

[201] *Compare* § 6.12.7 (Rules for Using Non-Remotely Delivered Anti-Personnel Mines Without Compliant SD/SDA Mechanisms).

[202] 2007 NWP 1-14M ¶9.2.3 ("The location of minefields must be carefully recorded to ensure accurate notification and to facilitate subsequent removal and/or deactivation."); 1997 NWP 9 ¶9.2.3 (same); 1989 NWP 9 ¶9.2.3 (same).

emplaced by belligerents in neutral waters.[203]

Naval mines may be employed to channelize neutral shipping, but not in a manner to deny transit passage of international straits or archipelagic sea lanes passage of archipelagic waters by such shipping.[204]

Mining of areas of indefinite extent in international waters is prohibited. Reasonably limited barred areas may be established by naval mines, provided neutral shipping retains an alternate route around or through such an area with reasonable assurance of safety.[205]

13.11.3.6 *Prohibition Against Mining Off Enemy Coasts and Ports Solely to Intercept Commercial Shipping*. Naval mines may not be emplaced off the coasts and ports of the enemy with the sole objective of intercepting commercial shipping.[206] Mining for some other purpose would not violate this rule.[207] For example, mines may otherwise be used in the strategic blockade of enemy ports, coasts, and waterways, even if commercial shipping is incidentally affected.[208]

13.11.3.7 *Neutralization of Naval Mines*. Anchored mines must become harmless as soon as they have broken their moorings.[209] In particular, it is forbidden to lay anchored

---

[203] 2007 NWP 1-14M ¶9.2.3 ("Mines may not be emplaced by belligerents in neutral waters."). *Refer to* § 15.7 (Neutral Waters).

[204] 2007 NWP 1-14M ¶9.2.3 ("Naval mines may be employed to channelize neutral shipping, but not in a manner to deny transit passage of international straits or archipelagic sea lanes passage of archipelagic waters by such shipping."); 1997 NWP 9 ¶9.2.3 (same); 1989 NWP 9 ¶9.2.3 ("Naval mines may be employed to channelize neutral shipping, but not in a manner to impede the transit passage of international straits or archipelagic sea lanes passage of archipelagic waters by such shipping.").

[205] 2007 NWP 1-14M ¶9.2.3 ("Mining of areas of indefinite extent in international waters is prohibited. Reasonably limited barred areas may be established by naval mines, provided neutral shipping retains an alternate route around or through such an area with reasonable assurance of safety."); 1997 NWP 9 ¶9.2.3 (same); 1989 NWP 9 ¶9.2.3 (same).

[206] HAGUE VIII art. 2 ("It is forbidden to lay automatic contact mines off the coast and ports of the enemy, with the sole object of intercepting commercial shipping."); 2007 NWP 1-14M ¶9.2.3 ("Naval mines may not be emplaced off the coasts and ports of the enemy with the sole objective of intercepting commercial shipping, but may otherwise be employed in the strategic blockade of enemy ports, coasts, and waterways."); 1997 NWP 9 ¶9.2.3 (same); 1989 NWP 9 ¶9.2.3 (same).

[207] WILLIAM H. BOOTHBY, WEAPONS AND THE LAW OF ARMED CONFLICT 283 (2009) ("If there is some other purpose to the laying of the mines, their use in these localities is lawful. Thus, if the purpose was to intercept all shipping, both commercial and military, the laying of the weapons would not breach this provision.").

[208] *For example*, Richard Nixon, *Address to the Nation on the Situation in Southeast Asia*, May 8, 1972, 1972 PUBLIC PAPERS OF THE PRESIDENTS 583, 585 ("I therefore concluded that Hanoi must be denied the weapons and supplies it needs to continue the aggression. In full coordination with the Republic of Vietnam, I have ordered the following measures which are being implemented as I am speaking to you. All entrances to North Vietnamese ports will be mined to prevent access to these ports and North Vietnamese naval operations from these ports. ... Countries with ships presently in North Vietnamese ports have already been notified that their ships will have three daylight periods to leave in safety. After that time, the mines will become active and any ships attempting to leave or enter these ports will do so at their own risk.").

[209] 2007 NWP ¶9.2.3 ("Anchored mines must become harmless as soon as they have broken their moorings."); 1997 NWP 9 ¶9.2.3 (same); 1989 NWP 9 ¶9.2.3 (same).

automatic contact mines that do not become harmless as soon as they have broken loose from their moorings.[210]

Unanchored mines not otherwise affixed or imbedded on the ocean floor must become harmless within an hour after loss of control over them.[211] In particular, it is forbidden to lay unanchored (*i.e.*, free-floating) automatic contact mines, except when they are so constructed as to become harmless one hour at most after the person who laid them ceases to control them.[212]

13.11.4 Post-Conflict Naval Demining Obligations. The removal of naval mines at the end of the conflict may be the subject of specific agreements among States.[213]

At the close of a war to which Hague VIII is applicable, Parties to Hague VIII have an obligation to remove the naval mines that they had laid, each State removing its own mines.[214] As regards anchored automatic contact mines laid by one of the belligerents off the coast of the other, their position must be notified to the other party by the State that laid them, and each State must proceed with the least possible delay to remove the mines in its own waters.[215]

13.12 TORPEDOES

It is forbidden to use torpedoes that do not become harmless when they miss their mark.[216] Such torpedoes may become a hazard to innocent shipping, and therefore torpedoes must be designed to become harmless when they have missed their mark.

For example, torpedoes have been designed to become harmless upon completion of their propulsion run, such as by sinking to the bottom.

13.12.1 Torpedoes – Notes on Terminology. In the 19th century, the term "torpedo" was

---

210 HAGUE VIII art. 1 ("It is forbidden … 2. To lay anchored automatic contact mines which do not become harmless as soon as they have broken loose from their moorings;").

211 2007 NWP ¶9.2.3 ("Unanchored mines not otherwise affixed or imbedded in the bottom must become harmless within an hour after loss of control over them."); 1997 NWP 9 ¶9.2.3 (same); 1989 NWP 9 ¶9.2.3 (same).

212 HAGUE VIII art. 1 ("It is forbidden … 1. To lay unanchored automatic contact mines, except when they are so constructed as to become harmless one hour at most after the person who laid them ceases to control them;").

213 *For example*, Protocol to the Agreement on Ending the War and Restoring Peace in Vietnam Concerning the Removal, Permanent Deactivation, or Destruction of Mines in the Territorial Waters, Ports, Harbors, and Waterways of the Democratic Republic of Vietnam, Jan. 27, 1973, 24 U.S.T. 1, art. 1 ("The United States shall clear all the mines it has placed in the territorial waters, ports, harbors, and waterways of the Democratic Republic of Vietnam. This mine clearing operation shall be accomplished by rendering the mines harmless through removal, permanent deactivation, or destruction.").

214 HAGUE VIII art. 5 ("At the close of the war, the Contracting Powers undertake to do their utmost to remove the mines which they had laid, each Power removing its own mines.").

215 HAGUE VIII art. 5 ("As regards anchored automatic contact mines laid by one of the belligerents off the coast of the other, their position must be notified to the other party by the Power which laid them, and each Power must proceed with the least possible delay to remove the mines in its own waters.").

216 HAGUE VIII art. 1 ("It is forbidden … 3. To use torpedoes which do not become harmless when they have missed their mark.").

used to refer to any explosive munition that operated by contact against the hull of a ship, including relatively stationary munitions that, in modern parlance, would be called mines.[217] However, by the time of the 1907 Hague VIII Convention, the term "torpedo" was used in the modern sense to refer to munitions that propelled through the water.[218]

13.13 DECEPTION BY NAVAL FORCES, INCLUDING THE USE OF ENEMY OR NEUTRAL FLAGS

In general, the rules concerning good faith, ruses, and perfidy also apply to naval warfare.[219] For example, it would be prohibited for a belligerent warship to convey falsely the appearance of a hospital ship.[220] On the other hand, a variety of deceptions are not prohibited, including camouflage, deceptive lighting, disguised electronic signatures, and dummy ships, among others.[221]

The rules concerning deception by belligerent warships, especially with respect to the flying of neutral flags or with respect to disguise as merchant vessels, may be considered more permissive than similar situations in land warfare.[222]

13.13.1 Belligerent Warship's Use of False Colors and Other Disguises. In particular, according to custom, it is permissible for a belligerent warship to use false colors and to disguise her outward appearance in other ways in order to deceive an enemy, provided that before going into action such warship shows her true colors.[223]

---

[217] *For example*, TAMARA MOSER MELIA, DAMN THE TORPEDOES: A SHORT HISTORY OF U.S. NAVAL MINE COUNTERMEASURES, 1777-1991, 3 (1991) ("At high tide on the morning of 5 August Farragut entered the bay. Farragut's officers had persuaded him to allow the sloop *Brooklyn*, hastily rigged with a rudimentary torpedo catcher on the bowsprit, to lead the advance in place of Farragut's flagship, *Hartford*. Contrary to Farragut's orders, monitor *Tecumseh* moved west of the red buoy where it struck and detonated one of the newly placed mines. As *Tecumseh* quickly went down, *Brooklyn* suddenly stopped and backed, stalling the fleet's advance. High in *Hartford*'s rigging Farragut watched *Tecumseh* sink and *Brooklyn* hesitate. From *Hartford*'s poop deck Lieutenant Watson heard the admiral's exchange with *Brooklyn*: 'Farragut hailed again and all that could be distinguished of her reply was something about torpedoes. 'Damn the torpedoes!' he instantly shouted, ordering *Hartford*'s captain 'Full speed ahead, Drayton.''").

[218] A. PEARCE HIGGINS, THE HAGUE PEACE CONFERENCES AND OTHER INTERNATIONAL CONFERENCES CONCERNING THE LAWS AND USAGES OF WAR. TEXT OF CONVENTIONS WITH COMMENTARIES 328 (1909) ("The word 'torpille' until recently appears to have meant any sort of receptacle containing an explosive intended to operate against the hull of a ship by contact either on or below the water line. Thus, there were *torpilles fizes*, *torpilles mouillees*, *torpilles mobiles*, and finally *torpilles automobiles*. It would appear that latterly the word has come to mean only 'automobile torpedo,' e.g. in the Convention now under consideration the word 'mine' is used when an automatic torpedo is not implied.").

[219] *Refer to* § 5.21 (Overview of Good Faith, Perfidy, and Ruses).

[220] *Refer to* § 5.24.2 (Distinctive Emblems of the Geneva Conventions (*e.g.*, Red Cross)); § 7.12.3 (Distinctive Marking and Other Identification of Hospital Ships and Coastal Rescue Craft).

[221] *Refer to* § 5.25.2 (Examples of Ruses).

[222] *Refer to* § 5.24.1 (Signs, Emblems, or Uniforms of a Neutral or Non-Belligerent State).

[223] *See, e.g.*, 2007 NWP 1-14M ¶12.3.1 ("Under the customary international law of naval warfare, it is permissible for a belligerent warship to fly false colors and disguise its outward appearance in other ways in order to deceive the enemy into believing the vessel is of neutral nationality or is other than a warship. However, it is unlawful for a warship to go into action without first showing her true colors."); 2007 NWP 1-14M ¶12.5.1 ("Naval surface and

For example, a belligerent warship may fly enemy or neutral colors and display enemy or neutral markings in order to deceive the enemy into believing the vessel is of enemy or neutral nationality or is not a warship.[224] Such deceptions may be used in order to facilitate the approach of enemy vessels or to escape enemy vessels.[225]

Warships, however, may not seek to claim falsely the status of vessels that are exempt from capture or destruction. These vessels include: (1) cartel vessels; (2) hospital ships; (3) vessels charged with religious, non-military scientific, or philanthropic missions; (4) vessels granted safe conduct; and (5) small coastal fishing vessels and small boats engaged in local coastal trade.[226]

---

subsurface forces may fly enemy colors and display enemy markings to deceive the enemy. Warships must, however, display their true colors prior to an actual armed engagement."); 1955 NWIP 10-2 ¶640a ("In particular, according to custom, it is permissible for a belligerent warship to use false colors and to disguise her outward appearance in other ways in order to deceive an enemy, provided that prior to going into action such warship shows her true colors.").

[224] *For example*, TUCKER, THE LAW OF WAR AND NEUTRALITY AT SEA 140 footnote 37 ("During World War II the Germans enjoyed a measurable degree of success through the skillful disguise they provided for their armed raiders. … The tactics of the armed raiders were to reveal their true identity only after having come within close enough range to overwhelm the victim (usually armed enemy merchant vessels) by surprise.— One of the most notable actions involving these armed raiders took place in November 1941 between the Australian cruiser *Sydney* and the German armed raider *Kormoran*. The disguised raider, when approached by the *Sydney*, identified herself as a Dutch merchant vessel. Before the Sydney could establish the truth or falsity of her claimed identity the *Kormoran* cast off her disguise and opened fire at a distance of 2,000 yards. As a result of the action the *Sydney* was destroyed with complete loss of officers and crew."); LAUTERPACT, II OPPENHEIM'S INTERNATIONAL LAW 510 (§211) ("On the other hand, the following is a perfectly legitimate ruse which is reported to have occurred during the World War: at the end of October 1914, the German cruiser *Emden*, hiding her identity by rigging up a dummy fourth funnel and flying the Japanese flag, passed the guardship of the harbor Penang in the Malay States, made no reply to its signals, came down at full speed on the Russian cruiser *Zhemshug*, and then, after lowering the Japanese flag and hoisting the German flag, opened fire and torpedoed her.").

[225] LAUTERPACT, II OPPENHEIM'S INTERNATIONAL LAW 509 (§211) ("As regards the use of a false flag, it is by most writers considered perfectly lawful for a man-of-war to use a neutral or enemy flag (1) when chasing an enemy vessel, (2) when trying to escape, and (3) for the purpose of drawing an enemy vessel into action. On the other hand, it is universally agreed that, immediately before an attack, a vessel must fly her national flag.").

[226] *Refer to* § 13.6 (Enemy Vessels Exempt From Capture or Destruction).

XIV – Air and Space Warfare

Chapter Contents

14.1 Introduction

This Chapter addresses the international law applicable to U.S. air and space operations during international armed conflict. This Chapter also discusses the application to air operations of some of the law of war rules discussed elsewhere in this manual.

Air Force publications have provided discussion of other aspects of public international law relating to air operations, including discussion of rules applicable during peacetime.[1]

14.1.1 Application of the 1944 Chicago Convention With Respect to Military Aircraft and With Respect to States' Rights During Armed Conflict. The 1944 Chicago Convention primarily addresses States' obligations regarding international civil aviation.[2] The 1944 Chicago Convention does not restrict State action during war.[3] In addition, the 1944 Chicago Convention generally is not applicable to State aircraft.[4] However, the 1944 Chicago Convention imposes requirements with respect to entry by State aircraft into foreign airspace and with respect to the issue of due regard for the safety of navigation of civil aircraft.[5]

14.1.1.1 *1944 Chicago Convention and Freedom of Action of States During Armed Conflict*. According to Article 89 of the 1944 Chicago Convention, "[i]n case of war, the provisions of this Convention shall not affect the freedom of action of any of the contracting

---

[1] *See, e.g.*, Department of the Air Force, The Judge Advocate General's School, *Air Force Operations and The Law* (3rd ed., 2014); 1976 AIR FORCE PAMPHLET 110-31.

[2] 1944 CHICAGO CONVENTION preamble ("THEREFORE, the undersigned governments having agreed on certain principles and arrangements in order that international civil aviation may be developed in a safe and orderly manner and that international air transport services may be established on the basis of equality of opportunity and operated soundly and economically; Have accordingly concluded this Convention to that end.").

[3] *Refer to* § 14.1.1.1 (1944 Chicago Convention and Freedom of Action of States During Armed Conflict).

[4] *Refer to* § 14.1.1.2 (1944 Chicago Convention and Military Aircraft or Other State Aircraft).

[5] *Refer to* § 14.1.1.3 (Requirement for State Consent Prior to Entry by Foreign State Aircraft); § 14.1.1.4 (Due Regard for the Safety of Navigation of Civil Aircraft).

States affected, whether as belligerents or as neutrals."[6] Article 89 may be understood as an example, reflected in this case in the Convention, of the application of the general principle that the law of war, as a body of law specially adapted to the circumstances of armed conflict, is the controlling body of law with respect to armed conflict.[7] Under Article 89, a State's rights under the law of war (and the law of neutrality) would prevail in the event of conflict with obligations under the 1944 Chicago Convention.

The provisions of the 1944 Chicago Convention may be relevant during armed conflict insofar as they articulate restrictions that continue to apply to civil aircraft. For example, neutral civil aircraft engaged in international navigation would still be required to seek permission from a foreign neutral State before carrying munitions of war or implements of war through that neutral State's airspace.[8]

The 1944 Chicago Convention's requirements with respect to entry by State aircraft into foreign airspace and with respect to the issue of due regard for the safety of navigation of civil aircraft are discussed below.[9]

14.1.1.2 *1944 Chicago Convention and Military Aircraft or Other State Aircraft*. The 1944 Chicago Convention provides generally that the Convention "shall be applicable only to civil aircraft, and shall not be applicable to state aircraft."[10] State aircraft include aircraft used in military service.[11] The United States has made statements interpreting this provision of the 1944 Chicago Convention.[12]

---

[6] 1944 CHICAGO CONVENTION art. 89 ("In case of war, the provisions of this Convention shall not affect the freedom of action of any of the contracting States affected, whether as belligerents or as neutrals.").

[7] *Refer to* § 1.3.2 (The Law of War's Relationship to Other Bodies of Law).

[8] *See, e.g.*, 1944 CHICAGO CONVENTION art. 35(a) ("(a) No munitions of war or implements of war may be carried in or above the territory of a State in aircraft engaged in international navigation, except by permission of such State. Each State shall determine by regulations what constitutes munitions of war or implements of war for the purposes of this Article, giving due consideration, for the purposes of uniformity, to such recommendations as the International Civil Aviation Organization may from time to time make.").

[9] *Refer to* § 14.1.1.3 (Requirement for State Consent Prior to Entry by Foreign State Aircraft); § 14.1.1.4 (Due Regard for the Safety of Navigation of Civil Aircraft).

[10] 1944 CHICAGO CONVENTION art. 3(a) ("This Convention shall be applicable only to civil aircraft, and shall not be applicable to state aircraft.").

[11] *Refer to* § 14.3.1 (State Versus Civil Aircraft).

[12] *See, e.g.*, Department of State Airgram CA-8085, Feb. 13, 1964, quoting U.S. Inter-Agency Group on International Aviation (IGIA) Doc. 88/1/1C, MS, Department of State, file POL 31 U.S., IX WHITEMAN'S DIGEST 430-31 ("The Chicago Convention expressly excludes state aircraft from its scope and thus from the scope of ICAO [International Civil Aviation Organization] responsibility. The United States intends that its state aircraft will follow the ICAO procedures set forth in Annex 2 ["Rules of the Air"] to the greatest extent practicable; however, the United States considers that state aircraft of any nation are subject to control and regulation exclusively by that nation (unless operating within airspace over which another nation has sovereignty). With respect to State aircraft, contracting States need not undertake any commitment, and the United States does not undertake any commitment, to other nations as to the rules and regulations which any specific state aircraft or class of state aircraft will follow, except when issuing regulations for their state aircraft, that 'they will have due regard for the safety of navigation of civil aircraft' (Article 3(d), Chicago Convention).").

The 1944 Chicago Convention, however, imposes obligations with respect to entry into foreign airspace by State aircraft and an obligation with respect to State aircraft and the safety of navigation of civil aircraft.[13]

14.1.1.3 *Requirement for State Consent Prior to Entry by Foreign State Aircraft*. The 1944 Chicago Convention provides that State aircraft (which include military aircraft) are not permitted to enter the airspace of another State without that State's consent.[14]

During armed conflict, the requirement for a State's consent to entry into its airspace would generally continue to apply with respect to neutral military aircraft seeking to enter the airspace of foreign States.

This requirement, however, clearly would not apply to belligerent military aircraft conducting operations in enemy airspacc.

The requirement for a State's consent to entry into its airspace may be characterized as applicable with respect to belligerent military aircraft and a neutral State's airspace; however, even if belligerent military aircraft enter neutral airspace with that neutral State's consent, such entry may involve violations of neutrality.[15]

There are exceptions to the requirement for State consent to entry into its airspace by State aircraft in certain cases of violations of neutrality.[16]

There is an exception during peacetime to the requirement for a State's consent to entry into its airspace by foreign State aircraft when such entry is due to distress and there is no reasonable safe alternative.[17]

14.1.1.4 *Due Regard for the Safety of Navigation of Civil Aircraft*. The 1944 Chicago Convention also provides that "[t]he contracting States undertake, when issuing regulations for their state aircraft, that they will have due regard for the safety of navigation of

---

[13] *Refer to* § 14.1.1.3 (Requirement for State Consent Prior to Entry by Foreign State Aircraft); § 14.1.1.4 (Due Regard for the Safety of Navigation of Civil Aircraft).

[14] 1944 CHICAGO CONVENTION art. 3(c) ("No state aircraft of a contracting State shall fly over the territory of another State or land thereon without authorization by special agreement or otherwise, and in accordance with the terms thereof.").

[15] *Refer to* § 15.10.2 (Prohibition on Entry by Belligerent Military Aircraft Into Neutral Airspace).

[16] *Refer to* § 15.4.2 (Belligerent Use of Self-Help When Neutral States Are Unable or Unwilling to Prevent Violations of Neutrality).

[17] *U.S. Response to Chinese Legal Views*, 2001 DIGEST OF UNITED STATES PRACTICE IN INTERNATIONAL LAW 703, 708 ("—Although we recognize that military aircraft normally require permission to enter the territorial airspace of another nation, international law recognizes a right of entry for foreign aircraft, state or civil, in circumstances such as these when such entry is due to distress and there is no reasonable safe alternative (Footnote 3 below). — Notwithstanding the ordinary rules requiring consent, a peacetime right to enter in distress for military aircraft is consistent with established international practice. — Such a right is clearly inferable both from analogous situations in which such a right exists (e.g., for civil aircraft under Article 25 of the Chicago Convention) and from basic humanitarian considerations.").

civil aircraft."[18] Assuming that an obligation to exercise due regard would be applicable during armed conflict, what regard would be due in any particular set of circumstances would depend on military necessity, and other principles and rules of the law of war, which are specially adapted to the circumstances of armed conflict. For example, the use of force against enemy civil aircraft that constitute military objectives and thus may be made the object of attack under the law of war would not be prohibited.[19]

As reflected in Article 89 of the 1944 Chicago Convention, the Convention does not restrict the freedom of action of States as belligerents or neutrals.[20] Nonetheless, as a practical matter, modern air warfare is often conducted in complex airspace, and U.S. forces have routinely and intensively coordinated flight operations with national civil aviation authorities. This coordination is important for a variety of purposes, including ensuring mission accomplishment, avoiding fratricide and mid-air collisions, and ensuring the safety of international civil aviation. DoD policy has required that, in the event of combat operations during armed conflict, aircraft commanders, consistent with military necessity, take measures to minimize hazards to civil air or surface traffic.[21]

Similarly, under the law of the sea, military operations must be conducted with due regard for the high seas freedom of overflight in international airspace.[22]

14.1.2 <u>Past Attempts to Conclude Treaties About Air Warfare</u>. Initial attempts to conclude agreements on the law of war governing means and methods in the air context were made during the 1899 and 1907 Hague Peace Conferences, before air power had become a significant factor in warfare. Extensive efforts were made in 1922-23 to adopt a code of laws specifically applicable only to air warfare; however, the proposed rules were not ratified by any State.[23] The United States has not ratified a treaty applicable solely to air operations during armed conflict, although the United States has ratified treaties that have included specific references to aspects of war in the air, such as protection for medical aircraft in the 1949 Geneva

---

[18] 1944 CHICAGO CONVENTION art. 3(d) ("The contracting States undertake, when issuing regulations for their state aircraft, that they will have due regard for the safety of navigation of civil aircraft.").

[19] *Refer to* § 14.8.3 (Attacks Against Civil Aircraft).

[20] *Refer to* § 14.1.1.1 (1944 Chicago Convention and Freedom of Action of States During Armed Conflict).

[21] DOD INSTRUCTION 4540.01, *Use of International Airspace by U.S. Military Aircraft and for Missile/Projectile Firings*, ¶4.2.3 (Mar. 28, 2007) ("In the event of combat operations in time of war, armed conflict, national emergency, situations requiring self-defense, or similar military contingencies, aircraft commanders shall, consistent with military necessity, take measures to minimize hazards to civil air or surface traffic. Such actions shall be of no greater extent or duration than required by military necessity."); DOD DIRECTIVE 4540.1, *Use of Airspace by U.S. Military Aircraft and Firings Over the High Seas*, ¶6b (Jan. 13, 1981) ("In the event of combat operations in time of war, armed conflict, national emergency, situations requiring self-defense, or similar military contingencies, departure from the operating procedures in this Directive may be required. In all such instances, however, all possible precautions shall be taken to minimize any hazard to the safety of other air and surface traffic and departure from procedures set forth in this Directive shall be of no greater extent or duration than is required to meet the contingency.").

[22] *Refer to* § 13.1.1 (The Law of the Sea During Armed Conflict).

[23] *Refer to* § 19.11 (1923 Hague Air and Radio Rules).

Conventions.[24]

14.2 LEGAL BOUNDARIES OF AIRSPACE

The legal classifications of airspace may be relevant to the application of the law of war and therefore may affect military operations during armed conflict by:

- determining whether airspace is neutral airspace;[25]
- determining the authority that a belligerent State has with respect to neutral aircraft in an area; or
- determining the authority that a neutral State has with respect to belligerent aircraft in an area.

14.2.1 Lateral Boundaries of Airspace. The lateral boundaries of the airspace are determined by the status of the land or water directly beneath them.

Airspace is often divided between *national airspace* (*i.e.*, airspace over a State's land territory, internal waters, territorial seas, and archipelagic waters), which is subject to the sovereignty of a State, and *international airspace*, which is not subject to the sovereignty of any State.[26] In addition, special rules apply to international straits and archipelagic sea lanes.[27]

The division between *national airspace* and *international airspace* is similar to the division between *national waters* and *international waters*.[28] One notable distinction, however, is that aircraft do not enjoy the same right of innocent passage over territorial seas that ships enjoy through territorial seas.[29]

14.2.1.1 *National Airspace*. Every State has complete and exclusive sovereignty over the airspace above its territory.[30] In other words, a State has sovereignty over the airspace that is above land or waters that are subject to its sovereignty.[31] Thus, a State's national airspace

---

[24] *Refer to* § 7.14 (Military Medical Aircraft); § 7.19 (Civilian Medical Aircraft).

[25] *Refer to* § 15.10 (Neutral Airspace).

[26] *Refer to* § 14.2.1.1 (National Airspace); § 14.2.1.2 (International Airspace).

[27] *Refer to* § 15.8 (Passage of Belligerent Vessels and Aircraft Through International Straits and Archipelagic Sea Lanes).

[28] *Refer to* § 13.2.2 (National Waters); § 13.2.3 (International Waters).

[29] *Refer to* § 13.2.2.4 (Innocent Passage of Foreign Vessels Through Territorial Seas and Archipelagic Waters).

[30] 1944 CHICAGO CONVENTION art. 1 ("The contracting States recognize that every State has complete and exclusive sovereignty over the airspace above its territory."). *Cf.* 49 U.S.C. § 40103 (a)(1) ("The United States Government has exclusive sovereignty of airspace of the United States.").

[31] *See, e.g.*, 1944 CHICAGO CONVENTION art. 2 ("For the purposes of this Convention the territory of a State shall be deemed to be the land areas and territorial waters adjacent thereto under the sovereignty, suzerainty, protection or mandate of such State."); Convention on the Territorial Sea and Contiguous Zone, art. 2, Apr. 29, 1958, 516 UNTS 205, 208 ("The sovereignty of a coastal State extends to the air space over the territorial sea as well as to its bed and subsoil."). *Consider* LOS CONVENTION art. 2(2) ("This sovereignty extends to the air space over the territorial sea

includes:

- airspace over that State's land territory, including its internal waters;[32]
- airspace over that State's territorial sea;[33] and
- airspace over that State's archipelagic sea.[34]

14.2.1.2 *International Airspace*. International airspace may be understood as all airspace that is not subject to the sovereignty of any State, including:[35]

- airspace over States' contiguous zones;[36]
- airspace over States' Exclusive Economic Zones;[37] and
- airspace over the high seas.[38]

14.2.2 Vertical Boundary Between Airspace and Outer Space. A State's sovereignty over its airspace does not extend to outer space, which is not subject to the sovereignty of any State.[39]

It is generally accepted that orbiting objects are in outer space.[40] The United States has

---

as well as to its bed and subsoil."); LOS CONVENTION art. 49(2) ("This sovereignty extends to the air space over the archipelagic waters, as well as to their bed and subsoil, and the resources contained therein.").

[32] *Refer to* § 13.2.2.1 (Internal Waters).

[33] *Refer to* § 13.2.2.2 (Territorial Seas).

[34] *Refer to* § 13.2.2.3 (Archipelagic Waters).

[35] *See, e.g.*, DOD DIRECTIVE 4500.54E, *DoD Foreign Clearance Program (FCP)*, Glossary (Dec. 28, 2009) ("international airspace. All airspace seaward of coastal states' national airspace, including airspace over contiguous zones, exclusive economic zones, and the high seas. International airspace is open to all aircraft of all nations. Military aircraft may operate in such areas free of interference or control by the coastal state.").

[36] *Refer to* § 13.2.3.2 (Contiguous Zones).

[37] *Refer to* § 13.2.3.3 (Exclusive Economic Zones (EEZs)).

[38] *Refer to* § 13.2.3.4 (High Seas).

[39] *Refer to* § 14.10.1 (Classification of Outer Space).

[40] *See, e.g.*, Department of the Air Force, The Judge Advocate General's School, *Air Force Operations and The Law*, 85 (3rd ed., 2014) ("According to this approach, the upper limit to airspace is above the highest altitude at which an aircraft can fly and below the lowest possible perigee of an earth satellite in orbit. The result is that anything in orbit or beyond can safely be regarded as being in outer space."); 2007 NWP 1-14M ¶¶1.10, 2.11.1 ("The upper limit of airspace subject to national jurisdiction has not been authoritatively defined by international law. International practice has established that airspace terminates at some point below the point at which artificial satellites can be placed in orbit without free-falling to earth. Outer space begins at that undefined point. … Although there is no legally defined boundary between the upper limit of national airspace and the lower limit of outer space, international law recognizes freedom of transit by man-made space objects at earth orbiting altitude and beyond. A generally acceptable definition is that outer space begins at the undefined upper limit of the earth's airspace and extends to infinity."); 2006 AUSTRALIAN MANUAL ¶8-2 ("While views differ as to the precise vertical and horizontal extent of airspace, for practical purposes, it can be said that the upper limit to a state's rights in airspace is above the highest altitude at which an aircraft can fly and below the lowest possible perigee of an earth

expressed the view that there is no legal or practical need to delimit or otherwise define a specific boundary between airspace and outer space.[41]

14.2.3 Flight Information Regions. Flight Information Regions (FIRs) are areas of airspace allocated by the International Civil Aviation Organization (ICAO). Every portion of airspace belongs to a defined flight information region. Within each flight information region, a flight information service and an alerting service are provided by the national authorities responsible for air traffic control. These services are the most basic levels of air traffic service, and they provide information to aviators necessary for the safe and efficient conduct of flights.[42]

A flight information region normally encompasses substantial areas of international airspace and does not necessarily reflect international or national airspace borders.[43]

---

satellite in orbit. The result is that anything in orbit or beyond can safely be regarded as in outer space."); 2004 UK MANUAL ¶12.13 ("Views differ as to the precise vertical and horizontal extent of airspace. For practical purposes, it can be said that the upper limit to a state's rights in airspace is above the highest altitude of what an aircraft can fly and below the lowest possible perigee of an earth satellite in orbit. The result is that anything in orbit or beyond can safely be regarded as in outer space.").

[41] Kenneth Hodgkins, U.S. Advisor to the United Nations, Legal Subcommittee (LSC) of the United Nations Committee on the Peaceful Uses of Outer Space (COPUOS) 719th Meeting [unedited transcript] (Apr. 8, 2005) ("As we have stated on previous occasions, the United States is firmly of the view that there is no need to seek a legal definition or delimitation for outer space. The current framework has presented no practical difficulties and, indeed, activities in outer space are flourishing. Given this situation, an attempt to define or delimit outer space would be an unnecessary theoretical exercise that could potentially complicate existing activities and that might not be able to anticipate continuing technological developments. The current framework has served us well and we should continue to operate under this framework until there is a demonstrated need and a practical basis for developing a definition or delimitation."); Stephen Mathias, U.S. Advisor to the United Nations, *U.S. Statements on Specific Agenda Items before the Legal Subcommittee of the Committee on the Peaceful Uses of Outer Space* (2003) ("At this time, the United States remains convinced that there is no need to seek a legal definition of delimitation for outer space. Activities in outer space and in airspace are flourishing and have raised no practical need for a definition or limitation between the spheres. In the absence of a real need, any attempt to develop a definition would be ill-advised as there would be no experience to call upon in agreeing upon any particular definition or delimitation."); *U.S. Statement before the Legal Subcommittee of the United Nations Committee on the Peaceful Uses of Outer Space regarding the Definition and Delimitation of Outer Space and the Character and Utilization of the Geostationary Orbit*, Apr. 4, 2001, 2001 DIGEST OF UNITED STATES PRACTICE IN INTERNATIONAL LAW 721 ("Our position continues to be that defining or delimiting outer space is not necessary. No legal or practical problems have arisen in the absence of such a definition. On the contrary, the differing legal regimes applicable in respect of airspace and outer space have operated well in their respective spheres. The lack of a definition or delimitation of outer space has not impeded the development of activities in either sphere. ... It would be dangerous for the Legal Subcommittee to agree to an artificial line between air space and outer space, when it cannot predict the consequences of such a line.").

[42] *Information Provided to U.S. Embassies in Rangoon and New Delhi Regarding Transit Through Flight Information Regions and International Airspace*, May 2007, 2007 DIGEST OF UNITED STATES PRACTICE IN INTERNATIONAL LAW 635, 636 ("A Flight Information Region, or FIR, is simply an area over which a civil aviation authority has responsibility for provision of flight information services. FIRs are allocated to coastal states by the International Civil Aviation Organization (ICAO) to facilitate the safety of civil aviation. Some FIRs encompass both national and international airspace. Civil aviation authorities may confuse responsibility for and authority over civil aviation in a FIR for sovereignty over the area.").

[43] DOD DIRECTIVE 4500.54E, *DoD Foreign Clearance Program (FCP)*, Glossary (Dec. 28, 2009) ("flight information region. An airspace of defined dimensions within which flight information service and alerting service are provided. A flight information region normally encompasses substantial areas of international airspace and does

Under Article 3 of the 1944 Chicago Convention, flight information region rules do not apply to State aircraft, including military aircraft, and military aircraft are free to operate in international airspace without the consent of or notice to coastal State authorities.[44] Thus, for example, a flight information region could not limit the rights of belligerent military aircraft during armed conflict.

14.2.4 Air Defense Identification Zone (ADIZ). In general terms, an ADIZ is an area of airspace over land or water in which the ready identification, location, and control of aircraft may be required in the interests of national security.[45] The United States has established ADIZs.[46]

14.2.4.1 *Establishment of an ADIZ*. The legal basis for a State to establish an ADIZ is its right to establish conditions and procedures for entry into its national airspace.[47]

---

not reflect international or national airspace borders. Responsibility for flight information region management is not the same as territorial authority; therefore, state aircraft are not to request aircraft diplomatic clearance to enter a flight information region if the aircraft will not enter national airspace. The International Civil Aviation Organization establishes flight information regions in accordance with the Convention on International Civil Aviation. Civil aviation authorities of designated nations administer them pursuant to International Civil Aviation Organization authority, rules, and procedures.").

[44] *Information Provided to U.S. Embassies in Rangoon and New Delhi Regarding Transit Through Flight Information Regions and International Airspace*, May 2007, 2007 DIGEST OF UNITED STATES PRACTICE IN INTERNATIONAL LAW 635-36 ("A coastal state may establish a FIR in international airspace consistent with the requirements of the 1944 Convention on International Civil Aviation (Chicago Convention), to which your country is a party; however, under Article 3 of that convention, FIR rules do not apply to state aircraft, including military aircraft. State aircraft, including military aircraft, operating in international airspace (whether within or outside a FIR) are free to operate without the consent of or notice to coastal state authorities and are not subject to the jurisdiction or control of the ATC authorities of those states. No notice to, clearance from, or approval of a coastal state is required to exercise such freedoms of navigation and overflight. The United States reaffirms its navigation and overflight rights in international airspace.").

[45] 14 CODE OF FEDERAL REGULATIONS § 99.3 ("*Air defense identification zone* (ADIZ) means an area of airspace over land or water in which the ready identification, location, and control of all aircraft (except for Department of Defense and law enforcement aircraft) is required in the interest of national security.").

[46] *See, e.g.*, Ian E. Rinehart & Bart Elias, *China's Air Defense Identification Zone (ADIZ)*, 2 (Congressional Research Service, Jan. 30, 2015) ("In 1948, the U.S. Air Force designated several offshore areas as 'active defense areas' or 'defense zones.' From these, the first ADIZs in the world were established in 1950, under an Executive order directing the Secretary of Commerce to exercise security control over aircraft. Various defense zones were redesignated as ADIZs (over Atlantic, Pacific, and Gulf of Mexico waters[)] the Alaska ADIZ, the Guam ADIZ, and the Hawaii ADIZ, are codified in Title 14, Part 99, of the Code of Federal Regulations, along with the procedural requirements for flights operating in these designated areas. They are predominantly located over water and typically do not extend to the shore, leaving a narrow strip of sovereign airspace parallel to the coastline that is not within the ADIZ."); 1955 NWIP 10-2 ¶422c endnote 16 ("It is apparent that the potential threat to the security of states presented by aircraft is considerably greater than the potential threat presented by vessels. However, there has not yet emerged a recognized practice of 'contiguous air space zones,' analogous to contiguous zones established on the high seas (see paragraph 413d), enabling states to exercise certain *legal controls* over aircraft flying outside territorial air space. The present system of Air Defense Identification Zones (ADIZ) employed by the United States extends to the air space above the open sea, and is limited to the purpose of identifying aircraft.").

[47] *See, e.g.*, 2007 NWP 1-14M ¶2.7.2.3 ("International law does not prohibit nations from establishing air defense identification zones (ADIZ) in the international airspace adjacent to their territorial airspace. The legal basis for ADIZ regulations is the right of a nation to establish reasonable conditions of entry into its territory. Accordingly,

The establishment of an ADIZ by a State does not constitute a claim to international airspace as its own. The ADIZ is merely a reference point for the initiation of identification procedures for aircraft on a course to enter national airspace.[48]

Because the establishment of an ADIZ by a State that extends to international airspace does not confer sovereignty over that airspace, the ADIZ, and its implementing regulations and operational practices, must respect the rights of other States to use international airspace.

The United States does not recognize the right of a State to apply its ADIZ laws and regulations to foreign aircraft, either civil aircraft or State aircraft, if those aircraft do not intend to enter the national airspace of that State.[49]

14.2.4.2 *Failure to Comply With Identification Requirements*. Failure by an aircraft to identify itself once it enters an ADIZ does not, of itself, entitle the declaring State to use force against that aircraft, although it may subject the aircraft to interception.[50] Depending on the circumstances, a persistent failure to comply with instructions may be evidence that the aircraft, in fact, poses a threat to the declaring State.[51]

Establishment of an ADIZ, like other warning zones, does not relieve the proclaiming State of its obligations under applicable international law, such as its obligation under the law of war to refrain from attacking aircraft that do not constitute lawful military objectives, or its obligation to refrain from attacks against civil aircraft under peacetime international law.[52]

---

an aircraft approaching national airspace can be required to identify itself while in international airspace as a condition of entry approval."); 1976 AIR FORCE PAMPHLET 110-31 ¶2-1g ("Civil aircraft on a course to penetrate United States airspace are required to identify themselves upon entry into the [Air Defense Identification] zone. This requirement is based on the right of every state to establish conditions and procedures for entry into its airspace."). *See also* 1944 CHICAGO CONVENTION art. 11 ("Subject to the provisions of this Convention, the laws and regulations of a contracting State relating to the admission to or departure from its territory of aircraft engaged in international air navigation, or to the operation and navigation of such aircraft while within its territory, shall be applied to the aircraft of all contracting States without distinction as to nationality, and shall be complied with by such aircraft upon entering or departing from or while within the territory of that State.").

[48] 1976 AIR FORCE PAMPHLET 110-31 ¶2-1g ("An air defense identification zone does not constitute a claim of sovereignty over airspace above the high seas. Such a zone is merely a reference point for initiation of identification procedures for aircraft on a course to penetrate national airspace.").

[49] *See, e.g.*, John Kerry, Secretary of State, Press Statement (Nov. 23, 2013) ("We don't support efforts by any State to apply its ADIZ procedures to foreign aircraft not intending to enter its national airspace. The United States does not apply its ADIZ procedures to foreign aircraft not intending to enter U.S. national airspace."); *U.S. Response to Chinese Legal Views*, 2001 DIGEST OF UNITED STATES PRACTICE IN INTERNATIONAL LAW 703, 707 ("The U.S. does not recognize the right of a coastal nation to apply its ADIZ procedures to foreign aircraft not intending to enter national airspace, and does not apply its ADIZ procedures to foreign aircraft not intending to enter U.S. airspace.").

[50] 1976 AIR FORCE PAMPHLET 110-31 ¶2-1g ("State aircraft on a course to penetrate United States airspace may be requested to identify themselves, and failing voluntary identification may be identified by intercept aircraft or otherwise as appropriate.").

[51] *Compare* § 14.5.2.1 (Failure to Comply by Civil Aircraft).

[52] *Refer to* § 13.9.2 (Use of Zones to Warn Vessels or Aircraft – War, Operational, Warning, and Safety Zones); § 14.8.3.1 (Protection of Civil Aircraft in Peacetime).

14.3 AIRCRAFT STATUS

14.3.1 State Versus Civil Aircraft. The 1944 Chicago Convention distinguishes between State aircraft and civil aircraft.[53]

Aircraft used in military, customs, and police services are deemed to be State aircraft for the purposes of the 1944 Chicago Convention.[54] More generally, State aircraft may be understood to include other aircraft operated by a government for sovereign, non-commercial purposes.[55] In U.S. practice, DoD contract aircraft have not qualified as State aircraft, unless specifically designated as such by the United States.[56]

The distinction between State aircraft and civil aircraft may be important for a variety of reasons. For example, the 1944 Chicago Convention generally does not apply to State aircraft.[57] In addition, enemy State aircraft are subject to seizure as war booty.[58] As another example, neutral State aircraft are not subject to visit and search or diversion.[59] And, although not necessary for an aircraft to constitute a military objective, the status of an aircraft as State aircraft

---

[53] 1944 CHICAGO CONVENTION art. 3(a) ("This Convention shall be applicable only to civil aircraft, and shall not be applicable to state aircraft."). *Consider* Commission of Jurists to Consider and Report Upon the Revision of the Rules of Warfare, *General Report, Part II: Rules of Aërial Warfare*, art. 2, Feb. 19, 1923, *reprinted in* 32 AJIL SUPPLEMENT: OFFICIAL DOCUMENTS 12, 12 (1938) ("The following shall be deemed to be public aircraft: (a) Military aircraft. (b) Non-military aircraft exclusively employed in the public service. All other aircraft shall be deemed to be private aircraft.").

[54] 1944 CHICAGO CONVENTION art. 3(b) ("Aircraft used in military, customs and police services shall be deemed to be state aircraft.").

[55] DOD DIRECTIVE 4500.54E, *DoD Foreign Clearance Program (FCP)*, Glossary (Dec. 28, 2009) ("state aircraft. Aircraft, including U.S. military aircraft, operated by a government for sovereign, non-commercial purposes.").

[56] *See, e.g.*, Secretary of State Cable 22631, *USG Policy Regarding Status of DOD Commercial Contract Aircraft* (Mar. 10, 2010) (The U.S. Government "has consistently taken the position that Department of Defense (DoD) commercial contract aircraft and other USG contract aircraft are not state aircraft unless the particular aircraft is specifically designated as such by the USG. The normal practice of the USG is not to designate contract aircraft as state aircraft."); 2007 NWP 1-14M ¶2.4.3 ("Auxiliary aircraft are State aircraft, other than military aircraft, that are owned by or under the exclusive control of the armed forces. Civilian owned and operated aircraft, the full capacity of which has been contracted by the DOD and used in the military service of the United States, qualify as 'auxiliary aircraft' if they are designated as 'State aircraft' by the United States. In those circumstances they too enjoy sovereign immunity from foreign search and inspection. As a matter of policy, however, the United States normally does not designate Air Mobility Command-charter aircraft as State aircraft."); Department of the Army, Office of the Judge Advocate General, *International and Operations Law: Payment of Fees Charged to State Aircraft*, 21 THE REPORTER 19, 20 (June 1994) ("The US government consistently has taken the position that Department of Defense contract aircraft do not qualify as state aircraft unless the particular aircraft is specifically designated as such by the US government. Although many SOFAs, base rights, and other agreements grant DoD contract aircraft the same rights of access, exit, and freedom from landing fees and similar charges enjoyed by US military aircraft, such agreements do not have the effect of declaring DoD contract aircraft to be military aircraft or any form of state aircraft.").

[57] *Refer to* § 14.1.1.2 (1944 Chicago Convention and Military Aircraft or Other State Aircraft).

[58] *Refer to* § 14.5.3 (Capture of Aircraft and Goods on Board Aircraft).

[59] *Refer to* § 15.13 (Belligerent Right of Visit and Search of Merchant Vessels and Civil Aircraft); 14.5.2 (Diversion of Aircraft).

may also be an important factor in determining that an aircraft constitutes a military objective.[60]

14.3.2 Nationality of Aircraft. State aircraft possess the nationality of the State that operates them. Civil aircraft possess the nationality of the State in which they are registered.[61]

The nationality of an aircraft may be important in assessing whether it constitutes an enemy or neutral aircraft.[62]

14.3.3 Status of Military Aircraft. Military aircraft may be understood as aircraft that are designated as such by a State that operates them. The United States has not ratified a treaty that requires certain qualifications before an aircraft may be designated as military aircraft.

In general, military aircraft are operated by commissioned units of the armed forces of a State, bearing the military markings of that State, and commanded by a member of the armed forces of that State.

In addition to combat aircraft such as fighters and bombers, other types of aircraft operated by the armed forces of a State may also be designated as military aircraft, such as transport, reconnaissance, and meteorological aircraft. Unmanned aircraft, *i.e.*, aircraft that are remotely piloted or controlled, may also be designated as military aircraft.

14.3.3.1 *Military Aircraft – Rights and Liabilities*. Of all aircraft, only military aircraft are entitled to engage in attacks in armed conflict.[63] Likewise, during armed conflict, enemy military aircraft generally constitute military objectives and, thus, may be made the object of attack, whether in the air or on the ground.[64] There may be exceptions to the general rule that enemy military aircraft are liable to being made the object of attack, such as in the case of enemy military medical aircraft or enemy military aircraft that have surrendered.[65]

---

[60] *Refer to* § 14.8.3 (Attacks Against Civil Aircraft); § 5.6 (Military Objectives).

[61] 1944 CHICAGO CONVENTION art. 17 ("Aircraft have the nationality of the State in which they are registered.").

[62] *Refer to* § 15.14 (Acquisition of Enemy Character by Neutral-Flagged Merchant Vessels and Neutral-Marked Civil Aircraft).

[63] *See, e.g.*, 2013 GERMAN MANUAL ¶1103 ("Only military aircraft are entitled to exercise belligerent rights and use military force in fighting military objectives of an adversary (**14** 13, 16 para.1)."); 2006 AUSTRALIAN MANUAL ¶8-14 ("[O]nly military aircraft can exercise the combat rights of a belligerent. Examples of such rights include attacking military objectives and overflying enemy territory."); 2004 UK MANUAL ¶12.34 ("Only military aircraft may carry out attacks."); 2001 CANADIAN MANUAL ¶704(3) ("Civil aircraft and state aircraft that are not military aircraft (for example, police or customs officials) may not engage in hostilities … ."); 1976 AIR FORCE PAMPHLET 110-31 ¶2-6d ("Only military aircraft may exercise such rights of belligerents as attacking and destroying military objectives or transporting troops in the adversary's national airspace or behind its lines."). *Consider* Commission of Jurists to Consider and Report Upon the Revision of the Rules of Warfare, *General Report, Part II: Rules of Aërial Warfare*, art. 16, Feb. 19, 1923, *reprinted in* 32 AJIL SUPPLEMENT: OFFICIAL DOCUMENTS 12, 19 (1938) ("No aircraft other than a belligerent military aircraft shall engage in hostilities in any form.").

[64] *Refer to* § 5.6.4.1 (Military Equipment and Bases).

[65] *Refer to* § 7.14 (Military Medical Aircraft); § 14.8.2 (Protection of Persons Who Surrender or Who Are Otherwise *Hors De Combat* on Board Enemy Aircraft).

Belligerent military aircraft generally may not enter neutral airspace.[66]

As State aircraft, military aircraft, like warships, are customarily accorded certain privileges and immunities by friendly foreign States.[67]

14.3.3.2 <u>*Military Aircraft – Markings*</u>. Military aircraft are customarily marked to signify both their nationality and military character.[68] Markings may help distinguish friend from foe and help preclude misidentification of aircraft as neutral or as civil.[69] However, circumstances may exist where such markings are superfluous.[70]

A single marking may be used to signify both an aircraft's nationality and its military character.[71]

---

[66] *Refer to* § 15.10.2 (Prohibition on Entry by Belligerent Military Aircraft Into Neutral Airspace).

[67] DoD DIRECTIVE 4500.54E, *DoD Foreign Clearance Program (FCP)*, ¶4 (Dec. 28, 2009) ("b. Consistent with U.S. Government policy, DoD aircraft shall not be subject to air navigation, overflight, or similar fees for transit through the national airspace of another country or through Flight Information Regions in international airspace. This policy is based upon the unique status of state aircraft, including U.S. military aircraft, in international law as instruments of a sovereign, and is consistent with international custom and practice. … c. DoD aircraft shall not be subject to search, seizure, and inspection (including customs, safety, and agriculture inspections) or any other exercise of jurisdiction by a foreign government over such aircraft, or the personnel, equipment, or cargo on board. DoD aircraft commanders shall not consent to the exercise of jurisdiction by foreign government authorities over U.S. military aircraft, except at the direction of the appropriate DoD Component headquarters."). *Consider* Convention Relating to the Regulation of Aerial Navigation, art. 32, Oct. 13, 1919, 11 LNTS 173, 195 ("No military aircraft of a contracting State shall fly over the territory of another contracting State nor land thereon without special authorisation. In case of such authorisation the military aircraft shall enjoy, in principle, in the absence of special stipulation, the privileges which are customarily accorded to foreign ships of war. A military aircraft which is forced to land or which is requested or summoned to land shall by reason thereof acquire no right to the privileges referred to in the above paragraph."); John Cobb Cooper, *A Study on the Legal Status of Aircraft*, *in* IVAN A. VLASIC, EXPLORATIONS IN AEROSPACE LAW 205, 243 (1968) ("It is felt that the rule stated in the Paris Convention that aircraft engaged in military services should, in the absence of stipulation to the contrary, be given the privileges of foreign warships when in national port is sound and may be considered as still part of international air law even though not restated in the Chicago Convention.").

[68] *Consider* Commission of Jurists to Consider and Report Upon the Revision of the Rules of Warfare, *General Report, Part II: Rules of Aërial Warfare*, art. 3, Feb. 19, 1923, *reprinted in* 32 AJIL SUPPLEMENT: OFFICIAL DOCUMENTS 12, 13 (1938) ("A military aircraft shall bear an external mark indicating its nationality and military character.").

[69] *For example*, SPAIGHT, AIR POWER AND WAR RIGHTS 82 ("Again and again one finds the fighting airmen of 1914-18 stating in their memoirs or diaries that they have been saved from attacking a friend or have been put on guard against a foe by seeing the distinguishing marks on the wings of the machines.").

[70] 1976 AIR FORCE PAMPHLET 110-31 ¶7-4 ("Military aircraft, as entities of combat in aerial warfare, are also required to be marked with appropriate signs of their nationality and military character. However, circumstances may exist where such markings are superfluous and are not required. An example is when no other aircraft except those belonging to a single state are flown. Such markings serve to distinguish friend from foe and serve to preclude misidentification as neutral or civilian aircraft. Accordingly, military aircraft may not bear markings of the enemy or markings of neutral aircraft while engaging in combat. Combatant markings should be prominently affixed to the exterior aircraft surfaces and be recognizable at a reasonable distance from any direction.").

[71] *For example*, 2004 UK MANUAL ¶12.10.4 ("In most air forces, the same marking indicates both nationality and military character, for example, the Royal Air Force roundel.").

14.3.3.3 *Military Aircraft – Command and Crew*. Military aircraft are commanded by members of the armed forces of that State.[72] The crew, however, may include civilian members, and such personnel are expressly entitled to POW status under the GPW.[73]

14.4 Status of Aircrew on Military Aircraft

14.4.1 Military Aircrew. Aircrew who are members of the armed forces of a State have the rights, duties, and liabilities of combatants.[74] For example, they are entitled to POW status if they fall into the power of the enemy during international armed conflict, and they have legal immunity from domestic law for acts done under military authority and in accordance with the law of war.

14.4.1.1 *Wearing of Uniform by Military Aircrew*. Military aircrew are required to distinguish themselves from the civilian population in the same manner as other combatants.[75] The wearing of flying clothing distinctive to the armed forces satisfies this requirement. In particular, military aircrew should wear military uniforms (including distinctive flying clothing) in case they become separated from the aircraft.[76]

14.4.2 Civilian Members of Military Aircrew and Other Persons Authorized to Accompany the Armed Forces. Civilian members of military aircrew fall into the category of persons authorized to accompany the armed forces.[77] Other civilians who are present on military aircraft or who support the operations of military aircraft may also fall into the category of persons authorized to accompany the armed forces, provided they have received such authorization.

As persons authorized to accompany the armed forces, civilian members of military aircrews are entitled to POW status if they fall into the power of the enemy during international armed conflict, and they have legal immunity from the enemy's domestic law for providing authorized support services to the armed forces. Civilians who work in or on military objectives, such as military aircraft, assume a certain risk of harm from attacks against military objectives.[78]

14.4.3 Downed Aircrew. There are a number of law of war issues related to downed

---

[72] *Consider* Commission of Jurists to Consider and Report Upon the Revision of the Rules of Warfare, *General Report, Part II: Rules of Aërial Warfare*, art. 14, Feb. 19, 1923, *reprinted in* 32 AJIL Supplement: Official Documents 12, 18 (1938) ("A military aircraft shall be under the command of a person duly commissioned or enlisted in the military service of the state;").

[73] *Refer to* § 4.15 (Persons Authorized to Accompany the Armed Forces).

[74] *Refer to* § 4.5 (Armed Forces of a State); § 4.4 (Rights, Duties, and Liabilities of Combatants).

[75] *Refer to* § 5.14.5 (Carrying Arms Openly and Wearing of Distinctive Emblems by the Armed Forces to Distinguish Themselves From the Civilian Population).

[76] *Consider* Commission of Jurists to Consider and Report Upon the Revision of the Rules of Warfare, *General Report, Part II: Rules of Aërial Warfare*, art. 15, Feb. 19, 1923, *reprinted in* 32 AJIL Supplement: Official Documents 12, 18 (1938) ("Members of the crew of a military aircraft shall wear a fixed distinctive emblem of such character as to be recognizable at a distance in case they become separated from their aircraft.").

[77] *Refer to* § 4.15 (Persons Authorized to Accompany the Armed Forces).

[78] *Refer to* § 5.12.3.3 (Civilian Workers Who Support Military Operations In or On Military Objectives).

aircrew.

14.4.3.1 *Protection of Aircrew While Parachuting From an Aircraft in Distress*. In general, aircrew parachuting from an aircraft in distress are treated as though they are *hors de combat*, *i.e.*, they must not be made the object of attack.[79] Aircrew parachuting from an aircraft in distress who engage in hostile acts or attempt to evade capture, either while descending or after reaching the ground, forfeit any protection from being made the object of attack.[80]

14.4.3.2 *Protection of Downed Aircrew at Sea*. Downed aircrew at sea are generally to be regarded as shipwrecked, as the definition of shipwrecked includes forced landings at sea by or from aircraft.[81] As shipwrecked persons, they must not be made the object of attack, and there are obligations to search for and collect them.[82]

14.4.3.3 *Rescue of Downed Aircrew*. The rescue of downed aircrew to prevent their capture by the adversary is generally regarded as a combat activity that enemy military forces may legitimately oppose.[83] Medical personnel, ships, or aircraft engaged in the rescue of downed aircrew must not hamper or interfere with the efforts of opposing military forces to capture downed aircrew or they will forfeit protection from being made the object of attack as a result.[84]

The United States has understood the prohibition against the use of riot control agents as a method of warfare not to prohibit the use of riot control agents to rescue downed aircrew in certain circumstances.[85]

14.4.3.4 *Downed Aircrew – Evasion From, and Capture by, the Enemy*. Downed aircrew may use enemy uniforms to evade capture by the enemy, but, in some cases, such use may risk liability to treatment as a spy.[86] Likewise, downed aircrew may use civilian clothes to evade capture by the enemy.[87]

If downed aircrew fall into the power of the enemy during international armed conflict,

---

[79] *Refer to* § 5.9.5 (Persons Parachuting From an Aircraft in Distress).

[80] *Refer to* § 5.9.5.1 (No Hostile Acts or Attempts to Evade Capture).

[81] *Refer to* § 7.3.1.2 (Shipwrecked).

[82] *Refer to* § 7.3.3 (Meaning of "Respect and Protection" of the Wounded, Sick, and Shipwrecked); § 7.4.1 (GWS-Sea Obligation Regarding the Search, Collection, and Affirmative Protection of the Wounded, Sick, Shipwrecked, and Dead).

[83] 2004 UK MANUAL ¶12.70.1 ("The use of, for example, military assets to rescue aircrew who have been 'downed' on territory under the control of the enemy is a combat activity. It is therefore legitimate for an enemy in such circumstances to attack the rescuers or by some other means to impede or prevent the rescue activity.").

[84] *Refer to* § 4.9.2.3 (Exclusively Engaged in Humanitarian Duties); § 7.12.2.3 (No Hampering the Movement of Combatants); § 7.14.2.2 (Search, Rescue, or Other Recovery Excluded).

[85] *Refer to* § 6.16.2 (Prohibition on Use of Riot Control Agents as a Method of Warfare).

[86] *Refer to* § 5.23.1.4 (Use of Enemy Uniforms to Evade Capture or Escape).

[87] *Refer to* § 5.25.3 (Examples of Other Deceptions That Are Not Prohibited). *Compare* § 9.25.2.2 (Only Disciplinary Punishments in Respect of an Act of Escape).

they are entitled to POW status.[88] Downed aircrew remain entitled to POW status even if they unsuccessfully attempt to escape capture by enemy forces or if they attack enemy forces upon reaching the ground. As POWs, downed aircrew are entitled to protection from violence from the civilian population and others.[89]

14.4.3.5 *Downed Aircrew in Neutral Territory*. Military aircrew forced to land in neutral territory due to navigational failure, combat damage, mechanical failure, or other emergencies are subject to internment by the neutral State for the duration of the conflict.[90]

14.5 MEASURES SHORT OF ATTACK: INTERCEPTION, DIVERSION, AND CAPTURE

14.5.1 Interception. During armed conflict, a party may choose to intercept an aircraft through a variety of ways, including closing to visual range or to a distance where the target aircraft is within the range of weapons systems. Interception of civil aircraft that are not military objectives should be exercised with due regard for the safety of such aircraft.[91]

14.5.1.1 *Purposes for Conducting Interception*. Interception may have a variety of purposes, including, for example:

- to assist in the obligation to distinguish between military objectives and civilian objects and the obligation to protect the civilian population,[92] such as by
  - warning a civil aircraft to refrain from entering an area of active operations; or
  - helping identify whether the aircraft constitutes a military objective;
- as part of the belligerent right of visit and search, including the belligerent right to enforce a blockade,[93] such as by
  - facilitating identification of an aircraft (*e.g.*, enemy or neutral);
  - forcing an aircraft to divert and land at a specific airfield for search or capture; or
- to be in a position to attack the aircraft.

14.5.1.2 *Airspace Where Interception May Be Conducted*. As a general rule, belligerent military aircraft may not intercept aircraft in neutral airspace.[94]

---

[88] *Refer to* § 9.3 (POW Status).

[89] *Refer to* § 9.5.2.2 (Protection Against Violence by the Civilian Population or Others).

[90] *Refer to* § 15.16 (Belligerent Forces Taking Refuge in Neutral Territory).

[91] *Refer to* § 14.1.1.4 (Due Regard for the Safety of Navigation of Civil Aircraft).

[92] *Refer to* § 2.5 (Distinction).

[93] *Refer to* § 15.13 (Belligerent Right of Visit and Search of Merchant Vessels and Civil Aircraft).

[94] *Refer to* § 15.10 (Neutral Airspace).

In addition, interception may not be conducted during passage through neutral international straits or neutral archipelagic sea lanes.[95]

14.5.2 Diversion of Aircraft. Diversion and search of civil aircraft may be conducted outside neutral airspace as part of the belligerent right of visit and search (*e.g.*, to help determine whether aircraft are liable to capture for carriage of contraband or for breach of blockade).[96] Interference with civil aircraft of neutral States must be justified by military necessity.

If, upon interception outside of neutral airspace, reasonable grounds exist for suspecting that the intercepted civil aircraft, its cargo, or its personnel are liable to capture,[97] then it may be directed to proceed to a belligerent airfield that is both reasonably accessible and suitable for the type of aircraft involved for visit and search.[98] Should such an airfield not be available, the intercepted civil aircraft may be diverted from its declared destination.[99]

Certain aircraft are exempt from the belligerent right to divert aircraft for purposes of visit and search: (1) neutral military aircraft; and (2) neutral civil aircraft accompanied by neutral military aircraft of the same nationality.[100]

14.5.2.1 *Failure to Comply by Civil Aircraft*. An enemy civil aircraft that persistently fails to comply with military instructions becomes a military objective subject to attack.[101]

Failure to comply with military instructions from intercepting aircraft does not in itself render a neutral or non-belligerent civil aircraft a military objective. However, it may provide strong evidence that the civil aircraft is in fact being used for a military or hostile purpose.

14.5.3 Capture of Aircraft and Goods on Board Aircraft. Enemy civil aircraft and goods

---

[95] *Refer to* § 15.8 (Passage of Belligerent Vessels and Aircraft Through International Straits and Archipelagic Sea Lanes).

[96] *Refer to* § 15.13.4.3 (Visit and Search of Civil Aircraft by Military Aircraft).

[97] *Refer to* § 15.15.1 (Grounds for the Capture of Neutral Vessels and Aircraft).

[98] *Consider* Commission of Jurists to Consider and Report Upon the Revision of the Rules of Warfare, *General Report, Part II: Rules of Aërial Warfare*, art. 50, Feb. 19, 1923, *reprinted in* 32 AJIL SUPPLEMENT: OFFICIAL DOCUMENTS 12, 44 (1938) ("Belligerent military aircraft have the right to order public non-military and private aircraft to alight in or proceed for visit and search to a suitable locality reasonably accessible. Refusal, after warning, to obey such orders to alight or to proceed to such a locality for examination exposes an aircraft to the risk of being fired upon.").

[99] 2007 NWP 1-14M ¶7.6.3 ("If, upon interception outside of neutral airspace, reasonable grounds exist for suspecting that the intercepted civilian aircraft is carrying contraband cargo or that, despite its neutral markings, it is, in fact, enemy, it may be directed to proceed for visit and search to a belligerent airfield that is both reasonably accessible and suitable for the type of aircraft involved. Should such an airfield not be available, the intercepted civilian aircraft may be diverted from its declared destination.").

[100] *Refer to* § 15.13.2 (Types of Neutral Vessels and Aircraft That Are Exempt From Visit and Search).

[101] *Refer to* § 14.8.3.2 (Forfeiture of Protection From Being Made the Object of Attack During Armed Conflict).

on board such aircraft may be captured outside neutral airspace.[102]

Any enemy State aircraft (including military, law enforcement, and customs aircraft), as public movable property, is subject to capture as war booty with ownership passing immediately to the captor government.[103] Similarly, prize procedure is not used for captured enemy warships.[104]

Neutral civil aircraft engaged in certain activity in violation of their neutral status are liable to capture.[105] Even if not liable to capture, neutral civil aircraft are subject to visit and search.[106]

14.6 Belligerent Control of Aviation in the Immediate Vicinity of Hostilities

Belligerents may prohibit or establish special restrictions upon flight activities in the immediate vicinity of hostilities to prevent such activities from jeopardizing military operations. In some cases, this right may be distinct from a belligerent State's right to establish airspace zones during armed conflict.[107]

As with the belligerent right to control the immediate area of naval operations, this right is based on a belligerent State's right to ensure the security of its forces and its right to conduct hostilities without interference from neutrals.[108] However, belligerent control of aviation in the immediate vicinity of hostilities may be applicable in the national airspace of belligerents.[109]

---

[102] *Consider* Commission of Jurists to Consider and Report Upon the Revision of the Rules of Warfare, *General Report, Part II: Rules of Aërial Warfare*, art. 49, Feb. 19, 1923, *reprinted in* 32 AJIL Supplement: Official Documents 12, 40 (1938) ("Private aircraft are liable to visit and search and to capture by belligerent military aircraft."); Commission of Jurists to Consider and Report Upon the Revision of the Rules of Warfare, *General Report, Part II: Rules of Aërial Warfare*, art. 52, Feb. 19, 1923, *reprinted in* 32 AJIL Supplement: Official Documents 12, 45 (1938) ("Enemy private aircraft are liable to capture in all circumstances.").

[103] *Refer to* § 5.17.3 (Enemy Movable Property on the Battlefield (War Booty)). *Consider* Commission of Jurists to Consider and Report Upon the Revision of the Rules of Warfare, *General Report, Part II: Rules of Aërial Warfare*, art. 32, Feb. 19, 1923, *reprinted in* 32 AJIL Supplement: Official Documents 12, 30 (1938) ("Enemy public aircraft, other than those treated on the same footing as private aircraft, shall be subject to confiscation without prize proceedings."); Program on Humanitarian Policy and Conflict Research at Harvard University, *Commentary on the HPCR Manual on International Law Applicable to Air and Missile Warfare*, 275 (U.I.136(a)) (2010) ("Enemy military, law-enforcement and customs aircraft are booty of war. Prize procedures do not apply to captured enemy military aircraft and other State aircraft, inasmuch as their ownership immediately passes to the captor government by virtue of capture.").

[104] *Refer to* § 13.4.3 (Captured Enemy Warships – No Prize Procedure).

[105] *Refer to* § 15.15.1 (Grounds for the Capture of Neutral Vessels and Aircraft).

[106] *Refer to* § 15.13 (Belligerent Right of Visit and Search of Merchant Vessels and Civil Aircraft).

[107] *Refer to* § 14.7 (Airspace Zones).

[108] *Refer to* § 13.8 (Belligerent Control of the Immediate Area of Naval Operations).

[109] *Refer to* § 14.2.1.1 (National Airspace).

14.7 Airspace Zones

During armed conflict, States may establish airspace zones and associated procedures intended to prohibit aircraft from entering or flying in designated areas, including areas in international airspace. Such zones may be established for a variety of purposes, including to decrease the risk of inadvertent attack of civil or neutral aircraft, to control the scope of the conflict, or to enhance the predictability and effectiveness of ongoing operations.

The legal rules that apply to the establishment and enforcement of a zone are discussed in connection with the establishment and enforcement of maritime zones.[110]

In some cases, such as with Air Defense Identification Zones, the zone may be established during peacetime.[111]

14.8 Attacks Against Military Objectives in the Air

The general rules on conducting attacks also apply to attacks against military objectives in the air.[112] In general, enemy military aircraft may be made the object of attack.

14.8.1 Medical Aircraft. Specific rules found in the 1949 Geneva Conventions address the protection of aircraft that are engaged exclusively in specified medical functions.[113]

14.8.2 Protection of Persons Who Surrender or Who Are Otherwise *Hors De Combat* on Board Enemy Aircraft. The general rules on the protection of persons who are *hors de combat* (such as those who have been incapacitated and those who have effectively surrendered) also apply to persons on board enemy aircraft.[114]

Although the capture of enemy military aircraft and aircrew may be of significant intelligence value, there are often significant practical obstacles to identifying when persons on board an aircraft are *hors de combat* and to accepting their surrender. Despite these practical difficulties, if surrender is offered in good faith and circumstances do not preclude enforcement, then surrender must be respected.[115] Persons who are conducting attacks against enemy military aircraft must assess in good faith whether surrender is offered in good faith and can feasibly be accepted based on the information that is available to them at the time.[116]

14.8.2.1 *Difficulty in Identifying Persons on Board Aircraft as Hors De Combat*. As a practical matter, it may be quite difficult to establish that persons on board enemy aircraft

---

[110] *Refer to* § 13.9 (Maritime and Airspace Zones: Exclusion, War, Operational, Warning, and Safety).

[111] *Refer to* § 14.2.4 (Air Defense Identification Zone (ADIZ)).

[112] *Refer to* § 5.4.2 (Overview of Rules in Conducting Attacks).

[113] *Refer to* § 7.14 (Military Medical Aircraft); § 7.19 (Civilian Medical Aircraft).

[114] *Refer to* § 5.9 (Persons Placed *Hors de Combat*).

[115] 1976 Air Force Pamphlet 110-31 ¶4-2d ("If surrender is offered in good faith so that circumstances do not preclude enforcement, then surrender must be respected.").

[116] *Refer to* § 5.3.2 (Decisions Must Be Made in Good Faith and Based on Information Available at the Time).

are *hors de combat* and may no longer be made the object of attack.

First, it is very difficult, if not impossible, to assess whether the enemy aircraft has actually been disabled and does not pose any threat. For example, aircraft may feign symptoms of distress to evade enemy attacks.[117] Moreover, even if an aircraft has been disabled in some respects, the aircraft may not have lost its means of combat, and weapons on board the aircraft may still pose a threat.

As a practical matter, it may also be difficult for the pilot of an attacking aircraft to know when an adversary is attempting to surrender or has surrendered. Broadcasting on the international GUARD frequency (aircraft emergency frequency), rocking the aircraft's wings, lowering the landing gear, and other signals (such as the flashing of navigational lights) are sometimes cited as indications of a pilot or aircrew's desire to surrender, but they are not recognized in law as signals of surrender. Consequently, absent an explicit message of offering surrender, an intention to surrender cannot be presumed from the conduct of the aircraft.

14.8.2.2 *Feasibility of Accepting Surrender by Enemy Aircraft*. In many circumstances, it may not be feasible to accept the surrender of enemy aircraft.[118] For example, it may not be possible to enforce surrender when the engagement takes place over enemy territory.[119]

14.8.3 Attacks Against Civil Aircraft. During armed conflict, civil aircraft are generally considered civilian objects, but may be made the object of attack, outside neutral territory, if they constitute a military objective.

14.8.3.1 *Protection of Civil Aircraft in Peacetime*. Under customary international law applicable during peacetime, States have an obligation to refrain from resorting to the use of weapons against civil aircraft in flight.[120] However, this obligation does not modify in any way

---

[117] *Refer to* § 5.25.3 (Examples of Other Deceptions That Are Not Prohibited).

[118] 1976 AIR FORCE PAMPHLET 110-31 ¶4-2d ("Surrenders in air combat are generally not offered. If surrender is offered, usually no way exists to enforce the surrender.").

[119] 2004 UK MANUAL ¶12.64 ("Although it is forbidden to kill or wound an enemy who, having laid down his arms, or having no longer means of defence, has surrendered at discretion in air-to-air combat, surrender is usually impracticable and occurs very infrequently."); 2004 UK MANUAL ¶12.64.1 ("In the special circumstances of air-to-air combat the continuation of an attack after an indication by the opponent of a wish to surrender is not inconsistent with the rule in paragraph 12.64, as the enemy pilot who remains in his aircraft cannot be said to have 'laid down his arms' or to have 'no longer a means of defence'. However, if the surrender is offered in good faith and in circumstances that do not prevent enforcement, for example, when the engagement has not taken place over enemy territory, it must be respected and accepted.").

[120] *See, e.g.*, Walter Dellinger, Assistant Attorney General, *United States Assistance to Countries that Shoot Down Civil Aircraft Involved in Drug Trafficking*, Jul. 14, 1994, 18 OPINIONS OF THE OFFICE OF LEGAL COUNSEL 148, 149-50 ("[T]he United States argued that the Soviet Union had violated both Article 3(d) and customary international legal norms in shooting down KAL 007. … We understand that the United States has not yet ratified Article 3 *bis*. There is, however, support for the view that the principle it announced is declaratory of customary international law."); U.N. SECURITY COUNCIL RESOLUTION 1067, U.N. Doc. S/RES/1067 (1996) ("6. Condemns the use of weapons against civil aircraft in flight as being incompatible with elementary considerations of humanity, the rules of customary international law as codified in article 3 bis of the Chicago Convention, … ."). *Consider* Protocol Relating to an Amendment to the Convention on International Civil Aviation (Article 3 bis), May 10, 1984, 2122

the rights and obligations of States set forth in the Charter of the United Nations.[121] Thus, a State's use of force against civil aircraft in the exercise of the inherent right of self-defense would be permitted.

14.8.3.2 *Forfeiture of Protection From Being Made the Object of Attack During Armed Conflict*. Civil aircraft may be made the object of attack, outside neutral territory, if the aircraft constitutes a military objective.[122]

In particular, civil aircraft forfeit any protection from being made the object of attack if they acquire the character of enemy military aircraft by:

- taking a direct part in the hostilities on the side of the enemy; or
- acting in any capacity as a naval or military auxiliary to the enemy's armed forces.[123]

In addition, enemy civil aircraft forfeit protection from being made the object of attack:[124]

- when persistently refusing to comply with directions from intercepting aircraft;[125]
- when flying under convoy of enemy warships or military aircraft;
- when armed with systems or weapons beyond that required for self-defense against

---

UNTS 346-47 ("The contracting States recognize that every State must refrain from resorting to the use of weapons against civil aircraft in flight and that, in case of interception, the lives of persons on board and the safety of aircraft must not be endangered. This provision shall not be interpreted as modifying in any way the rights and obligations of States set forth in the Charter of the United Nations.").

[121] *Consider* Protocol Relating to an Amendment to the Convention on International Civil Aviation (Article 3 bis), May 10, 1984, 2122 UNTS 346-47 ("The contracting States recognize that every State must refrain from resorting to the use of weapons against civil aircraft in flight and that, in case of interception, the lives of persons on board and the safety of aircraft must not be endangered. This provision shall not be interpreted as modifying in any way the rights and obligations of States set forth in the Charter of the United Nations.") (emphasis added). *Compare* § 13.1.1 (The Law of the Sea During Armed Conflict).

[122] *Refer to* § 5.6 (Military Objectives).

[123] *Refer to* § 15.14.2.1 (Acquiring the Character of an Enemy Warship or Military Aircraft).

[124] 2007 NWP 1-14M ¶8.8 ("Enemy merchant vessels and civil aircraft may be attacked and destroyed by military aircraft only under the following circumstances: 1. When persistently refusing to comply with directions from the intercepting aircraft 2. When sailing under convoy of enemy warships or military aircraft 3. When armed with systems or weapons beyond that required for self-defense against terrorism, piracy, or like threats 4. When incorporated into or assisting in any way the enemy's military intelligence system 5. When acting in any capacity as a naval or military auxiliary to an enemy's armed forces 6. When otherwise integrated into the enemy's war-fighting or war-sustaining effort."); 1989 NWP 9 ¶8.4 ("Enemy merchant vessels and civil aircraft may be attacked and destroyed by military aircraft only under the following circumstances: 1. When refusing to comply with directions from the intercepting aircraft 2. When assisting in any way the enemy's military intelligence system or acting in any capacity as auxiliaries to the enemy's armed forces 3. When sailing under convoy of enemy warships, escorted by enemy military aircraft, or armed 4. When otherwise integrated into the enemy's war-fighting or war-sustaining effort.").

[125] *Refer to* § 14.5.2.1 (Failure to Comply by Civil Aircraft).

terrorism, piracy, or like threats;

- when incorporated into or assisting the enemy's military intelligence system;[126] or
- when otherwise integrated into the enemy's war-fighting or war-sustaining effort.

14.8.3.3 *Attack of Civilian Passenger Aircraft*. If a civilian passenger aircraft constitutes a military objective and thus is liable to attack, any attack must comply with other applicable rules related to attacks.[127]

In particular, attacks against civilian passenger aircraft engaged in passenger service must comply with the requirement that the expected loss of life or injury to civilians, and damage to civilian objects incidental to the attack, must not be excessive in relation to the concrete and direct military advantage expected to be gained.[128]

14.9 AIR ATTACKS AGAINST MILITARY OBJECTIVES ON THE GROUND

The general rules on conducting attacks also apply to air attacks against military objectives on the ground.[129]

14.9.1 Prohibition Against Bombardment of Undefended Cities, Towns, and Villages. The aerial bombardment of towns, villages, dwellings, or buildings that are undefended is prohibited.[130] The phrase "by whatever means" was inserted in the Hague IV Regulations to clarify that bombing attacks by air were included in this rule.[131]

An "undefended" city, town, or village in this sense is a term of art. For example, a city may only be declared "undefended" if it is open for immediate physical occupation by opposing military ground forces.[132]

14.9.2 Selection of Weapons in Conducting Attacks From the Air Against Ground Military Objectives. It may be the case that commanders will have a variety of weapons with which to conduct a potential aerial bombardment.

Certain weapons are prohibited *per se*, and it is specifically provided that feasible

---

[126] *Consider* Commission of Jurists to Consider and Report Upon the Revision of the Rules of Warfare, *General Report, Part I: Rules for the Control of Radio in Time of War*, art. 6, Feb. 19, 1923, *reprinted in* 32 AJIL SUPPLEMENT: OFFICIAL DOCUMENTS 2, 7-8 (1938) ("1. The transmission by radio by a vessel or an aircraft, whether enemy or neutral, when on or over the high seas of military intelligence for the immediate use of a belligerent is to be deemed a hostile act and will render the vessel or aircraft liable to be fired upon.").

[127] *Refer to* § 5.4 (Rules on Conducting Assaults, Bombardments, and Other Attacks).

[128] *Refer to* § 5.12 (Proportionality – Prohibition on Attacks Expected to Cause Excessive Incidental Harm).

[129] *Refer to* § 5.4.2 (Overview of Rules in Conducting Attacks).

[130] *Refer to* § 5.15 (Undefended Cities, Towns, and Villages).

[131] *Refer to* § 5.15.2 ("By Whatever Means").

[132] *Refer to* § 5.15.3 (Declaration of a City as "Undefended").

precautions be taken in connection with certain weapons.[133] It must be emphasized, however, that the selection of the appropriate weapon for conducting an aerial bombardment remains primarily a military judgment rather than a legal one. In particular, there is no law of war requirement to use precision-guided weapons when non-precision-guided weapons may be used in compliance with the law of war.[134]

Commanders have a general obligation to take feasible precautions in planning and conducting attacks in order to reduce the risk of harm to the civilian population.[135] The selection of weapons may be among the available precautions that a commander could take in order to reduce the risk of harm to the civilian population.

14.9.3 Protection of Enemy Ground Forces Who Are *Hors de Combat*. When aircrew or aircraft operators assess that an enemy combatant has been placed *hors de combat*, they must refrain from making such persons the object of attack.[136]

In order to place a person *hors de combat*, the person's surrender must be (1) genuine; (2) clear and unconditional; and (3) under circumstances where it is feasible for the opposing party to accept the surrender.[137]

In many cases, it would not be feasible for a party that is conducting air operations to accept the surrender of an enemy person. In some cases, however, it may be appropriate, in order to facilitate such surrender, to communicate steps for enemy units to take to communicate clearly their intention to surrender.[138]

14.9.3.1 *Difficulty in Identifying Persons Placed Hors De Combat*. The identification by aircraft of an enemy combatant on the ground placed *hors de combat* may pose a particular challenge. It may be difficult for aircrew or aircraft operators to determine whether an enemy combatant is dead, injured, merely taking cover, or feigning injury or surrender to

---

[133] *Refer to* § 6.4 (Prohibited Weapons); § 5.2.3.4 (Requirements to Take Precautions Regarding Specific Weapons).

[134] *Refer to* § 5.11.6 (Weaponeering (E.g., Selecting Appropriate Weapons, Aim Points)).

[135] *Refer to* § 5.11 (Proportionality – Feasible Precautions in Planning and Conducting Attacks to Reduce the Risk of Harm to Protected Persons and Objects).

[136] *Refer to* § 5.9 (Persons Placed *Hors de Combat*).

[137] *Refer to* § 5.9.3 (Persons Who Have Surrendered).

[138] Captain M. Scott Holcomb, *View from the Legal Frontlines*, 4 CHICAGO JOURNAL OF INTERNATIONAL LAW 561, 566-67 (2003) ("In August 2002, I met with Commander Kenneth O'Rourke, the Chief of Operational Law at CENTCOM, and Lieutenant Commander Gregory Bart, the Special Operations Command Central ('SOCCENT') Staff Judge Advocate to develop legally supportable concepts that would achieve the commander's intent to either have Iraqi units assist Coalition forces or indicate a desire not to fight and remain in place, preferably in their barracks. … Consequently, we sketched an outline for an operational plan to encourage units to capitulate. Coalition forces would contact Iraqi units through various means including leaflet drops, radio broadcasts, and surrogates who would inform the commander of his opportunity to surrender with honor and preserve his unit. Iraqi units would receive these messages shortly before the air campaign started to give them time to perform the required actions, but not so much time that they would be subject to regime reprisals. If the unit performed certain observable actions, such as forming their vehicles in a square, then Special Forces would approach the unit and offer articles of capitulation for the surrender of the unit.").

avoid attack.[139] On the other hand, it may be difficult for enemy combatants on the ground to communicate clearly to aircraft that they wish genuinely to surrender unconditionally or that they have been incapacitated.

Aircrew or aircraft operators must assess in good faith whether persons have been placed *hors de combat* based on the information that is available to them at the time.[140]

14.9.3.2 Feasibility of Air Units to Accept the Surrender of Ground Forces. For a communication of surrender to place a person *hors de combat*, the person must make the surrender under circumstances where it is feasible for the opposing party to accept the surrender.[141] For example, it must be possible for the opposing party to take that person into custody.[142]

In many cases, it would not be feasible for the aircraft to land and take the person into custody or for nearby ground forces to take the person into custody.[143]

---

[139] *See* SPAIGHT, AIR POWER AND WAR RIGHTS 132 ("In the second world war also there were one or two instances in which ground forces showed the white flag to aircraft. ... Other circumstances are conceivable in which there could be no assurance that the display of a white flag was not a ruse to enable the enemy troops to escape after the immediate danger was past. In such circumstances it could he [sic] held that the airmen were under no obligation to discontinue their attack.").

[140] *Refer to* § 5.3.2 (Decisions Must Be Made in Good Faith and Based on Information Available at the Time).

[141] *Refer to* § 5.9.3.3 (Under Circumstances in Which It Is Feasible to Accept).

[142] *For example*, FINAL REPORT ON THE PERSIAN GULF WAR 381 ("During this attack, the two companies of 3/1 Attack Helicopter Battalion encountered minimal resistance in the form of T-55 tanks and BMPs, which they destroyed. The surprising aspect of this operation was that it was the first of many instances where hundreds of Iraqi soldiers ran out of their bunkers and attempted to surrender after seeing Army helicopters in their midst. Without the means to hold them, the aeroscout pilots played 'cowboys' to the 'herd' of Iraqi soldiers, hovering them into a tight circle until the lead ground elements of the Division's 1st Brigade arrived and secured them."); FINAL REPORT ON THE PERSIAN GULF WAR 212 ("In addition to direct support of NGFS missions, UAVs also were used to gather intelligence on Faylaka Island when national sensors were not available and weather prevented aircraft reconnaissance. Over Faylaka Island, *USS Wisconsin's* UAV recorded hundreds of Iraqi soldiers waving white flags – the first-ever surrender of enemy troops to an unmanned aircraft. After the cease-fire, UAVs monitored the coastline and outlying islands in reconnaissance support of occupying Coalition forces. Because UAVs were under direct tactical control of combat forces, they could respond quickly in dynamic situations. On one occasion, *USS Wisconsin's* UAV located two Iraqi patrol boats, which were sunk by aircraft directed to investigate.").

[143] *For example*, 101st Airborne ROE Card, Iraq (2003), *reprinted in* CENTER FOR LAW AND MILITARY OPERATIONS, THE JUDGE ADVOCATE GENERAL'S LEGAL CENTER & SCHOOL, U.S. ARMY, I LEGAL LESSONS LEARNED FROM AFGHANISTAN AND IRAQ: MAJOR COMBAT OPERATIONS (11 SEPTEMBER 2001 - 1 MAY 2003) 315, 316 (2004) ("**3. Facts**: An armed soldier sees you and throws his hands up to surrender. **Response**: Take the soldier prisoner, and treat as an EPW. (Note: aircraft are not in the position to accept surrender, in the foregoing scenario, a 101st ABD aircraft could fire upon the enemy soldier)."); SPAIGHT, AIR POWER AND WAR RIGHTS 131-32 ("Usually it is impossible for attacking airmen to take ground troops prisoners, and such a situation as that described by Lieut.-Col. Tennant as arising in Iraq in February, 1917, is probably more typical and normal than the cases quoted above. Lieut.-Col. Tennant describes how in the Turkish retreat towards Azizieh, after the forcing by General Maude's army of the Shumran Bend in the Tigris on 23 February, 1917, 'many of the waggons had hoisted the white flag,' while some of the flying Turks 'waved in token of surrender,' when the British aeroplanes attacked them with machine-guns. 'Flying along about 10 feet from the road I mowed down seven with one burst of machine-gun fire.' In such circumstances it is impossible to recognise the white flag. To try to do so would be to sacrifice the advantage of the destruction of a routed and demoralised foe.").

14.10 INTERNATIONAL LAW AND WARFARE IN OUTER SPACE

14.10.1 Classification of Outer Space. Outer space is governed by a separate legal regime than that for airspace.[144]

Outer space may be viewed as analogous to the high seas in certain respects.[145] For example, no State may claim sovereignty over outer space.[146] In addition, the space systems of all nations have rights of passage through space without interference.[147]

14.10.2 Application of International Law to Activities in Space.

14.10.2.1 *Treaties Specifically Addressing Space Activities*. The United States is a Party to certain treaties that address space activities. The Treaty on Principles Governing the Activities of States in the Exploration and Use of Outer Space, including the Moon and Other Celestial Bodies (Outer Space Treaty), imposes restrictions on certain military operations in outer space (*i.e.*, it does not exempt military spacecraft or military space activities from its purview).[148] The Outer Space Treaty provides for State responsibility for the activities of non-governmental entities in outer space, including the moon and other celestial bodies.[149]

Other treaties that specifically address space activities include:

- Agreement on the Rescue of Astronauts, the Return of Astronauts, and the Return of

---

[144] *Refer to* § 14.2.2 (Vertical Boundary Between Airspace and Outer Space).

[145] Arthur J. Goldberg, U.S. Ambassador to the United Nations, *Treaty on Outer Space: Hearings Before the Committee on Foreign Relations, U.S. Senate*, 90th Congress, First Session, 63 (Mar. 13, 1967) ("This is an attempt, once we leave airspace, and get to outer space, however you define the limits, this is an attempt to create in outer space the closest analogy and that is the high seas.").

[146] OUTER SPACE TREATY art. II ("Outer space, including the moon and other celestial bodies, is not subject to national appropriation by claim of sovereignty, by means of use or occupation, or by any other means.").

[147] *See, e.g.*, OUTER SPACE TREATY art. I ("Outer space, including the moon and other celestial bodies, shall be free for exploration and use by all States without discrimination of any kind, on a basis of equality and in accordance with international law, and there shall be free access to all areas of celestial bodies."); *National Space Policy of the United States of America*, 3 (Jun. 28, 2010) ("The United States considers the space systems of all nations to have the rights of passage through, and conduct of operations in, space without interference. Purposeful interference with space systems, including supporting infrastructure, will be considered an infringement of a nation's rights."); Presidential Directive/NSC-37, *National Space Policy*, ¶1.d (May 11, 1978) ("The space systems of any nation are national property and have the right of passage through and operations in space without interference. Purposeful interference with operational space systems shall be viewed as an infringement upon sovereign rights.").

[148] *Refer to* § 14.10.3 (Outer Space Treaty Restrictions on Military Activities).

[149] OUTER SPACE TREATY art. VI ("States Parties to the Treaty shall bear international responsibility for national activities in outer space, including the moon and other celestial bodies, whether such activities are carried on by governmental agencies or by non-governmental entities, and for assuring that national activities are carried out in conformity with the provisions set forth in the present Treaty. The activities of non-governmental entities in outer space, including the moon and other celestial bodies, shall require authorization and continuing supervision by the appropriate State Party to the Treaty.").

Objects Launched into Outer Space;[150]

- Convention on International Liability for Damage Caused by Space Objects;[151] and
- Convention on Registration of Objects Launched into Outer Space.[152]

Certain provisions of these treaties may not be applicable as between belligerents during international armed conflict.[153]

14.10.2.2 Application of General International Law to Activities and Use of Outer Space. The Outer Space Treaty reaffirms the duty of States Parties to comply with existing international law in carrying out activities in outer space. Article III of the Outer Space Treaty provides that "States Parties to the Treaty shall carry on activities in the exploration and use of outer space, including the moon and other celestial bodies, in accordance with international law, including the Charter of the United Nations, in the interest of maintaining international peace and security and promoting international cooperation and understanding."[154]

Although existing international law, such as the Charter of the United Nations, generally applies to States Parties' activities in outer space, international law that prescribes certain conditions for national claims of sovereignty does not apply to outer space because outer space is not subject to national appropriation.[155]

---

[150] Agreement on the Rescue of Astronauts, the Return of Astronauts, and the Return of Objects Launched into Outer Space, Apr. 22, 1968, 672 UNTS 119.

[151] Convention on International Liability for Damage Caused by Space Objects, Mar. 29, 1972, 961 UNTS 187.

[152] Convention on Registration of Objects Launched into Outer Space, Nov. 12, 1974, 1023 UNTS 15.

[153] Department of Defense, Office of the General Counsel, *An Assessment of International Legal Issues in Information Operations* (2nd ed., Nov. 1999), *reprinted in* 76 U.S. NAVAL WAR COLLEGE INTERNATIONAL LAW STUDIES 459, 494 (2002) ("During an international armed conflict between the two nations concerned, however, the law of armed conflict would apply unless it was trumped by the principle of noninterference with space systems. Resolution of this issue depends largely on whether the four space treaties will be considered to apply during an armed conflict. None of them has any specific provision that indicates whether the parties intended that the agreement apply in wartime. There appears to be a strong argument that the principle of noninterference established by these agreements is inconsistent with a state of hostilities, at least where the systems concerned are of such high military value that there is a strong military imperative for the adversary to be free to interfere with them, even to the extent of destroying the satellites in the system. As indicated in the discussion of treaty law in the introduction to this paper, the outcome of this debate may depend on the circumstances in which it first arises in practice.").

[154] OUTER SPACE TREATY art. III. *See also* Staff Report prepared for the use of the Committee on Aeronautical and Space Sciences, United States Senate, *Treaty on Principles Governing the Activities of States in the Exploration and Use of Outer Space, Including the Moon and Other Celestial Bodies: Analysis and Background Data*, 24 (Mar. 1967) ("This article makes clear that those nations which ratify the treaty will observe international law—and this includes the Charter of the United Nations—in order to promote international cooperation and peace. Thus that body of law, which has developed on the Earth in order to bring about harmonious relations between nations and settle disputes without resort to violence, would become applicable to outer space, the Moon, and other celestial bodies.").

[155] Staff Report prepared for the use of the Committee on Aeronautical and Space Sciences, United States Senate, *Treaty on Principles Governing the Activities of States in the Exploration and Use of Outer Space, Including the Moon and Other Celestial Bodies: Analysis and Background Data*, 24 (Mar. 1967) ("An exception would be

Certain treaties apply only in certain geographical locations (such as a State's own territory), and thus might not create obligations applicable to a State's activities in outer space. However, law of war treaties and the customary law of war are understood to regulate the conduct of hostilities, regardless of where they are conducted, which would include the conduct of hostilities in outer space. In this way, the application of the law of war to activities in outer space is the same as its application to activities in other environments, such as the land, sea, air, or cyber domains.

14.10.3 Outer Space Treaty Restrictions on Military Activities. The Outer Space Treaty imposes restrictions on certain military operations in outer space.

Other treaties may also impose restrictions on military activities in outer space. For example, the Treaty Banning Nuclear Testing in the Atmosphere, Oceans, and Outer Space (Limited Test Ban Treaty) prohibits nuclear weapon test explosions in outer space.[156]

14.10.3.1 *Restriction on Nuclear Weapons and Other Kinds of Weapons of Mass Destruction in Outer Space*. Article IV of the Outer Space Treaty provides that "States Parties to the Treaty undertake not to place in orbit around the Earth any objects carrying nuclear weapons or any other kinds of weapons of mass destruction, install such weapons on celestial bodies, or station such weapons in outer space in any other manner."[157]

The prohibition on placing weapons of mass destruction "in orbit around the earth" refers only to their placement in full orbit around the Earth; thus, the Outer Space Treaty does not ban the use of nuclear or other weapons of mass destruction that go into a fractional orbit or engage in suborbital flight.[158] For example, intercontinental ballistic missiles (ICBMs) will travel a portion of their trajectory in outer space; but because ICBMs would enter outer space only temporarily, their entry into outer space with nuclear warheads would not violate this prohibition.[159] By contrast, some arms control treaties have prohibited the production, testing, or

---

international law which provides certain conditions for national claims of sovereignty, this exception having been set forth in Article II."); OUTER SPACE TREATY art. II ("Outer space, including the moon and other celestial bodies, is not subject to national appropriation by claim of sovereignty, by means of use or occupation, or by any other means.").

[156] Treaty Banning Nuclear Weapon Tests in the Atmosphere, in Outer Space and Under Water, art. 1, Aug. 5, 1963, 480 UNTS 43, 45 ("Each of the Parties to this Treaty undertakes to prohibit, to prevent, and not to carry out any nuclear weapon test explosion, or any other nuclear explosion, at any place under its jurisdiction or control: (*a*) in the atmosphere; beyond its limits, including outer space; or under water, including territorial waters or high seas;").

[157] OUTER SPACE TREATY art. IV ("States Parties to the Treaty undertake not to place in orbit around the Earth any objects carrying nuclear weapons or any other kinds of weapons of mass destruction, install such weapons on celestial bodies, or station such weapons in outer space in any other manner.").

[158] *See* I NANDASIRI JASENTULIYANA & ROY S. LEE, MANUAL ON SPACE LAW 13-14 (1979) ("The phrase 'orbit around the earth' in the first paragraph of this Article means that an object must be placed in a full orbit around the earth before it comes within the prohibition of the Treaty. Therefore an object in a fractional orbit or suborbital flight is not intended to be covered. This was the clear intention of the drafters of this Article.").

[159] Staff Report prepared for the use of the Committee on Aeronautical and Space Sciences, United States Senate, *Treaty on Principles Governing the Activities of States in the Exploration and Use of Outer Space, Including the Moon and Other Celestial Bodies: Analysis and Background Data*, 26 (Mar. 1967) ("The treaty does not change the earthly situation with regard to ICBM's, but seeks to achieve on celestial bodies a form of demilitarization which is deemed feasible from military and political viewpoints.").

deployment of systems, including missiles, that place nuclear weapons or other weapons of mass destruction into either full earth orbit or a *fraction* of an earth orbit.[160]

In addition, this rule in Article IV of the Outer Space Treaty does not establish any prohibitions with respect to weapons that are not weapons of mass destruction (*e.g.*, anti-satellite laser weapons or other conventional weapons).[161]

14.10.3.2 *Restrictions on Military Activities on the Moon and Other Celestial Bodies*. Article IV of the Outer Space Treaty places certain prohibitions on military activities on the moon and other celestial bodies: (1) the establishment of military bases, installations, and fortifications; and (2) the testing of any type of weapons; and (3) the conduct of military maneuvers.[162]

These activities are prohibited only on the moon and other celestial bodies, not in outer space itself.

Article IV also recognizes the unimpeded right to: (1) the use of military personnel for scientific research or other peaceful purposes on outer space missions; and (2) the use of any equipment or facility necessary for the peaceful exploration of the moon and other celestial bodies.[163]

14.10.4 General Use of Outer Space for Peaceful Purposes. The United States has expressed the view that outer space should be used only for peaceful purposes.[164] This view is

---

[160] *For example*, Treaty Between the United States of America and the Union of Soviet Socialist Republics on the Reduction and Limitation of Strategic Offensive Arms, Jul. 31, 1991, U.S.-USSR, Article V(18)(c), S. TREATY DOC. NO. 102-20, which expired December 5, 2009.

[161] David A. Koplow, *ASAT-isfaction: Customary International Law and the Regulation of Anti-Satellite Weapons*, 30 MICHIGAN JOURNAL OF INTERNATIONAL LAW 1187, 1198 (2009) ("This provision does not impede the stationing of non-nuclear weapons (including conventional ASAT weapons) in space, nor does it affect a nuclear weapon that makes only a temporary transit of outer space, as when propelled by an intercontinental ballistic missile (ICBM) toward its target, rather than being 'stationed' in space.").

[162] OUTER SPACE TREATY art. IV ("The moon and other celestial bodies shall be used by all States Parties to the Treaty exclusively for peaceful purposes. The establishment of military bases, installations and fortifications, the testing of any type of weapons and the conduct of military maneuvers on celestial bodies shall be forbidden.").

[163] OUTER SPACE TREATY art. IV ("The use of military personnel for scientific research or for any other peaceful purposes shall not be prohibited. The use of any equipment or facility necessary for peaceful exploration of the moon and other celestial bodies shall also not be prohibited.").

[164] *See, e.g.*, *National Space Policy of the United States of America* 3 (Jun. 28, 2010) ("All nations have the right to explore and use space for peaceful purposes, and for the benefit of all humanity, in accordance with international law. Consistent with this principle, 'peaceful purposes' allows for space to be used for national and homeland security activities."); Albert Gore, Sr., U.S. Representative to the United Nations, U.N. General Assembly, 17th Sess., 1289th Mtg., U.N. Doc. A/C.1/PV.1289 (1962) ("It is the view of the United States that outer space should be used only for peaceful – that is non-aggressive and beneficial – purposes. The question of military activities in space cannot be divorced from the question of military activities on Earth. To banish these activities in both environments we must continue our efforts for general and complete disarmament with adequate safeguards. Until this is achieved, the test of any space activities must not be whether it is military or non-military, but whether or not it is consistent with the United Nations Charter and other obligations of law.").

consistent with the Preamble to the Outer Space Treaty.[165]

The United States has interpreted use of outer space for "peaceful purposes" to mean "non-aggressive and beneficial" purposes consistent with the Charter of the United Nations and other international law.[166] This interpretation of "peaceful purposes" is similar to the interpretation given to the reservation of the high seas for "peaceful purposes" in the LOS Convention.[167]

For example, observation or information-gathering from satellites in space is not an act of aggression under the Charter of the United Nations and, thus, would be a use of space for peaceful purposes.[168] Similarly, lawful military activities in self-defense (*e.g.*, missile early warning, use of weapon systems) would be consistent with the use of space for peaceful purposes, but aggressive activities that violate the Charter of the United Nations would not be permissible.[169]

Article IV of the Outer Space Treaty provides that "[t]he moon and other celestial bodies shall be used by all States Parties to the Treaty exclusively for peaceful purposes."[170] Article IV

---

[165] OUTER SPACE TREATY preamble ("Recognizing the common interest of all mankind in the progress of the exploration and use of outer space for peaceful purposes,").

[166] Senator Albert Gore, Sr., *Treaty on Outer Space: Hearings Before the Committee on Foreign Relations, U.S. Senate*, 90th Congress, First Session, 59 (Mar. 13, 1967) ("We interpret peaceful purposes as being non-aggressive and beneficial."). *See also* Staff Report prepared for the use of the Committee on Aeronautical and Space Sciences, United States Senate, *Treaty on Principles Governing the Activities of States in the Exploration and Use of Outer Space, Including the Moon and Other Celestial Bodies: Analysis and Background Data*, 11 (Mar. 1967) ("In Russian, the word for 'military' essentially means warlike rather than pertaining to the armed services of a country; in the United States, 'peaceful' is not regarded as the opposite of 'military'—we think of 'peaceful' as 'not aggressive.'"); CARL Q. CHRISTOL, THE MODERN INTERNATIONAL LAW OF OUTER SPACE 22 (1982) ("The expression 'peaceful purposes' is a legal term of art. At the beginning of the Space age several views were advanced as to its meaning, with one view being that military activities in the space environment could not be and were not peaceful. The opposing position, which today has gained general acceptance, is that nonaggressive military uses are peaceful. Thus, 'peaceful' has come to mean general space activity that is beneficial to and in the interests of all countries.").

[167] *Refer to* § 13.1.1 (The Law of the Sea During Armed Conflict).

[168] *See* Albert Gore, Sr., U.S. Representative to the United Nations, U.N. General Assembly, 17th Sess., 1289th Mtg., U.N. Doc. A/C.1/PV.1289 13 (1962) ("[A]ny nation may use space satellites for such purposes as observation and information-gathering. Observation from space is consistent with international law, just as is observation from the high seas."); Report by the Committee on Satellite Reconnaissance Policy, attached to Jul. 2, 1962 memorandum from Secretary Rusk to President Kennedy, *excerpted in* XXV FOREIGN RELATIONS OF THE UNITED STATES (1961-1963), 951-59 (2001) ("(b) It is well established that areas subject to the jurisdiction of a state may be observed from points outside that jurisdiction, *e.g.*, from a ship on the high seas. Observation from outer space, which is not subject to territorial claims, also cannot be considered to constitute a violation of international law.").

[169] CARL Q. CHRISTOL, THE INTERNATIONAL LAW OF OUTER SPACE 114 (1966) ("It may be concluded that both ballistic missiles, directly, and satellites, indirectly, have military utility. This does not automatically exclude them from the category of peaceful uses, since defensive and deterrent capabilities serve the cause of peace. It is only when such devices are intentionally used for aggressive purposes that they lose their peaceful status.").

[170] OUTER SPACE TREATY art. IV ("The moon and other celestial bodies shall be used by all States Parties to the Treaty exclusively for peaceful purposes.").

specifies restrictions on military operations on the moon and other celestial bodies.[171]

14.10.5 Outer Space Treaty Provisions on Cooperation, Mutual Assistance, and Potentially Harmful Interference. Article IX of the Outer Space Treaty provides that in the exploration and use of outer space, States Parties shall be guided by the principle of cooperation and mutual assistance and shall conduct all their activities in outer space with due regard to the corresponding interests of all other States Parties.[172] For example, States should conduct their activities in space with due regard for the rights of other States to have their space systems pass through, and conduct operations in, space without interference.

Article IX of the Outer Space Treaty also requires States Parties to undertake "appropriate international consultations" before proceeding with any activity or experiment planned by it or its nationals in outer space if that State Party has reason to believe that its activity or experiment would cause potentially harmful interference with the activities of other States Parties in the peaceful exploration and use of outer space.[173] Conversely, a State Party that has reason to believe that an activity or experiment planned by another State Party in outer space would cause potentially harmful interference with its activities in the peaceful exploration and use of outer space may request consultation concerning the activity or experiment.[174]

---

[171] *Refer to* § 14.10.3.2 (Restrictions on Military Activities on the Moon and Other Celestial Bodies).

[172] OUTER SPACE TREATY art. IX ("In the exploration and use of outer space, including the moon and other celestial bodies, States Parties to the Treaty shall be guided by the principle of cooperation and mutual assistance and shall conduct all their activities in outer space, including the moon and other celestial bodies, with due regard to the corresponding interests of all other States Parties to the Treaty.").

[173] OUTER SPACE TREATY art. IX ("If a State Party to the Treaty has reason to believe that an activity or experiment planned by it or its nationals in outer space, including the moon and other celestial bodies, would cause potentially harmful interference with activities of other States Parties in the peaceful exploration and use of outer space, including the moon and other celestial bodies, it shall undertake appropriate international consultations before proceeding with any such activity or experiment.").

[174] OUTER SPACE TREATY art. IX ("A State Party to the Treaty which has reason to believe that an activity or experiment planned by another State Party in outer space, including the moon and other celestial bodies, would cause potentially harmful interference with activities in the peaceful exploration and use of outer space, including the moon and other celestial bodies, may request consultation concerning the activity or experiment.").

XV – The Law of Neutrality

Chapter Contents

15.1 Introduction

This Chapter addresses the law of neutrality.

Issues of neutrality law can raise questions of national policy regarding an armed conflict.[1] In U.S. practice, such national policies would be developed through the National Security Council (NSC) process by the Department of State and other departments and agencies represented on the National Security Council.[2]

Some of the rules described in this Chapter were formulated long ago. Moreover, treaties concerning the law of neutrality might, by their terms, apply only to a limited set of international

---

[1] *Refer to* § 15.2.1.1 (Application of the Law of Neutrality and the National Policies of States Towards an Armed Conflict).

[2] *See, e.g.*, Barack Obama, Presidential Policy Directive – 1, *Organization of the National Security Council System*, Feb. 13, 2009.

armed conflicts, and the rules prescribed in those treaties might not reflect customary international law.[3] In addition, it may be important to consider the implications of more recent treaties that might be applicable to a specific legal issue. In particular, the Charter of the United Nations may, in certain respects, be understood to be consistent with, and, in other respects, to modify, rules reflected in the law of neutrality.[4]

15.1.1 Matters Addressed by the Law of Neutrality. The law of neutrality prescribes the legal relationship between belligerent States and neutral States. The law of neutrality regulates relations between: (1) belligerent States, vessels, aircraft, and persons; and (2) neutral States, vessels, aircraft, and persons. Under the law of neutrality, these categories of belligerents and neutrals have corresponding rights, duties, and liabilities. Special rules have been developed to address situations on land, at sea, and in the air.

Certain rules found in the law of neutrality have also been applied in other contexts that are closely analogous, such as a State's duties to prevent a non-State armed group's use of its territory for hostile expeditions against another State.[5]

15.1.2 Classification of States as Belligerent, Neutral, or Non-Belligerent.

15.1.2.1 *Belligerent State*. Belligerent State refers to a State that is engaged in an international armed conflict, whether or not a formal declaration of war has been made.[6]

15.1.2.2 *Neutral State*. Neutral State refers to a State that is not taking part in the armed conflict.[7] In some cases, States formally state their neutral status in relation to an armed conflict.[8]

15.1.2.3 *Non-Belligerent State*. The term "non-belligerent" or "non-belligerent State" has been used to refer to a State that is not participating in the armed conflict. The term "non-belligerent Power" is used in the 1949 Geneva Conventions.[9]

In addition, the term "non-belligerent" has been used to refer to States that sought to refrain from active participation in hostilities, but that did not adhere to the duties of strict impartiality to which neutrals have traditionally been required to adhere.[10] Such departure from

---

[3] *Refer to* § 15.1.4 (Application of Treaties on Neutrality and Customary International Law).

[4] *Refer to* § 15.2.3 (The Law of Neutrality Under the Charter of the United Nations).

[5] *Refer to* § 17.18 (Non-Intervention and Neutral Duties in NIAC).

[6] *Refer to* § 3.4.2.1 (Reasons for States to Seek to Deny the Existence of Hostilities).

[7] 1928 PAN AMERICAN MARITIME NEUTRALITY CONVENTION preamble ("Considering that neutrality is the juridical situation of states which do not take part in the hostilities, and that it creates rights and imposes obligations of impartiality, which should be regulated;").

[8] *Refer to* § 15.2.1.4 (Proclamations of Neutrality and Other Notifications of Neutral Status).

[9] *Refer to* § 15.16.3.1 (Provision of POW Treatment and Application of the GWS and GWS-Sea by Analogy).

[10] TUCKER, THE LAW OF WAR AND NEUTRALITY AT SEA 192 ("Thus one of the marked developments of the second World War was the emergence of so-called 'nonbelligerency,' a term used to indicate the position of states that refrained from active participation in hostilities while at the same time abandoning the duties heretofore imposed

the traditional duties of impartiality has, at times, been controversial.[11]

15.1.3 Purpose of the Law of Neutrality. The law of neutrality seeks to preserve friendly relations between belligerent and neutral States by permitting States to avoid taking sides in an armed conflict.[12] The law of neutrality also seeks to prevent additional States from being drawn into an armed conflict by establishing a clear distinction between belligerent and neutral States.[13] In particular, the law of neutrality seeks to minimize the effects of armed conflict on States that are not party to the conflict, including by lessening the effect of war on neutral commerce.

15.1.4 Application of Treaties on Neutrality and Customary International Law. The treaties that address neutrality may be limited in their application as a matter of treaty law, but provisions of these treaties may reflect customary international law.

For example, many of the treaties that address the law of neutrality were concluded before World War II, and have not been universally ratified by States.[14] Moreover, certain treaties only apply between the Parties to the treaty and, in some cases, only if all the belligerent States are also Parties to the treaty.[15] The principles reflected in those treaties, however, may still be applicable insofar as they reflect customary international law, even if they do not apply as a matter of treaty law.[16] However, if the factual circumstances of the current context are quite different from those underlying the formulation of the original treaty rule, it may be incorrect to assume that the particular treaty rule reflects (or should reflect) a rule of customary international law applicable to the current factual circumstances.

15.1.5 Domestic Neutrality Laws. States may have domestic legislation relating to the

---

upon non-participants."); *id.* at 198 ("It has already been observed that to the extent that this term has not been used merely as a synonym for the usual position occupied by non-participants it has served to indicate varying degrees of departure from the duties traditionally consequent upon a status of non-participation in war.").

[11] *Refer to* § 15.2.2 (Qualified Neutrality).

[12] Carl Salans, Deputy Legal Adviser, Department of State, comment to R.R. Baxter, *The Legal Consequences of the Unlawful Use of Force under the Charter*, 62 PROCEEDINGS OF THE AMERICAN SOCIETY OF INTERNATIONAL LAW AT ITS ANNUAL MEETING 68, 76 (1968) ("When armed conflict occurs, the purpose of international law ought to be to limit the scope of the conflict. This is also a purpose of the Charter. The law of neutrality serves that purpose. Small states, like Cambodia, would find themselves quickly engulfed in conflict if they had to act on a determination that one side or the other in hostilities was acting unlawfully. And nuclear states run another kind of risk if they have to take sides in every conflict.").

[13] Michael Bothe, *The Law of Neutrality, in* DIETER FLECK, THE HANDBOOK OF HUMANITARIAN LAW IN ARMED CONFLICTS 486 (¶1101) (1999) ("By establishing a clear distinction between neutral states and states parties to the conflict, international law prevents more states from being drawn into the conflict.").

[14] *See, e.g.*, 1928 PAN AMERICAN NEUTRALITY CONVENTION; HAGUE V; HAGUE XIII.

[15] *See, e.g.*, HAGUE V art. 20 ("The provisions of the present Convention do not apply except between Contracting Powers and then only if all the belligerents are parties to the Convention."); HAGUE XIII art. 28 ("The provisions of the present Convention do not apply except to the contracting Powers, and then only if all the belligerents are parties to the Convention."). *Consider* Declaration respecting maritime law signed by the Plenipotentiaries of Great Britain, Austria, France, Prussia, Russia, Sardinia, and Turkey, assembled in Congress at Paris, Apr. 16, 1856, *reprinted in* 1 AJIL SUPPLEMENT: OFFICIAL DOCUMENTS 89, 90 (1907) ("The present Declaration is not and shall not be binding, except between those Powers who have acceded, or shall accede to it.").

[16] *Refer to* § 1.8.1 (Relationship Between Treaties and Customary International Law).

law of neutrality.

In some cases, these statutes implement a State's obligations under the law of neutrality, such as its obligations as a neutral to prevent the arming of belligerent warships in neutral ports.[17] These statutes may also serve to implement a State's international obligations outside the context of international armed conflict, such as its peacetime obligations to prevent its territory from being used as a base of operations for hostile expeditions against friendly States.[18]

Domestic statutes may also implement the rights of States under the law of neutrality, such as the right of belligerents to conduct captures.[19]

Domestic neutrality statutes may also help implement a State's national policy with respect to neutrality. The law of neutrality permits neutral States a degree of policy discretion with respect to an armed conflict.[20] Some neutrality treaties recognize such domestic legislation.[21] Such legislation, however, must be applied impartially among belligerents.[22] In addition, a State may have an obligation to notify other States of its domestic neutrality

---

[17] *For example*, 18 U.S.C. § 961 ("Whoever, within the United States, increases or augments the force of any ship of war, cruiser, or other armed vessel which, at the time of her arrival within the United States, was a ship of war, cruiser, or armed vessel, in the service of any foreign prince or state, or of any colony, district, or people, or belonging to the subjects or citizens of any such prince or state, or of any colony, district, or people, the same being at war with any foreign prince or state, or of any colony, district, or people, with whom the United States is at peace, by adding to the number of guns of such vessel, or by changing those on board of her for guns of a larger caliber, or by adding thereto any equipment solely applicable to war, shall be fined under this title or imprisoned not more than one year, or both.").

[18] *For example*, 18 U.S.C. § 960 ("Whoever, within the United States, knowingly begins or sets on foot or provides or prepares a means for or furnishes the money for, or takes part in, any military or naval expedition or enterprise to be carried on from thence against the territory or dominion of any foreign prince or state, or of any colony, district, or people with whom the United States is at peace, shall be fined under this title or imprisoned for not more than three years, or both."). *Refer to* § 17.18 (Non-Intervention and Neutral Duties in NIAC).

[19] *For example*, 10 U.S.C. § 7651 ("(a) This chapter applies to all captures of vessels as prize during war by authority of the United States or adopted and ratified by the President. However, this chapter does not affect the right of the Army or the Air Force, while engaged in hostilities, to capture wherever found and without prize procedures--(1) enemy property; or (2) neutral property used or transported in violation of the obligations of neutrals under international law.").

[20] Cordell Hull, Secretary of State, *Statement at Department of State Press Conference*, Sept. 21, 1939, 1 DEPARTMENT OF STATE BULLETIN 280 (Sept. 23, 1939) ("I think that you will find from a careful analysis of the underlying principles of the law of neutrality that this Nation, or any neutral nation, has a right during a war to change its national policies whenever experience shows the necessity for such change for the protection of its interests and safety. I do not mean to be understood as saying that such action may be taken at the behest or in the interests of one of the contending belligerents, it being understood, of course, that any measures taken shall apply impartially to all belligerents.").

[21] *For example*, 1928 PAN AMERICAN MARITIME NEUTRALITY CONVENTION art. 5 ("When, according to the domestic law of the neutral state, the ship may not receive fuel until twenty-four hours after its arrival in port, the period of its stay may be extended an equal length of time.").

[22] HAGUE XIII preamble ("Seeing that it is desirable that the Powers should issue detailed enactments to regulate the results of the attitude of neutrality when adopted by them; Seeing that it is, for neutral Powers, an admitted duty to apply these rules impartially to the several belligerents;").

statutes.[23]

15.2 Application of the Law of Neutrality

The application of the law of neutrality may depend on a State's national policy towards an armed conflict. A State's obligations under *jus ad bellum*, including its obligations under the Charter of the United Nations, may alter significantly its rights and duties under the law of neutrality.

15.2.1 Armed Conflict and the Application of the Law of Neutrality.

15.2.1.1 *Application of the Law of Neutrality and the National Policies of States Towards an Armed Conflict*. Whether the law of neutrality governs a State's relations with belligerents in an armed conflict may depend on that State's national policy towards that armed conflict.[24] For example, if an armed conflict occurs, a State may choose to join the armed conflict, in which case it would no longer be neutral and the law of war rather than the law of neutrality would govern its relations with opposing belligerents.[25] Similarly, if two States conduct hostilities against one another, but refuse to recognize a state of armed conflict, third States may reject this position and invoke the law of neutrality to protect their rights in relation to the armed conflict.[26] In addition, outside States that recognize the belligerency of a rebel faction in a civil war may choose to apply the law of neutrality in their relations with the rebel faction and with the government.[27]

15.2.1.2 *Application of Certain Duties of Neutral States Only in Certain International Armed Conflicts*. The duties of neutral States to refrain from certain types of support to belligerent States do not apply to all armed conflicts to which *jus in bello* rules apply;

---

[23] HAGUE XIII art. 27 ("The Contracting Powers shall communicate to each other in due course all Laws, Proclamations, and other enactments regulating in their respective countries the status of belligerent warships in their ports and waters, by means of a communication addressed to the Government of the Netherlands, and forwarded immediately by that Government to the other Contracting Powers.").

[24] *Compare* § 3.4.1 (Intent-Based Test for Applying *Jus in Bello* Rules).

[25] Michael Bothe, *The Law of Neutrality*, *in* DIETER FLECK, THE HANDBOOK OF HUMANITARIAN LAW IN ARMED CONFLICTS 489 (¶1104) (1999) ("Traditional international law left to each state the sovereign decision of whether, at the outbreak of a conflict between other states, it would participate or remain neutral. … The distinction between participation and neutrality is a political, not military, decision. Where the law of neutrality requires decisions to be taken by military command, the government concerned must give political guidance and clarify the position which it takes in relation to a particular conflict.").

[26] TUCKER, THE LAW OF WAR AND NEUTRALITY AT SEA 199-200 ("Unlike the law governing the mutual behavior of combatants, a large part of which may be considered operative in any international armed conflict, the rules regulating the behavior of neutrals and belligerents remain strictly dependent for their operation upon the existence of a state of war. It may be, however, that states engaged in armed conflict are unwilling to issue a declaration of war or even to acknowledge the existence of a state of war. In such situations it would appear that the decision as to whether or not to recognize the existence of a state of war, and thereby to bring into force the law of neutrality, must rest principally with third states. The attitude of the parties engaged in armed conflict need not prove decisive for third states, the latter being at liberty either to accept the position of the contestants (i.e., the position that war does not exist) or to reject this position and to invoke the law of neutrality.").

[27] *Refer to* § 3.3.3.1 (Recognition by Outside States of a Rebel Faction as a Belligerent in a Civil War).

rather, such duties are only triggered in armed conflicts of a certain duration and intensity.[28] However, belligerent States have fundamental duties to respect the sovereignty of neutral States in all international armed conflicts.[29]

15.2.1.3 *Application of Certain Rules in the Law of Neutrality Outside the Context of International Armed Conflict*. Certain parts of the law of neutrality may be viewed as applicable outside the context of international armed conflict because certain duties that the law of neutrality imposes are also found in international law applicable in peacetime. For example, under the Charter of the United Nations, States must respect the sovereignty of other States.[30] Thus, States have duties of non-intervention and neutrality in relation to a non-international armed conflict against a friendly State.[31]

15.2.1.4 *Proclamations of Neutrality and Other Notifications of Neutral Status*. A formal declaration by nonparticipating States of their intention to adopt a neutral status generally would not be required for a State to retain its neutral status.[32] However, in light of the importance of national policy in determining whether the law of neutrality is applicable, States traditionally issued proclamations of neutrality in order to make known their neutral status in relation to a conflict.[33] These proclamations of neutrality would state the determination of the

---

[28] *See* Michael Bothe, *The Law of Neutrality*, *in* DIETER FLECK, THE HANDBOOK OF HUMANITARIAN LAW IN ARMED CONFLICTS 490-91 (¶1106) (1999) ("The law of neutrality leads to considerable modifications in the relationships between the neutral and the belligerent states, for instance as to the admissibility of exports, the sojurn of warships of the parties to the conflict in neutral waters, and the control of neutral trade. These fundamental changes are not triggered by every armed incident, but require an armed conflict of a certain duration and intensity. Thus, the threshold of application of the law of neutrality is probably higher than that for the rules of the law of war relating to the conduct of hostilities and the treatment of prisoners, which are applicable also in conflicts of less intensity.").

[29] *See* Legality of the Threat or Use of Nuclear Weapons, Advisory Opinion, 1996 I.C.J. (¶¶88-89) ("The Court will now turn to the principle of neutrality which was raised by several States. In the context of the advisory proceedings brought before the Court by the WHO concerning the *Legality of the Use by a State of Nuclear Weapons in Armed Conflict*, the position was put as follows by one State: 'The principle of neutrality, in its classic sense, was aimed at preventing the incursion of belligerent forces into neutral territory, or attacks on the persons or ships of neutrals. Thus: 'the territory of neutral powers is inviolable'; 'belligerents are bound to respect the sovereign rights of neutral powers ...' 'neutral states have equal interest in having their rights respected by belligerents ...'. It is clear, however, that the principle of neutrality applies with equal force to transborder incursions of armed forces and to the transborder damage caused to a neutral State by the use of a weapon in a belligerent State.' The principle so circumscribed is presented as an established part of the customary international law. The Court finds that as in the case of the principles of humanitarian law applicable in armed conflict, international law leaves no doubt that the principle of neutrality, whatever its content, which is of a fundamental character similar to that of the humanitarian principles and rules, is applicable (subject to the relevant provisions of the United Nations Charter), to all international armed conflict, whatever type of weapons might be used.") (citations omitted) (amendments in original).

[30] *Refer to* § 1.11.3 (Prohibition on Certain Uses of Force).

[31] *Refer to* § 17.18 (Non-Intervention and Neutral Duties in NIAC).

[32] *Compare* § 3.4.2.1 (Reasons for States to Seek to Deny the Existence of Hostilities).

[33] *For example*, Franklin D. Roosevelt, *Proclamation: Proclaiming the Neutrality of the United States in the War Between Germany and France; Poland; and The United Kingdom, India, Australia and New Zealand*, Sept. 5, 1939, 54 STAT. 2629 ("AND I do hereby give notice that all nationals of the United States and others who may claim the protection of this government, who may misconduct themselves in the premises, will do so at their peril, and that they can in no wise obtain any protection from the government of the United States against the consequences of their misconduct."); Woodrow Wilson, *Proclamation*, Aug. 18, 1914, 38 STAT. 2015 ("Whereas the United States is in

State to observe the duties of neutrality and warn its nationals of the penalties they would incur for joining or assisting a belligerent State.[34]

Although the practice of issuing formal proclamations of neutrality has declined, States have continued to make public statements of neutrality to indicate their national policy and legal status in relation to an armed conflict.[35] States may also communicate their neutral status through diplomatic channels or use other means they deem appropriate.

15.2.2 Qualified Neutrality. The United States has taken the position that certain duties of neutral States may be inapplicable under the doctrine of qualified neutrality.

The law of neutrality has traditionally required neutral States to observe a strict impartiality between parties to a conflict, regardless of which State was viewed as the aggressor

---

fact aware of the existence of a state of war between Belgium and Germany; And Whereas the United States is on terms of friendship and amity with the contending powers, and with the persons inhabiting their several dominions;"); George Washington, *Proclamation of Neutrality*, Apr. 22, 1793, *reprinted in* 32 THE WRITINGS OF GEORGE WASHINGTON FROM THE ORIGINAL MANUSCRIPT SOURCES 1745-1799, 430-31 (1939) ("Whereas it appears that a state of war exists between Austria, Prussia, Sardinia, Great Britain, and the United Netherlands, on the one part, and France on the other; and the duty and interest of the United States require, that they should with sincerity and good faith adopt and pursue a conduct friendly and impartial towards the belligerent powers: I have therefore thought fit by these presents, to declare the disposition of the United States to observe the conduct aforesaid towards those powers respectively; and to exhort and warn the citizens of the United States carefully to avoid all acts and proceedings whatsoever, which may in any manner tend to contravene such disposition. And I do hereby also make known, that whosoever of the citizens of the United States shall render himself liable to punishment or forfeiture under the law of nations, by committing, aiding or abetting hostilities against any of the said powers, or by carrying to any of them, those articles which are deemed contraband by the modern usage of nations, will not receive the protection of the United States against such punishment or forfeiture; and further that I have given instructions to those officers to whom it belongs, to cause prosecutions to be instituted against all persons, who shall, within the cognizance of the Courts of the United States, violate the law of nations, with respect to the powers at war, or any of them.").

[34] 1956 FM 27-10 (Change No. 1 1976) ¶514 ("When war occurs, neutral States usually issue proclamations of neutrality, in which they state their determination to observe the duties of neutrality and warn their nationals of the penalties they incur for joining or assisting a belligerent.").

[35] *For example*, FINAL REPORT ON THE PERSIAN GULF WAR 626 ("Iran and Jordan each issued proclamations of neutrality during the Persian Gulf crisis and, as described, refrained from active participation in the war."); Ronald Reagan, *Written Responses to Questions Submitted by Al-Qabas of Kuwait*, May 12, 1987, 1987-I PUBLIC PAPERS OF THE PRESIDENTS 529 ("The United States is neutral in the Iran-Iraq war."); Jimmy Carter, *Situation in Iraq and Iran: Remarks Concerning the Conflict*, Sept. 24, 1980, 1980-81-II PUBLIC PAPERS OF THE PRESIDENTS 1921, 1922 ("Let me repeat that we have not been and we will not become involved in the conflict between Iran and Iraq."); Royal Government of Laos, Statement of Jul. 9, 1962, *reprinted in* Burma, Cambodia Canada, People's Republic of China, Democratic Republic of Viet-Nam, etc., Declaration on the Neutrality of Laos, Jul. 23, 1962, 456 UNTS 301, 302-03 ("The Royal Government of Laos, Being resolved to follow the path of peace and neutrality in conformity with the interests and aspirations of the Laotian people, as well as the principles of the Joint Communiqué of Zurich dated June 22, 1961, and of the Geneva Agreements of 1954, in order to build a peaceful, neutral, independent, democratic, unified and prosperous Laos, Solemnly declares that: … (4) It will not enter into any military alliance or into any agreement, whether military or otherwise, which is inconsistent with the neutrality of the Kingdom of Laos; it will not allow the establishment of any foreign military base on Laotian territory, nor allow any country to use Laotian territory for military purposes or for the purposes of interference in the internal affairs of other countries, nor recognise the protection of any alliance or military coalition, including SEATO;").

in the armed conflict.[36] However, after treaties outlawed war as a matter of national policy, it was argued that neutral States could discriminate in favor of States that were victims of wars of aggression.[37] Thus, before its entry into World War II, the United States adopted a position of "qualified neutrality" in which neutral States had the right to support belligerent States that had been the victim of flagrant and illegal wars of aggression.[38] This position was controversial.[39]

15.2.3 <u>The Law of Neutrality Under the Charter of the United Nations</u>. The Charter of the United Nations may, in certain respects, be understood to be consistent with, and, in other respects, to modify, rules reflected in the law of neutrality.

15.2.3.1 <u>*Consistency Between the Rules in the Law of Neutrality and the Charter of the United Nations*</u>. In certain cases, the rules on the use of force prescribed in the Charter of the United Nations would be understood to be consistent with rules in the law of neutrality.[40]

---

[36] *Refer to* § 15.3.2 (Neutral Duties -- Abstention From Participation in Hostilities and Impartial Conduct Toward Contending Parties).

[37] LAUTERPACHT, II OPPENHEIM'S INTERNATIONAL LAW 221 (§61) ("Similarly, it is open to neutral States as a matter of legal right to give effect to their moral obligation to discriminate against the aggressor and to deny him, in their discretion, the right to exact from neutrals a full measure of impartiality. In some cases neutral States may, having regard to their own safety and the desire not to be involved in the war, continue to accord impartial treatment to the aggressor. But they need not do so wherever they feel in the position actively to assert the principle, as did the United States and other States before entering the Second World War, that the historic foundation of neutrality as an attitude of absolute impartiality has disappeared with the renunciation and the abolition of war as an instrument of national policy. With regard to States bound by the obligations of the Charter of the United Nations that legal faculty and that moral obligation assume the clear complexion of a legal duty.").

[38] *Address of Robert H. Jackson, Attorney General of the United States, Inter-American Bar Association, Havana, Cuba, March 27, 1941*, 35 AJIL 348, 353-54 (1941) ("Present aggressive wars are civil wars against the international community. Accordingly, as responsible members of that community, we can treat victims of aggression in the same way we treat legitimate governments when there is civil strife and a state of insurgency—that is to say, we are permitted to give to defending governments all the aid we choose. In the light of the flagrancy of current aggressions, which are apparent on their face, and which all right thinking people recognize for what they are, the United States and other states are entitled to assert a right of discriminatory action by reason of the fact that, since 1928 so far as it is concerned, the place of war and with it the place of neutrality in the international legal system have no longer been the same as they were prior to that date.").

[39] *See, e.g.*, Edwin Borchard, *War, Neutrality and Non-Belligerency*, 35 AJIL 618 (1941) ("At Havana on March 27, 1941, Attorney General Jackson delivered an address designed to prove that as a matter of *law* the United States was now obliged to render to England (and presumably others) all aid 'short of war,' while 'at the same time it is the declared determination of the government to avoid entry into the war as a belligerent.' Apparently convinced that United States military aid to one belligerent alone cannot be justified by the traditional international law, the Attorney General feels obliged first to explode as obsolete the international law conceptions of war and neutrality of the past two centuries, culminating in The Hague Conventions, and to maintain that a new international law has now been revealed in the Covenant of the League of Nations, the Kellogg Pact, the Budapest 'Articles of Interpretation' of 1934, and the Argentine Anti-War Treaty of 1933, all of which are alleged to make discrimination the new way of life for neutrals. The legislation of Congress requiring impartiality is not accorded even honorable mention. The 'new international law' is thus found in the vague and illusory monuments to the myth called 'collective security,' which crumbled under the impact of the first European crisis. It should be no surprise to the Attorney General that many international lawyers do not share his views on international law or how international law is created, or follow his unique construction of documents.").

[40] *See, e.g.*, BRUNO SIMMA, THE CHARTER OF THE UNITED NATIONS: A COMMENTARY 673 (1994) ("For the purpose of responding to an 'armed attack', the state acting in self-defence is allowed to trespass on foreign territory, even

For example, a neutral State's acts of participation in a war of aggression against another member of the United Nations would likely violate not only its duties under the law of neutrality,[41] but also the Charter's prohibition on the unlawful use of force.[42]

In the past, the law of neutrality was often viewed as not regulating a State's decision as to whether to adopt a position of neutrality or hostility towards another State.[43] Thus, under this view, the requirements of the law of neutrality could have been avoided by neutral States if they decided to enter the war or by belligerent States if they chose to declare war on a neutral.[44] The Charter of the United Nations clarifies that such decisions to resort to force may not be made without a proper legal basis.[45] Thus, insofar as provisions of the Charter are coincident with certain rules in the law of neutrality, such requirements of the Charter may not be evaded in the way that arguably certain requirements of the law of neutrality previously could have been evaded.

15.2.3.2 *Modification of Rules in the Law of Neutrality*. The Charter of the United Nations and decisions by the U.N. Security Council may, in certain circumstances,

---

when the attack cannot be attributed to the state from whose territory it is proceeding. It does not follow from the fact that the right of self-defence pursuant to Art. 51 is restricted to the case of an 'armed attack' that defensive measures may only affect the 'attacker'. Thus it is compatible with Art. 51 and the laws of neutrality when a warring state fights hostile armed forces undertaking an attack from neutral territory on the territory of the neutral state, provided that the state concerned is either unwilling or unable to curb the ongoing violation of its neutrality.").

[41] *Refer to* § 15.3.2 (Neutral Duties -- Abstention From Participation in Hostilities and Impartial Conduct Toward Contending Parties).

[42] *Refer to* § 1.11.3 (Prohibition on Certain Uses of Force).

[43] *See Editorial Comment: The Hague Conventions and the Neutrality of Belgium and Luxemburg*, 9 AJIL 959 (1915) ("[Articles of the Hague V] do not, however, guarantee neutrality, nor do they prevent a state from declaring war against a state wishing to remain neutral, which thus becomes a belligerent and loses the benefit of the convention. If the Hague conventions were violated by Germany in this matter it would appear to be a violation of the spirit, not of the letter, and indeed it is difficult to maintain that there was a violation even of the spirit, because international law in its present development apparently allows nations to go to war whenever they please, and the Hague conventions do not modify or abridge this provision of the law of nations.").

[44] *See* John Delatre Falconbridge, *The Right of a Belligerent to Make War Upon a Neutral*, 4 TRANSACTIONS OF THE GROTIUS SOCIETY 204, 209-11 (1918) ("The fifth [Hague] convention [of 1907] does not relate to the question of the right to convert the relation of belligerent and neutral into that of belligerent and belligerent, but simply defines the rights and obligations incidental to the former relation. … The fundamental proposition which has been left untouched by The Hague Conventions is that by the existing rules of international law one State may declare war against another State without any justifiable *casus belli,* and it commits no breach of law in so doing if it complies with the requirements relating to the declaration of war. Its action may be immoral, but it is not illegal unless there is a treaty forbidding such action (as there was in the case of Belgium).").

[45] *See* Michael Bothe, *The Law of Neutrality, in* DIETER FLECK, THE HANDBOOK OF HUMANITARIAN LAW IN ARMED CONFLICTS 489 (¶1104) (1999) ("Traditional international law left to each state the sovereign decision of whether, at the outbreak of a conflict between other states, it would participate or remain neutral. … At the outbreak of a conflict between two other states, a state is still free to participate or to remain neutral. Modern international law, however, limits the freedom of decision as to which side on which a state may become involved. Support granted to an aggressor is illegal, participation on the side of the victim of aggression, being collective self-defence, is permissible.").

qualify rights and obligations under the law of neutrality.[46]

For example, under the Charter of the United Nations, States may have obligations to support military operations that have been authorized by the U.N. Security Council.[47] In such circumstances, the obligations under the Charter would prevail over the obligations under the law of neutrality.[48] For example, a State that is not participating in the conflict that received in its territory military forces operating pursuant to a U.N. Security Council resolution might be required to return them, rather than to intern them under the law of neutrality.[49] Moreover, U.N. Security Council resolutions may obligate States to take measures that would not be required by neutrality law. For example, the U.N. Security Council may require States to impose restrictions on private conduct within their jurisdiction, such as to prevent private individuals from selling weapons to certain States or non-State armed groups.[50]

15.2.4 Neutrality Under Regional and Collective Self-Defense Arrangements. Regional and collective self-defense agreements may affect States' rights to maintain a neutral status because the States may be required to provide assistance or take military action in collective self-defense until the U.N. Security Council has taken measures necessary to maintain international peace and security.[51] The obligations by a State under such an agreement may prevail over the

---

[46] 1956 FM 27-10 (Change No. 1 1976) ¶513 ("Although these provisions of the Charter have not made it impossible for a State to remain neutral, the obligations which the Charter imposes have to a certain extent qualified the rights of States in this respect.").

[47] *Refer to* § 1.11.2.1 (U.N. Member State Obligations With Respect to U.N. Security Council Decisions).

[48] *For example*, FINAL REPORT ON THE PERSIAN GULF WAR 626 ("Neutrality in the Persian Gulf War was controlled in part by the 1907 Hague V Convention; but traditional concepts of neutral rights and duties are substantially modified when, as in this case, the United Nations authorizes collective action against an aggressor nation. It was the US position during the Persian Gulf crisis that, regardless of assertions of neutrality, all nations were obligated to avoid hindrance of Coalition operations undertaken pursuant to, or in conjunction with, UNSC decisions, and to provide whatever assistance possible. By virtue of UNSC Resolution 678 (29 November), members were requested 'to provide appropriate support for the actions undertaken' by nations pursuant to its authorization of use of all necessary means to uphold and implement prior resolutions. The language of UNSC Resolution 678 is consistent with Articles 2(5), 2(6), 25, and 49 of the UN Charter.").

[49] FINAL REPORT ON THE PERSIAN GULF WAR 628 ("Although the situation never arose, the United States advised Iran that, in light of UNSC Resolution 678, Iran would be obligated to return downed Coalition aircraft and aircrew, rather than intern them. This illustrates the modified nature of neutrality in these circumstances. It also was the US position that entry into Iranian (or Jordanian) airspace to rescue downed aviators would be consistent with its international obligations as a belligerent, particularly in light of Resolution 678.").

[50] *For example*, U.N. SECURITY COUNCIL RESOLUTION 1970, U.N. Doc. S/RES/1970, ¶9 (Feb. 26, 2011) ("Decides that all Member States shall immediately take the necessary measures to prevent the direct or indirect supply, sale or transfer to the Libyan Arab Jamahiriya, from or through their territories or by their nationals, or using their flag vessels or aircraft, of arms and related materiel of all types, including weapons and ammunition, military vehicles and equipment, paramilitary equipment, and spare parts for the aforementioned, and technical assistance, training, financial or other assistance, related to military activities or the provision, maintenance or use of any arms and related materiel, including the provision of armed mercenary personnel whether or not originating in their territories,"); U.N. SECURITY COUNCIL RESOLUTION 713, U.N. Doc S/RES/713 ¶6 (Sept. 25, 1991) ("Decides, under Chapter VII of the Charter of the United Nations, that all States shall, for the purposes of establishing peace and stability in Yugoslavia, immediately implement a general and complete embargo on all deliveries of weapons and military equipment to Yugoslavia until the Council decides otherwise following consultation between the Secretary- General and the Government of Yugoslavia;").

[51] *Refer to* § 1.11.5.5 (Right of Collective Self-Defense).

State's right under the customary law of neutrality to be impartial among the belligerents and to abstain from the armed conflict.

15.3 Overview of the Neutrality Law's Framework of Reciprocal Rights and Duties

The law of neutrality establishes a framework of reciprocal rights and duties for neutrals and belligerents.

15.3.1 Neutral Rights. Belligerent States are bound to respect the sovereign rights of neutral States (*e.g.*, the inviolability of a neutral State's territory).[52] The exercise by a neutral State of its rights under the law of neutrality may not be considered an unfriendly act by either of the belligerents.[53]

15.3.1.1 *Inviolability of Neutral Territory - Prohibition on Unauthorized Entry*. The territory of neutral States is inviolable.[54] The inviolability of neutral territory prohibits any unauthorized entry into the territory of a neutral State, its territorial waters, or the airspace over such areas by armed forces or instrumentalities of war.[55]

15.3.1.2 *Inviolability of Neutral Territory - Prohibition on Hostile Acts or Other Violations of Neutrality*. The inviolability of neutral territory also requires belligerent forces to refrain from committing hostile acts or other acts that, if knowingly permitted by a neutral State, would constitute a violation of neutrality in neutral territory (including neutral lands, neutral waters, and neutral airspace).[56] For example, belligerent warships may not exercise the belligerent right of visit and search, and may not capture vessels in neutral waters.[57]

However, belligerent forces may use force in self-defense or as part of self-help enforcement actions against enemy forces that have committed violations of neutrality when the

---

[52] HAGUE XIII art. 1 ("Belligerents are bound to respect the sovereign rights of neutral Powers and to abstain, in neutral territory or neutral waters, from any act which would, if knowingly permitted by any Power, constitute a violation of neutrality."); 1956 FM 27-10 (Change No. 1 1976) ¶512 ("It is the duty of belligerents to respect the territory and rights of neutral States.").

[53] HAGUE XIII art. 26 ("The exercise by a neutral Power of the rights laid down in the present convention can under no circumstances be considered as an unfriendly act by one or other belligerent who has accepted the Articles relating thereto.").

[54] HAGUE V art. 1 ("The territory of neutral Powers is inviolable.").

[55] 1956 FM 27-10 (Change No. 1 1976) ¶515 ("*b. Application of Rule*. The foregoing rule prohibits any unauthorized entry into the territory of a neutral State, its territorial waters, or the airspace over such areas by troops or instrumentalities of war.").

[56] 1928 PAN AMERICAN MARITIME NEUTRALITY CONVENTION art. 3 ("Belligerent states are obligated to refrain from performing acts of war in neutral waters or other acts which may constitute on the part of the State that tolerates them, a violation of neutrality."); HAGUE XIII art. 1 ("Belligerents are bound to respect the sovereign rights of neutral Powers and to abstain, in neutral territory or neutral waters, from any act which would, if knowingly permitted by any Power, constitute a violation of neutrality.").

[57] *Refer to* § 15.13.3 (Where Belligerents May Not Exercise the Right of Visit and Search); § 15.15 (Capture of Neutral Vessels and Aircraft).

neutral State is unwilling or unable to address such violations.[58]

15.3.2 Neutral Duties -- Abstention From Participation in Hostilities and Impartial Conduct Toward Contending Parties. The principal duties of a neutral State are to abstain from any participation in the conflict and to be impartial in conduct towards contending parties.[59]

Certain other duties may be viewed as a consequence of these principal duties, but different publicists have categorized these duties differently. For example, the duty of a neutral State to refrain from supporting one side in the conflict may be viewed as a function of its duty to abstain from participation in hostilities.[60] On the other hand, the duty of a neutral State to refrain from supporting one side in the conflict may also be viewed as a result of its duty of impartiality.[61]

The duties of a neutral State may also be classified in terms of: (1) abstention (obligations to refrain from taking certain actions); (2) prevention (obligations to take certain actions); and (3) acquiescence (obligations to accept certain actions by belligerents).[62]

15.3.2.1 *Duty to Refrain From Providing War-Related Goods and Services to Belligerents*. Neutral States have an obligation to refrain from providing war-related goods and services to belligerents.[63] A neutral State is prohibited from supplying a belligerent State in any manner, either directly or indirectly, with warships, ammunition, or war material of any kind.[64]

---

[58] *Refer to* § 15.4.2 (Belligerent Use of Self-Help When Neutral States Are Unable or Unwilling to Prevent Violations of Neutrality).

[59] The Three Friends, 166 U.S. 1, 52 (1897) ("Neutrality, strictly speaking, consists in abstinence from any participation in a public, private or civil war, and in impartiality of conduct toward both parties, … .").

[60] Michael Bothe, *The Law of Neutrality*, *in* DIETER FLECK, THE HANDBOOK OF HUMANITARIAN LAW IN ARMED CONFLICTS 485 (¶1101) (1999) ("The duty of non-participation means, above all, that the state must abstain from supporting a party to the conflict. This duty not to support also means that the neutral state is under a duty not to allow one party to the conflict to use the resources of the neutral state against the will of the opponent. Therefore, the defence of neutrality is part of the duty of non-participation.").

[61] LAUTERPACHT, II OPPENHEIM'S INTERNATIONAL LAW 654 (§294) ("Since neutrality is an attitude of impartiality, it excludes such assistance and succor to one of the belligerents as is detrimental to the other, and, further, such injuries to the one as benefit the other. But it requires, on the other hand, active measures from neutral States. For neutrals must prevent belligerents from making use of their neutral territories, and of their resources, for military and naval purposes during the war.").

[62] TUCKER, THE LAW OF WAR AND NEUTRALITY AT SEA 203 footnote 14 ("The duties of a neutral state may also be classified—and frequently are so classified—as duties of abstention, prevention and acquiesence [sic] (or toleration). Duties of abstention refer to acts the neutral state itself must refrain from performing; duties of prevention refer to acts the commission of which within its jurisdiction the neutral is obligated to prevent; and, finally, duties of acquiescence have reference to neutral obligations to permit belligerent measures of repression against neutral subjects found rendering certain acts of assistance to an enemy.").

[63] Philander C. Knox, Attorney General, *Neutrality—Military Supplies—Horses*, Apr. 4, 1902, 24 OPINIONS OF THE ATTORNEY GENERAL 15, 18 (1903) ("One of the rules of international law which seems to be now fully agreed upon is that a neutral nation shall not give aid to one of the belligerents in the carrying on of the war.").

[64] HAGUE XIII art. 6 ("The supply, in any manner, directly or indirectly, by a neutral Power to a belligerent Power, of war-ships, ammunition, or war material of any kind whatever, is forbidden.").

The neutral State is also prohibited from providing money or loans to a belligerent State.[65]

A neutral State also has a duty to refrain from placing its various governmental agencies at the disposal of a belligerent in such a way as to aid it directly or indirectly in the prosecution of the war.[66]

Although a neutral State may not supply war-related goods and services to belligerents, a neutral State is not called upon to prevent the export or transport, on behalf of one or other of the belligerents, of arms, munitions, or anything that can be of use to an armed force.[67] Commercial transactions between belligerent States and neutral corporations, companies, citizens, or persons resident in a neutral State are not prohibited.[68] A belligerent State may purchase from such corporations, companies, citizens, or persons supplies, munitions, or anything that may be of use to an armed force, which can be exported or transported without involving the neutral State.[69] The supply of services and goods to a belligerent State, however, must not convert neutral territory into a base of operations.[70]

If a neutral State prohibits the export or transport of arms, munitions, or anything that can be of use to an armed force, every measure of restriction or prohibition taken by a neutral State in regard to the provision of such supplies or munitions must be impartially applied by it to all

---

[65] 1928 PAN AMERICAN NEUTRALITY CONVENTION art. 16 ("The neutral state is forbidden: a) To deliver to the belligerent, directly or indirectly, or for any reason whatever, ships of war, munitions or any other war material; b) To grant it loans, or to open credits for it during the duration of war. Credits that a neutral state may give to facilitate the sale or exportation of its food products and raw materials are not included in this prohibition.").

[66] TUCKER, THE LAW OF WAR AND NEUTRALITY AT SEA 208 ("As Hyde has observed, 'the duty to abstain from giving aid is a broad one and covers a vast field of governmental activities;' for in addition to the prohibition against supplying belligerents with war materials of any kind the neutral is obligated, in general, 'to abstain from placing its various governmental agencies at the disposal of a belligerent in such a way as to aid it directly or indirectly in the prosecution of the war.' Thus in naval warfare, the public vessels of a neutral state must refrain from rendering services of any kind to belligerent naval units at sea.").

[67] 1928 PAN AMERICAN MARITIME NEUTRALITY CONVENTION art. 22 ("Neutral states are not obligated to prevent the export or transit at the expense of any one of the belligerents of arms, munitions and in general of anything which may be useful to their military forces."); HAGUE V art. 7 ("A neutral Power is not called upon to prevent the export or transport, on behalf of one or other of the belligerents, of arms, munitions of war, or, in general, of anything which can be of use to an army or a fleet."); HAGUE XIII art. 7 ("A neutral Power is not bound to prevent the export or transit, for the use of either belligerent, of arms, ammunitions, or, in general, of anything which could be of use to an army or fleet.").

[68] 1956 FM 27-10 (Change No. 1 1976) ¶527 ("Commercial transactions with belligerents by neutral corporations, companies, citizens, or persons resident in neutral territory are not prohibited."); 1928 PAN AMERICAN MARITIME NEUTRALITY CONVENTION art. 15 ("Of the acts of assistance coming from the neutral states, and the acts of commerce on the part of individuals, only the first are contrary to neutrality.").

[69] 1956 FM 27-10 (Change No. 1 1976) ¶527 ("A belligerent may purchase from such persons supplies, munitions, or anything that may be of use to an army or fleet, which can be exported or transported without involving the neutral State.").

[70] *Refer to* § 15.5.1 (Prohibition on Outfitting Hostile Expeditions With Supplies and Services for a Belligerent From Neutral Territory).

belligerent States.[71]

15.3.2.2 *Duty to Prevent Violations of Neutrality Within Its Jurisdiction*. A neutral State has certain obligations to prevent violations of its neutrality within its territory. A neutral State has an obligation to prevent violations of its neutrality committed by belligerent forces.[72] A neutral State also has an obligation to prevent violations of its neutrality committed by persons within its jurisdiction.[73]

15.3.2.3 *Public Expressions of Sympathy Are Not Violations of Neutrality*. Public expressions of sympathy for one belligerent or disapproval of another belligerent are not violations of duties of neutrality.[74]

15.3.2.4 *Authorized Humanitarian Assistance Is Not a Violation of Neutrality*. Humanitarian assistance given in accordance with international law is also not a violation of duties of neutrality.[75] For example, a neutral State's performing of the role of the Protecting Power in accordance with the 1949 Geneva Conventions is not regarded as unneutral conduct.[76]

15.3.3 Correlative or Reciprocal Nature of Rights and Duties Under the Law of Neutrality. The rights and duties of belligerents and neutrals under the law of neutrality may be

---

[71] HAGUE V art. 9 ("Every measure of restriction or prohibition taken by a neutral Power in regard to the matters referred to in Articles 7 and 8 must be impartially applied by it to both belligerents.").

[72] HAGUE XIII art. 25 ("A neutral Power is bound to exercise such surveillance as the means at its disposal allow to prevent any violation of the provisions of the above Articles occurring in its ports or roadsteads or in its waters."); HAGUE V art. 5 ("A neutral Power must not allow any of the acts referred to in Articles 2 to 4 to occur on its territory. It is not called upon to punish acts in violation of its neutrality unless the said acts have been committed on its own territory.").

[73] *See, e.g.*, Consultative Meeting of Foreign Ministers of the American Republics, *Final Act of the Meeting: V General Declaration of Neutrality of the American Republics*, ¶3, Oct. 3, 1939, 1 DEPARTMENT OF STATE BULLETIN 326, 327 (Oct. 7, 1939) (The American Republics resolve "[t]o declare that with regard to their status as neutrals, there exist certain standards recognized by the American Republics applicable in these circumstances and that in accordance with them they: ... (b) Shall prevent, in accordance with their internal legislations, the inhabitants of their territories from engaging in activities capable of affecting the neutral status of the American Republics."); Treaty between the United States and Great Britain, art. 6, May 8, 1871, 17 STAT. 863, 865 ("A neutral Government is bound – ... Thirdly, to exercise due diligence in its own ports and waters, and, as to all persons within its jurisdiction, to prevent any violation of the foregoing obligations and duties.").

[74] LAUTERPACHT, II OPPENHEIM'S INTERNATIONAL LAW 655 (§294) ("The required attitude of impartiality is not incompatible with sympathy with one belligerent, and disapproval of the other, so long as these feelings do not find expression in actions violating impartiality. Thus, not only public opinion and the press of a neutral State, but also its Government, may show their sympathy to one party or another without violating neutrality.").

[75] LAUTERPACHT, II OPPENHEIM'S INTERNATIONAL LAW 655 (§294) ("Moreover, acts of humanity on the part of neutrals and their subjects, such as the sending to military hospitals of doctors, medicine, provisions, dressing material, and the like, and the sending of clothes and money to prisoners of war, can never be construed as acts of partiality, even if these comforts are provided for the wounded and the prisoners of one belligerent only.").

[76] LESLIE C. GREEN, THE CONTEMPORARY LAW OF ARMED CONFLICT 269 (2nd ed., 2000) ("Frequently, as has been seen in the discussion concerning protecting powers, a neutral power is appointed to represent the interests of one belligerent in the territory of the adverse party or for some of its nationals to be appointed to the Fact Finding Commission called for in Protocol I in relation to the investigation of alleged breaches of the law of armed conflict. In neither case can a belligerent suggest that such action is in breach of the obligations of neutrality.").

understood as correlative or reciprocal.

The duties of neutrals often correspond to rights of belligerents, and rights of neutrals often correspond to the duties of belligerents.[77] For example, the duty of a neutral to abstain from hostilities is also a right of a belligerent not to have its adversary aided in hostilities by the neutral State. The right of a neutral State to have its territory be inviolable is also a duty of belligerent States to avoid conducting hostilities in neutral territory.

Similarly, the ability of a neutral to assert its rights may depend on whether it has fulfilled its corresponding neutral duties.[78] For example, the right of a neutral State to have its territory be inviolable may not be asserted to the extent it has failed in its duty to ensure that its territory is not used as a base of operations by a belligerent.

In light of the correlative nature of the rights and duties of belligerents and neutrals under the law of neutrality, a single rule in the law of neutrality may reflect multiple rights and duties of both belligerents and neutrals. For example, hostile acts are not to be committed on neutral territory. This rule involves the right of the neutral State for its territory to be inviolable, and involves a duty on the part of the neutral State to prevent such acts. This rule also reflects a duty of the belligerent State to refrain from such acts, and a right of the belligerent State not to have such acts conducted by an opposing belligerent.

15.4 Remedies for Violations of Neutrality Law

15.4.1 Distinction Between Violations of Neutral Duties and the End of Neutral Status. Violations of neutrality by belligerent or neutral States should be distinguished from the end of a State's neutral status. Rather, whether violations of neutrality result in the end of the neutral status of a State may depend on the national policies of that State and the belligerent States.[79]

Acts that are incompatible with the relationship between the neutral State and a belligerent State under the law of neutrality need not end the neutral State's neutrality and bring that State into the conflict as a belligerent. For example, despite Vichy France's violations of its neutral duties during World War II and despite the Allied invasion of French North Africa,

---

[77] Tucker, The Law of War and Neutrality at Sea 203 footnote 14 ("It is also helpful to observe that the duties of a neutral correspond to the rights of a belligerent, and that the rights of a neutral correspond to the duties of a belligerent. The neutral's duty to observe a strict impartiality corresponds to the belligerent's right to demand impartiality on the part of the neutral. At the same time, the neutral has a right to demand that the belligerent will act toward it in such a manner as to respect its position of impartiality, and there is no question but that the belligerent is under a duty to do so.").

[78] G. Sherston Baker, II Halleck's International Law 305 (28.1) (1908) ("The rights and duties of neutrality are correlative, and the former cannot be claimed, unless the latter are faithfully performed. If the neutral State fail to fulfil the obligations of neutrality, it cannot claim the privileges and exemptions incident to that condition. The rule is equally applicable to the citizens and subjects of a neutral State. So long as they faithfully perform the duties of neutrality, they are entitled to the rights and immunities of that condition. But for every violation of neutral duties, they are liable to the punishment of being treated in their persons or property as public enemies of the offended belligerent.").

[79] *Refer to* § 15.2.1.1 (Application of the Law of Neutrality and the National Policies of States Towards an Armed Conflict).

diplomatic relations persisted between the United States and France during World War II.[80]

15.4.2 Belligerent Use of Self-Help When Neutral States Are Unable or Unwilling to Prevent Violations of Neutrality. Should the neutral State be unable, or fail for any reason, to prevent violations of its neutrality by the forces of one belligerent entering or passing through its territory (including its lands, waters, and airspace), the other belligerent State may be justified in attacking the enemy forces on the neutral State's territory.[81] This view has been reflected in the military manuals of other States.[82] For example, consistent with the *jus ad bellum* requirements for self-defense, belligerent forces may act in self-defense when attacked or threatened with attack from enemy forces unlawfully present in neutral territory,[83] including by taking appropriate action to counter the use of neutral territory as a base of enemy operations when the

---

[80] DWIGHT D. EISENHOWER, CRUSADE IN EUROPE 86-88 (1997) ("Vichy France was a neutral country and during the entire period of the war the United States had maintained diplomatic connection with the French Government. Never, in all its history, had the United States been a party to an unprovoked attack upon a neutral country and even though Vichy was avowedly collaborating with Hitler, there is no doubt that American political leaders regarded the projected operation, from this viewpoint, with considerable distaste. … The Allied invasion of Africa was a most peculiar venture of armed forces in the field of international politics; we were invading a neutral country to create a friend.").

[81] 1956 FM 27-10 (Change No. 1 1976) ¶520 ("Should the neutral State be unable, or fail for any reason, to prevent violations of its neutrality by the troops of one belligerent entering or passing through its territory, the other belligerent State may be justified in attacking the enemy forces on this territory.").

[82] 2004 UK MANUAL ¶1.43a ("Neutral states must refrain from allowing their territory to be used by belligerent states for the purposes of military operations. If a neutral state is unable or unwilling to prevent the use of its territory for the purposes of such military operations, a belligerent state may become entitled to use force in self-defence against enemy forces operating from the territory of that neutral state. Whether or not they are so entitled will depend on the ordinary rules of the *jus ad bellum*."); 2006 AUSTRALIAN MANUAL ¶11.8 ("As a general rule of international law, all acts of hostility in neutral territory, including neutral land, neutral waters and neutral airspace are prohibited. A neutral state has a duty to prevent the use of its territory as a sanctuary or a base of operations by the belligerent forces of any side. If the neutral state is unable or unwilling to enforce effectively its right of inviolability, an aggrieved belligerent may resort to acts of hostility in neutral territory against enemy forces, including warships and military aircraft, making unlawful use of that territory. Belligerents are also authorised to act in self-defence when attacked or threatened with attack while in neutral territory or when attacked or threatened from neutral territory"); 2001 CANADIAN MANUAL ¶1304(3) ("A neutral state is permitted to resist any attempted violation of its borders by force and such resistance does not make the neutral a party to the conflict. If enemy forces enter neutral such territory and the neutral state is unwilling or unable to intern or expel them, the opposing party is entitled to attack them there, or to demand compensation from the neutral for this breach of neutrality."); 2002 GERMAN COMMANDER'S HANDBOOK: LEGAL BASES FOR THE OPERATIONS OF NAVAL FORCES ¶232 ("On the one hand, the parties to the conflict are obliged to respect the **inviolability of neural** [sic] **territory, neutral internal waters, neutral territorial seas** and the **neutral airspace** above these areas. Within and above these areas **all hostilities**, that is the use of armed force and of other measures of maritime war (including measures based on the law of prize) **are prohibited**. There is one **exception** to this principle which applies to measures of **self-defence**, that is the event that one of the parties to the conflict is attacked or endangered to be attacked in these areas. On the other hand, a neutral state is obliged to prevent the parties to the conflict from misusing these areas as **sanctuary** or **base of operations**. If it is unwilling or unable to do so, the other party to the conflict is entitled to take all measures necessary to terminate the misuse of neutral territory or neutral waters.").

[83] 2007 NWP 1-14M ¶7.3 ("If the neutral nation is unable or unwilling to enforce effectively its right of inviolability, an aggrieved belligerent may take such acts as are necessary in neutral territory to counter the activities of enemy forces, including warships and military aircraft, making unlawful use of that territory. Belligerents are also authorized to act in self-defense when attacked or threatened with attack while in neutral territory or when attacked or threatened from neutral territory.").

neutral State is unwilling or unable to prevent such violations.[84]

15.4.3 Neutral State's Use of Force to Defend Its Neutrality. A neutral State may also engage in self-help to prevent violations of neutrality on its territory. Such self-help is also an obligation of the neutral State.[85]

The fact that a neutral State resists, even by force, attempts to violate its neutrality cannot be regarded as a hostile act.[86] For example, a State whose territory is adjacent to a theater of war normally mobilizes a portion of its forces to prevent the forces of either belligerent from entering its territory, to intern such persons as may be permitted to enter, and generally to carry out its duties of neutrality.[87] Such military operations are not regarded as hostile acts against the belligerent State.

15.4.4 Redress of Certain Violations of Neutrality. In addition to the obligations to prevent violations of neutrality, a State may also have obligations to redress violations of neutrality that have been committed.

For example, violations of the law of neutrality may result in liability for payment of damages in certain cases.[88] As a case in point, if harm is caused in a neutral State by the

---

[84] *For example*, Richard Nixon, *Address to the Nation on the Situation in Southeast Asia*, Apr. 30, 1970, 1970 PUBLIC PAPERS OF THE PRESIDENTS 405, 406-08 ("American policy since then has been to scrupulously respect the neutrality of the Cambodian people. ... North Vietnam, however, has not respected that neutrality. For the past 5 years—as indicated on this map that you see here—North Vietnam has occupied military sanctuaries all along the Cambodian frontier with South Vietnam. Some of these extend up to 20 miles into Cambodia. The sanctuaries are in red and, as you note, they are on both sides of the border. They are used for hit and run attacks on American and South Vietnamese forces in South Vietnam. These Communist occupied territories contain major base camps, training sites, logistics facilities, weapons and ammunition factories, airstrips, and prisoner-of-war compounds. ... [T]his is the decision I have made. In cooperation with the armed forces of South Vietnam, attacks are being launched this week to clean out major enemy sanctuaries on the Cambodian-Vietnam border. ... This is not an invasion of Cambodia. The areas in which these attacks will be launched are completely occupied and controlled by North Vietnamese forces. Our purpose is not to occupy the areas. Once enemy forces are driven out of these sanctuaries and once their military supplies are destroyed, we will withdraw."); SPAIGHT, AIR POWER AND WAR RIGHTS 434 ("**Justifiable entry of neutral jurisdiction**.—The international law of neutrality is based on the principle that neutral States exclude *both* belligerent parties from entry into or passage through their territory. If that condition is not fulfilled, to advantage of one party and the detriment of the other, the latter is entitled, after protest, to take the action necessary to protect his interests. He is entitled to follow his enemy into neutral jurisdiction and to attack him there. It was for this reasons that Japan was able to justify her action in 1904 in cutting out the Russian cruiser *Reshitelni* from the Chinese harbor of Chifu when it became apparent that China was unable or unwilling to disarm the vessel in accordance with the requirements of international law. It was on the same principle that the British intervention in Syria in 1941 was justifiable. The Vichy authorities there were allowing German aircraft to use the Syrian airfields, and such use was particularly damaging to British interests at that time, in view of the revolt in Iraq.").

[85] *Refer to* § 15.3.2.2 (Duty to Prevent Violations of Neutrality Within Its Jurisdiction).

[86] HAGUE V art. 10 ("The fact of a neutral Power resisting, even by force, attempts to violate its neutrality cannot be regarded as a hostile act.").

[87] 1956 FM 27-10 (Change No. 1 1976) ¶519 ("In order to protect its neutrality, a State whose territory is adjacent to a theater of war normally mobilizes a portion of its forces to prevent troops of either belligerent from entering its territory, to intern such as may be permitted to enter, and generally to carry out its duties of neutrality.").

[88] *Refer to* § 18.16 (Compensation for Violations of the Law of War).

unauthorized entry of belligerent forces, the offending State may be required, according to the circumstances, to respond in damages.[89]

Similarly, when a ship has been captured in the territorial waters of a neutral State, the neutral State must employ, if the prize is still within its jurisdiction, the means at its disposal to release the prize with its officers and crew, and to intern the prize crew.[90] If the prize is no longer in the jurisdiction of the neutral power, the captor State, on the demand of the neutral State, must liberate the prize with its officers and crew.[91] The neutral State has a duty to make this demand.[92]

15.5 Prohibition on the Use of Neutral Territory as a Base of Operations

Neutral territory (including neutral lands, waters, and airspace) may not be used as a base of operations against belligerent forces.[93] For example, belligerent States are forbidden to use a neutral State's ports and waters as a base of naval operations against their adversaries,[94] and a neutral State has a corresponding obligation to prevent such use.[95]

---

[89] 1956 FM 27-10 (Change No. 1 1976) ¶515 ("If harm is caused in a neutral State by the unauthorized entry of a belligerent, the offending State may be required, according to the circumstances, to respond in damages.").

[90] Hague XIII art. 3 ("When a ship has been captured in the territorial waters of a neutral Power, this Power must employ, if the prize is still within its jurisdiction, the means at its disposal to release the prize with its officers and crew, and to intern the prize crew.").

[91] Hague XIII art. 3 ("If the prize is not in the jurisdiction of the neutral power, the captor Government, on the demand of that Power, must liberate the prize with its officers and crew.").

[92] William H. Taft, *Proclamation Regarding the Hague XIII*, Feb. 28, 1910, 36 Stat. 2415, 2438 ("And whereas the Senate of the United States of America by its resolution of April 17, 1908, (two-thirds of the Senators present concurring therein) did advise and consent to the adherence by the United States to the said Convention with the reservation and exclusion of its Article 23 and with the understanding that the last clause of Article 3 of the said Convention implies the duty of a neutral power to make the demand therein mentioned for the return of a ship captured within the neutral jurisdiction and no longer within that jurisdiction; And whereas the President of the United States of America, in pursuance of and in conformity with the aforesaid advice and consent of the Senate, did, on the 23rd day of February, 1909, declare the adherence of the United States to the said Convention;").

[93] Consultative Meeting of Foreign Ministers of the American Republics, *Final Act of the Meeting: V General Declaration of Neutrality of the American Republics*, ¶3, Oct. 3, 1939, 1 Department of State Bulletin 326, 327 (Oct. 7, 1939) (The American Republics resolve "[t]o declare that with regard to their status as neutrals, there exist certain standards recognized by the American Republics applicable in these circumstances and that in accordance with them they: (a) Shall prevent their respective terrestrial, maritime and aerial territories from being utilized as bases of belligerent operations."); 1955 NWIP 10-2 ¶442 ("Belligerents are forbidden to use neutral territory, territorial sea, or air space as a base for hostile operations.").

[94] 1928 Pan American Maritime Neutrality Convention art. 4 ("Under the terms of the preceding article, a belligerent state is forbidden: a) To make use of neutral waters as a base of naval operations against the enemy, or to renew or augment military supplies or the armament of its ships, or to complete the equipment of the latter;"); Hague XIII art. 5 ("Belligerents are forbidden to use neutral ports and waters as a base of naval operations against their adversaries, and in particular to erect wireless telegraphy stations or any apparatus for the purpose of communicating with the belligerent forces on land or sea.").

[95] *See, e.g.*, Treaty between the United States and Great Britain, art. 6, May 8, 1871, 17 Stat. 863, 865 ("A neutral Government is bound – Secondly, not to permit or suffer either belligerent to make use of its ports or waters as the base of naval operations against the other, or for the purpose of the renewal or augmentation of military supplies or

The prohibition against the use of neutral territory as a base of operations extends to any hostile expeditions against a belligerent State, and thus includes such expeditions by non-State actors.[96] For example, a neutral State has an obligation to prevent the arming of any vessel within its jurisdiction that is intended to engage in hostile operations against a State with which it is at peace and to prevent the departure from its jurisdiction of any vessel intended to engage in hostile operations that has been adapted entirely or partly within such jurisdiction for use in war.[97]

The prohibition on the use of neutral territory as a base of operations includes prohibitions against (1) outfitting hostile expeditions with supplies and services; (2) recruiting forces in neutral territory; (3) establishing military communications facilities in neutral territory; and (4) moving belligerent forces or convoys of military supplies on land.

15.5.1 Prohibition on Outfitting Hostile Expeditions With Supplies and Services for a Belligerent From Neutral Territory. It is forbidden to permit the use of the neutral State's territory for the fitting out of hostile expeditions.[98] As a case in point, a belligerent State's warships may not make use of a neutral State's ports, roadsteads, and territorial waters to replenish or increase their supplies of war materials or their armaments, or for completing their crews.[99]

15.5.2 Prohibition Against Recruiting and Forming Corps of Combatants. Units of combatants may not be formed nor may recruiting agencies be established on the territory of a neutral State to assist a belligerent State.[100] This means that the establishment of recruiting agencies, the enlistment of personnel, the formation and organization of hostile expeditions on a neutral State's territory, and the passage across its frontiers of organized bodies of personnel

---

arms, or the recruitment of men."). *Refer to* § 15.3.2.2 (Duty to Prevent Violations of Neutrality Within Its Jurisdiction).

[96] *Refer to* § 17.18.1 (Duty of Non-Belligerent States to Refrain From Supporting Hostilities by Non-State Armed Groups Against Other States).

[97] HAGUE XIII art. 8 ("A neutral Government is bound to employ the means at its disposal to prevent the fitting out or arming of any vessel within its jurisdiction which it has reason to believe is intended to cruise, or engage in hostile operations, against a Power with which that Government is at peace. It is also bound to display the same vigilance to prevent the departure from its jurisdiction of any vessel intended to cruise, or engage in hostile operations, which has been adapted entirely or partly within the said jurisdiction for use in war."); Treaty between the United States and Great Britain, art. 6, May 8, 1871, 17 STAT. 863, 865 ("A neutral Government is bound – First, to use due diligence to prevent the fitting out, arming, or equipping, within its jurisdiction, of any vessel which it has reasonable ground to believe is intended to cruise or to carry on war against a power with which it is at peace; and also to use like diligence to prevent the departure from its jurisdiction of any vessel intended to cruise or carry on war as above, such vessel having been specially adapted, in whole or in part, within such jurisdiction, to warlike use.").

[98] 1956 FM 27-10 (Change No. 1 1976) ¶526 ("It is also forbidden to permit the use of its territory for the fitting out of hostile expeditions.").

[99] HAGUE XIII art. 18 ("Belligerent war-ships may not make use of neutral ports, roadsteads, or territorial waters for replenishing or increasing their supplies of war material or their armament, or for completing their crews.").

[100] HAGUE V art. 4 ("Corps of combatants cannot be formed nor recruiting agencies opened on the territory of a neutral Power to assist the belligerents.").

intending to enlist are prohibited.[101]

15.5.2.1 *Exception for Authorized Medical Personnel*. This prohibition does not extend to medical personnel and units of voluntary aid societies of a neutral State who are duly authorized to provide medical assistance to a belligerent State.[102] In no circumstance shall such assistance by medical personnel and units of voluntary aid societies of the neutral State be considered as interference in the conflict.[103]

15.5.2.2 *Exception for Persons Crossing a Neutral State's Frontiers Separately to Assist a Belligerent State*. The prohibition against organizing units of combatants is directed against organized bodies, which only require being armed to become an immediate fighting force.[104] Thus, the responsibility of a neutral State is not engaged by the fact of persons crossing the frontier separately to offer their services to one of the belligerent States.[105] Individuals crossing the frontier singly or in small bands that are unorganized create no obligation on the neutral State.[106]

Neutral States shall not oppose the voluntary departure of nationals of belligerent States even though they leave simultaneously in great numbers; but they may oppose the voluntary departure of their own nationals going to enlist in the armed forces of belligerent States.[107] Neutral States are not required to enact legislation forbidding their nationals to join the armed forces of belligerent States.[108]

Neutral States, however, may not send regularly constituted military units across the

---

[101] 1956 FM 27-10 (Change No. 1 1976) ¶522b ("*Application of Rule*. The establishment of recruiting agencies, the enlistment of men, the formation and organization of hostile expeditions on neutral territory, and the passage across its frontiers of organized bodies of men intending to enlist are prohibited."); Consultative Meeting of Foreign Ministers of the American Republics, *Final Act of the Meeting: V General Declaration of Neutrality of the American Republics*, ¶3, Oct. 3, 1939, 1 DEPARTMENT OF STATE BULLETIN 326, 327 (Oct. 7, 1939) (The American Republics resolve "[t]o declare that with regard to their status as neutrals, there exist certain standards recognized by the American Republics applicable in these circumstances and that in accordance with them they: ... (c) Shall prevent on their respective territories the enlistment of persons to serve in the military, naval, or air forces of the belligerents;").

[102] 1956 FM 27-10 (Change No. 1 1976) ¶522c ("This prohibition does not extend to medical personnel and units of a voluntary aid society duly authorized to join one of the belligerents. (See *GWS, art. 27*; par. 229 herein.)").

[103] *Refer to* § 4.12 (Staff of a Recognized Aid Society of a Neutral Country).

[104] 1956 FM 27-10 (Change No. 1 1976) ¶524a ("The prohibition in Article 4, H. V (par. 522), is directed against organized bodies which only require to be armed to become an immediate fighting force.").

[105] HAGUE V art. 6 ("The responsibility of a neutral Power is not engaged by the fact of persons crossing the frontier separately to offer their services to one of the belligerents.").

[106] 1956 FM 27-10 (Change No. 1 1976) ¶524a ("Individuals crossing the frontier singly or in small bands that are unorganized create no obligation on the neutral State.").

[107] 1928 PAN AMERICAN MARITIME NEUTRALITY CONVENTION art. 23 ("Neutral states shall not oppose the voluntary departure of nationals of belligerent States even though they leave simultaneously in great numbers; but they may oppose the voluntary departure of their own nationals going to enlist in the armed forces.").

[108] 1956 FM 27-10 (Change No. 1 1976) ¶524a ("Neutral States are not required to enact legislation forbidding their nationals to join the armed forces of the belligerents.").

frontier in the guise of "volunteers" or small unorganized bands.[109]

15.5.3 Prohibition Against Establishment or Use of Belligerent Communications Facilities in Neutral Territory. Belligerent States are prohibited from erecting on the territory of a neutral State any apparatus for the purpose of communicating with belligerent forces on land or sea.[110] Belligerent States are prohibited from using any installation of this kind established by them before the armed conflict on the territory of a neutral State for purely military purposes, and which has not been opened for the service of public messages.[111]

15.5.3.1 *Use of Neutral Facilities by Belligerents Not Prohibited*. A neutral State does not, however, have to forbid or restrict the use on behalf of belligerent States of communications equipment and facilities belonging to the neutral State, or belonging to companies or private individuals.[112]

That a neutral State, if it so desires, may transmit messages by means of its communications facilities does not imply that the neutral State may use such facilities or permit their use to lend assistance to the belligerents on one side only.[113] Every measure of restriction or prohibition taken by a neutral State in regard to the use of its communications facilities and equipment must be impartially applied by it to all belligerent States.[114] It also must see to the same obligation being observed by companies or private individuals owning such communication equipment and facilities.[115]

---

[109] 1956 FM 27-10 (Change No. 1 1976) ¶524a ("The foregoing rules do not, however, permit a State professing to be neutral to send regularly constituted military units across the frontier in the guise of 'volunteers' or small unorganized bands.").

[110] HAGUE V art. 3 ("Belligerents are likewise forbidden to: (*a*.) Erect on the territory of a neutral Power a wireless telegraphy station or other apparatus for the purpose of communicating with belligerent forces on land or sea;"); HAGUE XIII art. 5 ("Belligerents are forbidden to use neutral ports and waters as a base of naval operations against their adversaries, and in particular to erect wireless telegraphy stations or any apparatus for the purpose of communicating with the belligerent forces on land or sea."); 1928 PAN AMERICAN MARITIME NEUTRALITY CONVENTION art. 4 ("Under the terms of the preceding article, a belligerent state is forbidden: ... b) To install in neutral waters radio-telegraph stations or any other apparatus which may serve as a means of communication with its military forces, or to make use of installations of this kind it may have established before the war and which may not have been opened to the public.").

[111] HAGUE V art. 3 ("Belligerents are likewise forbidden to: ... (*b*.) Use any installation of this kind established by them before the war on the territory of a neutral Power for purely military purposes, and which has not been opened for the service of public messages.").

[112] HAGUE V art. 8 ("A neutral Power is not called upon to forbid or restrict the use on behalf of the belligerents of telegraph or telephone cables or of wireless telegraphy apparatus belonging to it or to companies or private individuals.").

[113] 1956 FM 27-10 (Change No. 1 1976) ¶530 ("The liberty of a neutral State, if it so desires, to transmit messages by means of its telegraph, telephone, cable, radio, or other communications facilities does not imply the power so to use them or to permit their use as to lend assistance to the belligerents on one side only.").

[114] HAGUE V art. 9 ("Every measure of restriction or prohibition taken by a neutral Power in regard to the matters referred to in Articles 7 and 8 must be impartially applied by it to both belligerents.").

[115] HAGUE V art. 9 ("A neutral Power must see to the same obligations being observed by companies or private individuals owning telegraph or telephone cables or wireless telegraphy apparatus.").

15.5.4 Movement of Belligerent Forces and Convoys of Supplies Through Neutral Land Territory. Belligerent States are forbidden to move forces or convoys of either munitions of war or supplies across the land territory of a neutral State.[116] This rule only prohibits the official acts of a belligerent State in convoying or shipping munitions and supplies through a neutral State as part of an expedition; it does not prohibit the shipment of such supplies by private persons.[117]

However, a neutral State may authorize passage through its territory of the wounded and sick, including the overflight of its territory by certain medical aircraft.[118]

15.6 NEUTRAL PERSONS

15.6.1 Definition of Neutral Person. The nationals of a State that is not taking part in the war are considered neutral persons.[119]

15.6.2 Forfeiture of Protections of Neutral Status by a Neutral Person. A national of a neutral State would not retain the protections that a person would derive by virtue of the neutral status of his or her State of nationality if that person commits:

- hostile acts against a belligerent State; or
- acts in favor of a belligerent State, particularly if that person voluntarily enlists in the ranks of the armed forces of one of the parties to the armed conflict.[120]

For example, neutral persons who materially support one belligerent generally forfeit their neutral character or assume certain liabilities with respect to the other belligerent.[121]

15.6.2.1 *No More Severe Treatment Than Nationals of an Opposing Belligerent State*. A neutral person, however, shall not be more severely treated by the belligerent State as against whom that person has abandoned his or her neutrality than a national of the other

---

[116] HAGUE V art. 2 ("Belligerents are forbidden to move troops or convoys of either munitions of war or supplies across the territory of a neutral Power.").

[117] 1956 FM 27-10 (Change No. 1 1976) ¶517 ("A distinction must be drawn between the official acts of the belligerent State in convoying or shipping munitions and supplies through neutral territory as part of an expedition and the shipment of such supplies by private persons. The former is forbidden while the latter is not.").

[118] *Refer to* § 15.18 (Authorized Passage of Wounded and Sick Combatants Through Neutral Territory).

[119] HAGUE V art. 16 ("The nationals of a State which is not taking part in the war are considered as neutrals.").

[120] HAGUE V art. 17 ("A neutral cannot avail himself of his neutrality: (a.) If he commits hostile acts against a belligerent; (b.) If he commits acts in favor of a belligerent, particularly if he voluntarily enlists in the ranks of the armed force of one of the parties.").

[121] *See also* LAUTERPACHT, II OPPENHEIM'S INTERNATIONAL LAW 656 (§296) ("International Law is primarily a law between States. For this reason the rights and duties of neutrality are principally those of neutral States as such. ... At the same time, International Law renders unlawful certain activities of nationals of neutral States, like carriage of contraband or breach of blockade, without, however, imposing upon these States the duty to prevent or penalise such acts. These are punished by the belligerent against whom they are directed."); GREENSPAN, THE MODERN LAW OF LAND WARFARE 571 ("A neutral subject who indulges in partisan activity in favor of a belligerent usually loses the benefit of his neutral character in relation to the belligerent on the other side, as will be seen shortly. Therefore, while a neutral person is free to assist a belligerent, he generally does so at his own risk.").

belligerent State could be for the same act.[122]

Although a neutral person who takes certain actions may be liable to treatment as an unprivileged belligerent, the forfeiture of neutral protections does not necessarily result in that person being regarded as an unprivileged belligerent.

For example, if a national of a neutral State is a member of the armed forces of a belligerent State, that person would be entitled to all the protections that a member of the armed forces of the belligerent State would enjoy under the law of war, such as POW status if that person falls into the power of the enemy during international armed conflict.[123]

15.6.2.2 *Acts Not Considered in Favor of a Belligerent That Would Forfeit Protections of Neutral Status*. The followings acts would not be considered as committed in favor of a belligerent State that would forfeit a neutral person's protections of neutral status:

- furnishing supplies or making loans to a belligerent State, provided that the person who furnishes the supplies or who makes the loans lives neither in the territory of the belligerent State nor in the territory occupied by it, and that the supplies do not come from these territories; or

- rendering services in matters of police or civil administration.[124]

In addition, merely expressing sympathy for a belligerent's cause would not cause a person to forfeit one's neutral character, although incitement or recruitment would be treated differently.

Certain types of humanitarian assistance under the 1949 Geneva Conventions would also not be regarded as a violation of neutrality by the persons engaging in those activities.[125]

15.6.3 Neutral Persons in the Home Territory of a Belligerent. Neutral persons in the home territory of a belligerent State are not "protected persons" under the GC while their State of nationality has normal diplomatic relations with the belligerent State.[126]

In general, neutral persons residing permanently in the territory of a belligerent State,

---

[122] HAGUE V art. 17 ("In such a case, the neutral shall not be more severely treated by the belligerent as against whom he has abandoned his neutrality than a national of the other belligerent State could be for the same act.").

[123] *Refer to* § 4.4.4.1 (Nationals of Neutral States in Enemy Forces).

[124] HAGUE V art. 18 ("The following acts shall not be considered as committed in favour of one belligerent in the sense of Article 17, letter (b): (a.) Supplies furnished or loans made to one of the belligerents, provided that the person who furnishes the supplies or who makes the loans lives neither in the territory of the other party nor in the territory occupied by him, and that the supplies do not come from these territories; (b.) Services rendered in matters of police or civil administration.").

[125] *Refer to* § 4.12 (Staff of a Recognized Aid Society of a Neutral Country); § 7.12.1.3 (Authorized Neutral Civilian Hospital Ships).

[126] *Refer to* § 10.3.3.3 (Nationals of a Neutral State or Co-Belligerent State While Normal Diplomatic Representation Exists).

whether protected persons or not, are to a great extent regarded, both by that belligerent and the opposing side, like other residents of that territory, so long as they remain there.[127] By contrast, the neutral person who is a transient visitor in the territory of a belligerent is provided particular respect, so far as the hazards of war permit, and provided that the person's actions are consistent with that person's neutral character.[128]

15.6.4 Neutral Persons Resident in Occupied Territory. Neutral persons resident in occupied territory are not entitled to claim different treatment, in general, from that accorded the other inhabitants.[129] They must refrain from all participation in the war and from all hostile acts, and must observe strictly the rules of the Occupying Power.[130]

All nationals of neutral States, whether resident in or temporarily visiting an occupied territory, may be punished for offenses committed by them to the same extent and in the same manner as enemy nationals.[131] In addition, it may be possible to extradite nationals of neutral States who have committed offenses to their home States for prosecution. If nationals of neutral States are not "protected persons," they may be deported or expelled for just cause.[132]

In the event that such a person is arrested, suspicions must be verified by a serious inquiry, and the arrested neutral person must be given an opportunity to present a defense, and to communicate with his or her national consul if requested.[133] In addition, the minimum standards

---

[127] GREENSPAN, THE MODERN LAW OF LAND WARFARE 575 ("In general, neutrals residing permanently in the territory of a belligerent, whether protected persons or not, are to a great extent regarded, both by that belligerent and the opposing side, as sharing the lot and character of the people among whom they reside, so long as they continue there.").

[128] GREENSPAN, THE MODERN LAW OF LAND WARFARE 577-78 ("The neutral who is merely a transient visitor in the territory of a belligerent falls into a different category from the resident neutral; provided, of course, that his actions are consistent with his neutral character. Both his person and his property are entitled to particular respect from the belligerents, so far as the hazards of war permit.").

[129] 1956 FM 27-10 (Change No. 1 1976) ¶548 ("Neutral persons resident in occupied territory are not entitled to claim different treatment, in general, from that accorded the other inhabitants.").

[130] 1956 FM 27-10 (Change No. 1 1976) ¶548 ("They must refrain from all participation in the war, from all hostile acts, and observe strictly the rules of the occupant.").

[131] 1956 FM 27-10 (Change No. 1 1976) ¶550 ("All nationals of neutral powers, whether resident or temporarily visiting an occupied territory, may be punished for offenses committed by them to the same extent and in the same manner as enemy nationals.").

[132] 1958 UK MANUAL ¶691 note 1 ("If such neutrals are not 'protected persons' then they may be expelled or deported for just cause by the military or civil authorities of the Occupant.").

[133] In the Matter of the Claim of Madame Chevreau Against the United Kingdom, Arbitral Award, *reprinted in* 27 AJIL 153, 160 (1933) ("The principles involved in the present case which, among others, have been applied by different international commissions, may be briefly stated as follows: (1) The arbitrary arrest, detention or deportation of a foreigner may give rise to a claim in international law. But the claim is not justified if these measures were taken in good faith and upon reasonable suspicion, especially if a zone of military operations is involved. (2) In cases of arrest, suspicions must be verified by a serious inquiry, and the arrested person given an opportunity to defend himself against the suspicions directed against him, and particularly to communicate with the consul of his country if he requests it. If there is no inquiry, or if it is unnecessarily delayed, or, in general, if the detention is unnecessarily prolonged, there is ground for a claim.").

for humane treatment and for detention procedures would be applicable.[134]

15.6.4.1 *Protected Person Status of Neutral Persons in Occupied Territory*. Neutral persons, among other persons, who find themselves in the hands of an Occupying Power generally would be regarded as "protected persons" under the GC.[135] Neutral persons who travel to occupied territory for the purpose of fighting the Occupying Power are not regarded as "protected persons" under the GC.[136]

15.6.4.2 *Diplomatic Agents and Consular Personnel in Occupied Territory*. Diplomatic agents of neutral States must be treated with all courtesy and must be permitted such freedom of action as it is possible to allow, with due regard to the necessities of the war. The same is true of consular personnel of neutral States, except those who are enemy nationals.[137]

15.7 NEUTRAL WATERS

Belligerent States are forbidden to use a neutral State's ports and waters as a base of naval operations against their adversaries, and in particular to erect or employ any apparatus for communicating with belligerent forces on land or sea.[138] For example, a belligerent State's warships may not make use of a neutral State's ports, roadsteads, and territorial waters to replenish or increase their supplies of war materials or their armaments, or for completing their crews.[139]

---

[134] *Refer to* § 8.2 (Humane Treatment of Detainees); § 8.14 (Procedures for Detention).

[135] *See* Jack L. Goldsmith III, Assistant Attorney General, *"Protected Person" Status in Occupied Iraq Under the Fourth Geneva Convention*, Mar. 18, 2004, 28 OPINIONS OF THE OFFICE OF LEGAL COUNSEL 35, 45 ("Second, 'territory of a belligerent State' might refer to the *home* territory of the party to the conflict in whose hands the citizen of the neutral State finds himself. As applied to the armed conflict with Iraq, this interpretation would deny 'protected person[]' status to citizens of neutral States who find themselves in the territory of the United States, but not to those who find themselves in occupied Iraq. We conclude that the second interpretation is correct.") (amendment in original). *See also* II-A FINAL RECORD OF THE DIPLOMATIC CONFERENCE OF GENEVA OF 1949 793 ("A particularly delicate question was that of the position of the nationals of neutral States. The Drafting Committee had made a distinction between the position of neutrals in the home territory of belligerents and that of neutrals in occupied territory. In the former case, neutrals were protected by normal diplomatic representation; in the latter case, on the other hand, the diplomatic representatives concerned were only accredited to the Government of the occupied States, whereas authority rested with the Occupying Power. It followed that all neutrals in occupied territory must enjoy protection under the Convention, while neutrals in the home territory of a belligerent only required such protection if the State whose nationals they were had no normal diplomatic representation in the territory in question. The text drawn up by the Drafting Committee had taken account of the above considerations.").

[136] *Refer to* § 10.3.2.1 ("Find Themselves").

[137] 1956 FM 27-10 (Change No. 1 1976) ¶549 ("Diplomatic agents of neutral States must be treated with all courtesy and must be permitted such freedom of action as it is possible to allow, with due regard to the necessities of the war. The same is true of consular personnel of neutral States, except those who are enemy nationals.").

[138] HAGUE XIII art. 5 ("Belligerents are forbidden to use neutral ports and waters as a base of naval operations against their adversaries, and in particular to erect wireless telegraphy stations or any apparatus for the purpose of communicating with the belligerent forces on land or sea.").

[139] HAGUE XIII art. 18 ("Belligerent war-ships may not make use of neutral ports, roadsteads, or territorial waters for replenishing or increasing their supplies of war material or their armament, or for completing their crews.").

Belligerent State forces must refrain from acts of hostility in neutral waters, including the exercise of visit and search.[140]

The neutral State has an affirmative duty to police its waters to prevent violations of neutrality in its waters.[141] If a neutral State is unable or unwilling to detect and expel belligerent forces unlawfully present in its waters, the opposing belligerent State may undertake such self-help enforcement actions as may be necessary to terminate the violation of neutrality.

15.7.1 Waters That Are Considered Neutral. The waters that are subject to the sovereignty of a neutral State are considered neutral. Neutral waters may be understood to include the following waters belonging to a neutral State:

- the territorial sea, including up to 12 nautical miles;[142]
- archipelagic waters;[143] and
- ports, roadsteads, and internal waters.[144]

For the purpose of applying the law of neutrality, all ocean areas *not* subject to the territorial sovereignty of any State (*i.e.*, all waters seaward of neutral States' territorial seas) are not considered neutral waters. The following waters are not considered neutral waters:

- a neutral State's contiguous zone;[145]
- a neutral State's exclusive economic zone;[146] and
- the high seas.[147]

15.7.2 A Neutral State's Regulations Concerning Belligerent Warships and Prizes in Its Waters. A neutral State may adopt laws or regulations governing the presence of belligerent warships and their prizes in its waters.

A neutral State must apply impartially to opposing belligerents the conditions, restrictions, or prohibitions made by the neutral State in regard to the admission into its ports,

---

[140] *Refer to* § 15.13.3 (Where Belligerents May Not Exercise the Right of Visit and Search).

[141] Hague XIII art. 25 ("A neutral Power is bound to exercise such surveillance as the means at its disposal allow to prevent any violation of the provisions of the above Articles occurring in its ports or roadsteads or in its waters.").

[142] *Refer to* § 13.2.2.2 (Territorial Seas).

[143] *Refer to* § 13.2.2.3 (Archipelagic Waters).

[144] *Refer to* § 13.2.2.1 (Internal Waters).

[145] *Refer to* § 13.2.3.2 (Contiguous Zones).

[146] *Refer to* § 13.2.3.3 (Exclusive Economic Zones (EEZs)).

[147] *Refer to* § 13.2.3.4 (High Seas).

roadsteads, or territorial waters, of belligerent warships or of their prizes.[148] Nevertheless, a neutral Power may forbid a belligerent vessel that has failed to conform to the orders and regulations made by it, or that has violated neutrality, to enter its ports or roadsteads.[149]

15.7.3 <u>24-Hour Limit on Stay of Belligerent Warships in Neutral Waters</u>. In the absence of special provisions to the contrary in the legislation of a neutral State, a belligerent State's warships are generally prohibited from remaining in that neutral State's ports, roadsteads, or territorial waters for more than 24 hours.[150]

A belligerent warship may not prolong its stay in a neutral port beyond the permissible time except on account of damage or stress of weather. It must depart as soon as the cause of the delay is at an end.[151]

The regulations as to the question of the length of time that these vessels may remain in neutral ports, roadsteads, or waters, do not apply to warships devoted exclusively to religious, scientific, or philanthropic purposes.[152] Warships engaged in the collection of scientific data of potential military application would not be considered to be devoted exclusively to scientific purposes and would not be exempt.[153]

15.7.3.1 *<u>Notification to Belligerent Warships to Depart a Neutral State's Waters Upon Outbreak of Hostilities</u>*. If a neutral State, which has been informed of the outbreak of hostilities, learns that a belligerent State's warship is in one of the neutral State's ports or roadsteads, or in its territorial waters, it must notify such warship to depart within 24 hours or

---

[148] HAGUE XIII art. 9 ("A neutral Power must apply impartially to the two belligerents the conditions, restrictions, or prohibitions made by it in regard to the admission into its ports, roadsteads, or territorial waters, of belligerent war-ships or of their prizes.").

[149] HAGUE XIII art. 9 ("Nevertheless, a neutral Power may forbid a belligerent vessel which has failed to conform to the orders and regulations made by it, or which has violated neutrality, to enter its ports or roadsteads.").

[150] HAGUE XIII art. 12 ("In the absence of special provisions to the contrary in the legislation of a neutral Power, belligerent war-ships are not permitted to remain in the ports, roadsteads, or territorial waters of the said Power for more than twenty-four hours, except in cases covered by the present Convention."); 1928 PAN AMERICAN NEUTRALITY CONVENTION art. 5 ("Belligerent warships are forbidden to remain in the ports or waters of a neutral state more than twenty-four hours. This provision will be communicated to the ship as soon as it arrives in port or in the territorial waters, and if already there at the time of the declaration of war, as soon as the neutral state becomes aware of this declaration.").

[151] HAGUE XIII art. 14 ("A belligerent war-ship may not prolong its stay in a neutral port beyond the permissible time except on account of damage or stress of weather. It must depart as soon as the cause of the delay is at an end."). *See also* 1928 PAN AMERICAN NEUTRALITY CONVENTION art. 5 ("A ship may extend its stay in port more than twenty-four hours in case of damage or bad conditions at sea, but must depart as soon as the cause of the delay has ceased. When, according to the domestic law of the neutral state, the ship may not receive fuel until twenty-four hours after its arrival in port, the period of its stay may be extended an equal length of time.").

[152] HAGUE XIII art. 14 ("The regulations as to the question of the length of time which these vessels may remain in neutral ports, roadsteads, or waters, do not apply to war-ships devoted exclusively to religious, scientific, or philanthropic purposes."); 1928 PAN AMERICAN MARITIME NEUTRALITY CONVENTION art. 5 ("Vessels used exclusively for scientific, religious, or philanthropic purposes are exempted from the foregoing provisions.").

[153] 2007 NWP 1-14M ¶7.3.2.1 ("Warships engaged in the collection of scientific data of potential military application are not exempt."); 1997 NWP 9 ¶7.3.2.1 (same); 1989 NWP 9 ¶7.3.2.1 ("Vessels engaged in the collection of scientific data of potential military application are not exempt").

within the time prescribed by local regulations.[154]

15.7.4 Passage of Belligerent Warships and Prizes Through a Neutral State's Waters. A neutral State may allow the passage of belligerent warships and prizes through its waters. The neutrality of a State is not affected by the mere passage through its territorial waters of warships or prizes belonging to belligerents.[155]

A neutral State may, on a nondiscriminatory basis, suspend passage of belligerent warships and prizes through its waters (with the exception of international straits and archipelagic sea lanes).[156]

Although the general practice has been to close neutral territorial seas to belligerent submarines, a neutral State may elect to allow passage of submarines provided they do not engage in hostile acts while in territorial waters.[157]

Neutral States customarily authorize passage through their territorial sea of ships carrying the wounded, sick, and shipwrecked, whether or not those waters are otherwise closed to belligerent vessels.[158]

15.7.4.1 *Right of Entry in Distress for Belligerent Vessels*. Belligerent vessels, including warships, have a right of entry in distress whether caused by *force majeure* or damage resulting from enemy action.[159] The right of entry in distress does not prejudice the measures that a neutral State may take after entry has been granted, such as measures to intern the ship if it

---

[154] HAGUE XIII art. 13 ("If a Power which has been informed of the outbreak of hostilities learns that a belligerent war-ship is in one of its ports or roadsteads, or in its territorial waters, it must notify the said ship to depart within twenty-four hours or within the time prescribed by local regulations.").

[155] HAGUE XIII art. 10 ("The neutrality of a Power is not affected by the mere passage through its territorial waters of war-ships or prizes belonging to belligerents.").

[156] 2007 NWP 1-14M ¶7.3.4 ("A neutral nation may, on a nondiscriminatory basis, suspend passage of belligerent warships and prizes through its territorial seas, except in international straits."); 1997 NWP 9 ¶7.3.4 (same); 1989 NWP 9 ¶7.3.4.1 ("A neutral nation may, on a nondiscriminatory basis, close its territorial waters, except in international straits, to belligerent vessels.").

[157] 2007 NWP 1-14M ¶7.3.4 ("Although the general practice has been to close neutral territorial seas to belligerent submarines, a neutral nation may elect to allow passage of submarines."); 1997 NWP 9 ¶7.3.4 (same); 1989 NWP 9 ¶7.3.4.1 ("Although the general practice has been to close neutral territorial waters to belligerent submarines, a neutral nation may elect to allow passage of submarines, either surfaced or submerged.").

[158] 2007 NWP 1-14M ¶7.3.4 ("Neutral nations customarily authorize passage through their territorial sea of ships carrying the wounded, sick, and shipwrecked, whether or not those waters are otherwise closed to belligerent vessels."); 1997 NWP 9 ¶7.3.4 (same); 1989 NWP 9 ¶7.3.4.1 (same).

[159] TUCKER, THE LAW OF WAR AND NEUTRALITY AT SEA 240 ("It is generally recognized, however, that international practice requires that exception be made in the neutrality regulations of states to permit the entry of belligerent warships in distress. Entry in distress may result from weather or sea conditions, but it may also result from damage incurred in battle. Even pursuit by the enemy appears to give belligerent warships a right of entry. But this right of entry in distress cannot be held to prejudice the measures a neutral state may take once admission into its waters and ports has been granted.").

remains when it is not entitled to remain.[160]

15.8 Passage of Belligerent Vessels and Aircraft Through International Straits and Archipelagic Sea Lanes

Although a neutral State may suspend the passage of belligerent warships through its waters, a neutral State may not suspend, hamper, or otherwise impede the access of belligerent vessels and aircraft through international straits overlapped by neutral waters or archipelagic sea lanes of a neutral State.

Belligerent vessels and aircraft transiting through international straits overlapped by neutral waters or archipelagic sea lanes of a neutral State must adhere to certain requirements.

15.8.1 Passage of Belligerent Vessels and Aircraft Through International Straits Overlapped by Neutral Waters. All ships and aircraft (including those belonging to belligerent and neutral States) have a right of transit passage through, over, and under all straits used for international navigation.[161] Such passage by vessels carrying contraband of war or by belligerent warships is not regarded as compromising the neutrality of the State with water overlapping such straits.[162] Neutral States bordering international straits may not suspend, hamper, or otherwise impede the right of transit passage through international straits.[163]

Belligerent forces transiting through international straits overlapped by neutral waters must proceed without delay, must refrain from the threat or use of force against the neutral State, and must otherwise refrain from acts of hostility and other activities not incident to their transit.[164] For example, belligerent forces must refrain from exercising the right of visit and

---

[160] *Refer to* § 15.9.2 (Detention of Belligerent Ships That, and Personnel Who, Are Not Entitled to Remain in a Neutral Port).

[161] *See* 2007 NWP 1-14M ¶7.3.6 ("Customary international law as reflected in the 1982 LOS Convention provides that belligerent and neutral surface ships, submarines, and aircraft have a right of transit passage through, over, and under all straits used for international navigation."). *Consider* LOS CONVENTION art. 38(1) ("In straits referred to in article 37 [*i.e.*, straits that are used for international navigation between one part of the high seas or an exclusive economic zone and another part of the high seas or an exclusive economic zone], all ships and aircraft enjoy the right of transit passage, which shall not be impeded.").

[162] The S.S. Wimbledon, (United Kingdom, France, Japan v. Germany) (Judgment), 1923 P.C.I.J. (series A) No. 1, at 28 ("The precedents therefore afforded by the Suez and Panama Canals invalidate in advance the argument that Germany's neutrality would have necessarily been imperilled [sic] if her authorities had allowed the passage of the 'Wimbledon' through the Kiel Canal, because that vessel was carrying contraband of war consigned to a state then engaged in an armed conflict. Moreover they are merely illustrations of the general opinion according to which when an artificial waterway connecting two open seas has been permanently dedicated to the use of the whole world, such waterway is assimilated to natural straits in the sense that even the passage of a belligerent man-of-war does not compromise the neutrality of the sovereign State under whose jurisdiction the waters in question lie.").

[163] 2007 NWP 1-14M ¶7.3.6 ("Neutral nations cannot suspend, hamper, or otherwise impede this right of transit passage through international straits."). *Consider* LOS CONVENTION art. 44 ("States bordering straits shall not hamper transit passage and shall give appropriate publicity to any danger to navigation or overflight within or over the strait of which they have knowledge. There shall be no suspension of transit passage.").

[164] 2007 NWP 1-14M ¶7.3.6 ("Belligerent forces transiting through international straits overlapped by neutral waters must proceed without delay, must refrain from the threat or use of force against the neutral nation, and must otherwise refrain from acts of hostility and other activities not incident to their transit."). *Consider* LOS

search while transiting through international straits that are overlapped by neutral waters.[165]

Belligerent forces in transit may, however, take defensive measures consistent with their security, including the launching and recovery of military devices, screen formation steaming, and acoustic and electronic surveillance, and may respond in self-defense to a hostile act or a demonstration of hostile intent.[166]

15.8.2 Passage of Belligerent Vessels and Aircraft Through Archipelagic Sea Lanes of a Neutral State. Belligerent ships or aircraft, including surface warships, submarines, and military aircraft, retain the right of unimpeded archipelagic sea[167] lanes passage through, under, and over neutral archipelagic sea lanes.[168] Neutral archipelagic States shall not suspend or hamper the right of transit passage through their archipelagic sea lanes.[169]

Belligerent State forces exercising the right of archipelagic sea lanes passage must refrain from acts of hostility and other activities not incident to their transit.[170] For example, belligerent State forces must refrain from exercising the right of visit and search while exercising the right of archipelagic sea lanes passage.[171] Belligerent State forces exercising the right of archipelagic sea lanes passage may, however, engage in those activities that are incident to their normal mode of continuous and expeditious passage, and that are consistent with their security, including formation steaming, acoustic and electronic surveillance, and the launching and recovery of

---

CONVENTION art. 39(1) ("Ships and aircraft, while exercising the right of transit passage, shall: (a) proceed without delay through or over the strait; (b) refrain from any threat or use of force against the sovereignty, territorial integrity or political independence of States bordering the strait, or in any other manner in violation of the principles of international law embodied in the Charter of the United Nations; (c) refrain from any activities other than those incident to their normal modes of continuous and expeditious transit unless rendered necessary by force majeure or by distress.").

[165] *Refer to* § 15.13.3 (Where Belligerents May Not Exercise the Right of Visit and Search).

[166] 2007 NWP 1-14M ¶7.3.6 ("Belligerent forces in transit may, however, take defensive measures consistent with their security, including the launching and recovery of military devices, screen formation steaming, and acoustic and electronic surveillance, and may respond in self-defense to a hostile act or hostile intent.").

[167] *Refer to* § 13.2.2.3 (Archipelagic Waters).

[168] 2007 NWP 1-14M ¶7.3.7 ("Belligerent ships or aircraft, including surface warships, submarines and military aircraft, retain the right of unimpeded archipelagic sea lanes passage through, under, and over neutral archipelagic sea lanes."). *Consider* LOS CONVENTION art. 53(2) ("All ships and aircraft enjoy the right of archipelagic sea lanes passage in such sea lanes and air routes.").

[169] *Consider* LOS CONVENTION art. 54 ("Articles 39, 40, 42 and 44 apply mutatis mutandis to archipelagic sea lanes passage."); LOS CONVENTION art. 44 ("States bordering straits shall not hamper transit passage and shall give appropriate publicity to any danger to navigation or overflight within or over the strait of which they have knowledge. There shall be no suspension of transit passage.").

[170] *Consider* LOS CONVENTION art. 54 ("Articles 39, 40, 42 and 44 apply mutatis mutandis to archipelagic sea lanes passage."); LOS CONVENTION art. 39 ("Ships and aircraft, while exercising the right of transit passage, shall: (a) proceed without delay through or over the strait; (b) refrain from any threat or use of force against the sovereignty, territorial integrity or political independence of States bordering the strait, or in any other manner in violation of the principles of international law embodied in the Charter of the United Nations; (c) refrain from any activities other than those incident to their normal modes of continuous and expeditious transit unless rendered necessary by force majeure or by distress.").

[171] *Refer to* § 15.13.3 (Where Belligerents May Not Exercise the Right of Visit and Search).

military devices.[172]

15.9 Additional Rules Applicable to Neutral Ports, Roadsteads, and Internal Waters

In addition to the general rules applicable to neutral waters,[173] certain other rules apply to neutral ports, roadsteads, and internal waters.

15.9.1 Maximum Number of Belligerent Warships in One Neutral Port or Roadstead. In the absence of special provisions to the contrary in the legislation of a neutral State, the maximum number of warships belonging to a belligerent that may be in one of the ports or roadsteads of that neutral State simultaneously is three.[174]

15.9.2 Detention of Belligerent Ships That, and Personnel Who, Are Not Entitled to Remain in a Neutral Port. If, notwithstanding the notification of the neutral State, a belligerent ship of war does not leave a port where it is not entitled to remain, the neutral State is entitled to take such measures as it considers necessary to render the ship incapable of taking to sea during the war, and the commanding officer of the ship must facilitate the execution of such measures.[175]

When a belligerent ship is detained by a neutral Power, the officers and crew are likewise

---

[172] 2007 NWP 1-14M ¶7.3.7 ("Belligerent forces exercising the right of archipelagic sea lanes passage may engage in those activities that are incident to their normal mode of continuous and expeditious passage and are consistent with their security, including formation steaming, acoustic and electronic surveillance, and the launching and recovery of military devices."). *Consider* LOS CONVENTION art. 53(3) ("Archipelagic sea lanes passage means the exercise in accordance with this Convention of the rights of navigation and overflight in the normal mode solely for the purpose of continuous, expeditious and unobstructed transit between one part of the high seas or an exclusive economic zone and another part of the high seas or an exclusive economic zone.").

[173] *Refer to* § 15.7 (Neutral Waters).

[174] *See* Consultative Meeting of Foreign Ministers of the American Republics, *Final Act of the Meeting: V General Declaration of Neutrality of the American Republics*, ¶3, Oct. 3, 1939, 1 DEPARTMENT OF STATE BULLETIN 326, 327 (Oct. 7, 1939) (The American Republics resolve "[t]o declare that with regard to their status as neutrals, there exist certain standards recognized by the American Republics applicable in these circumstances and that in accordance with them they: ... (d) May determine, with regard to belligerent warships, that not more than three at a time be admitted in their own ports or waters and in any case they shall not be allowed to remain for more than twenty-four hours. Vessels engaged exclusively in scientific, religious or philanthropic missions may be exempted from this provision, as well as those which arrive in distress."); 1928 PAN AMERICAN NEUTRALITY CONVENTION art. 7 ("In the absence of a special provision of the local legislation, the maximum number of ships of war of a belligerent which may be in a neutral port at the same time shall be three."); HAGUE XIII art. 15 ("In the absence of special provisions to the contrary in the legislation of a neutral Power, the maximum number of war-ships belonging to a belligerent which may be in one of the ports or roadsteads of that Power simultaneously shall be three.").

[175] HAGUE XIII art. 24 ("If, notwithstanding the notification of the neutral Power, a belligerent ship of war does not leave a port where it is not entitled to remain, the neutral Power is entitled to take such measures as it considers necessary to render the ship incapable of taking the sea during the war, and the commanding officer of the ship must facilitate the execution of such measures."); 1928 PAN AMERICAN NEUTRALITY CONVENTION art. 6 ("The ship which does not conform to the foregoing rules may be interned by order of the neutral government. A ship shall be considered as interned from the moment it receives notice to that effect from the local neutral authority, even though a petition for reconsideration of the order has been interposed by the transgressing vessel, which shall remain under custody from the moment it receives the order.").

detained.[176]

The officers and crew thus detained may be left in the ship or kept either on another vessel or on land, and may be subjected to the measures of restriction that may appear necessary to impose upon them. A sufficient number of persons for looking after the vessel must, however, always be left on board. The officers may be left at liberty on giving their word not to quit the neutral territory without permission.[177]

15.9.3 Departure of Belligerent Warships in Relation to the Departure of Ships of the Opposing Belligerent. When warships of opposing belligerent States are present simultaneously in a neutral State's port or roadstead, a period of not less than 24 hours must elapse between the departure of the respective enemy warships.[178] The order of departure is determined by the order of arrival, unless the ship that arrived first is in such circumstances that an extension of its stay is permissible.[179]

A belligerent warship may not leave a neutral port or roadstead until 24 hours after the departure of a merchant ship flying the flag of its adversary.[180]

15.9.4 Supplies and Repairs of Belligerent Warships in Neutral Ports and Roadsteads.

15.9.4.1 *Food and Fuel for Belligerent Warships in Neutral Ports and Roadsteads*. A neutral State has discretion to issue and implement regulations regarding the supply of food and supplies for belligerent warships in its territory.[181] However, such regulations must be applied impartially among belligerent States.[182]

---

[176] HAGUE XIII art. 24 ("When a belligerent ship is detained by a neutral Power, the officers and crew are likewise detained.").

[177] HAGUE XIII art. 24 ("The officers and crew thus detained may be left in the ship or kept either on another vessel or on land, and may be subjected to the measures of restriction which it may appear necessary to impose upon them. A sufficient number of men for looking after the vessel must, however, be always left on board. The officers may be left at liberty on giving their word not to quit the neutral territory without permission."). *Refer to* § 15.16.4 (Parole of Belligerent Personnel Interned in Neutral Territory).

[178] *See* 1928 PAN AMERICAN NEUTRALITY CONVENTION art. 8 ("A ship of war may not depart from a neutral port within less than twenty-four hours after the departure of an enemy warship."); HAGUE XIII art. 16 ("When war-ships belonging to both belligerents are present simultaneously in a neutral port or roadstead, a period of not less than twenty-four hours must elapse between the departure of the ship belonging to one belligerent and the departure of the ship belonging to the other.").

[179] 1928 PAN AMERICAN NEUTRALITY CONVENTION art. 8 ("The one entering first shall depart first, unless it is in such condition as to warrant extending its stay."); HAGUE XIII art. 16 ("The order of departure is determined by the order of arrival, unless the ship which arrived first is so circumstanced that an extension of its stay is permissible.").

[180] HAGUE XIII art. 16 ("A belligerent war-ship may not leave a neutral port or roadstead until twenty-four hours after the departure of a merchant-ship flying the flag of its adversary.").

[181] 1928 PAN AMERICAN MARITIME NEUTRALITY CONVENTION art. 10 ("Belligerent warships may supply themselves with fuel and stores in neutral ports, under the conditions especially established by the local authority and in case there are no special provisions to that effect, they may supply themselves in the manner prescribed for provisioning in time of peace.").

[182] *Refer to* § 15.7.2 (A Neutral State's Regulations Concerning Belligerent Warships and Prizes in Its Waters).

A belligerent State's warships may take on food supplies and provisions in a neutral State's ports and roadsteads, but only to bring up their supplies to the peacetime standard.[183]

Similarly, a belligerent State's warship may only take on sufficient fuel to enable it to reach the nearest port in its own country.[184] The belligerent State's warship may, however, fill up its bunkers built to carry fuel when the neutral State has adopted this method of determining the amount of fuel to be supplied.[185]

15.9.4.2 _Repairs of Belligerent Warships in a Neutral State's Ports and Roadsteads_. A belligerent State's warships may only carry out such repairs in a neutral State's ports and roadsteads as are absolutely necessary to render the warships seaworthy; they may not add to or repair weapons systems, or enhance any other aspect of their war fighting capability.[186] The neutral State shall decide what repairs are necessary to restore seaworthiness; repairs must be accomplished with the least possible delay.[187]

If the 1928 Pan American Maritime Neutrality Convention is applicable, then damage found to have been produced by the enemy's fire must not be repaired.[188] However, whether such repairs are prohibited by customary international law is less clear.[189] Some States have allowed such repairs provided they are limited to rendering the ship sufficiently seaworthy to continue its voyage safely.[190]

---

[183] HAGUE XIII art. 19 ("Belligerent war-ships may only revictual in neutral ports or roadsteads to bring up their supplies to the peace standard.").

[184] HAGUE XIII art. 19 ("Similarly these vessels may only ship sufficient fuel to enable them to reach the nearest port in their own country.").

[185] HAGUE XIII art. 19 ("They may, on the other hand, fill up their bunkers built to carry fuel, when in neutral countries which have adopted this method of determining the amount of fuel to be supplied.").

[186] HAGUE XIII art. 17 ("In neutral ports and roadsteads belligerent war-ships may only carry out such repairs as are absolutely necessary to render them seaworthy, and may not add in any manner whatsoever to their fighting force."); 1928 PAN AMERICAN MARITIME NEUTRALITY CONVENTION art. 9 ("Damaged belligerent ships shall not be permitted to make repairs in neutral ports beyond those that are essential to the continuance of the voyage and which in no degree constitute an increase in its military strength.").

[187] HAGUE XIII art. 17 ("The local authorities of the neutral Power shall decide what repairs are necessary, and these must be carried out with the least possible delay."); 1928 PAN AMERICAN MARITIME NEUTRALITY CONVENTION art. 9 ("The neutral state shall ascertain the nature of the repairs to be made and will see that they are made as rapidly as possible.").

[188] 1928 PAN AMERICAN MARITIME NEUTRALITY CONVENTION art. 9 ("Damages which are found to have been produced by the enemy's fire shall in no case be repaired.").

[189] *See* TUCKER, THE LAW OF WAR AND NEUTRALITY AT SEA 244-45 ("But it is more than doubtful that the law presently forbids the repair of battle damage in neutral ports, and, in fact, some states when neutral still allow such repairs.").

[190] *For example*, TUCKER, THE LAW OF WAR AND NEUTRALITY AT SEA 245 footnote 2 ("As illustrated by the incident involving the German battleship *Admiral Graf Spee*. See Hackworth, *op. cit.*, Vol. VII, pp. 450-1. On December 13, 1939, the *Graf Spee* entered the Uruguayan port of Montevideo, following an engagement with British naval forces. A request was made to the Uruguayan authorities to permit the *Graf Spee* to remain fifteen days in port in order to repair damages suffered in battle and to restore the vessel's navigability. The Uruguayan authorities granted a seventy-two hour period of stay. Shortly before the expiration of this period the *Graf Spee* left

A belligerent warship damaged by enemy fire that will not (or cannot) be put to sea once the lawful period of stay has expired must be interned.[191]

15.9.5 Prizes in Neutral Ports or Roadsteads. A prize (*i.e.*, a captured neutral or enemy merchant ship) may only be brought into a neutral port or roadstead because of unseaworthiness, stress of weather, or want of fuel or provisions.[192] It must leave as soon as such circumstances that justified its entry cease.[193] Neutral ports may not be used as harbors of safety in which prizes may be kept indefinitely.[194]

If the prize does not leave as soon as such circumstances that justified it entry cease, the neutral State must order the prize to leave at once, and should it fail to do so, the neutral State must employ the means at its disposal to release it with its previous officers and crew, and to intern the prize crew.[195]

If a prize is brought into a neutral State's port under circumstances other than because of unseaworthiness, stress of weather, or want of fuel or provisions, the neutral State must release

---

Montevideo and was destroyed by its own crew in the Rio de la Plata. The British Government, while not insisting that Article 17 of Hague XIII clearly prohibited the repair of battle damage, did point to the widespread practice of states when neutral in forbidding the repair of battle damage in their ports. In accordance with this practice it was suggested that the *Graf Spee's* period of stay be limited to twenty-four hours. Uruguay maintained, however, that the scope of the neutral's duty required it only to prevent those repairs that would serve to augment the fighting force of a vessel but not repairs necessary for safety of navigation.—The incident is noteworthy as an example of the extent to which belligerents seemingly can make use of neutral ports without violating the prohibition against using neutral territory as a base of naval operations.").

[191] *Refer to* § 15.9.2 (Detention of Belligerent Ships That, and Personnel Who, Are Not Entitled to Remain in a Neutral Port).

[192] 1928 PAN AMERICAN MARITIME NEUTRALITY CONVENTION art. 17 ("Prizes cannot be taken to a neutral port except in case of unseaworthiness, stress of weather, or want of fuel or provisions."); HAGUE XIII art. 21 ("A prize may only be brought into a neutral port on account of unseaworthiness, stress of weather, or want of fuel or provisions.").

[193] 1928 PAN AMERICAN MARITIME NEUTRALITY CONVENTION art. 17 ("When the cause has disappeared, the prizes must leave immediately;"); HAGUE XIII art. 21 ("It must leave as soon as the circumstances which justified its entry are at an end.").

[194] The S.S. Appam, 243 U.S. 124, 148-49 (1917) ("It is familiar international law that the usual course after the capture of the *Appam* would have been to take her into a German port, where a prize court of that nation might have adjudicated her status, and, if it so determined, condemned the vessel as a prize of war. Instead of that, the vessel was neither taken to a German port nor to the nearest port accessible of a neutral power, but was ordered to, and did, proceed over a distance of more than 3,000 miles, with a view to laying up the captured ship in an American port. It was not the purpose to bring the vessel here within the privileges universally recognized in international law -- i.e., for necessary fuel or provisions, or because of stress of weather or necessity of repairs, and to leave as soon as the cause of such entry was satisfied or removed. ... The principles of international law recognized by this government, leaving the treaty aside, will not permit the ports of the United States to be thus used by belligerents. If such use were permitted, it would constitute of the ports of a neutral country harbors of safety into which prizes, captured by one of the belligerents, might be safely brought and indefinitely kept.").

[195] HAGUE XIII art. 21 ("If it does not [leave], the neutral Power must order it to leave at once; should it fail to obey, the neutral Power must employ the means at its disposal to release it with its officers and crew and to intern the prize crew."); 1928 PAN AMERICAN MARITIME NEUTRALITY CONVENTION art. 17 ("if none of the indicated conditions exist, the state shall suggest to them that they depart, and if not obeyed shall have recourse to the means at its disposal to disarm them with their officers and crew, or to intern the prize crew placed on board by the captor.").

the prize.[196] The prize crew should be interned and the vessel restored to its former crew.[197]

15.9.5.1 *Article 23 of Hague XIII – Prizes Sequestrated Pending Prize Court Decision*. Article 23 of Hague XIII permits a neutral State to allow prizes to enter its ports and roadsteads when they are brought there to be sequestrated pending the decision of a prize court.[198] However, the United States ratified Hague XIII subject to a reservation to Article 23.[199]

15.10 Neutral Airspace

In general, belligerent military aircraft may not enter neutral airspace except to address violations of neutrality by enemy forces when the neutral State is unwilling or unable to address such violations.

15.10.1 Airspace That Is Considered Neutral. The airspace over a neutral State's land territory and the neutral State's territorial and archipelagic waters is subject to the sovereignty of the neutral State and, thus, is considered neutral.[200]

The airspace over international waters, including the airspace over a neutral State's contiguous zone and exclusive economic zone, is not considered neutral airspace.[201]

15.10.2 Prohibition on Entry by Belligerent Military Aircraft Into Neutral Airspace. Belligerent military aircraft are forbidden to enter neutral airspace, subject to certain exceptions.[202]

---

[196] Hague XIII art. 22 ("A neutral Power must, similarly, release a prize brought into one of its ports under circumstances other than those referred to in Article 21."); 1928 Pan American Neutrality Convention art. 18 ("Outside of the cases provided for in Article 17, the neutral state must release the prizes which may have been brought into its territorial waters.").

[197] *Press Release*, Oct. 28, 1939, *German Capture of the American Steamer City of Flint*, 1 Department of State Bulletin 429, 432 ("A prize crew may take a captured ship into a neutral port without internment only in case of stress of weather, want of fuel and provisions, or necessity of repairs. In all other cases, the neutral is obligated to intern the prize crew and restore the vessel to her former crew.").

[198] Hague XIII art. 23 ("A neutral Power may allow prizes to enter its ports and roadsteads, whether under convoy or not, when they are brought there to be sequestrated pending the decision of a Prize Court. It may have the prize taken to another of its ports. If the prize is convoyed by a war-ship, the prize crew may go on board the convoying ship. If the prize is not under convoy, the prize crew are left at liberty.").

[199] William H. Taft, *Proclamation Regarding the Hague XIII*, Feb. 28, 1910, 36 Stat. 2415, 2438 ("And whereas the Senate of the United States of America by its resolution of April 17, 1908, (two-thirds of the Senators present concurring therein) did advise and consent to the adherence by the United States to the said Convention with the reservation and exclusion of its Article 23 and with the understanding that the last clause of Article 3 of the said Convention implies the duty of a neutral power to make the demand therein mentioned for the return of a ship captured within the neutral jurisdiction and no longer within that jurisdiction; And whereas the President of the United States of America, in pursuance of and in conformity with the aforesaid advice and consent of the Senate, did, on the 23rd day of February, 1909, declare the adherence of the United States to the said Convention;").

[200] *Refer to* § 14.2.1.1 (National Airspace).

[201] *Refer to* § 14.2.1.2 (International Airspace).

[202] Consultative Meeting of Foreign Ministers of the American Republics, *Final Act of the Meeting: V General Declaration of Neutrality of the American Republics*, ¶3, Oct. 3, 1939, 1 Department of State Bulletin 326, 327

Belligerent military aircraft have the right to pass through international straits overlapped by neutral waters and archipelagic sea lanes of a neutral State.[203]

Belligerent States' medical aircraft may enter neutral airspace subject to certain conditions.[204]

Belligerent aircraft in evident distress may be permitted to enter neutral airspace and to land in neutral territory under such safeguards as the neutral State may wish to impose. The neutral State must require such aircraft to land and must intern both aircraft and crew.[205] This situation would fall under the general duty of a neutral State with respect to the treatment of belligerent State forces that enter, or seek to enter, its territory.[206]

15.10.3 <u>Duties of Neutral States With Respect to Their Airspace</u>. As with other neutral territory, neutral States have an affirmative duty to prevent the violation of their airspace by belligerent military aircraft.[207] For example, if a belligerent military aircraft enters neutral airspace, the neutral State is obliged to use the means at its disposal to require the belligerent military aircraft to land within its territory.[208] After the aircraft lands, the neutral State must

---

(Oct. 7, 1939) (The American Republics resolve "[t]o declare that with regard to their status as neutrals, there exist certain standards recognized by the American Republics applicable in these circumstances and that in accordance with them they: ... (f) Shall regard as a contravention of their neutrality any flight by the military aircraft of a belligerent state over their own territory.").

[203] *Refer to* § 15.8 (Passage of Belligerent Vessels and Aircraft Through International Straits and Archipelagic Sea Lanes).

[204] *Refer to* § 15.18.2 (Medical Aircraft and Neutral Territory).

[205] 2007 NWP 1-14M ¶7.3.9 ("Belligerent aircraft in evident distress may be permitted to enter neutral airspace and to land in neutral territory under such safeguards as the neutral nation may wish to impose. The neutral nation must require such aircraft to land and must intern both aircraft and crew."). *See also* SPAIGHT, AIR POWER AND WAR RIGHTS 436 ("**The case of distress.**—It was agreed by the Commission of Jurists of 1922-23 that the obligation to prevent the entry of belligerent military aircraft was to be regarded as being subject to the neutral State's moral duty to grant succor to airmen in distress. As already explained, there is, in practice, some difficulty in differentiating between cases in which the reason for entry is genuine distress, or some similar cause such as engine failure or exhaustion of fuel which might lead to disaster, and those in which there is a deliberate attempt to penetrate in order to secure some military advantage or to escape from superior forces. The highest that one can put the neutral obligation is that asylum should be granted in all cases of evident distress, so far as the circumstances allow this obvious concession to humanitarian claims to be made.").

[206] *Refer to* § 15.16 (Belligerent Forces Taking Refuge in Neutral Territory).

[207] *See, e.g.*, TUCKER, THE LAW OF WAR AND NEUTRALITY AT SEA 251 ("The practices of states during World Wars I and II may be regarded as having firmly established both the right as well as the duty of the neutral state to forbid the entrance of belligerent military aircraft into its air space."); SPAIGHT, AIR POWER AND WAR RIGHTS 420 ("The important question whether the laws of neutrality allow belligerent military aircraft to come and go in neutral jurisdiction was answered by the practice of 1914-18 with a firm and unmistakable negative. The unanimity of the answer was remarkable. All the neutral States who had occasion to decide the question decided it in the same general way, and their decision gave rise to no protest on the part of the belligerents concerned, with one single exception, which the subsequent action and compliance of the State making it deprived of all its force.").

[208] *Consider* Commission of Jurists to Consider and Report Upon the Revision of the Rules of Warfare, *General Report, Part II: Rules of Aërial Warfare*, art. 42, Feb. 19, 1923, *reprinted in* 32 AJIL SUPPLEMENT: OFFICIAL DOCUMENTS 12, 36 (1938) ("A neutral government must use the means at its disposal to prevent the entry within its jurisdiction of belligerent military aircraft and to compel them to alight if they have entered such jurisdiction. A

intern the aircraft and its crew for the duration of the armed conflict.

If a neutral State is unable or unwilling to prevent the unlawful entry or use of its airspace by a belligerent State, the opposing belligerent State's forces may undertake such self-help enforcement measures as the circumstances may require.[209] For example, belligerents with missile defense capabilities may be justified in intercepting enemy missiles transiting neutral airspace if the neutral state cannot, or will not, prevent such airspace incursions.

15.11 Belligerent Right of Angary

The right of angary recognizes the right of belligerents to requisition (upon payment of just compensation) neutral property transiently within their territory, or in territory that they have occupied, where the property is urgently required for the conduct of the war.[210]

15.11.1 Neutral Property Transiently Within Belligerent Jurisdiction. The belligerent right of angary applies to property that is transiently within belligerent jurisdiction. For example, neutral ships have been subject of the exercise of the right of angary.[211]

The right of angary does not apply to property of neutral ownership that has acquired enemy character.[212]

---

neutral government shall use the means at its disposal to intern any belligerent military aircraft which is within its jurisdiction after having alighted for any reason whatsoever, together with its crew and the passengers, if any.").

[209] *Refer to* § 15.4.2 (Belligerent Use of Self-Help When Neutral States Are Unable or Unwilling to Prevent Violations of Neutrality).

[210] GREENSPAN, MODERN LAW OF LAND WARFARE 581 ("The right of angary, an ancient rule of international law, in its modern application recognizes the right of belligerents to requisition (upon payment of just compensation) neutral ships and other neutral property transiently within their territory, or in territory which they have occupied, where the property is urgently required for the conduct of the war.").

[211] *For example, Press Release: Swedish Motorship "Kungsholm,"* 5 DEPARTMENT OF STATE BULLETIN 519 (Dec. 13, 1941) ("The United States Government has exercised its right of angary to take over the Swedish motorship *Kungsholm*."); Woodrow Wilson, *Proclamation Concerning the Possession and Utilization of Netherlands Vessels*, Mar. 20, 1918, *reprinted in* 12 AJIL SUPPLEMENT: OFFICIAL DOCUMENTS 259-60 (1918) ("Whereas the law and practice of nations accords to a belligerent Power the right in time of military exigency and for purposes essential to the prosecution of the war, to take over and utilize neutral vessels lying within its jurisdiction: ... Now therefore I, Woodrow Wilson, President of the United States of America, in accordance with international law and practice, and by virtue of the Act of Congress aforesaid, and as Commander-in-Chief of the Army and Navy of the United States, do hereby find and proclaim that the imperative military needs of the United States require the immediate utilization of vessels of Netherlands registry, now lying within the territorial waters of the United States; and I do therefore authorize and empower the Secretary of the Navy to take over on behalf of the United States the possession of and to employ all such vessels of Netherlands registry as may be necessary for essential purposes connected with the prosecution of the war against the Imperial German Government. The vessels shall be manned, equipped, and operated by the Navy Department and the United States Shipping Board, as may be deemed expedient; and the United States Shipping Board shall make to the owners thereof full compensation, in accordance with the principles of international law.").

[212] LAUTERPACHT, II OPPENHEIM'S INTERNATIONAL LAW 761-62 (§365) ("In case property of subjects of neutral States is vested with enemy character, it is not neutral property in the strict sense of the term 'neutral,' and all rules respecting appropriation, utilization, and destruction of enemy property obviously apply to it. The object of the right of angary is, therefore, either such property of subjects of neutral States as retains its neutral character from its

15.11.2 Railway Material Coming From the Territory of a Neutral State. Railway material coming from the territory of a neutral State, whether it be the property of that State or of companies or private persons, and recognizable as such, shall not be requisitioned or utilized by a belligerent State except where and to the extent that it is absolutely necessary.[213] It shall be sent back as soon as possible to the country of origin.[214] A neutral State may likewise, in case of necessity, retain and utilize to an equal extent railway material coming from the territory of a belligerent State.[215] Compensation shall be paid by one party or the other in proportion to the railway material used, and to the period of usage.[216]

Railway materials would include, for example, railroad cars and locomotives.

This rule on railway material has sought to balance between the necessities of war (*i.e.*, that such material might be of great military utility) and the interests and rights of neutrals.[217] This rule also reflects a compromise between the different views of States.[218]

15.12 NEUTRAL COMMERCE AND CARRIAGE OF CONTRABAND

Although neutral States must not provide war-related goods and services to belligerents,

---

temporary position on belligerent territory, and which therefore is not vested with enemy character, or such neutral property on the open sea as has not acquired enemy character.").

[213] HAGUE V art. 19 ("Railway material coming from the territory of neutral Powers, whether it be the property of the said Powers or of Companies or private persons, and recognizable as such, shall not be requisitioned or utilized by a belligerent except where and to the extent that it is absolutely necessary.").

[214] HAGUE V art. 19 ("It shall be sent back as soon as possible to the country of origin.").

[215] HAGUE V art. 19 ("A neutral Power may likewise, in case of necessity, retain and utilize to an equal extent material coming from the territory of the belligerent Power.").

[216] HAGUE V art. 19 ("Compensation shall be paid by one party or the other in proportion to the material used, and to the period of usage.").

[217] Antonio S. de Bustamante, *The Hague Convention Concerning the Rights and Duties of Neutral Powers and Persons in Land Warfare*, 2 AJIL, 95, 119 (1908) ("The article in regard to railways – the only article saved in the chapter relating to foreign property – is useful to nations with land boundaries and is based on just terms, making the best equivalent for the necessities of war and in the interest and right of neutrals. Therefore, its acceptance brings great credit upon the delegation of Luxemburg. It is to be observed that the final redaction only relates to railway material coming from neutral states, belonging to the said states or to companies or private persons. It has no other purpose than to facilitate the return of the compensation or the payment for the use of the cars and locomotives of a country which may accidentally enter the other state through the occasions of ordinary traffic.").

[218] *See* A. PEARCE HIGGINS, THE HAGUE PEACE CONFERENCES AND OTHER INTERNATIONAL CONFERENCES CONCERNING THE LAWS AND USAGES OF WAR: TEXTS OF CONVENTIONS WITH COMMENTARIES 294 (1909) ("Article 19 replaces Article 54 of the Regulations of 1899 and is a compromise between contradictory views. Luxemburg and Belgium denied the right of belligerents to requisition and make use of neutral railway materials within their territory. Germany and Austria desired to have the right to use it admitted, on the understanding that an indemnity was paid for its use after the close of the war. France and Luxemburg as an alternative claimed both an indemnity and the right, in case of need, to retain and make use of a corresponding quantity of railway material coming from the territory of a belligerent state. The Conference took the middle course, allowing belligerents to requisition and use neutral railway material only when absolutely necessary, on condition that it be returned as soon as possible, the neutral being given the corresponding right over belligerent material within its territory, compensation to be paid by one party to the other in proportion to the material used and the period of use.").

neutral persons are not prohibited from such activity by the law of neutrality.[219] The law of neutrality's rules on neutral commerce and the carriage of contraband have sought to balance the right of neutral persons to conduct commerce free from unreasonable interference against the right of belligerent States to interdict the passage of war materials to the enemy.[220]

Neutral merchant vessels and civil aircraft engaged in legitimate neutral commerce are subject to visit and search, but generally may not be captured or destroyed by belligerent forces.[221] On the other hand, neutral merchant vessels and civil aircraft are subject to capture and other penalties if they engage in certain conduct.[222]

Contraband goods are liable to capture at any place beyond neutral territory, if their destination is the territory belonging to, or occupied by, an opposing belligerent State.[223]

15.12.1 Classes of Goods That May Be Considered Contraband. *Contraband* consists of goods that are destined for an enemy of a belligerent and that may be susceptible to use in armed conflict.[224] Items susceptible to use in armed conflict may be understood to include war-sustaining commerce, *i.e.*, commerce that indirectly but effectively supports and sustains the belligerent State's war fighting capability (*e.g.*, imports of raw materials used for the production of armaments and exports of products whose proceeds are used by the belligerent State to purchase arms and armaments).[225]

15.12.1.1 *Distinction Between Absolute and Conditional Contraband.* Whether

---

[219] *Refer to* § 15.3.2.1 (Duty to Refrain From Providing War-Related Goods and Services to Belligerents).

[220] TUCKER, THE LAW OF WAR AND NEUTRALITY AT SEA 182 ("It has long been customary to characterize the problems arising with respect to neutral commerce in terms of two conflicting rights: the right of the neutral state to insist upon continued freedom of commerce for its subjects despite the existence of war and the right of the belligerent to prevent neutral subjects from affording assistance to the military effort of an enemy. More accurate, perhaps, is the characterization of these problems in terms of conflicting interests rather than in terms of conflicting rights. Whereas the neutral's interest has been to suffer the least amount of belligerent interference in the trading activities of its subjects, the belligerent's interest has been to prevent neutrals from compensating for an enemy's weakness at sea.").

[221] *Refer to* § 15.13 (Belligerent Right of Visit and Search of Merchant Vessels and Civil Aircraft).

[222] *Refer to* § 15.15.1 (Grounds for the Capture of Neutral Vessels and Aircraft).

[223] 2007 NWP 1-14M ¶7.4.1.2 ("Contraband goods are liable to capture at any place beyond neutral territory, if their destination is the territory belonging to or occupied by the enemy."); 1998 NWP 9 ¶7.4.1.1 (same).

[224] 2007 NWP 1-14M ¶7.4.1 ("Contraband consists of goods destined for the enemy of a belligerent and that may be susceptible to use in armed conflict."); 1955 NWIP 10-2 ¶631a ("Contraband consists of all goods which are destined for an enemy and which may be susceptible of use in war.").

[225] *See* 2007 NWP 1-14M ¶7.4 ("For purposes of this publication, neutral commerce comprises all commerce between one neutral nation and another not involving materials of war or armaments ultimately destined for a belligerent nation, and all commerce between a neutral nation and a belligerent that does not involve the carriage of contraband or otherwise contribute to the belligerent's war-fighting/war-sustaining capability."); 1998 NWP 9 ¶7.4 footnote 88 ("Although war-sustaining commerce is not subject to precise definition, commerce that indirectly but effectively supports and sustains the belligerent's war-fighting capability properly falls within the scope of the term. Examples of war-sustaining commerce include imports of raw materials used for the production of armaments and exports of products the proceeds of which are used by the belligerent to purchase arms and armaments.") (internal citations omitted).

an item is susceptible to use in armed conflict may depend on the character of the item. Traditionally, contraband has been divided into two categories, *absolute* and *conditional*. *Absolute contraband* consisted of goods whose character is such that they are obviously destined for use in armed conflict, such as munitions, weapons, uniforms, and the like. *Conditional contraband* consisted of goods equally susceptible to either peaceful or warlike purposes, such as foodstuffs, construction materials, and fuel.[226]

Whether it is possible to distinguish between absolute contraband and conditional contraband may depend on the extent to which the enemy government controls imports and the scale of the conflict. For example, during World War II, belligerent States largely did not distinguish between absolute and conditional contraband because of the involvement of virtually the entire population in support of the war effort and because the belligerent States exercised governmental control over all imports.[227]

15.12.1.2 *Free Goods That Are Exempt From Capture as Contraband*. Certain goods qualify as "free goods," meaning that they are exempt from capture by belligerent States as contraband even though they are destined for enemy territory. Free goods include the following:

- equipment exclusively intended for the treatment of wounded and sick members of armed forces or for the prevention of disease, provided that the particulars regarding the voyage of such equipment have been notified to and approved by the opposing belligerent State;[228]

- consignments of certain types of relief goods (*e.g.*, medical supplies and religious

---

[226] 2007 NWP 1-14M ¶7.4.1 ("Contraband consists of goods destined for the enemy of a belligerent and that may be susceptible to use in armed conflict. Traditionally, contraband has been divided into two categories: absolute and conditional. Absolute contraband consisted of goods the character of which made it obvious that they were destined for use in armed conflict, such as munitions, weapons, uniforms, and the like. Conditional contraband consisted of goods equally susceptible to either peaceful or warlike purposes, such as foodstuffs, construction materials, and fuel."). *See also* The Peterhoff, 72 U.S. 28, 52-53 (1867) ("The classification of goods as contraband or not contraband has much perplexed text writers and jurists. A strictly accurate and satisfactory classification is perhaps impracticable; but that which is best supported by American and English decisions may be said to divide all merchandise into three classes. Of these classes, the first consists of articles manufactured and primarily and ordinarily used for military purposes in time of war; the second, of articles which may be and are used for purposes of war or peace, according to circumstances; and the third, of articles exclusively used for peaceful purposes. Merchandise of the first class, destined to a belligerent country or places occupied by the army or navy of a belligerent, is always contraband; merchandise of the second class is contraband only when actually destined to the military or naval use of a belligerent; while merchandise of the third class is not contraband at all, though liable to seizure and condemnation for violation of blockade or siege.").

[227] 2007 NWP 1-14M ¶7.4.1 ("The practice of belligerents during the Second World War collapsed the traditional distinction between absolute and conditional contraband. Because of the involvement of virtually the entire population in support of the war effort, the belligerents of both sides tended to exercise governmental control over all imports. Consequently, it became increasingly difficult to draw a meaningful distinction between goods destined for an enemy government and its armed forces and goods destined for consumption by the civilian populace. As a result, belligerents treated all imports directly or indirectly sustaining the war effort as contraband without making a distinction between absolute and conditional contraband.").

[228] *Refer to* § 7.13 (Chartered Medical Transport Ships).

materials for civilians; clothing and medicine for children under fifteen, expectant mothers, and maternity cases), under certain conditions;[229]

- certain types of relief consignments intended for the benefit of the population of occupied territory;[230]

- items destined for POWs, including individual parcels and collective relief shipments containing food, clothing, medical supplies, religious objects, and educational, cultural, and athletic articles;[231] and

- other goods that are specifically exempted from capture by an applicable treaty or by a special arrangement between belligerent States.[232]

In practice, neutral States have provided belligerent States of both sides with information regarding the nature, timing, and route of shipments of goods constituting exceptions to contraband, and obtained approval for their safe conduct and entry into belligerent owned or occupied territory.[233]

15.12.1.3 Contraband Lists. Belligerent States may declare contraband lists at the initiation of hostilities to notify neutral States of the type of goods considered to be absolute or conditional contraband, as well as those not considered to be contraband at all (*i.e.*, exempt or "free goods"). The precise nature of a belligerent State's contraband list may vary according to the circumstances of the conflict.[234]

---

[229] *Refer to* § 5.19.3 (Passage of Relief Consignments).

[230] *Refer to* § 11.17 (Relief).

[231] *Refer to* § 9.20.3 (Receipt of Individual and Collective Relief Shipments for POWs).

[232] *For example*, HAGUE XI art. 1 ("The postal correspondence of neutrals or belligerents, whatever its official or private character may be, found on the high seas on board a neutral or enemy ship, is inviolable. If the ship is detained, the correspondence is forwarded by the captor with the least possible delay."). *See also* TUCKER, THE LAW OF WAR AND NEUTRALITY AT SEA 91 ("From a formal point of view it must probably be concluded that these provisions remain binding today upon the parties to Hague Convention XI. On the other hand, it is difficult to avoid the conclusion that the events of the two World Wars have reduced the significance of these provisions almost to a vanishing point.").

[233] 1989 NWP 9 ¶7.4.1.2 ("It is customary for neutral nations to provide belligerents of both sides with information regarding the nature, timing, and route of shipments of goods constituting exceptions to contraband and to obtain approval for their safe conduct and entry into belligerent owned or occupied territory."). *Compare* § 5.19.3.1 (Technical Arrangements for the Passage and Distribution of Relief Consignments).

[234] 2007 NWP 1-14M ¶7.4.1 ("Belligerents may declare contraband lists at the initiation of hostilities to notify neutral nations of the type of goods considered to be absolute or conditional contraband, as well as those not considered to be contraband at all (i.e., exempt or "free goods"). The precise nature of a belligerent's contraband list may vary according to the circumstances of the conflict."); 1955 NWIP 10-2 ¶631b ("BELLIGERENT CONTRABAND DECLARATIONS. Upon the initiation of armed conflict, belligerents may declare contraband lists, setting forth therein the classification of articles to be regarded as contraband, as well as the distinction to be made between goods considered as absolute contraband and goods considered as conditional contraband. The precise nature of a belligerent's contraband list may vary according to the particular circumstances of the armed conflict.").

Although there has been no conflict of a similar scale and magnitude to World War II, in the years following the conclusion of that conflict State practice indicates that, to the extent international law may continue to require publication of contraband lists, the requirement may be satisfied by a listing of exempt goods.[235]

15.12.2 Requirement of Enemy Destination. Contraband goods are liable to capture at any place beyond neutral territory if their destination is the territory belonging to, or occupied by, the enemy.

15.12.2.1 *Ultimate Destination – Doctrine of Continuous Voyage*. It is immaterial whether the carriage of contraband is direct, involves transshipment, or requires overland transport.[236] Under the doctrine of continuous voyage, the ultimate destination is determinative, and contraband goods may be captured, even if there are neutral ports that are intended to be visited between the point of capture and the ultimate destination.[237]

15.12.2.2 *Presumption of Destination of Enemy Territory in Certain Cases*. When contraband is involved, a destination of enemy-owned or enemy-occupied territory may be presumed when:

- the neutral vessel is to call at an enemy port before arriving at a neutral port for which the goods are documented;
- the goods are documented to a neutral port serving as a port of transit to an enemy, even though they are consigned to a neutral; or
- the goods are consigned "to order" or to an unnamed consignee, but are destined for a neutral State in the vicinity of enemy territory.[238]

---

[235] 2007 NWP 1-14M ¶7.4.1 ("Though there has been no conflict of similar scale and magnitude since the Second World War, post–World War II-practice indicates that, to the extent international law may continue to require publication of contraband lists, the requirement may be satisfied by a listing of exempt goods.").

[236] 2007 NWP 1-14M ¶7.4.1.2 ("It is immaterial whether the carriage of contraband is direct, involves transshipment, or requires overland transport."); 1998 NWP 9 ¶7.4.1.1 (same). *Consider* 1909 DECLARATION OF LONDON art. 30 ("Absolute contraband is liable to capture if it is shown to be destined to territory belonging to or occupied by the enemy, or to the armed forces of the enemy. It is immaterial whether the carriage of the goods is direct or entails transhipment or a subsequent transport by land.").

[237] The Pedro, 175 U.S. 354, 365-66 (1899) ("In The Circassian, it was ruled that the intent to violate a blockade, found as a fact, was not disproved by evidence of a purpose to call at a neutral port, not reached at time of capture, with ulterior destination to the blockaded port. In The Bermuda, the actual destination to a belligerent port, whether ulterior or direct, was held to determine, the character of the transaction as a whole; that transhipment could not change the effect of the pursuit of a common object by a common plan; and that if the cargo was contraband its condemnation was justified, whether the voyage was to ports blockaded or to ports not blockaded; and so as to the vessel in the former case. And in The Springbok, it was held that an intention to tranship cargo at a neutral port did not save it when destined for a blockaded port; that as to cargo, both in law and intent, the voyage from London to the blockaded port was one voyage, and that the liability attached from the time of sailing if captured during any part of that voyage.").

[238] 2007 NWP 1-14M ¶7.4.1.2 ("When contraband is involved, a destination of enemy owned or occupied territory may be presumed when: 1. The neutral vessel is to call at an enemy port before arriving at a neutral port for which

These presumptions of enemy destination constitute sufficient cause for naval commanders to order a capture.[239] However, these presumptions may be rebuttable during subsequent prize court proceedings by an affirmative showing of innocent destination.[240]

These presumptions of the destination of enemy territory are not sufficient to establish that the property is destined for use by an enemy government or its armed forces, which would be necessary to establish a basis for the forfeiture of the property if the property is classified as conditional contraband.[241]

15.12.3 Certificate of Noncontraband Carriage. A certificate of noncontraband carriage is a document issued by a belligerent consular or other designated official to a neutral vessel (navicert) or neutral aircraft (aircert) certifying that the cargo being carried has been examined, usually at the initial place of departure, and has been found to be free of contraband. The purpose of such a navicert or aircert is to facilitate belligerent control of contraband goods with minimal interference and delay of neutral commerce.[242] The navicert or aircert may be viewed as a type of commercial passport.[243]

The certificate is not a guarantee that the vessel or aircraft will not be subject to visit and search or that cargo will not be seized. (Changed circumstances, such as a change in status of the

---

the goods are documented; 2. The goods are documented to a neutral port serving as a port of transit to an enemy, even though they are consigned to a neutral; or 3. The goods are consigned 'to order' or to an unnamed consignee, but are destined for a neutral nation in the vicinity of enemy territory."); 1998 NWP 9 ¶7.4.1.1 (substantially the same).

[239] 1955 NWIP 10-2 ¶631c(1) note 21 ("The circumstances creating a presumption of ultimate enemy destination enumerated in subparagraphs 631c 1 and 2 are of concern to operating naval commanders for the reason that circumstances held to create a presumption of enemy destination constitute sufficient cause for capture. Before a prize court each of these presumptions is rebuttable and whether or not a prize court will, in fact, condemn the captured cargo, and vessel (or aircraft), will depend upon a number of complex considerations with which an operating naval commander need not be concerned.").

[240] *See* TUCKER, THE LAW OF WAR AND NEUTRALITY AT SEA 272-73 ("In this connection the belligerent's task has been facilitated still further by the creation of a detailed set of presumptions governing hostile destination. Thus a presumption of enemy destination has been held to arise where goods are consigned 'to order,' or if the ships papers do not indicate the real consignee of the goods, or if goods are merely consigned to a dealer or agent and the ultimate buyer is unknown, or if the parties engaged in the transaction—though known—have or are suspected of having enemy connections. In any of the foregoing circumstances the inference of an ultimate enemy destination has been strong and could be displaced only by a positive showing that the goods in question had an innocent destination.").

[241] *Refer to* § 15.12.1.1 (Distinction Between Absolute and Conditional Contraband).

[242] 2007 NWP 1-14M ¶7.4.2 ("A certificate of noncontraband carriage is a document issued by a belligerent consular or other designated official to a neutral vessel (navicert) or neutral aircraft (aircert) certifying that the cargo being carried has been examined, usually at the initial place of departure, and has been found to be free of contraband. The purpose of such a navicert or aircert is to facilitate belligerent control of contraband goods with minimal interference and delay of neutral commerce."); 1998 NWP 9 ¶7.4.2 (same).

[243] *See* Malcolm Moos, *The Navicert in World War II*, 38 AJIL 115 (1944) ("In view of their favorable experience with the 'navicert' during World War I, its revival by the British in December 1939, occasioned no surprise. The term navicert is derived from the code word 'navicert,' and in essence is a commercial passport designed to facilitated the passage of consignments through the British blockade."). *Refer to* § 12.6 (Military Passports, Safe-Conducts, and Safeguards).

neutral vessel, between the time of issuance of the certificate and the time of interception at sea may cause it to be invalidated.) Conversely, the absence of a navicert or aircert is not, in itself, a valid ground for seizure of cargo.[244]

Navicerts and aircerts issued by one belligerent State do not limit the visit and search rights of an opposing belligerent State. When a neutral ship or aircraft accepts a navicert or aircert from one belligerent State, this may affect how the other belligerent State views the neutrality of that aircraft or vessel.[245]

A similar procedure was used during the Cuban Missile Crisis, when the United States issued clearance certificates (clearcerts).[246]

15.13 Belligerent Right of Visit and Search of Merchant Vessels and Civil Aircraft

Belligerent warships and military aircraft have a right of visit and search of merchant vessels and civil aircraft outside of neutral territory.

15.13.1 Purposes of Visit and Search. The belligerent right of visit and search may be viewed as a necessary part of the belligerent's right to capture enemy merchant vessels and civil aircraft, and to capture neutral merchant vessels and civil aircraft that have engaged in violations of neutrality.[247] Thus, for example, visit and search has been conducted with the object of:[248]

---

[244] 2007 NWP 1-14M ¶7.4.2 ("The certificate is not a guarantee that the vessel or aircraft will not be subject to visit and search or that cargo will not be seized. (Changed circumstances, such as a change in status of the neutral vessel, between the time of issuance of the certificate and the time of interception at sea may cause it to be invalidated.) Conversely, absence of a navicert or aircert is not, in itself, a valid ground for seizure of cargo."); 1998 NWP ¶7.4.2 (same).

[245] *See* TUCKER, THE LAW OF WAR AND NEUTRALITY AT SEA 322-23 ("In this connection a problem of considerable importance arises as a result of the attempt by belligerents to institute a system of passes for neutral shipping. In principle, it is clear that such devices as the navicert and ships warrant are intended to establish an effective control over the activities of neutral merchant vessels. Neutral merchant vessels by submitting to such a system thereby ease the belligerent's task of patrolling the high seas in search either of contraband carriers or of blockade runners. It seems reasonably well-established that a neutral merchant vessel in accepting a safe-conduct pass from a belligerent subjects itself to the control of the latter and performs an act of unneutral service. The same conclusion would appear warranted in the case of a neutral vessel that cooperates with a belligerent by voluntarily applying for, and accepting, a navicert or ship's warrant.").

[246] *Press Release: U.S. Acts To Avoid Delays for Ships Transiting Waters in Vicinity of Cuba,* Oct. 27, 1962, 47 DEPARTMENT OF STATE BULLETIN 747 (Nov. 12, 1962) ("The Department of State announced on October 27 the institution of a system of clearances to assist vessels which transit waters in the vicinity of Cuba and vessels destined for Cuban ports with cargoes containing no offensive weapons or associated materiel. The system, developed by the State, Defense, and Treasury Departments, is designed to avoid unnecessary delays and other difficulties arising out of the stoppage, inspection, or possible diversion of ships. The system is for the convenience of shipping, and clearances are obtainable upon application by ships' owners, agents, or officers. A vessel departing a United States port may obtain a special clearance from customs authorities at the port of departure. A vessel departing a foreign port may obtain the clearance from an American consulate.").

[247] *See, e.g.*, The Nereide, 13 U.S. 388, 427-28 (1815) ("Belligerents have a full and perfect right to capture enemy goods and articles going to their enemy which are contraband of war. To the exercise of that right the right of search is essential. It is a mean justified by the end. It has been truely denominated a right growing out of, and ancillary to the greater right of capture. Where this greater right may be legally exercised without search, the right of search can never arise or come into question.").

- ascertaining the character of the vessel or aircraft and nationality (including assessing whether a vessel or aircraft that is flagged to a neutral State has acquired enemy character by engaging in service to the enemy);[249]

- verifying whether it conveys contraband cargo;[250]

- verifying whether it has committed a breach of blockade;[251] or

- verifying whether the vessel or aircraft has committed another violation of neutrality making it liable to capture.[252]

15.13.2 Types of Neutral Vessels and Aircraft That Are Exempt From Visit and Search. Certain neutral vessels and aircraft are exempt from the belligerent right of visit and search: (1) neutral warships; (2) neutral State aircraft (including military aircraft); (3) ships of neutral States used only on government non-commercial service; and (4) neutral merchant vessels under convoy of neutral warships of the same nationality, and neutral aircraft accompanied by neutral military aircraft of the same nationality.

15.13.2.1 *Neutral Warships*. Neutral warships may not be subjected to visit and search because they have complete immunity from the jurisdiction of any State other than the flag State.[253]

15.13.2.2 *Neutral State Aircraft*. Neutral State aircraft (including military aircraft) are immune from visit and search by foreign States.[254]

15.13.2.3 *Ships of a Neutral State Used Only on Government Non-Commercial Service*. Ships owned or operated by a neutral State and used only on government non-commercial service may not be subjected to visit and search because they also have complete immunity from the jurisdiction of any State other than the flag State.[255]

---

[248] 1928 PAN AMERICAN MARITIME NEUTRALITY CONVENTION art. 1(1) ("Warships of the belligerents have the right to stop and visit on the high seas and in territorial waters that are not neutral any merchant ship with the object of ascertaining its character and nationality and of verifying whether it conveys cargo prohibited by international law or has committed any violation of blockade.").

[249] *Refer to* § 15.14 (Acquisition of Enemy Character by Neutral-Flagged Merchant Vessels and Neutral-Marked Civil Aircraft).

[250] *Refer to* § 15.12 (Neutral Commerce and Carriage of Contraband).

[251] *Refer to* § 13.10 (Blockade).

[252] *Refer to* § 15.15.1 (Grounds for the Capture of Neutral Vessels and Aircraft).

[253] *Consider* LOS CONVENTION art. 95 ("Warships on the high seas have complete immunity from the jurisdiction of any State other than the flag State.").

[254] *Refer to* § 14.3.1 (State Versus Civil Aircraft); 14.3.3.1 (Military Aircraft – Rights and Liabilities).

[255] *Consider* LOS CONVENTION art. 96 ("Ships owned or operated by a State and used only on government non-commercial service shall, on the high seas, have complete immunity from the jurisdiction of any State other than the flag State.").

15.13.2.4 *Neutral Merchant Vessels Under Convoy of Neutral Warships of the Same Nationality and Neutral Aircraft Accompanied by Neutral Military Aircraft of the Same Nationality*. Neutral merchant vessels under convoy of neutral warships of the same nationality are also exempt from visit and search.[256] However, the convoy commander may be required to provide in writing to the commanding officer of an intercepting belligerent State's warship information as to the character of the vessels and their cargoes that would otherwise be obtained by a visit and search.[257] Neutral merchant vessels under convoy of neutral warships of the same nationality are exempt from visit and search because the neutral State has provided an assurance that the neutral vessel is not engaged in violations of neutrality.[258]

If a convoy commander determines that a vessel under his or her charge possesses enemy character or carries contraband cargo, the commander is obliged to withdraw his or her protection from the offending vessel, making it liable to visit and search, and possible capture, by opposing belligerent warships.[259]

Neutral civil aircraft accompanied by neutral military aircraft of the same flag may also be exempt from visit and search if the following two elements are met:

- the flag State of a neutral military aircraft warrants that the neutral civil aircraft is not carrying contraband cargo; and
- the commander of the neutral military aircraft provides to the intercepting belligerent military aircraft upon request all information as to the character and cargo of the neutral

---

[256] *For example*, John H. McNeill, *Neutral Rights and Maritime Sanctions: The Effects of Two Gulf Wars*, 31 VIRGINIA JOURNAL OF INTERNATIONAL LAW 631, 635 (1991) ("And in July 1987, eleven Kuwaiti-owned tankers were registered under the U.S. flag and escorted by the U.S. Navy. To many, this reflagging procedure appeared to be a logical expedient, not for repudiating the rules concerning contraband, but rather for protecting these vessels against the attack-on-sight of neutral shipping, in addition to whatever U.S. foreign policy objectives the reflagging served. In effect, the U.S. relied upon the ancient doctrine of 'right of convoy' under which belligerents cannot visit and search convoyed ships and are to be satisfied with the declaration of the commander of the convoy that no cargo which can be considered contraband is on board the convoyed ships.").

[257] *Consider* 1909 DECLARATION OF LONDON art. 61 ("Neutral vessels under national convoy are exempt from search. The commander of a convoy gives, in writing, at the request of the commander of a belligerent warship, all information as to the character of the vessels and their cargoes, which could be obtained by search.").

[258] *See* General Report to the Conference, *reprinted in* JAMES BROWN SCOTT, THE DECLARATION OF LONDON FEBRUARY 26, 1909 177-78 (1920) ("The principle laid down is simple; a neutral vessel under the convoy of a warship of her own nationality is exempt from search. The reason for this rule is that the belligerent cruiser ought to be able to find in the assurances of the commander of the convoy as good a guaranty as would be afforded by the exercise of the right of search itself; in fact, she can not call in question the assurances given by the official representative of a neutral Government without displaying a lack of international courtesy.").

[259] *Consider* 1909 DECLARATION OF LONDON art. 62 ("If the commander of the belligerent warship has reason to suspect that the confidence of the commander of the convoy has been abused, he communicates his suspicions to him. In such a case it is for the commander of the convoy alone to investigate the matter. He must record the result of such investigation in a report, of which a copy is handed to the officer of the warship. If, in the opinion of the commander of the convoy, the facts shown in the report justify the capture of one or more vessels, the protection of the convoy must be withdrawn from such vessels.").

civil aircraft that would otherwise be obtained by a visit and search.[260]

15.13.3 Where Belligerents May Not Exercise the Right of Visit and Search. As an act of hostility, the belligerent right of visit and search may not be conducted within neutral territory (*e.g.*, a neutral State's territorial seas and neutral airspace).[261] This prohibition on the exercise of the belligerent right of visit and search extends to international straits overlapped by neutral territorial seas and to archipelagic sea lanes.[262]

15.13.4 Procedure for Visit and Search of Merchant Vessels and Aircraft. Belligerent States have discretion in formulating their procedures for conducting the visit and search of neutral merchant vessels and aircraft.[263] Generally, the belligerent warship or aircraft visits or intercepts the vessel or aircraft, shows its true colors, and provides a clear signal to the merchant vessel or civil aircraft that it is expected to submit to visit and search.[264]

During armed conflict, specific rules of engagement or other special instructions may be issued by the operational chain of command to provide guidance on the visit and search procedure to be carried out by U.S. warships and military aircraft when exercising the belligerent State's right of visit and search of merchant vessels and civil aircraft. For example, the issuance of certificates of non-contraband carriage may be part of such procedures.[265] In the absence of specific guidance from the operational chain of command, Military Department or Service

---

[260] 2007 NWP 1-14M ¶7.6.3 ("Neutral civilian aircraft accompanied by neutral military aircraft of the same flag are exempt from visit and search if the neutral military aircraft (1) warrants that the neutral civilian aircraft is not carrying contraband cargo and (2) provides to the intercepting belligerent military aircraft upon request such information as to the character and cargo of the neutral civilian aircraft as would otherwise be obtained in visit and search.").

[261] *See* HAGUE XIII art. 2 ("Any act of hostility, including capture and the exercise of the right of search, committed by belligerent war-ships in the territorial waters of a neutral Power, constitutes a violation of neutrality and is strictly forbidden."); 1928 PAN AMERICAN MARITIME NEUTRALITY CONVENTION art. 1(1) ("Warships of the belligerents have the right to stop and visit on the high seas and in territorial waters that are not neutral any merchant ship with the object of ascertaining its character and nationality and of verifying whether it conveys cargo prohibited by international law or has committed any violation of blockade.").

[262] *Refer to* § 15.8 (Passage of Belligerent Vessels and Aircraft Through International Straits and Archipelagic Sea Lanes).

[263] TUCKER, THE LAW OF WAR AND NEUTRALITY AT SEA 336 ("Customary international law does not lay down detailed rules governing the mode of conducting visit and search and belligerents have always enjoyed a certain discretion in this regard. In general, however, a substantial measure of uniformity came to characterize the traditional practices of states, and this uniformity was reflected in the special instructions issued by maritime powers to their naval forces.").

[264] TUCKER, THE LAW OF WAR AND NEUTRALITY AT SEA 336 ("Before calling upon a neutral merchantman to submit to visitation a belligerent warship is required to show its true colors. In addition, visitation must be preceded by a clear signal on the part of the warship that the merchant vessel is expected to stop and bring to. The notification of intention to visit may be accomplished by any of several means, e. g., by firing a blank charge, by international flag signal, or even by radio. Nor does international law prescribe the distance a belligerent warship must keep from the vessel being visited, which may vary according to the conditions of the sea, the size and character of the visiting warship, and many other factors.").

[265] *Refer to* § 15.12.3 (Certificate of Noncontraband Carriage).

regulations or guidance may provide the applicable procedures.[266]

15.13.4.1 *Use of Force During Visit and Search*. Merchant vessels or civil aircraft that comply with instructions given to them may not be made the object of attack; merchant ships or civil aircraft that refuse to comply may be stopped by force.[267] Merchant ships or civil aircraft that resist visit and search assume the risk of resulting damage.[268] Such vessels or aircraft also may be deemed to acquire the character of enemy merchant ships or civil aircraft.[269]

15.13.4.2 *Visit and Search of Merchant Vessels by Military Aircraft*. Belligerent military aircraft have a right to conduct visit and search of merchant vessels.[270]

Ordinarily, visit and search of a vessel by a belligerent State's aircraft is accomplished by directing and escorting the merchant vessel to the vicinity of a belligerent warship, which would carry out the visit and search at sea, or to a belligerent port.[271]

15.13.4.3 *Visit and Search of Civil Aircraft by Military Aircraft*. Belligerent military aircraft have a right to conduct visit and search of civil aircraft.[272] Such visit and search is conducted through interception and, if necessary, diversion.[273]

---

[266] *See, e.g.*, 2007 NWP 1-14M ¶7.6.1 ("In the absence of specific rules of engagement or other special instructions issued by the operational chain of command during a period of armed conflict, the following procedure should be carried out by U.S. warships exercising the belligerent right of visit and search of merchant vessels:").

[267] 1928 PAN AMERICAN MARITIME NEUTRALITY CONVENTION art. 1(1) ("If the merchant ship does not heed the signal to stop, it may be pursued by the warship and stopped by force; outside of such a case the ship cannot be attacked unless, after being hailed, it fails to observe the instructions given it.").

[268] *See* Eleanor, 15 U.S. 345, 358 (1817) ("To detain for examination is a right which a belligerant may exercise over every vessel, not a national vessel, that he meets with on the ocean. And whatever may be the injury that casually results to an individual from the act of another while pursuing the reasonable exercise of an established right, it is his misfortune. The law pronounces it damnum absque injuria, and the individual from whose act it proceeds is liable neither at law nor in the forum of conscience. And the principal right necessarily carries with it also all the means essential to its exercise. Thus, in the present case, a vessel must be pursued in order to be detained for examination. But if in the pursuit she had been dismasted, and upset or stranded, or run on shore and lost, it would have been an unfortunate case, but the pursuing vessel would have stood acquitted.").

[269] *Refer to* § 15.14.2.2 (Acquiring the Character of an Enemy Merchant Vessel or Civil Aircraft).

[270] 2007 NWP 1-14M ¶7.6.2 ("Although there is a right of visit and search by military aircraft, there is no established international practice as to how that right is to be exercised.").

[271] 2007 NWP 1-14M ¶7.6.2 ("Ordinarily, visit and search of a vessel by an aircraft is accomplished by directing and escorting the vessel to the vicinity of a belligerent warship, which will carry out the visit and search, or to a belligerent port.").

[272] 2007 NWP 1-14M ¶7.6.3 ("The right of a belligerent military aircraft to conduct visit and search of a civilian aircraft to ascertain its true identity (enemy or neutral), the nature of its cargo (contraband or 'free goods'), and the manner of its employment (innocent or hostile) is now well established in the law of armed conflict.").

[273] *Refer to* § 14.5.1 (Interception); § 14.5.2 (Diversion of Aircraft).

15.14 Acquisition of Enemy Character by Neutral-Flagged Merchant Vessels and Neutral-Marked Civil Aircraft

All vessels operating under an enemy flag, and all aircraft bearing enemy markings, possess enemy character. However, the fact that a ship flies a neutral flag, or that an aircraft bears neutral markings, does not necessarily establish the neutral character of the vessel or aircraft. Vessels or aircraft may acquire enemy character from (1) the ownership or control of the vessel or aircraft, or (2) their conduct.

15.14.1 Acquisition of Enemy Character by Vessels or Aircraft Through Belligerent Ownership or Control. Any merchant vessel or civil aircraft that is owned or controlled by an enemy State or person has enemy character, regardless of whether it is operating under a neutral flag or bears neutral markings.[274] A neutral flag or neutral markings cannot serve as a device to protect vessels or aircraft from seizure whose actual status indicates either continued ownership or control by individuals who themselves possess enemy character.[275] Such vessels may be subject to treatment as enemy merchant vessels or civil aircraft, including being subject to capture.[276]

15.14.2 Acquisition of Enemy Character by Vessels or Aircraft Through Conduct. Certain conduct by vessels or aircraft may lead them to acquire enemy character and make them liable to treatment as either (1) enemy warships or military aircraft, or (2) enemy merchant ships or civil aircraft.

Humanitarian assistance given to the wounded, sick, or shipwrecked of belligerent forces by neutral vessels does not lead to such vessels acquiring enemy character if such assistance is provided in accordance with the GWS-Sea.[277]

15.14.2.1 *Acquiring the Character of an Enemy Warship or Military Aircraft*. Neutral merchant vessels and civil aircraft acquire enemy character, and may be treated by a belligerent as enemy warships and military aircraft, when engaged in either of the following acts:[278]

---

[274] *See* 1955 NWIP 10-2 ¶501 ("Any merchant vessel or aircraft owned or controlled by or for an enemy State, enemy persons, or any enemy corporation possesses enemy character, regardless of whether or not such a vessel or aircraft operates under a neutral flag or bears neutral markings.").

[275] *See* TUCKER, THE LAW OF WAR AND NEUTRALITY AT SEA 75 ("For the practice of states is clear that even though entitled to fly a neutral flag—and thus possessing a neutral nationality—a vessel may nevertheless be considered as impressed with an enemy character. The neutral flag cannot serve as a device to protect vessels from seizure whose actual status indicates either continued ownership or control by individuals who themselves possess enemy character.").

[276] *Refer to* § 13.5 (Enemy Merchant Vessels).

[277] *Refer to* § 7.4.6 (Collection and Care of the Wounded, Sick, and Shipwrecked by Neutral Vessels); § 7.12.1.3 (Authorized Neutral Civilian Hospital Ships).

[278] *See, e.g.*, 2007 NWP 1-14M ¶7.5.1 ("Neutral merchant vessels and civil aircraft acquire enemy character and may be treated by a belligerent as enemy warships and military aircraft when engaged in either of the following acts: 1. Taking a direct part in the hostilities on the side of the enemy 2. Acting in any capacity as a naval or military auxiliary to the enemy's armed forces."); 1955 NWIP 10-2 ¶501a ("Neutral merchant vessels and aircraft acquire

- taking a direct part in the hostilities on the side of the enemy; or
- acting in any capacity as a naval or military auxiliary to the enemy's armed forces.[279]

For example, such vessels and aircraft may be made the object of attack outside of neutral territory.[280]

15.14.2.2 *Acquiring the Character of an Enemy Merchant Vessel or Civil Aircraft*. Neutral merchant vessels and civil aircraft acquire enemy character and may be treated by a belligerent as enemy merchant vessels or civil aircraft when engaged in either of the following acts:[281]

- operating directly under enemy control, orders, charter, employment, or direction; or
- resisting an attempt to establish identity, including resisting visit and search.[282]

For example, such vessels and aircraft may be captured and, under certain circumstances, destroyed.[283]

15.15 Capture of Neutral Vessels and Aircraft

Certain neutral merchant vessels and civil aircraft may be captured outside neutral territory.

15.15.1 Grounds for the Capture of Neutral Vessels and Aircraft. Neutral-flagged merchant vessels or neutral-marked civil aircraft that have acquired enemy character are liable to

---

enemy character and are liable to the same treatment as enemy warships and military aircraft (see paragraph 503a) when engaging in the following acts: 1. Taking a direct part in the hostilities on the side of an enemy; 2. Acting in any capacity as a naval or military auxiliary to an enemy's armed forces.").

[279] *See also* TUCKER, THE LAW OF WAR AND NEUTRALITY AT SEA 321 ("The general principle involved is reasonably clear, and no attempt need be made to enumerate all of the acts that may result in this assimilation to an enemy's armed forces. It is not the mere fact of assisting a belligerent that permits this severe treatment. Nor is it simply the consideration that the belligerent exercises a close control and direction over the neutral merchant vessel. The decisive consideration is rather that the services rendered are in direct support of the belligerent's military operations. It is this support, leading as it does to the identification of the neutral merchant vessel (or aircraft) with the belligerent's naval or military forces, that permits a treatment similar to that meted out to these forces.").

[280] *Refer to* § 13.4 (Enemy Warships).

[281] *See, e.g.*, 2007 NWP 1-14M ¶7.5.2 ("Neutral merchant vessels and civil aircraft acquire enemy character and may be treated by a belligerent as enemy merchant vessels or civil aircraft when engaged in either of the following acts: 1. Operating directly under enemy control, orders, charter, employment, or direction 2. Resisting an attempt to establish identity, including resisting visit and search."); 1955 NWIP 10-2 ¶501b ("Neutral merchant vessel and aircraft acquire enemy character and are liable to the same treatment as enemy merchant vessels and aircraft (see paragraph 503b), when engaging in the following acts: 1. Operating directly under enemy control, orders, charter, employment, or direction; 2. Resisting an attempt to establish identity, including visit and search.").

[282] *Refer to* § 15.13.4.1 (Use of Force During Visit and Search).

[283] *Refer to* § 13.5 (Enemy Merchant Vessels).

capture.[284] In addition, neutral merchant vessels and civil aircraft are, in general, liable to capture by a belligerent State's warships and military aircraft if performing any of the following acts:[285]

- carrying contraband;[286]
- carrying personnel in the military or public service of the enemy;[287]
- communicating information in the interest of the enemy;[288]
- breaching or attempting to breach a blockade;[289]
- violating regulations established by a belligerent within the immediate area of naval operations;[290]

---

[284] *Refer to* § 15.14 (Acquisition of Enemy Character by Neutral-Flagged Merchant Vessels and Neutral-Marked Civil Aircraft).

[285] 2007 NWP 1-14M ¶7.10 ("Neutral merchant vessels and civil aircraft are liable to capture by belligerent warships and military aircraft if engaged in any of the following activities: 1. Avoiding an attempt to establish identity 2. Resisting visit and search 3. Carrying contraband 4. Breaching or attempting to breach blockade 5. Presenting irregular or fraudulent papers; lacking necessary papers; or destroying, defacing, or concealing papers 6. Violating regulations established by a belligerent within the immediate area of naval operations 7. Carrying personnel in the military or public service of the enemy 8. Communicating information in the interest of the enemy."); 1955 NWIP 10-2 ¶503d ("NEUTRAL MERCHANT VESSELS AND AIRCRAFT are in general liable to capture if performing any of the following acts: 1. Carrying contraband (see paragraph 631d). 2. Breaking, or attempting to break, blockade (see paragraph 632g). 3. Carrying personnel in the military or public service of an enemy. 4. Transmitting information in the interest of an enemy. 5. Avoiding an attempt to establish identity, including visit and search. 6. Presenting irregular or fraudulent papers; lacking necessary papers; destroying, defacing, or concealing papers. 7. Violating regulations established by a belligerent within the immediate area of naval operations (see paragraph 430b).").

[286] *Refer to* § 15.12 (Neutral Commerce and Carriage of Contraband).

[287] *Cf.* 1928 PAN AMERICAN MARITIME NEUTRALITY CONVENTION art. 12 ("The neutral vessel shall be seized and in general subjected to the same treatment as enemy merchantmen: ... d) When actually and exclusively destined for transporting enemy troops ... ."). *Consider* 1909 DECLARATION OF LONDON art. 45 ("A neutral vessel will be condemned and will, in a general way, receive the same treatment as a neutral vessel liable to condemnation for carriage of contraband: (1) If she is on a voyage specially undertaken with a view to the transport of individual passengers who are embodied in the armed forces of the enemy, ... (2) If, to the knowledge of either the owner, the charterer, or the master, she is transporting a military detachment of the enemy, or one or more persons who, in the course of the voyage, directly assist the operations of the enemy.").

[288] *Cf.* 1928 PAN AMERICAN MARITIME NEUTRALITY CONVENTION art. 12 ("The neutral vessel shall be seized and in general subjected to the same treatment as enemy merchantmen: ... d) When actually and exclusively destined ... for the transmission of information on behalf of the enemy."). *Consider* 1909 DECLARATION OF LONDON art. 45 ("A neutral vessel will be condemned and will, in a general way, receive the same treatment as a neutral vessel liable to condemnation for carriage of contraband: (1) If she is on a voyage especially undertaken ... with a view to the transmission of intelligence in the interest of the enemy.").

[289] *Refer to* § 13.10.4 (Breach and Attempted Breach of Blockade).

[290] *Refer to* § 13.8 (Belligerent Control of the Immediate Area of Naval Operations).

- avoiding an attempt to establish identity, including visit and search;[291] or
- presenting irregular or fraudulent papers; lacking necessary papers; or destroying, defacing, or concealing papers.[292]

15.15.2 Procedure for Capture and Condemnation. Belligerent States have discretion in formulating their procedures for conducting the capture and condemnation of neutral merchant vessels and aircraft.[293] Prior exercise of the right of visit and search is not required for the capture of neutral-flagged vessels or neutral-marked aircraft that have acquired enemy status, if positive determination of status can be obtained by other means.[294]

Captured neutral merchant vessels and civil aircraft are sent to a port or airfield under a belligerent State's jurisdiction as a prize for adjudication by a prize court. Ordinarily, a belligerent State's warship will place a prize master and prize crew on board a captured vessel for this purpose. Should that be impracticable, the prize may be escorted into port by a belligerent State's warship or military aircraft. In the latter circumstances, the prize must obey the instructions of its escort or risk forcible measures.[295]

A prize may not be brought into a neutral port, except under emergency circumstances.[296] A prize court cannot be set up by a belligerent on neutral territory or on a vessel in neutral

---

[291] *Refer to* § 15.13.4 (Procedure for Visit and Search of Merchant Vessels and Aircraft).

[292] *See* Carrington v. Merchants' Ins. Co., 33 U.S. 495, 521-22 (1834) (Story, J.) ("The belligerent has a right to require a frank and bona fide conduct on the part of neutrals, in the course of their commerce in times of war; and if the latter will make use of fraud, and false papers, to elude the just rights of the belligerents, and to cloak their own illegal purposes, there is no injustice in applying to them the penalty of confiscation. The taint of the fraud travels with the party and his offending instrument during the whole course of the voyage, and until the enterprise has, in the understanding of the party himself, completely terminated. There are many analogous cases in the prize law, where fraud is followed by similar penalties. Thus, if a neutral will cover up enemy's property under false papers, which also cover his own property, prize courts will not disentangle the one from the other, but condemn the whole as good prize.").

[293] *See* 1928 PAN AMERICAN MARITIME NEUTRALITY CONVENTION art. 2 ("Both the detention of the vessel and its crew for violation of neutrality shall be made in accordance with the procedure which best suits the state effecting it and at the expense of the transgressing ship. Said state, except in the case of grave fault on its part, is not responsible for damages which the vessel may suffer.").

[294] 1955 NWIP 10-2 ¶502a ("Historically, visit and search was considered the only legally acceptable method for determining whether or not a merchant vessel was subject to capture. It is now recognized that changes in warfare have rendered this method either hazardous or impracticable in many situations. In the case of enemy merchant vessels and aircraft and neutral merchant vessels and aircraft acquiring enemy character as described in the preceding article, the belligerent right of capture (and, exceptionally, destruction as described in paragraph 503b) need not be preceded by visit and search, provided that a positive determination of status can be obtained by other methods.").

[295] 2007 NWP 1-14M ¶7.10 ("Captured vessels and aircraft are sent to a port or airfield under belligerent jurisdiction as a prize for adjudication by a prize court. Ordinarily, a belligerent warship will place a prize master and prize crew on board a captured vessel for this purpose. Should that be impracticable, the prize may be escorted into port by a belligerent warship or military aircraft. In the latter circumstances, the prize must obey the instructions of its escort or risk forcible measures."); 1998 NWP 9 ¶7.10 (substantially the same).

[296] *Refer to* § 15.9.5 (Prizes in Neutral Ports or Roadsteads).

waters.[297]

15.15.2.1 *Use of Force During Capture*. Neutral vessels or aircraft attempting to resist proper capture lay themselves open to forcible measures by a belligerent State's warships and military aircraft, and assume the risk of resulting damage.[298] The same rule applies to resistance during visit and search.[299]

15.15.3 Destruction of Neutral Prizes. Although the destruction of a neutral prize is not absolutely forbidden, it involves a much more serious responsibility than the destruction of an enemy prize.[300] Thus, a higher standard is applicable than for the destruction of enemy prizes.[301]

Every reasonable effort should be made to avoid destruction of captured neutral vessels and aircraft.[302] A capturing officer, therefore, should not order such destruction without being entirely satisfied that the prize can neither be sent to a belligerent State port or airfield nor, in his or her opinion, properly be released.[303]

Should it become necessary that the prize be destroyed, the capturing officer must provide for the safety of the passengers and crew.[304] In that event, all documents and papers relating to the prize should be preserved. If practicable, the personal effects of passengers should also be safeguarded.[305]

---

[297] HAGUE XIII art. 4 ("A Prize Court cannot be set up by a belligerent on neutral territory or on a vessel in neutral waters.").

[298] *See, e.g.*, 2007 NWP 1-14M ¶7.10 ("Neutral vessels or aircraft attempting to resist proper capture lay themselves open to forcible measures by belligerent warships and military aircraft and assume all risk of resulting damage."); 1989 NWP 9 ¶7.9 (same).

[299] *Refer to* § 15.13.4.1 (Use of Force During Visit and Search).

[300] 1955 NWIP 10-2 ¶509e ("Although the destruction of a neutral prize is not absolutely forbidden, it involves a much more serious responsibility than the destruction of an enemy prize.").

[301] *Refer to* § 13.5.1.3 (Destruction of Captured Enemy Merchant Vessels).

[302] 2006 AUSTRALIAN MANUAL ¶6.59 ("Every effort should be made to avoid destruction of a captured neutral vessel.").

[303] 1955 NWIP 10-2 ¶509e ("A capturing officer, therefore, should never order such destruction without being entirely satisfied that the military reasons therefore justify it, i.e. under circumstances such that a prize can neither be sent in nor, in his opinion, properly released.").

[304] 1928 PAN AMERICAN MARITIME NEUTRALITY CONVENTION art. 1(1) ("The ship shall not be rendered incapable of navigation before the crew and passengers have been placed in safety."); Treaty for the Limitation and Reduction of Naval Armament, art. 22, Apr. 22, 1930, 46 STAT. 2858, 2881-82 ("In particular, except in the case of persistent refusal to stop on being duly summoned, or of active resistance to visit or search, a warship, whether surface vessel or submarine, may not sink or render incapable of navigation a merchant vessel without having first placed passengers, crew and ship's papers in a place of safety. For this purpose the ship's boats are not regarded as a place of safety unless the safety of the passengers and crew is assured, in the existing sea and weather conditions, by the proximity of land, or the presence of another vessel which is in a position to take them on board."). *Consider Procès-Verbal* Relating to the Rules of Submarine Warfare Set Forth in Part IV of the Treaty of London of April 22, 1930, Nov. 6, 1936, 173 LNTS 353, 357 (same).

[305] 1955 NWIP 10-2 ¶509e ("Should the necessity for the destruction of a neutral prize arise, it is the duty of the capturing officer to provide for the safety of the passengers and crew. All documents and papers relating to a neutral

15.15.4 Personnel on Board Captured Neutral Vessels and Aircraft.

15.15.4.1 *Officers and Crews of Captured Neutral Merchant Vessels and Civil Aircraft*. The officers and crews of captured neutral merchant vessels and civil aircraft who are nationals of a neutral State should not be made POWs,[306] even if the vessel or aircraft has acquired the character of enemy merchant vessels or aircraft.[307] However, if the vessel or aircraft has acquired the character of an enemy warship or military aircraft,[308] the officers and crew may be held as POWs.[309]

15.15.4.2 *Enemy Nationals Found Onboard Neutral Merchant Vessels and Civil Aircraft*. Belligerents have a right to remove certain enemy persons from neutral vessels or aircraft, even if there are no grounds for the capture of the vessel or aircraft as prize.[310] Enemy nationals found onboard a neutral State's merchant vessels or civil aircraft as passengers who are:

- a current member of an enemy military force;[311]
- en route to join, or be incorporated into, an enemy's armed forces;
- employed in the public service of the enemy State; or

---

prize should be saved. If practicable, the personal effects of passengers should be saved. Every case of destruction of a neutral prize should be reported promptly to a higher command.").

[306] 1955 NWIP 10-2 ¶513a ("The officers and crews of captured neutral merchant vessels and aircraft who are nationals of a neutral State should not be made prisoners of war."). *See also* TUCKER, THE LAW OF WAR AND NEUTRALITY AT SEA 347 ("In seizing neutral vessels the belligerent incurs certain duties that have long enjoyed the sanction of state practice. Unless the neutral nationals serving as officers and crew of neutral vessels have taken a direct part in the hostilities they may not be treated as prisoners of war.").

[307] *Refer to* § 15.14.2.2 (Acquiring the Character of an Enemy Merchant Vessel or Civil Aircraft).

[308] *Refer to* § 15.14.2.1 (Acquiring the Character of an Enemy Warship or Military Aircraft).

[309] *See* 2007 NWP 1-14M ¶7.10.2 ("This rule applies equally to the officers and crews of neutral vessels and aircraft that assumed the character of enemy merchant vessels or aircraft by operating under enemy control or resisting visit and search. If, however, the neutral vessels or aircraft had taken a direct part in the hostilities on the side of the enemy or had served in any way as a naval or military auxiliary for the enemy, they thereby assumed the character of enemy warships or military aircraft and, upon capture, their officers and crew may be interned as prisoners of war."); 1955 NWIP 10-2 ¶513a endnote 41 ("This paragraph is applicable as well to the officers and crews, nationals of a neutral state, of captured neutral merchant vessels and aircraft which have acquired enemy character and which are liable to the same treatment as enemy merchant vessels and aircraft, as described in paragraph 501b. Hence, a distinction must be made between the treatment accorded to neutral merchant vessels acquiring enemy character, and the treatment accorded to the personnel of such vessels. There is a clear exception, however, in the case of personnel of neutral vessels and aircraft which take a direct part in the hostilities on the side of an enemy or which serve in any way as a naval or military auxiliary for an enemy.").

[310] TUCKER, THE LAW OF WAR AND NEUTRALITY AT SEA 328 ("Despite neutral opposition during World War I to conceding any belligerent right to remove enemy persons from neutral merchant vessels at sea, it would now seem that—in principle—the practice of states may be regarded as having sanctioned this belligerent measure.").

[311] *Consider* DECLARATION OF LONDON art. 47 ("Any individual embodied in the armed forces of the enemy who is found on board a neutral merchant vessel, may be made a prisoner of war, even though there be no ground for the capture of the vessel.").

- engaged in, or suspected of engagement in, service in the interests of the enemy State;[312]

also may be interned until a determination of their status has been made.[313]

15.16 Belligerent Forces Taking Refuge in Neutral Territory

Neutral States have rights and duties with respect to the treatment of belligerent State forces that enter, or seek to enter, their territory. Generally, a neutral State is required to intern a belligerent State's forces to ensure that they do not return to the armed conflict.[314]

15.16.1 Discretion of the Neutral State in Offering Asylum to Belligerent Forces Seeking Refuge. A neutral State has discretion in whether to permit belligerent forces seeking refuge to enter its territory.

---

[312] CDR Joe Munster, *Removal of Persons from Neutral Shipping*, THE JAG JOURNAL: THE OFFICE OF THE JUDGE ADVOCATE JOURNAL OF THE NAVY 3, 18 (Oct. 1952) ("It appears unlikely that the old rules concerning the removal of persons from neutral shipping can much longer survive, even extended to include reservists. With the increasing development of science it would appear foolhardly for a nation to permit an Oppenheimer, a Millikan, a Fermi, an Einstein, or any accomplished atomic or neuclear [sic] physicist to return to his own country, if that country be an opposing belligerent. An expert in guided missiles would be more important to a belligerent country than an ordinary soldier; and notwithstanding the expert is not 'embodied in the armed services' it would appear that the rules and regulations of international law must be amended to bring them into line with the requirements of belligerent necessity. It does not appear that neutrals can properly maintain that no persons other than those connected with the military, either entirely or in a reserve status, may be removed from neutral shipping.").

[313] 2007 NWP 1-14M ¶7.10.2 ("Enemy nationals found on board neutral merchant vessels and civil aircraft as passengers who are actually embodied in the military forces of the enemy, who are en route to serve in the enemy's armed forces, who are employed in the public service of the enemy, or who may be engaged in or suspected of service in the interests of the enemy may be made prisoners of war. All such enemy nationals may be removed from the neutral vessel or aircraft whether or not there is reason for its capture as a neutral prize."); 1955 NWIP 10-2 ¶513b ("Enemy nationals found on board neutral merchant vessels and aircraft as passengers who are actually embodied in the military forces of an enemy, or who are en route to serve in an enemy's military forces, or who are employed in the public service of an enemy, or who may be engaged in or suspected of service in the interests of an enemy may be made prisoners of war.").

[314] *For example*, I REPORT OF THE INTERNATIONAL COMMITTEE OF THE RED CROSS ON ITS ACTIVITIES DURING THE SECOND WORLD WAR (SEPTEMBER 1, 1939 - JUNE 30, 1947) 557 (1948) ("*Neutral States.* – The Swiss Government agreed, in June 1940, to receive on their territory and to intern 32,000 men of the 45th French Army Corps and 13,000 men of the 2nd Polish Division. After the repatriation of the French internees in January 1941, the Polish Division remained, and in 1943, the authorities interned 23,000 men of the Italian forces. In addition, individual internments during hostilities amounted to 7,000 combatants belonging to 37 different nationalities. In September 1939, *Rumania* received 20,000 men of the Polish forces, who were interned. *Hungary* received 36,000, *Lithuania* 14,000 and *Latvia* 1,600. Other neutral countries gave refuge to a limited number of military internees of various nationalities."); Ex parte Toscano, 208 F. 938, 939 (S.D. CA 1913) ("That for several days prior to April 13, 1913, an armed force of the Constitutionalist army attacked the same town of Naco, and on April 13, 1913, the petitioners and other Federalist troops occupying the said town were defeated and driven out of said town of Naco, and were pursued by the victorious Constitutionalist troops, and to avoid surrendering to the Constitutionalist force, the Federalist troops fled with their arms across the boundary line between the United States and Mexico, and sought refuge and asylum from the pursuing enemy in the United States. That immediately upon crossing the said neutral boundary and reaching United States soil, the said petitioners and other Federalist troops belonging to said belligerent army voluntarily surrendered themselves to the armed forces of the United States, which said armed forces of the United States, acting under authority of the President of the United States, thereupon disarmed said belligerent troops and detained and interned them pending the removal of said belligerent troops to a point within the territory of the United States at a distance from the theater of said civil war.").

15.16.1.1 *Neutral Right to Deny Access or to Impose Conditions on Belligerent Forces*. A neutral State is not bound to permit a belligerent State's forces to enter its territory.[315] The neutral State may impose conditions on belligerent forces seeking refuge in its territory.[316] In cases of large bodies of belligerent forces seeking refuge in neutral territory, these conditions will usually be stipulated in an agreement concluded by the representatives of the neutral State and the senior officer of the forces.[317]

15.16.1.2 *Neutral Duty to Disarm and Intern the Belligerent Forces*. If the belligerent forces are permitted to seek refuge in neutral territory, the neutral State must take appropriate measures to ensure that these forces will no longer participate in the armed conflict. If such measures were not taken, then the neutral State's territory might serve as an unlawful sanctuary or base of operations for the belligerent.[318]

Thus, belligerent forces received in neutral territory must be disarmed, and appropriate measures must be taken to prevent their leaving the neutral State.[319] In particular, a neutral State that receives on its territory personnel belonging to the belligerent forces shall intern them, as far as possible, at a distance from the theater of war.[320] For example, if belligerent military aircraft land in a neutral State, that State must intern the aircraft, aircrew, and accompanying military personnel for the duration of the war.[321]

15.16.2 Neutral Reception of the Wounded, Sick, and Shipwrecked. Like other belligerent personnel received in neutral land territory, the wounded, sick, and shipwrecked who are received within a neutral jurisdiction are also generally to be guarded so that they can no longer participate in hostilities.

However, ground transports of belligerent wounded and sick personnel may be authorized to pass through neutral land territory by special agreement.[322]

---

[315] 1956 FM 27-10 (Change No. 1 1976) ¶533 ("A neutral is not bound to permit belligerent troops to enter its territory.").

[316] 1956 FM 27-10 (Change No. 1 1976) ¶534 ("If troops or soldiers of a belligerent are permitted to seek refuge in neutral territory, the neutral is authorized to impose the terms upon which they may do so.").

[317] 1956 FM 27-10 (Change No. 1 1976) ¶534 ("In cases of large bodies of troops seeking refuge in neutral territory, these conditions will usually be stipulated in a convention drawn up by the representatives of the neutral power and the senior officer of the troops.").

[318] *Refer to* § 15.5 (Prohibition on the Use of Neutral Territory as a Base of Operations).

[319] 1956 FM 27-10 (Change No. 1 1976) ¶533 ("On the other hand, it may permit them to do so without violating its neutrality, but the troops must be interned or confined in places designated by the neutral. They must be disarmed and appropriate measures must be taken to prevent their leaving the neutral country.").

[320] HAGUE V art. 11 ("A neutral Power which receives on its territory troops belonging to the belligerent armies shall intern them, as far as possible, at a distance from the theatre of war.").

[321] FINAL REPORT ON THE PERSIAN GULF WAR 627 ("Under Article 11 of Hague V and traditional law of war principles regarding neutral rights and obligations, when belligerent military aircraft land in a nation not party to a conflict, the neutral must intern the aircraft, aircrew, and accompanying military personnel for the duration of the war.").

[322] *Refer to* § 15.18.1 (Authorized Ground Transports of Wounded and Sick Combatants Through Neutral Territory).

15.16.2.1 *Wounded, Sick, and Shipwrecked Landed in Neutral Ports*. Wounded, sick, or shipwrecked persons who are landed in neutral ports with the consent of the local authorities shall, failing arrangements to the contrary between the neutral State and the belligerent States, be so guarded by the neutral State, where so required by international law, that such persons cannot again take part in operations of war.[323]

The costs of hospital accommodation and internment shall be borne by the belligerent State on whom the wounded, sick, or shipwrecked persons depend.[324]

15.16.2.2 *Wounded, Sick, and Shipwrecked Taken Aboard a Neutral State's Warship or Aircraft*. If wounded, sick, or shipwrecked persons are taken on board a neutral State's warship or a neutral State's military aircraft, it shall be ensured, where so required by international law, that they can take no further part in operations of war.[325]

15.16.2.3 *Wounded and Sick Disembarked From Belligerent Medical Aircraft*. Unless otherwise agreed between the neutral State and the belligerent States, the wounded and sick who are disembarked, with the consent of the local authorities, on neutral territory by medical aircraft, shall be detained by the neutral State, where so required by international law, in such a manner that they cannot again take part in military operations.[326]

The cost of their accommodation and internment shall be borne by the State on which they depend.[327]

15.16.3 Conditions of Internment in a Neutral State. The neutral State may keep belligerent forces in camps and even confine them in military compounds or in places set apart for the purpose of internment.[328] Belligerent forces should be interned, as far as possible, at a

---

[323] GWS-SEA art. 17 ("Wounded, sick or shipwrecked persons who are landed in neutral ports with the consent of the local authorities, shall, failing arrangements to the contrary between the neutral and the belligerent Powers, be so guarded by the neutral Power, where so required by international law, that the said persons cannot again take part in operations of war.").

[324] GWS-SEA art. 17 ("The costs of hospital accommodation and internment shall be borne by the Power on whom the wounded, sick or shipwrecked persons depend.").

[325] GWS-SEA art. 15 ("If wounded, sick, or shipwrecked persons are taken on board a neutral warship or a neutral military aircraft, it shall be ensured, where so required by international law, that they can take no further part in operations of war.").

[326] GWS art. 37 ("Unless otherwise agreed between the neutral Power and the Parties to the conflict, the wounded and sick who are disembarked, with the consent of the local authorities, on neutral territory by medical aircraft, shall be detained by the neutral Power, where so required by international law, in such a manner that they cannot again take part in operations of war."); GWS-SEA art. 40 (same).

[327] GWS art. 37 ("The cost of their accommodation and internment shall be borne by the Power on which they depend."); GWS-SEA art. 40 (same).

[328] HAGUE V art. 11 ("It may keep them in camps and even confine them in fortresses or in places set apart for this purpose.").

distance from the theater of war.[329]

15.16.3.1 *Provision of POW Treatment and Application of the GWS and GWS-Sea by Analogy*. Under Article 4B(2) of the GPW, persons who are entitled to POW status if they fall into the power of the enemy during international armed conflict are generally entitled to POW treatment, as a minimum, if they are interned by a neutral State under its duties under international law.[330]

Provisions of the GWS and GWS-Sea apply by analogy to wounded and sick, to members of the medical personnel, and to chaplains of the armed forces of the parties to the conflict, who are received or interned in neutral territory, as well as to deceased persons of a State that is a party to a conflict found there.[331]

15.16.3.2 *Belligerent State Acting as the Protecting Power*. Where diplomatic relations exist between the parties to the conflict and the neutral or non-belligerent Power concerned, the parties to a conflict on whom these persons depend shall be allowed to perform towards them the functions of a Protecting Power as provided in the GPW, without prejudice to the functions that these parties normally exercise in conformity with diplomatic and consular usage and treaties.[332]

15.16.3.3 *Reimbursement of Expenses at the Conclusion of Peace*. In the absence of a special convention to the contrary, the neutral Power shall supply the interned with the food, clothing, and relief required by humanity.[333] At the conclusion of peace, the neutral Power's

---

[329] HAGUE V art. 11 ("A neutral Power which receives on its territory troops belonging to the belligerent armies shall intern them, as far as possible, at a distance from the theatre of war."). *Refer to* § 9.11.4.1 (Avoidance of the Combat Zone); § 9.11.3 (Location of POW Camps).

[330] GPW art. 4B ("The following shall likewise be treated as prisoners of war under the present Convention: ... (2) The persons belonging to one of the categories enumerated in the present Article, who have been received by neutral or non-belligerent Powers on their territory and whom these Powers are required to intern under international law, without prejudice to any more favourable treatment which these Powers may choose to give and with the exception of Articles 8, 10, 15, 30, fifth paragraph, 58-67, 92, 126 and, where diplomatic relations exist between the Parties to the conflict and the neutral or non-belligerent Power concerned, those Articles concerning the Protecting Power. Where such diplomatic relations exist, the Parties to a conflict on whom these persons depend shall be allowed to perform towards them the functions of a Protecting Power as provided in the present Convention, without prejudice to the functions which these Parties normally exercise in conformity with diplomatic and consular usage and treaties."). *Refer to* § 9.3.3 (Persons Entitled to POW Treatment).

[331] GWS art. 4 ("Neutral Powers shall apply by analogy the provisions of the present Convention to the wounded and sick, and to members of the medical personnel, and to chaplains of the armed forces of the Parties to the conflict, received or interned in their territory, as well as to dead persons found."); GWS-SEA art. 5 ("Neutral Powers shall apply by analogy the provisions of the present Convention to the wounded, sick and shipwrecked, and to members of the medical personnel and to chaplains of the armed forces of the Parties to the conflict received or interned in their territory, as well as to dead persons found.").

[332] GPW art. 4B(2) ("Where such diplomatic relations exist, the Parties to a conflict on whom these persons depend shall be allowed to perform towards them the functions of a Protecting Power as provided in the present Convention, without prejudice to the functions which these Parties normally exercise in conformity with diplomatic and consular usage and treaties.").

[333] HAGUE V art. 12 ("In the absence of a special convention to the contrary, the neutral Power shall supply the interned with the food, clothing, and relief required by humanity. At the conclusion of peace the expenses caused by the internment shall be made good.").

expenses incurred supporting the internment shall be made good.[334]

The provisions of the GPW regarding the costs of POW internment and the financial resources of POWs are not applicable to the situation of persons treated as POWs who have been interned by a neutral State.[335]

15.16.4 Parole of Belligerent Personnel Interned in Neutral Territory. The neutral State shall decide whether interned officers can be left at liberty on giving their parole not to leave the neutral territory without permission.[336]

Neutral States may release enlisted personnel on parole, prescribe penalties for violations of parole, and authorize personnel to depart neutral territory temporarily so long as these actions remain consistent with its obligations as a neutral State.[337] The granting of leave to an interned officer to return to his or her own country, however, would be considered an exceptional measure, and a neutral State inclined to grant such permission would be prudent in the first instance to obtain the consent of the opposing belligerent State.

A neutral State may demand the return of persons who have been released on parole but have left the neutral State in violation of their parole.[338] If such persons return to the State in

---

[334] *For example*, A. PEARCE HIGGINS, THE HAGUE PEACE CONFERENCES AND OTHER INTERNATIONAL CONFERENCES CONCERNING THE LAWS AND USAGES OF WAR: TEXTS OF CONVENTIONS WITH COMMENTARIES 293 footnote 2 (1909) ("The most striking example of internment occurred in 1871 during the Franco-Prussian war when over 80,000 French troops under General Clinchant entered Swiss territory and were interned for the remainder of the war; France at the conclusion of the war paid to Switzerland some 11 million francs for their maintenance.").

[335] *See* GPW art. 4B ("The following shall likewise be treated as prisoners of war under the present Convention: … (2) The persons belonging to one of the categories enumerated in the present Article, who have been received by neutral or non-belligerent Powers on their territory and whom these Powers are required to intern under international law, without prejudice to any more favourable treatment which these Powers may choose to give and with the exception of Articles 8, 10, 15, 30, fifth paragraph, 58-67, 92, 126 and, where diplomatic relations exist between the Parties to the conflict and the neutral or non-belligerent Power concerned, those Articles concerning the Protecting Power.") (emphasis added).

[336] HAGUE V art. 11 ("It shall decide whether officers can be left at liberty on giving their parole not to leave the neutral territory without permission.").

[337] *Cf.* JAMES BROWN SCOTT, THE PROCEEDINGS OF THE HAGUE PEACE CONFERENCES: I THE CONFERENCE OF 1907 147-48 (1920) ("Article 57, paragraph 3, of the [1899 Hague] Regulations leaves it to the neutral State to decide whether interned officers may be left at liberty on giving their parole *not to leave the neutral territory without permission*. It does not say upon what conditions a permission to leave this territory should be predicated; neither does it provide any penalty for violation of the parole. Finally, it does not mention either non-commissioned officers or private soldiers. The Japanese delegation proposed to fill this gap by deciding: (1) that the interned men, without distinction of rank, cannot be liberated nor permitted to reenter their country except with the consent of the adverse party under conditions fixed by it; (2) that the parole given in such cases to the neutral State would be equivalent to a parole given to the adverse party. Without ignoring the merits of this proposal, the Commission preferred to continue the existing text of the Regulations. It considered that permission given to an interned man to return temporarily to his country is something too exceptional to require regulation in express terms. There was no difficulty, moreover, in recognizing that the Japanese proposal conforms to recent precedents and contains a useful hint for a neutral State desirous of remaining entirely free from responsibility.").

[338] *For example*, Robert Lansing, *The Secretary of State to the German Ambassador*, Nov. 16, 1915, *reprinted in* JAMES BROWN SCOTT, DIPLOMATIC CORRESPONDENCE BETWEEN THE UNITED STATES AND GERMANY AUGUST 1, 1914 - APRIL 6, 1917, 163 (1918) ("It will be recalled that during the Russo-Japanese War, when the Russian Ship

whose armed forces they serve, that State is obliged to return them to the neutral State at its request.[339]

15.16.5 Military Equipment and Supplies of Belligerent Forces Taking Refuge. The munitions, arms, vehicles, equipment, and other supplies that the interned forces are allowed to bring with them into a neutral State are likewise detained by the neutral State. A belligerent State's military equipment and supplies, whether its own or captured, which are brought on to neutral territory must be returned at the end of the armed conflict to the State to which the items belong. Similarly, captured war material found in the possession of the belligerent forces that take refuge on neutral territory is the property of their State, regardless of its origin.[340]

15.16.6 Retention of Medical Personnel and Chaplains in a Neutral State. Medical and religious personnel serving with belligerent forces that are interned in neutral territory may be retained only in so far as the health and the numbers of such forces so require.[341] Subject to these requirements, they must be returned as soon as possible to the State to which they belong.[342] Chaplains are in the same position, their retention being dependent upon the spiritual needs of the interned forces.[343] Medical personnel and chaplains who are retained must be accorded similar treatment to those retained under the GPW.[344]

15.17 POWs or Internees Brought to, or Received by, a Neutral State

15.17.1 Escaped POWs Received by a Neutral State. POWs who have escaped to neutral

---

Lena was interned by the United States Authorities on the Pacific coast, three officers of that ship escaped and returned to Russia; and that upon the Government of the United States calling the matter to the attention of the Russian Government it immediately caused the escaped officers to return to American jurisdiction where they were interned for the remainder of the war. This precedent this Government regards as in accord with the best practice of nations and applicable to the cases which I have had the honor to present in this note.").

339 1956 FM 27-10 (Change No. 1 1976) ¶535 ("Officers and men interned in a neutral State may in the discretion of that State be released on their parole under conditions to be prescribed by the neutral State. If such persons leave the neutral State in violation of their parole, the State in whose armed forces they serve is obliged to return them to the neutral State at its request.").

340 *See* JAMES BROWN SCOTT, THE PROCEEDINGS OF THE HAGUE PEACE CONFERENCES: I THE CONFERENCE OF 1907 145 (1920) ("What becomes of the war material captured by troops and brought with them into the territory of a neutral State? This question was put by the Dutch delegation, which made the following motion: 'War material captured from the enemy by an armed force and brought with it while taking refuge on neutral territory shall be restored by the Government thereof to the State from which it was taken after the conclusion of peace.' But the Netherland delegation did not insist on its motion in the face of the objection made to it. On the one hand, the case of war material captured from the enemy cannot be assimilated to the case of prisoners of war. The capture of *matériel* creates for the captor an immediate right of ownership, which places this *matériel* on the same footing as the captor's own *matériel*. On the other hand, even if the captor's right to the property should become uncertain, owing to his taking refuge in the neutral territory, there would be no reason for making the neutral State the judge of the question and for imposing on it the invidious duty of examining the *matériel* brought into its territory by a belligerent force to see what has been taken from the enemy and what belongs to the force under some other title.").

341 *Refer to* § 7.9.1.2 (Medical and Religious Personnel Who May Be Retained).

342 *Refer to* § 7.9.4 (Return of Personnel Whose Retention Is Not Indispensable).

343 *Refer to* § 4.9.1.3 (Chaplains Attached to the Armed Forces).

344 *Refer to* § 7.9.5 (Rights and Privileges of Retained Personnel).

territory are deemed to have successfully escaped from the Detaining Power.[345]

A neutral State may deny the admission of escaped POWs or receive them. A neutral State that receives escaped POWs shall leave them at liberty. If it allows them to remain in its territory, it may assign them a place of residence.[346]

15.17.2 POWs Brought Into a Neutral State by Belligerent Forces Taking Refuge. POWs brought into a neutral State by belligerent forces that take refuge in the neutral State are treated like POWs who have escaped to neutral territory.[347] This means that the POWs regain their liberty from the belligerent forces that previously held them captive, and that if the neutral State allows them to remain on its territory, it may assign them a place of residence.

POWs brought into a neutral State by belligerent forces taking refuge are released from their captivity by the belligerent forces that previously held them because of a concern that the detention operations by the belligerent forces would constitute a form of continuation of hostilities on neutral territory and because the POWs probably would have been freed had the belligerent forces not taken refuge in neutral territory.[348]

15.17.3 POWs Brought to a Neutral State by Special Agreement Among the Neutral State and the Parties to a Conflict. POWs may be brought to a neutral State for internment by a special agreement among the neutral State and the parties to the conflict.[349] Wounded and sick POWs may also be brought to neutral countries for accommodation by a special agreement among the neutral State and the parties to the conflict.[350]

Such special agreements must not adversely affect the situation of POWs, nor restrict the

---

[345] *Refer to* § 9.25.1.1 (Types of Successful Escapes).

[346] HAGUE V art. 13 ("A neutral Power which receives escaped prisoners of war shall leave them at liberty. If it allows them to remain in its territory it may assign them a place of residence.").

[347] HAGUE V art. 13 ("A neutral Power which receives escaped prisoners of war shall leave them at liberty. If it allows them to remain in its territory it may assign them a place of residence. The same rule applies to prisoners of war brought by troops taking refuge in the territory of a neutral Power.").

[348] *See* JAMES BROWN SCOTT, THE PROCEEDINGS OF THE HAGUE PEACE CONFERENCES: I THE CONFERENCE OF 1907 144 (1920) ("Ought prisoners of war brought into the territory of a neutral State by belligerent troops who take refuge there, to become free, or should they be interned like the troops? Upon the motion of the Netherland delegation the Commission declared for the first solution. The only obstacle to the freedom of the prisoners here referred to lies in the actual power that the belligerent forces which captured them are exercising over them, and this actual power vanishes the moment the captor takes refuge in the territory of a neutral State. Moreover, troops taking this extreme step, do so in order to escape from an enemy who is pressing them, and from a capitulation whose effect would of course be to free the prisoners in their power."); Caleb Cushing, Attorney General, *Belligerent Asylum*, Apr. 28, 1855, 7 OPINIONS OF THE ATTORNEY GENERAL 122, 131 (1856) ("From all these premises, the consequences are inevitable in regard to the prisoners on board the Sitka. So long as they remained on board that ship, they were in the territory and jurisdiction of her sovereign. There, the neutral has no right to meddle with them. If, indeed, they be landed, then they pass from the jurisdiction of the belligerent to that of the neutral; they become practically free, because their detention is forcible, and force cannot be exercised on the neutral territory;").

[349] *Refer to* § 9.36.3 (Agreements to Intern POWs in Neutral Territory).

[350] *Refer to* § 9.36.2 (Accommodation in Neutral Countries).

rights that the GPW confers upon them.[351]

15.17.4 Certain Classes of Protected Persons Brought to a Neutral State by Special Agreement Among the Neutral State and the Parties to a Conflict. Certain classes of civilian internees may be brought to a neutral State for internment by a special agreement among the neutral State and the parties to the conflict.[352] Agreements may also be concluded for children under the age of fifteen who are orphaned or separated from their families to stay in neutral countries.[353]

Such special agreements must not adversely affect the situation of protected persons nor restrict the rights that the GC confers upon them.[354]

15.18 AUTHORIZED PASSAGE OF WOUNDED AND SICK COMBATANTS THROUGH NEUTRAL TERRITORY

Ground transports of wounded and sick combatants may pass through a neutral State's land territory with the permission of the neutral State. Subject to rules established by the neutral State, medical aircraft of belligerent States may fly over the territory of neutral States, land on it in case of necessity, or use it as a port of call.

15.18.1 Authorized Ground Transports of Wounded and Sick Combatants Through Neutral Territory. A neutral State may authorize the passage into its territory of wounded or sick persons belonging to belligerent forces, on condition that such transports shall carry neither personnel nor material of war.[355] In such a case, the neutral Power is bound to take whatever measures of safety and control are necessary for the purpose.[356]

However, if any such persons are committed to the care of the neutral State or remain in the neutral State's territory, they must be guarded so as to ensure they do not take part again in the war.[357]

15.18.1.1 *Discretion of the Neutral State to Authorize Such Passage*. The neutral State has the right, but not the obligation, to permit such passage; if provided, such passage

---

[351] *Refer to* § 9.1.2.2 (Special Agreements Under the GPW).

[352] *Refer to* § 10.9.6 (Agreements for the Release, Return, or Accommodation in a Neutral Country of Certain Classes of Internees).

[353] *Refer to* § 4.20.1.1 (Children Under Fifteen Who Are Orphaned or Separated).

[354] *Refer to* § 10.1.1.2 (Special Agreements Under the GC).

[355] HAGUE V art. 14 ("A neutral Power may authorize the passage into its territory of wounded or sick belonging to the belligerent armies, on condition that the trains bringing them shall carry neither personnel or material of war.").

[356] HAGUE V art. 14 ("In such a case, the neutral Power is bound to take whatever measures of safety and control are necessary for the purpose.").

[357] *Refer to* § 15.16.1.2 (Neutral Duty to Disarm and Intern the Belligerent Forces).

should be provided on an impartial basis to all belligerent States.[358]

It is not necessary to obtain the consent of the other belligerent States before permitting the passage of sick and wounded personnel, but it would be advisable to do so if considerable numbers are involved.[359]

15.18.1.2 *Personnel or Material of War Accompanying the Wounded or Sick*. A neutral State permitting the passage of sick and wounded into and through its territory must take measures of safety and control to ensure that combatants or military supplies do not accompany them. If combatants accompany the passage of the wounded and sick, they should be interned.[360] Similarly, any military supplies must be seized and placed in safe custody until the end of the conflict.[361]

Medical personnel and materials necessary for the care of the wounded and sick of a convoy of evacuation may be permitted to accompany the convoy.[362]

15.18.1.3 *Wounded and Sick POWs Brought Into Neutral Territory Under Authorized Ground Transports*. Wounded and sick POWs brought by one of the belligerents as part of a convoy of evacuation that is granted passage through neutral territory, and belonging to the hostile party, must be guarded by the neutral State so as to ensure they do not take part again in the operations of the war.[363]

Thus, wounded and sick and POWs brought into neutral territory by the Detaining Power as part of a convoy of evacuation granted right of passage through neutral territory are not treated like escaping POWs or POWs brought by belligerent forces seeking asylum in neutral territory

---

[358] 1956 FM 27-10 (Change No. 1 1976) ¶541 ("The neutral power is under no obligation to permit the passage of a convoy of sick and wounded through its territory, but when such a convoy is permitted to pass, the neutral must exercise control, must see that neither personnel nor material other than that necessary for the care of the sick and wounded is carried, and generally must accord impartiality of treatment to the belligerents."); 2004 UK MANUAL ¶8.162 ("It is under no obligation to do so but if the privilege is accorded, it must be given to all belligerent states impartially.").

[359] *For example*, 2004 UK MANUAL ¶8.162.1 footnote 427 ("After the battle of Sedan in the Franco-German war of 1870–71, the German General Staff wished to send railway trains conveying wounded to Germany through Belgium and Luxembourg. The French Minister of War protested. He argued, rightly, that this would free lines to bring forward fresh soldiers and ammunition. Belgium, after consulting the British government, decided that, if one of the belligerents objected, the giving of permission would be a breach of neutrality, and therefore refused it. Luxembourg took the opposite view and granted it. Under international law, Luxembourg was correct in its reasoning but, in view of the cogent arguments put forward by France, Belgium was right in its decision.").

[360] *Refer to* § 15.16.1.2 (Neutral Duty to Disarm and Intern the Belligerent Forces).

[361] *Refer to* § 15.16.5 (Military Equipment and Supplies of Belligerent Forces Taking Refuge).

[362] 1956 FM 27-10 (Change No. 1 1976) ¶545 ("Medical personnel and materials necessary for the care of the sick and wounded of a convoy of evacuation, permitted to pass through neutral territory under Article 14, *H. V* (par. 539), may be permitted to accompany the convoy.").

[363] HAGUE V art. 14 ("The wounded and sick brought under these conditions into neutral territory by one of the belligerents, and belonging to the hostile party, must be guarded by the neutral Power so as to ensure their not taking part again in the operations of the war.").

(*i.e.*, transported to their own country or liberated).[364] Instead, they are treated like other wounded, sick, and shipwrecked combatants who are received within neutral territory, and they must be guarded by the neutral State.[365]

15.18.1.4 *Wounded and Sick Combatants Committed to the Care of the Neutral State*. Wounded and sick combatants brought under these conditions into neutral territory by one of the belligerents, and who do not simply pass through neutral territory but are committed to the care of the neutral State, must be guarded by the neutral State so as to ensure they do not take part again in the operations of the war.[366]

15.18.2 Medical Aircraft and Neutral Territory. Subject to conditions and restrictions established by the neutral State, medical aircraft of belligerent States may fly over the territory of neutral States, land on it in case of necessity, or use it as a port of call.[367] Belligerent States shall give the neutral States previous notice of their passage over the neutral State and obey all summons to alight, on land or water.[368]

The neutral State may place conditions or restrictions on the passage or landing of medical aircraft on its territory.[369] Such conditions or restrictions shall be applied equally to all belligerent States.[370] Belligerent States' medical aircraft would be immune from attack only when flying on routes, at heights, and at times specifically agreed upon between the belligerent States and the neutral State concerned.[371]

As a general matter, the wounded and sick who are disembarked, with the consent of the local authorities, on neutral territory by medical aircraft, shall be detained by the neutral State, where so required by international law, in such a manner that they cannot again take part in military operations.[372]

---

[364] 1956 FM 27-10 (Change No. 1 1976) ¶543 ("Sick and wounded prisoners of war brought into neutral territory by the Detaining Power as part of a convoy of evacuation granted right of passage through neutral territory may not be transported to their own country or liberated, as are prisoners of war escaping into, or brought by troops seeking asylum in neutral territory, but must be detained by the neutral power, subject to the provisions contained in paragraphs 188 through 196.").

[365] *Refer to* § 15.16.2 (Neutral Reception of the Wounded, Sick, and Shipwrecked).

[366] HAGUE V art. 14 ("The wounded and sick brought under these conditions into neutral territory by one of the belligerents, and belonging to the hostile party, must be guarded by the neutral Power so as to ensure their not taking part again in the operations of the war. The same duty shall devolve on the neutral State with regard to wounded or sick of the other army who may be committed to its care.").

[367] GWS art. 37 ("Subject to the provisions of the second paragraph, medical aircraft of Parties to the conflict may fly over the territory of neutral Powers, land on it in case of necessity, or use it as a port of call."); GWS-SEA art. 40 (same).

[368] GWS art. 37 ("They shall give the neutral Powers previous notice of their passage over the said territory and obey all summons to alight, on land or water."); GWS-SEA art. 40 (same).

[369] GWS art. 37 ("The neutral Powers may, however, place conditions or restrictions on the passage or landing of medical aircraft on their territory."); GWS-SEA art. 40 (same).

[370] GWS art. 37 ("Such possible conditions or restrictions shall be applied equally to all Parties to the conflict."); GWS-SEA art. 40 (same).

[371] GWS art. 37 ("They will be immune from attack only when flying on routes, at heights and at times specifically agreed upon between the Parties to the conflict and the neutral Power concerned."); GWS-SEA art. 40 (same).

[372] *Refer to* § 15.16.2.3 (Wounded and Sick Disembarked From Belligerent Medical Aircraft).

XVI – Cyber Operations

Chapter Contents

16.1 Introduction

This Chapter addresses the law of war and cyber operations. It addresses how law of war principles and rules apply to relatively novel cyber capabilities and the cyber domain.

As a matter of U.S. policy, the United States has sought to work internationally to clarify how existing international law and norms, including law of war principles, apply to cyber operations.[1]

Precisely how the law of war applies to cyber operations is not well-settled, and aspects of the law in this area are likely to continue to develop, especially as new cyber capabilities are developed and States determine their views in response to such developments.[2]

---

[1] *See, e.g., United States Submission to the U.N. Group of Governmental Experts on Developments in the Field of Information and Telecommunications in the Context of International Security (2014–15)*, 1 ("But the challenge is not whether existing international law applies to State behavior in cyberspace. As the 2012–13 GGE affirmed, international law does apply, and such law is essential to regulating State conduct in this domain. The challenge is providing decision-makers with considerations that may be taken into account when determining how existing international law applies to cyber activities. Despite this challenge, history has shown that States, through consultation and cooperation, have repeatedly and successfully applied existing bodies of law to new technologies. It continues to be the U.S. view that all States will benefit from a stable international ICT [information and communication technologies] environment in which existing international law is the foundation for responsible State behavior in cyberspace."); Barack Obama, *International Strategy for Cyberspace: Prosperity, Security, and Openness in a Networked World*, 9 (May 2011) ("The development of norms for state conduct in cyberspace does not require a reinvention of customary international law, nor does it render existing international norms obsolete. Long-standing international norms guiding state behavior—in times of peace and conflict—also apply in cyberspace. Nonetheless, unique attributes of networked technology require additional work to clarify how these norms apply and what additional understandings might be necessary to supplement them. We will continue to work internationally to forge consensus regarding how norms of behavior apply to cyberspace, with the understanding that an important first step in such efforts is applying the broad expectations of peaceful and just interstate conduct to cyberspace."); DEPARTMENT OF DEFENSE, *Department of Defense Cyberspace Policy Report: A Report to Congress Pursuant to the National Defense Authorization Act for Fiscal Year 2011, Section 934*, 7-8 (Nov. 2011) ("The United States is actively engaged in the continuing development of norms of responsible state behavior in cyberspace, making clear that as a matter of U.S. policy, long-standing international norms guiding state behavior also apply equally in cyberspace. Among these, applying the tenets of the law of armed conflict are critical to this vision, although cyberspace's unique aspects may require clarifications in certain areas.").

[2] Department of Defense, Office of the General Counsel, *An Assessment of International Legal Issues in Information Operations* (2nd ed., Nov. 1999), *reprinted in* 76 U.S. NAVAL WAR COLLEGE INTERNATIONAL LAW STUDIES 459,

16.1.1 Cyberspace as a Domain. As a doctrinal matter, DoD has recognized cyberspace as an operational domain in which the armed forces must be able to defend and operate, just like the land, sea, air, and space domains.[3]

Cyberspace may be defined as "[a] global domain within the information environment consisting of interdependent networks of information technology infrastructures and resident data, including the Internet, telecommunications networks, computer systems, and embedded processors and controllers."[4]

16.1.2 Description of Cyber Operations. Cyberspace operations may be understood to be those operations that involve "[t]he employment of cyberspace capabilities where the primary purpose is to achieve objectives in or through cyberspace."[5] Cyber operations: (1) use cyber capabilities, such as computers, software tools, or networks; and (2) have a primary purpose of achieving objectives or effects in or through cyberspace.

16.1.2.1 *Examples of Cyber Operations*. Cyber operations include those operations that use computers to disrupt, deny, degrade, or destroy information resident in computers and computer networks, or the computers and networks themselves. Cyber operations can be a form of advance force operations, which precede the main effort in an objective area in order to prepare the objective for the main assault. For example, cyber operations may include reconnaissance (*e.g.*, mapping a network), seizure of supporting positions (*e.g.*, securing access to key network systems or nodes), and pre-emplacement of capabilities or weapons (*e.g.*, implanting cyber access tools or malicious code). In addition, cyber operations may be a method of acquiring foreign intelligence unrelated to specific military objectives, such as understanding

---

464-65 (2002) ("The international community ordinarily does not negotiate treaties to deal with problems until their consequences have begun to be felt. This is not all bad, since the solution can be tailored to the actual problems that have occurred, rather than to a range of hypothetical possibilities. One consequence, however, is that the resulting law, whether domestic or international, may be sharply influenced by the nature of the events that precipitate legal developments, together with all their attendant policy and political considerations. ... Similarly, we can make some educated guesses as to how the international legal system will respond to information operations, but the direction that response actually ends up taking may depend a great deal on the nature of the events that draw the nations' attention to the issue. If information operations techniques are seen as just another new technology that does not greatly threaten the nations' interests, no dramatic legal developments may occur. If they are seen as a revolutionary threat to the security of nations and the welfare of their citizens, it will be much more likely that efforts will be made to restrict or prohibit information operations by legal means. These are considerations that national leaders should understand in making decisions on using information operations techniques in the current formative period, but it should also be understood that the course of future events is often beyond the control of statesmen.").

[3] William J. Lynn III, Deputy Secretary of Defense, *Defending a New Domain: The Pentagon's Cyberstrategy*, 89 FOREIGN AFFAIRS 97, 101 (Sept./Oct. 2010) ("As a doctrinal matter, the Pentagon has formally recognized cyberspace as a new domain of warfare. Although cyberspace is a man-made domain, it has become just as critical to military operations as land, sea, air, and space. As such, the military must be able to defend and operate within it.").

[4] JOINT PUBLICATION 3-12, *Cyberspace Operations,* GL-4 (Feb. 5, 2013) ("(U) Cyberspace. A global domain within the information environment consisting of interdependent networks of information technology infrastructures and resident data, including the Internet, telecommunications networks, computer systems, and embedded processors and controllers.").

[5] JOINT PUBLICATION 3-0, *Joint Operations* (Aug. 11, 2011) ("cyberspace operations. The employment of cyberspace capabilities where the primary purpose is to achieve objectives in or through cyberspace.").

technological developments or gaining information about an adversary's military capabilities and intent.

16.1.2.2 *Examples of Operations That Would Not Be Regarded as Cyber Operations*. Cyber operations generally would not include activities that merely use computers or cyberspace without a primary purpose of achieving objectives or effects in or through cyberspace. For example, operations that use computer networks to facilitate command and control, operations that use air traffic control systems, and operations to distribute information broadly using computers would generally not be considered cyber operations.

Operations that target an adversary's cyberspace capabilities, but that are not achieved in or through cyberspace, would not be considered cyber operations. For example, the bombardment of a network hub, or the jamming of wireless communications, would not be considered cyber operations, even though they may achieve military objectives in cyberspace.

16.1.3 Cyber Operations – Notes on Terminology. DoD doctrine and terminology for cyber operations continue to develop.

16.1.3.1 *"Cyber" Versus "Cyberspace" as an Adjective*. The terms "cyber" and "cyberspace" when used as an adjective (*e.g.*, cyber attack, cyber defense, cyber operation) are generally used interchangeably.

16.1.3.2 *Cyber Attacks or Computer Network Attacks*. The term "attack" often has been used in a colloquial sense in discussing cyber operations to refer to many different types of hostile or malicious cyber activities, such as the defacement of websites, network intrusions, the theft of private information, or the disruption of the provision of internet services.

Operations described as "cyber attacks" or "computer network attacks," therefore, are not necessarily "attacks" for the purposes of applying rules on conducting attacks during the conduct of hostilities.[6] Similarly, operations described as "cyber attacks" or "computer network attacks" are not necessarily "armed attacks" for the purposes of triggering a State's inherent right of self-defense under *jus ad bellum*.[7]

16.2 Application of the Law of War to Cyber Operations

Specific law of war rules may apply to cyber operations, even though those rules were developed before cyber operations were possible. When no more specific law of war rule or other applicable rule applies, law of war principles provide a general guide for conduct during cyber operations in armed conflict.

16.2.1 Application of Specific Law of War Rules to Cyber Operations. Specific law of war rules may be applicable to cyber operations, even though these rules were developed long before cyber operations were possible.

---

[6] *Refer to* § 16.5.1 (Cyber Operations That Constitute "Attacks" for the Purpose of Applying Rules on Conducting Attacks).

[7] *Refer to* § 16.3.3 (Responding to Hostile or Malicious Cyber Operations).

The law of war affirmatively anticipates technological innovation and contemplates that its existing rules will apply to such innovation, including cyber operations.[8] Law of war rules may apply to new technologies because the rules often are not framed in terms of specific technological means. For example, the rules on conducting attacks do not depend on what type of weapon is used to conduct the attack. Thus, cyber operations may be subject to a variety of law of war rules depending on the rule and the nature of the cyber operation. For example, if the physical consequences of a cyber attack constitute the kind of physical damage that would be caused by dropping a bomb or firing a missile, that cyber attack would equally be subject to the same rules that apply to attacks using bombs or missiles.[9]

Cyber operations may pose challenging legal questions because of the variety of effects they can produce. For example, cyber operations could be a non-forcible means or method of conducting hostilities (such as information gathering), and would be regulated as such under rules applicable to non-forcible means and methods of warfare.[10] Other cyber operations could be used to create effects that amount to an attack and would be regulated under the rules on conducting attacks.[11] Moreover, another set of challenging issues may arise when considering whether a particular cyber operation might be regarded as a seizure or destruction of enemy property and should be assessed as such.[12]

16.2.2 Application of Law of War Principles as a General Guide to Cyber Operations. When no specific rule applies, the principles of the law of war form the general guide for conduct during war, including conduct during cyber operations.[13] For example, under the principle of humanity, suffering, injury, or destruction unnecessary to accomplish a legitimate military purpose must be avoided in cyber operations.[14]

---

[8] Harold Hongju Koh, Legal Adviser, Department of State, *International Law in Cyberspace: Remarks as Prepared for Delivery to the USCYBERCOM Inter-Agency Legal Conference (Sept. 18, 2012), reprinted in* 54 HARVARD INTERNATIONAL LAW JOURNAL ONLINE, 3 (Dec. 2012) ("**Cyberspace is not a 'law-free' zone where anyone can conduct hostile activities without rules or restraint.** Think of it this way. This is not the first time that technology has changed and that international law has been asked to deal with those changes. In particular, because the tools of conflict are constantly evolving, one relevant body of law—international humanitarian law, or the law of armed conflict—affirmatively anticipates technological innovation, and contemplates that its existing rules will apply to such innovation.").

[9] Harold Hongju Koh, Legal Adviser, Department of State, *International Law in Cyberspace: Remarks as Prepared for Delivery to the USCYBERCOM Inter-Agency Legal Conference (Sept. 18, 2012), reprinted in* 54 HARVARD INTERNATIONAL LAW JOURNAL ONLINE, 3-4 (Dec. 2012) ("In analyzing whether a cyber operation would constitute a use of force, most commentators focus on whether the direct physical injury and property damage resulting from the cyber event looks like that which would be considered a use of force if produced by kinetic weapons. For example, cyber activities that proximately result in death, injury, or significant destruction would likely be viewed as a use of force. ... Only a moment's reflection makes you realize that this is common sense: if the physical consequences of a cyber attack work the kind of physical damage that dropping a bomb or firing a missile would, that cyber attack should equally be considered a use of force.").

[10] *Refer to* § 5.26 (Non-Forcible Means and Methods of Warfare).

[11] *Refer to* § 5.4 (Rules on Conducting Assaults, Bombardments, and Other Attacks).

[12] *Refer to* § 5.17 (Seizure and Destruction of Enemy Property).

[13] *Refer to* § 2.1.2.2 (Law of War Principles as a General Guide).

[14] *Refer to* § 2.3 (Humanity).

Certain cyber operations may not have a clear kinetic parallel in terms of their capabilities and the effects they create.[15] Such operations may have implications that are quite different from those presented by attacks using traditional weapons, and those different implications may well yield different conclusions.[16]

16.3 CYBER OPERATIONS AND *JUS AD BELLUM*

Cyber operations may present issues under the law of war governing the resort to force (*i.e., jus ad bellum*).[17]

16.3.1 Prohibition on Cyber Operations That Constitute Illegal Uses of Force Under Article 2(4) of the Charter of the United Nations. Article 2(4) of the Charter of the United Nations states that "[a]ll Members shall refrain in their international relations from the threat or use of force against the territorial integrity or political independence of any state, or in any other manner inconsistent with the Purposes of the United Nations."[18]

Cyber operations may in certain circumstances constitute uses of force within the meaning of Article 2(4) of the Charter of the United Nations and customary international law.[19] For example, if cyber operations cause effects that, if caused by traditional physical means, would be regarded as a use of force under *jus ad bellum*, then such cyber operations would likely also be regarded as a use of force. Such operations may include cyber operations that: (1) trigger a nuclear plant meltdown; (2) open a dam above a populated area, causing destruction; or (3) disable air traffic control services, resulting in airplane crashes.[20] Similarly, cyber operations

[15] Harold Hongju Koh, Legal Adviser, Department of State, *International Law in Cyberspace: Remarks as Prepared for Delivery to the USCYBERCOM Inter-Agency Legal Conference (Sept. 18, 2012)*, *reprinted in* 54 HARVARD INTERNATIONAL LAW JOURNAL ONLINE, 7 (Dec. 2012) ("I have also noted some clear-cut cases where the physical effects of a hostile cyber action would be comparable to what a kinetic action could achieve: for example, a bomb might break a dam and flood a civilian population, but insertion of a line of malicious code from a distant computer might just as easily achieve that same result. As you all know, however, there are other types of cyber actions that do not have a clear kinetic parallel, which raise profound questions about exactly what we mean by 'force.'").

[16] Department of Defense, Office of the General Counsel, *An Assessment of International Legal Issues in Information Operations* (2nd ed., Nov. 1999), *reprinted in* 76 U.S. NAVAL WAR COLLEGE INTERNATIONAL LAW STUDIES 459, 490 (2002) ("In the process of reasoning by analogy to the law applicable to traditional weapons, it must always be kept in mind that computer network attacks are likely to present implications that are quite different from the implications presented by attacks with traditional weapons. These different implications may well yield different conclusions.").

[17] *Refer to* § 1.11 (*Jus ad Bellum*).

[18] U.N. CHARTER art. 2(4).

[19] Harold Hongju Koh, Legal Adviser, Department of State, *International Law in Cyberspace: Remarks as Prepared for Delivery to the USCYBERCOM Inter-Agency Legal Conference (Sept. 18, 2012)*, *reprinted in* 54 HARVARD INTERNATIONAL LAW JOURNAL ONLINE, 3 (Dec. 2012) ("Cyber activities may in certain circumstances constitute uses of force within the meaning of Article 2(4) of the UN Charter and customary international law.").

[20] Harold Hongju Koh, Legal Adviser, Department of State, *International Law in Cyberspace: Remarks as Prepared for Delivery to the USCYBERCOM Inter-Agency Legal Conference (Sept. 18, 2012)*, *reprinted in* 54 HARVARD INTERNATIONAL LAW JOURNAL ONLINE, 4 (Dec. 2012) ("Commonly cited examples of cyber activity that

that cripple a military's logistics systems, and thus its ability to conduct and sustain military operations, might also be considered a use of force under *jus ad bellum*.[21] Other factors, besides the effects of the cyber operation, may also be relevant to whether the cyber operation constitutes a use of force under *jus ad bellum*.[22]

Cyber operations that constitute uses of force within the meaning of Article 2(4) of the Charter of the United Nations and customary international law must have a proper legal basis in order not to violate *jus ad bellum* prohibitions on the resort to force.[23]

16.3.2 Peacetime Intelligence and Counterintelligence Activities. International law and long-standing international norms are applicable to State behavior in cyberspace,[24] and the question of the legality of peacetime intelligence and counterintelligence activities must be considered on a case-by-case basis. Generally, to the extent that cyber operations resemble traditional intelligence and counter-intelligence activities, such as unauthorized intrusions into computer networks solely to acquire information, then such cyber operations would likely be treated similarly under international law.[25] The United States conducts such activities via cyberspace, and such operations are governed by long-standing and well-established considerations, including the possibility that those operations could be interpreted as a hostile act.[26]

16.3.3 Responding to Hostile or Malicious Cyber Operations. A State's inherent right of self-defense, recognized in Article 51 of the Charter of the United Nations, may be triggered by

---

would constitute a use of force include, for example, (1) operations that trigger a nuclear plant meltdown, (2) operations that open a dam above a populated area causing destruction, or (3) operations that disable air traffic control resulting in airplane crashes.").

[21] Department of Defense, Office of the General Counsel, *An Assessment of International Legal Issues in Information Operations* (2nd ed., Nov. 1999), *reprinted in* 76 U.S. NAVAL WAR COLLEGE INTERNATIONAL LAW STUDIES 459, 483 (2002) ("Even if the systems attacked were unclassified military logistics systems, an attack on such systems might seriously threaten a nation's security. For example, corrupting the data in a nation's computerized systems for managing its military fuel, spare parts, transportation, troop mobilization, or medical supplies may seriously interfere with its ability to conduct military operations. In short, the consequences are likely to be more important than the means used.").

[22] Harold Hongju Koh, Legal Adviser, Department of State, *International Law in Cyberspace: Remarks as Prepared for Delivery to the USCYBERCOM Inter-Agency Legal Conference (Sept. 18, 2012)*, *reprinted in* 54 HARVARD INTERNATIONAL LAW JOURNAL ONLINE, 4 (Dec. 2012) ("In assessing whether an event constituted a use of force in or through cyberspace, we must evaluate factors including the context of the event, the actor perpetrating the action (recognizing challenging issues of attribution in cyberspace), the target and location, effects and intent, among other possible issues.").

[23] *Refer to* § 1.11.3 (Prohibition on Certain Uses of Force).

[24] *Refer to* § 16.1 (Introduction).

[25] Department of Defense, Office of the General Counsel, *An Assessment of International Legal Issues in Information Operations* (2nd ed., Nov. 1999), *reprinted in* 76 U.S. NAVAL WAR COLLEGE INTERNATIONAL LAW STUDIES 459, 518 (2002).

[26] DEPARTMENT OF DEFENSE, *Department of Defense Cyberspace Policy Report: A Report to Congress Pursuant to the National Defense Authorization Act for Fiscal Year 2011, Section 934*, 6-7 (Nov. 2011).

cyber operations that amount to an armed attack or imminent threat thereof.[27] As a matter of national policy, the United States has expressed the view that when warranted, it will respond to hostile acts in cyberspace as it would to any other threat to the country.[28]

Measures taken in the exercise of the right of national self-defense in response to an armed attack must be reported immediately to the U.N. Security Council in accordance with Article 51 of the Charter of the United Nations.[29]

16.3.3.1 Use of Force Versus Armed Attack. The United States has long taken the position that the inherent right of self-defense potentially applies against any illegal use of force.[30] Thus, any cyber operation that constitutes an illegal use of force against a State potentially gives rise to a right to take necessary and proportionate action in self-defense.[31]

16.3.3.2 No Legal Requirement for a Cyber Response to a Cyber Attack. There is no legal requirement that the response in self-defense to a cyber armed attack take the form of a cyber action, as long as the response meets the requirements of necessity and proportionality.[32]

---

[27] Harold Hongju Koh, Legal Adviser, Department of State, *International Law in Cyberspace: Remarks as Prepared for Delivery to the USCYBERCOM Inter-Agency Legal Conference (Sept. 18, 2012)*, *reprinted in* 54 HARVARD INTERNATIONAL LAW JOURNAL ONLINE, 4 (Dec. 2012) ("Question 4: *May a state ever respond to a computer network attack by exercising a right of national self-defense?* Answer 4: **Yes. A state's national right of self-defense, recognized in Article 51 of the UN Charter, may be triggered by computer network activities that amount to an armed attack or imminent threat thereof.**"); Barack Obama, *International Strategy for Cyberspace: Prosperity, Security, and Openness in a Networked World*, 10 (May 2011) ("**Right of Self-Defense:** Consistent with the United Nations Charter, states have an inherent right to self-defense that may be triggered by certain aggressive acts in cyberspace.").

[28] Barack Obama, *International Strategy for Cyberspace: Prosperity, Security, and Openness in a Networked World*, 14 (May 2011) ("When warranted, the United States will respond to hostile acts in cyberspace as we would to any other threat to our country. All states possess an inherent right to self-defense, and we recognize that certain hostile acts conducted through cyberspace could compel actions under the commitments we have with our military treaty partners. We reserve the right to use all necessary means—diplomatic, informational, military, and economic—as appropriate and consistent with applicable international law, in order to defend our Nation, our allies, our partners, and our interests. In so doing, we will exhaust all options before military force whenever we can; will carefully weigh the costs and risks of action against the costs of inaction; and will act in a way that reflects our values and strengthens our legitimacy, seeking broad international support whenever possible.").

[29] *Refer to* § 1.11.5.6 (Reporting to the U.N. Security Council).

[30] *Refer to* § 1.11.5.2 (Use of Force Versus Armed Attack).

[31] Harold Hongju Koh, Legal Adviser, Department of State, *International Law in Cyberspace: Remarks as Prepared for Delivery to the USCYBERCOM Inter-Agency Legal Conference (Sept. 18, 2012)*, *reprinted in* 54 HARVARD INTERNATIONAL LAW JOURNAL ONLINE, 7 (Dec. 2012) ("To cite just one example of this, the United States has for a long time taken the position that the inherent right of self-defense potentially applies against *any* illegal use of force. In our view, there is no threshold for a use of deadly force to qualify as an "armed attack" that may warrant a forcible response. But that is not to say that any illegal use of force triggers the right to use any and all force in response—such responses must still be *necessary* and of course *proportionate*.").

[32] Harold Hongju Koh, Legal Adviser, Department of State, *International Law in Cyberspace: Remarks as Prepared for Delivery to the USCYBERCOM Inter-Agency Legal Conference (Sept. 18, 2012)*, *reprinted in* 54 HARVARD INTERNATIONAL LAW JOURNAL ONLINE, 4 (Dec. 2012) ("There is no legal requirement that the response to a cyber armed attack take the form of a cyber action, as long as the response meets the requirements of necessity and proportionality.").

16.3.3.3 *Responses to Hostile or Malicious Cyber Acts That Do Not Constitute Uses of Force*. Although cyber operations that do not constitute uses of force under *jus ad bellum* would not permit injured States to use force in self-defense, those injured States may be justified in taking necessary and appropriate actions in response that do not constitute a use of force.[33] Such actions might include, for example, a diplomatic protest, an economic embargo, or other acts of retorsion.[34]

16.3.3.4 *Attribution and Self-Defense Against Cyber Operations*. Attribution may pose a difficult factual question in responding to hostile or malicious cyber operations because adversaries may be able to hide or disguise their activities or identities in cyberspace more easily than in the case of other types of operations.[35]

A State's right to take necessary and proportionate action in self-defense in response to an armed attack originating through cyberspace applies whether the attack is attributed to another State or to a non-State actor.[36]

16.3.3.5 *Authorities Under U.S. Law to Respond to Hostile Cyber Acts*. Decisions about whether to invoke a State's inherent right of self-defense would be made at the national level because they involve the State's rights and responsibilities under international law. For example, in the United States, such decisions would generally be made by the President.

The Standing Rules of Engagement for U.S. forces have addressed the authority of the U.S. armed forces to take action in self-defense in response to hostile acts or hostile intent,

---

[33] Department of Defense, Office of the General Counsel, *An Assessment of International Legal Issues in Information Operations* (2nd ed., Nov. 1999), *reprinted in* 76 U.S. NAVAL WAR COLLEGE INTERNATIONAL LAW STUDIES 459, 482 (2002) ("There is also a general recognition of the right of a nation whose rights under international law have been violated to take countermeasures against the offending state, in circumstances where neither the provocation nor the response involves the use of armed force. For example, an arbitral tribunal in 1978 ruled that the United States was entitled to suspend French commercial air flights into Los Angeles after the French had suspended U.S. commercial air flights into Paris. Discussions of the doctrine of countermeasures generally distinguish between countermeasures that would otherwise be violations of treaty obligations or of general principles of international law (in effect, reprisals not involving the use of armed force) and retorsions – actions that may be unfriendly or even damaging, but which do not violate any international legal obligation. The use of countermeasures is subject to the same requirements of necessity and proportionality as apply to self-defense.").

[34] *Refer to* § 18.17 (Retorsion).

[35] DEPARTMENT OF DEFENSE, *Department of Defense Cyberspace Policy Report: A Report to Congress Pursuant to the National Defense Authorization Act for Fiscal Year 2011, Section 934*, 4 (Nov. 2011) ("The same technical protocols of the Internet that have facilitated the explosive growth of cyberspace also provide some measure of anonymity. Our potential adversaries, both nations and non-state actors, clearly understand this dynamic and seek to use the challenge of attribution to their strategic advantage. The Department recognizes that deterring malicious actors from conducting cyber attacks is complicated by the difficulty of verifying the location from which an attack was launched and by the need to identify the attacker among a wide variety and high number of potential actors.").

[36] *United States Submission to the U.N. Group of Governmental Experts on Developments in the Field of Information and Telecommunications in the Context of International Security 2012-2013*, 2 ("As the United States noted in its 2010 submission to the GGE, the following established principles would apply in the context of an armed attack, whether it originated through cyberspace or not: • The right of self-defense against an imminent or actual armed attack applies whether the attacker is a State actor or a non-State actor."). *Refer to* § 1.11.5.4 (Right of Self-Defense Against Non-State Actors).

including such acts perpetrated in or through cyberspace.[37]

16.4 Cyber Operations and the Law of Neutrality

The law of neutrality may be important in certain cyber operations. For example, under the law of neutrality, belligerent States are bound to respect the sovereign rights of neutral States.[38] Because of the interconnected nature of cyberspace, cyber operations targeting networked information infrastructures in one State may create effects in another State that is not a party to the armed conflict.[39]

16.4.1 Cyber Operations That Use Communications Infrastructure in Neutral States. The law of neutrality has addressed the use of communications infrastructure in neutral States, and in certain circumstances, these rules would apply to cyber operations.

The use of communications infrastructure in neutral States may be implicated under the general rule that neutral territory may not serve as a base of operations for one belligerent against another.[40] In particular, belligerent States are prohibited from erecting on the territory of a neutral State any apparatus for the purpose of communicating with belligerent forces on land or sea, or from using any installation of this kind established by them before the armed conflict on the territory of a neutral State for purely military purposes, and which has not been opened for the service of public messages.[41]

However, merely relaying information through neutral communications infrastructure (provided that the facilities are made available impartially) generally would not constitute a violation of the law of neutrality that belligerent States would have an obligation to refrain from and that a neutral State would have an obligation to prevent.[42] This rule was developed because it was viewed as impractical for neutral States to censor or screen their publicly available

---

[37] *See, e.g.*, CHAIRMAN OF THE JOINT CHIEFS OF STAFF INSTRUCTION 3121.01B, *Standing Rules of Engagement/Standing Rules for the Use of Force for U.S. Forces*, ¶6b(1) (June 13, 2005), *reprinted in* INTERNATIONAL AND OPERATIONAL LAW DEPARTMENT, THE JUDGE ADVOCATE GENERAL'S LEGAL CENTER & SCHOOL, U.S. ARMY, OPERATIONAL LAW HANDBOOK 95 (2007) ("Unit commanders always retain the inherent right and obligation to exercise unit self-defense in response to a hostile act or demonstrated hostile intent. Unless otherwise directed by a unit commander as detailed below, military members may exercise individual self-defense in response to a hostile act or demonstrated hostile intent.").

[38] *Refer to* § 15.3.1 (Neutral Rights).

[39] Harold Hongju Koh, Legal Adviser, Department of State, *International Law in Cyberspace: Remarks as Prepared for Delivery to the USCYBERCOM Inter-Agency Legal Conference (Sept. 18, 2012)*, *reprinted in* 54 HARVARD INTERNATIONAL LAW JOURNAL ONLINE, 6 (Dec. 2012) ("States conducting activities in cyberspace must take into account the sovereignty of other states, including outside the context of armed conflict. The physical infrastructure that supports the Internet and cyber activities is generally located in sovereign territory and subject to the jurisdiction of the territorial state. Because of the interconnected, interoperable nature of cyberspace, operations targeting networked information infrastructures in one country may create effects in another country. Whenever a state contemplates conducting activities in cyberspace, the sovereignty of other states needs to be considered.").

[40] *Refer to* § 15.5 (Prohibition on the Use of Neutral Territory as a Base of Operations).

[41] *Refer to* § 15.5.3 (Prohibition Against Establishment or Use of Belligerent Communications Facilities in Neutral Territory).

[42] *Refer to* § 15.5.3.1 (Use of Neutral Facilities by Belligerents Not Prohibited).

communications infrastructure for belligerent traffic.[43] Thus, for example, it would not be prohibited for a belligerent State to route information through cyber infrastructure in a neutral State that is open for the service of public messages, and that neutral State would have no obligation to forbid such traffic. This rule would appear to be applicable even if the information that is being routed through neutral communications infrastructure may be characterized as a cyber weapon or otherwise could cause destructive effects in a belligerent State (but no destructive effects within the neutral State or States).[44]

16.5 CYBER OPERATIONS AND *JUS IN BELLO*

This section addresses *jus in bello* rules and cyber operations.

16.5.1 Cyber Operations That Constitute "Attacks" for the Purpose of Applying Rules on Conducting Attacks. If a cyber operation constitutes an attack, then the law of war rules on conducting attacks must be applied to those cyber operations.[45] For example, such operations

---

[43] Colonel Borel, *Report to the Conference from the Second Commission on Rights and Duties of Neutral States on Land*, *in* JAMES BROWN SCOTT, THE REPORTS TO THE HAGUE CONFERENCES OF 1899 AND 1907, 543 (1917) ("We are here dealing with cables or apparatus belonging either to a neutral State or to a company or individuals, the operation of which, for the transmission of news, has the character of a public service. There is no reason to compel the neutral State to restrict or prohibit the use by the belligerents of these means of communication. Were it otherwise, objections of a practical kind would be encountered, arising out of the considerable difficulties in exercising control, not to mention the confidential character of telegraphic correspondence and the rapidity necessary to this service. Through his Excellency Lord Reay, the British delegation requested that it be specified that 'the liberty of a neutral State to transmit messages, by means of its telegraph lines on land, its submarine cables or its wireless apparatus, does not imply that it has any right to use them or permit their use in order to render manifest assistance to one of the belligerents'. The justice of the idea thus stated was so great as to receive the unanimous approval of the Commission.").

[44] *See* DEPARTMENT OF DEFENSE, *Department of Defense Cyberspace Policy Report: A Report to Congress Pursuant to the National Defense Authorization Act for Fiscal Year 2011, Section 934*, 8 (Nov. 2011) ("***The issue of the legality of transporting cyber 'weapons' across the Internet through the infrastructure owned and/or located in neutral third countries without obtaining the equivalent of 'overflight rights.'*** There is currently no international consensus regarding the definition of a 'cyber weapon.' The often low cost of developing malicious code and the high number and variety of actors in cyberspace make the discovery and tracking of malicious cyber tools difficult. Most of the technology used in this context is inherently dual-use, and even software might be minimally repurposed for malicious action."); Department of Defense, Office of the General Counsel, *An Assessment of International Legal Issues in Information Operations* (2nd ed., Nov. 1999), *reprinted in* 76 U.S. NAVAL WAR COLLEGE INTERNATIONAL LAW STUDIES 459, 489 (2002) ("There need be less concern for the reaction of nations through whose territory or communications systems a destructive message may be routed. If only the nation's public communications systems are involved, the transited nation will normally not be aware of the routing such a message has taken. Even if it becomes aware of the transit of such a message and attributes it to the United States, there would be no established principle of international law that it could point to as being violated. As discussed above, even during an international armed conflict international law does not require a neutral nation to restrict the use of its public communications networks by belligerents. Nations generally consent to the free use of their communications networks on a commercial or reciprocal basis. Accordingly, use of a nation's communications networks as a conduit for an electronic attack would not be a violation of its sovereignty in the same way that would be a flight through its airspace by a military aircraft.").

[45] *Refer to* § 5.4 (Rules on Conducting Assaults, Bombardments, and Other Attacks).

must comport with the requirements of distinction and proportionality.[46]

For example, a cyber attack that would destroy enemy computer systems could not be directed against ostensibly civilian infrastructure, such as computer systems belonging to stock exchanges, banking systems, and universities, unless those computer systems met the test for being a military objective under the circumstances.[47] A cyber operation that would not constitute an attack, but would nonetheless seize or destroy enemy property, would have to be imperatively demanded by the necessities of war.[48]

16.5.1.1 *Assessing Incidental Injury or Damage During Cyber Operations*. The principle of proportionality prohibits attacks in which the expected loss of life or injury to civilians, and damage to civilian objects incidental to the attack, would be excessive in relation to the concrete and direct military advantage expected to be gained.[49]

For example, in applying this prohibition to cyber operations, it might be important to assess the potential effects of a cyber attack on computers that are not military objectives, such as private, civilian computers that hold no military significance, but that may be networked to computers that are valid military objectives.[50]

In assessing incidental injury or damage during cyber operations, it may be important to consider that remote harms and lesser forms of harm, such as mere inconveniences or temporary disruptions, need not be considered in assessing whether an attack is prohibited by the principle of proportionality.[51] For example, a minor, brief disruption of internet services to civilians that results incidentally from a cyber attack against a military objective generally would not need to be considered in a proportionality analysis.[52] In addition, the economic harms in the belligerent

---

[46] *Refer to* § 5.5 (Discrimination in Conducting Attacks); § 5.12 (Proportionality – Prohibition on Attacks Expected to Cause Excessive Incidental Harm).

[47] *Refer to* § 5.6 (Military Objectives).

[48] *Refer to* § 5.17.2 (Enemy Property – Military Necessity Standard).

[49] *Refer to* § 5.12 (Proportionality – Prohibition on Attacks Expected to Cause Excessive Incidental Harm).

[50] Harold Hongju Koh, Legal Adviser, Department of State, *International Law in Cyberspace: Remarks as Prepared for Delivery to the USCYBERCOM Inter-Agency Legal Conference (Sept. 18, 2012), reprinted in* 54 HARVARD INTERNATIONAL LAW JOURNAL ONLINE, 8 (Dec. 2012) ("As you all know, information and communications infrastructure is often shared between state militaries and private, civilian communities. The law of war requires that civilian infrastructure not be used to seek to immunize military objectives from attack, including in the cyber realm. But how, exactly, are the jus in bello rules to be implemented in cyberspace? Parties to an armed conflict will need to assess the potential effects of a cyber attack on computers that are not military objectives, such as private, civilian computers that hold no military significance, but may be networked to computers that are valid military objectives. Parties will also need to consider the harm to the civilian uses of such infrastructure in performing the necessary proportionality review. Any number of factual scenarios could arise, however, which will require a careful, fact-intensive legal analysis in each situation.").

[51] *Refer to* § 5.12.1.2 (Loss of Life, Injury, and Damage Versus Mere Inconveniences or Temporary Disruptions).

[52] *Cf.* Program on Humanitarian Policy and Conflict Research at Harvard University, *Commentary on the HPCR Manual on International Law Applicable to Air and Missile Warfare*, 28 (A.1.e.7) (2010) ("The definition of 'attacks' also covers 'non-kinetic' attacks (i.e. attacks that do not involve the physical transfer of energy, such as certain CNAs [computer network attacks]; see Rule 1(m)) that result in death, injury, damage or destruction of persons or objects. Admittedly, whether 'non-kinetic' operations rise to the level of an 'attack' in the context of the

State resulting from such disruptions, such as civilian businesses in the belligerent State being unable to conduct e-commerce, generally would not need to be considered in a proportionality analysis.[53]

Even if cyber operations that constitute attacks are not expected to result in excessive incidental loss of life or injury or damage such that the operation would be prohibited by the principle of proportionality, the party to the conflict nonetheless would be required to take feasible precautions to limit such loss of life or injury and damage in conducting those cyber operations.[54]

16.5.2 Cyber Operations That Do Not Amount to an "Attack" Under the Law of War. A cyber operation that does not constitute an attack is not restricted by the rules that apply to attacks.[55] Factors that would suggest that a cyber operation is not an "attack" include whether the operation causes only reversible effects or only temporary effects. Cyber operations that generally would not constitute attacks include:

- defacing a government webpage;
- a minor, brief disruption of internet services;
- briefly disrupting, disabling, or interfering with communications; and
- disseminating propaganda.

Since such operations generally would not be considered attacks under the law of war, they generally would not need to be directed at military objectives, and may be directed at civilians or civilian objects. Nonetheless, such operations must not be directed against enemy civilians or civilian objects unless the operations are militarily necessary.[56] Moreover, such operations should comport with the general principles of the law of war.[57] For example, even if a cyber operation is not an "attack" or does not cause any injury or damage that would need to be considered under the principle of proportionality in conducting attacks, that cyber operation still should not be conducted in a way that unnecessarily causes inconvenience to civilians or neutral persons.

16.5.3 Duty to Take Feasible Precautions and Cyber Operations. Parties to a conflict must take feasible precautions to reduce the risk of incidental harm to the civilian population and

---

law of international armed conflict is a controversial issue. There was agreement among the Group of Experts that the term 'attack' does not encompass CNAs that result in an inconvenience (such as temporary denial of internet access).").

[53] *Refer to* § 5.12.1.2 (Loss of Life, Injury, and Damage Versus Mere Inconveniences or Temporary Disruptions).

[54] *Refer to* § 16.5.3 (Duty to Take Feasible Precautions and Cyber Operations).

[55] *Refer to* § 5.4 (Rules on Conducting Assaults, Bombardments, and Other Attacks).

[56] *Refer to* § 5.2.2.1 (Non-Violent Measures That Are Militarily Necessary).

[57] *Refer to* § 16.2.2 (Application of Law of War Principles as a General Guide to Cyber Operations).

other protected persons and objects.[58] Parties to the conflict that employ cyber operations should take precautions to minimize the harm of their cyber activities on civilian infrastructure and users.[59]

The obligation to take feasible precautions may be of greater relevance in cyber operations than other law of war rules because this obligation applies to a broader set of activities than those to which other law of war rules apply. For example, the obligation to take feasible precautions to reduce the risk of incidental harm would apply to a party conducting an attack even if the attack would not be prohibited by the principle of proportionality.[60] In addition, the obligation to take feasible precautions applies even if a party is not conducting an attack because the obligation also applies to a party that is subject to attack.[61]

16.5.3.1 *Cyber Tools as Potential Measures to Reduce the Risk of Harm to Civilians or Civilian Objects*. In some cases, cyber operations that result in non-kinetic or reversible effects can offer options that help minimize unnecessary harm to civilians.[62] In this regard, cyber capabilities may in some circumstances be preferable, as a matter of policy, to kinetic weapons because their effects may be reversible, and they may hold the potential to accomplish military goals without any destructive kinetic effect at all.[63]

As with other precautions, the decision of which weapon to use will be subject to many practical considerations, including effectiveness, cost, and "fragility," *i.e.*, the possibility that once used an adversary may be able to devise defenses that will render a cyber tool ineffective in the future.[64] Thus, as with special kinetic weapons, such as precision-guided munitions that have

---

[58] *Refer to* § 5.2.3 (Affirmative Duties to Take Feasible Precautions for the Protection of Civilians and Other Protected Persons and Objects).

[59] *United States Submission to the U.N. Group of Governmental Experts on Developments in the Field of Information and Telecommunications in the Context of International Security 2012-2013*, 4 ("The law of war also requires warring States to take all practicable precautions, taking into account military and humanitarian considerations, to avoid and minimize incidental death, injury, and damage to civilians and civilian objects. In the context of hostilities involving information technologies in armed conflict, parties to the conflict should take precautions to minimize the harm of such cyber activities on civilian infrastructure and users.").

[60] *Refer to* § 5.10.5 (Relationship Between the Requirement to Take Feasible Precautions in Planning and Conducting Attacks and the Prohibition on Attacks Expected to Cause Excessive Incidental Harm).

[61] *Refer to* § 5.14 (Feasible Precautions to Reduce the Risk of Harm to Protected Persons and Objects by the Party Subject to Attack).

[62] *Refer to* § 5.11.6 (Weaponeering (E.g., Selecting Appropriate Weapons, Aim Points)).

[63] *United States Submission to the U.N. Group of Governmental Experts on Developments in the Field of Information and Telecommunications in the Context of International Security 2012-2013*, 4 ("Cyber operations that result in non-kinetic or reversible effects can be an important tool in creating options that minimize unnecessary harm to civilians. In this regard, cyber capabilities may in some circumstances be preferable, as a matter of policy, to kinetic weapons because their effects may be reversible, and they may hold the potential to accomplish military goals without any destructive kinetic effect at all.").

[64] Department of Defense, Office of the General Counsel, *An Assessment of International Legal Issues in Information Operations* (2nd ed., Nov. 1999), *reprinted in* 76 U.S. NAVAL WAR COLLEGE INTERNATIONAL LAW STUDIES 459, 490 (2002) ("Another possible implication of a defender's technological prowess may arise when a nation has the capacity for graduated self-defense measures. Some may argue that a nation having such capabilities must select a response that will do minimal damage. This is a variant of the argument that a nation possessing

the potential to produce less incidental damage than other kinetic weapons, cyber capabilities usually will not be the only type of weapon that is legally permitted.

16.5.4 Prohibition on Improper Use of Signs During Cyber Operations. Under the law of war, certain signs may not be used improperly.[65] These prohibitions may also be applicable during cyber operations. For example, it would not be permissible to conduct a cyber attack or to attempt to disable enemy internal communications by making use of communications that initiate non-hostile relations, such as prisoner exchanges or ceasefires.[66] Similarly, it would be prohibited to fabricate messages from an enemy's Head of State falsely informing that State's forces that an armistice or cease-fire had been signed.[67]

On the other hand, the restriction on the use of enemy flags, insignia, and uniforms only applies to concrete visual objects; it does not restrict the use of enemy codes, passwords, and countersigns.[68] Thus, for example, it would not be prohibited to disguise network traffic as though it came from enemy computers or to use enemy codes during cyber operations.

16.5.5 Use of Civilian Personnel to Support Cyber Operations. As with non-cyber operations, the law of war does not prohibit States from using civilian personnel to support their cyber operations, including support actions that may constitute taking a direct part in hostilities.[69]

Under the GPW, persons who are not members of the armed forces, but who are authorized to accompany them, are entitled to POW status.[70] This category was intended to include, *inter alia*, civilian personnel with special skills in operating military equipment who support and participate in military operations, such as civilian members of military aircrews.[71] It would include civilian cyber specialists who have been authorized to accompany the armed forces.

---

precision-guided munitions must always use them whenever there is a potential for collateral damage. That position has garnered little support among nations and has been strongly rejected by the United States. There is broad recognition that the risk of collateral damage is only one of many military considerations that must be balanced by military authorities planning an attack. One obvious consideration is that a military force that goes into a protracted conflict with a policy of always using precision-guided munitions whenever there is any potential for collateral damage will soon exhaust its supply of such munitions. Similarly, military authorities must be able to weigh all relevant military considerations in choosing a response in self-defense against computer network attacks. These considerations will include the probable effectiveness of the means at their disposal, the ability to assess their effects, and the "fragility" of electronic means of attack (i.e., once they are used, an adversary may be able to devise defenses that will render them ineffective in the future).").

[65] *Refer to* § 5.24 (Improper Use of Certain Signs).

[66] *Refer to* § 12.2 (Principle of Good Faith in Non-Hostile Relations).

[67] Department of Defense, Office of the General Counsel, *An Assessment of International Legal Issues in Information Operations* (2nd ed., Nov. 1999), *reprinted in* 76 U.S. NAVAL WAR COLLEGE INTERNATIONAL LAW STUDIES 459, 473 (2002) ("Perfidy: It may seem attractive for a combatant vessel or aircraft to avoid being attacked by broadcasting the agreed identification signals for a medical vessel or aircraft, but such actions would be a war crime. Similarly, it might be possible to use computer 'morphing' techniques to create an image of the enemy's chief of state informing his troops that an armistice or cease-fire agreement had been signed. If false, this would also be a war crime.").

[68] *Refer to* § 5.23.1.5 (Use of Enemy Codes, Passwords, and Countersigns Not Restricted).

[69] *Refer to* § 4.15.2.2 (Employment in Hostilities).

[70] *Refer to* § 4.15 (Persons Authorized to Accompany the Armed Forces).

[71] *Refer to* § 4.15 (Persons Authorized to Accompany the Armed Forces).

Civilians who take a direct part in hostilities forfeit protection from being made the object of attack.[72]

16.6 Legal Review of Weapons That Employ Cyber Capabilities

DoD policy requires the legal review of the acquisition of weapons or weapon systems.[73] This policy would include the review of weapons that employ cyber capabilities to ensure that they are not *per se* prohibited by the law of war.[74] Not all cyber capabilities, however, constitute a weapon or weapons system. Military Department regulations address what cyber capabilities require legal review.[75]

The law of war does not prohibit the development of novel cyber weapons. The customary law of war prohibitions on specific types of weapons result from State practice and *opinio juris* demonstrating that a type of weapon is illegal; the mere fact that a weapon is novel or employs new technology does not mean that the weapon is illegal.[76]

Although which issues may warrant legal analysis would depend on the characteristics of the weapon being assessed, a legal review of the acquisition or procurement of a weapon that employs cyber capabilities likely would assess whether the weapon is inherently indiscriminate.[77] For example, a destructive computer virus that was programmed to spread and destroy uncontrollably within civilian internet systems would be prohibited as an inherently indiscriminate weapon.[78]

---

[72] *Refer to* § 5.8 (Civilians Taking a Direct Part in Hostilities).

[73] *Refer to* § 6.2 (DoD Policy of Reviewing the Legality of Weapons).

[74] Harold Hongju Koh, Legal Adviser, Department of State, *International Law in Cyberspace: Remarks as Prepared for Delivery to the USCYBERCOM Inter-Agency Legal Conference (Sept. 18, 2012), reprinted in* 54 Harvard International Law Journal Online, 6 (Dec. 2012) ("States should undertake a legal review of weapons, including those that employ a cyber capability. Such a review should entail an analysis, for example, of whether a particular capability would be inherently indiscriminate, i.e., that it could not be used consistent with the principles of distinction and proportionality. The U.S. Government undertakes at least two stages of legal review of the use of weapons in the context of armed conflict: first, an evaluation of new weapons to determine whether their use would be per se prohibited by the law of war; and second, specific operations employing weapons are always reviewed to ensure that each particular operation is also compliant with the law of war.").

[75] *See, e.g.*, Department of the Army Regulation 27-53, *Review of Legality of Weapons Under International Law* (Jan. 1, 1979); Secretary of the Navy Instruction 5000.2E, *Department of the Navy Implementation and Operation of the Defense Acquisition System and the Joint Capabilities Integration and Development System* (Sept. 1, 2011); Department of the Air Force Instruction 51-402, *Legal Reviews of Weapons and Cyber Capabilities* (Jul. 27, 2011).

[76] *Refer to* § 6.2.1 (Review of New Types of Weapons).

[77] *Refer to* § 6.7 (Inherently Indiscriminate Weapons).

[78] *United States Submission to the U.N. Group of Governmental Experts on Developments in the Field of Information and Telecommunications in the Context of International Security 2012-2013*, 3 ("Weapons that cannot be directed at a specific military objective or whose effects cannot be controlled would be inherently indiscriminate, and per se unlawful under the law of armed conflict. In the traditional kinetic context, such inherently indiscriminate and unlawful weapons include, for example, biological weapons. Certain cyber tools could, in light of the interconnected nature of the network, be inherently indiscriminate in the sense that their effects cannot be predicted or controlled; a destructive virus that could spread uncontrollably within civilian internet systems might fall into this category. Attacks using such tools would be prohibited by the law of war.").

XVII – Non-International Armed Conflict (NIAC)

Chapter Contents

17.1 Introduction

This Chapter addresses the law of war rules applicable to armed conflict not of an international character, or non-international armed conflict (NIAC). Non-international armed conflicts are those armed conflicts that are not between States.[1] In particular, this Chapter addresses the rules applicable to State armed forces conducting military operations against non-State armed groups.

The application of the law of war to non-international armed conflict may be complex.[2] In U.S. practice, in certain cases, the rules applicable in international armed conflict have been applied as a matter of policy to military operations in non-international armed conflict.

17.1.1 Non-International Armed Conflict – Notes on Terminology. Non-international armed conflict is commonly referred to by the acronym "NIAC." Although there has been a range of views on what constitutes a non-international armed conflict, the intensity of the conflict and the organization of the parties are criteria that have been assessed to distinguish

[1] *Refer to* § 3.3.1 (International Armed Conflict and Non-International Armed Conflict).

[2] *Refer to* § 17.2 (Application of International Law to NIACs).

between non-international armed conflict and internal disturbances and tensions, such as riots, isolated and sporadic acts of violence, and other acts of a similar nature.[3]

A variety of terms have been used to describe factual situations that often may be characterized as non-international armed conflict.

17.1.1.1 *NIAC and Civil War*. Civil war is a classic example of a non-international armed conflict. For example, a non-international armed conflict could involve the open rebellion of segments of a nation's armed forces (sometimes called dissident armed forces) against the incumbent regime, each claiming to be the legitimate government.[4]

In some cases of civil war, the insurgent party has been recognized as a belligerent, and, at least in some respects, the law of international armed conflict would be applied by the States choosing to recognize the insurgent party as a belligerent.[5]

17.1.1.2 *NIAC and Internal Armed Conflict*. In some cases, the term internal armed conflict is used as a synonym for non-international armed conflict. Such usage may reflect a traditional definition of non-international armed conflict as only those armed conflicts occurring within the borders of a single State.[6] Non-international armed conflicts, however, are classified as such simply based on the status of the parties to the conflict, and sometimes occur in more than one State.[7] The mere fact that an armed conflict occurs in more than one State and thus may be characterized as international "in scope" does not render it "international in character."[8]

17.1.1.3 *Transnational or Internationalized NIACs*. Sometimes the terms of "transnational" or "internationalized" are used to describe certain non-international armed conflicts.

"Transnational" has been used to indicate that the non-international armed conflict takes place in more than one State.

---

[3] *Refer to* § 3.4.2.2 (Distinguishing Armed Conflict From Internal Disturbances and Tensions).

[4] *See, e.g.*, LIEBER CODE art. 150 ("Civil war is war between two or more portions of a country or state, each contending for the mastery of the whole, and each claiming to be the legitimate government. The term is also sometimes applied to war of rebellion, when the rebellious provinces or portions of the state are contiguous to those containing the seat of government.").

[5] *Refer to* § 3.3.3 (State Recognition of Armed Groups as Belligerents).

[6] *See, e.g.*, GC COMMENTARY 36 ("Speaking generally, it must be recognized that the conflicts referred to in Article 3 [of the GC] are armed conflicts, with armed forces on either side engaged in hostilities—conflicts, in short, which are in many respects similar to an international war, but take place within the confines of a single country.").

[7] *Refer to* § 3.3.1 (International Armed Conflict and Non-International Armed Conflict).

[8] Hamdan v. Rumsfeld, 548 U.S. 557, 630 (2006) ("The Court of Appeals thought, and the Government asserts, that Common Article 3 [of the 1949 Geneva Conventions] does not apply to Hamdan because the conflict with al Qaeda, being ''international in scope,'' does not qualify as a ''conflict not of an international character.'' 415 F. 3d, at 41. That reasoning is erroneous. The term 'conflict not of an international character' is used here in contradistinction to a conflict between nations.").

"Internationalized" has been used to indicate that multiple States may be involved in a non-international armed conflict.

17.1.1.4 NIAC and Guerilla or Unconventional Warfare. Guerrilla warfare may be understood to be military and paramilitary operations conducted in enemy-held or hostile territory by irregular, predominantly indigenous forces.[9] Guerrilla operations or unconventional warfare are common during non-international armed conflict. Such operations, however, are a method of warfare that has been employed in international armed conflicts and occupation as well.

17.1.1.5 NIAC and Rebellion or Insurrection. Rebellion, insurrection, or insurgency may also be types of non-international armed conflict.[10] Counter-insurgency operations generally occur in the context of non-international armed conflict, but could occur in the context of an international armed conflict and occupation as well.

17.1.1.6 NIAC and Terrorism. Issues surrounding terrorism and the activities of terrorist groups can arise in the contexts of non-international armed conflict, international armed conflict, and, of course, can arise outside the context of armed conflict altogether. Acts of terrorism are prohibited during international armed conflict and during non-international armed conflict.[11]

17.1.1.7 NIAC and Small Wars or Low-Intensity Conflict. Non-international armed conflict has sometimes been discussed using the term "low-intensity" conflict.[12] The term

---

[9] JOINT PUBLICATION 3-05.1, *Joint Special Operations Task Force Operations,* GL-11 (Apr. 26, 2007) ("**guerrilla warfare.** Military and paramilitary operations conducted in enemy-held or hostile territory by irregular, predominantly indigenous forces. Also called GW. (JP 3-05.1)"). *See also* FRANCIS LIEBER, GUERRILLA PARTIES CONSIDERED WITH REFERENCE TO THE LAWS AND USAGES OF WAR 7-8 (1862) ("[B]ut it may be stated here that whatever may be our final definition, it is universally understood in this country at the present time that a guerrilla party means an irregular band of armed men, carrying on an irregular war, not being able, according to their character as a guerrilla party, to carry on what the law terms a regular war. The irregularity of the guerrilla party consists in its origin, for it is either self-constituted or constituted by the call of a single individual, not according to the general law of levy, conscription, or volunteering; it consists in its disconnection with the army, as to its pay, provision, and movements, and it is irregular as to the permanency of the band, which may be dismissed and called again together at any time.").

[10] *See, e.g.,* LIEBER CODE art. 151 ("The term rebellion is applied to an insurrection of large extent, and is usually a war between the legitimate government of a country and portions of provinces of the same who seek to throw off their allegiance to it and set up a government of their own.").

[11] *Refer to* § 10.5.3.2 (Collective Penalties and Measures of Intimidation or Terrorism); § 17.6.5 (Prohibition on Acts of Terrorism).

[12] John M. Collins, *U.S. Low Intensity Conflicts, 1899-1990,* 4 (Congressional Research Service, Sept. 10, 1990) ("This survey locates LIC [Low-Intensity Conflict] on the conflict spectrum just above normal peacetime competition and just below any kind of armed combat that depletes U.S. forces slightly, if at all (Figures 1 and 2 graphically contrast LIC with mid- and high-intensity conflicts). Limitations on violence, rather than force levels and arsenals, determine the indistinct upper boundary of LIC. Large military formations conceivably could conduct low-intensity operations for limited objectives using the most lethal weapons (perhaps for signalling), provided few U.S. casualties and little U.S. damage ensued. The lower boundary, where nonviolent LICs abut normal peacetime competition, is equally inexact. Political, economic, technological, and psychological warfare, waged for deterrent, offensive, or defensive purposes, occupy prominent places. So do nonviolent military operations, typified by shows of force and peacekeeping. Insurgencies, counterinsurgencies, coups d'etat, transnational terrorism,

"small wars" has also been used in military doctrine to describe situations that may be characterized as non-international armed conflicts.[13] "Low-intensity conflict" and "small wars" are not synonymous with non-international armed conflict, but there is a high degree of overlap between those categories and non-international armed conflict.

17.1.2 Important Commonalities Between the Law Applicable to International Armed Conflict and the Law Applicable to Non-International Armed Conflict.

17.1.2.1 *Common Baseline Rules*. Certain baseline rules, in particular relating to the humane treatment of detainees, must be observed regardless of the character of the armed conflict.[14] The fact that certain baseline rules are common to international armed conflict and non-international armed conflict means that it may be unnecessary to determine the character of the armed conflict in order to assess whether the law has been violated.

17.1.2.2 *Foundational Principles of the Law of War*. The foundational principles of the law of war are common to both international armed conflict and non-international armed conflict.[15] Thus, reference to first principles in the law of war may be most useful in assessing the rules applicable during non-international armed conflict.[16]

17.1.2.3 *Rules for Conducting Operations Against Unprivileged Belligerents*. Rules for conducting operations against unprivileged belligerents are found in both the law applicable to international armed conflict and the law applicable to non-international armed

---

anti/counterterrorism, minor conventional wars, and narco conflict lie between those poles. Variations within each category, overlaps, and interlocks are virtually endless.").

[13] MARINE CORPS, *Small Wars Manual*, ¶1-1-¶1-2 (1940), *reprinted as* FLEET MARINE FORCE REFERENCE PUBLICATION 12-15 (1990) ("The ordinary expedition of the Marine Corps which does not involve a major effort in regular warfare against a first-rate power may be termed a small war. It is this type of routine active foreign duty of the Marine Corps in which this manual is primarily interested. Small wars represent the normal and frequent operations of the Marine Corps. During about 85 of the last 100 years, the Marine Corps has been engaged in small wars in different parts of the world. The Marine Corps has landed troops 180 times in 37 countries from 1800 to 1934. Every year during the past 36 years since the Spanish-American War, the Marine Corps has been engaged in active operations in the field. ... Most of the small wars of the United States have resulted from the obligation of the Government under the spirit of the Monroe Doctrine and have been undertaken to suppress lawlessness or insurrection. Punitive expeditions may be resorted to in some instances, but campaigns of conquest are contrary to the policy of the Government of the United States.").

[14] Military and Paramilitary Activities in and Against Nicaragua (Nicaragua v. United States), Merits, Judgment, 1986 I.C.J. 14, 114 (¶219) ("Because the minimum rules applicable to international and to non-international conflicts are identical, there is no need to address the question whether those actions must be looked at in the context of the rules which operate for the one or for the other category of conflict. The relevant principles are to be looked for in the provisions of Article 3 of each of the four Conventions of 12 August 1949, the text of which, identical in each Convention, expressly refers to conflicts not having an international character.").

[15] *See* Prosecutor v. Tadić, ICTY Appeals Chamber, IT-94-1-AR72, *Decision on the Defence Motion for Interlocutory Appeal on Jurisdiction*, ¶119 (Oct. 2, 1995) ("Indeed, elementary considerations of humanity and common sense make it preposterous that the use by States of weapons prohibited in armed conflicts between themselves be allowed when States try to put down rebellion by their own nationals on their own territory. What is inhumane, and consequently proscribed, in international wars, cannot but be inhumane and inadmissible in civil strife."). *Refer to* § 2.1 (Introduction).

[16] *Refer to* § 17.2.2.1 (Use of Law of War Principles to Discern Rules Applicable to NIAC).

conflict.[17] The rules for States conducting military operations against unprivileged belligerents in international armed conflict are not significantly different from the rules for States conducting military operations against non-State armed groups during non-international armed conflict.

17.1.3 Important Differences Between the Law Applicable to International Armed Conflict and the Law Applicable to Non-International Armed Conflict.

17.1.3.1 *Nationality and Territoriality Exclusions in the Law of International Armed Conflict*. Certain rules applicable to international armed conflict reflect concepts (*e.g.*, nationality and territory) that preclude the application of those rules to internal armed conflicts. For example, nationals who are in the power of their State of nationality would not be provided POW status under the GPW or protected person status under the GC.[18] Thus, even if the GPW and GC could otherwise be deemed applicable to a civil war, these exclusions based on nationality would limit the application of many of the provisions of the GPW and GC (as a matter of treaty law) to internal armed conflicts. In any case, it remains true that fundamental principles guaranteeing humane treatment (*e.g.*, Common Article 3 of the 1949 Geneva Conventions) would apply in any such circumstances.

Similarly, it is the essence of belligerent occupation that it should be exercised over foreign, enemy territory;[19] thus, occupation law rules would not apply to internal armed conflict.[20]

Certain non-international armed conflicts, however, are not internal armed conflicts.[21]

17.1.3.2 *Prevalence of Customary Law Applicable to NIAC as Opposed to Treaty Law*. There are fewer treaty provisions that address non-international armed conflict than that address international armed conflict.[22] Put another way, practitioners are generally more likely to encounter situations regulated by customary law in non-international armed conflict than in international armed conflict. Certain guidelines may be helpful in assessing customary international law applicable to non-international armed conflict.[23]

---

[17] *Refer to* § 4.3 (Lawful Combatants and Unprivileged Belligerents).

[18] *Refer to* § 4.4.4.2 (Nationals of a State Who Join Enemy Forces); § 10.3.3.1 (A State's Own Nationals).

[19] *Refer to* § 11.2.2.3 ("Of the Hostile Army" – Belligerent Occupation Applies to Enemy Territory).

[20] *See* Richard A. Baxter, *Ius in Bello Interno: The Present and Future Law*, *in* JOHN NORTON MOORE, LAW AND CIVIL WAR IN THE MODERN WORLD 518, 531 (1974) ("Other provisions of the [Fourth Geneva] Convention apply to 'territory of a party to the conflict' and to 'occupied territory.' In internal conflict, the lawful government and the insurgents will both maintain that there is only 'territory of a party to the conflict.' Territory cannot be belligerently occupied by the lawful government or the rebels. There is no starting point which divides territory into friendly and enemy areas, so that, when the latter type of area is occupied, it will be belligerently occupied. It surely cannot be maintained that the insurgents should be required to treat all territory over which they exercise control as being belligerently occupied or that the lawful government should be forced to treat territory liberated from the control of rebels as belligerently occupied. It is of the essence of belligerent occupation that it should be exercised over foreign, enemy territory. Such requirements as that of Article 43 of the Hague Regulations that the occupant must respect, 'unless absolutely prevented, the laws in force in the country' are simply unworkable in domestic conflict.").

[21] *Refer to* § 17.1.1.2 (NIAC and Internal Armed Conflict); § 17.1.1.3 (Transnational or Internationalized NIACs).

[22] *Refer to* § 17.2.1 (Treaties That Apply to NIAC).

[23] *Refer to* § 17.2.2 (Assessing Customary International Law Applicable to NIAC).

17.1.3.3 *Important Substantive Differences Between the Law Applicable to International Armed Conflict and the Law Applicable to Non-International Armed Conflict*. There are important substantive differences between the law applicable to international armed conflict and the law applicable to non-international armed conflict, including the following three examples.

First, the different circumstances that typically arise in non-international armed conflicts as compared to international armed conflicts may need to be considered in applying the principle of distinction.[24]

Second, States have greater latitude to compel enemy persons to switch allegiance or to serve the State in hostilities during non-international armed conflict than States have to compel enemy nationals during international armed conflict.[25]

Third, States have greater latitude to use their domestic law against enemy armed groups in non-international armed conflict than States have to use their domestic law against enemy forces or enemy nationals in international armed conflict.[26]

17.2 Application of International Law to NIACs

In some cases, there may be important substantive differences between the rules applicable in international armed conflict and the rules applicable in non-international armed conflict.[27] In some cases, only the general essence of a rule that applies during international armed conflict applies during non-international armed conflict, as opposed to the detailed provisions in some treaties relating to many aspects of international armed conflict.[28]

The extent to which the law of war rules that apply during international armed conflict must or should apply during non-international armed conflict has not been clearly defined as the law of war has developed.[29] The discretion afforded States in applying law of war rules to non-international armed conflicts results, in part, because treaty provisions applicable to international armed conflict have been presumed not to apply to non-international armed conflict unless explicitly made applicable. For example, in the 1949 Geneva Conventions, only Common Article 3 applies to non-international armed conflict.[30] The discretion afforded States in this

[24] *Refer to* § 17.5 (Principle of Distinction in NIAC).

[25] *Refer to* § 17.12.1 (Compelling Captured or Surrendered Enemy Personnel to Take Part in the Conflict).

[26] *Refer to* § 17.4.1 (Ability of a State to Use Its Domestic Law Against Non-State Armed Groups).

[27] *Refer to* § 17.1.3.3 (Important Substantive Differences Between the Law Applicable to International Armed Conflict and the Law Applicable to Non-International Armed Conflict).

[28] *See, e.g.*, Prosecutor v. Tadić, ICTY Appeals Chamber, IT-94-1-AR72, *Decision on the Defence Motion for Interlocutory Appeal on Jurisdiction*, ¶¶126-127 (Oct. 2, 1995) ("The emergence of the aforementioned general rules on internal armed conflicts does not imply that internal strife is regulated by general international law in all its aspects. Two particular limitations may be noted: (i) only a number of rules and principles governing international armed conflicts have gradually been extended to apply to internal conflicts; and (ii) this extension has not taken place in the form of a full and mechanical transplant of those rules to internal conflicts; rather, the general essence of those rules, and not the detailed regulation they may contain, has become applicable to internal conflicts.").

[29] *See, e.g.*, FRANCIS LIEBER, GUERRILLA PARTIES CONSIDERED WITH REFERENCE TO THE LAWS AND USAGES OF WAR 21 (1862) ("The application of the laws and usages of war to wars of insurrection or rebellion is always undefined, and depends on relaxations of municipal law, suggested by humanity or necessitated by the numbers engaged in the insurrection. The law of war, as acknowledged between independent belligerents, is, at times, not allowed to interfere with the municipal law of rebellion, or is allowed to do so only very partially, as was the case in Great Britain during the Stuart rebellion, in the middle of last century; at other times, again, measures are adopted in rebellions, by the victorious party or the legitimate government, more lenient even than the international law of war.").

[30] GC COMMENTARY 34 ("To borrow the phrase of one of the delegates, Article 3 is like a 'Convention in miniature'. It applies to non-international conflicts only, and will be the only Article applicable to them until such time as a special agreement between the Parties has brought into force between them all or part of the other provisions of the Convention.").

regard may also be understood to result from the wide range of circumstances that constitute non-international armed conflict. The United States has objected to efforts to make the applicability of the rules of international armed conflict turn on subjective and politicized criteria that would eliminate the distinction between international and non-international conflicts.[31]

In the sections that follow, which reflect the practice of the U.S. armed forces in applying the law of war to non-international armed conflict, the rules articulated may exceed the requirements of applicable customary international law and treaty law.

17.2.1 Treaties That Apply to NIAC. Relatively few treaties have provisions that expressly apply to non-international armed conflicts. Some treaties, however, may apply implicitly to non-international armed conflict.

17.2.1.1 *Treaties That Have Provisions That Explicitly Apply to NIAC*. Certain treaties to which the United States is a Party have provisions that explicitly apply to non-international armed conflict. These treaties include:

- the 1949 Geneva Conventions (*i.e.*, Common Article 3);[32]
- the 1954 Hague Cultural Property Convention;[33]
- the CCW Amended Mines Protocol;[34]
- the Amended CCW, including Protocols I, III, and IV;[35]
- the CCW Protocol V on Explosive Remnants of War;[36] and
- AP III.[37]

Treaties to which the United States is not a Party that have provisions applicable to "armed conflict not of an international character" include:

---

[31] *Refer to* § 3.3.4 (AP I Provision on National Liberation Movements).

[32] GPW art. 3 ("In the case of armed conflict not of an international character occurring in the territory of one of the High Contracting Parties … ."); GWS (same); GWS Sea (same); GC (same).

[33] 1954 HAGUE CULTURAL PROPERTY CONVENTION art. 19(1) ("In the event of an armed conflict not of an international character occurring within the territory of one of the High Contracting Parties, each party to the conflict shall be bound to apply, as a minimum, the provisions of the present Convention which relate to respect for cultural property.").

[34] CCW AMENDED MINES PROTOCOL art. 1 ("2. This Protocol shall apply, in addition to situations referred to in Article I of this Convention, to situations referred to in Article 3 common to the Geneva Conventions of 12 August 1949. This Protocol shall not apply to situations of internal disturbances and tensions, such as riots, isolated and sporadic acts of violence and other acts of a similar nature, as not being armed conflicts. 3. In case of armed conflicts not of an international character occurring in the territory of one of the High Contracting Parties, each party to the conflict shall be bound to apply the prohibitions and restrictions of this Protocol.").

[35] CCW AMENDED art. 1 ("2. This Convention and its annexed Protocols shall also apply, in addition to situations referred to in paragraph 1 of this Article, to situations referred to in Article 3 common to the Geneva Conventions of 12 August 1949. This Convention and its annexed Protocols shall not apply to situations of internal disturbances and tensions, such as riots, isolated and sporadic acts of violence, and other acts of a similar nature, as not being armed conflicts. 3. In case of armed conflicts not of an international character occurring in the territory of one of the High Contracting Parties, each party to the conflict shall be bound to apply the prohibitions and restrictions of this Convention and its annexed Protocols.").

[36] CCW PROTOCOL V ON EXPLOSIVE REMNANTS OF WAR art. 1(3) ("This Protocol shall apply to situations resulting from conflicts referred to in Article 1, paragraphs 1 to 6, of the Convention, as amended on 21 December 2001.").

[37] AP III art. 1 ("2. This Protocol reaffirms and supplements the provisions of the four Geneva Conventions of 12 August 1949 ('the Geneva Conventions') and, where applicable, of their two Additional Protocols of 8 June 1977 ('the 1977 Additional Protocols') relating to the distinctive emblems, namely the red cross, the red crescent and the red lion and sun, and shall apply in the same situations as those referred to in these provisions.").

- AP II;[38] and
- the Rome Statute of the International Criminal Court.[39]

17.2.1.2 *Implicit Application of Treaty Provisions to Situations in NIAC*. Some treaties may apply implicitly to certain situations in non-international armed conflict. For example, the Genocide Convention does not expressly refer to non-international armed conflict, but recognizes that acts of genocide are criminal "whether committed in time of peace or time of war" and whether they are committed by "constitutionally responsible rulers, public officials or private individuals."[40] Similarly, the Convention Against Torture recognizes that "No exceptional circumstances whatsoever, whether a state of war or a threat of war, internal political instability or any other public emergency, may be invoked as a justification of torture"; thus, the state of non-international armed conflict could not be justification for torture.[41]

The prohibitions in Article 1 of the Chemical Weapons Convention have been interpreted to apply to non-international armed conflict.[42]

In addition, the prohibitions and restrictions on acquisition and development of biological weapons in the Biological Weapons Convention effectively prevent the use of biological weapons by States in non-international armed conflict.[43]

Further, the obligations in the Child Soldiers Protocol relate implicitly to non-international armed conflict.[44]

17.2.1.3 *Human Rights Treaties and NIAC*. During an internal non-international armed conflict, a State would continue to be bound by applicable human rights treaty obligations.[45]

The applicability of human rights treaty obligations during non-international armed conflict may depend on a variety of factors. Such applicability depends on the terms of the particular treaty in question, and whether the State has exercised an authorized derogation from its provisions due to an emergency situation. The applicability of a human rights treaty obligation with respect to an individual, such as an obligation under the International Covenant on Civil and Political Rights, for example, may depend on whether the person is located outside

---

[38] AP II art. 1(1) ("This Protocol, which develops and supplements Article 3 common to the Geneva Conventions of 12 August 1949 without modifying its existing conditions of applications, shall apply to all armed conflicts which are not covered by Article 1 of the Protocol Additional to the Geneva Conventions of 12 August 1949, and relating to the Protection of Victims of International Armed Conflicts (Protocol I) and which take place in the territory of a High Contracting Party between its armed forces and dissident armed forces or other organized armed groups which, under responsible command, exercise such control over a part of its territory as to enable them to carry out sustained and concerted military operations and to implement this Protocol.").

[39] ROME STATUTE art. 8(2)(c) ("In the case of an armed conflict not of an international character, serious violations of article 3 common to the four Geneva Conventions …, namely, any of the following acts committed against persons taking no active part in the hostilities"); ROME STATUTE art. 8(2)(f) ("Paragraph 2(e) applies to armed conflicts not of an international character … .").

[40] Convention on the Prevention and Punishment of the Crime of Genocide, art. 1, Dec. 9, 1948, 78 UNTS 277, 280 ("The Contracting Parties confirm that genocide, whether committed in time of peace or in time of war, is a crime under international law which they undertake to prevent and to punish."); *id.* at art. 4 ("Persons committing genocide or any of the other acts enumerated in article III shall be punished, whether they are constitutionally responsible rulers, public officials or private individuals.").

[41] Convention against Torture and Other Cruel, Inhuman or Degrading Treatment or Punishment, art. 2(2), Dec. 10, 1984, 1465 UNTS 85, 114. *Refer to* § 1.6.3.4 (Convention Against Torture).

[42] *Refer to* § 6.8.3.2 (Prohibitions With Respect to Chemical Weapons).

[43] *Refer to* § 6.9.1 (Biological Weapons – Prohibition on Use as a Method of Warfare).

[44] *Refer to* § 4.20.5.2 (Child Soldiers Protocol).

[45] *Refer to* § 1.6.3 (Human Rights Treaties).

the territory of the State Party.[46] In addition, law of war rules constitute the *lex specialis* during situations of armed conflict, and as such, serve as the controlling body of law with regard to the conduct of hostilities and the protection of war victims.[47]

17.2.2 Assessing Customary International Law Applicable to NIAC. As a consequence of the fewer treaty provisions applicable to non-international armed conflict, many of the rules applicable to non-international armed conflict are found in customary international law. The following guidelines may be helpful in assessing the customary international law applicable to non-international armed conflict.

17.2.2.1 *Use of Law of War Principles to Discern Rules Applicable to NIAC*. The fundamental principles of the law of war also provide the foundation for the rules applicable during non-international armed conflict.[48] As during international armed conflict, the principles of the law of war form the general guide for conduct during non-international armed conflict, when no specific rule applies.[49]

However, the application of law of war principles may differ insofar as the circumstances in international armed conflicts may often be quite different from the circumstances in non-international armed conflicts.[50]

17.2.2.2 *Considered Absence of a Restriction in NIAC*. Under general principles of legal interpretation, when a rule mentions specific circumstances or conditions in which it applies, it may give rise to a presumption that the rule was not intended to apply in other related circumstances or conditions that are not specifically mentioned.[51]

---

[46] *Refer to* § 1.6.3.3 (International Covenant on Civil and Political Rights (ICCPR)).

[47] *Refer to* § 1.3.2 (The Law of War's Relationship to Other Bodies of Law).

[48] *Refer to* § 17.1.2.2 (Foundational Principles of the Law of War).

[49] *Refer to* § 2.1.2.2 (Law of War Principles as a General Guide).

[50] *Refer to* § 17.5 (Principle of Distinction in NIAC).

[51] *See, e.g.*, Tucker v. Alexandroff, 183 U.S. 424, 436 (1902) ("But whatever view might be taken of the question of delivering over foreign seamen in the absence of a treaty, we are of opinion that the treaty with Russia having contained a convention upon this subject, that convention must alone be looked to in determining the rights of the Russian authorities to the reclamation of the relator. Where the signatory powers have themselves fixed the terms upon which deserting seamen shall be surrendered, we have no right to enlarge those powers upon the principles of comity so as to embrace cases not contemplated by the treaty. Upon general principles applicable to the construction of written instruments, the enumeration of certain powers with respect to a particular subject-matter is a negation of all other analogous powers with respect to the same subject-matter. As observed by Lord Denham in Aspdin v. Austin, 'where parties have entered into written engagements with express stipulations, it is manifestly not desirable to extend them by any implications; the presumption is that, having expressed some, they have expressed all the conditions by which they intend to be bound under that instrument.' The rule is curtly stated in the familiar legal maxim, *Expressio unius est exclusio alterius*.") (internal citations omitted); The S.S. Wimbledon, (United Kingdom, France, Japan v. Germany) (Judgment), 1923 P.C.I.J. (series A) No. 1, at 23-24 ("Although the Kiel Canal, having been constructed by Germany in German territory, was, until 1919, an internal waterway of the state holding both banks, the Treaty has taken care not to assimilate it to the other internal navigable waterways of the German Empire. A special section has been created at the end of Part XII, dealing with ports, waterways and railways, and in this special section rules exclusively designed for the Kiel Canal have been inserted; these rules differ on more than one point from those to which other internal navigable waterways of the Empire are subjected by Articles 321 to 327. … The provisions relating to the Kiel Canal in the Treaty of Versailles are therefore self-contained; if they had to be supplemented and interpreted by the aid of those referring to the inland navigable waterways of Germany in the previous Sections of Part XII, they would lose their 'raison d'être', such repetitions as are found in them would be superfluous and there would be every justification for surprise at the fact that, in certain cases, when the provisions of Articles 321 to 327 might be applicable to the canal, the authors of the Treaty should have taken the trouble to repeat their terms or re-produce their substance.").

Thus, if a treaty addresses both international armed conflict and non-international armed conflict, and provides for a restriction in international armed conflict but does not provide for that restriction in non-international armed conflict, then this omission may, to some extent, reflect States' views that such restrictions were not applicable in non-international armed conflict.[52] Similarly, States negotiated and adopted AP I and AP II at the same diplomatic conference, and the omission from AP II of restrictions present in AP I may, to some extent, reflect States' views that such restrictions were not applicable in non-international armed conflict.[53]

17.2.2.3 Application of IAC Rules by Analogy. If an action is not prohibited by the law of war applicable to international armed conflict, it generally would not be prohibited by the law of war applicable to non-international armed conflict.

For example, analogous provisions of the GPW and GC may be helpful for understanding the baseline standards in international law for detention because the baseline standards applicable to all detainees during armed conflict (*e.g.*, Common Article 3 of the 1949 Geneva Conventions) are not more favorable than the treatment and protections applicable to POWs and civilian internees under the GPW and GC, respectively.[54] Thus, in some instances it may be appropriate

---

[52] *See, e.g.*, II OFFICIAL RECORDS OF THE UNITED NATIONS DIPLOMATIC CONFERENCE OF PLENIPOTENTIARIES ON THE ESTABLISHMENT OF AN INTERNATIONAL CRIMINAL COURT 157-58 (A/CONF.183/C.1/SR.4, ¶¶33-34) (2002) ("33. **Mr. van der Wind** (Netherlands), acting as Coordinator of part 2 of the draft Statute, said that the definition of war crimes was divided into four sections, of which sections A and B concerned norms applicable in international armed conflict and sections C and D those applicable in internal armed conflict. … 41. Under section D, subparagraph (*f*), the options were very similar to those proposed in section B, subparagraph (*t*), the differences in wording stemming from the fact that the norms applicable to international armed conflict and the sources used were somewhat different, as could be seen, for example, in options 2 and 3 which referred to armed forces or groups, and in the reference to allowing children to take part.").

[53] *See, e.g.*, XIV OFFICIAL RECORDS OF THE CDDH 67 (CDDH/III/SR.8, ¶¶67-72) ("Mr. ALDRICH (United States of America) said that article 46 was important for giving general guidance to military commanders in the conduct of their operations. … His delegation supported the amendments to article 26 of draft Protocol II in document CDDH/III/36. It was inappropriate to include the same detailed provisions in a protocol on non-international armed conflicts as in one on international armed conflicts."); XIV OFFICIAL RECORDS OF THE CDDH 179 (CDDH/III/SR.20, ¶53) (Mrs. DARIIMAA (Mongolia) said that the Working Group should consider the differences between article 28 of draft Protocol II and the corresponding article of draft Protocol I, since the practices and rules current in international and internal law were not the same. Unless that was taken into account, the Protocol would be inapplicable and might open the way to various forms of interference in the internal affairs of State."); XIV OFFICIAL RECORDS OF THE CDDH 73 (CDDH/III/SR.9, ¶14) ("Mr. BLISHCHENKO (Union of Soviet Socialist Republics) said that he wished to reply to certain delegations which had expressed the desire to see the same revisions in article 26 of draft Protocol II and in article 46 of draft Protocol I. He pointed out that there were differences between international and internal conflicts. With regard to the latter, it was essential to make rules that everyone could accept."); XV OFFICIAL RECORDS OF THE CDDH 460 (Committee III Report, CDDH/407/Rev.1, ¶40) ("The Committee was also aided in its task by the somewhat similar word done at the third session of the Conference by Committee I with respect to draft Protocol II. As a matter of drafting, the Committee adopted the texts of those parts of Articles 6 and 10 of draft Protocol II which it decided to include in Article 65. The rule applied was that the same text would be used unless there was reason for changing it inherent in the differences between international and non-international armed conflicts."); XI OFFICIAL RECORDS OF THE CDDH 248 (CDDH/II/SR.25, ¶¶16-18) ("Mr. IJAS (Indonesia) said that his delegation understood the concern of those who objected to draft Protocol II on the grounds that some of its provisions interfered in the internal affairs of States and were contrary to the principle of national sovereignty. … The provisions of Part III of draft Protocol II should not reproduce automatically those of the corresponding part of draft Protocol I, since they are concerned with different type of armed conflict. For example, article 16, paragraph 3 could give rise to serious problems if it was left as it stood."); XIV OFFICIAL RECORDS OF THE CDDH 312 (CDDH/III/SR.32, ¶15) ("Mr. WOLFE (Canada), referring to his delegation's amendment (CDDH/III/221), said that he thought it was dangerous to try to introduce in draft Protocol II a notion of perfidy which was only valid in international conflicts and very difficult to apply in internal conflicts.").

[54] *Refer to* § 8.1.4.4 (Analogous GPW and GC Provisions).

to implement measures during detention of persons during non-international armed conflict by analogy to the internment of POWs during international armed conflict or by analogy to the internment of protected persons in occupied territory.[55]

17.2.2.4 *Application of Law Enforcement Rules*. The law applicable to non-international armed conflict generally has been crafted to reflect baseline rules that States respect even in addressing common criminals.[56] Thus, if an action would be permissible under the domestic law enforcement rules of many States, it likely would be permissible as a matter of customary international law during non-international armed conflict.

17.2.3 Application of Humanitarian Rules and the Legal Status of the Parties to the Conflict. The application of humanitarian rules to enemy non-State armed groups does not affect the legal status of such groups.[57] For example, a State's decision to apply humanitarian rules in military operations against a non-State armed group would not constitute an implicit recognition of a government that such an armed group has purported to establish nor an implicit recognition of the legitimacy of the armed group's cause. Such application also would not implicitly provide the members of the armed group with any legal immunity from prosecution.

The principle that the application of humanitarian rules to an armed group does not affect the legal status of that armed group has been recognized in a number of treaties. For example, by its express terms, the application of Common Article 3 of the 1949 Geneva Conventions shall not affect the legal status of the parties to the conflict.[58] Also by express treaty terms, the application of the provisions of the CCW and its annexed Protocols to parties to a conflict that are not High Contracting Parties that have accepted the CCW or its annexed Protocols shall not change their legal status or the legal status of a disputed territory, either explicitly or implicitly.[59] Further, by the express terms of the 1954 Hague Cultural Property Convention, its provisions that relate to non-international armed conflict shall not affect the legal status of the parties to the conflict.[60]

[55] *Refer to* § 17.17.1.1 (Non-Punitive Detention in Non-International Armed Conflict).

[56] *See, e.g.*, GWS COMMENTARY 50 ("What Government would dare to claim before the world, in a case of civil disturbances which could justly be described as mere acts of banditry, that, Article 3 not being applicable, it was entitled to leave the wounded uncared for, to inflict torture and mutilations and to take hostages? However useful, therefore, the various conditions stated above may be, they are not indispensable, since no Government can object to respecting, in its dealings with internal enemies, whatever the nature of the conflict between it and them, a few essential rules which it in fact respects daily, under its own laws, even when dealing with common criminals.").

[57] *See* LIEBER CODE art. 152 ("When humanity induces the adoption of the rules of regular war toward rebels, whether the adoption is partial or entire, it does in no way whatever imply a partial or complete acknowledgement of their government, if they have set up one, or of them, as an independent and sovereign power. Neutrals have no right to make the adoption of the rules of war by the assailed government toward rebels the ground of their own acknowledgment of the revolted people as an independent power.").

[58] GWS art. 3 ("The application of the preceding provisions [in Article 3] shall not affect the legal status of the Parties to the conflict."); GWS-SEA art. 3 (same); GPW art. 3 (same); GC art. 3 (same).

[59] CCW AMENDED art. 1(6) ("The application of the provisions of this Convention and its annexed Protocols to parties to a conflict which are not High Contracting Parties that have accepted this Convention or its annexed Protocols, shall not change their legal status or the legal status of a disputed territory, either explicitly or implicitly."); CCW AMENDED MINES PROTOCOL art. 1(6) ("The application of the provisions of this Protocol to parties to a conflict, which are not High Contracting Parties that have accepted this Protocol, shall not change their legal status or the legal status of a disputed territory, either explicitly or implicitly."); CCW AMENDED MINES PROTOCOL art. 12(1)(b) ("The application of the provisions of this Article to parties to a conflict which are not High Contracting Parties shall not change their legal status or the legal status of a disputed territory, either explicitly or implicitly.").

[60] 1954 HAGUE CULTURAL PROPERTY CONVENTION art. 19(4) ("The application of the preceding provisions shall not affect the legal status of the parties to the conflict.").

17.2.4 Binding Force of the Law of War on Insurgents and Other Non-State Armed Groups. The law of war applicable in a non-international armed conflict is binding upon all parties to the armed conflict, including State armed forces and non-State armed groups. A variety of explanations have been offered for this principle.

Customary law of war rules are binding on a State, even if it is not a Party to a treaty containing the rule.[61] Similarly, customary law of war rules are binding on those parties to the armed conflict that intend to make war and to claim the rights of a belligerent, even if they are not States.[62]

Treaty provisions that address non-international armed conflict provide that they apply not only to the State, but to each party to the conflict.[63] In many cases, these treaty provisions would also be binding on non-State armed groups as a matter of customary international law.[64]

As a practical matter, non-State armed groups would often be bound by their State's treaty obligations due to the very fact that the leaders of those non-State armed groups would claim to be the State's legitimate representatives.[65] Other practical considerations, such as the

---

[61] *Refer to* § 1.8 (Customary International Law).

[62] *See* Trial of Henry Wirz, Argument of the Judge Advocate (Special Military Commission, Washington D.C., Oct. 20, 1865), *reprinted in* 40th Congress, House Executive Document No. 23, *A Congressionally Mandated Report Summarizing the Military Commission's Proceedings,* 722, 764 (Dec. 7, 1867) ("Whatever the form of government may have been to which the leaders of the confederacy, so-called, aspired; whatever of wrong and injustice they sought to embody in their system; with whatever of oppression and tyranny they sought to grind down their subjects, the moment they asked a place among nations they were bound to recognize and obey those laws international which are and of necessity must be applicable alike to all."); Chacon v. Eighty-Nine Bales of Cochineal, 5 F. Cas. 390, 394 (C.C.D. Va. 1821) (Marshall, C.J.) (whether an entity "be a state or not, if she is in a condition to make war, and to claim the character and rights of a belligerent, she is bound to respect the laws of war;"). *Refer to* § 3.4.1.2 (Non-State Armed Groups With the Intention of Conducting Hostilities).

[63] *See, e.g.*, GWS art. 3 ("In the case of armed conflict not of an international character occurring in the territory of one of the High Contracting Parties, each Party to the conflict shall be bound to apply, as a minimum, … ."); 1954 HAGUE CULTURAL PROPERTY CONVENTION ART. 19(1) ("In the event of an armed conflict not of an international character occurring within the territory of one of the High Contracting Parties, each party to the conflict shall be bound to apply, as a minimum, the provisions of the present Convention which relate to respect for cultural property."); CCW AMENDED MINES PROTOCOL art. 1(3) ("In case of armed conflicts not of an international character occurring in the territory of one of the High Contracting Parties, each party to the conflict shall be bound to apply the prohibitions and restrictions of this Protocol."); CCW AMENDED art. 1(3) ("In case of armed conflicts not of an international character occurring in the territory of one of the High Contracting Parties, each party to the conflict shall be bound to apply the prohibitions and restrictions of this Convention and its annexed Protocols.").

[64] Special Court for Sierra Leone Appeals Chamber, *Decision on Challenge to Jurisdiction: Lomé Accord Amnesty, SCSL-2004-15-AR72(E) and SCSL-2004-16-AR72(E)*, ¶47 (Mar. 13, 2004) ("It suffices to say, for the purpose of the present case, that no one has suggested that insurgents are bound because they have been vested with personality in international law of such a nature as to make it impossible for them to be a party to the Geneva Conventions. Rather, a convincing theory is that they are bound as a matter of international customary law to observe the obligations by common Article 3 which is aimed at the protection of humanity.").

[65] GWS COMMENTARY 51-52 ("On the other hand, what justification is there for the obligation on the adverse Party in revolt against the established authority? At the Diplomatic Conference doubt was expressed as to whether insurgents could be legally bound by a Convention which they had not themselves signed. But if the responsible authority at their head exercises effective sovereignty, it is bound by the very fact that it claims to represent the country, or part of the country. The 'authority' in question can only free itself from its obligations under the Convention by following the procedure for denunciation laid down in Article 63. But the denunciation would not be valid, and could not in point of fact be effected, unless the denouncing authority was recognized internationally as a competent Government. It should, moreover, be noted that under Article 63 denunciation does not take effect immediately.").

desire to be seen as legitimate, may also contribute to their compliance with the law of war.[66]

17.3 SPECIAL AGREEMENTS BETWEEN PARTIES TO THE CONFLICT

Parties to a conflict may enter into agreements to bring into force law of war rules.[67] For example, pursuant to Common Article 3 of the 1949 Geneva Conventions, the parties to the conflict should further endeavor to bring into force, by means of special agreements, all or part of the other provisions of the 1949 Geneva Conventions.[68] Similarly, pursuant to the 1954 Hague Cultural Property Convention, the parties to the conflict shall endeavor to bring into force, by means of special agreements, all or part of the other provisions of that Convention.[69]

Parties to a non-international armed conflict may wish to conclude agreements on these and a variety of other subjects, such as:

- temporary ceasefire agreements to collect the wounded;
- agreements to permit passage of medical or other relief supplies for the civilian population;
- agreements for the accommodation of detainees in other States;[70]

---

[66] GWS COMMENTARY 52 ("If an insurgent party applies Article 3, so much the better for the victims of the conflict. No one will complain. If it does not apply it, it will prove that those who regard its actions as mere acts of anarchy or brigandage are right."). *Refer to* § 18.2 (Prudential Reasons Supporting the Implementation and Enforcement of the Law of War).

[67] *For example*, Letter from James Robertson to George Washington (May 1, 1782) ("Sir, A Commission from the King appointing me Commander in Chief of his forces in this country having arrived by a late conveyance, I make it one of my first cares, to convince you of my wish to carry on the war agreeable to the rules which humanity formed, and the example of the politest nations recommended. I make this declaration of my resolution, in hope that I may find a similar inclination in you. To effect this, let us agree to prevent or punish every breach of the rules of war within the spheres of our command.") and, Letter from George Washington to James Robertson (May 5, 1782) ("Sincerely lamenting the cruel necessity, which alone can induce so distressing a measure in the present instance, I do assure your Excellency, I am as earnestly desirous as you can be, that the war may be carried on agreeable to the rules which humanity formed, and the example of the politest nations recommends, and shall be extremely happy in agreeing with you to prevent or punish every breach of the rules of war within the sphere of our respective commands."), *reprinted in* THE REMEMBRANCER; OR, IMPARTIAL REPOSITORY OF PUBLIC EVENTS FOR THE YEAR 1782, PART II, 156-57.

[68] GWS art. 3 ("The Parties to the conflict should further endeavour to bring into force, by means of special agreements, all or part of the other provisions of the present Convention."); GWS-SEA art. 3 (same); GPW art. 3 (same); GC art. 3 (same). *For example*, Bosnia and Herzegovina, Agreement No. 1 of May 22, 1992, *reprinted in* Marco Sassòli, Antoine A. Bouvier, Anne Quintin, *III How Does Law Protect In War? Cases and Documents*, Case No. 204: Former Yugoslavia, Special Agreements Between Parties to the Conflicts, 116-17 ¶2 (Mar. 2011) ("In accordance with the Article 3 of the four Geneva Conventions of August 12, 1949, the Parties agree to bring into force the following provisions … . Captured combatants shall enjoy the treatment provided for by the Third Geneva Convention."); U.N. COMMISSION ON HUMAN RIGHTS, *Report on the situation of human rights in Afghanistan prepared by the Special Rapporteur, Mr. Felix Ermacora, in accordance with Commission on Human Rights resolution 1984/55*, U.N. Doc. E/CN.4/1985/21, 28-29 ¶104 (Feb. 19, 1985) ("Apparently in 1982 an agreement on conditions for the internment of foreign prisoners was signed between the Afghan resistance movement and the International Committee of the Red Cross (ICRC) under which the resistance expressed its intention to respect the spirit of the provisions of the Geneva Convention relative to the Treatment of Prisoners of War. This involves the application of article 3 of the Geneva Conventions under which the parties to armed conflict can conclude agreements or make statements specifying that they will apply all or part of the other provisions of the Conventions. Analysing this agreement as calculated to set an example for better treatment of prisoners of war, witnesses stated that since then the resistance movements had endeavoured to ensure that foreign prisoners were not tortured or assassinated.").

[69] 1954 HAGUE CULTURAL PROPERTY CONVENTION art. 19(2) ("The parties to the Conflict shall endeavour to bring into force, by means of special agreements, all or part of the other provisions of the present Convention.").

[70] *For example*, International Committee of the Red Cross, *External Activities: Africa—Latin American—Asia—Middle East—Europe*, 24 INTERNATIONAL REVIEW OF THE RED CROSS 230, 239-40 (Jul.-Aug. 1984) ("Negotiations carried out by the ICRC with, successively, the USSR, the Afghan opposition movement, Pakistan and Switzerland

- agreements to establish hospital or safety zones;
- agreements for the cessation of hostilities; and
- agreements for post-conflict clearance of remnants of war.[71]

17.3.1 Communications Between Parties to the Conflict. The procedures that are used for non-hostile relations between belligerents during international armed conflict may also be applied by parties to a non-international armed conflict.[72]

As is the case during international armed conflict, parties to a non-international armed conflict may agree to specific means of communication between them.

17.4 A State's Use of Its Domestic Law and NIAC

17.4.1 Ability of a State to Use Its Domestic Law Against Non-State Armed Groups. A fundamental principle of the international legal order is the sovereign equality of States, which generally prohibits States from exercising sovereignty over one another.[73] However, the principle of the sovereign equality of States is not applicable in armed conflicts between a State and a non-State armed group. A State may exercise both sovereign and belligerent rights over non-State armed groups.[74] This means that a State may use not only its war powers to combat non-State armed groups, but it may also use its domestic law, including its ordinary criminal law, to combat non-State armed groups.

The limits imposed by international law on a State's action against non-State armed groups do not alter the basic principle that the State may exercise its sovereign powers against the non-State armed group.[75]

17.4.1.1 *A State's Power to Prosecute Hostile Activities*. An important consequence of the fact that States may exercise sovereignty over persons belonging to a non-State armed group is that a State may prosecute individuals for participating in hostilities against it. Such conduct frequently constitutes crimes under ordinary criminal law (*e.g.*, murder, assault, illegal destruction of property).

---

led to partial success. The parties agreed to the transfer and internment in a neutral country of Soviet soldiers detained by the Afghan opposition movements, in application, by analogy, of the Third Geneva Convention, relative to the treatment of prisoners of war. On the basis of this agreement, the ICRC has had access to some of the Soviet prisoners in the hands of the Afghan movements and has informed them, in the course of interviews without witness, of the possibility for transfer by the ICRC to Switzerland, where they would spend two years under the responsibility and watch of the Swiss government before returning to their country of origin. ... To date, eleven Soviet soldiers have accepted the proposal. The first three were transferred to Switzerland on 28 May 1982. Eight others arrived in August and October 1982, January and October 1983, and February and April 1984. One of them escaped to the Federal Republic of Germany in July 1983.").

[71] *Refer to* § 6.20.5 (Obligations Under the CCW Protocol V on Explosive Remnants of War That Are Triggered by the Cessation of Active Hostilities).

[72] *Refer to* § 12.3 (Methods for Communication Between Belligerents).

[73] *See* Jurisdictional Immunities of the State (Germany v. Italy: Greece intervening), Judgment, 2012 I.C.J. 99, 123 (¶57) ("The Court considers that the rule of State immunity occupies an important place in international law and international relations. It derives from the principle of sovereign equality of States, which, as Article 2, paragraph 1, of the Charter of the United Nations makes clear, is one of the fundamental principles of the international legal order.").

[74] The Prize Cases, 67 U.S. 635, 673 (1863) ("Now, it is a proposition never doubted, that the belligerent party who claims to be sovereign, may exercise both belligerent and sovereign rights, ...").

[75] CCW AMENDED art. 1(4) ("Nothing in this Convention or its annexed Protocols shall be invoked for the purpose of affecting the sovereignty of a State or the responsibility of the Government, by all legitimate means, to maintain or re-establish law and order in the State or to defend the national unity and territorial integrity of the State."). *Consider* AP II art. 3(1) ("Nothing in this Protocol shall be invoked for the purpose of affecting the sovereignty of a State or the responsibility of the government, by all legitimate means, to maintain or re-establish law and order in the State or to defend the national unity and territorial integrity of the State.").

Although, during international armed conflict, lawful combatants are afforded certain immunities from the enemy State's jurisdiction,[76] persons belonging to non-State armed groups lack any legal privilege or immunity from prosecution by a State that is engaged in hostilities against that group.

On the other hand, the non-State armed group lacks authority to prosecute members of the State armed forces. In addition, the non-State status of the armed group would not render inapplicable the privileges and immunities afforded lawful combatants and other State officials. Thus, for example, members of the armed forces of a State would continue to benefit from any privileges or immunities from the jurisdiction of foreign States that sought to exercise jurisdiction with respect to the actions of such State armed forces in a non-international armed conflict.[77]

17.4.1.2 Range of Activities Subject to Prosecution. A State may also use its domestic law to make punishable a wide range of activity that extend beyond the activities that constitute actual fighting against the State. For example, joining the non-State armed group, providing material support to the armed group, failing to report the treasonous activities of the armed group, and other conduct may be punishable under a State's domestic law.[78]

17.4.1.3 Other Sovereign Authorities. In addition to the power to criminalize certain conduct, a State may use its law and other regulatory powers in its effort to address the threat of non-State armed groups.

For example, the State could use its authority to tax, regulate, seize, or destroy property (*e.g.*, weapons, vehicles, food, and medical equipment) within its jurisdiction as part of its effort against the non-State armed group.[79] The use of these sovereign powers would be subject to domestic law restrictions, and might not depend on whether such action would be imperatively required by the necessities of war – the standard for the seizure of destruction of enemy property

[76] *Refer to* § 4.4.3 (Combatants - Legal Immunity From a Foreign State's Domestic Law).

[77] *For example*, Daniel Webster, *Letter to Mr. Fox*, Apr. 24, 1841, *reprinted in* THE DIPLOMATIC AND OFFICIAL PAPERS OF DANIEL WEBSTER, WHILE SECRETARY OF STATE 124 (1848) ("This doubt has occasioned the President some hesitation; but he inclines to take it for granted that the main purpose of the instruction was, to cause it to be signified to the government of the United States that the attack upon the steamboat 'Caroline' was an act of public force, done by the British colonial authorities [intended to address insurgents], and fully recognized by the queen's government at home; and that, consequently, no individual concerned in that transaction can, according to the just principles of the laws of nations, be held personally answerable in the ordinary courts of law as for a private offense; and that upon this avowal of her majesty's government, Alexander McLeod, now imprisoned on an indictment for murder alleged to have committed in that attack, ought to be released by such proceedings as are usual and are suitable to the case.").

[78] *For example*, 18 U.S.C. § 2339B(a)(1) ("Whoever knowingly provides material support or resources to a foreign terrorist organization, or attempts or conspires to do so, shall be fined under this title or imprisoned not more than 15 years, or both, and, if the death of any person results, shall be imprisoned for any term of years or for life. To violate this paragraph, a person must have knowledge that the organization is a designated terrorist organization (as defined in subsection (g)(6)), that the organization has engaged or engages in terrorist activity (as defined in section 212(a)(3)(B) of the Immigration and Nationality Act), or that the organization has engaged or engages in terrorism (as defined in section 140(d)(2) of the Foreign Relations Authorization Act, Fiscal Years 1988 and 1989)."); 18 U.S.C. § 2382 ("Whoever, owing allegiance to the United States and having knowledge of the commission of any treason against them, conceals and does not, as soon as may be, disclose and make known the same to the President or to some judge of the United States, or to the governor or to some judge or justice of a particular State, is guilty of misprision of treason and shall be fined under this title or imprisoned not more than seven years, or both.").

[79] *For example*, DEPARTMENT OF THE ARMY FIELD MANUAL 3-24.2, *Tactics in Counterinsurgency*, ¶3-170 (Apr. 2009) ("Resource control measures include control of select resources to include foodstuffs, medical supplies, and key equipment through: • Rationing or purchase permits • Registration of firearms. • Registration of automobiles and trucks. • Export and import restrictions.").

during international armed conflict.[80] In any event, however, it would not be permissible for the State to seek to starve civilians as a method of combat.[81]

17.4.2 Emergency Laws and Regulations. Many States have laws permitting the government to alter or suspend laws (such as a declaration of martial law, and the establishment of curfews and other controls on the movement of persons and traffic), to enact emergency regulations (such as the establishment of monetary or trade regulations, or the rationing of food, fuel, and other critical materials), and to take other steps to protect the public (such as the issuance of identification cards, the development of detention rules for members of non-State armed groups, and the establishment of special emergency courts).[82]

The full range of actions that a State may take under its domestic law during non-international armed conflict would depend on the content of that law, including applicable constitutional restrictions.[83]

17.4.3 Special Courts. As part of its emergency regulations, a State may establish special or emergency courts for cases involving unprivileged belligerents or other persons suspected of committing offenses related to the non-international armed conflict.

Such courts must be regularly constituted and afford all the judicial guarantees that are recognized as indispensable by civilized peoples.[84] Such courts may distinguish based on

---

[80] *Refer to* § 5.17.2 (Enemy Property – Military Necessity Standard).

[81] *Refer to* § 17.9.2 (Prohibition on Starvation of Civilians as a Method of Combat).

[82] *For example*, David Galula, *Pacification in Algeria, 1956-1958*, 21 (RAND Corporation, 2006) ("In the existing legal framework, proclamation of martial law was the only provision in case of disturbances endangering the security of the state. It would have entailed handing over all powers to the military authority and suspending private and public liberties. Government and Parliament considered this step too extreme. Hence they devised a new contingency, the so-called 'state of emergency,' which was declared for the first time for the Constantine area and for Kabylia in April 1955, and was extended to all Algeria in August 1955. Parliament voted a Special Powers Act (with the support of the Communists!), which gave the government a free hand for conducting its policy in Algeria by decree, notably in matters pertaining to economic development, economic and social reforms, territorial reorganization, public order, security of persons and property, and protection of the integrity of the territory. These special powers were vested in the existing government and would lapse with the end of its incumbency; the succeeding government would have to request an extension from the Parliament. The government in turn gave authority to the Minister-Resident (who by then had replaced the Governor General in Algiers) to regulate movements of persons and goods, assign places of residence, create forbidden zones, order searches, ban meetings, control the press, dissolve associations, collect reparations for willful damage and for aid given to the rebels, suspend or transfer civil servants, deprive elected representatives of their seats, postpone by-elections, and delegate certain civil powers to the military. Travel between France and Algeria was made subject to strict control (at least in theory)."); FRANK KITSON, GANGS AND COUNTER-GANGS 44 (1960) ("The legal code in Kenya in October 1952 was not very different from that in England. Certain acts such as theft or murder were illegal and if you committed them you were prosecuted. When the Emergency started some extra laws were made to fit the special circumstances. For example, it became illegal to administer the Mau Mau oath or to carry arms and certain areas of the forest were placed out of bounds. These extra laws, and there were many of them, were known as Emergency Regulations.").

[83] *For example*, FRANK KITSON, GANGS AND COUNTER-GANGS 289 (1960) ("No country which relies on the law of the land to regulate the lives of its citizens can afford to see that law flouted by its own government, even in an insurgency situation. In other words everything done by a government and its agents in combating insurgency must be legal. But this does not mean that the government must work within exactly the same set of laws during an insurgency as existed beforehand, because it is a function of a government when necessary. It does not mean that the law must be administered in exactly the same way during an uprising as it was in more peaceful times, because once again a government has the power to modify the way in which the law is administered if necessary, for the wellbeing of the people, although the exercise of such power is usually – and rightly – subject to considerable constitutional restraint.").

[84] *Refer to* § 8.16 (Criminal Procedure and Punishment).

nationality.[85] The procedures of such courts may deviate from those applicable during ordinary proceedings, but deviations should be warranted by practical need.[86]

17.4.4 Reintegration Programs and Amnesty. States have used reconciliation and reintegration programs during hostilities as alternatives to prosecution to seek to de-radicalize and rehabilitate violent extremists.[87]

Although amnesty is normally left to the discretion of the State, AP II provides that, at the end of hostilities, the authorities in power shall endeavor to grant the broadest possible amnesty to persons who have participated in the armed conflict, or those deprived of their liberty for reasons related to the armed conflict, whether they are interned or detained.[88]

17.5 PRINCIPLE OF DISTINCTION IN NIAC

As discussed below, the principle of distinction applies during non-international armed conflict. It may be important to note certain differences between the situations that typically arise in non-international armed conflict as compared to those typically arising in international armed conflict.

---

[85] *For example*, 10 U.S.C. § 948b ("(a) Purpose. –This chapter establishes procedures governing the use of military commissions to try alien unprivileged enemy belligerents for violations of the law of war and other offenses triable by military commission.") (emphasis added).

[86] *See* Hamdan v. Rumsfeld, 548 U.S. 557, 632-33 (2006) ("The Government offers only a cursory defense of Hamdan's military commission in light of Common Article 3. As Justice Kennedy explains, that defense fails because '[t]he regular military courts in our system are the courts-martial established by congressional statutes.' At a minimum, a military commission 'can be 'regularly constituted' by the standards of our military justice system only if some practical need explains deviations from court-martial practice.' As we have explained, no such need has been demonstrated here.") (internal citations omitted); *id.* at 645-46 (Kennedy, J., concurring) ("At a minimum a military commission like the one at issue--a commission specially convened by the President to try specific persons without express congressional authorization--can be 'regularly constituted' by the standards of our military justice system only if some practical need explains deviations from court-martial practice. … Relevant concerns, as noted earlier, relate to logistical constraints, accommodation of witnesses, security of the proceedings, and the like, not mere expedience or convenience. This determination, of course, must be made with due regard for the constitutional principle that congressional statutes can be controlling, including the congressional direction that the law of war has a bearing on the determination.").

[87] *For example*, Charles A. Allen, Deputy General Counsel, Department of Defense, *Alternatives to Prosecution for War Crimes in the War on Terrorism*, 17 TRANSNATIONAL LAW & CONTEMPORARY PROBLEMS 121, 131-34 (2008) ("In Pakistan, there is a reintegration program akin to the idea of 'it takes a village.' Village loyalties are paramount, and Pakistani leaders have found that returning a former combatant to his village and holding the village responsible for his conduct is a successful way to ensure that the person does not return to violence. Under this program, a village must agree to accept the return of the person and must pay the Government of Pakistan a 'retainer' equal to about $5000 that it forfeits if the individual returns to hostilities. … The Kingdom of Saudi Arabia uses a similar program, referred to as a 'counseling program,' to 'de-radicalize' and reintegrate former security prisoners back into society. … Prisoners who have not committed capital crimes or killings enter the program immediately after they are captured. Upon release, the former prisoners are then reconnected with their families and given psychological evaluation and counseling. After a few months of rehabilitation, they are brought into contact with moderate Islamic scholars and encouraged to enter into discussions about their beliefs. The moderate scholars are able to counter extremist views with the Koran and other authoritative texts to explain alternative interpretations that the former prisoner may not have heard before. Along with the counseling program, the Saudis try to convince the former combatants that they have a stake in a peaceful and stable government by encouraging them to marry, paying for their weddings and subsequent education for their children, and helping them to find suitable employment and housing.").

[88] *Consider* AP II art. 6(5) ("At the end of hostilities, the authorities in power shall endeavour to grant the broadest possible amnesty to persons who have participated in the armed conflict, or those deprived of their liberty for reasons related to the armed conflict, whether they are interned or detained.").

17.5.1 Discrimination in Conducting Attacks Against the Enemy in NIAC. Parties to a conflict must conduct attacks in accordance with the principle of distinction.[89]

As during international armed conflict, an adversary's failure to distinguish its forces from the civilian population does not relieve the attacking party of its obligations to discriminate in conducting attacks.[90] On the other hand – also as during international armed conflict – such conduct by the adversary does not increase the legal obligations on the attacking party to discriminate in conducting attacks against the enemy. For example, even though tactics used by non-State armed groups may make discriminating more difficult, State armed forces – though obligated to be discriminate – are not required to take additional protective measures to compensate for such tactics.

17.5.1.1 *Increased Difficulty in Identifying Enemy Forces and Other Military Objectives*. During international armed conflict, State armed forces generally are readily distinguishable from the civilian population. Traditionally, conventional armed forces would often confront one another, with the civilian population of each opposing State remaining to the rear of the lines separating their respective military forces.[91] During non-international armed conflict, however, discriminating in conducting attacks against the enemy may be more difficult because non-State armed groups often seek to blend in with the civilian population.[92]

17.5.1.2 *Different Support Structures for Non-State Armed Groups*. In addition to non-State armed groups, other military objectives may also be more difficult to identify because non-State armed groups often do not use military infrastructure (*e.g.*, military bases, logistics facilities) to conduct and sustain their operations. Rather, non-State armed groups may seek to use ostensibly civilian buildings and resources to conduct and sustain their operations. Denying non-State armed groups such support may be particularly important to the success of military operations and justifiable under the law of war.[93]

---

[89] *Refer to* § 17.7 (Rules on Conducting Attacks in NIAC).

[90] *Refer to* § 5.4.4 (Failure by the Defender to Separate or Distinguish Does Not Relieve the Attacker of the Duty to Discriminate in Conducting Attacks).

[91] *For example*, SYLVIE-STOYANKA JUNOD, INTERNATIONAL COMMITTEE OF THE RED CROSS, PROTECTION OF THE VICTIMS OF ARMED CONFLICT FALKLAND-MALVINAS ISLANDS: INTERNATIONAL HUMANITARIAN LAW AND HUMANITARIAN ACTION (1982) 26 (1984) ("The Falkland-Malvinas Islands' conflict provides a rare example of hostilities conducted by both sides with particular concern for the safety of the civilian population, as there were three civilian casualties. The instructions received both by the Argentine armed forces when disembarking on the island of South Georgia and on the archipelago, and by the British pilots and soldiers emanated from the desire to respect the civilian population. However, mention must also be made of the precautionary measures which were taken by the Parties to the civilian population in accordance with Part II of the Fourth Convention.").

[92] *For example*, Harold Hongju Koh, Legal Adviser, Department of State, *Address at the Annual Meeting of the American Society of International Law: The Obama Administration and International Law*, Mar. 25, 2010, 2010 DIGEST OF UNITED STATES PRACTICE IN INTERNATIONAL LAW 717 ("As recent events have shown, al-Qaeda has not abandoned its intent to attack the United States, and indeed continues to attack us. ... As you know, this is a conflict with an organized terrorist enemy that does not have conventional forces, but that plans and executes its attacks against us and our allies while hiding among civilian populations. That behavior simultaneously makes the application of international law more difficult and more critical for the protection of innocent civilians.").

[93] Christopher Paul, Colin P. Clarke, and Beth Grill, *Victory Has a Thousand Fathers: Sources of Success in Counterinsurgency*, 98 (RAND Corporation, 2010) ("The ability of insurgents to replenish and obtain personnel,

17.5.1.3 *Increased Strategic Importance of Minimizing Incidental Civilian Casualties*. For various reasons, there may be an increased emphasis by State armed forces on minimizing the risk of incidental civilian casualties, even beyond the requirements of the law of war.

The sympathy and support of the civilian population are frequently important objectives in non-international armed conflict.[94] In order to ensure such support, commanders and their forces may operate under rules of engagement that are more restrictive than what the law of war requires.[95]

17.5.2 Distinguishing State Forces From the Civilian Population in NIAC. During non-international armed conflict, as during international armed conflict, the principle of distinction prohibits the use of protected persons or objects to shield, favor, or impede military operations.[96] However, it may be important to consider certain differences in the circumstances arising in non-

---

materiel, financing, intelligence, and sanctuary (tangible support) perfectly predicts success or failure in the 30 COIN cases considered here. In all eight cases in which the COIN force prevailed, it also disrupted at least three insurgent support factors, while none of the COIN forces in the 22 losing cases managed to disrupt more than two."); Robert Wayne Gehring, *Protection of Civilian Infrastructures*, 42 LAW AND CONTEMPORARY PROBLEMS 86, 95 (1978) ("The importance of those who collect funds for the insurgent organization's operations, gather and analyze information about government forces, procure the necessary supplies from within or without the country, organize the delivery of the supplies to the military forces of the insurgency, and organize the recruitment of members of the local population cannot be overestimated. While these functions may be performed by military members of the movement, in many cases military training is not required or is not even an asset in their performance. One experienced observer, Sir Robert Thompson, believes that so long as the supporting organization remains intact, killing insurgents in the field is largely useless: the casualties will be replaced by new recruits. A study of characteristics that determined the outcome in forty-four revolutions of this century found the single most important factor was not battlefield success but whether the government was successful in interdicting the insurgents' supply of arms and ammunition. The government cannot rely upon success on the field of battle to bring its ultimate victory. It must starve the insurgent military forces by uncovering and neutralizing the civilian infrastructure supporting those military forces.").

[94] FRANK KITSON, BUNCH OF FIVE 59, 282, 289 (1977) ("The first aim of a government in an Emergency is to retain or regain the allegiance of the population. [...] There has never been much doubt that the main characteristic which distinguishes campaigns of insurgency from other forms of war is that they are primarily concerned with the struggle for men's minds, since only by succeeding in such a struggle with a large enough number of people can the rule of law be undermined and constitutional institutions overthrown.").

[95] *For example*, General Petraeus, *Unclassified Excerpts from Tactical Directive*, Aug. 1, 2010, *reprinted in* International Security Assistance Force – Afghanistan, Headquarters, *General Petraeus Issues Updated Tactical Directive: Emphasizes "Disciplined Use of Force,"* Aug. 4, 2010 ("We must continue – indeed, redouble – our efforts to reduce the loss of innocent civilian life to an absolute minimum. Every Afghan civilian death diminishes our cause. If we use excessive force or operate contrary to our counterinsurgency principles, tactical victories may prove to be strategic setbacks. We must never forget that the center of gravity in this struggle is the Afghan people; it is they who will ultimately determine the future of Afghanistan ... Prior to the use of fires, the commander approving the strike must determine that no civilians are present. If unable to assess the risk of civilian presence, fires are prohibited, except under of the following two conditions (specific conditions deleted due to operational security; however, they have to do with the risk to ISAF and Afghan forces). (NOTE) This directive, as with the previous version, does not prevent commanders from protecting the lives of their men and women as a matter of self-defense where it is determined no other options are available to effectively counter the threat.).") (ellipsis in original).

[96] *Refer to* § 17.6.3 (Prohibition on Using Protected Persons and Objects to Shield, Favor, or Impede Military Operations).

international armed conflict.

17.5.2.1 *Positioning Military Forces Near the Civilian Population to Win Their Support and to Protect Them*. During non-international armed conflict, insurgents or terrorists may seek to attack the civilian population, and the use of the State's forces to protect the civilian population from such attacks may be a key objective of State operations in non-international armed conflict.[97] Thus, positioning military forces near the civilian population may be essential to the protection of the civilian population, and States have not interpreted such practices to be inconsistent with the principle of distinction.[98]

17.5.2.2 *Role of Civilian Personnel, Including Law Enforcement Personnel, in Addressing Non-State Armed Groups*. Members of States' civilian agencies, such as judges, prosecutors, and police and other members of its law enforcement apparatus, often play a critical role in addressing non-State armed groups.[99] Although such personnel might be viewed by the adversary as "military objectives" or as taking a direct part in hostilities, States have not interpreted the principle of distinction to require the separation of such personnel from the civilian population in non-international armed conflict.

17.6 Respect and Humane Treatment of Persons Taking No Active Part in Hostilities in NIAC

All persons who do not take a direct part or who have ceased to take part in hostilities, whether or not their liberty has been restricted, are entitled to respect for their person, honor and convictions, and religious practices. They shall in all circumstances be treated humanely,

---

[97] *For example*, General David Petraeus, *Multi-National Force – Iraq Counterinsurgency Guidance*, 1 (Jun. 13, 2007) ("**1. Secure the people where they sleep.** Population security is our primary mission. And achieving population security promises to be an extremely long-term endeavor – a marathon, not a sprint – so focusing on this mission now is essential. Most extra-judicial killings occur at night and in people's homes, while most spectacular terrorist attacks occur during the day, where people shop, work and play – anywhere they gather publicly. These key areas must be secured. Once secured, an area cannot be abandoned; it must be permanently controlled and protected, 24 hours a day, or else the enemy will re-infiltrate and kill or intimidate those who have supported us. This protection must be kept up until the area can be effectively garrisoned and controlled by Iraqi police (ideally from the area being secured) and other security services. *We can't be everywhere – therefore you must assess your AOR, identify priority areas, work to secure them first, and then expand into other areas.*").

[98] *For example*, General David Petraeus, International Security Assistance Force/United States Forces-Afghanistan Headquarters, *COMISAF's Counterinsurgency Guidance*, 1 (Aug. 1, 2010) ("**Live among the people.** We can't commute to the fight. Position joint bases and combat outposts as close to those we're seeking to secure as is feasible. Decide on locations with input from our partners and after consultation with local citizens and informed by intelligence and security assessments.").

[99] *For example*, A.H. Peterson, G.C. Reinhardt and E.E. Conger, *Symposium on the Role of Airpower in Counterinsurgency and Unconventional Warfare: The Malayan Emergency*, 13 (RAND Corporation, Jul. 1963) ("COMMODORE GARRISSON: This Malayan campaign was run basically as a civilian operation by the civilian power. The first line of defense was the civilian Police, who received more equipment than the normal police. Any military operation had to be cleared with the civilian authority, who in effect called for military operations of a specific nature. I think this is the first thing to bear in mind. Police provided protection of the local population wherever possible. The true military forces went out to try to get the bandits.").

without any adverse distinction.[100]

In addition, the following prohibitions apply:

17.6.1 Prohibition on Declaring That No Quarter Be Given. It is prohibited to order that there shall be no survivors.[101]

17.6.2 Prohibition on the Taking of Hostages. The taking of hostages is prohibited.[102]

17.6.3 Prohibition on Using Protected Persons and Objects to Shield, Favor, or Impede Military Operations. It is prohibited to use civilians, persons placed *hors de combat*, or other protected persons to shield, favor, or impede military operations.[103]

17.6.4 Prohibition on Pillage. Pillage is prohibited.[104] There is an affirmative obligation to take measures to protect the wounded, sick, and shipwrecked from pillage, and the dead from being despoiled.[105]

17.6.5 Prohibition on Acts of Terrorism. It is prohibited to commit, or threaten to commit, acts of terrorism against persons who do not take a direct part or who have ceased to take part in hostilities.[106]

17.6.6 Prohibition on Offering of Rewards for Persons Dead or Alive. As during international armed conflict, it is prohibited to offer a reward for enemy persons to be turned over dead or alive.[107] On the other hand, as in international armed conflict, there is no prohibition against offering rewards for the apprehension of insurgents or for giving information

---

[100] *Consider* AP II art. 4(1) ("All persons who do not take a direct part or who have ceased to take part in hostilities, whether or not their liberty has been restricted, are entitled to respect for their person, honour and convictions and religious practices. They shall in all circumstances be treated humanely, without any adverse distinction.").

[101] *Consider* AP II art. 4(1) ("It is prohibited to order that there shall be no survivors."). *Refer to* § 5.4.7 (Prohibition Against Declaring That No Quarter Be Given).

[102] *See* GWS art. 3 (prohibiting "taking of hostages;"); GWS-SEA art. 3 (same); GPW art. 3 (same); GC art. 3 (same). *Consider* AP II art. 2 (prohibiting "taking of hostages;"). *Refer to* § 5.16.3 (Prohibition on Taking Hostages).

[103] *Refer to* § 5.16 (Prohibition on Using Protected Persons and Objects to Shield, Favor, or Impede Military Operations).

[104] *Consider* AP II art. 4(2)(g) (prohibiting pillage "at any time and in any place whatsoever" against "[a]ll persons who do not take a direct part or who have ceased to take part in hostilities, whether or not their liberty has been restricted"). *Refer to* § 5.17.4 (Pillage Prohibited).

[105] *Refer to* § 17.14.3 (Search, Collection, and Protection of the Wounded, Sick, Shipwrecked, and Dead).

[106] *Consider* AP II art. 4(2) (prohibiting with respect to all persons who do not take a direct part or who have ceased to take part in hostilities, whether or not their liberty has been restricted, "d) acts of terrorism" and "h) threats to commit any of the foregoing acts"). *Refer to* § 10.5.3.2 (Collective Penalties and Measures of Intimidation or Terrorism).

[107] *Refer to* § 5.26.3.1 (Prohibition on Offering Rewards for Enemy Persons Dead or Alive).

leading to the apprehension or killing of insurgents in combat.[108]

17.6.7 Prohibition on Collective Punishment. Collective punishments, whether administered by a court or through administrative measures, are prohibited.[109] Collective penalties are prohibited as a general matter.[110]

17.7 Rules on Conducting Attacks in NIAC

Parties to a conflict must conduct attacks in accordance with the principles of distinction and proportionality. In particular, the following rules must be observed:

- Combatants may not direct attacks against civilians, civilian objects, or other protected persons and objects.[111]
- The distinctive emblem must not be used while engaging in attacks.[112]
- Combatants must refrain from attacks in which the expected loss of life or injury to civilians, and damage to civilian objects incidental to the attack, would be excessive in relation to the concrete and direct military advantage expected to be gained.[113]
- Combatants must take feasible precautions in planning and conducting attacks to avoid incidental harm to civilians and civilian objects.[114]
- In conducting attacks, combatants must assess in good faith the information that is

---

[108] *See* 1958 UK Manual ¶116 note 1(b) ("If a government or military commander offers rewards for all or individual armed insurgents killed or wounded by the forces engaged in quelling the insurrection, such offers are open to the same objection as those set out above in respect of hostilities between belligerents, and are probable unlawful. On the other hand, there is no objection to offering rewards for the apprehension of insurgents or for giving information leading to the apprehension or killing of insurgents in combat. A State is entitled to secure the capture of armed rebels in order that they may be tried as such, or to kill or wound them in combat. However, the probable effect of the common Art. 3, when applicable, is to prohibit inducements being given to troops, police or civilians, to take the law into their own hands.").

[109] *Consider* AP II art. 4(2) ("Without prejudice to the generality of the foregoing, the following acts against the persons referred to in paragraph 1 [*i.e.*, all persons who do not take a direct part or who have ceased to take part in hostilities, whether or not their liberty has been restricted,] are and shall remain prohibited at any time and in any place whatsoever: … b) collective punishments;"); Bothe, Partsch, & Solf, New Rules 642 (AP II art. 4, ¶2.5) ("Paragraph 2 (b) prohibits 'collective punishments'. The Committee had proposed 'collective penalties'. The change of this wording was accepted in order to include not only penalties imposed by a court but also penalties imposed by administrative measures.").

[110] *Refer to* § 8.16.2.1 (Individual Penal Responsibility and No Collective Punishment).

[111] *Refer to* § 5.5 (Discrimination in Conducting Attacks).

[112] *Refer to* § 17.16.2 (Improper Use of the Distinctive Emblem).

[113] *Refer to* § 5.12 (Proportionality – Prohibition on Attacks Expected to Cause Excessive Incidental Harm).

[114] *Refer to* § 5.11 (Proportionality – Feasible Precautions in Planning and Conducting Attacks to Reduce the Risk of Harm to Protected Persons and Objects).

available to them.[115]

- Specific rules apply to the use of certain types of weapons.[116]

These rules apply to all parties to a non-international armed conflict, including persons belonging to non-State armed groups, and persons who decide to participate in hostilities of their own initiative. However, persons who belong to non-State armed groups, or who decide to participate in hostilities of their own initiative, may also be subject to the State's domestic law.[117]

17.7.1 AP II Rule on Works and Installations Containing Dangerous Forces. AP II provides that works or installations containing dangerous forces, namely dams, dykes, and nuclear electrical generating stations, shall not be made the object of attack, even where these objects are military objectives, if such attack may cause the release of dangerous forces and consequent severe losses among the civilian population.[118] The United States has objected to this rule in the context of international armed conflict and does not view it as reflecting customary international law in either international or non-international armed conflict insofar as the rule deviates from the regular application of the principles of distinction and proportionality.[119]

However, the Executive, in submitting AP II to the Senate for its advice and consent to ratification in 1987, did not recommend a reservation from or an understanding applicable to this provision of AP II based on an assessment that preserving the option to attack works or installations containing dangerous forces would not be as important in internal conflicts as preserving that option would be in international armed conflicts.[120]

---

[115] *Refer to* § 5.3 (Assessing Information Under the Law of War).

[116] *Refer to* § 17.13.2 (Certain Types of Weapons With Specific Rules on Use in NIAC).

[117] *Refer to* § 17.4 (A State's Use of Its Domestic Law and NIAC).

[118] *Consider* AP II art. 15 ("Works or installations containing dangerous forces, namely dams, dykes and nuclear electrical generating stations, shall not be made the object of attack, even where these objects are military objectives, if such attack may cause the release of dangerous forces and consequent severe losses among the civilian population.").

[119] *Refer to* § 5.13.1 (AP I Provisions on Works and Installations Containing Dangerous Forces).

[120] Michael J. Matheson, Deputy Legal Adviser, Department of State, *Remarks on the United States Position on the Relation of Customary International Law to the 1977 Protocols Additional to the 1949 Geneva Conventions at the Sixth Annual American Red Cross-Washington College of Law Conference on International Humanitarian Law* (Jan. 22, 1987), 2 AMERICAN UNIVERSITY JOURNAL OF INTERNATIONAL LAW AND POLICY 419, 434 (1987) ("Professor HAMILTON DESAUSSURE asked for an explanation of the apparent inconsistency between the United States rejection of the provisions in article 56 of Protocol I, relating to dams and dykes, and the simultaneous acceptance of article 15 of Protocol II, which contains similar provisions. Mr. MATHESON replied that the United States military based its objections on a pragmatic, real-world estimation of the difference between the two situations. The military perceives that in international conflicts, many situations may arise where it is important to attack and destroy parts of an electric power grid, such as a nuclear or hydroelectric generating station. In internal conflicts, on the other hand, such a significant real-world need will not exist. Preserving the military option in international conflicts where such facilities are more likely to become an object of military attack, therefore, is very important.").

17.8 Impartial Humanitarian Organizations and Humanitarian Activities During NIAC

An impartial humanitarian body, such as the International Committee of the Red Cross, may offer its services to the parties to the conflict.[121] The civilian population may, even on its own initiative, offer to collect and care for the wounded, sick, and shipwrecked.[122] Similarly, the United Nations Educational, Scientific and Cultural Organization may offer its services to the parties to the conflict.[123]

17.8.1 State Consent for Humanitarian Organizations. The activities of relief organizations are subject to the consent of the State concerned.[124]

States may withhold consent for, *inter alia*, legitimate military reasons, but should not arbitrarily withhold consent.[125] The safety of personnel of humanitarian organizations is a legitimate consideration for a government in consenting to their operations. Where a State has accepted the services of an impartial humanitarian organization, the State must not regard such service, such as the provision of medical care, as unlawful and subject to punishment.[126]

17.9 Protection of the Civilian Population in NIAC

17.9.1 Displacement of the Civilian Population. The displacement of the civilian population shall not be ordered for reasons related to the conflict unless the security of the

---

[121] GWS art. 3 ("An impartial humanitarian body, such as the International Committee of the Red Cross, may offer its services to the Parties to the conflict"); GWS-Sea art. 3 (same); GPW art. 3 (same); GC art. 3 (same). *Consider* AP II art. 18 ("Relief societies located in the territory of the High Contracting Party, such as Red Cross (Red Crescent, Red Lion and Sun) organizations, may offer their services for the performance of their traditional functions in relation to the victims of the armed conflict.").

[122] *Consider* AP II art. 18(1) ("The civilian population may, even on its own initiative, offer to collect and care for the wounded, sick and shipwrecked.").

[123] 1954 Hague Cultural Property Convention art. 19(3) ("The United Nations Educational, Scientific and Cultural Organization may offer its services to the parties to the conflict.").

[124] *Consider* AP II art. 18(2) ("If the civilian population is suffering undue hardship owing to a lack of the supplies essential for its survival, such as foodstuffs and medical supplies, relief actions for the civilian population which are of an exclusively humanitarian and impartial nature and which are conducted without any adverse distinction shall be undertaken subject to the consent of the High Contracting Party concerned.").

[125] *Detailed Analysis of Provisions*, Attachment 1 to George P. Shultz, *Letter of Submittal*, Dec. 13, 1986, Message from the President Transmitting AP II 6 ("For its part, the United States would expect that the requirement of consent [in article 18 of AP II] by the party concerned would not be implemented in an arbitrary manner, and that essential relief shipments would only be restricted or denied for the most compelling and legitimate reasons.").

[126] Principles Related to the Protection of Medical Care Provided by Impartial Humanitarian Organizations During Armed Conflict, ¶VI, attachment to Ash Carter, Secretary of Defense, *Memorandum re: Principles Related to the Protection of Medical Care Provided by Impartial Humanitarian Organizations During Armed Conflict*, Oct. 3, 2016 ("VI. Impartial humanitarian organizations may offer their services to any of the parties to the conflict. A. States should not arbitrarily withhold their consent to the activities of humanitarian organizations. B. Where a State has accepted the services of an impartial humanitarian organization, it must not regard such services, including the provision of medical care, as unlawful and subject to punishment.").

civilians involved or imperative military reasons so demand.[127] Should such displacements have to be carried out, all possible measures shall be taken in order that the civilian population may be received under satisfactory conditions of shelter, hygiene, health, safety, and nutrition.[128]

Civilians shall not be compelled to leave their own territory for reasons connected with the conflict.[129] A State must not compel civilians to leave its territory for reasons connected to the conflict, while insurgents that control territory must not compel civilians to leave the area under their authority.[130]

17.9.1.1 *Security of the Civilians Involved or Imperative Military Reasons*. Legitimate reasons to order the movement of the civilian population may include, for example:

- affording the civilian population greater protection from insurgents; and
- reducing the support provided to insurgents from elements of the civilian population.[131]

Legitimate reasons to order the movement of civilians do not include the use of individuals or groups of civilians around military objectives as involuntary human shields.[132]

17.9.2 Prohibition on Starvation of Civilians as a Method of Combat. Starvation of civilians as a method of combat is prohibited. It is therefore prohibited to attack, destroy, remove, or render useless, for that purpose, objects indispensable to the survival of the civilian population, such as foodstuffs, agricultural areas for the production of foodstuffs, crops,

---

[127] *Consider* AP II art. 17(1) ("The displacement of the civilian population shall not be ordered for reasons related to the conflict unless the security of the civilians involved or imperative military reasons so demand.").

[128] *Consider* AP II art. 17(1) ("Should such displacements have to be carried out, all possible measures shall be taken in order that the civilian population may be received under satisfactory conditions of shelter, hygiene, health, safety and nutrition.").

[129] *Consider* AP II art. 17(2) ("Civilians shall not be compelled to leave their own territory for reasons connected with the conflict.").

[130] *Cf.* ICRC AP COMMENTARY 1475 (¶4859) ("First, there is a question whether, within the meaning of this provision [in article 17 of AP II], the term 'territory' is equivalent to country. The ICRC draft referred to 'national territory'. Some amendments proposed substituting the formula 'across the frontiers of the country of origin'. It is clear that there was never any doubt in anyone's mind that the phrase was intended to refer to the whole of the territory of a country. However, the text states that it is prohibited to compel civilians to leave 'their own territory'. In fact, this formula appears to be better suited to all the possible cases which might arise in a situation covered by Protocol II, and to take into account, in particular, situations where the insurgent party is in control of an extensive part of the territory. In this case the insurgents, too, should respect the obligation laid down here, and not compel civilians to leave the area under their authority.").

[131] *For example*, Lt. Col. Jerome F. Bierly and Timothy W. Pleasant, *Malaya—A Case Study*, MARINE CORPS GAZETTE 46, 48 (Jul. 1990) ("The Briggs Plan called for the movement of the general population into protected areas. In all, a total of 410 villages were eventually moved into areas fortified against guerrilla attacks. This served two purposes: It helped to protect the populace from the attacks, and at the same time it cut off the majority of the food supply to the guerillas. Also, the Chinese population, from which the guerillas drew most of their support, was provided a situation in which they could participate in the local government and establish a degree of economic prosperity they had not previously enjoyed.").

[132] *Refer to* § 5.16 (Prohibition on Using Protected Persons and Objects to Shield, Favor, or Impede Military Operations).

livestock, drinking water installations and supplies, and irrigation works.[133]

17.9.2.1 *Starvation of Enemy Forces Not Prohibited*. It is only actions that are for the purpose of starving civilians as a method of combat that are prohibited under this rule; measures to starve enemy forces are not prohibited.[134] For example, States may institute general food control programs that involve the destruction of crops and the adequate provision of the civilian population with food.[135]

Military action intended to starve enemy forces, however, must not be taken where it is expected to result in incidental harm to the civilian population that is excessive in relation to the military advantage anticipated to be gained.[136]

Feasible precautions to reduce the risk of harm to the civilian population or other reasonable measures to mitigate the burden to the civilian population may also be warranted when seeking to starve enemy forces.[137]

17.10 PROTECTION OF CHILDREN IN NIAC

17.10.1 General Protection and Care of Children. Children shall be provided with the care and aid they require.[138]

Children shall receive an education, including religious and moral education, in keeping with the wishes of their parents, or in the absence of parents, of those responsible for their care.[139]

All appropriate steps shall be taken to facilitate the reunion of families temporarily

---

[133] *Consider* AP II art. 14 ("Starvation of civilians as a method of combat is prohibited. It is therefore prohibited to attack, destroy, remove or render useless, for that purpose, objects indispensable to the survival of the civilian population, such as food stuffs, agricultural areas for the production of foodstuffs, crops, livestock, drinking water installations and supplies and irrigation works.").

[134] *Refer to* § 5.20.1 (Starvation – Distinction).

[135] *For example*, R.W. Komer, *The Malayan Emergency in Retrospect: Organization of A Successful Counterinsurgency Effort*, 59 (RAND Corporation, Feb. 1972) ("In order to force the insurgents to make supply their major concern, the GOM turned to sizable food denial campaigns as the preferred form of security force operations. By July 1953 no less than 77 such operations had been mounted in the state of Negri Sembilan alone. … It did not take much 'seepage' to feed a guerrilla who could subsist on a daily ration of a handful of rice. But he could store without detection only about six to eight weeks' supply, and the number of people, time, and effort involved in a 'food lift' from village to jungle edge to deep jungle was such as to make the lift vulnerable to discovery.").

[136] *Refer to* § 5.20.2 (Starvation – Proportionality).

[137] *Refer to* § 5.20.2 (Starvation – Proportionality).

[138] *Consider* AP II art. 4(3) ("Children shall be provided with the care and aid they require, … .").

[139] *Consider* AP II art. 4(3)(a) ("they shall receive an education, including religious and moral education, in keeping with the wishes of their parents, or in the absence of parents, of those responsible for their care;").

separated.[140]

Measures shall be taken, if necessary, and whenever possible with the consent of their parents or persons who by law or custom are primarily responsible for their care, to remove children temporarily from the area in which hostilities are taking place to a safer area within the country and ensure that they are accompanied by persons responsible for their safety and well-being.[141]

The death penalty shall not be pronounced on persons who were under the age of eighteen years at the time of the offense and shall not be carried out on pregnant women or mothers of young children.[142]

17.10.2 Children and Participation in Non-International Armed Conflict. Children who have not attained the age of fifteen years shall neither be recruited in the armed forces or groups nor allowed to take part in hostilities.[143] Children who are captured and who have taken a direct part in hostilities remain entitled to the special protections afforded to children.[144]

The use or recruitment of child soldiers is an offense in U.S. law.[145] The United States has additional obligations as a Party to the Child Soldiers Protocol.[146]

17.11 PROTECTION OF CULTURAL PROPERTY IN NIAC

17.11.1 Application of Certain Provisions of the 1954 Hague Cultural Property Convention. In the event of an armed conflict not of an international character occurring within the territory of one of the Parties to the 1954 Hague Cultural Property Convention, each party to the conflict shall be bound to apply, as a minimum, the provisions of the 1954 Hague Cultural Property Convention that relate to respect for cultural property.[147]

---

[140] *Consider* AP II art. 4(3)(b) ("all appropriate steps shall be taken to facilitate the reunion of families temporarily separated;").

[141] *Consider* AP II art. 4(3)(e) ("[M]easures shall be taken, if necessary, and whenever possible with the consent of their parents or persons who by law or custom are primarily responsible for their care, to remove children temporarily from the area in which hostilities are taking place to a safer area within the country and ensure that they are accompanied by persons responsible for their safety and well-being.").

[142] *Refer to* § 8.16.2.4 (Limitations on the Death Penalty).

[143] *Consider* AP II art. 4(3)(c) ("[C]hildren who have not attained the age of fifteen years shall neither be recruited in the armed forces or groups nor allowed to take part in hostilities;"); ROME STATUTE art. 8(2)(e)(vii) (defining "war crime" to include "[c]onscripting or enlisting children under the age of fifteen years into armed forces or groups or using them to participate actively in hostilities" in non-international armed conflict).

[144] *Consider* AP II art. 4(3)(d) ("the special protection provided by this Article to children who have not attained the age of fifteen years shall remain applicable to them if they take a direct part in hostilities despite the provisions of sub-paragraph c) and are captured;").

[145] *Refer to* § 4.20.5.1 (U.S. Offense of Recruiting or Using Child Soldiers).

[146] *Refer to* § 4.20.5 (Child Soldiers); § 17.2.1.2 (Implicit Application of Treaty Provisions to Situations in NIAC).

[147] 1954 HAGUE CULTURAL PROPERTY CONVENTION art. 19(1) ("In the event of an armed conflict not of an international character occurring within the territory of one of the High Contracting Parties, each party to the

17.11.2 Obligations to Respect Cultural Property. The obligation to respect cultural property includes essentially negative duties, *i.e.*, duties to refrain from acts of hostility directed against cultural property and duties to refrain from the use of cultural property in support of military operations where such use is not imperatively necessary.[148]

For example, parties to a conflict must not direct acts of hostility against cultural property, its immediate surroundings, or appliances in use for its protection, unless such action is required by imperative military necessity.[149]

In addition, no use should be made of cultural property, its immediate surroundings, or appliances in use for its protection, for purposes that are likely to expose it to destruction or damage in the event of armed conflict, unless such action is required by imperative military necessity.[150]

17.12 Use of Captured or Surrendered Enemy Personnel in NIAC

In contrast to the rules during international armed conflict, State forces may use captured or surrendered enemy personnel in operations against enemy non-State armed groups. The cooperation of enemy personnel may not, however, be procured through illegal methods.

17.12.1 Compelling Captured or Surrendered Enemy Personnel to Take Part in the Conflict. During international armed conflict, it is prohibited to compel the nationals of the hostile party to take part in the operations of war directed against their own country.[151] Additional restrictions apply with respect to POWs, retained personnel, protected persons in the home territory of a belligerent, and protected persons in occupied territory.[152]

These rules, however, do not apply during non-international armed conflict. Under international law, a State may compel its nationals to serve in its armed forces and to fight against non-State armed groups.[153] For example, in contrast to POWs, captured insurgents who are nationals of that State could be required to serve in that State's armed forces or to take part in

---

conflict shall be bound to apply, as a minimum, the provisions of the present Convention which relate to respect for cultural property.").

[148] *Refer to* § 5.18.2 (Respect and Safeguarding of Cultural Property). *Consider* AP II art. 16 ("Without prejudice to the provisions of the Hague Convention for the Protection of Cultural Property in the Event of Armed Conflict of 14 May 1954, it is prohibited to commit any acts of hostility directed against historic monuments, works of art or places of worship which constitute the cultural or spiritual heritage of peoples, and to use them in support of the military effort.").

[149] *Refer to* § 5.18.5 (Refraining From Any Act of Hostility).

[150] *Refer to* § 5.18.3 (Refraining From Any Use for Purposes That Are Likely to Expose It to Destruction or Damage).

[151] *Refer to* § 5.27 (Prohibition Against Compelling Enemy Nationals to Take Part in the Operations of War Directed Against Their Own Country).

[152] *Refer to* § 9.19.2.3 (Labor Assignments That May Be Compelled); § 7.9.5.6 (No Other Compulsory Duties); § 10.7.3 (Compulsory Work for Protected Persons in a Belligerent's Home Territory); § 11.20.1.1 (Prohibition on Compulsory Service in an Occupying Power's Armed Forces).

[153] *Refer to* § 4.5.2.4 (Draftees).

operations directed against their former comrades.[154]

17.12.2 Methods of Gaining Cooperation. Inhumane treatment or other illegal methods (such as threats to commit unlawful acts) may not be used to gain the cooperation of captured enemy persons.[155]

However, a combination of threats of criminal punishment and inducements (*e.g.*, amnesty, monetary rewards) may be used to seek to gain the cooperation of captured enemy persons.[156] For example, law enforcement authorities often use the cooperation of members of criminal gangs or conspiracies to thwart and to prosecute the other participants or leaders in that criminal enterprise.[157]

17.13 WEAPONS IN NIAC

17.13.1 Prohibited Weapons in NIAC. The use of the following types of weapons is

---

[154] *For example*, Donald A. MacCuish and Spencer C. Tucker, *Pseudoforces*, *in* ENCYCLOPEDIA OF INSURGENCY AND COUNTERINSURGENCY: A NEW ERA OF MODERN WARFARE 452 (2013) ("Pseudoforces are military units made up of former insurgents who have been turned to work with counterinsurgency forces against their former colleagues. This is possible because insurgent rank and filers are generally not as committed as their ideologically bound leaders. Pseudoforces are a tremendous advantage in counterinsurgency operations. They can identify certain of the insurgents, are well familiar with the operational terrain and the villagers, and understand what motivates the insurgents and their supporters. They are of immense importance. Pseudoforces have played a role in virtually every insurgency since World War II (1939-1945). ... During the Dhofar campaigns in Oman (1970-1975), the British made extensive use of pseudoforces, employing some 1,600 in 21 different units based on tribal affiliations. The Portuguese also made extensive use of pseudoforces during the insurgencies in their African territories. Notable among these were the Flechas ('Arrows') in Angola."); MAJOR LAWRENCE M. GREENBERG, THE HUKBALAHAP INSURRECTION: A CASE STUDY OF A SUCCESSFUL ANTI-INSURGENCY OPERATION IN THE PHILIPPINES – 1946-1955 125 (1986) ("On the island of Panay, the Philippine Army tried a variation of the 'Force X' concept to break the local guerrilla structure. Accompanied by three military intelligence agents, a group of twenty former Huks were infiltrated into the island's interior. After three months of gathering information, establishing their cover as a bona fide Huk unit, and gaining the confidence of the island's Huk leadership, they hosted a 'by invitation only' barbecue for the Panay High Command. Between the ribs and potato salad, the covert government force sprang an ambush that killed or captured nearly all the Panay commanders and crippled the organization on the island for the duration of the campaign.").

[155] *Refer to* § 8.2 (Humane Treatment of Detainees); § 8.2.4 (Threats to Commit Inhumane Treatment).

[156] *For example*, DEPARTMENT OF THE ARMY FIELD MANUAL 3-24, *Counterinsurgency*, 1-19 (¶1-104) (Dec. 2006) ("Nothing is more demoralizing to insurgents than realizing that people inside their movement or trusted supporters among the public are deserting or providing information to government authorities. Counterinsurgents may attract deserters or informants by arousing fear of prosecution or by offering rewards.").

[157] *For example*, Benjamin Weiser, *Terrorist Has Cooperated With U.S. Since Secret Guilty Plea in 2011, Papers Show*, THE NEW YORK TIMES, Mar. 25, 2013 ("A Somali terrorist with ties to Al Qaeda whose capture and interrogation aboard a United States naval ship in 2011 fueled debate about the Obama administration's counterterrorism tactics secretly pleaded guilty in Manhattan and has been cooperating with the authorities, court documents released on Monday show. The terrorist, Ahmed Abdulkadir Warsame, served as a military commander with the Shabab in Somalia and worked as a liaison with Al Qaeda's branch in Yemen, including brokering a deal for the Shabab to buy weapons directly from the Qaeda group, the government has said. The newly unsealed court papers show Mr. Warsame pleaded guilty in a closed court proceeding in Manhattan in December 2011, about five months after he was brought to New York. After the plea, he met weekly with the government for hours at a time, disclosing intelligence information about his Shabab and Qaeda co-conspirators, who included 'high-level international terrorist operatives,' prosecutors said in one highly redacted letter dated March 2012.").

prohibited during non-international armed conflict:

- weapons calculated to cause superfluous injury;[158]
- inherently indiscriminate weapons;[159]
- poison, poisoned weapons, poisonous gases, and other chemical weapons;[160]
- biological weapons;[161]
- weapons that injure by fragments that are non-detectable by X-rays;[162]
- certain types of mines, booby-traps, and other devices;[163] and
- blinding lasers.[164]

17.13.2 Certain Types of Weapons With Specific Rules on Use in NIAC. Certain types of weapons are subject to specific rules that apply to their use by the U.S. armed forces in non-international armed conflict. These weapons include:

- mines, booby-traps, and other devices (except certain specific classes of prohibited mines, booby-traps, and other devices);[165]
- incendiary weapons;[166]
- laser weapons (except blinding lasers);[167] and
- explosive ordnance.[168]

17.14 Protection of the Wounded, Sick, Shipwrecked, and Dead in NIAC

17.14.1 Respect, Protection, Humane Treatment, and Medical Care of the Wounded,

---

[158] *Refer to* § 6.6 (Weapons Calculated to Cause Superfluous Injury).

[159] *Refer to* § 6.7 (Inherently Indiscriminate Weapons).

[160] *Refer to* § 6.8 (Poison, Poisoned Weapons, Poisonous Gases, and Other Chemical Weapons).

[161] *Refer to* § 6.9 (Biological Weapons).

[162] *Refer to* § 6.11 (Weapons Injuring by Fragments Not Detectable by X-Rays).

[163] *Refer to* § 6.12.4 (Prohibited Classes of Mines, Booby-Traps, and Other Devices).

[164] *Refer to* § 6.15.1 (Prohibition on "Blinding Laser" Weapons).

[165] *Refer to* § 6.12 (Landmines, Booby-Traps, and Other Devices).

[166] *Refer to* § 6.14 (Incendiary Weapons).

[167] *Refer to* § 6.15.2 (Feasible Precautions in the Employment of Laser Systems to Avoid the Incident of Permanent Blindness).

[168] *Refer to* § 6.19 (Explosive Ordnance).

<u>Sick, and Shipwrecked</u>. All the wounded, sick, and shipwrecked, whether or not they have taken part in the armed conflict, shall be respected and protected.[169]

17.14.1.1 *<u>Types of Persons Who Are Considered Wounded, Sick, and Shipwrecked in NIAC</u>*. The wounded, sick, and shipwrecked in non-international armed conflict may be understood to include:

- persons who have been rendered unconscious or otherwise have been incapacitated because of their wounds, sickness, or shipwreck;[170]
- persons who have surrendered as a consequence of their health; and[171]
- persons who have been shipwrecked (*i.e.*, helpless persons in distress at sea or stranded on the coast) from any cause, including forced landings at sea by or from aircraft.[172]

Of course, any person who commits hostile acts or attempts to evade capture forfeits protection as someone who is placed *hors de combat*.[173]

17.14.1.2 *<u>Meaning of "Respect and Protection" of the Wounded, Sick, and Shipwrecked</u>*. The wounded, sick, and shipwrecked must be respected and protected at all times. This means that they should not be knowingly attacked, fired upon, or unnecessarily interfered with.[174]

Persons who are part of armed forces or groups, however, are deemed to have accepted the risk of harm due to deliberate proximity to military objectives.[175] Although the presence of such persons does not serve to exempt nearby military objectives from attack due to the risk that such persons would be incidentally harmed, feasible precautions to reduce the risk of harm to such persons who are wounded, sick, or shipwrecked must be taken.[176]

The respect and protection afforded the wounded, sick, and shipwrecked do not immunize them from search, or other necessary security measures, or capture and detention, even if they are receiving medical care.[177]

---

169 *Consider* AP II art. 7(1) ("All the wounded, sick and shipwrecked, whether or not they have taken part in the armed conflict, shall be respected and protected.").

170 *Refer to* § 5.9.4 (Persons Rendered Unconscious or Otherwise Incapacitated by Wounds, Sickness, or Shipwreck).

171 *Refer to* § 5.9.3 (Persons Who Have Surrendered).

172 *Compare* § 7.3.1.2 (Shipwrecked).

173 *Refer to* § 5.9 (Persons Placed *Hors de Combat*).

174 *Compare* § 7.3.3 (Meaning of "Respect and Protection" of the Wounded, Sick, and Shipwrecked).

175 *Compare* § 7.3.3.1 (Incidental Harm Not Prohibited).

176 *Compare* § 5.10.1.2 (Proportionality in Conducting Attacks and Protected Military Personnel and Facilities).

177 *Compare* § 7.3.3.2 (Search and Other Security Measures Not Prohibited); § 7.3.3.3 (Capture of Wounded, Sick, and Shipwrecked Not Prohibited).

Booby-trapping the wounded or sick is expressly prohibited.[178]

17.14.2 Humane Treatment and Practicable Medical Care and Attention. In all circumstances, the wounded, sick, and shipwrecked shall be treated humanely and shall receive, to the fullest extent practicable and with the least possible delay, the medical care and attention required by their condition.[179] There shall be no distinction among them founded on any grounds other than medical ones.[180]

17.14.3 Search, Collection, and Protection of the Wounded, Sick, Shipwrecked, and Dead. Whenever circumstances permit, and particularly after an engagement, all possible measures shall be taken, without delay, to search for and collect the wounded, sick, and shipwrecked, to protect them against pillage and ill-treatment, to ensure their adequate care, and to search for the dead, prevent their being despoiled, and decently dispose of them.[181]

The obligations to search for, collect, and take affirmative steps to protect the wounded, sick, and shipwrecked are subject to practical limitations; military commanders are to judge what is possible, and to what extent they can commit their personnel to these duties.[182]

17.14.3.1 *Mistreatment and Booby-Trapping of the Dead Prohibited*. The mistreatment of the dead is prohibited.[183] In addition, the dead may not be booby-trapped.[184]

17.15 PROTECTION OF MEDICAL AND RELIGIOUS PERSONNEL AND MEDICAL TRANSPORTS IN NIAC

17.15.1 Protection of Medical and Religious Personnel. Medical and religious personnel

---

[178] *Refer to* § 6.12.4.9 (Certain Types of Prohibited Booby-Traps and Other Devices).

[179] *Consider* AP II art. 7(2) ("In all circumstances they shall be treated humanely and shall receive, to the fullest extent practicable and with the least possible delay, the medical care and attention required by their condition.").

[180] *Consider* AP II art. 7(2) ("There shall be no distinction among them founded on any grounds other than medical ones.").

[181] *Consider* AP II art. 8 ("Whenever circumstances permit, and particularly after an engagement, all possible measures shall be taken, without delay, to search for and collect the wounded, sick and shipwrecked, to protect them against pillage and ill-treatment, to ensure their adequate care, and to search for the dead, prevent their being despoiled, and decently dispose of them.").

[182] *Compare* § 7.4.4 (Practical Limitations on the Obligation to Search for, Collect, and Take Measures to Protect the Wounded, Sick, and Shipwrecked).

[183] *For example*, Karen Parrish, *Panetta Orders Investigation of Video, Vows Accountability*, AMERICAN FORCES PRESS SERVICE, Jan. 12, 2012 ("Defense Secretary Leon E. Panetta released a statement today strongly condemning the actions of a small group of Marines depicted in a video that began circulating online yesterday. The video shows four Marines apparently urinating over three enemy corpses in Afghanistan. The secretary's statement said he has seen the footage and finds the behavior depicted in it 'utterly deplorable.' 'I condemn it in the strongest possible terms,' Panetta said. 'I have ordered the Marine Corps and ISAF commander [Marine Corps] Gen. John Allen to immediately and fully investigate the incident. This conduct is entirely inappropriate for members of the United States military and does not reflect the standards or values our armed forces are sworn to uphold. Those found to have engaged in such conduct will be held accountable to the fullest extent.'"). *Compare* § 7.7.1.1 (No Disrespectful or Degrading Treatment of the Dead).

[184] *Refer to* § 6.12.4.9 (Certain Types of Prohibited Booby-Traps and Other Devices).

shall be respected and protected and shall be granted all available help for the performance of their duties. They shall not be compelled to carry out tasks that are not compatible with their humanitarian mission.[185]

17.15.1.1 *Types of Persons Who Are Considered Medical and Religious Personnel in NIAC*. Medical and religious personnel include those persons who are exclusively (*e.g.*, permanently) engaged in those duties.[186] For example, persons who intermittently take a direct part in hostilities are not considered medical and religious personnel.[187]

17.15.1.2 *Meaning of "Respect and Protection" of Medical and Religious Personnel*. The respect and protection accorded to medical and religious personnel mean that they must not knowingly be attacked, fired upon, or unnecessarily prevented from discharging their proper functions.[188]

Medical and religious personnel who are part of armed forces or groups, however, are deemed to have accepted the risk of harm due to their deliberate proximity to military objectives.[189] Although the presence of such personnel would not serve to exempt nearby military objectives from attack due to the risk that such personnel would be incidentally harmed, feasible precautions must be taken to reduce the risk of harm to such personnel.[190]

The respect and protection afforded medical and religious personnel do not immunize them from search, or from other necessary security measures, or from capture and detention.[191] AP II and applicable treaties to which the United States is a Party (such as the 1949 Geneva Conventions) do not afford medical and religious personnel belonging to non-State armed groups retained personnel status if captured.

17.15.2 Protection of Medical Units and Transports. Medical units and transports shall be respected and protected at all times and shall not be the object of attack.[192] The protection to which medical units and transports are entitled shall not cease unless they are used to commit hostile acts, outside their humanitarian function. Protection may, however, cease only after a warning has been given setting, whenever appropriate, a reasonable time-limit, and after such

---

185 *Consider* AP II art. 9(1) ("Medical and religious personnel shall be respected and protected and shall be granted all available help for the performance of their duties. They shall not be compelled to carry out tasks which are not compatible with their humanitarian mission.").

186 *Refer to* § 4.9.2.3 (Exclusively Engaged in Humanitarian Duties).

187 *Refer to* § 5.8.3 ("Taking a Direct Part in in Hostilities").

188 *Compare* § 7.8.2 (Meaning of "Respect and Protection" of Medical and Religious Personnel).

189 *Compare* § 7.8.2.1 (Incidental Harm Not Prohibited).

190 *Compare* § 5.10.1.2 (Proportionality in Conducting Attacks and Protected Military Personnel and Facilities).

191 *Compare* § 7.8.2.2 (Search and Other Security Measures Not Prohibited); § 7.8.2.3 (Capture Not Prohibited).

192 *Consider* AP II art. 11(1) ("Medical units and transports shall be respected and protected at all times and shall not be the object of attack.").

warning has remained unheeded.[193]

17.15.2.1 *Types of Units and Vehicles That Are Considered Medical Units and Transports*. Medical units and transports include those units and vehicles that are exclusively (*e.g.*, permanently) engaged in those activities.[194] For example, units and transports that intermittently are used in hostilities are not considered medical units and transports.

17.15.2.2 *Meaning of "Respect and Protection" of Medical Units and Transports*. The respect and protection accorded to medical units and transports mean that they must not knowingly be attacked, fired upon, or unnecessarily prevented from discharging their proper functions.[195]

Medical units and transports that are part of armed forces or groups, however, are deemed to have accepted the risk of harm due to their deliberate proximity to military objectives.[196] Although the presence of such medical units and transports would not serve to exempt nearby military objectives from attack due to the risk that such medical units and transports would be incidentally harmed, feasible precautions must be taken to reduce the risk of harm to such medical units and transports.[197]

The respect and protection afforded medical units and facilities does not immunize them from search or capture.[198]

17.16 Display of the Distinctive Emblem in NIAC

Under the direction of the competent authority concerned, the distinctive emblem of the red cross, red crescent, or red lion and sun on a white ground shall be displayed by medical and religious personnel and medical units, and on medical transports. It shall be respected in all circumstances. It shall not be used improperly.[199]

These rules also apply to the distinctive emblem of the red crystal.[200]

---

[193] *Consider* AP II art. 11(2) ("The protection to which medical units and transports are entitled shall not cease unless they are used to commit hostile acts, outside their humanitarian function. Protection may, however, cease only after a warning has been given setting, whenever appropriate, a reasonable time-limit, and after such warning has remained unheeded.").

[194] *Refer to* § 4.9.2.3 (Exclusively Engaged in Humanitarian Duties).

[195] *Compare* § 7.10.1 (Meaning of "Respect and Protection" of Military Medical Units and Facilities).

[196] *Compare* § 7.10.1.1 (Incidental Harm Not Prohibited).

[197] *Compare* § 5.10.1.2 (Proportionality in Conducting Attacks and Protected Military Personnel and Facilities).

[198] *Compare* § 7.10.1.2 (Search Not Prohibited); § 7.10.1.3 (Capture Not Prohibited).

[199] *Consider* AP II art. 12 ("Under the direction of the competent authority concerned, the distinctive emblem of the red cross, red crescent or red lion and sun on a white ground shall be displayed by medical and religious personnel and medical units, and on medical transports. It shall be respected in all circumstances. It shall not be used improperly.").

[200] *Refer to* § 7.15.1.3 (Red Crystal); § 17.2.1.1 (Treaties That Have Provisions That Explicitly Apply to NIAC).

17.16.1 Display of the Emblem Under the Direction of the Competent Authority Concerned. The display of the distinctive emblem is under the direction of the competent authority concerned, which authority may authorize the removal or obscuring of the distinctive emblem for tactical purposes, such as camouflage.[201] Similarly, it would be appropriate for the distinctive emblem to be removed if it is assessed that enemy forces will fail to respect the emblem and seek to attack medical personnel; display of the emblem in such circumstances would be deemed not to be feasible.[202]

17.16.2 Improper Use of the Distinctive Emblem. Improper use of the distinctive emblem includes use: (1) while engaging in attacks; (2) in order to shield, favor, or protect one's own military operations; or (3) to impede enemy military operations.[203]

17.17 DETENTION IN NIAC

17.17.1 State Authority to Detain. Law of war treaties have not limited the scope of whom a State may detain for reasons related to a non-international armed conflict, but have prescribed humane treatment for such persons.[204] A State's authority to conduct detention operations has often been understood as incident to the legal basis of the State to engage in operations against the non-State armed group.[205]

The precise legal requirements for a detention regime established by a State in non-international armed conflict would likely depend a great deal on its domestic law.

17.17.1.1 *Non-Punitive Detention in Non-International Armed Conflict*. Non-punitive detention may be conducted on a variety of legal theories under international law.[206] For example, although enemy non-State armed groups would not be entitled to POW status, a State may detain persons belonging to enemy armed groups, by analogy to the detention of POWs in international armed conflict. Similarly, although persons would not be protected persons under the GC, a State may detain persons for security reasons, by analogy to the

---

201 *Compare* § 7.15.2.1 (Removal or Obscuration of the Distinctive Emblem).

202 *Refer to* § 5.2.3.2 (What Precautions Are Feasible).

203 *Refer to* § 5.24 (Improper Use of Certain Signs).

204 AP II art. 5(1) ("In addition to the provisions of Article 4, the following provisions shall be respected as a minimum with regard to persons deprived of their liberty for reasons related to the armed conflict, whether they are interned or detained:").

205 *Refer to* § 8.1.3.1 (Detention Authority).

206 *For example*, FRANK KITSON, GANGS AND COUNTER-GANGS 45 (1960) ("There was one other legal means of getting at the Mau Mau. This was for the Police to submit a dossier giving a full list of all that was known against a person to the Governor, who could then sign an order for detention during the Emergency providing he was satisfied that such action was necessary in the interests of maintaining public order. This was a good idea as far as it went but the Governor could only sign a comparatively limited number. Certainly the system could not take care of all the committee members of all the committees though it was satisfactory for the most senior ones. It was an advance in another way, in that it all but recognized the status of prisoner of war by saying to a man 'You are not a criminal but you are on the wrong side. You must be restrained until this trouble is over.' It was of course contrary to the principles of British justice but it was merciful. In its extended form later in the Emergency it saved thousands of loyalist lives by reducing the number of Mau Mau, and probably saved many Mau Mau lives by locking up people who would otherwise have joined the gangs and been killed by the Security Forces.").

detention of protected persons in international armed conflict or occupation. Other legal rationales for the detention of persons in non-international armed conflict also may be available.

17.17.1.2 *Punitive Detention in Non-International Armed Conflict*. During non-international armed conflict, a State could also detain persons pursuant to its criminal law. For example, persons who support enemy non-State armed groups could be sentenced to a variety of offenses (*e.g.*, murder, criminal conspiracy, treason or other offenses against the State, material support to terrorism or terrorist organizations).

17.17.2 Detention by Non-State Armed Groups. Non-State armed groups typically would lack domestic legal authority to conduct detention operations. Their actions may be subject to prosecution under domestic statutes making punishable kidnapping, hostage taking, false imprisonment, interference with State officials, etc. Nonetheless, detention during non-international armed conflict by non-State armed groups is not prohibited by international law. In any case, non-State armed groups that conduct detention operations must provide humane treatment to detainees.

17.17.3 Humane Treatment and Other Applicable Requirements. All persons (including those belonging to the State or those belonging to non-State armed groups) who are detained by the adverse party are entitled to the protections of Common Article 3 of the 1949 Geneva Conventions, including humane treatment.[207] Although detainees are afforded humane treatment, they do not receive POW status.[208]

Chapter VIII addresses the baseline rules for the humane treatment of detainees that apply to all U.S. military operations, including those in non-international armed conflict.[209]

17.18 Non-Intervention and Neutral Duties in NIAC

17.18.1 Duty of Non-Belligerent States to Refrain From Supporting Hostilities by Non-State Armed Groups Against Other States. Under international law, principles of friendly relations and non-intervention require States to refrain from supporting non-State armed groups in hostilities against other States.[210]

---

[207] *Refer to* § 8.1.4.1 (Common Article 3 of the 1949 Geneva Conventions).

[208] *See, e.g.*, Bothe, Partsch, & Solf, New Rules 646 (AP II art. 5, ¶2.3) ("It must be emphasized in this connection that Protocol II does not confer a *special status* on members of the armed forces of either side captured by the adverse party similar to the status of a prisoner of war in an international armed conflict. The rebel does not enjoy any privilege with regard to acts committed during the rebellion."); ICRC AP Commentary 1386 (¶4570) ("Protocol II, following the example of common Article 3, does not grant a special status to members of the armed forces or armed groups who have fallen into enemy hands. They are not legally prisoners of war entitled to special protection; this is why it is so important that the rules laid down in this article [5 of AP II] establish minimum guarantees.").

[209] *Refer to* § 8.1.1 (Overview of Detention Rules in This Manual and the Scope of Chapter VIII).

[210] *See, e.g.*, *Declaration on Principles of International Law concerning Friendly Relations and Co-operation among States in accordance with the Charter of the United Nations*, annex to U.N. General Assembly Resolution 2625 (XXV), U.N. Doc. A/RES/2625(XXV) (1970) ("Every State has the duty to refrain from organizing or encouraging the organization of irregular forces or armed bands, including mercenaries, for incursion into the territory of another State. Every State has the duty to refrain from organizing, instigating, assisting or

These are closely analogous to the duties that neutral States have under the law of neutrality to refrain from supporting military operations against belligerents.[211]

In particular, States are required to take all reasonable steps to ensure that their territory is not used by non-State armed groups for purposes of armed activities—including planning, threatening, perpetrating, or providing material support for armed attacks—against other States and their interests.[212] The failure to fulfill this duty may have consequences in regard to whether other States that are threatened by these armed activities must seek the consent of that State before taking action in self-defense in that State's territory.[213]

Violations of law of war treaties applicable to non-international armed conflict by a State generally have not been understood to provide an independent basis in international law for a non-belligerent State to intervene against the violating State in that conflict.[214]

17.18.2 Duty of Belligerent States to Respect the Sovereignty of Other States. States that are engaged in hostilities against non-State armed groups must respect the sovereignty of other States.[215] In general, States must obtain the consent of a territorial State before conducting

---

participating in acts of civil strife or terrorist acts in another State or acquiescing in organized activities within its territory directed towards the commission of such acts, when the acts referred to in the present paragraph involve a threat or use of force.").

[211] *See, e.g.*, Christopher Greenwood, *International law and the 'war on terrorism,'* 78 INTERNATIONAL AFFAIRS 301, 313 (2002) ("By allowing Al-Qa'ida to operate from the territory which it controlled, the Taliban—and thus Afghanistan—violated the general duty of a state under international law not to allow its territory to be used as a base for attacks on other states. … At the very least, its position was analogous to that of a neutral state which allows a belligerent to mount military operations from its territory: even though it is not responsible for those operations, it exposes itself to the risk of lawful military action to put a stop to them. Similarly, where a state allows terrorist organizations to mount concerted operations against other states from its territory and refuses to take the action required by international law to put a stop to such operations, the victims of those operations are entitled to take action against those terrorists."); H. Lauterpacht, *Revolutionary Activities by Private Persons Against Foreign States*, 22 AJIL 105, 127 (1928) ("The nearest approach to what is believed to be the true juridical construction of the state's duty to prevent organized hostile expeditions from proceeding in times of peace against a friendly state will be found in the law of neutrality. … The two situations being closely analogous, it is only natural that they are regulated in Great Britain and in the United States in the same legal enactments. The law of hostile expeditions is nothing else than the law of neutrality in relation to an actual or impending civil war.").

[212] Daniel Bethlehem, *Principles Relevant to the Scope of a State's Right of Self-Defense Against an Imminent or Actual Armed Attack by Nonstate Actors*, 106 AJIL 1, 7 (2012) ("9. States are required to take all reasonable steps to ensure that their territory is not used by nonstate actors for purposes of armed activities—including planning, threatening, perpetrating, or providing material support for armed attacks—against other states and their interests.").

[213] *Refer to* § 17.18.2 (Duty of Belligerent States to Respect the Sovereignty of Other States).

[214] *See, e.g.*, CCW AMENDED art. 1(5) ("Nothing in this Convention or its annexed Protocols shall be invoked as a justification for intervening, directly or indirectly, for any reason whatever, in the armed conflict or in the internal or external affairs of the High Contracting Party in the territory of which that conflict occurs."). *Consider* AP II art. 2(2) ("Nothing in this Protocol shall be invoked as a justification for intervening, directly or indirectly, for any reason whatever, in the armed conflict or in the internal or external affairs of the High Contracting Party in the territory of which that conflict occurs."). *Refer to* § 1.11.4.4 (Humanitarian Intervention).

[215] *See, e.g.*, Jeh Charles Johnson, General Counsel, Department of Defense, *National Security Law, Lawyers, and Lawyering in the Obama Administration*, Feb. 22, 2012, 2012 DIGEST OF UNITED STATES PRACTICE IN INTERNATIONAL LAW 575, 577 ("Third: there is nothing in the wording of the 2001 AUMF or its legislative history that restricts this statutory authority to the 'hot' battlefields of Afghanistan. … The legal point is important because,

military operations against a non-State armed group in that State's territory.[216]

The consent of the territorial State, however, is not necessary when the U.N. Security Council has authorized the military operations.[217]

In addition, the United States has expressed the view that consent is not required when the territorial State is unwilling or unable to prevent its territory from being used by non-State armed groups as a base for launching attacks.[218] Other States have also expressed this view.[219]

---

in fact, over the last 10 years al Qaeda has not only become more decentralized, it has also, for the most part, migrated away from Afghanistan to other places where it can find safe haven. However, this legal conclusion too has its limits. It should not be interpreted to mean that we believe we are in any 'Global War on Terror,' or that we can use military force whenever we want, wherever we want. International legal principles, including respect for a state's sovereignty and the laws of war, impose important limits on our ability to act unilaterally, and on the way in which we can use force in foreign territories."); Harold Hongju Koh, Legal Adviser, Department of State, *Address at the Annual Meeting of the American Society of International Law: The Obama Administration and International Law* Mar. 25, 2010, 2010 DIGEST OF UNITED STATES PRACTICE IN INTERNATIONAL LAW 717-18 ("As recent events have shown, al-Qaeda has not abandoned its intent to attack the United States, and indeed continues to attack us. Thus, in this ongoing armed conflict, the United States has the authority under international law, and the responsibility to its citizens, to use force, including lethal force, to defend itself, including by targeting persons such as high-level al-Qaeda leaders who are planning attacks. ... Of course, whether a particular individual will be targeted in a particular location will depend upon considerations specific to each case, including those related to the imminence of the threat, the sovereignty of the other states involved, and the willingness and ability of those states to suppress the threat the target poses.").

[216] Daniel Bethlehem, *Principles Relevant to the Scope of a State's Right of Self-Defense Against an Imminent or Actual Armed Attack by Nonstate Actors*, 106 AJIL 1, 7 (2012) ("Subject to the following paragraphs, a state may not take armed action in self-defense against a nonstate actor in the territory or within the jurisdiction of another state ('the third state') without the consent of that state. The requirement for consent does not operate in circumstances in which there is an applicable resolution of the UN Security Council authorizing the use of armed force under Chapter VII of the Charter or other relevant and applicable legal provision of similar effect.").

[217] Daniel Bethlehem, *Principles Relevant to the Scope of a State's Right of Self-Defense Against an Imminent or Actual Armed Attack by Nonstate Actors*, 106 AJIL 1, 7 (2012) ("The requirement for consent does not operate in circumstances in which there is an applicable resolution of the UN Security Council authorizing the use of armed force under Chapter VII of the Charter or other relevant and applicable legal provision of similar effect."). *Refer to* § 1.11.4.2 (Use of Force Authorized by the U.N. Security Council Acting Under Chapter VII of the Charter of the United Nations).

[218] *See, e.g.*, Samantha J. Power, *Letter dated 23 September 2014 from the Permanent Representative of the United States of America to the United Nations addressed to the Secretary-General*, U.N. Doc. S/2014/695 (Sept. 23, 2014) ("ISIL and other terrorist groups in Syria are a threat not only to Iraq, but also to many other countries, including the United States and our partners in the region and beyond. States must be able to defend themselves, in accordance with the inherent right of individual and collective self-defence, as reflected in Article 51 of the Charter of the United Nations, when, as is the case here, the government of the State where the threat is located is unwilling or unable to prevent the use of its territory for such attacks. The Syrian regime has shown that it cannot and will not confront these safe havens effectively itself."); John B. Bellinger, III, Legal Adviser, Department of State, *Legal Issues in the War on Terrorism*, Oct. 31, 2006, 2006 DIGEST OF UNITED STATES PRACTICE IN INTERNATIONAL LAW 1104, 1109-10 ("Let me be very clear here: I am not suggesting that, because we remain in a state of armed conflict with al Qaida, the United States is free to use military force against al Qaida in any state where an al Qaida terrorist may seek shelter. The U.S. military does not plan to shoot terrorists on the streets of London. As a practical matter, though, a state must be responsible for preventing terrorists from using its territory as a base for launching attacks. And, as a legal matter, where a state is unwilling or unable to do so, it may be lawful for the targeted state to use military force in self-defense to address that threat."); Abraham Sofaer, *The Sixth Annual Waldemar A. Solf Lecture in International Law: Terrorism, the Law, and the National Defense*, 126 MILITARY LAW REVIEW 89, 108 (1989)

It may be unnecessary for a belligerent State to seek consent when there is a strong, reasonable, and objective basis for concluding that the seeking of consent would be likely to undermine materially the effectiveness of the action against the non-State armed group (*e.g.*, reasons of disclosure, delay, incapacity to act) or would increase the risk of armed attack, vulnerability to future attacks, or other development that would give rise to an independent imperative to act in self-defense.[220]

17.18.3 States' Support to Other States in Hostilities Against Non-State Armed Groups.

("The United States in fact supported the legality of a nation attacking a terrorist base from which attack on its citizens are being launched, if the host country is either unwilling or unable to stop the terrorists from using its territory for that purpose.").

[219] *For example*, Michael Grant, *Letter dated 31 March 2015 from the Chargé d'affaires a.i. of the Permanent Mission of Canada to the United Nations addressed to the President of the Security Council*, U.N. Doc. S/2015/221 (Mar. 31, 2015) ("ISIL also continues to pose a threat not only to Iraq, but also to Canada and Canadians, as well as to other countries in the region and beyond. In accordance with the inherent rights of individual and collective self-defence reflected in Article 51 of the United Nations Charter, States must be able to act in self-defence when the government of the State where a threat is located is unwilling or unable to prevent attacks emanating from its territory."); Russian Federation President V.V. Putin, Statement of Sept. 11, 2002, annexed to Sergey Lavrov, *Letter dated 11 September 2002 from the Permanent Representative of the Russian Federation to the United Nations addressed to the Secretary-General*, U.N. Doc. S/2002/1012 (Sept. 11, 2002) ("The Russian Federation firmly adheres to its international obligations and respects the sovereignty and integrity of other States, but it demands the same attitude towards itself. If the Georgian leadership is unable to establish a security zone in the area of the Georgian-Russian border, continues to ignore United Nations Security Council resolution 1373 (2001) of 28 September 2001, and does not put an end to the bandit sorties and attacks on adjoining areas in the Russian Federation, we reserve the right to act in accordance with Article 51 of the Charter of the United Nations, which lays down every Member State's inalienable right of individual or collective self-defence. ... None of this will be necessary, no measures or special operations will be needed if the Georgian leadership actually controls its own territory, carries out international obligations in combating international terrorism and prevents possible attacks by international terrorists from its territory against the territory of the Russian Federation."); Hayati Güven, *Letter Dated 24 July 1995 from the Charge D'affaires A.I. of the Permanent Mission of Turkey to the United Nations Addressed to the President of the Security Council*, U.N. Doc. S/1995/605 (Jul. 24, 1995) ("As Iraq has not been able to exercise its authority over the northern part of its country since 1991 for reasons well known, Turkey cannot ask the Government of Iraq to fulfil its obligation, under international law, to prevent the use of its territory for the staging of terrorist acts against Turkey. Under these circumstances, Turkey's resorting to legitimate measures which are imperative to its own security cannot be regarded as a violation of Iraq's sovereignty. No country could be expected to stand idle when its own territorial integrity is incessantly threatened by blatant cross-border attacks of a terrorist organization based and operating from a neighbouring country, if that country is unable to put an end to such attacks. The recent operations of limited time and scope were carried out within this framework, as explained to the world public."); *Statement of Mr. Blum, representative of Israel*, in U.N. Doc. S/PV.2292 ¶¶54-56 ("Members of the [Security] Council need scarcely be reminded that under international law, if a State is unwilling or unable to prevent the use of its territory to attack another State, that latter state is entitled to take all necessary measures in its own defence. The Government of Israel is in fact exercising the inherent right of self-defence enjoyed by every sovereign State, a right also preserved under Article 51 of the Charter of the United Nations. Israel's response to PLO terror is what any self-respecting sovereign State would do in similar circumstances. I must stress that Israel's actions are specifically directed against concentrations of PLO terrorists in Lebanon.").

[220] Daniel Bethlehem, *Principles Relevant to the Scope of a State's Right of Self-Defense Against an Imminent or Actual Armed Attack by Nonstate Actors*, 106 AJIL 1, 7 (2012) ("In such circumstances, in addition to the preceding requirements, there must also be a strong, reasonable, and objective basis for concluding that the seeking of consent would be likely to materially undermine the effectiveness of action in self-defense, whether for reasons of disclosure, delay, incapacity to act, or otherwise, or would increase the risk of armed attack, vulnerability to future attacks, or other development that would give rise to an independent imperative to act in self-defense.").

International law does not prohibit States from assisting other States in their armed conflicts against non-State armed groups. To the extent those States intend to conduct hostilities or actually do so, they may incur obligations under the law of war.[221] For example, a State that is conducting detention operations would have obligations to treat detainees (*e.g.*, persons belonging to non-State armed groups) humanely regardless of whether it considers itself a party to the non-international armed conflict.

17.18.4 Liability of Private Individuals for Supporting Non-State Armed Groups. Private individuals who support non-State armed groups that are preparing for, or engaged in, hostilities against a State may be subject to prosecution. Such conduct may be criminalized under a variety of domestic laws relating to treason, hostile expeditions against other States, material support to terrorism, or piracy.[222]

The State that is threatened by such activities may prosecute such individuals for treason or other offenses against the State.

States in which such conduct occurs may seek to prosecute such conduct for a variety of reasons, including its duties under international law to refrain from materially supporting hostilities against another State, and to repress terrorism or piracy.

---

[221] *Refer to* § 3.4 (When *Jus in Bello* Rules Apply).

[222] *Refer to* § 4.18.5 (Private Persons Who Engage in Hostilities and the Law of War).

XVIII – Implementation and Enforcement of the Law of War

Chapter Contents

18.1 Introduction

This Chapter addresses the implementation and enforcement of the law of war. It discusses activities that are undertaken in order to prevent violations of the law of war (such as training and the promulgation of policies, regulations, and orders). It discusses activities to respond to alleged violations, such as reporting, investigation, and corrective or punitive measures.

18.1.1 DoD Policy on Implementing and Enforcing the Law of War. DoD policy has addressed the policies and responsibilities for ensuring DoD compliance with the law of war obligations of the United States.[1] It has been DoD policy that:

- Members of the DoD Components comply with the law of war during all armed conflicts, however such conflicts are characterized, and in all other military operations;[2]
- The law of war obligations of the United States are observed and enforced by the DoD Components and DoD contractors assigned to, or accompanying, deployed armed forces;[3]
- An effective program to prevent violations of the law of war is implemented by the DoD Components.[4]

These policies follow a longer tradition of compliance with the law of war by U.S. armed forces.[5]

18.1.2 National Obligations to Implement and Enforce the Law of War. States, as Parties to treaties, have certain obligations to implement and enforce those treaties. These obligations may be written as a general obligation to undertake to respect and to ensure respect for the treaty.

In addition, treaties may provide for more specific obligations to help implement and enforce their provisions, such as obligations with respect to violations of the treaty or dissemination of the text of the treaty.

Different treaties may have different mechanisms to implement and to ensure compliance with that treaty.

---

[1] *See, e.g.*, DoD Directive 2311.01E, *DoD Law of War Program*, ¶1 (May 9, 2006, Certified Current as of Feb. 22, 2011) ("This Directive: 1.1. Reissues Reference (a) to update the policies and responsibilities ensuring DoD compliance with the law of war obligations of the United States."); DoD Directive 5100.77, *DoD Program for the Implementation of the Law of War*, ¶I (Nov. 5, 1974) ("This Directive provides policy guidance and assigns responsibilities within the Department of Defense for a program to insure implementation of the law of war.").

[2] *See, e.g.*, DoD Directive 2311.01E, *DoD Law of War Program*, ¶4.1 (May 9, 2006, Certified Current as of Feb. 22, 2011) ("Members of the DoD Components comply with the law of war during all armed conflicts, however such conflicts are characterized, and in all other military operations."); DoD Directive 5100.77, *DoD Law of War Program*, ¶5.3 (Dec. 9, 1998) ("The Heads of the DoD Components shall: 5.3.1. Ensure that the members of their DoD Components comply with the law of war during all armed conflicts, however such conflicts are characterized, and with the principles and spirit of the law of war during all other operations."); DoD Directive 5100.77, *DoD Law of War Program*, ¶E(1)(a) (Jul. 10, 1979) ("The Armed Forces of the United States shall comply with the law of war in the conduct of military operations and related activities in armed conflict, however such conflicts are characterized."); DoD Directive 5100.77, *DoD Program for the Implementation of the Law of War*, ¶V(A) (Nov. 5, 1974) ("The Armed Forces of the United States will comply with the law of war in the conduct of military operations and related activities in armed conflict however such conflicts are characterized.").

[3] DoD Directive 2311.01E, *DoD Law of War Program*, ¶4.2 (May 9, 2006, Certified Current as of Feb. 22, 2011) ("The law of war obligations of the United States are observed and enforced by the DoD Components and DoD contractors assigned to or accompanying deployed Armed Forces.").

[4] DoD Directive 2311.01E, *DoD Law of War Program*, ¶4.3 (May 9, 2006, Certified Current as of Feb. 22, 2011) ("An effective program to prevent violations of the law of war is implemented by the DoD Components.").

[5] *See, e.g.*, 1956 FM 27-10 (Change No. 1 1976) ¶7 ("In consequence, treaties relating to the law of war have a force equal to that of laws enacted by the Congress. Their provisions must be observed by both military and civilian personnel with the same strict regard for both the letter and spirit of the law which is required with respect to the Constitution and statutes enacted in pursuance thereof. … The unwritten or customary law of war is binding upon all nations. It will be strictly observed by United States forces, subject only to such exceptions as shall have been directed by competent authority by way of legitimate reprisals for illegal conduct of the enemy (see par. 497)."); U.S. Navy Regulations Article 0505 (1948) ("Observance of International Law. 1. In the event of war between nations with which the United States is at peace, a commander shall observe, and require his command to observe, the principles of international law. He shall make every effort consistent with those principles to preserve and protect the lives and property of citizens of the United States wherever situated. 2. When the United States is at war, he shall observe, and require his command to observe, the principles of international law and the rules of humane warfare. He shall respect the rights of neutrals as prescribed by international law and by pertinent provisions of treaties, and shall exact a like observance from neutrals.").

18.1.2.1 *General Treaty Obligations to Take Appropriate Actions to Implement and Enforce the Treaty – 1949 Geneva Conventions*. Parties to the 1949 Geneva Conventions undertake to respect and ensure respect for the conventions in all circumstances.[6] This is a general obligation to take the measures that the State deems appropriate in order to fulfill its obligations under the conventions. Although this provision does not reflect an obligation to ensure implementation of the conventions by other States or parties to a conflict, the United States, as a matter of policy, often seeks to promote adherence to the law of war by others.[7]

18.1.2.2 *General Treaty Obligations to Take Appropriate Actions to Implement and Enforce the Treaty – AP III*. Parties to AP III undertake to respect and to ensure respect for AP III in all circumstances.[8]

18.1.2.3 *General Treaty Obligations to Take Appropriate Actions to Implement and Enforce the Treaty – CCW Amended Mines Protocol*. Parties to the CCW Amended Mines Protocol shall take all appropriate steps, including legislative and other measures, to prevent and suppress violations of that Protocol by persons or on territory under its jurisdiction or control.[9]

18.1.2.4 *General Treaty Obligations to Take Appropriate Actions to Implement and Enforce the Treaty – Child Soldiers Protocol*. Each Party to the Child Soldiers Protocol shall take all necessary legal, administrative, and other measures to ensure the effective implementation and enforcement of the provisions of this Protocol within its jurisdiction.[10]

18.1.3 International or Multi-National Actions to Implement and Enforce the Law of War. States sometimes take actions on the international or multinational level to implement and enforce the law of war.

For example, NATO Standardization Agreements might specify common procedures to implement obligations under the 1949 Geneva Conventions for the treatment of POWs. States may investigate alleged violations of the law of war through international commissions of

---

[6] GWS art. 1 ("The High Contracting Parties undertake to respect and to ensure respect for the present Convention in all circumstances."); GWS-SEA art. 1 (same); GPW art. 1 (same); GC art. 1 (same).

[7] Brian Egan, Legal Adviser, Department of State, *Remarks to the American Society of International Law: International Law, Legal Diplomacy, and the Counter-ISIL Campaign*, Apr. 1, 2016 ("Some have argued that the obligation in Common Article 1 of the Geneva Conventions to 'ensure respect' for the Conventions legally requires us to undertake such steps and more vis-à-vis not only our partners, but all States and non-State actors engaged in armed conflict. Although we do not share this expansive interpretation of Common Article 1, as a matter of policy, we always seek to promote adherence to the law of armed conflict generally and encourage other States to do the same. As a matter of international law, we would look to the law of State responsibility and our partners' compliance with the law of armed conflict in assessing the lawfulness of our assistance to, and joint operations with, those military partners.").

[8] AP III art. 1(1) ("The High Contracting Parties undertake to respect and to ensure respect for this Protocol in all circumstances.").

[9] CCW AMENDED MINES PROTOCOL art. 14 ("1. Each High Contracting Party shall take all appropriate steps, including legislative and other measures, to prevent and suppress violations of this Protocol by persons or on territory under its jurisdiction or control. 2. The measures envisaged in paragraph I of this Article include appropriate measures to ensure the imposition of penal sanctions against persons who, in relation to an armed conflict and contrary to the provisions of this Protocol, wilfully kill or cause serious injury to civilians and to bring such persons to justice.").

[10] Optional Protocol to the Convention on the Rights of the Child on the Involvement of Children in Armed Conflict, art. 6(1), May 25, 2000, 2173 UNTS 222, 238 ("Each State Party shall take all necessary legal, administrative and other measures to ensure the effective implementation and enforcement of the provisions of this Protocol within its jurisdiction.").

inquiry.[11] As another example, States may establish international criminal tribunals to try enemy belligerents.[12]

18.1.4 Law of War Obligations and International Organizations. International organizations, such as the United Nations or NATO, are not Parties to law of war treaties, such as the 1949 Geneva Conventions. Thus, these organizations do not have obligations under those treaty instruments. However, the member States of international organizations are Parties to these treaties, and as a general matter, a State's obligations under law of war treaties would not be rendered inapplicable simply because its forces are part of an international or multinational force or are acting through an international organization.

18.1.5 Application of Implementation and Enforcement Measures Outside the Context of International Armed Conflict. Certain treaty obligations with respect to the implementation and enforcement of the law of war may not apply outside the context of international armed conflict.

Nonetheless, many of the domestic law, policies, and regulations that are used to implement and enforce the law of war are applicable outside the context of international armed conflict. Thus, for example, many of the provisions of the Uniform Code of Military Justice may be used to punish crimes that have been committed in the context of a non-international armed conflict or a military operation other than war.

18.2 Prudential Reasons Supporting the Implementation and Enforcement of the Law of War

The implementation and enforcement of the law of war have been supported by strong practical considerations. Compliance with the law of war is not only legally required but also in the strong self-interest of everyone subject to the law of war.[13]

18.2.1 Reinforcing Military Effectiveness. Conducting military operations in accordance with the law of war is not fighting with one hand tied behind one's back. Rather, law of war principles and rules are consistent with military doctrines for a profession of arms that are the basis for effective combat operations.[14]

For example, various military doctrines, such as accuracy of targeting, concentration of effort, maximization of military advantage, conservation of resources, avoidance of excessive collateral damage, and economy of force are not only fully consistent with compliance with the law of war, but also reinforce its observance. Use of indiscriminate and excessive force is costly, highly inefficient, and a waste of scarce resources.[15]

---

[11] *Refer to* § 18.14 (International Mechanisms to Investigate Alleged Law of War Violations).

[12] *Refer to* § 18.20.1 (Post-World War II International Military Tribunals).

[13] 1976 AIR FORCE PAMPHLET 110-31 ¶1-6 ("The law of armed conflict developed from an amalgam of social, political and military considerations. The primary basis for the law, and the principal reason for its respect, is that it generally serves the self-interest of everyone subject to its commands.").

[14] Christopher Greenwood, *Historical Development and Legal Basis*, *in* DIETER FLECK, THE HANDBOOK OF HUMANITARIAN LAW IN ARMED CONFLICTS 33 (¶132) (1999) ("It should not be assumed, however, that humanitarian law and military requirements will necessarily be opposed to one another. On the contrary, most rules of humanitarian law reflect good military practice, and adherence by armed forces to those rules is likely to reinforce discipline and good order within the forces concerned.").

[15] 1976 AIR FORCE PAMPHLET 110-31 ¶1-6b ("More importantly, various military doctrines, such as accuracy of targeting, concentration of effort, maximization of military advantage, conservation of resources, avoidance of excessive collateral damage, and economy of force are not only fully consistent with compliance with the law of armed conflict but reinforce its observance. Use of excessive force is not only costly and highly inefficient—and to be avoided for those reasons—it may also be a waste of scarce resources.").

Similarly, the necessity of discipline for an effective armed force reinforces the implementation and enforcement of the law of war. An undisciplined force is more likely to commit law of war violations, such as pillaging, detainee abuse, or atrocities against the civilian population.[16]

18.2.2 Encouraging Reciprocal Adherence by the Adversary. The requirement to comply with many law of war rules (such as the obligation to treat detainees humanely) does not depend on whether the enemy complies with that rule.[17]

Nevertheless, reciprocity may be a critical factor in the actual observance of the law of war. Adherence to law of war rules in conducting military operations can encourage an adversary also to comply with those law of war rules.[18] For example, humane treatment of enemy persons detained by U.S. forces can encourage enemy forces to treat detained U.S. persons humanely.[19] Conversely, the maltreatment of detained personnel by U.S. forces may have a dramatic and negative effect on how U.S. personnel in the hands of the enemy are treated and the degree to which the law of war is respected generally.[20]

18.2.3 Maintaining Public Support and Political Legitimacy. The implementation and enforcement of the law of war are also supported by the fact that violations of the law of war are counterproductive to the political goals sought to be achieved by military operations.[21] For example, violations of the law of war in counter-insurgency operations may diminish the support of the local population. Violations of the law of war may also diminish the support of the populace in democratic States, including the United States and other States that would otherwise support or participate in coalition operations. Violations of the law of war committed by one side may encourage third parties to support the opposing side.

18.3 Duties of Individual Members of the Armed Forces

Each member of the armed services has a duty to: (1) comply with the law of war in good faith; and (2) refuse to comply with clearly illegal orders to commit violations of the law of war.

18.3.1 Comply With the Law of War in Good Faith. Each member of the armed forces has a duty to comply with the law of war in good faith.[22] In practice, the obligation of individual

---

[16] *Compare* § 4.18.3 (Private Persons Who Engage in Hostilities – Lack of the Privileges of Combatant Status).

[17] *Refer to* § 3.6 (Reciprocity and Law of War Rules).

[18] 1976 Air Force Pamphlet 110-31 ¶10-1b ("The most important relevant treaties, the 1949 Geneva Conventions for the Protection of War Victims, are not formally conditioned on reciprocity. … Yet reciprocity is an implied condition in other rules and obligations including generally the law of armed conflict. It is moreover a critical factor in actual *observance* of the law of armed conflict. Reciprocity is also explicitly the basis for the doctrine of reprisals.").

[19] *Refer to* § 9.2.5 (Reciprocity in the Treatment of POWs).

[20] United States v. List, *et al.* (The Hostage Case), XI Trials of War Criminals Before the NMT 1274 ("It is almost inevitable that the murder of innocent members of the population, including the relatives and friends of the franc-tireurs, would generate a hatred that was bound to express itself in counterreprisals and acts of atrocity.").

[21] 1976 Air Force Pamphlet 110-31 ¶1-6a ("However, the application of military force has never been an end in itself. In many respects, the overall political context has increased in importance in recent years although that political context has always influenced the means of destruction or tactics used in warfare. Violations of the law of armed conflict have been recognized as counterproductive to the political goals sought to be achieved. For example, they may arouse public opinion and induce neutrals to become involved in the conflict on the adversary's side, such as the entry of the United States into World War I.").

[22] *Refer to* § 1.10.2 (Force of the Law of War Under U.S. Domestic Law).

service members to comply with the law of war in good faith is met when service members: (1) perform their duties as they have been trained and directed; and (2) apply the training on the law of war that they have received.[23]

The duty of each individual service member to comply with the law of war in good faith rests within a broader framework of law of war implementation by the U.S. armed forces.

18.3.1.1 *Implementation of International Obligations by Persons With the Authority to Make the Necessary Decisions and Judgments Required by International Law*. As a general matter, the persons within a party to a conflict who are responsible for implementing an obligation are those persons with the authority to make the necessary decisions and judgments required by that international obligation. It is not the case that every individual who belongs to a party to the conflict is responsible for implementing every obligation held by that party.

For example, certain law of war obligations only apply to commanders or to specialized units, such as units providing medical care, conducting detention operations, or engaging in the protection of cultural property. As a case in point, although the specific responsibilities that individual combatants have to implement the principle of proportionality will depend on their role and assigned military duties in planning or conducting an attack, commanders are responsible for making the decisions and judgments required by the principle of proportionality in conducting attacks.[24]

18.3.1.2 *Practical Ways in Which the Requirement to Comply With the Law of War in Good Faith is Met by Individual Service Members*. Individual service members are not expected to be experts in the law of war. The burden on individual members of the armed forces to know the relevant requirements of the law of war is addressed in practice through the following ways.

First, service members should receive training commensurate with their duties on the relevant requirements of the law of war.

Second, law of war requirements have also been incorporated into domestic law, policy, regulations, and orders, which often are reviewed by counsel for consistency with the law of war.[25] Moreover, in most cases, the requirements and standards in applicable policies, regulations, and orders will often impose higher standards than the requirements of the law of war.[26]

Third, when appropriate, service members should ask questions through appropriate channels and consult with the command legal adviser on issues relating to the law of war.

18.3.2 Refuse to Comply With Clearly Illegal Orders to Commit Law of War Violations. Members of the armed forces must refuse to comply with clearly illegal orders to commit law of war violations. In addition, orders should not be construed to authorize implicitly violations of law of war.

18.3.2.1 *Clearly Illegal Orders to Commit Law of War Violations*. The requirement to refuse to comply with orders to commit law of war violations applies to orders to perform conduct that is clearly illegal or orders that the subordinate knows, in fact, are illegal. For example, orders to fire upon the shipwrecked would be clearly illegal.[27] Similarly, orders to

---

[23] *Refer to* § 18.6.2 (Special Instruction or Training).

[24] *Refer to* § 5.10.2 (Responsibility of Commanders for Implementing the Principle of Proportionality in Conducting Attacks).

[25] *Refer to* § 18.7 (Instructions, Regulations, and Procedures to Implement and Enforce the Law of War).

[26] *Refer to* § 18.7.2.3 (Setting Higher Standards as a Matter of Policy).

[27] Judgement in Case of Lieutenants Dithmar and Boldt, Hospital Ship "Llandovery Castle" (Second Criminal Senate of the Imperial Court of Justice, Germany, Jul. 16, 1921), *reprinted in* 16 AJIL, 708, 721-22 (1922) ("It is certainly to

kill defenseless persons who have submitted to and are under effective physical control would also be clearly illegal.[28] On the other hand, the duty not to comply with orders that are clearly illegal would be limited in its application when the subordinate is not competent to evaluate whether the rule has been violated.[29]

Subordinates are not required to screen the orders of superiors for questionable points of legality, and may, absent specific knowledge to the contrary, presume that orders have been lawfully issued.[30]

18.3.2.2 Commands and Orders Should Not Be Understood as Implicitly Authorizing Violations of the Law of War. Commands and orders should not be understood as implicitly authorizing violations of the law of war where other interpretations are reasonably available.[31]

---

be urged in favor of the military subordinates, that they are under no obligation to question the order of their superior officer, and they can count upon its legality. But no such confidence can be held to exist, if such an order is universally known to everybody, including also the accused, to be without any doubt whatever against the law. This happens only in rare and exceptional cases. But this case was precisely one of them, for in the present instance, it was perfectly clear to the accused that killing defenceless people in the life-boats could be nothing else but a breach of the law. As naval officers by profession they were well aware, as the naval expert Saalwiachter has strikingly stated, that one is not legally authorized to kill defenceless people. They well knew that this was the case here. They quickly found out the facts by questioning the occupants in the boats when these were stopped. They could only have gathered, from the order given by Patzig, that he wished to make use of his subordinates to carry out a breach of the law. They should, therefore, have refused to obey.").

[28] United States v. Calley, 22 U.S.C.M.A. 534, 543-44 (C.M.A. 1973) ("In the stress of combat, a member of the armed forces cannot reasonably be expected to make a refined legal judgment and be held criminally responsible if he guesses wrong on a question as to which there may be considerable disagreement. But there is no disagreement as to the illegality of the order to kill in this case. For 100 years, it has been a settled rule of American law that even in war the summary killing of an enemy, who has submitted to, and is under, effective physical control, is murder.").

[29] *Refer to* § 5.10.2.3 (Duty Not to Comply With Clearly Illegal Orders and the Principle of Proportionality).

[30] United States v. von Leeb, *et al.* (The High Command Case), XI TRIAL OF WAR CRIMINALS BEFORE THE NMT 510-11 ("Orders are the basis upon which any army operates. It is basic to the discipline of an army that orders are issued to be carried out. Its discipline is built upon its principle. Without it, no army can be effective and it is certainly not incumbent upon a soldier in a subordinate position to screen the orders of superiors for questionable points of legality. Within certain limitations, he has the right to assume that the orders of his superiors and the state which he serves and which are issued to him are in conformity with international law. ... He has the right to presume, in the absence of specific knowledge to the contrary, that the legality of such orders has been properly determined before their issuance. He cannot be held criminally responsible for a mere error in judgment as to disputable legal questions."); WINTHROP, MILITARY LAW & PRECEDENTS 296-97 ("But for the inferior to assume to determine the question of the lawfulness of an order given him by a superior would of itself, as a general rule, amount to insubordination, and such an assumption carried into practice would subvert military discipline. Where the order is apparently regular and lawful on its face, he is not to go behind it to satisfy himself that his superior has proceeded with authority, but is to obey it according to its terms, the only exceptions recognized to the rule of obedience being cases of orders so manifestly beyond the legal power or discretion of the commander as to admit of no rational doubt of their unlawfulness. Except in such instances of palpable illegality, which must be of rare occurrence, the inferior should presume that the order was lawful and authorized and obey it accordingly, and in obeying it can scarcely fail to be held justified by a military court ... .").

[31] *See Basic Course in the Geneva Conventions of 1949 and Hague Convention No. IV of 1907: Lesson Plan—Second Hour*, ¶5b, Appendix A in DEPARTMENT OF THE ARMY SUBJECT SCHEDULE 27-1, *The Geneva Conventions of 1949 and Hague Convention No. IV of 1907*, 11 (Aug. 29, 1975) ("You should not presume that an order is criminal. If you think it is criminal, it is probably because the order is unclear. For example, while on patrol we capture a prisoner. On our return the patrol leader questions him. When the patrol leader finishes the questioning he tells you 'get rid of that man.' That order is not clear. The patrol leader undoubtedly means to take the man to the Detainee Collection Point. ... Rather than presume that an unclear order directs you to commit a crime, ask your superior for a clarification of the order. Above all, remember that if you are the leader, make your order clear and

For example, if a commander issues an order to attack a town, one should assume that the order directs attacks on military objectives located in that area.[32] Similarly, speeches by commanders before combat operations to rally members of their command should not be understood to authorize implicitly law of war violations against the enemy.[33]

18.4 Commanders' Duty to Implement and Enforce the Law of War

Military commanders have a duty to take appropriate measures as are within their power to control the forces under their command for the prevention of violations of the law of war.[34] For example, commanders have obligations to take appropriate measures to prevent pillage and

---

understandable. Don't put your subordinates in the position where they may think you are giving a criminal order.").

[32] *For example*, Prosecutor v. Gotovina and Markač, ICTY Appellate Chamber, IT-06-09-A, *Judgment*, ¶77 (Nov. 16, 2012) ("More specifically, the Trial Chamber relied on the Impact Analysis to discount Witness Rajčić's assertion that the 2 August Order called for shelling only lawful military targets. In addition, neither Witness Konings nor Witness Corn suggested that the only interpretation of the 2 August Order was as an instruction to commence indiscriminate attacks on the Four Towns. Given that the relevant portion of the 2 August Order was relatively short, and did not explicitly call for unlawful attacks on the Four Towns, the text of the 2 August Order could not, alone, reasonably be relied upon to support a finding that unlawful artillery attacks took place.").

[33] *For example*, L.C. Green, Superior Orders in National and International Law 131-32 (1976) ("The controversy arose over Patton's prepared remarks, which included these statements: 'The fact we are operating in enemy country does not permit us to forget our American tradition of respect for private property, non-combatants, and women. ...Attack rapidly, ruthlessly, viciously and without rest, and kill even civilians who have the stupidity to fight us.' Several days after the operation began, during which time the fighting was extremely fierce, a Captain Compton, who had lost several of his men, lined up forty-three captured Germans, some of whom were wearing civilian clothes, and had them executed by machine gun. At about the same time and in the same general location, a Sergeant West (of another company) shot and killed thirty-six Germans whom he was escorting to the prisoner-of-war cage in the rear. When General Patton learned of these incidents, he ordered both men court-martialed on charges of premeditated murder. At their trials, the two men asserted as a defence the orders issued by General Patton on June 27, 1943 in his preparatory speech. ... The defence's assertions prompted a subsequent inquiry into the speech given by Patton in which he was ultimately exonerated after producing the prepared text of the speech and delivering it orally to a board of investigating officers. Captain Compton and Sergeant West, however, were convicted as charged.") (first ellipsis in original).

[34] *See* In re Yamashita, 327 U.S. 1, 16 (1946) ("The question, then, is whether the law of war imposes on an army commander a duty to take such appropriate measures as are within his power to control the troops under his command for the prevention of the specified acts which are violations of the law of war and which are likely to attend the occupation of hostile territory by an uncontrolled soldiery, and whether he may be charged with personal responsibility for his failure to take such measures when violations result. ... These provisions [of the Hague IV Reg., the Hague X, and the 1929 GWS] plainly imposed on petitioner, who at the time specified was military governor of the Philippines as well as commander of the Japanese forces, an affirmative duty to take such measures as were within his power and appropriate in the circumstances to protect prisoners of war and the civilian population. This duty of a commanding officer has heretofore been recognized, and its breach penalized by our own military tribunals."); Elihu Root, Secretary of War, *Memorandum Transmitting the Record and Proceedings of the Trial of Brigadier General Jacob H. Smith*, Jul. 12, 1902, *reprinted in* H.C. Corbin, Adjutant General, Major General, U.S. Army, *General Orders, No. 80*, 2, 3 Jul. 16, 1902, General Orders and Circulars of the Adjutant General's Office, 1902 (1903) ("It is the duty of a general officer whose age and experience have brought him to high command not to incite his subordinates to acts of lawless violence, but to so explain to them the application of the laws of war and the limitations upon their conduct as to prevent transgressions upon their part and supplement their comparative inexperience by his wise control. In this General *Smith* has signally failed, and for this he has been justly convicted.").

to protect the wounded, sick, and shipwrecked within their control.[35]

18.4.1 Background on Commander's Duties to Implement and Enforce the Law of War. The law of war presupposes that its violation is to be avoided through the control of the operations of war by commanders who are to some extent responsible for their subordinates.[36] One of the requirements for armed forces to receive the privileges of combatant status is that they operate under a responsible command.[37] In addition, law of war treaties have specified that commanders must take appropriate measures to ensure that the provisions of those treaties are observed.[38]

18.4.2 Discipline of Subordinates. In carrying out their duties to implement and enforce the law of war, commanders may use disciplinary or penal measures.[39] Under international law, commanders have discretion about how to implement and enforce their law of war obligations; there is no absolute or automatic requirement under international law to punish particular offenders within their armed forces in a specific way.[40]

18.4.3 Duty to Investigate Reports of Alleged Law of War Violations. Commanders have a duty to investigate reports of alleged law of war violations committed by persons under

---

[35] *Refer to* § 5.17.4 (Pillage Prohibited); § 7.4 (Search, Collection, and Affirmative Protection of the Wounded, Sick, Shipwrecked, and Dead).

[36] In re Yamashita, 327 U.S. 1, 15 (1946) ("It is evident that the conduct of military operations by troops whose excesses are unrestrained by the orders or efforts of their commander would almost certainly result in violations which it is the purpose of the law of war to prevent. Its purpose to protect civilian populations and prisoners of war from brutality would largely be defeated if the commander of an invading army could, with impunity, neglect to take reasonable measures for their protection. Hence, the law of war presupposes that its violation is to be avoided through the control of the operations of war by commanders who are to some extent responsible for their subordinates."). *Consider* AP I art. 87(1) ("The High Contracting Parties and the Parties to the conflict shall require military commanders, with respect to members of the armed forces under their command and other persons under their control, to prevent and, where necessary, to suppress and to report to competent authorities breaches of the [Geneva] Conventions and of this Protocol.").

[37] *Refer to* § 4.6.3 (Being Commanded by a Person Responsible for His or Her Subordinates).

[38] *See, e.g.*, GWS art. 45 ("Each Party to the conflict, acting through its Commanders-in-Chief, shall ensure the detailed execution of the preceding Articles and provide for unforeseen cases, in conformity with the general principles of the present Convention."); GWS-SEA art. 46 (same). *Consider* HAGUE X art. 19 ("The Commanders-in-chief of the belligerent fleets must see that the above Articles are properly carried out; they will have also to see to cases not covered thereby, in accordance with the instructions of their respective Governments and in conformity with the general principles of the present Convention.").

[39] *Consider* AP I art. 87(3) ("The High Contracting Parties and Parties to the conflict shall require any commander who is aware that subordinates or other persons under his control are going to commit or have committed a breach of the Conventions or of this Protocol, to initiate such steps as are necessary to prevent such violations of the Conventions or this Protocol, and, where appropriate, to initiate disciplinary or penal action against violators thereof."). *Refer to* § 18.19 (Discipline in National Jurisdictions of Individuals for Violations of the Law of War).

[40] United States v. von Leeb, *et al.* (The High Command Case), XI TRIALS OF WAR CRIMINALS BEFORE THE NMT 524 ("With regard to the second aspect of this order, that is the obligation to prosecute soldiers who commit offences against the indigenous population, this obligation as a matter of International Law is considered doubtful. The duty imposed upon a military commander is the protection of the civilian population. Whether this protection be assured by the prosecution of soldiers charged with offences against the civilian population, or whether it be assured by disciplinary measures or otherwise, is immaterial from an international standpoint.").

their command or against persons to whom they have a legal duty to protect.[41]

18.4.4 Issuance of Guidance, Training of Subordinates, and Other Preventive or Corrective Measures. Apart from disciplinary measures, a variety of other measures may be appropriate to prevent or address violations of the law of war by subordinates. For example, commanders should ensure that members of the armed forces under their command are, commensurate with their duties, aware of their duties under the law of war.[42] After violations have occurred, retraining personnel or revising procedures may be appropriate, particularly where the underlying facts or nature of the violations do not warrant punitive measures.

18.5 Role of Judge Advocates and Legal Advisers

18.5.1 Legal Advisers. The United States has provided for legal advisers to advise military commanders on the law of war.[43] For example, DoD policy has required that each head of a DoD component make qualified legal advisers available at all levels of command to provide advice about law of war compliance during planning and execution of exercises and operations.[44]

18.5.1.1 *Review of Plans, Policies, Directives, and Rules of Engagement by Legal Advisers*. DoD policy has required that commanders of the combatant commands ensure that all plans, policies, directives, and rules of engagement, and those of subordinate commands and components, are reviewed by legal advisers to ensure their consistency with the law of war and DoD policy on the law of war.[45]

18.5.1.2 *Supervision of Administration of Programs to Address Enemy Violations of the Law of War*. DoD policy has required that commanders of the combatant commands

---

[41] *Refer to* § 18.13 (National Investigations of Alleged Violations of the Law of War).

[42] *Consider* AP I art. 87(2) ("In order to prevent and suppress breaches, High Contracting Parties and Parties to the conflict shall require that, commensurate with their level of responsibility, commanders ensure that members of the armed forces under their command are aware of their obligations under the Conventions and this Protocol.").

[43] *Consider* AP I art. 82 ("The High Contracting Parties at all times, and the Parties to the conflict in time of armed conflict, shall ensure that legal advisers are available, when necessary, to advise military commanders at the appropriate level on the application of the Conventions and this Protocol and on the appropriate instruction to be given to the armed forces on this subject.").

[44] DoD Directive 2311.01E, *DoD Law of War Program*, ¶5.1 (May 9, 2006, Certified Current as of Feb. 22, 2011) ("The Heads of the DoD Components shall: … [¶5.7.3] Make qualified legal advisers at all levels of command available to provide advice about law of war compliance during planning and execution of exercises and operations; and institute and implement programs to comply with the reporting requirements established in section 6."); DoD Directive 5100.77, *DoD Law of War Program*, ¶5.3 (Dec. 9, 1998) ("The Heads of the DoD Components shall: … [¶5.3.3] "Ensure that qualified legal advisers are immediately available at all levels of command to provide advice about law of war compliance during planning and execution of exercises and operations; and institute and implement programs to comply with the reporting requirements established in section 6., below.").

[45] DoD Directive 2311.01E, *DoD Law of War Program*, ¶5.11 (May 9, 2006, Certified Current as of Feb. 22, 2011) ("The Commanders of the Combatant Commands shall: …[¶5.11.8] Ensure all plans, policies, directives, and rules of engagement issued by the command and its subordinate commands and components are reviewed by legal advisers to ensure their consistency with this Directive and the law of war."); DoD Directive 5100.77, *DoD Law of War Program*, ¶5.8 (Dec. 9, 1998) ("The Commanders of the Combatant Commands shall: … [¶5.8.6] Ensure all plans, policies, directives, and rules of engagement issued by the command and its subordinate commands and components are reviewed by legal advisers to ensure their consistency with this Directive and the law of war.").

designate a command legal adviser to supervise the administration of those aspects of the command's program dealing with possible, suspected, or alleged enemy violations of the law of war.[46]

18.5.1.3 *Review of the Acquisition of Weapons*. DoD policy has required the legal review of the intended acquisition of weapons.[47]

18.5.2 Law of War Questions During Military Operations. During military operations, questions on the law of war from U.S. forces or coalition partners related to a specific issue should be referred through the operational chain of command for resolution. It may also be appropriate to refer questions to either the office of the Judge Advocate General of a Military Department, the Staff Judge Advocate to the Commandant of the Marines Corps, the General Counsel of a Military Department, the Legal Counsel to the Chairman of the Joint Chiefs of Staff, or the DoD General Counsel.

18.5.3 Role of the DoD Law of War Working Group. The DoD Law of War Working Group is a DoD internal mechanism for coordination on law of war issues. It consists of representatives of the General Counsel, Department of Defense; representatives, at the election of each, of the General Counsel of each Military Department, the Judge Advocate General of each Military Department, the Staff Judge Advocate to the Commandant of the Marine Corps, and the Legal Counsel to the Chairman of the Joint Chiefs of Staff.[48] The DoD Law of War Working Group develops and coordinates law of war initiatives and issues, manages other law of war matters as they arise, and provides advice to the DoD General Counsel on legal matters covered by DoD Directive 2311.01E.[49] This includes the preparation, review, and updating of

---

[46] DoD DIRECTIVE 2311.01E, *DoD Law of War Program*, ¶5.11 (May 9, 2006, Certified Current as of Feb. 22, 2011) ("The Commanders of the Combatant Commands shall: … [¶5.11.5] Designate the command legal adviser to supervise the administration of those aspects of this program dealing with possible, suspected, or alleged enemy violations of the law of war."); DoD DIRECTIVE 5100.77, *DoD Law of War Program*, ¶5.8 (Dec. 9, 1998) ("The Commanders of the Combatant Commands shall: … [¶5.8.3] Designate the command legal adviser to supervise the administration of those aspects of this program dealing with possible, suspected, or alleged enemy violations of the law of war.").

[47] *Refer to* § 6.2 (DoD Policy of Reviewing the Legality of Weapons).

[48] DoD DIRECTIVE 2311.01E, *DoD Law of War Program*, ¶5.1.4 (May 9, 2006, Certified Current as of Feb. 22, 2011) ("The General Counsel of the Department of Defense (GC, DoD) shall: Supervise and assign a chair for the DoD Law of War Working Group, consisting of representatives, at the election by each of the GC, DoD; the General Counsel of each Military Department; the Counsel to the Commandant of the Marine Corps; the Judge Advocate General of each Military Department; the Staff Judge Advocate to the Commandant of the Marine Corps; and the Legal Counsel to the Chairman of the Joint Chiefs of Staff."); DoD DIRECTIVE 5100.77, *DoD Law of War Program*, ¶5.1.2 (Dec. 9, 1998) ("The General Counsel of the Department of Defense shall: Establish a DoD Law of War Working Group consisting of representatives from the General Counsel of the Department of Defense (GC, DoD), the Legal Counsel to the Chairman of the Joint Chiefs of Staff, the International and Operational Law Division of the Office of the Judge Advocate General of each Military Department, and the Operational Law Branch of the Office of the Staff Judge Advocate to the Commandant of the Marine Corps.").

[49] DoD DIRECTIVE 2311.01E, *DoD Law of War Program*, ¶5.1.4 (May 9, 2006, Certified Current as of Feb. 22, 2011) ("The DoD Law of War Working Group shall develop and coordinate law of war initiatives and issues; support the research, preparation, review, and updating of the DoD Law of War Manual; manage other law of war matters as they arise; and provide advice to the General Counsel on legal matters covered by this Directive."); DoD DIRECTIVE 5100.77, *DoD Law of War Program*, ¶5.1.2 (Dec. 9, 1998) ("The DoD Law of War Working Group shall

this manual.

18.6 DISSEMINATION, STUDY, AND OTHER MEASURES TO FACILITATE UNDERSTANDING OF DUTIES UNDER THE LAW OF WAR

A basic step in implementing and enforcing the law of war is to ensure that people understand its requirements. Certain treaties require that Parties disseminate the text of that treaty and promote its study, especially by those personnel who are assigned to implement its obligations.

18.6.1 General Dissemination and Study of Treaties. Certain treaties require that Parties disseminate the treaty and promote study of that treaty by the armed forces and the civilian population.

18.6.1.1 *Dissemination and Study - 1949 Geneva Conventions*. Parties to 1949 Geneva Conventions undertake, in time of peace, as in time of war, to disseminate the text of those Conventions widely as possible in their respective countries, and in particular, to include the study of the Conventions in their programs of military and, if possible, civil instruction.[50] In addition to the entire population of the Party to the GPW, the GPW emphasizes that Parties' armed forces should know the principles of the GPW.[51] Similarly, the GWS and GWS-Sea emphasize that the armed fighting forces, medical personnel, and chaplains should know the principles of those treaties.[52]

18.6.1.2 *Dissemination and Study - CCW and Protocols*. Parties to the CCW also undertake, in time of peace as in time of armed conflict, to disseminate the CCW and those of its annexed Protocols by which they are bound as widely as possible in their respective countries and, in particular, to include the study of these instruments in their program of military instruction, so that those instruments may become known to their armed forces.[53]

---

develop and coordinate law of war initiatives and issues, manage other law of war matters as they arise, and provide advice to the General Counsel on legal matters covered by this Directive.").

[50] GC art. 144 ("The High Contracting Parties undertake, in time of peace as in time of war, to disseminate the text of the present Convention as widely as possible in their respective countries, and, in particular, to include the study thereof in their programmes of military and, if possible, civil instruction, so that the principles thereof may become known to the entire population.").

[51] GPW art. 127 (The High Contracting Parties undertake, in time of peace as in time of war, to disseminate the text of the present Convention as widely as possible in their respective countries, and, in particular, to include the study thereof in their programmes of military and, if possible, civil instruction, so that the principles thereof may become known to all their armed forces and to the entire population.").

[52] GWS art. 47 ("The High Contracting Parties undertake, in time of peace as in time of war, to disseminate the text of the present Convention as widely as possible in their respective countries, and, in particular, to include the study thereof in their programmes of military and, if possible, civil instruction, so that the principles thereof may become known to the entire population, in particular to the armed fighting forces, the medical personnel and the chaplains."); GWS-SEA art. 48 (same).

[53] CCW art. 6 ("The High Contracting Parties undertake, in time of peace as in time of armed conflict, to disseminate this Convention and those of its annexed Protocols by which they are bound as widely as possible in their respective countries and, in particular, to include the study thereof in their programmes of military instruction, so that those instruments may become known to their armed forces.").

18.6.1.3 *Dissemination and Study – AP III*. Parties to AP III undertake, in time of peace as in time of armed conflict, to disseminate this Protocol as widely as possible in their respective countries and, in particular, to include the study of it in their program of military instruction and to encourage the study of it by the civilian population, so that this instrument may become known to the armed forces and to the civilian population.[54]

18.6.1.4 *Dissemination and Study – 1954 Hague Cultural Property Convention*. Parties to the 1954 Hague Cultural Property Convention undertake, in time of peace as in time of armed conflict, to disseminate the text of the Convention and the Regulations for its execution as widely as possible in their respective countries. They undertake, in particular, to include the study thereof in their programs of military and, if possible, civilian training, so that its principles are made known to the whole population, especially the armed forces and personnel engaged in the protection of cultural property.[55]

18.6.1.5 *Dissemination and Study – Child Soldiers Protocol*. Parties to the Child Soldiers Protocol undertake to make the principles and provisions of the Child Soldiers Protocol widely known and promoted by appropriate means, to adults and children alike.[56]

18.6.2 Special Instruction or Training. In addition to requirements to disseminate and to promote the study of treaties, treaties also require States to ensure that members of the armed forces who have duties under those treaties are trained commensurate with those duties. DoD policy has required, as a general matter, that personnel are trained in the law of war commensurate with their duties.[57]

Training may involve not only classroom instruction or individualized study, but also, for example, unit training exercises.[58]

---

[54] AP III art. 7 ("The High Contracting Parties undertake, in time of peace as in time of armed conflict, to disseminate this Protocol as widely as possible in their respective countries and, in particular, to include the study thereof in their programmes of military instruction and to encourage the study thereof by the civilian population, so that this instrument may become known to the armed forces and to the civilian population.").

[55] 1954 HAGUE CULTURAL PROPERTY CONVENTION art. 25 ("The High Contracting Parties undertake, in time of peace as in time of armed conflict, to disseminate the text of the present Convention and the Regulations for its execution as widely as possible in their respective countries. They undertake, in particular, to include the study thereof in their programmes of military and, if possible, civilian training, so that its principles are made known to the whole population, especially the armed forces and personnel engaged in the protection of cultural property.").

[56] Optional Protocol to the Convention on the Rights of the Child on the Involvement of Children in Armed Conflict, art. 6(2), May 25, 2000, 2173 UNTS 222, 238 ("States Parties undertake to make the principles and provisions of the present Protocol widely known and promoted by appropriate means, to adults and children alike.").

[57] DOD DIRECTIVE 2311.01E, *DoD Law of War Program*, ¶5.8 (May 9, 2006, Certified Current as of Feb. 22, 2011) ("The Secretaries of the Military Departments shall develop internal policies and procedures consistent with this Directive in support of the DoD Law of War Program to: … 5.8.1. Provide directives, publications, instructions, and training so the principles and rules of the law of war will be known to members of their respective Departments. Such knowledge will be commensurate with each individual's duties and responsibilities.").

[58] *For example*, W. Hays Parks, *The United States Military and the Law of War: Inculcating an Ethos*, 69 SOCIAL RESEARCH 981, 995-96 (2002) ("The Army also maintains four permanent Combat Training Centers (CTCs). The CTCs-at Ft. Irwin, California; Ft. Polk, Louisiana; Ft. Leavenworth, Kansas; and Hohenfels, Germany-offer a variety of combat and peace operations training for Army units. Three of the CTCs are staffed with a full-time

In many cases, training on law of war requirements may not be classified as "law of war" training, or may be conducted without acknowledgment that the requirements are law of war requirements.[59] Rather, it may be the case that military forces would be trained according to military doctrines or regulations, which have incorporated law of war requirements and have been reviewed for consistency with the law of war.[60]

The 1949 Geneva Conventions, the CCW Amended Mines Protocol, and the CCW Protocol V on Explosive Remnants of War each have specific provisions relating to special instruction or training.

18.6.2.1 *Special Instructions or Training - 1949 Geneva Conventions*. The GPW and GC further provide that the military or other authorities who assume responsibilities for POWs or protected persons must possess the text of the GPW or the GC and be specially instructed as to its provisions.[61]

18.6.2.2 *Special Instructions or Training - CCW Amended Mines Protocol*. Each Party to the CCW Amended Mines Protocol shall require that armed forces personnel receive training commensurate with their duties and responsibilities to comply with the provisions of the

---

opposing force (the OPFOR), which 'engages' the training unit, as well as an observer-controller (OC) contingent. The OCs observe the mission, mentor the training unit's commanders and soldiers, and direct some of the activity that occurs during the training exercise. The Army Judge Advocate General's Corps has assigned Army judge advocates to serve as OCs at each of the CTCs. As part of their duties, these judge advocate OCs script events involving civilians, who, in turn, interact with the personnel of the unit being trained. These civilians, or role-players, serve critical training functions. For example, they may play the part of ICRC personnel who visit a training unit for the purpose of inspecting the unit's EPW holding facilities. They may also live in full-scale 'villages' on the battlefield, playing the role of civilians who find themselves caught up in the context of an ongoing conflict. The judge advocate observer-controllers monitor the training unit's interaction with these civilians, ensuring that commanders, staff, and individual soldiers understand and meet their law of war obligations. These 'villages' also include such structures as churches and historic sites. Thus, the unit also is 'tested' on law of war compliance as it relates to targeting and weaponeering considerations. Experience has shown this type of hands-on, realistic law of war training to be exceptionally effective.").

[59] *For example*, W. Hays Parks, *The United States Military and the Law of War: Inculcating an Ethos*, 69 SOCIAL RESEARCH 981, 982-83 (2002) ("Other training may cover law of war topics, or address law of war obligations, without necessarily referring to the law of war. An example is teaching a soldier how to handle an enemy prisoner of war (EPW). Once the prisoner of war has reached an EPW collection point, or a theater EPW camp, military police personnel working in each will go about their assigned duties to process and care for the prisoner of war. In all likelihood each soldier handling an EPW will have received training relative to his or her assigned duties. But the training of each will not necessarily be listed or categorized as 'law of war training,' since it is based on doctrine or regulations. Similarly, military medical personnel are trained to treat battlefield wounded and sick solely on the basis of medical priority. This training may be done without acknowledgment that it is a treaty requirement. The same may be said for training provided to combat engineers in laying minefields. The doctrine will have been reviewed for compliance with treaty requirements, and the mines employed will have been reviewed in compliance with the country's treaty obligations. The combat engineer will employ lawful mines in a manner consistent with his or her doctrine. It is unlikely this will be classified as law of war training.").

[60] *Refer to* § 18.7.2 (Reasons for Implementation Through Instructions, Regulations, and Procedures).

[61] GPW art. 127 ("Any military or other authorities, who in time of war assume responsibilities in respect of prisoners of war, must possess the text of the Convention and be specially instructed as to its provisions."); GC art. 144 ("Any civilian, military, police or other authorities, who in time of war assume responsibilities in respect of protected persons, must possess the text of the Convention and be specially instructed as to its provisions.").

CCW Amended Mines Protocol.[62]

18.6.2.3 *Special Instructions or Training - CCW Protocol V On Explosive Remnants of War*. Each Party to the CCW Protocol V on Explosive Remnants of War shall require that its personnel receive training consistent with the relevant provisions of this Protocol.[63]

18.7 INSTRUCTIONS, REGULATIONS, AND PROCEDURES TO IMPLEMENT AND ENFORCE THE LAW OF WAR

The law of war has traditionally been implemented through military instructions, regulations, and procedures. For example, the Lieber Code, one of the first codifications of the law of war, was called "Instructions for the Government of Armies of the United States in the Field," and was issued as a General Order.[64] Similarly, directives and regulations have been issued to implement law of war obligations relating to detainees and to establish higher standards as a matter of policy.[65]

18.7.1 Treaty Provisions Specifically Contemplating or Requiring Military Instructions, Regulations, and Procedures. Law of war treaties contemplate or in some cases require that such instructions will be issued. In some cases, the implementation of a treaty through military instructions or regulations may be understood as a part of the general requirements for States to take appropriate actions to implement and enforce their obligations under that treaty.[66]

18.7.1.1 *Instructions, Regulations, and Procedures – Hague Conventions on Land Warfare*. Parties to Hague IV shall issue instructions to their armed land forces, which shall be in conformity with the "Regulations respecting the Laws and Customs of War on Land" annexed

---

[62] CCW AMENDED MINES PROTOCOL art. 14(3) ("Each High Contracting Party shall also require that its armed forces issue relevant military instructions and operating procedures and that armed forces personnel receive training commensurate with their duties and responsibilities to comply with the provisions of this Protocol.").

[63] CCW PROTOCOL V ON EXPLOSIVE REMNANTS OF WAR art. 11(1) ("Each High Contracting Party shall require that its armed forces and relevant agencies or departments issue appropriate instructions and operating procedures and that its personnel receive training consistent with the relevant provisions of this Protocol.").

[64] *Refer to* § 19.3 (Lieber Code).

[65] *For example*, DOD DIRECTIVE 2310.01E, *DoD Detainee Program* (Aug. 19, 2014); DOD DIRECTIVE 2310.01E, *The Department of Defense Detainee Program* (Sept. 5, 2006); 1997 MULTI-SERVICE DETENTION REGULATION §1-1.*b* ("This regulation implements international law, both customary and codified, relating to EPW, RP, CI, and ODs which includes those persons held during military operations other than war. The principal treaties relevant to this regulation are: (1) The 1949 Geneva Convention Relative to the Amelioration of the Condition of the Wounded and Sick in Armed Forces in the Field (GWS). (2) The 1949 Geneva Convention Relative to the Amelioration of the Condition of the Wounded, Sick and Shipwrecked Members of the Armed Forces at Sea (GWS Sea). (3) The 1949 Geneva Convention Relative to the Treatment of Prisoners of War (GPW). (4) The 1949 Geneva Convention Relative to the Protection of Civilian Persons in Time of War (GC), and In the event of conflicts or discrepancies between this regulation and the Geneva Conventions, the provisions of the Geneva Conventions take precedence."). *Refer to* § 8.1.2 (DoD Policies and Regulations Regarding the Treatment of Detainees); § 9.1.3 (DoD Policies and Regulations for the Treatment of POWs); § 10.1.2 (DoD Policies and Regulations for the Treatment of Internees).

[66] *Refer to* § 18.1.2 (National Obligations to Implement and Enforce the Law of War).

to Hague IV.[67]

18.7.1.2 *Instructions, Regulations, and Procedures – 1949 Geneva Conventions*. The 1949 Geneva Conventions contemplate that Parties will adopt laws and regulations to ensure the proper application of the Conventions.[68] The requirement to issue implementing instructions may be understood as part of the general obligation of Parties to undertake to respect and to ensure respect for the Conventions.[69]

18.7.1.3 *Instructions, Regulations, and Procedures – CCW Amended Mines Protocol*. Each Party to the CCW Amended Mines Protocol shall require that its armed forces issue relevant military instructions and operating procedures.[70]

18.7.1.4 *Instructions, Regulations, and Procedures – 1954 Hague Cultural Property Convention*. Parties to the 1954 Hague Cultural Property Convention undertake to introduce in time of peace into their military regulations or instructions such provisions as may ensure observance of that Convention, and to foster in the members of their armed forces a spirit of respect for the culture and cultural property of all peoples.[71]

18.7.1.5 *Instructions, Regulations, and Procedures – CCW Protocol V on Explosive Remnants of War*. Each Party to the CCW Protocol V on Explosive Remnants of War shall require that its armed forces and relevant agencies or departments issue appropriate instructions and operating procedures.[72]

18.7.2 Reasons for Implementation Through Instructions, Regulations, and Procedures. In addition to cases in which instructions or regulations are required by a treaty, there are a number of reasons for implementing law of war obligations through instructions, regulations, and

---

[67] HAGUE IV art. 1 ("The Contracting Powers shall issue instructions to their armed land forces which shall be in conformity with the Regulations respecting the laws and customs of war on land, annexed to the present Convention."). *Cf.* 1899 HAGUE II art. 1 ("The High Contracting Parties shall issue instructions to their armed land forces, which shall be in conformity with the 'Regulations respecting the Laws and Customs of War on Land' annexed to the present Convention.").

[68] GWS art. 48 ("The High Contracting Parties shall communicate to one another through the Swiss Federal Council and, during hostilities, through the Protecting Powers, the official translations of the present Convention, as well as the laws and regulations which they may adopt to ensure the application thereof."); GWS-SEA art. 49 (same); GPW art. 128 (same); GC art. 145 (same).

[69] *Refer to* § 18.1.2.1 (General Treaty Obligations to Take Appropriate Actions to Implement and Enforce the Treaty – 1949 Geneva Conventions).

[70] CCW AMENDED MINES PROTOCOL art. 14(3) ("Each High Contracting Party shall also require that its armed forces issue relevant military instructions and operating procedures and that armed forces personnel receive training commensurate with their duties and responsibilities to comply with the provisions of this Protocol.").

[71] 1954 HAGUE CULTURAL PROPERTY CONVENTION art. 7 ("The High Contracting Parties undertake to introduce in time of peace into their military regulations or instructions such provisions as may ensure observance of the present Convention, and to foster in the members of their armed forces a spirit of respect for the culture and cultural property of all peoples.").

[72] CCW PROTOCOL V ON EXPLOSIVE REMNANTS OF WAR art. 11(1) ("Each High Contracting Party shall require that its armed forces and relevant agencies or departments issue appropriate instructions and operating procedures and that its personnel receive training consistent with the relevant provisions of this Protocol.").

other procedures.

18.7.2.1 *Re-characterizing National Obligations Into Rules for Individuals*. First, under the traditional view of international law, obligations are owed between States, and not as between States and individuals.[73] Thus, treaty provisions may need to be re-characterized from obligations that Parties to the treaty promise to one another into rules for individual conduct.

18.7.2.2 *Implementing the Rules in Non-Self-Executing Treaties*. The adoption of instructions, regulations, or procedures may assist in the implementation of non-self-executing treaties. When treaties or provisions of treaties are regarded as "non-self-executing," such provisions do not constitute enforceable domestic law even though the State has ratified them, but require further implementing action by the ratifying State.[74]

However, a State may adopt instructions, regulations, or procedures that are enforceable under its domestic law and that implement the rules reflected in a treaty. Thus, because such instructions, regulations, or procedures are enforceable domestically, the State can enforce the rules in the treaty, even though the treaty remains non-self-executing.

18.7.2.3 *Setting Higher Standards as a Matter of Policy*. In addition, States may choose to implement law of war obligations through instructions, regulations, and procedures because they wish to set a higher standard for their armed forces as a matter of policy. For example, rules of engagement are often more restrictive than relevant law of war requirements.[75] As another example, U.S. military operations are routinely subject to more restrictions and apply standards that are more protective of civilians than required by the law of war.[76]

Although failures to adhere to such more restrictive standards may be punishable under the UCMJ, such failures would not necessarily be violations of the law of war.

18.7.2.4 *Clarifying Ambiguities in the Law*. States may choose to implement law of war obligations through instructions, regulations, and procedures because they wish to clarify their interpretation of the obligations, which otherwise may not be clear because a treaty provision is ambiguous or because the obligation is reflected in customary international law.

18.7.2.5 *Ensuring Detailed Requirements Are Not Neglected, and Assistance in Training*. In cases in which treaty requirements are detailed and extensive, the promulgation of military instructions may also help ensure that treaty requirements are not omitted or neglected. Similarly, the promulgation of military instructions also assists in conducting training or special instruction.[77]

---

[73] *Refer to* § 1.10.1.3 (Predominately Inter-State Nature of International Obligations).

[74] *Refer to* § 1.10.2.1 (Force of Self-Executing and Non-Self-Executing Treaties Under U.S. Domestic Law).

[75] *Refer to* § 1.6.5 (Rules of Engagement (ROE)).

[76] *Refer to* § 5.1.2.1 (Applying Standards in the Conduct of Hostilities That Pose More Restrictions on Military Operations and That Are More Protective of Civilians Than Required By the Law of War).

[77] *Refer to* § 18.6.2 (Special Instruction or Training).

18.7.3 Enforcement of Law of War Obligations Through Military Instructions, Regulations, and Procedures. The implementation of law of war treaties and obligations through military instructions, regulations, and procedures has the effect of making such rules enforceable because military personnel are required to comply with duly issued instructions, regulations, and procedures. Military personnel may be punished for failure to comply with such orders and instructions.[78] Conduct that violates the law of war has often been punished through this mechanism.[79]

18.8 Considering Law of War Obligations in the Planning of Military Operations

Military commanders and planners should consider law of war obligations in the planning of military operations. DoD policy has required the review of plans by legal advisers to ensure their consistency with the law of war.[80]

It may be especially important to consider affirmative obligations imposed by the law of war. For example, military commanders and planners should plan for their medical facilities to consider needing to treat enemy wounded and sick. Similarly, the requirements to care for detainees should also be considered. Potential responsibilities as an Occupying Power should also be considered.

18.9 States' Obligations With Respect to Violations of the Law of War

States have certain obligations with respect to alleged violations of the law of war within their jurisdiction. In some cases, these obligations to address alleged violations of particular treaties may be understood as part of the general obligations to implement and enforce those treaties. In other cases, law of war treaties impose specific requirements on States with respect to alleged violations of obligations in those treaties.

18.9.1 State Responsibility for Violations of the Law of War by Its Armed Forces. A State may be responsible for violations of the law of war committed by persons forming part of its armed forces.[81] In particular, States are responsible for the treatment accorded protected

---

[78] *Refer to* § 18.19.3.1 (Uniform Code of Military Justice Offenses).

[79] *For example*, United States v. Harman, 68 M.J. 325, 326 (C.A.A.F. 2010) ("Contrary to her pleas, Appellant was convicted at a general court-martial, with officer and enlisted members, of conspiracy to maltreat subordinates; dereliction of duty by failing to protect Iraqi detainees from abuse, cruelty, and maltreatment; and four specifications of maltreatment under Articles 81, 92, and 93, Uniform Code of Military Justice (UCMJ), 10 U.S.C. §§ 881, 892, 893 (2006)."); Rear Admiral Richard G. Voge, *Too Much Accuracy*, PROCEEDINGS OF THE U.S. NAVAL INSTITUTE 257-59 (1950) ("[O]n April 9, 1945, to be exact, the Japanese government indignantly announced that the *Awa Maru*, on her return trip to Japan after carrying Red Cross supplies to Singapore and the Dutch East Indies, and travelling under a guarantee of safe conduct from the United States government, had been sunk by a U.S. submarine. … [T]he Navy announced that the *Awa Maru* had been sunk by the U.S.S. Queenfish, commanded by Commander Charles Elliot Loughlin, U.S. Navy, of North Wales, Pennsylvania. … Loughlin was brought to trial on three charges: Charge I. Culpable inefficiency in the performance of duty. Charge II. Disobeying the lawful order of his superior officer. Charge III. Negligence in obeying orders.").

[80] *Refer to* § 18.5.1.1 (Review of Plans, Policies, Directives, and Rules of Engagement by Legal Advisers).

[81] HAGUE IV art. 3 ("A belligerent party which violates the provisions of the said Regulations shall, if the case demands, be liable to pay compensation. It shall be responsible for all acts committed by persons forming part of its armed forces."); 1928 PAN AMERICAN NEUTRALITY CONVENTION art. 27 ("A belligerent shall indemnify the damage

persons under the GC by their agents.[82] State responsibility for violations of the law of war committed by its armed forces or other agents results from principles of State responsibility in international law that are not specific to the law of war.[83]

State responsibility for violations of the law of war results in obligations to compensate other States for violations.[84]

18.9.2 Breaches of the 1954 Hague Cultural Property Convention. Parties to the 1954 Hague Cultural Property Convention undertake to take, within the framework of their ordinary criminal jurisdiction, all necessary steps to prosecute and impose penal or disciplinary sanctions upon those persons, of whatever nationality, who commit or order to be committed a breach of the 1954 Hague Cultural Property Convention.[85]

18.9.3 Grave Breaches of the 1949 Geneva Conventions. Parties to the 1949 Geneva Conventions have certain obligations relating to grave breaches of the 1949 Geneva Conventions. These obligations have been interpreted as declaratory of the obligations of belligerents under customary international law to take measures for the punishment of war crimes committed by all persons, including members of a belligerent's armed forces.[86] These obligations do not affect the right of a belligerent, under customary international law, to try enemy personnel for war crimes other than grave breaches of the 1949 Geneva Conventions.[87]

---

caused by its violation of the foregoing provisions. It shall likewise be responsible for the acts of persons who may belong to its armed forces."). *Consider* AP I art. 91 ("A Party to the conflict which violates the provisions of the Conventions or of this Protocol shall, if the case demands, be liable to pay compensation. It shall be responsible for all acts committed by persons forming part of its armed forces.").

[82] *Refer to* § 10.3.5 (State Responsibility for Its Agents' Treatment of Protected Persons).

[83] *See, e.g.*, I RESTATEMENT (THIRD) OF FOREIGN RELATIONS LAW OF THE UNITED STATES 96 (§207) (1987) ("A state is responsible for any violation of its obligations under international law resulting from action or inaction by (a) the government of the state, (b) the government or authorities of any political subdivision of the state, or (c) any organ, agency, official, employee, or other agent of a government or of any political subdivision, acting within the scope of authority or under color of such authority.").

[84] *Refer to* § 18.16 (Compensation for Violations of the Law of War).

[85] 1954 HAGUE CULTURAL PROPERTY CONVENTION art. 28 ("The High Contracting Parties undertake to take, within the framework of their ordinary criminal jurisdiction, all necessary steps to prosecute and impose penal or disciplinary sanctions upon those persons, of whatever nationality, who commit or order to be committed a breach of the present Convention.").

[86] 1956 FM 27-10 (Change No. 1 1976) ¶506 ("*b. Declaratory Character of Above Principles.* The principles quoted in *a* [provisions of GWS art. 49, GWS-Sea art. 50, GPW art. 129, and GC art. 146], above, are declaratory of the obligations of belligerents under customary international law to take measures for the punishment of war crimes committed by all persons, including members of a belligerent's own armed forces."). *See also* Joyce A.C. Gutteridge, *The Geneva Conventions of 1949*, 26 BRITISH YEAR BOOK OF INTERNATIONAL LAW 294, 305 (1949) ("In accordance with the decision that there should be no attempt in the Geneva Conventions to embark, in however rudimentary a fashion, on the settlement of a procedure for dealing with war crimes, the Conventions do not attempt to provide for the trial of 'grave breaches' thereof by any international tribunal, but contemplate only trial and sentence by the regularly constituted courts of parties to the conflict.").

[87] Richard R. Baxter, *The Geneva Conventions of 1949*, 62 U.S. NAVAL WAR COLLEGE INTERNATIONAL LAW STUDIES 220, 223 (1980) ("It may cheer some of you to hear that the Conventions make no reference to war crimes—by that name. There was much controversy about this point at the Conference in 1949, and the upshot of it was that each of the four Conventions contains an article specifying certain atrocious acts, such as the torturing of prisoners and civilians, as 'grave breaches' of the Conventions. Judicial safeguards are provided for persons charged with such acts. Of course, these specific provisions do not affect the right of a belligerent, under customary international law, to try enemy personnel for war crimes other than 'grave breaches' of the treaties.").

Parties to the 1949 Geneva Conventions undertake to enact any legislation necessary to provide effective penal sanctions for persons committing, or ordering to be committed, any of the grave breaches of the 1949 Geneva Conventions.[88]

Each Party to the 1949 Geneva Conventions shall be under the obligation to search for persons alleged to have committed, or to have ordered to be committed, such grave breaches, and shall bring such persons, regardless of their nationality, before its own courts.[89] It may also, if it prefers, and in accordance with the provisions of its own legislation, hand such persons over for trial to another High Contracting Party concerned, provided such High Contracting Party has made out a *prima facie* case.[90]

No Party to the 1949 Geneva Conventions shall be allowed to absolve itself or any other Party of any liability incurred by itself or by another Party in respect of grave breaches of the 1949 Geneva Conventions.[91]

18.9.3.1 Acts Constituting Grave Breaches. The acts constituting "grave breaches" for the purpose of triggering these obligations are defined differently depending on the particular Geneva Convention. However, all of the Conventions include as grave breaches the following acts against persons protected by the respective Convention:

- willful killing;
- torture or inhuman treatment, including biological experiments; and
- willfully causing great suffering or serious injury to body or health.

The term "grave breaches" was deliberately chosen so as not to indicate that violations of those provisions of the 1949 Geneva Conventions were themselves crimes or that the 1949 Geneva Conventions created an international penal code.[92]

Grave breaches of the GWS and GWS-Sea are those involving any of the following acts, if committed against persons or property protected by the GWS or GWS-Sea:

- willful killing; torture or inhuman treatment, including biological experiments;
- willfully causing great suffering or serious injury to body or health; and

---

[88] GWS art. 49 ("The High Contracting Parties undertake to enact any legislation necessary to provide effective penal sanctions for persons committing, or ordering to be committed, any of the grave breaches of the present Convention defined in the following Article."); GWS-SEA art. 50 (same); GPW art. 129 (same); GC art. 146 (same).

[89] GWS art. 49 ("Each High Contracting Party shall be under the obligation to search for persons alleged to have committed, or to have ordered to be committed, such grave breaches, and shall bring such persons, regardless of their nationality, before its own courts."); GWS-SEA art. 50 (same); GPW art. 129 (same); GC art. 146 (same).

[90] GWS art. 49 ("It may also, if it prefers, and in accordance with the provisions of its own legislation, hand such persons over for trial to another High Contracting Party concerned, provided such High Contracting Party has made out a *prima facie* case."); GWS-SEA art. 50 (same); GPW art. 129 (same); GC art. 146 (same).

[91] GWS art. 51 ("No High Contracting Party shall be allowed to absolve itself or any other High Contracting Party of any liability incurred by itself or by another High Contracting Party in respect of breaches referred to in the preceding Article."); GWS-SEA art. 52 (same); GPW art. 131 (same); GC art. 148 (same).

[92] *See* II-B FINAL RECORD OF THE DIPLOMATIC CONFERENCE OF GENEVA OF 1949 356-57 ("Mr. SINCLAIR (United Kingdom): The Soviet proposal to substitute in these Articles the word 'crime' for the words 'grave breaches' has been very fully thrashed out both in the Special Committee and in the Joint Committee, and you will all have read the results in the Reports of those Committees and in particular in the Special Report on penal sanctions. It is not a question as to whether or not these grave breaches are crimes, it is simply a question of finding appropriate words for carrying out the intention behind these Articles which all the delegations who were responsible for framing those Articles were attempting to secure. That intention was to ensure that any persons who committed breaches of these Conventions would be suitably dealt with and punished according to the seriousness of the offenses that they

- extensive destruction and appropriation of property, not justified by military necessity and carried out unlawfully and wantonly.[93]

Grave breaches of the GPW are those involving any of the following acts, if committed against persons or property protected by the GPW:

- willful killing;
- torture or inhuman treatment, including biological experiments;
- willfully causing great suffering or serious injury to body or health;
- compelling a POW to serve in the forces of the hostile Power; and
- willfully depriving a POW of the rights of fair and regular trial prescribed in the GPW.[94]

Grave breaches of the GC are those involving any of the following acts, if committed against persons or property protected by the GC:

- willful killing;
- torture or inhuman treatment, including biological experiments;
- willfully causing great suffering or serious injury to body or health;
- unlawful deportation or transfer or unlawful confinement of a protected person;
- compelling a protected person to serve in the forces of a hostile Power;
- willfully depriving a protected person of the rights of fair and regular trial prescribed in the GC;
- taking of hostages; and
- extensive destruction and appropriation of property, not justified by military necessity and carried out unlawfully and wantonly.[95]

---

committed, and therefore it would have been quite inappropriate to have gone into the question of establishing a new penal code in these Articles. For that reason the proposal in the present Soviet amendment has been rejected throughout this Conference. … Mr. YINGLING (United States of America): I associate myself with the remarks which have been made by the Delegate of the United Kingdom. I see no need for repeating the arguments. This Convention is clearly not a penal statute, and the term 'crimes' is clearly inappropriate to express violations of this Convention, which will not be crimes until they are so made by domestic penal legislation.").

[93] GWS art. 50 ("Grave breaches to which the preceding Article relates shall be those involving any of the following acts, if committed against persons or property protected by the Convention: wilful killing, torture or inhuman treatment, including biological experiments, wilfully causing great suffering or serious injury to body or health, and extensive destruction and appropriation of property, not justified by military necessity and carried out unlawfully and wantonly."); GWS-SEA art. 51 (same).

[94] GPW art. 130 ("Grave breaches to which the preceding Article relates shall be those involving any of the following acts, if committed against persons or property protected by the Convention: wilful killing, torture or inhuman treatment, including biological experiments, wilfully causing great suffering or serious injury to body or health, compelling a prisoner of war to serve in the forces of the hostile Power, or wilfully depriving a prisoner of war of the rights of fair and regular trial prescribed in this Convention.").

[95] GC art. 147 ("Grave breaches to which the preceding Article relates shall be those involving any of the following acts, if committed against persons or property protected by the present Convention: wilful killing, torture or inhuman treatment, including biological experiments, wilfully causing great suffering or serious injury to body or health, unlawful deportation or transfer or unlawful confinement of a protected person, compelling a protected person to serve in the forces of a hostile Power, or wilfully depriving a protected person of the rights of fair and regular trial prescribed in the present Convention, taking of hostages and extensive destruction and appropriation of property, not justified by military necessity and carried out unlawfully and wantonly.").

18.9.3.2 *Applicability of Grave Breaches Obligations to Non-International Armed Conflict*. The text of the 1949 Geneva Conventions provides that grave breaches relate to violations "against persons or property protected by the Convention." Since Common Article 3 of the 1949 Convention protects persons against some of the acts described as grave breaches, the United States took the position that the obligations created by the grave breaches provisions of the 1949 Geneva Conventions could apply also to violations of Common Article 3.[96] An Appeals Chamber of the ICTY did not accept this view, and understood the grave breaches provisions of the 1949 Geneva Conventions only to create obligations applicable in international armed conflicts.[97] U.S. law makes punishable certain conduct that constitutes a "grave breach of common article 3."[98]

Regardless of whether the obligations in the grave breaches provisions apply with respect to violations of Common Article 3, serious violations of Common Article 3 may nonetheless be punishable.

18.9.3.3 *Suppression of All Acts Contrary to the Provisions of the 1949 Geneva Conventions*. Each High Contracting Party shall take measures necessary for the suppression of all acts contrary to the provisions of the 1949 Geneva Conventions other than the grave breaches.[99]

Such measures could include punishment of offenders. For example, if a U.S. Soldier steals the money that has been impounded from POWs and appropriates it for his or her own use, the theft would not constitute a grave breach of the 1949 Geneva Conventions, but would be an offense under the Uniform Code of Military Justice.[100]

---

[96] D. Stephen Mathias, Legal Counselor, Embassy of the United States, The Hague, The Netherlands, *Submission of the Government of the United States of America Concerning Certain Arguments Made by Counsel for the Accused in the Case of The Prosecutor of the Tribunal v. Dusan Tadic*, 35-36 (Jul. 17, 1995) ("For example, Article 130 of the 1949 Geneva Convention Relative to the Treatment of Prisoners of War defines 'grave breaches' as any of a series of specified acts 'if committed against persons or property protected by the Convention.' (This definition is included almost verbatim in Article 2 of the Tribunal Statute.) There is no special definition or usage in the Third Geneva Convention of the phrase 'persons protected by the Convention.' Insofar as Common Article 3 prohibits certain acts with respect to '[p]ersons taking no active part in hostilities' in cases of armed conflict not of an international character, it is consistent with the ordinary meaning of the Geneva Conventions to treat such persons as persons protected by the Conventions.").

[97] *See, e.g.*, Prosecutor v. Tadić, ICTY Appeals Chamber, IT-94-1-AR72, *Decision on the Defence Motion for Interlocutory Appeal on Jurisdiction*, ¶71 (Oct. 2, 1995) ("Article 2 refers to 'grave breaches' of the Geneva Conventions of 1949, which are widely understood to be committed only in international armed conflicts, so the reference in Article 2 would seem to suggest that the Article is limited to international armed conflicts.").

[98] 18 U.S.C. § 2441 ("(c) Definition.— As used in this section the term "war crime" means any conduct— …(3) which constitutes a grave breach of common Article 3 (as defined in subsection (d)) when committed in the context of and in association with an armed conflict not of an international character;").

[99] GWS art. 49 ("Each High Contracting Party shall take measures necessary for the suppression of all acts contrary to the provisions of the present Convention other than the grave breaches defined in the following Article."); GWS-SEA art. 50 (same); GPW art. 129 (same); GC art. 146 (same).

[100] *See, e.g.*, 10 U.S.C. § 903 ("(a) All persons subject to this chapter shall secure all public property taken from the enemy for the service of the United States, and shall give notice and turn over to the proper authority without delay all captured or abandoned property in their possession, custody, or control. (b) Any person subject to this chapter who—(1) fails to carry out the duties prescribed in subsection (a); (2) buys, sells, trades, or in any way deals in or disposes of captured or abandoned property, whereby he receives or expects any profit, benefit, or advantage to himself or another directly or indirectly connected with himself; or (3) engages in looting or pillaging; shall be punished as a court-martial may direct.").

Such measures may also be understood to include a wide range of measures, such as the promulgation or revision of policies and regulations, administrative or corrective measures, or retraining of personnel.[101]

18.9.4 CCW Amended Mines Protocol. Each Party to the CCW Amended Mines Protocol shall take all appropriate steps, including legislative and other measures, to prevent and suppress violations of the CCW Amended Mines Protocol by persons or on territory under its jurisdiction or control.[102] Such measures include appropriate measures to ensure the imposition of penal sanctions against persons who, in relation to an armed conflict and contrary to the provisions of the CCW Amended Mines Protocol, willfully kill or cause serious injury to civilians and to bring such persons to justice.[103]

Penal sanctions under Article 14 of the CCW Amended Mines Protocol only apply in a situation in which an individual: (1) knew, or should have known, that his or her action was prohibited under the CCW Amended Mines Protocol; (2) intended to kill or cause serious injury to a civilian; and (3) knew, or should have known, that the person he or she intended to kill or cause serious injury was a civilian.[104]

U.S. Federal law authorizes prosecutions for such conduct.[105]

18.9.5 War Crimes – Notes on Terminology. The term "war crime" has been used in different ways in different contexts. In contemporary parlance, the term "war crime" is most often used to mean serious violations of the law of war.

18.9.5.1 *War Crimes – Any Violation of the Law of War*. In some cases, the term "war crime" has been used as a technical expression for a violation of the law of war by any person; *i.e.*, under this usage, any violation of the law of war is a war crime.[106] This has been

[101] *Refer to* § 18.4.4 (Issuance of Guidance, Training of Subordinates, and Other Preventive or Corrective Measures); § 18.19.1 (Non-Judicial Punishment and Adverse or Corrective Administrative Actions); § 18.7 (Instructions, Regulations, and Procedures to Implement and Enforce the Law of War).

[102] *Refer to* § 18.1.2.3 (General Treaty Obligations to Take Appropriate Actions to Implement and Enforce the Treaty – CCW Amended Mines Protocol).

[103] CCW AMENDED MINES PROTOCOL art. 14 ("1. Each High Contracting Party shall take all appropriate steps, including legislative and other measures, to prevent and suppress violations of this Protocol by persons or on territory under its jurisdiction or control. 2. The measures envisaged in paragraph I of this Article include appropriate measures to ensure the imposition of penal sanctions against persons who, in relation to an armed conflict and contrary to the provisions of this Protocol, wilfully kill or cause serious injury to civilians and to bring such persons to justice.").

[104] United States, *Statement on Consent to Be Bound by the CCW Amended Mines Protocol,* May 24, 1999, 2065 UNTS 128, 129 ("The United States understands that - ... (B) Article 14 of the Amended Mines Protocol (insofar as it relates to penal sanctions) shall apply only in a situation in which an individual – (i) knew, or should have known, that his action was prohibited under the Amended Mines Protocol; (ii) intended to kill or cause serious injury to a civilian; and (iii) knew or should have known, that the person he intended to kill or cause serious injury was a civilian.").

[105] 18 U.S.C. § 2441 ("(a) Offense.— Whoever, whether inside or outside the United States, commits a war crime, in any of the circumstances described in subsection (b), shall be fined under this title or imprisoned for life or any term of years, or both, and if death results to the victim, shall also be subject to the penalty of death. ... (c) Definition.— As used in this section the term "war crime" means any conduct— ... (4) of a person who, in relation to an armed conflict and contrary to the provisions of the Protocol on Prohibitions or Restrictions on the Use of Mines, Booby-Traps and Other Devices as amended at Geneva on 3 May 1996 (Protocol II as amended on 3 May 1996), when the United States is a party to such Protocol, willfully kills or causes serious injury to civilians.").

[106] *See, e.g., Charter of the International Military Tribunal*, art. 6, annexed to Agreement by the Government of the United Kingdom of Great Britain and Northern Ireland, the Government of the United States of America, the Provisional Government of the French Republic and the Government of the Union of Soviet Socialist Republics for the Prosecution and Punishment of the Major War Criminals of the European Axis, Aug. 8, 1945, 82 UNTS 280,

longstanding U.S. military doctrine.[107]

Any violation of the law of war by members of the armed forces of a State could be made punishable by that State through its domestic law, including military law applicable to its armed forces. For example, under military law, violations of the law of war may be made punishable through military orders to comply with law of war requirements.[108] Commanders may also impose non-judicial punishment or take adverse administrative action to address minor violations.[109]

18.9.5.2 *War Crimes – Serious Violations of the Law of War*. Sometimes the term "war crime" is used to refer to particularly serious violations of the law of war. For example, this is generally the usage when the term "war crime" is defined for the purposes of a particular criminal statute.[110]

This usage of "war crime" is understood to exclude minor violations of the law of war. For example, if during an international armed conflict, military medical personnel perform their duties while wearing an armlet displaying the distinctive emblem affixed to their right arm – rather than to their left arm, as specified by Article 40 of the GWS, these personnel may be said to be violating the law of war. However, under this usage of "war crime," such violations generally would not be regarded as a "war crime."

18.9.5.3 *War Crimes – Serious Violations of Domestic Law Applicable During Armed Conflict*. The term "war crime" has also been used to describe offenses, such as espionage and unprivileged belligerency, that although not prohibited by international law, are properly liable to punishment by the belligerent against which they are directed.[111] Generally, this usage does not prevail today, although practitioners may find this usage in older sources.

---

288 ("The following acts, or any of them, are crimes coming within the jurisdiction of the Tribunal for which there shall be individual responsibility:– … (b) *War crimes:* namely, violations of the laws or customs of war. Such violations shall include, but not be limited to, murder, ill-treatment or deportation to slave labour or for any other purpose of civilian population of or in occupied territory, murder or ill-treatment of prisoners of war or persons on the seas, killing of hostages, plunder of public or private property, wanton destruction of cities, towns or villages, or devastation not justified by military necessity;").

[107] *See, e.g.*, U.S. MILITARY ASSISTANCE COMMAND VIETNAM DIRECTIVE 20-4, *Inspections and Investigations: War Crimes* ¶3.a (May 18, 1968) ("Every violation of the law of war is a war crime"); 1956 FM 27-10 (Change No. 1 1976) ¶499 ("The term 'war crime' is the technical expression for a violation of the law of war by any person or persons, military or civilian. Every violation of the law of war is a war crime."). *Cf.* 1958 UK MANUAL ¶624 ("The term 'war crime' is the technical expression for violations of the laws of warfare, whether committed by members of the armed forces or by civilians.").

[108] *Refer to* § 18.7.3 (Enforcement of Law of War Obligations Through Military Instructions, Regulations, and Procedures).

[109] *Refer to* § 18.19.1 (Non-Judicial Punishment and Adverse or Corrective Administrative Actions).

[110] *See, e.g.*, 18 U.S.C. § 2441 ("(a) Offense.— Whoever, whether inside or outside the United States, commits a war crime, in any of the circumstances described in subsection (b), shall be fined under this title or imprisoned for life or any term of years, or both, and if death results to the victim, shall also be subject to the penalty of death. … (c) Definition.— As used in this section the term "war crime" means any conduct— … .").

[111] 1958 UK MANUAL ¶624 ("The term 'war crime' is the technical expression for violations of the laws of warfare, whether committed by members of the armed forces or by civilians. It has also been customary to describe as war crimes such acts as espionage and so-called war treason which, although not prohibited by international law, are properly liable to punishment by the belligerent against which they are directed. However, the accuracy of the description of such acts as war crimes is doubtful."). *Refer to* § 4.19.4.1 (Unprivileged Belligerency and the Law of War – Notes on Terminology).

18.10 Methods for Responding to Violations of the Law of War by the Enemy

In the event of violation of the law of war, it may be possible for the injured State to resort to remedial action of the following types:

- publication of the facts, with a view to influencing public opinion against the offending belligerent;
- protests and demands to the offending party,[112] including demands for compensation or the punishment of enemy persons who have violated the law;[113]
- solicitation of the good offices, mediation, or intervention of neutral States for the purpose of making the enemy observe the law of war;[114]
- petition to the U.N. Security Council;[115]
- punishment of captured offenders as war criminals, either through national or international tribunals;[116]
- retorsion;[117] and
- reprisals.[118]

18.11 Protests and Demands to the Offending Party

An initial step in responding to law of war violations by the enemy is to issue a formal or informal complaint to the offending party.

18.11.1 Method of Transmitting Protests and Demands. In view of the lack of diplomatic relations between States involved in an armed conflict, complaints cannot normally be made through the usual diplomatic channels. However, other methods are available, depending on the degree of publicity required. The traditional method of complaining by *parlementaire* directly to the commander of the offending forces remains, although modern communications have meant that the message is more likely now to be transmitted through electronic means.[119]

Complaints also may be made through the Protecting Power, an impartial humanitarian organization performing the duties of a Protecting Power, or a Neutral State.[120]

---

[112] *Refer to* § 18.11 (Protests and Demands to the Offending Party).

[113] *Refer to* § 18.11.2 (Demands for Redress).

[114] *Refer to* § 18.15 (Protecting Power and Other Neutral Intermediaries).

[115] *Refer to* § 18.12 (U.N. Security Council and Enforcement of the Law of War).

[116] *Refer to* § 18.19 (Discipline in National Jurisdictions of Individuals for Violations of the Law of War); § 18.20 (Prosecution in International and Hybrid Courts).

[117] *Refer to* § 18.17 (Retorsion).

[118] *Refer to* § 18.18 (Reprisals).

[119] 2004 UK MANUAL ¶16.6 ("In view of the lack of diplomatic relations between states involved in an armed conflict, complaints cannot normally be made through the usual diplomatic channels. However, other methods are available, depending on the degree of publicity required. The traditional method of complaining under the protection of a flag of truce remains, although modern communications have meant that the message is more likely now to be transmitted by radio or television. Complaints may be made also through neutral states, whether or not the complainant also seeks their good offices to mediate with a view to making the adverse party observe the law of armed conflict."); 1956 FM 27-10 (Change No. 1 1976) ¶ 495b ("In the event of violation of the law of war, the injured party may legally resort to remedial action of the following types: ... b. Protest and demand for compensation and/or punishment of the individual offenders. Such communications may be sent through the protecting power, a humanitarian organization performing the duties of a protecting power, or a neutral state, or by parlementaire direct to the commander of the offending forces.").

[120] *Refer to* § 18.15 (Protecting Power and Other Neutral Intermediaries).

18.11.2 Demands for Redress. In addition to demands to cease committing violations, protests may also include demands for redress by the offending party. For example, a State may demand that a national investigation or international investigation be conducted.[121] A State may demand financial compensation or other reparations.[122] Similarly, a State may demand that offending individuals be held accountable for their offenses through judicial or other processes.[123]

18.12 U.N. SECURITY COUNCIL AND ENFORCEMENT OF THE LAW OF WAR

In some cases, the U.N. Security Council has determined that situations involving violations of the law of war constitute a threat to international peace and security.[124] The U.N. Security Council may take a variety actions to respond to such threats.

18.12.1 Investigation by the U.N. Security Council Under the Charter of the United Nations. Under the Charter of the United Nations, the U.N. Security Council may investigate any dispute, or any situation that might lead to international friction or give rise to a dispute, in order to determine whether the continuance of the dispute or situation is likely to endanger the maintenance of international peace and security.[125] This authority of the U.N. Security Council to investigate situations includes any such situations that involve violations of the law of war.

The U.N. Security Council has provided for the establishment of commissions of inquiry or commissions of experts to report on violations of the law of war.[126]

---

[121] *Refer to* § 18.13 (National Investigations of Alleged Violations of the Law of War); § 18.14 (International Mechanisms to Investigate Alleged Law of War Violations).

[122] *Refer to* § 18.16 (Compensation for Violations of the Law of War).

[123] *Refer to* § 18.19 (Discipline in National Jurisdictions of Individuals for Violations of the Law of War).

[124] U.N. SECURITY COUNCIL RESOLUTION 808, U.N. Doc S/RES/808 (Feb. 22, 1993) ("Expressing once again its grave alarm at continuing reports of widespread violations of international humanitarian law occurring within the territory of the former Yugoslavia, including reports of mass killings and the continuance of the practice of 'ethnic cleansing', Determining that this situation constitutes a threat to international peace and security."); U.N. SECURITY COUNCIL RESOLUTION 955, U.N. Doc S/RES/955 (Nov. 8, 1994) ("Expressing once again its grave concern at the reports indicating that genocide and other systematic, widespread and flagrant violations of international humanitarian law have been committed in Rwanda, Determining that this situation continues to constitute a threat to international peace and security,").

[125] U.N. CHARTER art. 34 ("The Security Council may investigate any dispute, or any situation which might lead to international friction or give rise to a dispute, in order to determine whether the continuance of the dispute or situation is likely to endanger the maintenance of international peace and security.").

[126] *For example*, U.N. SECURITY COUNCIL RESOLUTION 780, U.N. Doc S/RES/780 (Oct. 6, 1992) ("Requests the Secretary-General to establish, as a matter of urgency, an impartial Commission of Experts to examine and analyse the information submitted pursuant to resolution 771 (1992) and the present resolution, together with such further information as the Commission of Experts may obtain through its own investigations or efforts, of other persons or bodies pursuant to resolution 771 (1992), with a view to providing the Secretary-General with its conclusions on the evidence of grave breaches of the Geneva Conventions and other violations of international humanitarian law committed in the territory of the former Yugoslavia."); U.N. SECURITY COUNCIL RESOLUTION 935, U.N. Doc S/RES/935 (Jul. 1, 1994) ("Requests the Secretary-General to establish, as a matter of urgency, an impartial Commission of Experts to examine and analyse information submitted pursuant to the present resolution, together with such further information as the Commission of Experts may obtain through its own investigations or the efforts of other persons or bodies, including the information made available by the Special Rapporteur for Rwanda, with a view to providing the Secretary-General with its conclusions on the evidence of grave violations of international humanitarian law committed in the territory of Rwanda, including the evidence of possible acts of genocide."); U.N. SECURITY COUNCIL RESOLUTION 1564, U.N. Doc S/RES/1564 (Sept. 18, 2004) ("Requests that the Secretary- General rapidly establish an international commission of inquiry in order immediately to investigate reports of violations of international humanitarian law and human rights law in Darfur by all parties, to determine also whether or not acts of genocide have occurred, and to identify the perpetrators of such violations with a view to ensuring that those responsible are held accountable, calls on all parties to cooperate fully with such a commission, and further requests the Secretary-General, in conjunction with the Office of the High Commissioner for Human Rights, to take appropriate steps to increase the number of human rights monitors deployed to Darfur.").

18.12.2 Determining Liability and Determining That Compensation Should Be Paid. The U.N. Security Council may, in appropriate cases, affirm that States are liable for violations of international law and establish mechanisms to facilitate the payment of compensation for such violations.[127]

18.12.3 Authorizing the Use of Force. The U.N. Security Council has authorized the use of force in order to protect civilians who are being attacked in violation of the law of war.[128]

18.12.4 Authorizing International Criminal Tribunals. The U.N. Security Council has established international criminal tribunals for the purpose of prosecuting serious violations of international humanitarian law. The U.N. Security Council has exercised this authority to create the International Criminal Tribunal for the Former Yugoslavia and the International Criminal Tribunal for Rwanda.[129]

The Rome Statute of the International Criminal Court provides that the International Criminal Court may exercise its jurisdiction with respect to crimes when a situation is referred to the Prosecutor by the Security Council acting under Chapter VII of the Charter of the United

---

[127] *See, e.g.*, U.N. COMPENSATIONS COMMISSION GOVERNING COUNCIL, *Report and Recommendations Made by the Panel of Commissioners Appointed to Review the Well Blowout Control Claim (the "WBC Claim")*, U.N. Doc. S/AC.26/1996/R.27/Annex, 22 ¶ 68 (Dec. 18, 1996) ("The Security Council having determined, under Chapter VII of the Charter, that compensation in accordance with international law should be provided to foreign Governments, nationals and corporations for any direct loss, damage or injury sustained by them as a result of Iraq's unlawful invasion and occupation of Kuwait, in order to restore international peace and security, the issue of Iraq's liability has been resolved by the Security Council and constitutes part of the law applicable before the Commission."); *id.* at ¶67 ("According to paragraph 16 of Security Council resolution 687 (1991), which under article 31 of the Rules forms part of the law applicable before the Commission, 'Iraq . . . is liable under international law for any direct loss, damage, including environmental damage and the depletion of natural resources, or injury to foreign Governments, nationals and corporations, as a result of Iraq's unlawful invasion and occupation of Kuwait.' The Panel notes that, when making resolution 687 (1991), the Security Council acted under Chapter VII of the United Nations Charter, i.e., it exercised its powers under that Chapter to maintain and restore international peace and security.").

[128] U.N. SECURITY COUNCIL RESOLUTION 1973, U.N. Doc S/RES/1973 ¶4 (Mar. 17, 2011) ("Authorizes Member States that have notified the Secretary-General, acting nationally or through regional organizations or arrangements, and acting in cooperation with the Secretary-General, to take all necessary measures, notwithstanding paragraph 9 of resolution 1970 (2011), to protect civilians and civilian populated areas under threat of attack in the Libyan Arab Jamahiriya, including Benghazi, while excluding a foreign occupation force of any form on any part of Libyan territory, and requests the Member States concerned to inform the Secretary-General immediately of the measures they take pursuant to the authorization conferred by this paragraph which shall be immediately reported to the Security Council."); U.N. SECURITY COUNCIL RESOLUTION 1270, U.N. Doc S/RES/1270 ¶14 (Oct. 22, 1999) ("Acting under Chapter VII of the Charter of the United Nations, decides that in the discharge of its mandate UNAMSIL may take the necessary action to ensure the security and freedom of movement of its personnel and, within its capabilities and areas of deployment, to afford protection to civilians under imminent threat of physical violence, taking into account the responsibilities of the Government of Sierra Leone and ECOMOG;").

[129] U.N. SECURITY COUNCIL RESOLUTION 827, U.N. Doc S/RES/827 (May 25, 1993) ("Acting under Chapter VII of the Charter of the United Nations, ... 2. Decides hereby to establish an international tribunal for the sole purpose of prosecuting persons responsible for serious violations of international humanitarian law committed in the territory of the former Yugoslavia between 1 January 1991 and a date to be determined by the Security Council upon the restoration of peace and to this end to adopt the Statute of the International Tribunal annexed to the above-mentioned report;"); U.N. SECURITY COUNCIL RESOLUTION 955, U.N. Doc S/RES/955 (Nov. 8, 1994) ("Acting under Chapter VII of the Charter of the United Nations, 1. Decides hereby, having received the request of the Government of Rwanda (S/1994/1115), to establish an international tribunal for the sole purpose of prosecuting persons responsible for genocide and other serious violations of international humanitarian law committed in the territory of Rwanda and Rwandan citizens responsible for genocide and other such violations committed in the territory of neighbouring States, between 1 January 1994 and 31 December 1994 and to this end to adopt the Statute of the International Criminal Tribunal for Rwanda annexed hereto;").

Nations.[130] The U.N. Security Council has referred situations in Darfur and Libya to the Prosecutor of the International Criminal Court.[131] The United States has objected to certain aspects of the jurisdiction of the International Criminal Court, and there are certain restrictions in U.S. domestic law on support to the International Criminal Court.[132]

18.12.5 U.N. Security Council Role in Certain Treaties.

18.12.5.1 *U.N. Security Council Role in the Biological Weapons Convention and ENMOD Convention*. The Biological Weapons Convention and the ENMOD Convention provide that Parties to the treaties may lodge a complaint with the Security Council, when a Party believes that another Party is in breach of its obligations deriving from the provisions of that treaty.[133] These treaties provide that each Party undertakes to cooperate with any investigation that the Security Council may initiate.[134] In addition, these treaties impose an additional obligation on Parties to provide or support assistance to Parties that request assistance if the Security Council has made an appropriate decision.[135]

18.12.5.2 *U.N. Security Council and the Chemical Weapons Convention*. The Chemical Weapons Convention provides that the Conference of the States Parties shall, in cases of particular gravity, bring the issue, including relevant information and conclusions, to the attention of the U.N. General Assembly and the U.N. Security Council.[136]

---

[130] ROME STATUTE art. 13(b) ("The Court may exercise its jurisdiction with respect to a crime referred to in article 5 in accordance with the provisions of this Statute if: A situation in which one or more of such crimes appears to have been committed is referred to the Prosecutor by the Security Council acting under Chapter VII of the Charter of the United Nations;").

[131] U.N. SECURITY COUNCIL RESOLUTION 1593, U.N. Doc S/RES/1593 (Mar. 31, 2005) ("Decides to refer the situation in Darfur since 1 July 2002 to the Prosecutor of the International Criminal Court."); U.N. SECURITY COUNCIL RESOLUTION 1970, U.N. Doc S/RES/1970 (Feb. 26, 2011) ("Decides to refer the situation in the Libyan Arab Jamahiriya since 15 February 2011 to the Prosecutor of the International Criminal Court;").

[132] *Refer to* § 18.20.3 (The International Criminal Court (ICC) Created by the Rome Statute).

[133] BIOLOGICAL WEAPONS CONVENTION art. 6(1) ("Any State Party to this Convention which finds that any other State Party is acting in breach of obligations deriving from the provisions of the Convention may lodge a complaint with the Security Council of the United Nations. Such a complaint should include all possible evidence confirming its validity, as well as a request for its consideration by the Security Council."); ENMOD Convention art. 5(3) ("Any State Party to this Convention which has reason to believe that any other State Party is acting in breach of obligations deriving from the provisions of the Convention may lodge a complaint with the Security Council of the United Nations. Such a complaint should include all relevant information as well as all possible evidence supporting its validity.").

[134] BIOLOGICAL WEAPONS CONVENTION art. 6(2) ("Each State Party to this Convention undertakes to co-operate in carrying out any investigation which the Security Council may initiate, in accordance with the provisions of the Charter of the United Nations, on the basis of the complaint received by the Council. The Security Council shall inform the States Parties to the Convention of the results of the investigation."); ENMOD CONVENTION art. 5(4) ("Each State Party to this Convention undertakes to co-operate in carrying out any investigation which the Security Council may initiate, in accordance with the provisions of the Charter of the United Nations, on the basis of the complaint received by the Council. The Security Council shall inform the States Parties of the results of the investigation.").

[135] BIOLOGICAL WEAPONS CONVENTION art. 7 ("Each State Party to this Convention undertakes to provide or support assistance, in accordance with the United Nations Charter, to any Party to the Convention which so requests, if the Security Council decides that such Party has been exposed to danger as a result of violation of the Convention."); ENMOD CONVENTION art. 5(5) ("Each State Party to this Convention undertakes to provide or support assistance, in accordance with the provisions of the Charter of the United Nations, to any State Party which so requests, if the Security Council decides that such Party has been harmed or is likely to be harmed as a result of violation of the Convention.").

[136] CHEMICAL WEAPONS CONVENTION art. 12(4) ("The Conference shall, in cases of particular gravity, bring the issue, including relevant information and conclusions, to the attention of the United Nations General Assembly and the United Nations Security Council.").

18.12.5.3 U.N. Security Council Role in the Statute of the International Court of Justice. Under the Statute of the International Court of Justice, a party to a case may have recourse to the Security Council if an opposing party fails to perform the obligations incumbent upon it under a judgment rendered by the Court.[137]

18.13 NATIONAL INVESTIGATIONS OF ALLEGED VIOLATIONS OF THE LAW OF WAR

The duties to implement and enforce the law of war also imply duties to investigate reports of alleged violations of the law of war.[138] In addition to taking measures to meet the requirements of DoD policy, commanders may also take other measures they deem appropriate to ensure appropriate investigation and reporting of alleged violations of the law of war within their command.[139]

18.13.1 DoD Policy on Reporting Law of War Violations. DoD policy has required the reporting of possible, suspected, or alleged violations of the law of war for which there is credible information, or conduct during military operations other than war that would constitute a violation of the law of war if it occurred during armed conflict ("reportable incidents").[140] Such policy has been in addition to other DoD policies that address the reporting of criminal incidents.[141] Individual Military Services have implemented procedures to ensure that incidents, including war crimes, are promptly reported.[142]

---

[137] ICJ STATUTE art. 94(2) ("If any party to a case fails to perform the obligations incumbent upon it under a judgment rendered by the Court, the other party may have recourse to the Security Council, which may, if it deems necessary, make recommendations or decide upon measures to be taken to give effect to the judgment.").

[138] *See* United States v. List, *et al.* (The Hostage Case), XI TRIALS OF WAR CRIMINALS BEFORE THE NMT 1271 ("A commanding general of occupied territory is charged with the duty of maintaining peace and order, punishing crime, and protecting lives and property within the area of his command. His responsibility is coextensive with his area of command. He is charged with notice of occurrences taking place within that territory. He may require adequate reports of all occurrences that come within the scope of his power and, if such reports are incomplete or otherwise inadequate, he is obliged to require supplementary reports to apprize him of all the pertinent facts. If he fails to require and obtain complete information, the dereliction of duty rests upon him and he is in no position to plead his own dereliction as a defense. … Want of knowledge of the contents of reports made to him is not a defense. Reports to commanding generals are made for their special benefit. Any failure to acquaint themselves with the contents of such reports, or a failure to require additional reports where inadequacy appears on their face, constitutes a dereliction of duty which he cannot use in his own behalf.").

[139] *For example*, Defense Legal Policy Board, *Report of the Subcommittee on Military Justice in Combat Zones*, 54 (May 30, 2013) ("In 2009, USCENTCOM issued two fragmentary orders (FRAGOs) related to LOAC incident reports and 'legal reporting.' USCENTCOM issued the FRAGOs because of perceived 'lack of timely notifications and spotty recurring reports.' The FRAGOs established timeline requirements for reports and described the information expected to be included in LOAC reports. For example, the FRAGOs required reporting units with knowledge of a suspected LOAC violation to transmit information to USCENTCOM within two hours through the Service component and operational chains of command, irrespective of accuracy or detail. Follow-up was also required within 24-48 hours with expanded information. The FRAGOs also required formal and informal investigations to be forwarded to the USCENTCOM Staff Judge Advocate as soon as available and before submission to organizations outside the USCENTCOM area of responsibility (AOR). The FRAGOs mandated that initial and subsequent reports contain the '5 W's' of the incident and additional, operationally relevant data. Further, the FRAGOs clarified the USCENTCOM requirement for weekly Judge Advocate activity reports, and mandated that ARCENT (Army Central) maintain a generic email address to receive LOAC reports.").

[140] DOD DIRECTIVE 2311.01E, *DoD Law of War Program*, ¶3.2 (May 9, 2006, Certified Current as of Feb. 22, 2011) ("Reportable Incident. A possible, suspected, or alleged violation of the law of war, for which there is credible information, or conduct during military operations other than war that would constitute a violation of the law of war if it occurred during an armed conflict."); DOD DIRECTIVE 5100.77, *DoD Law of War Program*, ¶3.2 (Dec. 9, 1998) ("Reportable Incident. A possible, suspected, or alleged violation of the law of war.").

[141] *See, e.g.*, DOD DIRECTIVE 7730.47, *Defense Incident-Based Reporting System (DIBRS)* (Oct. 15, 1996); DOD INSTRUCTION 5240.4, *Reporting of Counterintelligence and Criminal Violations* (Sept. 22, 1992).

[142] *See, e.g.*, DEPARTMENT OF THE ARMY REGULATION 190-45, *Law Enforcement Reporting* (Mar. 30, 2007), Chapters 8 and 9.

18.13.1.1 *Requirement for All Military and U.S. Civilian Employees, Contractor Personnel, and Subcontractors Assigned to or Accompanying a DoD Component*. DoD policy has required that all military and U.S. civilian employees, contractor personnel, and subcontractors assigned to or accompanying a DoD Component shall report reportable incidents through their chain of command. Contracts shall require contractor employees to report reportable incidents to the commander of the unit they are accompanying or the installation to which they are assigned, or to the Combatant Commander.[143]

18.13.1.2 *Requirement for Unit Commanders*. DoD policy has required that the commander of any unit that obtains information about a reportable incident shall immediately report the incident through the applicable operational command and Military Department.[144]

18.13.2 DoD Policy on Investigating Law of War Violations. DoD policy has required that all reportable incidents be thoroughly investigated.[145] All the Military Departments and Services have regulations for the conduct of both formal and informal administrative investigations.[146]

In addition, DoD policy has required that higher authorities receiving an initial report request a formal investigation by the cognizant military criminal investigative organization.[147]

18.14 International Mechanisms to Investigate Alleged Law of War Violations

In some cases, international mechanisms, such as commissions of inquiry, may be used to

---

[143] DoD Directive 2311.01E, *DoD Law of War Program*, ¶6.3 (May 9, 2006, Certified Current as of Feb. 22, 2011) ("All military and U.S. civilian employees, contractor personnel, and subcontractors assigned to or accompanying a DoD Component shall report reportable incidents through their chain of command. Contracts shall require contractor employees to report reportable incidents to the commander of the unit they are accompanying or the installation to which they are assigned, or to the Combatant Commander. Such reports may be made through other channels, such as the military police, a judge advocate, or an inspector general. Reports made to officials other than those specified in this paragraph shall, nonetheless, be accepted and immediately forwarded through the recipient's chain of command.").

[144] DoD Directive 2311.01E, *DoD Law of War Program*, ¶6.4 (May 9, 2006, Certified Current as of Feb. 22, 2011) ("Initial Report. The commander of any unit that obtains information about a reportable incident shall immediately report the incident through the applicable operational command and Military Department. Reporting requirements are concurrent. The initial report shall be made through the most expeditious means available.").

[145] DoD Directive 2311.01E, *DoD Law of War Program*, ¶4.4 (May 9, 2006, Certified Current as of Feb. 22, 2011) ("All reportable incidents committed by or against U.S. personnel, enemy persons, or any other individual are reported promptly, investigated thoroughly, and, where appropriate, remedied by corrective action."); DoD Directive 5100.77, *DoD Law of War Program*, ¶4.3 (Dec. 9, 1998) ("All reportable incidents committed by or against U.S. or enemy persons are promptly reported, thoroughly investigated, and, where appropriate, remedied by corrective action."); DoD Directive 5100.77, *DoD Law of War Program*, ¶C(2) (Jul. 10, 1979) ("Alleged violations of the law of war, whether committed by or against U.S. or enemy personnel, are promptly reported, thoroughly investigated, and, whether appropriate, remedied by corrective action."); DoD Directive 5100.77, *DoD Program for the Implementation of the Law of War*, ¶II(C) (Nov. 5, 1974) ("Ensure that alleged violations of the law of war, whether committed by U. S. personnel or enemy personnel, are promptly reported, thoroughly investigated, and, where appropriate, remedied by corrective action.").

[146] *See, e.g.*, Department of the Navy Judge Advocate General Instruction 5800.7D, *Manual of the Judge Advocate General (JAGMAN)*, Chapter II (Mar. 15, 2004); Department of the Army Regulation 15-6, *Procedures for Investigating Officers and Boards of Officers* (Nov. 2, 2006).

[147] DoD Directive 2311.01E, *DoD Law of War Program*, ¶6.4 (May 9, 2006, Certified Current as of Feb. 22, 2011). Such organizations include U.S. Army Criminal Investigation Command (USACIDC/CID), Air Force Special Investigations Command (AFOSI/OSI), or the Naval Criminal Investigative Service (NCIS).

investigate alleged law of war violations. Commissions of inquiry might be established by treaty.[148] Commissions of inquiry might also be established by the U.N. Security Council.[149]

18.14.1 Inquiry Procedure in the 1949 Geneva Conventions. At the request of a party to the conflict, an inquiry shall be instituted, in a manner to be decided between the interested Parties, concerning any alleged violation of the 1949 Geneva Conventions.[150] If agreement has not been reached concerning the procedure for the inquiry, the Parties should agree on the choice of an "umpire" who will decide upon the procedure to be followed.[151] Once the violation has been established, the parties to the conflict "shall put an end to it and shall repress it with the least possible delay."[152]

18.14.1.1 *AP I – International Humanitarian Fact-Finding Commission (IHFFC)*. AP I provides for the establishment of an international fact-finding commission.[153] This commission is competent: (1) to inquire into any facts alleged to be a grave breach as defined in the 1949 Geneva Conventions and AP I or other serious violation of the 1949 Geneva Conventions or of AP I; and (2) to facilitate, through its good offices, the restoration of an attitude of respect for the Conventions and AP I.[154]

The commission operates on the basis of mutual consent. Any party to a conflict may ask the commission to conduct an inquiry; but, unless the States involved previously declared that they recognize *ipso facto* and without special agreement, in relation to any other Party to AP I accepting the same obligation, the competence of the Commission, the Commission will only investigate with the consent of the States involved.[155]

---

[148] *For example*, Treaty for the Settlement of disputes that may occur between the United States of America and Chile, art. 1, Jul. 24, 1914, 39 STAT. 1645, 1646 ("The High Contracting Parties agree that all disputes that may arise in the future between them, shall, when diplomatic methods of adjustment have failed, be submitted for investigation and report to an International Commission to be constituted in the manner prescribed in the next succeeding article; and they agree not to declare war or begin hostilities during such investigation, nor before all resources stipulated in this treaty have proved unsuccessful."); Convention for the Pacific Settlement of International Disputes, art. 9, Oct. 18, 1907, 36 STAT. 2199, 2214 ("In disputes of an international nature involving neither honour nor vital interests, and arising from a difference of opinion on points of fact, the Contracting Powers deem it expedient and desirable that the parties who have not been able to come to an agreement by means of diplomacy, should, as far as circumstances allow, institute an International Commission of Inquiry, to facilitate a solution of these disputes by elucidating the facts by means of an impartial and conscientious investigation."); Convention for the Pacific Settlement of International Disputes, art. 9, Jul. 29, 1899, 32 STAT. 1779, 1787 ("In differences of an international nature involving neither honour nor vital interests, and arising from a difference of opinion on points of fact, the Signatory Powers recommend that the parties, who have not been able to come to an agreement by means of diplomacy, should as far as circumstances allow, institute an International Commission of Inquiry, to facilitate a solution of these differences by elucidating the facts by means of an impartial and conscientious investigation.").

[149] *Refer to* § 18.12.1 (Investigation by the U.N. Security Council Under the Charter of the United Nations).

[150] GWS art. 52 ("At the request of a Party to the conflict, an enquiry shall be instituted, in a manner to be decided between the interested Parties, concerning any alleged violation of the Convention."); GWS-SEA art. 53 (same); GPW art. 132 (same); GC art. 149 (same).

[151] GWS art. 52 ("If agreement has not been reached concerning the procedure for the enquiry, the Parties should agree on the choice of an umpire who will decide upon the procedure to be followed."); GWS-SEA art. 53 (same); GPW art. 132 (same); GC art. 149 (same).

[152] GWS art. 52 ("Once the violation has been established, the Parties to the conflict shall put an end to it and shall repress it with the least possible delay."); GWS-SEA art. 53 (same); GPW art. 132 (same); GC art. 149 (same).

[153] AP I art. 90 ("An International Fact-Finding Commission 443 (hereinafter referred to as 'the Commission') consisting of fifteen members of high moral standing and acknowledged impartiality shall be established.").

[154] AP I art. 90(2)(c)(i-ii) ("The Commission shall be competent to: (i) Enquire into any facts alleged to be a grave breach as defined in the Conventions and this Protocol or other serious violation of the Conventions or of this Protocol; (ii) Facilitate, through its good offices, the restoration of an attitude of respect for the Conventions and this Protocol.").

Although the IHFFC was officially constituted in 1991, it has not been used in its first two decades.[156]

The United States has not ratified AP I, and has not recognized the competence of the IHFFC.

18.15 Protecting Power and Other Neutral Intermediaries

The Protecting Power is an organ for the implementation of the 1949 Geneva Conventions and the 1954 Hague Cultural Property Convention.

18.15.1 Background on the Protecting Power. Under international law, a State that lacks normal diplomatic relations with a second State may, with the consent of the second State, designate a third State act to protect the first State's interests as they relate to the second State.[157] This third State is often called a Protecting Power. A State could be a Protecting Power for the purposes of more than one treaty.

18.15.1.1 *Protecting Power Under the 1949 Geneva Conventions*. Under the 1949 Geneva Conventions, belligerents may designate neutral States as "Protecting Powers" to help implement the Geneva Conventions. Specifically, the 1949 Geneva Conventions provide that the Conventions shall be applied with the cooperation and under the scrutiny of the Protecting Powers whose duty it is to safeguard the interests of the parties to the conflict.[158]

The Detaining Power has an obligation to seek a Protecting Power if the wounded and sick, shipwrecked, medical personnel and chaplains, POWs, or protected persons under the GC in its custody do not benefit from one.[159] If such protection cannot be arranged, the 1949 Geneva Conventions contemplate that States will use the ICRC or another impartial humanitarian organization to assume the humanitarian functions performed by Protecting Powers.[160]

---

[155] AP I art. 90(2) ("(a) The High Contracting Parties may at the time of signing, ratifying or acceding to the Protocol, or at any other subsequent time, declare that they recognize ipso facto and without special agreement, in relation to any other High Contracting Party accepting the same obligation, the competence of the Commission to inquire into allegations by such other Party, as authorized by this Article; … (d) In other situations, the Commission shall institute an inquiry at the request of a Party to the conflict only with the consent of the other Party or Parties concerned;").

[156] Charles Garraway, *Fact-Finding and the International Humanitarian Fact-Finding Commission*, *in* MORTEN BERGSMO, QUALITY CONTROL IN FACT-FINDING 443 (Nov. 16, 2013) ("It is regrettable that in the two decades that the Commission has been established, it has never been called into action. In the early days, little was known of the Commission, but in recent years, a series of promotional activities have been undertaken to raise consciousness amongst States. In the view of the Commission, it has an important role to play in the modern world and is anxious to fulfil this.").

[157] Vienna Convention on Diplomatic Relations, art. 45, Apr. 18, 1961, 500 UNTS 95, 122 ("If diplomatic relations are broken off between two States, or if a mission is permanently or temporarily recalled: … (*c*) The sending State may entrust the protection of its interests and those of its nationals to a third State acceptable to the receiving State.").

[158] GWS art. 8 ("The present Convention shall be applied with the cooperation and under the scrutiny of the Protecting Powers whose duty it is to safeguard the interests of the Parties to the conflict."); GWS-SEA art. 8 (same); GPW art. 8 (same); GC art. 9 (same).

[159] *Refer to* § 18.15.2.2 (Obligation on the Detaining Power to Seek a Protecting Power if Persons Protected by the 1949 Geneva Conventions Do Not Benefit From One).

[160] *Refer to* § 18.15.2.3 (Impartial Humanitarian Organizations Assuming Humanitarian Functions Performed by Protecting Powers Under the 1949 Geneva Conventions).

18.15.1.2 *Protecting Power Under the 1954 Hague Cultural Property Convention*. The 1954 Hague Cultural Property Convention provides that it and the Regulations for its execution shall be applied with the co-operation of the Protecting Powers responsible for safeguarding the interests of the parties to the conflict.[161]

18.15.2 Appointment of a Protecting Power. Within a State, the appointment of a Protecting Power is a decision made by authorities at the national level. Among States, the appointment of a Protecting Power requires the consent of the States whose relations are to be transacted through the Protecting Power. For example, during an international armed conflict, the U.S. designation of a neutral State as its Protecting Power would require agreement of the enemy State, but the consent of States allied with the United States would not be required.

The State appointed to be a Protecting Power must be able to fulfill the Protecting Power's responsibilities.[162] This State should be neutral or non-belligerent with respect to the conflict in question.[163] However, the State need not be a traditionally neutral power, such as Sweden or Switzerland.[164] In cases where a State serving as a Protecting Power enters the armed conflict, another State may assume the responsibilities of the Protecting Power.[165] A State may serve as the Protecting Power for more than one side in an armed conflict.[166]

18.15.2.1 *Agreement for an Impartial and Effective Organization to Perform Protecting Power Duties Under the 1949 Geneva Conventions*. The Parties to the 1949 Geneva Conventions may at any time agree to entrust to an organization that offers all guarantees of impartiality and efficacy the duties incumbent on Protecting Powers by virtue of the 1949 Geneva Conventions.[167]

---

[161] 1954 HAGUE CULTURAL PROPERTY CONVENTION art. 21 ("The present Convention and the Regulations for its execution shall be applied with the co-operation of the Protecting Powers responsible for safeguarding the interests of the Parties to the conflict.").

[162] *See* GWS art. 10 (States and organizations fulfilling the duties of a Protecting Power "shall be required to act with a sense of responsibility towards the Party to the conflict on which persons protected by the present Convention depend, and shall be required to furnish sufficient assurances that it is in a position to undertake the appropriate functions and to discharge them impartially."); GWS-SEA art. 10 (same); GPW art. 10 (same); GC art. 11 (same).

[163] *See* GWS art. 10 (When persons protected by the Convention do not benefit from a Protecting Power, "the Detaining Power shall request a neutral State, or such an organization, to undertake the functions performed under the present Convention by a Protecting Power designated by the Parties to a conflict."); GWS-SEA art. 10 (same); GPW art. 10 (same); GC art. 11 (same). *Cf.* GWS art. 8 (contemplating that "Protecting Powers may appoint, apart from their diplomatic or consular staff, delegates from amongst their own nationals or the nationals of other neutral Powers) (emphasis added); GWS-SEA art. 8 (same); GPW art. 8 (same); GC art. 9 (same).

[164] For example, during the Franco-Prussian War (1870-71), "Great Britain was charged with the protection of the French in Germany; and the United States, Russia, and Switzerland acted as Protecting Powers in France for the various German States." LEVIE, POWS 256. At various times during World War II, "Spain acted as the Protecting Power for Japan in the continental United States, while Sweden acted for her in Hawaii, and Switzerland in American Samoa." LEVIE, POWS 257.

[165] *See* LEVIE, POWS 259 ("The practice was adopted that when a neutral which had been acting as a Protecting Power itself became embroiled in the conflict, a successor Protecting Power would be designated to fill the vacuum.").

[166] For example, during the "Sino-Japanese War (1894-95) each side requested the United States to act as its Protecting Power, and so we find the same State acting as the Protecting Power for each belligerent within the territory of the other." LEVIE, POWS 257.

[167] GWS art. 10 ("The High Contracting Parties may at any time agree to entrust to an organization which offers all guarantees of impartiality and efficacy the duties incumbent on the Protecting Powers by virtue of the present Convention."); GWS-SEA art. 11 (same); GPW art. 10 (same); GC art. 11 (same).

18.15.2.2 *Obligation on the Detaining Power to Seek a Protecting Power if Persons Protected by the 1949 Geneva Conventions Do Not Benefit From One*. When the wounded and sick, shipwrecked, medical personnel and chaplains, POWs, or protected persons under the GC do not benefit or cease to benefit from the activities of a Protecting Power or an impartial and effective organization that performs the duties of the Protecting Power, the Detaining Power shall request a neutral State or such an organization to undertake the functions performed under the 1949 Geneva Conventions by a Protecting Power designated by the parties to a conflict.[168]

18.15.2.3 *Impartial Humanitarian Organizations Assuming Humanitarian Functions Performed by Protecting Powers Under the 1949 Geneva Conventions*. If the protection of a Protecting Power or an impartial and effective organization that the performs the duties of the Protecting Power cannot be arranged, the 1949 Geneva Conventions contemplate that States will use the ICRC or another impartial humanitarian organization to assume the humanitarian functions performed by Protecting Powers.[169]

The ICRC has often performed such a role during armed conflict.[170]

18.15.3 Activities of the Protecting Power. A Protecting Power assists and verifies compliance with the 1949 Geneva Conventions. For example, under the GPW and GC, the Protecting Power transmits information between belligerents, monitors compliance by the Detaining Power, and takes an active role in promoting the welfare of POWs and protected persons.[171]

---

[168] GWS art. 10 ("When wounded and sick, or medical personnel and chaplains do not benefit or cease to benefit, no matter for what reason, by the activities of a Protecting Power or of an organization provided for in the first paragraph above, the Detaining Power shall request a neutral State, or such an organization, to undertake the functions performed under the present Convention by a Protecting Power designated by the Parties to a conflict."); GWS-SEA art. 10 ("When wounded, sick and shipwrecked, or medical personnel and chaplains do not benefit or cease to benefit, no matter for what reason, by the activities of a Protecting Power or of an organization provided for in the first paragraph above, the Detaining Power shall request a neutral State, or such an organization, to undertake the functions performed under the present Convention by a Protecting Power designated by the Parties to a conflict."); GPW art. 10 ("When prisoners of war do not benefit or cease to benefit, no matter for what reason, by the activities of a Protecting Power or of an organization provided for in the first paragraph above, the Detaining Power shall request a neutral State, or such an organization, to undertake the functions performed under the present Convention by a Protecting Power designated by the Parties to a conflict."); GC art. 11 ("When persons protected by the present Convention do not benefit or cease to benefit, no matter for what reason, by the activities of a Protecting Power or of an organization provided for in the first paragraph above, the Detaining Power shall request a neutral State, or such an organization, to undertake the functions performed under the present Convention by a Protecting Power designated by the Parties to a conflict.").

[169] *See* GWS art. 10 ("If protection cannot be arranged accordingly, the Detaining Power shall request or shall accept, subject to the provisions of this Article, the offer of the services of a humanitarian organization, such as the International Committee of the Red Cross, to assume the humanitarian functions performed by Protecting Powers under the present Convention."); GWS-SEA art. 10 (same); GPW art. 10 (same); GC art. 11 (same).

[170] *For example*, FINAL REPORT ON THE PERSIAN GULF WAR 617 (During the 1991 Persian Gulf War, "[t]he International Committee of the Red Cross (ICRC) was provided access to Coalition EPW facilities and reviewed their findings with Coalition representatives in periodic meetings in Riyadh, Saudi Arabia.").

[171] *Refer to* § 9.32 (Role of the Protecting Power in the GPW); § 10.32 (Role of the Protecting Power in the GC).

The Protecting Power's activities are conducted with the consent of the State on whose territory it serves and the State whose facilities it visits. For example, the delegates of the Protecting Power are subject to the approval of the Power with which they are to carry out their duties.[172] In addition, a Protecting Power must ensure that its delegation does not exceed its humanitarian responsibilities and takes into account the imperative necessities of security of the State wherein they carry out their duties.[173]

18.15.4 Lending of Good Offices to Assist in Dispute Resolution. The 1949 Geneva Conventions contemplate that Protecting Powers shall lend their good offices with a view to settling disagreements between the parties to the conflict regarding protected persons, particularly in cases regarding the application or interpretation of the 1949 Geneva Conventions.[174] Protecting Powers may propose to the parties to the conflict a representative of a neutral Power or the ICRC to participate in the meeting.[175] This mechanism developed from State practice during World War I.[176]

The 1954 Hague Cultural Property Convention also contemplates that Protecting Powers shall lend their good offices in all cases where they may deem it useful in the interests of cultural property, particularly if there is disagreement between the parties to the conflict as to the application or interpretation of the provisions of the 1954 Hague Cultural Property Convention or the Regulations for its execution.[177] The Director-General of the United Nations Educational, Scientific, and Cultural Organization can also have a role in this process.[178]

---

[172] *Refer to* § 4.25.1 (Appointment of Delegates of the Protecting Powers).

[173] *Refer to* § 4.25.2 (Duties of the Representatives or Delegates of the Protecting Power).

[174] *See* GWS art. 11 ("In cases where they deem it advisable in the interest of protected persons, particularly in cases of disagreement between the Parties to the conflict as to the application or interpretation of the provisions of the present Convention, the Protecting Powers shall lend their good offices with a view to settling the disagreement."); GWS-SEA art. 11 (same); GPW art. 11 (same); GC art. 12 (same).

[175] *See* GWS art. 11 ("The Protecting Powers may, if necessary, propose for approval by the Parties to the conflict a person belonging to a neutral Power, or delegated by the International Committee of the Red Cross, who shall be invited to take part in such a meeting."); GWS-SEA art. 11 (same); GPW art. 11 (same); GC art. 12 (same).

[176] *See* GPW COMMENTARY 125 ("This idea of arranging a meeting of the representatives of the Parties to the conflict on neutral territory suitably chosen is very largely the result of experience gained during the First World War, when such meetings, which were fairly frequent, led to the conclusion of special agreements on the treatment of prisoners of war and on other problems of a humanitarian nature.").

[177] REGULATIONS FOR THE EXECUTION OF THE 1954 HAGUE CULTURAL PROPERTY CONVENTION art. 22(1) ("The Protecting Powers shall lend their good offices in all cases where they may deem it useful in the interests of cultural property, particularly if there is disagreement between the Parties to the conflict as to the application or interpretation of the provisions of the present Convention or the Regulations for its execution.").

[178] REGULATIONS FOR THE EXECUTION OF THE 1954 HAGUE CULTURAL PROPERTY CONVENTION art. 22(2) ("For this purpose, each of the Protecting Powers may, either at the invitation of one Party, of the Director-General of the United Nations Educational, Scientific and Cultural Organization, or on its own initiative, propose to the Parties to the conflict a meeting of their representatives, and in particular of the authorities responsible for the protection of cultural property, if considered appropriate on suitably chosen neutral territory. The Parties to the conflict shall be bound to give effect to the proposals for meeting made to them. The Protecting Powers shall propose for approval by the Parties to the conflict a person belonging to a neutral Power or a person presented by the Director-General of the United Nations Educational, Scientific and Cultural Organization, which person shall be invited to take part in such a meeting in the capacity of Chairman.").

18.16 Compensation for Violations of the Law of War

A State that is responsible for an internationally wrongful act is under an obligation to make full reparation for the injury caused by that act.[179] This principle also applies to the law of war in that a State that violates the law of war shall, if the case demands, be liable to pay compensation.[180]

18.16.1 Agreements Between States Settling Claims. Claims may be addressed by international agreements between States.[181]

Peace treaties or other agreements concluded in connection with the cessation of hostilities have sometimes addressed liability for violations of the law of war committed during that conflict.[182] Parties to the 1949 Geneva Conventions, however, cannot absolve one another of liability for grave breaches of the Geneva Conventions.[183]

18.16.2 International Claims Commissions. Compensation claims have also been addressed by international claims commissions established by agreement by the Parties.[184] A claims commission may also be established by the U.N. Security Council.[185]

---

[179] U.N. International Law Commission, *Draft articles on Responsibility of States for Internationally Wrongful Acts, with commentaries*, art. 1 (2001) ("Every internationally wrongful act of a State entails the international responsibility of that State."); *id.* at art. 31(1) ("The responsible State is under an obligation to make full reparation for the injury caused by the internationally wrongful act.").

[180] HAGUE IV art. 3 ("A belligerent party which violates the provisions of the said Regulations shall, if the case demands, be liable to pay compensation. It shall be responsible for all acts committed by persons forming part of its armed forces.").

[181] *For example*, GREENSPAN, MODERN LAW OF LAND WARFARE 405 ("A recent example of the obligation of a state to pay compensation for war crimes for which it is responsible is the agreement on reparations signed at Luxembourg on September 10, 1952, between the Federal Republic of Germany (West Germany) and Israel. This agreement, together with the appended protocols, provides for the payment by Western Germany to Israel of 3,450,000,000 marks ($822,000,000 or £287,000,000) to make good, within the limits of its capacity, the material damage caused by the 'unspeakable criminal acts [which] were perpetrated against the Jewish people during the National Socialist régime of terror.'") (amendment in original); Dean Acheson, *The Secretary of State to the Swiss Minister*, Oct. 21, 1949, 64 STAT. B1097 ("I have the honor to refer to previous correspondence, and also to oral discussions between officials of your Government and the Government of the United States concerning claims asserted by your Government for compensation for losses and damages inflicted on persons and property in Switzerland during World War II by units of the United States armed forces in violation of neutral rights. On behalf of the United States Government, I wish to offer to your Government in full and final settlement of the balance due on all claims of the character referred to in the preceding paragraph the sum of 62,176,433.06 Swiss francs, which includes interest through October 21, 1949. The offer is made with the understanding that the Swiss Government accepts responsibility for making payment of the individual claims involved.").

[182] GREENSPAN, MODERN LAW OF LAND WARFARE 592 ("Even apart from express provision in the peace treaty for payment of indemnities or reparations, it will be recalled that compensation is payable in a proper case for violation of the rules of warfare. In general, although this last obligation extends beyond the termination of the war, a state may provide in the peace treaty for the extinguishment or restriction of its liability in this connection.").

[183] *Refer to* § 18.9.3 (Grave Breaches of the 1949 Geneva Conventions).

[184] *For example*, Agreement Between the Government of the State of Eritrea and the Government of the Federal Democratic Republic of Ethiopia, art. 5(1), Dec. 12, 2000, 2138 UNTS 93, 97 ("Consistent with the Framework Agreement, in which the parties commit themselves to addressing the negative socio-economic impact of the crisis on the civilian population, including the impact on those persons who have been deported, a neutral Claims Commission shall be established. The mandate of the Commission is to decide through binding arbitration all claims for loss, damage or injury by one Government against the other, and by nationals (including both natural and juridical persons) of one party against the Government of the other party or entities owned or controlled by the other party that are (a) related to the conflict that was the subject of the Framework Agreement, the Modalities for its Implementation and the Cessation of Hostilities Agreement, and (b) result from violations of international humanitarian law, including the 1949 Geneva Conventions, or other violations of international law. The Commission

18.16.3 Payment or Other Compensation *Ex Gratia*. In some cases, States may provide money or other compensation to other States where not legally required (or without an admission of legal liability or fault).[186] For example, although indemnification is not required for injuries or damage incidental to the lawful use of armed force, compensation may be provided as a humanitarian gesture.[187] Similarly, a State may institute mechanisms to make payments to foreign persons who have suffered loss from combat operations, even when no violation of law of war has occurred.

18.16.4 No Private Right to Compensation Under Customary International Law or the 1949 Geneva Conventions. The responsibility of States for violations of the law of war

---

shall not hear claims arising from the cost of military operations, preparing for military operations, or the use of force, except to the extent that such claims involve violations of international humanitarian law."); Treaty between the United States and Great Britain, art. 1, May 8, 1871, 17 STAT. 863, 863-64 ("Whereas differences have arisen between the Government of the United States and the Government of Her Britannic Majesty, and still exist, growing out of the Acts committed by the several vessels which have given rise to the claims generically known as the 'Alabama Claims.' And whereas Her Britannic Majesty has authorized Her High Commissioners and Plenipotentiaries to express, in a friendly spirit, the regret felt by Her Majesty's Government for the escape, under whatever circumstances, of the Alabama and other vessels from British ports, and for the depredations committed by those vessels: Now, in order to remove and adjust all complaints and claims on the part of the United States, and to provide for the speedy settlement of such claims, which are not admitted by Her Britannic Majesty's Government, the High Contracting Parties agree that all the said claims, growing out of acts committed by the aforesaid vessels and generically known as the 'Alabama Claims,' shall be referred to a Tribunal of Arbitration to be composed of five Arbitrators, … .").

[185] U.N. SECURITY COUNCIL RESOLUTION 687, U.N. Doc S/RES/687, ¶¶ 16-18 (Apr. 3, 1991) (establishing authority for the U.N. Compensation Commission to provide a reparation mechanism for violations of international law and "any direct loss, damage, including environmental damage and the depletion of natural resources, or injury to foreign governments, national and corporations, as a result of Iraq's unlawful invasion and occupation of Kuwait.").

[186] *For example*, *Communication of the United States Government*, Jul. 31, 1945, *reprinted in Offer of Ship to Replace "Awa Maru,"* 13 DEPARTMENT OF STATE BULLETIN 249, 249-50 (Aug. 12, 1945) ("'The United States Government realizes that the deplorable accidental sinking of the *Awa Maru* prevented the Japanese Government from giving immediate effect to its announced intention to continue to facilitate the shipment and distribution of relief supplies for Allied nationals. In order, therefore, to assist in overcoming this difficulty the United States Government makes the following offer to the Japanese Government, not as present indemnification for the *Awa Maru* (the suggestion having previously been made that owing to the complex nature of the question of indemnity, that matter might be deferred until the termination of hostilities) but as a replacement for the *Awa Maru* in its humanitarian service.' 'The United States Government is prepared immediately to transfer to the Japanese Government a vessel described below of approximately the same size and characteristics as the *Awa Maru*, conditioned upon the express agreement by the Japanese Government to use the vessel so transferred for the following purposes and no others … .'").

[187] *For example*, Abraham Sofaer, Legal Adviser, Department of State, *Compensation for Iranian Airbus Tragedy*, 88 DEPARTMENT OF STATE BULLETIN 58 (Oct. 1988) ("Principles of international law that govern potential liability for injuries and property damage arising out of military operations are generally well-established. **First,** indemnification is not required for injuries or damage incidental to the lawful use of armed force. **Second,** indemnification is required where the exercise of armed force is unlawful. **Third,** states may, nevertheless, pay compensation *ex gratia* without acknowledging, and irrespective of, legal liability. … In the case of the Iran Air incident, the damage caused in firing upon #655 was incidental to the lawful use of force. The Government of Iran should not have allowed gunboats to attack our vessels and aircraft. That government also should not have allowed a passenger airline to fly over a battle zone—especially not unless it was equipped and prepared to respond to our Navy's repeated warnings. The commander of the U.S.S. *Vincennes* evidently believed that his ship was under imminent threat of attack from a hostile aircraft, and he attempted repeatedly to identify or contact the aircraft before taking defensive action. Therefore, the United States does not accept legal responsibility for this incident and is not paying 'reparations,' a word which implies wrongdoing and is often associated with wartime activities. Instead, the President has decided to make an ex gratia payment as a humanitarian gesture to the families of the individuals who were on #655.").

committed by their agents is owed to other States.[188] The fact that such responsibility is owed to other States reflects the predominately inter-State nature of international obligations.[189] Customary international law and the 1949 Geneva Conventions do not provide a private right for individuals to claim compensation directly from a State; rather, such claims are made by other States.[190]

18.17 RETORSION

Retorsion is one of the measures that an injured party may use to seek to persuade an adversary to cease violations of the law of war.

Retorsion may be understood to mean unfriendly conduct, (1) which is not inconsistent with any international obligation of the State engaging in it, and (2) which is done in response to an internationally wrongful act.[191] Retorsion is frequently contrasted with reprisal, which involves measures that would otherwise be unlawful.[192]

Because retorsion, by definition, does not involve the resort to actions that would ordinarily be characterized as illegal, the stringent conditions that apply to reprisal do not apply to retorsion.[193]

Retorsion is a general remedy available to States under international law and is not specific to the law of war. Retorsion might be used by States before, or in connection with, military operations (*e.g.*, an economic embargo). Retorsion, however, could also be used to seek to compel an adversary to adhere to the law of war.

---

[188] *See, e.g.*, Johnson v. Eisentrager, 339 U.S. 763, 789 footnote 14 (1950) ("We are not holding that these prisoners have no right which the military authorities are bound to respect. The United States, by the Geneva Convention of July 27, 1929, 47 Stat. 2021, concluded with forty-six other countries, including the German Reich, an agreement upon the treatment to be accorded captives. These prisoners claim to be and are entitled to its protection. It is, however, the obvious scheme of the Agreement that responsibility for observance and enforcement of these rights is upon political and military authorities. Rights of alien enemies are vindicated under it only through protests and intervention of protecting powers as the rights of our citizens against foreign governments are vindicated only by Presidential intervention."); Juragua Iron Co. v. United States, 212 U.S. 297, 308 (1909) ("It is true that the army, under General Miles, was under a duty to observe the rules governing the conduct of independent nations when engaged in war — a duty for the proper performance of which the United States may have been responsible in its political capacity to the enemy government.").

[189] *Refer to* § 1.10.1.3 (Predominately Inter-State Nature of International Obligations).

[190] GC COMMENTARY 211 ("One other point should be made clear. The Convention does not give individual men and women the right to claim compensation. The State is answerable to another contracting State and not to the individual. On that point the recognized system was not in any way modified in 1949."); GC COMMENTARY 603 ("As regards material compensation for breaches of the Convention, it is inconceivable, at least as the law stands today, that claimants should be able to bring a direct action for damages against the State in whose service the person committing the breach was working. Only a State can make such claims on another State, and they form part, in general, of what is called 'war reparations.'").

[191] *See* U.N. International Law Commission, *Draft articles on Responsibility of States for Internationally Wrongful Acts, with commentaries*, 128 (2001) ("Countermeasures are to be contrasted with retorsion, i.e. 'unfriendly' conduct which is not inconsistent with any international obligation of the State engaging in it even though it may be a response to an internationally wrongful act. Acts of retorsion may include the prohibition of or limitations upon normal diplomatic relations or other contacts, embargoes of various kinds or withdrawal of voluntary aid programmes."); GWS COMMENTARY 342 ("A distinction is generally made between reprisals and retortion; the latter is also a form of retaliation, but the measures taken do not break the law, and are in reply to acts which are themselves generally admitted to be lawful. The acts in question on both sides are matters within the competence of the States concerned. A case of retortion would, for example, be the withdrawal by one belligerent from retained personnel of privileges accorded over and above those accorded under the convention, where the adverse Party had withdrawn privileges, whether in the same or in another connection, from the corresponding personnel in his hands.").

[192] *Refer to* § 18.18.1.2 (Acts That Would Otherwise Be Unlawful).

[193] *Refer to* § 18.18.2 (Conditions for Lawful Reprisals).

18.18 REPRISALS

Reprisals are extreme measures of coercion used to help enforce the law of war by seeking to persuade an adversary to cease violations.

States may resort to reprisals only when certain conditions are met. In addition, there are certain treaty prohibitions on reprisal, and practical considerations may counsel against their use.

18.18.1 Definition of Reprisal. Reprisals are acts taken against a party: (1) that would otherwise be unlawful; (2) in order to persuade that party to cease violating the law.[194]

For example, during the Civil War, the United States authorized reprisals against Confederate forces for murdering and enslaving captured Union soldiers.[195] Reprisals against POWs are now prohibited.[196]

18.18.1.1 *Reprisal – Notes on Terminology*. Some older sources used "reprisal" in a narrower sense only to refer to taking possession of property of the enemy in response to violations of the law of war.[197] Some older sources used the term "retaliation" to describe what is now commonly understood to be "reprisal."[198]

The term "countermeasures" is sometimes used to cover that part of the subject of reprisals not associated with armed conflict, with the term "reprisals" or "belligerent reprisals" sometimes reserved for action taken during international armed conflict.[199]

---

[194] *See* GC COMMENTARY 227 ("Reprisals are measures contrary to law, but which, when taken by one State with regard to another State to ensure the cessation of certain acts or to obtain compensation for them, are considered as lawful in the particular conditions under which they are carried out."); United States v. Ohlendorf, *et al.* (Einsatzgruppen Case), IV TRIALS OF WAR CRIMINALS BEFORE THE NMT 493 ("Reprisals in war are the commission of acts which, although illegal in themselves, may, under the specific circumstances of the given case, become justified because the guilty adversary has himself behaved illegally, and the action is taken in last resort, in order to prevent the adversary from behaving illegally in the future.").

[195] Abraham Lincoln, General Order No. 252, Jul. 31, 1863, *reprinted in* Thos. M. O'Brien & Oliver Diefendorf, UNITED STATES WAR DEPARTMENT, II GENERAL ORDERS OF THE WAR DEPARTMENT, EMBRACING THE YEARS 1861, 1862 & 1863, 323 (1864) ("It is the duty of every government to give protection to its citizens, of whatever class, color, or condition, and especially to those who are duly organized as soldiers in the public service. The law of nations and the usages and customs of war, as carried on by civilized powers, permit no distinction as to color in the treatment of prisoners of war as public enemies. To sell or enslave any captured person on account of his color, and for no offense against the laws of war, is a relapse into barbarism and a crime against the civilization of the age. The Government of the United States will give the same protection to all its soldiers, and if the enemy shall sell or enslave anyone because of his color the offense shall be punished by retaliation upon the enemy's prisoners in our possession. It is therefore ordered, That for every soldier of the United States killed in violation of the laws of war a rebel soldier shall be executed, and for every one enslaved by the enemy or sold into slavery a rebel soldier shall be placed at hard labor on the public works and continued at such labor until the other shall be released and receive the treatment due to a prisoner of war.").

[196] *Refer to* § 18.18.3.2 (Reprisals Prohibited by the 1949 Geneva Conventions).

[197] *See, e.g.*, WINTHROP, MILITARY LAW & PRECEDENTS 798 ("**Reprisal**. This further method, above specified, consists in the taking possession of property of the enemy or of his subjects, to be held as indemnity for injury inflicted in violation of the laws of war, or as security till a pecuniary indemnity be duly rendered.").

[198] LIEBER CODE art. 27 ("The law of war can no more wholly dispense with retaliation than can the law of nations, of which it is a branch. Yet civilized nations acknowledge retaliation as the sternest feature of war. A reckless enemy often leaves to his opponent no other means of securing himself against the repetition of barbarous outrage.").

[199] U.N. International Law Commission, *Draft articles on Responsibility of States for Internationally Wrongful Acts, with commentaries*, 128 (2001) ("As to terminology, traditionally the term 'reprisals' was used to cover otherwise unlawful action, including forcible action, taken by way of self-help in response to a breach. More recently, the term 'reprisals' has been limited to action taken in time of international armed conflict; i.e. it has been taken as equivalent to belligerent reprisals. The term 'countermeasures' covers that part of the subject of reprisals not associated with armed conflict, and in accordance with modern practice and judicial decisions the term is used in that sense in this chapter.").

18.18.1.2 *Acts That Would Otherwise Be Unlawful*. Reprisals involve acts that would otherwise be unlawful. For example, responding to illegal enemy action by withdrawing benefits extended to the enemy where such benefits are not legally required would not be characterized as a reprisal. Rather, such action would be characterized as retorsion, *i.e.*, unfriendly conduct that is not inconsistent with any international obligation of the State engaging in it even though it may be a response to an internationally wrongful act.[200]

18.18.1.3 *In Order to Persuade a Party to Cease Violating the Law*. Reprisals are intended to influence a party to cease committing violations at present and in the future. Reprisals are not revenge or collective punishment.

18.18.2 Conditions for Lawful Reprisals. Customary international law permits reprisals, subject to certain conditions.

18.18.2.1 *Careful Inquiry That Reprisals Are Justified*. Reprisals shall be resorted to only after a careful inquiry into the facts to determine that the enemy has, in fact, violated the law.[201] In many cases, whether a law of war rule has been violated will not be apparent to the opposing side or outside observers. For example, a bombardment that results in the death of civilians may be the result of good faith, reasonable, mistake or may have been justified by the importance of destroying the military objective against which the bombardment was directed.

18.18.2.2 *Exhaustion of Other Means of Securing the Adversary's Compliance With the Law of War*. Other means of securing compliance with the law of war should be exhausted before resorting to reprisals.[202] For example, consideration should be given to using protests and demands, retorsion, or reasonable notice of the threat to use reprisals before resorting to reprisals.[203]

18.18.2.3 *National-Level Authorization for Reprisal*. Reprisals require a variety of conditions and implicate the rights and duties of a State under international law.[204] Thus, the

---

[200] *Refer to* § 18.17 (Retorsion).

[201] LIEBER CODE art. 28 ("Retaliation will therefore never be resorted to as a measure of mere revenge, but only as a means of protective retribution, and moreover cautiously and unavoidably -- that is to say, retaliation shall only be resorted to after careful inquiry into the real occurrence and the character of the misdeeds that may demand retribution. Unjust or inconsiderate retaliation removes the belligerents farther and farther from the mitigating rules of regular war, and by rapid steps leads them nearer to the internecine wars of savages.").

[202] 1956 FM 27-10 (Change No. 1 1976) ¶497b ("*Priority of Other Remedies*. Other means of securing compliance with the law of war should normally be exhausted before resort is had to reprisals. This course should be pursued unless the safety of the troops requires immediate drastic action and the persons who actually committed the offenses cannot be secured.").

[203] *Refer to* § 18.10 (Methods for Responding to Violations of the Law of War by the Enemy).

[204] *See* Trial of Hans Albin Rauter, *Judgment*, XIV U.N. LAW REPORTS 89, 132 (Netherlands Special Court of Cassation, Jan. 12, 1949) ("In the proper sense one can speak of reprisals only when a State resorts, by means of its organs, to measures at variance with International Law, on account of the fact that its *opponent*—in this case the State with which it is at war—had begun, by means of one or more of its organs, to commit acts contrary to International Law, quite irrespective of the question as to what organ this may have been, Government or legislator, Commander of the Fleet, Commander of Land Forces, or of the Air Force, diplomat or colonial governor. The measures which the appellant describes ... as 'reprisals' bear an entirely different character, they are indeed retaliatory measures taken in time of war by the occupant of enemy territory as a retaliation not of unlawful acts *of the State* with which he is at war, but of hostile acts *of the population* of the territory in question or *of individual members* thereof, which, in accordance with the rights of occupation, he is not bound to suffer. Both types of 'reprisals' have this in common, that the right to take genuine reprisals as well as the alleged competence to take so called 'reprisals' may in principle belong only to the *State* which applies them, … .") (first ellipsis in original).

authority to conduct reprisal is generally held at the national level.[205] Service members and units are not to take reprisal action on their own initiative.

18.18.2.4 *Proportionality in Reprisal*. To be legal, reprisals must respond in a proportionate manner to the preceding illegal act by the party against which they are taken.[206] Identical reprisals are the easiest to justify as proportionate, because subjective comparisons are not involved.[207]

However, the acts resorted to by way of reprisal need not be identical nor of the same type as the violations committed by the enemy. A reprisal should not be unreasonable or excessive compared to the adversary's violation.[208]

18.18.2.5 *Public Announcement of Reprisals*. In order to fulfill their purpose of dissuading the adversary from further illegal conduct, reprisals must be made public and announced as such.[209]

18.18.3 Treaty Prohibitions on Reprisals. Although reprisals are generally permissible under customary international law, certain treaties have prohibited certain types of reprisals.

18.18.3.1 *Reprisals Prohibited by the CCW Amended Mines Protocol*. It is prohibited in all circumstances to direct mines, booby-traps, and other devices, either in offense, defense, or by way of reprisals, against the civilian population as such or against individual civilians or civilian objects.[210]

---

[205] *For example*, 2004 UK MANUAL ¶16.19.2 ("This means that reprisals taken in accordance with the statement are permissible by and against the United Kingdom. However, commanders and commanders-in-chief are not to take reprisal action on their own initiative. Requests for authority to take reprisal action must be submitted to the Ministry of Defence and require clearance at Cabinet level.").

[206] *Refer to* § 2.4 (Proportionality).

[207] Larry A. Hammond, Deputy Assistant Attorney General, *Possible Participation by the United States in Islamic Republic of Iran v. Pahlavi*, 4A OPINIONS OF THE OFFICE OF LEGAL COUNSEL 160, 163 (1980) ("Customary international law allows reprisals, which are breaches of a treaty's terms in response to a breach by another party. To be legal, reprisals must respond in a proportionate manner to a preceding illegal act by the party against whom they are taken. Identical reprisals are the easiest to justify as proportionate, because subjective comparisons are not involved. Thus, in the current crisis, the taking of Iranian diplomats as 'hostages' (or a lesser restriction on their freedom of movement that approaches imprisonment) would clearly be a proportionate response; reducing the immunity of Iranian diplomats from criminal prosecution would be more difficult to justify.").

[208] *See* Naulilaa Incident Arbitration, Portuguese-German Arbitral Tribunal, 1928, *reprinted and translated in* WILLIAM W. BISHOP, INTERNATIONAL LAW: CASES AND MATERIALS 904 (1971) ("The necessity of a proportion between the reprisals and the offense would appear to be recognized in the German answer. Even if one admitted that international law does not require that the reprisal be approximately measured by the offense, one should certainly consider as excessive, and thus illegal, reprisals out of all proportion with the act which motivated them. Now in this case ... there has been evident disproportion between the incident of Naulilaa and the six acts of reprisals which followed it. The arbiters conclude that the German aggressions of October, November and December, 1914, on the Angola frontier, cannot be considered as lawful reprisals for the Naulilaa incident ... , in view of the lack of sufficient occasion, of previous demand and of admissible proportion between the alleged offense and the reprisals taken.") (ellipses in original).

[209] Trial of Richard Wilhem Hermann Bruns and two others, III U.N. LAW REPORTS 15, 19 (By the Eidsivating Lagmannstrett and The Supreme Court of Norway, Mar. 20-Jul. 3, 1946) ("Reprisals were generally understood to aim at changing the adversary's conduct and forcing him to keep the general accepted rules of lawful warfare. If this aim were to be achieved, the reprisals must be made public and announced as such.").

[210] CCW AMENDED MINES PROTOCOL art. 3(7) ("It is prohibited in all circumstances to direct weapons to which this Article applies, either in offence, defence or by way of reprisals, against the civilian population as such or against individual civilians or civilian objects.").

18.18.3.2 _Reprisals Prohibited by the 1949 Geneva Conventions_. Reprisals against the wounded, sick, or shipwrecked persons, personnel, buildings, vessels, or equipment protected by the GWS or GWS-Sea are prohibited.[211] Such persons or property would include:

- combatant personnel who are wounded, sick, or shipwrecked;[212]
- medical personnel and chaplains;[213]
- medical units and facilities;[214] and
- hospital ships.[215]

Measures of reprisal against POWs are prohibited.[216]

Reprisals against protected persons under the GC and their property are prohibited.[217]

18.18.3.3 _Reprisals Prohibited by the 1954 Hague Cultural Property Convention_. Parties to the 1954 Hague Cultural Property Convention shall refrain from any act directed by way of reprisals against cultural property.[218] Cultural property is defined in the 1954 Hague Cultural Property Convention.[219]

18.18.3.4 _AP I Provisions on Reprisals_. AP I prohibits attacks by way of reprisal against:

- the civilian population or civilians;[220]
- civilian objects;[221]

---

[211] GWS art. 46 ("Reprisals against the wounded, sick, personnel, buildings or equipment protected by the Convention are prohibited."); GWS-SEA art. 47 ("Reprisals against the wounded, sick and shipwrecked persons, the personnel, the vessels or the equipment protected by the Convention are prohibited.").

[212] *Refer to* § 7.3.1 (Definitions of Wounded, Sick, and Shipwrecked).

[213] *Refer to* § 7.8 (Respect and Protection of Categories of Medical and Religious Personnel).

[214] *Refer to* § 7.10 (Military Medical Units and Facilities).

[215] *Refer to* § 7.12.1 (Types of Hospital Ships and Coastal Rescue Craft).

[216] GPW art. 13 ("Measures of reprisal against prisoners of war are prohibited."); The Dostler Case, Trial of General Anton Dostler, I U.N. LAW REPORTS 22, 31 (U.S. Military Commission, Rome, Oct. 8-12, 1945) ("under the law as codified by the 1929 Convention there can be no legitimate reprisals against prisoners of war. No soldier, and still less a Commanding General, can be heard to say that he considered the summary shooting of prisoners of war legitimate even as a reprisal."); Winston Churchill, Prime Minster, United Kingdom, *Oral Answers to Questions*, Oct. 13, 1942, HANSARD, 383 HOUSE OF COMMONS DEBATES § 1501 ("The Geneva Convention upon the treatment of prisoners of war does not attempt to regulate what happens in the actual fighting. It is confined solely to the treatment of prisoners who have been securely captured and are in the responsible charge of the hostile Government. Both His Majesty's Government and the German Government are bound by this Convention. The German Government by throwing into chains 1,370 British prisoners of war for whose proper treatment they are responsible have violated Article 2 of the aforesaid Convention. They are thus attempting to use prisoners of war as if they were hostages upon whom reprisals can be taken for occurrences on the field of battle with which the said prisoners can have had nothing to do. This action of the German Government affronts the sanctity of the Geneva Convention which His Majesty's Government have always been anxious to observe punctiliously."). *Refer to* § 9.3.2 (Persons Entitled to POW Status).

[217] GC art. 33 ("Reprisals against protected persons and their property are prohibited."). *Refer to* § 10.3 (Protected Person Status).

[218] 1954 HAGUE CULTURAL PROPERTY CONVENTION art. 4(4) ("They [High Contracting Parties] shall refrain from any act directed by way of reprisals against cultural property.").

[219] *Refer to* § 5.18.1 (Definition of Cultural Property).

[220] AP I art. 51(6) ("Attacks against the civilian population or civilians by way of reprisals are prohibited.").

[221] AP I art. 52 ("1. Civilian objects shall not be the object of attack or of reprisals. Civilian objects are all objects which are not military objectives as defined in paragraph 2.").

- objects indispensable to the survival of the civilian population such as foodstuffs, crops, livestock, drinking water installations and supplies, and irrigation works;[222]
- the natural environment;[223] and
- works and installations containing dangerous forces, namely dams, dykes, and nuclear electrical generating systems.[224]

The United States has expressed the view that AP I's provisions on reprisal are counter-productive and that they remove a significant deterrent that protects civilians and war victims on all sides of a conflict.[225] The United Kingdom has taken a reservation to AP I's prohibition on certain attacks by way of reprisal.[226] Egypt, Germany, and Italy also reserved the right to react to serious violations of AP I with any means permitted by international law to prevent further violations.[227]

---

[222] AP I art. 54 ("2. ...objects indispensable to the survival of the civilian population, such as foodstuffs, agricultural areas for the production of foodstuffs, crops, livestock, drinking water installations and supplies and irrigation works... 4. These objects shall not be made the object of reprisals.").

[223] AP I art. 55(2) ("Attacks against the natural environment by way of reprisals are prohibited.").

[224] AP I art. 56(1) ("Works or installations containing dangerous forces, namely dams, dykes and nuclear energy generating stations, shall not be made the object of attack, even where these objects are military objectives, if such attack may cause the release of dangerous forces and consequent severe losses among the civilian population."); AP I art. 56(4) ("It is prohibited to make any of the works, installations or military objects mentioned in paragraph 1 the object of reprisals.").

[225] *The Position of the United States on Current Law of War Agreements: Remarks of Judge Abraham D. Sofaer, Legal Adviser, United States Department of State, January 22, 1987*, 2 AMERICAN UNIVERSITY JOURNAL OF INTERNATIONAL LAW AND POLICY 460, 469 (1987) ("To take another example, article 51 of Protocol I prohibits any reprisal attacks against the civilian population, that is, attacks that would otherwise be forbidden but that are in response to the enemy's own violations of the law and are intended to deter future violations. Historically, reciprocity has been the major sanction underlying the laws of war. If article 51 were to come into force for the United States, an enemy could deliberately carry out attacks against friendly civilian populations, and the United States would be legally forbidden to reply in kind. As a practical matter, the United States might, for political or humanitarian reasons, decide in a particular case not to carry out retaliatory or reprisal attacks involving unfriendly civilian populations. To formally renounce even the option of such attacks, however, removes a significant deterrent that presently protects civilians and other war victims on all sides of a conflict.").

[226] United Kingdom, *Statement on Ratification of AP I*, Jan. 28, 1998, 2020 UNTS 75, 77-78 ("*(m) Re: Articles 51-55* The obligations of Article 51 and 55 are accepted on the basis that any adverse party against which the United Kingdom might be engaged will itself scrupulously observe those obligations. If an adverse party makes serious and deliberate attacks, in violation of Article 51 or Article 52 against the civilian population or civilians or against civilian objects, or, in violation of Articles 53, 54 and 55, on objects or items protected by those articles, the United Kingdom will regard itself as entitled to take measures otherwise prohibited by the Articles in question to the extent that it considers such measures necessary for the sole purpose of compelling the adverse party to cease committing violations under those Articles, but only after formal warning to the adverse party requiring cessation of the violations has been disregarded and then only after a decision taken at the highest level of government. Any measures thus taken by the United Kingdom will not be disproportionate to the violations giving rise thereto and will not involve any action prohibited by the Geneva Conventions of 1949, nor will such measures be continued after the violations have ceased. The United Kingdom will notify the Protecting Powers of any such formal warning given to an adverse party, and if that warning has been disregarded, of any measures taken as a result.").

[227] Egypt, *Statement on Ratification of AP I*, Oct. 9, 1992, 1712 UNTS 435, 439 ("The Arab Republic of Egypt, while declaring its commitment to respecting all the provisions of Protocols Additional I and II, wishes to emphasize, on the basis of reciprocity, that it upholds the right to react against any violation by any party of the obligations imposed by Protocols Additional I and II with all means admissible under international law in order to prevent any further violation."); Germany, *Statement on Ratification of AP I*, Feb. 14, 1991, 1607 UNTS 526, 529 ("The Federal Republic of Germany will react against serious and systematic violations of the obligations imposed by Additional Protocol I and in particular its Articles 51 and 52 with all means admissible under international law in order to prevent any further violation."); Italy, *Statement on Ratification of AP I*, Feb. 27, 1986, 1425 UNTS 438,440 ("Italy will react to serious and systematic violations by an enemy of the obligations imposed by Additional Protocol I and in particular its Articles 51 and 52 with all means admissible under international law in order to prevent any further violation.").

France has declared that it will apply the provisions of paragraph 8 of Article 51insofar as their interpretation does not constitute an obstacle to the use, according to international law, of the means which it considers indispensable for the protection of its civilian population against grave, clear and deliberate violations of the 1949 Geneva Conventions and of AP I by the enemy.[228]

18.18.4 Practical Considerations in the Use of Reprisals. Apart from the strict legal requirements for the resort to reprisal, it will be important to consider the potential practical consequences of the use of reprisals that may counsel strongly against taking such measures. Practical considerations, including longer-term military or political consequences, may include the following factors:

- Taking reprisals may divert valuable and scarce military resources from the military struggle and may not be as effective militarily as steady adherence to the law.
- Reprisals will usually have an adverse impact on the attitudes of governments not participating in the conflict.
- Reprisals may only strengthen enemy morale and will to resist.
- Reprisals frequently lead only to further unwanted escalation of the conflict by an adversary or a vicious cycle of counter-reprisals.
- Reprisals may render resources of an adversary less able to contribute to the rehabilitation of an area after the cessation of hostilities.[229]

18.19 Discipline in National Jurisdictions of Individuals for Violations of the Law of War

In most cases, individuals are disciplined in national jurisdictions for violations of the law of war. Corrective action may take the form of adverse or corrective administrative actions. Punishment may take the form of non-judicial punishment or judicial actions in military or civilian courts, depending on the circumstances. In some cases, prosecutions in national courts are carried out by charging violations of domestic law, but in other cases, prosecutions are carried out by charging violations of international law.

18.19.1 Non-Judicial Punishment and Adverse or Corrective Administrative Actions. In some cases, it may be appropriate to administer non-judicial punishment in order to punish and repress violations of the law of war. Non-judicial punishment of members of the armed forces is

---

[228] France, *Statement on Ratification of AP I, translated in* SCHINDLER & TOMAN, THE LAWS OF ARMED CONFLICTS: A COLLECTION OF CONVENTIONS, RESOLUTIONS, AND OTHER DOCUMENTS 800, 801 (2004) ("The Government of the French Republic declares that it will apply the provisions of paragraph 8 of Article 51 insofar as their interpretation does not constitute an obstacle to the use, according to international law, of the means which it considers indispensable for the protection of its civilian population against grave, clear and deliberate violations of the Geneva Conventions and of the Protocol by the enemy.").

[229] 1976 AIR FORCE PAMPHLET 110-31 ¶10-7d ("In addition to the legal requirements which regulate resort to reprisals, there are various practical factors which governments will consider before taking reprisals. The relative importance of these factors depends upon the degree and kind of armed conflict, the character of the adversary and its resources, and the importance of states not participating in hostilities. These considerations including the following: (1) Taking reprisals may divert valuable and scarce military resources from the military struggle and may not be as effective militarily as steady adherence to the law. (2) Reprisals will usually have an adverse impact on the attitudes of governments not participating in the conflict. (3) Reprisals may only strengthen enemy morale and will to resist. (4) Reprisals frequently lead only to further unwanted escalation of the conflict by an adversary. Accordingly, an adversary's ability to retaliate is an important factor. (5) Reprisals may render resources of an adversary less able to contribute to the rehabilitation of an area after the cessation of hostilities. (6) The threat of reprisals is usually more effective than their actual use. (7) Reprisals, to be effective, should be carried out speedily and must be kept under control. They will be ineffective if random, excessive or prolonged. (8) In any event, the decision to employ reprisals would be reached only as a matter of specific national policy. The immediate advantage sought, which is to stop current and deter future violations of the law by an adversary, must be weighed against the long range military and political consequences.").

authorized under the Uniform Code of Military Justice.[230]

In some cases, it may be appropriate to take adverse or corrective administrative action to repress violations of the law of war. Adverse and corrective administrative action for members of the armed forces is authorized by military regulations.[231]

18.19.2 Charging of Domestic Prosecutions as Violations of International Law or Domestic Law. In some cases, prosecutions in national courts for conduct constituting violations of the law of war are carried out by charging violations of ordinary domestic law or military law, and in other cases, such prosecutions are carried out by charging violations of international law. For example, the murder of a POW may be prosecuted under the ordinary criminal statutes prohibiting murder. On the other hand, the same conduct may be prosecuted under special criminal statutes that are framed in terms of "war crimes."[232]

The United States has no international law obligation to prosecute an offense as a "war crime" as opposed to an ordinary criminal offense.

Prosecutions in national courts remain domestic prosecutions for violations of domestic statutes, even when those domestic statutes were enacted pursuant to treaty obligations or are framed in terms of violations of international law (*e.g.*, war crimes).

In general, prosecutions of war crimes as such (*i.e.*, characterized as international law violations as opposed to violations of domestic law) have only been undertaken when a State seeks to punish enemy nationals or persons serving the interests of the enemy State. When members of a State's armed forces or other personnel violate the law of war, that State generally prosecutes those persons for offenses under ordinary domestic law or military law.[233]

18.19.3 U.S. Law That Can Be Used to Punish Violations of the Law of War. A number of U.S. statutes may be used to punish acts that constitute violations of the law of war. When violations of the law of war are committed within the United States, such acts usually constitute violations of Federal and State law and generally may be prosecuted under ordinary criminal statutes. However, a number of other Federal statutes may be used to prosecute conduct that

---

[230] 10 U.S.C. § 815.

[231] *See, e.g.*, MARINE CORPS ORDER P1900.16F, Change 2, *Marine Corps Separation and Retirement Manual* (Jun. 6, 2007) (providing general and specific bases, and procedures for involuntary administrative separations); DEPARTMENT OF THE NAVY JUDGE ADVOCATE GENERAL INSTRUCTION 5800.7F, *Manual of the Judge Advocate General*, §§ 0102-0105 (Jun. 26, 2012) (providing regulations for non-punitive administrative measures).

[232] *Refer to* § 18.19.3.8 (War Crimes Act).

[233] *For example*, GARY SOLIS, MARINES AND MILITARY LAW IN VIETNAM: TRIAL BY FIRE 32-33 (1989) ("No Marine was charged with the commission of a war crime, as such, in Vietnam. Rather, any 'violation of the law of war' committed by a Marine against a Vietnamese was charged as a violation of the UCMJ. For example, the murder of a civilian noncombatant was charged as a violation of Article 118, murder, rather than as a war crime in violation of the Geneva or Hague conventions."); 1956 FM 27-10 (Change No. 1 1976) ¶507b ("The United States normally punishes war crimes as such only if they are committed by enemy nationals or by persons serving the interests of the enemy State. Violations of the law of war committed by persons subject to the military law of the United States will usually constitute violations of the Uniform Code of Military Justice and, if so, will be prosecuted under that Code. Violations of the law of war committed within the United States by other persons will usually constitute violations of federal or state criminal law and preferably will be prosecuted under such law (see pars. 505 and 506)."); The Public Commission to Examine the Maritime Incident of 31 May 2010, *et. al* (The Turkel Commission), Second Report, Israel's Mechanisms for Examining and Investigating Complaints and Claims of Violations of the Laws of Armed Conflict According to International Law, 171 (Feb. 2013) ("As in the US, the charging practice in Canada appears to be to prosecute violations of the law of armed conflict by members of the armed forces as general criminal law offenses or military offenses under the Code of Service Discipline, rather than as specific offenses relating to the law of armed conflict."). *Compare* § 18.7.3 (Enforcement of Law of War Obligations Through Military Instructions, Regulations, and Procedures).

violates the law of war, even though that conduct does not occur within the United States. The application of any particular statute depends on the terms of that statute and the facts of a particular case.

18.19.3.1 Uniform Code of Military Justice Offenses. The principal way for the United States to punish members of the U.S. armed forces for violations of the law of war is through the Uniform Code of Military Justice.

Certain persons may be tried for violations of the Uniform Code of Military Justice, including, among others:

- members of a regular component of the U.S. armed forces;
- POWs in the custody of the U.S. armed forces;
- in time of declared war or contingency operations, persons serving with or accompanying an armed force in the field; and
- individuals belonging to one of the eight categories enumerated in Article 4 of the GPW who violate the law of war.[234]

Offenses under the Uniform Code of Military Justice that may be used to punish conduct that constitutes a violation of the law of war include, among others:

- cruelty and maltreatment;[235]
- murder;[236]
- rape and sexual assault;[237]
- failure to obey order or regulation;[238] and
- conduct prejudicial to good order and discipline.[239]

---

[234] 10 U.S.C. § 802 ("(a) The following persons are subject to this chapter: (1) Members of a regular component of the armed forces, including those awaiting discharge after expiration of their terms of enlistment; volunteers from the time of their muster or acceptance into the armed forces; inductees from the time of their actual induction into the armed forces; and other persons lawfully called or ordered into, or to duty in or for training in, the armed forces, from the dates when they are required by the terms of the call or order to obey it. … (9) Prisoners of war in custody of the armed forces. (10) In time of declared war or a contingency operation, persons serving with or accompanying an armed force in the field. … (13) Individuals belonging to one of the eight categories enumerated in Article 4 of the Convention Relative to the Treatment of Prisoners of War, done at Geneva August 12, 1949 (6 UST 3316), who violate the law of war.").

[235] 10 U.S.C. § 893 ("Any person subject to this chapter who is guilty of cruelty toward, or oppression or maltreatment of, any person subject to his orders shall be punished as a court-martial may direct.").

[236] 10 U.S.C. § 918.

[237] 10 U.S.C. § 920.

[238] *See* 10 U.S.C. § 892 ("Any person subject to this chapter who—(1) violates or fails to obey any lawful general order or regulation; (2) having knowledge of any other lawful order issued by a member of the armed forces, which it is his duty to obey, fails to obey the order; or (3) is derelict in the performance of his duties; shall be punished as a court-martial may direct."); 10 U.S.C. § 890 ("Any person subject to this chapter who— … (2) willfully disobeys a lawful command of his superior commissioned officer; shall be punished, if the offense is committed in time of war, by death or such other punishment as a court-martial may direct, and if the offense is committed at any other time, by such punishment, other than death, as a court-martial may direct.").

[239] 10 U.S.C. § 934 ("Though not specifically mentioned in this chapter, all disorders and neglects to the prejudice of good order and discipline in the armed forces, all conduct of a nature to bring discredit upon the armed forces, and crimes and offenses not capital, of which persons subject to this chapter may be guilty, shall be taken cognizance of by a general, special, or summary court-martial, according to the nature and degree of the offense, and shall be punished at the discretion of that court.").

18.19.3.2 <u>*Incorporation of Other Non-Capital Crimes and Offenses in the Uniform Code of Military Justice*</u>. Under the Uniform Code of Military Justice, "all disorders and neglects to the prejudice of good order and discipline in the armed forces, all conduct of a nature to bring discredit upon the armed forces, and crimes and offenses not capital," of which persons subject to the Uniform Code of Military Justice may be guilty, shall be taken cognizance of by a general, special, or summary court-martial, according to the nature and degree of the offense, and shall be punished at the discretion of that court.[240]

This provision may also be used to prosecute conduct that violates the law of war. However, the preemption doctrine prohibits application of this provision to conduct already covered by specific offenses in the Uniform Code of Military Justice.[241]

18.19.3.3 <u>*U.S. General Court-Martial Jurisdiction to Try and Punish Persons Under the Law of War*</u>. Under the Uniform Code of Military Justice, general courts-martial also have jurisdiction to try any person who by the law of war is subject to trial by a military tribunal and may adjudge any punishment permitted by the law of war.[242] For example, this authority could be used to try enemy combatants for violations of the law of war, because such trials are permitted by the law of war.

18.19.3.4 <u>*Title 18 Federal Crimes Punishing Conduct Outside the United States*</u>. Certain Federal statutes specify that they apply to conduct outside the United States and could be used to prosecute conduct that, in some circumstances, would constitute a violation of the law of war. These statutes may specify in detail the circumstances in which they authorize prosecution, which may vary from statute to statute.

These statutes include provisions prohibiting:

- torture;[243]
- genocide;[244]
- murder or manslaughter of foreign officials, official guests, or internationally protected persons;[245]
- piracy;[246]

---

[240] 10 U.S.C. § 934 ("Though not specifically mentioned in this chapter, all disorders and neglects to the prejudice of good order and discipline in the armed forces, all conduct of a nature to bring discredit upon the armed forces, and crimes and offenses not capital, of which persons subject to this chapter may be guilty, shall be taken cognizance of by a general, special, or summary court-martial, according to the nature and degree of the offense, and shall be punished at the discretion of that court.").

[241] MANUAL FOR COURTS-MARTIAL IV-102 (¶60.c.(5)(a)) (2012) ("The preemption doctrine prohibits application of Article 134 to conduct covered by Articles 80 through 132. For example, larceny is covered in Article 121, and if an element of that offense is lacking—for example, intent— there can be no larceny or larceny-type offense, either under Article 121 or, because of preemption, under Article 134. Article 134 cannot be used to create a new kind of larceny offense, one without the required intent, where Congress has already set the minimum requirements for such an offense in Article 121.").

[242] 10 U.S.C. § 818 ("General courts-martial also have jurisdiction to try any person who by the law of war is subject to trial by a military tribunal and may adjudge any punishment permitted by the law of war.").

[243] *See* 18 U.S.C. § 2340A(a) ("Whoever outside the United States commits or attempts to commit torture shall be fined under this title or imprisoned not more than 20 years, or both, and if death results to any person from conduct prohibited by this subsection, shall be punished by death or imprisoned for any term of years or for life.").

[244] 18 U.S.C. § 1091.

[245] 18 U.S.C. § 1116.

[246] 18 U.S.C. § 1651 ("Whoever, on the high seas, commits the crime of piracy as defined by the law of nations, and is afterwards brought into or found in the United States, shall be imprisoned for life.")

- acts of terrorism and material support to terrorists;[247]
- certain acts involving biological weapons;[248]
- certain acts involving chemical weapons;[249] and
- certain acts involving nuclear weapons.[250]

18.19.3.5 *Extraterritorial Application of Certain Federal Offenses Through MEJA*. U.S. law makes special provision for certain conduct that is committed outside the United States to be prosecuted as though it were committed inside the United States.

U.S. law, under the Military Extraterritorial Jurisdiction Act (MEJA), permits the United States to prosecute individuals who committed certain offenses outside the United States (i) while employed by or accompanying the U.S. armed forces overseas; or (ii) while a member of the U.S. armed forces subject to the Uniform Code of Military Justice.[251] MEJA cannot be used against a member of the Armed Forces who is subject to the Uniform Code of Military Justice unless (i) such member ceases to be subject to the Uniform Code of Military Justice; or (ii) an indictment or information charges that the member committed the offense with one or more other defendants, at least one of whom is not subject to the Uniform Code of Military Justice.[252] Provisions of MEJA have been implemented through DoD regulations.[253]

Among other things, MEJA provides a way for U.S. domestic law to be used to punish conduct that violates the law of war. For example, under MEJA, a former service member could be prosecuted for a murder committed while a member of the armed forces during armed conflict abroad, even though Uniform Code of Military Justice jurisdiction over that person has ceased.[254]

---

[247] 18 U.S.C. §§ 2332b, 2339A, 2339B.

[248] 18 U.S.C. § 175.

[249] 18 U.S.C. § 229.

[250] 18 U.S.C. § 831.

[251] 18 U.S.C. § 3261(a) ("Whoever engages in conduct outside the United States that would constitute an offense punishable by imprisonment for more than 1 year if the conduct had been engaged in within the special maritime and territorial jurisdiction of the United States—(1) while employed by or accompanying the Armed Forces outside the United States; or (2) while a member of the Armed Forces subject to chapter 47 of title 10 (the Uniform Code of Military Justice), shall be punished as provided for that offense.").

[252] 18 U.S.C. § 3261(d) ("No prosecution may be commenced against a member of the Armed Forces subject to chapter 47 of title 10 (the Uniform Code of Military Justice) under this section unless—(1) such member ceases to be subject to such chapter; or (2) an indictment or information charges that the member committed the offense with one or more other defendants, at least one of whom is not subject to such chapter.").

[253] DoD INSTRUCTION 5525.11, *Criminal Jurisdiction Over Civilians Employed By or Accompanying the Armed Forces Outside the United States, Certain Service Members, and Former Service Members*, ¶2.5 (Mar. 3, 2005) ("This Instruction: 1.1. Implements policies and procedures, and assigns responsibilities, under the "Military Extraterritorial Jurisdiction Act of 2000," as amended by Section 1088 of the "Ronald W. Reagan National Defense Authorization Act for Fiscal Year 2005" (reference (a)) (hereinafter the "Act") for exercising extraterritorial criminal jurisdiction over certain current and former members of the U.S. Armed Forces, and over civilians employed by or accompanying the U.S. Armed Forces outside the United States. 1.2. Implements Section 3266 of the Act.").

[254] *See, e.g.*, United States v. Green, 654 F.3d 637, 640-41 (6th Cir. 2011) ("Steven D. Green was convicted and sentenced to life in prison for participating in a sexual assault and multiple murders while stationed in Iraq as an infantryman in the United States Army. Before senior Army officials became aware that Green and three fellow servicemembers were involved in these crimes, Green was discharged due to a personality disorder. When officials discovered Green's involvement in the crimes, his three coconspirators were still on active duty in the Army and thus subject to the Uniform Code of Military Justice. They were tried by courts-martial and each sentenced to between 90 and 110 years imprisonment, which rendered them eligible for parole in ten years. However, the Army had no authority to court-martial Green because he had already been discharged. Thus, civilian prosecutors charged Green under the Military Extraterritorial Jurisdiction Act, which extends federal criminal jurisdiction to persons who commit criminal acts while a member of the Armed Forces but later cease to be subject to military jurisdiction. A

18.19.3.6 Special Maritime and Territorial Jurisdiction of the United States Under Title 18. U.S. law provides for certain offenses to be prosecuted if they are committed in the special maritime and territorial jurisdiction of the United States.[255] Such jurisdiction may include, for example, offenses committed by U.S. nationals on the premises of U.S. diplomatic, consular, military, or other U.S. Government missions or entities in foreign States.[256] This jurisdiction provides another method by which U.S. law may be used to punish conduct that violates the law of war.[257]

18.19.3.7 U.S. Military Commissions. U.S. statutes authorize the prosecution of alien unprivileged enemy belligerents for certain offenses.[258] The Secretary of Defense has promulgated additional rules of procedure and rules of evidence applicable to such proceedings.[259]

In the past, military commissions have been used by the United States and other States to prosecute enemy belligerents for violations of the law of war and for acts of unprivileged belligerency. Military commissions have also been used for the trial of offenses under U.S. law where local courts were not open and acting (*i.e.*, where martial law applies), and for the trial of violations of occupation ordinances. These military commissions have been regarded as instrumentalities for the more efficient execution of the war powers vested in Congress and the power vested in the President as Commander-in-chief in war.[260] Military commissions have been used instead of courts-martial because U.S. courts-martial have been adapted to the circumstances of disciplining members of the armed forces and have not been crafted with a view towards certain other offenses that are also committed during armed conflict.[261]

---

federal court jury convicted Green of a number of crimes, including murder and sexual assault, and the district court sentenced him to five consecutive life sentences.").

[255] *See, e.g.*, 18 U.S.C. § 1111 ("(b) Within the special maritime and territorial jurisdiction of the United States, Whoever is guilty of murder in the first degree shall be punished by death or by imprisonment for life; Whoever is guilty of murder in the second degree, shall be imprisoned for any term of years or for life.").

[256] 18 U.S.C. § 7 ("The term 'special maritime and territorial jurisdiction of the United States', as used in this title, includes: ... (9) With respect to offenses committed by or against a national of the United States as that term is used in section 101 of the Immigration and Nationality Act—(A) the premises of United States diplomatic, consular, military or other United States Government missions or entities in foreign States, including the buildings, parts of buildings, and land appurtenant or ancillary thereto or used for purposes of those missions or entities, irrespective of ownership;").

[257] *See, e.g.*, United States v. Passaro, 577 F.3d 207, 210-12 (4th Cir. 2009) ("This case arises from the conviction in a United States federal court of an American citizen for the brutal assault on an Afghan national in Afghanistan. A jury in the Eastern District of North Carolina found David A. Passaro, a Central Intelligence Agency civilian contractor, guilty of assault on Abdul Wali. The assault occurred in 2003 at Asadabad Firebase, a United States Army outpost in Afghanistan. ... The Government predicated federal criminal jurisdiction in this case on the special maritime and territorial jurisdiction statute.").

[258] 10 U.S.C. § 948c ("Any alien unprivileged enemy belligerent is subject to trial by military commission as set forth in this chapter.").

[259] DEPARTMENT OF DEFENSE, *Manual for Military Commissions* (Aug. 14, 2012); DEPARTMENT OF DEFENSE, *Manual for Military Commissions* (Apr. 27, 2010).

[260] WINTHROP, MILITARY LAW & PRECEDENTS 839 ("But, in general, it is those provisions of the Constitution which empower Congress to 'declare war' and 'raise armies,' and which, in authorizing the initiation of war, authorize the employment of all necessary and proper agencies for its due prosecution, from which this tribunal derives its original sanction. Its authority is thus the same as the authority for the making and waging of war and for the exercise of military government and martial law. The commission is simply an instrumentality for the more efficient execution of the war powers vested in Congress and the power vested in the President as Commander-in-chief in war.").

[261] WINTHROP, MILITARY LAW & PRECEDENTS 839 ("The *occasion* for the military commission arises principally from the fact that the jurisdiction of the court-martial proper, in our law, is restricted by statute almost exclusively to members of the military force and to certain specific offences defined in a written code. It does not extend to many criminal acts, especially of civilians, peculiar to time of war; and for the trial of these a different tribunal is required.

Similarly, the use of military commission proceedings continues to be appropriate in certain circumstances because the rules for such proceedings are specially adapted to reflect the realities of the battlefield and conducting investigations in a war zone.[262]

18.19.3.8 War Crimes Act. The War Crimes Act authorizes the prosecution of individuals for certain war crimes if the victim or the perpetrator is either a U.S. national or a member of the U.S. Armed Forces, whether inside or outside the United States.[263] Under this statute, an individual may be prosecuted for conduct:

- defined as a grave breach in any of the 1949 Geneva Conventions, or any protocol to such convention to which the United States is a Party;
- prohibited by Article 23, 25, 27, or 28 of the Annex to the Hague Convention IV, Respecting the Laws and Customs of War on Land, signed 18 October 1907;
- that constitutes a grave breach of common Article 3 (as defined in the statute) when committed in the context of and in association with an armed conflict not of an international character; or
- of a person who, in relation to an armed conflict and contrary to the provisions of the CCW Amended Mines Protocol, when the United States is a Party to such Protocol, willfully kills or causes serious injury to civilians.[264]

A commander indeed, where authorized to constitute a purely war-court, may designate it by any convenient name; he may style it a 'court-martial,' and, though not a court-martial proper, it will still be a legal body under the laws of war. But to employ the same name for the two kinds of court could scarcely but result in confusion and in questions as to jurisdiction and power of punishment.").

[262] Eric Holder, Attorney General, *Remarks at Northwestern University School of Law*, Mar. 5, 2012, 2012 DIGEST OF UNITED STATES PRACTICE IN INTERNATIONAL LAW 577, 579-80 ("Military commissions are also appropriate in proper circumstances, and we can use them as well to convict terrorists and disrupt their plots. ... It's important to note that the reformed commissions draw from the same fundamental protections of a fair trial that underlie our civilian courts. They provide a presumption of innocence and require proof of guilt beyond a reasonable doubt. They afford the accused the right to counsel – as well as the right to present evidence and cross-examine witnesses. They prohibit the use of statements obtained through torture or cruel, inhuman, or degrading treatment. And they secure the right to appeal to Article III judges – all the way to the United States Supreme Court. In addition, like our federal civilian courts, reformed commissions allow for the protection of sensitive sources and methods of intelligence gathering, and for the safety and security of participants. A key difference is that, in military commissions, evidentiary rules reflect the realities of the battlefield and of conducting investigations in a war zone. For example, statements may be admissible even in the absence of Miranda warnings, because we cannot expect military personnel to administer warnings to an enemy captured in battle. But instead, a military judge must make other findings – for instance, that the statement is reliable and that it was made voluntarily.").

[263] 18 U.S.C. § 2441 ("(a) Offense.— Whoever, whether inside or outside the United States, commits a war crime, in any of the circumstances described in subsection (b), shall be fined under this title or imprisoned for life or any term of years, or both, and if death results to the victim, shall also be subject to the penalty of death. (b) Circumstances.— The circumstances referred to in subsection (a) are that the person committing such war crime or the victim of such war crime is a member of the Armed Forces of the United States or a national of the United States (as defined in section 101 of the Immigration and Nationality Act).").

[264] 18 U.S.C. § 2441(c) ("c) Definition.— As used in this section the term "war crime" means any conduct— (1) defined as a grave breach in any of the international conventions signed at Geneva 12 August 1949, or any protocol to such convention to which the United States is a party; (2) prohibited by Article 23, 25, 27, or 28 of the Annex to the Hague Convention IV, Respecting the Laws and Customs of War on Land, signed 18 October 1907; (3) which constitutes a grave breach of common Article 3 (as defined in subsection (d)) when committed in the context of and in association with an armed conflict not of an international character; or (4) of a person who, in relation to an armed conflict and contrary to the provisions of the Protocol on Prohibitions or Restrictions on the Use of Mines, Booby-Traps and Other Devices as amended at Geneva on 3 May 1996 (Protocol II as amended on 3 May 1996), when the United States is a party to such Protocol, willfully kills or causes serious injury to civilians.").

18.19.4 U.S. Domestic Law and Policy on Military Jurisdiction.

18.19.4.1 *Limits on Military Jurisdiction Over U.S. Citizens Who Are Not Members of the Armed Forces*. As a matter of U.S. domestic law, the U.S. Constitution places certain limits on the use of military tribunals to punish U.S. citizens who are not members of the armed forces.[265] DoD policy addresses the use of the Uniform Code of Military Justice to try civilians serving with or accompanying the U.S. armed forces.[266] Such law and policy may dictate the forum for prosecution. For example, a person who has been discharged from the U.S. armed forces and is no longer subject to the Uniform Code of Military Justice would be prosecuted under the MEJA or the War Crimes Act rather than the Uniform Code of Military Justice.

18.19.4.2 *Efforts to Maximize Court-Martial Jurisdiction Over Persons Who Are Members of the Armed Forces*. Where the United States and a foreign State both claim jurisdiction over a service member's conduct, DoD policy has been to make efforts to maximize the exercise of court-martial jurisdiction over persons subject to the Uniform Code of Military Justice to the extent possible under applicable agreements.[267]

18.20 PROSECUTION IN INTERNATIONAL AND HYBRID COURTS

In some cases, the prosecution of individuals for violations of the law of war has been undertaken in international tribunals or hybrid tribunals that mix elements of national and international law.

The jurisdiction and procedures of these tribunals vary from tribunal to tribunal, and may depend on applicable treaties and customary international law. In general, the decisions of these tribunals are not binding as precedent on the United States, including U.S. courts.[268] However, in some cases, it may be appropriate to consider their decisions as persuasive authority.

18.20.1 Post-World War II International Military Tribunals. After World War II, the United Kingdom, France, the United States, and the Union of Soviet Socialist Republics sought to try the major European Axis war criminals. Established by the London Agreement of August 8, 1945, the International Military Tribunal at Nuremberg conducted the landmark Trial of Major War Criminals, with 21 defendants, in Nuremberg, Germany from November 1945 - October 1946.[269] A similar tribunal was established in Tokyo by U.S. General MacArthur in his role as

---

[265] *See, e.g.*, Reid v. Covert, 354 U.S. 1 (1956); Toth v. Quarles. 350 U.S. 11 (1955); Duncan v. Kahanamoku, 327 U.S. 304 (1946); Ex parte Milligan, 71 U.S. 2 (1866).

[266] *See, e.g.*, Robert Gates, Secretary of Defense, *Memorandum re: UCMJ Jurisdiction Over DoD Civilian Employees, DoD Contractor Personnel, and Other Persons Serving With or Accompanying the Armed Forces Overseas During Declared War and in Contingency Operations* (Mar. 10, 2008 incorporating Change 1 Sept. 23, 2010).

[267] *For example*, MANUAL FOR COURTS-MARTIAL II-10 (Discussion of R.C.M. 201(d)) (2012) ("As a matter of policy, efforts should be made to maximize the exercise of court-martial jurisdiction over persons subject to the code to the extent possible under applicable agreements."). *See also* DOD DIRECTIVE 5525.1, *DoD Status of Forces Policy and Information*, ¶3 (Aug. 7, 1979, Certified Current as of Nov. 21, 2003) ("It is the policy of the Department of Defense to protect, to the maximum extent possible, the rights of United States personnel who may be subject to criminal trial by foreign courts and imprisonment in foreign prisons.").

[268] *See, e.g.*, 18 U.S.C. 2441 note ("No foreign or international source of law shall supply a basis for a rule of decision in the courts of the United States in interpreting the prohibitions enumerated in subsection (d) of such section 2441.").

[269] Agreement by the Government of the United Kingdom of Great Britain and Northern Ireland, the Government of the United States of America, the Provisional Government of the French Republic and the Government of the Union of Soviet Socialist Republics for the Prosecution and Punishment of the Major War Criminals of the European Axis, art. 2, Aug. 8, 1945, 82 UNTS 280, 282 ("The constitution, jurisdiction and functions of the International Military Tribunal shall be those set out in the Charter annexed to this agreement, which Charter shall form an integral part of this Agreement.").

Supreme Allied Commander to try major Japanese war criminals in the Far East.[270]

18.20.2 International Criminal Tribunal for the Former Yugoslavia (ICTY) and International Criminal Tribunal for Rwanda (ICTR). The U.N. Security Council has used its authority under Chapter VII of the Charter of the United Nations to establish international criminal tribunals to prosecute persons responsible for serious violations of international humanitarian law committed in the territory of the former Yugoslavia since 1991, and in the territory of Rwanda, as well as Rwandan citizens responsible for genocide and other such violations committed in the territory of neighboring States, between January 1, 1994, and December 31, 1994.[271]

The United States has, through its membership in the U.N. Security Council, supported both the efforts of the ICTR and (also acting through NATO) the efforts of the ICTY.[272]

18.20.3 The International Criminal Court (ICC) Created by the Rome Statute. The Rome Statute of the ICC established the ICC, which sits in The Hague in the Netherlands.[273] The United States is not a Party to the Rome Statute.

The Rome Statute provides that the ICC "shall have the power to exercise its jurisdiction over persons for the most serious crimes of international concern" and "shall be complementary to national criminal jurisdictions."[274] The Rome Statute provides that the ICC has jurisdiction in accordance with the Statute with respect to:[275]

- the crime of genocide;
- crimes against humanity;
- war crimes; and
- the crime of aggression.

18.20.3.1 *Attempt to Assert Jurisdiction With Respect to Nationals of Non-Party States*. The ICC may exercise jurisdiction if a situation has been referred to it by the U.N. Security Council acting under Chapter VII of the Charter of the United Nations.[276] The Rome

---

[270] *See* Douglas MacArthur, Supreme Commander for the Allied Powers, *Special Proclamation: Establishment of an International Military Tribunal for the Far East*, Jan. 19, 1946, 4 BEVANS 20, 21 ("Now, therefore, I, Douglas MacArthur, as Supreme Commander for the Allied Powers, by virtue of the authority so conferred upon me, in order to implement the Term of Surrender which requires the meting out of stern justice to war criminals, do order and provide as follows: ARTICLE 1. There shall be established an International Military Tribunal for the Far East for the trial of those persons charged individually, or as members of organizations, or in both capacities, with offenses which include crimes against peace.").

[271] *Refer to* § 18.12.4 (Authorizing International Criminal Tribunals).

[272] For example, since the mid-1990s, as part of NATO's Operation JOINT ENDEAVOR, Operation JOINT GUARD and Operation JOINT FORGE, and as part of NATO's support to the European Union's Operation ALTHEA, the United States has conducted operations to apprehend, transfer, and support the prosecution of Persons Indicted for War Crimes (PIFWC) in the ICTY.

[273] *Refer to* § 19.23 (Rome Statute of the International Criminal Court).

[274] ROME STATUTE art. 1 ("An International Criminal Court ('the Court') is hereby established. It shall be a permanent institution and shall have the power to exercise its jurisdiction over persons for the most serious crimes of international concern, as referred to in this Statute, and shall be complementary to national criminal jurisdictions. The jurisdiction and functioning of the Court shall be governed by the provisions of this Statute.").

[275] ROME STATUTE art. 5 ("The jurisdiction of the Court shall be limited to the most serious crimes of concern to the international community as a whole. The Court has jurisdiction in accordance with this Statute with respect to the following crimes: (a) The crime of genocide; (b) Crimes against humanity; (c) War crimes; (d) The crime of aggression.").

[276] *Refer to* § 18.12.4 (Authorizing International Criminal Tribunals).

Statute also provides that the ICC may exercise its jurisdiction if one or more of the following States are Parties to the Rome Statute or have accepted the jurisdiction of the ICC on an *ad hoc* basis:

- the State on the territory of which the conduct in question occurred or, if the crime was committed on board a vessel or aircraft, the State of registration of that vessel or aircraft; or
- the State of which the person accused of the crime is a national.[277]

The first of these provisions creates the possibility that the ICC would seek to exercise jurisdiction with respect to the actions of nationals of States that have not ratified the Rome Statute, even if the U.N. Security Council has not referred the situation. The United States has a longstanding and continuing objection to any assertion of jurisdiction by the ICC with respect to nationals of States not Party to the Rome Statute in the absence of consent from such States or a referral by the Security Council.[278]

18.20.3.2 Article 98 Agreements. The Rome Statute provides that the ICC may not proceed with a request for surrender or assistance that would require the requested State to act inconsistently with its obligations under international law with respect to the State or diplomatic immunity of a person or property of a third State, unless the Court can first obtain the cooperation of that third State for the waiver of the immunity.[279] The Rome Statute also provides that the ICC may not proceed with a request for surrender that would require the requested State to act inconsistently with its obligations under international agreements pursuant to which the consent of a sending State is required to surrender a person of that State to the ICC, unless the ICC can first obtain the cooperation of the sending State for the giving of consent for the surrender.[280]

---

[277] ROME STATUTE art. 12 ("In the case of article 13, paragraph (a) or (c), the Court may exercise its jurisdiction if one or more of the following States are Parties to this Statute or have accepted the jurisdiction of the Court in accordance with paragraph 3: (a) The State on the territory of which the conduct in question occurred or, if the crime was committed on board a vessel or aircraft, the State of registration of that vessel or aircraft; (b) The State of which the person accused of the crime is a national.").

[278] *See, e.g.*, 22 U.S.C. § 7421(11) ("It is a fundamental principle of international law that a treaty is binding upon its parties only and that it does not create obligations for nonparties without their consent to be bound. The United States is not a party to the Rome Statute and will not be bound by any of its terms. The United States will not recognize the jurisdiction of the International Criminal Court over United States nationals."); William J. Clinton, *Statement on the Rome Treaty on the International Criminal Court*, Dec. 31, 2000, 2000-III PUBLIC PAPERS OF THE PRESIDENTS 2816 ("In particular, we are concerned that when the court comes into existence, it will not only exercise authority over personnel of states that have ratified the treaty, but also claim jurisdiction over personnel of states that have not."). *Cf.* Extracts from Comments by Governments on the Draft Convention on Genocide Prepared by the Secretary-General, *reprinted in* U.N. SECRETARY-GENERAL, *Historical Survey of the Question of International Criminal Jurisdiction*, U.N. Doc. A/CN.4/7/Rev.1, 137 (1949) (1. *United States of America* This article contains a broad jurisdictional provision. … A third reason for opposing the provision is that it would apparently seek to establish a rule of law applicable to nationals of States which have not consented to it, namely, such States as may not ratify the Convention.").

[279] ROME STATUTE art. 98(1) ("The Court may not proceed with a request for surrender or assistance which would require the requested State to act inconsistently with its obligations under international law with respect to the State or diplomatic immunity of a person or property of a third State, unless the Court can first obtain the cooperation of that third State for the waiver of the immunity.").

[280] ROME STATUTE art. 98(2) ("The Court may not proceed with a request for surrender which would require the requested State to act inconsistently with its obligations under international agreements pursuant to which the consent of a sending State is required to surrender a person of that State to the Court, unless the Court can first obtain the cooperation of the sending State for the giving of consent for the surrender.").

The United States has entered into agreements with numerous States, including Parties to the Rome Statute, that require U.S. consent before U.S. personnel may be surrendered by that State to the ICC.[281]

18.20.3.3 U.S. Law and Policy on Support to the ICC. U.S. law contains certain restrictions on support to the ICC or ICC activities within the United States.[282] U.S. policy is to work with the international community to prevent and call to account those responsible for the worst human rights abuses, including through support to the International Criminal Court, consistent with U.S. law and our commitment to protecting our personnel.[283]

18.20.3.4 ICC and the Crime of Aggression. As adopted in 1998, the Rome Statute does not define the crime of aggression, but provides that the ICC shall exercise jurisdiction over the crime of aggression once a provision is adopted in accordance with articles 121 and 123 of the Rome Statute defining the crime and setting out the conditions under which the ICC shall exercise jurisdiction with respect to this crime.[284] A 2010 Review Conference in Kampala, Uganda adopted amendments concerning the crime of aggression, but the amendments are subject to ratification or acceptance,[285] and certain conditions must be fulfilled before the

---

[281] Such agreements have been cited in certifications required under U.S. law before U.S. personnel are authorized to participate in certain U.N. peacekeeping and peace enforcement operations. *For example*, Barack Obama, *Certification Concerning U.S. Participation in the United Nations Multidimensional Integrated Stabilization Mission in Mali Consistent with Section 2005 of the American Servicemembers' Protection Act*, Jan. 31, 2014, 79 FEDERAL REGISTER 8079 (Feb. 10, 2014) ("By the authority vested in me as President by the Constitution and the laws of the United States of America, and consistent with section 2005 of the American Servicemembers' Protection Act of 2002 (22 U.S.C. 7424), concerning the participation of members of the Armed Forces of the United States in certain United Nations peacekeeping and peace enforcement operations, I hereby certify that members of the U.S. Armed Forces participating in the United Nations Multidimensional Integrated Stabilization Mission in Mali are without risk of criminal prosecution or other assertion of jurisdiction by the International Criminal Court (ICC) because the Republic of Mali has entered into an agreement in accordance with Article 98 of the Rome Statute preventing the ICC from proceeding against members of the Armed Forces of the United States present in that country.").

[282] *See, e.g.*, 22 U.S.C. §§ 7421-7433; 22 U.S.C. § 7401(b).

[283] Barak Obama, *National Security Strategy of the United States*, 22 (Feb. 2015) ("We will work with the international community to prevent and call to account those responsible for the worst human rights abuses, including through support to the International Criminal Court, consistent with U.S. law and our commitment to protecting our personnel."); Barak Obama, *National Security Strategy of the United States*, 48 (May 2010) ("Although the United States is not at present a party to the Rome Statute of the International Criminal Court (ICC), and will always protect U.S. personnel, we are engaging with State Parties to the Rome Statute on issues of concern and are supporting the ICC's prosecution of those cases that advance U.S. interests and values, consistent with the requirements of U.S. law."); Harold Hongju Koh, Legal Adviser, Department of State, *Remarks on international criminal justice at the Vera Institute of Justice in New York and at Leiden University, Campus The Hague*, 2012 DIGEST OF UNITED STATES PRACTICE IN INTERNATIONAL LAW 61, 67 ("So, while the United States will always protect U.S. personnel, we are engaging with States parties to the Rome Statute on issues of concern, and we have applied a pragmatic, case-by-case approach towards ICC issues.").

[284] ROME STATUTE art. 5(2) ("The Court shall exercise jurisdiction over the crime of aggression once a provision is adopted in accordance with articles 121 and 123 defining the crime and setting out the conditions under which the Court shall exercise jurisdiction with respect to this crime. Such a provision shall be consistent with the relevant provisions of the Charter of the United Nations.").

[285] *See* Resolution RC/Res.6, Review Conference of the Rome Statute of the International Criminal Court, Kampala, Uganda, Jun. 11, 2010 ("1. *Decides* to adopt, in accordance with article 5, paragraph 2, of the Rome Statute of the International Criminal Court (hereinafter: 'the Statute') the amendments to the Statute contained in annex I of the present resolution, which are subject to ratification or acceptance and shall enter into force in accordance with article 121, paragraph 5; and *notes* that any State Party may lodge a declaration referred to in article 15 *bis* prior to ratification or acceptance;").

ICC will be able to exercise jurisdiction with respect to the crime of aggression.[286] The United States has expressed the view that the definitions of "act of aggression" and "crime of aggression" in the Kampala amendments do not reflect customary international law.[287] The United States has expressed a broad range of other concerns about the Kampala amendments, including concerns regarding the possibility of the ICC exercising jurisdiction over the crime of aggression without a prior determination by the Security Council that a State has committed an act of aggression.[288]

18.20.4 Hybrid or Mixed Tribunals. In some cases, an international tribunal may mix elements of domestic and international law. For example, war crimes trials by national tribunals were conducted after World War II under the military government formed by the Allies to govern occupied Germany.[289]

More recently, hybrid tribunals have been established in Sierra Leone, Cambodia, and Lebanon. The Special Court for Sierra Leone was established by a treaty between Sierra Leone and the United Nations.[290] The Special Court applies both international and Sierra Leonean law.[291] Similarly, in Cambodia, the Extraordinary Chambers in the Courts of Cambodia (ECCC) was established under Cambodian domestic law, but regulated by an agreement between Cambodia and the United Nations.[292] The Special Tribunal for Lebanon was established

---

[286] *See, e.g.*, Article 15 *bis*, Amendments to the Rome Statute of the International Criminal Court on the Crime of Aggression, Annex I to Resolution RC/Res.6, Review Conference of the Rome Statute of the International Criminal Court, Kampala, Uganda, Jun. 11, 2010 ("2. The Court may exercise jurisdiction only with respect to crimes of aggression committed one year after the ratification or acceptance of the amendments by thirty States Parties. 3. The Court shall exercise jurisdiction over the crime of aggression in accordance with this article, subject to a decision to be taken after 1 January 2017 by the same majority of States Parties as is required for the adoption of an amendment to the Statute.").

[287] Harold Hongju Koh, Legal Adviser, Department of State, *Statement at the Review Conference of the International Criminal Court*, Jun. 4, 2010 ("[T]he definition of aggression does not truly reflect customary international law, i.e., widespread and consistent state practice followed out of a sense of legal obligation.").

[288] Sarah Sewall, Under Secretary for Civilian Security, Democracy, and Human Rights, *Remarks at the Annual Meeting of the American Society of International Law: The ICC Crime of Aggression and the Changing International Security Landscape*, Apr. 9, 2015 ("Many of our concerns – and many of the means of mitigating them – are linked to the uncertainty that still surrounds crucial aspects of the amendments and how they may be interpreted and applied. The definition of the crime itself, as adopted in Kampala, was ostensibly based on an earlier UN resolution that gave guidance to the Security Council on identifying acts of aggression. But the definition that the parties adopted stripped away the critical requirement that the assessment of a use of force 'must be considered in light of all the circumstances of each particular case,' and it shifted the role of applying this guidance and making these judgments – which inevitably involve political judgments – from the Security Council to a judicial body meant to remain above politics.").

[289] *See generally* DEPARTMENT OF THE ARMY PAMPHLET 27-161-2, *II International Law*, 224-33 (Oct. 23, 1962).

[290] *See* Agreement between the United Nations and the Government of Sierra Leone on the Establishment of a Special Court for Sierra Leone, *in* Appendix II to *Letter dated 6 March 2002 from the Secretary-General addressed to the President of the Security Council*, U.N. Doc S/2002/246, 17 (Mar. 8, 2002). *See also* U.N. SECURITY COUNCIL RESOLUTION 1315, U.N. Doc S/RES/1315 (Aug. 14, 2000) ("*Requests* the Secretary-General to negotiate an agreement with the Government of Sierra Leone to create an independent special court consistent with this resolution,").

[291] Statute of the Special Court for Sierra Leone, art. 1(1) Attachment to Agreement between the United Nations and the Government of Sierra Leone on the Establishment of a Special Court for Sierra Leone, *in* Appendix II to *Letter dated 6 March 2002 from the Secretary-General addressed to the President of the Security Council*, U.N. Doc S/2002/246, 17 (Mar. 8, 2002) ("There is hereby established a Special Court for Sierra Leone to prosecute persons who bear the greatest responsibility for serious violations of international humanitarian law and Sierra Leonean law committed in the territory of Sierra Leone since 30 November 1996.").

[292] *See* Harold Hongju Koh, Legal Adviser, Department of State, *Remarks on international criminal justice at the Vera Institute of Justice in New York and at Leiden University, Campus The Hague*, 2012 DIGEST OF UNITED

following an agreement between the United Nations and Lebanon to prosecute, *inter alia*, persons responsible for the February 2005 attack resulting in the death of former Lebanese Prime Minister Rafiq Hariri.[293]

18.21 LIMITS ON THE PUNISHMENT OF INDIVIDUALS UNDER THE LAW OF WAR

International law places certain limits on the authority of States, whether acting individually, or together with other States, to punish individuals for violations committed during armed conflict.

18.21.1 Jurisdiction Over War Crimes. States must have jurisdiction over an alleged offense to prosecute a person for committing war crimes or other punishable offenses committed during armed conflict.[294]

Jurisdiction over war crimes has traditionally been exercised by belligerents with respect to offenses committed by or against their nationals.[295] In addition, belligerents have also prosecuted war crimes committed by enemy nationals against nationals of allies and of co-

---

STATES PRACTICE IN INTERNATIONAL LAW 61, 66 ("Similarly, in Cambodia, the international community worked long and hard with domestic authorities to pursue accountability for atrocity crimes that took place decades ago. The Khmer Rouge Tribunal – formally, the Extraordinary Chambers in the Courts of Cambodia (ECCC) – was a different type of hybrid, established under domestic law but regulated by a UN-Cambodia agreement."). *See also* U.N. GENERAL ASSEMBLY, *Report of the Secretary-General on Khmer Rouge trials*, U.N. Doc A/60/565 (Nov. 25, 2005) ("On 28 April 2005 a notification was sent to the Government of Cambodia indicating that the legal requirements on the United Nations side for the entry into force of the Agreement between the United Nations and the Royal Government of Cambodia concerning the Prosecution under Cambodian Law of Crimes Committed during the Period of Democratic Kampuchea, done at Phnom Penh on 6 June 2003, had been complied with. The Agreement accordingly entered into force on 29 April 2005, the day after the notification, in accordance with its article 32. The Government of Cambodia had previously provided its notification under that article, on 16 November 2004.").

[293] Agreement between the United Nations and the Lebanese Republic on the establishment of a Special Tribunal for Lebanon, art. 1, Annex to U.N. SECURITY COUNCIL RESOLUTION 1757, U.N. Doc S/RES/1757 (2007) ("There is hereby established a Special Tribunal for Lebanon to prosecute persons responsible for the attack of 14 February 2005 resulting in the death of former Lebanese Prime Minister Rafiq Hariri and in the death or injury of other persons.").

[294] *See, e.g.*, United States v. Josef Altstoetter, *et al.* (Justice Case), III TRIALS OF WAR CRIMINALS BEFORE THE NMT 969-70 ("We are empowered to determine the guilt or innocence of persons accused of acts described as 'war crimes' and 'crimes against humanity' under rules of international law. At this point, in connection with cherished doctrines of national sovereignty, it is important to distinguish between the rules of common international law which are of universal and superior authority on the one hand, and the provisions for enforcement of those rules which are by no means universal on the other. ... This universality and superiority of international law does not necessarily imply universality of its enforcement.").

[295] United States v. Josef Altstoetter, *et al.* (Justice Case), III TRIALS OF WAR CRIMINALS BEFORE THE NMT 1189-90 (Separate Opinion of Judge Blair) ("[D]uring hostilities and before their formal termination belligerents have concurrent jurisdiction over war crimes committed by the captured enemy persons in their territory or against their nationals in time of war. ... After armistice or peace agreement the matter of punishment of war crimes is determined by the terms thereof."); United States v. Ohlendorf, *et al.* (Einsatzgruppen Case), IV TRIALS OF WAR CRIMINALS BEFORE THE NMT 460 (rejecting the defense counsel's argument that Russia's could not participate in the Tribunal instead explaining that "Russia's participation in the formulation of Control Council Law No. 10 is in accordance with every recognized principle of international law," because "[t]here is no authority which denies any belligerent nation jurisdiction over individuals in its actual custody charged with violation of international law" and "no one would be so bold as to suggest that what occurred between Germany and Russia from June 1941 to May 1945 was anything but war, and, being war, that Russia would not have the right to try the alleged violators of the rules of war on her territory and against her people.").

belligerents, and stateless persons.[296] Because jurisdiction over war crimes has sometimes been exercised by belligerents against enemy nationals without regard to the territorial location of the offense, it has sometimes been characterized as "universal" in character.[297]

In the past, neutral States generally did not exercise jurisdiction with respect to alleged law of war violations between belligerents.[298] For example, States have declined to exercise jurisdiction with respect to offenses committed by enemy nationals before those States became involved in an armed conflict with that State.[299]

---

[296] 1956 FM 27-10 (Change No. 1 1976) ¶507a ("The jurisdiction of United States military tribunals in connection with war crimes is not limited to offenses committed against nationals of the United States but extends also to all offenses of this nature committed against nationals of allies and of cobelligerents and stateless persons.").

[297] *See, e.g.*, TUCKER, THE LAW OF WAR AND NEUTRALITY AT SEA 155 footnote 12 ("It is generally agreed that post World War II practice has firmly established the so-called principle of 'universality of jurisdiction over war crimes,' thereby permitting belligerents to exercise jurisdiction over individuals accused of war crimes without regard to the place where an offense was committed or to the nationality of the victims. In its most general form this principle might well be interpreted to permit neutral states to try and punish war criminals who fall under their control. But there is no record of neutral states making such an attempt, and the right of neutrals to do so remains doubtful."); G. Brand, *The War Crimes Trials and the Laws of War*, 28 BRITISH YEAR BOOK OF INTERNATIONAL LAW 414, 416 (1951) ("Thus the doctrine of universality of war crimes is now generally accepted. Account has been taken of the crime itself rather than of (a) the nationality of the victim, provided that he has been, from the point of view of the court, an Allied national or could be treated as such; (b) the nationality of the accused, provided that he can be regarded as having identified himself with the enemy; or (c) the place of the offence."); Willard B. Cowles, *Universality of Jurisdiction over War Crimes*, 33 CALIFORNIA LAW REVIEW 177, 178 (1945) (describing the question of "whether the jurisdiction principle of universality is applicable to the punishment of war crimes" as "the question whether, under international law, a belligerent State has jurisdiction to punish an enemy war criminal in its custody when the victim of the war crime was a national of another State and the offense took place outside of territory under control of the punishing State.").

[298] La Amistad De Rues, 18 U.S. 385, 390 (1820) ("consider[ing] it no part of the duty of a neutral nation to interpose, upon the mere footing of the law of nations, to settle all the rights and wrongs which may grow out of a capture between belligerents" and noting that alleged law of war violations between belligerents "have never been held within the cognizance of the prize tribunals of neutral nations."); Juando v. Taylor, 13 F. Cas. 1179, 1189 (S.D.N.Y. 1818) (No. 7558) (explaining that "no suit or proceeding of any sort can be maintained in the courts of a neutral nation, by the subjects of one belligerent against the subjects of the other, for acts growing out of the war").

[299] *See* James Brown Scott and Robert Lansing, *Memorandum of Reservations Presented by the Representatives of the United States to the Report of the Commission on Responsibilities,* Annex II to the Report Presented to the Preliminary Peace Conference, Mar. 29, 1919, by the Commission on the Responsibility of the Authors of the War and on Enforcement of Penalties, *reprinted in* 14 AJIL 95, 147 (1920) ("It seemed elementary to the American representatives that a country could not take part in the trial and punishment of a violation of the laws and customs of war committed by Germany and her Allies before the particular country in question had become a party to the war against Germany and her Allies; that consequently the United States could not institute a military tribunal within its own jurisdiction to pass upon violations of the laws and customs of war, unless such violations were committed upon American persons or American property, and that the United States could not properly take part in the trial and punishment of persons accused of violations of the laws and customs of war committed by the military or civil authorities of Bulgaria or Turkey."). *Cf.* United States, *et al.* v. Göring, *et al.*, *Judgment*, I TRIAL OF THE MAJOR WAR CRIMINALS BEFORE THE IMT 254 ("To constitute Crimes against Humanity, the acts relied on before the outbreak of war must have been in execution of, or in connection with, any crime within the jurisdiction of the Tribunal. The Tribunal is of the opinion that revolting and horrible as many of these crimes were, it has not been satisfactorily proved that they were done in execution of, or in connection with, any such crime. The Tribunal therefore cannot make a general declaration that the acts before 1939 were Crimes against Humanity within the meaning of the Charter, but from the beginning of the war in 1939 War Crimes were committed on a vast scale, which were also Crimes against Humanity; and insofar as the inhumane acts charged in the Indictment, and committed after the beginning of the war, did not constitute War Crimes, they were all committed in execution of, or in connection with, the aggressive war, and therefore constituted Crimes against Humanity.").

Some have argued that States may exercise purely universal jurisdiction over war crimes, *i.e.*, jurisdiction to define and prescribe punishment based simply on the character of the offense as a war crime.[300] Until the 1990s, no such attempts were made by States to exercise jurisdiction on this basis.[301] Congress declined to authorize prosecutions for war crimes based on this principle.[302] Efforts by certain States to undertake prosecutions on the basis of this principle have been controversial.[303] Such prosecutions have generally not been successful unless the State concerned has consented.[304]

18.21.2 Tu Quoque. The international law doctrine *tu quoque* may be understood as an argument that a State does not have standing to complain about a practice in which it itself engages.[305]

---

[300] I RESTATEMENT (THIRD) OF FOREIGN RELATIONS LAW OF THE UNITED STATES 254 (§404, Reporters' Note 1) (1987) ("A state has jurisdiction to define and prescribe punishment for certain offenses recognized by the community of nations as of universal concern, such as piracy, slave trade, attacks on or hijacking of aircraft, genocide, war crimes, and perhaps certain acts of terrorism, even where none of the bases of jurisdiction indicated in § 402 is present."); *but see* I RESTATEMENT (THIRD) OF FOREIGN RELATIONS LAW OF THE UNITED STATES 257-58 (§404, Reporters' Note 3) (1987) ("The previous Restatement cited only piracy as an offense subject to universal jurisdiction. See § 34. Reporters' Note 2 of that section listed other crimes of universal interest but indicated they were not yet subject to universal jurisdiction as a matter of international law.").

[301] I RESTATEMENT (THIRD) OF FOREIGN RELATIONS LAW OF THE UNITED STATES 256 (1987) ("apparently no state has exercised such jurisdiction [over war crimes and genocide] in circumstances where no other basis for jurisdiction under § 402 was present."); Committee on the Judiciary, House of Representatives Report No. 104-698, 8 (Jul. 24, 1996) ("The Committee has been informed that there has never been a single case of a signatory country to the Geneva conventions exercising its own criminal jurisdiction over an alleged war criminal on the basis of universal jurisdiction.").

[302] *See* Committee on the Judiciary, House of Representatives Report No. 104-698, 8 (Jul. 24, 1996) ("The Committee decided that the expansion of H.R. 3680 to include universal jurisdiction would be an unwise [sic] at present. Domestic prosecution based on universal jurisdiction could draw the United States into conflicts in which this country has no place and where our national interests are slight. In addition, problems involving witnesses and evidence would likely be daunting. This does not mean that war criminals should go unpunished. There are ample alternative venues available which are more appropriate. Prosecutions can be handled by the nations involved or by international tribunal. If a war criminal is discovered in the United States, the federal government can extradite the individual upon request in order to facilitate prosecution overseas. The Committee is not presently aware that these alternative venues are inadequate to meet the task.").

[303] *See, e.g.*, Arrest Warrant of 11 April 2000 (Democratic Republic of the Congo v. Belgium), Judgment, 2002 I.C.J. 35, 43 (¶15) (Separate Opinion of President Guillaume) ("International criminal law has itself undergone considerable development and constitutes today an impressive legal corpus. It recognizes in many situations the possibility, or indeed the obligation, for a State other than that on whose territory the offence was committed to confer jurisdiction on its courts to prosecute the authors of certain crimes where they are present on its territory. International criminal courts have been created. But at no time has it been envisaged that jurisdiction should be conferred upon the courts of every State in the world to prosecute such crimes, whoever their authors and victims and irrespective of the place where the offender is to be found. To do this would, moreover, risk creating total judicial chaos. It would also be to encourage the arbitrary, for the benefit of the powerful, purportedly acting as agent for an ill-defined 'international community.' Contrary to what is advocated by certain publicists, such a development would represent not an advance in the law but a step backward.").

[304] Roman Anatolevich Kolodkin, Special Rapporteur, U.N. International Law Commission, *Second report on immunity of State officials from foreign criminal jurisdiction*, U.N. Doc A/CN.4/631, ¶16 (Jun. 10, 2010) ("It is noted that until now attempts to exercise universal jurisdiction that have been successful have just taken place in cases where the State concerned consented. In other cases, States usually react negatively to attempts to exercise foreign criminal jurisdiction even over their former Heads of State and Government, as they also do, however, in respect of other high-ranking officials. In the absence of cooperation with the State whose official a case concerns, the proper and legally correct criminal prosecution of such a person is practically impossible. On the whole, therefore, such attempts end up merely complicating relations between States.").

[305] Department of Defense, Office of the General Counsel, *An Assessment of International Legal Issues in Information Operations* 46 (May 1999) ("The lack of strong international legal sanctions for peacetime espionage

For example, it would seem unfair for a State to punish members of opposing military forces for committing acts that it considered lawful for members of its armed forces to perform.[306] On the other hand, as a general matter, the fact that criminal acts have been committed by opposing armed forces does not constitute a defense to criminal liability. In addition, as a general matter, the fact that members of its armed forces have committed a violation does not preclude a State from punishing captured members of opposing armed forces for such violations.[307] Similarly, the authority of a State to punish its own citizens, in accordance with municipal criminal law, for violations of international law is not affected by this rule.[308]

18.21.3 Fundamental Fairness Requirements.

18.21.3.1 *Fair Trial Requirements*. Any person charged with a crime under international law has the right to a fair trial on the facts and law.[309]

In all circumstances, persons who are accused of grave breaches of the 1949 Geneva Conventions shall benefit from safeguards of proper trial and defense, which shall not be less favorable than those provided by Article 105 and those following of the GPW.[310] In addition, other fundamental fair trial guarantees should be afforded.[311]

---

may also constitute an implicit application of the international law doctrine called "*tu quoque*" (roughly, a nation has no standing to complain about a practice in which it itself engages). Whatever the reasons, the international legal system generally imposes no sanctions upon nations for acts of espionage except for the political costs of public denunciation, which don't seem very onerous."). *See also* FRITS KALSHOVEN, BELLIGERENT REPRISALS 364 ("There is, however, another possible view of *tu quoque*, according to which this does not so much constitute a substantive justificatory ground as an argument of a procedural order, to the effect that a belligerent cannot charge his enemy with a particular form of illegal warfare if he has himself violated the same rule or rules, without this being justified as a reprisal. For this argument, it is not important whether the belligerent was the first to commit that violation, nor even whether he was aware that the enemy was guilty of the same illegal conduct: the contention is that the mere fact of his having infringed the identical norm precludes him from charging that particular illegality against the enemy.").

[306] United States, *et al.* v. Göring, *et al.*, *Judgment*, I TRIAL OF THE MAJOR WAR CRIMINALS BEFORE THE IMT 313 ("In view of all of the facts proved, and in particular of an order of the British Admiralty announced on 8 May 1940, according to which all vessels should be sunk at night in the Skagerrak, and the answer to interrogatories by Admiral Nimitz that unrestricted submarine warfare was carried on in the Pacific Ocean by the United States from the first day that nation entered the war, the sentence of Donitz is not assessed on the ground of his breaches of the international law of submarine warfare.").

[307] *See* United States v. von Leeb, *et al.* (The High Command Case), XI TRIALS OF WAR CRIMINALS BEFORE THE NMT 482 ("Under general principles of law, an accused does not exculpate himself from a crime by showing that another committed a similar crime, either before or after the alleged commission of the crime by the accused.").

[308] Sentence of the Bundesgerichtshof of Sept. 30, 1960, *reprinted in* FRITS KALSHOVEN, BELLIGERENT REPRISALS 365 footnote 15 (2005) (citing 32 International Law Reports 564) ("The rule of 'tu quoque' merely means that no State may accuse another State of violations of international law and exercise criminal jurisdiction over the latter's citizens in respect of such violations if it is itself guilty of similar violations against the other State or its allies. The right and duty of a State to hold its own citizens responsible, in accordance with municipal criminal law, for violations of international law is not affected by this rule.").

[309] U.N. International Law Commission, *Principles of International Law Recognized in the Charter of the Nürnberg Tribunal and in the Judgment of the Tribunal*, in *Report of the International Law Commission on its Second Session, 5 June to 29 July 1950*, (Document A/1316), *reprinted in* II YEARBOOK OF INTERNATIONAL LAW COMMISSION 1950, 374, 375 U.N. Doc. A/CN. 4/SER.A/1950/Add. 1 (Jun. 6, 1957) ("PRINCIPLE V Any person charged with a crime under international law has the right to a fair trial on the facts and law.").

[310] GWS art. 49 ("In all circumstances, the accused persons shall benefit by safeguards of proper trial and defence, which shall not be less favourable than those provided by Article 105 and those following of the Geneva Convention relative to the Treatment of Prisoners of War of August 12, 1949."); GWS-SEA art. 50 (same); GC art. 146 (same); GPW art. 129 ("In all circumstances, the accused persons shall benefit by safeguards of proper trial and defence, which shall not be less favourable than those provided by Article 105 and those following of the present Convention."). *Refer to* § 9.28.4 (Rights of Defense and Trial Procedure).

[311] *Refer to* § 8.16 (Criminal Procedure and Punishment).

18.21.3.2 *Punishment of Violations of the Law of War*. The punishment of war crimes may vary according to the particular forum in which the prosecution is brought. For example, what punishments are authorized may depend on a State's domestic law or the statute of an international criminal tribunal. In addition, special rules address the punishment of POWs and protected persons. However, the following principles apply, as a matter of international law, to the punishment of violations of the law of war:

- The punishment imposed for a violation of the law of war must be proportionate to the gravity of the offense.
- The death penalty may be imposed for grave breaches of the law.
- Corporal punishment is excluded.
- Punishments should be deterrent, and in imposing a sentence of imprisonment it is not necessary to take into consideration the end of the war, which does not of itself limit the imprisonment to be imposed.[312]

18.21.4 Limitations on the Trial and Punishment of Certain Classes of Persons.

18.21.4.1 *Limitations on the Trial and Punishment of POWs*. The trial and punishment of POWs must comport with the rules prescribed by the GPW.[313]

18.21.4.2 *Limitations on the Trial and Punishment of Protected Persons*. The trial and punishment of protected persons must comport with the rules prescribed by the GC.[314]

18.21.4.3 *Limitations on the Trial and Punishment of Persons Entitled to the Privileges of Combatant Status*. As a matter of international law, persons who are entitled to the privileges of combatant status have a certain legal immunity from the domestic law of foreign States.[315]

18.22 PRINCIPLES OF INDIVIDUAL CRIMINAL RESPONSIBILITY FOR CRIMES UNDER INTERNATIONAL LAW

Individual criminal responsibility exists for certain violations of the international law.

18.22.1 Individual Criminal Responsibility for Acts Constituting Crimes Under International Law. Any person who commits an act that constitutes a crime under international law is responsible therefor and liable to punishment.[316] International law imposes duties and liabilities on individuals as well as States, and individuals may be punished for violations of international law.[317]

---

312 1956 FM 27-10 (Change No. 1 1976) ¶508 ("The punishment imposed for a violation of the law of war must be proportionate to the gravity of the offense. The death penalty may be imposed for grave breaches of the law. Corporal punishment is excluded. Punishments should be deterrent, and in imposing a sentence of imprisonment it is not necessary to take into consideration the end of the war, which does not of itself limit the imprisonment to be imposed.").

313 *Refer to* § 9.26 (General Principles Applicable to POW Discipline); § 9.28 (Judicial Proceedings and Punishment).

314 *Refer to* § 10.27 (General Provisions Applicable to Both Judicial and Disciplinary Sanctions Regarding Internees); § 10.29 (Judicial Proceedings Regarding Protected Persons in Occupied Territory or Internees in a Belligerent's Home Territory).

315 *Refer to* § 4.4.3 (Combatants - Legal Immunity From a Foreign State's Domestic Law).

316 *See* U.N. International Law Commission, *Principles of International Law Recognized in the Charter of the Nürnberg Tribunal and in the Judgment of the Tribunal*, in *Report of the International Law Commission on its Second Session, 5 June to 29 July 1950*, (Document A/1316), *reprinted in* II YEARBOOK OF INTERNATIONAL LAW COMMISSION 1950, 374 U.N. Doc. A/CN. 4/SER.A/1950/Add. 1 (Jun. 6, 1957) ("PRINCIPLE I Any person who commits an act which constitutes a crime under international law is responsible therefor and liable to punishment.").

317 United States, *et al.* v. Göring, *et al.*, *Judgment*, I TRIAL OF THE MAJOR WAR CRIMINALS BEFORE THE IMT 223 ("That international law imposes duties and liabilities upon individuals as well as upon States has long been recognized. ... Many other authorities could be cited, but enough has been said to show that individuals can be punished for violations of international law. Crimes against international law are committed by men, not by abstract entities, and

18.22.2 Absence of Penalty Under Domestic Law Does Not Relieve a Person of Responsibility. The fact that internal law does not impose a penalty for an act that constitutes a crime under international law does not relieve the person who committed the act from responsibility under international law.[318]

For example, a State may lack domestic legislation that imposes any penalty for an act that violates international law. Nonetheless, just as a State's municipal law cannot excuse its failure to comply with its international legal obligations, a person is not relieved of responsibility for an act constituting a crime under international law because his or her State's municipal law does not impose any penalty for the offense.[319]

18.22.3 Official Position Does Not Relieve a Person of Responsibility. The fact that a person who committed an act which constitutes a crime under international law acted as Head of State or responsible Government official does not relieve him or her of responsibility under international law.[320]

This principle has been reflected in the statutes of international criminal tribunals.[321]

18.22.4 Acting Pursuant to Orders Does Not Relieve a Person of Responsibility. The fact that a person acted pursuant to orders of his or her Government or of a superior does not relieve that person from responsibility under international law, provided it was possible in fact for that person to make a moral choice.[322] This principle has been reflected in the statutes of international criminal tribunals.[323] It may also be understood as part of a broader principle that

---

only by punishing individuals who commit such crimes can the provisions of international law be enforced.") (citing Ex parte Quirin, 317 U.S. 1 (1942)). *Compare* § 10.3.5 (State Responsibility for Its Agents' Treatment of Protected Persons).

318 U.N. International Law Commission, *Principles of International Law Recognized in the Charter of the Nürnberg Tribunal and in the Judgment of the Tribunal*, in *Report of the International Law Commission on its Second Session, 5 June to 29 July 1950*, (Document A/1316), *reprinted in* II YEARBOOK OF INTERNATIONAL LAW COMMISSION 1950, 374 U.N. Doc. A/CN. 4/SER.A/1950/Add. 1 (Jun. 6, 1957) ("PRINCIPLE II The fact that internal law does not impose a penalty for an act which constitutes a crime under international law does not relieve the person who committed the act from responsibility under international law.").

319 *Refer to* § 1.10.1.4 (Force of International Law Notwithstanding a State's Domestic Law).

320 U.N. International Law Commission, *Principles of International Law Recognized in the Charter of the Nürnberg Tribunal and in the Judgment of the Tribunal*, in *Report of the International Law Commission on its Second Session, 5 June to 29 July 1950*, (Document A/1316), *reprinted in* II YEARBOOK OF INTERNATIONAL LAW COMMISSION 1950, 374, 375 U.N. Doc. A/CN. 4/SER.A/1950/Add. 1 (Jun. 6, 1957) ("PRINCIPLE III The fact that a person who committed an act which constitutes a crime under international law acted as Head of State or responsible Government official does not relieve him from responsibility under international law.").

321 *Charter of the International Military Tribunal*, art. 7, annexed to Agreement by the Government of the United Kingdom of Great Britain and Northern Ireland, the Government of the United States of America, the Provisional Government of the French Republic and the Government of the Union of Soviet Socialist Republics for the Prosecution and Punishment of the Major War Criminals of the European Axis, Aug. 8, 1945, 82 UNTS 280, 288 ("The official position of defendants, whether as Heads of State or responsible officials in Government Departments, shall not be considered as freeing them from responsibility or mitigating punishment."); ICTY STATUTE art. 7(2) ("The official position of any accused person, whether as Head of State or Government or as a responsible Government official, shall not relieve such person of criminal responsibility nor mitigate punishment.").

322 *See* U.N. International Law Commission, *Principles of International Law Recognized in the Charter of the Nürnberg Tribunal and in the Judgment of the Tribunal*, in *Report of the International Law Commission on its Second Session, 5 June to 29 July 1950*, (Document A/1316), *reprinted in* II YEARBOOK OF INTERNATIONAL LAW COMMISSION 1950, 374, 375 U.N. Doc. A/CN. 4/SER.A/1950/Add. 1 (Jun. 6, 1957) ("PRINCIPLE IV The fact that a person acted pursuant to order of his Government or of a superior does not relieve him from responsibility under international law, provided a moral choice was in fact possible to him.").

323 *Charter of the International Military Tribunal*, art. 8, annexed to Agreement by the Government of the United Kingdom of Great Britain and Northern Ireland, the Government of the United States of America, the Provisional

military personnel cannot justify committing unlawful acts by producing the order of their superior.[324]

Although it is clear that merely the fact that the act at issue was committed pursuant to superior orders does not constitute a defense to criminal responsibility under international law, the precise extent to which superior orders may constitute a defense or excuse may vary according to the forum in which a violation is tried.[325]

In cases in which the illegality of the order is not apparent, the subordinate might lack the wrongful intent necessary to the commission of the crime.[326] Subordinates, absent specific knowledge to the contrary, may presume orders to be lawful.[327] The acts of a subordinate done in compliance with an unlawful order given by a superior are generally excused unless the superior's order is one that a person of ordinary sense and understanding would, under the circumstances, know to be unlawful (*e.g.*, to torture or murder a detainee), or if the order in question is actually known to the accused to be unlawful.[328]

On the other hand, subordinates must refuse to comply with clearly illegal orders to

---

Government of the French Republic and the Government of the Union of Soviet Socialist Republics for the Prosecution and Punishment of the Major War Criminals of the European Axis, Aug. 8, 1945, 82 UNTS 280, 288 ("The fact that the Defendant acted pursuant to order of his Government or of a superior shall not free him from responsibility, but may be considered in mitigation of punishment if the Tribunal determines that justice so requires."); ICTY STATUTE art. 7(4) ("The fact that an accused person acted pursuant to an order of a Government or of a superior shall not relieve him of criminal responsibility, … ."); ICTR STATUTE art. 6(4) ("The fact that an accused person acted pursuant to an order of a Government or of a superior shall not relieve him [or her] of criminal responsibility … .").

[324] *See* Mitchell v. Harmony, 54 U.S. 115, 137 (1851) ("Consequently the order given was an order to do an illegal act; to commit a trespass upon the property of another; and can afford no justification to the person by whom it was executed. . . . And upon principle, independent of the weight of judicial decision, it can never be maintained that a military officer can justify himself for doing an unlawful act, by producing the order of his superior. The order may palliate, but it cannot justify.").

[325] LEVIE, POWS 389 ("The Commission of Experts convened by the ICRC in December 1948 in connection with the grave-breaches provisions which had been approved and the Resolution which had been adopted by the 1948 Stockholm Conference, drafted a proposed article relating solely to the defense of superior orders. The 1949 Diplomatic Conference did not include such a provision in the Convention as finally approved. Accordingly, this problem will once again have to be resolved on a national basis. Efforts to solve it on an international basis in related areas have been undertaken by various organs of the United Nations, but those efforts have complicated, rather than clarified, the problem. It is obvious that there is no clear and well-defined rule which will be applied to the defense of superior orders when it is advanced, as it undoubtedly will be, in future trials for violations of the grave breaches and other provisions of the 1949 Convention. However, it is believed that it may be safely stated that, as after World War II, the mere fact that the act complained of was committed pursuant to superior orders will not suffice as a defense.").

[326] United States v. List, *et al.* (The Hostage Case), XI TRIALS OF WAR CRIMINALS BEFORE THE NMT 1236 ("We are of the view, however, that if the illegality of the order was not known to the inferior, and he could not reasonably have been expected to know of its illegality, no wrongful intent necessary to the commission of a crime exists and the interior [sic] will be protected. But the general rule is that members of the armed forces are bound to obey only the lawful orders of their commanding officers and they cannot escape criminal liability by obeying a command which violates international law and outrages fundamental concepts of justice.").

[327] *Refer to* § 18.3.2.1 (Clearly Illegal Orders to Commit Law of War Violations).

[328] United States v. Calley, 22 U.S.C.M.A. 534, 542 (C.M.A. 1973) ("The acts of a subordinate done in compliance with an unlawful order given him by his superior are excused and impose no criminal liability upon him unless the superior's order is one which a man of ordinary sense and understanding would, under the circumstances, know to be unlawful, or if the order in question is actually know to the accused to be unlawful.").

commit violations of the law of war.[329]

That an offense was committed pursuant to superior orders may be considered in mitigation of punishment.[330] The degree to which superior orders should mitigate punishment would depend on the specific circumstances of the case.[331]

18.23 Theories of Individual Criminal Liability

Individuals may be held liable for violations of the law of war whether they have committed them directly or are complicit in the commission of such crimes.[332]

The theories of liability that apply to a law of war violation may vary depending on the particular forum (*e.g.*, U.S. Federal court, U.S. military commission, International Criminal Tribunal for the Former Yugoslavia) in which the violation is being adjudicated. Modes of liability for law of war offenses may include ordering, instigating or directly inciting, command responsibility, aiding and abetting, conspiracy, and joint criminal enterprise.

In some cases, these theories of liability may be viewed as ways of attributing an offense that is committed by one person to another person. In other cases, these theories of liability may be viewed as distinct offenses; for example, a first offense is committed by one person and a second offense is committed by another person that is somehow related to the first offense.

18.23.1 Ordering. A person who orders another person to commit an offense is generally punishable as though that person had committed the offense directly

---

[329] *Refer to* § 18.3.2 (Refuse to Comply With Clearly Illegal Orders to Commit Law of War Violations).

[330] *See, e.g.*, 1956 FM 27-10 (Change No. 1 1976) ¶509a ("In all cases where the order is held not to constitute a defense to an allegation of war crime, the fact that the individual was acting pursuant to orders may be considered in mitigation of punishment."); ICTY STATUTE art. 7(4) ("The fact that an accused person acted pursuant to an order of a Government or of a superior shall not relieve him of criminal responsibility, but may be considered in mitigation of punishment if the International Tribunal determines that justice so requires."); ICTR STATUTE art. 6(4).

[331] *For example*, Trial of Lieutenant-General Shigeru Sawada and Three Others, V U.N. LAW REPORTS 1, 7 (U.S. Military Commission, Shanghai, Feb. 27-Apr. 15, 1946) ("The offences of each of the accused resulted largely from obedience to the laws and instructions of their Government and their Military Superiors. They exercised no initiative to any marked degree. The preponderance of evidence shows beyond reasonable doubt that other officers, including high governmental and military officials, were responsible for the enactment of the *Ex Post Facto* 'Enemy Airmen's Law' and the issuance of special instructions as to how these American prisoners were to be treated, tried, sentenced and punished. The circumstances set forth above do not entirely absolve the accused from guilt. However, they do compel unusually strong mitigating consideration, applicable to each accused in various degrees.").

[332] U.N. International Law Commission, *Principles of International Law Recognized in the Charter of the Nürnberg Tribunal and in the Judgment of the Tribunal*, in *Report of the International Law Commission on its Second Session, 5 June to 29 July 1950*, (Document A/1316), *reprinted in* II YEARBOOK OF INTERNATIONAL LAW COMMISSION 1950, 374, 377 U.N. Doc. A/CN. 4/SER.A/1950/Add. 1 (Jun. 6, 1957) ("PRINCIPLE VII Complicity in the commission of a crime against peace, a war crime, or a crime against humanity as set forth in Principle VI is a crime under international law.").

This principle is reflected in the Uniform Code of Military Justice.[333] Statutes of international criminal tribunals have also reflected this mode of liability.[334]

18.23.2 Instigating or Directly Inciting. Instigating or direct incitement of an offense is punishable.[335] Statutes of international criminal tribunals have also reflected this mode of liability.[336]

18.23.3 Command Responsibility. Commanders have duties to take necessary and reasonable measures to ensure that their subordinates do not commit violations of the law of war.[337] Failures by commanders of their duties to take necessary and reasonable measures to ensure that their subordinates do not commit violations of the law of war can result in criminal responsibility.[338]

18.23.3.1 *Command Responsibility as a Distinct Offense*. Commanders may be punished directly for their failure to take necessary and reasonable measures to ensure that their subordinates do not commit violations of the law of war. For example, such failures may be punished under the Uniform Code of Military Justice as dereliction of duty or violation of orders to take such measures.[339]

---

[333] 10 U.S.C. § 877 ("Any person punishable under this chapter who— (1) commits an offense punishable by this chapter, or aids, abets, counsels, commands, or procures its commission; or (2) causes an act to be done which if directly performed by him would be punishable by this chapter; is a principal.").

[334] *See* ICTY STATUTE art. 7(1) ("A person who planned, instigated, ordered, committed or otherwise aided and abetted in the planning, preparation or execution of a crime referred to in articles 2 to 5 of the present Statute, shall be individually responsible for the crime."); ICTR STATUTE art. 6(1) ("A person who planned, instigated, ordered, committed or otherwise aided and abetted in the planning, preparation or execution of a crime referred to in Articles 2 to 4 of the present Statute, shall be individually responsible for the crime.").

[335] 1956 FM 27-10 (Change No. 1 1976) ¶500 ("Conspiracy, direct incitement, and attempts to commit, as well as complicity in the commission of, crimes against peace, crimes against humanity, and war crimes are punishable.").

[336] *See* ICTY STATUTE art. 7(1) ("A person who planned, instigated, ordered, committed or otherwise aided and abetted in the planning, preparation or execution of a crime referred to in articles 2 to 5 of the present Statute, shall be individually responsible for the crime."); ICTR STATUTE art. 6(1) ("A person who planned, instigated, ordered, committed or otherwise aided and abetted in the planning, preparation or execution of a crime referred to in Articles 2 to 4 of the present Statute, shall be individually responsible for the crime.").

[337] *Refer to* § 18.4 (Commanders' Duty to Implement and Enforce the Law of War).

[338] *See also* 1956 FM 27-10 (Change No. 1 1976) ¶501 ("In some cases, military commanders may be responsible for war crimes committed by subordinate members of the armed forces, or other persons subject to their control. Thus, for instance, when troops commit massacres and atrocities against the civilian population of occupied territory or against prisoners of war, the responsibility may rest not only with the actual perpetrators but also with the commander. Such a responsibility arises directly when the acts in question have been committed in pursuance of an order of the commander concerned. The commander is also responsible if he has actual knowledge, or should have knowledge, through reports received by him or through other means, that troops or other persons subject to his control are about to commit or have committed a war crime and he fails to take the necessary and reasonable steps to insure compliance with the law of war or to punish violators thereof."). *Consider* AP I art. 86(2) ("The fact that a breach of the Conventions or of this Protocol was committed by a subordinate does not absolve his superiors from penal or disciplinary responsibility, as the case may be, if they knew, or had information which should have enabled them to conclude in the circumstances at the time, that he was committing or was going to commit such a breach and if they did not take all feasible measures within their power to prevent or repress the breach.").

18.23.3.2 Command Responsibility as a Mode of Liability for an Offense. In some cases, the failure by commanders to fulfill their duties to take necessary and reasonable measures to ensure that their subordinates do not commit violations of the law of war are not punished directly as breaches of those duties, but instead by imputing responsibility for the offense committed by the subordinates to the commander.

Command responsibility as a mode of liability for an offense is reflected in U.S. statutes governing military commissions.[340] The statutes of international tribunals have also reflected command responsibility as a mode of liability.[341] In some cases, this theory of superior responsibility has been applied to civilian superiors.[342]

Command responsibility, as a mode of liability, is not a form of strict liability.[343] The commander's personal dereliction must have contributed to or failed to prevent the offense; there must be a personal neglect amounting to a wanton, immoral disregard of the action of his or her subordinates amounting to acquiescence in the crimes.[344]

---

339 *Refer to* § 18.19.3.1 (Uniform Code of Military Justice Offenses).

340 10 U.S.C. § 950q ("Any person is punishable under this chapter who— … (3) is a superior commander who, with regard to acts punishable under this chapter, knew, had reason to know, or should have known, that a subordinate was about to commit such acts or had done so and who failed to take the necessary and reasonable measures to prevent such acts or to punish the perpetrators thereof, is a principal.").

341 *See* ICTY STATUTE art. 7(3) ("The fact that any of the acts referred to in articles 2 to 5 of the present Statute was committed by a subordinate does not relieve his superior of criminal responsibility if he knew or had reason to know that the subordinate was about to commit such acts or had done so and the superior failed to take the necessary and reasonable measures to prevent such acts or to punish the perpetrators thereof."); ICTR STATUTE art. 6(3) (same); ROME STATUTE art. 28.

342 *See* Prosecutor v. Musema, ICTR Trial Chamber I, ICTR-96-13-A, *Judgment and Sentence*, ¶132 (Jan. 27, 2000) ("As to whether the form of individual criminal responsibility referred to under Article 6(3) of the Statute also applies to persons in both military and civilian authority, it is important to note that during the Tokyo Trials, civilian authorities were convicted of war crimes under this principle.").

343 *See also* Prosecutor v. Kordic and Cerkez, ICTY Trial Chamber, IT-95-14/2-T, *Judgment*, ¶369 (Feb. 26, 2001) ("It should be emphasised that the doctrine of command responsibility does not hold a superior responsible merely because he is in a position of authority as, for a superior to be held liable, it is necessary to prove that he 'knew or had reason to know' of the offences and failed to act to prevent or punish their occurrence. Superior responsibility, which is a type of imputed responsibility, is therefore not a form of strict liability.").

344 United States v. von Leeb, *et al.* (High Command Case), XI TRIALS OF WAR CRIMINALS BEFORE THE NMT 543 ("A high commander cannot keep completely informed of the details of military operations of subordinates and most assuredly not of every administrative measure. He has the right to assume that details entrusted to responsible subordinates will be legally executed. The President of the United States is Commander in Chief of its military forces. Criminal acts committed by those forces cannot in themselves be charged to him on the theory of subordination. The same is true of other high commanders in the chain of command. Criminality does not attach to every individual in this chain of command from that fact alone. There must be a personal dereliction. That can occur only where the act is directly traceable to him or where his failure to properly supervise his subordinates constitutes criminal negligence on his part. In the latter case it must be a personal neglect amounting to a wanton, immoral disregard of the action of his subordinates amounting to acquiescence. Any other interpretation of international law would go far beyond the basic principles of criminal law as known to civilized nations.").

345 Walter Dellinger, Assistant Attorney General, *United States Assistance to Countries that Shoot Down Civil Aircraft Involved in Drug Trafficking*, Jul. 14, 1994, 18 OPINIONS OF THE OFFICE OF LEGAL COUNSEL 148, 156 ("Aiding and abetting liability for a crime can be usefully analyzed as consisting of three elements: '[1] *knowledge* of the illegal activity that is being aided and abetted, [2] a *desire* to help the activity succeed, and [3] some *act* of helping.' All three elements must be present for aiding and abetting liability to attach.") (changes in original) (citation omitted).

18.23.4 Aiding and Abetting. The theory of aiding and abetting holds an individual liable for an offense committed by another based on certain assistance that the individual gave in relation to the crime. Aiding and abetting liability for a crime can be usefully analyzed as consisting of three elements: (1) knowledge of the illegal activity that is being aided and abetted; (2) a desire to help the activity succeed; and (3) some act of helping.[345]

This theory of liability is applicable in prosecutions in Federal court under title 18,[346] prosecutions under the Uniform Code of Military Justice,[347] and prosecutions by U.S. military commission.[348] This theory of liability has also been reflected in the statutes of international criminal tribunals.[349]

18.23.4.1 *Aiding and Abetting as a Principle of State Responsibility*. The principle of aiding and abetting is also reflected in principles of State responsibility.[350] As with the principle of aiding and abetting when applied to individuals, the aid or assistance must be given with a view to facilitating the commission of the wrongful act, and must actually do so, in order for the State giving the aid to incur liability.[351]

---

[346] 18 U.S.C. § 2 ("(a) Whoever commits an offense against the United States or aids, abets, counsels, commands, induces or procures its commission, is punishable as a principal. (b) Whoever willfully causes an act to be done which if directly performed by him or another would be an offense against the United States, is punishable as a principal.").

[347] 10 U.S.C. § 877 ("Principals. Any person punishable under this chapter who- (1) commits an offense punishable by this chapter, or aids, abets, counsels, commands, or procures its commission; or (2) causes an act to be done which if directly performed by him would be punishable by this chapter; is a principal.").

[348] 10 U.S.C § 950q ("Any person punishable under this chapter who—(1) commits an offense punishable by this chapter, or aids, abets, counsels, commands, or procures its commission; (2) causes an act to be done which if directly performed by him would be punishable by this chapter;").

[349] ICTY STATUTE art. 7(1) ("A person who planned, instigated, ordered, committed or otherwise aided and abetted in the planning, preparation or execution of a crime referred to in articles 2 to 5 of the present Statute, shall be individually responsible for the crime."); ICTR STATUTE art. 6(1) ("A person who planned, instigated, ordered, committed or otherwise aided and abetted in the planning, preparation or execution of a crime referred to in articles 2 to 4 of the present Statute, shall be individually responsible for the crime."); ROME STATUTE art. 25 ("In accordance with this Statute, a person shall be criminally responsible and liable for punishment for a crime within the jurisdiction of the Court if that person: … [¶3(c)] For the purpose of facilitating the commission of such a crime, aids, abets or otherwise assists in its commission or its attempted commission, including providing the means for its commission;").

[350] U.N. International Law Commission, *Draft articles on Responsibility of States for Internationally Wrongful Acts, with commentaries*, art. 16 (2001) ("A State which aids or assists another State in the commission of an internationally wrongful act by the latter is internationally responsible for doing so if: (a) that State does so with knowledge of the circumstances of the internationally wrongful act; and (b) the act would be internationally wrongful if committed by that State.").

[351] U.N. International Law Commission, *Draft articles on Responsibility of States for Internationally Wrongful Acts, with commentaries*, 66 (2001) ("The second requirement is that the aid or assistance must be given with a view to facilitating the commission of the wrongful act, and must actually do so. This limits the application of article 16 to those cases where the aid or assistance given is clearly linked to the subsequent wrongful conduct. A State is not responsible for aid or assistance under article 16 unless the relevant State organ intended, by the aid or assistance given, to facilitate the occurrence of the wrongful conduct and the internationally wrongful conduct is actually committed by the aided or assisted State. There is no requirement that the aid or assistance should have been essential to the performance of the internationally wrongful act; it is sufficient if it contributed significantly to that act.")

18.23.4.2 *Aiding and Abetting Certain Conduct as a Distinct Offense Instead of a Mode of Liability for an Offense*. In some cases, aiding certain conduct is a distinct offense as opposed to a mode of liability for an offense. These cases reflect circumstances in which (or a judgment that) there is a duty to refrain from aiding that conduct.[352]

18.23.5 Conspiracy. The essence of conspiracy is the combination of minds in an unlawful purpose.[353]

The United States has taken the position that conspiracy to violate the law of war is punishable.[354] The United States has used military tribunals to punish unprivileged belligerents for the offense of conspiracy to violate the law of war.[355]

---

[352] *See, e.g.*,10 U.S.C. § 904 (making punishable "aiding the enemy"); 10 U.S.C. § 950t(25) (making punishable by military commission "providing material support to terrorism"); 10 U.S.C. § 950t(26) (making punishable by military commission "wrongfully aiding the enemy"); 18 U.S.C. § 2339A (making punishable "[p]roviding material support to terrorists"); 18 U.S.C. § 2339B (making punishable "[p]roviding material support or resources to designated foreign terrorist organizations").

[353] Smith v. United States, 133 S. Ct. 714, 719 (2013) ("The essence of conspiracy is 'the combination of minds in an unlawful purpose.'") (quoting United States v. Hirsch, 100 U.S. 33, 34 (1879)).

[354] *See, e.g.*, 1956 FM 27-10 (Change No. 1 1976) ¶500 ("Conspiracy, direct incitement, and attempts to commit, as well as complicity in the commission of, crimes against peace, crimes against humanity, and war crimes are punishable."); Memorandum of Law from Tom C. Clark, Assistant Attorney General, to Major General Myron C. Kramer, Judge Advocate General, 6 (Mar. 12, 1945) ("In view of the statements of the authorities on military law set forth above, and the precedents established in the proceedings referred to above, it may be said to be well established that a conspiracy to commit an offense against the laws of war is itself an offense cognizable by a commission administering military judgment.").

[355] *See, e.g.*, Hamdan v. Rumsfeld, 548 U.S. 1, 23 (2006) (Thomas, J., dissenting) ("The Civil War experience provides further support for the President's conclusion that conspiracy to violate the laws of war is an offense cognizable before law-of-war military commissions. Indeed, in the highest profile case to be tried before a military commission relating to that war, namely, the trial of the men involved in the assassination of President Lincoln, the charge provided that those men had 'combin[ed], confederat[ed], and conspir[ed]...to kill and murder' President Lincoln."); Colepaugh v. Looney, 235 F.2d 429, 431 (10th Cir. 1956) ("January 11, 1945, by executive order, the President charged the petitioner with violation of the law of war and...to convene a military commission for trial of such offenses. The first charge specified: (1) ... the petitioner and one Gimpel, acting for the German Reich, secretly passed through, in civilian dress, contrary to the law of war, the military and naval lines of the United States for the purpose of committing espionage, sabotage and other hostile acts; and (2) that the accused ... appeared and remained in civil dress, contrary to the law of war behind the military lines of the United States for the purpose of committing espionage, sabotage and other hostile acts. The second charge alleged ... the petitioner and one Gimpel, acting for the German Reich, were, in time of war, found lurking and acting as spies in and about the fortifications, posts and encampments ... of the United States ..., for the purpose of obtaining intelligence and communicating it to the German Reich. The third charge alleged a conspiracy to commit the above substantive offenses."); Ex Parte Quirin, 317 U.S. 1, 23 (1942) ("On July 3, 1942, the Judge Advocate General's Department of the Army prepared and lodged with the Commission the following charges against petitioners, supported by specifications: 1. Violation of the law of war. 2. Violation of Article 81 of the Articles of War, defining the offense of relieving or attempting to relieve, or corresponding with or giving intelligence to, the enemy. 3. Violation of Article 82, defining the offense of spying. 4. Conspiracy to commit the offenses alleged in charges 1, 2 and 3."); *but see* Hamdan v. Rumsfeld, 548 U.S., 40-41 (2006) (Stevens, J., plurality) ("The crime of 'conspiracy' has rarely if ever been tried as such in this country by any law-of-war military commission not exercising some other form of jurisdiction, and does not appear in either the Geneva Conventions or the Hague Conventions—the major treaties on the law of war.").

[356] *See* 10 U.S.C. § 881 ("(a) Any person subject to this chapter who conspires with any other person to commit an offense under this chapter shall, if one or more of the conspirators does an act to effect the object of the conspiracy, be punished as a court-martial may direct. (b) Any person subject to this chapter who conspires with any other person to commit an offense under the law of war, and who knowingly does an overt act to effect the object of the conspiracy shall be punished, if death results to one or more of the victims, by death or such other punishment as a court martial or

Conspiracy is an offense under the Uniform Code of Military Justice.[356] Conspiracy is an offense under the Military Commissions Act of 2009.[357] Conspiracy to commit an offense is an offense under Title 18.[358]

The use of conspiracy may vary according the forum in which charges are brought. However, as a general matter, charges of conspiracy for violations of the law of war by persons belonging to the enemy should be restricted to cases of offenses in which an overt act has been committed because non-punitive measures, such as security detention, may be available to address threats.[359]

18.23.5.1 Conspiracy to Commit Genocide. The Genocide Convention provides that conspiracy to commit genocide shall be punishable.[360] Thus, mere agreement by perpetrators to commit genocide may be punishable even if no preparatory act has taken place.[361]

---

military commission may direct, and, if death does not result to any of the victims, by such punishment, other than death, as a court-martial or military commission may direct.").

[357] 10 U.S.C. § 950t(29) ("Any person subject to this chapter who conspires to commit one or more substantive offenses triable by military commission under this subchapter, and who knowingly does any overt act to effect the object of the conspiracy, shall be punished, if death results to one or more of the victims, by death or such other punishment as a military commission under this chapter may direct, and, if death does not result to any of the victims, by such punishment, other than death, as a military commission under this chapter may direct.").

[358] *See, e.g.*, 18 U.S.C. § 371 ("If two or more persons conspire either to commit any offense against the United States, or to defraud the United States, or any agency thereof in any manner or for any purpose, and one or more of such persons do any act to effect the object of the conspiracy, each shall be fined under this title or imprisoned not more than five years, or both. If, however, the offense, the commission of which is the object of the conspiracy, is a misdemeanor only, the punishment for such conspiracy shall not exceed the maximum punishment provided for such misdemeanor."); 18 U.S.C. § 2441 (including the act of conspiring to commit certain acts as punishable); 18 U.S.C. § 2442 (b) ("Whoever violates, or attempts or conspires to violate, subsection (a) shall be fined under this title or imprisoned not more than 20 years, or both and, if death of any person results, shall be fined under this title and imprisoned for any term of years or for life.").

[359] WINTHROP, MILITARY LAW & PRECEDENTS 841 ("It may be added that the jurisdiction of the military commission should be restricted to cases of offence consisting in *overt* acts, *i.e.* in unlawful commissions or actual attempts to commit, and not in intentions merely. Thus what would justify in war a precautionary arrest might not always justify a trial as for a specific offence.").

[360] Convention on the Prevention and Punishment of the Crime of Genocide, art. 3, Dec. 9, 1948, 78 UNTS 277, 280 ("The following acts shall be punishable: … (b) Conspiracy to commit genocide;…").

[361] *See* Prosecutor v. Musema, ICTR Trial Chamber I, ICTR-96-13-A, *Judgment and Sentence*, ¶185 (Jan. 27, 2000) ("The Chamber notes that the crime of conspiracy to commit genocide covered in the Statute is taken from the Genocide Convention. The 'Travaux Préparatoires' of the Genocide Convention suggest that the rationale for including such an offence was to ensure, in view of the serious nature of the crime of genocide, that the mere agreement to commit genocide should be punishable even if no preparatory act has taken place."); Ferdinand Nahimana, Jean-Bosco Barayagwiza, Hassan Ngeze v. The Prosecutor, ICTR Appeals Chamber, ICTR-99-52-A, *Judgment*, ¶894 (Nov. 28, 2007) ("Conspiracy to commit genocide under Article 2(3)(b) of the Statute has been defined as 'an agreement between two or more persons to commit the crime of genocide'. The existence of such an agreement between individuals to commit genocide (or 'concerted agreement to act') is its material element (actus reus); furthermore, the individuals involved in the agreement must have the intent to destroy in whole or in part a national, ethnical, racial or religious group as such (mens rea).").

[362] *Charter of the International Military Tribunal*, art. 6, annexed to Agreement by the Government of the United Kingdom of Great Britain and Northern Ireland, the Government of the United States of America, the Provisional Government of the French Republic and the Government of the Union of Soviet Socialist Republics for the Prosecution and Punishment of the Major War Criminals of the European Axis, Aug. 8, 1945, 82 UNTS 280, 288 ("The following acts, or any of them, are crimes coming within the jurisdiction of the Tribunal for which there shall be individual responsibility:– (a) *Crimes against peace:* namely, planning, preparation, initiation or waging of a war

18.23.5.2 Conspiracy to Commit Aggressive War. The International Military Tribunal at Nuremberg tried defendants for participation in a common plan or conspiracy to wage a war of aggression.[362] However, the International Military Tribunal declined to interpret its Charter to authorize prosecutions for conspiracy to commit war crimes and crimes against humanity.[363]

18.23.6 Other Group Criminality Theories – Joint Criminal Enterprise. In addition to conspiracy, analogous theories of group criminality have been applied to violations of the law of war and other violations of international law.[364] Under recognized principles common to the major legal systems of the world, persons who are connected with plans or enterprises involved in the commission of a crime, or who belong to an organization or group engaged in the commission of crime, may also be guilty of that crime.[365] Joining a criminal group may be punishable as a distinct offense separate from the atrocities committed by that criminal group.[366]

Three categories of group criminality or "joint criminal enterprise" may be identified, which vary according to the mental element (*mens rea*) of the defendant with respect to the crime that is committed:[367]

---

of aggression, or a war in violation of international treaties, agreements or assurances, or participation in a common plan or conspiracy for the accomplishment of any of the foregoing;").

[363] United States, *et al.* v. Göring, *et al.*, *Judgment*, I TRIAL OF THE MAJOR WAR CRIMINALS BEFORE THE IMT 226 ("Count One, however, charges not only the conspiracy to commit aggressive war, but also to commit War Crimes and Crimes against Humanity. But the Charter does not define as a separate crime any conspiracy except the one to commit acts of aggressive war.").

[364] *See, e.g.*, United States, *et al.* v. Göring, *et al.*, *Judgment*, I TRIAL OF THE MAJOR WAR CRIMINALS BEFORE THE IMT 256 ("If satisfied of the criminal guilt of any organisation or group, this Tribunal should not hesitate to declare it to be criminal because the theory of 'group criminality' is new, or because it might be unjustly applied by some subsequent tribunals. On the other hand, the Tribunal should make such declaration of criminality so far as possible in a manner to insure that innocent persons will not be punished. A criminal organisation is analogous to a criminal conspiracy in that the essence of both is cooperation for criminal purposes. There must be a group bound together and organized for a common purpose. The group must be formed or used in connection with the commission of crimes denounced by the Charter. Since the declaration with respect to the organisations and groups will, as has been pointed out, fix the criminality of its members, that definition should exclude persons who had no knowledge of the criminal purposes or acts of the organisation and those who were drafted by the State for membership, unless they were personally implicated in the commission of acts declared criminal by Article 6 of the Charter as members of the organisation. Membership alone is not enough to come within the scope of these declarations.").

[365] *See, e.g.*, United States v. Ohlendorf, *et al.* (Einsatzgruppen Case), IV TRIALS OF WAR CRIMINALS BEFORE THE NMT 372 ("In line with recognized principles common to all civilized legal systems, ¶ 2 of Article II of Control Council Law No. 10 specifies a number of types of connection with crime which are sufficient to establish guilt. Thus, not only are principals guilty but also accessories, those who take a consenting part in the commission of crime or are connected with plans or enterprises involved in its commission, those who order or abet crime, and those who belong to an organization or group engaged in the commission of crime.").

[366] James Speed, Attorney General, *Military Commissions*, July 1865, 11 OPINIONS OF THE ATTORNEY GENERAL 297, 312, 314 (1869) (noting that "to unite with banditti, jayhawkers, guerillas, or any other unauthorized marauders is a high offence against the laws of war; the offence is complete when the band is organized or joined. The atrocities committed by such a band do not constitute the offence, but make the reasons, and sufficient reasons they are, why such banditti are denounced by the laws of war.").

[367] Prosecutor v. Tadić, ICTY Appeals Chamber, IT-94-1-A, *Judgment*, ¶195 (Jul. 15, 1999) ("Many post-World War II cases concerning war crimes proceed upon the principle that when two or more persons act together to further a common criminal purpose, offences perpetrated by any of them may entail the criminal liability of all the members of the group. Close scrutiny of the relevant case law shows that broadly speaking, the notion of common purpose encompasses three distinct categories of collective criminality.").

- cases of co-perpetration where all participants in the common design possess the same criminal intent to commit a crime (and one or more of them actually perpetrate the crime, with intent);[368]
- cases where the requisite *mens rea* comprises knowledge of the nature of the system of ill-treatment (*e.g.*, a German concentration camp) and intent to further the common design of ill-treatment (such intent may be proved either directly or as a matter of inference from the nature of the accused's authority within the camp or organizational hierarchy);[369] and
- cases in which a "common purpose" exists because the following requirements concerning *mens rea* are fulfilled: (i) the intention to take part in a joint criminal enterprise and to further – individually and jointly – the criminal purposes of that enterprise; and (ii) the foreseeability of the possible commission by other members of the group of offenses that do not constitute the object of the common criminal purpose.[370]

---

[368] Prosecutor v. Tadić, ICTY Appeals Chamber, IT-94-1-A, *Judgment*, ¶220 (Jul. 15, 1999) ("In sum, the Appeals Chamber holds … that the notion of common design as a form of accomplice liability is firmly established in customary international law and in addition is upheld, albeit implicitly, in the Statute of the International Tribunal. As for the objective and subjective elements of the crime, the case law shows that the notion has been applied to three distinct categories of cases. First, in cases of co-perpetration, where all participants in the common design possess the same criminal intent to commit a crime (and one or more of them actually perpetrate the crime, with intent).").

[369] Prosecutor v. Tadić, ICTY Appeals Chamber, IT-94-1-A, *Judgment*, ¶220 (Jul. 15, 1999) ("Secondly, in the so-called 'concentration camp' cases, where the requisite *mens rea* comprises knowledge of the nature of the system of ill-treatment and intent to further the common design of ill-treatment. Such intent may be proved either directly or as a matter of inference from the nature of the accused's authority within the camp or organisational hierarchy."). *See also* Prosecutor v. Krnojelac, ICTY Appeals Chamber, IT-97-25-A, *Judgment*, ¶96 (Sept. 17, 2003) ("The Appeals Chamber notes that, with regard to the crimes considered within a systemic form of joint criminal enterprise, the intent of the participants other than the principal offenders presupposes personal knowledge of the system of ill-treatment (whether proven by express testimony or a matter of reasonable inference from the accused's position of authority) and the intent to further the concerted system of ill-treatment. Using these criteria, it is less important to prove that there was a more or less formal agreement between all the participants than to prove their involvement in the system. As the Appeals Chamber recalled in the *Tadic* Appeals Judgement, in his summary of the *Belsen* case the Judge Advocate summed up and approved the Prosecution's legal submissions in the following terms: 'The case for the Prosecution is that all the accused employed on the staff at Auschwitz knew that a system and a course of conduct was in force, and that, in one way or another, in furtherance of a common agreement to run the camp in a brutal way, all those people were taking part in that course of conduct.'").

[370] Prosecutor v. Tadić, ICTY Appeals Chamber, IT-94-1-A, *Judgment*, ¶220 (Jul. 15, 1999) ("With regard to the third category of cases, it is appropriate to apply the notion of 'common purpose' only where the following requirements concerning *mens rea* are fulfilled: (i) the intention to take part in a joint criminal enterprise and to further – individually and jointly – the criminal purposes of that enterprise; and (ii) the foreseeability of the possible commission by other members of the group of offences that do not constitute the object of the common criminal purpose. Hence, the participants must have had in mind the intent, for instance, to ill-treat prisoners of war (even if such a plan arose extemporaneously) and one or some members of the group must have actually killed them. In order for responsibility for the deaths to be imputable to the others, however, everyone in the group must have been able to *predict* this result. It should be noted that more than negligence is required. What is required is a state of mind in which a person, although he did not intend to bring about a certain result, was aware that the actions of the group were most likely to lead to that result but nevertheless willingly took that risk. In other words, the so-called *dolus eventualis* is required (also called 'advertent recklessness' in some national legal systems)."). *Cf.* Pinkerton v. United States, 328 U.S. 640, 647 (1946) ("A scheme to use the mails to defraud, which is joined in by more than one person, is a conspiracy. Yet all members are responsible, though only one did the mailing. The governing principle is the same when the substantive offense is committed by one of the conspirators in furtherance of the unlawful project. The criminal intent to do the act is established by the formation of the conspiracy. Each conspirator instigated the commission of the crime. The unlawful agreement contemplated precisely what was done. It was formed for the purpose. The act done was in execution of the enterprise. The rule which holds responsible one who counsels, procures, or commands another to commit a crime is founded on the same principle. That principle is recognized in the law of conspiracy when the overt act of one partner in crime is attributable to all.").

XIX Documentary Appendix – Notes on Treaties and Other Relevant Documents

Chapter Contents

19.1 Introduction

This appendix provides background information about certain treaties and other documents.

This appendix is intended to describe DoD views and practice relating to those documents as of the date of publication of this manual.

19.2 Lists of Treaties and Other Documents

This section lists: (1) law of war treaties to which the United States is a Party; (2) arms control agreements to which the United States is a Party that are of direct relevance to the law of war; (3) examples of treaties signed but not ratified by the United States; (4) examples of treaties that the United States has neither signed nor ratified; and (5) examples of treaties or documents of mainly historical value.

The categorization of a treaty as a "law of war" treaty or an "arms control" treaty is intended to help practitioners understand the context in which the treaty was concluded and its purposes. For example, a law of war treaty generally focuses on restrictions on the use of weapons during armed conflict, while an arms control treaty generally focuses on restricting development and acquisition of weapons.[1] Some treaties that are characterized below as law of war treaties have elements of arms control, and some treaties that are characterized below as arms control treaties have elements of the law of war.

Bold type within this section indicates an abbreviation used in this manual; a full list of abbreviations is provided at the beginning of the manual.[2]

19.2.1 Law of War Treaties to Which the United States Is a Party. Law of war treaties to which the United States is a Party include:

- Washington Convention Regarding the Rights of Neutrals at Sea of October 31, 1854.[3]
- Hague Convention for the Exemption of Hospital Ships, in Time of War, from the Payment of all Dues and Taxes Imposed for the Benefit of the State of December 21, 1904.[4]
- Hague Convention III of October 18, 1907, Relative to the Opening of Hostilities.[5]
- Hague Convention IV of October 18, 1907, Respecting the Laws and Customs of War on Land (**Hague IV**), and the Annex thereto, entitled Regulations Respecting the Laws and Customs of War on Land (**Hague IV Regulations**).[6]
- Hague Convention V of October 18, 1907, Respecting the Rights and Duties of Neutral Powers and Persons in Case of War on Land (**Hague V**).[7]
- Hague Convention VIII of October 18, 1907, Relative to the Laying of Automatic Submarine Contact Mines (**Hague VIII**).[8]
- Hague Convention IX of October 18, 1907, Concerning Bombardment by Naval Forces in Time of War (**Hague IX**).[9]
- Hague Convention XI of October 18, 1907, Relative to Certain Restrictions with Regard to the Exercise of the Right of Capture in Naval War (**Hague XI**).[10]
- Hague Convention XIII of October 18, 1907, Concerning the Rights and Duties of Neutral Powers in Naval War (**Hague XIII**).[11]
- 1928 Pan American Maritime Neutrality Convention.[12]

---

[1] *Refer to* § 1.6.2 (Arms Control).

[2] *Refer to* List of Abbreviations.

[3] Convention with Russia, Jul. 22, 1854, 10 STAT. 1105.

[4] *Refer to* § 7.12.4.3 (Relief From Taxation in Time of War).

[5] Convention Relative to the Opening of Hostilities, Oct. 18, 1907, 36 STAT. 2259.

[6] *Refer to* § 19.8.2 (Hague IV).

[7] Convention Respecting the Rights and Duties of Neutral Powers and Persons in Case of War on Land, Oct. 18, 1907, 36 STAT. 2310.

[8] *Refer to* § 13.11 (Naval Mines); § 13.12 (Torpedoes).

[9] Convention Concerning Bombardment by Naval Forces in Time of War, Oct. 18, 1907, 36 STAT. 2351.

[10] Convention Relative to Certain Restrictions With Regard to the Exercise of the Right of Capture in Naval War, Oct. 18, 1907, 36 STAT. 2396.

[11] Convention Concerning the Rights and Duties of Neutral Powers in Naval War, Oct. 18, 1907, 36 STAT. 2415.

- 1930 London Treaty for the Limitation and Reduction of Naval Armament.[13]
- Treaty on the Protection of Artistic and Scientific Institutions and Historic Monuments of April 15, 1935 (**Roerich Pact**).[14]
- Charter of the United Nations (**U.N. Charter**).[15]
- 1949 Geneva Conventions,[16] including the
  - Geneva Convention for the Amelioration of the Condition of the Wounded and Sick in Armed Forces in the Field of August 12, 1949 (**GWS**);[17]
  - Geneva Convention for the Amelioration of the Condition of Wounded, Sick and Shipwrecked Members of Armed Forces at Sea of August 12, 1949 (**GWS-Sea**);[18]
  - Geneva Convention Relative to the Treatment of Prisoners of War of August 12, 1949 (**GPW**);[19] and
  - Geneva Convention Relative to the Protection of Civilian Persons in Time of War of August 12, 1949 (**GC**).[20]
- Hague Convention for the Protection of Cultural Property in the Event of Armed Conflict of May 14, 1954 (**1954 Hague Cultural Property Convention**).[21]
- Convention on Prohibitions or Restrictions on the Use of Certain Conventional Weapons Which May Be Deemed to Be Excessively Injurious or to Have Indiscriminate Effects of October 10, 1980, its Protocols I, II, III, IV, and V, its Amended Protocol II, and its Amended Article 1 (**CCW**);[22]
  - CCW Amended Article 1;[23]
  - Protocol on Non-Detectable Fragments (Protocol I). Geneva, October 10, 1980 (**CCW Protocol I**);[24]
  - Protocol on Prohibitions or Restrictions on the Use of Mines, Booby-Traps and Other Devices as amended on May 3, 1996 (Protocol II to the 1980 CCW Convention as amended on May 3, 1996) (**CCW Amended Mines Protocol**);[25]
  - Protocol on Prohibitions or Restrictions on the Use of Incendiary Weapons (Protocol III). Geneva, October 10, 1980 (**CCW Protocol III on Incendiary Weapons**);[26]

---

[12] Pan American Maritime Neutrality Convention, Feb. 20, 1928, 47 STAT. 1989.

[13] *Refer to* § 19.14 (1930 London Treaty for the Limitation and Reduction of Naval Armament and 1936 London Protocol).

[14] *Refer to* § 19.15 (1935 Roerich Pact).

[15] *Refer to* § 1.11.2 (U.N. Charter Framework and the U.N. Security Council).

[16] *Refer to* § 19.16 (1949 Geneva Conventions).

[17] *Refer to* § 19.16.2 (GWS).

[18] *Refer to* § 19.16.3 (GWS-Sea).

[19] *Refer to* § 19.16.4 (GPW).

[20] *Refer to* § 19.16.5 (GC).

[21] *Refer to* § 19.17 (1954 Hague Cultural Property Convention).

[22] *Refer to* § 19.21 (CCW, CCW Amended Article 1, and CCW Protocols).

[23] *Refer to* § 19.21.1.1 (CCW Amended Scope of Application).

[24] *Refer to* § 19.21.2 (CCW Protocol I).

[25] *Refer to* § 19.21.3 (CCW Amended Mines Protocol).

  - Protocol on Blinding Laser Weapons (Protocol IV to the 1980 Convention), October 13, 1995 (**CCW Protocol IV on Blinding Laser Weapons**);[27] and
  - Protocol on Explosives Remnants of War (Protocol V to the 1980 Convention), November 28, 2004 (**CCW Protocol V on Explosive Remnants of War**).[28]
- Optional Protocol to the Convention on the Rights of the Child on the involvement of Children in Armed Conflict, May 25, 2000 (**Child Soldiers Protocol**).[29]
- Protocol Additional to the Geneva Conventions of 12 August 1949, and Relating to the Adoption of an Additional Distinctive Emblem (Protocol III), December 8, 2005 (**AP III**).[30]

19.2.2 Arms Control Agreements to Which the United States Is a Party That Are of Direct Relevance to the Law of War. The United States is a Party to the following treaties that contain restrictions on the use of weapons during armed conflict:

- Geneva Protocol for the Prohibition of the Use in War of Asphyxiating, Poisonous or Other Gases, and of Bacteriological Methods of Warfare of June 17, 1925 (**1925 Geneva Gas and Bacteriological Protocol**).[31]
- Convention on the Prohibition of Development, Production and Stockpiling of Bacteriological (Biological) and Toxin Weapons and on Their Destruction of April 10, 1972 (**Biological Weapons Convention**).[32]
- Convention on the Prohibition of Military or Any Other Hostile Use of Environmental Modification Techniques of May 18, 1977 (**ENMOD Convention**).[33]
- Convention on the Prohibition of the Development, Production, Stockpiling and Use of Chemical Weapons and on Their Destruction of January 13, 1993 (**Chemical Weapons Convention**).[34]

19.2.3 Examples of Treaties Signed but Not Ratified by the United States. This section is not comprehensive. It lists examples of treaties that the United States has signed, but not ratified.

A State that has signed a treaty is obliged to refrain from acts that would defeat the object and purpose of a treaty, until it shall have made its intention clear not to become a Party to the treaty.[35]

---

[26] *Refer to* § 19.21.4 (CCW Protocol III on Incendiary Weapons).

[27] *Refer to* § 19.21.5 (CCW Protocol IV on Blinding Laser Weapons).

[28] *Refer to* § 19.21.6 (CCW Protocol V on Explosive Remnants of War).

[29] *Refer to* § 4.20.5.2 (Child Soldiers Protocol).

[30] *Refer to* § 19.26 (AP III).

[31] *Refer to* § 19.12 (1925 Geneva Gas and Bacteriological Protocol).

[32] *Refer to* § 19.19 (Biological Weapons Convention).

[33] *Refer to* § 6.10 (Certain Environmental Modification Techniques).

[34] *Refer to* § 19.22 (Chemical Weapons Convention).

[35] *Consider* VCLT art. 18 ("A State is obliged to refrain from acts which would defeat the object and purpose of a treaty when: (a) It has signed the treaty or has exchanged instruments constituting the treaty subject to ratification, acceptance or approval, until it shall have made its intention clear not to become a party to the treaty; or (b) It has expressed its consent to be bound by the treaty, pending the entry into force of the treaty and provided that such entry into force is not unduly delayed."). *See also* William P. Rogers, *Letter of Submittal*, Oct. 18, 1971, MESSAGE

- *Procès-Verbal* Relating to the Rules of Submarine Warfare set forth in Part IV of the Treaty of London of April 22, 1930 (**1936 London Protocol**).[36]
- Vienna Convention on the Law of Treaties (**VCLT**).[37]
- Protocol (I) Additional to the Geneva Conventions of August 12, 1949, and Relating to the Protection of Victims of International Armed Conflicts of June 8, 1977 (**AP I**).[38]
- Protocol (II) Additional to the Geneva Conventions of August 12, 1949, and Relating to the Protection of Victims of Non-International Armed Conflicts of June 8, 1977 (**AP II**).[39]
- U.N. Convention on the Law of the Sea (**LOS Convention**).[40]
- Rome Statute of the International Criminal Court of July 17, 1998 (**Rome Statute**).[41]

19.2.4 Examples of Treaties That the United States Has Neither Signed Nor Ratified. This section is not comprehensive. It lists examples of law of war and arms control treaties that the United States has neither signed nor ratified:

- Declaration respecting maritime law signed by the Plenipotentiaries of Great Britain, Austria, France, Prussia, Russia, Sardinia, and Turkey, assembled in Congress at Paris, April 16, 1856.[42]
- Hague Declaration on Expanding Bullets of July 29, 1899.[43]
- Hague Convention VI Relating to the Status of Enemy Merchant Ships at the Outbreak of Hostilities of October 18, 1907.
- Hague Convention VII Relating to the Conversion of Merchant Ships into Warships of October 18, 1907.
- First Protocol to the Hague Convention of 1954 for the Protection of Cultural Property in the Event of Armed Conflict of May 14, 1954.
- Ottawa Convention on the Prohibition of the Use, Stockpiling, Production and Transfer of Anti-Personnel Mines and on Their Destruction of September 18, 1997.[44]

FROM THE PRESIDENT TRANSMITTING THE VCLT 2 ("Article 18 sets forth rules governing the obligation of States not to defeat the object and purpose of a treaty prior to its entry into force. That obligation is limited to (a) States that have signed a treaty or exchanged ad referendum instruments constituting a treaty, until such time as they make clear their intention not to become a party, and (b) States that have expressed consent to be bound, pending entry into force and provided such entry into force is not unduly delayed. This rule is widely recognized in customary international law.").

[36] *Refer to* § 19.14 (1930 London Treaty for the Limitation and Reduction of Naval Armament and 1936 London Protocol).

[37] *Refer to* § 19.18 (Vienna Convention on the Law of Treaties).

[38] *Refer to* § 19.20.1 (AP I).

[39] *Refer to* § 19.20.2 (AP II).

[40] *Refer to* § 13.1.2 (The United States and the LOS Convention).

[41] *Refer to* § 19.23 (Rome Statute of the International Criminal Court).

[42] *Refer to* § 19.4 (1856 Paris Declaration Respecting Maritime Law).

[43] *Refer to* § 19.7.1 (1899 Declaration on Expanding Bullets).

[44] *Refer to* § 6.12.14 (Ottawa Convention on Anti-Personnel Landmines).

- Second Protocol to the Hague Convention of 1954 for the Protection of Cultural Property in the Event of Armed Conflict of March 26, 1999.
- Convention on Cluster Munitions of May 30, 2008.[45]

19.2.5 Examples of Treaties or Documents of Mainly Historical Value. This section is not comprehensive. It lists examples of treaties and documents that are regarded as having mainly historical value:

- General Order No. 100, Instructions for the Government of Armies of the United States in the Field, 1863 (**Lieber Code**).[46]
- Geneva Convention for the Amelioration of the Wounded in Armies in the Field of August 22, 1864 (**1864 GWS**).[47]
- St. Petersburg Declaration Renouncing the Use, in Time of War, of Explosive Projectiles under 400 Grams Weight of December 11, 1868 (**1868 St. Petersburg Declaration**).[48]
- Hague Declaration (IV, 1) to Prohibit for the Term of Five Years the Launching of Projectiles and Explosives from Balloons, and Other Methods of a Similar Nature of July 29, 1899.[49]
- Hague Declaration on Asphyxiating Gases of July 29, 1899.[50]
- Hague Convention II with Respect to the Laws and Customs of War on Land, with Annex of Regulations of July 29, 1899 (**1899 Hague II**).[51]
- Hague Convention X for the Adaptation to Maritime Warfare of the Principles of the Geneva Convention of October 18, 1907 (**Hague X**).[52]
- Hague Declaration XIV Prohibiting the Discharge of Projectiles and Explosives from Balloons of October 18, 1907.[53]
- Washington Treaty Relating to the Use of Submarines and Noxious Gases in Warfare of February 6, 1922.[54]
- General Report of the Commission of Jurists to Consider and Report upon the Revision of the Rules of Warfare, Feb. 19, 1923 (**1923 Hague Air and Radio Rules**).[55]
- Geneva Convention Amelioration of the Condition of the Wounded and Sick of Armies in the Field of July 27, 1929 (**1929 GWS**).[56]
- Geneva Convention Relative to the Treatment of Prisoners of War of July 27, 1929 (**1929 GPW**).[57]

---

[45] *Refer to* § 6.13.4 (Convention on Cluster Munitions).

[46] *Refer to* § 19.3 (Lieber Code).

[47] *Refer to* § 19.5 (1864 GWS).

[48] *Refer to* § 19.6 (1868 St. Petersburg Declaration).

[49] *Refer to* § 19.7.3 (1899 and 1907 Declarations on the Discharge of Projectiles and Explosives From Balloons).

[50] *Refer to* § 19.7.2 (1899 Declaration on Asphyxiating Gases).

[51] *Refer to* § 19.8.1 (1899 Hague II).

[52] *Refer to* § 19.9 (1907 Hague X).

[53] *Refer to* § 19.7.3 (1899 and 1907 Declarations on the Discharge of Projectiles and Explosives From Balloons).

[54] *Refer to* § 19.10 (1922 Washington Treaty on Submarines and Noxious Gases).

[55] *Refer to* § 19.11 (1923 Hague Air and Radio Rules).

[56] *Refer to* § 19.13.1 (1929 GWS).

[57] *Refer to* § 19.13.2 (1929 GPW).

19.3 Lieber Code

General Order No. 100, Instructions for the Government of Armies of the United States in the Field, 1863, issued on April 24, 1863, is often called the "Lieber Code" because it was prepared by Francis Lieber.[58] It is an early example of the law of war being implemented through military instructions or regulations.[59]

The Lieber Code was the first comprehensive publication on the law of war for U.S. armed forces and is regarded as an important work of historical significance in the law of war.[60]

The Lieber Code established rules governing martial law, military jurisdiction, the treatment of spies and deserters, and the treatment of POWs. Many key law of war principles, such as the principle of military necessity, were codified in the Lieber Code.[61] However, parts of the Lieber Code reflect 19th century understandings of the law of war that have been modified by treaties that the United States has ratified or by subsequent customary international law. For example, the Lieber Code permitted the denial of quarter in certain circumstances.[62] However, denying quarter in those circumstances is no longer acceptable.[63]

The Lieber Code was prepared during the Civil War. The Confederate forces agreed with some provisions of the Lieber Code, but disagreed with others.[64]

---

[58] E. D. Townsend, Assistant Adjutant General, General Orders No. 100, *Instructions for the Government of Armies of the United States in the Field*, Apr. 24, 1863, *reprinted in* INSTRUCTIONS FOR THE GOVERNMENT OF ARMIES OF THE UNITED STATES IN THE FIELD, 2 (Government Printing Office, 1898) ("The following 'Instructions for the Government of Armies of the United States in the Field,' prepared by Francis Lieber, L.L.D., and revised by a Board of Officers, of which Major General E.A. Hitchcock is president, having been approved by the President of the United States, he commands that they be published for the information of all concerned.").

[59] *Refer to* § 18.7 (Instructions, Regulations, and Procedures to Implement and Enforce the Law of War).

[60] *See, e.g.*, Kononov v. Latvia, European Court of Human Rights, App. No. 36376/04, ¶63 (May 17, 2010) ("The Lieber Code 1863 is regarded as the first attempt to codify the laws and customs of war. Although only applicable to American forces, it represented a summary of the laws and customs of war existing at the time and was influential in later codifications."); Elihu Root, *Francis Lieber*, 7 AJIL 453, 457 (1913) ("In the Brussels Conference of 1874, convened at the instance of the Emperor of Russia for the purpose of codifying the laws and customs of war, the Russian delegate, Baron Jomini, as president of the conference, declared that the project of an international convention then presented had its origin in the rules of President Lincoln. The convention agreed upon at Brussels was not ratified, but in 1880 the Institute of International Law made the work of the Brussels Conference and the work of Lieber, which so far as it was of general application was incorporated in that convention, the basis of a manual of the laws of war upon land; and finally, in The Hague Conferences of 1899 and 1907, the conventions with respect to the laws and customs of war on land gave the adherence of the whole civilized world in substance and effect to those international rules which President Lincoln made binding upon the American armies fifty years ago.").

[61] *Refer to* § 2.2 (Military Necessity).

[62] LIEBER CODE art. 61 ("All troops of the enemy known or discovered to give no quarter in general, or to any portion of the army, receive none.").

[63] *Refer to* § 5.4.7 (Prohibition Against Declaring That No Quarter Be Given).

[64] James A. Seddon, Letter to Robert Ould, Jun. 24, 1863, *reprinted in* FRED C. AINSWORTH & JOSEPH W. KIRKLEY, VI THE WAR OF THE REBELLION: A COMPILATION OF THE OFFICIAL RECORDS OF THE UNION AND CONFEDERATE ARMIES, SERIES II, 41 (1899) ("Order No. 100 is a confused, unassorted, and undiscriminating compilation from the opinion of the publicists of the last two centuries, some of which are obsolete, others repudiated; and a military commander under this code may pursue a line of conduct in accordance with principles of justice, faith, and honor, or he may justify conduct correspondent with the warfare of the barbarous hordes who overran the Roman Empire, or who, in the Middle Ages, devastated the continent of Asia and menaced the civilization of Europe.").

The Lieber Code reflected rules for "regular war" or what today would be classified as international armed conflict. Such rules were applied to the Confederate forces for humanitarian reasons, even though the United States did not recognize the Confederacy as a legitimate government or State.[65] In this way, the Lieber Code is an example of the application of the doctrine of recognition of belligerency.[66]

19.4 1856 Paris Declaration Respecting Maritime Law

The 1856 Paris Declaration respecting Maritime Law is an early multilateral law of war treaty that was intended to be open to accession by all States, including States that did not participate in its negotiation.[67] This treaty illustrates how law of war treaties may be written with a view towards being able to be accepted and applied by all States.

The United States is not a Party to the 1856 Paris Declaration. The 1856 Paris Declaration's provision that blockades must be effective in order to be binding reflects customary international law.[68]

19.5 1864 GWS

The Geneva Convention for the Amelioration of the Wounded in Armies in the Field of August 22, 1864 (1864 GWS) was one of the earliest multilateral law of war treaties.[69]

The 1864 GWS provided for the use of the red cross as a distinctive emblem to help identify medical personnel.[70] It also provided for wounded and sick combatants to be collected and cared for regardless of the nation of their armed forces.[71]

The United States acceded to the 1864 GWS on March 1, 1882.[72] The 1864 GWS was replaced by the GWS in relations between the Parties to the GWS.[73]

---

[65] *Refer to* § 17.2.3 (Application of Humanitarian Rules and the Legal Status of the Parties to the Conflict).

[66] *Refer to* § 3.3.3.2 (Assertion of War Powers by a State Engaged in Hostilities Against a Non-State Armed Group).

[67] Declaration respecting maritime law signed by the Plenipotentiaries of Great Britain, Austria, France, Prussia, Russia, Sardinia, and Turkey, assembled in Congress at Paris, Apr. 16, 1856, *reprinted in* 1 AJIL Supplement: Official Documents 89 (1907) ("The Governments of the undersigned Plenipotentiaries engage to bring the present Declaration to the knowledge of the states which have not taken part in the Congress of Paris, and to invite them to accede to it. Convinced that the maxims which they now proclaim cannot but be received with gratitude by the whole world, the undersigned Plenipotentiaries doubt not that the efforts of their governments to obtain the general adoption thereof will be crowned with full success.").

[68] *Refer to* § 13.10.2.3 (Effectiveness of the Blockade).

[69] Convention for the Amelioration of the Wounded in Armies in the Field, Aug. 22, 1864, 22 Stat. 940.

[70] *Refer to* § 7.15.1.1 (Red Cross).

[71] *Refer to* § 7.5.2.2 (Affirmative Obligation to Provide Adequate Care).

[72] Chester A. Arthur, *Proclamation Regarding the 1864 GWS*, Jul. 26, 1882, 22 Stat. 940, 950-51 ("And whereas the President of the United States of America, by and with the advice and consent of the Senate, did, on the first day of March, one thousand eight hundred and eighty-two, declare that the United States accede to the said Convention of the 22d of August, 1864, and also accede to the said Convention of October 20, 1868; And whereas on the ninth day of June, one thousand eight hundred and eighty-two, the Federal Council of the Swiss Confederation, in virtue of the final provision of a certain minute of the exchange of the ratifications of the said Convention at Berne, December 22, 1864, did, by a formal declaration, accept the said adhesion of the United States of America, as well in the name of the Swiss Confederation as in that of the other contracting States; And whereas, furthermore, the government of the Swiss Confederation has informed the Government of the United States that the exchange of the ratifications of the aforesaid additional articles of 20th October, 1868, to which the United States of America have in like manner adhered as aforesaid, has not yet taken place between the contracting parties, and that these articles cannot be regarded as a treaty in full force and effect:").

[73] *Refer to* § 19.16.2.1 (Relationship Between the GWS and Earlier Conventions).

19.6 1868 ST. PETERSBURG DECLARATION

The Declaration Renouncing the Use, in Time of War, of Explosive Projectiles Weighing Under 400 Grams Weight (1868 St. Petersburg Declaration) was promulgated by an international conference held in St. Petersburg, Russia on December 11, 1868. The 1868 St. Petersburg Declaration prohibits Parties from, "in case of war among themselves, the employment, by their military or naval forces, of any projectile of less weight than four hundred grammes, which is explosive, or is charged with fulminating or inflammable substances."[74]

The United States is not a Party to the 1868 St. Petersburg Declaration.

The language in the Preamble of the 1868 St. Petersburg Declaration that notes that the "employment of arms which uselessly aggravate the sufferings of disabled men" would "be contrary to the laws of humanity" is an early statement of the prohibition against weapons calculated to cause unnecessary suffering, which is a principle that is found in treaties to which the United States is a Party and in customary international law.[75]

The prohibition in the Declaration against "any projectile of less weight than four hundred grammes, which is explosive, or is charged with fulminating or inflammable substances" does not reflect customary international law.[76] For example, for many decades without legal controversy, States have used, and continue to use, tracer ammunition, grenades, explosive bullets, or other projectiles of less weight than four hundred grams with a burning or explosive capability.[77]

19.7 1899 AND 1907 HAGUE DECLARATIONS ON WEAPONS

19.7.1 1899 Declaration on Expanding Bullets. The 1899 Declaration on Expanding Bullets prohibits Parties from using "bullets which expand or flatten easily in the human body, such as bullets with a hard envelope which does not entirely cover the core or is pierced with

---

[74] The Declaration of St. Petersburg, 1868, *reprinted in* 1 AJIL SUPPLEMENT: OFFICIAL DOCUMENTS 95, 96 (1907) ("The contracting parties engage, mutually, to renounce, in case of war among themselves, the employment, by their military or naval forces, of any projectile of less weight than four hundred grammes, which is explosive, or is charged with fulminating or inflammable substances.").

[75] *Refer to* § 6.6 (Weapons Calculated to Cause Superfluous Injury).

[76] U.S. RESPONSE TO ICRC CIHL STUDY 524 ("Since the St. Petersburg Declaration, there has been considerable State practice involving the anti-personnel use of exploding bullets, despite the ICRC's statement that governments have 'adhered' to the Declaration. Two participants in the ICRC-hosted 1974 Lucerne Meeting of Experts on certain weapons conventional weapons concluded: 'At present it is widely held that in view of the development in weapons technology and state practice the St. Petersburg Declaration cannot be interpreted literally, or in any case that it has not as such become declaratory of customary international law.... [T]he prohibition contained in it serves to illustrate the principle prohibiting the causing of unnecessary suffering, at least as it was contemplated in 1868.' U.S. legal reviews have detailed State practice contrary to the ICRC's statement and consistent with the conclusion contained in the above quotation.") (amendments to internal quote shown in U.S. Response to ICRC CIHL Study).

[77] *Consider* Commission of Jurists to Consider and Report Upon the Revision of the Rules of Warfare, *General Report, Part II: Rules of Aërial Warfare*, art. 18, Feb. 19, 1923, *reprinted in* 32 AJIL SUPPLEMENT: OFFICIAL DOCUMENTS 12, 21 (1938) ("The use of tracer, incendiary or explosive projectiles by or against an aircraft is not prohibited. This provision applies equally to states which are parties to the Declaration of St. Petersburg, 1868, and to those which are not."). *Refer to* § 6.5.4.3 (Exploding Bullets).

incisions."[78] The Declaration only creates obligations for Parties to the Declaration in international armed conflicts in which all the parties to the conflict are also Parties to the Declaration.[79]

The United States is not a Party to the 1899 Declaration on Expanding Bullets and does not regard the 1899 Declaration on Expanding Bullets as customary international law applicable in either international or non-international armed conflicts.[80]

19.7.2 1899 Declaration on Asphyxiating Gases. The 1899 Declaration on Asphyxiating Gases was concluded at The Hague on July 29, 1899.[81] This 1899 Declaration prohibits the use of projectiles the object of which is the diffusion of asphyxiating or deleterious gases.[82]

The United States did not ratify this declaration.

This declaration was followed by the 1922 Washington Treaty on Submarines and Noxious Gases, and the 1925 Geneva Gas and Bacteriological Protocol.[83] The United States is a Party to the 1925 Geneva Gas and Bacteriological Protocol and applies the broader prohibition in it on the use of asphyxiating, poisonous, or other gases, and all analogous liquids, materials, or devices.[84]

19.7.3 1899 and 1907 Declarations on the Discharge of Projectiles and Explosives From Balloons. In the 1899 Hague (IV, 1), Parties agreed to prohibit, for a term of five years, the launching of projectiles and explosives from balloons, or by other new methods of similar nature.[85] The United States deposited its instrument of ratification to the 1899 Hague Declaration (IV, 1) on September 4, 1900.[86]

---

[78] Declaration to Abstain From the Use of Bullets Which Expand or Flatten Easily in the Human Body, Jul. 29, 1899, *reprinted in* 1 AJIL SUPPLEMENT: OFFICIAL DOCUMENTS 155, 155-56 (1907) ("The Contracting Parties agree to abstain from the use of bullets which expand or flatten easily in the human body, such as bullets with a hard envelope which does not entirely cover the core, or is pierced with incisions.").

[79] Declaration to Abstain From the Use of Bullets Which Expand or Flatten Easily in the Human Body, Jul. 29, 1899, *reprinted in* 1 AJIL SUPPLEMENT: OFFICIAL DOCUMENTS 155, 156 (1907) ("The present Declaration is only binding for the Contracting Powers in the case of a war between two or more of them. It shall cease to be binding from the time when, in a war between the Contracting Powers, one of the belligerents is joined by a non-Contracting Power.").

[80] *Refer to* § 6.5.4.4 (Expanding Bullets).

[81] Declaration to Abstain From the Use of Projectiles the Object of Which Is the Diffusion of Asphyxiating or Deleterious Gases, Jul. 29, 1899, *reprinted in* 1 AJIL SUPPLEMENT: OFFICIAL DOCUMENTS 157, 158 (1907).

[82] Declaration to Abstain From the Use of Projectiles the Object of Which Is the Diffusion of Asphyxiating or Deleterious Gases, Jul. 29, 1899, *reprinted in* 1 AJIL SUPPLEMENT: OFFICIAL DOCUMENTS 157 (1907) ("The Contracting Powers agree to abstain from the use of projectiles the object of which is the diffusion of asphyxiating or deleterious gases.").

[83] *Refer to* § 19.10 (1922 Washington Treaty on Submarines and Noxious Gases); § 19.12 (1925 Geneva Gas and Bacteriological Protocol).

[84] *Refer to* § 6.8.2 (Asphyxiating, Poisonous, or Other Gases, and All Analogous Liquids, Materials, or Devices).

[85] Declaration Prohibiting for a Term of Five Years the Launching of Projectiles or Explosives from Balloons, or By Any Other New Methods of Similar Nature, Jul. 29, 1899, 32 STAT. 1839 ("The Contracting Powers agree to prohibit, for a term of five years, the launching of projectiles and explosives from balloons, or by other new methods of similar nature.").

[86] Theodore Roosevelt, *Proclamation Regarding the 1899 Declaration Prohibiting the Launching of Projectiles or Explosives from Balloons*, Nov. 1, 1901, 32 STAT. 1839, 1842 ("And Whereas, the said Declaration was duly ratified by the Government of the United States of America, by and with the advice and consent of the Senate thereof, and by the Governments of the other Powers aforesaid, with the exception of those of China and Turkey; And Whereas, in pursuance of a stipulation of the said Declaration, the ratifications thereof were deposited at the Hague on the 4th day of September, 1900, by the Plenipotentiaries of the Governments of the United States of America, Austria- Hungary, Belgium, Denmark, Spain, France, Italy, the Netherlands, Persia, Portugal, Roumania, Russia, Siam, Sweden and Norway, and Bulgaria . . . .").

The 1907 Hague Declaration (XIV) Prohibiting the Discharge of Projectiles and Explosives from Balloons sought to renew the expired 1899 Hague Declaration (IV, 1).[87] The United States deposited its instrument of ratification to the 1907 Hague Declaration (XIV) on November 27, 1909.[88] This treaty was intended to have effect until the end of the Third Hague Peace Conference.[89] The Third Hague Peace Conference never met due to the outbreak of World War I.[90] The application of the 1907 Hague Declaration (XIV) is limited, *inter alia*, due to its general participation clause providing that it only applies if all the parties to the conflict are also Parties to the Declaration.[91] During World War II, the War Department took the position that the 1907 Hague Declaration (XIV) is not binding and will not be observed.[92]

19.8 1899 HAGUE II AND 1907 HAGUE IV CONVENTIONS AND ANNEXED REGULATIONS REGARDING LAND WARFARE

19.8.1 1899 Hague II. The Hague Convention II with Respect to the Laws and Customs of War on Land of July 29, 1899 (1899 Hague II), with its annexed Regulations, was an early multilateral law of war treaty that contains provisions that were incorporated into later law of war treaties.

Article 1 of the 1899 Hague II Regulations addressed the criteria for militia and volunteer corps to qualify as lawful belligerents and for their members to be entitled to POW status if captured; these criteria are repeated in Article 4 of the GPW.[93] In addition, Articles 4-20 of the 1899 Hague II Regulations provide basic rules for the care and protection of POWs.

The United States deposited its instrument of ratification to the 1899 Hague II on April 5,

---

[87] Declaration (XIV) Prohibiting the Discharge of Projectiles and Explosives from Balloons, Oct. 18, 1907, 36 STAT. 2439 ("The Undersigned, Plenipotentiaries of the Powers invited to the Second International Peace Conference at The Hague, duly authorized to that effect by their Governments, inspired by the sentiments which found expression in the Declaration of St. Petersburg of the 29th November (11th December), 1868, and being desirous of renewing the declaration of The Hague of the 29th July, 1899, which was now expired,").

[88] William H. Taft, *Proclamation Regarding the 1907 Declaration Prohibiting the Discharge of Projectiles and Explosives from Balloons*, Feb. 28, 1910, 36 STAT. 2439, 2442-43 ("And whereas the said Declaration has been duly ratified by the Government of the United States of America, by and with the advice and consent of the Senate thereof, and by the Governments of China, Great Britain, the Netherlands, Bolivia, and Salvador, and the ratifications of the said Governments were, as provided for by the said Declaration, deposited by their respective plenipotentiaries with the Netherlands Government on November 27, 1909.").

[89] Declaration (XIV) Prohibiting the Discharge of Projectiles and Explosives from Balloons, Oct. 18, 1907, 36 STAT. 2439 ("The Contracting Powers agree to prohibit, for a period extending to the close of the Third Peace Conference, the discharge of projectiles and explosives from balloons or by other new methods of a similar nature.").

[90] SCHINDLER & TOMAN, THE LAWS OF ARMED CONFLICTS: A COLLECTION OF CONVENTIONS, RESOLUTIONS, AND OTHER DOCUMENTS 309 (2004) ("The Declaration of 1907 was to remain in force until the projected Third Peace Conference. This Conference never having met, the Declaration of 1907 is still formally in force today.").

[91] Declaration (XIV) Prohibiting the Discharge of Projectiles and Explosives from Balloons, Oct. 18, 1907, 36 STAT. 2439, 2440 ("The present Declaration is only binding on the Contracting Powers in a case of war between two or more of them. It shall cease to be binding from the time when, in a war between the Contracting Powers, one of the belligerents is joined by a non-Contracting Power.").

[92] WAR DEPARTMENT CIRCULAR NO. 136, § 1 (May 7, 1942) ("The Hague Declaration Number XIV, October 18, 1907, prohibiting the discharge of projectiles and explosives from balloons (H.D. XIV), is not binding and will not be observed.").

[93] *Refer to* § 4.6.1 (GPW 4A(2) Conditions in General).

1902.[94]

The 1899 Hague II was followed by Hague IV, which replaces the 1899 Hague II as between Parties to Hague IV.[95] Not all the States that ratified the 1899 Hague II have also ratified Hague IV.[96]

19.8.2 Hague IV. States sought to expand upon and clarify provisions of 1899 Hague II and the 1899 Hague II Regulations through the Hague Convention IV Respecting the Laws and Customs of War on Land of October 18, 1907 (Hague IV), and annexed Regulations (Hague IV Regulations).[97]

The United States deposited its instrument of ratification to Hague IV on November 27, 1909.[98]

19.8.2.1 *Hague IV and Customary International Law*. Provisions of Hague IV and Hague IV Regulations have been found to reflect customary international law.[99]

---

[94] Theodore Roosevelt, *Proclamation Regarding the 1899 Hague II*, Apr. 11, 1902, 32 STAT. 1803, 1825 ("And whereas the said Convention was duly ratified by the Government of the United States of America, by and with the advice and consent of the Senate thereof, and by the Governments of the other Powers aforesaid with the exception of Sweden and Norway and Turkey; And whereas, in pursuance of the stipulations of Article III of the said Convention the ratifications of the said Convention were deposited at the Hague … on the 5th Day of April, 1902, by the Plenipotentiary of the Government of the United States of America:").

[95] *Refer to* § 19.8.2.2 (Relationship Between the 1907 Hague IV and the 1899 Hague II).

[96] ADAM ROBERTS & RICHARD GUELFF, DOCUMENTS ON THE LAWS OF WAR 68-70 (3rd ed., 2000) ("[The 1907 Hague Convention] was intended to replace 1899 Hague Convention II as between states parties to both agreements. However, of the forty-six states which had become parties to the 1899 Convention, eighteen did not become parties to the 1907 Convention … . They or their successor states … remained formally bound by the 1899 Convention.").

[97] Convention (IV) Respecting the Laws and Customs of War on Land, Oct. 18, 1907, 36 STAT. 2277, 2279 (The Contracting Parties "[h]ave deemed it necessary to complete and explain in certain particulars the work of the First Peace Conference, which, following on the Brussels Conference of 1874, and inspired by the ideas dictated by a wise and generous forethought, adopted provisions intended to define and govern the usages of war on land.").

[98] William H. Taft, *Proclamation Regarding the Hague IV*, Feb. 28, 1907, 36 STAT. 2277, 2309 ("And whereas the said Convention has been duly ratified by the Government of the United States of America, by and with the advice and consent of the Senate thereof, and by the Governments of Austria-Hungary, Bolivia, Denmark, Germany, Great Britain, Mexico, the Netherlands, Russia, Salvador, and Sweden, and the ratifications of the said Governments were, under the provisions of Article 5 of the said Convention, deposited by their respective plenipotentiaries with the Netherlands Government on November 27, 1909;").

[99] *See, e.g.*, United States, *et al.* v. Göring, *et al.*, *Judgment*, I TRIAL OF THE MAJOR WAR CRIMINALS BEFORE THE IMT 253-54 (concluding that "by 1939 these rules laid down in [Hague IV] were recognized by all civilized nations, and were regarded as being declaratory of the laws and customs of war"); United States v. Krupp *et al.*, IX TRIALS OF WAR CRIMINALS BEFORE THE NMT 1340 (concurring in judgment "that the Hague Convention No. IV of 1907 to which Germany was a party had, by 1939, become customary law and was, therefore, binding on Germany not only as treaty law but also as customary law."); United States v. von Leeb, *et al.* (The High Command Case), XI TRIALS OF WAR CRIMINALS BEFORE THE NMT 535-38 (concluding that provisions of Hague IV Reg. and 1929 GPW reflected customary international law relating to the treatment of prisoners of war); United States, *et al.* v. Araki, *et al.*, *Majority Judgment*, International Military Tribunal for the Far East, 48,491, *reprinted in* NEIL BOISTER & ROBERT CRYER, DOCUMENTS ON THE TOKYO INTERNATIONAL MILITARY TRIBUNAL: CHARTER, INDICTMENT AND JUDGMENTS 102 (2008) (explaining that although certain treaties, such as Hague IV and Hague V, might not be applicable by their terms, "the Convention remains as good evidence of the customary law of nations, to be considered by the Tribunal along with all other available evidence in determining the customary law to be applied in any given situation.").

For example, Article 42 of the Hague IV Regulations, which provides a standard for when the law of belligerent occupation applies, is regarded as customary international law.[100]

19.8.2.2 *Relationship Between the 1907 Hague IV and the 1899 Hague II*. The Hague IV, duly ratified, shall as between its Parties be substituted for the 1899 Hague II. The 1899 Hague II remains in force as between its Parties that do not also ratify Hague IV.[101]

19.8.3 Martens Clause. The Preamble to the 1899 Hague II contains a clause known as the Martens Clause because of its association with a delegate to the Hague Peace Conference, F.F. de Martens:[102]

> Until a more complete code of the laws of war is issued, the High Contracting Parties think it right to declare that in cases not included in the Regulations adopted by them, populations and belligerents remain under the protection and empire of the principles of international law, as they result from the usages established between civilized nations, from the laws of humanity, and the requirements of the public conscience.[103]

A similar formulation was included in subsequent treaties, such as the Hague IV, the 1949 Geneva Conventions, and the CCW.[104]

The Martens Clause was a compromise following difficult and unresolved debates at the 1899 Hague Peace Conference about the status of resistance fighters in occupied territory.[105] However, the language of the clause is not limited to that specific context, and the Martens

---

[100] *Refer to* § 11.2.2 (Standard for Determining When Territory Is Considered Occupied).

[101] HAGUE IV art. 4 ("The present Convention, duly ratified, shall as between the Contracting Powers, be substituted for the Convention of the 29th July, 1899, respecting the Laws and Customs of War on Land. The Convention of 1899 remains in force as between the Powers which signed it, and which do not also ratify the present Convention.").

[102] Theodor Meron, *The Martens Clause, Principles of Humanity, and Dictates of Public Conscience*, 94 AJIL 78, 79 (2000) ("Proposed by the Russian delegate to the Hague Peace Conference, the eminent jurist F.F. de Martens, the clause has ancient antecedents rooted in natural law and chivalry.").

[103] 1899 HAGUE II preamble ("Until a more complete code of the laws of war is issued, the High Contracting Parties think it right to declare that in cases not included in the Regulations adopted by them, populations and belligerents remain under the protection and empire of the principles of international law, as they result from the usages established between civilized nations, from the laws of humanity, and the requirements of the public conscience").

[104] *See, e.g.*, HAGUE IV preamble ("Until a more complete code of the laws of war has been issued, the High Contracting Parties deem it expedient to declare that in cases not included in the Regulations adopted by them, the inhabitants and the belligerents remain under the protection and the rule of the principles of the law of nations, as they result from the usages established among civilized peoples, from the laws of humanity, and the dictates of the public conscience."); GWS art. 63 (providing that denunciation of the Convention "shall in no way impair the obligations which Parties to the conflict shall remain bound to fulfil by virtue of the principles of the law of nations, as they result from the usages established among civilized peoples, from the laws of humanity and the dictates of public conscience."); GWS-SEA art. 62 (same); GPW art. 142 (same); GC art. 158 (same); CCW preamble ("in cases not covered by this Convention and its annexed Protocols or by other international agreements, the civilian population and the combatants shall at all times remain under the protection and authority of the principles of international law derived from established custom, from the principles of humanity and from the dictates of public conscience,"). *Consider* AP I art. 1(2) ("In cases not covered by this Protocol or by other international agreements, civilians and combatants remain under the protection and authority of the principles of international law derived from established custom, from the principles of humanity and from the dictates of public conscience."); AP II preamble ("Recalling that, in cases not covered by the law in force, the human person remains under the protection of the principles of humanity and the dictates of the public conscience,").

[105] *See* ADAM ROBERTS & RICHARD GUELFF, DOCUMENTS ON THE LAWS OF WAR 9 (3rd ed., 2000) ("The wording of the Martens Clause was agreed at the 1899 Hague Peace Conference for a specific reason: it was a compromise

Clause has been cited in many other contexts.[106]

The Martens clause reflects the idea that when no specific rule applies, the principles of the law of war form the general guide for conduct during war.[107]

19.9 1907 Hague X

On November 27, 1909, the United States deposited its instrument of ratification to the 1907 Hague Convention (X) for the Adaption to Maritime Warfare of the Principles of the Geneva Convention of October 18, 1907.[108]

This treaty was followed by the GWS-Sea, which replaced it in relations between Parties to the GWS-Sea.[109]

19.10 1922 Washington Treaty on Submarines and Noxious Gases

The United States signed the Treaty Relating to the Use of Submarines and Noxious Gases in Warfare on February 6, 1922.[110] Article 6 of the treaty provided that the treaty shall take effect on the deposit of all the ratifications.[111] France did not ratify the treaty, and it did not enter into force.[112]

---

following difficult and unresolved debates about whether or not the inhabitants of occupied territory had a right of resistance."); United States v. Krupp, *et al.*, IX Trials of War Criminals Before the NMT 1340-41 ("It must also be pointed out that in the preamble to the Hague Convention No. IV, it is made abundantly clear that in cases not included in the Regulations, the inhabitants and the belligerents remain under the protection and the rule of the principles of the law of nations, as they result from the usages established among civilized peoples, from the laws of humanity and dictates of the public conscience. As the records of the Hague Peace Conferences of 1899 which enacted the Hague Regulations show, great emphasis was placed by the participants on the protection of invaded territories and the preamble just cited, also known as the "Mertens Clause," was inserted at the request of the Belgian delegate, Mertens, who was, as were others, not satisfied with the protection specifically guaranteed to belligerently occupied territory. Hence, not only the wording (which specifically mentions the 'inhabitants' before it mentions the 'belligerents') but also the discussions which took place at the time make it clear that it refers specifically to *belligerently occupied country*.").

[106] *See, e.g.*, Legality of the Threat or Use of Nuclear Weapons, Advisory Opinion, 1996 I.C.J. 226, 257 (¶78) ("The Court would likewise refer, in relation to these principles, to the Martens Clause, which was first included in the Hague Convention II with Respect to the Laws and Customs of War on Land of 1899 and which has proved to be an effective means of addressing the rapid evolution of military technology.").

[107] *Refer to* § 2.1.2.2 (Law of War Principles as a General Guide).

[108] William H. Taft, *Proclamation Regarding the Hague X*, Feb. 28, 1910, 36 Stat. 2371, 2395 ("And whereas the said Convention has been duly ratified by the Government of the United States of America, by and with the advice and consent of the Senate thereof, and by the Governments of Germany, Austria-Hungary, China, Denmark, Mexico, the Netherlands, Russia, Bolivia, and Salvador, and the ratifications of the said Governments were, under the provisions of Article 23 of the said Convention, deposited by their respective plenipotentiaries with the Netherlands Government on November 27, 1909.").

[109] *Refer to* § 19.16.3.1 (Relationship Between the 1907 Hague X and the GWS-Sea).

[110] Treaty in Relation to the Use of Submarines and Noxious Gases in Warfare, Feb. 6, 1922, *reprinted in* 16 AJIL Supplement: Official Documents 57, 60 (1922).

[111] Treaty in Relation to the Use of Submarines and Noxious Gases in Warfare, art. 6, Feb. 6, 1922, *reprinted in* 16 AJIL Supplement: Official Documents 57, 59 (1922) ("The present Treaty shall be ratified as soon as possible in accordance with the constitutional methods of the Signatory Powers and shall take effect on the deposit of all the ratifications, which shall take place at Washington.").

[112] Schinder & Toman, The Laws of Armed Conflicts 877 (1988) ("The Washington Conference of 1922 on the Limitation of Armaments, in which five of the victorious Powers of World War I took part, adopted the present Treaty, which due to the failure of France to ratify it, did not enter into force.").

The language of Article 5 of the 1922 Washington Treaty dealing with gas warfare corresponds to language in the 1925 Protocol for the Prohibition of the Use in War of Asphyxiating, Poisonous or Other Gases, and of Bacteriological Methods of Warfare signed at Geneva, June 17, 1925.[113] The 1925 Geneva Gas and Bacteriological Protocol, however, also prohibits bacteriological methods of warfare.[114]

19.11 1923 Hague Air and Radio Rules

In 1922, the Conference on the Limitation of Armament at Washington adopted a resolution for the appointment of a Commission representing the United States of America, the British Empire, France, Italy, and Japan, and later, the Netherlands, to consider the application of the existing law of war rules to new agencies of warfare and whether changes should be adopted.[115] It was agreed that the program of the Commission would be limited to the preparation of rules relating to aerial warfare, and to rules relating to the use of radio in time of war.[116] With John Bassett Moore as a U.S. Delegate and the President of the Commission, the Commission prepared a set of rules for the control of radio in time of war, as well as a set of rules for aerial warfare.[117]

The 1923 Hague Air Rules were not, however, subsequently adopted as a treaty by the United States.

Some provisions in the 1923 Hague Air Rules may reflect customary international law. For example, the 1923 Hague Air Rules recognize the permissibility of using tracer, incendiary, or explosive projectiles by or against aircraft, including by States that are Parties to the 1868 Declaration of St. Petersburg.[118]

---

[113] *Refer to* § 6.8.2 (Asphyxiating, Poisonous, or Other Gases, and All Analogous Liquids, Materials, or Devices).

[114] *Refer to* § 19.12 (1925 Geneva Gas and Bacteriological Protocol).

[115] Commission of Jurists to Consider and Report upon the Revision of the Rules of Warfare, *General Report*, Feb. 19, 1923, *reprinted in* 32 AJIL SUPPLEMENT: OFFICIAL DOCUMENTS 1 (1938) ("The Conference on the Limitation of Armament at Washington adopted at its sixth plenary session on the 4th February, 1922, a resolution for the appointment of a Commission representing the United States of America, the British Empire, France, Italy and Japan to consider the following questions: (a) *Do existing rules of international law adequately cover new methods of attack or defence resulting from the introduction or development, since The Hague Conference of 1907, of new agencies of warfare?* (b) *If not so, what changes in the existing rules ought to be adopted in consequence thereof as a part of the law of nations?* … With the unanimous concurrence of the Powers mentioned in the first of the above resolutions an invitation to participate in the work of the Commission was extended to and accepted by the Netherlands Government.").

[116] Commission of Jurists to Consider and Report upon the Revision of the Rules of Warfare, *General Report*, Feb. 19, 1923, *reprinted in* 32 AJIL SUPPLEMENT: OFFICIAL DOCUMENTS 1 (1938) ("It was also agreed that the programme of the Commission should be limited to the preparation of rules relating to aerial warfare, and to rules relating to the use of radio in time of war.").

[117] Commission of Jurists to Consider and Report upon the Revision of the Rules of Warfare, *General Report*, Feb. 19, 1923, *reprinted in* 32 AJIL SUPPLEMENT: OFFICIAL DOCUMENTS 1-2 (1938) ("The United States Government proposed that the Commission should meet on the 11th December, 1922, at The Hague, and the representatives of the six Powers mentioned above assembled on that date in the Palace of Peace. At the second meeting of the Commission the Honorable John Bassett Moore, First Delegate of the United States, was elected President of the Commission. The Commission has prepared a set of rules for the control of radio in time of war, which are contained in Part I of this report, and a set of rules for aërial warfare, which are contained in Part II of this report.").

[118] *Refer to* § 6.5.4.3 (Exploding Bullets); § 19.6 (1868 St. Petersburg Declaration).

Many of the other provisions in the 1923 Hague Air Rules, however, do not reflect customary international law. For example, the 1923 Hague Air Rules provide that the crew of military aircraft must be exclusively military.[119] The 1949 Geneva Conventions, however, contemplate that crews of military aircraft may include civilian members.[120] As another example, certain efforts in the 1923 Hague Air Rules to limit the effects of attacks also do not reflect customary international law.[121]

19.12 1925 Geneva Gas and Bacteriological Protocol

The Geneva Protocol for the Prohibition of the Use in War of Asphyxiating, Poisonous or Other Gases, and of Bacteriological Methods of Warfare, of June 17, 1925, prohibits the use of asphyxiating, poisonous, or other gases, and all analogous liquids, materials, or devices, and the use of bacteriological methods of warfare.[122]

This treaty followed the 1899 Declaration on Asphyxiating Gases and the 1922 Washington Treaty on Submarines and Noxious Gases.[123] This treaty also followed widespread use of chemical weapons in World War I.

On November 25, 1969, President Nixon announced the intention of the administration to seek Senate advice and consent to ratification of the 1925 Geneva Gas and Bacteriological Protocol as part of U.S. policies relating to chemical and biological weapons.[124] The United States deposited its instrument of ratification to the 1925 Geneva Gas and Bacteriological Protocol on April 10, 1975.[125]

---

[119] Commission of Jurists to Consider and Report Upon the Revision of the Rules of Warfare, *General Report, Part II: Rules of Aërial Warfare*, art. 14, Feb. 19, 1923, *reprinted in* 32 AJIL SUPPLEMENT: OFFICIAL DOCUMENTS 12, 18 (1938) ("A military aircraft shall be under the command of a person duly commissioned or enlisted in the military service of the state; the crew must be exclusively military.").

[120] *Refer to* § 14.3.3.3 (Military Aircraft – Command and Crew).

[121] J. Fred Buzhardt, DoD General Counsel, Letter to Senator Edward Kennedy, Sept. 22, 1972, *reprinted in* 67 AJIL 122, 123 (1973) ("In the application of the laws of war, it is important that there be a general understanding in the world community as to what shall be legitimate military objectives which may be attacked by air bombardment under the limitations imposed by treaty or by customary international law. Attempts to limit the effects of attacks in an unrealistic manner, by definition or otherwise, solely to the essential war making potential of enemy States have not been successful. For example, such attempts as the 1923 Hague Rules of Air Warfare, proposed by an International Commission of Jurists, and the 1956 *ICRC Draft Rules for the Limitation of the Dangers Incurred by the Civilian Population in Time of War* were not accepted by States and therefore do not reflect the laws of war either as customary international law or as adopted by treaty.").

[122] *Refer to* § 6.8.2 (Asphyxiating, Poisonous, or Other Gases, and All Analogous Liquids, Materials, or Devices); § 6.9.1 (Biological Weapons – Prohibition on Use as a Method of Warfare).

[123] *Refer to* § 19.7.2 (1899 Declaration on Asphyxiating Gases); § 19.10 (1922 Washington Treaty on Submarines and Noxious Gases).

[124] Richard Nixon, *Statement on Chemical and Biological Defense Policies and Programs*, Nov. 25, 1969, 1969 PUBLIC PAPERS OF THE PRESIDENTS 968 ("As to our chemical warfare program, the United States: —Reaffirms its oft-repeated renunciation of the first use of lethal chemical weapons. –Extends this renunciation to the first use of incapacitating chemicals. Consonant with these decisions, the administration will submit to the Senate, for its advice and consent to ratification, the Geneva Protocol of 1925 which prohibits the first use in war of 'asphyxiating, poisonous or other Gases and of Bacteriological Methods of Warfare.' The United States has long supported the principles and objectives of this Protocol. We take this step toward formal ratification to reinforce our continuing advocacy of international constraints on the use of these weapons.").

[125] 1925 Geneva Gas and Bacteriological Protocol, Apr. 10, 1975, 1541 UNTS 484 ("RATIFICATIONS Instruments deposited with the Government of France on: 10 April 1975 UNITED STATES OF AMERICA (With effect from 10 April 1975.)").

The United States took a reservation that the "Protocol shall cease to be binding on the government of the United States with respect to the use in war of asphyxiating, poisonous or other gases, and of all analogous liquids, materials, or devices, in regard to an enemy state if such state or any of its allies fails to respect the prohibitions laid down in this Protocol."[126] This reservation would permit use by the United States of chemical weapons and agents in response, but would not limit in any way the Protocol's prohibition with respect to biological weapons.[127] Other States, including France, Belgium, Canada, the USSR (now Russia), and the United Kingdom issued similar statements upon ratification.[128]

This treaty was followed by the Chemical Weapons Convention and Biological Weapons Convention, which, *inter alia*, place restrictions on the use, development, production, and possession of weapons addressed by the 1925 Geneva Gas and Bacteriological Protocol.[129]

19.13 1929 Geneva Conventions

19.13.1 1929 GWS. The United States deposited its instrument of ratification to the 1929 GWS on February 4, 1932.[130]

The 1929 GWS was replaced by the GWS in relations between Parties to the GWS.[131] All the Parties to the 1929 GWS have become Parties to the GWS.

19.13.2 1929 GPW. The United States deposited its instrument of ratification to the 1929 GPW on February 4, 1932.[132]

The 1929 GPW was replaced by the GPW in relations between Parties to the GPW.[133] All the Parties to the 1929 GPW have become Parties to the GPW.

---

[126] United States, *Statement on Ratification of the 1925 Geneva Gas and Bacteriological Protocol*, Apr. 10, 1975, 1541 UNTS 484 ("That the said Protocol shall cease to be binding on the Government of the United States with respect to the use in war of asphyxiating, poisonous or other gases, and of all analogous liquids, materials, or devices, in regard to an enemy State if such State or any of its allies fails to respect the prohibitions laid down in the Protocol.").

[127] William P. Rogers, *Letter of Submittal*, Aug. 11, 1970, Message from the President Transmitting the 1925 Geneva Gas and Bacteriological Protocol vi ("This reservation would permit the retaliatory use by the United States of chemical weapons and agents, but would not limit in any way the Protocol's prohibition with respect to biological weapons.").

[128] France, *Statement on Ratification of the 1925 Geneva Gas and Bacteriological Protocol*, May 9, 1926, 94 LNTS 67 ("The said Protocol shall *ipso facto* cease to be binding on the Government of the French Republic in regard to any enemy State whose armed forces or whose Allies fail to respect the prohibitions laid down in the Protocol."); Belgium, *Statement on Ratification of the 1925 Geneva Gas and Bacteriological Protocol*, Dec. 4, 1928, 94 LNTS 67 ("(2) The said Protocol shall *ipso facto* cease to be binding on the Belgian Government in regard to any enemy State whose armed forces or whose Allies fail to respect the prohibitions laid down in the Protocol."); Canada, *Statement on Ratification of the 1925 Geneva Gas and Bacteriological Protocol*, May 6, 1930, 94 LNTS 71 ("The said Protocol shall cease to be binding on His Britannic Majesty towards any State at enmity with Him whose armed forces, or whose allies *de jure* or in fact fail to respect the prohibitions laid down in the Protocol."); Union of Soviet Socialist Republics, *Statement on Accession to the 1925 Geneva Gas and Bacteriological Protocol*, Apr. 5, 1928, 94 LNTS 71 ("(2) The said Protocol shall cease to be binding on the Government of the Union of Soviet Socialist Republics in regard to all enemy States whose armed forces or whose Allies *de jure* or in fact do not respect the restrictions which are the object of this Protocol."); British Empire, *Statement on Ratification of the 1925 Geneva Gas and Bacteriological Protocol*, Apr. 9, 1930, 94 LNTS 69 ("The said Protocol shall cease to be binding on His Britannic Majesty towards any Power at enmity with Him whose armed forces, or the armed forces of whose allies, fail to respect the prohibitions laid down in the Protocol.").

[129] *Refer to* § 19.22 (Chemical Weapons Convention); § 19.19 (Biological Weapons Convention).

[130] Herbert Hoover, *Proclamation Regarding the 1929 GPW*, Aug. 4, 1932, 47 Stat. 2021, 2073 ("And whereas, the said Convention has been duly ratified on the part of the United States of America and the instrument of ratification of the United States of America was deposited with the Government of Switzerland on February 4, 1932; And whereas, in accordance with Article 92 thereof, the said Convention became effective in respect of the United States of America six months after the deposit of its instrument of ratification, namely, on August 4, 1932;").

Provisions of the 1929 GPW were found to reflect customary international law by war crimes tribunals after World War II.[134] The 1929 GPW may be relevant to understanding provisions of the 1949 GPW because some provisions of the 1949 GPW were drawn from the 1929 GW or reflect an effort to improve upon the 1929 GPW.

19.14 1930 LONDON TREATY FOR THE LIMITATION AND REDUCTION OF NAVAL ARMAMENT AND 1936 LONDON PROTOCOL

Article 22 of the 1930 London Treaty for the Limitation and Reduction of Naval Armament (1930 London Treaty) and the 1936 London Protocol set forth identical rules regarding submarine warfare, and the obligations of surface warships and submarines with respect to the sinking of merchant vessels, including the obligation to put merchant vessels' passengers and crew in a place of safety.[135]

The United States deposited its instrument of ratification to the 1930 London Treaty on October 27, 1930.[136] Although other aspects of the treaty expired on December 31, 1936, Article 22 remains in force.[137] Signatories to the 1930 London Treaty desired that as many States as possible accept the rules in Article 22; thus, they concluded the 1936 London Protocol with the same language as that in Article 22 and invited other States to accede to the 1936 London Protocol.[138] The United States signed the 1936 Protocol on November 6, 1936.[139]

---

[131] *Refer to* § 19.16.2.1 (Relationship Between the GWS and Earlier Conventions).

[132] Herbert Hoover, *Proclamation Regarding the 1929 GWS*, Aug. 4, 1932, 47 STAT. 2074, 2101 ("And whereas, the said Convention has been duly ratified on the part of the United States of America and the instrument of ratification of the United States of America was deposited with the Government of Switzerland on February 4, 1932: And whereas, in accordance with Article 33 thereof, the said Convention became effective in respect of the United States of America six months after the deposit of its instrument of ratification, namely, on August 4, 1932;").

[133] *Refer to* § 19.16.4.1 (Relationship Between the GPW and the 1929 GPW).

[134] *Refer to* § 9.1.1 (Brief History of POW Law).

[135] *Refer to* § 13.7.1 (General Principle – Same Rules Applicable to Both Submarine and Surface Warships); § 13.5.2 (Attack of Enemy Merchant Vessels); § 15.15.3 (Destruction of Neutral Prizes).

[136] Herbert Hoover, *Proclamation Regarding the 1930 Treaty for the Limitation and Reduction of Naval Armament*, Jan. 1, 1931, 46 STAT. 2858, 2885 ("AND WHEREAS the ratification by the United States of America, subject to the understandings, set forth therein, … deposited at London on the 27th day of October, one thousand nine hundred and thirty,").

[137] Treaty for the Limitation and Reduction of Naval Armament art. 23, Apr. 22, 1930, 46 STAT. 2858, 2882 ("The present Treaty shall remain in force until the 31st December, 1936, subject to the following exceptions: (1) Part IV shall remain in force without limit of time; (2) the provisions of Articles 3, 4 and 5, and of Article 11 and Annex II to Part II so far as they relate to aircraft carriers, shall remain in force for the same period as the Washington Treaty.").

[138] *Procès-Verbal* Relating to the Rules of Submarine Warfare Set Forth in Part IV of the Treaty of London of April 22, 1930, preamble, Nov. 6, 1936, 173 LNTS 353, 355 ("And whereas all the signatories of the said Treaty desire that as great a number of Powers as possible should accept the rules contained in the said Part IV as established rules of international law; The undersigned, representatives of their respective Governments, bearing in mind the said Article 22 of the Treaty, hereby request the Government of the United Kingdom of Great Britain and Northern Ireland forthwith to communicate the said rules, as annexed hereto, to the Governments of all Powers which are not signatories of the said Treaty, with an invitation to accede thereto definitely and without limit of time.").

[139] *Procès-Verbal* Relating to the Rules of Submarine Warfare Set Forth in Part IV of the Treaty of London of April 22, 1930, Nov. 6, 1936, 173 LNTS 353, 357 ("Signed in London, the 6th day of November, nineteen hundred and thirty-six. For the Government of the United States of America: Robert Worth BINGHAM.").

19.15 1935 ROERICH PACT

The 1935 Roerich Pact was concluded in Washington on April 15, 1935.[140] It provides for the respect and protection of "historic monuments, museums, scientific, artistic, educational and cultural institutions" and their personnel in time of peace as well as in war.[141] Such institutions and personnel receive protection as cultural property under the 1954 Hague Cultural Property or the general protection afforded civilian objects and persons.[142]

The United States deposited its instrument of ratification to the 1935 Roerich Pact on July 13, 1935.[143]

This treaty was followed by the 1954 Hague Cultural Property Convention.[144] All Parties to the Roerich Pact are Parties to the 1954 Hague Cultural Property Convention.

The 1954 Hague Cultural Property Convention is supplementary to the Roerich Pact, but the distinctive emblem of the 1954 Hague Cultural Property Convention is to be used instead of the distinguishing flag described in Article III of the 1935 Roerich Pact, in situations where the 1954 Hague Cultural Property Convention and the Regulations for its execution provide for the use of this distinctive emblem.[145]

19.16 1949 GENEVA CONVENTIONS

The four 1949 Geneva Conventions were adopted at a Diplomatic Conference at Geneva on August 12, 1949. More than 193 States have ratified the 1949 Geneva Conventions.[146]

The United States signed each of the 1949 Geneva Conventions on August 12, 1949. The United States deposited its instrument of ratification to each convention on August 2, 1955.[147]

The United States has viewed many of the protections embodied in the 1949 Geneva Conventions as reflecting appropriate U.S. practice in armed conflict regardless of formal treaty

---

[140] Pan American Treaty on the Protection of Artistic and Scientific Institutions and Historic Monuments, Apr. 15, 1935, 49 STAT. 3267.

[141] ROERICH PACT art. 1 ("The historic monuments, museums, scientific, artistic, educational and cultural institutions shall be considered as neutral and as such respected and protected by belligerents. The same respect and protection shall be due to the personnel of the institutions mentioned above. The same respect and protection shall be accorded to the historic monuments, museums, scientific, artistic, educational and cultural institutions in time of peace as well as in war."). *Refer to* § 5.18.1.1 (Definition of Cultural Property – Notes on Terminology).

[142] *Refer to* § 5.18 (Protection of Cultural Property During Hostilities); § 5.5 (Discrimination in Conducting Attacks).

[143] Franklin D. Roosevelt, *Proclamation Regarding the Roerich Pact*, Oct. 25, 1935, 49 STAT. 3267, 3274 ("AND WHEREAS the said Treaty has been duly ratified by the United States of America, whose instrument of ratification was deposited with the Pan American Union on July 13, 1935;").

[144] *Refer to* § 19.17 (1954 Hague Cultural Property Convention).

[145] *Refer to* § 19.17.1.2 (Relationship Between the 1935 Roerich Pact and the 1954 Hague Cultural Property Convention).

[146] *See* DEPARTMENT OF STATE, *Treaties in Force: A List of Treaties and Other International Agreements of the United States in Force on January 1, 2013*, 465-66 (2013).

[147] 213 UNTS 378 (GWS Ratification, "*Instrument deposited with the Swiss Federal Council on:* 2 August 1955 UNITED STATES OF AMERICA (To take effect on 2 February 1956.)"); 213 UNTS 382 (GWS-Sea Ratification, "*Instrument deposited with the Swiss Federal Council on:* 2 August 1955 UNITED STATES OF AMERICA (To take effect on 2 February 1956.)"); 213 UNTS 383 (GPW Ratification, "*Instrument deposited with the Swiss Federal Council on:* 2 August 1955 UNITED STATES OF AMERICA (To take effect on 2 February 1956.)"); 213 UNTS 384 (GC Ratification, "*Instrument deposited with the Swiss Federal Council on:* 2 August 1955 UNITED STATES OF AMERICA (To take effect on 2 February 1956.)").

obligations.[148]

The 1949 Geneva Conventions followed earlier multilateral treaties that addressed the same subjects, including the 1864 GWS, the 1907 Hague X, the 1899 and 1907 Hague Conventions on the Law of Land Warfare, and the 1929 Geneva Conventions.[149]

The Commentaries to the 1949 Geneva Conventions, published by the International Committee of the Red Cross, under the general editorship of Jean S. Pictet, have often been helpful in understanding the provisions of the 1949 Geneva Conventions and have often been cited in this manual. As noted by the International Committee of the Red Cross, however, these Commentaries are not an official interpretation of the 1949 Geneva Conventions, which only participant States would be qualified to give.[150]

19.16.1 Common Provisions in the 1949 Geneva Conventions. The four 1949 Geneva Conventions contain a number of common provisions, *i.e.*, provisions that are substantively the same (if not identical in text) among the conventions.

The four Geneva Conventions have this duplication, in part, because each convention is designed to be effective, even if a State only ratifies that particular convention.[151] For example, the list of persons entitled to receive POW status in Article 4 of the GPW is repeated in the GWS and GWS-Sea.[152]

19.16.1.1 *Common Terms in the 1949 Geneva Conventions – Notes on Terminology*. In the 1949 Geneva Conventions, "Power" generally refers to a State.[153]

---

[148] *See* SENATE EXECUTIVE REPORT 84-9, *Geneva Conventions for the Protection of War Victims: Report of the Committee on Foreign Relations on Executives D, E, F, and G*, 82nd Congress, First Session, 32 (Jun. 27, 1955) ("Our Nation has everything to gain and nothing to lose by being a party to the conventions now before the Senate, and by encouraging their most widespread adoption. As emphasized in this report, the requirements of the four conventions to a very great degree reflect the actual policies of the United States in World War II. The practices which they bind nations to follow impose no burden upon us that we would not voluntarily assume in a future conflict without the injunctions of formal treaty obligations.").

[149] *Refer to* § 19.5 (1864 GWS); § 19.9 (1907 Hague X); § 19.8 (1899 Hague II and 1907 Hague IV Conventions and Annexed Regulations Regarding Land Warfare); § 19.13 (1929 Geneva Conventions).

[150] *See, e.g.*, GWS COMMENTARY Foreword ("Although published by the International Committee, the Commentary is the personal work of its authors. The Committee, moreoever, whenever called upon for an opinion on a provision of an international Convention, always takes care to emphasize that only the participant States are qualified, through consultation between themselves, to give an oficial and, as it were, authentic interpretation of an intergovernmental treaty.").

[151] *See, e.g.*, II-B FINAL RECORD OF THE DIPLOMATIC CONFERENCE OF GENEVA OF 1949 257 ("Mr. NAJAR (Israel): ... We have a number of Conventions here, with different signatories, which constitute distinct legal instruments. It is not at all surprising that one more of them should contain Articles of a more or less similar character; but one Convention is distinguished from another by being a self-contained legal instrument, and by its signatories."); *id.* at 283 ("Mr. FILIPPOV (Union of Soviet Socialist Republics): ... In the amendment submitted to us an allusion is made to Article 20 of the Wounded and Sick Convention. This reference seems to us inadmissible, as the Prisoners of War Convention is an entirely independent document and the allusions in its Articles to other Conventions, in particular the Wounded and Sick, might involve difficulties if the Parties to the conflict were not signatories to both Conventions.").

[152] *Refer to* § 7.3.2 (Persons Entitled to Protection as Wounded, Sick, or Shipwrecked Under the GWS and GWS-Sea).

[153] Jack L. Goldsmith III, Assistant Attorney General, *"Protected Person" Status in Occupied Iraq Under the Fourth Geneva Convention*, Mar. 18, 2004, 28 OPINIONS OF THE OFFICE OF LEGAL COUNSEL 35, 39 ("Finally, al Qaeda is not a 'Power[] in conflict' that can 'accept[] and appl[y]' GC4 within the meaning of article 2(3). *See, e.g.*, G.I.A.D. Draper, *The Red Cross Conventions* 16 (1958) (arguing that 'in the context of Article 2, para. 3, 'Powers' means States capable then and there of becoming Contracting Parties to these Conventions either by ratification or by accession'); 2B *Final Record of the Diplomatic Conference of Geneva of 1949*, at 108

In the 1949 Geneva Conventions, the *Detaining Power* refers to the State that holds the POW or internee.[154]

In the 1949 Geneva Conventions, the *Protecting Power* refers to a neutral State that helps implement the Conventions.[155]

19.16.1.2 Common Article 2 of the 1949 Geneva Conventions. Common Article 2 of the four 1949 Geneva Conventions declares that the provisions of each convention apply "to all cases of declared war or of any other armed conflict which may arise between two or more of the High Contracting Parties, even if the state of war is not recognized by one of them."[156] This language is used to help explain when the law of war applies.[157]

Common Article 2 also provides that each convention "shall also apply to all cases of partial or total occupation of the territory of a High Contracting Party, even if the said occupation meets with no armed resistance."[158] Common Article 2, thus, helps explain that the law of belligerent occupation is applicable, even if the occupying forces are not opposed by force.[159]

The 1954 Hague Cultural Property Convention repeats language used in Common Article 2, and the CCW incorporates language from Common Article 2 by reference.

19.16.1.3 Common Article 3 of the 1949 Geneva Conventions. Common Article 3 to the 1949 Geneva Conventions has been described as a "Convention in miniature" that addresses non-international armed conflict.[160] It was the first provision in a multilateral law of war treaty that addressed humane treatment during non-international armed conflict to gain widespread ratification by States.[161]

Although Common Article 3 only applies by its terms to non-international armed conflicts, Common Article 3 reflects a minimum yardstick of humane treatment protections that apply more broadly, including during international armed conflict.[162]

(explaining that article 2(3) would impose an 'obligation to recognize that the Convention be applied to the non-Contracting adverse *State*, in so far as the latter accepted and applied the provisions thereof') (emphasis added) ('*Final Record*'); *supra* note 4, at 23 (using 'non-Contracting State' interchangeably with 'non-Contracting Power' and 'non-Contracting Party').").

[154] *Refer to* § 9.1.2.1 (GPW – Notes on Terminology); § 10.1.1.1 (GC – Notes on Terminology).

[155] *Refer to* § 18.15.1.1 (Protecting Power Under the 1949 Geneva Conventions).

[156] GWS art. 2 ("In addition to the provisions which shall be implemented in peacetime, the present Convention shall apply to all cases of declared war or of any other armed conflict which may arise between two or more of the High Contracting Parties, even if the state of war is not recognized by one of them."); GWS-SEA art. 2 (same); GPW art. 2 (same); GC art. 2 (same).

[157] *Refer to* § 3.4 (When *Jus in Bello* Rules Apply).

[158] GWS art. 2 ("The Convention shall also apply to all cases of partial or total occupation of the territory of a High Contracting Party, even if the said occupation meets with no armed resistance."); GWS-SEA art. 2 (same); GPW art. 2 (same); GC art. 2 (same).

[159] *Refer to* § 11.2.2.3 ("Of the Hostile Army" – Belligerent Occupation Applies to Enemy Territory).

[160] GPW COMMENTARY 34 ("To borrow the phrase of one of the delegates, Article 3 is like a 'Convention in miniature'. It applies to non-international conflicts only, and will be the only Article applicable to them until such time as a special agreement between the Parties has brought into force between them all or part of the other provisions of the Convention.").

[161] *Refer to* § 17.2.1.1 (Treaties That Have Provisions That Explicitly Apply to NIAC).

[162] *Refer to* § 8.1.4.1 (Common Article 3 of the 1949 Geneva Conventions).

19.16.1.4 *POW Status and the 1949 Geneva Conventions*. Article 4 of the GPW explains which persons are entitled to receive POW status under the GPW.[163] This provision is mirrored in the GWS and GWS-Sea, as those conventions are intended to protect persons who are entitled to POW status under the GPW.[164]

The GC excludes from its protection those persons who are entitled to POW status under the GPW.[165]

19.16.1.5 *Retained Personnel and the 1949 Geneva Conventions*. Retained personnel are addressed by both the GPW and the GWS.[166]

19.16.2 GWS. The GWS is often called the first Geneva Convention.[167] The GWS addresses the following subjects on land: (1) the protection of the wounded, sick, and dead; (2) the rights, duties, and liabilities of military medical and religious personnel; and (3) the protection of military medical units, facilities, and transports.[168]

19.16.2.1 *Relationship Between the GWS and Earlier Conventions*. The GWS replaces the Conventions of August 22, 1864, July 6, 1906, and July 27, 1929, in relations between the Parties to the GWS.[169]

19.16.3 GWS-Sea. The GWS-Sea is often called the second Geneva Convention.[170] The GWS-Sea addresses the following subjects at sea: (1) the protection of the wounded, sick, shipwrecked, and dead; (2) the rights, duties, and liabilities of military medical and religious personnel; and (3) the protection of military medical units, facilities, and transports.[171]

19.16.3.1 *Relationship Between the 1907 Hague X and the GWS-Sea*. The GWS-Sea replaces the Hague X in relations between the Parties to the GWS-Sea.[172]

19.16.4 GPW. The GPW is often called the third Geneva Convention.[173] The GPW addresses the protection of POWs.[174]

19.16.4.1 *Relationship Between the GPW and the 1929 GPW*. The GPW replaces the 1929 GPW in relations between the Parties to the GPW.[175]

---

[163] *Refer to* § 9.3.2 (Persons Entitled to POW Status).

[164] *Refer to* § 7.3.2 (Persons Entitled to Protection as Wounded, Sick, or Shipwrecked Under the GWS and GWS-Sea).

[165] *Refer to* § 10.3.2.3 (Not Protected by the GWS, GWS-Sea, or the GPW).

[166] *Refer to* § 7.9.1.2 (Medical and Religious Personnel Who May Be Retained).

[167] Geneva Convention for the Amelioration of the Condition of the Wounded and Sick in Armed Forces in the Field of August 12, 1949, 75 UNTS 31.

[168] *Refer to* § 7.1.1 (Interpretation and Application of Provisions Relating to Medical Issues in the GWS, GWS-Sea, GPW, and GC).

[169] GWS art. 59 ("The present Convention replaces the Conventions of 22 August 1864, 6 July 1906, and 27 July 1929, in relations between the High Contracting Parties.").

[170] Geneva Convention for the Amelioration of the Condition of Wounded, Sick and Shipwrecked Members of Armed Forces at Sea of August 12, 1949, 75 UNTS 85.

[171] *Refer to* § 7.1.1 (Interpretation and Application of Provisions Relating to Medical Issues in the GWS, GWS-Sea, GPW, and GC).

[172] GWS-SEA art. 58 ("The present Convention replaces the Xth Hague Convention of October 18, 1907, for the adaptation to Maritime Warfare of the principles of the Geneva Convention of 1906, in relations between the High Contracting Parties.").

[173] Geneva Convention Relative to the Treatment of Prisoners of War of August 12, 1949, 75 UNTS 135.

[174] *Refer to* § 9.1.2 (Interpretation and Application of the GPW).

[175] GPW art. 134 ("The present Convention replaces the Convention of July 27, 1929, in relations between the High Contracting Parties.").

19.16.4.2 *Relationship Between the GPW and the 1899 Hague II or 1907 Hague IV*. In the relations between States that are bound by the 1899 Hague II or the 1907 Hague IV, and that are Parties to the GPW, the GPW shall be complementary to Chapter II of the Regulations annexed to the 1899 Hague II or the 1907 Hague IV.[176]

19.16.5 GC. The GC is often called the fourth Geneva Convention.[177] The GC addresses the protection of civilians in the hands of a party a conflict, including civilian internees.[178] The GC also addresses belligerent occupation.

19.16.5.1 *Application of Different Parts of the GC*. Different parts of the GC apply to different situations.

In general, the GC uses the concept of protected person to define the individuals who are entitled to receive its protections.[179] The provisions of Part II of the GC (articles 13-26) are wider in application; they do not only apply to those persons who are protected persons under the GC.[180] These provisions cover the whole of the populations of the countries in conflict.[181]

Section I (articles 27-34) of Part III of the GC includes provisions that are common to the home territories of the parties to the conflict and to occupied territories.

Section II (articles 35-46) of Part III of the GC addresses aliens in the home territory of a party to the conflict.

Section III (articles 47-78) of Part III of the GC addresses occupied territories.

Section IV (articles 79-135) of Part III of the GC provides regulations for the treatment of internees.

19.16.5.2 *Relationship Between the GC and the 1899 Hague II and the 1907 Hague IV Conventions*. In the relations between States that are bound by the 1899 Hague II, or the 1907 Hague IV, and that are Parties to the GC, the GC shall be supplementary to Sections II (Articles 22-41 – Hostilities) and III (Articles 42-56 – Military Authority Over the Territory of the Hostile State) of the Regulations annexed to the 1899 Hague II or the 1907 Hague IV.[182]

---

[176] GPW art. 135 ("In the relations between the Powers which are bound by the Hague Convention respecting the Laws and Customs of War on Land, whether that of July 29, 1899, or that of October 18, 1907, and which are parties to the present Convention, this last Convention shall be complementary to Chapter II of the Regulations annexed to the above-mentioned Conventions of the Hague.").

[177] Geneva Convention Relative to the Protection of Civilian Persons in Time of War of August 12, 1949, 75 UNTS 287.

[178] *Refer to* § 10.1.1 (Interpretation and Application of the GC).

[179] *Refer to* § 10.3 (Protected Person Status).

[180] *Refer to* § 10.3.3 (Categories of Nationals Specifically Excluded From the Definition of Protected Person Under the GC).

[181] GC art. 13 ("The provisions of Part II cover the whole of the populations of the countries in conflict, without any adverse distinction based, in particular, on race, nationality, religion or political opinion, and are intended to alleviate the sufferings caused by war.").

[182] GC art. 154 ("In the relations between the Powers who are bound by The Hague Conventions respecting the Laws and Customs of War on Land, whether that of July 29, 1899, or that of October 18, 1907, and who are parties to the present Convention, this last Convention shall be supplementary to Sections II and III of the Regulations annexed to the above mentioned Conventions of The Hague.").

19.17 1954 Hague Cultural Property Convention

The 1954 Hague Cultural Property Convention addresses the protection of cultural property during international armed conflict.[183] It addresses personnel who are engaged in duties related to the protection of cultural property.[184] It also has provisions that apply during occupation.[185] Some provisions of the 1954 Hague Cultural Property Convention apply to non-international armed conflict.[186]

The 1954 Hague Cultural Property Convention was adopted at a diplomatic conference on May 14, 1954.[187] The United States deposited its instrument of ratification to the Hague Cultural Property Convention on March 13, 2009, and stated four understandings.[188]

Two Protocols to the 1954 Hague Cultural Property Convention have been adopted.[189] The United States has neither signed nor ratified either one.

19.17.1 Relationship Between the 1954 Hague Cultural Property Convention and Earlier Treaties.

19.17.1.1 *Relationship Between the 1954 Hague Cultural Property Convention and Certain 1899 and 1907 Hague Conventions*. In the relations between States that are bound by the Conventions of The Hague concerning the Laws and Customs of War on Land (IV) (Hague IV) and Concerning Naval Bombardment in Time of War (Hague IX), whether those of July 29, 1899, or those of October 18, 1907, and that are Parties to the 1954 Hague Cultural Property Convention, the 1954 Hague Cultural Property Convention shall be supplementary to the Hague IX Convention and to the Regulations annexed to the Hague IV Convention.[190]

19.17.1.2 *Relationship Between the 1935 Roerich Pact and the 1954 Hague Cultural Property Convention*. In the relations between States that are bound by the 1935 Roerich Pact and that are Parties to the 1954 Hague Cultural Property Convention, the 1954 Hague Cultural Property Convention shall be supplementary to the Roerich Pact and shall substitute for the distinguishing flag described in Article III of the Roerich Pact the emblem

---

[183] *Refer to* § 5.18 (Protection of Cultural Property).

[184] *Refer to* § 4.14 (Personnel Engaged in Duties Related to the Protection of Cultural Property).

[185] *Refer to* § 11.19 (Protection of Cultural Property During Occupation).

[186] *Refer to* § 17.2.1.1 (Treaties That Have Provisions That Explicitly Apply to NIAC); § 17.11 (Protection of Cultural Property in NIAC).

[187] Convention for the Protection of Cultural Property in the Event of Armed Conflict, May 14, 1954, 249 UNTS 240.

[188] 2575 UNTS 7 ("Ratification (with declarations) **United States of America** *Deposit of instrument with the Director-General of the United Nations Educational, Scientific and Cultural Organization: 13 March 2009*").

[189] Protocol for the Protection of Cultural Property in the Event of Armed Conflict, May 14, 1954, 249 UNTS 358; Second Protocol to The Hague Convention of 1954 for the Protection of Cultural Property in the Event of Armed Conflict, Mar. 26, 1999, 2253 UNTS 172.

[190] 1954 Hague Cultural Property Convention art. 36(1) ("In the relations between Powers which are bound by the Conventions of The Hague concerning the Laws and Customs of War on Land (IV) and concerning Naval Bombardment in Time of War (IX), whether those of 29 July, 1899 or those of 18 October, 1907, and which are Parties to the present Convention, this last Convention shall be supplementary to the aforementioned Convention (IX) and to the Regulations annexed to the aforementioned Convention (IV) and shall substitute for the emblem described in Article 5 of the aforementioned Convention (IX) the emblem described in Article 16 of the present Convention, in cases in which the present Convention and the Regulations for its execution provide for the use of this distinctive emblem.").

defined in Article 16 of the 1954 Hague Cultural Property Convention—in cases in which the 1954 Hague Cultural Property Convention and the Regulations for its execution provide for the use of this distinctive emblem.[191]

19.18 Vienna Convention on the Law of Treaties

The Vienna Convention on the Law of Treaties (VCLT) was adopted on May 23, 1969, by the U.N. Conference on the Law of Treaties.

The United States signed the VCLT on April 24, 1970. President Nixon transmitted the VCLT to the Senate for its advice and consent to ratification on November 22, 1971.[192]

The United States is not a Party to the VCLT but has viewed many of its provisions as reflecting customary international law.

19.19 Biological Weapons Convention

After negotiations at the Conference of the Committee on Disarmament at Geneva and at the United Nations, the Biological Weapons Convention was opened for signature on April 10, 1972.[193]

The United States deposited its instrument of ratification on March 26, 1975.[194]

The Biological Weapons Convention followed the 1925 Geneva Gas and Bacteriological Protocol.[195]

In implementation of the Biological Weapons Convention, Congress enacted legislation prohibiting development, production, transfer, acquisition, or possession of a biological agent, toxin, or delivery system for use as a weapon.[196]

---

[191] 1954 Hague Cultural Property Convention art. 36(2) ("In the relations between Powers which are bound by the Washington Pact of l 5 April 1935 for the Protection of Artistic and Scientific Institutions and of Historic Monuments (Roerich Pact) and which are Parties to the present Convention, the latter Convention shall be supplementary to the Roerich Pact and shall substitute for the distinguishing flag described in Article III of the Pact the emblem defined in Article 16 of the present Convention, in cases in which the present Convention and the Regulations for its execution provide for the use of this distinctive emblem.").

[192] Richard Nixon, *Letter of Transmittal*, Nov. 22, 1971, Message from the President Transmitting the VCLT III.

[193] Convention on the Prohibition of the Development, Production and Stockpiling of Bacteriological (Biological) and Toxin Weapons and on Their Destruction, 1015 UNTS 164.

[194] 1015 UNTS 165.

[195] *Refer to* § 19.12 (1925 Geneva Gas and Bacteriological Protocol).

[196] 18 U.S.C. § 175 ("Prohibitions with respect to biological weapons. (a) In general. -- Whoever knowingly develops, produces, stockpiles, transfers, acquires, retains, or possesses any biological agent, toxin, or delivery system for use as a weapon, or knowingly assists a foreign state or any organization to do so, or attempts, threatens, or conspires to do the same, shall be fined under this title or imprisoned for life or any term of years, or both. There is extraterritorial Federal jurisdiction over an offense under this section committed by or against a national of the United States. (b) Additional offense. -- Whoever knowingly possesses any biological agent, toxin, or delivery system of a type or in a quantity that, under the circumstances, is not reasonably justified by a prophylactic, protective, bona fide research, or other peaceful purpose, shall be fined under this title, imprisoned not more than 10 years, or both. In this subsection, the terms 'biological agent' and 'toxin' do not encompass any biological agent or toxin that is in its naturally occurring environment, if the biological agent or toxin has not been cultivated, collected, or otherwise extracted from its natural source. (c) Definition. -- For purposes of this section, the term 'for use as a weapon' includes the development, production, transfer, acquisition, retention, or possession of any biological agent, toxin, or delivery system for other than prophylactic, protective, bona fide research, or other peaceful purposes.").

19.20 1977 ADDITIONAL PROTOCOLS TO THE 1949 GENEVA CONVENTIONS

A diplomatic conference between 1974 and 1977 negotiated two protocols to the 1949 Geneva Conventions that addressed international armed conflict (AP I) and non-international armed conflict (AP II).

Because these treaties were negotiated at the same time, they may provide information on States' views on differences between the rules applicable in international armed conflict and the rules applicable in non-international armed conflict.[197]

19.20.1 AP I. Protocol (I) Additional to the Geneva Conventions, and Relating to the Protection of Victims of International Armed Conflicts (AP I) contains rules on the conduct of hostilities during international armed conflict that are intended to supplement the 1949 Geneva Conventions.[198] For example, AP I provides additional protections for the wounded and sick, and provides for the establishment of an international humanitarian fact-finding commission.[199] AP I, however, does not apply to the use of nuclear weapons.[200]

The United States signed AP I and stated two understandings.[201] As explained below, AP I is a significant law of war treaty that the United States has decided not to ratify.

On January 28, 1987, President Reagan informed the Senate that AP I would not be submitted for the Senate's advice and consent to ratification because it is "fundamentally and irreconcilably flawed."[202] However, President Reagan noted that the United States would support "the positive provisions of Protocol I that could be of real humanitarian benefit if generally observed by parties to international armed conflicts."[203]

This manual references AP I provisions, some of which are consistent with DoD practice. Unless explicitly noted, no determinations are made about whether any of these AP I provisions reflect customary international law.

19.20.1.1 Examples of AP I Provisions Incorporated Into Other Treaties That the

---

[197] *Refer to* § 17.2.2.2 (Considered Absence of a Restriction in NIAC).

[198] Protocol (I) Additional to the Geneva Conventions of August 12, 1949, and Relating to the Protection of Victims of International Armed Conflicts of June 8, 1977.

[199] *Refer to* § 7.20 (AP I Provisions on the Wounded, Sick, and Shipwrecked); § 18.14.1.1 (AP I – International Humanitarian Fact-Finding Commission (IHFFC)).

[200] *Refer to* § 6.18.3 (AP I Provisions and Nuclear Weapons).

[201] United States, *Statement on Signature of AP I*, 1125 UNTS 404, 434 ("1. It is the understanding of the United States of America that the rules established by this Protocol were not intended to have any effect on and do not regulate or prohibit the use of nuclear weapons. 2. It is the understanding of the United States of America that the phrase 'military deployment preceding the launching of an attack' in Article 44, paragraph 3, means any movement towards a place from which an attack is to be launched.").

[202] Ronald Reagan, *Letter of Transmittal*, Jan. 29, 1987, MESSAGE FROM THE PRESIDENT TRANSMITTING AP II III-IV ("Like all other efforts associated with the International Committee of the Red Cross, this agreement has certain meritorious elements. But Protocol I is fundamentally and irreconcilably flawed. It contains provisions that would undermine humanitarian law and endanger civilians in war. ... These problems are so fundamental in character that they cannot be remedied through reservations, and I therefore have decided not to submit the Protocol to the Senate in any form, and I would invite an expression of the sense of the Senate that it shares this view. Finally, the Joint Chiefs of Staff have also concluded that a number of the provisions of the Protocol are militarily unacceptable.").

[203] Ronald Reagan, *Letter of Transmittal*, Jan. 29, 1987, MESSAGE FROM THE PRESIDENT TRANSMITTING AP II IV ("In this case, for example, we can reject Protocol I as a reference for humanitarian law, and at the same time devise an alternative reference for the positive provisions of Protocol I that could be of real humanitarian benefit if generally observed by parties to international armed conflicts. We are therefore in the process of consulting with our allies to develop appropriate methods for incorporating these positive provisions into the rules that govern our military operations, and as customary international law.").

United States Has Accepted. Some AP I provisions have been incorporated into later treaties to which the United States is a Party. For example, AP I's definition of military objective in Article 51(2) is substantially similar to the definition in Article 2(6) of CCW Amended Mines Protocol and Article 1(3) of CCW Protocol III on Incendiary Weapons.[204] Similarly, requirements under the Child Soldiers Protocol and U.S. law are comparable to AP I's requirements with respect to child soldiers.[205]

19.20.1.2 Examples of AP I Provisions That Are Consistent With Longstanding U.S. Practice. Certain provisions of AP I may not reflect customary international law, but may be consistent with longstanding U.S. practice. For example, AP I requires that Parties to AP I ensure that legal advisers are available to advise military commanders, and the United States has long employed legal advisers in this role.[206] Similarly, AP I requires that Parties to AP I undertake a legal review of, *inter alia*, new weapons, and the DoD policy and practice of conducting weapons reviews preceded this provision of AP I.[207]

19.20.1.3 Examples of AP I Provisions That the United States Has Supported. The United States has expressed support for certain AP I provisions. For example, United States has supported and sought to promote as a matter of national policy fundamental guarantees for the treatment of persons detained during international armed conflict that are reflected in Article 75 of AP I.[208]

19.20.1.4 Examples of AP I Provisions Based on a Principle That the U.S. Supports, Even Though the Provision Is Not Necessarily Customary International Law Nor Militarily Acceptable in All Respects. In some cases, the United States has supported a principle underlying an AP I provision, but the provision may not be customary international law or militarily acceptable in all respects. For example, the United States has supported the principle recognized in AP I that journalism is generally to be regarded as a civilian activity.[209]

Even where the United States has expressed support for an underlying customary principle that AP I provisions are based upon, the United States may disagree that the language of the provision reflects customary international law. For example, with regard to "direct participation in hostilities," the United States has supported the customary principle underlying Article 51(3) of AP I, but has disagreed that the language of that provision reflects customary international law.[210] Similarly, the intricacy of the provisions of AP I on objects indispensable to the survival of the civilian population make it doubtful that such provisions could be characterized as customary international law, although the United States has supported the principle that the starvation of civilians not be used as a method of warfare.[211] In addition, although the United States has supported the principle that civilian civil defense organizations and their personnel be respected and protected as civilians, a number of military operational problems have been identified with respect to the system of protection for civil defense established by AP I.[212]

---

[204] *Refer to* § 5.6.3 (Objects That Are Military Objectives).

[205] *Refer to* § 4.20.5.1 (U.S. Offense of Recruiting or Using Child Soldiers).

[206] *Refer to* § 18.5 (Role of Judge Advocates and Legal Advisers).

[207] *Refer to* § 6.2.3 (AP I Requirement for Legal Review of a New Weapon, Means, or Method of Warfare).

[208] *Refer to* § 8.1.4.2 (Article 75 of AP I and Relevant AP II Provisions).

[209] *Refer to* § 4.24.1 (Status of Journalists – Generally Civilian).

[210] *Refer to* § 5.8.1.2 (AP I, Article 51(3) Provision on Direct Participation in Hostilities).

[211] *Refer to* § 5.20.4 (AP I Provision on Objects Indispensable to the Survival of the Civilian Population); § 5.20.1 (Starvation – Distinction).

[212] *Refer to* § 4.22 (AP I Provisions on Civil Defense Personnel).

19.20.1.5 <u>*Examples of AP I Provisions to Which the United States Has Objected*</u>. The United States has objected to certain provisions of AP I. For example, the United States has objected to AP I provisions on:

- national liberation movements;[213]
- mercenaries;[214]
- works and installations containing dangerous forces;[215]
- criteria for lawful combatant status;[216]
- the obligation of combatants to distinguish themselves;[217]
- environmental protection;[218]
- presumptions in favor of civilian status in conducting attacks;[219]
- prohibiting the use of enemy flags, insignia, or uniforms to shield, favor, protect, or impede military operations;[220] and
- reprisals.[221]

19.20.2 <u>AP II</u>. Protocol (II) Additional to the Geneva Conventions, and Relating to the Protection of Victims of Non-International Armed Conflict (AP II) addresses certain types of non-international armed conflicts.[222] AP II reaffirmed, elaborated upon, and supplemented the protections contained in Common Article 3 of the 1949 Geneva Conventions.[223]

19.20.2.1 <u>*The United States and AP II*</u>. The United States is not a Party to AP II.

The United States signed AP II and stated one understanding on December 12, 1977.[224] President Reagan transmitted AP II to the Senate for its advice and consent to ratification on January 29, 1987.[225]

After the Supreme Court's decision in *Hamdan v. Rumsfeld*, 548 U.S. 557 (2006), the Bush Administration moved AP II down on the Executive's treaty priority list, indicating that it did not seek Senate action on the treaty at that time, so that the Administration could study the

---

213 *Refer to* § 3.3.4 (AP I Provision on National Liberation Movements).

214 *Refer to* § 4.21.1 (Treaties on Mercenaries).

215 *Refer to* § 5.13.1 (AP I Provisions on Works and Installations Containing Dangerous Forces).

216 *Refer to* § 4.6.1.2 (AP I and the GPW 4A(2) Conditions).

217 *Refer to* § 5.4.8.2 (AP I Obligation for Combatants to Distinguish Themselves During Attacks or Military Operations Preparatory to an Attack).

218 *Refer to* § 6.10.3.1 (AP I Provisions on Environmental Protection).

219 *Refer to* § 5.4.3.2 (AP I Presumptions in Favor of Civilian Status in Conducting Attacks).

220 *Refer to* § 5.23.3 (AP I and the Use of Enemy Flags, Insignia, or Uniforms to Shield, Favor, Protect, or Impede Military Operations).

221 *Refer to* § 18.18.3.4 (AP I Provisions on Reprisals).

222 Protocol (II) Additional to the Geneva Conventions of August 12, 1949, and Relating to the Protection of Victims of Non-International Armed Conflicts of June 8, 1977.

223 *Refer to* § 19.16.1.3 (Common Article 3 of the 1949 Geneva Conventions).

224 United States, *Statement on Signature of AP II*, 1125 UNTS 699 ("It is the understanding of the United States of America that the terms used in Part III of this Protocol which are the same as the terms defined in Article 8 of Protocol I shall so far as relevant be construed in the same sense as those definitions.").

225 Ronald Reagan, *Letter of Transmittal*, Jan. 29, 1987, MESSAGE FROM THE PRESIDENT TRANSMITTING AP II III.

treaty in light of the decision. On March 7, 2011, after interagency review, the Obama Administration urged the Senate to act as soon as practicable on AP II.[226]

Although the United States is not a Party to AP II, reviews have concluded that the provisions of AP II are consistent with U.S. practice, and that any issues could be addressed with reservations, understandings, and declarations.[227]

19.20.2.2 *AP II's Requirements for Its Application*. By its terms, AP II does not apply to all armed conflicts not of an international character. Instead, according to its terms, AP II only applies to armed conflicts that are not covered by Article 1 of AP I and that take place in the territory of a Party to AP II between its armed forces and dissident armed forces or other organized armed groups, which, under responsible command, exercise such control over a part of its territory as to enable them to carry out sustained and concerted military operations and to implement AP II.[228]

This threshold limits the application of AP II to a subset of armed conflicts that would be covered by Common Article 3 of the 1949 Geneva Conventions. For example, AP II would only cover conflicts in which dissident armed forces or other organized armed groups are organized and disciplined like regular armed forces.[229] In addition, non-State armed groups must be in a position to implement AP II before it is deemed to apply to all parties to the conflict.[230]

---

[226] The White House, Office of the Press Secretary, *Fact Sheet: New Actions on Guantánamo and Detainee Policy*, Mar. 7, 2011 ("Additional Protocol II, which contains detailed humane treatment standards and fair trial guarantees that apply in the context of non-international armed conflicts, was originally submitted to the Senate for approval by President Reagan in 1987. The Administration urges the Senate to act as soon as practicable on this Protocol, to which 165 States are a party. An extensive interagency review concluded that United States military practice is already consistent with the Protocol's provisions.").

[227] George P. Shultz, *Letter of Submittal*, Dec. 13, 1986, MESSAGE FROM THE PRESIDENT TRANSMITTING AP II VIII ("With the above caveats, the obligations contained in Protocol II are no more than a restatement of the rules of conduct with which U.S. military forces would almost certainly comply as a matter of national policy, constitutional and legal protections, and common decency."); Hillary Rodham Clinton, Secretary of State and Robert Gates, Secretary of Defense, *Letter to Senators Kerry and Lugar*, Mar. 7, 2011 ("We have now completed a comprehensive interagency review of Protocol II, and, subject to reservations, understandings, and declarations that were submitted to the Senate in 1987, along with refinements and additions that we will submit, assess it to be consistent with current military practice and beneficial to our national security and foreign policy interests.").

[228] AP II art. 1(1) ("This Protocol, which develops and supplements Article 3 common to the Geneva Conventions of 12 August 1949 without modifying its existing conditions of application, shall apply to all armed conflicts which are not covered by Article 1 of the Protocol Additional to the Geneva Conventions of 12 August 1949, and relating to the Protection of Victims of International Armed Conflicts (Protocol I) and which take place in the territory of a High Contracting Party between its armed forces and dissident armed forces or other organized armed groups which, under responsible command, exercise such control over a part of its territory as to enable them to carry out sustained and concerted military operations and to implement this Protocol.").

[229] BOTHE, PARTSCH, & SOLF, NEW RULES 626 (AP II art. 1, ¶2.5) ("Regarding the concept of 'organized armed groups' the ICRC delivered the following statement during the negotiations in Working Group B of Committee I: The expression does not mean any armed band acting under a leader. Such armed groups must be structured and possess organs, and must therefore have a system for allocating authority and responsibility: they must also be subject to rules of internal discipline. Consequently the expression 'organized armed groups' does not imply any appreciable difference in degree of organization from that of regular armed forces.").

[230] ICRC AP COMMENTARY 1353 (¶4470) ("This is the fundamental criterion which justifies the other elements of the definition: being under responsible command and in control of a part of the territory concerned, the insurgents must be in a position to implement the Protocol. The threshold for application therefore seems fairly high. Yet, apart from the fact that it reflects the desire of the Diplomatic Conference, it must be admitted that this threshold has a degree of realism. The conditions laid down in this paragraph 1, as analysed above, correspond with actual circumstances in which the parties may reasonably be expected to apply the rules developed in the Protocol, since they have the minimum infrastructure required therefor.").

Although AP II specifies more strict requirements for its application, President Reagan, in submitting AP II to the Senate for its advice and consent to ratification, recommended that the United States take the position that it would apply AP II to all armed conflicts that would be covered by Common Article 3 of the 1949 Geneva Conventions.[231]

19.21 CCW, CCW AMENDED ARTICLE 1, AND CCW PROTOCOLS

19.21.1 CCW. The Convention on Certain Conventional Weapons (CCW) and Protocols I, II, and III were adopted at Geneva on October 10, 1980. Subsequent conferences adopted: (1) an amended Protocol II; (2) Protocols IV and V; and (3) an amendment to apply the CCW and Protocols I, II, III, and IV to non-international armed conflicts.

Protocols to the CCW are subject to ratification or other acceptance by a State before such protocols enter into force for that State. Additional protocols that have been adopted by a Conference of States Parties enter into force as provided in paragraphs 3 and 4 of Article 5 of the CCW.[232] Paragraphs 3 and 4 of Article 5 of the CCW provide, *inter alia*, that each of the CCW's Protocols may only enter into force for a State after that State has notified its consent to be bound by it.[233] Thus, a State's notification of its consent to be bound by a Protocol is a prerequisite to the Protocol's entry into force for that State.

Similarly, amendments to the CCW or its Protocols are subject to ratification or other acceptance by a State before such amendments enter into force for that State. Amendments to the CCW or its Protocols are adopted and enter into force in the same manner as the CCW and its Protocols.[234] As discussed above, a State must provide notification of its consent to be bound by a CCW Protocol before that Protocol's entry into force for that State. Similarly, the CCW is subject to ratification or other acceptance by States.[235] And, the CCW only enters into force for

---

[231] George P. Shultz, *Letter of Submittal*, Dec. 13, 1986, MESSAGE FROM THE PRESIDENT TRANSMITTING AP II VIII ("We are therefore recommending that U.S. ratification be subject to an understanding declaring that the United States will apply the Protocol to all conflicts covered by Article 3 common to the 1949 Conventions ... . This understanding will also have the effect of treating as non-international these so-called 'wars of national liberation' described in Article 1(4) of Protocol I which fail to meet the traditional test of an international conflict.").

[232] CCW art. 8(2)(b) (Additional protocols to the CCW adopted at a conference convened under Article 8(2) "shall enter into force as provided in paragraphs 3 and 4 of Article 5 of this Convention."); CCW art. 8(2)(b) (Additional protocols to the CCW adopted at a conference convened under Article 8(3) "shall enter into force as provided in paragraphs 3 and 4 of Article 5 of this Convention.").

[233] CCW art. 5 ("3. Each of the Protocols annexed to this Convention shall enter into force six months after the date by which twenty States have notified their consent to be bound by it in accordance with paragraph 3 or 4 of Article 4 of this Convention. 4. For any State which notifies its consent to be bound by a Protocol annexed to this Convention after the date by which twenty States have notified their consent to be bound by it, the Protocol shall enter into force six months after the date on which that State has notified its consent so to be bound."). *See also* CCW art. 4 ("3. Expressions of consent to be bound by any of the Protocols annexed to this Convention shall be optional for each State, provided that at the time of the deposit of its instrument of ratification, acceptance or approval of this Convention or of accession thereto, that State shall notify the Depositary of its consent to be bound by any two or more of these Protocols. 4. At any time after the deposit of its instrument of ratification, acceptance or approval of this Convention or of accession thereto, a State may notify the Depositary of its consent to be bound by any annexed Protocol by which it is not already bound.").

[234] CCW art. 8(1)(b) (Amendments to the CCW or its protocols adopted at a conference convened under Article 8(1) "shall be adopted and shall enter into force in the same manner as this Convention and the annexed Protocols, ..."); CCW art. 8(3)(a) (Amendments to the CCW or its protocols adopted at a conference convened under Article 8(3) "shall be adopted and enter into force in accordance with subparagraph 1 (b) above.")).

[235] CCW art. 4 ("1. This Convention is subject to ratification, acceptance or approval by the Signatories. Any State which has not signed this Convention may accede to it.").

a State after that State has deposited its instrument of ratification or other acceptance.[236] Thus, a State's acceptance of any amendment to the CCW or its Protocols is a prerequisite to that amendment's entry into force for that State.

The United States is a Party to the: (1) CCW; (2) CCW Protocol I; (3) CCW Amended Mines Protocol; (4) CCW Protocol III on Incendiary Weapons; (5) CCW Protocol IV on Blinding Laser Weapons; and (6) CCW Protocol V on Explosive Remnants of War. The United States deposited its instrument of ratification to the CCW and accepted Protocols I and II on March 25, 1995. The United States provided notification of its consent to be bound by the CCW Amended Mines Protocol on May 24, 1999. The United States deposited its instrument of ratification to the Amendment to Article 1 of the CCW, and provided notification of its consent to be bound by Protocols III, IV, and V, on January 21, 2009.

19.21.1.1 *CCW Amended Scope of Application*. For the United States, the CCW and its Protocols apply to non-international armed conflict.[237]

On December 21, 2001, Parties to the CCW adopted an amendment to Article 1 of the CCW that modified the application of the CCW and Protocols I, II, III, and IV to apply to non-international armed conflicts.[238] The CCW Amended Mines Protocol and CCW Protocol V on Explosive Remnants of War also apply to non-international armed conflicts.[239]

The amended scope of the CCW does not prejudice additional protocols to the CCW adopted after January 1, 2002, which may apply, exclude, or modify the scope of their application in relation to Article 1 of the CCW.[240]

The United States deposited its instrument of ratification to the amendment to Article 1 of the CCW on January 21, 2009.[241]

U.S. policy before the entry into force for the United States of the amendment to Article 1 of the CCW was to apply the CCW, Protocol I, Protocol II, and CCW Protocol IV on Blinding Laser Weapons to non-international armed conflict. At the time of the deposit of U.S. instruments of ratification of the CCW, CCW Protocol I, and CCW Protocol II, the United States declared its intent to apply the provisions of those instruments to all armed conflicts referred to in Articles 2 and 3 of the GPW, *i.e.*, both international and non-international armed conflicts.[242]

---

[236] *See* CCW art. 5 ("1. This Convention shall enter into force six months after the date of deposit of the twentieth instrument of ratification, acceptance, approval or accession. 2. For any State which deposits its instrument of ratification, acceptance, approval or accession after the date of the deposit of the twentieth instrument of ratification, acceptance, approval or accession, this Convention shall enter into force six months after the date on which that State has deposited its instrument of ratification, acceptance, approval or accession.").

[237] *Refer to* § 17.2.1.1 (Treaties That Have Provisions That Explicitly Apply to NIAC).

[238] *Amendment to the Convention on Prohibitions or Restrictions on the Use of Certain Conventional Weapons Which May be Deemed to be Excessively Injurious or to have Indiscriminate Effects – Overview*, 3, MESSAGE FROM THE PRESIDENT TRANSMITTING AP III, CCW AMENDED ARTICLE 1, AND CCW PROTOCOL V ON EXPLOSIVE REMNANTS OF WAR 9 ("By its terms, this paragraph means that the amended scope provision automatically applies to CCW Protocols I, II, III, and IV.").

[239] *Refer to* § 17.2.1.1 (Treaties That Have Provisions That Explicitly Apply to NIAC).

[240] CCW AMENDED art. 1 ("The provisions of paragraphs 2 to 6 of this Article shall not prejudice additional Protocols adopted after January 1, 2002, which may apply, exclude or modify the scope of their application in relation to this Article.").

[241] 2562 UNTS 39 (*RATIFICATION* **United States of America** *Deposit of instrument with the Secretary-General of the United Nations: 21 January 2009*).

[242] United States, *Statement on Ratification of the CCW, Accepting Protocols I & II*, Mar. 24, 1995, 1861 UNTS 482, 482-83 ("The United States declares, with reference to the scope of application defined in Article 1 of the Convention, that the United States will apply the provisions of the Convention, Protocol I, and Protocol II to all armed conflicts referred to in Articles 2 and 3 common to the Geneva Conventions for the Protection of War Victims of August 12, 1949.").

Similarly, before the United States ratified the amendment to Article 1 of the CCW, U.S. policy was to apply the CCW Protocol on Blinding Laser Weapons to all armed conflicts and in peacetime.[243]

19.21.1.2 U.S. Reservation to Article 7(4)(b) of the CCW. The United States took a reservation to Article 7(4)(b) of the CCW.[244]

Article 7(4) of the CCW provides:

> This Convention, and the annexed Protocols by which a High Contracting Party is bound, shall apply with respect to an armed conflict against that High Contracting Party of the type referred to in Article 1, paragraph 4, of Additional Protocol I to the Geneva Conventions of 12 August 1949 for the Protection of War Victims:
>
> ...
>
> (b) where the High Contracting Party is not a party to Additional Protocol I and an authority of the type referred to in subparagraph (a) above accepts and applies the obligations of the Geneva Conventions and of this Convention and the relevant annexed Protocols in relation to that conflict. Such an acceptance and application shall have in relation to that conflict the following effects:
>
> (i) the Geneva Conventions and this Convention and its relevant annexed Protocols are brought into force for the parties to the conflict with immediate effect;
>
> (ii) the said authority assumes the same rights and obligations as those which have been assumed by a High Contracting Party to the Geneva Conventions, this Convention and its relevant annexed Protocols; and
>
> (iii) the Geneva Conventions, this Convention and its relevant annexed Protocols are equally binding upon all parties to the conflict.
>
> The High Contracting Party and the authority may also agree to accept and apply the obligations of Additional Protocol I to the Geneva Conventions on a reciprocal basis.

The U.S. reservation to Article 7(4)(b) of the CCW is consistent with the longstanding objections of the United States to Article 1(4) of AP I regarding national liberation movements.[245]

19.21.1.3 CCW and Customary International Law. The restrictions and prohibitions in the CCW and its Protocols on weapons generally have not been based on the premise that such restrictions or prohibitions are warranted because the weapons at issue are calculated to cause superfluous injury or are inherently indiscriminate.[246] Rather, the CCW and Protocols have been drafted on the basis that they are largely new contractual rules, and not a

---

[243] *Article-by-Article Analysis of CCW Protocol IV on Blinding Laser Weapons*, 3-4, Enclosure C to Warren Christopher, *Letter of Submittal*, Dec. 7, 1996, MESSAGE FROM THE PRESIDENT TRANSMITTING THE CCW AMENDED MINES PROTOCOL, PROTOCOL III ON INCENDIARY WEAPONS, AND PROTOCOL IV ON BLINDING LASER WEAPONS 43-44 ("The United States favored an expanded scope of application for the Blinding Laser Weapons Protocol. As a matter of policy, the United States will refrain from the use of laser weapons prohibited by the Protocol. Therefore, while the Blinding Laser Weapons Protocol does not legally apply to all armed conflicts, it is U.S. policy to apply the Protocol to all such conflicts, however, they may be characterized, and in peacetime.").

[244] United States, *Statement on Ratification of the CCW, Accepting Protocols I & II*, Mar. 24, 1995, 1861 UNTS 482 ("(1) *Reservation*. Article 7 (4) (b) of the Convention shall not apply with respect to the United States.").

[245] *Refer to* § 3.3.4 (AP I Provision on National Liberation Movements).

[246] George Aldrich, Ambassador, Chairman of the Delegation, *Report of the United States Delegation to the United Nations Conference on Prohibitions or Restrictions of Use of Certain Conventional Weapons Which May be Deemed to be Excessively Injurious or to have Indiscriminate Effects, Second Session, Geneva, Switzerland,*

restatement of existing customary international law.[247]

19.21.2 CCW Protocol I. CCW Protocol I prohibits the use of weapons whose primary effect is to injure by fragments not detectable by X-rays.[248]

CCW Protocol I was adopted by the first CCW Conference in 1980. The United States accepted CCW Protocol I on March 24, 1995, when it deposited its instrument of ratification to the CCW.[249]

19.21.3 CCW Amended Mines Protocol. The CCW Amended Mines Protocol addresses landmines, booby-traps, and other devices.[250]

CCW Protocol II on Mines, Booby-traps and Other Devices was adopted by the first CCW Conference in 1980. The United States accepted CCW Protocol II on March 24, 1995, when it deposited its instrument of ratification to the CCW.[251]

CCW Protocol II was later substantially amended by the first Review Conference of CCW States Parties, which concluded its work on May 3, 1996. The CCW Amended Mines Protocol includes more detailed restrictions on the use of mines, booby-traps, and other devices, and prohibitions on specific types of such devices. The CCW Amended Mines Protocol also applies to non-international armed conflicts.[252] The CCW Amended Mines Protocol has provisions that are to be observed at all times, *e.g.*, provisions that are to be implemented in peace-time.[253]

Before the United States accepted the CCW Amended Mines Protocol, U.S. policy was to

---

September 15-October 10, 1980, 16 (Jan. 15, 1981) ("Finally, it is significant to note that the Conference ended with no finding that these restrictions and prohibitions were imposed because of any agreed belief or finding that they were in fact excessively injurious or had indiscriminate effects. Thus the adoption of this Convention in no way affects the legality, under the customary and conventional law of war, of past uses of these weapons in the modes to be restricted or prohibited. The restrictions and prohibitions contained in the Convention were recognized by the Conference as being primarily new contractual rules which would only bind parties in the future.").

247 United States, *Statement on Signature of the CCW*, Apr. 8, 1982, 1342 UNTS 255 ("As indicated in the negotiating record of the 1980 Conference, the prohibitions and restrictions contained in the Convention and its Protocols are of course new contractual rules (with the exception of certain provisions which restate existing international law) which will only bind States upon their ratification of, or accession to, the Convention and their consent to be bound by the Protocols in question.").

248 *Refer to* § 6.11 (Weapons Injuring by Fragments Not Detectable by X-Rays).

249 1861 UNTS 482 ("*Instrument deposited on:* 24 March 1995 UNITED STATES OF AMERICA (With effect from 24 September 1995. Accepting Protocols I and II.)").

250 *Refer to* § 6.12 (Landmines, Booby-Traps, and Other Devices).

251 1861 UNTS 482 ("*Instrument deposited on:* 24 March 1995 UNITED STATES OF AMERICA (With effect from 24 September 1995. Accepting Protocols I and II.)").

252 *Refer to* § 17.2.1.1 (Treaties That Have Provisions That Explicitly Apply to NIAC).

253 *Article-by-Article Analysis of CCW Amended Mines Protocol,* 3-4, Enclosure A to Warren Christopher, *Letter of Submittal*, Dec. 7, 1996, MESSAGE FROM THE PRESIDENT TRANSMITTING THE CCW AMENDED MINES PROTOCOL, PROTOCOL III ON INCENDIARY WEAPONS, AND PROTOCOL IV ON BLINDING LASER WEAPONS 3-4 ("Finally, it was understood that certain provisions of the amended Protocol must be observed at all times. A statement to this effect was made part of the negotiating record by the delegation of Belgium, speaking on behalf of 24 other delegations, including the U.S. delegation, at the final plenary session of the Review Conference and was not contested by any other delegation. This conclusion is supported, as well, by the scope of the Convention itself which makes clear that it and its annexed Protocols shall apply in situations referred to in Article 2 common to the Geneva Conventions of 12 August 1949. Common Article 2 refers specifically to provisions which shall be implemented in peace-time, a recognition that certain provisions must be observed at all times if they are to be implemented in good faith. Among the provisions of the amended Protocol that must be so observed are: the provisions regarding the recording, marking, monitoring and protection of areas containing mines; provisions of Article 8 regarding transfers; and provisions of Articles 13 and 14 regarding consultations and compliance. A statement to this effect was made part of the negotiating record by the U.S. Delegation, and was not contested by any other delegation.").

observe the requirements of the CCW Amended Mines Protocol to the fullest extent possible.[254]

The CCW Amended Mines Protocol entered into force on December 3, 1998.[255] The United States provided notification of its consent to be bound by the CCW Amended Mines Protocol with declarations and a reservation on May 24, 1999.[256]

19.21.4 CCW Protocol III on Incendiary Weapons. CCW Protocol III on Incendiary Weapons places certain restrictions on the use of incendiary weapons.[257]

CCW Protocol III on Incendiary Weapons was adopted by the first CCW Conference in 1980. The United States provided notification of its consent to be bound by CCW Protocol III on Incendiary Weapons on January 21, 2009, with a reservation and an understanding.[258]

19.21.5 CCW Protocol IV on Blinding Laser Weapons. CCW Protocol IV on Blinding Laser Weapons prohibits the use of blinding laser weapons and requires that feasible precautions be taken in the employment of laser systems to avoid causing permanent blindness.[259]

States Parties to the CCW adopted CCW Protocol IV on Blinding Laser Weapons at the first Review Conference of CCW States Parties, which concluded its work on May 3, 1996.[260] This Protocol was consistent with DoD policy on blinding lasers before the Protocol was adopted.[261]

---

[254] Review Conference of the States Parties to the Convention on Prohibitions or Restrictions on the Use of Certain Conventional Weapons Which May be Deemed to be Excessively Injurious or to Have Indiscriminate Effects, *Summary Record of the 14th Meeting (Second Part),* Second resumed session, Geneva, Apr. 22 – May 3, 1996, CCW/CONF.I/SR.14/Add.1, May 9, 1996, ¶¶6-8 ("Mr. MATHESON (United States of America) said that the revised Protocol II on land-mines was a significant advance that would, if widely observed, result in a substantial decrease in civilian casualties and be an important first step towards the elimination of such mines. … While such a commitment did not legally bind the United States or prejudice the Senate's consideration of the amended Protocol, it was his country's policy, pending the entry into force of the Protocol, to observe all of its restrictions to the fullest extent possible from the time of adoption.").

[255] 2048 UNTS 93 ("**Entry into force:** 3 December 1998, in accordance with article 2 of the Protocol").

[256] 2065 UNTS 128 ("*CONSENT TO BE BOUND (WITH DECLARATIONS AND RESERVATION)* **United States of America** *Notification effected with the Secretary-General of the United Nations: 24 May 1999*").

[257] *Refer to* § 6.14 (Incendiary Weapons).

[258] United States, *Statement on Consent to Be Bound by CCW Protocol III on Incendiary Weapons*, Jan. 21, 2009, 2562 UNTS 36, 37 ("It is the understanding of the United States of America that any decision by any military commander, military personnel, or any other person responsible for planning, authorizing or executing military action shall only be judged on the basis of that person's assessment of the information reasonably available to the person at the time the person planned, authorized, or executed the action under review, and shall not be judged on the basis of information that comes to light after the action under review was taken."). *Refer to* § 6.14.3.2 (U.S. Reservation to CCW Protocol III on Incendiary Weapons).

[259] *Refer to* § 6.15 (Laser Weapons).

[260] Additional Protocol to the Convention on Prohibitions or Restrictions on the Use of Certain Conventional Weapons which may be deemed to be Excessively Injurious or to have Indiscriminate Effects (Protocol IV, entitled Protocol on Blinding Laser Weapons), Oct. 13, 1995, 2024 UNTS 163.

[261] William J. Perry, Secretary of Defense, *DOD Policy on Blinding Lasers*, Jan. 17, 1997 (amending policy statement of Aug. 29, 1995) ("The Department of Defense prohibits the use of lasers specifically designed to cause permanent blindness and supports negotiations to prohibit the use of such weapons. However, laser systems are absolutely vital to our modern military. Among other things, they are currently used for detection, targeting, range-finding, communications and target destruction. They provide a critical technological edge to U.S. forces and allow our forces to fight, win and survive on an increasingly lethal battlefield. In addition, lasers provide significant humanitarian benefits. They allow weapon systems to be increasingly discriminate, thereby reducing collateral damage to civilian lives and property. The Department of Defense recognizes that accidental or incidental eye injuries may occur on the battlefield as the result of the use of lasers not specifically designed to cause permanent blindness. Therefore, we continue to strive, through training and doctrine, to minimize these injuries.").

The United States provided notification of its consent to be bound by CCW Protocol IV on Blinding Laser Weapons on January 21, 2009, with an understanding.[262]

U.S. legal reviews before CCW Protocol IV was adopted concluded that the use of a laser for the purpose of blinding an enemy combatant would not constitute unnecessary suffering under the law of war.[263] Similarly, the restrictions in CCW Protocol IV on Blinding Laser Weapons may be characterized as arms control obligations in that these restrictions do not establish that the use of lasers as anti-personnel weapons, including for the purpose of blinding, is prohibited by the rule against weapons calculated to cause unnecessary suffering nor otherwise prohibited by the customary law of war.[264]

19.21.6 CCW Protocol V on Explosive Remnants of War. CCW Protocol V on Explosive Remnants of War addresses explosive ordnance and explosive remnants of war.[265] CCW Protocol V on Explosive Remnants of War contains no restrictions or prohibitions on the use of these weapons; rather, it addresses what must be done with respect to unexploded munitions that threaten civilians and post-conflict reconstruction.[266] CCW Protocol V on Explosive Remnants of War addresses primarily the steps to be taken before or after hostilities, not during them, and it includes a Technical Annex of suggested best practices for greater munitions reliability.[267]

---

262 United States, *Statement on Consent to Be Bound to CCW Protocol IV on Blinding Laser Weapons*, Jan. 21, 2009, 2562 UNTS 38 ("It is the understanding of the United States of America with respect to Article 2 that any decision by any military commander, military personnel, or any other person responsible for planning, authorizing or executing military action shall only be judged on the basis of that person's assessment of the information reasonably available to the person at the time the person planned, authorized or executed the action under review, and shall not be judged on the basis of information that comes to light after the action under review was taken.").

263 Major General Hugh R. Overholt, The Judge Advocate General, Army, *Memorandum of Law: Use of Lasers as Antipersonnel Weapons*, ¶7, Sept. 29, 1988, *reprinted in* THE ARMY LAWYER 3, 4 (Nov. 1988) ("The fundamental issue with which this review is concerned is whether the use of a laser for the purpose of blinding an enemy soldier would constitute unnecessary suffering. The conclusion is that it would not.").

264 W. Hays Parks, Special Assistant to The Judge Advocate General of the Army for Law of War Matters, *Memorandum of Law: Travaux Preparatoires and Legal Analysis of Blinding Laser Weapons Protocol*, *reprinted in* THE ARMY LAWYER 33, 36 (Jun. 1997) ("As the delegate from Sweden observed in the fourth and final meeting of the Laser Working Group on 6 October 1995, Protocol IV is a unique step in combining law of war and arms control mechanisms. The first sentence of Article 1 follows arms control lines by creating a national obligation to forego the use on the battlefield of a laser weapon of the type described in the balance of the sentence, rather than establishing that an antipersonnel laser weapon is inconsistent with the law of war prohibition on unnecessary suffering. … Neither the prohibition in Article 1 nor anything else in Protocol IV establishes, nor was it intended to establish, that an individual, intentional act of blinding by a laser constitutes unnecessary suffering or is otherwise a violation of the law of war, for several reasons.").

265 *Refer to* § 6.19 (Explosive Ordnance); § 6.20 (Explosive Remnants of War).

266 *Overview and Article by Article Analysis of CCW Protocol V on Explosive Remnants of War* 1-2, MESSAGE FROM THE PRESIDENT TRANSMITTING AP III, CCW AMENDED ARTICLE 1, AND CCW PROTOCOL V ON EXPLOSIVE REMNANTS OF WAR 11-12 ("Protocol V is the first international agreement specifically aimed at reducing the humanitarian threat posed by unexploded and abandoned munitions of all types remaining on the battlefield after the end of armed conflicts. Protocol V contains no restrictions or prohibitions on the use of these weapons; rather, it addresses what must be done with respect to unexploded munitions that threaten civilians and post-conflict reconstruction.").

267 *Overview and Article-by-Article Analysis of CCW Protocol V on Explosive Remnants of War* 1-2, MESSAGE FROM THE PRESIDENT TRANSMITTING AP III, CCW AMENDED ARTICLE 1, AND CCW PROTOCOL V ON EXPLOSIVE REMNANTS OF WAR 11-12 ("The Protocol deals primarily with steps to be taken before or after hostilities, not during them. Protocol V also includes a Technical Annex of suggested best practices that states Parties to the Protocol are encouraged to follow on a voluntary basis in order to achieve greater munitions reliability.").

CCW Protocol V on Explosive Remnants of War was adopted on November 28, 2003.[268]

The United States provided notification of its consent to be bound by CCW Protocol V on Explosive Remnants of War on January 21, 2009.[269] The United States expressed its understanding relating to future arrangements in connection with the settlement of armed conflicts.[270]

19.22 Chemical Weapons Convention

The Chemical Weapons Convention creates extensive obligations for States with respect to the use and possession of chemical weapons.[271]

Article 22 of the Chemical Weapons Convention prohibits reservations to the Convention and prohibits reservations to the Convention's Annexes incompatible with its object and purpose.[272]

During the negotiation of the Chemical Weapons Convention, President George H.W. Bush on May 13, 1991, announced that the United States was formally forswearing the use of chemical weapons for any reason, including retaliation, against any State, effective when the Convention entered into force.[273]

The United States signed the Chemical Weapons Convention on January 13, 1993, and President Clinton submitted it to the Senate for its advice and consent to ratification on November 23, 1993.[274] In transmitting the Chemical Weapons Convention to the Senate for its advice and consent to ratification, President Clinton notified the Senate that the administration was reviewing the effect of the Convention's prohibition on the use of riot control agents as a method of warfare on Executive Order No. 11850, which specified the current policy of the United States with regard to the use of riot control agents in war, and would submit the results of that review separately to the Senate.[275] The review concluded that under then-current interpretations of the Chemical Weapons Convention, certain uses of riot control agents authorized under Executive Order 11850 would no longer be permissible and that a new

---

[268] Protocol on Explosive Remnants of War to the Convention on Prohibitions or Restrictions on the Use of Certain Conventional Weapons which may be deemed to be Excessively Injurious or to have Indiscriminate Effects (Protocol V), Nov. 28, 2003, 2399 UNTS 100-177.

[269] 2562 UNTS 39, 40 ("*Receipt of notification by the Secretary-General of the United Nations: 21 January 2009*").

[270] *Refer to* § 6.20.5 (Obligations Under the CCW Protocol V on Explosive Remnants of War That Are Triggered by the Cessation of Active Hostilities).

[271] *Refer to* § 6.8.3 (Chemical Weapons).

[272] Chemical Weapons Convention art. 22 ("The Articles of this Convention shall not be subject to reservations. The Annexes of this Convention shall not be subject to reservations incompatible with its object and purpose.").

[273] George H. W. Bush, *Statement on Chemical Weapons,* May 13, 1991, 1991-I Public Papers of the Presidents 503 ("To demonstrate the United States commitment to banning chemical weapons, we are formally forswearing the use of chemical weapons for any reason, including retaliation, against any state, effective when the convention enters into force, and will propose that all states follow suit.").

[274] William J. Clinton, *Letter of Transmittal*, Nov. 23, 1993, Message from the President Transmitting the Chemical Weapons Convention iii ("The Convention was opened for signature and was signed by the United States at Paris on January 13, 1993.").

[275] William J. Clinton, *Letter of Transmittal*, Nov. 23, 1993, Message from the President Transmitting the Chemical Weapons Convention v ("The Administration is reviewing the impact of the Convention's prohibition on the use of riot control agents as a method of warfare on Executive Order No. 11850, which specifies the current policy of the United States with regard to the use of riot control agents in war. The results of the review will be submitted separately to the Senate.").

Executive Order on riot control agents would be issued.[276] The Senate, as a condition of its advice and consent to ratification, required that the President certify to Congress that the United States is not restricted by the Chemical Weapons Convention in its use of riot control agents in certain cases and that Executive Order 11850 would not be modified.[277] President Clinton provided this certification on April 25, 1997.[278]

The United States ratified the Chemical Weapons Convention on April 25, 1997, with one condition that relates to the Annex on Implementation and Verification.[279] The treaty requires that sixty-five nations become Party to it before it enters into force, which occurred on April 29, 1997.[280]

---

[276] William J. Clinton, *Message to the Senate on the Impact of the Chemical Weapons Convention on the Use of Riot Control Agents*, Jun. 23, 1994, 1994-I PUBLIC PAPERS OF THE PRESIDENTS 1127, 1128 ("—The CWC does prohibit the use of RCAs solely against combatants. In addition, according to the current international understanding, the CWC's prohibition on the use of RCAs as a 'method of warfare' also precludes the use of RCAs even for humanitarian purposes in situations where combatants and noncombatants are intermingled, such as the rescue of downed air crews, passengers, and escaping prisoners and situations where civilians are being used to mask or screen attacks. However, were the international understanding of this issue to change, the United States would not consider itself bound by this position. Upon receiving the advice and consent of the Senate to ratification of the Chemical Weapons Convention, a new Executive order outlining U.S. policy on the use of RCAs under the Convention will be issued.").

[277] Senate, *Conditions to Ratification of the Chemical Weapons Convention*, Senate Resolution 75, 105th Congress, 143 CONGRESSIONAL RECORD S3651, S3657 (1997) ("(26) Riot control agents: (A) Permitted uses. — Prior to the deposit of the United States instrument of ratification, the President shall certify to Congress that the United States is not restricted by the Convention in its use of riot control agents, including the use against combatants who are parties to a conflict, in any of the following cases: (i) UNITED STATES NOT A PARTY. — The conduct of peacetime military operations within an area of ongoing armed conflict when the United States is not a party to the conflict (such as recent use of the United States Armed Forces in Somalia, Bosnia, and Rwanda). (ii) CONSENSUAL PEACEKEEPING. — Consensual peacekeeping operations when the use of force is authorized by the receiving state, including operations pursuant to Chapter VI of the United Nations Charter. (iii) CHAPTER VII PEACEKEEPING. — Peacekeeping operations when force is authorized by the Security Council under Chapter VII of the United Nations Charter. (B) Implementation. — The President shall take no measure, and prescribe no rule or regulation, which would alter or eliminate Executive Order 11850 of April 8, 1975. (C) Definition. — In this paragraph, the term 'riot control agent' has the meaning given the term in Article II(7) of the Convention.").

[278] William J. Clinton, *Message to the Congress on the Chemical Weapons Convention*, Apr. 25, 1997, 1997-I PUBLIC PAPERS OF THE PRESIDENTS 495, 495-97 ("In accordance with the resolution of advice and consent to ratification of the Convention on the Prohibition of the Development, Production, Stockpiling and Use of Chemical Weapons and on Their Destruction, adopted by the Senate of the United States on April 24, 1997, I hereby certify that: ... In connection with Condition (26), Riot Control Agents, the United States is not restricted by the Convention in its use of riot control agents, including the use against combatants who are parties to a conflict, in any of the following cases: (i) the conduct of peacetime military operations within an area of ongoing armed conflict when the United States is not a party to the conflict (such as recent use of the United States Armed Forces in Somalia, Bosnia, and Rwanda); (ii) consensual peacekeeping operations when the use of force is authorized by the receiving state, including operations pursuant to Chapter VI of the United Nations Charter; and (iii) peacekeeping operations when force is authorized by the Security Council under Chapter VII of the United Nations Charter. ... In accordance with Condition (26) on Riot Control Agents, I have certified that the United States is not restricted by the Convention in its use of riot control agents in various peacetime and peacekeeping operations. These are situations in which the United States is not engaged in a use of force of a scope, duration and intensity that would trigger the laws of war with respect to U.S. forces.").

[279] United States, *Declaration Made on Ratification of the Chemical Weapons Convention*, Apr. 29, 1997, 1975 UNTS 475 ("Subject to the condition which relates to the Annex on Implementation and Verification, that no sample collected in the United States pursuant to the Convention will be transferred for analysis to any laboratory outside the territory of the United States.").

[280] Convention on the Prohibition of the Development, Production, Stockpiling and Use of Chemical Weapons and on Their Destruction, Jan. 13, 1993, 1974 UNTS 317 footnote 1 ("Came into force on 29 April 1997, in accordance with article XXI:"). *See also* CHEMICAL WEAPONS CONVENTION art. 21 ("This Convention shall enter into force 180 days after the date of the deposit of the 65th instrument of ratification, but in no case earlier than two years after its opening for signature.").

In implementation of the Chemical Weapons Convention, Congress enacted laws prohibiting, *inter alia*, development, production, acquisition, transfer directly or indirectly, receipt, stockpiling, retention, possession, use, or threat of use of any chemical weapon.[281]

19.23 ROME STATUTE OF THE INTERNATIONAL CRIMINAL COURT

The Rome Statute of the International Criminal Court ("Rome Statute") establishes the International Criminal Court ("ICC") at The Hague, Netherlands.[282] Under the Rome Statute, the ICC may investigate and prosecute certain international crimes (*e.g.*, genocide, war crimes) in certain situations.[283]

The United States signed the Rome Statute on December 31, 2000, but President Clinton did not submit the treaty to the Senate for its advice and consent to ratification. Because of "significant flaws," President Clinton recommended that his successor not submit the Rome Statute to the Senate until the United States' fundamental concerns with the treaty were addressed.[284] In particular, the United States has expressed concern that the ICC would claim jurisdiction over personnel of States that have not ratified the Rome Statute.[285] In addition, for example, concerns have been raised that the ICC would not provide U.S. persons accused of war crimes with the procedural protections that they are afforded under U.S. domestic law.[286]

On May 6, 2002, the United States filed a letter with the U.N. Secretary General, the depositary for the Rome Statute, indicating that it "does not intend to become a party to the treaty," and that "[a]ccordingly, the United States has no legal obligations arising from its signature on December 31, 2000."[287] The United States participated as an observer in the Rome Statute's first Review conference in Kampala, Uganda, May 30-June 11, 2010, and has supported ICC efforts in certain cases.[288] The Department of State Legal Adviser has noted that U.S. policy is explicitly not to frustrate the object and purpose of the Rome Statute.[289]

---

[281] 18 U.S.C.S. § 229 ("(a) Unlawful conduct. Except as provided in subsection (b), it shall be unlawful for any person knowingly— (1) to develop, produce, otherwise acquire, transfer directly or indirectly, receive, stockpile, retain, own, possess, or use, or threaten to use, any chemical weapon; or (2) to assist or induce, in any way, any person to violate paragraph (1), or to attempt or conspire to violate paragraph (1). (b) Exempted agencies and persons. (1) In general. Subsection (a) does not apply to the retention, ownership, possession, transfer, or receipt of a chemical weapon by a department, agency, or other entity of the United States, or by a person described in paragraph (2), pending destruction of the weapon. (2) Exempted persons. A person referred to in paragraph (1) is— (A) any person, including a member of the Armed Forces of the United States, who is authorized by law or by an appropriate officer of the United States to retain, own, possess, transfer, or receive the chemical weapon; or (B) in an emergency situation, any otherwise nonculpable person if the person is attempting to destroy or seize the weapon.").

[282] Rome Statute of the International Criminal Court, Jul. 17, 1998, 2187 UNTS 90.

[283] *Refer to* § 18.20.3 (The International Criminal Court (ICC) Created by the Rome Statute).

[284] William J. Clinton, *Statement on the Rome Treaty on the International Criminal Court*, Dec. 31, 2000, 2000-III PUBLIC PAPERS OF THE PRESIDENTS 2816.

[285] *Refer to* § 18.20.3.1 (Attempt to Assert Jurisdiction With Respect to Nationals of Non-Party States).

[286] *See, e.g.*, 22 U.S.C. § 7421 ("Congress makes the following findings: … (7) Any American prosecuted by the International Criminal Court will, under the Rome Statute, be denied procedural protections to which all Americans are entitled under the Bill of Rights to the United States Constitution, such as the right to trial by jury.").

[287] John Bolton, Letter to Kofi Anan, U.N. Treaty Collection Depository Notification, C.N.434.2002, May 6, 2002.

[288] *Refer to* § 18.20.3.3 (U.S. Law and Policy on Support to the ICC).

[289] Harold Hongju Koh, Legal Adviser, Department of State, *Remarks on international criminal justice at the Vera Institute of Justice in New York and at Leiden University, Campus The Hague*, 2012 DIGEST OF UNITED STATES PRACTICE IN INTERNATIONAL LAW 61, 68 ("Putting all of this together, as I made clear more than two years ago in a speech at New York University, 'What you quite explicitly do not see from this Administration is U.S. hostility towards the Court. You do not see what international lawyers might call a concerted effort to frustrate the object and purpose of the Rome Statute. That is explicitly not the policy of this administration. Because although the United States is not a party to the Rome Statute, we share with the States parties a deep and abiding interest in seeing the Court successfully complete the important prosecutions it has already begun.'").

19.24 1999 U.N. SECRETARY GENERAL'S BULLETIN FOR U.N. FORCES

The U.N. Secretary General has promulgated a bulletin for the purpose of setting out fundamental principles and rules of international humanitarian law applicable to United Nations forces conducting operations under United Nations command.[290] The bulletin is not a legally binding instrument, although, in many cases, the rules reflected in the bulletin reflect law of war rules that are binding upon the United States as a matter of treaty or customary international law. The bulletin has been the subject of criticism by States.[291]

19.25 2005 ICRC STUDY ON CUSTOMARY INTERNATIONAL HUMANITARIAN LAW

There is no list of treaty provisions (or other codification) that the United States has agreed reflects the entirety of the customary international law of war.[292]

In 2005, the International Committee of the Red Cross published a study on customary international humanitarian law (ICRC CIHL Study), which has been criticized for its methodology and formulation of certain specific rules.[293] The United States likewise has expressed serious concerns about the methodology used in the ICRC CIHL Study and has stated that it is not in a position to accept without further analysis the Study's conclusions that certain rules related to the law of war in fact reflect customary international law.[294]

19.26 AP III

A third additional protocol to the 1949 Geneva Conventions was adopted on December 8, 2005.[295] AP III recognizes a red crystal as an additional distinctive emblem for the same purposes as the distinctive emblems of the Geneva Conventions.[296]

The United States deposited its instrument of ratification to AP III on March 8, 2007, without making any statements of reservation, declaration, or understanding.[297]

---

[290] U.N. SECRETARIAT, *Secretary-General's Bulletin: Observance by United Nations Forces of International Humanitarian Law*, U.N. Doc. ST/SGB/1999/13 (Aug. 6, 1999) ("The Secretary-General, for the purpose of setting out fundamental principles and rules of international humanitarian law applicable to United Nations forces conducting operations under United Nations command and control, promulgates the following:").

[291] Report of the Special Committee on Peacekeeping Operations, *Comprehensive review of the whole question of peacekeeping operations in all their aspects*, U.N. Doc. A/54/839 ¶82 (Mar. 20, 2000) ("The Special Committee notes the Secretary-General's comments on the guidelines on compliance with international humanitarian law by United Nations peacekeepers. The Committee expresses concern about the lack of consultation with Member States by the Secretariat before finalizing Secretary-General's Bulletin ST/SGB/1999/13. It requests further clarification on the Bulletin's legal status, and stresses that it must accurately reflect the terms of international humanitarian law. It requests the Secretary-General to carry out consultations on the Bulletin with the Special Committee.").

[292] *Refer to* § 1.8 (Customary International Law).

[293] *See, e.g.*, Daniel Bethlehem, *The Methodological framework of the Study*, ELIZABETH WILMSHURST & SUSAN BREAU, PERSPECTIVES ON THE ICRC STUDY ON CUSTOMARY INTERNATIONAL HUMANITARIAN LAW 4 (2007) ("Without detracting from this genuine appreciation, it is necessary and appropriate to draw attention to some important misgivings about the Study, as regards both methodology and the formulation of certain specific Rules.").

[294] U.S. RESPONSE TO ICRC CIHL STUDY 514 ("Given the Study's large scope, we have not yet been able to complete a detailed review of its conclusions. We recognize that a significant number of the rules set forth in the Study are applicable in international armed conflict because they have achieved universal status, either as a matter of treaty law or – as with many provisions derived from the Hague Regulations of 1907 – customary law. Nonetheless, it is important to make clear – both to you and to the greater international community – that, based upon our review thus far, we are concerned about the methodology used to ascertain rules and about whether the authors have proffered sufficient facts and evidence to support those rules. Accordingly, the United States is not in a position to accept without further analysis the Study's conclusions that particular rules related to the laws and customs of war in fact reflect customary international law.").

[295] Protocol additional to the Geneva Conventions of 12 August 1949, and relating to the Adoption of an Additional Distinctive Emblem (Protocol III), Dec. 8, 2005, 2404 UNTS 1.

[296] *Refer to* § 7.15.1.3 (Red Crystal).

[297] 2444 UNTS 287 ("RATIFICATION **United States of America** *Deposit of instrument with the Government of Switzerland: 8 March 2007*").

CPSIA information can be obtained
at www.ICGtesting.com
Printed in the USA
BVHW080843141222
654220BV00005B/143

9 780997 87831